THE SPORT AMERICANA ®

PRICE GUIDE

NO. 12

By
DR. JAMES BECKETT

About the Author

Jim Beckett, the leading authority on sport card values in the United States, maintains a wide range of activities in the world of sports. He possesses one of the finest collections of sports cards and autographs in the world, has made numerous appearances on radio and television, and has been frequently cited in many national publications. He was awarded the first "Special Achievement Award" for Contributions to the Hobby by the National Sports Collectors Convention in 1980 and the "Jock-Jasperson Award" for Hobby Dedication in 1983.

Dr. Beckett is the author of *The Sport Americana Baseball Card Price Guide, The Official Price Guide to Baseball Cards, The Sport Americana Football, Hockey, Basketball and Boxing Price Guide, The Official Price Guide to Football Cards, The Official Price Guide to Hockey and Basketball Cards, The Sport Americana Price Guide to Baseball Collectibles, The Sport Americana Baseball Memorabilia and Autograph Price Guide*, and *The Sport Americana Alphabetical Baseball Card Checklist*. In addition, he is the founder, author, and editor of *Beckett Baseball Card Monthly, Beckett Basketball Card Magazine, Beckett Football Card Magazine*, magazines dedicated to advancing the card collecting hobby.

Jim Beckett received his Ph.D. in Statistics from Southern Methodist University in 1975. He resides in Dallas with his wife Patti and their daughters, Christina, Rebecca, and Melissa.

Acknowledgments

A great deal of hard work went into this volume, and it could not have been done without help from many people. Our thanks are extended to each and every one of you.

Those who have worked closely with us on this and many other books, have again proven themselves invaluable -- Frank and Vivian Barning (*Baseball Hobby News*), Chris Benjamin, Sy Berger (Topps), Card Collectors Co., Cartophilium (Andrew Pywowarczuk), Ira Cetron, Mike Cramer (Pacific Trading Cards), Bill and Diane Dodge, Richard Duglin (Baseball Cards-n-More), Steve Freedman, Gervise Ford, Larry and Jeff Fritsch, Tony Galovich (American Card Exchange), Georgia Music and Sports (Dick DeCourcy and Floyd Parr), Bill Goodwin (St. Louis Baseball Cards), Mike and Howard Gordon, John Greenwald, Wayne Grove, Bill Haber, Bill Henderson, Danny Hitt, Tom Imboden, Allan Kaye (*Baseball Card News*), Rick Keplinger, David Kohler (SportsCards Plus), Don Lepore, Paul Lewicki, Neil Lewis (Leaf), Lew Lipset, Norman and Ken Liss (Topps), Major League Marketing (Dan Shedrick, Tom Day, George Martin), Mid-Atlantic Coin Exchange (Bill Bossert), David "Otis" Miller, Dick Millerd, Brian Morris, Paul Mullen and Vincent Murray (Fleer), Ralph Nozaki, Optigraphics (Anne Flavin and Ed Fick), Jack Pollard, Gavin Riley, Alan Rosen (Mr. Mint), John Rumierz, San Diego Sport Collectibles (Bill Goepner and Nacho Arredondo), Kevin Savage (Sports Gallery), Mike Schechter, Barry Sloate, John Spalding, Phil Spector (Scoreboard, Inc.), Sports Collectors Store, Frank Steele, Murvin Sterling, Lee Temanson, Ed Twombly (New England Bullpen), Gary Walter, Kit Young, and Ted Zanidakis. Finally we owe a special acknowledgment to Dennis W. Eckes, "Mr. Sport Americana." The success of the *Beckett Price Guides* has always been the result of a team effort.

This Price Guide is our best one yet and you can thank all of the contributors (listed above and below) as well as our staff here for that. But two people on our staff here have made direct and important specific contributions to this work. Theo Chen has done many things to help, e.g., he's done a great job on Readers Write freeing me up for more attention to pricing, and has in fact provided most of the R/W answers which I then only need to review. He's also primarily responsible for the paragraph descriptions for the new sets this year. B.A. Murry's contribution has been significant with respect to virtually all aspects of pricing cards. It is very difficult to be "accurate" -- one can only do one's best, but this job is especially difficult since we're shooting at a moving target as prices are fluctuating all the time. Having two full-time pricing experts has definitely proven to be better than one, and I thank B.A. for coming on board and making a difference resulting in more accurate prices for you our readers.

Many people have provided price input, illustrative material, checklist verifications, errata, and/or background information. We should like to individually thank AbD Cards (Dale Wesolewski), Carl Abrams, Jerry Adamic, Ron Adelson, Tony Adkins, A.J.'s Sport Stop, Ercu Aktay, Bob Alexander, Jay Alicea, All Star Sports Collectibles, Jason Allen, Paul Allen, Kent W. Alverson, Pat Alvey, Doug Amerman, Jon Andell, Read Andersen, Dennis Anderson, Roberto Ansourian, Ric Apter, Mark Argo (Olde South Cards), Neil Armstrong (World Series Cards), Troy Arnold, Hury Askotzky, Sammy Ayres, B&F Sports Cards, Joel Bachman, Josh Bakk, Ball Four Cards, Brad Bane, Joe Barney, Fernando Barriga, Ed Barry (Ed's Collectibles), Bob Bartosz (Baseball Card Shop), Bay State Cards (Lenny DeAngelico), Tom Beckley, Karen Bell, Jason Beloro, Chris Berbermeyer, Carl Berg, Frank Bernatt, Bernie's Bullpen, Curtis

Bethea, Beulah Sports, BH Baseball Cards, Darin Blang, Eddy Blaw, Levi Bleam, Bob Boffa, Moni Boling, Tim Bond (Tim's Cards & Comics), Bobby Bono, Charlie Botello, Travis Boyer, Randy Bradford, Peter T. Brennan, David Brewer, John Brigandi, Chuck Brooks, Casey Brough, Richard Brown, Derek Brusko, William Bryfia, Hans Buchsteiner, Eric Bush, Patrick Buss, California Card Co., David Call (9th Inning Baseball Card Shop), Joe Callahan, Jim Carballido, Paul C. Carpenter, Michael Cary, Sandy Chan, David Chang, Dwight Chapin, Erick Chapman, Chris Charles, Jared Chasteen, Ray Cherry, Wayne Christian, Dick Cianciotto, Cincinnati Baseball Cards, Terry Circle, Ron Citrenbaum, James Clark, Alexander Clarke, Daniel Cleaveland, Ronald Cochran, Barry Colla, Collectibles Unlimited (John Alward and Deb Ingram), Collection de Sport AZ (Ronald Villaneuve), Ryan Collins, Nathan Cooper, Curt Cooter, Steve Corbin, S. Alan Corlew, Douglas Covelli, Matt Craig, Taylor Crane, Chad Cripe, James Critzer, John Curtis, Allen Custer.

Paul Dainesi, Eugene Dalager, Dave Dame, Don Daniel III, Cameron Davis, Kevin Davis, Paul R. Davis, Ben Deaton, Jason Decena, Jeff Dickenson, Howard J. Didier Jr., Ken Diemer, Andrew Dilg, Ken Dinerman (California Cruizers), D.L. Ditto, George Doherty, George Dolence, Richard Dolloff (Dolloff Coin Center), George Dougherty, Jonathon Drye, Irving Eichenthal, Karen Ellison, Doak Ewing, Matthew Falewicz, Josh Feinkind, Tom Feldman, Eric Fellows, Chuck Ferrero, David Festberg, Jay Finglass, Danny Fitzgerald, Doug Flatau, Roger Flood, Kirk Fogg, Fremont Fong, Perry Fong, Tim Fong, Tommy Fox, Andrew France, Walter Franklin, Steve Freeburne, Mark Friedman, Robert Garren, David Garrett, Mike Garrett, Willie George Jr., Stanley Gilbert, Bob Gill, Timothy Gilman, Deric Glissmeyer, Dick Goddard, Steve Gold (AU Sports), Greg Goldstein (Dragon's Den), Jeff Goldstein, Jerry Goodman, Jim Goodreid, Robert Gottberg, Keith Gradwohl, Grauer's Collectables, Stephen Grave, Justin Greenwald, Gabe Greer, Alex Gregg, Al Gritter, Bob Gullic, and Steve Gungormez.

Chris Hackman, Hall's Nostalgia, Hershell Hanks, A.R. Hanson, Mike Harrigan, Chris Hathaway, Aaron Hecht, Billy Heffner, Joel Hellman, Mark Hellman, Stacy Henderson, Dennis Henry, John Higley, James Hilgert, Zack Hill, Scott Hill, Curtis Hoggatt, Home Plate of Utah (Ken Edick), Joan Hoole, David Horie, Rich Hovoroka, Jimmy Howell, David A. Hunt, Keith Huskamp, Matt and Marc Hutcheson, Heath Ingersoll, Richard Iozia, Ryan Jansen, Paul Jastrzembski, Nancy Jennings, JJ's Budget Baseball Cards, Bryan D. Johnson, Jay Johnson, Kevin M. Johnson, Jack L.Johnstone, Stewart W. Jones, Steve Juon, Dave Jurgensmeier, Aaron Kalina, Eric Karabagli, Jay and Mary Kasper, Frank Katen, Neil Katz, Tim Kelley, Mike Kelly, Paul M. Kelly, Justin Kerstetter, Phil Kidel, Leroy King, Chad Kisner, Richard Klein, Rob H. Klein, Eric Knodel, David Kohler, Jim Kohlmeyer, Ernie Kohlstruk, Koinz and Kards, David Koslik, David Kreskai, William and Curt Kruschwitz, Michael Kullkewski, Thomas Kunnecke, Jared Kvapil, Andy Kwang, John Kyranos, Tim Langan, Shawn Larson, Jason Lassic, Dan Lavin, Sylvia Leasure, Phil Lee, Morley Leeking, Michael Lenart, Glenn Lerch, Irv Lerner, Dale E. Loebs, Mike London, Damian Lopez, Ray Luangsuwan, and Jeff Lupke.

David Macaray, Robert Macasinag, Jim Macie, Mark Macrae, Adam Magary, Paul Manning, Andy Mar, Paul Marchant, Dick Marshall, Bill Mastro, P.M. Mathis, Jeffrey Maxey, Dr. William McAvoy, Alex McCollum, Mike McConnell, Scott McCoy, Michael McDonald (The Sports Page), Dan McIlhargey, Ryan McKee, Reed McKenney, Scott McKevitt, Tony McLaughlin, Michael McLean, Scott McNutt, W. Terry McPherson,

BILL HENDERSON'S CARDS
"King of the Commons"

"ALWAYS BUYING"
Call or Write
for Quote

**2320 RUGER AVE. PG12
JANESVILLE, WISCONSIN 53545
1-608-755-0922**

"ALWAYS BUYING"
Call or Write
for Quote

	HI # OR SCARCE SERIES		COMMONS EACH		EX/MT TO MINT CONDITION GROUP LOTS FOR SALE				VG+ to EX Condition		
					50 Diff.	100 Diff.	300 Asst.	500 Asst.	50	100	200 Different
1948 BOWMAN	(37-48)	25.00	15.00								
1949 BOWMAN	(145-240)	80.00	15.00		675.				400.		
50-51 BOWMAN	50 (1-72) 51 (253-324)	50.00	15.00	51 (2-36) 20.00	675.				400.		
1952 TOPPS	(311-407)	P.O.R.	30.00	(2-80) 60.00	1350.				800.		
1952 BOWMAN	(217-252)	30.00	15.00	(2-36) 20.00	675.				400.		
1953 TOPPS	(220-280)	80.00	20.00	(2-165) 30.00	900.				600.		
1953 BOWMAN	(129-160)	40.00	30.00	(113-128) 50.00	1350.				800.		
1954 TOPPS			12.00	(51-75) 25.00	540.				360.		
1954 BOWMAN			7.00	(129-224) 8.00	315.	600.			210.		
1955 TOPPS	(161-210)	18.00	7.00	(151-160) 12.00	315.				210.		
1955 BOWMAN	(225-320)	15.-20. Umps	6.00	(2-96) 8.00	270.	500.			180.	350.	
1956 TOPPS			7.00	(181-260) 12.00	315.				210.	400.	
1957 TOPPS	(265-352)	17.50	5.00	(353-407) 5.00	220.	420.			155.	300.	
1958 TOPPS			3.50	(1-110) 5.00	155.	300.	850.		105.	200.	
1959 TOPPS	(507-572)	12.50	3.00	(1-110) 4.00	135.	260.	750.		90.	175.	385.
1960 TOPPS	(523-572)	12.50	1.75	(441-506) 3.50	85.	165.	450.	750.	52.	100.	190.
1961 TOPPS	(523-589)	25.00	1.50	(371-522) 2.00	65.	125.	360.	700.	45.	80.	155.
1962 TOPPS	(523-590)	12.50	1.50	(371-522) 2.00	65.	125.	360.		45.	80.	155.
1963 TOPPS	(447-576)	8.00	1.00	(197-446) 2.00	45.	90.			32.	60.	
1964 TOPPS	(523-587)	7.50	1.00	(371-522) 2.00	45.	90.			32.	60.	115.
1965 TOPPS	(447-522) 3.00 (523-598) 5.00		1.00	(371-446) 1.50	45.	90.			32.	60.	115.
1966 TOPPS	(523-598)	15.00	1.00	(447-522) 4.00	45.	90.			32.	60.	115.
1967 TOPPS	(534-609)	10.00	1.00	(458-533) 4.00	45.	90.			32.	60.	115.
1968 TOPPS			.75	(458-533) 1.00	35.	65.			23.	45.	85.
1969 TOPPS	(589-664)	1.00	.60	(219-327) 1.00	28.	55.	155.		18.	35.	65.
1970 TOPPS	(634-720)	2.50	.45	(547-633) 1.25	22.	42.	120.	190.	14.	26.	50.
1971 TOPPS	(644-752)	2.50	.45	(524-643) 1.50	22.	42.	120.	190.	14.	26.	50.
1972 TOPPS	(657-787)	3.00	.45	(526-656) 1.50	22.	42.	*120.	190.	14.	26.	50.
1973 TOPPS	(528-660)	2.00	.35	(397-528) .60	16.	32.	*90.		12.	22.	40.
1974 TOPPS			.35		16.	32.	*90.	*150.		22.	40.
1975 TOPPS	(8-132 .50)		.35		16.	32.	*90.			22.	40.
1976-77			.20			18.	*50.	*85.		10.	18.
1978-1980			.15			13.	*38.	*65.		8.	15.
1981 thru 1990 Topps, Fleer or Donrus			.10			8.	*22.	*35.		5.	10.
Specify Year & Company except below						Per Yr.	Per Yr.	Per Yr.			
1984-86 DONRUS			.15			7.	13.	*38.	*60.			

SPECIAL IN VG+ to EX
CONDITION-POSTPAID

250	58-62	300.00
500	58-62	550.00
250	60-69	170.00
500	60-69	320.00
1000	60-69	600.00
250	70-79	50.00
500	70-79	90.00
1000	70-79	160.00
250	80-84	15.00
500	80-84	28.00
1000	80-84	55.00

*These lots are all different.
Special 1 Different from each year 1949-80 - $130.00 postpaid.
Special 100 Different from each year 1956-80 - $2600.00 postpaid.
Special 10 Different from each year 1956-80 - $280.00 postpaid.
All lot groups are my choice only.
All assorted lots will contain as many different as possible.
Please list alternates whenever possible.
Send your want list and I will fill them at the above price for commons. High numbers, specials, scarce series, and stars extra.
You can use your Master Card or Visa to charge your purchases.
Minimum order $7.50 - Postage and handling .50 per 100 cards (minimum $1.75)
Also interested in purchasing your collection.
Groups include various years of my choice.
ANY CARD NOT LISTED ON PRICE SHEET IS PRICED AT BECKETT-SPORTS AMERICANA PRICE GUIDE XII

SETS AVAILABLE
Topps 1988, 1989, 1990
19.95 ea. + 2.50 UPS
6 for 19.75 ea. + 9.00 UPS
18 for 19.25 ea. + 20.00 UPS
54 for 18.75 ea. + 60.00 UPS
MIX OR MATCH

Mendal Mearkle, Raj Mehta, Ken Melanson, Randy Messel, Blake Meyer (Lone Star Sportscards), Joe Michalowicz, Eric Miller, Cary Miller, Linda Miller, Wayne Miller, Dick Millerd, Patrick Montagu, Leland Morris, Bill Morton, Brian Munger, Zachary Myles, Edward Nazzaro (The Collector), Lloyd Neider, Robby Nelson, James W. Niels, Rusty Nighbert, Will Norris, Neal Obermeyer, Mike O'Brien, Keith Olbermann, Oldies and Goodies, Scott Orgera, Ron Oser, Jeff Osner, Jamie O'Sullivan, Tom Overson, Nelson Paine, Jason Parker, Gary Parnell, John Pash, Clay Pasternack, Mark Patzschke, Bernie Paul, Mark A. Paulson, Michael Pensabene, Michael Perrotta, Trevor Perry, Jeff Pfeil, Tom Pfirrmann, John Phillips, Mark L. Phillips, Dan Piepenbrock, Curtis Pires, Bob Poet, Edward Pope, Seth Poppel, Mark Porath, Chip Porter, Michael Poynter, Don Prestia, Kelby Joe Price, Jeff Prillaman (Southern Cards), Donald Prindle, and James Quintong.

David Rae, Sam Ramirez, Victor Ramos, Rick Rapa and Barry Sanders (Atlanta Sports Cards), R.W. Ray, Dylan Reach, Steve Reardon, Matt Reghitto, Tom Reid, Paula Ann Reinke, Frank J. Retcho, Jeff Reynolds, Stephen Ricci, Dave Ring, Al Rocca, Jeff Rockholt, Doug Rodman, Carlyle Rood, Avi Rosenfeld, Rick Ross, Clifton Rouse, Deedrick Rowe III, George Rusnak, Gregory Russell, Terry Sack, Todd Sackmann, Harry Sacks, Joe Sak, Jennifer Salems, John San Martino Jr., Gary Sawatzki, Evan Schenkman, Bruce Schwartz, David Seaverns, Tom Shanyfelt, Gerry Shebib, Farr N. Shepherd, Wayne Sherman, Tom Sherry, Rey Silva, Rick Sinchak, Bob Singer, Robert Smathers, Art Smith, Brian W. Smith, Chad Smith, Michael Snowden, Fred Mo Snyder, Brian E. South, Martin Spitzer, Linda Spitzer, Howard Staples, John Stephens, Kim A. Stigall, Tim Strandberg, Edward Strauss, Richard Strobino, Jon Strohl, Alan Sugahara, Superior Sport Card, Matt Swarner, J. and A. Swenson, Ian Taylor, Jason Terry, Jim Thompson, Carl Thrower, Joshua Tjiong, Karrie Tompkins, Dan Trimble, Dr. Ralph Triplette, Howard Tung, Ralph Turkenkopf, Jim Turner, Matt Tyson, Andrew Uzarowski, Todd Van Der Kruik, Mark Vanden Busch, Jeff Varnado, Michael Vrooman, Tom R. Walton, Greg Watanabe, Joe Webb, Mark Weber, R.R. Webster, Douglas Weddleton, Tony Weiand, Josh Weis, Andy Wemmer, Melvin D. Werling, Bill Wesslund, Richard West, Mark Whiteside, Timothy Wiley, Matt Wilgenbush, Jeff Williams, Mark Willis, Andy Wilson, David Wilson, Eric Wilson, Jesse Wilson, Opry Winston, John Witmer, Dylan Wolfe, Kyle Wolfe, Jay Wolt (Cavalcade of Sports), Lawrence Wong, Leon Wong, Pete Wooten, Vida Yancy, Chris Yang, Mike Yanke, Dan Yaw, Sandy Yelnick, Yesterday's Heroes, V.P. Young Jr., Eddy Yuan, Robert Zanze, and Chris Ziemba.

Every year we make active solicitations for input to that year's edition and we are particularly appreciative of help (large and small) provided for this volume. While we receive many inquiries, comments, and questions regarding material within this book -- and, in fact, each and every one is read and digested -- time constraints prevent us from personally replying. We hope that the letters will continue, and that even though no reply is received, you will feel that you are making significant contributions to the hobby through your interest and comments.

Special thanks go the staff of *Beckett Publications* for their help. Editorial Director Fred Reed was very helpful with the editing of the introductory section, the production of the advertising pages, and the supervision of the extensive production support team. He was ably assisted by Jeff Amano, Therese Bellar, Michael Bolduc, Lou Cather, Theo

Chen, Susan Elliott, Julie Fulton, Pepper Hastings, Sara Jenks, Jay Johnson, Tricia Jones, Rudy Klancnik, Frances Knight, Omar Mediano, and Reed Poole. The rest of the overall operations of *Beckett Monthly* were skillfully directed by Claire Backus and Joe Galindo. Working with them were Nancy Barton, Lisa Borden, Chris Calandro, Mary Campana, Paige Crosby, Jan Dickerson, Louise Ebaugh, Mary Gregory, Julie Grove, Beth Hartke, Laura Kelley, Monte King, Debbie Kingsbury, Amy Kirk, Renee MacElvaine, Glen Morante, Ruth Price, Cindy Struble, Mark Whitesell, and Jay Yarid. James and Sandi Beane performed several major system programming jobs for us this year in order to help us accomplish our work faster and more accurately. The whole *Beckett Publications* team has my thanks for jobs well done. Thank you, everyone.

I also thank my family, especially my wife, Patti, and daughters, Christina, Rebecca, and Melissa, for putting up with me again.

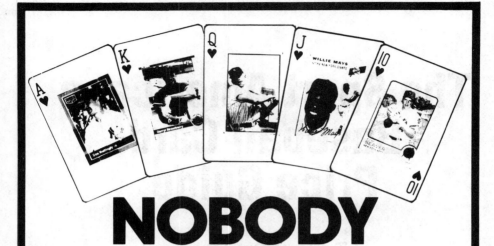

The Sport Americana Baseball Card Price Guide

Table of Contents

THE BASEBALL CARD SHOW

"The Baseball Card Show" is the only show of its kind. It is the weekly video magazine of the hobby. Aired each week during Prime Time, 7:30 to 8:00 pm, on Manhattan Cable Television, Channel 23, it features current hobby news — the new card sets, what's hot and what's not, interviews with former players and card company spokesmen, reviews of older card sets and hobby history, and much more. It is your show and it's on now in the country's largest metropolitan area.

THE BASEBALL CARD SHOW

Monday Nights
7:30 to 8:00 pm

Manhattan Cable TV
CHANNEL 23

Interesting in sponsoring "The Baseball Card Show" in your local area? Give us a call at (212) 873-6999.

Interested in spot commercials on "The Baseball Card Show" in the Manhattan area with its many millions of viewers? Call us at (212) 873-6999.

CONSIDERING INVESTING IN BASEBALL CARDS?

If so, consider the following:

1. We offer a variety of investment programs to fit any investor, starting at $2000.

2. We only deal in the finest cards on today's market. We thus only sell the finest cards. If you want 1990s or the hot card of the week, we can't help you. But if you're looking for rare or classic cards from 1909-1980 we definitely can be of service.

3. We offer a daily cash **BUY-SELL** market for hundreds of the top cards on today's market. Thus we can help you when you're ready to liquidate as well.

4. We publish THE BASEBALL CARD INVESTMENT REPORT, the industry's #1 newsletter for the serious investor. This will help you keep on top of the fast moving card market. Send $3 for a sample issue or $40 for a six-issue subscription.

5. Our track record for making profits for our clients is unsurpassed. **EVERY** client who has followed our advice has made a minimum of 48% net profit per year! Many have done double that and more. Our program works and we can make it work for you as well.

6. We are specialists in the investment card market. With over 18 years experience, you know you're dealing with experienced and knowledgeable people who understand the market from the financial viewpoint.

7. Looking to sell your cards? Look no further. We are **ALWAYS** serious buyers for the finest cards on the market. **NO ONE CONSISTENTLY PAYS MORE FOR YOUR NEAR MINT OR MINT GRADE SPORTS CARDS AND PREMIUM MEMORABILIA. WE PAY FULL GUIDE PRICE AND MORE FOR MANY ITEMS.** Here are just a few of our current buying prices for premimum quality cards:
   T-206 Wagner $200,000; 1933 Goudey Babe Ruths $4,000; 1951 Bowman Mickey Mantle $9,000; 1954 Hank Aaron $2,500; 1967 Tom Seaver $1,400; 1969 Reggie Jackson $550; 1973 Mike Schmidt $600.

If you have anything choice you're considering selling immediately, call us **TODAY** for our immediate top dollar offer. We can also sell your items through our consignment or auction plans as well, to get you even more for your cards. Call for details.

If you've been seriously considering investing in rare baseball cards and want to know how to get started correctly, call Tony Galovich today at **714-662-2273**. I will gladly answer any questions you may have without obligation. Please also ask for our free information packet to further help you and of course will explain how our investment programs can work for you to make serious money in the exciting world of baseball cards.

AMERICAN CARD EXCHANGE
TONY GALOVICH

P.O. Box 9625 • Newport Beach, CA 92660 • (714) 662-2273

Paying Top Dollar

- Our 10,000+ store and mail order customers need your cards.
- We have a six figure bank balance to support our buying commitment.
- All transactions and payments are mailed within 24 hours.

We Want To Buy!

We will pay cash for the following:

Large & small collections — Star cards — Baseball sets
Unopened boxes & cases — Football, Basketball, Hockey sets
Hartland statues — All Sports Memorabilia
Tobacco cards etc.

- Please feel **free to call** and discuss any transactions!

FREE
1990 illustrated catalog is available. Included in it is a variety of material 1910-1980s, including stars, complete sets, unopened material, rookie cards, Hartlands, bulk lots, etc. Please send two 25-cent stamps.

SportsCards Plus
14038 Beach Blvd. B-1
Westminster, CA 92683
(714) 895-4401 • Fax (714) 891-8078
Call David Kohler or Joe Kohler

Preface

Isn't it great? Every year this book gets bigger and bigger with all the new sets coming out. But even more exciting is that every year there are more collectors, more shows, more stores, and ... more interest in the cards we love so much. This edition has been enhanced and expanded from the previous edition. The cards you collect -- who they are, what they look like, where they are from, and (most important to many of you) what their current values are -- are enumerated within. Many of the features contained in the other *Beckett Price Guides* have been incorporated into this volume since condition grading, nomenclature, and many other aspects of collecting are common to the card hobby in general. We hope you find the book both interesting and useful in your collecting pursuits.

The Beckett Guide has been successful where other attempts have failed because it is complete, current, and valid. This *Price Guide* contains not just one, but three, prices by condition for all the baseball cards in the issues listed. These account for almost all the baseball cards in existence. The prices were added to the card lists just prior to printing and reflect not the author's opinions or desires but the going retail prices for each card, based on the marketplace (sports memorabilia conventions and shows, hobby papers, current mail order catalogs, local club meetings, auction results, and other firsthand reportings of actually realized prices).

What is the BEST Price Guide available (on the market) today? Of course card sellers will prefer the Price Guide with the highest prices as the best -- while card buyers will naturally prefer the one with the lowest prices. Accuracy, however, is the true test. Use the Price Guide used by more collectors and dealers than all the others combined. Look for the Beckett name. I won't put my name on anything I won't stake my reputation on. Not the lowest and not the highest -- but the most accurate, with integrity.

To facilitate your use of this book, read the complete introductory section in the pages following before going to the pricing pages. Every collectible field has its own terminology; we've tried to capture most of these terms and definitions in our glossary. Please read carefully the section on grading and the condition of your cards as you will not be able to determine which price column is appropriate for a given card without first knowing its condition.

Welcome to the world of baseball cards.

Sincerely, Dr. James Beckett

BASEBALL CARD CENTER

19190 TOLEDO BLADE BLVD.
PORT CHARLOTTE, FL 33948
813-624-4020

TWO LOCATIONS

2245-B WINKLER AVE.
FORT MYERS, FL 33901
813-278-3232

LICENSED PRO SPORT & COLLEGIATE MERCHANDISE

MERCHANDISE LINES

Come to the
FUN STORE!!

HOURS:
MON.-THURS. 10-9
FRI.-SAT.   10-10
SUN.   1-5

VISIT OUR STORES
WHEN IN FLORIDA.

WE BUY CARDS

. . . . MORE THAN JUST A CARD SHOP!

Introduction

Welcome to the exciting world of baseball card collecting, America's fastest-growing avocation. You have made a good choice in buying this book, since it will open up to you the entire panorama of this field in the simplest, most concise way.

It is estimated that nearly a third of a million different baseball cards have been issued during the past century. And the number of total cards put out by all manufacturers last year has been estimated at several billion with an initial retail value of more than $300 million. Sales of older cards by dealers may account for a like amount. With all that cardboard available in the marketplace, it should be no surprise that several million sports fans like you collect baseball cards today, and that number is growing by hundreds of thousands each year.

The growth of *Beckett Baseball Card Monthly* is another indication of this rising crescendo of popularity for baseball cards. Founded less than five years ago by Dr. James Beckett, the author of this price guide, *Beckett Monthly* has grown to the pinnacle of the baseball card hobby with more than a half million readers anxiously awaiting each enjoyable issue.

So collecting baseball cards -- while still pursued as a hobby with youthful exuberance by kids in the neighborhood -- has also taken on the trappings of an industry, with thousands of full- and part-time card dealers, as well as vendors of supplies, clubs and conventions. In fact, each year since 1980 thousands of hobbyists have assembled for a National Sports Collectors Convention, at which hundreds of dealers have displayed their wares, seminars have been conducted, autographs penned by sports notables, and millions of cards changed hands. These colossal affairs have been staged in Los Angeles, Detroit, St. Louis, Chicago, New York, Anaheim, Arlington (TX), San Francisco, Atlantic City, Chicago, and this year back in Arlington, Texas at the Convention Center. So baseball card collecting really is national in scope!

This increasing interest has been reflected in card values. As more collectors compete for available supplies, card prices (especially for premium-grade cards) rise. A national publication indicated a "very strong advance" in baseball card prices during the past decade, and a quick perusal of prices in this book compared to the figures in earlier editions of this price guide will quickly confirm this. Which brings us back around again to the book you have in your hands. Many prices have literally doubled! It is the best annual guide available to this exciting world of baseball cards. Read it and use it. May your enjoyment and your card collection increase in the coming months and years.

How to Collect

Each collection is personal and reflects the individuality of its owner. There are no set rules on how to collect cards. Since card collecting is a hobby or leisure pastime, what you collect, how much you collect, and how much time and money you spend collecting are entirely up to you. The funds you have available for collecting and your own personal taste should determine how you collect. Information and ideas presented here are intended to help you get the most enjoyment from this hobby.

It is impossible to collect every card ever produced. Therefore, beginners as well as intermediate and advanced collectors usually specialize in some way. One of the reasons this hobby is popular is that individual collectors can define and tailor their collecting methods to match their own tastes. To give you some ideas of the various approaches to collecting, we will list some of the more popular areas of specialization.

Many collectors select complete sets from particular years. For example, they may concentrate on assembling complete sets from all the years since their birth or since they became avid sports fans. They may try to collect a card for every player during that specified period of time.

Many others wish to acquire only certain players. Usually such players are the superstars of the sport, but occasionally collectors will specialize in all the cards of players who attended certain colleges or came from certain towns. Some collectors are only interested in the first cards or rookie cards of certain players. A handy guide for collectors interested in pursuing the hobby this way is the just-released *Sport Americana Alphabetical Checklist No. 4.*

Another fun way to collect cards is by team. Most fans have a favorite team, and it is natural for that loyalty to be translated into a desire for cards of the players on that favorite team. For most of the recent years, team sets (all the cards from a given team for that year) are readily available at a reasonable price. *The Sport Americana Team Baseball Card Checklist* will open up this field to the collector.

Obtaining Cards

Several avenues are open to card collectors. Cards can be purchased in the traditional way at the local candy, grocery, or drug stores, with the bubble gum or other products included. In recent years, it has also become possible to purchase complete sets of baseball cards through mail order advertisers found in traditional sports media publications, such as *The Sporting News*, *Baseball Digest*, *Street & Smith* yearbooks, and others. These sets are also advertised in the card collecting periodicals. Many collectors will begin by subscribing to at least one of the hobby periodicals, all with good up-to-date information. In fact, subscription offers can be found in the advertising section of this book.

Most serious card collectors obtain old (and new) cards from one or more of several main sources: (1) trading or buying from other collectors or dealers; (2) responding to sale or auction ads in the hobby publications; and/or (3) attending sports collectibles shows or conventions. We advise that you try all three methods since each has its own distinct advantages: (1) trading is a great way to make new friends; (2) hobby periodicals help you keep up with what's going on in the hobby (including when and where the conventions are happening); and (3) shows provide enjoyment and the

★ ★ ★ ★ ★ ★ ★ ★ ★ ★ ★ ★ ★ ★ ★ ★ ★ ★

THE LONGEST RUNNING CARD SHOWS IN LAS VEGAS

Are Promoted By

Joel Hellmann
J.J.'s Baseball Cards
Harbour Mall
William S. Canning Blvd.
Fall River, MA 02720
(508) 677-3143

&

Bob Byer
Triple Play Sportscards
114 N. Gaffey
Suite E
San Pedro, CA 90731
(213) 831-1551

Future Shows:
November 3 & 4, 1990
February 2 & 3, 1991

A N N O U N C I N G

THE FIRST ANNUAL NATIONAL ALL COLLECTABLES SHOW

July 11-15, 1990

Featuring the top dealers from around the country in Sportcards, Records, Comics, Movie Collectables and much more!

Super Star Guests • Seminars • Contests

Auction benefiting MDA & Lou Gehrig's Disease (ALS)
Triple-A All-Star Game in **Las Vegas on July 11, 1990**

For more information regarding the
All Collectables Show call:

(213) 831-1551 or (508) 677-9480

★ ★ ★ ★ ★ ★ ★ ★ ★ ★ ★ ★ ★ ★ ★ ★ ★ ★

opportunity to view millions of collectibles under one roof, in addition to meeting some of the hundreds or even thousands of other collectors with similar interests who also attend the shows.

Preserving Your Cards

Cards are fragile. They must be handled properly in order to retain their value. Careless handling can easily result in creased or bent cards. It is, however, not recommended that tweezers or tongs be used to pick up your cards since such utensils might mar or indent card surfaces and thus reduce those cards' conditions and values. In general, your cards should be handled directly as little as possible. This is sometimes easier to say than to do. Although there are still many who use custom boxes, storage trays, or even shoe boxes, plastic sheets are the preferred method of storing cards. A collection stored in plastic pages in a three-ring album allows you to view your collection at any time without the need to touch the card itself. For a large collection, some collectors may use a combination of the above methods.

When purchasing plastic sheets for your cards, be sure that you find the pocket size that fits the cards snugly. Don't put your 1951 Bowmans in a sheet designed to fit 1981 Topps. Most hobby and collectibles shops and virtually all collectors' conventions will have these plastic pages available in quantity for the various sizes offered or you can purchase them directly from the advertisers in this book. Also remember that pocket size isn't the only factor to consider when looking for plastic sheets. Some collectors concerned with long term storage of their cards in plastic sheets are cautious to avoid sheets containing PVC and request non-PVC sheets from their dealer.

Damp, sunny and/or hot conditions -- no, this is not a weather forecast -- are three elements to avoid in extremes if you are interested in preserving your collection. Too much (or too little) humidity can cause gradual deterioration of a card. Direct, bright sun (or fluorescent light) over time will bleach out the color of a card. Extreme heat accelerates the decomposition of the card. On the other hand, many cards have lasted more than 50 years without much scientific intervention. Be cautious, even if the above factors typically present a problem only in the extreme. It never hurts to be prudent.

Collecting/Investing

Collecting individual players and collecting complete sets are both popular vehicles for investment and speculation. Most investors and speculators stock up on complete sets or on quantities of players they think have good investment potential. There is obviously no guarantee in this book, or anywhere else for that matter, that cards will outperform the stock market or other investment alternatives in the future. After all, baseball cards do not pay quarterly dividends and cards cannot be sold at their "current values" as easily as stocks or bonmds. Nevertheless, investors have noticed a favorable trend in the past performance of baseball and other sports collectibles, and certain cards and sets have outperformed just about any other investment in some years.

Some of the obvious questions are: Which cards? When to buy? When to sell? The best investment you can make is in your own education. The more you know about your collection and the hobby, the more informed the decisions you will be able to make. We're not selling investment tips. We're selling information about the current value of baseball cards. It's up to you to use that information to your best advantage.

Nomenclature

Each hobby has its own language to describe its area of interest. The nomenclature traditionally used for trading cards is derived from the *American Card Catalog*, published in 1960 by Nostalgia Press. That catalog, written by Jefferson Burdick (who is called the "Father of Card Collecting" for his pioneering work), uses letter and number designations for each separate set of cards.

The letter used in the ACC designation refers to the generic type of card. While both sport and non-sport issues are classified in the ACC, we shall confine ourselves to the sport issues. The following list defines the letters and their meanings as used by the American Card Catalog.

(none) or N - 19th Century U.S. Tobacco
B - Blankets
D - Bakery Inserts Including Bread
E - Early Candy and Gum
F - Food Inserts
H - Advertising
M - Periodicals
PC - Postcards
R - Candy and Gum Cards 1930 to Present
T - 20th Century U.S. Tobacco
UO - Gas and Oil Inserts
V - Canadian Candy
W - Exhibits, Strip Cards, Team Issues

Following the letter prefix and an optional hyphen are one-, two-, or three-digit numbers, 1-999. These typically represent the company or entity issuing the cards. In several cases, the ACC number is extended by an additional hyphen and another one- or two-digit numerical suffix. For example, the 1957 Topps regular series baseball card issue carries an ACC designation of R414-11. The "R" indicates a Candy or Gum Card produced since 1930. The "414" is the ACC designation for Topps Chewing Gum baseball card issues, and the "11" is the ACC designation for the 1957 regular issue (Topps' eleventh baseball set).

Like other traditional methods of identification, this system provides order to the process of cataloging cards; however, most serious collectors learn the ACC designation of the popular sets by repetition and familiarity, rather than by attempting to "figure out" what they might or should be.

From 1948 forward, collectors and dealers commonly refer to all sets by their year, maker, type of issue, and any other distinguishing characteristic. For example, such a characteristic could be an unusual issue or one of several regular issues put out by a specific maker in a single year. Regional issues are usually referred to by year, maker, and sometimes by title or theme of the set.

Glossary/Legend

Our glossary defines terms frequently used in the card collecting hobby. Many of these terms are also common to other types of sports memorabilia collecting. Some terms may have several meanings depending on use.

AAS - Action All Stars, a postcard-size set issued by the Donruss Company.

ACC - Acronym for *American Card Catalog*.

ALL STAR CARD - A card portraying an All Star Player of the previous year that says "All Star" on its face.

ALPH - Alphabetical.

AS - Abbreviation for All Star (card).

ATG - All Time Great card.

BLANKET - A felt square (normally 5" to 6") portraying a baseball player.

BOX - Card issued on a box or a card depicting a Boxer.

BRICK - A group of 50 or more cards having common characteristics, that is intended to be bought, sold, or traded as a unit.

CABINETS - Popular and highly valuable photographs on thick card stock produced in the 19th and early 20th century.

CHECKLIST - A list of the cards contained in a particular set. The list is always in numerical order if the cards are numbered. Some unnumbered sets are artificially numbered in alphabetical order, by team and alphabetically within the team, or by uniform number for convenience.

CHECKLIST CARD - A card that lists in order the cards and players in the set or series. Older checklist cards in Mint condition that have not been checked off or marked off are very desirable.

CL - Abbreviation for Checklist.

COA - Abbreviation for Coach.

COIN - A small disc of metal or plastic portraying a player in its center.

COLLECTOR - A person who engages in the hobby of collecting cards primarily for his own enjoyment, with any profit motive being secondary.

COLLECTOR ISSUE - A set produced for the sake of the card itself with no product or service sponsor. It derives its name from the fact that most of these sets are produced for sale directly to the hobby market.

COMBINATION CARD - A single card depicting two or more players (but not a team card).

COMMON CARD - The typical card of any set; it has no premium value accruing from subject matter, numerical scarcity, popular demand, or anomaly.

COM - Card issued by the Post Cereal Company through their mail-in offer.

CONVENTION - A large weekend gathering of dealers and collectors at a single location for the purpose of buying, selling, and sometimes trading sports memorabilia items. Conventions are open to the public and sometimes feature celebrities, door prizes, films, contests, etc. They are frequently referred to simply as "shows."

CONVENTION ISSUE - A set produced in conjunction with a sports collectibles convention to commemorate or promote the show.

COR - Correct or corrected card.

COUPON - See Tab.

CREASE - A wrinkle on the card, usually caused by bending the card. Creases are a common (and serious) defect from careless handling.

CY - Cy Young Award.

DEALER - A person who engages in buying, selling, and trading sports collectibles or supplies. A dealer may also be a collector, but as a dealer, he anticipates a profit.

DIE-CUT - A card with part of its stock partially cut, allowing one or more parts to be folded or removed. After removal or appropriate folding, the remaining part of the card can frequently be made to stand up.

DISC - A circular-shaped card.

DISPLAY CARD - A sheet, usually containing three to nine cards, that is printed and used by the manufacturer to advertise and/or display the packages containing his products and cards. The backs of display cards are blank or contain advertisements.

DK - Diamond King (artwork produced by Perez-Steele for Donruss).

DP - Double Print (a card that was printed in double the quantity compared to the other cards in the same series).

ERA - Earned Run Average.

ERR - Error card (see also COR).

ERROR CARD - A card with erroneous information, spelling, or depiction on either side of the card. Most errors are not corrected by the producing card company.

EXHIBIT - The generic name given to thick-stock, postcard-size cards with single color obverse pictures. The name is derived from the Exhibit Supply Co. of Chicago, the principal manufacturer of this type of card. These are also known as Arcade cards since they were found in many arcades.

FDP - First Draft Pick.

FULL SHEET - A complete sheet of cards that has not been cut up into individual cards by the manufacturer. Also called an uncut sheet.

HALL OF FAMER - (HOF'er) A card that portrays a player who has been inducted into the Hall of Fame.

HIGH NUMBER - The cards in the last series of numbers in a year in which such higher-numbered cards were printed or distributed in significantly lesser amounts than the lower-numbered cards. The high-number designation refers to a scarcity of the high-numbered cards. Not all years have high numbers in terms of this definition.

HOC - House of Collectibles.

HOF - Hall of Fame.

HOR - Horizontal pose on card as opposed to the standard vertical orientation found on most cards.

HR - Home Run.

IA - In Action (type of card).

INSERT - A card of a different type, e.g., a poster, or any other sports collectible contained and sold in the same package along with a card or cards of a major set.

ISSUE - Synonymous with set, but usually used in conjunction with a manufacturer, e.g., a Topps issue.

K - Strikeout.

KP - Kid Picture (a sub-series issued in the Topps Baseball sets of 1972 and 1973).

LAYERING - The separation or peeling of one or more layers of the card stock, usually at the corner of the card.

LEGITIMATE ISSUE - A set produced to promote or boost sales of a product or service, e.g., bubble gum, cereal, cigarettes, etc. Most collector issues are not legitimate issues in this sense.

LHP - Left Handed Pitcher.

LID - A circular-shaped card (possibly with tab) that forms the top of the container for the product being promoted.

LL - Living Legends (Donruss 1984) or large letters.

MAJOR SET - A set produced by a national manufacturer of cards containing a large number of cards. Usually 100 or more different cards comprise the set.

MG - Abbreviation for Manager.

MINI - A small card; specifically, a Topps baseball card of identical design but smaller dimensions than the regular Topps issue of 1975.

ML - Major League.

MVP - Most Valuable Player.

NNOF - No Name on Front (see 1949 Bowman).

NOF - Name on Front (see 1949 Bowman).

NON-SPORT CARD - A card from a set whose major theme is a subject other than a sports subject. A card of a sports figure or event that is part of a non-sport set is still a non-sport card, e.g., while the "Look 'N' See" non-sport card set contains a card of Babe Ruth, a sports figure, that card is a non-sport card.

NOTCHING - The grooving of the card, usually caused by fingernails, rubber bands, or bumping card edges against other objects.

NY - New York.

OBVERSE - The front, face, or pictured side of the card.

OLY - Olympics (see 1985 Topps Baseball and 1988 Topps Traded sets; the members of the U.S. Olympic Baseball teams were featured subsets in both of these sets).

OPT - Option.

P - Pitcher or Pitching pose.

P1 - First Printing.

P2 - Second Printing.

P3 - Third Printing.

PANEL - An extended card that is composed of two or more individual cards. Often the panel forms the back part of the container for the product being promoted, e.g., a Hostess panel, a Bazooka panel, an Esskay Meat panel.

PCL - Pacific Coast League.

PG - Price Guide.

PLASTIC SHEET - A clear, plastic page that is punched for insertion into a binder (with standard three-ring spacing) containing pockets for displaying cards. Many different styles of sheets exist with pockets of varying sizes to hold the many differing card formats.

PREMIUM - A card, sometimes on photographic stock, that is purchased or obtained in conjunction with/or redemption for another card or product. The premium is not packaged in the same unit as the primary item.

PUZZLE CARD - A card whose back contains a part of a picture which, when joined correctly with other puzzle cards, forms the completed picture.

PUZZLE PIECE - A die-cut piece designed to interlock with similar pieces.

PVC - Polyvinyl Chloride, a substance used to make many of the popular card display protective sheets. Non-PVC sheets are considered preferable for long term storage of cards.

RARE - A card or series of cards of very limited availability. Unfortunately, "rare" is a subjective term sometimes used indiscriminately. "Rare" cards are harder to obtain than "scarce" cards.

RB - Record Breaker card.

REGIONAL - A card or set of cards issued and distributed only in a limited geographical area of the country.

REVERSE - The back or narrative side of the card.

RHP - Right-Handed Pitcher.

ROY - Rookie of the Year.

RP - Relief Pitcher.

RR - Rated Rookies (a subset featured in the Donruss Baseball sets).

SA - Super Action or Sport Americana.

SASE - Self-Addressed, Stamped Envelope.

SB - Stolen Bases.

SCARCE - A card or series of cards of limited availability. This subjective term is sometimes used indiscriminately to promote or hype value. "Scarce" cards are not as difficult to obtain as "rare" cards.

SCR - Script name on back (see 1949 Bowman Baseball).

SEMI-HIGH - A card from the next to last series of a sequentially issued set. It has more value than an average card and generally less value than a high number. A card is not called a semi-high unless the next to last series in which it exists has an additional premium attached to it.

SERIES - The entire set of cards issued by a particular producer in a particular year, e.g., the 1971 Topps series. Also, within a particular set, series can refer to a group of (consecutively numbered) cards printed at the same time, e.g., the first series of the 1957 Topps issue (numbers 1 through 88).

SET - One each of the entire run of cards of the same type produced by a particular manufacturer during a single year. In other words, if you have a (complete) set of 1976 Topps then you have every card from number 1 up through and including number 660, i.e., all the different cards that were produced.

SKIP-NUMBERED - A set that has many unissued card numbers between the lowest number in the set and the highest number in the set, e.g., the 1948 Leaf baseball set contains 98 cards skip-numbered from number 1 to number 168. A major set in which a few numbers were not printed is not considered to be skip-numbered.

SO - Strikeouts.

SP - Single or Short Print (a card which was printed in lesser quantity compared to the other cards in the same series; see also DP and TP).

SPECIAL CARD - A card that portrays something other than a single player or team, for example, a card that portrays the previous year's statistical leaders or the results from the previous year's post-season action.

SS - Shortstop.

STAMP - Adhesive-backed papers depicting a player. The stamp may be individual or in a sheet of many stamps. Moisture must be applied to the adhesive in order for the stamp to be attached to another surface.

STAR CARD - A card that portrays a player of some repute, usually determined by his ability; however, sometimes referring to sheer popularity.

STICKER - A card with a removable layer that can be affixed to (stuck onto) another surface.

STOCK - The cardboard or paper on which the card is printed.

STRIP CARDS - A sheet or strip of cards, particularly popular in the 1920s and 1930s, with the individual cards usually separated by broken or dotted lines.

SUPERSTAR CARD - A card that portrays a superstar, e.g., a Hall of Fame member or one with strong Hall of Fame potential.

SV - Super Veteran (see 1982 Topps).

TAB - A card portion set off from the rest of the card, usually with perforations, that may be removed without damaging the central character or event depicted by the card.

TBC - Turn Back the Clock cards.

TC - Team Checklist cards (see 1989 and 1990 Upper Deck).

TEAM CARD - A card that depicts an entire team.

TEST SET - A set, usually containing a small number of cards, issued by a national card producer and distributed in a limited section or sections of the country. Presumably, the purpose of a test set is to test market appeal for a particular type of card.

TL - Team Leader card.

TP - Triple Print (a card that was printed in triple the quantity compared to the other cards in the same series).

TR - Trade or Traded.

TRIMMED - A card cut down from its original size. Trimmed cards are undesirable to most collectors.

VARIATION - One of two or more cards from the same series with the same number (or player with identical pose if the series is unnumbered) differing from one another by some aspect, the different feature stemming from the printing or stock of the card. This can be caused when the manufacturer of the cards notices an error in one (or more) of the cards, makes the changes, and then resumes the print run. In this case there will be two versions or variations of the same card. Sometimes one of the variations is relatively scarce.

VERT - Vertical pose on card.

WAS - Washington.

WS - World Series card.

Business of Baseball Card Collecting

Determining Value

Why are some cards more valuable than others? Obviously, the economic laws of supply and demand are applicable to card collecting just as they are to any other field where a commodity is bought, sold, or traded in a free unregulated market.

Supply (the number of cards available on the market) is less than the total number of cards originally produced since attrition diminishes that original quantity. Each year a percentage of cards are typically thrown away, destroyed, or otherwise lost to collectors. This percentage is much smaller today than it was in the past because more and more people have become increasingly aware of the value of their cards. For those who collect only "Mint" condition cards, the supply of older cards can be quite small indeed. Until recently, collectors were not so conscious of the need to preserve the condition of their cards. For this reason, it is difficult to know exactly how many 1953 Topps are currently available, Mint or otherwise. It is generally accepted that there are fewer 1953 Topps available than 1963, 1973, or 1983 Topps cards. If demand were equal for each of these sets, the law of supply and demand would increase the price for the least available sets. Demand, however, is not equal for all sets, so price correlations can be complicated.

The demand for a card is influenced by many factors. These include: (1) the age of the card; (2) the number of cards printed; (3) the player(s) portrayed on the card; (4) the attractiveness and popularity of the set; and perhaps most important, (5) the physical condition of the card.

In general, (1) the older the card, (2) the fewer the number of the cards printed, (3) the more famous the player, (4) the more attractive and popular the set, or (5) the better the condition of the card, the higher the value of the card will be. There are exceptions to all but one of these factors: the condition of the card. Given two cards similar in all respects except condition, the one in the best condition will ALWAYS be valued higher.

While there are certain guidelines that help to establish the value of a card, the exceptions and peculiarities make any simple, direct mathematical formula to determine card values impossible.

Regional Variation

Two types of price variations exist among the sections of the country where a card is bought or sold. The first is the general price variation on all cards bought and sold in one geographical area as compared to another. Card prices are slightly higher on the East and West coasts, and slightly lower in the middle of the country. Although prices may vary from the East to the West, or from the Southwest to the Midwest, the prices listed in this guide are nonetheless presented as a consensus of all sections of this large and diverse country.

Still, prices for a particular player's cards may well be higher in his home team's area than in other regions. This exhibits the second type of regional price variation in which local players are favored over those from distant areas. For example, an Al Kaline card would be valued higher in Detroit than in Cincinnati because Kaline played in Detroit; therefore, the demand there for Al Kaline cards is higher than it is in Cincinnati. On the other hand, a Johnny Bench card would be priced higher in Cincinnati where he played than in Detroit for similar reasons. Sometimes even common player cards command such a premium from hometown collectors.

Set Prices

A somewhat paradoxical situation exists in the price of a complete set versus the combined cost of the individual cards in the set. In nearly every case, the sum of the prices for the individual cards is higher than the cost for the complete set. This is especially prevalent in the cards of the past few years. The reasons for this apparent anomaly stem from the habits of collectors and from the carrying costs to dealers. Today each card in a set is normally produced in the same quantity as all others in its set. However, many collectors pick up only stars, superstars, and particular teams. As a result, the dealer is left with a shortage of certain player cards and an abundance of others. He therefore incurs an expense in simply "carrying" these less desirable cards in stock. On the other hand, if he sells a complete set, he gets rid of large numbers of cards at one time. For this reason, he is often willing to receive less money for a complete set. By doing this, he recovers all of his costs and also receives some profit.

The disparity between the price of the complete set and that for the sum of the individual cards has also been influenced by the fact that the major manufacturers are now pre-collating card sets. Since "pulling" individual cards from the sets of all three manufacturers involves a specific type of labor (and cost), the singles or star card market is not affected significantly by pre-collation.

Set prices also do not include rare card varieties, unless specifically stated. Of course, the prices for sets do include one example of each type for the given set, but this is the least expensive variety.

Scarce Series

Scarce series occur because cards issued before 1974 were made available to the public each year in several series of finite numbers of cards, rather than all cards of the set being available for purchase at one time. At some point during the year, usually toward the end of the baseball season, interest in current year baseball cards waned. Consequently, the manufacturers produced smaller numbers of these later series of cards. Nearly all nationwide issues from post-World War II manufacturers (1948 to 1973) exhibit these series variations. In the past Topps, for example, may have issued series consisting of many different numbers of cards, including 55, 66, 80, 88, and others. Recently Topps has settled on what is now their standard sheet size of 132 cards, six of which comprise its 792-card set.

While the number of cards within a given series is usually the same as the number of cards on one printed sheet, this is not always the case. For example, Bowman used 36 cards on its standard printed sheets, but in 1948 substituted 12 cards during later print runs of that year's baseball cards. Twelve of the cards from the initial sheet of 36 cards were removed and replaced by 12 different cards giving, in effect, a first series of 36 cards and a second series of 12 new cards. This replacement produced a scarcity of 24 cards -- the 12 cards removed from the original sheet and the 12 new cards added to the sheet. A full sheet of 1948 Bowman cards (second printing) shows that card numbers 37 through 48 have replaced 12 of the cards on the first printing sheet.

The Topps Gum Company has also created scarcities and/or excesses of certain cards in many of their sets. Topps, however, has most frequently gone the other direction by double printing some of the cards. Double printing causes an abundance of cards of the players who are on the same sheet more than one time. During the years from 1978 to 1981, Topps double printed 66 cards out of their large 726-card set. The Topps' practice of double printing cards in earlier years is the most logical explanation for the known scarcities of particular cards in some of these Topps sets.

Recently Donruss has always been short-printing or double-printing certain cards in its major sets. Ostensibly this is due to their addition of Bonus MVP cards in their regular issue wax packs.

We are always looking for information or photographs of printing sheets of cards for research. Each year we try to update the hobby's knowledge of distribution anomalies. Please let us know at the address in this book if you have first-hand knowledge that would be helpful in this pursuit.

Grading Your Cards

Each hobby has its own grading terminology -- stamps, coins, comic books, beer cans, right down the line. Collectors of sports cards are no exception. The one invariable criterion for determining the value of a card is its condition: the better the condition of the card, the more valuable it is. However, condition grading is very subjective. Individual card dealers and collectors differ in the strictness of their grading, but the stated condition of a card should be determined without regard to whether it is being bought or sold.

The physical defects which lower the condition of a card are usually quite apparent, but each individual places his own estimation (negative value in this case) on these defects. We present the condition guide for use in determining values listed in this price guide in the hopes that excess subjectivity can be minimized.

The defects listed in the condition guide below are those either placed in the card at the time of printing -- uneven borders, focus -- or those defects that can occur to a card under normal handling -- corner sharpness, gloss, edge wear, light creases -- and finally, environmental conditions -- browning. Other defects to cards are caused by human carelessness and in all cases should be noted separately and in addition to the condition grade. Among the more common alterations are heavy creases, tape, tape stains, rubber band marks, water damage, smoke damage, trimming, paste, tears, writing, pin or tack holes, any back damage, and missing parts (tabs, tops, coupons, backgrounds).

Centering

It is important to define in words and pictures what is meant by certain frequently used hobby terms relating to grading cards. The adjacent pictures portray various stages of centering. Centering can range from well-centered to slightly off-centered to off-centered to badly off-centered to miscut.

Slightly Off-Centered: A slightly off-center card is one which upon close inspection is found to have one border bigger than the opposite border. This degree is only offensive to a purist.

Off-Centered: An off-center card has one border which is noticeably more than twice as wide as the opposite border.

Badly Off-Centered: A badly off-center card has virtually no border on one side of the card.

Miscut: A miscut card actually shows part of the adjacent card in its larger border and consequently a corresponding amount of its card is cut off.

Corner Wear

Degrees of corner wear generate several common terms used and useful to accurate grading. The wear on card corners can be expressed as fuzzy corners, corner wear or slightly rounded corners, rounded corners, badly rounded corners.

Fuzzy Corners: Fuzzy corners still come to a right angle (to a point) but the point has begun to fray slightly.

Corner Wear or Slightly Rounded Corners: The slight fraying of the corners has increased to where there is no longer a point to the corner. Nevertheless the corner is still reasonably sharp. There may be evidence of some slight loss of color in the corner also.

Rounded Corners: The corner is definitely no longer sharp but is not badly rounded.

Badly Rounded Corners: The corner is rounded to an objectionable degree. Excessive wear and rough handling are evident.

Creases

The third, and perhaps most frequent, common defect is the crease; the degree of creasing in a card is very difficult to show in a drawing or picture. On giving the specific condition of an expensive card for sale, the seller should note any creases additionally. Creases can be categorized as to severity according to the following scale.

Light Crease: A light crease is a crease which is barely noticeable on close inspection. In fact when cards are in plastic sheets or holders, a light crease may not be seen (until the card is taken out of the holder). A light crease on the front is much more serious than a light crease on the card back only.

Medium Crease: A medium crease is noticeable when held and studied at arm's length by the naked eye, but does not overly detract from the appearance of the card. It is an obvious crease, but not one that breaks the picture surface of the card.

Heavy Crease: A heavy crease is one which has torn or broken through the card's picture surface, e.g., puts a tear in the photo surface.

Alterations

Deceptive Trimming: Deceptive trimming occurs when someone alters the card in order (1) to shave off edge wear, (2) to improve the sharpness of the corners, or (3) to improve centering -- obviously their objective is to falsely increase the perceived value of the card to an unsuspecting buyer. The shrinkage is usually only evident if the trimmed card is compared to an adjacent full-sized card or if the trimmed card is itself measured.

Obvious Trimming: Obvious trimming is noticeable and unfortunate. It is usually performed by non-collectors who give no thought to the present or future value of their cards.

CENTERING

WELL-CENTERED

SLIGHTLY OFF-CENTERED

OFF-CENTERED

BADLY OFF-CENTERED

MISCUT

CORNER WEAR

The partial cards shown at the right have been photographed at 300%. This was done in order to magnify each card's corner wear to such a degree that differences could be shown on a printed page.

The 1962 Topps Mickey Mantle card definitely has a rounded corner. Some may say that this corner is badly rounded, but that is a judgment call.

The 1962 Topps Hank Aaron card has a slightly rounded corner. Note that there is definite corner wear evident by the fraying and that there is no longer a sharp point to which the corner converges.

The 1962 Topps Gil Hodges card has corner wear; it is slightly better than the Aaron card above. Nevertheless some collectors might classify this Hodges corner as slightly rounded.

The 1962 Topps Manager's Dream card showing Mantle and Mays has slight corner wear. This is not a fuzzy corner as very slight wear is noticeable on the card's photo surface.

The 1962 Topps Don Mossi card has very slight corner wear such that it might be called a fuzzy corner. A close look at the original card shows that the corner is not perfect, but almost. However, note that corner wear is somewhat academic on this card. As you can plainly see, the heavy crease going across his name breaks through the photo surface.

Deceptively Retouched Borders: This occurs when the borders (especially on those cards with dark borders) are touched up on the edges and corners with magic marker of appropriate color in order to make the card appear to be mint.

Categorization of Defects

A "Micro Defect" would be fuzzy corners, slight off-centering, printer's lines, printer's spots, slightly out of focus, or slight loss of original gloss. A NrMT card may have one micro defect. An Ex-MT card may have two or more micro defects.

A "Minor Defect" would be corner wear or slight rounding, off-centering, light crease on back, wax or gum stains on reverse, loss of original gloss, writing or tape marks on back, or rubber band marks. An Excellent card may have minor defects.

A "Major Defect" would be rounded corner(s), badly off-centering, crease(s), deceptive trimming, deceptively retouched borders, pin hole, staple hole, incidental writing or tape marks on front, warping, water stains, or sun fading. A VG card may have one major defect. A Good card may have two or more major defects.

A "Catastrophic Defect" is the worst kind of defect and would include such defects as badly rounded corner(s), miscutting, heavy crease(s), obvious trimming, punch hole, tack hole, tear(s), corner missing or clipped, destructive writing on front. A Fair card may have one catastrophic defect. A Poor card has two or more catastrophic defects.

Condition Guide

MINT (M OR MT) - A card with no defects. The card has sharp corners, even borders, original gloss or shine on the surface, sharp focus of the picture, smooth edges, no signs of wear, and white borders. A Mint card (that is, a card that is worth a "Mint" price) does NOT have printers' lines or other printing defects or other serious quality control problems that should have been discovered by the producing card company before distribution. Note also that there is no allowance made for the age of the card.

NEAR MINT (NrMT) - A card with a micro defect. Any of the following would be sufficient to lower the grade of a card from Mint to the Near Mint category: layering at some of the corners (fuzzy corners), a very small amount of the original gloss lost, very minor wear on the edges, slightly off-center borders, slight wear visible only on close inspection, slight off-whiteness of the borders.

EXCELLENT-MINT (EX-MT) - A card with micro defects, but no minor defects. Two or three of the following would be sufficient to lower the grade of a card from Mint to the Excellent-Mint category: layering at some of the corners (fuzzy corners), a very small amount of the original gloss lost, minor wear on the edges, slightly off-center borders, slight wear visible only on close inspection, slight off-whiteness of the borders.

EXCELLENT (EX OR E) - A card with minor defects. Any of the following would be sufficient to lower the grade of a card from Mint to the Excellent category: slight rounding at some of the corners, a small amount of the original gloss lost, minor wear on the edges, off-center borders, wear visible only on close inspection; off-whiteness of the borders.

VERY GOOD (VG) - A card that has been handled but not abused: Some rounding at all corners, slight layering or scuffing at one or two corners, slight notching on edges, gloss lost from the surface but not scuffed, borders might be somewhat uneven but some white is visible on all borders, noticeable yellowing or browning of borders, pictures may be slightly off focus.

GOOD (G) - A well-handled card, rounding and some layering at the corners, scuffing at the corners and minor scuffing on the face, borders noticeably uneven and browning, loss of gloss on the face, notching on the edges.

FAIR (F) - Round and layering corners, brown and dirty borders, frayed edges, noticeable scuffing on the face, white not visible on one or more borders, cloudy focus.

POOR (P) - An abused card: The lowest grade of card, frequently some major physical alteration has been performed on the card, collectible only as a filler until a better-condition replacement can be obtained.

Categories between these major condition grades are frequently used, such as Very Good to Excellent (VG-E), Fair to Good (F-G), etc. Such grades indicate a card with all qualities at least in the lower of the two categories, but with several qualities in the higher of the two categories. In the case of EX-MT, it essentially refers to a card which is halfway between Excellent and Mint.

Unopened "Mint" cards and factory-collated sets are considered Mint in their unknown (and presumed perfect) state. However, once opened or broken out, each of these cards is graded (and valued) in its own right by taking into account any quality control defects (such as off-centering, printer's lines, machine creases, or gum stains) that may be present in spite of the fact that the card has never been handled.

Cards before 1980 which are priced in the Price Guide in a top condition of NrMT, are obviously worth an additional premium when offered in strict Mint condition. This additional premium increases relative to the age and scarcity of the card. For example, Mint cards from the late '70s may bring only a 10% premium for Mint (above NrMT), whereas high demand (or condition rarity) cards from early vintage sets can be sold for as much as double (and occasionally even more) the NrMT price when offered in strict Mint condition.

Cards before 1946 which are priced in the Price Guide in a top condition of Ex-MT, are obviously worth an additional premium when offered in strict Near Mint or better condition. This additional premium increases relative to the age and scarcity of the card.

Selling Your Cards

Just about every collector sells cards or will sell cards eventually. Someday you may be interested in selling your duplicates or maybe even your whole collection. You may sell to other collectors, friends, or dealers. You may even sell cards you purchased from a certain dealer back to that same dealer. In any event, it helps to know some of the mechanics of the typical transaction between buyer and seller.

Dealers will buy cards in order to resell them to other collectors who are interested in the cards. Dealers will always pay a higher percentage for items which (in their opinion) can be resold quickly, and a much lower percentage for those items which are perceived as having low demand and hence are slow moving. In either case, dealers must buy at a price that allows for the expense of doing business and a fair margin for profit.

If you have cards for sale, the best advice we can give is that you get three offers for your cards and take the best offer, all things considered. Note, the "best" offer may not be the one for the highest amount. And remember, if a dealer really wants your cards, he won't let you get away without making his best competitive offer. Another alternative is to take your cards to a nearby convention and either auction them off in the show auction or offer them for sale to some of the dealers present.

Many people think nothing of going into a department store and paying $15 for an item of clothing for which the store paid $5. But, if you were selling your $15 card to a dealer and he offered you only $5 for it, you might think his mark-up unreasonable. To complete the analogy: most department stores (and card dealers) that pay $10 for $15 items eventually go out of business. An exception to this is when the dealer knows that a willing buyer for the merchandise you are attempting to sell is only a phone call away. Then an offer of 2/3 or maybe 70% of the book value will still allow him to make a reasonable profit due to the short time he will need to hold the merchandise. Nevertheless, most cards and collections will bring offers in the range of 25% to 50% of retail price. Material from the past five to ten years or so is very plentiful. Don't be surprised if your best offer is only 20% of the book value for these recent years.

Interesting Notes

The numerically first card of an issue is the single card most likely to obtain excessive wear. Consequently, you will typically find the price on the number one card (in Mint condition) somewhat higher than might otherwise be the case. Similarly, but to a lesser extent (because normally the less important, reverse side of the card is the one exposed), the numerically last card in an issue is also prone to abnormal wear. This extra wear and tear occurs because the first and last cards are exposed to the elements (human element included) more than any other cards. They are generally end cards in any brick formations, rubber bandings, stackings on wet surfaces, and like activities.

Sports cards have no intrinsic value. The value of a card, like the value of other collectibles, can only be determined by you and your enjoyment in viewing and possessing these cardboard swatches.

Remember, the buyer ultimately determines the price of each baseball card. You are the determining price factor because you have the ability to say "No" to the price of any card by not exchanging your hard-earned money for a given card. When the cost of a trading card exceeds the enjoyment you will receive from it, your answer should be "No." We assess and report the prices. You set them!

We are always interested in receiving the price input of collectors and dealers from around the country. We happily credit major contributors. We welcome your opinions, since your contributions assist us in ensuring a better guide each year. If you would like to join our survey list for the next editions of this book and others authored by Dr. Beckett, please send your name and address to Dr. James Beckett, 4887 Alpha Road, Suite 200, Dallas, Texas 75244.

Advertising

Within this price guide you will find advertisements for sports memorabilia material, mail order, and retail sports collectibles establishments. All advertisements were accepted in good faith based on the advertiser's reputation; however, neither the author, publisher, distributors, nor the other advertisers in the price guide accept any responsibility for any particular advertiser not complying with the terms of his or her ad.

Readers should also be aware that prices in advertisements are subject to change over the annual period before a new edition of this volume is issued each spring. When replying to an advertisement late in the baseball year, the reader should take this into account, and contact the dealer by phone or in writing for up-to-date price information. Should you come into contact with any of the advertisers in this guide as a result of their advertisement herein, please mention to them this source as your contact.

Additional Reading

With the increase in popularity of the hobby in recent years, there has been a corresponding increase in available literature. Below is a list of the books and periodicals which receive our highest recommendation and which we hope will further advance your knowledge and enjoyment of our great hobby.

The Sport Americana Price Guide to Baseball Collectibles by Dr. James Beckett (Second Edition, $12.95, released 1988, published by Edgewater Book Company) -- the complete guide/checklist with up to date values for box cards, coins, labels, Canadian cards, stamps, stickers, pins, etc.

The Sport Americana Football, Hockey, Basketball and Boxing Card Price Guide by Dr. James Beckett (Sixth Edition, $14.95, released 1989, published by Edgewater Book Company) -- the most comprehensive price guide/checklist ever issued on football and other non-baseball sports cards. No serious hobbyist should be without it.

The Official Price Guide to Football Cards by Dr. James Beckett (Ninth Edition, $5.95, released 1989, published by The House of Collectibles) -- an abridgement of the *Sport Americana Price Guide* listed above in a convenient and economical pocket-size format providing Dr. Beckett's pricing of the major football sets since 1948.

The Official Price Guide to Hockey and Basketball Cards by Dr. James Beckett (First Edition, $5.95, released 1989, published by The House of Collectibles) -- an abridgement of the *Sport Americana Price Guide* listed above in a convenient, economical size providing Dr. Beckett's pricing of major hockey and basketball sets since 1948.

The Sport Americana Baseball Memorabilia and Autograph Price Guide by Dr. James Beckett and Dennis W. Eckes (First Edition, $8.95, released 1982, co-published by Den's Collectors Den and Edgewater Book Company) -- the most complete book ever produced on baseball memorabilia other than baseball cards. This book presents in an illustrated, logical fashion information on baseball memorabilia and autographs which had been heretofore unavailable to the collector.

The Sport Americana Alphabetical Baseball Card Checklist by Dr. James Beckett (Fourth Edition, $12.95, released 1990, published by Edgewater Book Company) -- an alphabetical listing, by last names of players portrayed on cards, of virtually all baseball cards (Major and Minor Leagues) produced up through the 1990 major sets.

The Sport Americana Price Guide to the Non-Sports Cards by Christopher

Benjamin and Dennis W. Eckes (Third Edition (Part Two), $12.95, released 1988, published by Edgewater Book Company) -- the definitive guide to all popular non-sports American tobacco and bubble gum cards. In addition to cards, illustrations and prices for wrappers are also included. Part Two covers non-sports cards from 1961 through 1987.

The Sport Americana Baseball Address List by Jack Smalling and Dennis W. Eckes (Fifth Edition, $10.95, released 1988, published by Edgewater Book Company) -- the definitive guide for autograph hunters giving addresses and deceased information for virtually all major league baseball players past and present.

The Sport Americana Baseball Card Team Checklist by Jeff Fritsch and Dennis W. Eckes (Fifth Edition, $12.95, released 1990, published by Edgwater Book Company) -- includes all Topps, Bowman, Donruss, Fleer, Score, Play Ball, Goudey, and Upper Deck cards, with the players portrayed on the cards listed with the teams for whom they played. The book is invaluable to the collector who specializes in an individual team because it is the most complete baseball card team checklist available.

The Encyclopedia of Baseball Cards, Volume I: 19th Century Cards by Lew Lipset ($11.95, released 1983, published by the author) -- everything you ever wanted to know about 19th century cards.

The Encyclopedia of Baseball Cards, Volume II: Early Gum and Candy Cards by Lew Lipset ($10.95, released 1984, published by the author) -- everything you ever wanted to know about Early Candy and Gum cards.

The Encyclopedia of Baseball Cards, Volume III: 20th Century Tobacco Cards, 1909-1932 by Lew Lipset ($12.95, released 1986, published by the author) -- everything you ever wanted to know about old tobacco cards.

Beckett Baseball Card Monthly authored and edited by Dr. James Beckett -- contains the most extensive and accepted monthly price guide, feature articles, "who's hot and who's not" section, convention calendar, and numerous letters to and responses from the editor. Published 12 times annually, it is the hobby's largest paid circulation periodical. **Beckett Football Card Magazine** (eight times a year) and **Beckett Basketball Card Magazine** (six times a year) are both very similar to **Beckett Baseball Card Monthly** in style and content.

Errata

There are thousands of names, more than 100,000 prices, and untold other words in this book. There are going to be a few typographical errors, a few misspellings, and possibly, a number or two out of place. If you catch a blooper, drop me a note directly or in care of the publisher, and we will fix it up in the next year's edition.

Prices in this Guide

Prices found in this guide reflect current retail rates just prior to printing this book. They do not reflect FOR SALE prices by the author, the publisher, the distributors, the advertisers, or any card dealers associated with this guide. No one is obligated in any way to buy, sell, or trade his or her cards based on these prices. The price listings were compiled by the author from actual buy/sell transactions at sports conventions, buy/sell advertisements in the hobby papers, for sale prices from dealer catalogs and price lists, and discussions with leading hobbyists in the U.S. and Canada. Prices are in U.S. dollars.

1962 American Tract Society

I RECOMMEND JESUS CHRIST

As a teenage boy I chose athletics as my god. Although I didn't fall on my knees each day before a carved image of a baseball player, I might just as well have, because baseball occupied the very throne of my life.

Near the end of my junior year in high school, I removed baseball from the throne of my life and replaced it with the only person who is worthy of our worship and trust Jesus Christ, the Son of God and Saviour of the world. I accepted, by faith, what He accomplished when He died on the cross nearly 2,000 years ago. He paid the penalty for my sin and enabled me to be restored to that perfect relationship with God that had been broken by sin.

It is impossible for us to earn the right to once again reunited with God as His children. Rather, this right is offered to us as a gift if we believe in Jesus Christ and accept Him as the Saviour and Lord of our life. This is Christianity; not a religion, not a church, but a relationship with Jesus Christ that restores the shine, vitality, and meaning to life.

"As many as received him [Christ], to them gave he power to become the sons of God, even to them that believe on his name" (John 1:12).

St. Augustine said: "Thou hast made us for thyself O God, and restless are our hearts until they rest in thee."

May I recommend Jesus Christ to you?
— Jerry Kindall

American Tract Society — a non-profit organization Publishers of Christian Literature since 1825
Oradell, New Jersey   Tracard No. 51

These cards are quite attractive and feature the "pure card" concept that is always popular with collectors, i.e., no borders or anything else on the card front to detract from the color photo. The cards are numbered on the back and are actually part of a much larger set with a Christian theme. The set features Christian ballplayers giving first-person testimonies on the card backs telling how Jesus Christ has changed their lives. These cards are sometimes referred to as "Tracards." The cards measure approximately 2 3/4" by 3 1/2". The set price below refers to only one of each player, not including any variations.

	NRMT	VG-E	GOOD
COMPLETE SET (4)	16.00	8.00	1.60
COMMON PLAYER	4.00	2.00	.40
☐ 43A Bobby Richardson (black print on back)	8.00	4.00	.80
☐ 43B Bobby Richardson (blue print on back)	8.00	4.00	.80
☐ 43C Bobby Richardson (black print on back with Play Ball in red)	8.00	4.00	.80
☐ 43D Bobby Richardson (black print on back with exclamation point after Play Ball)	8.00	4.00	.80
☐ 51A Jerry Kindall (portrait from chest up, black print on back)	4.00	2.00	.40
☐ 51B Jerry Kindall (on one knee with bat, blue print on back)	4.00	2.00	.40
☐ 52A Felipe Alou (on one knee looking up, black print on back)	5.00	2.50	.50
☐ 52B Felipe Alou (on one knee looking up, blue print on back)	5.00	2.50	.50
☐ 52C Felipe Alou (batting pose)	5.00	2.50	.50
☐ 66 Al Worthington (black print on back)	4.00	2.00	.40

1948 Babe Ruth Story

The 1948 Babe Ruth Story set of 28 black and white numbered cards (measuring 2" by 2 1/2") was issued by the Philadelphia Chewing Gum Company to commemorate the 1949 movie of the same name starring William Bendix, Claire Trevor, and Charles Bickford. Babe Ruth himself appears on several cards. The last 12 cards (17 to 28) are more difficult to obtain than other cards in the set and are also more desirable in that most picture actual players as well as actors from the movie. Supposedly these last

12 cards were issued much later after the first 16 cards had already been released and distributed. The ACC designation for this set is R421.

	NRMT	VG-E	GOOD
COMPLETE SET	1050.00	500.00	125.00
COMMON PLAYER (1-16)	12.50	6.25	1.25
COMMON PLAYER (17-28)	40.00	20.00	4.00
☐ 1 The Babe Ruth Story In the Making (Babe Ruth shown with William Bendix)	100.00	15.00	3.00
☐ 2 Bat Boy Becomes the Babe	12.50	6.25	1.25
☐ 3 Claire Hodgson played by Claire Trevor	12.50	6.25	1.25
☐ 4 Babe Ruth played by William Bendix; Claire Hodgson played by Claire Trevor	12.50	6.25	1.25
☐ 5 Brother Matthias played by Charles Bickford	12.50	6.25	1.25
☐ 6 Phil Conrad played by Sam Levene	12.50	6.25	1.25
☐ 7 Night Club Singer played by Gertrude Niesen	12.50	6.25	1.25
☐ 8 Baseball's Famous Deal	12.50	6.25	1.25
☐ 9 Babe Ruth played by William Bendix; Mrs.Babe Ruth played by Claire Trevor	12.50	6.25	1.25
☐ 10 Actors for Babe Ruth, Mrs. Babe Ruth, and Brother Matthias	12.50	6.25	1.25
☐ 11 Babe Ruth played by William Bendix; Miller Huggins played by Fred Lightner	12.50	6.25	1.25
☐ 12 Babe Ruth played by William Bendix; Johnny Sylvester played by George Marshall	12.50	6.25	1.25
☐ 13 Actors for Mr., Mrs. and Johnny Sylvester	12.50	6.25	1.25
☐ 14 When A Feller Needs A Friend	12.50	6.25	1.25
☐ 15 Dramatic Home Run	12.50	6.25	1.25
☐ 16 The Homer That Set the Record	12.50	6.25	1.25
☐ 17 The Slap That Started Baseball's Most Famous Career	40.00	20.00	4.00
☐ 18 The Babe Plays Santa Claus	40.00	20.00	4.00
☐ 19 Actors for Ed Barrow, Jacob Ruppert, and Miller Huggins	40.00	20.00	4.00
☐ 20 Broken Window Paid Off	40.00	20.00	4.00
☐ 21 Regardless of the Generation/ Babe Ruth	40.00	20.00	4.00
☐ 22 Charley Grimm and William Bendix	40.00	20.00	4.00
☐ 23 Ted Lyons and William Bendix	50.00	25.00	5.00
☐ 24 Lefty Gomez, William Bendix, and Bucky Harris	60.00	30.00	6.00
☐ 25 Babe Ruth and William Bendix	125.00	60.00	12.50
☐ 26 Babe Ruth and William Bendix	125.00	60.00	12.50
☐ 27 Babe Ruth and Claire Trevor	125.00	60.00	12.50

☐ 28 William Bendix, Babe 125.00   60.00   12.50
        Ruth, Claire Trevor

1934-36 Batter-Up

The 1934-36 Batter-Up set issued by National Chicle contains 192 blank-backed die-cut cards. Numbers 1 to 80 are 2 3/8" by 3 1/4" in size while 81 to 192 are 2 3/8" by 3". The latter are more difficult to find than the former. The pictures come in basic black and white or in tints of blue, brown, green, purple, red, or sepia. There are three combination cards (each featuring two players per card) in the high series (98, 111, and 115). The ACC designation for the set is R318. Cards with backs removed are graded fair at best.

		EX-MT	VG-E	GOOD
COMPLETE SET (192)		18000.00	9000.00	2000.00
COMMON PLAYER (1-80)		40.00	20.00	4.00
COMMON PLAYER (81-192)		80.00	40.00	8.00

		EX-MT	VG-E	GOOD
☐	1 Wally Berger	75.00	25.00	5.00
☐	2 Ed Brandt	40.00	20.00	4.00
☐	3 Al Lopez	100.00	50.00	10.00
☐	4 Dick Bartell	40.00	20.00	4.00
☐	5 Carl Hubbell	150.00	75.00	15.00
☐	6 Bill Terry	150.00	75.00	15.00
☐	7 Pepper Martin	60.00	30.00	6.00
☐	8 Jim Bottomley	100.00	50.00	10.00
☐	9 Tom Bridges	50.00	25.00	5.00
☐	10 Rick Ferrell	100.00	50.00	10.00
☐	11 Ray Benge	40.00	20.00	4.00
☐	12 Wes Ferrell	50.00	25.00	5.00
☐	13 Chalmer Cissell	40.00	20.00	4.00
☐	14 Pie Traynor	150.00	75.00	15.00
☐	15 Leroy Mahaffey	40.00	20.00	4.00
☐	16 Chick Hafey	100.00	50.00	10.00
☐	17 Lloyd Waner	100.00	50.00	10.00
☐	18 Jack Burns	40.00	20.00	4.00
☐	19 Buddy Myer	40.00	20.00	4.00
☐	20 Bob Johnson	50.00	25.00	5.00
☐	21 Arky Vaughan	100.00	50.00	10.00
☐	22 Red Rolfe	50.00	25.00	5.00
☐	23 Lefty Gomez	150.00	75.00	15.00
☐	24 Earl Averill	100.00	50.00	10.00
☐	25 Mickey Cochrane	150.00	75.00	15.00
☐	26 Van Lingle Mungo	50.00	25.00	5.00
☐	27 Mel Ott	150.00	75.00	15.00
☐	28 Jimmy Foxx	175.00	85.00	18.00
☐	29 Jimmy Dykes	50.00	25.00	5.00
☐	30 Bill Dickey	175.00	85.00	18.00
☐	31 Lefty Grove	175.00	85.00	18.00
☐	32 Joe Cronin	150.00	75.00	15.00
☐	33 Frank Frisch	150.00	75.00	15.00
☐	34 Al Simmons	125.00	60.00	12.50
☐	35 Rogers Hornsby	175.00	85.00	18.00
☐	36 Ted Lyons	100.00	50.00	10.00
☐	37 Rabbit Maranville	100.00	50.00	10.00
☐	38 Jimmy Wilson	40.00	20.00	4.00
☐	39 Willie Kamm	40.00	20.00	4.00
☐	40 Bill Hallahan	40.00	20.00	4.00
☐	41 Gus Suhr	40.00	20.00	4.00
☐	42 Charlie Gehringer	125.00	60.00	12.50

		EX-MT	VG-E	GOOD
☐	43 Joe Heving	40.00	20.00	4.00
☐	44 Adam Comorosky	40.00	20.00	4.00
☐	45 Tony Lazzeri	75.00	37.50	7.50
☐	46 Sam Leslie	40.00	20.00	4.00
☐	47 Bob Smith	40.00	20.00	4.00
☐	48 Willis Hudlin	40.00	20.00	4.00
☐	49 Carl Reynolds	40.00	20.00	4.00
☐	50 Fred Schulte	40.00	20.00	4.00
☐	51 Cookie Lavagetto	50.00	25.00	5.00
☐	52 Hal Schumacher	40.00	20.00	4.00
☐	53 Roger Cramer	50.00	25.00	5.00
☐	54 Sylvester Johnson	40.00	20.00	4.00
☐	55 Ollie Bejma	40.00	20.00	4.00
☐	56 Sam Byrd	40.00	20.00	4.00
☐	57 Hank Greenberg	175.00	85.00	18.00
☐	58 Bill Knickerbocker	40.00	20.00	4.00
☐	59 Bill Urbanski	40.00	20.00	4.00
☐	60 Eddie Morgan	40.00	20.00	4.00
☐	61 Rabbit McNair	40.00	20.00	4.00
☐	62 Ben Chapman	50.00	25.00	5.00
☐	63 Roy Johnson	40.00	20.00	4.00
☐	64 Dizzy Dean	300.00	150.00	30.00
☐	65 Zeke Bonura	40.00	20.00	4.00
☐	66 Fred Marberry	40.00	20.00	4.00
☐	67 Gus Mancuso	40.00	20.00	4.00
☐	68 Joe Vosmik	40.00	20.00	4.00
☐	69 Earl Grace	40.00	20.00	4.00
☐	70 Tony Piet	40.00	20.00	4.00
☐	71 Rollie Hemsley	40.00	20.00	4.00
☐	72 Fred Fitzsimmons	40.00	20.00	4.00
☐	73 Hack Wilson	150.00	75.00	15.00
☐	74 Chick Fullis	40.00	20.00	4.00
☐	75 Fred Frankhouse	40.00	20.00	4.00
☐	76 Ethan Allen	40.00	20.00	4.00
☐	77 Heine Manush	100.00	50.00	10.00
☐	78 Rip Collins	40.00	20.00	4.00
☐	79 Tony Cuccinello	40.00	20.00	4.00
☐	80 Joe Kuhel	40.00	20.00	4.00
☐	81 Tom Bridges	90.00	45.00	9.00
☐	82 Clint Brown	80.00	40.00	8.00
☐	83 Albert Blanche	80.00	40.00	8.00
☐	84 Boze Berger	80.00	40.00	8.00
☐	85 Goose Goslin	175.00	85.00	18.00
☐	86 Lefty Gomez	250.00	125.00	25.00
☐	87 Joe Glenn	80.00	40.00	8.00
☐	88 Cy Blanton	80.00	40.00	8.00
☐	89 Tom Carey	80.00	40.00	8.00
☐	90 Ralph Birkofer	80.00	40.00	8.00
☐	91 Fred Gabler	80.00	40.00	8.00
☐	92 Dick Coffman	80.00	40.00	8.00
☐	93 Ollie Bejma	80.00	40.00	8.00
☐	94 Leroy Parmelee	80.00	40.00	8.00
☐	95 Carl Reynolds	80.00	40.00	8.00
☐	96 Ben Cantwell	80.00	40.00	8.00
☐	97 Curtis Davis	80.00	40.00	8.00
☐	98 Webb and Wally Moses	100.00	50.00	10.00
☐	99 Ray Benge	80.00	40.00	8.00
☐100	Pie Traynor	200.00	100.00	20.00
☐101	Phil Cavarretta	90.00	45.00	9.00
☐102	Pep Young	80.00	40.00	8.00
☐103	Willis Hudlin	80.00	40.00	8.00
☐104	Mickey Haslin	80.00	40.00	8.00
☐105	Oswald Bluege	80.00	40.00	8.00
☐106	Paul Andrews	80.00	40.00	8.00
☐107	Ed Brandt	80.00	40.00	8.00
☐108	Don Taylor	80.00	40.00	8.00
☐109	Thornton Lee	80.00	40.00	8.00
☐110	Hal Schumacher	80.00	40.00	8.00
☐111	Hayes and Ted Lyons	150.00	75.00	15.00
☐112	Odell Hale	80.00	40.00	8.00
☐113	Earl Averill	175.00	85.00	18.00
☐114	Italo Chelini	80.00	40.00	8.00
☐115	Andrews and	150.00	75.00	15.00
	Jim Bottomley			
☐116	Bill Walker	80.00	40.00	8.00
☐117	Bill Dickey	300.00	150.00	30.00
☐118	Gerald Walker	80.00	40.00	8.00
☐119	Ted Lyons	175.00	85.00	18.00
☐120	Eldon Auker	80.00	40.00	8.00
☐121	Bill Hallahan	80.00	40.00	8.00
☐122	Fred Lindstrom	175.00	85.00	18.00
☐123	Oral Hildebrand	80.00	40.00	8.00
☐124	Luke Appling	175.00	85.00	18.00
☐125	Pepper Martin	100.00	50.00	10.00
☐126	Rick Ferrell	175.00	85.00	18.00
☐127	Ival Goodman	80.00	40.00	8.00
☐128	Joe Kuhel	80.00	40.00	8.00
☐129	Ernie Lombardi	175.00	85.00	18.00
☐130	Charlie Gehringer	250.00	125.00	25.00
☐131	Van Lingle Mungo	90.00	45.00	9.00
☐132	Larry French	80.00	40.00	8.00
☐133	Buddy Myer	80.00	40.00	8.00
☐134	Mel Harder	100.00	50.00	10.00
☐135	Augie Galan	80.00	40.00	8.00
☐136	Gabby Hartnett	175.00	85.00	18.00

☐ 137	Stan Hack	90.00	45.00	9.00
☐ 138	Billy Herman	175.00	85.00	18.00
☐ 139	Bill Jurges	80.00	40.00	8.00
☐ 140	Bill Lee	80.00	40.00	8.00
☐ 141	Zeke Bonura	80.00	40.00	8.00
☐ 142	Tony Piet	80.00	40.00	8.00
☐ 143	Paul Dean	100.00	50.00	10.00
☐ 144	Jimmy Foxx	350.00	175.00	35.00
☐ 145	Joe Medwick	200.00	100.00	20.00
☐ 146	Rip Collins	80.00	40.00	8.00
☐ 147	Mel Almada	80.00	40.00	8.00
☐ 148	Allan Cooke	80.00	40.00	8.00
☐ 149	Moe Berg	125.00	60.00	12.50
☐ 150	Dolph Camilli	80.00	40.00	8.00
☐ 151	Oscar Melillo	80.00	40.00	8.00
☐ 152	Bruce Campbell	80.00	40.00	8.00
☐ 153	Lefty Grove	300.00	150.00	30.00
☐ 154	Johnny Murphy	90.00	45.00	9.00
☐ 155	Luke Sewell	90.00	45.00	9.00
☐ 156	Leo Durocher	200.00	100.00	20.00
☐ 157	Lloyd Waner	175.00	85.00	18.00
☐ 158	Gus Bush	80.00	40.00	8.00
☐ 159	Jimmy Dykes	90.00	45.00	9.00
☐ 160	Steve O'Neill	80.00	40.00	8.00
☐ 161	General Crowder	80.00	40.00	8.00
☐ 162	Joe Cascarella	80.00	40.00	8.00
☐ 163	Daniel (Bud) Hafey	80.00	40.00	8.00
☐ 164	Gilly Campbell	80.00	40.00	8.00
☐ 165	Ray Hayworth	80.00	40.00	8.00
☐ 166	Frank Demaree	80.00	40.00	8.00
☐ 167	John Babich	80.00	40.00	8.00
☐ 168	Marvin Owen	80.00	40.00	8.00
☐ 169	Ralph Kress	80.00	40.00	8.00
☐ 170	Mule Haas	80.00	40.00	8.00
☐ 171	Frank Higgins	80.00	40.00	8.00
☐ 172	Wally Berger	90.00	45.00	9.00
☐ 173	Frank Frisch	200.00	100.00	20.00
☐ 174	Wes Ferrell	90.00	45.00	9.00
☐ 175	Pete Fox	80.00	40.00	8.00
☐ 176	John Vergez	80.00	40.00	8.00
☐ 177	Billy Rogell	80.00	40.00	8.00
☐ 178	Don Brennan	80.00	40.00	8.00
☐ 179	Jim Bottomley	175.00	85.00	18.00
☐ 180	Travis Jackson	175.00	85.00	18.00
☐ 181	Red Rolfe	100.00	50.00	10.00
☐ 182	Frank Crosetti	125.00	60.00	12.50
☐ 183	Joe Cronin	175.00	85.00	18.00
☐ 184	Schoolboy Rowe	100.00	50.00	10.00
☐ 185	Chuck Klein	200.00	100.00	20.00
☐ 186	Lon Warneke	80.00	40.00	8.00
☐ 187	Gus Suhr	80.00	40.00	8.00
☐ 188	Ben Chapman	90.00	45.00	9.00
☐ 189	Clint Brown	80.00	40.00	8.00
☐ 190	Paul Derringer	100.00	50.00	10.00
☐ 191	John Burns	80.00	40.00	8.00
☐ 192	John Broaca	125.00	50.00	10.00

1988 Bazooka

There are 22 cards in the set; cards are standard size, 2 1/2" by 3 1/2". The cards have extra thick white borders. Card backs are printed in blue and red on white card stock. Cards are numbered on the back; they were numbered by Topps alphabetically. The word "Bazooka" only appears faintly as background for the statistics on the back of the card. Cards were available inside specially marked boxes of Bazooka gum retailing for from 59 cents to 99

cents. The emphasis in the player selection for this set is on the emerging young stars of baseball.

		MINT	EXC	G-VG
COMPLETE SET (22)		10.00	5.00	1.00
COMMON PLAYER (1-22)		.30	.15	.03
☐ 1	George Bell	.40	.20	.04
☐ 2	Wade Boggs	.90	.45	.09
☐ 3	Jose Canseco	1.50	.75	.15
☐ 4	Roger Clemens	.75	.35	.07
☐ 5	Vince Coleman	.50	.25	.05
☐ 6	Eric Davis	.90	.45	.09
☐ 7	Tony Fernandez	.30	.15	.03
☐ 8	Dwight Gooden	.75	.35	.07
☐ 9	Tony Gwynn	.60	.30	.06
☐ 10	Wally Joyner	.50	.25	.05
☐ 11	Don Mattingly	1.50	.75	.15
☐ 12	Willie McGee	.30	.15	.03
☐ 13	Mark McGwire	1.00	.50	.10
☐ 14	Kirby Puckett	.90	.45	.09
☐ 15	Tim Raines	.40	.20	.04
☐ 16	Dave Righetti	.30	.15	.03
☐ 17	Cal Ripken	.50	.25	.05
☐ 18	Juan Samuel	.30	.15	.03
☐ 19	Ryne Sandberg	.50	.25	.05
☐ 20	Benny Santiago	.40	.20	.04
☐ 21	Darryl Strawberry	1.00	.50	.10
☐ 22	Todd Worrell	.30	.15	.03

1989 Bazooka Shining Stars

The 1989 Bazooka Shining Stars set contains 22 standard-size (2 1/2 by 3 1/2 inch) cards. The fronts have white borders and a large yellow stripe; the vertically-oriented backs are pink, red and white and have career stats. The cards were inserted one per box of Bazooka Gum.

		MINT	EXC	G-VG
COMPLETE SET (22)		10.00	5.00	1.00
COMMON PLAYER (1-22)		.30	.15	.03
☐ 1	Tim Belcher	.40	.20	.04
☐ 2	Damon Berryhill	.40	.20	.04
☐ 3	Wade Boggs	.90	.45	.09
☐ 4	Jay Buhner	.30	.15	.03
☐ 5	Jose Canseco	1.50	.75	.15
☐ 6	Vince Coleman	.40	.20	.04
☐ 7	Cecil Espy	.30	.15	.03
☐ 8	Dave Gallagher	.30	.15	.03
☐ 9	Ron Gant	.40	.20	.04
☐ 10	Kirk Gibson	.40	.20	.04
☐ 11	Paul Gibson	.30	.15	.03
☐ 12	Mark Grace	1.50	.75	.15
☐ 13	Tony Gwynn	.60	.30	.06
☐ 14	Rickey Henderson	.75	.35	.07
☐ 15	Orel Hershiser	.60	.30	.06
☐ 16	Gregg Jefferies	.75	.35	.07
☐ 17	Ricky Jordan	.75	.35	.07
☐ 18	Chris Sabo	.50	.25	.05
☐ 19	Gary Sheffield	.60	.30	.06
☐ 20	Darryl Strawberry	1.00	.50	.10
☐ 21	Frank Viola	.40	.20	.04
☐ 22	Walt Weiss	.40	.20	.04

1958 Bell Brand

The 1958 Bell Brand Potato Chips set of 10 unnumbered cards features members of the Los Angeles Dodgers exclusively. Each card has a 1/4" dark green border, and the Gino Cimoli, Johnny Podres, and Duke Snider cards are more difficult to find; they are marked with an SP (short printed) in the checklist below. The cards measure 3" by 4". This set marks the first year for the Dodgers in Los Angeles and includes a Campanella card despite the fact that he never played for the team in California. The ACC designation is F339-1.

		NRMT	VG-E	GOOD
COMPLETE SET (10)		1100.00	550.00	125.00
COMMON PLAYER (1-10)		40.00	20.00	4.00
☐ 1	Roy Campanella	125.00	60.00	12.50
☐ 2	Gino Cimoli SP	150.00	75.00	15.00
☐ 3	Don Drysdale	90.00	45.00	9.00
☐ 4	Jim Gilliam	40.00	20.00	4.00
☐ 5	Gil Hodges	75.00	37.50	7.50
☐ 6	Sandy Koufax	125.00	60.00	12.50
☐ 7	Johnny Podres SP	150.00	75.00	15.00
☐ 8	Pee Wee Reese	90.00	45.00	9.00
☐ 9	Duke Snider SP	250.00	125.00	25.00
☐ 10	Don Zimmer	40.00	20.00	4.00

1960 Bell Brand

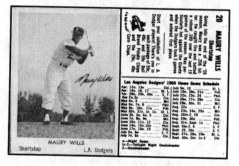

Shortstop   L.A. Dodgers

The 1960 Bell Brand Potato Chips set of 20 full color, numbered cards features Los Angeles Dodgers only. Because these cards, measuring 2 1/2" by 3 1/2", were issued in packages of potato chips, many cards suffered from stains. Clem Labine, Johnny Klippstein, and Walter Alston are somewhat more difficult to obtain than other cards in the set; they are marked with SP (short printed) in the checklist below. The ACC designation for this set is F339- 2.

		NRMT	VG-E	GOOD
COMPLETE SET (20)		750.00	350.00	90.00
COMMON PLAYER (1-20)		16.00	8.00	1.60
☐ 1	Norm Larker	16.00	8.00	1.60
☐ 2	Duke Snider	60.00	30.00	6.00
☐ 3	Danny McDevitt	16.00	8.00	1.60
☐ 4	Jim Gilliam	20.00	10.00	2.00
☐ 5	Rip Repulski	16.00	8.00	1.60
☐ 6	Clem Labine SP	100.00	50.00	10.00
☐ 7	John Roseboro	16.00	8.00	1.60
☐ 8	Carl Furillo	25.00	12.50	2.50
☐ 9	Sandy Koufax	90.00	45.00	9.00
☐ 10	Joe Pignatano	16.00	8.00	1.60
☐ 11	Chuck Essegian	16.00	8.00	1.60
☐ 12	John Klippstein SP	100.00	50.00	10.00
☐ 13	Ed Roebuck	16.00	8.00	1.60
☐ 14	Don Demeter	16.00	8.00	1.60
☐ 15	Roger Craig	25.00	12.50	2.50
☐ 16	Stan Williams	16.00	8.00	1.60

☐ 17	Don Zimmer	20.00	10.00	2.00
☐ 18	Walt Alston SP	150.00	75.00	15.00
☐ 19	Johnny Podres	25.00	12.50	2.50
☐ 20	Maury Wills	35.00	17.50	3.50

1961 Bell Brand

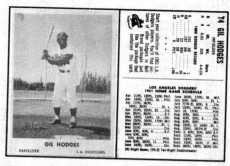

INFIELDER   L.A. DODGERS

The 1961 Bell Brand Potato Chips set of 20 full color cards features Los Angeles Dodger players only and is numbered by the uniform numbers of the players. The cards are slightly smaller (2 7/16" by 3 1/2") than the 1960 Bell Brand cards and are on thinner paper stock. The ACC designation is F339-3.

		NRMT	VG-E	GOOD
COMPLETE SET (20)		375.00	175.00	40.00
COMMON PLAYER (1-51)		12.00	6.00	1.20
☐ 3	Willie Davis	15.00	7.50	1.50
☐ 4	Duke Snider	45.00	22.50	4.50
☐ 5	Norm Larker	12.00	6.00	1.20
☐ 8	John Roseboro	12.00	6.00	1.20
☐ 9	Wally Moon	12.00	6.00	1.20
☐ 11	Bob Lillis	12.00	6.00	1.20
☐ 12	Tom Davis	15.00	7.50	1.50
☐ 14	Gil Hodges	25.00	12.50	2.50
☐ 16	Don Demeter	12.00	6.00	1.20
☐ 19	Jim Gilliam	12.00	6.00	1.20
☐ 22	John Podres	15.00	7.50	1.50
☐ 24	Walt Alston MG	25.00	12.50	2.50
☐ 30	Maury Wills	25.00	12.50	2.50
☐ 32	Sandy Koufax	75.00	37.50	7.50
☐ 34	Norm Sherry	12.00	6.00	1.20
☐ 37	Ed Roebuck	12.00	6.00	1.20
☐ 38	Roger Craig	18.00	9.00	1.80
☐ 40	Stan Williams	12.00	6.00	1.20
☐ 43	Charlie Neal	12.00	6.00	1.20
☐ 51	Larry Sherry	12.00	6.00	1.20

1962 Bell Brand

PITCHER   L.A. DODGERS

The 1962 Bell Brand Potato Chips set of 20 full color cards features Los Angeles Dodger players only and is numbered by the uniform numbers of the players.

These cards were printed on a high quality glossy paper, much better than the previous two years, virtually eliminating the grease stains. This set is distinguished by a 1962 Home schedule on the backs of the cards. The cards measure 2 7/16" by 3 1/2", the same size as the year before. The ACC designation is F339-4.

	NRMT	VG-E	GOOD
COMPLETE SET (20)	375.00	175.00	40.00
COMMON PLAYER (1-56)	12.00	6.00	1.20

		NRMT	VG-E	GOOD
☐ 3	Willie Davis	15.00	7.50	1.50
☐ 4	Duke Snider	45.00	22.50	4.50
☐ 6	Ron Fairly	12.00	6.00	1.20
☐ 8	John Roseboro	12.00	6.00	1.20
☐ 9	Wally Moon	12.00	6.00	1.20
☐ 12	Tom Davis	15.00	7.50	1.50
☐ 16	Ron Perranoski	12.00	6.00	1.20
☐ 19	Jim Gilliam	15.00	7.50	1.50
☐ 20	Daryl Spencer	12.00	6.00	1.20
☐ 22	John Podres	15.00	7.50	1.50
☐ 24	Walt Alston MG	25.00	12.50	2.50
☐ 25	Frank Howard	15.00	7.50	1.50
☐ 30	Maury Wills	25.00	12.50	2.50
☐ 32	Sandy Koufax	75.00	37.50	7.50
☐ 34	Norm Sherry	12.00	6.00	1.20
☐ 37	Ed Roebuck	12.00	6.00	1.20
☐ 40	Stan Williams	12.00	6.00	1.20
☐ 51	Larry Sherry	12.00	6.00	1.20
☐ 53	Don Drysdale	30.00	15.00	3.00
☐ 56	Lee Walls	12.00	6.00	1.20

1951 Berk Ross

The 1951 Berk Ross set consists of 72 cards (each measuring 2 1/16" by 2 1/2") with tinted photographs, divided evenly into four series (designated in the checklist as A, B, C and D). The cards were marketed in boxes containing two card panels, without gum, and the set includes stars of other sports as well as baseball players. Intact panels are worth 20% more than the sum of the individual cards. The ACC designation is W532-1. In every series the first ten cards are baseball players; the set has a heavy emphasis on Yankees and Phillies players as they were in the World Series the year before.

		NRMT	VG-E	GOOD
COMPLETE SET (72)		600.00	300.00	60.00
COMMON BASEBALL		6.00	3.00	.60
COMMON FOOTBALL		6.00	3.00	.60
COMMON OTHERS		4.00	2.00	.40
☐ A1	Al Rosen	9.00	4.50	.90
☐ A2	Bob Lemon	13.50	6.50	1.50
☐ A3	Phil Rizzuto	16.00	8.00	1.60
☐ A4	Hank Bauer	9.00	4.50	.90
☐ A5	Billy Johnson	6.00	3.00	.60
☐ A6	Jerry Coleman	6.00	3.00	.60
☐ A7	Johnny Mize	16.00	8.00	1.60
☐ A8	Dom DiMaggio	9.00	4.50	.90
☐ A9	Richie Ashburn	12.50	6.25	1.25
☐ A10	Del Ennis	6.00	3.00	.60
☐ A11	Bob Cousy	9.00	4.50	.90
☐ A12	Dick Schnittker	4.00	2.00	.40

		NRMT	VG-E	GOOD
☐ A13	Ezzard Charles	4.00	2.00	.40
☐ A14	Leon Hart	6.00	3.00	.60
☐ A15	James Martin	6.00	3.00	.60
☐ A16	Ben Hogan	6.00	3.00	.60
☐ A17	Bill Durnan	6.00	3.00	.60
☐ A18	Bill Quackenbush	4.00	2.00	.40
☐ B1	Stan Musial	65.00	32.50	6.50
☐ B2	Warren Spahn	20.00	10.00	2.00
☐ B3	Tom Henrich	9.00	4.50	.90
☐ B4	Yogi Berra	40.00	20.00	4.00
☐ B5	Joe DiMaggio	100.00	50.00	10.00
☐ B6	Bobby Brown	9.00	4.50	.90
☐ B7	Granny Hamner	6.00	3.00	.60
☐ B8	Willie Jones	6.00	3.00	.60
☐ B9	Stan Lopata	6.00	3.00	.60
☐ B10	Mike Goliat	6.00	3.00	.60
☐ B11	Sherman White	6.00	3.00	.60
☐ B12	Joe Maxim	4.00	2.00	.40
☐ B13	Ray Robinson	7.50	3.75	.75
☐ B14	Doak Walker	9.00	4.50	.90
☐ B15	Emil Sitko	4.00	2.00	.40
☐ B16	Jack Stewart	4.00	2.00	.40
☐ B17	Dick Button	8.00	3.00	.60
☐ B18	Melvin Patton	4.00	2.00	.40
☐ C1	Ralph Kiner	16.00	8.00	1.60
☐ C2	Bill Goodman	6.00	3.00	.60
☐ C3	Allie Reynolds	9.00	4.50	.90
☐ C4	Vic Raschi	7.50	3.75	.75
☐ C5	Joe Page	7.50	3.75	.75
☐ C6	Eddie Lopat	9.00	4.50	.90
☐ C7	Andy Seminick	6.00	3.00	.60
☐ C8	Dick Sisler	6.00	3.00	.60
☐ C9	Eddie Waitkus	6.00	3.00	.60
☐ C10	Ken Heintzelman	6.00	3.00	.60
☐ C11	Paul Unruh	4.00	2.00	.40
☐ C12	Jake LaMotta	7.50	3.75	.75
☐ C13	Ike Williams	4.00	2.00	.40
☐ C14	Wade Walker	4.00	2.00	.40
☐ C15	Rodney Franz	4.00	2.00	.40
☐ C16	Sid Abel	6.00	3.00	.60
☐ C17	Claire Sherman	4.00	2.00	.40
☐ C18	Jesse Owens	6.00	3.00	.60
☐ D1	Gene Woodling	7.50	3.75	.75
☐ D2	Cliff Mapes	6.00	3.00	.60
☐ D3	Fred Sanford	6.00	3.00	.60
☐ D4	Tommy Byrne	6.00	3.00	.60
☐ D5	Whitey Ford	20.00	10.00	2.00
☐ D6	Jim Konstanty	6.00	3.00	.60
☐ D7	Russ Meyer	6.00	3.00	.60
☐ D8	Robin Roberts	16.00	8.00	1.60
☐ D9	Curt Simmons	7.50	3.75	.75
☐ D10	Sam Jethroe	6.00	3.00	.60
☐ D11	Bill Sharman	6.00	3.00	.60
☐ D12	Sandy Saddler	4.00	2.00	.40
☐ D13	Margaret DuPont	4.00	2.00	.40
☐ D14	Arnold Galiffa	6.00	3.00	.60
☐ D15	Charlie Justice	7.50	3.75	.75
☐ D16	Glen Cunningham	4.00	2.00	.40
☐ D17	Gregory Rice	4.00	2.00	.40
☐ D18	Harrison Dillard	4.00	2.00	.40

1952 Berk Ross

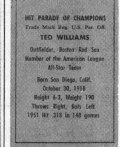

The 1952 Berk Ross set of 72 unnumbered, tinted photocards, each measuring 2" by 3", seems to have been patterned after the highly successful 1951 Bowman set. The reverses of Ewell Blackwell and Nellie Fox are transposed while Phil Rizzuto comes with two different poses. There is a card of Joe DiMaggio even though he retired after the 1951 season. The ACC designation for this set is W532-2, and the cards have been assigned numbers in the alphabetical checklist below.

			NRMT	VG-E	GOOD
	COMPLETE SET (72)		3750.00	1750.00	425.00
	COMMON PLAYER (1-71)		10.00	5.00	1.00
☐	1	Richie Ashburn	30.00	15.00	3.00
☐	2	Hank Bauer	15.00	7.50	1.50
☐	3	Yogi Berra	125.00	60.00	12.50
☐	4	Ewell Blackwell	20.00	10.00	2.00
		(photo actually Nellie Fox)			
☐	5	Bobby Brown	15.00	7.50	1.50
☐	6	Jim Busby	10.00	5.00	1.00
☐	7	Roy Campanella	125.00	60.00	12.50
☐	8	Chico Carrasquel	10.00	5.00	1.00
☐	9	Jerry Coleman	10.00	5.00	1.00
☐	10	Joe Collins	10.00	5.00	1.00
☐	11	Alvin Dark	15.00	7.50	1.50
☐	12	Dom DiMaggio	15.00	7.50	1.50
☐	13	Joe DiMaggio	650.00	325.00	65.00
☐	14	Larry Doby	20.00	10.00	2.00
☐	15	Bobby Doerr	45.00	22.50	4.50
☐	16	Bob Elliott	10.00	5.00	1.00
☐	17	Del Ennis	10.00	5.00	1.00
☐	18	Ferris Fain	10.00	5.00	1.00
☐	19	Bob Feller	80.00	40.00	8.00
☐	20	Nellie Fox	20.00	10.00	2.00
		(photo actually Ewell Blackwell)			
☐	21	Ned Garver	10.00	5.00	1.00
☐	22	Clint Hartung	10.00	5.00	1.00
☐	23	Jim Hearn	10.00	5.00	1.00
☐	24	Gil Hodges	45.00	22.50	4.50
☐	25	Monte Irvin	35.00	17.50	3.50
☐	26	Larry Jansen	10.00	5.00	1.00
☐	27	Sheldon Jones	10.00	5.00	1.00
☐	28	George Kell	35.00	17.50	3.50
☐	29	Monte Kennedy	10.00	5.00	1.00
☐	30	Ralph Kiner	45.00	22.50	4.50
☐	31	Dave Koslo	10.00	5.00	1.00
☐	32	Bob Kuzava	10.00	5.00	1.00
☐	33	Bob Lemon	35.00	17.50	3.50
☐	34	Whitey Lockman	10.00	5.00	1.00
☐	35	Ed Lopat	20.00	10.00	2.00
☐	36	Sal Maglie	15.00	7.50	1.50
☐	37	Mickey Mantle	1000.00	500.00	100.00
☐	38	Billy Martin	45.00	22.50	4.50
☐	39	Willie Mays	400.00	200.00	40.00
☐	40	Gil McDougald	15.00	7.50	1.50
☐	41	Minnie Minoso	15.00	7.50	1.50
☐	42	Johnny Mize	45.00	22.50	4.50
☐	43	Tom Morgan	10.00	5.00	1.00
☐	44	Don Mueller	10.00	5.00	1.00
☐	45	Stan Musial	200.00	100.00	20.00
☐	46	Don Newcombe	20.00	10.00	2.00
☐	47	Ray Noble	10.00	5.00	1.00
☐	48	Joe Ostrowski	10.00	5.00	1.00
☐	49	Mel Parnell	15.00	7.50	1.50
☐	50	Vic Raschi	15.00	7.50	1.50
☐	51	Pee Wee Reese	65.00	32.50	6.50
☐	52	Allie Reynolds	20.00	10.00	2.00
☐	53	Bill Rigney	10.00	5.00	1.00
☐	54A	Phil Rizzuto	45.00	22.50	4.50
		(bunting)			
☐	54B	Phil Rizzuto	45.00	22.50	4.50
		(swinging)			
☐	55	Robin Roberts	35.00	17.50	3.50
☐	56	Eddie Robinson	10.00	5.00	1.00
☐	57	Jackie Robinson	200.00	100.00	20.00
☐	58	Preacher Roe	15.00	7.50	1.50
☐	59	Johnny Sain	15.00	7.50	1.50
☐	60	Red Schoendienst	35.00	17.50	3.50
☐	61	Duke Snider	150.00	75.00	15.00
☐	62	George Spencer	10.00	5.00	1.00
☐	63	Eddie Stanky	15.00	7.50	1.50
☐	64	Hank Thompson	10.00	5.00	1.00
☐	65	Bobby Thomson	15.00	7.50	1.50
☐	66	Vic Wertz	10.00	5.00	1.00
☐	67	Wally Westlake	10.00	5.00	1.00
☐	68	Wes Westrum	10.00	5.00	1.00
☐	69	Ted Williams	300.00	150.00	30.00
☐	70	Gene Woodling	10.00	5.00	1.00
☐	71	Gus Zernial	10.00	5.00	1.00

1986 Big League Chew

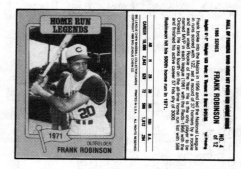

This 12-card set was produced by Big League Chew and was inserted in with their packages of chewing gum, which were shaped and styled after a pouch of chewing tobacco. The cards were found one per pouch of shredded chewing gum or were available through a mail-in offer of two coupons and 2.00 for a complete set. The players featured are members of the 500 career home run club. The backs are printed in blue ink on white card stock. The cards are standard size, 2 1/2" by 3 1/2" and are subtitled "Home Run Legends." The front of each card shows a year inside a small flag; the year is the year that player passed 500 homers.

			MINT	EXC	G-VG
	COMPLETE SET (12)		5.00	2.50	.50
	COMMON PLAYER (1-12)		.30	.15	.03
☐	1	Hank Aaron	.50	.25	.05
☐	2	Babe Ruth	1.00	.50	.10
☐	3	Willie Mays	.50	.25	.05
☐	4	Frank Robinson	.40	.20	.04
☐	5	Harmon Killebrew	.30	.15	.03
☐	6	Mickey Mantle	1.00	.50	.10
☐	7	Jimmie Foxx	.30	.15	.03
☐	8	Ted Williams	.50	.25	.05
☐	9	Ernie Banks	.40	.20	.04
☐	10	Eddie Mathews	.30	.15	.03
☐	11	Mel Ott	.30	.15	.03
☐	12	500 HR Members	.30	.15	.03

1987 Boardwalk and Baseball

This 33-card set was produced by Topps for distribution by the "Boardwalk and Baseball" Theme Park located near Orlando, Florida. The cards are standard size, 2 1/2" by 3 1/2", and come in a custom blue collector box. The full-color fronts are surrounded by a pink and black frame border. The card backs are printed in pink and black on white card stock. The set is subtitled "Top Run Makers." Hence no pitchers are included in the set. The checklist for the set is given on the back panel of the box.

	MINT	EXC	G-VG
COMPLETE SET (33)	6.00	3.00	.60
COMMON PLAYER (1-33)	.10	.05	.01
□ 1 Mike Schmidt	.60	.30	.06
□ 2 Eddie Murray	.30	.15	.03
□ 3 Dale Murphy	.35	.17	.03
□ 4 Dave Winfield	.25	.12	.02
□ 5 Jim Rice	.20	.10	.02
□ 6 Cecil Cooper	.10	.05	.01
□ 7 Dwight Evans	.15	.07	.01
□ 8 Rickey Henderson	.40	.20	.04
□ 9 Robin Yount	.40	.20	.04
□ 10 Andre Dawson	.20	.10	.02
□ 11 Gary Carter	.20	.10	.02
□ 12 Keith Hernandez	.20	.10	.02
□ 13 George Brett	.35	.17	.03
□ 14 Bill Buckner	.10	.05	.01
□ 15 Tony Armas	.10	.05	.01
□ 16 Harold Baines	.15	.07	.01
□ 17 Don Baylor	.10	.05	.01
□ 18 Steve Garvey	.25	.12	.02
□ 19 Lance Parrish	.15	.07	.01
□ 20 Dave Parker	.10	.05	.01
□ 21 Buddy Bell	.10	.05	.01
□ 22 Cal Ripken	.40	.20	.04
□ 23 Bob Horner	.10	.05	.01
□ 24 Tim Raines	.25	.12	.02
□ 25 Jack Clark	.20	.10	.02
□ 26 Leon Durham	.10	.05	.01
□ 27 Pedro Guerrero	.15	.07	.01
□ 28 Kent Hrbek	.20	.10	.02
□ 29 Kirk Gibson	.30	.15	.03
□ 30 Ryne Sandberg	.35	.17	.03
□ 31 Wade Boggs	.60	.30	.06
□ 32 Don Mattingly	1.00	.50	.10
□ 33 Darryl Strawberry	.50	.25	.05

1987 Bohemian Padres

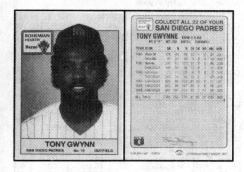

The Bohemian Hearth Bread Company issued this 22-card set of San Diego Padres. The cards measure 2 1/2" by 3 1/2" and feature a distinctive yellow border on the front of the cards. Card backs provide career year-by-year statistics.

	MINT	EXC	G-VG
COMPLETE SET (22)	40.00	20.00	4.00
COMMON PLAYER	.65	.30	.06
□ 1 Garry Templeton	.75	.35	.07
□ 4 Joe Cora	.75	.35	.07
□ 5 Randy Ready	.75	.35	.07
□ 6 Steve Garvey	5.00	2.50	.50
□ 7 Kevin Mitchell	5.00	2.50	.50
□ 8 John Kruk	2.00	1.00	.20
□ 9 Benito Santiago	5.00	2.50	.50
□ 10 Larry Bowa MG	1.00	.50	.10
□ 11 Tim Flannery	.65	.30	.06
□ 14 Carmelo Martinez	1.00	.50	.10
□ 16 Marvell Wynne	.65	.30	.06
□ 19 Tony Gwynn	10.00	5.00	1.00
□ 21 James Steels	.65	.30	.06

□ 22 Stan Jefferson	1.00	.50	.10
□ 30 Eric Show	1.00	.50	.10
□ 31 Ed Whitson	.75	.35	.07
□ 34 Storm Davis	2.00	1.00	.20
□ 37 Craig Lefferts	.75	.35	.07
□ 40 Andy Hawkins	1.00	.50	.10
□ 41 Lance McCullers	1.00	.50	.10
□ 43 Dave Dravecky	2.00	1.00	.20
□ 54 Rich Gossage	2.00	1.00	.20

1947 Bond Bread

The 1947 Bond Bread Jackie Robinson set features 13 unnumbered cards of Jackie in different action or portrait poses; each card measures 2 1/4" by 3 1/2". Card number 7, which is the only card in the set to contain a facsimile autograph, was apparently issued in greater quantity than other cards in the set. Several of the cards have a horizontal format; these are marked in the checklist below by HOR. The ACC designation is D302.

	NRMT	VG-E	GOOD
COMPLETE SET (13)	4200.00	2000.00	450.00
COMMON PLAYER (1-13)	350.00	175.00	35.00
□ 1 Sliding into base, cap, ump in photo, HOR	350.00	175.00	35.00
□ 2 Running down 3rd base line	350.00	175.00	35.00
□ 3 Batting, bat behind head, facing camera	350.00	175.00	35.00
□ 4 Moving towards second, throw almost to glove, HOR	350.00	175.00	35.00
□ 5 Taking throw at first, HOR	350.00	175.00	35.00
□ 6 Jumping high in the air for ball	350.00	175.00	35.00
□ 7 Profile with glove in front of head; facsimile autograph)	250.00	125.00	25.00
□ 8 Leaping over second base, ready to throw	350.00	175.00	35.00
□ 9 Portrait, holding glove over head	350.00	175.00	35.00
□ 10 Portrait, holding bat perpendicular to body	350.00	175.00	35.00
□ 11 Reaching for throw, glove near ankle	350.00	175.00	35.00
□ 12 Leaping for throw, no scoreboard in background	350.00	175.00	35.00

		NRMT	VG-E	GOOD
☐ 13	Portrait, holding .... bat parallel to body	350.00	175.00	35.00

☐ 45	Hank Sauer	33.00	16.00	3.50
☐ 46	Herman Wehmeier	21.00	10.50	2.10
☐ 47	Bobby Thomson	50.00	25.00	5.00
☐ 48	Dave Koslo	50.00	12.00	2.50

1948 Bowman

The 48-card Bowman set of 1948 was the first major set of the post-war period. Each 2 1/16" by 2 1/2" card had a black and white photo of a current player, with his biographical information printed in black ink on a gray back. Due to the printing process and the 36-card sheet size upon which Bowman was then printing, the 12 cards marked with an SP in the checklist are scarcer numerically, as they were removed from the printing sheet in order to make room for the 12 high numbers (37-48). Many cards are found with over-printed, transposed, or blank backs. The set features the Rookie Cards of Hall of Famers Yogi Berra, Ralph Kiner, Stan Musial, Red Schoendienst, and Warren Spahn.

	NRMT	VG-E	GOOD
COMPLETE SET	2700.00	1300.00	450.00
COMMON PLAYER (1-36)	14.00	7.00	1.40
COMMON PLAYER (37-48)	21.00	10.50	2.10
COMMON PLAYER SP	30.00	15.00	3.00

☐ 1	Bob Elliott	75.00	10.00	2.00
☐ 2	Ewell Blackwell	27.00	13.50	2.70
☐ 3	Ralph Kiner	125.00	50.00	10.00
☐ 4	Johnny Mize	70.00	35.00	7.00
☐ 5	Bob Feller	135.00	65.00	13.50
☐ 6	Yogi Berra	400.00	200.00	40.00
☐ 7	Pete Reiser SP	40.00	20.00	4.00
☐ 8	Phil Rizzuto SP	175.00	85.00	18.00
☐ 9	Walker Cooper	14.00	7.00	1.40
☐ 10	Buddy Rosar	14.00	7.00	1.40
☐ 11	Johnny Lindell	14.00	7.00	1.40
☐ 12	Johnny Sain	35.00	17.50	3.50
☐ 13	Willard Marshall SP	30.00	15.00	3.00
☐ 14	Allie Reynolds	35.00	17.50	3.50
☐ 15	Eddie Joost	14.00	7.00	1.40
☐ 16	Jack Lohrke SP	30.00	15.00	3.00
☐ 17	Enos Slaughter	70.00	35.00	7.00
☐ 18	Warren Spahn	200.00	100.00	20.00
☐ 19	Tommy Henrich	22.00	11.00	2.20
☐ 20	Buddy Kerr SP	30.00	15.00	3.00
☐ 21	Ferris Fain	18.00	9.00	1.80
☐ 22	Floyd Bevens SP	30.00	15.00	3.00
☐ 23	Larry Jansen	16.00	8.00	1.60
☐ 24	Dutch Leonard SP	30.00	15.00	3.00
☐ 25	Barney McCosky	14.00	7.00	1.40
☐ 26	Frank Shea SP	30.00	15.00	3.00
☐ 27	Sid Gordon	14.00	7.00	1.40
☐ 28	Emil Verban SP	30.00	15.00	3.00
☐ 29	Joe Page SP	33.00	16.00	3.50
☐ 30	Whitey Lockman SP	33.00	16.00	3.50
☐ 31	Bill McCahan	14.00	7.00	1.40
☐ 32	Bill Rigney	16.00	8.00	1.60
☐ 33	Bill Johnson	14.00	7.00	1.40
☐ 34	Sheldon Jones SP	30.00	15.00	3.00
☐ 35	Snuffy Stirnweiss	18.00	9.00	1.80
☐ 36	Stan Musial	600.00	300.00	60.00
☐ 37	Clint Hartung	21.00	10.50	2.10
☐ 38	Red Schoendienst	100.00	50.00	10.00
☐ 39	Augie Galan	21.00	10.50	2.10
☐ 40	Marty Marion	50.00	25.00	5.00
☐ 41	Rex Barney	21.00	10.50	2.10
☐ 42	Ray Poat	21.00	10.50	2.10
☐ 43	Bruce Edwards	21.00	10.50	2.10
☐ 44	Johnny Wyrostek	21.00	10.50	2.10

1949 Bowman

The cards in this 240-card set measure 2 1/16" by 2 1/2". In 1949 Bowman took an intermediate step between black and white and full color with this set of tinted photos on colored backgrounds. Collectors should note the series price variations which reflect some inconsistencies in the printing process. There are four major varieties in name printing which are noted in the checklist below: NOF: name on front; NNOF: no name on front; PR: printed name on back; and SCR: script name on back. These variations resulted when Bowman used twelve of the lower numbers to fill out the last press sheet of 36 cards adding to numbers 217-240. Cards 1-3 and 5-73 can be found with either gray or white backs. The set features the Rookie Cards of Hall of Famers Roy Campanella, Bob Lemon, Robin Roberts, Duke Snider, and Early Wynn.

	NRMT	VG-E	GOOD
COMPLETE SET	15000.00	7000.00	1800.00
COMMON CARD 1-3/5-36/73 ..	14.00	7.00	1.40
COMMON CARD (37-72)	15.00	7.50	1.50
COMMON CARD (4/74-108)	13.00	6.50	1.30
COMMON CARD (109-144)	12.00	6.00	1.20
COMMON CARD (145-180)	80.00	40.00	8.00
COMMON CARD (181-216)	75.00	37.50	7.50
COMMON CARD (217-240)	75.00	37.50	7.50

☐ 1	Vern Bickford	70.00	8.00	1.50
☐ 2	Whitey Lockman	16.00	8.00	1.60
☐ 3	Bob Porterfield	14.00	7.00	1.40
☐ 4A	Jerry Priddy NNOF	13.00	6.50	1.30
☐ 4B	Jerry Priddy NOF	40.00	20.00	4.00
☐ 5	Hank Sauer	18.00	9.00	1.80
☐ 6	Phil Cavarretta	18.00	9.00	1.80
☐ 7	Joe Dobson	14.00	7.00	1.40
☐ 8	Murry Dickson	14.00	7.00	1.40
☐ 9	Ferris Fain	18.00	9.00	1.80
☐ 10	Ted Gray	14.00	7.00	1.40
☐ 11	Lou Boudreau	50.00	22.50	4.50
☐ 12	Cass Michaels	14.00	7.00	1.40
☐ 13	Bob Chesnes	14.00	7.00	1.40
☐ 14	Curt Simmons	25.00	12.50	2.50
☐ 15	Ned Garver	14.00	7.00	1.40
☐ 16	Al Kozar	14.00	7.00	1.40
☐ 17	Earl Torgeson	14.00	7.00	1.40
☐ 18	Bobby Thomson	21.00	10.50	2.10
☐ 19	Bobby Brown	30.00	15.00	3.00
☐ 20	Gene Hermanski	14.00	7.00	1.40
☐ 21	Frank Baumholtz	14.00	7.00	1.40
☐ 22	Peanuts Lowrey	14.00	7.00	1.40
☐ 23	Bobby Doerr	60.00	30.00	6.00
☐ 24	Stan Musial	450.00	225.00	45.00
☐ 25	Carl Scheib	14.00	7.00	1.40
☐ 26	George Kell	50.00	22.50	4.50
☐ 27	Bob Feller	110.00	55.00	11.00
☐ 28	Don Kolloway	14.00	7.00	1.40
☐ 29	Ralph Kiner	60.00	30.00	6.00
☐ 30	Andy Seminick	14.00	7.00	1.40
☐ 31	Dick Kokos	14.00	7.00	1.40
☐ 32	Eddie Yost	14.00	7.00	1.40
☐ 33	Warren Spahn	110.00	55.00	11.00
☐ 34	Dave Koslo	14.00	7.00	1.40

☐	35	Vic Raschi	35.00	17.50	3.50
☐	36	Pee Wee Reese	110.00	50.00	10.00
☐	37	Johnny Wyrostek	15.00	7.50	1.50
☐	38	Emil Verban	15.00	7.50	1.50
☐	39	Billy Goodman	18.00	9.00	1.80
☐	40	Red Munger	15.00	7.50	1.50
☐	41	Lou Brissie	15.00	7.50	1.50
☐	42	Hoot Evers	15.00	7.50	1.50
☐	43	Dale Mitchell	18.00	9.00	1.80
☐	44	Dave Philley	15.00	7.50	1.50
☐	45	Wally Westlake	15.00	7.50	1.50
☐	46	Robin Roberts	165.00	75.00	15.00
☐	47	Johnny Sain	25.00	12.50	2.50
☐	48	Willard Marshall	15.00	7.50	1.50
☐	49	Frank Shea	15.00	7.50	1.50
☐	50	Jackie Robinson	600.00	300.00	60.00
☐	51	Herman Wehmeier	15.00	7.50	1.50
☐	52	Johnny Schmitz	15.00	7.50	1.50
☐	53	Jack Kramer	15.00	7.50	1.50
☐	54	Marty Marion	22.00	11.00	2.20
☐	55	Eddie Joost	15.00	7.50	1.50
☐	56	Pat Mullin	15.00	7.50	1.50
☐	57	Gene Bearden	15.00	7.50	1.50
☐	58	Bob Elliott	18.00	9.00	1.80
☐	59	Jack Lohrke	15.00	7.50	1.50
☐	60	Yogi Berra	250.00	125.00	25.00
☐	61	Rex Barney	15.00	7.50	1.50
☐	62	Grady Hatton	15.00	7.50	1.50
☐	63	Andy Pafko	18.00	9.00	1.80
☐	64	Dom DiMaggio	22.00	11.00	2.20
☐	65	Enos Slaughter	60.00	30.00	6.00
☐	66	Elmer Valo	15.00	7.50	1.50
☐	67	Alvin Dark	22.00	11.00	2.20
☐	68	Sheldon Jones	15.00	7.50	1.50
☐	69	Tommy Henrich	22.00	11.00	2.20
☐	70	Carl Furillo	45.00	22.50	4.50
☐	71	Vern Stephens	18.00	9.00	1.80
☐	72	Tommy Holmes	18.00	9.00	1.80
☐	73	Billy Cox	22.00	11.00	2.20
☐	74	Tom McBride	13.00	6.50	1.30
☐	75	Eddie Mayo	13.00	6.50	1.30
☐	76	Bill Nicholson	13.00	6.50	1.30
☐	77	Ernie Bonham	13.00	6.50	1.30
☐	78A	Sam Zoldak NNOF	13.00	6.50	1.30
☐	78B	Sam Zoldak NOF	40.00	20.00	4.00
☐	79	Ron Northey	13.00	6.50	1.30
☐	80	Bill McCahan	13.00	6.50	1.30
☐	81	Virgil Stallcup	13.00	6.50	1.30
☐	82	Joe Page	20.00	10.00	2.00
☐	83A	Bob Scheffing NNOF	13.00	6.50	1.30
☐	83B	Bob Scheffing NOF	40.00	20.00	4.00
☐	84	Roy Campanella	500.00	250.00	50.00
☐	85A	Johnny Mize NNOF	60.00	30.00	6.00
☐	85B	Johnny Mize NOF	120.00	60.00	12.00
☐	86	Johnny Pesky	15.00	7.50	1.50
☐	87	Randy Gumpert	13.00	6.50	1.30
☐	88A	Bill Salkeld NNOF	13.00	6.50	1.30
☐	88B	Bill Salkeld NOF	40.00	20.00	4.00
☐	89	Mizell Platt	13.00	6.50	1.30
☐	90	Gil Coan	13.00	6.50	1.30
☐	91	Dick Wakefield	13.00	6.50	1.30
☐	92	Willie Jones	13.00	6.50	1.30
☐	93	Ed Stevens	13.00	6.50	1.30
☐	94	Mickey Vernon	22.00	11.00	2.20
☐	95	Howie Pollet	13.00	6.50	1.30
☐	96	Taft Wright	13.00	6.50	1.30
☐	97	Danny Litwhiler	13.00	6.50	1.30
☐	98A	Phil Rizzuto NNOF	80.00	40.00	8.00
☐	98B	Phil Rizzuto NOF	160.00	80.00	16.00
☐	99	Frank Gustine	13.00	6.50	1.30
☐	100	Gil Hodges	165.00	80.00	16.00
☐	101	Sid Gordon	13.00	6.50	1.30
☐	102	Stan Spence	13.00	6.50	1.30
☐	103	Joe Tipton	13.00	6.50	1.30
☐	104	Eddie Stanky	20.00	10.00	2.00
☐	105	Bill Kennedy	13.00	6.50	1.30
☐	106	Jake Early	13.00	6.50	1.30
☐	107	Eddie Lake	13.00	6.50	1.30
☐	108	Ken Heintzelman	13.00	6.50	1.30
☐	109A	Ed Fitzgerald SCR	12.00	6.00	1.20
☐	109B	Ed Fitzgerald PR	35.00	17.50	3.50
☐	110	Early Wynn	100.00	50.00	10.00
☐	111	Red Schoendienst	60.00	30.00	6.00
☐	112	Sam Chapman	12.00	6.00	1.20
☐	113	Ray LaManno	12.00	6.00	1.20
☐	114	Allie Reynolds	25.00	12.50	2.50
☐	115	Dutch Leonard	12.00	6.00	1.20
☐	116	Joe Hatton	12.00	6.00	1.20
☐	117	Walker Cooper	12.00	6.00	1.20
☐	118	Sam Mele	12.00	6.00	1.20
☐	119	Floyd Baker	12.00	6.00	1.20
☐	120	Cliff Fannin	12.00	6.00	1.20
☐	121	Mark Christman	12.00	6.00	1.20
☐	122	George Vico	12.00	6.00	1.20
☐	123	Johnny Blatnick	12.00	6.00	1.20
☐	124A	Danny Murtaugh SCR	12.00	6.00	1.20
☐	124B	Danny Murtaugh PR	35.00	17.50	3.50
☐	125	Ken Keltner	14.00	7.00	1.40
☐	126A	Al Brazle SCR	12.00	6.00	1.20
☐	126B	Al Brazle PR	35.00	17.50	3.50
☐	127A	Hank Majeski SCR	12.00	6.00	1.20
☐	127B	Hank Majeski PR	35.00	17.50	3.50
☐	128	Johnny VanderMeer	20.00	10.00	2.00
☐	129	Bill Johnson	12.00	6.00	1.20
☐	130	Harry Walker	12.00	6.00	1.20
☐	131	Paul Lehner	12.00	6.00	1.20
☐	132A	Al Evans SCR	12.00	6.00	1.20
☐	132B	Al Evans PR	35.00	17.50	3.50
☐	133	Aaron Robinson	12.00	6.00	1.20
☐	134	Hank Borowy	12.00	6.00	1.20
☐	135	Stan Rojek	12.00	6.00	1.20
☐	136	Hank Edwards	12.00	6.00	1.20
☐	137	Ted Wilks	12.00	6.00	1.20
☐	138	Buddy Rosar	12.00	6.00	1.20
☐	139	Hank Arft	12.00	6.00	1.20
☐	140	Ray Scarborough	12.00	6.00	1.20
☐	141	Ulysses Lupien	12.00	6.00	1.20
☐	142	Eddie Waitkus	14.00	7.00	1.40
☐	143A	Bob Dillinger SCR	12.00	6.00	1.20
☐	143B	Bob Dillinger PR	35.00	17.50	3.50
☐	144	Mickey Haefner	12.00	6.00	1.20
☐	145	Sylvester Donnelly	80.00	40.00	8.00
☐	146	Mike McCormick	80.00	40.00	8.00
☐	147	Bert Singleton	80.00	40.00	8.00
☐	148	Bob Swift	80.00	40.00	8.00
☐	149	Roy Partee	80.00	40.00	8.00
☐	150	Allie Clark	80.00	40.00	8.00
☐	151	Mickey Harris	80.00	40.00	8.00
☐	152	Clarence Maddern	80.00	40.00	8.00
☐	153	Phil Masi	80.00	40.00	8.00
☐	154	Clint Hartung	80.00	40.00	8.00
☐	155	Mickey Guerra	80.00	40.00	8.00
☐	156	Al Zarilla	80.00	40.00	8.00
☐	157	Walt Masterson	80.00	40.00	8.00
☐	158	Harry Brecheen	90.00	45.00	9.00
☐	159	Glen Moulder	80.00	40.00	8.00
☐	160	Jim Blackburn	80.00	40.00	8.00
☐	161	Jocko Thompson	80.00	40.00	8.00
☐	162	Preacher Roe	125.00	60.00	12.50
☐	163	Clyde McCullough	80.00	40.00	8.00
☐	164	Vic Wertz	90.00	45.00	9.00
☐	165	Snuffy Stirnweiss	90.00	45.00	9.00
☐	166	Mike Tresh	80.00	40.00	8.00
☐	167	Babe Martin	80.00	40.00	8.00
☐	168	Doyle Lade	80.00	40.00	8.00
☐	169	Jeff Heath	80.00	40.00	8.00
☐	170	Bill Rigney	90.00	45.00	9.00
☐	171	Dick Fowler	80.00	40.00	8.00
☐	172	Eddie Pellagrini	80.00	40.00	8.00
☐	173	Eddie Stewart	80.00	40.00	8.00
☐	174	Terry Moore	100.00	50.00	10.00
☐	175	Luke Appling	125.00	60.00	12.50
☐	176	Ken Raffensberger	80.00	40.00	8.00
☐	177	Stan Lopata	80.00	40.00	8.00
☐	178	Tom Brown	80.00	40.00	8.00
☐	179	Hugh Casey	90.00	45.00	9.00
☐	180	Connie Berry	80.00	40.00	8.00
☐	181	Gus Niarhos	75.00	37.50	7.50
☐	182	Hal Peck	75.00	37.50	7.50
☐	183	Lou Stringer	75.00	37.50	7.50
☐	184	Bob Chipman	75.00	37.50	7.50
☐	185	Pete Reiser	90.00	45.00	9.00
☐	186	Buddy Kerr	75.00	37.50	7.50
☐	187	Phil Marchildon	75.00	37.50	7.50
☐	188	Karl Drews	75.00	37.50	7.50
☐	189	Earl Wooten	75.00	37.50	7.50
☐	190	Jim Hearn	75.00	37.50	7.50
☐	191	Joe Haynes	75.00	37.50	7.50
☐	192	Harry Gumbert	75.00	37.50	7.50
☐	193	Ken Trinkle	75.00	37.50	7.50
☐	194	Ralph Branca	100.00	50.00	10.00
☐	195	Eddie Bockman	75.00	37.50	7.50
☐	196	Fred Hutchinson	90.00	45.00	9.00
☐	197	Johnny Lindell	75.00	37.50	7.50
☐	198	Steve Gromek	75.00	37.50	7.50
☐	199	Tex Hughson	75.00	37.50	7.50
☐	200	Jess Dobernic	75.00	37.50	7.50
☐	201	Sibby Sisti	75.00	37.50	7.50
☐	202	Larry Jansen	90.00	45.00	9.00
☐	203	Barney McCosky	75.00	37.50	7.50
☐	204	Bob Savage	75.00	37.50	7.50
☐	205	Dick Sisler	75.00	37.50	7.50
☐	206	Bruce Edwards	75.00	37.50	7.50
☐	207	Johnny Hopp	90.00	45.00	9.00
☐	208	Dizzy Trout	90.00	45.00	9.00
☐	209	Charlie Keller	100.00	50.00	10.00
☐	210	Joe Gordon	100.00	50.00	10.00
☐	211	Boo Ferriss	75.00	37.50	7.50
☐	212	Ralph Hamner	75.00	37.50	7.50
☐	213	Red Barrett	75.00	37.50	7.50

		NRMT	VG-E	GOOD
☐ 214	Richie Ashburn	500.00	250.00	50.00
☐ 215	Kirby Higbe	75.00	37.50	7.50
☐ 216	Schoolboy Rowe	90.00	45.00	9.00
☐ 217	Marino Pieretti	75.00	37.50	7.50
☐ 218	Dick Kryhoski	75.00	37.50	7.50
☐ 219	Virgil"Fire" Trucks	90.00	45.00	9.00
☐ 220	Johnny McCarthy	75.00	37.50	7.50
☐ 221	Bob Muncrief	75.00	37.50	7.50
☐ 222	Alex Kellner	75.00	37.50	7.50
☐ 223	Bobby Hofman	75.00	37.50	7.50
☐ 224	Satchell Paige	1200.00	100.00	20.00
☐ 225	Gerry Coleman	90.00	45.00	9.00
☐ 226	Duke Snider	1000.00	500.00	100.00
☐ 227	Fritz Ostermueller	75.00	37.50	7.50
☐ 228	Jackie Mayo	75.00	37.50	7.50
☐ 229	Ed Lopat	125.00	60.00	12.50
☐ 230	Augie Galan	75.00	37.50	7.50
☐ 231	Earl Johnson	75.00	37.50	7.50
☐ 232	George McQuinn	75.00	37.50	7.50
☐ 233	Larry Doby	125.00	60.00	12.50
☐ 234	Rip Sewell	75.00	37.50	7.50
☐ 235	Jim Russell	75.00	37.50	7.50
☐ 236	Fred Sanford	75.00	37.50	7.50
☐ 237	Monte Kennedy	75.00	37.50	7.50
☐ 238	Bob Lemon	225.00	110.00	22.00
☐ 239	Frank McCormick	90.00	45.00	9.00
☐ 240	Babe Young	125.00	60.00	12.50
	(photo actually			
	Bobby Young)			

1950 Bowman

The cards in this 252-card set measure 2 1/16" by 2 1/2". This set, marketed in 1950 by Bowman, represented a major improvement in terms of quality over their previous efforts. Each card was a beautifully colored line drawing developed from a simple photograph. The first 72 cards are the scarcest in the set, while the final 72 cards may be found with or without the copyright line. This was the only Bowman sports set to carry the famous "5-Star" logo.

		NRMT	VG-E	GOOD
COMPLETE SET		8000.00	4000.00	900.00
COMMON PLAYER (1-72)		36.00	18.00	3.60
COMMON PLAYER (73-252)		13.00	6.50	1.30
☐ 1	Mel Parnell	200.00	20.00	4.00
☐ 2	Vern Stephens	40.00	20.00	4.00
☐ 3	Dom DiMaggio	45.00	22.50	4.50
☐ 4	Gus Zernial	45.00	22.50	4.50
☐ 5	Bob Kuzava	36.00	18.00	3.60
☐ 6	Bob Feller	135.00	65.00	13.50
☐ 7	Jim Hegan	40.00	20.00	4.00
☐ 8	George Kell	70.00	35.00	7.00
☐ 9	Vic Wertz	40.00	20.00	4.00
☐ 10	Tommy Henrich	45.00	22.50	4.50
☐ 11	Phil Rizzuto	110.00	55.00	11.00
☐ 12	Joe Page	45.00	22.50	4.50
☐ 13	Ferris Fain	40.00	20.00	4.00
☐ 14	Alex Kellner	36.00	18.00	3.60
☐ 15	Al Kozar	36.00	18.00	3.60
☐ 16	Roy Sievers	45.00	22.50	4.50
☐ 17	Sid Hudson	36.00	18.00	3.60
☐ 18	Eddie Robinson	36.00	18.00	3.60
☐ 19	Warren Spahn	135.00	65.00	13.50
☐ 20	Bob Elliott	40.00	20.00	4.00
☐ 21	Pee Wee Reese	125.00	60.00	12.50
☐ 22	Jackie Robinson	500.00	250.00	50.00
☐ 23	Don Newcombe	80.00	40.00	8.00
☐ 24	Johnny Schmitz	36.00	18.00	3.60

☐ 25	Hank Sauer	40.00	20.00	4.00
☐ 26	Grady Hatton	36.00	18.00	3.60
☐ 27	Herman Wehmeier	36.00	18.00	3.60
☐ 28	Bobby Thomson	45.00	22.50	4.50
☐ 29	Eddie Stanky	40.00	20.00	4.00
☐ 30	Eddie Waitkus	36.00	18.00	3.60
☐ 31	Del Ennis	40.00	20.00	4.00
☐ 32	Robin Roberts	100.00	50.00	10.00
☐ 33	Ralph Kiner	80.00	40.00	8.00
☐ 34	Murry Dickson	36.00	18.00	3.60
☐ 35	Enos Slaughter	80.00	40.00	8.00
☐ 36	Eddie Kazak	36.00	18.00	3.60
☐ 37	Luke Appling	60.00	30.00	6.00
☐ 38	Bill Wight	36.00	18.00	3.60
☐ 39	Larry Doby	50.00	25.00	5.00
☐ 40	Bob Lemon	80.00	40.00	8.00
☐ 41	Hoot Evers	36.00	18.00	3.60
☐ 42	Art Houtteman	36.00	18.00	3.60
☐ 43	Bobby Doerr	70.00	35.00	7.00
☐ 44	Joe Dobson	36.00	18.00	3.60
☐ 45	Al Zarilla	36.00	18.00	3.60
☐ 46	Yogi Berra	350.00	175.00	35.00
☐ 47	Jerry Coleman	45.00	22.50	4.50
☐ 48	Lou Brissie	36.00	18.00	3.60
☐ 49	Elmer Valo	36.00	18.00	3.60
☐ 50	Dick Kokos	36.00	18.00	3.60
☐ 51	Ned Garver	36.00	18.00	3.60
☐ 52	Sam Mele	36.00	18.00	3.60
☐ 53	Clyde Vollmer	36.00	18.00	3.60
☐ 54	Gil Coan	36.00	18.00	3.60
☐ 55	Buddy Kerr	36.00	18.00	3.60
☐ 56	Del Crandall	45.00	22.50	4.50
☐ 57	Vern Bickford	36.00	18.00	3.60
☐ 58	Carl Furillo	50.00	25.00	5.00
☐ 59	Ralph Branca	45.00	22.50	4.50
☐ 60	Andy Pafko	40.00	20.00	4.00
☐ 61	Bob Rush	36.00	18.00	3.60
☐ 62	Ted Kluszewski	50.00	25.00	5.00
☐ 63	Ewell Blackwell	40.00	20.00	4.00
☐ 64	Alvin Dark	45.00	22.50	4.50
☐ 65	Dave Koslo	36.00	18.00	3.60
☐ 66	Larry Jansen	40.00	20.00	4.00
☐ 67	Willie Jones	36.00	18.00	3.60
☐ 68	Curt Simmons	40.00	20.00	4.00
☐ 69	Wally Westlake	36.00	18.00	3.60
☐ 70	Bob Chesnes	36.00	18.00	3.60
☐ 71	Red Schoendienst	75.00	37.50	7.50
☐ 72	Howie Pollet	36.00	18.00	3.60
☐ 73	Willard Marshall	13.00	6.50	1.30
☐ 74	Johnny Antonelli	20.00	10.00	2.00
☐ 75	Roy Campanella	250.00	125.00	25.00
☐ 76	Rex Barney	13.00	6.50	1.30
☐ 77	Duke Snider	250.00	125.00	25.00
☐ 78	Mickey Owen	15.00	7.50	1.50
☐ 79	Johnny VanderMeer	20.00	10.00	2.00
☐ 80	Howard Fox	13.00	6.50	1.30
☐ 81	Ron Northey	13.00	6.50	1.30
☐ 82	Whitey Lockman	15.00	7.50	1.50
☐ 83	Sheldon Jones	13.00	6.50	1.30
☐ 84	Richie Ashburn	50.00	25.00	5.00
☐ 85	Ken Heintzelman	13.00	6.50	1.30
☐ 86	Stan Rojek	13.00	6.50	1.30
☐ 87	Bill Werle	13.00	6.50	1.30
☐ 88	Marty Marion	20.00	10.00	2.00
☐ 89	Red Munger	13.00	6.50	1.30
☐ 90	Harry Brecheen	15.00	7.50	1.50
☐ 91	Cass Michaels	13.00	6.50	1.30
☐ 92	Hank Majeski	13.00	6.50	1.30
☐ 93	Gene Bearden	13.00	6.50	1.30
☐ 94	Lou Boudreau	40.00	20.00	4.00
☐ 95	Aaron Robinson	13.00	6.50	1.30
☐ 96	Virgil Trucks	15.00	7.50	1.50
☐ 97	Maurice McDermott	13.00	6.50	1.30
☐ 98	Ted Williams	600.00	275.00	55.00
☐ 99	Billy Goodman	15.00	7.50	1.50
☐ 100	Vic Raschi	22.00	11.00	2.20
☐ 101	Bobby Brown	25.00	12.50	2.50
☐ 102	Billy Johnson	13.00	6.50	1.30
☐ 103	Eddie Joost	13.00	6.50	1.30
☐ 104	Sam Chapman	13.00	6.50	1.30
☐ 105	Bob Dillinger	13.00	6.50	1.30
☐ 106	Cliff Fannin	13.00	6.50	1.30
☐ 107	Sam Dente	13.00	6.50	1.30
☐ 108	Ray Scarborough	13.00	6.50	1.30
☐ 109	Sid Gordon	13.00	6.50	1.30
☐ 110	Tommy Holmes	15.00	7.50	1.50
☐ 111	Walker Cooper	13.00	6.50	1.30
☐ 112	Gil Hodges	70.00	35.00	7.00
☐ 113	Gene Hermanski	13.00	6.50	1.30
☐ 114	Wayne Terwilliger	13.00	6.50	1.30
☐ 115	Roy Smalley	13.00	6.50	1.30
☐ 116	Virgil Stallcup	13.00	6.50	1.30
☐ 117	Bill Rigney	13.00	6.50	1.30
☐ 118	Clint Hartung	13.00	6.50	1.30
☐ 119	Dick Sisler	13.00	6.50	1.30

		NRMT	VG-E	GOOD
☐ 120	John Thompson	13.00	6.50	1.30
☐ 121	Andy Seminick	13.00	6.50	1.30
☐ 122	Johnny Hopp	15.00	7.50	1.50
☐ 123	Dino Restelli	13.00	6.50	1.30
☐ 124	Clyde McCullough	13.00	6.50	1.30
☐ 125	Del Rice	13.00	6.50	1.30
☐ 126	Al Brazle	13.00	6.50	1.30
☐ 127	Dave Philley	13.00	6.50	1.30
☐ 128	Phil Masi	13.00	6.50	1.30
☐ 129	Joe Gordon	18.00	9.00	1.80
☐ 130	Dale Mitchell	15.00	7.50	1.50
☐ 131	Steve Gromek	13.00	6.50	1.30
☐ 132	James "Mickey" Vernon	15.00	7.50	1.50
☐ 133	Don Kolloway	13.00	6.50	1.30
☐ 134	Paul Trout	13.00	6.50	1.30
☐ 135	Pat Mullin	13.00	6.50	1.30
☐ 136	Warren Rosar	13.00	6.50	1.30
☐ 137	Johnny Pesky	15.00	7.50	1.50
☐ 138	Allie Reynolds	25.00	12.50	2.50
☐ 139	Johnny Mize	60.00	30.00	6.00
☐ 140	Pete Suder	13.00	6.50	1.30
☐ 141	Joe Coleman	13.00	6.50	1.30
☐ 142	Sherm Lollar	15.00	7.50	1.50
☐ 143	Eddie Stewart	13.00	6.50	1.30
☐ 144	Al Evans	13.00	6.50	1.30
☐ 145	Jack Graham	13.00	6.50	1.30
☐ 146	Floyd Baker	13.00	6.50	1.30
☐ 147	Mike Garcia	15.00	7.50	1.50
☐ 148	Early Wynn	50.00	25.00	5.00
☐ 149	Bob Swift	13.00	6.50	1.30
☐ 150	George Vico	13.00	6.50	1.30
☐ 151	Fred Hutchinson	15.00	7.50	1.50
☐ 152	Ellis Kinder	13.00	6.50	1.30
☐ 153	Walt Masterson	13.00	6.50	1.30
☐ 154	Gus Niarhos	13.00	6.50	1.30
☐ 155	Frank Shea	13.00	6.50	1.30
☐ 156	Fred Sanford	13.00	6.50	1.30
☐ 157	Mike Guerra	13.00	6.50	1.30
☐ 158	Paul Lehner	13.00	6.50	1.30
☐ 159	Joe Tipton	13.00	6.50	1.30
☐ 160	Mickey Harris	13.00	6.50	1.30
☐ 161	Sherry Robertson	13.00	6.50	1.30
☐ 162	Eddie Yost	13.00	6.50	1.30
☐ 163	Earl Torgeson	13.00	6.50	1.30
☐ 164	Sibby Sisti	13.00	6.50	1.30
☐ 165	Bruce Edwards	13.00	6.50	1.30
☐ 166	Joe Hatton	13.00	6.50	1.30
☐ 167	Preacher Roe	25.00	12.50	2.50
☐ 168	Bob Scheffing	13.00	6.50	1.30
☐ 169	Hank Edwards	13.00	6.50	1.30
☐ 170	Dutch Leonard	13.00	6.50	1.30
☐ 171	Harry Gumbert	13.00	6.50	1.30
☐ 172	Peanuts Lowrey	13.00	6.50	1.30
☐ 173	Lloyd Merriman	13.00	6.50	1.30
☐ 174	Hank Thompson	15.00	7.50	1.50
☐ 175	Monte Kennedy	13.00	6.50	1.30
☐ 176	Sylvester Donnelly	13.00	6.50	1.30
☐ 177	Hank Borowy	13.00	6.50	1.30
☐ 178	Ed Fitzgerald	13.00	6.50	1.30
☐ 179	Chuck Diering	13.00	6.50	1.30
☐ 180	Harry Walker	13.00	6.50	1.30
☐ 181	Marino Pieretti	13.00	6.50	1.30
☐ 182	Sam Zoldak	13.00	6.50	1.30
☐ 183	Mickey Haefner	13.00	6.50	1.30
☐ 184	Randy Gumpert	13.00	6.50	1.30
☐ 185	Howie Judson	13.00	6.50	1.30
☐ 186	Ken Keltner	15.00	7.50	1.50
☐ 187	Lou Stringer	13.00	6.50	1.30
☐ 188	Earl Johnson	13.00	6.50	1.30
☐ 189	Owen Friend	13.00	6.50	1.30
☐ 190	Ken Wood	13.00	6.50	1.30
☐ 191	Dick Starr	13.00	6.50	1.30
☐ 192	Bob Chipman	13.00	6.50	1.30
☐ 193	Pete Reiser	15.00	7.50	1.50
☐ 194	Billy Cox	15.00	7.50	1.50
☐ 195	Phil Cavarretta	15.00	7.50	1.50
☐ 196	Doyle Lade	13.00	6.50	1.30
☐ 197	Johnny Wyrostek	13.00	6.50	1.30
☐ 198	Danny Litwhiler	13.00	6.50	1.30
☐ 199	Jack Kramer	13.00	6.50	1.30
☐ 200	Kirby Higbe	13.00	6.50	1.30
☐ 201	Pete Castiglione	13.00	6.50	1.30
☐ 202	Cliff Chambers	13.00	6.50	1.30
☐ 203	Danny Murtaugh	13.00	6.50	1.30
☐ 204	Granny Hamner	13.00	6.50	1.30
☐ 205	Mike Goliat	13.00	6.50	1.30
☐ 206	Stan Lopata	13.00	6.50	1.30
☐ 207	Max Lanier	13.00	6.50	1.30
☐ 208	Jim Hearn	13.00	6.50	1.30
☐ 209	Johnny Lindell	13.00	6.50	1.30
☐ 210	Ted Gray	13.00	6.50	1.30
☐ 211	Charley Keller	15.00	7.50	1.50
☐ 212	Jerry Priddy	13.00	6.50	1.30
☐ 213	Carl Scheib	13.00	6.50	1.30
☐ 214	Dick Fowler	13.00	6.50	1.30
☐ 215	Ed Lopat	25.00	12.50	2.50
☐ 216	Bob Porterfield	13.00	6.50	1.30
☐ 217	Casey Stengel MG	100.00	50.00	10.00
☐ 218	Cliff Mapes	15.00	7.50	1.50
☐ 219	Hank Bauer	45.00	22.50	4.50
☐ 220	Leo Durocher MG	40.00	20.00	4.00
☐ 221	Don Mueller	24.00	12.00	2.40
☐ 222	Bobby Morgan	13.00	6.50	1.30
☐ 223	Jim Russell	13.00	6.50	1.30
☐ 224	Jack Banta	13.00	6.50	1.30
☐ 225	Eddie Sawyer MG	15.00	7.50	1.50
☐ 226	Jim Konstanty	24.00	12.00	2.40
☐ 227	Bob Miller	13.00	6.50	1.30
☐ 228	Bill Nicholson	13.00	6.50	1.30
☐ 229	Frank Frisch	40.00	20.00	4.00
☐ 230	Bill Serena	13.00	6.50	1.30
☐ 231	Preston Ward	13.00	6.50	1.30
☐ 232	Al Rosen	45.00	22.50	4.50
☐ 233	Allie Clark	13.00	6.50	1.30
☐ 234	Bobby Shantz	21.00	10.50	2.10
☐ 235	Harold Gilbert	13.00	6.50	1.30
☐ 236	Bob Cain	13.00	6.50	1.30
☐ 237	Bill Salkeld	13.00	6.50	1.30
☐ 238	Vernal Jones	13.00	6.50	1.30
☐ 239	Bill Howerton	13.00	6.50	1.30
☐ 240	Eddie Lake	13.00	6.50	1.30
☐ 241	Neil Berry	13.00	6.50	1.30
☐ 242	Dick Kryhoski	13.00	6.50	1.30
☐ 243	Johnny Groth	13.00	6.50	1.30
☐ 244	Dale Coogan	13.00	6.50	1.30
☐ 245	Al Papai	13.00	6.50	1.30
☐ 246	Walt Dropo	21.00	10.50	2.10
☐ 247	Irv Noren	15.00	7.50	1.50
☐ 248	Sam Jethroe	15.00	7.50	1.50
☐ 249	Snuffy Stirnweiss	15.00	7.50	1.50
☐ 250	Ray Coleman	13.00	6.50	1.30
☐ 251	John Moss	13.00	6.50	1.30
☐ 252	Billy DeMars	70.00	8.00	1.50

1951 Bowman

The cards in this 324-card set measure 2 1/16" by 3 1/8". Many of the obverses of the cards appearing in the 1951 Bowman set are enlargements of those appearing in the previous year. The high number series (253-324) is highly valued and contains the true "Rookie" cards of Mickey Mantle and Willie Mays. Card number 195 depicts Paul Richards in caricature. George Kell's card (#46) incorrectly lists him as being in the "1941" Bowman series. Player names are found printed in a panel on the front of the card. These cards were supposedly also sold in sheets in variety stores in the Philadelphia area.

		NRMT	VG-E	GOOD
COMPLETE SET (324)		16000.00	8000.00	2000.00
COMMON PLAYER (1-36)		16.00	8.00	1.60
COMMON PLAYER (37-72)		13.00	6.50	1.30
COMMON PLAYER (73-252)		12.00	6.00	1.20
COMMON PLAYER (253-324)		45.00	22.50	4.50
☐ 1	Whitey Ford	1200.00	150.00	30.00
☐ 2	Yogi Berra	350.00	175.00	35.00
☐ 3	Robin Roberts	60.00	30.00	6.00
☐ 4	Del Ennis	18.00	9.00	1.80
☐ 5	Dale Mitchell	18.00	9.00	1.80
☐ 6	Don Newcombe	30.00	15.00	3.00
☐ 7	Gil Hodges	60.00	30.00	6.00

☐	8	Paul Lehner	16.00	8.00	1.60	☐ 102	Dutch Leonard	12.00	6.00	1.20
☐	9	Sam Chapman	16.00	8.00	1.60	☐ 103	Andy Pafko	15.00	7.50	1.50
☐	10	Red Schoendienst	60.00	30.00	6.00	☐ 104	Virgil Trucks	15.00	7.50	1.50
☐	11	Red Munger	16.00	8.00	1.60	☐ 105	Don Kolloway	12.00	6.00	1.20
☐	12	Hank Majeski	16.00	8.00	1.60	☐ 106	Pat Mullin	12.00	6.00	1.20
☐	13	Eddie Stanky	20.00	10.00	2.00	☐ 107	Johnny Wyrostek	12.00	6.00	1.20
☐	14	Alvin Dark	22.00	11.00	2.20	☐ 108	Virgil Stallcup	12.00	6.00	1.20
☐	15	Johnny Pesky	18.00	9.00	1.80	☐ 109	Allie Reynolds	25.00	12.50	2.50
☐	16	Maurice McDermott	16.00	8.00	1.60	☐ 110	Bobby Brown	25.00	12.50	2.50
☐	17	Pete Castiglione	16.00	8.00	1.60	☐ 111	Curt Simmons	15.00	7.50	1.50
☐	18	Gil Coan	16.00	8.00	1.60	☐ 112	Willie Jones	12.00	6.00	1.20
☐	19	Sid Gordon	16.00	8.00	1.60	☐ 113	Bill Nicholson	12.00	6.00	1.20
☐	20	Del Crandell	20.00	10.00	2.00	☐ 114	Sam Zoldak	12.00	6.00	1.20
		(sic, Crandall)				☐ 115	Steve Gromek	12.00	6.00	1.20
☐	21	Snuffy Stirnweiss	18.00	9.00	1.80	☐ 116	Bruce Edwards	12.00	6.00	1.20
☐	22	Hank Sauer	18.00	9.00	1.80	☐ 117	Eddie Miksis	12.00	6.00	1.20
☐	23	Hoot Evers	16.00	8.00	1.60	☐ 118	Preacher Roe	25.00	12.50	2.50
☐	24	Ewell Blackwell	20.00	10.00	2.00	☐ 119	Eddie Joost	12.00	6.00	1.20
☐	25	Vic Raschi	22.00	11.00	2.20	☐ 120	Joe Coleman	12.00	6.00	1.20
☐	26	Phil Rizzuto	65.00	32.50	6.50	☐ 121	Jerry Staley	12.00	6.00	1.20
☐	27	Jim Konstanty	18.00	9.00	1.80	☐ 122	Joe Garagiola	100.00	50.00	10.00
☐	28	Eddie Waitkus	16.00	8.00	1.60	☐ 123	Howie Judson	12.00	6.00	1.20
☐	29	Allie Clark	16.00	8.00	1.60	☐ 124	Gus Niarhos	12.00	6.00	1.20
☐	30	Bob Feller	100.00	50.00	10.00	☐ 125	Bill Rigney	12.00	6.00	1.20
☐	31	Roy Campanella	225.00	110.00	22.00	☐ 126	Bobby Thomson	25.00	12.50	2.50
☐	32	Duke Snider	180.00	90.00	18.00	☐ 127	Sal Maglie	35.00	17.50	3.50
☐	33	Bob Hooper	16.00	8.00	1.60	☐ 128	Ellis Kinder	12.00	6.00	1.20
☐	34	Marty Marion	20.00	10.00	2.00	☐ 129	Matt Batts	12.00	6.00	1.20
☐	35	Al Zarilla	16.00	8.00	1.60	☐ 130	Tom Saffell	12.00	6.00	1.20
☐	36	Joe Dobson	16.00	8.00	1.60	☐ 131	Cliff Chambers	12.00	6.00	1.20
☐	37	Whitey Lockman	16.00	8.00	1.60	☐ 132	Cass Michaels	12.00	6.00	1.20
☐	38	Al Evans	13.00	6.50	1.30	☐ 133	Sam Dente	12.00	6.00	1.20
☐	39	Ray Scarborough	13.00	6.50	1.30	☐ 134	Warren Spahn	90.00	45.00	9.00
☐	40	Gus Bell	20.00	10.00	2.00	☐ 135	Walker Cooper	12.00	6.00	1.20
☐	41	Eddie Yost	13.00	6.50	1.30	☐ 136	Ray Coleman	12.00	6.00	1.20
☐	42	Vern Bickford	13.00	6.50	1.30	☐ 137	Dick Starr	12.00	6.00	1.20
☐	43	Billy DeMars	13.00	6.50	1.30	☐ 138	Phil Cavarretta	15.00	7.50	1.50
☐	44	Roy Smalley	13.00	6.50	1.30	☐ 139	Doyle Lade	12.00	6.00	1.20
☐	45	Art Houtteman	13.00	6.50	1.30	☐ 140	Eddie Lake	12.00	6.00	1.20
☐	46	George Kell 1941	50.00	25.00	5.00	☐ 141	Fred Hutchinson	15.00	7.50	1.50
☐	47	Grady Hatton	13.00	6.50	1.30	☐ 142	Aaron Robinson	12.00	6.00	1.20
☐	48	Ken Raffensberger	13.00	6.50	1.30	☐ 143	Ted Kluszewski	25.00	12.50	2.50
☐	49	Jerry Coleman	16.00	8.00	1.60	☐ 144	Herman Wehmeier	12.00	6.00	1.20
☐	50	Johnny Mize	50.00	25.00	5.00	☐ 145	Fred Sanford	12.00	6.00	1.20
☐	51	Andy Seminick	13.00	6.50	1.30	☐ 146	Johnny Hopp	15.00	7.50	1.50
☐	52	Dick Sisler	13.00	6.50	1.30	☐ 147	Ken Heintzelman	12.00	6.00	1.20
☐	53	Bob Lemon	45.00	22.50	4.50	☐ 148	Granny Hamner	12.00	6.00	1.20
☐	54	Ray Boone	16.00	8.00	1.60	☐ 149	Bubba Church	12.00	6.00	1.20
☐	55	Gene Hermanski	13.00	6.50	1.30	☐ 150	Mike Garcia	15.00	7.50	1.50
☐	56	Ralph Branca	20.00	10.00	2.00	☐ 151	Larry Doby	21.00	10.50	2.10
☐	57	Alex Kellner	13.00	6.50	1.30	☐ 152	Cal Abrams	12.00	6.00	1.20
☐	58	Enos Slaughter	50.00	25.00	5.00	☐ 153	Rex Barney	12.00	6.00	1.20
☐	59	Randy Gumpert	13.00	6.50	1.30	☐ 154	Pete Suder	12.00	6.00	1.20
☐	60	Chico Carrasquel	13.00	6.50	1.30	☐ 155	Lou Brissie	12.00	6.00	1.20
☐	61	Jim Hearn	13.00	6.50	1.30	☐ 156	Del Rice	12.00	6.00	1.20
☐	62	Lou Boudreau	40.00	20.00	4.00	☐ 157	Al Brazle	12.00	6.00	1.20
☐	63	Bob Dillinger	13.00	6.50	1.30	☐ 158	Chuck Diering	12.00	6.00	1.20
☐	64	Bill Werle	13.00	6.50	1.30	☐ 159	Eddie Stewart	12.00	6.00	1.20
☐	65	Mickey Vernon	18.00	9.00	1.80	☐ 160	Phil Masi	12.00	6.00	1.20
☐	66	Bob Elliott	16.00	8.00	1.60	☐ 161	Wes Westrum	12.00	6.00	1.20
☐	67	Roy Sievers	16.00	8.00	1.60	☐ 162	Larry Jansen	12.00	6.00	1.20
☐	68	Dick Kokos	13.00	6.50	1.30	☐ 163	Monte Kennedy	12.00	6.00	1.20
☐	69	Johnny Schmitz	13.00	6.50	1.30	☐ 164	Bill Wight	12.00	6.00	1.20
☐	70	Ron Northey	13.00	6.50	1.30	☐ 165	Ted Williams	450.00	225.00	45.00
☐	71	Jerry Priddy	13.00	6.50	1.30	☐ 166	Stan Rojek	12.00	6.00	1.20
☐	72	Lloyd Merriman	13.00	6.50	1.30	☐ 167	Murry Dickson	12.00	6.00	1.20
☐	73	Tommy Byrne	15.00	7.50	1.50	☐ 168	Sam Mele	12.00	6.00	1.20
☐	74	Billy Johnson	15.00	7.50	1.50	☐ 169	Sid Hudson	12.00	6.00	1.20
☐	75	Russ Meyer	12.00	6.00	1.20	☐ 170	Sibby Sisti	12.00	6.00	1.20
☐	76	Stan Lopata	12.00	6.00	1.20	☐ 171	Buddy Kerr	12.00	6.00	1.20
☐	77	Mike Goliat	12.00	6.00	1.20	☐ 172	Ned Garver	12.00	6.00	1.20
☐	78	Early Wynn	45.00	22.50	4.50	☐ 173	Hank Arft	12.00	6.00	1.20
☐	79	Jim Hegan	15.00	7.50	1.50	☐ 174	Mickey Owen	15.00	7.50	1.50
☐	80	Pee Wee Reese	90.00	45.00	9.00	☐ 175	Wayne Terwilliger	12.00	6.00	1.20
☐	81	Carl Furillo	27.00	13.50	2.70	☐ 176	Vic Wertz	15.00	7.50	1.50
☐	82	Joe Tipton	12.00	6.00	1.20	☐ 177	Charlie Keller	15.00	7.50	1.50
☐	83	Carl Scheib	12.00	6.00	1.20	☐ 178	Ted Gray	12.00	6.00	1.20
☐	84	Barney McCosky	12.00	6.00	1.20	☐ 179	Danny Litwhiler	12.00	6.00	1.20
☐	85	Eddie Kazak	12.00	6.00	1.20	☐ 180	Howie Fox	12.00	6.00	1.20
☐	86	Harry Brecheen	15.00	7.50	1.50	☐ 181	Casey Stengel MG	80.00	40.00	8.00
☐	87	Floyd Baker	12.00	6.00	1.20	☐ 182	Tom Ferrick	12.00	6.00	1.20
☐	88	Eddie Robinson	12.00	6.00	1.20	☐ 183	Hank Bauer	25.00	12.50	2.50
☐	89	Hank Thompson	15.00	7.50	1.50	☐ 184	Eddie Sawyer MG	15.00	7.50	1.50
☐	90	Dave Koslo	12.00	6.00	1.20	☐ 185	Jimmy Bloodworth	12.00	6.00	1.20
☐	91	Clyde Vollmer	12.00	6.00	1.20	☐ 186	Richie Ashburn	45.00	22.50	4.50
☐	92	Vern Stephens	15.00	7.50	1.50	☐ 187	Al Rosen	22.00	11.00	2.20
☐	93	Danny O'Connell	12.00	6.00	1.20	☐ 188	Bobby Avila	15.00	7.50	1.50
☐	94	Clyde McCullough	12.00	6.00	1.20	☐ 189	Erv Palica	12.00	6.00	1.20
☐	95	Sherry Robertson	12.00	6.00	1.20	☐ 190	Joe Hatton	12.00	6.00	1.20
☐	96	Sandy Consuegra	12.00	6.00	1.20	☐ 191	Billy Hitchcock	12.00	6.00	1.20
☐	97	Bob Kuzava	12.00	6.00	1.20	☐ 192	Hank Wyse	12.00	6.00	1.20
☐	98	Willard Marshall	12.00	6.00	1.20	☐ 193	Ted Wilks	12.00	6.00	1.20
☐	99	Earl Torgeson	12.00	6.00	1.20	☐ 194	Peanuts Lowrey	12.00	6.00	1.20
☐	100	Sherm Lollar	15.00	7.50	1.50	☐ 195	Paul Richards	15.00	7.50	1.50
☐	101	Owen Friend	12.00	6.00	1.20		(caricature)			

☐ 196	Billy Pierce	22.00	11.00	2.20
☐ 197	Bob Cain	12.00	6.00	1.20
☐ 198	Monte Irvin	75.00	37.50	7.50
☐ 199	Sheldon Jones	12.00	6.00	1.20
☐ 200	Jack Kramer	12.00	6.00	1.20
☐ 201	Steve O'Neill	12.00	6.00	1.20
☐ 202	Mike Guerra	12.00	6.00	1.20
☐ 203	Vernon Law	20.00	10.00	2.00
☐ 204	Vic Lombardi	12.00	6.00	1.20
☐ 205	Mickey Grasso	12.00	6.00	1.20
☐ 206	Conrado Marrero	12.00	6.00	1.20
☐ 207	Billy Southworth	12.00	6.00	1.20
☐ 208	Blix Donnelly	12.00	6.00	1.20
☐ 209	Ken Wood	12.00	6.00	1.20
☐ 210	Les Moss	12.00	6.00	1.20
☐ 211	Hal Jeffcoat	12.00	6.00	1.20
☐ 212	Bob Rush	12.00	6.00	1.20
☐ 213	Neil Berry	12.00	6.00	1.20
☐ 214	Bob Swift	12.00	6.00	1.20
☐ 215	Ken Peterson	12.00	6.00	1.20
☐ 216	Connie Ryan	12.00	6.00	1.20
☐ 217	Joe Page	18.00	9.00	1.80
☐ 218	Ed Lopat	25.00	12.50	2.50
☐ 219	Gene Woodling	27.00	13.50	2.70
☐ 220	Bob Miller	12.00	6.00	1.20
☐ 221	Dick Whitman	12.00	6.00	1.20
☐ 222	Thurman Tucker	12.00	6.00	1.20
☐ 223	Johnny VanderMeer	20.00	10.00	2.00
☐ 224	Billy Cox	15.00	7.50	1.50
☐ 225	Dan Bankhead	15.00	7.50	1.50
☐ 226	Jimmy Dykes	15.00	7.50	1.50
☐ 227	Bobby Schantz	18.00	9.00	1.80
	(sic, Shantz)			
☐ 228	Cloyd Boyer	15.00	7.50	1.50
☐ 229	Bill Howerton	12.00	6.00	1.20
☐ 230	Max Lanier	12.00	6.00	1.20
☐ 231	Luis Aloma	12.00	6.00	1.20
☐ 232	Nelson Fox	75.00	30.00	6.00
☐ 233	Leo Durocher MG	40.00	20.00	4.00
☐ 234	Clint Hartung	12.00	6.00	1.20
☐ 235	Jack Lohrke	12.00	6.00	1.20
☐ 236	Warren Rosar	12.00	6.00	1.20
☐ 237	Billy Goodman	15.00	7.50	1.50
☐ 238	Pete Reiser	18.00	9.00	1.80
☐ 239	Bill MacDonald	12.00	6.00	1.20
☐ 240	Joe Haynes	12.00	6.00	1.20
☐ 241	Irv Noren	12.00	6.00	1.20
☐ 242	Sam Jethroe	12.00	6.00	1.20
☐ 243	Johnny Antonelli	15.00	7.50	1.50
☐ 244	Cliff Fannin	12.00	6.00	1.20
☐ 245	John Berardino	15.00	7.50	1.50
☐ 246	Bill Serena	12.00	6.00	1.20
☐ 247	Bob Ramazotti	12.00	6.00	1.20
☐ 248	Johnny Klippstein	12.00	6.00	1.20
☐ 249	Johnny Groth	12.00	6.00	1.20
☐ 250	Hank Borowy	12.00	6.00	1.20
☐ 251	Willard Ramsdell	12.00	6.00	1.20
☐ 252	Dixie Howell	12.00	6.00	1.20
☐ 253	Mickey Mantle	5000.00	2000.00	500.00
☐ 254	Jackie Jensen	100.00	50.00	10.00
☐ 255	Milo Candini	45.00	22.50	4.50
☐ 256	Ken Sylvestri	45.00	22.50	4.50
☐ 257	Birdie Tebbetts	55.00	27.50	5.50
☐ 258	Luke Easter	55.00	27.50	5.50
☐ 259	Chuck Dressen MG	55.00	27.50	5.50
☐ 260	Carl Erskine	85.00	42.50	8.50
☐ 261	Wally Moses	55.00	27.50	5.50
☐ 262	Gus Zernial	55.00	27.50	5.50
☐ 263	Howie Pollet	45.00	22.50	4.50
☐ 264	Don Richmond	45.00	22.50	4.50
☐ 265	Steve Bilko	45.00	22.50	4.50
☐ 266	Harry Dorish	45.00	22.50	4.50
☐ 267	Ken Holcombe	45.00	22.50	4.50
☐ 268	Don Mueller	55.00	27.50	5.50
☐ 269	Ray Noble	45.00	22.50	4.50
☐ 270	Willard Nixon	45.00	22.50	4.50
☐ 271	Tommy Wright	45.00	22.50	4.50
☐ 272	Billy Meyer MG	45.00	22.50	4.50
☐ 273	Danny Murtaugh	45.00	22.50	4.50
☐ 274	George Metkovich	45.00	22.50	4.50
☐ 275	Bucky Harris MG	65.00	32.50	6.50
☐ 276	Frank Quinn	45.00	22.50	4.50
☐ 277	Roy Hartsfield	45.00	22.50	4.50
☐ 278	Norman Roy	45.00	22.50	4.50
☐ 279	Jim Delsing	45.00	22.50	4.50
☐ 280	Frank Overmire	45.00	22.50	4.50
☐ 281	Al Widmar	45.00	22.50	4.50
☐ 282	Frank Frisch	75.00	37.50	7.50
☐ 283	Walt Dubiel	45.00	22.50	4.50
☐ 284	Gene Bearden	45.00	22.50	4.50
☐ 285	Johnny Lipon	45.00	22.50	4.50
☐ 286	Bob Usher	45.00	22.50	4.50
☐ 287	Jim Blackburn	45.00	22.50	4.50
☐ 288	Bobby Adams	45.00	22.50	4.50
☐ 289	Cliff Mapes	55.00	27.50	5.50

☐ 290	Bill Dickey	150.00	75.00	15.00
☐ 291	Tommy Henrich	65.00	32.50	6.50
☐ 292	Eddie Pellegrini	45.00	22.50	4.50
☐ 293	Ken Johnson	45.00	22.50	4.50
☐ 294	Jocko Thompson	45.00	22.50	4.50
☐ 295	Al Lopez MG	75.00	37.50	7.50
☐ 296	Bob Kennedy	55.00	27.50	5.50
☐ 297	Dave Philley	45.00	22.50	4.50
☐ 298	Joe Astroth	45.00	22.50	4.50
☐ 299	Clyde King	55.00	27.50	5.50
☐ 300	Hal Rice	45.00	22.50	4.50
☐ 301	Tommy Glaviano	45.00	22.50	4.50
☐ 302	Jim Busby	45.00	22.50	4.50
☐ 303	Marv Rotblatt	45.00	22.50	4.50
☐ 304	Al Gettell	45.00	22.50	4.50
☐ 305	Willie Mays	1700.00	600.00	150.00
☐ 306	Jim Piersall	90.00	45.00	9.00
☐ 307	Walt Masterson	45.00	22.50	4.50
☐ 308	Ted Beard	45.00	22.50	4.50
☐ 309	Mel Queen	45.00	22.50	4.50
☐ 310	Erv Dusak	45.00	22.50	4.50
☐ 311	Mickey Harris	45.00	22.50	4.50
☐ 312	Gene Mauch	55.00	27.50	5.50
☐ 313	Ray Mueller	45.00	22.50	4.50
☐ 314	Johnny Sain	55.00	27.50	5.50
☐ 315	Zack Taylor	45.00	22.50	4.50
☐ 316	Duane Pillette	45.00	22.50	4.50
☐ 317	Smokey Burgess	55.00	27.50	5.50
☐ 318	Warren Hacker	45.00	22.50	4.50
☐ 319	Red Rolfe	55.00	27.50	5.50
☐ 320	Hal White	45.00	22.50	4.50
☐ 321	Earl Johnson	45.00	22.50	4.50
☐ 322	Luke Sewell	55.00	27.50	5.50
☐ 323	Joe Adcock	65.00	32.50	6.50
☐ 324	Johnny Pramesa	85.00	25.00	5.00

1952 Bowman

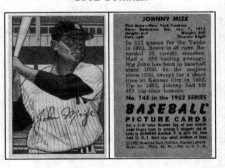

The cards in this 252-card set measure 2 1/16" by 3 1/8". While the Bowman set of 1952 retained the card size introduced in 1951, it employed a modification of color tones from the two preceding years. The cards also appeared with a facsimile autograph on the front and, for the first time since 1949, premium advertising on the back. The 1952 set was sold in sheets as well as in gum packs. Artwork for 15 cards that were never issued was recently discovered.

		NRMT	VG-E	GOOD
COMPLETE SET (252)		8200.00	4100.00	900.00
COMMON PLAYER (1-36)		16.00	8.00	1.60
COMMON PLAYER (37-144)		14.00	7.00	1.40
COMMON PLAYER (145-180)		13.00	6.50	1.30
COMMON PLAYER (181-216)		12.00	6.00	1.20
COMMON PLAYER (217-252)		27.00	13.50	2.70

☐ 1	Yogi Berra	600.00	150.00	30.00
☐ 2	Bobby Thomson	25.00	12.50	2.50
☐ 3	Fred Hutchinson	20.00	10.00	2.00
☐ 4	Robin Roberts	50.00	25.00	5.00
☐ 5	Minnie Minoso	40.00	20.00	4.00
☐ 6	Virgil Stallcup	16.00	8.00	1.60
☐ 7	Mike Garcia	18.00	9.00	1.80
☐ 8	Pee Wee Reese	90.00	45.00	9.00
☐ 9	Vern Stephens	18.00	9.00	1.80
☐ 10	Bob Hooper	16.00	8.00	1.60
☐ 11	Ralph Kiner	45.00	22.50	4.50

□	#	Name			
□	12	Max Surkont	16.00	8.00	1.60
□	13	Cliff Mapes	16.00	8.00	1.60
□	14	Cliff Chambers	16.00	8.00	1.60
□	15	Sam Mele	16.00	8.00	1.60
□	16	Turk Lown	16.00	8.00	1.60
□	17	Ed Lopat	25.00	12.50	2.50
□	18	Don Mueller	18.00	9.00	1.80
□	19	Bob Cain	16.00	8.00	1.60
□	20	Willie Jones	16.00	8.00	1.60
□	21	Nellie Fox	35.00	17.50	3.50
□	22	Willard Ramsdell	16.00	8.00	1.60
□	23	Bob Lemon	45.00	22.50	4.50
□	24	Carl Furillo	27.00	13.50	2.70
□	25	Mickey McDermott	16.00	8.00	1.60
□	26	Eddie Joost	16.00	8.00	1.60
□	27	Joe Garagiola	60.00	30.00	6.00
□	28	Roy Hartsfield	16.00	8.00	1.60
□	29	Ned Garver	16.00	8.00	1.60
□	30	Red Schoendienst	50.00	25.00	5.00
□	31	Eddie Yost	16.00	8.00	1.60
□	32	Eddie Miksis	16.00	8.00	1.60
□	33	Gil McDougald	40.00	20.00	4.00
□	34	Alvin Dark	20.00	10.00	2.00
□	35	Granny Hamner	14.00	7.00	1.40
□	36	Cass Michaels	14.00	7.00	1.40
□	37	Vic Raschi	18.00	9.00	1.80
□	38	Whitey Lockman	16.00	8.00	1.60
□	39	Vic Wertz	16.00	8.00	1.60
□	40	Bubba Church	14.00	7.00	1.40
□	41	Chico Carrasquel	14.00	7.00	1.40
□	42	Johnny Wyrostek	14.00	7.00	1.40
□	43	Bob Feller	80.00	40.00	8.00
□	44	Roy Campanella	175.00	85.00	18.00
□	45	Johnny Pesky	16.00	8.00	1.60
□	46	Carl Scheib	14.00	7.00	1.40
□	47	Pete Castiglione	14.00	7.00	1.40
□	48	Vern Bickford	14.00	7.00	1.40
□	49	Jim Hearn	14.00	7.00	1.40
□	50	Jerry Staley	14.00	7.00	1.40
□	51	Gil Coan	14.00	7.00	1.40
□	52	Phil Rizzuto	55.00	27.50	5.50
□	53	Richie Ashburn	40.00	20.00	4.00
□	54	Billy Pierce	18.00	9.00	1.80
□	55	Ken Raffensberger	14.00	7.00	1.40
□	56	Clyde King	16.00	8.00	1.60
□	57	Clyde Vollmer	14.00	7.00	1.40
□	58	Hank Majeski	14.00	7.00	1.40
□	59	Murry Dickson	14.00	7.00	1.40
□	60	Sid Gordon	14.00	7.00	1.40
□	61	Tommy Byrne	14.00	7.00	1.40
□	62	Joe Presko	14.00	7.00	1.40
□	63	Irv Noren	14.00	7.00	1.40
□	64	Roy Smalley	14.00	7.00	1.40
□	65	Hank Bauer	21.00	10.50	2.10
□	66	Sal Maglie	20.00	10.00	2.00
□	67	Johnny Groth	14.00	7.00	1.40
□	68	Jim Busby	14.00	7.00	1.40
□	69	Joe Adcock	18.00	9.00	1.80
□	70	Carl Erskine	21.00	10.50	2.10
□	71	Vernon Law	16.00	8.00	1.60
□	72	Earl Torgeson	14.00	7.00	1.40
□	73	Gerry Coleman	16.00	8.00	1.60
□	74	Wes Westrum	14.00	7.00	1.40
□	75	George Kell	40.00	20.00	4.00
□	76	Del Ennis	16.00	8.00	1.60
□	77	Eddie Robinson	14.00	7.00	1.40
□	78	Lloyd Merriman	14.00	7.00	1.40
□	79	Lou Brissie	14.00	7.00	1.40
□	80	Gil Hodges	50.00	25.00	5.00
□	81	Billy Goodman	16.00	8.00	1.60
□	82	Gus Zernial	16.00	8.00	1.60
□	83	Howie Pollet	14.00	7.00	1.40
□	84	Sam Jethroe	14.00	7.00	1.40
□	85	Marty Marion	20.00	10.00	2.00
□	86	Cal Abrams	14.00	7.00	1.40
□	87	Mickey Vernon	18.00	9.00	1.80
□	88	Bruce Edwards	14.00	7.00	1.40
□	89	Billy Hitchcock	14.00	7.00	1.40
□	90	Larry Jansen	14.00	7.00	1.40
□	91	Don Kolloway	14.00	7.00	1.40
□	92	Eddie Waitkus	14.00	7.00	1.40
□	93	Paul Richards	16.00	8.00	1.60
□	94	Luke Sewell	16.00	8.00	1.60
□	95	Luke Easter	16.00	8.00	1.60
□	96	Ralph Branca	20.00	10.00	2.00
□	97	Willard Marshall	14.00	7.00	1.40
□	98	Jimmy Dykes	16.00	8.00	1.60
□	99	Clyde McCullough	14.00	7.00	1.40
□	100	Sibby Sisti	14.00	7.00	1.40
□	101	Mickey Mantle	1500.00	600.00	150.00
□	102	Peanuts Lowrey	14.00	7.00	1.40
□	103	Joe Haynes	14.00	7.00	1.40
□	104	Hal Jeffcoat	14.00	7.00	1.40
□	105	Bobby Brown	22.00	11.00	2.20
□	106	Randy Gumpert	14.00	7.00	1.40
□	107	Del Rice	14.00	7.00	1.40
□	108	George Metkovich	14.00	7.00	1.40
□	109	Tom Morgan	14.00	7.00	1.40
□	110	Max Lanier	14.00	7.00	1.40
□	111	Hoot Evers	14.00	7.00	1.40
□	112	Smokey Burgess	16.00	8.00	1.60
□	113	Al Zarilla	14.00	7.00	1.40
□	114	Frank Hiller	14.00	7.00	1.40
□	115	Larry Doby	20.00	10.00	2.00
□	116	Duke Snider	150.00	75.00	15.00
□	117	Bill Wight	14.00	7.00	1.40
□	118	Ray Murray	14.00	7.00	1.40
□	119	Bill Howerton	14.00	7.00	1.40
□	120	Chet Nichols	14.00	7.00	1.40
□	121	Al Corwin	14.00	7.00	1.40
□	122	Billy Johnson	14.00	7.00	1.40
□	123	Sid Hudson	14.00	7.00	1.40
□	124	Birdie Tebbetts	16.00	8.00	1.60
□	125	Howie Fox	14.00	7.00	1.40
□	126	Phil Cavarretta	16.00	8.00	1.60
□	127	Dick Sisler	14.00	7.00	1.40
□	128	Don Newcombe	21.00	10.50	2.10
□	129	Gus Niarhos	14.00	7.00	1.40
□	130	Allie Clark	14.00	7.00	1.40
□	131	Bob Swift	14.00	7.00	1.40
□	132	Dave Cole	14.00	7.00	1.40
□	133	Dick Kryhoski	14.00	7.00	1.40
□	134	Al Brazle	14.00	7.00	1.40
□	135	Mickey Harris	14.00	7.00	1.40
□	136	Gene Hermanski	14.00	7.00	1.40
□	137	Stan Rojek	14.00	7.00	1.40
□	138	Ted Wilks	14.00	7.00	1.40
□	139	Jerry Priddy	14.00	7.00	1.40
□	140	Ray Scarborough	14.00	7.00	1.40
□	141	Hank Edwards	14.00	7.00	1.40
□	142	Early Wynn	40.00	20.00	4.00
□	143	Sandy Consuegra	14.00	7.00	1.40
□	144	Joe Hatton	14.00	7.00	1.40
□	145	Johnny Mize	50.00	25.00	5.00
□	146	Leo Durocher MG	36.00	18.00	3.60
□	147	Marlin Stuart	13.00	6.50	1.30
□	148	Ken Heintzelman	13.00	6.50	1.30
□	149	Howie Judson	13.00	6.50	1.30
□	150	Herman Wehmeier	13.00	6.50	1.30
□	151	Al Rosen	20.00	10.00	2.00
□	152	Billy Cox	16.00	8.00	1.60
□	153	Fred Hatfield	13.00	6.50	1.30
□	154	Ferris Fain	15.00	7.50	1.50
□	155	Billy Meyer	13.00	6.50	1.30
□	156	Warren Spahn	75.00	37.50	7.50
□	157	Jim Delsing	13.00	6.50	1.30
□	158	Bucky Harris MG	27.00	13.50	2.70
□	159	Dutch Leonard	13.00	6.50	1.30
□	160	Eddie Stanky	16.00	8.00	1.60
□	161	Jackie Jensen	25.00	12.50	2.50
□	162	Monte Irvin	40.00	20.00	4.00
□	163	Johnny Lipon	13.00	6.50	1.30
□	164	Connie Ryan	13.00	6.50	1.30
□	165	Saul Rogovin	13.00	6.50	1.30
□	166	Bobby Adams	13.00	6.50	1.30
□	167	Bobby Avila	15.00	7.50	1.50
□	168	Preacher Roe	22.00	11.00	2.20
□	169	Walt Dropo	15.00	7.50	1.50
□	170	Joe Astroth	13.00	6.50	1.30
□	171	Mel Queen	13.00	6.50	1.30
□	172	Ebba St.Claire	13.00	6.50	1.30
□	173	Gene Bearden	13.00	6.50	1.30
□	174	Mickey Grasso	13.00	6.50	1.30
□	175	Randy Jackson	13.00	6.50	1.30
□	176	Harry Brecheen	13.00	6.50	1.30
□	177	Gene Woodling	18.00	9.00	1.80
□	178	Dave Williams	16.00	8.00	1.60
□	179	Pete Suder	13.00	6.50	1.30
□	180	Ed Fitzgerald	13.00	6.50	1.30
□	181	Joe Collins	15.00	7.50	1.50
□	182	Dave Koslo	12.00	6.00	1.20
□	183	Pat Mullin	12.00	6.00	1.20
□	184	Curt Simmons	15.00	7.50	1.50
□	185	Eddie Stewart	12.00	6.00	1.20
□	186	Frank Smith	12.00	6.00	1.20
□	187	Jim Hegan	14.00	7.00	1.40
□	188	Charlie Dressen MG	15.00	7.50	1.50
□	189	Jim Piersall	18.00	9.00	1.80
□	190	Dick Fowler	12.00	6.00	1.20
□	191	Bob Friend	18.00	9.00	1.80
□	192	John Cusick	12.00	6.00	1.20
□	193	Bobby Young	12.00	6.00	1.20
□	194	Bob Porterfield	12.00	6.00	1.20
□	195	Frank Baumholtz	12.00	6.00	1.20
□	196	Stan Musial	400.00	200.00	40.00
□	197	Charlie Silvera	12.00	6.00	1.20
□	198	Chuck Diering	12.00	6.00	1.20
□	199	Ted Gray	12.00	6.00	1.20
□	200	Ken Silvestri	12.00	6.00	1.20
□	201	Ray Coleman	12.00	6.00	1.20

☐ 202	Harry Perkowski	12.00	6.00	1.20
☐ 203	Steve Gromek	12.00	6.00	1.20
☐ 204	Andy Pafko	14.00	7.00	1.40
☐ 205	Walt Masterson	12.00	6.00	1.20
☐ 206	Elmer Valo	12.00	6.00	1.20
☐ 207	George Strickland	12.00	6.00	1.20
☐ 208	Walker Cooper	12.00	6.00	1.20
☐ 209	Dick Littlefield	12.00	6.00	1.20
☐ 210	Archie Wilson	12.00	6.00	1.20
☐ 211	Paul Minner	12.00	6.00	1.20
☐ 212	Solly Hemus	12.00	6.00	1.20
☐ 213	Monte Kennedy	12.00	6.00	1.20
☐ 214	Ray Boone	12.00	6.00	1.20
☐ 215	Sheldon Jones	12.00	6.00	1.20
☐ 216	Matt Batts	12.00	6.00	1.20
☐ 217	Casey Stengel MG	125.00	60.00	12.50
☐ 218	Willie Mays	800.00	400.00	80.00
☐ 219	Neil Berry	27.00	13.50	2.70
☐ 220	Russ Meyer	27.00	13.50	2.70
☐ 221	Lou Kretlow	27.00	13.50	2.70
☐ 222	Dixie Howell	27.00	13.50	2.70
☐ 223	Harry Simpson	27.00	13.50	2.70
☐ 224	Johnny Schmitz	27.00	13.50	2.70
☐ 225	Del Wilber	27.00	13.50	2.70
☐ 226	Alex Kellner	27.00	13.50	2.70
☐ 227	Clyde Sukeforth	27.00	13.50	2.70
☐ 228	Bob Chipman	27.00	13.50	2.70
☐ 229	Hank Arft	27.00	13.50	2.70
☐ 230	Frank Shea	27.00	13.50	2.70
☐ 231	Dee Fondy	27.00	13.50	2.70
☐ 232	Enos Slaughter	65.00	32.50	6.50
☐ 233	Bob Kuzava	27.00	13.50	2.70
☐ 234	Fred Fitzsimmons	27.00	13.50	2.70
☐ 235	Steve Souchock	27.00	13.50	2.70
☐ 236	Tommy Brown	27.00	13.50	2.70
☐ 237	Sherm Lollar	32.00	16.00	3.20
☐ 238	Roy McMillan	32.00	16.00	3.20
☐ 239	Dale Mitchell	32.00	16.00	3.20
☐ 240	Billy Loes	32.00	16.00	3.20
☐ 241	Mel Parnell	32.00	16.00	3.20
☐ 242	Everett Kell	27.00	13.50	2.70
☐ 243	Red Munger	27.00	13.50	2.70
☐ 244	Lew Burdette	50.00	25.00	5.00
☐ 245	George Schmees	27.00	13.50	2.70
☐ 246	Jerry Snyder	27.00	13.50	2.70
☐ 247	Johnny Pramesa	27.00	13.50	2.70
☐ 248	Bill Werle	27.00	13.50	2.70
☐ 249	Hank Thompson	32.00	16.00	3.20
☐ 250	Ike Delock	27.00	13.50	2.70
☐ 251	Jack Lohrke	27.00	13.50	2.70
☐ 252	Frank Crosetti CO	125.00	25.00	5.00

1953 Bowman Color

The cards in this 160-card set measure 2 1/2" by 3 3/4". The 1953 Bowman Color set, considered by many to be the best looking set of the modern era, contains Kodachrome photographs with no names or facsimile autographs on the face. Numbers 113 to 160 are somewhat more difficult to obtain. There are two cards of Al Corwin (126 and 149).

	NRMT	VG-E	GOOD
COMPLETE SET (160)	10000.00	5000.00	1250.00
COMMON PLAYER (1-96)	25.00	12.50	2.50
COMMON PLAYER (97-112)	28.00	14.00	2.80
COMMON PLAYER (113-128)	45.00	22.50	4.50
COMMON PLAYER (129-160)	33.00	16.00	3.50

☐ 1	Dave Williams	100.00	15.00	3.00

☐ 2	Vic Wertz	28.00	14.00	2.80
☐ 3	Sam Jethroe	25.00	12.50	2.50
☐ 4	Art Houtteman	25.00	12.50	2.50
☐ 5	Sid Gordon	25.00	12.50	2.50
☐ 6	Joe Ginsberg	25.00	12.50	2.50
☐ 7	Harry Chiti	25.00	12.50	2.50
☐ 8	Al Rosen	35.00	17.50	3.50
☐ 9	Phil Rizzuto	75.00	37.50	7.50
☐ 10	Richie Ashburn	50.00	25.00	5.00
☐ 11	Bobby Shantz	30.00	15.00	3.00
☐ 12	Carl Erskine	35.00	17.50	3.50
☐ 13	Gus Zernial	28.00	14.00	2.80
☐ 14	Billy Loes	28.00	14.00	2.80
☐ 15	Jim Busby	25.00	12.50	2.50
☐ 16	Bob Friend	28.00	14.00	2.80
☐ 17	Jerry Staley	25.00	12.50	2.50
☐ 18	Nellie Fox	48.00	24.00	5.00
☐ 19	Alvin Dark	30.00	15.00	3.00
☐ 20	Don Lenhardt	25.00	12.50	2.50
☐ 21	Joe Garagiola	50.00	25.00	5.00
☐ 22	Bob Porterfield	25.00	12.50	2.50
☐ 23	Herman Wehmeier	25.00	12.50	2.50
☐ 24	Jackie Jensen	32.00	16.00	3.20
☐ 25	Hoot Evers	25.00	12.50	2.50
☐ 26	Roy McMillan	25.00	12.50	2.50
☐ 27	Vic Raschi	32.00	16.00	3.20
☐ 28	Smokey Burgess	28.00	14.00	2.80
☐ 29	Bobby Avila	28.00	14.00	2.80
☐ 30	Phil Cavarretta	28.00	14.00	2.80
☐ 31	Jimmy Dykes	28.00	14.00	2.80
☐ 32	Stan Musial	425.00	200.00	42.00
☐ 33	Pee Wee Reese HOR	225.00	110.00	22.00
☐ 34	Gil Coan	25.00	12.50	2.50
☐ 35	Maurice McDermott	25.00	12.50	2.50
☐ 36	Minnie Minoso	35.00	17.50	3.50
☐ 37	Jim Wilson	25.00	12.50	2.50
☐ 38	Harry Byrd	25.00	12.50	2.50
☐ 39	Paul Richards MG	28.00	14.00	2.80
☐ 40	Larry Doby	35.00	17.50	3.50
☐ 41	Sammy White	25.00	12.50	2.50
☐ 42	Tommy Brown	25.00	12.50	2.50
☐ 43	Mike Garcia	28.00	14.00	2.80
☐ 44	Berra/Bauer/Mantle	350.00	175.00	35.00
☐ 45	Walt Dropo	28.00	14.00	2.80
☐ 46	Roy Campanella	225.00	110.00	22.00
☐ 47	Ned Garver	25.00	12.50	2.50
☐ 48	Hank Sauer	28.00	14.00	2.80
☐ 49	Eddie Stanky	30.00	15.00	3.00
☐ 50	Lou Kretlow	25.00	12.50	2.50
☐ 51	Monte Irvin	50.00	25.00	5.00
☐ 52	Marty Marion	32.00	16.00	3.20
☐ 53	Del Rice	25.00	12.50	2.50
☐ 54	Chico Carrasquel	25.00	12.50	2.50
☐ 55	Leo Durocher MG	45.00	22.50	4.50
☐ 56	Bob Cain	25.00	12.50	2.50
☐ 57	Lou Boudreau MG	50.00	25.00	5.00
☐ 58	Willard Marshall	25.00	12.50	2.50
☐ 59	Mickey Mantle	1400.00	500.00	150.00
☐ 60	Granny Hamner	25.00	12.50	2.50
☐ 61	George Kell	50.00	25.00	5.00
☐ 62	Ted Kluszewski	35.00	17.50	3.50
☐ 63	Gil McDougald	35.00	17.50	3.50
☐ 64	Curt Simmons	30.00	15.00	3.00
☐ 65	Robin Roberts	55.00	27.50	5.50
☐ 66	Mel Parnell	28.00	14.00	2.80
☐ 67	Mel Clark	25.00	12.50	2.50
☐ 68	Allie Reynolds	35.00	17.50	3.50
☐ 69	Charlie Grimm MG	28.00	14.00	2.80
☐ 70	Clint Courtney	25.00	12.50	2.50
☐ 71	Paul Minner	25.00	12.50	2.50
☐ 72	Ted Gray	25.00	12.50	2.50
☐ 73	Billy Pierce	28.00	14.00	2.80
☐ 74	Don Mueller	28.00	14.00	2.80
☐ 75	Saul Rogovin	25.00	12.50	2.50
☐ 76	Jim Hearn	25.00	12.50	2.50
☐ 77	Mickey Grasso	25.00	12.50	2.50
☐ 78	Carl Furillo	35.00	17.50	3.50
☐ 79	Ray Boone	28.00	14.00	2.80
☐ 80	Ralph Kiner	60.00	30.00	6.00
☐ 81	Enos Slaughter	60.00	30.00	6.00
☐ 82	Joe Astroth	25.00	12.50	2.50
☐ 83	Jack Daniels	25.00	12.50	2.50
☐ 84	Hank Bauer	35.00	17.50	3.50
☐ 85	Solly Hemus	25.00	12.50	2.50
☐ 86	Harry Simpson	25.00	12.50	2.50
☐ 87	Harry Perkowski	25.00	12.50	2.50
☐ 88	Joe Dobson	25.00	12.50	2.50
☐ 89	Sandy Consuegra	25.00	12.50	2.50
☐ 90	Joe Nuxhall	28.00	14.00	2.80
☐ 91	Steve Souchock	25.00	12.50	2.50
☐ 92	Gil Hodges	100.00	50.00	10.00
☐ 93	Phil Rizzuto and Billy Martin	200.00	100.00	20.00
☐ 94	Bob Addis	25.00	12.50	2.50
☐ 95	Wally Moses	28.00	14.00	2.80

		NRMT	VG-E	GOOD
☐	96 Sal Maglie	32.00	16.00	3.20
☐	97 Eddie Mathews	150.00	75.00	15.00
☐	98 Hector Rodriguez	28.00	14.00	2.80
☐	99 Warren Spahn	110.00	55.00	11.00
☐	100 Bill Wight	28.00	14.00	2.80
☐	101 Red Schoendienst	75.00	37.50	7.50
☐	102 Jim Hegan	30.00	15.00	3.00
☐	103 Del Ennis	30.00	15.00	3.00
☐	104 Luke Easter	30.00	15.00	3.00
☐	105 Eddie Joost	28.00	14.00	2.80
☐	106 Ken Raffensberger	28.00	14.00	2.80
☐	107 Alex Kellner	28.00	14.00	2.80
☐	108 Bobby Adams	28.00	14.00	2.80
☐	109 Ken Wood	28.00	14.00	2.80
☐	110 Bob Rush	28.00	14.00	2.80
☐	111 Jim Dyck	28.00	14.00	2.80
☐	112 Toby Atwell	28.00	14.00	2.80
☐	113 Karl Drews	45.00	22.50	4.50
☐	114 Bob Feller	250.00	125.00	25.00
☐	115 Cloyd Boyer	45.00	22.50	4.50
☐	116 Eddie Yost	45.00	22.50	4.50
☐	117 Duke Snider	500.00	250.00	50.00
☐	118 Billy Martin	250.00	125.00	25.00
☐	119 Dale Mitchell	45.00	22.50	4.50
☐	120 Marlin Stuart	45.00	22.50	4.50
☐	121 Yogi Berra	500.00	250.00	50.00
☐	122 Bill Serena	45.00	22.50	4.50
☐	123 Johnny Lipon	45.00	22.50	4.50
☐	124 Charlie Dressen MG	55.00	27.50	5.50
☐	125 Fred Hatfield	45.00	22.50	4.50
☐	126 Al Corwin	45.00	22.50	4.50
☐	127 Dick Kryhoski	45.00	22.50	4.50
☐	128 Whitey Lockman	45.00	22.50	4.50
☐	129 Russ Meyer	33.00	16.00	3.50
☐	130 Cass Michaels	33.00	16.00	3.50
☐	131 Connie Ryan	33.00	16.00	3.50
☐	132 Fred Hutchinson	40.00	20.00	4.00
☐	133 Willie Jones	33.00	16.00	3.50
☐	134 Johnny Pesky	36.00	18.00	3.60
☐	135 Bobby Morgan	33.00	16.00	3.50
☐	136 Jim Brideweser	33.00	16.00	3.50
☐	137 Sam Dente	33.00	16.00	3.50
☐	138 Bubba Church	33.00	16.00	3.50
☐	139 Pete Runnels	36.00	18.00	3.60
☐	140 Al Brazle	33.00	16.00	3.50
☐	141 Frank Shea	33.00	16.00	3.50
☐	142 Larry Miggins	33.00	16.00	3.50
☐	143 Al Lopez MG	65.00	32.50	6.50
☐	144 Warren Hacker	33.00	16.00	3.50
☐	145 George Shuba	36.00	18.00	3.60
☐	146 Early Wynn	110.00	55.00	11.00
☐	147 Clem Koshorek	33.00	16.00	3.50
☐	148 Billy Goodman	36.00	18.00	3.60
☐	149 Al Corwin	33.00	16.00	3.50
☐	150 Carl Scheib	33.00	16.00	3.50
☐	151 Joe Adcock	40.00	20.00	4.00
☐	152 Clyde Vollmer	33.00	16.00	3.50
☐	153 Whitey Ford	375.00	175.00	37.00
☐	154 Turk Lown	33.00	16.00	3.50
☐	155 Allie Clark	33.00	16.00	3.50
☐	156 Max Surkont	33.00	16.00	3.50
☐	157 Sherm Lollar	36.00	18.00	3.60
☐	158 Howard Fox	33.00	16.00	3.50
☐	159 Mickey Vernon (photo actually Floyd Baker)	40.00	20.00	4.00
☐	160 Cal Abrams	60.00	20.00	4.00

1953 Bowman BW

The cards in this 64-card set measure 2 1/2" by 3 3/4". Some collectors believe that the high cost of producing the 1953 color series forced Bowman to issue this set in black and white, since the two sets are identical in design except for the element of color. This set was also produced in fewer numbers than its color counterpart, and is popular among collectors for the challenge involved in completing it.

		NRMT	VG-E	GOOD
	COMPLETE SET (64)	2250.00	1100.00	300.00
	COMMON PLAYER (1-64)	28.00	14.00	2.80
☐	1 Gus Bell	100.00	15.00	3.00
☐	2 Willard Nixon	28.00	14.00	2.80
☐	3 Bill Rigney	28.00	14.00	2.80

		NRMT	VG-E	GOOD
☐	4 Pat Mullin	28.00	14.00	2.80
☐	5 Dee Fondy	28.00	14.00	2.80
☐	6 Ray Murray	28.00	14.00	2.80
☐	7 Andy Seminick	28.00	14.00	2.80
☐	8 Pete Suder	28.00	14.00	2.80
☐	9 Walt Masterson	28.00	14.00	2.80
☐	10 Dick Sisler	28.00	14.00	2.80
☐	11 Dick Gernert	28.00	14.00	2.80
☐	12 Randy Jackson	28.00	14.00	2.80
☐	13 Joe Tipton	28.00	14.00	2.80
☐	14 Bill Nicholson	28.00	14.00	2.80
☐	15 Johnny Mize	100.00	50.00	10.00
☐	16 Stu Miller	33.00	16.00	3.50
☐	17 Virgil Trucks	33.00	16.00	3.50
☐	18 Billy Hoeft	33.00	16.00	3.50
☐	19 Paul LaPalme	28.00	14.00	2.80
☐	20 Eddie Robinson	28.00	14.00	2.80
☐	21 Clarence Podbielan	28.00	14.00	2.80
☐	22 Matt Batts	28.00	14.00	2.80
☐	23 Wilmer Mizell	33.00	16.00	3.50
☐	24 Del Wilber	28.00	14.00	2.80
☐	25 Johnny Sain	50.00	25.00	5.00
☐	26 Preacher Roe	50.00	25.00	5.00
☐	27 Bob Lemon	90.00	45.00	9.00
☐	28 Hoyt Wilhelm	100.00	50.00	10.00
☐	29 Sid Hudson	28.00	14.00	2.80
☐	30 Walker Cooper	28.00	14.00	2.80
☐	31 Gene Woodling	40.00	20.00	4.00
☐	32 Rocky Bridges	28.00	14.00	2.80
☐	33 Bob Kuzava	28.00	14.00	2.80
☐	34 Ebba St.Claire	28.00	14.00	2.80
☐	35 Johnny Wyrostek	28.00	14.00	2.80
☐	36 Jim Piersall	40.00	20.00	4.00
☐	37 Hal Jeffcoat	28.00	14.00	2.80
☐	38 Dave Cole	28.00	14.00	2.80
☐	39 Casey Stengel MG	275.00	135.00	27.00
☐	40 Larry Jansen	33.00	16.00	3.50
☐	41 Bob Ramazotti	28.00	14.00	2.80
☐	42 Howie Judson	28.00	14.00	2.80
☐	43 Hal Bevan	28.00	14.00	2.80
☐	44 Jim Delsing	28.00	14.00	2.80
☐	45 Irv Noren	33.00	16.00	3.50
☐	46 Bucky Harris	50.00	25.00	5.00
☐	47 Jack Lohrke	28.00	14.00	2.80
☐	48 Steve Ridzik	28.00	14.00	2.80
☐	49 Floyd Baker	28.00	14.00	2.80
☐	50 Dutch Leonard	28.00	14.00	2.80
☐	51 Lou Burdette	40.00	20.00	4.00
☐	52 Ralph Branca	36.00	18.00	3.60
☐	53 Morrie Martin	28.00	14.00	2.80
☐	54 Bill Miller	28.00	14.00	2.80
☐	55 Don Johnson	28.00	14.00	2.80
☐	56 Roy Smalley	28.00	14.00	2.80
☐	57 Andy Pafko	33.00	16.00	3.50
☐	58 Jim Konstanty	33.00	16.00	3.50
☐	59 Duane Pillette	28.00	14.00	2.80
☐	60 Billy Cox	33.00	16.00	3.50
☐	61 Tom Gorman	28.00	14.00	2.80
☐	62 Keith Thomas	28.00	14.00	2.80
☐	63 Steve Gromek	28.00	14.00	2.80
☐	64 Andy Hansen	45.00	15.00	3.00

1954 Bowman

The cards in this 224-card set measure 2 1/2" by 3 3/4". A contractual problem apparently resulted in the deletion of the number 66 Ted Williams card from this Bowman set, thereby creating a scarcity which

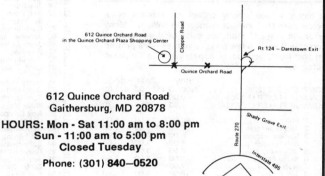

is highly valued among collectors. The set price below does NOT include number 66 Williams. Many errors in players' statistics exist (and some were corrected) while a few players' names were printed on the front, instead of appearing as a facsimile autograph.

	NRMT	VG-E	GOOD
COMPLETE SET (224)	3600.00	1800.00	425.00
COMMON PLAYER (1-128)	6.00	3.00	.60
COMMON PLAYER (129-224)	7.00	3.50	.70

		NRMT	VG-E	GOOD
☐	1 Phil Rizzuto	160.00	25.00	5.00
☐	2 Jackie Jensen	10.00	5.00	1.00
☐	3 Marion Fricano	6.00	3.00	.60
☐	4 Bob Hooper	6.00	3.00	.60
☐	5 Billy Hunter	6.00	3.00	.60
☐	6 Nellie Fox	16.00	8.00	1.60
☐	7 Walt Dropo	7.00	3.50	.70
☐	8 Jim Busby	6.00	3.00	.60
☐	9 Davey Williams	7.00	3.50	.70
☐	10 Carl Erskine	10.00	5.00	1.00
☐	11 Sid Gordon	6.00	3.00	.60
☐	12 Roy McMillan	6.00	3.00	.60
☐	13 Paul Minner	6.00	3.00	.60
☐	14 Jerry Staley	6.00	3.00	.60
☐	15 Richie Ashburn	22.00	11.00	2.20
☐	16 Jim Wilson	6.00	3.00	.60
☐	17 Tom Gorman	6.00	3.00	.60
☐	18 Hoot Evers	6.00	3.00	.60
☐	19 Bobby Shantz	8.00	4.00	.80
☐	20 Art Houtteman	6.00	3.00	.60
☐	21 Vic Wertz	7.00	3.50	.70
☐	22 Sam Mele	6.00	3.00	.60
☐	23 Harvey Kuenn	22.00	11.00	2.20
☐	24 Bob Porterfield	6.00	3.00	.60
☐	25 Wes Westrum	6.00	3.00	.60
☐	26 Billy Cox	7.00	3.50	.70
☐	27 Dick Cole	6.00	3.00	.60
☐	28 Jim Greengrass	6.00	3.00	.60
☐	29 Johnny Klippstein	6.00	3.00	.60
☐	30 Del Rice	6.00	3.00	.60
☐	31 Smoky Burgess	7.00	3.50	.70
☐	32 Del Crandall	7.00	3.50	.70
☐	33A Vic Raschi (no mention of trade on back)	10.00	5.00	1.00
☐	33B Vic Raschi (traded to St.Louis)	20.00	10.00	2.00
☐	34 Sammy White	6.00	3.00	.60
☐	35 Eddie Joost	6.00	3.00	.60
☐	36 George Strickland	6.00	3.00	.60
☐	37 Dick Kokos	6.00	3.00	.60
☐	38 Minnie Minoso	10.00	5.00	1.00
☐	39 Ned Garver	6.00	3.00	.60
☐	40 Gil Coan	6.00	3.00	.60
☐	41 Alvin Dark	8.00	4.00	.80
☐	42 Billy Loes	6.00	3.00	.60
☐	43 Bob Friend	7.00	3.50	.70
☐	44 Harry Perkowski	6.00	3.00	.60
☐	45 Ralph Kiner	30.00	15.00	3.00
☐	46 Rip Repulski	6.00	3.00	.60
☐	47 Granny Hamner	6.00	3.00	.60
☐	48 Jack Dittmer	6.00	3.00	.60
☐	49 Harry Byrd	6.00	3.00	.60
☐	50 George Kell	25.00	12.50	2.50
☐	51 Alex Kellner	6.00	3.00	.60
☐	52 Joe Ginsberg	6.00	3.00	.60
☐	53 Don Lenhardt	6.00	3.00	.60
☐	54 Chico Carrasquel	6.00	3.00	.60
☐	55 Jim Delsing	6.00	3.00	.60
☐	56 Maurice McDermott	6.00	3.00	.60
☐	57 Hoyt Wilhelm	25.00	12.50	2.50
☐	58 Pee Wee Reese	45.00	22.50	4.50
☐	59 Bob Schultz	6.00	3.00	.60
☐	60 Fred Baczewski	6.00	3.00	.60
☐	61 Eddie Miksis	6.00	3.00	.60
☐	62 Enos Slaughter	28.00	14.00	2.80
☐	63 Earl Torgeson	6.00	3.00	.60
☐	64 Eddie Mathews	40.00	20.00	4.00
☐	65 Mickey Mantle	750.00	375.00	75.00
☐	66A Ted Williams	2700.00	1200.00	300.00
☐	66B Jim Piersall	100.00	50.00	10.00
☐	67 Carl Scheib	6.00	3.00	.60
☐	68 Bobby Avila	7.00	3.50	.70
☐	69 Clint Courtney	6.00	3.00	.60
☐	70 Willard Marshall	6.00	3.00	.60
☐	71 Ted Gray	6.00	3.00	.60
☐	72 Eddie Yost	6.00	3.00	.60
☐	73 Don Mueller	7.00	3.50	.70
☐	74 Jim Gilliam	10.00	5.00	1.00
☐	75 Max Surkont	6.00	3.00	.60
☐	76 Joe Nuxhall	7.00	3.50	.70
☐	77 Bob Rush	6.00	3.00	.60
☐	78 Sal Yvars	6.00	3.00	.60
☐	79 Curt Simmons	7.00	3.50	.70
☐	80 Johnny Logan	7.00	3.50	.70
☐	81 Jerry Coleman	7.00	3.50	.70
☐	82 Billy Goodman	7.00	3.50	.70
☐	83 Ray Murray	6.00	3.00	.60
☐	84 Larry Doby	10.00	5.00	1.00
☐	85 Jim Dyck	6.00	3.00	.60
☐	86 Harry Dorish	6.00	3.00	.60
☐	87 Don Lund	6.00	3.00	.60
☐	88 Tom Umphlett	6.00	3.00	.60
☐	89 Willie Mays	275.00	135.00	27.00
☐	90 Roy Campanella	110.00	55.00	11.00
☐	91 Cal Abrams	6.00	3.00	.60
☐	92 Ken Raffensberger	6.00	3.00	.60
☐	93 Bill Serena	6.00	3.00	.60
☐	94 Solly Hemus	6.00	3.00	.60
☐	95 Robin Roberts	27.00	13.50	2.70
☐	96 Joe Adcock	7.00	3.50	.70
☐	97 Gil McDougald	10.00	5.00	1.00
☐	98 Ellis Kinder	6.00	3.00	.60
☐	99 Pete Suder	6.00	3.00	.60
☐	100 Mike Garcia	7.00	3.50	.70
☐	101 Don Larsen	22.00	11.00	2.20
☐	102 Billy Pierce	8.00	4.00	.80
☐	103 Steve Souchock	6.00	3.00	.60
☐	104 Frank Shea	6.00	3.00	.60
☐	105 Sal Maglie	9.00	4.50	.90
☐	106 Clem Labine	7.00	3.50	.70
☐	107 Paul LaPalme	6.00	3.00	.60
☐	108 Bobby Adams	6.00	3.00	.60
☐	109 Roy Smalley	6.00	3.00	.60
☐	110 Red Schoendienst	27.00	13.50	2.70
☐	111 Murry Dickson	6.00	3.00	.60
☐	112 Andy Pafko	7.00	3.50	.70
☐	113 Allie Reynolds	13.00	6.50	1.30
☐	114 Willard Nixon	6.00	3.00	.60
☐	115 Don Bollweg	6.00	3.00	.60
☐	116 Luke Easter	7.00	3.50	.70
☐	117 Dick Kryhoski	6.00	3.00	.60
☐	118 Bob Boyd	6.00	3.00	.60
☐	119 Fred Hatfield	6.00	3.00	.60
☐	120 Mel Hoderlein	6.00	3.00	.60
☐	121 Ray Katt	6.00	3.00	.60
☐	122 Carl Furillo	13.00	6.50	1.30
☐	123 Toby Atwell	6.00	3.00	.60
☐	124 Gus Bell	7.00	3.50	.70
☐	125 Warren Hacker	6.00	3.00	.60
☐	126 Cliff Chambers	6.00	3.00	.60
☐	127 Del Ennis	7.00	3.50	.70
☐	128 Ebba St.Claire	6.00	3.00	.60
☐	129 Hank Bauer	14.00	7.00	1.40
☐	130 Milt Bolling	7.00	3.50	.70
☐	131 Joe Astroth	7.00	3.50	.70
☐	132 Bob Feller	65.00	32.50	6.50
☐	133 Duane Pillette	7.00	3.50	.70
☐	134 Luis Aloma	7.00	3.50	.70
☐	135 Johnny Pesky	8.00	4.00	.80
☐	136 Clyde Vollmer	7.00	3.50	.70
☐	137 Al Corwin	7.00	3.50	.70
☐	138 Gil Hodges	40.00	20.00	4.00
☐	139 Preston Ward	7.00	3.50	.70
☐	140 Saul Rogovin	7.00	3.50	.70
☐	141 Joe Garagiola	33.00	16.00	3.50
☐	142 Al Brazle	7.00	3.50	.70
☐	143 Willie Jones	7.00	3.50	.70
☐	144 Ernie Johnson	7.00	3.50	.70
☐	145 Billy Martin	50.00	25.00	5.00
☐	146 Dick Gernert	7.00	3.50	.70
☐	147 Joe DeMaestri	7.00	3.50	.70
☐	148 Dale Mitchell	8.00	4.00	.80
☐	149 Bob Young	7.00	3.50	.70

☐ 150	Cass Michaels	7.00	3.50	.70
☐ 151	Pat Mullin	7.00	3.50	.70
☐ 152	Mickey Vernon	9.00	4.50	.90
☐ 153	Whitey Lockman	8.00	4.00	.80
☐ 154	Don Newcombe	13.00	6.50	1.30
☐ 155	Frank Thomas	8.00	4.00	.80
☐ 156	Rocky Bridges	7.00	3.50	.70
☐ 157	Turk Lown	7.00	3.50	.70
☐ 158	Stu Miller	8.00	4.00	.80
☐ 159	Johnny Lindell	7.00	3.50	.70
☐ 160	Danny O'Connell	7.00	3.50	.70
☐ 161	Yogi Berra	120.00	60.00	12.00
☐ 162	Ted Lepcio	7.00	3.50	.70
☐ 163A	Dave Philley	8.00	4.00	.80
	(no mention of			
	trade on back)			
☐ 163B	Dave Philley	18.00	9.00	1.80
	(traded to			
	Cleveland)			
☐ 164	Early Wynn	25.00	12.50	2.50
☐ 165	Johnny Groth	7.00	3.50	.70
☐ 166	Sandy Consuegra	7.00	3.50	.70
☐ 167	Billy Hoeft	7.00	3.50	.70
☐ 168	Ed Fitzgerald	7.00	3.50	.70
☐ 169	Larry Jansen	8.00	4.00	.80
☐ 170	Duke Snider	110.00	55.00	11.00
☐ 171	Carlos Bernier	7.00	3.50	.70
☐ 172	Andy Seminick	7.00	3.50	.70
☐ 173	Dee Fondy	7.00	3.50	.70
☐ 174	Pete Castiglione	7.00	3.50	.70
☐ 175	Mel Clark	7.00	3.50	.70
☐ 176	Vern Bickford	7.00	3.50	.70
☐ 177	Whitey Ford	70.00	35.00	7.00
☐ 178	Del Wilber	7.00	3.50	.70
☐ 179	Morrie Martin	7.00	3.50	.70
☐ 180	Joe Tipton	7.00	3.50	.70
☐ 181	Les Moss	7.00	3.50	.70
☐ 182	Sherm Lollar	8.00	4.00	.80
☐ 183	Matt Batts	7.00	3.50	.70
☐ 184	Mickey Grasso	7.00	3.50	.70
☐ 185	Daryl Spencer	7.00	3.50	.70
☐ 186	Russ Meyer	7.00	3.50	.70
☐ 187	Vernon Law	8.00	4.00	.80
☐ 188	Frank Smith	7.00	3.50	.70
☐ 189	Randy Jackson	7.00	3.50	.70
☐ 190	Joe Presko	7.00	3.50	.70
☐ 191	Karl Drews	7.00	3.50	.70
☐ 192	Lou Burdette	9.00	4.50	.90
☐ 193	Eddie Robinson	7.00	3.50	.70
☐ 194	Sid Hudson	7.00	3.50	.70
☐ 195	Bob Cain	7.00	3.50	.70
☐ 196	Bob Lemon	25.00	12.50	2.50
☐ 197	Lou Kretlow	7.00	3.50	.70
☐ 198	Virgil Trucks	8.00	4.00	.80
☐ 199	Steve Gromek	7.00	3.50	.70
☐ 200	Conrado Marrero	7.00	3.50	.70
☐ 201	Bobby Thomson	9.00	4.50	.90
☐ 202	George Shuba	8.00	4.00	.80
☐ 203	Vic Janowicz	8.00	4.00	.80
☐ 204	Jack Collum	7.00	3.50	.70
☐ 205	Hal Jeffcoat	7.00	3.50	.70
☐ 206	Steve Bilko	7.00	3.50	.70
☐ 207	Stan Lopata	7.00	3.50	.70
☐ 208	Johnny Antonelli	8.00	4.00	.80
☐ 209	Gene Woodling	9.00	4.50	.90
☐ 210	Jim Piersall	10.00	5.00	1.00
☐ 211	Al Robertson	7.00	3.50	.70
☐ 212	Owen Friend	7.00	3.50	.70
☐ 213	Dick Littlefield	7.00	3.50	.70
☐ 214	Ferris Fain	8.00	4.00	.80
☐ 215	Johnny Bucha	7.00	3.50	.70
☐ 216	Jerry Snyder	7.00	3.50	.70
☐ 217	Hank Thompson	8.00	4.00	.80
☐ 218	Preacher Roe	11.00	5.50	1.10
☐ 219	Hal Rice	7.00	3.50	.70
☐ 220	Hobie Landrith	7.00	3.50	.70
☐ 221	Frank Baumholtz	7.00	3.50	.70
☐ 222	Memo Luna	7.00	3.50	.70
☐ 223	Steve Ridzik	7.00	3.50	.70
☐ 224	Bill Bruton	20.00	5.00	1.00

1955 Bowman

The cards in this 320-card set measure 2 1/2" by 3 3/4". The Bowman set of 1955 is known as the "TV set" because each player photograph is cleverly shown within a television set design. The set contains umpire cards, some transposed pictures (e.g.,

Johnsons and Bollings), an incorrect spelling for Harvey Kuenn, and a traded line for Palica (all of which are noted in the checklist below). Some three-card advertising strips exist.

		NRMT	VG-E	GOOD
COMPLETE SET (320)		4400.00	2200.00	525.00
COMMON PLAYER (1-96)		6.00	3.00	.60
COMMON PLAYER (97-224)		4.00	2.00	.40
COMMON PLAYER (225-320)		12.00	6.00	1.20
COMMON UMPIRES (225-320)		16.00	8.00	1.60
☐ 1	Hoyt Wilhelm	100.00	10.00	2.00
☐ 2	Alvin Dark	8.00	4.00	.80
☐ 3	Joe Coleman	6.00	3.00	.60
☐ 4	Eddie Waitkus	6.00	3.00	.60
☐ 5	Jim Robertson	6.00	3.00	.60
☐ 6	Pete Suder	6.00	3.00	.60
☐ 7	Gene Baker	6.00	3.00	.60
☐ 8	Warren Hacker	6.00	3.00	.60
☐ 9	Gil McDougald	10.00	5.00	1.00
☐ 10	Phil Rizzuto	40.00	20.00	4.00
☐ 11	Bill Bruton	7.00	3.50	.70
☐ 12	Andy Pafko	7.00	3.50	.70
☐ 13	Clyde Vollmer	6.00	3.00	.60
☐ 14	Gus Keriazakos	6.00	3.00	.60
☐ 15	Frank Sullivan	6.00	3.00	.60
☐ 16	Jim Piersall	9.00	4.50	.90
☐ 17	Del Ennis	7.00	3.50	.70
☐ 18	Stan Lopata	6.00	3.00	.60
☐ 19	Bobby Avila	7.00	3.50	.70
☐ 20	Al Smith	6.00	3.00	.60
☐ 21	Don Hoak	7.00	3.50	.70
☐ 22	Roy Campanella	90.00	45.00	9.00
☐ 23	Al Kaline	100.00	50.00	10.00
☐ 24	Al Aber	6.00	3.00	.60
☐ 25	Minnie Minoso	10.00	5.00	1.00
☐ 26	Virgil Trucks	7.00	3.50	.70
☐ 27	Preston Ward	6.00	3.00	.60
☐ 28	Dick Cole	6.00	3.00	.60
☐ 29	Red Schoendienst	22.00	11.00	2.20
☐ 30	Bill Sarni	6.00	3.00	.60
☐ 31	Johnny Temple	7.00	3.50	.70
☐ 32	Wally Post	7.00	3.50	.70
☐ 33	Nellie Fox	16.00	8.00	1.60
☐ 34	Clint Courtney	6.00	3.00	.60
☐ 35	Bill Tuttle	6.00	3.00	.60
☐ 36	Wayne Belardi	6.00	3.00	.60
☐ 37	Pee Wee Reese	45.00	22.50	4.50
☐ 38	Early Wynn	20.00	10.00	2.00
☐ 39	Bob Darnell	6.00	3.00	.60
☐ 40	Vic Wertz	7.00	3.50	.70
☐ 41	Mel Clark	6.00	3.00	.60
☐ 42	Bob Greenwood	6.00	3.00	.60
☐ 43	Bob Buhl	6.00	3.00	.60
☐ 44	Danny O'Connell	6.00	3.00	.60
☐ 45	Tom Umphlett	6.00	3.00	.60
☐ 46	Mickey Vernon	8.00	4.00	.80
☐ 47	Sammy White	6.00	3.00	.60
☐ 48A	Milt Bolling ERR	8.00	4.00	.80
	(name on back is			
	Frank Bolling)			
☐ 48B	Milt Bolling COR	25.00	10.00	2.00
☐ 49	Jim Greengrass	6.00	3.00	.60
☐ 50	Hobie Landrith	6.00	3.00	.60
☐ 51	Elvin Tappe	6.00	3.00	.60
☐ 52	Hal Rice	6.00	3.00	.60
☐ 53	Alex Kellner	6.00	3.00	.60
☐ 54	Don Bollweg	6.00	3.00	.60
☐ 55	Cal Abrams	6.00	3.00	.60
☐ 56	Billy Cox	7.00	3.50	.70
☐ 57	Bob Friend	8.00	4.00	.80

☐ 58	Frank Thomas	7.00	3.50	.70
☐ 59	Whitey Ford	60.00	30.00	6.00
☐ 60	Enos Slaughter	22.00	11.00	2.20
☐ 61	Paul LaPalme	6.00	3.00	.60
☐ 62	Royce Lint	6.00	3.00	.60
☐ 63	Irv Noren	7.00	3.50	.70
☐ 64	Curt Simmons	7.00	3.50	.70
☐ 65	Don Zimmer	16.00	8.00	1.60
☐ 66	George Shuba	7.00	3.50	.70
☐ 67	Don Larsen	13.00	6.50	1.30
☐ 68	Elston Howard	22.00	11.00	2.20
☐ 69	Billy Hunter	6.00	3.00	.60
☐ 70	Lou Burdette	9.00	4.50	.90
☐ 71	Dave Jolly	6.00	3.00	.60
☐ 72	Chet Nichols	6.00	3.00	.60
☐ 73	Eddie Yost	6.00	3.00	.60
☐ 74	Jerry Snyder	6.00	3.00	.60
☐ 75	Brooks Lawrence	6.00	3.00	.60
☐ 76	Tom Poholsky	6.00	3.00	.60
☐ 77	Jim McDonald	6.00	3.00	.60
☐ 78	Gil Coan	6.00	3.00	.60
☐ 79	Willie Miranda	6.00	3.00	.60
☐ 80	Lou Limmer	6.00	3.00	.60
☐ 81	Bobby Morgan	6.00	3.00	.60
☐ 82	Lee Walls	6.00	3.00	.60
☐ 83	Max Surkont	6.00	3.00	.60
☐ 84	George Freese	6.00	3.00	.60
☐ 85	Cass Michaels	6.00	3.00	.60
☐ 86	Ted Gray	6.00	3.00	.60
☐ 87	Randy Jackson	6.00	3.00	.60
☐ 88	Steve Bilko	6.00	3.00	.60
☐ 89	Lou Boudreau MG	20.00	10.00	2.00
☐ 90	Art Ditmar	6.00	3.00	.60
☐ 91	Dick Marlowe	6.00	3.00	.60
☐ 92	George Zuverink	6.00	3.00	.60
☐ 93	Andy Seminick	6.00	3.00	.60
☐ 94	Hank Thompson	7.00	3.50	.70
☐ 95	Sal Maglie	9.00	4.50	.90
☐ 96	Ray Narleski	6.00	3.00	.60
☐ 97	Johnny Podres	10.00	5.00	1.00
☐ 98	Jim Gilliam	10.00	5.00	1.00
☐ 99	Jerry Coleman	7.00	3.50	.70
☐ 100	Tom Morgan	6.00	3.00	.60
☐ 101A	Don Johnson ERR	7.00	3.50	.70
	(photo actually Ernie Johnson)			
☐ 101B	Don Johnson COR	20.00	8.00	1.60
☐ 102	Bobby Thomson	8.00	4.00	.80
☐ 103	Eddie Mathews	33.00	16.00	3.50
☐ 104	Bob Porterfield	4.00	2.00	.40
☐ 105	Johnny Schmitz	4.00	2.00	.40
☐ 106	Del Rice	4.00	2.00	.40
☐ 107	Solly Hemus	4.00	2.00	.40
☐ 108	Lou Kretlow	4.00	2.00	.40
☐ 109	Vern Stephens	5.00	2.50	.50
☐ 110	Bob Miller	4.00	2.00	.40
☐ 111	Steve Ridzik	4.00	2.00	.40
☐ 112	Granny Hamner	4.00	2.00	.40
☐ 113	Bob Hall	4.00	2.00	.40
☐ 114	Vic Janowicz	5.00	2.50	.50
☐ 115	Roger Bowman	4.00	2.00	.40
☐ 116	Sandy Consuegra	4.00	2.00	.40
☐ 117	Johnny Groth	4.00	2.00	.40
☐ 118	Bobby Adams	4.00	2.00	.40
☐ 119	Joe Astroth	4.00	2.00	.40
☐ 120	Ed Burtschy	4.00	2.00	.40
☐ 121	Rufus Crawford	4.00	2.00	.40
☐ 122	Al Corwin	4.00	2.00	.40
☐ 123	Marv Grissom	4.00	2.00	.40
☐ 124	Johnny Antonelli	6.00	3.00	.60
☐ 125	Paul Giel	4.00	2.00	.40
☐ 126	Billy Goodman	5.00	2.50	.50
☐ 127	Hank Majeski	4.00	2.00	.40
☐ 128	Mike Garcia	6.00	3.00	.60
☐ 129	Hal Naragon	4.00	2.00	.40
☐ 130	Richie Ashburn	16.00	8.00	1.60
☐ 131	Willard Marshall	4.00	2.00	.40
☐ 132A	Harvey Kueen ERR	8.00	4.00	.80
	(sic, Kuenn)			
☐ 132B	Harvey Kuenn COR	20.00	10.00	2.00
☐ 133	Charles King	4.00	2.00	.40
☐ 134	Bob Feller	55.00	27.50	5.50
☐ 135	Lloyd Merriman	4.00	2.00	.40
☐ 136	Rocky Bridges	4.00	2.00	.40
☐ 137	Bob Talbot	4.00	2.00	.40
☐ 138	Davey Williams	5.00	2.50	.50
☐ 139	Shantz Brothers	6.00	3.00	.60
	Wilmer and Bobby			
☐ 140	Bobby Shantz	6.00	3.00	.60
☐ 141	Wes Westrum	5.00	2.50	.50
☐ 142	Rudy Regalado	4.00	2.00	.40
☐ 143	Don Newcombe	9.00	4.50	.90
☐ 144	Art Houtteman	4.00	2.00	.40
☐ 145	Bob Nieman	4.00	2.00	.40
☐ 146	Don Liddle	4.00	2.00	.40
☐ 147	Sam Mele	4.00	2.00	.40
☐ 148	Bob Chakales	4.00	2.00	.40
☐ 149	Cloyd Boyer	4.00	2.00	.40
☐ 150	Billy Klaus	4.00	2.00	.40
☐ 151	Jim Brideweser	4.00	2.00	.40
☐ 152	Johnny Klippstein	4.00	2.00	.40
☐ 153	Eddie Robinson	4.00	2.00	.40
☐ 154	Frank Lary	6.00	3.00	.60
☐ 155	Jerry Staley	4.00	2.00	.40
☐ 156	Jim Hughes	4.00	2.00	.40
☐ 157A	Ernie Johnson ERR	5.00	2.50	.50
	(photo actually Don Johnson)			
☐ 157B	Ernie Johnson COR	20.00	8.00	1.60
☐ 158	Gil Hodges	30.00	15.00	3.00
☐ 159	Harry Byrd	5.00	2.50	.50
☐ 160	Bill Skowron	12.00	6.00	1.20
☐ 161	Matt Batts	4.00	2.00	.40
☐ 162	Charlie Maxwell	4.00	2.00	.40
☐ 163	Sid Gordon	4.00	2.00	.40
☐ 164	Toby Atwell	4.00	2.00	.40
☐ 165	Maurice McDermott	4.00	2.00	.40
☐ 166	Jim Busby	4.00	2.00	.40
☐ 167	Bob Grim	6.00	3.00	.60
☐ 168	Yogi Berra	90.00	45.00	9.00
☐ 169	Carl Furillo	10.00	5.00	1.00
☐ 170	Carl Erskine	9.00	4.50	.90
☐ 171	Robin Roberts	22.00	11.00	2.20
☐ 172	Willie Jones	4.00	2.00	.40
☐ 173	Chico Carrasquel	4.00	2.00	.40
☐ 174	Sherm Lollar	5.00	2.50	.50
☐ 175	Wilmer Shantz	4.00	2.00	.40
☐ 176	Joe DeMaestri	4.00	2.00	.40
☐ 177	Willard Nixon	4.00	2.00	.40
☐ 178	Tom Brewer	4.00	2.00	.40
☐ 179	Hank Aaron	180.00	90.00	18.00
☐ 180	Johnny Logan	5.00	2.50	.50
☐ 181	Eddie Miksis	4.00	2.00	.40
☐ 182	Bob Rush	4.00	2.00	.40
☐ 183	Ray Katt	4.00	2.00	.40
☐ 184	Willie Mays	180.00	90.00	18.00
☐ 185	Vic Raschi	7.00	3.50	.70
☐ 186	Alex Grammas	4.00	2.00	.40
☐ 187	Fred Hatfield	4.00	2.00	.40
☐ 188	Ned Garver	4.00	2.00	.40
☐ 189	Jack Collum	4.00	2.00	.40
☐ 190	Fred Baczewski	4.00	2.00	.40
☐ 191	Bob Lemon	20.00	10.00	2.00
☐ 192	George Strickland	4.00	2.00	.40
☐ 193	Howie Judson	4.00	2.00	.40
☐ 194	Joe Nuxhall	5.00	2.50	.50
☐ 195A	Erv Palica	5.00	2.50	.50
	(without trade)			
☐ 195B	Erv Palica	20.00	8.00	1.60
	(with trade)			
☐ 196	Russ Meyer	4.00	2.00	.40
☐ 197	Ralph Kiner	24.00	12.00	2.40
☐ 198	Dave Pope	4.00	2.00	.40
☐ 199	Vernon Law	6.00	3.00	.60
☐ 200	Dick Littlefield	4.00	2.00	.40
☐ 201	Allie Reynolds	11.00	5.50	1.10
☐ 202	Mickey Mantle	400.00	200.00	40.00
☐ 203	Steve Gromek	4.00	2.00	.40
☐ 204A	Frank Bolling ERR	5.00	2.50	.50
	(name on back is Milt Bolling)			
☐ 204B	Frank Bolling COR	20.00	8.00	1.60
☐ 205	Rip Repulski	4.00	2.00	.40
☐ 206	Ralph Beard	4.00	2.00	.40
☐ 207	Frank Shea	4.00	2.00	.40
☐ 208	Ed Fitzgerald	4.00	2.00	.40
☐ 209	Smokey Burgess	5.00	2.50	.50
☐ 210	Earl Torgeson	4.00	2.00	.40
☐ 211	Sonny Dixon	4.00	2.00	.40
☐ 212	Jack Dittmer	4.00	2.00	.40
☐ 213	George Kell	20.00	10.00	2.00
☐ 214	Billy Pierce	6.00	3.00	.60
☐ 215	Bob Kuzava	4.00	2.00	.40
☐ 216	Preacher Roe	8.00	4.00	.80
☐ 217	Del Crandall	5.00	2.50	.50
☐ 218	Joe Adcock	6.00	3.00	.60
☐ 219	Whitey Lockman	5.00	2.50	.50
☐ 220	Jim Hearn	4.00	2.00	.40
☐ 221	Hector Brown	4.00	2.00	.40
☐ 222	Russ Kemmerer	4.00	2.00	.40
☐ 223	Hal Jeffcoat	4.00	2.00	.40
☐ 224	Dee Fondy	4.00	2.00	.40
☐ 225	Paul Richards	14.00	7.00	1.40
☐ 226	W. McKinley UMP	16.00	8.00	1.60
☐ 227	Frank Baumholtz	12.00	6.00	1.20
☐ 228	John Phillips	12.00	6.00	1.20
☐ 229	Jim Brosnan	14.00	7.00	1.40
☐ 230	Al Brazle	12.00	6.00	1.20
☐ 231	Jim Konstanty	14.00	7.00	1.40
☐ 232	Birdie Tebbetts	14.00	7.00	1.40

☐ 233	Bill Serena	12.00	6.00	1.20
☐ 234	Dick Bartell	12.00	6.00	1.20
☐ 235	J. Paparella UMP	16.00	8.00	1.60
☐ 236	Murry Dickson	12.00	6.00	1.20
☐ 237	Johnny Wyrostek	12.00	6.00	1.20
☐ 238	Eddie Stanky	16.00	8.00	1.60
☐ 239	Edwin Rommel UMP	16.00	8.00	1.60
☐ 240	Billy Loes	14.00	7.00	1.40
☐ 241	Johnny Pesky	14.00	7.00	1.40
☐ 242	Ernie Banks	300.00	150.00	30.00
☐ 243	Gus Bell	14.00	7.00	1.40
☐ 244	Duane Pillette	12.00	6.00	1.20
☐ 245	Bill Miller	12.00	6.00	1.20
☐ 246	Hank Bauer	24.00	12.00	2.40
☐ 247	Dutch Leonard	12.00	6.00	1.20
☐ 248	Harry Dorish	12.00	6.00	1.20
☐ 249	Billy Gardner	14.00	7.00	1.40
☐ 250	Larry Napp UMP	16.00	8.00	1.60
☐ 251	Stan Jok	12.00	6.00	1.20
☐ 252	Roy Smalley	12.00	6.00	1.20
☐ 253	Jim Wilson	12.00	6.00	1.20
☐ 254	Bennett Flowers	12.00	6.00	1.20
☐ 255	Pete Runnels	14.00	7.00	1.40
☐ 256	Owen Friend	12.00	6.00	1.20
☐ 257	Tom Alston	12.00	6.00	1.20
☐ 258	John Stevens UMP	16.00	8.00	1.60
☐ 259	Don Mossi	16.00	8.00	1.60
☐ 260	Edwin Hurley UMP	16.00	8.00	1.60
☐ 261	Walt Moryn	12.00	6.00	1.20
☐ 262	Jim Lemon	14.00	7.00	1.40
☐ 263	Eddie Joost	12.00	6.00	1.20
☐ 264	Bill Henry	12.00	6.00	1.20
☐ 265	Albert Barlick UMP	50.00	25.00	5.00
☐ 266	Mike Fornieles	12.00	6.00	1.20
☐ 267	Jim Honochick UMP	50.00	25.00	5.00
☐ 268	Roy Lee Hawes	12.00	6.00	1.20
☐ 269	Joe Amalfitano	12.00	6.00	1.20
☐ 270	Chico Fernandez	12.00	6.00	1.20
☐ 271	Bob Hooper	12.00	6.00	1.20
☐ 272	John Flaherty UMP	16.00	8.00	1.60
☐ 273	Bubba Church	12.00	6.00	1.20
☐ 274	Jim Delsing	12.00	6.00	1.20
☐ 275	William Grieve UMP	16.00	8.00	1.60
☐ 276	Ike Delock	12.00	6.00	1.20
☐ 277	Ed Runge UMP	20.00	10.00	2.00
☐ 278	Charlie Neal	18.00	9.00	1.80
☐ 279	Hank Soar UMP	16.00	8.00	1.60
☐ 280	Clyde McCullough	12.00	6.00	1.20
☐ 281	Charles Berry UMP	16.00	8.00	1.60
☐ 282	Phil Cavarretta	16.00	8.00	1.60
☐ 283	Nestor Chylak UMP	16.00	8.00	1.60
☐ 284	Bill Jackowski UMP	16.00	8.00	1.60
☐ 285	Walt Dropo	14.00	7.00	1.40
☐ 286	Frank Secory UMP	16.00	8.00	1.60
☐ 287	Ron Mrozinski	12.00	6.00	1.20
☐ 288	Dick Smith	12.00	6.00	1.20
☐ 289	Arthur Gore UMP	16.00	8.00	1.60
☐ 290	Hershell Freeman	12.00	6.00	1.20
☐ 291	Frank Dascoli UMP	16.00	8.00	1.60
☐ 292	Marv Blaylock	12.00	6.00	1.20
☐ 293	Thomas Gorman UMP	16.00	8.00	1.60
☐ 294	Wally Moses	14.00	7.00	1.40
☐ 295	Lee Ballanfant UMP	16.00	8.00	1.60
☐ 296	Bill Virdon	30.00	15.00	3.00
☐ 297	Dusty Boggess UMP	16.00	8.00	1.60
☐ 298	Charlie Grimm	14.00	7.00	1.40
☐ 299	Lon Warneke UMP	16.00	8.00	1.60
☐ 300	Tommy Byrne	14.00	7.00	1.40
☐ 301	William Engeln UMP	16.00	8.00	1.60
☐ 302	Frank Malzone	20.00	10.00	2.00
☐ 303	Jocko Conlan UMP	65.00	32.50	6.50
☐ 304	Harry Chiti	12.00	6.00	1.20
☐ 305	Frank Umont UMP	16.00	8.00	1.60
☐ 306	Bob Cerv	20.00	10.00	2.00
☐ 307	Babe Pinelli UMP	20.00	10.00	2.00
☐ 308	Al Lopez MG	40.00	20.00	4.00
☐ 309	Hal Dixon UMP	16.00	8.00	1.60
☐ 310	Ken Lehman	12.00	6.00	1.20
☐ 311	Lawrence Goetz UMP	16.00	8.00	1.60
☐ 312	Bill Wight	12.00	6.00	1.20
☐ 313	Augie Donatelli UMP	25.00	12.50	2.50
☐ 314	Dale Mitchell	14.00	7.00	1.40
☐ 315	Cal Hubbard UMP	55.00	27.50	5.50
☐ 316	Marion Fricano	12.00	6.00	1.20
☐ 317	William Summers UMP	16.00	8.00	1.60
☐ 318	Sid Hudson	12.00	6.00	1.20
☐ 319	Al Schroll	12.00	6.00	1.20
☐ 320	George Susce Jr.	25.00	7.00	1.50

1989 Bowman

The 1989 Bowman set, which was actually produced by Topps, contains 484 cards measuring 2 1/2 by 3 3/4 inches. The fronts have white-bordered color photos with facsimile autographs and small Bowman logos. The backs are scarlet and feature charts detailing 1988 player performances vs. each team. The set is arranged in alphabetical team order. The player selection is concentrated on prospects and "name" players. The cards were released in midseason 1989 in wax, rack and cello pack formats.

		MINT	EXC	G-VG
COMPLETE SET (484)		25.00	12.50	2.50
COMMON PLAYER (1-484)		.03	.01	.00
☐	1 Oswald Peraza	.10	.02	.01
☐	2 Brian Holton	.08	.04	.01
☐	3 Jose Bautista	.08	.04	.01
☐	4 Pete Harnisch	.10	.05	.01
☐	5 Dave Schmidt	.03	.01	.00
☐	6 Gregg Olson	.75	.35	.07
☐	7 Jeff Ballard	.15	.07	.01
☐	8 Bob Melvin	.03	.01	.00
☐	9 Cal Ripken	.15	.07	.01
☐	10 Randy Milligan	.10	.05	.01
☐	11 Juan Bell	.20	.10	.02
☐	12 Billy Ripken	.03	.01	.00
☐	13 Jim Traber	.03	.01	.00
☐	14 Pete Stanicek	.08	.04	.01
☐	15 Steve Finley	.30	.15	.03
☐	16 Larry Sheets	.03	.01	.00
☐	17 Phil Bradley	.06	.03	.00
☐	18 Brady Anderson	.20	.10	.02
☐	19 Lee Smith	.03	.01	.00
☐	20 Tom Fischer	.08	.04	.01
☐	21 Mike Boddicker	.03	.01	.00
☐	22 Rob Murphy	.03	.01	.00
☐	23 Wes Gardner	.03	.01	.00
☐	24 John Dopson	.18	.09	.01
☐	25 Bob Stanley	.03	.01	.00
☐	26 Roger Clemens	.30	.15	.03
☐	27 Rich Gedman	.03	.01	.00
☐	28 Marty Barrett	.03	.01	.00
☐	29 Luis Rivera	.03	.01	.00
☐	30 Jody Reed	.03	.01	.00
☐	31 Nick Esasky	.08	.04	.01
☐	32 Wade Boggs	.50	.25	.05
☐	33 Jim Rice	.12	.06	.01
☐	34 Mike Greenwell	.60	.30	.06
☐	35 Dwight Evans	.10	.05	.01
☐	36 Ellis Burks	.25	.12	.02
☐	37 Mark Clear	.03	.01	.00
☐	38 Kirk McCaskill	.03	.01	.00
☐	39 Jim Abbott	2.00	1.00	.20
☐	40 Bryan Harvey	.20	.10	.02
☐	41 Bert Blyleven	.08	.04	.01
☐	42 Mike Witt	.06	.03	.00
☐	43 Bob McClure	.03	.01	.00
☐	44 Bill Schroeder	.03	.01	.00
☐	45 Lance Parrish	.08	.04	.01
☐	46 Dick Schofield	.03	.01	.00
☐	47 Wally Joyner	.15	.07	.01
☐	48 Jack Howell	.03	.01	.00
☐	49 Johnny Ray	.06	.03	.00
☐	50 Chili Davis	.06	.03	.00
☐	51 Tony Armas	.06	.03	.00

□	#	Name			
□	52	Claudell Washington	.06	.03	.00
□	53	Brian Downing	.03	.01	.00
□	54	Devon White	.12	.06	.01
□	55	Bobby Thigpen	.06	.03	.00
□	56	Bill Long	.03	.01	.00
□	57	Jerry Reuss	.03	.01	.00
□	58	Shawn Hillegas	.03	.01	.00
□	59	Melido Perez	.08	.04	.01
□	60	Jeff Bittiger	.10	.05	.01
□	61	Jack McDowell	.10	.05	.01
□	62	Carlton Fisk	.10	.05	.01
□	63	Steve Lyons	.03	.01	.00
□	64	Ozzie Guillen	.06	.03	.00
□	65	Robin Ventura	1.00	.50	.10
□	66	Fred Manrique	.03	.01	.00
□	67	Dan Pasqua	.03	.01	.00
□	68	Ivan Calderon	.06	.03	.00
□	69	Ron Kittle	.08	.04	.01
□	70	Daryl Boston	.03	.01	.00
□	71	Dave Gallagher	.20	.10	.02
□	72	Harold Baines	.08	.04	.01
□	73	Charles Nagy	.20	.10	.02
□	74	John Farrell	.03	.01	.00
□	75	Kevin Wickander	.10	.05	.01
□	76	Greg Swindell	.08	.04	.01
□	77	Mike Walker	.10	.05	.01
□	78	Doug Jones	.06	.03	.00
□	79	Rich Yett	.03	.01	.00
□	80	Tom Candiotti	.03	.01	.00
□	81	Jesse Orosco	.03	.01	.00
□	82	Bud Black	.03	.01	.00
□	83	Andy Allanson	.03	.01	.00
□	84	Pete O'Brien	.06	.03	.00
□	85	Jerry Browne	.06	.03	.00
□	86	Brook Jacoby	.06	.03	.00
□	87	Mark Lewis	.20	.10	.02
□	88	Luis Aguayo	.03	.01	.00
□	89	Cory Snyder	.08	.04	.01
□	90	Oddibe McDowell	.06	.03	.00
□	91	Joe Carter	.12	.06	.01
□	92	Frank Tanana	.03	.01	.00
□	93	Jack Morris	.08	.04	.01
□	94	Doyle Alexander	.03	.01	.00
□	95	Steve Searcy	.20	.10	.02
□	96	Randy Bockus	.08	.04	.01
□	97	Jeff Robinson	.06	.03	.00
□	98	Mike Henneman	.06	.03	.00
□	99	Paul Gibson	.08	.04	.01
□	100	Frank Williams	.03	.01	.00
□	101	Matt Nokes	.08	.04	.01
□	102	Ricco Brogna	.10	.05	.01
□	103	Lou Whitaker	.08	.04	.01
□	104	Al Pedrique	.03	.01	.00
□	105	Alan Trammell	.12	.06	.01
□	106	Chris Brown	.03	.01	.00
□	107	Pat Sheridan	.03	.01	.00
□	108	Gary Pettis	.03	.01	.00
□	109	Keith Moreland	.03	.01	.00
□	110	Mel Stottlemyre Jr.	.20	.10	.02
□	111	Bret Saberhagen	.15	.07	.01
□	112	Floyd Bannister	.03	.01	.00
□	113	Jeff Montgomery	.12	.06	.01
□	114	Steve Farr	.03	.01	.00
□	115	Tom Gordon UER (front shows autograph of Don Gordon)	1.00	.50	.10
□	116	Charlie Leibrandt	.03	.01	.00
□	117	Mark Gubicza	.08	.04	.01
□	118	Mike Macfarlane	.10	.05	.01
□	119	Bob Boone	.08	.04	.01
□	120	Kurt Stillwell	.03	.01	.00
□	121	George Brett	.20	.10	.02
□	122	Frank White	.06	.03	.00
□	123	Kevin Seitzer	.18	.09	.01
□	124	Willie Wilson	.06	.03	.00
□	125	Pat Tabler	.03	.01	.00
□	126	Bo Jackson	.85	.40	.08
□	127	Hugh Walker	.12	.06	.01
□	128	Danny Tartabull	.08	.04	.01
□	129	Teddy Higuera	.06	.03	.00
□	130	Don August	.06	.03	.00
□	131	Juan Nieves	.03	.01	.00
□	132	Mike Birkbeck	.03	.01	.00
□	133	Dan Plesac	.06	.03	.00
□	134	Chris Bosio	.06	.03	.00
□	135	Bill Wegman	.03	.01	.00
□	136	Chuck Crim	.03	.01	.00
□	137	B.J. Surhoff	.08	.04	.01
□	138	Joey Meyer	.06	.03	.00
□	139	Dale Sveum	.03	.01	.00
□	140	Paul Molitor	.10	.05	.01
□	141	Jim Gantner	.03	.01	.00
□	142	Gary Sheffield	1.00	.50	.10
□	143	Greg Brock	.03	.01	.00
□	144	Robin Yount	.20	.10	.02
□	145	Glenn Braggs	.06	.03	.00
□	146	Rob Deer	.06	.03	.00
□	147	Fred Toliver	.03	.01	.00
□	148	Jeff Reardon	.08	.04	.01
□	149	Allan Anderson	.06	.03	.00
□	150	Frank Viola	.10	.05	.01
□	151	Shane Rawley	.03	.01	.00
□	152	Juan Berenguer	.03	.01	.00
□	153	Johnny Ard	.15	.07	.01
□	154	Tim Laudner	.03	.01	.00
□	155	Brian Harper	.03	.01	.00
□	156	Al Newman	.03	.01	.00
□	157	Kent Hrbek	.10	.05	.01
□	158	Gary Gaetti	.08	.04	.01
□	159	Wally Backman	.03	.01	.00
□	160	Gene Larkin	.03	.01	.00
□	161	Greg Gagne	.03	.01	.00
□	162	Kirby Puckett	.40	.20	.04
□	163	Dan Gladden	.03	.01	.00
□	164	Randy Bush	.03	.01	.00
□	165	Dave LaPoint	.03	.01	.00
□	166	Andy Hawkins	.03	.01	.00
□	167	Dave Righetti	.08	.04	.01
□	168	Lance McCullers	.03	.01	.00
□	169	Jimmy Jones	.03	.01	.00
□	170	Al Leiter	.10	.05	.01
□	171	John Candelaria	.06	.03	.00
□	172	Don Slaught	.03	.01	.00
□	173	Jamie Quirk	.03	.01	.00
□	174	Rafael Santana	.03	.01	.00
□	175	Mike Pagliarulo	.06	.03	.00
□	176	Don Mattingly	.85	.40	.08
□	177	Ken Phelps	.06	.03	.00
□	178	Steve Sax	.08	.04	.01
□	179	Dave Winfield	.12	.06	.01
□	180	Stan Jefferson	.03	.01	.00
□	181	Rickey Henderson	.25	.12	.02
□	182	Bob Brower	.03	.01	.00
□	183	Roberto Kelly	.25	.12	.02
□	184	Curt Young	.03	.01	.00
□	185	Gene Nelson	.03	.01	.00
□	186	Bob Welch	.06	.03	.00
□	187	Rick Honeycutt	.03	.01	.00
□	188	Dave Stewart	.10	.05	.01
□	189	Mike Moore	.06	.03	.00
□	190	Dennis Eckersley	.08	.04	.01
□	191	Eric Plunk	.03	.01	.00
□	192	Storm Davis	.06	.03	.00
□	193	Terry Steinbach	.10	.05	.01
□	194	Ron Hassey	.03	.01	.00
□	195	Stan Royer	.12	.06	.01
□	196	Walt Weiss	.20	.10	.02
□	197	Mark McGwire	.60	.30	.06
□	198	Carney Lansford	.08	.04	.01
□	199	Glenn Hubbard	.03	.01	.00
□	200	Dave Henderson	.03	.01	.00
□	201	Jose Canseco	.85	.40	.08
□	202	Dave Parker	.08	.04	.01
□	203	Scott Bankhead	.06	.03	.00
□	204	Tom Niedenfuer	.03	.01	.00
□	205	Mark Langston	.12	.06	.01
□	206	Erik Hanson	.20	.10	.02
□	207	Mike Jackson	.03	.01	.00
□	208	Dave Valle	.03	.01	.00
□	209	Scott Bradley	.03	.01	.00
□	210	Harold Reynolds	.06	.03	.00
□	211	Tino Martinez	.75	.35	.07
□	212	Rich Renteria	.10	.05	.01
□	213	Rey Quinones	.03	.01	.00
□	214	Jim Presley	.03	.01	.00
□	215	Alvin Davis	.08	.04	.01
□	216	Edgar Martinez	.10	.05	.01
□	217	Darnell Coles	.03	.01	.00
□	218	Jeffrey Leonard	.06	.03	.00
□	219	Jay Buhner	.15	.07	.01
□	220	Ken Griffey Jr.	3.00	1.50	.30
□	221	Drew Hall	.03	.01	.00
□	222	Bobby Witt	.06	.03	.00
□	223	Jamie Moyer	.03	.01	.00
□	224	Charlie Hough	.03	.01	.00
□	225	Nolan Ryan	.60	.30	.06
□	226	Jeff Russell	.06	.03	.00
□	227	Jim Sundberg	.03	.01	.00
□	228	Julio Franco	.08	.04	.01
□	229	Buddy Bell	.06	.03	.00
□	230	Scott Fletcher	.03	.01	.00
□	231	Jeff Kunkel	.03	.01	.00
□	232	Steve Buechele	.03	.01	.00
□	233	Monty Fariss	.15	.07	.01
□	234	Rick Leach	.03	.01	.00
□	235	Ruben Sierra	.30	.15	.03
□	236	Cecil Espy	.08	.04	.01
□	237	Rafael Palmeiro	.10	.05	.01
□	238	Pete Incaviglia	.08	.04	.01
□	239	Dave Stieb	.08	.04	.01

240	Jeff Musselman	.03	.01	.00
241	Mike Flanagan	.03	.01	.00
242	Todd Stottlemyre	.12	.06	.01
243	Jimmy Key	.06	.03	.00
244	Tony Castillo	.10	.05	.01
245	Alex Sanchez	.20	.10	.02
246	Tom Henke	.06	.03	.00
247	John Cerutti	.03	.01	.00
248	Ernie Whitt	.03	.01	.00
249	Bob Brenly	.03	.01	.00
250	Rance Mulliniks	.03	.01	.00
251	Kelly Gruber	.06	.03	.00
252	Ed Sprague	.20	.10	.02
253	Fred McGriff	.20	.10	.02
254	Tony Fernandez	.10	.05	.01
255	Tom Lawless	.03	.01	.00
256	George Bell	.12	.06	.01
257	Jesse Barfield	.08	.04	.01
258	Roberto Alomar w/Dad	.20	.10	.02
259	Ken Griffey Jr./Sr.	.65	.30	.06
260	Cal Ripken Jr./Sr.	.08	.04	.01
261	M.Stottlemyre Jr./Sr.	.08	.04	.01
262	Zane Smith	.03	.01	.00
263	Charlie Puleo	.03	.01	.00
264	Derek Lilliquist	.20	.10	.02
265	Paul Assenmacher	.03	.01	.00
266	John Smoltz	.40	.20	.04
267	Tom Glavine	.06	.03	.00
268	Steve Avery	.40	.20	.04
269	Pete Smith	.08	.04	.01
270	Jody Davis	.03	.01	.00
271	Bruce Benedict	.03	.01	.00
272	Andres Thomas	.03	.01	.00
273	Gerald Perry	.06	.03	.00
274	Ron Gant	.15	.07	.01
275	Darrell Evans	.06	.03	.00
276	Dale Murphy	.15	.07	.01
277	Dion James	.03	.01	.00
278	Lonnie Smith	.06	.03	.00
279	Geronimo Berroa	.03	.01	.00
280	Steve Wilson	.15	.07	.01
281	Rick Sutcliffe	.08	.04	.01
282	Kevin Coffman	.08	.04	.01
283	Mitch Williams	.08	.04	.01
284	Greg Maddux	.10	.05	.01
285	Paul Kilgus	.03	.01	.00
286	Mike Harkey	.20	.10	.02
287	Lloyd McClendon	.08	.04	.01
288	Damon Berryhill	.25	.12	.02
289	Ty Griffin	.85	.40	.08
290	Ryne Sandberg	.15	.07	.01
291	Mark Grace	2.25	1.10	.22
292	Curt Wilkerson	.03	.01	.00
293	Vance Law	.03	.01	.00
294	Shawon Dunston	.06	.03	.00
295	Jerome Walton	3.50	1.75	.35
296	Mitch Webster	.03	.01	.00
297	Dwight Smith	1.50	.75	.15
298	Andre Dawson	.12	.06	.01
299	Jeff Sellers	.03	.01	.00
300	Jose Rijo	.03	.01	.00
301	John Franco	.06	.03	.00
302	Rick Mahler	.03	.01	.00
303	Ron Robinson	.03	.01	.00
304	Danny Jackson	.06	.03	.00
305	Rob Dibble	.20	.10	.02
306	Tom Browning	.08	.04	.01
307	Bo Diaz	.03	.01	.00
308	Manny Trillo	.03	.01	.00
309	Chris Sabo	.45	.22	.04
310	Ron Oester	.03	.01	.00
311	Barry Larkin	.12	.06	.01
312	Todd Benzinger	.03	.01	.00
313	Paul O'Neill	.08	.04	.01
314	Kal Daniels	.10	.05	.01
315	Joel Youngblood	.03	.01	.00
316	Eric Davis	.30	.15	.03
317	Dave Smith	.03	.01	.00
318	Mark Portugal	.03	.01	.00
319	Brian Meyer	.10	.05	.01
320	Jim Deshaies	.03	.01	.00
321	Juan Agosto	.03	.01	.00
322	Mike Scott	.12	.06	.01
323	Rick Rhoden	.03	.01	.00
324	Jim Clancy	.03	.01	.00
325	Larry Andersen	.03	.01	.00
326	Alex Trevino	.03	.01	.00
327	Alan Ashby	.03	.01	.00
328	Craig Reynolds	.03	.01	.00
329	Bill Doran	.06	.03	.00
330	Rafael Ramirez	.03	.01	.00
331	Glenn Davis	.10	.05	.01
332	Willie Ansley	.25	.12	.02
333	Gerald Young	.03	.01	.00
334	Cameron Drew	.18	.09	.01
335	Jay Howell	.06	.03	.00
336	Tim Belcher	.20	.10	.02
337	Fernando Valenzuela	.10	.05	.01
338	Ricky Horton	.03	.01	.00
339	Tim Leary	.06	.03	.00
340	Bill Bene	.12	.06	.01
341	Orel Hershiser	.20	.10	.02
342	Mike Scioscia	.03	.01	.00
343	Rick Dempsey	.03	.01	.00
344	Willie Randolph	.06	.03	.00
345	Alfredo Griffin	.03	.01	.00
346	Eddie Murray	.10	.05	.01
347	Mickey Hatcher	.03	.01	.00
348	Mike Sharperson	.03	.01	.00
349	John Shelby	.03	.01	.00
350	Mike Marshall	.08	.04	.01
351	Kirk Gibson	.10	.05	.01
352	Mike Davis	.00	.00	.00
353	Bryn Smith	.06	.03	.00
354	Pascual Perez	.08	.04	.01
355	Kevin Gross	.03	.01	.00
356	Andy McGaffigan	.03	.01	.00
357	Brian Holman	.08	.04	.01
358	Dave Wainhouse	.10	.05	.01
359	Dennis Martinez	.06	.03	.00
360	Tim Burke	.06	.03	.00
361	Nelson Santovenia	.15	.07	.01
362	Tim Wallach	.08	.04	.01
363	Spike Owen	.03	.01	.00
364	Rex Hudler	.03	.01	.00
365	Andres Galarraga	.10	.05	.01
366	Otis Nixon	.03	.01	.00
367	Hubie Brooks	.06	.03	.00
368	Mike Aldrete	.03	.01	.00
369	Tim Raines	.10	.05	.01
370	Dave Martinez	.03	.01	.00
371	Bob Ojeda	.06	.03	.00
372	Ron Darling	.08	.04	.01
373	Wally Whitehurst	.20	.10	.02
374	Randy Myers	.06	.03	.00
375	David Cone	.15	.07	.01
376	Dwight Gooden	.25	.12	.02
377	Sid Fernandez	.08	.04	.01
378	Dave Proctor	.12	.06	.01
379	Gary Carter	.12	.06	.01
380	Keith Miller	.03	.01	.00
381	Gregg Jefferies	1.00	.50	.10
382	Tim Teufel	.03	.01	.00
383	Kevin Elster	.06	.03	.00
384	Dave Magadan	.08	.04	.01
385	Keith Hernandez	.10	.05	.01
386	Mookie Wilson	.06	.03	.00
387	Darryl Strawberry	.40	.20	.04
388	Kevin McReynolds	.10	.05	.01
389	Mark Carreon	.10	.05	.01
390	Jeff Parrett	.10	.05	.01
391	Mike Maddux	.03	.01	.00
392	Don Carman	.03	.01	.00
393	Bruce Ruffin	.03	.01	.00
394	Ken Howell	.03	.01	.00
395	Steve Bedrosian	.08	.04	.01
396	Floyd Youmans	.03	.01	.00
397	Larry McWilliams	.03	.01	.00
398	Pat Combs	.60	.30	.06
399	Steve Lake	.03	.01	.00
400	Dickie Thon	.06	.03	.00
401	Ricky Jordan	1.00	.50	.10
402	Mike Schmidt	.30	.15	.03
403	Tom Herr	.03	.01	.00
404	Chris James	.06	.03	.00
405	Juan Samuel	.08	.04	.01
406	Von Hayes	.08	.04	.01
407	Ron Jones	.25	.12	.02
408	Curt Ford	.03	.01	.00
409	Bob Walk	.03	.01	.00
410	Jeff Robinson	.06	.03	.00
411	Jim Gott	.03	.01	.00
412	Mike Dunne	.06	.03	.00
413	John Smiley	.06	.03	.00
414	Bob Kipper	.03	.01	.00
415	Brian Fisher	.03	.01	.00
416	Doug Drabek	.06	.03	.00
417	Mike LaValliere	.03	.01	.00
418	Ken Oberkfell	.03	.01	.00
419	Sid Bream	.03	.01	.00
420	Austin Manahan	.10	.05	.01
421	Jose Lind	.03	.01	.00
422	Bobby Bonilla	.08	.04	.01
423	Glenn Wilson	.03	.01	.00
424	Andy Van Slyke	.10	.05	.01
425	Gary Redus	.03	.01	.00
426	Barry Bonds	.08	.04	.01
427	Don Heinkel	.03	.01	.00
428	Ken Dayley	.03	.01	.00
429	Todd Worrell	.08	.04	.01

☐ 430	Brad DuVall	.10	.05	.01
☐ 431	Jose DeLeon	.06	.03	.00
☐ 432	Joe Magrane	.08	.04	.01
☐ 433	John Ericks	.20	.10	.02
☐ 434	Frank DiPino	.03	.01	.00
☐ 435	Tony Pena	.06	.03	.00
☐ 436	Ozzie Smith	.10	.05	.01
☐ 437	Terry Pendleton	.03	.01	.00
☐ 438	Jose Oquendo	.03	.01	.00
☐ 439	Tim Jones	.08	.04	.01
☐ 440	Pedro Guerrero	.10	.05	.01
☐ 441	Milt Thompson	.03	.01	.00
☐ 442	Willie McGee	.08	.04	.01
☐ 443	Vince Coleman	.10	.05	.01
☐ 444	Tom Brunansky	.08	.04	.01
☐ 445	Walt Terrell	.03	.01	.00
☐ 446	Eric Show	.03	.01	.00
☐ 447	Mark Davis	.12	.06	.01
☐ 448	Andy Benes	.85	.40	.08
☐ 449	Ed Whitson	.03	.01	.00
☐ 450	Dennis Rasmussen	.03	.01	.00
☐ 451	Bruce Hurst	.08	.04	.01
☐ 452	Pat Clements	.03	.01	.00
☐ 453	Benito Santiago	.12	.06	.01
☐ 454	Sandy Alomar Jr.	.75	.35	.07
☐ 455	Garry Templeton	.06	.03	.00
☐ 456	Jack Clark	.10	.05	.01
☐ 457	Tim Flannery	.03	.01	.00
☐ 458	Roberto Alomar	.25	.12	.02
☐ 459	Carmelo Martinez	.03	.01	.00
☐ 460	John Kruk	.06	.03	.00
☐ 461	Tony Gwynn	.20	.10	.02
☐ 462	Jerald Clark	.20	.10	.02
☐ 463	Don Robinson	.03	.01	.00
☐ 464	Craig Lefferts	.06	.03	.00
☐ 465	Kelly Downs	.06	.03	.00
☐ 466	Rick Reuschel	.06	.03	.00
☐ 467	Scott Garrelts	.06	.03	.00
☐ 468	Wil Tejada	.03	.01	.00
☐ 469	Kirt Manwaring	.08	.04	.01
☐ 470	Terry Kennedy	.03	.01	.00
☐ 471	Jose Uribe	.03	.01	.00
☐ 472	Royce Clayton	.10	.05	.01
☐ 473	Robby Thompson	.03	.01	.00
☐ 474	Kevin Mitchell	.30	.15	.03
☐ 475	Ernie Riles	.03	.01	.00
☐ 476	Will Clark	.85	.40	.08
☐ 477	Donell Nixon	.03	.01	.00
☐ 478	Candy Maldonado	.03	.01	.00
☐ 479	Tracy Jones	.03	.01	.00
☐ 480	Brett Butler	.06	.03	.00
☐ 481	Checklist	.06	.01	.00
☐ 482	Checklist	.06	.01	.00
☐ 483	Checklist	.06	.01	.00
☐ 484	Checklist	.06	.01	.00

1989 Bowman Reprint Inserts

EDWIN "Duke" SNIDER

The 1989 Bowman Reprint Inserts set contains 11 cards measuring 2 1/2 by 3 3/4 inches. The fronts depict reproduced actual size "classic" Bowman cards, which are noted as reprints. The backs are devoted to a sweepstakes entry form. One of these reprint cards was included in each 1989 Bowman wax pack thus making these "reprints" quite easy to find. Since the cards are unnumbered, they are ordered below in alphabetical order by player's name

and year within player.

		MINT	EXC	G-VG
COMPLETE SET (11)		2.00	.75	.10
COMMON PLAYER (1-11)		.15	.06	.01
☐ 1	Richie Ashburn '49	.15	.06	.01
☐ 2	Yogi Berra '48	.20	.10	.02
☐ 3	Whitey Ford '51	.20	.10	.02
☐ 4	Gil Hodges '49	.20	.10	.02
☐ 5	Mickey Mantle '51	.25	.10	.02
☐ 6	Mickey Mantle '53	.25	.10	.02
☐ 7	Willie Mays '51	.20	.10	.02
☐ 8	Satchel Paige '49	.20	.10	.02
☐ 9	Jackie Robinson '50	.20	.10	.02
☐ 10	Duke Snider '49	.20	.10	.02
☐ 11	Ted Williams '54	.20	.10	.02

1977 Burger King Yankees

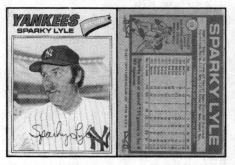

The cards in this 24-card set measure 2 1/2" by 3 1/2". The cards in this set marked with an asterisk have different poses than those cards in the regular 1977 Topps set. The checklist card is unnumbered and the Piniella card was issued subsequent to the original printing. The complete set price below refers to all 24 cards listed, including Piniella.

		NRMT	VG-E	GOOD
COMPLETE SET (24)		40.00	20.00	4.00
COMMON PLAYER (1-23)		.35	.17	.03
☐ 1	Yankees Team Billy Martin MG	1.00	.50	.10
☐ 2	Thurman Munson * (facsimile autograph misspelled)	6.00	3.00	.60
☐ 3	Fran Healy	.35	.17	.03
☐ 4	Jim Hunter	2.50	1.25	.25
☐ 5	Ed Figueroa *	.35	.17	.03
☐ 6	Don Gullett * (mouth closed)	.50	.25	.05
☐ 7	Mike Torrez *	.50	.25	.05
☐ 8	Ken Holtzman	.35	.17	.03
☐ 9	Dick Tidrow	.35	.17	.03
☐ 10	Sparky Lyle	.50	.25	.05
☐ 11	Ron Guidry	2.00	1.00	.20
☐ 12	Chris Chambliss	.50	.25	.05
☐ 13	Willie Randolph * (no rookie trophy)	1.00	.50	.10
☐ 14	Bucky Dent * (shown as White Sox in 1977 Topps)	1.00	.50	.10
☐ 15	Graig Nettles * (closer photo than in 1977 Topps)	1.50	.75	.15
☐ 16	Fred Stanley	.35	.17	.03
☐ 17	Reggie Jackson * (looking up with bat)	7.50	3.75	.75
☐ 18	Mickey Rivers	.50	.25	.05
☐ 19	Roy White	.35	.17	.03
☐ 20	Jim Wynn * (shown as Brave in 1977 Topps)	.50	.25	.05
☐ 21	Paul Blair * (shown as Oriole in 1977 Topps)	.50	.25	.05
☐ 22	Carlos May *	.35	.17	.03

		NRMT	VG-E	GOOD
☐ 23	Lou Piniella	20.00	10.00	2.00
☐ xx	Checklist card	.15	.02	.00
	(unnumbered)			

1978 Burger King Astros

JESUS ALOU

The cards in this 23-card set measure 2 1/2" by 3 1/2". Released in local Houston Burger King outlets during the 1978 season, this Houston Astros series contains the standard 22 numbered player cards and one unnumbered checklist. The player poses found to differ from the regular Topps issue are marked with astericks.

		NRMT	VG-E	GOOD
COMPLETE SET (23)		11.00	5.50	1.10
COMMON PLAYER (1-23)		.35	.17	.03
☐ 1	Bill Virdon MG	.75	.35	.07
☐ 2	Joe Ferguson	.35	.17	.03
☐ 3	Ed Herrmann	.35	.17	.03
☐ 4	J.R. Richard	.90	.45	.09
☐ 5	Joe Niekro	1.00	.50	.10
☐ 6	Floyd Bannister	1.00	.50	.10
☐ 7	Joaquin Andujar	.90	.45	.09
☐ 8	Ken Forsch	.45	.22	.04
☐ 9	Mark Lemongello	.35	.17	.03
☐ 10	Joe Sambito	.45	.22	.04
☐ 11	Gene Pentz	.35	.17	.03
☐ 12	Bob Watson	.60	.30	.06
☐ 13	Julio Gonzales	.35	.17	.03
☐ 14	Enos Cabell	.35	.17	.03
☐ 15	Roger Metzger	.35	.17	.03
☐ 16	Art Howe	.75	.35	.07
☐ 17	Jose Cruz	.90	.45	.09
☐ 18	Cesar Cedeno	.75	.35	.07
☐ 19	Terry Puhl	.60	.30	.06
☐ 20	Wilbur Howard	.35	.17	.03
☐ 21	Dave Bergman *	.45	.22	.04
☐ 22	Jesus Alou *	.45	.22	.04
☐ 23	Checklist card	.05	.02	.00
	(unnumbered)			

1978 Burger King Rangers

The cards in this 23-card set measure 2 1/2" by 3 1/2". This set of 22 numbered player cards (featuring the Texas Rangers) and one unnumbered checklist was issued regionally by Burger King in 1978. Astericks denote poses different from those found in the regular Topps cards of this year.

		NRMT	VG-E	GOOD
COMPLETE SET (23)		11.00	5.50	1.10
COMMON PLAYER (1-23)		.35	.17	.03
☐ 1	Billy Hunter MG	.35	.17	.03
☐ 2	Jim Sundberg	.60	.30	.06
☐ 3	John Ellis	.35	.17	.03
☐ 4	Doyle Alexander	.75	.35	.07
☐ 5	Jon Matlack *	.60	.30	.06
☐ 6	Dock Ellis	.45	.22	.04

DOYLE ALEXANDER

		NRMT	VG-E	GOOD
☐ 7	Doc Medich	.45	.22	.04
☐ 8	Fergie Jenkins *	1.50	.75	.15
☐ 9	Len Barker	.35	.17	.03
☐ 10	Reggie Cleveland *	.35	.17	.03
☐ 11	Mike Hargrove	.60	.30	.06
☐ 12	Bump Wills	.35	.17	.03
☐ 13	Toby Harrah	.75	.35	.07
☐ 14	Bert Campaneris	.60	.30	.06
☐ 15	Sandy Alomar	.35	.17	.03
☐ 16	Kurt Bevacqua	.35	.17	.03
☐ 17	Al Oliver *	.90	.45	.09
☐ 18	Juan Beniquez	.45	.22	.04
☐ 19	Claudell Washington	.75	.35	.07
☐ 20	Richie Zisk	.45	.22	.04
☐ 21	John Lowenstein *	.35	.17	.03
☐ 22	Bobby Thompson *	.35	.17	.03
☐ 23	Checklist card	.05	.02	.00
	(unnumbered)			

1978 Burger King Tigers

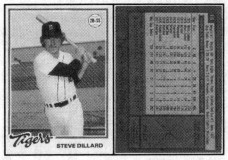

STEVE DILLARD

The cards in this 23-card set measure 2 1/2" by 3 1/2". Twenty-three color cards, 22 players and one numbered checklist, comprise the 1978 Burger King Tigers set issued in the Detroit area. The cards marked with an asterisk contain photos different from those appearing on the Topps regular issue cards of that year. For example, Jack Morris and Lou Whitaker (in the 1978 Topps regular issue cards) each appear on rookie prospect cards with three other young players; whereas in this Burger King set, each has his own individual card.

		NRMT	VG-E	GOOD
COMPLETE SET (23)		42.00	18.00	4.00
COMMON PLAYER (1-23)		.35	.17	.03
☐ 1	Ralph Houk MG	.60	.30	.06
☐ 2	Milt May	.35	.17	.03
☐ 3	John Wockenfuss	.35	.17	.03
☐ 4	Mark Fidrych	.75	.35	.07
☐ 5	Dave Rozema	.35	.17	.03
☐ 6	Jack Billingham *	.35	.17	.03
☐ 7	Jim Slaton *	.35	.17	.03
☐ 8	Jack Morris *	9.00	4.50	.90
☐ 9	John Hiller	.60	.30	.06
☐ 10	Steve Foucault	.35	.17	.03

☐ 11	Milt Wilcox	.35	.17	.03
☐ 12	Jason Thompson	.60	.30	.06
☐ 13	Lou Whitaker *	9.00	4.50	.90
☐ 14	Aurelio Rodriguez	.35	.17	.03
☐ 15	Alan Trammell *	16.00	8.00	1.60
☐ 16	Steve Dillard *	.35	.17	.03
☐ 17	Phil Mankowski	.35	.17	.03
☐ 18	Steve Kemp	.60	.30	.06
☐ 19	Ron LeFlore	.45	.22	.04
☐ 20	Tim Corcoran	.35	.17	.03
☐ 21	Mickey Stanley	.45	.22	.04
☐ 22	Rusty Staub	1.00	.50	.10
☐ 23	Checklist card (unnumbered)	.05	.02	.00

1978 Burger King Yankees

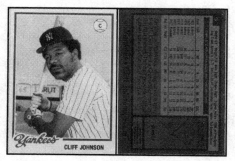

CLIFF JOHNSON

The cards in this 23-card set measure 2 1/2" by 3 1/2". These cards were distributed in packs of three players plus a checklist at Burger King's New York area outlets. Cards with an asterisk have different poses than those in the Topps regular issue.

		NRMT	VG-E	GOOD
COMPLETE SET (23)		10.00	5.00	1.00
COMMON PLAYER (1-23)		.20	.10	.02

☐ 1	Billy Martin MG	.75	.35	.07
☐ 2	Thurman Munson	3.00	1.50	.30
☐ 3	Cliff Johnson	.20	.10	.02
☐ 4	Ron Guidry	1.25	.60	.12
☐ 5	Ed Figueroa	.20	.10	.02
☐ 6	Dick Tidrow	.20	.10	.02
☐ 7	Jim Hunter	1.50	.75	.15
☐ 8	Don Gullett	.25	.12	.02
☐ 9	Sparky Lyle	.40	.20	.04
☐ 10	Rich Gossage *	.90	.45	.09
☐ 11	Rawly Eastwick *	.20	.10	.02
☐ 12	Chris Chambliss	.25	.12	.02
☐ 13	Willie Randolph	.60	.30	.06
☐ 14	Graig Nettles	.75	.35	.07
☐ 15	Bucky Dent	.60	.30	.06
☐ 16	Jim Spencer *	.20	.10	.02
☐ 17	Fred Stanley	.20	.10	.02
☐ 18	Lou Piniella	.40	.20	.04
☐ 19	Roy White	.25	.12	.02
☐ 20	Mickey Rivers	.25	.12	.02
☐ 21	Reggie Jackson	3.50	1.75	.35
☐ 22	Paul Blair	.20	.10	.02
☐ 23	Checklist card (unnumbered)	.05	.02	.00

1979 Burger King Phillies

The cards in this 23-card set measure 2 1/2" by 3 1/2". The 1979 Burger King Phillies set follows the regular format of 22 player cards and one unnumbered checklist card. The asterisk indicates where the pose differs from the Topps card of that year.

		NRMT	VG-E	GOOD
COMPLETE SET (23)		7.00	3.50	.70
COMMON PLAYER (1-23)		.10	.05	.01

TUG McGRAW P
PHILLIES

☐ 1	Danny Ozark MG *	.10	.05	.01
☐ 2	Bob Boone	.50	.25	.05
☐ 3	Tim McCarver	.50	.25	.05
☐ 4	Steve Carlton	2.00	1.00	.20
☐ 5	Larry Christenson	.10	.05	.01
☐ 6	Dick Ruthven	.10	.05	.01
☐ 7	Ron Reed	.10	.05	.01
☐ 8	Randy Lerch	.10	.05	.01
☐ 9	Warren Brusstar	.10	.05	.01
☐ 10	Tug McGraw	.30	.15	.03
☐ 11	Nino Espinosa *	.10	.05	.01
☐ 12	Doug Bird *	.10	.05	.01
☐ 13	Pete Rose *	2.50	1.25	.25
☐ 14	Manny Trillo *	.15	.07	.01
☐ 15	Larry Bowa	.40	.20	.04
☐ 16	Mike Schmidt	2.50	1.25	.25
☐ 17	Pete Mackanin *	.10	.05	.01
☐ 18	Jose Cardenal	.10	.05	.01
☐ 19	Greg Luzinski	.40	.20	.04
☐ 20	Garry Maddox	.15	.07	.01
☐ 21	Bake McBride	.10	.05	.01
☐ 22	Greg Gross *	.10	.05	.01
☐ 23	Checklist card (unnumbered)	.05	.02	.00

1979 Burger King Yankees

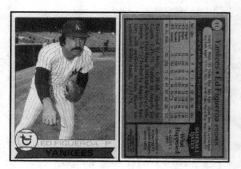

ED FIGUEROA P
YANKEES

The cards in this 23-card set measure 2 1/2" X 3 1/2". There are 22 numbered cards and one unnumbered checklist in the 1979 Burger King Yankee set. The poses of Guidry, Tiant, John and Beniquez, each marked with an asterisk below, are different from their poses appearing in the regular Topps issue. The team card has a picture of Lemon rather than Martin.

		NRMT	VG-E	GOOD
COMPLETE SET (23)		7.00	3.50	.70
COMMON PLAYER (1-23)		.10	.05	.01

☐ 1	Yankees Team: Bob Lemon MG *	.50	.25	.05
☐ 2	Thurman Munson	2.00	1.00	.20
☐ 3	Cliff Johnson	.10	.05	.01
☐ 4	Ron Guidry *	1.00	.50	.10

			MINT	EXC	G-VG
☐	5	Jay Johnstone	.25	.12	.02
☐	6	Jim Hunter	1.00	.50	.10
☐	7	Jim Beattie	.10	.05	.01
☐	8	Luis Tiant *	.25	.12	.02
☐	9	Tommy John *	.75	.35	.07
☐	10	Rich Gossage	.60	.30	.06
☐	11	Ed Figueroa	.10	.05	.01
☐	12	Chris Chambliss	.15	.07	.01
☐	13	Willie Randolph	.40	.20	.04
☐	14	Bucky Dent	.40	.20	.04
☐	15	Graig Nettles	.50	.25	.05
☐	16	Fred Stanley	.10	.05	.01
☐	17	Jim Spencer	.10	.05	.01
☐	18	Lou Piniella	.30	.15	.03
☐	19	Roy White	.15	.07	.01
☐	20	Mickey Rivers	.15	.07	.01
☐	21	Reggie Jackson	2.50	1.25	.25
☐	22	Juan Beniquez *	.20	.10	.02
☐	23	Checklist card (unnumbered)	.05	.02	.00

1980 Burger King Phillies

The cards in this 23-card set measure 2 1/2" by 3 1/2". The 1980 edition of Burger King Phillies follows the established pattern of 22 numbered player cards and one unnumbered checklist. Cards marked with asterisks contain poses different from those found in the regular 1980 Topps cards. This was the first Burger King set to carry the Burger King logo and hence does not generate the same confusion that the three previous years do for collectors trying to distinguish Burger King cards from the very similar Topps cards of the same years.

			MINT	EXC	G-VG
	COMPLETE SET (23)		6.00	3.00	.60
	COMMON PLAYER (1-23)		.10	.05	.01
☐	1	Dallas Green MG *	.30	.15	.03
☐	2	Bob Boone	.40	.20	.04
☐	3	Keith Moreland *	.75	.35	.07
☐	4	Pete Rose	2.50	1.25	.25
☐	5	Manny Trillo	.15	.07	.01
☐	6	Mike Schmidt	2.50	1.25	.25
☐	7	Larry Bowa	.35	.17	.03
☐	8	John Vukovich *	.10	.05	.01
☐	9	Bake McBride	.10	.05	.01
☐	10	Garry Maddox	.15	.07	.01
☐	11	Greg Luzinski	.25	.12	.02
☐	12	Greg Gross	.10	.05	.01
☐	13	Del Unser	.10	.05	.01
☐	14	Lonnie Smith *	.50	.25	.05
☐	15	Steve Carlton	1.50	.75	.15
☐	16	Larry Christenson	.10	.05	.01
☐	17	Nino Espinosa	.10	.05	.01
☐	18	Randy Lerch	.10	.05	.01
☐	19	Dick Ruthven	.10	.05	.01
☐	20	Tug McGraw	.30	.15	.03
☐	21	Ron Reed	.10	.05	.01
☐	22	Kevin Saucier *	.10	.05	.01
☐	23	Checklist card (unnumbered)	.05	.02	.00

1980 Burger King Pitch/Hit/Run

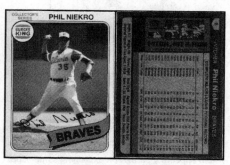

The cards in this 34-card set measure 2 1/2" by 3 1/2". The "Pitch, Hit, and Run" set was a promotion introduced by Burger King in 1980. The cards carry a Burger King logo on the front and those marked by an asterisk in the checklist contain a different photo from that found in the regularly issued Topps series. Cards 1-11 are pitchers, 12-22 are hitters, and 23-33 are speedsters. Within each subgroup, the players are numbered corresponding to the alphabetical order of their names. The unnumbered checklist card was triple printed and is the least valuable card in the set.

			MINT	EXC	G-VG
	COMPLETE SET (34)		12.00	6.00	1.20
	COMMON PLAYER (1-34)		.10	.05	.01
☐	1	Vida Blue *	.10	.05	.01
☐	2	Steve Carlton	1.25	.60	.12
☐	3	Rollie Fingers	.50	.25	.05
☐	4	Ron Guidry *	.30	.15	.03
☐	5	Jerry Koosman *	.15	.07	.01
☐	6	Phil Niekro	.50	.25	.05
☐	7	Jim Palmer *	1.00	.50	.10
☐	8	J.R. Richard	.10	.05	.01
☐	9	Nolan Ryan *	2.50	1.25	.25
☐	10	Tom Seaver *	1.25	.60	.12
☐	11	Bruce Sutter	.15	.07	.01
☐	12	Don Baylor	.15	.07	.01
☐	13	George Brett	1.00	.50	.10
☐	14	Rod Carew	.75	.35	.07
☐	15	George Foster	.15	.07	.01
☐	16	Keith Hernandez *	.60	.30	.06
☐	17	Reggie Jackson *	1.50	.75	.15
☐	18	Fred Lynn *	.20	.10	.02
☐	19	Dave Parker	.25	.12	.02
☐	20	Jim Rice	.40	.20	.04
☐	21	Pete Rose	2.00	1.00	.20
☐	22	Dave Winfield *	1.00	.50	.10
☐	23	Bobby Bonds *	.15	.07	.01
☐	24	Enos Cabell *	.10	.05	.01
☐	25	Cesar Cedeno *	.10	.05	.01
☐	26	Julio Cruz	.10	.05	.01
☐	27	Ron LeFlore *	.10	.05	.01
☐	28	Dave Lopes *	.10	.05	.01
☐	29	Omar Moreno *	.10	.05	.01
☐	30	Joe Morgan *	1.00	.50	.10
☐	31	Bill North	.10	.05	.01
☐	32	Frank Taveras	.10	.05	.01
☐	33	Willie Wilson	.15	.07	.01
☐	34	Unnumbered Checklist	.05	.02	.00

1982 Burger King Indians

The cards in this 12-card set measure 3" by 5". Tips From The Dugout is the series title of this set issued on a one card per week basis by the Burger King chain in the Cleveland area. Each card contains a black and white photo of manager Dave Garcia or coaches Goryl, McCraw, Queen and Sommers, under

whom appears a paragraph explaining some aspect of inside baseball. The photo and "Tip" are set upon a large yellow area surrounded by green borders. The cards are not numbered and are blank-backed. The logos of Burger King and WUAB-TV appear at the base of the card.

	MINT	EXC	G-VG
COMPLETE SET (12)	6.00	3.00	.60
COMMON PLAYER (1-12)	.55	.25	.05
☐ 1 Dave Garcia: .... Be in the Game	.55	.25	.05
☐ 2 Dave Garcia: .... Sportsmanship	.55	.25	.05
☐ 3 Johnny Goryl: .... Rounding Bases	.55	.25	.05
☐ 4 Johnny Goryl: .... 3B Running	.55	.25	.05
☐ 5 Tom McCraw: .... Follow Thru	.55	.25	.05
☐ 6 Tom McCraw: .... Selecting a Bat	.55	.25	.05
☐ 7 Tom McCraw: .... Watch the Ball	.55	.25	.05
☐ 8 Mel Queen: .... Master One Pitch	.55	.25	.05
☐ 9 Mel Queen: .... Warm Up	.55	.25	.05
☐ 10 Dennis Sommers: .... Protect Fingers	.55	.25	.05
☐ 11 Dennis Sommers: .... Tagging 1st Base	.55	.25	.05
☐ 12 Dennis Sommers	.55	.25	.05

1986 Burger King All Pro

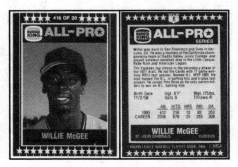

This 20-card set was distributed in Burger King restaurants across the country. They were produced as panels of three where the middle card was actually a special discount coupon card. The folded panel was given with the purchase of a Whopper. Each individual card measures 2 1/2" by 3 1/2". The team logos have been airbrushed from the pictures. The

cards are numbered on the front at the top.

	MINT	EXC	G-VG
COMPLETE SET (20)	6.00	3.00	.60
COMMON PLAYER (1-20)	.20	.10	.02
☐ 1 Tony Pena	.20	.10	.02
☐ 2 Dave Winfield	.40	.20	.04
☐ 3 Fernando Valenzuela	.30	.15	.03
☐ 4 Pete Rose	.80	.40	.08
☐ 5 Mike Schmidt	.80	.40	.08
☐ 6 Steve Carlton	.50	.25	.05
☐ 7 Glenn Wilson	.20	.10	.02
☐ 8 Jim Rice	.30	.15	.03
☐ 9 Wade Boggs	.80	.40	.08
☐ 10 Juan Samuel	.20	.10	.02
☐ 11 Dale Murphy	.50	.25	.05
☐ 12 Reggie Jackson	.70	.35	.07
☐ 13 Kirk Gibson	.40	.20	.04
☐ 14 Eddie Murray	.40	.20	.04
☐ 15 Cal Ripken	.50	.25	.05
☐ 16 Willie McGee	.30	.15	.03
☐ 17 Dwight Gooden	.60	.30	.06
☐ 18 Steve Garvey	.50	.25	.05
☐ 19 Don Mattingly	1.00	.50	.10
☐ 20 George Brett	.60	.30	.06

1987 Burger King All-Pro

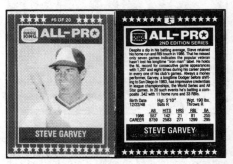

This 20-card set consists of 10 panels of two cards each joined together along with a promotional coupon. Individual cards measure 2 1/2" by 3 1/2" whereas the panels measure 3 1/2" by 7 5/8". MSA (Mike Schechter Associates produced the cards for Burger King; there are no Major League logos on the cards. The cards are numbered on the front. The set card numbering is almost (but not quite) in alphabetical order by player's name.

	MINT	EXC	G-VG
COMPLETE SET (20)	5.00	2.50	.50
COMMON PLAYER (1-20)	.20	.10	.02
☐ 1 Wade Boggs	.80	.40	.08
☐ 2 Gary Carter	.40	.20	.04
☐ 3 Will Clark	1.00	.50	.10
☐ 4 Roger Clemens	.70	.35	.07
☐ 5 Steve Garvey	.40	.20	.04
☐ 6 Ron Darling	.30	.15	.03
☐ 7 Pedro Guerrero	.30	.15	.03
☐ 8 Von Hayes	.20	.10	.02
☐ 9 Rickey Henderson	.60	.30	.06
☐ 10 Keith Hernandez	.30	.15	.03
☐ 11 Wally Joyner	.50	.25	.05
☐ 12 Mike Krukow	.20	.10	.02
☐ 13 Don Mattingly	1.00	.50	.10
☐ 14 Ozzie Smith	.40	.20	.04
☐ 15 Tony Pena	.20	.10	.02
☐ 16 Jim Rice	.30	.15	.03
☐ 17 Mike Schmidt	.80	.40	.08
☐ 18 Ryne Sandberg	.50	.25	.05
☐ 19 Darryl Strawberry	.60	.30	.06
☐ 20 Fernando Valenzuela	.30	.15	.03

1988 Chef Boyardee

This 24-card set was distributed as a perforated sheet of four rows and six columns of cards in return for ten proofs of puchase of Chef Boyardeee products. The card photos on the fronts are in full color with a light blue border but are not shown with team logos. The card backs are numbered and printed in red and blue on gray card stock. Individual cards measure approximately 2 1/2" by 3 1/2" and show the Chef Boyardee logo in the upper right corner of the obverse. Card backs feature year-by-year season statistics since 1984.

		MINT	EXC	G-VG
COMPLETE SET (24)		16.00	8.00	1.60
COMMON PLAYER (1-24)		.40	.20	.04
□ 1	Mark McGwire	1.25	.60	.12
□ 2	Eric Davis	.90	.45	.09
□ 3	Jack Morris	.40	.20	.04
□ 4	George Bell	.50	.25	.05
□ 5	Ozzie Smith	.60	.30	.06
□ 6	Tony Gwynn	.75	.35	.07
□ 7	Cal Ripken	.75	.35	.07
□ 8	Todd Worrell	.40	.20	.04
□ 9	Larry Parrish	.40	.20	.04
□ 10	Gary Carter	.50	.25	.05
□ 11	Ryne Sandberg	.60	.30	.06
□ 12	Keith Hernandez	.50	.25	.05
□ 13	Kirby Puckett	1.00	.50	.10
□ 14	Mike Schmidt	1.25	.60	.12
□ 15	Frank Viola	.50	.25	.05
□ 16	Don Mattingly	2.00	1.00	.20
□ 17	Dale Murphy	.75	.35	.07
□ 18	Andre Dawson	.50	.25	.05
□ 19	Mike Scott	.40	.20	.04
□ 20	Rickey Henderson	.90	.45	.09
□ 21	Jim Rice	.50	.25	.05
□ 22	Wade Boggs	1.25	.60	.12
□ 23	Roger Clemens	1.00	.50	.10
□ 24	Fernando Valenzuela	.50	.25	.05

1985 CIGNA Phillies

This colorful 16-card set (measuring 2 5/8" by 4 1/8") features the Philadelphia Phillies and was also sponsored by CIGNA Corporation. Cards are numbered on the back and contain a safety tip as such the set is frequently categorized and referenced as a safety set. Cards are also numbered by uniform number on the front.

		MINT	EXC	G-VG
COMPLETE SET (16)		6.00	3.00	.60
COMMON PLAYER (1-16)		.20	.10	.02
□ 1	Juan Samuel	.50	.25	.05
□ 2	Von Hayes	.50	.25	.05
□ 3	Ozzie Virgil	.30	.15	.03
□ 4	Mike Schmidt	2.50	1.25	.25
□ 5	Greg Gross	.20	.10	.02

□ 6	Tim Corcoran	.20	.10	.02
□ 7	Jerry Koosman	.30	.15	.03
□ 8	Jeff Stone	.20	.10	.02
□ 9	Glenn Wilson	.30	.15	.03
□ 10	Steve Jeltz	.20	.10	.02
□ 11	Garry Maddox	.20	.10	.02
□ 12	Steve Carlton	1.25	.60	.12
□ 13	John Denny	.25	.12	.02
□ 14	Kevin Gross	.40	.20	.04
□ 15	Shane Rawley	.30	.15	.03
□ 16	Charlie Hudson	.30	.15	.03

1986 CIGNA Phillies

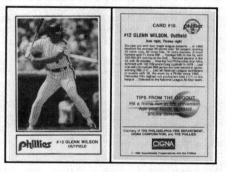

This 16-card set was sponsored by CIGNA Corp. and was given away by the Philadelphia area Fire Departments. Cards measure 2 3/4" by 4 1/8" and feature full color fronts. The card backs are printed in maroon and black on white card stock. Although the uniform numbers are given on the front of the card, the cards are numbered on the back in the order listed below.

		MINT	EXC	G-VG
COMPLETE SET (16)		6.00	3.00	.60
COMMON PLAYER (1-16)		.20	.10	.02
□ 1	Juan Samuel	.50	.25	.05
□ 2	Don Carman	.30	.15	.03
□ 3	Von Hayes	.50	.25	.05
□ 4	Kent Tekulve	.30	.15	.03
□ 5	Greg Gross	.20	.10	.02
□ 6	Shane Rawley	.30	.15	.03
□ 7	Darren Daulton	.20	.10	.02
□ 8	Kevin Gross	.30	.15	.03
□ 9	Steve Jeltz	.20	.10	.02
□ 10	Mike Schmidt	2.50	1.25	.25
□ 11	Steve Bedrosian	.75	.35	.07
□ 12	Gary Redus	.30	.15	.03
□ 13	Charles Hudson	.30	.15	.03
□ 14	John Russell	.20	.10	.02
□ 15	Fred Toliver	.20	.10	.02
□ 16	Glenn Wilson	.30	.15	.03

1985 Circle K

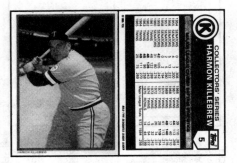

The cards in this 33-card set measure 2 1/2" by 3 1/2" and were issued with accompanying box. In 1985, Topps produced this set for Circle K; cards were printed in Ireland. Cards are numbered on the back according to each player's rank on the all-time career Home Run list. The backs are printed in blue and red on white card stock. The card fronts are glossy and each player is named in the lower left corner. Most of the obverses are in color, although the older vintage players are pictured in black and white. Joe DiMaggio was not included in the set; card #31 does not exist. It was intended to be DiMaggio but he apparently would not consent to be included in the set.

		MINT	EXC	G-VG
COMPLETE SET (33)		5.00	2.50	.50
COMMON PLAYER (1-34)		.10	.05	.01
☐ 1	Hank Aaron	.50	.25	.05
☐ 2	Babe Ruth	.90	.45	.09
☐ 3	Willie Mays	.50	.25	.05
☐ 4	Frank Robinson	.20	.10	.02
☐ 5	Harmon Killebrew	.15	.07	.01
☐ 6	Mickey Mantle	1.00	.50	.10
☐ 7	Jimmie Foxx	.15	.07	.01
☐ 8	Willie McCovey	.20	.10	.02
☐ 9	Ted Williams	.40	.20	.04
☐ 10	Ernie Banks	.20	.10	.02
☐ 11	Eddie Mathews	.15	.07	.01
☐ 12	Mel Ott	.15	.07	.01
☐ 13	Reggie Jackson	.50	.25	.05
☐ 14	Lou Gehrig	.50	.25	.05
☐ 15	Stan Musial	.35	.17	.03
☐ 16	Willie Stargell	.20	.10	.02
☐ 17	Carl Yastrzemski	.50	.25	.05
☐ 18	Billy Williams	.15	.07	.01
☐ 19	Mike Schmidt	.50	.25	.05
☐ 20	Duke Snider	.30	.15	.03
☐ 21	Al Kaline	.20	.10	.02
☐ 22	Johnny Bench	.35	.17	.03
☐ 23	Frank Howard	.10	.05	.01
☐ 24	Orlando Cepeda	.10	.05	.01
☐ 25	Norm Cash	.10	.05	.01
☐ 26	Dave Kingman	.10	.05	.01
☐ 27	Rocky Colavito	.10	.05	.01
☐ 28	Tony Perez	.10	.05	.01
☐ 29	Gil Hodges	.10	.05	.01
☐ 30	Ralph Kiner	.10	.05	.01
☐ 31	Joe DiMaggio (not included in set, card does not exist)	.00	.00	.00
☐ 32	Johnny Mize	.15	.07	.01
☐ 33	Yogi Berra	.30	.15	.03
☐ 34	Lee May	.10	.05	.01

1987 Classic Game

George Brett

This 100-card set was actually distributed as part of a trivia board game. The card backs contain several trivia questions (and answers) which are used to play the game. A dark green border frames the full color photo. The games were produced by Game Time, Ltd. and were available in toy stores as well as from card dealers.

		MINT	EXC	G-VG
COMPLETE SET (100)		35.00	17.50	3.50
COMMON PLAYER (1-100)		.10	.05	.01
☐ 1	Pete Rose	1.25	.50	.10
☐ 2	Len Dykstra	.15	.07	.01
☐ 3	Darryl Strawberry	1.00	.50	.10
☐ 4	Keith Hernandez	.25	.12	.02
☐ 5	Gary Carter	.25	.12	.02
☐ 6	Wally Joyner	.75	.35	.07
☐ 7	Andres Thomas	.10	.05	.01
☐ 8	Pat Dodson	.10	.05	.01
☐ 9	Kirk Gibson	.30	.15	.03
☐ 10	Don Mattingly	1.25	.60	.12
☐ 11	Dave Winfield	.30	.15	.03
☐ 12	Rickey Henderson	.40	.20	.04
☐ 13	Dan Pasqua	.10	.05	.01
☐ 14	Don Baylor	.10	.05	.01
☐ 15	Bo Jackson (swinging bat in Auburn FB uniform)	15.00	7.50	1.50
☐ 16	Pete Incaviglia	.40	.20	.04
☐ 17	Kevin Bass	.10	.05	.01
☐ 18	Barry Larkin	.40	.20	.04
☐ 19	Dave Magadan	.15	.07	.01
☐ 20	Steve Sax	.20	.10	.02
☐ 21	Eric Davis	1.00	.50	.10
☐ 22	Mike Pagliarulo	.10	.05	.01
☐ 23	Fred Lynn	.15	.07	.01
☐ 24	Reggie Jackson	.75	.35	.07
☐ 25	Larry Parrish	.10	.05	.01
☐ 26	Tony Gwynn	.60	.30	.06
☐ 27	Steve Garvey	.50	.25	.05
☐ 28	Glenn Davis	.30	.15	.03
☐ 29	Tim Raines	.30	.15	.03
☐ 30	Vince Coleman	.30	.15	.03
☐ 31	Willie McGee	.15	.07	.01
☐ 32	Ozzie Smith	.25	.12	.02
☐ 33	Dave Parker	.15	.07	.01
☐ 34	Tony Pena	.10	.05	.01
☐ 35	Ryne Sandberg	.35	.17	.03
☐ 36	Brett Butler	.15	.07	.01
☐ 37	Dale Murphy	.50	.25	.05
☐ 38	Bob Horner	.10	.05	.01
☐ 39	Pedro Guerrero	.20	.10	.02
☐ 40	Brook Jacoby	.10	.05	.01
☐ 41	Carlton Fisk	.25	.12	.02
☐ 42	Harold Baines	.15	.07	.01
☐ 43	Rob Deer	.10	.05	.01
☐ 44	Robin Yount	.60	.30	.06
☐ 45	Paul Molitor	.20	.10	.02
☐ 46	Jose Canseco	1.50	.75	.15
☐ 47	George Brett	.60	.30	.06
☐ 48	Jim Presley	.10	.05	.01
☐ 49	Rich Gedman	.10	.05	.01
☐ 50	Lance Parrish	.15	.07	.01
☐ 51	Eddie Murray	.30	.15	.03
☐ 52	Cal Ripken	.35	.17	.03
☐ 53	Kent Hrbek	.20	.10	.02
☐ 54	Gary Gaetti	.20	.10	.02

☐ 55	Kirby Puckett	1.00	.50	.10
☐ 56	George Bell	.25	.12	.02
☐ 57	Tony Fernandez	.20	.10	.02
☐ 58	Jesse Barfield	.15	.07	.01
☐ 59	Jim Rice	.20	.10	.02
☐ 60	Wade Boggs	1.00	.50	.10
☐ 61	Marty Barrett	.10	.05	.01
☐ 62	Mike Schmidt	1.00	.50	.10
☐ 63	Von Hayes	.15	.07	.01
☐ 64	Jeff Leonard	.10	.05	.01
☐ 65	Chris Brown	.10	.05	.01
☐ 66	Dave Smith	.10	.05	.01
☐ 67	Mike Krukow	.10	.05	.01
☐ 68	Ron Guidry	.20	.10	.02
☐ 69	Rob Woodward	.10	.05	.01
☐ 70	Rob Murphy	.10	.05	.01
☐ 71	Andres Galarraga	.30	.15	.03
☐ 72	Dwight Gooden	.75	.35	.07
☐ 73	Bob Ojeda	.15	.07	.01
☐ 74	Sid Fernandez	.15	.07	.01
☐ 75	Jesse Orosco	.10	.05	.01
☐ 76	Roger McDowell	.15	.07	.01
☐ 77	John Tudor	.20	.10	.02
	(misspelled Tutor)			
☐ 78	Tom Browning	.15	.07	.01
☐ 79	Rick Aguilera	.15	.07	.01
☐ 80	Lance McCullers	.15	.07	.01
☐ 81	Mike Scott	.25	.12	.02
☐ 82	Nolan Ryan	1.50	.75	.15
☐ 83	Bruce Hurst	.20	.10	.02
☐ 84	Roger Clemens	.75	.35	.07
☐ 85	Oil Can Boyd	.10	.05	.01
☐ 86	Dave Righetti	.15	.07	.01
☐ 87	Dennis Rasmussen	.15	.07	.01
☐ 88	Bret Saberhagen	.40	.20	.04
☐ 89	Mark Langston	.30	.15	.03
☐ 90	Jack Morris	.20	.10	.02
☐ 91	Fernando Valenzuela	.20	.10	.02
☐ 92	Orel Hershiser	.60	.30	.06
☐ 93	Rick Honeycutt	.10	.05	.01
☐ 94	Jeff Reardon	.20	.10	.02
☐ 95	John Habyan	.10	.05	.01
☐ 96	Goose Gossage	.15	.07	.01
☐ 97	Todd Worrell	.20	.10	.02
☐ 98	Floyd Youmans	.10	.05	.01
☐ 99	Don Aase	.10	.05	.01
☐ 100	John Franco	.20	.10	.02

☐ 102	Eric Davis	.75	.35	.07
☐ 103	Pete Rose	1.00	.50	.10
☐ 104	Don Mattingly	1.25	.60	.12
☐ 105	Wade Boggs	1.00	.50	.10
☐ 106	Dale Murphy	.30	.15	.03
☐ 107	Glenn Davis	.20	.10	.02
☐ 108	Wally Joyner	.50	.25	.05
☐ 109	Bo Jackson	1.25	.60	.12
☐ 110	Cory Snyder	.20	.10	.02
☐ 111	Jim Lindeman	.10	.05	.01
☐ 112	Kirby Puckett	.75	.35	.07
☐ 113	Barry Bonds	.20	.10	.02
☐ 114	Roger Clemens	.60	.30	.06
☐ 115	Oddibe McDowell	.10	.05	.01
☐ 116	Bret Saberhagen	.25	.12	.02
☐ 117	Joe Magrane	.15	.07	.01
☐ 118	Scott Fletcher	.10	.05	.01
☐ 119	Mark McLemore	.10	.05	.01
☐ 120	Who Me (Joe Niekro)	.10	.05	.01
☐ 121	Mark McGwire	1.00	.50	.10
☐ 122	Darryl Strawberry	.75	.35	.07
☐ 123	Mike Scott	.15	.07	.01
☐ 124	Andre Dawson	.20	.10	.02
☐ 125	Jose Canseco	1.25	.60	.12
☐ 126	Kevin McReynolds	.25	.12	.02
☐ 127	Joe Carter	.20	.10	.02
☐ 128	Casey Candaele	.10	.05	.01
☐ 129	Matt Nokes	.35	.17	.03
☐ 130	Kal Daniels	.30	.15	.03
☐ 131	Pete Incaviglia	.20	.10	.02
☐ 132	Benito Santiago	.50	.25	.05
☐ 133	Barry Larkin	.30	.15	.03
☐ 134	Gary Pettis	.10	.05	.01
☐ 135	B.J. Surhoff	.15	.07	.01
☐ 136	Juan Nieves	.10	.05	.01
☐ 137	Jim Deshaies	.10	.05	.01
☐ 138	Pete O'Brien	.15	.07	.01
☐ 139	Kevin Seitzer	.75	.35	.07
☐ 140	Devon White	.25	.12	.02
☐ 141	Rob Deer	.15	.07	.01
☐ 142	Kurt Stillwell	.15	.07	.01
☐ 143	Edwin Correa	.10	.05	.01
☐ 144	Dion James	.10	.05	.01
☐ 145	Danny Tartabull	.35	.17	.03
☐ 146	Jerry Browne	.15	.07	.01
☐ 147	Ted Higuera	.15	.07	.01
☐ 148	Jack Clark	.20	.10	.02
☐ 149	Ruben Sierra	1.00	.50	.10
☐ 150	McGwire/Eric Davis	.90	.45	.09

1987 Classic Update Yellow

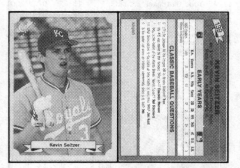

Kevin Seitzer

This 50-card set was actually distributed as part of an update to a trivia board game, but (unlike the original Classic game) was sold without the game. The set is sometimes referred to as the "Travel Edition" of the game. The card backs contain several trivia questions (and answers) which are used to play the game. A yellow border frames the full color photo. The games were produced by Game Time, Ltd. and were available in toy stores as well as from card dealers. Cards are numbered beginning with 101, as they are an extension of the original set.

	MINT	EXC	G-VG
COMPLETE SET (50)	10.00	5.00	1.00
COMMON PLAYER (101-150)	.10	.05	.01
☐ 101 Mike Schmidt	1.00	.50	.10

1988 Classic Red

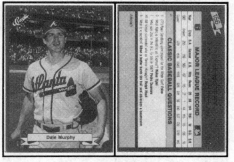

Dale Murphy

This 50-card red-bordered set was actually distributed as part of an update to a trivia board game, but (unlike the original Classic game) was sold without the game. The card backs contain several trivia questions (and answers) which are used to play the game. A red border frames the full color photo. The games were produced by Game Time, Ltd. and were available in toy stores as well as from card dealers. Cards are numbered beginning with 151 as they are an extension of the original sets.

	MINT	EXC	G-VG
COMPLETE SET (50)	10.00	5.00	1.00
COMMON PLAYER (151-200)	.10	.05	.01
☐ 151 Mark McGwire and	1.25	.60	.12

	Don Mattingly			
☐ 152	Don Mattingly	1.25	.60	.12
☐ 153	Mark McGwire	.75	.35	.07
☐ 154	Eric Davis	.75	.35	.07
☐ 155	Wade Boggs	1.00	.50	.10
☐ 156	Dale Murphy	.50	.25	.05
☐ 157	Andre Dawson	.30	.15	.03
☐ 158	Roger Clemens	.75	.35	.07
☐ 159	Kevin Seitzer	.50	.25	.05
☐ 160	Benito Santiago	.50	.25	.05
☐ 161	Kal Daniels	.30	.15	.03
☐ 162	John Kruk	.20	.10	.02
☐ 163	Bill Ripken	.15	.07	.01
☐ 164	Kirby Puckett	.75	.35	.07
☐ 165	Jose Canseco	1.50	.75	.15
☐ 166	Matt Nokes	.30	.15	.03
☐ 167	Mike Schmidt	1.00	.50	.10
☐ 168	Tim Raines	.25	.12	.02
☐ 169	Ryne Sandberg	.35	.17	.03
☐ 170	Dave Winfield	.25	.12	.02
☐ 171	Dwight Gooden	.50	.25	.05
☐ 172	Bret Saberhagen	.25	.12	.02
☐ 173	Willie McGee	.20	.10	.02
☐ 174	Jack Morris	.15	.07	.01
☐ 175	Jeff Leonard	.10	.05	.01
☐ 176	Cal Ripken	.35	.17	.03
☐ 177	Pete Incaviglia	.20	.10	.02
☐ 178	Devon White	.20	.10	.02
☐ 179	Nolan Ryan	1.25	.60	.12
☐ 180	Ruben Sierra	.75	.35	.07
☐ 181	Todd Worrell	.15	.07	.01
☐ 182	Glenn Davis	.20	.10	.02
☐ 183	Frank Viola	.20	.10	.02
☐ 184	Cory Snyder	.20	.10	.02
☐ 185	Tracy Jones	.10	.05	.01
☐ 186	Terry Steinbach	.20	.10	.02
☐ 187	Julio Franco	.20	.10	.02
☐ 188	Larry Sheets	.10	.05	.01
☐ 189	John Marzano	.10	.05	.01
☐ 190	Kevin Elster	.15	.07	.01
☐ 191	Vincente Palacios	.10	.05	.01
☐ 192	Kent Hrbek	.20	.10	.02
☐ 193	Eric Bell	.10	.05	.01
☐ 194	Kelly Downs	.15	.07	.01
☐ 195	Jose Lind	.15	.07	.01
☐ 196	Dave Stewart	.25	.12	.02
☐ 197	Mark McGwire and Jose Canseco	1.25	.60	.12
☐ 198	Phil Niekro Cleveland Indians	.20	.10	.02
☐ 199	Phil Niekro Toronto Blue Jays	.20	.10	.02
☐ 200	Phil Niekro Atlanta Braves	.20	.10	.02

		MINT	EXC	G-VG
COMPLETE SET (50)		10.00	5.00	1.00
COMMON PLAYER (201-250)		.10	.05	.01
☐ 201	Eric Davis and Dale Murphy	1.00	.50	.10
☐ 202	B.J. Surhoff	.20	.10	.02
☐ 203	John Kruk	.20	.10	.02
☐ 204	Sam Horn	.15	.07	.01
☐ 205	Jack Clark	.20	.10	.02
☐ 206	Wally Joyner	.40	.20	.04
☐ 207	Matt Nokes	.30	.15	.03
☐ 208	Bo Jackson	1.25	.60	.12
☐ 209	Darryl Strawberry	.75	.35	.07
☐ 210	Ozzie Smith	.25	.12	.02
☐ 211	Don Mattingly	1.25	.60	.12
☐ 212	Mark McGwire	1.00	.50	.10
☐ 213	Eric Davis	.75	.35	.07
☐ 214	Wade Boggs	1.00	.50	.10
☐ 215	Dale Murphy	.50	.25	.05
☐ 216	Andre Dawson	.25	.12	.02
☐ 217	Roger Clemens	.50	.25	.05
☐ 218	Kevin Seitzer	.35	.17	.03
☐ 219	Benito Santiago	.40	.20	.04
☐ 220	Tony Gwynn	.50	.25	.05
☐ 221	Mike Scott	.20	.10	.02
☐ 222	Steve Bedrosian	.15	.07	.01
☐ 223	Vince Coleman	.25	.12	.02
☐ 224	Rick Sutcliffe	.15	.07	.01
☐ 225	Will Clark	1.25	.60	.12
☐ 226	Pete Rose	1.00	.50	.10
☐ 227	Mike Greenwell	1.25	.60	.12
☐ 228	Ken Caminiti	.15	.07	.01
☐ 229	Ellis Burks	.75	.35	.07
☐ 230	Dave Magadan	.20	.10	.02
☐ 231	Alan Trammell	.20	.10	.02
☐ 232	Paul Molitor	.20	.10	.02
☐ 233	Gary Gaetti	.20	.10	.02
☐ 234	Rickey Henderson	.60	.30	.06
☐ 235	Danny Tartabull (photo actually Hal McRae)	.30	.15	.03
☐ 236	Bobby Bonilla	.20	.10	.02
☐ 237	Mike Dunne	.10	.05	.01
☐ 238	Al Leiter	.15	.07	.01
☐ 239	John Farrell	.15	.07	.01
☐ 240	Joe Magrane	.25	.12	.02
☐ 241	Mike Henneman	.15	.07	.01
☐ 242	George Bell	.25	.12	.02
☐ 243	Gregg Jeffries	1.25	.60	.12
☐ 244	Jay Buhner	.30	.15	.03
☐ 245	Todd Benzinger	.15	.07	.01
☐ 246	Matt Williams	.50	.25	.05
☐ 247	Mark McGwire and Don Mattingly	1.50	.75	.15
☐ 248	George Brett	.50	.25	.05
☐ 249	Jimmy Key	.10	.05	.01
☐ 250	Mark Langston	.25	.12	.02

1988 Classic Blue

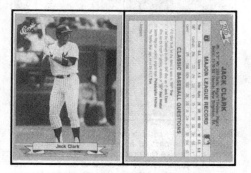

This 50-card blue-bordered set was actually distributed as part of an update to a trivia board game, but (unlike the original Classic game) was sold without the game. The card backs contain several trivia questions (and answers) which are used to play the game. A blue border frames the full color photo. The games were produced by Game Time, Ltd. and were available in toy stores as well as from card dealers. Cards are numbered beginning with 201 as they are an extension of the original sets.

1989 Classic Light Blue

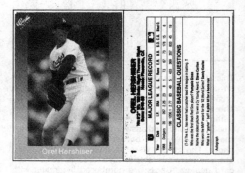

The 1989 Classic set contains 100 standard- size (2 1/2 by 3 1/2 inch) cards. The fronts of these cards have light blue borders. The backs feature 1988 and lifetime stats. The cards were distributed with a baseball boardgame. Supposedly there were 150,000 sets produced.

		MINT	EXC	G-VG
	COMPLETE SET (100)	14.00	7.00	1.40
	COMMON PLAYER (1-100)	.10	.05	.01
☐ 1	Orel Hershiser	.40	.20	.04
☐ 2	Wade Boggs	.75	.35	.07
☐ 3	Jose Canseco	1.00	.50	.10
☐ 4	Mark McGwire	.75	.35	.07
☐ 5	Don Mattingly	1.00	.50	.10
☐ 6	Gregg Jefferies	.75	.35	.07
☐ 7	Dwight Gooden	.50	.25	.05
☐ 8	Darryl Strawberry	.75	.35	.07
☐ 9	Eric Davis	.60	.30	.06
☐ 10	Joey Meyer	.10	.05	.01
☐ 11	Joe Carter	.15	.07	.01
☐ 12	Paul Molitor	.15	.07	.01
☐ 13	Mark Grace	1.00	.50	.10
☐ 14	Kurt Stillwell	.10	.05	.01
☐ 15	Kirby Puckett	.60	.30	.06
☐ 16	Keith Miller	.10	.05	.01
☐ 17	Glenn Davis	.20	.10	.02
☐ 18	Will Clark	1.00	.50	.10
☐ 19	Cory Snyder	.20	.10	.02
☐ 20	Jose Lind	.10	.05	.01
☐ 21	Andres Thomas	.10	.05	.01
☐ 22	Dave Smith	.10	.05	.01
☐ 23	Mike Scott	.20	.10	.02
☐ 24	Kevin McReynolds	.20	.10	.02
☐ 25	B.J. Surhoff	.15	.07	.01
☐ 26	Mackey Sasser	.15	.07	.01
☐ 27	Chad Kreuter	.10	.05	.01
☐ 28	Hal Morris	.15	.07	.01
☐ 29	Wally Joyner	.30	.15	.03
☐ 30	Tony Gwynn	.50	.25	.05
☐ 31	Kevin Mitchell	.50	.25	.05
☐ 32	Dave Winfield	.30	.15	.03
☐ 33	Billy Bean	.10	.05	.01
☐ 34	Steve Bedrosian	.15	.07	.01
☐ 35	Ron Gant	.15	.07	.01
☐ 36	Len Dykstra	.15	.07	.01
☐ 37	Andre Dawson	.20	.10	.02
☐ 38	Brett Butler	.15	.07	.01
☐ 39	Rob Deer	.15	.07	.01
☐ 40	Tommy John	.20	.10	.02
☐ 41	Gary Gaetti	.15	.07	.01
☐ 42	Tim Raines	.25	.12	.02
☐ 43	George Bell	.20	.10	.02
☐ 44	Dwight Evans	.15	.07	.01
☐ 45	Dennis Martinez	.10	.05	.01
☐ 46	Andres Galarraga	.25	.12	.02
☐ 47	George Brett	.50	.25	.05
☐ 48	Mike Schmidt	1.00	.50	.10
☐ 49	Dave Stieb	.15	.07	.01
☐ 50	Rickey Henderson	.50	.25	.05
☐ 51	Craig Biggio	.25	.12	.02
☐ 52	Mark Lemke	.10	.05	.01
☐ 53	Chris Sabo	.20	.10	.02
☐ 54	Jeff Treadway	.10	.05	.01
☐ 55	Kent Hrbek	.20	.10	.02
☐ 56	Cal Ripken	.30	.15	.03
☐ 57	Tim Belcher	.20	.10	.02
☐ 58	Ozzie Smith	.25	.12	.02
☐ 59	Keith Hernandez	.20	.10	.02
☐ 60	Pedro Guerrero	.20	.10	.02
☐ 61	Greg Swindell	.20	.10	.02
☐ 62	Bret Saberhagen	.35	.17	.03
☐ 63	John Tudor	.15	.07	.01
☐ 64	Gary Carter	.25	.12	.02
☐ 65	Kevin Seitzer	.25	.12	.02
☐ 66	Jesse Barfield	.15	.07	.01
☐ 67	Luis Medina	.15	.07	.01
☐ 68	Walt Weiss	.30	.15	.03
☐ 69	Terry Steinbach	.20	.10	.02
☐ 70	Barry Larkin	.25	.12	.02
☐ 71	Pete Rose	1.00	.50	.10
☐ 72	Luis Salazar	.10	.05	.01
☐ 73	Benito Santiago	.30	.15	.03
☐ 74	Kal Daniels	.20	.10	.02
☐ 75	Kevin Elster	.15	.07	.01
☐ 76	Rob Dibble	.20	.10	.02
☐ 77	Bobby Witt	.15	.07	.01
☐ 78	Steve Searcy	.15	.07	.01
☐ 79	Sandy Alomar Jr.	.50	.25	.05
☐ 80	Chili Davis	.15	.07	.01
☐ 81	Alvin Davis	.15	.07	.01
☐ 82	Charlie Leibrandt	.10	.05	.01
☐ 83	Robin Yount	.75	.35	.07
☐ 84	Mark Carreon	.10	.05	.01
☐ 85	Pascual Perez	.15	.07	.01
☐ 86	Dennis Rasmussen	.10	.05	.01
☐ 87	Ernie Riles	.10	.05	.01
☐ 88	Melido Perez	.15	.07	.01
☐ 89	Doug Jones	.15	.07	.01
☐ 90	Dennis Eckersley	.25	.12	.02
☐ 91	Bob Welch	.10	.05	.01
☐ 92	Bob Milacki	.15	.07	.01
☐ 93	Jeff Robinson	.15	.07	.01
☐ 94	Mike Henneman	.10	.05	.01
☐ 95	Randy Johnson	.15	.07	.01
☐ 96	Ron Jones	.15	.07	.01
☐ 97	Jack Armstrong	.15	.07	.01
☐ 98	Willie McGee	.15	.07	.01
☐ 99	Ryne Sandberg	.30	.15	.03
☐ 100	David Cone/Jackson	.30	.15	.03

1989 Classic Travel Orange

Roger Clemens

The 1989 Classic Travel Orange set contains 50 standard-size (2 1/2 by 3 1/2 inch) cards. The fronts of the cards have orange borders. The backs feature 1988 and lifetime stats. This subset of cards were distributed as a set in blister packs as "Travel Update I" subsets. Supposedly there were 150,000 sets produced.

		MINT	EXC	G-VG
	COMPLETE SET (50)	10.00	5.00	1.00
	COMMON PLAYER (101-150)	.10	.05	.01
☐ 101	Gary Sheffield	.75	.35	.07
☐ 102	Wade Boggs	.75	.35	.07
☐ 103	Jose Canseco	1.00	.50	.10
☐ 104	Mark McGwire	.75	.35	.07
☐ 105	Orel Hershiser	.50	.25	.05
☐ 106	Don Mattingly	1.00	.50	.10
☐ 107	Dwight Gooden	.50	.25	.05
☐ 108	Darryl Strawberry	.60	.30	.06
☐ 109	Eric Davis	.60	.30	.06
☐ 110	Hensley Meulens	.50	.25	.05
☐ 111	Andy Van Slyke	.15	.07	.01
☐ 112	Al Leiter	.15	.07	.01
☐ 113	Matt Nokes	.15	.07	.01
☐ 114	Mike Krukow	.10	.05	.01
☐ 115	Tony Fernandez	.15	.07	.01
☐ 116	Fred McGriff	.40	.20	.04
☐ 117	Barry Bonds	.15	.07	.01
☐ 118	Gerald Perry	.10	.05	.01
☐ 119	Roger Clemens	.50	.25	.05
☐ 120	Kirk Gibson	.20	.10	.02
☐ 121	Greg Maddux	.15	.07	.01
☐ 122	Bo Jackson	1.00	.50	.10
☐ 123	Danny Jackson	.15	.07	.01
☐ 124	Dale Murphy	.30	.15	.03
☐ 125	David Cone	.30	.15	.03
☐ 126	Tom Browning	.15	.07	.01
☐ 127	Roberto Alomar	.20	.10	.02
☐ 128	Alan Trammell	.15	.07	.01
☐ 129	Ricky Jordan UER (misspelled Jordon on card back)	1.00	.50	.10
☐ 130	Ramon Martinez	.30	.15	.03
☐ 131	Ken Griffey Jr.	1.50	.75	.15
☐ 132	Gregg Olson	.50	.25	.05
☐ 133	Carlos Quintana	.20	.10	.02
☐ 134	Dave West	.20	.10	.02
☐ 135	Cameron Drew	.15	.07	.01
☐ 136	Teddy Higuera	.15	.07	.01
☐ 137	Sil Campusano	.15	.07	.01
☐ 138	Mark Gubicza	.15	.07	.01
☐ 139	Mike Boddicker	.10	.05	.01
☐ 140	Paul Gibson	.10	.05	.01
☐ 141	Jose Rijo	.10	.05	.01

		MINT	EXC	G-VG
☐ 142	John Costello	.10	.05	.01
☐ 143	Cecil Espy	.10	.05	.01
☐ 144	Frank Viola	.20	.10	.02
☐ 145	Erik Hanson	.15	.07	.01
☐ 146	Juan Samuel	.15	.07	.01
☐ 147	Harold Reynolds	.15	.07	.01
☐ 148	Joe Magrane	.20	.10	.02
☐ 149	Mike Greenwell	.75	.35	.07
☐ 150	Darryl Strawberry and Will Clark	1.00	.50	.10

1989 Classic Travel Purple

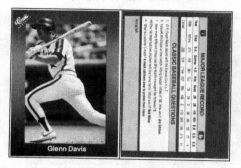

Glenn Davis

The 1989 Classic "Travel Update II" set contains 50 standard-size (2 1/2 by 3 1/2 inch) cards. The fronts have purple (and gray) borders. The set features "two sport" cards of Bo Jackson and Deion Sanders. The cards were distributed as a set in blister packs.

		MINT	EXC	G-VG
COMPLETE SET (50)		10.00	5.00	1.00
COMMON PLAYER (151-200)		.10	.05	.01
☐ 151	Jim Abbott	1.00	.50	.10
☐ 152	Ellis Burks	.50	.25	.05
☐ 153	Mike Schmidt	.75	.35	.07
☐ 154	Gregg Jefferies	.75	.35	.07
☐ 155	Mark Grace	1.00	.50	.10
☐ 156	Jerome Walton	1.50	.75	.15
☐ 157	Bo Jackson	1.00	.50	.10
☐ 158	Jack Clark	.20	.10	.02
☐ 159	Tom Glavine	.15	.07	.01
☐ 160	Eddie Murray	.25	.12	.02
☐ 161	John Dopson	.15	.07	.01
☐ 162	Ruben Sierra	.60	.30	.06
☐ 163	Rafael Palmeiro	.20	.10	.02
☐ 164	Nolan Ryan	1.00	.50	.10
☐ 165	Barry Larkin	.20	.10	.02
☐ 166	Tommy Herr	.10	.05	.01
☐ 167	Roberto Kelly	.20	.10	.02
☐ 168	Glenn Davis	.20	.10	.02
☐ 169	Glenn Braggs	.15	.07	.01
☐ 170	Juan Bell	.20	.10	.02
☐ 171	Todd Burns	.15	.07	.01
☐ 172	Derek Lilliquist	.15	.07	.01
☐ 173	Orel Hershiser	.30	.15	.03
☐ 174	John Smoltz	.25	.12	.02
☐ 175	Guillen/Burks	.30	.15	.03
☐ 176	Kirby Puckett	.60	.30	.06
☐ 177	Robin Ventura	.50	.25	.05
☐ 178	Allan Anderson	.15	.07	.01
☐ 179	Steve Sax	.20	.10	.02
☐ 180	Will Clark	1.00	.50	.10
☐ 181	Mike Devereaux	.15	.07	.01
☐ 182	Tom Gordon	.75	.35	.07
☐ 183	Rob Murphy	.10	.05	.01
☐ 184	Pete O'Brien	.15	.07	.01
☐ 185	Cris Carpenter	.10	.05	.01
☐ 186	Tom Brunansky	.15	.07	.01
☐ 187	Bob Boone	.20	.10	.02
☐ 188	Lou Whitaker	.20	.10	.02
☐ 189	Dwight Gooden	.50	.25	.05
☐ 190	Mark McGwire	.75	.35	.07
☐ 191	John Smiley	.15	.07	.01
☐ 192	Tommy Gregg	.10	.05	.01
☐ 193	Ken Griffey Jr.	1.50	.75	.15
☐ 194	Bruce Hurst	.15	.07	.01
☐ 195	Greg Swindell	.15	.07	.01
☐ 196	Nelson Liriano	.10	.05	.01

		MINT	EXC	G-VG
☐ 197	Randy Myers	.15	.07	.01
☐ 198	Kevin Mitchell	.50	.25	.05
☐ 199	Dante Bichette	.10	.05	.01
☐ 200	Deion Sanders	1.00	.50	.10

1990 Classic Game

Will Clark

The 1990 Classic Game set contains 150 standard-size (2 1/2 by 3 1/2 inch) cards, the largest Classic set to date in terms of player selection. The front borders are blue with magenta splotches. The backs feature 1989 and career total stats. The cards were distributed as a set in blister packs. According to distributors of the set, supposedly there were 200,000 sets produced. Supposedly the Sanders "correction" was made at Sanders own request; less than 10% of the sets contain the first version and hence it has the higher value in the checklist below.

		MINT	EXC	G-VG
COMPLETE SET (150)		15.00	7.50	1.50
COMMON PLAYER (1-150)		.10	.05	.01
☐ 1	Nolan Ryan	1.00	.50	.10
☐ 2	Bo Jackson	1.00	.50	.10
☐ 3	Gregg Olson	.50	.25	.05
☐ 4	Tom Gordon	.50	.25	.05
☐ 5	Robin Ventura	.50	.25	.05
☐ 6	Will Clark	1.00	.50	.10
☐ 7	Ruben Sierra	.50	.25	.05
☐ 8	Mark Grace	.75	.35	.07
☐ 9	Luis De Los Santos	.20	.10	.02
☐ 10	Bernie Williams	.35	.17	.03
☐ 11	Eric Davis	.50	.25	.05
☐ 12	Carney Lansford	.20	.10	.02
☐ 13	John Smoltz	.20	.10	.02
☐ 14	Gary Sheffield	.50	.25	.05
☐ 15	Kent Mercker	.30	.15	.03
☐ 16	Don Mattingly	1.00	.50	.10
☐ 17	Tony Gwynn	.50	.25	.05
☐ 18	Ozzie Smith	.20	.10	.02
☐ 19	Fred McGriff	.30	.15	.03
☐ 20	Ken Griffey Jr.	1.00	.50	.10
☐ 21A	Deion Sanders (identified only as "Prime Time" on front)	3.00	1.25	.25
☐ 21B	Deion Sanders (identified as Deion "Prime Time" Sanders on front of card)	1.00	.50	.10
☐ 22	Jose Canseco	1.00	.50	.10
☐ 23	Mitch Williams	.15	.07	.01
☐ 24	Cal Ripken	.25	.12	.02
☐ 25	Bob Geren	.20	.10	.02
☐ 26	Wade Boggs	.75	.35	.07
☐ 27	Ryne Sandberg	.30	.15	.03
☐ 28	Kirby Puckett	.60	.30	.06
☐ 29	Mike Scott	.20	.10	.02
☐ 30	Dwight Smith	.60	.30	.06
☐ 31	Craig Worthington	.20	.10	.02
☐ 32	Ricky Jordan UER (misspelled Jordon on card front)	1.00	.50	.10
☐ 33	Darryl Strawberry	.60	.30	.06
☐ 34	Jerome Walton	1.00	.50	.10
☐ 35	John Olerud	1.00	.50	.10
☐ 36	Tom Glavine	.15	.07	.01

☐ 37	Rickey Henderson	.50	.25	.05
☐ 38	Rolando Roomes	.15	.07	.01
☐ 39	Mickey Tettleton	.15	.07	.01
☐ 40	Jim Abbott	.75	.35	.07
☐ 41	Dave Righetti	.15	.07	.01
☐ 42	Mike LaValliere	.10	.05	.01
☐ 43	Rob Dibble	.15	.07	.01
☐ 44	Pete Harnisch	.10	.05	.01
☐ 45	Jose Offerman	.50	.25	.05
☐ 46	Walt Weiss	.20	.10	.02
☐ 47	Mike Greenwell	.50	.25	.05
☐ 48	Barry Larkin	.25	.12	.02
☐ 49	Dave Gallagher	.15	.07	.01
☐ 50	Junior Felix	.25	.12	.02
☐ 51	Roger Clemens	.50	.25	.05
☐ 52	Lonnie Smith	.15	.07	.01
☐ 53	Jerry Browne	.15	.07	.01
☐ 54	Greg Briley	.25	.12	.02
☐ 55	Delino Deshields	.30	.15	.03
☐ 56	Carmelo Martinez	.10	.05	.01
☐ 57	Craig Biggio	.25	.12	.02
☐ 58	Dwight Gooden	.40	.20	.04
☐ 59	Bo Jackson,	1.00	.50	.10
	Ruben Sierra, and			
	Mark McGwire			
☐ 60	Greg Vaughn	1.00	.50	.10
☐ 61	Roberto Alomar	.20	.10	.02
☐ 62	Steve Bedrosian	.15	.07	.01
☐ 63	Devon White	.15	.07	.01
☐ 64	Kevin Mitchell	.40	.20	.04
☐ 65	Marquis Grissom	.50	.25	.05
☐ 66	Brian Holman	.10	.05	.01
☐ 67	Julio Franco	.15	.07	.01
☐ 68	Dave West	.20	.10	.02
☐ 69	Harold Baines	.15	.07	.01
☐ 70	Eric Anthony	1.00	.50	.10
☐ 71	Glenn Davis	.20	.10	.02
☐ 72	Mark Langston	.20	.10	.02
☐ 73	Matt Williams	.40	.20	.04
☐ 74	Rafael Palmeiro	.20	.10	.02
☐ 75	Pete Rose Jr.	.50	.25	.05
☐ 76	Ramon Martinez	.20	.10	.02
☐ 77	Dwight Evans	.15	.07	.01
☐ 78	Mackey Sasser	.15	.07	.01
☐ 79	Mike Schooler	.15	.07	.01
☐ 80	Dennis Cook	.10	.05	.01
☐ 81	Orel Hershiser	.35	.17	.03
☐ 82	Barry Bonds	.15	.07	.01
☐ 83	Geronimo Berroa	.10	.05	.01
☐ 84	George Bell	.15	.07	.01
☐ 85	Andre Dawson	.20	.10	.02
☐ 86	John Franco	.15	.07	.01
☐ 87	W.Clark/T.Gwynn	.75	.35	.07
☐ 88	Glenallen Hill	.25	.12	.02
☐ 89	Jeff Ballard	.20	.10	.02
☐ 90	Todd Zeile	1.00	.50	.10
☐ 91	Frank Viola	.15	.07	.01
☐ 92	Ozzie Guillen	.15	.07	.01
☐ 93	Jeffrey Leonard	.10	.05	.01
☐ 94	Dave Smith	.10	.05	.01
☐ 95	Dave Parker	.15	.07	.01
☐ 96	Jose Gonzalez	.10	.05	.01
☐ 97	Dave Stieb	.15	.07	.01
☐ 98	Charlie Hayes	.15	.07	.01
☐ 99	Jesse Barfield	.15	.07	.01
☐ 100	Joey Belle	.50	.25	.05
☐ 101	Jeff Reardon	.15	.07	.01
☐ 102	Bruce Hurst	.15	.07	.01
☐ 103	Luis Medina	.15	.07	.01
☐ 104	Mike Moore	.15	.07	.01
☐ 105	Vince Coleman	.20	.10	.02
☐ 106	Alan Trammell	.15	.07	.01
☐ 107	Randy Myers	.15	.07	.01
☐ 108	Frank Tanana	.10	.05	.01
☐ 109	Craig Lefferts	.10	.05	.01
☐ 110	John Wetteland	.25	.12	.02
☐ 111	Chris Gwynn	.15	.07	.01
☐ 112	Mark Carreon	.10	.05	.01
☐ 113	Von Hayes	.15	.07	.01
☐ 114	Doug Jones	.15	.07	.01
☐ 115	Andres Galarraga	.25	.12	.02
☐ 116	Carlton Fisk	.25	.12	.02
☐ 117	Paul O'Neill	.20	.10	.02
☐ 118	Tim Raines	.25	.12	.02
☐ 119	Tom Brunansky	.15	.07	.01
☐ 120	Andy Benes	.60	.30	.06
☐ 121	Mark Portugal	.10	.05	.01
☐ 122	Willie Randolph	.15	.07	.01
☐ 123	Jeff Blauser	.10	.05	.01
☐ 124	Don August	.10	.05	.01
☐ 125	Chuck Cary	.15	.07	.01
☐ 126	John Smiley	.15	.07	.01
☐ 127	Terry Mulholland	.10	.05	.01
☐ 128	Harold Reynolds	.15	.07	.01
☐ 129	Hubie Brooks	.15	.07	.01

☐ 130	Ben McDonald	1.00	.50	.10
☐ 131	Kevin Ritz	.15	.07	.01
☐ 132	Luis Quinones	.10	.05	.01
☐ 133	Hensley Meulens UER (Misspelled Muelens on card front)	.25	.12	.02
☐ 134	Bill Spiers	.35	.17	.03
☐ 135	Andy Hawkins	.15	.07	.01
☐ 136	Alvin Davis	.15	.07	.01
☐ 137	Lee Smith	.15	.07	.01
☐ 138	Joe Carter	.15	.07	.01
☐ 139	Bret Saberhagen	.25	.12	.02
☐ 140	Sammy Sosa	.40	.20	.04
☐ 141	Matt Nokes	.20	.10	.02
☐ 142	Bert Blyleven	.20	.10	.02
☐ 143	Bobby Bonilla	.20	.10	.02
☐ 144	Howard Johnson	.25	.12	.02
☐ 145	Joe Magrane	.20	.10	.02
☐ 146	Pedro Guerrero	.20	.10	.02
☐ 147	Robin Yount	.50	.25	.05
☐ 148	Dan Gladden	.10	.05	.01
☐ 149	Steve Sax	.20	.10	.02
☐ 150	Will Clark and Kevin Mitchell	.75	.35	.07

1988 CMC Don Mattingly

This 20-card set featuring Don Mattingly was distributed as part of a Collecting Kit produced by Collector's Marketing Corp. The cards themselves measure approximately 2 1/2" by 3 1/2" and have a light blue border. The card backs describe some aspect of Mattingly's career. Also in the kit were plastic sheets, a small album, a record, a booklet, and information on how to join Don's Fan Club. The set price below is for the whole kit as well as the cards.

		MINT	EXC	G-VG
COMPLETE SET (20)		10.00	5.00	1.00
COMMON PLAYER (1-20)		.60	.30	.06
☐ 1	Game Face	.60	.30	.06
☐ 2	Columbus Clippers	.60	.30	.06
☐ 3	1983 Spring Camp	.60	.30	.06
☐ 4	AL Batting Crown	.60	.30	.06
☐ 5	1981 All-Star Outfielder	.60	.30	.06
☐ 6	The Batting Tee	.60	.30	.06
☐ 7	AL MVP Honors	.60	.30	.06
☐ 8	Gold Glove Winner	.60	.30	.06
☐ 9	Batting Practice	.60	.30	.06
☐ 10	Yankee Records	.60	.30	.06
☐ 11	Baseball On His Mind	.60	.30	.06
☐ 12	Big Home Runs	.60	.30	.06
☐ 13	Hustle and Determination	.60	.30	.06
☐ 14	Delivering In The Clutch	.60	.30	.06
☐ 15	A Slick First Baseman	.60	.30	.06
☐ 16	Keep Playing Hard	.60	.30	.06
☐ 17	Mattingly's Eight-Game Streak	.60	.30	.06
☐ 18	The Textbook Swing	.60	.30	.06
☐ 19	It's Time To Go Forward	.60	.30	.06
☐ 20	Surehanded First Baseman	.60	.30	.06

1989 CMC Jose Canseco

The 1989 CMC Jose Canseco Collector's Kit set contains 20 numbered standard-size (2 1/2 by 3 1/2 inch) cards. The front borders are Oakland A's green and yellow. The backs are green and white, and feature narratives and facsimile signatures. The cards were distributed as a set in a box along with an album and a booklet as well as other elements by CMC, Collectors Marketing Corporation. Since all the cards in the set feature the same player, cards in the checklist below are differentiated by some other characteristic of the particular card.

	MINT	EXC	G-VG
COMPLETE SET (20)	10.00	5.00	1.00
COMMON PLAYER (1-20)	.60	.30	.06
☐ 1 Looking up with .... yellow jersey	.60	.30	.06
☐ 2 Posing with bat from .... the waist up	.60	.30	.06
☐ 3 Portrait with green .... cap	.60	.30	.06
☐ 4 Follow-through on .... swing (catcher visible)	.60	.30	.06
☐ 5 Running the bases	.60	.30	.06
☐ 6 Warming up with bat .... over head	.60	.30	.06
☐ 7 Sitting in dugout .... holding bat	.60	.30	.06
☐ 8 Standing in outfield .... with sunglasses up	.60	.30	.06
☐ 9 Batting stance ready .... for pitch	.60	.30	.06
☐ 10 Taking a lead off .... first base	.60	.30	.06
☐ 11 Looking to the side .... (elephant logo on left shoulder)	.60	.30	.06
☐ 12 Bashing with Mark .... McGwire after homer	.60	.30	.06
☐ 13 Looking up witrh green .... batting glove in foreground	.60	.30	.06
☐ 14 Stretching to catch .... fly ball	.60	.30	.06
☐ 15 Follow through on .... swing (no catcher visible)	.60	.30	.06
☐ 16 Standing at plate .... glaring at pitcher	.60	.30	.06
☐ 17 Follow through on .... swing (stain on pants)	.60	.30	.06
☐ 18 Signing autographs .... for the fans at the ballpark	.60	.30	.06
☐ 19 Waiting at first base .... with hands on hips	.60	.30	.06
☐ 20 Admiring his hit at .... plate with tongue out	.60	.30	.06

1989 CMC Mickey Mantle

The 1989 CMC Mickey Mantle Collector's Kit set contains 20 numbered standard-size (2 1/2 by 3 1/2 inch) cards. The fronts and backs are white, red and navy. The backs feature narratives and facsimile signatures. The cards were distributed as a set in a box along with an album and a booklet as well as other elements by CMC, Collectors Marketing Corporation. Since all the cards in the set feature the same player, cards in the checklist below are differentiated by some other characteristic of the particular card. Some of the cards in this set are sepia- tone photos as the action predates the widespread use of color film.

	MINT	EXC	G-VG
COMPLETE SET (20)	10.00	5.00	1.00
COMMON PLAYER (1-20)	.60	.30	.06
☐ 1 Standing with bat on .... left shoulder	.60	.30	.06
☐ 2 Batting stance lefty .... (back to camera)	.60	.30	.06
☐ 3 Looking intense in .... the field (waist up)	.60	.30	.06
☐ 4 Follow through on .... lefty swing	.60	.30	.06
☐ 5 Half smile (head and .... shoulders)	.60	.30	.06
☐ 6 Posing with bat .... alongside Roger Maris	.60	.30	.06
☐ 7 Holding up his 1962 .... contract (wearing suit and tie)	.60	.30	.06
☐ 8 Receiving 1962 MVP .... form Joe Cronin	.60	.30	.06
☐ 9 Batting stance lefty .... (catcher's glove in picture)	.60	.30	.06
☐ 10 Posing with Roger .... Maris and Yogi Berra	.60	.30	.06
☐ 11 Looking away with eyes ... closed, holding bat	.60	.30	.06
☐ 12 Swinging righty at .... pitch	.60	.30	.06
☐ 13 Starting to run to .... first base	.60	.30	.06
☐ 14 Mickey Mantle Day, ... September 18, 1965	.60	.30	.06
☐ 15 Shaking hands with .... Joe DiMaggio at Yankee Stadium	.60	.30	.06
☐ 16 Giving speech at .... Yankee Stadium	.60	.30	.06
☐ 17 Backing away from .... plate after pitch	.60	.30	.06
☐ 18 Getting ready at .... plate with bat in right hand	.60	.30	.06
☐ 19 Holding bat in both .... hands parallel to ground	.60	.30	.06
☐ 20 Waiting for pitch with .... bat on shoulder (lefty)	.60	.30	.06

1989 CMC Babe Ruth

The 1989 CMC Babe Ruth Collector's Kit set contains 20 numbered standard-size (2 1/2 by 3 1/2 inch) cards. The front borders are white, red and navy. The backs are blue and white, and feature narratives and facsimile signatures. The cards were distributed as a set in a box along with an album and a booklet as well as other elements by CMC, Collectors Marketing Corporation. Since all the cards in the set feature the same player, cards in the checklist below are differentiated by some other characteristic of the particular card. All of the cards in this set are sepia-tone photos as the action predates the widespread use of color film.

	MINT	EXC	G-VG
COMPLETE SET (20)	10.00	5.00	1.00
COMMON PLAYER (1-20)	.60	.30	.06
☐ 1 Smiling holding .... three bats	.60	.30	.06
☐ 2 Posing in Red Sox .... uniform (head and shoulders)	.60	.30	.06
☐ 3 Looking up (waist up)	.60	.30	.06
☐ 4 Holding nine bats .... in front of him	.60	.30	.06
☐ 5 Golfing swing follow .... through	.60	.30	.06
☐ 6 Oldtimers' game photo .... holding two bats	.60	.30	.06
☐ 7 Follow through .... looking up (in Japan)	.60	.30	.06
☐ 8 Looking dapper in .... fur coat	.60	.30	.06
☐ 9 Babe Ruth Day, ... April 27, 1947	.60	.30	.06
☐ 10 Bust photo with .... no background	.60	.30	.06
☐ 11 Practicing swing .... (photo from knees up)	.60	.30	.06
☐ 12 Watching his hit after .... swing (knees up)	.60	.30	.06
☐ 13 Follow through on .... swing, starting to first base	.60	.30	.06
☐ 14 Practice swing with .... photographers in background	.60	.30	.06
☐ 15 Posing with .... Jacob Ruppert	.60	.30	.06
☐ 16 Follow through .... from waist up	.60	.30	.06
☐ 17 Shaking hands with .... Miller Huggins	.60	.30	.06
☐ 18 Signing autographs .... for the kids	.60	.30	.06
☐ 19 Sitting wearing .... Braves uniform	.60	.30	.06
☐ 20 Hall of Fame Plaque	.60	.30	.06

1981 Coke

The cards in this 132-card set measure 2 1/2" by 3 1/2". In 1981, Topps produced 11 sets of 12 cards each for the Coca-Cola Company. Each set features 11 star players for a particular team plus an advertising card with the team name on the front. Although the cards are numbered in the upper right corner of the back from 1 to 11, they are re-numbered below within team, i.e., Boston Red Sox (1-12), Chicago Cubs (13-24), Chicago White Sox (25-36), Cincinnati Reds (37-48), Detroit Tigers (49-60), Houston Astros (61- 72), Kansas City Royals (73-84), New York Mets (85-96), Philadelphia Phillies (97-108), Pittsburgh Pirates (109- 120), and St. Louis Cardinals (121-132). Within each team the player actually numbered #1 (on the card back) is the first player below and the player numbered #11 is the last in that team's list. These player cards are quite similar to the 1981 Topps issue but feature a Coca-Cola logo on both the front and the back. The advertising card for each team features, on its back, an offer for obtaining an uncut sheet of 1981 Topps cards. These promotional cards were actually issued by Coke in only a few of the cities, and most of these cards have reached collectors hands through dealers who have purchased the cards through suppliers.

	MINT	EXC	G-VG
COMPLETE SET (132)	25.00	12.50	2.50
COMMON PLAYER	.06	.03	.00
COMMON CHECKLIST	.03	.01	.00
☐ 1 Tom Burgmeier	.06	.03	.00
☐ 2 Dennis Eckersley	.75	.35	.07
☐ 3 Dwight Evans	.60	.30	.06
☐ 4 Bob Stanley	.10	.05	.01
☐ 5 Glenn Hoffman	.06	.03	.00
☐ 6 Carney Lansford	.50	.25	.05
☐ 7 Frank Tanana	.15	.07	.01
☐ 8 Tony Perez	.50	.25	.05
☐ 9 Jim Rice	.90	.45	.09
☐ 10 Dave Stapleton	.06	.03	.00
☐ 11 Carl Yastrzemski	2.50	1.25	.25
☐ 12 Red Sox Checklist .... (unnumbered)	.03	.01	.00
☐ 13 Tim Blackwell	.06	.03	.00
☐ 14 Bill Buckner	.20	.10	.02
☐ 15 Ivan DeJesus	.06	.03	.00
☐ 16 Leon Durham	.20	.10	.02
☐ 17 Steve Henderson	.06	.03	.00
☐ 18 Mike Krukow	.10	.05	.01
☐ 19 Ken Reitz	.06	.03	.00
☐ 20 Rick Reuschel	.35	.17	.03
☐ 21 Scot Thompson	.06	.03	.00
☐ 22 Dick Tidrow	.06	.03	.00
☐ 23 Mike Tyson	.06	.03	.00
☐ 24 Cubs Checklist .... (unnumbered)	.03	.01	.00
☐ 25 Britt Burns	.10	.05	.01
☐ 26 Todd Cruz	.06	.03	.00
☐ 27 Rich Dotson	.30	.15	.03
☐ 28 Jim Essian	.06	.03	.00

☐	29	Ed Farmer	.06	.03	.00
☐	30	Lamar Johnson	.06	.03	.00
☐	31	Ron LeFlore	.10	.05	.01
☐	32	Chet Lemon	.10	.05	.01
☐	33	Bob Molinaro	.06	.03	.00
☐	34	Jim Morrison	.06	.03	.00
☐	35	Wayne Nordhagen	.06	.03	.00
☐	36	White Sox Checklist	.03	.01	.00
		(unnumbered)			
☐	37	Johnny Bench	2.00	1.00	.20
☐	38	Dave Collins	.10	.05	.01
☐	39	Dave Concepcion	.20	.10	.02
☐	40	Dan Driessen	.06	.03	.00
☐	41	George Foster	.30	.15	.03
☐	42	Ken Griffey	.20	.10	.02
☐	43	Tom Hume	.06	.03	.00
☐	44	Ray Knight	.15	.07	.01
☐	45	Ron Oester	.10	.05	.01
☐	46	Tom Seaver	1.50	.75	.15
☐	47	Mario Soto	.10	.05	.01
☐	48	Reds Checklist	.03	.01	.00
		(unnumbered)			
☐	49	Champ Summers	.06	.03	.00
☐	50	Al Cowens	.06	.03	.00
☐	51	Rich Hebner	.06	.03	.00
☐	52	Steve Kemp	.10	.05	.01
☐	53	Aurelio Lopez	.06	.03	.00
☐	54	Jack Morris	.75	.35	.07
☐	55	Lance Parrish	.75	.35	.07
☐	56	Johnny Wockenfuss	.06	.03	.00
☐	57	Alan Trammell	1.25	.60	.12
☐	58	Lou Whitaker	1.00	.50	.10
☐	59	Kirk Gibson	2.50	1.25	.25
☐	60	Tigers Checklist	.03	.01	.00
		(unnumbered)			
☐	61	Alan Ashby	.06	.03	.00
☐	62	Cesar Cedeno	.10	.05	.01
☐	63	Jose Cruz	.15	.07	.01
☐	64	Art Howe	.15	.07	.01
☐	65	Rafael Landestoy	.06	.03	.00
☐	66	Joe Niekro	.20	.10	.02
☐	67	Terry Puhl	.10	.05	.01
☐	68	J.R. Richard	.15	.07	.01
☐	69	Nolan Ryan	3.00	1.50	.30
☐	70	Joe Sambito	.10	.05	.01
☐	71	Don Sutton	1.00	.50	.10
☐	72	Astros Checklist	.03	.01	.00
		(unnumbered)			
☐	73	Willie Aikens	.10	.05	.01
☐	74	George Brett	1.50	.75	.15
☐	75	Larry Gura	.10	.05	.01
☐	76	Dennis Leonard	.10	.05	.01
☐	77	Hal McRae	.10	.05	.01
☐	78	Amos Otis	.15	.07	.01
☐	79	Dan Quisenberry	.20	.10	.02
☐	80	U.L. Washington	.06	.03	.00
☐	81	John Wathan	.15	.07	.01
☐	82	Frank White	.20	.10	.02
☐	83	Willie Wilson	.20	.10	.02
☐	84	Royals Checklist	.03	.01	.00
		(unnumbered)			
☐	85	Neil Allen	.10	.05	.01
☐	86	Doug Flynn	.06	.03	.00
☐	87	Dave Kingman	.25	.12	.02
☐	88	Randy Jones	.06	.03	.00
☐	89	Pat Zachry	.06	.03	.00
☐	90	Lee Mazzilli	.10	.05	.01
☐	91	Rusty Staub	.20	.10	.02
☐	92	Craig Swan	.06	.03	.00
☐	93	Frank Taveras	.06	.03	.00
☐	94	Alex Trevino	.06	.03	.00
☐	95	Joel Youngblood	.06	.03	.00
☐	96	Mets Checklist	.03	.01	.00
		(unnumbered)			
☐	97	Bob Boone	.30	.15	.03
☐	98	Larry Bowa	.25	.12	.02
☐	99	Steve Carlton	1.25	.60	.12
☐	100	Greg Luzinski	.20	.10	.02
☐	101	Garry Maddox	.10	.05	.01
☐	102	Bake McBride	.06	.03	.00
☐	103	Tug McGraw	.25	.12	.02
☐	104	Pete Rose	2.00	1.00	.20
☐	105	Mike Schmidt	2.50	1.25	.25
☐	106	Lonnie Smith	.20	.10	.02
☐	107	Manny Trillo	.06	.03	.00
☐	108	Phillies Checklist	.03	.01	.00
		(unnumbered)			
☐	109	Jim Bibby	.06	.03	.00
☐	110	John Candelaria	.10	.05	.01
☐	111	Mike Easler	.10	.05	.01
☐	112	Tim Foli	.06	.03	.00
☐	113	Phil Garner	.10	.05	.01
☐	114	Bill Madlock	.20	.10	.02
☐	115	Omar Moreno	.06	.03	.00
☐	116	Ed Ott	.06	.03	.00

☐	117	Dave Parker	.60	.30	.06
☐	118	Willie Stargell	1.00	.50	.10
☐	119	Kent Tekulve	.10	.05	.01
☐	120	Pirates Checklist	.03	.01	.00
		(unnumbered)			
☐	121	Bob Forsch	.10	.05	.01
☐	122	George Hendrick	.10	.05	.01
☐	123	Keith Hernandez	.75	.35	.07
☐	124	Tom Herr	.15	.07	.01
☐	125	Sixto Lezcano	.06	.03	.00
☐	126	Ken Oberkfell	.06	.03	.00
☐	127	Darrell Porter	.10	.05	.01
☐	128	Tony Scott	.06	.03	.00
☐	129	Lary Sorensen	.06	.03	.00
☐	130	Bruce Sutter	.20	.10	.02
☐	131	Garry Templeton	.10	.05	.01
☐	132	Cardinals Checklist	.03	.01	.00
		(unnumbered)			

1982 Coke Red Sox

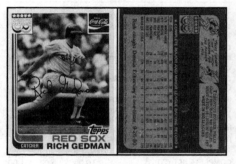

The cards in this 22-card set measure 2 1/2" by 3 1/2". This set of Boston Red Sox ballplayers was issued locally in the Boston area as a joint promotion by Brigham's Ice Cream Stores and Coca-Cola. The pictures are identical to those in the Topps regular 1982 issue, except that the colors are brighter and the Brigham and Coke logos appear inside the frame line. The reverses are done in red, black and gray, in contrast to the Topps set, and the number appears to the right of the position listing. The cards were initally distributed in three-card cello packs with an ice cream or Coca-Cola purchase but later became available as sets within the hobby. The unnumbered title or advertising card carries a premium offer on the reverse.

			MINT	EXC	G-VG
COMPLETE SET (23)			6.00	3.00	.60
COMMON PLAYER (1-23)			.06	.03	.00
☐	1	Gary Allenson	.06	.03	.00
☐	2	Tom Burgmeier	.06	.03	.00
☐	3	Mark Clear	.10	.05	.01
☐	4	Steve Crawford	.06	.03	.00
☐	5	Dennis Eckersley	.75	.35	.07
☐	6	Dwight Evans	.75	.35	.07
☐	7	Rich Gedman	.60	.30	.06
☐	8	Garry Hancock	.06	.03	.00
☐	9	Glen Hoffman	.06	.03	.00
☐	10	Carney Lansford	.50	.25	.05
☐	11	Rick Miller	.06	.03	.00
☐	12	Reid Nichols	.06	.03	.00
☐	13	Bob Ojeda	.25	.12	.02
☐	14	Tony Perez	.50	.25	.05
☐	15	Chuck Rainey	.06	.03	.00
☐	16	Jerry Remy	.06	.03	.00
☐	17	Jim Rice	.90	.45	.09
☐	18	Bob Stanley	.15	.07	.01
☐	19	Dave Stapleton	.06	.03	.00
☐	20	Mike Torrez	.10	.05	.01
☐	21	John Tudor	.35	.17	.03
☐	22	Carl Yastrzemski	2.50	1.25	.25
☐	23	Title Card	.03	.01	.00
		(unnumbered)			

1982 Coke Reds

The cards in this 22-card set measure 2 1/2" by 3 1/2". The 1982 Coca-Cola Cincinnati Reds set, issued in conjunction with Topps, contains 22 cards of current Reds players. Although the cards of 15 players feature the exact photo used in the Topps' regular issue, the Coke photos have better coloration and appear sharper than their Topps counterparts. Six players, Cedeno, Harris, Hurdle, Kern, Krenchicki, and Trevino are new to the Redleg uniform via trades, while Joel Householder had formerly appeared on the Reds' 1982 Topps "Future Stars" card. The cards are numbered 1 to 22 on the red and gray reverse, and the Coke logo appears on both sides of the card. There is an unnumbered title card which contains a premium offer on the reverse.

		MINT	EXC	G-VG
	COMPLETE SET (23)	6.00	3.00	.60
	COMMON PLAYER (1-23)	.06	.03	.00
☐ 1	Johnny Bench	2.00	1.00	.20
☐ 2	Bruce Berenyi	.06	.03	.00
☐ 3	Larry Biittner	.06	.03	.00
☐ 4	Cesar Cedeno	.10	.05	.01
☐ 5	Dave Concepcion	.25	.12	.02
☐ 6	Dan Driessen	.10	.05	.01
☐ 7	Greg Harris	.20	.10	.02
☐ 8	Paul Householder	.06	.03	.00
☐ 9	Tom Hume	.06	.03	.00
☐ 10	Clint Hurdle	.06	.03	.00
☐ 11	Jim Kern	.06	.03	.00
☐ 12	Wayne Krenchicki	.06	.03	.00
☐ 13	Rafael Landestoy	.06	.03	.00
☐ 14	Charlie Leibrandt	.25	.12	.02
☐ 15	Mike O'Berry	.06	.03	.00
☐ 16	Ron Oester	.10	.05	.01
☐ 17	Frank Pastore	.06	.03	.00
☐ 18	Joe Price	.06	.03	.00
☐ 19	Tom Seaver	2.00	1.00	.20
☐ 20	Mario Soto	.15	.07	.01
☐ 21	Alex Trevino	.06	.03	.00
☐ 22	Mike Vail	.06	.03	.00
☐ 23	Title Card	.03	.01	.00
	(unnumbered)			

1985 Coke White Sox

This 30-card set features present and past Chicago White Sox players and personnel. Cards measure 2 5/8" by 4 1/8" and feature a red band at the bottom of the card. Within the red band are the White Sox logo, the player's name, position, uniform number, and a small oval portrait of an all-time White Sox Great at a similar position. the cards were available two at a time at Tuesday night White Sox home

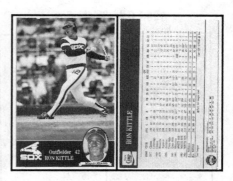

games or as a complete set through membership in the Coca-Cola White Sox Fan Club. The cards below are numbered by uniform number; the last three cards are unnumbered.

		MINT	EXC	G-VG
	COMPLETE SET (30)	11.00	5.50	1.10
	COMMON PLAYER	.25	.12	.02
☐ 0	Oscar Gamble	.25	.12	.02
	Zeke Bonura			
☐ 1	Scott Fletcher	.50	.25	.05
	Luke Appling			
☐ 3	Harold Baines	.90	.45	.09
	Bill Melton			
☐ 5	Luis Salazar	.25	.12	.02
	Chico Carrasquel			
☐ 7	Marc Hill	.25	.12	.02
	Sherm Lollar			
☐ 8	Daryl Boston	.25	.12	.02
	Jim Landis			
☐ 10	Tony LaRussa	.60	.30	.06
	Al Lopez			
☐ 12	Julio Cruz	.40	.20	.04
	Nellie Fox			
☐ 13	Ozzie Guillen	1.25	.60	.12
	Luis Aparicio			
☐ 17	Jerry Hairston	.25	.12	.02
	Smoky Burgess			
☐ 20	Joe DeSa	.25	.12	.02
	Carlos May			
☐ 22	Joel Skinner	.25	.12	.02
	J.C. Martin			
☐ 23	Rudy Law	.25	.12	.02
	Bill Skowron			
☐ 24	Floyd Bannister	.40	.20	.04
	Red Faber			
☐ 29	Greg Walker	.60	.30	.06
	Dick Allen			
☐ 30	Gene Nelson	.40	.20	.04
	Early Wynn			
☐ 32	Tim Hulett	.25	.12	.02
	Pete Ward			
☐ 34	Richard Dotson	.50	.25	.05
	Ed Walsh			
☐ 37	Dan Spillner	.25	.12	.02
	Thornton Lee			
☐ 40	Britt Burns	.25	.12	.02
	Gary Peters			
☐ 41	Tom Seaver	1.50	.75	.15
	Ted Lyons			
☐ 40	Ron Kittle	.50	.25	.05
	Minnie Minoso			
☐ 43	Bob James	.35	.17	.03
	Hoyt Wilhelm			
☐ 44	Tom Paciorek	.35	.17	.03
	Eddie Collins			
☐ 46	Tim Lollar	.25	.12	.02
	Billy Pierce			
☐ 50	Juan Agosto	.25	.12	.02
	Wilbur Wood			
☐ 72	Carlton Fisk	1.00	.50	.10
	Ray Schalk			
☐ xx	Comiskey Park	.25	.12	.02
	(unnumbered)			
☐ xx	Nancy Faust	.25	.12	.02
	(park organist)			
	(unnumbered)			
☐ xx	Ribbie and Roobarb	.25	.12	.02
	(unnumbered)			

1986 Coke White Sox

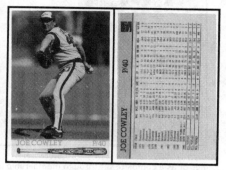

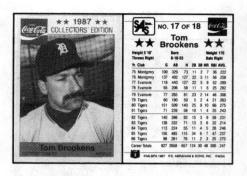

This colorful 30-card set features a borderless photo on top of a blue-on-white name, position, and uniform number. Card backs provide complete major and minor season-by-season career statistical information. Since the cards are unnumbered, they are numbered below according to uniform number. The cards measure approximately 2 5/8" by 4". The five unnumbered non-player cards are listed at the end of the checklist below.

	MINT	EXC	G-VG
COMPLETE SET (30)	10.00	5.00	1.00
COMMON PLAYER	.20	.10	.02

		MINT	EXC	G-VG
☐ 1	Wayne Tolleson	.20	.10	.02
☐ 3	Harold Baines	1.00	.50	.10
☐ 7	Marc Hill	.20	.10	.02
☐ 8	Daryl Boston	.20	.10	.02
☐ 12	Julio Cruz	.20	.10	.02
☐ 13	Ozzie Guillen	.75	.35	.07
☐ 17	Jerry Hairston	.20	.10	.02
☐ 19	Floyd Bannister	.30	.15	.03
☐ 20	Reid Nichols	.20	.10	.02
☐ 22	Joel Skinner	.20	.10	.02
☐ 24	Dave Schmidt	.30	.15	.03
☐ 26	Bobby Bonilla	1.00	.50	.10
☐ 29	Greg Walker	.50	.25	.05
☐ 30	Gene Nelson	.30	.15	.03
☐ 32	Tim Hulett	.20	.10	.02
☐ 33	Neil Allen	.20	.10	.02
☐ 34	Richard Dotson	.40	.20	.04
☐ 40	Joe Cowley	.20	.10	.02
☐ 41	Tom Seaver	1.25	.60	.12
☐ 42	Ron Kittle	.50	.25	.05
☐ 43	Bob James	.20	.10	.02
☐ 44	John Cangelosi	.30	.15	.03
☐ 50	Juan Agosto	.20	.10	.02
☐ 52	Joel Davis	.30	.15	.03
☐ 72	Carlton Fisk	1.00	.50	.10
☐ xx	Nancy Faust ORG (unnumbered)	.20	.10	.02
☐ xx	Ken "Hawk" Harrelson (unnumbered)	.30	.15	.03
☐ xx	Tony LaRussa MG (unnumbered)	.30	.15	.03
☐ xx	Minnie Minoso CO (unnumbered)	.30	.15	.03
☐ xx	Ribbie and Roobarb (unnumbered)	.20	.10	.02

1987 Coke Tigers

Coca-Cola in collaboration with S. Abraham and Sons issued a set of 18 cards featuring the Detroit Tigers. The cards are numbered on the back. The cards are distinguished by the bright yellow border framing the full-color picture of the player on the front. The cards were issued in panels of four: three player cards and a team logo card. The cards measure the standard 2 1/2" by 3 1/2" and were produced by MSA, Mike Schechter Associates.

	MINT	EXC	G-VG
COMPLETE SET (18)	5.00	2.50	.50
COMMON PLAYER (1-18)	.20	.10	.02

		MINT	EXC	G-VG
☐ 1	Kirk Gibson	.75	.35	.07
☐ 2	Larry Herndon	.20	.10	.02
☐ 3	Walt Terrell	.30	.15	.03
☐ 4	Alan Trammell	.75	.35	.07
☐ 5	Frank Tanana	.30	.15	.03
☐ 6	Pat Sheridan	.20	.10	.02
☐ 7	Jack Morris	.50	.25	.05
☐ 8	Mike Heath	.20	.10	.02
☐ 9	Dave Bergman	.20	.10	.02
☐ 10	Chet Lemon	.30	.15	.03
☐ 11	Dwight Lowry	.20	.10	.02
☐ 12	Dan Petry	.20	.10	.02
☐ 13	Darrell Evans	.30	.15	.03
☐ 14	Darnell Coles	.20	.10	.02
☐ 15	Willie Hernandez	.30	.15	.03
☐ 16	Lou Whitaker	.50	.25	.05
☐ 17	Tom Brookens	.20	.10	.02
☐ 18	John Grubb	.20	.10	.02

1987 Coke White Sox

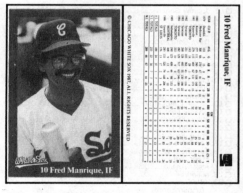

This colorful 30-card set features a card front with a blue-bordered photo and name, position, and uniform number. Card backs provide complete major and minor season-by-season career statistical information. Since the cards are unnumbered, they are numbered below in uniform number order. The cards measure approximately 2 5/8" by 4". The three unnumbered non-player cards are listed at the end. The card set, sponsored by Coca-Cola, is an exclusive for fan club members who join (for 10.00) in 1987.

	MINT	EXC	G-VG
COMPLETE SET (30)	9.00	4.50	.90
COMMON PLAYER (1-30)	.20	.10	.02

		MINT	EXC	G-VG
☐ 1	Jerry Royster 1	.20	.10	.02

				MINT	EXC	G-VG
☐	2	Harold Baines 3	....	.75	.35	.07
☐	3	Ron Karkovice 5	....	.20	.10	.02
☐	4	Daryl Boston 8	....	.20	.10	.02
☐	5	Fred Manrique 10	....	.30	.15	.03
☐	6	Steve Lyons 12	....	.20	.10	.02
☐	7	Ozzie Guillen 13	....	.50	.25	.05
☐	8	Russ Morman 14	....	.20	.10	.02
☐	9	Donnie Hill 15	....	.20	.10	.02
☐	10	Jim Fregosi MG 16	....	.30	.15	.03
☐	11	Jerry Hairston 17	....	.20	.10	.02
☐	12	Floyd Bannister 19	....	.30	.15	.03
☐	13	Gary Redus 21	....	.30	.15	.03
☐	14	Ivan Calderon 22	....	.50	.25	.05
☐	15	Ron Hassey 25	....	.30	.15	.03
☐	16	Jose DeLeon 26	....	.40	.20	.04
☐	17	Greg Walker 29	....	.50	.25	.05
☐	18	Tim Hulett 32	....	.20	.10	.02
☐	19	Neil Allen 33	....	.30	.15	.03
☐	20	Richard Dotson 34	....	.30	.15	.03
☐	21	Ray Searage 36	....	.20	.10	.02
☐	22	Bobby Thigpen 37	....	.60	.30	.06
☐	23	Jim Winn 40	....	.20	.10	.02
☐	24	Bob James 43	....	.20	.10	.02
☐	25	Joel McKeon 50	....	.20	.10	.02
☐	26	Joel Davis 52	....	.20	.10	.02
☐	27	Carlton Fisk 72	....	1.00	.50	.10
☐	28	Nancy Faust ORG	....	.20	.10	.02
		(unnumbered)				
☐	29	Minnie Minoso	....	.30	.15	.03
		(unnumbered)				
☐	30	Robbie and Roobarb	....	.20	.10	.02
		(unnumbered)				

1988 Coke Padres

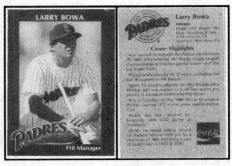

#10 Manager

These cards were actually issued as two separate promotions. The first eight cards were issued as a perforated sheet (approximately 7 1/2" by 10 1/2") as a Coca Cola Junior Padres Club promotion. The other 12 cards were issued later on specific game days to members of the Junior Padres Club. All the cards are standard size, 2 1/2" by 3 1/2" and are unnumbered. Cards that were on the perforated panel are indicated by PAN in the checklist below. Since the cards are unnumbered, they are listed below by uniform number, which is featured prominently on the card fronts.

				MINT	EXC	G-VG
	COMPLETE SET (21)		....	30.00	15.00	3.00
	COMMON PANEL PLAYER		....	.50	.25	.05
	COMMON NON-PAN PLAYER		....	1.00	.50	.10
☐	1	Garry Templeton PAN	....	.50	.25	.05
☐	5	Randy Ready PAN	....	.50	.25	.05
☐	7	Keith Moreland	....	1.00	.50	.10
☐	8	John Kruk	....	1.50	.75	.15
☐	9	Benito Santiago	....	5.00	2.50	.50
☐	10	Larry Bowa MG PAN	....	.50	.25	.05
☐	11	Tim Flannery PAN	....	.50	.25	.05
☐	14	Carmelo Martinez	....	1.00	.50	.10
☐	15	Jack McKeon MG	....	1.00	.50	.10
☐	19	Tony Gwynn	....	10.00	5.00	1.00
☐	22	Stan Jefferson	....	1.50	.75	.15
☐	27	Mark Parent	....	1.00	.50	.10
☐	30	Eric Show	....	1.50	.75	.15
☐	31	Eddie Whitson	....	1.50	.75	.15

				MINT	EXC	G-VG
☐	35	Chris Brown PAN	....	.75	.35	.07
☐	41	Lance McCullers	....	1.50	.75	.15
☐	45	Jimmy Jones PAN	....	.75	.35	.07
☐	48	Mark Davis PAN	....	2.50	1.25	.25
☐	51	Greg Booker	....	1.00	.50	.10
☐	55	Mark Grant PAN	....	.50	.25	.05
☐	xx	Padres Logo PAN	....	.50	.25	.05
		(program explanation on reverse)				

1988 Coke White Sox

This colorful 30-card set features a card front with a red-bordered photo and name and position. Card backs provide a narrative without any statistical tables. Since the cards are unnumbered, they are numbered below in alphabetical order according to the subject's name or card's title. The cards measure approximately 2 5/8" by 3 1/2". The card set, sponsored by Coca-Cola, was for fan club members who join (for 10.00) in 1988. The cards were also given out at the May 22nd game at Comiskey Park. These cards do not even list the player's uniform number anywhere on the card. Card backs are printed in black and gray on thin white card stock.

				MINT	EXC	G-VG
	COMPLETE SET (30)		....	6.00	3.00	.60
	COMMON PLAYER (1-30)		....	.15	.07	.01
☐	1	Harold Baines	....	.45	.22	.04
☐	2	Daryl Boston	....	.15	.07	.01
☐	3	Ivan Calderon	....	.35	.17	.03
☐	4	Comiskey Park	....	.15	.07	.01
☐	5	John Davis	....	.25	.12	.02
☐	6	Nancy Faust	....	.15	.07	.01
		(organist)				
☐	7	Jim Fregosi MG	....	.25	.12	.02
☐	8	Carlton Fisk	....	.75	.35	.07
☐	9	Ozzie Guillen	....	.35	.17	.03
☐	10	Donnie Hill	....	.15	.07	.01
☐	11	Rick Horton	....	.25	.12	.02
☐	12	Lance Johnson	....	.25	.12	.02
☐	13	Dave LaPoint	....	.25	.12	.02
☐	14	Bill Long	....	.15	.07	.01
☐	15	Steve Lyons	....	.15	.07	.01
☐	16	Jack McDowell	....	.25	.12	.02
☐	17	Fred Manrique	....	.15	.07	.01
☐	18	Minnie Minoso	....	.35	.17	.03
☐	19	Dan Pasqua	....	.25	.12	.02
☐	20	John Pawlowski	....	.15	.07	.01
☐	21	Melido Perez	....	.35	.17	.03
☐	22	Billy Pierce	....	.25	.12	.02
☐	23	Jerry Reuss	....	.25	.12	.02
☐	24	Gary Redus	....	.25	.12	.02
☐	25	Ribbie and Roobarb	....	.15	.07	.01
☐	26	Mark Salas	....	.15	.07	.01
☐	27	Jose Segura	....	.25	.12	.02
☐	28	Bobby Thigpen	....	.35	.17	.03
☐	29	Greg Walker	....	.35	.17	.03
☐	30	Kenny Williams	....	.25	.12	.02

1989 Coke Padres

These cards were actually issued as two separate promotions. The first nine cards were issued as a perforated sheet (approximately 7 1/2" by 10 1/2") as a Coca Cola Junior Padres Club promotion. The other 12 cards were issued later on specific game days to members of the Junior Padres Club. All the cards are standard size, 2 1/2" by 3 1/2" and are unnumbered. Cards that were on the perforated panel are indicated by PAN in the checklist below. Since the cards are unnumbered, they are listed below in alphabetical order by subject. Marvell Wynne was planned for the set but was not issued since he was traded before the set was released; Walt Terrell also is tougher to find due to his mid-season trade.

		MINT	EXC	G-VG
COMPLETE SET (21)		25.00	12.50	2.50
COMMON PLAYER (1-21)		1.00	.50	.10
COMMON PLAYER PAN		.50	.25	.05
□ 1	Roberto Alomar PAN	.75	.35	.07
□ 2	Jack Clark	2.00	1.00	.20
□ 3	Mark Davis	5.00	2.50	.50
□ 4	Tim Flannery	1.00	.50	.10
□ 5	Mark Grant	1.00	.50	.10
□ 6	Tony Gwynn	9.00	4.50	.90
□ 7	Bruce Hurst	2.00	1.00	.20
□ 8	Chris James	1.50	.75	.15
□ 9	Carmelo Martinez PAN	.50	.25	.05
□ 10	Jack McKeon MG PAN	.50	.25	.05
□ 11	Mark Parent	1.00	.50	.10
□ 12	Dennis Rasmussen PAN	.50	.25	.05
□ 13	Randy Ready PAN	.50	.25	.05
□ 14	Leon Bip Roberts	1.00	.50	.10
□ 15	Luis Salazar	1.00	.50	.10
□ 16	Benito Santiago	2.50	1.25	.25
□ 17	Eric Show PAN	.75	.35	.07
□ 18	Gary Templeton PAN	.75	.35	.07
□ 19	Walt Terrell SP	3.00	1.50	.30
□ 20	Ed Whitson PAN	.75	.35	.07
□ xx	Padres Logo PAN	.50	.25	.05

1989 Coke White Sox

The 1989 Coke Chicago White Sox set contains 30 cards measuring 2 5/8" by 3 1/2". The players in the set represent the White Sox opening day roster. The fronts are blue. The horizontally-oriented backs are gray and white, and feature biographical information. The set was a promotional give-away August 10, 1989 at the Baseball Card Night game against the Oakland A's to the first 15,000 fans. The set includes a special "New Comiskey Park, 1991" card. The complete set was also available with (10.00) membership in the Chi-Sox Fan Club.

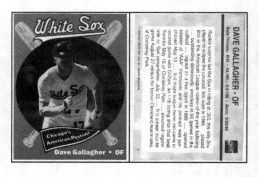

		MINT	EXC	G-VG
COMPLETE SET (30)		6.00	3.00	.60
COMMON PLAYER (1-30)		.15	.07	.01
□ 1	New Comiskey Park 1991	.15	.07	.01
□ 2	Comiskey Park	.15	.07	.01
□ 3	Jeff Torborg MG	.25	.12	.02
□ 4	Coaching Staff	.15	.07	.01
□ 5	Harold Baines	.50	.25	.05
□ 6	Daryl Boston	.15	.07	.01
□ 7	Ivan Calderon	.35	.17	.03
□ 8	Carlton Fisk	.75	.35	.07
□ 9	Dave Gallagher	.25	.12	.02
□ 10	Ozzie Guillen	.35	.17	.03
□ 11	Shawn Hillegas	.15	.07	.01
□ 12	Barry Jones	.15	.07	.01
□ 13	Ron Karkovice	.15	.07	.01
□ 14	Eric King	.15	.07	.01
□ 15	Ron Kittle	.25	.12	.02
□ 16	Bill Long	.15	.07	.01
□ 17	Steve Lyons	.15	.07	.01
□ 18	Donn Pall	.15	.07	.01
□ 19	Dan Pasqua	.15	.07	.01
□ 20	Ken Patterson	.15	.07	.01
□ 21	Melido Perez	.25	.12	.02
□ 22	Jerry Reuss	.15	.07	.01
□ 23	Billy Joe Robidoux	.15	.07	.01
□ 24	Steve Rosenberg	.15	.07	.01
□ 25	Jeff Schaefer	.15	.07	.01
□ 26	Bobby Thigpen	.25	.12	.02
□ 27	Greg Walker	.25	.12	.02
□ 28	Eddie Williams	.15	.07	.01
□ 29	Nancy Faust (organist)	.15	.07	.01
□ 30	Minnie Minoso	.25	.12	.02

1914 Cracker Jack

The cards in this 144-card set measure 2 1/4" by 3". This "Series of colored pictures of Famous Ball Players and Managers" was issued in packages of Cracker Jack in 1914. The cards have tinted photos set against red backgrounds and many are found with caramel stains. The set also contains Federal League players. The company claims to have printed

15 million cards. The 1914 series can be distinguished from the 1915 issue by the advertising found on the back of the cards. The ACC catalog number is E145-1.

		EX-MT	VG-E	GOOD
	COMPLETE SET (144)	27500.	13500.	3250.
	COMMON PLAYER (1-144)	100.00	50.00	10.00
☐ 1	Otto Knabe	100.00	50.00	10.00
☐ 2	Frank Baker	300.00	150.00	30.00
☐ 3	Joe Tinker	225.00	110.00	22.00
☐ 4	Larry Doyle	100.00	50.00	10.00
☐ 5	Ward Miller	100.00	50.00	10.00
☐ 6	Eddie Plank (Phila. AL)	300.00	150.00	30.00
☐ 7	Eddie Collins (Phila. AL)	300.00	150.00	30.00
☐ 8	Rube Oldring	100.00	50.00	10.00
☐ 9	Artie Hoffman	100.00	50.00	10.00
☐ 10	John McInnis	125.00	60.00	12.50
☐ 11	George Stovall	100.00	50.00	10.00
☐ 12	Connie Mack	350.00	175.00	35.00
☐ 13	Art Wilson	100.00	50.00	10.00
☐ 14	Sam Crawford	225.00	110.00	22.00
☐ 15	Reb Russell	100.00	50.00	10.00
☐ 16	Howie Camnitz	100.00	50.00	10.00
☐ 17	Roger Bresnahan (Catcher)	225.00	110.00	22.00
☐ 18	Johnny Evers	225.00	110.00	22.00
☐ 19	Chief Bender (Phila. AL)	300.00	150.00	30.00
☐ 20	Cy Falkenberg	100.00	50.00	10.00
☐ 21	Heine Zimmerman	100.00	50.00	10.00
☐ 22	Joe Wood	150.00	75.00	15.00
☐ 23	Charles Comiskey	250.00	125.00	25.00
☐ 24	George Mullen	100.00	50.00	10.00
☐ 25	Michael Simon	100.00	50.00	10.00
☐ 26	James Scott	100.00	50.00	10.00
☐ 27	Bill Carrigan	100.00	50.00	10.00
☐ 28	Jack Barry	100.00	50.00	10.00
☐ 29	Vean Gregg (Cleve)	125.00	60.00	12.50
☐ 30	Ty Cobb	3200.00	1500.00	350.00
☐ 31	Heine Wagner	100.00	50.00	10.00
☐ 32	Mordecai Brown	225.00	110.00	22.00
☐ 33	Amos Strunk	100.00	50.00	10.00
☐ 34	Ira Thomas	100.00	50.00	10.00
☐ 35	Harry Hooper	225.00	110.00	22.00
☐ 36	Ed Walsh	225.00	110.00	22.00
☐ 37	Grover Alexander	450.00	225.00	45.00
☐ 38	Red Dooin (Phila. NL)	100.00	50.00	10.00
☐ 39	Chick Gandil	150.00	75.00	15.00
☐ 40	Jimmy Austin (St.L. AL)	100.00	50.00	10.00
☐ 41	Tommy Leach	100.00	50.00	10.00
☐ 42	Al Bridwell	100.00	50.00	10.00
☐ 43	Rube Marquard (NY NL)	250.00	125.00	25.00
☐ 44	Charles Tesreau	100.00	50.00	10.00
☐ 45	Fred Luderus	100.00	50.00	10.00
☐ 46	Bob Groom	100.00	50.00	10.00
☐ 47	Josh Devore (Phila. NL)	100.00	50.00	10.00
☐ 48	Harry Lord	200.00	100.00	20.00
☐ 49	John Miller	100.00	50.00	10.00
☐ 50	John Hummell	100.00	50.00	10.00
☐ 51	Nap Rucker	100.00	50.00	10.00
☐ 52	Zach Wheat	225.00	110.00	22.00
☐ 53	Otto Miller	100.00	50.00	10.00
☐ 54	Marty O'Toole	100.00	50.00	10.00
☐ 55	Dick Hoblitzel (Cinc.)	100.00	50.00	10.00
☐ 56	Clyde Milan	100.00	50.00	10.00
☐ 57	Walter Johnson	1000.00	500.00	100.00
☐ 58	Wally Schang	100.00	50.00	10.00
☐ 59	Harry Gessler	100.00	50.00	10.00
☐ 60	Rollie Zeider	175.00	85.00	18.00
☐ 61	Ray Schalk	225.00	110.00	22.00
☐ 62	Jay Cashion	200.00	100.00	20.00
☐ 63	Babe Adams	100.00	50.00	10.00
☐ 64	Jimmy Archer	100.00	50.00	10.00
☐ 65	Tris Speaker	500.00	250.00	50.00
☐ 66	Napoleon Lajoie (Cleve.)	600.00	300.00	60.00
☐ 67	Otis Crandall	100.00	50.00	10.00
☐ 68	Honus Wagner	1000.00	500.00	100.00
☐ 69	John McGraw	300.00	150.00	30.00
☐ 70	Fred Clarke	225.00	110.00	22.00
☐ 71	Chief Meyers	100.00	50.00	10.00
☐ 72	John Boehling	100.00	50.00	10.00
☐ 73	Max Carey	225.00	110.00	22.00
☐ 74	Frank Owens	100.00	50.00	10.00
☐ 75	Miller Huggins	225.00	110.00	22.00
☐ 76	Claude Hendrix	100.00	50.00	10.00
☐ 77	Hugh Jennings	225.00	110.00	22.00
☐ 78	Fred Merkle	125.00	60.00	12.50
☐ 79	Ping Bodie	100.00	50.00	10.00
☐ 80	Ed Ruelbach	100.00	50.00	10.00
☐ 81	J.C. Delehanty	100.00	50.00	10.00
☐ 82	Gavvy Cravath	125.00	60.00	12.50
☐ 83	Russ Ford	100.00	50.00	10.00
☐ 84	E.E. Knetzer	100.00	50.00	10.00
☐ 85	Buck Herzog	100.00	50.00	10.00
☐ 86	Burt Shotten	100.00	50.00	10.00
☐ 87	Forrest Cady	100.00	50.00	10.00
☐ 88	Christy Mathewson (Pitching)	1250.00	125.00	25.00
☐ 89	Lawrence Cheney	100.00	50.00	10.00
☐ 90	Frank Smith	100.00	50.00	10.00
☐ 91	Roger Peckinpaugh	100.00	50.00	10.00
☐ 92	Al Demaree (N.Y. NL)	100.00	50.00	10.00
☐ 93	Derrill Pratt (Throwing)	200.00	100.00	20.00
☐ 94	Eddie Cicotte	150.00	75.00	15.00
☐ 95	Ray Keating	100.00	50.00	10.00
☐ 96	Beals Becker	100.00	50.00	10.00
☐ 97	John (Rube) Benton	100.00	50.00	10.00
☐ 98	Frank LaPorte	100.00	50.00	10.00
☐ 99	Frank Chance	750.00	375.00	75.00
☐ 100	Thomas Seaton	100.00	50.00	10.00
☐ 101	Frank Schulte	100.00	50.00	10.00
☐ 102	Ray Fisher	100.00	50.00	10.00
☐ 103	Joe Jackson	2500.00	250.00	50.00
☐ 104	Vic Saier	100.00	50.00	10.00
☐ 105	James Lavender	100.00	50.00	10.00
☐ 106	Joe Birmingham	100.00	50.00	10.00
☐ 107	Tom Downey	100.00	50.00	10.00
☐ 108	Sherwood Magee (Phila. NL)	100.00	50.00	10.00
☐ 109	Fred Blanding	100.00	50.00	10.00
☐ 110	Bob Bescher	100.00	50.00	10.00
☐ 111	Jim Callahan	200.00	100.00	20.00
☐ 112	Ed Sweeney	100.00	50.00	10.00
☐ 113	George Suggs	100.00	50.00	10.00
☐ 114	Geo. J. Moriarty	100.00	50.00	10.00
☐ 115	Addison Brennan	100.00	50.00	10.00
☐ 116	Rollie Zeider	100.00	50.00	10.00
☐ 117	Ted Easterly	100.00	50.00	10.00
☐ 118	Ed Konetchy (Pitts.)	100.00	50.00	10.00
☐ 119	George Perring	100.00	50.00	10.00
☐ 120	Mike Doolan	100.00	50.00	10.00
☐ 121	Perdue (Boston NL)	100.00	50.00	10.00
☐ 122	Owen Bush	100.00	50.00	10.00
☐ 123	Slim Sallee	100.00	50.00	10.00
☐ 124	Earl Moore	100.00	50.00	10.00
☐ 125	Bert Niehoff	100.00	50.00	10.00
☐ 126	Walter Blair	100.00	50.00	10.00
☐ 127	Butch Schmidt	100.00	50.00	10.00
☐ 128	Steve Evans	100.00	50.00	10.00
☐ 129	Ray Caldwell	100.00	50.00	10.00
☐ 130	Ivy Wingo	100.00	50.00	10.00
☐ 131	George Baumgardner	100.00	50.00	10.00
☐ 132	Les Nunamaker	100.00	50.00	10.00
☐ 133	Branch Rickey	300.00	150.00	30.00
☐ 134	Armando Marsans (Cincinnati)	100.00	50.00	10.00
☐ 135	Bill Killefer	100.00	50.00	10.00
☐ 136	Rabbit Maranville	225.00	110.00	22.00
☐ 137	William Rariden	100.00	50.00	10.00
☐ 138	Hank Gowdy	100.00	50.00	10.00
☐ 139	Rebel Oakes	100.00	50.00	10.00
☐ 140	Danny Murphy	100.00	50.00	10.00
☐ 141	Cy Barger	100.00	50.00	10.00
☐ 142	Eugene Packard	100.00	50.00	10.00
☐ 143	Jake Daubert	125.00	60.00	12.50
☐ 144	James C. Walsh	125.00	60.00	12.50

1915 Cracker Jack

The cards in this 176-card set measure 2 1/4" by 3". When turned over in a lateral motion, a 1915 "series of 176" Cracker Jack card shows the back printing upside-down. Cards were available in boxes of Cracker Jack or from the company for "100 Cracker Jack coupons, or one coupon and 25 cents." An album was available for "50 coupons or one coupon and 10 cents." Because of this send-in offer, the 1915 Cracker Jack cards are noticeably easier to find than the 1914 Cracker Jack cards, although obviously neither set is plentiful. The set essentially

duplicates E145-1 (1914 Cracker Jack) except for some additional cards and new poses. Players in the Federal League are indicated by FED in the checklist below. The ACC designation is E145- 2.

		EX-MT	VG-E	GOOD
COMPLETE SET (176)		21000.	10000.	2250.
COMMON PLAYER (1-144)		70.00	35.00	7.50
COMMON PLAYER (145-176)		90.00	45.00	9.00
☐ 1	Otto Knabe	70.00	35.00	7.50
☐ 2	Frank Baker	225.00	110.00	22.00
☐ 3	Joe Tinker	175.00	85.00	18.00
☐ 4	Larry Doyle	70.00	35.00	7.50
☐ 5	Ward Miller	70.00	35.00	7.50
☐ 6	Eddie Plank	225.00	110.00	22.00
	(St.L. FED)			
☐ 7	Eddie Collins	225.00	110.00	22.00
	(Chicago AL)			
☐ 8	Rube Oldring	70.00	35.00	7.50
☐ 9	Artie Hoffman	70.00	35.00	7.50
☐ 10	John McInnis	90.00	45.00	9.00
☐ 11	George Stovall	70.00	35.00	7.50
☐ 12	Connie Mack	300.00	150.00	30.00
☐ 13	Art Wilson	70.00	35.00	7.50
☐ 14	Sam Crawford	175.00	85.00	18.00
☐ 15	Reb Russell	70.00	35.00	7.50
☐ 16	Howie Camnitz	70.00	35.00	7.50
☐ 17	Roger Bresnahan	175.00	85.00	18.00
☐ 18	Johnny Evers	175.00	85.00	18.00
☐ 19	Chief Bender	225.00	110.00	22.00
	(Baltimore FED)			
☐ 20	Cy Falkenberg	70.00	35.00	7.50
☐ 21	Heine Zimmerman	70.00	35.00	7.50
☐ 22	Joe Wood	125.00	60.00	12.50
☐ 23	Charles Comiskey	200.00	100.00	20.00
☐ 24	George Mullen	70.00	35.00	7.50
☐ 25	Michael Simon	70.00	35.00	7.50
☐ 26	James Scott	70.00	35.00	7.50
☐ 27	Bill Carrigan	70.00	35.00	7.50
☐ 28	Jack Barry	70.00	35.00	7.50
☐ 29	Vean Gregg	90.00	45.00	9.00
	(Boston AL)			
☐ 30	Ty Cobb	2500.00	1200.00	300.00
☐ 31	Heine Wagner	70.00	35.00	7.50
☐ 32	Mordecai Brown	175.00	85.00	18.00
☐ 33	Amos Strunk	70.00	35.00	7.50
☐ 34	Ira Thomas	70.00	35.00	7.50
☐ 35	Harry Hooper	175.00	85.00	18.00
☐ 36	Ed Walsh	175.00	85.00	18.00
☐ 37	Grover C. Alexander	350.00	175.00	35.00
☐ 38	Red Dooin (Cinc.)	70.00	35.00	7.50
☐ 39	Chick Gandil	125.00	60.00	12.50
☐ 40	Jimmy Austin	70.00	35.00	7.50
	(Pitts. FED)			
☐ 41	Tommy Leach	70.00	35.00	7.50
☐ 42	Al Bridwell	70.00	35.00	7.50
☐ 43	Rube Marquard	200.00	100.00	20.00
	(Brooklyn FED)			
☐ 44	Charles Tesreau	70.00	35.00	7.50
☐ 45	Fred Luderus	70.00	35.00	7.50
☐ 46	Bob Groom	70.00	35.00	7.50
☐ 47	Josh Devore	70.00	35.00	7.50
	(Boston NL)			
☐ 48	Steve O'Neill	70.00	35.00	7.50
☐ 49	John Miller	70.00	35.00	7.50
☐ 50	John Hummell	70.00	35.00	7.50
☐ 51	Nap Rucker	70.00	35.00	7.50
☐ 52	Zach Wheat	175.00	85.00	18.00
☐ 53	Otto Miller	70.00	35.00	7.50
☐ 54	Marty O'Toole	70.00	35.00	7.50
☐ 55	Dick Hoblitzel	70.00	35.00	7.50
	(Boston AL)			
☐ 56	Clyde Milan	70.00	35.00	7.50
☐ 57	Walter Johnson	800.00	400.00	80.00
☐ 58	Wally Schang	70.00	35.00	7.50
☐ 59	Harry Gessler	70.00	35.00	7.50
☐ 60	Oscar Dugey	70.00	35.00	7.50
☐ 61	Ray Schalk	175.00	85.00	18.00
☐ 62	Willie Mitchell	70.00	35.00	7.50
☐ 63	Babe Adams	70.00	35.00	7.50
☐ 64	Jimmy Archer	70.00	35.00	7.50
☐ 65	Tris Speaker	400.00	200.00	40.00
☐ 66	Napoleon Lajoie	450.00	225.00	45.00
	(Phila. AL)			
☐ 67	Otis Crandall	70.00	35.00	7.50
☐ 68	Honus Wagner	800.00	400.00	80.00
☐ 69	John McGraw	225.00	110.00	22.00
☐ 70	Fred Clarke	175.00	85.00	18.00
☐ 71	Chief Meyers	70.00	35.00	7.50
☐ 72	John Boehling	70.00	35.00	7.50
☐ 73	Max Carey	175.00	85.00	18.00
☐ 74	Frank Owens	70.00	35.00	7.50
☐ 75	Miller Huggins	175.00	85.00	18.00
☐ 76	Claude Hendrix	70.00	35.00	7.50
☐ 77	Hugh Jennings	175.00	85.00	18.00
☐ 78	Fred Merkle	90.00	45.00	9.00
☐ 79	Ping Bodie	70.00	35.00	7.50
☐ 80	Ed Ruelbach	70.00	35.00	7.50
☐ 81	J.C. Delehanty	70.00	35.00	7.50
☐ 82	Gavvy Cravath	90.00	45.00	9.00
☐ 83	Russ Ford	70.00	35.00	7.50
☐ 84	E.E. Knetzer	70.00	35.00	7.50
☐ 85	Buck Herzog	70.00	35.00	7.50
☐ 86	Burt Shotten	70.00	35.00	7.50
☐ 87	Forrest Cady	70.00	35.00	7.50
☐ 88	Christy Mathewson	900.00	450.00	90.00
	(Portrait)			
☐ 89	Lawrence Cheney	70.00	35.00	7.50
☐ 90	Frank Smith	70.00	35.00	7.50
☐ 91	Roger Peckinpaugh	70.00	35.00	7.50
☐ 92	Al Demaree	70.00	35.00	7.50
	(Phila. NL)			
☐ 93	Derrill Pratt	90.00	45.00	9.00
	(Portrait)			
☐ 94	Eddie Cicotte	125.00	60.00	12.50
☐ 95	Ray Keating	70.00	35.00	7.50
☐ 96	Beals Becker	70.00	35.00	7.50
☐ 97	John (Rube) Benton	70.00	35.00	7.50
☐ 98	Frank LaPorte	70.00	35.00	7.50
☐ 99	Hal Chase	200.00	100.00	20.00
☐ 100	Thomas Seaton	70.00	35.00	7.50
☐ 101	Frank Schulte	70.00	35.00	7.50
☐ 102	Ray Fisher	70.00	35.00	7.50
☐ 103	Joe Jackson	2000.00	1000.00	200.00
☐ 104	Vic Saier	70.00	35.00	7.50
☐ 105	James Lavender	70.00	35.00	7.50
☐ 106	Joe Birmingham	70.00	35.00	7.50
☐ 107	Thomas Downey	70.00	35.00	7.50
☐ 108	Sherwood Magee	70.00	35.00	7.50
	(Boston NL)			
☐ 109	Fred Blanding	70.00	35.00	7.50
☐ 110	Bob Bescher	70.00	35.00	7.50
☐ 111	Herbie Moran	70.00	35.00	7.50
☐ 112	Ed Sweeney	70.00	35.00	7.50
☐ 113	George Suggs	70.00	35.00	7.50
☐ 114	Geo. J. Moriarty	70.00	35.00	7.50
☐ 115	Addison Brennan	70.00	35.00	7.50
☐ 116	Rollie Zeider	70.00	35.00	7.50
☐ 117	Ted Easterly	70.00	35.00	7.50
☐ 118	Ed Konetchy	70.00	35.00	7.50
	(Pitts. FED)			
☐ 119	George Perring	70.00	35.00	7.50
☐ 120	Mike Doolan	70.00	35.00	7.50
☐ 121	Perdue (St.L. NL)	70.00	35.00	7.50
☐ 122	Owen Bush	70.00	35.00	7.50
☐ 123	Slim Sallee	70.00	35.00	7.50
☐ 124	Earl Moore	70.00	35.00	7.50
☐ 125	Bert Niehoff	70.00	35.00	7.50
	(Phila. NL)			
☐ 126	Walter Blair	70.00	35.00	7.50
☐ 127	Butch Schmidt	70.00	35.00	7.50
☐ 128	Steve Evans	70.00	35.00	7.50
☐ 129	Ray Caldwell	70.00	35.00	7.50
☐ 130	Ivy Wingo	70.00	35.00	7.50
☐ 131	Geo. Baumgardner	70.00	35.00	7.50
☐ 132	Les Nunamaker	70.00	35.00	7.50
☐ 133	Branch Rickey	225.00	110.00	22.00
☐ 134	Armando Marsans	70.00	35.00	7.50
	(St.L. FED)			
☐ 135	William Killefer	70.00	35.00	7.50
☐ 136	Rabbit Maranville	175.00	85.00	18.00
☐ 137	William Rariden	70.00	35.00	7.50
☐ 138	Hank Gowdy	70.00	35.00	7.50
☐ 139	Rebel Oakes	70.00	35.00	7.50
☐ 140	Danny Murphy	70.00	35.00	7.50
☐ 141	Cy Barger	70.00	35.00	7.50
☐ 142	Eugene Packard	70.00	35.00	7.50
☐ 143	Jake Daubert	90.00	45.00	9.00

☐ 144	James C. Walsh	70.00	35.00	7.50
☐ 145	Ted Cather	90.00	45.00	9.00
☐ 146	George Tyler	90.00	45.00	9.00
☐ 147	Lee Magee	90.00	45.00	9.00
☐ 148	Owen Wilson	90.00	45.00	9.00
☐ 149	Hal Janvrin	90.00	45.00	9.00
☐ 150	Doc Johnston	90.00	45.00	9.00
☐ 151	George Whitted	90.00	45.00	9.00
☐ 152	George McQuillen	90.00	45.00	9.00
☐ 153	Bill James	90.00	45.00	9.00
☐ 154	Dick Rudolph	90.00	45.00	9.00
☐ 155	Joe Connolly	90.00	45.00	9.00
☐ 156	Jean Dubuc	90.00	45.00	9.00
☐ 157	George Kaiserling	90.00	45.00	9.00
☐ 158	Fritz Maisel	90.00	45.00	9.00
☐ 159	Heine Groh	90.00	45.00	9.00
☐ 160	Benny Kauff	90.00	45.00	9.00
☐ 161	Ed Rousch	225.00	110.00	22.00
☐ 162	George Stallings	90.00	45.00	9.00
☐ 163	Bert Whaling	90.00	45.00	9.00
☐ 164	Bob Shawkey	125.00	60.00	12.50
☐ 165	Eddie Murphy	90.00	45.00	9.00
☐ 166	Joe Bush	125.00	60.00	12.50
☐ 167	Clark Griffith	225.00	110.00	22.00
☐ 168	Vin Campbell	90.00	45.00	9.00
☐ 169	Raymond Collins	90.00	45.00	9.00
☐ 170	Hans Lobert	90.00	45.00	9.00
☐ 171	Earl Hamilton	90.00	45.00	9.00
☐ 172	Erskine Mayer	90.00	45.00	9.00
☐ 173	Tilly Walker	90.00	45.00	9.00
☐ 174	Robert Veach	90.00	45.00	9.00
☐ 175	Joseph Benz	90.00	45.00	9.00
☐ 176	Jim Vaughn	125.00	60.00	12.50

1982 Cracker Jack

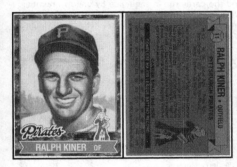

The cards in this 16-card set measure 2 1/2" by 3 1/2"; cards came in two sheets of 8 cards, plus an advertising card with a title in the center, which measured 7 1/2" by 10 1/2". Cracker Jack reentered the baseball card market for the first time since 1915 to promote the first "Old Timers Baseball Classic" held July 19, 1982. The color player photos have a Cracker Jack border and have either green (NL) or red (AL) frame lines and name panels. The Cracker Jack logo appears on both sides of each card, with AL players numbered 1-8 and NL players numbered 9-16. Of the 16 ballplayers pictured, five did not appear at the game. At first, the two sheets were available only through the mail but are now commonly found in hobby circles. The set was prepared for Cracker Jack by Topps. The prices below reflect individual card prices; the price for complete panels would be about the same as the sum of the card prices for those players on the panel due to the easy availability of uncut sheets.

		MINT	EXC	G-VG
COMPLETE SET (16)		7.00	3.50	.70
COMMON PLAYER (1-16)		.15	.07	.01
☐ 1	Larry Doby	.15	.07	.01
☐ 2	Bob Feller	.65	.30	.06
☐ 3	Whitey Ford	.65	.30	.06

☐ 4	Al Kaline	.65	.30	.06
☐ 5	Harmon Killebrew	.35	.17	.03
☐ 6	Mickey Mantle	2.00	1.00	.20
☐ 7	Tony Oliva	.15	.07	.01
☐ 8	Brooks Robinson	.65	.30	.06
☐ 9	Hank Aaron	1.00	.50	.10
☐ 10	Ernie Banks	.65	.30	.06
☐ 11	Ralph Kiner	.40	.20	.04
☐ 12	Ed Mathews	.30	.15	.03
☐ 13	Willie Mays	1.00	.50	.10
☐ 14	Robin Roberts	.30	.15	.03
☐ 15	Duke Snider	.65	.30	.06
☐ 16	Warren Spahn	.50	.25	.05

1980-83 Cramer Legends

This 124-card set is actually four 30-card subsets plus a four-card wax box bottom panel. The set was distributed by series over several years beginning in 1980 with the first 30 cards. The set was produced by Pacific Trading Cards and is frequently referred to as Cramer Legends for the founder of Pacific Trading cards, Mike Cramer. Cards are standard size, 2 1/2" by 3 1/2" and are golden-toned. Even though the wax box cards are numbered from 121-124 and called "series 5", the set is considered complete without them.

		MINT	EXC	G-VG
COMPLETE SET (120)		12.50	6.25	1.25
COMMON PLAYER (1-120)		.10	.05	.01
COMMON PLAYER (121-124)		.20	.10	.02
☐ 1	Babe Ruth	1.00	.30	.06
☐ 2	Heinie Manush	.10	.05	.01
☐ 3	Rabbit Maranville	.10	.05	.01
☐ 4	Earl Averill	.10	.05	.01
☐ 5	Joe DiMaggio	.60	.30	.06
☐ 6	Mickey Mantle	.80	.40	.08
☐ 7	Hank Aaron	.30	.15	.03
☐ 8	Stan Musial	.25	.12	.02
☐ 9	Bill Terry	.10	.05	.01
☐ 10	Sandy Koufax	.25	.12	.02
☐ 11	Ernie Lombardi	.10	.05	.01
☐ 12	Dizzy Dean	.20	.10	.02
☐ 13	Lou Gehrig	.50	.25	.05
☐ 14	Walter Alston	.10	.05	.01
☐ 15	Jackie Robinson	.25	.12	.02
☐ 16	Jimmie Foxx	.10	.05	.01
☐ 17	Billy Southworth	.10	.05	.01
☐ 18	Honus Wagner	.20	.10	.02
☐ 19	Duke Snider	.20	.10	.02
☐ 20	Rogers Hornsby	.20	.10	.02
☐ 21	Paul Waner	.10	.05	.01
☐ 22	Luke Appling	.10	.05	.01
☐ 23	Billy Herman	.10	.05	.01
☐ 24	Lloyd Waner	.10	.05	.01
☐ 25	Fred Hutchinson	.10	.05	.01
☐ 26	Eddie Collins	.10	.05	.01
☐ 27	Lefty Grove	.20	.10	.02
☐ 28	Chuck Connors	.20	.10	.02
☐ 29	Lefty O'Doul	.10	.05	.01
☐ 30	Hank Greenberg	.15	.07	.01
☐ 31	Ty Cobb	.50	.25	.05
☐ 32	Enos Slaughter	.10	.05	.01
☐ 33	Ernie Banks	.20	.10	.02
☐ 34	Christy Mathewson	.20	.10	.02

☐ 35	Mel Ott	.10	.05	.01
☐ 36	Pie Traynor	.10	.05	.01
☐ 37	Clark Griffith	.10	.05	.01
☐ 38	Mickey Cochrane	.10	.05	.01
☐ 39	Joe Cronin	.10	.05	.01
☐ 40	Leo Durocher	.10	.05	.01
☐ 41	Home Run Baker	.10	.05	.01
☐ 42	Joe Tinker	.10	.05	.01
☐ 43	John McGraw	.10	.05	.01
☐ 44	Bill Dickey	.10	.05	.01
☐ 45	Walter Johnson	.20	.10	.02
☐ 46	Frankie Frisch	.10	.05	.01
☐ 47	Casey Stengel	.20	.10	.02
☐ 48	Willie Mays	.35	.17	.03
☐ 49	Johnny Mize	.10	.05	.01
☐ 50	Roberto Clemente	.20	.10	.02
☐ 51	Burleigh Grimes	.10	.05	.01
☐ 52	Pee Wee Reese	.15	.07	.01
☐ 53	Bob Feller	.20	.10	.02
☐ 54	Brooks Robinson	.20	.10	.02
☐ 55	Sam Crawford	.10	.05	.01
☐ 56	Robin Roberts	.15	.07	.01
☐ 57	Warren Spahn	.20	.10	.02
☐ 58	Joe McCarthy	.10	.05	.01
☐ 59	Jocko Conlan	.10	.05	.01
☐ 60	Satchel Paige	.20	.10	.02
☐ 61	Ted Williams	.25	.12	.02
☐ 62	George Kelly	.10	.05	.01
☐ 63	Gil Hodges	.10	.05	.01
☐ 64	Jim Bottomley	.10	.05	.01
☐ 65	Al Kaline	.20	.10	.02
☐ 66	Harvey Kuenn	.10	.05	.01
☐ 67	Yogi Berra	.20	.10	.02
☐ 68	Nellie Fox	.10	.05	.01
☐ 69	Harmon Killebrew	.15	.07	.01
☐ 70	Ed Roush	.10	.05	.01
☐ 71	Mordecai Brown	.10	.05	.01
☐ 72	Gabby Hartnett	.10	.05	.01
☐ 73	Early Wynn	.10	.05	.01
☐ 74	Nap Lajoie	.10	.05	.01
☐ 75	Charlie Grimm	.10	.05	.01
☐ 76	Joe Garagiola	.20	.10	.02
☐ 77	Ted Lyons	.10	.05	.01
☐ 78	Mickey Vernon	.10	.05	.01
☐ 79	Lou Boudreau	.10	.05	.01
☐ 80	Al Dark	.10	.05	.01
☐ 81	Ralph Kiner	.15	.07	.01
☐ 82	Phil Rizzuto	.15	.07	.01
☐ 83	Stan Hack	.10	.05	.01
☐ 84	Frank Chance	.10	.05	.01
☐ 85	Ray Schalk	.10	.05	.01
☐ 86	Bill McKechnie	.10	.05	.01
☐ 87	Travis Jackson	.10	.05	.01
☐ 88	Pete Reiser	.10	.05	.01
☐ 89	Carl Hubbell	.10	.05	.01
☐ 90	Roy Campanella	.20	.10	.02
☐ 91	Cy Young	.10	.05	.01
☐ 92	Kiki Cuyler	.10	.05	.01
☐ 93	Chief Bender	.10	.05	.01
☐ 94	Richie Ashburn	.20	.10	.02
☐ 95	Riggs Stephenson	.10	.05	.01
☐ 96	Minnie Minoso	.10	.05	.01
☐ 97	Hack Wilson	.10	.05	.01
☐ 98	Al Lopez	.10	.05	.01
☐ 99	Willie Keeler	.10	.05	.01
☐ 100	Fred Lindstrom	.10	.05	.01
☐ 101	Roger Maris	.25	.12	.02
☐ 102	Roger Bresnahan	.10	.05	.01
☐ 103	Monty Stratton	.10	.05	.01
☐ 104	Goose Goslin	.10	.05	.01
☐ 105	Earl Combs	.10	.05	.01
☐ 106	Pepper Martin	.10	.05	.01
☐ 107	Joe Jackson	.40	.20	.04
☐ 108	George Sisler	.10	.05	.01
☐ 109	Red Ruffing	.10	.05	.01
☐ 110	Johnny Vander Meer	.10	.05	.01
☐ 111	Herb Pennock	.10	.05	.01
☐ 112	Chuck Klein	.10	.05	.01
☐ 113	Paul Derringer	.10	.05	.01
☐ 114	Addie Joss	.10	.05	.01
☐ 115	Bobby Thomson	.10	.05	.01
☐ 116	Chick Hafey	.10	.05	.01
☐ 117	Lefty Gomez	.15	.07	.01
☐ 118	George Kell	.10	.05	.01
☐ 119	Al Simmons	.10	.05	.01
☐ 120	Bob Lemon	.10	.05	.01
☐ 121	Hoyt Wilhelm (wax box card)	.25	.12	.02
☐ 122	Arky Vaughan (wax box card)	.20	.10	.02
☐ 123	Frank Robinson (wax box card)	.30	.15	.03
☐ 124	Grover Alexander (wax box card)	.20	.10	.02

1982 Cubs Red Lobster

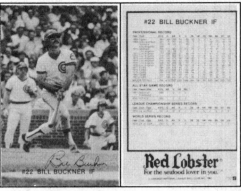

#22 BILL BUCKNER IF

Red Lobster
For the seafood lover in you.

The cards in this 28-card set measure 2 1/4" by 3 1/2". This set of Chicago Cubs players was co-produced by the Cubs and Chicago-area Red Lobster restaurants and was introduced as a promotional giveaway on August 20, 1982, at Wrigley Field. The cards contain borderless color photos of 25 players, manager Lee Elia, the coaching staff, and a team picture. A facsimile autograph appears on the front, and the cards run in sequence by uniform number. While the coaches have a short biographical sketch on back, the player cards simply list the individual's professional record.

		MINT	EXC	G-VG
	COMPLETE SET (28)	12.50	6.25	1.25
	COMMON PLAYER	.20	.10	.02
☐ 1	Larry Bowa	.50	.25	.05
☐ 4	Lee Elia MG	.20	.10	.02
☐ 6	Keith Moreland	.30	.15	.03
☐ 7	Jody Davis	.40	.20	.04
☐ 10	Leon Durham	.30	.15	.03
☐ 15	Junior Kennedy	.20	.10	.02
☐ 17	Bump Wills	.20	.10	.02
☐ 18	Scot Thompson	.20	.10	.02
☐ 21	Jay Johnstone	.30	.15	.03
☐ 22	Bill Buckner	.50	.25	.05
☐ 23	Ryne Sandberg	7.50	3.75	.75
☐ 24	Jerry Morales	.20	.10	.02
☐ 25	Gary Woods	.20	.10	.02
☐ 28	Steve Henderson	.20	.10	.02
☐ 29	Bob Molinaro	.20	.10	.02
☐ 31	Fergie Jenkins	1.00	.50	.10
☐ 33	Al Ripley	.20	.10	.02
☐ 34	Randy Martz	.20	.10	.02
☐ 36	Mike Proly	.20	.10	.02
☐ 37	Ken Kravec	.20	.10	.02
☐ 38	Willie Hernandez	.40	.20	.04
☐ 39	Bill Campbell	.20	.10	.02
☐ 41	Dick Tidrow	.20	.10	.02
☐ 46	Lee Smith	.75	.35	.07
☐ 47	Doug Bird	.20	.10	.02
☐ 48	Dickie Noles	.20	.10	.02
☐ xx	Team Picture (unnumbered)	.40	.20	.04
☐ xx	Coaches Card (unnumbered)	.30	.15	.03

1983 Cubs Thorn Apple Valley

This set of 28 Chicago Cubs features full-color action photos on the front and was sponsored by Thorn Apple Valley. The cards measure 2 1/4" by 3 1/2". The backs provide year-by-year statistics. The cards are unnumbered except for uniform number; they are listed below by uniform with the special cards listed at the end.

	MINT	EXC	G-VG
COMPLETE SET (28)	10.00	5.00	1.00

was much better attended that year. There actually were two additional cards produced (in limited quantities) later which some collectors consider part of this set; these late issue cards show four Cubs rookies on each card.

		MINT	EXC	G-VG
COMPLETE SET (28)		15.00	7.50	1.50
COMMON PLAYER		.40	.20	.04
☐ 1	Larry Bowa	.75	.35	.07
☐ 6	Keith Moreland	.50	.25	.05
☐ 7	Jody Davis	.50	.25	.05
☐ 10	Leon Durham	.50	.25	.05
☐ 11	Ron Cey	.50	.25	.05
☐ 15	Ron Hassey	.40	.20	.04
☐ 18	Richie Hebner	.40	.20	.04
☐ 19	Dave Owen	.40	.20	.04
☐ 20	Bob Dernier	.40	.20	.04
☐ 21	Jay Johnstone	.60	.30	.06
☐ 23	Ryne Sandberg	3.50	1.75	.35
☐ 24	Scott Sanderson	.50	.25	.05
☐ 25	Gary Woods	.40	.20	.04
☐ 27	Thad Bosley	.40	.20	.04
☐ 28	Henry Cotto	.40	.20	.04
☐ 34	Steve Trout	.50	.25	.05
☐ 36	Gary Matthews	.50	.25	.05
☐ 39	George Frazier	.40	.20	.04
☐ 40	Rick Sutcliffe	1.00	.50	.10
☐ 41	Warren Brusstar	.40	.20	.04
☐ 42	Rich Bordi	.40	.20	.04
☐ 43	Dennis Eckersley	1.00	.50	.10
☐ 44	Dick Ruthven	.40	.20	.04
☐ 46	Lee Smith	.60	.30	.06
☐ 47	Rick Reuschel	.80	.40	.08
☐ 49	Tim Stoddard	.40	.20	.04
☐ xx	Coaches (unnumbered)	.40	.20	.04
☐ xx	Jim Frey MG (unnumbered)	.40	.20	.04

COMMON PLAYER		.25	.12	.02
☐ 1	Larry Bowa	.45	.22	.04
☐ 6	Keith Moreland	.35	.17	.03
☐ 7	Jody Davis	.35	.17	.03
☐ 10	Leon Durham	.35	.17	.03
☐ 11	Ron Cey	.45	.22	.04
☐ 16	Steve Lake	.25	.12	.02
☐ 20	Thad Bosley	.25	.12	.02
☐ 21	Jay Johnstone	.35	.17	.03
☐ 22	Bill Buckner	.45	.22	.04
☐ 23	Ryne Sandberg	3.00	1.50	.30
☐ 24	Jerry Morales	.25	.12	.02
☐ 25	Gary Woods	.25	.12	.02
☐ 27	Mel Hall	.60	.30	.06
☐ 29	Tom Veryzer	.25	.12	.02
☐ 30	Chuck Rainey	.25	.12	.02
☐ 31	Fergie Jenkins	.75	.35	.07
☐ 32	Craig Lefferts	.35	.17	.03
☐ 33	Joe Carter	2.50	1.25	.25
☐ 34	Steve Trout	.25	.12	.02
☐ 36	Mike Proly	.25	.12	.02
☐ 39	Bill Campbell	.25	.12	.02
☐ 41	Warren Brusstar	.25	.12	.02
☐ 44	Dick Ruthven	.25	.12	.02
☐ 46	Lee Smith	.45	.22	.04
☐ 48	Dickie Noles	.25	.12	.02
☐ xx	Manager/Coaches .... Lee Elia MG Ruben Amaro Billy Connors Duffy Dyer Fred Koenig John Vukovich (unnumbered)	.25	.12	.02
☐ xx	Team Photo .... (unnumbered)	.25	.12	.02

1985 Cubs Seven-Up

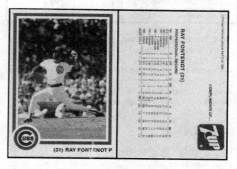

(31) RAY FONTENOT P

This 28-card set was distributed on August 14th at Wrigley Field for the game against the Expos. The cards measure 2 1/2" by 3 1/2" and were distributed wrapped in cellophane. The cards are unnumbered except for uniform number. The card backs are printed in black on white with a 7-Up logo in the upper right hand corner.

		MINT	EXC	G-VG
COMPLETE SET (28)		7.50	3.75	.75
COMMON PLAYER		.15	.07	.01
☐ 1	Larry Bowa	.35	.17	.03
☐ 6	Keith Moreland	.25	.12	.02
☐ 7	Jody Davis	.25	.12	.02
☐ 10	Leon Durham	.25	.12	.02
☐ 11	Ron Cey	.25	.12	.02
☐ 15	Davey Lopes	.25	.12	.02
☐ 16	Steve Lake	.15	.07	.01
☐ 18	Rich Hebner	.15	.07	.01
☐ 20	Bob Dernier	.15	.07	.01
☐ 21	Scott Sanderson	.15	.07	.01
☐ 22	Billy Hatcher	.25	.12	.02
☐ 23	Ryne Sandberg	2.50	1.25	.25

1984 Cubs Seven-Up

This 28-card set was sponsored by 7-Up. The cards are in full color and measure 2 1/4" by 3 1/2". The card backs are printed in black on white card stock. This set is tougher to find than the other similar Cubs sets since the Cubs were more successful (on the field) in 1984 winning their division, that is, virtually all of the cards printed were distributed during the "Baseball Card Day" promotion (August 12th) which

□ 24	Brian Dayett	.15	.07	.01
□ 25	Gary Woods	.15	.07	.01
□ 27	Thad Bosley	.15	.07	.01
□ 28	Chris Speier	.15	.07	.01
□ 31	Ray Fontenot	.15	.07	.01
□ 34	Steve Trout	.15	.07	.01
□ 36	Gary Matthews	.25	.12	.02
□ 39	George Frazier	.15	.07	.01
□ 40	Rick Sutcliffe	.60	.30	.06
□ 41	Warren Brusstar	.15	.07	.01
□ 42	Lary Sorensen	.15	.07	.01
□ 43	Dennis Eckersley	.60	.30	.06
□ 44	Dick Ruthven	.15	.07	.01
□ 46	Lee Smith	.35	.17	.03
□ xx	Jim Frey MG	.15	.07	.01
	(unnumbered)			
□ xx	Cubs Coaching Staff	.15	.07	.01
	Ruben Amaro			
	Billy Connors			
	Johnny Oates			
	John Vukovich			
	Don Zimmer			
	(unnumbered)			

1986 Cubs Gatorade

(11) RON CEY, IF

This 28-card set was given out at Wrigley Field on the Cubs' special "baseball card" promotion held July 17th for the game against the Giants. The set was sponsored by Gatorade. The cards are unnumbered except for uniform number. Card backs feature blue print on white card stock. The cards measure 2 7/8" by 4 1/4" and are in full color.

		MINT	EXC	G-VG
COMPLETE SET (28)		7.50	3.75	.75
COMMON PLAYER		.10	.05	.01
□ 4	Gene Michael MG	.20	.10	.02
□ 6	Keith Moreland	.25	.12	.02
□ 7	Jody Davis	.25	.12	.02
□ 10	Leon Durham	.25	.12	.02
□ 11	Ron Cey	.25	.12	.02
□ 12	Shawon Dunston	.75	.35	.07
□ 15	Davey Lopes	.20	.10	.02
□ 16	Terry Francona	.10	.05	.01
□ 18	Steve Christmas	.15	.07	.01
□ 19	Manny Trillo	.10	.05	.01
□ 20	Bob Dernier	.10	.05	.01
□ 21	Scott Sanderson	.10	.05	.01
□ 22	Jerry Mumphrey	.10	.05	.01
□ 23	Ryne Sandberg	2.00	1.00	.20
□ 27	Thad Bosley	.10	.05	.01
□ 28	Chris Speier	.10	.05	.01
□ 29	Steve Lake	.10	.05	.01
□ 31	Ray Fontenot	.10	.05	.01
□ 34	Steve Trout	.10	.05	.01
□ 36	Gary Matthews	.20	.10	.02
□ 39	George Frazier	.10	.05	.01
□ 40	Rick Sutcliffe	.50	.25	.05
□ 43	Dennis Eckersley	.60	.30	.06
□ 46	Lee Smith	.25	.12	.02
□ 48	Jay Baller	.10	.05	.01
□ 49	Jamie Moyer	.20	.10	.02
□ 50	Guy Hoffman	.10	.05	.01
□ xx	Coaches Card	.10	.05	.01
	(unnumbered)			

1987 Cubs David Berg

(6) KEITH MORELAND, OF/IF

This 28-card set was given out at Wrigley Field on the Cubs' special "baseball card" promotion held July 29th. The set was sponsored by David Berg Pure Beef Hot Dogs. The cards are unnumbered except for uniform number. Card backs feature red and blue print on white card stock. The cards measure 2 7/8" by 4 1/4" and are in full color.

		MINT	EXC	G-VG
COMPLETE SET (28)		7.50	3.75	.75
COMMON PLAYER		.15	.07	.01
□ 1	Dave Martinez	.25	.12	.02
□ 4	Gene Michael MG	.20	.10	.02
□ 6	Keith Moreland	.25	.12	.02
□ 7	Jody Davis	.25	.12	.02
□ 8	Andre Dawson	1.25	.60	.12
□ 10	Leon Durham	.20	.10	.02
□ 11	Jim Sundberg	.15	.07	.01
□ 12	Shawon Dunston	.40	.20	.04
□ 19	Manny Trillo	.15	.07	.01
□ 20	Bob Dernier	.15	.07	.01
□ 21	Scott Sanderson	.15	.07	.01
□ 22	Jerry Mumphrey	.15	.07	.01
□ 23	Ryne Sandberg	1.50	.75	.15
□ 24	Brian Dayett	.15	.07	.01
□ 29	Chico Walker	.25	.12	.02
□ 31	Greg Maddux	.75	.35	.07
□ 33	Frank DiPino	.15	.07	.01
□ 34	Steve Trout	.15	.07	.01
□ 36	Gary Matthews	.25	.12	.02
□ 37	Ed Lynch	.15	.07	.01
□ 39	Ron Davis	.15	.07	.01
□ 40	Rick Sutcliffe	.40	.20	.04
□ 46	Lee Smith	.25	.12	.02
□ 47	Dickie Noles	.15	.07	.01
□ 49	Jamie Moyer	.25	.12	.02
□ xx	Coaching Staff	.15	.07	.01

1988 Cubs David Berg

This 27-card set was given out at Wrigley Field with every paid admission on the Cubs' special "baseball card" promotion held August 24th. The set was sponsored by David Berg Pure Beef Hot Dogs and the Venture store chain. The cards are unnumbered except for uniform number. Card backs feature primarily black print on white card stock. The cards measure approximately 2 7/8" by 4 1/4" and are in full color.

		MINT	EXC	G-VG
COMPLETE SET (27)		7.50	3.75	.75
COMMON PLAYER		.15	.07	.01
□ 2	Vance Law	.25	.12	.02
□ 4	Don Zimmer MG	.35	.17	.03
□ 7	Jody Davis	.25	.12	.02
□ 8	Andre Dawson	.60	.30	.06

☐	9	Damon Berryhill	.60	.30	.06
☐	12	Shawon Dunston	.45	.22	.04
☐	17	Mark Grace	1.50	.75	.15
☐	18	Angel Salazar	.15	.07	.01
☐	19	Manny Trillo	.15	.07	.01
☐	21	Scott Sanderson	.15	.07	.01
☐	22	Jerry Mumphrey	.15	.07	.01
☐	23	Ryne Sandberg	1.00	.50	.10
☐	24	Gary Varsho	.25	.12	.02
☐	25	Rafael Palmeiro	.75	.35	.07
☐	28	Mitch Webster	.15	.07	.01
☐	30	Darrin Jackson	.25	.12	.02
☐	31	Greg Maddux	.50	.25	.05
☐	32	Calvin Schiraldi	.20	.10	.02
☐	33	Frank DiPino	.15	.07	.01
☐	37	Pat Perry	.15	.07	.01
☐	40	Rick Sutcliffe	.35	.17	.03
☐	41	Jeff Pico	.15	.07	.01
☐	45	Al Nipper	.15	.07	.01
☐	49	Jamie Moyer	.25	.12	.02
☐	50	Les Lancaster	.15	.07	.01
☐	54	Rich Gossage	.25	.12	.02
☐	xx	Cubs Coaching Staff	.15	.07	.01
		Joe Altobelli CO			
		Chuck Cottier CO			
		Larry Cox CO			
		Jose Martinez CO			
		Dick Pole CO			

1989 Cubs Marathon

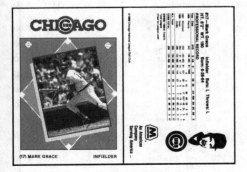

The 1989 Marathon Cubs set features 25 cards measuring 2 3/4 by 4 1/4 inches. The fronts are green and white, and feature facsimile autographs. The backs show black and white mug shots and career stats. The set was given away at the August 10, 1989 Cubs home game. The cards are numbered by the players' uniform numbers.

			MINT	EXC	G-VG
COMPLETE SET (25)			7.50	3.75	.75
COMMON PLAYER			.15	.07	.01
☐	2	Vance Law	.15	.07	.01
☐	4	Don Zimmer MG	.35	.17	.03

☐	7	Joe Girardi	.35	.17	.03
☐	8	Andre Dawson	.50	.25	.05
☐	9	Damon Berryhill	.50	.25	.05
☐	10	Lloyd McClendon	.25	.12	.02
☐	12	Shawon Dunston	.35	.17	.03
☐	15	Domingo Ramos	.15	.07	.01
☐	17	Mark Grace	1.00	.50	.10
☐	18	Dwight Smith	.75	.35	.07
☐	19	Curt Wilkerson	.15	.07	.01
☐	20	Jerome Walton	1.25	.60	.12
☐	21	Scott Sanderson	.15	.07	.01
☐	23	Ryne Sandberg	1.00	.50	.10
☐	28	Mitch Williams	.25	.12	.02
☐	31	Greg Maddux	.35	.17	.03
☐	32	Calvin Schiraldi	.15	.07	.01
☐	33	Mitch Webster	.15	.07	.01
☐	36	Mike Bielecki	.25	.12	.02
☐	39	Paul Kilgus	.15	.07	.01
☐	40	Rick Sutcliffe	.35	.17	.03
☐	41	Jeff Pico	.15	.07	.01
☐	44	Steve Wilson	.25	.12	.02
☐	50	Les Lancaster	.25	.12	.02
☐	xx	Cubs Coaches	.15	.07	.01

1954 Dan Dee

The cards in this 29-card set measure 2 1/2" by 3 5/8". Most of the cards marketed by Dan Dee in bags of potato chips in 1954 depict players from the Indians or Pirates. The Pirate players in the set are much tougher to find than the Cleveland Indians players. The pictures used for Yankee players were also employed in the Briggs and Stahl-Meyer sets. Dan Dee cards have a waxed surface, but are commonly found with product stains. Paul Smith and Walker Cooper are considered the known scarcities. The ACC designation for this set is F342.

			NRMT	VG-E	GOOD
COMPLETE SET (29)			3500.00	1750.00	400.00
COMMON PLAYER (1-29)			45.00	22.50	4.50
COMMON PIRATE PLAYER			65.00	32.50	6.50
☐	1	Bobby Avila	45.00	22.50	4.50
☐	2	Hank Bauer	65.00	32.50	6.50
☐	3	Walker Cooper	300.00	150.00	30.00
		Pittsburgh Pirates			
☐	4	Larry Doby	65.00	32.50	6.50
☐	5	Luke Easter	45.00	22.50	4.50
☐	6	Bob Feller	200.00	100.00	20.00
☐	7	Bob Friend	90.00	45.00	9.00
		Pittsburgh Pirates			
☐	8	Mike Garcia	45.00	22.50	4.50
☐	9	Sid Gordon	65.00	32.50	6.50
		Pittsburgh Pirates			
☐	10	Jim Hegan	45.00	22.50	4.50
☐	11	Gil Hodges	150.00	75.00	15.00
☐	12	Art Houtteman	45.00	22.50	4.50
☐	13	Monte Irvin	100.00	50.00	10.00
☐	14	Paul LaPalme	65.00	32.50	6.50
		Pittsburgh Pirates			
☐	15	Bob Lemon	100.00	50.00	10.00
☐	16	Al Lopez	100.00	50.00	10.00
☐	17	Mickey Mantle	900.00	450.00	90.00
☐	18	Dale Mitchell	45.00	22.50	4.50
☐	19	Phil Rizzuto	150.00	75.00	15.00
☐	20	Curt Roberts	65.00	32.50	6.50

	Pittsburgh Pirates			
☐ 21	Al Rosen	65.00	32.50	6.50
☐ 22	Red Schoendienst	125.00	60.00	12.50
☐ 23	Paul Smith	450.00	225.00	45.00
	Pittsburgh Pirates			
☐ 24	Duke Snider	200.00	100.00	20.00
☐ 25	George Strickland	45.00	22.50	4.50
☐ 26	Max Surkont	65.00	32.50	6.50
	Pittsburgh Pirates			
☐ 27	Frank Thomas	100.00	50.00	10.00
	Pittsburgh Pirates			
☐ 28	Wally Westlake	45.00	22.50	4.50
☐ 29	Early Wynn	100.00	50.00	10.00

1933 Delong

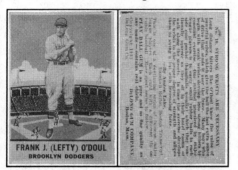

FRANK J. (LEFTY) O'DOUL
BROOKLYN DODGERS

The cards in this 24-card set measures 2" by 3". The 1933 Delong Gum set of 24 multi-colored cards was, along with the 1933 Goudey Big League series, one of the first baseball card sets issued with chewing gum. It was the only card set issued by this company. The reverse text was written by Austen Lake, who also wrote the sports tips found on the Diamond Stars series which began in 1934, leading to speculation that Delong was bought out by National Chicle. The ACC designation for this set is R333.

		EX-MT	VG-E	GOOD
COMPLETE SET (24)		9000.00	4500.00	1000.00
COMMON PLAYER (1-24)		175.00	85.00	18.00
☐ 1	Marty McManus	175.00	85.00	18.00
☐ 2	Al Simmons	300.00	150.00	30.00
☐ 3	Oscar Melillo	175.00	85.00	18.00
☐ 4	William Terry	350.00	175.00	35.00
☐ 5	Charlie Gehringer	350.00	175.00	35.00
☐ 6	Mickey Cochrane	350.00	175.00	35.00
☐ 7	Lou Gehrig	2800.00	1350.00	300.00
☐ 8	Kiki Cuyler	300.00	150.00	30.00
☐ 9	Bill Urbanski	175.00	85.00	18.00
☐ 10	Lefty O'Doul	200.00	100.00	20.00
☐ 11	Fred Lindstrom	300.00	150.00	30.00
☐ 12	Pie Traynor	350.00	175.00	35.00
☐ 13	Rabbit Maranville	300.00	150.00	30.00
☐ 14	Lefty Gomez	350.00	175.00	35.00
☐ 15	Riggs Stephenson	200.00	100.00	20.00
☐ 16	Lon Warneke	175.00	85.00	18.00
☐ 17	Pepper Martin	200.00	100.00	20.00
☐ 18	Jim Dykes	175.00	85.00	18.00
☐ 19	Chick Hafey	300.00	150.00	30.00
☐ 20	Joe Vosmik	175.00	85.00	18.00
☐ 21	Jimmie Foxx	600.00	300.00	60.00
☐ 22	Chuck Klein	350.00	175.00	35.00
☐ 23	Lefty Grove	450.00	225.00	45.00
☐ 24	Goose Goslin	300.00	150.00	30.00

1934-36 Diamond Stars

The cards in this 108-card set measure 2 3/8" by 2 7/8". The Diamond Stars set produced by National Chicle from 1934-36 is also commonly known as

R327 (ACC). The year of production can be determined by the statistics contained on the back of the card. There are at least 168 possible front/back combinations counting blue (B) and green (G) backs over all three years. The last twelve cards are repeat players and are quite scarce. A blank backed proof sheet of 12 additional cards was recently discovered and has been reproduced from this original artwork and assigned numbers and text by Sport Americana. The checklist below lists the year(s) and back color(s) for the cards. Cards 32 through 72 were issued only in 1935 with green ink on back. Cards 73 through 84 were issued three ways: 35B, 35G, and 36B. Card numbers 85 through 108 were issued only in 1936 with blue ink on back. The complete set price below refers to the set of all variations listed explicitly below.

		EX-MT	VG-E	GOOD
COMPLETE SET (114)		14000.00	7000.00	1750.00
COMMON PLAYER (1-31)		45.00	22.50	4.50
COMMON PLAYER (32-72)		50.00	25.00	5.00
COMMON PLAYER (73-84)		60.00	30.00	6.00
COMMON PLAYER (85-96)		90.00	45.00	9.00
COMMON PLAYER (97-108)		300.00	150.00	30.00
☐ 1	Lefty Grove .... (34G, 35G)	750.00	75.00	15.00
☐ 2A	Al Simmons .... (34G, 35G) (Sox on uniform)	125.00	60.00	12.50
☐ 2B	Al Simmons .... (36B) (No name on uniform)	175.00	85.00	18.00
☐ 3	Rabbit Maranville .... (34G, 35G)	100.00	50.00	10.00
☐ 4	Buddy Myer .... (34G, 35G, 36B)	45.00	22.50	4.50
☐ 5	Tommy Bridges .... (34G, 35G, 36B)	45.00	22.50	4.50
☐ 6	Max Bishop .... (34G, 35G)	45.00	22.50	4.50
☐ 7	Lew Fonseca .... (34G, 35G)	45.00	22.50	4.50
☐ 8	Joe Vosmik .... (34G, 35G, 36B)	45.00	22.50	4.50
☐ 9	Mickey Cochrane .... (34G, 35G, 36B)	125.00	60.00	12.50
☐ 10A	Leroy Mahaffey .... (34G, 35G) (A's on uniform)	45.00	22.50	4.50
☐ 10B	Leroy Mahaffey .... (36B) (No name on uniform)	75.00	37.50	7.50
☐ 11	Bill Dickey .... (34G, 35G)	200.00	100.00	20.00
☐ 12	F. Walker 34G, 35G, 36B)	45.00	22.50	4.50
☐ 13	George Blaeholder .... (34G, 35G)	45.00	22.50	4.50
☐ 14	Bill Terry .... (34G, 35G)	125.00	60.00	12.50
☐ 15	Dick Bartell .... (34G, 35G)	45.00	22.50	4.50
☐ 16	Lloyd Waner .... (34G, 35G, 36B)	100.00	50.00	10.00
☐ 17	Frank Frisch .... (34G, 35G)	125.00	60.00	12.50
☐ 18	Chick Hafey .... (34G, 35G)	100.00	50.00	10.00
☐ 19	Van Lingle Mungo	45.00	22.50	4.50

	(34G, 35G)			
☐ 20	Frank Hogan	45.00	22.50	4.50
	(34G, 35G)			
☐ 21	Johnny Vergez	45.00	22.50	4.50
	(34G, 35G)			
☐ 22	Jimmy Wilson	45.00	22.50	4.50
	(34G, 35G, 36B)			
☐ 23	Bill Hallahan	45.00	22.50	4.50
	(34G, 35G)			
☐ 24	Earl Adams	45.00	22.50	4.50
	(34G, 35G)			
☐ 25	Wally Berger	60.00	30.00	6.00
	(35G)			
☐ 26	Pepper Martin	60.00	30.00	6.00
	35G, 36B)			
☐ 27	Pie Traynor (35G)	150.00	75.00	15.00
☐ 28	Al Lopez (35G)	125.00	60.00	12.50
☐ 29	Red Rolfe (35G)	60.00	30.00	6.00
☐ 30A	Heine Manush	125.00	60.00	12.50
	(35G)			
	(W on sleeve)			
☐ 30B	Heine Manush	175.00	85.00	18.00
	(36B)			
	(No W on sleeve)			
☐ 31	Kiki Cuyler	100.00	50.00	10.00
	(35G, 36B)			
☐ 32	Sam Rice	100.00	50.00	10.00
☐ 33	Schoolboy Rowe	50.00	25.00	5.00
☐ 34	Stan Hack	50.00	25.00	5.00
☐ 35	Earl Averill	100.00	50.00	10.00
☐ 36A	"Earnie" Lombardi	200.00	100.00	20.00
	(sic, Ernie)			
☐ 36B	"Ernie" Lombardi	100.00	50.00	10.00
☐ 37	Billy Urbanski	50.00	25.00	5.00
☐ 38	Ben Chapman	60.00	30.00	6.00
☐ 39	Carl Hubbell	125.00	60.00	12.50
☐ 40	Blondy Ryan	50.00	25.00	5.00
☐ 41	Harvey Hendrick	50.00	25.00	5.00
☐ 42	Jimmy Dykes	60.00	30.00	6.00
☐ 43	Ted Lyons	100.00	50.00	10.00
☐ 44	Rogers Hornsby	300.00	150.00	30.00
☐ 45	Jo Jo White	50.00	25.00	5.00
☐ 46	Red Lucas	50.00	25.00	5.00
☐ 47	Bob Bolton	50.00	25.00	5.00
☐ 48	Rick Ferrell	100.00	50.00	10.00
☐ 49	Buck Jordan	50.00	25.00	5.00
☐ 50	Mel Ott	200.00	100.00	20.00
☐ 51	Burgess Whitehead	50.00	25.00	5.00
☐ 52	Tuck Stainback	50.00	25.00	5.00
☐ 53	Oscar Melillo	50.00	25.00	5.00
☐ 54A	"Hank" Greenburg	350.00	175.00	35.00
	(sic, Greenberg)			
☐ 54B	"Hank" Greenberg	175.00	85.00	18.00
☐ 55	Tony Cuccinello	50.00	25.00	5.00
☐ 56	Gus Suhr	50.00	25.00	5.00
☐ 57	Cy Blanton	50.00	25.00	5.00
☐ 58	Glenn Myatt	50.00	25.00	5.00
☐ 59	Jim Bottomley	100.00	50.00	10.00
☐ 60	Red Ruffing	125.00	60.00	12.50
☐ 61	Bill Werber	50.00	25.00	5.00
☐ 62	Fred Frankhouse	50.00	25.00	5.00
☐ 63	Travis Jackson	100.00	50.00	10.00
☐ 64	Jimmy Foxx	300.00	150.00	30.00
☐ 65	Zeke Bonura	50.00	25.00	5.00
☐ 66	Ducky Medwick	125.00	60.00	12.50
☐ 67	Marvin Owen	50.00	25.00	5.00
☐ 68	Sam Leslie	50.00	25.00	5.00
☐ 69	Earl Grace	50.00	25.00	5.00
☐ 70	Hal Trosky	60.00	30.00	6.00
☐ 71	Ossie Bluege	50.00	25.00	5.00
☐ 72	Tony Piet	50.00	25.00	5.00
☐ 73	Fritz Ostermueller	60.00	30.00	6.00
☐ 74	Tony Lazzeri	90.00	45.00	9.00
☐ 75	Jack Burns	60.00	30.00	6.00
☐ 76	Billy Rogell	60.00	30.00	6.00
☐ 77	Charlie Gehringer	150.00	75.00	15.00
☐ 78	Joe Kuhel	60.00	30.00	6.00
☐ 79	Willis Hudlin	60.00	30.00	6.00
☐ 80	Lou Chiozza	60.00	30.00	6.00
☐ 81	Bill Delancey	60.00	30.00	6.00
☐ 82A	Johnny Babich	60.00	30.00	6.00
	(Dodgers on uniform; 35G, 35B)			
☐ 82B	Johnny Babich	90.00	45.00	9.00
	(No name on uniform; 36B)			
☐ 83	Paul Waner	150.00	75.00	15.00
☐ 84	Sam Byrd	60.00	30.00	6.00
☐ 85	Moose Solters	90.00	45.00	9.00
☐ 86	Frank Crosetti	125.00	60.00	12.50
☐ 87	Steve O'Neill	90.00	45.00	9.00
☐ 88	George Selkirk	125.00	60.00	12.50
☐ 89	Joe Stripp	90.00	45.00	9.00
☐ 90	Ray Hayworth	90.00	45.00	9.00
☐ 91	Bucky Harris	175.00	85.00	18.00
☐ 92	Ethan Allen	90.00	45.00	9.00
☐ 93	General Crowder	90.00	45.00	9.00
☐ 94	Wes Ferrell	125.00	60.00	12.50
☐ 95	Luke Appling	200.00	100.00	20.00
☐ 96	Lew Riggs	90.00	45.00	9.00
☐ 97	Al Lopez	500.00	250.00	50.00
☐ 98	Schoolboy Rowe	350.00	175.00	35.00
☐ 99	Pie Traynor	600.00	300.00	60.00
☐ 100	Earl Averill	500.00	250.00	50.00
☐ 101	Dick Bartell	300.00	150.00	30.00
☐ 102	Van Lingle Mungo	300.00	150.00	30.00
☐ 103	Bill Dickey	750.00	375.00	75.00
☐ 104	Red Rolfe	300.00	150.00	30.00
☐ 105	Ernie Lombardi	500.00	250.00	50.00
☐ 106	Red Lucas	300.00	150.00	30.00
☐ 107	Stan Hack	300.00	150.00	30.00
☐ 108	Wally Berger	350.00	175.00	35.00

1988 Domino's Tigers

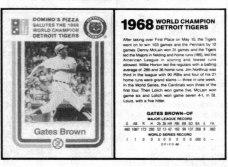

This rather unattractive set commemorates the 20th anniversary of the Detroit Tigers' World Championship season in 1968. The card stock used is rather thin. The cards measure approximately 2 1/2" by 3 1/2". There are a number of errors in the set including biographical errors, misspellings, and photo misidentifications. Players are pictured in black and white inside a red and blue horseshoe. The numerous factual errors in the set detract from the set's collectibility in the eyes of many collectors.

		MINT	EXC	G-VG
COMPLETE SET (28)		6.00	3.00	.60
COMMON PLAYER (1-28)		.10	.05	.01
☐ 1	Gates Brown	.15	.07	.01
☐ 2	Norm Cash	.25	.12	.02
☐ 3	Wayne Comer	.10	.05	.01
☐ 4	Pat Dobson	.15	.07	.01
☐ 5	Bill Freehan	.20	.10	.02
☐ 6	Ernie Harwell	.15	.07	.01
	(announcer)			
☐ 7	John Hiller	.15	.07	.01
☐ 8	Willie Horton	.15	.07	.01
☐ 9	Al Kaline	.90	.45	.09
☐ 10	Fred Lasher	.10	.05	.01
☐ 11	Mickey Lolich	.30	.15	.03
☐ 12	Tom Matchick	.10	.05	.01
☐ 13	Ed Mathews	.60	.30	.06
☐ 14	Dick McAuliffe	.10	.05	.01
☐ 15	Denny McLain	.35	.17	.03
☐ 16	Don McMahon	.15	.07	.01
☐ 17	Jim Northrup	.15	.07	.01
☐ 18	Ray Oyler	.10	.05	.01
☐ 19	Daryl Patterson	.10	.05	.01
☐ 20	Jim Price	.10	.05	.01
☐ 21	Joe Sparma	.10	.05	.01
☐ 22	Mickey Stanley	.20	.10	.02
☐ 23	Dick Tracewski	.10	.05	.01
☐ 24	Jon Warden	.10	.05	.01
☐ 25	Don Wert	.10	.05	.01
☐ 26	Earl Wilson	.15	.07	.01
☐ 27	Pizza Buck Coupon	.10	.05	.01
☐ 28	Title Card	.10	.05	.01
	Old Timers Game 1988			

1981 Donruss

The cards in this 605-card set measure 2 1/2" by 3 1/2". In 1981 Donruss launched itself into the baseball card market with a set containing 600 numbered cards and five unnumbered checklists. Even though the five checklist cards are unnumbered, they are numbered below (601-605) for convenience in reference. The cards are printed on thin stock and more than one pose exists for several popular players. The numerous errors of the first print run were later corrected by the company. These are marked P1 and P2 in the checklist below.

		MINT	EXC	G-VG
	COMPLETE SET (P1)	33.00	15.00	3.00
	COMPLETE SET (P2)	27.00	13.50	2.70
	COMMON PLAYER (1-605)	.03	.01	.00
☐	1 Ozzie Smith	.75	.15	.03
☐	2 Rollie Fingers	.35	.17	.03
☐	3 Rick Wise	.03	.01	.00
☐	4 Gene Richards	.03	.01	.00
☐	5 Alan Trammell	.45	.22	.04
☐	6 Tom Brookens	.03	.01	.00
☐	7A Duffy Dyer P1 1980 batting average has decimal point	.10	.05	.01
☐	7B Duffy Dyer P2 1980 batting average has no decimal point	.06	.03	.00
☐	8 Mark Fidrych	.10	.05	.01
☐	9 Dave Rozema	.03	.01	.00
☐	10 Ricky Peters	.03	.01	.00
☐	11 Mike Schmidt	1.50	.75	.15
☐	12 Willie Stargell	.40	.20	.04
☐	13 Tim Foli	.03	.01	.00
☐	14 Manny Sanguillen	.06	.03	.00
☐	15 Grant Jackson	.03	.01	.00
☐	16 Eddie Solomon	.03	.01	.00
☐	17 Omar Moreno	.03	.01	.00
☐	18 Joe Morgan	.45	.22	.04
☐	19 Rafael Landestoy	.03	.01	.00
☐	20 Bruce Bochy	.03	.01	.00
☐	21 Joe Sambito	.03	.01	.00
☐	22 Manny Trillo	.03	.01	.00
☐	23A Dave Smith P1 Line box around stats is not complete	.35	.17	.03
☐	23B Dave Smith P2 Box totally encloses stats at top	.35	.17	.03
☐	24 Terry Puhl	.06	.03	.00
☐	25 Bump Wills	.03	.01	.00
☐	26A John Ellis P1 ERR Photo on front shows Danny Walton	.60	.30	.06
☐	26B John Ellis P2 COR	.10	.05	.01
☐	27 Jim Kern	.03	.01	.00
☐	28 Richie Zisk	.06	.03	.00
☐	29 John Mayberry	.06	.03	.00
☐	30 Bob Davis	.03	.01	.00
☐	31 Jackson Todd	.03	.01	.00
☐	32 Alvis Woods	.03	.01	.00
☐	33 Steve Carlton	.65	.30	.06
☐	34 Lee Mazzilli	.03	.01	.00
☐	35 John Stearns	.03	.01	.00
☐	36 Roy Lee Jackson	.03	.01	.00
☐	37 Mike Scott	1.00	.50	.10

☐	38 Lamar Johnson	.03	.01	.00
☐	39 Kevin Bell	.03	.01	.00
☐	40 Ed Farmer	.03	.01	.00
☐	41 Ross Baumgarten	.03	.01	.00
☐	42 Leo Sutherland	.03	.01	.00
☐	43 Dan Meyer	.03	.01	.00
☐	44 Ron Reed	.03	.01	.00
☐	45 Mario Mendoza	.03	.01	.00
☐	46 Rick Honeycutt	.03	.01	.00
☐	47 Glenn Abbott	.03	.01	.00
☐	48 Leon Roberts	.03	.01	.00
☐	49 Rod Carew	.65	.30	.06
☐	50 Bert Campaneris	.06	.03	.00
☐	51A Tom Donahue P1 ERR Name on front misspelled Donahue	.15	.07	.01
☐	51B Tom Donohue P2 COR	.10	.05	.01
☐	52 Dave Frost	.03	.01	.00
☐	53 Ed Halicki	.03	.01	.00
☐	54 Dan Ford	.03	.01	.00
☐	55 Garry Maddox	.06	.03	.00
☐	56A Steve Garvey P1 "Surpassed 25 HR"	1.25	.60	.12
☐	56B Steve Garvey P2 "Surpassed 21 HR"	.65	.30	.06
☐	57 Bill Russell	.06	.03	.00
☐	58 Don Sutton	.30	.15	.03
☐	59 Reggie Smith	.10	.05	.01
☐	60 Rick Monday	.06	.03	.00
☐	61 Ray Knight	.10	.05	.01
☐	62 Johnny Bench	.75	.35	.07
☐	63 Mario Soto	.10	.05	.01
☐	64 Doug Bair	.03	.01	.00
☐	65 George Foster	.20	.10	.02
☐	66 Jeff Burroughs	.06	.03	.00
☐	67 Keith Hernandez	.35	.17	.03
☐	68 Tom Herr	.15	.07	.01
☐	69 Bob Forsch	.06	.03	.00
☐	70 John Fulgham	.03	.01	.00
☐	71A Bobby Bonds P1 ERR 986 lifetime HR	.40	.20	.04
☐	71B Bobby Bonds P2 COR 326 lifetime HR	.15	.07	.01
☐	72A Rennie Stennett P1 "breaking broke leg"	.10	.05	.01
☐	72B Rennie Stennett P2 Word "broke" deleted	.06	.03	.00
☐	73 Joe Strain	.03	.01	.00
☐	74 Ed Whitson	.06	.03	.00
☐	75 Tom Griffin	.03	.01	.00
☐	76 Billy North	.03	.01	.00
☐	77 Gene Garber	.03	.01	.00
☐	78 Mike Hargrove	.06	.03	.00
☐	79 Dave Rosello	.03	.01	.00
☐	80 Ron Hassey	.06	.03	.00
☐	81 Sid Monge	.03	.01	.00
☐	82A Joe Charboneau P1 '78 highlights, "For some reason"	.15	.07	.01
☐	82B Joe Charboneau P2 phrase "For some reason" deleted	.10	.05	.01
☐	83 Cecil Cooper	.15	.07	.01
☐	84 Sal Bando	.06	.03	.00
☐	85 Moose Haas	.06	.03	.00
☐	86 Mike Caldwell	.03	.01	.00
☐	87A Larry Hisle P1 '77 highlights, line ends with "28 RBI"	.15	.07	.01
☐	87B Larry Hisle P2 correct line "28 HR"	.10	.05	.01
☐	88 Luis Gomez	.03	.01	.00
☐	89 Larry Parrish	.06	.03	.00
☐	90 Gary Carter	.50	.25	.05
☐	91 Bill Gullickson	.25	.12	.02
☐	92 Fred Norman	.03	.01	.00
☐	93 Tommy Hutton	.03	.01	.00
☐	94 Carl Yastrzemski	1.00	.50	.10
☐	95 Glenn Hoffman	.03	.01	.00
☐	96 Dennis Eckersley	.25	.12	.02
☐	97A Tom Burgmeier P1 ERR Throws: Right	.10	.05	.01
☐	97B Tom Burgmeier P2 COR Throws: Left	.06	.03	.00
☐	98 Win Remmerswaal	.03	.01	.00
☐	99 Bob Horner	.15	.07	.01
☐	100 George Brett	.90	.45	.09
☐	101 Dave Chalk	.03	.01	.00
☐	102 Dennis Leonard	.06	.03	.00
☐	103 Renie Martin	.03	.01	.00
☐	104 Amos Otis	.10	.05	.01
☐	105 Graig Nettles	.15	.07	.01
☐	106 Eric Soderholm	.03	.01	.00
☐	107 Tommy John	.20	.10	.02

☐ 108 Tom Underwood	.03	.01	.00
☐ 109 Lou Piniella	.10	.05	.01
☐ 110 Mickey Klutts	.03	.01	.00
☐ 111 Bobby Murcer	.10	.05	.01
☐ 112 Eddie Murray	.80	.40	.08
☐ 113 Rick Dempsey	.06	.03	.00
☐ 114 Scott McGregor	.06	.03	.00
☐ 115 Ken Singleton	.10	.05	.01
☐ 116 Gary Roenicke	.03	.01	.00
☐ 117 Dave Revering	.03	.01	.00
☐ 118 Mike Norris	.03	.01	.00
☐ 119 Rickey Henderson	3.00	1.50	.30
☐ 120 Mike Heath	.03	.01	.00
☐ 121 Dave Cash	.03	.01	.00
☐ 122 Randy Jones	.03	.01	.00
☐ 123 Eric Rasmussen	.03	.01	.00
☐ 124 Jerry Mumphrey	.03	.01	.00
☐ 125 Richie Hebner	.03	.01	.00
☐ 126 Mark Wagner	.03	.01	.00
☐ 127 Jack Morris	.30	.15	.03
☐ 128 Dan Petry	.10	.05	.01
☐ 129 Bruce Robbins	.03	.01	.00
☐ 130 Champ Summers	.03	.01	.00
☐ 131A Pete Rose P1	2.00	1.00	.20
last line ends with "see card 251"			
☐ 131B Pete Rose P2	1.25	.60	.12
last line corrected "see card 371"			
☐ 132 Willie Stargell	.40	.20	.04
☐ 133 Ed Ott	.03	.01	.00
☐ 134 Jim Bibby	.03	.01	.00
☐ 135 Bert Blyleven	.20	.10	.02
☐ 136 Dave Parker	.30	.15	.03
☐ 137 Bill Robinson	.06	.03	.00
☐ 138 Enos Cabell	.03	.01	.00
☐ 139 Dave Bergman	.03	.01	.00
☐ 140 J.R. Richard	.10	.05	.01
☐ 141 Ken Forsch	.03	.01	.00
☐ 142 Larry Bowa UER	.15	.07	.01
(shortshop on front)			
☐ 143 Frank LaCorte UER	.03	.01	.00
(photo actually Randy Niemann)			
☐ 144 Denny Walling	.03	.01	.00
☐ 145 Buddy Bell	.15	.07	.01
☐ 146 Ferguson Jenkins	.20	.10	.02
☐ 147 Danny Darwin	.03	.01	.00
☐ 148 John Grubb	.03	.01	.00
☐ 149 Alfredo Griffin	.10	.05	.01
☐ 150 Jerry Garvin	.03	.01	.00
☐ 151 Paul Mirabella	.03	.01	.00
☐ 152 Rick Bosetti	.03	.01	.00
☐ 153 Dick Ruthven	.03	.01	.00
☐ 154 Frank Taveras	.03	.01	.00
☐ 155 Craig Swan	.03	.01	.00
☐ 156 Jeff Reardon	.75	.35	.07
☐ 157 Steve Henderson	.03	.01	.00
☐ 158 Jim Morrison	.03	.01	.00
☐ 159 Glenn Borgmann	.03	.01	.00
☐ 160 LaMarr Hoyt	.25	.12	.02
☐ 161 Rich Wortham	.03	.01	.00
☐ 162 Thad Bosley	.03	.01	.00
☐ 163 Julio Cruz	.03	.01	.00
☐ 164A Del Unser P1	.10	.05	.01
no "3B" heading			
☐ 164B Del Unser P2	.06	.03	.00
Batting record on back corrected ("3B")			
☐ 165 Jim Anderson	.03	.01	.00
☐ 166 Jim Beattie	.03	.01	.00
☐ 167 Shane Rawley	.06	.03	.00
☐ 168 Joe Simpson	.03	.01	.00
☐ 169 Rod Carew	.65	.30	.06
☐ 170 Fred Patek	.06	.03	.00
☐ 171 Frank Tanana	.10	.05	.01
☐ 172 Alfredo Martinez	.03	.01	.00
☐ 173 Chris Knapp	.03	.01	.00
☐ 174 Joe Rudi	.06	.03	.00
☐ 175 Greg Luzinski	.15	.07	.01
☐ 176 Steve Garvey	.65	.30	.06
☐ 177 Joe Ferguson	.03	.01	.00
☐ 178 Bob Welch	.15	.07	.01
☐ 179 Dusty Baker	.10	.05	.01
☐ 180 Rudy Law	.03	.01	.00
☐ 181 Dave Concepcion	.15	.07	.01
☐ 182 Johnny Bench	.75	.35	.07
☐ 183 Mike LaCoss	.03	.01	.00
☐ 184 Ken Griffey	.12	.06	.01
☐ 185 Dave Collins	.03	.01	.00
☐ 186 Brian Asselstine	.03	.01	.00
☐ 187 Garry Templeton	.10	.05	.01
☐ 188 Mike Phillips	.03	.01	.00
☐ 189 Pete Vuckovich	.06	.03	.00
☐ 190 John Urrea	.03	.01	.00
☐ 191 Tony Scott	.03	.01	.00
☐ 192 Darrell Evans	.15	.07	.01
☐ 193 Milt May	.03	.01	.00
☐ 194 Bob Knepper	.06	.03	.00
☐ 195 Randy Moffitt	.03	.01	.00
☐ 196 Larry Herndon	.03	.01	.00
☐ 197 Rick Camp	.03	.01	.00
☐ 198 Andre Thornton	.06	.03	.00
☐ 199 Tom Veryzer	.03	.01	.00
☐ 200 Gary Alexander	.03	.01	.00
☐ 201 Rick Waits	.03	.01	.00
☐ 202 Rick Manning	.03	.01	.00
☐ 203 Paul Molitor	.35	.17	.03
☐ 204 Jim Gantner	.06	.03	.00
☐ 205 Paul Mitchell	.03	.01	.00
☐ 206 Reggie Cleveland	.03	.01	.00
☐ 207 Sixto Lezcano	.03	.01	.00
☐ 208 Bruce Benedict	.03	.01	.00
☐ 209 Rodney Scott	.03	.01	.00
☐ 210 John Tamargo	.03	.01	.00
☐ 211 Bill Lee	.06	.03	.00
☐ 212 Andre Dawson	.40	.20	.04
☐ 213 Rowland Office	.03	.01	.00
☐ 214 Carl Yastrzemski	1.00	.50	.10
☐ 215 Jerry Remy	.03	.01	.00
☐ 216 Mike Torrez	.03	.01	.00
☐ 217 Skip Lockwood	.03	.01	.00
☐ 218 Fred Lynn	.20	.10	.02
☐ 219 Chris Chambliss	.10	.05	.01
☐ 220 Willie Aikens	.03	.01	.00
☐ 221 John Wathan	.10	.05	.01
☐ 222 Dan Quisenberry	.15	.07	.01
☐ 223 Willie Wilson	.15	.07	.01
☐ 224 Clint Hurdle	.03	.01	.00
☐ 225 Bob Watson	.06	.03	.00
☐ 226 Jim Spencer	.03	.01	.00
☐ 227 Ron Guidry	.20	.10	.02
☐ 228 Reggie Jackson	1.00	.50	.10
☐ 229 Oscar Gamble	.06	.03	.00
☐ 230 Jeff Cox	.03	.01	.00
☐ 231 Luis Tiant	.10	.05	.01
☐ 232 Rich Dauer	.03	.01	.00
☐ 233 Dan Graham	.03	.01	.00
☐ 234 Mike Flanagan	.10	.05	.01
☐ 235 John Lowenstein	.03	.01	.00
☐ 236 Benny Ayala	.03	.01	.00
☐ 237 Wayne Gross	.03	.01	.00
☐ 238 Rick Langford	.03	.01	.00
☐ 239 Tony Armas	.10	.05	.01
☐ 240A Bob Lacy P1 ERR	.30	.15	.03
Name misspelled Bob "Lacy"			
☐ 240B Bob Lacey P2 COR	.10	.05	.01
☐ 241 Gene Tenace	.06	.03	.00
☐ 242 Bob Shirley	.03	.01	.00
☐ 243 Gary Lucas	.06	.03	.00
☐ 244 Jerry Turner	.03	.01	.00
☐ 245 John Wockenfuss	.03	.01	.00
☐ 246 Stan Papi	.03	.01	.00
☐ 247 Milt Wilcox	.03	.01	.00
☐ 248 Dan Schatzeder	.03	.01	.00
☐ 249 Steve Kemp	.10	.05	.01
☐ 250 Jim Lentine	.03	.01	.00
☐ 251 Pete Rose	1.25	.60	.12
☐ 252 Bill Madlock	.15	.07	.01
☐ 253 Dale Berra	.03	.01	.00
☐ 254 Kent Tekulve	.06	.03	.00
☐ 255 Enrique Romo	.03	.01	.00
☐ 256 Mike Easler	.06	.03	.00
☐ 257 Chuck Tanner MG	.06	.03	.00
☐ 258 Art Howe	.10	.05	.01
☐ 259 Alan Ashby	.03	.01	.00
☐ 260 Nolan Ryan	1.75	.85	.17
☐ 261A Vern Ruhle P1 ERR	.60	.30	.06
Photo on front actually Ken Forsch			
☐ 261B Vern Ruhle P2 COR	.10	.05	.01
☐ 262 Bob Boone	.20	.10	.02
☐ 263 Cesar Cedeno	.10	.05	.01
☐ 264 Jeff Leonard	.15	.07	.01
☐ 265 Pat Putnam	.03	.01	.00
☐ 266 Jon Matlack	.06	.03	.00
☐ 267 Dave Rajsich	.03	.01	.00
☐ 268 Billy Sample	.03	.01	.00
☐ 269 Damaso Garcia	.10	.05	.01
☐ 270 Tom Buskey	.03	.01	.00
☐ 271 Joey McLaughlin	.03	.01	.00
☐ 272 Barry Bonnell	.03	.01	.00
☐ 273 Tug McGraw	.10	.05	.01
☐ 274 Mike Jorgensen	.03	.01	.00
☐ 275 Pat Zachry	.03	.01	.00
☐ 276 Neil Allen	.06	.03	.00
☐ 277 Joel Youngblood	.03	.01	.00
☐ 278 Greg Pryor	.03	.01	.00
☐ 279 Britt Burns	.15	.07	.01

☐ 280	Rich Dotson	.35	.17	.03
☐ 281	Chet Lemon	.06	.03	.00
☐ 282	Rusty Kuntz	.03	.01	.00
☐ 283	Ted Cox	.03	.01	.00
☐ 284	Sparky Lyle	.10	.05	.01
☐ 285	Larry Cox	.03	.01	.00
☐ 286	Floyd Bannister	.06	.03	.00
☐ 287	Byron McLaughlin	.03	.01	.00
☐ 288	Rodney Craig	.03	.01	.00
☐ 289	Bobby Grich	.10	.05	.01
☐ 290	Dickie Thon	.10	.05	.01
☐ 291	Mark Clear	.06	.03	.00
☐ 292	Dave Lemanczyk	.03	.01	.00
☐ 293	Jason Thompson	.03	.01	.00
☐ 294	Rick Miller	.03	.01	.00
☐ 295	Lonnie Smith	.15	.07	.01
☐ 296	Ron Cey	.10	.05	.01
☐ 297	Steve Yeager	.03	.01	.00
☐ 298	Bobby Castillo	.03	.01	.00
☐ 299	Manny Mota	.06	.03	.00
☐ 300	Jay Johnstone	.06	.03	.00
☐ 301	Dan Driessen	.03	.01	.00
☐ 302	Joe Nolan	.03	.01	.00
☐ 303	Paul Householder	.03	.01	.00
☐ 304	Harry Spilman	.03	.01	.00
☐ 305	Cesar Geronimo	.03	.01	.00
☐ 306A	Gary Mathews P1 ERR . Name misspelled	.30	.15	.03
☐ 306B	Gary Matthews P2 COR	.10	.05	.01
☐ 307	Ken Reitz	.03	.01	.00
☐ 308	Ted Simmons	.15	.07	.01
☐ 309	John Littlefield	.03	.01	.00
☐ 310	George Frazier	.03	.01	.00
☐ 311	Dane Iorg	.03	.01	.00
☐ 312	Mike Ivie	.03	.01	.00
☐ 313	Dennis Littlejohn	.03	.01	.00
☐ 314	Gary Lavelle	.03	.01	.00
☐ 315	Jack Clark	.30	.15	.03
☐ 316	Jim Wohlford	.03	.01	.00
☐ 317	Rick Matula	.03	.01	.00
☐ 318	Toby Harrah	.06	.03	.00
☐ 319A	Dwane Kuiper P1 ERR .. Name misspelled	.15	.07	.01
☐ 319B	Duane Kuiper P2 COR .	.10	.05	.01
☐ 320	Len Barker	.03	.01	.00
☐ 321	Victor Cruz	.03	.01	.00
☐ 322	Dell Alston	.03	.01	.00
☐ 323	Robin Yount	1.00	.50	.10
☐ 324	Charlie Moore	.03	.01	.00
☐ 325	Lary Sorensen	.03	.01	.00
☐ 326A	Gorman Thomas P1 2nd line on back: "30 HR mark 4th"	.30	.15	.03
☐ 326B	Gorman Thomas P2 "30 HR mark 3rd"	.10	.05	.01
☐ 327	Bob Rodgers MG	.06	.03	.00
☐ 328	Phil Niekro	.30	.15	.03
☐ 329	Chris Speier	.03	.01	.00
☐ 330A	Steve Rodgers P1 ERR Name misspelled	.30	.15	.03
☐ 330B	Steve Rogers P2 COR ..	.10	.05	.01
☐ 331	Woodie Fryman	.03	.01	.00
☐ 332	Warren Cromartie	.03	.01	.00
☐ 333	Jerry White	.03	.01	.00
☐ 334	Tony Perez	.20	.10	.02
☐ 335	Carlton Fisk	.40	.20	.04
☐ 336	Dick Drago	.03	.01	.00
☐ 337	Steve Renko	.03	.01	.00
☐ 338	Jim Rice	.30	.15	.03
☐ 339	Jerry Royster	.03	.01	.00
☐ 340	Frank White	.10	.05	.01
☐ 341	Jamie Quirk	.03	.01	.00
☐ 342A	Paul Spittorff P1 ERR ... Name misspelled	.15	.07	.01
☐ 342B	Paul Splittorff P2 COR	.10	.05	.01
☐ 343	Marty Pattin	.03	.01	.00
☐ 344	Pete LaCock	.03	.01	.00
☐ 345	Willie Randolph	.10	.05	.01
☐ 346	Rick Cerone	.06	.03	.00
☐ 347	Rich Gossage	.20	.10	.02
☐ 348	Reggie Jackson	1.00	.50	.10
☐ 349	Ruppert Jones	.03	.01	.00
☐ 350	Dave McKay	.03	.01	.00
☐ 351	Yogi Berra CO	.20	.10	.02
☐ 352	Doug DeCinces	.06	.03	.00
☐ 353	Jim Palmer	.60	.30	.06
☐ 354	Tippy Martinez	.03	.01	.00
☐ 355	Al Bumbry	.03	.01	.00
☐ 356	Earl Weaver MG	.10	.05	.01
☐ 357A	Bob Picciolo P1 ERR .... Name misspelled	.15	.07	.01
☐ 357B	Rob Picciolo P2 COR ...	.06	.03	.00
☐ 358	Matt Keough	.03	.01	.00
☐ 359	Dwayne Murphy	.03	.01	.00
☐ 360	Brian Kingman	.03	.01	.00
☐ 361	Bill Fahey	.03	.01	.00
☐ 362	Steve Mura	.03	.01	.00
☐ 363	Dennis Kinney	.03	.01	.00
☐ 364	Dave Winfield	.50	.25	.05
☐ 365	Lou Whitaker	.30	.15	.03
☐ 366	Lance Parrish	.25	.12	.02
☐ 367	Tim Corcoran	.03	.01	.00
☐ 368	Pat Underwood	.03	.01	.00
☐ 369	Al Cowens	.06	.03	.00
☐ 370	Sparky Anderson MG	.10	.05	.01
☐ 371	Pete Rose	1.25	.60	.12
☐ 372	Phil Garner	.03	.01	.00
☐ 373	Steve Nicosia	.03	.01	.00
☐ 374	John Candelaria	.10	.05	.01
☐ 375	Don Robinson	.06	.03	.00
☐ 376	Lee Lacy	.03	.01	.00
☐ 377	John Milner	.03	.01	.00
☐ 378	Craig Reynolds	.03	.01	.00
☐ 379A	Luis Pujois P1 ERR Name misspelled	.15	.07	.01
☐ 379B	Luis Pujols P2 COR	.06	.03	.00
☐ 380	Joe Niekro	.10	.05	.01
☐ 381	Joaquin Andujar	.10	.05	.01
☐ 382	Keith Moreland	.30	.15	.03
☐ 383	Jose Cruz	.10	.05	.01
☐ 384	Bill Virdon MG	.06	.03	.00
☐ 385	Jim Sundberg	.06	.03	.00
☐ 386	Doc Medich	.03	.01	.00
☐ 387	Al Oliver	.12	.06	.01
☐ 388	Jim Norris	.03	.01	.00
☐ 389	Bob Bailor	.03	.01	.00
☐ 390	Ernie Whitt	.10	.05	.01
☐ 391	Otto Velez	.03	.01	.00
☐ 392	Roy Howell	.03	.01	.00
☐ 393	Bob Walk	.30	.15	.03
☐ 394	Doug Flynn	.03	.01	.00
☐ 395	Pete Falcone	.03	.01	.00
☐ 396	Tom Hausman	.03	.01	.00
☐ 397	Elliott Maddox	.03	.01	.00
☐ 398	Mike Squires	.03	.01	.00
☐ 399	Marvis Foley	.03	.01	.00
☐ 400	Steve Trout	.06	.03	.00
☐ 401	Wayne Nordhagen	.03	.01	.00
☐ 402	Tony LaRussa MG	.06	.03	.00
☐ 403	Bruce Bochte	.03	.01	.00
☐ 404	Bake McBride	.03	.01	.00
☐ 405	Jerry Narron	.03	.01	.00
☐ 406	Rob Dressler	.03	.01	.00
☐ 407	Dave Heaverlo	.03	.01	.00
☐ 408	Tom Paciorek	.03	.01	.00
☐ 409	Carney Lansford	.25	.10	.02
☐ 410	Brian Downing	.06	.03	.00
☐ 411	Don Aase	.03	.01	.00
☐ 412	Jim Barr	.03	.01	.00
☐ 413	Don Baylor	.15	.07	.01
☐ 414	Jim Fregosi	.06	.03	.00
☐ 415	Dallas Green MG	.10	.05	.01
☐ 416	Dave Lopes	.10	.05	.01
☐ 417	Jerry Reuss	.06	.03	.00
☐ 418	Rick Sutcliffe	.30	.15	.03
☐ 419	Derrel Thomas	.03	.01	.00
☐ 420	Tom Lasorda MG	.10	.05	.01
☐ 421	Charles Leibrandt	.30	.15	.03
☐ 422	Tom Seaver	.60	.30	.06
☐ 423	Ron Oester	.06	.03	.00
☐ 424	Junior Kennedy	.03	.01	.00
☐ 425	Tom Seaver	.60	.30	.06
☐ 426	Bobby Cox MG	.03	.01	.00
☐ 427	Leon Durham	.30	.15	.03
☐ 428	Terry Kennedy	.06	.03	.00
☐ 429	Silvio Martinez	.03	.01	.00
☐ 430	George Hendrick	.06	.03	.00
☐ 431	Red Schoendienst MG	.15	.07	.01
☐ 432	Johnnie LeMaster	.03	.01	.00
☐ 433	Vida Blue	.10	.05	.01
☐ 434	John Montefusco	.06	.03	.00
☐ 435	Terry Whitfield	.03	.01	.00
☐ 436	Dave Bristol MG	.03	.01	.00
☐ 437	Dale Murphy	1.25	.60	.12
☐ 438	Jerry Dybzinski	.03	.01	.00
☐ 439	Jorge Orta	.03	.01	.00
☐ 440	Wayne Garland	.03	.01	.00
☐ 441	Miguel Dilone	.03	.01	.00
☐ 442	Dave Garcia MG	.03	.01	.00
☐ 443	Don Money	.03	.01	.00
☐ 444A	Buck Martinez P1 ERR . (reverse negative)	.15	.07	.01
☐ 444B	Buck Martinez P2 COR	.06	.03	.00
☐ 445	Jerry Augustine	.03	.01	.00
☐ 446	Ben Oglivie	.06	.03	.00
☐ 447	Jim Slaton	.03	.01	.00
☐ 448	Doyle Alexander	.10	.05	.01

☐ 449	Tony Bernazard	.06	.03	.00
☐ 450	Scott Sanderson	.06	.03	.00
☐ 451	David Palmer	.06	.03	.00
☐ 452	Stan Bahnsen	.03	.01	.00
☐ 453	Dick Williams MG	.06	.03	.00
☐ 454	Rick Burleson	.06	.03	.00
☐ 455	Gary Allenson	.03	.01	.00
☐ 456	Bob Stanley	.03	.01	.00
☐ 457A	John Tudor P1 ERR lifetime W-L "9.7"	1.25	.60	.12
☐ 457B	John Tudor P2 COR corrected "9-7"	1.00	.50	.10
☐ 458	Dwight Evans	.25	.12	.02
☐ 459	Glenn Hubbard	.03	.01	.00
☐ 460	U.L. Washington	.03	.01	.00
☐ 461	Larry Gura	.06	.03	.00
☐ 462	Rich Gale	.03	.01	.00
☐ 463	Hal McRae	.06	.03	.00
☐ 464	Jim Frey MG	.03	.01	.00
☐ 465	Bucky Dent	.12	.06	.01
☐ 466	Dennis Werth	.03	.01	.00
☐ 467	Ron Davis	.03	.01	.00
☐ 468	Reggie Jackson	1.00	.50	.10
☐ 469	Bobby Brown	.03	.01	.00
☐ 470	Mike Davis	.25	.12	.02
☐ 471	Gaylord Perry	.30	.15	.03
☐ 472	Mark Belanger	.06	.03	.00
☐ 473	Jim Palmer	.65	.30	.06
☐ 474	Sammy Stewart	.03	.01	.00
☐ 475	Tim Stoddard	.03	.01	.00
☐ 476	Steve Stone	.06	.03	.00
☐ 477	Jeff Newman	.03	.01	.00
☐ 478	Steve McCatty	.03	.01	.00
☐ 479	Billy Martin MG	.20	.10	.02
☐ 480	Mitchell Page	.03	.01	.00
☐ 481	Cy Young Winner 1980 .. Steve Carlton	.30	.15	.03
☐ 482	Bill Buckner	.15	.07	.01
☐ 483A	Ivan DeJesus P1 ERR lifetime hits "702"	.10	.05	.01
☐ 483B	Ivan DeJesus P2 COR .. lifetime hits "642"	.06	.03	.00
☐ 484	Cliff Johnson	.03	.01	.00
☐ 485	Lenny Randle	.03	.01	.00
☐ 486	Larry Milbourne	.03	.01	.00
☐ 487	Roy Smalley	.03	.01	.00
☐ 488	John Castino	.03	.01	.00
☐ 489	Ron Jackson	.03	.01	.00
☐ 490A	Dave Roberts P1 Career Highlights: "Showed pop in"	.10	.05	.01
☐ 490B	Dave Roberts P2 "Declared himself"	.06	.03	.00
☐ 491	MVP: George Brett	.60	.30	.06
☐ 492	Mike Cubbage	.03	.01	.00
☐ 493	Rob Wilfong	.03	.01	.00
☐ 494	Danny Goodwin	.03	.01	.00
☐ 495	Jose Morales	.03	.01	.00
☐ 496	Mickey Rivers	.06	.03	.00
☐ 497	Mike Edwards	.03	.01	.00
☐ 498	Mike Sadek	.03	.01	.00
☐ 499	Lenn Sakata	.03	.01	.00
☐ 500	Gene Michael MG	.03	.01	.00
☐ 501	Dave Roberts	.03	.01	.00
☐ 502	Steve Dillard	.03	.01	.00
☐ 503	Jim Essian	.03	.01	.00
☐ 504	Rance Mulliniks	.03	.01	.00
☐ 505	Darrell Porter	.03	.01	.00
☐ 506	Joe Torre MG	.10	.05	.01
☐ 507	Terry Crowley	.03	.01	.00
☐ 508	Bill Travers	.03	.01	.00
☐ 509	Nelson Norman	.03	.01	.00
☐ 510	Bob McClure	.03	.01	.00
☐ 511	Steve Howe	.10	.05	.01
☐ 512	Dave Rader	.03	.01	.00
☐ 513	Mick Kelleher	.03	.01	.00
☐ 514	Kiko Garcia	.03	.01	.00
☐ 515	Larry Biittner	.03	.01	.00
☐ 516A	Willie Norwood P1 Career Highlights "Spent most of"	.10	.05	.01
☐ 516B	Willie Norwood P2 "Traded to Seattle"	.06	.03	.00
☐ 517	Bo Diaz	.06	.03	.00
☐ 518	Juan Beniquez	.03	.01	.00
☐ 519	Scot Thompson	.03	.01	.00
☐ 520	Jim Tracy	.03	.01	.00
☐ 521	Carlos Lezcano	.03	.01	.00
☐ 522	Joe Amalfitano MG	.03	.01	.00
☐ 523	Preston Hanna	.03	.01	.00
☐ 524A	Ray Burris P1 Career Highlights: "Went on ..."	.10	.05	.01
☐ 524B	Ray Burris P2 "Drafted by ..."	.06	.03	.00

☐ 525	Broderick Perkins	.03	.01	.00
☐ 526	Mickey Hatcher	.10	.05	.01
☐ 527	John Goryl MG	.03	.01	.00
☐ 528	Dick Davis	.03	.01	.00
☐ 529	Butch Wynegar	.03	.01	.00
☐ 530	Sal Butera	.03	.01	.00
☐ 531	Jerry Koosman	.10	.05	.01
☐ 532A	Geoff Zahn P1 Career Highlights: "Was 2nd in"	.10	.05	.01
☐ 532B	Geoff Zahn P2 "Signed a 3 year"	.06	.03	.00
☐ 533	Dennis Martinez	.10	.05	.01
☐ 534	Gary Thomasson	.03	.01	.00
☐ 535	Steve Macko	.03	.01	.00
☐ 536	Jim Kaat	.20	.10	.02
☐ 537	Best Hitters George Brett Rod Carew	1.25	.60	.12
☐ 538	Tim Raines	5.00	2.50	.50
☐ 539	Keith Smith	.03	.01	.00
☐ 540	Ken Macha	.03	.01	.00
☐ 541	Burt Hooton	.03	.01	.00
☐ 542	Butch Hobson	.03	.01	.00
☐ 543	Bill Stein	.03	.01	.00
☐ 544	Dave Stapleton	.03	.01	.00
☐ 545	Bob Pate	.03	.01	.00
☐ 546	Doug Corbett	.06	.03	.00
☐ 547	Darrell Jackson	.03	.01	.00
☐ 548	Pete Redfern	.03	.01	.00
☐ 549	Roger Erickson	.03	.01	.00
☐ 550	Al Hrabosky	.06	.03	.00
☐ 551	Dick Tidrow	.03	.01	.00
☐ 552	Dave Ford	.03	.01	.00
☐ 553	Dave Kingman	.15	.07	.01
☐ 554A	Mike Vail P1 Career Highlights: "After two ..."	.10	.05	.01
☐ 554B	Mike Vail P2 "Traded to ..."	.06	.03	.00
☐ 555A	Jerry Martin P1 Career Highlights: "Overcame a ..."	.10	.05	.01
☐ 555B	Jerry Martin P2 "Traded to ..."	.06	.03	.00
☐ 556A	Jesus Figueroa P1 Career Highlights: "Had an ..."	.10	.05	.01
☐ 556B	Jesus Figueroa P2 "Traded to ..."	.06	.03	.00
☐ 557	Don Stanhouse	.03	.01	.00
☐ 558	Barry Foote	.03	.01	.00
☐ 559	Tim Blackwell	.03	.01	.00
☐ 560	Bruce Sutter	.20	.10	.02
☐ 561	Rick Reuschel	.20	.10	.02
☐ 562	Lynn McGlothen	.03	.01	.00
☐ 563A	Bob Owchinko P1 Career Highlights: "Traded to ..."	.10	.05	.01
☐ 563B	Bob Owchinko P2 "Involved in a ..."	.06	.03	.00
☐ 564	John Verhoeven	.03	.01	.00
☐ 565	Ken Landreaux	.03	.01	.00
☐ 566A	Glen Adams P1 ERR Name misspelled	.15	.07	.01
☐ 566B	Glenn Adams P2 COR ..	.06	.03	.00
☐ 567	Hosken Powell	.03	.01	.00
☐ 568	Dick Noles	.03	.01	.00
☐ 569	Danny Ainge	.40	.20	.04
☐ 570	Bobby Mattick MG	.03	.01	.00
☐ 571	Joe Lefebvre	.06	.03	.00
☐ 572	Bobby Clark	.03	.01	.00
☐ 573	Dennis Lamp	.03	.01	.00
☐ 574	Randy Lerch	.03	.01	.00
☐ 575	Mookie Wilson	.50	.25	.05
☐ 576	Ron LeFlore	.06	.03	.00
☐ 577	Jim Dwyer	.03	.01	.00
☐ 578	Bill Castro	.03	.01	.00
☐ 579	Greg Minton	.03	.01	.00
☐ 580	Mark Littell	.03	.01	.00
☐ 581	Andy Hassler	.03	.01	.00
☐ 582	Dave Stieb	.35	.17	.03
☐ 583	Ken Oberkfell	.03	.01	.00
☐ 584	Larry Bradford	.03	.01	.00
☐ 585	Fred Stanley	.03	.01	.00
☐ 586	Bill Caudill	.03	.01	.00
☐ 587	Doug Capilla	.03	.01	.00
☐ 588	George Riley	.03	.01	.00
☐ 589	Willie Hernandez	.15	.07	.01
☐ 590	MVP: Mike Schmidt	.75	.35	.07
☐ 591	Cy Young Winner 1980: Steve Stone	.06	.03	.00
☐ 592	Rick Sofield	.03	.01	.00
☐ 593	Bombo Rivera	.03	.01	.00
☐ 594	Gary Ward	.06	.03	.00

		MINT	EXC	G-VG
☐ 595A	Dave Edwards P1 .... Career Highlights: "Sidelined the"	.10	.05	.01
☐ 595B	Dave Edwards P2 .... "Traded to ..."	.06	.03	.00
☐ 596	Mike Proly	.03	.01	.00
☐ 597	Tommy Boggs	.03	.01	.00
☐ 598	Greg Gross	.03	.01	.00
☐ 599	Elias Sosa	.03	.01	.00
☐ 600	Pat Kelly	.03	.01	.00
☐ 601A	Checklist 1 P1 ERR ..... unnumbered (51 Donahue)	.10	.05	.01
☐ 601B	Checklist 1 P2 COR ..... unnumbered (51 Donohue)	.75	.35	.07
☐ 602	Checklist 2 .... unnumbered	.10	.05	.01
☐ 603A	Checklist 3 P1 ERR ...... unnumbered (306 Mathews)	.10	.05	.01
☐ 603B	Checklist 3 P2 COR ..... unnumbered (306 Matthews)	.10	.05	.01
☐ 604A	Checklist 4 P1 ERR ...... unnumbered (379 Pujois)	.10	.05	.01
☐ 604B	Checklist 4 P2 COR ..... unnumbered (379 Pujols)	.10	.05	.01
☐ 605A	Checklist 5 P1 ERR ...... unnumbered (566 Glen Adams)	.10	.05	.01
☐ 605B	Checklist 5 P2 COR ..... unnumbered (566 Glenn Adams)	.10	.05	.01

1982 Donruss

The 1982 Donruss set contains 653 numbered cards and the seven unnumbered checklists; each card measures 2 1/2" by 3 1/2". The first 26 cards of this set are entitled Donruss Diamond Kings (DK) and feature the artwork of Dick Perez of Perez-Steele Galleries. The set was marketed with puzzle pieces rather than with bubble gum. There are 63 pieces to the puzzle, which when put together make a collage of Babe Ruth entitled "Hall of Fame Diamond King." The card stock in this year's Donruss cards is considerably thicker than that of the 1981 cards. The seven unnumbered checklist cards are arbitrarily assigned numbers 654 through 660 and are listed at the end of the list below.

		MINT	EXC	G-VG
COMPLETE SET (660)		35.00	17.50	3.50
COMMON PLAYER (1-660)		.03	.01	.00
☐ 1	Pete Rose DK	1.75	.50	.10
☐ 2	Gary Carter DK	.45	.22	.04
☐ 3	Steve Garvey DK	.50	.25	.05
☐ 4	Vida Blue DK	.08	.04	.01
☐ 5A	Alan Trammel DK ERR . (name misspelled)	1.50	.75	.15
☐ 5B	Alan Trammell DK .... COR	.40	.20	.04

		MINT	EXC	G-VG
☐ 6	Len Barker DK	.06	.03	.00
☐ 7	Dwight Evans DK	.20	.10	.02
☐ 8	Rod Carew DK	.50	.25	.05
☐ 9	George Hendrick DK	.06	.03	.00
☐ 10	Phil Niekro DK	.25	.12	.02
☐ 11	Richie Zisk DK	.06	.03	.00
☐ 12	Dave Parker DK	.20	.10	.02
☐ 13	Nolan Ryan DK	1.00	.50	.10
☐ 14	Ivan DeJesus DK	.06	.03	.00
☐ 15	George Brett DK	.75	.35	.07
☐ 16	Tom Seaver DK	.50	.25	.05
☐ 17	Dave Kingman DK	.10	.05	.01
☐ 18	Dave Winfield DK	.45	.22	.04
☐ 19	Mike Norris DK	.06	.03	.00
☐ 20	Carlton Fisk DK	.20	.10	.02
☐ 21	Ozzie Smith DK	.25	.12	.02
☐ 22	Roy Smalley DK	.06	.03	.00
☐ 23	Buddy Bell DK	.08	.04	.01
☐ 24	Ken Singleton DK	.08	.04	.01
☐ 25	John Mayberry DK	.06	.03	.00
☐ 26	Gorman Thomas DK	.08	.04	.01
☐ 27	Earl Weaver MG	.06	.03	.00
☐ 28	Rollie Fingers	.20	.10	.02
☐ 29	Sparky Anderson MG	.06	.03	.00
☐ 30	Dennis Eckersley	.20	.09	.02
☐ 31	Dave Winfield	.50	.25	.05
☐ 32	Burt Hooton	.03	.01	.00
☐ 33	Rick Waits	.03	.01	.00
☐ 34	George Brett	.80	.40	.08
☐ 35	Steve McCatty	.03	.01	.00
☐ 36	Steve Rogers	.03	.01	.00
☐ 37	Bill Stein	.03	.01	.00
☐ 38	Steve Renko	.03	.01	.00
☐ 39	Mike Squires	.03	.01	.00
☐ 40	George Hendrick	.06	.03	.00
☐ 41	Bob Knepper	.08	.04	.01
☐ 42	Steve Carlton	.60	.30	.06
☐ 43	Larry Biittner	.03	.01	.00
☐ 44	Chris Welsh	.03	.01	.00
☐ 45	Steve Nicosia	.03	.01	.00
☐ 46	Jack Clark	.25	.12	.02
☐ 47	Chris Chambliss	.06	.03	.00
☐ 48	Ivan DeJesus	.03	.01	.00
☐ 49	Lee Mazzilli	.03	.01	.00
☐ 50	Julio Cruz	.03	.01	.00
☐ 51	Pete Redfern	.03	.01	.00
☐ 52	Dave Stieb	.20	.10	.02
☐ 53	Doug Corbett	.03	.01	.00
☐ 54	Jorge Bell	6.50	3.25	.65
☐ 55	Joe Simpson	.03	.01	.00
☐ 56	Rusty Staub	.12	.06	.01
☐ 57	Hector Cruz	.03	.01	.00
☐ 58	Claudell Washington	.08	.04	.01
☐ 59	Enrique Romo	.03	.01	.00
☐ 60	Gary Lavelle	.03	.01	.00
☐ 61	Tim Flannery	.03	.01	.00
☐ 62	Joe Nolan	.03	.01	.00
☐ 63	Larry Bowa	.15	.07	.01
☐ 64	Sixto Lezcano	.03	.01	.00
☐ 65	Joe Sambito	.03	.01	.00
☐ 66	Bruce Kison	.03	.01	.00
☐ 67	Wayne Nordhagen	.03	.01	.00
☐ 68	Woodie Fryman	.03	.01	.00
☐ 69	Billy Sample	.03	.01	.00
☐ 70	Amos Otis	.08	.04	.01
☐ 71	Matt Keough	.03	.01	.00
☐ 72	Toby Harrah	.06	.03	.00
☐ 73	Dave Righetti	1.50	.75	.15
☐ 74	Carl Yastrzemski	1.00	.50	.10
☐ 75	Bob Welch	.10	.05	.01
☐ 76A	Alan Trammel ERR .... (name misspelled)	1.50	.75	.15
☐ 76B	Alan Trammell CORR ...	.40	.20	.04
☐ 77	Rick Dempsey	.03	.01	.00
☐ 78	Paul Molitor	.25	.12	.02
☐ 79	Dennis Martinez	.08	.04	.01
☐ 80	Jim Slaton	.03	.01	.00
☐ 81	Champ Summers	.03	.01	.00
☐ 82	Carney Lansford	.20	.07	.01
☐ 83	Barry Foote	.03	.01	.00
☐ 84	Steve Garvey	.50	.25	.05
☐ 85	Rick Manning	.03	.01	.00
☐ 86	John Wathan	.06	.03	.00
☐ 87	Brian Kingman	.03	.01	.00
☐ 88	Andre Dawson	.35	.17	.03
☐ 89	Jim Kern	.03	.01	.00
☐ 90	Bobby Grich	.08	.04	.01
☐ 91	Bob Forsch	.03	.01	.00
☐ 92	Art Howe	.08	.04	.01
☐ 93	Marty Bystrom	.03	.01	.00
☐ 94	Ozzie Smith	.40	.20	.04
☐ 95	Dave Parker	.25	.12	.02
☐ 96	Doyle Alexander	.03	.01	.00
☐ 97	Al Hrabosky	.06	.03	.00
☐ 98	Frank Taveras	.03	.01	.00

99	Tim Blackwell	.03	.01	.00
100	Floyd Bannister	.06	.03	.00
101	Alfredo Griffin	.08	.04	.01
102	Dave Engle	.03	.01	.00
103	Mario Soto	.06	.03	.00
104	Ross Baumgarten	.03	.01	.00
105	Ken Singleton	.08	.04	.01
106	Ted Simmons	.15	.07	.01
107	Jack Morris	.20	.10	.02
108	Bob Watson	.06	.03	.00
109	Dwight Evans	.20	.10	.02
110	Tom Lasorda MG	.08	.04	.01
111	Bert Blyleven	.20	.10	.02
112	Dan Quisenberry	.12	.06	.01
113	Rickey Henderson	1.50	.75	.15
114	Gary Carter	.45	.22	.04
115	Brian Downing	.06	.03	.00
116	Al Oliver	.10	.05	.01
117	LaMarr Hoyt	.06	.03	.00
118	Cesar Cedeno	.08	.04	.01
119	Keith Moreland	.03	.01	.00
120	Bob Shirley	.03	.01	.00
121	Terry Kennedy	.03	.01	.00
122	Frank Pastore	.03	.01	.00
123	Gene Garber	.03	.01	.00
124	Tony Pena	.35	.17	.03
125	Allen Ripley	.03	.01	.00
126	Randy Martz	.03	.01	.00
127	Richie Zisk	.03	.01	.00
128	Mike Scott	.40	.20	.04
129	Lloyd Moseby	.25	.12	.02
130	Rob Wilfong	.03	.01	.00
131	Tim Stoddard	.03	.01	.00
132	Gorman Thomas	.10	.05	.01
133	Dan Petry	.06	.03	.00
134	Bob Stanley	.03	.01	.00
135	Lou Piniella	.12	.06	.01
136	Pedro Guerrero	.60	.30	.06
137	Len Barker	.03	.01	.00
138	Rich Gale	.03	.01	.00
139	Wayne Gross	.03	.01	.00
140	Tim Wallach	1.00	.50	.10
141	Gene Mauch MG	.03	.01	.00
142	Doc Medich	.03	.01	.00
143	Tony Bernazard	.03	.01	.00
144	Bill Virdon MG	.03	.01	.00
145	John Littlefield	.03	.01	.00
146	Dave Bergman	.03	.01	.00
147	Dick Davis	.03	.01	.00
148	Tom Seaver	.50	.25	.05
149	Matt Sinatro	.03	.01	.00
150	Chuck Tanner MG	.03	.01	.00
151	Leon Durham	.06	.03	.00
152	Gene Tenace	.03	.01	.00
153	Al Bumbry	.03	.01	.00
154	Mark Brouhard	.03	.01	.00
155	Rick Peters	.03	.01	.00
156	Jerry Remy	.03	.01	.00
157	Rick Reuschel	.15	.07	.01
158	Steve Howe	.03	.01	.00
159	Alan Bannister	.03	.01	.00
160	U.L. Washington	.03	.01	.00
161	Rick Langford	.03	.01	.00
162	Bill Gullickson	.06	.03	.00
163	Mark Wagner	.03	.01	.00
164	Geoff Zahn	.03	.01	.00
165	Ron LeFlore	.06	.03	.00
166	Dane Iorg	.03	.01	.00
167	Joe Niekro	.10	.05	.01
168	Pete Rose	1.25	.60	.12
169	Dave Collins	.03	.01	.00
170	Rick Wise	.03	.01	.00
171	Jim Bibby	.03	.01	.00
172	Larry Herndon	.03	.01	.00
173	Bob Horner	.15	.07	.01
174	Steve Dillard	.03	.01	.00
175	Mookie Wilson	.12	.06	.01
176	Dan Meyer	.03	.01	.00
177	Fernando Arroyo	.03	.01	.00
178	Jackson Todd	.03	.01	.00
179	Darrell Jackson	.03	.01	.00
180	Alvis Woods	.03	.01	.00
181	Jim Anderson	.03	.01	.00
182	Dave Kingman	.15	.07	.01
183	Steve Henderson	.03	.01	.00
184	Brian Asselstine	.03	.01	.00
185	Rod Scurry	.03	.01	.00
186	Fred Breining	.03	.01	.00
187	Danny Boone	.03	.01	.00
188	Junior Kennedy	.03	.01	.00
189	Sparky Lyle	.10	.05	.01
190	Whitey Herzog MG	.06	.03	.00
191	Dave Smith	.08	.04	.01
192	Ed Ott	.03	.01	.00
193	Greg Luzinski	.12	.06	.01
194	Bill Lee	.06	.03	.00
195	Don Zimmer MG	.06	.03	.00
196	Hal McRae	.06	.03	.00
197	Mike Norris	.03	.01	.00
198	Duane Kuiper	.03	.01	.00
199	Rick Cerone	.03	.01	.00
200	Jim Rice	.30	.15	.03
201	Steve Yeager	.03	.01	.00
202	Tom Brookens	.03	.01	.00
203	Jose Morales	.03	.01	.00
204	Roy Howell	.03	.01	.00
205	Tippy Martinez	.03	.01	.00
206	Moose Haas	.03	.01	.00
207	Al Cowens	.03	.01	.00
208	Dave Stapleton	.03	.01	.00
209	Bucky Dent	.12	.06	.01
210	Ron Cey	.10	.05	.01
211	Jorge Orta	.03	.01	.00
212	Jamie Quirk	.03	.01	.00
213	Jeff Jones	.03	.01	.00
214	Tim Raines	1.00	.50	.10
215	Jon Matlack	.03	.01	.00
216	Rod Carew	.50	.25	.05
217	Jim Kaat	.15	.07	.01
218	Joe Pittman	.03	.01	.00
219	Larry Christenson	.03	.01	.00
220	Juan Bonilla	.03	.01	.00
221	Mike Easler	.03	.01	.00
222	Vida Blue	.08	.04	.01
223	Rick Camp	.03	.01	.00
224	Mike Jorgensen	.03	.01	.00
225	Jody Davis	.35	.17	.03
226	Mike Parrott	.03	.01	.00
227	Jim Clancy	.03	.01	.00
228	Hosken Powell	.03	.01	.00
229	Tom Hume	.03	.01	.00
230	Britt Burns	.03	.01	.00
231	Jim Palmer	.60	.30	.06
232	Bob Rodgers MG	.03	.01	.00
233	Milt Wilcox	.03	.01	.00
234	Dave Revering	.03	.01	.00
235	Mike Torrez	.03	.01	.00
236	Robert Castillo	.03	.01	.00
237	Von Hayes	1.00	.50	.10
238	Renie Martin	.03	.01	.00
239	Dwayne Murphy	.03	.01	.00
240	Rodney Scott	.03	.01	.00
241	Fred Patek	.03	.01	.00
242	Mickey Rivers	.06	.03	.00
243	Steve Trout	.03	.01	.00
244	Jose Cruz	.10	.05	.01
245	Manny Trillo	.03	.01	.00
246	Lary Sorensen	.03	.01	.00
247	Dave Edwards	.03	.01	.00
248	Dan Driessen	.03	.01	.00
249	Tommy Boggs	.03	.01	.00
250	Dale Berra	.03	.01	.00
251	Ed Whitson	.06	.03	.00
252	Lee Smith	.60	.30	.06
253	Tom Paciorek	.03	.01	.00
254	Pat Zachry	.03	.01	.00
255	Luis Leal	.03	.01	.00
256	John Castino	.03	.01	.00
257	Rich Dauer	.03	.01	.00
258	Cecil Cooper	.15	.07	.01
259	Dave Rozema	.03	.01	.00
260	John Tudor	.20	.10	.02
261	Jerry Mumphrey	.03	.01	.00
262	Jay Johnstone	.06	.03	.00
263	Bo Diaz	.06	.03	.00
264	Dennis Leonard	.06	.03	.00
265	Jim Spencer	.03	.01	.00
266	John Milner	.03	.01	.00
267	Don Aase	.03	.01	.00
268	Jim Sundberg	.06	.03	.00
269	Lamar Johnson	.03	.01	.00
270	Frank LaCorte	.03	.01	.00
271	Barry Evans	.03	.01	.00
272	Enos Cabell	.03	.01	.00
273	Del Unser	.03	.01	.00
274	George Foster	.12	.06	.01
275	Brett Butler	.75	.35	.07
276	Lee Lacy	.03	.01	.00
277	Ken Reitz	.03	.01	.00
278	Keith Hernandez	.35	.17	.03
279	Doug DeCinces	.06	.03	.00
280	Charlie Moore	.03	.01	.00
281	Lance Parrish	.20	.10	.02
282	Ralph Houk MG	.03	.01	.00
283	Rich Gossage	.20	.10	.02
284	Jerry Reuss	.06	.03	.00
285	Mike Stanton	.03	.01	.00
286	Frank White	.06	.03	.00
287	Bob Owchinko	.03	.01	.00
288	Scott Sanderson	.03	.01	.00

☐ 289	Bump Wills	.03	.01	.00
☐ 290	Dave Frost	.03	.01	.00
☐ 291	Chet Lemon	.06	.03	.00
☐ 292	Tito Landrum	.03	.01	.00
☐ 293	Vern Ruhle	.03	.01	.00
☐ 294	Mike Schmidt	1.00	.50	.10
☐ 295	Sam Mejias	.03	.01	.00
☐ 296	Gary Lucas	.03	.01	.00
☐ 297	John Candelaria	.08	.04	.01
☐ 298	Jerry Martin	.03	.01	.00
☐ 299	Dale Murphy	.90	.45	.09
☐ 300	Mike Lum	.03	.01	.00
☐ 301	Tom Hausman	.03	.01	.00
☐ 302	Glenn Abbott	.03	.01	.00
☐ 303	Roger Erickson	.03	.01	.00
☐ 304	Otto Velez	.03	.01	.00
☐ 305	Danny Goodwin	.03	.01	.00
☐ 306	John Mayberry	.06	.03	.00
☐ 307	Lenny Randle	.03	.01	.00
☐ 308	Bob Bailor	.03	.01	.00
☐ 309	Jerry Morales	.03	.01	.00
☐ 310	Rufino Linares	.03	.01	.00
☐ 311	Kent Tekulve	.06	.03	.00
☐ 312	Joe Morgan	.35	.17	.03
☐ 313	John Urrea	.03	.01	.00
☐ 314	Paul Householder	.03	.01	.00
☐ 315	Garry Maddox	.06	.03	.00
☐ 316	Mike Ramsey	.03	.01	.00
☐ 317	Alan Ashby	.03	.01	.00
☐ 318	Bob Clark	.03	.01	.00
☐ 319	Tony LaRussa MG	.06	.03	.00
☐ 320	Charlie Lea	.03	.01	.00
☐ 321	Danny Darwin	.03	.01	.00
☐ 322	Cesar Geronimo	.03	.01	.00
☐ 323	Tom Underwood	.03	.01	.00
☐ 324	Andre Thornton	.06	.03	.00
☐ 325	Rudy May	.03	.01	.00
☐ 326	Frank Tanana	.08	.04	.01
☐ 327	Dave Lopes	.08	.04	.01
☐ 328	Richie Hebner	.03	.01	.00
☐ 329	Mike Flanagan	.08	.04	.01
☐ 330	Mike Caldwell	.03	.01	.00
☐ 331	Scott McGregor	.06	.03	.00
☐ 332	Jerry Augustine	.03	.01	.00
☐ 333	Stan Papi	.03	.01	.00
☐ 334	Rick Miller	.03	.01	.00
☐ 335	Graig Nettles	.12	.06	.01
☐ 336	Dusty Baker	.06	.03	.00
☐ 337	Dave Garcia MG	.03	.01	.00
☐ 338	Larry Gura	.06	.03	.00
☐ 339	Cliff Johnson	.03	.01	.00
☐ 340	Warren Cromartie	.03	.01	.00
☐ 341	Steve Comer	.03	.01	.00
☐ 342	Rick Burleson	.06	.03	.00
☐ 343	John Martin	.03	.01	.00
☐ 344	Craig Reynolds	.03	.01	.00
☐ 345	Mike Proly	.03	.01	.00
☐ 346	Ruppert Jones	.03	.01	.00
☐ 347	Omar Moreno	.03	.01	.00
☐ 348	Greg Minton	.03	.01	.00
☐ 349	Rick Mahler	.25	.12	.02
☐ 350	Alex Trevino	.03	.01	.00
☐ 351	Mike Krukow	.06	.03	.00
☐ 352A	Shane Rawley ERR (photo actually Jim Anderson)	.75	.35	.07
☐ 352B	Shane Rawley COR	.10	.05	.01
☐ 353	Garth Iorg	.03	.01	.00
☐ 354	Pete Mackanin	.03	.01	.00
☐ 355	Paul Moskau	.03	.01	.00
☐ 356	Richard Dotson	.06	.03	.00
☐ 357	Steve Stone	.06	.03	.00
☐ 358	Larry Hisle	.06	.03	.00
☐ 359	Aurelio Lopez	.03	.01	.00
☐ 360	Oscar Gamble	.03	.01	.00
☐ 361	Tom Burgmeier	.03	.01	.00
☐ 362	Terry Forster	.06	.03	.00
☐ 363	Joe Charboneau	.06	.03	.00
☐ 364	Ken Brett	.03	.01	.00
☐ 365	Tony Armas	.08	.04	.01
☐ 366	Chris Speier	.03	.01	.00
☐ 367	Fred Lynn	.20	.10	.02
☐ 368	Buddy Bell	.12	.06	.01
☐ 369	Jim Essian	.03	.01	.00
☐ 370	Terry Puhl	.03	.01	.00
☐ 371	Greg Gross	.03	.01	.00
☐ 372	Bruce Sutter	.15	.07	.01
☐ 373	Joe Lefebvre	.03	.01	.00
☐ 374	Ray Knight	.08	.04	.01
☐ 375	Bruce Benedict	.03	.01	.00
☐ 376	Tim Foli	.03	.01	.00
☐ 377	Al Holland	.03	.01	.00
☐ 378	Ken Kravec	.03	.01	.00
☐ 379	Jeff Burroughs	.03	.01	.00
☐ 380	Pete Falcone	.03	.01	.00
☐ 381	Ernie Whitt	.06	.03	.00
☐ 382	Brad Havens	.03	.01	.00
☐ 383	Terry Crowley	.03	.01	.00
☐ 384	Don Money	.03	.01	.00
☐ 385	Dan Schatzeder	.03	.01	.00
☐ 386	Gary Allenson	.03	.01	.00
☐ 387	Yogi Berra MG	.15	.07	.01
☐ 388	Ken Landreaux	.03	.01	.00
☐ 389	Mike Hargrove	.06	.03	.00
☐ 390	Darryl Motley	.06	.03	.00
☐ 391	Dave McKay	.03	.01	.00
☐ 392	Stan Bahnsen	.03	.01	.00
☐ 393	Ken Forsch	.03	.01	.00
☐ 394	Mario Mendoza	.03	.01	.00
☐ 395	Jim Morrison	.03	.01	.00
☐ 396	Mike Ivie	.03	.01	.00
☐ 397	Broderick Perkins	.03	.01	.00
☐ 398	Darrell Evans	.12	.06	.01
☐ 399	Ron Reed	.03	.01	.00
☐ 400	Johnny Bench	.65	.30	.06
☐ 401	Steve Bedrosian	1.00	.50	.10
☐ 402	Bill Robinson	.06	.03	.00
☐ 403	Bill Buckner	.12	.06	.01
☐ 404	Ken Oberkfell	.03	.01	.00
☐ 405	Cal Ripken Jr.	8.50	4.25	.85
☐ 406	Jim Gantner	.03	.01	.00
☐ 407	Kirk Gibson	1.75	.85	.17
☐ 408	Tony Perez	.18	.09	.01
☐ 409	Tommy John	.18	.09	.01
☐ 410	Dave Stewart	3.75	1.85	.37
☐ 411	Dan Spillner	.03	.01	.00
☐ 412	Willie Aikens	.03	.01	.00
☐ 413	Mike Heath	.03	.01	.00
☐ 414	Ray Burris	.03	.01	.00
☐ 415	Leon Roberts	.03	.01	.00
☐ 416	Mike Witt	.75	.35	.07
☐ 417	Bob Molinaro	.03	.01	.00
☐ 418	Steve Braun	.03	.01	.00
☐ 419	Nolan Ryan	1.75	.85	.17
☐ 420	Tug McGraw	.10	.05	.01
☐ 421	Dave Concepcion	.12	.06	.01
☐ 422A	Juan Eichelberger ERR (photo actually Gary Lucas)	.65	.30	.06
☐ 422B	Juan Eichelberger COR	.08	.04	.01
☐ 423	Rick Rhoden	.08	.04	.01
☐ 424	Frank Robinson MG	.15	.07	.01
☐ 425	Eddie Miller	.03	.01	.00
☐ 426	Bill Caudill	.03	.01	.00
☐ 427	Doug Flynn	.03	.01	.00
☐ 428	Larry Andersen UER (misspelled Anderson on card front)	.03	.01	.00
☐ 429	Al Williams	.03	.01	.00
☐ 430	Jerry Garvin	.03	.01	.00
☐ 431	Glenn Adams	.03	.01	.00
☐ 432	Barry Bonnell	.03	.01	.00
☐ 433	Jerry Narron	.03	.01	.00
☐ 434	John Stearns	.03	.01	.00
☐ 435	Mike Tyson	.03	.01	.00
☐ 436	Glenn Hubbard	.03	.01	.00
☐ 437	Eddie Solomon	.03	.01	.00
☐ 438	Jeff Leonard	.08	.04	.01
☐ 439	Randy Bass	.06	.03	.00
☐ 440	Mike LaCoss	.03	.01	.00
☐ 441	Gary Matthews	.06	.03	.00
☐ 442	Mark Littell	.03	.01	.00
☐ 443	Don Sutton	.30	.15	.03
☐ 444	John Harris	.03	.01	.00
☐ 445	Vada Pinson CO	.06	.03	.00
☐ 446	Elias Sosa	.03	.01	.00
☐ 447	Charlie Hough	.06	.03	.00
☐ 448	Willie Wilson	.12	.06	.01
☐ 449	Fred Stanley	.03	.01	.00
☐ 450	Tom Veryzer	.03	.01	.00
☐ 451	Ron Davis	.03	.01	.00
☐ 452	Mark Clear	.03	.01	.00
☐ 453	Bill Russell	.06	.03	.00
☐ 454	Lou Whitaker	.25	.12	.02
☐ 455	Dan Graham	.03	.01	.00
☐ 456	Reggie Cleveland	.03	.01	.00
☐ 457	Sammy Stewart	.03	.01	.00
☐ 458	Pete Vuckovich	.08	.04	.01
☐ 459	John Wockenfuss	.03	.01	.00
☐ 460	Glenn Hoffman	.03	.01	.00
☐ 461	Willie Randolph	.10	.05	.01
☐ 462	Fernando Valenzuela	.90	.45	.09
☐ 463	Ron Hassey	.03	.01	.00
☐ 464	Paul Splittorff	.03	.01	.00
☐ 465	Rob Picciolo	.03	.01	.00
☐ 466	Larry Parrish	.06	.03	.00
☐ 467	Johnny Grubb	.03	.01	.00
☐ 468	Dan Ford	.03	.01	.00
☐ 469	Silvio Martinez	.03	.01	.00

470	Kiko Garcia	.03	.01	.00
471	Bob Boone	.15	.07	.01
472	Luis Salazar	.10	.05	.01
473	Randy Niemann	.03	.01	.00
474	Tom Griffin	.03	.01	.00
475	Phil Niekro	.30	.15	.03
476	Hubie Brooks	.40	.20	.04
477	Dick Tidrow	.03	.01	.00
478	Jim Beattie	.03	.01	.00
479	Damaso Garcia	.06	.03	.00
480	Mickey Hatcher	.06	.03	.00
481	Joe Price	.03	.01	.00
482	Ed Farmer	.03	.01	.00
483	Eddie Murray	.50	.25	.05
484	Ben Oglivie	.06	.03	.00
485	Kevin Saucier	.03	.01	.00
486	Bobby Murcer	.10	.05	.01
487	Bill Campbell	.03	.01	.00
488	Reggie Smith	.08	.04	.01
489	Wayne Garland	.03	.01	.00
490	Jim Wright	.03	.01	.00
491	Billy Martin MG	.20	.10	.02
492	Jim Fanning MG	.03	.01	.00
493	Don Baylor	.15	.07	.01
494	Rick Honeycutt	.03	.01	.00
495	Carlton Fisk	.35	.17	.03
496	Denny Walling	.03	.01	.00
497	Bake McBride	.03	.01	.00
498	Darrell Porter	.03	.01	.00
499	Gene Richards	.03	.01	.00
500	Ron Oester	.03	.01	.00
501	Ken Dayley	.20	.10	.02
502	Jason Thompson	.03	.01	.00
503	Milt May	.03	.01	.00
504	Doug Bird	.03	.01	.00
505	Bruce Bochte	.03	.01	.00
506	Neil Allen	.06	.03	.00
507	Joey McLaughlin	.03	.01	.00
508	Butch Wynegar	.03	.01	.00
509	Gary Roenicke	.03	.01	.00
510	Robin Yount	1.00	.50	.10
511	Dave Tobik	.03	.01	.00
512	Rich Gedman	.40	.20	.04
513	Gene Nelson	.08	.04	.01
514	Rick Monday	.06	.03	.00
515	Miguel Dilone	.03	.01	.00
516	Clint Hurdle	.03	.01	.00
517	Jeff Newman	.03	.01	.00
518	Grant Jackson	.03	.01	.00
519	Andy Hassler	.03	.01	.00
520	Pat Putnam	.03	.01	.00
521	Greg Pryor	.03	.01	.00
522	Tony Scott	.03	.01	.00
523	Steve Mura	.03	.01	.00
524	Johnnie LeMaster	.03	.01	.00
525	Dick Ruthven	.03	.01	.00
526	John McNamara MG	.06	.03	.00
527	Larry McWilliams	.03	.01	.00
528	Johnny Ray	.75	.35	.07
529	Pat Tabler	.60	.30	.06
530	Tom Herr	.10	.05	.01
531A	San Diego Chicken (with TM)	.90	.45	.09
531B	San Diego Chicken (without TM)	.75	.35	.07
532	Sal Butera	.03	.01	.00
533	Mike Griffin	.03	.01	.00
534	Kelvin Moore	.03	.01	.00
535	Reggie Jackson	.75	.35	.07
536	Ed Romero	.03	.01	.00
537	Derrel Thomas	.03	.01	.00
538	Mike O'Berry	.03	.01	.00
539	Jack O'Connor	.03	.01	.00
540	Bob Ojeda	.60	.30	.06
541	Roy Lee Jackson	.03	.01	.00
542	Lynn Jones	.03	.01	.00
543	Gaylord Perry	.30	.15	.03
544A	Phil Garner ERR (reverse negative)	.75	.35	.07
544B	Phil Garner COR	.10	.05	.01
545	Garry Templeton	.08	.04	.01
546	Rafael Ramirez	.03	.01	.00
547	Jeff Reardon	.20	.07	.01
548	Ron Guidry	.25	.12	.02
549	Tim Laudner	.25	.12	.02
550	John Henry Johnson	.03	.01	.00
551	Chris Bando	.03	.01	.00
552	Bobby Brown	.03	.01	.00
553	Larry Bradford	.03	.01	.00
554	Scott Fletcher	.40	.20	.04
555	Jerry Royster	.03	.01	.00
556	Shooty Babbitt (spelled Babbitt on front)	.03	.01	.00
557	Kent Hrbek	3.00	1.50	.30
558	Yankee Winners / Ron Guidry / Tommy John	.12	.06	.01
559	Mark Bomback	.03	.01	.00
560	Julio Valdez	.03	.01	.00
561	Buck Martinez	.03	.01	.00
562	Mike Marshall (Dodger hitter)	1.00	.50	.10
563	Rennie Stennett	.03	.01	.00
564	Steve Crawford	.03	.01	.00
565	Bob Babcock	.03	.01	.00
566	Johnny Podres CO	.06	.03	.00
567	Paul Serna	.03	.01	.00
568	Harold Baines	.75	.35	.07
569	Dave LaRoche	.03	.01	.00
570	Lee May	.03	.01	.00
571	Gary Ward	.06	.03	.00
572	John Denny	.06	.03	.00
573	Roy Smalley	.03	.01	.00
574	Bob Brenly	.20	.10	.02
575	Bronx Bombers / Reggie Jackson / Dave Winfield	.45	.22	.04
576	Luis Pujols	.03	.01	.00
577	Butch Hobson	.03	.01	.00
578	Harvey Kuenn MG	.06	.03	.00
579	Cal Ripken Sr. CO	.08	.04	.01
580	Juan Berenguer	.03	.01	.00
581	Benny Ayala	.03	.01	.00
582	Vance Law	.20	.10	.02
583	Rick Leach	.03	.01	.00
584	George Frazier	.03	.01	.00
585	Phillies Finest / Pete Rose / Mike Schmidt	1.00	.50	.10
586	Joe Rudi	.06	.03	.00
587	Juan Beniquez	.03	.01	.00
588	Luis DeLeon	.06	.03	.00
589	Craig Swan	.03	.01	.00
590	Dave Chalk	.03	.01	.00
591	Billy Gardner MG	.03	.01	.00
592	Sal Bando	.06	.03	.00
593	Bert Campaneris	.06	.03	.00
594	Steve Kemp	.06	.03	.00
595A	Randy Lerch ERR (Braves)	.65	.30	.06
595B	Randy Lerch COR (Brewers)	.06	.03	.00
596	Bryan Clark	.03	.01	.00
597	Dave Ford	.03	.01	.00
598	Mike Scioscia	.25	.12	.02
599	John Lowenstein	.03	.01	.00
600	Rene Lachemann MG	.06	.03	.00
601	Mick Kelleher	.03	.01	.00
602	Ron Jackson	.03	.01	.00
603	Jerry Koosman	.08	.04	.01
604	Dave Goltz	.03	.01	.00
605	Ellis Valentine	.03	.01	.00
606	Lonnie Smith	.10	.05	.01
607	Joaquin Andujar	.10	.05	.01
608	Garry Hancock	.03	.01	.00
609	Jerry Turner	.03	.01	.00
610	Bob Bonner	.03	.01	.00
611	Jim Dwyer	.03	.01	.00
612	Terry Bulling	.03	.01	.00
613	Joel Youngblood	.03	.01	.00
614	Larry Milbourne	.03	.01	.00
615	Gene Roof (name on front is Phil Roof)	.06	.03	.00
616	Keith Drumwright	.03	.01	.00
617	Dave Rosello	.03	.01	.00
618	Rickey Keeton	.03	.01	.00
619	Dennis Lamp	.03	.01	.00
620	Sid Monge	.03	.01	.00
621	Jerry White	.03	.01	.00
622	Luis Aguayo	.03	.01	.00
623	Jamie Easterly	.03	.01	.00
624	Steve Sax	2.75	1.35	.27
625	Dave Roberts	.03	.01	.00
626	Rick Bosetti	.03	.01	.00
627	Terry Francona	.08	.04	.01
628	Pride of Reds / Tom Seaver / Johnny Bench	.50	.25	.05
629	Paul Mirabella	.03	.01	.00
630	Rance Mulliniks	.03	.01	.00
631	Kevin Hickey	.03	.01	.00
632	Reid Nichols	.03	.01	.00
633	Dave Geisel	.03	.01	.00
634	Ken Griffey	.10	.05	.01
635	Bob Lemon MG	.10	.05	.01
636	Orlando Sanchez	.03	.01	.00
637	Bill Almon	.03	.01	.00
638	Danny Ainge	.15	.07	.01

☐ 639	Willie Stargell	.40	.20	.04
☐ 640	Bob Sykes	.03	.01	.00
☐ 641	Ed Lynch	.06	.03	.00
☐ 642	John Ellis	.03	.01	.00
☐ 643	Ferguson Jenkins	.15	.07	.01
☐ 644	Lenn Sakata	.03	.01	.00
☐ 645	Julio Gonzalez	.03	.01	.00
☐ 646	Jesse Orosco	.06	.03	.00
☐ 647	Jerry Dybzinski	.03	.01	.00
☐ 648	Tommy Davis	.06	.03	.00
☐ 649	Ron Gardenhire	.06	.03	.00
☐ 650	Felipe Alou CO	.06	.03	.00
☐ 651	Harvey Haddix CO	.03	.01	.00
☐ 652	Willie Upshaw	.06	.03	.00
☐ 653	Bill Madlock	.10	.05	.01
☐ 654A	DK Checklist (unnumbered) (with Trammel)	.25	.03	.01
☐ 654B	DK Checklist (unnumbered) (with Trammell)	.12	.02	.00
☐ 655	Checklist 1 (unnumbered)	.08	.01	.00
☐ 656	Checklist 2 (unnumbered)	.08	.01	.00
☐ 657	Checklist 3 (unnumbered)	.08	.01	.00
☐ 658	Checklist 4 (unnumbered)	.08	.01	.00
☐ 659	Checklist 5 (unnumbered)	.08	.01	.00
☐ 660	Checklist 6 (unnumbered)	.08	.01	.00

1983 Donruss

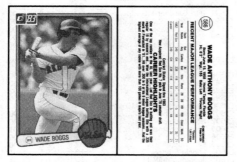

The cards in this 660-card set measure 2 1/2" by 3 1/2". The 1983 Donruss baseball set, issued with a 63-piece Diamond King puzzle, again leads off with a 26-card Diamond Kings (DK) series. Of the remaining 634 cards, two are combination cards, one portrays the San Diego Chicken, one shows the completed Ty Cobb puzzle, and seven are unnumbered checklist cards. The seven unnumbered checklist cards are arbitrarily assigned numbers 654 through 660 and are listed at the end of the list below. The Donruss logo and the year of issue are shown in the upper left corner of the obverse. The card backs have black print on yellow and white and are numbered on a small ball design. The complete set price below includes only the more common of each variation pair.

	MINT	EXC	G-VG
COMPLETE SET (660)	65.00	32.50	6.50
COMMON PLAYER (1-660)	.03	.01	.00

☐ 1	Fern.Valenzuela DK	.50	.10	.02
☐ 2	Rollie Fingers DK	.20	.10	.02
☐ 3	Reggie Jackson DK	.50	.25	.05
☐ 4	Jim Palmer DK	.35	.17	.03
☐ 5	Jack Morris DK	.15	.07	.01
☐ 6	George Foster DK	.10	.05	.01
☐ 7	Jim Sundberg DK	.06	.03	.00
☐ 8	Willie Stargell DK	.35	.17	.03
☐ 9	Dave Stieb DK	.15	.07	.01

☐ 10	Joe Niekro DK	.08	.04	.01
☐ 11	Rickey Henderson DK	.75	.35	.07
☐ 12	Dale Murphy DK	.60	.30	.06
☐ 13	Toby Harrah DK	.06	.03	.00
☐ 14	Bill Buckner DK	.08	.04	.01
☐ 15	Willie Wilson DK	.10	.05	.01
☐ 16	Steve Carlton DK	.40	.20	.04
☐ 17	Ron Guidry DK	.20	.10	.02
☐ 18	Steve Rogers DK	.06	.03	.00
☐ 19	Kent Hrbek DK	.40	.20	.04
☐ 20	Keith Hernandez DK	.30	.15	.03
☐ 21	Floyd Bannister DK	.06	.03	.00
☐ 22	Johnny Bench DK	.50	.25	.05
☐ 23	Britt Burns DK	.06	.03	.00
☐ 24	Joe Morgan DK	.35	.17	.03
☐ 25	Carl Yastrzemski DK	.80	.40	.08
☐ 26	Terry Kennedy DK	.06	.03	.00
☐ 27	Gary Roenicke	.03	.01	.00
☐ 28	Dwight Bernard	.03	.01	.00
☐ 29	Pat Underwood	.03	.01	.00
☐ 30	Gary Allenson	.03	.01	.00
☐ 31	Ron Guidry	.18	.09	.01
☐ 32	Burt Hooton	.03	.01	.00
☐ 33	Chris Bando	.03	.01	.00
☐ 34	Vida Blue	.08	.04	.00
☐ 35	Rickey Henderson	.90	.45	.09
☐ 36	Ray Burris	.03	.01	.00
☐ 37	John Butcher	.03	.01	.00
☐ 38	Don Aase	.03	.01	.00
☐ 39	Jerry Koosman	.08	.04	.01
☐ 40	Bruce Sutter	.15	.07	.01
☐ 41	Jose Cruz	.08	.04	.01
☐ 42	Pete Rose	1.00	.50	.10
☐ 43	Cesar Cedeno	.06	.03	.00
☐ 44	Floyd Chiffer	.03	.01	.00
☐ 45	Larry McWilliams	.03	.01	.00
☐ 46	Alan Fowlkes	.03	.01	.00
☐ 47	Dale Murphy	.85	.40	.08
☐ 48	Doug Bird	.03	.01	.00
☐ 49	Hubie Brooks	.10	.05	.01
☐ 50	Floyd Bannister	.03	.01	.00
☐ 51	Jack O'Connor	.03	.01	.00
☐ 52	Steve Senteney	.03	.01	.00
☐ 53	Gary Gaetti	3.00	1.50	.30
☐ 54	Damaso Garcia	.03	.01	.00
☐ 55	Gene Nelson	.03	.01	.00
☐ 56	Mookie Wilson	.10	.05	.01
☐ 57	Allen Ripley	.03	.01	.00
☐ 58	Bob Horner	.15	.07	.01
☐ 59	Tony Pena	.15	.07	.01
☐ 60	Gary Lavelle	.03	.01	.00
☐ 61	Tim Lollar	.03	.01	.00
☐ 62	Frank Pastore	.03	.01	.00
☐ 63	Garry Maddox	.06	.03	.00
☐ 64	Bob Forsch	.03	.01	.00
☐ 65	Harry Spilman	.03	.01	.00
☐ 66	Geoff Zahn	.03	.01	.00
☐ 67	Salome Barojas	.03	.01	.00
☐ 68	David Palmer	.03	.01	.00
☐ 69	Charlie Hough	.06	.03	.00
☐ 70	Dan Quisenberry	.12	.06	.01
☐ 71	Tony Armas	.06	.03	.00
☐ 72	Rick Sutcliffe	.15	.07	.01
☐ 73	Steve Balboni	.06	.03	.00
☐ 74	Jerry Remy	.03	.01	.00
☐ 75	Mike Scioscia	.06	.03	.00
☐ 76	John Wockenfuss	.03	.01	.00
☐ 77	Jim Palmer	.40	.20	.04
☐ 78	Rollie Fingers	.20	.10	.02
☐ 79	Joe Nolan	.03	.01	.00
☐ 80	Pete Vuckovich	.06	.03	.00
☐ 81	Rick Leach	.03	.01	.00
☐ 82	Rick Miller	.03	.01	.00
☐ 83	Graig Nettles	.12	.06	.01
☐ 84	Ron Cey	.10	.05	.01
☐ 85	Miguel Dilone	.03	.01	.00
☐ 86	John Wathan	.06	.03	.00
☐ 87	Kelvin Moore	.03	.01	.00
☐ 88A	Byrn Smith ERR (sic, Bryn)	.50	.25	.05
☐ 88B	Bryn Smith COR	1.00	.50	.10
☐ 89	Dave Hostetler	.06	.03	.00
☐ 90	Rod Carew	.50	.22	.04
☐ 91	Lonnie Smith	.12	.06	.01
☐ 92	Bob Knepper	.06	.03	.00
☐ 93	Marty Bystrom	.03	.01	.00
☐ 94	Chris Welsh	.03	.01	.00
☐ 95	Jason Thompson	.03	.01	.00
☐ 96	Tom O'Malley	.03	.01	.00
☐ 97	Phil Niekro	.25	.12	.02
☐ 98	Neil Allen	.03	.01	.00
☐ 99	Bill Buckner	.10	.05	.01
☐ 100	Ed VandeBerg	.03	.01	.00
☐ 101	Jim Clancy	.03	.01	.00
☐ 102	Robert Castillo	.03	.01	.00

☐ 103	Bruce Berenyi	.03	.01	.00
☐ 104	Carlton Fisk	.35	.17	.03
☐ 105	Mike Flanagan	.08	.04	.01
☐ 106	Cecil Cooper	.15	.07	.01
☐ 107	Jack Morris	.20	.10	.02
☐ 108	Mike Morgan	.06	.03	.00
☐ 109	Luis Aponte	.03	.01	.00
☐ 110	Pedro Guerrero	.30	.15	.03
☐ 111	Len Barker	.03	.01	.00
☐ 112	Willie Wilson	.12	.06	.01
☐ 113	Dave Beard	.03	.01	.00
☐ 114	Mike Gates	.03	.01	.00
☐ 115	Reggie Jackson	.50	.25	.05
☐ 116	George Wright	.03	.01	.00
☐ 117	Vance Law	.06	.03	.00
☐ 118	Nolan Ryan	1.25	.60	.12
☐ 119	Mike Krukow	.06	.03	.00
☐ 120	Ozzie Smith	.35	.17	.03
☐ 121	Broderick Perkins	.03	.01	.00
☐ 122	Tom Seaver	.40	.20	.04
☐ 123	Chris Chambliss	.06	.03	.00
☐ 124	Chuck Tanner MG	.03	.01	.00
☐ 125	Johnnie LeMaster	.03	.01	.00
☐ 126	Mel Hall	.75	.35	.07
☐ 127	Bruce Bochte	.03	.01	.00
☐ 128	Charlie Puleo	.03	.01	.00
☐ 129	Luis Leal	.03	.01	.00
☐ 130	John Pacella	.03	.01	.00
☐ 131	Glenn Gulliver	.03	.01	.00
☐ 132	Don Money	.03	.01	.00
☐ 133	Dave Rozema	.03	.01	.00
☐ 134	Bruce Hurst	.40	.20	.04
☐ 135	Rudy May	.03	.01	.00
☐ 136	Tom Lasorda MG	.06	.03	.00
☐ 137	Dan Spillner UER (photo actually Ed Whitson)	.06	.03	.00
☐ 138	Jerry Martin	.03	.01	.00
☐ 139	Mike Norris	.03	.01	.00
☐ 140	Al Oliver	.08	.04	.01
☐ 141	Daryl Sconiers	.03	.01	.00
☐ 142	Lamar Johnson	.03	.01	.00
☐ 143	Harold Baines	.25	.12	.02
☐ 144	Alan Ashby	.03	.01	.00
☐ 145	Garry Templeton	.06	.03	.00
☐ 146	Al Holland	.03	.01	.00
☐ 147	Bo Diaz	.03	.01	.00
☐ 148	Dave Concepcion	.10	.05	.01
☐ 149	Rick Camp	.03	.01	.00
☐ 150	Jim Morrison	.03	.01	.00
☐ 151	Randy Martz	.03	.01	.00
☐ 152	Keith Hernandez	.30	.15	.03
☐ 153	John Lowenstein	.03	.01	.00
☐ 154	Mike Caldwell	.03	.01	.00
☐ 155	Milt Wilcox	.03	.01	.00
☐ 156	Rich Gedman	.08	.04	.01
☐ 157	Rich Gossage	.15	.07	.01
☐ 158	Jerry Reuss	.06	.03	.00
☐ 159	Ron Hassey	.03	.01	.00
☐ 160	Larry Gura	.06	.03	.00
☐ 161	Dwayne Murphy	.03	.01	.00
☐ 162	Woodie Fryman	.03	.01	.00
☐ 163	Steve Comer	.03	.01	.00
☐ 164	Ken Forsch	.03	.01	.00
☐ 165	Dennis Lamp	.03	.01	.00
☐ 166	David Green	.03	.01	.00
☐ 167	Terry Puhl	.03	.01	.00
☐ 168	Mike Schmidt	1.00	.50	.10
☐ 169	Eddie Milner	.08	.04	.01
☐ 170	John Curtis	.03	.01	.00
☐ 171	Don Robinson	.03	.01	.00
☐ 172	Rich Gale	.03	.01	.00
☐ 173	Steve Bedrosian	.25	.12	.02
☐ 174	Willie Hernandez	.10	.05	.01
☐ 175	Ron Gardenhire	.03	.01	.00
☐ 176	Jim Beattie	.03	.01	.00
☐ 177	Tim Laudner	.03	.01	.00
☐ 178	Buck Martinez	.03	.01	.00
☐ 179	Kent Hrbek	.50	.25	.05
☐ 180	Alfredo Griffin	.06	.03	.00
☐ 181	Larry Andersen	.03	.01	.00
☐ 182	Pete Falcone	.03	.01	.00
☐ 183	Jody Davis	.08	.04	.01
☐ 184	Glenn Hubbard	.03	.01	.00
☐ 185	Dale Berra	.03	.01	.00
☐ 186	Greg Minton	.03	.01	.00
☐ 187	Gary Lucas	.03	.01	.00
☐ 188	Dave Van Gorder	.03	.01	.00
☐ 189	Bob Dernier	.03	.01	.00
☐ 190	Willie McGee	1.25	.60	.12
☐ 191	Dickie Thon	.03	.01	.00
☐ 192	Bob Boone	.15	.07	.01
☐ 193	Britt Burns	.03	.01	.00
☐ 194	Jeff Reardon	.15	.07	.01
☐ 195	Jon Matlack	.03	.01	.00
☐ 196	Don Slaught	.30	.15	.03
☐ 197	Fred Stanley	.03	.01	.00
☐ 198	Rick Manning	.03	.01	.00
☐ 199	Dave Righetti	.25	.12	.02
☐ 200	Dave Stapleton	.03	.01	.00
☐ 201	Steve Yeager	.03	.01	.00
☐ 202	Enos Cabell	.03	.01	.00
☐ 203	Sammy Stewart	.03	.01	.00
☐ 204	Moose Haas	.03	.01	.00
☐ 205	Lenn Sakata	.03	.01	.00
☐ 206	Charlie Moore	.03	.01	.00
☐ 207	Alan Trammell	.30	.15	.03
☐ 208	Jim Rice	.30	.15	.03
☐ 209	Roy Smalley	.03	.01	.00
☐ 210	Bill Russell	.06	.03	.00
☐ 211	Andre Thornton	.06	.03	.00
☐ 212	Willie Aikens	.03	.01	.00
☐ 213	Dave McKay	.03	.01	.00
☐ 214	Tim Blackwell	.03	.01	.00
☐ 215	Buddy Bell	.08	.04	.01
☐ 216	Doug DeCinces	.06	.03	.00
☐ 217	Tom Herr	.08	.04	.01
☐ 218	Frank LaCorte	.03	.01	.00
☐ 219	Steve Carlton	.35	.17	.03
☐ 220	Terry Kennedy	.03	.01	.00
☐ 221	Mike Easler	.03	.01	.00
☐ 222	Jack Clark	.25	.12	.02
☐ 223	Gene Garber	.03	.01	.00
☐ 224	Scott Holman	.03	.01	.00
☐ 225	Mike Proly	.03	.01	.00
☐ 226	Terry Bulling	.03	.01	.00
☐ 227	Jerry Garvin	.03	.01	.00
☐ 228	Ron Davis	.03	.01	.00
☐ 229	Tom Hume	.03	.01	.00
☐ 230	Marc Hill	.03	.01	.00
☐ 231	Dennis Martinez	.06	.03	.00
☐ 232	Jim Gantner	.03	.01	.00
☐ 233	Larry Pashnick	.03	.01	.00
☐ 234	Dave Collins	.03	.01	.00
☐ 235	Tom Burgmeier	.03	.01	.00
☐ 236	Ken Landreaux	.03	.01	.00
☐ 237	John Denny	.08	.04	.01
☐ 238	Hal McRae	.06	.03	.00
☐ 239	Matt Keough	.03	.01	.00
☐ 240	Doug Flynn	.03	.01	.00
☐ 241	Fred Lynn	.18	.09	.01
☐ 242	Billy Sample	.03	.01	.00
☐ 243	Tom Paciorek	.03	.01	.00
☐ 244	Joe Sambito	.03	.01	.00
☐ 245	Sid Monge	.03	.01	.00
☐ 246	Ken Oberkfell	.03	.01	.00
☐ 247	Joe Pittman UER (photo actually Juan Eichelberger)	.06	.03	.00
☐ 248	Mario Soto	.06	.03	.00
☐ 249	Claudell Washington	.08	.04	.01
☐ 250	Rick Rhoden	.06	.03	.00
☐ 251	Darrell Evans	.10	.05	.01
☐ 252	Steve Henderson	.03	.01	.00
☐ 253	Manny Castillo	.03	.01	.00
☐ 254	Craig Swan	.03	.01	.00
☐ 255	Joey McLaughlin	.03	.01	.00
☐ 256	Pete Redfern	.03	.01	.00
☐ 257	Ken Singleton	.08	.04	.01
☐ 258	Robin Yount	.65	.30	.06
☐ 259	Elias Sosa	.03	.01	.00
☐ 260	Bob Ojeda	.10	.05	.01
☐ 261	Bobby Murcer	.08	.04	.01
☐ 262	Candy Maldonado	.40	.20	.04
☐ 263	Rick Waits	.03	.01	.00
☐ 264	Greg Pryor	.03	.01	.00
☐ 265	Bob Owchinko	.03	.01	.00
☐ 266	Chris Speier	.03	.01	.00
☐ 267	Bruce Kison	.03	.01	.00
☐ 268	Mark Wagner	.03	.01	.00
☐ 269	Steve Kemp	.03	.01	.00
☐ 270	Phil Garner	.03	.01	.00
☐ 271	Gene Richards	.03	.01	.00
☐ 272	Renie Martin	.03	.01	.00
☐ 273	Dave Roberts	.03	.01	.00
☐ 274	Dan Driessen	.03	.01	.00
☐ 275	Rufino Linares	.03	.01	.00
☐ 276	Lee Lacy	.03	.01	.00
☐ 277	Ryne Sandberg	8.00	4.00	.80
☐ 278	Darrell Porter	.03	.01	.00
☐ 279	Cal Ripken	1.25	.60	.12
☐ 280	Jamie Easterly	.03	.01	.00
☐ 281	Bill Fahey	.03	.01	.00
☐ 282	Glenn Hoffman	.03	.01	.00
☐ 283	Willie Randolph	.08	.04	.01
☐ 284	Fernando Valenzuela	.30	.15	.03
☐ 285	Alan Bannister	.03	.01	.00
☐ 286	Paul Splittorff	.03	.01	.00
☐ 287	Joe Rudi	.06	.03	.00
☐ 288	Bill Gullickson	.03	.01	.00

☐ 289 Danny Darwin	.03	.01	.00
☐ 290 Andy Hassler	.03	.01	.00
☐ 291 Ernesto Escarrega	.03	.01	.00
☐ 292 Steve Mura	.03	.01	.00
☐ 293 Tony Scott	.03	.01	.00
☐ 294 Manny Trillo	.03	.01	.00
☐ 295 Greg Harris	.03	.01	.00
☐ 296 Luis DeLeon	.03	.01	.00
☐ 297 Kent Tekulve	.06	.03	.00
☐ 298 Atlee Hammaker	.06	.03	.00
☐ 299 Bruce Benedict	.03	.01	.00
☐ 300 Fergie Jenkins	.15	.07	.01
☐ 301 Dave Kingman	.10	.05	.01
☐ 302 Bill Caudill	.03	.01	.00
☐ 303 John Castino	.03	.01	.00
☐ 304 Ernie Whitt	.06	.03	.00
☐ 305 Randy Johnson	.03	.01	.00
☐ 306 Garth Iorg	.03	.01	.00
☐ 307 Gaylord Perry	.25	.12	.02
☐ 308 Ed Lynch	.03	.01	.00
☐ 309 Keith Moreland	.03	.01	.00
☐ 310 Rafael Ramirez	.03	.01	.00
☐ 311 Bill Madlock	.08	.04	.01
☐ 312 Milt May	.03	.01	.00
☐ 313 John Montefusco	.06	.03	.00
☐ 314 Wayne Krenchicki	.03	.01	.00
☐ 315 George Vukovich	.03	.01	.00
☐ 316 Joaquin Andujar	.08	.04	.01
☐ 317 Craig Reynolds	.03	.01	.00
☐ 318 Rick Burleson	.06	.03	.00
☐ 319 Richard Dotson	.06	.03	.00
☐ 320 Steve Rogers	.03	.01	.00
☐ 321 Dave Schmidt	.15	.07	.01
☐ 322 Bud Black	.20	.10	.02
☐ 323 Jeff Burroughs	.06	.03	.00
☐ 324 Von Hayes	.20	.10	.02
☐ 325 Butch Wynegar	.03	.01	.00
☐ 326 Carl Yastrzemski	.80	.40	.08
☐ 327 Ron Roenicke	.03	.01	.00
☐ 328 Howard Johnson	9.00	4.50	.90
☐ 329 Rick Dempsey	.03	.01	.00
☐ 330A Jim Slaton (bio printed black on white)	.06	.03	.00
☐ 330B Jim Slaton (bio printed black on yellow)	.15	.07	.01
☐ 331 Benny Ayala	.03	.01	.00
☐ 332 Ted Simmons	.12	.06	.01
☐ 333 Lou Whitaker	.25	.12	.02
☐ 334 Chuck Rainey	.03	.01	.00
☐ 335 Lou Piniella	.12	.06	.01
☐ 336 Steve Sax	.50	.25	.05
☐ 337 Toby Harrah	.06	.03	.00
☐ 338 George Brett	.65	.30	.06
☐ 339 Dave Lopes	.08	.04	.01
☐ 340 Gary Carter	.35	.17	.03
☐ 341 John Grubb	.03	.01	.00
☐ 342 Tim Foli	.03	.01	.00
☐ 343 Jim Kaat	.12	.06	.01
☐ 344 Mike LaCoss	.03	.01	.00
☐ 345 Larry Christenson	.03	.01	.00
☐ 346 Juan Bonilla	.03	.01	.00
☐ 347 Omar Moreno	.03	.01	.00
☐ 348 Chili Davis	.30	.15	.03
☐ 349 Tommy Boggs	.03	.01	.00
☐ 350 Rusty Staub	.10	.05	.01
☐ 351 Bump Wills	.03	.01	.00
☐ 352 Rick Sweet	.03	.01	.00
☐ 353 Jim Gott	.30	.15	.03
☐ 354 Terry Felton	.03	.01	.00
☐ 355 Jim Kern	.03	.01	.00
☐ 356 Bill Almon	.03	.01	.00
☐ 357 Tippy Martinez	.03	.01	.00
☐ 358 Roy Howell	.03	.01	.00
☐ 359 Dan Petry	.03	.01	.00
☐ 360 Jerry Mumphrey	.03	.01	.00
☐ 361 Mark Clear	.03	.01	.00
☐ 362 Mike Marshall	.25	.12	.02
☐ 363 Lary Sorensen	.03	.01	.00
☐ 364 Amos Otis	.08	.04	.01
☐ 365 Rick Langford	.03	.01	.00
☐ 366 Brad Mills	.03	.01	.00
☐ 367 Brian Downing	.06	.03	.00
☐ 368 Mike Richardt	.03	.01	.00
☐ 369 Aurelio Rodriguez	.03	.01	.00
☐ 370 Dave Smith	.06	.03	.00
☐ 371 Tug McGraw	.10	.05	.01
☐ 372 Doug Bair	.03	.01	.00
☐ 373 Ruppert Jones	.03	.01	.00
☐ 374 Alex Trevino	.03	.01	.00
☐ 375 Ken Dayley	.06	.03	.00
☐ 376 Rod Scurry	.03	.01	.00
☐ 377 Bob Brenly	.03	.01	.00
☐ 378 Scot Thompson	.03	.01	.00
☐ 379 Julio Cruz	.03	.01	.00
☐ 380 John Stearns	.03	.01	.00
☐ 381 Dale Murray	.03	.01	.00
☐ 382 Frank Viola	3.75	1.85	.37
☐ 383 Al Bumbry	.03	.01	.00
☐ 384 Ben Oglivie	.06	.03	.00
☐ 385 Dave Tobik	.03	.01	.00
☐ 386 Bob Stanley	.03	.01	.00
☐ 387 Andre Robertson	.03	.01	.00
☐ 388 Jorge Orta	.03	.01	.00
☐ 389 Ed Whitson	.06	.03	.00
☐ 390 Don Hood	.03	.01	.00
☐ 391 Tom Underwood	.03	.01	.00
☐ 392 Tim Wallach	.18	.09	.01
☐ 393 Steve Renko	.03	.01	.00
☐ 394 Mickey Rivers	.06	.03	.00
☐ 395 Greg Luzinski	.10	.05	.01
☐ 396 Art Howe	.08	.04	.01
☐ 397 Alan Wiggins	.10	.05	.01
☐ 398 Jim Barr	.03	.01	.00
☐ 399 Ivan DeJesus	.03	.01	.00
☐ 400 Tom Lawless	.06	.03	.00
☐ 401 Bob Walk	.06	.03	.00
☐ 402 Jimmy Smith	.03	.01	.00
☐ 403 Lee Smith	.10	.05	.01
☐ 404 George Hendrick	.06	.03	.00
☐ 405 Eddie Murray	.45	.22	.04
☐ 406 Marshall Edwards	.03	.01	.00
☐ 407 Lance Parrish	.20	.10	.02
☐ 408 Carney Lansford	.20	.07	.01
☐ 409 Dave Winfield	.40	.20	.04
☐ 410 Bob Welch	.08	.04	.01
☐ 411 Larry Milbourne	.03	.01	.00
☐ 412 Dennis Leonard	.06	.03	.00
☐ 413 Dan Meyer	.03	.01	.00
☐ 414 Charlie Lea	.03	.01	.00
☐ 415 Rick Honeycutt	.03	.01	.00
☐ 416 Mike Witt	.15	.07	.01
☐ 417 Steve Trout	.03	.01	.00
☐ 418 Glenn Brummer	.03	.01	.00
☐ 419 Denny Walling	.03	.01	.00
☐ 420 Gary Matthews	.06	.03	.00
☐ 421 Charlie Leibrandt UER (Liebrandt on front of card)	.06	.03	.00
☐ 422 Juan Eichelberger UER (photo actually Joe Pittman)	.06	.03	.00
☐ 423 Matt Guante	.06	.03	.00
☐ 424 Bill Laskey	.03	.01	.00
☐ 425 Jerry Royster	.03	.01	.00
☐ 426 Dickie Noles	.03	.01	.00
☐ 427 George Foster	.15	.07	.01
☐ 428 Mike Moore	1.50	.75	.15
☐ 429 Gary Ward	.06	.03	.00
☐ 430 Barry Bonnell	.03	.01	.00
☐ 431 Ron Washington	.03	.01	.00
☐ 432 Rance Mulliniks	.03	.01	.00
☐ 433 Mike Stanton	.03	.01	.00
☐ 434 Jesse Orosco	.06	.03	.00
☐ 435 Larry Bowa	.10	.05	.01
☐ 436 Biff Pocoroba	.03	.01	.00
☐ 437 Johnny Ray	.12	.06	.01
☐ 438 Joe Morgan	.30	.15	.03
☐ 439 Eric Show	.35	.17	.03
☐ 440 Larry Biittner	.03	.01	.00
☐ 441 Greg Gross	.03	.01	.00
☐ 442 Gene Tenace	.03	.01	.00
☐ 443 Danny Heep	.03	.01	.00
☐ 444 Bobby Clark	.03	.01	.00
☐ 445 Kevin Hickey	.03	.01	.00
☐ 446 Scott Sanderson	.03	.01	.00
☐ 447 Frank Tanana	.08	.04	.01
☐ 448 Cesar Geronimo	.03	.01	.00
☐ 449 Jimmy Sexton	.03	.01	.00
☐ 450 Mike Hargrove	.03	.01	.00
☐ 451 Doyle Alexander	.06	.03	.00
☐ 452 Dwight Evans	.18	.09	.01
☐ 453 Terry Forster	.06	.03	.00
☐ 454 Tom Brookens	.03	.01	.00
☐ 455 Rich Dauer	.03	.01	.00
☐ 456 Rob Picciolo	.03	.01	.00
☐ 457 Terry Crowley	.03	.01	.00
☐ 458 Ned Yost	.03	.01	.00
☐ 459 Kirk Gibson	.40	.20	.04
☐ 460 Reid Nichols	.03	.01	.00
☐ 461 Oscar Gamble	.03	.01	.00
☐ 462 Dusty Baker	.06	.03	.00
☐ 463 Jack Perconte	.03	.01	.00
☐ 464 Frank White	.08	.04	.01
☐ 465 Mickey Klutts	.03	.01	.00
☐ 466 Warren Cromartie	.03	.01	.00
☐ 467 Larry Parrish	.06	.03	.00
☐ 468 Bobby Grich	.06	.03	.00
☐ 469 Dane Iorg	.03	.01	.00

☐ 470	Joe Niekro	.10	.05	.01
☐ 471	Ed Farmer	.03	.01	.00
☐ 472	Tim Flannery	.03	.01	.00
☐ 473	Dave Parker	.20	.10	.02
☐ 474	Jeff Leonard	.08	.04	.01
☐ 475	Al Hrabosky	.06	.03	.00
☐ 476	Ron Hodges	.03	.01	.00
☐ 477	Leon Durham	.06	.03	.00
☐ 478	Jim Essian	.03	.01	.00
☐ 479	Roy Lee Jackson	.03	.01	.00
☐ 480	Brad Havens	.03	.01	.00
☐ 481	Joe Price	.03	.01	.00
☐ 482	Tony Bernazard	.03	.01	.00
☐ 483	Scott McGregor	.06	.03	.00
☐ 484	Paul Molitor	.18	.09	.01
☐ 485	Mike Ivie	.03	.01	.00
☐ 486	Ken Griffey	.10	.05	.01
☐ 487	Dennis Eckersley	.20	.10	.02
☐ 488	Steve Garvey	.40	.20	.04
☐ 489	Mike Fischlin	.03	.01	.00
☐ 490	U.L. Washington	.03	.01	.00
☐ 491	Steve McCatty	.03	.01	.00
☐ 492	Roy Johnson	.03	.01	.00
☐ 493	Don Baylor	.12	.06	.01
☐ 494	Bobby Johnson	.03	.01	.00
☐ 495	Mike Squires	.03	.01	.00
☐ 496	Bert Roberge	.03	.01	.00
☐ 497	Dick Ruthven	.03	.01	.00
☐ 498	Tito Landrum	.03	.01	.00
☐ 499	Sixto Lezcano	.03	.01	.00
☐ 500	Johnny Bench	.50	.25	.05
☐ 501	Larry Whisenton	.03	.01	.00
☐ 502	Manny Sarmiento	.03	.01	.00
☐ 503	Fred Breining	.03	.01	.00
☐ 504	Bill Campbell	.03	.01	.00
☐ 505	Todd Cruz	.03	.01	.00
☐ 506	Bob Bailor	.03	.01	.00
☐ 507	Dave Stieb	.18	.09	.01
☐ 508	Al Williams	.03	.01	.00
☐ 509	Dan Ford	.03	.01	.00
☐ 510	Gorman Thomas	.08	.04	.01
☐ 511	Chet Lemon	.06	.03	.00
☐ 512	Mike Torrez	.03	.01	.00
☐ 513	Shane Rawley	.03	.01	.00
☐ 514	Mark Belanger	.06	.03	.00
☐ 515	Rodney Craig	.03	.01	.00
☐ 516	Onix Concepcion	.03	.01	.00
☐ 517	Mike Heath	.03	.01	.00
☐ 518	Andre Dawson	.35	.17	.03
☐ 519	Luis Sanchez	.03	.01	.00
☐ 520	Terry Bogener	.03	.01	.00
☐ 521	Rudy Law	.03	.01	.00
☐ 522	Ray Knight	.06	.03	.00
☐ 523	Joe Lefebvre	.03	.01	.00
☐ 524	Jim Wohlford	.03	.01	.00
☐ 525	Julio Franco	4.00	2.00	.40
☐ 526	Ron Oester	.03	.01	.00
☐ 527	Rick Mahler	.03	.01	.00
☐ 528	Steve Nicosia	.03	.01	.00
☐ 529	Junior Kennedy	.03	.01	.00
☐ 530A	Whitey Herzog MG (bio printed black on white)	.10	.05	.01
☐ 530B	Whitey Herzog MG (bio printed black on yellow)	.10	.05	.01
☐ 531A	Don Sutton (blue border on photo)	.40	.20	.04
☐ 531B	Don Sutton (green border on photo)	.40	.20	.04
☐ 532	Mark Brouhard	.03	.01	.00
☐ 533A	Sparky Anderson MG (bio printed black on white)	.10	.05	.01
☐ 533B	Sparky Anderson MG (bio printed black on yellow)	.10	.05	.01
☐ 534	Roger LaFrancois	.03	.01	.00
☐ 535	George Frazier	.03	.01	.00
☐ 536	Tom Niedenfuer	.06	.03	.00
☐ 537	Ed Glynn	.03	.01	.00
☐ 538	Lee May	.06	.03	.00
☐ 539	Bob Kearney	.03	.01	.00
☐ 540	Tim Raines	.50	.25	.05
☐ 541	Paul Mirabella	.03	.01	.00
☐ 542	Luis Tiant	.08	.04	.01
☐ 543	Ron LeFlore	.06	.03	.00
☐ 544	Dave LaPoint	.35	.17	.03
☐ 545	Randy Moffitt	.03	.01	.00
☐ 546	Luis Aguayo	.03	.01	.00
☐ 547	Brad Lesley	.03	.01	.00
☐ 548	Luis Salazar	.03	.01	.00
☐ 549	John Candelaria	.06	.03	.00
☐ 550	Dave Bergman	.03	.01	.00
☐ 551	Bob Watson	.06	.03	.00
☐ 552	Pat Tabler	.10	.05	.01
☐ 553	Brent Gaff	.03	.01	.00
☐ 554	Al Cowens	.03	.01	.00
☐ 555	Tom Brunansky	.60	.30	.06
☐ 556	Lloyd Moseby	.10	.05	.01
☐ 557A	Pascual Perez ERR (Twins in glove)	2.00	1.00	.20
☐ 557B	Pascual Perez COR (Braves in glove)	.20	.10	.02
☐ 558	Willie Upshaw	.03	.01	.00
☐ 559	Richie Zisk	.03	.01	.00
☐ 560	Pat Zachry	.03	.01	.00
☐ 561	Jay Johnstone	.06	.03	.00
☐ 562	Carlos Diaz	.03	.01	.00
☐ 563	John Tudor	.12	.06	.01
☐ 564	Frank Robinson MG	.15	.07	.01
☐ 565	Dave Edwards	.03	.01	.00
☐ 566	Paul Householder	.03	.01	.00
☐ 567	Ron Reed	.03	.01	.00
☐ 568	Mike Ramsey	.03	.01	.00
☐ 569	Kiko Garcia	.03	.01	.00
☐ 570	Tommy John	.15	.07	.01
☐ 571	Tony LaRussa MG	.06	.03	.00
☐ 572	Joel Youngblood	.03	.01	.00
☐ 573	Wayne Tolleson	.15	.07	.01
☐ 574	Keith Creel	.03	.01	.00
☐ 575	Billy Martin MG	.15	.07	.01
☐ 576	Jerry Dybzinski	.03	.01	.00
☐ 577	Rick Cerone	.03	.01	.00
☐ 578	Tony Perez	.15	.07	.01
☐ 579	Greg Brock	.30	.15	.03
☐ 580	Glenn Wilson	.35	.17	.03
☐ 581	Tim Stoddard	.03	.01	.00
☐ 582	Bob McClure	.03	.01	.00
☐ 583	Jim Dwyer	.03	.01	.00
☐ 584	Ed Romero	.03	.01	.00
☐ 585	Larry Herndon	.03	.01	.00
☐ 586	Wade Boggs	18.00	9.00	1.80
☐ 587	Jay Howell	.06	.03	.00
☐ 588	Dave Stewart	.50	.25	.05
☐ 589	Bert Blyleven	.20	.10	.02
☐ 590	Dick Howser MG	.06	.03	.00
☐ 591	Wayne Gross	.03	.01	.00
☐ 592	Terry Francona	.03	.01	.00
☐ 593	Don Werner	.03	.01	.00
☐ 594	Bill Stein	.03	.01	.00
☐ 595	Jesse Barfield	.75	.35	.07
☐ 596	Bob Molinaro	.03	.01	.00
☐ 597	Mike Vail	.03	.01	.00
☐ 598	Tony Gwynn	12.50	6.00	1.20
☐ 599	Gary Rajsich	.03	.01	.00
☐ 600	Jerry Ujdur	.03	.01	.00
☐ 601	Cliff Johnson	.03	.01	.00
☐ 602	Jerry White	.03	.01	.00
☐ 603	Bryan Clark	.03	.01	.00
☐ 604	Joe Ferguson	.03	.01	.00
☐ 605	Guy Sularz	.03	.01	.00
☐ 606A	Ozzie Virgil (green border on photo)	.10	.05	.01
☐ 606B	Ozzie Virgil (orange border on photo)	.10	.05	.01
☐ 607	Terry Harper	.03	.01	.00
☐ 608	Harvey Kuenn MG	.06	.03	.00
☐ 609	Jim Sundberg	.03	.01	.00
☐ 610	Willie Stargell	.35	.17	.03
☐ 611	Reggie Smith	.08	.04	.01
☐ 612	Rob Wilfong	.03	.01	.00
☐ 613	The Niekro Brothers Joe Niekro Phil Niekro	.12	.06	.01
☐ 614	Lee Elia MG	.03	.01	.00
☐ 615	Mickey Hatcher	.06	.03	.00
☐ 616	Jerry Hairston	.03	.01	.00
☐ 617	John Martin	.03	.01	.00
☐ 618	Wally Backman	.20	.10	.02
☐ 619	Storm Davis	.60	.30	.06
☐ 620	Alan Knicely	.03	.01	.00
☐ 621	John Stuper	.03	.01	.00
☐ 622	Matt Sinatro	.03	.01	.00
☐ 623	Geno Petralli	.15	.07	.01
☐ 624	Duane Walker	.03	.01	.00
☐ 625	Dick Williams MG	.03	.01	.00
☐ 626	Pat Corrales MG	.03	.01	.00
☐ 627	Vern Ruhle	.03	.01	.00
☐ 628	Joe Torre MG	.08	.04	.01
☐ 629	Anthony Johnson	.03	.01	.00
☐ 630	Steve Howe	.03	.01	.00
☐ 631	Gary Woods	.03	.01	.00
☐ 632	LaMarr Hoyt	.08	.04	.01
☐ 633	Steve Swisher	.03	.01	.00
☐ 634	Terry Leach	.25	.12	.02

☐ 635	Jeff Newman	.03	.01	.00
☐ 636	Brett Butler	.12	.06	.01
☐ 637	Gary Gray	.03	.01	.00
☐ 638	Lee Mazzilli	.03	.01	.00
☐ 639A	Ron Jackson ERR	12.00	6.00	1.20
	(A's in glove)			
☐ 639B	Ron Jackson COR	.15	.07	.01
	(Angels in glove, red border on photo)			
☐ 639C	Ron Jackson COR	.50	.25	.05
	(Angels in glove, green border on photo)			
☐ 640	Juan Beniquez	.03	.01	.00
☐ 641	Dave Rucker	.03	.01	.00
☐ 642	Luis Pujols	.03	.01	.00
☐ 643	Rick Monday	.06	.03	.00
☐ 644	Hosken Powell	.03	.01	.00
☐ 645	The Chicken	.15	.07	.01
☐ 646	Dave Engle	.03	.01	.00
☐ 647	Dick Davis	.03	.01	.00
☐ 648	Frank Robinson	.15	.07	.01
	Vida Blue Joe Morgan			
☐ 649	Al Chambers	.03	.01	.00
☐ 650	Jesus Vega	.03	.01	.00
☐ 651	Jeff Jones	.03	.01	.00
☐ 652	Marvis Foley	.03	.01	.00
☐ 653	Ty Cobb Puzzle Card	.03	.01	.00
☐ 654A	Dick Perez/Diamond King Checklist (unnumbered) (word "checklist" omitted from back)	.15	.02	.01
☐ 654B	Dick Perez/Diamond King Checklist (unnumbered) (word "checklist" is on back)	.15	.02	.01
☐ 655	Checklist 1 (unnumbered)	.07	.01	.00
☐ 656	Checklist 2 (unnumbered)	.07	.01	.00
☐ 657	Checklist 3 (unnumbered)	.07	.01	.00
☐ 658	Checklist 4 (unnumbered)	.07	.01	.00
☐ 659	Checklist 5 (unnumbered)	.07	.01	.00
☐ 660	Checklist 6 (unnumbered)	.07	.01	.00

1983 Donruss Action All-Stars

 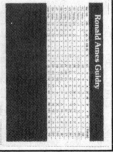

The cards in this 60-card set measure 3 1/2" by 5". The 1983 Action All-Stars series depicts 60 major leaguers in a distinctive new style. Each card contains a large close-up on the left and an action photo on the right. Team affiliations appear as part of the background design, and the cards have cranberry color borders. The backs contain the card number, the player's major league line record, and biographical material. A 63-piece Mickey Mantle puzzle (three pieces on one card per pack) was marketed as an insert premium.

		MINT	EXC	G-VG
	COMPLETE SET (60)	6.00	3.00	.60
	COMMON PLAYER (1-60)	.05	.02	.00
☐ 1	Eddie Murray	.30	.15	.03
☐ 2	Dwight Evans	.15	.07	.01
☐ 3A	Reggie Jackson ERR (red screen on back covers some stats)	1.00	.50	.10
☐ 3B	Reggie Jackson COR	.75	.35	.07
☐ 4	Greg Luzinski	.10	.05	.01
☐ 5	Larry Herndon	.05	.02	.00
☐ 6	Al Oliver	.10	.05	.01
☐ 7	Bill Buckner	.10	.05	.01
☐ 8	Jason Thompson	.05	.02	.00
☐ 9	Andre Dawson	.20	.10	.02
☐ 10	Greg Minton	.05	.02	.00
☐ 11	Terry Kennedy	.05	.02	.00
☐ 12	Phil Niekro	.20	.10	.02
☐ 13	Willie Wilson	.10	.05	.01
☐ 14	Johnny Bench	.40	.20	.04
☐ 15	Ron Guidry	.10	.05	.01
☐ 16	Hal McRae	.05	.02	.00
☐ 17	Damaso Garcia	.05	.02	.00
☐ 18	Gary Ward	.05	.02	.00
☐ 19	Cecil Cooper	.10	.05	.01
☐ 20	Keith Hernandez	.20	.10	.02
☐ 21	Ron Cey	.05	.02	.00
☐ 22	Rickey Henderson	.50	.25	.05
☐ 23	Nolan Ryan	1.00	.50	.10
☐ 24	Steve Carlton	.35	.17	.03
☐ 25	John Stearns	.05	.02	.00
☐ 26	Jim Sundberg	.05	.02	.00
☐ 27	Joaquin Andujar	.05	.02	.00
☐ 28	Gaylord Perry	.20	.10	.02
☐ 29	Jack Clark	.20	.10	.02
☐ 30	Bill Madlock	.05	.02	.00
☐ 31	Pete Rose	.65	.30	.06
☐ 32	Mookie Wilson	.05	.02	.00
☐ 33	Rollie Fingers	.15	.07	.01
☐ 34	Lonnie Smith	.10	.05	.01
☐ 35	Tony Pena	.05	.02	.00
☐ 36	Dave Winfield	.20	.10	.02
☐ 37	Tim Lollar	.05	.02	.00
☐ 38	Rod Carew	.35	.17	.03
☐ 39	Toby Harrah	.05	.02	.00
☐ 40	Buddy Bell	.05	.02	.00
☐ 41	Bruce Sutter	.10	.05	.01
☐ 42	George Brett	.45	.22	.04
☐ 43	Carlton Fisk	.30	.15	.03
☐ 44	Carl Yastrzemski	.75	.35	.07
☐ 45	Dale Murphy	.40	.20	.04
☐ 46	Bob Horner	.10	.05	.01
☐ 47	Dave Concepcion	.05	.02	.00
☐ 48	Dave Stieb	.10	.05	.01
☐ 49	Kent Hrbek	.20	.10	.02
☐ 50	Lance Parrish	.10	.05	.01
☐ 51	Joe Niekro	.10	.05	.01
☐ 52	Cal Ripken	.35	.17	.03
☐ 53	Fernando Valenzuela	.25	.12	.02
☐ 54	Richie Zisk	.05	.02	.00
☐ 55	Leon Durham	.05	.02	.00
☐ 56	Robin Yount	.50	.25	.05
☐ 57	Mike Schmidt	.90	.45	.09
☐ 58	Gary Carter	.30	.15	.03
☐ 59	Fred Lynn	.10	.05	.01
☐ 60	Checklist Card	.05	.02	.00

1983 Donruss HOF Heroes

The cards in this 44-card set measure 2 1/2" by 3 1/2". Although it was issued with the same Mantle puzzle as the Action All Stars set, the Donruss Hall of Fame Heroes set is completely different in content and design. Of the 44 cards in the set, 42 are Dick Perez artwork portraying Hall of Fame members, while one card depicts the completed Mantle puzzle and the last card is a checklist. The red, white, and blue backs contain the card number and a short player biography. The cards were packaged 8 cards plus one puzzle card (3 pieces) for 30 cents in the summer of 1983.

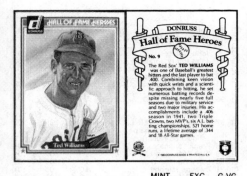

	MINT	EXC	G-VG
COMPLETE SET (44)	5.00	2.50	.50
COMMON PLAYER (1-44)	.05	.02	.00

		MINT	EXC	G-VG
☐	1 Ty Cobb	.50	.25	.05
☐	2 Walter Johnson	.15	.07	.01
☐	3 Christy Mathewson	.15	.07	.01
☐	4 Josh Gibson	.15	.07	.01
☐	5 Honus Wagner	.15	.07	.01
☐	6 Jackie Robinson	.15	.07	.01
☐	7 Mickey Mantle	.80	.40	.08
☐	8 Luke Appling	.05	.02	.00
☐	9 Ted Williams	.20	.10	.02
☐	10 Johnny Mize	.05	.02	.00
☐	11 Satchel Paige	.10	.05	.01
☐	12 Lou Boudreau	.05	.02	.00
☐	13 Jimmie Foxx	.10	.05	.01
☐	14 Duke Snider	.15	.07	.01
☐	15 Monte Irvin	.05	.02	.00
☐	16 Hank Greenberg	.05	.02	.00
☐	17 Roberto Clemente	.15	.07	.01
☐	18 Al Kaline	.15	.07	.01
☐	19 Frank Robinson	.15	.07	.01
☐	20 Joe Cronin	.05	.02	.00
☐	21 Burleigh Grimes	.05	.02	.00
☐	22 The Waner Brothers Paul Waner Lloyd Waner	.05	.02	.00
☐	23 Grover Alexander	.05	.02	.00
☐	24 Yogi Berra	.20	.10	.02
☐	25 Cool Papa Bell	.05	.02	.00
☐	26 Bill Dickey	.05	.02	.00
☐	27 Cy Young	.10	.05	.01
☐	28 Charlie Gehringer	.05	.02	.00
☐	29 Dizzy Dean	.15	.07	.01
☐	30 Bob Lemon	.05	.02	.00
☐	31 Red Ruffing	.05	.02	.00
☐	32 Stan Musial	.20	.10	.02
☐	33 Carl Hubbell	.10	.05	.01
☐	34 Hank Aaron	.25	.12	.02
☐	35 John McGraw	.05	.02	.00
☐	36 Bob Feller	.15	.07	.01
☐	37 Casey Stengel	.10	.05	.01
☐	38 Ralph Kiner	.10	.05	.01
☐	39 Roy Campanella	.15	.07	.01
☐	40 Mel Ott	.10	.05	.01
☐	41 Robin Roberts	.10	.05	.01
☐	42 Early Wynn	.05	.02	.00
☐	43 Mantle Puzzle Card	.05	.02	.00
☐	44 Checklist Card	.05	.02	.00

1984 Donruss

The 1984 Donruss set contains a total of 660 cards, each measuring 2 1/2" by 3 1/2"; however, only 658 are numbered. The first 26 cards in the set are again Diamond Kings (DK), although the drawings this year were styled differently and are easily differentiated from other DK issues. A new feature, Rated Rookies (RR), was introduced with this set with Bill Madden's 20 selections comprising numbers 27 through 46. Two "Living Legend" cards designated A (featuring Gaylord Perry and Rollie Fingers) and B (featuring Johnny Bench and Carl Yastrzemski) were issued as bonus cards in wax packs, but were not issued in the vending sets sold to hobby dealers. The seven

unnumbered checklist cards are arbitrarily assigned numbers 652 through 658 and are listed at the end of the list below. The designs on the fronts of the Donruss cards changed considerably from the past two years. The backs contain statistics and are printed in green and black ink. The cards were distributed with a 63-piece puzzle of Duke Snider. There are no extra variation cards included in the complete set price below.

	MINT	EXC	G-VG
COMPLETE SET (658)	275.00	125.00	25.00
COMMON PLAYER (1-658)	.10	.05	.01

		MINT	EXC	G-VG
☐	1A Robin Yount DK ERR (Perez Steel)	1.25	.60	.12
☐	1B Robin Yount DK COR	2.00	1.00	.20
☐	2A Dave Concepcion DK ERR (Perez Steel)	.15	.07	.01
☐	2B Dave Concepcion DK COR	.25	.12	.02
☐	3A Dwayne Murphy DK ERR (Perez Steel)	.15	.07	.01
☐	3B Dwayne Murphy DK COR	.25	.12	.02
☐	4A John Castino DK ERR (Perez Steel)	.15	.07	.01
☐	4B John Castino DK COR	.25	.12	.02
☐	5A Leon Durham DK ERR (Perez Steel)	.15	.07	.01
☐	5B Leon Durham DK COR	.25	.12	.02
☐	6A Rusty Staub DK ERR (Perez Steel)	.15	.07	.01
☐	6B Rusty Staub DK COR	.25	.12	.02
☐	7A Jack Clark DK ERR (Perez Steel)	.30	.15	.03
☐	7B Jack Clark DK COR	.50	.25	.05
☐	8A Dave Dravecky DK ERR (Perez Steel)	.15	.07	.01
☐	8B Dave Dravecky DK COR	.25	.12	.02
☐	9A Al Oliver DK ERR (Perez Steel)	.15	.07	.01
☐	9B Al Oliver DK COR	.25	.12	.02
☐	10A Dave Righetti DK ERR (Perez Steel)	.20	.10	.02
☐	10B Dave Righetti DK COR	.30	.15	.03
☐	11A Hal McRae DK ERR (Perez Steel)	.15	.07	.01
☐	11B Hal McRae DK COR	.25	.12	.02
☐	12A Ray Knight DK ERR (Perez Steel)	.15	.07	.01
☐	12B Ray Knight DK COR	.25	.12	.02
☐	13A Bruce Sutter DK ERR (Perez Steel)	.15	.07	.01
☐	13B Bruce Sutter DK COR	.25	.12	.02
☐	14A Bob Horner DK ERR (Perez Steel)	.15	.07	.01
☐	14B Bob Horner DK COR	.25	.12	.02
☐	15A Lance Parrish DK ERR (Perez Steel)	.25	.12	.02
☐	15B Lance Parrish DK COR	.35	.17	.03
☐	16A Matt Young DK ERR (Perez Steel)	.15	.07	.01
☐	16B Matt Young DK COR	.25	.12	.02
☐	17A Fred Lynn DK ERR (Perez Steel) (A's logo on back)	.20	.10	.02
☐	17B Fred Lynn DK COR	.30	.15	.03
☐	18A Ron Kittle DK ERR	.20	.10	.02

    (Perez Steel)
☐ 18B Ron Kittle DK COR ...... .30 .15 .03
☐ 19A Jim Clancy DK ERR ...... .15 .07 .01
    (Perez Steel)
☐ 19B Jim Clancy DK COR .... .25 .12 .02
☐ 20A Bill Madlock DK ERR .... .15 .07 .01
    (Perez Steel)
☐ 20B Bill Madlock DK COR .... .25 .12 .02
☐ 21A Larry Parrish DK .... .15 .07 .01
    ERR (Perez Steel)
☐ 21B Larry Parrish DK .... .25 .12 .02
    COR
☐ 22A Eddie Murray DK ERR .. .90 .45 .09
    (Perez Steel)
☐ 22B Eddie Murray DK COR . 1.50 .75 .15
☐ 23A Mike Schmidt DK ERR . 1.25 .60 .12
    (Perez Steel)
☐ 23B Mike Schmidt DK COR . 2.00 1.00 .20
☐ 24A Pedro Guerrero DK ...... .35 .17 .03
    ERR (Perez Steel)
☐ 24B Pedro Guerrero DK ...... .50 .25 .05
    COR
☐ 25A Andre Thornton DK ...... .15 .07 .01
    ERR (Perez Steel)
☐ 25B Andre Thornton DK ...... .25 .12 .02
    COR
☐ 26A Wade Boggs DK ERR .... 3.50 1.75 .35
    (Perez Steel)
☐ 26B Wade Boggs DK COR ... 5.50 2.75 .55
☐ 27 Joel Skinner RR .... .25 .12 .02
☐ 28 Tommy Dunbar RR .... .15 .07 .01
☐ 29A Mike Stenhouse RR ...... .25 .12 .02
    ERR (no back number)
☐ 29B Mike Stenhouse RR ...... 3.00 1.50 .30
    COR (number on back)
☐ 30A Ron Darling RR ERR ..... 6.00 3.00 .60
    (no number on back)
☐ 30B Ron Darling RR COR 16.00 8.00 1.60
☐ 31 Dion James RR .... .60 .30 .06
☐ 32 Tony Fernandez RR .... 8.00 4.00 .80
☐ 33 Angel Salazar RR .... .15 .07 .01
☐ 34 Kevin McReynolds RR 11.00 5.50 1.10
☐ 35 Dick Schofield RR .... .60 .30 .06
☐ 36 Brad Komminsk RR .... .35 .17 .03
☐ 37 Tim Teufel RR .... .40 .20 .04
☐ 38 Doug Frobel RR .... .15 .07 .01
☐ 39 Greg Gagne RR .... .35 .17 .03
☐ 40 Mike Fuentes RR .... .15 .07 .01
☐ 41 Joe Carter RR 15.00 7.50 1.50
☐ 42 Mike Brown RR .... .15 .07 .01
    (Angels OF)
☐ 43 Mike Jeffcoat RR .... .15 .07 .01
☐ 44 Sid Fernandez RR .... 7.00 3.50 .70
☐ 45 Brian Dayett RR .... .20 .10 .02
☐ 46 Chris Smith RR .... .15 .07 .01
☐ 47 Eddie Murray .... 1.00 .50 .10
☐ 48 Robin Yount .... 1.50 .75 .15
☐ 49 Lance Parrish .... .35 .17 .03
☐ 50 Jim Rice .... .45 .22 .04
☐ 51 Dave Winfield .... .85 .40 .08
☐ 52 Fernando Valenzuela ...... .45 .22 .04
☐ 53 George Brett .... 1.25 .60 .12
☐ 54 Rickey Henderson .... 2.00 1.00 .20
☐ 55 Gary Carter .... .65 .30 .06
☐ 56 Buddy Bell .... .15 .07 .01
☐ 57 Reggie Jackson .... 1.50 .75 .15
☐ 58 Harold Baines .... .35 .17 .03
☐ 59 Ozzie Smith .... .75 .30 .06
☐ 60 Nolan Ryan .... 3.25 1.60 .32
☐ 61 Pete Rose .... 2.50 1.25 .25
☐ 62 Ron Oester .... .10 .05 .01
☐ 63 Steve Garvey .... .90 .45 .09
☐ 64 Jason Thompson .... .10 .05 .01
☐ 65 Jack Clark .... .35 .17 .03
☐ 66 Dale Murphy .... 1.50 .75 .15
☐ 67 Leon Durham .... .15 .07 .01
☐ 68 Darryl Strawberry 36.00 18.00 3.60
☐ 69 Richie Zisk .... .10 .05 .01
☐ 70 Kent Hrbek .... .60 .30 .06
☐ 71 Dave Stieb .... .25 .12 .02
☐ 72 Ken Schrom .... .10 .05 .01
☐ 73 George Bell .... 1.75 .85 .17
☐ 74 John Moses .... .15 .07 .01
☐ 75 Ed Lynch .... .10 .05 .01
☐ 76 Chuck Rainey .... .10 .05 .01
☐ 77 Biff Pocoroba .... .10 .05 .01
☐ 78 Cecilio Guante .... .10 .05 .01
☐ 79 Jim Barr .... .10 .05 .01
☐ 80 Kurt Bevacqua .... .10 .05 .01
☐ 81 Tom Foley .... .10 .05 .01
☐ 82 Joe Lefebvre .... .10 .05 .01
☐ 83 Andy Van Slyke .... 4.00 2.00 .40
☐ 84 Bob Lillis MG .... .10 .05 .01
☐ 85 Ricky Adams .... .10 .05 .01
☐ 86 Jerry Hairston .... .10 .05 .01

☐ 87 Bob James .... .20 .10 .02
☐ 88 Joe Altobelli MG .... .10 .05 .01
☐ 89 Ed Romero .... .10 .05 .01
☐ 90 John Grubb .... .10 .05 .01
☐ 91 John Henry Johnson .... .10 .05 .01
☐ 92 Juan Espino .... .10 .05 .01
☐ 93 Candy Maldonado .... .20 .10 .02
☐ 94 Andre Thornton .... .15 .07 .01
☐ 95 Onix Concepcion .... .10 .05 .01
☐ 96 Donnie Hill .... .15 .07 .01
    (listed as P, should be 2B)
☐ 97 Andre Dawson UER .... .75 .35 .07
    (wrong middle name, should be Nolan)
☐ 98 Frank Tanana .... .15 .07 .01
☐ 99 Curt Wilkerson .... .15 .07 .01
☐ 100 Larry Gura .... .10 .05 .01
☐ 101 Dwayne Murphy .... .10 .05 .01
☐ 102 Tom Brennan .... .10 .05 .01
☐ 103 Dave Righetti .... .30 .15 .03
☐ 104 Steve Sax .... .50 .25 .05
☐ 105 Dan Petry .... .10 .05 .01
☐ 106 Cal Ripken .... 1.75 .85 .17
☐ 107 Paul Molitor .... .30 .15 .03
☐ 108 Fred Lynn .... .25 .12 .02
☐ 109 Neil Allen .... .10 .05 .01
☐ 110 Joe Niekro .... .15 .07 .01
☐ 111 Steve Carlton .... .90 .45 .09
☐ 112 Terry Kennedy .... .10 .05 .01
☐ 113 Bill Madlock .... .20 .10 .02
☐ 114 Chili Davis .... .20 .10 .02
☐ 115 Jim Gantner .... .10 .05 .01
☐ 116 Tom Seaver .... 1.00 .50 .10
☐ 117 Bill Buckner .... .20 .10 .02
☐ 118 Bill Caudill .... .10 .05 .01
☐ 119 Jim Clancy .... .10 .05 .01
☐ 120 John Castino .... .10 .05 .01
☐ 121 Dave Concepcion .... .20 .10 .02
☐ 122 Greg Luzinski .... .20 .10 .02
☐ 123 Mike Boddicker .... .20 .10 .02
☐ 124 Pete Ladd .... .10 .05 .01
☐ 125 Juan Berenguer .... .10 .05 .01
☐ 126 John Montefusco .... .10 .05 .01
☐ 127 Ed Jurak .... .10 .05 .01
☐ 128 Tom Niedenfuer .... .15 .07 .01
☐ 129 Bert Blyleven .... .25 .10 .02
☐ 130 Bud Black .... .10 .05 .01
☐ 131 Gorman Heimueller .... .10 .05 .01
☐ 132 Dan Schatzeder .... .10 .05 .01
☐ 133 Ron Jackson .... .10 .05 .01
☐ 134 Tom Henke .... .90 .45 .09
☐ 135 Kevin Hickey .... .10 .05 .01
☐ 136 Mike Scott .... .60 .30 .06
☐ 137 Bo Diaz .... .10 .05 .01
☐ 138 Glenn Brummer .... .10 .05 .01
☐ 139 Sid Monge .... .10 .05 .01
☐ 140 Rich Gale .... .10 .05 .01
☐ 141 Brett Butler .... .20 .10 .02
☐ 142 Brian Harper .... .30 .15 .03
☐ 143 John Rabb .... .10 .05 .01
☐ 144 Gary Woods .... .10 .05 .01
☐ 145 Pat Putnam .... .10 .05 .01
☐ 146 Jim Acker .... .15 .07 .01
☐ 147 Mickey Hatcher .... .15 .07 .01
☐ 148 Todd Cruz .... .10 .05 .01
☐ 149 Tom Tellmann .... .10 .05 .01
☐ 150 John Wockenfuss .... .10 .05 .01
☐ 151 Wade Boggs 11.00 5.50 1.10
☐ 152 Don Baylor .... .20 .10 .02
☐ 153 Bob Welch .... .15 .07 .01
☐ 154 Alan Bannister .... .10 .05 .01
☐ 155 Willie Aikens .... .10 .05 .01
☐ 156 Jeff Burroughs .... .10 .05 .01
☐ 157 Bryan Little .... .10 .05 .01
☐ 158 Bob Boone .... .25 .12 .02
☐ 159 Dave Hostetler .... .10 .05 .01
☐ 160 Jerry Dybzinski .... .10 .05 .01
☐ 161 Mike Madden .... .10 .05 .01
☐ 162 Luis DeLeon .... .10 .05 .01
☐ 163 Willie Hernandez .... .25 .12 .02
☐ 164 Frank Pastore .... .10 .05 .01
☐ 165 Rick Camp .... .10 .05 .01
☐ 166 Lee Mazzilli .... .10 .05 .01
☐ 167 Scot Thompson .... .10 .05 .01
☐ 168 Bob Forsch .... .10 .05 .01
☐ 169 Mike Flanagan .... .15 .07 .01
☐ 170 Rick Manning .... .10 .05 .01
☐ 171 Chet Lemon .... .15 .07 .01
☐ 172 Jerry Remy .... .10 .05 .01
☐ 173 Ron Guidry .... .25 .12 .02
☐ 174 Pedro Guerrero .... .50 .25 .05
☐ 175 Willie Wilson .... .20 .10 .02
☐ 176 Carney Lansford .... .25 .12 .02
☐ 177 Al Oliver .... .20 .10 .02

☐ 178	Jim Sundberg	.10	.05	.01
☐ 179	Bobby Grich	.15	.07	.01
☐ 180	Rich Dotson	.15	.07	.01
☐ 181	Joaquin Andujar	.15	.07	.01
☐ 182	Jose Cruz	.15	.07	.01
☐ 183	Mike Schmidt	3.25	1.50	.30
☐ 184	Gary Redus	.40	.20	.04
☐ 185	Garry Templeton	.15	.07	.01
☐ 186	Tony Pena	.20	.10	.02
☐ 187	Greg Minton	.10	.05	.01
☐ 188	Phil Niekro	.40	.20	.04
☐ 189	Ferguson Jenkins	.25	.12	.02
☐ 190	Mookie Wilson	.20	.10	.02
☐ 191	Jim Beattie	.10	.05	.01
☐ 192	Gary Ward	.15	.07	.01
☐ 193	Jesse Barfield	.40	.20	.04
☐ 194	Pete Filson	.10	.05	.01
☐ 195	Roy Lee Jackson	.10	.05	.01
☐ 196	Rick Sweet	.10	.05	.01
☐ 197	Jesse Orosco	.10	.05	.01
☐ 198	Steve Lake	.10	.05	.01
☐ 199	Ken Dayley	.10	.05	.01
☐ 200	Manny Sarmiento	.10	.05	.01
☐ 201	Mark Davis	1.50	.75	.15
☐ 202	Tim Flannery	.10	.05	.01
☐ 203	Bill Scherrer	.10	.05	.01
☐ 204	Al Holland	.10	.05	.01
☐ 205	Dave Von Ohlen	.10	.05	.01
☐ 206	Mike LaCoss	.10	.05	.01
☐ 207	Juan Beniquez	.10	.05	.01
☐ 208	Juan Agosto	.20	.10	.02
☐ 209	Bobby Ramos	.10	.05	.01
☐ 210	Al Bumbry	.10	.05	.01
☐ 211	Mark Brouhard	.10	.05	.01
☐ 212	Howard Bailey	.10	.05	.01
☐ 213	Bruce Hurst	.35	.17	.03
☐ 214	Bob Shirley	.10	.05	.01
☐ 215	Pat Zachry	.10	.05	.01
☐ 216	Julio Franco	1.25	.60	.12
☐ 217	Mike Armstrong	.10	.05	.01
☐ 218	Dave Beard	.10	.05	.01
☐ 219	Steve Rogers	.10	.05	.01
☐ 220	John Butcher	.10	.05	.01
☐ 221	Mike Smithson	.15	.07	.01
☐ 222	Frank White	.15	.07	.01
☐ 223	Mike Heath	.10	.05	.01
☐ 224	Chris Bando	.10	.05	.01
☐ 225	Roy Smalley	.10	.05	.01
☐ 226	Dusty Baker	.15	.07	.01
☐ 227	Lou Whitaker	.35	.17	.03
☐ 228	John Lowenstein	.10	.05	.01
☐ 229	Ben Oglivie	.15	.07	.01
☐ 230	Doug DeCinces	.15	.07	.01
☐ 231	Lonnie Smith	.20	.10	.02
☐ 232	Ray Knight	.15	.07	.01
☐ 233	Gary Matthews	.15	.07	.01
☐ 234	Juan Bonilla	.10	.05	.01
☐ 235	Rod Scurry	.10	.05	.01
☐ 236	Atlee Hammaker	.10	.05	.01
☐ 237	Mike Caldwell	.10	.05	.01
☐ 238	Keith Hernandez	.45	.22	.04
☐ 239	Larry Bowa	.15	.07	.01
☐ 240	Tony Bernazard	.10	.05	.01
☐ 241	Damaso Garcia	.10	.05	.01
☐ 242	Tom Brunansky	.35	.17	.03
☐ 243	Dan Driessen	.10	.05	.01
☐ 244	Ron Kittle	.30	.15	.03
☐ 245	Tim Stoddard	.10	.05	.01
☐ 246	Bob L. Gibson (Brewers Pitcher)	.15	.07	.01
☐ 247	Marty Castillo	.10	.05	.01
☐ 248	Don Mattingly UER ("traiing" on back)	65.00	32.50	6.50
☐ 249	Jeff Newman	.10	.05	.01
☐ 250	Alejandro Pena	.60	.30	.06
☐ 251	Toby Harrah	.15	.07	.01
☐ 252	Cesar Geronimo	.10	.05	.01
☐ 253	Tom Underwood	.10	.05	.01
☐ 254	Doug Flynn	.10	.05	.01
☐ 255	Andy Hassler	.10	.05	.01
☐ 256	Odell Jones	.10	.05	.01
☐ 257	Rudy Law	.10	.05	.01
☐ 258	Harry Spilman	.10	.05	.01
☐ 259	Marty Bystrom	.10	.05	.01
☐ 260	Dave Rucker	.10	.05	.01
☐ 261	Ruppert Jones	.10	.05	.01
☐ 262	Jeff R. Jones (Reds OF)	.10	.05	.01
☐ 263	Gerald Perry	1.50	.75	.15
☐ 264	Gene Tenace	.10	.05	.01
☐ 265	Brad Wellman	.10	.05	.01
☐ 266	Dickie Noles	.10	.05	.01
☐ 267	Jamie Allen	.10	.05	.01
☐ 268	Jim Gott	.15	.07	.01
☐ 269	Ron Davis	.10	.05	.01
☐ 270	Benny Ayala	.10	.05	.01
☐ 271	Ned Yost	.10	.05	.01
☐ 272	Dave Rozema	.10	.05	.01
☐ 273	Dave Stapleton	.10	.05	.01
☐ 274	Lou Piniella	.20	.10	.02
☐ 275	Jose Morales	.10	.05	.01
☐ 276	Broderick Perkins	.10	.05	.01
☐ 277	Butch Davis	.15	.07	.01
☐ 278	Tony Phillips	.35	.17	.03
☐ 279	Jeff Reardon	.20	.10	.02
☐ 280	Ken Forsch	.10	.05	.01
☐ 281	Pete O'Brien	1.50	.75	.15
☐ 282	Tom Paciorek	.10	.05	.01
☐ 283	Frank LaCorte	.10	.05	.01
☐ 284	Tim Lollar	.10	.05	.01
☐ 285	Greg Gross	.10	.05	.01
☐ 286	Alex Trevino	.10	.05	.01
☐ 287	Gene Garber	.10	.05	.01
☐ 288	Dave Parker	.40	.20	.04
☐ 289	Lee Smith	.20	.10	.02
☐ 290	Dave LaPoint	.15	.07	.01
☐ 291	John Shelby	.45	.22	.04
☐ 292	Charlie Moore	.10	.05	.01
☐ 293	Alan Trammell	.60	.30	.06
☐ 294	Tony Armas	.15	.07	.01
☐ 295	Shane Rawley	.10	.05	.01
☐ 296	Greg Brock	.15	.07	.01
☐ 297	Hal McRae	.15	.07	.01
☐ 298	Mike Davis	.10	.05	.01
☐ 299	Tim Raines	.75	.35	.07
☐ 300	Bucky Dent	.20	.10	.02
☐ 301	Tommy John	.30	.15	.03
☐ 302	Carlton Fisk	.50	.25	.05
☐ 303	Darrell Porter	.10	.05	.01
☐ 304	Dickie Thon	.15	.07	.01
☐ 305	Garry Maddox	.10	.05	.01
☐ 306	Cesar Cedeno	.15	.07	.01
☐ 307	Gary Lucas	.10	.05	.01
☐ 308	Johnny Ray	.20	.10	.02
☐ 309	Andy McGaffigan	.10	.05	.01
☐ 310	Claudell Washington	.15	.07	.01
☐ 311	Ryne Sandberg	3.00	1.50	.30
☐ 312	George Foster	.25	.12	.02
☐ 313	Spike Owen	.30	.15	.03
☐ 314	Gary Gaetti	1.00	.50	.10
☐ 315	Willie Upshaw	.15	.07	.01
☐ 316	Al Williams	.10	.05	.01
☐ 317	Jorge Orta	.10	.05	.01
☐ 318	Orlando Mercado	.10	.05	.01
☐ 319	Junior Ortiz	.10	.05	.01
☐ 320	Mike Proly	.10	.05	.01
☐ 321	Randy Johnson	.10	.05	.01
☐ 322	Jim Morrison	.10	.05	.01
☐ 323	Max Venable	.10	.05	.01
☐ 324	Tony Gwynn	5.00	2.50	.50
☐ 325	Duane Walker	.10	.05	.01
☐ 326	Ozzie Virgil	.10	.05	.01
☐ 327	Jeff Lahti	.10	.05	.01
☐ 328	Bill Dawley	.15	.07	.01
☐ 329	Rob Wilfong	.10	.05	.01
☐ 330	Marc Hill	.10	.05	.01
☐ 331	Ray Burris	.10	.05	.01
☐ 332	Allan Ramirez	.10	.05	.01
☐ 333	Chuck Porter	.10	.05	.01
☐ 334	Wayne Krenchicki	.10	.05	.01
☐ 335	Gary Allenson	.10	.05	.01
☐ 336	Bobby Meacham	.15	.07	.01
☐ 337	Joe Beckwith	.10	.05	.01
☐ 338	Rick Sutcliffe	.35	.17	.03
☐ 339	Mark Huismann	.15	.07	.01
☐ 340	Tim Conroy	.15	.07	.01
☐ 341	Scott Sanderson	.10	.05	.01
☐ 342	Larry Biittner	.10	.05	.01
☐ 343	Dave Stewart	.60	.30	.06
☐ 344	Darryl Motley	.10	.05	.01
☐ 345	Chris Codiroli	.15	.07	.01
☐ 346	Rich Behenna	.10	.05	.01
☐ 347	Andre Robertson	.10	.05	.01
☐ 348	Mike Marshall	.25	.12	.02
☐ 349	Larry Herndon	.10	.05	.01
☐ 350	Rich Dauer	.10	.05	.01
☐ 351	Cecil Cooper	.15	.07	.01
☐ 352	Rod Carew	.90	.45	.09
☐ 353	Willie McGee	.40	.20	.04
☐ 354	Phil Garner	.10	.05	.01
☐ 355	Joe Morgan	.60	.30	.06
☐ 356	Luis Salazar	.15	.07	.01
☐ 357	John Candelaria	.15	.07	.01
☐ 358	Bill Laskey	.10	.05	.01
☐ 359	Bob McClure	.10	.05	.01
☐ 360	Dave Kingman	.20	.10	.02
☐ 361	Ron Cey	.15	.07	.01
☐ 362	Matt Young	.15	.07	.01
☐ 363	Lloyd Moseby	.20	.10	.02
☐ 364	Frank Viola	1.25	.60	.12

☐ 365	Eddie Milner	.10	.05	.01
☐ 366	Floyd Bannister	.10	.05	.01
☐ 367	Dan Ford	.10	.05	.01
☐ 368	Moose Haas	.10	.05	.01
☐ 369	Doug Bair	.10	.05	.01
☐ 370	Ray Fontenot	.10	.05	.01
☐ 371	Luis Aponte	.10	.05	.01
☐ 372	Jack Fimple	.10	.05	.01
☐ 373	Neal Heaton	.30	.15	.03
☐ 374	Greg Pryor	.10	.05	.01
☐ 375	Wayne Gross	.10	.05	.01
☐ 376	Charlie Lea	.10	.05	.01
☐ 377	Steve Lubratich	.10	.05	.01
☐ 378	Jon Matlack	.10	.05	.01
☐ 379	Julio Cruz	.10	.05	.01
☐ 380	John Mizerock	.10	.05	.01
☐ 381	Kevin Gross	.50	.25	.05
☐ 382	Mike Ramsey	.10	.05	.01
☐ 383	Doug Gwosdz	.10	.05	.01
☐ 384	Kelly Paris	.15	.07	.01
☐ 385	Pete Falcone	.10	.05	.01
☐ 386	Milt May	.10	.05	.01
☐ 387	Fred Breining	.10	.05	.01
☐ 388	Craig Lefferts	.30	.15	.03
☐ 389	Steve Henderson	.10	.05	.01
☐ 390	Randy Moffitt	.10	.05	.01
☐ 391	Ron Washington	.10	.05	.01
☐ 392	Gary Roenicke	.10	.05	.01
☐ 393	Tom Candiotti	.35	.17	.03
☐ 394	Larry Pashnick	.10	.05	.01
☐ 395	Dwight Evans	.35	.17	.03
☐ 396	Goose Gossage	.25	.12	.02
☐ 397	Derrel Thomas	.10	.05	.01
☐ 398	Juan Eichelberger	.10	.05	.01
☐ 399	Leon Roberts	.10	.05	.01
☐ 400	Dave Lopes	.15	.07	.01
☐ 401	Bill Gullickson	.10	.05	.01
☐ 402	Geoff Zahn	.10	.05	.01
☐ 403	Billy Sample	.10	.05	.01
☐ 404	Mike Squires	.10	.05	.01
☐ 405	Craig Reynolds	.10	.05	.01
☐ 406	Eric Show	.15	.07	.01
☐ 407	John Denny	.15	.07	.01
☐ 408	Dann Bilardello	.10	.05	.01
☐ 409	Bruce Benedict	.10	.05	.01
☐ 410	Kent Tekulve	.15	.07	.01
☐ 411	Mel Hall	.25	.12	.02
☐ 412	John Stuper	.10	.05	.01
☐ 413	Rick Dempsey	.10	.05	.01
☐ 414	Don Sutton	.40	.20	.04
☐ 415	Jack Morris	.35	.17	.03
☐ 416	John Tudor	.30	.15	.03
☐ 417	Willie Randolph	.20	.10	.02
☐ 418	Jerry Reuss	.15	.07	.01
☐ 419	Don Slaught	.15	.07	.01
☐ 420	Steve McCatty	.10	.05	.01
☐ 421	Tim Wallach	.25	.12	.02
☐ 422	Larry Parrish	.15	.07	.01
☐ 423	Brian Downing	.15	.07	.01
☐ 424	Britt Burns	.10	.05	.01
☐ 425	David Green	.10	.05	.01
☐ 426	Jerry Mumphrey	.10	.05	.01
☐ 427	Ivan DeJesus	.10	.05	.01
☐ 428	Mario Soto	.10	.05	.01
☐ 429	Gene Richards	.10	.05	.01
☐ 430	Dale Berra	.10	.05	.01
☐ 431	Darrell Evans	.20	.10	.02
☐ 432	Glenn Hubbard	.10	.05	.01
☐ 433	Jody Davis	.15	.07	.01
☐ 434	Danny Heep	.10	.05	.01
☐ 435	Ed Nunez	.20	.10	.02
☐ 436	Bobby Castillo	.10	.05	.01
☐ 437	Ernie Whitt	.15	.07	.01
☐ 438	Scott Ullger	.10	.05	.01
☐ 439	Doyle Alexander	.15	.07	.01
☐ 440	Domingo Ramos	.10	.05	.01
☐ 441	Craig Swan	.10	.05	.01
☐ 442	Warren Brusstar	.10	.05	.01
☐ 443	Len Barker	.10	.05	.01
☐ 444	Mike Easler	.10	.05	.01
☐ 445	Renie Martin	.10	.05	.01
☐ 446	Dennis Rasmussen	.65	.30	.06
☐ 447	Ted Power	.15	.07	.01
☐ 448	Charles Hudson	.25	.12	.02
☐ 449	Danny Cox	.65	.30	.06
☐ 450	Kevin Bass	.20	.10	.02
☐ 451	Daryl Sconiers	.10	.05	.01
☐ 452	Scott Fletcher	.20	.10	.02
☐ 453	Bryn Smith	.20	.10	.02
☐ 454	Jim Dwyer	.10	.05	.01
☐ 455	Rob Picciolo	.10	.05	.01
☐ 456	Enos Cabell	.10	.05	.01
☐ 457	Dennis Boyd	.65	.30	.06
☐ 458	Butch Wynegar	.10	.05	.01
☐ 459	Burt Hooton	.10	.05	.01
☐ 460	Ron Hassey	.10	.05	.01
☐ 461	Danny Jackson	2.00	1.00	.20
☐ 462	Bob Kearney	.10	.05	.01
☐ 463	Terry Francona	.10	.05	.01
☐ 464	Wayne Tolleson	.10	.05	.01
☐ 465	Mickey Rivers	.10	.05	.01
☐ 466	John Wathan	.10	.05	.01
☐ 467	Bill Almon	.10	.05	.01
☐ 468	George Vukovich	.10	.05	.01
☐ 469	Steve Kemp	.15	.07	.01
☐ 470	Ken Landreaux	.10	.05	.01
☐ 471	Milt Wilcox	.10	.05	.01
☐ 472	Tippy Martinez	.10	.05	.01
☐ 473	Ted Simmons	.20	.10	.02
☐ 474	Tim Foli	.10	.05	.01
☐ 475	George Hendrick	.15	.07	.01
☐ 476	Terry Puhl	.10	.05	.01
☐ 477	Von Hayes	.25	.12	.02
☐ 478	Bobby Brown	.10	.05	.01
☐ 479	Lee Lacy	.10	.05	.01
☐ 480	Joel Youngblood	.10	.05	.01
☐ 481	Jim Slaton	.10	.05	.01
☐ 482	Mike Fitzgerald	.10	.05	.01
☐ 483	Keith Moreland	.10	.05	.01
☐ 484	Ron Roenicke	.10	.05	.01
☐ 485	Luis Leal	.10	.05	.01
☐ 486	Bryan Oelkers	.10	.05	.01
☐ 487	Bruce Berenyi	.10	.05	.01
☐ 488	LaMarr Hoyt	.15	.07	.01
☐ 489	Joe Nolan	.10	.05	.01
☐ 490	Marshall Edwards	.10	.05	.01
☐ 491	Mike Laga	.10	.05	.01
☐ 492	Rick Cerone	.10	.05	.01
☐ 493	Rick Miller	.10	.05	.01
	(listed as Mike			
	on card front)			
☐ 494	Rick Honeycutt	.10	.05	.01
☐ 495	Mike Hargrove	.15	.07	.01
☐ 496	Joe Simpson	.10	.05	.01
☐ 497	Keith Atherton	.10	.05	.01
☐ 498	Chris Welsh	.10	.05	.01
☐ 499	Bruce Kison	.10	.05	.01
☐ 500	Bobby Johnson	.10	.05	.01
☐ 501	Jerry Koosman	.20	.10	.02
☐ 502	Frank DiPino	.10	.05	.01
☐ 503	Tony Perez	.30	.15	.03
☐ 504	Ken Oberkfell	.10	.05	.01
☐ 505	Mark Thurmond	.15	.07	.01
☐ 506	Joe Price	.10	.05	.01
☐ 507	Pascual Perez	.30	.15	.03
☐ 508	Marvell Wynne	.15	.07	.01
☐ 509	Mike Krukow	.15	.07	.01
☐ 510	Dick Ruthven	.10	.05	.01
☐ 511	Al Cowens	.10	.05	.01
☐ 512	Cliff Johnson	.10	.05	.01
☐ 513	Randy Bush	.25	.12	.02
☐ 514	Sammy Stewart	.10	.05	.01
☐ 515	Bill Schroeder	.15	.07	.01
☐ 516	Aurelio Lopez	.10	.05	.01
☐ 517	Mike Brown	.15	.07	.01
	(Red Sox pitcher)			
☐ 518	Graig Nettles	.20	.10	.02
☐ 519	Dave Sax	.10	.05	.01
☐ 520	Jerry Willard	.10	.05	.01
☐ 521	Paul Splittorff	.10	.05	.01
☐ 522	Tom Burgmeier	.10	.05	.01
☐ 523	Chris Speier	.10	.05	.01
☐ 524	Bobby Clark	.10	.05	.01
☐ 525	George Wright	.10	.05	.01
☐ 526	Dennis Lamp	.10	.05	.01
☐ 527	Tony Scott	.10	.05	.01
☐ 528	Ed Whitson	.10	.05	.01
☐ 529	Ron Reed	.10	.05	.01
☐ 530	Charlie Puleo	.10	.05	.01
☐ 531	Jerry Royster	.10	.05	.01
☐ 532	Don Robinson	.10	.05	.01
☐ 533	Steve Trout	.10	.05	.01
☐ 534	Bruce Sutter	.20	.10	.02
☐ 535	Bob Horner	.20	.10	.02
☐ 536	Pat Tabler	.20	.10	.02
☐ 537	Chris Chambliss	.15	.07	.01
☐ 538	Bob Ojeda	.20	.10	.02
☐ 539	Alan Ashby	.10	.05	.01
☐ 540	Jay Johnstone	.15	.07	.01
☐ 541	Bob Dernier	.10	.05	.01
☐ 542	Brook Jacoby	1.25	.60	.12
☐ 543	U.L. Washington	.10	.05	.01
☐ 544	Danny Darwin	.10	.05	.01
☐ 545	Kiko Garcia	.10	.05	.01
☐ 546	Vance Law UER	.15	.07	.01
	(listed as P			
	on card front)			
☐ 547	Tug McGraw	.20	.10	.02
☐ 548	Dave Smith	.15	.07	.01
☐ 549	Len Matuszek	.10	.05	.01

☐ 550	Tom Hume	.10	.05	.01
☐ 551	Dave Dravecky	.60	.30	.06
☐ 552	Rick Rhoden	.15	.07	.01
☐ 553	Duane Kuiper	.10	.05	.01
☐ 554	Rusty Staub	.20	.10	.02
☐ 555	Bill Campbell	.10	.05	.01
☐ 556	Mike Torrez	.10	.05	.01
☐ 557	Dave Henderson	.30	.15	.03
☐ 558	Len Whitehouse	.10	.05	.01
☐ 559	Barry Bonnell	.10	.05	.01
☐ 560	Rick Lysander	.10	.05	.01
☐ 561	Garth Iorg	.10	.05	.01
☐ 562	Bryan Clark	.10	.05	.01
☐ 563	Brian Giles	.10	.05	.01
☐ 564	Vern Ruhle	.10	.05	.01
☐ 565	Steve Bedrosian	.30	.15	.03
☐ 566	Larry McWilliams	.10	.05	.01
☐ 567	Jeff Leonard UER	.20	.10	.02
	(listed as P			
	on card front)			
☐ 568	Alan Wiggins	.10	.05	.01
☐ 569	Jeff Russell	.75	.35	.07
☐ 570	Salome Barojas	.10	.05	.01
☐ 571	Dane Iorg	.10	.05	.01
☐ 572	Bob Knepper	.15	.07	.01
☐ 573	Gary Lavelle	.10	.05	.01
☐ 574	Gorman Thomas	.15	.07	.01
☐ 575	Manny Trillo	.10	.05	.01
☐ 576	Jim Palmer	1.00	.50	.10
☐ 577	Dale Murray	.10	.05	.01
☐ 578	Tom Brookens	.10	.05	.01
☐ 579	Rich Gedman	.15	.07	.01
☐ 580	Bill Doran	1.00	.50	.10
☐ 581	Steve Yeager	.10	.05	.01
☐ 582	Dan Spillner	.10	.05	.01
☐ 583	Dan Quisenberry	.20	.10	.02
☐ 584	Rance Mulliniks	.10	.05	.01
☐ 585	Storm Davis	.20	.10	.02
☐ 586	Dave Schmidt	.15	.07	.01
☐ 587	Bill Russell	.15	.07	.01
☐ 588	Pat Sheridan	.25	.12	.02
☐ 589	Rafael Ramirez	.15	.07	.01
	ERR (A's on front)			
☐ 590	Bud Anderson	.10	.05	.01
☐ 591	George Frazier	.10	.05	.01
☐ 592	Lee Tunnell	.15	.07	.01
☐ 593	Kirk Gibson	.65	.30	.06
☐ 594	Scott McGregor	.15	.07	.01
☐ 595	Bob Bailor	.10	.05	.01
☐ 596	Tommy Herr	.15	.07	.01
☐ 597	Luis Sanchez	.10	.05	.01
☐ 598	Dave Engle	.10	.05	.01
☐ 599	Craig McMurtry	.15	.07	.01
☐ 600	Carlos Diaz	.10	.05	.01
☐ 601	Tom O'Malley	.10	.05	.01
☐ 602	Nick Esasky	3.50	1.75	.35
☐ 603	Ron Hodges	.10	.05	.01
☐ 604	Ed VandeBerg	.10	.05	.01
☐ 605	Alfredo Griffin	.15	.07	.01
☐ 606	Glenn Hoffman	.10	.05	.01
☐ 607	Hubie Brooks	.25	.12	.02
☐ 608	Richard Barnes UER	.10	.05	.01
	(photo actually			
	Neal Heaton)			
☐ 609	Greg Walker	.50	.25	.05
☐ 610	Ken Singleton	.15	.07	.01
☐ 611	Mark Clear	.10	.05	.01
☐ 612	Buck Martinez	.10	.05	.01
☐ 613	Ken Griffey	.20	.10	.02
☐ 614	Reid Nichols	.10	.05	.01
☐ 615	Doug Sisk	.10	.05	.01
☐ 616	Bob Brenly	.10	.05	.01
☐ 617	Joey McLaughlin	.10	.05	.01
☐ 618	Glenn Wilson	.15	.07	.01
☐ 619	Bob Stoddard	.10	.05	.01
☐ 620	Lenn Sakata UER	.10	.05	.01
	(listed as Len			
	on card front)			
☐ 621	Mike Young	.25	.12	.02
☐ 622	John Stefero	.15	.07	.01
☐ 623	Carmelo Martinez	.30	.15	.03
☐ 624	Dave Bergman	.10	.05	.01
☐ 625	Runnin' Reds	.20	.10	.02
	(sic, Redbirds)			
	David Green			
	Willie McGee			
	Lonnie Smith			
	Ozzie Smith			
☐ 626	Rudy May	.10	.05	.01
☐ 627	Matt Keough	.10	.05	.01
☐ 628	Jose DeLeon	.75	.35	.07
☐ 629	Jim Essian	.10	.05	.01
☐ 630	Darnell Coles	.40	.20	.04
☐ 631	Mike Warren	.15	.07	.01
☐ 632	Del Crandall MG	.10	.05	.01

☐ 633	Dennis Martinez	.15	.07	.01
☐ 634	Mike Moore	.25	.12	.02
☐ 635	Lary Sorensen	.10	.05	.01
☐ 636	Ricky Nelson	.10	.05	.01
☐ 637	Omar Moreno	.10	.05	.01
☐ 638	Charlie Hough	.15	.07	.01
☐ 639	Dennis Eckersley	.30	.12	.03
☐ 640	Walt Terrell	.60	.30	.06
☐ 641	Denny Walling	.10	.05	.01
☐ 642	Dave Anderson	.25	.12	.02
☐ 643	Jose Oquendo	.75	.35	.07
☐ 644	Bob Stanley	.10	.05	.01
☐ 645	Dave Geisel	.10	.05	.01
☐ 646	Scott Garrelts	1.00	.50	.10
☐ 647	Gary Pettis	.50	.25	.05
☐ 648	Duke Snider	.10	.05	.01
	Puzzle Card			
☐ 649	Johnnie LeMaster	.10	.05	.01
☐ 650	Dave Collins	.10	.05	.01
☐ 651	The Chicken	.20	.10	.02
☐ 652	DK Checklist	.10	.01	.00
	(unnumbered)			
☐ 653	Checklist 1-130	.08	.01	.00
	(unnumbered)			
☐ 654	Checklist 131-234	.08	.01	.00
	(unnumbered)			
☐ 655	Checklist 235-338	.08	.01	.00
	(unnumbered)			
☐ 656	Checklist 339-442	.08	.01	.00
	(unnumbered)			
☐ 657	Checklist 443-546	.08	.01	.00
	(unnumbered)			
☐ 658	Checklist 547-651	.08	.01	.00
	(unnumbered)			
☐ A	Living Legends A	3.00	1.50	.30
	Gaylord Perry			
	Rollie Fingers			
☐ B	Living Legends B	7.00	3.50	.70
	Carl Yastrzemski			
	Johnny Bench			

1984 Donruss Action All-Stars

The cards in this 60-card set measure 3 1/2" by 5". For the second year in a row, Donruss issued a postcard-size card set. The set was distributed with a 63-piece Ted Williams puzzle. Unlike last year, when the fronts of the cards contained both an action and a portrait shot of the player, the fronts of this year's cards contain only an action photo. On the backs, the top section contains the card number and a full-color portrait of the player pictured on the front. The bottom half features the player's career statistics.

		MINT	EXC	G-VG
COMPLETE SET (60)		6.00	3.00	.60
COMMON PLAYER (1-60)		.05	.02	.00
☐ 1	Gary Lavelle	.05	.02	.00
☐ 2	Willie McGee	.15	.07	.01
☐ 3	Tony Pena	.05	.02	.00
☐ 4	Lou Whitaker	.15	.07	.01
☐ 5	Robin Yount	.45	.22	.04
☐ 6	Doug DeCinces	.05	.02	.00
☐ 7	John Castino	.05	.02	.00
☐ 8	Terry Kennedy	.05	.02	.00

	9	Rickey Henderson	.50	.25	.05
☐	10	Bob Horner	.15	.07	.01
☐	11	Harold Baines	.15	.07	.01
☐	12	Buddy Bell	.05	.02	.00
☐	13	Fernando Valenzuela	.20	.10	.02
☐	14	Nolan Ryan	1.00	.50	.10
☐	15	Andre Thornton	.05	.02	.00
☐	16	Gary Redus	.05	.02	.00
☐	17	Pedro Guerrero	.20	.10	.02
☐	18	Andre Dawson	.20	.10	.02
☐	19	Dave Stieb	.10	.05	.01
☐	20	Cal Ripken	.35	.17	.03
☐	21	Ken Griffey	.10	.05	.01
☐	22	Wade Boggs	1.00	.50	.10
☐	23	Keith Hernandez	.25	.12	.02
☐	24	Steve Carlton	.35	.17	.03
☐	25	Hal McRae	.05	.02	.00
☐	26	John Lowenstein	.05	.02	.00
☐	27	Fred Lynn	.10	.05	.01
☐	28	Bill Buckner	.10	.05	.01
☐	29	Chris Chambliss	.05	.02	.00
☐	30	Richie Zisk	.05	.02	.00
☐	31	Jack Clark	.20	.10	.02
☐	32	George Hendrick	.05	.02	.00
☐	33	Bill Madlock	.05	.02	.00
☐	34	Lance Parrish	.10	.05	.01
☐	35	Paul Molitor	.20	.10	.02
☐	36	Reggie Jackson	.60	.30	.06
☐	37	Kent Hrbek	.20	.10	.02
☐	38	Steve Garvey	.40	.20	.04
☐	39	Carney Lansford	.15	.07	.01
☐	40	Dale Murphy	.45	.22	.04
☐	41	Greg Luzinski	.10	.05	.01
☐	42	Larry Parrish	.05	.02	.00
☐	43	Ryne Sandberg	.50	.25	.05
☐	44	Dickie Thon	.05	.02	.00
☐	45	Bert Blyleven	.15	.07	.01
☐	46	Ron Oester	.05	.02	.00
☐	47	Dusty Baker	.05	.02	.00
☐	48	Steve Rogers	.05	.02	.00
☐	49	Jim Clancy	.05	.02	.00
☐	50	Eddie Murray	.30	.15	.03
☐	51	Ron Guidry	.20	.10	.02
☐	52	Jim Rice	.20	.10	.02
☐	53	Tom Seaver	.40	.20	.04
☐	54	Pete Rose	.75	.35	.07
☐	55	George Brett	.45	.22	.04
☐	56	Dan Quisenberry	.10	.05	.01
☐	57	Mike Schmidt	.90	.45	.09
☐	58	Ted Simmons	.10	.05	.01
☐	59	Dave Righetti	.15	.07	.01
☐	60	Checklist Card	.05	.02	.00

1984 Donruss Champions

The cards in this 60-card set measure 3 1/2" by 5". The 1984 Donruss Champions set is a hybrid photo/artwork issue. Grand Champions, listed GC in the checklist below, feature the artwork of Dick Perez of Perez-Steele Galleries. Current players in the set feature photographs. The theme of this postcard-size set features a Grand Champion and those current players that are directly behind him in a baseball statistical category, for example, Season Home Runs (1-7), Career Home Runs (8-13), Season Batting Average (14-19), Career Batting Average (20-25), Career Hits (26-30), Career Victories (31-

36), Career Strikeouts (37-42), Most Valuable Players (43-49), World Series stars (50-54), and All-Star heroes (55-59). The cards were issued in cello packs with pieces of the Duke Snider puzzle.

			MINT	EXC	G-VG
	COMPLETE SET (60)		6.00	3.00	.60
	COMMON PLAYER (1-60)		.05	.02	.00
☐	1	Babe Ruth GC	1.00	.50	.10
☐	2	George Foster	.10	.05	.01
☐	3	Dave Kingman	.10	.05	.01
☐	4	Jim Rice	.20	.10	.02
☐	5	Gorman Thomas	.05	.02	.00
☐	6	Ben Oglivie	.05	.02	.00
☐	7	Jeff Burroughs	.05	.02	.00
☐	8	Hank Aaron GC	.30	.15	.03
☐	9	Reggie Jackson	.50	.25	.05
☐	10	Carl Yastrzemski	.60	.30	.06
☐	11	Mike Schmidt	.75	.35	.07
☐	12	Graig Nettles	.10	.05	.01
☐	13	Greg Luzinski	.05	.02	.00
☐	14	Ted Williams GC	.35	.17	.03
☐	15	George Brett	.40	.20	.04
☐	16	Wade Boggs	.75	.35	.07
☐	17	Hal McRae	.05	.02	.00
☐	18	Bill Buckner	.10	.05	.01
☐	19	Eddie Murray	.25	.12	.02
☐	20	Rogers Hornsby GC	.10	.05	.01
☐	21	Rod Carew	.30	.15	.03
☐	22	Bill Madlock	.05	.02	.00
☐	23	Lonnie Smith	.10	.05	.01
☐	24	Cecil Cooper	.10	.05	.01
☐	25	Ken Griffey	.10	.05	.01
☐	26	Ty Cobb GC	.40	.20	.04
☐	27	Pete Rose	.60	.30	.06
☐	28	Rusty Staub	.05	.02	.00
☐	29	Tony Perez	.15	.07	.01
☐	30	Al Oliver	.10	.05	.01
☐	31	Cy Young GC	.10	.05	.01
☐	32	Gaylord Perry	.15	.07	.01
☐	33	Ferguson Jenkins	.10	.05	.01
☐	34	Phil Niekro	.20	.10	.02
☐	35	Jim Palmer	.30	.15	.03
☐	36	Tommy John	.10	.05	.01
☐	37	Walter Johnson GC	.15	.07	.01
☐	38	Steve Carlton	.30	.15	.03
☐	39	Nolan Ryan	.75	.35	.07
☐	40	Tom Seaver	.40	.20	.04
☐	41	Don Sutton	.15	.07	.01
☐	42	Bert Blyleven	.15	.07	.01
☐	43	Frank Robinson GC	.15	.07	.01
☐	44	Joe Morgan	.25	.12	.02
☐	45	Rollie Fingers	.15	.07	.01
☐	46	Keith Hernandez	.20	.10	.02
☐	47	Robin Yount	.35	.17	.03
☐	48	Cal Ripken	.35	.17	.03
☐	49	Dale Murphy	.35	.17	.03
☐	50	Mickey Mantle GC	1.00	.50	.10
☐	51	Johnny Bench	.45	.22	.04
☐	52	Carlton Fisk	.25	.12	.02
☐	53	Tug McGraw	.05	.02	.00
☐	54	Paul Molitor	.15	.07	.01
☐	55	Carl Hubbell GC	.10	.05	.01
☐	56	Steve Garvey	.30	.15	.03
☐	57	Dave Parker	.15	.07	.01
☐	58	Gary Carter	.20	.10	.02
☐	59	Fred Lynn	.10	.05	.01
☐	60	Checklist Card	.05	.02	.00

1985 Donruss

The cards in this 660-card set measure 2 1/2" by 3 1/2". The 1985 Donruss regular issue cards have fronts that feature jet black borders on which orange lines have been placed. The fronts contain the standard team logo, player's name, position, and Donruss logo. The cards were distributed with puzzle pieces from a Dick Perez rendition of Lou Gehrig. The first 26 cards of the set feature Diamond Kings (DK), for the fourth year in a row; the artwork on the Diamond Kings was again produced by the Perez-Steele Galleries. Cards 27-46 feature Rated Rookies (RR). The unnumbered checklist cards are arbitrarily numbered below as numbers 654 through 660. This

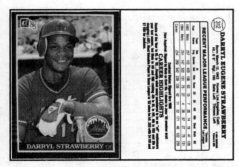

set is noted for containing the Rookie Cards of Roger Clemens, Alvin Davis, Eric Davis, Dwight Gooden, Orel Hershiser, Mark Langston, Kirby Puckett, Bret Saberhagen, and Danny Tartabull.

		MINT	EXC	G-VG
	COMPLETE SET (660)	150.00	70.00	14.00
	COMMON PLAYER (1-660)	.06	.03	.00
☐ 1	Ryne Sandberg DK	.60	.12	.02
☐ 2	Doug DeCinces DK	.10	.05	.01
☐ 3	Richard Dotson DK	.10	.05	.01
☐ 4	Bert Blyleven DK	.15	.07	.01
☐ 5	Lou Whitaker DK	.20	.10	.02
☐ 6	Dan Quisenberry DK	.15	.07	.01
☐ 7	Don Mattingly DK	6.00	3.00	.60
☐ 8	Carney Lansford DK	.15	.07	.01
☐ 9	Frank Tanana DK	.10	.05	.01
☐ 10	Willie Upshaw DK	.10	.05	.01
☐ 11	Claudell Washington DK	.10	.05	.01
☐ 12	Mike Marshall DK	.15	.07	.01
☐ 13	Joaquin Andujar DK	.10	.05	.01
☐ 14	Cal Ripken DK	.40	.20	.04
☐ 15	Jim Rice DK	.25	.12	.02
☐ 16	Don Sutton DK	.25	.12	.02
☐ 17	Frank Viola DK	.40	.20	.04
☐ 18	Alvin Davis DK	.40	.20	.04
☐ 19	Mario Soto DK	.10	.05	.01
☐ 20	Jose Cruz DK	.10	.05	.01
☐ 21	Charlie Lea DK	.10	.05	.01
☐ 22	Jesse Orosco DK	.10	.05	.01
☐ 23	Juan Samuel DK	.30	.15	.03
☐ 24	Tony Pena DK	.15	.07	.01
☐ 25	Tony Gwynn DK	.75	.35	.07
☐ 26	Bob Brenly DK	.10	.05	.01
☐ 27	Danny Tartabull RR	5.00	2.50	.50
☐ 28	Mike Bielecki RR	.75	.35	.07
☐ 29	Steve Lyons RR	.15	.07	.01
☐ 30	Jeff Reed RR	.10	.05	.01
☐ 31	Tony Brewer RR	.10	.05	.01
☐ 32	John Morris RR	.15	.07	.01
☐ 33	Daryl Boston RR	.20	.10	.02
☐ 34	Al Pulido RR	.10	.05	.01
☐ 35	Steve Kiefer RR	.15	.07	.01
☐ 36	Larry Sheets RR	.35	.17	.03
☐ 37	Scott Bradley RR	.30	.15	.03
☐ 38	Calvin Schiraldi RR	.25	.12	.02
☐ 39	Shawon Dunston RR	2.50	1.25	.25
☐ 40	Charlie Mitchell RR	.10	.05	.01
☐ 41	Billy Hatcher RR	.45	.22	.04
☐ 42	Russ Stephans RR	.10	.05	.01
☐ 43	Alejandro Sanchez RR	.10	.05	.01
☐ 44	Steve Jeltz RR	.10	.05	.01
☐ 45	Jim Traber RR	.25	.12	.02
☐ 46	Doug Loman RR	.15	.07	.01
☐ 47	Eddie Murray	.45	.22	.04
☐ 48	Robin Yount	.70	.35	.07
☐ 49	Lance Parrish	.25	.12	.02
☐ 50	Jim Rice	.30	.15	.03
☐ 51	Dave Winfield	.40	.20	.04
☐ 52	Fernando Valenzuela	.25	.12	.02
☐ 53	George Brett	.70	.35	.07
☐ 54	Dave Kingman	.12	.06	.01
☐ 55	Gary Carter	.35	.17	.03
☐ 56	Buddy Bell	.12	.06	.01
☐ 57	Reggie Jackson	.60	.30	.06
☐ 58	Harold Baines	.25	.12	.02
☐ 59	Ozzie Smith	.35	.17	.03
☐ 60	Nolan Ryan	1.75	.85	.17
☐ 61	Mike Schmidt	1.50	.75	.15
☐ 62	Dave Parker	.20	.10	.02
☐ 63	Tony Gwynn	1.50	.75	.15
☐ 64	Tony Pena	.12	.06	.01
☐ 65	Jack Clark	.25	.12	.02
☐ 66	Dale Murphy	.75	.35	.07
☐ 67	Ryne Sandberg	.60	.30	.06
☐ 68	Keith Hernandez	.35	.17	.03
☐ 69	Alvin Davis	4.00	2.00	.40
☐ 70	Kent Hrbek	.35	.17	.03
☐ 71	Willie Upshaw	.06	.03	.00
☐ 72	Dave Engle	.06	.03	.00
☐ 73	Alfredo Griffin	.10	.05	.01
☐ 74A	Jack Perconte (Career Highlights takes four lines)	.15	.07	.01
☐ 74B	Jack Perconte (Career Highlights takes three lines)	.15	.07	.01
☐ 75	Jesse Orosco	.06	.03	.00
☐ 76	Jody Davis	.10	.05	.01
☐ 77	Bob Horner	.12	.06	.01
☐ 78	Larry McWilliams	.06	.03	.00
☐ 79	Joel Youngblood	.06	.03	.00
☐ 80	Alan Wiggins	.06	.03	.00
☐ 81	Ron Oester	.06	.03	.00
☐ 82	Ozzie Virgil	.06	.03	.00
☐ 83	Ricky Horton	.20	.10	.02
☐ 84	Bill Doran	.15	.07	.01
☐ 85	Rod Carew	.50	.25	.05
☐ 86	LaMarr Hoyt	.10	.05	.01
☐ 87	Tim Wallach	.12	.06	.01
☐ 88	Mike Flanagan	.10	.05	.01
☐ 89	Jim Sundberg	.06	.03	.00
☐ 90	Chet Lemon	.10	.05	.01
☐ 91	Bob Stanley	.06	.03	.00
☐ 92	Willie Randolph	.12	.06	.01
☐ 93	Bill Russell	.10	.05	.01
☐ 94	Julio Franco	.40	.20	.04
☐ 95	Dan Quisenberry	.15	.07	.01
☐ 96	Bill Caudill	.06	.03	.00
☐ 97	Bill Gullickson	.06	.03	.00
☐ 98	Danny Darwin	.06	.03	.00
☐ 99	Curtis Wilkerson	.06	.03	.00
☐ 100	Bud Black	.06	.03	.00
☐ 101	Tony Phillips	.06	.03	.00
☐ 102	Tony Bernazard	.06	.03	.00
☐ 103	Jay Howell	.10	.05	.01
☐ 104	Burt Hooton	.06	.03	.00
☐ 105	Milt Wilcox	.06	.03	.00
☐ 106	Rich Dauer	.06	.03	.00
☐ 107	Don Sutton	.25	.12	.02
☐ 108	Mike Witt	.10	.05	.01
☐ 109	Bruce Sutter	.12	.06	.01
☐ 110	Enos Cabell	.06	.03	.00
☐ 111	John Denny	.10	.05	.01
☐ 112	Dave Dravecky	.15	.07	.01
☐ 113	Marvell Wynne	.06	.03	.00
☐ 114	Johnnie LeMaster	.06	.03	.00
☐ 115	Chuck Porter	.06	.03	.00
☐ 116	John Gibbons	.10	.05	.01
☐ 117	Keith Moreland	.06	.03	.00
☐ 118	Darnell Coles	.10	.05	.01
☐ 119	Dennis Lamp	.06	.03	.00
☐ 120	Ron Davis	.06	.03	.00
☐ 121	Nick Esasky	.25	.12	.02
☐ 122	Vance Law	.10	.05	.01
☐ 123	Gary Roenicke	.06	.03	.00
☐ 124	Bill Schroeder	.06	.03	.00
☐ 125	Dave Rozema	.06	.03	.00
☐ 126	Bobby Meacham	.06	.03	.00
☐ 127	Marty Barrett	.35	.17	.03
☐ 128	R.J. Reynolds	.25	.12	.02
☐ 129	Ernie Camacho UER (photo actually Rich Thompson)	.06	.03	.00
☐ 130	Jorge Orta	.06	.03	.00
☐ 131	Lary Sorensen	.06	.03	.00
☐ 132	Terry Francona	.06	.03	.00
☐ 133	Fred Lynn	.15	.07	.01
☐ 134	Bob Jones	.06	.03	.00
☐ 135	Jerry Hairston	.06	.03	.00
☐ 136	Kevin Bass	.12	.06	.01
☐ 137	Garry Maddox	.10	.05	.01
☐ 138	Dave LaPoint	.10	.05	.01
☐ 139	Kevin McReynolds	1.00	.50	.10
☐ 140	Wayne Krenchicki	.06	.03	.00
☐ 141	Rafael Ramirez	.06	.03	.00
☐ 142	Rod Scurry	.06	.03	.00
☐ 143	Greg Minton	.06	.03	.00
☐ 144	Tim Stoddard	.06	.03	.00
☐ 145	Steve Henderson	.06	.03	.00
☐ 146	George Bell	.65	.30	.06
☐ 147	Dave Meier	.06	.03	.00
☐ 148	Sammy Stewart	.06	.03	.00
☐ 149	Mark Brouhard	.06	.03	.00
☐ 150	Larry Herndon	.06	.03	.00
☐ 151	Oil Can Boyd	.10	.05	.01
☐ 152	Brian Dayett	.06	.03	.00

☐ 153	Tom Niedenfuer	.06	.03	.00	☐ 246	Tom Tellmann	.06	.03	.00
☐ 154	Brook Jacoby	.12	.06	.01	☐ 247	Howard Johnson	2.00	1.00	.20
☐ 155	Onix Concepcion	.06	.03	.00	☐ 248	Ray Fontenot	.06	.03	.00
☐ 156	Tim Conroy	.06	.03	.00	☐ 249	Tony Armas	.10	.05	.01
☐ 157	Joe Hesketh	.15	.07	.01	☐ 250	Candy Maldonado	.10	.05	.01
☐ 158	Brian Downing	.10	.05	.01	☐ 251	Mike Jeffcoat	.06	.03	.00
☐ 159	Tommy Dunbar	.06	.03	.00	☐ 252	Dane Iorg	.06	.03	.00
☐ 160	Marc Hill	.06	.03	.00	☐ 253	Bruce Bochte	.06	.03	.00
☐ 161	Phil Garner	.06	.03	.00	☐ 254	Pete Rose	1.50	.75	.15
☐ 162	Jerry Davis	.06	.03	.00	☐ 255	Don Aase	.06	.03	.00
☐ 163	Bill Campbell	.06	.03	.00	☐ 256	George Wright	.06	.03	.00
☐ 164	John Franco	2.00	1.00	.20	☐ 257	Britt Burns	.06	.03	.00
☐ 165	Len Barker	.06	.03	.00	☐ 258	Mike Scott	.40	.20	.04
☐ 166	Benny Distefano	.10	.05	.01	☐ 259	Len Matuszek	.06	.03	.00
☐ 167	George Frazier	.06	.03	.00	☐ 260	Dave Rucker	.06	.03	.00
☐ 168	Tito Landrum	.06	.03	.00	☐ 261	Craig Lefferts	.10	.05	.01
☐ 169	Cal Ripken	.60	.30	.06	☐ 262	Jay Tibbs	.12	.06	.01
☐ 170	Cecil Cooper	.12	.06	.01	☐ 263	Bruce Benedict	.06	.03	.00
☐ 171	Alan Trammell	.30	.15	.03	☐ 264	Don Robinson	.06	.03	.00
☐ 172	Wade Boggs	5.50	2.75	.55	☐ 265	Gary Lavelle	.06	.03	.00
☐ 173	Don Baylor	.15	.07	.01	☐ 266	Scott Sanderson	.06	.03	.00
☐ 174	Pedro Guerrero	.30	.15	.03	☐ 267	Matt Young	.06	.03	.00
☐ 175	Frank White	.10	.05	.01	☐ 268	Ernie Whitt	.06	.03	.00
☐ 176	Rickey Henderson	.90	.45	.09	☐ 269	Houston Jimenez	.06	.03	.00
☐ 177	Charlie Lea	.06	.03	.00	☐ 270	Ken Dixon	.10	.05	.01
☐ 178	Pete O'Brien	.15	.07	.01	☐ 271	Pete Ladd	.06	.03	.00
☐ 179	Doug DeCinces	.10	.05	.01	☐ 272	Juan Berenguer	.06	.03	.00
☐ 180	Ron Kittle	.20	.10	.02	☐ 273	Roger Clemens	15.00	7.50	1.50
☐ 181	George Hendrick	.10	.05	.01	☐ 274	Rick Cerone	.06	.03	.00
☐ 182	Joe Niekro	.10	.05	.01	☐ 275	Dave Anderson	.06	.03	.00
☐ 183	Juan Samuel	1.00	.50	.10	☐ 276	George Vukovich	.06	.03	.00
☐ 184	Mario Soto	.06	.03	.00	☐ 277	Greg Pryor	.06	.03	.00
☐ 185	Goose Gossage	.15	.07	.01	☐ 278	Mike Warren	.06	.03	.00
☐ 186	Johnny Ray	.12	.06	.01	☐ 279	Bob James	.06	.03	.00
☐ 187	Bob Brenly	.06	.03	.00	☐ 280	Bobby Grich	.10	.05	.01
☐ 188	Craig McMurtry	.06	.03	.00	☐ 281	Mike Mason	.06	.03	.00
☐ 189	Leon Durham	.10	.05	.01	☐ 282	Ron Reed	.06	.03	.00
☐ 190	Dwight Gooden	13.50	6.00	1.25	☐ 283	Alan Ashby	.06	.03	.00
☐ 191	Barry Bonnell	.06	.03	.00	☐ 284	Mark Thurmond	.06	.03	.00
☐ 192	Tim Teufel	.10	.05	.01	☐ 285	Joe Lefebvre	.06	.03	.00
☐ 193	Dave Stieb	.15	.07	.01	☐ 286	Ted Power	.06	.03	.00
☐ 194	Mickey Hatcher	.06	.03	.00	☐ 287	Chris Chambliss	.10	.05	.01
☐ 195	Jesse Barfield	.25	.12	.02	☐ 288	Lee Tunnell	.06	.03	.00
☐ 196	Al Cowens	.06	.03	.00	☐ 289	Rich Bordi	.06	.03	.00
☐ 197	Hubie Brooks	.10	.05	.01	☐ 290	Glenn Brummer	.06	.03	.00
☐ 198	Steve Trout	.06	.03	.00	☐ 291	Mike Boddicker	.10	.05	.01
☐ 199	Glenn Hubbard	.06	.03	.00	☐ 292	Rollie Fingers	.20	.10	.02
☐ 200	Bill Madlock	.10	.05	.01	☐ 293	Lou Whitaker	.25	.12	.02
☐ 201	Jeff Robinson (Giants pitcher)	.35	.17	.03	☐ 294	Dwight Evans	.18	.09	.01
☐ 202	Eric Show	.06	.03	.00	☐ 295	Don Mattingly	15.00	7.50	1.50
☐ 203	Dave Concepcion	.10	.05	.01	☐ 296	Mike Marshall	.15	.07	.01
☐ 204	Ivan DeJesus	.06	.03	.00	☐ 297	Willie Wilson	.12	.06	.01
☐ 205	Neil Allen	.06	.03	.00	☐ 298	Mike Heath	.06	.03	.00
☐ 206	Jerry Mumphrey	.06	.03	.00	☐ 299	Tim Raines	.50	.25	.05
☐ 207	Mike Brown (Angels OF)	.06	.03	.00	☐ 300	Larry Parrish	.10	.05	.01
☐ 208	Carlton Fisk	.30	.15	.03	☐ 301	Geoff Zahn	.06	.03	.00
☐ 209	Bryn Smith	.12	.06	.01	☐ 302	Rich Dotson	.10	.05	.01
☐ 210	Tippy Martinez	.06	.03	.00	☐ 303	David Green	.06	.03	.00
☐ 211	Dion James	.10	.05	.01	☐ 304	Jose Cruz	.10	.05	.01
☐ 212	Willie Hernandez	.10	.05	.01	☐ 305	Steve Carlton	.50	.25	.05
☐ 213	Mike Easler	.06	.03	.00	☐ 306	Gary Redus	.06	.03	.00
☐ 214	Ron Guidry	.20	.10	.02	☐ 307	Steve Garvey	.50	.25	.05
☐ 215	Rick Honeycutt	.06	.03	.00	☐ 308	Jose DeLeon	.10	.05	.01
☐ 216	Brett Butler	.10	.05	.01	☐ 309	Randy Lerch	.06	.03	.00
☐ 217	Larry Gura	.06	.03	.00	☐ 310	Claudell Washington	.10	.05	.01
☐ 218	Ray Burris	.06	.03	.00	☐ 311	Lee Smith	.10	.05	.01
☐ 219	Steve Rogers	.06	.03	.00	☐ 312	Darryl Strawberry	5.00	2.50	.50
☐ 220	Frank Tanana	.10	.05	.01	☐ 313	Jim Beattie	.06	.03	.00
☐ 221	Ned Yost	.06	.03	.00	☐ 314	John Butcher	.06	.03	.00
☐ 222	Bret Saberhagen	10.00	5.00	1.00	☐ 315	Damaso Garcia	.06	.03	.00
☐ 223	Mike Davis	.10	.05	.01	☐ 316	Mike Smithson	.06	.03	.00
☐ 224	Bert Blyleven	.20	.10	.02	☐ 317	Luis Leal	.06	.03	.00
☐ 225	Steve Kemp	.10	.05	.01	☐ 318	Ken Phelps	.45	.22	.04
☐ 226	Jerry Reuss	.10	.05	.01	☐ 319	Wally Backman	.10	.05	.01
☐ 227	Darrell Evans	.15	.07	.01	☐ 320	Ron Cey	.10	.05	.01
☐ 228	Wayne Gross	.06	.03	.00	☐ 321	Brad Komminsk	.06	.03	.00
☐ 229	Jim Gantner	.06	.03	.00	☐ 322	Jason Thompson	.06	.03	.00
☐ 230	Bob Boone	.15	.07	.01	☐ 323	Frank Williams	.12	.06	.01
☐ 231	Lonnie Smith	.12	.06	.01	☐ 324	Tim Lollar	.06	.03	.00
☐ 232	Frank DiPino	.06	.03	.00	☐ 325	Eric Davis	18.00	9.00	1.80
☐ 233	Jerry Koosman	.10	.05	.01	☐ 326	Von Hayes	.15	.07	.01
☐ 234	Graig Nettles	.15	.07	.01	☐ 327	Andy Van Slyke	.50	.25	.05
☐ 235	John Tudor	.15	.07	.01	☐ 328	Craig Reynolds	.06	.03	.00
☐ 236	John Rabb	.06	.03	.00	☐ 329	Dick Schofield	.10	.05	.01
☐ 237	Rick Manning	.06	.03	.00	☐ 330	Scott Fletcher	.10	.05	.01
☐ 238	Mike Fitzgerald	.06	.03	.00	☐ 331	Jeff Reardon	.12	.06	.01
☐ 239	Gary Matthews	.10	.05	.01	☐ 332	Rick Dempsey	.06	.03	.00
☐ 240	Jim Presley	.90	.45	.09	☐ 333	Ben Oglivie	.10	.05	.01
☐ 241	Dave Collins	.06	.03	.00	☐ 334	Dan Petry	.06	.03	.00
☐ 242	Gary Gaetti	.40	.20	.04	☐ 335	Jackie Gutierrez	.06	.03	.00
☐ 243	Dann Bilardello	.06	.03	.00	☐ 336	Dave Righetti	.15	.07	.01
☐ 244	Rudy Law	.06	.03	.00	☐ 337	Alejandro Pena	.10	.05	.01
☐ 245	John Lowenstein	.06	.03	.00	☐ 338	Mel Hall	.12	.06	.01
					☐ 339	Pat Sheridan	.06	.03	.00
					☐ 340	Keith Atherton	.06	.03	.00

☐ 341	David Palmer	.06	.03	.00
☐ 342	Gary Ward	.10	.05	.01
☐ 343	Dave Stewart	.35	.17	.03
☐ 344	Mark Gubicza	2.50	1.25	.25
☐ 345	Carney Lansford	.15	.07	.01
☐ 346	Jerry Willard	.06	.03	.00
☐ 347	Ken Griffey	.12	.06	.01
☐ 348	Franklin Stubbs	.35	.17	.03
☐ 349	Aurelio Lopez	.06	.03	.00
☐ 350	Al Bumbry	.06	.03	.00
☐ 351	Charlie Moore	.06	.03	.00
☐ 352	Luis Sanchez	.06	.03	.00
☐ 353	Darrell Porter	.06	.03	.00
☐ 354	Bill Dawley	.06	.03	.00
☐ 355	Charles Hudson	.06	.03	.00
☐ 356	Garry Templeton	.10	.05	.01
☐ 357	Cecilio Guante	.06	.03	.00
☐ 358	Jeff Leonard	.12	.06	.01
☐ 359	Paul Molitor	.20	.10	.02
☐ 360	Ron Gardenhire	.06	.03	.00
☐ 361	Larry Bowa	.10	.05	.01
☐ 362	Bob Kearney	.06	.03	.00
☐ 363	Garth Iorg	.06	.03	.00
☐ 364	Tom Brunansky	.25	.12	.02
☐ 365	Brad Gulden	.06	.03	.00
☐ 366	Greg Walker	.10	.05	.01
☐ 367	Mike Young	.10	.05	.01
☐ 368	Rick Waits	.06	.03	.00
☐ 369	Doug Bair	.06	.03	.00
☐ 370	Bob Shirley	.06	.03	.00
☐ 371	Bob Ojeda	.10	.05	.01
☐ 372	Bob Welch	.10	.05	.01
☐ 373	Neal Heaton	.06	.03	.00
☐ 374	Danny Jackson UER (photo actually Frank Wills)	.40	.20	.04
☐ 375	Donnie Hill	.06	.03	.00
☐ 376	Mike Stenhouse	.06	.03	.00
☐ 377	Bruce Kison	.06	.03	.00
☐ 378	Wayne Tolleson	.06	.03	.00
☐ 379	Floyd Bannister	.06	.03	.00
☐ 380	Vern Ruhle	.06	.03	.00
☐ 381	Tim Corcoran	.06	.03	.00
☐ 382	Kurt Kepshire	.06	.03	.00
☐ 383	Bobby Brown	.06	.03	.00
☐ 384	Dave Van Gorder	.06	.03	.00
☐ 385	Rick Mahler	.06	.03	.00
☐ 386	Lee Mazzilli	.06	.03	.00
☐ 387	Bill Laskey	.06	.03	.00
☐ 388	Thad Bosley	.06	.03	.00
☐ 389	Al Chambers	.06	.03	.00
☐ 390	Tony Fernandez	.75	.35	.07
☐ 391	Ron Washington	.06	.03	.00
☐ 392	Bill Swaggerty	.06	.03	.00
☐ 393	Bob L. Gibson	.06	.03	.00
☐ 394	Marty Castillo	.06	.03	.00
☐ 395	Steve Crawford	.06	.03	.00
☐ 396	Clay Christiansen	.06	.03	.00
☐ 397	Bob Bailor	.06	.03	.00
☐ 398	Mike Hargrove	.10	.05	.01
☐ 399	Charlie Leibrandt	.06	.03	.00
☐ 400	Tom Burgmeier	.06	.03	.00
☐ 401	Razor Shines	.10	.05	.01
☐ 402	Rob Wilfong	.06	.03	.00
☐ 403	Tom Henke	.15	.07	.01
☐ 404	Al Jones	.06	.03	.00
☐ 405	Mike LaCoss	.06	.03	.00
☐ 406	Luis DeLeon	.06	.03	.00
☐ 407	Greg Gross	.06	.03	.00
☐ 408	Tom Hume	.06	.03	.00
☐ 409	Rick Camp	.06	.03	.00
☐ 410	Milt May	.06	.03	.00
☐ 411	Henry Cotto	.10	.05	.01
☐ 412	David Von Ohlen	.06	.03	.00
☐ 413	Scott McGregor	.10	.05	.01
☐ 414	Ted Simmons	.12	.06	.01
☐ 415	Jack Morris	.18	.09	.01
☐ 416	Bill Buckner	.10	.05	.01
☐ 417	Butch Wynegar	.06	.03	.00
☐ 418	Steve Sax	.30	.15	.03
☐ 419	Steve Balboni	.06	.03	.00
☐ 420	Dwayne Murphy	.06	.03	.00
☐ 421	Andre Dawson	.35	.17	.03
☐ 422	Charlie Hough	.10	.05	.01
☐ 423	Tommy John	.15	.07	.01
☐ 424A	Tom Seaver ERR (photo actually Floyd Bannister)	1.00	.50	.10
☐ 424B	Tom Seaver COR	10.00	5.00	1.00
☐ 425	Tommy Herr	.10	.05	.01
☐ 426	Terry Puhl	.06	.03	.00
☐ 427	Al Holland	.06	.03	.00
☐ 428	Eddie Milner	.06	.03	.00
☐ 429	Terry Kennedy	.06	.03	.00
☐ 430	John Candelaria	.10	.05	.01
☐ 431	Manny Trillo	.06	.03	.00
☐ 432	Ken Oberkfell	.06	.03	.00
☐ 433	Rick Sutcliffe	.20	.10	.02
☐ 434	Ron Darling	.90	.45	.09
☐ 435	Spike Owen	.06	.03	.00
☐ 436	Frank Viola	.45	.22	.04
☐ 437	Lloyd Moseby	.12	.06	.01
☐ 438	Kirby Puckett	20.00	10.00	2.00
☐ 439	Jim Clancy	.06	.03	.00
☐ 440	Mike Moore	.12	.06	.01
☐ 441	Doug Sisk	.06	.03	.00
☐ 442	Dennis Eckersley	.20	.10	.02
☐ 443	Gerald Perry	.18	.09	.01
☐ 444	Dale Berra	.06	.03	.00
☐ 445	Dusty Baker	.10	.05	.01
☐ 446	Ed Whitson	.06	.03	.00
☐ 447	Cesar Cedeno	.10	.05	.01
☐ 448	Rick Schu	.18	.09	.01
☐ 449	Joaquin Andujar	.10	.05	.01
☐ 450	Mark Bailey	.10	.05	.01
☐ 451	Ron Romanick	.10	.05	.01
☐ 452	Julio Cruz	.06	.03	.00
☐ 453	Miguel Dilone	.06	.03	.00
☐ 454	Storm Davis	.12	.06	.01
☐ 455	Jaime Cocanower	.10	.05	.01
☐ 456	Barbaro Garbey	.06	.03	.00
☐ 457	Rich Gedman	.10	.05	.01
☐ 458	Phil Niekro	.25	.12	.02
☐ 459	Mike Scioscia	.10	.05	.01
☐ 460	Pat Tabler	.10	.05	.01
☐ 461	Darryl Motley	.06	.03	.00
☐ 462	Chris Codiroli	.06	.03	.00
☐ 463	Doug Flynn	.06	.03	.00
☐ 464	Billy Sample	.06	.03	.00
☐ 465	Mickey Rivers	.06	.03	.00
☐ 466	John Wathan	.06	.03	.00
☐ 467	Bill Krueger	.06	.03	.00
☐ 468	Andre Thornton	.10	.05	.01
☐ 469	Rex Hudler	.18	.09	.01
☐ 470	Sid Bream	.35	.17	.03
☐ 471	Kirk Gibson	.35	.17	.03
☐ 472	John Shelby	.06	.03	.00
☐ 473	Moose Haas	.06	.03	.00
☐ 474	Doug Corbett	.06	.03	.00
☐ 475	Willie McGee	.35	.17	.03
☐ 476	Bob Knepper	.10	.05	.01
☐ 477	Kevin Gross	.06	.03	.00
☐ 478	Carmelo Martinez	.06	.03	.00
☐ 479	Kent Tekulve	.10	.05	.01
☐ 480	Chili Davis	.10	.05	.01
☐ 481	Bobby Clark	.06	.03	.00
☐ 482	Mookie Wilson	.12	.06	.01
☐ 483	Dave Owen	.06	.03	.00
☐ 484	Ed Nunez	.06	.03	.00
☐ 485	Rance Mulliniks	.06	.03	.00
☐ 486	Ken Schrom	.06	.03	.00
☐ 487	Jeff Russell	.06	.03	.00
☐ 488	Tom Paciorek	.06	.03	.00
☐ 489	Dan Ford	.06	.03	.00
☐ 490	Mike Caldwell	.06	.03	.00
☐ 491	Scottie Earl	.06	.03	.00
☐ 492	Jose Rijo	.45	.22	.04
☐ 493	Bruce Hurst	.15	.07	.01
☐ 494	Ken Landreaux	.06	.03	.00
☐ 495	Mike Fischlin	.06	.03	.00
☐ 496	Don Slaught	.06	.03	.00
☐ 497	Steve McCatty	.06	.03	.00
☐ 498	Gary Lucas	.06	.03	.00
☐ 499	Gary Pettis	.10	.05	.01
☐ 500	Marvis Foley	.06	.03	.00
☐ 501	Mike Squires	.06	.03	.00
☐ 502	Jim Pankovits	.06	.03	.00
☐ 503	Luis Aguayo	.06	.03	.00
☐ 504	Ralph Citarella	.06	.03	.00
☐ 505	Bruce Bochy	.06	.03	.00
☐ 506	Bob Owchinko	.06	.03	.00
☐ 507	Pascual Perez	.15	.07	.01
☐ 508	Lee Lacy	.06	.03	.00
☐ 509	Atlee Hammaker	.06	.03	.00
☐ 510	Bob Dernier	.06	.03	.00
☐ 511	Ed VandeBerg	.06	.03	.00
☐ 512	Cliff Johnson	.06	.03	.00
☐ 513	Len Whitehouse	.06	.03	.00
☐ 514	Dennis Martinez	.10	.05	.01
☐ 515	Ed Romero	.06	.03	.00
☐ 516	Rusty Kuntz	.06	.03	.00
☐ 517	Rick Miller	.06	.03	.00
☐ 518	Dennis Rasmussen	.15	.07	.01
☐ 519	Steve Yeager	.06	.03	.00
☐ 520	Chris Bando	.06	.03	.00
☐ 521	U.L. Washington	.06	.03	.00
☐ 522	Curt Young	.35	.17	.03
☐ 523	Angel Salazar	.06	.03	.00
☐ 524	Curt Kaufman	.06	.03	.00
☐ 525	Odell Jones	.06	.03	.00

□	#	Name			
□	526	Juan Agosto	.06	.03	.00
□	527	Denny Walling	.06	.03	.00
□	528	Andy Hawkins	.25	.12	.02
□	529	Sixto Lezcano	.06	.03	.00
□	530	Skeeter Barnes	.06	.03	.00
□	531	Randy Johnson	.06	.03	.00
□	532	Jim Morrison	.06	.03	.00
□	533	Warren Brusstar	.06	.03	.00
□	534A	Jeff Pendleton ERR (wrong first name)	.75	.35	.07
□	534B	Terry Pendleton COR	3.50	1.75	.35
□	535	Vic Rodriguez	.10	.05	.01
□	536	Bob McClure	.06	.03	.00
□	537	Dave Bergman	.06	.03	.00
□	538	Mark Clear	.06	.03	.00
□	539	Mike Pagliarulo	.90	.45	.09
□	540	Terry Whitfield	.06	.03	.00
□	541	Joe Beckwith	.06	.03	.00
□	542	Jeff Burroughs	.06	.03	.00
□	543	Dan Schatzeder	.06	.03	.00
□	544	Donnie Scott	.06	.03	.00
□	545	Jim Slaton	.06	.03	.00
□	546	Greg Luzinski	.12	.06	.01
□	547	Mark Salas	.12	.06	.01
□	548	Dave Smith	.06	.03	.00
□	549	John Wockenfuss	.06	.03	.00
□	550	Frank Pastore	.06	.03	.00
□	551	Tim Flannery	.06	.03	.00
□	552	Rick Rhoden	.10	.05	.01
□	553	Mark Davis	.30	.15	.03
□	554	Jeff Dedmon	.10	.05	.01
□	555	Gary Woods	.06	.03	.00
□	556	Danny Heep	.06	.03	.00
□	557	Mark Langston	7.50	3.75	.75
□	558	Darrell Brown	.06	.03	.00
□	559	Jimmy Key	1.75	.85	.17
□	560	Rick Lysander	.06	.03	.00
□	561	Doyle Alexander	.10	.05	.01
□	562	Mike Stanton	.06	.03	.00
□	563	Sid Fernandez	.75	.35	.07
□	564	Richie Hebner	.06	.03	.00
□	565	Alex Trevino	.06	.03	.00
□	566	Brian Harper	.06	.03	.00
□	567	Dan Gladden	.45	.22	.04
□	568	Luis Salazar	.10	.05	.01
□	569	Tom Foley	.06	.03	.00
□	570	Larry Andersen	.06	.03	.00
□	571	Danny Cox	.10	.05	.01
□	572	Joe Sambito	.06	.03	.00
□	573	Juan Beniquez	.06	.03	.00
□	574	Joel Skinner	.06	.03	.00
□	575	Randy St.Claire	.06	.03	.00
□	576	Floyd Rayford	.06	.03	.00
□	577	Roy Howell	.06	.03	.00
□	578	John Grubb	.06	.03	.00
□	579	Ed Jurak	.06	.03	.00
□	580	John Montefusco	.06	.03	.00
□	581	Orel Hershiser	11.00	5.50	1.10
□	582	Tom Waddell	.10	.05	.01
□	583	Mark Huismann	.06	.03	.00
□	584	Joe Morgan	.30	.15	.03
□	585	Jim Wohlford	.06	.03	.00
□	586	Dave Schmidt	.10	.05	.01
□	587	Jeff Kunkel	.10	.05	.01
□	588	Hal McRae	.10	.05	.01
□	589	Bill Almon	.06	.03	.00
□	590	Carmen Castillo	.06	.03	.00
□	591	Omar Moreno	.06	.03	.00
□	592	Ken Howell	.15	.07	.01
□	593	Tom Brookens	.06	.03	.00
□	594	Joe Nolan	.06	.03	.00
□	595	Willie Lozado	.10	.05	.01
□	596	Tom Nieto	.10	.05	.01
□	597	Walt Terrell	.06	.03	.00
□	598	Al Oliver	.10	.05	.01
□	599	Shane Rawley	.06	.03	.00
□	600	Denny Gonzalez	.10	.05	.01
□	601	Mark Grant	.10	.05	.01
□	602	Mike Armstrong	.06	.03	.00
□	603	George Foster	.12	.06	.01
□	604	Dave Lopes	.10	.05	.01
□	605	Salome Barojas	.06	.03	.00
□	606	Roy Lee Jackson	.06	.03	.00
□	607	Pete Filson	.06	.03	.00
□	608	Duane Walker	.06	.03	.00
□	609	Glenn Wilson	.10	.05	.01
□	610	Rafael Santana	.25	.12	.02
□	611	Roy Smith	.10	.05	.01
□	612	Ruppert Jones	.06	.03	.00
□	613	Joe Cowley	.06	.03	.00
□	614	Al Nipper UER (photo actually Mike Brown)	.20	.10	.02
□	615	Gene Nelson	.06	.03	.00
□	616	Joe Carter	2.25	1.10	.22

□	#	Name			
□	617	Ray Knight	.10	.05	.01
□	618	Chuck Rainey	.06	.03	.00
□	619	Dan Driessen	.06	.03	.00
□	620	Daryl Sconiers	.06	.03	.00
□	621	Bill Stein	.06	.03	.00
□	622	Roy Smalley	.06	.03	.00
□	623	Ed Lynch	.06	.03	.00
□	624	Jeff Stone	.12	.06	.01
□	625	Bruce Berenyi	.06	.03	.00
□	626	Kelvin Chapman	.10	.05	.01
□	627	Joe Price	.06	.03	.00
□	628	Steve Bedrosian	.15	.07	.01
□	629	Vic Mata	.10	.05	.01
□	630	Mike Krukow	.06	.03	.00
□	631	Phil Bradley	1.00	.50	.10
□	632	Jim Gott	.10	.05	.01
□	633	Randy Bush	.10	.05	.01
□	634	Tom Browning	1.50	.75	.15
□	635	Lou Gehrig Puzzle Card	.06	.03	.00
□	636	Reid Nichols	.06	.03	.00
□	637	Dan Pasqua	.65	.30	.06
□	638	German Rivera	.10	.05	.01
□	639	Don Schulze	.06	.03	.00
□	640A	Mike Jones (Career Highlights, takes five lines)	.10	.05	.01
□	640B	Mike Jones (Career Highlights, takes four lines)	.10	.05	.01
□	641	Pete Rose	1.00	.50	.10
□	642	Wade Rowdon	.10	.05	.01
□	643	Jerry Narron	.06	.03	.00
□	644	Darrell Miller	.10	.05	.01
□	645	Tim Hulett	.10	.05	.01
□	646	Andy McGaffigan	.06	.03	.00
□	647	Kurt Bevacqua	.06	.03	.00
□	648	John Russell	.10	.05	.01
□	649	Ron Robinson	.20	.10	.02
□	650	Donnie Moore	.06	.03	.00
□	651A	Two for the Title Dave Winfield Don Mattingly (yellow letters)	5.00	2.50	.50
□	651B	Two for the Title Dave Winfield Don Mattingly (white letters)	7.50	3.75	.75
□	652	Tim Laudner	.06	.03	.00
□	653	Steve Farr	.30	.15	.03
□	654	DK Checklist 1-26 (unnumbered)	.09	.01	.00
□	655	Checklist 27-130 (unnumbered)	.07	.01	.00
□	656	Checklist 131-234 (unnumbered)	.07	.01	.00
□	657	Checklist 235-338 (unnumbered)	.07	.01	.00
□	658	Checklist 339-442 (unnumbered)	.07	.01	.00
□	659	Checklist 443-546 (unnumbered)	.07	.01	.00
□	660	Checklist 547-653 (unnumbered)	.07	.01	.00

1985 Donruss Wax Box Cards

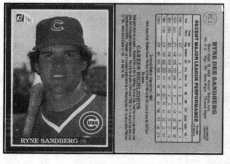

The boxes in which the wax packs (of the 1985 Donruss regular issue baseball cards) were contained feature four baseball cards, with backs.

The complete set price of the regular issue set does not include these cards; they are considered a separate set. The cards measure the standard 2 1/2" by 3 1/2" and are styled the same as the regular Donruss cards. The cards are numbered but with the prefix PC before the number. The value of the panel uncut is slightly greater, perhaps by 25% greater, than the value of the individual cards cut up carefully.

	MINT	EXC	G-VG
COMPLETE SET (4)	5.00	2.50	.50
COMMON PLAYER	.05	.02	.00
☐ PC1 Dwight Gooden	4.50	2.25	.45
☐ PC2 Ryne Sandberg	.75	.35	.07
☐ PC3 Ron Kittle	.15	.07	.01
☐ PUZ Lou Gehrig	.05	.02	.00
Puzzle Card			

1985 Donruss Super DK's

The cards in this 28-card set measure 4 15/16 by 6 3/4". The 1985 Donruss Diamond Kings Supers set contains enlarged cards of the first 26 cards of the Donruss regular set of this year. In addition, the Diamond Kings checklist card, a card of artist Dick Perez, and a Lou Gehrig puzzle card are included in the set. The set was the brain-child of the Perez-Steele Galleries and could be obtained via a write-in offer on the wrappers of the Donruss regular cards of this year. The Gehrig puzzle card is actually a 12-piece jigsaw puzzle. The back of the checklist card is blank; however, the Dick Perez card back gives a short history of Dick Perez and the Perez-Steele Galleries. The offer for obtaining this set was detailed on the wax pack wrappers; three wrappers plus 9.00 was required for this mail-in offer.

	MINT	EXC	G-VG
COMPLETE SET (28)	11.00	5.50	1.10
COMMON PLAYER (1-26)	.20	.10	.02
☐ 1 Ryne Sandberg	1.00	.50	.10
☐ 2 Doug DeCinces	.20	.10	.02
☐ 3 Richard Dotson	.20	.10	.02
☐ 4 Bert Blyleven	.30	.15	.03
☐ 5 Lou Whitaker	.40	.20	.04
☐ 6 Dan Quisenberry	.20	.10	.02
☐ 7 Don Mattingly	5.00	2.50	.50
☐ 8 Carney Lansford	.40	.20	.04
☐ 9 Frank Tanana	.20	.10	.02
☐ 10 Willie Upshaw	.20	.10	.02
☐ 11 Claudell Washington	.20	.10	.02
☐ 12 Mike Marshall	.30	.15	.03
☐ 13 Joaquin Andujar	.20	.10	.02
☐ 14 Cal Ripken	1.00	.50	.10
☐ 15 Jim Rice	.40	.20	.04
☐ 16 Don Sutton	.40	.20	.04
☐ 17 Frank Viola	.50	.25	.05
☐ 18 Alvin Davis	.50	.25	.05
☐ 19 Mario Soto	.20	.10	.02
☐ 20 Jose Cruz	.20	.10	.02

		MINT	EXC	G-VG
☐ 21	Charlie Lea	.20	.10	.02
☐ 22	Jesse Orosco	.20	.10	.02
☐ 23	Juan Samuel	.30	.15	.03
☐ 24	Tony Pena	.20	.10	.02
☐ 25	Tony Gwynn	1.25	.60	.12
☐ 26	Bob Brenly	.20	.10	.02
☐ 27	Checklist Card (unnumbered)	.10	.05	.01
☐ 28	Dick Perez (unnumbered) (History of DK's)	.10	.05	.01

1985 Donruss Action All-Stars

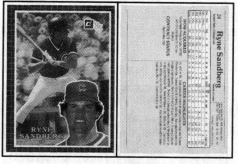

The cards in this 60-card set measure 3 1/2" by 5". For the third year in a row, Donruss issued a set of Action All-Stars. This set features action photos on the obverse which also contains a portrait inset of the player. The backs, unlike the year before, do not contain a full color picture of the player but list, if space is available, full statistical data, biographical data, career highlights, and acquisition and contract status. The cards were issued with a Lou Gehrig puzzle card.

		MINT	EXC	G-VG
COMPLETE SET (60)		6.00	3.00	.60
COMMON PLAYER (1-60)		.05	.02	.00
☐ 1	Tim Raines	.30	.15	.03
☐ 2	Jim Gantner	.05	.02	.00
☐ 3	Mario Soto	.05	.02	.00
☐ 4	Spike Owen	.05	.02	.00
☐ 5	Lloyd Moseby	.10	.05	.01
☐ 6	Damaso Garcia	.05	.02	.00
☐ 7	Cal Ripken	.30	.15	.03
☐ 8	Dan Quisenberry	.10	.05	.01
☐ 9	Eddie Murray	.25	.12	.02
☐ 10	Tony Pena	.05	.02	.00
☐ 11	Buddy Bell	.10	.05	.01
☐ 12	Dave Winfield	.20	.10	.02
☐ 13	Ron Kittle	.10	.05	.01
☐ 14	Rich Gossage	.10	.05	.01
☐ 15	Dwight Evans	.15	.07	.01
☐ 16	Alvin Davis	.15	.07	.01
☐ 17	Mike Schmidt	.75	.35	.07
☐ 18	Pascual Perez	.10	.05	.01
☐ 19	Tony Gwynn	.50	.25	.05
☐ 20	Nolan Ryan	.75	.35	.07
☐ 21	Robin Yount	.35	.17	.03
☐ 22	Mike Marshall	.15	.07	.01
☐ 23	Brett Butler	.10	.05	.01
☐ 24	Ryne Sandberg	.35	.17	.03
☐ 25	Dale Murphy	.50	.25	.05
☐ 26	George Brett	.50	.25	.05
☐ 27	Jim Rice	.20	.10	.02
☐ 28	Ozzie Smith	.25	.12	.02
☐ 29	Larry Parrish	.05	.02	.00
☐ 30	Jack Clark	.20	.10	.02
☐ 31	Manny Trillo	.05	.02	.00
☐ 32	Dave Kingman	.10	.05	.01
☐ 33	Geoff Zahn	.05	.02	.00
☐ 34	Pedro Guerrero	.20	.10	.02
☐ 35	Dave Parker	.15	.07	.01
☐ 36	Rollie Fingers	.15	.07	.01
☐ 37	Fernando Valenzuela	.20	.10	.02
☐ 38	Wade Boggs	.75	.35	.07

☐ 39	Reggie Jackson	.60	.30	.06
☐ 40	Kent Hrbek	.25	.12	.02
☐ 41	Keith Hernandez	.25	.12	.02
☐ 42	Lou Whitaker	.15	.07	.01
☐ 43	Tom Herr	.05	.02	.00
☐ 44	Alan Trammell	.20	.10	.02
☐ 45	Butch Wynegar	.05	.02	.00
☐ 46	Leon Durham	.05	.02	.00
☐ 47	Dwight Gooden	1.25	.60	.12
☐ 48	Don Mattingly	1.50	.75	.15
☐ 49	Phil Niekro	.20	.10	.02
☐ 50	Johnny Ray	.10	.05	.01
☐ 51	Doug DeCinces	.05	.02	.00
☐ 52	Willie Upshaw	.05	.02	.00
☐ 53	Lance Parrish	.10	.05	.01
☐ 54	Jody Davis	.05	.02	.00
☐ 55	Steve Carlton	.30	.15	.03
☐ 56	Juan Samuel	.15	.07	.01
☐ 57	Gary Carter	.20	.10	.02
☐ 58	Harold Baines	.10	.05	.01
☐ 59	Eric Show	.05	.02	.00
☐ 60	Checklist Card	.05	.02	.00

1985 Donruss Highlights

Dale Murphy

National League Player of the Month April

Before the '85 National League season was even one month old, fans were fitting Dale Murphy for a place in the record books alongside Hack Wilson who, in '30 set National League records of 56 homers and 190 RBI. The reason for such lofty comparisons was obvious. Murphy tied a major league record for most RBI in one month with 29 in April of '85. In addition, the Atlanta Braves' perennial All-Star centerfielder and two-time winner of the Most Valuable Player Award, hit nine homers. His batting average for the month was .380, including 8 doubles, 62 total bases and 17 runs scored in just 19 games. Along with his offensive stats, Murphy kept his consecutive games playing streak going through 515 entering May.

DALE MURPHY N.L. PLAYER OF THE MONTH—APRIL

© 1985 LEAF-DONRUSS   MADE & PRINTED IN U.S.A.

NO. 5

This 56-card set features the players and pitchers of the month for each league as well as a number of highlight cards commemorating the 1985 season. The Donruss Company dedicated the last two cards to their own selections for Rookies of the Year (ROY). This set proved to be more popular than the Donruss Company had predicted, as their first and only print run was exhausted before card dealers' initial orders were filled.

	MINT	EXC	G-VG
COMPLETE SET (56)	25.00	12.50	2.50
COMMON PLAYER (1-56)	.10	.05	.01

☐ 1	Tom Seaver: Sets Opening Day Record	.50	.25	.05
☐ 2	Rollie Fingers: Sets AL Save Mark	.20	.10	.02
☐ 3	Mike Davis: AL Player April	.10	.05	.01
☐ 4	Charlie Leibrandt: AL Pitcher April	.10	.05	.01
☐ 5	Dale Murphy: NL Player April	.75	.35	.07
☐ 6	Fernando Valenzuela: NL Pitcher April	.25	.12	.02
☐ 7	Larry Bowa: NL Shortstop Record	.10	.05	.01
☐ 8	Dave Concepcion: Joins Reds' 2000 Hit Club	.10	.05	.01
☐ 9	Tony Perez: Eldest Grand Slammer	.15	.07	.01
☐ 10	Pete Rose: NL Career Run Leader	1.25	.60	.12
☐ 11	George Brett: AL Player May	.75	.35	.07
☐ 12	Dave Stieb: AL Pitcher May	.15	.07	.01
☐ 13	Dave Parker: NL Player May	.15	.07	.01
☐ 14	Andy Hawkins: NL Pitcher May	.10	.05	.01
☐ 15	Andy Hawkins: Records	.10	.05	.01

	11th Straight Win			
☐ 16	Von Hayes: Two Homers in First Inning	.15	.07	.01
☐ 17	Rickey Henderson: AL Player June	.75	.35	.07
☐ 18	Jay Howell: AL Pitcher June	.10	.05	.01
☐ 19	Pedro Guerrero: NL Player June	.20	.10	.02
☐ 20	John Tudor: NL Pitcher June	.15	.07	.01
☐ 21	Hernandez/Carter: Marathon Game Iron Men	.25	.12	.02
☐ 22	Nolan Ryan: Records 4000th K	1.25	.60	.12
☐ 23	LaMarr Hoyt: All-Star Game MVP	.10	.05	.01
☐ 24	Oddibe McDowell: 1st Ranger to Hit for Cycle	.25	.12	.02
☐ 25	George Brett: AL Player July	.75	.35	.07
☐ 26	Bret Saberhagen: AL Pitcher July	.75	.35	.07
☐ 27	Keith Hernandez: NL Player July	.25	.12	.02
☐ 28	Fernando Valenzuela: NL Pitcher July	.25	.12	.02
☐ 29	W.McGee/V.Coleman: Record Setting Base Stealers	.75	.35	.07
☐ 30	Tom Seaver: Notches 300th Career Win	.35	.17	.03
☐ 31	Rod Carew: Strokes 3000th Hit	.35	.17	.03
☐ 32	Dwight Gooden: Establishes Met Record	1.25	.60	.12
☐ 33	Dwight Gooden: Achieves Strikeout Milestone	1.25	.60	.12
☐ 34	Eddie Murray: Explodes for 9 RBI	.35	.17	.03
☐ 35	Don Baylor: AL Career HBP Leader	.15	.07	.01
☐ 36	Don Mattingly: AL Player August	2.50	1.25	.25
☐ 37	Dave Righetti: AL Pitcher August	.15	.07	.01
☐ 38	Willie McGee: NL Player August	.25	.12	.02
☐ 39	Shane Rawley: NL Pitcher August	.10	.05	.01
☐ 40	Pete Rose: Ty-Breaking Hit	1.25	.60	.12
☐ 41	Andre Dawson: Hits 3 HR's Drives in 8 Runs	.25	.12	.02
☐ 42	Rickey Henderson: Sets Yankee Theft Mark	.75	.35	.07
☐ 43	Tom Browning: 20 Wins in Rookie Season	.20	.10	.02
☐ 44	Don Mattingly: Yankee Milestone for Hits	2.50	1.25	.25
☐ 45	Don Mattingly: AL Player September	2.50	1.25	.25
☐ 46	Charlie Leibrandt: AL Pitcher September	.10	.05	.01
☐ 47	Gary Carter: NL Player September	.25	.12	.02
☐ 48	Dwight Gooden: NL Pitcher September	1.25	.60	.12
☐ 49	Wade Boggs: Major League Record Setter	2.00	1.00	.20
☐ 50	Phil Niekro: Hurls Shutout for 300th Win	.20	.10	.02
☐ 51	Darrell Evans: Venerable HR King	.10	.05	.01
☐ 52	Willie McGee: NL Switch-Hitting Record	.20	.10	.02
☐ 53	Dave Winfield: Equals DiMaggio Feat	.30	.15	.03
☐ 54	Vince Coleman: Donruss NL ROY	2.00	1.00	.20
☐ 55	Ozzie Guillen: Donruss AL ROY	.50	.25	.05
☐ 56	Checklist Card (unnumbered)	.10	.05	.01

1986 Donruss

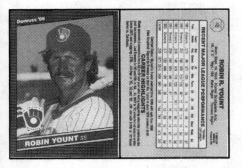

The cards in this 660-card set measure 2 1/2" by 3 1/2". The 1986 Donruss regular issue cards have fronts that feature blue borders. The fronts contain the standard team logo, player's name, position, and Donruss logo. The cards were distributed with puzzle pieces from a Dick Perez rendition of Hank Aaron. The first 26 cards of the set are Diamond Kings (DK), for the fifth year in a row; the artwork on the Diamond Kings was again produced by the Perez-Steele Galleries. Cards 27-46 again feature Rated Rookies (RR); Danny Tartabull is included in this subset for the second year in a row. The unnumbered checklist cards are arbitrarily numbered below as numbers 654 through 660.

	MINT	EXC	G-VG
COMPLETE SET (660)	130.00	65.00	13.00
COMMON PLAYER (1-660)	.05	.02	.00

		MINT	EXC	G-VG
☐	1 Kirk Gibson DK	.35	.08	.01
☐	2 Goose Gossage DK	.12	.06	.01
☐	3 Willie McGee DK	.15	.07	.01
☐	4 George Bell DK	.18	.09	.01
☐	5 Tony Armas DK	.08	.04	.01
☐	6 Chili Davis DK	.08	.04	.01
☐	7 Cecil Cooper DK	.10	.05	.01
☐	8 Mike Boddicker DK	.08	.04	.01
☐	9 Dave Lopes DK	.08	.04	.01
☐	10 Bill Doran DK	.08	.04	.01
☐	11 Bret Saberhagen DK	.50	.25	.05
☐	12 Brett Butler DK	.08	.04	.01
☐	13 Harold Baines DK	.12	.06	.01
☐	14 Mike Davis DK	.08	.04	.01
☐	15 Tony Perez DK	.12	.06	.01
☐	16 Willie Randolph DK	.08	.04	.01
☐	17 Bob Boone DK	.10	.05	.01
☐	18 Orel Hershiser DK	.90	.45	.09
☐	19 Johnny Ray DK	.08	.04	.01
☐	20 Gary Ward DK	.08	.04	.01
☐	21 Rick Mahler DK	.08	.04	.01
☐	22 Phil Bradley DK	.10	.05	.01
☐	23 Jerry Koosman DK	.08	.04	.01
☐	24 Tom Brunansky DK	.12	.06	.01
☐	25 Andre Dawson DK	.25	.12	.02
☐	26 Dwight Gooden DK	1.00	.50	.10
☐	27 Kal Daniels RR	3.50	1.75	.35
☐	28 Fred McGriff RR	15.00	7.50	1.50
☐	29 Cory Snyder RR	2.25	1.10	.22
☐	30 Jose Guzman RR	.25	.12	.02
☐	31 Ty Gainey RR	.10	.05	.01
☐	32 Johnny Abrego RR	.08	.04	.01
☐	33A Andres Galarraga RR (no accent)	4.00	2.00	.40
☐	33B Andre's Galarraga RR (accent over e)	6.00	3.00	.60
☐	34 Dave Shipanoff RR	.08	.04	.01
☐	35 Mark McLemore RR	.10	.05	.01
☐	36 Marty Clary RR	.10	.05	.01
☐	37 Paul O'Neill RR	1.75	.85	.17
☐	38 Danny Tartabull RR	1.00	.50	.10
☐	39 Jose Canseco RR	50.00	25.00	5.00
☐	40 Juan Nieves RR	.30	.15	.03
☐	41 Lance McCullers RR	.40	.20	.04
☐	42 Rick Surhoff RR	.10	.05	.01
☐	43 Todd Worrell RR	.90	.45	.09
☐	44 Bob Kipper RR	.10	.05	.01
☐	45 John Habyan RR	.10	.05	.01
☐	46 Mike Woodard RR	.10	.05	.01
☐	47 Mike Boddicker	.08	.04	.01
☐	48 Robin Yount	.50	.25	.05
☐	49 Lou Whitaker	.15	.07	.01
☐	50 Oil Can Boyd	.08	.04	.01
☐	51 Rickey Henderson	.60	.30	.06
☐	52 Mike Marshall	.12	.06	.01
☐	53 George Brett	.50	.25	.05
☐	54 Dave Kingman	.10	.05	.01
☐	55 Hubie Brooks	.10	.05	.01
☐	56 Oddibe McDowell	.25	.12	.02
☐	57 Doug DeCinces	.08	.04	.01
☐	58 Britt Burns	.05	.02	.00
☐	59 Ozzie Smith	.30	.15	.03
☐	60 Jose Cruz	.08	.04	.01
☐	61 Mike Schmidt	.90	.45	.09
☐	62 Pete Rose	.75	.35	.07
☐	63 Steve Garvey	.40	.20	.04
☐	64 Tony Pena	.08	.04	.01
☐	65 Chili Davis	.08	.04	.01
☐	66 Dale Murphy	.50	.25	.05
☐	67 Ryne Sandberg	.40	.20	.04
☐	68 Gary Carter	.30	.15	.03
☐	69 Alvin Davis	.30	.15	.03
☐	70 Kent Hrbek	.25	.12	.02
☐	71 George Bell	.30	.15	.03
☐	72 Kirby Puckett	4.00	2.00	.40
☐	73 Lloyd Moseby	.10	.05	.01
☐	74 Bob Kearney	.05	.02	.00
☐	75 Dwight Gooden	2.75	1.35	.27
☐	76 Gary Matthews	.08	.04	.01
☐	77 Rick Mahler	.05	.02	.00
☐	78 Benny Distefano	.05	.02	.00
☐	79 Jeff Leonard	.10	.05	.01
☐	80 Kevin McReynolds	.50	.25	.05
☐	81 Ron Oester	.05	.02	.00
☐	82 John Russell	.05	.02	.00
☐	83 Tommy Herr	.08	.04	.01
☐	84 Jerry Mumphrey	.05	.02	.00
☐	85 Ron Romanick	.05	.02	.00
☐	86 Daryl Boston	.05	.02	.00
☐	87 Andre Dawson	.30	.15	.03
☐	88 Eddie Murray	.35	.17	.03
☐	89 Dion James	.05	.02	.00
☐	90 Chet Lemon	.08	.04	.01
☐	91 Bob Stanley	.05	.02	.00
☐	92 Willie Randolph	.08	.04	.01
☐	93 Mike Scioscia	.08	.04	.01
☐	94 Tom Waddell	.05	.02	.00
☐	95 Danny Jackson	.25	.12	.02
☐	96 Mike Davis	.08	.04	.01
☐	97 Mike Fitzgerald	.05	.02	.00
☐	98 Gary Ward	.08	.04	.01
☐	99 Pete O'Brien	.08	.04	.01
☐	100 Bret Saberhagen	1.75	.85	.17
☐	101 Alfredo Griffin	.08	.04	.01
☐	102 Brett Butler	.08	.04	.01
☐	103 Ron Guidry	.15	.07	.01
☐	104 Jerry Reuss	.08	.04	.01
☐	105 Jack Morris	.15	.07	.01
☐	106 Rick Dempsey	.05	.02	.00
☐	107 Ray Burris	.05	.02	.00
☐	108 Brian Downing	.08	.04	.01
☐	109 Willie McGee	.15	.07	.01
☐	110 Bill Doran	.10	.05	.01
☐	111 Kent Tekulve	.05	.02	.00
☐	112 Tony Gwynn	1.00	.50	.10
☐	113 Marvell Wynne	.05	.02	.00
☐	114 David Green	.05	.02	.00
☐	115 Jim Gantner	.05	.02	.00
☐	116 George Foster	.12	.06	.01
☐	117 Steve Trout	.05	.02	.00
☐	118 Mark Langston	.90	.45	.09
☐	119 Tony Fernandez	.25	.12	.02
☐	120 John Butcher	.05	.02	.00
☐	121 Ron Robinson	.05	.02	.00
☐	122 Dan Spillner	.05	.02	.00
☐	123 Mike Young	.08	.04	.01
☐	124 Paul Molitor	.15	.07	.01
☐	125 Kirk Gibson	.25	.12	.02
☐	126 Ken Griffey	.10	.05	.01
☐	127 Tony Armas	.08	.04	.01
☐	128 Mariano Duncan	.15	.07	.01
☐	129 Pat Tabler	.08	.04	.01
☐	130 Frank White	.08	.04	.01
☐	131 Carney Lansford	.12	.06	.01
☐	132 Vance Law	.08	.04	.01
☐	133 Dick Schofield	.08	.04	.01
☐	134 Wayne Tolleson	.05	.02	.00
☐	135 Greg Walker	.08	.04	.01
☐	136 Denny Walling	.05	.02	.00
☐	137 Ozzie Virgil	.05	.02	.00
☐	138 Ricky Horton	.05	.02	.00
☐	139 LaMarr Hoyt	.08	.04	.01

☐ 140	Wayne Krenchicki	.05	.02	.00	☐ 234	Eric Show	.08	.04	.01
☐ 141	Glenn Hubbard	.05	.02	.00	☐ 235	Jose DeLeon	.05	.02	.00
☐ 142	Cecilio Guante	.05	.02	.00	☐ 236	Jose Uribe	.30	.15	.03
☐ 143	Mike Krukow	.05	.02	.00	☐ 237	Moose Haas	.05	.02	.00
☐ 144	Lee Smith	.08	.04	.01	☐ 238	Wally Backman	.05	.02	.00
☐ 145	Edwin Nunez	.05	.02	.00	☐ 239	Dennis Eckersley	.15	.07	.01
☐ 146	Dave Stieb	.12	.06	.01	☐ 240	Mike Moore	.10	.05	.01
☐ 147	Mike Smithson	.05	.02	.00	☐ 241	Damaso Garcia	.05	.02	.00
☐ 148	Ken Dixon	.05	.02	.00	☐ 242	Tim Teufel	.05	.02	.00
☐ 149	Danny Darwin	.05	.02	.00	☐ 243	Dave Concepcion	.10	.05	.01
☐ 150	Chris Pittaro	.05	.02	.00	☐ 244	Floyd Bannister	.05	.02	.00
☐ 151	Bill Buckner	.08	.04	.01	☐ 245	Fred Lynn	.15	.07	.01
☐ 152	Mike Pagliarulo	.10	.05	.01	☐ 246	Charlie Moore	.05	.02	.00
☐ 153	Bill Russell	.08	.04	.01	☐ 247	Walt Terrell	.05	.02	.00
☐ 154	Brook Jacoby	.10	.05	.01	☐ 248	Dave Winfield	.30	.15	.03
☐ 155	Pat Sheridan	.05	.02	.00	☐ 249	Dwight Evans	.15	.07	.01
☐ 156	Mike Gallego	.05	.02	.00	☐ 250	Dennis Powell	.08	.04	.01
☐ 157	Jim Wohlford	.05	.02	.00	☐ 251	Andre Thornton	.08	.04	.01
☐ 158	Gary Pettis	.05	.02	.00	☐ 252	Onix Concepcion	.05	.02	.00
☐ 159	Toby Harrah	.08	.04	.01	☐ 253	Mike Heath	.05	.02	.00
☐ 160	Richard Dotson	.08	.04	.01	☐ 254A	David Palmer ERR	.10	.05	.01
☐ 161	Bob Knepper	.08	.04	.01		(position 2B)			
☐ 162	Dave Dravecky	.10	.05	.01	☐ 254B	David Palmer COR	.60	.30	.06
☐ 163	Greg Gross	.05	.02	.00		(position P)			
☐ 164	Eric Davis	3.50	1.75	.35	☐ 255	Donnie Moore	.05	.02	.00
☐ 165	Gerald Perry	.12	.06	.01	☐ 256	Curtis Wilkerson	.05	.02	.00
☐ 166	Rick Rhoden	.08	.04	.01	☐ 257	Julio Cruz	.05	.02	.00
☐ 167	Keith Moreland	.05	.02	.00	☐ 258	Nolan Ryan	.90	.45	.09
☐ 168	Jack Clark	.25	.12	.02	☐ 259	Jeff Stone	.05	.02	.00
☐ 169	Storm Davis	.10	.05	.01	☐ 260	John Tudor	.12	.06	.01
☐ 170	Cecil Cooper	.10	.05	.01	☐ 261	Mark Thurmond	.05	.02	.00
☐ 171	Alan Trammell	.25	.12	.02	☐ 262	Jay Tibbs	.05	.02	.00
☐ 172	Roger Clemens	3.50	1.75	.35	☐ 263	Rafael Ramirez	.05	.02	.00
☐ 173	Don Mattingly	5.00	2.50	.50	☐ 264	Larry McWilliams	.05	.02	.00
☐ 174	Pedro Guerrero	.25	.12	.02	☐ 265	Mark Davis	.15	.07	.01
☐ 175	Willie Wilson	.10	.05	.01	☐ 266	Bob Dernier	.05	.02	.00
☐ 176	Dwayne Murphy	.05	.02	.00	☐ 267	Matt Young	.05	.02	.00
☐ 177	Tim Raines	.30	.15	.03	☐ 268	Jim Clancy	.05	.02	.00
☐ 178	Larry Parrish	.05	.02	.00	☐ 269	Mickey Hatcher	.05	.02	.00
☐ 179	Mike Witt	.08	.04	.01	☐ 270	Sammy Stewart	.05	.02	.00
☐ 180	Harold Baines	.15	.07	.01	☐ 271	Bob L. Gibson	.05	.02	.00
☐ 181	Vince Coleman	2.25	1.10	.22	☐ 272	Nelson Simmons	.05	.02	.00
	(BA 2.67 on back)				☐ 273	Rich Gedman	.05	.02	.00
☐ 182	Jeff Heathcock	.05	.02	.00	☐ 274	Butch Wynegar	.05	.02	.00
☐ 183	Steve Carlton	.30	.15	.03	☐ 275	Ken Howell	.05	.02	.00
☐ 184	Mario Soto	.05	.02	.00	☐ 276	Mel Hall	.10	.05	.01
☐ 185	Goose Gossage	.12	.06	.01	☐ 277	Jim Sundberg	.05	.02	.00
☐ 186	Johnny Ray	.08	.04	.01	☐ 278	Chris Codiroli	.05	.02	.00
☐ 187	Dan Gladden	.08	.04	.01	☐ 279	Herm Winningham	.10	.05	.01
☐ 188	Bob Horner	.15	.07	.01	☐ 280	Rod Carew	.35	.17	.03
☐ 189	Rick Sutcliffe	.15	.07	.01	☐ 281	Don Slaught	.05	.02	.00
☐ 190	Keith Hernandez	.25	.12	.02	☐ 282	Scott Fletcher	.05	.02	.00
☐ 191	Phil Bradley	.10	.05	.01	☐ 283	Bill Dawley	.05	.02	.00
☐ 192	Tom Brunansky	.15	.07	.01	☐ 284	Andy Hawkins	.10	.05	.01
☐ 193	Jesse Barfield	.25	.12	.02	☐ 285	Glenn Wilson	.08	.04	.01
☐ 194	Frank Viola	.35	.17	.03	☐ 286	Nick Esasky	.12	.06	.01
☐ 195	Willie Upshaw	.05	.02	.00	☐ 287	Claudell Washington	.08	.04	.01
☐ 196	Jim Beattie	.05	.02	.00	☐ 288	Lee Mazzilli	.05	.02	.00
☐ 197	Darryl Strawberry	2.50	1.25	.25	☐ 289	Jody Davis	.05	.02	.00
☐ 198	Ron Cey	.10	.05	.01	☐ 290	Darrell Porter	.05	.02	.00
☐ 199	Steve Bedrosian	.12	.06	.01	☐ 291	Scott McGregor	.05	.02	.00
☐ 200	Steve Kemp	.08	.04	.01	☐ 292	Ted Simmons	.10	.05	.01
☐ 201	Manny Trillo	.05	.02	.00	☐ 293	Aurelio Lopez	.05	.02	.00
☐ 202	Garry Templeton	.08	.04	.01	☐ 294	Marty Barrett	.10	.05	.01
☐ 203	Dave Parker	.15	.07	.01	☐ 295	Dale Berra	.05	.02	.00
☐ 204	John Denny	.08	.04	.01	☐ 296	Greg Brock	.05	.02	.00
☐ 205	Terry Pendleton	.08	.04	.01	☐ 297	Charlie Leibrandt	.05	.02	.00
☐ 206	Terry Puhl	.05	.02	.00	☐ 298	Bill Krueger	.05	.02	.00
☐ 207	Bobby Grich	.08	.04	.01	☐ 299	Bryn Smith	.10	.05	.01
☐ 208	Ozzie Guillen	.60	.30	.06	☐ 300	Burt Hooton	.05	.02	.00
☐ 209	Jeff Reardon	.10	.05	.01	☐ 301	Stu Cliburn	.08	.04	.01
☐ 210	Cal Ripken	.45	.22	.04	☐ 302	Luis Salazar	.05	.02	.00
☐ 211	Bill Schroeder	.05	.02	.00	☐ 303	Ken Dayley	.05	.02	.00
☐ 212	Dan Petry	.05	.02	.00	☐ 304	Frank DiPino	.05	.02	.00
☐ 213	Jim Rice	.20	.10	.02	☐ 305	Von Hayes	.12	.06	.01
☐ 214	Dave Righetti	.12	.06	.01	☐ 306	Gary Redus	.05	.02	.00
☐ 215	Fernando Valenzuela	.25	.12	.02	☐ 307	Craig Lefferts	.08	.04	.01
☐ 216	Julio Franco	.20	.10	.02	☐ 308	Sammy Khalifa	.08	.04	.01
☐ 217	Darryl Motley	.05	.02	.00	☐ 309	Scott Garrelts	.12	.06	.01
☐ 218	Dave Collins	.05	.02	.00	☐ 310	Rick Cerone	.05	.02	.00
☐ 219	Tim Wallach	.10	.05	.01	☐ 311	Shawon Dunston	.35	.17	.03
☐ 220	George Wright	.05	.02	.00	☐ 312	Howard Johnson	.60	.30	.06
☐ 221	Tommy Dunbar	.05	.02	.00	☐ 313	Jim Presley	.10	.05	.01
☐ 222	Steve Balboni	.05	.02	.00	☐ 314	Gary Gaetti	.25	.12	.02
☐ 223	Jay Howell	.08	.04	.01	☐ 315	Luis Leal	.05	.02	.00
☐ 224	Joe Carter	.60	.30	.06	☐ 316	Mark Salas	.05	.02	.00
☐ 225	Ed Whitson	.05	.02	.00	☐ 317	Bill Caudill	.05	.02	.00
☐ 226	Orel Hershiser	2.00	1.00	.20	☐ 318	Dave Henderson	.10	.05	.01
☐ 227	Willie Hernandez	.10	.05	.01	☐ 319	Rafael Santana	.05	.02	.00
☐ 228	Lee Lacy	.05	.02	.00	☐ 320	Leon Durham	.08	.04	.01
☐ 229	Rollie Fingers	.15	.07	.01	☐ 321	Bruce Sutter	.12	.06	.01
☐ 230	Bob Boone	.12	.06	.01	☐ 322	Jason Thompson	.05	.02	.00
☐ 231	Joaquin Andujar	.10	.05	.01	☐ 323	Bob Brenly	.05	.02	.00
☐ 232	Craig Reynolds	.05	.02	.00	☐ 324	Carmelo Martinez	.05	.02	.00
☐ 233	Shane Rawley	.05	.02	.00	☐ 325	Eddie Milner	.05	.02	.00

☐ 326	Juan Samuel	.15	.07	.01
☐ 327	Tom Nieto	.05	.02	.00
☐ 328	Dave Smith	.08	.04	.01
☐ 329	Urbano Lugo	.05	.02	.00
☐ 330	Joel Skinner	.05	.02	.00
☐ 331	Bill Gullickson	.05	.02	.00
☐ 332	Floyd Rayford	.05	.02	.00
☐ 333	Ben Oglivie	.08	.04	.01
☐ 334	Lance Parrish	.15	.07	.01
☐ 335	Jackie Gutierrez	.05	.02	.00
☐ 336	Dennis Rasmussen	.10	.05	.01
☐ 337	Terry Whitfield	.05	.02	.00
☐ 338	Neal Heaton	.05	.02	.00
☐ 339	Jorge Orta	.05	.02	.00
☐ 340	Donnie Hill	.05	.02	.00
☐ 341	Joe Hesketh	.05	.02	.00
☐ 342	Charlie Hough	.08	.04	.01
☐ 343	Dave Rozema	.05	.02	.00
☐ 344	Greg Pryor	.05	.02	.00
☐ 345	Mickey Tettleton	.60	.30	.06
☐ 346	George Vukovich	.05	.02	.00
☐ 347	Don Baylor	.10	.05	.01
☐ 348	Carlos Diaz	.05	.02	.00
☐ 349	Barbaro Garbey	.05	.02	.00
☐ 350	Larry Sheets	.08	.04	.01
☐ 351	Ted Higuera	1.50	.75	.15
☐ 352	Juan Beniquez	.05	.02	.00
☐ 353	Bob Forsch	.05	.02	.00
☐ 354	Mark Bailey	.05	.02	.00
☐ 355	Larry Andersen	.05	.02	.00
☐ 356	Terry Kennedy	.05	.02	.00
☐ 357	Don Robinson	.05	.02	.00
☐ 358	Jim Gott	.05	.02	.00
☐ 359	Earnie Riles	.25	.12	.02
☐ 360	John Christensen	.05	.02	.00
☐ 361	Ray Fontenot	.05	.02	.00
☐ 362	Spike Owen	.05	.02	.00
☐ 363	Jim Acker	.05	.02	.00
☐ 364	Ron Davis	.08	.04	.01
☐ 365	Tom Hume	.05	.02	.00
☐ 366	Carlton Fisk	.30	.15	.03
☐ 367	Nate Snell	.05	.02	.00
☐ 368	Rick Manning	.05	.02	.00
☐ 369	Darrell Evans	.10	.05	.01
☐ 370	Ron Hassey	.05	.02	.00
☐ 371	Wade Boggs	3.00	1.50	.30
☐ 372	Rick Honeycutt	.05	.02	.00
☐ 373	Chris Bando	.05	.02	.00
☐ 374	Bud Black	.05	.02	.00
☐ 375	Steve Henderson	.05	.02	.00
☐ 376	Charlie Lea	.05	.02	.00
☐ 377	Reggie Jackson	.50	.25	.05
☐ 378	Dave Schmidt	.08	.04	.01
☐ 379	Bob James	.05	.02	.00
☐ 380	Glenn Davis	3.75	1.85	.37
☐ 381	Tim Corcoran	.05	.02	.00
☐ 382	Danny Cox	.10	.05	.01
☐ 383	Tim Flannery	.05	.02	.00
☐ 384	Tom Browning	.20	.10	.02
☐ 385	Rick Camp	.05	.02	.00
☐ 386	Jim Morrison	.05	.02	.00
☐ 387	Dave LaPoint	.08	.04	.01
☐ 388	Dave Lopes	.08	.04	.01
☐ 389	Al Cowens	.05	.02	.00
☐ 390	Doyle Alexander	.08	.04	.01
☐ 391	Tim Laudner	.05	.02	.00
☐ 392	Don Aase	.05	.02	.00
☐ 393	Jaime Cocanower	.05	.02	.00
☐ 394	Randy O'Neal	.05	.02	.00
☐ 395	Mike Easler	.05	.02	.00
☐ 396	Scott Bradley	.05	.02	.00
☐ 397	Tom Niedenfuer	.05	.02	.00
☐ 398	Jerry Willard	.05	.02	.00
☐ 399	Lonnie Smith	.10	.05	.01
☐ 400	Bruce Bochte	.05	.02	.00
☐ 401	Terry Francona	.05	.02	.00
☐ 402	Jim Slaton	.05	.02	.00
☐ 403	Bill Stein	.05	.02	.00
☐ 404	Tim Hulett	.05	.02	.00
☐ 405	Alan Ashby	.05	.02	.00
☐ 406	Tim Stoddard	.05	.02	.00
☐ 407	Garry Maddox	.05	.02	.00
☐ 408	Ted Power	.05	.02	.00
☐ 409	Len Barker	.05	.02	.00
☐ 410	Denny Gonzalez	.05	.02	.00
☐ 411	George Frazier	.05	.02	.00
☐ 412	Andy Van Slyke	.25	.12	.02
☐ 413	Jim Dwyer	.05	.02	.00
☐ 414	Paul Householder	.05	.02	.00
☐ 415	Alejandro Sanchez	.05	.02	.00
☐ 416	Steve Crawford	.05	.02	.00
☐ 417	Dan Pasqua	.10	.05	.01
☐ 418	Enos Cabell	.05	.02	.00
☐ 419	Mike Jones	.05	.02	.00
☐ 420	Steve Kiefer	.05	.02	.00
☐ 421	Tim Burke	.35	.17	.03
☐ 422	Mike Mason	.05	.02	.00
☐ 423	Ruppert Jones	.05	.02	.00
☐ 424	Jerry Hairston	.05	.02	.00
☐ 425	Tito Landrum	.05	.02	.00
☐ 426	Jeff Calhoun	.05	.02	.00
☐ 427	Don Carman	.25	.12	.02
☐ 428	Tony Perez	.12	.06	.01
☐ 429	Jerry Davis	.05	.02	.00
☐ 430	Bob Walk	.05	.02	.00
☐ 431	Brad Wellman	.05	.02	.00
☐ 432	Terry Forster	.08	.04	.01
☐ 433	Billy Hatcher	.10	.05	.01
☐ 434	Clint Hurdle	.05	.02	.00
☐ 435	Ivan Calderon	.65	.30	.06
☐ 436	Pete Filson	.05	.02	.00
☐ 437	Tom Henke	.10	.05	.01
☐ 438	Dave Engle	.05	.02	.00
☐ 439	Tom Filer	.05	.02	.00
☐ 440	Gorman Thomas	.10	.05	.01
☐ 441	Rick Aguilera	.35	.17	.03
☐ 442	Scott Sanderson	.05	.02	.00
☐ 443	Jeff Dedmon	.05	.02	.00
☐ 444	Joe Orsulak	.10	.05	.01
☐ 445	Atlee Hammaker	.05	.02	.00
☐ 446	Jerry Royster	.05	.02	.00
☐ 447	Buddy Bell	.10	.05	.01
☐ 448	Dave Rucker	.05	.02	.00
☐ 449	Ivan DeJesus	.05	.02	.00
☐ 450	Jim Pankovits	.05	.02	.00
☐ 451	Jerry Narron	.05	.02	.00
☐ 452	Bryan Little	.05	.02	.00
☐ 453	Gary Lucas	.05	.02	.00
☐ 454	Dennis Martinez	.08	.04	.01
☐ 455	Ed Romero	.05	.02	.00
☐ 456	Bob Melvin	.10	.05	.01
☐ 457	Glenn Hoffman	.05	.02	.00
☐ 458	Bob Shirley	.05	.02	.00
☐ 459	Bob Welch	.08	.04	.01
☐ 460	Carmen Castillo	.05	.02	.00
☐ 461	Dave Leeper (outfielder)	.08	.04	.01
☐ 462	Tim Birtsas	.10	.05	.01
☐ 463	Randy St.Claire	.05	.02	.00
☐ 464	Chris Welsh	.05	.02	.00
☐ 465	Greg Harris	.05	.02	.00
☐ 466	Lynn Jones	.05	.02	.00
☐ 467	Dusty Baker	.08	.04	.01
☐ 468	Roy Smith	.05	.02	.00
☐ 469	Andre Robertson	.05	.02	.00
☐ 470	Ken Landreaux	.05	.02	.00
☐ 471	Dave Bergman	.05	.02	.00
☐ 472	Gary Roenicke	.05	.02	.00
☐ 473	Pete Vuckovich	.05	.02	.00
☐ 474	Kirk McCaskill	.60	.30	.06
☐ 475	Jeff Lahti	.05	.02	.00
☐ 476	Mike Scott	.35	.17	.03
☐ 477	Darren Daulton	.15	.07	.01
☐ 478	Graig Nettles	.10	.05	.01
☐ 479	Bill Almon	.05	.02	.00
☐ 480	Greg Minton	.05	.02	.00
☐ 481	Randy Ready	.05	.02	.00
☐ 482	Len Dykstra	.75	.35	.07
☐ 483	Thad Bosley	.05	.02	.00
☐ 484	Harold Reynolds	.60	.30	.06
☐ 485	Al Oliver	.10	.05	.01
☐ 486	Roy Smalley	.05	.02	.00
☐ 487	John Franco	.20	.10	.02
☐ 488	Juan Agosto	.05	.02	.00
☐ 489	Al Pulido	.05	.02	.00
☐ 490	Bill Wegman	.10	.05	.01
☐ 491	Frank Tanana	.08	.04	.01
☐ 492	Brian Fisher	.20	.10	.02
☐ 493	Mark Clear	.05	.02	.00
☐ 494	Len Matuszek	.05	.02	.00
☐ 495	Ramon Romero	.05	.02	.00
☐ 496	John Wathan	.05	.02	.00
☐ 497	Rob Picciolo	.05	.02	.00
☐ 498	U.L. Washington	.05	.02	.00
☐ 499	John Candelaria	.08	.04	.01
☐ 500	Duane Walker	.05	.02	.00
☐ 501	Gene Nelson	.05	.02	.00
☐ 502	John Mizerock	.05	.02	.00
☐ 503	Luis Aguayo	.05	.02	.00
☐ 504	Kurt Kepshire	.05	.02	.00
☐ 505	Ed Wojna	.10	.05	.01
☐ 506	Joe Price	.05	.02	.00
☐ 507	Milt Thompson	.30	.15	.03
☐ 508	Junior Ortiz	.05	.02	.00
☐ 509	Vida Blue	.08	.04	.01
☐ 510	Steve Engel	.05	.02	.00
☐ 511	Karl Best	.05	.02	.00
☐ 512	Cecil Fielder	.20	.10	.02
☐ 513	Frank Eufemia	.08	.04	.01
☐ 514	Tippy Martinez	.05	.02	.00

☐ 515	Billy Jo Robidoux	.10	.05	.01
☐ 516	Bill Scherrer	.05	.02	.00
☐ 517	Bruce Hurst	.15	.07	.01
☐ 518	Rich Bordi	.05	.02	.00
☐ 519	Steve Yeager	.05	.02	.00
☐ 520	Tony Bernazard	.05	.02	.00
☐ 521	Hal McRae	.08	.04	.01
☐ 522	Jose Rijo	.08	.04	.01
☐ 523	Mitch Webster	.30	.15	.03
☐ 524	Jack Howell	.35	.17	.03
☐ 525	Alan Bannister	.05	.02	.00
☐ 526	Ron Kittle	.10	.05	.01
☐ 527	Phil Garner	.05	.02	.00
☐ 528	Kurt Bevacqua	.05	.02	.00
☐ 529	Kevin Gross	.05	.02	.00
☐ 530	Bo Diaz	.05	.02	.00
☐ 531	Ken Oberkfell	.05	.02	.00
☐ 532	Rick Reuschel	.12	.06	.01
☐ 533	Ron Meridith	.08	.04	.01
☐ 534	Steve Braun	.05	.02	.00
☐ 535	Wayne Gross	.05	.02	.00
☐ 536	Ray Searage	.05	.02	.00
☐ 537	Tom Brookens	.05	.02	.00
☐ 538	Al Nipper	.05	.02	.00
☐ 539	Billy Sample	.05	.02	.00
☐ 540	Steve Sax	.20	.10	.02
☐ 541	Dan Quisenberry	.10	.05	.01
☐ 542	Tony Phillips	.05	.02	.00
☐ 543	Floyd Youmans	.30	.15	.03
☐ 544	Steve Buechele	.25	.12	.02
☐ 545	Craig Gerber	.05	.02	.00
☐ 546	Joe DeSa	.05	.02	.00
☐ 547	Brian Harper	.05	.02	.00
☐ 548	Kevin Bass	.08	.04	.01
☐ 549	Tom Foley	.05	.02	.00
☐ 550	Dave Van Gorder	.05	.02	.00
☐ 551	Bruce Bochy	.05	.02	.00
☐ 552	R.J. Reynolds	.05	.02	.00
☐ 553	Chris Brown	.20	.10	.02
☐ 554	Bruce Benedict	.05	.02	.00
☐ 555	Warren Brusstar	.05	.02	.00
☐ 556	Danny Heep	.05	.02	.00
☐ 557	Darnell Coles	.05	.02	.00
☐ 558	Greg Gagne	.08	.04	.01
☐ 559	Ernie Whitt	.08	.04	.01
☐ 560	Ron Washington	.05	.02	.00
☐ 561	Jimmy Key	.15	.07	.01
☐ 562	Billy Swift	.10	.05	.01
☐ 563	Ron Darling	.30	.15	.03
☐ 564	Dick Ruthven	.05	.02	.00
☐ 565	Zane Smith	.25	.12	.02
☐ 566	Sid Bream	.05	.02	.00
☐ 567A	Joel Youngblood ERR (position P)	.10	.05	.01
☐ 567B	Joel Youngblood COR (position IF)	.60	.30	.06
☐ 568	Mario Ramirez	.05	.02	.00
☐ 569	Tom Runnels	.05	.02	.00
☐ 570	Rick Schu	.05	.02	.00
☐ 571	Bill Campbell	.05	.02	.00
☐ 572	Dickie Thon	.05	.02	.00
☐ 573	Al Holland	.05	.02	.00
☐ 574	Reid Nichols	.05	.02	.00
☐ 575	Bert Roberge	.05	.02	.00
☐ 576	Mike Flanagan	.08	.04	.01
☐ 577	Tim Leary	.35	.17	.03
☐ 578	Mike Laga	.05	.02	.00
☐ 579	Steve Lyons	.05	.02	.00
☐ 580	Phil Niekro	.20	.10	.02
☐ 581	Gilberto Reyes	.10	.05	.01
☐ 582	Jamie Easterly	.05	.02	.00
☐ 583	Mark Gubicza	.20	.10	.02
☐ 584	Stan Javier	.25	.12	.02
☐ 585	Bill Laskey	.05	.02	.00
☐ 586	Jeff Russell	.10	.05	.01
☐ 587	Dickie Noles	.05	.02	.00
☐ 588	Steve Farr	.08	.04	.01
☐ 589	Steve Ontiveros	.10	.05	.01
☐ 590	Mike Hargrove	.05	.02	.00
☐ 591	Marty Bystrom	.05	.02	.00
☐ 592	Franklin Stubbs	.08	.04	.01
☐ 593	Larry Herndon	.05	.02	.00
☐ 594	Bill Swaggerty	.05	.02	.00
☐ 595	Carlos Ponce	.05	.02	.00
☐ 596	Pat Perry	.10	.05	.01
☐ 597	Ray Knight	.08	.04	.01
☐ 598	Steve Lombardozzi	.12	.06	.01
☐ 599	Brad Havens	.05	.02	.00
☐ 600	Pat Clements	.10	.05	.01
☐ 601	Joe Niekro	.08	.04	.01
☐ 602	Hank Aaron Puzzle Card			
☐ 603	Dwayne Henry	.08	.04	.01
☐ 604	Mookie Wilson	.08	.04	.01
☐ 605	Buddy Biancalana	.05	.02	.00

☐ 606	Rance Mulliniks	.05	.02	.00
☐ 607	Alan Wiggins	.05	.02	.00
☐ 608	Joe Cowley	.05	.02	.00
☐ 609A	Tom Seaver (green borders on name)	.50	.25	.05
☐ 609B	Tom Seaver (yellow borders on name)	1.50	.75	.15
☐ 610	Neil Allen	.05	.02	.00
☐ 611	Don Sutton	.25	.12	.02
☐ 612	Fred Toliver	.10	.05	.01
☐ 613	Jay Baller	.08	.04	.01
☐ 614	Marc Sullivan	.08	.04	.01
☐ 615	John Grubb	.05	.02	.00
☐ 616	Bruce Kison	.05	.02	.00
☐ 617	Bill Madlock	.10	.05	.01
☐ 618	Chris Chambliss	.08	.04	.01
☐ 619	Dave Stewart	.30	.15	.03
☐ 620	Tim Lollar	.05	.02	.00
☐ 621	Gary Lavelle	.05	.02	.00
☐ 622	Charles Hudson	.05	.02	.00
☐ 623	Joel Davis	.10	.05	.01
☐ 624	Joe Johnson	.10	.05	.01
☐ 625	Sid Fernandez	.25	.12	.02
☐ 626	Dennis Lamp	.05	.02	.00
☐ 627	Terry Harper	.05	.02	.00
☐ 628	Jack Lazorko	.05	.02	.00
☐ 629	Roger McDowell	.50	.25	.05
☐ 630	Mark Funderburk	.10	.05	.01
☐ 631	Ed Lynch	.05	.02	.00
☐ 632	Rudy Law	.05	.02	.00
☐ 633	Roger Mason	.10	.05	.01
☐ 634	Mike Felder	.12	.06	.01
☐ 635	Ken Schrom	.05	.02	.00
☐ 636	Bob Ojeda	.08	.04	.01
☐ 637	Ed VandeBerg	.05	.02	.00
☐ 638	Bobby Meacham	.05	.02	.00
☐ 639	Cliff Johnson	.05	.02	.00
☐ 640	Garth Iorg	.05	.02	.00
☐ 641	Dan Driessen	.05	.02	.00
☐ 642	Mike Brown OF	.05	.02	.00
☐ 643	John Shelby	.05	.02	.00
☐ 644	Pete Rose (Ty-Breaking)	.35	.17	.03
☐ 645	The Knuckle Brothers Phil Niekro Joe Niekro	.10	.05	.01
☐ 646	Jesse Orosco	.05	.02	.00
☐ 647	Billy Beane	.12	.06	.01
☐ 648	Cesar Cedeno	.08	.04	.01
☐ 649	Bert Blyleven	.12	.06	.01
☐ 650	Max Venable	.05	.02	.00
☐ 651	Fleet Feet Vince Coleman Willie McGee	.30	.15	.03
☐ 652	Calvin Schiraldi	.08	.04	.01
☐ 653	King of Kings (Pete Rose)	.75	.35	.07
☐ 654	CL: Diamond Kings (unnumbered)	.08	.01	.00
☐ 655A	CL 1: 27-130 (unnumbered) (45 Beane ERR)	.10	.01	.00
☐ 655B	CL 1: 27-130 (unnumbered) (45 Habyan COR)	.50	.05	.01
☐ 656	CL 2: 131-234 (unnumbered)	.06	.01	.00
☐ 657	CL 3: 235-338 (unnumbered)	.06	.01	.00
☐ 658	CL 4: 339-442 (unnumbered)	.06	.01	.00
☐ 659	CL 5: 443-546 (unnumbered)	.06	.01	.00
☐ 660	CL 6: 547-653 (unnumbered)	.06	.01	.00

1986 Donruss Wax Box Cards

The cards in this 4-card set measure the standard 2 1/2" by 3 1/2". Cards have essentially the same design as the 1986 Donruss regular issue set. The cards were printed on the bottoms of the regular issue wax pack boxes. The four cards (PC4 to PC6 plus a Hank Aaron puzzle card) are considered a separate set in their own right and are not typically included in a complete set of the regular issue 1986

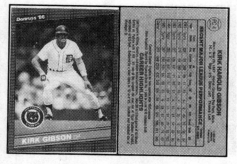

Donruss cards. The value of the panel uncut is slightly greater, perhaps by 25% greater, than the value of the individual cards cut up carefully.

	MINT	EXC	G-VG
COMPLETE SET (4)	.60	.30	.06
COMMON PLAYERS	.05	.02	.00
☐ PC4 Kirk Gibson	.50	.25	.05
☐ PC5 Willie Hernandez	.10	.05	.01
☐ PC6 Doug DeCinces	.10	.05	.01
☐ PUZ Hank Aaron Puzzle Card	.05	.02	.00

1986 Donruss All-Stars

The cards in this 60-card set measure 3 1/2" by 5". Players featured were involved in the 1985 All-Star game played in Minnesota. Cards are very similar in design to the 1986 Donruss regular issue set. The backs give each player's All-Star game statistics and have an orange-yellow border.

	MINT	EXC	G-VG
COMPLETE SET (60)	6.00	3.00	.60
COMMON PLAYERS (1-60)	.05	.02	.00
☐ 1 Tony Gwynn	.35	.17	.03
☐ 2 Tommy Herr	.05	.02	.00
☐ 3 Steve Garvey	.30	.15	.03
☐ 4 Dale Murphy	.45	.22	.04
☐ 5 Darryl Strawberry	.60	.30	.06
☐ 6 Graig Nettles	.10	.05	.01
☐ 7 Terry Kennedy	.05	.02	.00
☐ 8 Ozzie Smith	.20	.10	.02
☐ 9 LaMarr Hoyt	.05	.02	.00
☐ 10 Rickey Henderson	.45	.22	.04
☐ 11 Lou Whitaker	.15	.07	.01
☐ 12 George Brett	.40	.20	.04
☐ 13 Eddie Murray	.30	.15	.03
☐ 14 Cal Ripken	.30	.15	.03
☐ 15 Dave Winfield	.20	.10	.02
☐ 16 Jim Rice	.20	.10	.02
☐ 17 Carlton Fisk	.25	.12	.02
☐ 18 Jack Morris	.10	.05	.01
☐ 19 Jose Cruz	.05	.02	.00
☐ 20 Tim Raines	.20	.10	.02

☐ 21 Nolan Ryan	.75	.35	.07
☐ 22 Tony Pena	.05	.02	.00
☐ 23 Jack Clark	.15	.07	.01
☐ 24 Dave Parker	.10	.05	.01
☐ 25 Tim Wallach	.05	.02	.00
☐ 26 Ozzie Virgil	.05	.02	.00
☐ 27 Fernando Valenzuela	.20	.10	.02
☐ 28 Dwight Gooden	.75	.35	.07
☐ 29 Glenn Wilson	.05	.02	.00
☐ 30 Garry Templeton	.05	.02	.00
☐ 31 Goose Gossage	.10	.05	.01
☐ 32 Ryne Sandberg	.30	.15	.03
☐ 33 Jeff Reardon	.10	.05	.01
☐ 34 Pete Rose	.90	.45	.09
☐ 35 Scott Garrelts	.05	.02	.00
☐ 36 Willie McGee	.15	.07	.01
☐ 37 Ron Darling	.15	.07	.01
☐ 38 Dick Williams MG	.05	.02	.00
☐ 39 Paul Molitor	.20	.10	.02
☐ 40 Damaso Garcia	.05	.02	.00
☐ 41 Phil Bradley	.10	.05	.01
☐ 42 Dan Petry	.05	.02	.00
☐ 43 Willie Hernandez	.10	.05	.01
☐ 44 Tom Brunansky	.10	.05	.01
☐ 45 Alan Trammell	.20	.10	.02
☐ 46 Donnie Moore	.05	.02	.00
☐ 47 Wade Boggs	.90	.45	.09
☐ 48 Ernie Whitt	.05	.02	.00
☐ 49 Harold Baines	.10	.05	.01
☐ 50 Don Mattingly	1.25	.60	.12
☐ 51 Gary Ward	.05	.02	.00
☐ 52 Bert Blyleven	.15	.07	.01
☐ 53 Jimmy Key	.10	.05	.01
☐ 54 Cecil Cooper	.10	.05	.01
☐ 55 Dave Stieb	.10	.05	.01
☐ 56 Rich Gedman	.05	.02	.00
☐ 57 Jay Howell	.05	.02	.00
☐ 58 Sparky Anderson MG	.05	.02	.00
☐ 59 Minneapolis Metrodome	.05	.02	.00
☐ 60 Checklist Card (unnumbered)	.05	.02	.00

1986 Donruss All-Star Box

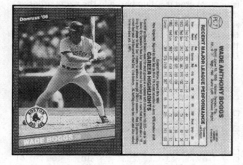

The cards in this 4-card set measure the standard 2 1/2" by 3 1/2" in spite of the fact that they form the bottom of the wax pack box for the larger Donruss All-Star cards. These box cards have essentially the same design as the 1986 Donruss regular issue set. The cards were printed on the bottoms of the Donruss All-Star (3 1/2" by 5") wax pack boxes. The four cards (PC7 to PC9 plus a Hank Aaron puzzle card) are considered a separate set in their own right and are not typically included in a complete set of the regular issue 1986 Donruss All-Star (or regular) cards. The value of the panel uncut is slightly greater, perhaps by 25% greater, than the value of the individual cards cut up carefully.

	MINT	EXC	G-VG
COMPLETE SET (4)	1.00	.50	.10
COMMON PLAYERS	.05	.02	.00
☐ PC7 Wade Boggs	.90	.45	.09
☐ PC8 Lee Smith	.10	.05	.01
☐ PC9 Cecil Cooper	.10	.05	.01

☐ PUZ Hank Aaron .... .05 .02 .00
Puzzle Card

1986 Donruss Pop-Ups

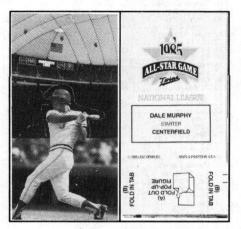

This set is the companion of the 1986 Donruss All-Star (60) set; as such it features the first 18 cards of that set (the All-Star starting line-ups) in a pop-up, die-cut type of card. These cards (measuring (2 1/2" by 5") can be "popped up" to feature a standing card showing the player in action in front of the Metrodome ballpark background. Although this set is unnumbered it is numbered in the same order as its companion set, presumably according to the respective batting orders of the starting line-ups. The first nine numbers below are National Leaguers and the last nine are American Leaguers. See also the Donruss All-Star checklist card which contains a checklist for the Pop-Ups as well.

	MINT	EXC	G-VG
COMPLETE SET (18)	4.00	2.00	.40
COMMON PLAYERS (1-18)	.10	.05	.01

		MINT	EXC	G-VG
☐	1 Tony Gwynn	.40	.20	.04
☐	2 Tommy Herr	.10	.05	.01
☐	3 Steve Garvey	.40	.20	.04
☐	4 Dale Murphy	.40	.20	.04
☐	5 Darryl Strawberry	.60	.30	.06
☐	6 Graig Nettles	.10	.05	.01
☐	7 Terry Kennedy	.10	.05	.01
☐	8 Ozzie Smith	.20	.10	.02
☐	9 LaMarr Hoyt	.10	.05	.01
☐	10 Rickey Henderson	.50	.25	.05
☐	11 Lou Whitaker	.20	.10	.02
☐	12 George Brett	.50	.25	.05
☐	13 Eddie Murray	.30	.15	.03
☐	14 Cal Ripken	.40	.20	.04
☐	15 Dave Winfield	.20	.10	.02
☐	16 Jim Rice	.20	.10	.02
☐	17 Carlton Fisk	.20	.10	.02
☐	18 Jack Morris	.10	.05	.01

1986 Donruss Super DK's

This 29-card set of large Diamond Kings features the full-color artwork of Dick Perez. The set could be obtained from Perez-Steele Galleries by sending three Donruss wrappers and 9.00. The cards measure 4 7/8" by 6 13/16" and are identical in design to the Diamond King cards in the Donruss regular issue.

	MINT	EXC	G-VG
COMPLETE SET (29)	10.00	5.00	1.00
COMMON PLAYER (1-27)	.20	.10	.02

		MINT	EXC	G-VG
☐	1 Kirk Gibson	.50	.25	.05
☐	2 Goose Gossage	.30	.15	.03
☐	3 Willie McGee	.30	.15	.03
☐	4 George Bell	.30	.15	.03
☐	5 Tony Armas	.20	.10	.02
☐	6 Chili Davis	.20	.10	.02
☐	7 Cecil Cooper	.20	.10	.02
☐	8 Mike Boddicker	.20	.10	.02
☐	9 Dave Lopes	.20	.10	.02
☐	10 Bill Doran	.20	.10	.02
☐	11 Bret Saberhagen	.60	.30	.06
☐	12 Brett Butler	.20	.10	.02
☐	13 Harold Baines	.30	.15	.03
☐	14 Mike Davis	.20	.10	.02
☐	15 Tony Perez	.30	.15	.03
☐	16 Willie Randolph	.30	.15	.03
☐	17 Bob Boone	.30	.15	.03
☐	18 Orel Hershiser	1.00	.50	.10
☐	19 Johnny Ray	.30	.15	.03
☐	20 Gary Ward	.20	.10	.02
☐	21 Rick Mahler	.20	.10	.02
☐	22 Phil Bradley	.30	.15	.03
☐	23 Jerry Koosman	.30	.15	.03
☐	24 Tom Brunansky	.30	.15	.03
☐	25 Andre Dawson	.50	.25	.05
☐	26 Dwight Gooden	1.25	.60	.12
☐	27 Pete Rose	1.25	.60	.12
	King of Kings			
☐	28 Checklist Card	.10	.05	.01
	(unnumbered)			
☐	29 Aaron Large Puzzle	.20	.10	.02
	(unnumbered)			

1986 Donruss Rookies

The 1986 Donruss "The Rookies" set features 56 cards plus a 15-piece puzzle of Hank Aaron. Cards are in full color and are standard size, 2 1/2" by 3 1/2". The set was distributed in a small green box with gold lettering. Although the set was wrapped in cellophane, the top card was #1 Joyner, resulting in a percentage of (Joyner) cards arriving in less than perfect condition. Card fronts are similar in design to the 1986 Donruss regular issue except for the presence of "The Rookies" logo in the lower left corner and a bluish green border instead of a blue border.

	MINT	EXC	G-VG
COMPLETE SET (56)	50.00	25.00	5.00
COMMON PLAYER (1-56)	.08	.04	.01

		MINT	EXC	G-VG
☐ 1	Wally Joyner	4.00	2.00	.40
☐ 2	Tracy Jones	.35	.17	.03
☐ 3	Allan Anderson	.45	.22	.04
☐ 4	Ed Correa	.20	.10	.02
☐ 5	Reggie Williams	.15	.07	.01
☐ 6	Charlie Kerfeld	.15	.07	.01
☐ 7	Andres Galarraga	1.00	.50	.10
☐ 8	Bob Tewksbury	.15	.07	.01
☐ 9	Al Newman	.15	.07	.01
☐ 10	Andres Thomas	.25	.12	.02
☐ 11	Barry Bonds	1.50	.75	.15
☐ 12	Juan Nieves	.15	.07	.01
☐ 13	Mark Eichhorn	.15	.07	.01
☐ 14	Dan Plesac	.35	.17	.03
☐ 15	Cory Snyder	1.00	.50	.10
☐ 16	Kelly Gruber	.45	.22	.04
☐ 17	Kevin Mitchell	7.00	3.50	.70
☐ 18	Steve Lombardozzi	.08	.04	.01
☐ 19	Mitch Williams	.60	.30	.06
☐ 20	John Cerutti	.30	.15	.03
☐ 21	Todd Worrell	.45	.22	.04
☐ 22	Jose Canseco	9.00	4.50	.90
☐ 23	Pete Incaviglia	.85	.40	.08
☐ 24	Jose Guzman	.15	.07	.01
☐ 25	Scott Bailes	.15	.07	.01
☐ 26	Greg Mathews	.25	.12	.02
☐ 27	Eric King	.20	.10	.02
☐ 28	Paul Assenmacher	.15	.07	.01
☐ 29	Jeff Sellers	.20	.10	.02
☐ 30	Bobby Bonilla	1.50	.75	.15
☐ 31	Doug Drabek	.45	.22	.04
☐ 32	Will Clark	13.50	6.00	1.25
☐ 33	Bip Roberts	.25	.12	.02
☐ 34	Jim Deshaies	.45	.22	.04
☐ 35	Mike LaValliere	.25	.12	.02
☐ 36	Scott Bankhead	.30	.15	.03
☐ 37	Dale Sveum	.25	.12	.02
☐ 38	Bo Jackson	11.00	5.50	1.10
☐ 39	Rob Thompson	.45	.22	.04
☐ 40	Eric Plunk	.25	.12	.02
☐ 41	Bill Bathe	.15	.07	.01
☐ 42	John Kruk	.50	.25	.05
☐ 43	Andy Allanson	.15	.07	.01
☐ 44	Mark Portugal	.25	.12	.02
☐ 45	Danny Tartabull	.85	.40	.08
☐ 46	Bob Kipper	.08	.04	.01
☐ 47	Gene Walter	.15	.07	.01
☐ 48	Rey Quinones	.20	.10	.02
☐ 49	Bobby Witt	.45	.22	.04
☐ 50	Bill Mooneyham	.15	.07	.01
☐ 51	John Cangelosi	.15	.07	.01
☐ 52	Ruben Sierra	7.50	3.75	.75
☐ 53	Rob Woodward	.15	.07	.01
☐ 54	Ed Hearn	.15	.07	.01
☐ 55	Joel McKeon	.15	.07	.01
☐ 56	Checklist card	.08	.01	.00

1986 Donruss Highlights

Donruss' second edition of Highlights was released late in 1986. These glossy-coated cards are standard size, measuring 2 1/2" by 3 1/2". Cards commemorate events during the 1986 season, as well as players and pitchers of the month from each league. The set was distributed in its own red, white, blue, and gold box along with a small Hank Aaron puzzle. Card fronts are similar to the regular 1986 Donruss issue except that the Highlights logo is positioned in the lower left-hand corner and the borders are in gold instead of blue. The backs are printed in black and gold on white card stock.

	MINT	EXC	G-VG
COMPLETE SET (56)	9.00	4.50	.90
COMMON PLAYER (1-56)	.06	.03	.00

		MINT	EXC	G-VG
☐ 1	Will Clark Homers in First At-Bat	1.00	.50	.10
☐ 2	Jose Rijo Oakland Milestone for Strikeouts	.06	.03	.00
☐ 3	George Brett Royals' All-Time Hit Man	.25	.12	.02
☐ 4	Mike Schmidt Phillies RBI Leader	.65	.30	.06
☐ 5	Roger Clemens KKKKKKKKKK KKKKKKKKKK	.40	.20	.04
☐ 6	Roger Clemens AL Pitcher April	.40	.20	.04
☐ 7	Kirby Puckett AL Player April	.50	.25	.05
☐ 8	Dwight Gooden NL Pitcher April	.40	.20	.04
☐ 9	Johnny Ray NL Player April	.06	.03	.00
☐ 10	Reggie Jackson Eclipses Mantle HR Record	.40	.20	.04
☐ 11	Wade Boggs First Five Hit Game of Career	.65	.30	.06
☐ 12	Don Aase AL Pitcher May	.06	.03	.00
☐ 13	Wade Boggs AL Player May	.65	.30	.06
☐ 14	Jeff Reardon NL Pitcher May	.06	.03	.00
☐ 15	Hubie Brooks NL Player May	.06	.03	.00
☐ 16	Don Sutton Notches 300th	.10	.05	.01
☐ 17	Roger Clemens Starts 14-0	.40	.20	.04
☐ 18	Roger Clemens AL Pitcher June	.40	.20	.04
☐ 19	Kent Hrbek AL Player June	.15	.07	.01
☐ 20	Rick Rhoden NL Pitcher June	.06	.03	.00
☐ 21	Kevin Bass NL Player June	.06	.03	.00
☐ 22	Bob Horner Blasts four HRs in one Game	.10	.05	.01
☐ 23	Wally Joyner Starting All-Star Rookie	.50	.25	.05
☐ 24	Darryl Strawberry Starts Third Straight All-Star Game	.50	.25	.05
☐ 25	Fernando Valenzuela Ties All-Star Game Record	.15	.07	.01
☐ 26	Roger Clemens All-Star Game MVP	.40	.20	.04
☐ 27	Jack Morris AL Pitcher July	.10	.05	.01
☐ 28	Scott Fletcher AL Player July	.06	.03	.00
☐ 29	Todd Worrell NL Pitcher July	.10	.05	.01
☐ 30	Eric Davis NL Player July	.65	.30	.06
☐ 31	Bert Blyleven Records 3000th Strikeout	.15	.07	.01

☐ 32 Bobby Doerr '86 HOF Inductee	.15	.07	.01
☐ 33 Ernie Lombardi '86 HOF Inductee	.15	.07	.01
☐ 34 Willie McCovey '86 HOF Inductee	.25	.12	.02
☐ 35 Steve Carlton Notches 4000th K	.25	.12	.02
☐ 36 Mike Schmidt Surpasses DiMaggio Record	.65	.30	.06
☐ 37 Juan Samuel Records 3rd "Quadruple Double"	.10	.05	.01
☐ 38 Mike Witt AL Pitcher August	.10	.05	.01
☐ 39 Doug DeCinces AL Player August	.06	.03	.00
☐ 40 Bill Gullickson NL Pitcher August	.06	.03	.00
☐ 41 Dale Murphy NL Player August	.30	.15	.03
☐ 42 Joe Carter Sets Tribe Offensive Record	.15	.07	.01
☐ 43 Bo Jackson Longest HR in Royals Stadium	1.50	.75	.15
☐ 44 Joe Cowley Majors 1st No- Hitter in 2 Years	.06	.03	.00
☐ 45 Jim Deshaies Sets ML Strikeout Record	.06	.03	.00
☐ 46 Mike Scott No Hitter Clinches Division	.15	.07	.01
☐ 47 Bruce Hurst AL Pitcher September	.10	.05	.01
☐ 48 Don Mattingly AL Player September	1.00	.50	.10
☐ 49 Mike Krukow NL Pitcher September	.06	.03	.00
☐ 50 Steve Sax NL Player September	.15	.07	.01
☐ 51 John Cangelosi AL Rookie Steals Record	.10	.05	.01
☐ 52 Dave Righetti ML Save Mark	.10	.05	.01
☐ 53 Don Mattingly Yankee Record for Hits and Doubles	1.25	.60	.12
☐ 54 Todd Worrell Donruss NL ROY	.15	.07	.01
☐ 55 Jose Canseco Donruss AL ROY	1.50	.75	.15
☐ 56 Checklist Card	.06	.03	.00

1987 Donruss

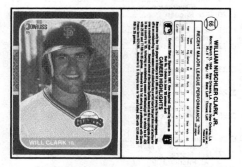

This 660-card set was distributed along with a puzzle of Roberto Clemente. The checklist cards are numbered throughout the set as multiples of 100. The wax pack boxes again contain a separate four cards printed on the bottom of the box. Cards measure 2 1/2" by 3 1/2" and feature a black and gold border on the front; the backs are also done in

black and gold on white card stock. The popular Diamond King subset returns for the sixth consecutive year. Some of the Diamond King (1-26) selections are repeats from prior years; Perez-Steele Galleries has indicated that a five-year rotation will be maintained in order to avoid depleting the pool of available worthy "kings" on some of the teams. Three of the Diamond Kings have a variation (on the reverse) where the yellow strip behind the words "Donruss Diamond Kings" is not printed and hence the background is white.

		MINT	EXC	G-VG
COMPLETE SET (660)		75.00	35.00	7.00
COMMON PLAYER (1-660)		.04	.02	.00
☐ 1	Wally Joyner DK	1.00	.15	.03
☐ 2	Roger Clemens DK	.60	.30	.06
☐ 3	Dale Murphy DK	.40	.20	.04
☐ 4	Darryl Strawberry DK	.50	.25	.05
☐ 5	Ozzie Smith DK	.15	.07	.01
☐ 6	Jose Canseco DK	1.50	.75	.15
☐ 7	Charlie Hough DK	.07	.03	.01
☐ 8	Brook Jacoby DK	.07	.03	.01
☐ 9	Fred Lynn DK	.12	.06	.01
☐ 10	Rick Rhoden DK	.07	.03	.01
☐ 11	Chris Brown DK	.07	.03	.01
☐ 12	Von Hayes DK	.10	.05	.01
☐ 13	Jack Morris DK	.12	.06	.01
☐ 14A	Kevin McReynolds DK .. (yellow strip missing on back)	1.00	.50	.10
☐ 14B	Kevin McReynolds DK ..	.30	.15	.03
☐ 15	George Brett DK	.40	.20	.04
☐ 16	Ted Higuera DK	.15	.07	.01
☐ 17	Hubie Brooks DK	.07	.03	.01
☐ 18	Mike Scott DK	.15	.07	.01
☐ 19	Kirby Puckett DK	.40	.20	.04
☐ 20	Dave Winfield DK	.25	.12	.02
☐ 21	Lloyd Moseby DK	.07	.03	.01
☐ 22A	Eric Davis DK (yellow strip missing on back)	3.00	1.50	.30
☐ 22B	Eric Davis DK	1.00	.50	.10
☐ 23	Jim Presley DK	.07	.03	.01
☐ 24	Keith Moreland DK	.07	.03	.01
☐ 25A	Greg Walker DK (yellow strip missing on back)	.75	.35	.07
☐ 25B	Greg Walker DK	.12	.06	.01
☐ 26	Steve Sax DK	.15	.07	.01
☐ 27	DK Checklist 1-26	.07	.01	.00
☐ 28	B.J. Surhoff RR	.45	.22	.04
☐ 29	Randy Myers RR	.60	.30	.06
☐ 30	Ken Gerhart RR	.15	.07	.01
☐ 31	Benito Santiago RR	1.50	.75	.15
☐ 32	Greg Swindell RR	1.50	.75	.15
☐ 33	Mike Birkbeck RR	.15	.07	.01
☐ 34	Terry Steinbach RR	.75	.35	.07
☐ 35	Bo Jackson RR	9.00	4.50	.90
☐ 36	Greg Maddux RR	1.50	.75	.15
☐ 37	Jim Lindeman RR	.15	.07	.01
☐ 38	Devon White RR	1.25	.60	.12
☐ 39	Eric Bell RR	.10	.05	.01
☐ 40	Willie Fraser RR	.10	.05	.01
☐ 41	Jerry Browne RR	.50	.25	.05
☐ 42	Chris James RR	.90	.45	.09
☐ 43	Rafael Palmeiro RR	2.00	1.00	.20
☐ 44	Pat Dodson RR	.15	.07	.01
☐ 45	Duane Ward RR	.20	.10	.02
☐ 46	Mark McGwire RR	8.00	4.00	.80
☐ 47	Bruce Fields RR (photo actually Darnell Coles)	.10	.05	.01
☐ 48	Eddie Murray	.25	.12	.02
☐ 49	Ted Higuera	.18	.09	.01
☐ 50	Kirk Gibson	.25	.12	.02
☐ 51	Oil Can Boyd	.07	.03	.01
☐ 52	Don Mattingly	2.25	1.10	.22
☐ 53	Pedro Guerrero	.15	.07	.01
☐ 54	George Brett	.30	.15	.03
☐ 55	Jose Rijo	.07	.03	.01
☐ 56	Tim Raines	.25	.12	.02
☐ 57	Ed Correa	.12	.06	.01
☐ 58	Mike Witt	.07	.03	.01
☐ 59	Greg Walker	.07	.03	.01
☐ 60	Ozzie Smith	.20	.10	.02
☐ 61	Glenn Davis	.30	.15	.03
☐ 62	Glenn Wilson	.04	.02	.00
☐ 63	Tom Browning	.10	.05	.01
☐ 64	Tony Gwynn	.50	.25	.05

□	#	Name			
□	65	R.J. Reynolds	.04	.02	.00
□	66	Will Clark	12.00	6.00	1.20
□	67	Ozzie Virgil	.04	.02	.00
□	68	Rick Sutcliffe	.10	.05	.01
□	69	Gary Carter	.25	.12	.02
□	70	Mike Moore	.07	.03	.01
□	71	Bert Blyleven	.12	.06	.01
□	72	Tony Fernandez	.15	.07	.01
□	73	Kent Hrbek	.15	.07	.01
□	74	Lloyd Moseby	.07	.03	.01
□	75	Alvin Davis	.12	.06	.01
□	76	Keith Hernandez	.20	.10	.02
□	77	Ryne Sandberg	.25	.12	.02
□	78	Dale Murphy	.40	.20	.04
□	79	Sid Bream	.04	.02	.00
□	80	Chris Brown	.04	.02	.00
□	81	Steve Garvey	.25	.12	.02
□	82	Mario Soto	.04	.02	.00
□	83	Shane Rawley	.04	.02	.00
□	84	Willie McGee	.10	.05	.01
□	85	Jose Cruz	.07	.03	.01
□	86	Brian Downing	.07	.03	.01
□	87	Ozzie Guillen	.07	.03	.01
□	88	Hubie Brooks	.07	.03	.01
□	89	Cal Ripken	.30	.15	.03
□	90	Juan Nieves	.07	.03	.01
□	91	Lance Parrish	.10	.05	.01
□	92	Jim Rice	.18	.09	.01
□	93	Ron Guidry	.12	.06	.01
□	94	Fernando Valenzuela	.18	.09	.01
□	95	Andy Allanson	.07	.03	.01
□	96	Willie Wilson	.10	.05	.01
□	97	Jose Canseco	6.50	3.25	.65
□	98	Jeff Reardon	.10	.05	.01
□	99	Bobby Witt	.30	.15	.03
□	100	Checklist	.07	.01	.00
□	101	Jose Guzman	.04	.02	.00
□	102	Steve Balboni	.04	.02	.00
□	103	Tony Phillips	.04	.02	.00
□	104	Brook Jacoby	.07	.03	.01
□	105	Dave Winfield	.30	.15	.03
□	106	Orel Hershiser	.40	.20	.04
□	107	Lou Whitaker	.12	.06	.01
□	108	Fred Lynn	.12	.06	.01
□	109	Bill Wegman	.04	.02	.00
□	110	Donnie Moore	.04	.02	.00
□	111	Jack Clark	.18	.09	.01
□	112	Bob Knepper	.07	.03	.01
□	113	Von Hayes	.07	.03	.01
□	114	Bip Roberts	.12	.06	.01
□	115	Tony Pena	.07	.03	.01
□	116	Scott Garrelts	.07	.03	.01
□	117	Paul Molitor	.12	.06	.01
□	118	Darryl Strawberry	.75	.35	.07
□	119	Shawon Dunston	.12	.06	.01
□	120	Jim Presley	.07	.03	.01
□	121	Jesse Barfield	.15	.07	.01
□	122	Gary Gaetti	.15	.07	.01
□	123	Kurt Stillwell	.30	.15	.03
□	124	Joel Davis	.04	.02	.00
□	125	Mike Boddicker	.07	.03	.01
□	126	Robin Yount	.40	.20	.04
□	127	Alan Trammell	.20	.10	.02
□	128	Dave Righetti	.10	.05	.01
□	129	Dwight Evans	.10	.05	.01
□	130	Mike Scioscia	.04	.02	.00
□	131	Julio Franco	.12	.06	.01
□	132	Bret Saberhagen	.35	.17	.03
□	133	Mike Davis	.04	.02	.00
□	134	Joe Hesketh	.04	.02	.00
□	135	Wally Joyner	1.75	.85	.17
□	136	Don Slaught	.04	.02	.00
□	137	Daryl Boston	.04	.02	.00
□	138	Nolan Ryan	.50	.25	.05
□	139	Mike Schmidt	.50	.25	.05
□	140	Tommy Herr	.07	.03	.01
□	141	Garry Templeton	.07	.03	.01
□	142	Kal Daniels	.75	.35	.07
□	143	Billy Sample	.04	.02	.00
□	144	Johnny Ray	.07	.03	.01
□	145	Rob Thompson	.30	.15	.03
□	146	Bob Dernier	.04	.02	.00
□	147	Danny Tartabull	.30	.15	.03
□	148	Ernie Whitt	.04	.02	.00
□	149	Kirby Puckett	1.00	.50	.10
□	150	Mike Young	.04	.02	.00
□	151	Ernest Riles	.04	.02	.00
□	152	Frank Tanana	.07	.03	.01
□	153	Rich Gedman	.04	.02	.00
□	154	Willie Randolph	.07	.03	.01
□	155	Bill Madlock	.07	.03	.01
□	156	Joe Carter	.30	.15	.03
□	157	Danny Jackson	.10	.05	.01
□	158	Carney Lansford	.10	.05	.01
□	159	Bryn Smith	.07	.03	.01
□	160	Gary Pettis	.04	.02	.00
□	161	Oddibe McDowell	.10	.05	.01
□	162	John Cangelosi	.10	.05	.01
□	163	Mike Scott	.20	.10	.02
□	164	Eric Show	.07	.03	.01
□	165	Juan Samuel	.12	.06	.01
□	166	Nick Esasky	.10	.05	.01
□	167	Zane Smith	.07	.03	.01
□	168	Mike Brown (Pirates OF)	.04	.02	.00
□	169	Keith Moreland	.04	.02	.00
□	170	John Tudor	.10	.05	.01
□	171	Ken Dixon	.04	.02	.00
□	172	Jim Gantner	.04	.02	.00
□	173	Jack Morris	.12	.06	.01
□	174	Bruce Hurst	.12	.06	.01
□	175	Dennis Rasmussen	.07	.03	.01
□	176	Mike Marshall	.10	.05	.01
□	177	Dan Quisenberry	.10	.05	.01
□	178	Eric Plunk	.07	.03	.01
□	179	Tim Wallach	.07	.03	.01
□	180	Steve Buechele	.04	.02	.00
□	181	Don Sutton	.15	.07	.01
□	182	Dave Schmidt	.07	.03	.01
□	183	Terry Pendleton	.07	.03	.01
□	184	Jim Deshaies	.35	.17	.03
□	185	Steve Bedrosian	.12	.06	.01
□	186	Pete Rose	.55	.27	.05
□	187	Dave Dravecky	.10	.05	.01
□	188	Rick Reuschel	.10	.05	.01
□	189	Dan Gladden	.07	.03	.01
□	190	Rick Mahler	.04	.02	.00
□	191	Thad Bosley	.04	.02	.00
□	192	Ron Darling	.18	.09	.01
□	193	Matt Young	.04	.02	.00
□	194	Tom Brunansky	.12	.06	.01
□	195	Dave Stieb	.10	.05	.01
□	196	Frank Viola	.15	.07	.01
□	197	Tom Henke	.07	.03	.01
□	198	Karl Best	.04	.02	.00
□	199	Dwight Gooden	.75	.35	.07
□	200	Checklist	.07	.01	.00
□	201	Steve Trout	.04	.02	.00
□	202	Rafael Ramirez	.04	.02	.00
□	203	Bob Walk	.04	.02	.00
□	204	Roger Mason	.04	.02	.00
□	205	Terry Kennedy	.04	.02	.00
□	206	Ron Oester	.04	.02	.00
□	207	John Russell	.04	.02	.00
□	208	Greg Mathews	.20	.10	.02
□	209	Charlie Kerfeld	.04	.02	.00
□	210	Reggie Jackson	.40	.20	.04
□	211	Floyd Bannister	.04	.02	.00
□	212	Vance Law	.04	.02	.00
□	213	Rich Bordi	.04	.02	.00
□	214	Dan Plesac	.30	.15	.03
□	215	Dave Collins	.04	.02	.00
□	216	Bob Stanley	.04	.02	.00
□	217	Joe Niekro	.07	.03	.01
□	218	Tom Niedenfuer	.04	.02	.00
□	219	Brett Butler	.07	.03	.01
□	220	Charlie Leibrandt	.04	.02	.00
□	221	Steve Ontiveros	.04	.02	.00
□	222	Tim Burke	.07	.03	.01
□	223	Curtis Wilkerson	.04	.02	.00
□	224	Pete Incaviglia	.75	.35	.07
□	225	Lonnie Smith	.07	.03	.01
□	226	Chris Codiroli	.04	.02	.00
□	227	Scott Bailes	.10	.05	.01
□	228	Rickey Henderson	.40	.20	.04
□	229	Ken Howell	.04	.02	.00
□	230	Darnell Coles	.04	.02	.00
□	231	Don Aase	.04	.02	.00
□	232	Tim Leary	.10	.05	.01
□	233	Bob Boone	.10	.05	.01
□	234	Ricky Horton	.04	.02	.00
□	235	Mark Bailey	.04	.02	.00
□	236	Kevin Gross	.04	.02	.00
□	237	Lance McCullers	.07	.03	.01
□	238	Cecilio Guante	.04	.02	.00
□	239	Bob Melvin	.04	.02	.00
□	240	Billy Jo Robidoux	.04	.02	.00
□	241	Roger McDowell	.07	.03	.01
□	242	Leon Durham	.07	.03	.01
□	243	Ed Nunez	.04	.02	.00
□	244	Jimmy Key	.10	.05	.01
□	245	Mike Smithson	.04	.02	.00
□	246	Bo Diaz	.04	.02	.00
□	247	Carlton Fisk	.18	.09	.01
□	248	Larry Sheets	.07	.03	.01
□	249	Juan Castillo	.04	.02	.00
□	250	Eric King	.12	.06	.01
□	251	Doug Drabek	.30	.15	.03
□	252	Wade Boggs	1.50	.75	.15
□	253	Mariano Duncan	.04	.02	.00

#	Name			
☐ 254	Pat Tabler	.07	.03	.01
☐ 255	Frank White	.07	.03	.01
☐ 256	Alfredo Griffin	.07	.03	.01
☐ 257	Floyd Youmans	.07	.03	.01
☐ 258	Rob Wilfong	.04	.02	.00
☐ 259	Pete O'Brien	.07	.03	.01
☐ 260	Tim Hulett	.04	.02	.00
☐ 261	Dickie Thon	.04	.02	.00
☐ 262	Darren Daulton	.04	.02	.00
☐ 263	Vince Coleman	.40	.20	.04
☐ 264	Andy Hawkins	.07	.03	.01
☐ 265	Eric Davis	1.50	.75	.15
☐ 266	Andres Thomas	.18	.09	.01
☐ 267	Mike Diaz	.10	.05	.01
☐ 268	Chili Davis	.07	.03	.01
☐ 269	Jody Davis	.04	.02	.00
☐ 270	Phil Bradley	.07	.03	.01
☐ 271	George Bell	.25	.12	.02
☐ 272	Keith Atherton	.04	.02	.00
☐ 273	Storm Davis	.07	.03	.01
☐ 274	Rob Deer	.25	.12	.02
☐ 275	Walt Terrell	.04	.02	.00
☐ 276	Roger Clemens	1.50	.75	.15
☐ 277	Mike Easler	.04	.02	.00
☐ 278	Steve Sax	.15	.07	.01
☐ 279	Andre Thornton	.07	.03	.01
☐ 280	Jim Sundberg	.04	.02	.00
☐ 281	Bill Bathe	.07	.03	.01
☐ 282	Jay Tibbs	.04	.02	.00
☐ 283	Dick Schofield	.04	.02	.00
☐ 284	Mike Mason	.04	.02	.00
☐ 285	Jerry Hairston	.04	.02	.00
☐ 286	Bill Doran	.07	.03	.01
☐ 287	Tim Flannery	.04	.02	.00
☐ 288	Gary Redus	.04	.02	.00
☐ 289	John Franco	.10	.05	.01
☐ 290	Paul Assenmacher	.07	.03	.01
☐ 291	Joe Orsulak	.04	.02	.00
☐ 292	Lee Smith	.07	.03	.01
☐ 293	Mike Laga	.04	.02	.00
☐ 294	Rick Dempsey	.04	.02	.00
☐ 295	Mike Felder	.07	.03	.01
☐ 296	Tom Brookens	.04	.02	.00
☐ 297	Al Nipper	.04	.02	.00
☐ 298	Mike Pagliarulo	.07	.03	.01
☐ 299	Franklin Stubbs	.07	.03	.01
☐ 300	Checklist	.07	.01	.00
☐ 301	Steve Farr	.04	.02	.00
☐ 302	Bill Mooneyham	.07	.03	.01
☐ 303	Andres Galarraga	.40	.20	.04
☐ 304	Scott Fletcher	.07	.03	.01
☐ 305	Jack Howell	.07	.03	.01
☐ 306	Russ Morman	.10	.05	.01
☐ 307	Todd Worrell	.15	.07	.01
☐ 308	Dave Smith	.07	.03	.01
☐ 309	Jeff Stone	.04	.02	.00
☐ 310	Ron Robinson	.04	.02	.00
☐ 311	Bruce Bochy	.04	.02	.00
☐ 312	Jim Winn	.04	.02	.00
☐ 313	Mark Davis	.12	.06	.01
☐ 314	Jeff Dedmon	.04	.02	.00
☐ 315	Jamie Moyer	.15	.07	.01
☐ 316	Wally Backman	.04	.02	.00
☐ 317	Ken Phelps	.07	.03	.01
☐ 318	Steve Lombardozzi	.04	.02	.00
☐ 319	Rance Mulliniks	.04	.02	.00
☐ 320	Tim Laudner	.04	.02	.00
☐ 321	Mark Eichhorn	.10	.05	.01
☐ 322	Lee Guetterman	.12	.06	.01
☐ 323	Sid Fernandez	.12	.06	.01
☐ 324	Jerry Mumphrey	.04	.02	.00
☐ 325	David Palmer	.04	.02	.00
☐ 326	Bill Almon	.04	.02	.00
☐ 327	Candy Maldonado	.07	.03	.01
☐ 328	John Kruk	.35	.17	.03
☐ 329	John Denny	.04	.02	.00
☐ 330	Milt Thompson	.07	.03	.01
☐ 331	Mike LaValliere	.20	.10	.02
☐ 332	Alan Ashby	.04	.02	.00
☐ 333	Doug Corbett	.04	.02	.00
☐ 334	Ron Karkovice	.07	.03	.01
☐ 335	Mitch Webster	.04	.02	.00
☐ 336	Lee Lacy	.04	.02	.00
☐ 337	Glenn Braggs	.50	.25	.05
☐ 338	Dwight Lowry	.10	.05	.01
☐ 339	Don Baylor	.07	.03	.01
☐ 340	Brian Fisher	.07	.03	.01
☐ 341	Reggie Williams	.10	.05	.01
☐ 342	Tom Candiotti	.04	.02	.00
☐ 343	Rudy Law	.04	.02	.00
☐ 344	Curt Young	.04	.02	.00
☐ 345	Mike Fitzgerald	.04	.02	.00
☐ 346	Ruben Sierra	5.50	2.75	.55
☐ 347	Mitch Williams	.45	.22	.04
☐ 348	Jorge Orta	.04	.02	.00
☐ 349	Mickey Tettleton	.12	.06	.01
☐ 350	Ernie Camacho	.04	.02	.00
☐ 351	Ron Kittle	.10	.05	.01
☐ 352	Ken Landreaux	.04	.02	.00
☐ 353	Chet Lemon	.04	.02	.00
☐ 354	John Shelby	.04	.02	.00
☐ 355	Mark Clear	.04	.02	.00
☐ 356	Doug DeCinces	.07	.03	.01
☐ 357	Ken Dayley	.04	.02	.00
☐ 358	Phil Garner	.04	.02	.00
☐ 359	Steve Jeltz	.04	.02	.00
☐ 360	Ed Whitson	.04	.02	.00
☐ 361	Barry Bonds	1.00	.50	.10
☐ 362	Vida Blue	.07	.03	.01
☐ 363	Cecil Cooper	.07	.03	.01
☐ 364	Bob Ojeda	.07	.03	.01
☐ 365	Dennis Eckersley	.12	.06	.01
☐ 366	Mike Morgan	.07	.03	.01
☐ 367	Willie Upshaw	.04	.02	.00
☐ 368	Allan Anderson	.35	.17	.03
☐ 369	Bill Gullickson	.04	.02	.00
☐ 370	Bobby Thigpen	.30	.15	.03
☐ 371	Juan Beniquez	.04	.02	.00
☐ 372	Charlie Moore	.04	.02	.00
☐ 373	Dan Petry	.04	.02	.00
☐ 374	Rod Scurry	.04	.02	.00
☐ 375	Tom Seaver	.30	.15	.03
☐ 376	Ed VandeBerg	.04	.02	.00
☐ 377	Tony Bernazard	.04	.02	.00
☐ 378	Greg Pryor	.04	.02	.00
☐ 379	Dwayne Murphy	.04	.02	.00
☐ 380	Andy McGaffigan	.04	.02	.00
☐ 381	Kirk McCaskill	.04	.02	.00
☐ 382	Greg Harris	.04	.02	.00
☐ 383	Rich Dotson	.07	.03	.01
☐ 384	Craig Reynolds	.04	.02	.00
☐ 385	Greg Gross	.04	.02	.00
☐ 386	Tito Landrum	.04	.02	.00
☐ 387	Craig Lefferts	.07	.03	.01
☐ 388	Dave Parker	.12	.06	.01
☐ 389	Bob Horner	.10	.05	.01
☐ 390	Pat Clements	.04	.02	.00
☐ 391	Jeff Leonard	.07	.03	.01
☐ 392	Chris Speier	.04	.02	.00
☐ 393	John Moses	.04	.02	.00
☐ 394	Garth Iorg	.04	.02	.00
☐ 395	Greg Gagne	.04	.02	.00
☐ 396	Nate Snell	.04	.02	.00
☐ 397	Bryan Clutterbuck	.07	.03	.01
☐ 398	Darrell Evans	.07	.03	.01
☐ 399	Steve Crawford	.04	.02	.00
☐ 400	Checklist	.07	.01	.00
☐ 401	Phil Lombardi	.12	.06	.01
☐ 402	Rick Honeycutt	.04	.02	.00
☐ 403	Ken Schrom	.04	.02	.00
☐ 404	Bud Black	.04	.02	.00
☐ 405	Donnie Hill	.04	.02	.00
☐ 406	Wayne Krenchicki	.04	.02	.00
☐ 407	Chuck Finley	.50	.25	.05
☐ 408	Toby Harrah	.04	.02	.00
☐ 409	Steve Lyons	.04	.02	.00
☐ 410	Kevin Bass	.07	.03	.01
☐ 411	Marvell Wynne	.04	.02	.00
☐ 412	Ron Roenicke	.04	.02	.00
☐ 413	Tracy Jones	.20	.10	.02
☐ 414	Gene Garber	.04	.02	.00
☐ 415	Mike Bielecki	.12	.06	.01
☐ 416	Frank DiPino	.04	.02	.00
☐ 417	Andy Van Slyke	.20	.10	.02
☐ 418	Jim Dwyer	.04	.02	.00
☐ 419	Ben Oglivie	.07	.03	.01
☐ 420	Dave Bergman	.04	.02	.00
☐ 421	Joe Sambito	.04	.02	.00
☐ 422	Bob Tewksbury	.10	.05	.01
☐ 423	Len Matuszek	.04	.02	.00
☐ 424	Mike Kingery	.12	.06	.01
☐ 425	Dave Kingman	.07	.03	.01
☐ 426	Al Newman	.07	.03	.01
☐ 427	Gary Ward	.04	.02	.00
☐ 428	Ruppert Jones	.04	.02	.00
☐ 429	Harold Baines	.10	.05	.01
☐ 430	Pat Perry	.04	.02	.00
☐ 431	Terry Puhl	.04	.02	.00
☐ 432	Don Carman	.04	.02	.00
☐ 433	Eddie Milner	.04	.02	.00
☐ 434	LaMarr Hoyt	.07	.03	.01
☐ 435	Rick Rhoden	.07	.03	.01
☐ 436	Jose Uribe	.04	.02	.00
☐ 437	Ken Oberkfell	.04	.02	.00
☐ 438	Ron Davis	.04	.02	.00
☐ 439	Jesse Orosco	.04	.02	.00
☐ 440	Scott Bradley	.04	.02	.00
☐ 441	Randy Bush	.04	.02	.00
☐ 442	John Cerutti	.20	.10	.02
☐ 443	Roy Smalley	.04	.02	.00

☐ 444	Kelly Gruber	.10	.05	.01
☐ 445	Bob Kearney	.04	.02	.00
☐ 446	Ed Hearn	.07	.03	.01
☐ 447	Scott Sanderson	.04	.02	.00
☐ 448	Bruce Benedict	.04	.02	.00
☐ 449	Junior Ortiz	.04	.02	.00
☐ 450	Mike Aldrete	.20	.10	.02
☐ 451	Kevin McReynolds	.30	.15	.03
☐ 452	Rob Murphy	.25	.12	.02
☐ 453	Kent Tekulve	.04	.02	.00
☐ 454	Curt Ford	.07	.03	.01
☐ 455	Dave Lopes	.07	.03	.01
☐ 456	Bob Grich	.07	.03	.01
☐ 457	Jose DeLeon	.07	.03	.01
☐ 458	Andre Dawson	.25	.12	.02
☐ 459	Mike Flanagan	.07	.03	.01
☐ 460	Joey Meyer	.45	.22	.04
☐ 461	Chuck Cary	.15	.07	.01
☐ 462	Bill Buckner	.07	.03	.01
☐ 463	Bob Shirley	.04	.02	.00
☐ 464	Jeff Hamilton	.25	.12	.02
☐ 465	Phil Niekro	.15	.07	.01
☐ 466	Mark Gubicza	.12	.06	.01
☐ 467	Jerry Willard	.04	.02	.00
☐ 468	Bob Sebra	.10	.05	.01
☐ 469	Larry Parrish	.04	.02	.00
☐ 470	Charlie Hough	.07	.03	.01
☐ 471	Hal McRae	.07	.03	.01
☐ 472	Dave Leiper	.07	.03	.01
☐ 473	Mel Hall	.10	.05	.01
☐ 474	Dan Pasqua	.07	.03	.01
☐ 475	Bob Welch	.07	.03	.01
☐ 476	Johnny Grubb	.04	.02	.00
☐ 477	Jim Traber	.07	.03	.01
☐ 478	Chris Bosio	.35	.17	.03
☐ 479	Mark McLemore	.04	.02	.00
☐ 480	John Morris	.04	.02	.00
☐ 481	Billy Hatcher	.07	.03	.01
☐ 482	Dan Schatzeder	.04	.02	.00
☐ 483	Rich Gossage	.10	.05	.01
☐ 484	Jim Morrison	.04	.02	.00
☐ 485	Bob Brenly	.04	.02	.00
☐ 486	Bill Schroeder	.04	.02	.00
☐ 487	Mookie Wilson	.07	.03	.01
☐ 488	Dave Martinez	.20	.10	.02
☐ 489	Harold Reynolds	.07	.03	.01
☐ 490	Jeff Hearron	.07	.03	.01
☐ 491	Mickey Hatcher	.04	.02	.00
☐ 492	Barry Larkin	2.25	1.10	.22
☐ 493	Bob James	.04	.02	.00
☐ 494	John Habyan	.04	.02	.00
☐ 495	Jim Adduci	.10	.05	.01
☐ 496	Mike Heath	.04	.02	.00
☐ 497	Tim Stoddard	.04	.02	.00
☐ 498	Tony Armas	.07	.03	.01
☐ 499	Dennis Powell	.04	.02	.00
☐ 500	Checklist	.07	.01	.00
☐ 501	Chris Bando	.04	.02	.00
☐ 502	David Cone	3.75	1.85	.37
☐ 503	Jay Howell	.07	.03	.01
☐ 504	Tom Foley	.04	.02	.00
☐ 505	Ray Chadwick	.07	.03	.01
☐ 506	Mike Loynd	.07	.03	.01
☐ 507	Neil Allen	.04	.02	.00
☐ 508	Danny Darwin	.04	.02	.00
☐ 509	Rick Schu	.04	.02	.00
☐ 510	Jose Oquendo	.04	.02	.00
☐ 511	Gene Walter	.04	.02	.00
☐ 512	Terry McGriff	.15	.07	.01
☐ 513	Ken Griffey	.10	.05	.01
☐ 514	Benny Distefano	.04	.02	.00
☐ 515	Terry Mulholland	.07	.03	.01
☐ 516	Ed Lynch	.04	.02	.00
☐ 517	Bill Swift	.07	.03	.01
☐ 518	Manny Lee	.07	.03	.01
☐ 519	Andre David	.04	.02	.00
☐ 520	Scott McGregor	.07	.03	.01
☐ 521	Rick Manning	.04	.02	.00
☐ 522	Willie Hernandez	.07	.03	.01
☐ 523	Marty Barrett	.07	.03	.01
☐ 524	Wayne Tolleson	.04	.02	.00
☐ 525	Jose Gonzalez	.20	.10	.02
☐ 526	Cory Snyder	.60	.30	.06
☐ 527	Buddy Biancalana	.04	.02	.00
☐ 528	Moose Haas	.04	.02	.00
☐ 529	Wilfredo Tejada	.07	.03	.01
☐ 530	Stu Cliburn	.04	.02	.00
☐ 531	Dale Mohorcic	.15	.07	.01
☐ 532	Ron Hassey	.04	.02	.00
☐ 533	Ty Gainey	.04	.02	.00
☐ 534	Jerry Royster	.04	.02	.00
☐ 535	Mike Maddux	.15	.07	.01
☐ 536	Ted Power	.04	.02	.00
☐ 537	Ted Simmons	.10	.05	.01
☐ 538	Rafael Belliard	.07	.03	.01
☐ 539	Chico Walker	.07	.03	.01
☐ 540	Bob Forsch	.04	.02	.00
☐ 541	John Stefero	.04	.02	.00
☐ 542	Dale Sveum	.18	.09	.01
☐ 543	Mark Thurmond	.04	.02	.00
☐ 544	Jeff Sellers	.15	.07	.01
☐ 545	Joel Skinner	.04	.02	.00
☐ 546	Alex Trevino	.04	.02	.00
☐ 547	Randy Kutcher	.07	.03	.01
☐ 548	Joaquin Andujar	.07	.03	.01
☐ 549	Casey Candaele	.10	.05	.01
☐ 550	Jeff Russell	.10	.05	.01
☐ 551	John Candelaria	.07	.03	.01
☐ 552	Joe Cowley	.04	.02	.00
☐ 553	Danny Cox	.07	.03	.01
☐ 554	Denny Walling	.04	.02	.00
☐ 555	Bruce Ruffin	.15	.07	.01
☐ 556	Buddy Bell	.07	.03	.01
☐ 557	Jimmy Jones	.25	.12	.02
☐ 558	Bobby Bonilla	1.00	.50	.10
☐ 559	Jeff Robinson (Giants pitcher)	.10	.05	.01
☐ 560	Ed Olwine	.06	.03	.00
☐ 561	Glenallen Hill	.90	.45	.09
☐ 562	Lee Mazzilli	.04	.02	.00
☐ 563	Mike Brown (pitcher)	.04	.02	.00
☐ 564	George Frazier	.04	.02	.00
☐ 565	Mike Sharperson	.07	.03	.01
☐ 566	Mark Portugal	.20	.10	.02
☐ 567	Rick Leach	.04	.02	.00
☐ 568	Mark Langston	.30	.15	.03
☐ 569	Rafael Santana	.04	.02	.00
☐ 570	Manny Trillo	.04	.02	.00
☐ 571	Cliff Speck	.07	.03	.01
☐ 572	Bob Kipper	.04	.02	.00
☐ 573	Kelly Downs	.30	.15	.03
☐ 574	Randy Asadoor	.07	.03	.01
☐ 575	Dave Magadan	1.00	.50	.10
☐ 576	Marvin Freeman	.15	.07	.01
☐ 577	Jeff Lahti	.04	.02	.00
☐ 578	Jeff Calhoun	.04	.02	.00
☐ 579	Gus Polidor	.04	.02	.00
☐ 580	Gene Nelson	.04	.02	.00
☐ 581	Tim Teufel	.04	.02	.00
☐ 582	Odell Jones	.04	.02	.00
☐ 583	Mark Ryal	.07	.03	.01
☐ 584	Randy O'Neal	.04	.02	.00
☐ 585	Mike Greenwell	9.00	4.50	.90
☐ 586	Ray Knight	.07	.03	.01
☐ 587	Ralph Bryant	.10	.05	.01
☐ 588	Carmen Castillo	.04	.02	.00
☐ 589	Ed Wojna	.04	.02	.00
☐ 590	Stan Javier	.07	.03	.01
☐ 591	Jeff Musselman	.15	.07	.01
☐ 592	Mike Stanley	.15	.07	.01
☐ 593	Darrell Porter	.04	.02	.00
☐ 594	Drew Hall	.10	.05	.01
☐ 595	Rob Nelson	.15	.07	.01
☐ 596	Bryan Oelkers	.04	.02	.00
☐ 597	Scott Nielsen	.15	.07	.01
☐ 598	Brian Holton	.18	.09	.01
☐ 599	Kevin Mitchell	5.00	2.50	.50
☐ 600	Checklist	.07	.01	.00
☐ 601	Jackie Gutierrez	.04	.02	.00
☐ 602	Barry Jones	.12	.06	.01
☐ 603	Jerry Narron	.04	.02	.00
☐ 604	Steve Lake	.04	.02	.00
☐ 605	Jim Pankovits	.04	.02	.00
☐ 606	Ed Romero	.04	.02	.00
☐ 607	Dave LaPoint	.07	.03	.01
☐ 608	Don Robinson	.04	.02	.00
☐ 609	Mike Krukow	.04	.02	.00
☐ 610	Dave Valle	.04	.02	.00
☐ 611	Len Dykstra	.10	.05	.01
☐ 612	Roberto Clemente Puzzle Card	.07	.03	.01
☐ 613	Mike Trujillo	.04	.02	.00
☐ 614	Damaso Garcia	.04	.02	.00
☐ 615	Neal Heaton	.04	.02	.00
☐ 616	Juan Berenguer	.04	.02	.00
☐ 617	Steve Carlton	.20	.10	.02
☐ 618	Gary Lucas	.04	.02	.00
☐ 619	Geno Petralli	.04	.02	.00
☐ 620	Rick Aguilera	.04	.02	.00
☐ 621	Fred McGriff	3.00	1.50	.30
☐ 622	Dave Henderson	.07	.03	.01
☐ 623	Dave Clark	.35	.17	.03
☐ 624	Angel Salazar	.04	.02	.00
☐ 625	Randy Hunt	.04	.02	.00
☐ 626	John Gibbons	.04	.02	.00
☐ 627	Kevin Brown	.65	.30	.06
☐ 628	Bill Dawley	.04	.02	.00
☐ 629	Aurelio Lopez	.04	.02	.00
☐ 630	Charles Hudson	.04	.02	.00

☐ 631	Ray Soff	.07	.03	.01
☐ 632	Ray Hayward	.07	.03	.01
☐ 633	Spike Owen	.04	.02	.00
☐ 634	Glenn Hubbard	.04	.02	.00
☐ 635	Kevin Elster	.60	.30	.06
☐ 636	Mike LaCoss	.04	.02	.00
☐ 637	Dwayne Henry	.04	.02	.00
☐ 638	Rey Quinones	.20	.10	.02
☐ 639	Jim Clancy	.04	.02	.00
☐ 640	Larry Andersen	.04	.02	.00
☐ 641	Calvin Schiraldi	.07	.03	.01
☐ 642	Stan Jefferson	.25	.12	.02
☐ 643	Marc Sullivan	.04	.02	.00
☐ 644	Mark Grant	.04	.02	.00
☐ 645	Cliff Johnson	.04	.02	.00
☐ 646	Howard Johnson	.30	.15	.03
☐ 647	Dave Sax	.04	.02	.00
☐ 648	Dave Stewart	.15	.07	.01
☐ 649	Danny Heep	.04	.02	.00
☐ 650	Joe Johnson	.04	.02	.00
☐ 651	Bob Brower	.15	.07	.01
☐ 652	Rob Woodward	.04	.02	.00
☐ 653	John Mizerock	.04	.02	.00
☐ 654	Tim Pyznarski	.10	.05	.01
☐ 655	Luis Aquino	.07	.03	.01
☐ 656	Mickey Brantley	.15	.07	.01
☐ 657	Doyle Alexander	.07	.03	.01
☐ 658	Sammy Stewart	.04	.02	.00
☐ 659	Jim Acker	.04	.02	.00
☐ 660	Pete Ladd	.07	.03	.01

1987 Donruss Wax Box Cards

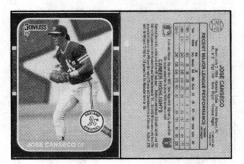

The cards in this 4-card set measure the standard 2 1/2" by 3 1/2". Cards have essentially the same design as the 1987 Donruss regular issue set. The cards were printed on the bottoms of the regular issue wax pack boxes. The four cards (PC10 to PC12 plus a Roberto Clemente puzzle card) are considered a separate set in their own right and are not typically included in a complete set of the regular issue 1987 Donruss cards. The value of the panel uncut is slightly greater, perhaps by 25% greater, than the value of the individual cards cut up carefully.

		MINT	EXC	G-VG
COMPLETE SET (4)		1.50	.75	.15
COMMON PLAYER		.05	.02	.00
☐ PC10	Dale Murphy	.30	.15	.03
☐ PC11	Jeff Reardon	.15	.07	.01
☐ PC12	Jose Canseco	1.25	.60	.12
☐ PUZ	Roberto Clemente (Puzzle Card)	.05	.02	.00

1987 Donruss Super DK's

This 28-card set was available through a mail-in offer detailed on the wax packs. The set was sent in return for 8.00 and three wrappers plus 1.50 postage and handling. The set features the popular Diamond King

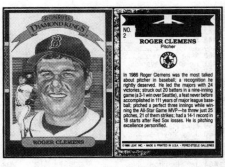

subseries in large (approximately 4 7/8" by 6 13/16") form. Dick Perez of Perez-Steele Galleries did another outstanding job on the artwork. The cards are essentially a large version of the Donruss regular issue Diamond Kings.

		MINT	EXC	G-VG
COMPLETE SET (28)		11.00	5.50	1.10
COMMON PLAYER (1-26)		.15	.07	.01
☐ 1	Wally Joyner	1.00	.50	.10
☐ 2	Roger Clemens	1.00	.50	.10
☐ 3	Dale Murphy	.50	.25	.05
☐ 4	Darryl Strawberry	.75	.35	.07
☐ 5	Ozzie Smith	.35	.17	.03
☐ 6	Jose Canseco	2.50	1.25	.25
☐ 7	Charlie Hough	.15	.07	.01
☐ 8	Brook Jacoby	.15	.07	.01
☐ 9	Fred Lynn	.20	.10	.02
☐ 10	Rick Rhoden	.15	.07	.01
☐ 11	Chris Brown	.15	.07	.01
☐ 12	Von Hayes	.20	.10	.02
☐ 13	Jack Morris	.25	.12	.02
☐ 14	Kevin McReynolds	.35	.17	.03
☐ 15	George Brett	.50	.25	.05
☐ 16	Ted Higuera	.25	.12	.02
☐ 17	Hubie Brooks	.15	.07	.01
☐ 18	Mike Scott	.30	.15	.03
☐ 19	Kirby Puckett	1.00	.50	.10
☐ 20	Dave Winfield	.40	.20	.04
☐ 21	Lloyd Moseby	.15	.07	.01
☐ 22	Eric Davis	1.00	.50	.10
☐ 23	Jim Presley	.15	.07	.01
☐ 24	Keith Moreland	.15	.07	.01
☐ 25	Greg Walker	.15	.07	.01
☐ 26	Steve Sax	.25	.12	.02
☐ 27	DK Checklist 1-26	.10	.05	.01
☐ 28	Roberto Clemente Large Puzzle (unnumbered)	.25	.12	.02

1987 Donruss All-Stars

This 60-card set features cards measuring 3 1/2" by 5". Card fronts are in full color with a black border. The card backs are printed in black and blue on white card stock. Cards are numbered on the back. Card backs feature statistical information about the player's performance in past All-Star games. The set was distributed in packs which also contained a Pop-Up.

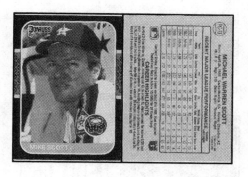

		MINT	EXC	G-VG
	COMPLETE SET (60)	6.00	3.00	.60
	COMMON PLAYER (1-60)	.05	.02	.00
☐ 1	Wally Joyner	.50	.25	.05
☐ 2	Dave Winfield	.25	.12	.02
☐ 3	Lou Whitaker	.15	.07	.01
☐ 4	Kirby Puckett	.60	.30	.06
☐ 5	Cal Ripken	.35	.17	.03
☐ 6	Rickey Henderson	.45	.22	.04
☐ 7	Wade Boggs	.75	.35	.07
☐ 8	Roger Clemens	.60	.30	.06
☐ 9	Lance Parrish	.10	.05	.01
☐ 10	Dick Howser MG	.05	.02	.00
☐ 11	Keith Hernandez	.20	.10	.02
☐ 12	Darryl Strawberry	.50	.25	.05
☐ 13	Ryne Sandberg	.30	.15	.03
☐ 14	Dale Murphy	.35	.17	.03
☐ 15	Ozzie Smith	.25	.12	.02
☐ 16	Tony Gwynn	.40	.20	.04
☐ 17	Mike Schmidt	.75	.35	.07
☐ 18	Dwight Gooden	.60	.30	.06
☐ 19	Gary Carter	.25	.12	.02
☐ 20	Whitey Herzog MG	.05	.02	.00
☐ 21	Jose Canseco	1.00	.50	.10
☐ 22	John Franco	.10	.05	.01
☐ 23	Jesse Barfield	.10	.05	.01
☐ 24	Rick Rhoden	.05	.02	.00
☐ 25	Harold Baines	.10	.05	.01
☐ 26	Sid Fernandez	.10	.05	.01
☐ 27	George Brett	.40	.20	.04
☐ 28	Steve Sax	.15	.07	.01
☐ 29	Jim Presley	.10	.05	.01
☐ 30	Dave Smith	.05	.02	.00
☐ 31	Eddie Murray	.25	.12	.02
☐ 32	Mike Scott	.20	.10	.02
☐ 33	Don Mattingly	1.00	.50	.10
☐ 34	Dave Parker	.20	.10	.02
☐ 35	Tony Fernandez	.15	.07	.01
☐ 36	Tim Raines	.30	.15	.03
☐ 37	Brook Jacoby	.10	.05	.01
☐ 38	Chili Davis	.10	.05	.01
☐ 39	Rich Gedman	.05	.02	.00
☐ 40	Kevin Bass	.05	.02	.00
☐ 41	Frank White	.05	.02	.00
☐ 42	Glenn Davis	.20	.10	.02
☐ 43	Willie Hernandez	.10	.05	.01
☐ 44	Chris Brown	.05	.02	.00
☐ 45	Jim Rice	.20	.10	.02
☐ 46	Tony Pena	.05	.02	.00
☐ 47	Don Aase	.05	.02	.00
☐ 48	Hubie Brooks	.05	.02	.00
☐ 49	Charlie Hough	.05	.02	.00
☐ 50	Jody Davis	.10	.05	.01
☐ 51	Mike Witt	.10	.05	.01
☐ 52	Jeff Reardon	.10	.05	.01
☐ 53	Ken Schrom	.05	.02	.00
☐ 54	Fernando Valenzuela	.20	.10	.02
☐ 55	Dave Righetti	.15	.07	.01
☐ 56	Shane Rawley	.05	.02	.00
☐ 57	Ted Higuera	.15	.07	.01
☐ 58	Mike Krukow	.05	.02	.00
☐ 59	Lloyd Moseby	.10	.05	.01
☐ 60	Checklist Card	.05	.02	.00

1987 Donruss All-Star Box

The cards in this 4-card set measure the standard 2 1/2" by 3 1/2" in spite of the fact that they form the bottom of the wax pack box for the larger Donruss All-Star cards. These box cards have essentially the same design as the 1987 Donruss regular issue set. The cards were printed on the bottoms of the Donruss All-Star (3 1/2" by 5") wax pack boxes. The four cards (PC13 to PC15 plus a Roberto Clemente puzzle card) are considered a separate set in their own right and are not typically included in a complete set of the 1987 Donruss All-Star (or regular) cards. The value of the panel uncut is slightly greater, perhaps by 25% greater, than the value of the individual cards cut up carefully.

		MINT	EXC	G-VG
	COMPLETE SET (4)	.75	.35	.07
	COMMON PLAYERS	.05	.02	.00
☐	PC13 Mike Scott	.20	.10	.02
☐	PC14 Roger Clemens	.60	.30	.06
☐	PC15 Mike Krukow	.05	.02	.00
☐	PUZ Roberto Clemente Puzzle Card	.05	.02	.00

1987 Donruss Pop-Ups

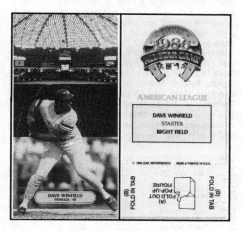

This 20-card set features "fold-out" cards measuring 2 1/2" by 5". Card fronts are in full color. Cards are unnumbered but are listed in the same order as the Donruss All-Stars on the All-Star checklist card. Card backs present essentially no information about the player. The set was distributed in packs which also contained All-Star cards (3 1/2" by 5").

		MINT	EXC	G-VG
	COMPLETE SET (20)	4.00	2.00	.40
	COMMON PLAYER (1-20)	.10	.05	.01
☐ 1	Wally Joyner	.50	.25	.05
☐ 2	Dave Winfield	.25	.12	.02
☐ 3	Lou Whitaker	.15	.07	.01
☐ 4	Kirby Puckett	.60	.30	.06
☐ 5	Cal Ripken	.35	.17	.03
☐ 6	Rickey Henderson	.45	.22	.04
☐ 7	Wade Boggs	.75	.35	.07
☐ 8	Roger Clemens	.60	.30	.06
☐ 9	Lance Parrish	.10	.05	.01
☐ 10	Dick Howser MG	.10	.05	.01
☐ 11	Keith Hernandez	.20	.10	.02
☐ 12	Darryl Strawberry	.50	.25	.05
☐ 13	Ryne Sandberg	.30	.15	.03

		MINT	EXC	G-VG
☐ 14	Dale Murphy	.35	.17	.03
☐ 15	Ozzie Smith	.25	.12	.02
☐ 16	Tony Gwynn	.40	.20	.04
☐ 17	Mike Schmidt	.75	.35	.07
☐ 18	Dwight Gooden	.60	.30	.06
☐ 19	Gary Carter	.25	.12	.02
☐ 20	Whitey Herzog MG	.10	.05	.01

1987 Donruss Opening Day

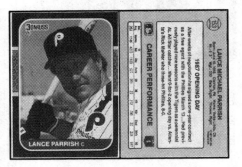

This innovative set of 272 cards features a card for
each of the players in the starting line-ups of all the
teams on Opening Day 1987. Cards are the standard
size, 2 1/2" by 3 1/2", and are packaged as a
complete set in a specially designed box. Cards are
very similar in design to the 1987 regular Donruss
issue except that these "OD" cards have a maroon
border instead of a black border. The set features the
first card in a Major League uniform of Joey Cora,
Mark Davidson, Donnell Nixon, Bob Patterson, and
Alonzo Powell. Teams in the same city share a
checklist card. A 15-piece puzzle of Roberto
Clemente is also included with every complete set.
The error on Bobby Bonds was corrected very early
in the press run; supposedly less than one percent
of the sets have the error.

		MINT	EXC	G-VG
COMPLETE SET (272)		18.00	9.00	1.80
COMMON PLAYER (1-248)		.05	.02	.00
COMMON LOGO (249-272)		.03	.01	.00

		MINT	EXC	G-VG
☐ 1	Doug DeCinces	.05	.02	.00
☐ 2	Mike Witt	.10	.05	.01
☐ 3	George Hendrick	.05	.02	.00
☐ 4	Dick Schofield	.05	.02	.00
☐ 5	Devon White	.60	.30	.06
☐ 6	Butch Wynegar	.05	.02	.00
☐ 7	Wally Joyner	1.00	.50	.10
☐ 8	Mark McLemore	.05	.02	.00
☐ 9	Brian Downing	.05	.02	.00
☐ 10	Gary Pettis	.05	.02	.00
☐ 11	Bill Doran	.10	.05	.01
☐ 12	Phil Garner	.05	.02	.00
☐ 13	Jose Cruz	.10	.05	.01
☐ 14	Kevin Bass	.10	.05	.01
☐ 15	Mike Scott	.20	.10	.02
☐ 16	Glenn Davis	.25	.12	.02
☐ 17	Alan Ashby	.05	.02	.00
☐ 18	Billy Hatcher	.10	.05	.01
☐ 19	Craig Reynolds	.05	.02	.00
☐ 20	Carney Lansford	.20	.10	.02
☐ 21	Mike Davis	.05	.02	.00
☐ 22	Reggie Jackson	.50	.25	.05
☐ 23	Mickey Tettleton	.20	.10	.02
☐ 24	Jose Canseco	2.50	1.25	.25
☐ 25	Rob Nelson	.05	.02	.00
☐ 26	Tony Phillips	.05	.02	.00
☐ 27	Dwayne Murphy	.05	.02	.00
☐ 28	Alfredo Griffin	.05	.02	.00
☐ 29	Curt Young	.05	.02	.00
☐ 30	Willie Upshaw	.05	.02	.00
☐ 31	Mike Sharperson	.05	.02	.00
☐ 32	Rance Mulliniks	.05	.02	.00
☐ 33	Ernie Whitt	.05	.02	.00
☐ 34	Jesse Barfield	.15	.07	.01

		MINT	EXC	G-VG
☐ 35	Tony Fernandez	.15	.07	.01
☐ 36	Lloyd Moseby	.10	.05	.01
☐ 37	Jimmy Key	.10	.05	.01
☐ 38	Fred McGriff	.75	.35	.07
☐ 39	George Bell	.25	.12	.02
☐ 40	Dale Murphy	.35	.17	.03
☐ 41	Rick Mahler	.05	.02	.00
☐ 42	Ken Griffey	.10	.05	.01
☐ 43	Andres Thomas	.05	.02	.00
☐ 44	Dion James	.05	.02	.00
☐ 45	Ozzie Virgil	.05	.02	.00
☐ 46	Ken Oberkfell	.05	.02	.00
☐ 47	Gary Roenicke	.05	.02	.00
☐ 48	Glenn Hubbard	.05	.02	.00
☐ 49	Bill Schroeder	.05	.02	.00
☐ 50	Greg Brock	.05	.02	.00
☐ 51	Billy Jo Robidoux	.05	.02	.00
☐ 52	Glenn Braggs	.25	.12	.02
☐ 53	Jim Gantner	.05	.02	.00
☐ 54	Paul Molitor	.15	.07	.01
☐ 55	Dale Sveum	.10	.05	.01
☐ 56	Ted Higuera	.15	.07	.01
☐ 57	Rob Deer	.10	.05	.01
☐ 58	Robin Yount	.45	.22	.04
☐ 59	Jim Lindeman	.10	.05	.01
☐ 60	Vince Coleman	.30	.15	.03
☐ 61	Tommy Herr	.05	.02	.00
☐ 62	Terry Pendleton	.15	.07	.01
☐ 63	John Tudor	.15	.07	.01
☐ 64	Tony Pena	.10	.05	.01
☐ 65	Ozzie Smith	.25	.12	.02
☐ 66	Tito Landrum	.05	.02	.00
☐ 67	Jack Clark	.20	.10	.02
☐ 68	Bob Dernier	.05	.02	.00
☐ 69	Rick Sutcliffe	.10	.05	.01
☐ 70	Andre Dawson	.25	.12	.02
☐ 71	Keith Moreland	.05	.02	.00
☐ 72	Jody Davis	.05	.02	.00
☐ 73	Brian Dayett	.05	.02	.00
☐ 74	Leon Durham	.05	.02	.00
☐ 75	Ryne Sandberg	.25	.12	.02
☐ 76	Shawon Dunston	.20	.10	.02
☐ 77	Mike Marshall	.15	.07	.01
☐ 78	Bill Madlock	.05	.02	.00
☐ 79	Orel Hershiser	.60	.30	.06
☐ 80	Mike Ramsey	.10	.05	.01
☐ 81	Ken Landreaux	.05	.02	.00
☐ 82	Mike Scioscia	.05	.02	.00
☐ 83	Franklin Stubbs	.05	.02	.00
☐ 84	Mariano Duncan	.05	.02	.00
☐ 85	Steve Sax	.15	.07	.01
☐ 86	Mitch Webster	.05	.02	.00
☐ 87	Reid Nichols	.05	.02	.00
☐ 88	Tim Wallach	.10	.05	.01
☐ 89	Floyd Youmans	.10	.05	.01
☐ 90	Andres Galarraga	.35	.17	.03
☐ 91	Hubie Brooks	.10	.05	.01
☐ 92	Jeff Reed	.05	.02	.00
☐ 93	Alonzo Powell	.10	.05	.01
☐ 94	Vance Law	.05	.02	.00
☐ 95	Bob Brenly	.05	.02	.00
☐ 96	Will Clark	2.50	1.25	.25
☐ 97	Chili Davis	.10	.05	.01
☐ 98	Mike Krukow	.05	.02	.00
☐ 99	Jose Uribe	.05	.02	.00
☐ 100	Chris Brown	.05	.02	.00
☐ 101	Rob Thompson	.10	.05	.01
☐ 102	Candy Maldonado	.10	.05	.01
☐ 103	Jeff Leonard	.10	.05	.01
☐ 104	Tom Candiotti	.05	.02	.00
☐ 105	Chris Bando	.05	.02	.00
☐ 106	Cory Snyder	.40	.20	.04
☐ 107	Pat Tabler	.05	.02	.00
☐ 108	Andre Thornton	.05	.02	.00
☐ 109	Joe Carter	.20	.10	.02
☐ 110	Tony Bernazard	.05	.02	.00
☐ 111	Julio Franco	.15	.07	.01
☐ 112	Brook Jacoby	.10	.05	.01
☐ 113	Brett Butler	.10	.05	.01
☐ 114	Donnell Nixon	.10	.05	.01
☐ 115	Alvin Davis	.20	.10	.02
☐ 116	Mark Langston	.35	.17	.03
☐ 117	Harold Reynolds	.10	.05	.01
☐ 118	Ken Phelps	.05	.02	.00
☐ 119	Mike Kingery	.05	.02	.00
☐ 120	Dave Valle	.05	.02	.00
☐ 121	Rey Quinones	.05	.02	.00
☐ 122	Phil Bradley	.10	.05	.01
☐ 123	Jim Presley	.10	.05	.01
☐ 124	Keith Hernandez	.20	.10	.02
☐ 125	Kevin McReynolds	.25	.12	.02
☐ 126	Rafael Santana	.05	.02	.00
☐ 127	Bob Ojeda	.10	.05	.01
☐ 128	Darryl Strawberry	.90	.45	.09
☐ 129	Mookie Wilson	.05	.02	.00

☐ 130	Gary Carter	.20	.10	.02
☐ 131	Tim Teufel	.05	.02	.00
☐ 132	Howard Johnson	.25	.12	.02
☐ 133	Cal Ripken	.35	.17	.03
☐ 134	Rick Burleson	.05	.02	.00
☐ 135	Fred Lynn	.10	.05	.01
☐ 136	Eddie Murray	.20	.10	.02
☐ 137	Ray Knight	.05	.02	.00
☐ 138	Alan Wiggins	.05	.02	.00
☐ 139	John Shelby	.05	.02	.00
☐ 140	Mike Boddicker	.05	.02	.00
☐ 141	Ken Gerhart	.10	.05	.01
☐ 142	Terry Kennedy	.05	.02	.00
☐ 143	Steve Garvey	.30	.15	.03
☐ 144	Marvell Wynne	.05	.02	.00
☐ 145	Kevin Mitchell	1.00	.50	.10
☐ 146	Tony Gwynn	.75	.35	.07
☐ 147	Joey Cora	.10	.05	.01
☐ 148	Benito Santiago	1.00	.50	.10
☐ 149	Eric Show	.10	.05	.01
☐ 150	Garry Templeton	.10	.05	.01
☐ 151	Carmelo Martinez	.05	.02	.00
☐ 152	Von Hayes	.10	.05	.01
☐ 153	Lance Parrish	.10	.05	.01
☐ 154	Milt Thompson	.05	.02	.00
☐ 155	Mike Easler	.05	.02	.00
☐ 156	Juan Samuel	.15	.07	.01
☐ 157	Steve Jeltz	.05	.02	.00
☐ 158	Glenn Wilson	.10	.05	.01
☐ 159	Shane Rawley	.05	.02	.00
☐ 160	Mike Schmidt	.75	.35	.07
☐ 161	Andy Van Slyke	.20	.10	.02
☐ 162	Johnny Ray	.10	.05	.01
☐ 163A	Barry Bonds ERR	150.00	75.00	15.00
	(photo actually			
	Johnny Ray)			
☐ 163B	Barry Bonds COR	.30	.15	.03
☐ 164	Junior Ortiz	.05	.02	.00
☐ 165	Rafael Belliard	.05	.02	.00
☐ 166	Bob Patterson	.10	.05	.01
☐ 167	Bobby Bonilla	.30	.15	.03
☐ 168	Sid Bream	.05	.02	.00
☐ 169	Jim Morrison	.05	.02	.00
☐ 170	Jerry Browne	.10	.05	.01
☐ 171	Scott Fletcher	.05	.02	.00
☐ 172	Ruben Sierra	1.50	.75	.15
☐ 173	Larry Parrish	.05	.02	.00
☐ 174	Pete O'Brien	.10	.05	.01
☐ 175	Pete Incaviglia	.35	.17	.03
☐ 176	Don Slaught	.05	.02	.00
☐ 177	Oddibe McDowell	.10	.05	.01
☐ 178	Charlie Hough	.05	.02	.00
☐ 179	Steve Buechele	.05	.02	.00
☐ 180	Bob Stanley	.05	.02	.00
☐ 181	Wade Boggs	1.00	.50	.10
☐ 182	Jim Rice	.20	.10	.02
☐ 183	Bill Buckner	.10	.05	.01
☐ 184	Dwight Evans	.15	.07	.01
☐ 185	Spike Owen	.05	.02	.00
☐ 186	Don Baylor	.10	.05	.01
☐ 187	Marc Sullivan	.05	.02	.00
☐ 188	Marty Barrett	.10	.05	.01
☐ 189	Dave Henderson	.10	.05	.01
☐ 190	Bo Diaz	.05	.02	.00
☐ 191	Barry Larkin	.75	.35	.07
☐ 192	Kal Daniels	.45	.22	.04
☐ 193	Terry Francona	.05	.02	.00
☐ 194	Tom Browning	.15	.07	.01
☐ 195	Ron Oester	.05	.02	.00
☐ 196	Buddy Bell	.10	.05	.01
☐ 197	Eric Davis	1.00	.50	.10
☐ 198	Dave Parker	.15	.07	.01
☐ 199	Steve Balboni	.05	.02	.00
☐ 200	Danny Tartabull	.25	.12	.02
☐ 201	Ed Hearn	.05	.02	.00
☐ 202	Buddy Biancalana	.05	.02	.00
☐ 203	Danny Jackson	.20	.10	.02
☐ 204	Frank White	.10	.05	.01
☐ 205	Bo Jackson	2.50	1.25	.25
☐ 206	George Brett	.35	.17	.03
☐ 207	Kevin Seitzer	1.00	.50	.10
☐ 208	Willie Wilson	.10	.05	.01
☐ 209	Orlando Mercado	.05	.02	.00
☐ 210	Darrell Evans	.10	.05	.01
☐ 211	Larry Herndon	.05	.02	.00
☐ 212	Jack Morris	.15	.07	.01
☐ 213	Chet Lemon	.05	.02	.00
☐ 214	Mike Heath	.05	.02	.00
☐ 215	Darnell Coles	.05	.02	.00
☐ 216	Alan Trammell	.25	.12	.02
☐ 217	Terry Harper	.05	.02	.00
☐ 218	Lou Whitaker	.15	.07	.01
☐ 219	Gary Gaetti	.20	.10	.02
☐ 220	Tom Nieto	.05	.02	.00
☐ 221	Kirby Puckett	.75	.35	.07

☐ 222	Tom Brunansky	.15	.07	.01
☐ 223	Greg Gagne	.05	.02	.00
☐ 224	Dan Gladden	.05	.02	.00
☐ 225	Mark Davidson	.10	.05	.01
☐ 226	Bert Blyleven	.15	.07	.01
☐ 227	Steve Lombardozzi	.05	.02	.00
☐ 228	Kent Hrbek	.25	.12	.02
☐ 229	Gary Redus	.05	.02	.00
☐ 230	Ivan Calderon	.10	.05	.01
☐ 231	Tim Hulett	.05	.02	.00
☐ 232	Carlton Fisk	.25	.12	.02
☐ 233	Greg Walker	.10	.05	.01
☐ 234	Ron Karkovice	.05	.02	.00
☐ 235	Ozzie Guillen	.15	.07	.01
☐ 236	Harold Baines	.15	.07	.01
☐ 237	Donnie Hill	.05	.02	.00
☐ 238	Rich Dotson	.10	.05	.01
☐ 239	Mike Pagliarulo	.10	.05	.01
☐ 240	Joel Skinner	.05	.02	.00
☐ 241	Don Mattingly	1.50	.75	.15
☐ 242	Gary Ward	.05	.02	.00
☐ 243	Dave Winfield	.25	.12	.02
☐ 244	Dan Pasqua	.10	.05	.01
☐ 245	Wayne Tolleson	.05	.02	.00
☐ 246	Willie Randolph	.10	.05	.01
☐ 247	Dennis Rasmussen	.10	.05	.01
☐ 248	Rickey Henderson	.45	.22	.04
☐ 249	Angels Logo	.03	.01	.00
☐ 250	Astros Logo	.03	.01	.00
☐ 251	A's Logo	.03	.01	.00
☐ 252	Blue Jays Logo	.03	.01	.00
☐ 253	Braves Logo	.03	.01	.00
☐ 254	Brewers Logo	.03	.01	.00
☐ 255	Cardinals Logo	.03	.01	.00
☐ 256	Dodgers Logo	.03	.01	.00
☐ 257	Expos Logo	.03	.01	.00
☐ 258	Giants Logo	.03	.01	.00
☐ 259	Indians Logo	.03	.01	.00
☐ 260	Mariners Logo	.03	.01	.00
☐ 261	Orioles Logo	.03	.01	.00
☐ 262	Padres Logo	.03	.01	.00
☐ 263	Phillies Logo	.03	.01	.00
☐ 264	Pirates Logo	.03	.01	.00
☐ 265	Rangers Logo	.03	.01	.00
☐ 266	Red Sox Logo	.03	.01	.00
☐ 267	Reds Logo	.03	.01	.00
☐ 268	Royals Logo	.03	.01	.00
☐ 269	Tigers Logo	.03	.01	.00
☐ 270	Twins Logo	.03	.01	.00
☐ 271	Chicago Logos	.03	.01	.00
☐ 272	New York Logos	.03	.01	.00

1987 Donruss Rookies

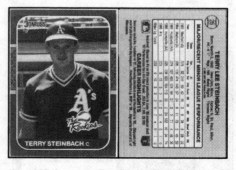

The 1987 Donruss "The Rookies" set features 56 cards plus a 15-piece puzzle of Roberto Clemente. Cards are in full color and are standard size, 2 1/2" by 3 1/2". The set was distributed in a small green and black box with gold lettering. Card fronts are similar in design to the 1987 Donruss regular issue except for the presence of "The Rookies" logo in the lower left corner and a green border instead of a black border.

	MINT	EXC	G-VG
COMPLETE SET (56)	20.00	9.00	1.80
COMMON PLAYER (1-56)	.06	.03	.00

☐ 1	Mark McGwire	3.00	1.00	.20
☐ 2	Eric Bell	.06	.03	.00
☐ 3	Mark Williamson	.12	.06	.01
☐ 4	Mike Greenwell	3.50	1.75	.35
☐ 5	Ellis Burks	2.50	1.25	.25
☐ 6	DeWayne Buice	.12	.06	.01
☐ 7	Mark McLemore	.06	.03	.00
☐ 8	Devon White	.45	.22	.04
☐ 9	Willie Fraser	.06	.03	.00
☐ 10	Les Lancaster	.20	.10	.02
☐ 11	Ken Williams	.25	.12	.02
☐ 12	Matt Nokes	.60	.30	.06
☐ 13	Jeff Robinson	.35	.17	.03
	(Tigers pitcher)			
☐ 14	Bo Jackson	3.50	1.75	.35
☐ 15	Kevin Seitzer	1.25	.60	.12
☐ 16	Billy Ripken	.25	.12	.02
☐ 17	B.J. Surhoff	.15	.07	.01
☐ 18	Chuck Crim	.12	.06	.01
☐ 19	Mike Birkbeck	.06	.03	.00
☐ 20	Chris Bosio	.15	.07	.01
☐ 21	Les Straker	.12	.06	.01
☐ 22	Mark Davidson	.12	.06	.01
☐ 23	Gene Larkin	.35	.17	.03
☐ 24	Ken Gerhart	.10	.05	.01
☐ 25	Luis Polonia	.30	.15	.03
☐ 26	Terry Steinbach	.25	.12	.02
☐ 27	Mickey Brantley	.15	.07	.01
☐ 28	Mike Stanley	.10	.05	.01
☐ 29	Jerry Browne	.10	.05	.01
☐ 30	Todd Benzinger	.45	.22	.04
☐ 31	Fred McGriff	2.00	1.00	.20
☐ 32	Mike Henneman	.30	.15	.03
☐ 33	Casey Candaele	.10	.05	.01
☐ 34	Dave Magadan	.25	.12	.02
☐ 35	David Cone	1.00	.50	.10
☐ 36	Mike Jackson	.20	.10	.02
☐ 37	John Mitchell	.15	.07	.01
☐ 38	Mike Dunne	.25	.12	.02
☐ 39	John Smiley	.35	.17	.03
☐ 40	Joe Magrane	1.50	.75	.15
☐ 41	Jim Lindeman	.10	.05	.01
☐ 42	Shane Mack	.20	.10	.02
☐ 43	Stan Jefferson	.12	.06	.01
☐ 44	Benito Santiago	.60	.30	.06
☐ 45	Matt Williams	3.00	1.50	.30
☐ 46	Dave Meads	.10	.05	.01
☐ 47	Rafael Palmeiro	.75	.35	.07
☐ 48	Bill Long	.12	.06	.01
☐ 49	Bob Brower	.10	.05	.01
☐ 50	James Steels	.10	.05	.01
☐ 51	Paul Noce	.12	.06	.01
☐ 52	Greg Maddux	.45	.22	.04
☐ 53	Jeff Musselman	.10	.05	.01
☐ 54	Brian Holton	.10	.05	.01
☐ 55	Chuck Jackson	.12	.06	.01
☐ 56	Checklist Card	.06	.01	.00

1987 Donruss Highlights

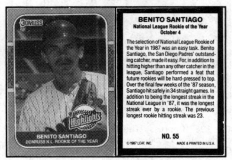

BENITO SANTIAGO
National League Rookie of the Year
October 4

The selection of National League Rookie of the Year in 1987 was an easy task. Benito Santiago, the San Diego Padres' outstanding catcher, made it easy. For, in addition to hitting higher than any other catcher in the league, Santiago performed a feat that future rookies will be hard-pressed to top. Over the final few weeks of the '87 season, Santiago hit safely in 34 straight games. In addition to being the longest streak in the National League in '87, it was the longest streak ever by a rookie. The previous longest rookie hitting streak was 23.

NO. 55

BENITO SANTIAGO
DONRUSS N.L. ROOKIE OF THE YEAR
© 1987 LEAF, INC.   MADE & PRINTED IN U.S.A.

Donruss' third (and last) edition of Highlights was released late in 1987. The cards are standard size, measuring 2 1/2" by 3 1/2", and are glossy in appearance. Cards commemorate events during the 1987 season, as well as players and pitchers of the month from each league. The set was distributed in its own red, black, blue, and gold box along with a small Roberto Clemente puzzle. Card fronts are

similar to the regular 1987 Donruss issue except that the Highlights logo is positioned in the lower right-hand corner and the borders are in blue instead of black. The backs are printed in black and gold on white card stock.

		MINT	EXC	G-VG
COMPLETE SET (56)		8.00	4.00	.80
COMMON PLAYER (1-56)		.06	.03	.00
☐ 1	Juan Nieves	.06	.03	.00
	First No-Hitter			
☐ 2	Mike Schmidt	.45	.22	.04
	Hits 500th Homer			
☐ 3	Eric Davis	.35	.17	.03
	NL Player April			
☐ 4	Sid Fernandez	.10	.05	.01
	NL Pitcher April			
☐ 5	Brian Downing	.06	.03	.00
	AL Player April			
☐ 6	Bret Saberhagen	.25	.12	.02
	AL Pitcher April			
☐ 7	Tim Raines	.15	.07	.01
	Free Agent Returns			
☐ 8	Eric Davis	.35	.17	.03
	NL Player May			
☐ 9	Steve Bedrosian	.10	.05	.01
	NL Pitcher May			
☐ 10	Larry Parrish	.06	.03	.00
	AL Player May			
☐ 11	Jim Clancy	.06	.03	.00
	AL Pitcher May			
☐ 12	Tony Gwynn	.25	.12	.02
	NL Player June			
	ERR (over "20" hits)			
☐ 13	Orel Hershiser	.35	.17	.03
	NL Pitcher June			
☐ 14	Wade Boggs	.50	.25	.05
	AL Player June			
☐ 15	Steve Ontiveros	.06	.03	.00
	AL Pitcher June			
☐ 16	Tim Raines	.15	.07	.01
	All Star Game Hero			
☐ 17	Don Mattingly	.75	.35	.07
	Consecutive Game Homerun Streak			
☐ 18	Ray Dandridge	.15	.07	.01
	1987 HOF Inductee			
☐ 19	Jim "Catfish" Hunter	.15	.07	.01
	1987 HOF Inductee			
☐ 20	Billy Williams	.15	.07	.01
	1987 HOF Inductee			
☐ 21	Bo Diaz	.06	.03	.00
	NL Player July			
☐ 22	Floyd Youmans	.06	.03	.00
	NL Pitcher July			
☐ 23	Don Mattingly	.75	.35	.07
	AL Player July			
☐ 24	Frank Viola	.15	.07	.01
	AL Pitcher July			
☐ 25	Bobby Witt	.15	.07	.01
	Strikes Out Four Batters in One Inning			
☐ 26	Kevin Seitzer	.45	.22	.04
	Ties AL 9-Inning Game Hit Mark			
☐ 27	Mark McGwire	.90	.45	.09
	Sets Rookie HR Record			
☐ 28	Andre Dawson	.20	.10	.02
	Sets Cubs' 1st Year Homer Mark			
☐ 29	Paul Molitor	.15	.07	.01
	Hits in 39 Straight Games			
☐ 30	Kirby Puckett	.50	.25	.05
	Record Weekend			
☐ 31	Andre Dawson	.20	.10	.02
	NL Player August			
☐ 32	Doug Drabek	.06	.03	.00
	NL Pitcher August			
☐ 33	Dwight Evans	.10	.05	.01
	AL Player August			
☐ 34	Mark Langston	.20	.10	.02
	AL Pitcher August			
☐ 35	Wally Joyner	.25	.12	.02
	100 RBI in 1st Two Major League Seasons			
☐ 36	Vince Coleman	.20	.10	.02
	100 SB in 1st Three Major League Seasons			
☐ 37	Eddie Murray	.20	.10	.02
	Orioles' All Time Homer King			

☐ 38	Cal Ripken .... Ends Consecutive Innings Streak	.20	.10	.02
☐ 39	Blue Jays .... Hit Record 10 Homers In One Game (McGriff/Ducey/Whitt)	.06	.03	.00
☐ 40	McGwire/Canseco .... Equal A's RBI Marks	1.00	.50	.10
☐ 41	Bob Boone .... Sets All-Time Catching Record	.10	.05	.01
☐ 42	Darryl Strawberry .... Sets Mets' One-Season Home Run Mark	.35	.17	.03
☐ 43	Howard Johnson .... NL's All-Time Switchhit HR King	.25	.12	.02
☐ 44	Wade Boggs .... Five Straight 200 Hit Seasons	.50	.25	.05
☐ 45	Benito Santiago .... Eclipses Rookie Game Hitting Streak	.35	.17	.03
☐ 46	Mark McGwire .... Eclipses Jackson's A's HR Record	.90	.45	.09
☐ 47	Kevin Seitzer .... 13th Rookie to Collect 200 Hits	.45	.22	.04
☐ 48	Don Mattingly .... Sets Slam Record	1.00	.50	.10
☐ 49	Darryl Strawberry .... NL Player September	.40	.20	.04
☐ 50	Pascual Perez .... NL Pitcher September	.10	.05	.01
☐ 51	Alan Trammell .... AL Player September	.15	.07	.01
☐ 52	Doyle Alexander .... AL Pitcher September	.06	.03	.00
☐ 53	Nolan Ryan .... Strikeout King Again	1.00	.50	.10
☐ 54	Mark McGwire .... Donruss AL ROY	1.00	.50	.10
☐ 55	Benito Santiago .... Donruss NL ROY	.50	.25	.05
☐ 56	Checklist Card	.06	.03	.00

1988 Donruss

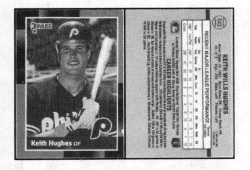

Keith Hughes OF

This 660-card set was distributed along with a puzzle of Stan Musial. The six regular checklist cards are numbered throughout the set as multiples of 100. Cards measure 2 1/2" by 3 1/2" and feature a distinctive black and blue border on the front. The popular Diamond King subset returns for the seventh consecutive year. Rated Rookies are featured again as cards 28-47. Cards marked as SP (short printed) from 648-660 are more difficult to find than the other 13 SP's in the lower 600s. These 26 cards listed as SP were apparently pulled from the printing sheet to make room for the 26 Bonus MVP cards. Six of the checklist cards were done two different ways to reflect the inclusion or exclusion of the Bonus MVP cards in the wax packs. In the checklist below, the A variations (for the checklist cards) are from the wax packs and the B variations are from the factory-collated sets.

		MINT	EXC	G-VG
COMPLETE SET (660)		28.00	14.00	2.80
COMMON PLAYER (1-647)		.03	.01	.00
COMMON PLAYER (648-660)		.08	.04	.01
☐	1 Mark McGwire DK	.65	.15	.03
☐	2 Tim Raines DK	.15	.07	.01
☐	3 Benito Santiago DK	.15	.07	.01
☐	4 Alan Trammell DK	.12	.06	.01
☐	5 Danny Tartabull DK	.10	.05	.01
☐	6 Ron Darling DK	.10	.05	.01
☐	7 Paul Molitor DK	.12	.06	.01
☐	8 Devon White DK	.12	.06	.01
☐	9 Andre Dawson DK	.15	.07	.01
☐	10 Julio Franco DK	.10	.05	.01
☐	11 Scott Fletcher DK	.06	.03	.00
☐	12 Tony Fernandez DK	.10	.05	.01
☐	13 Shane Rawley DK	.06	.03	.00
☐	14 Kal Daniels DK	.10	.05	.01
☐	15 Jack Clark DK	.12	.06	.01
☐	16 Dwight Evans DK	.12	.06	.01
☐	17 Tommy John DK	.12	.06	.01
☐	18 Andy Van Slyke DK	.12	.06	.01
☐	19 Gary Gaetti DK	.10	.05	.01
☐	20 Mark Langston DK	.15	.07	.01
☐	21 Will Clark DK	.60	.30	.06
☐	22 Glenn Hubbard DK	.06	.03	.00
☐	23 Billy Hatcher DK	.06	.03	.00
☐	24 Bob Welch DK	.08	.04	.01
☐	25 Ivan Calderon DK	.08	.04	.01
☐	26 Cal Ripken Jr. DK	.20	.10	.02
☐	27 DK Checklist 1-26	.06	.01	.00
☐	28 Mackey Sasser RR	.20	.10	.02
☐	29 Jeff Treadway RR	.30	.15	.03
☐	30 Mike Campbell RR	.18	.09	.01
☐	31 Lance Johnson RR	.18	.09	.01
☐	32 Nelson Liriano RR	.20	.10	.02
☐	33 Shawn Abner RR	.18	.09	.01
☐	34 Roberto Alomar RR	1.00	.40	.07
☐	35 Shawn Hillegas RR	.18	.09	.01
☐	36 Joey Meyer RR	.12	.06	.01
☐	37 Kevin Elster RR	.15	.07	.01
☐	38 Jose Lind RR	.20	.10	.02
☐	39 Kirt Manwaring RR	.20	.10	.02
☐	40 Mark Grace RR	4.00	2.00	.40
☐	41 Jody Reed RR	.35	.17	.03
☐	42 John Farrell RR	.25	.12	.02
☐	43 Al Leiter RR	.50	.25	.05
☐	44 Gary Thurman RR	.20	.10	.02
☐	45 Vicente Palacios RR	.12	.06	.01
☐	46 Eddie Williams RR	.15	.07	.01
☐	47 Jack McDowell RR	.15	.07	.01
☐	48 Ken Dixon	.03	.01	.00
☐	49 Mike Birkbeck	.03	.01	.00
☐	50 Eric King	.03	.01	.00
☐	51 Roger Clemens	.50	.25	.05
☐	52 Pat Clements	.03	.01	.00
☐	53 Fernando Valenzuela	.12	.06	.01
☐	54 Mark Gubicza	.10	.05	.01
☐	55 Jay Howell	.03	.01	.00
☐	56 Floyd Youmans	.03	.01	.00
☐	57 Ed Correa	.03	.01	.00
☐	58 DeWayne Buice	.08	.04	.01
☐	59 Jose DeLeon	.03	.01	.00
☐	60 Danny Cox	.03	.01	.00
☐	61 Nolan Ryan	.40	.20	.04
☐	62 Steve Bedrosian	.08	.04	.01
☐	63 Tom Browning	.08	.04	.01
☐	64 Mark Davis	.12	.06	.01
☐	65 R.J. Reynolds	.03	.01	.00
☐	66 Kevin Mitchell	.45	.22	.04
☐	67 Ken Oberkfell	.03	.01	.00
☐	68 Rick Sutcliffe	.08	.04	.01
☐	69 Dwight Gooden	.45	.22	.04
☐	70 Scott Bankhead	.12	.06	.01
☐	71 Bert Blyleven	.10	.05	.01
☐	72 Jimmy Key	.06	.03	.00
☐	73 Les Straker	.08	.04	.01
☐	74 Jim Clancy	.03	.01	.00
☐	75 Mike Moore	.06	.03	.00
☐	76 Ron Darling	.08	.04	.01
☐	77 Ed Lynch	.03	.01	.00
☐	78 Dale Murphy	.25	.12	.02
☐	79 Doug Drabek	.06	.03	.00
☐	80 Scott Garrelts	.06	.03	.00
☐	81 Ed Whitson	.03	.01	.00
☐	82 Rob Murphy	.03	.01	.00
☐	83 Shane Rawley	.03	.01	.00
☐	84 Greg Mathews	.03	.01	.00
☐	85 Jim Deshaies	.03	.01	.00
☐	86 Mike Witt	.06	.03	.00

☐ 87	Donnie Hill	.03	.01	.00
☐ 88	Jeff Reed	.03	.01	.00
☐ 89	Mike Boddicker	.03	.01	.00
☐ 90	Ted Higuera	.08	.04	.01
☐ 91	Walt Terrell	.03	.01	.00
☐ 92	Bob Stanley	.03	.01	.00
☐ 93	Dave Righetti	.08	.04	.01
☐ 94	Orel Hershiser	.20	.10	.02
☐ 95	Chris Bando	.03	.01	.00
☐ 96	Bret Saberhagen	.20	.10	.02
☐ 97	Curt Young	.03	.01	.00
☐ 98	Tim Burke	.06	.03	.00
☐ 99	Charlie Hough	.03	.01	.00
☐ 100A	Checklist 28-137	.06	.01	.00
☐ 100B	Checklist 28-133	.06	.01	.00
☐ 101	Bobby Witt	.06	.03	.00
☐ 102	George Brett	.25	.12	.02
☐ 103	Mickey Tettleton	.06	.03	.00
☐ 104	Scott Bailes	.03	.01	.00
☐ 105	Mike Pagliarulo	.06	.03	.00
☐ 106	Mike Scioscia	.03	.01	.00
☐ 107	Tom Brookens	.03	.01	.00
☐ 108	Ray Knight	.06	.03	.00
☐ 109	Dan Plesac	.06	.03	.00
☐ 110	Wally Joyner	.40	.20	.04
☐ 111	Bob Forsch	.03	.01	.00
☐ 112	Mike Scott	.15	.07	.01
☐ 113	Kevin Gross	.03	.01	.00
☐ 114	Benito Santiago	.30	.15	.03
☐ 115	Bob Kipper	.03	.01	.00
☐ 116	Mike Krukow	.03	.01	.00
☐ 117	Chris Bosio	.06	.03	.00
☐ 118	Sid Fernandez	.08	.04	.01
☐ 119	Jody Davis	.03	.01	.00
☐ 120	Mike Morgan	.06	.03	.00
☐ 121	Mark Eichhorn	.03	.01	.00
☐ 122	Jeff Reardon	.08	.04	.01
☐ 123	John Franco	.08	.04	.01
☐ 124	Richard Dotson	.03	.01	.00
☐ 125	Eric Bell	.03	.01	.00
☐ 126	Juan Nieves	.03	.01	.00
☐ 127	Jack Morris	.10	.05	.01
☐ 128	Rick Rhoden	.03	.01	.00
☐ 129	Rich Gedman	.03	.01	.00
☐ 130	Ken Howell	.03	.01	.00
☐ 131	Brook Jacoby	.06	.03	.00
☐ 132	Danny Jackson	.08	.04	.01
☐ 133	Gene Nelson	.03	.01	.00
☐ 134	Neal Heaton	.03	.01	.00
☐ 135	Willie Fraser	.03	.01	.00
☐ 136	Jose Guzman	.03	.01	.00
☐ 137	Ozzie Guillen	.06	.03	.00
☐ 138	Bob Knepper	.03	.01	.00
☐ 139	Mike Jackson	.12	.06	.01
☐ 140	Joe Magrane	.50	.25	.05
☐ 141	Jimmy Jones	.06	.03	.00
☐ 142	Ted Power	.03	.01	.00
☐ 143	Ozzie Virgil	.03	.01	.00
☐ 144	Felix Fermin	.08	.04	.01
☐ 145	Kelly Downs	.06	.03	.00
☐ 146	Shawon Dunston	.08	.04	.01
☐ 147	Scott Bradley	.03	.01	.00
☐ 148	Dave Stieb	.08	.04	.01
☐ 149	Frank Viola	.12	.06	.01
☐ 150	Terry Kennedy	.03	.01	.00
☐ 151	Bill Wegman	.03	.01	.00
☐ 152	Matt Nokes	.40	.20	.04
☐ 153	Wade Boggs	.80	.40	.08
☐ 154	Wayne Tolleson	.03	.01	.00
☐ 155	Mariano Duncan	.03	.01	.00
☐ 156	Julio Franco	.10	.05	.01
☐ 157	Charlie Leibrandt	.03	.01	.00
☐ 158	Terry Steinbach	.12	.06	.01
☐ 159	Mike Fitzgerald	.03	.01	.00
☐ 160	Jack Lazorko	.03	.01	.00
☐ 161	Mitch Williams	.03	.01	.00
☐ 162	Greg Walker	.06	.03	.00
☐ 163	Alan Ashby	.03	.01	.00
☐ 164	Tony Gwynn	.35	.17	.03
☐ 165	Bruce Ruffin	.03	.01	.00
☐ 166	Ron Robinson	.03	.01	.00
☐ 167	Zane Smith	.03	.01	.00
☐ 168	Junior Ortiz	.03	.01	.00
☐ 169	Jamie Moyer	.03	.01	.00
☐ 170	Tony Pena	.08	.04	.01
☐ 171	Cal Ripken	.20	.10	.02
☐ 172	B.J. Surhoff	.10	.05	.01
☐ 173	Lou Whitaker	.10	.05	.01
☐ 174	Ellis Burks	1.50	.75	.15
☐ 175	Ron Guidry	.10	.05	.01
☐ 176	Steve Sax	.12	.06	.01
☐ 177	Danny Tartabull	.20	.10	.02
☐ 178	Carney Lansford	.08	.04	.01
☐ 179	Casey Candaele	.03	.01	.00
☐ 180	Scott Fletcher	.03	.01	.00
☐ 181	Mark McLemore	.03	.01	.00
☐ 182	Ivan Calderon	.06	.03	.00
☐ 183	Jack Clark	.12	.06	.01
☐ 184	Glenn Davis	.15	.07	.01
☐ 185	Luis Aguayo	.03	.01	.00
☐ 186	Bo Diaz	.03	.01	.00
☐ 187	Stan Jefferson	.03	.01	.00
☐ 188	Sid Bream	.03	.01	.00
☐ 189	Bob Brenly	.03	.01	.00
☐ 190	Dion James	.03	.01	.00
☐ 191	Leon Durham	.03	.01	.00
☐ 192	Jesse Orosco	.03	.01	.00
☐ 193	Alvin Davis	.10	.05	.01
☐ 194	Gary Gaetti	.10	.05	.01
☐ 195	Fred McGriff	.45	.22	.04
☐ 196	Steve Lombardozzi	.03	.01	.00
☐ 197	Rance Mulliniks	.03	.01	.00
☐ 198	Rey Quinones	.03	.01	.00
☐ 199	Gary Carter	.15	.07	.01
☐ 200A	Checklist 138-247	.06	.01	.00
☐ 200B	Checklist 134-239	.06	.01	.00
☐ 201	Keith Moreland	.03	.01	.00
☐ 202	Ken Griffey	.08	.04	.01
☐ 203	Tommy Gregg	.18	.09	.01
☐ 204	Will Clark	1.50	.75	.15
☐ 205	John Kruk	.08	.04	.01
☐ 206	Buddy Bell	.06	.03	.00
☐ 207	Von Hayes	.08	.04	.01
☐ 208	Tommy Herr	.03	.01	.00
☐ 209	Craig Reynolds	.03	.01	.00
☐ 210	Gary Pettis	.03	.01	.00
☐ 211	Harold Baines	.08	.04	.01
☐ 212	Vance Law	.03	.01	.00
☐ 213	Ken Gerhart	.03	.01	.00
☐ 214	Jim Gantner	.03	.01	.00
☐ 215	Chet Lemon	.03	.01	.00
☐ 216	Dwight Evans	.10	.05	.01
☐ 217	Don Mattingly	1.25	.60	.12
☐ 218	Franklin Stubbs	.03	.01	.00
☐ 219	Pat Tabler	.06	.03	.00
☐ 220	Bo Jackson	1.00	.50	.10
☐ 221	Tony Phillips	.03	.01	.00
☐ 222	Tim Wallach	.06	.03	.00
☐ 223	Ruben Sierra	.50	.25	.05
☐ 224	Steve Buechele	.03	.01	.00
☐ 225	Frank White	.06	.03	.00
☐ 226	Alfredo Griffin	.06	.03	.00
☐ 227	Greg Swindell	.12	.06	.01
☐ 228	Willie Randolph	.06	.03	.00
☐ 229	Mike Marshall	.10	.05	.01
☐ 230	Alan Trammell	.15	.07	.01
☐ 231	Eddie Murray	.15	.07	.01
☐ 232	Dale Sveum	.03	.01	.00
☐ 233	Dick Schofield	.03	.01	.00
☐ 234	Jose Oquendo	.03	.01	.00
☐ 235	Bill Doran	.06	.03	.00
☐ 236	Milt Thompson	.03	.01	.00
☐ 237	Marvell Wynne	.03	.01	.00
☐ 238	Bobby Bonilla	.15	.07	.01
☐ 239	Chris Speier	.03	.01	.00
☐ 240	Glenn Braggs	.06	.03	.00
☐ 241	Wally Backman	.03	.01	.00
☐ 242	Ryne Sandberg	.20	.10	.02
☐ 243	Phil Bradley	.06	.03	.00
☐ 244	Kelly Gruber	.06	.03	.00
☐ 245	Tom Brunansky	.10	.05	.01
☐ 246	Ron Oester	.03	.01	.00
☐ 247	Bobby Thigpen	.08	.04	.01
☐ 248	Fred Lynn	.10	.05	.01
☐ 249	Paul Molitor	.12	.06	.01
☐ 250	Darrell Evans	.08	.04	.01
☐ 251	Gary Ward	.03	.01	.00
☐ 252	Bruce Hurst	.10	.05	.01
☐ 253	Bob Welch	.06	.03	.00
☐ 254	Joe Carter	.15	.07	.01
☐ 255	Willie Wilson	.06	.03	.00
☐ 256	Mark McGwire	1.25	.60	.12
☐ 257	Mitch Webster	.03	.01	.00
☐ 258	Brian Downing	.03	.01	.00
☐ 259	Mike Stanley	.06	.03	.00
☐ 260	Carlton Fisk	.12	.06	.01
☐ 261	Billy Hatcher	.06	.03	.00
☐ 262	Glenn Wilson	.03	.01	.00
☐ 263	Ozzie Smith	.15	.07	.01
☐ 264	Randy Ready	.03	.01	.00
☐ 265	Kurt Stillwell	.03	.01	.00
☐ 266	David Palmer	.03	.01	.00
☐ 267	Mike Diaz	.03	.01	.00
☐ 268	Rob Thompson	.03	.01	.00
☐ 269	Andre Dawson	.15	.07	.01
☐ 270	Lee Guetterman	.03	.01	.00
☐ 271	Willie Upshaw	.03	.01	.00
☐ 272	Randy Bush	.03	.01	.00
☐ 273	Larry Sheets	.06	.03	.00
☐ 274	Rob Deer	.08	.04	.01

☐ 275	Kirk Gibson	.18	.09	.01	☐ 368	Kirby Puckett	.50	.25	.05
☐ 276	Marty Barrett	.06	.03	.00	☐ 369	Eric Davis	.50	.25	.05
☐ 277	Rickey Henderson	.25	.12	.02	☐ 370	Gary Redus	.03	.01	.00
☐ 278	Pedro Guerrero	.15	.07	.01	☐ 371	Dave Schmidt	.03	.01	.00
☐ 279	Brett Butler	.06	.03	.00	☐ 372	Mark Clear	.03	.01	.00
☐ 280	Kevin Seitzer	.75	.35	.07	☐ 373	Dave Bergman	.03	.01	.00
☐ 281	Mike Davis	.03	.01	.00	☐ 374	Charles Hudson	.03	.01	.00
☐ 282	Andres Galarraga	.25	.12	.02	☐ 375	Calvin Schiraldi	.03	.01	.00
☐ 283	Devon White	.18	.09	.01	☐ 376	Alex Trevino	.03	.01	.00
☐ 284	Pete O'Brien	.06	.03	.00	☐ 377	Tom Candiotti	.03	.01	.00
☐ 285	Jerry Hairston	.03	.01	.00	☐ 378	Steve Farr	.03	.01	.00
☐ 286	Kevin Bass	.06	.03	.00	☐ 379	Mike Gallego	.03	.01	.00
☐ 287	Carmelo Martinez	.03	.01	.00	☐ 380	Andy McGaffigan	.03	.01	.00
☐ 288	Juan Samuel	.08	.04	.01	☐ 381	Kirk McCaskill	.03	.01	.00
☐ 289	Kal Daniels	.15	.07	.01	☐ 382	Oddibe McDowell	.06	.03	.00
☐ 290	Albert Hall	.03	.01	.00	☐ 383	Floyd Bannister	.03	.01	.00
☐ 291	Andy Van Slyke	.12	.06	.01	☐ 384	Denny Walling	.03	.01	.00
☐ 292	Lee Smith	.06	.03	.00	☐ 385	Don Carman	.03	.01	.00
☐ 293	Vince Coleman	.15	.07	.01	☐ 386	Todd Worrell	.08	.04	.01
☐ 294	Tom Niedenfuer	.03	.01	.00	☐ 387	Eric Show	.03	.01	.00
☐ 295	Robin Yount	.20	.10	.02	☐ 388	Dave Parker	.10	.05	.01
☐ 296	Jeff Robinson	.30	.15	.03	☐ 389	Rick Mahler	.03	.01	.00
	(Tigers pitcher)				☐ 390	Mike Dunne	.08	.04	.01
☐ 297	Todd Benzinger	.30	.15	.03	☐ 391	Candy Maldonado	.06	.03	.00
☐ 298	Dave Winfield	.20	.10	.02	☐ 392	Bob Dernier	.03	.01	.00
☐ 299	Mickey Hatcher	.03	.01	.00	☐ 393	Dave Valle	.03	.01	.00
☐ 300A	Checklist 248-357	.06	.01	.00	☐ 394	Ernie Whitt	.03	.01	.00
☐ 300B	Checklist 240-345	.06	.01	.00	☐ 395	Juan Berenguer	.03	.01	.00
☐ 301	Bud Black	.03	.01	.00	☐ 396	Mike Young	.03	.01	.00
☐ 302	Jose Canseco	1.25	.60	.12	☐ 397	Mike Felder	.03	.01	.00
☐ 303	Tom Foley	.03	.01	.00	☐ 398	Willie Hernandez	.06	.03	.00
☐ 304	Pete Incaviglia	.15	.07	.01	☐ 399	Jim Rice	.12	.06	.01
☐ 305	Bob Boone	.08	.04	.01	☐ 400A	Checklist 358-467	.06	.01	.00
☐ 306	Bill Long	.08	.04	.01	☐ 400B	Checklist 346-451	.06	.01	.00
☐ 307	Willie McGee	.10	.05	.01	☐ 401	Tommy John	.10	.05	.01
☐ 308	Ken Caminiti	.18	.09	.01	☐ 402	Brian Holton	.03	.01	.00
☐ 309	Darren Daulton	.03	.01	.00	☐ 403	Carmen Castillo	.03	.01	.00
☐ 310	Tracy Jones	.08	.04	.01	☐ 404	Jamie Quirk	.03	.01	.00
☐ 311	Greg Booker	.03	.01	.00	☐ 405	Dwayne Murphy	.03	.01	.00
☐ 312	Mike LaValliere	.03	.01	.00	☐ 406	Jeff Parrett	.15	.07	.01
☐ 313	Chili Davis	.06	.03	.00	☐ 407	Don Sutton	.12	.06	.01
☐ 314	Glenn Hubbard	.03	.01	.00	☐ 408	Jerry Browne	.06	.03	.00
☐ 315	Paul Noce	.08	.04	.01	☐ 409	Jim Winn	.03	.01	.00
☐ 316	Keith Hernandez	.15	.07	.01	☐ 410	Dave Smith	.03	.01	.00
☐ 317	Mark Langston	.12	.06	.01	☐ 411	Shane Mack	.10	.05	.01
☐ 318	Keith Atherton	.03	.01	.00	☐ 412	Greg Gross	.03	.01	.00
☐ 319	Tony Fernandez	.10	.05	.01	☐ 413	Nick Esasky	.08	.04	.01
☐ 320	Kent Hrbek	.12	.06	.01	☐ 414	Damaso Garcia	.03	.01	.00
☐ 321	John Cerutti	.03	.01	.00	☐ 415	Brian Fisher	.03	.01	.00
☐ 322	Mike Kingery	.03	.01	.00	☐ 416	Brian Dayett	.03	.01	.00
☐ 323	Dave Magadan	.10	.05	.01	☐ 417	Curt Ford	.03	.01	.00
☐ 324	Rafael Palmeiro	.25	.12	.02	☐ 418	Mark Williamson	.08	.04	.01
☐ 325	Jeff Dedmon	.03	.01	.00	☐ 419	Bill Schroeder	.03	.01	.00
☐ 326	Barry Bonds	.20	.10	.02	☐ 420	Mike Henneman	.20	.10	.02
☐ 327	Jeffrey Leonard	.06	.03	.00	☐ 421	John Marzano	.08	.04	.01
☐ 328	Tim Flannery	.03	.01	.00	☐ 422	Ron Kittle	.08	.04	.01
☐ 329	Dave Concepcion	.06	.03	.00	☐ 423	Matt Young	.03	.01	.00
☐ 330	Mike Schmidt	.35	.17	.03	☐ 424	Steve Balboni	.03	.01	.00
☐ 331	Bill Dawley	.03	.01	.00	☐ 425	Luis Polonia	.15	.07	.01
☐ 332	Larry Andersen	.03	.01	.00	☐ 426	Randy St.Claire	.03	.01	.00
☐ 333	Jack Howell	.03	.01	.00	☐ 427	Greg Harris	.03	.01	.00
☐ 334	Ken Williams	.15	.07	.01	☐ 428	Johnny Ray	.06	.03	.00
☐ 335	Bryn Smith	.06	.03	.00	☐ 429	Ray Searage	.03	.01	.00
☐ 336	Billy Ripken	.15	.07	.01	☐ 430	Ricky Horton	.03	.01	.00
☐ 337	Greg Brock	.03	.01	.00	☐ 431	Gerald Young	.30	.15	.03
☐ 338	Mike Heath	.03	.01	.00	☐ 432	Rick Schu	.03	.01	.00
☐ 339	Mike Greenwell	1.25	.60	.12	☐ 433	Paul O'Neill	.08	.04	.01
☐ 340	Claudell Washington	.06	.03	.00	☐ 434	Rich Gossage	.08	.04	.01
☐ 341	Jose Gonzalez	.03	.01	.00	☐ 435	John Cangelosi	.03	.01	.00
☐ 342	Mel Hall	.06	.03	.00	☐ 436	Mike LaCoss	.03	.01	.00
☐ 343	Jim Eisenreich	.06	.03	.00	☐ 437	Gerald Perry	.06	.03	.00
☐ 344	Tony Bernazard	.03	.01	.00	☐ 438	Dave Martinez	.06	.03	.00
☐ 345	Tim Raines	.18	.09	.01	☐ 439	Darryl Strawberry	.45	.22	.04
☐ 346	Bob Brower	.03	.01	.00	☐ 440	John Moses	.03	.01	.00
☐ 347	Larry Parrish	.03	.01	.00	☐ 441	Greg Gagne	.03	.01	.00
☐ 348	Thad Bosley	.03	.01	.00	☐ 442	Jesse Barfield	.10	.05	.01
☐ 349	Dennis Eckersley	.10	.05	.01	☐ 443	George Frazier	.03	.01	.00
☐ 350	Cory Snyder	.12	.06	.01	☐ 444	Garth Iorg	.03	.01	.00
☐ 351	Rick Cerone	.03	.01	.00	☐ 445	Ed Nunez	.03	.01	.00
☐ 352	John Shelby	.03	.01	.00	☐ 446	Rick Aguilera	.03	.01	.00
☐ 353	Larry Herndon	.03	.01	.00	☐ 447	Jerry Mumphrey	.03	.01	.00
☐ 354	John Habyan	.03	.01	.00	☐ 448	Rafael Ramirez	.03	.01	.00
☐ 355	Chuck Crim	.06	.03	.00	☐ 449	John Smiley	.35	.17	.03
☐ 356	Gus Polidor	.03	.01	.00	☐ 450	Atlee Hammaker	.03	.01	.00
☐ 357	Ken Dayley	.03	.01	.00	☐ 451	Lance McCullers	.06	.03	.00
☐ 358	Danny Darwin	.03	.01	.00	☐ 452	Guy Hoffman	.03	.01	.00
☐ 359	Lance Parrish	.10	.05	.01	☐ 453	Chris James	.08	.04	.01
☐ 360	James Steels	.08	.04	.01	☐ 454	Terry Pendleton	.03	.01	.00
☐ 361	Al Pedrique	.08	.04	.01	☐ 455	Dave Meads	.08	.04	.01
☐ 362	Mike Aldrete	.03	.01	.00	☐ 456	Bill Buckner	.08	.04	.01
☐ 363	Juan Castillo	.03	.01	.00	☐ 457	John Pawlowski	.08	.04	.01
☐ 364	Len Dykstra	.06	.03	.00	☐ 458	Bob Sebra	.03	.01	.00
☐ 365	Luis Quinones	.06	.03	.00	☐ 459	Jim Dwyer	.03	.01	.00
☐ 366	Jim Presley	.06	.03	.00	☐ 460	Jay Aldrich	.08	.04	.01
☐ 367	Lloyd Moseby	.06	.03	.00	☐ 461	Frank Tanana	.03	.01	.00

☐ 462	Oil Can Boyd	.03	.01	.00
☐ 463	Dan Pasqua	.03	.01	.00
☐ 464	Tim Crews	.08	.04	.01
☐ 465	Andy Allanson	.03	.01	.00
☐ 466	Bill Pecota	.08	.04	.01
☐ 467	Steve Ontiveros	.03	.01	.00
☐ 468	Hubie Brooks	.08	.04	.01
☐ 469	Paul Kilgus	.12	.06	.01
☐ 470	Dale Mohorcic	.03	.01	.00
☐ 471	Dan Quisenberry	.08	.04	.01
☐ 472	Dave Stewart	.12	.06	.01
☐ 473	Dave Clark	.06	.03	.00
☐ 474	Joel Skinner	.03	.01	.00
☐ 475	Dave Anderson	.03	.01	.00
☐ 476	Dan Petry	.03	.01	.00
☐ 477	Carl Nichols	.08	.04	.01
☐ 478	Ernest Riles	.03	.01	.00
☐ 479	George Hendrick	.03	.01	.00
☐ 480	John Morris	.03	.01	.00
☐ 481	Manny Hernandez	.08	.04	.01
☐ 482	Jeff Stone	.03	.01	.00
☐ 483	Chris Brown	.03	.01	.00
☐ 484	Mike Bielecki	.08	.04	.01
☐ 485	Dave Dravecky	.08	.04	.01
☐ 486	Rick Manning	.03	.01	.00
☐ 487	Bill Almon	.03	.01	.00
☐ 488	Jim Sundberg	.03	.01	.00
☐ 489	Ken Phelps	.06	.03	.00
☐ 490	Tom Henke	.06	.03	.00
☐ 491	Dan Gladden	.06	.03	.00
☐ 492	Barry Larkin	.25	.12	.02
☐ 493	Fred Manrique	.10	.05	.01
☐ 494	Mike Griffin	.03	.01	.00
☐ 495	Mark Knudson	.10	.05	.01
☐ 496	Bill Madlock	.06	.03	.00
☐ 497	Tim Stoddard	.03	.01	.00
☐ 498	Sam Horn	.15	.07	.01
☐ 499	Tracy Woodson	.18	.09	.01
☐ 500A	Checklist 468-577	.06	.01	.00
☐ 500B	Checklist 452-557	.06	.01	.00
☐ 501	Ken Schrom	.03	.01	.00
☐ 502	Angel Salazar	.03	.01	.00
☐ 503	Eric Plunk	.03	.01	.00
☐ 504	Joe Hesketh	.03	.01	.00
☐ 505	Greg Minton	.03	.01	.00
☐ 506	Geno Petralli	.03	.01	.00
☐ 507	Bob James	.03	.01	.00
☐ 508	Robbie Wine	.08	.04	.01
☐ 509	Jeff Calhoun	.03	.01	.00
☐ 510	Steve Lake	.03	.01	.00
☐ 511	Mark Grant	.03	.01	.00
☐ 512	Frank Williams	.03	.01	.00
☐ 513	Jeff Blauser	.25	.12	.02
☐ 514	Bob Walk	.03	.01	.00
☐ 515	Craig Lefferts	.06	.03	.00
☐ 516	Manny Trillo	.03	.01	.00
☐ 517	Jerry Reed	.03	.01	.00
☐ 518	Rick Leach	.03	.01	.00
☐ 519	Mark Davidson	.12	.06	.01
☐ 520	Jeff Ballard	.35	.17	.03
☐ 521	Dave Stapleton	.06	.03	.00
☐ 522	Pat Sheridan	.03	.01	.00
☐ 523	Al Nipper	.03	.01	.00
☐ 524	Steve Trout	.03	.01	.00
☐ 525	Jeff Hamilton	.06	.03	.00
☐ 526	Tommy Hinzo	.08	.04	.01
☐ 527	Lonnie Smith	.06	.03	.00
☐ 528	Greg Cadaret	.20	.10	.02
☐ 529	Bob McClure ("Rob" on front)	.03	.01	.00
☐ 530	Chuck Finley	.06	.03	.00
☐ 531	Jeff Russell	.06	.03	.00
☐ 532	Steve Lyons	.03	.01	.00
☐ 533	Terry Puhl	.03	.01	.00
☐ 534	Eric Nolte	.12	.06	.01
☐ 535	Kent Tekulve	.03	.01	.00
☐ 536	Pat Pacillo	.08	.04	.01
☐ 537	Charlie Puleo	.03	.01	.00
☐ 538	Tom Prince	.10	.05	.01
☐ 539	Greg Maddux	.18	.09	.01
☐ 540	Jim Lindeman	.03	.01	.00
☐ 541	Pete Stanicek	.15	.07	.01
☐ 542	Steve Kiefer	.03	.01	.00
☐ 543A	Jim Morrison ERR (no decimal before lifetime average)	.25	.12	.02
☐ 543B	Jim Morrison COR	.06	.03	.00
☐ 544	Spike Owen	.03	.01	.00
☐ 545	Jay Buhner	.45	.22	.04
☐ 546	Mike Devereaux	.25	.12	.02
☐ 547	Jerry Don Gleaton	.03	.01	.00
☐ 548	Jose Rijo	.03	.01	.00
☐ 549	Dennis Martinez	.03	.01	.00
☐ 550	Mike Loynd	.03	.01	.00
☐ 551	Darrell Miller	.03	.01	.00
☐ 552	Dave LaPoint	.03	.01	.00
☐ 553	John Tudor	.08	.04	.01
☐ 554	Rocky Childress	.08	.04	.01
☐ 555	Wally Ritchie	.08	.04	.01
☐ 556	Terry McGriff	.06	.03	.00
☐ 557	Dave Leiper	.03	.01	.00
☐ 558	Jeff Robinson (Pirates pitcher)	.08	.04	.01
☐ 559	Jose Uribe	.03	.01	.00
☐ 560	Ted Simmons	.08	.04	.01
☐ 561	Les Lancaster	.15	.07	.01
☐ 562	Keith Miller (New York Mets)	.20	.10	.02
☐ 563	Harold Reynolds	.06	.03	.00
☐ 564	Gene Larkin	.25	.12	.02
☐ 565	Cecil Fielder	.03	.01	.00
☐ 566	Roy Smalley	.03	.01	.00
☐ 567	Duane Ward	.03	.01	.00
☐ 568	Bill Wilkinson	.10	.05	.01
☐ 569	Howard Johnson	.15	.07	.01
☐ 570	Frank DiPino	.03	.01	.00
☐ 571	Pete Smith	.15	.07	.01
☐ 572	Darnell Coles	.03	.01	.00
☐ 573	Don Robinson	.03	.01	.00
☐ 574	Rob Nelson	.03	.01	.00
☐ 575	Dennis Rasmussen	.06	.03	.00
☐ 576	Steve Jeltz	.03	.01	.00
☐ 577	Tom Pagnozzi	.10	.05	.01
☐ 578	Ty Gainey	.03	.01	.00
☐ 579	Gary Lucas	.03	.01	.00
☐ 580	Ron Hassey	.03	.01	.00
☐ 581	Herm Winningham	.03	.01	.00
☐ 582	Rene Gonzales	.10	.05	.01
☐ 583	Brad Komminsk	.03	.01	.00
☐ 584	Doyle Alexander	.03	.01	.00
☐ 585	Jeff Sellers	.03	.01	.00
☐ 586	Bill Gullickson	.03	.01	.00
☐ 587	Tim Belcher	.40	.20	.04
☐ 588	Doug Jones	.30	.15	.03
☐ 589	Melido Perez	.25	.12	.02
☐ 590	Rick Honeycutt	.03	.01	.00
☐ 591	Pascual Perez	.08	.04	.01
☐ 592	Curt Wilkerson	.03	.01	.00
☐ 593	Steve Howe	.03	.01	.00
☐ 594	John Davis	.12	.06	.01
☐ 595	Storm Davis	.08	.04	.01
☐ 596	Sammy Stewart	.03	.01	.00
☐ 597	Neil Allen	.03	.01	.00
☐ 598	Alejandro Pena	.06	.03	.00
☐ 599	Mark Thurmond	.03	.01	.00
☐ 600A	Checklist 578-BC26	.06	.01	.00
☐ 600B	Checklist 558-660	.06	.01	.00
☐ 601	Jose Mesa	.12	.06	.01
☐ 602	Don August	.12	.06	.01
☐ 603	Terry Leach SP	.10	.05	.01
☐ 604	Tom Newell	.12	.06	.01
☐ 605	Randall Byers SP	.20	.10	.02
☐ 606	Jim Gott	.03	.01	.00
☐ 607	Harry Spilman	.03	.01	.00
☐ 608	John Candelaria	.06	.03	.00
☐ 609	Mike Brumley	.15	.07	.01
☐ 610	Mickey Brantley	.06	.03	.00
☐ 611	Jose Nunez SP	.20	.10	.02
☐ 612	Tom Nieto	.03	.01	.00
☐ 613	Rick Reuschel	.06	.03	.00
☐ 614	Lee Mazzilli SP	.08	.04	.01
☐ 615	Scott Lusader	.12	.06	.01
☐ 616	Bobby Meacham	.03	.01	.00
☐ 617	Kevin McReynolds SP	.15	.07	.01
☐ 618	Gene Garber	.03	.01	.00
☐ 619	Barry Lyons SP	.25	.12	.02
☐ 620	Randy Myers	.10	.05	.01
☐ 621	Donnie Moore	.03	.01	.00
☐ 622	Domingo Ramos	.03	.01	.00
☐ 623	Ed Romero	.03	.01	.00
☐ 624	Greg Myers	.12	.06	.01
☐ 625	Ripken Family	.08	.04	.01
☐ 626	Pat Perry	.03	.01	.00
☐ 627	Andres Thomas SP	.10	.05	.01
☐ 628	Matt Williams SP	1.25	.60	.12
☐ 629	Dave Hengel	.12	.06	.01
☐ 630	Jeff Musselman SP	.08	.04	.01
☐ 631	Tim Laudner	.03	.01	.00
☐ 632	Bob Ojeda SP	.10	.05	.01
☐ 633	Rafael Santana	.03	.01	.00
☐ 634	Wes Gardner	.20	.10	.02
☐ 635	Roberto Kelly SP	1.00	.50	.10
☐ 636	Mike Flanagan SP	.08	.04	.01
☐ 637	Jay Bell	.20	.10	.02
☐ 638	Bob Melvin	.03	.01	.00
☐ 639	Damon Berryhill	.45	.22	.04
☐ 640	David Wells SP	.25	.12	.02
☐ 641	Puzzle Card (Stan Musial)	.03	.01	.00
☐ 642	Doug Sisk	.03	.01	.00

☐	643	Keith Hughes	.18	.09	.01
☐	644	Tom Glavine	.35	.17	.03
☐	645	Al Newman	.03	.01	.00
☐	646	Scott Sanderson	.03	.01	.00
☐	647	Scott Terry	.12	.06	.01
☐	648	Tim Teufel SP	.08	.04	.01
☐	649	Garry Templeton SP	.10	.05	.01
☐	650	Manny Lee SP	.08	.04	.01
☐	651	Roger McDowell SP	.10	.05	.01
☐	652	Mookie Wilson SP	.10	.05	.01
☐	653	David Cone SP	.60	.30	.06
☐	654	Ron Gant SP	.60	.30	.06
☐	655	Joe Price SP	.08	.04	.01
☐	656	George Bell SP	.20	.10	.02
☐	657	Gregg Jefferies SP	4.00	2.00	.40
☐	658	Todd Stottlemyre SP	.35	.17	.03
☐	659	Geronimo Berroa SP	.35	.17	.03
☐	660	Jerry Royster SP	.08	.04	.01

1988 Donruss Bonus MVP's

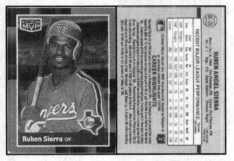

Ruben Sierra OF

This 26-card set was distributed along with the regular 1988 Donruss issue as random inserts with the rack and wax packs. These bonus cards are numbered with the prefix BC for bonus cards and were supposedly produced in the same quantities as the other 660 regular issue cards. The "most valuable" player was selected from each of the 26 teams. Cards measure 2 1/2" by 3 1/2" and feature the same distinctive black and blue border on the front as the regular issue. The cards are distinguished by the MVP logo in the upper left corner of the obverse. The last 13 cards numerically are considered to be somewhat tougher to find than the first 13 cards.

		MINT	EXC	G-VG
COMPLETE SET (26)		7.50	3.75	.75
COMMON CARD (BC1-BC13)		.05	.02	.00
COMMON CARD (BC14-BC26) ..		.10	.05	.01
☐	BC1 Cal Ripken	.25	.12	.02
☐	BC2 Eric Davis	.40	.20	.04
☐	BC3 Paul Molitor	.10	.05	.01
☐	BC4 Mike Schmidt	.40	.20	.04
☐	BC5 Ivan Calderon	.05	.02	.00
☐	BC6 Tony Gwynn	.30	.15	.03
☐	BC7 Wade Boggs	.50	.25	.05
☐	BC8 Andy Van Slyke	.10	.05	.01
☐	BC9 Joe Carter	.10	.05	.01
☐	BC10 Andre Dawson	.15	.07	.01
☐	BC11 Alan Trammell	.10	.05	.01
☐	BC12 Mike Scott	.10	.05	.01
☐	BC13 Wally Joyner	.20	.10	.02
☐	BC14 Dale Murphy	.25	.12	.02
☐	BC15 Kirby Puckett	.45	.22	.04
☐	BC16 Pedro Guerrero	.10	.05	.01
☐	BC17 Kevin Seitzer	.30	.15	.03
☐	BC18 Tim Raines	.15	.07	.01
☐	BC19 George Bell	.15	.07	.01
☐	BC20 Darryl Strawberry	.45	.22	.04
☐	BC21 Don Mattingly	.75	.35	.07
☐	BC22 Ozzie Smith	.15	.07	.01
☐	BC23 Mark McGwire	.60	.30	.06
☐	BC24 Will Clark	.90	.45	.09
☐	BC25 Alvin Davis	.10	.05	.01
☐	BC26 Ruben Sierra	.35	.17	.03

1988 Donruss Super DK's

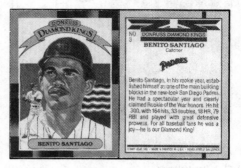

This 26-player card set was available through a mail-in offer detailed on the wax packs. The set was sent in return for 8.00 and three wrappers plus 1.50 postage and handling. The set features the popular Diamond King subseries in large (approximately 4 7/8" by 6 13/16") form. Dick Perez of Perez-Steele Galleries did another outstanding job on the artwork. The cards are essentially a large version of the Donruss regular issue Diamond Kings.

		MINT	EXC	G-VG
COMPLETE SET (26)		10.00	5.00	1.00
COMMON PLAYER (1-26)		.15	.07	.01
☐	1 Mark McGwire DK	1.50	.75	.15
☐	2 Tim Raines DK	.40	.20	.04
☐	3 Benito Santiago DK	.75	.35	.07
☐	4 Alan Trammell DK	.30	.15	.03
☐	5 Danny Tartabull DK	.40	.20	.04
☐	6 Ron Darling DK	.25	.12	.02
☐	7 Paul Molitor DK	.25	.12	.02
☐	8 Devon White DK	.35	.17	.03
☐	9 Andre Dawson DK	.30	.15	.03
☐	10 Julio Franco DK	.25	.12	.02
☐	11 Scott Fletcher DK	.15	.07	.01
☐	12 Tony Fernandez DK	.25	.12	.02
☐	13 Shane Rawley DK	.15	.07	.01
☐	14 Kal Daniels DK	.35	.17	.03
☐	15 Jack Clark DK	.35	.17	.03
☐	16 Dwight Evans DK	.25	.12	.02
☐	17 Tommy John DK	.25	.12	.02
☐	18 Andy Van Slyke DK	.25	.12	.02
☐	19 Gary Gaetti DK	.35	.17	.03
☐	20 Mark Langston DK	.35	.17	.03
☐	21 Will Clark DK	1.50	.75	.15
☐	22 Glenn Hubbard DK	.15	.07	.01
☐	23 Billy Hatcher DK	.15	.07	.01
☐	24 Bob Welch DK	.15	.07	.01
☐	25 Ivan Calderon DK	.25	.12	.02
☐	26 Cal Ripken Jr. DK	.60	.30	.06

1988 Donruss All-Stars

This 64-card set features cards measuring standard size, 2 1/2" by 3 1/2". Card fronts are in full color with a solid blue and black border. The card backs are printed in black and blue on white card stock. Cards are numbered on the back inside a blue star in the upper right hand corner. Card backs feature statistical information about the player's performance in past All-Star games. The set was distributed in packs which also contained a Pop-Up. The AL Checklist card #32 has two uncorrected errors on it, Wade Boggs is erroneously listed as the AL Leftfielder and Dan Plesac is erroneously listed as being the Tigers Pitcher.

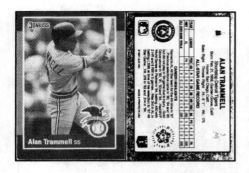

	MINT	EXC	G-VG
COMPLETE SET (64)	7.50	3.75	.75
COMMON PLAYER (1-64)	.10	.05	.01

		MINT	EXC	G-VG
☐	1 Don Mattingly	.75	.35	.07
☐	2 Dave Winfield	.25	.12	.02
☐	3 Willie Randolph	.15	.07	.01
☐	4 Rickey Henderson	.40	.20	.04
☐	5 Cal Ripken	.30	.15	.03
☐	6 George Bell	.20	.10	.02
☐	7 Wade Boggs	.75	.35	.07
☐	8 Bret Saberhagen	.30	.15	.03
☐	9 Terry Kennedy	.10	.05	.01
☐	10 John McNamara MG	.10	.05	.01
☐	11 Jay Howell	.10	.05	.01
☐	12 Harold Baines	.15	.07	.01
☐	13 Harold Reynolds	.10	.05	.01
☐	14 Bruce Hurst	.15	.07	.01
☐	15 Kirby Puckett	.40	.20	.04
☐	16 Matt Nokes	.20	.10	.02
☐	17 Pat Tabler	.10	.05	.01
☐	18 Dan Plesac	.10	.05	.01
☐	19 Mark McGwire	.75	.35	.07
☐	20 Mike Witt	.10	.05	.01
☐	21 Larry Parrish	.10	.05	.01
☐	22 Alan Trammell	.20	.10	.02
☐	23 Dwight Evans	.10	.05	.01
☐	24 Jack Morris	.15	.07	.01
☐	25 Tony Fernandez	.15	.07	.01
☐	26 Mark Langston	.25	.12	.02
☐	27 Kevin Seitzer	.45	.22	.04
☐	28 Tom Henke	.10	.05	.01
☐	29 Dave Righetti	.15	.07	.01
☐	30 Oakland Stadium	.10	.05	.01
☐	31 Wade Boggs	.75	.35	.07
☐	32 AL Checklist	.10	.05	.01
☐	33 Jack Clark	.20	.10	.02
☐	34 Darryl Strawberry	.40	.20	.04
☐	35 Ryne Sandberg	.30	.15	.03
☐	36 Andre Dawson	.25	.12	.02
☐	37 Ozzie Smith	.25	.12	.02
☐	38 Eric Davis	.50	.25	.05
☐	39 Mike Schmidt	.60	.30	.06
☐	40 Mike Scott	.20	.10	.02
☐	41 Gary Carter	.20	.10	.02
☐	42 Davey Johnson MG	.10	.05	.01
☐	43 Rick Sutcliffe	.10	.05	.01
☐	44 Willie McGee	.15	.07	.01
☐	45 Hubie Brooks	.10	.05	.01
☐	46 Dale Murphy	.30	.15	.03
☐	47 Bo Diaz	.10	.05	.01
☐	48 Pedro Guerrero	.20	.10	.02
☐	49 Keith Hernandez	.20	.10	.02
☐	50 Ozzie Virgil UER	.10	.05	.01
	(Phillies logo			
	on card back,			
	wrong birth year)			
☐	51 Tony Gwynn	.35	.17	.03
☐	52 Rick Reuschel UER	.10	.05	.01
	(Pirates logo			
	on card back)			
☐	53 John Franco	.15	.07	.01
☐	54 Jeffrey Leonard	.10	.05	.01
☐	55 Juan Samuel	.15	.07	.01
☐	56 Orel Hershiser	.50	.25	.05
☐	57 Tim Raines	.25	.12	.02
☐	58 Sid Fernandez	.15	.07	.01
☐	59 Tim Wallach	.10	.05	.01
☐	60 Lee Smith	.10	.05	.01
☐	61 Steve Bedrosian	.10	.05	.01
☐	62 Tim Raines	.25	.12	.02
☐	63 Ozzie Smith	.20	.10	.02
☐	64 NL Checklist	.10	.05	.01

1988 Donruss Pop-Ups

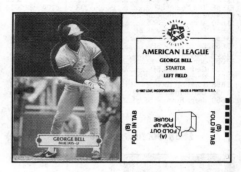

This 20-card set features "fold-out" cards measuring standard size, 2 1/2" by 3 1/2". Card fronts are in full color. Cards are unnumbered but are listed in the same order as the Donruss All-Stars on the All-Star checklist card. Card backs present essentially no information about the player. The set was distributed in packs which also contained All-Star cards. In order to remain in mint condition, the cards should not be popped up.

		MINT	EXC	G-VG
COMPLETE SET (20)		4.00	2.00	.40
COMMON PLAYER (1-20)		.10	.05	.01

		MINT	EXC	G-VG
☐	1 Don Mattingly	.75	.35	.07
☐	2 Dave Winfield	.25	.12	.02
☐	3 Willie Randolph	.15	.07	.01
☐	4 Rickey Henderson	.40	.20	.04
☐	5 Cal Ripken	.30	.15	.03
☐	6 George Bell	.20	.10	.02
☐	7 Wade Boggs	.75	.35	.07
☐	8 Bret Saberhagen	.30	.15	.03
☐	9 Terry Kennedy	.10	.05	.01
☐	10 John McNamara MG	.10	.05	.01
☐	11 Jack Clark	.20	.10	.02
☐	12 Darryl Strawberry	.40	.20	.04
☐	13 Ryne Sandberg	.30	.15	.03
☐	14 Andre Dawson	.25	.12	.02
☐	15 Ozzie Smith	.25	.12	.02
☐	16 Eric Davis	.50	.25	.05
☐	17 Mike Schmidt	.60	.30	.06
☐	18 Mike Scott	.20	.10	.02
☐	19 Gary Carter	.20	.10	.02
☐	20 Davey Johnson MG	.10	.05	.01

1988 Donruss Rookies

The 1988 Donruss "The Rookies" set features 56 cards plus a 15-piece puzzle of Stan Musial. Cards are in full color and are standard size, 2 1/2" by 3 1/2". The set was distributed in a small green and black box with gold lettering. Card fronts are similar in design to the 1988 Donruss regular issue except for the presence of "The Rookies" logo in the lower right corner and a green and black border instead of a blue and black border on the fronts.

		MINT	EXC	G-VG
COMPLETE SET (56)		13.00	6.50	1.30
COMMON PLAYER (1-56)		.06	.03	.00

		MINT	EXC	G-VG
☐	1 Mark Grace	4.00	1.00	.20
☐	2 Mike Campbell	.10	.05	.01
☐	3 Todd Frohwirth	.10	.05	.01
☐	4 Dave Stapleton	.06	.03	.00
☐	5 Shawn Abner	.10	.05	.01

☐	6	Jose Cecena	.10	.05	.01
☐	7	Dave Gallagher	.35	.17	.03
☐	8	Mark Parent	.15	.07	.01
☐	9	Cecil Espy	.15	.07	.01
☐	10	Pete Smith	.10	.05	.01
☐	11	Jay Buhner	.20	.10	.02
☐	12	Pat Borders	.25	.12	.02
☐	13	Doug Jennings	.25	.12	.02
☐	14	Brady Anderson	.35	.17	.03
☐	15	Pete Stanicek	.10	.05	.01
☐	16	Roberto Kelly	.40	.20	.04
☐	17	Jeff Treadway	.10	.05	.01
☐	18	Walt Weiss	1.25	.60	.12
☐	19	Paul Gibson	.10	.05	.01
☐	20	Tim Crews	.06	.03	.00
☐	21	Melido Perez	.15	.07	.01
☐	22	Steve Peters	.15	.07	.01
☐	23	Craig Worthington	.50	.25	.05
☐	24	John Trautwein	.15	.07	.01
☐	25	DeWayne Vaughn	.10	.05	.01
☐	26	David Wells	.10	.05	.01
☐	27	Al Leiter	.15	.07	.01
☐	28	Tim Belcher	.25	.12	.02
☐	29	Johnny Paredes	.15	.07	.01
☐	30	Chris Sabo	1.25	.60	.12
☐	31	Damon Berryhill	.25	.12	.02
☐	32	Randy Milligan	.20	.10	.02
☐	33	Gary Thurman	.15	.07	.01
☐	34	Kevin Elster	.20	.10	.02
☐	35	Roberto Alomar	.30	.15	.03
☐	36	Edgar Martinez UER (photo actually Edwin Nunez)	.25	.12	.02
☐	37	Todd Stottlemyre	.15	.07	.01
☐	38	Joey Meyer	.10	.05	.01
☐	39	Carl Nichols	.06	.03	.00
☐	40	Jack McDowell	.10	.05	.01
☐	41	Jose Bautista	.15	.07	.01
☐	42	Sil Campusano	.25	.12	.02
☐	43	John Dopson	.20	.10	.02
☐	44	Jody Reed	.15	.07	.01
☐	45	Darrin Jackson	.15	.07	.01
☐	46	Mike Capel	.12	.06	.01
☐	47	Ron Gant	.20	.10	.02
☐	48	John Davis	.06	.03	.00
☐	49	Kevin Coffman	.10	.05	.01
☐	50	Cris Carpenter	.25	.12	.02
☐	51	Mackey Sasser	.10	.05	.01
☐	52	Luis Alicea	.10	.05	.01
☐	53	Bryan Harvey	.25	.12	.02
☐	54	Steve Ellsworth	.15	.07	.01
☐	55	Mike Macfarlane	.20	.10	.02
☐	56	Checklist Card	.06	.01	.00

1988 Donruss Athletics Book

The 1988 Donruss Athletics Team Book set features 27 cards (three pages with nine cards on each page) plus a large full-page puzzle of Stan Musial. Cards are in full color and are standard size, 2 1/2" by 3 1/2". The set was distributed as a four-page book; although the puzzle page was perforated, the card pages were not. The cover of the "Team Collection" book is primarily bright red. Card fronts are very similar in design to the 1988 Donruss regular issue. The card numbers on the backs are the same for those players

that are the same as in the regular Donruss set; the new players pictured are numbered on the back as "NEW." The book is usually sold intact. When cut from the book into individual cards, these cards are distinguishable from the regular 1988 Donruss cards since these have a 1988 copyright on the back whereas the regular issue has a 1987 copyright on the back.

			MINT	EXC	G-VG
COMPLETE SET (27)			5.00	2.50	.50
COMMON PLAYER			.10	.05	.01
☐	97	Curt Young	.10	.05	.01
☐	133	Gene Nelson	.10	.05	.01
☐	158	Terry Steinbach	.25	.12	.02
☐	178	Carney Lansford	.25	.12	.02
☐	221	Tony Phillips	.10	.05	.01
☐	256	Mark McGwire	1.00	.50	.10
☐	302	Jose Canseco	1.50	.75	.15
☐	349	Dennis Eckersley	.35	.17	.03
☐	379	Mike Gallego	.10	.05	.01
☐	425	Luis Polonia	.10	.05	.01
☐	467	Steve Ontiveros	.10	.05	.01
☐	472	Dave Stewart	.35	.17	.03
☐	503	Eric Plunk	.10	.05	.01
☐	528	Greg Cadaret	.10	.05	.01
☐	590	Rick Honeycutt	.10	.05	.01
☐	595	Storm Davis	.20	.10	.02
☐	NEW	Don Baylor	.15	.07	.01
☐	NEW	Ron Hassey	.10	.05	.01
☐	NEW	Dave Henderson	.15	.07	.01
☐	NEW	Glenn Hubbard	.10	.05	.01
☐	NEW	Stan Javier	.10	.05	.01
☐	NEW	Doug Jennings	.25	.12	.02
☐	NEW	Edward Jurak	.10	.05	.01
☐	NEW	Dave Parker	.20	.10	.02
☐	NEW	Walt Weiss	.75	.35	.07
☐	NEW	Bob Welch	.15	.07	.01
☐	NEW	Matt Young	.10	.05	.01

1988 Donruss Cubs Team Book

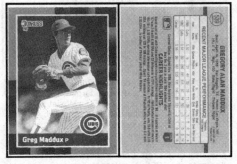

The 1988 Donruss Cubs Team Book set features 27 cards (three pages with nine cards on each page) plus a large full-page puzzle of Stan Musial. Cards are in full color and are standard size, 2 1/2" by 3 1/2". The set was distributed as a four-page book; although the puzzle page was perforated, the card pages were not. The cover of the "Team Collection" book is primarily bright red. Card fronts are very similar in design to the 1988 Donruss regular issue. The card numbers on the backs are the same for those players that are the same as in the regular Donruss set; the new players pictured are numbered on the back as "NEW." The book is usually sold intact. When cut from the book into individual cards, these cards are distinguishable from the regular 1988 Donruss cards since these have a 1988 copyright on the back whereas the regular issue has a 1987 copyright on the back.

		MINT	EXC	G-VG
COMPLETE SET (27)		5.00	2.50	.50
COMMON PLAYER		.10	.05	.01
☐ 40	Mark Grace	2.00	1.00	.20
☐ 68	Rick Sutcliffe	.20	.10	.02
☐ 119	Jody Davis	.15	.07	.01
☐ 146	Shawon Dunston	.25	.12	.02
☐ 169	Jamie Moyer	.15	.07	.01
☐ 191	Leon Durham	.15	.07	.01
☐ 242	Ryne Sandberg	.40	.20	.04
☐ 269	Andre Dawson	.40	.20	.04
☐ 315	Paul Noce	.15	.07	.01
☐ 324	Rafael Palmeiro	.60	.30	.06
☐ 438	Dave Martinez	.15	.07	.01
☐ 447	Jerry Mumphrey	.10	.05	.01
☐ 488	Jim Sundberg	.10	.05	.01
☐ 516	Manny Trillo	.10	.05	.01
☐ 539	Greg Maddux	.35	.17	.03
☐ 561	Les Lancaster	.10	.05	.01
☐ 570	Frank DiPino	.10	.05	.01
☐ 639	Damon Berryhill	.35	.17	.03
☐ 646	Scott Sanderson	.10	.05	.01
☐ NEW	Mike Bielecki	.20	.10	.02
☐ NEW	Rich Gossage	.15	.07	.01
☐ NEW	Drew Hall	.15	.07	.01
☐ NEW	Darrin Jackson	.20	.10	.02
☐ NEW	Vance Law	.10	.05	.01
☐ NEW	Al Nipper	.10	.05	.01
☐ NEW	Angel Salazar	.10	.05	.01
☐ NEW	Calvin Schiraldi	.10	.05	.01

1988 Donruss Mets Team Book

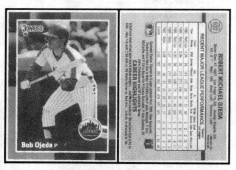

Bob Ojeda P

The 1988 Donruss Mets Team Book set features 27 cards (three pages with nine cards on each page) plus a large full-page puzzle of Stan Musial. Cards are in full color and are standard size, 2 1/2" by 3 1/2". The set was distributed as a four-page book; although the puzzle page was perforated, the card pages were not. The cover of the "Team Collection" book is primarily bright red. Card fronts are very similar in design to the 1988 Donruss regular issue. The card numbers on the backs are the same for those players that are the same as in the regular Donruss set; the new players pictured are numbered on the back as

"NEW." The book is usually sold intact. When cut from the book into individual cards, these cards are distinguishable from the regular 1988 Donruss cards since these have a 1988 copyright on the back whereas the regular issue has a 1987 copyright on the back.

		MINT	EXC	G-VG
COMPLETE SET (27)		5.00	2.50	.50
COMMON PLAYER		.10	.05	.01
☐ 37	Kevin Elster	.15	.07	.01
☐ 69	Dwight Gooden	.50	.25	.05
☐ 76	Ron Darling	.20	.10	.02
☐ 118	Sid Fernandez	.20	.10	.02
☐ 199	Gary Carter	.25	.12	.02
☐ 241	Wally Backman	.10	.05	.01
☐ 316	Keith Hernandez	.25	.12	.02
☐ 323	Dave Magadan	.20	.10	.02
☐ 364	Lee Dykstra	.15	.07	.01
☐ 439	Darryl Strawberry	.75	.35	.07
☐ 446	Rick Aguilera	.15	.07	.01
☐ 562	Keith Miller	.15	.07	.01
☐ 569	Howard Johnson	.30	.15	.03
☐ 603	Terry Leach	.15	.07	.01
☐ 614	Lee Mazzilli	.10	.05	.01
☐ 617	Kevin McReynolds	.25	.12	.02
☐ 619	Barry Lyons	.10	.05	.01
☐ 620	Randy Myers	.20	.10	.02
☐ 632	Bob Ojeda	.15	.07	.01
☐ 648	Tim Teufel	.10	.05	.01
☐ 651	Roger McDowell	.15	.07	.01
☐ 652	Mookie Wilson	.15	.07	.01
☐ 653	David Cone	.40	.20	.04
☐ 657	Greg Jefferies	1.25	.60	.12
☐ NEW	Jeff Innis	.20	.10	.02
☐ NEW	Mackey Sasser	.15	.07	.01
☐ NEW	Gene Walter	.10	.05	.01

1988 Donruss Red Sox Team Book

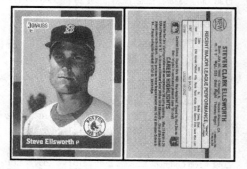

Steve Ellsworth P

The 1988 Donruss Red Sox Team Book set features 27 cards (three pages with nine cards on each page) plus a large full-page puzzle of Stan Musial. Cards are in full color and are standard size, 2 1/2" by 3 1/2". The set was distributed as a four-page book; although the puzzle page was perforated, the card pages were not. The cover of the "Team Collection" book is primarily bright red. Card fronts are very similar in design to the 1988 Donruss regular issue. The card numbers on the backs are the same for those players that are the same as in the regular Donruss set; the new players pictured are numbered on the back as "NEW." The book is usually sold intact. When cut from the book into individual cards, these cards are distinguishable from the regular 1988 Donruss cards since these have a 1988 copyright on the back whereas the regular issue has a 1987 copyright on the back.

	MINT	EXC	G-VG
COMPLETE SET (27)	5.00	2.50	.50
COMMON PLAYER	.10	.05	.01

☐ 41	Jody Reed	.20	.10	.02
☐ 51	Roger Clemens	.60	.30	.06
☐ 92	Bob Stanley	.10	.05	.01
☐ 129	Rich Gedman	.10	.05	.01
☐ 153	Wade Boggs	1.00	.50	.10
☐ 174	Ellis Burks	1.00	.50	.10
☐ 216	Dwight Evans	.20	.10	.02
☐ 252	Bruce Hurst	.25	.12	.02
☐ 276	Marty Barrett	.15	.07	.01
☐ 297	Todd Benzinger	.20	.10	.02
☐ 339	Mike Greenwell	1.25	.60	.12
☐ 399	Jim Rice	.25	.12	.02
☐ 421	John Marzano	.10	.05	.01
☐ 462	Oil Can Boyd	.15	.07	.01
☐ 498	Sam Horn	.15	.07	.01
☐ 544	Spike Owen	.10	.05	.01
☐ 585	Jeff Sellers	.10	.05	.01
☐ 623	Ed Romero	.10	.05	.01
☐ 634	Wes Gardner	.15	.07	.01
☐ NEW	Brady Anderson	.25	.12	.02
☐ NEW	Rick Cerone	.10	.05	.01
☐ NEW	Steve Ellsworth	.15	.07	.01
☐ NEW	Dennis Lamp	.10	.05	.01
☐ NEW	Kevin Romine	.10	.05	.01
☐ NEW	Lee Smith	.15	.07	.01
☐ NEW	Mike Smithson	.10	.05	.01
☐ NEW	John Trautwein	.15	.07	.01

1988 Donruss Yankees Team Book

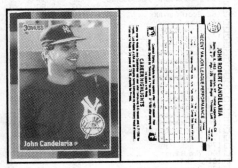

John Candelaria P

The 1988 Donruss Yankees Team Book set features 27 cards (three pages with nine cards on each page) plus a large full-page puzzle of Stan Musial. Cards are in full color and are standard size, 2 1/2" by 3 1/2". The set was distributed as a four-page book; although the puzzle page was perforated, the card pages were not. The cover of the "Team Collection" book is primarily bright red. Card fronts are very similar in design to the 1988 Donruss regular issue. The card numbers on the backs are the same for those players that are the same as in the regular Donruss set; the new players pictured are numbered on the back as "NEW." The book is usually kept intact. When cut from the book into individual cards, these cards are distinguishable from the regular 1988 Donruss cards since these have a 1988 copyright on the back whereas the regular issue has a 1987 copyright on the back.

	MINT	EXC	G-VG
COMPLETE SET (27)	5.00	2.50	.50
COMMON PLAYER	.10	.05	.01

☐ 43	Al Leiter	.15	.07	.01
☐ 93	Dave Righetti	.20	.10	.02
☐ 105	Mike Pagliarulo	.15	.07	.01
☐ 128	Rick Rhoden	.10	.05	.01
☐ 175	Ron Guidry	.25	.12	.02
☐ 217	Don Mattingly	1.50	.75	.15
☐ 228	Willie Randolph	.20	.10	.02
☐ 251	Gary Ward	.10	.05	.01
☐ 277	Rickey Henderson	.60	.30	.06
☐ 278	Dave Winfield	.35	.17	.03
☐ 340	Claudell Washington	.15	.07	.01

☐ 374	Charles Hudson	.10	.05	.01
☐ 401	Tommy John	.20	.10	.02
☐ 474	Joel Skinner	.10	.05	.01
☐ 497	Tim Stoddard	.10	.05	.01
☐ 545	Jay Buhner	.25	.12	.02
☐ 616	Bobby Meacham	.10	.05	.01
☐ 635	Roberto Kelly	.50	.25	.05
☐ NEW	John Candelaria	.15	.07	.01
☐ NEW	Jack Clark	.25	.12	.02
☐ NEW	Jose Cruz	.15	.07	.01
☐ NEW	Richard Dotson	.15	.07	.01
☐ NEW	Cecilo Guante	.10	.05	.01
☐ NEW	Lee Guetterman	.15	.07	.01
☐ NEW	Rafael Santana	.10	.05	.01
☐ NEW	Steve Shields	.10	.05	.01
☐ NEW	Don Slaught	.10	.05	.01

1988 Donruss Baseball's Best

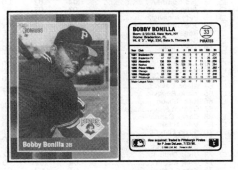

Bobby Bonilla 3B

This innovative set of 336 cards was released by Donruss very late in the 1988 season to be sold in large national retail chains as a complete packaged set. Cards are the standard size, 2 1/2" by 3 1/2", and are packaged as a complete set in a specially designed box. Cards are very similar in design to the 1988 regular Donruss issue except that these cards have orange and black borders instead of blue and black borders. Six (2 1/2" by 3 1/2") 15-piece puzzles of Stan Musial are also included with every complete set.

	MINT	EXC	G-VG
COMPLETE SET (336)	20.00	10.00	2.00
COMMON PLAYER (1-336)	.04	.02	.00

☐ 1	Don Mattingly	1.00	.50	.10
☐ 2	Ron Gant	.35	.17	.03
☐ 3	Bob Boone	.10	.05	.01
☐ 4	Mark Grace	1.25	.60	.12
☐ 5	Andy Allanson	.04	.02	.00
☐ 6	Kal Daniels	.10	.05	.01
☐ 7	Floyd Bannister	.04	.02	.00
☐ 8	Alan Ashby	.04	.02	.00
☐ 9	Marty Barrett	.07	.03	.01
☐ 10	Tim Belcher	.15	.07	.01
☐ 11	Harold Baines	.10	.05	.01
☐ 12	Hubie Brooks	.07	.03	.01
☐ 13	Doyle Alexander	.04	.02	.00
☐ 14	Gary Carter	.20	.10	.02
☐ 15	Glenn Braggs	.10	.05	.01
☐ 16	Steve Bedrosian	.10	.05	.01
☐ 17	Barry Bonds	.20	.10	.02
☐ 18	Bert Blyleven	.10	.05	.01
☐ 19	Tom Brunansky	.10	.05	.01
☐ 20	John Candelaria	.04	.02	.00
☐ 21	Shawn Abner	.10	.05	.01
☐ 22	Jose Canseco	1.25	.60	.12
☐ 23	Brett Butler	.07	.03	.01
☐ 24	Scott Bradley	.04	.02	.00
☐ 25	Ivan Calderon	.07	.03	.01
☐ 26	Rich Gossage	.10	.05	.01
☐ 27	Brian Downing	.04	.02	.00
☐ 28	Jim Rice	.15	.07	.01
☐ 29	Dion James	.04	.02	.00
☐ 30	Terry Kennedy	.04	.02	.00
☐ 31	George Bell	.15	.07	.01
☐ 32	Scott Fletcher	.04	.02	.00

☐ 33	Bobby Bonilla	.15	.07	.01
☐ 34	Tim Burke	.04	.02	.00
☐ 35	Darrell Evans	.07	.03	.01
☐ 36	Mike Davis	.04	.02	.00
☐ 37	Shawon Dunston	.10	.05	.01
☐ 38	Kevin Bass	.07	.03	.01
☐ 39	George Brett	.25	.12	.02
☐ 40	David Cone	.30	.15	.03
☐ 41	Ron Darling	.10	.05	.01
☐ 42	Roberto Alomar	.35	.17	.03
☐ 43	Dennis Eckersley	.15	.07	.01
☐ 44	Vince Coleman	.20	.10	.02
☐ 45	Sid Bream	.04	.02	.00
☐ 46	Gary Gaetti	.15	.07	.01
☐ 47	Phil Bradley	.07	.03	.01
☐ 48	Jim Clancy	.04	.02	.00
☐ 49	Jack Clark	.15	.07	.01
☐ 50	Mike Krukow	.04	.02	.00
☐ 51	Henry Cotto	.04	.02	.00
☐ 52	Rich Dotson	.04	.02	.00
☐ 53	Jim Gantner	.04	.02	.00
☐ 54	John Franco	.07	.03	.01
☐ 55	Pete Incaviglia	.15	.07	.01
☐ 56	Joe Carter	.15	.07	.01
☐ 57	Roger Clemens	.50	.25	.05
☐ 58	Gerald Perry	.04	.02	.00
☐ 59	Jack Howell	.04	.02	.00
☐ 60	Vance Law	.04	.02	.00
☐ 61	Jay Bell	.04	.02	.00
☐ 62	Eric Davis	.50	.25	.05
☐ 63	Gene Garber	.04	.02	.00
☐ 64	Glenn Davis	.15	.07	.01
☐ 65	Wade Boggs	.75	.35	.07
☐ 66	Kirk Gibson	.20	.10	.02
☐ 67	Carlton Fisk	.20	.10	.02
☐ 68	Casey Candaele	.04	.02	.00
☐ 69	Mike Heath	.04	.02	.00
☐ 70	Kevin Elster	.10	.05	.01
☐ 71	Greg Brock	.04	.02	.00
☐ 72	Don Carman	.04	.02	.00
☐ 73	Doug Drabek	.07	.03	.01
☐ 74	Greg Gagne	.04	.02	.00
☐ 75	Danny Cox	.07	.03	.01
☐ 76	Rickey Henderson	.35	.17	.03
☐ 77	Chris Brown	.04	.02	.00
☐ 78	Terry Steinbach	.10	.05	.01
☐ 79	Will Clark	1.25	.60	.12
☐ 80	Mickey Brantley	.07	.03	.01
☐ 81	Ozzie Guillen	.10	.05	.01
☐ 82	Greg Maddux	.15	.07	.01
☐ 83	Kirk McCaskill	.04	.02	.00
☐ 84	Dwight Evans	.15	.07	.01
☐ 85	Ozzie Virgil	.04	.02	.00
☐ 86	Mike Morgan	.07	.03	.01
☐ 87	Tony Fernandez	.10	.05	.01
☐ 88	Jose Guzman	.04	.02	.00
☐ 89	Mike Dunne	.07	.03	.01
☐ 90	Andres Galarraga	.25	.12	.02
☐ 91	Mike Henneman	.07	.03	.01
☐ 92	Alfredo Griffin	.04	.02	.00
☐ 93	Rafael Palmeiro	.20	.10	.02
☐ 94	Jim Deshaies	.04	.02	.00
☐ 95	Mark Gubicza	.10	.05	.01
☐ 96	Dwight Gooden	.50	.25	.05
☐ 97	Howard Johnson	.20	.10	.02
☐ 98	Mark Davis	.20	.10	.02
☐ 99	Dave Stewart	.20	.10	.02
☐ 100	Joe Magrane	.15	.07	.01
☐ 101	Brian Fisher	.04	.02	.00
☐ 102	Kent Hrbek	.15	.07	.01
☐ 103	Kevin Gross	.04	.02	.00
☐ 104	Tom Henke	.07	.03	.01
☐ 105	Mike Pagliarulo	.07	.03	.01
☐ 106	Kelly Downs	.04	.02	.00
☐ 107	Alvin Davis	.10	.05	.01
☐ 108	Willie Randolph	.10	.05	.01
☐ 109	Rob Deer	.10	.05	.01
☐ 110	Bo Diaz	.04	.02	.00
☐ 111	Paul Kilgus	.04	.02	.00
☐ 112	Tom Candiotti	.04	.02	.00
☐ 113	Dale Murphy	.30	.15	.03
☐ 114	Rick Mahler	.04	.02	.00
☐ 115	Wally Joyner	.40	.20	.04
☐ 116	Ryne Sandberg	.30	.15	.03
☐ 117	John Farrell	.10	.05	.01
☐ 118	Nick Esasky	.10	.05	.01
☐ 119	Bo Jackson	1.25	.60	.12
☐ 120	Bill Doran	.07	.03	.01
☐ 121	Ellis Burks	.75	.35	.07
☐ 122	Pedro Guerrero	.15	.07	.01
☐ 123	Dave LaPoint	.07	.03	.01
☐ 124	Neal Heaton	.04	.02	.00
☐ 125	Willie Hernandez	.07	.03	.01
☐ 126	Roger McDowell	.07	.03	.01
☐ 127	Ted Higuera	.07	.03	.01
☐ 128	Von Hayes	.10	.05	.01
☐ 129	Mike LaValliere	.04	.02	.00
☐ 130	Dan Gladden	.04	.02	.00
☐ 131	Willie McGee	.10	.05	.01
☐ 132	Al Leiter	.10	.05	.01
☐ 133	Mark Grant	.04	.02	.00
☐ 134	Bob Welch	.07	.03	.01
☐ 135	Dave Dravecky	.10	.05	.01
☐ 136	Mark Langston	.20	.10	.02
☐ 137	Dan Pasqua	.07	.03	.01
☐ 138	Rick Sutcliffe	.10	.05	.01
☐ 139	Dan Petry	.04	.02	.00
☐ 140	Rich Gedman	.07	.03	.01
☐ 141	Ken Griffey Sr.	.10	.05	.01
☐ 142	Eddie Murray	.20	.10	.02
☐ 143	Jimmy Key	.07	.03	.01
☐ 144	Dale Mohorcic	.04	.02	.00
☐ 145	Jose Lind	.07	.03	.01
☐ 146	Dennis Martinez	.07	.03	.01
☐ 147	Chet Lemon	.04	.02	.00
☐ 148	Orel Hershiser	.35	.17	.03
☐ 149	Dave Martinez	.04	.02	.00
☐ 150	Billy Hatcher	.07	.03	.01
☐ 151	Charlie Leibrandt	.04	.02	.00
☐ 152	Keith Hernandez	.15	.07	.01
☐ 153	Kevin McReynolds	.20	.10	.02
☐ 154	Tony Gwynn	.35	.17	.03
☐ 155	Stan Javier	.04	.02	.00
☐ 156	Tony Pena	.04	.02	.00
☐ 157	Andy Van Slyke	.10	.05	.01
☐ 158	Gene Larkin	.07	.03	.01
☐ 159	Chris James	.07	.03	.01
☐ 160	Fred McGriff	.35	.17	.03
☐ 161	Rick Rhoden	.07	.03	.01
☐ 162	Scott Garrelts	.07	.03	.01
☐ 163	Mike Campbell	.07	.03	.01
☐ 164	Dave Righetti	.10	.05	.01
☐ 165	Paul Molitor	.15	.07	.01
☐ 166	Danny Jackson	.10	.05	.01
☐ 167	Pete O'Brien	.10	.05	.01
☐ 168	Julio Franco	.15	.07	.01
☐ 169	Mark McGwire	.75	.35	.07
☐ 170	Zane Smith	.07	.03	.01
☐ 171	Johnny Ray	.07	.03	.01
☐ 172	Lester Lancaster	.07	.03	.01
☐ 173	Mel Hall	.10	.05	.01
☐ 174	Tracy Jones	.07	.03	.01
☐ 175	Kevin Seitzer	.35	.17	.03
☐ 176	Bob Knepper	.04	.02	.00
☐ 177	Mike Greenwell	1.25	.60	.12
☐ 178	Mike Marshall	.10	.05	.01
☐ 179	Melido Perez	.15	.07	.01
☐ 180	Tim Raines	.20	.10	.02
☐ 181	Jack Morris	.10	.05	.01
☐ 182	Darryl Strawberry	.50	.25	.05
☐ 183	Robin Yount	.35	.17	.03
☐ 184	Lance Parrish	.10	.05	.01
☐ 185	Darnell Coles	.04	.02	.00
☐ 186	Kirby Puckett	.50	.25	.05
☐ 187	Terry Pendleton	.04	.02	.00
☐ 188	Don Slaught	.04	.02	.00
☐ 189	Jimmy Jones	.07	.03	.01
☐ 190	Dave Parker	.15	.07	.01
☐ 191	Mike Aldrete	.04	.02	.00
☐ 192	Mike Moore	.07	.03	.01
☐ 193	Greg Walker	.07	.03	.01
☐ 194	Calvin Schiraldi	.04	.02	.00
☐ 195	Dick Schofield	.04	.02	.00
☐ 196	Jody Reed	.10	.05	.01
☐ 197	Pete Smith	.07	.03	.01
☐ 198	Cal Ripken	.25	.12	.02
☐ 199	Lloyd Moseby	.10	.05	.01
☐ 200	Ruben Sierra	.35	.17	.03
☐ 201	R.J. Reynolds	.04	.02	.00
☐ 202	Bryn Smith	.07	.03	.01
☐ 203	Gary Pettis	.04	.02	.00
☐ 204	Steve Sax	.15	.07	.01
☐ 205	Frank DiPino	.04	.02	.00
☐ 206	Mike Scott	.15	.07	.01
☐ 207	Kurt Stillwell	.07	.03	.01
☐ 208	Mookie Wilson	.07	.03	.01
☐ 209	Lee Mazzilli	.04	.02	.00
☐ 210	Lance McCullers	.07	.03	.01
☐ 211	Rick Honeycutt	.04	.02	.00
☐ 212	John Tudor	.10	.05	.01
☐ 213	Jim Gott	.04	.02	.00
☐ 214	Frank Viola	.15	.07	.01
☐ 215	Juan Samuel	.10	.05	.01
☐ 216	Jesse Barfield	.15	.07	.01
☐ 217	Claudell Washington	.07	.03	.01
☐ 218	Rick Reuschel	.10	.05	.01
☐ 219	Jim Presley	.07	.03	.01
☐ 220	Tommy John	.15	.07	.01
☐ 221	Dan Plesac	.07	.03	.01
☐ 222	Barry Larkin	.20	.10	.02

☐ 223	Mike Stanley	.04	.02	.00
☐ 224	Cory Snyder	.15	.07	.01
☐ 225	Andre Dawson	.20	.10	.02
☐ 226	Ken Oberkfell	.04	.02	.00
☐ 227	Devon White	.15	.07	.01
☐ 228	Jamie Moyer	.07	.03	.01
☐ 229	Brook Jacoby	.07	.03	.01
☐ 230	Rob Murphy	.07	.03	.01
☐ 231	Bret Saberhagen	.25	.12	.02
☐ 232	Nolan Ryan	.60	.30	.06
☐ 233	Bruce Hurst	.10	.05	.01
☐ 234	Jesse Orosco	.04	.02	.00
☐ 235	Bobby Thigpen	.07	.03	.01
☐ 236	Pascual Perez	.07	.03	.01
☐ 237	Matt Nokes	.10	.05	.01
☐ 238	Bob Ojeda	.07	.03	.01
☐ 239	Joey Meyer	.07	.03	.01
☐ 240	Shane Rawley	.04	.02	.00
☐ 241	Jeff Robinson	.07	.03	.01
☐ 242	Jeff Reardon	.10	.05	.01
☐ 243	Ozzie Smith	.15	.07	.01
☐ 244	Dave Winfield	.20	.10	.02
☐ 245	John Kruk	.10	.05	.01
☐ 246	Carney Lansford	.15	.07	.01
☐ 247	Candy Maldonado	.07	.03	.01
☐ 248	Ken Phelps	.07	.03	.01
☐ 249	Ken Williams	.07	.03	.01
☐ 250	Al Nipper	.04	.02	.00
☐ 251	Mark McLemore	.04	.02	.00
☐ 252	Lee Smith	.07	.03	.01
☐ 253	Albert Hall	.04	.02	.00
☐ 254	Billy Ripken	.07	.03	.01
☐ 255	Kelly Gruber	.07	.03	.01
☐ 256	Charlie Hough	.04	.02	.00
☐ 257	John Smiley	.07	.03	.01
☐ 258	Tim Wallach	.10	.05	.01
☐ 259	Frank Tanana	.07	.03	.01
☐ 260	Mike Scioscia	.04	.02	.00
☐ 261	Damon Berryhill	.15	.07	.01
☐ 262	Dave Smith	.04	.02	.00
☐ 263	Willie Wilson	.07	.03	.01
☐ 264	Len Dykstra	.07	.03	.01
☐ 265	Randy Myers	.07	.03	.01
☐ 266	Keith Moreland	.04	.02	.00
☐ 267	Eric Plunk	.04	.02	.00
☐ 268	Todd Worrell	.10	.05	.01
☐ 269	Bob Walk	.04	.02	.00
☐ 270	Keith Atherton	.04	.02	.00
☐ 271	Mike Schmidt	.50	.25	.05
☐ 272	Mike Flanagan	.04	.02	.00
☐ 273	Rafael Santana	.04	.02	.00
☐ 274	Rob Thompson	.07	.03	.01
☐ 275	Rey Quinones	.04	.02	.00
☐ 276	Cecilio Guante	.04	.02	.00
☐ 277	B.J. Surhoff	.10	.05	.01
☐ 278	Chris Sabo	.45	.22	.04
☐ 279	Mitch Williams	.10	.05	.01
☐ 280	Greg Swindell	.10	.05	.01
☐ 281	Alan Trammell	.15	.07	.01
☐ 282	Storm Davis	.10	.05	.01
☐ 283	Chuck Finley	.07	.03	.01
☐ 284	Dave Stieb	.10	.05	.01
☐ 285	Scott Bailes	.04	.02	.00
☐ 286	Larry Sheets	.07	.03	.01
☐ 287	Danny Tartabull	.15	.07	.01
☐ 288	Checklist Card	.04	.02	.00
☐ 289	Todd Benzinger	.10	.05	.01
☐ 290	John Shelby	.04	.02	.00
☐ 291	Steve Lyons	.04	.02	.00
☐ 292	Mitch Webster	.04	.02	.00
☐ 293	Walt Terrell	.04	.02	.00
☐ 294	Pete Stanicek	.04	.02	.00
☐ 295	Chris Bosio	.07	.03	.01
☐ 296	Milt Thompson	.04	.02	.00
☐ 297	Fred Lynn	.10	.05	.01
☐ 298	Juan Berenguer	.04	.02	.00
☐ 299	Ken Dayley	.04	.02	.00
☐ 300	Joel Skinner	.04	.02	.00
☐ 301	Benito Santiago	.35	.17	.03
☐ 302	Ron Hassey	.04	.02	.00
☐ 303	Jose Uribe	.04	.02	.00
☐ 304	Harold Reynolds	.07	.03	.01
☐ 305	Dale Sveum	.04	.02	.00
☐ 306	Glenn Wilson	.04	.02	.00
☐ 307	Mike Witt	.07	.03	.01
☐ 308	Ron Robinson	.04	.02	.00
☐ 309	Denny Walling	.04	.02	.00
☐ 310	Joe Orsulak	.04	.02	.00
☐ 311	David Wells	.04	.02	.00
☐ 312	Steve Buechele	.04	.02	.00
☐ 313	Jose Oquendo	.04	.02	.00
☐ 314	Floyd Youmans	.04	.02	.00
☐ 315	Lou Whitaker	.10	.05	.01
☐ 316	Fernando Valenzuela	.15	.07	.01
☐ 317	Mike Boddicker	.07	.03	.01
☐ 318	Gerald Young	.07	.03	.01
☐ 319	Frank White	.07	.03	.01
☐ 320	Bill Wegman	.04	.02	.00
☐ 321	Tom Niedenfuer	.04	.02	.00
☐ 322	Ed Whitson	.04	.02	.00
☐ 323	Curt Young	.04	.02	.00
☐ 324	Greg Mathews	.04	.02	.00
☐ 325	Doug Jones	.10	.05	.01
☐ 326	Tommy Herr	.07	.03	.01
☐ 327	Kent Tekulve	.04	.02	.00
☐ 328	Rance Mulliniks	.04	.02	.00
☐ 329	Checklist Card	.04	.02	.00
☐ 330	Craig Lefferts	.04	.02	.00
☐ 331	Franklin Stubbs	.04	.02	.00
☐ 332	Rick Cerone	.04	.02	.00
☐ 333	Dave Schmidt	.04	.02	.00
☐ 334	Larry Parrish	.04	.02	.00
☐ 335	Tom Browning	.10	.05	.01
☐ 336	Checklist Card	.04	.02	.00

1989 Donruss

This 660-card set was distributed along with a puzzle of Warren Spahn. The six regular checklist cards are numbered throughout the set as multiples of 100. Cards measure 2 1/2" by 3 1/2" and feature a distinctive black side border with an alternating coating. The popular Diamond King subset returns for the eighth consecutive year. Rated Rookies are featured again as cards 28-47. The Donruss '89 logo appears in the lower left corner of every obverse. There are two variations which occur throughout most of the set. On the card backs "Denotes Led League" can be found with one asterisk to the left or with an asterisk on each side. On the card fronts the horizontal lines on the left and right borders can be glossy or non-glossy. Since both of these variation types are relatively minor and seem equally common, there is no premium value for either type. Rather than short-printing 26 cards in order to make room for printing the Bonus MVP's this year, Donruss apparently chose to double print 106 cards. These double prints are listed below by DP.

		MINT	EXC	G-VG
COMPLETE SET (660)		25.00	12.50	2.50
COMMON PLAYER (1-660)		.03	.01	.00
☐	1 Mike Greenwell DK	.50	.10	.02
☐	2 Bobby Bonilla DK DP	.08	.04	.01
☐	3 Pete Incaviglia DK	.08	.04	.01
☐	4 Chris Sabo DK DP	.12	.06	.01
☐	5 Robin Yount DK	.15	.06	.01
☐	6 Tony Gwynn DK DP	.15	.06	.01
☐	7 Carlton Fisk DK	.12	.06	.01
	(OF on back)			
☐	8 Cory Snyder DK	.10	.05	.01
☐	9 David Cone DK UER	.15	.06	.01
	(sic, "hurdlers")			
☐	10 Kevin Seitzer DK	.12	.06	.01
☐	11 Rick Reuschel DK	.08	.04	.01
☐	12 Johnny Ray DK	.08	.04	.01
☐	13 Dave Schmidt DK	.06	.03	.00
☐	14 Andres Galarraga DK	.10	.05	.01

☐	15	Kirk Gibson DK	.12	.06	.01	☐	105	Ryne Sandberg	.15	.07	.01
☐	16	Fred McGriff DK	.15	.07	.01	☐	106	Dennis Martinez	.06	.03	.00
☐	17	Mark Grace DK	.75	.35	.07	☐	107	Pete O'Brien	.06	.03	.00
☐	18	Jeff Robinson DT DK	.08	.04	.01	☐	108	Dick Schofield	.03	.01	.00
☐	19	Vince Coleman DK DP	.08	.04	.01	☐	109	Henry Cotto	.03	.01	.00
☐	20	Dave Henderson DK	.06	.03	.00	☐	110	Mike Marshall	.08	.04	.01
☐	21	Harold Reynolds DK	.06	.03	.00	☐	111	Keith Moreland	.03	.01	.00
☐	22	Gerald Perry DK	.06	.03	.00	☐	112	Tom Brunansky	.08	.04	.01
☐	23	Frank Viola DK	.12	.06	.01	☐	113	Kelly Gruber UER	.06	.03	.00
☐	24	Steve Bedrosian DK	.08	.04	.01			(wrong birthdate)			
☐	25	Glenn Davis DK	.12	.06	.01	☐	114	Brook Jacoby	.06	.03	.00
☐	26	Don Mattingly DK UER	.60	.30	.06	☐	115	Keith Brown	.10	.05	.01
		(doesn't mention Don's				☐	116	Matt Nokes	.08	.04	.01
		previous DK in 1985)				☐	117	Keith Hernandez	.10	.05	.01
☐	27	DK Checklist DP	.06	.01	.00	☐	118	Bob Forsch	.03	.01	.00
☐	28	Sandy Alomar Jr. RR	1.25	.60	.12	☐	119	Bert Blyleven UER	.08	.04	.01
☐	29	Steve Searcy RR	.20	.10	.02			(... 3000 strikeouts in			
☐	30	Cameron Drew RR	.20	.10	.02			1987, should be 1986)			
☐	31	Gary Sheffield RR	1.50	.75	.15	☐	120	Willie Wilson	.06	.03	.00
☐	32	Erik Hanson RR	.20	.10	.02	☐	121	Tommy Gregg	.03	.01	.00
☐	33	Ken Griffey Jr. RR	3.75	1.85	.37	☐	122	Jim Rice	.10	.05	.01
☐	34	Greg Harris RR	.20	.10	.02	☐	123	Bob Knepper	.03	.01	.00
		San Diego Padres				☐	124	Danny Jackson	.06	.03	.00
☐	35	Gregg Jefferies RR	1.50	.75	.15	☐	125	Eric Plunk	.03	.01	.00
☐	36	Luis Medina RR	.25	.12	.02	☐	126	Brian Fisher	.03	.01	.00
☐	37	Carlos Quintana RR	.30	.15	.03	☐	127	Mike Pagliarulo	.06	.03	.00
☐	38	Felix Jose RR	.25	.12	.02	☐	128	Tony Gwynn	.20	.10	.02
☐	39	Cris Carpenter RR	.20	.10	.02	☐	129	Lance McCullers	.03	.01	.00
☐	40	Ron Jones RR	.30	.15	.03	☐	130	Andres Galarraga	.10	.05	.01
☐	41	Dave West RR	.35	.17	.03	☐	131	Jose Uribe	.03	.01	.00
☐	42	Randy Johnson RR	.25	.12	.02	☐	132	Kirk Gibson UER	.12	.06	.01
☐	43	Mike Harkey RR	.30	.15	.03			(wrong birthdate)			
☐	44	Pete Harnisch RR	.15	.07	.01	☐	133	David Palmer	.03	.01	.00
☐	45	Tom Gordon RR DP	1.00	.50	.10	☐	134	R.J. Reynolds	.03	.01	.00
☐	46	Gregg Olson RR DP	1.00	.50	.10	☐	135	Greg Walker	.06	.03	.00
☐	47	Alex Sanchez RR DP	.20	.10	.02	☐	136	Kirk McCaskill UER	.03	.01	.00
☐	48	Ruben Sierra	.25	.12	.02			(wrong birthdate)			
☐	49	Rafael Palmeiro	.10	.05	.01	☐	137	Shawon Dunston	.08	.04	.01
☐	50	Ron Gant	.10	.05	.01	☐	138	Andy Allanson	.03	.01	.00
☐	51	Cal Ripken	.15	.07	.01	☐	139	Rob Murphy	.03	.01	.00
☐	52	Wally Joyner	.15	.07	.01	☐	140	Mike Aldrete	.03	.01	.00
☐	53	Gary Carter	.12	.06	.01	☐	141	Terry Kennedy	.03	.01	.00
☐	54	Andy Van Slyke	.10	.05	.01	☐	142	Scott Fletcher	.03	.01	.00
☐	55	Robin Yount	.18	.09	.01	☐	143	Steve Balboni	.03	.01	.00
☐	56	Pete Incaviglia	.10	.05	.01	☐	144	Bret Saberhagen	.15	.07	.01
☐	57	Greg Brock	.03	.01	.00	☐	145	Ozzie Virgil	.03	.01	.00
☐	58	Melido Perez	.06	.03	.00	☐	146	Dale Sveum	.03	.01	.00
☐	59	Craig Lefferts	.06	.03	.00	☐	147	Darryl Strawberry	.40	.20	.04
☐	60	Gary Pettis	.03	.01	.00	☐	148	Harold Baines	.08	.04	.01
☐	61	Danny Tartabull	.10	.05	.01	☐	149	George Bell	.12	.06	.01
☐	62	Guillermo Hernandez	.06	.03	.00	☐	150	Dave Parker	.08	.04	.01
☐	63	Ozzie Smith	.12	.06	.01	☐	151	Bobby Bonilla	.10	.05	.01
☐	64	Gary Gaetti	.08	.04	.01	☐	152	Mookie Wilson	.06	.03	.00
☐	65	Mark Davis	.12	.06	.01	☐	153	Ted Power	.03	.01	.00
☐	66	Lee Smith	.06	.03	.00	☐	154	Nolan Ryan	.30	.15	.03
☐	67	Dennis Eckersley	.10	.05	.01	☐	155	Jeff Reardon	.06	.03	.00
☐	68	Wade Boggs	.50	.25	.05	☐	156	Tim Wallach	.06	.03	.00
☐	69	Mike Scott	.10	.05	.01	☐	157	Jamie Moyer	.03	.01	.00
☐	70	Fred McGriff	.18	.09	.01	☐	158	Rich Gossage	.08	.04	.01
☐	71	Tom Browning	.08	.04	.01	☐	159	Dave Winfield	.12	.06	.01
☐	72	Claudell Washington	.06	.03	.00	☐	160	Von Hayes	.08	.04	.01
☐	73	Mel Hall	.06	.03	.00	☐	161	Willie McGee	.08	.04	.01
☐	74	Don Mattingly	.85	.40	.08	☐	162	Rich Gedman	.03	.01	.00
☐	75	Steve Bedrosian	.08	.04	.01	☐	163	Tony Pena	.06	.03	.00
☐	76	Juan Samuel	.08	.04	.01	☐	164	Mike Morgan	.06	.03	.00
☐	77	Mike Scioscia	.03	.01	.00	☐	165	Charlie Hough	.03	.01	.00
☐	78	Dave Righetti	.08	.04	.01	☐	166	Mike Stanley	.03	.01	.00
☐	79	Alfredo Griffin	.03	.01	.00	☐	167	Andre Dawson	.12	.06	.01
☐	80	Eric Davis UER	.30	.15	.03	☐	168	Joe Boever	.08	.04	.01
		(165 games in 1988,				☐	169	Pete Stanicek	.03	.01	.00
		should be 135)				☐	170	Bob Boone	.08	.04	.01
☐	81	Juan Berenguer	.03	.01	.00	☐	171	Ron Darling	.08	.04	.01
☐	82	Todd Worrell	.08	.04	.01	☐	172	Bob Walk	.03	.01	.00
☐	83	Joe Carter	.12	.06	.01	☐	173	Rob Deer	.06	.03	.00
☐	84	Steve Sax	.10	.05	.01	☐	174	Steve Buechele	.03	.01	.00
☐	85	Frank White	.06	.03	.00	☐	175	Ted Higuera	.06	.03	.00
☐	86	John Kruk	.06	.03	.00	☐	176	Ozzie Guillen	.06	.03	.00
☐	87	Rance Mulliniks	.03	.01	.00	☐	177	Candy Maldonado	.03	.01	.00
☐	88	Alan Ashby	.03	.01	.00	☐	178	Doyle Alexander	.03	.01	.00
☐	89	Charlie Leibrandt	.03	.01	.00	☐	179	Mark Gubicza	.08	.04	.01
☐	90	Frank Tanana	.03	.01	.00	☐	180	Alan Trammell	.12	.06	.01
☐	91	Jose Canseco	1.00	.50	.10	☐	181	Vince Coleman	.10	.05	.01
☐	92	Barry Bonds	.08	.04	.01	☐	182	Kirby Puckett	.30	.15	.03
☐	93	Harold Reynolds	.06	.03	.00	☐	183	Chris Brown	.03	.01	.00
☐	94	Mark McLemore	.03	.01	.00	☐	184	Marty Barrett	.03	.01	.00
☐	95	Mark McGwire	.50	.25	.05	☐	185	Stan Javier	.03	.01	.00
☐	96	Eddie Murray	.12	.06	.01	☐	186	Mike Greenwell	.65	.30	.06
☐	97	Tim Raines	.12	.06	.01	☐	187	Billy Hatcher	.03	.01	.00
☐	98	Rob Thompson	.03	.01	.00	☐	188	Jimmy Key	.06	.03	.00
☐	99	Kevin McReynolds	.10	.05	.01	☐	189	Nick Esasky	.06	.03	.00
☐	100	Checklist	.06	.01	.00	☐	190	Don Slaught	.03	.01	.00
☐	101	Carlton Fisk	.10	.05	.01	☐	191	Cory Snyder	.10	.05	.01
☐	102	Dave Martinez	.03	.01	.00	☐	192	John Candelaria	.06	.03	.00
☐	103	Glenn Braggs	.06	.03	.00	☐	193	Mike Schmidt	.25	.12	.02
☐	104	Dale Murphy	.18	.09	.01	☐	194	Kevin Gross	.03	.01	.00

☐ 195	John Tudor	.08	.04	.01
☐ 196	Neil Allen	.03	.01	.00
☐ 197	Orel Hershiser	.20	.10	.02
☐ 198	Kal Daniels	.08	.04	.01
☐ 199	Kent Hrbek	.10	.05	.01
☐ 200	Checklist	.06	.01	.00
☐ 201	Joe Magrane	.08	.04	.01
☐ 202	Scott Bailes	.03	.01	.00
☐ 203	Tim Belcher	.08	.04	.01
☐ 204	George Brett	.20	.10	.02
☐ 205	Benito Santiago	.15	.07	.01
☐ 206	Tony Fernandez	.10	.05	.01
☐ 207	Gerald Young	.06	.03	.00
☐ 208	Bo Jackson	.75	.35	.07
☐ 209	Chet Lemon	.03	.01	.00
☐ 210	Storm Davis	.06	.03	.00
☐ 211	Doug Drabek	.06	.03	.00
☐ 212	Mickey Brantley UER (photo actually Nelson Simmons)	.06	.03	.00
☐ 213	Devon White	.10	.05	.01
☐ 214	Dave Stewart	.10	.05	.01
☐ 215	Dave Schmidt	.03	.01	.00
☐ 216	Bryn Smith	.03	.01	.00
☐ 217	Brett Butler	.06	.03	.00
☐ 218	Bob Ojeda	.06	.03	.00
☐ 219	Steve Rosenberg	.10	.05	.01
☐ 220	Hubie Brooks	.06	.03	.00
☐ 221	B.J. Surhoff	.06	.03	.00
☐ 222	Rick Mahler	.03	.01	.00
☐ 223	Rick Sutcliffe	.08	.04	.01
☐ 224	Neal Heaton	.03	.01	.00
☐ 225	Mitch Williams	.08	.04	.01
☐ 226	Chuck Finley	.06	.03	.00
☐ 227	Mark Langston	.12	.06	.01
☐ 228	Jesse Orosco	.03	.01	.00
☐ 229	Ed Whitson	.03	.01	.00
☐ 230	Terry Pendleton	.03	.01	.00
☐ 231	Lloyd Moseby	.06	.03	.00
☐ 232	Greg Swindell	.08	.04	.01
☐ 233	John Franco	.08	.04	.01
☐ 234	Jack Morris	.10	.05	.01
☐ 235	Howard Johnson	.15	.07	.01
☐ 236	Glenn Davis	.12	.06	.01
☐ 237	Frank Viola	.15	.07	.01
☐ 238	Kevin Seitzer	.15	.07	.01
☐ 239	Gerald Perry	.06	.03	.00
☐ 240	Dwight Evans	.08	.04	.01
☐ 241	Jim Deshaies	.03	.01	.00
☐ 242	Bo Diaz	.03	.01	.00
☐ 243	Carney Lansford	.08	.04	.01
☐ 244	Mike LaValliere	.03	.01	.00
☐ 245	Rickey Henderson	.25	.12	.02
☐ 246	Roberto Alomar	.20	.10	.02
☐ 247	Jimmy Jones	.03	.01	.00
☐ 248	Pascual Perez	.08	.04	.01
☐ 249	Will Clark	.75	.35	.07
☐ 250	Fernando Valenzuela	.10	.05	.01
☐ 251	Shane Rawley	.03	.01	.00
☐ 252	Sid Bream	.03	.01	.00
☐ 253	Steve Lyons	.03	.01	.00
☐ 254	Brian Downing	.03	.01	.00
☐ 255	Mark Grace	1.50	.75	.15
☐ 256	Tom Candiotti	.03	.01	.00
☐ 257	Barry Larkin	.12	.06	.01
☐ 258	Mike Krukow	.03	.01	.00
☐ 259	Billy Ripken	.03	.01	.00
☐ 260	Cecilio Guante	.03	.01	.00
☐ 261	Scott Bradley	.03	.01	.00
☐ 262	Floyd Bannister	.03	.01	.00
☐ 263	Pete Smith	.03	.01	.00
☐ 264	Jim Gantner UER (wrong birtdate)	.03	.01	.00
☐ 265	Roger McDowell	.06	.03	.00
☐ 266	Bobby Thigpen	.06	.03	.00
☐ 267	Jim Clancy	.03	.01	.00
☐ 268	Terry Steinbach	.10	.05	.01
☐ 269	Mike Dunne	.06	.03	.00
☐ 270	Dwight Gooden	.25	.12	.02
☐ 271	Mike Heath	.03	.01	.00
☐ 272	Dave Smith	.03	.01	.00
☐ 273	Keith Atherton	.03	.01	.00
☐ 274	Tim Burke	.06	.03	.00
☐ 275	Damon Berryhill	.10	.05	.01
☐ 276	Vance Law	.03	.01	.00
☐ 277	Rich Dotson	.03	.01	.00
☐ 278	Lance Parrish	.08	.04	.01
☐ 279	Denny Walling	.03	.01	.00
☐ 280	Roger Clemens	.25	.12	.02
☐ 281	Greg Mathews	.03	.01	.00
☐ 282	Tom Niedenfuer	.03	.01	.00
☐ 283	Paul Kilgus	.03	.01	.00
☐ 284	Jose Guzman	.03	.01	.00
☐ 285	Calvin Schiraldi	.03	.01	.00
☐ 286	Charlie Puleo UER	.03	.01	.00
	(career ERA 4.24, should be 4.23)			
☐ 287	Joe Orsulak	.03	.01	.00
☐ 288	Jack Howell	.03	.01	.00
☐ 289	Kevin Elster	.06	.03	.00
☐ 290	Jose Lind	.03	.01	.00
☐ 291	Paul Molitor	.10	.05	.01
☐ 292	Cecil Espy	.10	.05	.01
☐ 293	Bill Wegman	.03	.01	.00
☐ 294	Dan Pasqua	.03	.01	.00
☐ 295	Scott Garrelts UER (wrong birthdate)	.06	.03	.00
☐ 296	Walt Terrell	.03	.01	.00
☐ 297	Ed Hearn	.03	.01	.00
☐ 298	Lou Whitaker	.08	.04	.01
☐ 299	Ken Dayley	.03	.01	.00
☐ 300	Checklist	.06	.01	.00
☐ 301	Tommy Herr	.03	.01	.00
☐ 302	Mike Brumley	.03	.01	.00
☐ 303	Ellis Burks	.30	.15	.03
☐ 304	Curt Young UER (wrong birthdate)	.03	.01	.00
☐ 305	Jody Reed	.06	.03	.00
☐ 306	Bill Doran	.06	.03	.00
☐ 307	David Wells	.03	.01	.00
☐ 308	Ron Robinson	.03	.01	.00
☐ 309	Rafael Santana	.03	.01	.00
☐ 310	Julio Franco	.08	.04	.01
☐ 311	Jack Clark	.10	.05	.01
☐ 312	Chris James	.06	.03	.00
☐ 313	Milt Thompson	.03	.01	.00
☐ 314	John Shelby	.03	.01	.00
☐ 315	Al Leiter	.08	.04	.01
☐ 316	Mike Davis	.03	.01	.00
☐ 317	Chris Sabo	.50	.25	.05
☐ 318	Greg Gagne	.03	.01	.00
☐ 319	Jose Oquendo	.03	.01	.00
☐ 320	John Farrell	.03	.01	.00
☐ 321	Franklin Stubbs	.03	.01	.00
☐ 322	Kurt Stillwell	.03	.01	.00
☐ 323	Shawn Abner	.06	.03	.00
☐ 324	Mike Flanagan	.06	.03	.00
☐ 325	Kevin Bass	.06	.03	.00
☐ 326	Pat Tabler	.06	.03	.00
☐ 327	Mike Henneman	.03	.01	.00
☐ 328	Rick Honeycutt	.03	.01	.00
☐ 329	John Smiley	.03	.01	.00
☐ 330	Rey Quinones	.03	.01	.00
☐ 331	Johnny Ray	.06	.03	.00
☐ 332	Bob Welch	.06	.03	.00
☐ 333	Larry Sheets	.03	.01	.00
☐ 334	Jeff Parrett	.03	.01	.00
☐ 335	Rick Reuschel UER (for Don Robinson, should be Jeff)	.08	.04	.01
☐ 336	Randy Myers	.08	.04	.01
☐ 337	Ken Williams	.03	.01	.00
☐ 338	Andy McGaffigan	.03	.01	.00
☐ 339	Joey Meyer	.06	.03	.00
☐ 340	Dion James	.03	.01	.00
☐ 341	Les Lancaster	.03	.01	.00
☐ 342	Tom Foley	.03	.01	.00
☐ 343	Geno Petralli	.03	.01	.00
☐ 344	Dan Petry	.03	.01	.00
☐ 345	Alvin Davis	.08	.04	.01
☐ 346	Mickey Hatcher	.03	.01	.00
☐ 347	Marvell Wynne	.03	.01	.00
☐ 348	Danny Cox	.03	.01	.00
☐ 349	Dave Stieb	.08	.04	.01
☐ 350	Jay Bell	.03	.01	.00
☐ 351	Jeff Treadway	.06	.03	.00
☐ 352	Luis Salazar	.03	.01	.00
☐ 353	Len Dykstra	.06	.03	.00
☐ 354	Juan Agosto	.03	.01	.00
☐ 355	Gene Larkin	.06	.03	.00
☐ 356	Steve Farr	.03	.01	.00
☐ 357	Paul Assenmacher	.03	.01	.00
☐ 358	Todd Benzinger	.03	.01	.00
☐ 359	Larry Andersen	.03	.01	.00
☐ 360	Paul O'Neill	.08	.04	.01
☐ 361	Ron Hassey	.03	.01	.00
☐ 362	Jim Gott	.03	.01	.00
☐ 363	Ken Phelps	.06	.03	.00
☐ 364	Tim Flannery	.03	.01	.00
☐ 365	Randy Ready	.03	.01	.00
☐ 366	Nelson Santovenia	.15	.07	.01
☐ 367	Kelly Downs	.06	.03	.00
☐ 368	Danny Heep	.03	.01	.00
☐ 369	Phil Bradley	.06	.03	.00
☐ 370	Jeff Robinson (Pittsburgh Pirates)	.06	.03	.00
☐ 371	Ivan Calderon	.06	.03	.00
☐ 372	Mike Witt	.06	.03	.00
☐ 373	Greg Maddux	.10	.05	.01
☐ 374	Carmen Castillo	.03	.01	.00

☐ 375	Jose Rijo	.03	.01	.00
☐ 376	Joe Price	.03	.01	.00
☐ 377	Rene C. Gonzales	.03	.01	.00
☐ 378	Oddibe McDowell	.06	.03	.00
☐ 379	Jim Presley	.03	.01	.00
☐ 380	Brad Wellman	.03	.01	.00
☐ 381	Tom Glavine	.06	.03	.00
☐ 382	Dan Plesac	.06	.03	.00
☐ 383	Wally Backman	.03	.01	.00
☐ 384	Dave Gallagher	.20	.10	.02
☐ 385	Tom Henke	.06	.03	.00
☐ 386	Luis Polonia	.03	.01	.00
☐ 387	Junior Ortiz	.03	.01	.00
☐ 388	David Cone	.20	.10	.02
☐ 389	Dave Bergman	.03	.01	.00
☐ 390	Danny Darwin	.03	.01	.00
☐ 391	Dan Gladden	.03	.01	.00
☐ 392	John Dopson	.15	.07	.01
☐ 393	Frank DiPino	.03	.01	.00
☐ 394	Al Nipper	.03	.01	.00
☐ 395	Willie Randolph	.06	.03	.00
☐ 396	Don Carman	.03	.01	.00
☐ 397	Scott Terry	.03	.01	.00
☐ 398	Rick Cerone	.03	.01	.00
☐ 399	Tom Pagnozzi	.03	.01	.00
☐ 400	Checklist	.06	.01	.00
☐ 401	Mickey Tettleton	.06	.03	.00
☐ 402	Curtis Wilkerson	.03	.01	.00
☐ 403	Jeff Russell	.06	.03	.00
☐ 404	Pat Perry	.03	.01	.00
☐ 405	Jose Alvarez	.08	.04	.01
☐ 406	Rick Schu	.03	.01	.00
☐ 407	Sherman Corbett	.08	.04	.01
☐ 408	Dave Magadan	.08	.04	.01
☐ 409	Bob Kipper	.03	.01	.00
☐ 410	Don August	.06	.03	.00
☐ 411	Bob Brower	.03	.01	.00
☐ 412	Chris Bosio	.03	.01	.00
☐ 413	Jerry Reuss	.03	.01	.00
☐ 414	Atlee Hammaker	.03	.01	.00
☐ 415	Jim Walewander	.08	.04	.01
☐ 416	Mike Macfarlane	.12	.06	.01
☐ 417	Pat Sheridan	.03	.01	.00
☐ 418	Pedro Guerrero	.10	.05	.01
☐ 419	Allan Anderson	.06	.03	.00
☐ 420	Mark Parent	.12	.06	.01
☐ 421	Bob Stanley	.03	.01	.00
☐ 422	Mike Gallego	.03	.01	.00
☐ 423	Bruce Hurst	.08	.04	.01
☐ 424	Dave Meads	.03	.01	.00
☐ 425	Jesse Barfield	.08	.04	.01
☐ 426	Rob Dibble	.25	.12	.02
☐ 427	Joel Skinner	.03	.01	.00
☐ 428	Ron Kittle	.08	.04	.01
☐ 429	Rick Rhoden	.03	.01	.00
☐ 430	Bob Dernier	.03	.01	.00
☐ 431	Steve Jeltz	.03	.01	.00
☐ 432	Rick Dempsey	.03	.01	.00
☐ 433	Roberto Kelly	.15	.07	.01
☐ 434	Dave Anderson	.03	.01	.00
☐ 435	Herm Winningham	.03	.01	.00
☐ 436	Al Newman	.03	.01	.00
☐ 437	Jose DeLeon	.06	.03	.00
☐ 438	Doug Jones	.06	.03	.00
☐ 439	Brian Holton	.03	.01	.00
☐ 440	Jeff Montgomery	.15	.07	.01
☐ 441	Dickie Thon	.03	.01	.00
☐ 442	Cecil Fielder	.03	.01	.00
☐ 443	John Fishel	.10	.05	.01
☐ 444	Jerry Don Gleaton	.03	.01	.00
☐ 445	Paul Gibson	.10	.05	.01
☐ 446	Walt Weiss	.40	.20	.04
☐ 447	Glenn Wilson	.03	.01	.00
☐ 448	Mike Moore	.06	.03	.00
☐ 449	Chili Davis	.06	.03	.00
☐ 450	Dave Henderson	.06	.03	.00
☐ 451	Jose Bautista	.08	.04	.01
☐ 452	Rex Hudler	.03	.01	.00
☐ 453	Bob Brenly	.03	.01	.00
☐ 454	Mackey Sasser	.08	.04	.01
☐ 455	Daryl Boston	.03	.01	.00
☐ 456	Mike Fitzgerald	.03	.01	.00
	Montreal Expos			
☐ 457	Jeffrey Leonard	.06	.03	.00
☐ 458	Bruce Sutter	.08	.04	.01
☐ 459	Mitch Webster	.03	.01	.00
☐ 460	Joe Hesketh	.03	.01	.00
☐ 461	Bobby Witt	.06	.03	.00
☐ 462	Stew Cliburn	.03	.01	.00
☐ 463	Scott Bankhead	.06	.03	.00
☐ 464	Ramon Martinez	.35	.17	.03
☐ 465	Dave Leiper	.03	.01	.00
☐ 466	Luis Alicea	.10	.05	.01
☐ 467	John Cerutti	.03	.01	.00
☐ 468	Ron Washington	.03	.01	.00
☐ 469	Jeff Reed	.03	.01	.00
☐ 470	Jeff Robinson	.06	.03	.00
	Detroit Tigers			
☐ 471	Sid Fernandez	.08	.04	.01
☐ 472	Terry Puhl	.03	.01	.00
☐ 473	Charlie Lea	.03	.01	.00
☐ 474	Israel Sanchez	.08	.04	.01
☐ 475	Bruce Benedict	.03	.01	.00
☐ 476	Oil Can Boyd	.06	.03	.00
☐ 477	Craig Reynolds	.03	.01	.00
☐ 478	Frank Williams	.03	.01	.00
☐ 479	Greg Cadaret	.03	.01	.00
☐ 480	Randy Kramer	.10	.05	.01
☐ 481	Dave Eiland	.10	.05	.01
☐ 482	Eric Show	.03	.01	.00
☐ 483	Garry Templeton	.06	.03	.00
☐ 484	Wallace Johnson	.03	.01	.00
☐ 485	Kevin Mitchell	.35	.17	.03
☐ 486	Tim Crews	.03	.01	.00
☐ 487	Mike Maddux	.03	.01	.00
☐ 488	Dave LaPoint	.03	.01	.00
☐ 489	Fred Manrique	.03	.01	.00
☐ 490	Greg Minton	.03	.01	.00
☐ 491	Doug Dascenzo UER	.25	.12	.02
	(photo actually Damon Berryhill)			
☐ 492	Willie Upshaw	.03	.01	.00
☐ 493	Jack Armstrong	.25	.12	.02
☐ 494	Kirt Manwaring	.03	.01	.00
☐ 495	Jeff Ballard	.08	.04	.01
☐ 496	Jeff Kunkel	.03	.01	.00
☐ 497	Mike Campbell	.03	.01	.00
☐ 498	Gary Thurman	.03	.01	.00
☐ 499	Zane Smith	.03	.01	.00
☐ 500	Checklist DP	.06	.01	.00
☐ 501	Mike Birkbeck	.03	.01	.00
☐ 502	Terry Leach	.06	.03	.00
☐ 503	Shawn Hillegas	.03	.01	.00
☐ 504	Manny Lee	.03	.01	.00
☐ 505	Doug Jennings	.20	.10	.02
☐ 506	Ken Oberkfell	.03	.01	.00
☐ 507	Tim Teufel	.03	.01	.00
☐ 508	Tom Brookens	.03	.01	.00
☐ 509	Rafael Ramirez	.03	.01	.00
☐ 510	Fred Toliver	.03	.01	.00
☐ 511	Brian Holman	.10	.05	.01
☐ 512	Mike Bielecki	.08	.04	.01
☐ 513	Jeff Pico	.10	.05	.01
☐ 514	Charles Hudson	.03	.01	.00
☐ 515	Bruce Ruffin	.03	.01	.00
☐ 516	Larry McWilliams UER	.03	.01	.00
	(New Richland, should be North Richland)			
☐ 517	Jeff Sellers	.03	.01	.00
☐ 518	John Costello	.10	.05	.01
☐ 519	Brady Anderson	.25	.12	.02
☐ 520	Craig McMurtry	.03	.01	.00
☐ 521	Ray Hayward DP	.03	.01	.00
☐ 522	Drew Hall DP	.03	.01	.00
☐ 523	Mark Lemke DP	.10	.05	.01
☐ 524	Oswald Peraza DP	.08	.04	.01
☐ 525	Bryan Harvey DP	.15	.07	.01
☐ 526	Rick Aguilera DP	.03	.01	.00
☐ 527	Tom Prince DP	.03	.01	.00
☐ 528	Mark Clear DP	.03	.01	.00
☐ 529	Jerry Browne DP	.03	.01	.00
☐ 530	Juan Castillo DP	.03	.01	.00
☐ 531	Jack McDowell DP	.06	.03	.00
☐ 532	Chris Speier DP	.03	.01	.00
☐ 533	Darrell Evans DP	.06	.03	.00
☐ 534	Luis Aquino DP	.03	.01	.00
☐ 535	Eric King DP	.03	.01	.00
☐ 536	Ken Hill DP	.12	.06	.01
☐ 537	Randy Bush DP	.03	.01	.00
☐ 538	Shane Mack DP	.03	.01	.00
☐ 539	Tom Bolton DP	.06	.03	.00
☐ 540	Gene Nelson DP	.03	.01	.00
☐ 541	Wes Gardner DP	.03	.01	.00
☐ 542	Ken Caminiti DP	.03	.01	.00
☐ 543	Duane Ward DP	.03	.01	.00
☐ 544	Norm Charlton DP	.10	.05	.01
☐ 545	Hal Morris DP	.15	.07	.01
☐ 546	Rich Yett DP	.03	.01	.00
☐ 547	Hensley Meulens DP	.50	.25	.05
☐ 548	Greg Harris DP	.03	.01	.00
	Philadelphia Phillies			
☐ 549	Darren Daulton DP	.03	.01	.00
	(posing as right-handed hitter)			
☐ 550	Jeff Hamilton DP	.03	.01	.00
☐ 551	Luis Aguayo DP	.03	.01	.00
☐ 552	Tim Leary DP	.06	.03	.00
	(resembles M.Marshall)			
☐ 553	Ron Oester DP	.03	.01	.00
☐ 554	Steve Lombardozzi DP	.03	.01	.00

☐ 555	Tim Jones DP	.08	.04	.01
☐ 556	Bud Black DP	.03	.01	.00
☐ 557	Alejandro Pena DP	.03	.01	.00
☐ 558	Jose DeJesus DP	.08	.04	.01
☐ 559	Dennis Rasmussen DP	.03	.01	.00
☐ 560	Pat Borders DP	.10	.05	.01
☐ 561	Craig Biggio DP	.35	.17	.03
☐ 562	Luis De Los Santos DP	.15	.07	.01
☐ 563	Fred Lynn DP	.06	.03	.00
☐ 564	Todd Burns DP	.20	.10	.02
☐ 565	Felix Fermin DP	.03	.01	.00
☐ 566	Darnell Coles DP	.03	.01	.00
☐ 567	Willie Fraser DP	.03	.01	.00
☐ 568	Glenn Hubbard DP	.03	.01	.00
☐ 569	Craig Worthington DP	.35	.17	.03
☐ 570	Johnny Paredes DP	.08	.04	.01
☐ 571	Don Robinson DP	.03	.01	.00
☐ 572	Barry Lyons DP	.03	.01	.00
☐ 573	Bill Long DP	.03	.01	.00
☐ 574	Tracy Jones DP	.03	.01	.00
☐ 575	Juan Nieves DP	.03	.01	.00
☐ 576	Andres Thomas DP	.03	.01	.00
☐ 577	Rolando Roomes DP	.25	.12	.02
☐ 578	Luis Rivera UER DP (wrong birthdate)	.03	.01	.00
☐ 579	Chad Kreuter DP	.10	.05	.01
☐ 580	Tony Armas DP	.03	.01	.00
☐ 581	Jay Buhner	.10	.05	.01
☐ 582	Ricky Horton DP	.03	.01	.00
☐ 583	Andy Hawkins DP	.03	.01	.00
☐ 584	Sil Campusano	.20	.10	.02
☐ 585	Dave Clark	.06	.03	.00
☐ 586	Van Snider DP	.20	.10	.02
☐ 587	Todd Frohwirth DP	.03	.01	.00
☐ 588	Puzzle Card DP Warren Spahn	.03	.01	.00
☐ 589	William Brennan	.12	.06	.01
☐ 590	German Gonzalez	.10	.05	.01
☐ 591	Ernie Whitt DP	.03	.01	.00
☐ 592	Jeff Blauser	.03	.01	.00
☐ 593	Spike Owen DP	.03	.01	.00
☐ 594	Matt Williams	.25	.12	.02
☐ 595	Lloyd McClendon DP	.08	.04	.01
☐ 596	Steve Ontiveros	.03	.01	.00
☐ 597	Scott Medvin	.12	.06	.01
☐ 598	Hipolito Pena DP	.08	.04	.01
☐ 599	Jerald Clark DP	.20	.10	.02
☐ 600A	Checklist Card DP 635 Kurt Schilling	.25	.03	.01
☐ 600B	Checklist Card DP 635 Curt Schilling (MVP's not listed on checklist card)	.06	.01	.00
☐ 600C	Checklist Card DP 635 Curt Schilling (MVP's listed following #660)	.06	.01	.00
☐ 601	Carmelo Martinez DP	.03	.01	.00
☐ 602	Mike LaCoss	.03	.01	.00
☐ 603	Mike Devereaux	.06	.03	.00
☐ 604	Alex Madrid DP	.08	.04	.01
☐ 605	Gary Redus DP	.03	.01	.00
☐ 606	Lance Johnson	.03	.01	.00
☐ 607	Terry Clark DP	.08	.04	.01
☐ 608	Manny Trillo DP	.03	.01	.00
☐ 609	Scott Jordan	.10	.05	.01
☐ 610	Jay Howell DP	.03	.01	.00
☐ 611	Francisco Melendez	.20	.10	.02
☐ 612	Mike Boddicker	.03	.01	.00
☐ 613	Kevin Brown DP	.08	.04	.01
☐ 614	Dave Valle	.03	.01	.00
☐ 615	Tim Laudner DP	.03	.01	.00
☐ 616	Andy Nezelek UER (wrong birthdate)	.20	.10	.02
☐ 617	Chuck Crim	.03	.01	.00
☐ 618	Jack Savage DP	.08	.04	.01
☐ 619	Adam Peterson	.08	.04	.01
☐ 620	Todd Stottlemyre	.08	.04	.01
☐ 621	Lance Blankenship	.20	.10	.02
☐ 622	Miguel Garcia DP	.08	.04	.01
☐ 623	Keith Miller DP New York Mets	.03	.01	.00
☐ 624	Ricky Jordan DP	1.25	.60	.12
☐ 625	Ernest Riles DP	.03	.01	.00
☐ 626	John Moses DP	.03	.01	.00
☐ 627	Nelson Liriano DP	.03	.01	.00
☐ 628	Mike Smithson DP	.03	.01	.00
☐ 629	Scott Sanderson	.03	.01	.00
☐ 630	Dale Mohorcic	.03	.01	.00
☐ 631	Marvin Freeman DP	.03	.01	.00
☐ 632	Mike Young DP	.03	.01	.00
☐ 633	Dennis Lamp	.03	.01	.00
☐ 634	Dante Bichette DP	.18	.09	.01
☐ 635	Curt Schilling DP	.10	.05	.01
☐ 636	Scott May DP	.10	.05	.01

☐ 637	Mike Schooler	.35	.17	.03
☐ 638	Rick Leach	.03	.01	.00
☐ 639	Tom Lampkin UER (Throws Left, should be Throws Right)	.10	.05	.01
☐ 640	Brian Meyer	.10	.05	.01
☐ 641	Brian Harper	.03	.01	.00
☐ 642	John Smoltz	.50	.25	.05
☐ 643	Jose: 40/40 Club (Jose Canseco)	.50	.25	.05
☐ 644	Bill Schroeder	.03	.01	.00
☐ 645	Edgar Martinez	.10	.05	.01
☐ 646	Dennis Cook	.25	.12	.02
☐ 647	Barry Jones	.03	.01	.00
☐ 648	Orel: 59 and Counting (Orel Hershiser)	.15	.07	.01
☐ 649	Rod Nichols	.10	.05	.01
☐ 650	Jody Davis	.03	.01	.00
☐ 651	Bob Milacki	.25	.12	.02
☐ 652	Mike Jackson	.03	.01	.00
☐ 653	Derek Lilliquist	.30	.15	.03
☐ 654	Paul Mirabella	.03	.01	.00
☐ 655	Mike Diaz	.03	.01	.00
☐ 656	Jeff Musselman	.03	.01	.00
☐ 657	Jerry Reed	.03	.01	.00
☐ 658	Kevin Blankenship	.15	.07	.01
☐ 659	Wayne Tolleson	.03	.01	.00
☐ 660	Eric Hetzel	.12	.06	.01

1989 Donruss Bonus MVP's

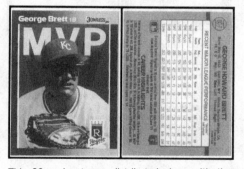

This 26-card set was distributed along with the regular 1989 Donruss issue as random inserts with the rack and wax packs. These bonus cards are numbered with the prefix BC for bonus cards and were supposedly produced in the same quantities as the other 660 regular issue cards. The 'most valuable" player was selected from each of the 26 teams. Cards measure 2 1/2" by 3 1/2" and feature the same distinctive side border as the regular issue. The cards are distinguished by the bold MVP logo in the upper background of the obverse. Four of these cards were double printed with respect to the other cards in the set; these four are denoted by DP in the checklist below.

		MINT	EXC	G-VG
	COMPLETE SET (26)	6.00	3.00	.60
	COMMON CARD (BC1-BC26)	.07	.03	.01
☐ BC1	Kirby Puckett	.30	.15	.03
☐ BC2	Mike Scott	.12	.06	.01
☐ BC3	Joe Carter	.12	.06	.01
☐ BC4	Orel Hershiser	.20	.10	.02
☐ BC5	Jose Canseco	.60	.30	.06
☐ BC6	Darryl Strawberry	.35	.17	.03
☐ BC7	George Brett	.20	.10	.02
☐ BC8	Andre Dawson	.12	.06	.01
☐ BC9	Paul Molitor UER (Brewers logo missing the word Milwaukee)	.12	.06	.01
☐ BC10	Andy Van Slyke	.10	.05	.01
☐ BC11	Dave Winfield	.12	.06	.01
☐ BC12	Kevin Gross	.07	.03	.01
☐ BC13	Mike Greenwell	.40	.20	.04
☐ BC14	Ozzie Smith	.12	.06	.01

			MINT	EXC	G-VG
☐	BC15	Cal Ripken	.15	.07	.01
☐	BC16	Andres Galarraga	.10	.05	.01
☐	BC17	Alan Trammell	.12	.06	.01
☐	BC18	Kal Daniels	.10	.05	.01
☐	BC19	Fred McGriff	.15	.07	.01
☐	BC20	Tony Gwynn	.20	.10	.02
☐	BC21	Wally Joyner DP	.10	.05	.01
☐	BC22	Will Clark DP	.50	.25	.05
☐	BC23	Ozzie Guillen	.07	.03	.01
☐	BC24	Gerald Perry DP	.07	.03	.01
☐	BC25	Alvin Davis DP	.10	.05	.01
☐	BC26	Ruben Sierra	.25	.12	.02

1989 Donruss Super DK's

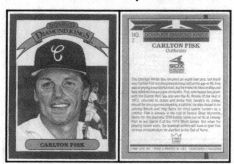

This 26-player card set was available through a mail-in offer detailed on the wax packs. The set was sent in return for 8.00 and three wrappers plus 2.00 postage and handling. The set features the popular Diamond King subseries in large (approximately 4 7/8" by 6 13/16") form. Dick Perez of Perez-Steele Galleries did another outstanding job on the artwork. The cards are essentially a large version of the Donruss regular issue Diamond Kings.

			MINT	EXC	G-VG
	COMPLETE SET (26)		10.00	5.00	1.00
	COMMON PLAYER (1-26)		.15	.07	.01
☐	1	Mike Greenwell DK	1.00	.50	.10
☐	2	Bobby Bonilla DK	.25	.12	.02
☐	3	Pete Incaviglia DK	.25	.12	.02
☐	4	Chris Sabo DK	.75	.35	.07
☐	5	Robin Yount DK	.60	.30	.06
☐	6	Tony Gwynn DK	.60	.30	.06
☐	7	Carlton Fisk DK	.30	.15	.03
☐	8	Cory Snyder DK	.30	.15	.03
☐	9	David Cone DK	.40	.20	.04
☐	10	Kevin Seitzer DK	.40	.20	.04
☐	11	Rick Reuschel DK	.20	.10	.02
☐	12	Johnny Ray DK	.15	.07	.01
☐	13	Dave Schmidt DK	.15	.07	.01
☐	14	Andres Galarraga DK	.30	.15	.03
☐	15	Kirk Gibson DK	.45	.22	.04
☐	16	Fred McGriff DK	.50	.25	.05
☐	17	Mark Grace DK	1.50	.75	.15
☐	18	Jeff Robinson DT DK	.20	.10	.02
☐	19	Vince Coleman DK	.35	.17	.03
☐	20	Dave Henderson DK	.15	.07	.01
☐	21	Harold Reynolds DK	.20	.10	.02
☐	22	Gerald Perry DK	.20	.10	.02
☐	23	Frank Viola DK	.30	.15	.03
☐	24	Steve Bedrosian DK	.20	.10	.02
☐	25	Glenn Davis DK	.40	.20	.04
☐	26	Don Mattingly DK	1.50	.75	.15

1989 Donruss All-Stars

These All-Stars are standard size, 2 1/2" by 3 1/2" and very similar in design to the regular issue of 1989 Donruss. The set is distinguished by the presence of the respective League logos in the lower right corner

of each obverse. The cards are numbered on the backs. The players chosen for the set are essentially the participants at the previous year's All-Star Game. Individual wax packs of All Stars (suggested retail price of 35 cents) contained one Pop-Up, five All-Star cards, and a Warren Spahn puzzle card.

			MINT	EXC	G-VG
	COMPLETE SET (64)		7.50	3.75	.75
	COMMON PLAYER (1-64)		.07	.03	.01
☐	1	Mark McGwire	.75	.35	.07
☐	2	Jose Canseco	1.00	.50	.10
☐	3	Paul Molitor	.15	.07	.01
☐	4	Rickey Henderson	.35	.17	.03
☐	5	Cal Ripken Jr.	.25	.12	.02
☐	6	Dave Winfield	.20	.10	.02
☐	7	Wade Boggs	.75	.35	.07
☐	8	Frank Viola	.15	.07	.01
☐	9	Terry Steinbach	.10	.05	.01
☐	10	Tom Kelly MG	.07	.03	.01
☐	11	George Brett	.35	.17	.03
☐	12	Doyle Alexander	.07	.03	.01
☐	13	Gary Gaetti	.15	.07	.01
☐	14	Roger Clemens	.50	.25	.05
☐	15	Mike Greenwell	1.00	.50	.10
☐	16	Dennis Eckersley	.20	.10	.02
☐	17	Carney Lansford	.15	.07	.01
☐	18	Mark Gubicza	.15	.07	.01
☐	19	Tim Laudner	.07	.03	.01
☐	20	Doug Jones	.10	.05	.01
☐	21	Don Mattingly	1.00	.50	.10
☐	22	Dan Plesac	.10	.05	.01
☐	23	Kirby Puckett	.60	.30	.06
☐	24	Jeff Reardon	.10	.05	.01
☐	25	Johnny Ray	.10	.05	.01
☐	26	Jeff Russell	.10	.05	.01
☐	27	Harold Reynolds	.07	.03	.01
☐	28	Dave Stieb	.10	.05	.01
☐	29	Kurt Stillwell	.07	.03	.01
☐	30	Jose Canseco	1.25	.60	.12
☐	31	Terry Steinbach	.10	.05	.01
☐	32	AL Checklist	.07	.03	.01
☐	33	Will Clark	1.25	.60	.12
☐	34	Darryl Strawberry	.75	.35	.07
☐	35	Ryne Sandberg	.35	.17	.03
☐	36	Andre Dawson	.25	.12	.02
☐	37	Ozzie Smith	.25	.12	.02
☐	38	Vince Coleman	.20	.10	.02
☐	39	Bobby Bonilla	.15	.07	.01
☐	40	Dwight Gooden	.50	.25	.05
☐	41	Gary Carter	.25	.12	.02
☐	42	Whitey Herzog MG	.07	.03	.01
☐	43	Shawon Dunston	.15	.07	.01
☐	44	David Cone	.35	.17	.03
☐	45	Andres Galarraga	.25	.12	.02
☐	46	Mark Davis	.07	.03	.01
☐	47	Barry Larkin	.25	.12	.02
☐	48	Kevin Gross	.07	.03	.01
☐	49	Vance Law	.07	.03	.01
☐	50	Orel Hershiser	.50	.25	.05
☐	51	Willie McGee	.15	.07	.01
☐	52	Danny Jackson	.10	.05	.01
☐	53	Rafael Palmeiro	.20	.10	.02
☐	54	Bob Knepper	.07	.03	.01
☐	55	Lance Parrish	.10	.05	.01
☐	56	Greg Maddux	.15	.07	.01
☐	57	Gerald Perry	.07	.03	.01
☐	58	Bob Walk	.07	.03	.01
☐	59	Chris Sabo	.35	.17	.03
☐	60	Todd Worrell	.15	.07	.01
☐	61	Andy Van Slyke	.15	.07	.01
☐	62	Ozzie Smith	.25	.12	.02

		MINT	EXC	G-VG
☐ 63	Riverfront Stadium	.07	.03	.01
☐ 64	NL Checklist	.07	.03	.01

1989 Donruss Pop-Ups

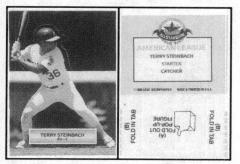

These Pop-Ups are borderless and standard size, 2 1/2" by 3 1/2". The cards are unnumbered; however the All Star checklist card lists the same numbers as the All Star cards. Those numbers are used below for reference. The players chosen for the set are essentially the starting lineups for the previous year's All-Star Game. Individual wax packs of All Stars (suggested retail price of 35 cents) contained one Pop-Up, five All-Star cards, and a puzzle card.

		MINT	EXC	G-VG
COMPLETE SET (20)		4.00	2.00	.40
COMMON PLAYER		.10	.05	.01
☐ 1	Mark McGwire	.75	.35	.07
☐ 2	Jose Canseco	1.00	.50	.10
☐ 3	Paul Molitor	.15	.07	.01
☐ 4	Rickey Henderson	.35	.17	.03
☐ 5	Cal Ripken Jr.	.25	.12	.02
☐ 6	Dave Winfield	.20	.10	.02
☐ 7	Wade Boggs	.75	.35	.07
☐ 8	Frank Viola	.15	.07	.01
☐ 9	Terry Steinbach	.10	.05	.01
☐ 10	Tom Kelly MG	.10	.05	.01
☐ 33	Will Clark	1.25	.60	.12
☐ 34	Darryl Strawberry	.75	.35	.07
☐ 35	Ryne Sandberg	.35	.17	.03
☐ 36	Andre Dawson	.25	.12	.02
☐ 37	Ozzie Smith	.25	.12	.02
☐ 38	Vince Coleman	.20	.10	.02
☐ 39	Bobby Bonilla	.15	.07	.01
☐ 40	Dwight Gooden	.50	.25	.05
☐ 41	Gary Carter	.25	.12	.02
☐ 42	Whitey Herzog MG	.10	.05	.01

1989 Donruss Traded

The 1989 Donruss Traded set contains 56 standard-size (2 1/2 by 3 1/2 inch) cards. The fronts have yellowish-orange borders; the backs are yellow and feature recent statistics. The cards were distributed as a boxed set. The set was never very popular with collectors since it included (as the name implies) only traded players rather than rookies.

		MINT	EXC	G-VG
COMPLETE SET (56)		5.00	2.50	.50
COMMON PLAYER (1-55)		.05	.02	.00
☐ 1	Jeffrey Leonard	.10	.05	.01
☐ 2	Jack Clark	.15	.07	.01
☐ 3	Kevin Gross	.05	.02	.00
☐ 4	Tommy Herr	.10	.05	.01
☐ 5	Bob Boone	.15	.07	.01

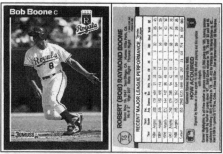

		MINT	EXC	G-VG
☐ 6	Rafael Palmeiro	.25	.12	.02
☐ 7	John Dopson	.05	.02	.00
☐ 8	Willie Randolph	.10	.05	.01
☐ 9	Chris Brown	.05	.02	.00
☐ 10	Wally Backman	.05	.02	.00
☐ 11	Steve Ontiveros	.05	.02	.00
☐ 12	Eddie Murray	.15	.07	.01
☐ 13	Lance McCullers	.05	.02	.00
☐ 14	Spike Owen	.05	.02	.00
☐ 15	Rob Murphy	.05	.02	.00
☐ 16	Pete O'Brien	.10	.05	.01
☐ 17	Ken Williams	.05	.02	.00
☐ 18	Nick Esasky	.15	.07	.01
☐ 19	Nolan Ryan	1.25	.60	.12
☐ 20	Brian Holton	.05	.02	.00
☐ 21	Mike Moore	.10	.05	.01
☐ 22	Joel Skinner	.05	.02	.00
☐ 23	Steve Sax	.15	.07	.01
☐ 24	Rick Mahler	.05	.02	.00
☐ 25	Mike Aldrete	.05	.02	.00
☐ 26	Jesse Orosco	.05	.02	.00
☐ 27	Dave LaPoint	.05	.02	.00
☐ 28	Walt Terrell	.05	.02	.00
☐ 29	Eddie Williams	.05	.02	.00
☐ 30	Mike Devereaux	.05	.02	.00
☐ 31	Julio Franco	.15	.07	.01
☐ 32	Jim Clancy	.05	.02	.00
☐ 33	Felix Fermin	.05	.02	.00
☐ 34	Curt Wilkerson	.05	.02	.00
☐ 35	Bert Blyleven	.15	.07	.01
☐ 36	Mel Hall	.10	.05	.01
☐ 37	Eric King	.05	.02	.00
☐ 38	Mitch Williams	.10	.05	.01
☐ 39	Jamie Moyer	.05	.02	.00
☐ 40	Rick Rhoden	.05	.02	.00
☐ 41	Phil Bradley	.10	.05	.01
☐ 42	Paul Kilgus	.05	.02	.00
☐ 43	Milt Thompson	.05	.02	.00
☐ 44	Jerry Browne	.10	.05	.01
☐ 45	Bruce Hurst	.10	.05	.01
☐ 46	Claudell Washington	.10	.05	.01
☐ 47	Todd Benzinger	.10	.05	.01
☐ 48	Steve Balboni	.05	.02	.00
☐ 49	Oddibe McDowell	.10	.05	.01
☐ 50	Charles Hudson	.05	.02	.00
☐ 51	Ron Kittle	.10	.05	.01
☐ 52	Andy Hawkins	.05	.02	.00
☐ 53	Tom Brookens	.05	.02	.00
☐ 54	Tom Niedenfuer	.05	.02	.00
☐ 55	Jeff Parrett	.05	.02	.00
☐ 56	Checklist Card	.05	.02	.00

1989 Donruss Grand Slammers

The 1989 Donruss Grand Slammers set contains 12 standard-size (2 1/2 by 3 1/2 inch) cards. Each card in the set can be found with five different colored border combinations, but no color combination of borders appears to be scarcer than any other. The set includes cards for each player who hit one or more grand slams in 1988. The backs detail the players' grand slams. The cards were distributed one per cello pack.

	MINT	EXC	G-VG
COMPLETE SET (12)	4.00	2.00	.40
COMMON PLAYER (1-12)	.10	.05	.01

			MINT	EXC	G-VG
☐	1	Jose Canseco	1.00	.50	.10
☐	2	Mike Marshall	.15	.07	.01
☐	3	Walt Weiss	.20	.10	.02
☐	4	Kevin McReynolds	.20	.10	.02
☐	5	Mike Greenwell	.60	.30	.06
☐	6	Dave Winfield	.30	.15	.03
☐	7	Mark McGwire	.60	.30	.06
☐	8	Keith Hernandez	.20	.10	.02
☐	9	Franklin Stubbs	.10	.05	.01
☐	10	Danny Tartabull	.20	.10	.02
☐	11	Jesse Barfield	.20	.10	.02
☐	12	Ellis Burks	.30	.15	.03

1989 Donruss Baseball's Best

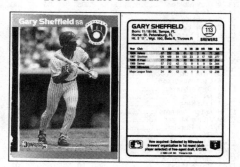

The 1989 Donruss Baseball's Best set contains 336 standard-size (2 1/2 by 3 1/2 inch) glossy cards. The fronts are green and yellow, and the backs feature career highlight information. The backs are green, and feature vertically-oriented career stats. The cards were distributed as a set in a blister pack through various retail and department store chains.

			MINT	EXC	G-VG
		COMPLETE SET (336)	20.00	10.00	2.00
		COMMON PLAYER (1-336)	.04	.02	.00
☐	1	Don Mattingly	1.00	.50	.10
☐	2	Tom Glavine	.10	.05	.01
☐	3	Bert Blyleven	.10	.05	.01
☐	4	Andre Dawson	.15	.07	.01
☐	5	Pete O'Brien	.07	.03	.01
☐	6	Eric Davis	.45	.22	.04
☐	7	George Brett	.35	.17	.03
☐	8	Glenn Davis	.20	.10	.02
☐	9	Ellis Burks	.30	.15	.03
☐	10	Kirk Gibson	.20	.10	.02
☐	11	Carlton Fisk	.20	.10	.02
☐	12	Andres Galarraga	.20	.10	.02
☐	13	Alan Trammell	.15	.07	.01
☐	14	Dwight Gooden	.40	.20	.04
☐	15	Paul Molitor	.15	.07	.01
☐	16	Roger McDowell	.07	.03	.01
☐	17	Doug Drabek	.07	.03	.01
☐	18	Kent Hrbek	.15	.07	.01
☐	19	Vince Coleman	.20	.10	.02
☐	20	Steve Sax	.15	.07	.01
☐	21	Roberto Alomar	.20	.10	.02
☐	22	Carney Lansford	.15	.07	.01
☐	23	Will Clark	1.00	.50	.10
☐	24	Alvin Davis	.10	.05	.01
☐	25	Bobby Thigpen	.07	.03	.01
☐	26	Ryne Sandberg	.25	.12	.02
☐	27	Devon White	.10	.05	.01
☐	28	Mike Greenwell	.60	.30	.06
☐	29	Dale Murphy	.35	.17	.03
☐	30	Jeff Ballard	.10	.05	.01
☐	31	Kelly Gruber	.07	.03	.01
☐	32	Julio Franco	.10	.05	.01
☐	33	Bobby Bonilla	.10	.05	.01
☐	34	Tim Wallach	.07	.03	.01
☐	35	Lou Whitaker	.10	.05	.01
☐	36	Jay Howell	.07	.03	.01
☐	37	Greg Maddux	.10	.05	.01
☐	38	Bill Doran	.07	.03	.01
☐	39	Danny Tartabull	.15	.07	.01
☐	40	Darryl Strawberry	.40	.20	.04
☐	41	Ron Darling	.10	.05	.01
☐	42	Tony Gwynn	.30	.15	.03
☐	43	Mark McGwire	.60	.30	.06
☐	44	Ozzie Smith	.20	.10	.02
☐	45	Andy Van Slyke	.10	.05	.01
☐	46	Juan Berenguer	.04	.02	.00
☐	47	Von Hayes	.10	.05	.01
☐	48	Tony Fernandez	.10	.05	.01
☐	49	Eric Plunk	.04	.02	.00
☐	50	Ernest Riles	.04	.02	.00
☐	51	Harold Reynolds	.07	.03	.01
☐	52	Andy Hawkins	.04	.02	.00
☐	53	Robin Yount	.35	.17	.03
☐	54	Danny Jackson	.10	.05	.01
☐	55	Nolan Ryan	.75	.35	.07
☐	56	Joe Carter	.15	.07	.01
☐	57	Jose Canseco	1.00	.50	.10
☐	58	Jody Davis	.04	.02	.00
☐	59	Lance Parrish	.07	.03	.01
☐	60	Mitch Williams	.07	.03	.01
☐	61	Brook Jacoby	.07	.03	.01
☐	62	Tom Browning	.07	.03	.01
☐	63	Kurt Stillwell	.04	.02	.00
☐	64	Rafael Ramirez	.04	.02	.00
☐	65	Roger Clemens	.40	.20	.04
☐	66	Mike Scioscia	.04	.02	.00
☐	67	Dave Gallagher	.07	.03	.01
☐	68	Mark Langston	.20	.10	.02
☐	69	Chet Lemon	.04	.02	.00
☐	70	Kevin McReynolds	.10	.05	.01
☐	71	Rob Deer	.07	.03	.01
☐	72	Tommy Herr	.07	.03	.01
☐	73	Barry Bonds	.10	.05	.01
☐	74	Frank Viola	.15	.07	.01
☐	75	Pedro Guerrero	.15	.07	.01
☐	76	Dave Righetti	.10	.05	.01
☐	77	Bruce Hurst	.07	.03	.01
☐	78	Rickey Henderson	.35	.17	.03
☐	79	Robby Thompson	.04	.02	.00
☐	80	Randy Johnson	.07	.03	.01
☐	81	Harold Baines	.10	.05	.01
☐	82	Calvin Schiraldi	.04	.02	.00
☐	83	Kirk McCaskill	.04	.02	.00
☐	84	Lee Smith	.07	.03	.01
☐	85	John Smoltz	.10	.05	.01
☐	86	Mickey Tettleton	.10	.05	.01
☐	87	Jimmy Key	.07	.03	.01
☐	88	Rafael Palmeiro	.15	.07	.01
☐	89	Sid Bream	.04	.02	.00
☐	90	Dennis Martinez	.07	.03	.01
☐	91	Frank Tanana	.04	.02	.00
☐	92	Eddie Murray	.20	.10	.02
☐	93	Shawon Dunston	.10	.05	.01
☐	94	Mike Scott	.15	.07	.01
☐	95	Bret Saberhagen	.20	.10	.02
☐	96	David Cone	.20	.10	.02
☐	97	Kevin Elster	.07	.03	.01
☐	98	Jack Clark	.15	.07	.01
☐	99	Dave Stewart	.20	.10	.02
☐	100	Jose Oquendo	.04	.02	.00
☐	101	Jose Lind	.04	.02	.00
☐	102	Gary Gaetti	.10	.05	.01
☐	103	Ricky Jordan	.25	.12	.02
☐	104	Fred McGriff	.30	.15	.03
☐	105	Don Slaught	.04	.02	.00
☐	106	Jose Uribe	.04	.02	.00
☐	107	Jeffrey Leonard	.07	.03	.01
☐	108	Lee Guetterman	.04	.02	.00
☐	109	Chris Bosio	.07	.03	.01
☐	110	Barry Larkin	.20	.10	.02
☐	111	Ruben Sierra	.35	.17	.03
☐	112	Greg Swindell	.10	.05	.01
☐	113	Gary Sheffield	.50	.25	.05
☐	114	Lonnie Smith	.07	.03	.01
☐	115	Chili Davis	.04	.02	.00

□ 116	Damon Berryhill	.10	.05	.01
□ 117	Tom Candiotti	.04	.02	.00
□ 118	Kal Daniels	.10	.05	.01
□ 119	Mark Gubicza	.10	.05	.01
□ 120	Jim Deshaies	.04	.02	.00
□ 121	Dwight Evans	.10	.05	.01
□ 122	Mike Morgan	.07	.03	.01
□ 123	Dan Pasqua	.04	.02	.00
□ 124	Bryn Smith	.07	.03	.01
□ 125	Doyle Alexander	.04	.02	.00
□ 126	Howard Johnson	.15	.07	.01
□ 127	Chuck Crim	.04	.02	.00
□ 128	Darren Daulton	.04	.02	.00
□ 129	Jeff Robinson	.07	.03	.01
□ 130	Kirby Puckett	.40	.20	.04
□ 131	Joe Magrane	.10	.05	.01
□ 132	Jesse Barfield	.10	.05	.01
□ 133	Mark Davis	.20	.10	.02
□ 134	Dennis Eckersley	.15	.07	.01
□ 135	Mike Krukow	.04	.02	.00
□ 136	Jay Buhner	.10	.05	.01
□ 137	Ozzie Guillen	.07	.03	.01
□ 138	Rick Sutcliffe	.07	.03	.01
□ 139	Wally Joyner	.20	.10	.02
□ 140	Wade Boggs	.50	.25	.05
□ 141	Jeff Treadway	.04	.02	.00
□ 142	Cal Ripken	.25	.12	.02
□ 143	Dave Stieb	.10	.05	.01
□ 144	Pete Incaviglia	.10	.05	.01
□ 145	Bob Walk	.04	.02	.00
□ 146	Nelson Santovenia	.07	.03	.01
□ 147	Mike Heath	.04	.02	.00
□ 148	Willie Randolph	.07	.03	.01
□ 149	Paul Kilgus	.04	.02	.00
□ 150	Billy Hatcher	.04	.02	.00
□ 151	Steve Farr	.04	.02	.00
□ 152	Gregg Jefferies	.75	.35	.07
□ 153	Randy Myers	.07	.03	.01
□ 154	Garry Templeton	.07	.03	.01
□ 155	Walt Weiss	.15	.07	.01
□ 156	Terry Pendleton	.04	.02	.00
□ 157	John Smiley	.07	.03	.01
□ 158	Greg Gagne	.04	.02	.00
□ 159	Len Dykstra	.07	.03	.01
□ 160	Nelson Liriano	.04	.02	.00
□ 161	Alvaro Espinoza	.04	.02	.00
□ 162	Rick Reuschel	.10	.05	.01
□ 163	Omar Vizquel UER (photo actually Darnell Coles)	.15	.07	.01
□ 164	Clay Parker	.07	.03	.01
□ 165	Dan Plesac	.07	.03	.01
□ 166	John Franco	.10	.05	.01
□ 167	Scott Fletcher	.04	.02	.00
□ 168	Cory Snyder	.10	.05	.01
□ 169	Bo Jackson	1.00	.50	.10
□ 170	Tommy Gregg	.07	.03	.01
□ 171	Jim Abbott	1.00	.50	.10
□ 172	Jerome Walton	1.50	.75	.15
□ 173	Doug Jones	.07	.03	.01
□ 174	Todd Benzinger	.07	.03	.01
□ 175	Frank White	.07	.03	.01
□ 176	Craig Biggio	.20	.10	.02
□ 177	John Dopson	.04	.02	.00
□ 178	Alfredo Griffin	.04	.02	.00
□ 179	Melido Perez	.07	.03	.01
□ 180	Tim Burke	.07	.03	.01
□ 181	Matt Nokes	.10	.05	.01
□ 182	Gary Carter	.20	.10	.02
□ 183	Ted Higuera	.10	.05	.01
□ 184	Ken Howell	.04	.02	.00
□ 185	Rey Quinones	.04	.02	.00
□ 186	Wally Backman	.04	.02	.00
□ 187	Tom Brunansky	.10	.05	.01
□ 188	Steve Balboni	.04	.02	.00
□ 189	Marvell Wynne	.04	.02	.00
□ 190	Dave Henderson	.04	.02	.00
□ 191	Don Robinson	.04	.02	.00
□ 192	Ken Griffey Jr.	1.50	.75	.15
□ 193	Ivan Calderon	.07	.03	.01
□ 194	Mike Bielecki	.07	.03	.01
□ 195	Johnny Ray	.07	.03	.01
□ 196	Rob Murphy	.04	.02	.00
□ 197	Andres Thomas	.04	.02	.00
□ 198	Phil Bradley	.07	.03	.01
□ 199	Junior Felix	.35	.17	.03
□ 200	Jeff Russell	.07	.03	.01
□ 201	Mike LaValliere	.04	.02	.00
□ 202	Kevin Gross	.04	.02	.00
□ 203	Keith Moreland	.04	.02	.00
□ 204	Mike Marshall	.10	.05	.01
□ 205	Dwight Smith	.75	.35	.07
□ 206	Jim Clancy	.04	.02	.00
□ 207	Kevin Seitzer	.15	.07	.01
□ 208	Keith Hernandez	.15	.07	.01
□ 209	Bob Ojeda	.07	.03	.01
□ 210	Ed Whitson	.04	.02	.00
□ 211	Tony Phillips	.04	.02	.00
□ 212	Milt Thompson	.04	.02	.00
□ 213	Randy Kramer	.04	.02	.00
□ 214	Randy Bush	.04	.02	.00
□ 215	Randy Ready	.04	.02	.00
□ 216	Duane Ward	.04	.02	.00
□ 217	Jimmy Jones	.07	.03	.01
□ 218	Scott Garrelts	.07	.03	.01
□ 219	Scott Bankhead	.07	.03	.01
□ 220	Lance McCullers	.07	.03	.01
□ 221	B.J. Surhoff	.07	.03	.01
□ 222	Chris Sabo	.15	.07	.01
□ 223	Steve Buechele	.04	.02	.00
□ 224	Joel Skinner	.04	.02	.00
□ 225	Orel Hershiser	.30	.15	.03
□ 226	Derek Lilliquist	.10	.05	.01
□ 227	Claudell Washington	.07	.03	.01
□ 228	Lloyd McClendon	.04	.02	.00
□ 229	Felix Fermin	.04	.02	.00
□ 230	Paul O'Neill	.10	.05	.01
□ 231	Charlie Leibrandt	.04	.02	.00
□ 232	Dave Smith	.04	.02	.00
□ 233	Bob Stanley	.04	.02	.00
□ 234	Tim Belcher	.10	.05	.01
□ 235	Eric King	.04	.02	.00
□ 236	Spike Owen	.04	.02	.00
□ 237	Mike Henneman	.04	.02	.00
□ 238	Juan Samuel	.10	.05	.01
□ 239	Greg Brock	.04	.02	.00
□ 240	John Kruk	.10	.05	.01
□ 241	Glenn Wilson	.07	.03	.01
□ 242	Jeff Reardon	.07	.03	.01
□ 243	Todd Worrell	.10	.05	.01
□ 244	Dave LaPoint	.04	.02	.00
□ 245	Walt Terrell	.04	.02	.00
□ 246	Mike Moore	.07	.03	.01
□ 247	Kelly Downs	.04	.02	.00
□ 248	Dave Valle	.04	.02	.00
□ 249	Ron Kittle	.10	.05	.01
□ 250	Steve Wilson	.07	.03	.01
□ 251	Dick Schofield	.04	.02	.00
□ 252	Marty Barrett	.07	.03	.01
□ 253	Dion James	.04	.02	.00
□ 254	Bob Milacki	.10	.05	.01
□ 255	Ernie Whitt	.04	.02	.00
□ 256	Kevin Brown	.10	.05	.01
□ 257	R.J. Reynolds	.04	.02	.00
□ 258	Tim Raines	.20	.10	.02
□ 259	Frank Williams	.04	.02	.00
□ 260	Jose Gonzalez	.04	.02	.00
□ 261	Mitch Webster	.04	.02	.00
□ 262	Ken Caminiti	.04	.02	.00
□ 263	Bob Boone	.10	.05	.01
□ 264	Dave Magadan	.10	.05	.01
□ 265	Rick Aguilera	.04	.02	.00
□ 266	Chris James	.07	.03	.01
□ 267	Bob Welch	.07	.03	.01
□ 268	Ken Dayley	.04	.02	.00
□ 269	Junior Ortiz	.04	.02	.00
□ 270	Allan Anderson	.07	.03	.01
□ 271	Steve Jeltz	.04	.02	.00
□ 272	George Bell	.15	.07	.01
□ 273	Roberto Kelly	.20	.10	.02
□ 274	Brett Butler	.07	.03	.01
□ 275	Mike Schooler	.10	.05	.01
□ 276	Ken Phelps	.07	.03	.01
□ 277	Glenn Braggs	.10	.05	.01
□ 278	Jose Rijo	.04	.02	.00
□ 279	Bobby Witt	.07	.03	.01
□ 280	Jerry Browne	.07	.03	.01
□ 281	Kevin Mitchell	.45	.22	.04
□ 282	Craig Worthington	.20	.10	.02
□ 283	Greg Minton	.04	.02	.00
□ 284	Nick Esasky	.10	.05	.01
□ 285	John Farrell	.07	.03	.01
□ 286	Rick Mahler	.04	.02	.00
□ 287	Tom Gordon	.50	.25	.05
□ 288	Gerald Young	.10	.05	.01
□ 289	Jody Reed	.04	.02	.00
□ 290	Jeff Hamilton	.04	.02	.00
□ 291	Gerald Perry	.04	.02	.00
□ 292	Hubie Brooks	.07	.03	.01
□ 293	Bo Diaz	.04	.02	.00
□ 294	Terry Puhl	.04	.02	.00
□ 295	Jim Gantner	.04	.02	.00
□ 296	Jeff Parrett	.04	.02	.00
□ 297	Mike Boddicker	.04	.02	.00
□ 298	Dan Gladden	.04	.02	.00
□ 299	Tony Pena	.07	.03	.01
□ 300	Checklist Card	.04	.02	.00
□ 301	Tom Henke	.07	.03	.01
□ 302	Pascual Perez	.07	.03	.01
□ 303	Steve Bedrosian	.07	.03	.01

		MINT	EXC	G-VG
☐ 304	Ken Hill	.07	.03	.01
☐ 305	Jerry Reuss	.04	.02	.00
☐ 306	Jim Eisenreich	.07	.03	.01
☐ 307	Jack Howell	.04	.02	.00
☐ 308	Rick Cerone	.04	.02	.00
☐ 309	Tim Leary	.07	.03	.01
☐ 310	Joe Orsulak	.04	.02	.00
☐ 311	Jim Dwyer	.04	.02	.00
☐ 312	Geno Petralli	.04	.02	.00
☐ 313	Rick Honeycutt	.04	.02	.00
☐ 314	Tom Foley	.04	.02	.00
☐ 315	Kenny Rogers	.04	.02	.00
☐ 316	Mike Flanagan	.04	.02	.00
☐ 317	Bryan Harvey	.10	.05	.01
☐ 318	Billy Ripken	.04	.02	.00
☐ 319	Jeff Montgomery	.10	.05	.01
☐ 320	Erik Hanson	.07	.03	.01
☐ 321	Brian Downing	.04	.02	.00
☐ 322	Gregg Olson	.50	.25	.05
☐ 323	Terry Steinbach	.10	.05	.01
☐ 324	Sammy Sosa	.40	.20	.04
☐ 325	Gene Harris	.15	.07	.01
☐ 326	Mike Devereaux	.07	.03	.01
☐ 327	Dennis Cook	.07	.03	.01
☐ 328	David Wells	.04	.02	.00
☐ 329	Checklist Card	.04	.02	.00
☐ 330	Kirt Manwaring	.07	.03	.01
☐ 331	Jim Presley	.04	.02	.00
☐ 332	Checklist Card	.04	.02	.00
☐ 333	Chuck Finley	.07	.03	.01
☐ 334	Rob Dibble	.10	.05	.01
☐ 335	Cecil Espy	.07	.03	.01
☐ 336	Dave Parker	.10	.05	.01
☐ 24	German Gonzalez	.07	.03	.01
☐ 25	Craig Worthington	.35	.17	.03
☐ 26	Jerome Walton	4.50	2.25	.45
☐ 27	Gary Wayne	.20	.10	.02
☐ 28	Tim Jones	.10	.05	.01
☐ 29	Dante Bichette	.10	.05	.01
☐ 30	Alexis Infante	.15	.07	.01
☐ 31	Ken Hill	.10	.05	.01
☐ 32	Dwight Smith	1.50	.75	.15
☐ 33	Luis de los Santos	.15	.07	.01
☐ 34	Eric Yelding	.15	.07	.01
☐ 35	Gregg Olson	1.00	.50	.10
☐ 36	Phil Stephenson	.20	.10	.02
☐ 37	Ken Patterson	.10	.05	.01
☐ 38	Rick Wrona	.30	.15	.03
☐ 39	Mike Brumley	.10	.05	.01
☐ 40	Cris Carpenter	.10	.05	.01
☐ 41	Jeff Brantley	.20	.10	.02
☐ 42	Ron Jones	.20	.10	.02
☐ 43	Randy Johnson	.10	.05	.01
☐ 44	Kevin Brown	.15	.07	.01
☐ 45	Ramon Martinez	.20	.10	.02
☐ 46	Greg W.Harris	.15	.07	.01
☐ 47	Steve Finley	.30	.15	.03
☐ 48	Randy Kramer	.10	.05	.01
☐ 49	Erik Hanson	.15	.07	.01
☐ 50	Matt Merullo	.15	.07	.01
☐ 51	Mike Devereaux	.10	.05	.01
☐ 52	Clay Parker	.25	.12	.02
☐ 53	Omar Vizquel	.30	.15	.03
☐ 54	Derek Lilliquist	.15	.07	.01
☐ 55	Junior Felix	1.00	.50	.10
☐ 56	Checklist	.07	.01	.00

1989 Donruss Rookies

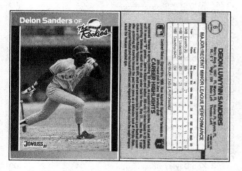

The 1989 Donruss Rookies set contains 56 standard-size (2 1/2 by 3 1/2 inch) cards. The fronts have green and black borders; the backs are green and feature career highlights. The cards were distributed as a boxed set.

		MINT	EXC	G-VG
COMPLETE SET (56)		27.00	13.50	2.70
COMMON PLAYER (1-56)		.07	.03	.01
☐ 1	Gary Sheffield	1.00	.50	.10
☐ 2	Gregg Jefferies	1.00	.50	.10
☐ 3	Ken Griffey Jr.	3.00	1.50	.30
☐ 4	Tom Gordon	1.00	.50	.10
☐ 5	Billy Spiers	.35	.17	.03
☐ 6	Deion Sanders	1.25	.60	.12
☐ 7	Donn Pall	.10	.05	.01
☐ 8	Steve Carter	.20	.10	.02
☐ 9	Francisco Oliveras	.10	.05	.01
☐ 10	Steve Wilson	.15	.07	.01
☐ 11	Bob Geren	.45	.22	.04
☐ 12	Tony Castillo	.15	.07	.01
☐ 13	Kenny Rogers	.15	.07	.01
☐ 14	Carlos Martinez	.20	.10	.02
☐ 15	Edgar Martinez	.10	.05	.01
☐ 16	Jim Abbott	2.50	1.25	.25
☐ 17	Torey Lovullo	.15	.07	.01
☐ 18	Mark Carreon	.10	.05	.01
☐ 19	Geronimo Berroa	.07	.03	.01
☐ 20	Luis Medina	.15	.07	.01
☐ 21	Sandy Alomar Jr.	.50	.25	.05
☐ 22	Bob Milacki	.15	.07	.01
☐ 23	Joe Girardi	.35	.17	.03

1990 Donruss Preview

The 1990 Donruss Preview set contains 12 standard-size (2 1/2 by 3 1/2 inch) cards. The bright red borders are exactly like the regular 1990 Donruss cards, but the photos are different. The horizontally-oriented backs are plain white with career highlights in black lettering. Two cards were sent to each dealer in the Donruss dealer network thus making it quite difficult to put together a set.

		MINT	EXC	G-VG
COMPLETE SET (12)		200.00	.00	.00
COMMON PLAYER (1-12)		10.00	5.00	1.00
☐ 1	Todd Zeile	25.00	10.00	2.00
☐ 2	Ben McDonald	25.00	10.00	2.00
☐ 3	Bo Jackson	35.00	14.00	2.50
☐ 4	Will Clark	35.00	14.00	2.50
☐ 5	Dave Stewart	10.00	5.00	1.00
☐ 6	Kevin Mitchell	15.00	7.00	1.50
☐ 7	Nolan Ryan	35.00	14.00	2.50
☐ 8	Howard Johnson	15.00	7.00	1.50
☐ 9	Tony Gwynn	15.00	7.00	1.50
☐ 10	Jerome Walton	25.00	10.00	2.00
☐ 11	Wade Boggs	25.00	10.00	2.00
☐ 12	Kirby Puckett	25.00	10.00	2.00

1990 Donruss

The 1990 Donruss set contains 716 standard-size (2 1/2 by 3 1/2 inch) cards. The front borders are bright red. The horizontally-oriented backs are amber. Cards numbered 1-26 are Diamond Kings; cards numbered 28-47 are Rated Rookies. Card #716 was added to the set shortly after the set's initial production, necessitating the checklist variation on card #700. The set is the largest ever produced by Donruss, unfortunately it is also has a large number of errors which were corrected after the cards were released. Every All-Star selection in the set has two versions, the statistical heading on the back is either "Recent Major League Performance" or "All-Star Game Performance."

	MINT	EXC	G-VG
COMPLETE SET (716)	24.00	12.00	2.40
COMMON PLAYER (1-716)	.03	.01	.00

		MINT	EXC	G-VG
☐ 1	Bo Jackson DK	.50	.20	.04
☐ 2	Steve Sax DK	.08	.04	.01
☐ 3A	Ruben Sierra DK ERR (no small line on top border on card back)	1.50	.50	.07
☐ 3B	Ruben Sierra DK COR	.30	.10	.02
☐ 4	Ken Griffey Jr. DK	.50	.25	.05
☐ 5	Mickey Tettleton DK	.06	.03	.00
☐ 6	Dave Stewart DK	.08	.04	.01
☐ 7	Jim Deshaies DK	.06	.03	.00
☐ 8	John Smoltz DK	.08	.04	.01
☐ 9	Mike Bielecki DK	.06	.03	.00
☐ 10A	Brian Downing DK ERR (reverse negative)	1.50	.60	.15
☐ 10B	Brian Downing DK COR	.10	.03	.01
☐ 11	Kevin Mitchell DK	.15	.07	.01
☐ 12	Kelly Gruber DK	.06	.03	.00
☐ 13	Joe Magrane DK	.08	.04	.01
☐ 14	John Franco DK	.08	.04	.01
☐ 15	Ozzie Guillen DK	.06	.03	.00
☐ 16	Lou Whitaker DK	.08	.04	.01
☐ 17	John Smiley DK	.06	.03	.00
☐ 18	Howard Johnson DK	.10	.05	.01
☐ 19	Willie Randolph DK	.06	.03	.00
☐ 20	Chris Bosio DK	.06	.03	.00
☐ 21	Tommy Herr DK	.06	.03	.00
☐ 22	Dan Gladden DK	.06	.03	.00
☐ 23	Ellis Burks DK	.15	.07	.01
☐ 24	Pete O'Brien DK	.06	.03	.00
☐ 25	Bryn Smith DK	.06	.03	.00
☐ 26	Ed Whitson DK	.06	.03	.00
☐ 27	DK Checklist	.06	.01	.00
☐ 28	Robin Ventura	.50	.25	.05
☐ 29	Todd Zeile	1.25	.60	.12
☐ 30	Sandy Alomar Jr.	.25	.12	.02
☐ 31	Kent Mercker	.35	.17	.03
☐ 32	Ben McDonald	1.75	.85	.17
☐ 33A	Juan Gonzalez ERR (reverse negative)	5.00	2.50	.50
☐ 33B	Juan Gonzalez COR	.75	.35	.07
☐ 34	Eric Anthony	1.50	.75	.15
☐ 35	Mike Fetters	.20	.10	.02
☐ 36	Marquis Grissom	.50	.25	.05
☐ 37	Greg Vaughn	1.25	.60	.12
☐ 38	Brian Dubois	.15	.07	.01
☐ 39	Steve Avery	.35	.17	.03
☐ 40	Mark Gardner	.15	.07	.01
☐ 41	Andy Benes	.40	.20	.04
☐ 42	Delino DeShields	.35	.17	.03
☐ 43	Scott Coolbaugh	.25	.12	.02
☐ 44	Pat Combs	.35	.17	.03
☐ 45	Alex Sanchez	.10	.05	.01
☐ 46	Kelly Mann	.15	.07	.01
☐ 47	Julio Machado	.20	.10	.02
☐ 48	Pete Incaviglia	.08	.04	.01
☐ 49	Shawon Dunston	.08	.04	.01
☐ 50	Jeff Treadway	.03	.01	.00
☐ 51	Jeff Ballard	.06	.03	.00
☐ 52	Claudell Washington	.06	.03	.00
☐ 53	Juan Samuel	.08	.04	.01
☐ 54	John Smiley	.06	.03	.00
☐ 55	Rob Deer	.06	.03	.00
☐ 56	Geno Petralli	.03	.01	.00
☐ 57	Chris Bosio	.06	.03	.00
☐ 58	Carlton Fisk	.10	.05	.01
☐ 59	Kirt Manwaring	.03	.01	.00
☐ 60	Chet Lemon	.03	.01	.00
☐ 61	Bo Jackson	.50	.25	.05
☐ 62	Doyle Alexander	.03	.01	.00
☐ 63	Pedro Guerrero	.08	.04	.01
☐ 64	Allan Anderson	.06	.03	.00
☐ 65	Greg Harris	.03	.01	.00
☐ 66	Mike Greenwell	.25	.12	.02
☐ 67	Walt Weiss	.08	.04	.01
☐ 68	Wade Boggs	.25	.12	.02
☐ 69	Jim Clancy	.03	.01	.00
☐ 70	Junior Felix	.35	.17	.03
☐ 71	Barry Larkin	.10	.05	.01
☐ 72	Dave LaPoint	.03	.01	.00
☐ 73	Joel Skinner	.03	.01	.00
☐ 74	Jesse Barfield	.08	.04	.01
☐ 75	Tommy Herr	.03	.01	.00
☐ 76	Ricky Jordan	.20	.10	.02
☐ 77	Eddie Murray	.10	.05	.01
☐ 78	Steve Sax	.08	.04	.01
☐ 79	Tim Belcher	.06	.03	.00
☐ 80	Danny Jackson	.06	.03	.00
☐ 81	Kent Hrbek	.08	.04	.01
☐ 82	Milt Thompson	.03	.01	.00
☐ 83	Brook Jacoby	.06	.03	.00
☐ 84	Mike Marshall	.08	.04	.01
☐ 85	Kevin Seitzer	.08	.04	.01
☐ 86	Tony Gwynn	.20	.10	.02
☐ 87	Dave Stieb	.08	.04	.01
☐ 88	Dave Smith	.03	.01	.00
☐ 89	Bret Saberhagen	.10	.05	.01
☐ 90	Alan Trammell	.08	.04	.01
☐ 91	Tony Phillips	.03	.01	.00
☐ 92	Doug Drabek	.03	.01	.00
☐ 93	Jeffrey Leonard	.06	.03	.00
☐ 94	Wally Joyner	.08	.04	.01
☐ 95	Carney Lansford	.08	.04	.01
☐ 96	Cal Ripken	.12	.06	.01
☐ 97	Andres Galarraga	.08	.04	.01
☐ 98	Kevin Mitchell	.20	.10	.02
☐ 99	Howard Johnson	.10	.05	.01
☐ 100	Checklist Card	.06	.01	.00
☐ 101	Melido Perez	.03	.01	.00
☐ 102	Spike Owen	.03	.01	.00
☐ 103	Paul Molitor	.08	.04	.01
☐ 104	Geronimo Berroa	.03	.01	.00
☐ 105	Ryne Sandberg	.12	.06	.01
☐ 106	Bryn Smith	.06	.03	.00
☐ 107	Steve Buechele	.03	.01	.00
☐ 108	Jim Abbott	.75	.35	.07
☐ 109	Alvin Davis	.08	.04	.01
☐ 110	Lee Smith	.06	.03	.00
☐ 111	Roberto Alomar	.08	.04	.01
☐ 112	Rick Reuschel	.06	.03	.00
☐ 113	Kelly Gruber	.06	.03	.00
☐ 114	Joe Carter	.10	.05	.01
☐ 115	Jose Rijo	.03	.01	.00
☐ 116	Greg Minton	.03	.01	.00
☐ 117	Bob Ojeda	.06	.03	.00
☐ 118	Glenn Davis	.10	.05	.01
☐ 119	Jeff Reardon	.06	.03	.00
☐ 120	Kurt Stillwell	.03	.01	.00
☐ 121	John Smoltz	.10	.05	.01
☐ 122	Dwight Evans	.08	.04	.01
☐ 123	Eric Yelding	.10	.05	.01
☐ 124	John Franco	.08	.04	.01
☐ 125	Jose Canseco	.50	.25	.05
☐ 126	Barry Bonds	.08	.04	.01
☐ 127	Lee Guetterman	.03	.01	.00
☐ 128	Jack Clark	.08	.04	.01
☐ 129	Dave Valle	.03	.01	.00
☐ 130	Hubie Brooks	.06	.03	.00
☐ 131	Ernest Riles	.03	.01	.00
☐ 132	Mike Morgan	.03	.01	.00
☐ 133	Steve Jeltz	.03	.01	.00
☐ 134	Jeff Robinson	.06	.03	.00
☐ 135	Ozzie Guillen	.06	.03	.00

COMPLETE BASEBALL CARD SETS

REGULAR ISSUES
1990 Topps (792) $25.00
1989 Topps (792) 26.00
1988 Topps (792) 25.00
1987 Topps (792) 35.00
1986 Topps (792) 35.00
All 5 above Topps Sets 135.00
1985 Topps (792) 100.00
1984 Topps (792) 100.00
1989 Bowman (484) 23.00
1990 Fleer (660) 28.00
1989 Fleer (660) 30.00
1988 Fleer (660) 35.00
1986 Fleer (660) 100.00
1990 Donruss (716) 28.00
1989 Donruss (660) 30.00
1988 Donruss (660) 35.00
1990 Score (714) 23.00
1989 Score (660) 22.00
1988 Score (660) 24.00
1990 Sportflics (225) 40.00
1989 Sportflics (225) 42.00
1988 Sportflics (225) 50.00
1987 Sportflics (200) 32.00

TRADED OR UPDATE ISSUES
1989 Topps (132) $15.00
1988 Topps (132) 26.00
1987 Topps (132) 14.00
1985 Topps (132) 16.00
1982 Topps (132) 32.00
1989 Fleer (132) 22.00
1988 Fleer (132) 13.00
1987 Fleer (132) 18.00
1986 Fleer (132) 34.00
1985 Fleer (132) 16.00
1989 Score (110) 15.00
1988 Score (110) 38.00
1989 Donruss (56) 7.00
1989 Upper Deck (100) 50.00
1987 Topps Tiffany (132) 35.00
1988 Fleer Tin (132) 25.00
1987 Fleer Tin (132) 25.00

ROOKIE SETS
1989 Donruss (56) $28.00
1988 Donruss (56) 14.00
1987 Donruss (56) 20.00
1987 Sportflics-Pt. 1 (25) 12.00
1987 Sportflics-Pt. 2 (25) 12.00
1986 Sportflics (50) 13.00
1989 Topps (22) 10.00

TOPPS GLOSSY ALL-STARS
All 22 cards per set
1990, 1989, 1988 . . . .$5.00 each
1985, 1984 . . . . .6.00 each

CANADIAN ISSUES
1990 O.P.C. (792) $32.00
1989 O.P.C. (396) .16.00
1988 O.P.C. (396) .16.00
1984 O.P.C. (396) .40.00
1988 Leaf (264) 16.00

MINI SETS
1988 Fleer (120) $14.00
1987 Fleer (120) .10.00
1986 Fleer (120) .12.00

DONRUSS ALL-STAR SETS
60 or 64 cards per set
1989, 1988, 1987, 1986 . . . .$9.00 each

DONRUSS POP-UP SETS
18 or 20 cards per set
1989, 1988, 1987, 1986 . . . .$5.00 each

DONRUSS LARGE DIAMOND KINGS (5″ x 7″)
28 cards per set
1990, 1989, 1988, 1986, 1985 . . . .$12.00 each

OTHER ISSUES
1990 Topps Major League Debut (152) $16.00
1989 Topps 'Big' Cards (330) 32.00
1989 Score Young Superstars
    Series 1 (40) .11.00
    Series 2 (40) .11.00
    Both Series 1 & 2 . . . . .20.00
1989 Score Masters (42) 13.00
1988 Topps 'Big' Cards (264) 30.00
1988 Topps United Kingdom (88) 10.00
1988 Topps Glossy Send In (60) 12.00
1988 Score Young Superstars
    Series 1 (40) .12.00
    Series 2 (40) .12.00
    Both Series 1 & 2 . . . . .22.00
1987 Topps Tiffany (792) 120.00
1987 Donruss Opening Day (272) 18.00
1987 Sportflics Team Preview (26) 7.00
1987 Sportflics Rookie Packs (10) 10.00
1987 Sportflics Superstar Sheets (4) 15.00
1987 Donruss Highlights (56) 5.00
1986 Topps Supers (60) 8.00
1985 Topps Pete Rose (120) 18.00
1985 Donruss Highlights (56) 28.00
1982 Topps Stickers (260 + album) 10.00
1982 Fleer Stamps (Box of 600) 10.00
1981 Topps Stickers (262 + album) 10.00

BILL DODGE
P.O. BOX 40154
BAY VILLAGE, OH 44140
Phone: (216) 835-4146

#	Player	Price1	Price2	Price3	#	Player	Price1	Price2	Price3
☐ 136	Chili Davis	.06	.03	.00	☐ 231	Jimmy Key	.06	.03	.00
☐ 137	Mitch Webster	.03	.01	.00	☐ 232	John Farrell	.03	.01	.00
☐ 138	Jerry Browne	.03	.01	.00	☐ 233	Eric Davis	.20	.10	.02
☐ 139	Bo Diaz	.03	.01	.00	☐ 234	Johnny Ray	.06	.03	.00
☐ 140	Robby Thompson	.03	.01	.00	☐ 235	Darryl Strawberry	.25	.12	.02
☐ 141	Craig Worthington	.10	.05	.01	☐ 236	Bill Doran	.06	.03	.00
☐ 142	Julio Franco	.08	.04	.01	☐ 237	Greg Gagne	.03	.01	.00
☐ 143	Brian Holman	.03	.01	.00	☐ 238	Jim Eisenreich	.03	.01	.00
☐ 144	George Brett	.12	.06	.01	☐ 239	Tommy Gregg	.03	.01	.00
☐ 145	Tom Glavine	.06	.03	.00	☐ 240	Marty Barrett	.03	.01	.00
☐ 146	Robin Yount	.25	.12	.02	☐ 241	Rafael Ramirez	.03	.01	.00
☐ 147	Gary Carter	.08	.04	.01	☐ 242	Chris Sabo	.08	.04	.01
☐ 148	Ron Kittle	.06	.03	.00	☐ 243	Dave Henderson	.03	.01	.00
☐ 149	Tony Fernandez	.08	.04	.01	☐ 244	Andy Van Slyke	.08	.04	.01
☐ 150	Dave Stewart	.08	.04	.01	☐ 245	Alvaro Espinoza	.03	.01	.00
☐ 151	Gary Gaetti	.08	.04	.01	☐ 246	Garry Templeton	.06	.03	.00
☐ 152	Kevin Elster	.06	.03	.00	☐ 247	Gene Harris	.15	.07	.01
☐ 153	Gerald Perry	.03	.01	.00	☐ 248	Kevin Gross	.03	.01	.00
☐ 154	Jesse Orosco	.03	.01	.00	☐ 249	Brett Butler	.06	.03	.00
☐ 155	Wally Backman	.03	.01	.00	☐ 250	Willie Randolph	.06	.03	.00
☐ 156	Dennis Martinez	.03	.01	.00	☐ 251	Roger McDowell	.06	.03	.00
☐ 157	Rick Sutcliffe	.08	.04	.01	☐ 252	Rafael Belliard	.03	.01	.00
☐ 158	Greg Maddux	.08	.04	.01	☐ 253	Steve Rosenberg	.03	.01	.00
☐ 159	Andy Hawkins	.03	.01	.00	☐ 254	Jack Howell	.03	.01	.00
☐ 160	John Kruk	.06	.03	.00	☐ 255	Marvell Wynne	.03	.01	.00
☐ 161	Jose Oquendo	.03	.01	.00	☐ 256	Tom Candiotti	.03	.01	.00
☐ 162	John Dopson	.03	.01	.00	☐ 257	Todd Benzinger	.03	.01	.00
☐ 163	Joe Magrane	.08	.04	.01	☐ 258	Don Robinson	.03	.01	.00
☐ 164	Bill Ripken	.03	.01	.00	☐ 259	Phil Bradley	.06	.03	.00
☐ 165	Fred Manrique	.03	.01	.00	☐ 260	Cecil Espy	.03	.01	.00
☐ 166	Nolan Ryan	.25	.12	.02	☐ 261	Scott Bankhead	.06	.03	.00
☐ 167	Damon Berryhill	.08	.04	.01	☐ 262	Frank White	.06	.03	.00
☐ 168	Dale Murphy	.12	.06	.01	☐ 263	Andres Thomas	.03	.01	.00
☐ 169	Mickey Tettleton	.06	.03	.00	☐ 264	Glenn Braggs	.06	.03	.00
☐ 170	Kirk McCaskill	.03	.01	.00	☐ 265	David Cone	.08	.04	.01
☐ 171	Dwight Gooden	.20	.10	.02	☐ 266	Bobby Thigpen	.06	.03	.00
☐ 172	Jose Lind	.03	.01	.00	☐ 267	Nelson Liriano	.03	.01	.00
☐ 173	B.J. Surhoff	.06	.03	.00	☐ 268	Terry Steinbach	.08	.04	.01
☐ 174	Ruben Sierra	.25	.12	.02	☐ 269	Kirby Puckett	.25	.12	.02
☐ 175	Dan Plesac	.06	.03	.00	☐ 270	Gregg Jefferies	.35	.17	.03
☐ 176	Dan Pasqua	.03	.01	.00	☐ 271	Jeff Blauser	.03	.01	.00
☐ 177	Kelly Downs	.03	.01	.00	☐ 272	Cory Snyder	.08	.04	.01
☐ 178	Matt Nokes	.06	.03	.00	☐ 273	Roy Smith	.03	.01	.00
☐ 179	Luis Aquino	.03	.01	.00	☐ 274	Tom Foley	.03	.01	.00
☐ 180	Frank Tanana	.03	.01	.00	☐ 275	Mitch Williams	.06	.03	.00
☐ 181	Tony Pena	.06	.03	.00	☐ 276	Paul Kilgus	.03	.01	.00
☐ 182	Dan Gladden	.03	.01	.00	☐ 277	Don Slaught	.03	.01	.00
☐ 183	Bruce Hurst	.06	.03	.00	☐ 278	Von Hayes	.08	.04	.01
☐ 184	Roger Clemens	.25	.12	.02	☐ 279	Vince Coleman	.08	.04	.01
☐ 185	Mark McGwire	.25	.12	.02	☐ 280	Mike Boddicker	.03	.01	.00
☐ 186	Rob Murphy	.03	.01	.00	☐ 281	Ken Dayley	.03	.01	.00
☐ 187	Jim Deshaies	.03	.01	.00	☐ 282	Mike Devereaux	.03	.01	.00
☐ 188	Fred McGriff	.12	.06	.01	☐ 283	Kenny Rogers	.10	.05	.01
☐ 189	Rob Dibble	.06	.03	.00	☐ 284	Jeff Russell	.06	.03	.00
☐ 190	Don Mattingly	.50	.25	.05	☐ 285	Jerome Walton	1.00	.50	.10
☐ 191	Felix Fermin	.03	.01	.00	☐ 286	Derek Lilliquist	.03	.01	.00
☐ 192	Roberto Kelly	.10	.05	.01	☐ 287	Joe Orsulak	.03	.01	.00
☐ 193	Dennis Cook	.08	.04	.01	☐ 288	Dick Schofield	.03	.01	.00
☐ 194	Darren Daulton	.03	.01	.00	☐ 289	Ron Darling	.08	.04	.01
☐ 195	Alfredo Griffin	.03	.01	.00	☐ 290	Bobby Bonilla	.08	.04	.01
☐ 196	Eric Plunk	.03	.01	.00	☐ 291	Jim Gantner	.03	.01	.00
☐ 197	Orel Hershiser	.10	.05	.01	☐ 292	Bobby Witt	.06	.03	.00
☐ 198	Paul O'Neill	.08	.04	.01	☐ 293	Greg Brock	.03	.01	.00
☐ 199	Randy Bush	.03	.01	.00	☐ 294	Ivan Calderon	.06	.03	.00
☐ 200	Checklist Card	.06	.01	.00	☐ 295	Steve Bedrosian	.08	.04	.01
☐ 201	Ozzie Smith	.10	.05	.01	☐ 296	Mike Henneman	.03	.01	.00
☐ 202	Pete O'Brien	.06	.03	.00	☐ 297	Tom Gordon	.40	.20	.04
☐ 203	Jay Howell	.03	.01	.00	☐ 298	Lou Whitaker	.08	.04	.01
☐ 204	Mark Gubicza	.08	.04	.01	☐ 299	Terry Pendleton	.03	.01	.00
☐ 205	Ed Whitson	.03	.01	.00	☐ 300	Checklist Card	.06	.01	.00
☐ 206	George Bell	.08	.04	.01	☐ 301	Juan Berenguer	.03	.01	.00
☐ 207	Mike Scott	.08	.04	.01	☐ 302	Mark Davis	.08	.04	.01
☐ 208	Charlie Leibrandt	.03	.01	.00	☐ 303	Nick Esasky	.06	.03	.00
☐ 209	Mike Heath	.03	.01	.00	☐ 304	Rickey Henderson	.20	.10	.02
☐ 210	Dennis Eckersley	.08	.04	.01	☐ 305	Rick Cerone	.03	.01	.00
☐ 211	Mike LaValliere	.03	.01	.00	☐ 306	Craig Biggio	.10	.05	.01
☐ 212	Darnell Coles	.03	.01	.00	☐ 307	Duane Ward	.03	.01	.00
☐ 213	Lance Parrish	.08	.04	.01	☐ 308	Tom Browning	.06	.03	.00
☐ 214	Mike Moore	.06	.03	.00	☐ 309	Walt Terrell	.03	.01	.00
☐ 215	Steve Finley	.12	.06	.01	☐ 310	Greg Swindell	.08	.04	.01
☐ 216	Tim Raines	.10	.05	.01	☐ 311	Dave Righetti	.08	.04	.01
☐ 217	Scott Garrelts	.06	.03	.00	☐ 312	Mike Maddux	.03	.01	.00
☐ 218	Kevin McReynolds	.08	.04	.01	☐ 313	Len Dykstra	.06	.03	.00
☐ 219	Dave Gallagher	.03	.01	.00	☐ 314	Jose Gonzalez	.03	.01	.00
☐ 220	Tim Wallach	.06	.03	.00	☐ 315	Steve Balboni	.03	.01	.00
☐ 221	Chuck Crim	.03	.01	.00	☐ 316	Mike Scioscia	.03	.01	.00
☐ 222	Lonnie Smith	.06	.03	.00	☐ 317	Ron Oester	.03	.01	.00
☐ 223	Andre Dawson	.10	.05	.01	☐ 318	Gary Wayne	.10	.05	.01
☐ 224	Nelson Santovenia	.06	.03	.00	☐ 319	Todd Worrell	.08	.04	.01
☐ 225	Rafael Palmeiro	.08	.04	.01	☐ 320	Doug Jones	.06	.03	.00
☐ 226	Devon White	.08	.04	.01	☐ 321	Jeff Hamilton	.06	.03	.00
☐ 227	Harold Reynolds	.06	.03	.00	☐ 322	Danny Tartabull	.08	.04	.01
☐ 228	Ellis Burks	.15	.07	.01	☐ 323	Chris James	.06	.03	.00
☐ 229	Mark Parent	.03	.01	.00	☐ 324	Mike Flanagan	.03	.01	.00
☐ 230	Will Clark	.50	.25	.05	☐ 325	Gerald Young	.03	.01	.00

DEN'S
COLLECTORS DEN

PLASTIC CARD PROTECTING PAGES
LARGEST SELECTION IN THE HOBBY

FINEST QUALITY PLASTIC SHEETS

DEN'S COLLECTORS DEN

HOME OF SPORT AMERICANA

Featuring:
NON—MIGRATING PLASTIC IN ALL SHEETS
PLASTIC THAT DOES NOT STICK TOGETHER
STIFFNESS TO RESIST CARD CURLING
INTELLIGENT DESIGN
RESISTANCE TO CRACKING
FULL COVERAGE OF CARDS, PHOTOS, ENVELOPES

DEPT. PG12
P.O. BOX 606, LAUREL, MD 20725

SEND ONLY $ 1.00 for DEN'S BIG CATALOGUE CATALOGUE sent FREE with each ORDER

NO   MIX   &   MATCH

STYLE	POCKETS CAPACITY	RECOMMENDED FOR	PRICE EACH (Does not include Post. & Hand.)			
			1—24	25—99	100—299	300 plus
9	9 / 18	TOPPS (1957 to present), FLEER, DONRUSS SCORE, SPORTFLICS, TCMA, LEAF (1960), All standard 2½" X 3½" cards, SIDE LOAD	.25	.23	.21	.19
9T	9 / 18	SAME AS STYLE 9 ABOVE, TOP LOAD	.25	.23	.21	.19
8	8 / 16	TOPPS (1952—1956, 1988 Big), BOWMAN (1953—1955)	.25	.23	.21	.19
12	12 / 24	BOWMAN (1948—1950), TOPPS (1951), TOPPS (Stickers), FLEER (Minis & Stickers)	.25	.23	.21	.19
1	1 / 2	PHOTOGRAPHS (8" X 10")	.25	.23	.21	.19
2	2 / 4	PHOTOGRAPHS (5" X 7"), TOPPS (1984, 1985 & 1986 Supers)	.25	.23	.21	.19
4	4 / 8	POSTCARDS, EXHIBITS, PEREZ—STEELE (Hall of Fame postcards), DONRUSS (1983—1987 All-Stars), TOPPS (1964,70,71 Supers)	.25	.23	.21	.19
6P	6 / 12	POLICE AND SAFETY CARDS (All sports)	.25	.23	.21	.19
18	18 / 36	T206 and most other T CARDS, BAZOOKA (1963—1967 Individual cards), Many 19th Century cards (N Cards)	.40	.40	35	.35
9G	9 / 18	GOUDEY, DIAMOND STARS, LEAF (1948)	.40	.40	.35	.35
9PB	9 / 18	PLAY BALL, BOWMAN (1951-52), All GUM, INC. Cards, TOPPS (Minis), DOUBLE PLAY	.40	.40	.35	.35
1C	1 / 2	TURKEY RED (T3), PRESS GUIDES, PEREZ—STEELE (Greatest Moments), Many WRAPPERS (Sport & non-sport)	.40	.40	.35	.35
3	3 / 6	3—CARD PANELS (Hostess, Star, Zeller's)	.40	.40	.35	.35
6V	6 / 12	TOPPS (Double Headers, Greatest Moments, 1951 Connie Mack, Current All-Stars, Team, 1965 Football and Hockey, Bucks, 1969—1970 Basketball, T201 (Mecca Double folders), T202 (Hassan Triple folders), DADS (Hockey), DONRUSS (1986—87 Pop—Ups)	.40	.40	.35	.35
6D	6 / 12	RED MAN (With or without tabs), DISCS, KAHN'S (1955—1967)	.40	.40	.35	.35
1Y	1 / 1	YEARBOOKS, PROGRAMS, MAGAZINES, Pocket Size is 9" X 12"	.40	.40	.35	.35
1S	1 / 2	MAGAZINE PAGES and PHOTOS, SMALL PROGRAMS, CRACKER JACK (1982 sheets), Pocket Size is 8½" X 11"	.40	.40	.35	.35
10	10 / 10	MATCHBOOK COVERS (Standard 20 match)	.40	.40	.35	.35
3E	3 / 3	FIRST DAY COVERS, BASEBALL COM—MEMORATIVE ENVELOPES	.40	.40	.35	.35
3L	3 / 6	SQUIRT PANELS, PEPSI (1963), FLEER (Stamps in strips)	.40	.40	.35	.35

☐ 326	Bob Boone	.08	.04	.01
☐ 327	Frank Williams	.03	.01	.00
☐ 328	Dave Parker	.08	.04	.01
☐ 329	Sid Bream	.03	.01	.00
☐ 330	Mike Schooler	.06	.03	.00
☐ 331	Bert Blyleven	.08	.04	.01
☐ 332	Bob Welch	.06	.03	.00
☐ 333	Bob Milacki	.06	.03	.00
☐ 334	Tim Burke	.06	.03	.00
☐ 335	Jose Uribe	.03	.01	.00
☐ 336	Randy Myers	.03	.01	.00
☐ 337	Eric King	.03	.01	.00
☐ 338	Mark Langston	.10	.05	.01
☐ 339	Teddy Higuera	.06	.03	.00
☐ 340	Oddibe McDowell	.06	.03	.00
☐ 341	Lloyd McClendon	.03	.01	.00
☐ 342	Pascual Perez	.06	.03	.00
☐ 343	Kevin Brown	.08	.04	.01
☐ 344	Chuck Finley	.06	.03	.00
☐ 345	Erik Hanson	.03	.01	.00
☐ 346	Rich Gedman	.03	.01	.00
☐ 347	Bip Roberts	.03	.01	.00
☐ 348	Matt Williams	.12	.06	.01
☐ 349	Tom Henke	.06	.03	.00
☐ 350	Brad Komminsk	.03	.01	.00
☐ 351	Jeff Reed	.03	.01	.00
☐ 352	Brian Downing	.03	.01	.00
☐ 353	Frank Viola	.08	.04	.01
☐ 354	Terry Puhl	.03	.01	.00
☐ 355	Brian Harper	.03	.01	.00
☐ 356	Steve Farr	.03	.01	.00
☐ 357	Joe Boever	.03	.01	.00
☐ 358	Danny Heep	.03	.01	.00
☐ 359	Larry Andersen	.03	.01	.00
☐ 360	Rolando Roomes	.06	.03	.00
☐ 361	Mike Gallego	.03	.01	.00
☐ 362	Bob Kipper	.03	.01	.00
☐ 363	Clay Parker	.10	.05	.01
☐ 364	Mike Pagliarulo	.06	.03	.00
☐ 365	Ken Griffey Jr. UER	1.00	.50	.10
	(signed through 1990, should be 1991)			
☐ 366	Rex Hudler	.03	.01	.00
☐ 367	Pat Sheridan	.03	.01	.00
☐ 368	Kirk Gibson	.08	.04	.01
☐ 369	Jeff Parrett	.03	.01	.00
☐ 370	Bob Walk	.03	.01	.00
☐ 371	Ken Patterson	.08	.04	.01
☐ 372	Bryan Harvey	.03	.01	.00
☐ 373	Mike Bielecki	.06	.03	.00
☐ 374	Tom Magrann	.12	.06	.01
☐ 375	Rick Mahler	.03	.01	.00
☐ 376	Craig Lefferts	.03	.01	.00
☐ 377	Gregg Olson	.25	.12	.02
☐ 378	Jamie Moyer	.03	.01	.00
☐ 379	Randy Johnson	.03	.01	.00
☐ 380	Jeff Montgomery	.06	.03	.00
☐ 381	Marty Clary	.03	.01	.00
☐ 382	Bill Spiers	.20	.08	.01
☐ 383	Dave Magadan	.08	.04	.01
☐ 384	Greg Hibbard	.10	.05	.01
☐ 385	Ernie Whitt	.03	.01	.00
☐ 386	Rick Honeycutt	.03	.01	.00
☐ 387	Dave West	.06	.03	.00
☐ 388	Keith Hernandez	.08	.04	.01
☐ 389	Jose Alvarez	.03	.01	.00
☐ 390	Joey Belle	.50	.25	.05
☐ 391	Rick Aguilera	.03	.01	.00
☐ 392	Mike Fitzgerald	.03	.01	.00
☐ 393	Dwight Smith	.50	.25	.05
☐ 394	Steve Wilson	.10	.05	.01
☐ 395	Bob Geren	.12	.06	.01
☐ 396	Randy Ready	.03	.01	.00
☐ 397	Ken Hill	.03	.01	.00
☐ 398	Jody Reed	.03	.01	.00
☐ 399	Tom Brunansky	.08	.04	.01
☐ 400	Checklist Card	.06	.01	.00
☐ 401	Rene Gonzales	.03	.01	.00
☐ 402	Harold Baines	.08	.04	.01
☐ 403	Cecilio Guante	.03	.01	.00
☐ 404	Joe Girardi	.10	.05	.01
☐ 405	Sergio Valdez	.10	.05	.01
☐ 406	Mark Williamson	.03	.01	.00
☐ 407	Glenn Hoffman	.03	.01	.00
☐ 408	Jeff Innis	.08	.04	.01
☐ 409	Randy Kramer	.03	.01	.00
☐ 410	Charlie O'Brien	.03	.01	.00
☐ 411	Charlie Hough	.03	.01	.00
☐ 412	Gus Polidor	.03	.01	.00
☐ 413	Ron Karkovice	.03	.01	.00
☐ 414	Trevor Wilson	.10	.05	.01
☐ 415	Kevin Ritz	.15	.07	.01
☐ 416	Gary Thurman	.03	.01	.00
☐ 417	Jeff Robinson	.06	.03	.00
☐ 418	Scott Terry	.03	.01	.00
☐ 419	Tim Laudner	.03	.01	.00
☐ 420	Dennis Rasmussen	.03	.01	.00
☐ 421	Luis Rivera	.03	.01	.00
☐ 422	Jim Corsi	.06	.03	.00
☐ 423	Dennis Lamp	.03	.01	.00
☐ 424	Ken Caminiti	.03	.01	.00
☐ 425	David Wells	.03	.01	.00
☐ 426	Norm Charlton	.03	.01	.00
☐ 427	Deion Sanders	.50	.25	.05
☐ 428	Dion James	.03	.01	.00
☐ 429	Chuck Cary	.06	.03	.00
☐ 430	Ken Howell	.03	.01	.00
☐ 431	Steve Lake	.03	.01	.00
☐ 432	Kal Daniels	.08	.04	.01
☐ 433	Lance McCullers	.03	.01	.00
☐ 434	Lenny Harris	.10	.05	.01
☐ 435	Scott Scudder	.15	.07	.01
☐ 436	Gene Larkin	.03	.01	.00
☐ 437	Dan Quisenberry	.06	.03	.00
☐ 438	Steve Olin	.08	.04	.01
☐ 439	Mickey Hatcher	.03	.01	.00
☐ 440	Willie Wilson	.06	.03	.00
☐ 441	Mark Grant	.03	.01	.00
☐ 442	Mookie Wilson	.06	.03	.00
☐ 443	Alex Trevino	.03	.01	.00
☐ 444	Pat Tabler	.03	.01	.00
☐ 445	Dave Bergman	.03	.01	.00
☐ 446	Todd Burns	.06	.03	.00
☐ 447	R.J. Reynolds	.03	.01	.00
☐ 448	Jay Buhner	.08	.04	.01
☐ 449	Lee Stevens	.20	.10	.02
☐ 450	Ron Hassey	.03	.01	.00
☐ 451	Bob Melvin	.03	.01	.00
☐ 452	Dave Martinez	.03	.01	.00
☐ 453	Greg Litton	.20	.10	.02
☐ 454	Mark Carreon	.06	.03	.00
☐ 455	Scott Fletcher	.03	.01	.00
☐ 456	Otis Nixon	.03	.01	.00
☐ 457	Tony Fossas	.10	.05	.01
☐ 458	John Russell	.03	.01	.00
☐ 459	Paul Assenmacher	.03	.01	.00
☐ 460	Zane Smith	.03	.01	.00
☐ 461	Jack Daugherty	.12	.06	.01
☐ 462	Rich Monteleone	.10	.05	.01
☐ 463	Greg Briley	.20	.10	.02
☐ 464	Mike Smithson	.03	.01	.00
☐ 465	Benito Santiago	.08	.04	.01
☐ 466	Jeff Brantley	.10	.05	.01
☐ 467	Jose Nunez	.03	.01	.00
☐ 468	Scott Bailes	.03	.01	.00
☐ 469	Ken Griffey Sr.	.08	.04	.01
☐ 470	Bob McClure	.03	.01	.00
☐ 471	Mackey Sasser	.06	.03	.00
☐ 472	Glenn Wilson	.03	.01	.00
☐ 473	Kevin Tapani	.15	.07	.01
☐ 474	Bill Buckner	.06	.03	.00
☐ 475	Ron Gant	.06	.03	.00
☐ 476	Kevin Romine	.03	.01	.00
☐ 477	Juan Agosto	.03	.01	.00
☐ 478	Herm Winningham	.03	.01	.00
☐ 479	Storm Davis	.06	.03	.00
☐ 480	Jeff King	.08	.04	.01
☐ 481	Kevin Mmahat	.12	.06	.01
☐ 482	Carmelo Martinez	.03	.01	.00
☐ 483	Omar Vizquel	.12	.06	.01
☐ 484	Jim Dwyer	.03	.01	.00
☐ 485	Bob Knepper	.03	.01	.00
☐ 486	Dave Anderson	.03	.01	.00
☐ 487	Ron Jones	.06	.03	.00
☐ 488	Jay Bell	.03	.01	.00
☐ 489	Sammy Sosa	.35	.17	.03
☐ 490	Kent Anderson	.10	.05	.01
☐ 491	Domingo Ramos	.03	.01	.00
☐ 492	Dave Clark	.06	.03	.00
☐ 493	Tim Birtsas	.03	.01	.00
☐ 494	Ken Oberkfell	.03	.01	.00
☐ 495	Larry Sheets	.03	.01	.00
☐ 496	Jeff Kunkel	.03	.01	.00
☐ 497	Jim Presley	.03	.01	.00
☐ 498	Mike Macfarlane	.03	.01	.00
☐ 499	Pete Smith	.03	.01	.00
☐ 500	Checklist Card	.06	.01	.00
☐ 501	Gary Sheffield	.35	.17	.03
☐ 502	Terry Bross	.12	.06	.01
☐ 503	Jerry Kutzler	.12	.06	.01
☐ 504	Lloyd Moseby	.06	.03	.00
☐ 505	Curt Young	.03	.01	.00
☐ 506	Al Newman	.03	.01	.00
☐ 507	Keith Miller	.03	.01	.00
☐ 508	Mike Stanton	.20	.10	.02
☐ 509	Rich Yett	.03	.01	.00
☐ 510	Tim Drummond	.12	.06	.01
☐ 511	Joe Hesketh	.03	.01	.00
☐ 512	Rick Wrona	.20	.10	.02
☐ 513	Luis Salazar	.03	.01	.00

☐ 514	Hal Morris	.03	.01	.00
☐ 515	Terry Mulholland	.03	.01	.00
☐ 516	John Morris	.03	.01	.00
☐ 517	Carlos Quintana	.03	.01	.00
☐ 518	Frank DiPino	.03	.01	.00
☐ 519	Randy Milligan	.10	.05	.01
☐ 520	Chad Kreuter	.03	.01	.00
☐ 521	Mike Jeffcoat	.03	.01	.00
☐ 522	Mike Harkey	.06	.03	.00
☐ 523	Andy Nezelek UER (wrong birth year)	.03	.01	.00
☐ 524	Dave Schmidt	.03	.01	.00
☐ 525	Tony Armas	.06	.03	.00
☐ 526	Barry Lyons	.03	.01	.00
☐ 527	Rick Reed	.10	.05	.01
☐ 528	Jerry Reuss	.03	.01	.00
☐ 529	Dean Palmer	.30	.15	.03
☐ 530	Jeff Peterek	.12	.06	.01
☐ 531	Carlos Martinez	.20	.10	.02
☐ 532	Atlee Hammaker	.03	.01	.00
☐ 533	Mike Brumley	.03	.01	.00
☐ 534	Terry Leach	.03	.01	.00
☐ 535	Doug Strange	.12	.06	.01
☐ 536	Jose DeLeon	.06	.03	.00
☐ 537	Shane Rawley	.03	.01	.00
☐ 538	Joey Cora	.06	.03	.00
☐ 539	Eric Hetzel	.03	.01	.00
☐ 540	Gene Nelson	.03	.01	.00
☐ 541	Wes Gardner	.03	.01	.00
☐ 542	Mark Portugal	.03	.01	.00
☐ 543	Al Leiter	.06	.03	.00
☐ 544	Jack Armstrong	.06	.03	.00
☐ 545	Greg Cadaret	.03	.01	.00
☐ 546	Rod Nichols	.03	.01	.00
☐ 547	Luis Polonia	.03	.01	.00
☐ 548	Charlie Hayes	.08	.04	.01
☐ 549	Dickie Thon	.03	.01	.00
☐ 550	Tim Crews	.03	.01	.00
☐ 551	Dave Winfield	.10	.05	.01
☐ 552	Mike Davis	.03	.01	.00
☐ 553	Ron Robinson	.03	.01	.00
☐ 554	Carmen Castillo	.03	.01	.00
☐ 555	John Costello	.03	.01	.00
☐ 556	Bud Black	.03	.01	.00
☐ 557	Rick Dempsey	.03	.01	.00
☐ 558	Jim Acker	.03	.01	.00
☐ 559	Eric Show	.03	.01	.00
☐ 560	Pat Borders	.03	.01	.00
☐ 561	Danny Darwin	.03	.01	.00
☐ 562	Rick Luecken	.10	.05	.01
☐ 563	Edwin Nunez	.03	.01	.00
☐ 564	Felix Jose	.03	.01	.00
☐ 565	John Cangelosi	.03	.01	.00
☐ 566	Bill Swift	.03	.01	.00
☐ 567	Bill Schroeder	.03	.01	.00
☐ 568	Stan Javier	.03	.01	.00
☐ 569	Jim Traber	.03	.01	.00
☐ 570	Wallace Johnson	.03	.01	.00
☐ 571	Donell Nixon	.03	.01	.00
☐ 572	Sid Fernandez	.08	.04	.01
☐ 573	Lance Johnson	.03	.01	.00
☐ 574	Andy McGaffigan	.03	.01	.00
☐ 575	Mark Knudson	.03	.01	.00
☐ 576	Tommy Greene	.35	.17	.03
☐ 577	Mark Grace	.35	.17	.03
☐ 578	Larry Walker	.20	.10	.02
☐ 579	Mike Stanley	.03	.01	.00
☐ 580	Mike Witt	.06	.03	.00
☐ 581	Scott Bradley	.03	.01	.00
☐ 582	Greg Harris	.03	.01	.00
☐ 583	Kevin Hickey	.03	.01	.00
☐ 584	Lee Mazzilli	.03	.01	.00
☐ 585	Jeff Pico	.03	.01	.00
☐ 586	Joe Oliver	.12	.06	.01
☐ 587	Willie Fraser	.03	.01	.00
☐ 588	Carl Yastrzemski PUZ Puzzle Card	.06	.03	.00
☐ 589	Kevin Bass	.06	.03	.00
☐ 590	John Moses	.03	.01	.00
☐ 591	Tom Pagnozzi	.03	.01	.00
☐ 592	Tony Castillo	.08	.04	.01
☐ 593	Jerald Clark	.03	.01	.00
☐ 594	Dan Schatzeder	.03	.01	.00
☐ 595	Luis Quinones	.03	.01	.00
☐ 596	Pete Harnisch	.03	.01	.00
☐ 597	Gary Redus	.03	.01	.00
☐ 598	Mel Hall	.06	.03	.00
☐ 599	Rick Schu	.03	.01	.00
☐ 600	Checklist Card	.06	.01	.00
☐ 601	Mike Kingery	.03	.01	.00
☐ 602	Terry Kennedy	.03	.01	.00
☐ 603	Mike Sharperson	.03	.01	.00
☐ 604	Don Carman	.03	.01	.00
☐ 605	Jim Gott	.03	.01	.00
☐ 606	Donn Pall	.08	.04	.01
☐ 607	Rance Mulliniks	.03	.01	.00
☐ 608	Curt Wilkerson	.03	.01	.00
☐ 609	Mike Felder	.03	.01	.00
☐ 610	Guillermo Hernandez	.06	.03	.00
☐ 611	Candy Maldonado	.03	.01	.00
☐ 612	Mark Thurmond	.03	.01	.00
☐ 613	Rick Leach	.03	.01	.00
☐ 614	Jerry Reed	.03	.01	.00
☐ 615	Franklin Stubbs	.03	.01	.00
☐ 616	Billy Hatcher	.03	.01	.00
☐ 617	Don August	.03	.01	.00
☐ 618	Tim Teufel	.03	.01	.00
☐ 619	Shawn Hillegas	.03	.01	.00
☐ 620	Manny Lee	.03	.01	.00
☐ 621	Gary Ward	.03	.01	.00
☐ 622	Mark Guthrie	.12	.06	.01
☐ 623	Jeff Musselman	.03	.01	.00
☐ 624	Mark Lemke	.03	.01	.00
☐ 625	Fernando Valenzuela	.10	.05	.01
☐ 626	Paul Sorrento	.15	.07	.01
☐ 627	Glenallen Hill	.15	.07	.01
☐ 628	Les Lancaster	.03	.01	.00
☐ 629	Vance Law	.03	.01	.00
☐ 630	Randy Velarde	.06	.03	.00
☐ 631	Todd Frohwirth	.03	.01	.00
☐ 632	Willie McGee	.08	.04	.01
☐ 633	Dennis Boyd	.06	.03	.00
☐ 634	Cris Carpenter	.03	.01	.00
☐ 635	Brian Holton	.03	.01	.00
☐ 636	Tracy Jones	.03	.01	.00
☐ 637A	Terry Steinbach AS (Recent Major League Performance)	.50	.25	.05
☐ 637B	Terry Steinbach AS (All-Star Game Performance)	.10	.05	.01
☐ 638	Brady Anderson	.06	.03	.00
☐ 639	Jack Morris	.08	.04	.01
☐ 640	Jaime Navarro	.15	.07	.01
☐ 641	Darrin Jackson	.03	.01	.00
☐ 642	Mike Dyer	.15	.07	.01
☐ 643	Mike Schmidt	.25	.12	.02
☐ 644	Henry Cotto	.03	.01	.00
☐ 645	John Cerutti	.03	.01	.00
☐ 646	Francisco Cabrera	.20	.10	.02
☐ 647	Scott Sanderson	.03	.01	.00
☐ 648	Brian Meyer	.03	.01	.00
☐ 649	Ray Searage	.03	.01	.00
☐ 650A	Bo Jackson AS (Recent Major League Performance)	2.00	1.00	.20
☐ 650B	Bo Jackson AS (All-Star Game Performance)	.50	.20	.04
☐ 651	Steve Lyons	.03	.01	.00
☐ 652	Mike LaCoss	.03	.01	.00
☐ 653	Ted Power	.03	.01	.00
☐ 654A	Howard Johnson AS (Recent Major League Performance)	.75	.35	.07
☐ 654B	Howard Johnson AS (All-Star Game Performance)	.15	.07	.01
☐ 655	Mauro Gozzo	.15	.07	.01
☐ 656	Mike Blowers	.20	.10	.02
☐ 657	Paul Gibson	.03	.01	.00
☐ 658	Neal Heaton	.03	.01	.00
☐ 659A	Nolan Ryan 5000K (#665 King of Kings back) ERR	10.00	5.00	1.00
☐ 659B	Nolan Ryan 5000K COR	.75	.35	.07
☐ 660A	Harold Baines AS (black line through star on front; Recent Major League Performance)	10.00	4.00	.75
☐ 660B	Harold Baines AS (black line through star on front; All-Star Game Performance)	10.00	4.00	.75
☐ 660C	Harold Baines AS (black line behind star on front; Recent Major League Performance)	10.00	4.00	.75
☐ 660D	Harold Baines AS (black line behind star on front; All-Star Game Performance)	.15	.07	.01
☐ 661	Gary Pettis	.03	.01	.00
☐ 662	Clint Zavaras	.12	.06	.01
☐ 663A	Rick Reuschel AS (Recent Major League Performance)	.50	.25	.05

☐ 663B Rick Reuschel AS .... (All-Star Game Performance)	.10	.05	.01
☐ 664 Alejandro Pena	.03	.01	.00
☐ 665A Nolan Ryan KING .... (#659 5000 K back) ERR	10.00	5.00	1.00
☐ 665B Nolan Ryan KING COR .	.75	.35	.07
☐ 666 Ricky Horton	.03	.01	.00
☐ 667 Curt Schilling	.03	.01	.00
☐ 668 Bill Landrum	.03	.01	.00
☐ 669 Todd Stottlemyre	.06	.03	.00
☐ 670 Tim Leary	.06	.03	.00
☐ 671 John Wetteland	.25	.12	.02
☐ 672 Calvin Schiraldi	.03	.01	.00
☐ 673A Ruben Sierra AS .... (Recent Major League Performance)	1.00	.50	.10
☐ 673B Ruben Sierra AS .... (All-Star Game Performance)	.20	.10	.02
☐ 674A Pedro Guerrero AS ...... (Recent Major League Performance)	.50	.25	.05
☐ 674B Pedro Guerrero AS ...... (All-Star Game Performance)	.10	.05	.01
☐ 675 Ken Phelps	.03	.01	.00
☐ 676A Cal Ripken AS .... (Recent Major League Performance)	.75	.35	.07
☐ 676B Cal Ripken AS .... (All-Star Game Performance)	.15	.07	.01
☐ 677 Denny Walling	.03	.01	.00
☐ 678 Goose Gossage	.06	.03	.00
☐ 679 Gary Mielke	.10	.05	.01
☐ 680 Bill Bathe	.03	.01	.00
☐ 681 Tom Lawless	.03	.01	.00
☐ 682 Xavier Hernandez	.12	.06	.01
☐ 683A Kirby Puckett AS .... (Recent Major League Performance)	1.00	.50	.10
☐ 683B Kirby Puckett AS .... (All-Star Game Performance)	.20	.10	.02
☐ 684 Mariano Duncan	.03	.01	.00
☐ 685 Ramon Martinez	.08	.04	.01
☐ 686 Tim Jones	.03	.01	.00
☐ 687 Tom Filer	.03	.01	.00
☐ 688 Steve Lombardozzi	.03	.01	.00
☐ 689 Bernie Williams	.40	.20	.04
☐ 690 Chip Hale	.15	.07	.01
☐ 691 Beau Allred	.15	.07	.01
☐ 692A Ryne Sandberg AS .... (Recent Major League Performance)	1.00	.50	.10
☐ 692B Ryne Sandberg AS .... (All-Star Game Performance)	.20	.10	.02
☐ 693 Jeff Huson	.12	.06	.01
☐ 694 Curt Ford	.03	.01	.00
☐ 695A Eric Davis AS .... (Recent Major League Performance)	1.00	.50	.10
☐ 695B Eric Davis AS .... (All-Star Game Performance)	.20	.10	.02
☐ 696 Scott Lusader	.03	.01	.00
☐ 697A Mark McGwire AS .... (Recent Major League Performance)	1.00	.50	.10
☐ 697B Mark McGwire AS .... (All-Star Game Performance)	.20	.10	.02
☐ 698 Steve Cummings	.12	.06	.01
☐ 699 George Canale	.20	.10	.02
☐ 700A Checklist Card .... (#716 not listed)	1.00	.50	.02
☐ 700B Checklist Card .... (#716 listed)	.10	.05	.00
☐ 701A Julio Franco AS .... (Recent Major League Performance)	.50	.25	.05
☐ 701B Julio Franco AS .... (All-Star Game Performance)	.10	.05	.01
☐ 702 Dave Johnson (P)	.15	.07	.01
☐ 703A Dave Stewart AS .... (Recent Major League Performance)	.50	.25	.05
☐ 703B Dave Stewart AS .... (All-Star Game Performance)	.10	.05	.01

☐ 704 Dave Justice	.20	.10	.02
☐ 705A Tony Gwynn AS .... (Recent Major League Performance)	.75	.35	.07
☐ 705B Tony Gwynn AS .... (All-Star Game Performance)	.15	.07	.01
☐ 706 Greg Myers	.03	.01	.00
☐ 707A Will Clark AS .... (Recent Major League Performance)	2.00	1.00	.20
☐ 707B Will Clark AS .... (All-Star Game Performance)	.40	.20	.04
☐ 708A Benito Santiago AS ...... (Recent Major League Performance)	.50	.25	.05
☐ 708B Benito Santiago AS ...... (All-Star Game Performance)	.10	.05	.01
☐ 709 Larry McWilliams	.03	.01	.00
☐ 710A Ozzie Smith AS .... (Recent Major League Performance)	.50	.25	.05
☐ 710B Ozzie Smith AS .... (All-Star Game Performance)	.10	.05	.01
☐ 711 John Olerud	2.50	1.00	.20
☐ 712A Wade Boggs AS .... (Recent Major League Performance)	1.00	.50	.10
☐ 712B Wade Boggs AS .... (All-Star Game Performance)	.20	.10	.02
☐ 713 Gary Eave	.12	.06	.01
☐ 714 Bob Tewksbury	.03	.01	.00
☐ 715A Kevin Mitchell AS .... (Recent Major League Performance)	.75	.35	.07
☐ 715B Kevin Mitchell AS .... (All-Star Game Performance)	.15	.07	.01
☐ 716 Bart Giamatti	1.00	.50	.10

1990 Donruss Bonus MVP's

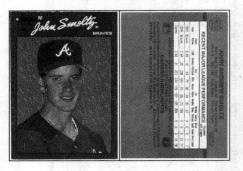

The 1990 Donruss Bonus MVP's set contains 26 standard-size (2 1/2 by 3 1/2 inch) cards. The front borders are bright red. The horizontally-oriented backs are amber. These cards were randomly distributed in all 1990 Donruss unopened pack formats. The slection of players in the set is Donruss' opinion of each team's MVP. The complete set price below does not include any variation cards.

	MINT	EXC	G-VG
COMPLETE SET (26)	5.00	2.50	.50
COMMON CARD (BC1-BC26)	.05	.02	.00
☐ BC1 Bo Jackson	.40	.20	.04
☐ BC2 Howard Johnson	.10	.05	.01
☐ BC3 Dave Stewart	.08	.04	.01
☐ BC4 Tony Gwynn	.15	.07	.01
☐ BC5 Orel Hershiser	.12	.06	.01
☐ BC6 Pedro Guerrero	.08	.04	.01
☐ BC7 Tim Raines	.10	.05	.01
☐ BC8 Kirby Puckett	.20	.10	.02

☐ BC9	Alvin Davis	.08	.04	.01
☐ BC10	Ryne Sandberg	.12	.06	.01
☐ BC11	Kevin Mitchell	.12	.06	.01
☐ BC12	John Smoltz UER	.75	.30	.06
	(photo actually			
	Tom Glavine)			
☐ BC13	George Bell	.08	.04	.01
☐ BC14	Julio Franco	.08	.04	.01
☐ BC15	Paul Molitor	.08	.04	.01
☐ BC16	Bobby Bonilla	.08	.04	.01
☐ BC17	Mike Greenwell	.15	.07	.01
☐ BC18	Cal Ripken	.12	.06	.01
☐ BC19	Carlton Fisk	.10	.05	.01
☐ BC20	Chili Davis	.05	.02	.00
☐ BC21	Glenn Davis	.08	.04	.01
☐ BC22	Steve Sax	.08	.04	.01
☐ BC23	Eric Davis	.15	.07	.01
☐ BC24	Greg Swindell	.08	.04	.01
☐ BC25	Von Hayes	.08	.04	.01
☐ BC26	Alan Trammell	.10	.05	.01

1990 Donruss Super DK's

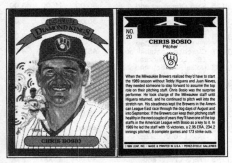

This 26-player card set was available through a mail-in offer detailed on the wax packs. The set was sent in return for 10.00 and three wrappers plus 2.00 postage and handling. The set features the popular Diamond King subseries in large (approximately 4 7/8" by 6 13/16") form. Dick Perez of Perez-Steele Galleries did another outstanding job on the artwork. The cards are essentially a large version of the Donruss regular issue Diamond Kings.

	MINT	EXC	G-VG
COMPLETE SET (26)	10.00	5.00	1.00
COMMON PLAYER (1-26)	.15	.07	.01

☐ 1	Bo Jackson DK	1.50	.75	.15
☐ 2	Steve Sax DK	.20	.10	.02
☐ 3	Ruben Sierra DK	.40	.20	.04
☐ 4	Ken Griffey Jr. DK	1.25	.60	.12
☐ 5	Mickey Tettleton DK	.15	.07	.01
☐ 6	Dave Stewart DK	.25	.12	.02
☐ 7	Jim Deshaies DK	.15	.07	.01
☐ 8	John Smoltz DK	.25	.12	.02
☐ 9	Mike Bielecki DK	.15	.07	.01
☐ 10	Brian Downing DK	.15	.07	.01
☐ 11	Kevin Mitchell DK	.40	.20	.04
☐ 12	Kelly Gruber DK	.15	.07	.01
☐ 13	Joe Magrane DK	.20	.10	.02
☐ 14	John Franco DK	.20	.10	.02
☐ 15	Ozzie Guillen DK	.20	.10	.02
☐ 16	Lou Whitaker DK	.20	.10	.02
☐ 17	John Smiley DK	.15	.07	.01
☐ 18	Howard Johnson DK	.30	.15	.03
☐ 19	Willie Randolph DK	.20	.10	.02
☐ 20	Chris Bosio DK	.15	.07	.01
☐ 21	Tommy Herr DK	.15	.07	.01
☐ 22	Dan Gladden DK	.15	.07	.01
☐ 23	Ellis Burks DK	.35	.17	.03
☐ 24	Pete O'Brien DK	.20	.10	.02
☐ 25	Bryn Smith DK	.20	.10	.02
☐ 26	Ed Whitson DK	.15	.07	.01

1986 Dorman's Cheese

This 20-card set was issued in panels of two cards. The individual cards measure 1 1/2" by 2" whereas the panels measure 3" by 2". Team logos have been removed from the photos as these cards were not licensed by Major League Baseball (team owners). The backs contain a minimum of information.

	MINT	EXC	G-VG
COMPLETE SET (20)	20.00	10.00	2.00
COMMON PLAYER (1-20)	.75	.35	.07

☐ 1	George Brett	1.25	.60	.12
☐ 2	Jack Morris	.75	.35	.07
☐ 3	Gary Carter	.90	.45	.09
☐ 4	Cal Ripken	1.00	.50	.10
☐ 5	Dwight Gooden	1.25	.60	.12
☐ 6	Kent Hrbek	.90	.45	.09
☐ 7	Rickey Henderson	1.25	.60	.12
☐ 8	Mike Schmidt	1.50	.75	.15
☐ 9	Keith Hernandez	.90	.45	.09
☐ 10	Dale Murphy	1.00	.50	.10
☐ 11	Reggie Jackson	1.00	.50	.10
☐ 12	Eddie Murray	.90	.45	.09
☐ 13	Don Mattingly	3.00	1.50	.30
☐ 14	Ryne Sandberg	1.00	.50	.10
☐ 15	Willie McGee	.75	.35	.07
☐ 16	Robin Yount	1.25	.60	.12
☐ 17	Rick Sutcliffe	.75	.35	.07
☐ 18	Wade Boggs	2.00	1.00	.20
☐ 19	Dave Winfield	1.00	.50	.10
☐ 20	Jim Rice	.90	.45	.09

1941 Double Play

The cards in this 75-card set measure 2 1/2" by 3 1/8". The 1941 Double Play set, listed as R330 in the American Card Catalog, was a blank-backed issue distributed by Gum Products. It consists of 75 numbered cards (two consecutive numbers per card), each depicting two players in sepia tone photographs. Cards 81-100 contain action poses, and the last 50 numbers of the set are slightly harder to find. Cards that have been cut in half to form "singles" have a greatly reduced value.

	EX-MT	VG-E	GOOD
COMPLETE SET (150)	4000.00	2000.00	500.00
COMMON PAIRS (1-100)	24.00	12.00	2.40
COMMON PAIRS (101-150)	30.00	15.00	3.00

☐ 1	Larry French and	24.00	12.00	2.40
	2 Vance Page			
☐ 3	Billy Herman and	30.00	15.00	3.00
	4 Stan Hack			

☐	5 Lonnie Frey and .... 6 Johnny VanderMeer	30.00	15.00	3.00
☐	7 Paul Derringer and .... 8 Bucky Walters	30.00	15.00	3.00
☐	9 Frank McCormick and .... 10 Bill Werber	24.00	12.00	2.40
☐	11 Jimmy Ripple and .... 12 Ernie Lombardi	30.00	15.00	3.00
☐	13 Alex Kampouris and ...... 14 Whitlow Wyatt	24.00	12.00	2.40
☐	15 Mickey Owen and .... 16 Paul Waner	35.00	17.50	3.50
☐	17 Cookie Lavagetto and .... 18 Pete Reiser	24.00	12.00	2.40
☐	19 James Wasdell and .... 20 Dolf Camilli	24.00	12.00	2.40
☐	21 Dixie Walker and .... 22 Joe Medwick	30.00	15.00	3.00
☐	23 Pee Wee Reese and .... 24 Kirby Higbe	125.00	60.00	12.50
☐	25 Harry Danning and .... 26 Cliff Melton	24.00	12.00	2.40
☐	27 Harry Gumbert and .... 28 Burgess Whitehead	24.00	12.00	2.40
☐	29 Joe Orengo and .... 30 Joe Moore	24.00	12.00	2.40
☐	31 Mel Ott and .... 32 Norman Young	75.00	37.50	7.50
☐	33 Lee Handley and .... 34 Arky Vaughan	35.00	17.50	3.50
☐	35 Bob Klinger and .... 36 Stanley Brown	24.00	12.00	2.40
☐	37 Terry Moore and .... 38 Gus Mancuso	24.00	12.00	2.40
☐	39 Johnny Mize and .... 40 Enos Slaughter	125.00	60.00	12.50
☐	41 Johnny Cooney and .... 42 Sibby Sisti	24.00	12.00	2.40
☐	43 Max West and .... 44 Carvel Rowell	24.00	12.00	2.40
☐	45 Danny Litwhiler and .... 46 Merrill May	24.00	12.00	2.40
☐	47 Frank Hayes and .... 48 Al Brancato	24.00	12.00	2.40
☐	49 Bob Johnson and .... 50 Bill Nagel	24.00	12.00	2.40
☐	51 Buck Newsom and .... 52 Hank Greenberg	50.00	25.00	5.00
☐	53 Barney McCosky and ..... 54 Charlie Gehringer	50.00	25.00	5.00
☐	55 Mike Higgins and .... 56 Dick Bartell	24.00	12.00	2.40
☐	57 Ted Williams and .... 58 Jim Tabor	300.00	150.00	30.00
☐	59 Joe Cronin and .... 60 Jimmie Foxx	150.00	75.00	15.00
☐	61 Lefty Gomez and .... 62 Phil Rizzuto	200.00	100.00	20.00
☐	63 Joe DiMaggio and .... 64 Charlie Keller	500.00	250.00	50.00
☐	65 Red Rolfe and .... 66 Bill Dickey	100.00	50.00	10.00
☐	67 Joe Gordon and .... 68 Red Ruffing	75.00	37.50	7.50
☐	69 Mike Tresh and .... 70 Luke Appling	35.00	17.50	3.50
☐	71 Moose Solters and .... 72 Johnny Rigney	24.00	12.00	2.40
☐	73 Buddy Myer and .... 74 Ben Chapman	24.00	12.00	2.40
☐	75 Cecil Travis and .... 76 George Case	24.00	12.00	2.40
☐	77 Joe Krakauskas and ...... 78 Bob Feller	100.00	50.00	10.00
☐	79 Ken Keltner and .... 80 Hal Trosky	24.00	12.00	2.40
☐	81 Ted Williams and .... 82 Joe Cronin	350.00	175.00	35.00
☐	83 Joe Gordon and .... 84 Charlie Keller	35.00	17.50	3.50
☐	85 Hank Greenberg and ...... 86 Red Ruffing	150.00	75.00	15.00
☐	87 Hal Trosky and .... 88 George Case	24.00	12.00	2.40
☐	89 Mel Ott and .... 90 Burgess Whitehead	75.00	37.50	7.50
☐	91 Harry Danning and .... 92 Harry Gumbert	24.00	12.00	2.40
☐	93 Norman Young and .... 94 Cliff Melton	24.00	12.00	2.40
☐	95 Jimmy Ripple and .... 96 Bucky Walters	24.00	12.00	2.40
☐	97 Stanley Jack and .... 98 Bob Klinger	24.00	12.00	2.40
☐	99 Johnny Mize and	45.00	22.50	4.50

	100 Dan Litwhiler			
☐	101 Dom Dallesandro and ..... 102 Augie Galan	30.00	15.00	3.00
☐	103 Bill Lee and .... 104 Phil Cavarretta	30.00	15.00	3.00
☐	105 Lefty Grove and .... 106 Bobby Doerr	150.00	75.00	15.00
☐	107 Frank Pytlak and .... 108 Dom DiMaggio	35.00	17.50	3.50
☐	109 Jerry Priddy and .... 110 Johnny Murphy	30.00	15.00	3.00
☐	111 Tommy Henrich and ...... 112 Marius Russo	35.00	17.50	3.50
☐	113 Frank Crosetti and .... 114 John Sturm	35.00	17.50	3.50
☐	115 Ival Goodman and .... 116 Myron McCormick	30.00	15.00	3.00
☐	117 Eddie Joost and .... 118 Ernie Koy	30.00	15.00	3.00
☐	119 Lloyd Waner and .... 120 Hank Majeski	45.00	22.50	4.50
☐	121 Buddy Hassett and .... 122 Eugene Moore	30.00	15.00	3.00
☐	123 Nick Etten and .... 124 John Rizzo	30.00	15.00	3.00
☐	125 Sam Chapman and .... 126 Wally Moses	30.00	15.00	3.00
☐	127 Johnny Babich and .... 128 Dick Siebert	30.00	15.00	3.00
☐	129 Nelson Potter and .... 130 Benny McCoy	30.00	15.00	3.00
☐	131 Clarence Campbell and .. 132 Lou Boudreau	45.00	22.50	4.50
☐	133 Rollie Hemsley and .... 134 Mel Harder	35.00	17.50	3.50
☐	135 Gerald Walker and .... 136 Joe Heving	30.00	15.00	3.00
☐	137 Johnny Rucker and .... 138 Ace Adams	30.00	15.00	3.00
☐	139 Morris Arnovich and .... 140 Carl Hubbell	75.00	37.50	7.50
☐	141 Lew Riggs and .... 142 Leo Durocher	45.00	22.50	4.50
☐	143 Fred Fitzsimmons and .... 144 Joe Vosmik	30.00	15.00	3.00
☐	145 Frank Crespi and .... 146 Jim Brown	30.00	15.00	3.00
☐	147 Don Heffner and .... 148 Harland Clift	30.00	15.00	3.00
☐	149 Debs Garms and .... 150 Elbert Fletcher	30.00	15.00	3.00

1950 Drake's

The cards in this 36-card set measure 2 1/2" by 2 1/2". The 1950 Drake's Cookies set contains numbered black and white cards. The players are pictured inside a simulated television screen and the caption "TV Baseball Series" appears on the cards. The players selected for this set show a heavy representation of players from New York teams. The ACC designation for this set is D358.

		NRMT	VG-E	GOOD
	COMPLETE SET (36)	3000.00	1500.00	350.00
	COMMON PLAYER (1-36)	45.00	22.50	4.50
☐	1 Preacher Roe	65.00	32.50	6.50
☐	2 Clint Hartung	45.00	22.50	4.50
☐	3 Earl Torgeson	45.00	22.50	4.50
☐	4 Lou Brissie	45.00	22.50	4.50
☐	5 Duke Snider	250.00	125.00	25.00
☐	6 Roy Campanella	300.00	150.00	30.00
☐	7 Sheldon Jones	45.00	22.50	4.50

			MINT	EXC	G-VG
☐	8	Whitey Lockman	45.00	22.50	4.50
☐	9	Bobby Thomson	65.00	32.50	6.50
☐	10	Dick Sisler	45.00	22.50	4.50
☐	11	Gil Hodges	150.00	75.00	15.00
☐	12	Eddie Waitkus	45.00	22.50	4.50
☐	13	Bobby Kerr	45.00	22.50	4.50
☐	14	Warren Spahn	200.00	100.00	20.00
☐	15	Buddy Kerr	45.00	22.50	4.50
☐	16	Sid Gordon	45.00	22.50	4.50
☐	17	Willard Marshall	45.00	22.50	4.50
☐	18	Carl Furillo	75.00	37.50	7.50
☐	19	Pee Wee Reese	200.00	100.00	20.00
☐	20	Alvin Dark	65.00	32.50	6.50
☐	21	Del Ennis	45.00	22.50	4.50
☐	22	Ed Stanky	55.00	27.50	5.50
☐	23	Tom Henrich	65.00	32.50	6.50
☐	24	Yogi Berra	300.00	150.00	30.00
☐	25	Phil Rizzuto	175.00	85.00	18.00
☐	26	Jerry Coleman	45.00	22.50	4.50
☐	27	Joe Page	45.00	22.50	4.50
☐	28	Allie Reynolds	65.00	32.50	6.50
☐	29	Ray Scarborough	45.00	22.50	4.50
☐	30	Birdie Tebbetts	45.00	22.50	4.50
☐	31	Maurice McDermott	45.00	22.50	4.50
☐	32	Johnny Pesky	45.00	22.50	4.50
☐	33	Dom DiMaggio	75.00	37.50	7.50
☐	34	Vern Stephens	55.00	27.50	5.50
☐	35	Bob Elliott	45.00	22.50	4.50
☐	36	Enos Slaughter	175.00	85.00	18.00

			MINT	EXC	G-VG
☐	19	Dave Kingman	.10	.05	.01
☐	20	Cesar Cedeno	.05	.02	.00
☐	21	Joe Charboneau	.05	.02	.00
☐	22	George Hendrick	.05	.02	.00
☐	23	Gary Carter	.25	.12	.02
☐	24	Al Oliver	.10	.05	.01
☐	25	Bruce Bochte	.05	.02	.00
☐	26	Jerry Mumphrey	.05	.02	.00
☐	27	Steve Kemp	.05	.02	.00
☐	28	Bob Watson	.05	.02	.00
☐	29	John Castino	.05	.02	.00
☐	30	Tony Armas	.05	.02	.00
☐	31	John Mayberry	.05	.02	.00
☐	32	Carlton Fisk	.25	.12	.02
☐	33	Lee Mazzilli	.05	.02	.00

1982 Drake's

The cards in this 33-card set measure 2 1/2" by 3 1/2". The 1982 Drake's Big Hitters series cards each has the title "2nd Annual Collectors' Edition" in a ribbon design at the top of the picture area. Each color player photo has "photo mount" designs in the corners, red for the AL and green for the NL. The reverses are green and blue, the same as the regular 1982 Topps format, and the photos are larger than those of the previous year. Of the 33 hitters featured, 19 represent the National League. There are 21 returnees from the 1981 set and only one photo, that of Kennedy, is the same as that appearing in the regular Topps issue. The Drake's logo appears centered in the bottom border on the obverse.

1981 Drake's

The cards in this 33-card set measure 2 1/2" by 3 1/2". The 1981 Drake's Bakeries set contains National and American League stars. Produced in conjunction with Topps and released to the public in Drake's Cakes, this set features red frames for American League players and blue frames for National League players. A Drake's Cakes logo with the words "Big Hitters" appears on the lower front of each card. The backs are quite similar to the 1981 Topps backs but contain the Drake's logo, a different card number, and a short paragraph entitled "What Makes a Big Hitter?" at the top of the card.

			MINT	EXC	G-VG
	COMPLETE SET (33)		7.00	3.50	.70
	COMMON PLAYER (1-33)		.05	.02	.00
☐	1	Carl Yastrzemski	1.00	.50	.10
☐	2	Rod Carew	.50	.25	.05
☐	3	Pete Rose	1.00	.50	.10
☐	4	Dave Parker	.20	.10	.02
☐	5	George Brett	.60	.30	.06
☐	6	Eddie Murray	.45	.22	.04
☐	7	Mike Schmidt	1.00	.50	.10
☐	8	Jim Rice	.25	.12	.02
☐	9	Fred Lynn	.15	.07	.01
☐	10	Reggie Jackson	.75	.35	.07
☐	11	Steve Garvey	.45	.22	.04
☐	12	Ken Singleton	.05	.02	.00
☐	13	Bill Buckner	.05	.02	.00
☐	14	Dave Winfield	.30	.15	.03
☐	15	Jack Clark	.20	.10	.02
☐	16	Cecil Cooper	.10	.05	.01
☐	17	Bob Horner	.10	.05	.01
☐	18	George Foster	.10	.05	.01

			MINT	EXC	G-VG
	COMPLETE SET (33)		8.00	4.00	.80
	COMMON PLAYER (1-33)		.05	.02	.00
☐	1	Tony Armas	.05	.02	.00
☐	2	Buddy Bell	.10	.05	.01
☐	3	Johnny Bench	.75	.35	.07
☐	4	George Brett	.60	.30	.06
☐	5	Bill Buckner	.05	.02	.00
☐	6	Rod Carew	.45	.22	.04
☐	7	Gary Carter	.35	.17	.03
☐	8	Jack Clark	.20	.10	.02
☐	9	Cecil Cooper	.10	.05	.01
☐	10	Jose Cruz	.05	.02	.00
☐	11	Dwight Evans	.15	.07	.01
☐	12	Carlton Fisk	.25	.12	.02
☐	13	George Foster	.10	.05	.01
☐	14	Steve Garvey	.45	.22	.04
☐	15	Kirk Gibson	.45	.22	.04
☐	16	Mike Hargrove	.10	.05	.01
☐	17	George Hendrick	.05	.02	.00
☐	18	Bob Horner	.15	.07	.01
☐	19	Reggie Jackson	.75	.35	.07
☐	20	Terry Kennedy	.05	.02	.00
☐	21	Dave Kingman	.10	.05	.01
☐	22	Greg Luzinski	.10	.05	.01
☐	23	Bill Madlock	.05	.02	.00
☐	24	John Mayberry	.05	.02	.00
☐	25	Eddie Murray	.45	.22	.04
☐	26	Graig Nettles	.10	.05	.01
☐	27	Jim Rice	.25	.12	.02
☐	28	Pete Rose	.80	.40	.08
☐	29	Mike Schmidt	.80	.40	.08

				MINT	EXC	G-VG
☐	30	Ken Singleton	....	.05	.02	.00
☐	31	Dave Winfield	....	.30	.15	.03
☐	32	Butch Wynegar	....	.05	.02	.00
☐	33	Richie Zisk	....	.05	.02	.00

1983 Drake's

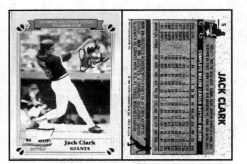

The cards in this 33-card series measure 2 1/2" by 3 1/2". For the third year in a row, Drake's Cakes, in conjunction with Topps, issued a set entitled Big Hitters. The fronts appear very similar to those of the previous two years with slight variations on the framelines and player identification sections. The backs are the same as the Topps backs of this year except for the card number and the Drake's logo.

			MINT	EXC	G-VG
COMPLETE SET (33)		....	6.00	3.00	.60
COMMON PLAYER (1-33)		....	.05	.02	.00
☐	1	Don Baylor	.10	.05	.01
☐	2	Bill Buckner	.10	.05	.01
☐	3	Rod Carew	.40	.20	.04
☐	4	Gary Carter	.35	.17	.03
☐	5	Jack Clark	.20	.10	.02
☐	6	Cecil Cooper	.10	.05	.01
☐	7	Dwight Evans	.15	.07	.01
☐	8	George Foster	.10	.05	.01
☐	9	Pedro Guerrero	.20	.10	.02
☐	10	George Hendrick	.05	.02	.00
☐	11	Bob Horner	.15	.07	.01
☐	12	Reggie Jackson	.65	.30	.06
☐	13	Steve Kemp	.05	.02	.00
☐	14	Dave Kingman	.10	.05	.01
☐	15	Bill Madlock	.05	.02	.00
☐	16	Gary Matthews	.05	.02	.00
☐	17	Hal McRae	.05	.02	.00
☐	18	Dale Murphy	.50	.25	.05
☐	19	Eddie Murray	.45	.22	.04
☐	20	Ben Oglivie	.05	.02	.00
☐	21	Al Oliver	.10	.05	.01
☐	22	Jim Rice	.25	.12	.02
☐	23	Cal Ripken	.40	.20	.04
☐	24	Pete Rose	.90	.45	.09
☐	25	Mike Schmidt	.90	.45	.09
☐	26	Ken Singleton	.05	.02	.00
☐	27	Gorman Thomas	.05	.02	.00
☐	28	Jason Thompson	.05	.02	.00
☐	29	Mookie Wilson	.10	.05	.01
☐	30	Willie Wilson	.10	.05	.01
☐	31	Dave Winfield	.35	.17	.03
☐	32	Carl Yastrzemski	.90	.45	.09
☐	33	Robin Yount	.60	.30	.06

1984 Drake's

The cards in this 33-card set measure 2 1/2" by 3 1/2". The Fourth Annual Collectors Edition of baseball cards produced by Drake's Cakes in conjunction with Topps continued this now annual set entitled Big Hitters. As in previous years, the front

contains a frameline in which the title of the set, the Drake's logo, and the player's name, his team, and position appear. The cards all feature the player in a batting action pose. While the cards fronts are different from the Topps fronts of this year, the backs differ only in the card number and the use of the Drake's logo instead of the Topps logo.

			MINT	EXC	G-VG
COMPLETE SET (33)		....	7.00	3.50	.70
COMMON PLAYER (1-33)		....	.05	.02	.00
☐	1	Don Baylor	.10	.05	.01
☐	2	Wade Boggs	1.00	.50	.10
☐	3	George Brett	.60	.30	.06
☐	4	Bill Buckner	.05	.02	.00
☐	5	Rod Carew	.40	.20	.04
☐	6	Gary Carter	.35	.17	.03
☐	7	Ron Cey	.05	.02	.00
☐	8	Cecil Cooper	.10	.05	.01
☐	9	Andre Dawson	.25	.12	.02
☐	10	Steve Garvey	.40	.20	.04
☐	11	Pedro Guerrero	.20	.10	.02
☐	12	George Hendrick	.05	.02	.00
☐	13	Keith Hernandez	.20	.10	.02
☐	14	Bob Horner	.15	.07	.01
☐	15	Reggie Jackson	.60	.30	.06
☐	16	Steve Kemp	.05	.02	.00
☐	17	Ron Kittle	.10	.05	.01
☐	18	Greg Luzinski	.10	.05	.01
☐	19	Fred Lynn	.10	.05	.01
☐	20	Bill Madlock	.05	.02	.00
☐	21	Gary Matthews	.05	.02	.00
☐	22	Dale Murphy	.50	.25	.05
☐	23	Eddie Murray	.40	.20	.04
☐	24	Al Oliver	.10	.05	.01
☐	25	Jim Rice	.25	.12	.02
☐	26	Cal Ripken	.40	.20	.04
☐	27	Pete Rose	.90	.45	.09
☐	28	Mike Schmidt	.90	.45	.09
☐	29	Darryl Strawberry	1.50	.75	.15
☐	30	Alan Trammell	.20	.10	.02
☐	31	Mookie Wilson	.05	.02	.00
☐	32	Dave Winfield	.30	.15	.03
☐	33	Robin Yount	.60	.30	.06

1985 Drake's

The cards in this 44-card set measure 2 1/2" by 3 1/2". The Fifth Annual Collectors Edition of baseball cards produced by Drake's Cakes in conjunction with Topps continued this apparently annual set with a new twist, for the first time, 11 pitchers were included. The "Big Hitters" are numbered 1-33 and the pitchers are numbered 34- 44; each subgroup is ordered alphabetically. The cards are numbered in the upper right corner of the backs of the cards. The complete set could be obtained directly from the company by sending 2.95 with four proofs of purchase.

	MINT	EXC	G-VG
COMPLETE SET (44)	12.00	6.00	1.20

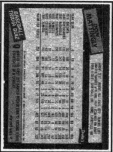

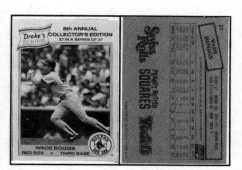

COMMON PLAYER (1-33)	.05	.02	.00
COMMON PLAYER (34-44)	.10	.05	.01

☐	1 Tony Armas	.05	.02	.00
☐	2 Harold Baines	.10	.05	.01
☐	3 Don Baylor	.10	.05	.01
☐	4 George Brett	.60	.30	.06
☐	5 Gary Carter	.35	.17	.03
☐	6 Ron Cey	.05	.02	.00
☐	7 Jose Cruz	.05	.02	.00
☐	8 Alvin Davis	.15	.07	.01
☐	9 Chili Davis	.05	.02	.00
☐	10 Dwight Evans	.15	.07	.01
☐	11 Steve Garvey	.40	.20	.04
☐	12 Kirk Gibson	.35	.17	.03
☐	13 Pedro Guerrero	.20	.10	.02
☐	14 Tony Gwynn	.45	.22	.04
☐	15 Keith Hernandez	.25	.12	.02
☐	16 Kent Hrbek	.20	.10	.02
☐	17 Reggie Jackson	.65	.30	.06
☐	18 Gary Matthews	.05	.02	.00
☐	19 Don Mattingly	1.25	.60	.12
☐	20 Dale Murphy	.50	.25	.05
☐	21 Eddie Murray	.40	.20	.04
☐	22 Dave Parker	.15	.07	.01
☐	23 Lance Parrish	.10	.05	.01
☐	24 Tim Raines	.25	.12	.02
☐	25 Jim Rice	.25	.12	.02
☐	26 Cal Ripken	.40	.20	.04
☐	27 Juan Samuel	.15	.07	.01
☐	28 Ryne Sandberg	.35	.17	.03
☐	29 Mike Schmidt	.90	.45	.09
☐	30 Darryl Strawberry	.90	.45	.09
☐	31 Alan Trammell	.25	.12	.02
☐	32 Dave Winfield	.30	.15	.03
☐	33 Robin Yount	.50	.25	.05
☐	34 Mike Boddicker	.10	.05	.01
☐	35 Steve Carlton	.35	.17	.03
☐	36 Dwight Gooden	1.00	.50	.10
☐	37 Willie Hernandez	.10	.05	.01
☐	38 Mark Langston	.25	.12	.02
☐	39 Dan Quisenberry	.10	.05	.01
☐	40 Dave Righetti	.15	.07	.01
☐	41 Tom Seaver	.40	.20	.04
☐	42 Bob Stanley	.10	.05	.01
☐	43 Rick Sutcliffe	.10	.05	.01
☐	44 Bruce Sutter	.15	.07	.01

1986 Drake's

This set of 37 cards was distributed as back panels of various Drake's snack products. Each individual card measures 2 1/2" by 3 1/2". Each specially marked package features two, three, or four cards on the back. The set is easily recognized by the Drake's logo and "6th Annual Collector's Edition" at the top of the obverse. Cards are numbered on the front and the back. Cards below are coded based on the product upon which they appeared, for example, Apple Pies (AP), Cherry Pies (CP), Chocolate Donut Delites (CDD), Coffee Cake Jr. (CCJ), Creme Shortcakes (CS), Devil Dogs (DD), Fudge Brownies (FUD), Funny Bones (FB), Peanut Butter Squares (PBS), Powdered Sugar Donut Delites (PSDD), Ring Ding Jr. (RDJ), Sunny Doodles (SD), Swiss Rolls (SR),

Yankee Doodles (YD), and Yodels (Y). The last nine cards are pitchers. Complete panels would be valued approximately 25% higher than the individual card prices listed below.

		MINT	EXC	G-VG
COMPLETE SET (37)		30.00	15.00	3.00
COMMON PLAYER (1-37)		.30	.15	.03

☐	1	Gary Carter Y	.60	.30	.06
☐	2	Dwight Evans Y	.40	.20	.04
☐	3	Reggie Jackson SR	1.00	.50	.10
☐	4	Dave Parker SR	.40	.20	.04
☐	5	Rickey Henderson FB	1.00	.50	.10
☐	6	Pedro Guerrero FB	.40	.20	.04
☐	7	Don Mattingly YD	3.00	1.50	.30
☐	8	Mike Marshall YD	.40	.20	.04
☐	9	Keith Moreland YD	.30	.15	.03
☐	10	Keith Hernandez CS	.50	.25	.05
☐	11	Cal Ripken CS	.75	.35	.07
☐	12	Dale Murphy RDJ	.90	.45	.09
☐	13	Jim Rice RDJ	.40	.20	.04
☐	14	George Brett CCJ	.75	.35	.07
☐	15	Tim Raines CCJ	.50	.25	.05
☐	16	Darryl Strawberry DD	1.25	.60	.12
☐	17	Bill Buckner DD	.30	.15	.03
☐	18	Dave Winfield AP	.50	.25	.05
☐	19	Ryne Sandberg AP	.60	.30	.06
☐	20	Steve Balboni AP	.30	.15	.03
☐	21	Tommy Herr AP	.30	.15	.03
☐	22	Pete Rose CP	1.25	.60	.12
☐	23	Willie McGee CP	.40	.20	.04
☐	24	Harold Baines CP	.40	.20	.04
☐	25	Eddie Murray CP	.60	.30	.06
☐	26	Mike Schmidt SD/FUD	1.50	.75	.15
☐	27	Wade Boggs SD/FUD	2.00	1.00	.20
☐	28	Kirk Gibson SD/FUD	.60	.30	.06
☐	29	Bret Saberhagen PBS	.75	.35	.07
☐	30	John Tudor PBS	.40	.20	.04
☐	31	Orel Hershiser PBS	.75	.35	.07
☐	32	Ron Guidry CDD	.40	.20	.04
☐	33	Nolan Ryan CDD	2.00	1.00	.20
☐	34	Dave Stieb CDD	.40	.20	.04
☐	35	Dwight Gooden SDD	1.00	.50	.10
☐	36	Fern.Valenzuela SDD	.50	.25	.05
☐	37	Tom Browning SDD	.40	.20	.04

1987 Drake's

This 33-card set features 25 top hitters and eight top pitchers. Cards were printed in groups of two, three, or four on the backs of Drake's bakery products. Individual cards measure 2 1/2" by 3 1/2" and tout the 7th annual edition. Card backs feature year-by-year season statistics. The cards are numbered such that the pitchers are listed numerically last. Complete panels would be valued approximately 25% higher than the individual card prices listed below.

		MINT	EXC	G-VG
COMPLETE SET (33)		27.00	13.50	2.70
COMMON PLAYER (1-33)		.30	.15	.03

☐	1	Darryl Strawberry	1.25	.60	.12

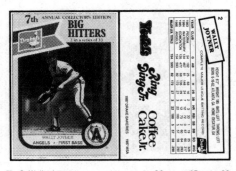

Doodles, 22-24 Powdered Sugar Donuts, 25-27 Chocolate Donuts, 28-29 Yodels, and 30-33 Apple Pies. Complete panels would be valued approximately 25% higher than the individual card prices listed below.

		MINT	EXC	G-VG
COMPLETE SET (33)		27.00	13.50	2.70
COMMON PLAYER (1-33)		.30	.15	.03
☐ 1	Don Mattingly	2.50	1.25	.25
☐ 2	Tim Raines	.50	.25	.05
☐ 3	Darryl Strawberry	1.25	.60	.12
☐ 4	Wade Boggs	2.00	1.00	.20
☐ 5	Keith Hernandez	.50	.25	.05
☐ 6	Mark McGwire	1.00	.50	.10
☐ 7	Rickey Henderson	1.00	.50	.10
☐ 8	Mike Schmidt	2.00	1.00	.20
☐ 9	Dwight Evans	.40	.20	.04
☐ 10	Gary Carter	.50	.25	.05
☐ 11	Paul Molitor	.40	.20	.04
☐ 12	Dave Winfield	.60	.30	.06
☐ 13	Alan Trammell	.50	.25	.05
☐ 14	Tony Gwynn	.75	.35	.07
☐ 15	Dale Murphy	.75	.35	.07
☐ 16	Andre Dawson	.40	.20	.04
☐ 17	Von Hayes	.30	.15	.03
☐ 18	Willie Randolph	.30	.15	.03
☐ 19	Kirby Puckett	1.00	.50	.10
☐ 20	Juan Samuel	.30	.15	.03
☐ 21	Eddie Murray	.75	.35	.07
☐ 22	George Bell	.40	.20	.04
☐ 23	Larry Sheets	.30	.15	.03
☐ 24	Eric Davis	.90	.45	.09
☐ 25	Cal Ripken	.60	.30	.06
☐ 26	Pedro Guerrero	.40	.20	.04
☐ 27	Will Clark	2.00	1.00	.20
☐ 28	Dwight Gooden	.90	.45	.09
☐ 29	Frank Viola	.50	.25	.05
☐ 30	Roger Clemens	.75	.35	.07
☐ 31	Rick Sutcliffe	.40	.20	.04
☐ 32	Jack Morris	.40	.20	.04
☐ 33	John Tudor	.40	.20	.04

☐ 2	Wally Joyner	.90	.45	.09
☐ 3	Von Hayes	.30	.15	.03
☐ 4	Jose Canseco	2.00	1.00	.20
☐ 5	Dave Winfield	.60	.30	.06
☐ 6	Cal Ripken	.75	.35	.07
☐ 7	Keith Moreland	.30	.15	.03
☐ 8	Don Mattingly	2.50	1.25	.25
☐ 9	Willie McGee	.40	.20	.04
☐ 10	Keith Hernandez	.50	.25	.05
☐ 11	Tony Gwynn	.90	.45	.09
☐ 12	Rickey Henderson	1.00	.50	.10
☐ 13	Dale Murphy	.90	.45	.09
☐ 14	George Brett	.90	.45	.09
☐ 15	Jim Rice	.50	.25	.05
☐ 16	Wade Boggs	2.00	1.00	.20
☐ 17	Kevin Bass	.30	.15	.03
☐ 18	Dave Parker	.40	.20	.04
☐ 19	Kirby Puckett	1.00	.50	.10
☐ 20	Gary Carter	.50	.25	.05
☐ 21	Ryne Sandberg	.60	.30	.06
☐ 22	Harold Baines	.40	.20	.04
☐ 23	Mike Schmidt	2.00	1.00	.20
☐ 24	Eddie Murray	.60	.30	.06
☐ 25	Steve Sax	.40	.20	.04
☐ 26	Dwight Gooden	.75	.35	.07
☐ 27	Jack Morris	.40	.20	.04
☐ 28	Ron Darling	.40	.20	.04
☐ 29	Fernando Valenzuela	.50	.25	.05
☐ 30	John Tudor	.40	.20	.04
☐ 31	Roger Clemens	.75	.35	.07
☐ 32	Nolan Ryan	2.00	1.00	.20
☐ 33	Mike Scott	.50	.25	.05

1988 Drake's

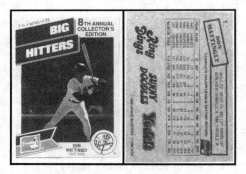

This 33-card set features 27 top hitters and six top pitchers. Cards were printed in groups of two, three, or four on the backs of Drake's bakery products. Individual cards measure approximately 2 1/2" by 3 1/2" and tout the 8th annual edition. Card backs feature year-by-year season statistics. The cards are numbered such that the pitchers are listed numerically last. The product affiliations are as follows, 1-2 Ring Dings, 3-4 Devil Dogs, 5-6 Coffee Cakes, 7-9 Yankee Doodles, 10-11 Funny Bones, 12-14 Fudge Brownies, 15-18 Cherry Pies, 19-21 Sunny

1966 East Hills Pirates

The 1966 East Hills Pirates set consists of 25 large (3 1/4" by 4 1/4"), full color photos of Pittsburgh Pirate ballplayers. These blank-backed cards are numbered in the lower right corner according to the uniform number of the individual depicted. The set was distributed by various stores located in the East Hills Shopping Center. The ACC catalog number for this set is F405.

		NRMT	VG-E	GOOD
COMPLETE SET (25)		30.00	15.00	3.00
COMMON PLAYER (1-45)		.40	.20	.04
☐ 3	Harry Walker MG	.60	.30	.06
☐ 7	Bob Bailey	.40	.20	.04
☐ 8	Willie Stargell	7.50	3.75	.75
☐ 9	Bill Mazeroski	2.50	1.25	.25

		NRMT	VG-E	GOOD
☐ 10	Jim Pagliaroni	.40	.20	.04
☐ 11	Jose Pagan	.40	.20	.04
☐ 12	Jerry May	.40	.20	.04
☐ 14	Gene Alley	.60	.30	.06
☐ 15	Manny Mota	.75	.35	.07
☐ 16	Andy Rodgers	.40	.20	.04
☐ 17	Donn Clendenon	.60	.30	.06
☐ 18	Matty Alou	.75	.35	.07
☐ 19	Pete Mikkelsen	.40	.20	.04
☐ 20	Jesse Gonder	.40	.20	.04
☐ 21	Bob Clemente	15.00	7.50	1.50
☐ 22	Woody Fryman	.40	.20	.04
☐ 24	Jerry Lynch	.40	.20	.04
☐ 25	Tommie Sisk	.40	.20	.04
☐ 26	Roy Face	1.25	.60	.12
☐ 28	Steve Blass	.60	.30	.06
☐ 32	Vernon Law	1.00	.50	.10
☐ 34	Al McBean	.40	.20	.04
☐ 39	Bob Veale	.60	.30	.06
☐ 43	Don Cardwell	.40	.20	.04
☐ 45	Gene Michael	.60	.30	.06

1959 Fleer

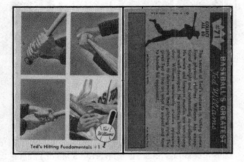

Ted's Hitting Fundamentals ● 1

The cards in this 80-card set measure 2 1/2" by 3 1/2". The 1959 Fleer set, designated as R418-1 in the ACC, portrays the life of Ted Williams. The wording of the wrapper, "Baseball's Greatest Series," has led to speculation that Fleer contemplated similar sets honoring other baseball immortals, but chose to develop instead the format of the 1960 and 1961 issues. Card number 68, which was withdrawn early in production, is considered scarce and has even been counterfeited; the fake has a rosy coloration and a cross-hatch pattern visible over the picture area.

		NRMT	VG-E	GOOD
COMPLETE SET (80)		600.00	300.00	60.00
COMMON CARDS (1-80)		3.00	1.50	.30
☐ 1	The Early Years	15.00	2.00	.40
☐ 2	Ted's Idol Babe Ruth	10.00	5.00	1.00
☐ 3	Practice Makes Perfect	3.00	1.50	.30
☐ 4	Learns Fine Points	3.00	1.50	.30
☐ 5	Ted's Fame Spreads	3.00	1.50	.30
☐ 6	Ted Turns Pro	3.00	1.50	.30
☐ 7	From Mound to Plate	3.00	1.50	.30
☐ 8	1937 First Full Season	3.00	1.50	.30
☐ 9	First Step to Majors	3.00	1.50	.30
☐ 10	Gunning as Pastime	3.00	1.50	.30
☐ 11	First Spring Training (with Jimmie Foxx)	6.00	3.00	.60
☐ 12	Burning Up Minors	3.00	1.50	.30
☐ 13	1939 Shows Will Stay	3.00	1.50	.30
☐ 14	Outstanding Rookie '39	3.00	1.50	.30
☐ 15	Licks Sophomore Jinx	3.00	1.50	.30
☐ 16	1941 Greatest Year	3.00	1.50	.30
☐ 17	How Ted Hit .400	3.00	1.50	.30
☐ 18	1941 All Star Hero	3.00	1.50	.30
☐ 19	Ted Wins Triple Crown	3.00	1.50	.30
☐ 20	On to Naval Training	3.00	1.50	.30
☐ 21	Honors for Williams	3.00	1.50	.30
☐ 22	1944 Ted Solos	3.00	1.50	.30
☐ 23	Williams Wins Wings	3.00	1.50	.30
☐ 24	1945 Sharpshooter	3.00	1.50	.30
☐ 25	1945 Ted Discharged	3.00	1.50	.30
☐ 26	Off to Flying Start	3.00	1.50	.30
☐ 27	7/9/46 One Man Show	3.00	1.50	.30
☐ 28	The Williams Shift	3.00	1.50	.30
☐ 29	Ted Hits for Cycle	3.00	1.50	.30
☐ 30	Beating Williams Shift	3.00	1.50	.30
☐ 31	Sox Lose Series	3.00	1.50	.30
☐ 32	Most Valuable Player	3.00	1.50	.30
☐ 33	Another Triple Crown	3.00	1.50	.30
☐ 34	Runs Scored Record	3.00	1.50	.30
☐ 35	Sox Miss Pennant	3.00	1.50	.30
☐ 36	Banner Year for Ted	3.00	1.50	.30
☐ 37	1949 Sox Miss Again	3.00	1.50	.30
☐ 38	1949 Power Rampage	3.00	1.50	.30
☐ 39	1950 Great Start	3.00	1.50	.30
☐ 40	Ted Crashes into Wall	3.00	1.50	.30
☐ 41	1950 Ted Recovers	3.00	1.50	.30
☐ 42	Slowed by Injury	3.00	1.50	.30
☐ 43	Double Play Lead	3.00	1.50	.30
☐ 44	Back to Marines	3.00	1.50	.30
☐ 45	Farewell to Baseball	3.00	1.50	.30
☐ 46	Ready for Combat	3.00	1.50	.30
☐ 47	Ted Crash Lands Jet	3.00	1.50	.30
☐ 48	1953 Ted Returns	3.00	1.50	.30
☐ 49	Smash Return	3.00	1.50	.30
☐ 50	1954 Spring Injury	3.00	1.50	.30
☐ 51	Ted is Patched Up	3.00	1.50	.30
☐ 52	1954 Ted's Comeback	3.00	1.50	.30
☐ 53	Comeback is Success	3.00	1.50	.30
☐ 54	Ted Hooks Big One	3.00	1.50	.30
☐ 55	Retirement "No Go"	3.00	1.50	.30
☐ 56	2000th Hit	3.00	1.50	.30
☐ 57	400th Homer	3.00	1.50	.30
☐ 58	Williams Hits .388	3.00	1.50	.30
☐ 59	Hot September for Ted	3.00	1.50	.30
☐ 60	More Records for Ted	3.00	1.50	.30
☐ 61	1957 Outfielder Ted	3.00	1.50	.30
☐ 62	1958 Sixth Batting Title	3.00	1.50	.30
☐ 63	Ted's All-Star Record	3.00	1.50	.30
☐ 64	Daughter and Daddy	3.00	1.50	.30
☐ 65	1958 August 30	3.00	1.50	.30
☐ 66	1958 Powerhouse	3.00	1.50	.30
☐ 67	Two Famous Fishermen	6.00	3.00	.60
☐ 68	Ted Signs for 1959	350.00	175.00	35.00
☐ 69	A Future Ted Williams	3.00	1.50	.30
☐ 70	Williams and Thorpe	6.00	3.00	.60
☐ 71	Hitting Fund. 1	3.00	1.50	.30
☐ 72	Hitting Fund. 2	3.00	1.50	.30
☐ 73	Hitting Fund. 3	3.00	1.50	.30
☐ 74	Here's How	3.00	1.50	.30
☐ 75	Williams' Value to Sox	3.00	1.50	.30
☐ 76	On Base Record	3.00	1.50	.30
☐ 77	Ted Relaxes	3.00	1.50	.30
☐ 78	Honors for Williams	3.00	1.50	.30
☐ 79	Where Ted Stands	3.00	1.50	.30
☐ 80	Ted's Goals for 1959	6.00	3.00	.60

1960 Fleer

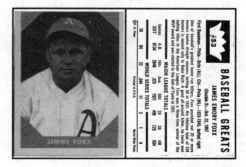

The cards in this 79-card set measure 2 1/2" by 3 1/2". The cards from the 1960 Fleer series of Baseball Greats are sometimes mistaken for 1930s cards by collectors not familiar with this set. The cards each contain a tinted photo of a baseball immortal, and were issued in one series. There are no known scarcities, although a number 80 card (Pepper Martin reverse with Eddie Collins obverse) exists (this is not considered part of the set). The catalog designation for 1960 Fleer is R418-2. The cards were printed on a 96-card sheet with 17 double prints. These are noted in the checklist below by DP. On the sheet the (second) Eddie Collins card is typically found in the #80 position.

		NRMT	VG-E	GOOD
COMPLETE SET (79)		300.00	150.00	30.00
COMMON PLAYER (1-79)		2.00	1.00	.20
COMMON PLAYER DP		1.25	.60	.12
☐ 1	Napoleon Lajoie DP	10.00	1.00	.20
☐ 2	Christy Mathewson	7.50	3.75	.75
☐ 3	George H. Ruth	50.00	25.00	5.00
☐ 4	Carl Hubbell	3.00	1.50	.30
☐ 5	Grover Alexander	3.00	1.50	.30
☐ 6	Walter Johnson DP	5.00	2.50	.50
☐ 7	Charles A. Bender	2.00	1.00	.20
☐ 8	Roger P. Bresnahan	2.00	1.00	.20
☐ 9	Mordecai P. Brown	2.00	1.00	.20
☐ 10	Tristram Speaker	3.00	1.50	.30
☐ 11	Arky Vaughan DP	1.25	.60	.12
☐ 12	Zachariah Wheat	2.00	1.00	.20
☐ 13	George Sisler	2.00	1.00	.20
☐ 14	Connie Mack	3.00	1.50	.30
☐ 15	Clark C. Griffith	2.00	1.00	.20
☐ 16	Louis Boudreau DP	2.00	1.00	.20
☐ 17	Ernest Lombardi	2.00	1.00	.20
☐ 18	Henry Manush	2.00	1.00	.20
☐ 19	Martin Marion	2.00	1.00	.20
☐ 20	Edward Collins DP	1.25	.60	.12
☐ 21	James Maranville DP	1.25	.60	.12
☐ 22	Joseph Medwick	2.00	1.00	.20
☐ 23	Edward Barrow	2.00	1.00	.20
☐ 24	Gordon Cochrane	3.00	1.50	.30
☐ 25	James J. Collins	2.00	1.00	.20
☐ 26	Robert Feller DP	6.00	3.00	.60
☐ 27	Lucius Appling	3.00	1.50	.30
☐ 28	Lou Gehrig	25.00	12.50	2.50
☐ 29	Charles Hartnett	2.00	1.00	.20
☐ 30	Charles Klein	2.00	1.00	.20
☐ 31	Anthony Lazzeri DP	1.25	.60	.12
☐ 32	Aloysius Simmons	2.00	1.00	.20
☐ 33	Wilbert Robinson	2.00	1.00	.20
☐ 34	Edgar Rice	2.00	1.00	.20
☐ 35	Herbert Pennock	2.00	1.00	.20
☐ 36	Melvin Ott DP	2.00	1.00	.20
☐ 37	Frank O'Doul	2.00	1.00	.20
☐ 38	John Mize	3.00	1.50	.30
☐ 39	Edmund Miller	2.00	1.00	.20
☐ 40	Joseph Tinker	2.00	1.00	.20
☐ 41	John Baker DP	1.25	.60	.12
☐ 42	Tyrus Cobb	25.00	12.50	2.50
☐ 43	Paul Derringer	2.00	1.00	.20
☐ 44	Adrian Anson	2.00	1.00	.20
☐ 45	James Bottomley	2.00	1.00	.20
☐ 46	Edward S. Plank DP	1.25	.60	.12
☐ 47	Denton (Cy) Young	5.00	2.50	.50
☐ 48	Hack Wilson	3.00	1.50	.30
☐ 49	Edward Walsh UER	2.00	1.00	.20
	(photo actually Ed Walsh Jr.)			
☐ 50	Frank Chance	2.00	1.00	.20
☐ 51	Arthur Vance DP	1.25	.60	.12
☐ 52	William Terry	3.00	1.50	.30
☐ 53	James Foxx	5.00	2.50	.50
☐ 54	Vernon Gomez	3.00	1.50	.30
☐ 55	Branch Rickey	2.00	1.00	.20
☐ 56	Raymond Schalk DP	1.25	.60	.12
☐ 57	John Evers	2.00	1.00	.20
☐ 58	Charles Gehringer	3.00	1.50	.30
☐ 59	Burleigh Grimes	2.00	1.00	.20
☐ 60	Robert (Lefty) Grove	4.00	2.00	.40
☐ 61	George Waddell DP	1.25	.60	.12
☐ 62	John (Honus) Wagner	7.50	3.75	.75
☐ 63	Charles(Red) Ruffing	2.00	1.00	.20
☐ 64	Kenesaw M. Landis	2.00	1.00	.20
☐ 65	Harry Heilmann	2.00	1.00	.20
☐ 66	John McGraw DP	2.00	1.00	.20
☐ 67	Hugh Jennings	2.00	1.00	.20
☐ 68	Harold Newhouser	2.00	1.00	.20
☐ 69	Waite Hoyt	2.00	1.00	.20
☐ 70	Louis (Bobo) Newsom	2.00	1.00	.20
☐ 71	Earl Averill DP	1.25	.60	.12
☐ 72	Theodore Williams	40.00	20.00	4.00
☐ 73	Warren Giles	2.00	1.00	.20
☐ 74	Ford Frick	2.00	1.00	.20
☐ 75	Hazen (Kiki) Cuyler	2.00	1.00	.20
☐ 76	Paul Waner DP	1.25	.60	.12
☐ 77	Harold(Pie) Traynor	2.00	1.00	.20
☐ 78	Lloyd Waner	2.00	1.00	.20
☐ 79	Ralph Kiner	4.00	2.00	.40
☐ 80	Pepper Martin SP	500.00	250.00	50.00
	(Eddie Collins pictured on obverse)			

1961 Fleer

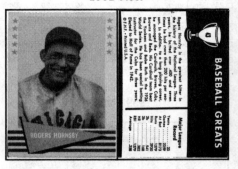

The cards in this 154-card set measure 2 1/2" by 3 1/2". In 1961, Fleer continued its Baseball Greats format by issuing this series of cards. The set was released in two distinct series, 1-88 and 89-154 (of which the latter is more difficult to obtain). The players within each series are conveniently numbered in alphabetical order. It appears that this set continued to be issued the following year by Fleer. The catalog number for this set is F418-3. In each first series pack Fleer inserted a Major League team decal and a pennant sticker honoring past World Series winners.

		NRMT	VG-E	GOOD
COMPLETE SET (154)		600.00	300.00	60.00
COMMON PLAYER (1-88)		1.50	.75	.15
COMMON PLAYER (89-154)		3.00	1.50	.30
☐ 1	Baker/Cobb/Wheat	15.00	2.50	.50
	(checklist back)			
☐ 2	Grover C. Alexander	3.00	1.50	.30
☐ 3	Nick Altrock	1.50	.75	.15
☐ 4	Cap Anson	1.50	.75	.15
☐ 5	Earl Averill	1.50	.75	.15
☐ 6	Frank Baker	1.50	.75	.15
☐ 7	Dave Bancroft	1.50	.75	.15
☐ 8	Chief Bender	1.50	.75	.15
☐ 9	Jim Bottomley	1.50	.75	.15
☐ 10	Roger Bresnahan	1.50	.75	.15
☐ 11	Mordecai Brown	1.50	.75	.15
☐ 12	Max Carey	1.50	.75	.15
☐ 13	Jack Chesbro	1.50	.75	.15
☐ 14	Ty Cobb	25.00	12.50	2.50
☐ 15	Mickey Cochrane	2.50	1.25	.25
☐ 16	Eddie Collins	1.50	.75	.15
☐ 17	Earle Combs	1.50	.75	.15
☐ 18	Charles Comiskey	1.50	.75	.15
☐ 19	Kiki Cuyler	1.50	.75	.15
☐ 20	Paul Derringer	1.50	.75	.15
☐ 21	Howard Ehmke	1.50	.75	.15
☐ 22	W. Evans	1.50	.75	.15
☐ 23	Johnny Evers	1.50	.75	.15
☐ 24	Urban Faber	1.50	.75	.15
☐ 25	Bob Feller	7.50	3.75	.75
☐ 26	Wes Ferrell	1.50	.75	.15
☐ 27	Lew Fonseca	1.50	.75	.15
☐ 28	Jimmy Foxx	5.00	2.50	.50
☐ 29	Ford Frick	1.50	.75	.15
☐ 30	Frank Frisch	2.50	1.25	.25
☐ 31	Lou Gehrig	25.00	12.50	2.50
☐ 32	Charlie Gehringer	2.50	1.25	.25
☐ 33	Warren Giles	1.50	.75	.15
☐ 34	Lefty Gomez	2.50	1.25	.25
☐ 35	Goose Goslin	1.50	.75	.15
☐ 36	Clark Griffith	1.50	.75	.15
☐ 37	Burleigh Grimes	1.50	.75	.15
☐ 38	Lefty Grove	3.00	1.50	.30
☐ 39	Chick Hafey	1.50	.75	.15

☐ 40	Jesse Haines	1.50	.75	.15
☐ 41	Gabby Hartnett	1.50	.75	.15
☐ 42	Harry Heilmann	1.50	.75	.15
☐ 43	Rogers Hornsby	4.00	2.00	.40
☐ 44	Waite Hoyt	1.50	.75	.15
☐ 45	Carl Hubbell	2.50	1.25	.25
☐ 46	Miller Huggins	1.50	.75	.15
☐ 47	Hugh Jennings	1.50	.75	.15
☐ 48	Ban Johnson	1.50	.75	.15
☐ 49	Walter Johnson	7.50	3.75	.75
☐ 50	Ralph Kiner	3.50	1.75	.35
☐ 51	Chuck Klein	1.50	.75	.15
☐ 52	Johnny Kling	1.50	.75	.15
☐ 53	K.M. Landis	1.50	.75	.15
☐ 54	Tony Lazzeri	1.50	.75	.15
☐ 55	Ernie Lombardi	1.50	.75	.15
☐ 56	Dolf Luque	1.50	.75	.15
☐ 57	Heine Manush	1.50	.75	.15
☐ 58	Marty Marion	1.50	.75	.15
☐ 59	Christy Mathewson	7.50	3.75	.75
☐ 60	John McGraw	2.50	1.25	.25
☐ 61	Joe Medwick	1.50	.75	.15
☐ 62	E. (Bing) Miller	1.50	.75	.15
☐ 63	Johnny Mize	3.50	1.75	.35
☐ 64	John Mostil	1.50	.75	.15
☐ 65	Art Nehf	1.50	.75	.15
☐ 66	Hal Newhouser	1.50	.75	.15
☐ 67	D. (Bobo) Newsom	1.50	.75	.15
☐ 68	Mel Ott	2.50	1.25	.25
☐ 69	Allie Reynolds	1.50	.75	.15
☐ 70	Sam Rice	1.50	.75	.15
☐ 71	Eppa Rixey	1.50	.75	.15
☐ 72	Edd Roush	1.50	.75	.15
☐ 73	Schoolboy Rowe	1.50	.75	.15
☐ 74	Red Ruffing	1.50	.75	.15
☐ 75	Babe Ruth	50.00	25.00	5.00
☐ 76	Joe Sewell	1.50	.75	.15
☐ 77	Al Simmons	1.50	.75	.15
☐ 78	George Sisler	1.50	.75	.15
☐ 79	Tris Speaker	3.00	1.50	.30
☐ 80	Fred Toney	1.50	.75	.15
☐ 81	Dazzy Vance	1.50	.75	.15
☐ 82	Jim Vaughn	1.50	.75	.15
☐ 83	Ed Walsh	1.50	.75	.15
☐ 84	Lloyd Waner	1.50	.75	.15
☐ 85	Paul Waner	1.50	.75	.15
☐ 86	Zack Wheat	1.50	.75	.15
☐ 87	Hack Wilson	2.50	1.25	.25
☐ 88	Jimmy Wilson	1.50	.75	.15
☐ 89	Sisler and Traynor	12.00	2.50	.50
	(checklist back)			
☐ 90	Babe Adams	3.00	1.50	.30
☐ 91	Dale Alexander	3.00	1.50	.30
☐ 92	Jim Bagby	3.00	1.50	.30
☐ 93	Ossie Bluege	3.00	1.50	.30
☐ 94	Lou Boudreau	6.00	3.00	.60
☐ 95	Tom Bridges	3.00	1.50	.30
☐ 96	Donie Bush	3.00	1.50	.30
☐ 97	Dolph Camilli	3.00	1.50	.30
☐ 98	Frank Chance	4.50	2.25	.45
☐ 99	Jimmy Collins	4.50	2.25	.45
☐ 100	Stan Coveleskie	4.50	2.25	.45
☐ 101	Hugh Critz	3.00	1.50	.30
☐ 102	Alvin Crowder	3.00	1.50	.30
☐ 103	Joe Dugan	3.00	1.50	.30
☐ 104	Bibb Falk	3.00	1.50	.30
☐ 105	Rick Ferrell	4.50	2.25	.45
☐ 106	Art Fletcher	3.00	1.50	.30
☐ 107	Dennis Galehouse	3.00	1.50	.30
☐ 108	Chick Galloway	3.00	1.50	.30
☐ 109	Mule Haas	3.00	1.50	.30
☐ 110	Stan Hack	3.00	1.50	.30
☐ 111	Bump Hadley	3.00	1.50	.30
☐ 112	Billy B. Hamilton	4.50	2.25	.45
☐ 113	Joe Hauser	3.00	1.50	.30
☐ 114	Babe Herman	3.00	1.50	.30
☐ 115	Travis Jackson	6.00	3.00	.60
☐ 116	Eddie Joost	3.00	1.50	.30
☐ 117	Addie Joss	6.00	3.00	.60
☐ 118	Joe Judge	3.00	1.50	.30
☐ 119	Joe Kuhel	3.00	1.50	.30
☐ 120	Napoleon Lajoie	9.00	4.50	.90
☐ 121	Dutch Leonard	3.00	1.50	.30
☐ 122	Ted Lyons	4.50	2.25	.45
☐ 123	Connie Mack	9.00	4.50	.90
☐ 124	Rabbit Maranville	4.50	2.25	.45
☐ 125	Fred Marberry	3.00	1.50	.30
☐ 126	Joe McGinnity	6.00	3.00	.60
☐ 127	Oscar Melillo	3.00	1.50	.30
☐ 128	Ray Mueller	3.00	1.50	.30
☐ 129	Kid Nichols	4.50	2.25	.45
☐ 130	Lefty O'Doul	3.00	1.50	.30
☐ 131	Bob O'Farrell	3.00	1.50	.30
☐ 132	Roger Peckinpaugh	3.00	1.50	.30
☐ 133	Herb Pennock	4.50	2.25	.45

☐ 134	George Pipgras	3.00	1.50	.30
☐ 135	Eddie Plank	6.00	3.00	.60
☐ 136	Ray Schalk	4.50	2.25	.45
☐ 137	Hal Schumacher	3.00	1.50	.30
☐ 138	Luke Sewell	3.00	1.50	.30
☐ 139	Bob Shawkey	3.00	1.50	.30
☐ 140	Riggs Stephenson	3.00	1.50	.30
☐ 141	Billy Sullivan	3.00	1.50	.30
☐ 142	Bill Terry	7.50	3.75	.75
☐ 143	Joe Tinker	4.50	2.25	.45
☐ 144	Pie Traynor	6.00	3.00	.60
☐ 145	Hal Trosky	3.00	1.50	.30
☐ 146	George Uhle	3.00	1.50	.30
☐ 147	Johnny VanderMeer	4.50	2.25	.45
☐ 148	Arky Vaughan	4.50	2.25	.45
☐ 149	Rube Waddell	4.50	2.25	.45
☐ 150	Honus Wagner	25.00	12.50	2.50
☐ 151	Dixie Walker	3.00	1.50	.30
☐ 152	Ted Williams	50.00	25.00	5.00
☐ 153	Cy Young	15.00	7.50	1.50
☐ 154	Ross Young	9.00	4.50	.90

1963 Fleer

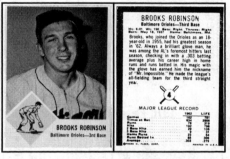

BROOKS ROBINSON
Baltimore Orioles—3rd Base

The cards in this 66-card set measure 2 1/2" by 3 1/2". The Fleer set of current baseball players was marketed in 1963 in a gum card-style waxed wrapper package which contained a cherry cookie instead of gum. The cards were printed in sheets of 66 with the scarce card of Adcock apparently being replaced by the unnumbered checklist card for the final press run. The complete set price includes the checklist card. The catalog designation for this set is R418-4.

		NRMT	VG-E	GOOD
COMPLETE SET (67)		750.00	375.00	75.00
COMMON PLAYER (1-66)		2.50	1.25	.25

☐ 1	Steve Barber	5.00	1.25	.25
☐ 2	Ron Hansen	2.50	1.25	.25
☐ 3	Milt Pappas	3.00	1.50	.30
☐ 4	Brooks Robinson	27.00	13.50	2.70
☐ 5	Willie Mays	50.00	25.00	5.00
☐ 6	Lou Clinton	2.50	1.25	.25
☐ 7	Bill Monbouquette	2.50	1.25	.25
☐ 8	Carl Yastrzemski	50.00	25.00	5.00
☐ 9	Ray Herbert	2.50	1.25	.25
☐ 10	Jim Landis	2.50	1.25	.25
☐ 11	Dick Donovan	2.50	1.25	.25
☐ 12	Tito Francona	2.50	1.25	.25
☐ 13	Jerry Kindall	2.50	1.25	.25
☐ 14	Frank Lary	3.00	1.50	.30
☐ 15	Dick Howser	4.00	2.00	.40
☐ 16	Jerry Lumpe	2.50	1.25	.25
☐ 17	Norm Siebern	2.50	1.25	.25
☐ 18	Don Lee	2.50	1.25	.25
☐ 19	Albie Pearson	2.50	1.25	.25
☐ 20	Bob Rodgers	3.00	1.50	.30
☐ 21	Leon Wagner	2.50	1.25	.25
☐ 22	Jim Kaat	6.00	3.00	.60
☐ 23	Vic Power	2.50	1.25	.25
☐ 24	Rich Rollins	2.50	1.25	.25
☐ 25	Bobby Richardson	5.00	2.50	.50
☐ 26	Ralph Terry	3.00	1.50	.30
☐ 27	Tom Cheney	2.50	1.25	.25
☐ 28	Chuck Cottier	2.50	1.25	.25
☐ 29	Jim Piersall	3.50	1.75	.35
☐ 30	Dave Stenhouse	2.50	1.25	.25

		NRMT	VG-E	GOOD
☐ 31	Glen Hobbie	2.50	1.25	.25
☐ 32	Ron Santo	5.00	2.50	.50
☐ 33	Gene Freese	2.50	1.25	.25
☐ 34	Vada Pinson	4.00	2.00	.40
☐ 35	Bob Purkey	2.50	1.25	.25
☐ 36	Joe Amalfitano	2.50	1.25	.25
☐ 37	Bob Aspromonte	2.50	1.25	.25
☐ 38	Dick Farrell	2.50	1.25	.25
☐ 39	Al Spangler	2.50	1.25	.25
☐ 40	Tommy Davis	3.50	1.75	.35
☐ 41	Don Drysdale	18.00	9.00	1.80
☐ 42	Sandy Koufax	50.00	25.00	5.00
☐ 43	Maury Wills	30.00	14.00	2.70
☐ 44	Frank Bolling	2.50	1.25	.25
☐ 45	Warren Spahn	18.00	9.00	1.80
☐ 46	Joe Adcock SP	85.00	42.50	8.50
☐ 47	Roger Craig	4.00	2.00	.40
☐ 48	Al Jackson	2.50	1.25	.25
☐ 49	Rod Kanehl	2.50	1.25	.25
☐ 50	Ruben Amaro	2.50	1.25	.25
☐ 51	Johnny Callison	3.00	1.50	.30
☐ 52	Clay Dalrymple	2.50	1.25	.25
☐ 53	Don Demeter	2.50	1.25	.25
☐ 54	Art Mahaffey	2.50	1.25	.25
☐ 55	Smokey Burgess	3.00	1.50	.30
☐ 56	Roberto Clemente	50.00	25.00	5.00
☐ 57	Roy Face	3.50	1.75	.35
☐ 58	Vern Law	3.00	1.50	.30
☐ 59	Bill Mazeroski	5.00	2.50	.50
☐ 60	Ken Boyer	5.00	2.50	.50
☐ 61	Bob Gibson	18.00	9.00	1.80
☐ 62	Gene Oliver	2.50	1.25	.25
☐ 63	Bill White	5.00	2.50	.50
☐ 64	Orlando Cepeda	6.00	3.00	.60
☐ 65	Jim Davenport	2.50	1.25	.25
☐ 66	Billy O'Dell	3.00	1.50	.30
☐ 67	Checklist card (unnumbered)	250.00	50.00	10.00

1970 Fleer World Series

This set of 66 cards was distributed by Fleer. The cards are standard size, 2 1/2" by 3 1/2" and are in crude color on the front with light blue printing on white card stock on the back. All the years are represented except for 1904 when no World Series was played. In the list below, the winning series team is listed first. The year of the Series on the obverse is inside a white baseball.

		NRMT	VG-E	GOOD
COMPLETE SET (66)		25.00	12.50	2.50
COMMON PLAYER (1-66)		.35	.17	.03
☐ 1	1903 Red Sox/Pirates	.35	.17	.03
☐ 2	1905 Giants/A's (Christy Mathewson)	.45	.22	.04
☐ 3	1906 White Sox/Cubs	.35	.17	.03
☐ 4	1907 Cubs/Tigers	.35	.17	.03
☐ 5	1908 Cubs/Tigers (Tinker/Evers/Chance)	.45	.22	.04
☐ 6	1909 Pirates/Tigers (Wagner/Cobb)	.55	.27	.05
☐ 7	1910 A's/Cubs (Bender/Coombs)	.35	.17	.03
☐ 8	1911 A's/Giants (John McGraw)	.35	.17	.03
☐ 9	1912 Red Sox/Giants	.35	.17	.03
☐ 10	1913 A's/Giants	.35	.17	.03
☐ 11	1914 Braves/A's	.35	.17	.03
☐ 12	1915 Red Sox/Phillies (Babe Ruth)	.85	.40	.08
☐ 13	1916 Red Sox/Dodgers (Babe Ruth)	.85	.40	.08
☐ 14	1917 White Sox/Giants	.35	.17	.03
☐ 15	1918 Red Sox/Cubs	.35	.17	.03
☐ 16	1919 Reds/White Sox	.35	.17	.03
☐ 17	1920 Indians/Dodgers (Stan Coveleski)	.35	.17	.03
☐ 18	1921 Giants/Yankees (Commissioner Landis)	.35	.17	.03
☐ 19	1922 Giants/Yankees	.35	.17	.03
☐ 20	1923 Yankees/Giants (Babe Ruth)	.85	.40	.08
☐ 21	1924 Senators/Giants (John McGraw)	.35	.17	.03
☐ 22	1925 Pirates/Senators (Walter Johnson)	.45	.22	.04
☐ 23	1926 Cardinals/Yankees (Alexander/Lazzeri)	.35	.17	.03
☐ 24	1927 Yankees/Pirates	.35	.17	.03
☐ 25	1928 Yankees/Cardinals (Ruth/Gehrig)	.85	.40	.08
☐ 26	1929 A's/Cubs	.35	.17	.03
☐ 27	1930 A's/Cardinals	.35	.17	.03
☐ 28	1931 Cardinals/A's (Pepper Martin)	.35	.17	.03
☐ 29	1932 Yankees/Cubs (Ruth/Gehrig)	.85	.40	.08
☐ 30	1933 Giants/Senators (Mel Ott)	.45	.22	.04
☐ 31	1934 Cardinals/Tigers	.35	.17	.03
☐ 32	1935 Tigers/Cubs (Gehringer/Bridges)	.45	.22	.04
☐ 33	1936 Yankees/Giants	.35	.17	.03
☐ 34	1937 Yankees/Giants (Carl Hubbell)	.35	.17	.03
☐ 35	1938 Yankees/Cubs (Lou Gehrig)	.65	.30	.06
☐ 36	1939 Yankees/Reds	.35	.17	.03
☐ 37	1940 Reds/Tigers	.35	.17	.03
☐ 38	1941 Yankees/Dodgers	.35	.17	.03
☐ 39	1942 Cardinals/Yankees	.35	.17	.03
☐ 40	1943 Yankees/Cardinals	.35	.17	.03
☐ 41	1944 Cardinals/Browns	.35	.17	.03
☐ 42	1945 Tigers/Cubs (Hank Greenberg)	.35	.17	.03
☐ 43	1946 Cardinals/Red Sox (Enos Slaughter)	.35	.17	.03
☐ 44	1947 Yankees/Dodgers (Al Gionfriddo)	.35	.17	.03
☐ 45	1948 Indians/Braves	.35	.17	.03
☐ 46	1949 Yankees/Dodgers (Reynolds/Roe)	.35	.17	.03
☐ 47	1950 Yankees/Phillies	.35	.17	.03
☐ 48	1951 Yankees/Giants	.35	.17	.03
☐ 49	1952 Yankees/Dodgers (Mize/Snider)	.55	.27	.05
☐ 50	1953 Yankees/Dodgers (Carl Erskine)	.35	.17	.03
☐ 51	1954 Giants/Indians (Johnny Antonelli)	.35	.17	.03
☐ 52	1955 Dodgers/Yankees (Johnny Podres)	.35	.17	.03
☐ 53	1956 Yankees/Dodgers	.35	.17	.03
☐ 54	1957 Braves/Yankees (Lew Burdette)	.35	.17	.03
☐ 55	1958 Yankees/Braves (Bob Turley)	.35	.17	.03
☐ 56	1959 Dodgers/Wh.Sox (Chuck Essegian)	.35	.17	.03
☐ 57	1960 Pirates/Yankees	.35	.17	.03
☐ 58	1961 Yankees/Reds (Whitey Ford)	.45	.22	.04
☐ 59	1962 Yankees/Giants	.35	.17	.03
☐ 60	1963 Dodgers/Yankees (Moose Skowron)	.35	.17	.03
☐ 61	1964 Cardinals/Yankees (Bobby Richardson)	.45	.22	.04
☐ 62	1965 Dodgers/Twins	.35	.17	.03
☐ 63	1966 Orioles/Dodgers	.35	.17	.03
☐ 64	1967 Cardinals/Red Sox	.35	.17	.03
☐ 65	1968 Tigers/Cardinals	.35	.17	.03
☐ 66	1969 Mets/Orioles	.45	.22	.04

YOU CAN HELP: Your input is solicited for future editions of this guide. Write the author at 4887 Alpha Rd., Suite 200, Dallas, Texas 75244.

1971 Fleer World Series

This set of 68 cards was distributed by Fleer. The cards are standard size, 2 1/2" by 3 1/2" and are in crude color on the front with brown printing on white card stock on the back. All the years are represented in this set as 1904 when no World Series was played is represented by a card explaining why there was no World Series that year. In the list below, the winning series team is listed first. The year of the Series on the obverse is inside a white square over the official World Series logo.

		NRMT	VG-E	GOOD
COMPLETE SET (68)		25.00	12.50	2.50
COMMON PLAYER (1-68)		.35	.17	.03
☐ 1	1903 Red Sox/Pirates ..... (Cy Young)	.45	.22	.04
☐ 2	1904 NO Series .... (John McGraw)	.45	.22	.04
☐ 3	1905 Giants/A's .... (Mathewson, Bender, and McGinnity)	.45	.22	.04
☐ 4	1906 White Sox/Cubs	.35	.17	.03
☐ 5	1907 Cubs/Tigers	.35	.17	.03
☐ 6	1908 Cubs/Tigers .... (Ty Cobb)	.65	.30	.06
☐ 7	1909 Pirates/Tigers	.35	.17	.03
☐ 8	1910 A's/Cubs .... (Eddie Collins)	.35	.17	.03
☐ 9	1911 A's/Giants .... (Home Run Baker)	.35	.17	.03
☐10	1912 Red Sox/Giants	.35	.17	.03
☐11	1913 A's/Giants .... (Christy Mathewson)	.45	.22	.04
☐12	1914 Braves/A's	.35	.17	.03
☐13	1915 Red Sox/Phillies	.35	.17	.03
	(Grover Alexander)			
☐14	1916 Red Sox/Dodgers	.35	.17	.03
☐15	1917 White Sox/Giants ... (Red Faber)	.35	.17	.03
☐16	1918 Red Sox/Cubs .... (Babe Ruth)	.85	.40	.08
☐17	1919 Reds/White Sox	.35	.17	.03
☐18	1920 Indians/Dodgers	.35	.17	.03
☐19	1921 Giants/Yankees ...... (Waite Hoyt)	.35	.17	.03
☐20	1922 Giants/Yankees	.35	.17	.03
☐21	1923 Yankees/Giants ...... (Herb Pennock)	.35	.17	.03
☐22	1924 Senators/Giants ..... (Walter Johnson)	.45	.22	.04
☐23	1925 Pirates/Senators .... (Cuyler/W.Johnson)	.45	.22	.04
☐24	1926 Cardinals/Yankees . (Rogers Hornsby)	.45	.22	.04
☐25	1927 Yankees/Pirates	.35	.17	.03
☐26	1928 Yankees/Cardinals . (Lou Gehrig)	.65	.30	.06
☐27	1929 A's/Cubs	.35	.17	.03
☐28	1930 A's/Cardinals .... (Jimmie Foxx)	.45	.22	.04
☐29	1931 Cardinals/A's .... (Pepper Martin)	.35	.17	.03
☐30	1932 Yankees/Cubs .... (Babe Ruth)	.85	.40	.08
☐31	1933 Giants/Senators ..... (Carl Hubbell)	.35	.17	.03

☐32	1934 Cardinals/Tigers	.35	.17	.03
☐33	1935 Tigers/Cubs .... (Mickey Cochrane)	.45	.22	.04
☐34	1936 Yankees/Giants ...... (Red Rolfe)	.35	.17	.03
☐35	1937 Yankees/Giants ...... (Tony Lazzeri)	.35	.17	.03
☐36	1938 Yankees/Cubs	.35	.17	.03
☐37	1939 Yankees/Reds	.35	.17	.03
☐38	1940 Reds/Tigers	.35	.17	.03
☐39	1941 Yankees/Dodgers ...	.35	.17	.03
☐40	1942 Cardinals/Yankees .	.35	.17	.03
☐41	1943 Yankees/Cardinals .	.35	.17	.03
☐42	1944 Cardinals/Browns ...	.35	.17	.03
☐43	1945 Tigers/Cubs .... (Hank Greenberg)	.35	.17	.03
☐44	1946 Cardinals/Red Sox . (Enos Slaughter)	.35	.17	.03
☐45	1947 Yankees/Dodgers ...	.35	.17	.03
☐46	1948 Indians/Braves	.35	.17	.03
☐47	1949 Yankees/Dodgers ... (Preacher Roe)	.35	.17	.03
☐48	1950 Yankees/Phillies ..... (Allie Reynolds)	.35	.17	.03
☐49	1951 Yankees/Giants ...... (Ed Lopat)	.35	.17	.03
☐50	1952 Yankees/Dodgers ... (Johnny Mize)	.45	.22	.04
☐51	1953 Yankees/Dodgers ...	.35	.17	.03
☐52	1954 Giants/Indians	.35	.17	.03
☐53	1955 Dodgers/Yankees ... (Duke Snider)	.45	.22	.04
☐54	1956 Yankees/Dodgers ...	.35	.17	.03
☐55	1957 Braves/Yankees	.35	.17	.03
☐56	1958 Yankees/Braves ..... (Hank Bauer)	.35	.17	.03
☐57	1959 Dodgers/Wh.Sox .... (Duke Snider)	.45	.22	.04
☐58	1960 Pirates/Yankees	.35	.17	.03
☐59	1961 Yankees/Reds .... (Whitey Ford)	.45	.22	.04
☐60	1962 Yankees/Giants	.35	.17	.03
☐61	1963 Dodgers/Yankees ...	.35	.17	.03
☐62	1964 Cardinals/Yankees .	.35	.17	.03
☐63	1965 Dodgers/Twins	.35	.17	.03
☐64	1966 Orioles/Dodgers	.35	.17	.03
☐65	1967 Cardinals/Red Sox .	.35	.17	.03
☐66	1968 Tigers/Cardinals	.35	.17	.03
☐67	1969 Mets/Orioles	.45	.22	.04
☐68	1970 Orioles/Reds	.45	.22	.04

1972 Fleer Famous Feats

This Fleer set of 40 cards features the artwork of sports artist R.G. Laughlin. The set is titled "Baseball's Famous Feats." The cards are numbered both on the front and back. The backs are printed in light blue on white card stock. The cards measure approximately 2 1/2" by 4". This set was licensed by Major League Baseball.

		NRMT	VG-E	GOOD
COMPLETE SET (40)		12.00	6.00	1.20
COMMON PLAYER (1-40)		.35	.17	.03
☐ 1	Joe McGinnity	.35	.17	.03

			NRMT	VG-E	GOOD
☐	2	Rogers Hornsby	.45	.22	.04
☐	3	Christy Mathewson	.55	.27	.05
☐	4	Dazzy Vance	.35	.17	.03
☐	5	Lou Gehrig	.75	.35	.07
☐	6	Jim Bottomley	.35	.17	.03
☐	7	Johnny Evers	.35	.17	.03
☐	8	Walter Johnson	.55	.27	.05
☐	9	Hack Wilson	.35	.17	.03
☐	10	Wilbert Robinson	.35	.17	.03
☐	11	Cy Young	.45	.22	.04
☐	12	Rudy York	.35	.17	.03
☐	13	Grover C. Alexander	.35	.17	.03
☐	14	Fred Toney and Hippo Vaughan	.35	.17	.03
☐	15	Ty Cobb	.75	.35	.07
☐	16	Jimmie Foxx	.45	.22	.04
☐	17	Hub Leonard	.35	.17	.03
☐	18	Eddie Collins	.35	.17	.03
☐	19	Joe Oeschger and Leon Cadore	.35	.17	.03
☐	20	Babe Ruth	1.00	.50	.10
☐	21	Honus Wagner	.55	.27	.05
☐	22	Red Rolfe	.35	.17	.03
☐	23	Ed Walsh	.35	.17	.03
☐	24	Paul Waner	.35	.17	.03
☐	25	Mel Ott	.45	.22	.04
☐	26	Eddie Plank	.35	.17	.03
☐	27	Sam Crawford	.35	.17	.03
☐	28	Napoleon Lajoie	.45	.22	.04
☐	29	Ed Reulbach	.35	.17	.03
☐	30	Pinky Higgins	.35	.17	.03
☐	31	Bill Klem	.45	.22	.04
☐	32	Tris Speaker	.45	.22	.04
☐	33	Hank Gowdy	.35	.17	.03
☐	34	Lefty O'Doul	.35	.17	.03
☐	35	Lloyd Waner	.35	.17	.03
☐	36	Chuck Klein	.35	.17	.03
☐	37	Deacon Phillippe	.35	.17	.03
☐	38	Ed Delahanty	.35	.17	.03
☐	39	Jack Chesbro	.35	.17	.03
☐	40	Willie Keeler	.35	.17	.03

			NRMT	VG-E	GOOD
☐	7	Four 20-Game Winners But No Pennant	.35	.17	.03
☐	8	Dummy Hoy Umpires Signal Strikes	.35	.17	.03
☐	9	Fourteeen Hits in One Inning	.35	.17	.03
☐	10	Yankees Not Shut Out For Two Years	.35	.17	.03
☐	11	Buck Weaver 17 Straight Fouls	.35	.17	.03
☐	12	George Sisler Greatest Thrill Was as a Pitcher	.35	.17	.03
☐	13	Wrong-Way Baserunner	.35	.17	.03
☐	14	Kiki Cuyler Sits Out Series	.35	.17	.03
☐	15	Grounder Climbed Wall	.35	.17	.03
☐	16	Gabby Street Washington Monument	.35	.17	.03
☐	17	Mel Ott Ejected Twice	.35	.17	.03
☐	18	Shortest Pitching Career	.35	.17	.03
☐	19	Three Homers in One Inning	.35	.17	.03
☐	20	Bill Byron Singing Umpire	.35	.17	.03
☐	21	Fred Clarke Walking Steal of Home	.35	.17	.03
☐	22	Christy Mathewson 373rd Win Discovered	.45	.22	.04
☐	23	Hitting Through the Unglaub Arc	.35	.17	.03
☐	24	Jim O'Rourke Catching at 52	.35	.17	.03
☐	25	Fired for Striking Out in Series	.35	.17	.03
☐	26	Eleven Run Inning on One Hit	.35	.17	.03
☐	27	58 Innings in 3 Days	.35	.17	.03
☐	28	Homer on Warm-Up Pitch	.35	.17	.03
☐	29	Giants Win 26 Straight But Finish Fourth	.35	.17	.03
☐	30	Player Who Stole First Base	.35	.17	.03
☐	31	Ernie Shore Perfect Game in Relief	.35	.17	.03
☐	32	Greatest Comeback	.35	.17	.03
☐	33	All-Time Flash-In-The-Pan	.35	.17	.03
☐	34	Pruett Fanned Ruth 19 out of 31	.65	.30	.06
☐	35	Fixed Batting Race Cobb/Lajoie	.65	.30	.06
☐	36	Wild-Pitch Rebound Play	.35	.17	.03
☐	37	17 Straight Scoring Innings	.35	.17	.03
☐	38	Wildest Opening Day	.35	.17	.03
☐	39	Baseball's Strike One	.35	.17	.03
☐	40	Opening Day No Hitter That Didn't Count	.35	.17	.03
☐	41	Jimmie Foxx Six Straight Walks in One Game	.45	.22	.04
☐	42	Entire Team Hit and Scored in Inning	.35	.17	.03

1973 Fleer Wildest Days

The Star Who Sat Out The World Series!

It's often the unhappy lot of a star player to miss the World Series due to an injury —but in 1927 a healthy star sat out the fall classic. Kiki Cuyler, a future Hall-of-Famer, had broken up the '25 Series with a bases-clearing double off Walter Johnson in the final game. While missing much of the '27 season with an injury, he still hit over .300. But he had quarreled with his new manager, Donie Bush, over being moved from third to second in the batting order—where Kiki didn't want to hit. He was fined once for not sliding. Both were stubborn, and Bush traded Cuyler before the next season. Despite Pittsburgh chants of "We want Cuyler!" he never appeared in the '27 Series.

No. 14 of 42 CARDS by R. G. Laughlin.
©1973 Fleer Corp., Phila., Pa. 19141

This Fleer set of 42 cards is titled "Baseball's Wildest Days and Plays" and features the artwork of sports artist R.G. Laughlin. The cards are numbered on the back. The backs are printed in dark red on white card stock. The cards measure approximately 2 1/2" by 4". This set was not licensed by Major League Baseball.

			NRMT	VG-E	GOOD
	COMPLETE SET (42)		12.00	6.00	1.20
	COMMON PLAYER (1-42)		.35	.17	.03
☐	1	Cubs and Phillies Score 49 Runs in Game	.35	.17	.03
☐	2	Frank Chance Five HBP's in One Day	.35	.17	.03
☐	3	Jim Thorpe Homered into 3 States	.65	.30	.06
☐	4	Eddie Gaedel Midget in Majors	.35	.17	.03
☐	5	Most Tied Game Ever	.35	.17	.03
☐	6	Seven Errors in	.35	.17	.03

1974 Fleer Baseball Firsts

This Fleer set of 42 cards is titled "Baseball Firsts" and features the artwork of sports artist R.G. Laughlin. The cards are numbered on the back. The backs are printed in black on gray card stock. The cards measure approximately 2 1/2" by 4". This set was not licensed by Major League Baseball.

			NRMT	VG-E	GOOD
	COMPLETE SET (42)		8.00	4.00	.80
	COMMON PLAYER (1-42)		.20	.10	.02
☐	1	Slide	.20	.10	.02
☐	2	Spring Training	.20	.10	.02
☐	3	Bunt	.20	.10	.02
☐	4	Catcher's Mask	.20	.10	.02

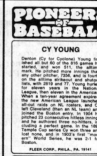

☐	5	Four Straight Homers	.60	.30	.06
		(Lou Gehrig)			
☐	6	Radio Broadcast	.20	.10	.02
☐	7	Numbered Uniforms	.20	.10	.02
☐	8	Shin Guards	.20	.10	.02
☐	9	Players Association	.20	.10	.02
☐	10	Knuckleball	.20	.10	.02
☐	11	Player With Glasses	.20	.10	.02
☐	12	Baseball Cards	.75	.35	.07
☐	13	Standardized Rules	.20	.10	.02
☐	14	Grand Slam	.20	.10	.02
☐	15	Player Fined	.20	.10	.02
☐	16	Presidential Opener	.20	.10	.02
☐	17	Player Transaction	.20	.10	.02
☐	18	All-Star Game	.20	.10	.02
☐	19	Scoreboard	.20	.10	.02
☐	20	Cork Center Ball	.20	.10	.02
☐	21	Scorekeeping	.20	.10	.02
☐	22	Domed Stadium	.20	.10	.02
☐	23	Batting Helmet	.20	.10	.02
☐	24	Fatality	.20	.10	.02
☐	25	Unassisted Triple Play	.20	.10	.02
☐	26	Home Run At Night	.20	.10	.02
☐	27	Black Major Leaguer	.30	.15	.03
☐	28	Pinch Hitter	.20	.10	.02
☐	29	Million-Dollar	.20	.10	.02
		World Series			
☐	30	Tarpaulin	.20	.10	.02
☐	31	Team Initials	.20	.10	.02
☐	32	Pennant Playoff	.20	.10	.02
☐	33	Glove	.20	.10	.02
☐	34	Curve Ball	.20	.10	.02
☐	35	Night Game	.20	.10	.02
☐	36	Admission Charge	.20	.10	.02
☐	37	Farm System	.20	.10	.02
☐	38	Telecast	.20	.10	.02
☐	39	Commissioner	.20	.10	.02
☐	40	.400 Hitter	.20	.10	.02
☐	41	World Series	.20	.10	.02
☐	42	Player Into Service	.20	.10	.02

1975 Fleer Pioneers

This 28-card set of brown and white sepia-toned photos of old timers is subtitled "Pioneers of Baseball. The graphics artwork was done by R.G. Laughlin. The cards measure 2 1/2" by 4". The card backs are a narrative about the particular player. The cards are numbered on the back at the bottom.

	NRMT	VG-E	GOOD
COMPLETE SET (28)	10.00	5.00	1.00
COMMON PLAYER (1-28)	.35	.17	.03

☐	1	Cap Anson	.75	.35	.07
☐	2	Harry Wright	.45	.22	.04
☐	3	Buck Ewing	.45	.22	.04
☐	4	A.G. Spalding	.45	.22	.04
☐	5	Old Hoss Radbourn	.45	.22	.04
☐	6	Dan Brouthers	.45	.22	.04
☐	7	Roger Bresnahan	.45	.22	.04
☐	8	Mike Kelly	.45	.22	.04
☐	9	Ned Hanlon	.35	.17	.03
☐	10	Ed Delahanty	.45	.22	.04
☐	11	Pud Galvin	.45	.22	.04

☐	12	Amos Rusie	.45	.22	.04
☐	13	Tommy McCarthy	.45	.22	.04
☐	14	Ty Cobb	1.00	.50	.10
☐	15	John McGraw	.45	.22	.04
☐	16	Home Run Baker	.45	.22	.04
☐	17	Johnny Evers	.45	.22	.04
☐	18	Nap Lajoie	.45	.22	.04
☐	19	Cy Young	.60	.30	.06
☐	20	Eddie Collins	.45	.22	.04
☐	21	John Glasscock	.35	.17	.03
☐	22	Hal Chase	.35	.17	.03
☐	23	Mordecai Brown	.45	.22	.04
☐	24	Jake Daubert	.35	.17	.03
☐	25	Mike Donlin	.35	.17	.03
☐	26	John Clarkson	.45	.22	.04
☐	27	Buck Herzog	.35	.17	.03
☐	28	Art Nehf	.35	.17	.03

1981 Fleer

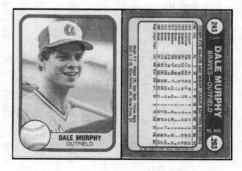

The cards in this 660-card set measure 2 1/2" by 3 1/2". This issue of cards marks Fleer's first entry into the current player baseball card market since 1963. Players from the same team are conveniently grouped together by number in the set. The teams are ordered (by 1980 standings) as follows: Philadelphia (1-27), Kansas City (28-50), Houston (51-78), New York Yankees (79-109), Los Angeles (110-141), Montreal (142-168), Baltimore (169-195), Cincinnati (196-220), Boston (221-241), Atlanta (242-267), California (268-290), Chicago Cubs (291-315), New York Mets (316-338), Chicago White Sox (339-350 and 352-359), Pittsburgh (360-386), Cleveland (387-408), Toronto (409-431), San Francisco (432-458), Detroit (459-483), San Diego (484-506), Milwaukee (507-527), St. Louis (528-550), Minnesota (551-571), Oakland (351 and 572-594), Seattle (595-616), and Texas (617-637). Cards 638-660 feature specials and checklists. The cards of pitchers in this set erroneously show a heading (on the card backs) of "Batting Record" over their printings: the two following the primary run were designed to correct numerous errors. The variations caused by these multiple printings are noted in the checklist below (P1, P2, or P3). The C. Nettles variation was corrected before the end of the first printing and thus is not included in the complete set consideration for a P1 (first printing) set.

		MINT	EXC	G-VG
	COMPLETE SET (P1)	33.00	16.00	3.00
	COMPLETE SET (P2)	27.00	13.50	2.70
	COMPLETE SET (P3)	30.00	15.00	3.00
	COMMON PLAYER (1-660)	.03	.01	.00
☐ 1	Pete Rose	2.00	.50	.10
☐ 2	Larry Bowa	.15	.07	.01
☐ 3	Manny Trillo	.03	.01	.00
☐ 4	Bob Boone	.20	.10	.02
☐ 5	Mike Schmidt	1.25	.60	.12
	See also 640A			
☐ 6A	Steve Carlton P1	.75	.35	.07
	Pitcher of Year			
	See also 660A			
	Back "1066 Cardinals"			
☐ 6B	Steve Carlton P2	.65	.30	.06
	Pitcher of Year			
	Back "1066 Cardinals"			
☐ 6C	Steve Carlton P3	2.00	1.00	.20
	"1966 Cardinals"			
☐ 7	Tug McGraw	.10	.05	.01
	See 657A			
☐ 8	Larry Christenson	.03	.01	.00
☐ 9	Bake McBride	.03	.01	.00
☐ 10	Greg Luzinski	.12	.06	.01
☐ 11	Ron Reed	.03	.01	.00
☐ 12	Dickie Noles	.03	.01	.00
☐ 13	Keith Moreland	.30	.15	.03
☐ 14	Bob Walk	.30	.15	.03
☐ 15	Lonnie Smith	.15	.07	.01
☐ 16	Dick Ruthven	.03	.01	.00
☐ 17	Sparky Lyle	.10	.05	.01
☐ 18	Greg Gross	.03	.01	.00
☐ 19	Garry Maddox	.06	.03	.00
☐ 20	Nino Espinosa	.03	.01	.00
☐ 21	George Vukovich	.03	.01	.00
☐ 22	John Vukovich	.03	.01	.00
☐ 23	Ramon Aviles	.03	.01	.00
☐ 24A	Ken Saucier P1	.06		
	Name on front "Ken"			
☐ 24B	Ken Saucier P2	.06	.03	.00
	Name on front "Ken"			
☐ 24C	Kevin Saucier P3	.35	.17	.03
	Name on front "Kevin"			
☐ 25	Randy Lerch	.03	.01	.00
☐ 26	Del Unser	.03	.01	.00
☐ 27	Tim McCarver	.15	.07	.01
☐ 28	George Brett	1.00	.50	.10
	See also 655A			
☐ 29	Willie Wilson	.15	.07	.01
	See also 653A			
☐ 30	Paul Splittorff	.03	.01	.00
☐ 31	Dan Quisenberry	.15	.07	.01
☐ 32A	Amos Otis P1	.10	.05	.01
	Batting Pose			
	"Outfield"			
	(32 on back)			
☐ 32B	Amos Otis P2	.10	.05	.01
	"Series Starter"			
	(483 on back)			
☐ 33	Steve Busby	.03	.01	.00
☐ 34	U.L. Washington	.03	.01	.00
☐ 35	Dave Chalk	.03	.01	.00
☐ 36	Darrell Porter	.03	.01	.00
☐ 37	Marty Pattin	.03	.01	.00
☐ 38	Larry Gura	.06	.03	.00
☐ 39	Renie Martin	.03	.01	.00
☐ 40	Rich Gale	.03	.01	.00
☐ 41A	Hal McRae P1	.50	.25	.05
	"Royals" on front			
	in black letters			
☐ 41B	Hal McRae P2	.10	.05	.01
	"Royals" on front			
	in blue letters			
☐ 42	Dennis Leonard	.06	.03	.00
☐ 43	Willie Aikens	.06	.03	.00
☐ 44	Frank White	.10	.05	.01
☐ 45	Clint Hurdle	.03	.01	.00
☐ 46	John Wathan	.10	.05	.01
☐ 47	Pete LaCock	.03	.01	.00
☐ 48	Rance Mulliniks	.03	.01	.00
☐ 49	Jeff Twitty	.03	.01	.00
☐ 50	Jamie Quirk	.03	.01	.00
☐ 51	Art Howe	.10	.05	.01
☐ 52	Ken Forsch	.03	.01	.00
☐ 53	Vern Ruhle	.03	.01	.00
☐ 54	Joe Niekro	.10	.05	.01
☐ 55	Frank LaCorte	.03	.01	.00
☐ 56	J.R. Richard	.10	.05	.01
☐ 57	Nolan Ryan	1.75	.85	.17
☐ 58	Enos Cabell	.03	.01	.00
☐ 59	Cesar Cedeno	.10	.05	.01
☐ 60	Jose Cruz	.10	.05	.01
☐ 61	Bill Virdon MG	.06	.03	.01
☐ 62	Terry Puhl	.06	.03	.00
☐ 63	Joaquin Andujar	.10	.05	.01
☐ 64	Alan Ashby	.03	.01	.00
☐ 65	Joe Sambito	.03	.01	.00
☐ 66	Denny Walling	.03	.01	.00
☐ 67	Jeff Leonard	.15	.07	.01
☐ 68	Luis Pujols	.03	.01	.00
☐ 69	Bruce Bochy	.03	.01	.00
☐ 70	Rafael Landestoy	.03	.01	.00
☐ 71	Dave Smith	.35	.17	.03
☐ 72	Danny Heep	.20	.10	.02
☐ 73	Julio Gonzalez	.03	.01	.00
☐ 74	Craig Reynolds	.03	.01	.00
☐ 75	Gary Woods	.03	.01	.00
☐ 76	Dave Bergman	.03	.01	.00
☐ 77	Randy Niemann	.03	.01	.00
☐ 78	Joe Morgan	.40	.20	.04
☐ 79	Reggie Jackson	1.00	.50	.10
	See 650A			
☐ 80	Bucky Dent	.12	.06	.01
☐ 81	Tommy John	.20	.10	.02
☐ 82	Luis Tiant	.10	.05	.01
☐ 83	Rick Cerone	.06	.03	.00
☐ 84	Dick Howser MG	.10	.05	.01
☐ 85	Lou Piniella	.12	.06	.01
☐ 86	Ron Davis	.03	.01	.00
☐ 87A	Craig Nettles P1	11.00	5.50	1.10
	ERR (Name on back			
	misspelled "Craig")			
☐ 87B	Graig Nettles P2 COR	.30	.15	.03
	"Graig"			
☐ 88	Ron Guidry	.20	.10	.02
☐ 89	Rich Gossage	.20	.10	.02
☐ 90	Rudy May	.03	.01	.00
☐ 91	Gaylord Perry	.30	.15	.03
☐ 92	Eric Soderholm	.03	.01	.00
☐ 93	Bob Watson	.06	.03	.00
☐ 94	Bobby Murcer	.10	.05	.01
☐ 95	Bobby Brown	.03	.01	.00
☐ 96	Jim Spencer	.03	.01	.00
☐ 97	Tom Underwood	.03	.01	.00
☐ 98	Oscar Gamble	.03	.01	.00
☐ 99	Johnny Oates	.03	.01	.00
☐ 100	Fred Stanley	.03	.01	.00
☐ 101	Ruppert Jones	.03	.01	.00
☐ 102	Dennis Werth	.03	.01	.00
☐ 103	Joe Lefebvre	.06	.03	.00
☐ 104	Brian Doyle	.03	.01	.00
☐ 105	Aurelio Rodriguez	.03	.01	.00
☐ 106	Doug Bird	.03	.01	.00
☐ 107	Mike Griffin	.03	.01	.00
☐ 108	Tim Lollar	.03	.01	.00
☐ 109	Willie Randolph	.10	.05	.01
☐ 110	Steve Garvey	.65	.30	.06
☐ 111	Reggie Smith	.10	.05	.01
☐ 112	Don Sutton	.30	.15	.03
☐ 113	Burt Hooton	.03	.01	.00
☐ 114A	Dave Lopes P1	.50	.25	.05
	Small hand on back			
☐ 114B	Dave Lopes P2	.10	.05	.01
	No hand			
☐ 115	Dusty Baker	.06	.03	.00
☐ 116	Tom Lasorda MG	.10	.05	.01
☐ 117	Bill Russell	.06	.03	.00
☐ 118	Jerry Reuss	.06	.03	.00
☐ 119	Terry Forster	.06	.03	.00
☐ 120A	Bob Welch P1	.20	.10	.02
	Name on back			
	is "Bob"			
☐ 120B	Bob Welch P2	.20	.10	.02
	Name on back			
	is "Robert"			
☐ 121	Don Stanhouse	.03	.01	.00
☐ 122	Rick Monday	.03	.01	.00
☐ 123	Derrel Thomas	.03	.01	.00
☐ 124	Joe Ferguson	.03	.01	.00
☐ 125	Rick Sutcliffe	.30	.15	.03
☐ 126A	Ron Cey P1	.50	.25	.05
	Small hand on back			
☐ 126B	Ron Cey P2	.10	.05	.01
	No hand			
☐ 127	Dave Goltz	.03	.01	.00
☐ 128	Jay Johnstone	.06	.03	.00

☐ 129	Steve Yeager	.03	.01	.00
☐ 130	Gary Weiss	.03	.01	.00
☐ 131	Mike Scioscia	.60	.30	.06
☐ 132	Vic Davalillo	.03	.01	.00
☐ 133	Doug Rau	.03	.01	.00
☐ 134	Pepe Frias	.03	.01	.00
☐ 135	Mickey Hatcher	.10	.05	.01
☐ 136	Steve Howe	.10	.05	.01
☐ 137	Robert Castillo	.03	.01	.00
☐ 138	Gary Thomasson	.03	.01	.00
☐ 139	Rudy Law	.03	.01	.00
☐ 140	Fernand Valenzuela	4.50	2.25	.45
	(sic, Fernando)			
☐ 141	Manny Mota	.06	.03	.00
☐ 142	Gary Carter	.50	.25	.05
☐ 143	Steve Rogers	.06	.03	.00
☐ 144	Warren Cromartie	.03	.01	.00
☐ 145	Andre Dawson	.40	.20	.04
☐ 146	Larry Parrish	.06	.03	.00
☐ 147	Rowland Office	.03	.01	.00
☐ 148	Ellis Valentine	.03	.01	.00
☐ 149	Dick Williams MG	.03	.01	.00
☐ 150	Bill Gullickson	.25	.12	.02
☐ 151	Elias Sosa	.03	.01	.00
☐ 152	John Tamargo	.03	.01	.00
☐ 153	Chris Speier	.03	.01	.00
☐ 154	Ron LeFlore	.06	.03	.00
☐ 155	Rodney Scott	.03	.01	.00
☐ 156	Stan Bahnsen	.03	.01	.00
☐ 157	Bill Lee	.06	.03	.00
☐ 158	Fred Norman	.03	.01	.00
☐ 159	Woodie Fryman	.03	.01	.00
☐ 160	David Palmer	.06	.03	.00
☐ 161	Jerry White	.03	.01	.00
☐ 162	Roberto Ramos	.03	.01	.00
☐ 163	John D'Acquisto	.03	.01	.00
☐ 164	Tommy Hutton	.03	.01	.00
☐ 165	Charlie Lea	.20	.10	.02
☐ 166	Scott Sanderson	.06	.03	.00
☐ 167	Ken Macha	.03	.01	.00
☐ 168	Tony Bernazard	.06	.03	.00
☐ 169	Jim Palmer	.60	.30	.06
☐ 170	Steve Stone	.06	.03	.00
☐ 171	Mike Flanagan	.10	.05	.01
☐ 172	Al Bumbry	.03	.01	.00
☐ 173	Doug DeCinces	.06	.03	.00
☐ 174	Scott McGregor	.06	.03	.00
☐ 175	Mark Belanger	.06	.03	.00
☐ 176	Tim Stoddard	.03	.01	.00
☐ 177A	Rick Dempsey P1	.50	.25	.05
	Small hand on front			
☐ 177B	Rick Dempsey P2	.10	.05	.01
	No hand			
☐ 178	Earl Weaver MG	.06	.03	.00
☐ 179	Tippy Martinez	.03	.01	.00
☐ 180	Dennis Martinez	.10	.05	.01
☐ 181	Sammy Stewart	.03	.01	.00
☐ 182	Rich Dauer	.03	.01	.00
☐ 183	Lee May	.06	.03	.00
☐ 184	Eddie Murray	.75	.35	.07
☐ 185	Benny Ayala	.03	.01	.00
☐ 186	John Lowenstein	.03	.01	.00
☐ 187	Gary Roenicke	.03	.01	.00
☐ 188	Ken Singleton	.10	.05	.01
☐ 189	Dan Graham	.03	.01	.00
☐ 190	Terry Crowley	.03	.01	.00
☐ 191	Kiko Garcia	.03	.01	.00
☐ 192	Dave Ford	.03	.01	.00
☐ 193	Mark Corey	.03	.01	.00
☐ 194	Lenn Sakata	.03	.01	.00
☐ 195	Doug DeCinces	.06	.03	.00
☐ 196	Johnny Bench	.75	.35	.07
☐ 197	Dave Concepcion	.15	.07	.01
☐ 198	Ray Knight	.10	.05	.01
☐ 199	Ken Griffey	.10	.05	.01
☐ 200	Tom Seaver	.60	.30	.06
☐ 201	Dave Collins	.03	.01	.00
☐ 202A	George Foster P1	.15	.07	.01
	Slugger			
	Number on back 216			
☐ 202B	George Foster P2	.15	.07	.01
	Slugger			
	Number on back 202			
☐ 203	Junior Kennedy	.03	.01	.00
☐ 204	Frank Pastore	.03	.01	.00
☐ 205	Dan Driessen	.03	.01	.00
☐ 206	Hector Cruz	.03	.01	.00
☐ 207	Paul Moskau	.03	.01	.00
☐ 208	Charlie Leibrandt	.30	.15	.03
☐ 209	Harry Spilman	.03	.01	.00
☐ 210	Joe Price	.06	.03	.00
☐ 211	Tom Hume	.03	.01	.00
☐ 212	Joe Nolan	.03	.01	.00
☐ 213	Doug Bair	.03	.01	.00
☐ 214	Mario Soto	.10	.05	.01
☐ 215A	Bill Bonham P1	.50	.25	.05
	Small hand on back			
☐ 215B	Bill Bonham P2	.06	.03	.00
	No hand			
☐ 216	George Foster	.15	.07	.01
	See #202			
☐ 217	Paul Householder	.03	.01	.00
☐ 218	Ron Oester	.06	.03	.00
☐ 219	Sam Mejias	.03	.01	.00
☐ 220	Sheldon Burnside	.03	.01	.00
☐ 221	Carl Yastrzemski	1.00	.50	.10
☐ 222	Jim Rice	.30	.15	.03
☐ 223	Fred Lynn	.20	.10	.02
☐ 224	Carlton Fisk	.40	.20	.04
☐ 225	Rick Burleson	.06	.03	.00
☐ 226	Dennis Eckersley	.25	.12	.02
☐ 227	Butch Hobson	.03	.01	.00
☐ 228	Tom Burgmeier	.03	.01	.00
☐ 229	Garry Hancock	.03	.01	.00
☐ 230	Don Zimmer MG	.06	.03	.00
☐ 231	Steve Renko	.03	.01	.00
☐ 232	Dwight Evans	.25	.12	.02
☐ 233	Mike Torrez	.06	.03	.00
☐ 234	Bob Stanley	.03	.01	.00
☐ 235	Jim Dwyer	.03	.01	.00
☐ 236	Dave Stapleton	.03	.01	.00
☐ 237	Glen Hoffman	.03	.01	.00
☐ 238	Jerry Remy	.03	.01	.00
☐ 239	Dick Drago	.03	.01	.00
☐ 240	Bill Campbell	.03	.01	.00
☐ 241	Tony Perez	.20	.10	.02
☐ 242	Phil Niekro	.30	.15	.03
☐ 243	Dale Murphy	1.25	.60	.12
☐ 244	Bob Horner	.15	.07	.01
☐ 245	Jeff Burroughs	.03	.01	.00
☐ 246	Rick Camp	.03	.01	.00
☐ 247	Bobby Cox MG	.03	.01	.00
☐ 248	Bruce Benedict	.03	.01	.00
☐ 249	Gene Garber	.03	.01	.00
☐ 250	Jerry Royster	.03	.01	.00
☐ 251A	Gary Matthews P1	.50	.25	.05
	Small hand on back			
☐ 251B	Gary Matthews P2	.10	.05	.01
	No hand			
☐ 252	Chris Chambliss	.10	.05	.01
☐ 253	Luis Gomez	.03	.01	.00
☐ 254	Bill Nahorodny	.03	.01	.00
☐ 255	Doyle Alexander	.06	.03	.00
☐ 256	Brian Asselstine	.03	.01	.00
☐ 257	Biff Pocoroba	.03	.01	.00
☐ 258	Mike Lum	.03	.01	.00
☐ 259	Charlie Spikes	.03	.01	.00
☐ 260	Glenn Hubbard	.03	.01	.00
☐ 261	Tommy Boggs	.03	.01	.00
☐ 262	Al Hrabosky	.06	.03	.00
☐ 263	Rick Matula	.03	.01	.00
☐ 264	Preston Hanna	.03	.01	.00
☐ 265	Larry Bradford	.03	.01	.00
☐ 266	Rafael Ramirez	.25	.12	.02
☐ 267	Larry McWilliams	.03	.01	.00
☐ 268	Rod Carew	.65	.30	.06
☐ 269	Bobby Grich	.10	.05	.01
☐ 270	Carney Lansford	.25	.10	.02
☐ 271	Don Baylor	.15	.07	.01
☐ 272	Joe Rudi	.06	.03	.00
☐ 273	Dan Ford	.03	.01	.00
☐ 274	Jim Fregosi	.06	.03	.00
☐ 275	Dave Frost	.03	.01	.00
☐ 276	Frank Tanana	.10	.05	.01
☐ 277	Dickie Thon	.10	.05	.01
☐ 278	Jason Thompson	.03	.01	.00
☐ 279	Rick Miller	.03	.01	.00
☐ 280	Bert Campaneris	.06	.03	.00
☐ 281	Tom Donohue	.03	.01	.00
☐ 282	Brian Downing	.06	.03	.00
☐ 283	Fred Patek	.03	.01	.00
☐ 284	Bruce Kison	.03	.01	.00
☐ 285	Dave LaRoche	.03	.01	.00
☐ 286	Don Aase	.03	.01	.00
☐ 287	Jim Barr	.03	.01	.00
☐ 288	Alfredo Martinez	.03	.01	.00
☐ 289	Larry Harlow	.03	.01	.00
☐ 290	Andy Hassler	.03	.01	.00
☐ 291	Dave Kingman	.15	.07	.01
☐ 292	Bill Buckner	.12	.06	.01
☐ 293	Rick Reuschel	.20	.10	.02
☐ 294	Bruce Sutter	.20	.10	.02
☐ 295	Jerry Martin	.03	.01	.00
☐ 296	Scot Thompson	.03	.01	.00
☐ 297	Ivan DeJesus	.03	.01	.00
☐ 298	Steve Dillard	.03	.01	.00
☐ 299	Dick Tidrow	.03	.01	.00
☐ 300	Randy Martz	.03	.01	.00
☐ 301	Lenny Randle	.03	.01	.00
☐ 302	Lynn McGlothen	.03	.01	.00

☐ 303	Cliff Johnson	.03	.01	.00	☐ 386	John Milner	.03	.01	.00
☐ 304	Tim Blackwell	.03	.01	.00	☐ 387	Mike Hargrove	.06	.03	.00
☐ 305	Dennis Lamp	.03	.01	.00	☐ 388	Jorge Orta	.03	.01	.00
☐ 306	Bill Caudill	.03	.01	.00	☐ 389	Toby Harrah	.06	.03	.00
☐ 307	Carlos Lezcano	.03	.01	.00	☐ 390	Tom Veryzer	.03	.01	.00
☐ 308	Jim Tracy	.03	.01	.00	☐ 391	Miguel Dilone	.03	.01	.00
☐ 309	Doug Capilla	.03	.01	.00	☐ 392	Dan Spillner	.03	.01	.00
☐ 310	Willie Hernandez	.15	.07	.01	☐ 393	Jack Brohamer	.03	.01	.00
☐ 311	Mike Vail	.03	.01	.00	☐ 394	Wayne Garland	.03	.01	.00
☐ 312	Mike Krukow	.06	.03	.00	☐ 395	Sid Monge	.03	.01	.00
☐ 313	Barry Foote	.03	.01	.00	☐ 396	Rick Waits	.03	.01	.00
☐ 314	Larry Biittner	.03	.01	.00	☐ 397	Joe Charboneau	.10	.05	.01
☐ 315	Mike Tyson	.03	.01	.00	☐ 398	Gary Alexander	.03	.01	.00
☐ 316	Lee Mazzilli	.03	.01	.00	☐ 399	Jerry Dybzinski	.03	.01	.00
☐ 317	John Stearns	.03	.01	.00	☐ 400	Mike Stanton	.03	.01	.00
☐ 318	Alex Trevino	.03	.01	.00	☐ 401	Mike Paxton	.03	.01	.00
☐ 319	Craig Swan	.03	.01	.00	☐ 402	Gary Gray	.03	.01	.00
☐ 320	Frank Taveras	.03	.01	.00	☐ 403	Rick Manning	.03	.01	.00
☐ 321	Steve Henderson	.03	.01	.00	☐ 404	Bo Diaz	.06	.03	.00
☐ 322	Neil Allen	.06	.03	.00	☐ 405	Ron Hassey	.03	.01	.00
☐ 323	Mark Bomback	.03	.01	.00	☐ 406	Ross Grimsley	.03	.01	.00
☐ 324	Mike Jorgensen	.03	.01	.00	☐ 407	Victor Cruz	.03	.01	.00
☐ 325	Joe Torre MG	.10	.05	.01	☐ 408	Len Barker	.03	.01	.00
☐ 326	Elliott Maddox	.03	.01	.00	☐ 409	Bob Bailor	.03	.01	.00
☐ 327	Pete Falcone	.03	.01	.00	☐ 410	Otto Velez	.03	.01	.00
☐ 328	Ray Burris	.03	.01	.00	☐ 411	Ernie Whitt	.10	.05	.01
☐ 329	Claudell Washington	.06	.03	.00	☐ 412	Jim Clancy	.06	.03	.00
☐ 330	Doug Flynn	.03	.01	.00	☐ 413	Barry Bonnell	.03	.01	.00
☐ 331	Joel Youngblood	.03	.01	.00	☐ 414	Dave Stieb	.35	.17	.03
☐ 332	Bill Almon	.03	.01	.00	☐ 415	Damaso Garcia	.10	.05	.01
☐ 333	Tom Hausman	.03	.01	.00	☐ 416	John Mayberry	.06	.03	.00
☐ 334	Pat Zachry	.03	.01	.00	☐ 417	Roy Howell	.03	.01	.00
☐ 335	Jeff Reardon	.75	.35	.07	☐ 418	Danny Ainge	.45	.22	.04
☐ 336	Wally Backman	.35	.17	.03	☐ 419A	Jesse Jefferson P1	.06	.03	.00
☐ 337	Dan Norman	.03	.01	.00		Back says Pirates			
☐ 338	Jerry Morales	.03	.01	.00	☐ 419B	Jesse Jefferson P2	.06	.03	.00
☐ 339	Ed Farmer	.03	.01	.00		Back says Pirates			
☐ 340	Bob Molinaro	.03	.01	.00	☐ 419C	Jesse Jefferson P3	.35	.17	.03
☐ 341	Todd Cruz	.03	.01	.00		Back says Blue Jays			
☐ 342A	Britt Burns P1	.40	.20	.04	☐ 420	Joey McLaughlin	.03	.01	.00
	Small hand on front				☐ 421	Lloyd Moseby	.75	.35	.07
☐ 342B	Britt Burns P2	.20	.10	.02	☐ 422	Alvis Woods	.03	.01	.00
	No hand				☐ 423	Garth Iorg	.03	.01	.00
☐ 343	Kevin Bell	.03	.01	.00	☐ 424	Doug Ault	.03	.01	.00
☐ 344	Tony LaRussa MG	.06	.03	.00	☐ 425	Ken Schrom	.06	.03	.00
☐ 345	Steve Trout	.06	.03	.00	☐ 426	Mike Willis	.03	.01	.00
☐ 346	Harold Baines	2.25	1.10	.22	☐ 427	Steve Braun	.03	.01	.00
☐ 347	Richard Wortham	.03	.01	.00	☐ 428	Bob Davis	.03	.01	.00
☐ 348	Wayne Nordhagen	.03	.01	.00	☐ 429	Jerry Garvin	.03	.01	.00
☐ 349	Mike Squires	.03	.01	.00	☐ 430	Alfredo Griffin	.10	.05	.01
☐ 350	Lamar Johnson	.03	.01	.00	☐ 431	Bob Mattick MG	.03	.01	.00
☐ 351	Rickey Henderson	3.00	1.50	.30	☐ 432	Vida Blue	.10	.05	.01
☐ 352	Francisco Barrios	.03	.01	.00	☐ 433	Jack Clark	.30	.15	.03
☐ 353	Thad Bosley	.03	.01	.00	☐ 434	Willie McCovey	.35	.17	.03
☐ 354	Chet Lemon	.06	.03	.00	☐ 435	Mike Ivie	.03	.01	.00
☐ 355	Bruce Kimm	.03	.01	.00	☐ 436A	Darrel Evans P1 ERR	.40	.20	.04
☐ 356	Richard Dotson	.35	.17	.03		Name on front "Darrel"			
☐ 357	Jim Morrison	.03	.01	.00	☐ 436B	Darrell Evans P2	.15	.07	.01
☐ 358	Mike Proly	.03	.01	.00		Name on front			
☐ 359	Greg Pryor	.03	.01	.00		"Darrell"			
☐ 360	Dave Parker	.25	.12	.02	☐ 437	Terry Whitfield	.03	.01	.00
☐ 361	Omar Moreno	.03	.01	.00	☐ 438	Rennie Stennett	.03	.01	.00
☐ 362A	Kent Tekulve P1	.15	.07	.01	☐ 439	John Montefusco	.06	.03	.00
	Back "1071 Waterbury" and "1078 Pirates"				☐ 440	Jim Wohlford	.03	.01	.00
☐ 362B	Kent Tekulve P2	.10	.05	.01	☐ 441	Bill North	.03	.01	.00
	"1971 Waterbury" and "1978 Pirates"				☐ 442	Milt May	.03	.01	.00
					☐ 443	Max Venable	.03	.01	.00
☐ 363	Willie Stargell	.40	.20	.04	☐ 444	Ed Whitson	.06	.03	.00
☐ 364	Phil Garner	.03	.01	.00	☐ 445	Al Holland	.06	.03	.00
☐ 365	Ed Ott	.03	.01	.00	☐ 446	Randy Moffitt	.03	.01	.00
☐ 366	Don Robinson	.06	.03	.00	☐ 447	Bob Knepper	.06	.03	.00
☐ 367	Chuck Tanner MG	.06	.03	.00	☐ 448	Gary Lavelle	.03	.01	.00
☐ 368	Jim Rooker	.03	.01	.00	☐ 449	Greg Minton	.03	.01	.00
☐ 369	Dale Berra	.03	.01	.00	☐ 450	Johnnie LeMaster	.03	.01	.00
☐ 370	Jim Bibby	.03	.01	.00	☐ 451	Larry Herndon	.03	.01	.00
☐ 371	Steve Nicosia	.03	.01	.00	☐ 452	Rich Murray	.03	.01	.00
☐ 372	Mike Easler	.06	.03	.00	☐ 453	Joe Pettini	.03	.01	.00
☐ 373	Bill Robinson	.06	.03	.00	☐ 454	Allen Ripley	.03	.01	.00
☐ 374	Lee Lacy	.03	.01	.00	☐ 455	Dennis Littlejohn	.03	.01	.00
☐ 375	John Candelaria	.10	.05	.01	☐ 456	Tom Griffin	.03	.01	.00
☐ 376	Manny Sanguillen	.06	.03	.00	☐ 457	Alan Hargesheimer	.03	.01	.00
☐ 377	Rick Rhoden	.06	.03	.00	☐ 458	Joe Strain	.03	.01	.00
☐ 378	Grant Jackson	.03	.01	.00	☐ 459	Steve Kemp	.06	.03	.00
☐ 379	Tim Foli	.03	.01	.00	☐ 460	Sparky Anderson MG	.10	.05	.01
☐ 380	Rod Scurry	.03	.01	.00	☐ 461	Alan Trammell	.45	.22	.04
☐ 381	Bill Madlock	.12	.06	.01	☐ 462	Mark Fidrych	.10	.05	.01
☐ 382A	Kurt Bevacqua P1 ERR	.20	.10	.02	☐ 463	Lou Whitaker	.30	.15	.03
	(P on cap backwards)				☐ 464	Dave Rozema	.03	.01	.00
☐ 382B	Kurt Bevacqua P2 COR	.06	.03	.00	☐ 465	Milt Wilcox	.03	.01	.00
					☐ 466	Champ Summers	.03	.01	.00
					☐ 467	Lance Parrish	.25	.12	.02
☐ 383	Bert Blyleven	.20	.10	.02	☐ 468	Dan Petry	.10	.05	.01
☐ 384	Eddie Solomon	.03	.01	.00	☐ 469	Pat Underwood	.03	.01	.00
☐ 385	Enrique Romo	.03	.01	.00	☐ 470	Rick Peters	.03	.01	.00
					☐ 471	Al Cowens	.03	.01	.00

□ 472	John Wockenfuss	.03	.01	.00
□ 473	Tom Brookens	.03	.01	.00
□ 474	Richie Hebner	.03	.01	.00
□ 475	Jack Morris	.25	.12	.02
□ 476	Jim Lentine	.03	.01	.00
□ 477	Bruce Robbins	.03	.01	.00
□ 478	Mark Wagner	.03	.01	.00
□ 479	Tim Corcoran	.03	.01	.00
□ 480A	Stan Papi P1	.15	.07	.01
	Front as Pitcher			
□ 480B	Stan Papi P2	.10	.05	.01
	Front as Shortstop			
□ 481	Kirk Gibson	3.75	1.85	.37
□ 482	Dan Schatzeder	.03	.01	.00
□ 483A	Amos Otis P1	.10	.05	.01
	See card 32			
□ 483B	Amos Otis P2	.10	.05	.01
	See card 32			
□ 484	Dave Winfield	.50	.25	.05
□ 485	Rollie Fingers	.35	.17	.03
□ 486	Gene Richards	.03	.01	.00
□ 487	Randy Jones	.03	.01	.00
□ 488	Ozzie Smith	.50	.25	.05
□ 489	Gene Tenace	.03	.01	.00
□ 490	Bill Fahey	.03	.01	.00
□ 491	John Curtis	.03	.01	.00
□ 492	Dave Cash	.03	.01	.00
□ 493A	Tim Flannery P1	.15	.07	.01
	Batting right			
□ 493B	Tim Flannery P2	.06	.03	.00
	Batting left			
□ 494	Jerry Mumphrey	.03	.01	.00
□ 495	Bob Shirley	.03	.01	.00
□ 496	Steve Mura	.03	.01	.00
□ 497	Eric Rasmussen	.03	.01	.00
□ 498	Broderick Perkins	.03	.01	.00
□ 499	Barry Evans	.03	.01	.00
□ 500	Chuck Baker	.03	.01	.00
□ 501	Luis Salazar	.15	.07	.01
□ 502	Gary Lucas	.06	.03	.00
□ 503	Mike Armstrong	.06	.03	.00
□ 504	Jerry Turner	.03	.01	.00
□ 505	Dennis Kinney	.03	.01	.00
□ 506	Willie Montanez	.03	.01	.00
□ 507	Gorman Thomas	.10	.05	.01
□ 508	Ben Oglivie	.06	.03	.00
□ 509	Larry Hisle	.06	.03	.00
□ 510	Sal Bando	.06	.03	.00
□ 511	Robin Yount	1.00	.50	.10
□ 512	Mike Caldwell	.03	.01	.00
□ 513	Sixto Lezcano	.03	.01	.00
□ 514A	Bill Travers P1 ERR	.20	.10	.02
	"Jerry Augustine"			
	with Augustine back			
□ 514B	Bill Travers P2 COR	.10	.05	.01
□ 515	Paul Molitor	.35	.17	.03
□ 516	Moose Haas	.03	.01	.00
□ 517	Bill Castro	.03	.01	.00
□ 518	Jim Slaton	.03	.01	.00
□ 519	Lary Sorensen	.03	.01	.00
□ 520	Bob McClure	.03	.01	.00
□ 521	Charlie Moore	.03	.01	.00
□ 522	Jim Gantner	.06	.03	.00
□ 523	Reggie Cleveland	.03	.01	.00
□ 524	Don Money	.03	.01	.00
□ 525	Bill Travers	.03	.01	.00
□ 526	Buck Martinez	.03	.01	.00
□ 527	Dick Davis	.03	.01	.00
□ 528	Ted Simmons	.15	.07	.01
□ 529	Garry Templeton	.10	.05	.01
□ 530	Ken Reitz	.03	.01	.00
□ 531	Tony Scott	.03	.01	.00
□ 532	Ken Oberkfell	.03	.01	.00
□ 533	Bob Sykes	.03	.01	.00
□ 534	Keith Smith	.03	.01	.00
□ 535	John Littlefield	.03	.01	.00
□ 536	Jim Kaat	.20	.10	.02
□ 537	Bob Forsch	.03	.01	.00
□ 538	Mike Phillips	.03	.01	.00
□ 539	Terry Landrum	.06	.03	.00
□ 540	Leon Durham	.30	.15	.03
□ 541	Terry Kennedy	.06	.03	.00
□ 542	George Hendrick	.06	.03	.00
□ 543	Dane Iorg	.03	.01	.00
□ 544	Mark Littell	.03	.01	.00
□ 545	Keith Hernandez	.35	.17	.03
□ 546	Silvio Martinez	.03	.01	.00
□ 547A	Don Hood P1 ERR	.20	.10	.02
	"Pete Vuckovich"			
	with Vuckovich back			
□ 547B	Don Hood P2 COR	.10	.05	.01
□ 548	Bobby Bonds	.12	.06	.01
□ 549	Mike Ramsey	.03	.01	.00
□ 550	Tom Herr	.15	.07	.01
□ 551	Roy Smalley	.03	.01	.00
□ 552	Jerry Koosman	.10	.05	.01
□ 553	Ken Landreaux	.03	.01	.00
□ 554	John Castino	.03	.01	.00
□ 555	Doug Corbett	.06	.03	.00
□ 556	Bombo Rivera	.03	.01	.00
□ 557	Ron Jackson	.03	.01	.00
□ 558	Butch Wynegar	.03	.01	.00
□ 559	Hosken Powell	.03	.01	.00
□ 560	Pete Redfern	.03	.01	.00
□ 561	Roger Erickson	.03	.01	.00
□ 562	Glenn Adams	.03	.01	.00
□ 563	Rick Sofield	.03	.01	.00
□ 564	Geoff Zahn	.03	.01	.00
□ 565	Pete Mackanin	.03	.01	.00
□ 566	Mike Cubbage	.03	.01	.00
□ 567	Darrell Jackson	.03	.01	.00
□ 568	Dave Edwards	.03	.01	.00
□ 569	Rob Wilfong	.03	.01	.00
□ 570	Sal Butera	.03	.01	.00
□ 571	Jose Morales	.03	.01	.00
□ 572	Rick Langford	.03	.01	.00
□ 573	Mike Norris	.03	.01	.00
□ 574	Rickey Henderson	3.00	1.50	.30
□ 575	Tony Armas	.10	.05	.01
□ 576	Dave Revering	.03	.01	.00
□ 577	Jeff Newman	.03	.01	.00
□ 578	Bob Lacey	.03	.01	.00
□ 579	Brian Kingman	.03	.01	.00
□ 580	Mitchell Page	.03	.01	.00
□ 581	Billy Martin MG	.20	.10	.02
□ 582	Rob Picciolo	.03	.01	.00
□ 583	Mike Heath	.03	.01	.00
□ 584	Mickey Klutts	.03	.01	.00
□ 585	Orlando Gonzalez	.03	.01	.00
□ 586	Mike Davis	.25	.12	.02
□ 587	Wayne Gross	.03	.01	.00
□ 588	Matt Keough	.03	.01	.00
□ 589	Steve McCatty	.03	.01	.00
□ 590	Dwayne Murphy	.03	.01	.00
□ 591	Mario Guerrero	.03	.01	.00
□ 592	Dave McKay	.03	.01	.00
□ 593	Jim Essian	.03	.01	.00
□ 594	Dave Heaverlo	.03	.01	.00
□ 595	Maury Wills MG	.10	.05	.01
□ 596	Juan Beniquez	.03	.01	.00
□ 597	Rodney Craig	.03	.01	.00
□ 598	Jim Anderson	.03	.01	.00
□ 599	Floyd Bannister	.06	.03	.00
□ 600	Bruce Bochte	.03	.01	.00
□ 601	Julio Cruz	.03	.01	.00
□ 602	Ted Cox	.03	.01	.00
□ 603	Dan Meyer	.03	.01	.00
□ 604	Larry Cox	.03	.01	.00
□ 605	Bill Stein	.03	.01	.00
□ 606	Steve Garvey	.65	.30	.06
□ 607	Dave Roberts	.03	.01	.00
□ 608	Leon Roberts	.03	.01	.00
□ 609	Reggie Walton	.03	.01	.00
□ 610	Dave Edler	.03	.01	.00
□ 611	Larry Milbourne	.03	.01	.00
□ 612	Kim Allen	.03	.01	.00
□ 613	Mario Mendoza	.03	.01	.00
□ 614	Tom Paciorek	.03	.01	.00
□ 615	Glenn Abbott	.03	.01	.00
□ 616	Joe Simpson	.03	.01	.00
□ 617	Mickey Rivers	.06	.03	.00
□ 618	Jim Kern	.03	.01	.00
□ 619	Jim Sundberg	.06	.03	.00
□ 620	Richie Zisk	.06	.03	.00
□ 621	Jon Matlack	.03	.01	.00
□ 622	Ferguson Jenkins	.15	.07	.01
□ 623	Pat Corrales MG	.06	.03	.00
□ 624	Ed Figueroa	.03	.01	.00
□ 625	Buddy Bell	.15	.07	.01
□ 626	Al Oliver	.12	.06	.01
□ 627	Doc Medich	.03	.01	.00
□ 628	Bump Wills	.03	.01	.00
□ 629	Rusty Staub	.12	.06	.01
□ 630	Pat Putnam	.03	.01	.00
□ 631	John Grubb	.03	.01	.00
□ 632	Danny Darwin	.03	.01	.00
□ 633	Ken Clay	.03	.01	.00
□ 634	Jim Norris	.03	.01	.00
□ 635	John Butcher	.06	.03	.00
□ 636	Dave Roberts	.03	.01	.00
□ 637	Billy Sample	.03	.01	.00
□ 638	Carl Yastrzemski	1.00	.50	.10
□ 639	Cecil Cooper	.15	.07	.01
□ 640A	Mike Schmidt P1	1.50	.75	.15
	(Portrait)			
	"Third Base"			
	(number on back 5)			
□ 640B	Mike Schmidt P2	1.25	.60	.12
	"1980 Home Run King"			
	(640 on back)			

☐ 641A CL: Phils/Royals P1 ..... 41 is Hal McRae	.10	.05	.01
☐ 641B CL: Phils/Royals P2 .... 41 is Hal McRae, Double Threat	.10	.05	.01
☐ 642 CL: Astros/Yankees	.08	.04	.01
☐ 643 CL: Expos/Dodgers	.08	.04	.01
☐ 644A CL: Reds/Orioles P1 .... 202 is George Foster	.10	.05	.01
☐ 644B CL: Reds/Orioles P2 ... 202 is Foster Slugger	.10	.05	.01
☐ 645A Rose/Bowa/Schmidt .. Triple Threat P1 (No number on back)	2.00	1.00	.20
☐ 645B Rose/Bowa/Schmidt .. Triple Threat P2 (Back numbered 645)	1.00	.50	.10
☐ 646 CL: Braves/Red Sox	.08	.04	.01
☐ 647 CL: Cubs/Angels	.08	.04	.01
☐ 648 CL: Mets/White Sox	.08	.04	.01
☐ 649 CL: Indians/Pirates	.08	.04	.01
☐ 650A Reggie Jackson .... Mr. Baseball P1 Number on back 79	1.25	.60	.12
☐ 650B Reggie Jackson .... Mr. Baseball P2 Number on back 650	1.00	.50	.10
☐ 651 CL: Giants/Blue Jays	.08	.04	.01
☐ 652A CL: Tigers/Padres P1 .. 483 is listed	.10	.05	.01
☐ 652B CL: Tigers/Padres P2 .. 483 is deleted	.10	.05	.01
☐ 653A Willie Wilson P1 .... Most Hits Most Runs Number on back 29	.10	.05	.01
☐ 653B Willie Wilson P2 .... Most Hits Most Runs Number on back 653	.10	.05	.01
☐ 654A CL:Brewers/Cards P1 .. 514 Jerry Augustine 547 Pete Vuckovich	.10	.05	.01
☐ 654B CL:Brewers/Cards P2 . 514 Billy Travers 547 Don Hood	.10	.05	.01
☐ 655A George Brett P1 .... .390 Average Number on back 28	1.25	.60	.12
☐ 655B George Brett P2 .... .390 Average Number on back 655	.90	.45	.09
☐ 656 CL: Twins/Oakland A's ..	.08	.04	.01
☐ 657A Tug McGraw P1 .... Game Saver Number on back 7	.10	.05	.01
☐ 657B Tug McGraw P2 .... Game Saver Number on back 657	.10	.05	.01
☐ 658 CL: Rangers/Mariners ...	.08	.04	.01
☐ 659A Checklist P1 .... of Special Cards Last lines on front Wilson Most Hits	.10	.05	.01
☐ 659B Checklist P2 .... of Special Cards Last lines on front Otis Series Starter	.10	.05	.01
☐ 660A Steve Carlton P1 .... Golden Arm Back "1066 Cardinals" Number on back 6	.80	.40	.08
☐ 660B Steve Carlton P2 .... Golden Arm Number on back 660 Back "1066 Cardinals"	.65	.30	.06
☐ 660C Steve Carlton P3 .... Golden Arm "1966 Cardinals"	2.00	1.00	.20

1981 Fleer Sticker Cards

The stickers in this 128-sticker set measure 2 1/2" by 3 1/2". The 1981 Fleer Baseball Star Stickers consist of numbered cards with peelable, full-color sticker fronts and three unnumbered checklists. The backs of the numbered player cards are the same as the 1981 Fleer regular issue cards except for the numbers, while the checklist cards (cards 126-128 below) have sticker fronts of Jackson (1-42), Brett (43-83), and Schmidt (84-125).

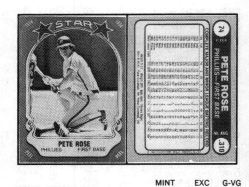

	MINT	EXC	G-VG
COMPLETE SET (128)	45.00	22.50	4.50
COMMON PLAYER (1-128)	.15	.07	.01

			MINT	EXC	G-VG
☐	1	Steve Garvey	2.00	.50	.10
☐	2	Ron LeFlore	.15	.07	.01
☐	3	Ron Cey	.20	.10	.02
☐	4	Dave Revering	.15	.07	.01
☐	5	Tony Armas	.15	.07	.01
☐	6	Mike Norris	.15	.07	.01
☐	7	Steve Kemp	.20	.10	.02
☐	8	Bruce Bochte	.15	.07	.01
☐	9	Mike Schmidt	3.50	1.75	.35
☐	10	Scott McGregor	.20	.10	.02
☐	11	Buddy Bell	.25	.12	.02
☐	12	Carney Lansford	.30	.15	.03
☐	13	Carl Yastrzemski	3.00	1.50	.30
☐	14	Ben Oglivie	.15	.07	.01
☐	15	Willie Stargell	1.25	.60	.12
☐	16	Cecil Cooper	.20	.10	.02
☐	17	Gene Richards	.15	.07	.01
☐	18	Jim Kern	.15	.07	.01
☐	19	Jerry Koosman	.20	.10	.02
☐	20	Larry Bowa	.25	.12	.02
☐	21	Kent Tekulve	.15	.07	.01
☐	22	Dan Driessen	.15	.07	.01
☐	23	Phil Niekro	.75	.35	.07
☐	24	Dan Quisenberry	.25	.12	.02
☐	25	Dave Winfield	1.50	.75	.15
☐	26	Dave Parker	.60	.30	.06
☐	27	Rick Langford	.15	.07	.01
☐	28	Amos Otis	.20	.10	.02
☐	29	Bill Buckner	.20	.10	.02
☐	30	Al Bumbry	.15	.07	.01
☐	31	Bake McBride	.15	.07	.01
☐	32	Mickey Rivers	.15	.07	.01
☐	33	Rick Burleson	.20	.10	.02
☐	34	Dennis Eckersley	.40	.20	.04
☐	35	Cesar Cedeno	.20	.10	.02
☐	36	Enos Cabell	.15	.07	.01
☐	37	Johnny Bench	3.00	1.50	.30
☐	38	Robin Yount	3.00	1.50	.30
☐	39	Mark Belanger	.15	.07	.01
☐	40	Rod Carew	2.00	1.00	.20
☐	41	George Foster	.60	.30	.06
☐	42	Lee Mazzilli	.15	.07	.01
☐	43	Triple Threat: .... Pete Rose Larry Bowa Mike Schmidt	2.50	1.25	.25
☐	44	J.R. Richard	.20	.10	.02
☐	45	Lou Piniella	.20	.10	.02
☐	46	Ken Landreaux	.15	.07	.01
☐	47	Rollie Fingers	.60	.30	.06
☐	48	Joaquin Andujar	.20	.10	.02
☐	49	Tom Seaver	2.00	1.00	.20
☐	50	Bobby Grich	.20	.10	.02
☐	51	Jon Matlack	.15	.07	.01
☐	52	Jack Clark	.50	.25	.05
☐	53	Jim Rice	.90	.45	.09
☐	54	Rickey Henderson	3.00	1.50	.30
☐	55	Roy Smalley	.15	.07	.01
☐	56	Mike Flanagan	.20	.10	.02
☐	57	Steve Rogers	.15	.07	.01
☐	58	Carlton Fisk	.60	.30	.06
☐	59	Don Sutton	.60	.30	.06
☐	60	Ken Griffey	.25	.12	.02
☐	61	Burt Hooton	.15	.07	.01
☐	62	Dusty Baker	.20	.10	.02
☐	63	Vida Blue	.20	.10	.02
☐	64	Al Oliver	.20	.10	.02
☐	65	Jim Bibby	.15	.07	.01

☐	66	Tony Perez	.40	.20	.04
☐	67	Davy Lopes	.20	.10	.02
☐	68	Bill Russell	.15	.07	.01
☐	69	Larry Parrish	.15	.07	.01
☐	70	Garry Maddox	.15	.07	.01
☐	71	Phil Garner	.15	.07	.01
☐	72	Graig Nettles	.35	.17	.03
☐	73	Gary Carter	1.50	.75	.15
☐	74	Pete Rose	4.50	2.25	.45
☐	75	Greg Luzinski	.25	.12	.02
☐	76	Ron Guidry	.50	.25	.05
☐	77	Gorman Thomas	.20	.10	.02
☐	78	Jose Cruz	.20	.10	.02
☐	79	Bob Boone	.35	.17	.03
☐	80	Bruce Sutter	.25	.12	.02
☐	81	Chris Chambliss	.20	.10	.02
☐	82	Paul Molitor	.60	.30	.06
☐	83	Tug McGraw	.25	.12	.02
☐	84	Ferguson Jenkins	.45	.22	.04
☐	85	Steve Carlton	1.75	.85	.17
☐	86	Miguel Dilone	.15	.07	.01
☐	87	Reggie Smith	.25	.12	.02
☐	88	Rick Cerone	.15	.07	.01
☐	89	Alan Trammell	1.00	.50	.10
☐	90	Doug DeCinces	.25	.12	.02
☐	91	Sparky Lyle	.25	.12	.02
☐	92	Warren Cromartie	.15	.07	.01
☐	93	Rick Reuschel	.40	.20	.04
☐	94	Larry Hisle	.15	.07	.01
☐	95	Paul Splittorff	.20	.10	.02
☐	96	Manny Trillo	.15	.07	.01
☐	97	Frank White	.25	.12	.02
☐	98	Fred Lynn	.50	.25	.05
☐	99	Bob Horner	.50	.25	.05
☐	100	Omar Moreno	.15	.07	.01
☐	101	Dave Concepcion	.20	.10	.02
☐	102	Larry Gura	.15	.07	.01
☐	103	Ken Singleton	.20	.10	.02
☐	104	Steve Stone	.15	.07	.01
☐	105	Richie Zisk	.15	.07	.01
☐	106	Willie Wilson	.25	.12	.02
☐	107	Willie Randolph	.25	.12	.02
☐	108	Nolan Ryan	4.00	2.00	.40
☐	109	Joe Morgan	1.50	.75	.15
☐	110	Bucky Dent	.50	.25	.05
☐	111	Dave Kingman	.35	.17	.03
☐	112	John Castino	.15	.07	.01
☐	113	Joe Rudi	.15	.07	.01
☐	114	Ed Farmer	.15	.07	.01
☐	115	Reggie Jackson	2.50	1.25	.25
☐	116	George Brett	2.50	1.25	.25
☐	117	Eddie Murray	1.50	.75	.15
☐	118	Rich Gossage	.40	.20	.04
☐	119	Dale Murphy	2.00	1.00	.20
☐	120	Ted Simmons	.25	.12	.02
☐	121	Tommy John	.50	.25	.05
☐	122	Don Baylor	.40	.20	.04
☐	123	Andre Dawson	1.50	.75	.15
☐	124	Jim Palmer	1.50	.75	.15
☐	125	Garry Templeton	.20	.10	.02
☐	126	CL 1: Reggie Jackson	1.25	.60	.12
☐	127	CL 2: George Brett	1.25	.60	.12
☐	128	CL 3: Mike Schmidt	2.50	1.25	.25

1982 Fleer

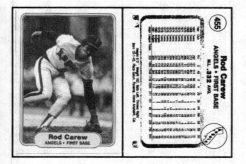

Rod Carew
ANGELS • FIRST BASE

The cards in this 660-card set measure 2 1/2" by 3 1/2". The 1982 Fleer set is again ordered by teams; in fact the players within each team are listed in alphabetical order. The teams are ordered (by 1981 standings) as follows: Los Angeles (1-29), New York Yankees (30-56), Cincinnati (57-84), Oakland (85-109), St. Louis (110-132), Milwaukee (133-156), Baltimore (157-182), Montreal (183-211), Houston (212-237), Philadelphia (238- 262), Detroit (263-286), Boston (287-312), Texas (313-334), Chicago White Sox (335-358), Cleveland (359-382), San Francisco (383-403), Kansas City (404-427), Atlanta (428- 449), California (450-474), Pittsburgh (475-501), Seattle (502-519), New York Mets (520-544), Minnesota (545-565), San Diego (566-585), Chicago Cubs (586-607), and Toronto (608- 627). Cards numbered 628 through 646 are special cards highlighting some of the stars and leaders of the 1981 season. The last 14 cards in the set (647-660) are checklist cards. The backs feature player statistics and a full-color team logo in the upper right-hand corner of each card. The complete set price below does not include any of the more valuable variation cards listed.

		MINT	EXC	G-VG
COMPLETE SET (660)		35.00	17.50	3.50
COMMON PLAYER (1-660)		.03	.01	.00

☐	1	Dusty Baker	.12	.03	.01
☐	2	Robert Castillo	.03	.01	.00
☐	3	Ron Cey	.10	.05	.01
☐	4	Terry Forster	.06	.03	.00
☐	5	Steve Garvey	.50	.25	.05
☐	6	Dave Goltz	.03	.01	.00
☐	7	Pedro Guerrero	.45	.22	.04
☐	8	Burt Hooton	.03	.01	.00
☐	9	Steve Howe	.03	.01	.00
☐	10	Jay Johnstone	.06	.03	.00
☐	11	Ken Landreaux	.03	.01	.00
☐	12	Dave Lopes	.08	.04	.01
☐	13	Mike Marshall	1.25	.60	.12
☐	14	Bobby Mitchell	.03	.01	.00
☐	15	Rick Monday	.03	.01	.00
☐	16	Tom Niedenfuer	.20	.10	.02
☐	17	Ted Power	.20	.10	.02
☐	18	Jerry Reuss	.06	.03	.00
☐	19	Ron Roenicke	.03	.01	.00
☐	20	Bill Russell	.06	.03	.00
☐	21	Steve Sax	2.75	1.35	.27
☐	22	Mike Scioscia	.10	.05	.01
☐	23	Reggie Smith	.08	.04	.01
☐	24	Dave Stewart	3.75	1.85	.37
☐	25	Rick Sutcliffe	.20	.10	.02
☐	26	Derrel Thomas	.03	.01	.00
☐	27	Fernando Valenzuela	.60	.30	.06
☐	28	Bob Welch	.08	.04	.01
☐	29	Steve Yeager	.03	.01	.00
☐	30	Bobby Brown	.03	.01	.00
☐	31	Rick Cerone	.03	.01	.00
☐	32	Ron Davis	.03	.01	.00
☐	33	Bucky Dent	.10	.05	.01
☐	34	Barry Foote	.03	.01	.00
☐	35	George Frazier	.03	.01	.00
☐	36	Oscar Gamble	.03	.01	.00
☐	37	Rich Gossage	.20	.10	.02
☐	38	Ron Guidry	.20	.10	.02
☐	39	Reggie Jackson	.75	.35	.07
☐	40	Tommy John	.18	.09	.01
☐	41	Rudy May	.03	.01	.00
☐	42	Larry Milbourne	.03	.01	.00
☐	43	Jerry Mumphrey	.03	.01	.00
☐	44	Bobby Murcer	.08	.04	.01
☐	45	Gene Nelson	.20	.10	.02
☐	46	Graig Nettles	.12	.06	.01
☐	47	Johnny Oates	.03	.01	.00
☐	48	Lou Piniella	.10	.05	.01
☐	49	Willie Randolph	.08	.04	.01
☐	50	Rick Reuschel	.15	.07	.01
☐	51	Dave Revering	.03	.01	.00
☐	52	Dave Righetti	1.50	.75	.15
☐	53	Aurelio Rodriguez	.03	.01	.00
☐	54	Bob Watson	.06	.03	.00
☐	55	Dennis Werth	.03	.01	.00
☐	56	Dave Winfield	.50	.25	.05
☐	57	Johnny Bench	.65	.30	.06
☐	58	Bruce Berenyi	.03	.01	.00
☐	59	Larry Biittner	.03	.01	.00
☐	60	Scott Brown	.03	.01	.00
☐	61	Dave Collins	.03	.01	.00
☐	62	Geoff Combe	.03	.01	.00
☐	63	Dave Concepcion	.10	.05	.01

☐ 64	Dan Driessen	.03	.01	.00	☐ 159	Al Bumbry	.03	.01	.00
☐ 65	Joe Edelen	.03	.01	.00	☐ 160	Terry Crowley	.03	.01	.00
☐ 66	George Foster	.15	.07	.01	☐ 161	Rich Dauer	.03	.01	.00
☐ 67	Ken Griffey	.10	.05	.01	☐ 162	Doug DeCinces	.06	.03	.00
☐ 68	Paul Householder	.03	.01	.00	☐ 163	Rick Dempsey	.03	.01	.00
☐ 69	Tom Hume	.03	.01	.00	☐ 164	Jim Dwyer	.03	.01	.00
☐ 70	Junior Kennedy	.03	.01	.00	☐ 165	Mike Flanagan	.08	.04	.01
☐ 71	Ray Knight	.08	.04	.01	☐ 166	Dave Ford	.03	.01	.00
☐ 72	Mike LaCoss	.03	.01	.00	☐ 167	Dan Graham	.03	.01	.00
☐ 73	Rafael Landestoy	.03	.01	.00	☐ 168	Wayne Krenchicki	.03	.01	.00
☐ 74	Charlie Leibrandt	.06	.03	.00	☐ 169	John Lowenstein	.03	.01	.00
☐ 75	Sam Mejias	.03	.01	.00	☐ 170	Dennis Martinez	.08	.04	.01
☐ 76	Paul Moskau	.03	.01	.00	☐ 171	Tippy Martinez	.03	.01	.00
☐ 77	Joe Nolan	.03	.01	.00	☐ 172	Scott McGregor	.06	.03	.00
☐ 78	Mike O'Berry	.03	.01	.00	☐ 173	Jose Morales	.03	.01	.00
☐ 79	Ron Oester	.03	.01	.00	☐ 174	Eddie Murray	.50	.25	.05
☐ 80	Frank Pastore	.03	.01	.00	☐ 175	Jim Palmer	.45	.22	.04
☐ 81	Joe Price	.03	.01	.00	☐ 176	Cal Ripken	8.50	4.25	.85
☐ 82	Tom Seaver	.50	.25	.05	☐ 177	Gary Roenicke	.03	.01	.00
☐ 83	Mario Soto	.06	.03	.00	☐ 178	Lenn Sakata	.03	.01	.00
☐ 84	Mike Vail	.03	.01	.00	☐ 179	Ken Singleton	.08	.04	.01
☐ 85	Tony Armas	.06	.03	.00	☐ 180	Sammy Stewart	.03	.01	.00
☐ 86	Shooty Babitt	.03	.01	.00	☐ 181	Tim Stoddard	.03	.01	.00
☐ 87	Dave Beard	.03	.01	.00	☐ 182	Steve Stone	.06	.03	.00
☐ 88	Rick Bosetti	.03	.01	.00	☐ 183	Stan Bahnsen	.03	.01	.00
☐ 89	Keith Drumwright	.03	.01	.00	☐ 184	Ray Burris	.03	.01	.00
☐ 90	Wayne Gross	.03	.01	.00	☐ 185	Gary Carter	.45	.22	.04
☐ 91	Mike Heath	.03	.01	.00	☐ 186	Warren Cromartie	.03	.01	.00
☐ 92	Rickey Henderson	1.50	.75	.15	☐ 187	Andre Dawson	.40	.20	.04
☐ 93	Cliff Johnson	.03	.01	.00	☐ 188	Terry Francona	.08	.04	.01
☐ 94	Jeff Jones	.03	.01	.00	☐ 189	Woodie Fryman	.03	.01	.00
☐ 95	Matt Keough	.03	.01	.00	☐ 190	Bill Gullickson	.06	.03	.00
☐ 96	Brian Kingman	.03	.01	.00	☐ 191	Grant Jackson	.03	.01	.00
☐ 97	Mickey Klutts	.03	.01	.00	☐ 192	Wallace Johnson	.06	.03	.00
☐ 98	Rick Langford	.03	.01	.00	☐ 193	Charlie Lea	.06	.03	.00
☐ 99	Steve McCatty	.03	.01	.00	☐ 194	Bill Lee	.06	.03	.00
☐ 100	Dave McKay	.03	.01	.00	☐ 195	Jerry Manuel	.03	.01	.00
☐ 101	Dwayne Murphy	.03	.01	.00	☐ 196	Brad Mills	.03	.01	.00
☐ 102	Jeff Newman	.03	.01	.00	☐ 197	John Milner	.03	.01	.00
☐ 103	Mike Norris	.03	.01	.00	☐ 198	Rowland Office	.03	.01	.00
☐ 104	Bob Owchinko	.03	.01	.00	☐ 199	David Palmer	.03	.01	.00
☐ 105	Mitchell Page	.03	.01	.00	☐ 200	Larry Parrish	.06	.03	.00
☐ 106	Rob Picciolo	.03	.01	.00	☐ 201	Mike Phillips	.03	.01	.00
☐ 107	Jim Spencer	.03	.01	.00	☐ 202	Tim Raines	2.00	1.00	.20
☐ 108	Fred Stanley	.03	.01	.00	☐ 203	Bobby Ramos	.03	.01	.00
☐ 109	Tom Underwood	.03	.01	.00	☐ 204	Jeff Reardon	.20	.07	.01
☐ 110	Joaquin Andujar	.08	.04	.01	☐ 205	Steve Rogers	.06	.03	.00
☐ 111	Steve Braun	.03	.01	.00	☐ 206	Scott Sanderson	.03	.01	.00
☐ 112	Bob Forsch	.03	.01	.00	☐ 207	Rodney Scott UER	.20	.10	.02
☐ 113	George Hendrick	.06	.03	.00		(photo actually			
☐ 114	Keith Hernandez	.35	.17	.03		Tim Raines)			
☐ 115	Tom Herr	.08	.04	.01	☐ 208	Elias Sosa	.03	.01	.00
☐ 116	Dane Iorg	.03	.01	.00	☐ 209	Chris Speier	.03	.01	.00
☐ 117	Jim Kaat	.15	.07	.01	☐ 210	Tim Wallach	1.00	.50	.10
☐ 118	Tito Landrum	.03	.01	.00	☐ 211	Jerry White	.03	.01	.00
☐ 119	Sixto Lezcano	.03	.01	.00	☐ 212	Alan Ashby	.03	.01	.00
☐ 120	Mark Littell	.03	.01	.00	☐ 213	Cesar Cedeno	.08	.04	.01
☐ 121	John Martin	.03	.01	.00	☐ 214	Jose Cruz	.08	.04	.01
☐ 122	Silvio Martinez	.03	.01	.00	☐ 215	Kiko Garcia	.03	.01	.00
☐ 123	Ken Oberkfell	.03	.01	.00	☐ 216	Phil Garner	.03	.01	.00
☐ 124	Darrell Porter	.03	.01	.00	☐ 217	Danny Heep	.03	.01	.00
☐ 125	Mike Ramsey	.03	.01	.00	☐ 218	Art Howe	.08	.04	.01
☐ 126	Orlando Sanchez	.03	.01	.00	☐ 219	Bob Knepper	.08	.04	.01
☐ 127	Bob Shirley	.03	.01	.00	☐ 220	Frank LaCorte	.03	.01	.00
☐ 128	Lary Sorensen	.03	.01	.00	☐ 221	Joe Niekro	.10	.05	.01
☐ 129	Bruce Sutter	.15	.07	.01	☐ 222	Joe Pittman	.03	.01	.00
☐ 130	Bob Sykes	.03	.01	.00	☐ 223	Terry Puhl	.03	.01	.00
☐ 131	Garry Templeton	.08	.04	.01	☐ 224	Luis Pujols	.03	.01	.00
☐ 132	Gene Tenace	.03	.01	.00	☐ 225	Craig Reynolds	.03	.01	.00
☐ 133	Jerry Augustine	.03	.01	.00	☐ 226	J.R. Richard	.08	.04	.01
☐ 134	Sal Bando	.06	.03	.00	☐ 227	Dave Roberts	.03	.01	.00
☐ 135	Mark Brouhard	.03	.01	.00	☐ 228	Vern Ruhle	.03	.01	.00
☐ 136	Mike Caldwell	.03	.01	.00	☐ 229	Nolan Ryan	1.75	.85	.17
☐ 137	Reggie Cleveland	.03	.01	.00	☐ 230	Joe Sambito	.03	.01	.00
☐ 138	Cecil Cooper	.15	.07	.01	☐ 231	Tony Scott	.03	.01	.00
☐ 139	Jamie Easterly	.03	.01	.00	☐ 232	Dave Smith	.08	.04	.01
☐ 140	Marshall Edwards	.03	.01	.00	☐ 233	Harry Spilman	.03	.01	.00
☐ 141	Rollie Fingers	.20	.10	.02	☐ 234	Don Sutton	.30	.15	.03
☐ 142	Jim Gantner	.03	.01	.00	☐ 235	Dickie Thon	.06	.03	.00
☐ 143	Moose Haas	.03	.01	.00	☐ 236	Denny Walling	.03	.01	.00
☐ 144	Larry Hisle	.06	.03	.00	☐ 237	Gary Woods	.03	.01	.00
☐ 145	Roy Howell	.03	.01	.00	☐ 238	Luis Aguayo	.03	.01	.00
☐ 146	Rickey Keeton	.03	.01	.00	☐ 239	Ramon Aviles	.03	.01	.00
☐ 147	Randy Lerch	.03	.01	.00	☐ 240	Bob Boone	.15	.07	.01
☐ 148	Paul Molitor	.25	.12	.02	☐ 241	Larry Bowa	.12	.06	.01
☐ 149	Don Money	.03	.01	.00	☐ 242	Warren Brusstar	.03	.01	.00
☐ 150	Charlie Moore	.03	.01	.00	☐ 243	Steve Carlton	.60	.30	.06
☐ 151	Ben Oglivie	.06	.03	.00	☐ 244	Larry Christenson	.03	.01	.00
☐ 152	Ted Simmons	.12	.06	.01	☐ 245	Dick Davis	.03	.01	.00
☐ 153	Jim Slaton	.03	.01	.00	☐ 246	Greg Gross	.03	.01	.00
☐ 154	Gorman Thomas	.08	.04	.01	☐ 247	Sparky Lyle	.10	.05	.01
☐ 155	Robin Yount	1.00	.50	.10	☐ 248	Garry Maddox	.06	.03	.00
☐ 156	Pete Vuckovich	.08	.04	.01	☐ 249	Gary Matthews	.06	.03	.00
☐ 157	Benny Ayala	.03	.01	.00	☐ 250	Bake McBride	.03	.01	.00
☐ 158	Mark Belanger	.06	.03	.00	☐ 251	Tug McGraw	.10	.05	.01

☐ 252	Keith Moreland	.03	.01	.00
☐ 253	Dickie Noles	.03	.01	.00
☐ 254	Mike Proly	.03	.01	.00
☐ 255	Ron Reed	.03	.01	.00
☐ 256	Pete Rose	1.25	.60	.12
☐ 257	Dick Ruthven	.03	.01	.00
☐ 258	Mike Schmidt	1.00	.50	.10
☐ 259	Lonnie Smith	.12	.06	.01
☐ 260	Manny Trillo	.03	.01	.00
☐ 261	Del Unser	.03	.01	.00
☐ 262	George Vukovich	.03	.01	.00
☐ 263	Tom Brookens	.03	.01	.00
☐ 264	George Cappuzzello	.03	.01	.00
☐ 265	Marty Castillo	.03	.01	.00
☐ 266	Al Cowens	.03	.01	.00
☐ 267	Kirk Gibson	.75	.35	.07
☐ 268	Richie Hebner	.03	.01	.00
☐ 269	Ron Jackson	.03	.01	.00
☐ 270	Lynn Jones	.03	.01	.00
☐ 271	Steve Kemp	.06	.03	.00
☐ 272	Rick Leach	.03	.01	.00
☐ 273	Aurelio Lopez	.03	.01	.00
☐ 274	Jack Morris	.20	.10	.02
☐ 275	Kevin Saucier	.03	.01	.00
☐ 276	Lance Parrish	.20	.10	.02
☐ 277	Rick Peters	.03	.01	.00
☐ 278	Dan Petry	.03	.01	.00
☐ 279	Dave Rozema	.03	.01	.00
☐ 280	Stan Papi	.03	.01	.00
☐ 281	Dan Schatzeder	.03	.01	.00
☐ 282	Champ Summers	.03	.01	.00
☐ 283	Alan Trammell	.35	.17	.03
☐ 284	Lou Whitaker	.25	.12	.02
☐ 285	Milt Wilcox	.03	.01	.00
☐ 286	John Wockenfuss	.03	.01	.00
☐ 287	Gary Allenson	.03	.01	.00
☐ 288	Tom Burgmeier	.03	.01	.00
☐ 289	Bill Campbell	.03	.01	.00
☐ 290	Mark Clear	.03	.01	.00
☐ 291	Steve Crawford	.03	.01	.00
☐ 292	Dennis Eckersley	.20	.10	.02
☐ 293	Dwight Evans	.20	.10	.02
☐ 294	Rich Gedman	.35	.17	.03
☐ 295	Garry Hancock	.03	.01	.00
☐ 296	Glenn Hoffman	.03	.01	.00
☐ 297	Bruce Hurst	.65	.30	.06
☐ 298	Carney Lansford	.25	.12	.02
☐ 299	Rick Miller	.03	.01	.00
☐ 300	Reid Nichols	.03	.01	.00
☐ 301	Bob Ojeda	.60	.30	.06
☐ 302	Tony Perez	.18	.09	.01
☐ 303	Chuck Rainey	.03	.01	.00
☐ 304	Jerry Remy	.03	.01	.00
☐ 305	Jim Rice	.30	.15	.03
☐ 306	Joe Rudi	.06	.03	.00
☐ 307	Bob Stanley	.03	.01	.00
☐ 308	Dave Stapleton	.03	.01	.00
☐ 309	Frank Tanana	.06	.03	.00
☐ 310	Mike Torrez	.03	.01	.00
☐ 311	John Tudor	.20	.10	.02
☐ 312	Carl Yastrzemski	1.00	.50	.10
☐ 313	Buddy Bell	.10	.05	.01
☐ 314	Steve Comer	.03	.01	.00
☐ 315	Danny Darwin	.03	.01	.00
☐ 316	John Ellis	.03	.01	.00
☐ 317	John Grubb	.03	.01	.00
☐ 318	Rick Honeycutt	.03	.01	.00
☐ 319	Charlie Hough	.06	.03	.00
☐ 320	Ferguson Jenkins	.15	.07	.01
☐ 321	John Henry Johnson	.03	.01	.00
☐ 322	Jim Kern	.03	.01	.00
☐ 323	Jon Matlack	.03	.01	.00
☐ 324	Doc Medich	.03	.01	.00
☐ 325	Mario Mendoza	.03	.01	.00
☐ 326	Al Oliver	.10	.05	.01
☐ 327	Pat Putnam	.03	.01	.00
☐ 328	Mickey Rivers	.06	.03	.00
☐ 329	Leon Roberts	.03	.01	.00
☐ 330	Billy Sample	.03	.01	.00
☐ 331	Bill Stein	.03	.01	.00
☐ 332	Jim Sundberg	.06	.03	.00
☐ 333	Mark Wagner	.03	.01	.00
☐ 334	Bump Wills	.03	.01	.00
☐ 335	Bill Almon	.03	.01	.00
☐ 336	Harold Baines	.35	.17	.03
☐ 337	Ross Baumgarten	.03	.01	.00
☐ 338	Tony Bernazard	.03	.01	.00
☐ 339	Britt Burns	.06	.03	.00
☐ 340	Richard Dotson	.06	.03	.00
☐ 341	Jim Essian	.03	.01	.00
☐ 342	Ed Farmer	.03	.01	.00
☐ 343	Carlton Fisk	.35	.17	.03
☐ 344	Kevin Hickey	.03	.01	.00
☐ 345	LaMarr Hoyt	.06	.03	.00
☐ 346	Lamar Johnson	.03	.01	.00
☐ 347	Jerry Koosman	.08	.04	.01
☐ 348	Rusty Kuntz	.03	.01	.00
☐ 349	Dennis Lamp	.03	.01	.00
☐ 350	Ron LeFlore	.06	.03	.00
☐ 351	Chet Lemon	.06	.03	.00
☐ 352	Greg Luzinski	.10	.05	.01
☐ 353	Bob Molinaro	.03	.01	.00
☐ 354	Jim Morrison	.03	.01	.00
☐ 355	Wayne Nordhagen	.03	.01	.00
☐ 356	Greg Pryor	.03	.01	.00
☐ 357	Mike Squires	.03	.01	.00
☐ 358	Steve Trout	.03	.01	.00
☐ 359	Alan Bannister	.03	.01	.00
☐ 360	Len Barker	.03	.01	.00
☐ 361	Bert Blyleven	.20	.07	.01
☐ 362	Joe Charboneau	.06	.03	.00
☐ 363	John Denny	.06	.03	.00
☐ 364	Bo Diaz	.03	.01	.00
☐ 365	Miguel Dilone	.03	.01	.00
☐ 366	Jerry Dybzinski	.03	.01	.00
☐ 367	Wayne Garland	.03	.01	.00
☐ 368	Mike Hargrove	.06	.03	.00
☐ 369	Toby Harrah	.06	.03	.00
☐ 370	Ron Hassey	.03	.01	.00
☐ 371	Von Hayes	1.00	.50	.10
☐ 372	Pat Kelly	.03	.01	.00
☐ 373	Duane Kuiper	.03	.01	.00
☐ 374	Rick Manning	.03	.01	.00
☐ 375	Sid Monge	.03	.01	.00
☐ 376	Jorge Orta	.03	.01	.00
☐ 377	Dave Rosello	.03	.01	.00
☐ 378	Dan Spillner	.03	.01	.00
☐ 379	Mike Stanton	.03	.01	.00
☐ 380	Andre Thornton	.06	.03	.00
☐ 381	Tom Veryzer	.03	.01	.00
☐ 382	Rick Waits	.03	.01	.00
☐ 383	Doyle Alexander	.06	.03	.00
☐ 384	Vida Blue	.08	.04	.01
☐ 385	Fred Breining	.03	.01	.00
☐ 386	Enos Cabell	.03	.01	.00
☐ 387	Jack Clark	.25	.12	.02
☐ 388	Darrell Evans	.12	.06	.01
☐ 389	Tom Griffin	.03	.01	.00
☐ 390	Larry Herndon	.03	.01	.00
☐ 391	Al Holland	.03	.01	.00
☐ 392	Gary Lavelle	.03	.01	.00
☐ 393	Johnnie LeMaster	.03	.01	.00
☐ 394	Jerry Martin	.03	.01	.00
☐ 395	Milt May	.03	.01	.00
☐ 396	Greg Minton	.03	.01	.00
☐ 397	Joe Morgan	.35	.17	.03
☐ 398	Joe Pettini	.03	.01	.00
☐ 399	Allen Ripley	.03	.01	.00
☐ 400	Billy Smith	.03	.01	.00
☐ 401	Rennie Stennett	.03	.01	.00
☐ 402	Ed Whitson	.06	.03	.00
☐ 403	Jim Wohlford	.03	.01	.00
☐ 404	Willie Aikens	.03	.01	.00
☐ 405	George Brett	.80	.40	.08
☐ 406	Ken Brett	.03	.01	.00
☐ 407	Dave Chalk	.03	.01	.00
☐ 408	Rich Gale	.03	.01	.00
☐ 409	Cesar Geronimo	.03	.01	.00
☐ 410	Larry Gura	.06	.03	.00
☐ 411	Clint Hurdle	.03	.01	.00
☐ 412	Mike Jones	.03	.01	.00
☐ 413	Dennis Leonard	.06	.03	.00
☐ 414	Renie Martin	.03	.01	.00
☐ 415	Lee May	.06	.03	.00
☐ 416	Hal McRae	.06	.03	.00
☐ 417	Darryl Motley	.06	.03	.00
☐ 418	Rance Mulliniks	.03	.01	.00
☐ 419	Amos Otis	.08	.04	.01
☐ 420	Ken Phelps	.50	.25	.05
☐ 421	Jamie Quirk	.03	.01	.00
☐ 422	Dan Quisenberry	.15	.07	.01
☐ 423	Paul Splittorff	.03	.01	.00
☐ 424	U.L. Washington	.03	.01	.00
☐ 425	John Wathan	.06	.03	.00
☐ 426	Frank White	.08	.04	.01
☐ 427	Willie Wilson	.12	.06	.01
☐ 428	Brian Asselstine	.03	.01	.00
☐ 429	Bruce Benedict	.03	.01	.00
☐ 430	Tommy Boggs	.03	.01	.00
☐ 431	Larry Bradford	.03	.01	.00
☐ 432	Rick Camp	.03	.01	.00
☐ 433	Chris Chambliss	.08	.04	.01
☐ 434	Gene Garber	.03	.01	.00
☐ 435	Preston Hanna	.03	.01	.00
☐ 436	Bob Horner	.15	.07	.01
☐ 437	Glenn Hubbard	.03	.01	.00
☐ 438A	All Hrabosky ERR (height 5'1", All on reverse)	20.00	10.00	2.00
☐ 438B	Al Hrabosky ERR	1.25	.60	.12

	(height 5'1")			
□ 438C	Al Hrabosky	.10	.05	.01
	(height 5'10")			
□ 439	Rufino Linares	.06	.03	.00
□ 440	Rick Mahler	.25	.12	.02
□ 441	Ed Miller	.03	.01	.00
□ 442	John Montefusco	.06	.03	.00
□ 443	Dale Murphy	.90	.45	.09
□ 444	Phil Niekro	.30	.15	.03
□ 445	Gaylord Perry	.30	.15	.03
□ 446	Biff Pocoroba	.03	.01	.00
□ 447	Rafael Ramirez	.03	.01	.00
□ 448	Jerry Royster	.03	.01	.00
□ 449	Claudell Washington	.08	.04	.01
□ 450	Don Aase	.03	.01	.00
□ 451	Don Baylor	.15	.07	.01
□ 452	Juan Beniquez	.03	.01	.00
□ 453	Rick Burleson	.06	.03	.00
□ 454	Bert Campaneris	.06	.03	.00
□ 455	Rod Carew	.50	.25	.05
□ 456	Bob Clark	.03	.01	.00
□ 457	Brian Downing	.06	.03	.00
□ 458	Dan Ford	.03	.01	.00
□ 459	Ken Forsch	.03	.01	.00
□ 460A	Dave Frost (5 mm space before ERA)	.40	.20	.04
□ 460B	Dave Frost (1 mm space)	.06	.03	.00
□ 461	Bobby Grich	.08	.04	.01
□ 462	Larry Harlow	.03	.01	.00
□ 463	John Harris	.03	.01	.00
□ 464	Andy Hassler	.03	.01	.00
□ 465	Butch Hobson	.03	.01	.00
□ 466	Jesse Jefferson	.03	.01	.00
□ 467	Bruce Kison	.03	.01	.00
□ 468	Fred Lynn	.20	.10	.02
□ 469	Angel Moreno	.03	.01	.00
□ 470	Ed Ott	.03	.01	.00
□ 471	Fred Patek	.03	.01	.00
□ 472	Steve Renko	.03	.01	.00
□ 473	Mike Witt	.75	.35	.07
□ 474	Geoff Zahn	.03	.01	.00
□ 475	Gary Alexander	.03	.01	.00
□ 476	Dale Berra	.03	.01	.00
□ 477	Kurt Bevacqua	.03	.01	.00
□ 478	Jim Bibby	.03	.01	.00
□ 479	John Candelaria	.08	.04	.01
□ 480	Victor Cruz	.03	.01	.00
□ 481	Mike Easler	.06	.03	.00
□ 482	Tim Foli	.03	.01	.00
□ 483	Lee Lacy	.03	.01	.00
□ 484	Vance Law	.20	.10	.02
□ 485	Bill Madlock	.12	.06	.01
□ 486	Willie Montanez	.03	.01	.00
□ 487	Omar Moreno	.03	.01	.00
□ 488	Steve Nicosia	.03	.01	.00
□ 489	Dave Parker	.25	.12	.02
□ 490	Tony Pena	.35	.17	.03
□ 491	Pascual Perez	.30	.15	.03
□ 492	Johnny Ray	.75	.35	.07
□ 493	Rick Rhoden	.06	.03	.00
□ 494	Bill Robinson	.06	.03	.00
□ 495	Don Robinson	.06	.03	.00
□ 496	Enrique Romo	.03	.01	.00
□ 497	Rod Scurry	.03	.01	.00
□ 498	Eddie Solomon	.03	.01	.00
□ 499	Willie Stargell	.40	.20	.04
□ 500	Kent Tekulve	.06	.03	.00
□ 501	Jason Thompson	.03	.01	.00
□ 502	Glenn Abbott	.03	.01	.00
□ 503	Jim Anderson	.03	.01	.00
□ 504	Floyd Bannister	.03	.01	.00
□ 505	Bruce Bochte	.03	.01	.00
□ 506	Jeff Burroughs	.06	.03	.00
□ 507	Bryan Clark	.03	.01	.00
□ 508	Ken Clay	.03	.01	.00
□ 509	Julio Cruz	.03	.01	.00
□ 510	Dick Drago	.03	.01	.00
□ 511	Gary Gray	.03	.01	.00
□ 512	Dan Meyer	.03	.01	.00
□ 513	Jerry Narron	.03	.01	.00
□ 514	Tom Paciorek	.03	.01	.00
□ 515	Casey Parsons	.03	.01	.00
□ 516	Lenny Randle	.03	.01	.00
□ 517	Shane Rawley	.06	.03	.00
□ 518	Joe Simpson	.03	.01	.00
□ 519	Richie Zisk	.03	.01	.00
□ 520	Neil Allen	.06	.03	.00
□ 521	Bob Bailor	.03	.01	.00
□ 522	Hubie Brooks	.40	.20	.04
□ 523	Mike Cubbage	.03	.01	.00
□ 524	Pete Falcone	.03	.01	.00
□ 525	Doug Flynn	.03	.01	.00
□ 526	Tom Hausman	.03	.01	.00
□ 527	Ron Hodges	.03	.01	.00
□ 528	Randy Jones	.03	.01	.00
□ 529	Mike Jorgensen	.03	.01	.00
□ 530	Dave Kingman	.12	.06	.01
□ 531	Ed Lynch	.06	.03	.00
□ 532	Mike Marshall (screwball pitcher)	.06	.03	.00
□ 533	Lee Mazzilli	.03	.01	.00
□ 534	Dyar Miller	.03	.01	.00
□ 535	Mike Scott	.50	.25	.05
□ 536	Rusty Staub	.10	.05	.01
□ 537	John Stearns	.03	.01	.00
□ 538	Craig Swan	.03	.01	.00
□ 539	Frank Taveras	.03	.01	.00
□ 540	Alex Trevino	.03	.01	.00
□ 541	Ellis Valentine	.03	.01	.00
□ 542	Mookie Wilson	.10	.05	.01
□ 543	Joel Youngblood	.03	.01	.00
□ 544	Pat Zachry	.03	.01	.00
□ 545	Glenn Adams	.03	.01	.00
□ 546	Fernando Arroyo	.03	.01	.00
□ 547	John Verhoeven	.03	.01	.00
□ 548	Sal Butera	.03	.01	.00
□ 549	John Castino	.03	.01	.00
□ 550	Don Cooper	.03	.01	.00
□ 551	Doug Corbett	.03	.01	.00
□ 552	Dave Engle	.03	.01	.00
□ 553	Roger Erickson	.03	.01	.00
□ 554	Danny Goodwin	.03	.01	.00
□ 555A	Darrell Jackson (black cap)	1.00	.50	.10
□ 555B	Darrell Jackson (red cap with T)	.10	.05	.01
□ 555C	Darrell Jackson (red cap, no emblem)	5.00	2.50	.50
□ 556	Pete Mackanin	.03	.01	.00
□ 557	Jack O'Connor	.03	.01	.00
□ 558	Hosken Powell	.03	.01	.00
□ 559	Pete Redfern	.03	.01	.00
□ 560	Roy Smalley	.03	.01	.00
□ 561	Chuck Baker UER (shortstop on front)	.03	.01	.00
□ 562	Gary Ward	.06	.03	.00
□ 563	Rob Wilfong	.03	.01	.00
□ 564	Al Williams	.03	.01	.00
□ 565	Butch Wynegar	.03	.01	.00
□ 566	Randy Bass	.06	.03	.00
□ 567	Juan Bonilla	.03	.01	.00
□ 568	Danny Boone	.03	.01	.00
□ 569	John Curtis	.03	.01	.00
□ 570	Juan Eichelberger	.03	.01	.00
□ 571	Barry Evans	.03	.01	.00
□ 572	Tim Flannery	.03	.01	.00
□ 573	Ruppert Jones	.03	.01	.00
□ 574	Terry Kennedy	.03	.01	.00
□ 575	Joe Lefebvre	.03	.01	.00
□ 576A	John Littlefield ERR (left handed)	150.00	75.00	15.00
□ 576B	John Littlefield COR (right handed)	.06	.03	.00
□ 577	Gary Lucas	.03	.01	.00
□ 578	Steve Mura	.03	.01	.00
□ 579	Broderick Perkins	.03	.01	.00
□ 580	Gene Richards	.03	.01	.00
□ 581	Luis Salazar	.06	.03	.00
□ 582	Ozzie Smith	.35	.17	.03
□ 583	John Urrea	.03	.01	.00
□ 584	Chris Welsh	.03	.01	.00
□ 585	Rick Wise	.03	.01	.00
□ 586	Doug Bird	.03	.01	.00
□ 587	Tim Blackwell	.03	.01	.00
□ 588	Bobby Bonds	.10	.05	.01
□ 589	Bill Buckner	.10	.05	.01
□ 590	Bill Caudill	.03	.01	.00
□ 591	Hector Cruz	.03	.01	.00
□ 592	Jody Davis	.35	.17	.03
□ 593	Ivan DeJesus	.03	.01	.00
□ 594	Steve Dillard	.03	.01	.00
□ 595	Leon Durham	.06	.03	.00
□ 596	Rawly Eastwick	.03	.01	.00
□ 597	Steve Henderson	.03	.01	.00
□ 598	Mike Krukow	.06	.03	.00
□ 599	Mike Lum	.03	.01	.00
□ 600	Randy Martz	.03	.01	.00
□ 601	Jerry Morales	.03	.01	.00
□ 602	Ken Reitz	.03	.01	.00
□ 603A	Lee Smith ERR (Cubs logo reversed)	1.25	.60	.12
□ 603B	Lee Smith COR	.65	.30	.06
□ 604	Dick Tidrow	.03	.01	.00
□ 605	Jim Tracy	.03	.01	.00
□ 606	Mike Tyson	.03	.01	.00
□ 607	Ty Waller	.03	.01	.00
□ 608	Danny Ainge	.15	.07	.01
□ 609	Jorge Bell	6.50	3.25	.65
□ 610	Mark Bomback	.03	.01	.00

☐ 611	Barry Bonnell	.03	.01	.00
☐ 612	Jim Clancy	.03	.01	.00
☐ 613	Damaso Garcia	.03	.01	.00
☐ 614	Jerry Garvin	.03	.01	.00
☐ 615	Alfredo Griffin	.06	.03	.00
☐ 616	Garth Iorg	.03	.01	.00
☐ 617	Luis Leal	.03	.01	.00
☐ 618	Ken Macha	.03	.01	.00
☐ 619	John Mayberry	.06	.03	.00
☐ 620	Joey McLaughlin	.03	.01	.00
☐ 621	Lloyd Moseby	.15	.07	.01
☐ 622	Dave Stieb	.20	.10	.02
☐ 623	Jackson Todd	.03	.01	.00
☐ 624	Willie Upshaw	.03	.01	.00
☐ 625	Otto Velez	.03	.01	.00
☐ 626	Ernie Whitt	.06	.03	.00
☐ 627	Alvis Woods	.03	.01	.00
☐ 628	All Star Game	.06	.03	.00
	Cleveland, Ohio			
☐ 629	All Star Infielders	.06	.03	.00
	Frank White and			
	Bucky Dent			
☐ 630	Big Red Machine	.08	.04	.01
	Dan Driessen			
	Dave Concepcion			
	George Foster			
☐ 631	Bruce Sutter	.08	.04	.01
	Top NL Relief Pitcher			
☐ 632	"Steve and Carlton"	.20	.10	.02
	Steve Carlton and			
	Carlton Fisk			
☐ 633	Carl Yastrzemski	.35	.17	.03
	3000th Game			
☐ 634	Dynamic Duo	.35	.17	.03
	Johnny Bench and			
	Tom Seaver			
☐ 635	West Meets East	.20	.10	.02
	Fernando Valenzuela			
	and Gary Carter			
☐ 636A	Fernando Valenzuela: ...	.60	.30	.06
	NL SO King ("he" NL)			
☐ 636B	Fernando Valenzuela: ...	.25	.12	.02
	NL SO King ("the" NL)			
☐ 637	Mike Schmidt	.35	.17	.03
	Home Run King			
☐ 638	NL All Stars	.15	.07	.01
	Gary Carter and			
	Dave Parker			
☐ 639	Perfect Game	.06	.03	.00
	Len Barker and			
	Bo Diaz			
	(catcher actually			
	Ron Hassey)			
☐ 640	Pete and Re-Pete	1.50	.75	.15
	Pete Rose and Son			
☐ 641	Phillies Finest	.35	.17	.03
	Lonnie Smith			
	Mike Schmidt			
	Steve Carlton			
☐ 642	Red Sox Reunion	.08	.04	.01
	Fred Lynn and			
	Dwight Evans			
☐ 643	Rickey Henderson	.30	.15	.03
	Most Hits and Runs			
☐ 644	Rollie Fingers	.10	.05	.01
	Most Saves AL			
☐ 645	Tom Seaver	.20	.10	.02
	Most 1981 Wins			
☐ 646A	Yankee Powerhouse	.75	.35	.07
	Reggie Jackson and			
	Dave Winfield			
	(comma on back			
	after outfielder)			
☐ 646B	Yankee Powerhouse	.40	.20	.04
	Reggie Jackson and			
	Dave Winfield			
	(no comma)			
☐ 647	CL: Yankees/Dodgers	.08	.01	.00
☐ 648	CL: A's/Reds	.07	.01	.00
☐ 649	CL: Cards/Brewers	.07	.01	.00
☐ 650	CL: Expos/Orioles	.07	.01	.00
☐ 651	CL: Astros/Phillies	.07	.01	.00
☐ 652	CL: Tigers/Red Sox	.07	.01	.00
☐ 653	CL: Rangers/White Sox .	.07	.01	.00
☐ 654	CL: Giants/Indians	.07	.01	.00
☐ 655	CL: Royals/Braves	.07	.01	.00
☐ 656	CL: Angels/Pirates	.07	.01	.00
☐ 657	CL: Mariners/Mets	.07	.01	.00
☐ 658	CL: Padres/Twins	.07	.01	.00
☐ 659	CL: Blue Jays/Cubs	.07	.01	.00
☐ 660	Specials Checklist	.10	.01	.00

1983 Fleer

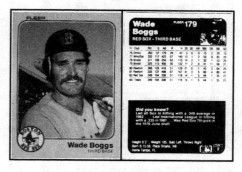

Wade Boggs
THIRD BASE

The cards in this 660-card set measure 2 1/2" by 3 1/2". In 1983, for the third straight year, Fleer has produced a baseball series numbering 660 cards. Of these, 1-628 are player cards, 629-646 are special cards, and 647-660 are checklist cards. The player cards are again ordered alphabetically within team. The team order relates back to each team's on-field performance during the previous year, i.e., World Champion Cardinals (1-25), AL Champion Brewers (26-51), Baltimore (52-75), California (76-103), Kansas City (104-128), Atlanta (129-152), Philadelphia (153- 176), Boston (177-200), Los Angeles (201-227), Chicago White Sox (228-251), San Francisco (252-276), Montreal (277-301), Pittsburgh (302-326), Detroit (327-351), San Diego (352- 375), New York Yankees (376-399), Cleveland (400-423), Toronto (424-444), Houston (445-469), Seattle (470-489), Chicago Cubs (490-512), Oakland (513-535), New York Mets (536-561), Texas (562-583), Cincinnati (584-606), and Minnesota (607-628). The front of each card has a colorful team logo at bottom left and the player's name and position at lower right. The reverses are done in shades of brown on white. The cards are numbered on the back next to a small black and white photo of the player.

		MINT	EXC	G-VG
COMPLETE SET (660)		65.00	32.50	6.50
COMMON PLAYER (1-660)		.03	.01	.00
☐	1 Joaquin Andujar	.12	.03	.01
☐	2 Doug Bair	.03	.01	.00
☐	3 Steve Braun	.03	.01	.00
☐	4 Glenn Brummer	.03	.01	.00
☐	5 Bob Forsch	.03	.01	.00
☐	6 David Green	.03	.01	.00
☐	7 George Hendrick	.06	.03	.00
☐	8 Keith Hernandez	.30	.15	.03
☐	9 Tom Herr	.08	.04	.01
☐	10 Dane Iorg	.03	.01	.00
☐	11 Jim Kaat	.12	.06	.01
☐	12 Jeff Lahti	.03	.01	.00
☐	13 Tito Landrum	.03	.01	.00
☐	14 Dave LaPoint	.35	.17	.03
☐	15 Willie McGee	1.25	.60	.12
☐	16 Steve Mura	.03	.01	.00
☐	17 Ken Oberkfell	.03	.01	.00
☐	18 Darrell Porter	.03	.01	.00
☐	19 Mike Ramsey	.03	.01	.00
☐	20 Gene Roof	.03	.01	.00
☐	21 Lonnie Smith	.10	.05	.01
☐	22 Ozzie Smith	.35	.17	.03
☐	23 John Stuper	.03	.01	.00
☐	24 Bruce Sutter	.12	.06	.01
☐	25 Gene Tenace	.03	.01	.00
☐	26 Jerry Augustine	.03	.01	.00
☐	27 Dwight Bernard	.03	.01	.00
☐	28 Mark Brouhard	.03	.01	.00
☐	29 Mike Caldwell	.03	.01	.00
☐	30 Cecil Cooper	.10	.05	.01
☐	31 Jamie Easterly	.03	.01	.00
☐	32 Marshall Edwards	.03	.01	.00

☐	33	Rollie Fingers	.18	.09	.01	☐	127	Frank White	.08	.04	.01
☐	34	Jim Gantner	.03	.01	.00	☐	128	Willie Wilson	.12	.06	.01
☐	35	Moose Haas	.03	.01	.00	☐	129	Steve Bedrosian	.40	.20	.04
☐	36	Roy Howell	.03	.01	.00	☐	130	Bruce Benedict	.03	.01	.00
☐	37	Pete Ladd	.03	.01	.00	☐	131	Tommy Boggs	.03	.01	.00
☐	38	Bob McClure	.03	.01	.00	☐	132	Brett Butler	.10	.05	.01
☐	39	Doc Medich	.03	.01	.00	☐	133	Rick Camp	.03	.01	.00
☐	40	Paul Molitor	.18	.09	.01	☐	134	Chris Chambliss	.06	.03	.00
☐	41	Don Money	.03	.01	.00	☐	135	Ken Dayley	.06	.03	.00
☐	42	Charlie Moore	.03	.01	.00	☐	136	Gene Garber	.03	.01	.00
☐	43	Ben Oglivie	.06	.03	.00	☐	137	Terry Harper	.03	.01	.00
☐	44	Ed Romero	.03	.01	.00	☐	138	Bob Horner	.15	.07	.01
☐	45	Ted Simmons	.12	.06	.01	☐	139	Glenn Hubbard	.03	.01	.00
☐	46	Jim Slaton	.03	.01	.00	☐	140	Rufino Linares	.03	.01	.00
☐	47	Don Sutton	.30	.15	.03	☐	141	Rick Mahler	.03	.01	.00
☐	48	Gorman Thomas	.08	.04	.01	☐	142	Dale Murphy	.85	.40	.08
☐	49	Pete Vuckovich	.06	.03	.00	☐	143	Phil Niekro	.25	.12	.02
☐	50	Ned Yost	.03	.01	.00	☐	144	Pascual Perez	.10	.05	.01
☐	51	Robin Yount	.65	.30	.06	☐	145	Biff Pocoroba	.03	.01	.00
☐	52	Benny Ayala	.03	.01	.00	☐	146	Rafael Ramirez	.03	.01	.00
☐	53	Bob Bonner	.03	.01	.00	☐	147	Jerry Royster	.03	.01	.00
☐	54	Al Bumbry	.03	.01	.00	☐	148	Ken Smith	.03	.01	.00
☐	55	Terry Crowley	.03	.01	.00	☐	149	Bob Walk	.06	.03	.00
☐	56	Storm Davis	.65	.30	.06	☐	150	Claudell Washington	.08	.04	.01
☐	57	Rich Dauer	.03	.01	.00	☐	151	Bob Watson	.06	.03	.00
☐	58	Rick Dempsey	.06	.03	.00	☐	152	Larry Whisenton	.03	.01	.00
		(posing batting lefty)				☐	153	Porfirio Altamirano	.03	.01	.00
☐	59	Jim Dwyer	.03	.01	.00	☐	154	Marty Bystrom	.03	.01	.00
☐	60	Mike Flanagan	.06	.03	.00	☐	155	Steve Carlton	.35	.17	.03
☐	61	Dan Ford	.03	.01	.00	☐	156	Larry Christenson	.03	.01	.00
☐	62	Glenn Gulliver	.03	.01	.00	☐	157	Ivan DeJesus	.03	.01	.00
☐	63	John Lowenstein	.03	.01	.00	☐	158	John Denny	.08	.04	.01
☐	64	Dennis Martinez	.06	.03	.00	☐	159	Bob Dernier	.03	.01	.00
☐	65	Tippy Martinez	.03	.01	.00	☐	160	Bo Diaz	.03	.01	.00
☐	66	Scott McGregor	.06	.03	.00	☐	161	Ed Farmer	.03	.01	.00
☐	67	Eddie Murray	.45	.22	.04	☐	162	Greg Gross	.03	.01	.00
☐	68	Joe Nolan	.03	.01	.00	☐	163	Mike Krukow	.06	.03	.00
☐	69	Jim Palmer	.45	.22	.04	☐	164	Garry Maddox	.03	.01	.00
☐	70	Cal Ripken Jr.	1.25	.60	.12	☐	165	Gary Matthews	.06	.03	.00
☐	71	Gary Roenicke	.03	.01	.00	☐	166	Tug McGraw	.10	.05	.01
☐	72	Lenn Sakata	.03	.01	.00	☐	167	Bob Molinaro	.03	.01	.00
☐	73	Ken Singleton	.08	.04	.01	☐	168	Sid Monge	.03	.01	.00
☐	74	Sammy Stewart	.03	.01	.00	☐	169	Ron Reed	.03	.01	.00
☐	75	Tim Stoddard	.03	.01	.00	☐	170	Bill Robinson	.03	.01	.00
☐	76	Don Aase	.03	.01	.00	☐	171	Pete Rose	1.00	.50	.10
☐	77	Don Baylor	.12	.06	.01	☐	172	Dick Ruthven	.03	.01	.00
☐	78	Juan Beniquez	.03	.01	.00	☐	173	Mike Schmidt	1.00	.50	.10
☐	79	Bob Boone	.15	.07	.01	☐	174	Manny Trillo	.03	.01	.00
☐	80	Rick Burleson	.06	.03	.00	☐	175	Ozzie Virgil	.03	.01	.00
☐	81	Rod Carew	.50	.22	.04	☐	176	George Vukovich	.03	.01	.00
☐	82	Bobby Clark	.03	.01	.00	☐	177	Gary Allenson	.03	.01	.00
☐	83	Doug Corbett	.03	.01	.00	☐	178	Luis Aponte	.03	.01	.00
☐	84	John Curtis	.03	.01	.00	☐	179	Wade Boggs	18.00	9.00	1.80
☐	85	Doug DeCinces	.06	.03	.00	☐	180	Tom Burgmeier	.03	.01	.00
☐	86	Brian Downing	.06	.03	.00	☐	181	Mark Clear	.03	.01	.00
☐	87	Joe Ferguson	.03	.01	.00	☐	182	Dennis Eckersley	.20	.10	.02
☐	88	Tim Foli	.03	.01	.00	☐	183	Dwight Evans	.18	.09	.01
☐	89	Ken Forsch	.03	.01	.00	☐	184	Rich Gedman	.08	.04	.01
☐	90	Dave Goltz	.03	.01	.00	☐	185	Glenn Hoffman	.03	.01	.00
☐	91	Bobby Grich	.06	.03	.00	☐	186	Bruce Hurst	.20	.10	.02
☐	92	Andy Hassler	.03	.01	.00	☐	187	Carney Lansford	.20	.07	.01
☐	93	Reggie Jackson	.50	.25	.05	☐	188	Rick Miller	.03	.01	.00
☐	94	Ron Jackson	.03	.01	.00	☐	189	Reid Nichols	.03	.01	.00
☐	95	Tommy John	.15	.07	.01	☐	190	Bob Ojeda	.10	.05	.01
☐	96	Bruce Kison	.03	.01	.00	☐	191	Tony Perez	.15	.07	.01
☐	97	Fred Lynn	.18	.09	.01	☐	192	Chuck Rainey	.03	.01	.00
☐	98	Ed Ott	.03	.01	.00	☐	193	Jerry Remy	.03	.01	.00
☐	99	Steve Renko	.03	.01	.00	☐	194	Jim Rice	.25	.12	.02
☐	100	Luis Sanchez	.03	.01	.00	☐	195	Bob Stanley	.03	.01	.00
☐	101	Rob Wilfong	.03	.01	.00	☐	196	Dave Stapleton	.03	.01	.00
☐	102	Mike Witt	.15	.07	.01	☐	197	Mike Torrez	.03	.01	.00
☐	103	Geoff Zahn	.03	.01	.00	☐	198	John Tudor	.12	.06	.01
☐	104	Willie Aikens	.03	.01	.00	☐	199	Julio Valdez	.03	.01	.00
☐	105	Mike Armstrong	.03	.01	.00	☐	200	Carl Yastrzemski	.80	.40	.08
☐	106	Vida Blue	.06	.03	.00	☐	201	Dusty Baker	.06	.03	.00
☐	107	Bud Black	.20	.10	.02	☐	202	Joe Beckwith	.03	.01	.00
☐	108	George Brett	.65	.30	.06	☐	203	Greg Brock	.30	.15	.03
☐	109	Bill Castro	.03	.01	.00	☐	204	Ron Cey	.10	.05	.01
☐	110	Onix Concepcion	.03	.01	.00	☐	205	Terry Forster	.06	.03	.00
☐	111	Dave Frost	.03	.01	.00	☐	206	Steve Garvey	.45	.22	.04
☐	112	Cesar Geronimo	.03	.01	.00	☐	207	Pedro Guerrero	.30	.15	.03
☐	113	Larry Gura	.03	.01	.00	☐	208	Burt Hooton	.03	.01	.00
☐	114	Steve Hammond	.03	.01	.00	☐	209	Steve Howe	.03	.01	.00
☐	115	Don Hood	.03	.01	.00	☐	210	Ken Landreaux	.03	.01	.00
☐	116	Dennis Leonard	.06	.03	.00	☐	211	Mike Marshall	.25	.12	.02
☐	117	Jerry Martin	.03	.01	.00	☐	212	Candy Maldonado	.45	.22	.04
☐	118	Lee May	.06	.03	.00	☐	213	Rick Monday	.06	.03	.00
☐	119	Hal McRae	.06	.03	.00	☐	214	Tom Niedenfuer	.03	.01	.00
☐	120	Amos Otis	.08	.04	.01	☐	215	Jorge Orta	.03	.01	.00
☐	121	Greg Pryor	.03	.01	.00	☐	216	Jerry Reuss	.06	.03	.00
☐	122	Dan Quisenberry	.12	.06	.01	☐	217	Ron Roenicke	.03	.01	.00
☐	123	Don Slaught	.30	.15	.03	☐	218	Vicente Romo	.03	.01	.00
☐	124	Paul Splittorff	.03	.01	.00	☐	219	Bill Russell	.06	.03	.00
☐	125	U.L. Washington	.03	.01	.00	☐	220	Steve Sax	.50	.25	.05
☐	126	John Wathan	.06	.03	.00	☐	221	Mike Scioscia	.06	.03	.00

☐ 222	Dave Stewart	.50	.25	.05	☐ 317	Johnny Ray	.15	.07	.01
☐ 223	Derrel Thomas	.03	.01	.00	☐ 318	Rick Rhoden	.06	.03	.00
☐ 224	Fernando Valenzuela	.30	.15	.03	☐ 319	Don Robinson	.03	.01	.00
☐ 225	Bob Welch	.08	.04	.01	☐ 320	Enrique Romo	.03	.01	.00
☐ 226	Ricky Wright	.03	.01	.00	☐ 321	Manny Sarmiento	.03	.01	.00
☐ 227	Steve Yeager	.03	.01	.00	☐ 322	Rod Scurry	.03	.01	.00
☐ 228	Bill Almon	.03	.01	.00	☐ 323	Jimmy Smith	.03	.01	.00
☐ 229	Harold Baines	.25	.12	.02	☐ 324	Willie Stargell	.35	.17	.03
☐ 230	Salome Barojas	.03	.01	.00	☐ 325	Jason Thompson	.03	.01	.00
☐ 231	Tony Bernazard	.03	.01	.00	☐ 326	Kent Tekulve	.06	.03	.00
☐ 232	Britt Burns	.03	.01	.00	☐ 327	Tom Brookens	.03	.01	.00
☐ 233	Richard Dotson	.06	.03	.00	☐ 328	Enos Cabell	.03	.01	.00
☐ 234	Ernesto Escarrega	.03	.01	.00	☐ 329	Kirk Gibson	.40	.20	.04
☐ 235	Carlton Fisk	.30	.15	.03	☐ 330	Larry Herndon	.03	.01	.00
☐ 236	Jerry Hairston	.03	.01	.00	☐ 331	Mike Ivie	.03	.01	.00
☐ 237	Kevin Hickey	.03	.01	.00	☐ 332	Howard Johnson	9.00	4.50	.90
☐ 238	LaMarr Hoyt	.06	.03	.00	☐ 333	Lynn Jones	.03	.01	.00
☐ 239	Steve Kemp	.06	.03	.00	☐ 334	Rick Leach	.03	.01	.00
☐ 240	Jim Kern	.03	.01	.00	☐ 335	Chet Lemon	.06	.03	.00
☐ 241	Ron Kittle	1.00	.50	.10	☐ 336	Jack Morris	.20	.10	.02
☐ 242	Jerry Koosman	.08	.04	.01	☐ 337	Lance Parrish	.20	.10	.02
☐ 243	Dennis Lamp	.03	.01	.00	☐ 338	Larry Pashnick	.03	.01	.00
☐ 244	Rudy Law	.03	.01	.00	☐ 339	Dan Petry	.03	.01	.00
☐ 245	Vance Law	.06	.03	.00	☐ 340	Dave Rozema	.03	.01	.00
☐ 246	Ron LeFlore	.06	.03	.00	☐ 341	Dave Rucker	.03	.01	.00
☐ 247	Greg Luzinski	.10	.05	.01	☐ 342	Elias Sosa	.03	.01	.00
☐ 248	Tom Paciorek	.03	.01	.00	☐ 343	Dave Tobik	.03	.01	.00
☐ 249	Aurelio Rodriguez	.03	.01	.00	☐ 344	Alan Trammell	.30	.15	.03
☐ 250	Mike Squires	.03	.01	.00	☐ 345	Jerry Turner	.03	.01	.00
☐ 251	Steve Trout	.03	.01	.00	☐ 346	Jerry Ujdur	.03	.01	.00
☐ 252	Jim Barr	.03	.01	.00	☐ 347	Pat Underwood	.03	.01	.00
☐ 253	Dave Bergman	.03	.01	.00	☐ 348	Lou Whitaker	.25	.12	.02
☐ 254	Fred Breining	.03	.01	.00	☐ 349	Milt Wilcox	.03	.01	.00
☐ 255	Bob Brenly	.03	.01	.00	☐ 350	Glenn Wilson	.35	.17	.03
☐ 256	Jack Clark	.25	.12	.02	☐ 351	John Wockenfuss	.03	.01	.00
☐ 257	Chili Davis	.25	.12	.02	☐ 352	Kurt Bevacqua	.03	.01	.00
☐ 258	Darrell Evans	.10	.05	.01	☐ 353	Juan Bonilla	.03	.01	.00
☐ 259	Alan Fowlkes	.03	.01	.00	☐ 354	Floyd Chiffer	.03	.01	.00
☐ 260	Rich Gale	.03	.01	.00	☐ 355	Luis DeLeon	.03	.01	.00
☐ 261	Atlee Hammaker	.03	.01	.00	☐ 356	Dave Dravecky	.75	.35	.07
☐ 262	Al Holland	.03	.01	.00	☐ 357	Dave Edwards	.03	.01	.00
☐ 263	Duane Kuiper	.03	.01	.00	☐ 358	Juan Eichelberger	.03	.01	.00
☐ 264	Bill Laskey	.03	.01	.00	☐ 359	Tim Flannery	.03	.01	.00
☐ 265	Gary Lavelle	.03	.01	.00	☐ 360	Tony Gwynn	12.50	6.00	1.20
☐ 266	Johnnie LeMaster	.03	.01	.00	☐ 361	Ruppert Jones	.03	.01	.00
☐ 267	Renie Martin	.03	.01	.00	☐ 362	Terry Kennedy	.03	.01	.00
☐ 268	Milt May	.03	.01	.00	☐ 363	Joe Lefebvre	.03	.01	.00
☐ 269	Greg Minton	.03	.01	.00	☐ 364	Sixto Lezcano	.03	.01	.00
☐ 270	Joe Morgan	.30	.15	.03	☐ 365	Tim Lollar	.03	.01	.00
☐ 271	Tom O'Malley	.06	.03	.00	☐ 366	Gary Lucas	.03	.01	.00
☐ 272	Reggie Smith	.06	.03	.00	☐ 367	John Montefusco	.03	.01	.00
☐ 273	Guy Sularz	.03	.01	.00	☐ 368	Broderick Perkins	.03	.01	.00
☐ 274	Champ Summers	.03	.01	.00	☐ 369	Joe Pittman	.03	.01	.00
☐ 275	Max Venable	.03	.01	.00	☐ 370	Gene Richards	.03	.01	.00
☐ 276	Jim Wohlford	.03	.01	.00	☐ 371	Luis Salazar	.03	.01	.00
☐ 277	Ray Burris	.03	.01	.00	☐ 372	Eric Show	.35	.17	.03
☐ 278	Gary Carter	.30	.15	.03	☐ 373	Garry Templeton	.08	.04	.01
☐ 279	Warren Cromartie	.03	.01	.00	☐ 374	Chris Welsh	.03	.01	.00
☐ 280	Andre Dawson	.35	.17	.03	☐ 375	Alan Wiggins	.10	.05	.01
☐ 281	Terry Francona	.03	.01	.00	☐ 376	Rick Cerone	.03	.01	.00
☐ 282	Doug Flynn	.03	.01	.00	☐ 377	Dave Collins	.03	.01	.00
☐ 283	Woodie Fryman	.03	.01	.00	☐ 378	Roger Erickson	.03	.01	.00
☐ 284	Bill Gullickson	.03	.01	.00	☐ 379	George Frazier	.03	.01	.00
☐ 285	Wallace Johnson	.06	.03	.00	☐ 380	Oscar Gamble	.03	.01	.00
☐ 286	Charlie Lea	.03	.01	.00	☐ 381	Goose Gossage	.15	.07	.01
☐ 287	Randy Lerch	.03	.01	.00	☐ 382	Ken Griffey	.10	.05	.01
☐ 288	Brad Mills	.03	.01	.00	☐ 383	Ron Guidry	.18	.09	.01
☐ 289	Dan Norman	.03	.01	.00	☐ 384	Dave LaRoche	.03	.01	.00
☐ 290	Al Oliver	.08	.04	.01	☐ 385	Rudy May	.03	.01	.00
☐ 291	David Palmer	.03	.01	.00	☐ 386	John Mayberry	.06	.03	.00
☐ 292	Tim Raines	.50	.25	.05	☐ 387	Lee Mazzilli	.03	.01	.00
☐ 293	Jeff Reardon	.12	.06	.01	☐ 388	Mike Morgan	.06	.03	.00
☐ 294	Steve Rogers	.03	.01	.00	☐ 389	Jerry Mumphrey	.03	.01	.00
☐ 295	Scott Sanderson	.03	.01	.00	☐ 390	Bobby Murcer	.10	.05	.01
☐ 296	Dan Schatzeder	.03	.01	.00	☐ 391	Graig Nettles	.12	.06	.01
☐ 297	Bryn Smith	.50	.25	.05	☐ 392	Lou Piniella	.10	.05	.01
☐ 298	Chris Speier	.03	.01	.00	☐ 393	Willie Randolph	.08	.04	.01
☐ 299	Tim Wallach	.18	.09	.01	☐ 394	Shane Rawley	.06	.03	.00
☐ 300	Jerry White	.03	.01	.00	☐ 395	Dave Righetti	.25	.12	.02
☐ 301	Joel Youngblood	.03	.01	.00	☐ 396	Andre Robertson	.03	.01	.00
☐ 302	Ross Baumgarten	.03	.01	.00	☐ 397	Roy Smalley	.03	.01	.00
☐ 303	Dale Berra	.03	.01	.00	☐ 398	Dave Winfield	.40	.20	.04
☐ 304	John Candelaria	.06	.03	.00	☐ 399	Butch Wynegar	.03	.01	.00
☐ 305	Dick Davis	.03	.01	.00	☐ 400	Chris Bando	.03	.01	.00
☐ 306	Mike Easler	.03	.01	.00	☐ 401	Alan Bannister	.03	.01	.00
☐ 307	Richie Hebner	.03	.01	.00	☐ 402	Len Barker	.03	.01	.00
☐ 308	Lee Lacy	.03	.01	.00	☐ 403	Tom Brennan	.03	.01	.00
☐ 309	Bill Madlock	.08	.04	.01	☐ 404	Carmelo Castillo	.06	.03	.00
☐ 310	Larry McWilliams	.03	.01	.00	☐ 405	Miguel Dilone	.03	.01	.00
☐ 311	John Milner	.03	.01	.00	☐ 406	Jerry Dybzinski	.03	.01	.00
☐ 312	Omar Moreno	.03	.01	.00	☐ 407	Mike Fischlin	.03	.01	.00
☐ 313	Jim Morrison	.03	.01	.00	☐ 408	Ed Glynn UER	.03	.01	.00
☐ 314	Steve Nicosia	.03	.01	.00		(photo actually			
☐ 315	Dave Parker	.18	.09	.01		Bud Anderson)			
☐ 316	Tony Pena	.15	.07	.01	☐ 409	Mike Hargrove	.06	.03	.00

□	#	Name			
□	410	Toby Harrah	.06	.03	.00
□	411	Ron Hassey	.03	.01	.00
□	412	Von Hayes	.18	.09	.01
□	413	Rick Manning	.03	.01	.00
□	414	Bake McBride	.03	.01	.00
□	415	Larry Milbourne	.03	.01	.00
□	416	Bill Nahorodny	.03	.01	.00
□	417	Jack Perconte	.03	.01	.00
□	418	Lary Sorensen	.03	.01	.00
□	419	Dan Spillner	.03	.01	.00
□	420	Rick Sutcliffe	.15	.07	.01
□	421	Andre Thornton	.06	.03	.00
□	422	Rick Waits	.03	.01	.00
□	423	Eddie Whitson	.06	.03	.00
□	424	Jesse Barfield	.75	.35	.07
□	425	Barry Bonnell	.03	.01	.00
□	426	Jim Clancy	.03	.01	.00
□	427	Damaso Garcia	.03	.01	.00
□	428	Jerry Garvin	.03	.01	.00
□	429	Alfredo Griffin	.06	.03	.00
□	430	Garth Iorg	.03	.01	.00
□	431	Roy Lee Jackson	.03	.01	.00
□	432	Luis Leal	.03	.01	.00
□	433	Buck Martinez	.03	.01	.00
□	434	Joey McLaughlin	.03	.01	.00
□	435	Lloyd Moseby	.10	.05	.01
□	436	Rance Mulliniks	.03	.01	.00
□	437	Dale Murray	.03	.01	.00
□	438	Wayne Nordhagen	.03	.01	.00
□	439	Geno Petralli	.15	.07	.01
□	440	Hosken Powell	.03	.01	.00
□	441	Dave Stieb	.15	.07	.01
□	442	Willie Upshaw	.03	.01	.00
□	443	Ernie Whitt	.06	.03	.00
□	444	Alvis Woods	.03	.01	.00
□	445	Alan Ashby	.03	.01	.00
□	446	Jose Cruz	.08	.04	.01
□	447	Kiko Garcia	.03	.01	.00
□	448	Phil Garner	.03	.01	.00
□	449	Danny Heep	.03	.01	.00
□	450	Art Howe	.08	.04	.01
□	451	Bob Knepper	.06	.03	.00
□	452	Alan Knicely	.03	.01	.00
□	453	Ray Knight	.08	.04	.01
□	454	Frank LaCorte	.03	.01	.00
□	455	Mike LaCoss	.03	.01	.00
□	456	Randy Moffitt	.03	.01	.00
□	457	Joe Niekro	.10	.05	.01
□	458	Terry Puhl	.03	.01	.00
□	459	Luis Pujols	.03	.01	.00
□	460	Craig Reynolds	.03	.01	.00
□	461	Bert Roberge	.03	.01	.00
□	462	Vern Ruhle	.03	.01	.00
□	463	Nolan Ryan	1.25	.60	.12
□	464	Joe Sambito	.03	.01	.00
□	465	Tony Scott	.03	.01	.00
□	466	Dave Smith	.06	.03	.00
□	467	Harry Spilman	.03	.01	.00
□	468	Dickie Thon	.03	.01	.00
□	469	Denny Walling	.03	.01	.00
□	470	Larry Andersen	.03	.01	.00
□	471	Floyd Bannister	.03	.01	.00
□	472	Jim Beattie	.03	.01	.00
□	473	Bruce Bochte	.03	.01	.00
□	474	Manny Castillo	.03	.01	.00
□	475	Bill Caudill	.03	.01	.00
□	476	Bryan Clark	.03	.01	.00
□	477	Al Cowens	.03	.01	.00
□	478	Julio Cruz	.03	.01	.00
□	479	Todd Cruz	.03	.01	.00
□	480	Gary Gray	.03	.01	.00
□	481	Dave Henderson	.35	.17	.03
□	482	Mike Moore	1.50	.75	.15
□	483	Gaylord Perry	.25	.12	.02
□	484	Dave Revering	.03	.01	.00
□	485	Joe Simpson	.03	.01	.00
□	486	Mike Stanton	.03	.01	.00
□	487	Rick Sweet	.03	.01	.00
□	488	Ed VandeBerg	.03	.01	.00
□	489	Richie Zisk	.03	.01	.00
□	490	Doug Bird	.03	.01	.00
□	491	Larry Bowa	.10	.05	.01
□	492	Bill Buckner	.10	.05	.01
□	493	Bill Campbell	.03	.01	.00
□	494	Jody Davis	.08	.04	.01
□	495	Leon Durham	.06	.03	.00
□	496	Steve Henderson	.03	.01	.00
□	497	Willie Hernandez	.10	.05	.01
□	498	Ferguson Jenkins	.15	.07	.01
□	499	Jay Johnstone	.06	.03	.00
□	500	Junior Kennedy	.03	.01	.00
□	501	Randy Martz	.03	.01	.00
□	502	Jerry Morales	.03	.01	.00
□	503	Keith Moreland	.03	.01	.00
□	504	Dickie Noles	.03	.01	.00
□	505	Mike Proly	.03	.01	.00
□	506	Allen Ripley	.03	.01	.00
□	507	Ryne Sandberg	8.00	4.00	.80
□	508	Lee Smith	.10	.05	.01
□	509	Pat Tabler	.30	.15	.03
□	510	Dick Tidrow	.03	.01	.00
□	511	Bump Wills	.03	.01	.00
□	512	Gary Woods	.03	.01	.00
□	513	Tony Armas	.06	.03	.00
□	514	Dave Beard	.03	.01	.00
□	515	Jeff Burroughs	.06	.03	.00
□	516	John D'Acquisto	.03	.01	.00
□	517	Wayne Gross	.03	.01	.00
□	518	Mike Heath	.03	.01	.00
□	519	Rickey Henderson	.90	.45	.09
□	520	Cliff Johnson	.03	.01	.00
□	521	Matt Keough	.03	.01	.00
□	522	Brian Kingman	.03	.01	.00
□	523	Rick Langford	.03	.01	.00
□	524	Dave Lopes	.08	.04	.01
□	525	Steve McCatty	.03	.01	.00
□	526	Dave McKay	.03	.01	.00
□	527	Dan Meyer	.03	.01	.00
□	528	Dwayne Murphy	.03	.01	.00
□	529	Jeff Newman	.03	.01	.00
□	530	Mike Norris	.03	.01	.00
□	531	Bob Owchinko	.03	.01	.00
□	532	Joe Rudi	.06	.03	.00
□	533	Jimmy Sexton	.03	.01	.00
□	534	Fred Stanley	.03	.01	.00
□	535	Tom Underwood	.03	.01	.00
□	536	Neil Allen	.03	.01	.00
□	537	Wally Backman	.08	.04	.01
□	538	Bob Bailor	.03	.01	.00
□	539	Hubie Brooks	.10	.05	.01
□	540	Carlos Diaz	.03	.01	.00
□	541	Pete Falcone	.03	.01	.00
□	542	George Foster	.12	.06	.01
□	543	Ron Gardenhire	.03	.01	.00
□	544	Brian Giles	.03	.01	.00
□	545	Ron Hodges	.03	.01	.00
□	546	Randy Jones	.03	.01	.00
□	547	Mike Jorgensen	.03	.01	.00
□	548	Dave Kingman	.12	.06	.01
□	549	Ed Lynch	.03	.01	.00
□	550	Jesse Orosco	.03	.01	.00
□	551	Rick Ownbey	.03	.01	.00
□	552	Charlie Puleo	.03	.01	.00
□	553	Gary Rajsich	.03	.01	.00
□	554	Mike Scott	.30	.15	.03
□	555	Rusty Staub	.10	.05	.01
□	556	John Stearns	.03	.01	.00
□	557	Craig Swan	.03	.01	.00
□	558	Ellis Valentine	.03	.01	.00
□	559	Tom Veryzer	.03	.01	.00
□	560	Mookie Wilson	.10	.05	.01
□	561	Pat Zachry	.03	.01	.00
□	562	Buddy Bell	.10	.05	.01
□	563	John Butcher	.03	.01	.00
□	564	Steve Comer	.03	.01	.00
□	565	Danny Darwin	.03	.01	.00
□	566	Bucky Dent	.10	.05	.01
□	567	John Grubb	.03	.01	.00
□	568	Rick Honeycutt	.03	.01	.00
□	569	Dave Hostetler	.06	.03	.00
□	570	Charlie Hough	.06	.03	.00
□	571	Lamar Johnson	.03	.01	.00
□	572	Jon Matlack	.03	.01	.00
□	573	Paul Mirabella	.03	.01	.00
□	574	Larry Parrish	.06	.03	.00
□	575	Mike Richardt	.03	.01	.00
□	576	Mickey Rivers	.06	.03	.00
□	577	Billy Sample	.03	.01	.00
□	578	Dave Schmidt	.15	.07	.01
□	579	Bill Stein	.03	.01	.00
□	580	Jim Sundberg	.03	.01	.00
□	581	Frank Tanana	.08	.04	.01
□	582	Mark Wagner	.03	.01	.00
□	583	George Wright	.03	.01	.00
□	584	Johnny Bench	.60	.30	.06
□	585	Bruce Berenyi	.03	.01	.00
□	586	Larry Biittner	.03	.01	.00
□	587	Cesar Cedeno	.08	.04	.01
□	588	Dave Concepcion	.10	.05	.01
□	589	Dan Driessen	.03	.01	.00
□	590	Greg Harris	.03	.01	.00
□	591	Ben Hayes	.03	.01	.00
□	592	Paul Householder	.03	.01	.00
□	593	Tom Hume	.03	.01	.00
□	594	Wayne Krenchicki	.03	.01	.00
□	595	Rafael Landestoy	.03	.01	.00
□	596	Charlie Leibrandt	.03	.01	.00
□	597	Eddie Milner	.08	.04	.01
□	598	Ron Oester	.03	.01	.00
□	599	Frank Pastore	.03	.01	.00

□ 600	Joe Price	.03	.01	.00
□ 601	Tom Seaver	.40	.20	.04
□ 602	Bob Shirley	.03	.01	.00
□ 603	Mario Soto	.06	.03	.00
□ 604	Alex Trevino	.03	.01	.00
□ 605	Mike Vail	.03	.01	.00
□ 606	Duane Walker	.03	.01	.00
□ 607	Tom Brunansky	.60	.30	.06
□ 608	Bobby Castillo	.03	.01	.00
□ 609	John Castino	.03	.01	.00
□ 610	Ron Davis	.03	.01	.00
□ 611	Lenny Faedo	.03	.01	.00
□ 612	Terry Felton	.03	.01	.00
□ 613	Gary Gaetti	3.00	1.50	.30
□ 614	Mickey Hatcher	.06	.03	.00
□ 615	Brad Havens	.03	.01	.00
□ 616	Kent Hrbek	1.25	.60	.12
□ 617	Randy Johnson	.03	.01	.00
□ 618	Tim Laudner	.06	.03	.00
□ 619	Jeff Little	.03	.01	.00
□ 620	Bobby Mitchell	.03	.01	.00
□ 621	Jack O'Connor	.03	.01	.00
□ 622	John Pacella	.03	.01	.00
□ 623	Pete Redfern	.03	.01	.00
□ 624	Jesus Vega	.03	.01	.00
□ 625	Frank Viola	3.75	1.85	.37
□ 626	Ron Washington	.06	.03	.00
□ 627	Gary Ward	.06	.03	.00
□ 628	Al Williams	.03	.01	.00
□ 629	Red Sox All-Stars Carl Yastrzemski Dennis Eckersley Mark Clear	.25	.12	.02
□ 630	"300 Career Wins" Gaylord Perry and Terry Bulling 5/6/82	.10	.05	.01
□ 631	Pride of Venezuela Dave Concepcion and Manny Trillo	.06	.03	.00
□ 632	All-Star Infielders Robin Yount and Buddy Bell	.15	.07	.01
□ 633	Mr.Vet and Mr.Rookie Dave Winfield and Kent Hrbek	.20	.10	.02
□ 634	Fountain of Youth Willie Stargell and Pete Rose	.60	.30	.06
□ 635	Big Chiefs Toby Harrah and Andre Thornton	.06	.03	.00
□ 636	Smith Brothers Ozzie and Lonnie	.08	.04	.01
□ 637	Base Stealers' Threat Bo Diaz and Gary Carter	.10	.05	.01
□ 638	All-Star Catchers Carlton Fisk and Gary Carter	.12	.06	.01
□ 639	The Silver Shoe Rickey Henderson	.30	.15	.03
□ 640	Home Run Threats Ben Oglivie and Reggie Jackson	.18	.09	.01
□ 641	Two Teams Same Day Joel Youngblood August 4, 1982	.06	.03	.00
□ 642	Last Perfect Game Ron Hassey and Len Barker	.06	.03	.00
□ 643	Black and Blue Bud Black	.06	.03	.00
□ 644	Black and Blue Vida Blue	.06	.03	.00
□ 645	Speed and Power Reggie Jackson	.25	.12	.02
□ 646	Speed and Power Rickey Henderson	.30	.15	.03
□ 647	CL: Cards/Brewers	.07	.01	.00
□ 648	CL: Orioles/Angels	.07	.01	.00
□ 649	CL: Royals/Braves	.07	.01	.00
□ 650	CL: Phillies/Red Sox	.07	.01	.00
□ 651	CL: Dodgers/White Sox	.07	.01	.00
□ 652	CL: Giants/Expos	.07	.01	.00
□ 653	CL: Pirates/Tigers	.07	.01	.00
□ 654	CL: Padres/Yankees	.07	.01	.00
□ 655	CL: Indians/Blue Jays	.07	.01	.00
□ 656	CL: Astros/Mariners	.07	.01	.00
□ 657	CL: Cubs/A's	.07	.01	.00
□ 658	CL: Mets/Rangers	.07	.01	.00
□ 659	CL: Reds/Twins	.07	.01	.00
□ 660	CL: Specials/Teams	.09	.01	.00

1984 Fleer

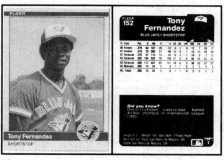

The cards in this 660-card set measure 2 1/2" by 3 1/2". The 1984 Fleer card set featured fronts with full-color team logos along with the player's name and position and the Fleer identification. The set features many imaginative photos, several multi-player cards, and many more action shots than the 1983 card set. The backs are quite similar to the 1983 backs except that blue rather than brown ink is used. The player cards are alphabetized within team and the teams are ordered by their 1983 season finish and won-lost record, e.g., Baltimore (1-23), Philadelphia (24-49), Chicago White Sox (50-73), Detroit (74-95), Los Angeles (96-118), New York Yankees (119-144), Toronto (145-169), Atlanta (170-193), Milwaukee (194-219), Houston (220-244), Pittsburgh (245-269), Montreal (270-293), San Diego (294-317), St. Louis (318-340), Kansas City (341-364), San Francisco (365-387), Boston (388-412), Texas (413-435), Oakland (436-461), Cincinnati (462-485), Chicago (486-507), California (508-532), Cleveland (533-555), Minnesota (556-579), New York Mets (580-603), and Seattle (604-625). Specials (626-646) and checklist cards (647-660) make up the end of the set.

		MINT	EXC	G-VG
COMPLETE SET (660)		135.00	60.00	12.00
COMMON PLAYER (1-660)		.06	.03	.00
□	1 Mike Boddicker	.20	.04	.01
□	2 Al Bumbry	.06	.03	.00
□	3 Todd Cruz	.06	.03	.00
□	4 Rich Dauer	.06	.03	.00
□	5 Storm Davis	.15	.07	.01
□	6 Rick Dempsey	.06	.03	.00
□	7 Jim Dwyer	.06	.03	.00
□	8 Mike Flanagan	.10	.05	.01
□	9 Dan Ford	.06	.03	.00
□	10 John Lowenstein	.06	.03	.00
□	11 Dennis Martinez	.10	.05	.01
□	12 Tippy Martinez	.06	.03	.00
□	13 Scott McGregor	.10	.05	.01
□	14 Eddie Murray	.55	.27	.05
□	15 Joe Nolan	.06	.03	.00
□	16 Jim Palmer	.50	.25	.05
□	17 Cal Ripken	1.00	.50	.10
□	18 Gary Roenicke	.06	.03	.00
□	19 Lenn Sakata	.06	.03	.00
□	20 John Shelby	.35	.17	.03
□	21 Ken Singleton	.10	.05	.01
□	22 Sammy Stewart	.06	.03	.00
□	23 Tim Stoddard	.06	.03	.00
□	24 Marty Bystrom	.06	.03	.00
□	25 Steve Carlton	.50	.25	.05
□	26 Ivan DeJesus	.06	.03	.00
□	27 John Denny	.10	.05	.01
□	28 Bob Dernier	.06	.03	.00
□	29 Bo Diaz	.06	.03	.00
□	30 Kiko Garcia	.06	.03	.00
□	31 Greg Gross	.06	.03	.00
□	32 Kevin Gross	.35	.17	.03
□	33 Von Hayes	.20	.10	.02
□	34 Willie Hernandez	.20	.10	.02

□	#	Player			
□	35	Al Holland	.06	.03	.00
□	36	Charles Hudson	.25	.12	.02
□	37	Joe Lefebvre	.06	.03	.00
□	38	Sixto Lezcano	.06	.03	.00
□	39	Garry Maddox	.06	.03	.00
□	40	Gary Matthews	.10	.05	.01
□	41	Len Matuszek	.06	.03	.00
□	42	Tug McGraw	.10	.05	.01
□	43	Joe Morgan	.35	.17	.03
□	44	Tony Perez	.25	.12	.02
□	45	Ron Reed	.06	.03	.00
□	46	Pete Rose	1.25	.60	.12
□	47	Juan Samuel	3.50	1.75	.35
□	48	Mike Schmidt	2.25	1.10	.22
□	49	Ozzie Virgil	.06	.03	.00
□	50	Juan Agosto	.20	.10	.02
□	51	Harold Baines	.25	.12	.02
□	52	Floyd Bannister	.06	.03	.00
□	53	Salome Barojas	.06	.03	.00
□	54	Britt Burns	.06	.03	.00
□	55	Julio Cruz	.06	.03	.00
□	56	Richard Dotson	.10	.05	.01
□	57	Jerry Dybzinski	.06	.03	.00
□	58	Carlton Fisk	.40	.20	.04
□	59	Scott Fletcher	.25	.12	.02
□	60	Jerry Hairston	.06	.03	.00
□	61	Kevin Hickey	.06	.03	.00
□	62	Marc Hill	.06	.03	.00
□	63	LaMarr Hoyt	.10	.05	.01
□	64	Ron Kittle	.20	.10	.02
□	65	Jerry Koosman	.10	.05	.01
□	66	Dennis Lamp	.06	.03	.00
□	67	Rudy Law	.06	.03	.00
□	68	Vance Law	.10	.05	.01
□	69	Greg Luzinski	.10	.05	.01
□	70	Tom Paciorek	.06	.03	.00
□	71	Mike Squires	.06	.03	.00
□	72	Dick Tidrow	.06	.03	.00
□	73	Greg Walker	.45	.22	.04
□	74	Glenn Abbott	.06	.03	.00
□	75	Howard Bailey	.06	.03	.00
□	76	Doug Bair	.06	.03	.00
□	77	Juan Berenguer	.06	.03	.00
□	78	Tom Brookens	.06	.03	.00
□	79	Enos Cabell	.06	.03	.00
□	80	Kirk Gibson	.45	.22	.04
□	81	John Grubb	.06	.03	.00
□	82	Larry Herndon	.06	.03	.00
□	83	Wayne Krenchicki	.06	.03	.00
□	84	Rick Leach	.06	.03	.00
□	85	Chet Lemon	.10	.05	.01
□	86	Aurelio Lopez	.06	.03	.00
□	87	Jack Morris	.20	.10	.02
□	88	Lance Parrish	.25	.12	.02
□	89	Dan Petry	.06	.03	.00
□	90	Dave Rozema	.06	.03	.00
□	91	Alan Trammell	.40	.20	.04
□	92	Lou Whitaker	.30	.15	.03
□	93	Milt Wilcox	.06	.03	.00
□	94	Glenn Wilson	.10	.05	.01
□	95	John Wockenfuss	.06	.03	.00
□	96	Dusty Baker	.10	.05	.01
□	97	Joe Beckwith	.06	.03	.00
□	98	Greg Brock	.10	.05	.01
□	99	Jack Fimple	.06	.03	.00
□	100	Pedro Guerrero	.40	.20	.04
□	101	Rick Honeycutt	.06	.03	.00
□	102	Burt Hooton	.06	.03	.00
□	103	Steve Howe	.06	.03	.00
□	104	Ken Landreaux	.06	.03	.00
□	105	Mike Marshall	.20	.10	.02
□	106	Rick Monday	.10	.05	.01
□	107	Jose Morales	.06	.03	.00
□	108	Tom Niedenfuer	.10	.05	.01
□	109	Alejandro Pena	.40	.20	.04
□	110	Jerry Reuss	.10	.05	.01
□	111	Bill Russell	.10	.05	.01
□	112	Steve Sax	.35	.17	.03
□	113	Mike Scioscia	.10	.05	.01
□	114	Derrel Thomas	.06	.03	.00
□	115	Fernando Valenzuela	.30	.15	.03
□	116	Bob Welch	.10	.05	.01
□	117	Steve Yeager	.06	.03	.00
□	118	Pat Zachry	.06	.03	.00
□	119	Don Baylor	.15	.07	.01
□	120	Bert Campaneris	.10	.05	.01
□	121	Rick Cerone	.06	.03	.00
□	122	Ray Fontenot	.06	.03	.00
□	123	George Frazier	.06	.03	.00
□	124	Oscar Gamble	.06	.03	.00
□	125	Goose Gossage	.20	.10	.02
□	126	Ken Griffey	.15	.07	.01
□	127	Ron Guidry	.25	.12	.02
□	128	Jay Howell	.30	.15	.03
□	129	Steve Kemp	.10	.05	.01
□	130	Matt Keough	.06	.03	.00
□	131	Don Mattingly	36.00	18.00	3.60
□	132	John Montefusco	.06	.03	.00
□	133	Omar Moreno	.06	.03	.00
□	134	Dale Murray	.06	.03	.00
□	135	Graig Nettles	.15	.07	.01
□	136	Lou Piniella	.10	.05	.01
□	137	Willie Randolph	.15	.07	.01
□	138	Shane Rawley	.06	.03	.00
□	139	Dave Righetti	.20	.10	.02
□	140	Andre Robertson	.06	.03	.00
□	141	Bob Shirley	.06	.03	.00
□	142	Roy Smalley	.06	.03	.00
□	143	Dave Winfield	.40	.20	.04
□	144	Butch Wynegar	.06	.03	.00
□	145	Jim Acker	.10	.05	.01
□	146	Doyle Alexander	.10	.05	.01
□	147	Jesse Barfield	.30	.15	.03
□	148	Jorge Bell	1.25	.60	.12
□	149	Barry Bonnell	.06	.03	.00
□	150	Jim Clancy	.06	.03	.00
□	151	Dave Collins	.06	.03	.00
□	152	Tony Fernandez	4.50	2.25	.45
□	153	Damaso Garcia	.06	.03	.00
□	154	Dave Geisel	.06	.03	.00
□	155	Jim Gott	.20	.10	.02
□	156	Alfredo Griffin	.10	.05	.01
□	157	Garth Iorg	.06	.03	.00
□	158	Roy Lee Jackson	.06	.03	.00
□	159	Cliff Johnson	.06	.03	.00
□	160	Luis Leal	.06	.03	.00
□	161	Buck Martinez	.06	.03	.00
□	162	Joey McLaughlin	.06	.03	.00
□	163	Randy Moffitt	.06	.03	.00
□	164	Lloyd Moseby	.15	.07	.01
□	165	Rance Mulliniks	.06	.03	.00
□	166	Jorge Orta	.06	.03	.00
□	167	Dave Stieb	.20	.10	.02
□	168	Willie Upshaw	.10	.05	.01
□	169	Ernie Whitt	.10	.05	.01
□	170	Len Barker	.06	.03	.00
□	171	Steve Bedrosian	.20	.10	.02
□	172	Bruce Benedict	.06	.03	.00
□	173	Brett Butler	.15	.07	.01
□	174	Rick Camp	.06	.03	.00
□	175	Chris Chambliss	.10	.05	.01
□	176	Ken Dayley	.06	.03	.00
□	177	Pete Falcone	.06	.03	.00
□	178	Terry Forster	.10	.05	.01
□	179	Gene Garber	.06	.03	.00
□	180	Terry Harper	.06	.03	.00
□	181	Bob Horner	.15	.07	.01
□	182	Glenn Hubbard	.06	.03	.00
□	183	Randy Johnson	.06	.03	.00
□	184	Craig McMurtry	.10	.05	.01
□	185	Donnie Moore	.06	.03	.00
□	186	Dale Murphy	1.00	.50	.10
□	187	Phil Niekro	.25	.12	.02
□	188	Pascual Perez	.20	.10	.02
□	189	Biff Pocoroba	.06	.03	.00
□	190	Rafael Ramirez	.06	.03	.00
□	191	Jerry Royster	.06	.03	.00
□	192	Claudell Washington	.10	.05	.01
□	193	Bob Watson	.10	.05	.01
□	194	Jerry Augustine	.06	.03	.00
□	195	Mark Brouhard	.06	.03	.00
□	196	Mike Caldwell	.06	.03	.00
□	197	Tom Candiotti	.30	.15	.03
□	198	Cecil Cooper	.15	.07	.01
□	199	Rollie Fingers	.20	.10	.02
□	200	Jim Gantner	.06	.03	.00
□	201	Bob L. Gibson	.10	.05	.01
□	202	Moose Haas	.06	.03	.00
□	203	Roy Howell	.06	.03	.00
□	204	Pete Ladd	.06	.03	.00
□	205	Rick Manning	.06	.03	.00
□	206	Bob McClure	.06	.03	.00
□	207	Paul Molitor	.20	.10	.02
□	208	Don Money	.06	.03	.00
□	209	Charlie Moore	.06	.03	.00
□	210	Ben Oglivie	.10	.05	.01
□	211	Chuck Porter	.06	.03	.00
□	212	Ed Romero	.06	.03	.00
□	213	Ted Simmons	.15	.07	.01
□	214	Jim Slaton	.06	.03	.00
□	215	Don Sutton	.30	.15	.03
□	216	Tom Tellmann	.06	.03	.00
□	217	Pete Vuckovich	.10	.05	.01
□	218	Ned Yost	.06	.03	.00
□	219	Robin Yount	1.00	.50	.10
□	220	Alan Ashby	.06	.03	.00
□	221	Kevin Bass	.15	.07	.01
□	222	Jose Cruz	.10	.05	.01
□	223	Bill Dawley	.10	.05	.01
□	224	Frank DiPino	.06	.03	.00

#	Name			
225	Bill Doran	.75	.35	.07
226	Phil Garner	.06	.03	.00
227	Art Howe	.10	.05	.01
228	Bob Knepper	.10	.05	.01
229	Ray Knight	.10	.05	.01
230	Frank LaCorte	.06	.03	.00
231	Mike LaCoss	.06	.03	.00
232	Mike Madden	.06	.03	.00
233	Jerry Mumphrey	.06	.03	.00
234	Joe Niekro	.10	.05	.01
235	Terry Puhl	.06	.03	.00
236	Luis Pujols	.06	.03	.00
237	Craig Reynolds	.06	.03	.00
238	Vern Ruhle	.06	.03	.00
239	Nolan Ryan	2.50	1.25	.25
240	Mike Scott	.40	.20	.04
241	Tony Scott	.06	.03	.00
242	Dave Smith	.10	.05	.01
243	Dickie Thon	.06	.03	.00
244	Denny Walling	.06	.03	.00
245	Dale Berra	.06	.03	.00
246	Jim Bibby	.06	.03	.00
247	John Candelaria	.10	.05	.01
248	Jose DeLeon	.45	.22	.04
249	Mike Easler	.10	.05	.01
250	Cecilio Guante	.06	.03	.00
251	Richie Hebner	.06	.03	.00
252	Lee Lacy	.06	.03	.00
253	Bill Madlock	.15	.07	.01
254	Milt May	.06	.03	.00
255	Lee Mazzilli	.06	.03	.00
256	Larry McWilliams	.06	.03	.00
257	Jim Morrison	.06	.03	.00
258	Dave Parker	.20	.10	.02
259	Tony Pena	.15	.07	.01
260	Johnny Ray	.15	.07	.01
261	Rick Rhoden	.10	.05	.01
262	Don Robinson	.06	.03	.00
263	Manny Sarmiento	.06	.03	.00
264	Rod Scurry	.06	.03	.00
265	Kent Tekulve	.10	.05	.01
266	Gene Tenace	.06	.03	.00
267	Jason Thompson	.06	.03	.00
268	Lee Tunnell	.10	.05	.01
269	Marvell Wynne	.10	.05	.01
270	Ray Burris	.06	.03	.00
271	Gary Carter	.40	.20	.04
272	Warren Cromartie	.06	.03	.00
273	Andre Dawson	.35	.17	.03
274	Doug Flynn	.06	.03	.00
275	Terry Francona	.06	.03	.00
276	Bill Gullickson	.06	.03	.00
277	Bob James	.15	.07	.01
278	Charlie Lea	.06	.03	.00
279	Bryan Little	.06	.03	.00
280	Al Oliver	.10	.05	.01
281	Tim Raines	.50	.25	.05
282	Bobby Ramos	.06	.03	.00
283	Jeff Reardon	.15	.07	.01
284	Steve Rogers	.06	.03	.00
285	Scott Sanderson	.06	.03	.00
286	Dan Schatzeder	.06	.03	.00
287	Bryn Smith	.15	.07	.01
288	Chris Speier	.06	.03	.00
289	Manny Trillo	.06	.03	.00
290	Mike Vail	.06	.03	.00
291	Tim Wallach	.15	.07	.01
292	Chris Welsh	.06	.03	.00
293	Jim Wohlford	.06	.03	.00
294	Kurt Bevacqua	.06	.03	.00
295	Juan Bonilla	.06	.03	.00
296	Bobby Brown	.06	.03	.00
297	Luis DeLeon	.06	.03	.00
298	Dave Dravecky	.15	.07	.01
299	Tim Flannery	.06	.03	.00
300	Steve Garvey	.50	.25	.05
301	Tony Gwynn	3.50	1.75	.35
302	Andy Hawkins	.60	.30	.06
303	Ruppert Jones	.06	.03	.00
304	Terry Kennedy	.10	.05	.01
305	Tim Lollar	.06	.03	.00
306	Gary Lucas	.06	.03	.00
307	Kevin McReynolds	6.50	3.25	.65
308	Sid Monge	.06	.03	.00
309	Mario Ramirez	.06	.03	.00
310	Gene Richards	.06	.03	.00
311	Luis Salazar	.06	.03	.00
312	Eric Show	.10	.05	.01
313	Elias Sosa	.06	.03	.00
314	Garry Templeton	.10	.05	.01
315	Mark Thurmond	.10	.05	.01
316	Ed Whitson	.06	.03	.00
317	Alan Wiggins	.06	.03	.00
318	Neil Allen	.06	.03	.00
319	Joaquin Andujar	.10	.05	.01
320	Steve Braun	.06	.03	.00
321	Glenn Brummer	.06	.03	.00
322	Bob Forsch	.06	.03	.00
323	David Green	.06	.03	.00
324	George Hendrick	.10	.05	.01
325	Tom Herr	.10	.05	.01
326	Dane Iorg	.06	.03	.00
327	Jeff Lahti	.06	.03	.00
328	Dave LaPoint	.10	.05	.01
329	Willie McGee	.30	.15	.03
330	Ken Oberkfell	.06	.03	.00
331	Darrell Porter	.06	.03	.00
332	Jamie Quirk	.06	.03	.00
333	Mike Ramsey	.06	.03	.00
334	Floyd Rayford	.06	.03	.00
335	Lonnie Smith	.15	.07	.01
336	Ozzie Smith	.50	.20	.04
337	John Stuper	.06	.03	.00
338	Bruce Sutter	.15	.07	.01
339	Andy Van Slyke	2.50	1.25	.25
340	Dave Von Ohlen	.06	.03	.00
341	Willie Aikens	.06	.03	.00
342	Mike Armstrong	.06	.03	.00
343	Bud Black	.06	.03	.00
344	George Brett	1.00	.50	.10
345	Onix Concepcion	.06	.03	.00
346	Keith Creel	.06	.03	.00
347	Larry Gura	.06	.03	.00
348	Don Hood	.06	.03	.00
349	Dennis Leonard	.10	.05	.01
350	Hal McRae	.10	.05	.01
351	Amos Otis	.10	.05	.01
352	Gaylord Perry	.25	.12	.02
353	Greg Pryor	.06	.03	.00
354	Dan Quisenberry	.15	.07	.01
355	Steve Renko	.06	.03	.00
356	Leon Roberts	.06	.03	.00
357	Pat Sheridan	.20	.10	.02
358	Joe Simpson	.06	.03	.00
359	Don Slaught	.06	.03	.00
360	Paul Splittorff	.06	.03	.00
361	U.L. Washington	.06	.03	.00
362	John Wathan	.06	.03	.00
363	Frank White	.10	.05	.01
364	Willie Wilson	.15	.07	.01
365	Jim Barr	.06	.03	.00
366	Dave Bergman	.06	.03	.00
367	Fred Breining	.06	.03	.00
368	Bob Brenly	.06	.03	.00
369	Jack Clark	.30	.15	.03
370	Chili Davis	.15	.07	.01
371	Mark Davis	.75	.35	.07
372	Darrell Evans	.15	.07	.01
373	Atlee Hammaker	.06	.03	.00
374	Mike Krukow	.10	.05	.01
375	Duane Kuiper	.06	.03	.00
376	Bill Laskey	.06	.03	.00
377	Gary Lavelle	.06	.03	.00
378	Johnnie LeMaster	.06	.03	.00
379	Jeff Leonard	.10	.05	.01
380	Randy Lerch	.06	.03	.00
381	Renie Martin	.06	.03	.00
382	Andy McGaffigan	.06	.03	.00
383	Greg Minton	.06	.03	.00
384	Tom O'Malley	.06	.03	.00
385	Max Venable	.06	.03	.00
386	Brad Wellman	.06	.03	.00
387	Joel Youngblood	.06	.03	.00
388	Gary Allenson	.06	.03	.00
389	Luis Aponte	.06	.03	.00
390	Tony Armas	.10	.05	.01
391	Doug Bird	.06	.03	.00
392	Wade Boggs	8.00	4.00	.80
393	Dennis Boyd	.45	.22	.04
394	Mike Brown (Red Sox pitcher)	.10	.05	.01
395	Mark Clear	.06	.03	.00
396	Dennis Eckersley	.25	.12	.02
397	Dwight Evans	.25	.12	.02
398	Rich Gedman	.10	.05	.01
399	Glenn Hoffman	.06	.03	.00
400	Bruce Hurst	.25	.12	.02
401	John Henry Johnson	.06	.03	.00
402	Ed Jurak	.06	.03	.00
403	Rick Miller	.06	.03	.00
404	Jeff Newman	.06	.03	.00
405	Reid Nichols	.06	.03	.00
406	Bob Ojeda	.10	.05	.01
407	Jerry Remy	.06	.03	.00
408	Jim Rice	.25	.12	.02
409	Bob Stanley	.06	.03	.00
410	Dave Stapleton	.06	.03	.00
411	John Tudor	.15	.07	.01
412	Carl Yastrzemski	1.00	.50	.10
413	Buddy Bell	.15	.07	.01

□ 414	Larry Biittner	.06	.03	.00
□ 415	John Butcher	.06	.03	.00
□ 416	Danny Darwin	.06	.03	.00
□ 417	Bucky Dent	.15	.07	.01
□ 418	Dave Hostetler	.06	.03	.00
□ 419	Charlie Hough	.10	.05	.01
□ 420	Bobby Johnson	.06	.03	.00
□ 421	Odell Jones	.06	.03	.00
□ 422	Jon Matlack	.06	.03	.00
□ 423	Pete O'Brien	1.00	.50	.10
□ 424	Larry Parrish	.10	.05	.01
□ 425	Mickey Rivers	.10	.05	.01
□ 426	Billy Sample	.06	.03	.00
□ 427	Dave Schmidt	.10	.05	.01
□ 428	Mike Smithson	.10	.05	.01
□ 429	Bill Stein	.06	.03	.00
□ 430	Dave Stewart	.50	.25	.05
□ 431	Jim Sundberg	.06	.03	.00
□ 432	Frank Tanana	.10	.05	.01
□ 433	Dave Tobik	.06	.03	.00
□ 434	Wayne Tolleson	.10	.05	.01
□ 435	George Wright	.06	.03	.00
□ 436	Bill Almon	.06	.03	.00
□ 437	Keith Atherton	.06	.03	.00
□ 438	Dave Beard	.06	.03	.00
□ 439	Tom Burgmeier	.06	.03	.00
□ 440	Jeff Burroughs	.10	.05	.01
□ 441	Chris Codiroli	.10	.05	.01
□ 442	Tim Conroy	.10	.05	.01
□ 443	Mike Davis	.10	.05	.01
□ 444	Wayne Gross	.06	.03	.00
□ 445	Garry Hancock	.06	.03	.00
□ 446	Mike Heath	.06	.03	.00
□ 447	Rickey Henderson	1.50	.75	.15
□ 448	Donnie Hill	.10	.05	.01
□ 449	Bob Kearney	.06	.03	.00
□ 450	Bill Krueger	.10	.05	.01
□ 451	Rick Langford	.06	.03	.00
□ 452	Carney Lansford	.15	.07	.01
□ 453	Dave Lopes	.10	.05	.01
□ 454	Steve McCatty	.06	.03	.00
□ 455	Dan Meyer	.06	.03	.00
□ 456	Dwayne Murphy	.06	.03	.00
□ 457	Mike Norris	.06	.03	.00
□ 458	Ricky Peters	.06	.03	.00
□ 459	Tony Phillips	.25	.12	.02
□ 460	Tom Underwood	.06	.03	.00
□ 461	Mike Warren	.10	.05	.01
□ 462	Johnny Bench	.90	.45	.09
□ 463	Bruce Berenyi	.06	.03	.00
□ 464	Dann Bilardello	.06	.03	.00
□ 465	Cesar Cedeno	.10	.05	.01
□ 466	Dave Concepcion	.15	.07	.01
□ 467	Dan Driessen	.06	.03	.00
□ 468	Nick Esasky	2.50	1.25	.25
□ 469	Rich Gale	.06	.03	.00
□ 470	Ben Hayes	.06	.03	.00
□ 471	Paul Householder	.06	.03	.00
□ 472	Tom Hume	.06	.03	.00
□ 473	Alan Knicely	.06	.03	.00
□ 474	Eddie Milner	.06	.03	.00
□ 475	Ron Oester	.06	.03	.00
□ 476	Kelly Paris	.10	.05	.01
□ 477	Frank Pastore	.06	.03	.00
□ 478	Ted Power	.06	.03	.00
□ 479	Joe Price	.06	.03	.00
□ 480	Charlie Puleo	.06	.03	.00
□ 481	Gary Redus	.25	.12	.02
□ 482	Bill Scherrer	.06	.03	.00
□ 483	Mario Soto	.06	.03	.00
□ 484	Alex Trevino	.06	.03	.00
□ 485	Duane Walker	.06	.03	.00
□ 486	Larry Bowa	.10	.05	.01
□ 487	Warren Brusstar	.06	.03	.00
□ 488	Bill Buckner	.10	.05	.01
□ 489	Bill Campbell	.06	.03	.00
□ 490	Ron Cey	.10	.05	.01
□ 491	Jody Davis	.10	.05	.01
□ 492	Leon Durham	.10	.05	.01
□ 493	Mel Hall	.30	.15	.03
□ 494	Ferguson Jenkins	.20	.10	.02
□ 495	Jay Johnstone	.10	.05	.01
□ 496	Craig Lefferts	.30	.15	.03
□ 497	Carmelo Martinez	.25	.12	.02
□ 498	Jerry Morales	.06	.03	.00
□ 499	Keith Moreland	.06	.03	.00
□ 500	Dickie Noles	.06	.03	.00
□ 501	Mike Proly	.06	.03	.00
□ 502	Chuck Rainey	.06	.03	.00
□ 503	Dick Ruthven	.06	.03	.00
□ 504	Ryne Sandberg	2.25	1.10	.22
□ 505	Lee Smith	.15	.07	.01
□ 506	Steve Trout	.06	.03	.00
□ 507	Gary Woods	.06	.03	.00
□ 508	Juan Beniquez	.06	.03	.00
□ 509	Bob Boone	.20	.10	.02
□ 510	Rick Burleson	.10	.05	.01
□ 511	Rod Carew	.50	.25	.05
□ 512	Bobby Clark	.06	.03	.00
□ 513	John Curtis	.06	.03	.00
□ 514	Doug DeCinces	.10	.05	.01
□ 515	Brian Downing	.10	.05	.01
□ 516	Tim Foli	.06	.03	.00
□ 517	Ken Forsch	.06	.03	.00
□ 518	Bobby Grich	.10	.05	.01
□ 519	Andy Hassler	.06	.03	.00
□ 520	Reggie Jackson	.75	.35	.07
□ 521	Ron Jackson	.06	.03	.00
□ 522	Tommy John	.18	.09	.01
□ 523	Bruce Kison	.06	.03	.00
□ 524	Steve Lubratich	.06	.03	.00
□ 525	Fred Lynn	.20	.10	.02
□ 526	Gary Pettis	.35	.17	.03
□ 527	Luis Sanchez	.06	.03	.00
□ 528	Daryl Sconiers	.06	.03	.00
□ 529	Ellis Valentine	.06	.03	.00
□ 530	Rob Wilfong	.06	.03	.00
□ 531	Mike Witt	.10	.05	.01
□ 532	Geoff Zahn	.06	.03	.00
□ 533	Bud Anderson	.06	.03	.00
□ 534	Chris Bando	.06	.03	.00
□ 535	Alan Bannister	.06	.03	.00
□ 536	Bert Blyleven	.20	.10	.02
□ 537	Tom Brennan	.06	.03	.00
□ 538	Jamie Easterly	.06	.03	.00
□ 539	Juan Eichelberger	.06	.03	.00
□ 540	Jim Essian	.06	.03	.00
□ 541	Mike Fischlin	.06	.03	.00
□ 542	Julio Franco	1.50	.75	.15
□ 543	Mike Hargrove	.10	.05	.01
□ 544	Toby Harrah	.10	.05	.01
□ 545	Ron Hassey	.06	.03	.00
□ 546	Neal Heaton	.25	.12	.02
□ 547	Bake McBride	.06	.03	.00
□ 548	Broderick Perkins	.06	.03	.00
□ 549	Lary Sorensen	.06	.03	.00
□ 550	Dan Spillner	.06	.03	.00
□ 551	Rick Sutcliffe	.25	.12	.02
□ 552	Pat Tabler	.15	.07	.01
□ 553	Gorman Thomas	.10	.05	.01
□ 554	Andre Thornton	.10	.05	.01
□ 555	George Vukovich	.06	.03	.00
□ 556	Darrell Brown	.06	.03	.00
□ 557	Tom Brunansky	.30	.15	.03
□ 558	Randy Bush	.25	.12	.02
□ 559	Bobby Castillo	.06	.03	.00
□ 560	John Castino	.06	.03	.00
□ 561	Ron Davis	.06	.03	.00
□ 562	Dave Engle	.06	.03	.00
□ 563	Lenny Faedo	.06	.03	.00
□ 564	Pete Filson	.06	.03	.00
□ 565	Gary Gaetti	.90	.45	.09
□ 566	Mickey Hatcher	.10	.05	.01
□ 567	Kent Hrbek	.50	.25	.05
□ 568	Rusty Kuntz	.06	.03	.00
□ 569	Tim Laudner	.06	.03	.00
□ 570	Rick Lysander	.06	.03	.00
□ 571	Bobby Mitchell	.06	.03	.00
□ 572	Ken Schrom	.06	.03	.00
□ 573	Ray Smith	.06	.03	.00
□ 574	Tim Teufel	.30	.15	.03
□ 575	Frank Viola	1.00	.50	.10
□ 576	Gary Ward	.10	.05	.01
□ 577	Ron Washington	.06	.03	.00
□ 578	Len Whitehouse	.06	.03	.00
□ 579	Al Williams	.06	.03	.00
□ 580	Bob Bailor	.06	.03	.00
□ 581	Mark Bradley	.10	.05	.01
□ 582	Hubie Brooks	.15	.07	.01
□ 583	Carlos Diaz	.06	.03	.00
□ 584	George Foster	.15	.07	.01
□ 585	Brian Giles	.06	.03	.00
□ 586	Danny Heep	.06	.03	.00
□ 587	Keith Hernandez	.35	.17	.03
□ 588	Ron Hodges	.06	.03	.00
□ 589	Scott Holman	.06	.03	.00
□ 590	Dave Kingman	.15	.07	.01
□ 591	Ed Lynch	.06	.03	.00
□ 592	Jose Oquendo	.60	.30	.06
□ 593	Jesse Orosco	.06	.03	.00
□ 594	Junior Ortiz	.06	.03	.00
□ 595	Tom Seaver	.60	.30	.06
□ 596	Doug Sisk	.06	.03	.00
□ 597	Rusty Staub	.15	.07	.01
□ 598	John Stearns	.06	.03	.00
□ 599	Darryl Strawberry	24.00	12.00	2.40
□ 600	Craig Swan	.06	.03	.00
□ 601	Walt Terrell	.50	.25	.05
□ 602	Mike Torrez	.06	.03	.00
□ 603	Mookie Wilson	.15	.07	.01

☐ 604	Jamie Allen	.06	.03	.00
☐ 605	Jim Beattie	.06	.03	.00
☐ 606	Tony Bernazard	.06	.03	.00
☐ 607	Manny Castillo	.06	.03	.00
☐ 608	Bill Caudill	.06	.03	.00
☐ 609	Bryan Clark	.06	.03	.00
☐ 610	Al Cowens	.06	.03	.00
☐ 611	Dave Henderson	.20	.10	.02
☐ 612	Steve Henderson	.06	.03	.00
☐ 613	Orlando Mercado	.06	.03	.00
☐ 614	Mike Moore	.25	.12	.02
☐ 615	Ricky Nelson UER	.15	.07	.01
	(Jamie Nelson's			
	stats on back)			
☐ 616	Spike Owen	.25	.12	.02
☐ 617	Pat Putnam	.06	.03	.00
☐ 618	Ron Roenicke	.06	.03	.00
☐ 619	Mike Stanton	.06	.03	.00
☐ 620	Bob Stoddard	.06	.03	.00
☐ 621	Rick Sweet	.06	.03	.00
☐ 622	Roy Thomas	.06	.03	.00
☐ 623	Ed VandeBerg	.06	.03	.00
☐ 624	Matt Young	.10	.05	.01
☐ 625	Richie Zisk	.06	.03	.00
☐ 626	Fred Lynn	.10	.05	.01
	1982 AS Game RB			
☐ 627	Manny Trillo	.10	.05	.01
	1983 AS Game RB			
☐ 628	Steve Garvey	.20	.10	.02
	NL Iron Man			
☐ 629	Rod Carew	.20	.10	.02
	AL Batting Runner-Up			
☐ 630	Wade Boggs	.60	.30	.06
	AL Batting Champion			
☐ 631	Tim Raines: Letting	.20	.10	.02
	Go of the Raines			
☐ 632	Al Oliver	.10	.05	.01
	Double Trouble			
☐ 633	Steve Sax	.15	.07	.01
	AS Second Base			
☐ 634	Dickie Thon	.10	.05	.01
	AS Shortstop			
☐ 635	Ace Firemen	.10	.05	.01
	Dan Quisenberry			
	and Tippy Martinez			
☐ 636	Reds Reunited	.40	.20	.04
	Joe Morgan			
	Pete Rose			
	Tony Perez			
☐ 637	Backstop Stars	.10	.05	.01
	Lance Parrish			
	Bob Boone			
☐ 638	Geo.Brett and G.Perry	.15	.07	.01
	Pine Tar 7/24/83			
☐ 639	1983 No Hitters	.10	.05	.01
	Dave Righetti			
	Mike Warren			
	Bob Forsch			
☐ 640	Bench and Yaz	.75	.35	.07
	Retiring Superstars			
☐ 641	Gaylord Perry	.15	.07	.01
	Going Out In Style			
☐ 642	Steve Carlton	.20	.10	.02
	300 Club and			
	Strikeout Record			
☐ 643	Altobelli and Owens	.10	.05	.01
	WS Managers			
☐ 644	Rick Dempsey	.10	.05	.01
	World Series MVP			
☐ 645	Mike Boddicker	.10	.05	.01
	WS Rookie Winner			
☐ 646	Scott McGregor	.10	.05	.01
	WS Clincher			
☐ 647	CL: Orioles/Royals	.08	.01	.00
☐ 648	CL: Phillies/Giants	.07	.01	.00
☐ 649	CL: White Sox/Red Sox	.07	.01	.00
☐ 650	CL: Tigers/Rangers	.07	.01	.00
☐ 651	CL: Dodgers/A's	.07	.01	.00
☐ 652	CL: Yankees/Reds	.07	.01	.00
☐ 653	CL: Blue Jays/Cubs	.07	.01	.00
☐ 654	CL: Braves/Angels	.07	.01	.00
☐ 655	CL: Brewers/Indians	.07	.01	.00
☐ 656	CL: Astros/Twins	.07	.01	.00
☐ 657	CL: Pirates/Mets	.07	.01	.00
☐ 658	CL: Expos/Mariners	.07	.01	.00
☐ 659	CL: Padres/Specials	.07	.01	.00
☐ 660	CL: Cardinals/Teams	.08	.01	.00

SURVEY CONTRIBUTORS: Prices typically increase over time, let us know of price changes you observe.

1984 Fleer Update

The cards in this 132-card set measure 2 1/2" by 3 1/2". For the first time, the Fleer Gum Company issued a traded, extended, or update set. The purpose of the set was the same as the traded sets issued by Topps over the past four years, i.e., to portray players with their proper team for the current year and to portray rookies who were not in their regular issue. Like the Topps Traded sets of the past four years, the Fleer Update sets were distributed through hobby channels only. The set was quite popular with collectors, and apparently, the print run was relatively short, as the set was quickly in short supply and exhibited a rapid and dramatic price increase. The cards are numbered on the back with a U prefix; the order corresponds to the alphabetical order of the subjects' names. Collectors are urged to be careful if purchasing single cards of Clemens, Darling, Gooden, Puckett, Rose, or Saberhagen as these specific cards have been illegally reprinted. These fakes are blurry when compared to the real thing.

		MINT	EXC	G-VG
COMPLETE SET (132)		375.00	175.00	37.00
COMMON PLAYER (1-132)		.20	.10	.02
☐ 1U	Willie Aikens	.30	.15	.03
☐ 2U	Luis Aponte	.20	.10	.02
☐ 3U	Mark Bailey	.30	.15	.03
☐ 4U	Bob Bailor	.20	.10	.02
☐ 5U	Dusty Baker	.30	.15	.03
☐ 6U	Steve Balboni	.30	.15	.03
☐ 7U	Alan Bannister	.20	.10	.02
☐ 8U	Marty Barrett	3.50	1.75	.35
☐ 9U	Dave Beard	.20	.10	.02
☐ 10U	Joe Beckwith	.20	.10	.02
☐ 11U	Dave Bergman	.20	.10	.02
☐ 12U	Tony Bernazard	.20	.10	.02
☐ 13U	Bruce Bochte	.20	.10	.02
☐ 14U	Barry Bonnell	.20	.10	.02
☐ 15U	Phil Bradley	4.00	2.00	.40
☐ 16U	Fred Breining	.20	.10	.02
☐ 17U	Mike Brown	.20	.10	.02
	(Angels OF)			
☐ 18U	Bill Buckner	.40	.20	.04
☐ 19U	Ray Burris	.20	.10	.02
☐ 20U	John Butcher	.20	.10	.02
☐ 21U	Brett Butler	.40	.20	.04
☐ 22U	Enos Cabell	.20	.10	.02
☐ 23U	Bill Campbell	.20	.10	.02
☐ 24U	Bill Caudill	.20	.10	.02
☐ 25U	Bobby Clark	.20	.10	.02
☐ 26U	Bryan Clark	.20	.10	.02
☐ 27U	Roger Clemens	85.00	42.50	8.50
☐ 28U	Jaime Cocanower	.30	.15	.03
☐ 29U	Ron Darling	9.00	4.50	.90
☐ 30U	Alvin Davis	11.00	5.50	1.10
☐ 31U	Bob Dernier	.20	.10	.02
☐ 32U	Carlos Diaz	.20	.10	.02
☐ 33U	Mike Easler	.20	.10	.02
☐ 34U	Dennis Eckersley	1.00	.50	.10
☐ 35U	Jim Essian	.20	.10	.02
☐ 36U	Darrell Evans	.40	.20	.04
☐ 37U	Mike Fitzgerald	.30	.15	.03

☐	38U	Tim Foli	.20	.10	.02
☐	39U	John Franco	8.00	4.00	.80
☐	40U	George Frazier	.20	.10	.02
☐	41U	Rich Gale	.20	.10	.02
☐	42U	Barbaro Garbey	.30	.15	.03
☐	43U	Dwight Gooden	75.00	37.50	7.50
☐	44U	Goose Gossage	.75	.35	.07
☐	45U	Wayne Gross	.20	.10	.02
☐	46U	Mark Gubicza	7.00	3.50	.70
☐	47U	Jackie Gutierrez	.30	.15	.03
☐	48U	Toby Harrah	.30	.15	.03
☐	49U	Ron Hassey	.30	.15	.03
☐	50U	Richie Hebner	.20	.10	.02
☐	51U	Willie Hernandez	.60	.30	.06
☐	52U	Ed Hodge	.20	.10	.02
☐	53U	Ricky Horton	.50	.25	.05
☐	54U	Art Howe	.30	.15	.03
☐	55U	Dane Iorg	.20	.10	.02
☐	56U	Brook Jacoby	2.00	1.00	.20
☐	57U	Dion James	.60	.30	.06
☐	58U	Mike Jeffcoat	.30	.15	.03
☐	59U	Ruppert Jones	.20	.10	.02
☐	60U	Bob Kearney	.20	.10	.02
☐	61U	Jimmy Key	5.00	2.50	.50
☐	62U	Dave Kingman	.40	.20	.04
☐	63U	Brad Komminsk	.40	.20	.04
☐	64U	Jerry Koosman	.30	.15	.03
☐	65U	Wayne Krenchicki	.20	.10	.02
☐	66U	Rusty Kuntz	.20	.10	.02
☐	67U	Frank LaCorte	.20	.10	.02
☐	68U	Dennis Lamp	.20	.10	.02
☐	69U	Tito Landrum	.30	.15	.03
☐	70U	Mark Langston	24.00	12.00	2.40
☐	71U	Rick Leach	.20	.10	.02
☐	72U	Craig Lefferts	.40	.20	.04
☐	73U	Gary Lucas	.20	.10	.02
☐	74U	Jerry Martin	.20	.10	.02
☐	75U	Carmelo Martinez	.30	.15	.03
☐	76U	Mike Mason	.30	.15	.03
☐	77U	Gary Matthews	.30	.15	.03
☐	78U	Andy McGaffigan	.20	.10	.02
☐	79U	Joey McLaughlin	.20	.10	.02
☐	80U	Joe Morgan	4.00	2.00	.40
☐	81U	Darryl Motley	.30	.15	.03
☐	82U	Graig Nettles	.90	.45	.09
☐	83U	Phil Niekro	2.50	1.25	.25
☐	84U	Ken Oberkfell	.20	.10	.02
☐	85U	Al Oliver	.40	.20	.04
☐	86U	Jorge Orta	.20	.10	.02
☐	87U	Amos Otis	.30	.15	.03
☐	88U	Bob Owchinko	.20	.10	.02
☐	89U	Dave Parker	2.00	1.00	.20
☐	90U	Jack Perconte	.20	.10	.02
☐	91U	Tony Perez	1.50	.75	.15
☐	92U	Gerald Perry	1.75	.85	.17
☐	93U	Kirby Puckett	110.00	55.00	11.00
☐	94U	Shane Rawley	.30	.15	.03
☐	95U	Floyd Rayford	.20	.10	.02
☐	96U	Ron Reed	.20	.10	.02
☐	97U	R.J. Reynolds	1.25	.60	.12
☐	98U	Gene Richards	.20	.10	.02
☐	99U	Jose Rijo	3.00	1.50	.30
☐	100U	Jeff Robinson	1.25	.60	.12
		(Giants pitcher)			
☐	101U	Ron Romanick	.30	.15	.03
☐	102U	Pete Rose	15.00	7.50	1.50
☐	103U	Bret Saberhagen	30.00	15.00	3.00
☐	104U	Scott Sanderson	.40	.20	.04
☐	105U	Dick Schofield	.65	.30	.06
☐	106U	Tom Seaver	8.00	4.00	.80
☐	107U	Jim Slaton	.20	.10	.02
☐	108U	Mike Smithson	.20	.10	.02
☐	109U	Lary Sorensen	.20	.10	.02
☐	110U	Tim Stoddard	.20	.10	.02
☐	111U	Jeff Stone	.40	.20	.04
☐	112U	Champ Summers	.20	.10	.02
☐	113U	Jim Sundberg	.30	.15	.03
☐	114U	Rick Sutcliffe	.75	.35	.07
☐	115U	Craig Swan	.30	.15	.03
☐	116U	Derrel Thomas	.20	.10	.02
☐	117U	Gorman Thomas	.40	.20	.04
☐	118U	Alex Trevino	.20	.10	.02
☐	119U	Manny Trillo	.20	.10	.02
☐	120U	John Tudor	.50	.25	.05
☐	121U	Tom Underwood	.20	.10	.02
☐	122U	Mike Vail	.20	.10	.02
☐	123U	Tom Waddell	.30	.15	.03
☐	124U	Gary Ward	.30	.15	.03
☐	125U	Terry Whitfield	.20	.10	.02
☐	126U	Curtis Wilkerson	.30	.15	.03
☐	127U	Frank Williams	.50	.25	.05
☐	128U	Glenn Wilson	.30	.15	.03
☐	129U	John Wockenfuss	.20	.10	.02
☐	130U	Ned Yost	.20	.10	.02
☐	131U	Mike Young	.50	.25	.05

☐ 132U Checklist: 1-132 .... .20 .03 .01

1985 Fleer

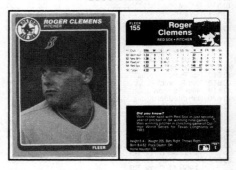

The cards in this 660-card set measure 2 1/2" by 3 1/2". The 1985 Fleer set features fronts which contain the team logo along with the player's name and position. The borders enclosing the photo are color-coded to correspond to the player's team. In each case, the color is one of the standard colors of that team, e.g., orange for Baltimore, red for St. Louis, etc. The backs feature the same name, number, and statistics format that Fleer has been using over the past few years. The cards are ordered alphabetically within team. The teams are ordered based on their respective performance during the prior year, e.g., World Champion Detroit Tigers (1-25), NL Champion San Diego (26-48), Chicago Cubs (49-71), New York Mets (72-95), Toronto (96-119), New York Yankees (120-147), Boston (148- 169), Baltimore (170-195), Kansas City (196-218), St. Louis (219-243), Philadelphia (244-269), Minnesota (270-292), California (293-317), Atlanta (318-342), Houston (343-365), Los Angeles (366-391), Montreal (392-413), Oakland (414- 436), Cleveland (437-460), Pittsburgh (461-481), Seattle (482-505), Chicago White Sox (506-530), Cincinnati (531- 554), Texas (555-575), Milwaukee (576-601), and San Francisco (602-625). Specials (626-643), Rookie pairs (644- 653), and checklist cards (654-660) complete the set. The black and white photo on the reverse is included for the third straight year. This set is noted for containing the Rookie Cards of Roger Clemens, Alvin Davis, Eric Davis, Glenn Davis, Dwight Gooden, Orel Hershiser, Mark Langston, Kirby Puckett, Bret Saberhagen, and Danny Tartabull.

			MINT	EXC	G-VG
	COMPLETE SET (660)		125.00	60.00	12.00
	COMMON PLAYER (1-660)		.05	.02	.00
☐	1	Doug Bair	.10	.02	.01
☐	2	Juan Berenguer	.05	.02	.00
☐	3	Dave Bergman	.05	.02	.00
☐	4	Tom Brookens	.05	.02	.00
☐	5	Marty Castillo	.05	.02	.00
☐	6	Darrell Evans	.12	.06	.01
☐	7	Barbaro Garbey	.05	.02	.00
☐	8	Kirk Gibson	.30	.15	.03
☐	9	John Grubb	.05	.02	.00
☐	10	Willie Hernandez	.12	.06	.01
☐	11	Larry Herndon	.05	.02	.00
☐	12	Howard Johnson	2.00	1.00	.20
☐	13	Ruppert Jones	.05	.02	.00
☐	14	Rusty Kuntz	.05	.02	.00
☐	15	Chet Lemon	.08	.04	.01
☐	16	Aurelio Lopez	.05	.02	.00
☐	17	Sid Monge	.05	.02	.00
☐	18	Jack Morris	.18	.09	.01
☐	19	Lance Parrish	.20	.10	.02

#	Player			
☐ 20	Dan Petry	.05	.02	.00
☐ 21	Dave Rozema	.05	.02	.00
☐ 22	Bill Scherrer	.05	.02	.00
☐ 23	Alan Trammell	.30	.15	.03
☐ 24	Lou Whitaker	.25	.12	.02
☐ 25	Milt Wilcox	.05	.02	.00
☐ 26	Kurt Bevacqua	.05	.02	.00
☐ 27	Greg Booker	.05	.02	.00
☐ 28	Bobby Brown	.05	.02	.00
☐ 29	Luis DeLeon	.05	.02	.00
☐ 30	Dave Dravecky	.15	.07	.01
☐ 31	Tim Flannery	.05	.02	.00
☐ 32	Steve Garvey	.40	.20	.04
☐ 33	Goose Gossage	.15	.07	.01
☐ 34	Tony Gwynn	1.50	.75	.15
☐ 35	Greg Harris	.05	.02	.00
☐ 36	Andy Hawkins	.10	.05	.01
☐ 37	Terry Kennedy	.05	.02	.00
☐ 38	Craig Lefferts	.08	.04	.01
☐ 39	Tim Lollar	.05	.02	.00
☐ 40	Carmelo Martinez	.05	.02	.00
☐ 41	Kevin McReynolds	1.00	.50	.10
☐ 42	Graig Nettles	.12	.06	.01
☐ 43	Luis Salazar	.08	.04	.01
☐ 44	Eric Show	.08	.04	.01
☐ 45	Garry Templeton	.08	.04	.01
☐ 46	Mark Thurmond	.05	.02	.00
☐ 47	Ed Whitson	.05	.02	.00
☐ 48	Alan Wiggins	.05	.02	.00
☐ 49	Rich Bordi	.05	.02	.00
☐ 50	Larry Bowa	.10	.05	.01
☐ 51	Warren Brusstar	.05	.02	.00
☐ 52	Ron Cey	.10	.05	.01
☐ 53	Henry Cotto	.15	.07	.01
☐ 54	Jody Davis	.08	.04	.01
☐ 55	Bob Dernier	.05	.02	.00
☐ 56	Leon Durham	.08	.04	.01
☐ 57	Dennis Eckersley	.18	.09	.01
☐ 58	George Frazier	.05	.02	.00
☐ 59	Richie Hebner	.05	.02	.00
☐ 60	Dave Lopes	.08	.04	.01
☐ 61	Gary Matthews	.08	.04	.01
☐ 62	Keith Moreland	.05	.02	.00
☐ 63	Rick Reuschel	.12	.06	.01
☐ 64	Dick Ruthven	.05	.02	.00
☐ 65	Ryne Sandberg	.60	.30	.06
☐ 66	Scott Sanderson	.05	.02	.00
☐ 67	Lee Smith	.10	.05	.01
☐ 68	Tim Stoddard	.05	.02	.00
☐ 69	Rick Sutcliffe	.15	.07	.01
☐ 70	Steve Trout	.05	.02	.00
☐ 71	Gary Woods	.05	.02	.00
☐ 72	Wally Backman	.08	.04	.01
☐ 73	Bruce Berenyi	.05	.02	.00
☐ 74	Hubie Brooks	.10	.05	.01
☐ 75	Kelvin Chapman	.08	.04	.01
☐ 76	Ron Darling	1.25	.60	.12
☐ 77	Sid Fernandez	1.25	.60	.12
☐ 78	Mike Fitzgerald	.05	.02	.00
☐ 79	George Foster	.12	.06	.01
☐ 80	Brent Gaff	.05	.02	.00
☐ 81	Ron Gardenhire	.05	.02	.00
☐ 82	Dwight Gooden	12.00	6.00	1.20
☐ 83	Tom Gorman	.05	.02	.00
☐ 84	Danny Heep	.05	.02	.00
☐ 85	Keith Hernandez	.30	.15	.03
☐ 86	Ray Knight	.10	.05	.01
☐ 87	Ed Lynch	.05	.02	.00
☐ 88	Jose Oquendo	.08	.04	.01
☐ 89	Jesse Orosco	.05	.02	.00
☐ 90	Rafael Santana	.25	.12	.02
☐ 91	Doug Sisk	.05	.02	.00
☐ 92	Rusty Staub	.12	.06	.01
☐ 93	Darryl Strawberry	4.50	2.25	.45
☐ 94	Walt Terrell	.08	.04	.01
☐ 95	Mookie Wilson	.10	.05	.01
☐ 96	Jim Acker	.05	.02	.00
☐ 97	Willie Aikens	.05	.02	.00
☐ 98	Doyle Alexander	.08	.04	.01
☐ 99	Jesse Barfield	.30	.15	.03
☐ 100	George Bell	.50	.25	.05
☐ 101	Jim Clancy	.05	.02	.00
☐ 102	Dave Collins	.05	.02	.00
☐ 103	Tony Fernandez	.45	.22	.04
☐ 104	Damaso Garcia	.05	.02	.00
☐ 105	Jim Gott	.05	.02	.00
☐ 106	Alfredo Griffin	.08	.04	.01
☐ 107	Garth Iorg	.05	.02	.00
☐ 108	Roy Lee Jackson	.05	.02	.00
☐ 109	Cliff Johnson	.05	.02	.00
☐ 110	Jimmy Key	1.25	.60	.12
☐ 111	Dennis Lamp	.05	.02	.00
☐ 112	Rick Leach	.05	.02	.00
☐ 113	Luis Leal	.05	.02	.00
☐ 114	Buck Martinez	.05	.02	.00
☐ 115	Lloyd Moseby	.10	.05	.01
☐ 116	Rance Mulliniks	.05	.02	.00
☐ 117	Dave Stieb	.15	.07	.01
☐ 118	Willie Upshaw	.05	.02	.00
☐ 119	Ernie Whitt	.05	.02	.00
☐ 120	Mike Armstrong	.05	.02	.00
☐ 121	Don Baylor	.12	.06	.01
☐ 122	Marty Bystrom	.05	.02	.00
☐ 123	Rick Cerone	.05	.02	.00
☐ 124	Joe Cowley	.05	.02	.00
☐ 125	Brian Dayett	.05	.02	.00
☐ 126	Tim Foli	.05	.02	.00
☐ 127	Ray Fontenot	.05	.02	.00
☐ 128	Ken Griffey	.12	.06	.01
☐ 129	Ron Guidry	.15	.07	.01
☐ 130	Toby Harrah	.05	.02	.00
☐ 131	Jay Howell	.08	.04	.01
☐ 132	Steve Kemp	.08	.04	.01
☐ 133	Don Mattingly	12.00	6.00	1.20
☐ 134	Bobby Meacham	.05	.02	.00
☐ 135	John Montefusco	.05	.02	.00
☐ 136	Omar Moreno	.05	.02	.00
☐ 137	Dale Murray	.05	.02	.00
☐ 138	Phil Niekro	.25	.12	.02
☐ 139	Mike Pagliarulo	.75	.35	.07
☐ 140	Willie Randolph	.10	.05	.01
☐ 141	Dennis Rasmussen	.25	.12	.02
☐ 142	Dave Righetti	.18	.09	.01
☐ 143	Jose Rijo	.45	.22	.04
☐ 144	Andre Robertson	.05	.02	.00
☐ 145	Bob Shirley	.05	.02	.00
☐ 146	Dave Winfield	.35	.17	.03
☐ 147	Butch Wynegar	.05	.02	.00
☐ 148	Gary Allenson	.05	.02	.00
☐ 149	Tony Armas	.08	.04	.01
☐ 150	Marty Barrett	.35	.17	.03
☐ 151	Wade Boggs	4.00	2.00	.40
☐ 152	Dennis Boyd	.10	.05	.01
☐ 153	Bill Buckner	.10	.05	.01
☐ 154	Mark Clear	.05	.02	.00
☐ 155	Roger Clemens	12.00	6.00	1.20
☐ 156	Steve Crawford	.05	.02	.00
☐ 157	Mike Easler	.05	.02	.00
☐ 158	Dwight Evans	.18	.09	.01
☐ 159	Rich Gedman	.10	.05	.01
☐ 160	Jackie Gutierrez	.15	.07	.01
	(W.Boggs on deck)			
☐ 161	Bruce Hurst	.15	.07	.01
☐ 162	John Henry Johnson	.05	.02	.00
☐ 163	Rick Miller	.05	.02	.00
☐ 164	Reid Nichols	.05	.02	.00
☐ 165	Al Nipper	.12	.06	.01
☐ 166	Bob Ojeda	.10	.05	.01
☐ 167	Jerry Remy	.05	.02	.00
☐ 168	Jim Rice	.25	.12	.02
☐ 169	Bob Stanley	.05	.02	.00
☐ 170	Mike Boddicker	.10	.05	.01
☐ 171	Al Bumbry	.05	.02	.00
☐ 172	Todd Cruz	.05	.02	.00
☐ 173	Rich Dauer	.05	.02	.00
☐ 174	Storm Davis	.12	.06	.01
☐ 175	Rick Dempsey	.05	.02	.00
☐ 176	Jim Dwyer	.05	.02	.00
☐ 177	Mike Flanagan	.08	.04	.01
☐ 178	Dan Ford	.05	.02	.00
☐ 179	Wayne Gross	.05	.02	.00
☐ 180	John Lowenstein	.05	.02	.00
☐ 181	Dennis Martinez	.08	.04	.01
☐ 182	Tippy Martinez	.05	.02	.00
☐ 183	Scott McGregor	.08	.04	.01
☐ 184	Eddie Murray	.40	.20	.04
☐ 185	Joe Nolan	.05	.02	.00
☐ 186	Floyd Rayford	.05	.02	.00
☐ 187	Cal Ripken	.60	.30	.06
☐ 188	Gary Roenicke	.05	.02	.00
☐ 189	Lenn Sakata	.05	.02	.00
☐ 190	John Shelby	.05	.02	.00
☐ 191	Ken Singleton	.08	.04	.01
☐ 192	Sammy Stewart	.05	.02	.00
☐ 193	Bill Swaggerty	.08	.04	.01
☐ 194	Tom Underwood	.05	.02	.00
☐ 195	Mike Young	.15	.07	.01
☐ 196	Steve Balboni	.05	.02	.00
☐ 197	Joe Beckwith	.05	.02	.00
☐ 198	Bud Black	.05	.02	.00
☐ 199	George Brett	.60	.30	.06
☐ 200	Onix Concepcion	.05	.02	.00
☐ 201	Mark Gubicza	2.00	1.00	.20
☐ 202	Larry Gura	.05	.02	.00
☐ 203	Mark Huismann	.05	.02	.00
☐ 204	Dane Iorg	.05	.02	.00
☐ 205	Danny Jackson	.85	.40	.08
☐ 206	Charlie Leibrandt	.05	.02	.00
☐ 207	Hal McRae	.08	.04	.01
☐ 208	Darryl Motley	.05	.02	.00

#	Player			
☐ 209	Jorge Orta	.05	.02	.00
☐ 210	Greg Pryor	.05	.02	.00
☐ 211	Dan Quisenberry	.12	.06	.01
☐ 212	Bret Saberhagen	8.00	4.00	.80
☐ 213	Pat Sheridan	.05	.02	.00
☐ 214	Don Slaught	.05	.02	.00
☐ 215	U.L. Washington	.05	.02	.00
☐ 216	John Wathan	.05	.02	.00
☐ 217	Frank White	.08	.04	.01
☐ 218	Willie Wilson	.12	.06	.01
☐ 219	Neil Allen	.05	.02	.00
☐ 220	Joaquin Andujar	.08	.04	.01
☐ 221	Steve Braun	.05	.02	.00
☐ 222	Danny Cox	.10	.05	.01
☐ 223	Bob Forsch	.05	.02	.00
☐ 224	David Green	.05	.02	.00
☐ 225	George Hendrick	.08	.04	.01
☐ 226	Tom Herr	.08	.04	.01
☐ 227	Ricky Horton	.20	.10	.02
☐ 228	Art Howe	.08	.04	.01
☐ 229	Mike Jorgensen	.05	.02	.00
☐ 230	Kurt Kepshire	.08	.04	.01
☐ 231	Jeff Lahti	.05	.02	.00
☐ 232	Tito Landrum	.05	.02	.00
☐ 233	Dave LaPoint	.08	.04	.01
☐ 234	Willie McGee	.30	.15	.03
☐ 235	Tom Nieto	.05	.02	.00
☐ 236	Terry Pendleton	.45	.22	.04
☐ 237	Darrell Porter	.05	.02	.00
☐ 238	Dave Rucker	.05	.02	.00
☐ 239	Lonnie Smith	.12	.06	.01
☐ 240	Ozzie Smith	.35	.15	.03
☐ 241	Bruce Sutter	.12	.06	.01
☐ 242	Andy Van Slyke UER (Bats Right, Throws Left)	.50	.25	.05
☐ 243	Dave Von Ohlen	.05	.02	.00
☐ 244	Larry Andersen	.05	.02	.00
☐ 245	Bill Campbell	.05	.02	.00
☐ 246	Steve Carlton	.40	.20	.04
☐ 247	Tim Corcoran	.05	.02	.00
☐ 248	Ivan DeJesus	.05	.02	.00
☐ 249	John Denny	.08	.04	.01
☐ 250	Bo Diaz	.05	.02	.00
☐ 251	Greg Gross	.05	.02	.00
☐ 252	Kevin Gross	.08	.04	.01
☐ 253	Von Hayes	.18	.09	.01
☐ 254	Al Holland	.05	.02	.00
☐ 255	Charles Hudson	.05	.02	.00
☐ 256	Jerry Koosman	.08	.04	.01
☐ 257	Joe Lefebvre	.05	.02	.00
☐ 258	Sixto Lezcano	.05	.02	.00
☐ 259	Garry Maddox	.08	.04	.01
☐ 260	Len Matuszek	.05	.02	.00
☐ 261	Tug McGraw	.10	.05	.01
☐ 262	Al Oliver	.10	.05	.01
☐ 263	Shane Rawley	.05	.02	.00
☐ 264	Juan Samuel	.35	.17	.03
☐ 265	Mike Schmidt	.80	.40	.08
☐ 266	Jeff Stone	.12	.06	.01
☐ 267	Ozzie Virgil	.05	.02	.00
☐ 268	Glenn Wilson	.08	.04	.01
☐ 269	John Wockenfuss	.05	.02	.00
☐ 270	Darrell Brown	.05	.02	.00
☐ 271	Tom Brunansky	.20	.10	.02
☐ 272	Randy Bush	.08	.04	.01
☐ 273	John Butcher	.05	.02	.00
☐ 274	Bobby Castillo	.05	.02	.00
☐ 275	Ron Davis	.05	.02	.00
☐ 276	Dave Engle	.05	.02	.00
☐ 277	Pete Filson	.05	.02	.00
☐ 278	Gary Gaetti	.35	.17	.03
☐ 279	Mickey Hatcher	.05	.02	.00
☐ 280	Ed Hodge	.05	.02	.00
☐ 281	Kent Hrbek	.35	.17	.03
☐ 282	Houston Jimenez	.05	.02	.00
☐ 283	Tim Laudner	.05	.02	.00
☐ 284	Rick Lysander	.05	.02	.00
☐ 285	Dave Meier	.05	.02	.00
☐ 286	Kirby Puckett	18.00	9.00	1.80
☐ 287	Pat Putnam	.05	.02	.00
☐ 288	Ken Schrom	.05	.02	.00
☐ 289	Mike Smithson	.05	.02	.00
☐ 290	Tim Teufel	.05	.02	.00
☐ 291	Frank Viola	.40	.20	.04
☐ 292	Ron Washington	.05	.02	.00
☐ 293	Don Aase	.05	.02	.00
☐ 294	Juan Beniquez	.05	.02	.00
☐ 295	Bob Boone	.12	.06	.01
☐ 296	Mike Brown (Angels OF)	.05	.02	.00
☐ 297	Rod Carew	.40	.20	.04
☐ 298	Doug Corbett	.05	.02	.00
☐ 299	Doug DeCinces	.08	.04	.01
☐ 300	Brian Downing	.08	.04	.01

#	Player			
☐ 301	Ken Forsch	.05	.02	.00
☐ 302	Bobby Grich	.08	.04	.01
☐ 303	Reggie Jackson	.50	.25	.05
☐ 304	Tommy John	.15	.07	.01
☐ 305	Curt Kaufman	.08	.04	.01
☐ 306	Bruce Kison	.05	.02	.00
☐ 307	Fred Lynn	.15	.07	.01
☐ 308	Gary Pettis	.08	.04	.01
☐ 309	Ron Romanick	.05	.02	.00
☐ 310	Luis Sanchez	.05	.02	.00
☐ 311	Dick Schofield	.10	.05	.01
☐ 312	Daryl Sconiers	.05	.02	.00
☐ 313	Jim Slaton	.05	.02	.00
☐ 314	Derrel Thomas	.05	.02	.00
☐ 315	Rob Wilfong	.05	.02	.00
☐ 316	Mike Witt	.10	.05	.01
☐ 317	Geoff Zahn	.05	.02	.00
☐ 318	Len Barker	.05	.02	.00
☐ 319	Steve Bedrosian	.15	.07	.01
☐ 320	Bruce Benedict	.05	.02	.00
☐ 321	Rick Camp	.05	.02	.00
☐ 322	Chris Chambliss	.08	.04	.01
☐ 323	Jeff Dedmon	.08	.04	.01
☐ 324	Terry Forster	.08	.04	.01
☐ 325	Gene Garber	.05	.02	.00
☐ 326	Albert Hall	.10	.05	.01
☐ 327	Terry Harper	.05	.02	.00
☐ 328	Bob Horner	.12	.06	.01
☐ 329	Glenn Hubbard	.05	.02	.00
☐ 330	Randy Johnson	.05	.02	.00
☐ 331	Brad Komminsk	.08	.04	.01
☐ 332	Rick Mahler	.05	.02	.00
☐ 333	Craig McMurtry	.05	.02	.00
☐ 334	Donnie Moore	.05	.02	.00
☐ 335	Dale Murphy	.60	.30	.06
☐ 336	Ken Oberkfell	.05	.02	.00
☐ 337	Pascual Perez	.12	.06	.01
☐ 338	Gerald Perry	.30	.15	.03
☐ 339	Rafael Ramirez	.05	.02	.00
☐ 340	Jerry Royster	.05	.02	.00
☐ 341	Alex Trevino	.05	.02	.00
☐ 342	Claudell Washington	.08	.04	.01
☐ 343	Alan Ashby	.05	.02	.00
☐ 344	Mark Bailey	.08	.04	.01
☐ 345	Kevin Bass	.10	.05	.01
☐ 346	Enos Cabell	.05	.02	.00
☐ 347	Jose Cruz	.10	.05	.01
☐ 348	Bill Dawley	.05	.02	.00
☐ 349	Frank DiPino	.05	.02	.00
☐ 350	Bill Doran	.15	.07	.01
☐ 351	Phil Garner	.05	.02	.00
☐ 352	Bob Knepper	.08	.04	.01
☐ 353	Mike LaCoss	.05	.02	.00
☐ 354	Jerry Mumphrey	.05	.02	.00
☐ 355	Joe Niekro	.10	.05	.01
☐ 356	Terry Puhl	.05	.02	.00
☐ 357	Craig Reynolds	.05	.02	.00
☐ 358	Vern Ruhle	.05	.02	.00
☐ 359	Nolan Ryan	1.50	.75	.15
☐ 360	Joe Sambito	.05	.02	.00
☐ 361	Mike Scott	.35	.17	.03
☐ 362	Dave Smith	.08	.04	.01
☐ 363	Julio Solano	.08	.04	.01
☐ 364	Dickie Thon	.05	.02	.00
☐ 365	Denny Walling	.05	.02	.00
☐ 366	Dave Anderson	.05	.02	.00
☐ 367	Bob Bailor	.05	.02	.00
☐ 368	Greg Brock	.08	.04	.01
☐ 369	Carlos Diaz	.05	.02	.00
☐ 370	Pedro Guerrero	.30	.15	.03
☐ 371	Orel Hershiser	10.00	5.00	1.00
☐ 372	Rick Honeycutt	.05	.02	.00
☐ 373	Burt Hooton	.05	.02	.00
☐ 374	Ken Howell	.15	.07	.01
☐ 375	Ken Landreaux	.05	.02	.00
☐ 376	Candy Maldonado	.10	.05	.01
☐ 377	Mike Marshall	.15	.07	.01
☐ 378	Tom Niedenfuer	.08	.04	.01
☐ 379	Alejandro Pena	.08	.04	.01
☐ 380	Jerry Reuss	.08	.04	.01
☐ 381	R.J. Reynolds	.25	.12	.02
☐ 382	German Rivera	.08	.04	.01
☐ 383	Bill Russell	.08	.04	.01
☐ 384	Steve Sax	.25	.12	.02
☐ 385	Mike Scioscia	.08	.04	.01
☐ 386	Franklin Stubbs	.30	.15	.03
☐ 387	Fernando Valenzuela	.25	.12	.02
☐ 388	Bob Welch	.10	.05	.01
☐ 389	Terry Whitfield	.05	.02	.00
☐ 390	Steve Yeager	.05	.02	.00
☐ 391	Pat Zachry	.05	.02	.00
☐ 392	Fred Breining	.05	.02	.00
☐ 393	Gary Carter	.30	.15	.03
☐ 394	Andre Dawson	.30	.15	.03
☐ 395	Miguel Dilone	.05	.02	.00

☐ 396	Dan Driessen	.05	.02	.00	☐ 491	Bob Kearney	.05	.02	.00
☐ 397	Doug Flynn	.05	.02	.00	☐ 492	Mark Langston	5.00	2.50	.50
☐ 398	Terry Francona	.05	.02	.00	☐ 493	Larry Milbourne	.05	.02	.00
☐ 399	Bill Gullickson	.05	.02	.00	☐ 494	Paul Mirabella	.05	.02	.00
☐ 400	Bob James	.05	.02	.00	☐ 495	Mike Moore	.15	.07	.01
☐ 401	Charlie Lea	.05	.02	.00	☐ 496	Edwin Nunez	.05	.02	.00
☐ 402	Bryan Little	.05	.02	.00	☐ 497	Spike Owen	.05	.02	.00
☐ 403	Gary Lucas	.05	.02	.00	☐ 498	Jack Perconte	.05	.02	.00
☐ 404	David Palmer	.05	.02	.00	☐ 499	Ken Phelps	.10	.05	.01
☐ 405	Tim Raines	.35	.17	.03	☐ 500	Jim Presley	.75	.35	.07
☐ 406	Mike Ramsey	.05	.02	.00	☐ 501	Mike Stanton	.05	.02	.00
☐ 407	Jeff Reardon	.12	.06	.01	☐ 502	Bob Stoddard	.05	.02	.00
☐ 408	Steve Rogers	.05	.02	.00	☐ 503	Gorman Thomas	.10	.05	.01
☐ 409	Dan Schatzeder	.05	.02	.00	☐ 504	Ed VandeBerg	.05	.02	.00
☐ 410	Bryn Smith	.10	.05	.01	☐ 505	Matt Young	.05	.02	.00
☐ 411	Mike Stenhouse	.05	.02	.00	☐ 506	Juan Agosto	.05	.02	.00
☐ 412	Tim Wallach	.12	.06	.01	☐ 507	Harold Baines	.20	.10	.02
☐ 413	Jim Wohlford	.05	.02	.00	☐ 508	Floyd Bannister	.05	.02	.00
☐ 414	Bill Almon	.05	.02	.00	☐ 509	Britt Burns	.05	.02	.00
☐ 415	Keith Atherton	.05	.02	.00	☐ 510	Julio Cruz	.05	.02	.00
☐ 416	Bruce Bochte	.05	.02	.00	☐ 511	Richard Dotson	.08	.04	.01
☐ 417	Tom Burgmeier	.05	.02	.00	☐ 512	Jerry Dybzinski	.05	.02	.00
☐ 418	Ray Burris	.05	.02	.00	☐ 513	Carlton Fisk	.25	.12	.02
☐ 419	Bill Caudill	.05	.02	.00	☐ 514	Scott Fletcher	.08	.04	.01
☐ 420	Chris Codiroli	.05	.02	.00	☐ 515	Jerry Hairston	.05	.02	.00
☐ 421	Tim Conroy	.05	.02	.00	☐ 516	Marc Hill	.05	.02	.00
☐ 422	Mike Davis	.08	.04	.01	☐ 517	LaMarr Hoyt	.08	.04	.01
☐ 423	Jim Essian	.05	.02	.00	☐ 518	Ron Kittle	.15	.07	.01
☐ 424	Mike Heath	.05	.02	.00	☐ 519	Rudy Law	.05	.02	.00
☐ 425	Rickey Henderson	.75	.35	.07	☐ 520	Vance Law	.08	.04	.01
☐ 426	Donnie Hill	.05	.02	.00	☐ 521	Greg Luzinski	.10	.05	.01
☐ 427	Dave Kingman	.10	.05	.01	☐ 522	Gene Nelson	.05	.02	.00
☐ 428	Bill Krueger	.05	.02	.00	☐ 523	Tom Paciorek	.05	.02	.00
☐ 429	Carney Lansford	.12	.06	.01	☐ 524	Ron Reed	.05	.02	.00
☐ 430	Steve McCatty	.05	.02	.00	☐ 525	Bert Roberge	.05	.02	.00
☐ 431	Joe Morgan	.25	.12	.02	☐ 526	Tom Seaver	.30	.15	.03
☐ 432	Dwayne Murphy	.05	.02	.00	☐ 527	Roy Smalley	.05	.02	.00
☐ 433	Tony Phillips	.05	.02	.00	☐ 528	Dan Spillner	.05	.02	.00
☐ 434	Lary Sorensen	.05	.02	.00	☐ 529	Mike Squires	.05	.02	.00
☐ 435	Mike Warren	.05	.02	.00	☐ 530	Greg Walker	.10	.05	.01
☐ 436	Curt Young	.30	.15	.03	☐ 531	Cesar Cedeno	.08	.04	.01
☐ 437	Luis Aponte	.05	.02	.00	☐ 532	Dave Concepcion	.10	.05	.01
☐ 438	Chris Bando	.05	.02	.00	☐ 533	Eric Davis	16.00	8.00	1.60
☐ 439	Tony Bernazard	.05	.02	.00	☐ 534	Nick Esasky	.25	.12	.02
☐ 440	Bert Blyleven	.15	.07	.01	☐ 535	Tom Foley	.05	.02	.00
☐ 441	Brett Butler	.10	.05	.01	☐ 536	John Franco	1.50	.75	.15
☐ 442	Ernie Camacho	.05	.02	.00	☐ 537	Brad Gulden	.05	.02	.00
☐ 443	Joe Carter	3.00	1.50	.30	☐ 538	Tom Hume	.05	.02	.00
☐ 444	Carmelo Castillo	.05	.02	.00	☐ 539	Wayne Krenchicki	.05	.02	.00
☐ 445	Jamie Easterly	.05	.02	.00	☐ 540	Andy McGaffigan	.05	.02	.00
☐ 446	Steve Farr	.30	.15	.03	☐ 541	Eddie Milner	.05	.02	.00
☐ 447	Mike Fischlin	.05	.02	.00	☐ 542	Ron Oester	.05	.02	.00
☐ 448	Julio Franco	.40	.20	.04	☐ 543	Bob Owchinko	.05	.02	.00
☐ 449	Mel Hall	.12	.06	.01	☐ 544	Dave Parker	.18	.09	.01
☐ 450	Mike Hargrove	.08	.04	.01	☐ 545	Frank Pastore	.05	.02	.00
☐ 451	Neal Heaton	.05	.02	.00	☐ 546	Tony Perez	.18	.09	.01
☐ 452	Brook Jacoby	.25	.12	.02	☐ 547	Ted Power	.05	.02	.00
☐ 453	Mike Jeffcoat	.05	.02	.00	☐ 548	Joe Price	.05	.02	.00
☐ 454	Don Schulze	.08	.04	.01	☐ 549	Gary Redus	.05	.02	.00
☐ 455	Roy Smith	.08	.04	.01	☐ 550	Pete Rose	1.00	.50	.10
☐ 456	Pat Tabler	.10	.05	.01	☐ 551	Jeff Russell	.30	.15	.03
☐ 457	Andre Thornton	.08	.04	.01	☐ 552	Mario Soto	.05	.02	.00
☐ 458	George Vukovich	.05	.02	.00	☐ 553	Jay Tibbs	.10	.05	.01
☐ 459	Tom Waddell	.08	.04	.01	☐ 554	Duane Walker	.05	.02	.00
☐ 460	Jerry Willard	.05	.02	.00	☐ 555	Alan Bannister	.05	.02	.00
☐ 461	Dale Berra	.05	.02	.00	☐ 556	Buddy Bell	.10	.05	.01
☐ 462	John Candelaria	.08	.04	.01	☐ 557	Danny Darwin	.05	.02	.00
☐ 463	Jose DeLeon	.08	.04	.01	☐ 558	Charlie Hough	.08	.04	.01
☐ 464	Doug Frobel	.05	.02	.00	☐ 559	Bobby Jones	.05	.02	.00
☐ 465	Cecilio Guante	.05	.02	.00	☐ 560	Odell Jones	.05	.02	.00
☐ 466	Brian Harper	.15	.07	.01	☐ 561	Jeff Kunkel	.08	.04	.01
☐ 467	Lee Lacy	.05	.02	.00	☐ 562	Mike Mason	.08	.04	.01
☐ 468	Bill Madlock	.10	.05	.01	☐ 563	Pete O'Brien	.10	.05	.01
☐ 469	Lee Mazzilli	.05	.02	.00	☐ 564	Larry Parrish	.08	.04	.01
☐ 470	Larry McWilliams	.05	.02	.00	☐ 565	Mickey Rivers	.08	.04	.01
☐ 471	Jim Morrison	.05	.02	.00	☐ 566	Billy Sample	.05	.02	.00
☐ 472	Tony Pena	.12	.06	.01	☐ 567	Dave Schmidt	.08	.04	.01
☐ 473	Johnny Ray	.08	.04	.01	☐ 568	Donnie Scott	.05	.02	.00
☐ 474	Rick Rhoden	.08	.04	.01	☐ 569	Dave Stewart	.35	.17	.03
☐ 475	Don Robinson	.05	.02	.00	☐ 570	Frank Tanana	.08	.04	.01
☐ 476	Rod Scurry	.05	.02	.00	☐ 571	Wayne Tolleson	.05	.02	.00
☐ 477	Kent Tekulve	.08	.04	.01	☐ 572	Gary Ward	.08	.04	.01
☐ 478	Jason Thompson	.05	.02	.00	☐ 573	Curtis Wilkerson	.05	.02	.00
☐ 479	John Tudor	.15	.07	.01	☐ 574	George Wright	.05	.02	.00
☐ 480	Lee Tunnell	.05	.02	.00	☐ 575	Ned Yost	.05	.02	.00
☐ 481	Marvell Wynne	.05	.02	.00	☐ 576	Mark Brouhard	.05	.02	.00
☐ 482	Salome Barojas	.05	.02	.00	☐ 577	Mike Caldwell	.05	.02	.00
☐ 483	Dave Beard	.05	.02	.00	☐ 578	Bobby Clark	.05	.02	.00
☐ 484	Jim Beattie	.05	.02	.00	☐ 579	Jaime Cocanower	.05	.02	.00
☐ 485	Barry Bonnell	.05	.02	.00	☐ 580	Cecil Cooper	.12	.06	.01
☐ 486	Phil Bradley	1.00	.50	.10	☐ 581	Rollie Fingers	.15	.07	.01
☐ 487	Al Cowens	.05	.02	.00	☐ 582	Jim Gantner	.05	.02	.00
☐ 488	Alvin Davis	3.00	1.50	.30	☐ 583	Moose Haas	.05	.02	.00
☐ 489	Dave Henderson	.12	.06	.01	☐ 584	Dion James	.10	.05	.01
☐ 490	Steve Henderson	.05	.02	.00	☐ 585	Pete Ladd	.05	.02	.00

☐ 586	Rick Manning	.05	.02	.00
☐ 587	Bob McClure	.05	.02	.00
☐ 588	Paul Molitor	.20	.10	.02
☐ 589	Charlie Moore	.05	.02	.00
☐ 590	Ben Oglivie	.08	.04	.01
☐ 591	Chuck Porter	.05	.02	.00
☐ 592	Randy Ready	.20	.10	.02
☐ 593	Ed Romero	.05	.02	.00
☐ 594	Bill Schroeder	.05	.02	.00
☐ 595	Ray Searage	.05	.02	.00
☐ 596	Ted Simmons	.12	.06	.01
☐ 597	Jim Sundberg	.05	.02	.00
☐ 598	Don Sutton	.25	.12	.02
☐ 599	Tom Tellmann	.05	.02	.00
☐ 600	Rick Waits	.05	.02	.00
☐ 601	Robin Yount	.60	.30	.06
☐ 602	Dusty Baker	.08	.04	.01
☐ 603	Bob Brenly	.05	.02	.00
☐ 604	Jack Clark	.20	.10	.02
☐ 605	Chili Davis	.10	.05	.01
☐ 606	Mark Davis	.25	.12	.02
☐ 607	Dan Gladden	.40	.20	.04
☐ 608	Atlee Hammaker	.05	.02	.00
☐ 609	Mike Krukow	.05	.02	.00
☐ 610	Duane Kuiper	.05	.02	.00
☐ 611	Bob Lacey	.05	.02	.00
☐ 612	Bill Laskey	.05	.02	.00
☐ 613	Gary Lavelle	.05	.02	.00
☐ 614	Johnnie LeMaster	.05	.02	.00
☐ 615	Jeff Leonard	.10	.05	.01
☐ 616	Randy Lerch	.05	.02	.00
☐ 617	Greg Minton	.05	.02	.00
☐ 618	Steve Nicosia	.05	.02	.00
☐ 619	Gene Richards	.05	.02	.00
☐ 620	Jeff Robinson (Giants pitcher)	.35	.17	.03
☐ 621	Scot Thompson	.05	.02	.00
☐ 622	Manny Trillo	.05	.02	.00
☐ 623	Brad Wellman	.05	.02	.00
☐ 624	Frank Williams	.15	.07	.01
☐ 625	Joel Youngblood	.05	.02	.00
☐ 626	Cal Ripken IA	.20	.10	.02
☐ 627	Mike Schmidt IA	.35	.17	.03
☐ 628	Giving The Signs Sparky Anderson	.05	.02	.00
☐ 629	AL Pitcher's Nightmare Dave Winfield Rickey Henderson	.25	.12	.02
☐ 630	NL Pitcher's Nightmare Mike Schmidt Ryne Sandberg	.30	.15	.03
☐ 631	NL All-Stars Darryl Strawberry Gary Carter Steve Garvey Ozzie Smith	.25	.12	.02
☐ 632	A-S Winning Battery Gary Carter Charlie Lea	.10	.05	.01
☐ 633	NL Pennant Clinchers Steve Garvey Goose Gossage	.12	.06	.01
☐ 634	NL Rookie Phenoms Dwight Gooden Juan Samuel	.90	.45	.09
☐ 635	Toronto's Big Guns Willie Upshaw	.05	.02	.00
☐ 636	Toronto's Big Guns Lloyd Moseby	.08	.04	.01
☐ 637	HOLLAND: Al Holland	.05	.02	.00
☐ 638	TUNNELL: Lee Tunnell	.05	.02	.00
☐ 639	500th Homer Reggie Jackson	.30	.15	.03
☐ 640	4000th Hit Pete Rose	.45	.22	.04
☐ 641	Father and Son Cal Ripken Jr. and Sr.	.12	.06	.01
☐ 642	Cubs: Division Champs	.05	.02	.00
☐ 643	Two Perfect Games and One No-Hitter: Mike Witt David Palmer Jack Morris	.08	.04	.01
☐ 644	Willie Lozado and Vic Mata	.10	.05	.01
☐ 645	Kelly Gruber and Randy O'Neal	.90	.45	.09
☐ 646	Jose Roman and Joel Skinner	.10	.05	.01
☐ 647	Steve Kiefer and Danny Tartabull	4.00	2.00	.40
☐ 648	Rob Deer and Alejandro Sanchez	1.25	.60	.12
☐ 649	Billy Hatcher and Shawon Dunston	2.25	1.10	.22
☐ 650	Ron Robinson and Mike Bielecki	.75	.35	.07
☐ 651	Zane Smith and Paul Zuvella	.35	.17	.03
☐ 652	Joe Hesketh and Glenn Davis	9.00	4.50	.90
☐ 653	John Russell and Steve Jeltz	.12	.06	.01
☐ 654	CL: Tigers/Padres and Cubs/Mets	.07	.01	.00
☐ 655	CL: Blue Jays/Yankees and Red Sox/Orioles	.07	.01	.00
☐ 656	CL: Royals/Cardinals and Phillies/Twins	.07	.01	.00
☐ 657	CL: Angels/Braves and Astros/Dodgers	.07	.01	.00
☐ 658	CL: Expos/A's and Indians/Pirates	.07	.01	.00
☐ 659	CL: Mariners/Wh.Sox and Reds/Rangers	.07	.01	.00
☐ 660	CL: Brewers/Giants and Special Cards	.10	.01	.00

1985 Fleer Limited Edition

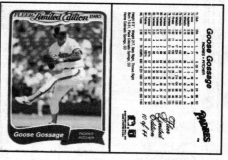

This 44-card set features standard size cards (2 1/2" by 3 1/2") which were distributed as a complete set in a colorful box. The back of the box gives a complete checklist of the cards in the set. The cards are ordered alphabetically by the player's name. Backs of the cards are yellow and white whereas the fronts show a picture of the player inside a red banner-type border.

		MINT	EXC	G-VG
	COMPLETE SET (44)	5.00	2.50	.50
	COMMON PLAYER (1-44)	.05	.02	.00
☐ 1	Buddy Bell	.05	.02	.00
☐ 2	Bert Blyleven	.15	.07	.01
☐ 3	Wade Boggs	1.00	.50	.10
☐ 4	George Brett	.50	.25	.05
☐ 5	Rod Carew	.40	.20	.04
☐ 6	Steve Carlton	.35	.17	.03
☐ 7	Alvin Davis	.15	.07	.01
☐ 8	Andre Dawson	.25	.12	.02
☐ 9	Steve Garvey	.30	.15	.03
☐ 10	Goose Gossage	.10	.05	.01
☐ 11	Tony Gwynn	.40	.20	.04
☐ 12	Keith Hernandez	.20	.10	.02
☐ 13	Kent Hrbek	.20	.10	.02
☐ 14	Reggie Jackson	.50	.25	.05
☐ 15	Dave Kingman	.10	.05	.01
☐ 16	Ron Kittle	.10	.05	.01
☐ 17	Mark Langston	.20	.10	.02
☐ 18	Jeff Leonard	.05	.02	.00
☐ 19	Bill Madlock	.05	.02	.00
☐ 20	Don Mattingly	1.25	.60	.12
☐ 21	Jack Morris	.15	.07	.01
☐ 22	Dale Murphy	.40	.20	.04
☐ 23	Eddie Murray	.30	.15	.03
☐ 24	Tony Pena	.05	.02	.00
☐ 25	Dan Quisenberry	.10	.05	.01
☐ 26	Tim Raines	.20	.10	.02
☐ 27	Jim Rice	.20	.10	.02
☐ 28	Cal Ripken	.35	.17	.03
☐ 29	Pete Rose	.75	.35	.07
☐ 30	Nolan Ryan	1.25	.60	.12

☐ 31	Ryne Sandberg	.35	.17	.03
☐ 32	Steve Sax	.15	.07	.01
☐ 33	Mike Schmidt	1.00	.50	.10
☐ 34	Tom Seaver	.35	.17	.03
☐ 35	Ozzie Smith	.25	.12	.02
☐ 36	Mario Soto	.05	.02	.00
☐ 37	Dave Stieb	.10	.05	.01
☐ 38	Darryl Strawberry	.60	.30	.06
☐ 39	Rick Sutcliffe	.10	.05	.01
☐ 40	Alan Trammell	.20	.10	.02
☐ 41	Willie Upshaw	.05	.02	.00
☐ 42	Fernando Valenzuela	.20	.10	.02
☐ 43	Dave Winfield	.25	.12	.02
☐ 44	Robin Yount	.45	.22	.04

1985 Fleer Update

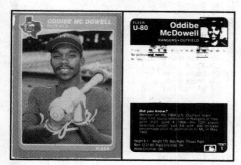

This 132-card set was issued late in the collecting year and features new players and players on new teams compared to the 1985 Fleer regular issue cards. Cards measure 2 1/2" by 3 1/2" and were distributed together as a complete set within a special box. The cards are numbered with a U prefix and are ordered alphabetically by the player's name. This set features the Extended Rookie Cards of Vince Coleman, Ozzie Guillen, Teddy Higuera, and Mickey Tettleton.

		MINT	EXC	G-VG
COMPLETE SET (132)		16.00	8.00	1.60
COMMON PLAYER (1-132)		.06	.03	.00
☐	U1 Don Aase	.10	.02	.01
☐	U2 Bill Almon	.06	.03	.00
☐	U3 Dusty Baker	.10	.05	.01
☐	U4 Dale Berra	.06	.03	.00
☐	U5 Karl Best	.10	.05	.01
☐	U6 Tim Birtsas	.12	.06	.01
☐	U7 Vida Blue	.10	.05	.01
☐	U8 Rich Bordi	.06	.03	.00
☐	U9 Daryl Boston	.10	.05	.01
☐	U10 Hubie Brooks	.25	.12	.02
☐	U11 Chris Brown	.20	.10	.02
☐	U12 Tom Browning	1.25	.60	.12
☐	U13 Al Bumbry	.06	.03	.00
☐	U14 Tim Burke	.50	.25	.05
☐	U15 Ray Burris	.06	.03	.00
☐	U16 Jeff Burroughs	.06	.03	.00
☐	U17 Ivan Calderon	.75	.35	.07
☐	U18 Jeff Calhoun	.10	.05	.01
☐	U19 Bill Campbell	.06	.03	.00
☐	U20 Don Carman	.25	.12	.02
☐	U21 Gary Carter	.75	.35	.07
☐	U22 Bobby Castillo	.06	.03	.00
☐	U23 Bill Caudill	.06	.03	.00
☐	U24 Rick Cerone	.10	.05	.01
☐	U25 Jack Clark	.35	.17	.03
☐	U26 Pat Clements	.10	.05	.01
☐	U27 Stewart Cliburn	.10	.05	.01
☐	U28 Vince Coleman	4.50	2.25	.45
☐	U29 Dave Collins	.06	.03	.00
☐	U30 Fritz Connally	.10	.05	.01
☐	U31 Henry Cotto	.06	.03	.00
☐	U32 Danny Darwin	.06	.03	.00
☐	U33 Darren Daulton	.15	.07	.01
☐	U34 Jerry Davis	.10	.05	.01
☐	U35 Brian Dayett	.10	.05	.01
☐	U36 Ken Dixon	.12	.06	.01

☐ U37	Tommy Dunbar	.06	.03	.00
☐ U38	Mariano Duncan	.25	.12	.02
☐ U39	Bob Fallon	.10	.05	.01
☐ U40	Brian Fisher	.25	.12	.02
☐ U41	Mike Fitzgerald	.06	.03	.00
☐ U42	Ray Fontenot	.06	.03	.00
☐ U43	Greg Gagne	.30	.15	.03
☐ U44	Oscar Gamble	.06	.03	.00
☐ U45	Jim Gott	.10	.05	.01
☐ U46	David Green	.06	.03	.00
☐ U47	Alfredo Griffin	.10	.05	.01
☐ U48	Ozzie Guillen	1.25	.60	.12
☐ U49	Toby Harrah	.10	.05	.01
☐ U50	Ron Hassey	.06	.03	.00
☐ U51	Rickey Henderson	2.00	1.00	.20
☐ U52	Steve Henderson	.06	.03	.00
☐ U53	George Hendrick	.10	.05	.01
☐ U54	Teddy Higuera	2.00	1.00	.20
☐ U55	Al Holland	.06	.03	.00
☐ U56	Burt Hooton	.06	.03	.00
☐ U57	Jay Howell	.15	.07	.01
☐ U58	LaMarr Hoyt	.10	.05	.01
☐ U59	Tim Hulett	.10	.05	.01
☐ U60	Bob James	.10	.05	.01
☐ U61	Cliff Johnson	.06	.03	.00
☐ U62	Howard Johnson	2.25	1.10	.22
☐ U63	Ruppert Jones	.06	.03	.00
☐ U64	Steve Kemp	.10	.05	.01
☐ U65	Bruce Kison	.06	.03	.00
☐ U66	Mike LaCoss	.06	.03	.00
☐ U67	Lee Lacy	.06	.03	.00
☐ U68	Dave LaPoint	.10	.05	.01
☐ U69	Gary Lavelle	.06	.03	.00
☐ U70	Vance Law	.10	.05	.01
☐ U71	Manny Lee	.12	.06	.01
☐ U72	Sixto Lezcano	.06	.03	.00
☐ U73	Tim Lollar	.06	.03	.00
☐ U74	Urbano Lugo	.10	.05	.01
☐ U75	Fred Lynn	.25	.12	.02
☐ U76	Steve Lyons	.10	.05	.01
☐ U77	Mickey Mahler	.06	.03	.00
☐ U78	Ron Mathis	.10	.05	.01
☐ U79	Len Matuszek	.06	.03	.00
☐ U80	Oddibe McDowell UER . (part of bio actually Roger's)	.65	.30	.06
☐ U81	Roger McDowell UER ... (part of bio actually Oddibe's)	.85	.40	.08
☐ U82	Donnie Moore	.06	.03	.00
☐ U83	Ron Musselman	.10	.05	.01
☐ U84	Al Oliver	.15	.07	.01
☐ U85	Joe Orsulak	.20	.10	.02
☐ U86	Dan Pasqua	.40	.20	.04
☐ U87	Chris Pittaro	.10	.05	.01
☐ U88	Rick Reuschel	.25	.12	.02
☐ U89	Earnie Riles	.25	.12	.02
☐ U90	Jerry Royster	.06	.03	.00
☐ U91	Dave Rozema	.06	.03	.00
☐ U92	Dave Rucker	.06	.03	.00
☐ U93	Vern Ruhle	.06	.03	.00
☐ U94	Mark Salas	.12	.06	.01
☐ U95	Luis Salazar	.10	.05	.01
☐ U96	Joe Sambito	.06	.03	.00
☐ U97	Billy Sample	.06	.03	.00
☐ U98	Alejandro Sanchez	.10	.05	.01
☐ U99	Calvin Schiraldi	.20	.10	.02
☐ U100	Rick Schu	.15	.07	.01
☐ U101	Larry Sheets	.30	.15	.03
☐ U102	Ron Shephard	.10	.05	.01
☐ U103	Nelson Simmons	.10	.05	.01
☐ U104	Don Slaught	.06	.03	.00
☐ U105	Roy Smalley	.06	.03	.00
☐ U106	Lonnie Smith	.20	.10	.02
☐ U107	Nate Snell	.10	.05	.01
☐ U108	Lary Sorensen	.06	.03	.00
☐ U109	Chris Speier	.06	.03	.00
☐ U110	Mike Stenhouse	.10	.05	.01
☐ U111	Tim Stoddard	.06	.03	.00
☐ U112	John Stuper	.06	.03	.00
☐ U113	Jim Sundberg	.10	.05	.01
☐ U114	Bruce Sutter	.20	.10	.02
☐ U115	Don Sutton	.50	.25	.05
☐ U116	Bruce Tanner	.10	.05	.01
☐ U117	Kent Tekulve	.10	.05	.01
☐ U118	Walt Terrell	.15	.07	.01
☐ U119	Mickey Tettleton	1.00	.50	.10
☐ U120	Rich Thompson	.10	.05	.01
☐ U121	Louis Thornton	.10	.05	.01
☐ U122	Alex Trevino	.06	.03	.00
☐ U123	John Tudor	.20	.10	.02
☐ U124	Jose Uribe	.35	.17	.03
☐ U125	Dave Valle	.10	.05	.01
☐ U126	Dave Von Ohlen	.06	.03	.00
☐ U127	Curt Wardle	.10	.05	.01

			MINT	EXC	G-VG
☐	U128	U.L. Washington	.06	.03	.00
☐	U129	Ed Whitson	.10	.05	.01
☐	U130	Herm Winningham	.15	.07	.01
☐	U131	Rich Yett	.10	.05	.01
☐	U132	Checklist U1-U132	.06	.01	.00

1986 Fleer

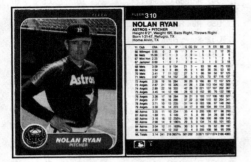

The cards in this 660-card set measure 2 1/2" by 3 1/2". The 1986 Fleer set features fronts which contain the team logo along with the player's name and position. The player cards are alphabetized within team and the teams are ordered by their 1985 season finish and won- lost record, e.g., Kansas City (1-25), St. Louis (26-49), Toronto (50-73), New York Mets (74-97), New York Yankees (98-122), Los Angeles (123-147), California (148-171), Cincinnati (172-196), Chicago White Sox (197-220), Detroit (221-243), Montreal (244-267), Baltimore (268-291), Houston (292-314), San Diego (315-338), Boston (339-360), Chicago Cubs (361-385), Minnesota (386-409), Oakland (410-432), Philadelphia (433-457), Seattle (458-481), Milwaukee (482- 506), Atlanta (507-532), San Francisco (533-555), Texas (556-578), Cleveland (579-601), and Pittsburgh (602-625). Specials (626-643), Rookie pairs (644-653), and checklist cards (654-660) complete the set. The border enclosing the photo is dark blue. The backs feature the same name, number, and statistics format that Fleer has been using over the past few years. The Dennis and Tippy Martinez cards were apparently switched in the set numbering, as their adjacent numbers (279 and 280) were reversed on the Orioles checklist card.

			MINT	EXC	G-VG
COMPLETE SET (660)			100.00	50.00	10.00
COMMON PLAYER (1-660)			.05	.02	.00

			MINT	EXC	G-VG
☐	1	Steve Balboni	.10	.02	.01
☐	2	Joe Beckwith	.05	.02	.00
☐	3	Buddy Biancalana	.05	.02	.00
☐	4	Bud Black	.05	.02	.00
☐	5	George Brett	.45	.22	.04
☐	6	Onix Concepcion	.05	.02	.00
☐	7	Steve Farr	.08	.04	.01
☐	8	Mark Gubicza	.20	.10	.02
☐	9	Dane Iorg	.05	.02	.00
☐	10	Danny Jackson	.20	.10	.02
☐	11	Lynn Jones	.05	.02	.00
☐	12	Mike Jones	.05	.02	.00
☐	13	Charlie Leibrandt	.05	.02	.00
☐	14	Hal McRae	.08	.04	.01
☐	15	Omar Moreno	.05	.02	.00
☐	16	Darryl Motley	.05	.02	.00
☐	17	Jorge Orta	.05	.02	.00
☐	18	Dan Quisenberry	.12	.06	.01
☐	19	Bret Saberhagen	1.25	.60	.12
☐	20	Pat Sheridan	.05	.02	.00
☐	21	Lonnie Smith	.10	.05	.01
☐	22	Jim Sundberg	.05	.02	.00

			MINT	EXC	G-VG
☐	23	John Wathan	.05	.02	.00
☐	24	Frank White	.08	.04	.01
☐	25	Willie Wilson	.10	.05	.01
☐	26	Joaquin Andujar	.08	.04	.01
☐	27	Steve Braun	.05	.02	.00
☐	28	Bill Campbell	.05	.02	.00
☐	29	Cesar Cedeno	.08	.04	.01
☐	30	Jack Clark	.25	.12	.02
☐	31	Vince Coleman	2.25	1.10	.22
☐	32	Danny Cox	.10	.05	.01
☐	33	Ken Dayley	.05	.02	.00
☐	34	Ivan DeJesus	.05	.02	.00
☐	35	Bob Forsch	.05	.02	.00
☐	36	Brian Harper	.05	.02	.00
☐	37	Tom Herr	.08	.04	.01
☐	38	Ricky Horton	.05	.02	.00
☐	39	Kurt Kepshire	.05	.02	.00
☐	40	Jeff Lahti	.05	.02	.00
☐	41	Tito Landrum	.05	.02	.00
☐	42	Willie McGee	.15	.07	.01
☐	43	Tom Nieto	.05	.02	.00
☐	44	Terry Pendleton	.08	.04	.01
☐	45	Darrell Porter	.05	.02	.00
☐	46	Ozzie Smith	.25	.12	.02
☐	47	John Tudor	.15	.07	.01
☐	48	Andy Van Slyke	.25	.12	.02
☐	49	Todd Worrell	.90	.45	.09
☐	50	Jim Acker	.05	.02	.00
☐	51	Doyle Alexander	.08	.04	.01
☐	52	Jesse Barfield	.20	.10	.02
☐	53	George Bell	.30	.15	.03
☐	54	Jeff Burroughs	.05	.02	.00
☐	55	Bill Caudill	.05	.02	.00
☐	56	Jim Clancy	.05	.02	.00
☐	57	Tony Fernandez	.25	.12	.02
☐	58	Tom Filer	.05	.02	.00
☐	59	Damaso Garcia	.05	.02	.00
☐	60	Tom Henke	.25	.12	.02
☐	61	Garth Iorg	.05	.02	.00
☐	62	Cliff Johnson	.05	.02	.00
☐	63	Jimmy Key	.12	.06	.01
☐	64	Dennis Lamp	.05	.02	.00
☐	65	Gary Lavelle	.05	.02	.00
☐	66	Buck Martinez	.05	.02	.00
☐	67	Lloyd Moseby	.10	.05	.01
☐	68	Rance Mulliniks	.05	.02	.00
☐	69	Al Oliver	.10	.05	.01
☐	70	Dave Stieb	.12	.06	.01
☐	71	Louis Thornton	.10	.05	.01
☐	72	Willie Upshaw	.05	.02	.00
☐	73	Ernie Whitt	.05	.02	.00
☐	74	Rick Aguilera	.35	.17	.03
☐	75	Wally Backman	.05	.02	.00
☐	76	Gary Carter	.30	.15	.03
☐	77	Ron Darling	.25	.12	.02
☐	78	Len Dykstra	.75	.35	.07
☐	79	Sid Fernandez	.15	.07	.01
☐	80	George Foster	.12	.06	.01
☐	81	Dwight Gooden	2.25	1.10	.22
☐	82	Tom Gorman	.05	.02	.00
☐	83	Danny Heep	.05	.02	.00
☐	84	Keith Hernandez	.25	.12	.02
☐	85	Howard Johnson	.40	.20	.04
☐	86	Ray Knight	.08	.04	.01
☐	87	Terry Leach	.15	.07	.01
☐	88	Ed Lynch	.05	.02	.00
☐	89	Roger McDowell	.45	.22	.04
☐	90	Jesse Orosco	.05	.02	.00
☐	91	Tom Paciorek	.05	.02	.00
☐	92	Ronn Reynolds	.05	.02	.00
☐	93	Rafael Santana	.05	.02	.00
☐	94	Doug Sisk	.05	.02	.00
☐	95	Rusty Staub	.10	.05	.01
☐	96	Darryl Strawberry	2.00	1.00	.20
☐	97	Mookie Wilson	.10	.05	.01
☐	98	Neil Allen	.05	.02	.00
☐	99	Don Baylor	.10	.05	.01
☐	100	Dale Berra	.05	.02	.00
☐	101	Rich Bordi	.05	.02	.00
☐	102	Marty Bystrom	.05	.02	.00
☐	103	Joe Cowley	.05	.02	.00
☐	104	Brian Fisher	.20	.10	.02
☐	105	Ken Griffey	.10	.05	.01
☐	106	Ron Guidry	.15	.07	.01
☐	107	Ron Hassey	.05	.02	.00
☐	108	Rickey Henderson	.60	.30	.06
☐	109	Don Mattingly	4.00	2.00	.40
☐	110	Bobby Meacham	.05	.02	.00
☐	111	John Montefusco	.05	.02	.00
☐	112	Phil Niekro	.18	.09	.01
☐	113	Mike Pagliarulo	.10	.05	.01
☐	114	Dan Pasqua	.12	.06	.01
☐	115	Willie Randolph	.10	.05	.01
☐	116	Dave Righetti	.12	.06	.01
☐	117	Andre Robertson	.05	.02	.00

☐ 118	Billy Sample	.05	.02	.00	☐ 213	Gene Nelson	.05	.02	.00
☐ 119	Bob Shirley	.05	.02	.00	☐ 214	Reid Nichols	.05	.02	.00
☐ 120	Ed Whitson	.05	.02	.00	☐ 215	Luis Salazar	.05	.02	.00
☐ 121	Dave Winfield	.30	.15	.03	☐ 216	Tom Seaver	.35	.17	.03
☐ 122	Butch Wynegar	.05	.02	.00	☐ 217	Dan Spillner	.05	.02	.00
☐ 123	Dave Anderson	.05	.02	.00	☐ 218	Bruce Tanner	.08	.04	.01
☐ 124	Bob Bailor	.05	.02	.00	☐ 219	Greg Walker	.08	.04	.01
☐ 125	Greg Brock	.05	.02	.00	☐ 220	Dave Wehrmeister	.05	.02	.00
☐ 126	Enos Cabell	.05	.02	.00	☐ 221	Juan Berenguer	.05	.02	.00
☐ 127	Bobby Castillo	.05	.02	.00	☐ 222	Dave Bergman	.05	.02	.00
☐ 128	Carlos Diaz	.05	.02	.00	☐ 223	Tom Brookens	.05	.02	.00
☐ 129	Mariano Duncan	.20	.10	.02	☐ 224	Darrell Evans	.10	.05	.01
☐ 130	Pedro Guerrero	.20	.10	.02	☐ 225	Barbaro Garbey	.05	.02	.00
☐ 131	Orel Hershiser	1.75	.85	.17	☐ 226	Kirk Gibson	.25	.12	.02
☐ 132	Rick Honeycutt	.05	.02	.00	☐ 227	John Grubb	.05	.02	.00
☐ 133	Ken Howell	.05	.02	.00	☐ 228	Willie Hernandez	.10	.05	.01
☐ 134	Ken Landreaux	.05	.02	.00	☐ 229	Larry Herndon	.05	.02	.00
☐ 135	Bill Madlock	.10	.05	.01	☐ 230	Chet Lemon	.08	.04	.01
☐ 136	Candy Maldonado	.10	.05	.01	☐ 231	Aurelio Lopez	.05	.02	.00
☐ 137	Mike Marshall	.12	.06	.01	☐ 232	Jack Morris	.15	.07	.01
☐ 138	Len Matuszek	.05	.02	.00	☐ 233	Randy O'Neal	.05	.02	.00
☐ 139	Tom Niedenfuer	.05	.02	.00	☐ 234	Lance Parrish	.15	.07	.01
☐ 140	Alejandro Pena	.08	.04	.01	☐ 235	Dan Petry	.05	.02	.00
☐ 141	Jerry Reuss	.08	.04	.01	☐ 236	Alejandro Sanchez	.05	.02	.00
☐ 142	Bill Russell	.08	.04	.01	☐ 237	Bill Scherrer	.05	.02	.00
☐ 143	Steve Sax	.18	.09	.01	☐ 238	Nelson Simmons	.08	.04	.01
☐ 144	Mike Scioscia	.08	.04	.01	☐ 239	Frank Tanana	.08	.04	.01
☐ 145	Fernando Valenzuela	.25	.12	.02	☐ 240	Walt Terrell	.05	.02	.00
☐ 146	Bob Welch	.08	.04	.01	☐ 241	Alan Trammell	.25	.12	.02
☐ 147	Terry Whitfield	.05	.02	.00	☐ 242	Lou Whitaker	.15	.07	.01
☐ 148	Juan Beniquez	.05	.02	.00	☐ 243	Milt Wilcox	.05	.02	.00
☐ 149	Bob Boone	.12	.06	.01	☐ 244	Hubie Brooks	.10	.05	.01
☐ 150	John Candelaria	.08	.04	.01	☐ 245	Tim Burke	.35	.17	.03
☐ 151	Rod Carew	.30	.15	.03	☐ 246	Andre Dawson	.30	.15	.03
☐ 152	Stewart Cliburn	.08	.04	.01	☐ 247	Mike Fitzgerald	.05	.02	.00
☐ 153	Doug DeCinces	.08	.04	.01	☐ 248	Terry Francona	.05	.02	.00
☐ 154	Brian Downing	.08	.04	.01	☐ 249	Bill Gullickson	.05	.02	.00
☐ 155	Ken Forsch	.05	.02	.00	☐ 250	Joe Hesketh	.05	.02	.00
☐ 156	Craig Gerber	.05	.02	.00	☐ 251	Bill Laskey	.05	.02	.00
☐ 157	Bobby Grich	.08	.04	.01	☐ 252	Vance Law	.05	.02	.00
☐ 158	George Hendrick	.08	.04	.01	☐ 253	Charlie Lea	.05	.02	.00
☐ 159	Al Holland	.05	.02	.00	☐ 254	Gary Lucas	.05	.02	.00
☐ 160	Reggie Jackson	.40	.20	.04	☐ 255	David Palmer	.05	.02	.00
☐ 161	Ruppert Jones	.05	.02	.00	☐ 256	Tim Raines	.30	.15	.03
☐ 162	Urbano Lugo	.05	.02	.00	☐ 257	Jeff Reardon	.10	.05	.01
☐ 163	Kirk McCaskill	.60	.30	.06	☐ 258	Bert Roberge	.05	.02	.00
☐ 164	Donnie Moore	.05	.02	.00	☐ 259	Dan Schatzeder	.05	.02	.00
☐ 165	Gary Pettis	.05	.02	.00	☐ 260	Bryn Smith	.10	.05	.01
☐ 166	Ron Romanick	.05	.02	.00	☐ 261	Randy St.Claire	.05	.02	.00
☐ 167	Dick Schofield	.05	.02	.00	☐ 262	Scot Thompson	.05	.02	.00
☐ 168	Daryl Sconiers	.05	.02	.00	☐ 263	Tim Wallach	.10	.05	.01
☐ 169	Jim Slaton	.05	.02	.00	☐ 264	U.L. Washington	.05	.02	.00
☐ 170	Don Sutton	.18	.09	.01	☐ 265	Mitch Webster	.30	.15	.03
☐ 171	Mike Witt	.10	.05	.01	☐ 266	Herm Winningham	.10	.05	.01
☐ 172	Buddy Bell	.10	.05	.01	☐ 267	Floyd Youmans	.30	.15	.03
☐ 173	Tom Browning	.25	.12	.02	☐ 268	Don Aase	.05	.02	.00
☐ 174	Dave Concepcion	.10	.05	.01	☐ 269	Mike Boddicker	.08	.04	.01
☐ 175	Eric Davis	3.00	1.50	.30	☐ 270	Rich Dauer	.05	.02	.00
☐ 176	Bo Diaz	.05	.02	.00	☐ 271	Storm Davis	.10	.05	.01
☐ 177	Nick Esasky	.12	.06	.01	☐ 272	Rick Dempsey	.05	.02	.00
☐ 178	John Franco	.15	.07	.01	☐ 273	Ken Dixon	.05	.02	.00
☐ 179	Tom Hume	.05	.02	.00	☐ 274	Jim Dwyer	.05	.02	.00
☐ 180	Wayne Krenchicki	.05	.02	.00	☐ 275	Mike Flanagan	.08	.04	.01
☐ 181	Andy McGaffigan	.05	.02	.00	☐ 276	Wayne Gross	.05	.02	.00
☐ 182	Eddie Milner	.05	.02	.00	☐ 277	Lee Lacy	.05	.02	.00
☐ 183	Ron Oester	.05	.02	.00	☐ 278	Fred Lynn	.15	.07	.01
☐ 184	Dave Parker	.15	.07	.01	☐ 279	Tippy Martinez	.05	.02	.00
☐ 185	Frank Pastore	.05	.02	.00	☐ 280	Dennis Martinez	.08	.04	.01
☐ 186	Tony Perez	.15	.07	.01	☐ 281	Scott McGregor	.08	.04	.01
☐ 187	Ted Power	.05	.02	.00	☐ 282	Eddie Murray	.30	.15	.03
☐ 188	Joe Price	.05	.02	.00	☐ 283	Floyd Rayford	.05	.02	.00
☐ 189	Gary Redus	.05	.02	.00	☐ 284	Cal Ripken	.40	.20	.04
☐ 190	Ron Robinson	.05	.02	.00	☐ 285	Gary Roenicke	.05	.02	.00
☐ 191	Pete Rose	.75	.35	.07	☐ 286	Larry Sheets	.15	.07	.01
☐ 192	Mario Soto	.05	.02	.00	☐ 287	John Shelby	.05	.02	.00
☐ 193	John Stuper	.05	.02	.00	☐ 288	Nate Snell	.08	.04	.01
☐ 194	Jay Tibbs	.05	.02	.00	☐ 289	Sammy Stewart	.05	.02	.00
☐ 195	Dave Van Gorder	.05	.02	.00	☐ 290	Alan Wiggins	.05	.02	.00
☐ 196	Max Venable	.05	.02	.00	☐ 291	Mike Young	.08	.04	.01
☐ 197	Juan Agosto	.05	.02	.00	☐ 292	Alan Ashby	.05	.02	.00
☐ 198	Harold Baines	.12	.06	.01	☐ 293	Mark Bailey	.05	.02	.00
☐ 199	Floyd Bannister	.05	.02	.00	☐ 294	Kevin Bass	.08	.04	.01
☐ 200	Britt Burns	.05	.02	.00	☐ 295	Jeff Calhoun	.08	.04	.01
☐ 201	Julio Cruz	.05	.02	.00	☐ 296	Jose Cruz	.08	.04	.01
☐ 202	Joel Davis	.10	.05	.01	☐ 297	Glenn Davis	1.25	.60	.12
☐ 203	Richard Dotson	.08	.04	.01	☐ 298	Bill Dawley	.05	.02	.00
☐ 204	Carlton Fisk	.25	.12	.02	☐ 299	Frank DiPino	.05	.02	.00
☐ 205	Scott Fletcher	.08	.04	.01	☐ 300	Bill Doran	.10	.05	.01
☐ 206	Ozzie Guillen	.45	.22	.04	☐ 301	Phil Garner	.05	.02	.00
☐ 207	Jerry Hairston	.05	.02	.00	☐ 302	Jeff Heathcock	.05	.02	.00
☐ 208	Tim Hulett	.05	.02	.00	☐ 303	Charlie Kerfeld	.08	.04	.01
☐ 209	Bob James	.05	.02	.00	☐ 304	Bob Knepper	.08	.04	.01
☐ 210	Ron Kittle	.10	.05	.01	☐ 305	Ron Mathis	.08	.04	.01
☐ 211	Rudy Law	.05	.02	.00	☐ 306	Jerry Mumphrey	.05	.02	.00
☐ 212	Bryan Little	.05	.02	.00	☐ 307	Jim Pankovits	.05	.02	.00

☐ 308	Terry Puhl	.05	.02	.00	☐ 403	Ken Schrom	.05	.02	.00
☐ 309	Craig Reynolds	.05	.02	.00	☐ 404	Roy Smalley	.05	.02	.00
☐ 310	Nolan Ryan	.80	.40	.08	☐ 405	Mike Smithson	.05	.02	.00
☐ 311	Mike Scott	.35	.17	.03	☐ 406	Mike Stenhouse	.05	.02	.00
☐ 312	Dave Smith	.08	.04	.01	☐ 407	Tim Teufel	.05	.02	.00
☐ 313	Dickie Thon	.05	.02	.00	☐ 408	Frank Viola	.30	.15	.03
☐ 314	Denny Walling	.05	.02	.00	☐ 409	Ron Washington	.05	.02	.00
☐ 315	Kurt Bevacqua	.05	.02	.00	☐ 410	Keith Atherton	.05	.02	.00
☐ 316	Al Bumbry	.05	.02	.00	☐ 411	Dusty Baker	.08	.04	.01
☐ 317	Jerry Davis	.05	.02	.00	☐ 412	Tim Birtsas	.10	.05	.01
☐ 318	Luis DeLeon	.05	.02	.00	☐ 413	Bruce Bochte	.05	.02	.00
☐ 319	Dave Dravecky	.12	.06	.01	☐ 414	Chris Codiroli	.05	.02	.00
☐ 320	Tim Flannery	.05	.02	.00	☐ 415	Dave Collins	.05	.02	.00
☐ 321	Steve Garvey	.35	.17	.03	☐ 416	Mike Davis	.05	.02	.00
☐ 322	Goose Gossage	.12	.06	.01	☐ 417	Alfredo Griffin	.08	.04	.01
☐ 323	Tony Gwynn	.75	.35	.07	☐ 418	Mike Heath	.05	.02	.00
☐ 324	Andy Hawkins	.10	.05	.01	☐ 419	Steve Henderson	.05	.02	.00
☐ 325	LaMarr Hoyt	.08	.04	.01	☐ 420	Donnie Hill	.05	.02	.00
☐ 326	Roy Lee Jackson	.05	.02	.00	☐ 421	Jay Howell	.08	.04	.01
☐ 327	Terry Kennedy	.05	.02	.00	☐ 422	Tommy John	.15	.07	.01
☐ 328	Craig Lefferts	.08	.04	.01	☐ 423	Dave Kingman	.12	.06	.01
☐ 329	Carmelo Martinez	.05	.02	.00	☐ 424	Bill Krueger	.05	.02	.00
☐ 330	Lance McCullers	.35	.17	.03	☐ 425	Rick Langford	.05	.02	.00
☐ 331	Kevin McReynolds	.35	.17	.03	☐ 426	Carney Lansford	.12	.06	.01
☐ 332	Graig Nettles	.10	.05	.01	☐ 427	Steve McCatty	.05	.02	.00
☐ 333	Jerry Royster	.05	.02	.00	☐ 428	Dwayne Murphy	.05	.02	.00
☐ 334	Eric Show	.08	.04	.01	☐ 429	Steve Ontiveros	.10	.05	.01
☐ 335	Tim Stoddard	.05	.02	.00	☐ 430	Tony Phillips	.05	.02	.00
☐ 336	Garry Templeton	.08	.04	.01	☐ 431	Jose Rijo	.10	.05	.01
☐ 337	Mark Thurmond	.05	.02	.00	☐ 432	Mickey Tettleton	.60	.30	.06
☐ 338	Ed Wojna	.08	.04	.01	☐ 433	Luis Aguayo	.05	.02	.00
☐ 339	Tony Armas	.08	.04	.01	☐ 434	Larry Andersen	.05	.02	.00
☐ 340	Marty Barrett	.10	.05	.01	☐ 435	Steve Carlton	.25	.12	.02
☐ 341	Wade Boggs	2.50	1.25	.25	☐ 436	Don Carman	.20	.10	.02
☐ 342	Dennis Boyd	.08	.04	.01	☐ 437	Tim Corcoran	.05	.02	.00
☐ 343	Bill Buckner	.10	.05	.01	☐ 438	Darren Daulton	.12	.06	.01
☐ 344	Mark Clear	.05	.02	.00	☐ 439	John Denny	.08	.04	.01
☐ 345	Roger Clemens	3.00	1.50	.30	☐ 440	Tom Foley	.05	.02	.00
☐ 346	Steve Crawford	.05	.02	.00	☐ 441	Greg Gross	.05	.02	.00
☐ 347	Mike Easler	.05	.02	.00	☐ 442	Kevin Gross	.05	.02	.00
☐ 348	Dwight Evans	.15	.07	.01	☐ 443	Von Hayes	.10	.05	.01
☐ 349	Rich Gedman	.08	.04	.01	☐ 444	Charles Hudson	.05	.02	.00
☐ 350	Jackie Gutierrez	.05	.02	.00	☐ 445	Garry Maddox	.05	.02	.00
☐ 351	Glenn Hoffman	.05	.02	.00	☐ 446	Shane Rawley	.05	.02	.00
☐ 352	Bruce Hurst	.15	.07	.01	☐ 447	Dave Rucker	.05	.02	.00
☐ 353	Bruce Kison	.05	.02	.00	☐ 448	John Russell	.05	.02	.00
☐ 354	Tim Lollar	.05	.02	.00	☐ 449	Juan Samuel	.15	.07	.01
☐ 355	Steve Lyons	.05	.02	.00	☐ 450	Mike Schmidt	.75	.35	.07
☐ 356	Al Nipper	.05	.02	.00	☐ 451	Rick Schu	.05	.02	.00
☐ 357	Bob Ojeda	.08	.04	.01	☐ 452	Dave Shipanoff	.08	.04	.01
☐ 358	Jim Rice	.20	.10	.02	☐ 453	Dave Stewart	.25	.12	.02
☐ 359	Bob Stanley	.05	.02	.00	☐ 454	Jeff Stone	.05	.02	.00
☐ 360	Mike Trujillo	.05	.02	.00	☐ 455	Kent Tekulve	.05	.02	.00
☐ 361	Thad Bosley	.05	.02	.00	☐ 456	Ozzie Virgil	.05	.02	.00
☐ 362	Warren Brusstar	.05	.02	.00	☐ 457	Glenn Wilson	.08	.04	.01
☐ 363	Ron Cey	.08	.04	.01	☐ 458	Jim Beattie	.05	.02	.00
☐ 364	Jody Davis	.05	.02	.00	☐ 459	Karl Best	.08	.04	.01
☐ 365	Bob Dernier	.05	.02	.00	☐ 460	Barry Bonnell	.05	.02	.00
☐ 366	Shawon Dunston	.25	.12	.02	☐ 461	Phil Bradley	.12	.06	.01
☐ 367	Leon Durham	.08	.04	.01	☐ 462	Ivan Calderon	.65	.30	.06
☐ 368	Dennis Eckersley	.15	.07	.01	☐ 463	Al Cowens	.05	.02	.00
☐ 369	Ray Fontenot	.05	.02	.00	☐ 464	Alvin Davis	.25	.12	.02
☐ 370	George Frazier	.05	.02	.00	☐ 465	Dave Henderson	.08	.04	.01
☐ 371	Billy Hatcher	.10	.05	.01	☐ 466	Bob Kearney	.05	.02	.00
☐ 372	Dave Lopes	.08	.04	.01	☐ 467	Mark Langston	.60	.30	.06
☐ 373	Gary Matthews	.08	.04	.01	☐ 468	Bob Long	.05	.02	.00
☐ 374	Ron Meredith	.05	.02	.00	☐ 469	Mike Moore	.10	.05	.01
☐ 375	Keith Moreland	.05	.02	.00	☐ 470	Edwin Nunez	.05	.02	.00
☐ 376	Reggie Patterson	.05	.02	.00	☐ 471	Spike Owen	.05	.02	.00
☐ 377	Dick Ruthven	.05	.02	.00	☐ 472	Jack Perconte	.05	.02	.00
☐ 378	Ryne Sandberg	.30	.15	.03	☐ 473	Jim Presley	.10	.05	.01
☐ 379	Scott Sanderson	.05	.02	.00	☐ 474	Donnie Scott	.05	.02	.00
☐ 380	Lee Smith	.08	.04	.01	☐ 475	Bill Swift	.10	.05	.01
☐ 381	Lary Sorensen	.05	.02	.00	☐ 476	Danny Tartabull	.65	.30	.06
☐ 382	Chris Speier	.05	.02	.00	☐ 477	Gorman Thomas	.10	.05	.01
☐ 383	Rick Sutcliffe	.12	.06	.01	☐ 478	Roy Thomas	.05	.02	.00
☐ 384	Steve Trout	.05	.02	.00	☐ 479	Ed VandeBerg	.05	.02	.00
☐ 385	Gary Woods	.05	.02	.00	☐ 480	Frank Wills	.08	.04	.01
☐ 386	Bert Blyleven	.15	.07	.01	☐ 481	Matt Young	.05	.02	.00
☐ 387	Tom Brunansky	.15	.07	.01	☐ 482	Ray Burris	.05	.02	.00
☐ 388	Randy Bush	.05	.02	.00	☐ 483	Jaime Cocanower	.05	.02	.00
☐ 389	John Butcher	.05	.02	.00	☐ 484	Cecil Cooper	.10	.05	.01
☐ 390	Ron Davis	.05	.02	.00	☐ 485	Danny Darwin	.05	.02	.00
☐ 391	Dave Engle	.05	.02	.00	☐ 486	Rollie Fingers	.15	.07	.01
☐ 392	Frank Eufemia	.05	.02	.00	☐ 487	Jim Gantner	.05	.02	.00
☐ 393	Pete Filson	.05	.02	.00	☐ 488	Bob L. Gibson	.05	.02	.00
☐ 394	Gary Gaetti	.20	.10	.02	☐ 489	Moose Haas	.05	.02	.00
☐ 395	Greg Gagne	.10	.05	.01	☐ 490	Teddy Higuera	1.25	.60	.12
☐ 396	Mickey Hatcher	.05	.02	.00	☐ 491	Paul Householder	.05	.02	.00
☐ 397	Kent Hrbek	.25	.12	.02	☐ 492	Pete Ladd	.05	.02	.00
☐ 398	Tim Laudner	.05	.02	.00	☐ 493	Rick Manning	.05	.02	.00
☐ 399	Rick Lysander	.05	.02	.00	☐ 494	Bob McClure	.05	.02	.00
☐ 400	Dave Meier	.05	.02	.00	☐ 495	Paul Molitor	.18	.09	.01
☐ 401	Kirby Puckett	3.50	1.75	.35	☐ 496	Charlie Moore	.05	.02	.00
☐ 402	Mark Salas	.05	.02	.00	☐ 497	Ben Oglivie	.08	.04	.01

☐ 498	Randy Ready	.05	.02	.00
☐ 499	Earnie Riles	.20	.10	.02
☐ 500	Ed Romero	.05	.02	.00
☐ 501	Bill Schroeder	.05	.02	.00
☐ 502	Ray Searage	.05	.02	.00
☐ 503	Ted Simmons	.10	.05	.01
☐ 504	Pete Vuckovich	.08	.04	.01
☐ 505	Rick Waits	.05	.02	.00
☐ 506	Robin Yount	.40	.20	.04
☐ 507	Len Barker	.05	.02	.00
☐ 508	Steve Bedrosian	.12	.06	.01
☐ 509	Bruce Benedict	.05	.02	.00
☐ 510	Rick Camp	.05	.02	.00
☐ 511	Rick Cerone	.05	.02	.00
☐ 512	Chris Chambliss	.08	.04	.01
☐ 513	Jeff Dedmon	.05	.02	.00
☐ 514	Terry Forster	.08	.04	.01
☐ 515	Gene Garber	.05	.02	.00
☐ 516	Terry Harper	.05	.02	.00
☐ 517	Bob Horner	.12	.06	.01
☐ 518	Glenn Hubbard	.05	.02	.00
☐ 519	Joe Johnson	.10	.05	.01
☐ 520	Brad Komminsk	.05	.02	.00
☐ 521	Rick Mahler	.05	.02	.00
☐ 522	Dale Murphy	.50	.25	.05
☐ 523	Ken Oberkfell	.05	.02	.00
☐ 524	Pascual Perez	.12	.06	.01
☐ 525	Gerald Perry	.10	.05	.01
☐ 526	Rafael Ramirez	.05	.02	.00
☐ 527	Steve Shields	.08	.04	.01
☐ 528	Zane Smith	.10	.05	.01
☐ 529	Bruce Sutter	.12	.06	.01
☐ 530	Milt Thompson	.30	.15	.03
☐ 531	Claudell Washington	.08	.04	.01
☐ 532	Paul Zuvella	.05	.02	.00
☐ 533	Vida Blue	.08	.04	.01
☐ 534	Bob Brenly	.05	.02	.00
☐ 535	Chris Brown	.18	.09	.01
☐ 536	Chili Davis	.10	.05	.01
☐ 537	Mark Davis	.15	.07	.01
☐ 538	Rob Deer	.35	.17	.03
☐ 539	Dan Driessen	.05	.02	.00
☐ 540	Scott Garrelts	.30	.15	.03
☐ 541	Dan Gladden	.08	.04	.01
☐ 542	Jim Gott	.08	.04	.01
☐ 543	David Green	.05	.02	.00
☐ 544	Atlee Hammaker	.05	.02	.00
☐ 545	Mike Jeffcoat	.05	.02	.00
☐ 546	Mike Krukow	.05	.02	.00
☐ 547	Dave LaPoint	.08	.04	.01
☐ 548	Jeff Leonard	.08	.04	.01
☐ 549	Greg Minton	.05	.02	.00
☐ 550	Alex Trevino	.05	.02	.00
☐ 551	Manny Trillo	.05	.02	.00
☐ 552	Jose Uribe	.30	.15	.03
☐ 553	Brad Wellman	.05	.02	.00
☐ 554	Frank Williams	.05	.02	.00
☐ 555	Joel Youngblood	.05	.02	.00
☐ 556	Alan Bannister	.05	.02	.00
☐ 557	Glenn Brummer	.05	.02	.00
☐ 558	Steve Buechele	.25	.12	.02
☐ 559	Jose Guzman	.25	.12	.02
☐ 560	Toby Harrah	.05	.02	.00
☐ 561	Greg Harris	.05	.02	.00
☐ 562	Dwayne Henry	.08	.04	.01
☐ 563	Burt Hooton	.05	.02	.00
☐ 564	Charlie Hough	.08	.04	.01
☐ 565	Mike Mason	.05	.02	.00
☐ 566	Oddibe McDowell	.20	.10	.02
☐ 567	Dickie Noles	.05	.02	.00
☐ 568	Pete O'Brien	.10	.05	.01
☐ 569	Larry Parrish	.05	.02	.00
☐ 570	Dave Rozema	.05	.02	.00
☐ 571	Dave Schmidt	.08	.04	.01
☐ 572	Don Slaught	.05	.02	.00
☐ 573	Wayne Tolleson	.05	.02	.00
☐ 574	Duane Walker	.05	.02	.00
☐ 575	Gary Ward	.08	.04	.01
☐ 576	Chris Welsh	.05	.02	.00
☐ 577	Curtis Wilkerson	.05	.02	.00
☐ 578	George Wright	.05	.02	.00
☐ 579	Chris Bando	.05	.02	.00
☐ 580	Tony Bernazard	.05	.02	.00
☐ 581	Brett Butler	.08	.04	.01
☐ 582	Ernie Camacho	.05	.02	.00
☐ 583	Joe Carter	.60	.30	.06
☐ 584	Carmen Castillo	.05	.02	.00
☐ 585	Jamie Easterly	.05	.02	.00
☐ 586	Julio Franco	.20	.10	.02
☐ 587	Mel Hall	.10	.05	.01
☐ 588	Mike Hargrove	.08	.04	.01
☐ 589	Neal Heaton	.05	.02	.00
☐ 590	Brook Jacoby	.10	.05	.01
☐ 591	Otis Nixon	.15	.07	.01
☐ 592	Jerry Reed	.05	.02	.00

☐ 593	Vern Ruhle	.05	.02	.00
☐ 594	Pat Tabler	.08	.04	.01
☐ 595	Rich Thompson	.05	.02	.00
☐ 596	Andre Thornton	.08	.04	.01
☐ 597	Dave Von Ohlen	.05	.02	.00
☐ 598	George Vukovich	.05	.02	.00
☐ 599	Tom Waddell	.05	.02	.00
☐ 600	Curt Wardle	.05	.02	.00
☐ 601	Jerry Willard	.05	.02	.00
☐ 602	Bill Almon	.05	.02	.00
☐ 603	Mike Bielecki	.10	.05	.01
☐ 604	Sid Bream	.08	.04	.01
☐ 605	Mike Brown OF	.05	.02	.00
☐ 606	Pat Clements	.10	.05	.01
☐ 607	Jose DeLeon	.08	.04	.01
☐ 608	Denny Gonzalez	.05	.02	.00
☐ 609	Cecilio Guante	.05	.02	.00
☐ 610	Steve Kemp	.08	.04	.01
☐ 611	Sammy Khalifa	.08	.04	.01
☐ 612	Lee Mazzilli	.05	.02	.00
☐ 613	Larry McWilliams	.05	.02	.00
☐ 614	Jim Morrison	.05	.02	.00
☐ 615	Joe Orsulak	.12	.06	.01
☐ 616	Tony Pena	.10	.05	.01
☐ 617	Johnny Ray	.10	.05	.01
☐ 618	Rick Reuschel	.10	.05	.01
☐ 619	R.J. Reynolds	.05	.02	.00
☐ 620	Rick Rhoden	.08	.04	.01
☐ 621	Don Robinson	.05	.02	.00
☐ 622	Jason Thompson	.05	.02	.00
☐ 623	Lee Tunnell	.05	.02	.00
☐ 624	Jim Winn	.05	.02	.00
☐ 625	Marvell Wynne	.05	.02	.00
☐ 626	Dwight Gooden IA	.40	.20	.04
☐ 627	Don Mattingly IA	1.50	.75	.15
☐ 628	4192 (Pete Rose)	.40	.20	.04
☐ 629	3000 Career Hits — Rod Carew	.20	.10	.02
☐ 630	300 Career Wins — Tom Seaver, Phil Niekro	.15	.07	.01
☐ 631	Ouch (Don Baylor)	.08	.04	.01
☐ 632	Instant Offense — Darryl Strawberry, Tim Raines	.25	.12	.02
☐ 633	Shortstops Supreme — Cal Ripken, Alan Trammell	.12	.06	.01
☐ 634	Boggs and "Hero" — Wade Boggs, George Brett	.50	.25	.05
☐ 635	Braves Dynamic Duo — Bob Horner, Dale Murphy	.15	.07	.01
☐ 636	Cardinal Ignitors — Willie McGee, Vince Coleman	.15	.07	.01
☐ 637	Terror on Basepaths — Vince Coleman	.20	.10	.02
☐ 638	Charlie Hustle / Dr.K — Pete Rose, Dwight Gooden	.75	.35	.07
☐ 639	1984 and 1985 AL Batting Champs — Wade Boggs, Don Mattingly	1.75	.85	.17
☐ 640	NL West Sluggers — Dale Murphy, Steve Garvey, Dave Parker	.15	.07	.01
☐ 641	Staff Aces — Fernando Valenzuela, Dwight Gooden	.30	.15	.03
☐ 642	Blue Jay Stoppers — Jimmy Key, Dave Stieb	.08	.04	.01
☐ 643	AL All-Star Backstops — Carlton Fisk, Rich Gedman	.08	.04	.01
☐ 644	Gene Walter and Benito Santiago	4.50	2.25	.45
☐ 645	Mike Woodard and Collin Ward	.10	.05	.01
☐ 646	Kal Daniels and Paul O'Neill	4.00	2.00	.40
☐ 647	Andres Galarraga and Fred Toliver	3.00	1.50	.30
☐ 648	Bob Kipper and Curt Ford	.10	.05	.01
☐ 649	Jose Canseco and Eric Plunk	35.00	17.50	3.50
☐ 650	Mark McLemore and Gus Polidor	.10	.05	.01
☐ 651	Rob Woodward and Mickey Brantley	.35	.17	.03

		MINT	EXC	G-VG
☐ 652	Billy Jo Robidoux and .... Mark Funderburk	.10	.05	.01
☐ 653	Cecil Fielder and .... Cory Snyder	2.25	1.10	.22
☐ 654	CL: Royals/Cardinals ..... Blue Jays/Mets	.08	.01	.00
☐ 655	CL: Yankees/Dodgers .... Angels/Reds	.08	.01	.00
☐ 656	CL: White Sox/Tigers ..... Expos/Orioles (279 Dennis, 280 Tippy)	.08	.01	.00
☐ 657	CL: Astros/Padres .... Red Sox/Cubs	.08	.01	.00
☐ 658	CL: Twins/A's .... Phillies/Mariners	.08	.01	.00
☐ 659	CL: Brewers/Braves ...... Giants/Rangers	.08	.01	.00
☐ 660	CL: Indians/Pirates .... Special Cards	.08	.01	.00

1986 Fleer Wax Box Cards

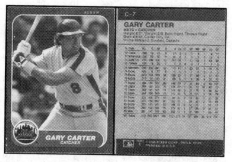

The cards in this 8-card set measure the standard 2 1/2" by 3 1/2" and were found on the bottom of the Fleer regular issue wax pack and cello pack boxes as four-card panel. Cards have essentially the same design as the 1986 Fleer regular issue set. These 8 cards (C1 to C8) are considered a separate set in their own right and are not typically included in a complete set of the regular issue 1986 Fleer cards. The value of the panel uncut is slightly greater, perhaps by 25% greater, than the value of the individual cards cut up carefully.

		MINT	EXC	G-VG
COMPLETE SET (8)	....	1.25	.60	.12
COMMON PLAYERS	....	.05	.02	.00
☐ C1	Royals Logo	.05	.02	.00
☐ C2	George Brett	.35	.17	.03
☐ C3	Ozzie Guillen	.15	.07	.01
☐ C4	Dale Murphy	.50	.25	.05
☐ C5	Cardinals Logo	.05	.02	.00
☐ C6	Tom Browning	.15	.07	.01
☐ C7	Gary Carter	.20	.10	.02
☐ C8	Carlton Fisk	.20	.10	.02

1986 Fleer All-Star Inserts

Fleer selected a 12-card (Major League) All-Star team to be included as inserts in their 39 cent wax packs and 59 cent cello packs. However they were randomly inserted in such a way that not all wax packs contain the insert. Cards measure 2 1/2" by 3 1/2" and feature attractive red backgrounds (American Leaguers) and blue backgrounds (National Leaguers). The 12 selections cover each position, left and right-handed starting pitchers, a reliever, and a designated hitter.

Dwight Gooden
METS • RIGHT HAND PITCHER

		MINT	EXC	G-VG
COMPLETE SET (12)	....	17.50	7.50	1.50
COMMON PLAYER (1-12)	....	.30	.15	.03
☐ 1	Don Mattingly .... First Base	9.00	4.50	.90
☐ 2	Tom Herr .... Second Base	.30	.15	.03
☐ 3	George Brett .... Third Base	1.00	.50	.10
☐ 4	Gary Carter .... Catcher	.75	.35	.07
☐ 5	Cal Ripken .... Shortstop	1.00	.50	.10
☐ 6	Dave Parker .... Outfield	.40	.20	.04
☐ 7	Rickey Henderson .... Outfield	2.00	1.00	.20
☐ 8	Pedro Guerrero .... Outfield	.40	.20	.04
☐ 9	Dan Quisenberry .... Relief Pitcher	.30	.15	.03
☐ 10	Dwight Gooden .... Right-Hand Pitcher	3.00	1.50	.30
☐ 11	Gorman Thomas .... Designated Hitter	.30	.15	.03
☐ 12	John Tudor .... Left-Hand Pitcher	.30	.15	.03

1986 Fleer Future HOF

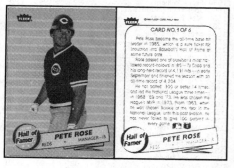

PETE ROSE
REDS • MANAGER-1B

These attractive cards were issued as inserts with the Fleer three-packs. They are the same size as the regular issue (2 1/2" by 3 1/2") and feature players that Fleer predicts will be "Future Hall of Famers." The card backs describe career highlights, records, and honors won by the player. The cards are numbered on the back; Pete Rose is given the honor of being card #1.

		MINT	EXC	G-VG
COMPLETE SET (6)	....	7.50	3.75	.75
COMMON PLAYER (1-6)	....	1.00	.50	.10
☐ 1	Pete Rose	2.00	1.00	.20

			MINT	EXC	G-VG
		Cincinnati Reds			
☐	2	Steve Carlton	1.00	.50	.10
		Philadelphia Phillies			
☐	3	Tom Seaver	1.00	.50	.10
		Chicago White Sox			
☐	4	Rod Carew	1.00	.50	.10
		California Angels			
☐	5	Nolan Ryan	2.50	1.25	.25
		Houston Astros			
☐	6	Reggie Jackson	1.25	.60	.12
		California Angels			

1986 Fleer League Leaders

This 44-card set is also sometimes referred to as the Walgreen's set. Although the set was distributed through Walgreen's, there is no mention on the cards or box of that fact. The cards are easily recognizable by the fact that they contain the phrase "Fleer League Leaders" at the top of the obverse. Both sides of the cards are designed with a blue stripe on white pattern. The checklist for the set is given on the outside of the red, white, blue, and gold box in which the set was packaged. Cards are numbered on the back and measure the standard 2 1/2" by 3 1/2".

			MINT	EXC	G-VG
	COMPLETE SET (44)		5.00	2.50	.50
	COMMON PLAYER (1-44)		.10	.05	.01
☐	1	Wade Boggs	.75	.35	.07
☐	2	George Brett	.40	.20	.04
☐	3	Jose Canseco	1.25	.60	.12
☐	4	Rod Carew	.30	.15	.03
☐	5	Gary Carter	.20	.10	.02
☐	6	Jack Clark	.20	.10	.02
☐	7	Vince Coleman	.35	.17	.03
☐	8	Jose Cruz	.10	.05	.01
☐	9	Alvin Davis	.15	.07	.01
☐	10	Mariano Duncan	.10	.05	.01
☐	11	Leon Durham	.10	.05	.01
☐	12	Carlton Fisk	.20	.10	.02
☐	13	Julio Franco	.10	.05	.01
☐	14	Scott Garrelts	.10	.05	.01
☐	15	Steve Garvey	.30	.15	.03
☐	16	Dwight Gooden	.45	.22	.04
☐	17	Ozzie Guillen	.15	.07	.01
☐	18	Willie Hernandez	.10	.05	.01
☐	19	Bob Horner	.15	.07	.01
☐	20	Kent Hrbek	.20	.10	.02
☐	21	Charlie Leibrandt	.10	.05	.01
☐	22	Don Mattingly	1.00	.50	.10
☐	23	Oddibe McDowell	.15	.07	.01
☐	24	Willie McGee	.20	.10	.02
☐	25	Keith Moreland	.10	.05	.01
☐	26	Lloyd Moseby	.10	.05	.01
☐	27	Dale Murphy	.35	.17	.03
☐	28	Phil Niekro	.20	.10	.02
☐	29	Joe Orsulak	.10	.05	.01
☐	30	Dave Parker	.20	.10	.02
☐	31	Lance Parrish	.15	.07	.01
☐	32	Kirby Puckett	.50	.25	.05
☐	33	Tim Raines	.25	.12	.02
☐	34	Earnie Riles	.10	.05	.01
☐	35	Cal Ripken	.30	.15	.03
☐	36	Pete Rose	.60	.30	.06

			MINT	EXC	G-VG
☐	37	Bret Saberhagen	.30	.15	.03
☐	38	Juan Samuel	.15	.07	.01
☐	39	Ryne Sandberg	.30	.15	.03
☐	40	Tom Seaver	.30	.15	.03
☐	41	Lee Smith	.10	.05	.01
☐	42	Ozzie Smith	.20	.10	.02
☐	43	Dave Stieb	.15	.07	.01
☐	44	Robin Yount	.35	.17	.03

1986 Fleer Limited Edition

The 44-card boxed set was produced by Fleer for McCrory's. The cards are standard size 2 1/2" by 3 1/2" and have green and yellow borders. Card backs are printed in red and black on white card stock. Cards are numbered on the back; the back of the original box gives a complete checklist of the players in the set. The set box also contains six logo stickers.

			MINT	EXC	G-VG
	COMPLETE SET (44)		5.00	2.50	.50
	COMMON PLAYER (1-44)		.10	.05	.01
☐	1	Doyle Alexander	.10	.05	.01
☐	2	Joaquin Andujar	.10	.05	.01
☐	3	Harold Baines	.15	.07	.01
☐	4	Wade Boggs	.75	.35	.07
☐	5	Phil Bradley	.15	.07	.01
☐	6	George Brett	.35	.17	.03
☐	7	Hubie Brooks	.10	.05	.01
☐	8	Chris Brown	.10	.05	.01
☐	9	Tom Brunansky	.15	.07	.01
☐	10	Gary Carter	.25	.12	.02
☐	11	Vince Coleman	.30	.15	.03
☐	12	Cecil Cooper	.15	.07	.01
☐	13	Jose Cruz	.10	.05	.01
☐	14	Mike Davis	.10	.05	.01
☐	15	Carlton Fisk	.20	.10	.02
☐	16	Julio Franco	.15	.07	.01
☐	17	Damaso Garcia	.10	.05	.01
☐	18	Rich Gedman	.10	.05	.01
☐	19	Kirk Gibson	.35	.17	.03
☐	20	Dwight Gooden	.50	.25	.05
☐	21	Pedro Guerrero	.20	.10	.02
☐	22	Tony Gwynn	.40	.20	.04
☐	23	Rickey Henderson	.50	.25	.05
☐	24	Orel Hershiser	.50	.25	.05
☐	25	LaMarr Hoyt	.10	.05	.01
☐	26	Reggie Jackson	.50	.25	.05
☐	27	Don Mattingly	1.00	.50	.10
☐	28	Oddibe McDowell	.15	.07	.01
☐	29	Willie McGee	.20	.10	.02
☐	30	Paul Molitor	.20	.10	.02
☐	31	Dale Murphy	.35	.17	.03
☐	32	Eddie Murray	.25	.12	.02
☐	33	Dave Parker	.20	.10	.02
☐	34	Tony Pena	.10	.05	.01
☐	35	Jeff Reardon	.15	.07	.01
☐	36	Cal Ripken	.30	.15	.03
☐	37	Pete Rose	.60	.30	.06
☐	38	Bret Saberhagen	.30	.15	.03
☐	39	Juan Samuel	.15	.07	.01
☐	40	Ryne Sandberg	.30	.15	.03
☐	41	Mike Schmidt	.75	.35	.07
☐	42	Lee Smith	.10	.05	.01
☐	43	Don Sutton	.20	.10	.02
☐	44	Lou Whitaker	.20	.10	.02

1986 Fleer Mini

The Fleer "Classic Miniatures" set consists of 120 small cards with all new pictures of the players as compared to the 1986 Fleer regular issue. The cards are only 1 13/16" by 2 9/16", making them one of the smallest (in size) produced in recent memory. Card backs provide career year-by-year statistics. The complete set was distributed in a red, white, and silver box along with 18 logo stickers. The card numbering is done in team order as is the usual Fleer style.

		MINT	EXC	G-VG
COMPLETE SET (120)		12.00	6.00	1.20
COMMON PLAYER (1-120)		.05	.02	.00
☐	1 George Brett	.30	.15	.03
☐	2 Dan Quisenberry	.10	.05	.01
☐	3 Bret Saberhagen	.30	.15	.03
☐	4 Lonnie Smith	.10	.05	.01
☐	5 Willie Wilson	.10	.05	.01
☐	6 Jack Clark	.20	.10	.02
☐	7 Vince Coleman	.30	.15	.03
☐	8 Tom Herr	.05	.02	.00
☐	9 Willie McGee	.15	.07	.01
☐	10 Ozzie Smith	.20	.10	.02
☐	11 John Tudor	.10	.05	.01
☐	12 Jesse Barfield	.15	.07	.01
☐	13 George Bell	.20	.10	.02
☐	14 Tony Fernandez	.15	.07	.01
☐	15 Damaso Garcia	.05	.02	.00
☐	16 Dave Stieb	.10	.05	.01
☐	17 Gary Carter	.20	.10	.02
☐	18 Ron Darling	.10	.05	.01
☐	19A Dwight Gooden	1.00	.50	.10
	(R on Mets logo)			
☐	19B Dwight Gooden	1.00	.50	.10
	(no R on Mets logo)			
☐	20 Keith Hernandez	.20	.10	.02
☐	21 Darryl Strawberry	.50	.25	.05
☐	22 Ron Guidry	.15	.07	.01
☐	23 Rickey Henderson	.40	.20	.04
☐	24 Don Mattingly	1.50	.75	.15
☐	25 Dave Righetti	.15	.07	.01
☐	26 Dave Winfield	.20	.10	.02
☐	27 Mariano Duncan	.05	.02	.00
☐	28 Pedro Guerrero	.15	.07	.01
☐	29 Bill Madlock	.05	.02	.00
☐	30 Mike Marshall	.10	.05	.01
☐	31 Fernando Valenzuela	.15	.07	.01
☐	32 Reggie Jackson	.35	.17	.03
☐	33 Gary Pettis	.05	.02	.00
☐	34 Ron Romanick	.05	.02	.00
☐	35 Don Sutton	.15	.07	.01
☐	36 Mike Witt	.10	.05	.01
☐	37 Buddy Bell	.10	.05	.01
☐	38 Tom Browning	.10	.05	.01
☐	39 Dave Parker	.15	.07	.01
☐	40 Pete Rose	.65	.30	.06
☐	41 Mario Soto	.05	.02	.00
☐	42 Harold Baines	.10	.05	.01
☐	43 Carlton Fisk	.20	.10	.02
☐	44 Ozzie Guillen	.10	.05	.01
☐	45 Ron Kittle	.10	.05	.01
☐	46 Tom Seaver	.25	.12	.02
☐	47 Kirk Gibson	.25	.12	.02
☐	48 Jack Morris	.10	.05	.01
☐	49 Lance Parrish	.10	.05	.01
☐	50 Alan Trammell	.15	.07	.01
☐	51 Lou Whitaker	.15	.07	.01
☐	52 Hubie Brooks	.10	.05	.01
☐	53 Andre Dawson	.20	.10	.02
☐	54 Tim Raines	.20	.10	.02
☐	55 Bryn Smith	.10	.05	.01
☐	56 Tim Wallach	.10	.05	.01
☐	57 Mike Boddicker	.10	.05	.01
☐	58 Eddie Murray	.20	.10	.02
☐	59 Cal Ripken	.30	.15	.03
☐	60 John Shelby	.05	.02	.00
☐	61 Mike Young	.05	.02	.00
☐	62 Jose Cruz	.05	.02	.00
☐	63 Glenn Davis	.25	.12	.02
☐	64 Phil Garner	.05	.02	.00
☐	65 Nolan Ryan	1.00	.50	.10
☐	66 Mike Scott	.15	.07	.01
☐	67 Steve Garvey	.20	.10	.02
☐	68 Goose Gossage	.10	.05	.01
☐	69 Tony Gwynn	.30	.15	.03
☐	70 Andy Hawkins	.05	.02	.00
☐	71 Garry Templeton	.05	.02	.00
☐	72 Wade Boggs	.90	.45	.09
☐	73 Roger Clemens	.75	.35	.07
☐	74 Dwight Evans	.15	.07	.01
☐	75 Rich Gedman	.05	.02	.00
☐	76 Jim Rice	.20	.10	.02
☐	77 Shawon Dunston	.10	.05	.01
☐	78 Leon Durham	.05	.02	.00
☐	79 Keith Moreland	.05	.02	.00
☐	80 Ryne Sandberg	.20	.10	.02
☐	81 Rick Sutcliffe	.10	.05	.01
☐	82 Bert Blyleven	.15	.07	.01
☐	83 Tom Brunansky	.10	.05	.01
☐	84 Kent Hrbek	.15	.07	.01
☐	85 Kirby Puckett	.45	.22	.04
☐	86 Bruce Bochte	.05	.02	.00
☐	87 Jose Canseco	2.00	1.00	.20
☐	88 Mike Davis	.05	.02	.00
☐	89 Jay Howell	.05	.02	.00
☐	90 Dwayne Murphy	.05	.02	.00
☐	91 Steve Carlton	.25	.12	.02
☐	92 Von Hayes	.10	.05	.01
☐	93 Juan Samuel	.15	.07	.01
☐	94 Mike Schmidt	.75	.35	.07
☐	95 Glenn Wilson	.05	.02	.00
☐	96 Phil Bradley	.10	.05	.01
☐	97 Alvin Davis	.10	.05	.01
☐	98 Jim Presley	.05	.02	.00
☐	99 Danny Tartabull	.20	.10	.02
☐	100 Cecil Cooper	.10	.05	.01
☐	101 Paul Molitor	.15	.07	.01
☐	102 Ernie Riles	.05	.02	.00
☐	103 Robin Yount	.50	.25	.05
☐	104 Bob Horner	.10	.05	.01
☐	105 Dale Murphy	.30	.15	.03
☐	106 Bruce Sutter	.10	.05	.01
☐	107 Claudell Washington	.05	.02	.00
☐	108 Chris Brown	.05	.02	.00
☐	109 Chili Davis	.05	.02	.00
☐	110 Scott Garrelts	.05	.02	.00
☐	111 Oddibe McDowell	.10	.05	.01
☐	112 Pete O'Brien	.10	.05	.01
☐	113 Gary Ward	.05	.02	.00
☐	114 Brett Butler	.10	.05	.01
☐	115 Julio Franco	.10	.05	.01
☐	116 Brook Jacoby	.10	.05	.01
☐	117 Mike Brown OF	.05	.02	.00
☐	118 Joe Orsulak	.05	.02	.00
☐	119 Tony Pena	.10	.05	.01
☐	120 R.J. Reynolds	.05	.02	.00

1986 Fleer Sluggers/Pitchers

Fleer produced this 44-card boxed set although it was primarily distributed by Kress, McCrory, Newberry, T.G.Y., and other similar stores. The set features 22 sluggers and 22 pitchers and is subtitled "Baseball's Best". Cards are standard-size, 2 1/2" by 3 1/2", and were packaged in a red, white, blue, and yellow custom box along with six logo stickers. The set checklist is given on the back of the box.

		MINT	EXC	G-VG
COMPLETE SET (44)		7.50	3.75	.75
COMMON PLAYER (1-44)		.10	.05	.01
☐	1 Bert Blyleven	.15	.07	.01
☐	2 Wade Boggs	.75	.35	.07

printed on the bottom of the counter display box which held 24 small boxed sets; hence theoretically these box cards are 1/24 as plentiful as the regular boxed set cards. These 6 cards, numbered M1 to M5 with one blank-back (unnumbered) card, are considered a separate set in their own right and are not typically included in a complete set of the 1986 Fleer Sluggers vs. Pitchers set of 44. The value of the panels uncut is slightly greater, perhaps by 25% greater, than the value of the individual cards cut up carefully.

			MINT	EXC	G-VG
	COMPLETE SET		2.50	1.25	.25
	COMMON PLAYERS		.10	.05	.01
☐	M1	Harold Baines	.15	.07	.01
☐	M2	Steve Carlton	.75	.35	.07
☐	M3	Gary Carter	.50	.25	.05
☐	M4	Vince Coleman	.75	.35	.07
☐	M5	Kirby Puckett	1.00	.50	.10
☐	xx	Team Logo (unnumbered, blank back)	.10	.05	.01

☐	3	George Brett	.35	.17	.03
☐	4	Tom Browning	.10	.05	.01
☐	5	Jose Canseco	2.50	1.25	.25
☐	6	Will Clark	2.50	1.25	.25
☐	7	Roger Clemens	.60	.30	.06
☐	8	Alvin Davis	.15	.07	.01
☐	9	Julio Franco	.15	.07	.01
☐	10	Kirk Gibson	.30	.15	.03
☐	11	Dwight Gooden	.50	.25	.05
☐	12	Goose Gossage	.15	.07	.01
☐	13	Pedro Guerrero	.20	.10	.02
☐	14	Ron Guidry	.15	.07	.01
☐	15	Tony Gwynn	.35	.17	.03
☐	16	Orel Hershiser	.50	.25	.05
☐	17	Kent Hrbek	.20	.10	.02
☐	18	Reggie Jackson	.40	.20	.04
☐	19	Wally Joyner	1.25	.60	.12
☐	20	Charlie Leibrandt	.10	.05	.01
☐	21	Don Mattingly	1.00	.50	.10
☐	22	Willie McGee	.20	.10	.02
☐	23	Jack Morris	.15	.07	.01
☐	24	Dale Murphy	.35	.17	.03
☐	25	Eddie Murray	.25	.12	.02
☐	26	Jeff Reardon	.10	.05	.01
☐	27	Rick Reuschel	.15	.07	.01
☐	28	Cal Ripken	.30	.15	.03
☐	29	Pete Rose	.60	.30	.06
☐	30	Nolan Ryan	1.00	.50	.10
☐	31	Bret Saberhagen	.30	.15	.03
☐	32	Ryne Sandberg	.25	.12	.02
☐	33	Mike Schmidt	.75	.35	.07
☐	34	Tom Seaver	.30	.15	.03
☐	35	Bryn Smith	.10	.05	.01
☐	36	Mario Soto	.10	.05	.01
☐	37	Dave Stieb	.15	.07	.01
☐	38	Darryl Strawberry	.60	.30	.06
☐	39	Rick Sutcliffe	.15	.07	.01
☐	40	John Tudor	.15	.07	.01
☐	41	Fernando Valenzuela	.20	.10	.02
☐	42	Bobby Witt	.20	.10	.02
☐	43	Mike Witt	.15	.07	.01
☐	44	Robin Yount	.35	.17	.03

1986 Fleer Slug/Pitch Box Cards

The cards in this 6-card set each measure the standard 2 1/2" by 3 1/2". Cards have essentially the same design as the 1986 Fleer Sluggers vs. Pitchers set of Baseball's Best. The cards were

1986 Fleer Sticker Cards

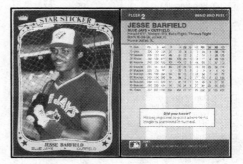

The stickers in this 132-sticker card set are standard card size, 2 1/2" by 3 1/2". The card photo on the front is surrounded by a yellow border and a cranberry frame. The backs are printed in blue and black on white card stock. The backs contain year-by-year statistical information. They are numbered on the back in the upper left-hand corner.

			MINT	EXC	G-VG
	COMPLETE SET (132)		28.00	14.00	2.80
	COMMON PLAYER (1-132)		.05	.02	.00
☐	1	Harold Baines	.15	.07	.01
☐	2	Jesse Barfield	.15	.07	.01
☐	3	Don Baylor	.10	.05	.01
☐	4	Juan Beniquez	.05	.02	.00
☐	5	Tim Birtsas	.05	.02	.00
☐	6	Bert Blyleven	.15	.07	.01
☐	7	Bruce Bochte	.05	.02	.00
☐	8	Wade Boggs	1.25	.60	.12
☐	9	Dennis Boyd	.10	.05	.01
☐	10	Phil Bradley	.10	.05	.01
☐	11	George Brett	.75	.35	.07
☐	12	Hubie Brooks	.10	.05	.01
☐	13	Chris Brown	.05	.02	.00
☐	14	Tom Browning	.15	.07	.01
☐	15	Tom Brunansky	.15	.07	.01
☐	16	Bill Buckner	.10	.05	.01
☐	17	Britt Burns	.05	.02	.00
☐	18	Brett Butler	.10	.05	.01
☐	19	Jose Canseco	3.00	1.50	.30
☐	20	Rod Carew	.40	.20	.04
☐	21	Steve Carlton	.40	.20	.04
☐	22	Don Carman	.10	.05	.01
☐	23	Gary Carter	.30	.15	.03
☐	24	Jack Clark	.20	.10	.02
☐	25	Vince Coleman	1.00	.50	.10
☐	26	Cecil Cooper	.10	.05	.01

☐ 27	Jose Cruz	.05	.02	.00
☐ 28	Ron Darling	.15	.07	.01
☐ 29	Alvin Davis	.20	.10	.02
☐ 30	Jody Davis	.05	.02	.00
☐ 31	Mike Davis	.05	.02	.00
☐ 32	Andre Dawson	.25	.12	.02
☐ 33	Mariano Duncan	.10	.05	.01
☐ 34	Shawon Dunston	.10	.05	.01
☐ 35	Leon Durham	.05	.02	.00
☐ 36	Darrell Evans	.10	.05	.01
☐ 37	Tony Fernandez	.15	.07	.01
☐ 38	Carlton Fisk	.25	.12	.02
☐ 39	John Franco	.10	.05	.01
☐ 40	Julio Franco	.10	.05	.01
☐ 41	Damaso Garcia	.05	.02	.00
☐ 42	Scott Garrelts	.10	.05	.01
☐ 43	Steve Garvey	.40	.20	.04
☐ 44	Rich Gedman	.05	.02	.00
☐ 45	Kirk Gibson	.35	.17	.03
☐ 46	Dwight Gooden	1.00	.50	.10
☐ 47	Pedro Guerrero	.20	.10	.02
☐ 48	Ron Guidry	.15	.07	.01
☐ 49	Ozzie Guillen	.15	.07	.01
☐ 50	Tony Gwynn	.45	.22	.04
☐ 51	Andy Hawkins	.05	.02	.00
☐ 52	Von Hayes	.10	.05	.01
☐ 53	Rickey Henderson	.75	.35	.07
☐ 54	Tom Henke	.10	.05	.01
☐ 55	Keith Hernandez	.25	.12	.02
☐ 56	Willie Hernandez	.10	.05	.01
☐ 57	Tommy Herr	.05	.02	.00
☐ 58	Orel Hershiser	.60	.30	.06
☐ 59	Teddy Higuera	.40	.20	.04
☐ 60	Bob Horner	.15	.07	.01
☐ 61	Charlie Hough	.05	.02	.00
☐ 62	Jay Howell	.05	.02	.00
☐ 63	LaMarr Hoyt	.05	.02	.00
☐ 64	Kent Hrbek	.20	.10	.02
☐ 65	Reggie Jackson	.50	.25	.05
☐ 66	Bob James	.05	.02	.00
☐ 67	Dave Kingman	.10	.05	.01
☐ 68	Ron Kittle	.10	.05	.01
☐ 69	Charlie Leibrandt	.05	.02	.00
☐ 70	Fred Lynn	.15	.07	.01
☐ 71	Mike Marshall	.15	.07	.01
☐ 72	Don Mattingly	2.50	1.25	.25
☐ 73	Oddibe McDowell	.15	.07	.01
☐ 74	Willie McGee	.20	.10	.02
☐ 75	Scott McGregor	.05	.02	.00
☐ 76	Paul Molitor	.20	.10	.02
☐ 77	Charlie Moore	.05	.02	.00
☐ 78	Keith Moreland	.05	.02	.00
☐ 79	Jack Morris	.15	.07	.01
☐ 80	Dale Murphy	.50	.25	.05
☐ 81	Eddie Murray	.40	.20	.04
☐ 82	Phil Niekro	.25	.12	.02
☐ 83	Joe Orsulak	.05	.02	.00
☐ 84	Dave Parker	.15	.07	.01
☐ 85	Lance Parrish	.15	.07	.01
☐ 86	Larry Parrish	.05	.02	.00
☐ 87	Tony Pena	.10	.05	.01
☐ 88	Gary Pettis	.10	.05	.01
☐ 89	Jim Presley	.10	.05	.01
☐ 90	Kirby Puckett	1.00	.50	.10
☐ 91	Dan Quisenberry	.10	.05	.01
☐ 92	Tim Raines	.20	.10	.02
☐ 93	Johnny Ray	.10	.05	.01
☐ 94	Jeff Reardon	.10	.05	.01
☐ 95	Rick Reuschel	.15	.07	.01
☐ 96	Jim Rice	.20	.10	.02
☐ 97	Dave Righetti	.15	.07	.01
☐ 98	Earnie Riles	.05	.02	.00
☐ 99	Cal Ripken	.45	.22	.04
☐ 100	Ron Romanick	.05	.02	.00
☐ 101	Pete Rose	1.00	.50	.10
☐ 102	Nolan Ryan	1.50	.75	.15
☐ 103	Bret Saberhagen	.50	.25	.05
☐ 104	Mark Salas	.05	.02	.00
☐ 105	Juan Samuel	.15	.07	.01
☐ 106	Ryne Sandberg	.45	.22	.04
☐ 107	Mike Schmidt	1.25	.60	.12
☐ 108	Mike Scott	.20	.10	.02
☐ 109	Tom Seaver	.35	.17	.03
☐ 110	Bryn Smith	.10	.05	.01
☐ 111	Dave Smith	.05	.02	.00
☐ 112	Lonnie Smith	.10	.05	.01
☐ 113	Ozzie Smith	.25	.12	.02
☐ 114	Mario Soto	.05	.02	.00
☐ 115	Dave Stieb	.10	.05	.01
☐ 116	Darryl Strawberry	.75	.35	.07
☐ 117	Bruce Sutter	.10	.05	.01
☐ 118	Garry Templeton	.05	.02	.00
☐ 119	Gorman Thomas	.10	.05	.01
☐ 120	Andre Thornton	.05	.02	.00
☐ 121	Alan Trammell	.25	.12	.02
☐ 122	John Tudor	.15	.07	.01
☐ 123	Fernando Valenzuela	.20	.10	.02
☐ 124	Frank Viola	.20	.10	.02
☐ 125	Gary Ward	.05	.02	.00
☐ 126	Lou Whitaker	.15	.07	.01
☐ 127	Frank White	.10	.05	.01
☐ 128	Glenn Wilson	.05	.02	.00
☐ 129	Willie Wilson	.15	.07	.01
☐ 130	Dave Winfield	.30	.15	.03
☐ 131	Robin Yount	.50	.25	.05
☐ 132	Checklist Card	1.00	.50	.10
	Dwight Gooden			
	Dale Murphy			

1986 Fleer Sticker Wax Box

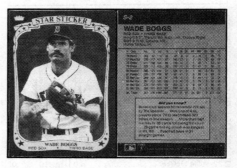

The bottoms of the Star Sticker wax boxes contained a set of four cards done in a similar format to the stickers; these cards (they are not stickers but truly cards) are numbered with the prefix S and are considered a separate set. Each individual card measures 2 1/2" by 3 1/2". The value of the panel uncut is slightly greater, perhaps by 25% greater, than the value of the individual cards cut up carefully.

		MINT	EXC	G-VG
COMPLETE SET (4)		1.50	.75	.15
COMMON PLAYER (S1-S4)		.10	.05	.01
☐ S1	Team Logo	.10	.05	.01
	(checklist back)			
☐ S2	Wade Boggs	1.00	.50	.10
☐ S3	Steve Garvey	.35	.17	.03
☐ S4	Dave Winfield	.35	.17	.03

1986 Fleer Update

This 132-card set was distributed by Fleer to dealers as a complete set within a custom box. In addition to the complete set of 132 cards, the box also contains 25 Team Logo Stickers. The card fronts look very similar to the 1986 Fleer regular issue. The cards are numbered (with a U prefix) alphabetically according to player's last name. Cards measure the standard size, 2 1/2" by 3 1/2".

		MINT	EXC	G-VG
	COMPLETE SET (132)	33.00	15.00	3.00
	COMMON PLAYER (1-132)	.06	.03	.00
☐	U1 Mike Aldrete	.25	.06	.01
☐	U2 Andy Allanson	.15	.07	.01
☐	U3 Neil Allen	.06	.03	.00
☐	U4 Joaquin Andujar	.10	.05	.01
☐	U5 Paul Assenmacher	.15	.07	.01
☐	U6 Scott Bailes	.15	.07	.01
☐	U7 Jay Baller	.10	.05	.01
☐	U8 Scott Bankhead	.35	.17	.03
☐	U9 Bill Bathe	.10	.05	.01
☐	U10 Don Baylor	.10	.05	.01
☐	U11 Billy Beane	.15	.07	.01
☐	U12 Steve Bedrosian	.15	.07	.01
☐	U13 Juan Beniquez	.06	.03	.00
☐	U14 Barry Bonds	1.25	.60	.12
☐	U15 Bobby Bonilla UER	1.25	.60	.12
	(wrong birthday)			
☐	U16 Rich Bordi	.06	.03	.00
☐	U17 Bill Campbell	.06	.03	.00
☐	U18 Tom Candiotti	.10	.05	.01
☐	U19 John Cangelosi	.15	.07	.01
☐	U20 Jose Canseco UER	8.00	4.00	.80
	(headings on back			
	for a pitcher)			
☐	U21 Chuck Cary	.20	.10	.02
☐	U22 Juan Castillo	.10	.05	.01
☐	U23 Rick Cerone	.10	.05	.01
☐	U24 John Cerutti	.25	.12	.02
☐	U25 Will Clark	12.00	6.00	1.20
☐	U26 Mark Clear	.06	.03	.00
☐	U27 Darnell Coles	.10	.05	.01
☐	U28 Dave Collins	.06	.03	.00
☐	U29 Tim Conroy	.06	.03	.00
☐	U30 Ed Correa	.15	.07	.01
☐	U31 Joe Cowley	.06	.03	.00
☐	U32 Bill Dawley	.06	.03	.00
☐	U33 Rob Deer	.20	.10	.02
☐	U34 John Denny	.10	.05	.01
☐	U35 Jim Deshaies	.35	.17	.03
☐	U36 Doug Drabek	.35	.17	.03
☐	U37 Mike Easler	.06	.03	.00
☐	U38 Mark Eichhorn	.10	.05	.01
☐	U39 Dave Engle	.06	.03	.00
☐	U40 Mike Fischlin	.06	.03	.00
☐	U41 Scott Fletcher	.10	.05	.01
☐	U42 Terry Forster	.10	.05	.01
☐	U43 Terry Francona	.06	.03	.00
☐	U44 Andres Galarraga	.90	.45	.09
☐	U45 Lee Guetterman	.20	.10	.02
☐	U46 Bill Gullickson	.06	.03	.00
☐	U47 Jackie Gutierrez	.06	.03	.00
☐	U48 Moose Haas	.06	.03	.00
☐	U49 Billy Hatcher	.10	.05	.01
☐	U50 Mike Heath	.06	.03	.00
☐	U51 Guy Hoffman	.06	.03	.00
☐	U52 Tom Hume	.06	.03	.00
☐	U53 Pete Incaviglia	.75	.35	.07
☐	U54 Dane Iorg	.06	.03	.00
☐	U55 Chris James	.80	.40	.08
☐	U56 Stan Javier	.25	.12	.02
☐	U57 Tommy John	.15	.07	.01
☐	U58 Tracy Jones	.35	.17	.03
☐	U59 Wally Joyner	2.50	1.25	.25
☐	U60 Wayne Krenchicki	.06	.03	.00
☐	U61 John Kruk	.45	.22	.04
☐	U62 Mike LaCoss	.06	.03	.00
☐	U63 Pete Ladd	.06	.03	.00
☐	U64 Dave LaPoint	.10	.05	.01
☐	U65 Mike LaValliere	.25	.12	.02
☐	U66 Rudy Law	.06	.03	.00
☐	U67 Dennis Leonard	.10	.05	.01
☐	U68 Steve Lombardozzi	.10	.05	.01
☐	U69 Aurelio Lopez	.06	.03	.00
☐	U70 Mickey Mahler	.06	.03	.00
☐	U71 Candy Maldonado	.10	.05	.01
☐	U72 Roger Mason	.10	.05	.01
☐	U73 Greg Mathews	.25	.12	.02
☐	U74 Andy McGaffigan	.06	.03	.00
☐	U75 Joel McKeon	.10	.05	.01
☐	U76 Kevin Mitchell	6.50	3.25	.65
☐	U77 Bill Mooneyham	.10	.05	.01
☐	U78 Omar Moreno	.06	.03	.00
☐	U79 Jerry Mumphrey	.06	.03	.00
☐	U80 Al Newman	.10	.05	.01
☐	U81 Phil Niekro	.35	.17	.03
☐	U82 Randy Niemann	.06	.03	.00
☐	U83 Juan Nieves	.15	.07	.01

☐	U84 Bob Ojeda	.15	.07	.01
☐	U85 Rick Ownbey	.06	.03	.00
☐	U86 Tom Paciorek	.06	.03	.00
☐	U87 David Palmer	.06	.03	.00
☐	U88 Jeff Parrett	.35	.17	.03
☐	U89 Pat Perry	.15	.07	.01
☐	U90 Dan Plesac	.35	.17	.03
☐	U91 Darrell Porter	.06	.03	.00
☐	U92 Luis Quinones	.15	.07	.01
☐	U93 Rey Quinones	.20	.10	.02
☐	U94 Gary Redus	.06	.03	.00
☐	U95 Jeff Reed	.10	.05	.01
☐	U96 Bip Roberts	.25	.12	.02
☐	U97 Billy Jo Robidoux	.10	.05	.01
☐	U98 Gary Roenicke	.06	.03	.00
☐	U99 Ron Roenicke	.06	.03	.00
☐	U100 Angel Salazar	.06	.03	.00
☐	U101 Joe Sambito	.06	.03	.00
☐	U102 Billy Sample	.06	.03	.00
☐	U103 Dave Schmidt	.10	.05	.01
☐	U104 Ken Schrom	.06	.03	.00
☐	U105 Ruben Sierra	6.50	3.25	.65
☐	U106 Ted Simmons	.20	.10	.02
☐	U107 Sammy Stewart	.06	.03	.00
☐	U108 Kurt Stillwell	.30	.15	.03
☐	U109 Dale Sveum	.25	.12	.02
☐	U110 Tim Teufel	.10	.05	.01
☐	U111 Bob Tewksbury	.15	.07	.01
☐	U112 Andres Thomas	.25	.12	.02
☐	U113 Jason Thompson	.06	.03	.00
☐	U114 Milt Thompson	.10	.05	.01
☐	U115 Robby Thompson	.40	.20	.04
☐	U116 Jay Tibbs	.06	.03	.00
☐	U117 Fred Toliver	.10	.05	.01
☐	U118 Wayne Tolleson	.06	.03	.00
☐	U119 Alex Trevino	.06	.03	.00
☐	U120 Manny Trillo	.06	.03	.00
☐	U121 Ed VandeBerg	.06	.03	.00
☐	U122 Ozzie Virgil	.06	.03	.00
☐	U123 Tony Walker	.10	.05	.01
☐	U124 Gene Walter	.10	.05	.01
☐	U125 Duane Ward	.20	.10	.02
☐	U126 Jerry Willard	.06	.03	.00
☐	U127 Mitch Williams	.50	.25	.05
☐	U128 Reggie Williams	.10	.05	.01
☐	U129 Bobby Witt	.40	.20	.04
☐	U130 Marvell Wynne	.06	.03	.00
☐	U131 Steve Yeager	.06	.03	.00
☐	U132 Checklist 1-132	.06	.01	.00

1987 Fleer

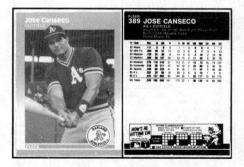

This 660-card set features a distinctive blue border which fades to white on the card fronts. The backs are printed in blue, red, and pink on white card stock. The bottom of the card back shows an innovative graph of the player's ability, e.g., "He's got the stuff" for pitchers and "How he's hitting 'em," for hitters. Cards are numbered on the back and are again the standard 2 1/2" by 3 1/2". Cards are again organized numerically by teams, i.e., World Champion Mets (1-25), Boston Red Sox (26-48), Houston Astros (49-72), California Angels (73-95), New York Yankees (96-120), Texas Rangers (121-143), Detroit Tigers (144-168), Philadelphia Phillies (169-192), Cincinnati Reds (193-218), Toronto Blue

Jays (219-240), Cleveland Indians (241-263), San Francisco Giants (264-288), St. Louis Cardinals (289-312), Montreal Expos (313-337), Milwaukee Brewers (338-361), Kansas City Royals (362-384), Oakland A's (385-410), San Diego Padres (411-435), Los Angeles Dodgers (436-460), Baltimore Orioles (461-483), Chicago White Sox (484-508), Atlanta Braves (509-532), Minnesota Twins (533-554), Chicago Cubs (555-578), Seattle Mariners (579-600), and Pittsburgh Pirates (601-624). The last 36 cards in the set consist of Specials (625-643), Rookie Pairs (644-653), and checklists (654-660). Fleer also produced a "limited" edition version of this set with glossy coating and packaged in a "tin." However this tin set was apparently not limited enough (estimated between 75,000 and 100,000 1987 tin sets produced by Fleer) since the price of the "tin" glossy cards is now the same as the regular set.

	MINT	EXC	G-VG
COMPLETE SET (660)	95.00	40.00	9.00
COMMON PLAYER (1-660)	.05	.02	.00

		MINT	EXC	G-VG
☐	1 Rick Aguilera	.10	.03	.01
☐	2 Richard Anderson	.08	.04	.01
☐	3 Wally Backman	.05	.02	.00
☐	4 Gary Carter	.25	.12	.02
☐	5 Ron Darling	.18	.09	.01
☐	6 Len Dykstra	.12	.06	.01
☐	7 Kevin Elster	.65	.30	.06
☐	8 Sid Fernandez	.12	.06	.01
☐	9 Dwight Gooden	1.00	.50	.10
☐	10 Ed Hearn	.08	.04	.01
☐	11 Danny Heep	.05	.02	.00
☐	12 Keith Hernandez	.25	.12	.02
☐	13 Howard Johnson	.30	.15	.03
☐	14 Ray Knight	.08	.04	.01
☐	15 Lee Mazzilli	.05	.02	.00
☐	16 Roger McDowell	.08	.04	.01
☐	17 Kevin Mitchell	9.00	4.50	.90
☐	18 Randy Niemann	.05	.02	.00
☐	19 Bob Ojeda	.08	.04	.01
☐	20 Jesse Orosco	.05	.02	.00
☐	21 Rafael Santana	.05	.02	.00
☐	22 Doug Sisk	.05	.02	.00
☐	23 Darryl Strawberry	1.00	.50	.10
☐	24 Tim Teufel	.05	.02	.00
☐	25 Mookie Wilson	.08	.04	.01
☐	26 Tony Armas	.08	.04	.01
☐	27 Marty Barrett	.08	.04	.01
☐	28 Don Baylor	.10	.05	.01
☐	29 Wade Boggs	1.50	.75	.15
☐	30 Oil Can Boyd	.08	.04	.01
☐	31 Bill Buckner	.08	.04	.01
☐	32 Roger Clemens	1.50	.75	.15
☐	33 Steve Crawford	.05	.02	.00
☐	34 Dwight Evans	.12	.06	.01
☐	35 Rich Gedman	.05	.02	.00
☐	36 Dave Henderson	.08	.04	.01
☐	37 Bruce Hurst	.12	.06	.01
☐	38 Tim Lollar	.05	.02	.00
☐	39 Al Nipper	.05	.02	.00
☐	40 Spike Owen	.05	.02	.00
☐	41 Jim Rice	.18	.09	.01
☐	42 Ed Romero	.05	.02	.00
☐	43 Joe Sambito	.05	.02	.00
☐	44 Calvin Schiraldi	.05	.02	.00
☐	45 Tom Seaver	.35	.17	.03
☐	46 Jeff Sellers	.15	.07	.01
☐	47 Bob Stanley	.05	.02	.00
☐	48 Sammy Stewart	.05	.02	.00
☐	49 Larry Andersen	.05	.02	.00
☐	50 Alan Ashby	.05	.02	.00
☐	51 Kevin Bass	.10	.05	.01
☐	52 Jeff Calhoun	.05	.02	.00
☐	53 Jose Cruz	.10	.05	.01
☐	54 Danny Darwin	.05	.02	.00
☐	55 Glenn Davis	.35	.17	.03
☐	56 Jim Deshaies	.35	.17	.03
☐	57 Bill Doran	.10	.05	.01
☐	58 Phil Garner	.05	.02	.00
☐	59 Billy Hatcher	.08	.04	.01
☐	60 Charlie Kerfeld	.05	.02	.00
☐	61 Bob Knepper	.08	.04	.01
☐	62 Dave Lopes	.08	.04	.01
☐	63 Aurelio Lopez	.05	.02	.00
☐	64 Jim Pankovits	.05	.02	.00
☐	65 Terry Puhl	.05	.02	.00
☐	66 Craig Reynolds	.05	.02	.00
☐	67 Nolan Ryan	.90	.45	.09
☐	68 Mike Scott	.25	.12	.02
☐	69 Dave Smith	.08	.04	.01
☐	70 Dickie Thon	.05	.02	.00
☐	71 Tony Walker	.08	.04	.01
☐	72 Denny Walling	.05	.02	.00
☐	73 Bob Boone	.12	.06	.01
☐	74 Rick Burleson	.08	.04	.01
☐	75 John Candelaria	.08	.04	.01
☐	76 Doug Corbett	.05	.02	.00
☐	77 Doug DeCinces	.08	.04	.01
☐	78 Brian Downing	.08	.04	.01
☐	79 Chuck Finley	.75	.35	.07
☐	80 Terry Forster	.08	.04	.01
☐	81 Bob Grich	.08	.04	.01
☐	82 George Hendrick	.08	.04	.01
☐	83 Jack Howell	.15	.07	.01
☐	84 Reggie Jackson	.45	.22	.04
☐	85 Ruppert Jones	.05	.02	.00
☐	86 Wally Joyner	2.50	1.25	.25
☐	87 Gary Lucas	.05	.02	.00
☐	88 Kirk McCaskill	.10	.05	.01
☐	89 Donnie Moore	.05	.02	.00
☐	90 Gary Pettis	.05	.02	.00
☐	91 Vern Ruhle	.05	.02	.00
☐	92 Dick Schofield	.05	.02	.00
☐	93 Don Sutton	.15	.07	.01
☐	94 Rob Wilfong	.05	.02	.00
☐	95 Mike Witt	.08	.04	.01
☐	96 Doug Drabek	.45	.22	.04
☐	97 Mike Easler	.05	.02	.00
☐	98 Mike Fischlin	.05	.02	.00
☐	99 Brian Fisher	.05	.02	.00
☐	100 Ron Guidry	.12	.06	.01
☐	101 Rickey Henderson	.50	.25	.05
☐	102 Tommy John	.15	.07	.01
☐	103 Ron Kittle	.10	.05	.01
☐	104 Don Mattingly	2.50	1.25	.25
☐	105 Bobby Meacham	.05	.02	.00
☐	106 Joe Niekro	.10	.05	.01
☐	107 Mike Pagliarulo	.08	.04	.01
☐	108 Dan Pasqua	.08	.04	.01
☐	109 Willie Randolph	.08	.04	.01
☐	110 Dennis Rasmussen	.08	.04	.01
☐	111 Dave Righetti	.10	.05	.01
☐	112 Gary Roenicke	.05	.02	.00
☐	113 Rod Scurry	.05	.02	.00
☐	114 Bob Shirley	.05	.02	.00
☐	115 Joel Skinner	.05	.02	.00
☐	116 Tim Stoddard	.05	.02	.00
☐	117 Bob Tewksbury	.10	.05	.01
☐	118 Wayne Tolleson	.05	.02	.00
☐	119 Claudell Washington	.08	.04	.01
☐	120 Dave Winfield	.25	.12	.02
☐	121 Steve Buechele	.05	.02	.00
☐	122 Ed Correa	.15	.07	.01
☐	123 Scott Fletcher	.08	.04	.01
☐	124 Jose Guzman	.08	.04	.01
☐	125 Toby Harrah	.05	.02	.00
☐	126 Greg Harris	.05	.02	.00
☐	127 Charlie Hough	.08	.04	.01
☐	128 Pete Incaviglia	1.00	.50	.10
☐	129 Mike Mason	.05	.02	.00
☐	130 Oddibe McDowell	.10	.05	.01
☐	131 Dale Mohorcic	.15	.07	.01
☐	132 Pete O'Brien	.10	.05	.01
☐	133 Tom Paciorek	.05	.02	.00
☐	134 Larry Parrish	.05	.02	.00
☐	135 Geno Petralli	.05	.02	.00
☐	136 Darrell Porter	.05	.02	.00
☐	137 Jeff Russell	.10	.05	.01
☐	138 Ruben Sierra	9.00	4.50	.90
☐	139 Don Slaught	.05	.02	.00
☐	140 Gary Ward	.05	.02	.00
☐	141 Curtis Wilkerson	.05	.02	.00
☐	142 Mitch Williams	.65	.30	.06
☐	143 Bobby Witt	.35	.17	.03
☐	144 Dave Bergman	.05	.02	.00
☐	145 Tom Brookens	.05	.02	.00
☐	146 Bill Campbell	.05	.02	.00
☐	147 Chuck Cary	.25	.12	.02
☐	148 Darnell Coles	.08	.04	.01
☐	149 Dave Collins	.05	.02	.00
☐	150 Darrell Evans	.10	.05	.01
☐	151 Kirk Gibson	.25	.12	.02
☐	152 John Grubb	.05	.02	.00
☐	153 Willie Hernandez	.10	.05	.01
☐	154 Larry Herndon	.05	.02	.00
☐	155 Eric King	.15	.07	.01
☐	156 Chet Lemon	.05	.02	.00
☐	157 Dwight Lowry	.10	.05	.01
☐	158 Jack Morris	.12	.06	.01
☐	159 Randy O'Neal	.05	.02	.00
☐	160 Lance Parrish	.12	.06	.01
☐	161 Dan Petry	.05	.02	.00

☐ 162	Pat Sheridan	.05	.02	.00	☐ 256	Dickie Noles	.05	.02	.00
☐ 163	Jim Slaton	.05	.02	.00	☐ 257	Bryan Oelkers	.05	.02	.00
☐ 164	Frank Tanana	.08	.04	.01	☐ 258	Ken Schrom	.05	.02	.00
☐ 165	Walt Terrell	.05	.02	.00	☐ 259	Don Schulze	.05	.02	.00
☐ 166	Mark Thurmond	.05	.02	.00	☐ 260	Cory Snyder	.75	.35	.07
☐ 167	Alan Trammell	.18	.09	.01	☐ 261	Pat Tabler	.10	.05	.01
☐ 168	Lou Whitaker	.12	.06	.01	☐ 262	Andre Thornton	.08	.04	.01
☐ 169	Luis Aguayo	.05	.02	.00	☐ 263	Rich Yett	.05	.02	.00
☐ 170	Steve Bedrosian	.12	.06	.01	☐ 264	Mike Aldrete	.20	.10	.02
☐ 171	Don Carman	.05	.02	.00	☐ 265	Juan Berenguer	.05	.02	.00
☐ 172	Darren Daulton	.05	.02	.00	☐ 266	Vida Blue	.08	.04	.01
☐ 173	Greg Gross	.05	.02	.00	☐ 267	Bob Brenly	.05	.02	.00
☐ 174	Kevin Gross	.05	.02	.00	☐ 268	Chris Brown	.05	.02	.00
☐ 175	Von Hayes	.10	.05	.01	☐ 269	Will Clark	35.00	17.50	3.50
☐ 176	Charles Hudson	.05	.02	.00	☐ 270	Chili Davis	.10	.05	.01
☐ 177	Tom Hume	.05	.02	.00	☐ 271	Mark Davis	.15	.07	.01
☐ 178	Steve Jeltz	.05	.02	.00	☐ 272	Kelly Downs	.35	.17	.03
☐ 179	Mike Maddux	.15	.07	.01	☐ 273	Scott Garrelts	.08	.04	.01
☐ 180	Shane Rawley	.05	.02	.00	☐ 274	Dan Gladden	.08	.04	.01
☐ 181	Gary Redus	.05	.02	.00	☐ 275	Mike Krukow	.05	.02	.00
☐ 182	Ron Roenicke	.05	.02	.00	☐ 276	Randy Kutcher	.10	.05	.01
☐ 183	Bruce Ruffin	.18	.09	.01	☐ 277	Mike LaCoss	.05	.02	.00
☐ 184	John Russell	.05	.02	.00	☐ 278	Jeff Leonard	.08	.04	.01
☐ 185	Juan Samuel	.12	.06	.01	☐ 279	Candy Maldonado	.08	.04	.01
☐ 186	Dan Schatzeder	.05	.02	.00	☐ 280	Roger Mason	.05	.02	.00
☐ 187	Mike Schmidt	.80	.40	.08	☐ 281	Bob Melvin	.05	.02	.00
☐ 188	Rick Schu	.05	.02	.00	☐ 282	Greg Minton	.05	.02	.00
☐ 189	Jeff Stone	.05	.02	.00	☐ 283	Jeff Robinson	.10	.05	.01
☐ 190	Kent Tekulve	.05	.02	.00		(Giants pitcher)			
☐ 191	Milt Thompson	.08	.04	.01	☐ 284	Harry Spilman	.05	.02	.00
☐ 192	Glenn Wilson	.05	.02	.00	☐ 285	Robby Thompson	.35	.17	.03
☐ 193	Buddy Bell	.10	.05	.01	☐ 286	Jose Uribe	.05	.02	.00
☐ 194	Tom Browning	.12	.06	.01	☐ 287	Frank Williams	.05	.02	.00
☐ 195	Sal Butera	.05	.02	.00	☐ 288	Joel Youngblood	.05	.02	.00
☐ 196	Dave Concepcion	.10	.05	.01	☐ 289	Jack Clark	.20	.10	.02
☐ 197	Kal Daniels	.80	.40	.08	☐ 290	Vince Coleman	.40	.20	.04
☐ 198	Eric Davis	1.50	.75	.15	☐ 291	Tim Conroy	.05	.02	.00
☐ 199	John Denny	.08	.04	.01	☐ 292	Danny Cox	.08	.04	.01
☐ 200	Bo Diaz	.05	.02	.00	☐ 293	Ken Dayley	.05	.02	.00
☐ 201	Nick Esasky	.10	.05	.01	☐ 294	Curt Ford	.08	.04	.01
☐ 202	John Franco	.10	.05	.01	☐ 295	Bob Forsch	.05	.02	.00
☐ 203	Bill Gullickson	.05	.02	.00	☐ 296	Tom Herr	.08	.04	.01
☐ 204	Barry Larkin	3.50	1.75	.35	☐ 297	Ricky Horton	.05	.02	.00
☐ 205	Eddie Milner	.05	.02	.00	☐ 298	Clint Hurdle	.05	.02	.00
☐ 206	Rob Murphy	.30	.15	.03	☐ 299	Jeff Lahti	.05	.02	.00
☐ 207	Ron Oester	.05	.02	.00	☐ 300	Steve Lake	.05	.02	.00
☐ 208	Dave Parker	.15	.07	.01	☐ 301	Tito Landrum	.05	.02	.00
☐ 209	Tony Perez	.15	.07	.01	☐ 302	Mike LaValliere	.20	.10	.02
☐ 210	Ted Power	.05	.02	.00	☐ 303	Greg Mathews	.20	.10	.02
☐ 211	Joe Price	.05	.02	.00	☐ 304	Willie McGee	.12	.06	.01
☐ 212	Ron Robinson	.05	.02	.00	☐ 305	Jose Oquendo	.05	.02	.00
☐ 213	Pete Rose	.60	.30	.06	☐ 306	Terry Pendleton	.08	.04	.01
☐ 214	Mario Soto	.05	.02	.00	☐ 307	Pat Perry	.05	.02	.00
☐ 215	Kurt Stillwell	.45	.22	.04	☐ 308	Ozzie Smith	.20	.10	.02
☐ 216	Max Venable	.05	.02	.00	☐ 309	Ray Soff	.08	.04	.01
☐ 217	Chris Welsh	.05	.02	.00	☐ 310	John Tudor	.10	.05	.01
☐ 218	Carl Willis	.08	.04	.01	☐ 311	Andy Van Slyke	.25	.12	.02
☐ 219	Jesse Barfield	.18	.09	.01		ERR (Bats R, Throws L)			
☐ 220	George Bell	.35	.17	.03	☐ 312	Todd Worrell	.20	.10	.02
☐ 221	Bill Caudill	.05	.02	.00	☐ 313	Dann Bilardello	.05	.02	.00
☐ 222	John Cerutti	.30	.15	.03	☐ 314	Hubie Brooks	.08	.04	.01
☐ 223	Jim Clancy	.05	.02	.00	☐ 315	Tim Burke	.08	.04	.01
☐ 224	Mark Eichhorn	.10	.05	.01	☐ 316	Andre Dawson	.30	.15	.03
☐ 225	Tony Fernandez	.25	.12	.02	☐ 317	Mike Fitzgerald	.05	.02	.00
☐ 226	Damaso Garcia	.05	.02	.00	☐ 318	Tom Foley	.05	.02	.00
☐ 227	Kelly Gruber ERR	.10	.05	.01	☐ 319	Andres Galarraga	.35	.17	.03
	(wrong birth year)				☐ 320	Joe Hesketh	.05	.02	.00
☐ 228	Tom Henke	.08	.04	.01	☐ 321	Wallace Johnson	.05	.02	.00
☐ 229	Garth Iorg	.05	.02	.00	☐ 322	Wayne Krenchicki	.05	.02	.00
☐ 230	Joe Johnson	.05	.02	.00	☐ 323	Vance Law	.05	.02	.00
☐ 231	Cliff Johnson	.05	.02	.00	☐ 324	Dennis Martinez	.08	.04	.01
☐ 232	Jimmy Key	.10	.05	.01	☐ 325	Bob McClure	.05	.02	.00
☐ 233	Dennis Lamp	.05	.02	.00	☐ 326	Andy McGaffigan	.05	.02	.00
☐ 234	Rick Leach	.05	.02	.00	☐ 327	Al Newman	.08	.04	.01
☐ 235	Buck Martinez	.05	.02	.00	☐ 328	Tim Raines	.25	.12	.02
☐ 236	Lloyd Moseby	.08	.04	.01	☐ 329	Jeff Reardon	.10	.05	.01
☐ 237	Rance Mulliniks	.05	.02	.00	☐ 330	Luis Rivera	.08	.04	.01
☐ 238	Dave Stieb	.10	.05	.01	☐ 331	Bob Sebra	.10	.05	.01
☐ 239	Willie Upshaw	.05	.02	.00	☐ 332	Bryn Smith	.10	.05	.01
☐ 240	Ernie Whitt	.05	.02	.00	☐ 333	Jay Tibbs	.05	.02	.00
☐ 241	Andy Allanson	.08	.04	.01	☐ 334	Tim Wallach	.10	.05	.01
☐ 242	Scott Bailes	.10	.05	.01	☐ 335	Mitch Webster	.05	.02	.00
☐ 243	Chris Bando	.05	.02	.00	☐ 336	Jim Wohlford	.05	.02	.00
☐ 244	Tony Bernazard	.05	.02	.00	☐ 337	Floyd Youmans	.08	.04	.01
☐ 245	John Butcher	.05	.02	.00	☐ 338	Chris Bosio	.45	.22	.04
☐ 246	Brett Butler	.08	.04	.01	☐ 339	Glenn Braggs	.75	.35	.07
☐ 247	Ernie Camacho	.05	.02	.00	☐ 340	Rick Cerone	.05	.02	.00
☐ 248	Tom Candiotti	.05	.02	.00	☐ 341	Mark Clear	.05	.02	.00
☐ 249	Joe Carter	.35	.17	.03	☐ 342	Bryan Clutterbuck	.08	.04	.01
☐ 250	Carmen Castillo	.05	.02	.00	☐ 343	Cecil Cooper	.10	.05	.01
☐ 251	Julio Franco	.15	.07	.01	☐ 344	Rob Deer	.30	.15	.03
☐ 252	Mel Hall	.10	.05	.01	☐ 345	Jim Gantner	.05	.02	.00
☐ 253	Brook Jacoby	.08	.04	.01	☐ 346	Ted Higuera	.15	.07	.01
☐ 254	Phil Niekro	.18	.09	.01	☐ 347	John Henry Johnson	.05	.02	.00
☐ 255	Otis Nixon	.10	.05	.01	☐ 348	Tim Leary	.30	.15	.03

#	Player				#	Player			
349	Rick Manning	.05	.02	.00	444	Ken Landreaux	.05	.02	.00
350	Paul Molitor	.12	.06	.01	445	Bill Madlock	.07	.03	.01
351	Charlie Moore	.05	.02	.00	446	Mike Marshall	.10	.05	.01
352	Juan Nieves	.15	.07	.01	447	Len Matuszek	.05	.02	.00
353	Ben Oglivie	.08	.04	.01	448	Tom Niedenfuer	.05	.02	.00
354	Dan Plesac	.35	.17	.03	449	Alejandro Pena	.08	.04	.01
355	Ernest Riles	.05	.02	.00	450	Dennis Powell	.05	.02	.00
356	Billy Jo Robidoux	.05	.02	.00	451	Jerry Reuss	.05	.02	.00
357	Bill Schroeder	.05	.02	.00	452	Bill Russell	.05	.02	.00
358	Dale Sveum	.18	.09	.01	453	Steve Sax	.15	.07	.01
359	Gorman Thomas	.10	.05	.01	454	Mike Scioscia	.08	.04	.01
360	Bill Wegman	.08	.04	.01	455	Franklin Stubbs	.05	.02	.00
361	Robin Yount	.45	.22	.04	456	Alex Trevino	.05	.02	.00
362	Steve Balboni	.05	.02	.00	457	Fernando Valenzuela	.18	.09	.01
363	Scott Bankhead	.20	.10	.02	458	Ed VandeBerg	.05	.02	.00
364	Buddy Biancalana	.05	.02	.00	459	Bob Welch	.08	.04	.01
365	Bud Black	.05	.02	.00	460	Reggie Williams	.08	.04	.01
366	George Brett	.45	.22	.04	461	Don Aase	.05	.02	.00
367	Steve Farr	.08	.04	.01	462	Juan Beniquez	.05	.02	.00
368	Mark Gubicza	.15	.07	.01	463	Mike Boddicker	.08	.04	.01
369	Bo Jackson	18.00	9.00	1.80	464	Juan Bonilla	.05	.02	.00
370	Danny Jackson	.12	.06	.01	465	Rich Bordi	.05	.02	.00
371	Mike Kingery	.12	.06	.01	466	Storm Davis	.08	.04	.01
372	Rudy Law	.05	.02	.00	467	Rick Dempsey	.05	.02	.00
373	Charlie Leibrandt	.05	.02	.00	468	Ken Dixon	.05	.02	.00
374	Dennis Leonard	.05	.02	.00	469	Jim Dwyer	.05	.02	.00
375	Hal McRae	.08	.04	.01	470	Mike Flanagan	.08	.04	.01
376	Jorge Orta	.05	.02	.00	471	Jackie Gutierrez	.05	.02	.00
377	Jamie Quirk	.05	.02	.00	472	Brad Havens	.05	.02	.00
378	Dan Quisenberry	.10	.05	.01	473	Lee Lacy	.05	.02	.00
379	Bret Saberhagen	.45	.22	.04	474	Fred Lynn	.12	.06	.01
380	Angel Salazar	.05	.02	.00	475	Scott McGregor	.08	.04	.01
381	Lonnie Smith	.10	.05	.01	476	Eddie Murray	.25	.12	.02
382	Jim Sundberg	.05	.02	.00	477	Tom O'Malley	.05	.02	.00
383	Frank White	.08	.04	.01	478	Cal Ripken Jr.	.30	.15	.03
384	Willie Wilson	.10	.05	.01	479	Larry Sheets	.08	.04	.01
385	Joaquin Andujar	.08	.04	.01	480	John Shelby	.05	.02	.00
386	Doug Bair	.05	.02	.00	481	Nate Snell	.05	.02	.00
387	Dusty Baker	.08	.04	.01	482	Jim Traber	.05	.02	.00
388	Bruce Bochte	.05	.02	.00	483	Mike Young	.05	.02	.00
389	Jose Canseco	8.00	4.00	.80	484	Neil Allen	.05	.02	.00
390	Chris Codiroli	.05	.02	.00	485	Harold Baines	.12	.06	.01
391	Mike Davis	.05	.02	.00	486	Floyd Bannister	.05	.02	.00
392	Alfredo Griffin	.08	.04	.01	487	Daryl Boston	.05	.02	.00
393	Moose Haas	.05	.02	.00	488	Ivan Calderon	.12	.06	.01
394	Donnie Hill	.05	.02	.00	489	John Cangelosi	.10	.05	.01
395	Jay Howell	.08	.04	.01	490	Steve Carlton	.20	.10	.02
396	Dave Kingman	.10	.05	.01	491	Joe Cowley	.05	.02	.00
397	Carney Lansford	.12	.06	.01	492	Julio Cruz	.05	.02	.00
398	Dave Leiper	.08	.04	.01	493	Bill Dawley	.05	.02	.00
399	Bill Mooneyham	.08	.04	.01	494	Jose DeLeon	.05	.02	.00
400	Dwayne Murphy	.05	.02	.00	495	Richard Dotson	.08	.04	.01
401	Steve Ontiveros	.05	.02	.00	496	Carlton Fisk	.20	.10	.02
402	Tony Phillips	.05	.02	.00	497	Ozzie Guillen	.10	.05	.01
403	Eric Plunk	.05	.02	.00	498	Jerry Hairston	.05	.02	.00
404	Jose Rijo	.08	.04	.01	499	Ron Hassey	.05	.02	.00
405	Terry Steinbach	1.25	.60	.12	500	Tim Hulett	.05	.02	.00
406	Dave Stewart	.18	.09	.01	501	Bob James	.05	.02	.00
407	Mickey Tettleton	.20	.10	.02	502	Steve Lyons	.05	.02	.00
408	Dave Von Ohlen	.05	.02	.00	503	Joel McKeon	.10	.05	.01
409	Jerry Willard	.05	.02	.00	504	Gene Nelson	.05	.02	.00
410	Curt Young	.05	.02	.00	505	Dave Schmidt	.05	.02	.00
411	Bruce Bochy	.05	.02	.00	506	Ray Searage	.05	.02	.00
412	Dave Dravecky	.10	.05	.01	507	Bobby Thigpen	.35	.17	.03
413	Tim Flannery	.05	.02	.00	508	Greg Walker	.08	.04	.01
414	Steve Garvey	.30	.15	.03	509	Jim Acker	.05	.02	.00
415	Goose Gossage	.10	.05	.01	510	Doyle Alexander	.08	.04	.01
416	Tony Gwynn	.60	.30	.06	511	Paul Assenmacher	.08	.04	.01
417	Andy Hawkins	.08	.04	.01	512	Bruce Benedict	.05	.02	.00
418	LaMarr Hoyt	.08	.04	.01	513	Chris Chambliss	.08	.04	.01
419	Terry Kennedy	.05	.02	.00	514	Jeff Dedmon	.05	.02	.00
420	John Kruk	.45	.22	.04	515	Gene Garber	.05	.02	.00
421	Dave LaPoint	.08	.04	.01	516	Ken Griffey	.10	.05	.01
422	Craig Lefferts	.08	.04	.01	517	Terry Harper	.05	.02	.00
423	Carmelo Martinez	.05	.02	.00	518	Bob Horner	.12	.06	.01
424	Lance McCullers	.08	.04	.01	519	Glenn Hubbard	.05	.02	.00
425	Kevin McReynolds	.30	.15	.03	520	Rick Mahler	.05	.02	.00
426	Graig Nettles	.10	.05	.01	521	Omar Moreno	.05	.02	.00
427	Bip Roberts	.20	.10	.02	522	Dale Murphy	.40	.20	.04
428	Jerry Royster	.05	.02	.00	523	Ken Oberkfell	.05	.02	.00
429	Benito Santiago	1.00	.50	.10	524	Ed Olwine	.08	.04	.01
430	Eric Show	.08	.04	.01	525	David Palmer	.05	.02	.00
431	Bob Stoddard	.05	.02	.00	526	Rafael Ramirez	.05	.02	.00
432	Garry Templeton	.08	.04	.01	527	Billy Sample	.05	.02	.00
433	Gene Walter	.05	.02	.00	528	Ted Simmons	.10	.05	.01
434	Ed Whitson	.05	.02	.00	529	Zane Smith	.08	.04	.01
435	Marvell Wynne	.05	.02	.00	530	Bruce Sutter	.10	.05	.01
436	Dave Anderson	.05	.02	.00	531	Andres Thomas	.25	.12	.02
437	Greg Brock	.05	.02	.00	532	Ozzie Virgil	.05	.02	.00
438	Enos Cabell	.05	.02	.00	533	Allan Anderson	.45	.22	.04
439	Mariano Duncan	.05	.02	.00	534	Keith Atherton	.05	.02	.00
440	Pedro Guerrero	.15	.07	.01	535	Billy Beane	.08	.04	.01
441	Orel Hershiser	.40	.20	.04	536	Bert Blyleven	.12	.06	.01
442	Rick Honeycutt	.05	.02	.00	537	Tom Brunansky	.12	.06	.01
443	Ken Howell	.05	.02	.00	538	Randy Bush	.05	.02	.00

☐ 539	George Frazier	.05	.02	.00
☐ 540	Gary Gaetti	.15	.07	.01
☐ 541	Greg Gagne	.05	.02	.00
☐ 542	Mickey Hatcher	.05	.02	.00
☐ 543	Neal Heaton	.05	.02	.00
☐ 544	Kent Hrbek	.15	.07	.01
☐ 545	Roy Lee Jackson	.05	.02	.00
☐ 546	Tim Laudner	.05	.02	.00
☐ 547	Steve Lombardozzi	.05	.02	.00
☐ 548	Mark Portugal	.25	.12	.02
☐ 549	Kirby Puckett	1.75	.85	.17
☐ 550	Jeff Reed	.05	.02	.00
☐ 551	Mark Salas	.05	.02	.00
☐ 552	Roy Smalley	.05	.02	.00
☐ 553	Mike Smithson	.05	.02	.00
☐ 554	Frank Viola	.18	.09	.01
☐ 555	Thad Bosley	.05	.02	.00
☐ 556	Ron Cey	.08	.04	.01
☐ 557	Jody Davis	.05	.02	.00
☐ 558	Ron Davis	.05	.02	.00
☐ 559	Bob Dernier	.05	.02	.00
☐ 560	Frank DiPino	.05	.02	.00
☐ 561	Shawon Dunston UER	.15	.07	.01
	(wrong birth year listed on card back)			
☐ 562	Leon Durham	.08	.04	.01
☐ 563	Dennis Eckersley	.12	.06	.01
☐ 564	Terry Francona	.05	.02	.00
☐ 565	Dave Gumpert	.05	.02	.00
☐ 566	Guy Hoffman	.05	.02	.00
☐ 567	Ed Lynch	.05	.02	.00
☐ 568	Gary Matthews	.05	.02	.00
☐ 569	Keith Moreland	.05	.02	.00
☐ 570	Jamie Moyer	.15	.07	.01
☐ 571	Jerry Mumphrey	.05	.02	.00
☐ 572	Ryne Sandberg	.35	.17	.03
☐ 573	Scott Sanderson	.05	.02	.00
☐ 574	Lee Smith	.08	.04	.01
☐ 575	Chris Speier	.05	.02	.00
☐ 576	Rick Sutcliffe	.10	.05	.01
☐ 577	Manny Trillo	.05	.02	.00
☐ 578	Steve Trout	.05	.02	.00
☐ 579	Karl Best	.05	.02	.00
☐ 580	Scott Bradley	.05	.02	.00
☐ 581	Phil Bradley	.08	.04	.01
☐ 582	Mickey Brantley	.08	.04	.01
☐ 583	Mike Brown	.05	.02	.00
	(Mariners pitcher)			
☐ 584	Alvin Davis	.18	.09	.01
☐ 585	Lee Guetterman	.20	.10	.02
☐ 586	Mark Huismann	.05	.02	.00
☐ 587	Bob Kearney	.05	.02	.00
☐ 588	Pete Ladd	.05	.02	.00
☐ 589	Mark Langston	.35	.17	.03
☐ 590	Mike Moore	.10	.05	.01
☐ 591	Mike Morgan	.08	.04	.01
☐ 592	John Moses	.05	.02	.00
☐ 593	Ken Phelps	.08	.04	.01
☐ 594	Jim Presley	.10	.05	.01
☐ 595	Rey Quinones UER	.20	.10	.02
	(Quinonez on front)			
☐ 596	Harold Reynolds	.08	.04	.01
☐ 597	Billy Swift	.05	.02	.00
☐ 598	Danny Tartabull	.35	.17	.03
☐ 599	Steve Yeager	.05	.02	.00
☐ 600	Matt Young	.05	.02	.00
☐ 601	Bill Almon	.05	.02	.00
☐ 602	Rafael Belliard	.08	.04	.01
☐ 603	Mike Bielecki	.12	.06	.01
☐ 604	Barry Bonds	1.50	.75	.15
☐ 605	Bobby Bonilla	1.50	.75	.15
☐ 606	Sid Bream	.05	.02	.00
☐ 607	Mike Brown	.05	.02	.00
	(Pirates OF)			
☐ 608	Pat Clements	.05	.02	.00
☐ 609	Mike Diaz	.10	.05	.01
☐ 610	Cecilio Guante	.05	.02	.00
☐ 611	Barry Jones	.10	.05	.01
☐ 612	Bob Kipper	.05	.02	.00
☐ 613	Larry McWilliams	.05	.02	.00
☐ 614	Jim Morrison	.05	.02	.00
☐ 615	Joe Orsulak	.05	.02	.00
☐ 616	Junior Ortiz	.05	.02	.00
☐ 617	Tony Pena	.08	.04	.01
☐ 618	Johnny Ray	.08	.04	.01
☐ 619	Rick Reuschel	.10	.05	.01
☐ 620	R.J. Reynolds	.05	.02	.00
☐ 621	Rick Rhoden	.08	.04	.01
☐ 622	Don Robinson	.05	.02	.00
☐ 623	Bob Walk	.05	.02	.00
☐ 624	Jim Winn	.05	.02	.00
☐ 625	Youthful Power	.60	.30	.06
	Pete Incaviglia Jose Canseco			
☐ 626	300 Game Winners	.10	.05	.01

	Don Sutton Phil Niekro			
☐ 627	AL Firemen	.07	.03	.01
	Dave Righetti Don Aase			
☐ 628	Rookie All-Stars	1.25	.60	.12
	Wally Joyner Jose Canseco			
☐ 629	Magic Mets	.50	.25	.05
	Gary Carter Sid Fernandez Dwight Gooden Keith Hernandez Darryl Strawberry			
☐ 630	NL Best Righties	.08	.04	.01
	Mike Scott Mike Krukow			
☐ 631	Sensational Southpaws	.10	.05	.01
	Fernando Valenzuela John Franco			
☐ 632	Count'Em	.08	.04	.01
	Bob Horner			
☐ 633	AL Pitcher's Nightmare	.75	.35	.07
	Jose Canseco Jim Rice Kirby Puckett			
☐ 634	All-Star Battery	.25	.12	.02
	Gary Carter Roger Clemens			
☐ 635	4000 Strikeouts	.15	.07	.01
	Steve Carlton			
☐ 636	Big Bats at First	.15	.07	.01
	Glenn Davis Eddie Murray			
☐ 637	On Base	.35	.17	.03
	Wade Boggs Keith Hernandez			
☐ 638	Sluggers Left Side	1.00	.50	.10
	Don Mattingly Darryl Strawberry			
☐ 639	Former MVP's	.12	.06	.01
	Dave Parker Ryne Sandberg			
☐ 640	Dr. K , Super K	.65	.30	.06
	Dwight Gooden Roger Clemens			
☐ 641	AL West Stoppers	.08	.04	.01
	Mike Witt Charlie Hough			
☐ 642	Doubles and Triples	.10	.05	.01
	Juan Samuel Tim Raines			
☐ 643	Outfielders with Punch	.10	.05	.01
	Harold Baines Jesse Barfield			
☐ 644	Dave Clark and	2.50	1.25	.25
	Greg Swindell			
☐ 645	Ron Karkovice and	.10	.05	.01
	Russ Morman			
☐ 646	Devon White and	1.50	.75	.15
	Willie Fraser			
☐ 647	Mike Stanley and	.45	.22	.04
	Jerry Browne			
☐ 648	Dave Magadan and	1.00	.50	.10
	Phil Lombardi			
☐ 649	Jose Gonzalez and	.25	.12	.02
	Ralph Bryant			
☐ 650	Jimmy Jones and	.20	.10	.02
	Randy Asadoor			
☐ 651	Tracy Jones and	.30	.15	.03
	Marvin Freeman			
☐ 652	John Stefero and	5.00	2.50	.50
	Kevin Seitzer			
☐ 653	Rob Nelson and	.15	.07	.01
	Steve Fireovid			
☐ 654	CL: Mets/Red Sox Astros/Angels	.08	.01	.00
☐ 655	CL: Yankees/Rangers Tigers/Phillies	.08	.01	.00
☐ 656	CL: Reds/Blue Jays Indians/Giants ERR (230/231 wrong)	.08	.01	.00
☐ 657	CL: Cardinals/Expos Brewers/Royals	.08	.01	.00
☐ 658	CL: A's/Padres Dodgers/Orioles	.08	.01	.00
☐ 659	CL: White Sox/Braves Twins/Cubs	.08	.01	.00
☐ 660	CL: Mariners/Pirates Special Cards ERR (580/581 wrong)	.08	.01	.00

1987 Fleer Wax Box Cards

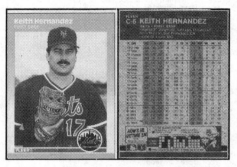

The cards in this 16-card set measure the standard 2 1/2" by 3 1/2". Cards have essentially the same design as the 1987 Fleer regular issue set. The cards were printed on the bottoms of the regular issue wax pack boxes. These 16 cards (C1 to C16) are considered a separate set in their own right and are not typically included in a complete set of the regular issue 1987 Fleer cards. The value of the panel uncut is slightly greater, perhaps by 25% greater, than the value of the individual cards cut up carefully.

	MINT	EXC	G-VG
COMPLETE SET (16)	4.00	2.00	.40
COMMON CARDS (C1-C16)	.05	.02	.00
☐ C1 Mets Logo	.05	.02	.00
☐ C2 Jesse Barfield	.15	.07	.01
☐ C3 George Brett	.35	.17	.03
☐ C4 Dwight Gooden	.60	.30	.06
☐ C5 Boston Logo	.05	.02	.00
☐ C6 Keith Hernandez	.20	.10	.02
☐ C7 Wally Joyner	.90	.45	.09
☐ C8 Dale Murphy	.40	.20	.04
☐ C9 Astros Logo	.05	.02	.00
☐ C10 Dave Parker	.15	.07	.01
☐ C11 Kirby Puckett	.60	.30	.06
☐ C12 Dave Righetti	.15	.07	.01
☐ C13 Angels Logo	.05	.02	.00
☐ C14 Ryne Sandberg	.30	.15	.03
☐ C15 Mike Schmidt	.75	.35	.07
☐ C16 Robin Yount	.50	.25	.05

1987 Fleer All-Star Inserts

This 12-card set was distributed as an insert in packs of the Fleer regular issue. The cards are 2 1/2" by 3 1/2" and designed with a color player photo superimposed on a gray or black background with yellow stars. The player's name, team, and position are printed in orange on black or gray at the bottom of the obverse. The card backs are done

predominantly in gray, red, and black. Cards are numbered on the back in the upper right hand corner.

	MINT	EXC	G-VG
COMPLETE SET (12)	14.00	7.00	1.40
COMMON PLAYER (1-12)	.25	.12	.02
☐ 1 Don Mattingly .... First Base	6.00	3.00	.60
☐ 2 Gary Carter .... Catcher	.90	.45	.09
☐ 3 Tony Fernandez .... Shortstop	.40	.20	.04
☐ 4 Steve Sax .... Second Base	.40	.20	.04
☐ 5 Kirby Puckett .... Outfield	2.00	1.00	.20
☐ 6 Mike Schmidt .... Third Base	2.00	1.00	.20
☐ 7 Mike Easler .... Designated Hitter	.25	.12	.02
☐ 8 Todd Worrell .... Relief Pitcher	.40	.20	.04
☐ 9 George Bell .... Outfield	.50	.25	.05
☐ 10 Fernando Valenzuela .... Left Hand Starter	.50	.25	.05
☐ 11 Roger Clemens .... Right Hand Starter	2.00	1.00	.20
☐ 12 Tim Raines .... Outfield	.75	.35	.07

1987 Fleer Headliners

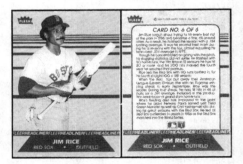

This six-card set was distributed as a special insert in rack packs as well as with three-pack wax pack rack packs. The obverse features the player photo against a beige background with irregular red stripes. Cards are 2 1/2" by 3 1/2". The cards are numbered on the back. The checklist below also lists each player's team affiliation.

	MINT	EXC	G-VG
COMPLETE SET (6)	7.50	3.75	.75
COMMON PLAYER (1-6)	.60	.30	.06
☐ 1 Wade Boggs .... Boston Red Sox	2.50	1.25	.25
☐ 2 Jose Canseco .... Oakland Athletics	3.00	1.50	.30
☐ 3 Dwight Gooden .... New York Mets	1.00	.50	.10
☐ 4 Rickey Henderson .... New York Yankees	1.00	.50	.10
☐ 5 Keith Hernandez .... New York Mets	.60	.30	.06
☐ 6 Jim Rice .... Boston Red Sox	.60	.30	.06

1987 Fleer Sticker Cards

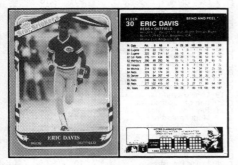

These Star Stickers were distributed as a separate issue by Fleer with five star stickers and a logo sticker in each wax pack. The 132-card (sticker) set features 2 1/2" by 3 1/2" full-color fronts and even statistics on the sticker back, which is an indication that the Fleer Company understands that these stickers are rarely used as stickers but more like traditional cards. The card fronts are surrounded by a green border and the backs are printed in green and yellow on white card stock.

	MINT	EXC	G-VG
COMPLETE SET (132)	25.00	12.50	2.50
COMMON PLAYER (1-132)	.05	.02	.00

		MINT	EXC	G-VG
☐	1 Don Aase	.05	.02	.00
☐	2 Harold Baines	.10	.05	.01
☐	3 Floyd Bannister	.05	.02	.00
☐	4 Jesse Barfield	.15	.07	.01
☐	5 Marty Barrett	.05	.02	.00
☐	6 Kevin Bass	.05	.02	.00
☐	7 Don Baylor	.10	.05	.01
☐	8 Steve Bedrosian	.10	.05	.01
☐	9 George Bell	.20	.10	.02
☐	10 Bert Blyleven	.15	.07	.01
☐	11 Mike Boddicker	.10	.05	.01
☐	12 Wade Boggs	1.50	.75	.15
☐	13 Phil Bradley	.10	.05	.01
☐	14 Sid Bream	.05	.02	.00
☐	15 George Brett	.45	.22	.04
☐	16 Hubie Brooks	.10	.05	.01
☐	17 Tom Brunansky	.15	.07	.01
☐	18 Tom Candiotti	.05	.02	.00
☐	19 Jose Canseco	2.50	1.25	.25
☐	20 Gary Carter	.30	.15	.03
☐	21 Joe Carter	.20	.10	.02
☐	22 Will Clark	2.50	1.25	.25
☐	23 Mark Clear	.05	.02	.00
☐	24 Roger Clemens	.75	.35	.07
☐	25 Vince Coleman	.35	.17	.03
☐	26 Jose Cruz	.10	.05	.01
☐	27 Ron Darling	.15	.07	.01
☐	28 Alvin Davis	.10	.05	.01
☐	29 Chili Davis	.10	.05	.01
☐	30 Eric Davis	1.00	.50	.10
☐	31 Glenn Davis	.30	.15	.03
☐	32 Mike Davis	.05	.02	.00
☐	33 Andre Dawson	.30	.15	.03
☐	34 Doug DeCinces	.05	.02	.00
☐	35 Brian Downing	.05	.02	.00
☐	36 Shawon Dunston	.15	.07	.01
☐	37 Mark Eichhorn	.05	.02	.00
☐	38 Dwight Evans	.20	.10	.02
☐	39 Tony Fernandez	.15	.07	.01
☐	40 Bob Forsch	.05	.02	.00
☐	41 John Franco	.10	.05	.01
☐	42 Julio Franco	.10	.05	.01
☐	43 Gary Gaetti	.20	.10	.02
☐	44 Gene Garber	.05	.02	.00
☐	45 Scott Garrelts	.10	.05	.01
☐	46 Steve Garvey	.45	.22	.04
☐	47 Kirk Gibson	.35	.17	.03
☐	48 Dwight Gooden	.75	.35	.07
☐	49 Ken Griffey Sr.	.10	.05	.01
☐	50 Ozzie Guillen	.10	.05	.01
☐	51 Bill Gullickson	.05	.02	.00
☐	52 Tony Gwynn	.50	.25	.05
☐	53 Mel Hall	.10	.05	.01
☐	54 Greg Harris	.05	.02	.00
☐	55 Von Hayes	.10	.05	.01
☐	56 Rickey Henderson	.75	.35	.07
☐	57 Tom Henke	.10	.05	.01
☐	58 Keith Hernandez	.20	.10	.02
☐	59 Willie Hernandez	.10	.05	.01
☐	60 Ted Higuera	.15	.07	.01
☐	61 Bob Horner	.15	.07	.01
☐	62 Charlie Hough	.05	.02	.00
☐	63 Jay Howell	.05	.02	.00
☐	64 Kent Hrbek	.20	.10	.02
☐	65 Bruce Hurst	.15	.07	.01
☐	66 Pete Incaviglia	.25	.12	.02
☐	67 Bob James	.05	.02	.00
☐	68 Wally Joyner	1.00	.50	.10
☐	69 Mike Krukow	.05	.02	.00
☐	70 Mark Langston	.25	.12	.02
☐	71 Carney Lansford	.15	.07	.01
☐	72 Fred Lynn	.15	.07	.01
☐	73 Bill Madlock	.05	.02	.00
☐	74 Don Mattingly	2.50	1.25	.25
☐	75 Kirk McCaskill	.05	.02	.00
☐	76 Lance McCullers	.05	.02	.00
☐	77 Oddibe McDowell	.10	.05	.01
☐	78 Paul Molitor	.20	.10	.02
☐	79 Keith Moreland	.05	.02	.00
☐	80 Jack Morris	.15	.07	.01
☐	81 Jim Morrison	.05	.02	.00
☐	82 Jerry Mumphrey	.05	.02	.00
☐	83 Dale Murphy	.40	.20	.04
☐	84 Eddie Murray	.35	.17	.03
☐	85 Ben Oglivie	.05	.02	.00
☐	86 Bob Ojeda	.10	.05	.01
☐	87 Jesse Orosco	.05	.02	.00
☐	88 Dave Parker	.15	.07	.01
☐	89 Larry Parrish	.05	.02	.00
☐	90 Tony Pena	.05	.02	.00
☐	91 Jim Presley	.10	.05	.01
☐	92 Kirby Puckett	1.00	.50	.10
☐	93 Dan Quisenberry	.10	.05	.01
☐	94 Tim Raines	.25	.12	.02
☐	95 Dennis Rasmussen	.05	.02	.00
☐	96 Shane Rawley	.05	.02	.00
☐	97 Johnny Ray	.10	.05	.01
☐	98 Jeff Reardon	.10	.05	.01
☐	99 Jim Rice	.20	.10	.02
☐	100 Dave Righetti	.15	.07	.01
☐	101 Cal Ripken Jr.	.40	.20	.04
☐	102 Pete Rose	.75	.35	.07
☐	103 Nolan Ryan	1.50	.75	.15
☐	104 Juan Samuel	.15	.07	.01
☐	105 Ryne Sandberg	.30	.15	.03
☐	106 Steve Sax	.15	.07	.01
☐	107 Mike Schmidt	1.25	.60	.12
☐	108 Mike Scott	.20	.10	.02
☐	109 Dave Smith	.05	.02	.00
☐	110 Lee Smith	.10	.05	.01
☐	111 Lonnie Smith	.10	.05	.01
☐	112 Ozzie Smith	.20	.10	.02
☐	113 Cory Snyder	.25	.12	.02
☐	114 Darryl Strawberry	.60	.30	.06
☐	115 Don Sutton	.20	.10	.02
☐	116 Kent Tekulve	.05	.02	.00
☐	117 Andres Thomas	.05	.02	.00
☐	118 Alan Trammell	.25	.12	.02
☐	119 John Tudor	.15	.07	.01
☐	120 Fernando Valenzuela	.20	.10	.02
☐	121 Bob Welch	.10	.05	.01
☐	122 Lou Whitaker	.15	.07	.01
☐	123 Frank White	.10	.05	.01
☐	124 Reggie Williams	.05	.02	.00
☐	125 Willie Wilson	.10	.05	.01
☐	126 Dave Winfield	.25	.12	.02
☐	127 Mike Witt	.10	.05	.01
☐	128 Todd Worrell	.20	.10	.02
☐	129 Curt Young	.05	.02	.00
☐	130 Robin Yount	.75	.35	.07
☐	131 Checklist	2.00	1.00	.20
	Jose Canseco			
	Don Mattingly			
☐	132 Checklist	2.00	1.00	.20
	Bo Jackson			
	Eric Davis			

ADVERTISER INDEX: Found at the end of the Table of Contents. Be sure to let our advertisers know that you saw their ad in this publication.

1987 Fleer Sticker Wax Box

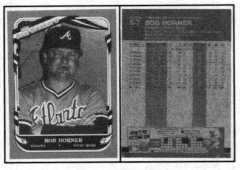

The bottoms of the Star Sticker wax boxes contained two different sets of four cards done in a similar format to the stickers; these cards (they are not stickers but truly cards) are numbered with the prefix S and are considered a separate set. The value of the panels uncut is slightly greater, perhaps by 25% greater, than the value of the individual cards cut up carefully.

	MINT	EXC	G-VG
COMPLETE SET (8)	2.25	1.10	.22
COMMON PLAYER (S1-S8)	.10	.05	.01
☐ S1 Detroit Logo	.10	.05	.01
☐ S2 Wade Boggs	.75	.35	.07
☐ S3 Bert Blyleven	.15	.07	.01
☐ S4 Jose Cruz	.10	.05	.01
☐ S5 Glenn Davis	.20	.10	.02
☐ S6 Phillies Logo	.10	.05	.01
☐ S7 Bob Horner	.15	.07	.01
☐ S8 Don Mattingly	1.25	.60	.12

1987 Fleer Award Winners

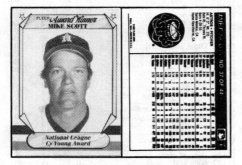

This small set of 44 cards was (mass)- produced for 7-Eleven stores by Fleer. The cards measure the standard 2 1/2" by 3 1/2" and feature full color fronts and yellow, white, and black backs. The card fronts are distinguished by their yellow frame around the player's full-color photo. The box for the cards describes the set as the "1987 Limited Edition Baseball's Award Winners." The checklist for the set is given on the back of the set box.

	MINT	EXC	G-VG
COMPLETE SET (44)	4.00	2.00	.40
COMMON PLAYER (1-44)	.05	.02	.00
☐ 1 Marty Barrett	.05	.02	.00
☐ 2 George Bell	.10	.05	.01
☐ 3 Bert Blyleven	.10	.05	.01

☐ 4 Bob Boone	.10	.05	.01
☐ 5 John Candelaria	.05	.02	.00
☐ 6 Jose Canseco	1.00	.50	.10
☐ 7 Gary Carter	.20	.10	.02
☐ 8 Joe Carter	.15	.07	.01
☐ 9 Roger Clemens	.45	.22	.04
☐ 10 Cecil Cooper	.05	.02	.00
☐ 11 Eric Davis	.60	.30	.06
☐ 12 Tony Fernandez	.10	.05	.01
☐ 13 Scott Fletcher	.05	.02	.00
☐ 14 Bob Forsch	.05	.02	.00
☐ 15 Dwight Gooden	.40	.20	.04
☐ 16 Ron Guidry	.10	.05	.01
☐ 17 Ozzie Guillen	.10	.05	.01
☐ 18 Bill Gullickson	.05	.02	.00
☐ 19 Tony Gwynn	.40	.20	.04
☐ 20 Bob Knepper	.05	.02	.00
☐ 21 Ray Knight	.05	.02	.00
☐ 22 Mark Langston	.15	.07	.01
☐ 23 Candy Maldonado	.05	.02	.00
☐ 24 Don Mattingly	1.00	.50	.10
☐ 25 Roger McDowell	.15	.07	.01
☐ 26 Dale Murphy	.35	.17	.03
☐ 27 Dave Parker	.15	.07	.01
☐ 28 Lance Parrish	.10	.05	.01
☐ 29 Gary Pettis	.05	.02	.00
☐ 30 Kirby Puckett	.50	.25	.05
☐ 31 Johnny Ray	.10	.05	.01
☐ 32 Dave Righetti	.10	.05	.01
☐ 33 Cal Ripken	.30	.15	.03
☐ 34 Bret Saberhagen	.20	.10	.02
☐ 35 Ryne Sandberg	.30	.15	.03
☐ 36 Mike Schmidt	.75	.35	.07
☐ 37 Mike Scott	.15	.07	.01
☐ 38 Ozzie Smith	.20	.10	.02
☐ 39 Robbie Thompson	.10	.05	.01
☐ 40 Fernando Valenzuela	.20	.10	.02
☐ 41 Mitch Webster UER	.05	.02	.00
(Mike on front)			
☐ 42 Frank White	.05	.02	.00
☐ 43 Mike Witt	.10	.05	.01
☐ 44 Todd Worrell	.15	.07	.01

1987 Fleer Exciting Stars

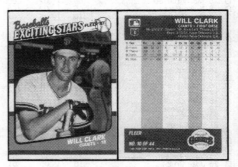

This small 44-card boxed set was produced by Fleer for distribution by the Cumberland Farm stores. The cards measure the standard 2 1/2" by 3 1/2" and feature full color fronts. The set is titled "Baseball's Exciting Stars." Each individual boxed set includes the 44 cards and 6 logo stickers. The checklist for the set is found on the back panel of the box.

	MINT	EXC	G-VG
COMPLETE SET (44)	5.00	2.50	.50
COMMON PLAYER (1-44)	.10	.05	.01
☐ 1 Don Aase	.10	.05	.01
☐ 2 Rick Aguilera	.15	.07	.01
☐ 3 Jesse Barfield	.15	.07	.01
☐ 4 Wade Boggs	.75	.35	.07
☐ 5 Dennis"Oil Can" Boyd	.15	.07	.01
☐ 6 Sid Bream	.10	.05	.01
☐ 7 Jose Canseco	1.25	.60	.12
☐ 8 Steve Carlton	.30	.15	.03
☐ 9 Gary Carter	.25	.12	.02
☐ 10 Will Clark	1.25	.60	.12
☐ 11 Roger Clemens	.50	.25	.05
☐ 12 Danny Cox	.10	.05	.01

		MINT	EXC	G-VG
□ 13	Alvin Davis	.15	.07	.01
□ 14	Eric Davis	.60	.30	.06
□ 15	Rob Deer	.15	.07	.01
□ 16	Brian Downing	.10	.05	.01
□ 17	Gene Garber	.10	.05	.01
□ 18	Steve Garvey	.30	.15	.03
□ 19	Dwight Gooden	.45	.22	.04
□ 20	Mark Gubicza	.20	.10	.02
□ 21	Mel Hall	.15	.07	.01
□ 22	Terry Harper	.10	.05	.01
□ 23	Von Hayes	.15	.07	.01
□ 24	Rickey Henderson	.40	.20	.04
□ 25	Tom Henke	.15	.07	.01
□ 26	Willie Hernandez	.15	.07	.01
□ 27	Ted Higuera	.15	.07	.01
□ 28	Rick Honeycutt	.10	.05	.01
□ 29	Kent Hrbek	.20	.10	.02
□ 30	Wally Joyner	.50	.25	.05
□ 31	Charlie Kerfeld	.10	.05	.01
□ 32	Fred Lynn	.15	.07	.01
□ 33	Don Mattingly	1.00	.50	.10
□ 34	Tim Raines	.25	.12	.02
□ 35	Dennis Rasmussen	.10	.05	.01
□ 36	Johnny Ray	.15	.07	.01
□ 37	Jim Rice	.20	.10	.02
□ 38	Pete Rose	.65	.30	.06
□ 39	Lee Smith	.10	.05	.01
□ 40	Cory Snyder	.20	.10	.02
□ 41	Darryl Strawberry	.60	.30	.06
□ 42	Kent Tekulve	.10	.05	.01
□ 43	Willie Wilson	.15	.07	.01
□ 44	Bobby Witt	.15	.07	.01

		MINT	EXC	G-VG
□ 20	Willie Hernandez	.10	.05	.01
□ 21	Ted Higuera	.10	.05	.01
□ 22	Wally Joyner	.40	.20	.04
□ 23	Bob Knepper	.05	.02	.00
□ 24	Mike Krukow	.05	.02	.00
□ 25	Jeff Leonard	.05	.02	.00
□ 26	Don Mattingly	1.00	.50	.10
□ 27	Kirk McCaskill	.05	.02	.00
□ 28	Kevin McReynolds	.15	.07	.01
□ 29	Jim Morrison	.05	.02	.00
□ 30	Dale Murphy	.35	.17	.03
□ 31	Pete O'Brien	.10	.05	.01
□ 32	Bob Ojeda	.10	.05	.01
□ 33	Larry Parrish	.05	.02	.00
□ 34	Ken Phelps	.05	.02	.00
□ 35	Dennis Rasmussen	.05	.02	.00
□ 36	Ernest Riles	.05	.02	.00
□ 37	Cal Ripken	.35	.17	.03
□ 38	Ron Robinson	.05	.02	.00
□ 39	Steve Sax	.15	.07	.01
□ 40	Mike Schmidt	.75	.35	.07
□ 41	John Tudor	.10	.05	.01
□ 42	Fernando Valenzuela	.20	.10	.02
□ 43	Mike Witt	.10	.05	.01
□ 44	Curt Young	.05	.02	.00

1987 Fleer Hottest Stars

This 44-card boxed set was produced by Fleer for distribution by Revco stores all over the country. The cards measure the standard 2 1/2" by 3 1/2" and feature full color fronts and red, white, and black backs. The card fronts are easily distinguished by their solid red outside borders and and white and blue inner borders framing the player's picture. The box for the cards proclaims "1987 Limited Edition Baseball's Hottest Stars" and is styled in the same manner and color scheme as the cards themselves. The checklist for the set is given on the back of the set box.

1987 Fleer Game Winners

This small 44-card boxed set was produced by Fleer for distribution by several store chains, including Bi-Mart, Pay'n'Save, Mott's, M.E.Moses, and Winn's. The cards measure the standard 2 1/2" by 3 1/2" and feature full color fronts. The set is titled "Baseball's Game Winners." Each individual boxed set includes the 44 cards and 6 logo stickers. The checklist for the set is found on the back panel of the box.

		MINT	EXC	G-VG
COMPLETE SET (44)		4.00	2.00	.40
COMMON PLAYER (1-44)		.05	.02	.00
□ 1	Harold Baines	.10	.05	.01
□ 2	Don Baylor	.10	.05	.01
□ 3	George Bell	.15	.07	.01
□ 4	Tony Bernazard	.05	.02	.00
□ 5	Wade Boggs	.75	.35	.07
□ 6	George Brett	.35	.17	.03
□ 7	Hubie Brooks	.05	.02	.00
□ 8	Jose Canseco	1.00	.50	.10
□ 9	Gary Carter	.20	.10	.02
□ 10	Roger Clemens	.45	.22	.04
□ 11	Eric Davis	.60	.30	.06
□ 12	Glenn Davis	.20	.10	.02
□ 13	Shawon Dunston	.10	.05	.01
□ 14	Mark Eichhorn	.05	.02	.00
□ 15	Gary Gaetti	.15	.07	.01
□ 16	Steve Garvey	.30	.15	.03
□ 17	Kirk Gibson	.30	.15	.03
□ 18	Dwight Gooden	.40	.20	.04
□ 19	Von Hayes	.10	.05	.01

		MINT	EXC	G-VG
COMPLETE SET (44)		5.00	2.50	.50
COMMON PLAYER (1-44)		.10	.05	.01
□ 1	Joaquin Andujar	.10	.05	.01
□ 2	Harold Baines	.15	.07	.01
□ 3	Kevin Bass	.10	.05	.01
□ 4	Don Baylor	.15	.07	.01
□ 5	Barry Bonds	.25	.12	.02
□ 6	George Brett	.40	.20	.04
□ 7	Tom Brunansky	.15	.07	.01
□ 8	Brett Butler	.15	.07	.01
□ 9	Jose Canseco	1.25	.60	.12
□ 10	Roger Clemens	.50	.25	.05
□ 11	Ron Darling	.20	.10	.02
□ 12	Eric Davis	.60	.30	.06
□ 13	Andre Dawson	.25	.12	.02
□ 14	Doug DeCinces	.10	.05	.01
□ 15	Leon Durham	.10	.05	.01
□ 16	Mark Eichhorn	.10	.05	.01
□ 17	Scott Garrelts	.15	.07	.01
□ 18	Dwight Gooden	.50	.25	.05
□ 19	Dave Henderson	.10	.05	.01
□ 20	Rickey Henderson	.50	.25	.05
□ 21	Keith Hernandez	.20	.10	.02
□ 22	Ted Higuera	.15	.07	.01

		MINT	EXC	G-VG
☐ 23	Bob Horner	.15	.07	.01
☐ 24	Pete Incaviglia	.20	.10	.02
☐ 25	Wally Joyner	.45	.22	.04
☐ 26	Mark Langston	.20	.10	.02
☐ 27	Don Mattingly UER	1.25	.60	.12
	(Pirates logo on back)			
☐ 28	Dale Murphy	.35	.17	.03
☐ 29	Kirk McCaskill	.10	.05	.01
☐ 30	Willie McGee	.15	.07	.01
☐ 31	Dave Righetti	.15	.07	.01
☐ 32	Pete Rose	.60	.30	.06
☐ 33	Bruce Ruffin	.10	.05	.01
☐ 34	Steve Sax	.20	.10	.02
☐ 35	Mike Schmidt	.75	.35	.07
☐ 36	Larry Sheets	.10	.05	.01
☐ 37	Eric Show	.10	.05	.01
☐ 38	Dave Smith	.10	.05	.01
☐ 39	Cory Snyder	.20	.10	.02
☐ 40	Frank Tanana	.10	.05	.01
☐ 41	Alan Trammell	.20	.10	.02
☐ 42	Reggie Williams	.10	.05	.01
☐ 43	Mookie Wilson	.10	.05	.01
☐ 44	Todd Worrell	.20	.10	.02

		MINT	EXC	G-VG
☐ 27	Dave Kingman	.15	.07	.01
☐ 28	Don Mattingly	1.00	.50	.10
☐ 29	Willie McGee	.15	.07	.01
☐ 30	Donnie Moore	.10	.05	.01
☐ 31	Keith Moreland	.10	.05	.01
☐ 32	Eddie Murray	.25	.12	.02
☐ 33	Mike Pagliarulo	.15	.07	.01
☐ 34	Larry Parrish	.10	.05	.01
☐ 35	Tony Pena	.10	.05	.01
☐ 36	Kirby Puckett	.50	.25	.05
☐ 37	Pete Rose	.60	.30	.06
☐ 38	Juan Samuel	.20	.10	.02
☐ 39	Ryne Sandberg	.25	.12	.02
☐ 40	Mike Schmidt	.75	.35	.07
☐ 41	Darryl Strawberry	.60	.30	.06
☐ 42	Greg Walker	.15	.07	.01
☐ 43	Bob Welch	.10	.05	.01
☐ 44	Todd Worrell	.20	.10	.02

1987 Fleer Baseball All-Stars

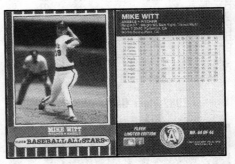

This small set of 44 cards was produced for Ben Franklin stores by Fleer. The cards measure the standard 2 1/2" by 3 1/2" and feature full color fronts and red, white, and blue backs. The card fronts are easily distinguished by their white vertical stripes over a bright red background. The box for the cards proclaims "Limited Edition Baseball All-Stars" and is styled in the same manner and color scheme as the cards themselves. The checklist for the set is given on the back of the set box.

1987 Fleer League Leaders

This small set of 44 cards was produced for Walgreens by Fleer. The cards measure the standard 2 1/2" by 3 1/2" and feature full color fronts and red, white, and blue backs. The card fronts are easily distinguished by their light blue vertical stripes over a white background. The box for the cards proclaims a "Walgreens Exclusive" and is styled in the same manner and color scheme as the cards themselves. The checklist for the set is given on the back of the set box.

		MINT	EXC	G-VG
COMPLETE SET (44)		5.00	2.50	.50
COMMON PLAYER (1-44)		.10	.05	.01
☐ 1	Jesse Barfield	.15	.07	.01
☐ 2	Mike Boddicker	.10	.05	.01
☐ 3	Wade Boggs	.75	.35	.07
☐ 4	Phil Bradley	.15	.07	.01
☐ 5	George Brett	.40	.20	.04
☐ 6	Hubie Brooks	.10	.05	.01
☐ 7	Chris Brown	.10	.05	.01
☐ 8	Jose Canseco	1.00	.50	.10
☐ 9	Joe Carter	.20	.10	.02
☐ 10	Roger Clemens	.50	.25	.05
☐ 11	Vince Coleman	.35	.17	.03
☐ 12	Joe Cowley	.10	.05	.01
☐ 13	Kal Daniels	.20	.10	.02
☐ 14	Glenn Davis	.20	.10	.02
☐ 15	Jody Davis	.10	.05	.01
☐ 16	Darrell Evans	.15	.07	.01
☐ 17	Dwight Evans	.20	.10	.02
☐ 18	John Franco	.10	.05	.01
☐ 19	Julio Franco	.15	.07	.01
☐ 20	Dwight Gooden	.45	.22	.04
☐ 21	Goose Gossage	.15	.07	.01
☐ 22	Tom Herr	.10	.05	.01
☐ 23	Ted Higuera	.15	.07	.01
☐ 24	Bob Horner	.15	.07	.01
☐ 25	Pete Incaviglia	.20	.10	.02
☐ 26	Wally Joyner	.45	.22	.04

		MINT	EXC	G-VG
COMPLETE SET (44)		5.00	2.50	.50
COMMON PLAYER (1-44)		.10	.05	.01
☐ 1	Harold Baines	.15	.07	.01
☐ 2	Jesse Barfield	.15	.07	.01
☐ 3	Wade Boggs	.75	.35	.07
☐ 4	Dennis "Oil Can" Boyd	.15	.07	.01
☐ 5	Scott Bradley	.10	.05	.01
☐ 6	Jose Canseco	1.00	.50	.10
☐ 7	Gary Carter	.25	.12	.02
☐ 8	Joe Carter	.20	.10	.02
☐ 9	Mark Clear	.10	.05	.01
☐ 10	Roger Clemens	.50	.25	.05
☐ 11	Jose Cruz	.10	.05	.01
☐ 12	Chili Davis	.10	.05	.01
☐ 13	Jody Davis	.10	.05	.01
☐ 14	Rob Deer	.10	.05	.01
☐ 15	Brian Downing	.10	.05	.01
☐ 16	Sid Fernandez	.15	.07	.01
☐ 17	John Franco	.15	.07	.01
☐ 18	Andres Galarraga	.25	.12	.02
☐ 19	Dwight Gooden	.45	.22	.04
☐ 20	Tony Gwynn	.45	.22	.04
☐ 21	Charlie Hough	.10	.05	.01
☐ 22	Bruce Hurst	.15	.07	.01
☐ 23	Wally Joyner	.45	.22	.04
☐ 24	Carney Lansford	.20	.10	.02
☐ 25	Fred Lynn	.15	.07	.01
☐ 26	Don Mattingly	1.00	.50	.10
☐ 27	Willie McGee	.15	.07	.01
☐ 28	Jack Morris	.15	.07	.01
☐ 29	Dale Murphy	.35	.17	.03
☐ 30	Bob Ojeda	.10	.05	.01
☐ 31	Tony Pena	.10	.05	.01
☐ 32	Kirby Puckett	.50	.25	.05

		MINT	EXC	G-VG
☐ 33	Dan Quisenberry	.15	.07	.01
☐ 34	Tim Raines	.25	.12	.02
☐ 35	Willie Randolph	.15	.07	.01
☐ 36	Cal Ripken	.35	.17	.03
☐ 37	Pete Rose	.50	.25	.05
☐ 38	Nolan Ryan	1.00	.50	.10
☐ 39	Juan Samuel	.15	.07	.01
☐ 40	Mike Schmidt	.75	.35	.07
☐ 41	Ozzie Smith	.20	.10	.02
☐ 42	Andres Thomas	.10	.05	.01
☐ 43	Fernando Valenzuela	.20	.10	.02
☐ 44	Mike Witt	.15	.07	.01

1987 Fleer Limited Edition

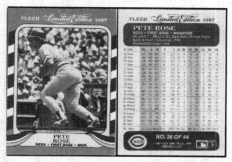

This 44-card boxed set was (mass) produced by Fleer for distribution by McCrory's and is sometimes referred to as the McCrory's set. The numerical checklist on the back of the box shows that the set is numbered alphabetically. The cards measure 2 1/2" by 3 1/2".

		MINT	EXC	G-VG
COMPLETE SET (44)		4.00	2.00	.40
COMMON PLAYER (1-44)		.05	.02	.00
☐ 1	Floyd Bannister	.05	.02	.00
☐ 2	Marty Barrett	.05	.02	.00
☐ 3	Steve Bedrosian	.10	.05	.01
☐ 4	George Bell	.15	.07	.01
☐ 5	George Brett	.30	.15	.03
☐ 6	Jose Canseco	1.00	.50	.10
☐ 7	Joe Carter	.15	.07	.01
☐ 8	Will Clark	1.00	.50	.10
☐ 9	Roger Clemens	.50	.25	.05
☐ 10	Vince Coleman	.25	.12	.02
☐ 11	Glenn Davis	.15	.07	.01
☐ 12	Mike Davis	.05	.02	.00
☐ 13	Len Dykstra	.10	.05	.01
☐ 14	John Franco	.10	.05	.01
☐ 15	Julio Franco	.10	.05	.01
☐ 16	Steve Garvey	.30	.15	.03
☐ 17	Kirk Gibson	.30	.15	.03
☐ 18	Dwight Gooden	.50	.25	.05
☐ 19	Tony Gwynn	.40	.20	.04
☐ 20	Keith Hernandez	.20	.10	.02
☐ 21	Teddy Higuera	.10	.05	.01
☐ 22	Kent Hrbek	.15	.07	.01
☐ 23	Wally Joyner	.40	.20	.04
☐ 24	Mike Krukow	.05	.02	.00
☐ 25	Mike Marshall	.10	.05	.01
☐ 26	Don Mattingly	1.00	.50	.10
☐ 27	Oddibe McDowell	.10	.05	.01
☐ 28	Jack Morris	.10	.05	.01
☐ 29	Lloyd Moseby	.05	.02	.00
☐ 30	Dale Murphy	.35	.17	.03
☐ 31	Eddie Murray	.25	.12	.02
☐ 32	Tony Pena	.05	.02	.00
☐ 33	Jim Presley	.05	.02	.00
☐ 34	Jeff Reardon	.05	.02	.00
☐ 35	Jim Rice	.15	.07	.01
☐ 36	Pete Rose	.50	.25	.05
☐ 37	Mike Schmidt	.75	.35	.07
☐ 38	Mike Scott	.15	.07	.01
☐ 39	Lee Smith	.05	.02	.00
☐ 40	Lonnie Smith	.10	.05	.01
☐ 41	Gary Ward	.05	.02	.00
☐ 42	Dave Winfield	.25	.12	.02
☐ 43	Todd Worrell	.15	.07	.01

		MINT	EXC	G-VG
☐ 44	Robin Yount	.45	.22	.04

1987 Fleer Limited Box Cards

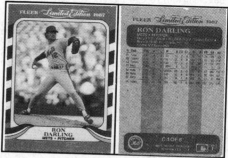

The cards in this 6-card set each measure the standard 2 1/2" by 3 1/2". Cards have essentially the same design as the 1987 Fleer Limited Edition cards which were distributed by McCrory's. The cards were printed on the bottom of the counter display box which held 24 small boxed sets; hence theoretically these box cards are 1/24 as plentiful as the regular boxed set cards. These 6 cards, numbered C1 to C6, are considered a separate set in their own right and are not typically included in a complete set of the 1987 Fleer Limited Edition set of 44. The value of the panels uncut is slightly greater, perhaps by 25% greater, than the value of the individual cards cut up carefully.

		MINT	EXC	G-VG
COMPLETE SET (6)		1.25	.60	.12
COMMON PLAYERS (C1-C6)		.10	.05	.01
☐ C1	Ron Darling (box bottom card)	.25	.12	.02
☐ C2	Bill Buckner (box bottom card)	.15	.07	.01
☐ C3	John Candelaria (box bottom card)	.15	.07	.01
☐ C4	Jack Clark (box bottom card)	.35	.17	.03
☐ C5	Bret Saberhagen (box bottom card)	.50	.25	.05
☐ C6	Team Logo (box bottom card; checklist back)	.10	.05	.01

1987 Fleer Mini

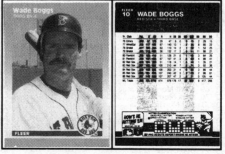

The 1987 Fleer "Classic Miniatures" set consists of 120 small cards with all new pictures of the players as compared to the 1987 Fleer regular issue. The cards are only 1 13/16" by 2 9/16", making them one of the smallest cards available. Card backs provide career year-by-year statistics. The complete set was distributed in a blue, red, white, and silver box along with 18 logo stickers. The card numbering is by alphabetical order.

	MINT	EXC	G-VG
COMPLETE SET (120)	9.00	4.50	.90
COMMON PLAYER (1-120)	.05	.02	.00
☐ 1 Don Aase	.05	.02	.00
☐ 2 Joaquin Andujar	.05	.02	.00
☐ 3 Harold Baines	.10	.05	.01
☐ 4 Jesse Barfield	.15	.07	.01
☐ 5 Kevin Bass	.05	.02	.00
☐ 6 Don Baylor	.10	.05	.01
☐ 7 George Bell	.15	.07	.01
☐ 8 Tony Bernazard	.05	.02	.00
☐ 9 Bert Blyleven	.10	.05	.01
☐ 10 Wade Boggs	.75	.35	.07
☐ 11 Phil Bradley	.10	.05	.01
☐ 12 Sid Bream	.05	.02	.00
☐ 13 George Brett	.35	.17	.03
☐ 14 Hubie Brooks	.05	.02	.00
☐ 15 Chris Brown	.05	.02	.00
☐ 16 Tom Candiotti	.05	.02	.00
☐ 17 Jose Canseco	1.00	.50	.10
☐ 18 Gary Carter	.20	.10	.02
☐ 19 Joe Carter	.15	.07	.01
☐ 20 Roger Clemens	.45	.22	.04
☐ 21 Vince Coleman	.20	.10	.02
☐ 22 Cecil Cooper	.10	.05	.01
☐ 23 Ron Darling	.15	.07	.01
☐ 24 Alvin Davis	.10	.05	.01
☐ 25 Chili Davis	.10	.05	.01
☐ 26 Eric Davis	.60	.30	.06
☐ 27 Glenn Davis	.20	.10	.02
☐ 28 Mike Davis	.05	.02	.00
☐ 29 Doug DeCinces	.05	.02	.00
☐ 30 Rob Deer	.10	.05	.01
☐ 31 Jim Deshaies	.05	.02	.00
☐ 32 Bo Diaz	.05	.02	.00
☐ 33 Richard Dotson	.05	.02	.00
☐ 34 Brian Downing	.05	.02	.00
☐ 35 Shawon Dunston	.10	.05	.01
☐ 36 Mark Eichhorn	.05	.02	.00
☐ 37 Dwight Evans	.10	.05	.01
☐ 38 Tony Fernandez	.10	.05	.01
☐ 39 Julio Franco	.10	.05	.01
☐ 40 Gary Gaetti	.15	.07	.01
☐ 41 Andres Galarraga	.25	.12	.02
☐ 42 Scott Garrelts	.10	.05	.01
☐ 43 Steve Garvey	.25	.12	.02
☐ 44 Kirk Gibson	.25	.12	.02
☐ 45 Dwight Gooden	.45	.22	.04
☐ 46 Ken Griffey Sr.	.10	.05	.01
☐ 47 Mark Gubicza	.10	.05	.01
☐ 48 Ozzie Guillen	.10	.05	.01
☐ 49 Bill Gullickson	.05	.02	.00
☐ 50 Tony Gwynn	.40	.20	.04
☐ 51 Von Hayes	.10	.05	.01
☐ 52 Rickey Henderson	.45	.22	.04
☐ 53 Keith Hernandez	.20	.10	.02
☐ 54 Willie Hernandez	.10	.05	.01
☐ 55 Ted Higuera	.10	.05	.01
☐ 56 Charlie Hough	.05	.02	.00
☐ 57 Kent Hrbek	.15	.07	.01
☐ 58 Pete Incaviglia	.15	.07	.01
☐ 59 Wally Joyner	.40	.20	.04
☐ 60 Bob Knepper	.05	.02	.00
☐ 61 Mike Krukow	.05	.02	.00
☐ 62 Mark Langston	.20	.10	.02
☐ 63 Carney Lansford	.15	.07	.01
☐ 64 Jim Lindeman	.05	.02	.00
☐ 65 Bill Madlock	.05	.02	.00
☐ 66 Don Mattingly	1.00	.50	.10
☐ 67 Kirk McCaskill	.05	.02	.00
☐ 68 Lance McCullers	.05	.02	.00
☐ 69 Keith Moreland	.05	.02	.00
☐ 70 Jack Morris	.10	.05	.01
☐ 71 Jim Morrison	.05	.02	.00
☐ 72 Lloyd Moseby	.05	.02	.00
☐ 73 Jerry Mumphrey	.05	.02	.00
☐ 74 Dale Murphy	.35	.17	.03
☐ 75 Eddie Murray	.30	.15	.03
☐ 76 Pete O'Brien	.10	.05	.01
☐ 77 Bob Ojeda	.10	.05	.01
☐ 78 Jesse Orosco	.05	.02	.00
☐ 79 Dan Pasqua	.05	.02	.00
☐ 80 Dave Parker	.15	.07	.01
☐ 81 Larry Parrish	.05	.02	.00
☐ 82 Jim Presley	.05	.02	.00
☐ 83 Kirby Puckett	.50	.25	.05
☐ 84 Dan Quisenberry	.10	.05	.01
☐ 85 Tim Raines	.25	.12	.02
☐ 86 Dennis Rasmussen	.05	.02	.00
☐ 87 Johnny Ray	.10	.05	.01
☐ 88 Jeff Reardon	.10	.05	.01
☐ 89 Jim Rice	.20	.10	.02
☐ 90 Dave Righetti	.10	.05	.01
☐ 91 Earnest Riles	.05	.02	.00
☐ 92 Cal Ripken	.30	.15	.03
☐ 93 Ron Robinson	.05	.02	.00
☐ 94 Juan Samuel	.10	.05	.01
☐ 95 Ryne Sandberg	.25	.12	.02
☐ 96 Steve Sax	.15	.07	.01
☐ 97 Mike Schmidt	.75	.35	.07
☐ 98 Ken Schrom	.05	.02	.00
☐ 99 Mike Scott	.20	.10	.02
☐ 100 Ruben Sierra	.60	.30	.06
☐ 101 Lee Smith	.10	.05	.01
☐ 102 Ozzie Smith	.15	.07	.01
☐ 103 Cory Snyder	.15	.07	.01
☐ 104 Kent Tekulve	.05	.02	.00
☐ 105 Andres Thomas	.05	.02	.00
☐ 106 Rob Thompson	.05	.02	.00
☐ 107 Alan Trammell	.20	.10	.02
☐ 108 John Tudor	.10	.05	.01
☐ 109 Fernando Valenzuela	.15	.07	.01
☐ 110 Greg Walker	.05	.02	.00
☐ 111 Mitch Webster	.05	.02	.00
☐ 112 Lou Whitaker	.15	.07	.01
☐ 113 Frank White	.05	.02	.00
☐ 114 Reggie Williams	.05	.02	.00
☐ 115 Glenn Wilson	.05	.02	.00
☐ 116 Willie Wilson	.10	.05	.01
☐ 117 Dave Winfield	.25	.12	.02
☐ 118 Mike Witt	.10	.05	.01
☐ 119 Todd Worrell	.15	.07	.01
☐ 120 Floyd Youmans	.05	.02	.00

1987 Fleer Record Setters

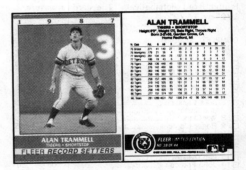

This 44-card boxed set was produced by Fleer for distribution by Eckerd's Drug Stores and is sometimes referred to as the Eckerd's set. Six team logo stickers are included in the box with the complete set. The numerical checklist on the back of the box shows that the set is numbered alphabetically. The cards measure 2 1/2" by 3 1/2".

	MINT	EXC	G-VG
COMPLETE SET (44)	5.00	2.50	.50
COMMON PLAYER (1-44)	.05	.02	.00
☐ 1 George Brett	.35	.17	.03
☐ 2 Chris Brown	.05	.02	.00
☐ 3 Jose Canseco UER	1.25	.60	.12
(3 of 444 on back)			
☐ 4 Roger Clemens	.60	.30	.06
☐ 5 Alvin Davis UER	.10	.05	.01
(5 of 441 on back, upside down one)			
☐ 6 Shawon Dunston	.10	.05	.01
☐ 7 Tony Fernandez	.10	.05	.01
☐ 8 Carlton Fisk UER	.20	.10	.02
(8 of 44' on back)			
☐ 9 Gary Gaetti UER	.15	.07	.01
(9 of 444 on back)			
☐ 10 Gene Garber	.05	.02	.00

		MINT	EXC	G-VG
☐ 11	Rich Gedman	.05	.02	.00
☐ 12	Dwight Gooden	.50	.25	.05
☐ 13	Ozzie Guillen	.10	.05	.01
☐ 14	Bill Gullickson	.05	.02	.00
☐ 15	Billy Hatcher	.05	.02	.00
☐ 16	Orel Hershiser	.45	.22	.04
☐ 17	Wally Joyner	.40	.20	.04
☐ 18	Ray Knight	.05	.02	.00
☐ 19	Craig Lefferts	.05	.02	.00
☐ 20	Don Mattingly	1.00	.50	.10
☐ 21	Kevin Mitchell	.50	.25	.05
☐ 22	Lloyd Moseby	.05	.02	.00
☐ 23	Dale Murphy	.30	.15	.03
☐ 24	Eddie Murray	.25	.12	.02
☐ 25	Phil Niekro	.15	.07	.01
☐ 26	Ben Oglivie	.05	.02	.00
☐ 27	Jesse Orosco	.05	.02	.00
☐ 28	Joe Orsulak	.05	.02	.00
☐ 29	Larry Parrish	.05	.02	.00
☐ 30	Tim Raines	.20	.10	.02
☐ 31	Shane Rawley	.05	.02	.00
☐ 32	Dave Righetti	.10	.05	.01
☐ 33	Pete Rose	.60	.30	.06
☐ 34	Steve Sax	.15	.07	.01
☐ 35	Mike Schmidt	.75	.35	.07
☐ 36	Mike Scott	.15	.07	.01
☐ 37	Don Sutton	.15	.07	.01
☐ 38	Alan Trammell	.20	.10	.02
☐ 39	John Tudor	.10	.05	.01
☐ 40	Gary Ward	.05	.02	.00
☐ 41	Lou Whitaker	.10	.05	.01
☐ 42	Willie Wilson	.10	.05	.01
☐ 43	Todd Worrell	.15	.07	.01
☐ 44	Floyd Youmans	.05	.02	.00

		MINT	EXC	G-VG
☐ 17	Tony Gwynn	.35	.17	.03
☐ 18	Rickey Henderson	.45	.22	.04
☐ 19	Tom Henke	.10	.05	.01
☐ 20	Ted Higuera	.15	.07	.01
☐ 21	Pete Incaviglia	.20	.10	.02
☐ 22	Wally Joyner	.40	.20	.04
☐ 23	Jeff Leonard	.10	.05	.01
☐ 24	Joe Magrane	.20	.10	.02
☐ 25	Don Mattingly	1.00	.50	.10
☐ 26	Mark McGwire	1.00	.50	.10
☐ 27	Jack Morris	.15	.07	.01
☐ 28	Dale Murphy	.35	.17	.03
☐ 29	Dave Parker	.15	.07	.01
☐ 30	Ken Phelps	.10	.05	.01
☐ 31	Kirby Puckett	.40	.20	.04
☐ 32	Tim Raines	.25	.12	.02
☐ 33	Jeff Reardon	.10	.05	.01
☐ 34	Dave Righetti	.15	.07	.01
☐ 35	Cal Ripken	.30	.15	.03
☐ 36	Bret Saberhagen	.30	.15	.03
☐ 37	Mike Schmidt	.75	.35	.07
☐ 38	Mike Scott	.20	.10	.02
☐ 39	Kevin Seitzer	.75	.35	.07
☐ 40	Darryl Strawberry	.60	.30	.06
☐ 41	Rick Sutcliffe	.15	.07	.01
☐ 42	Pat Tabler	.15	.07	.01
☐ 43	Fernando Valenzuela	.20	.10	.02
☐ 44	Mike Witt	.15	.07	.01

1987 Fleer Sluggers/Pitchers

Fleer produced this 44-card boxed set although it was primarily distributed by McCrory, McLellan, Newberry, H.L.Green, T.G.Y., and other similar stores. The set features 28 sluggers and 16 pitchers and is subtitled "Baseball's Best". Cards are standard-size, 2 1/2" by 3 1/2", and were packaged in a red, white, blue, and yellow custom box along with six logo stickers. The set checklist is given on the back of the box. The checklist on the back of the set box misspells McGwire as McGuire.

		MINT	EXC	G-VG
COMPLETE SET (44)		5.00	2.50	.50
COMMON PLAYER (1-44)		.10	.05	.01
☐ 1	Kevin Bass	.10	.05	.01
☐ 2	Jesse Barfield	.15	.07	.01
☐ 3	George Bell	.20	.10	.02
☐ 4	Wade Boggs	.75	.35	.07
☐ 5	Sid Bream	.10	.05	.01
☐ 6	George Brett	.35	.17	.03
☐ 7	Ivan Calderon	.15	.07	.01
☐ 8	Jose Canseco	1.00	.50	.10
☐ 9	Jack Clark	.20	.10	.02
☐ 10	Roger Clemens	.50	.25	.05
☐ 11	Eric Davis	.60	.30	.06
☐ 12	Andre Dawson	.25	.12	.02
☐ 13	Sid Fernandez	.15	.07	.01
☐ 14	John Franco	.15	.07	.01
☐ 15	Dwight Gooden	.40	.20	.04
☐ 16	Pedro Guerrero	.20	.10	.02

1987 Fleer Slug/Pitch Box Cards

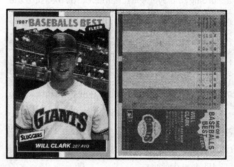

The cards in this 6-card set each measure the standard 2 1/2" by 3 1/2". Cards have essentially the same design as the 1987 Fleer Sluggers vs. Pitchers set of Baseball's Best. The cards were printed on the bottom of the counter display box which held 24 small boxed sets; hence theoretically these box cards are 1/24 as plentiful as the regular boxed set cards. These 6 cards, numbered M1 to M5 with one blank-back (unnumbered) card, are considered a separate set in their own right and are not typically included in a complete set of the 1987 Fleer Sluggers vs. Pitchers set of 44. The value of the panels uncut is slightly greater, perhaps by 25% greater, than the value of the individual cards cut up carefully.

		MINT	EXC	G-VG
COMPLETE SET (6)		2.50	1.25	.25
COMMON PLAYERS (M1-M5)		.10	.05	.01
☐ M1	Steve Bedrosian (box bottom card)	.15	.07	.01
☐ M2	Will Clark (box bottom card)	1.00	.50	.10
☐ M3	Vince Coleman (box bottom card)	.45	.22	.04
☐ M4	Bo Jackson (box bottom card)	1.00	.50	.10
☐ M5	Cory Snyder (box bottom card)	.35	.17	.03
☐ xx	Team Logo (box bottom card, unnumbered, blank back)	.10	.05	.01

1987 Fleer Update

This 132-card set was distributed by Fleer to dealers as a complete set within a custom box. In addition to the complete set of 132 cards, the box also contains 25 Team Logo stickers. The card fronts look very similar to the 1987 Fleer regular issue. The cards are numbered (with a U prefix) alphabetically according to player's last name. Cards measure the standard size, 2 1/2" by 3 1/2". Fleer misalphabetized Jim Winn in their set numbering by putting him ahead of the next four players listed. Fleer also produced a "limited" edition version of this set with glossy coating and packaged in a "tin." However this tin set was apparently not limited enough (estimated between 75,000 and 100,000 1987 update tin sets produced by Fleer) since the price of the "tin" glossy cards is now the same as the regular set.

		MINT	EXC	G-VG
COMPLETE SET (132)		18.00	8.50	1.70
COMMON PLAYER (1-132)		.06	.03	.00
☐	U1 Scott Bankhead	.15	.04	.01
☐	U2 Eric Bell	.10	.05	.01
☐	U3 Juan Beniquez	.06	.03	.00
☐	U4 Juan Berenguer	.06	.03	.00
☐	U5 Mike Birkbeck	.15	.07	.01
☐	U6 Randy Bockus	.10	.05	.01
☐	U7 Greg Booker	.06	.03	.00
☐	U8 Thad Bosley	.06	.03	.00
☐	U9 Greg Brock	.06	.03	.00
☐	U10 Bob Brower	.12	.06	.01
☐	U11 Chris Brown	.10	.05	.01
☐	U12 Jerry Browne	.06	.03	.00
☐	U13 Ralph Bryant	.10	.05	.01
☐	U14 DeWayne Buice	.10	.05	.01
☐	U15 Ellis Burks	2.50	1.25	.25
☐	U16 Casey Candaele	.10	.05	.01
☐	U17 Steve Carlton	.35	.17	.03
☐	U18 Juan Castillo	.06	.03	.00
☐	U19 Chuck Crim	.10	.05	.01
☐	U20 Mark Davidson	.12	.06	.01
☐	U21 Mark Davis	.20	.10	.02
☐	U22 Storm Davis	.15	.07	.01
☐	U23 Bill Dawley	.06	.03	.00
☐	U24 Andre Dawson	.35	.17	.03
☐	U25 Brian Dayett	.06	.03	.00
☐	U26 Rick Dempsey	.06	.03	.00
☐	U27 Ken Dowell	.10	.05	.01
☐	U28 Dave Dravecky	.15	.07	.01
☐	U29 Mike Dunne	.20	.10	.02
☐	U30 Dennis Eckersley	.30	.15	.03
☐	U31 Cecil Fielder	.10	.05	.01
☐	U32 Brian Fisher	.10	.05	.01
☐	U33 Willie Fraser	.10	.05	.01
☐	U34 Ken Gerhart	.12	.06	.01
☐	U35 Jim Gott	.10	.05	.01
☐	U36 Dan Gladden	.10	.05	.01
☐	U37 Mike Greenwell	4.00	2.00	.40
☐	U38 Cecilio Guante	.06	.03	.00
☐	U39 Albert Hall	.06	.03	.00
☐	U40 Atlee Hammaker	.06	.03	.00
☐	U41 Mickey Hatcher	.06	.03	.00
☐	U42 Mike Heath	.06	.03	.00
☐	U43 Neal Heaton	.06	.03	.00
☐	U44 Mike Henneman	.30	.15	.03
☐	U45 Guy Hoffman	.10	.05	.01
☐	U46 Charles Hudson	.06	.03	.00
☐	U47 Chuck Jackson	.12	.06	.01
☐	U48 Mike Jackson	.15	.07	.01
☐	U49 Reggie Jackson	.50	.25	.05
☐	U50 Chris James	.30	.15	.03
☐	U51 Dion James	.10	.05	.01
☐	U52 Stan Javier	.10	.05	.01
☐	U53 Stan Jefferson	.20	.10	.02
☐	U54 Jimmy Jones	.12	.06	.01
☐	U55 Tracy Jones	.15	.07	.01
☐	U56 Terry Kennedy	.06	.03	.00
☐	U57 Mike Kingery	.10	.05	.01
☐	U58 Ray Knight	.10	.05	.01
☐	U59 Gene Larkin	.35	.17	.03
☐	U60 Mike LaValliere	.10	.05	.01
☐	U61 Jack Lazorko	.10	.05	.01
☐	U62 Terry Leach	.12	.06	.01
☐	U63 Rick Leach	.06	.03	.00
☐	U64 Craig Lefferts	.10	.05	.01
☐	U65 Jim Lindeman	.12	.06	.01
☐	U66 Bill Long	.12	.06	.01
☐	U67 Mike Loynd	.10	.05	.01
☐	U68 Greg Maddux	1.00	.50	.10
☐	U69 Bill Madlock	.12	.06	.01
☐	U70 Dave Magadan	.35	.17	.03
☐	U71 Joe Magrane	1.25	.60	.12
☐	U72 Fred Manrique	.12	.06	.01
☐	U73 Mike Mason	.06	.03	.00
☐	U74 Lloyd McClendon	.30	.15	.03
☐	U75 Fred McGriff	2.25	1.10	.22
☐	U76 Mark McGwire	3.00	1.50	.30
☐	U77 Mark McLemore	.06	.03	.00
☐	U78 Kevin McReynolds	.30	.15	.03
☐	U79 Dave Meads	.10	.05	.01
☐	U80 Greg Minton	.06	.03	.00
☐	U81 John Mitchell	.15	.07	.01
☐	U82 Kevin Mitchell	2.00	1.00	.20
☐	U83 John Morris	.06	.03	.00
☐	U84 Jeff Musselman	.15	.07	.01
☐	U85 Randy Myers	.50	.25	.05
☐	U86 Gene Nelson	.06	.03	.00
☐	U87 Joe Niekro	.15	.07	.01
☐	U88 Tom Nieto	.06	.03	.00
☐	U89 Reid Nichols	.06	.03	.00
☐	U90 Matt Nokes	.50	.25	.05
☐	U91 Dickie Noles	.06	.03	.00
☐	U92 Edwin Nunez	.06	.03	.00
☐	U93 Jose Nunez	.15	.07	.01
☐	U94 Paul O'Neill	.30	.15	.03
☐	U95 Jim Paciorek	.10	.05	.01
☐	U96 Lance Parrish	.12	.06	.01
☐	U97 Bill Pecota	.12	.06	.01
☐	U98 Tony Pena	.12	.06	.01
☐	U99 Luis Polonia	.30	.15	.03
☐	U100 Randy Ready	.10	.05	.01
☐	U101 Jeff Reardon	.15	.07	.01
☐	U102 Gary Redus	.06	.03	.00
☐	U103 Rick Rhoden	.10	.05	.01
☐	U104 Wally Ritchie	.10	.05	.01
☐	U105 Jeff Robinson (wrong Jeff's stats on back)	.35	.17	.03
☐	U106 Mark Salas	.06	.03	.00
☐	U107 Dave Schmidt	.10	.05	.01
☐	U108 Kevin Seitzer ERR (wrong birth year)	1.00	.50	.10
☐	U109 John Shelby	.06	.03	.00
☐	U110 John Smiley	.40	.20	.04
☐	U111 Lary Sorensen	.06	.03	.00
☐	U112 Chris Speier	.06	.03	.00
☐	U113 Randy St.Claire	.06	.03	.00
☐	U114 Jim Sundberg	.06	.03	.00
☐	U115 B.J. Surhoff	.35	.17	.03
☐	U116 Greg Swindell	.60	.30	.06
☐	U117 Danny Tartabull	.35	.17	.03
☐	U118 Dorn Taylor	.10	.05	.01
☐	U119 Lee Tunnell	.06	.03	.00
☐	U120 Ed VandeBerg	.06	.03	.00
☐	U121 Andy Van Slyke	.20	.10	.02
☐	U122 Gary Ward	.10	.05	.01
☐	U123 Devon White	.35	.17	.03
☐	U124 Alan Wiggins	.06	.03	.00
☐	U125 Bill Wilkinson	.10	.05	.01
☐	U126 Jim Winn	.06	.03	.00
☐	U127 Frank Williams	.06	.03	.00
☐	U128 Ken Williams	.15	.07	.01
☐	U129 Matt Williams	2.50	1.25	.25
☐	U130 Herm Winningham	.10	.05	.01
☐	U131 Matt Young	.06	.03	.00
☐	U132 Checklist	.06	.01	.00

1987 Fleer World Series

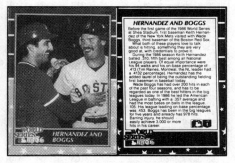

HERNANDEZ AND BOGGS

Before the first game of the 1986 World Series at Shea Stadium, first baseman Keith Hernandez of the New York Mets visited with Wade Boggs, third baseman of the Boston Red Sox. What both of these players love to talk about is hitting, something they are very good at, with credentials to prove it.

During the 1986 season Keith Hernandez batted .310, fifth best among all National League players. Of equal importance were his 94 walks and his on-base percentage of .413 (Tim Raines, Montreal, the NL leader had a .4132 percentage). Hernandez has the added laurel of being the outstanding fielding first baseman in baseball today.

Wade Boggs has had over 200 hits in each of the past four seasons, and has to be regarded as one of the best hitters in the big leagues today. In 1986 he led the American League in batting with a .357 average and had the most bases on balls in the league, 105. His league leading on-base percentage was .453. Boggs has been in the big leagues for five years and already has 978 hits. Barring injury, he should easily achieve 3,000 or more hits in his career.

This 12-card set of 2 1/2" by 3 1/2" cards features highlights of the previous year's World Series between the Mets and the Red Sox. The sets were packaged as a complete set insert with the collated sets (of the 1987 Fleer regular issue) which were sold by Fleer directly to hobby card dealers; they were not available in the general retail candy store outlets.

	MINT	EXC	G-VG
COMPLETE SET (12)	4.00	2.00	.40
COMMON PLAYER (1-12)	.25	.12	.02
☐ 1 Bruce Hurst .... Left Hand Finesse Beats Mets	.35	.17	.03
☐ 2 Keith Hernandez and .... Wade Boggs	.60	.30	.06
☐ 3 Roger Clemens HOR	.75	.35	.07
☐ 4 Clutch Hitting .... (Gary Carter)	.35	.17	.03
☐ 5 Ron Darling .... Picks Up Slack	.35	.17	.03
☐ 6 Marty Barrett .... .433 Series BA	.25	.12	.02
☐ 7 Dwight Gooden	.60	.30	.06
☐ 8 Strategy at Work .... (Mets Conference)	.25	.12	.02
☐ 9 Dewey Evans .... (Congratulated by Rich Gedman)	.35	.17	.03
☐ 10 One Strike From .... Boston Victory (Dave Henderson)	.25	.12	.02
☐ 11 Series Home Run Duo ...... (Ray Knight and Darryl Strawberry)	.35	.17	.03
☐ 12 Ray Knight .... (Series MVP)	.25	.12	.02

1988 Fleer

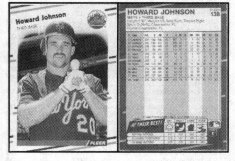

HOWARD JOHNSON   138
METS • THIRD BASE

This 660-card set features a distinctive white background with red and blue diagonal stripes across the card. The backs are printed in gray and red on white card stock. The bottom of the card back shows an innovative breakdown of the player's demonstrated ability with respect to day, night, home, and road games. Cards are numbered on the back and are again the standard 2 1/2" by 3 1/2". Cards are again organized numerically by teams, i.e., World Champion Twins (1-25), St. Louis Cardinals (26-50), Detroit Tigers (51-75), San Francisco Giants (76-101), Toronto Blue Jays (102-126), New York Mets (127-154), Milwaukee Brewers (155-178), Montreal Expos (179-201), New York Yankees (202-226), Cincinnati Reds (227-250), Kansas City Royals (251- 274), Oakland A's (275-296), Philadelphia Phillies (297- 320), Pittsburgh Pirates (321-342), Boston Red Sox (343- 367), Seattle Mariners (368-390), Chicago White Sox (391- 413), Chicago Cubs (414-436), Houston Astros (437-460), Texas Rangers (461-483), California Angels (484-507), Los Angeles Dodgers (508-530), Atlanta Braves (531-552), Baltimore Orioles (553-575), San Diego Padres (576-599), and Cleveland Indians (600-621). The last 39 cards in the set consist of Specials (622-640), Rookie Pairs (641-653), and checklists (654-660). Cards 90 and 91 are incorrectly numbered on the checklist card #654. Fleer also produced a "limited" edition version of this set with glossy coating and packaged in a "tin." However this tin set was apparently not limited enough (estimated between 40,000 and 60,000 1988 tin sets produced by Fleer) since the price of the "tin" glossy cards is now only double the price of the regular set.

	MINT	EXC	G-VG
COMPLETE SET (660)	32.00	16.00	3.20
COMMON PLAYER (1-660)	.03	.01	.00
☐ 1 Keith Atherton	.10	.02	.01
☐ 2 Don Baylor	.08	.04	.01
☐ 3 Juan Berenguer	.03	.01	.00
☐ 4 Bert Blyleven	.08	.04	.01
☐ 5 Tom Brunansky	.10	.05	.01
☐ 6 Randy Bush	.03	.01	.00
☐ 7 Steve Carlton	.18	.09	.01
☐ 8 Mark Davidson	.10	.05	.01
☐ 9 George Frazier	.03	.01	.00
☐ 10 Gary Gaetti	.12	.06	.01
☐ 11 Greg Gagne	.03	.01	.00
☐ 12 Dan Gladden	.06	.03	.00
☐ 13 Kent Hrbek	.12	.06	.01
☐ 14 Gene Larkin	.25	.12	.02
☐ 15 Tim Laudner	.03	.01	.00
☐ 16 Steve Lombardozzi	.03	.01	.00
☐ 17 Al Newman	.03	.01	.00
☐ 18 Joe Niekro	.06	.03	.00
☐ 19 Kirby Puckett	.60	.30	.06
☐ 20 Jeff Reardon	.08	.04	.01
☐ 21A Dan Schatzeder ERR .... (misspelled Schatzader on card front)	.15	.07	.01
☐ 21B Dan Schatzeder COR ...	.06	.03	.00
☐ 22 Roy Smalley	.03	.01	.00
☐ 23 Mike Smithson	.03	.01	.00
☐ 24 Les Straker	.10	.05	.01
☐ 25 Frank Viola	.15	.07	.01
☐ 26 Jack Clark	.15	.07	.01
☐ 27 Vince Coleman	.18	.09	.01
☐ 28 Danny Cox	.03	.01	.00
☐ 29 Bill Dawley	.03	.01	.00
☐ 30 Ken Dayley	.03	.01	.00
☐ 31 Doug DeCinces	.06	.03	.00
☐ 32 Curt Ford	.03	.01	.00
☐ 33 Bob Forsch	.03	.01	.00
☐ 34 David Green	.03	.01	.00
☐ 35 Tom Herr	.03	.01	.00
☐ 36 Ricky Horton	.03	.01	.00
☐ 37 Lance Johnson	.18	.09	.01
☐ 38 Steve Lake	.03	.01	.00
☐ 39 Jim Lindeman	.06	.03	.00
☐ 40 Joe Magrane	.75	.35	.07
☐ 41 Greg Mathews	.03	.01	.00
☐ 42 Willie McGee	.10	.05	.01
☐ 43 John Morris	.03	.01	.00
☐ 44 Jose Oquendo	.03	.01	.00

☐ 45	Tony Pena	.06	.03	.00
☐ 46	Terry Pendleton	.03	.01	.00
☐ 47	Ozzie Smith	.15	.07	.01
☐ 48	John Tudor	.08	.04	.01
☐ 49	Lee Tunnell	.03	.01	.00
☐ 50	Todd Worrell	.10	.05	.01
☐ 51	Doyle Alexander	.03	.01	.00
☐ 52	Dave Bergman	.03	.01	.00
☐ 53	Tom Brookens	.03	.01	.00
☐ 54	Darrell Evans	.08	.04	.01
☐ 55	Kirk Gibson	.20	.10	.02
☐ 56	Mike Heath	.03	.01	.00
☐ 57	Mike Henneman	.25	.12	.02
☐ 58	Willie Hernandez	.06	.03	.00
☐ 59	Larry Herndon	.03	.01	.00
☐ 60	Eric King	.03	.01	.00
☐ 61	Chet Lemon	.03	.01	.00
☐ 62	Scott Lusader	.15	.07	.01
☐ 63	Bill Madlock	.06	.03	.00
☐ 64	Jack Morris	.10	.05	.01
☐ 65	Jim Morrison	.03	.01	.00
☐ 66	Matt Nokes	.40	.20	.04
☐ 67	Dan Petry	.03	.01	.00
☐ 68A	Jeff Robinson ERR Detroit Tigers (stats for other Jeff Robinson on card back)	1.00	.50	.10
☐ 68B	Jeff Robinson COR Detroit Tigers	.40	.20	.04
☐ 69	Pat Sheridan	.03	.01	.00
☐ 70	Nate Snell	.03	.01	.00
☐ 71	Frank Tanana	.03	.01	.00
☐ 72	Walt Terrell	.03	.01	.00
☐ 73	Mark Thurmond	.03	.01	.00
☐ 74	Alan Trammell	.15	.07	.01
☐ 75	Lou Whitaker	.12	.06	.01
☐ 76	Mike Aldrete	.03	.01	.00
☐ 77	Bob Brenly	.03	.01	.00
☐ 78	Will Clark	3.50	1.75	.35
☐ 79	Chili Davis	.06	.03	.00
☐ 80	Kelly Downs	.06	.03	.00
☐ 81	Dave Dravecky	.08	.04	.01
☐ 82	Scott Garrelts	.06	.03	.00
☐ 83	Atlee Hammaker	.03	.01	.00
☐ 84	Dave Henderson	.06	.03	.00
☐ 85	Mike Krukow	.03	.01	.00
☐ 86	Mike LaCoss	.03	.01	.00
☐ 87	Craig Lefferts	.06	.03	.00
☐ 88	Jeff Leonard	.06	.03	.00
☐ 89	Candy Maldonado	.06	.03	.00
☐ 90	Eddie Milner	.03	.01	.00
☐ 91	Bob Melvin	.03	.01	.00
☐ 92	Kevin Mitchell	1.00	.50	.10
☐ 93	Jon Perlman	.08	.04	.01
☐ 94	Rick Reuschel	.08	.04	.01
☐ 95	Don Robinson	.03	.01	.00
☐ 96	Chris Speier	.03	.01	.00
☐ 97	Harry Spilman	.03	.01	.00
☐ 98	Robbie Thompson	.06	.03	.00
☐ 99	Jose Uribe	.03	.01	.00
☐ 100	Mark Wasinger	.15	.07	.01
☐ 101	Matt Williams	2.00	1.00	.20
☐ 102	Jesse Barfield	.12	.06	.01
☐ 103	George Bell	.18	.09	.01
☐ 104	Juan Beniquez	.03	.01	.00
☐ 105	John Cerutti	.03	.01	.00
☐ 106	Jim Clancy	.03	.01	.00
☐ 107	Rob Ducey	.20	.10	.02
☐ 108	Mark Eichhorn	.03	.01	.00
☐ 109	Tony Fernandez	.10	.05	.01
☐ 110	Cecil Fielder	.03	.01	.00
☐ 111	Kelly Gruber	.06	.03	.00
☐ 112	Tom Henke	.06	.03	.00
☐ 113A	Garth Iorg ERR (misspelled Iorq on card front)	.15	.07	.01
☐☐ 113B	Garth Iorg COR	.06	.03	.00
☐ 114	Jimmy Key	.06	.03	.00
☐ 115	Rick Leach	.03	.01	.00
☐ 116	Manny Lee	.06	.03	.00
☐ 117	Nelson Liriano	.25	.12	.02
☐ 118	Fred McGriff	1.75	.85	.17
☐ 119	Lloyd Moseby	.06	.03	.00
☐ 120	Rance Mulliniks	.03	.01	.00
☐ 121	Jeff Musselman	.08	.04	.01
☐ 122	Jose Nunez	.15	.07	.01
☐ 123	Dave Stieb	.08	.04	.01
☐ 124	Willie Upshaw	.03	.01	.00
☐ 125	Duane Ward	.08	.04	.01
☐ 126	Ernie Whitt	.03	.01	.00
☐ 127	Rick Aguilera	.03	.01	.00
☐ 128	Wally Backman	.03	.01	.00
☐ 129	Mark Carreon	.12	.06	.01
☐ 130	Gary Carter	.15	.07	.01
☐ 131	David Cone	1.25	.60	.12
☐ 132	Ron Darling	.10	.05	.01
☐ 133	Len Dykstra	.08	.04	.01
☐ 134	Sid Fernandez	.08	.04	.01
☐ 135	Dwight Gooden	.60	.30	.06
☐ 136	Keith Hernandez	.18	.09	.01
☐ 137	Gregg Jefferies	4.00	2.00	.40
☐ 138	Howard Johnson	.20	.10	.02
☐ 139	Terry Leach	.06	.03	.00
☐ 140	Barry Lyons	.25	.12	.02
☐ 141	Dave Magadan	.12	.06	.01
☐ 142	Roger McDowell	.06	.03	.00
☐ 143	Kevin McReynolds	.15	.07	.01
☐ 144	Keith Miller (New York Mets)	.20	.10	.02
☐ 145	John Mitchell	.15	.07	.01
☐ 146	Randy Myers	.35	.17	.03
☐ 147	Bob Ojeda	.06	.03	.00
☐ 148	Jesse Orosco	.03	.01	.00
☐ 149	Rafael Santana	.03	.01	.00
☐ 150	Doug Sisk	.03	.01	.00
☐ 151	Darryl Strawberry	.50	.25	.05
☐ 152	Tim Teufel	.03	.01	.00
☐ 153	Gene Walter	.03	.01	.00
☐ 154	Mookie Wilson	.06	.03	.00
☐ 155	Jay Aldrich	.08	.04	.01
☐ 156	Chris Bosio	.06	.03	.00
☐ 157	Glenn Braggs	.08	.04	.01
☐ 158	Greg Brock	.03	.01	.00
☐ 159	Juan Castillo	.06	.03	.00
☐ 160	Mark Clear	.03	.01	.00
☐ 161	Cecil Cooper	.08	.04	.01
☐ 162	Chuck Crim	.10	.05	.01
☐ 163	Rob Deer	.08	.04	.01
☐ 164	Mike Felder	.03	.01	.00
☐ 165	Jim Gantner	.03	.01	.00
☐ 166	Ted Higuera	.10	.05	.01
☐ 167	Steve Kiefer	.03	.01	.00
☐ 168	Rick Manning	.03	.01	.00
☐ 169	Paul Molitor	.12	.06	.01
☐ 170	Juan Nieves	.03	.01	.00
☐ 171	Dan Plesac	.06	.03	.00
☐ 172	Earnest Riles	.03	.01	.00
☐ 173	Bill Schroeder	.03	.01	.00
☐ 174	Steve Stanicek	.12	.06	.01
☐ 175	B.J. Surhoff	.15	.07	.01
☐ 176	Dale Sveum	.03	.01	.00
☐ 177	Bill Wegman	.03	.01	.00
☐ 178	Robin Yount	.30	.15	.03
☐ 179	Hubie Brooks	.08	.04	.01
☐ 180	Tim Burke	.06	.03	.00
☐ 181	Casey Candaele	.03	.01	.00
☐ 182	Mike Fitzgerald	.03	.01	.00
☐ 183	Tom Foley	.03	.01	.00
☐ 184	Andres Galarraga	.25	.12	.02
☐ 185	Neal Heaton	.03	.01	.00
☐ 186	Wallace Johnson	.03	.01	.00
☐ 187	Vance Law	.03	.01	.00
☐ 188	Dennis Martinez	.03	.01	.00
☐ 189	Bob McClure	.03	.01	.00
☐ 190	Andy McGaffigan	.03	.01	.00
☐ 191	Reid Nichols	.03	.01	.00
☐ 192	Pascual Perez	.08	.04	.01
☐ 193	Tim Raines	.20	.10	.02
☐ 194	Jeff Reed	.03	.01	.00
☐ 195	Bob Sebra	.03	.01	.00
☐ 196	Bryn Smith	.06	.03	.00
☐ 197	Randy St.Claire	.03	.01	.00
☐ 198	Tim Wallach	.08	.04	.01
☐ 199	Mitch Webster	.03	.01	.00
☐ 200	Herm Winningham	.03	.01	.00
☐ 201	Floyd Youmans	.03	.01	.00
☐ 202	Brad Arnsberg	.10	.05	.01
☐ 203	Rick Cerone	.03	.01	.00
☐ 204	Pat Clements	.03	.01	.00
☐ 205	Henry Cotto	.03	.01	.00
☐ 206	Mike Easler	.03	.01	.00
☐ 207	Ron Guidry	.08	.04	.01
☐ 208	Bill Gullickson	.03	.01	.00
☐ 209	Rickey Henderson	.30	.15	.03
☐ 210	Charles Hudson	.03	.01	.00
☐ 211	Tommy John	.10	.05	.01
☐ 212	Roberto Kelly	1.00	.50	.10
☐ 213	Ron Kittle	.08	.04	.01
☐ 214	Don Mattingly	1.50	.75	.15
☐ 215	Bobby Meacham	.03	.01	.00
☐ 216	Mike Pagliarulo	.06	.03	.00
☐ 217	Dan Pasqua	.03	.01	.00
☐ 218	Willie Randolph	.06	.03	.00
☐ 219	Rick Rhoden	.03	.01	.00
☐ 220	Dave Righetti	.08	.04	.01
☐ 221	Jerry Royster	.03	.01	.00
☐ 222	Tim Stoddard	.03	.01	.00
☐ 223	Wayne Tolleson	.03	.01	.00
☐ 224	Gary Ward	.03	.01	.00
☐ 225	Claudell Washington	.06	.03	.00

226	Dave Winfield	.25	.12	.02
227	Buddy Bell	.08	.04	.01
228	Tom Browning	.08	.04	.01
229	Dave Concepcion	.08	.04	.01
230	Kal Daniels	.18	.09	.01
231	Eric Davis	.75	.35	.07
232	Bo Diaz	.03	.01	.00
233	Nick Esasky	.08	.04	.01
234	John Franco	.08	.04	.01
235	Guy Hoffman	.03	.01	.00
236	Tom Hume	.03	.01	.00
237	Tracy Jones	.03	.01	.00
238	Bill Landrum	.25	.12	.02
239	Barry Larkin	.30	.15	.03
240	Terry McGriff	.10	.05	.01
241	Rob Murphy	.03	.01	.00
242	Ron Oester	.03	.01	.00
243	Dave Parker	.10	.05	.01
244	Pat Perry	.03	.01	.00
245	Ted Power	.03	.01	.00
246	Dennis Rasmussen	.06	.03	.00
247	Ron Robinson	.03	.01	.00
248	Kurt Stillwell	.06	.03	.00
249	Jeff Treadway	.30	.15	.03
250	Frank Williams	.03	.01	.00
251	Steve Balboni	.03	.01	.00
252	Bud Black	.03	.01	.00
253	Thad Bosley	.03	.01	.00
254	George Brett	.30	.15	.03
255	John Davis	.15	.07	.01
256	Steve Farr	.03	.01	.00
257	Gene Garber	.03	.01	.00
258	Jerry Don Gleaton	.03	.01	.00
259	Mark Gubicza	.10	.05	.01
260	Bo Jackson	2.50	1.25	.25
261	Danny Jackson	.08	.04	.01
262	Ross Jones	.08	.04	.01
263	Charlie Leibrandt	.03	.01	.00
264	Bill Pecota	.08	.04	.01
265	Melido Perez	.25	.12	.02
266	Jamie Quirk	.03	.01	.00
267	Dan Quisenberry	.08	.04	.01
268	Bret Saberhagen	.25	.12	.02
269	Angel Salazar	.03	.01	.00
270	Kevin Seitzer UER (wrong birth year)	.45	.22	.04
271	Danny Tartabull	.20	.10	.02
272	Gary Thurman	.25	.12	.02
273	Frank White	.06	.03	.00
274	Willie Wilson	.06	.03	.00
275	Tony Bernazard	.03	.01	.00
276	Jose Canseco	1.75	.85	.17
277	Mike Davis	.03	.01	.00
278	Storm Davis	.08	.04	.01
279	Dennis Eckersley	.12	.06	.01
280	Alfredo Griffin	.06	.03	.00
281	Rick Honeycutt	.03	.01	.00
282	Jay Howell	.06	.03	.00
283	Reggie Jackson	.30	.15	.03
284	Dennis Lamp	.03	.01	.00
285	Carney Lansford	.10	.05	.01
286	Mark McGwire	2.50	1.25	.25
287	Dwayne Murphy	.03	.01	.00
288	Gene Nelson	.03	.01	.00
289	Steve Ontiveros	.03	.01	.00
290	Tony Phillips	.03	.01	.00
291	Eric Plunk	.03	.01	.00
292	Luis Polonia	.25	.12	.02
293	Rick Rodriguez	.08	.04	.01
294	Terry Steinbach	.10	.05	.01
295	Dave Stewart	.12	.06	.01
296	Curt Young	.03	.01	.00
297	Luis Aguayo	.03	.01	.00
298	Steve Bedrosian	.08	.04	.01
299	Jeff Calhoun	.03	.01	.00
300	Don Carman	.03	.01	.00
301	Todd Frohwirth	.15	.07	.01
302	Greg Gross	.03	.01	.00
303	Kevin Gross	.03	.01	.00
304	Von Hayes	.08	.04	.01
305	Keith Hughes	.18	.09	.01
306	Mike Jackson	.15	.07	.01
307	Chris James	.15	.07	.01
308	Steve Jeltz	.03	.01	.00
309	Mike Maddux	.03	.01	.00
310	Lance Parrish	.10	.05	.01
311	Shane Rawley	.03	.01	.00
312	Wally Ritchie	.08	.04	.01
313	Bruce Ruffin	.03	.01	.00
314	Juan Samuel	.08	.04	.01
315	Mike Schmidt	.40	.20	.04
316	Rick Schu	.03	.01	.00
317	Jeff Stone	.03	.01	.00
318	Kent Tekulve	.03	.01	.00
319	Milt Thompson	.03	.01	.00
320	Glenn Wilson	.03	.01	.00
321	Rafael Belliard	.03	.01	.00
322	Barry Bonds	.20	.10	.02
323	Bobby Bonilla UER (wrong birth year)	.20	.10	.02
324	Sid Bream	.03	.01	.00
325	John Cangelosi	.03	.01	.00
326	Mike Diaz	.03	.01	.00
327	Doug Drabek	.06	.03	.00
328	Mike Dunne	.10	.05	.01
329	Brian Fisher	.03	.01	.00
330	Brett Gideon	.10	.05	.01
331	Terry Harper	.03	.01	.00
332	Bob Kipper	.03	.01	.00
333	Mike LaValliere	.03	.01	.00
334	Jose Lind	.20	.10	.02
335	Junior Ortiz	.03	.01	.00
336	Vincent Palacios	.08	.04	.01
337	Bob Patterson	.08	.04	.01
338	Al Pedrique	.08	.04	.01
339	R.J. Reynolds	.03	.01	.00
340	John Smiley	.25	.12	.02
341	Andy Van Slyke UER (wrong batting and throwing listed)	.15	.07	.01
342	Bob Walk	.03	.01	.00
343	Marty Barrett	.06	.03	.00
344	Todd Benzinger	.40	.20	.04
345	Wade Boggs	1.00	.50	.10
346	Tom Bolton	.15	.07	.01
347	Oil Can Boyd	.06	.03	.00
348	Ellis Burks	1.75	.85	.17
349	Roger Clemens	.75	.35	.07
350	Steve Crawford	.08	.04	.01
351	Dwight Evans	.10	.05	.01
352	Wes Gardner	.20	.10	.02
353	Rich Gedman	.03	.01	.00
354	Mike Greenwell	2.50	1.25	.25
355	Sam Horn	.20	.10	.02
356	Bruce Hurst	.10	.05	.01
357	John Marzano	.10	.05	.01
358	Al Nipper	.03	.01	.00
359	Spike Owen	.03	.01	.00
360	Jody Reed	.40	.20	.04
361	Jim Rice	.15	.07	.01
362	Ed Romero	.03	.01	.00
363	Kevin Romine	.10	.05	.01
364	Joe Sambito	.03	.01	.00
365	Calvin Schiraldi	.03	.01	.00
366	Jeff Sellers	.03	.01	.00
367	Bob Stanley	.03	.01	.00
368	Scott Bankhead	.08	.04	.01
369	Phil Bradley	.06	.03	.00
370	Scott Bradley	.03	.01	.00
371	Mickey Brantley	.06	.03	.00
372	Mike Campbell	.15	.07	.01
373	Alvin Davis	.10	.05	.01
374	Lee Guetterman	.03	.01	.00
375	Dave Hengel	.12	.06	.01
376	Mike Kingery	.03	.01	.00
377	Mark Langston	.12	.06	.01
378	Edgar Martinez	.25	.12	.02
379	Mike Moore	.08	.04	.01
380	Mike Morgan	.06	.03	.00
381	John Moses	.03	.01	.00
382	Donnell Nixon	.15	.07	.01
383	Edwin Nunez	.03	.01	.00
384	Ken Phelps	.06	.03	.00
385	Jim Presley	.06	.03	.00
386	Rey Quinones	.03	.01	.00
387	Jerry Reed	.03	.01	.00
388	Harold Reynolds	.06	.03	.00
389	Dave Valle	.06	.03	.00
390	Bill Wilkinson	.10	.05	.01
391	Harold Baines	.10	.05	.01
392	Floyd Bannister	.03	.01	.00
393	Daryl Boston	.03	.01	.00
394	Ivan Calderon	.06	.03	.00
395	Jose DeLeon	.06	.03	.00
396	Richard Dotson	.03	.01	.00
397	Carlton Fisk	.12	.06	.01
398	Ozzie Guillen	.06	.03	.00
399	Ron Hassey	.03	.01	.00
400	Donnie Hill	.03	.01	.00
401	Bob James	.03	.01	.00
402	Dave LaPoint	.03	.01	.00
403	Bill Lindsey	.08	.04	.01
404	Bill Long	.08	.04	.01
405	Steve Lyons	.03	.01	.00
406	Fred Manrique	.10	.05	.01
407	Jack McDowell	.20	.10	.02
408	Gary Redus	.03	.01	.00
409	Ray Searage	.03	.01	.00
410	Bobby Thigpen	.08	.04	.01
411	Greg Walker	.06	.03	.00

☐ 412	Ken Williams	.15	.07	.01	☐ 496	Kirk McCaskill	.03	.01	.00
☐ 413	Jim Winn	.03	.01	.00	☐ 497	Mark McLemore	.03	.01	.00
☐ 414	Jody Davis	.03	.01	.00	☐ 498	Darrell Miller	.03	.01	.00
☐ 415	Andre Dawson	.20	.10	.02	☐ 499	Greg Minton	.03	.01	.00
☐ 416	Brian Dayett	.03	.01	.00	☐ 500	Donnie Moore	.03	.01	.00
☐ 417	Bob Dernier	.03	.01	.00	☐ 501	Gus Polidor	.03	.01	.00
☐ 418	Frank DiPino	.03	.01	.00	☐ 502	Johnny Ray	.06	.03	.00
☐ 419	Shawon Dunston	.08	.04	.01	☐ 503	Mark Ryal	.06	.03	.00
☐ 420	Leon Durham	.03	.01	.00	☐ 504	Dick Schofield	.03	.01	.00
☐ 421	Les Lancaster	.20	.10	.02	☐ 505	Don Sutton	.12	.06	.01
☐ 422	Ed Lynch	.03	.01	.00	☐ 506	Devon White	.15	.07	.01
☐ 423	Greg Maddux	.75	.35	.07	☐ 507	Mike Witt	.06	.03	.00
☐ 424	Dave Martinez	.10	.05	.01	☐ 508	Dave Anderson	.03	.01	.00
☐ 425A	Keith Moreland ERR	4.00	2.00	.40	☐ 509	Tim Belcher	.50	.25	.05
	(photo actually				☐ 510	Ralph Bryant	.03	.01	.00
	Jody Davis)				☐ 511	Tim Crews	.08	.04	.01
☐ 425B	Keith Moreland COR	.15	.07	.01	☐ 512	Mike Devereaux	.30	.15	.03
	(bat on shoulder)				☐ 513	Mariano Duncan	.03	.01	.00
☐ 426	Jamie Moyer	.03	.01	.00	☐ 514	Pedro Guerrero	.15	.07	.01
☐ 427	Jerry Mumphrey	.03	.01	.00	☐ 515	Jeff Hamilton	.12	.06	.01
☐ 428	Paul Noce	.10	.05	.01	☐ 516	Mickey Hatcher	.03	.01	.00
☐ 429	Rafael Palmeiro	.65	.30	.06	☐ 517	Brad Havens	.03	.01	.00
☐ 430	Wade Rowdon	.08	.04	.01	☐ 518	Orel Hershiser	.25	.12	.02
☐ 431	Ryne Sandberg	.25	.12	.02	☐ 519	Shawn Hillegas	.15	.07	.01
☐ 432	Scott Sanderson	.03	.01	.00	☐ 520	Ken Howell	.03	.01	.00
☐ 433	Lee Smith	.06	.03	.00	☐ 521	Tim Leary	.08	.04	.01
☐ 434	Jim Sundberg	.03	.01	.00	☐ 522	Mike Marshall	.10	.05	.01
☐ 435	Rick Sutcliffe	.08	.04	.01	☐ 523	Steve Sax	.15	.07	.01
☐ 436	Manny Trillo	.03	.01	.00	☐ 524	Mike Scioscia	.03	.01	.00
☐ 437	Juan Agosto	.03	.01	.00	☐ 525	Mike Sharperson	.06	.03	.00
☐ 438	Larry Andersen	.03	.01	.00	☐ 526	John Shelby	.03	.01	.00
☐ 439	Alan Ashby	.03	.01	.00	☐ 527	Franklin Stubbs	.03	.01	.00
☐ 440	Kevin Bass	.06	.03	.00	☐ 528	Fernando Valenzuela	.12	.06	.01
☐ 441	Ken Caminiti	.30	.15	.03	☐ 529	Bob Welch	.06	.03	.00
☐ 442	Rocky Childress	.08	.04	.01	☐ 530	Matt Young	.03	.01	.00
☐ 443	Jose Cruz	.06	.03	.00	☐ 531	Jim Acker	.03	.01	.00
☐ 444	Danny Darwin	.03	.01	.00	☐ 532	Paul Assenmacher	.03	.01	.00
☐ 445	Glenn Davis	.15	.07	.01	☐ 533	Jeff Blauser	.30	.15	.03
☐ 446	Jim Deshaies	.03	.01	.00	☐ 534	Joe Boever	.20	.10	.02
☐ 447	Bill Doran	.06	.03	.00	☐ 535	Martin Clary	.06	.03	.00
☐ 448	Ty Gainey	.03	.01	.00	☐ 536	Kevin Coffman	.10	.05	.01
☐ 449	Billy Hatcher	.06	.03	.00	☐ 537	Jeff Dedmon	.03	.01	.00
☐ 450	Jeff Heathcock	.03	.01	.00	☐ 538	Ron Gant	.60	.30	.06
☐ 451	Bob Knepper	.06	.03	.00	☐ 539	Tom Glavine	.40	.20	.04
☐ 452	Rob Mallicoat	.08	.04	.01	☐ 540	Ken Griffey	.08	.04	.01
☐ 453	Dave Meads	.08	.04	.01	☐ 541	Albert Hall	.03	.01	.00
☐ 454	Craig Reynolds	.03	.01	.00	☐ 542	Glenn Hubbard	.03	.01	.00
☐ 455	Nolan Ryan	.50	.25	.05	☐ 543	Dion James	.03	.01	.00
☐ 456	Mike Scott	.15	.07	.01	☐ 544	Dale Murphy	.30	.15	.03
☐ 457	Dave Smith	.03	.01	.00	☐ 545	Ken Oberkfell	.03	.01	.00
☐ 458	Denny Walling	.03	.01	.00	☐ 546	David Palmer	.03	.01	.00
☐ 459	Robbie Wine	.08	.04	.01	☐ 547	Gerald Perry	.06	.03	.00
☐ 460	Gerald Young	.30	.15	.03	☐ 548	Charlie Puleo	.03	.01	.00
☐ 461	Bob Brower	.08	.04	.01	☐ 549	Ted Simmons	.08	.04	.01
☐ 462A	Jerry Browne ERR	4.00	2.00	.40	☐ 550	Zane Smith	.03	.01	.00
	(photo actually				☐ 551	Andres Thomas	.03	.01	.00
	Bob Brower,				☐ 552	Ozzie Virgil	.03	.01	.00
	white player)				☐ 553	Don Aase	.03	.01	.00
☐ 462B	Jerry Browne COR	.15	.07	.01	☐ 554	Jeff Ballard	.45	.22	.04
	(black player)				☐ 555	Eric Bell	.06	.03	.00
☐ 463	Steve Buechele	.03	.01	.00	☐ 556	Mike Boddicker	.03	.01	.00
☐ 464	Edwin Correa	.03	.01	.00	☐ 557	Ken Dixon	.03	.01	.00
☐ 465	Cecil Espy	.15	.07	.01	☐ 558	Jim Dwyer	.03	.01	.00
☐ 466	Scott Fletcher	.03	.01	.00	☐ 559	Ken Gerhart	.06	.03	.00
☐ 467	Jose Guzman	.03	.01	.00	☐ 560	Rene Gonzales	.10	.05	.01
☐ 468	Greg Harris	.03	.01	.00	☐ 561	Mike Griffin	.03	.01	.00
☐ 469	Charlie Hough	.03	.01	.00	☐ 562	John Habyan UER	.08	.04	.01
☐ 470	Pete Incaviglia	.15	.07	.01		(misspelled Hayban on			
☐ 471	Paul Kilgus	.12	.06	.01		both sides of card)			
☐ 472	Mike Loynd	.03	.01	.00	☐ 563	Terry Kennedy	.03	.01	.00
☐ 473	Oddibe McDowell	.06	.03	.00	☐ 564	Ray Knight	.06	.03	.00
☐ 474	Dale Mohorcic	.03	.01	.00	☐ 565	Lee Lacy	.03	.01	.00
☐ 475	Pete O'Brien	.06	.03	.00	☐ 566	Fred Lynn	.10	.05	.01
☐ 476	Larry Parrish	.03	.01	.00	☐ 567	Eddie Murray	.15	.07	.01
☐ 477	Geno Petralli	.03	.01	.00	☐ 568	Tom Niedenfuer	.03	.01	.00
☐ 478	Jeff Russell	.06	.03	.00	☐ 569	Bill Ripken	.15	.07	.01
☐ 479	Ruben Sierra	.75	.35	.07	☐ 570	Cal Ripken Jr.	.25	.12	.02
☐ 480	Mike Stanley	.03	.01	.00	☐ 571	Dave Schmidt	.03	.01	.00
☐ 481	Curtis Wilkerson	.03	.01	.00	☐ 572	Larry Sheets	.06	.03	.00
☐ 482	Mitch Williams	.08	.04	.01	☐ 573	Pete Stanicek	.20	.10	.02
☐ 483	Bobby Witt	.06	.03	.00	☐ 574	Mark Williamson	.08	.04	.01
☐ 484	Tony Armas	.06	.03	.00	☐ 575	Mike Young	.03	.01	.00
☐ 485	Bob Boone	.08	.04	.01	☐ 576	Shawn Abner	.15	.07	.01
☐ 486	Bill Buckner	.06	.03	.00	☐ 577	Greg Booker	.03	.01	.00
☐ 487	DeWayne Buice	.10	.05	.01	☐ 578	Chris Brown	.03	.01	.00
☐ 488	Brian Downing	.03	.01	.00	☐ 579	Keith Comstock	.08	.04	.01
☐ 489	Chuck Finley	.08	.04	.01	☐ 580	Joey Cora	.10	.05	.01
☐ 490	Willie Fraser UER	.03	.01	.00	☐ 581	Mark Davis	.12	.06	.01
	(wrong bio stats,				☐ 582	Tim Flannery	.03	.01	.00
	for George Hendrick)					(with surfboard)			
☐ 491	Jack Howell	.03	.01	.00	☐ 583	Goose Gossage	.08	.04	.01
☐ 492	Ruppert Jones	.03	.01	.00	☐ 584	Mark Grant	.03	.01	.00
☐ 493	Wally Joyner	.50	.25	.05	☐ 585	Tony Gwynn	.35	.17	.03
☐ 494	Jack Lazorko	.03	.01	.00	☐ 586	Andy Hawkins	.03	.01	.00
☐ 495	Gary Lucas	.03	.01	.00	☐ 587	Stan Jefferson	.15	.07	.01

☐ 588	Jimmy Jones	.06	.03	.00
☐ 589	John Kruk	.08	.04	.01
☐ 590	Shane Mack	.12	.06	.01
☐ 591	Carmelo Martinez	.03	.01	.00
☐ 592	Lance McCullers UER (6'11" tall)	.06	.03	.00
☐ 593	Eric Nolte	.12	.06	.01
☐ 594	Randy Ready	.03	.01	.00
☐ 595	Luis Salazar	.03	.01	.00
☐ 596	Benito Santiago	.40	.20	.04
☐ 597	Eric Show	.03	.01	.00
☐ 598	Garry Templeton	.06	.03	.00
☐ 599	Ed Whitson	.03	.01	.00
☐ 600	Scott Bailes	.03	.01	.00
☐ 601	Chris Bando	.03	.01	.00
☐ 602	Jay Bell	.20	.10	.02
☐ 603	Brett Butler	.06	.03	.00
☐ 604	Tom Candiotti	.03	.01	.00
☐ 605	Joe Carter	.20	.10	.02
☐ 606	Carmen Castillo	.03	.01	.00
☐ 607	Brian Dorsett	.10	.05	.01
☐ 608	John Farrell	.25	.12	.02
☐ 609	Julio Franco	.10	.05	.01
☐ 610	Mel Hall	.03	.01	.00
☐ 611	Tommy Hinzo	.10	.05	.01
☐ 612	Brook Jacoby	.06	.03	.00
☐ 613	Doug Jones	.35	.17	.03
☐ 614	Ken Schrom	.03	.01	.00
☐ 615	Cory Snyder	.15	.07	.01
☐ 616	Sammy Stewart	.03	.01	.00
☐ 617	Greg Swindell	.20	.10	.02
☐ 618	Pat Tabler	.06	.03	.00
☐ 619	Ed VandeBerg	.03	.01	.00
☐ 620	Eddie Williams	.18	.09	.01
☐ 621	Rich Yett	.03	.01	.00
☐ 622	Slugging Sophomores Wally Joyner Cory Snyder	.12	.06	.01
☐ 623	Dominican Dynamite George Bell Pedro Guerrero	.10	.05	.01
☐ 624	Oakland's Power Team Mark McGwire Jose Canseco	.75	.35	.07
☐ 625	Classic Relief Dave Righetti Dan Plesac	.10	.05	.01
☐ 626	All Star Righties Bret Saberhagen Mike Witt Jack Morris	.10	.05	.01
☐ 627	Game Closers John Franco Steve Bedrosian	.08	.04	.01
☐ 628	Masters/Double Play Ozzie Smith Ryne Sandberg	.12	.06	.01
☐ 629	Rookie Record Setter Mark McGwire	.40	.20	.04
☐ 630	Changing the Guard Mike Greenwell Ellis Burks Todd Benzinger	.75	.35	.07
☐ 631	NL Batting Champs Tony Gwynn Tim Raines	.18	.09	.01
☐ 632	Pitching Magic Mike Scott Orel Hershiser	.12	.06	.01
☐ 633	Big Bats at First Pat Tabler Mark McGwire	.25	.12	.02
☐ 634	Hitting King/Thief Tony Gwynn Vince Coleman	.12	.06	.01
☐ 635	Slugging Shortstops Tony Fernandez Cal Ripken Alan Trammell	.10	.05	.01
☐ 636	Tried/True Sluggers Mike Schmidt Gary Carter	.12	.06	.01
☐ 637	Crunch Time Darryl Strawberry Eric Davis	.35	.17	.03
☐ 638	AL All-Stars Matt Nokes Kirby Puckett	.15	.07	.01
☐ 639	NL All-Stars Keith Hernandez Dale Murphy	.10	.05	.01
☐ 640	The O's Brothers Billy Ripken Cal Ripken	.08	.04	.01
☐ 641	Mark Grace and	7.50	3.75	.75

	Darrin Jackson			
☐ 642	Damon Berryhill and Jeff Montgomery	1.25	.60	.12
☐ 643	Felix Fermin and Jesse Reid	.12	.06	.01
☐ 644	Greg Myers and Greg Tabor	.15	.07	.01
☐ 645	Joey Meyer and Jim Eppard	.15	.07	.01
☐ 646	Adam Peterson and Randy Velarde	.12	.06	.01
☐ 647	Peter Smith and Chris Gwynn	.35	.17	.03
☐ 648	Tom Newell and Greg Jelks	.12	.06	.01
☐ 649	Mario Diaz and Clay Parker	.35	.17	.03
☐ 650	Jack Savage and Todd Simmons	.15	.07	.01
☐ 651	John Burkett and Kirt Manwaring	.20	.10	.02
☐ 652	Dave Otto and Walt Weiss	1.25	.60	.12
☐ 653	Jeff King and Randell Byers	.35	.17	.03
☐ 654	CL: Twins/Cards Tigers/Giants UER (90 Bob Melvin, 91 Eddie Milner)	.06	.01	.00
☐ 655	CL: Blue Jays/Mets Brewers/Expos UER (Mets listed before Blue Jays on card)	.06	.01	.00
☐ 656	CL: Yankees/Reds Royals/A's	.06	.01	.00
☐ 657	CL: Phillies/Pirates Red Sox/Mariners	.06	.01	.00
☐ 658	CL: White Sox/Cubs Astros/Rangers	.06	.01	.00
☐ 659	CL: Angels/Dodgers Braves/Orioles	.06	.01	.00
☐ 660	CL: Padres/Indians Rookies/Specials	.06	.01	.00

1988 Fleer Wax Box Cards

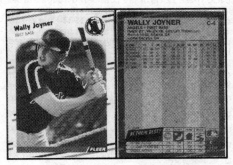

The cards in this 16-card set measure the standard 2 1/2" by 3 1/2". Cards have essentially the same design as the 1988 Fleer regular issue set. The cards were printed on the bottoms of the regular issue wax pack boxes. These 16 cards (C1 to C16) are considered a separate set in their own right and are not typically included in a complete set of the regular issue 1988 Fleer cards. The value of the panel uncut is slightly greater, perhaps by 25% greater, than the value of the individual cards cut up carefully.

		MINT	EXC	G-VG
COMPLETE SET (16)		3.00	1.50	.30
COMMON PLAYER (C1-C16)		.05	.02	.00
☐ C1	Cardinals Logo	.05	.02	.00
☐ C2	Dwight Evans	.10	.05	.01
☐ C3	Andres Galarraga	.20	.10	.02
☐ C4	Wally Joyner	.40	.20	.04
☐ C5	Twins Logo	.05	.02	.00
☐ C6	Dale Murphy	.30	.15	.03
☐ C7	Kirby Puckett	.50	.25	.05

☐	C8	Shane Rawley	.05	.02	.00
☐	C9	Giants Logo	.05	.02	.00
☐	C10	Ryne Sandberg	.25	.12	.02
☐	C11	Mike Schmidt	.60	.30	.06
☐	C12	Kevin Seitzer	.50	.25	.05
☐	C13	Tigers Logo	.05	.02	.00
☐	C14	Dave Stewart	.15	.07	.01
☐	C15	Tim Wallach	.10	.05	.01
☐	C16	Todd Worrell	.15	.07	.01

1988 Fleer All-Star Inserts

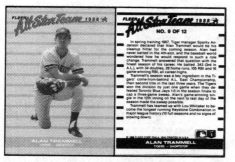

The cards in this 12-card set measure the standard 2 1/2" by 3 1/2". These cards were inserted (randomly) in wax and cello packs of the 1988 Fleer regular issue set. The cards show the player silhouetted against a light green background with dark green stripes. The player's name, team, and position are printed in yellow at the bottom of the obverse. The card backs are done predominantly in green, white, and black. Cards are numbered on the back. These 12 cards are considered a separate set in their own right and are not typically included in a complete set of the regular issue 1988 Fleer cards. The players are the "best" at each position, three pitchers, eight position players, and a designated hitter.

		MINT	EXC	G-VG
COMPLETE SET (12)		12.50	6.25	1.25
COMMON PLAYERS (1-12)		.25	.12	.02
☐ 1	Matt Nokes Catcher	.50	.25	.05
☐ 2	Tom Henke Relief Pitcher	.25	.12	.02
☐ 3	Ted Higuera Left Hand Pitcher	.35	.17	.03
☐ 4	Roger Clemens Right Hand Pitcher	2.00	1.00	.20
☐ 5	George Bell Outfielder	.50	.25	.05
☐ 6	Andre Dawson Outfielder	.50	.25	.05
☐ 7	Eric Davis Outfielder	2.00	1.00	.20
☐ 8	Wade Boggs Third Baseman	3.00	1.50	.30
☐ 9	Alan Trammell Shortstop	.75	.35	.07
☐ 10	Juan Samuel Second Baseman	.35	.17	.03
☐ 11	Jack Clark First Baseman	.50	.25	.05
☐ 12	Paul Molitor Designated Hitter	.50	.25	.05

TELL FRIENDS: Share your fun with your friends. Tell them about this publication and Beckett Baseball Card Monthly.

1988 Fleer Headliners

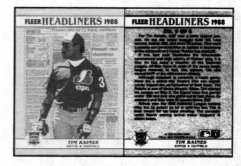

This six-card set was distributed as a special insert in rack packs. The obverse features the player photo superimposed on a gray newsprint background. Cards are 2 1/2" by 3 1/2". The cards are printed in red, black, and white on the back describing why that particular player made headlines the previous season. The cards are numbered on the back.

		MINT	EXC	G-VG
COMPLETE SET (6)		7.50	3.75	.75
COMMON PLAYER (1-6)		.60	.30	.06
☐ 1	Don Mattingly New York Yankees	3.00	1.50	.30
☐ 2	Mark McGwire Oakland Athletics	2.00	1.00	.20
☐ 3	Jack Morris Detroit Tigers	.60	.30	.06
☐ 4	Darryl Strawberry New York Mets	1.25	.60	.12
☐ 5	Dwight Gooden New York Mets	1.00	.50	.10
☐ 6	Tim Raines Montreal Expos	.80	.40	.08

1988 Fleer Update

This 132-card set was distributed by Fleer to dealers as a complete set within a custom box. In addition to the complete set of 132 cards, the box also contains 25 Team Logo stickers. The card fronts look very similar to the 1987 Fleer regular issue. The cards are numbered (with a U prefix) alphabetically according to player's last name. Cards measure the standard size, 2 1/2" by 3 1/2". This was the first Fleer Update set to adopt the Fleer "alphabetical within team" numbering system. Fleer also produced a "limited" edition version of this set with glossy coating and packaged in a "tin." However this tin set was apparently not limited enough (estimated between 40,000 and 60,000 1988 update tin sets produced by Fleer) since the price of the "tin" glossy cards is now only double the price of the regular set.

		MINT	EXC	G-VG
	COMPLETE SET (132)	13.50	6.00	1.25
	COMMON PLAYER (1-132)	.05	.02	.00
☐	U1 Jose Bautista	.15	.07	.01
☐	U2 Joe Orsulak	.05	.02	.00
☐	U3 Doug Sisk	.05	.02	.00
☐	U4 Craig Worthington	.50	.25	.05
☐	U5 Mike Boddicker	.08	.04	.01
☐	U6 Rick Cerone	.05	.02	.00
☐	U7 Larry Parrish	.05	.02	.00
☐	U8 Lee Smith	.08	.04	.01
☐	U9 Mike Smithson	.05	.02	.00
☐	U10 John Trautwein	.10	.05	.01
☐	U11 Sherman Corbett	.12	.06	.01
☐	U12 Chili Davis	.08	.04	.01
☐	U13 Jim Eppard	.05	.02	.00
☐	U14 Bryan Harvey	.25	.12	.02
☐	U15 John Davis	.05	.02	.00
☐	U16 Dave Gallagher	.35	.17	.03
☐	U17 Ricky Horton	.05	.02	.00
☐	U18 Dan Pasqua	.05	.02	.00
☐	U19 Melido Perez	.12	.06	.01
☐	U20 Jose Segura	.12	.06	.01
☐	U21 Andy Allanson	.05	.02	.00
☐	U22 Jon Perlman	.05	.02	.00
☐	U23 Domingo Ramos	.08	.04	.01
☐	U24 Rick Rodriguez	.05	.02	.00
☐	U25 Willie Upshaw	.05	.02	.00
☐	U26 Paul Gibson	.12	.06	.01
☐	U27 Don Heinkel	.12	.06	.01
☐	U28 Ray Knight	.08	.04	.01
☐	U29 Gary Pettis	.08	.04	.01
☐	U30 Luis Salazar	.05	.02	.00
☐	U31 Mike MacFarlane	.18	.09	.01
☐	U32 Jeff Montgomery	.15	.07	.01
☐	U33 Ted Power	.05	.02	.00
☐	U34 Israel Sanchez	.12	.06	.01
☐	U35 Kurt Stillwell	.08	.04	.01
☐	U36 Pat Tabler	.08	.04	.01
☐	U37 Don August	.15	.07	.01
☐	U38 Darryl Hamilton	.25	.12	.02
☐	U39 Jeff Leonard	.08	.04	.01
☐	U40 Joey Meyer	.10	.05	.01
☐	U41 Allan Anderson	.12	.06	.01
☐	U42 Brian Harper	.05	.02	.00
☐	U43 Tom Herr	.05	.02	.00
☐	U44 Charlie Lea	.05	.02	.00
☐	U45 John Moses (listed as Hohn on checklist card)	.05	.02	.00
☐	U46 John Candelaria	.08	.04	.01
☐	U47 Jack Clark	.15	.07	.01
☐	U48 Richard Dotson	.05	.02	.00
☐	U49 Al Leiter	.25	.12	.02
☐	U50 Rafael Santana	.05	.02	.00
☐	U51 Don Slaught	.05	.02	.00
☐	U52 Todd Burns	.35	.17	.03
☐	U53 Dave Henderson	.08	.04	.01
☐	U54 Doug Jennings	.25	.12	.02
☐	U55 Dave Parker	.15	.07	.01
☐	U56 Walt Weiss	.60	.30	.06
☐	U57 Bob Welch	.08	.04	.01
☐	U58 Henry Cotto	.05	.02	.00
☐	U59 Mario Diaz UER (listed as Marion on card front)	.08	.04	.01
☐	U60 Mike Jackson	.08	.04	.01
☐	U61 Bill Swift	.08	.04	.01
☐	U62 Jose Cecena	.10	.05	.01
☐	U63 Ray Hayward	.10	.05	.01
☐	U64 Jim Steels UER (listed as Jim Steele on card back)	.10	.05	.01
☐	U65 Pat Borders	.20	.10	.02
☐	U66 Sil Campusano	.25	.12	.02
☐	U67 Mike Flanagan	.08	.04	.01
☐	U68 Todd Stottlemyre	.25	.12	.02
☐	U69 David Wells	.15	.07	.01
☐	U70 Jose Alvarez	.12	.06	.01
☐	U71 Paul Runge	.05	.02	.00
☐	U72 Cesar Jimenez (card intended for German Jiminez, it's his photo)	.15	.07	.01
☐	U73 Pete Smith	.12	.06	.01
☐	U74 John Smoltz	1.75	.85	.17
☐	U75 Damon Berryhill	.30	.15	.03
☐	U76 Goose Gossage	.12	.06	.01
☐	U77 Mark Grace	3.50	1.75	.35
☐	U78 Darrin Jackson	.12	.06	.01
☐	U79 Vance Law	.05	.02	.00
☐	U80 Jeff Pico	.15	.07	.01
☐	U81 Gary Varsho	.20	.10	.02
☐	U82 Tim Birtsas	.05	.02	.00
☐	U83 Rob Dibble	.50	.25	.05
☐	U84 Danny Jackson	.12	.06	.01
☐	U85 Paul O'Neill	.15	.07	.01
☐	U86 Jose Rijo	.10	.05	.01
☐	U87 Chris Sabo	1.00	.50	.10
☐	U88 John Fishel	.15	.07	.01
☐	U89 Craig Biggio	1.00	.50	.10
☐	U90 Terry Puhl	.05	.02	.00
☐	U91 Rafael Ramirez	.05	.02	.00
☐	U92 Louie Meadows	.10	.05	.01
☐	U93 Kirk Gibson	.25	.12	.02
☐	U94 Alfredo Griffin	.08	.04	.01
☐	U95 Jay Howell	.08	.04	.01
☐	U96 Jesse Orosco	.05	.02	.00
☐	U97 Alejandro Pena	.05	.02	.00
☐	U98 Tracy Woodson	.20	.10	.02
☐	U99 John Dopson	.20	.10	.02
☐	U100 Brian Holman	.20	.10	.02
☐	U101 Rex Hudler	.05	.02	.00
☐	U102 Jeff Parrett	.08	.04	.01
☐	U103 Nelson Santovenia	.25	.12	.02
☐	U104 Kevin Elster	.15	.07	.01
☐	U105 Jeff Innis	.20	.10	.02
☐	U106 Mackey Sasser	.15	.07	.01
☐	U107 Phil Bradley	.08	.04	.01
☐	U108 Danny Clay	.12	.06	.01
☐	U109 Greg Harris	.05	.02	.00
☐	U110 Ricky Jordan	3.00	1.50	.30
☐	U111 David Palmer	.05	.02	.00
☐	U112 Jim Gott	.08	.04	.01
☐	U113 Tommy Gregg UER (photo actually Randy Milligan)	.25	.12	.02
☐	U114 Barry Jones	.05	.02	.00
☐	U115 Randy Milligan	.25	.12	.02
☐	U116 Luis Alicea	.12	.06	.01
☐	U117 Tom Brunansky	.10	.05	.01
☐	U118 John Costello	.15	.07	.01
☐	U119 Jose DeLeon	.08	.04	.01
☐	U120 Bob Horner	.10	.05	.01
☐	U121 Scott Terry	.12	.06	.01
☐	U122 Roberto Alomar	.50	.25	.05
☐	U123 Dave Leiper	.05	.02	.00
☐	U124 Keith Moreland	.05	.02	.00
☐	U125 Mark Parent	.15	.07	.01
☐	U126 Dennis Rasmussen	.08	.04	.01
☐	U127 Randy Bockus	.05	.02	.00
☐	U128 Brett Butler	.10	.05	.01
☐	U129 Donell Nixon	.08	.04	.01
☐	U130 Earnest Riles	.05	.02	.00
☐	U131 Roger Samuels	.12	.06	.01
☐	U132 Checklist U1-U132	.05	.01	.00

1988 Fleer Award Winners

This small set of 44 cards was produced for 7-Eleven stores by Fleer. The cards measure the standard 2 1/2" by 3 1/2" and feature full color fronts and red, white, and blue backs. The card fronts are distinguished by the red, white, and blue frame around the player's full-color photo. The box for the cards describes the set as the "1988 Limited Edition Baseball Award Winners." The checklist for the set is given on the back of the set box.

		MINT	EXC	G-VG
COMPLETE SET (44)		4.00	2.00	.40
COMMON PLAYER (1-44)		.05	.02	.00
☐ 1	Steve Bedrosian	.10	.05	.01
☐ 2	George Bell	.15	.07	.01
☐ 3	Wade Boggs	.65	.30	.06
☐ 4	Jose Canseco	1.00	.50	.10
☐ 5	Will Clark	1.00	.50	.10
☐ 6	Roger Clemens	.50	.25	.05
☐ 7	Kal Daniels	.10	.05	.01
☐ 8	Eric Davis	.50	.25	.05
☐ 9	Andre Dawson	.20	.10	.02
☐ 10	Mike Dunne	.05	.02	.00
☐ 11	Dwight Evans	.10	.05	.01
☐ 12	Carlton Fisk	.15	.07	.01
☐ 13	Julio Franco	.10	.05	.01
☐ 14	Dwight Gooden	.35	.17	.03
☐ 15	Pedro Guerrero	.15	.07	.01
☐ 16	Tony Gwynn	.30	.15	.03
☐ 17	Orel Hershiser	.30	.15	.03
☐ 18	Tom Henke	.05	.02	.00
☐ 19	Ted Higuera	.10	.05	.01
☐ 20	Charlie Hough	.05	.02	.00
☐ 21	Wally Joyner	.25	.12	.02
☐ 22	Jimmy Key	.05	.02	.00
☐ 23	Don Mattingly	1.00	.50	.10
☐ 24	Mark McGwire	.65	.30	.06
☐ 25	Paul Molitor	.10	.05	.01
☐ 26	Jack Morris	.10	.05	.01
☐ 27	Dale Murphy	.30	.15	.03
☐ 28	Terry Pendleton	.05	.02	.00
☐ 29	Kirby Puckett	.40	.20	.04
☐ 30	Tim Raines	.20	.10	.02
☐ 31	Jeff Reardon	.10	.05	.01
☐ 32	Harold Reynolds	.05	.02	.00
☐ 33	Dave Righetti	.10	.05	.01
☐ 34	Benito Santiago	.25	.12	.02
☐ 35	Mike Schmidt	.60	.30	.06
☐ 36	Mike Scott	.15	.07	.01
☐ 37	Kevin Seitzer	.25	.12	.02
☐ 38	Larry Sheets	.05	.02	.00
☐ 39	Ozzie Smith	.15	.07	.01
☐ 40	Darryl Strawberry	.50	.25	.05
☐ 41	Rick Sutcliffe	.10	.05	.01
☐ 42	Danny Tartabull	.20	.10	.02
☐ 43	Alan Trammell	.15	.07	•01
☐ 44	Tim Wallach	.05	.02	.00

☐ 2	Wade Boggs	.75	.35	.07
☐ 3	Bobby Bonilla	.20	.10	.02
☐ 4	George Brett	.40	.20	.04
☐ 5	Jose Canseco	1.25	.60	.12
☐ 6	Jack Clark	.20	.10	.02
☐ 7	Will Clark	1.25	.60	.12
☐ 8	Roger Clemens	.60	.30	.06
☐ 9	Eric Davis	.60	.30	.06
☐ 10	Andre Dawson	.25	.12	.02
☐ 11	Julio Franco	.15	.07	.01
☐ 12	Dwight Gooden	.50	.25	.05
☐ 13	Tony Gwynn	.45	.22	.04
☐ 14	Orel Hershiser	.45	.22	.04
☐ 15	Teddy Higuera	.15	.07	.01
☐ 16	Charlie Hough	.10	.05	.01
☐ 17	Kent Hrbek	.20	.10	.02
☐ 18	Bruce Hurst	.15	.07	.01
☐ 19	Wally Joyner	.35	.17	.03
☐ 20	Mark Langston	.20	.10	.02
☐ 21	Dave LaPoint	.10	.05	.01
☐ 22	Candy Maldonado	.10	.05	.01
☐ 23	Don Mattingly	1.00	.50	.10
☐ 24	Roger McDowell	.10	.05	.01
☐ 25	Mark McGwire	.75	.35	.07
☐ 26	Jack Morris	.15	.07	.01
☐ 27	Dale Murphy	.35	.17	.03
☐ 28	Eddie Murray	.35	.17	.03
☐ 29	Matt Nokes	.20	.10	.02
☐ 30	Kirby Puckett	.40	.20	.04
☐ 31	Tim Raines	.20	.10	.02
☐ 32	Willie Randolph	.15	.07	.01
☐ 33	Jeff Reardon	.15	.07	.01
☐ 34	Nolan Ryan	1.00	.50	.10
☐ 35	Juan Samuel	.15	.07	.01
☐ 36	Mike Schmidt	.75	.35	.07
☐ 37	Mike Scott	.15	.07	.01
☐ 38	Kevin Seitzer	.30	.15	.03
☐ 39	Ozzie Smith	.20	.10	.02
☐ 40	Darryl Strawberry	.60	.30	.06
☐ 41	Rick Sutcliffe	.15	.07	.01
☐ 42	Alan Trammell	.20	.10	.02
☐ 43	Tim Wallach	.10	.05	.01
☐ 44	Dave Winfield	.25	.12	.02

1988 Fleer Baseball MVP

This small 44-card boxed set was produced by Fleer for distribution by the Toys'r'Us stores. The cards measure the standard 2 1/2" by 3 1/2" and feature full color fronts. The set is titled "Baseball MVP." Each individual boxed set includes the 44 cards and 6 logo stickers. The checklist for the set is found on the back panel of the box. The card fronts have a vanilla-yellow and blue border. The box refers to Toys'r'Us but there is no mention of Toys'r'Us anywhere on the cards themselves.

		MINT	EXC	G-VG
COMPLETE SET (44)		5.00	2.50	.50
COMMON PLAYER (1-44)		.10	.05	.01
☐ 1	George Bell	.20	.10	.02
☐ 2	Wade Boggs	.75	.35	.07
☐ 3	Jose Canseco	1.25	.60	.12
☐ 4	Ivan Calderon	.15	.07	.01
☐ 5	Will Clark	1.25	.60	.12
☐ 6	Roger Clemens	.60	.30	.06
☐ 7	Vince Coleman	.25	.12	.02

1988 Fleer Baseball All-Stars

This small boxed set of 44 cards was produced exclusively for Ben Franklin Stores. The cards measure the standard 2 1/2" by 3 1/2" and feature full color fronts and white and blue backs. The card fronts are distinguished by the yellow and blue striped background behind the player's full-color photo. The box for the cards describes the set as the "1988 Fleer Baseball All-Stars." The checklist for the set is given on the back of the set box.

		MINT	EXC	G-VG
COMPLETE SET (44)		5.00	2.50	.50
COMMON PLAYER (1-44)		.10	.05	.01
☐ 1	George Bell	.20	.10	.02

☐	8	Eric Davis	.60	.30	.06
☐	9	Andre Dawson	.25	.12	.02
☐	10	Dave Dravecky	.15	.07	.01
☐	11	Mike Dunne	.10	.05	.01
☐	12	Dwight Evans	.15	.07	.01
☐	13	Sid Fernandez	.15	.07	.01
☐	14	Tony Fernandez	.15	.07	.01
☐	15	Julio Franco	.15	.07	.01
☐	16	Dwight Gooden	.40	.20	.04
☐	17	Tony Gwynn	.35	.17	.03
☐	18	Ted Higuera	.15	.07	.01
☐	19	Charlie Hough	.10	.05	.01
☐	20	Wally Joyner	.35	.17	.03
☐	21	Mark Langston	.20	.10	.02
☐	22	Don Mattingly	1.00	.50	.10
☐	23	Mark McGwire	.75	.35	.07
☐	24	Jack Morris	.15	.07	.01
☐	25	Dale Murphy	.35	.17	.03
☐	26	Kirby Puckett	.45	.22	.04
☐	27	Tim Raines	.20	.10	.02
☐	28	Willie Randolph	.15	.07	.01
☐	29	Ryne Sandberg	.25	.12	.02
☐	30	Benito Santiago	.30	.15	.03
☐	31	Mike Schmidt	.75	.35	.07
☐	32	Mike Scott	.15	.07	.01
☐	33	Kevin Seitzer	.30	.15	.03
☐	34	Larry Sheets	.10	.05	.01
☐	35	Ozzie Smith	.20	.10	.02
☐	36	Dave Stewart	.25	.12	.02
☐	37	Darryl Strawberry	.60	.30	.06
☐	38	Rick Sutcliffe	.15	.07	.01
☐	39	Alan Trammell	.20	.10	.02
☐	40	Fernando Valenzuela	.20	.10	.02
☐	41	Frank Viola	.20	.10	.02
☐	42	Tim Wallach	.10	.05	.01
☐	43	Dave Winfield	.25	.12	.02
☐	44	Robin Yount	.50	.25	.05

☐	14	Julio Franco	.15	.07	.01
☐	15	Dwight Gooden	.50	.25	.05
☐	16	Mike Greenwell	1.00	.50	.10
☐	17	Tony Gwynn	.35	.17	.03
☐	18	Von Hayes	.15	.07	.01
☐	19	Tom Henke	.10	.05	.01
☐	20	Orel Hershiser	.45	.22	.04
☐	21	Teddy Higuera	.15	.07	.01
☐	22	Brook Jacoby	.15	.07	.01
☐	23	Wally Joyner	.35	.17	.03
☐	24	Jimmy Key	.15	.07	.01
☐	25	Don Mattingly	1.00	.50	.10
☐	26	Mark McGwire	.75	.35	.07
☐	27	Jack Morris	.15	.07	.01
☐	28	Dale Murphy	.30	.15	.03
☐	29	Matt Nokes	.20	.10	.02
☐	30	Kirby Puckett	.40	.20	.04
☐	31	Tim Raines	.20	.10	.02
☐	32	Ryne Sandberg	.25	.12	.02
☐	33	Benito Santiago	.30	.15	.03
☐	34	Mike Schmidt	.75	.35	.07
☐	35	Mike Scott	.15	.07	.01
☐	36	Kevin Seitzer	.30	.15	.03
☐	37	Larry Sheets	.10	.05	.01
☐	38	Ruben Sierra	.60	.30	.06
☐	39	Darryl Strawberry	.60	.30	.06
☐	40	Rick Sutcliffe	.15	.07	.01
☐	41	Danny Tartabull	.25	.12	.02
☐	42	Alan Trammell	.20	.10	.02
☐	43	Fernando Valenzuela	.15	.07	.01
☐	44	Devon White	.20	.10	.02

1988 Fleer Hottest Stars

This 44-card boxed set was produced by Fleer for exclusive distribution by Revco Discount Drug stores all over the country. The cards measure the standard 2 1/2" by 3 1/2" and feature full color fronts and red, white, and blue backs. The card fronts are easily distinguished by the flaming baseball in the lower right corner which says "Fleer Baseball's Hottest Stars." The player's picture is framed in red fading from orange down to yellow. The box for the cards proclaims "1988 Limited Edition Baseball's Hottest Stars" and is styled in blue, red, and yellow. The checklist for the set is given on the back of the set box. The box refers to Revco but there is no mention of Revco anywhere on the cards themselves.

1988 Fleer Exciting Stars

This small boxed set of 44 cards was produced exclusively for Cumberland Farm Stores. The cards measure the standard 2 1/2" by 3 1/2" and feature full color fronts and red, white, and blue backs. The card fronts are distinguished by the framing of the player's full-color photo with a blue border and a red and white bar stripe across the middle. The box for the cards describes the set as the "1988 Fleer Baseball's Exciting Stars." The checklist for the set is given on the back of the set box.

	MINT	EXC	G-VG
COMPLETE SET (44)	5.00	2.50	.50
COMMON PLAYER (1-44)	.10	.05	.01

☐	1	Harold Baines	.15	.07	.01
☐	2	Kevin Bass	.10	.05	.01
☐	3	George Bell	.20	.10	.02
☐	4	Wade Boggs	.75	.35	.07
☐	5	Mickey Brantley	.10	.05	.01
☐	6	Sid Bream	.10	.05	.01
☐	7	Jose Canseco	1.25	.60	.12
☐	8	Jack Clark	.20	.10	.02
☐	9	Will Clark	1.25	.60	.12
☐	10	Roger Clemens	.60	.30	.06
☐	11	Vince Coleman	.25	.12	.02
☐	12	Eric Davis	.60	.30	.06
☐	13	Andre Dawson	.25	.12	.02

	MINT	EXC	G-VG
COMPLETE SET (44)	5.00	2.50	.50
COMMON PLAYER (1-44)	.10	.05	.01

☐	1	George Bell	.20	.10	.02
☐	2	Wade Boggs	.75	.35	.07
☐	3	Bobby Bonilla	.20	.10	.02
☐	4	George Brett	.35	.17	.03
☐	5	Jose Canseco	1.25	.60	.12
☐	6	Will Clark	1.25	.60	.12
☐	7	Roger Clemens	.60	.30	.06
☐	8	Eric Davis	.60	.30	.06
☐	9	Andre Dawson	.20	.10	.02
☐	10	Tony Fernandez	.15	.07	.01
☐	11	Julio Franco	.10	.05	.01
☐	12	Gary Gaetti	.15	.07	.01
☐	13	Dwight Gooden	.40	.20	.04

		MINT	EXC	G-VG
☐ 14	Mike Greenwell	1.00	.50	.10
☐ 15	Tony Gwynn	.35	.17	.03
☐ 16	Rickey Henderson	.40	.20	.04
☐ 17	Keith Hernandez	.20	.10	.02
☐ 18	Tom Herr	.10	.05	.01
☐ 19	Orel Hershiser	.40	.20	.04
☐ 20	Ted Higuera	.15	.07	.01
☐ 21	Wally Joyner	.35	.17	.03
☐ 22	Jimmy Key	.10	.05	.01
☐ 23	Mark Langston	.20	.10	.02
☐ 24	Don Mattingly	1.00	.50	.10
☐ 25	Jack McDowell	.15	.07	.01
☐ 26	Mark McGwire	.75	.35	.07
☐ 27	Kevin Mitchell	.50	.25	.05
☐ 28	Jack Morris	.15	.07	.01
☐ 29	Dale Murphy	.35	.17	.03
☐ 30	Kirby Puckett	.40	.20	.04
☐ 31	Tim Raines	.20	.10	.02
☐ 32	Shane Rawley	.10	.05	.01
☐ 33	Benito Santiago	.35	.17	.03
☐ 34	Mike Schmidt	.75	.35	.07
☐ 35	Mike Scott	.15	.07	.01
☐ 36	Kevin Seitzer	.30	.15	.03
☐ 37	Larry Sheets	.10	.05	.01
☐ 38	Ruben Sierra	.60	.30	.06
☐ 39	Dave Smith	.10	.05	.01
☐ 40	Ozzie Smith	.20	.10	.02
☐ 41	Darryl Strawberry	.60	.30	.06
☐ 42	Rick Sutcliffe	.15	.07	.01
☐ 43	Pat Tabler	.10	.05	.01
☐ 44	Alan Trammell	.20	.10	.02

		MINT	EXC	G-VG
☐ 20	Ted Higuera	.15	.07	.01
☐ 21	Kent Hrbek	.20	.10	.02
☐ 22	Wally Joyner	.35	.17	.03
☐ 23	Jimmy Key	.10	.05	.01
☐ 24	Mark Langston	.20	.10	.02
☐ 25	Don Mattingly	1.00	.50	.10
☐ 26	Mark McGwire	.75	.35	.07
☐ 27	Paul Molitor	.20	.10	.02
☐ 28	Jack Morris	.15	.07	.01
☐ 29	Dale Murphy	.35	.17	.03
☐ 30	Kirby Puckett	.40	.20	.04
☐ 31	Tim Raines	.20	.10	.02
☐ 32	Rick Reuschel	.15	.07	.01
☐ 33	Bret Saberhagen	.30	.15	.03
☐ 34	Benito Santiago	.30	.15	.03
☐ 35	Mike Schmidt	.75	.35	.07
☐ 36	Mike Scott	.15	.07	.01
☐ 37	Kevin Seitzer	.30	.15	.03
☐ 38	Larry Sheets	.10	.05	.01
☐ 39	Ruben Sierra	.60	.30	.06
☐ 40	Darryl Strawberry	.60	.30	.06
☐ 41	Rick Sutcliffe	.15	.07	.01
☐ 42	Alan Trammell	.20	.10	.02
☐ 43	Andy Van Slyke	.15	.07	.01
☐ 44	Todd Worrell	.15	.07	.01

1988 Fleer League Leaders

ANDRES GALARRAGA
MONTREAL EXPOS • FIRST BASE

NO. 14 OF 44

This small boxed set of 44 cards was produced exclusively for Walgreen Drug Stores. The cards measure the standard 2 1/2" by 3 1/2" and feature full color fronts and pink, white, and blue backs. The card fronts are distinguished by the blue solid and striped background behind the player's full-color photo. The box for the cards describes the set as the "1988 Fleer Baseball's League Leaders." The checklist for the set is given on the back of the set box.

		MINT	EXC	G-VG
		5.00	2.50	.50
COMPLETE SET (44)				
COMMON PLAYER (1-44)		.10	.05	.01
☐ 1	George Bell	.20	.10	.02
☐ 2	Wade Boggs	.75	.35	.07
☐ 3	Ivan Calderon	.15	.07	.01
☐ 4	Jose Canseco	1.25	.60	.12
☐ 5	Will Clark	1.25	.60	.12
☐ 6	Roger Clemens	.60	.30	.06
☐ 7	Vince Coleman	.25	.12	.02
☐ 8	Eric Davis	.60	.30	.06
☐ 9	Andre Dawson	.25	.12	.02
☐ 10	Bill Doran	.15	.07	.01
☐ 11	Dwight Evans	.15	.07	.01
☐ 12	Julio Franco	.15	.07	.01
☐ 13	Gary Gaetti	.15	.07	.01
☐ 14	Andres Galarraga	.20	.10	.02
☐ 15	Dwight Gooden	.50	.25	.05
☐ 16	Tony Gwynn	.40	.20	.04
☐ 17	Tom Henke	.10	.05	.01
☐ 18	Keith Hernandez	.20	.10	.02
☐ 19	Orel Hershiser	.40	.20	.04

1988 Fleer Mini

The 1988 Fleer "Classic Miniatures" set consists of 120 small cards with all new pictures of the players as compared to the 1988 Fleer regular issue. The cards are only 1 13/16" by 2 9/16", making them one of the smallest cards available. Card backs provide career year-by-year statistics. The complete set was distributed in a green, red, white, and silver box along with 18 logo stickers. The card numbering is by team order.

		MINT	EXC	G-VG
COMPLETE SET (120)		10.00	5.00	1.00
COMMON PLAYER (1-120)		.05	.02	.00
☐ 1	Eddie Murray	.20	.10	.02
☐ 2	Dave Schmidt	.05	.02	.00
☐ 3	Larry Sheets	.05	.02	.00
☐ 4	Wade Boggs	.75	.35	.07
☐ 5	Roger Clemens	.50	.25	.05
☐ 6	Dwight Evans	.10	.05	.01
☐ 7	Mike Greenwell	.75	.35	.07
☐ 8	Sam Horn	.10	.05	.01
☐ 9	Lee Smith	.05	.02	.00
☐ 10	Brian Downing	.05	.02	.00
☐ 11	Wally Joyner	.35	.17	.03
☐ 12	Devon White	.20	.10	.02
☐ 13	Mike Witt	.10	.05	.01
☐ 14	Ivan Calderon	.10	.05	.01
☐ 15	Ozzie Guillen	.10	.05	.01
☐ 16	Jack McDowell	.10	.05	.01
☐ 17	Kenny Williams	.10	.05	.01
☐ 18	Joe Carter	.15	.07	.01
☐ 19	Julio Franco	.10	.05	.01
☐ 20	Pat Tabler	.05	.02	.00
☐ 21	Doyle Alexander	.05	.02	.00
☐ 22	Jack Morris	.10	.05	.01
☐ 23	Matt Nokes	.15	.07	.01
☐ 24	Walt Terrell	.05	.02	.00
☐ 25	Alan Trammell	.15	.07	.01
☐ 26	Bret Saberhagen	.25	.12	.02
☐ 27	Kevin Seitzer	.30	.15	.03
☐ 28	Danny Tartabull	.20	.10	.02
☐ 29	Gary Thurman	.10	.05	.01

☐	30	Ted Higuera	.10	.05	.01
☐	31	Paul Molitor	.15	.07	.01
☐	32	Dan Plesac	.10	.05	.01
☐	33	Robin Yount	.40	.20	.04
☐	34	Gary Gaetti	.15	.07	.01
☐	35	Kent Hrbek	.15	.07	.01
☐	36	Kirby Puckett	.40	.20	.04
☐	37	Jeff Reardon	.10	.05	.01
☐	38	Frank Viola	.15	.07	.01
☐	39	Jack Clark	.15	.07	.01
☐	40	Rickey Henderson	.40	.20	.04
☐	41	Don Mattingly	1.00	.50	.10
☐	42	Willie Randolph	.10	.05	.01
☐	43	Dave Righetti	.10	.05	.01
☐	44	Dave Winfield	.25	.12	.02
☐	45	Jose Canseco	1.25	.60	.12
☐	46	Mark McGwire	.75	.35	.07
☐	47	Dave Parker	.15	.07	.01
☐	48	Dave Stewart	.15	.07	.01
☐	49	Walt Weiss	.35	.17	.03
☐	50	Bob Welch	.05	.02	.00
☐	51	Mickey Brantley	.05	.02	.00
☐	52	Mark Langston	.15	.07	.01
☐	53	Harold Reynolds	.05	.02	.00
☐	54	Scott Fletcher	.05	.02	.00
☐	55	Charlie Hough	.05	.02	.00
☐	56	Pete Incaviglia	.15	.07	.01
☐	57	Larry Parrish	.05	.02	.00
☐	58	Ruben Sierra	.50	.25	.05
☐	59	George Bell	.20	.10	.02
☐	60	Mark Eichhorn	.05	.02	.00
☐	61	Tony Fernandez	.10	.05	.01
☐	62	Tom Henke	.05	.02	.00
☐	63	Jimmy Key	.10	.05	.01
☐	64	Dion James	.05	.02	.00
☐	65	Dale Murphy	.30	.15	.03
☐	66	Zane Smith	.05	.02	.00
☐	67	Andre Dawson	.20	.10	.02
☐	68	Mark Grace	1.50	.75	.15
☐	69	Jerry Mumphrey	.05	.02	.00
☐	70	Ryne Sandberg	.25	.12	.02
☐	71	Rick Sutcliffe	.10	.05	.01
☐	72	Kal Daniels	.15	.07	.01
☐	73	Eric Davis	.75	.35	.07
☐	74	John Franco	.05	.02	.00
☐	75	Ron Robinson	.05	.02	.00
☐	76	Jeff Treadway	.10	.05	.01
☐	77	Kevin Bass	.05	.02	.00
☐	78	Glenn Davis	.20	.10	.02
☐	79	Nolan Ryan	1.00	.50	.10
☐	80	Mike Scott	.15	.07	.01
☐	81	Dave Smith	.05	.02	.00
☐	82	Kirk Gibson	.25	.12	.02
☐	83	Pedro Guerrero	.15	.07	.01
☐	84	Orel Hershiser	.40	.20	.04
☐	85	Steve Sax	.15	.07	.01
☐	86	Fernando Valenzuela	.15	.07	.01
☐	87	Tim Burke	.10	.05	.01
☐	88	Andres Galarraga	.25	.12	.02
☐	89	Neal Heaton	.05	.02	.00
☐	90	Tim Raines	.25	.12	.02
☐	91	Tim Wallach	.05	.02	.00
☐	92	Dwight Gooden	.45	.22	.04
☐	93	Keith Hernandez	.20	.10	.02
☐	94	Gregg Jefferies	1.50	.75	.15
☐	95	Howard Johnson	.20	.10	.02
☐	96	Roger McDowell	.10	.05	.01
☐	97	Darryl Strawberry	.50	.25	.05
☐	98	Steve Bedrosian	.10	.05	.01
☐	99	Von Hayes	.10	.05	.01
☐	100	Shane Rawley	.05	.02	.00
☐	101	Juan Samuel	.10	.05	.01
☐	102	Mike Schmidt	.75	.35	.07
☐	103	Bobby Bonilla	.15	.07	.01
☐	104	Mike Dunne	.05	.02	.00
☐	105	Andy Van Slyke	.10	.05	.01
☐	106	Vince Coleman	.20	.10	.02
☐	107	Bob Horner	.15	.07	.01
☐	108	Willie McGee	.15	.07	.01
☐	109	Ozzie Smith	.15	.07	.01
☐	110	John Tudor	.10	.05	.01
☐	111	Todd Worrell	.15	.07	.01
☐	112	Tony Gwynn	.35	.17	.03
☐	113	John Kruk	.15	.07	.01
☐	114	Lance McCullers	.05	.02	.00
☐	115	Benito Santiago	.35	.17	.03
☐	116	Will Clark	1.25	.60	.12
☐	117	Jeff Leonard	.05	.02	.00
☐	118	Candy Maldonado	.05	.02	.00
☐	119	Kirt Manwaring	.10	.05	.01
☐	120	Don Robinson	.05	.02	.00

1988 Fleer Record Setters

This small boxed set of 44 cards was produced exclusively for Eckerd's Drug Stores. The cards measure the standard 2 1/2" by 3 1/2" and feature full color fronts and red, white, and blue backs. The card fronts are distinguished by the red and blue frame around the player's full-color photo. The box for the cards describes the set as the "1988 Baseball Record Setters." The checklist for the set is given on the back of the set box.

		MINT	EXC	G-VG
COMPLETE SET (44)		5.00	2.50	.50
COMMON PLAYER (1-44)		.10	.05	.01
☐ 1	Jesse Barfield	.20	.10	.02
☐ 2	George Bell	.20	.10	.02
☐ 3	Wade Boggs	.75	.35	.07
☐ 4	Jose Canseco	1.25	.60	.12
☐ 5	Jack Clark	.20	.10	.02
☐ 6	Will Clark	1.25	.60	.12
☐ 7	Roger Clemens	.60	.30	.06
☐ 8	Alvin Davis	.15	.07	.01
☐ 9	Eric Davis	.60	.30	.06
☐ 10	Andre Dawson	.25	.12	.02
☐ 11	Mike Dunne	.10	.05	.01
☐ 12	John Franco	.10	.05	.01
☐ 13	Julio Franco	.15	.07	.01
☐ 14	Dwight Gooden	.50	.25	.05
☐ 15	Mark Gubicza	.15	.07	.01
	(listed as Gubiczo on box checklist)			
☐ 16	Ozzie Guillen	.15	.07	.01
☐ 17	Tony Gwynn	.40	.20	.04
☐ 18	Orel Hershiser	.40	.20	.04
☐ 19	Teddy Higuera	.15	.07	.01
☐ 20	Howard Johnson UER	.20	.10	.02
	(missing '87 stats on card back)			
☐ 21	Wally Joyner	.35	.17	.03
☐ 22	Jimmy Key	.15	.07	.01
☐ 23	Jeff Leonard	.10	.05	.01
☐ 24	Don Mattingly	1.00	.50	.10
☐ 25	Mark McGwire	.75	.35	.07
☐ 26	Jack Morris	.15	.07	.01
☐ 27	Dale Murphy	.35	.17	.03
☐ 28	Larry Parrish	.10	.05	.01
☐ 29	Kirby Puckett	.45	.22	.04
☐ 30	Tim Raines	.20	.10	.02
☐ 31	Harold Reynolds	.10	.05	.01
☐ 32	Dave Righetti	.15	.07	.01
☐ 33	Cal Ripken	.25	.12	.02
☐ 34	Benito Santiago	.25	.12	.02
☐ 35	Mike Schmidt	.75	.35	.07
☐ 36	Mike Scott	.15	.07	.01
☐ 37	Kevin Seitzer	.30	.15	.03
☐ 38	Ozzie Smith	.20	.10	.02
☐ 39	Darryl Strawberry	.60	.30	.06
☐ 40	Rick Sutcliffe	.15	.07	.01
☐ 41	Alan Trammell	.20	.10	.02
☐ 42	Frank Viola	.20	.10	.02
☐ 43	Mitch Williams	.15	.07	.01
☐ 44	Todd Worrell	.15	.07	.01

1988 Fleer Sluggers/Pitchers

Fleer produced this 44-card boxed set although it was primarily distributed by McCrory, McLellan, J.J Newberry, H.L.Green, T.G.Y., and other similar stores. The set is subtitled "Baseball's Best". Cards are standard- size, 2 1/2" by 3 1/2", and were packaged in a green custom box along with six logo stickers. The set checklist is given on the back of the box. The bottoms of the boxes which held the individual set boxes also contained a panel of six cards; these box bottom cards were numbered C1 through C6.

		MINT	EXC	G-VG
COMPLETE SET (44)		5.00	2.50	.50
COMMON PLAYER (1-44)		.10	.05	.01
☐ 1	George Bell	.20	.10	.02
☐ 2	Wade Boggs	.75	.35	.07
☐ 3	Bobby Bonilla	.20	.10	.02
☐ 4	Tom Brunansky	.15	.07	.01
☐ 5	Ellis Burks	.75	.35	.07
☐ 6	Jose Canseco	1.25	.60	.12
☐ 7	Joe Carter	.20	.10	.02
☐ 8	Will Clark	1.25	.60	.12
☐ 9	Roger Clemens	.60	.30	.06
☐ 10	Eric Davis	.60	.30	.06
☐ 11	Glenn Davis	.20	.10	.02
☐ 12	Andre Dawson	.25	.12	.02
☐ 13	Dennis Eckersley	.20	.10	.02
☐ 14	Andres Galarraga	.25	.12	.02
☐ 15	Dwight Gooden	.50	.25	.05
☐ 16	Pedro Guerrero	.20	.10	.02
☐ 17	Tony Gwynn	.35	.17	.03
☐ 18	Orel Hershiser	.35	.17	.03
☐ 19	Ted Higuera	.15	.07	.01
☐ 20	Pete Incaviglia	.15	.07	.01
☐ 21	Danny Jackson	.10	.05	.01
☐ 22	Doug Jennings	.15	.07	.01
☐ 23	Mark Langston	.20	.10	.02
☐ 24	Dave LaPoint	.10	.05	.01
☐ 25	Mike LaValliere	.10	.05	.01
☐ 26	Don Mattingly	1.00	.50	.10
☐ 27	Mark McGwire	.75	.35	.07
☐ 28	Dale Murphy	.35	.17	.03
☐ 29	Ken Phelps	.10	.05	.01
☐ 30	Kirby Puckett	.40	.20	.04
☐ 31	Johnny Ray	.15	.07	.01
☐ 32	Jeff Reardon	.15	.07	.01
☐ 33	Dave Righetti	.15	.07	.01
☐ 34	Cal Ripken UER (misspelled Ripkin on card front)	.30	.15	.03
☐ 35	Chris Sabo	.45	.22	.04
☐ 36	Mike Schmidt	.75	.35	.07
☐ 37	Mike Scott	.15	.07	.01
☐ 38	Kevin Seitzer	.30	.15	.03
☐ 39	Dave Stewart	.20	.10	.02
☐ 40	Darryl Strawberry	.60	.30	.06
☐ 41	Greg Swindell	.20	.10	.02
☐ 42	Frank Tanana	.10	.05	.01
☐ 43	Dave Winfield	.25	.12	.02
☐ 44	Todd Worrell	.15	.07	.01

1988 Fleer Slug/Pitch Box Cards

The cards in this 6-card set each measure the standard 2 1/2" by 3 1/2". Cards have essentially the same design as the 1988 Fleer Sluggers vs. Pitchers set of Baseball's Best. The cards were printed on the bottom of the counter display box which held 24 small boxed sets; hence theoretically these box cards are 1/24 as plentiful as the regular boxed set cards. These 6 cards, numbered C1 to C6 are considered a separate set in their own right and are not typically included in a complete set of the 1988 Fleer Sluggers vs. Pitchers set of 44. The value of the panels uncut is slightly greater, perhaps by 25% greater, than the value of the individual cards cut up carefully.

		MINT	EXC	G-VG
COMPLETE SET (6)		1.25	.60	.12
COMMON PLAYERS (C1-C6)		.10	.05	.01
☐ C1	Ron Darling (box bottom card)	.15	.07	.01
☐ C2	Rickey Henderson (box bottom card)	.60	.30	.06
☐ C3	Carney Lansford (box bottom card)	.15	.07	.01
☐ C4	Rafael Palmeiro (box bottom card)	.25	.12	.02
☐ C5	Frank Viola (box bottom card)	.25	.12	.02
☐ C6	Twins Logo (checklist back) (box bottom card)	.10	.05	.01

1988 Fleer Sticker Cards

These Star Stickers were distributed as a separate issue by Fleer, with five star stickers and a logo sticker in each wax pack. The 132-card (sticker) set features 2 1/2" by 3 1/2" full-color fronts and even statistics on the sticker back, which is an indication that the Fleer Company understands that these stickers are rarely used as stickers but more like traditional cards. The card fronts are surrounded by a silver-gray border and the backs are printed in red and black on white card stock.

		MINT	EXC	G-VG
COMPLETE SET (132)		20.00	10.00	2.00
COMMON PLAYER (1-132)		.05	.02	.00

☐	1 Mike Boddicker	.10	.05	.01
☐	2 Eddie Murray	.20	.10	.02
☐	3 Cal Ripken	.25	.12	.02
☐	4 Larry Sheets	.05	.02	.00
☐	5 Wade Boggs	1.50	.75	.15
☐	6 Ellis Burks	1.00	.50	.10
☐	7 Roger Clemens	.90	.45	.09
☐	8 Dwight Evans	.10	.05	.01
☐	9 Mike Greenwell	1.00	.50	.10
☐	10 Bruce Hurst	.10	.05	.01
☐	11 Brian Downing	.05	.02	.00
☐	12 Wally Joyner	.50	.25	.05
☐	13 Mike Witt	.10	.05	.01
☐	14 Ivan Calderon	.10	.05	.01
☐	15 Jose DeLeon	.10	.05	.01
☐	16 Ozzie Guillen	.10	.05	.01
☐	17 Bobby Thigpen	.15	.07	.01
☐	18 Joe Carter	.15	.07	.01
☐	19 Julio Franco	.15	.07	.01
☐	20 Brook Jacoby	.10	.05	.01
☐	21 Cory Snyder	.20	.10	.02
☐	22 Pat Tabler	.05	.02	.00
☐	23 Doyle Alexander	.05	.02	.00
☐	24 Kirk Gibson	.25	.12	.02
☐	25 Mike Henneman	.10	.05	.01
☐	26 Jack Morris	.15	.07	.01
☐	27 Matt Nokes	.20	.10	.02
☐	28 Walt Terrell	.05	.02	.00
☐	29 Alan Trammell	.25	.12	.02
☐	30 George Brett	.45	.22	.04
☐	31 Charlie Leibrandt	.05	.02	.00
☐	32 Bret Saberhagen	.30	.15	.03
☐	33 Kevin Seitzer	.35	.17	.03
☐	34 Danny Tartabull	.25	.12	.02
☐	35 Frank White	.10	.05	.01
☐	36 Rob Deer	.10	.05	.01
☐	37 Ted Higuera	.10	.05	.01
☐	38 Paul Molitor	.15	.07	.01
☐	39 Dan Plesac	.10	.05	.01
☐	40 Robin Yount	.45	.22	.04
☐	41 Bert Blyleven	.15	.07	.01
☐	42 Tom Brunansky	.15	.07	.01
☐	43 Gary Gaetti	.15	.07	.01
☐	44 Kent Hrbek	.20	.10	.02
☐	45 Kirby Puckett	.60	.30	.06
☐	46 Jeff Reardon	.10	.05	.01
☐	47 Frank Viola	.15	.07	.01
☐	48 Don Mattingly	2.00	1.00	.20
☐	49 Mike Pagliarulo	.10	.05	.01
☐	50 Willie Randolph	.10	.05	.01
☐	51 Rick Rhoden	.05	.02	.00
☐	52 Dave Righetti	.15	.07	.01
☐	53 Dave Winfield	.25	.12	.02
☐	54 Jose Canseco	2.00	1.00	.20
☐	55 Carney Lansford	.15	.07	.01
☐	56 Mark McGwire	1.00	.50	.10
☐	57 Dave Stewart	.15	.07	.01
☐	58 Curt Young	.05	.02	.00
☐	59 Alvin Davis	.10	.05	.01
☐	60 Mark Langston	.20	.10	.02
☐	61 Ken Phelps	.05	.02	.00
☐	62 Harold Reynolds	.05	.02	.00
☐	63 Scott Fletcher	.05	.02	.00
☐	64 Charlie Hough	.05	.02	.00
☐	65 Pete Incaviglia	.20	.10	.02
☐	66 Oddibe McDowell	.10	.05	.01
☐	67 Pete O'Brien	.10	.05	.01
☐	68 Larry Parrish	.05	.02	.00
☐	69 Ruben Sierra	.75	.35	.07
☐	70 Jesse Barfield	.15	.07	.01
☐	71 George Bell	.20	.10	.02
☐	72 Tony Fernandez	.15	.07	.01
☐	73 Tom Henke	.05	.02	.00
☐	74 Jimmy Key	.10	.05	.01
☐	75 Lloyd Moseby	.10	.05	.01
☐	76 Dion James	.05	.02	.00
☐	77 Dale Murphy	.40	.20	.04
☐	78 Zane Smith	.05	.02	.00
☐	79 Andre Dawson	.25	.12	.02
☐	80 Ryne Sandberg	.30	.15	.03
☐	81 Rick Sutcliffe	.10	.05	.01
☐	82 Kal Daniels	.15	.07	.01
☐	83 Eric Davis	.90	.45	.09
☐	84 John Franco	.10	.05	.01
☐	85 Kevin Bass	.05	.02	.00
☐	86 Glenn Davis	.15	.07	.01
☐	87 Bill Doran	.10	.05	.01
☐	88 Nolan Ryan	1.25	.60	.12
☐	89 Mike Scott	.15	.07	.01
☐	90 Dave Smith	.05	.02	.00
☐	91 Pedro Guerrero	.20	.10	.02
☐	92 Orel Hershiser	.45	.22	.04
☐	93 Steve Sax	.15	.07	.01
☐	94 Fernando Valenzuela	.15	.07	.01
☐	95 Tim Burke	.10	.05	.01
☐	96 Andres Galarraga	.25	.12	.02
☐	97 Tim Raines	.25	.12	.02
☐	98 Tim Wallach	.10	.05	.01
☐	99 Mitch Webster	.05	.02	.00
☐	100 Ron Darling	.10	.05	.01
☐	101 Sid Fernandez	.10	.05	.01
☐	102 Dwight Gooden	.50	.25	.05
☐	103 Keith Hernandez	.20	.10	.02
☐	104 Howard Johnson	.20	.10	.02
☐	105 Roger McDowell	.05	.02	.00
☐	106 Darryl Strawberry	.75	.35	.07
☐	107 Steve Bedrosian	.10	.05	.01
☐	108 Von Hayes	.10	.05	.01
☐	109 Shane Rawley	.05	.02	.00
☐	110 Juan Samuel	.15	.07	.01
☐	111 Mike Schmidt	.75	.35	.07
☐	112 Milt Thompson	.05	.02	.00
☐	113 Sid Bream	.05	.02	.00
☐	114 Bobby Bonilla	.15	.07	.01
☐	115 Mike Dunne	.05	.02	.00
☐	116 Any Van Slyke	.10	.05	.01
☐	117 Vince Coleman	.20	.10	.02
☐	118 Willie McGee	.15	.07	.01
☐	119 Terry Pendleton	.15	.07	.01
☐	120 Ozzie Smith	.15	.07	.01
☐	121 John Tudor	.10	.05	.01
☐	122 Todd Worrell	.15	.07	.01
☐	123 Tony Gwynn	.45	.22	.04
☐	124 John Kruk	.15	.07	.01
☐	125 Benito Santiago	.45	.22	.04
☐	126 Will Clark	2.00	1.00	.20
☐	127 Dave Dravecky	.15	.07	.01
☐	128 Jeff Leonard	.05	.02	.00
☐	129 Candy Maldonado	.05	.02	.00
☐	130 Rick Reuschel	.10	.05	.01
☐	131 Don Robinson	.05	.02	.00
☐	132 Checklist Card	.05	.02	.00

1988 Fleer Sticker Box Cards

The bottoms of the Star Sticker wax boxes contained two different sets of four cards done in a similar format to the stickers; these cards (they are not stickers but truly cards) are numbered with the prefix S and are considered a separate set. The value of the panels uncut is slightly greater, perhaps by 25% greater, than the value of the individual cards cut up carefully.

		MINT	EXC	G-VG
COMPLETE SET (8)		2.50	1.25	.25
COMMON PLAYER		.10	.05	.01

☐	S1 Don Baylor (wax box card)	.15	.07	.01
☐	S2 Gary Carter	.35	.17	.03

		MINT	EXC	G-VG
	(wax box card)			
☐ S3	Ron Guidry	.20	.10	.02
	(wax box card)			
☐ S4	Rickey Henderson	.60	.30	.06
	(wax box card)			
☐ S5	Kevin Mitchell	.50	.25	.05
	(wax box card)			
☐ S6	Mark McGwire and	1.00	.50	.10
	Eric Davis			
	(wax box card)			
☐ S7	Giants Logo	.10	.05	.01
	(wax box card)			
☐ S8	Detroit Logo	.10	.05	.01
	(wax box card)			

☐ 35	Kevin Seitzer	.25	.12	.02
☐ 36	Ruben Sierra	.50	.25	.05
☐ 37	Cory Snyder	.20	.10	.02
☐ 38	Darryl Strawberry	.50	.25	.05
☐ 39	Rick Sutcliffe	.10	.05	.01
☐ 40	Danny Tartabull	.20	.10	.02
☐ 41	Alan Trammell	.15	.07	.01
☐ 42	Kenny Williams	.10	.05	.01
☐ 43	Mike Witt	.10	.05	.01
☐ 44	Robin Yount	.35	.17	.03

1988 Fleer Superstars Box Cards

1988 Fleer Superstars

Fleer produced this 44-card boxed set although it was primarily distributed by McCrory, McLellan, J.J Newberry, H.L.Green, T.G.Y., and other similar stores. The set is subtitled "Fleer Superstars." Cards are standard-size, 2 1/2" by 3 1/2", and were packaged in a red, white, blue, and yellow custom box along with six logo stickers. The set checklist is given on the back of the box. The bottoms of the boxes which held the individual set boxes also contained a panel of six cards; these box bottom cards were numbered C1 through C6.

The cards in this 6-card set each measure the standard 2 1/2" by 3 1/2". Cards have essentially the same design as the 1988 Fleer Superstars set. The cards were printed on the bottom of the counter display box which held 24 small boxed sets; hence theoretically these box cards are 1/24 as plentiful as the regular boxed set cards. These 6 cards, numbered C1 to C6 are considered a separate set in their own right and are not typically included in a complete set of the 1988 Fleer Superstars set of 44. The value of the panels uncut is slightly greater, perhaps by 25% greater, than the value of the individual cards cut up carefully.

		MINT	EXC	G-VG
COMPLETE SET (44)		4.00	2.00	.40
COMMON PLAYER (1-44)		.05	.02	.00
☐ 1	Steve Bedrosian	.10	.05	.01
☐ 2	George Bell	.15	.07	.01
☐ 3	Wade Boggs	.60	.30	.06
☐ 4	Barry Bonds	.15	.07	.01
☐ 5	Jose Canseco	1.00	.50	.10
☐ 6	Joe Carter	.15	.07	.01
☐ 7	Jack Clark	.15	.07	.01
☐ 8	Will Clark	1.00	.50	.10
☐ 9	Roger Clemens	.50	.25	.05
☐ 10	Alvin Davis	.10	.05	.01
☐ 11	Eric Davis	.50	.25	.05
☐ 12	Glenn Davis	.15	.07	.01
☐ 13	Andre Dawson	.20	.10	.02
☐ 14	Dwight Gooden	.35	.17	.03
☐ 15	Orel Hershiser	.35	.17	.03
☐ 16	Teddy Higuera	.10	.05	.01
☐ 17	Kent Hrbek	.15	.07	.01
☐ 18	Wally Joyner	.25	.12	.02
☐ 19	Jimmy Key	.10	.05	.01
☐ 20	John Kruk	.10	.05	.01
☐ 21	Jeff Leonard	.05	.02	.00
☐ 22	Don Mattingly	1.00	.50	.10
☐ 23	Mark McGwire	.65	.30	.06
☐ 24	Kevin McReynolds	.15	.07	.01
☐ 25	Dale Murphy	.30	.15	.03
☐ 26	Matt Nokes	.15	.07	.01
☐ 27	Terry Pendleton	.05	.02	.00
☐ 28	Kirby Puckett	.40	.20	.04
☐ 29	Tim Raines	.20	.10	.02
☐ 30	Rick Rhoden	.05	.02	.00
☐ 31	Cal Ripken Jr.	.25	.12	.02
☐ 32	Benito Santiago	.25	.12	.02
☐ 33	Mike Schmidt	.75	.35	.07
☐ 34	Mike Scott	.15	.07	.01

		MINT	EXC	G-VG
COMPLETE SET (6)		1.50	.75	.15
COMMON PLAYER (C1-C6)		.10	.05	.01
☐ C1	Pete Incaviglia	.25	.12	.02
	(box bottom card)			
☐ C2	Rickey Henderson	.75	.35	.07
	(box bottom card)			
☐ C3	Tony Fernandez	.20	.10	.02
	(box bottom card)			
☐ C4	Shane Rawley	.10	.05	.01
	(box bottom card)			
☐ C5	Ryne Sandberg	.35	.17	.03
	(box bottom card)			
☐ C6	Cardinals Logo	.10	.05	.01
	(checklist back)			
	(box bottom card)			

1988 Fleer Team Leaders

This 44-card boxed set was produced by Fleer for exclusive distribution by Kay Bee Toys and is sometimes referred to as the Fleer Kay Bee set. Six team logo stickers are included in the box with the complete set. The numerical checklist on the back of the box shows that the set is numbered alphabetically. The cards measure 2 1/2" by 3 1/2" and have a distinctive red border on the fronts. The Kay Bee logo is printed in the lower right corner of the obverse of each card.

	MINT	EXC	G-VG
COMPLETE SET (44)	5.00	2.50	.50
COMMON PLAYER (1-44)	.10	.05	.01

		MINT	EXC	G-VG
☐ 1	George Bell	.20	.10	.02
☐ 2	Wade Boggs	.75	.35	.07
☐ 3	Jose Canseco	1.25	.60	.12
☐ 4	Will Clark	1.25	.60	.12
☐ 5	Roger Clemens	.60	.30	.06
☐ 6	Eric Davis	.60	.30	.06
☐ 7	Andre Dawson	.20	.10	.02
☐ 8	Julio Franco	.15	.07	.01
☐ 9	Andres Galarraga	.20	.10	.02
☐ 10	Dwight Gooden	.50	.25	.05
☐ 11	Tony Gwynn	.40	.20	.04
☐ 12	Tom Henke	.10	.05	.01
☐ 13	Orel Hershiser	.40	.20	.04
☐ 14	Kent Hrbek	.20	.10	.02
☐ 15	Ted Higuera	.15	.07	.01
☐ 16	Wally Joyner	.30	.15	.03
☐ 17	Jimmy Key	.10	.05	.01
☐ 18	Mark Langston	.20	.10	.02
☐ 19	Don Mattingly	1.25	.60	.12
☐ 20	Willie McGee	.15	.07	.01
☐ 21	Mark McGwire	.75	.35	.07
☐ 22	Paul Molitor	.15	.07	.01
☐ 23	Jack Morris	.15	.07	.01
☐ 24	Dale Murphy	.30	.15	.03
☐ 25	Larry Parrish	.10	.05	.01
☐ 26	Kirby Puckett	.45	.22	.04
☐ 27	Tim Raines	.20	.10	.02
☐ 28	Jeff Reardon	.10	.05	.01
☐ 29	Dave Righetti	.15	.07	.01
☐ 30	Cal Ripken	.30	.15	.03
☐ 31	Don Robinson	.10	.05	.01
☐ 32	Bret Saberhagen	.30	.15	.03
☐ 33	Juan Samuel	.15	.07	.01
☐ 34	Mike Schmidt	.75	.35	.07
☐ 35	Mike Scott	.15	.07	.01
☐ 36	Kevin Seitzer	.30	.15	.03
☐ 37	Dave Smith	.10	.05	.01
☐ 38	Ozzie Smith	.20	.10	.02
☐ 39	Zane Smith	.10	.05	.01
☐ 40	Darryl Strawberry	.60	.30	.06
☐ 41	Rick Sutcliffe	.15	.07	.01
☐ 42	Bobby Thigpen	.15	.07	.01
☐ 43	Alan Trammell	.20	.10	.02
☐ 44	Andy Van Slyke	.15	.07	.01

1988 Fleer World Series

This 12-card set of 2 1/2" by 3 1/2" cards features highlights of the previous year's World Series between the Minnesota Twins and the St. Louis Cardinals. The sets were packaged as a complete set insert with the collated sets (of the 1988 Fleer regular issue) which were sold by Fleer directly to hobby card dealers; they were not available in the general retail candy store outlets.

	MINT	EXC	G-VG
COMPLETE SET (12)	4.00	2.00	.40
COMMON PLAYER (1-12)	.25	.12	.02

		MINT	EXC	G-VG
☐ 1	Dan Gladden	.25	.12	.02

		MINT	EXC	G-VG
☐ 2	Randy Bush Cardinals "Bush" Wacked	.25	.12	.02
☐ 3	John Tudor Masterful Performance in Game 3	.35	.17	.03
☐ 4	Ozzie Smith The Wizard	.75	.35	.07
☐ 5	Todd Worrell and Tony Pena Throw Smoke	.25	.12	.02
☐ 6	Vince Coleman Cardinal Attack	.50	.25	.05
☐ 7	Tom Herr/Dan Driessen Herr's Wallop	.25	.12	.02
☐ 8	Kirby Puckett Kirby's Bat Comes Alive	.90	.45	.09
☐ 9	Kent Hrbek Hrbek's Slam Forces Game 7	.50	.25	.05
☐ 10	Tom Herr Out at First	.25	.12	.02
☐ 11	Don Baylor Game 7's Play At The Plate	.25	.12	.02
☐ 12	Frank Viola Series MVP, 16 K's	.60	.30	.06

1989 Fleer

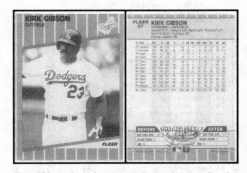

This 660-card set features a distinctive gray border background with white and yellow trim. The backs are printed in gray, black, and yellow on white card stock. The bottom of the card back shows an innovative breakdown of the player's demonstrated ability with respect to his performance before and after the All-Star break. Cards are numbered on the back and are again the standard 2 1/2" by 3 1/2". Cards are again organized numerically by teams and alphabetically within teams: Oakland A's (1-26), New York Mets (27-52), Los Angeles Dodgers (53-77), Boston Red Sox (78-101), Minnesota Twins (102-127), Detroit Tigers (128- 151), Cincinnati Reds (152-175), Milwaukee Brewers (176- 200),

Pittsburgh Pirates (201-224), Toronto Blue Jays (225- 248), New York Yankees (249-274), Kansas City Royals (275- 298), San Diego Padres (299-322), San Francisco Giants (323- 347), Houston Astros (348-370), Montreal Expos (371-395), Cleveland Indians (396-417), Chicago Cubs (418-442), St. Louis Cardinals (443-466), California Angels (467-490), Chicago White Sox (491-513), Texas Rangers (514-537), Seattle Mariners (538-561), Philadelphia Phillies (562-584), Atlanta Braves (585-605), and Baltimore Orioles (606-627). However pairs 148/149, 153/154, 272/273, 283/284, and 367/368 were apparently mis-alphabetized by Fleer. The last 33 cards in the set consist of Specials (628-639), Rookie Pairs (640-653), and checklists (654-660). Due to the early beginning of production of this set, it seems Fleer "presumed" that the A's would win the World Series since they are listed as the first team in the numerical order; in fact, Fleer had the Mets over the underdog (but eventual World Champion) Dodgers as well. Approximately half of the California Angels players have white rather than yellow halos. Certain Oakland A's player cards have red instead of green lines for front photo borders. Checklist cards are available either with or without positions listed for each player. Fleer also produced a "limited" edition version of this set with glossy coating and packaged in a "tin." However this tin set was apparently not limited enough (estimated between 30,000 and 45,000 1989 tin sets produced by Fleer) since the price of the "tin" glossy cards is now only double the price of the regular set.

		MINT	EXC	G-VG
COMPLETE SET (660)		30.00	15.00	3.00
COMMON PLAYER (1-660)		.03	.01	.00

			MINT	EXC	G-VG
☐	1	Don Baylor	.10	.02	.01
☐	2	Lance Blankenship	.25	.12	.02
☐	3	Todd Burns UER (wrong birthdate; before/after All-Star stats missing)	.35	.17	.03
☐	4	Greg Cadaret (All-Star Break stats show 3 losses, should be 2)	.10	.05	.01
☐	5	Jose Canseco	1.25	.60	.12
☐	6	Storm Davis	.06	.03	.00
☐	7	Dennis Eckersley	.10	.05	.01
☐	8	Mike Gallego	.03	.01	.00
☐	9	Ron Hassey	.03	.01	.00
☐	10	Dave Henderson	.06	.03	.00
☐	11	Rick Honeycutt	.03	.01	.00
☐	12	Glenn Hubbard	.03	.01	.00
☐	13	Stan Javier	.03	.01	.00
☐	14	Doug Jennings	.25	.12	.02
☐	15	Felix Jose	.30	.15	.03
☐	16	Carney Lansford	.08	.04	.01
☐	17	Mark McGwire	.60	.30	.06
☐	18	Gene Nelson	.03	.01	.00
☐	19	Dave Parker	.08	.04	.01
☐	20	Eric Plunk	.03	.01	.00
☐	21	Luis Polonia	.03	.01	.00
☐	22	Terry Steinbach	.08	.04	.01
☐	23	Dave Stewart	.10	.05	.01
☐	24	Walt Weiss	.25	.12	.02
☐	25	Bob Welch	.06	.03	.00
☐	26	Curt Young	.03	.01	.00
☐	27	Rick Aguilera	.03	.01	.00
☐	28	Wally Backman	.03	.01	.00
☐	29	Mark Carreon UER (after All-Star Break batting 7.14)	.03	.01	.00
☐	30	Gary Carter	.12	.06	.01
☐	31	David Cone	.20	.10	.02
☐	32	Ron Darling	.08	.04	.01
☐	33	Len Dykstra	.06	.03	.00
☐	34	Kevin Elster	.06	.03	.00
☐	35	Sid Fernandez	.08	.04	.01
☐	36	Dwight Gooden	.30	.15	.03
☐	37	Keith Hernandez	.12	.06	.01
☐	38	Gregg Jefferies	1.50	.75	.15
☐	39	Howard Johnson	.15	.07	.01

			MINT	EXC	G-VG
☐	40	Terry Leach	.06	.03	.00
☐	41	Dave Magadan UER (bio says 15 doubles, should be 13)	.08	.04	.01
☐	42	Bob McClure	.03	.01	.00
☐	43	Roger McDowell UER (led Mets with 58, should be 62)	.06	.03	.00
☐	44	Kevin McReynolds	.12	.06	.01
☐	45	Keith Miller	.03	.01	.00
		New York Mets			
☐	46	Randy Myers	.08	.04	.01
☐	47	Bob Ojeda	.06	.03	.00
☐	48	Mackey Sasser	.12	.06	.01
☐	49	Darryl Strawberry	.40	.20	.04
☐	50	Tim Teufel	.03	.01	.00
☐	51	Dave West	.40	.20	.04
☐	52	Mookie Wilson	.06	.03	.00
☐	53	Dave Anderson	.03	.01	.00
☐	54	Tim Belcher	.12	.06	.01
☐	55	Mike Davis	.03	.01	.00
☐	56	Mike Devereaux	.06	.03	.00
☐	57	Kirk Gibson	.15	.07	.01
☐	58	Alfredo Griffin	.03	.01	.00
☐	59	Chris Gwynn	.06	.03	.00
☐	60	Jeff Hamilton	.03	.01	.00
☐	61A	Danny Heep (Home: Lake Hills)	.90	.45	.09
☐	61B	Danny Heep (Home: San Antonio)	.15	.07	.01
☐	62	Orel Hershiser	.25	.12	.02
☐	63	Brian Holton	.03	.01	.00
☐	64	Jay Howell	.03	.01	.00
☐	65	Tim Leary	.06	.03	.00
☐	66	Mike Marshall	.08	.04	.01
☐	67	Ramon Martinez	.45	.22	.04
☐	68	Jesse Orosco	.03	.01	.00
☐	69	Alejandro Pena	.03	.01	.00
☐	70	Steve Sax	.10	.05	.01
☐	71	Mike Scioscia	.03	.01	.00
☐	72	Mike Sharperson	.03	.01	.00
☐	73	John Shelby	.03	.01	.00
☐	74	Franklin Stubbs	.03	.01	.00
☐	75	John Tudor	.08	.04	.01
☐	76	Fernando Valenzuela	.12	.06	.01
☐	77	Tracy Woodson	.10	.05	.01
☐	78	Marty Barrett	.03	.01	.00
☐	79	Todd Benzinger	.03	.01	.00
☐	80	Mike Boddicker UER (Rochester in '76, should be '78)	.03	.01	.00
☐	81	Wade Boggs	.60	.30	.06
☐	82	"Oil Can" Boyd	.03	.01	.00
☐	83	Ellis Burks	.35	.17	.03
☐	84	Rick Cerone	.03	.01	.00
☐	85	Roger Clemens	.30	.15	.03
☐	86	Steve Curry	.10	.05	.01
☐	87	Dwight Evans	.08	.04	.01
☐	88	Wes Gardner	.03	.01	.00
☐	89	Rich Gedman	.03	.01	.00
☐	90	Mike Greenwell	.90	.45	.09
☐	91	Bruce Hurst	.10	.05	.01
☐	92	Dennis Lamp	.03	.01	.00
☐	93	Spike Owen	.03	.01	.00
☐	94	Larry Parrish UER (before All-Star Break batting 1.90)	.03	.01	.00
☐	95	Carlos Quintana	.35	.17	.03
☐	96	Jody Reed	.06	.03	.00
☐	97	Jim Rice	.10	.05	.01
☐	98A	Kevin Romine ERR (photo actually Randy Kutcher batting)	.80	.40	.08
☐	98B	Kevin Romine COR (arms folded)	.40	.20	.04
☐	99	Lee Smith	.06	.03	.00
☐	100	Mike Smithson	.03	.01	.00
☐	101	Bob Stanley	.03	.01	.00
☐	102	Allan Anderson	.06	.03	.00
☐	103	Keith Atherton	.03	.01	.00
☐	104	Juan Berenguer	.03	.01	.00
☐	105	Bert Blyleven	.08	.04	.01
☐	106	Eric Bullock UER (Bats/Throws Right, should be Left)	.12	.06	.01
☐	107	Randy Bush	.03	.01	.00
☐	108	John Christensen	.03	.01	.00
☐	109	Mark Davidson	.03	.01	.00
☐	110	Gary Gaetti	.08	.04	.01
☐	111	Greg Gagne	.03	.01	.00
☐	112	Dan Gladden	.03	.01	.00
☐	113	German Gonzalez	.08	.04	.01
☐	114	Brian Harper	.03	.01	.00
☐	115	Tom Herr	.03	.01	.00
☐	116	Kent Hrbek	.10	.05	.01

☐ 117	Gene Larkin	.06	.03	.00
☐ 118	Tim Laudner	.03	.01	.00
☐ 119	Charlie Lea	.03	.01	.00
☐ 120	Steve Lombardozzi	.03	.01	.00
☐ 121A	John Moses (Home: Tempe)	.90	.45	.09
☐ 121B	John Moses (Home: Phoenix)	.15	.07	.01
☐ 122	Al Newman	.03	.01	.00
☐ 123	Mark Portugal	.03	.01	.00
☐ 124	Kirby Puckett	.35	.17	.03
☐ 125	Jeff Reardon	.08	.04	.01
☐ 126	Fred Toliver	.03	.01	.00
☐ 127	Frank Viola	.15	.07	.01
☐ 128	Doyle Alexander	.03	.01	.00
☐ 129	Dave Bergman	.03	.01	.00
☐ 130A	Tom Brookens ERR (Mike Heath back)	2.00	1.00	.20
☐ 130B	Tom Brookens COR	.15	.07	.01
☐ 131	Paul Gibson	.10	.05	.01
☐ 132A	Mike Heath ERR (Tom Brookens back)	2.00	1.00	.20
☐ 132B	Mike Heath COR	.15	.07	.01
☐ 133	Don Heinkel	.08	.04	.01
☐ 134	Mike Henneman	.03	.01	.00
☐ 135	Guillermo Hernandez	.06	.03	.00
☐ 136	Eric King	.03	.01	.00
☐ 137	Chet Lemon	.03	.01	.00
☐ 138	Fred Lynn UER ('74, '75 stats missing)	.10	.05	.01
☐ 139	Jack Morris	.10	.05	.01
☐ 140	Matt Nokes	.10	.05	.01
☐ 141	Gary Pettis	.03	.01	.00
☐ 142	Ted Power	.03	.01	.00
☐ 143	Jeff M. Robinson Detroit Tigers	.08	.04	.01
☐ 144	Luis Salazar	.03	.01	.00
☐ 145	Steve Searcy	.25	.12	.02
☐ 146	Pat Sheridan	.03	.01	.00
☐ 147	Frank Tanana	.03	.01	.00
☐ 148	Alan Trammell	.15	.07	.01
☐ 149	Walt Terrell	.03	.01	.00
☐ 150	Jim Walewander	.10	.05	.01
☐ 151	Lou Whitaker	.08	.04	.01
☐ 152	Tim Birtsas	.03	.01	.00
☐ 153	Tom Browning	.08	.04	.01
☐ 154	Keith Brown	.10	.05	.01
☐ 155	Norm Charlton	.15	.07	.01
☐ 156	Dave Concepcion	.08	.04	.01
☐ 157	Kal Daniels	.08	.04	.01
☐ 158	Eric Davis	.35	.17	.03
☐ 159	Bo Diaz	.03	.01	.00
☐ 160	Rob Dibble	.30	.15	.03
☐ 161	Nick Esasky	.08	.04	.01
☐ 162	John Franco	.08	.04	.01
☐ 163	Danny Jackson	.08	.04	.01
☐ 164	Barry Larkin	.15	.07	.01
☐ 165	Rob Murphy	.03	.01	.00
☐ 166	Paul O'Neill	.08	.04	.01
☐ 167	Jeff Reed	.03	.01	.00
☐ 168	Jose Rijo	.03	.01	.00
☐ 169	Ron Robinson	.03	.01	.00
☐ 170	Chris Sabo	.60	.30	.06
☐ 171	Candy Sierra	.10	.05	.01
☐ 172	Van Snider	.25	.12	.02
☐ 173A	Jeff Treadway (target registration mark above head on front in light blue)	10.00	4.50	.75
☐ 173B	Jeff Treadway (no target on front)	.10	.05	.01
☐ 174	Frank Williams (after All-Star Break stats are jumbled)	.03	.01	.00
☐ 175	Herm Winningham	.03	.01	.00
☐ 176	Jim Adduci	.03	.01	.00
☐ 177	Don August	.06	.03	.00
☐ 178	Mike Birkbeck	.03	.01	.00
☐ 179	Chris Bosio	.06	.03	.00
☐ 180	Glenn Braggs	.06	.03	.00
☐ 181	Greg Brock	.03	.01	.00
☐ 182	Mark Clear	.03	.01	.00
☐ 183	Chuck Crim	.03	.01	.00
☐ 184	Rob Deer	.06	.03	.00
☐ 185	Tom Filer	.03	.01	.00
☐ 186	Jim Gantner	.03	.01	.00
☐ 187	Darryl Hamilton	.25	.12	.02
☐ 188	Ted Higuera	.06	.03	.00
☐ 189	Odell Jones	.03	.01	.00
☐ 190	Jeffrey Leonard	.06	.03	.00
☐ 191	Joey Meyer	.06	.03	.00
☐ 192	Paul Mirabella	.03	.01	.00
☐ 193	Paul Molitor	.10	.05	.01
☐ 194	Charlie O'Brien	.10	.05	.01
☐ 195	Dan Plesac	.06	.03	.00
☐ 196	Gary Sheffield	1.50	.75	.15
☐ 197	B.J. Surhoff	.08	.04	.01
☐ 198	Dale Sveum	.03	.01	.00
☐ 199	Bill Wegman	.03	.01	.00
☐ 200	Robin Yount	.18	.09	.01
☐ 201	Rafael Belliard	.03	.01	.00
☐ 202	Barry Bonds	.10	.05	.01
☐ 203	Bobby Bonilla	.10	.05	.01
☐ 204	Sid Bream	.03	.01	.00
☐ 205	Benny Distefano	.03	.01	.00
☐ 206	Doug Drabek	.06	.03	.00
☐ 207	Mike Dunne	.06	.03	.00
☐ 208	Felix Fermin	.03	.01	.00
☐ 209	Brian Fisher	.03	.01	.00
☐ 210	Jim Gott	.03	.01	.00
☐ 211	Bob Kipper	.03	.01	.00
☐ 212	Dave LaPoint	.03	.01	.00
☐ 213	Mike LaValliere	.03	.01	.00
☐ 214	Jose Lind	.03	.01	.00
☐ 215	Junior Ortiz	.03	.01	.00
☐ 216	Vicente Palacios	.03	.01	.00
☐ 217	Tom Prince	.08	.04	.01
☐ 218	Gary Redus	.03	.01	.00
☐ 219	R.J. Reynolds	.03	.01	.00
☐ 220	Jeff Robinson Pittsburgh Pirates	.06	.03	.00
☐ 221	John Smiley	.06	.03	.00
☐ 222	Andy Van Slyke	.10	.05	.01
☐ 223	Bob Walk	.03	.01	.00
☐ 224	Glenn Wilson	.03	.01	.00
☐ 225	Jesse Barfield	.08	.04	.01
☐ 226	George Bell	.12	.06	.01
☐ 227	Pat Borders	.12	.06	.01
☐ 228	John Cerutti	.03	.01	.00
☐ 229	Jim Clancy	.03	.01	.00
☐ 230	Mark Eichhorn	.03	.01	.00
☐ 231	Tony Fernandez	.10	.05	.01
☐ 232	Cecil Fielder	.03	.01	.00
☐ 233	Mike Flanagan	.03	.01	.00
☐ 234	Kelly Gruber	.06	.03	.00
☐ 235	Tom Henke	.06	.03	.00
☐ 236	Jimmy Key	.06	.03	.00
☐ 237	Rick Leach	.03	.01	.00
☐ 238	Manny Lee UER (bio says regular shortstop, what about Tony Fernandez?)	.03	.01	.00
☐ 239	Nelson Liriano	.03	.01	.00
☐ 240	Fred McGriff	.20	.10	.02
☐ 241	Lloyd Moseby	.06	.03	.00
☐ 242	Rance Mulliniks	.03	.01	.00
☐ 243	Jeff Musselman	.03	.01	.00
☐ 244	Dave Stieb	.08	.04	.01
☐ 245	Todd Stottlemyre	.15	.07	.01
☐ 246	Duane Ward	.03	.01	.00
☐ 247	David Wells	.08	.04	.01
☐ 248	Ernie Whitt UER (HR total 21, should be 121)	.03	.01	.00
☐ 249	Luis Aguayo	.03	.01	.00
☐ 250A	Neil Allen (Home: Sarasota, FL)	2.00	1.00	.20
☐ 250B	Neil Allen (Home: Syosset, NY)	.25	.12	.02
☐ 251	John Candelaria	.06	.03	.00
☐ 252	Jack Clark	.12	.06	.01
☐ 253	Richard Dotson	.03	.01	.00
☐ 254	Rickey Henderson	.25	.12	.02
☐ 255	Tommy John	.10	.05	.01
☐ 256	Roberto Kelly	.20	.10	.02
☐ 257	Al Leiter	.15	.07	.01
☐ 258	Don Mattingly	1.00	.50	.10
☐ 259	Dale Mohorcic	.03	.01	.00
☐ 260	Hal Morris	.20	.10	.02
☐ 261	Scott Nielsen	.03	.01	.00
☐ 262	Mike Pagliarulo UER (wrong birthdate)	.06	.03	.00
☐ 263	Hipolito Pena	.12	.06	.01
☐ 264	Ken Phelps	.06	.03	.00
☐ 265	Willie Randolph	.06	.03	.00
☐ 266	Rick Rhoden	.03	.01	.00
☐ 267	Dave Righetti	.08	.04	.01
☐ 268	Rafael Santana	.03	.01	.00
☐ 269	Steve Shields	.03	.01	.00
☐ 270	Joel Skinner	.03	.01	.00
☐ 271	Don Slaught	.03	.01	.00
☐ 272	Claudell Washington	.06	.03	.00
☐ 273	Gary Ward	.03	.01	.00
☐ 274	Dave Winfield	.15	.07	.01
☐ 275	Luis Aquino	.03	.01	.00
☐ 276	Floyd Bannister	.03	.01	.00
☐ 277	George Brett	.20	.10	.02
☐ 278	Bill Buckner	.06	.03	.00
☐ 279	Nick Capra	.08	.04	.01
☐ 280	Jose DeJesus	.08	.04	.01

☐ 281	Steve Farr	.03	.01	.00
☐ 282	Jerry Don Gleaton	.03	.01	.00
☐ 283	Mark Gubicza	.08	.04	.01
☐ 284	Tom Gordon UER	1.25	.60	.12
	(16.2 innings in '88, should be 15.2)			
☐ 285	Bo Jackson	.90	.45	.09
☐ 286	Charlie Leibrandt	.03	.01	.00
☐ 287	Mike Macfarlane	.15	.07	.01
☐ 288	Jeff Montgomery	.08	.04	.01
☐ 289	Bill Pecota UER	.03	.01	.00
	(photo actually Brad Wellman)			
☐ 290	Jamie Quirk	.03	.01	.00
☐ 291	Bret Saberhagen	.15	.07	.01
☐ 292	Kevin Seitzer	.15	.07	.01
☐ 293	Kurt Stillwell	.03	.01	.00
☐ 294	Pat Tabler	.06	.03	.00
☐ 295	Danny Tartabull	.10	.05	.01
☐ 296	Gary Thurman	.03	.01	.00
☐ 297	Frank White	.06	.03	.00
☐ 298	Willie Wilson	.06	.03	.00
☐ 299	Roberto Alomar	.40	.20	.04
☐ 300	Sandy Alomar Jr. UER	1.50	.75	.15
	(wrong birthdate)			
☐ 301	Chris Brown	.03	.01	.00
☐ 302	Mike Brumley UER	.08	.04	.01
	(133 hits in '88, should be 134)			
☐ 303	Mark Davis	.12	.06	.01
☐ 304	Mark Grant	.03	.01	.00
☐ 305	Tony Gwynn	.25	.12	.02
☐ 306	Greg W. Harris San Diego Padres	.20	.10	.02
☐ 307	Andy Hawkins	.03	.01	.00
☐ 308	Jimmy Jones	.06	.03	.00
☐ 309	John Kruk	.06	.03	.00
☐ 310	Dave Leiper	.03	.01	.00
☐ 311	Carmelo Martinez	.03	.01	.00
☐ 312	Lance McCullers	.06	.03	.00
☐ 313	Keith Moreland	.03	.01	.00
☐ 314	Dennis Rasmussen	.06	.03	.00
☐ 315	Randy Ready UER	.03	.01	.00
	(1214 games in '88, should be 114)			
☐ 316	Benito Santiago	.18	.09	.01
☐ 317	Eric Show	.03	.01	.00
☐ 318	Todd Simmons	.06	.03	.00
☐ 319	Garry Templeton	.06	.03	.00
☐ 320	Dickie Thon	.03	.01	.00
☐ 321	Ed Whitson	.03	.01	.00
☐ 322	Marvell Wynne	.03	.01	.00
☐ 323	Mike Aldrete	.03	.01	.00
☐ 324	Brett Butler	.06	.03	.00
☐ 325	Will Clark UER	1.00	.50	.10
	(three consecutive 100 RBI seasons)			
☐ 326	Kelly Downs UER	.06	.03	.00
	('88 stats missing)			
☐ 327	Dave Dravecky	.08	.04	.01
☐ 328	Scott Garrelts	.06	.03	.00
☐ 329	Atlee Hammaker	.03	.01	.00
☐ 330	Charlie Hayes	.30	.15	.03
☐ 331	Mike Krukow	.03	.01	.00
☐ 332	Craig Lefferts	.06	.03	.00
☐ 333	Candy Maldonado	.06	.03	.00
☐ 334	Kirt Manwaring UER	.03	.01	.00
	(Bats Rights)			
☐ 335	Bob Melvin	.03	.01	.00
☐ 336	Kevin Mitchell	.40	.20	.04
☐ 337	Donell Nixon	.03	.01	.00
☐ 338	Tony Perezchica	.12	.06	.01
☐ 339	Joe Price	.03	.01	.00
☐ 340	Rick Reuschel	.06	.03	.00
☐ 341	Earnest Riles	.03	.01	.00
☐ 342	Don Robinson	.03	.01	.00
☐ 343	Chris Speier	.03	.01	.00
☐ 344	Robby Thompson UER	.03	.01	.00
	(West Plam Beach)			
☐ 345	Jose Uribe	.03	.01	.00
☐ 346	Matt Williams	.30	.15	.03
☐ 347	Trevor Wilson	.15	.07	.01
☐ 348	Juan Agosto	.03	.01	.00
☐ 349	Larry Andersen	.03	.01	.00
☐ 350A	Alan Ashby ERR	3.00	1.50	.30
	(Throws Rig)			
☐ 350B	Alan Ashby COR	.06	.03	.00
☐ 351	Kevin Bass	.06	.03	.00
☐ 352	Buddy Bell	.06	.03	.00
☐ 353	Craig Biggio	.75	.35	.07
☐ 354	Danny Darwin	.03	.01	.00
☐ 355	Glenn Davis	.10	.05	.01
☐ 356	Jim Deshaies	.03	.01	.00
☐ 357	Bill Doran	.06	.03	.00
☐ 358	John Fishel	.10	.05	.01
☐ 359	Billy Hatcher	.03	.01	.00
☐ 360	Bob Knepper	.03	.01	.00
☐ 361	Louie Meadows UER	.08	.04	.01
	(bio says 10 EBH's and 6 SB's in '88, should be 3 and 4)			
☐ 362	Dave Meads	.03	.01	.00
☐ 363	Jim Pankovits	.03	.01	.00
☐ 364	Terry Puhl	.03	.01	.00
☐ 365	Rafael Ramirez	.03	.01	.00
☐ 366	Craig Reynolds	.03	.01	.00
☐ 367	Mike Scott	.12	.06	.01
	(card # listed as 368 on Astros CL)			
☐ 368	Nolan Ryan	.35	.17	.03
	(card # listed as 367 on Astros CL)			
☐ 369	Dave Smith	.03	.01	.00
☐ 370	Gerald Young	.06	.03	.00
☐ 371	Hubie Brooks	.06	.03	.00
☐ 372	Tim Burke	.06	.03	.00
☐ 373	John Dopson	.25	.12	.02
☐ 374	Mike Fitzgerald Montreal Expos	.03	.01	.00
☐ 375	Tom Foley	.03	.01	.00
☐ 376	Andres Galarraga UER	.12	.06	.01
	(Home: Caracus)			
☐ 377	Neal Heaton	.03	.01	.00
☐ 378	Joe Hesketh	.03	.01	.00
☐ 379	Brian Holman	.15	.07	.01
☐ 380	Rex Hudler	.03	.01	.00
☐ 381	Randy Johnson UER	.25	.12	.02
	(innings for '85 and '86 shown as 27 and 120, should be 27.1 and 119.2)			
☐ 382	Wallace Johnson	.03	.01	.00
☐ 383	Tracy Jones	.03	.01	.00
☐ 384	Dave Martinez	.03	.01	.00
☐ 385	Dennis Martinez	.06	.03	.00
☐ 386	Andy McGaffigan	.03	.01	.00
☐ 387	Otis Nixon	.03	.01	.00
☐ 388	Johnny Paredes	.10	.05	.01
☐ 389	Jeff Parrett	.10	.05	.01
☐ 390	Pascual Perez	.08	.04	.01
☐ 391	Tim Raines	.15	.07	.01
☐ 392	Luis Rivera	.03	.01	.00
☐ 393	Nelson Santovenia	.25	.12	.02
☐ 394	Bryn Smith	.06	.03	.00
☐ 395	Tim Wallach	.08	.04	.01
☐ 396	Andy Allanson UER	.03	.01	.00
	(1214 hits in '88, should be 114)			
☐ 397	Rod Allen	.15	.07	.01
☐ 398	Scott Bailes	.03	.01	.00
☐ 399	Tom Candiotti	.03	.01	.00
☐ 400	Joe Carter	.12	.06	.01
☐ 401	Carmen Castillo UER	.03	.01	.00
	(after All-Star Break batting 2.50)			
☐ 402	Dave Clark UER	.08	.04	.01
	(card front shows position as Rookie; after All-Star Break batting 3.14)			
☐ 403	John Farrell UER	.03	.01	.00
	(typo in runs allowed in '88)			
☐ 404	Julio Franco	.08	.04	.01
☐ 405	Don Gordon	.08	.04	.01
☐ 406	Mel Hall	.06	.03	.00
☐ 407	Brad Havens	.03	.01	.00
☐ 408	Brook Jacoby	.06	.03	.00
☐ 409	Doug Jones	.06	.03	.00
☐ 410	Jeff Kaiser	.10	.05	.01
☐ 411	Luis Medina	.30	.15	.03
☐ 412	Cory Snyder	.10	.05	.01
☐ 413	Greg Swindell	.10	.05	.01
☐ 414	Ron Tingley UER	.10	.05	.01
	(hit HR in first ML at-bat, should be first AL at-bat)			
☐ 415	Willie Upshaw	.03	.01	.00
☐ 416	Ron Washington	.03	.01	.00
☐ 417	Rich Yett	.03	.01	.00
☐ 418	Damon Berryhill	.10	.05	.01
☐ 419	Mike Bielecki	.06	.03	.00
☐ 420	Doug Dascenzo	.15	.07	.01
☐ 421	Jody Davis UER	.03	.01	.00
	(Braves stats for '88 missing)			
☐ 422	Andre Dawson	.12	.06	.01
☐ 423	Frank DiPino	.03	.01	.00
☐ 424	Shawon Dunston	.08	.04	.01
☐ 425	Goose Gossage	.08	.04	.01

☐ 426	Mark Grace UER (Minor League stats for '88 missing)	2.00	1.00	.20
☐ 427	Mike Harkey	.30	.15	.03
☐ 428	Darrin Jackson	.08	.04	.01
☐ 429	Les Lancaster	.03	.01	.00
☐ 430	Vance Law	.03	.01	.00
☐ 431	Greg Maddux	.12	.06	.01
☐ 432	Jamie Moyer	.03	.01	.00
☐ 433	Al Nipper	.03	.01	.00
☐ 434	Rafael Palmeiro UER (170 hits in '88, should be 178)	.12	.06	.01
☐ 435	Pat Perry	.03	.01	.00
☐ 436	Jeff Pico	.10	.05	.01
☐ 437	Ryne Sandberg	.15	.07	.01
☐ 438	Calvin Schiraldi	.03	.01	.00
☐ 439	Rick Sutcliffe	.08	.04	.01
☐ 440A	Manny Trillo ERR (Throws Rig)	3.00	1.50	.30
☐ 440B	Manny Trillo COR	.06	.03	.00
☐ 441	Gary Varsho UER (wrong birthdate; .303 should be .302; 11/28 should be 9/19)	.15	.07	.01
☐ 442	Mitch Webster	.03	.01	.00
☐ 443	Luis Alicea	.10	.05	.01
☐ 444	Tom Brunansky	.08	.04	.01
☐ 445	Vince Coleman UER (third straight with 83, should be fourth straight with 81)	.12	.06	.01
☐ 446	John Costello	.12	.06	.01
☐ 447	Danny Cox	.03	.01	.00
☐ 448	Ken Dayley	.03	.01	.00
☐ 449	Jose DeLeon	.06	.03	.00
☐ 450	Curt Ford	.03	.01	.00
☐ 451	Pedro Guerrero	.10	.05	.01
☐ 452	Bob Horner	.08	.04	.01
☐ 453	Tim Jones	.10	.05	.01
☐ 454	Steve Lake	.03	.01	.00
☐ 455	Joe Magrane UER (Des Moines, IO)	.08	.04	.01
☐ 456	Greg Mathews	.03	.01	.00
☐ 457	Willie McGee	.08	.04	.00
☐ 458	Larry McWilliams	.03	.01	.00
☐ 459	Jose Oquendo	.03	.01	.00
☐ 460	Tony Pena	.06	.03	.00
☐ 461	Terry Pendleton	.03	.01	.00
☐ 462	Steve Peters	.10	.05	.01
☐ 463	Ozzie Smith	.12	.06	.01
☐ 464	Scott Terry	.03	.01	.00
☐ 465	Denny Walling	.03	.01	.00
☐ 466	Todd Worrell	.08	.04	.01
☐ 467	Tony Armas UER (before All-Star Break batting 2.39)	.06	.03	.00
☐ 468	Dante Bichette	.20	.10	.02
☐ 469	Bob Boone	.08	.04	.01
☐ 470	Terry Clark	.12	.06	.01
☐ 471	Stew Cliburn	.03	.01	.00
☐ 472	Mike Cook UER (TM near Angels logo missing from front)	.10	.05	.01
☐ 473	Sherman Corbett	.10	.05	.01
☐ 474	Chili Davis	.06	.03	.00
☐ 475	Brian Downing	.03	.01	.00
☐ 476	Jim Eppard	.03	.01	.00
☐ 477	Chuck Finley	.06	.03	.00
☐ 478	Willie Fraser	.03	.01	.00
☐ 479	Bryan Harvey (ML record shows 0-0, should be 7-5)	.20	.10	.02
☐ 480	Jack Howell	.03	.01	.00
☐ 481	Wally Joyner UER (Yorba Linda, GA)	.20	.10	.02
☐ 482	Jack Lazorko	.03	.01	.00
☐ 483	Kirk McCaskill	.03	.01	.00
☐ 484	Mark McLemore	.03	.01	.00
☐ 485	Greg Minton	.03	.01	.00
☐ 486	Dan Petry	.03	.01	.00
☐ 487	Johnny Ray	.06	.03	.00
☐ 488	Dick Schofield	.03	.01	.00
☐ 489	Devon White	.10	.05	.01
☐ 490	Mike Witt	.06	.03	.00
☐ 491	Harold Baines	.08	.04	.01
☐ 492	Daryl Boston	.03	.01	.00
☐ 493	Ivan Calderon UER ('80 stats shifted)	.08	.04	.01
☐ 494	Mike Diaz	.03	.01	.00
☐ 495	Carlton Fisk	.10	.05	.01
☐ 496	Dave Gallagher	.25	.12	.02
☐ 497	Ozzie Guillen	.06	.03	.00
☐ 498	Shawn Hillegas	.03	.01	.00
☐ 499	Lance Johnson	.03	.01	.00
☐ 500	Barry Jones	.03	.01	.00
☐ 501	Bill Long	.03	.01	.00
☐ 502	Steve Lyons	.03	.01	.00
☐ 503	Fred Manrique	.03	.01	.00
☐ 504	Jack McDowell	.08	.04	.01
☐ 505	Donn Pall	.08	.04	.01
☐ 506	Kelly Paris	.03	.01	.00
☐ 507	Dan Pasqua	.03	.01	.00
☐ 508	Ken Patterson	.10	.05	.01
☐ 509	Melido Perez	.08	.04	.01
☐ 510	Jerry Reuss	.03	.01	.00
☐ 511	Mark Salas	.03	.01	.00
☐ 512	Bobby Thigpen UER ('86 ERA 4.69, should be 4.68)	.06	.03	.00
☐ 513	Mike Woodard	.03	.01	.00
☐ 514	Bob Brower	.03	.01	.00
☐ 515	Steve Buechele	.03	.01	.00
☐ 516	Jose Cecena	.08	.04	.01
☐ 517	Cecil Espy	.08	.04	.01
☐ 518	Scott Fletcher	.03	.01	.00
☐ 519	Cecilio Guante ('87 Yankee stats are off-centered)	.03	.01	.00
☐ 520	Jose Guzman	.03	.01	.00
☐ 521	Ray Hayward	.06	.03	.00
☐ 522	Charlie Hough	.03	.01	.00
☐ 523	Pete Incaviglia	.10	.05	.01
☐ 524	Mike Jeffcoat	.03	.01	.00
☐ 525	Paul Kilgus	.03	.01	.00
☐ 526	Chad Kreuter	.15	.07	.01
☐ 527	Jeff Kunkel	.03	.01	.00
☐ 528	Oddibe McDowell	.06	.03	.00
☐ 529	Pete O'Brien	.06	.03	.00
☐ 530	Geno Petralli	.03	.01	.00
☐ 531	Jeff Russell	.06	.03	.00
☐ 532	Ruben Sierra	.30	.15	.03
☐ 533	Mike Stanley	.03	.01	.00
☐ 534A	Ed VandeBerg ERR (Throws Lef)	3.00	1.50	.30
☐ 534B	Ed VandeBerg COR	.06	.03	.00
☐ 535	Curtis Wilkerson ERR (pitcher headings at bottom)	.06	.03	.00
☐ 536	Mitch Williams	.08	.04	.01
☐ 537	Bobby Witt UER ('85 ERA .643, should be 6.43)	.06	.03	.00
☐ 538	Steve Balboni	.03	.01	.00
☐ 539	Scott Bankhead	.06	.03	.00
☐ 540	Scott Bradley	.03	.01	.00
☐ 541	Mickey Brantley	.06	.03	.00
☐ 542	Jay Buhner	.20	.10	.02
☐ 543	Mike Campbell	.03	.01	.00
☐ 544	Darnell Coles	.03	.01	.00
☐ 545	Henry Cotto	.03	.01	.00
☐ 546	Alvin Davis	.08	.04	.01
☐ 547	Mario Diaz	.03	.01	.00
☐ 548	Ken Griffey Jr.	5.00	2.50	.50
☐ 549	Erik Hanson	.25	.12	.02
☐ 550	Mike Jackson UER (Lifetime ERA 3.345, should be 3.45)	.03	.01	.00
☐ 551	Mark Langston	.12	.06	.01
☐ 552	Edgar Martinez	.08	.04	.01
☐ 553	Bill McGuire	.10	.05	.01
☐ 554	Mike Moore	.06	.03	.00
☐ 555	Jim Presley	.03	.01	.00
☐ 556	Rey Quinones	.03	.01	.00
☐ 557	Jerry Reed	.03	.01	.00
☐ 558	Harold Reynolds	.06	.03	.00
☐ 559	Mike Schooler	.35	.17	.03
☐ 560	Bill Swift	.03	.01	.00
☐ 561	Dave Valle	.03	.01	.00
☐ 562	Steve Bedrosian	.08	.04	.01
☐ 563	Phil Bradley	.06	.03	.00
☐ 564	Don Carman	.03	.01	.00
☐ 565	Bob Dernier	.03	.01	.00
☐ 566	Marvin Freeman	.03	.01	.00
☐ 567	Todd Frohwirth	.03	.01	.00
☐ 568	Greg Gross	.03	.01	.00
☐ 569	Kevin Gross	.03	.01	.00
☐ 570	Greg Harris Philadelphia Phillies	.03	.01	.00
☐ 571	Von Hayes	.08	.04	.01
☐ 572	Chris James	.08	.04	.01
☐ 573	Steve Jeltz	.03	.01	.00
☐ 574	Ron Jones UER (Led IL in '88 with 85, should be 75)	.35	.17	.03
☐ 575	Ricky Jordan	1.75	.85	.17
☐ 576	Mike Maddux	.03	.01	.00
☐ 577	David Palmer	.03	.01	.00
☐ 578	Lance Parrish	.08	.04	.01

☐ 579	Shane Rawley	.03	.01	.00
☐ 580	Bruce Ruffin	.03	.01	.00
☐ 581	Juan Samuel	.08	.04	.01
☐ 582	Mike Schmidt	.35	.17	.03
☐ 583	Kent Tekulve	.03	.01	.00
☐ 584	Milt Thompson UER	.03	.01	.00
	(19 hits in '88,			
	should be 109)			
☐ 585	Jose Alvarez	.10	.05	.01
☐ 586	Paul Assenmacher	.03	.01	.00
☐ 587	Bruce Benedict	.03	.01	.00
☐ 588	Jeff Blauser	.03	.01	.00
☐ 589	Terry Blocker	.12	.06	.01
☐ 590	Ron Gant	.10	.05	.01
☐ 591	Tom Glavine	.03	.01	.00
☐ 592	Tommy Gregg	.12	.06	.01
☐ 593	Albert Hall	.03	.01	.00
☐ 594	Dion James	.03	.01	.00
☐ 595	Rick Mahler	.03	.01	.00
☐ 596	Dale Murphy	.25	.12	.02
☐ 597	Gerald Perry	.06	.03	.00
☐ 598	Charlie Puleo	.03	.01	.00
☐ 599	Ted Simmons	.08	.04	.01
☐ 600	Pete Smith	.03	.01	.00
☐ 601	Zane Smith	.03	.01	.00
☐ 602	John Smoltz	.60	.30	.06
☐ 603	Bruce Sutter	.08	.04	.01
☐ 604	Andres Thomas	.03	.01	.00
☐ 605	Ozzie Virgil	.03	.01	.00
☐ 606	Brady Anderson	.30	.15	.03
☐ 607	Jeff Ballard	.08	.04	.01
☐ 608	Jose Bautista	.08	.04	.01
☐ 609	Ken Gerhart	.03	.01	.00
☐ 610	Terry Kennedy	.03	.01	.00
☐ 611	Eddie Murray	.12	.06	.01
☐ 612	Carl Nichols	.08	.04	.01
	(before All-Star Break			
	batting 1.88)			
☐ 613	Tom Niedenfuer	.03	.01	.00
☐ 614	Joe Orsulak	.03	.01	.00
☐ 615	Oswald Peraza UER	.10	.05	.01
	(shown as Oswaldo)			
☐ 616A	Bill Ripken ERR	18.00	9.00	1.80
	(Rick Face written			
	on knob of bat)			
☐ 616B	Bill Ripken	40.00	20.00	4.00
	(bat knob			
	whited out)			
☐ 616C	Bill Ripken	18.00	9.00	1.80
	(words on bat knob			
	scribbled out)			
☐ 616D	Bill Ripken	.75	.35	.07
	(black box covering			
	bat knob			
☐ 617	Cal Ripken Jr.	.15	.07	.01
☐ 618	Dave Schmidt	.03	.01	.00
☐ 619	Rick Schu	.03	.01	.00
☐ 620	Larry Sheets	.03	.01	.00
☐ 621	Doug Sisk	.03	.01	.00
☐ 622	Pete Stanicek	.03	.01	.00
☐ 623	Mickey Tettleton	.08	.04	.01
☐ 624	Jay Tibbs	.03	.01	.00
☐ 625	Jim Traber	.03	.01	.00
☐ 626	Mark Williamson	.03	.01	.00
☐ 627	Craig Worthington	.50	.25	.05
☐ 628	Speed/Power	.60	.30	.06
	Jose Canseco			
☐ 629	Pitcher Perfect	.06	.03	.00
	Tom Browning			
☐ 630	Like Father/Like Sons ...	.25	.12	.02
	Roberto Alomar			
	Sandy Alomar Jr.			
	(names on card listed			
	in wrong order) UER			
☐ 631	NL All Stars UER	.20	.10	.02
	Will Clark			
	Rafael Palmeiro			
	(Gallaraga, sic;			
	Clark 3 consecutive			
	100 RBI seasons;			
	third with 102 RBI's)			
☐ 632	Homeruns - Coast	.30	.15	.03
	to Coast UER			
	Darryl Strawberry			
	Will Clark (Homeruns			
	should be two words)			
☐ 633	Hot Corners - Hot	.20	.10	.02
	Hitters UER			
	Wade Boggs			
	Carney Lansford			
	(Boggs hit .366 in '86,			
	should be '88)			
☐ 634	Triple A's	.35	.17	.03
	Jose Canseco			
	Terry Steinbach			

	Mark McGwire			
☐ 635	Dual Heat	.20	.10	.02
	Mark Davis			
	Dwight Gooden			
☐ 636	NL Pitching Power UER .	.08	.04	.01
	Danny Jackson			
	David Cone			
	(Hersheiser, sic)			
☐ 637	Cannon Arms UER	.08	.04	.01
	Chris Sabo			
	Bobby Bonilla			
	(Bobby Bonds, sic)			
☐ 638	Double Trouble UER	.06	.03	.00
	Andres Galarraga			
	(misspelled Gallaraga			
	on card back)			
	Gerald Perry			
☐ 639	Power Center	.20	.10	.02
	Kirby Puckett			
	Eric Davis			
☐ 640	Steve Wilson and	.20	.10	.02
	Cameron Drew			
☐ 641	Kevin Brown and	.20	.10	.02
	Kevin Reimer			
☐ 642	Brad Pounders and	.20	.10	.02
	Jerald Clark			
☐ 643	Mike Capel and	.20	.10	.02
	Drew Hall			
☐ 644	Joe Girardi and	.40	.20	.04
	Rolando Roomes			
☐ 645	Lenny Harris and	.20	.10	.02
	Marty Brown			
☐ 646	Luis De Los Santos	.20	.10	.02
	and Jim Campbell			
☐ 647	Randy Kramer and	.15	.07	.01
	Miguel Garcia			
☐ 648	Torey Lovullo and	.15	.07	.01
	Robert Palacios			
☐ 649	Jim Corsi and	.25	.12	.02
	Bob Milacki			
☐ 650	Grady Hall and	.15	.07	.01
	Mike Rochford			
☐ 651	Terry Taylor and	.20	.10	.02
	Vance Lovelace			
☐ 652	Ken Hill and	.50	.25	.05
	Dennis Cook			
☐ 653	Scott Service and	.20	.10	.02
	Shane Turner			
☐ 654	CL: Oakland/Mets	.06	.01	.00
	Dodgers/Red Sox			
	(10 Henderson;			
	68 Jess Orosco)			
☐ 655	CL: Twins/Tigers	.06	.01	.00
	Reds/Brewers			
	(179 Boslo)			
☐ 656	CL: Pirates/Blue Jays	.06	.01	.00
	Yankees/Royals			
	(225 Jess Barfield)			
☐ 657	CL: Padres/Giants	.06	.01	.00
	Astros/Expos			
	(367/368 wrong)			
☐ 658	CL: Indians/Cubs	.06	.01	.00
	Cardinals/Angels			
	(449 Deleon)			
☐ 659	CL: White Sox/Rangers .	.06	.01	.00
	Mariners/Phillies			
☐ 660	CL: Braves/Orioles	.06	.01	.00
	Specials/Checklists			
	(632 hyphenated diff-			
	erently and 650 Hali;			
	595 Rich Mahler;			
	619 Rich Schu)			

1989 Fleer Wax Box Cards

The cards in this 28-card set measure the standard 2 1/2" by 3 1/2". Cards have essentially the same design as the 1989 Fleer regular issue set. The cards were printed on the bottoms of the regular issue wax pack boxes. These 28 cards (C1 to C28) are considered a separate set in their own right and are not typically included in a complete set of the regular issue 1989 Fleer cards. The value of the panel uncut is slightly greater, perhaps by 25% greater, than the value of the individual cards cut up carefully. The wax box cards are further distinguished by the gray card stock used.

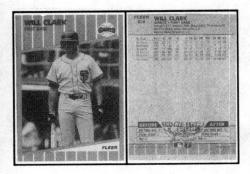

		MINT	EXC	G-VG
	COMPLETE SET (28)	5.00	2.50	.50
	COMMON PLAYER (C1-C28)	.05	.02	.00
☐ C1	Mets Logo	.05	.02	.00
☐ C2	Wade Boggs	.50	.25	.05
☐ C3	George Brett	.30	.15	.03
☐ C4	Jose Canseco UER ('88 strikeouts 121 and career strikeouts 49, should be 128 and 491)	1.00	.50	.10
☐ C5	A's Logo	.05	.02	.00
☐ C6	Will Clark	1.00	.50	.10
☐ C7	David Cone	.25	.12	.02
☐ C8	Andres Galarraga UER (career average .289 should be .269)	.20	.10	.02
☐ C9	Dodgers Logo	.05	.02	.00
☐ C10	Kirk Gibson	.25	.12	.02
☐ C11	Mike Greenwell	.65	.30	.06
☐ C12	Tony Gwynn	.30	.15	.03
☐ C13	Tigers Logo	.05	.02	.00
☐ C14	Orel Hershiser	.25	.12	.02
☐ C15	Danny Jackson	.10	.05	.01
☐ C16	Wally Joyner	.30	.15	.03
☐ C17	Red Sox Logo	.05	.02	.00
☐ C18	Yankees Logo	.05	.02	.00
☐ C19	Fred McGriff	.25	.12	.02
☐ C20	Kirby Puckett	.45	.22	.04
☐ C21	Chris Sabo	.30	.15	.03
☐ C22	Kevin Seitzer	.20	.10	.02
☐ C23	Pirates Logo	.05	.02	.00
☐ C24	Astros Logo	.05	.02	.00
☐ C25	Darryl Strawberry	.35	.17	.03
☐ C26	Alan Trammell	.20	.10	.02
☐ C27	Andy Van Slyke	.15	.07	.01
☐ C28	Frank Viola	.15	.07	.01

1989 Fleer All Star Inserts

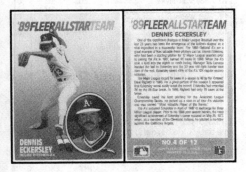

This twelve-card subset was randomly inserted in Fleer wax packs (15 regular cards) and Fleer value packs (36 regular cards). The players selected are the 1989 Fleer Major League All-Star team. One player has been selected for each position along with a DH and three pitchers. The cards are attractively

designed and are standard size, 2 1/2" by 3 1/2". The cards are numbered on the backs and feature a distinctive green background on the card fronts.

		MINT	EXC	G-VG
	COMPLETE SET (12)	12.50	6.25	1.25
	COMMON PLAYER (1-12)	.30	.15	.03
☐ 1	Bobby Bonilla Third Baseman	.50	.25	.05
☐ 2	Jose Canseco Outfielder	3.50	1.75	.35
☐ 3	Will Clark First Baseman	3.50	1.75	.35
☐ 4	Dennis Eckersley Relief Pitcher	.60	.30	.06
☐ 5	Julio Franco Second Baseman	.50	.25	.05
☐ 6	Mike Greenwell Outfielder	2.50	1.25	.25
☐ 7	Orel Hershiser Righthand Pitcher	1.00	.50	.10
☐ 8	Paul Molitor Designated Hitter	.50	.25	.05
☐ 9	Mike Scioscia Catcher	.30	.15	.03
☐ 10	Darryl Strawberry Outfielder	1.25	.60	.12
☐ 11	Alan Trammell Shortstop	.50	.25	.05
☐ 12	Frank Viola Lefthand Pitcher	.50	.25	.05

1989 Fleer For The Record

This six-card subset was distributed randomly (as an insert) in Fleer rack packs. These cards are standard size, 2 1/2" by 3 1/2" and are quite attractive. The set is subtitled "For The Record" and commemorates record-breaking events for those players from the previous season. The cards are numbered on the backs. The card backs are printed in red, black, and gray on white card stock.

		MINT	EXC	G-VG
	COMPLETE SET (6)	7.50	3.75	.75
	COMMON PLAYER (1-6)	.60	.30	.06
☐ 1	Wade Boggs Boston Red Sox	2.00	1.00	.20
☐ 2	Roger Clemens Boston Red Sox	1.50	.75	.15
☐ 3	Andres Galarraga Montreal Expos	.60	.30	.06
☐ 4	Kirk Gibson Los Angeles Dodgers	1.00	.50	.10
☐ 5	Greg Maddux Chicago Cubs	.60	.30	.06
☐ 6	Don Mattingly UER New York Yankees (won batting title '83, should say '84)	2.50	1.25	.25

1989 Fleer Baseball All-Stars

The 1989 Fleer Baseball All-Stars set contains 44 standard-size (2 1/2 by 3 1/2 inch) cards. The fronts are yellowish beige with salmon pinstripes; the vertically-oriented backs are red, white and pink and feature career stats. The cards were distributed through Ben Franklin stores as a boxed set.

		MINT	EXC	G-VG
COMPLETE SET (44)		5.00	2.50	.50
COMMON PLAYER (1-44)		.05	.02	.00
☐	1 Doyle Alexander	.05	.02	.00
☐	2 George Bell	.15	.07	.01
☐	3 Wade Boggs	.65	.30	.06
☐	4 Bobby Bonilla	.10	.05	.01
☐	5 Jose Canseco	1.00	.50	.10
☐	6 Will Clark	1.00	.50	.10
☐	7 Roger Clemens	.50	.25	.05
☐	8 Vince Coleman	.25	.12	.02
☐	9 David Cone	.25	.12	.02
☐	10 Mark Davis	.15	.07	.01
☐	11 Andre Dawson	.20	.10	.02
☐	12 Dennis Eckersley	.15	.07	.01
☐	13 Andres Galarraga	.20	.10	.02
☐	14 Kirk Gibson	.25	.12	.02
☐	15 Dwight Gooden	.45	.22	.04
☐	16 Mike Greenwell	.75	.35	.07
☐	17 Mark Gubicza	.15	.07	.01
☐	18 Ozzie Guillen	.10	.05	.01
☐	19 Tony Gwynn	.35	.17	.03
☐	20 Rickey Henderson	.45	.22	.04
☐	21 Orel Hershiser	.35	.17	.03
☐	22 Danny Jackson	.10	.05	.01
☐	23 Doug Jones	.05	.02	.00
☐	24 Ricky Jordan	.50	.25	.05
☐	25 Bob Knepper	.05	.02	.00
☐	26 Barry Larkin	.15	.07	.01
☐	27 Vance Law	.05	.02	.00
☐	28 Don Mattingly	1.00	.50	.10
☐	29 Mark McGwire	.75	.35	.07
☐	30 Paul Molitor	.15	.07	.01
☐	31 Gerald Perry	.05	.02	.00
☐	32 Kirby Puckett	.45	.22	.04
☐	33 Johnny Ray	.10	.05	.01
☐	34 Harold Reynolds	.05	.02	.00
☐	35 Cal Ripken	.35	.17	.03
☐	36 Don Robinson	.05	.02	.00
☐	37 Ruben Sierra	.50	.25	.05
☐	38 Dave Smith	.05	.02	.00
☐	39 Darryl Strawberry	.50	.25	.05
☐	40 Dave Stieb	.10	.05	.01
☐	41 Alan Trammell	.15	.07	.01
☐	42 Andy Van Slyke	.10	.05	.01
☐	43 Frank Viola	.15	.07	.01
☐	44 Dave Winfield	.20	.10	.02

1989 Fleer Baseball MVP's

The 1989 Fleer Baseball MVP's set contains 44 standard-size (2 1/2 by 3 1/2 inch) cards. The fronts and backs are green and yellow. The horizontally-oriented backs feature career stats. The cards were distributed through Toys 'R' Us stores as a boxed set.

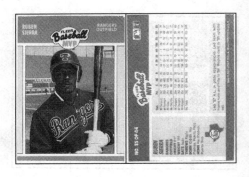

		MINT	EXC	G-VG
COMPLETE SET (44)		5.00	2.50	.50
COMMON PLAYER (1-44)		.05	.02	.00
☐	1 Steve Bedrosian	.10	.05	.01
☐	2 George Bell	.15	.07	.01
☐	3 Wade Boggs	.75	.35	.07
☐	4 George Brett	.35	.17	.03
☐	5 Hubie Brooks	.10	.05	.01
☐	6 Jose Canseco	1.00	.50	.10
☐	7 Will Clark	1.00	.50	.10
☐	8 Roger Clemens	.60	.30	.06
☐	9 Eric Davis	.60	.30	.06
☐	10 Glenn Davis	.20	.10	.02
☐	11 Andre Dawson	.20	.10	.02
☐	12 Andres Galarraga	.20	.10	.02
☐	13 Kirk Gibson	.20	.10	.02
☐	14 Dwight Gooden	.40	.20	.04
☐	15 Mark Grace	1.00	.50	.10
☐	16 Mike Greenwell	.75	.35	.07
☐	17 Tony Gwynn	.35	.17	.03
☐	18 Bryan Harvey	.15	.07	.01
☐	19 Orel Hershiser	.35	.17	.03
☐	20 Ted Higuera	.10	.05	.01
☐	21 Danny Jackson	.10	.05	.01
☐	22 Mike Jackson	.05	.02	.00
☐	23 Doug Jones	.05	.02	.00
☐	24 Greg Maddux	.15	.07	.01
☐	25 Mike Marshall	.10	.05	.01
☐	26 Don Mattingly	1.00	.50	.10
☐	27 Fred McGriff	.25	.12	.02
☐	28 Mark McGwire	.75	.35	.07
☐	29 Kevin McReynolds	.15	.07	.01
☐	30 Jack Morris	.10	.05	.01
☐	31 Gerald Perry	.05	.02	.00
☐	32 Kirby Puckett	.45	.22	.04
☐	33 Chris Sabo	.35	.17	.03
☐	34 Mike Scott	.15	.07	.01
☐	35 Ruben Sierra	.50	.25	.05
☐	36 Darryl Strawberry	.50	.25	.05
☐	37 Danny Tartabull	.15	.07	.01
☐	38 Bobby Thigpen	.10	.05	.01
☐	39 Alan Trammell	.15	.07	.01
☐	40 Andy Van Slyke	.10	.05	.01
☐	41 Frank Viola	.15	.07	.01
☐	42 Walt Weiss	.15	.07	.01
☐	43 Dave Winfield	.20	.10	.02
☐	44 Todd Worrell	.10	.05	.01

1989 Fleer Exciting Stars

The 1989 Fleer Exciting Stars set contains 44 standard-size (2 1/2 by 3 1/2 inch) cards. The fronts have baby blue borders; the backs are pink and blue. The vertically-oriented backs feature career stats. The cards were distributed as a boxed set.

		MINT	EXC	G-VG
COMPLETE SET (44)		5.00	2.50	.50
COMMON PLAYER (1-44)		.05	.02	.00
☐	1 Harold Baines	.10	.05	.01
☐	2 Wade Boggs	.75	.35	.07
☐	3 Jose Canseco	1.00	.50	.10
☐	4 Joe Carter	.15	.07	.01
☐	5 Will Clark	1.00	.50	.10

			MINT	EXC	G-VG
	COMPLETE SET (44)		5.00	2.50	.50
	COMMON PLAYER (1-44)		.05	.02	.00
☐	1	George Bell	.15	.07	.01
☐	2	Wade Boggs	.75	.35	.07
☐	3	Barry Bonds	.15	.07	.01
☐	4	Tom Brunansky	.15	.07	.01
☐	5	Jose Canseco	1.00	.50	.10
☐	6	Joe Carter	.15	.07	.01
☐	7	Will Clark	1.00	.50	.10
☐	8	Roger Clemens	.60	.30	.06
☐	9	David Cone	.25	.12	.02
☐	10	Eric Davis	.60	.30	.06
☐	11	Glenn Davis	.20	.10	.02
☐	12	Andre Dawson	.20	.10	.02
☐	13	Dennis Eckersley	.15	.07	.01
☐	14	John Franco	.10	.05	.01
☐	15	Gary Gaetti	.10	.05	.01
☐	16	Andres Galarraga	.20	.10	.02
☐	17	Kirk Gibson	.20	.10	.02
☐	18	Dwight Gooden	.40	.20	.04
☐	19	Mike Greenwell	.75	.35	.07
☐	20	Tony Gwynn	.35	.17	.03
☐	21	Bryan Harvey	.15	.07	.01
☐	22	Orel Hershiser	.35	.17	.03
☐	23	Ted Higuera	.10	.05	.01
☐	24	Danny Jackson	.10	.05	.01
☐	25	Ricky Jordan	.50	.25	.05
☐	26	Don Mattingly	1.00	.50	.10
☐	27	Fred McGriff	.25	.12	.02
☐	28	Mark McGwire	.75	.35	.07
☐	29	Kevin McReynolds	.15	.07	.01
☐	30	Gerald Perry	.05	.02	.00
☐	31	Kirby Puckett	.45	.22	.04
☐	32	Johnny Ray	.10	.05	.01
☐	33	Harold Reynolds	.05	.02	.00
☐	34	Cal Ripken Jr.	.30	.15	.03
☐	35	Ryne Sandberg	.30	.15	.03
☐	36	Kevin Seitzer	.20	.10	.02
☐	37	Ruben Sierra	.50	.25	.05
☐	38	Darryl Strawberry	.50	.25	.05
☐	39	Bobby Thigpen	.10	.05	.01
☐	40	Alan Trammell	.15	.07	.01
☐	41	Andy Van Slyke	.10	.05	.01
☐	42	Frank Viola	.15	.07	.01
☐	43	Dave Winfield	.20	.10	.02
☐	44	Robin Yount	.40	.20	.04

☐	6	Roger Clemens	.60	.30	.06
☐	7	Vince Coleman	.25	.12	.02
☐	8	David Cone	.25	.12	.02
☐	9	Eric Davis	.60	.30	.06
☐	10	Glenn Davis	.20	.10	.02
☐	11	Andre Dawson	.20	.10	.02
☐	12	Dwight Evans	.15	.07	.01
☐	13	Andres Galarraga	.20	.10	.02
☐	14	Kirk Gibson	.20	.10	.02
☐	15	Dwight Gooden	.40	.20	.04
☐	16	Jim Gott	.05	.02	.00
☐	17	Mark Grace	1.00	.50	.10
☐	18	Mike Greenwell	.75	.35	.07
☐	19	Mark Gubicza	.15	.07	.01
☐	20	Tony Gwynn	.35	.17	.03
☐	21	Rickey Henderson	.45	.22	.04
☐	22	Tom Henke	.05	.02	.00
☐	23	Mike Henneman	.05	.02	.00
☐	24	Orel Hershiser	.35	.17	.03
☐	25	Danny Jackson	.10	.05	.01
☐	26	Gregg Jefferies	.75	.35	.07
☐	27	Ricky Jordan	.50	.25	.05
☐	28	Wally Joyner	.25	.12	.02
☐	29	Mark Langston	.15	.07	.01
☐	30	Tim Leary	.10	.05	.01
☐	31	Don Mattingly	1.00	.50	.10
☐	32	Mark McGwire	.75	.35	.07
☐	33	Dale Murphy	.35	.17	.03
☐	34	Kirby Puckett	.45	.22	.04
☐	35	Chris Sabo	.35	.17	.03
☐	36	Kevin Seitzer	.20	.10	.02
☐	37	Ruben Sierra	.50	.25	.05
☐	38	Ozzie Smith	.15	.07	.01
☐	39	Dave Stewart	.15	.07	.01
☐	40	Darryl Strawberry	.50	.25	.05
☐	41	Alan Trammell	.15	.07	.01
☐	42	Frank Viola	.15	.07	.01
☐	43	Dave Winfield	.20	.10	.02
☐	44	Robin Yount	.35	.17	.03

1989 Fleer League Leaders

Will Clark — GIANTS FIRST BASE

The 1989 Fleer League Leaders set contains 44 standard-size (2 1/2 by 3 1/2 inch) cards. The fronts are red and yellow; the horizontally-oriented backs are light blue and red, and feature career stats. The cards were distributed through Woolworth stores as a boxed set.

			MINT	EXC	G-VG
	COMPLETE SET (44)		5.00	2.50	.50
	COMMON PLAYER (1-44)		.05	.02	.00
☐	1	Allan Anderson	.10	.05	.01
☐	2	Wade Boggs	.75	.35	.07
☐	3	Jose Canseco	1.00	.50	.10
☐	4	Will Clark	1.00	.50	.10
☐	5	Roger Clemens	.60	.30	.06
☐	6	Vince Coleman	.25	.12	.02
☐	7	David Cone	.25	.12	.02
☐	8	Kal Daniels	.15	.07	.01

1989 Fleer Heroes of Baseball

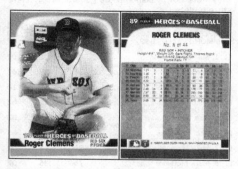

Roger Clemens — RED SOX PITCHER

The 1989 Fleer Heroes of Baseball set contains 44 standard-size (2 1/2 by 3 1/2 inch) cards. The fronts and backs are red, white and blue. The vertically-oriented backs feature career stats. The cards were distributed through Woolworth stores as a boxed set.

		MINT	EXC	G-VG
☐ 9	Chili Davis	.10	.05	.01
☐ 10	Eric Davis	.60	.30	.06
☐ 11	Glenn Davis	.20	.10	.02
☐ 12	Andre Dawson	.20	.10	.02
☐ 13	John Franco	.10	.05	.01
☐ 14	Andres Galarraga	.20	.10	.02
☐ 15	Kirk Gibson	.20	.10	.02
☐ 16	Dwight Gooden	.40	.20	.04
☐ 17	Mark Grace	1.00	.50	.10
☐ 18	Mike Greenwell	.75	.35	.07
☐ 19	Tony Gwynn	.35	.17	.03
☐ 20	Orel Hershiser	.35	.17	.03
☐ 21	Pete Incaviglia	.15	.07	.01
☐ 22	Danny Jackson	.10	.05	.01
☐ 23	Gregg Jefferies	.75	.35	.07
☐ 24	Joe Magrane	.20	.10	.02
☐ 25	Don Mattingly	1.00	.50	.10
☐ 26	Fred McGriff	.35	.17	.03
☐ 27	Mark McGwire	.75	.35	.07
☐ 28	Dale Murphy	.35	.17	.03
☐ 29	Dan Plesac	.10	.05	.01
☐ 30	Kirby Puckett	.45	.22	.04
☐ 31	Harold Reynolds	.10	.05	.01
☐ 32	Cal Ripken Jr.	.30	.15	.03
☐ 33	Jeff Robinson	.10	.05	.01
☐ 34	Mike Scott	.15	.07	.01
☐ 35	Ozzie Smith	.15	.07	.01
☐ 36	Dave Stewart	.15	.07	.01
☐ 37	Darryl Strawberry	.50	.25	.05
☐ 38	Greg Swindell	.15	.07	.01
☐ 39	Bobby Thigpen	.10	.05	.01
☐ 40	Alan Trammell	.15	.07	.01
☐ 41	Andy Van Slyke	.10	.05	.01
☐ 42	Frank Viola	.15	.07	.01
☐ 43	Dave Winfield	.20	.10	.02
☐ 44	Robin Yount	.40	.20	.04

		MINT	EXC	G-VG
☐ 19	Mark Grace	1.00	.50	.10
☐ 20	Mike Greenwell	.75	.35	.07
☐ 21	Tony Gwynn	.35	.17	.03
☐ 22	Rickey Henderson	.45	.22	.04
☐ 23	Orel Hershiser	.35	.17	.03
☐ 24	Ted Higuera	.10	.05	.01
☐ 25	Gregg Jefferies	.75	.35	.07
☐ 26	Wally Joyner	.25	.12	.02
☐ 27	Mark Langston	.15	.07	.01
☐ 28	Greg Maddux	.15	.07	.01
☐ 29	Don Mattingly	1.00	.50	.10
☐ 30	Fred McGriff	.35	.17	.03
☐ 31	Mark McGwire	.75	.35	.07
☐ 32	Dan Plesac	.10	.05	.01
☐ 33	Kirby Puckett	.45	.22	.04
☐ 34	Jeff Reardon	.10	.05	.01
☐ 35	Chris Sabo	.35	.17	.03
☐ 36	Mike Schmidt	.75	.35	.07
☐ 37	Mike Scott	.15	.07	.01
☐ 38	Cory Snyder	.15	.07	.01
☐ 39	Darryl Strawberry	.50	.25	.05
☐ 40	Alan Trammell	.15	.07	.01
☐ 41	Frank Viola	.15	.07	.01
☐ 42	Walt Weiss	.15	.07	.01
☐ 43	Dave Winfield	.20	.10	.02
☐ 44	Todd Worrell UER	.10	.05	.01
	(statistical headings on back for hitter)			

1989 Fleer Super Stars

The 1989 Fleer Super Stars set contains 44 standard-size (2 1/2 by 3 1/2 inch) cards. The fronts are red and beige; the horizontally-oriented backs are yellow, and feature career stats. The cards were distributed as a boxed set.

		MINT	EXC	G-VG
	COMPLETE SET (44)	5.00	2.50	.50
	COMMON PLAYER (1-44)	.05	.02	.00
☐ 1	Roberto Alomar	.25	.12	.02
☐ 2	Harold Baines	.10	.05	.01
☐ 3	Tim Belcher	.15	.07	.01
☐ 4	Wade Boggs	.75	.35	.07
☐ 5	George Brett	.35	.17	.03
☐ 6	Jose Canseco	1.00	.50	.10
☐ 7	Gary Carter	.20	.10	.02
☐ 8	Will Clark	1.00	.50	.10
☐ 9	Roger Clemens	.60	.30	.06
☐ 10	Kal Daniels UER (reverse negative photo on front)	.10	.05	.01
☐ 11	Eric Davis	.60	.30	.06
☐ 12	Andre Dawson	.20	.10	.02
☐ 13	Tony Fernandez	.15	.07	.01
☐ 14	Scott Fletcher	.05	.02	.00
☐ 15	Andres Galarraga	.20	.10	.02
☐ 16	Kirk Gibson	.20	.10	.02
☐ 17	Dwight Gooden	.40	.20	.04
☐ 18	Jim Gott	.05	.02	.00

1989 Fleer World Series

This 12-card set of 2 1/2" by 3 1/2" cards features highlights of the previous year's World Series between the Dodgers and the Athletics. The sets were packaged as a complete set insert with the collated sets (of the 1989 Fleer regular issue) which were sold by Fleer directly to hobby card dealers; they were not available in the general retail candy store outlets.

		MINT	EXC	G-VG
	COMPLETE SET (12)	4.00	2.00	.40
	COMMON PLAYER (1-12)	.25	.12	.02
☐ 1	Mickey Hatcher Dodgers' Secret Weapon	.25	.12	.02
☐ 2	Tim Belcher Rookie Starts Series	.35	.17	.03
☐ 3	Jose Canseco Canseco Slams L.A.	1.00	.50	.10
☐ 4	Mike Scioscia Dramatic Comeback	.25	.12	.02
☐ 5	Kirk Gibson Gibson Steals The Show	.75	.35	.07
☐ 6	Orel Hershiser Bulldog	.60	.30	.06
☐ 7	Mike Marshall One Swing, Three RBI's	.35	.17	.03
☐ 8	Mark McGwire Game-Winning Homer	.75	.35	.07
☐ 9	Steve Sax Sax's Speed Wins Game 4	.35	.17	.03
☐ 10	Walt Weiss Series Caps Award-Winning Year	.35	.17	.03
☐ 11	Orel Hershiser Series MVP Uses	.60	.30	.06

Shutout Magic
☐ 12 Dodger Blue, ... .25 .12 .02
World Champs

1989 Fleer Update

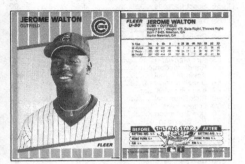

The 1989 Fleer Update set contains 132 standard-size (2 1/2 by 3 1/2 inch) cards. The fronts are gray with white pinstripes. The vertically-oriented backs show lifetime stats and performance "Before and After the All-Star Break." The set does not include a card of 1989 AL Rookie of the Year Gregg Olson, but contains the first major card of Greg Vaughn and special cards for Nolan Ryan's 5,000th strikeout and Mike Schmidt's retirement. Fleer did not produce a "limited" edition version of this set.

		MINT	EXC	G-VG
	COMPLETE SET (132)	20.00	10.00	2.00
	COMMON PLAYER (1-132)	.06	.03	.00
☐ U1	Phil Bradley	.15	.03	.01
☐ U2	Mike Devereaux	.10	.05	.01
☐ U3	Steve Finley	.30	.15	.03
☐ U4	Kevin Hickey	.06	.03	.00
☐ U5	Brian Holton	.10	.05	.01
☐ U6	Bob Milacki	.15	.07	.01
☐ U7	Randy Milligan	.10	.05	.01
☐ U8	John Dopson	.10	.05	.01
☐ U9	Nick Esasky	.15	.07	.01
☐ U10	Rob Murphy	.10	.05	.01
☐ U11	Jim Abbott	2.50	1.25	.25
☐ U12	Bert Blyleven	.15	.07	.01
☐ U13	Jeff Manto	.30	.15	.03
☐ U14	Bob McClure	.06	.03	.00
☐ U15	Lance Parrish	.10	.05	.01
☐ U16	Lee Stevens	.50	.25	.05
☐ U17	Claudell Washington	.10	.05	.01
☐ U18	Mark Davis	.25	.12	.02
☐ U19	Eric King	.10	.05	.01
☐ U20	Ron Kittle	.15	.07	.01
☐ U21	Matt Merullo	.20	.10	.02
☐ U22	Steve Rosenberg	.15	.07	.01
☐ U23	Robin Ventura	1.50	.75	.15
☐ U24	Keith Atherton	.06	.03	.00
☐ U25	Joey Belle	1.00	.50	.10
☐ U26	Jerry Browne	.10	.05	.01
☐ U27	Felix Fermin	.06	.03	.00
☐ U28	Brad Komminsk	.10	.05	.01
☐ U29	Pete O'Brien	.10	.05	.01
☐ U30	Mike Brumley	.10	.05	.01
☐ U31	Tracy Jones	.10	.05	.01
☐ U32	Mike Schwabe	.15	.07	.01
☐ U33	Gary Ward	.06	.03	.00
☐ U34	Frank Williams	.06	.03	.00
☐ U35	Kevin Appier	.20	.10	.02
☐ U36	Bob Boone	.15	.07	.01
☐ U37	Luis de los Santos	.20	.10	.02
☐ U38	Jim Eisenreich	.10	.05	.01
☐ U39	Jaime Navarro	.40	.20	.04

☐ U40	Bill Spiers	.35	.17	.03
☐ U41	Greg Vaughn	3.00	1.50	.30
☐ U42	Randy Veres	.15	.07	.01
☐ U43	Wally Backman	.06	.03	.00
☐ U44	Shane Rawley	.06	.03	.00
☐ U45	Steve Balboni	.06	.03	.00
☐ U46	Jesse Barfield	.15	.07	.01
☐ U47	Alvaro Espinoza	.10	.05	.01
☐ U48	Bob Geren	.45	.22	.04
☐ U49	Mel Hall	.10	.05	.01
☐ U50	Andy Hawkins	.10	.05	.01
☐ U51	Hensley Meulens	.50	.25	.05
☐ U52	Steve Sax	.15	.07	.01
☐ U53	Deion Sanders	1.25	.60	.12
☐ U54	Rickey Henderson	.40	.20	.04
☐ U55	Mike Moore	.15	.07	.01
☐ U56	Tony Phillips	.10	.05	.01
☐ U57	Greg Briley	.75	.35	.07
☐ U58	Gene Harris	.30	.15	.03
☐ U59	Randy Johnson	.15	.07	.01
☐ U60	Jeffrey Leonard	.10	.05	.01
☐ U61	Dennis Powell	.06	.03	.00
☐ U62	Omar Vizquel	.25	.12	.02
☐ U63	Kevin Brown	.15	.07	.01
☐ U64	Julio Franco	.15	.07	.01
☐ U65	Jamie Moyer	.06	.03	.00
☐ U66	Rafael Palmeiro	.15	.07	.01
☐ U67	Nolan Ryan	1.50	.60	.12
☐ U68	Francisco Cabrera	.30	.15	.03
☐ U69	Junior Felix	.90	.50	.10
☐ U70	Al Leiter	.10	.05	.01
☐ U71	Alex Sanchez	.20	.10	.02
☐ U72	Geronimo Berroa	.06	.03	.00
☐ U73	Derek Lilliquist	.20	.10	.02
☐ U74	Lonnie Smith	.15	.07	.01
☐ U75	Jeff Treadway	.10	.05	.01
☐ U76	Paul Kilgus	.06	.03	.00
☐ U77	Lloyd McClendon	.10	.05	.01
☐ U78	Scott Sanderson	.06	.03	.00
☐ U79	Dwight Smith	1.50	.75	.15
☐ U80	Jerome Walton	4.50	2.25	.45
☐ U81	Mitch Williams	.20	.10	.02
☐ U82	Steve Wilson	.10	.05	.01
☐ U83	Todd Benzinger	.10	.05	.01
☐ U84	Ken Griffey Sr.	.15	.07	.01
☐ U85	Rick Mahler	.06	.03	.00
☐ U86	Rolando Roomes	.15	.07	.01
☐ U87	Scott Scudder	.30	.15	.03
☐ U88	Jim Clancy	.06	.03	.00
☐ U89	Rick Rhoden	.06	.03	.00
☐ U90	Dan Schatzeder	.06	.03	.00
☐ U91	Mike Morgan	.10	.05	.01
☐ U92	Eddie Murray	.15	.07	.01
☐ U93	Willie Randolph	.10	.05	.01
☐ U94	Ray Searage	.06	.03	.00
☐ U95	Mike Aldrete	.06	.03	.00
☐ U96	Kevin Gross	.10	.05	.01
☐ U97	Mark Langston	.25	.12	.02
☐ U98	Spike Owen	.06	.03	.00
☐ U99	Zane Smith	.06	.03	.00
☐ U100	Don Aase	.06	.03	.00
☐ U101	Barry Lyons	.06	.03	.00
☐ U102	Juan Samuel	.15	.07	.01
☐ U103	Wally Whitehurst	.20	.10	.02
☐ U104	Dennis Cook	.15	.07	.01
☐ U105	Len Dykstra	.15	.07	.01
☐ U106	Charlie Hayes	.15	.07	.01
☐ U107	Tommy Herr	.06	.03	.00
☐ U108	Ken Howell	.06	.03	.00
☐ U109	John Kruk	.10	.05	.01
☐ U110	Roger McDowell	.10	.05	.01
☐ U111	Terry Mulholland	.06	.03	.00
☐ U112	Jeff Parrett	.10	.05	.01
☐ U113	Neal Heaton	.06	.03	.00
☐ U114	Jeff King	.15	.07	.01
☐ U115	Randy Kramer	.10	.05	.01
☐ U116	Bill Landrum	.10	.05	.01
☐ U117	Cris Carpenter	.10	.05	.01
☐ U118	Frank DiPino	.06	.03	.00
☐ U119	Ken Hill	.10	.05	.01
☐ U120	Dan Quisenberry	.10	.05	.01
☐ U121	Milt Thompson	.06	.03	.00
☐ U122	Todd Zeile	3.00	1.50	.30
☐ U123	Jack Clark	.12	.06	.01
☐ U124	Bruce Hurst	.12	.06	.01
☐ U125	Mark Parent	.06	.03	.00
☐ U126	Bip Roberts	.06	.03	.00
☐ U127	Jeff Brantley UER	.25	.12	.02
	(photo actually			
	Joe Kmak)			
☐ U128	Terry Kennedy	.06	.03	.00
☐ U129	Mike LaCoss	.06	.03	.00
☐ U130	Greg Litton	.30	.15	.03
☐ U131	Mike Schmidt	1.50	.60	.12
☐ U132	Checklist 1-132	.06	.01	.00

1990 Fleer

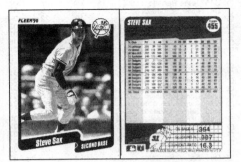

The 1990 Fleer set contains 660 standard- size (2 1/2 by 3 1/2 inch) cards. The outer front borders are white; the inner, ribbon-like borders are different depending on the team. The vertically-oriented backs are white, red, pink and navy. The set is again ordered numerically by teams, followed by combination cards, rookie prospect pairs, and checklists. Just as with the 1989 set, Fleer incorrectly anticipated the outcome of the 1989 Playoffs according to the team ordering. The A's, listed first, did win the World Series, but their opponents were the Giants, not the Cubs.

	MINT	EXC	G-VG
COMPLETE SET (660)	24.00	12.00	2.40
COMMON PLAYER (1-660)	.03	.01	.00

		MINT	EXC	G-VG
☐	1 Lance Blankenship	.10	.02	.01
☐	2 Todd Burns	.06	.03	.00
☐	3 Jose Canseco	.50	.25	.05
☐	4 Jim Corsi	.03	.01	.00
☐	5 Storm Davis	.06	.03	.00
☐	6 Dennis Eckersley	.08	.04	.01
☐	7 Mike Gallego	.03	.01	.00
☐	8 Ron Hassey	.03	.01	.00
☐	9 Dave Henderson	.03	.01	.00
☐	10 Rickey Henderson	.25	.12	.02
☐	11 Rick Honeycutt	.03	.01	.00
☐	12 Stan Javier	.03	.01	.00
☐	13 Felix Jose	.03	.01	.00
☐	14 Carney Lansford	.08	.04	.01
☐	15 Mark McGwire	.25	.12	.02
☐	16 Mike Moore	.06	.03	.00
☐	17 Gene Nelson	.03	.01	.00
☐	18 Dave Parker	.08	.04	.01
☐	19 Tony Phillips	.03	.01	.00
☐	20 Terry Steinbach	.06	.03	.00
☐	21 Dave Stewart	.08	.04	.01
☐	22 Walt Weiss	.08	.04	.01
☐	23 Bob Welch	.06	.03	.00
☐	24 Curt Young	.03	.01	.00
☐	25 Paul Assenmacher	.03	.01	.00
☐	26 Damon Berryhill	.08	.04	.01
☐	27 Mike Bielecki	.06	.03	.00
☐	28 Kevin Blankenship	.08	.04	.01
☐	29 Andre Dawson	.10	.05	.01
☐	30 Shawon Dunston	.06	.03	.00
☐	31 Joe Girardi	.08	.04	.01
☐	32 Mark Grace	.35	.17	.03
☐	33 Mike Harkey	.06	.03	.00
☐	34 Paul Kilgus	.03	.01	.00
☐	35 Les Lancaster	.03	.01	.00
☐	36 Vance Law	.03	.01	.00
☐	37 Greg Maddux	.06	.03	.00
☐	38 Lloyd McClendon	.03	.01	.00
☐	39 Jeff Pico	.03	.01	.00
☐	40 Ryne Sandberg	.15	.07	.01
☐	41 Scott Sanderson	.03	.01	.00
☐	42 Dwight Smith	.50	.25	.05
☐	43 Rick Sutcliffe	.06	.03	.00
☐	44 Jerome Walton	1.25	.60	.12
☐	45 Mitch Webster	.03	.01	.00
☐	46 Curt Wilkerson	.03	.01	.00
☐	47 Dean Wilkins	.15	.07	.01
☐	48 Mitch Williams	.06	.03	.00
☐	49 Steve Wilson	.03	.01	.00
☐	50 Steve Bedrosian	.06	.03	.00
☐	51 Mike Benjamin	.12	.06	.01
☐	52 Jeff Brantley	.12	.06	.01
☐	53 Brett Butler	.06	.03	.00
☐	54 Will Clark	.50	.25	.05
☐	55 Kelly Downs	.03	.01	.00
☐	56 Scott Garrelts	.06	.03	.00
☐	57 Atlee Hammaker	.03	.01	.00
☐	58 Terry Kennedy	.03	.01	.00
☐	59 Mike LaCoss	.03	.01	.00
☐	60 Craig Lefferts	.03	.01	.00
☐	61 Greg Litton	.20	.10	.02
☐	62 Candy Maldonado	.03	.01	.00
☐	63 Kirt Manwaring	.06	.03	.00
☐	64 Randy McCament	.12	.06	.01
☐	65 Kevin Mitchell	.20	.10	.02
☐	66 Donell Nixon	.03	.01	.00
☐	67 Ken Oberkfell	.03	.01	.00
☐	68 Rick Reuschel	.06	.03	.00
☐	69 Ernest Riles	.03	.01	.00
☐	70 Don Robinson	.03	.01	.00
☐	71 Pat Sheridan	.03	.01	.00
☐	72 Chris Speier	.03	.01	.00
☐	73 Robby Thompson	.03	.01	.00
☐	74 Jose Uribe	.03	.01	.00
☐	75 Matt Williams	.12	.06	.01
☐	76 George Bell	.10	.05	.01
☐	77 Pat Borders	.03	.01	.00
☐	78 John Cerutti	.03	.01	.00
☐	79 Junior Felix	.35	.17	.03
☐	80 Tony Fernandez	.08	.04	.01
☐	81 Mike Flanagan	.03	.01	.00
☐	82 Mauro Gozzo	.20	.10	.02
☐	83 Kelly Gruber	.06	.03	.00
☐	84 Tom Henke	.06	.03	.00
☐	85 Jimmy Key	.06	.03	.00
☐	86 Manny Lee	.03	.01	.00
☐	87 Nelson Liriano	.03	.01	.00
☐	88 Lee Mazzilli	.03	.01	.00
☐	89 Fred McGriff	.12	.06	.01
☐	90 Lloyd Moseby	.06	.03	.00
☐	91 Rance Mulliniks	.03	.01	.00
☐	92 Alex Sanchez	.12	.06	.01
☐	93 Dave Stieb	.08	.04	.01
☐	94 Todd Stottlemyre	.06	.03	.00
☐	95 Duane Ward	.03	.01	.00
☐	96 David Wells	.03	.01	.00
☐	97 Ernie Whitt	.03	.01	.00
☐	98 Frank Wills	.03	.01	.00
☐	99 Mookie Wilson	.06	.03	.00
☐	100 Kevin Appier	.12	.06	.01
☐	101 Luis Aquino	.03	.01	.00
☐	102 Bob Boone	.08	.04	.01
☐	103 George Brett	.12	.06	.01
☐	104 Jose DeJesus	.03	.01	.00
☐	105 Luis De Los Santos	.03	.01	.00
☐	106 Jim Eisenreich	.03	.01	.00
☐	107 Steve Farr	.03	.01	.00
☐	108 Tom Gordon	.40	.20	.04
☐	109 Mark Gubicza	.08	.04	.01
☐	110 Bo Jackson	.50	.25	.05
☐	111 Terry Leach	.03	.01	.00
☐	112 Charlie Leibrandt	.03	.01	.00
☐	113 Rick Luecken	.12	.06	.01
☐	114 Mike Macfarlane	.03	.01	.00
☐	115 Jeff Montgomery	.06	.03	.00
☐	116 Bret Saberhagen	.10	.05	.01
☐	117 Kevin Seitzer	.08	.04	.01
☐	118 Kurt Stillwell	.03	.01	.00
☐	119 Pat Tabler	.03	.01	.00
☐	120 Danny Tartabull	.08	.04	.01
☐	121 Gary Thurman	.03	.01	.00
☐	122 Frank White	.06	.03	.00
☐	123 Willie Wilson	.06	.03	.00
☐	124 Matt Winters	.12	.06	.01
☐	125 Jim Abbott	1.00	.50	.10
☐	126 Tony Armas	.06	.03	.00
☐	127 Dante Bichette	.03	.01	.00
☐	128 Bert Blyleven	.08	.04	.01
☐	129 Chili Davis	.06	.03	.00
☐	130 Brian Downing	.03	.01	.00
☐	131 Mike Fetters	.12	.06	.01
☐	132 Chuck Finley	.06	.03	.00
☐	133 Willie Fraser	.03	.01	.00
☐	134 Bryan Harvey	.03	.01	.00
☐	135 Jack Howell	.03	.01	.00
☐	136 Wally Joyner	.10	.05	.01
☐	137 Jeff Manto	.15	.07	.01
☐	138 Kirk McCaskill	.03	.01	.00
☐	139 Bob McClure	.03	.01	.00
☐	140 Greg Minton	.03	.01	.00
☐	141 Lance Parrish	.08	.04	.01
☐	142 Dan Petry	.03	.01	.00

☐ 143	Johnny Ray	.06	.03	.00	☐ 238	Dave Smith	.03	.01	.00
☐ 144	Dick Schofield	.03	.01	.00	☐ 239	Alex Trevino	.03	.01	.00
☐ 145	Lee Stevens	.25	.12	.02	☐ 240	Glenn Wilson	.03	.01	.00
☐ 146	Claudell Washington	.06	.03	.00	☐ 241	Gerald Young	.03	.01	.00
☐ 147	Devon White	.08	.04	.01	☐ 242	Tom Brunansky	.08	.04	.01
☐ 148	Mike Witt	.06	.03	.00	☐ 243	Cris Carpenter	.03	.01	.00
☐ 149	Roberto Alomar	.08	.04	.01	☐ 244	Alex Cole	.15	.07	.01
☐ 150	Sandy Alomar Jr.	.30	.15	.03	☐ 245	Vince Coleman	.08	.04	.01
☐ 151	Andy Benes	.50	.25	.05	☐ 246	John Costello	.03	.01	.00
☐ 152	Jack Clark	.08	.04	.01	☐ 247	Ken Dayley	.03	.01	.00
☐ 153	Pat Clements	.03	.01	.00	☐ 248	Jose DeLeon	.06	.03	.00
☐ 154	Joey Cora	.03	.01	.00	☐ 249	Frank DiPino	.03	.01	.00
☐ 155	Mark Davis	.08	.04	.01	☐ 250	Pedro Guerrero	.08	.04	.01
☐ 156	Mark Grant	.03	.01	.00	☐ 251	Ken Hill	.03	.01	.00
☐ 157	Tony Gwynn	.15	.07	.01	☐ 252	Joe Magrane	.08	.04	.01
☐ 158	Greg W. Harris	.03	.01	.00	☐ 253	Willie McGee	.08	.04	.01
☐ 159	Bruce Hurst	.08	.04	.01	☐ 254	John Morris	.03	.01	.00
☐ 160	Darrin Jackson	.03	.01	.00	☐ 255	Jose Oquendo	.03	.01	.00
☐ 161	Chris James	.06	.03	.00	☐ 256	Tony Pena	.06	.03	.00
☐ 162	Carmelo Martinez	.03	.01	.00	☐ 257	Terry Pendleton	.03	.01	.00
☐ 163	Mike Pagliarulo	.06	.03	.00	☐ 258	Ted Power	.03	.01	.00
☐ 164	Mark Parent	.08	.04	.01	☐ 259	Dan Quisenberry	.06	.03	.00
☐ 165	Dennis Rasmussen	.03	.01	.00	☐ 260	Ozzie Smith	.08	.04	.01
☐ 166	Bip Roberts	.03	.01	.00	☐ 261	Scott Terry	.03	.01	.00
☐ 167	Benito Santiago	.08	.04	.01	☐ 262	Milt Thompson	.03	.01	.00
☐ 168	Calvin Schiraldi	.03	.01	.00	☐ 263	Denny Walling	.03	.01	.00
☐ 169	Eric Show	.03	.01	.00	☐ 264	Todd Worrell	.08	.04	.01
☐ 170	Garry Templeton	.06	.03	.00	☐ 265	Todd Zeile	1.50	.75	.15
☐ 171	Ed Whitson	.03	.01	.00	☐ 266	Marty Barrett	.03	.01	.00
☐ 172	Brady Anderson	.03	.01	.00	☐ 267	Mike Boddicker	.03	.01	.00
☐ 173	Jeff Ballard	.06	.03	.00	☐ 268	Wade Boggs	.25	.12	.02
☐ 174	Phil Bradley	.06	.03	.00	☐ 269	Ellis Burks	.15	.07	.01
☐ 175	Mike Devereaux	.03	.01	.00	☐ 270	Rick Cerone	.03	.01	.00
☐ 176	Steve Finley	.12	.06	.01	☐ 271	Roger Clemens	.25	.12	.02
☐ 177	Pete Harnisch	.08	.04	.01	☐ 272	John Dopson	.03	.01	.00
☐ 178	Kevin Hickey	.03	.01	.00	☐ 273	Nick Esasky	.06	.03	.00
☐ 179	Brian Holton	.03	.01	.00	☐ 274	Dwight Evans	.08	.04	.01
☐ 180	Ben McDonald	2.00	1.00	.20	☐ 275	Wes Gardner	.03	.01	.00
☐ 181	Bob Melvin	.03	.01	.00	☐ 276	Rich Gedman	.03	.01	.00
☐ 182	Bob Milacki	.10	.05	.01	☐ 277	Mike Greenwell	.20	.10	.02
☐ 183	Randy Milligan	.08	.04	.01	☐ 278	Danny Heep	.03	.01	.00
☐ 184	Gregg Olson	.30	.15	.03	☐ 279	Eric Hetzel	.08	.04	.01
☐ 185	Joe Orsulak	.03	.01	.00	☐ 280	Dennis Lamp	.03	.01	.00
☐ 186	Bill Ripken	.03	.01	.00	☐ 281	Rob Murphy	.03	.01	.00
☐ 187	Cal Ripken	.15	.07	.01	☐ 282	Joe Price	.03	.01	.00
☐ 188	Dave Schmidt	.03	.01	.00	☐ 283	Carlos Quintana	.06	.03	.00
☐ 189	Larry Sheets	.03	.01	.00	☐ 284	Jody Reed	.03	.01	.00
☐ 190	Mickey Tettleton	.06	.03	.00	☐ 285	Luis Rivera	.03	.01	.00
☐ 191	Mark Thurmond	.03	.01	.00	☐ 286	Kevin Romine	.03	.01	.00
☐ 192	Jay Tibbs	.03	.01	.00	☐ 287	Lee Smith	.06	.03	.00
☐ 193	Jim Traber	.03	.01	.00	☐ 288	Mike Smithson	.03	.01	.00
☐ 194	Mark Williamson	.03	.01	.00	☐ 289	Bob Stanley	.03	.01	.00
☐ 195	Craig Worthington	.10	.05	.01	☐ 290	Harold Baines	.08	.04	.01
☐ 196	Don Aase	.03	.01	.00	☐ 291	Kevin Brown	.08	.04	.01
☐ 197	Blaine Beatty	.15	.07	.01	☐ 292	Steve Buechele	.03	.01	.00
☐ 198	Mark Carreon	.03	.01	.00	☐ 293	Scott Coolbaugh	.30	.15	.03
☐ 199	Gary Carter	.08	.04	.01	☐ 294	Jack Daugherty	.12	.06	.01
☐ 200	David Cone	.08	.04	.01	☐ 295	Cecil Espy	.03	.01	.00
☐ 201	Ron Darling	.08	.04	.01	☐ 296	Julio Franco	.08	.04	.01
☐ 202	Kevin Elster	.06	.03	.00	☐ 297	Juan Gonzalez	.75	.35	.07
☐ 203	Sid Fernandez	.08	.04	.01	☐ 298	Cecilio Guante	.03	.01	.00
☐ 204	Dwight Gooden	.20	.10	.02	☐ 299	Drew Hall	.03	.01	.00
☐ 205	Keith Hernandez	.08	.04	.01	☐ 300	Charlie Hough	.03	.01	.00
☐ 206	Jeff Innis	.10	.05	.01	☐ 301	Pete Incaviglia	.08	.04	.01
☐ 207	Gregg Jefferies	.35	.17	.03	☐ 302	Mike Jeffcoat	.03	.01	.00
☐ 208	Howard Johnson	.10	.05	.01	☐ 303	Chad Kreuter	.03	.01	.00
☐ 209	Barry Lyons	.03	.01	.00	☐ 304	Jeff Kunkel	.03	.01	.00
☐ 210	Dave Magadan	.06	.03	.00	☐ 305	Rick Leach	.03	.01	.00
☐ 211	Kevin McReynolds	.08	.04	.01	☐ 306	Fred Manrique	.03	.01	.00
☐ 212	Jeff Musselman	.03	.01	.00	☐ 307	Jamie Moyer	.03	.01	.00
☐ 213	Randy Myers	.06	.03	.00	☐ 308	Rafael Palmeiro	.08	.04	.01
☐ 214	Bob Ojeda	.06	.03	.00	☐ 309	Geno Petralli	.03	.01	.00
☐ 215	Juan Samuel	.06	.03	.00	☐ 310	Kevin Reimer	.03	.01	.00
☐ 216	Mackey Sasser	.06	.03	.00	☐ 311	Kenny Rogers	.10	.05	.01
☐ 217	Darryl Strawberry	.25	.12	.02	☐ 312	Jeff Russell	.06	.03	.00
☐ 218	Tim Teufel	.03	.01	.00	☐ 313	Nolan Ryan	.30	.15	.03
☐ 219	Frank Viola	.08	.04	.01	☐ 314	Ruben Sierra	.20	.10	.02
☐ 220	Juan Agosto	.03	.01	.00	☐ 315	Bobby Witt	.06	.03	.00
☐ 221	Larry Andersen	.03	.01	.00	☐ 316	Chris Bosio	.06	.03	.00
☐ 222	Eric Anthony	1.75	.85	.17	☐ 317	Glenn Braggs	.06	.03	.00
☐ 223	Kevin Bass	.06	.03	.00	☐ 318	Greg Brock	.03	.01	.00
☐ 224	Craig Biggio	.10	.05	.01	☐ 319	Chuck Crim	.03	.01	.00
☐ 225	Ken Caminiti	.03	.01	.00	☐ 320	Rob Deer	.06	.03	.00
☐ 226	Jim Clancy	.03	.01	.00	☐ 321	Mike Felder	.03	.01	.00
☐ 227	Danny Darwin	.03	.01	.00	☐ 322	Tom Filer	.03	.01	.00
☐ 228	Glenn Davis	.10	.05	.01	☐ 323	Tony Fossas	.10	.05	.01
☐ 229	Jim Deshaies	.03	.01	.00	☐ 324	Jim Gantner	.03	.01	.00
☐ 230	Bill Doran	.06	.03	.00	☐ 325	Darryl Hamilton	.03	.01	.00
☐ 231	Bob Forsch	.03	.01	.00	☐ 326	Teddy Higuera	.06	.03	.00
☐ 232	Brian Meyer	.08	.04	.01	☐ 327	Mark Knudson	.08	.04	.01
☐ 233	Terry Puhl	.03	.01	.00	☐ 328	Bill Krueger	.03	.01	.00
☐ 234	Rafael Ramirez	.03	.01	.00	☐ 329	Tim McIntosh	.12	.06	.01
☐ 235	Rick Rhoden	.03	.01	.00	☐ 330	Paul Molitor	.08	.04	.01
☐ 236	Dan Schatzeder	.03	.01	.00	☐ 331	Jaime Navarro	.15	.07	.01
☐ 237	Mike Scott	.08	.04	.01	☐ 332	Charlie O'Brien	.03	.01	.00

☐ 333	Jeff Peterek	.12	.06	.01	☐ 428	Luis Quinones	.03	.01	.00
☐ 334	Dan Plesac	.06	.03	.00	☐ 429	Jeff Reed	.03	.01	.00
☐ 335	Jerry Reuss	.03	.01	.00	☐ 430	Jose Rijo	.03	.01	.00
☐ 336	Gary Sheffield	.30	.15	.03	☐ 431	Ron Robinson	.03	.01	.00
☐ 337	Bill Spiers	.30	.15	.03	☐ 432	Rolando Roomes	.08	.04	.01
☐ 338	B.J. Surhoff	.06	.03	.00	☐ 433	Chris Sabo	.08	.04	.01
☐ 339	Greg Vaughn	1.50	.75	.15	☐ 434	Scott Scudder	.15	.07	.01
☐ 340	Robin Yount	.25	.12	.02	☐ 435	Herm Winningham	.03	.01	.00
☐ 341	Hubie Brooks	.06	.03	.00	☐ 436	Steve Balboni	.03	.01	.00
☐ 342	Tim Burke	.06	.03	.00	☐ 437	Jesse Barfield	.08	.04	.01
☐ 343	Mike Fitzgerald	.03	.01	.00	☐ 438	Mike Blowers	.20	.10	.02
☐ 344	Tom Foley	.03	.01	.00	☐ 439	Tom Brookens	.03	.01	.00
☐ 345	Andres Galarraga	.08	.04	.01	☐ 440	Greg Cadaret	.03	.01	.00
☐ 346	Damaso Garcia	.03	.01	.00	☐ 441	Alvaro Espinoza	.03	.01	.00
☐ 347	Marquis Grissom	.60	.30	.06	☐ 442	Bob Geren	.15	.07	.01
☐ 348	Kevin Gross	.03	.01	.00	☐ 443	Lee Guetterman	.03	.01	.00
☐ 349	Joe Hesketh	.03	.01	.00	☐ 444	Mel Hall	.06	.03	.00
☐ 350	Jeff Huson	.12	.06	.01	☐ 445	Andy Hawkins	.03	.01	.00
☐ 351	Wallace Johnson	.03	.01	.00	☐ 446	Roberto Kelly	.10	.05	.01
☐ 352	Mark Langston	.10	.05	.01	☐ 447	Don Mattingly	.50	.25	.05
☐ 353	Dave Martinez	.03	.01	.00	☐ 448	Lance McCullers	.03	.01	.00
☐ 354	Dennis Martinez	.03	.01	.00	☐ 449	Hensley Meulens	.20	.10	.02
☐ 355	Andy McGaffigan	.03	.01	.00	☐ 450	Dale Mohorcic	.03	.01	.00
☐ 356	Otis Nixon	.03	.01	.00	☐ 451	Clay Parker	.03	.01	.00
☐ 357	Spike Owen	.03	.01	.00	☐ 452	Eric Plunk	.03	.01	.00
☐ 358	Pascual Perez	.06	.03	.00	☐ 453	Dave Righetti	.08	.04	.01
☐ 359	Tim Raines	.10	.05	.01	☐ 454	Deion Sanders	.50	.25	.05
☐ 360	Nelson Santovenia	.03	.01	.00	☐ 455	Steve Sax	.08	.04	.01
☐ 361	Bryn Smith	.06	.03	.00	☐ 456	Don Slaught	.03	.01	.00
☐ 362	Zane Smith	.03	.01	.00	☐ 457	Walt Terrell	.03	.01	.00
☐ 363	Larry Walker	.25	.12	.02	☐ 458	Dave Winfield	.10	.05	.01
☐ 364	Tim Wallach	.06	.03	.00	☐ 459	Jay Bell	.03	.01	.00
☐ 365	Rick Aguilera	.03	.01	.00	☐ 460	Rafael Belliard	.03	.01	.00
☐ 366	Allan Anderson	.06	.03	.00	☐ 461	Barry Bonds	.08	.04	.01
☐ 367	Wally Backman	.03	.01	.00	☐ 462	Bobby Bonilla	.08	.04	.01
☐ 368	Doug Baker	.03	.01	.00	☐ 463	Sid Bream	.03	.01	.00
☐ 369	Juan Berenguer	.03	.01	.00	☐ 464	Benny Distefano	.03	.01	.00
☐ 370	Randy Bush	.03	.01	.00	☐ 465	Doug Drabek	.03	.01	.00
☐ 371	Carmen Castillo	.03	.01	.00	☐ 466	Jim Gott	.03	.01	.00
☐ 372	Mike Dyer	.15	.07	.01	☐ 467	Billy Hatcher	.03	.01	.00
☐ 373	Gary Gaetti	.08	.04	.01	☐ 468	Neal Heaton	.03	.01	.00
☐ 374	Greg Gagne	.03	.01	.00	☐ 469	Jeff King	.06	.03	.00
☐ 375	Dan Gladden	.03	.01	.00	☐ 470	Bob Kipper	.03	.01	.00
☐ 376	German Gonzalez	.06	.03	.00	☐ 471	Randy Kramer	.03	.01	.00
☐ 377	Brian Harper	.03	.01	.00	☐ 472	Bill Landrum	.03	.01	.00
☐ 378	Kent Hrbek	.08	.04	.01	☐ 473	Mike LaValliere	.03	.01	.00
☐ 379	Gene Larkin	.03	.01	.00	☐ 474	Jose Lind	.03	.01	.00
☐ 380	Tim Laudner	.03	.01	.00	☐ 475	Junior Ortiz	.03	.01	.00
☐ 381	John Moses	.03	.01	.00	☐ 476	Gary Redus	.03	.01	.00
☐ 382	Al Newman	.03	.01	.00	☐ 477	Rick Reed	.12	.06	.01
☐ 383	Kirby Puckett	.20	.10	.02	☐ 478	R.J. Reynolds	.03	.01	.00
☐ 384	Shane Rawley	.03	.01	.00	☐ 479	Jeff Robinson	.06	.03	.00
☐ 385	Jeff Reardon	.06	.03	.00	☐ 480	John Smiley	.06	.03	.00
☐ 386	Roy Smith	.03	.01	.00	☐ 481	Andy Van Slyke	.08	.04	.01
☐ 387	Gary Wayne	.12	.06	.01	☐ 482	Bob Walk	.03	.01	.00
☐ 388	Dave West	.06	.03	.00	☐ 483	Andy Allanson	.03	.01	.00
☐ 389	Tim Belcher	.06	.03	.00	☐ 484	Scott Bailes	.03	.01	.00
☐ 390	Tim Crews	.03	.01	.00	☐ 485	Joey Belle	.50	.25	.05
☐ 391	Mike Davis	.03	.01	.00	☐ 486	Bud Black	.03	.01	.00
☐ 392	Rick Dempsey	.03	.01	.00	☐ 487	Jerry Browne	.03	.01	.00
☐ 393	Kirk Gibson	.08	.04	.01	☐ 488	Tom Candiotti	.03	.01	.00
☐ 394	Jose Gonzalez	.03	.01	.00	☐ 489	Joe Carter	.10	.05	.01
☐ 395	Alfredo Griffin	.03	.01	.00	☐ 490	Dave Clark	.03	.01	.00
☐ 396	Jeff Hamilton	.03	.01	.00	☐ 491	John Farrell	.03	.01	.00
☐ 397	Lenny Harris	.03	.01	.00	☐ 492	Felix Fermin	.03	.01	.00
☐ 398	Mickey Hatcher	.03	.01	.00	☐ 493	Brook Jacoby	.06	.03	.00
☐ 399	Orel Hershiser	.10	.05	.01	☐ 494	Dion James	.03	.01	.00
☐ 400	Jay Howell	.03	.01	.00	☐ 495	Doug Jones	.06	.03	.00
☐ 401	Mike Marshall	.08	.04	.01	☐ 496	Brad Komminsk	.03	.01	.00
☐ 402	Ramon Martinez	.08	.04	.01	☐ 497	Rod Nichols	.06	.03	.00
☐ 403	Mike Morgan	.03	.01	.00	☐ 498	Pete O'Brien	.06	.03	.00
☐ 404	Eddie Murray	.10	.05	.01	☐ 499	Steve Olin	.10	.05	.01
☐ 405	Alejandro Pena	.03	.01	.00	☐ 500	Jesse Orosco	.03	.01	.00
☐ 406	Willie Randolph	.06	.03	.00	☐ 501	Joel Skinner	.03	.01	.00
☐ 407	Mike Scioscia	.03	.01	.00	☐ 502	Cory Snyder	.08	.04	.01
☐ 408	Ray Searage	.03	.01	.00	☐ 503	Greg Swindell	.08	.04	.01
☐ 409	Fernando Valenzuela	.10	.05	.01	☐ 504	Rich Yett	.03	.01	.00
☐ 410	Jose Vizcaino	.25	.12	.02	☐ 505	Scott Bankhead	.06	.03	.00
☐ 411	John Wetteland	.25	.12	.02	☐ 506	Scott Bradley	.03	.01	.00
☐ 412	Jack Armstrong	.10	.05	.01	☐ 507	Greg Briley	.25	.12	.02
☐ 413	Todd Benzinger	.03	.01	.00	☐ 508	Jay Buhner	.06	.03	.00
☐ 414	Tim Birtsas	.03	.01	.00	☐ 509	Darnell Coles	.03	.01	.00
☐ 415	Tom Browning	.06	.03	.00	☐ 510	Keith Comstock	.03	.01	.00
☐ 416	Norm Charlton	.03	.01	.00	☐ 511	Henry Cotto	.03	.01	.00
☐ 417	Eric Davis	.20	.10	.02	☐ 512	Alvin Davis	.08	.04	.01
☐ 418	Rob Dibble	.06	.03	.00	☐ 513	Ken Griffey Jr.	1.00	.50	.10
☐ 419	John Franco	.06	.03	.00	☐ 514	Erik Hanson	.03	.01	.00
☐ 420	Ken Griffey Sr.	.06	.03	.00	☐ 515	Gene Harris	.15	.07	.01
☐ 421	Chris Hammond	.12	.06	.01	☐ 516	Brian Holman	.03	.01	.00
☐ 422	Danny Jackson	.06	.03	.00	☐ 517	Mike Jackson	.03	.01	.00
☐ 423	Barry Larkin	.10	.05	.01	☐ 518	Randy Johnson	.03	.01	.00
☐ 424	Tim Leary	.06	.03	.00	☐ 519	Jeffrey Leonard	.03	.01	.00
☐ 425	Rick Mahler	.03	.01	.00	☐ 520	Edgar Martinez	.03	.01	.00
☐ 426	Joe Oliver	.12	.06	.01	☐ 521	Dennis Powell	.03	.01	.00
☐ 427	Paul O'Neill	.08	.04	.01	☐ 522	Jim Presley	.03	.01	.00

☐ 523 Jerry Reed	.03	.01	.00
☐ 524 Harold Reynolds	.06	.03	.00
☐ 525 Mike Schooler	.06	.03	.00
☐ 526 Bill Swift	.03	.01	.00
☐ 527 Dave Valle	.03	.01	.00
☐ 528 Omar Vizquel	.15	.07	.01
☐ 529 Ivan Calderon	.06	.03	.00
☐ 530 Carlton Fisk	.10	.05	.01
☐ 531 Scott Fletcher	.03	.01	.00
☐ 532 Dave Gallagher	.03	.01	.00
☐ 533 Ozzie Guillen	.06	.03	.00
☐ 534 Greg Hibbard	.12	.06	.01
☐ 535 Shawn Hillegas	.03	.01	.00
☐ 536 Lance Johnson	.03	.01	.00
☐ 537 Eric King	.03	.01	.00
☐ 538 Ron Kittle	.06	.03	.00
☐ 539 Steve Lyons	.03	.01	.00
☐ 540 Carlos Martinez	.20	.10	.02
☐ 541 Tom McCarthy	.10	.05	.01
☐ 542 Matt Merullo	.10	.05	.01
☐ 543 Donn Pall	.03	.01	.00
☐ 544 Dan Pasqua	.03	.01	.00
☐ 545 Ken Patterson	.03	.01	.00
☐ 546 Melido Perez	.06	.03	.00
☐ 547 Steve Rosenberg	.08	.04	.01
☐ 548 Sammy Sosa	.40	.20	.04
☐ 549 Bobby Thigpen	.06	.03	.00
☐ 550 Robin Ventura	.50	.25	.05
☐ 551 Greg Walker	.03	.01	.00
☐ 552 Don Carman	.03	.01	.00
☐ 553 Pat Combs	.40	.20	.04
☐ 554 Dennis Cook	.06	.03	.00
☐ 555 Darren Daulton	.03	.01	.00
☐ 556 Len Dykstra	.06	.03	.00
☐ 557 Curt Ford	.03	.01	.00
☐ 558 Charlie Hayes	.06	.03	.00
☐ 559 Von Hayes	.08	.04	.01
☐ 560 Tommy Herr	.03	.01	.00
☐ 561 Ken Howell	.03	.01	.00
☐ 562 Steve Jeltz	.03	.01	.00
☐ 563 Ron Jones	.06	.03	.00
☐ 564 Ricky Jordan UER (duplicate line of statistics on back)	.50	.25	.05
☐ 565 John Kruk	.06	.03	.00
☐ 566 Steve Lake	.03	.01	.00
☐ 567 Roger McDowell	.06	.03	.00
☐ 568 Terry Mulholland	.03	.01	.00
☐ 569 Dwayne Murphy	.03	.01	.00
☐ 570 Jeff Parrett	.03	.01	.00
☐ 571 Randy Ready	.03	.01	.00
☐ 572 Bruce Ruffin	.03	.01	.00
☐ 573 Dickie Thon	.03	.01	.00
☐ 574 Jose Alvarez	.03	.01	.00
☐ 575 Geronimo Berroa	.08	.04	.01
☐ 576 Jeff Blauser	.03	.01	.00
☐ 577 Joe Boever	.03	.01	.00
☐ 578 Marty Clary	.03	.01	.00
☐ 579 Jody Davis	.03	.01	.00
☐ 580 Mark Eichhorn	.03	.01	.00
☐ 581 Darrell Evans	.06	.03	.00
☐ 582 Ron Gant	.06	.03	.00
☐ 583 Tom Glavine	.06	.03	.00
☐ 584 Tommy Greene	.40	.20	.04
☐ 585 Tommy Gregg	.03	.01	.00
☐ 586 Dave Justice	.20	.10	.02
☐ 587 Mark Lemke	.08	.04	.01
☐ 588 Derek Lilliquist	.08	.04	.01
☐ 589 Oddibe McDowell	.06	.03	.00
☐ 590 Kent Mercker	.40	.20	.04
☐ 591 Dale Murphy	.12	.06	.01
☐ 592 Gerald Perry	.06	.03	.00
☐ 593 Lonnie Smith	.06	.03	.00
☐ 594 Pete Smith	.03	.01	.00
☐ 595 John Smoltz	.08	.04	.01
☐ 596 Mike Stanton	.20	.10	.02
☐ 597 Andres Thomas	.03	.01	.00
☐ 598 Jeff Treadway	.03	.01	.00
☐ 599 Doyle Alexander	.03	.01	.00
☐ 600 Dave Bergman	.03	.01	.00
☐ 601 Brian Dubois	.12	.06	.01
☐ 602 Paul Gibson	.03	.01	.00
☐ 603 Mike Heath	.03	.01	.00
☐ 604 Mike Henneman	.03	.01	.00
☐ 605 Guillermo Hernandez	.06	.03	.00
☐ 606 Shawn Holman	.12	.06	.01
☐ 607 Tracy Jones	.03	.01	.00
☐ 608 Chet Lemon	.03	.01	.00
☐ 609 Fred Lynn	.08	.04	.01
☐ 610 Jack Morris	.08	.04	.01
☐ 611 Matt Nokes	.03	.01	.00
☐ 612 Gary Pettis	.03	.01	.00
☐ 613 Kevin Ritz	.15	.07	.01
☐ 614 Jeff Robinson	.06	.03	.00
☐ 615 Steve Searcy	.03	.01	.00

☐ 616 Frank Tanana	.03	.01	.00
☐ 617 Alan Trammell	.08	.04	.01
☐ 618 Gary Ward	.03	.01	.00
☐ 619 Lou Whitaker	.08	.04	.01
☐ 620 Frank Williams	.03	.01	.00
☐ 621A George Brett '80 ERR (had 10 .390 hitting seasons)	5.00	2.00	.40
☐ 621A George Brett '80 COR	.20	.08	.01
☐ 622 Fern.Valenzuela '81	.08	.03	.01
☐ 623 Dale Murphy '82	.12	.06	.01
☐ 624 Cal Ripken '83	.12	.06	.01
☐ 625 Ryne Sandberg '84	.12	.06	.01
☐ 626 Don Mattingly '85	.35	.17	.03
☐ 627 Roger Clemens '86	.12	.06	.01
☐ 628 George Bell '87	.08	.04	.01
☐ 629 Jose Canseco '88 UER (Reggie won MVP in '83, should say '73)	.50	.25	.05
☐ 630 Will Clark '89	.35	.17	.03
☐ 631 Game Savers Mark Davis Mitch Williams	.08	.04	.01
☐ 632 Boston Igniters Wade Boggs Mike Greenwell	.20	.10	.02
☐ 633 Starter and Stopper Mark Gubicza Jeff Russell	.06	.03	.00
☐ 634 League's Best Shortstops Tony Fernandez Cal Ripken	.08	.04	.01
☐ 635 Human Dynamos Kirby Puckett Bo Jackson	.25	.12	.02
☐ 636 300 Strikeout Club Nolan Ryan Mike Scott	.15	.07	.01
☐ 637 The Dynamic Duo Will Clark Kevin Mitchell	.20	.10	.02
☐ 638 AL All-Stars Don Mattingly Mark McGwire	.25	.12	.02
☐ 639 NL East Rivals Howard Johnson Ryne Sandberg	.10	.05	.01
☐ 640 Rudy Seanez Colin Charland	.20	.10	.02
☐ 641 George Canale Kevin Maas	.30	.15	.03
☐ 642 Kelly Mann Dave Hansen	.20	.10	.02
☐ 643 Greg Smith Stu Tate	.20	.10	.02
☐ 644 Tom Drees Dan Howitt	.30	.15	.03
☐ 645 Mike Roesler Derrick May	.25	.12	.02
☐ 646 Scott Hemond Mark Gardner	.20	.10	.02
☐ 647 John Orton Scott Leius	.20	.10	.02
☐ 648 Rich Monteleone Dana Williams	.20	.10	.02
☐ 649 Mike Huff Steve Frey	.20	.10	.02
☐ 650 Chuck McElroy Moises Alou	.20	.10	.02
☐ 651 Bobby Rose Mike Hartley	.20	.10	.02
☐ 652 Matt Kinzer Wayne Edwards	.20	.10	.02
☐ 653 Delino DeShields Jason Grimsley	.40	.20	.04
☐ 654 CL: A's/Cubs Giants/Blue Jays	.06	.01	.00
☐ 655 CL: Royals/Angels Padres/Orioles	.06	.01	.00
☐ 656 CL: Mets/Astros Cards/Red Sox	.06	.01	.00
☐ 657 CL: Rangers/Brewers Expos/Twins	.06	.01	.00
☐ 658 CL: Dodgers/Reds Yankees/Pirates	.06	.01	.00
☐ 659 CL: Indians/Mariners White Sox/Phillies	.06	.01	.00
☐ 660 CL: Braves/Tigers Specials/Checklists	.06	.01	.00

1990 Fleer Wax Box Cards

The 1990 Fleer wax box cards comprise seven different box bottoms with four cards each, for a total of 28 standard-size (2 1/2 by 3 1/2 inch) cards. The outer front borders are white; the inner, ribbon-like borders are different depending on the team. The vertically-oriented backs are gray. The cards are numbered with a C prefix.

	MINT	EXC	G-VG
COMPLETE SET (28)	6.00	3.00	.60
COMMON PLAYER (C1-C28)	.05	.02	.00

			MINT	EXC	G-VG
☐	C1	Giants Logo	.05	.02	.00
☐	C2	Tim Belcher	.10	.05	.01
☐	C3	Roger Clemens	.50	.25	.05
☐	C4	Eric Davis	.50	.25	.05
☐	C5	Glenn Davis	.20	.10	.02
☐	C6	Cubs Logo	.05	.02	.00
☐	C7	John Franco	.10	.05	.01
☐	C8	Mike Greenwell	.65	.30	.06
☐	C9	A's Logo	.05	.02	.00
☐	C10	Ken Griffey Jr.	1.00	.50	.10
☐	C11	Pedro Guerrero	.15	.07	.01
☐	C12	Tony Gwynn	.35	.17	.03
☐	C13	Blue Jays Logo	.05	.02	.00
☐	C14	Orel Hershiser	.30	.15	.03
☐	C15	Bo Jackson	1.00	.50	.10
☐	C16	Howard Johnson	.20	.10	.02
☐	C17	Mets Logo	.05	.02	.00
☐	C18	Cardinals Logo	.05	.02	.00
☐	C19	Don Mattingly	1.00	.50	.10
☐	C20	Mark McGwire	.75	.35	.07
☐	C21	Kevin Mitchell	.40	.20	.04
☐	C22	Kirby Puckett	.40	.20	.04
☐	C23	Royals Logo	.05	.02	.00
☐	C24	Orioles Logo	.05	.02	.00
☐	C25	Ruben Sierra	.50	.25	.05
☐	C26	Dave Stewart	.15	.07	.01
☐	C27	Jerome Walton	1.00	.50	.10
☐	C28	Robin Yount	.40	.20	.04

1990 Fleer All-Star Inserts

The 1990 Fleer All-Star insert set includes 12 standard-size (2 1/2 by 3 1/2 inch) cards. The fronts are white with a light gray screen and bright red stripes. The vertically-oriented backs are red, pink and white. The player selection for the set is Fleer's opinion of the best Major Leaguer at each position. Cards were individually distributed as an insert in 33-card cellos and random wax packs.

	MINT	EXC	G-VG
COMPLETE SET (12)	12.00	6.00	1.20
COMMON PLAYER (1-12)	.25	.12	.02

			MINT	EXC	G-VG
☐	1	Harold Baines .... Designated Hitter	.35	.17	.03
☐	2	Will Clark .... First Base	3.00	1.50	.30
☐	3	Mark Davis	.50	.25	.05

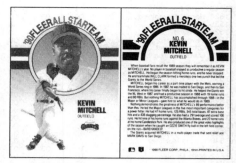

			MINT	EXC	G-VG
		Relief Pitcher			
☐	4	Howard Johnson .... Third Base	.50	.25	.05
☐	5	Joe Magrane .... Left Handed Pitcher	.50	.25	.05
☐	6	Kevin Mitchell .... Outfielder	1.00	.50	.10
☐	7	Kirby Puckett .... Outfielder	1.25	.60	.12
☐	8	Cal Ripken .... Shortstop	1.00	.50	.10
☐	9	Ryne Sandberg .... Second Base	1.00	.50	.10
☐	10	Mike Scott .... Right Handed Pitcher	.50	.25	.05
☐	11	Ruben Sierra .... Outfielder	1.25	.60	.12
☐	12	Mickey Tettleton .... Catcher	.35	.17	.03

1990 Fleer League Standouts

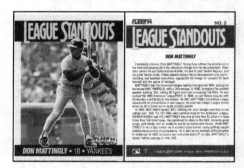

This six-card subset was distributed randomly (as an insert) in Fleer's 45-card rack packs. These cards are standard size, 2 1/2" by 3 1/2" and are quite attractive. The set is subtitled "Standouts" and commemorates outstanding events for those players from the previous season. The cards are numbered on the backs. The card backs are printed on white card stock.

	MINT	EXC	G-VG
COMPLETE SET (6)	6.00	2.00	.40
COMMON PLAYER (1-6)	.75	.25	.05

			MINT	EXC	G-VG
☐	1	Barry Larkin .... Cincinnati Reds	.75	.25	.05
☐	2	Don Mattingly .... New York Yankees	2.00	.90	.15
☐	3	Darryl Strawberry .... New York Mets	1.00	.40	.08
☐	4	Jose Canseco .... Oakland A's	2.00	.90	.15
☐	5	Wade Boggs .... Boston Red Sox	1.50	.60	.12
☐	6	Mark Grace .... Chicago Cubs	1.50	.60	.12

1987 French Bray Orioles

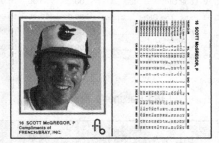

16 SCOTT McGREGOR, P
Compliments of
FRENCH/BRAY, INC.

The 1987 French Bray set contains 30 cards (featuring members of the Baltimore Orioles) measuring 2 1/4 by 3 inches. The fronts have facial photos with white and orange borders; the horizontally-oriented backs are white and feature career stats. The cards were given away in perforated sheet form on Photo Card Day at the Orioles home game on July 26, 1987. A large team photo was also included as one of the three panels in this perforated card set. The cards are unnumbered except for uniform number.

		MINT	EXC	G-VG
COMPLETE SET (30)		10.00	5.00	1.00
COMMON PLAYER		.20	.10	.02
☐ 2	Alan Wiggins	.20	.10	.02
☐ 3	Bill Ripken	.30	.15	.03
☐ 6	Floyd Rayford	.20	.10	.02
☐ 7	Cal Ripken Sr. MG	.30	.15	.03
☐ 8	Cal Ripken Jr.	1.25	.60	.12
☐ 9	Jim Dwyer	.20	.10	.02
☐ 10	Terry Crowley CO	.20	.10	.02
☐ 15	Terry Kennedy	.20	.10	.02
☐ 16	Scott McGregor	.30	.15	.03
☐ 18	Larry Sheets	.30	.15	.03
☐ 19	Fred Lynn	.40	.20	.04
☐ 20	Frank Robinson CO	1.00	.50	.10
☐ 24	Dave Schmidt	.30	.15	.03
☐ 25	Ray Knight	.30	.15	.03
☐ 27	Lee Lacy	.20	.10	.02
☐ 31	Mark Wiley CO	.20	.10	.02
☐ 32	Mark Williamson	.20	.10	.02
☐ 33	Eddie Murray	.75	.35	.07
☐ 38	Ken Gerhart	.30	.15	.03
☐ 39	Ken Dixon	.20	.10	.02
☐ 40	Jimmy Williams CO	.20	.10	.02
☐ 42	Mike Griffin	.20	.10	.02
☐ 43	Mike Young	.20	.10	.02
☐ 44	Elrod Hendricks CO	.20	.10	.02
☐ 45	Eric Bell	.20	.10	.02
☐ 46	Mike Flanagan	.30	.15	.03
☐ 49	Tom Niedenfuer	.20	.10	.02
☐ 52	Mike Boddicker	.30	.15	.03
☐ 54	John Habyan	.20	.10	.02
☐ 57	Tony Arnold	.20	.10	.02

1988 French Bray Orioles

This set was distributed as a perforated set of 30 full-color cards attached to a large team photo on July 31, 1988, the Baltimore Orioles' Photo Card Day. The cards measure approximately 2 1/4" by 3 1/16". Card backs are simply done in black and white with statistics but no narrative or any personal information. Cards are unnumbered except for uniform number. Card front have a thin orange inner border and have the French Bray (Printing and Graphic Communication) logo in the lower right corner.

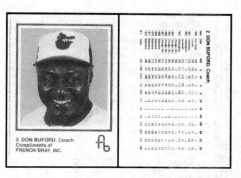

2 DON BUFORD, Coach
Compliments of
FRENCH/BRAY, INC.

		MINT	EXC	G-VG
COMPLETE SET (30)		8.00	4.00	.80
COMMON PLAYER		.20	.10	.02
☐ 2	Don Buford CO	.20	.10	.02
☐ 6	Joe Orsulak	.30	.15	.03
☐ 7	Bill Ripken	.40	.20	.04
☐ 8	Cal Ripken	1.00	.50	.10
☐ 9	Jim Dwyer	.20	.10	.02
☐ 10	Terry Crowley CO	.20	.10	.02
☐ 12	Mike Morgan	.30	.15	.03
☐ 14	Mickey Tettleton	.50	.25	.05
☐ 15	Terry Kennedy	.20	.10	.02
☐ 17	Pete Stanicek	.20	.10	.02
☐ 18	Larry Sheets	.30	.15	.03
☐ 19	Fred Lynn	.50	.25	.05
☐ 20	Frank Robinson MG	.75	.35	.07
☐ 23	Ozzie Peraza	.30	.15	.03
☐ 24	Dave Schmidt	.30	.15	.03
☐ 25	Rick Schu	.20	.10	.02
☐ 28	Jim Traber	.20	.10	.02
☐ 31	Herm Starrette CO	.20	.10	.02
☐ 33	Eddie Murray	.75	.35	.07
☐ 34	Jeff Ballard	.50	.25	.05
☐ 38	Ken Gerhart	.30	.15	.03
☐ 40	Minnie Mendoza CO	.20	.10	.02
☐ 41	Don Aase	.20	.10	.02
☐ 44	Elrod Hendricks CO	.20	.10	.02
☐ 47	John Hart CO	.20	.10	.02
☐ 48	Jose Bautista	.20	.10	.02
☐ 49	Tom Niedenfuer	.20	.10	.02
☐ 52	Mike Boddicker	.30	.15	.03
☐ 53	Jay Tibbs	.20	.10	.02
☐ 88	Rene Gonzales	.20	.10	.02

1989 French Bray Orioles

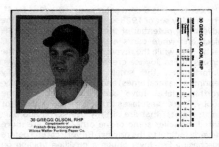

30 GREGG OLSON, RHP
Compliments of
French-Bray, Incorporated
Wilcox Walter Furlong Paper Co.

The 1989 French Bray Orioles set contains 31 cards measuring 2 1/4 by 3 inches. The fronts have facial photos with orange and white borders; the backs are white and feature career stats. The set was given away at a Baltimore home game. The cards are numbered by the players' uniform numbers.

		MINT	EXC	G-VG
COMPLETE SET (31)		8.00	4.00	.80
COMMON PLAYER		.20	.10	.02
☐ 3	Bill Ripken	.30	.15	.03

☐ 6	Joe Orsulak	.30	.15	.03
☐ 7	Cal Ripken Sr. CO	.30	.15	.03
☐ 8	Cal Ripken Jr.	1.00	.50	.10
☐ 9	Brady Anderson	.40	.20	.04
☐ 10	Steve Finley	.40	.20	.04
☐ 11	Craig Worthington	.50	.25	.05
☐ 12	Mike Devereaux	.30	.15	.03
☐ 14	Mickey Tettleton	.50	.25	.05
☐ 15	Randy Milligan	.40	.20	.04
☐ 16	Phil Bradley	.40	.20	.04
☐ 18	Bob Milacki	.40	.20	.04
☐ 19	Larry Sheets	.30	.15	.03
☐ 20	Frank Robinson MG	1.00	.50	.10
☐ 21	Mark Thurmond	.20	.10	.02
☐ 23	Kevin Hickey	.20	.10	.02
☐ 24	Dave Schmidt	.30	.15	.03
☐ 28	Jim Traber	.20	.10	.02
☐ 29	Jeff Ballard	.40	.20	.04
☐ 30	Gregg Olson	1.00	.50	.10
☐ 31	Al Jackson	.20	.10	.02
☐ 32	Mark Williamson	.20	.10	.02
☐ 36	Bob Melvin	.20	.10	.02
☐ 37	Brian Holton	.20	.10	.02
☐ 40	Tom McCraw CO	.20	.10	.02
☐ 42	Pete Harnisch	.20	.10	.02
☐ 43	Francisco Melendez	.30	.15	.03
☐ 44	Elrod Hendricks CO	.20	.10	.02
☐ 46	Johnny Oates CO	.20	.10	.02
☐ 48	Jose Bautista	.20	.10	.02
☐ 88	Rene Gonzales	.30	.15	.03

1928 Fro Joy

George Herman ("Babe") Ruth

The cards in this 6-card set measure 2 1/16" by 4". The Fro Joy set of 1928 was designed to exploit the advertising potential of the mighty Babe Ruth. Six black and white cards explained specific baseball techniques while the reverse advertising extolled the virtues of Fro Joy ice cream and ice cream cones. Unfortunately this small set has been illegally reprinted (several times) and many of these virtually-worthless fakes have been introduced into the hobby. The easiest fakes to spot are those cards (or uncut sheets) that are slightly over-sized and blue tinted; however some of the other fakes are more cleverly faithful to the original. Be very careful before purchasing Fro-Joys; obtain a qualified opinion on authenticity from an experienced dealer (preferably one who is unrelated to the dealer trying to sell you his cards). You might also show the cards (before you commit to purchase them) to an experienced printer who can advise you on the true age of the paper stock. One dealer has been quoted as saying that 99% of the Fro Joys are fakes.

	EX-MT	VG-E	GOOD
COMPLETE SET (6)	650.00	325.00	65.00
COMMON PLAYER (1-6)	100.00	50.00	10.00

☐ 1	George Herman (Babe) Ruth	150.00	75.00	15.00
☐ 2	Look Out, Mr. Pitcher	100.00	50.00	10.00
☐ 3	Bang; The Babe Lines one out	100.00	50.00	10.00
☐ 4	When the Babe Comes Out	100.00	50.00	10.00
☐ 5	Babe Ruth's Grip	100.00	50.00	10.00
☐ 6	Ruth is a Crack Fielder	100.00	50.00	10.00

1983 Gardner's Brewers

The cards in this 22-card set measure 2 1/2" by 3 1/2". The 1983 Gardner's Brewers set features Milwaukee Brewer players and manager Harvey Kuenn. Topps printed the set for the Madison (Wisconsin) bakery, hence, the backs are identical to the 1983 Topps backs except for the card number. The fronts of the cards, however, feature all new photos and include the Gardner's logo and the Brewers' logo. Many of the cards are grease laden, as they were issued with packages of bread and hamburger and hot-dog buns.

		MINT	EXC	G-VG
COMPLETE SET (22)		25.00	12.50	2.50
COMMON PLAYER (1-22)		.40	.20	.04
☐ 1	Harvey Kuenn MG	1.00	.50	.10
☐ 2	Dwight Bernard	.50	.25	.05
☐ 3	Mark Brouhard	.50	.25	.05
☐ 4	Mike Caldwell	.75	.35	.07
☐ 5	Cecil Cooper	1.50	.75	.15
☐ 6	Marshall Edwards	.50	.25	.05
☐ 7	Rollie Fingers	5.00	2.50	.50
☐ 8	Jim Gantner	.75	.35	.07
☐ 9	Moose Haas	.75	.35	.07
☐ 10	Bob McClure	.50	.25	.05
☐ 11	Paul Molitor	4.00	2.00	.40
☐ 12	Don Money	.75	.35	.07
☐ 13	Charlie Moore	.75	.35	.07
☐ 14	Ben Oglivie	.75	.35	.07
☐ 15	Ed Romero	.50	.25	.05
☐ 16	Ted Simmons	1.50	.75	.15
☐ 17	Jim Slaton	.75	.35	.07
☐ 18	Don Sutton	3.00	1.50	.30
☐ 19	Gorman Thomas	1.00	.50	.10
☐ 20	Pete Vuckovich	.75	.35	.07
☐ 21	Ned Yost	.50	.25	.05
☐ 22	Robin Yount	9.00	4.50	.90

1984 Gardner's Brewers

The cards in this 22-card set measure 2 1/2" by 3 1/2". For the second year in a row, the Gardner Bakery Company issued a set of cards available in packages of Gardner Bakery products. The set was manufactured by Topps, and the backs of the cards

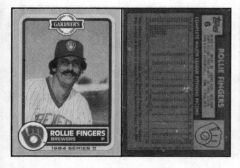

are identical to the Topps cards of this year except for the numbers. The Gardner logo appears on the fronts of the cards with the player's name, position abbreviation, the name Brewers, and the words 1984 Series II.

		MINT	EXC	G-VG
COMPLETE SET (22)		9.00	4.50	.90
COMMON PLAYER (1-22)		.30	.15	.03
☐ 1	Rene Lachemann MG	.40	.20	.04
☐ 2	Mark Brouhard	.30	.15	.03
☐ 3	Mike Caldwell	.40	.20	.04
☐ 4	Bobby Clark	.30	.15	.03
☐ 5	Cecil Cooper	.75	.35	.07
☐ 6	Rollie Fingers	2.00	1.00	.20
☐ 7	Jim Gantner	.50	.25	.05
☐ 8	Moose Haas	.40	.20	.04
☐ 9	Roy Howell	.30	.15	.03
☐ 10	Pete Ladd	.30	.15	.03
☐ 11	Rick Manning	.30	.15	.03
☐ 12	Bob McClure	.30	.15	.03
☐ 13	Paul Molitor	2.00	1.00	.20
☐ 14	Charlie Moore	.40	.20	.04
☐ 15	Ben Oglivie	.50	.25	.05
☐ 16	Ed Romero	.30	.15	.03
☐ 17	Ted Simmons	1.00	.50	.10
☐ 18	Jim Sundberg	.40	.20	.04
☐ 19	Don Sutton	1.75	.85	.17
☐ 20	Tom Tellman	.30	.15	.03
☐ 21	Pete Vuckovich	.50	.25	.05
☐ 22	Robin Yount	4.00	2.00	.40

1985 Gardner's Brewers

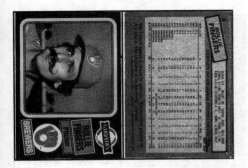

The cards in this 22-card set measure 2 1/2" by 3 1/2". For the third year in a row, the Gardner Bakery Company issued a set of cards available in packages of Gardner Bakery products. The set was manufactured by Topps, and the backs of the cards are identical to the Topps cards of this year except for the card numbers and copyright information. The Gardner logo appears on the fronts of the cards with the player's name, position abbreviation, and the name Brewers.

		MINT	EXC	G-VG
COMPLETE SET (22)		9.00	4.50	.90
COMMON PLAYER (1-22)		.30	.15	.03
☐ 1	George Bamberger MG	.40	.20	.04
☐ 2	Mark Brouhard	.30	.15	.03
☐ 3	Bobby Clark	.30	.15	.03
☐ 4	Jaime Cocanower	.30	.15	.03
☐ 5	Cecil Cooper	.90	.45	.09
☐ 6	Rollie Fingers	2.00	1.00	.20
☐ 7	Jim Gantner	.50	.25	.05
☐ 8	Moose Haas	.40	.20	.04
☐ 9	Dion James	.30	.15	.03
☐ 10	Pete Ladd	.30	.15	.03
☐ 11	Rick Manning	.30	.15	.03
☐ 12	Bob McClure	.30	.15	.03
☐ 13	Paul Molitor	2.00	1.00	.20
☐ 14	Charlie Moore	.40	.20	.04
☐ 15	Ben Oglivie	.40	.20	.04
☐ 16	Chuck Porter	.30	.15	.03
☐ 17	Ed Romero	.30	.15	.03
☐ 18	Bill Schroeder	.40	.20	.04
☐ 19	Ted Simmons	1.00	.50	.10
☐ 20	Tom Tellman	.30	.15	.03
☐ 21	Pete Vuckovich	.50	.25	.05
☐ 22	Robin Yount	4.00	2.00	.40

1989 Gardner's Brewers

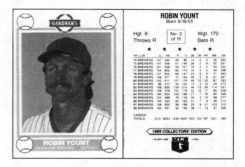

The 1989 Gardner's Brewers set contains 15 standard-size (2 1/2 by 3 1/2 inch) cards. The fronts feature airbrushed mugshots with sky blue backgrounds and white borders. The backs are white and feature career stats. One card was distributed in each specially marked Gardner's bakery product.

		MINT	EXC	G-VG
COMPLETE SET (15)		6.00	3.00	.60
COMMON PLAYER (1-15)		.25	.12	.02
☐ 1	Paul Molitor	1.25	.60	.12
☐ 2	Robin Yount	2.50	1.25	.25
☐ 3	Jim Gantner	.35	.17	.03
☐ 4	Rob Deer	.35	.17	.03
☐ 5	B.J. Surhoff	.35	.17	.03
☐ 6	Dale Sveum	.25	.12	.02
☐ 7	Ted Higuera	.35	.17	.03
☐ 8	Dan Plesac	.35	.17	.03
☐ 9	Bill Wegman	.25	.12	.02
☐ 10	Juan Nieves	.25	.12	.02
☐ 11	Greg Brock	.25	.12	.02
☐ 12	Glenn Braggs	.35	.17	.03
☐ 13	Joey Meyer	.25	.12	.02
☐ 14	Ernest Riles	.25	.12	.02
☐ 15	Don August	.25	.12	.02

1987 Gatorade Indians

Gatorade sponsored this perforated set of 30 full-color cards of the Cleveland Indians. The cards measure 2 1/8" by 3" (or 3 1/8") and feature the

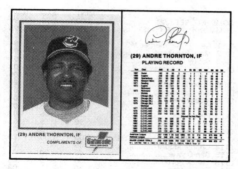

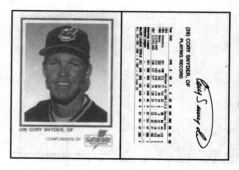

Gatorade logo prominently on the fronts of the cards. The cards were distributed as a tri-folded sheet (each part approximately 9 5/8" by 11 3/16") on April 25th at the stadium during the game against the Yankees. The large team photo is approximately 11 3/16" by 9 5/8". Card backs for the individual players contain year-by-year stats for that player.

	MINT	EXC	G-VG
COMPLETE SET (30)	9.00	4.50	.90
COMMON PLAYER	.25	.12	.02

		MINT	EXC	G-VG
☐ 2	Brett Butler	.50	.25	.05
☐ 4	Tony Bernazard	.35	.17	.03
☐ 6	Andy Allanson	.35	.17	.03
☐ 7	Pat Corrales MG	.25	.12	.02
☐ 8	Carmen Castillo	.25	.12	.02
☐ 10	Pat Tabler	.35	.17	.03
☐ 11	Jamie Easterly	.25	.12	.02
☐ 12	Dave Clark	.35	.17	.03
☐ 13	Ernie Camacho	.25	.12	.02
☐ 14	Julio Franco	.75	.35	.07
☐ 17	Junior Noboa	.25	.12	.02
☐ 18	Ken Schrom	.25	.12	.02
☐ 20	Otis Nixon	.25	.12	.02
☐ 21	Greg Swindell	.75	.35	.07
☐ 22	Frank Wills	.25	.12	.02
☐ 23	Chris Bando	.25	.12	.02
☐ 24	Rick Dempsey	.25	.12	.02
☐ 26	Brook Jacoby	.50	.25	.05
☐ 27	Mel Hall	.50	.25	.05
☐ 28	Cory Snyder	.75	.35	.07
☐ 29	Andre Thornton	.35	.17	.03
☐ 30	Joe Carter	1.00	.50	.10
☐ 35	Phil Niekro	1.00	.50	.10
☐ 36	Ed VandeBerg	.25	.12	.02
☐ 42	Rich Yett	.25	.12	.02
☐ 43	Scott Bailes	.25	.12	.02
☐ 46	Doug Jones	.50	.25	.05
☐ 49	Tom Candiotti	.25	.12	.02
☐ 54	Tom Waddell	.25	.12	.02
☐ xx	Indians MG/Coaches	.25	.12	.02
	Bobby Bonds 25			
	Johnny Goryl 45			
	Pat Corrales MG 7			
	Doc Edwards 32			
	Jack Aker 1			
☐ xx	Team Photo	.75	.35	.07
	(large size)			

1988 Gatorade Indians

This set was distributed as 30 perforated player cards attached to a large team photo of the Cleveland Indians. The cards measure approximately 2 1/4" by 3". Card backs are oriented either horizontally or vertically. Card backs are printed in red, blue, and black on white card stock. Card backs contain a facsimile autograph of the player. Cards are not arranged on the sheet in any order. The cards are unnumbered except for uniform number, which is given on the front and back of each card. The Gatorade logo is on the front of every card in the lower right corner.

	MINT	EXC	G-VG
COMPLETE SET (30)	7.00	3.50	.70
COMMON PLAYER	.20	.10	.02

		MINT	EXC	G-VG
☐ 2	Tom Spencer CO	.20	.10	.02
☐ 6	Andy Allanson	.20	.10	.02
☐ 7	Luis Isaac CO	.20	.10	.02
☐ 8	Carmen Castillo	.20	.10	.02
☐ 9	Charlie Manuel CO	.20	.10	.02
☐ 10	Pat Tabler	.30	.15	.03
☐ 11	Doug Jones	.40	.20	.04
☐ 14	Julio Franco	.50	.25	.05
☐ 15	Ron Washington	.20	.10	.02
☐ 16	Jay Bell	.30	.15	.03
☐ 17	Bill Laskey	.20	.10	.02
☐ 20	Willie Upshaw	.20	.10	.02
☐ 21	Greg Swindell	.50	.25	.05
☐ 23	Chris Bando	.20	.10	.02
☐ 25	Dave Clark	.30	.15	.03
☐ 26	Brook Jacoby	.30	.15	.03
☐ 27	Mel Hall	.40	.20	.04
☐ 28	Cory Snyder	.60	.30	.06
☐ 30	Joe Carter	.75	.35	.07
☐ 31	Dan Schatzeder	.20	.10	.02
☐ 32	Doc Edwards MG	.20	.10	.02
☐ 33	Ron Kittle	.30	.15	.03
☐ 35	Mark Wiley CO	.20	.10	.02
☐ 42	Rich Yett	.20	.10	.02
☐ 43	Scott Bailes	.20	.10	.02
☐ 45	John Goryl CO	.20	.10	.02
☐ 47	Jeff Kaiser	.20	.10	.02
☐ 49	Tom Candiotti	.30	.15	.03
☐ 50	Jeff Dedmon	.20	.10	.02
☐ 52	John Farrell	.40	.20	.04

1953 Glendale

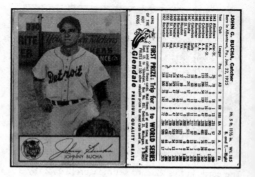

The cards in this 28-card set measure 2 5/8" by 3 3/4". The 1953 Glendale Meats set of full-color, unnumbered cards features Detroit Tiger ballplayers exclusively and was distributed one per package of Glendale Meats in the Detroit area. The back contains the complete major and minor league record through the 1952 season. The scarcer cards of the set command higher prices, with the Houtteman card being the most difficult to find.

There is an album associated with the set (which also is quite scarce now). The ACC designation for this scarce regional set is F151. Since the cards are unnumbered, they are ordered below alphabetically.

		NRMT	VG-E	GOOD
COMPLETE SET (28)		5000.00	2500.00	500.00
COMMON PLAYER (1-28)		125.00	60.00	12.50

			NRMT	VG-E	GOOD
☐	1	Matt Batts	125.00	60.00	12.50
☐	2	Johnny Bucha	125.00	60.00	12.50
☐	3	Frank Carswell	125.00	60.00	12.50
☐	4	Jim Delsing	125.00	60.00	12.50
☐	5	Walt Dropo	150.00	75.00	15.00
☐	6	Hal Erickson	125.00	60.00	12.50
☐	7	Paul Foytack	125.00	60.00	12.50
☐	8	Owen Friend	125.00	60.00	12.50
☐	9	Ned Garver	125.00	60.00	12.50
☐	10	Joe Ginsberg	300.00	150.00	30.00
☐	11	Ted Gray	125.00	60.00	12.50
☐	12	Fred Hatfield	125.00	60.00	12.50
☐	13	Ray Herbert	125.00	60.00	12.50
☐	14	Bill Hitchcock	125.00	60.00	12.50
☐	15	Bill Hoeft	200.00	100.00	20.00
☐	16	Art Houtteman	2100.00	900.00	225.00
☐	17	Milt Jordan	150.00	75.00	15.00
☐	18	Harvey Kuenn	350.00	175.00	35.00
☐	19	Don Lund	125.00	60.00	12.50
☐	20	Dave Madison	125.00	60.00	12.50
☐	21	Dick Marlowe	125.00	60.00	12.50
☐	22	Pat Mullin	125.00	60.00	12.50
☐	23	Bob Nieman	125.00	60.00	12.50
☐	24	Johnny Pesky	150.00	75.00	15.00
☐	25	Jerry Priddy	125.00	60.00	12.50
☐	26	Steve Souchock	125.00	60.00	12.50
☐	27	Russ Sullivan	125.00	60.00	12.50
☐	28	Bill Wight	150.00	75.00	15.00

1961 Golden Press

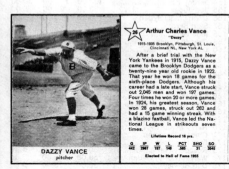

The cards in this 33-card set measure 2 1/2" by 3 1/2". The 1961 Golden Press set of full color cards features members of Baseball's Hall of Fame. The cards came in a booklet with perforations for punching the cards out of the book. The catalog designation is W524. The price for the full book intact is 25% higher than the complete set price listed.

		NRMT	VG-E	GOOD
COMPLETE SET (33)		50.00	25.00	5.00
COMMON PLAYER (1-33)		.50	.25	.05

			NRMT	VG-E	GOOD
☐	1	Mel Ott	1.50	.75	.15
☐	2	Grover C. Alexander	1.50	.75	.15
☐	3	Babe Ruth	15.00	7.50	1.50
☐	4	Hank Greenberg	1.00	.50	.10
☐	5	Bill Terry	.75	.35	.07
☐	6	Carl Hubbell	.75	.35	.07
☐	7	Rogers Hornsby	2.00	1.00	.20
☐	8	Dizzy Dean	4.00	2.00	.40
☐	9	Joe DiMaggio	10.00	5.00	1.00
☐	10	Charlie Gehringer	.75	.35	.07
☐	11	Gabby Hartnett	.50	.25	.05
☐	12	Mickey Cochrane	.75	.35	.07
☐	13	George Sisler	.65	.30	.06
☐	14	Joe Cronin	.65	.30	.06
☐	15	Pie Traynor	.65	.30	.06

			NRMT	VG-E	GOOD
☐	16	Lou Gehrig	10.00	5.00	1.00
☐	17	Lefty Grove	1.50	.75	.15
☐	18	Chief Bender	.50	.25	.05
☐	19	Frankie Frisch	.65	.30	.06
☐	20	Al Simmons	.50	.25	.05
☐	21	Home Run Baker	.50	.25	.05
☐	22	Jimmy Foxx	1.50	.75	.15
☐	23	John McGraw	.75	.35	.07
☐	24	Christy Mathewson	3.00	1.50	.30
☐	25	Ty Cobb	10.00	5.00	1.00
☐	26	Dazzy Vance	.50	.25	.05
☐	27	Bill Dickey	.75	.35	.07
☐	28	Eddie Collins	.50	.25	.05
☐	29	Walter Johnson	3.00	1.50	.30
☐	30	Tris Speaker	1.50	.75	.15
☐	31	Nap Lajoie	1.50	.75	.15
☐	32	Honus Wagner	3.00	1.50	.30
☐	33	Cy Young	2.00	1.00	.20

1933 Goudey

The cards in this 240-card set measure 2 3/8" by 2 7/8". The 1933 Goudey set, designated R319 by the ACC, was that company's first baseball issue. The four Babe Ruth and two Lou Gehrig cards in the set are extremely popular with collectors. Card number 106, Napoleon Lajoie, was not printed in 1933, and was circulated to a limited number of collectors in 1934 upon request (it was printed along with the 1934 Goudey cards). An album was offered to house the 1933 set. Several minor leaguers are depicted. Card number 1 (Bengough) is very rarely found in mint condition; in fact, as a general rule all the first series cards are more difficult to find in Mint condition. Players with more than one card are also sometimes differentiated below by their pose: BAT (Batting), FIELD (Fielding), PIT (Pitching), THROW (Throwing). One of the Babe Ruth cards was double printed (DP) apparently in place of the Lajoie and hence is easier to obtain than the others. Due to the scarcity of the Lajoie card, the set is considered complete at 239 cards and is priced as such below.

		EX-MT	VG-E	GOOD
COMPLETE SET (239)		33000.	15000.	3500.
COMMON PLAYER (1-40)		70.00	35.00	7.50
COMMON PLAYER (41-44)		50.00	25.00	5.00
COMMON PLAYER (45-52)		70.00	35.00	7.50
COMMON PLAYER (53-240)		50.00	25.00	5.00

			EX-MT	VG-E	GOOD
☐	1	Benny Bengough	1000.00	60.00	10.00
☐	2	Dazzy Vance	150.00	75.00	15.00
☐	3	Hugh Critz	70.00	35.00	7.50
☐	4	Heine Schuble	70.00	35.00	7.50
☐	5	Babe Herman	100.00	50.00	10.00
☐	6	Jimmy Dykes	90.00	45.00	9.00
☐	7	Ted Lyons	150.00	75.00	15.00
☐	8	Roy Johnson	70.00	35.00	7.50
☐	9	Dave Harris	70.00	35.00	7.50
☐	10	Glenn Myatt	70.00	35.00	7.50
☐	11	Billy Rogell	70.00	35.00	7.50
☐	12	George Pipgras	70.00	35.00	7.50
☐	13	Lafayette Thompson	70.00	35.00	7.50
☐	14	Henry Johnson	70.00	35.00	7.50
☐	15	Victor Sorrell	70.00	35.00	7.50
☐	16	George Blaeholder	70.00	35.00	7.50
☐	17	Watson Clark	70.00	35.00	7.50

☐	18	Muddy Ruel	70.00	35.00	7.50
☐	19	Bill Dickey	300.00	150.00	30.00
☐	20	Bill Terry THROW	200.00	100.00	20.00
☐	21	Phil Collins	70.00	35.00	7.50
☐	22	Pie Traynor	200.00	100.00	20.00
☐	23	Kiki Cuyler	150.00	75.00	15.00
☐	24	Horace Ford	70.00	35.00	7.50
☐	25	Paul Waner	150.00	75.00	15.00
☐	26	Chalmer Cissell	70.00	35.00	7.50
☐	27	George Connally	70.00	35.00	7.50
☐	28	Dick Bartell	70.00	35.00	7.50
☐	29	Jimmy Foxx	300.00	150.00	30.00
☐	30	Frank Hogan	70.00	35.00	7.50
☐	31	Tony Lazzeri	125.00	60.00	12.50
☐	32	Bud Clancy	70.00	35.00	7.50
☐	33	Ralph Kress	70.00	35.00	7.50
☐	34	Bob O'Farrell	70.00	35.00	7.50
☐	35	Al Simmons	200.00	100.00	20.00
☐	36	Tommy Thevenow	70.00	35.00	7.50
☐	37	Jimmy Wilson	70.00	35.00	7.50
☐	38	Fred Bickell	70.00	35.00	7.50
☐	39	Mark Koenig	70.00	35.00	7.50
☐	40	Taylor Douthit	70.00	35.00	7.50
☐	41	Gus Mancuso	50.00	25.00	5.00
☐	42	Eddie Collins	100.00	50.00	10.00
☐	43	Lew Fonseca	50.00	25.00	5.00
☐	44	Jim Bottomley	100.00	50.00	10.00
☐	45	Larry Benton	70.00	35.00	7.50
☐	46	Ethan Allen	70.00	35.00	7.50
☐	47	Heine Manush BAT	150.00	75.00	15.00
☐	48	Marty McManus	70.00	35.00	7.50
☐	49	Frank Frisch	200.00	100.00	20.00
☐	50	Ed Brandt	70.00	35.00	7.50
☐	51	Charlie Grimm	90.00	45.00	9.00
☐	52	Andy Cohen	70.00	35.00	7.50
☐	53	Babe Ruth	3500.00	1750.00	400.00
☐	54	Ray Kremer	50.00	25.00	5.00
☐	55	Pat Malone	50.00	25.00	5.00
☐	56	Charlie Ruffing	125.00	60.00	12.50
☐	57	Earl Clark	50.00	25.00	5.00
☐	58	Lefty O'Doul	70.00	35.00	7.50
☐	59	Bing Miller	50.00	25.00	5.00
☐	60	Waite Hoyt	100.00	50.00	10.00
☐	61	Max Bishop	50.00	25.00	5.00
☐	62	Pepper Martin	70.00	35.00	7.50
☐	63	Joe Cronin BAT	125.00	60.00	12.50
☐	64	Burleigh Grimes	100.00	50.00	10.00
☐	65	Milt Gaston	50.00	25.00	5.00
☐	66	George Grantham	50.00	25.00	5.00
☐	67	Guy Bush	50.00	25.00	5.00
☐	68	Horace Lisenbee	50.00	25.00	5.00
☐	69	Randy Moore	50.00	25.00	5.00
☐	70	Floyd (Pete) Scott	50.00	25.00	5.00
☐	71	Robert J. Burke	50.00	25.00	5.00
☐	72	Owen Carroll	50.00	25.00	5.00
☐	73	Jess Haines	100.00	50.00	10.00
☐	74	Eppa Rixey	100.00	50.00	10.00
☐	75	Willie Kamm	50.00	25.00	5.00
☐	76	Mickey Cochrane	150.00	75.00	15.00
☐	77	Adam Comorosky	50.00	25.00	5.00
☐	78	Jack Quinn	50.00	25.00	5.00
☐	79	Red Faber	100.00	50.00	10.00
☐	80	Clyde Manion	50.00	25.00	5.00
☐	81	Sam Jones	50.00	25.00	5.00
☐	82	Dibrell Williams	50.00	25.00	5.00
☐	83	Pete Jablonowski	50.00	25.00	5.00
☐	84	Glenn Spencer	50.00	25.00	5.00
☐	85	Heine Sand	50.00	25.00	5.00
☐	86	Phil Todt	50.00	25.00	5.00
☐	87	Frank O'Rourke	50.00	25.00	5.00
☐	88	Russell Rollings	50.00	25.00	5.00
☐	89	Tris Speaker	300.00	150.00	30.00
☐	90	Jess Petty	50.00	25.00	5.00
☐	91	Tom Zachary	50.00	25.00	5.00
☐	92	Lou Gehrig	1750.00	800.00	200.00
☐	93	John Welch	50.00	25.00	5.00
☐	94	Bill Walker	50.00	25.00	5.00
☐	95	Alvin Crowder	50.00	25.00	5.00
☐	96	Willis Hudlin	50.00	25.00	5.00
☐	97	Joe Morrissey	50.00	25.00	5.00
☐	98	Walter Berger	60.00	30.00	6.00
☐	99	Tony Cuccinello	60.00	30.00	6.00
☐	100	George Uhle	50.00	25.00	5.00
☐	101	Richard Coffman	50.00	25.00	5.00
☐	102	Travis Jackson	100.00	50.00	10.00
☐	103	Earl Combs	100.00	50.00	10.00
☐	104	Fred Marberry	50.00	25.00	5.00
☐	105	Bernie Friberg	50.00	25.00	5.00
☐	106	Napoleon Lajoie	12500.	5000.00	1250.00
		(not issued until 1934)			
☐	107	Heine Manush	100.00	50.00	10.00
☐	108	Joe Kuhel	50.00	25.00	5.00
☐	109	Joe Cronin	125.00	60.00	12.50
☐	110	Goose Goslin	100.00	50.00	10.00

☐	111	Monte Weaver	50.00	25.00	5.00
☐	112	Fred Schulte	50.00	25.00	5.00
☐	113	Oswald Bluege	50.00	25.00	5.00
☐	114	Luke Sewell	60.00	30.00	6.00
☐	115	Cliff Heathcote	50.00	25.00	5.00
☐	116	Eddie Morgan	50.00	25.00	5.00
☐	117	Rabbit Maranville	100.00	50.00	10.00
☐	118	Val Picinich	50.00	25.00	5.00
☐	119	Rogers Hornsby FIELD	300.00	150.00	30.00
☐	120	Carl Reynolds	50.00	25.00	5.00
☐	121	Walter Stewart	50.00	25.00	5.00
☐	122	Alvin Crowder	50.00	25.00	5.00
☐	123	Jack Russell	50.00	25.00	5.00
☐	124	Earl Whitehill	50.00	25.00	5.00
☐	125	Bill Terry	200.00	100.00	20.00
☐	126	Joe Moore	50.00	25.00	5.00
☐	127	Mel Ott	225.00	110.00	22.00
☐	128	Chuck Klein	150.00	75.00	15.00
☐	129	Hal Schumacher PIT	50.00	25.00	5.00
☐	130	Fred Fitzsimmons	50.00	25.00	5.00
☐	131	Fred Frankhouse	50.00	25.00	5.00
☐	132	Jim Elliott	50.00	25.00	5.00
☐	133	Fred Lindstrom	100.00	50.00	10.00
☐	134	Sam Rice	100.00	50.00	10.00
☐	135	Woody English	50.00	25.00	5.00
☐	136	Flint Rhem	50.00	25.00	5.00
☐	137	Fred (Red) Lucas	50.00	25.00	5.00
☐	138	Herb Pennock	100.00	50.00	10.00
☐	139	Ben Cantwell	50.00	25.00	5.00
☐	140	Bump Hadley	50.00	25.00	5.00
☐	141	Ray Benge	50.00	25.00	5.00
☐	142	Paul Richards	60.00	30.00	6.00
☐	143	Glenn Wright	50.00	25.00	5.00
☐	144	Babe Ruth BAT DP	3000.00	1500.00	350.00
☐	145	George Walberg	50.00	25.00	5.00
☐	146	Walter Stewart PIT	50.00	25.00	5.00
☐	147	Leo Durocher	100.00	50.00	10.00
☐	148	Eddie Farrell	50.00	25.00	5.00
☐	149	Babe Ruth	3500.00	1750.00	350.00
☐	150	Ray Kolp	50.00	25.00	5.00
☐	151	Jake Flowers	50.00	25.00	5.00
☐	152	Zack Taylor	50.00	25.00	5.00
☐	153	Buddy Myer	50.00	25.00	5.00
☐	154	Jimmy Foxx	300.00	150.00	30.00
☐	155	Joe Judge	50.00	25.00	5.00
☐	156	Danny MacFayden	50.00	25.00	5.00
☐	157	Sam Byrd	50.00	25.00	5.00
☐	158	Moe Berg	90.00	45.00	9.00
☐	159	Oswald Bluege	50.00	25.00	5.00
☐	160	Lou Gehrig	1750.00	800.00	200.00
☐	161	Al Spohrer	50.00	25.00	5.00
☐	162	Leo Mangum	50.00	25.00	5.00
☐	163	Luke Sewell	60.00	30.00	6.00
☐	164	Lloyd Waner	100.00	50.00	10.00
☐	165	Joe Sewell	100.00	50.00	10.00
☐	166	Sam West	50.00	25.00	5.00
☐	167	Jack Russell	50.00	25.00	5.00
☐	168	Goose Goslin	100.00	50.00	10.00
☐	169	Al Thomas	50.00	25.00	5.00
☐	170	Harry McCurdy	50.00	25.00	5.00
☐	171	Charlie Jamieson	50.00	25.00	5.00
☐	172	Billy Hargrave	50.00	25.00	5.00
☐	173	Roscoe Holm	50.00	25.00	5.00
☐	174	Warren(Curly) Ogden	50.00	25.00	5.00
☐	175	Dan Howley	50.00	25.00	5.00
☐	176	John Ogden	50.00	25.00	5.00
☐	177	Walter French	50.00	25.00	5.00
☐	178	Jackie Warner	50.00	25.00	5.00
☐	179	Fred Leach	50.00	25.00	5.00
☐	180	Eddie Moore	50.00	25.00	5.00
☐	181	Babe Ruth	3500.00	1750.00	350.00
☐	182	Andy High	50.00	25.00	5.00
☐	183	George Walberg	50.00	25.00	5.00
☐	184	Charley Berry	50.00	25.00	5.00
☐	185	Bob Smith	50.00	25.00	5.00
☐	186	John Schulte	50.00	25.00	5.00
☐	187	Heine Manush	100.00	50.00	10.00
☐	188	Rogers Hornsby	300.00	150.00	30.00
☐	189	Joe Cronin	125.00	60.00	12.50
☐	190	Fred Schulte	50.00	25.00	5.00
☐	191	Ben Chapman	60.00	30.00	6.00
☐	192	Walter Brown	50.00	25.00	5.00
☐	193	Lynford Lary	50.00	25.00	5.00
☐	194	Earl Averill	100.00	50.00	10.00
☐	195	Evar Swanson	50.00	25.00	5.00
☐	196	Leroy Mahaffey	50.00	25.00	5.00
☐	197	Rick Ferrell	100.00	50.00	10.00
☐	198	Jack Burns	50.00	25.00	5.00
☐	199	Tom Bridges	60.00	30.00	6.00
☐	200	Bill Hallahan	50.00	25.00	5.00
☐	201	Ernie Orsatti	50.00	25.00	5.00
☐	202	Gabby Hartnett	100.00	50.00	10.00
☐	203	Lon Warneke	50.00	25.00	5.00
☐	204	Riggs Stephenson	60.00	30.00	6.00
☐	205	Heine Meine	50.00	25.00	5.00

Brian Morris

226 North Fullerton Avenue
Montclair, NJ 07042
201-509-8484

Please include SASE with all inquiries.

Specializing in Hartland Statues, Scarce,
Rare and Unusual Issues and single cards,
as well as Topps, Bowman, Play Balls,
Goudeys and Tobacco cards.

**Building quality investment portfolios
for collectors and investors.**

✦ **If you're a Team collector,**
✦ **If you're a Superstar collector,**
✦ **If you're a Hall of Fame collector,**
✦ **If you're a Type card collector,**

**Try me, I may be able to help your
collection grow.**

I also am buying any issues listed in this
book in Mint condition prior to 1979 for
70-100% of the values printed. I also will buy
cards prior to 1959 in lesser conditions.

		EX-MT	VG-E	GOOD
☐ 206	Gus Suhr	50.00	25.00	5.00
☐ 207	Mel Ott BAT	225.00	110.00	22.00
☐ 208	Bernie James	50.00	25.00	5.00
☐ 209	Adolfo Luque	50.00	25.00	5.00
☐ 210	Virgil Davis	50.00	25.00	5.00
☐ 211	Hack Wilson	200.00	100.00	20.00
☐ 212	Billy Urbanski	50.00	25.00	5.00
☐ 213	Earl Adams	50.00	25.00	5.00
☐ 214	John Kerr	50.00	25.00	5.00
☐ 215	Russ Van Atta	50.00	25.00	5.00
☐ 216	Vernon Gomez	300.00	150.00	30.00
☐ 217	Frank Crosetti	90.00	45.00	9.00
☐ 218	Wes Ferrell	60.00	30.00	6.00
☐ 219	Mule Haas	50.00	25.00	5.00
☐ 220	Lefty Grove	350.00	175.00	35.00
☐ 221	Dale Alexander	50.00	25.00	5.00
☐ 222	Charley Gehringer	200.00	100.00	20.00
☐ 223	Dizzy Dean	600.00	300.00	60.00
☐ 224	Frank Demaree	50.00	25.00	5.00
☐ 225	Bill Jurges	50.00	25.00	5.00
☐ 226	Charley Root	50.00	25.00	5.00
☐ 227	Billy Herman	100.00	50.00	10.00
☐ 228	Tony Piet	50.00	25.00	5.00
☐ 229	Floyd(Arky) Vaughan	100.00	50.00	10.00
☐ 230	Carl Hubbell PIT	175.00	85.00	18.00
☐ 231	Joe Moore FIELD	50.00	25.00	5.00
☐ 232	Lefty O'Doul	60.00	30.00	6.00
☐ 233	Johnny Vergez	50.00	25.00	5.00
☐ 234	Carl Hubbell	175.00	85.00	18.00
☐ 235	Fred Fitzsimmons	60.00	30.00	6.00
☐ 236	George Davis	50.00	25.00	5.00
☐ 237	Gus Mancuso	50.00	25.00	5.00
☐ 238	Hugh Critz	50.00	25.00	5.00
☐ 239	Leroy Parmelee	50.00	25.00	5.00
☐ 240	Hal Schumacher	100.00	30.00	6.00

1934 Goudey

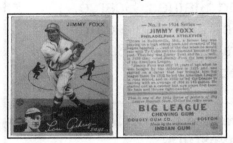

The cards in this 96-card set measure 2 3/8" by 2 7/8". The 1934 Goudey set of color cards carries the ACC catalog number R320. Cards 1-48 are considered to be the easiest to find (although card number 1, Foxx, is very scarce in mint condition) while 73-96 are much more difficult to find. Cards of this 1934 Goudey series are slightly less abundant than cards of the 1933 Goudey set. Of the 96 cards, 84 contain a "Lou Gehrig Says" line on the front in a blue design, while 12 of the high series contain a "Chuck Klein Says" line in a red design. These Chuck Klein cards are indicated in the checklist below by CK and are in fact the 12 National Leaguers in the high series.

	EX-MT	VG-E	GOOD
COMPLETE SET (96)	15000.00	7500.00	1750.00
COMMON PLAYER (1-48)	50.00	25.00	5.00
COMMON PLAYER (49-72)	75.00	37.50	7.50
COMMON PLAYER (73-96)	200.00	100.00	20.00

☐ 1	Jimmy Foxx	600.00	150.00	30.00
☐ 2	Mickey Cochrane	150.00	75.00	15.00
☐ 3	Charlie Grimm	60.00	30.00	6.00
☐ 4	Woody English	50.00	25.00	5.00
☐ 5	Ed Brandt	50.00	25.00	5.00
☐ 6	Dizzy Dean	500.00	250.00	50.00
☐ 7	Leo Durocher	75.00	37.50	7.50
☐ 8	Tony Piet	50.00	25.00	5.00
☐ 9	Ben Chapman	60.00	30.00	6.00
☐ 10	Chuck Klein	100.00	50.00	10.00
☐ 11	Paul Waner	100.00	50.00	10.00

☐ 12	Carl Hubbell	150.00	75.00	15.00
☐ 13	Frank Frisch	150.00	75.00	15.00
☐ 14	Willie Kamm	50.00	25.00	5.00
☐ 15	Alvin Crowder	50.00	25.00	5.00
☐ 16	Joe Kuhel	50.00	25.00	5.00
☐ 17	Hugh Critz	50.00	25.00	5.00
☐ 18	Heinie Manush	100.00	50.00	10.00
☐ 19	Lefty Grove	200.00	100.00	20.00
☐ 20	Frank Hogan	50.00	25.00	5.00
☐ 21	Bill Terry	150.00	75.00	15.00
☐ 22	Arky Vaughan	100.00	50.00	10.00
☐ 23	Charlie Gehringer	150.00	75.00	15.00
☐ 24	Ray Benge	50.00	25.00	5.00
☐ 25	Roger Cramer	60.00	30.00	6.00
☐ 26	Gerald Walker	50.00	25.00	5.00
☐ 27	Luke Appling	100.00	50.00	10.00
☐ 28	Ed Coleman	50.00	25.00	5.00
☐ 29	Larry French	50.00	25.00	5.00
☐ 30	Julius Solters	50.00	25.00	5.00
☐ 31	Buck Jordan	50.00	25.00	5.00
☐ 32	Blondy Ryan	50.00	25.00	5.00
☐ 33	Frank Hurst	50.00	25.00	5.00
☐ 34	Chick Hafey	100.00	50.00	10.00
☐ 35	Ernie Lombardi	100.00	50.00	10.00
☐ 36	Walter Betts	50.00	25.00	5.00
☐ 37	Lou Gehrig	2000.00	1000.00	250.00
☐ 38	Oral Hildebrand	50.00	25.00	5.00
☐ 39	Fred Walker	50.00	25.00	5.00
☐ 40	John Stone	50.00	25.00	5.00
☐ 41	George Earnshaw	50.00	25.00	5.00
☐ 42	John Allen	50.00	25.00	5.00
☐ 43	Dick Porter	50.00	25.00	5.00
☐ 44	Tom Bridges	60.00	30.00	6.00
☐ 45	Oscar Melillo	50.00	25.00	5.00
☐ 46	Joe Stripp	50.00	25.00	5.00
☐ 47	John Frederick	50.00	25.00	5.00
☐ 48	Tex Carleton	50.00	25.00	5.00
☐ 49	Sam Leslie	75.00	37.50	7.50
☐ 50	Walter Beck	75.00	37.50	7.50
☐ 51	Rip Collins	75.00	37.50	7.50
☐ 52	Herman Bell	75.00	37.50	7.50
☐ 53	George Watkins	75.00	37.50	7.50
☐ 54	Wesley Schulmerich	75.00	37.50	7.50
☐ 55	Ed Holley	75.00	37.50	7.50
☐ 56	Mark Koenig	75.00	37.50	7.50
☐ 57	Bill Swift	75.00	37.50	7.50
☐ 58	Earl Grace	75.00	37.50	7.50
☐ 59	Joe Mowry	75.00	37.50	7.50
☐ 60	Lynn Nelson	75.00	37.50	7.50
☐ 61	Lou Gehrig	2250.00	1000.00	250.00
☐ 62	Hank Greenberg	225.00	110.00	22.00
☐ 63	Minter Hayes	75.00	37.50	7.50
☐ 64	Frank Grube	75.00	37.50	7.50
☐ 65	Cliff Bolton	75.00	37.50	7.50
☐ 66	Mel Harder	90.00	45.00	9.00
☐ 67	Bob Weiland	75.00	37.50	7.50
☐ 68	Bob Johnson	90.00	45.00	9.00
☐ 69	John Marcum	75.00	37.50	7.50
☐ 70	Pete Fox	75.00	37.50	7.50
☐ 71	Lyle Tinning	75.00	37.50	7.50
☐ 72	Arndt Jorgens	75.00	37.50	7.50
☐ 73	Ed Wells	200.00	100.00	20.00
☐ 74	Bob Boken	200.00	100.00	20.00
☐ 75	Bill Werber	200.00	100.00	20.00
☐ 76	Hal Trosky	225.00	110.00	22.00
☐ 77	Joe Vosmik	200.00	100.00	20.00
☐ 78	Pinky Higgins	225.00	110.00	22.00
☐ 79	Ed Durham	200.00	100.00	20.00
☐ 80	Marty McManus CK	200.00	100.00	20.00
☐ 81	Bob Brown CK	200.00	100.00	20.00
☐ 82	Bill Hallahan CK	200.00	100.00	20.00
☐ 83	Jim Mooney CK	200.00	100.00	20.00
☐ 84	Paul Derringer CK	225.00	110.00	22.00
☐ 85	Adam Comorosky CK	200.00	100.00	20.00
☐ 86	Lloyd Johnson CK	200.00	100.00	20.00
☐ 87	George Darrow CK	200.00	100.00	20.00
☐ 88	Homer Peel CK	200.00	100.00	20.00
☐ 89	Linus Frey CK	200.00	100.00	20.00
☐ 90	Ki-Ki Cuyler CK	400.00	200.00	40.00
☐ 91	Dolph Camilli CK	225.00	110.00	22.00
☐ 92	Steve Larkin	200.00	100.00	20.00
☐ 93	Fred Ostermueller	200.00	100.00	20.00
☐ 94	Red Rolfe	225.00	110.00	22.00
☐ 95	Myril Hoag	200.00	100.00	20.00
☐ 96	James DeShong	250.00	100.00	20.00

1935 Goudey

PICTURE 1   CARD B

The cards in this 36-card set (the number of different front pictures) measure 2 3/8" by 2 7/8". The 1935 Goudey set is sometimes called the Goudey Puzzle Set, the Goudey 4-in-1's, or R321 (ACC). There are 36 different card fronts but 114 different front/back combinations. The card number in the checklist refers to the back puzzle number, as the backs can be arranged to form a puzzle picturing a player or team. To avoid the confusion caused by two different fronts having the same back number, the rarer cards have been arbitrarily given a "1" prefix. The scarcer puzzle cards are hence all listed at the numerical end of the list below, i.e. rare puzzle 1 is listed as number 11, rare puzzle 2 is listed as number 12, etc. The BLUE in the checklist refers to a card with a blue border, as most cards have a red border. The set price below includes all the cards listed. The following is the list of the puzzle back pictures: 1) Detroit Tigers; 2) Chuck Klein; 3) Frankie Frisch; 4) Mickey Cochrane; 5) Joe Cronin; 6) Jimmy Foxx; 7) Al Simmons; 8) Cleveland Indians; and 9) Washington Senators.

	EX-MT	VG-E	GOOD
COMPLETE SET (114)	15000.00	7000.00	1750.00
COMMON CARDS (1-9)	50.00	25.00	5.00
COMMON CARDS (11-17)	100.00	50.00	10.00

		EX-MT	VG-E	GOOD
☐ 1A	F.Frisch/Dizzy Dean Orsatti/Carleton	150.00	75.00	15.00
☐ 1B	Mahaffey/Jimmie Foxx Williams/Higgins	100.00	50.00	10.00
☐ 1C	Heine Manush/Lary Weaver/Hadley	65.00	32.50	6.50
☐ 1D	Cochrane/C.Gehringer Bridges/Rogell	100.00	50.00	10.00
☐ 1E	Paul Waner/Bush W.Hoyt/Lloyd Waner	100.00	50.00	10.00
☐ 1F	B.Grimes/Chuck Klein K.Cuyler/English	100.00	50.00	10.00
☐ 1G	Leslie/Frey Joe Stripp/Clark	50.00	25.00	5.00
☐ 1H	Piet/Comorosky Bottomley/Adams	65.00	32.50	6.50
☐ 1I	Earnshaw/Dykes Luke Sewell/Appling	65.00	32.50	6.50
☐ 1J	Babe Ruth/McManus Brandt/Maranville	900.00	450.00	90.00
☐ 1K	Bill Terry/Schumacher Mancuso/T.Jackson	100.00	50.00	10.00
☐ 1L	Kamm/Hildebrand Averill/Trosky	65.00	32.50	6.50
☐ 2A	F.Frisch/Dizzy Dean Orsatti/Carleton	150.00	75.00	15.00
☐ 2B	Mahaffey/Jimmie Foxx Williams/Higgins	100.00	50.00	10.00
☐ 2C	Heine Manush/Lary Weaver/Hadley	65.00	32.50	6.50
☐ 2D	Cochrane/C.Gehringer Bridges/Rogell	100.00	50.00	10.00
☐ 2E	Kamm/Hildebrand Earl Averill/Trosky	65.00	32.50	6.50
☐ 2F	Earnshaw/Dykes Luke Sewell/Appling	65.00	32.50	6.50
☐ 3A	Babe Ruth/McManus Brandt/Maranville	900.00	450.00	90.00
☐ 3B	Bill Terry/Schumacher Mancuso/T.Jackson	100.00	50.00	10.00

		EX-MT	VG-E	GOOD
☐ 3C	Paul Waner/Bush W.Hoyt/Lloyd Waner	100.00	50.00	10.00
☐ 3D	B.Grimes/Chuck Klein K.Cuyler/English	100.00	50.00	10.00
☐ 3E	Leslie/Frey Joe Stripp/Clark	50.00	25.00	5.00
☐ 3F	Piet/Comorosky Jim Bottomley/Adams	65.00	32.50	6.50
☐ 4A	Critz/D.Bartell BLUE Mel Ott/Mancuso	100.00	50.00	10.00
☐ 4B	Pie Traynor/Lucas BLUE Tom Thevenow/Wright	65.00	32.50	6.50
☐ 4C	Berry/Burke BLUE Kress/Dazzy Vance	65.00	32.50	6.50
☐ 4D	R.Ruffing/Malone BLUE Lazzeri/Bill Dickey	150.00	75.00	15.00
☐ 4E	Moore/Hogan BLUE Frankhouse/Brandt	50.00	25.00	5.00
☐ 4F	Martin/O'Farrell BLUE Byrd/MacFayden	50.00	25.00	5.00
☐ 5A	Ruel/Al Simmons Kamm/M.Cochrane	100.00	50.00	10.00
☐ 5B	Willis Hudlin/Myatt Comorosky/Bottomley	65.00	32.50	6.50
☐ 5C	Paul Waner/Bush W.Hoyt/Lloyd Waner	100.00	50.00	10.00
☐ 5D	West/Oscar Melillo Blaeholder/Coffman	50.00	25.00	5.00
☐ 5E	Leslie/Frey Joe Stripp/Clark	50.00	25.00	5.00
☐ 5F	Schuble/Marberry Goose Goslin/Crowder	65.00	32.50	6.50
☐ 6A	Ruel/Al Simmons Kamm/M.Cochrane	100.00	50.00	10.00
☐ 6B	Willis Hudlin/Myatt Comorosky/Bottomley	65.00	32.50	6.50
☐ 6C	Wilson/Allen Jonnard/Brickell	50.00	25.00	5.00
☐ 6D	West/Oscar Melillo Blaeholder/Coffman	50.00	25.00	5.00
☐ 6E	Joe Cronin/Reynolds Bishop/Cissell	65.00	32.50	6.50
☐ 6F	Schuble/Marberry Goose Goslin/Crowder	65.00	32.50	6.50
☐ 7A	Critz/Bartell BLUE Mel Ott/Mancuso	100.00	50.00	10.00
☐ 7B	Pie Traynor/Lucas BLUE Tom Thevenow/Wright	65.00	32.50	6.50
☐ 7C	Berry/Burke BLUE Kress/Dazzy Vance	65.00	32.50	6.50
☐ 7D	R.Ruffing/Malone BLUE Lazzeri/Bill Dickey	150.00	75.00	15.00
☐ 7E	Moore/Hogan BLUE Frankhouse/Brandt	50.00	25.00	5.00
☐ 7F	Martin/O'Farrell BLUE Byrd/MacFayden	50.00	25.00	5.00
☐ 8A	M.Koenig/Fitzsimmons Benge/Zachary	50.00	25.00	5.00
☐ 8B	Hayes/Ted Lyons Haas/Zeke Bonura	65.00	32.50	6.50
☐ 8C	Burns/Rollie Hemsley Grube/Weiland	50.00	25.00	5.00
☐ 8D	Campbell/Meyers Goodman/Kampouris	50.00	25.00	5.00
☐ 8E	DeShong/Allen Red Rolfe/Walker	50.00	25.00	5.00
☐ 8F	P.Fox/Hank Greenberg Walker/Rowe	80.00	40.00	8.00
☐ 8G	Werber/Rick Ferrell W.Ferrell/Ostermueller	65.00	32.50	6.50
☐ 8H	Joe Kuhel/Whitehill Meyer/Stone	50.00	25.00	5.00
☐ 8I	J.Vosmik/Knickerbocker Mel Harder/Stewart	50.00	25.00	5.00
☐ 8J	Johnson/Coleman Marcum/Cramer	50.00	25.00	5.00
☐ 8K	Herman/Suhr Padden/Blanton	50.00	25.00	5.00
☐ 8L	Spohrer/Rhem Cantwell/Benton	50.00	25.00	5.00
☐ 8M	M.Koenig/Fitzsimmons Benge/Zachary	50.00	25.00	5.00
☐ 9B	Hayes/Ted Lyons Haas/Zeke Bonura	65.00	32.50	6.50
☐ 9C	Burns/Rollie Hemsley Grube/Weiland	50.00	25.00	5.00
☐ 9D	Campbell/Meyers Goodman/Kampouris	50.00	25.00	5.00
☐ 9E	DeShong/Allen Red Rolfe/Walker	50.00	25.00	5.00
☐ 9F	P.Fox/Hank Greenberg Walker/Rowe	80.00	40.00	8.00
☐ 9G	Werber/Rick Ferrell W.Ferrell/Ostermueller	65.00	32.50	6.50
☐ 9H	Joe Kuhel/Whitehill	50.00	25.00	5.00

	Meyer/Stone			
☐ 9I	J.Vosmik/Knickerbocker ..	50.00	25.00	5.00
	Mel Harder/Stewart			
☐ 9J	Johnson/Coleman	50.00	25.00	5.00
	Marcum/Cramer			
☐ 9K	Herman/Suhr	50.00	25.00	5.00
	Padden/Blanton			
☐ 9L	Spohrer/Rhem	50.00	25.00	5.00
	Cantwell/Benton			
☐ 11E	Wilson/Allen	100.00	50.00	10.00
	Jonnard/Brickell			
☐ 11F	West/Melillo	100.00	50.00	10.00
	Blaeholder/Coffman			
☐ 11G	Joe Cronin/Reynolds	150.00	75.00	15.00
	Bishop/Cissel			
☐ 11H	Schuble/Marberry	125.00	60.00	12.50
	Goose Goslin/Crowder			
☐ 11J	Ruel/Al Simmons	175.00	85.00	18.00
	Kamm/M.Cochrane			
☐ 11K	Hudlin/Myatt	125.00	60.00	12.50
	Comorosky/Bottomley			
☐ 12A	Critz/Bartell BLUE	150.00	75.00	15.00
	Mel Ott/Mancuso			
☐ 12B	P.Traynor/Lucas BLUE ..	125.00	60.00	12.50
	Thevenow/Wright			
☐ 12C	Berry/Burke BLUE	125.00	60.00	12.50
	Kress/D.Vance			
☐ 12D	Ruffing/Malone BLUE	250.00	125.00	25.00
	Lazzeri/Bill Dickey			
☐ 12E	Moore/Hogan BLUE	100.00	50.00	10.00
	Frankhouse/Brandt			
☐ 12F	Martin/O'Farrell BLUE ...	100.00	50.00	10.00
	Byrd/MacFayden			
☐ 13A	Ruel/Al Simmons	175.00	85.00	18.00
	Kamm/M.Cochrane			
☐ 13B	Hudlin/Myatt	125.00	60.00	12.50
	Comorosky/Bottomley			
☐ 13C	Wilson/Allen	100.00	50.00	10.00
	Jonnard/Brickell			
☐ 13D	West/Oscar Melillo	100.00	50.00	10.00
	Blaeholder/Coffman			
☐ 13E	Joe Cronin/Reynolds	125.00	60.00	12.50
	Bishop/Cissell			
☐ 13F	Schuble/Marberry	125.00	60.00	12.50
	Goose Goslin/Crowder			
☐ 14A	Babe Ruth/McManus	2000.00	1000.00	250.00
	Brandt/Maranville			
☐ 14B	Bill Terry/Schumacher ..	150.00	75.00	15.00
	Mancuso/T.Jackson			
☐ 14C	Paul Waner/Bush	150.00	75.00	15.00
	W.Hoyt/Lloyd Waner			
☐ 14D	B.Grimes/Chuck Klein ...	150.00	75.00	15.00
	K.Cuyler/English			
☐ 14E	Leslie/Frey	100.00	50.00	10.00
	Joe Stripp/Clark			
☐ 14F	Piet/Comorosky	125.00	60.00	12.50
	Jim Bottomley/Adams			
☐ 15A	Babe Ruth/McManus	2000.00	1000.00	250.00
	Brandt/Maranville			
☐ 15B	Bill Terry/Schumacher ..	150.00	75.00	15.00
	Mancuso/T.Jackson			
☐ 15C	Wilson/Allen	100.00	50.00	10.00
	Jonnard/Brickell			
☐ 15D	B.Grimes/Chuck Klein ...	150.00	75.00	15.00
	K.Cuyler/English			
☐ 15E	Joe Cronin/Reynolds	125.00	60.00	12.50
	Bishop/Cissell			
☐ 15F	Piet/Comorosky	125.00	60.00	12.50
	Jim Bottomley/Adams			
☐ 16A	F.Frisch/Dizzy Dean	250.00	125.00	25.00
	E.Orsatti/Carleton			
☐ 16B	Mahaffey/Jimmie Foxx ..	150.00	75.00	15.00
	Williams/Higgins			
☐ 16C	Heine Manush/Lary	125.00	60.00	12.50
	Weaver/Hadley			
☐ 16D	Cochrane/C.Gehringer ..	175.00	85.00	18.00
	Tom Bridges/Rogell			
☐ 16E	Kamm/Hildebrand	125.00	60.00	12.50
	Earl Averill/Trosky			
☐ 16F	G.Earnshaw/Dykes	125.00	60.00	12.50
	Luke Sewell/Appling			
☐ 17A	F.Frisch/Dizzy Dean	250.0A	125.00	25.00
	E.Orsatti/Carleton			
☐ 17B	Mahaffey/Jimmie Foxx ..	150.00	75.00	15.00
	Williams/Higgins			
☐ 17C	Heine Manush/Lary	125.00	60.00	12.50
	Weaver/Hadley			
☐ 17D	Cochrane/C.Gehringer ..	175.00	85.00	18.00
	Tom Bridges/Rogell			
☐ 17E	Kamm/Hildebrand	125.00	60.00	12.50
	Earl Averill/Trosky			
☐ 17F	G.Earnshaw/Dykes	125.00	60.00	12.50
	Luke Sewell/Appling			

1936 Goudey

The cards in this 25-card black and white set measure 2 3/8" by 2 7/8". In contrast to the color artwork of its previous sets, the 1936 Goudey set contained a simple black and white player photograph. A facsimile autograph appeared within the picture area. Each card was issued with a number of different "game situation" backs, and there may be as many as 200 different front/back combinations. The ACC designation is R322.

		EX-MT	VG-E	GOOD
COMPLETE SET (25)		1500.00	750.00	175.00
COMMON PLAYER (1-25)		35.00	17.50	3.50
☐ 1	Wally Berger	35.00	17.50	3.50
☐ 2	Zeke Bonura	35.00	17.50	3.50
☐ 3	Stan Bordagaray	35.00	17.50	3.50
☐ 4	Bill Brubaker	35.00	17.50	3.50
☐ 5	Dolph Camilli	35.00	17.50	3.50
☐ 6	Clyde Castleman	35.00	17.50	3.50
☐ 7	Mickey Cochrane	150.00	75.00	15.00
☐ 8	Joe Coscarart	35.00	17.50	3.50
☐ 9	Frank Crosetti	55.00	27.50	5.50
☐ 10	Kiki Cuyler	80.00	40.00	8.00
☐ 11	Paul Derringer	45.00	22.50	4.50
☐ 12	Jimmy Dykes	45.00	22.50	4.50
☐ 13	Rick Ferrell	80.00	40.00	8.00
☐ 14	Lefty Gomez	150.00	75.00	15.00
☐ 15	Hank Greenberg	150.00	75.00	15.00
☐ 16	Bucky Harris	80.00	40.00	8.00
☐ 17	Rollie Hemsley	35.00	17.50	3.50
☐ 18	Pinky Higgins	35.00	17.50	3.50
☐ 19	Oral Hildebrand	35.00	17.50	3.50
☐ 20	Chuck Klein	100.00	50.00	10.00
☐ 21	Pepper Martin	45.00	22.50	4.50
☐ 22	Bobo Newsom	35.00	17.50	3.50
☐ 23	Joe Vosmik	35.00	17.50	3.50
☐ 24	Paul Waner	80.00	40.00	8.00
☐ 25	Bill Werber	35.00	17.50	3.50

1938 Goudey Heads Up

The cards in this 48-card set measure 2 3/8" by 2 7/8". The 1938 Goudey set is commonly referred to as the Heads-Up set, or R323 (ACC). These very popular but difficult to obtain cards came in two series of the same 24 players. The first series, numbers 241-264, is distinguished from the second series, numbers 265-288, in that the second contains etched cartoons and comments surrounding the player picture. Although the set starts with number 241, it is not a continuation of the 1933 Goudey set, but a separate set in its own right.

		EX-MT	VG-E	GOOD
COMPLETE SET (48)		13500.00	6500.00	1500.00
COMMON PLAYER (241-264)		80.00	40.00	8.00
COMMON PLAYER (265-288)		100.00	50.00	10.00
☐ 241	Charlie Gehringer	300.00	150.00	30.00
☐ 242	Pete Fox	80.00	40.00	8.00
☐ 243	Joe Kuhel	80.00	40.00	8.00
☐ 244	Frank Demaree	80.00	40.00	8.00
☐ 245	Frank Pytlak	80.00	40.00	8.00
☐ 246	Ernie Lombardi	175.00	85.00	18.00
☐ 247	Joe Vosmik	80.00	40.00	8.00
☐ 248	Dick Bartell	80.00	40.00	8.00
☐ 249	Jimmie Foxx	400.00	200.00	40.00
☐ 250	Joe DiMaggio	3000.00	1500.00	350.00
☐ 251	Bump Hadley	80.00	40.00	8.00
☐ 252	Zeke Bonura	80.00	40.00	8.00
☐ 253	Hank Greenberg	350.00	175.00	35.00
☐ 254	Van Lingle Mungo	80.00	40.00	8.00
☐ 255	Moose Solters	80.00	40.00	8.00
☐ 256	Vernon Kennedy	80.00	40.00	8.00
☐ 257	Al Lopez	175.00	85.00	18.00
☐ 258	Bobby Doerr	300.00	150.00	30.00
☐ 259	Billy Werber	80.00	40.00	8.00
☐ 260	Rudy York	80.00	40.00	8.00
☐ 261	Rip Radcliff	80.00	40.00	8.00
☐ 262	Joe Medwick	250.00	125.00	25.00
☐ 263	Marvin Owen	80.00	40.00	8.00
☐ 264	Bob Feller	600.00	300.00	60.00
☐ 265	Charlie Gehringer	350.00	175.00	35.00
☐ 266	Pete Fox	100.00	50.00	10.00
☐ 267	Joe Kuhel	100.00	50.00	10.00
☐ 268	Frank Demaree	100.00	50.00	10.00
☐ 269	Frank Pytlak	100.00	50.00	10.00
☐ 270	Ernie Lombardi	225.00	110.00	22.00
☐ 271	Joe Vosmik	100.00	50.00	10.00
☐ 272	Dick Bartell	100.00	50.00	10.00
☐ 273	Jimmie Foxx	450.00	225.00	45.00
☐ 274	Joe DiMaggio	3250.00	1500.00	350.00
☐ 275	Bump Hadley	100.00	50.00	10.00
☐ 276	Zeke Bonura	100.00	50.00	10.00
☐ 277	Hank Greenberg	400.00	200.00	40.00
☐ 278	Van Lingle Mungo	100.00	50.00	10.00
☐ 279	Moose Solters	100.00	50.00	10.00
☐ 280	Vernon Kennedy	100.00	50.00	10.00
☐ 281	Al Lopez	225.00	110.00	22.00
☐ 282	Bobby Doerr	350.00	175.00	35.00
☐ 283	Billy Werber	100.00	50.00	10.00
☐ 284	Rudy York	100.00	50.00	10.00
☐ 285	Rip Radcliff	100.00	50.00	10.00
☐ 286	Joe Medwick	300.00	150.00	30.00
☐ 287	Marvin Owen	100.00	50.00	10.00
☐ 288	Bob Feller	700.00	350.00	70.00

1981 Granny Goose

This set is the hardest to obtain of the three years Granny Goose issued cards of the Oakland A's. The Revering card was supposedly destroyed by the printer soon after he was traded away and hence is in shorter supply than the other 14 cards in the set.

Wayne Gross is also supposedly available in lesser quantity compared to the other players. Cards are standard size (2 1/2" by 3 1/2") and were issued in bags of potato chips. Cards are numbered on the front and back by the player's uniform number.

		MINT	EXC	G-VG
COMPLETE SET (15)		75.00	37.50	7.50
COMMON PLAYER		1.00	.50	.10
☐ 1	Billy Martin MG	7.50	3.75	.75
☐ 2	Mike Heath	1.00	.50	.10
☐ 5	Jeff Newman	1.00	.50	.10
☐ 6	Mitchell Page	1.00	.50	.10
☐ 8	Rob Picciolo	1.00	.50	.10
☐ 10	Wayne Gross	6.00	3.00	.60
☐ 13	Dave Revering SP	35.00	17.50	3.50
☐ 17	Mike Norris	1.00	.50	.10
☐ 20	Tony Armas	2.00	1.00	.20
☐ 21	Dwayne Murphy	2.00	1.00	.20
☐ 22	Rick Langford	1.50	.75	.15
☐ 27	Matt Keough	1.00	.50	.10
☐ 35	Rickey Henderson	25.00	12.50	2.50
☐ 39	Dave McKay	1.00	.50	.10
☐ 54	Steve McCatty	1.00	.50	.10

1982 Granny Goose

 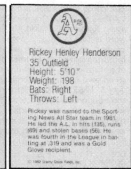

The cards in this 15-card set measure 2 1/2" by 3 1/2". Granny Goose Foods, Inc., a California based company, repeated its successful promotional idea of 1981 by issuing a new set of Oakland A's baseball cards for 1982. Each color player picture is surrounded by white borders and has trim and lettering done in Oakland's green and yellow colors. The cards are numbered according to the uniform number of the player, and the backs carry vital statistics done in black print on a white background. The cards were distributed in packages of potato chips and were also handed out on Fan Appreciation Day at the stadium. Although Picciolo was traded, his card was not withdrawn (as was Revering last year) and, therefore, its value is no greater than other cards in the set.

		MINT	EXC	G-VG
COMPLETE SET (15)		15.00	7.50	1.50
COMMON PLAYER (1-15)		.40	.20	.04
☐ 1	Tony Armas	.75	.35	.07
☐ 2	Wayne Gross	.40	.20	.04
☐ 3	Mike Heath	.40	.20	.04
☐ 4	Rickey Henderson	9.00	4.50	.90
☐ 5	Cliff Johnson	.40	.20	.04
☐ 6	Matt Keough	.40	.20	.04
☐ 7	Rick Langford	.40	.20	.04
☐ 8	Davey Lopes	.75	.35	.07
☐ 9	Billy Martin MG	2.00	1.00	.20
☐ 10	Steve McCatty	.40	.20	.04
☐ 11	Dwayne Murphy	.75	.35	.07
☐ 12	Jeff Newman	.40	.20	.04
☐ 13	Mike Norris	.40	.20	.04

☐ 14 Rob Picciolo .... .40   .20   .04
☐ 15 Fred Stanley .... .40   .20   .04

1983 Granny Goose

The cards in this 15-card set measure 2 1/2" by 4 1/4". The 1983 Granny Goose Potato Chips set again features Oakland A's players. The cards that were issued in bags of potato chips have a tear off coupon on the bottom with a scratch off section featuring prizes. In addition to their release in bags of potato chips, the Granny Goose cards were also given away to fans attending the Oakland game of July 3, 1983. These give away cards did not contain the coupon on the bottom. Prices listed below are for cards without the detachable tabs that came on the bottom of the cards; cards with tabs intact are valued 50% higher than the prices below.

	MINT	EXC	G-VG
COMPLETE SET (15)	12.00	6.00	1.20
COMMON PLAYER	.40	.20	.04
☐ 2 Mike Heath	.40	.20	.04
☐ 4 Carney Lansford	1.50	.75	.15
☐ 10 Wayne Gross	.40	.20	.04
☐ 14 Steve Boros MG	.40	.20	.04
☐ 15 Davey Lopes	.75	.35	.07
☐ 16 Mike Davis	.75	.35	.07
☐ 17 Mike Norris	.40	.20	.04
☐ 21 Dwayne Murphy	.75	.35	.07
☐ 22 Rick Langford	.40	.20	.04
☐ 27 Matt Keough	.40	.20	.04
☐ 31 Tom Underwood	.40	.20	.04
☐ 33 Dave Beard	.40	.20	.04
☐ 35 Rickey Henderson	7.50	3.75	.75
☐ 39 Tom Burgmeier	.40	.20	.04
☐ 54 Steve McCatty	.40	.20	.04

1958 Hires

The cards in this 66-card set measure 2 5/16" by 3 1/2" or 2 5/16" by 7" with tabs. The 1958 Hires Root Beer set of numbered, colored cards was issued with detachable coupons as inserts with Hires Root Beer cartons. Cards with the coupon still intact are worth double the prices listed below. The card front picture is surrounded with a wood grain effect which makes it look like the player is seen through a knot hole. The numbering of this set is rather strange in that it begins with 10 and skips 69.

	NRMT	VG-E	GOOD
COMPLETE SET (66)	1250.00	600.00	125.00

PEE WEE REESE
INFIELD—LOS ANGELES DODGERS

JOIN THE HIRES BASEBALL CLUB TODAY!

Learn how to play baseball from the BIG LEAGUERS! How to pitch! Catch! Judge plays! Just paste 10c to the Hires bottle cap picture on the reverse side and send with 2 Hires bottle caps to:

CHARLES E. HIRES COMPANY
P. O. Box 500, Haddonfield, New Jersey

LOOK WHAT YOU GET:

1 Hires "How To Play Baseball Book".

2 Valuable membership card.

Printed in U. S. A.

COMMON PLAYER (10-76)	9.00	4.50	.90
☐ 10 Richie Ashburn	35.00	17.50	3.50
☐ 11 Chico Carrasquel	9.00	4.50	.90
☐ 12 Dave Philley	9.00	4.50	.90
☐ 13 Don Newcombe	15.00	7.50	1.50
☐ 14 Wally Post	9.00	4.50	.90
☐ 15 Rip Repulski	9.00	4.50	.90
☐ 16 Chico Fernandez	9.00	4.50	.90
☐ 17 Larry Doby	15.00	7.50	1.50
☐ 18 Hector Brown	9.00	4.50	.90
☐ 19 Danny O'Connell	9.00	4.50	.90
☐ 20 Granny Hamner	9.00	4.50	.90
☐ 21 Dick Groat	12.00	6.00	1.20
☐ 22 Ray Narleski	9.00	4.50	.90
☐ 23 Pee Wee Reese	60.00	30.00	6.00
☐ 24 Bob Friend	12.00	6.00	1.20
☐ 25 Willie Mays	250.00	125.00	25.00
☐ 26 Bob Nieman	9.00	4.50	.90
☐ 27 Frank Thomas	9.00	4.50	.90
☐ 28 Curt Simmons	12.00	6.00	1.20
☐ 29 Stan Lopata	9.00	4.50	.90
☐ 30 Bob Skinner	9.00	4.50	.90
☐ 31 Ron Kline	9.00	4.50	.90
☐ 32 Willie Miranda	9.00	4.50	.90
☐ 33 Bobby Avila	9.00	4.50	.90
☐ 34 Clem Labine	12.00	6.00	1.20
☐ 35 Ray Jablonski	9.00	4.50	.90
☐ 36 Bill Mazeroski	15.00	7.50	1.50
☐ 37 Billy Gardner	9.00	4.50	.90
☐ 38 Pete Runnels	12.00	6.00	1.20
☐ 39 Jack Sanford	9.00	4.50	.90
☐ 40 Dave Sisler	9.00	4.50	.90
☐ 41 Don Zimmer	15.00	7.50	1.50
☐ 42 Johnny Podres	15.00	7.50	1.50
☐ 43 Dick Farrell	9.00	4.50	.90
☐ 44 Hank Aaron	250.00	125.00	25.00
☐ 45 Bill Virdon	15.00	7.50	1.50
☐ 46 Bobby Thomson	15.00	7.50	1.50
☐ 47 Willard Nixon	9.00	4.50	.90
☐ 48 Billy Loes	9.00	4.50	.90
☐ 49 Hank Sauer	12.00	6.00	1.20
☐ 50 Johnny Antonelli	12.00	6.00	1.20
☐ 51 Daryl Spencer	9.00	4.50	.90
☐ 52 Ken Lehman	9.00	4.50	.90
☐ 53 Sammy White	9.00	4.50	.90
☐ 54 Charley Neal	12.00	6.00	1.20
☐ 55 Don Drysdale	45.00	22.50	4.50
☐ 56 Jackie Jensen	15.00	7.50	1.50
☐ 57 Ray Katt	9.00	4.50	.90
☐ 58 Frank Sullivan	9.00	4.50	.90
☐ 59 Roy Face	12.00	6.00	1.20

		NRMT	VG-E	GOOD
☐ 60	Willie Jones	9.00	4.50	.90
☐ 61	Duke Snider	100.00	50.00	10.00
☐ 62	Whitey Lockman	9.00	4.50	.90
☐ 63	Gino Cimoli	9.00	4.50	.90
☐ 64	Marv Grissom	9.00	4.50	.90
☐ 65	Gene Baker	9.00	4.50	.90
☐ 66	George Zuverink	9.00	4.50	.90
☐ 67	Ted Kluszewski	18.00	9.00	1.80
☐ 68	Jim Busby	9.00	4.50	.90
☐ 69	Not Issued	0.00	.00	.00
☐ 70	Curt Barclay	9.00	4.50	.90
☐ 71	Hank Foiles	9.00	4.50	.90
☐ 72	Gene Stephens	9.00	4.50	.90
☐ 73	Al Worthington	9.00	4.50	.90
☐ 74	Al Walker	9.00	4.50	.90
☐ 75	Bob Boyd	9.00	4.50	.90
☐ 76	Al Pilarcik	9.00	4.50	.90

1958 Hires Test

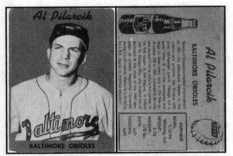

The cards in this 8-card test set measure 2 5/16" by 3 1/2" or 2 5/16" by 7" with tabs. The 1958 Hires Root Beer test set features unnumbered, color cards. The card front photos are shown on a yellow or orange back ground instead of the wood grain background used in the Hires regular set. The cards contain a detachable coupon just as the regular Hires issue does. Cards were test marketed on a very limited basis in a few cities. Cards with the coupon still intact are worth double the prices in the checklist below. The checklist below is ordered alphabetically.

		NRMT	VG-E	GOOD
COMPLETE SET (8)		1000.00	500.00	125.00
COMMON PLAYER (1-8)		90.00	45.00	9.00
☐ 1	Johnny Antonelli	100.00	50.00	10.00
☐ 2	Jim Busby	90.00	45.00	9.00
☐ 3	Chico Fernandez	90.00	45.00	9.00
☐ 4	Bob Friend	100.00	50.00	10.00
☐ 5	Vern Law	100.00	50.00	10.00
☐ 6	Stan Lopata	90.00	45.00	9.00
☐ 7	Willie Mays	400.00	200.00	40.00
☐ 8	Al Pilarcik	90.00	45.00	9.00

1959 Home Run Derby

This 20-card set was produced in 1959 by American Motors to publicize a TV program. The cards are black and white and blank backed. The cards measure approximately 3 1/8" by 5 1/4". The cards are unnumbered and are ordered alphabetically below for convenience. During 1988, the 19 player cards in this set were publicly reprinted.

		NRMT	VG-E	GOOD
COMPLETE SET (20)		2500.00	1200.00	250.00
COMMON PLAYER (1-20)		40.00	20.00	4.00
☐ 1	Hank Aaron	300.00	150.00	30.00

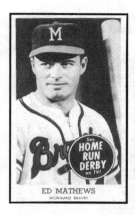

ED MATHEWS
MILWAUKEE BRAVES

☐ 2	Bob Allison	40.00	20.00	4.00
☐ 3	Ernie Banks	125.00	60.00	12.50
☐ 4	Ken Boyer	60.00	30.00	6.00
☐ 5	Bob Cerv	40.00	20.00	4.00
☐ 6	Rocky Colavito	60.00	30.00	6.00
☐ 7	Gil Hodges	90.00	45.00	9.00
☐ 8	Jackie Jensen	60.00	30.00	6.00
☐ 9	Al Kaline	150.00	75.00	15.00
☐ 10	Harmon Killebrew	125.00	60.00	12.50
☐ 11	Jim Lemon	40.00	20.00	4.00
☐ 12	Mickey Mantle	800.00	400.00	80.00
☐ 13	Ed Mathews	125.00	60.00	12.50
☐ 14	Willie Mays	300.00	150.00	30.00
☐ 15	Wally Post	40.00	20.00	4.00
☐ 16	Frank Robinson	125.00	60.00	12.50
☐ 17	Mark Scott	40.00	20.00	4.00
	(TV show host)			
☐ 18	Duke Snider	200.00	100.00	20.00
☐ 19	Dick Stuart	40.00	20.00	4.00
☐ 20	Gus Triandos	40.00	20.00	4.00

1947 Homogenized Bond

The cards in this 48-card set measure 2 1/4" by 3 1/2". The 1947 W571/D305 Homogenized Bread are sets of unnumbered cards containing 44 baseball players and four boxers. The W571 set exists in two styles. Style one is identical to the D305 set except for the back printing while style two has perforated edges and movie stars depicted on the backs. The second style of W571 cards contains only 13 cards. The four boxers in the checklist below are indicated by BOX. The checklist below is ordered alphabetically. There are 24 cards in the set which were definitely produced in greater supply. These 24 (marked by DP below) are quite a bit more common than the other 24 cards in the set.

	NRMT	VG-E	GOOD
COMPLETE SET	550.00	250.00	50.00
COMMON PLAYER (1-48)	7.50	3.75	.75
COMMON BOXER	3.00	1.50	.30
COMMON DP BASEBALL	3.00	1.50	.30
COMMON DP BOXER	1.50	.75	.15

			NRMT	VG-E	GOOD
☐	1	Rex Barney	7.50	3.75	.75
☐	2	Larry Berra	50.00	25.00	5.00
☐	3	Ewell Blackwell DP	3.00	1.50	.30
☐	4	Lou Boudreau DP	6.00	3.00	.60
☐	5	Ralph Branca	9.00	4.50	.90
☐	6	Harry Brecheen DP	3.00	1.50	.30
☐	7	Primo Carnera BOX DP	1.50	.75	.15
☐	8	Marcel Cerdan BOX	3.00	1.50	.30
☐	9	Dom DiMaggio	10.00	5.00	1.00
☐	10	Joe DiMaggio	100.00	50.00	10.00
☐	11	Bobby Doerr DP	6.00	3.00	.60
☐	12	Bruce Edwards	7.50	3.75	.75
☐	13	Bob Elliott DP	3.00	1.50	.30
☐	14	Del Ennis DP	3.00	1.50	.30
☐	15	Bob Feller DP	12.50	6.25	1.25
☐	16	Carl Furillo	12.00	6.00	1.20
☐	17	Joe Gordon DP	3.00	1.50	.30
☐	18	Sid Gordon	7.50	3.75	.75
☐	19	Joe Hatten	7.50	3.75	.75
☐	20	Gil Hodges	30.00	15.00	3.00
☐	21	Tommy Holmes DP	3.00	1.50	.30
☐	22	Larry Jansen	7.50	3.75	.75
☐	23	Sheldon Jones	7.50	3.75	.75
☐	24	Edwin Joost	7.50	3.75	.75
☐	25	Charlie Keller	9.00	4.50	.90
☐	26	Ken Keltner DP	3.00	1.50	.30
☐	27	Buddy Kerr	7.50	3.75	.75
☐	28	Ralph Kiner DP	9.00	4.50	.90
☐	29	Jake LaMotta BOX	6.00	3.00	.60
☐	30	John Lindell	7.50	3.75	.75
☐	31	Whitey Lockman	7.50	3.75	.75
☐	32	Joe Louis BOX DP	7.50	3.75	.75
☐	33	Willard Marshall	7.50	3.75	.75
☐	34	Johnny Mize DP	9.00	4.50	.90
☐	35	Stan Musial DP	35.00	17.50	3.50
☐	36	Andy Pafko DP	3.00	1.50	.30
☐	37	Johnny Pesky DP	3.00	1.50	.30
☐	38	Pee Wee Reese	35.00	17.50	3.50
☐	39	Phil Rizzuto DP	12.00	6.00	1.20
☐	40	Aaron Robinson DP	3.00	1.50	.30
☐	41	Jackie Robinson DP	45.00	22.50	4.50
☐	42	John Sain DP	6.00	3.00	.60
☐	43	Enos Slaughter DP	9.00	4.50	.90
☐	44	Vern Stephens DP	3.00	1.50	.30
☐	45	George Tebbetts	7.50	3.75	.75
☐	46	Bobby Thomson	9.00	4.50	.90
☐	47	Johnny VanderMeer	9.00	4.50	.90
☐	48	Ted Williams DP	40.00	20.00	4.00

1975 Hostess

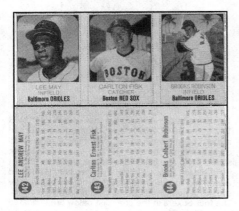

LEE MAY — Baltimore ORIOLES
CARLTON FISK — CATCHER — Boston RED SOX
BROOKS ROBINSON — INFIELD — Baltimore ORIOLES

The cards in this 150-card set measure 2 1/4" by 3 1/4" individually or 3 1/4" by 7 1/4" as panels of three. The 1975 Hostess set was issued in panels of

three cards each on the backs of family-size packages of Hostess cakes. Card number 125, Bill Madlock, was listed correctly as an infielder and incorrectly as a pitcher. Number 11, Burt Hooton, and number 89, Doug Rader, are spelled two different ways. Some panels are more difficult to find than others as they were issued only on the backs of less popular Hostess products. These scarcer panels are shown with asterisks in the checklist. Although complete panel prices are not explicitly listed, they would generally have a value 25% greater than the sum of the values of the individual players on that panel.

			NRMT	VG-E	GOOD
COMPLETE INDIV.SET			175.00	85.00	18.00
COMMON PLAYER (1-150)			.45	.22	.04
☐	1	Bob Tolan	.45	.22	.04
☐	2	Cookie Rojas	.45	.22	.04
☐	3	Darrell Evans	.75	.35	.07
☐	4	Sal Bando	.60	.30	.06
☐	5	Joe Morgan	3.50	1.75	.35
☐	6	Mickey Lolich	.75	.35	.07
☐	7	Don Sutton	2.50	1.25	.25
☐	8	Bill Melton	.45	.22	.04
☐	9	Tim Foli	.45	.22	.04
☐	10	Joe LaHoud	.45	.22	.04
☐	11A	Bert Hooten (sic)	1.00	.50	.10
☐	11B	Burt Hooton	1.00	.50	.10
☐	12	Paul Blair	.45	.22	.04
☐	13	Jim Barr	.45	.22	.04
☐	14	Toby Harrah	.60	.30	.06
☐	15	John Milner	.45	.22	.04
☐	16	Ken Holtzman	.60	.30	.06
☐	17	Cesar Cedeno	.60	.30	.06
☐	18	Dwight Evans	1.25	.60	.12
☐	19	Willie McCovey	3.00	1.50	.30
☐	20	Tony Oliva	1.00	.50	.10
☐	21	Manny Sanguillen	.60	.30	.06
☐	22	Mickey Rivers	.45	.22	.04
☐	23	Lou Brock	3.00	1.50	.30
☐	24	Graig Nettles (Craig on front)	1.50	.75	.15
☐	25	Jim Wynn	.60	.30	.06
☐	26	George Scott	.45	.22	.04
☐	27	Greg Luzinski	.60	.30	.06
☐	28	Bert Campaneris	.60	.30	.06
☐	29	Pete Rose	10.00	5.00	1.00
☐	30	Buddy Bell	.75	.35	.07
☐	31	Gary Matthews	.60	.30	.06
☐	32	Freddie Patek	.45	.22	.04
☐	33	Mike Lum	.45	.22	.04
☐	34	Ellie Rodriguez	.45	.22	.04
☐	35	Milt May (photo actually Lee May)	.60	.30	.06
☐	36	Willie Horton	.60	.30	.06
☐	37	Dave Winfield	4.00	2.00	.40
☐	38	Tom Grieve	.60	.30	.06
☐	39	Barry Foote	.45	.22	.04
☐	40	Joe Rudi	.60	.30	.06
☐	41	Bake McBride	.45	.22	.04
☐	42	Mike Cuellar	.60	.30	.06
☐	43	Garry Maddox	.60	.30	.06
☐	44	Carlos May	.45	.22	.04
☐	45	Bud Harrelson	.45	.22	.04
☐	46	Dave Chalk	.45	.22	.04
☐	47	Dave Concepcion	.75	.35	.07
☐	48	Carl Yastrzemski	8.00	4.00	.80
☐	49	Steve Garvey	4.50	2.25	.45
☐	50	Amos Otis	.60	.30	.06
☐	51	Rick Reuschel	.75	.35	.07
☐	52	Rollie Fingers	1.50	.75	.15
☐	53	Bob Watson	.60	.30	.06
☐	54	John Ellis	.45	.22	.04
☐	55	Bob Bailey	.45	.22	.04
☐	56	Rod Carew	4.50	2.25	.45
☐	57	Rich Hebner	.45	.22	.04
☐	58	Nolan Ryan	9.00	4.50	.90
☐	59	Reggie Smith	.60	.30	.06
☐	60	Joe Coleman	.45	.22	.04
☐	61	Ron Cey	.60	.30	.06
☐	62	Darrell Porter	.45	.22	.04
☐	63	Steve Carlton	4.50	2.25	.45
☐	64	Gene Tenace	.45	.22	.04
☐	65	Jose Cardenal	.45	.22	.04
☐	66	Bill Lee	.45	.22	.04
☐	67	Dave Lopes	.60	.30	.06
☐	68	Wilbur Wood	.60	.30	.06
☐	69	Steve Renko	.45	.22	.04

☐ 70	Joe Torre	.75	.35	.07
☐ 71	Ted Sizemore	.45	.22	.04
☐ 72	Bobby Grich	.60	.30	.06
☐ 73	Chris Speier	.45	.22	.04
☐ 74	Bert Blyleven	1.00	.50	.10
☐ 75	Tom Seaver	4.50	2.25	.45
☐ 76	Nate Colbert	.45	.22	.04
☐ 77	Don Kessinger	.60	.30	.06
☐ 78	George Medich	.45	.22	.04
☐ 79	Andy Messersmith *	.60	.30	.06
☐ 80	Robin Yount *	12.00	6.00	1.20
☐ 81	Al Oliver *	.90	.45	.09
☐ 82	Bill Singer *	.60	.30	.06
☐ 83	Johnny Bench *	7.50	3.75	.75
☐ 84	Gaylord Perry *	2.50	1.25	.25
☐ 85	Dave Kingman *	.90	.45	.09
☐ 86	Ed Herrmann *	.60	.30	.06
☐ 87	Ralph Garr *	.60	.30	.06
☐ 88	Reggie Jackson *	7.50	3.75	.75
☐ 89A	Doug Radar ERR *	1.00	.50	.10
	(sic, Rader)			
☐ 89B	Doug Rader COR *	2.00	1.00	.20
☐ 90	Elliott Maddox *	.60	.30	.06
☐ 91	Bill Russell *	.75	.35	.07
☐ 92	John Mayberry *	.60	.30	.06
☐ 93	Dave Cash *	.60	.30	.06
☐ 94	Jeff Burroughs *	.60	.30	.06
☐ 95	Ted Simmons *	1.00	.50	.10
☐ 96	Joe Decker *	.60	.30	.06
☐ 97	Bill Buckner *	.90	.45	.09
☐ 98	Bobby Darwin *	.60	.30	.06
☐ 99	Phil Niekro *	3.00	1.50	.30
☐ 100	Jim Sundberg *	.60	.30	.06
☐ 101	Greg Gross	.45	.22	.04
☐ 102	Luis Tiant	.75	.35	.07
☐ 103	Glenn Beckert	.45	.22	.04
☐ 104	Hal McRae	.60	.30	.06
☐ 105	Mike Jorgensen	.45	.22	.04
☐ 106	Mike Hargrove	.60	.30	.06
☐ 107	Don Gullett	.60	.30	.06
☐ 108	Tito Fuentes	.45	.22	.04
☐ 109	John Grubb	.45	.22	.04
☐ 110	Jim Kaat	1.00	.50	.10
☐ 111	Felix Millan	.45	.22	.04
☐ 112	Don Money	.45	.22	.04
☐ 113	Rick Monday	.60	.30	.06
☐ 114	Dick Bosman	.45	.22	.04
☐ 115	Roger Metzger	.45	.22	.04
☐ 116	Fergie Jenkins	1.00	.50	.10
☐ 117	Dusty Baker	.60	.30	.06
☐ 118	Billy Champion *	.60	.30	.06
☐ 119	Bob Gibson *	3.50	1.75	.35
☐ 120	Bill Freehan *	.75	.35	.07
☐ 121	Cesar Geronimo	.45	.22	.04
☐ 122	Jorge Orta	.45	.22	.04
☐ 123	Cleon Jones	.45	.22	.04
☐ 124	Steve Busby	.60	.30	.06
☐ 125A	Bill Madlock ERR	1.50	.75	.15
	(pitcher)			
☐ 125B	Bill Madlock COR	1.50	.75	.15
	(infielder)			
☐ 126	Jim Palmer	3.50	1.75	.35
☐ 127	Tony Perez	1.00	.50	.10
☐ 128	Larry Hisle	.60	.30	.06
☐ 129	Rusty Staub	.60	.30	.06
☐ 130	Hank Aaron *	9.00	4.50	.90
☐ 131	Rennie Stennett *	.60	.30	.06
☐ 132	Rico Petrocelli *	.60	.30	.06
☐ 133	Mike Schmidt *	9.00	4.50	.90
☐ 134	Sparky Lyle *	.75	.35	.07
☐ 135	Willie Stargell *	3.00	1.50	.30
☐ 136	Ken Henderson *	.45	.22	.04
☐ 137	Willie Montanez *	.45	.22	.04
☐ 138	Thurman Munson *	4.00	2.00	.40
☐ 139	Richie Zisk *	.60	.30	.06
☐ 140	George Hendrick *	.60	.30	.06
☐ 141	Bobby Murcer *	.75	.35	.07
☐ 142	Lee May *	.60	.30	.06
☐ 143	Carlton Fisk *	2.00	1.00	.20
☐ 144	Brooks Robinson *	3.00	1.50	.30
☐ 145	Bobby Bonds *	.75	.35	.07
☐ 146	Gary Sutherland *	.45	.22	.04
☐ 147	Oscar Gamble *	.60	.30	.06
☐ 148	Jim Hunter *	2.00	1.00	.20
☐ 149	Tug McGraw *	.75	.35	.07
☐ 150	Dave McNally	.60	.30	.06

GET THE EDGE: Subscribe to Beckett Baseball Card Monthly today and keep up with this exciting hobby.

1975 Hostess Twinkie

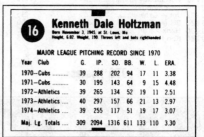

The cards in this 60-card set measure 2 1/4" by 3 1/4". The 1975 Hostess Twinkie set was issued on a limited basis in the far western part of the country. The set contains the same numbers as the regular set to number 36; however, the set is skip numbered after number 36. The cards were issued as the backs for 25-cent Twinkies packs. The fronts are indistinguishable from the regular Hostess cards; however the card backs are different in that the Twinkie cards have a thick black bar in the middle of the reverse.

		NRMT	VG-E	GOOD
COMPLETE SET (60)		90.00	45.00	9.00
COMMON PLAYER		.75	.35	.07

☐	1	Bob Tolan	.75	.35	.07
☐	2	Cookie Rojas	.75	.35	.07
☐	3	Darrell Evans	1.00	.50	.10
☐	4	Sal Bando	.90	.45	.09
☐	5	Joe Morgan	3.50	1.75	.35
☐	6	Mickey Lolich	1.00	.50	.10
☐	7	Don Sutton	2.50	1.25	.25
☐	8	Bill Melton	.75	.35	.07
☐	9	Tim Foli	.75	.35	.07
☐	10	Joe LaHoud	.75	.35	.07
☐	11	Bert Hooten (sic)	1.00	.50	.10
☐	12	Paul Blair	.75	.35	.07
☐	13	Jim Barr	.75	.35	.07
☐	14	Toby Harrah	.90	.45	.09
☐	15	John Milner	.75	.35	.07
☐	16	Ken Holtzman	.90	.45	.09
☐	17	Cesar Cedeno	.90	.45	.09
☐	18	Dwight Evans	1.25	.60	.12
☐	19	Willie McCovey	3.00	1.50	.30
☐	20	Tony Oliva	1.00	.50	.10
☐	21	Manny Sanguillen	.90	.45	.09
☐	22	Mickey Rivers	.75	.35	.07
☐	23	Lou Brock	3.00	1.50	.30
☐	24	Graig Nettles	1.50	.75	.15
		(Craig on front)			
☐	25	Jim Wynn	.75	.35	.07
☐	26	George Scott	.75	.35	.07
☐	27	Greg Luzinski	.90	.45	.09
☐	28	Bert Campaneris	.90	.45	.09
☐	29	Pete Rose	10.00	5.00	1.00
☐	30	Buddy Bell	1.00	.50	.10
☐	31	Gary Matthews	.90	.45	.09
☐	32	Freddie Patek	.75	.35	.07
☐	33	Mike Lum	.75	.35	.07
☐	34	Ellie Rodriguez	.75	.35	.07
☐	35	Milt May	.90	.45	.09
		(Lee May picture)			
☐	36	Willie Horton	.90	.45	.09
☐	40	Joe Rudi	.90	.45	.09
☐	43	Garry Maddox	.75	.35	.07
☐	46	Dave Chalk	.75	.35	.07
☐	49	Steve Garvey	4.50	2.25	.45
☐	52	Rollie Fingers	1.50	.75	.15
☐	58	Nolan Ryan	9.00	4.50	.90
☐	61	Ron Cey	.90	.45	.09
☐	64	Gene Tenace	.75	.35	.07
☐	65	Jose Cardenal	.75	.35	.07
☐	67	Dave Lopes	.90	.45	.09
☐	68	Wilbur Wood	.90	.45	.09
☐	73	Chris Speier	.75	.35	.07
☐	77	Don Kessinger	.90	.45	.09
☐	79	Andy Messersmith	.90	.45	.09
☐	80	Robin Yount	10.00	5.00	1.00
☐	82	Bill Singer	.75	.35	.07

☐ 103	Glenn Beckert	.75	.35	.07
☐ 110	Jim Kaat	1.00	.50	.10
☐ 112	Don Money	.75	.35	.07
☐ 113	Rick Monday	.90	.45	.09
☐ 122	Jorge Orta	.75	.35	.07
☐ 125	Bill Madlock	1.00	.50	.10
☐ 130	Hank Aaron	8.00	4.00	.80
☐ 136	Ken Henderson	.75	.35	.07

1976 Hostess

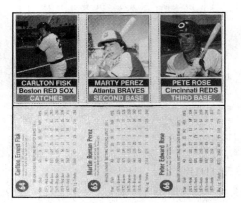

CARLTON FISK	Boston RED SOX — CATCHER
MARTY PEREZ	Atlanta BRAVES — SECOND BASE
PETE ROSE	Cincinnati REDS — THIRD BASE

The cards in this 150-card set measure 2 1/4" by 3 1/4" individually or 3 1/4" by 7 1/4" as panels of three. The 1976 Hostess set contains full-color, numbered cards issued in panels of three cards each on family-size packages of Hostess cakes. Scarcer panels (those only found on less popular Hostess products) are listed in the checklist below with asterisks. Complete panels of three have a value 25% more than the sum of the individual cards on the panel. Nine additional numbers (151-159) were apparently planned but never actually issued. These exist as proof cards and are quite scarce, e.g., 151 Ferguson Jenkins, 152 Mike Cuellar, 153 Tom Murphy, 154 Al Cowens, 155 Barry Foote, 156 Steve Carlton, 157 Richie Zisk, 158 Ken Holtzman, and 159 Cliff Johnson.

	NRMT	VG-E	GOOD
COMPLETE INDIV.SET(150)	175.00	85.00	18.00
COMMON PLAYER (1-150)	.45	.22	.04

☐ 1	Fred Lynn	1.25	.60	.12
☐ 2	Joe Morgan	3.00	1.50	.30
☐ 3	Phil Niekro	2.50	1.25	.25
☐ 4	Gaylord Perry	2.00	1.00	.20
☐ 5	Bob Watson	.60	.30	.06
☐ 6	Bill Freehan	.60	.30	.06
☐ 7	Lou Brock	3.00	1.50	.30
☐ 8	Al Fitzmorris	.45	.22	.04
☐ 9	Rennie Stennett	.45	.22	.04
☐ 10	Tony Oliva	1.00	.50	.10
☐ 11	Robin Yount	8.00	4.00	.80
☐ 12	Rick Manning	.45	.22	.04
☐ 13	Bobby Grich	.60	.30	.06
☐ 14	Terry Forster	.60	.30	.06
☐ 15	Dave Kingman	.75	.35	.07
☐ 16	Thurman Munson	4.00	2.00	.40
☐ 17	Rick Reuschel	.75	.35	.07
☐ 18	Bobby Bonds	.75	.35	.07
☐ 19	Steve Garvey	4.00	2.00	.40
☐ 20	Vida Blue	.60	.30	.06
☐ 21	Dave Rader	.45	.22	.04
☐ 22	Johnny Bench	5.00	2.50	.50
☐ 23	Luis Tiant	.75	.35	.07
☐ 24	Darrell Evans	.75	.35	.07
☐ 25	Larry Dierker	.45	.22	.04
☐ 26	Willie Horton	.60	.30	.06
☐ 27	John Ellis	.45	.22	.04
☐ 28	Al Cowens	.45	.22	.04

☐ 29	Jerry Reuss	.45	.22	.04
☐ 30	Reggie Smith	.60	.30	.06
☐ 31	Bobby Darwin *	.60	.30	.06
☐ 32	Fritz Peterson *	.60	.30	.06
☐ 33	Rod Carew *	4.00	2.00	.40
☐ 34	Carlos May *	.60	.30	.06
☐ 35	Tom Seaver *	4.50	2.25	.45
☐ 36	Brooks Robinson *	4.00	2.00	.40
☐ 37	Jose Cardenal	.45	.22	.04
☐ 38	Ron Blomberg	.45	.22	.04
☐ 39	Leroy Stanton	.45	.22	.04
☐ 40	Dave Cash	.45	.22	.04
☐ 41	John Montefusco	.60	.30	.06
☐ 42	Bob Tolan	.45	.22	.04
☐ 43	Carl Morton	.45	.22	.04
☐ 44	Rick Burleson	.60	.30	.06
☐ 45	Don Gullett	.60	.30	.06
☐ 46	Vern Ruhle	.45	.22	.04
☐ 47	Cesar Cedeno	.60	.30	.06
☐ 48	Toby Harrah	.60	.30	.06
☐ 49	Willie Stargell	3.00	1.50	.30
☐ 50	Al Hrabosky	.60	.30	.06
☐ 51	Amos Otis	.60	.30	.06
☐ 52	Bud Harrelson	.45	.22	.04
☐ 53	Jim Hughes	.45	.22	.04
☐ 54	George Scott	.45	.22	.04
☐ 55	Mike Vail *	.60	.30	.06
☐ 56	Jim Palmer *	4.00	2.00	.40
☐ 57	Jorge Orta *	.60	.30	.06
☐ 58	Chris Chambliss *	.75	.35	.07
☐ 59	Dave Chalk *	.60	.30	.06
☐ 60	Ray Burris *	.60	.30	.06
☐ 61	Bert Campaneris *	.75	.35	.07
☐ 62	Gary Carter *	6.00	3.00	.60
☐ 63	Ron Cey *	.75	.35	.07
☐ 64	Carlton Fisk *	2.00	1.00	.20
☐ 65	Marty Perez *	.60	.30	.06
☐ 66	Pete Rose *	10.00	5.00	1.00
☐ 67	Roger Metzger *	.60	.30	.06
☐ 68	Jim Sundberg *	.60	.30	.06
☐ 69	Ron LeFlore *	.60	.30	.06
☐ 70	Ted Sizemore *	.60	.30	.06
☐ 71	Steve Busby *	.75	.35	.07
☐ 72	Manny Sanguillen *	.75	.35	.07
☐ 73	Larry Hisle *	.60	.30	.06
☐ 74	Pete Broberg *	.60	.30	.06
☐ 75	Boog Powell *	.90	.45	.09
☐ 76	Ken Singleton *	.75	.35	.07
☐ 77	Rich Gossage *	1.25	.60	.12
☐ 78	Jerry Grote *	.60	.30	.06
☐ 79	Nolan Ryan *	9.00	4.50	.90
☐ 80	Rick Monday *	.75	.35	.07
☐ 81	Graig Nettles *	.90	.45	.09
☐ 82	Chris Speier	.45	.22	.04
☐ 83	Dave Winfield	3.00	1.50	.30
☐ 84	Mike Schmidt	8.00	4.00	.80
☐ 85	Buzz Capra	.45	.22	.04
☐ 86	Tony Perez	.90	.45	.09
☐ 87	Dwight Evans	.90	.45	.09
☐ 88	Mike Hargrove	.60	.30	.06
☐ 89	Joe Coleman	.45	.22	.04
☐ 90	Greg Gross	.45	.22	.04
☐ 91	John Mayberry	.60	.30	.06
☐ 92	John Candelaria	.75	.35	.07
☐ 93	Bake McBride	.45	.22	.04
☐ 94	Hank Aaron	7.00	3.50	.70
☐ 95	Buddy Bell	.60	.30	.06
☐ 96	Steve Braun	.45	.22	.04
☐ 97	Jon Matlack	.60	.30	.06
☐ 98	Lee May	.60	.30	.06
☐ 99	Wilbur Wood	.60	.30	.06
☐ 100	Bill Madlock	.75	.35	.07
☐ 101	Frank Tanana	.60	.30	.06
☐ 102	Mickey Rivers	.45	.22	.04
☐ 103	Mike Ivie	.45	.22	.04
☐ 104	Rollie Fingers	1.25	.60	.12
☐ 105	Dave Lopes	.60	.30	.06
☐ 106	George Foster	1.00	.50	.10
☐ 107	Denny Doyle	.45	.22	.04
☐ 108	Earl Williams	.45	.22	.04
☐ 109	Tom Veryzer	.45	.22	.04
☐ 110	J.R. Richard	.60	.30	.06
☐ 111	Jeff Burroughs	.45	.22	.04
☐ 112	Al Oliver	.75	.35	.07
☐ 113	Ted Simmons	.75	.35	.07
☐ 114	George Brett	8.00	4.00	.80
☐ 115	Frank Duffy	.45	.22	.04
☐ 116	Bert Blyleven	.90	.45	.09
☐ 117	Darrell Porter	.45	.22	.04
☐ 118	Don Baylor	.75	.35	.07
☐ 119	Bucky Dent	.75	.35	.07
☐ 120	Felix Millan	.45	.22	.04
☐ 121	Mike Cuellar	.60	.30	.06
☐ 122	Gene Tenace	.45	.22	.04
☐ 123	Bobby Murcer	.60	.30	.06

		NRMT	VG-E	GOOD
☐ 124	Willie McCovey	2.00	1.00	.20
☐ 125	Greg Luzinski	.60	.30	.06
☐ 126	Larry Parrish	.45	.22	.04
☐ 127	Jim Rice	3.50	1.75	.35
☐ 128	Dave Concepcion	.75	.35	.07
☐ 129	Jim Wynn	.60	.30	.06
☐ 130	Tom Grieve	.60	.30	.06
☐ 131	Mike Cosgrove	.45	.22	.04
☐ 132	Dan Meyer	.45	.22	.04
☐ 133	Dave Parker	2.00	1.00	.20
☐ 134	Don Kessinger	.60	.30	.06
☐ 135	Hal McRae	.60	.30	.06
☐ 136	Don Money	.45	.22	.04
☐ 137	Dennis Eckersley	1.50	.75	.15
☐ 138	Fergie Jenkins	.90	.45	.09
☐ 139	Mike Torrez	.60	.30	.06
☐ 140	Jerry Morales	.45	.22	.04
☐ 141	Jim Hunter	2.00	1.00	.20
☐ 142	Gary Matthews	.60	.30	.06
☐ 143	Randy Jones	.60	.30	.06
☐ 144	Mike Jorgensen	.45	.22	.04
☐ 145	Larry Bowa	.75	.35	.07
☐ 146	Reggie Jackson	5.00	2.50	.50
☐ 147	Steve Yeager	.45	.22	.04
☐ 148	Dave May	.45	.22	.04
☐ 149	Carl Yastrzemski	7.00	3.50	.70
☐ 150	Cesar Geronimo	.45	.22	.04

1976 Hostess Twinkie

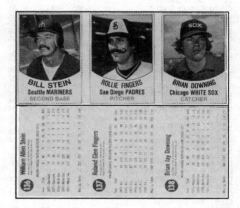

The cards in this 60-card set measure 2 1/4" by 3 1/4". The 1976 Hostess Twinkies set contains the first 60 cards of the 1976 Hostess set. These cards were issued as backs on 25-cent Twinkie packages as in the 1975 Twinkies set. The fronts are indistinguishable from the regular Hostess cards; however the card backs are different in that the Twinkie cards have a thick black bar in the middle of the reverse.

		NRMT	VG-E	GOOD
COMPLETE SET (60)		90.00	45.00	9.00
COMMON PLAYER (1-60)		.75	.35	.07
☐ 1	Fred Lynn	1.25	.60	.12
☐ 2	Joe Morgan	3.00	1.50	.30
☐ 3	Phil Niekro	2.50	1.25	.25
☐ 4	Gaylord Perry	2.00	1.00	.20
☐ 5	Bob Watson	.90	.45	.09
☐ 6	Bill Freehan	.90	.45	.09
☐ 7	Lou Brock	3.00	1.50	.30
☐ 8	Al Fitzmorris	.75	.35	.07
☐ 9	Rennie Stennett	.75	.35	.07
☐ 10	Tony Oliva	1.00	.50	.10
☐ 11	Robin Yount	8.00	4.00	.80
☐ 12	Rick Manning	.75	.35	.07
☐ 13	Bobby Grich	.90	.45	.09
☐ 14	Terry Forster	.90	.45	.09
☐ 15	Dave Kingman	1.00	.50	.10
☐ 16	Thurman Munson	4.00	2.00	.40
☐ 17	Rick Reuschel	1.00	.50	.10
☐ 18	Bobby Bonds	1.00	.50	.10
☐ 19	Steve Garvey	4.00	2.00	.40
☐ 20	Vida Blue	.90	.45	.09
☐ 21	Dave Rader	.75	.35	.07
☐ 22	Johnny Bench	5.00	2.50	.50
☐ 23	Luis Tiant	.90	.45	.09
☐ 24	Darrell Evans	1.00	.50	.10
☐ 25	Larry Dierker	.75	.35	.07
☐ 26	Willie Horton	.75	.35	.07
☐ 27	John Ellis	.75	.35	.07
☐ 28	Al Cowens	.75	.35	.07
☐ 29	Jerry Reuss	.75	.35	.07
☐ 30	Reggie Smith	.90	.45	.09
☐ 31	Bobby Darwin	.75	.35	.07
☐ 32	Fritz Peterson	.75	.35	.07
☐ 33	Rod Carew	4.00	2.00	.40
☐ 34	Carlos May	.75	.35	.07
☐ 35	Tom Seaver	4.50	2.25	.45
☐ 36	Brooks Robinson	4.00	2.00	.40
☐ 37	Jose Cardenal	.75	.35	.07
☐ 38	Ron Blomberg	.75	.35	.07
☐ 39	Leroy Stanton	.75	.35	.07
☐ 40	Dave Cash	.75	.35	.07
☐ 41	John Montefusco	.75	.35	.07
☐ 42	Bob Tolan	.75	.35	.07
☐ 43	Carl Morton	.75	.35	.07
☐ 44	Rick Burleson	.90	.45	.09
☐ 45	Don Gullett	.90	.45	.09
☐ 46	Vern Ruhle	.75	.35	.07
☐ 47	Cesar Cedeno	.90	.45	.09
☐ 48	Toby Harrah	.90	.45	.09
☐ 49	Willie Stargell	3.00	1.50	.30
☐ 50	Al Hrabosky	.90	.45	.09
☐ 51	Amos Otis	.90	.45	.09
☐ 52	Bud Harrelson	.75	.35	.07
☐ 53	Jim Hughes	.75	.35	.07
☐ 54	George Scott	.75	.35	.07
☐ 55	Mike Vail	.75	.35	.07
☐ 56	Jim Palmer	4.00	2.00	.40
☐ 57	Jorge Orta	.75	.35	.07
☐ 58	Chris Chambliss	.90	.45	.09
☐ 59	Dave Chalk	.75	.35	.07
☐ 60	Ray Burris	.75	.35	.07

1977 Hostess

The cards in this 150-card set measure 2 1/4" by 3 1/4" individually or 3 1/4" by 7 1/4" as panels of three. The 1977 Hostess set contains full-color, numbered cards issued in panels of three cards each with Hostess family-size cake products. Scarcer panels are listed in the checklist below with asterisks. Although complete panel prices are not explicitly listed below, they would generally have a value 25% greater than the sum of the individual players on the panel. There were 10 additional cards proofed, but not produced or distributed; they are 151 Ed Kranepool, 152 Ross Grimsley, 153 Ken Brett, 154 Rowland Office, 155 Rick Wise, 156 Paul Splittorff, 157 Gerald Augustine, 158 Ken Forsch, 159 Jerry Reuss (Reuss is also #119), and 160 Nelson Briles. There is also a complete variation set that was available one card per Twinkie package. Common cards in this Twinkie set are worth double the prices listed below, although the stars are only worth about 20% more. The Twinkie cards are distinguished by the thick printing bar or band printed on the card backs just below the statistics.

		NRMT	VG-E	GOOD
	COMPLETE IND.SET (150)	175.00	85.00	18.00
	COMMON PLAYER (1-150)	.45	.22	.04
☐	1 Jim Palmer	3.00	1.50	.30
☐	2 Joe Morgan	3.00	1.50	.30
☐	3 Reggie Jackson	5.00	2.50	.50
☐	4 Carl Yastrzemski	7.00	3.50	.70
☐	5 Thurman Munson	4.00	2.00	.40
☐	6 Johnny Bench	5.00	2.50	.50
☐	7 Tom Seaver	4.00	2.00	.40
☐	8 Pete Rose	9.00	4.50	.90
☐	9 Rod Carew	4.00	2.00	.40
☐	10 Luis Tiant	.75	.35	.07
☐	11 Phil Garner	.45	.22	.04
☐	12 Sixto Lezcano	.45	.22	.04
☐	13 Mike Torrez	.45	.22	.04
☐	14 Dave Lopes	.60	.30	.06
☐	15 Doug DeCinces	.60	.30	.06
☐	16 Jim Spencer	.45	.22	.04
☐	17 Hal McRae	.60	.30	.06
☐	18 Mike Hargrove	.60	.30	.06
☐	19 Willie Montanez *	.60	.30	.06
☐	20 Roger Metzger *	.60	.30	.06
☐	21 Dwight Evans	1.50	.75	.15
☐	22 Steve Rogers *	.75	.35	.07
☐	23 Jim Rice *	3.50	1.75	.35
☐	24 Pete Falcone *	.60	.30	.06
☐	25 Greg Luzinski *	.90	.45	.09
☐	26 Randy Jones *	.60	.30	.06
☐	27 Willie Stargell *	3.50	1.75	.35
☐	28 John Hiller *	.60	.30	.06
☐	29 Bobby Murcer *	.75	.35	.07
☐	30 Rick Monday *	.60	.30	.06
☐	31 John Montefusco *	.60	.30	.06
☐	32 Lou Brock *	3.50	1.75	.35
☐	33 Bill North *	.60	.30	.06
☐	34 Robin Yount *	6.50	3.25	.65
☐	35 Steve Garvey *	5.00	2.50	.50
☐	36 George Brett *	6.50	3.25	.65
☐	37 Toby Harrah *	.60	.30	.06
☐	38 Jerry Royster *	.60	.30	.06
☐	39 Bob Watson *	.60	.30	.06
☐	40 George Foster	.90	.45	.09
☐	41 Gary Carter	3.50	1.75	.35
☐	42 John Denny	.60	.30	.06
☐	43 Mike Schmidt	7.50	3.75	.75
☐	44 Dave Winfield	3.00	1.50	.30
☐	45 Al Oliver	.75	.35	.07
☐	46 Mark Fidrych	.60	.30	.06
☐	47 Larry Herndon	.45	.22	.04
☐	48 Dave Goltz	.45	.22	.04
☐	49 Jerry Morales	.45	.22	.04
☐	50 Ron LeFlore	.60	.30	.06
☐	51 Fred Lynn	1.00	.50	.10
☐	52 Vida Blue	.60	.30	.06
☐	53 Rick Manning	.45	.22	.04
☐	54 Bill Buckner	.75	.35	.07
☐	55 Lee May	.60	.30	.06
☐	56 John Mayberry	.60	.30	.06
☐	57 Darrell Chaney	.45	.22	.04
☐	58 Cesar Cedeno	.60	.30	.06
☐	59 Ken Griffey	.75	.35	.07
☐	60 Dave Kingman	.75	.35	.07
☐	61 Ted Simmons	.90	.45	.09
☐	62 Larry Bowa	.60	.30	.06
☐	63 Frank Tanana	.60	.30	.06
☐	64 Jason Thompson	.60	.30	.06
☐	65 Ken Brett	.45	.22	.04
☐	66 Roy Smalley	.60	.30	.06
☐	67 Ray Burris	.45	.22	.04
☐	68 Rick Burleson	.60	.30	.06
☐	69 Buddy Bell	.75	.35	.07
☐	70 Don Sutton	2.00	1.00	.20
☐	71 Mark Belanger	.60	.30	.06
☐	72 Dennis Leonard	.60	.30	.06
☐	73 Gaylord Perry	2.00	1.00	.20
☐	74 Dick Ruthven	.45	.22	.04
☐	75 Jose Cruz	.60	.30	.06
☐	76 Cesar Geronimo	.45	.22	.04
☐	77 Jerry Koosman	.75	.35	.07
☐	78 Garry Templeton	.75	.35	.07
☐	79 Jim Hunter	2.50	1.25	.25
☐	80 John Candelaria	.60	.30	.06
☐	81 Nolan Ryan	8.00	4.00	.80
☐	82 Rusty Staub	.75	.35	.07
☐	83 Jim Barr	.45	.22	.04
☐	84 Butch Wynegar	.45	.22	.04
☐	85 Jose Cardenal	.45	.22	.04
☐	86 Claudell Washington	.60	.30	.06
☐	87 Bill Travers	.45	.22	.04
☐	88 Rick Waits	.45	.22	.04
☐	89 Ron Cey	.60	.30	.06
☐	90 Al Bumbry	.45	.22	.04
☐	91 Bucky Dent	.75	.35	.07
☐	92 Amos Otis	.60	.30	.06
☐	93 Tom Grieve	.60	.30	.06
☐	94 Enos Cabell	.45	.22	.04
☐	95 Dave Concepcion	.75	.35	.07
☐	96 Felix Millan	.45	.22	.04
☐	97 Bake McBride	.45	.22	.04
☐	98 Chris Chambliss	.60	.30	.06
☐	99 Butch Metzger	.45	.22	.04
☐	100 Rennie Stennett	.45	.22	.04
☐	101 Dave Roberts	.45	.22	.04
☐	102 Lyman Bostock	.60	.30	.06
☐	103 Rick Reuschel	.75	.35	.07
☐	104 Carlton Fisk	1.50	.75	.15
☐	105 Jim Slaton	.45	.22	.04
☐	106 Dennis Eckersley	1.00	.50	.10
☐	107 Ken Singleton	.60	.30	.06
☐	108 Ralph Garr	.45	.22	.04
☐	109 Freddie Patek *	.60	.30	.06
☐	110 Jim Sundberg *	.60	.30	.06
☐	111 Phil Niekro *	2.00	1.00	.20
☐	112 J.R. Richard *	.60	.30	.06
☐	113 Gary Nolan *	.60	.30	.06
☐	114 Jon Matlack *	.60	.30	.06
☐	115 Keith Hernandez *	4.00	2.00	.40
☐	116 Graig Nettles *	1.00	.50	.10
☐	117 Steve Carlton *	4.00	2.00	.40
☐	118 Bill Madlock *	1.25	.60	.12
☐	119 Jerry Reuss *	.60	.30	.06
☐	120 Aurelio Rodriguez *	.60	.30	.06
☐	121 Dan Ford *	.60	.30	.06
☐	122 Ray Fosse *	.60	.30	.06
☐	123 George Hendrick *	.60	.30	.06
☐	124 Alan Ashby	.45	.22	.04
☐	125 Joe Lis	.45	.22	.04
☐	126 Sal Bando	.60	.30	.06
☐	127 Richie Zisk	.60	.30	.06
☐	128 Rich Gossage	.75	.35	.07
☐	129 Don Baylor	.60	.30	.06
☐	130 Dave McKay	.45	.22	.04
☐	131 Bob Grich	.60	.30	.06
☐	132 Dave Pagan	.45	.22	.04
☐	133 Dave Cash	.45	.22	.04
☐	134 Steve Braun	.45	.22	.04
☐	135 Dan Meyer	.45	.22	.04
☐	136 Bill Stein	.45	.22	.04
☐	137 Rollie Fingers	1.50	.75	.15
☐	138 Brian Downing	.60	.30	.06
☐	139 Bill Singer	.45	.22	.04
☐	140 Doyle Alexander	.60	.30	.06
☐	141 Gene Tenace	.45	.22	.04
☐	142 Gary Matthews	.60	.30	.06
☐	143 Don Gullett	.60	.30	.06
☐	144 Wayne Garland	.45	.22	.04
☐	145 Pete Broberg	.45	.22	.04
☐	146 Joe Rudi	.60	.30	.06
☐	147 Glenn Abbott	.45	.22	.04
☐	148 George Scott	.45	.22	.04
☐	149 Bert Campaneris	.60	.30	.06
☐	150 Andy Messersmith	.60	.30	.06

1978 Hostess

The cards in this 150-card set measure 2 1/4" by 3 1/4" individually or 3 1/4" by 7 1/4" as panels of three. The 1978 Hostess set contains full-color, numbered cards issued in panels of three cards each on family packages of Hostess cake products. Scarcer panels are listed in the checklist with asterisks. The 1978 Hostess panels are considered by some collectors to be somewhat more difficult to obtain than Hostess panels of other years. Although complete panel prices are not explicitly listed below, they would generally have a value 25% greater than the sum of the individual players on the panel. There is additional interest in Eddie Murray #31, since this card corresponds to his "rookie" year in cards.

		NRMT	VG-E	GOOD
	COMPLETE IND.SET (150)	175.00	85.00	18.00
	COMMON PLAYER (1-150)	.45	.22	.04
☐	1 Butch Hobson	.45	.22	.04
☐	2 George Foster	.90	.45	.09
☐	3 Bob Forsch	.60	.30	.06

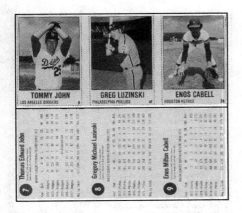

TOMMY JOHN — LOS ANGELES DODGERS p
GREG LUZINSKI — PHILADELPHIA PHILLIES of
ENOS CABELL — HOUSTON ASTROS 3b

☐ 73	Willie McCovey	2.00	1.00	.20
☐ 74	Bert Blyleven	.90	.45	.09
☐ 75	Ken Singleton	.60	.30	.06
☐ 76	Bill North	.45	.22	.04
☐ 77	Jason Thompson	.60	.30	.06
☐ 78	Dennis Eckersley	1.00	.50	.10
☐ 79	Jim Sundberg	.60	.30	.06
☐ 80	Jerry Koosman	.60	.30	.06
☐ 81	Bruce Bochte	.45	.22	.04
☐ 82	George Hendrick	.45	.22	.04
☐ 83	Nolan Ryan	7.50	3.75	.75
☐ 84	Roy Howell	.45	.22	.04
☐ 85	Roger Metzger	.45	.22	.04
☐ 86	Doc Medich	.45	.22	.04
☐ 87	Joe Morgan	3.00	1.50	.30
☐ 88	Dennis Leonard	.60	.30	.06
☐ 89	Willie Randolph	.75	.35	.07
☐ 90	Bobby Murcer	.60	.30	.06
☐ 91	Rick Manning	.45	.22	.04
☐ 92	J.R. Richard	.60	.30	.06
☐ 93	Ron Cey	.60	.30	.06
☐ 94	Sal Bando	.60	.30	.06
☐ 95	Ron LeFlore	.60	.30	.06
☐ 96	Dave Goltz	.45	.22	.04
☐ 97	Dan Meyer	.45	.22	.04
☐ 98	Chris Chambliss	.60	.30	.06
☐ 99	Biff Pocoroba	.45	.22	.04
☐ 100	Oscar Gamble	.60	.30	.06
☐ 101	Frank Tanana	.60	.30	.06
☐ 102	Len Randle	.45	.22	.04
☐ 103	Tommy Hutton	.45	.22	.04
☐ 104	John Candelaria	.60	.30	.06
☐ 105	George Orta	.45	.22	.04
☐ 106	Ken Reitz	.45	.22	.04
☐ 107	Bill Campbell	.45	.22	.04
☐ 108	Dave Concepcion	.75	.35	.07
☐ 109	Joe Ferguson	.45	.22	.04
☐ 110	Mickey Rivers	.60	.30	.06
☐ 111	Paul Splittorff	.60	.30	.06
☐ 112	Dave Lopes	.60	.30	.06
☐ 113	Mike Schmidt	7.00	3.50	.70
☐ 114	Joe Rudi	.60	.30	.06
☐ 115	Milt May	.45	.22	.04
☐ 116	Jim Palmer	3.00	1.50	.30
☐ 117	Bill Madlock	.90	.45	.09
☐ 118	Roy Smalley	.60	.30	.06
☐ 119	Cecil Cooper	.90	.45	.09
☐ 120	Rick Langford	.45	.22	.04
☐ 121	Ruppert Jones	.60	.30	.06
☐ 122	Phil Niekro	1.50	.75	.15
☐ 123	Toby Harrah	.60	.30	.06
☐ 124	Chet Lemon	.60	.30	.06
☐ 125	Gene Tenace	.45	.22	.04
☐ 126	Steve Henderson	.45	.22	.04
☐ 127	Mike Torrez	.45	.22	.04
☐ 128	Pete Rose	9.00	4.50	.90
☐ 129	John Denny	.60	.30	.06
☐ 130	Darrell Porter	.60	.30	.06
☐ 131	Rick Reuschel	.75	.35	.07
☐ 132	Graig Nettles	.75	.35	.07
☐ 133	Garry Maddox	.45	.22	.04
☐ 134	Mike Flanagan	.60	.30	.06
☐ 135	Dave Parker	2.00	1.00	.20
☐ 136	Terry Whitfield	.45	.22	.04
☐ 137	Wayne Garland	.45	.22	.04
☐ 138	Robin Yount	6.00	3.00	.60
☐ 139	Gaylord Perry	1.50	.75	.15
☐ 140	Rod Carew	3.50	1.75	.35
☐ 141	Greg Gross	.45	.22	.04
☐ 142	Barry Bonnell	.45	.22	.04
☐ 143	Willie Montanez	.45	.22	.04
☐ 144	Rollie Fingers	1.50	.75	.15
☐ 145	Lyman Bostock	.60	.30	.06
☐ 146	Gary Carter	3.50	1.75	.35
☐ 147	Ron Blomberg	.45	.22	.04
☐ 148	Bob Bailor	.45	.22	.04
☐ 149	Tom Seaver	4.00	2.00	.40
☐ 150	Thurman Munson	3.50	1.75	.35

☐ 4	Tony Perez	.90	.45	.09
☐ 5	Bruce Sutter	.90	.45	.09
☐ 6	Hal McRae	.40	.20	.04
☐ 7	Tommy John	1.00	.50	.10
☐ 8	Greg Luzinski	.60	.30	.06
☐ 9	Enos Cabell	.45	.22	.04
☐ 10	Doug DeCinces	.60	.30	.06
☐ 11	Willie Stargell	2.00	1.00	.20
☐ 12	Ed Halicki	.45	.22	.04
☐ 13	Larry Hisle	.45	.22	.04
☐ 14	Jim Slaton	.45	.22	.04
☐ 15	Buddy Bell	.75	.35	.07
☐ 16	Earl Williams	.45	.22	.04
☐ 17	Glenn Abbott	.45	.22	.04
☐ 18	Dan Ford	.45	.22	.04
☐ 19	Gary Matthews	.60	.30	.06
☐ 20	Eric Soderholm	.45	.22	.04
☐ 21	Bump Wills	.45	.22	.04
☐ 22	Keith Hernandez	2.50	1.25	.25
☐ 23	Dave Cash	.45	.22	.04
☐ 24	George Scott	.45	.22	.04
☐ 25	Ron Guidry	1.50	.75	.15
☐ 26	Dave Kingman	.75	.35	.07
☐ 27	George Brett	6.00	3.00	.60
☐ 28	Bob Watson *	.60	.30	.06
☐ 29	Bob Boone *	1.00	.50	.10
☐ 30	Reggie Smith *	.75	.35	.07
☐ 31	Eddie Murray *	12.00	6.00	1.20
☐ 32	Gary Lavelle *	.60	.30	.06
☐ 33	Rennie Stennett *	.60	.30	.06
☐ 34	Duane Kuiper *	.60	.30	.06
☐ 35	Sixto Lezcano *	.60	.30	.06
☐ 36	Dave Rozema *	.60	.30	.06
☐ 37	Butch Wynegar *	.60	.30	.06
☐ 38	Mitchell Page *	.60	.30	.06
☐ 39	Bill Stein *	.60	.30	.06
☐ 40	Elliott Maddox	.45	.22	.04
☐ 41	Mike Hargrove	.60	.30	.06
☐ 42	Bobby Bonds	.75	.35	.07
☐ 43	Garry Templeton	.60	.30	.06
☐ 44	Johnny Bench	4.50	2.25	.45
☐ 45	Jim Rice	3.00	1.50	.30
☐ 46	Bill Buckner	.60	.30	.06
☐ 47	Reggie Jackson	4.50	2.25	.45
☐ 48	Freddie Patek	.45	.22	.04
☐ 49	Steve Carlton	3.50	1.75	.35
☐ 50	Cesar Cedeno	.60	.30	.06
☐ 51	Steve Yeager	.45	.22	.04
☐ 52	Phil Garner	.45	.22	.04
☐ 53	Lee May	.60	.30	.06
☐ 54	Darrell Evans	.75	.35	.07
☐ 55	Steve Kemp	.60	.30	.06
☐ 56	Dusty Baker	.60	.30	.06
☐ 57	Ray Fosse	.45	.22	.04
☐ 58	Manny Sanguillen	.60	.30	.06
☐ 59	Tom Johnson	.45	.22	.04
☐ 60	Lee Stanton	.45	.22	.04
☐ 61	Jeff Burroughs	.60	.30	.06
☐ 62	Bobby Grich	.60	.30	.06
☐ 63	Dave Winfield	3.00	1.50	.30
☐ 64	Dan Driessen	.60	.30	.06
☐ 65	Ted Simmons	.75	.35	.07
☐ 66	Jerry Remy	.45	.22	.04
☐ 67	Al Cowens	.60	.30	.06
☐ 68	Sparky Lyle	.75	.35	.07
☐ 69	Manny Trillo	.60	.30	.06
☐ 70	Don Sutton	2.00	1.00	.20
☐ 71	Larry Bowa	.60	.30	.06
☐ 72	Jose Cruz	.60	.30	.06

1979 Hostess

The cards in this 150-card set measure 3 1/4" by 7 1/4" as panels of three. The 1979 Hostess set contains full color, numbered cards issued in panels of three cards each on the backs of family sized Hostess cake products. Scarcer panels are listed in the checklist below with asterisks. Although complete panel prices are not explicitly listed below

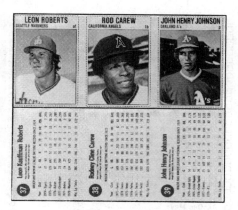

LEON ROBERTS	ROD CAREW	JOHN HENRY JOHNSON
SEATTLE MARINERS of	CALIFORNIA ANGELS 1b	OAKLAND A's p
37	38	39

they would generally have a value 25% greater than
the sum of the individual players on the panel. There
is additional interest in Ozzie Smith #102 since this
card corresponds to his "rookie" year in cards.

	NRMT	VG-E	GOOD
COMPLETE INDIV. SET	175.00	85.00	18.00
COMMON PLAYER (1-150)	.45	.22	.04

			NRMT	VG-E	GOOD
☐	1	John Denny	.60	.30	.06
☐	2	Jim Rice	3.00	1.50	.30
☐	3	Doug Bair	.45	.22	.04
☐	4	Darrell Porter	.45	.22	.04
☐	5	Ross Grimsley	.45	.22	.04
☐	6	Bobby Murcer	.60	.30	.06
☐	7	Lee Mazzilli	.45	.22	.04
☐	8	Steve Garvey	3.50	1.75	.35
☐	9	Mike Schmidt	6.50	3.25	.65
☐	10	Terry Whitfield	.45	.22	.04
☐	11	Jim Palmer	3.00	1.50	.30
☐	12	Omar Moreno	.45	.22	.04
☐	13	Duane Kuiper	.45	.22	.04
☐	14	Mike Caldwell	.45	.22	.04
☐	15	Steve Kemp	.45	.22	.04
☐	16	Dave Goltz	.45	.22	.04
☐	17	Mitchell Page	.45	.22	.04
☐	18	Bill Stein	.45	.22	.04
☐	19	Gene Tenace	.45	.22	.04
☐	20	Jeff Burroughs	.45	.22	.04
☐	21	Francisco Barrios	.45	.22	.04
☐	22	Mike Torrez	.45	.22	.04
☐	23	Ken Reitz	.45	.22	.04
☐	24	Gary Carter	3.00	1.50	.30
☐	25	Al Hrabosky	.60	.30	.06
☐	26	Thurman Munson	3.50	1.75	.35
☐	27	Bill Buckner	.60	.30	.06
☐	28	Ron Cey *	.75	.35	.07
☐	29	J.R. Richard *	.60	.30	.06
☐	30	Greg Luzinski *	.90	.45	.09
☐	31	Ed Ott *	.60	.30	.06
☐	32	Dennis Martinez *	.75	.35	.07
☐	33	Darrell Evans *	.75	.35	.07
☐	34	Ron LeFlore	.45	.22	.04
☐	35	Rick Waits	.45	.22	.04
☐	36	Cecil Cooper	.75	.35	.07
☐	37	Leon Roberts	.45	.22	.04
☐	38	Rod Carew	3.50	1.75	.35
☐	39	John Henry Johnson	.45	.22	.04
☐	40	Chet Lemon	.45	.22	.04
☐	41	Craig Swan	.45	.22	.04
☐	42	Gary Matthews	.45	.22	.04
☐	43	Lamar Johnson	.45	.22	.04
☐	44	Ted Simmons	.90	.45	.09
☐	45	Ken Griffey	.75	.35	.07
☐	46	Fred Patek	.45	.22	.04
☐	47	Frank Tanana	.45	.22	.04
☐	48	Goose Gossage	.90	.45	.09
☐	49	Burt Hooton	.45	.22	.04
☐	50	Ellis Valentine	.45	.22	.04
☐	51	Ken Forsch	.45	.22	.04
☐	52	Bob Knepper	.45	.22	.04
☐	53	Dave Parker	2.00	1.00	.20
☐	54	Doug DeCinces	.60	.30	.06
☐	55	Robin Yount	5.00	2.50	.50
☐	56	Rusty Staub	.60	.30	.06
☐	57	Gary Alexander	.45	.22	.04
☐	58	Julio Cruz	.45	.22	.04
☐	59	Matt Keough	.45	.22	.04
☐	60	Roy Smalley	.45	.22	.04
☐	61	Joe Morgan	3.00	1.50	.30
☐	62	Phil Niekro	2.00	1.00	.20
☐	63	Don Baylor	.60	.30	.06
☐	64	Dwight Evans	.90	.45	.09
☐	65	Tom Seaver	3.50	1.75	.35
☐	66	George Hendrick	.45	.22	.04
☐	67	Rick Reuschel	.60	.30	.06
☐	68	George Brett	5.00	2.50	.50
☐	69	Lou Piniella	.75	.35	.07
☐	70	Enos Cabell	.45	.22	.04
☐	71	Steve Carlton	3.50	1.75	.35
☐	72	Reggie Smith	.60	.30	.06
☐	73	Rick Dempsey *	.60	.30	.06
☐	74	Vida Blue *	.60	.30	.06
☐	75	Phil Garner *	.60	.30	.06
☐	76	Rick Manning *	.60	.30	.06
☐	77	Mark Fidrych *	.75	.35	.07
☐	78	Mario Guerrero *	.60	.30	.06
☐	79	Bob Stinson *	.60	.30	.06
☐	80	Al Oliver *	.90	.45	.09
☐	81	Doug Flynn *	.60	.30	.06
☐	82	John Mayberry	.60	.30	.06
☐	83	Gaylord Perry	1.50	.75	.15
☐	84	Joe Rudi	.60	.30	.06
☐	85	Dave Concepcion	.75	.35	.07
☐	86	John Candelaria	.60	.30	.06
☐	87	Pete Vuckovich	.60	.30	.06
☐	88	Ivan DeJesus	.45	.22	.04
☐	89	Ron Guidry	1.50	.75	.15
☐	90	Hal McRae	.60	.30	.06
☐	91	Cesar Cedeno	.60	.30	.06
☐	92	Don Sutton	2.00	1.00	.20
☐	93	Andre Thornton	.60	.30	.06
☐	94	Roger Erickson	.45	.22	.04
☐	95	Larry Hisle	.60	.30	.06
☐	96	Jason Thompson	.60	.30	.06
☐	97	Jim Sundberg	.60	.30	.06
☐	98	Bob Horner	1.50	.75	.15
☐	99	Ruppert Jones	.45	.22	.04
☐	100	Willie Montanez	.45	.22	.04
☐	101	Nolan Ryan	6.00	3.00	.60
☐	102	Ozzie Smith	12.00	5.00	1.00
☐	103	Eric Soderholm	.45	.22	.04
☐	104	Willie Stargell	2.00	1.00	.20
☐	105A	Bob Bailor ERR	.60	.30	.06
		(reverse negative)			
☐	105B	Bob Bailor COR	.90	.45	.09
☐	106	Carlton Fisk	1.50	.75	.15
☐	107	George Foster	.90	.45	.09
☐	108	Keith Hernandez	2.50	1.25	.25
☐	109	Dennis Leonard	.60	.30	.06
☐	110	Graig Nettles	.75	.35	.07
☐	111	Jose Cruz	.60	.30	.06
☐	112	Bobby Grich	.60	.30	.06
☐	113	Bob Boone	.90	.45	.09
☐	114	Dave Lopes	.60	.30	.06
☐	115	Eddie Murray	4.50	2.25	.45
☐	116	Jack Clark	2.50	1.25	.25
☐	117	Lou Whitaker	1.50	.75	.15
☐	118	Miguel Dilone	.45	.22	.04
☐	119	Sal Bando	.60	.30	.06
☐	120	Reggie Jackson	4.50	2.25	.45
☐	121	Dale Murphy	8.00	4.00	.80
☐	122	Jon Matlack	.45	.22	.04
☐	123	Bruce Bochte	.45	.22	.04
☐	124	John Stearns	.45	.22	.04
☐	125	Dave Winfield	3.00	1.50	.30
☐	126	Jorge Orta	.45	.22	.04
☐	127	Garry Templeton	.45	.22	.04
☐	128	Johnny Bench	3.50	1.75	.35
☐	129	Butch Hobson	.45	.22	.04
☐	130	Bruce Sutter	.90	.45	.09
☐	131	Bucky Dent	.75	.35	.07
☐	132	Amos Otis	.60	.30	.06
☐	133	Bert Blyleven	.90	.45	.09
☐	134	Larry Bowa	.60	.30	.06
☐	135	Ken Singleton	.60	.30	.06
☐	136	Sixto Lezcano	.45	.22	.04
☐	137	Roy Howell	.45	.22	.04
☐	138	Bill Madlock	.90	.45	.09
☐	139	Dave Revering	.45	.22	.04
☐	140	Richie Zisk	.60	.30	.06
☐	141	Butch Wynegar	.45	.22	.04
☐	142	Alan Ashby	.45	.22	.04
☐	143	Sparky Lyle	.75	.35	.07
☐	144	Pete Rose	9.00	4.50	.90
☐	145	Dennis Eckersley	1.00	.50	.10
☐	146	Dave Kingman	.75	.35	.07
☐	147	Buddy Bell	.60	.30	.06
☐	148	Mike Hargrove	.60	.30	.06
☐	149	Jerry Koosman	.60	.30	.06
☐	150	Toby Harrah	.60	.30	.06

1985 Hostess Braves

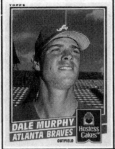

The cards in this 22-card set measure 2 1/2" by 3 1/2" and feature players of the Atlanta Braves. Cards were produced by Topps for Hostess (Continental Baking Co.) and are quite attractive. The card backs are similar in design to the 1985 Topps regular issue; however all photos are different from those that Topps used as these were apparently taken during Spring Training. Cards were available in boxes of Hostess products in packs of four (three players and a contest card).

	MINT	EXC	G-VG
COMPLETE SET (22)	8.00	4.00	.80
COMMON PLAYER (1-22)	.25	.12	.02

		MINT	EXC	G-VG
☐ 1	Eddie Haas MG	.25	.12	.02
☐ 2	Len Barker	.25	.12	.02
☐ 3	Steve Bedrosian	.75	.35	.07
☐ 4	Bruce Benedict	.25	.12	.02
☐ 5	Rick Camp	.25	.12	.02
☐ 6	Rick Cerone	.25	.12	.02
☐ 7	Chris Chambliss	.35	.17	.03
☐ 8	Terry Forster	.45	.22	.04
☐ 9	Gene Garber	.25	.12	.02
☐ 10	Albert Hall	.25	.12	.02
☐ 11	Bob Horner	.75	.35	.07
☐ 12	Glenn Hubbard	.35	.17	.03
☐ 13	Brad Komminsk	.35	.17	.03
☐ 14	Rick Mahler	.35	.17	.03
☐ 15	Craig McMurtry	.25	.12	.02
☐ 16	Dale Murphy	4.00	2.00	.40
☐ 17	Ken Oberkfell	.25	.12	.02
☐ 18	Pascual Perez	.45	.22	.04
☐ 19	Gerald Perry	.45	.22	.04
☐ 20	Rafael Ramirez	.25	.12	.02
☐ 21	Bruce Sutter	.60	.30	.06
☐ 22	Claudell Washington	.45	.22	.04

1953 Johnston Cookies

The cards in this 25-card set measure 2 9/16" by 3 5/8". The 1953 Johnston's Cookies set of numbered cards features Milwaukee Braves players only. This set is the most plentiful of the three Johnston's Cookies sets and no known scarcities exist. The ACC designation for this set is D356-1.

	NRMT	VG-E	GOOD
COMPLETE SET (25)	250.00	125.00	25.00
COMMON PLAYER (1-25)	7.50	3.75	.75

		NRMT	VG-E	GOOD
☐ 1	Charlie Grimm MG	9.00	4.50	.90
☐ 2	John Antonelli	9.00	4.50	.90
☐ 3	Vern Bickford	7.50	3.75	.75
☐ 4	Bob Buhl	7.50	3.75	.75
☐ 5	Lew Burdette	12.50	6.25	1.25
☐ 6	Dave Cole	7.50	3.75	.75
☐ 7	Ernie Johnson	9.00	4.50	.90
☐ 8	Dave Jolly	7.50	3.75	.75
☐ 9	Don Liddle	7.50	3.75	.75
☐ 10	Warren Spahn	40.00	20.00	4.00

☐ 11	Max Surkont	7.50	3.75	.75
☐ 12	Jim Wilson	7.50	3.75	.75
☐ 13	Sibbi Sisti	7.50	3.75	.75
☐ 14	Walker Cooper	7.50	3.75	.75
☐ 15	Del Crandall	9.00	4.50	.90
☐ 16	Ebba St.Claire	7.50	3.75	.75
☐ 17	Joe Adcock	10.00	5.00	1.00
☐ 18	George Crowe	7.50	3.75	.75
☐ 19	Jack Dittmer	7.50	3.75	.75
☐ 20	Johnny Logan	9.00	4.50	.90
☐ 21	Ed Mathews	40.00	20.00	4.00
☐ 22	Bill Bruton	9.00	4.50	.90
☐ 23	Sid Gordon	7.50	3.75	.75
☐ 24	Andy Pafko	9.00	4.50	.90
☐ 25	Jim Pendleton	7.50	3.75	.75

1954 Johnston Cookies

The cards in this 35-card set measure 2" by 3 7/8". The 1954 Johnston's Cookies set of color cards of Milwaukee Braves are numbered according to the player's uniform number, except for the non-players, Lacks and Taylor, who are found at the end of the set. The Bobby Thomson card was withdrawn early in the year after his injury and is scarce. The ACC catalog number for this set is D356-2.

	NRMT	VG-E	GOOD
COMPLETE SET (35)	900.00	450.00	90.00
COMMON PLAYER (1-50)	10.00	5.00	1.00

		NRMT	VG-E	GOOD
☐ 1	Del Crandall	12.00	6.00	1.20
☐ 3	Jim Pendleton	10.00	5.00	1.00
☐ 4	Danny O'Connell	10.00	5.00	1.00
☐ 5	Hank Aaron	350.00	175.00	35.00
☐ 6	Jack Dittmer	10.00	5.00	1.00
☐ 9	Joe Adcock	12.00	6.00	1.20
☐ 10	Bob Buhl	10.00	5.00	1.00
☐ 11	Phil Paine	10.00	5.00	1.00

☐ 12	Ben Johnson	10.00	5.00	1.00
☐ 13	Sibbi Sisti	10.00	5.00	1.00
☐ 15	Charles Gorin	10.00	5.00	1.00
☐ 16	Chet Nichols	10.00	5.00	1.00
☐ 17	Dave Jolly	10.00	5.00	1.00
☐ 19	Jim Wilson	10.00	5.00	1.00
☐ 20	Ray Crone	10.00	5.00	1.00
☐ 21	Warren Spahn	50.00	25.00	5.00
☐ 22	Gene Conley	10.00	5.00	1.00
☐ 23	Johnny Logan	12.00	6.00	1.20
☐ 24	Charlie White	10.00	5.00	1.00
☐ 27	George Metkovich	10.00	5.00	1.00
☐ 28	Johnny Cooney	10.00	5.00	1.00
☐ 29	Paul Burris	10.00	5.00	1.00
☐ 31	Bucky Walters	12.00	6.00	1.20
☐ 32	Ernie Johnson	12.00	6.00	1.20
☐ 33	Lou Burdette	20.00	10.00	2.00
☐ 34	Bob Thomson	200.00	100.00	20.00
☐ 35	Bob Keely	10.00	5.00	1.00
☐ 38	Bill Bruton	12.00	6.00	1.20
☐ 40	Charlie Grimm MG	12.00	6.00	1.20
☐ 41	Eddie Mathews	50.00	25.00	5.00
☐ 42	Sam Calderone	10.00	5.00	1.00
☐ 47	Joey Jay	10.00	5.00	1.00
☐ 48	Andy Pafko	10.00	5.00	1.00
☐ 49	Dr. Charles Lacks (unnumbered)	10.00	5.00	1.00
☐ 50	Joseph F. Taylor (unnumbered)	10.00	5.00	1.00

☐ 22	Gene Conley P3	18.00	9.00	1.80
☐ 23	Johnny Logan P4	21.00	10.50	2.10
☐ 24	Charlie White P2	18.00	9.00	1.80
☐ 28	Johnny Cooney P4	18.00	9.00	1.80
☐ 30	Roy Smalley P3	18.00	9.00	1.80
☐ 31	Bucky Walters P6	21.00	10.50	2.10
☐ 32	Ernie Johnson P5	18.00	9.00	1.80
☐ 33	Lew Burdette P1	30.00	15.00	3.00
☐ 34	Bobby Thomson P6	24.00	12.00	2.40
☐ 35	Bob Keely P1	18.00	9.00	1.80
☐ 38	Bill Bruton P4	21.00	10.50	2.10
☐ 39	George Crowe P3	18.00	9.00	1.80
☐ 40	Charlie Grimm MG P6	21.00	10.50	2.10
☐ 41	Eddie Mathews P5	75.00	37.50	7.50
☐ 44	Hank Aaron P1	300.00	150.00	30.00
☐ 47	Joey Jay P2	18.00	9.00	1.80
☐ 48	Andy Pafko P2 P4	18.00	9.00	1.80
☐ 49	Dr. Charles Leaks P2 (unnumbered)	18.00	9.00	1.80
☐ 50	Duffy Lewis P5 (unnumbered)	18.00	9.00	1.80
☐ 51	Joe Taylor P3 (unnumbered)	18.00	9.00	1.80

1955 Johnston Cookies

The cards in this 35-card set measure 2 3/4" by 4". This set of Milwaukee Braves issued in 1955 by Johnston Cookies are numbered by the uniform number of the player depicted, except for non-players Lacks, Lewis and Taylor. The cards were issued in strips of six which accounts for the rouletted edges found on single cards. They are larger in size than the two previous sets but are printed on thinner cardboard. Each player in the checklist has been marked to show on which panel or strip he appeared (Pafko appears twice). A complete panel of six cards is worth 25% more than the sum of the individual players. The ACC designation for this set is D356-3.

		NRMT	VG-E	GOOD
COMPLETE SET (35)		1000.00	500.00	100.00
COMMON PLAYER (1-51)		18.00	9.00	1.80
☐ 1	Del Crandall P1	21.00	10.50	2.10
☐ 3	Jim Pendleton P3	18.00	9.00	1.80
☐ 4	Danny O'Connell P1	18.00	9.00	1.80
☐ 6	Jack Dittmer P6	18.00	9.00	1.80
☐ 9	Joe Adcock P2	21.00	10.50	2.10
☐ 10	Bob Buhl P6	18.00	9.00	1.80
☐ 11	Phil Paine P5	18.00	9.00	1.80
☐ 12	Ray Crone P5	18.00	9.00	1.80
☐ 15	Charlie Gorin P1	18.00	9.00	1.80
☐ 16	Dave Jolly P4	18.00	9.00	1.80
☐ 17	Chet Nichols P2	18.00	9.00	1.80
☐ 18	Chuck Tanner P5	24.00	12.00	2.40
☐ 19	Jim Wilson P6	18.00	9.00	1.80
☐ 20	Dave Koslo P4	18.00	9.00	1.80
☐ 21	Warren Spahn P3	75.00	37.50	7.50

1955 Kahn's

Compliments of Kahn's Wieners
"THE WIENER THE WORLD AWAITED"

The cards in this 6-card set measure 3 1/4" by 4". The 1955 Kahn's Wieners set received very limited distribution. The cards were supposedly given away at an amusement park. The set portrays the players in street clothes rather than in uniform and hence are sometimes referred to as "street clothes" Kahn's. All Kahn's sets from 1955 through 1963 are black and white and contain a 1/2" tab. Cards with the tab still intact are worth approximately 50% more than cards without the tab. Cards feature a facsimile autograph of the player on the front. Cards are blank-backed. Cincinnati Redlegs players only are featured.

		NRMT	VG-E	GOOD
COMPLETE SET (6)		3000.00	1500.00	300.00
COMMON PLAYER (1-6)		450.00	225.00	45.00
☐ 1	Gus Bell (street clothes)	750.00	375.00	75.00
☐ 2	Ted Kluszewski (street clothes)	750.00	375.00	75.00
☐ 3	Roy McMillan (street clothes)	450.00	225.00	45.00
☐ 4	Joe Nuxhall (street clothes)	450.00	225.00	45.00
☐ 5	Wally Post (street clothes)	450.00	225.00	45.00
☐ 6	Johnny Temple (street clothes)	450.00	225.00	45.00

1956 Kahn's

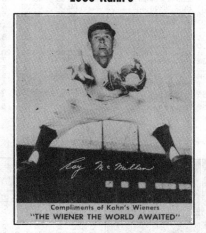

Compliments of Kahn's Wieners
"THE WIENER THE WORLD AWAITED"

The cards in this 15-card set measure 3 1/4" by 4". The 1956 Kahn's set was the first set to be issued with Kahn's meat products. The cards are blank backed. The set is distinguished by the old style, short sleeve shirts on the players and the existence of backgounds (Kahn's cards of later years utilize a blank background). Cards which have the tab still intact are worth approximately 50% more than cards without the tab. Cincinnati Redlegs players only are featured.

	NRMT	VG-E	GOOD
COMPLETE SET (15)	1400.00	700.00	150.00
COMMON PLAYER (1-15)	75.00	37.50	7.50

			NRMT	VG-E	GOOD
☐	1	Ed Bailey	75.00	37.50	7.50
☐	2	Gus Bell	90.00	45.00	9.00
☐	3	Joe Black	90.00	45.00	9.00
☐	4	Smoky Burgess	90.00	45.00	9.00
☐	5	Art Fowler	75.00	37.50	7.50
☐	6	Hershel Freeman	75.00	37.50	7.50
☐	7	Ray Jablonski	75.00	37.50	7.50
☐	8	John Klippstein	75.00	37.50	7.50
☐	9	Ted Kluszewski	150.00	75.00	15.00
☐	10	Brooks Lawrence	75.00	37.50	7.50
☐	11	Roy McMillan	75.00	37.50	7.50
☐	12	Joe Nuxhall	90.00	45.00	9.00
☐	13	Wally Post	75.00	37.50	7.50
☐	14	Frank Robinson	300.00	150.00	30.00
☐	15	Johnny Temple	90.00	45.00	9.00

1957 Kahn's

The cards in this 29-card set measure 3 1/4" by 4". The 1957 Kahn's Wieners set contains black and white, blank backed, unnumbered cards. The set features the Cincinnati Redlegs and Pittsburgh Pirates only. The cards feature a light background. Each card features a facsimile autograph of the player on the front. The Groat card exists with a "Richard Groat" autograph and also exists with the printed name "Dick Groat" on the card. The ACC designation is D155-3.

	NRMT	VG-E	GOOD
COMPLETE SET (29)	2500.00	1200.00	250.00
COMMON PLAYER (1-29)	60.00	30.00	6.00

			NRMT	VG-E	GOOD
☐	1	Tom Acker	60.00	30.00	6.00
☐	2	Ed Bailey	60.00	30.00	6.00
☐	3	Gus Bell	75.00	37.50	7.50
☐	4	Smoky Burgess	75.00	37.50	7.50

Compliments of Kahn's Wieners
"THE WIENER THE WORLD AWAITED"

			NRMT	VG-E	GOOD
☐	5	Robert Clemente	500.00	250.00	50.00
☐	6	George Crowe	60.00	30.00	6.00
☐	7	Elroy Face	90.00	45.00	9.00
☐	8	Hershel Freeman	60.00	30.00	6.00
☐	9	Bob Friend	75.00	37.50	7.50
☐	10	Dick Groat	90.00	45.00	9.00
☐	11	Richard Groat	175.00	85.00	18.00
☐	12	Don Gross	60.00	30.00	6.00
☐	13	Warren Hacker	60.00	30.00	6.00
☐	14	Don Hoak	60.00	30.00	6.00
☐	15	Hal Jeffcoat	60.00	30.00	6.00
☐	16	Ron Kline	60.00	30.00	6.00
☐	17	John Klippstein	60.00	30.00	6.00
☐	18	Ted Kluszewski	125.00	60.00	12.50
☐	19	Brooks Lawrence	60.00	30.00	6.00
☐	20	Dale Long	75.00	37.50	7.50
☐	21	Bill Mazeroski	125.00	60.00	12.50
☐	22	Roy McMillan	60.00	30.00	6.00
☐	23	Joe Nuxhall	75.00	37.50	7.50
☐	24	Wally Post	60.00	30.00	6.00
☐	25	Frank Robinson	225.00	110.00	22.00
☐	26	John Temple	75.00	37.50	7.50
☐	27	Frank Thomas	75.00	37.50	7.50
☐	28	Bob Thurman	60.00	30.00	6.00
☐	29	Lee Walls	60.00	30.00	6.00

1958 Kahn's

MY GREATEST THRILL IN BASEBALL
By FRANK ROBINSON

In 1956, my rookie year in the big leagues, I was named by Birdie Tebbetts to start the season in left field for the Cincinnati Redlegs. Everybody had told me that Opening Day in Cincinnati was almost a national holiday, and it was really the truth.

When I came out on the field the park was overflowing with fans. They were even sitting on the terrace in back of my left field position.

My first time at bat in the major leagues came that day, and I doubled off the center-field wall. That was my big moment in baseball, the one I'll always remember.

Compliments of Kahn's Wieners
"THE WIENER THE WORLD AWAITED"

The cards in this 29-card set measure 3 1/4" by 4". The 1958 Kahn's Wieners set of unnumbered, black and white cards features Cincinnati Redlegs, Philadelphia Phillies, and Pittsburgh Pirates. The backs present a story for each player entitled "My Greatest Thrill in Baseball". A method of distinguishing 1958 Kahn's from 1959 Kahn's is that the word Wieners is found on the front of the 1958 but not on the front of the 1959 cards. Cards of Wally Post, Charlie Rabe, and Frank Thomas are somewhat more difficult to find and are marked with an asterisk in the checklist below.

	NRMT	VG-E	GOOD
COMPLETE SET (29)	2800.00	1400.00	300.00
COMMON PLAYER (1-29)	50.00	25.00	5.00

		NRMT	VG-E	GOOD
☐ 1	Ed Bailey	50.00	25.00	5.00
☐ 2	Gene Baker	50.00	25.00	5.00
☐ 3	Gus Bell	60.00	30.00	6.00
☐ 4	Smoky Burgess	60.00	30.00	6.00
☐ 5	Roberto Clemente	450.00	225.00	45.00
☐ 6	George Crowe	50.00	25.00	5.00
☐ 7	Elroy Face	75.00	37.50	7.50
☐ 8	Hank Foiles	50.00	25.00	5.00
☐ 9	Dee Fondy	50.00	25.00	5.00
☐ 10	Bob Friend	60.00	30.00	6.00
☐ 11	Dick Groat	75.00	37.50	7.50
☐ 12	Harvey Haddix	60.00	30.00	6.00
☐ 13	Don Hoak	50.00	25.00	5.00
☐ 14	Hal Jeffcoat	50.00	25.00	5.00
☐ 15	Ron Kline	50.00	25.00	5.00
☐ 16	Ted Kluszewski	100.00	50.00	10.00
☐ 17	Vernon Law	60.00	30.00	6.00
☐ 18	Brooks Lawrence	50.00	25.00	5.00
☐ 19	Bill Mazeroski	90.00	45.00	9.00
☐ 20	Roy McMillan	50.00	25.00	5.00
☐ 21	Joe Nuxhall	60.00	30.00	6.00
☐ 22	Wally Post *	300.00	150.00	30.00
☐ 23	John Powers	50.00	25.00	5.00
☐ 24	Bob Purkey	50.00	25.00	5.00
☐ 25	Charlie Rabe *	300.00	150.00	30.00
☐ 26	Frank Robinson	200.00	100.00	20.00
☐ 27	Bob Skinner	50.00	25.00	5.00
☐ 28	Johnny Temple	60.00	30.00	6.00
☐ 29	Frank Thomas *	300.00	150.00	30.00

☐ 24	Minnie Minoso	90.00	45.00	9.00
☐ 25	Russ Nixon	60.00	30.00	6.00
☐ 26	Joe Nuxhall	60.00	30.00	6.00
☐ 27	Jim Perry	75.00	37.50	7.50
☐ 28	Vada Pinson	75.00	37.50	7.50
☐ 29	Vic Power	50.00	25.00	5.00
☐ 30	Bob Purkey	50.00	25.00	5.00
☐ 31	Frank Robinson	200.00	100.00	20.00
☐ 32	Herb Score	75.00	37.50	7.50
☐ 33	Bob Skinner	50.00	25.00	5.00
☐ 34	George Strickland	50.00	25.00	5.00
☐ 35	Dick Stuart	60.00	30.00	6.00
☐ 36	Johnny Temple	50.00	25.00	5.00
☐ 37	Frank Thomas	60.00	30.00	6.00
☐ 38	George Witt	50.00	25.00	5.00

1960 Kahn's

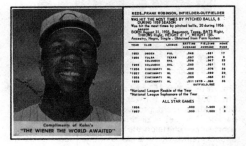

Compliments of Kahn's
"THE WIENER THE WORLD AWAITED"

The cards in this 42-card set measure 3 1/4" by 4". The 1960 Kahn's set features players of the Chicago Cubs, Chicago White Sox, Cincinnati Redlegs, Cleveland Indians, Pittsburgh Pirates, and St. Louis Cardinals. The backs give vital player information and records through the 1959 season. Kline appears with either St. Louis or Pittsburgh. The Harvey Kuenn card (asterisked below) appears with a blank back, and is scarce.

		NRMT	VG-E	GOOD
COMPLETE SET (43)		1750.00	850.00	200.00
COMMON PLAYER (1-42)		24.00	12.00	2.40
☐ 1	Ed Bailey	24.00	12.00	2.40
☐ 2	Gary Bell	24.00	12.00	2.40
☐ 3	Gus Bell	28.00	14.00	2.80
☐ 4	Smoky Burgess	28.00	14.00	2.80
☐ 5	Gino Cimoli	24.00	12.00	2.40
☐ 6	Roberto Clemente	300.00	150.00	30.00
☐ 7	Roy Face	32.00	16.00	3.20
☐ 8	Tito Francona	24.00	12.00	2.40
☐ 9	Bob Friend	28.00	14.00	2.80
☐ 10	Jim Grant	24.00	12.00	2.40
☐ 11	Dick Groat	32.00	16.00	3.20
☐ 12	Harvey Haddix	28.00	14.00	2.80
☐ 13	Woodie Held	24.00	12.00	2.40
☐ 14	Bill Henry	24.00	12.00	2.40
☐ 15	Don Hoak	24.00	12.00	2.40
☐ 16	Jay Hook	24.00	12.00	2.40
☐ 17	Eddie Kasko	24.00	12.00	2.40
☐ 18A	Ron Kline (Pittsburgh)	45.00	22.50	4.50
☐ 18B	Ron Kline (St. Louis)	45.00	22.50	4.50
☐ 19	Ted Kluszewski	50.00	25.00	5.00
☐ 20	Harvey Kuenn (blank back)	300.00	150.00	30.00
☐ 21	Vernon Law	28.00	14.00	2.80
☐ 22	Brooks Lawrence	24.00	12.00	2.40
☐ 23	Jerry Lynch	24.00	12.00	2.40
☐ 24	Billy Martin	60.00	30.00	6.00
☐ 25	Bill Mazeroski	40.00	20.00	4.00
☐ 26	Cal McLish	24.00	12.00	2.40
☐ 27	Roy McMillan	24.00	12.00	2.40
☐ 28	Don Newcombe	32.00	16.00	3.20
☐ 29	Russ Nixon	28.00	14.00	2.80
☐ 30	Joe Nuxhall	28.00	14.00	2.80
☐ 31	Jim O'Toole	24.00	12.00	2.40
☐ 32	Jim Perry	28.00	14.00	2.80
☐ 33	Vada Pinson	32.00	16.00	3.20
☐ 34	Vic Power	24.00	12.00	2.40

1959 Kahn's

THE TOUGHEST PLAY
I HAVE TO MAKE
by FRANKIE ROBINSON

"The toughest play I have to make as a first baseman is fielding a hard hit grounder to my right when there's a man on first. I have to stay close to the bag to hold the man on until the ball is pitched. That means I have to move fast to stop the ball and still be in position to make a play, either to second for a double play or to first for one out."

Compliments of Kahn's
"THE WIENER THE WORLD AWAITED"

The cards in this 38-card set measure 3 1/4" by 4". The 1959 Kahn's set features Cincinnati, Cleveland, and Pittsburgh players. The backs feature stories entitled "The Toughest Play I have to Make," or "The Toughest Batter I Have To Face." The Brodowski card is very scarce while Haddix, Held and McLish are considered quite difficult to obtain; these scarcities are the asterisked cards in the checklist below.

		NRMT	VG-E	GOOD
COMPLETE SET (38)		4000.00	2000.00	500.00
COMMON PLAYER (1-38)		50.00	25.00	5.00
☐ 1	Ed Bailey	50.00	25.00	5.00
☐ 2	Gary Bell	50.00	25.00	5.00
☐ 3	Gus Bell	60.00	30.00	6.00
☐ 4	Dick Brodowski *	500.00	250.00	50.00
☐ 5	Smoky Burgess	60.00	30.00	6.00
☐ 6	Roberto Clemente	450.00	225.00	45.00
☐ 7	Rocky Colavito	100.00	50.00	10.00
☐ 8	Elroy Face	75.00	37.50	7.50
☐ 9	Bob Friend	60.00	30.00	6.00
☐ 10	Joe Gordon	60.00	30.00	6.00
☐ 11	Jim Grant	50.00	25.00	5.00
☐ 12	Dick Groat	75.00	37.50	7.50
☐ 13	Harvey Haddix * (blank back)	350.00	175.00	35.00
☐ 14	Woodie Held *	350.00	175.00	35.00
☐ 15	Don Hoak	50.00	25.00	5.00
☐ 16	Ron Kline	50.00	25.00	5.00
☐ 17	Ted Kluszewski	90.00	45.00	9.00
☐ 18	Vernon Law	60.00	30.00	6.00
☐ 19	Jerry Lynch	50.00	25.00	5.00
☐ 20	Billy Martin	125.00	60.00	12.50
☐ 21	Bill Mazeroski	90.00	45.00	9.00
☐ 22	Cal McLish *	350.00	175.00	35.00
☐ 23	Roy McMillan	50.00	25.00	5.00

		NRMT	VG-E	GOOD
☐ 35	Bob Purkey	24.00	12.00	2.40
☐ 36	Frank Robinson	150.00	75.00	15.00
☐ 37	Herb Score	32.00	16.00	3.20
☐ 38	Bob Skinner	24.00	12.00	2.40
☐ 39	Dick Stuart	28.00	14.00	2.80
☐ 40	Johnny Temple	28.00	14.00	2.80
☐ 41	Frank Thomas	28.00	14.00	2.80
☐ 42	Lee Walls	24.00	12.00	2.40

1961 Kahn's

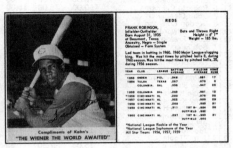

Compliments of Kahn's
"THE WIENER THE WORLD AWAITED"

The cards in this 43-card set measure 3 1/4" by 4". The 1961 Kahn's Wieners set of black and white, unnumbered cards features players from Cincinnati, Cleveland, and Pittsburgh. This year was the first year Kahn's made complete sets available to the public; hence they are more available, especially in the better condition grades, than the Kahn's of the previous years. The backs give vital player information and year by year career statistics through 1960. The ACC designation is F155-7.

		NRMT	VG-E	GOOD
COMPLETE SET (43)		675.00	300.00	75.00
COMMON PLAYER (1-43)		12.00	6.00	1.20
☐ 1	John Antonelli	12.00	6.00	1.20
☐ 2	Ed Bailey	12.00	6.00	1.20
☐ 3	Gary Bell	12.00	6.00	1.20
☐ 4	Gus Bell	12.00	6.00	1.20
☐ 5	Jim Brosnan	12.00	6.00	1.20
☐ 6	Smoky Burgess	15.00	7.50	1.50
☐ 7	Gino Cimoli	12.00	6.00	1.20
☐ 8	Roberto Clemente	200.00	100.00	20.00
☐ 9	Gordie Coleman	12.00	6.00	1.20
☐ 10	Jimmy Dykes	12.00	6.00	1.20
☐ 11	Roy Face	15.00	7.50	1.50
☐ 12	Tito Francona	12.00	6.00	1.20
☐ 13	Gene Freese	12.00	6.00	1.20
☐ 14	Bob Friend	12.00	6.00	1.20
☐ 15	Jim Grant	12.00	6.00	1.20
☐ 16	Dick Groat	18.00	9.00	1.80
☐ 17	Harvey Haddix	12.00	6.00	1.20
☐ 18	Woodie Held	12.00	6.00	1.20
☐ 19	Don Hoak	12.00	6.00	1.20
☐ 20	Jay Hook	12.00	6.00	1.20
☐ 21	Joey Jay	12.00	6.00	1.20
☐ 22	Eddie Kasko	12.00	6.00	1.20
☐ 23	Willie Kirkland	12.00	6.00	1.20
☐ 24	Vernon Law	12.00	6.00	1.20
☐ 25	Jerry Lynch	12.00	6.00	1.20
☐ 26	Jim Maloney	15.00	7.50	1.50
☐ 27	Bill Mazeroski	20.00	10.00	2.00
☐ 28	Wilmer Mizell	12.00	6.00	1.20
☐ 29	Rocky Nelson	12.00	6.00	1.20
☐ 30	Jim O'Toole	12.00	6.00	1.20
☐ 31	Jim Perry	15.00	7.50	1.50
☐ 32	Bubba Phillips	12.00	6.00	1.20
☐ 33	Vada Pinson	18.00	9.00	1.80
☐ 34	Wally Post	12.00	6.00	1.20
☐ 35	Vic Power	12.00	6.00	1.20
☐ 36	Bob Purkey	12.00	6.00	1.20
☐ 37	Frank Robinson	90.00	45.00	9.00
☐ 38	John Romano	12.00	6.00	1.20
☐ 39	Dick Schofield	12.00	6.00	1.20
☐ 40	Bob Skinner	12.00	6.00	1.20
☐ 41	Hal Smith	12.00	6.00	1.20
☐ 42	Dick Stuart	15.00	7.50	1.50
☐ 43	Johnny Temple	12.00	6.00	1.20

1962 Kahn's

Compliments of Kahn's
"THE WIENER THE WORLD AWAITED"

The cards in this 38-card set measure 3 1/4" by 4". The 1962 Kahn's Wieners set of black and white, unnumbered cards features Cincinnati, Cleveland, Minnesota, and Pittsburgh players. Card numbers 1 Bell, 33 Power, and 34 Purkey exist in two different forms; these variations are listed in the checklist below. The backs of the cards contain career information. The ACC designation is F155-8. The set price below includes the set with all variation cards.

		NRMT	VG-E	GOOD
COMPLETE SET (41)		1000.00	500.00	100.00
COMMON PLAYER (1-38)		10.00	5.00	1.00
☐ 1A	Gary Bell	100.00	50.00	10.00
	(with fat man)			
☐ 1B	Gary Bell	35.00	17.50	3.50
	(no fat man)			
☐ 2	Jim Brosnan	10.00	5.00	1.00
☐ 3	Smoky Burgess	12.00	6.00	1.20
☐ 4	Chico Cardenas	10.00	5.00	1.00
☐ 5	Roberto Clemente	150.00	75.00	15.00
☐ 6	Ty Cline	10.00	5.00	1.00
☐ 7	Gordon Coleman	10.00	5.00	1.00
☐ 8	Dick Donovan	10.00	5.00	1.00
☐ 9	John Edwards	10.00	5.00	1.00
☐ 10	Tito Francona	10.00	5.00	1.00
☐ 11	Gene Freese	10.00	5.00	1.00
☐ 12	Bob Friend	12.00	6.00	1.20
☐ 13	Joe Gibbon	100.00	50.00	10.00
☐ 14	Jim Grant	10.00	5.00	1.00
☐ 15	Dick Groat	15.00	7.50	1.50
☐ 16	Harvey Haddix	12.00	6.00	1.20
☐ 17	Woodie Held	10.00	5.00	1.00
☐ 18	Bill Henry	10.00	5.00	1.00
☐ 19	Don Hoak	10.00	5.00	1.00
☐ 20	Ken Hunt	10.00	5.00	1.00
☐ 21	Joey Jay	10.00	5.00	1.00
☐ 22	Eddie Kasko	10.00	5.00	1.00
☐ 23	Willie Kirkland	10.00	5.00	1.00
☐ 24	Barry Latman	10.00	5.00	1.00
☐ 25	Jerry Lynch	10.00	5.00	1.00
☐ 26	Jim Maloney	12.00	6.00	1.20
☐ 27	Bill Mazeroski	16.00	8.00	1.60
☐ 28	Jim O'Toole	10.00	5.00	1.00
☐ 29	Jim Perry	12.00	6.00	1.20
☐ 30	Bubba Phillips	10.00	5.00	1.00
☐ 31	Vada Pinson	15.00	7.50	1.50
☐ 32	Wally Post	10.00	5.00	1.00
☐ 33A	Vic Power (Indians)	35.00	17.50	3.50
☐ 33B	Vic Power (Twins)	100.00	50.00	10.00
☐ 34A	Bob Purkey	35.00	17.50	3.50
	(with autograph)			
☐ 34B	Bob Purkey	100.00	50.00	10.00
	(no autograph)			
☐ 35	Frank Robinson	75.00	37.50	7.50
☐ 36	John Romano	10.00	5.00	1.00
☐ 37	Dick Stuart	12.00	6.00	1.20

☐ 38 Bill Virdon 15.00   7.50   1.50

1962 Kahn's Atlanta

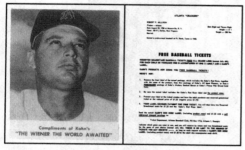

Compliments of Kahn's
"THE WIENER THE WORLD AWAITED"

The cards in this 24-card set measure 3 1/4" by 4". The 1962 Kahn's Wieners Atlanta set features unnumbered, black and white cards of the Atlanta Crackers of the International League. The backs contain player statistical information as well as instructions on how to obtain free tickets. The ACC designation is F155-9.

		NRMT	VG-E	GOOD
COMPLETE SET (24)	....	350.00	175.00	35.00
COMMON PLAYER (1-24)	....	12.00	6.00	1.20

			NRMT	VG-E	GOOD
☐	1	Jim Beauchamp	15.00	7.50	1.50
☐	2	Gerry Buchek	12.00	6.00	1.20
☐	3	Bob Burda	12.00	6.00	1.20
☐	4	Dick Dietz	15.00	7.50	1.50
☐	5	Bob Duliba	12.00	6.00	1.20
☐	6	Harry Fanok	12.00	6.00	1.20
☐	7	Phil Gagliano	15.00	7.50	1.50
☐	8	John Glenn	12.00	6.00	1.20
☐	9	Leroy Gregory	12.00	6.00	1.20
☐	10	Dick Hughes	12.00	6.00	1.20
☐	11	Johnny Kucks	15.00	7.50	1.50
☐	12	Johnny Lewis	12.00	6.00	1.20
☐	13	Tim McCarver	60.00	30.00	6.00
☐	14	Bob Milliken	12.00	6.00	1.20
☐	15	Joe M. Morgan	25.00	12.50	2.50
☐	16	Ron Plaza	12.00	6.00	1.20
☐	17	Bob Sadowski	12.00	6.00	1.20
☐	18	Jim Saul	12.00	6.00	1.20
☐	19	Willard Schmidt	12.00	6.00	1.20
☐	20	Joe Schultz	12.00	6.00	1.20
☐	21	Mike Shannon	25.00	12.50	2.50
☐	22	Paul Toth	12.00	6.00	1.20
☐	23	Lou Vickery	12.00	6.00	1.20
☐	24	Fred Whitfield	15.00	7.50	1.50

1963 Kahn's

Compliments of Kahn's
"THE WIENER THE WORLD AWAITED"

The cards in this 30-card set measure 3 1/4" by 4". The 1963 Kahn's Wieners set of black and white, unnumbered cards features players from Cincinnati, Cleveland, St. Louis, Pittsburgh and the New York

Yankees. The cards feature a white border around the picture of the players. The backs contain career information. The ACC designation is F155-10.

		NRMT	VG-E	GOOD
COMPLETE SET (30)	....	500.00	250.00	50.00
COMMON PLAYER (1-30)	....	10.00	5.00	1.00

			NRMT	VG-E	GOOD
☐	1	Bob Bailey	10.00	5.00	1.00
☐	2	Don Blasingame	10.00	5.00	1.00
☐	3	Clete Boyer	12.00	6.00	1.20
☐	4	Smoky Burgess	10.00	5.00	1.00
☐	5	Chico Cardenas	10.00	5.00	1.00
☐	6	Roberto Clemente	150.00	75.00	15.00
☐	7	Donn Clendenon	12.00	6.00	1.20
☐	8	Gordon Coleman	10.00	5.00	1.00
☐	9	John Edwards	10.00	5.00	1.00
☐	10	Gene Freese	10.00	5.00	1.00
☐	11	Bob Friend	10.00	5.00	1.00
☐	12	Joe Gibbon	10.00	5.00	1.00
☐	13	Dick Groat	15.00	7.50	1.50
☐	14	Harvey Haddix	12.00	6.00	1.20
☐	15	Elston Howard	18.00	9.00	1.80
☐	16	Joey Jay	10.00	5.00	1.00
☐	17	Eddie Kasko	10.00	5.00	1.00
☐	18	Tony Kubek	22.00	11.00	2.20
☐	19	Jerry Lynch	10.00	5.00	1.00
☐	20	Jim Maloney	12.00	6.00	1.20
☐	21	Bill Mazeroski	16.00	8.00	1.60
☐	22	Joe Nuxhall	12.00	6.00	1.20
☐	23	Jim O'Toole	10.00	5.00	1.00
☐	24	Vada Pinson	15.00	7.50	1.50
☐	25	Bob Purkey	10.00	5.00	1.00
☐	26	Bobby Richardson	22.00	11.00	2.20
☐	27	Frank Robinson	75.00	37.50	7.50
☐	28	Bill Stafford	10.00	5.00	1.00
☐	29	Ralph Terry	12.00	6.00	1.20
☐	30	Bill Virdon	12.00	6.00	1.20

1964 Kahn's

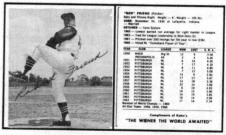

Compliments of Kahn's
"THE WIENER THE WORLD AWAITED"

The cards in this 31-card set measure 3" by 3 1/2". The 1964 Kahn's set marks the beginning of the full color cards and the elimination of the tabs which existed on previous Kahn's cards. The set of unnumbered cards contains player information through the 1963 season on the backs. The set features Cincinnati, Cleveland and Pittsburgh players.

		NRMT	VG-E	GOOD
COMPLETE SET (31)	....	750.00	375.00	75.00
COMMON PLAYER (1-31)	....	10.00	5.00	1.00

			NRMT	VG-E	GOOD
☐	1	Max Alvis	10.00	5.00	1.00
☐	2	Bob Bailey	10.00	5.00	1.00
☐	3	Chico Cardenas	10.00	5.00	1.00
☐	4	Roberto Clemente	150.00	75.00	15.00
☐	5	Donn Clendenon	12.00	6.00	1.20
☐	6	Vic Davalillo	10.00	5.00	1.00
☐	7	Dick Donovan	10.00	5.00	1.00
☐	8	John Edwards	10.00	5.00	1.00
☐	9	Bob Friend	12.00	6.00	1.20
☐	10	Jim Grant	10.00	5.00	1.00
☐	11	Tommy Harper	10.00	5.00	1.00
☐	12	Woodie Held	10.00	5.00	1.00
☐	13	Joey Jay	10.00	5.00	1.00
☐	14	Jack Kralick	10.00	5.00	1.00
☐	15	Jerry Lynch	10.00	5.00	1.00
☐	16	Jim Maloney	12.00	6.00	1.20
☐	17	Bill Mazeroski	16.00	8.00	1.60

		NRMT	VG-E	GOOD
☐ 18	Alvin McBean	10.00	5.00	1.00
☐ 19	Joe Nuxhall	12.00	6.00	1.20
☐ 20	Jim Pagliaroni	10.00	5.00	1.00
☐ 21	Vada Pinson	15.00	7.50	1.50
☐ 22	Bob Purkey	10.00	5.00	1.00
☐ 23	Pedro Ramos	10.00	5.00	1.00
☐ 24	Frank Robinson	75.00	37.50	7.50
☐ 25	John Romano	10.00	5.00	1.00
☐ 26	Pete Rose	350.00	175.00	35.00
☐ 27	John Tsitouris	10.00	5.00	1.00
☐ 28	Bob Veale	10.00	5.00	1.00
☐ 29	Bill Virdon	12.00	6.00	1.20
☐ 30	Leon Wagner	10.00	5.00	1.00
☐ 31	Fred Whitfield	10.00	5.00	1.00

1965 Kahn's

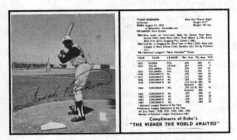

The cards in this 45-card set measure 3" by 3 1/2". The 1965 Kahn's set contains full color, unnumbered cards. The set features Cincinnati, Cleveland, Pittsburgh, and Milwaukee players. Backs contain statistical information through the 1964 season.

		NRMT	VG-E	GOOD
COMPLETE SET (45)		900.00	425.00	100.00
COMMON PLAYER (1-45)		10.00	5.00	1.00
☐ 1	Henry Aaron	150.00	75.00	15.00
☐ 2	Max Alvis	10.00	5.00	1.00
☐ 3	Joe Azcue	10.00	5.00	1.00
☐ 4	Bob Bailey	10.00	5.00	1.00
☐ 5	Frank Bolling	10.00	5.00	1.00
☐ 6	Chico Cardenas	10.00	5.00	1.00
☐ 7	Rico Carty	15.00	7.50	1.50
☐ 8	Donn Clendenon	12.00	6.00	1.20
☐ 9	Tony Cloninger	10.00	5.00	1.00
☐ 10	Gordon Coleman	10.00	5.00	1.00
☐ 11	Vic Davalillo	10.00	5.00	1.00
☐ 12	John Edwards	10.00	5.00	1.00
☐ 13	Sammy Ellis	10.00	5.00	1.00
☐ 14	Bob Friend	12.00	6.00	1.20
☐ 15	Tommy Harper	10.00	5.00	1.00
☐ 16	Chuck Hinton	10.00	5.00	1.00
☐ 17	Dick Howser	15.00	7.50	1.50
☐ 18	Joey Jay	10.00	5.00	1.00
☐ 19	Deron Johnson	10.00	5.00	1.00
☐ 20	Jack Kralick	10.00	5.00	1.00
☐ 21	Denver LeMaster	10.00	5.00	1.00
☐ 22	Jerry Lynch	10.00	5.00	1.00
☐ 23	Jim Maloney	12.00	6.00	1.20
☐ 24	Lee Maye	10.00	5.00	1.00
☐ 25	Bill Mazeroski	16.00	8.00	1.60
☐ 26	Alvin McBean	10.00	5.00	1.00
☐ 27	Bill McCool	10.00	5.00	1.00
☐ 28	Sam McDowell	12.00	6.00	1.20
☐ 29	Don McMahon	10.00	5.00	1.00
☐ 30	Denis Menke	10.00	5.00	1.00
☐ 31	Joe Nuxhall	12.00	6.00	1.20
☐ 32	Gene Oliver	10.00	5.00	1.00
☐ 33	Jim O'Toole	10.00	5.00	1.00
☐ 34	Jim Pagliaroni	10.00	5.00	1.00
☐ 35	Vada Pinson	15.00	7.50	1.50
☐ 36	Frank Robinson	75.00	37.50	7.50
☐ 37	Pete Rose	250.00	125.00	25.00
☐ 38	Willie Stargell	100.00	50.00	10.00
☐ 39	Ralph Terry	12.00	6.00	1.20
☐ 40	Luis Tiant	15.00	7.50	1.50
☐ 41	Joe Torre	16.00	8.00	1.60
☐ 42	John Tsitouris	10.00	5.00	1.00
☐ 43	Bob Veale	10.00	5.00	1.00
☐ 44	Bill Virdon	12.00	6.00	1.20
☐ 45	Leon Wagner	10.00	5.00	1.00

1966 Kahn's

The cards in this 32-card set measure 2 13/16" by 4". 1966 Kahn's full color, unnumbered set features players from Atlanta, Cincinnati, Cleveland, and Pittsburgh. The set is identified by yellow and white vertical stripes and the name Kahn's written in red across a red rose at the top. The cards contain a 1 5/16" ad in the form of a tab. Cards with the ad (tab) are worth twice as much as cards without the ad, i.e., double the prices below.

		NRMT	VG-E	GOOD
COMPLETE SET (32)		500.00	250.00	50.00
COMMON PLAYER (1-32)		7.00	3.50	.70
☐ 1	Henry Aaron (portrait, no wind-breaker under jersey)	75.00	37.50	7.50
☐ 2	Felipe Alou: Braves (full pose, batting screen in background)	9.00	4.50	.90
☐ 3	Max Alvis: Indians (kneeling, full pose, with bat, no patch on jersey)	7.00	3.50	.70
☐ 4	Bob Bailey	7.00	3.50	.70
☐ 5	Wade Blasingame	7.00	3.50	.70
☐ 6	Frank Bolling	7.00	3.50	.70
☐ 7	Chico Cardenas: Reds (fielding, feet at base)	7.00	3.50	.70
☐ 8	Roberto Clemente	75.00	37.50	7.50
☐ 9	Tony Cloninger: Braves (pitching, foulpole in background)	7.00	3.50	.70
☐ 10	Vic Davalillo	7.00	3.50	.70
☐ 11	John Edwards: Reds (catching)	7.00	3.50	.70
☐ 12	Sam Ellis: Reds (white hat)	7.00	3.50	.70
☐ 13	Pedro Gonzalez	7.00	3.50	.70
☐ 14	Tommy Harper: Reds (arm cocked)	7.00	3.50	.70
☐ 15	Deron Johnson: Reds (batting with batting cage in background)	7.00	3.50	.70
☐ 16	Mack Jones	7.00	3.50	.70
☐ 17	Denver Lemaster	7.00	3.50	.70
☐ 18	Jim Maloney: Reds (pitching, white hat)	9.00	4.50	.90
☐ 19	Bill Mazeroski: Pirates (throwing)	11.00	5.50	1.10
☐ 20	Bill McCool: Reds (white hat)	7.00	3.50	.70
☐ 21	Sam McDowell: Indians (kneeling)	9.00	4.50	.90
☐ 22	Denis Menke: Braves (white windbreaker under jersey)	7.00	3.50	.70
☐ 23	Joe Nuxhall	9.00	4.50	.90
☐ 24	Jim Pagliaroni Pirates (catching)	7.00	3.50	.70
☐ 25	Milt Pappas	9.00	4.50	.90

		NRMT	VG-E	GOOD
☐ 26	Vada Pinson: Reds (fielding, ball on ground)	11.00	5.50	1.10
☐ 27	Pete Rose: Reds (with glove)	125.00	60.00	12.50
☐ 28	Sonny Siebert: Indians (pitching, signature at feet)	7.00	3.50	.70
☐ 29	Willie Stargell: Pirates (batting, clouds in sky)	40.00	20.00	4.00
☐ 30	Joe Torre: Braves (catching with hand on mask)	11.00	5.50	1.10
☐ 31	Bob Veale: Pirates (hands at knee with glasses)	7.00	3.50	.70
☐ 32	Fred Whitfield	7.00	3.50	.70

1967 Kahn's

TONY PEREZ

The cards in this 41-player set measure 2 13/16" by 4". The 1967 Kahn's set of full color, unnumbered cards is almost identical in style to the 1966 issue. Different meat products had different background colors (yellow and white stripes, red and white stripes, etc.). The set features players from Atlanta, Cincinnati, Cleveland, New York Mets and Pittsburgh. Cards with the ads (see 1966 set) are worth twice as much as cards without the ad, i.e., double the prices below. The complete set price below includes all variations.

		NRMT	VG-E	GOOD
	COMPLETE SET (51)	700.00	350.00	70.00
	COMMON PLAYER (1-41)	7.00	3.50	.70
☐ 1A	Henry Aaron: Braves (swinging pose, batting glove, ball, and hat on ground)	75.00	37.50	7.50
☐ 1B	Henry Aaron: Braves (swinging pose, batting glove, ball, and hat on ground; Cut Along Dotted Lines printed on lower tab)	125.00	60.00	12.50
☐ 2	Gene Alley: Pirates (portrait)	7.00	3.50	.70
☐ 3	Felipe Alou: Braves (full pose, bat on shoulder)	9.00	4.50	.90
☐ 4A	Matty Alou: Pirates (portrait with bat, "Matio Rojas Alou"; yellow stripes)	9.00	4.50	.90
☐ 4B	Matty Alou: Pirates (portrait with bat, "Matio Rojas Alou"; red stripes)	11.00	5.50	1.10
☐ 5	Max Alvis: Indians (fielding, hands on knees)	7.00	3.50	.70

		NRMT	VG-E	GOOD
☐ 6A	Ken Boyer (batting righthanded; autograph at waist)	11.00	5.50	1.10
☐ 6B	Ken Boyer (batting righthanded; autograph at shoulders; Cut Along Dotted Lines printed on lower tab)	15.00	7.50	1.50
☐ 7	Chico Cardenas: Reds (fielding, hand on knee)	7.00	3.50	.70
☐ 8	Rico Carty	9.00	4.50	.90
☐ 9	Tony Cloninger: Braves (pitching, no foul-pole in background)	7.00	3.50	.70
☐ 10	Tommy Davis	9.00	4.50	.90
☐ 11	John Edwards: Reds (kneeling with bat)	7.00	3.50	.70
☐ 12A	Sam Ellis: Reds (all red hat)	7.00	3.50	.70
☐ 12B	Sam Ellis: Reds (all red hat) Cut Along Dotted Lines printed on lower tab)	9.00	4.50	.90
☐ 13	Jack Fisher	7.00	3.50	.70
☐ 14	Steve Hargan: Indians (pitching, no clouds, blue sky)	7.00	3.50	.70
☐ 15	Tommy Harper: Reds (fielding, glove on ground)	7.00	3.50	.70
☐ 16A	Tommy Helms (batting righthanded; top of bat visible)	7.00	3.50	.70
☐ 16B	Tommy Helms (batting righthanded; bat chopped above hat; Cut Along Dotted Lines printed on lower tab)	9.00	4.50	.90
☐ 17	Deron Johnson: Reds (batting, blue sky)	7.00	3.50	.70
☐ 18	Ken Johnson	7.00	3.50	.70
☐ 19	Cleon Jones	7.00	3.50	.70
☐ 20A	Ed Kranepool (ready for throw; yellow stripes)	9.00	4.50	.90
☐ 20B	Ed Kranepool (ready for throw; red stripes)	11.00	5.50	1.10
☐ 21A	Jim Maloney: Reds (pitching, red hat, follow thru delivery; yellow stripes)	9.00	4.50	.90
☐ 21B	Jim Maloney: Reds (pitching, red hat, follow thru delivery; red stripes)	11.00	5.50	1.10
☐ 22	Lee May: Reds (hands on knee)	9.00	4.50	.90
☐ 23A	Bill Mazeroski: Pirates (portrait; autograph below waist)	11.00	5.50	1.10
☐ 23B	Bill Mazeroski: Pirates (portrait; autograph above waist; Cut Along Dotted Lines printed on lower tab)	15.00	7.50	1.50
☐ 24	Bill McCool: Reds (red hat, left hand out)	7.00	3.50	.70
☐ 25	Sam McDowell: Indians (pitching, left hand under glove)	9.00	4.50	.90
☐ 26	Denis Menke: Braves (blue sleeves)	7.00	3.50	.70
☐ 27	Jim Pagliaroni: Pirates (catching, no chest protector)	7.00	3.50	.70
☐ 28	Don Pavletich	7.00	3.50	.70
☐ 29	Tony Perez: Reds (throwing)	20.00	10.00	2.00
☐ 30	Vada Pinson: Reds (ready to throw)	11.00	5.50	1.10
☐ 31	Dennis Ribant	7.00	3.50	.70
☐ 32	Pete Rose: Reds (batting)	125.00	60.00	12.50
☐ 33	Art Shamsky: Reds	7.00	3.50	.70
☐ 34	Bob Shaw	7.00	3.50	.70
☐ 35	Sonny Siebert: Indians (pitching, signature at knees)	7.00	3.50	.70
☐ 36	Willie Stargell: Pirates (batting, no clouds)	40.00	20.00	4.00
☐ 37A	Joe Torre: Braves (catching, mask	11.00	5.50	1.10

		NRMT	VG-E	GOOD
☐ 37B	Joe Torre: Braves .... (catching, mask on ground; Cut Along Dotted Lines printed on lower tab)	15.00	7.50	1.50
☐ 38	Bob Veale: Pirates .... (portrait, hands not shown)	7.00	3.50	.70
☐ 39	Leon Wagner: Indians .... (fielding)	7.00	3.50	.70
☐ 40A	Fred Whitfield .... (batting lefthanded)	7.00	3.50	.70
☐ 40B	Fred Whitfield .... (batting lefthanded; Cut Along Dotted Lines printed on lower tab)	9.00	4.50	.90
☐ 41	Woody Woodward	9.00	4.50	.90

1968 Kahn's

The cards in this 50-card set contain two different sizes. The smaller of the two sizes, which contains 12 cards, is 2 13/16" by 3 1/4" with the ad tab and 2 13/16" by 1 7/8" without the ad tab. The larger size, which contains 38 cards, measures 2 13/16" by 3 7/8" with the ad tab and 2 13/16" by 2 11/16" without the ad tab. The 1968 Kahn's set of full color, blank backed, unnumbered cards features players from Atlanta, Chicago Cubs, Chicago White Sox, Cincinnati, Cleveland, Detroit, New York Mets, and Pittsburgh. In the set of 12, listed with the letter A in the checklist, Maloney exists with either yellow or yellow and green stripes at the top of the card. The large set of 38, listed with a letter B in the checklist, contains five cards which exist in two variations. The variations in this large set have either yellow or red stripes at the top of the cards, with Maloney being an exception. Maloney has either a yellow stripe or a Blue Mountain ad at the top. Cards with the ad tabs (see other Kahn's sets) are worth twice as much as cards without the ad, i.e., double the prices below.

	NRMT	VG-E	GOOD
COMPLETE SET (50)	750.00	375.00	90.00
COMMON PLAYER	7.00	3.50	.70

		NRMT	VG-E	GOOD
☐ A1	Hank Aaron	75.00	37.50	7.50
☐ A2	Gene Alley	7.00	3.50	.70
☐ A3	Max Alvis	7.00	3.50	.70
☐ A4	Clete Boyer	9.00	4.50	.90
☐ A5	Chico Cardenas	7.00	3.50	.70
☐ A6	Bill Freehan	10.00	5.00	1.00
☐ A7	Jim Maloney (2)	9.00	4.50	.90
☐ A8	Lee May	7.00	3.50	.70
☐ A9	Bill Mazeroski	11.00	5.50	1.10
☐ A10	Vada Pinson	11.00	5.50	1.10
☐ A11	Joe Torre	11.00	5.50	1.10
☐ A12	Bob Veale	7.00	3.50	.70

		NRMT	VG-E	GOOD
☐ B1	Hank Aaron: Braves .... (full pose, batting bat cocked)	75.00	37.50	7.50
☐ B2	Tommy Agee	7.00	3.50	.70
☐ B3	Gene Alley: Pirates .... (fielding, full pose)	7.00	3.50	.70
☐ B4	Felipe Alou (full .... pose, batting, swinging, player in background)	9.00	4.50	.90
☐ B5	Matty Alou: Pirates .... (portrait with bat, "Matio Alou" (2)	9.00	4.50	.90
☐ B6	Max Alvis (fielding, ... glove on ground)	7.00	3.50	.70
☐ B7	Gerry Arrigo: Reds .... (pitching, follow thru delivery)	7.00	3.50	.70
☐ B8	John Bench	250.00	125.00	25.00
☐ B9	Clete Boyer	9.00	4.50	.90
☐ B10	Larry Brown	7.00	3.50	.70
☐ B11	Leo Cardenas: Reds .... (leaping in the air)	7.00	3.50	.70
☐ B12	Bill Freehan	9.00	4.50	.90
☐ B13	Steve Hargan: .... Indians (pitching, clouds in background)	7.00	3.50	.70
☐ B14	Joel Horlen: White .... Sox (portrait)	7.00	3.50	.70
☐ B15	Tony Horton: Indians ..... (portrait, signed Anthony)	7.00	3.50	.70
☐ B16	Willie Horton	7.00	3.50	.70
☐ B17	Ferguson Jenkins	16.00	8.00	1.60
☐ B18	Deron Johnson: .... Braves	7.00	3.50	.70
☐ B19	Mack Jones: Reds	7.00	3.50	.70
☐ B20	Bob Lee	7.00	3.50	.70
☐ B21	Jim Maloney: Reds .... (red hat, pitching hands up) (2)	9.00	4.50	.90
☐ B22	Lee May: Reds .... (batting)	9.00	4.50	.90
☐ B23	Bill Mazeroski: .... Pirates (fielding, hands in front of body)	11.00	5.50	1.10
☐ B24	Dick McAuliffe	7.00	3.50	.70
☐ B25	Bill McCool (red .... hat, left hand down)	7.00	3.50	.70
☐ B26	Sam McDowell: .... Indians (pitching, left hand over glove (2)	9.00	4.50	.90
☐ B27	Tony Perez (fielding .... ball in glove (2)	20.00	10.00	2.00
☐ B28	Gary Peters: White .... Sox (portrait)	7.00	3.50	.70
☐ B29	Vada Pinson: Reds .... (batting)	11.00	5.50	1.10
☐ B30	Chico Ruiz	7.00	3.50	.70
☐ B31	Ron Santo: Cubs .... (batting, follow thru (2)	11.00	5.50	1.10
☐ B32	Art Shamsky: Mets	7.00	3.50	.70
☐ B33	Luis Tiant: Indians .... (hands over head)	10.00	5.00	1.00
☐ B34	Joe Torre: Braves .... (batting)	11.00	5.50	1.10
☐ B35	Bob Veale: Pirates .... (hands chest high)	7.00	3.50	.70
☐ B36	Leon Wagner: Indians .... (batting)	7.00	3.50	.70
☐ B37	Billy Williams: Cubs .... (bat behind back)	35.00	17.50	3.50
☐ B38	Earl Wilson	7.00	3.50	.70

1969 Kahn's

The cards in this 25-card set contain two different sizes. The three small cards (see 1968 description) measure 2 13/16" by 3 1/4" and the 22 large cards (see 1968 description) measure 2 13/16" by 3 15/16". The 1969 Kahn's Wieners set of full color, unnumbered cards features players from Atlanta, Chicago Cubs, Chicago White Sox, Cincinnati, Cleveland, Pittsburgh, and St. Louis. The small cards

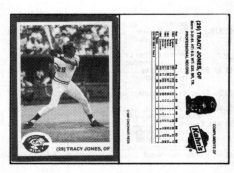

have the letter A in the checklist while the large cards have the letter B in the checklist. Four of the larger cards exist in two variations (red or yellow color stripes at the top of the card). These variations are identified in the checklist below. Cards with the ad tabs (see other Kahn's sets) are worth twice as much as cards without the ad, i.e., double the prices below.

		NRMT	VG-E	GOOD
	COMPLETE SET (25)	350.00	175.00	35.00
	COMMON PLAYER	7.00	3.50	.70
☐ A1	Hank Aaron (portrait)	75.00	37.50	7.50
☐ A2	Jim Maloney (pitching, hands at side)	9.00	4.50	.90
☐ A3	Tony Perez (glove on)	16.00	8.00	1.60
☐ B1	Hank Aaron	75.00	37.50	7.50
☐ B2	Matty Alou (batting)	9.00	4.50	.90
☐ B3	Max Alvis ('69 patch)	7.00	3.50	.70
☐ B4	Gerry Arrigo (leg up)	7.00	3.50	.70
☐ B5	Steve Blass	9.00	4.50	.90
☐ B6	Clay Carroll	7.00	3.50	.70
☐ B7	Tony Cloninger: Reds	7.00	3.50	.70
☐ B8	George Culver	7.00	3.50	.70
☐ B9	Joel Horlen (pitching)	7.00	3.50	.70
☐ B10	Tony Horton (batting)	7.00	3.50	.70
☐ B11	Alex Johnson	7.00	3.50	.70
☐ B12	Jim Maloney	9.00	4.50	.90
☐ B13	Lee May (foot on bag) (2)	9.00	4.50	.90
☐ B14	Bill Mazeroski (hands on knees) (2)	11.00	5.50	1.10
☐ B15	Sam McDowell (leg up) (2)	9.00	4.50	.90
☐ B16	Tony Perez	16.00	8.00	1.60
☐ B17	Gary Peters (pitching)	7.00	3.50	.70
☐ B18	Ron Santo (emblem) (2)	11.00	5.50	1.10
☐ B19	Luis Tiant (glove at knee)	10.00	5.00	1.00
☐ B20	Joe Torre: Cardinals	11.00	5.50	1.10
☐ B21	Bob Veale (hands at knees, no glasses)	7.00	3.50	.70
☐ B22	Billy Williams (bat behind head)	35.00	17.50	3.50

1987 Kahn's Weiners Reds

This 30-card set was issued to the first 20,000 fans at the August 2nd game between the Reds and the San Francisco Giants at Riverfront Stadium. Cards are standard size, 2 1/2" by 3 1/2". The cards are unnumbered except for uniform number and feature full-color photos bordered in red and white on the front. The Kahn's logo is printed in red in the corner of the reverse.

		MINT	EXC	G-VG
	COMPLETE SET (30)	18.00	9.00	1.80
	COMMON PLAYER	.40	.20	.04
☐ 6	Bo Diaz	.50	.25	.05
☐ 10	Terry Francona	.50	.25	.05
☐ 11	Kurt Stillwell	.60	.30	.06
☐ 12	Nick Esasky	.75	.35	.07
☐ 13	Dave Concepcion	.75	.35	.07
☐ 15	Barry Larkin	2.50	1.25	.25
☐ 16	Ron Oester	.50	.25	.05
☐ 21	Paul O'Neill	1.00	.50	.10
☐ 23	Lloyd McClendon	.50	.25	.05
☐ 25	Buddy Bell	.60	.30	.06
☐ 28	Kal Daniels	2.00	1.00	.20
☐ 29	Tracy Jones	.60	.30	.06
☐ 30	Guy Hoffman	.40	.20	.04
☐ 31	John Franco	1.00	.50	.10
☐ 32	Tom Browning	.75	.35	.07
☐ 33	Ron Robinson	.50	.25	.05
☐ 34	Bill Gullickson	.50	.25	.05
☐ 35	Pat Pacillo	.50	.25	.05
☐ 39	Dave Parker	1.00	.50	.10
☐ 43	Bill Landrum	.40	.20	.04
☐ 44	Eric Davis	4.50	2.25	.45
☐ 46	Rob Murphy	.60	.30	.06
☐ 47	Frank Williams	.50	.25	.05
☐ 48	Ted Power	.40	.20	.04
☐ xx	Pete Rose MG	1.50	.75	.15
☐ xx	Coaches Card	.50	.25	.05
	Scott Breeden			
	Billy DeMars			
	Tommy Helms			
	Bruce Kimm			
	Jim Lett			
	Tony Perez			
☐ xx	Ad Card Save 25 cents on Corn Dogs	.40	.20	.04
☐ xx	Ad Card Save 30 cents on Smokeys	.40	.20	.04

1988 Kahn's Mets

These 32-card sets were issued to the first 48,000 fans at the June 30th game between the Mets and the Houston Astros at Shea Stadium. The set includes 30 players, a team card, and a discount coupon card (to be redeemed at the grocery store). Cards are standard size, 2 1/2" by 3 1/2". The cards are unnumbered except for uniform number and feature full-color photos bordered in blue and orange on the front. The Kahn's logo is printed in red in the corner of the reverse.

		MINT	EXC	G-VG
	COMPLETE SET (32)	14.00	7.00	1.40
	COMMON PLAYER	.30	.15	.03
☐ 1	Mookie Wilson	.50	.25	.05

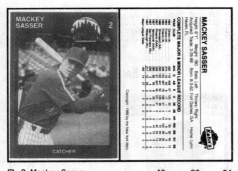

☐	2	Mackey Sasser	.40	.20	.04
☐	3	Bud Harrelson CO	.30	.15	.03
☐	4	Lenny Dykstra	.40	.20	.04
☐	5	Davey Johnson MG	.40	.20	.04
☐	6	Wally Backman	.40	.20	.04
☐	8	Gary Carter	.75	.35	.07
☐	11	Tim Teufel	.30	.15	.03
☐	12	Ron Darling	.60	.30	.06
☐	13	Lee Mazzilli	.30	.15	.03
☐	15	Rick Aguilera	.30	.15	.03
☐	16	Dwight Gooden	1.00	.50	.10
☐	17	Keith Hernandez	.75	.35	.07
☐	18	Darryl Strawberry	1.50	.75	.15
☐	19	Bob Ojeda	.50	.25	.05
☐	20	Howard Johnson	.75	.35	.07
☐	21	Kevin Elster	.40	.20	.04
☐	22	Kevin McReynolds	1.00	.50	.10
☐	26	Terry Leach	.30	.15	.03
☐	28	Bill Robinson CO	.30	.15	.03
☐	29	Dave Magadan	.50	.25	.05
☐	30	Mel Stottlemyre CO	.40	.20	.04
☐	31	Gene Walter	.30	.15	.03
☐	33	Barry Lyons	.30	.15	.03
☐	34	Sam Perlozzo CO	.30	.15	.03
☐	42	Roger McDowell	.40	.20	.04
☐	44	David Cone	1.00	.50	.10
☐	48	Randy Myers	.50	.25	.05
☐	50	Sid Fernandez	.50	.25	.05
☐	52	Greg Pavlick	.30	.15	.03
☐	x	Team Photo Card .... (unnumbered)	.30	.15	.03
☐	x	Discount Coupon .... (unnumbered)	.30	.15	.03

1988 Kahn's Reds

These 26-card sets were issued to fans at the August 14th game between the Reds and the Atlanta Braves at Riverfront Stadium. Cards are standard size, 2 1/2" by 3 1/2". The cards are unnumbered except for uniform number and feature full-color photos bordered in red and white on the front. The Kahn's logo is printed in red in the corner of the reverse. The cards are numbered below by uniform number which is listed parenthetically on the front of the cards.

			MINT	EXC	G-VG
COMPLETE SET (26)			14.00	7.00	1.40
COMMON PLAYER			.30	.15	.03
☐	6	Bo Diaz	.30	.15	.03
☐	8	Terry McGriff	.40	.20	.04
☐	9	Eddie Milner	.30	.15	.03
☐	10	Leon Durham	.30	.15	.03
☐	11	Barry Larkin	1.25	.60	.12
☐	12	Nick Esasky	.60	.30	.06
☐	13	Dave Concepcion	.50	.25	.05
☐	14	Pete Rose MG	1.00	.50	.10
☐	15	Jeff Treadway	.50	.25	.05
☐	17	Chris Sabo	2.00	1.00	.20
☐	20	Danny Jackson	.60	.30	.06
☐	21	Paul O'Neill	.75	.35	.07
☐	22	Dave Collins	.30	.15	.03
☐	27	Jose Rijo	.30	.15	.03
☐	28	Kal Daniels	.75	.35	.07
☐	29	Tracy Jones	.30	.15	.03
☐	30	Lloyd McClendon	.40	.20	.04
☐	31	John Franco	.50	.25	.05
☐	32	Tom Browning	.50	.25	.05
☐	33	Ron Robinson	.30	.15	.03
☐	40	Jack Armstrong	.50	.25	.05
☐	44	Eric Davis	1.25	.60	.12
☐	46	Rob Murphy	.40	.20	.04
☐	47	Frank Williams	.30	.15	.03
☐	48	Tim Birtsas	.30	.15	.03
☐	xx	Reds Coaches	.30	.15	.03
		Lee May CO			
		Tony Perez CO			
		Bruce Kimm CO			
		Tommy Helms CO			
		Jim Lett CO			
		Scott Breeden CO			

1989 Kahn's Cooperstown

The 1989 Kahn's Cooperstown set contains 11 standard-size (2 1/2 by 3 1/2 inch) cards. This set is sometimes referenced as Hillshire Farms or Kahn's Cooperstown Collection. All players included in the set are members (for the most part they are recent inductees) of the Hall of Fame. The pictures are actually paintings and are surrounded by gold borders. The fronts resemble plaques and also have facsimile autographs. The cards were available from the company via a send-in offer. A set of cards was available in return for three proofs of purchase (and 1.00 postage and handling) from Hillshire Farms. The last card in the set is actually a coupon card for Kahn's products; this card is not even considered part of the set by some collectors. A related promotion offered two coin cards (coins laminated on cards) featuring Johnny Bench and Carl Yastrzemski. These coin cards are approximately 5 1/2" by 3 3/4" and are blank backed.

			MINT	EXC	G-VG
COMPLETE SET (12)			8.00	4.00	.80
COMMON PLAYER (1-11)			.50	.25	.05
☐	1	Cool Papa Bell	.50	.25	.05
☐	2	Johnny Bench	1.25	.60	.12
☐	3	Lou Brock	.75	.35	.07

			MINT	EXC	G-VG
☐	4	Whitey Ford	.75	.35	.07
☐	5	Bob Gibson	.75	.35	.07
☐	6	Billy Herman	.60	.30	.06
☐	7	Harmon Killebrew	.75	.35	.07
☐	8	Eddie Mathews	1.00	.50	.10
☐	9	Brooks Robinson	1.00	.50	.10
☐	10	Willie Stargell	1.00	.50	.10
☐	11	Carl Yastrzemski	1.25	.60	.12
☐	12	Coupon Card	.50	.25	.05

1989 Kahn's Mets

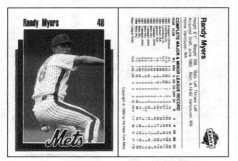

The 1989 Kahn's Mets set contains 36 (32 original and 4 update) standard-size (2 1/2 by 3 1/2 inch) cards. The fronts have color photos with Mets' colored borders (blue, orange and white). The horizontally-oriented backs have career stats. The cards were available from Kahn's by sending three UPC symbols from Kahn's products and a coupon appearing in certain local newspapers. There was also a small late-season update set of Kahn's Mets showing new Mets players arriving in mid-season trades, e.g., Jeff Innis, Keith Miller, Jeff Musselman, and Frank Viola. This "Update" subset was distributed at a different Mets Baseball Card Night game than the main set. These update cards are given the prefix U in the checklist below.

			MINT	EXC	G-VG
	COMPLETE SET (32)		10.00	5.00	1.00
	COMPLETE UPDATE SET (4)		2.50	1.00	.20
	COMMON PLAYER		.25	.12	.02
	COMMON UPDATE PLAYER		.60	.20	.04
☐	1	Mookie Wilson	.45	.22	.04
☐	2	Mackey Sasser	.35	.17	.03
☐	3	Bud Harrelson CO	.25	.12	.02
☐	5	Dave Johnson MG	.35	.17	.03
☐	7	Juan Samuel	.45	.22	.04
☐	8	Gary Carter	.75	.35	.07
☐	9	Gregg Jefferies	1.00	.50	.10
☐	11	Tim Teufel	.25	.12	.02
☐	12	Ron Darling	.45	.22	.04
☐	13	Lee Mazzilli	.25	.12	.02
☐	16	Dwight Gooden	1.00	.50	.10
☐	17	Keith Hernandez	.45	.22	.04
☐	18	Darryl Strawberry	1.00	.50	.10
☐	19	Bob Ojeda	.35	.17	.03
☐	20	Howard Johnson	.75	.35	.07
☐	21	Kevin Elster	.35	.17	.03
☐	22	Kevin McReynolds	.45	.22	.04
☐	28	Bill Robinson CO	.25	.12	.02
☐	29	Dave Magadan	.35	.17	.03
☐	30	Mel Stottlemyre CO	.35	.17	.03
☐	32	Mark Carreon	.25	.12	.02
☐	33	Barry Lyons	.25	.12	.02
☐	34	Sam Perlozzo CO	.25	.12	.02
☐	38	Rick Aguilera	.25	.12	.02
☐	44	David Cone	.45	.22	.04
☐	46	Dave West	.35	.17	.03
☐	48	Randy Myers	.35	.17	.03
☐	49	Don Aase	.25	.12	.02
☐	50	Sid Fernandez	.45	.22	.04
☐	52	Greg Pavlick CO	.25	.12	.02
☐	xx	Mets Team Photo	.25	.12	.02
☐	xx	Sponsors Card	.25	.12	.02

			MINT	EXC	G-VG
☐	U1	Jeff Innis	.60	.20	.04
☐	U2	Keith Miller	.60	.20	.04
☐	U3	Jeff Musselman	.60	.20	.04
☐	U4	Frank Viola	1.00	.40	.08

1989 Kahn's Reds

The 1989 Kahn's Reds set contains 28 standard-size (2 1/2 by 3 1/2 inch) cards; each card features a member of the Cincinnati Reds. The fronts have color photos with red borders. The horizontally-oriented backs have career stats.

			MINT	EXC	G-VG
	COMPLETE SET (28)		12.00	6.00	1.20
	COMMON PLAYER		.30	.15	.03
☐	6	Bo Diaz	.30	.15	.03
☐	7	Lenny Harris	.40	.20	.04
☐	11	Barry Larkin	1.00	.50	.10
☐	12	Joel Youngblood	.30	.15	.03
☐	14	Pete Rose MG	1.00	.50	.10
☐	16	Ron Oester	.30	.15	.03
☐	17	Chris Sabo	.50	.25	.05
☐	20	Danny Jackson	.50	.25	.05
☐	21	Paul O'Neill	.75	.35	.07
☐	25	Todd Benzinger	.50	.25	.05
☐	27	Jose Rijo	.40	.20	.04
☐	28	Kal Daniels	.60	.30	.06
☐	29	Herm Winningham	.30	.15	.03
☐	30	Ken Griffey Sr.	.50	.25	.05
☐	31	John Franco	.50	.25	.05
☐	32	Tom Browning	.50	.25	.05
☐	33	Ron Robinson	.30	.15	.03
☐	34	Jeff Reed	.30	.15	.03
☐	36	Rolando Roomes	.40	.20	.04
☐	37	Norm Charlton	.30	.15	.03
☐	42	Rick Mahler	.30	.15	.03
☐	43	Kent Tekulve	.30	.15	.03
☐	44	Eric Davis	1.00	.50	.10
☐	48	Tim Birtsas	.30	.15	.03
☐	49	Rob Dibble	.50	.25	.05
☐	xx	Coaches Card	.30	.15	.03
☐	xx	Sponsors Card	.30	.15	.03
☐	xx	Sponsors Card	.30	.15	.03

1986 Kay-Bee Young Stars

This 33-card, standard-sized (2 1/2" by 3 1/2") set was produced by Topps, although manufactured in Northern Ireland. This boxed set retailed in Kay-Bee stores for 1.99; the checklist was listed on the back of the box. The set is subtitled "Young Superstars of Baseball" and does indeed feature many young players. The cards are numbered on the back; the set card numbering is alphabetical by player's name.

			MINT	EXC	G-VG
	COMPLETE SET (33)		5.00	2.50	.50
	COMMON PLAYER (1-33)		.10	.05	.01
☐	1	Rick Aguilera	.15	.07	.01

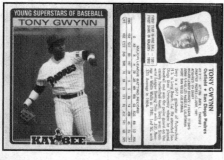

☐ 2	Chris Brown	.10	.05	.01
☐ 3	Tom Browning	.15	.07	.01
☐ 4	Tom Brunansky	.15	.07	.01
☐ 5	Vince Coleman	.25	.12	.02
☐ 6	Ron Darling	.15	.07	.01
☐ 7	Alvin Davis	.15	.07	.01
☐ 8	Mariano Duncan	.10	.05	.01
☐ 9	Shawon Dunston	.15	.07	.01
☐ 10	Sid Fernandez	.15	.07	.01
☐ 11	Tony Fernandez	.20	.10	.02
☐ 12	Brian Fisher	.10	.05	.01
☐ 13	John Franco	.15	.07	.01
☐ 14	Julio Franco	.20	.10	.02
☐ 15	Dwight Gooden	.75	.35	.07
☐ 16	Ozzie Guillen	.15	.07	.01
☐ 17	Tony Gwynn	.45	.22	.04
☐ 18	Jimmy Key	.15	.07	.01
☐ 19	Don Mattingly	1.00	.50	.10
☐ 20	Oddibe McDowell	.15	.07	.01
☐ 21	Roger McDowell	.10	.05	.01
☐ 22	Dan Pasqua	.10	.05	.01
☐ 23	Terry Pendleton	.10	.05	.01
☐ 24	Jim Presley	.10	.05	.01
☐ 25	Kirby Puckett	.75	.35	.07
☐ 26	Earnie Riles	.10	.05	.01
☐ 27	Bret Saberhagen	.35	.17	.03
☐ 28	Mark Salas	.10	.05	.01
☐ 29	Juan Samuel	.15	.07	.01
☐ 30	Jeff Stone	.10	.05	.01
☐ 31	Darryl Strawberry	.75	.35	.07
☐ 32	Andy Van Slyke	.20	.10	.02
☐ 33	Frank Viola	.20	.10	.02

1987 Kay-Bee Superstars

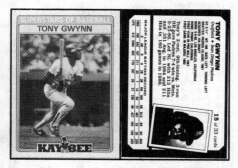

This small 33-card boxed set was produced by Topps for Kay-Bee Toy Stores. The set is subtitled "Super Stars of Baseball" and measures the standard 2 1/2" by 3 1/2" with full-color fronts. The card backs are printed in blue and black on white card stock. The checklist for the set is printed on the back panel of the yellow box.

		MINT	EXC	G-VG
COMPLETE SET (33)		5.00	2.50	.50
COMMON PLAYER (1-33)		.10	.05	.01
☐ 1	Harold Baines	.10	.05	.01

☐ 2	Jesse Barfield	.15	.07	.01
☐ 3	Don Baylor	.10	.05	.01
☐ 4	Wade Boggs	.60	.30	.06
☐ 5	George Brett	.40	.20	.04
☐ 6	Hubie Brooks	.10	.05	.01
☐ 7	Jose Canseco	1.00	.50	.10
☐ 8	Gary Carter	.20	.10	.02
☐ 9	Joe Carter	.20	.10	.02
☐ 10	Roger Clemens	.50	.25	.05
☐ 11	Vince Coleman	.25	.12	.02
☐ 12	Glenn Davis	.20	.10	.02
☐ 13	Dwight Gooden	.40	.20	.04
☐ 14	Pedro Guerrero	.20	.10	.02
☐ 15	Tony Gwynn	.40	.20	.04
☐ 16	Rickey Henderson	.45	.22	.04
☐ 17	Keith Hernandez	.20	.10	.02
☐ 18	Wally Joyner	.40	.20	.04
☐ 19	Don Mattingly	1.00	.50	.10
☐ 20	Jack Morris	.20	.10	.02
☐ 21	Dale Murphy	.35	.17	.03
☐ 22	Eddie Murray	.25	.12	.02
☐ 23	Dave Parker	.20	.10	.02
☐ 24	Kirby Puckett	.50	.25	.05
☐ 25	Tim Raines	.20	.10	.02
☐ 26	Jim Rice	.20	.10	.02
☐ 27	Dave Righetti	.15	.07	.01
☐ 28	Ryne Sandberg	.30	.15	.03
☐ 29	Mike Schmidt	.60	.30	.06
☐ 30	Mike Scott	.20	.10	.02
☐ 31	Darryl Strawberry	.50	.25	.05
☐ 32	Fernando Valenzuela	.20	.10	.02
☐ 33	Dave Winfield	.25	.12	.02

1988 Kay-Bee Superstars

This small 33-card boxed set was produced by Topps for Kay-Bee Toy Stores. The set is subtitled "Superstars of Baseball" and measures the standard 2 1/2" by 3 1/2" with full-color fronts. The card backs are printed in blue and green on white card stock. The checklist for the set is printed on the back panel of the box. These cards are numbered on the back.

		MINT	EXC	G-VG
COMPLETE SET (33)		4.00	2.00	.40
COMMON PLAYER (1-33)		.10	.05	.01
☐ 1	George Bell	.20	.10	.02
☐ 2	Wade Boggs	.60	.30	.06
☐ 3	Jose Canseco	1.00	.50	.10
☐ 4	Joe Carter	.20	.10	.02
☐ 5	Jack Clark	.20	.10	.02
☐ 6	Alvin Davis	.15	.07	.01
☐ 7	Eric Davis	.60	.30	.06
☐ 8	Andre Dawson	.20	.10	.02
☐ 9	Darrell Evans	.10	.05	.01
☐ 10	Dwight Evans	.15	.07	.01
☐ 11	Gary Gaetti	.15	.07	.01
☐ 12	Pedro Guerrero	.20	.10	.02
☐ 13	Tony Gwynn	.35	.17	.03
☐ 14	Howard Johnson	.25	.12	.02
☐ 15	Wally Joyner	.30	.15	.03
☐ 16	Don Mattingly	1.00	.50	.10
☐ 17	Willie McGee	.20	.10	.02
☐ 18	Mark McGwire	.75	.35	.07
☐ 19	Paul Molitor	.20	.10	.02
☐ 20	Dale Murphy	.30	.15	.03

		MINT	EXC	G-VG
☐ 21	Dave Parker	.15	.07	.01
☐ 22	Lance Parrish	.15	.07	.01
☐ 23	Kirby Puckett	.50	.25	.05
☐ 24	Tim Raines	.25	.12	.02
☐ 25	Cal Ripken	.30	.15	.03
☐ 26	Juan Samuel	.15	.07	.01
☐ 27	Mike Schmidt	.60	.30	.06
☐ 28	Ruben Sierra	.50	.25	.05
☐ 29	Darryl Strawberry	.60	.30	.06
☐ 30	Danny Tartabull	.25	.12	.02
☐ 31	Alan Trammell	.20	.10	.02
☐ 32	Tim Wallach	.10	.05	.01
☐ 33	Dave Winfield	.25	.12	.02

1989 Kay-Bee

The 1989 Kay-Bee set contains 33 standard-size (2 1/2 by 3 1/2 inch) glossy cards. The fronts have magenta and yellow borders. The horizontally oriented backs are brown and yellow. The cards were distributed as boxed sets through Kay-Bee toy stores.

		MINT	EXC	G-VG
COMPLETE SET (33)		4.00	2.00	.40
COMMON PLAYER (1-33)		.10	.05	.01
☐ 1	Wade Boggs	.60	.30	.06
☐ 2	George Brett	.30	.15	.03
☐ 3	Jose Canseco	1.00	.50	.10
☐ 4	Gary Carter	.20	.10	.02
☐ 5	Jack Clark	.20	.10	.02
☐ 6	Will Clark	1.00	.50	.10
☐ 7	Roger Clemens	.50	.25	.05
☐ 8	Eric Davis	.50	.25	.05
☐ 9	Andre Dawson	.20	.10	.02
☐ 10	Dwight Evans	.15	.07	.01
☐ 11	Carlton Fisk	.20	.10	.02
☐ 12	Andres Galarraga	.20	.10	.02
☐ 13	Kirk Gibson	.20	.10	.02
☐ 14	Dwight Gooden	.40	.20	.04
☐ 15	Mike Greenwell	.60	.30	.06
☐ 16	Pedro Guerrero	.20	.10	.02
☐ 17	Tony Gwynn	.35	.17	.03
☐ 18	Rickey Henderson	.40	.20	.04
☐ 19	Orel Hershiser	.30	.15	.03
☐ 20	Don Mattingly	1.00	.50	.10
☐ 21	Mark McGwire	.60	.30	.06
☐ 22	Dale Murphy	.30	.15	.03
☐ 23	Eddie Murray	.25	.12	.02
☐ 24	Kirby Puckett	.50	.25	.05
☐ 25	Tim Raines	.20	.10	.02
☐ 26	Ryne Sandberg	.30	.15	.03
☐ 27	Mike Schmidt	.60	.30	.06
☐ 28	Ozzie Smith	.20	.10	.02
☐ 29	Darryl Strawberry	.50	.25	.05
☐ 30	Alan Trammell	.20	.10	.02
☐ 31	Frank Viola	.15	.07	.01
☐ 32	Dave Winfield	.20	.10	.02
☐ 33	Robin Yount	.50	.25	.05

1970 Kellogg's

The cards in this 75-card set measure 2 1/4" by 3 1/2". The 1970 Kellogg's set was Kellogg's first venture into the baseball card producing field. The design incorporates a brilliant color photo of the player set against an indistinct background, which is then covered with a layer of plastic to simulate a 3-D look. Cards 16-30 seem to be in shorter supply than the other cards in the set.

		NRMT	VG-E	GOOD
COMPLETE SET (75)		125.00	60.00	12.50
COMMON PLAYER (1-75)		1.00	.50	.10
☐ 1	Ed Kranepool	1.00	.50	.10
☐ 2	Pete Rose	15.00	7.50	1.50
☐ 3	Cleon Jones	1.00	.50	.10
☐ 4	Willie McCovey	4.00	2.00	.40
☐ 5	Mel Stottlemyre	1.50	.75	.15
☐ 6	Frank Howard	1.50	.75	.15
☐ 7	Tom Seaver	8.00	4.00	.80
☐ 8	Don Sutton	2.50	1.25	.25
☐ 9	Jim Wynn	1.50	.75	.15
☐ 10	Jim Maloney	1.50	.75	.15
☐ 11	Tommie Agee	1.00	.50	.10
☐ 12	Willie Mays	10.00	5.00	1.00
☐ 13	Juan Marichal	3.50	1.75	.35
☐ 14	Dave McNally	1.50	.75	.15
☐ 15	Frank Robinson	4.00	2.00	.40
☐ 16	Carlos May	1.00	.50	.10
☐ 17	Bill Singer	1.00	.50	.10
☐ 18	Rick Reichardt	1.00	.50	.10
☐ 19	Boog Powell	1.50	.75	.15
☐ 20	Gaylord Perry	3.50	1.75	.35
☐ 21	Brooks Robinson	6.00	3.00	.60
☐ 22	Luis Aparicio	4.00	2.00	.40
☐ 23	Joel Horlen	1.00	.50	.10
☐ 24	Mike Epstein	1.00	.50	.10
☐ 25	Tom Haller	1.00	.50	.10
☐ 26	Willie Crawford	1.00	.50	.10
☐ 27	Roberto Clemente	10.00	5.00	1.00
☐ 28	Matty Alou	1.00	.50	.10
☐ 29	Willie Stargell	4.50	2.25	.45
☐ 30	Tim Cullen	1.00	.50	.10
☐ 31	Randy Hundley	1.00	.50	.10
☐ 32	Reggie Jackson	10.00	5.00	1.00
☐ 33	Rich Allen	1.00	.50	.10
☐ 34	Tim McCarver	1.50	.75	.15
☐ 35	Ray Culp	1.00	.50	.10
☐ 36	Jim Fregosi	1.50	.75	.15
☐ 37	Billy Williams	3.50	1.75	.35
☐ 38	Johnny Odom	1.00	.50	.10
☐ 39	Bert Campaneris	1.50	.75	.15
☐ 40	Ernie Banks	5.00	2.50	.50
☐ 41	Chris Short	1.00	.50	.10
☐ 42	Ron Santo	1.50	.75	.15
☐ 43	Glenn Beckert	1.00	.50	.10
☐ 44	Lou Brock	4.00	2.00	.40
☐ 45	Larry Hisle	1.00	.50	.10
☐ 46	Reggie Smith	1.50	.75	.15
☐ 47	Rod Carew	5.00	2.50	.50
☐ 48	Curt Flood	1.50	.75	.15
☐ 49	Jim Lonborg	1.50	.75	.15
☐ 50	Sam McDowell	1.50	.75	.15
☐ 51	Sal Bando	1.50	.75	.15
☐ 52	Al Kaline	5.00	2.50	.50
☐ 53	Gary Nolan	1.00	.50	.10

		NRMT	VG-E	GOOD
☐ 54	Rico Petrocelli	1.00	.50	.10
☐ 55	Ollie Brown	1.00	.50	.10
☐ 56	Luis Tiant	1.50	.75	.15
☐ 57	Bill Freehan	1.50	.75	.15
☐ 58	Johnny Bench	10.00	5.00	1.00
☐ 59	Joe Pepitone	1.50	.75	.15
☐ 60	Bobby Murcer	1.50	.75	.15
☐ 61	Harmon Killebrew	3.50	1.75	.35
☐ 62	Don Wilson	1.00	.50	.10
☐ 63	Tony Oliva	2.00	1.00	.20
☐ 64	Jim Perry	1.50	.75	.15
☐ 65	Mickey Lolich	1.50	.75	.15
☐ 66	Jose Laboy	1.00	.50	.10
☐ 67	Dean Chance	1.00	.50	.10
☐ 68	Ken Harrelson	1.50	.75	.15
☐ 69	Willie Horton	1.00	.50	.10
☐ 70	Wally Bunker	1.00	.50	.10
☐ 71	Bob Gibson	4.00	2.00	.40
☐ 72	Joe Morgan	4.00	2.00	.40
☐ 73	Denny McLain	1.50	.75	.15
☐ 74	Tommy Harper	1.00	.50	.10
☐ 75	Don Mincher	1.00	.50	.10

1971 Kellogg's

The cards in this 75-card set measure 2 1/4" by 3 1/2". The 1971 set of 3-D cards marketed by the Kellogg Company is the scarcest of all that company's issues. It was distributed as single cards, one in each package of cereal, without the usual complete set mail-in offer. In addition, card dealers were unable to obtain this set in quantity, as they have in other years. All the cards are available with and without the copyright notice on the back; the version without carries a slight premium for most numbers. Prices listed below are for the more common variety with copyright.

		NRMT	VG-E	GOOD
COMPLETE SET (75)		750.00	375.00	75.00
COMMON PLAYER (1-75)		6.50	3.25	.65
☐ 1	Wayne Simpson	6.50	3.25	.65
☐ 2	Tom Seaver	25.00	12.50	2.50
☐ 3	Jim Perry	7.50	3.75	.75
☐ 4	Bob Robertson	6.50	3.25	.65
☐ 5	Roberto Clemente	30.00	15.00	3.00
☐ 6	Gaylord Perry	15.00	7.50	1.50
☐ 7	Felipe Alou	7.50	3.75	.75
☐ 8	Denis Menke	6.50	3.25	.65
☐ 9	Don Kessinger	7.50	3.75	.75
☐ 10	Willie Mays	35.00	17.50	3.50
☐ 11	Jim Hickman	6.50	3.25	.65
☐ 12	Tony Oliva	10.00	5.00	1.00
☐ 13	Manny Sanguillen	7.50	3.75	.75
☐ 14	Frank Howard	7.50	3.75	.75
☐ 15	Frank Robinson	20.00	10.00	2.00
☐ 16	Willie Davis	7.50	3.75	.75
☐ 17	Lou Brock	20.00	10.00	2.00
☐ 18	Cesar Tovar	6.50	3.25	.65
☐ 19	Luis Aparicio	15.00	7.50	1.50
☐ 20	Boog Powell	10.00	5.00	1.00
☐ 21	Dick Selma	6.50	3.25	.65
☐ 22	Danny Walton	6.50	3.25	.65
☐ 23	Carl Morton	6.50	3.25	.65

		NRMT	VG-E	GOOD
☐ 24	Sonny Siebert	6.50	3.25	.65
☐ 25	Jim Merritt	6.50	3.25	.65
☐ 26	Jose Cardenal	6.50	3.25	.65
☐ 27	Don Mincher	6.50	3.25	.65
☐ 28	Clyde Wright	6.50	3.25	.65
☐ 29	Les Cain	6.50	3.25	.65
☐ 30	Danny Cater	6.50	3.25	.65
☐ 31	Don Sutton	15.00	7.50	1.50
☐ 32	Chuck Dobson	6.50	3.25	.65
☐ 33	Willie McCovey	20.00	10.00	2.00
☐ 34	Mike Epstein	6.50	3.25	.65
☐ 35	Paul Blair	6.50	3.25	.65
☐ 36	Gary Nolan	6.50	3.25	.65
☐ 37	Sam McDowell	7.50	3.75	.75
☐ 38	Amos Otis	7.50	3.75	.75
☐ 39	Ray Fosse	6.50	3.25	.65
☐ 40	Mel Stottlemyre	7.50	3.75	.75
☐ 41	Clarence Gaston	7.50	3.75	.75
☐ 42	Dick Dietz	6.50	3.25	.65
☐ 43	Roy White	7.50	3.75	.75
☐ 44	Al Kaline	25.00	12.50	2.50
☐ 45	Carlos May	6.50	3.25	.65
☐ 46	Tommie Agee	6.50	3.25	.65
☐ 47	Tommy Harper	6.50	3.25	.65
☐ 48	Larry Dierker	6.50	3.25	.65
☐ 49	Mike Cuellar	6.50	3.25	.65
☐ 50	Ernie Banks	25.00	12.50	2.50
☐ 51	Bob Gibson	18.00	9.00	1.80
☐ 52	Reggie Smith	7.50	3.75	.75
☐ 53	Matty Alou	7.50	3.75	.75
☐ 54	Alex Johnson	6.50	3.25	.65
☐ 55	Harmon Killebrew	18.00	9.00	1.80
☐ 56	Bill Grabarkewitz	6.50	3.25	.65
☐ 57	Richie Allen	10.00	5.00	1.00
☐ 58	Tony Perez	12.00	6.00	1.20
☐ 59	Dave McNally	7.50	3.75	.75
☐ 60	Jim Palmer	25.00	12.50	2.50
☐ 61	Billy Williams	18.00	9.00	1.80
☐ 62	Joe Torre	10.00	5.00	1.00
☐ 63	Jim Northrup	7.50	3.75	.75
☐ 64	Jim Fregosi	7.50	3.75	.75
☐ 65	Pete Rose	60.00	30.00	6.00
☐ 66	Bud Harrelson	6.50	3.25	.65
☐ 67	Tony Taylor	6.50	3.25	.65
☐ 68	Willie Stargell	20.00	10.00	2.00
☐ 69	Tony Horton	7.50	3.75	.75
☐ 70	Claude Osteen	6.50	3.25	.65
☐ 71	Glenn Beckert	6.50	3.25	.65
☐ 72	Nate Colbert	6.50	3.25	.65
☐ 73	Rick Monday	7.50	3.75	.75
☐ 74	Tommy John	12.00	6.00	1.20
☐ 75	Chris Short	6.50	3.25	.65

1972 Kellogg's

The cards in this 54-card set measure 2 1/8" by 3 1/4". The dimensions of the cards in the 1972 Kellogg's set were reduced in comparison to those of the 1971 series. In addition, the length of the set was set at 54 cards rather than the 75 of the previous year. The cards of this Kellogg's set are characterized by the diagonal bands found on the obverse.

	NRMT	VG-E	GOOD
COMPLETE SET (54)	60.00	30.00	6.00
COMMON PLAYER (1-54)	.60	.30	.06

☐	1	Tom Seaver	7.50	3.75	.75
☐	2	Amos Otis	.75	.35	.07
☐	3	Willie Davis	.75	.35	.07
☐	4	Wilbur Wood	.60	.30	.06
☐	5	Bill Parsons	.60	.30	.06
☐	6	Pete Rose	15.00	7.50	1.50
☐	7	Willie McCovey	3.50	1.75	.35
☐	8	Ferguson Jenkins	1.00	.50	.10
☐	9	Vida Blue	.75	.35	.07
☐	10	Joe Torre	1.00	.50	.10
☐	11	Merv Rettenmund	.60	.30	.06
☐	12	Bill Melton	.60	.30	.06
☐	13	Jim Palmer	4.00	2.00	.40
☐	14	Doug Rader	.75	.35	.07
☐	15	Dave Roberts	.60	.30	.06
☐	16	Bobby Murcer	.75	.35	.07
☐	17	Wes Parker	.75	.35	.07
☐	18	Joe Coleman	.60	.30	.06
☐	19	Manny Sanguillen	.75	.35	.07
☐	20	Reggie Jackson	9.00	4.50	.90
☐	21	Ralph Garr	.60	.30	.06
☐	22	Jim Hunter	2.50	1.25	.25
☐	23	Rick Wise	.60	.30	.06
☐	24	Glenn Beckert	.60	.30	.06
☐	25	Tony Oliva	1.50	.75	.15
☐	26	Bob Gibson	3.50	1.75	.35
☐	27	Mike Cuellar	.60	.30	.06
☐	28	Chris Speier	.60	.30	.06
☐	29	Dave McNally	.60	.30	.06
☐	30	Leo Cardenas	.60	.30	.06
☐	31	Bill Freehan	.75	.35	.07
☐	32	Bud Harrelson	.60	.30	.06
☐	33	Sam McDowell	.75	.35	.07
☐	34	Claude Osteen	.60	.30	.06
☐	35	Reggie Smith	.75	.35	.07
☐	36	Sonny Siebert	.60	.30	.06
☐	37	Lee May	.75	.35	.07
☐	38	Mickey Lolich	1.00	.50	.10
☐	39	Cookie Rojas	.60	.30	.06
☐	40	Dick Drago	.60	.30	.06
☐	41	Nate Colbert	.60	.30	.06
☐	42	Andy Messersmith	.75	.35	.07
☐	43	Dave Johnson	1.00	.50	.10
☐	44	Steve Blass	.75	.35	.07
☐	45	Bob Robertson	.60	.30	.06
☐	46	Billy Williams	3.50	1.75	.35
☐	47	Juan Marichal	3.50	1.75	.35
☐	48	Lou Brock	4.00	2.00	.40
☐	49	Roberto Clemente	8.00	4.00	.80
☐	50	Mel Stottlemyre	.75	.35	.07
☐	51	Don Wilson	.60	.30	.06
☐	52	Sal Bando	.75	.35	.07
☐	53	Willie Stargell	3.50	1.75	.35
☐	54	Willie Mays	9.00	4.50	.90

1972 Kellogg's ATG

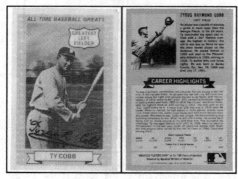

The cards in this 15-card set measure 2 1/4" by 3 1/2". The 1972 All-Time Greats 3-D set was issued with Kellogg's Danish Go Rounds. The set contains two different cards of Babe Ruth. The set is a reissue of a 1970 set issued by Rold Gold Pretzels to commemorate baseball's first 100 years. The Rold Gold cards are copyrighted 1970 on the reverse and are valued at approximately double the prices listed below.

			NRMT	VG-E	GOOD
COMPLETE SET (15)			15.00	7.50	1.50
COMMON PLAYER (1-15)			.50	.25	.05
☐	1	Walter Johnson	1.25	.60	.12
☐	2	Rogers Hornsby	.75	.35	.07
☐	3	John McGraw	.50	.25	.05
☐	4	Mickey Cochrane	.60	.30	.06
☐	5	George Sisler	.60	.30	.06
☐	6	Babe Ruth	3.50	1.75	.35
☐	7	Lefty Grove	.75	.35	.07
☐	8	Pie Traynor	.50	.25	.05
☐	9	Honus Wagner	1.25	.60	.12
☐	10	Eddie Collins	.50	.25	.05
☐	11	Tris Speaker	.75	.35	.07
☐	12	Cy Young	.90	.45	.09
☐	13	Lou Gehrig	2.00	1.00	.20
☐	14	Babe Ruth	3.50	1.75	.35
☐	15	Ty Cobb	2.00	1.00	.20

1973 Kellogg's 2D

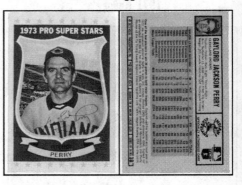

The cards in this 54-card set measure 2 1/4" by 3 1/2". The 1973 Kellogg's set is the only non-3D set produced by the Kellogg Company. Apparently Kellogg's decided to have the cards produced through Visual Panographics rather than by Xograph, as in the other years. The complete set could be obtained from the company through a box-top redemption procedure. The card size is slightly larger than the previous year.

			NRMT	VG-E	GOOD
COMPLETE SET (54)			60.00	30.00	6.00
COMMON PLAYER (1-54)			.60	.30	.06
☐	1	Amos Otis	.75	.35	.07
☐	2	Ellie Rodriguez	.60	.30	.06
☐	3	Mickey Lolich	1.00	.50	.10
☐	4	Tony Oliva	1.25	.60	.12
☐	5	Don Sutton	2.00	1.00	.20
☐	6	Pete Rose	15.00	7.50	1.50
☐	7	Steve Carlton	5.00	2.50	.50
☐	8	Bobby Bonds	.90	.45	.09
☐	9	Wilbur Wood	.60	.30	.06
☐	10	Billy Williams	3.00	1.50	.30
☐	11	Steve Blass	.75	.35	.07
☐	12	Jon Matlack	.75	.35	.07
☐	13	Cesar Cedeno	.75	.35	.07
☐	14	Bob Gibson	3.00	1.50	.30
☐	15	Sparky Lyle	1.00	.50	.10
☐	16	Nolan Ryan	10.00	5.00	1.00
☐	17	Jim Palmer	4.00	2.00	.40
☐	18	Ray Fosse	.60	.30	.06
☐	19	Bobby Murcer	.75	.35	.07
☐	20	Jim Hunter	2.00	1.00	.20
☐	21	Tom McCraw	.60	.30	.06
☐	22	Reggie Jackson	7.50	3.75	.75
☐	23	Bill Stoneman	.60	.30	.06
☐	24	Lou Piniella	.75	.35	.07
☐	25	Willie Stargell	3.50	1.75	.35
☐	26	Dick Allen	.90	.45	.09
☐	27	Carlton Fisk	3.00	1.50	.30
☐	28	Ferguson Jenkins	1.00	.50	.10

			NRMT	VG-E	GOOD
☐ 29	Phil Niekro		2.00	1.00	.20
☐ 30	Gary Nolan		.60	.30	.06
☐ 31	Joe Torre		.90	.45	.09
☐ 32	Bobby Tolan		.60	.30	.06
☐ 33	Nate Colbert		.60	.30	.06
☐ 34	Joe Morgan		3.50	1.75	.35
☐ 35	Bert Blyleven		1.00	.50	.10
☐ 36	Joe Rudi		.75	.35	.07
☐ 37	Ralph Garr		.60	.30	.06
☐ 38	Gaylord Perry		2.00	1.00	.20
☐ 39	Bobby Grich		.75	.35	.07
☐ 40	Lou Brock		3.00	1.50	.30
☐ 41	Pete Broberg		.60	.30	.06
☐ 42	Manny Sanguillen		.75	.35	.07
☐ 43	Willie Davis		.75	.35	.07
☐ 44	Dave Kingman		.90	.45	.09
☐ 45	Carlos May		.60	.30	.06
☐ 46	Tom Seaver		4.50	2.25	.45
☐ 47	Mike Cuellar		.60	.30	.06
☐ 48	Joe Coleman		.60	.30	.06
☐ 49	Claude Osteen		.60	.30	.06
☐ 50	Steve Kline		.60	.30	.06
☐ 51	Rod Carew		4.00	2.00	.40
☐ 52	Al Kaline		4.00	2.00	.40
☐ 53	Larry Dierker		.60	.30	.06
☐ 54	Ron Santo		.90	.45	.09

			NRMT	VG-E	GOOD
☐ 29	John Mayberry		.40	.20	.04
☐ 30	Rod Carew		4.00	2.00	.40
☐ 31	Ken Holtzman		.50	.25	.05
☐ 32	Billy Williams		2.00	1.00	.20
☐ 33	Dick Allen		.75	.35	.07
☐ 34	Wilbur Wood		.50	.25	.05
☐ 35	Danny Thompson		.40	.20	.04
☐ 36	Joe Morgan		3.00	1.50	.30
☐ 37	Willie Stargell		3.00	1.50	.30
☐ 38	Pete Rose		12.00	6.00	1.20
☐ 39	Bobby Bonds		.60	.30	.06
☐ 40	Chris Speier		.40	.20	.04
☐ 41	Sparky Lyle		.75	.35	.07
☐ 42	Cookie Rojas		.40	.20	.04
☐ 43	Tommy Davis		.50	.25	.05
☐ 44	Jim Hunter		2.00	1.00	.20
☐ 45	Willie Davis		.60	.30	.06
☐ 46	Bert Blyleven		.90	.45	.09
☐ 47	Pat Kelly		.40	.20	.04
☐ 48	Ken Singleton		.60	.30	.06
☐ 49	Manny Mota		.50	.25	.05
☐ 50	Dave Johnson		.75	.35	.07
☐ 51	Sal Bando		.50	.25	.05
☐ 52	Tom Seaver		4.50	2.25	.45
☐ 53	Felix Millan		.40	.20	.04
☐ 54	Ron Blomberg		.40	.20	.04

1974 Kellogg's

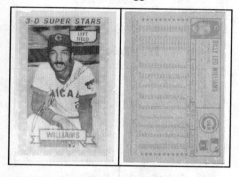

The cards in this 54-card set measure 2 1/8" by 3 1/4". In 1974 the Kellogg's set returned to its 3-D format; it also returned to the smaller-size card. Complete sets could be obtained from the company through a box-top offer. The cards are numbered on the back.

			NRMT	VG-E	GOOD
	COMPLETE SET (54)		50.00	25.00	5.00
	COMMON PLAYER (1-54)		.40	.20	.04
☐ 1	Bob Gibson		2.50	1.25	.25
☐ 2	Rick Monday		.50	.25	.05
☐ 3	Joe Coleman		.40	.20	.04
☐ 4	Bert Campaneris		.50	.25	.05
☐ 5	Carlton Fisk		1.50	.75	.15
☐ 6	Jim Palmer		3.00	1.50	.30
☐ 7	Ron Santo		.75	.35	.07
☐ 8	Nolan Ryan		8.00	4.00	.80
☐ 9	Greg Luzinski		.60	.30	.06
☐ 10	Buddy Bell		.60	.30	.06
☐ 11	Bob Watson		.50	.25	.05
☐ 12	Bill Singer		.40	.20	.04
☐ 13	Dave May		.40	.20	.04
☐ 14	Jim Brewer		.40	.20	.04
☐ 15	Manny Sanguillen		.50	.25	.05
☐ 16	Jeff Burroughs		.50	.25	.05
☐ 17	Amos Otis		.50	.25	.05
☐ 18	Ed Goodson		.40	.20	.04
☐ 19	Nate Colbert		.40	.20	.04
☐ 20	Reggie Jackson		7.00	3.50	.70
☐ 21	Ted Simmons		.75	.35	.07
☐ 22	Bobby Murcer		.60	.30	.06
☐ 23	Willie Horton		.50	.25	.05
☐ 24	Orlando Cepeda		1.00	.50	.10
☐ 25	Ron Hunt		.40	.20	.04
☐ 26	Wayne Twitchell		.40	.20	.04
☐ 27	Ron Fairly		.40	.20	.04
☐ 28	Johnny Bench		6.00	3.00	.60

1975 Kellogg's

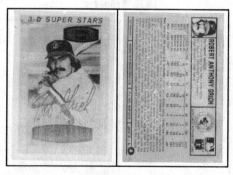

The cards in this 57-card set measure 2 1/8" by 3 1/4". The 1975 Kellogg's 3-D set could be obtained card by card in cereal boxes or as a set from a box-top offer from the company. Card number 44, Jim Hunter, exists with the A's emblem or the Yankees emblem on the back of the card.

			NRMT	VG-E	GOOD
	COMPLETE SET (57)		150.00	75.00	15.00
	COMMON PLAYER (1-57)		.75	.35	.07
☐ 1	Roy White		.75	.35	.07
☐ 2	Ross Grimsley		.75	.35	.07
☐ 3	Reggie Smith		1.00	.50	.10
☐ 4	Bob Grich		1.00	.50	.10
☐ 5	Greg Gross		.75	.35	.07
☐ 6	Bob Watson		.90	.45	.09
☐ 7	Johnny Bench		9.00	4.50	.90
☐ 8	Jeff Burroughs		.75	.35	.07
☐ 9	Elliott Maddox		.75	.35	.07
☐ 10	Jon Matlack		.75	.35	.07
☐ 11	Pete Rose		18.00	9.00	1.80
☐ 12	Lee Stanton		.75	.35	.07
☐ 13	Bake McBride		.75	.35	.07
☐ 14	Jorge Orta		.75	.35	.07
☐ 15	Al Oliver		1.00	.50	.10
☐ 16	John Briggs		.75	.35	.07
☐ 17	Steve Garvey		6.50	3.25	.65
☐ 18	Brooks Robinson		5.00	2.50	.50
☐ 19	John Hiller		.75	.35	.07
☐ 20	Lynn McGlothen		.75	.35	.07
☐ 21	Cleon Jones		.75	.35	.07
☐ 22	Fergie Jenkins		1.50	.75	.15
☐ 23	Bill North		.75	.35	.07
☐ 24	Steve Busby		.75	.35	.07
☐ 25	Richie Zisk		.90	.45	.09
☐ 26	Nolan Ryan		12.50	6.00	1.20
☐ 27	Joe Morgan		4.00	2.00	.40
☐ 28	Joe Rudi		.90	.45	.09

		NRMT	VG-E	GOOD
☐ 29	Jose Cardenal	.75	.35	.07
☐ 30	Andy Messersmith	.75	.35	.07
☐ 31	Willie Montanez	.75	.35	.07
☐ 32	Bill Buckner	1.00	.50	.10
☐ 33	Rod Carew	6.00	3.00	.60
☐ 34	Lou Piniella	1.00	.50	.10
☐ 35	Ralph Garr	.75	.35	.07
☐ 36	Mike Marshall	.75	.35	.07
☐ 37	Garry Maddox	.75	.35	.07
☐ 38	Dwight Evans	1.50	.75	.15
☐ 39	Lou Brock	5.00	2.50	.50
☐ 40	Ken Singleton	.90	.45	.09
☐ 41	Steve Braun	.75	.35	.07
☐ 42	Rich Allen	1.00	.50	.10
☐ 43	John Grubb	.75	.35	.07
☐ 44	Jim Hunter (2)	4.00	2.00	.40
☐ 45	Gaylord Perry	2.50	1.25	.25
☐ 46	George Hendrick	.90	.45	.09
☐ 47	Sparky Lyle	.90	.45	.09
☐ 48	Dave Cash	.75	.35	.07
☐ 49	Luis Tiant	.90	.45	.09
☐ 50	Cesar Geronimo	.75	.35	.07
☐ 51	Carl Yastrzemski	15.00	7.50	1.50
☐ 52	Ken Brett	.75	.35	.07
☐ 53	Hal McRae	.90	.45	.09
☐ 54	Reggie Jackson	12.50	6.00	1.20
☐ 55	Rollie Fingers	3.00	1.50	.30
☐ 56	Mike Schmidt	12.50	6.00	1.20
☐ 57	Richie Hebner	.75	.35	.07

		NRMT	VG-E	GOOD
☐ 23	Al Hrabosky	.50	.25	.05
☐ 24	Carl Yastrzemski	7.00	3.50	.70
☐ 25	Jim Kaat	.90	.45	.09
☐ 26	Marty Perez	.40	.20	.04
☐ 27	Bob Watson	.50	.25	.05
☐ 28	Eric Soderholm	.40	.20	.04
☐ 29	Bill Lee	.50	.25	.05
☐ 30	Frank Tanana	.50	.25	.05
☐ 31	Fred Lynn	1.50	.75	.15
☐ 32	Tom Seaver	4.00	2.00	.40
☐ 33	Steve Busby	.50	.25	.05
☐ 34	Gary Carter	3.50	1.75	.35
☐ 35	Rick Wise	.40	.20	.04
☐ 36	Johnny Bench	5.00	2.50	.50
☐ 37	Jim Palmer	2.50	1.25	.25
☐ 38	Bobby Murcer	.60	.30	.06
☐ 39	Von Joshua	.40	.20	.04
☐ 40	Lou Brock	3.00	1.50	.30
☐ 41	Mickey Rivers (2)	.50	.25	.05
☐ 42	Manny Sanguillen	.50	.25	.05
☐ 43	Jerry Reuss	.40	.20	.04
☐ 44	Ken Griffey	.60	.30	.06
☐ 45	Jorge Orta	.40	.20	.04
☐ 46	John Mayberry	.40	.20	.04
☐ 47	Vida Blue (2)	.50	.25	.05
☐ 48	Rod Carew	3.50	1.75	.35
☐ 49	Jon Matlack	.50	.25	.05
☐ 50	Boog Powell	.75	.35	.07
☐ 51	Mike Hargrove	.50	.25	.05
☐ 52	Paul Lindblad	.40	.20	.04
☐ 53	Thurman Munson	4.00	2.00	.40
☐ 54	Steve Garvey	3.50	1.75	.35
☐ 55	Pete Rose	12.00	6.00	1.20
☐ 56	Greg Gross	.40	.20	.04
☐ 57	Ted Simmons	.75	.35	.07

1976 Kellogg's

The cards in this 57-card set measure 2 1/8" by 3 1/4". The 1976 Kellogg's 3-D set could be obtained card by card in cereal boxes or as a set from the company for box-tops. Card number 6, that of Clay Carroll, exists with both a Reds or White Sox emblem on the back. Cards 1-3 (marked in the checklist below with SP) were apparently printed apart from the other 54 and are in shorter supply.

	NRMT	VG-E	GOOD
COMPLETE SET	75.00	37.50	7.50
COMMON PLAYER (1-3) SP	9.00	4.50	.90
COMMON PLAYER (4-57)	.40	.20	.04

		NRMT	VG-E	GOOD
☐ 1	Steve Hargan SP	9.00	4.50	.90
☐ 2	Claudell Washington SP	9.00	4.50	.90
☐ 3	Don Gullett SP	9.00	4.50	.90
☐ 4	Randy Jones	.50	.25	.05
☐ 5	Jim Hunter	2.00	1.00	.20
☐ 6	Clay Carroll (2)	.60	.30	.06
☐ 7	Joe Rudi	.50	.25	.05
☐ 8	Reggie Jackson	6.00	3.00	.60
☐ 9	Felix Millan	.40	.20	.04
☐ 10	Jim Rice	3.00	1.50	.30
☐ 11	Bert Blyleven	.75	.35	.07
☐ 12	Ken Singleton	.50	.25	.05
☐ 13	Don Sutton	1.50	.75	.15
☐ 14	Joe Morgan	3.50	1.75	.35
☐ 15	Dave Parker	1.50	.75	.15
☐ 16	Dave Cash	.40	.20	.04
☐ 17	Ron LeFlore	.40	.20	.04
☐ 18	Greg Luzinski	.60	.30	.06
☐ 19	Dennis Eckersley	1.50	.75	.15
☐ 20	Bill Madlock	.80	.40	.08
☐ 21	George Scott	.40	.20	.04
☐ 22	Willie Stargell	2.50	1.25	.25

1977 Kellogg's

The cards in this 57-card set measure 2 1/8" by 3 1/4". The 1977 Kellogg's series of 3-D baseball player cards could be obtained card by card from cereal boxes or by sending in box-tops and money. Each player's picture appears in miniature form on the reverse, an idea begun in 1971 and replaced in subsequent years by the use of a picture of the Kellogg's mascot.

	NRMT	VG-E	GOOD
COMPLETE SET (57)	50.00	25.00	5.00
COMMON PLAYER (1-57)	.35	.17	.03

		NRMT	VG-E	GOOD
☐ 1	George Foster	.80	.40	.08
☐ 2	Bert Campaneris	.45	.22	.04
☐ 3	Fergie Jenkins	.80	.40	.08
☐ 4	Dock Ellis	.35	.17	.03
☐ 5	John Montefusco	.35	.17	.03
☐ 6	George Brett	7.00	3.50	.70
☐ 7	John Candelaria	.45	.22	.04
☐ 8	Fred Norman	.35	.17	.03
☐ 9	Bill Travers	.35	.17	.03
☐ 10	Hal McRae	.45	.22	.04
☐ 11	Doug Rau	.35	.17	.03
☐ 12	Greg Luzinski	.45	.22	.04
☐ 13	Ralph Garr	.35	.17	.03
☐ 14	Steve Garvey	3.50	1.75	.35
☐ 15	Rick Manning	.35	.17	.03
☐ 16	Lyman Bostock	.45	.22	.04
☐ 17	Randy Jones	.35	.17	.03

☐ 18	Ron Cey	.45	.22	.04
☐ 19	Dave Parker	1.00	.50	.10
☐ 20	Pete Rose	9.00	4.50	.90
☐ 21	Wayne Garland	.35	.17	.03
☐ 22	Bill North	.35	.17	.03
☐ 23	Thurman Munson	3.00	1.50	.30
☐ 24	Tom Poquette	.35	.17	.03
☐ 25	Ron LeFlore	.45	.22	.04
☐ 26	Mark Fidrych	.45	.22	.04
☐ 27	Sixto Lezcano	.35	.17	.03
☐ 28	Dave Winfield	2.50	1.25	.25
☐ 29	Jerry Koosman	.45	.22	.04
☐ 30	Mike Hargrove	.35	.17	.03
☐ 31	Willie Montanez	.35	.17	.03
☐ 32	Don Stanhouse	.35	.17	.03
☐ 33	Jay Johnstone	.45	.22	.04
☐ 34	Bake McBride	.35	.17	.03
☐ 35	Dave Kingman	.60	.30	.06
☐ 36	Fred Patek	.35	.17	.03
☐ 37	Garry Maddox	.35	.17	.03
☐ 38	Ken Reitz	.35	.17	.03
☐ 39	Bobby Grich	.45	.22	.04
☐ 40	Cesar Geronimo	.35	.17	.03
☐ 41	Jim Lonborg	.45	.22	.04
☐ 42	Ed Figueroa	.35	.17	.03
☐ 43	Bill Madlock	.75	.35	.07
☐ 44	Jerry Remy	.35	.17	.03
☐ 45	Frank Tanana	.45	.22	.04
☐ 46	Al Oliver	.75	.35	.07
☐ 47	Charlie Hough	.45	.22	.04
☐ 48	Lou Piniella	.60	.30	.06
☐ 49	Ken Griffey	.60	.30	.06
☐ 50	Jose Cruz	.45	.22	.04
☐ 51	Rollie Fingers	1.50	.75	.15
☐ 52	Chris Chambliss	.45	.22	.04
☐ 53	Rod Carew	3.50	1.75	.35
☐ 54	Andy Messersmith	.45	.22	.04
☐ 55	Mickey Rivers	.45	.22	.04
☐ 56	Butch Wynegar	.45	.22	.04
☐ 57	Steve Carlton	3.50	1.75	.35

☐ 14	Paul Dade	.35	.17	.03
☐ 15	Jeff Burroughs	.35	.17	.03
☐ 16	Jose Cruz	.45	.22	.04
☐ 17	Mickey Rivers	.45	.22	.04
☐ 18	John Candelaria	.45	.22	.04
☐ 19	Ellis Valentine	.35	.17	.03
☐ 20	Hal McRae	.45	.22	.04
☐ 21	Dave Rozema	.35	.17	.03
☐ 22	Lenny Randle	.35	.17	.03
☐ 23	Willie McCovey	2.00	1.00	.20
☐ 24	Ron Cey	.45	.22	.04
☐ 25	Eddie Murray	10.00	5.00	1.00
☐ 26	Larry Bowa	.45	.22	.04
☐ 27	Tom Seaver	4.00	2.00	.40
☐ 28	Garry Maddox	.35	.17	.03
☐ 29	Rod Carew	3.00	1.50	.30
☐ 30	Thurman Munson	3.50	1.75	.35
☐ 31	Gary Templeton	.45	.22	.04
☐ 32	Eric Soderholm	.35	.17	.03
☐ 33	Greg Luzinski	.45	.22	.04
☐ 34	Reggie Smith	.45	.22	.04
☐ 35	Dave Goltz	.35	.17	.03
☐ 36	Tommy John	.75	.35	.07
☐ 37	Ralph Garr	.35	.17	.03
☐ 38	Alan Bannister	.35	.17	.03
☐ 39	Bob Bailor	.35	.17	.03
☐ 40	Reggie Jackson	4.50	2.25	.45
☐ 41	Cecil Cooper	.45	.22	.04
☐ 42	Burt Hooton	.35	.17	.03
☐ 43	Sparky Lyle	.45	.22	.04
☐ 44	Steve Ontiveros	.35	.17	.03
☐ 45	Rick Reuschel	.60	.30	.06
☐ 46	Lyman Bostock	.45	.22	.04
☐ 47	Mitchell Page	.35	.17	.03
☐ 48	Bruce Sutter	.60	.30	.06
☐ 49	Jim Rice	2.00	1.00	.20
☐ 50	Ken Forsch	.35	.17	.03
☐ 51	Nolan Ryan	6.00	3.00	.60
☐ 52	Dave Parker	1.25	.60	.12
☐ 53	Bert Blyleven	.60	.30	.06
☐ 54	Frank Tanana	.45	.22	.04
☐ 55	Ken Singleton	.45	.22	.04
☐ 56	Mike Hargrove	.45	.22	.04
☐ 57	Don Sutton	1.50	.75	.15

1978 Kellogg's

The cards in this 57-card set measure 2 1/8" by 3 1/4". This 1978 3-D Kellogg's series marks the first year in which Tony the Tiger appears on the reverse of each card next to the team and MLB logos. Once again the set could be obtained as individually wrapped cards in cereal boxes or as a set via a mail-in offer.

		NRMT	VG-E	GOOD
COMPLETE SET (57)		45.00	22.50	4.50
COMMON PLAYER (1-57)		.35	.17	.03

☐ 1	Steve Carlton	3.00	1.50	.30
☐ 2	Bucky Dent	.60	.30	.06
☐ 3	Mike Schmidt	6.00	3.00	.60
☐ 4	Ken Griffey	.45	.22	.04
☐ 5	Al Cowens	.35	.17	.03
☐ 6	George Brett	5.00	2.50	.50
☐ 7	Lou Brock	2.50	1.25	.25
☐ 8	Rich Gossage	.75	.35	.07
☐ 9	Tom Johnson	.35	.17	.03
☐ 10	George Foster	.75	.35	.07
☐ 11	Dave Winfield	2.50	1.25	.25
☐ 12	Dan Meyer	.35	.17	.03
☐ 13	Chris Chambliss	.45	.22	.04

1979 Kellogg's

The cards in this 60-card set measure 1 15/16" by 3 1/4". The 1979 edition of Kellogg's 3-D baseball cards have a 3/16" reduced width from the previous year; a nicely designed curved panel above the picture gives this set a distinctive appearance. The set contains the largest number of cards issued in a Kellogg's set since the 1971 series.

		NRMT	VG-E	GOOD
COMPLETE SET (60)		30.00	15.00	3.00
COMMON PLAYER (1-60)		.25	.12	.02

☐ 1	Bruce Sutter	.50	.25	.05
☐ 2	Ted Simmons	.50	.25	.05
☐ 3	Ross Grimsley	.25	.12	.02
☐ 4	Wayne Nordhagen	.25	.12	.02
☐ 5	Jim Palmer	2.00	1.00	.20
☐ 6	John Henry Johnson	.25	.12	.02
☐ 7	Jason Thompson	.25	.12	.02
☐ 8	Pat Zachry	.25	.12	.02
☐ 9	Dennis Eckersley	1.00	.50	.10

☐ 10	Paul Splittorff	.25	.12	.02
☐ 11	Ron Guidry	1.25	.60	.12
☐ 12	Jeff Burroughs	.25	.12	.02
☐ 13	Rod Carew	2.50	1.25	.25
☐ 14	Buddy Bell	.35	.17	.03
☐ 15	Jim Rice	2.00	1.00	.20
☐ 16	Garry Maddox	.25	.12	.02
☐ 17	Willie McCovey	1.50	.75	.15
☐ 18	Steve Carlton	2.50	1.25	.25
☐ 19	J.R. Richard	.35	.17	.03
☐ 20	Paul Molitor	1.25	.60	.12
☐ 21	Dave Parker	1.25	.60	.12
☐ 22	Pete Rose	7.00	3.50	.70
☐ 23	Vida Blue	.35	.17	.03
☐ 24	Richie Zisk	.25	.12	.02
☐ 25	Darrell Porter	.25	.12	.02
☐ 26	Dan Driessen	.25	.12	.02
☐ 27	Geoff Zahn	.25	.12	.02
☐ 28	Phil Niekro	1.25	.60	.12
☐ 29	Tom Seaver	3.00	1.50	.30
☐ 30	Fred Lynn	.75	.35	.07
☐ 31	Bill Bonham	.25	.12	.02
☐ 32	George Foster	.50	.25	.05
☐ 33	Terry Puhl	.25	.12	.02
☐ 34	John Candelaria	.35	.17	.03
☐ 35	Bob Knepper	.25	.12	.02
☐ 36	Fred Patek	.25	.12	.02
☐ 37	Chris Chambliss	.35	.17	.03
☐ 38	Bob Forsch	.25	.12	.02
☐ 39	Ken Griffey	.35	.17	.03
☐ 40	Jack Clark	1.50	.75	.15
☐ 41	Dwight Evans	1.00	.50	.10
☐ 42	Lee Mazzilli	.25	.12	.02
☐ 43	Mario Guerrero	.25	.12	.02
☐ 44	Larry Bowa	.35	.17	.03
☐ 45	Carl Yastrzemski	5.00	2.50	.50
☐ 46	Reggie Jackson	5.00	2.50	.50
☐ 47	Rick Reuschel	.50	.25	.05
☐ 48	Mike Flanagan	.35	.17	.03
☐ 49	Gaylord Perry	1.50	.75	.15
☐ 50	George Brett	4.00	2.00	.40
☐ 51	Craig Reynolds	.25	.12	.02
☐ 52	Dave Lopes	.35	.17	.03
☐ 53	Bill Almon	.25	.12	.02
☐ 54	Roy Howell	.25	.12	.02
☐ 55	Frank Tanana	.35	.17	.03
☐ 56	Doug Rau	.25	.12	.02
☐ 57	Rick Monday	.35	.17	.03
☐ 58	Jon Matlack	.25	.12	.02
☐ 59	Ron Jackson	.25	.12	.02
☐ 60	Jim Sundberg	.25	.12	.02

☐ 4	Ron Guidry	.75	.35	.07
☐ 5	Bert Blyleven	.60	.30	.06
☐ 6	Dave Kingman	.40	.20	.04
☐ 7	Jeff Newman	.20	.10	.02
☐ 8	Steve Rogers	.30	.15	.03
☐ 9	George Brett	3.50	1.75	.35
☐ 10	Bruce Sutter	.50	.25	.05
☐ 11	Gorman Thomas	.30	.15	.03
☐ 12	Darrell Porter	.20	.10	.02
☐ 13	Roy Smalley	.20	.10	.02
☐ 14	Steve Carlton	2.50	1.25	.25
☐ 15	Jim Palmer	2.50	1.25	.25
☐ 16	Bob Bailor	.20	.10	.02
☐ 17	Jason Thompson	.20	.10	.02
☐ 18	Graig Nettles	.40	.20	.04
☐ 19	Ron Cey	.40	.20	.04
☐ 20	Nolan Ryan	5.00	2.50	.50
☐ 21	Ellis Valentine	.20	.10	.02
☐ 22	Larry Hisle	.20	.10	.02
☐ 23	Dave Parker	.75	.35	.07
☐ 24	Eddie Murray	2.00	1.00	.20
☐ 25	Willie Stargell	1.50	.75	.15
☐ 26	Reggie Jackson	3.50	1.75	.35
☐ 27	Carl Yastrzemski	3.50	1.75	.35
☐ 28	Andre Thornton	.20	.10	.02
☐ 29	Dave Lopes	.30	.15	.03
☐ 30	Ken Singleton	.30	.15	.03
☐ 31	Steve Garvey	2.00	1.00	.20
☐ 32	Dave Winfield	2.00	1.00	.20
☐ 33	Steve Kemp	.30	.15	.03
☐ 34	Claudell Washington	.30	.15	.03
☐ 35	Pete Rose	6.00	3.00	.60
☐ 36	Cesar Cedeno	.30	.15	.03
☐ 37	John Stearns	.20	.10	.02
☐ 38	Lee Mazzilli	.20	.10	.02
☐ 39	Larry Bowa	.30	.15	.03
☐ 40	Fred Lynn	.60	.30	.06
☐ 41	Carlton Fisk	1.00	.50	.10
☐ 42	Vida Blue	.30	.15	.03
☐ 43	Keith Hernandez	1.25	.60	.12
☐ 44	Jim Rice	1.50	.75	.15
☐ 45	Ted Simmons	.40	.20	.04
☐ 46	Chet Lemon	.30	.15	.03
☐ 47	Ferguson Jenkins	.60	.30	.06
☐ 48	Gary Matthews	.30	.15	.03
☐ 49	Tom Seaver	2.50	1.25	.25
☐ 50	George Foster	.50	.25	.05
☐ 51	Phil Niekro	1.00	.50	.10
☐ 52	Johnny Bench	3.00	1.50	.30
☐ 53	Buddy Bell	.40	.20	.04
☐ 54	Lance Parrish	.75	.35	.07
☐ 55	Joaquin Andujar	.30	.15	.03
☐ 56	Don Baylor	.30	.15	.03
☐ 57	Jack Clark	1.00	.50	.10
☐ 58	J.R. Richard	.30	.15	.03
☐ 59	Bruce Bochte	.20	.10	.02
☐ 60	Rod Carew	2.50	1.25	.25

1980 Kellogg's

The cards in this 60-card set measure 1 7/8" by 3 1/4". The 1980 Kellogg's 3-D set is quite similar to, but smaller (narrower) than, the other recent Kellogg's issues. Sets could be obtained card by card from cereal boxes or as a set from a box-top offer from the company.

	MINT	EXC	G-VG
COMPLETE SET (60)	25.00	12.50	2.50
COMMON PLAYER (1-60)	.20	.10	.02
☐ 1 Ross Grimsley	.20	.10	.02
☐ 2 Mike Schmidt	5.00	2.50	.50
☐ 3 Mike Flanagan	.30	.15	.03

1981 Kellogg's

The cards in this 66-card set measure 2 1/2" by 3 1/2". The 1981 Kellogg's set witnessed an increase in both the size of the card and the size of the set. For the first time, cards were not packed in cereal sizes but available only by mail-in procedure. The offer for the card set was advertised on boxes of Kellogg's Corn Flakes. The cards were printed on a different stock than in previous years, presumably to prevent the cracking problem which has plagued all Kellogg's 3-D issues. At the end of the promotion, the remainder of the sets not distributed (to cereal-eaters), were "sold" into the organized hobby, thus creating a situation where the set is relatively plentiful compared to other years of Kellogg's.

		MINT	EXC	G-VG
	COMPLETE SET (66)	9.00	4.50	.90
	COMMON PLAYER (1-66)	.07	.03	.01
☐ 1	George Foster	.15	.07	.01
☐ 2	Jim Palmer	.50	.25	.05
☐ 3	Reggie Jackson	1.00	.50	.10
☐ 4	Al Oliver	.10	.05	.01
☐ 5	Mike Schmidt	1.25	.60	.12
☐ 6	Nolan Ryan	1.50	.75	.15
☐ 7	Bucky Dent	.15	.07	.01
☐ 8	George Brett	1.00	.50	.10
☐ 9	Jim Rice	.30	.15	.03
☐ 10	Steve Garvey	.45	.22	.04
☐ 11	Willie Stargell	.35	.17	.03
☐ 12	Phil Niekro	.25	.12	.02
☐ 13	Dave Parker	.20	.10	.02
☐ 14	Cesar Cedeno	.10	.05	.01
☐ 15	Don Baylor	.10	.05	.01
☐ 16	J.R. Richard	.07	.03	.01
☐ 17	Tony Perez	.10	.05	.01
☐ 18	Eddie Murray	.60	.30	.06
☐ 19	Chet Lemon	.07	.03	.01
☐ 20	Ben Oglivie	.07	.03	.01
☐ 21	Dave Winfield	.40	.20	.04
☐ 22	Joe Morgan	.40	.20	.04
☐ 23	Vida Blue	.10	.05	.01
☐ 24	Willie Wilson	.10	.05	.01
☐ 25	Steve Henderson	.07	.03	.01
☐ 26	Rod Carew	.40	.20	.04
☐ 27	Garry Templeton	.07	.03	.01
☐ 28	Dave Concepcion	.10	.05	.01
☐ 29	Dave Lopes	.07	.03	.01
☐ 30	Ken Landreaux	.07	.03	.01
☐ 31	Keith Hernandez	.30	.15	.03
☐ 32	Cecil Cooper	.10	.05	.01
☐ 33	Rickey Henderson	.75	.35	.07
☐ 34	Frank White	.07	.03	.01
☐ 35	George Hendrick	.07	.03	.01
☐ 36	Reggie Smith	.10	.05	.01
☐ 37	Tug McGraw	.10	.05	.01
☐ 38	Tom Seaver	.50	.25	.05
☐ 39	Ken Singleton	.10	.05	.01
☐ 40	Fred Lynn	.15	.07	.01
☐ 41	Rich Gossage	.10	.05	.01
☐ 42	Terry Puhl	.07	.03	.01
☐ 43	Larry Bowa	.10	.05	.01
☐ 44	Phil Garner	.07	.03	.01
☐ 45	Ron Guidry	.20	.10	.02
☐ 46	Lee Mazzilli	.07	.03	.01
☐ 47	Dave Kingman	.10	.05	.01
☐ 48	Carl Yastrzemski	1.00	.50	.10
☐ 49	Rick Burleson	.07	.03	.01
☐ 50	Steve Carlton	.50	.25	.05
☐ 51	Alan Trammell	.30	.15	.03
☐ 52	Tommy John	.15	.07	.01
☐ 53	Paul Molitor	.25	.12	.02
☐ 54	Joe Charbonneau	.07	.03	.01
☐ 55	Rick Langford	.07	.03	.01
☐ 56	Bruce Sutter	.10	.05	.01
☐ 57	Robin Yount	.75	.35	.07
☐ 58	Steve Stone	.07	.03	.01
☐ 59	Larry Gura	.07	.03	.01
☐ 60	Mike Flanagan	.07	.03	.01
☐ 61	Bob Horner	.15	.07	.01
☐ 62	Bruce Bochte	.07	.03	.01
☐ 63	Pete Rose	1.00	.50	.10
☐ 64	Buddy Bell	.10	.05	.01
☐ 65	Johnny Bench	.75	.35	.07
☐ 66	Mike Hargrove	.10	.05	.01

1982 Kellogg's

The cards in this 64-card set measure 2 1/8" by 3 1/4". The 1982 version of 3-D cards prepared for the Kellogg Company by Visual Panographics, Inc., is not only smaller in physical dimensions from the 1981 series (which was standard card size at 2 1/2" by 3 1/2") but is also two cards shorter in length (64 in

'82 and 66 in '81). In addition, while retaining the policy of not inserting single cards into cereal packages and offering the sets through box-top mail-ins only, the Kellogg Company accepted box tops from four types of cereals, as opposed to only one type the previous year. Each card features a color 3-D ballplayer picture with a vertical line of white stars on each side set upon a blue background. The player's name and the word Kellogg's are printed in red on the obverse, and the card number is found on the bottom right of the reverse.

		MINT	EXC	G-VG
	COMPLETE SET (64)	14.00	7.00	1.40
	COMMON PLAYER (1-64)	.09	.04	.01
☐ 1	Richie Zisk	.09	.04	.01
☐ 2	Bill Buckner	.15	.07	.01
☐ 3	George Brett	1.00	.50	.10
☐ 4	Rickey Henderson	1.00	.50	.10
☐ 5	Jack Morris	.15	.07	.01
☐ 6	Ozzie Smith	.45	.22	.04
☐ 7	Rollie Fingers	.15	.07	.01
☐ 8	Tom Seaver	.60	.30	.06
☐ 9	Fernando Valuenzuela	.40	.20	.04
☐ 10	Hubie Brooks	.15	.07	.01
☐ 11	Nolan Ryan	1.25	.60	.12
☐ 12	Dave Winfield	.35	.17	.03
☐ 13	Bob Horner	.20	.10	.02
☐ 14	Reggie Jackson	1.00	.50	.10
☐ 15	Burt Hooton	.09	.04	.01
☐ 16	Mike Schmidt	1.25	.60	.12
☐ 17	Bruce Sutter	.15	.07	.01
☐ 18	Pete Rose	1.00	.50	.10
☐ 19	Dave Kingman	.15	.07	.01
☐ 20	Neil Allen	.09	.04	.01
☐ 21	Don Sutton	.30	.15	.03
☐ 22	Dave Concepcion	.15	.07	.01
☐ 23	Keith Hernandez	.25	.12	.02
☐ 24	Gary Carter	.35	.17	.03
☐ 25	Carlton Fisk	.30	.15	.03
☐ 26	Ron Guidry	.20	.10	.02
☐ 27	Steve Carlton	.35	.17	.03
☐ 28	Robin Yount	.75	.35	.07
☐ 29	John Castino	.09	.04	.01
☐ 30	Johnny Bench	.75	.35	.07
☐ 31	Bob Knepper	.09	.04	.01
☐ 32	Rich Gossage	.15	.07	.01
☐ 33	Buddy Bell	.15	.07	.01
☐ 34	Art Howe	.15	.07	.01
☐ 35	Tony Armas	.15	.07	.01
☐ 36	Phil Niekro	.25	.12	.02
☐ 37	Len Barker	.09	.04	.01
☐ 38	Bob Grich	.15	.07	.01
☐ 39	Steve Kemp	.09	.04	.01
☐ 40	Kirk Gibson	.40	.20	.04
☐ 41	Carney Lansford	.25	.12	.02
☐ 42	Jim Palmer	.45	.22	.04
☐ 43	Carl Yastrzemski	1.00	.50	.10
☐ 44	Rick Burleson	.09	.04	.01
☐ 45	Dwight Evans	.20	.10	.02
☐ 46	Ron Cey	.15	.07	.01
☐ 47	Steve Garvey	.45	.22	.04
☐ 48	Dave Parker	.20	.10	.02
☐ 49	Mike Easler	.09	.04	.01
☐ 50	Dusty Baker	.09	.04	.01
☐ 51	Rod Carew	.40	.20	.04
☐ 52	Chris Chambliss	.15	.07	.01
☐ 53	Tim Raines	.40	.20	.04
☐ 54	Chet Lemon	.09	.04	.01

		MINT	EXC	G-VG
☐ 55	Bill Madlock	.15	.07	.01
☐ 56	George Foster	.15	.07	.01
☐ 57	Dwayne Murphy	.09	.04	.01
☐ 58	Ken Singleton	.15	.07	.01
☐ 59	Mike Norris	.09	.04	.01
☐ 60	Cecil Cooper	.15	.07	.01
☐ 61	Al Oliver	.15	.07	.01
☐ 62	Willie Wilson	.15	.07	.01
☐ 63	Vida Blue	.15	.07	.01
☐ 64	Eddie Murray	.50	.25	.05

1983 Kellogg's

The cards in this 60-card set measure 1 7/8" by 3 1/4". For the 14th year in a row, the Kellogg Company issued a card set of Major League players. The set of 3-D cards contains the photo, player's autograph, Kellogg's logo, and name and position of the player on the front of the card. The backs feature the player's team logo, career statistics, player biography, and a narrative on the player's career.

		MINT	EXC	G-VG
COMPLETE SET (60)		14.00	7.00	1.40
COMMON PLAYER (1-60)		.09	.04	.01
☐ 1	Rod Carew	.45	.22	.04
☐ 2	Rollie Fingers	.25	.12	.02
☐ 3	Reggie Jackson	.90	.45	.09
☐ 4	George Brett	1.00	.50	.10
☐ 5	Hal McRae	.15	.07	.01
☐ 6	Pete Rose	1.00	.50	.10
☐ 7	Fernando Valenzuela	.35	.17	.03
☐ 8	Rickey Henderson	.90	.45	.09
☐ 9	Carl Yastrzemski	1.00	.50	.10
☐ 10	Rich Gossage	.15	.07	.01
☐ 11	Eddie Murray	.45	.22	.04
☐ 12	Buddy Bell	.15	.07	.01
☐ 13	Jim Rice	.30	.15	.03
☐ 14	Robin Yount	.75	.35	.07
☐ 15	Dave Winfield	.35	.17	.03
☐ 16	Harold Baines	.20	.10	.02
☐ 17	Garry Templeton	.09	.04	.01
☐ 18	Bill Madlock	.15	.07	.01
☐ 19	Pete Vuckovich	.09	.04	.01
☐ 20	Pedro Guerrero	.20	.10	.02
☐ 21	Ozzie Smith	.30	.15	.03
☐ 22	George Foster	.15	.07	.01
☐ 23	Willie Wilson	.15	.07	.01
☐ 24	Johnny Ray	.15	.07	.01
☐ 25	George Hendrick	.09	.04	.01
☐ 26	Andre Thornton	.09	.04	.01
☐ 27	Leon Durham	.09	.04	.01
☐ 28	Cecil Cooper	.15	.07	.01
☐ 29	Don Baylor	.15	.07	.01
☐ 30	Lonnie Smith	.15	.07	.01
☐ 31	Nolan Ryan	1.25	.60	.12
☐ 32	Dan Quisenberry	.15	.07	.01
☐ 33	Len Barker	.09	.04	.01
☐ 34	Neil Allen	.09	.04	.01
☐ 35	Jack Morris	.20	.10	.02
☐ 36	Dave Stieb	.15	.07	.01
☐ 37	Bruce Sutter	.15	.07	.01
☐ 38	Jim Sundberg	.09	.04	.01
☐ 39	Jim Palmer	.50	.25	.05
☐ 40	Lance Parrish	.20	.10	.02
☐ 41	Floyd Bannister	.09	.04	.01
☐ 42	Larry Gura	.09	.04	.01

☐ 43	Britt Burns	.09	.04	.01
☐ 44	Toby Harrah	.09	.04	.01
☐ 45	Steve Carlton	.40	.20	.04
☐ 46	Greg Minton	.09	.04	.01
☐ 47	Gorman Thomas	.15	.07	.01
☐ 48	Jack Clark	.25	.12	.02
☐ 49	Keith Hernandez	.25	.12	.02
☐ 50	Greg Luzinski	.15	.07	.01
☐ 51	Fred Lynn	.15	.07	.01
☐ 52	Dale Murphy	.65	.30	.06
☐ 53	Kent Hrbek	.35	.17	.03
☐ 54	Bob Horner	.20	.10	.02
☐ 55	Gary Carter	.35	.17	.03
☐ 56	Carlton Fisk	.30	.15	.03
☐ 57	Dave Concepcion	.15	.07	.01
☐ 58	Mike Schmidt	1.25	.60	.12
☐ 59	Bill Buckner	.15	.07	.01
☐ 60	Bob Grich	.15	.07	.01

1982 K-Mart

The cards in this 44-card set measure 2 1/2" by 3 1/2". This set was produced by Topps for K Mart's 20th Anniversary Celebration. The set features Topps cards of National and American League MVP's from 1962 through 1981. The backs highlight individual MVP winning performances. The dual National League MVP winners of 1979 and special cards commemorating the accomplishments of Drysdale (scoreless consecutive innings pitched streak), Aaron (home run record), and Rose (National League most hits lifetime record) round out the set. The 1975 Fred Lynn card is an original construction from the multi-player "Rookie Outfielders" card of Lynn of 1975. The Maury Wills card #2, similarly, was created after the fact as Maury was not originally included in the 1962 Topps set. The set was "Mass" produced for K-Mart distribution as a complete set in a box. Some collectors consider this to be one of the most plentiful sets ever produced.

		MINT	EXC	G-VG
COMPLETE SET (44)		1.25	.60	.12
COMMON PLAYER (1-44)		.01	.00	.00
☐ 1	Mickey Mantle: 62AL	.25	.12	.02
☐ 2	Maury Wills: 62NL	.02	.01	.00
☐ 3	Elston Howard: 63AL	.01	.00	.00
☐ 4	Sandy Koufax: 63NL	.06	.03	.00
☐ 5	Brooks Robinson: 64AL	.04	.02	.00
☐ 6	Ken Boyer: 64NL	.01	.00	.00
☐ 7	Zoilo Versalles: 65AL	.01	.00	.00
☐ 8	Willie Mays: 65NL	.08	.04	.01
☐ 9	Frank Robinson: 66AL	.03	.01	.00
☐ 10	Bob Clemente: 66NL	.06	.03	.00
☐ 11	Carl Yastrzemski: 67AL	.08	.04	.01
☐ 12	Orlando Cepeda: 67NL	.01	.00	.00
☐ 13	Denny McLain: 68AL	.01	.00	.00
☐ 14	Bob Gibson: 68NL	.03	.01	.00
☐ 15	Harmon Killebrew: 69AL	.02	.01	.00
☐ 16	Willie McCovey: 69NL	.03	.01	.00
☐ 17	Boog Powell: 70AL	.01	.00	.00
☐ 18	Johnny Bench: 70NL	.05	.02	.00

			MINT	EXC	G-VG
☐ 19	Vida Blue: 71AL		.01	.00	.00
☐ 20	Joe Torre: 71NL		.01	.00	.00
☐ 21	Rich Allen: 72AL		.01	.00	.00
☐ 22	Johnny Bench: 72NL		.05	.02	.00
☐ 23	Reggie Jackson: 73AL		.05	.02	.00
☐ 24	Pete Rose: 73NL		.08	.04	.01
☐ 25	Jeff Burroughs: 74AL		.01	.00	.00
☐ 26	Steve Garvey: 74NL		.04	.02	.00
☐ 27	Fred Lynn: 75AL		.02	.01	.00
☐ 28	Joe Morgan: 75NL		.03	.01	.00
☐ 29	Thurman Munson: 76AL		.04	.02	.00
☐ 30	Joe Morgan: 76NL		.03	.01	.00
☐ 31	Rod Carew: 77AL		.04	.02	.00
☐ 32	George Foster: 77NL		.01	.00	.00
☐ 33	Jim Rice: 78AL		.02	.01	.00
☐ 34	Dave Parker: 78NL		.01	.00	.00
☐ 35	Don Baylor: 79AL		.01	.00	.00
☐ 36	Keith Hernandez: 79NL		.02	.01	.00
☐ 37	Willie Stargell: 79NL		.03	.01	.00
☐ 38	George Brett: 80AL		.05	.02	.00
☐ 39	Mike Schmidt: 80NL		.06	.03	.00
☐ 40	Rollie Fingers: 81AL		.02	.01	.00
☐ 41	Mike Schmidt: 81NL		.06	.03	.00
☐ 42	'68 HL: Don Drysdale (scoreless innings)		.02	.01	.00
☐ 43	'74 HL: Hank Aaron (home run record)		.07	.03	.01
☐ 44	'81 HL: Pete Rose (NL most hits)		.10	.05	.01

1987 K-Mart

Topps produced this 33-card boxed set for K-Mart. The set celebrates K-Mart's 25th anniversary and is subtitled, "Stars of the Decades." Card fronts feature a color photo of the player oriented diagonally. Cards measure 2 1/2" by 3 1/2" and are numbered on the back. Card backs provide statistics for the player's best decade.

			MINT	EXC	G-VG
	COMPLETE SET (33)		4.50	2.25	.45
	COMMON PLAYER (1-33)		.10	.05	.01
☐ 1	Hank Aaron		.35	.17	.03
☐ 2	Roberto Clemente		.30	.15	.03
☐ 3	Bob Gibson		.10	.05	.01
☐ 4	Harmon Killebrew		.10	.05	.01
☐ 5	Mickey Mantle		1.00	.50	.10
☐ 6	Juan Marichal		.10	.05	.01
☐ 7	Roger Maris		.30	.15	.03
☐ 8	Willie Mays		.35	.17	.03
☐ 9	Brooks Robinson		.15	.07	.01
☐ 10	Frank Robinson		.15	.07	.01
☐ 11	Carl Yastrzemski		.35	.17	.03
☐ 12	Johnny Bench		.25	.12	.02
☐ 13	Lou Brock		.15	.07	.01
☐ 14	Rod Carew		.15	.07	.01
☐ 15	Steve Carlton		.15	.07	.01
☐ 16	Reggie Jackson		.25	.12	.02
☐ 17	Jim Palmer		.20	.10	.02
☐ 18	Jim Rice		.10	.05	.01
☐ 19	Pete Rose		.50	.25	.05
☐ 20	Nolan Ryan		.50	.25	.05
☐ 21	Tom Seaver		.25	.12	.02
☐ 22	Willie Stargell		.15	.07	.01
☐ 23	Wade Boggs		.50	.25	.05
☐ 24	George Brett		.25	.12	.02
☐ 25	Gary Carter		.15	.07	.01

			MINT	EXC	G-VG
☐ 26	Dwight Gooden		.35	.17	.03
☐ 27	Rickey Henderson		.35	.17	.03
☐ 28	Don Mattingly		.75	.35	.07
☐ 29	Dale Murphy		.25	.12	.02
☐ 30	Eddie Murray		.20	.10	.02
☐ 31	Mike Schmidt		.50	.25	.05
☐ 32	Darryl Strawberry		.35	.17	.03
☐ 33	Fernando Valenzuela		.15	.07	.01

1988 K-Mart Memorable Moments

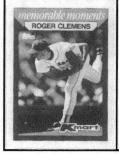 

Topps produced this 33-card boxed set exclusively for K-Mart. The set is subtitled, "Memorable Moments." Card fronts feature a color photo of the player with the K-Mart logo in lower right corner. Cards measure 2 1/2" by 3 1/2" and are numbered on the back. Card backs provide details for that player's "memorable moment." The set is packaged in a bright yellow and green box with a checklist on the back panel of the box.

			MINT	EXC	G-VG
	COMPLETE SET (33)		4.50	2.25	.45
	COMMON PLAYER (1-33)		.10	.05	.01
☐ 1	George Bell		.15	.07	.01
☐ 2	Wade Boggs		.50	.25	.05
☐ 3	George Brett		.30	.15	.03
☐ 4	Jose Canseco		.90	.45	.09
☐ 5	Jack Clark		.15	.07	.01
☐ 6	Will Clark		.90	.45	.09
☐ 7	Roger Clemens		.40	.20	.04
☐ 8	Vince Coleman		.20	.10	.02
☐ 9	Andre Dawson		.20	.10	.02
☐ 10	Dwight Gooden		.30	.15	.03
☐ 11	Pedro Guerrero		.15	.07	.01
☐ 12	Tony Gwynn		.30	.15	.03
☐ 13	Rickey Henderson		.35	.17	.03
☐ 14	Keith Hernandez		.20	.10	.02
☐ 15	Don Mattingly		.90	.45	.09
☐ 16	Mark McGwire		.60	.30	.06
☐ 17	Paul Molitor		.15	.07	.01
☐ 18	Dale Murphy		.30	.15	.03
☐ 19	Tim Raines		.20	.10	.02
☐ 20	Dave Righetti		.15	.07	.01
☐ 21	Cal Ripken		.25	.12	.02
☐ 22	Pete Rose		.60	.30	.06
☐ 23	Nolan Ryan		.90	.45	.09
☐ 24	Benny Santiago		.25	.12	.02
☐ 25	Mike Schmidt		.75	.35	.07
☐ 26	Mike Scott		.15	.07	.01
☐ 27	Kevin Seitzer		.20	.10	.02
☐ 28	Ozzie Smith		.20	.10	.02
☐ 29	Darryl Strawberry		.45	.22	.04
☐ 30	Rick Sutcliffe		.10	.05	.01
☐ 31	Fernando Valenzuela		.15	.07	.01
☐ 32	Todd Worrell		.10	.05	.01
☐ 33	Robin Yount		.45	.22	.04

ADD TO YOUR SET: Write for current availability and prices for back editions of Sport Americana series, as well as back issues of Beckett Monthly.

1989 K-Mart Career Batting Leaders

The 1989 K-Mart Career Batting Leaders set contains 22 standard-size (2 1/2 by 3 1/2 inch) glossy cards. The fronts are bright red. The set depicts the 22 veterans with the highest lifetime batting averages. The cards were distributed one per Topps blister pack. These blister packs were sold exclusively through K-Mart stores.

		MINT	EXC	G-VG
COMPLETE SET (22)		5.00	2.00	.40
COMMON PLAYER (1-22)		.10	.05	.01
☐ 1	Wade Boggs	.60	.25	.05
☐ 2	Tony Gwynn	.35	.15	.03
☐ 3	Don Mattingly	.75	.35	.07
☐ 4	Kirby Puckett	.50	.25	.05
☐ 5	George Brett	.30	.15	.03
☐ 6	Pedro Guerrero	.20	.10	.02
☐ 7	Tim Raines	.20	.10	.02
☐ 8	Keith Hernandez	.20	.10	.02
☐ 9	Jim Rice	.20	.10	.02
☐ 10	Paul Molitor	.15	.07	.01
☐ 11	Eddie Murray	.20	.10	.02
☐ 12	Willie McGee	.10	.05	.01
☐ 13	Dave Parker	.15	.07	.01
☐ 14	Julio Franco	.15	.07	.01
☐ 15	Rickey Henderson	.40	.20	.04
☐ 16	Kent Hrbek	.20	.10	.02
☐ 17	Willie Wilson	.10	.05	.01
☐ 18	Johnny Ray	.10	.05	.01
☐ 19	Pat Tabler	.10	.05	.01
☐ 20	Carney Lansford	.15	.07	.01
☐ 21	Robin Yount	.50	.20	.04
☐ 22	Alan Trammell	.15	.07	.01

1989 K-Mart Dream Team

The 1989 K-Mart Dream Team set contains 33 standard-size (2 1/2 by 3 1/2 inch) glossy cards. The fronts are blue. The cards were distributed as a boxed set through K-Mart stores.

		MINT	EXC	G-VG
COMPLETE SET (33)		4.00	2.00	.40
COMMON PLAYER (1-33)		.10	.05	.01
☐ 1	Mark Grace	.75	.35	.07
☐ 2	Ron Gant	.20	.10	.02
☐ 3	Chris Sabo	.30	.15	.03
☐ 4	Walt Weiss	.20	.10	.02
☐ 5	Jay Buhner	.15	.07	.01
☐ 6	Cecil Espy	.10	.05	.01
☐ 7	Dave Gallagher	.15	.07	.01
☐ 8	Damon Berryhill	.20	.10	.02
☐ 9	Tim Belcher	.15	.07	.01
☐ 10	Paul Gibson	.10	.05	.01
☐ 11	Gregg Jefferies	.75	.35	.07
☐ 12	Don Mattingly	.75	.35	.07
☐ 13	Harold Reynolds	.10	.05	.01
☐ 14	Wade Boggs	.45	.22	.04
☐ 15	Cal Ripken	.30	.15	.03
☐ 16	Kirby Puckett	.45	.22	.04
☐ 17	George Bell	.20	.10	.02
☐ 18	Jose Canseco	.75	.35	.07
☐ 19	Terry Steinbach	.15	.07	.01
☐ 20	Roger Clemens	.40	.20	.04
☐ 21	Mark Langston	.20	.10	.02
☐ 22	Harold Baines	.15	.07	.01
☐ 23	Will Clark	.75	.35	.07
☐ 24	Ryne Sandberg	.25	.12	.02
☐ 25	Tim Wallach	.10	.05	.01
☐ 26	Shawon Dunston	.10	.05	.01
☐ 27	Tim Raines	.20	.10	.02
☐ 28	Darryl Strawberry	.40	.20	.04
☐ 29	Tony Gwynn	.30	.15	.03
☐ 30	Tony Pena	.10	.05	.01
☐ 31	Dwight Gooden	.30	.15	.03
☐ 32	Fernando Valenzuela	.20	.10	.02
☐ 33	Pedro Guerrero	.15	.07	.01

1990 K-Mart Career Batting Leaders

The 1990 K-Mart Career Batting Leaders set contains 22 standard-size (2 1/2 by 3 1/2 inch) cards. The front borders are emerald green, and the backs are white, blue and evergreen. This set, like the 1989 set of the same name, depicts the 22 major leaguers with the highest lifetime batting averages (minimum 765 games). The card numbers correspond to the player's rank in terms of career batting average. Many of the photos are the same as those from the 1989 set. The cards were distributed one per special Topps blister pack available only at K-Mart stores and were produced by Topps. The K-Mart logo does not appear anywhere on the cards themselves, although there is a Topps logo on the front and back of each card.

		MINT	EXC	G-VG
COMPLETE SET (22)		5.00	2.00	.50
COMMON PLAYER (1-22)		.10	.05	.01
☐ 1	Wade Boggs	.60	.25	.05
☐ 2	Tony Gwynn	.35	.15	.03
☐ 3	Kirby Puckett	.50	.25	.05
☐ 4	Don Mattingly	.75	.35	.07
☐ 5	George Brett	.30	.15	.03
☐ 6	Pedro Guerrero	.20	.10	.02
☐ 7	Tim Raines	.20	.10	.02

			NRMT	VG-E	GOOD
☐	8	Paul Molitor	.15	.07	.01
☐	9	Jim Rice	.20	.10	.02
☐	10	Keith Hernandez	.20	.10	.02
☐	11	Julio Franco	.15	.07	.01
☐	12	Carney Lansford	.15	.07	.01
☐	13	Dave Parker	.15	.07	.01
☐	14	Willie McGee	.10	.05	.01
☐	15	Robin Yount	.50	.20	.04
☐	16	Tony Fernandez	.10	.05	.01
☐	17	Eddie Murray	.20	.10	.02
☐	18	Johnny Ray	.10	.05	.01
☐	19	Lonnie Smith	.10	.05	.01
☐	20	Phil Bradley	.10	.05	.01
☐	21	Rickey Henderson	.40	.20	.04
☐	22	Kent Hrbek	.20	.10	.02

1960 Lake to Lake

The cards in this 28-card set measure 2 1/2" by 3 1/4". The 1960 Lake to Lake set of unnumbered, blue tinted cards features Milwaukee Braves players only. For some reason, this set of Braves does not include Eddie Mathews. The cards were issued on milk cartons by Lake to Lake Dairy. Most cards have staple holes in the upper right corner. The backs are in red and give details and prizes associated with the card promotion. Cards with staple holes can be considered very good to excellent at best. The ACC designation is F102-1. For some unknown reason Eddie Mathews was not included in this set.

			NRMT	VG-E	GOOD
		COMPLETE SET (28)	1000.00	500.00	100.00
		COMMON PLAYER (1-28)	12.00	6.00	1.20
☐	1	Hank Aaron	250.00	125.00	25.00
☐	2	Joe Adcock	16.00	8.00	1.60
☐	3	Ray Boone	125.00	60.00	12.50
☐	4	Bill Bruton	250.00	125.00	25.00
☐	5	Bob Buhl	12.00	6.00	1.20
☐	6	Lew Burdette	18.00	9.00	1.80
☐	7	Chuck Cottier	12.00	6.00	1.20
☐	8	Wes Covington	12.00	6.00	1.20
☐	9	Del Crandall	14.00	7.00	1.40
☐	10	Chuck Dressen	12.00	6.00	1.20
☐	11	Bob Giggie	12.00	6.00	1.20
☐	12	Joey Jay	12.00	6.00	1.20
☐	13	Johnny Logan	14.00	7.00	1.40
☐	14	Felix Mantilla	12.00	6.00	1.20
☐	15	Lee Maye	12.00	6.00	1.20
☐	16	Don McMahon	12.00	6.00	1.20
☐	17	George Myatt CO	12.00	6.00	1.20
☐	18	Andy Pafko	12.00	6.00	1.20
☐	19	Juan Pizarro	12.00	6.00	1.20
☐	20	Mel Roach	12.00	6.00	1.20
☐	21	Bob Rush	12.00	6.00	1.20
☐	22	Bob Scheffing	12.00	6.00	1.20
☐	23	Red Schoendienst	40.00	20.00	4.00
☐	24	Warren Spahn	50.00	25.00	5.00
☐	25	Al Spangler	12.00	6.00	1.20
☐	26	Frank Torre	12.00	6.00	1.20

			NRMT	VG-E	GOOD
☐	27	Carlton Willey	12.00	6.00	1.20
☐	28	Whit Wyatt CO	12.00	6.00	1.20

1948-49 Leaf

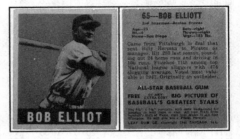

The cards in this 98-card set measure 2 3/8" by 2 7/8". The 1948-49 Leaf set was the first post-war baseball series issued in color. This effort was not entirely successful due to a lack of refinement which resulted in many color variations and cards out of register. In addition, the set was skip numbered from 1-168, with 49 of the 98 cards printed in limited quantities (marked with an asterisk in the checklist). Cards 102 and 136 have variations, and cards are sometimes found with overprinted or incorrect backs.

			NRMT	VG-E	GOOD
		COMPLETE SET (98)	25000.	12000.	3200.
		COMMON NUMBERS	20.00	10.00	2.00
		COMMON * NUMBERS	350.00	175.00	35.00
☐	1	Joe DiMaggio	1500.00	500.00	100.00
☐	3	Babe Ruth	1650.00	750.00	200.00
☐	4	Stan Musial	400.00	200.00	40.00
☐	5	Virgil Trucks *	350.00	175.00	35.00
☐	8	Satchel Paige *	1800.00	900.00	200.00
☐	10	Dizzy Trout	20.00	10.00	2.00
☐	11	Phil Rizzuto	100.00	50.00	10.00
☐	13	Cass Michaels *	350.00	175.00	35.00
☐	14	Billy Johnson	20.00	10.00	2.00
☐	17	Frank Overmire	20.00	10.00	2.00
☐	19	Johnny Wyrostek *	350.00	175.00	35.00
☐	20	Hank Sauer *	350.00	175.00	35.00
☐	22	Al Evans	20.00	10.00	2.00
☐	26	Sam Chapman	20.00	10.00	2.00
☐	27	Mickey Harris	20.00	10.00	2.00
☐	28	Jim Hegan	20.00	10.00	2.00
☐	29	Elmer Valo	20.00	10.00	2.00
☐	30	Billy Goodman *	350.00	175.00	35.00
☐	31	Lou Brissie	20.00	10.00	2.00
☐	32	Warren Spahn	150.00	75.00	15.00
☐	33	Peanuts Lowrey *	350.00	175.00	35.00
☐	36	Al Zarilla *	350.00	175.00	35.00
☐	38	Ted Kluszewski	40.00	20.00	4.00
☐	39	Ewell Blackwell	30.00	15.00	3.00
☐	42	Kent Peterson	20.00	10.00	2.00
☐	43	Ed Stevens *	350.00	175.00	35.00
☐	45	Ken Keltner *	350.00	175.00	35.00
☐	46	Johnny Mize	100.00	50.00	10.00
☐	47	George Vico	20.00	10.00	2.00
☐	48	Johnny Schmitz *	350.00	175.00	35.00
☐	49	Del Ennis	20.00	10.00	2.00
☐	50	Dick Wakefield	20.00	10.00	2.00
☐	51	Al Dark *	400.00	200.00	40.00
☐	53	Johnny VanderMeer	30.00	15.00	3.00
☐	54	Bobby Adams *	350.00	175.00	35.00
☐	55	Tommy Henrich *	400.00	200.00	40.00
☐	56	Larry Jansen	20.00	10.00	2.00
☐	57	Bob McCall	20.00	10.00	2.00
☐	59	Luke Appling	50.00	25.00	5.00
☐	61	Jake Early	20.00	10.00	2.00
☐	62	Eddie Joost *	350.00	175.00	35.00
☐	63	Barney McCosky *	350.00	175.00	35.00
☐	65	Robert Elliott	20.00	10.00	2.00
		(misspelled Elliot on card front)			
☐	66	Orval Grove *	350.00	175.00	35.00
☐	68	Eddie Miller *	350.00	175.00	35.00
☐	70	Honus Wagner	200.00	100.00	20.00

☐ 72	Hank Edwards	20.00	10.00	2.00
☐ 73	Pat Seerey	20.00	10.00	2.00
☐ 75	Dom DiMaggio *	450.00	225.00	45.00
☐ 76	Ted Williams *	400.00	200.00	40.00
☐ 77	Roy Smalley	20.00	10.00	2.00
☐ 78	Hoot Evers *	350.00	175.00	35.00
☐ 79	Jackie Robinson *	400.00	200.00	40.00
☐ 81	Whitey Kurowski *	350.00	175.00	35.00
☐ 82	Johnny Lindell	20.00	10.00	2.00
☐ 83	Bobby Doerr *	100.00	50.00	10.00
☐ 84	Sid Hudson	20.00	10.00	2.00
☐ 85	Dave Philley *	350.00	175.00	35.00
☐ 86	Ralph Weigel	20.00	10.00	2.00
☐ 88	Frank Gustine *	350.00	175.00	35.00
☐ 91	Ralph Kiner *	100.00	50.00	10.00
☐ 93	Bob Feller *	1250.00	600.00	150.00
☐ 95	George Stirnweiss	20.00	10.00	2.00
☐ 97	Marty Marion	30.00	15.00	3.00
☐ 98	Hal Newhouser *	450.00	225.00	45.00
☐ 102A	Gene Hermansk (sic) ...	200.00	100.00	20.00
☐ 102B	Gene Hermanski	20.00	10.00	2.00
☐ 104	Eddie Stewart *	350.00	175.00	35.00
☐ 106	Lou Boudreau *	90.00	45.00	9.00
☐ 108	Matt Batts *	350.00	175.00	35.00
☐ 111	Jerry Priddy	20.00	10.00	2.00
☐ 113	Dutch Leonard *	350.00	175.00	35.00
☐ 117	Joe Gordon	25.00	12.50	2.50
☐ 120	George Kell *	600.00	300.00	60.00
☐ 121	Johnny Pesky *	350.00	175.00	35.00
☐ 123	Cliff Fannin *	350.00	175.00	35.00
☐ 125	Andy Pafko	20.00	10.00	2.00
☐ 127	Enos Slaughter *	650.00	325.00	65.00
☐ 128	Buddy Rosar	20.00	10.00	2.00
☐ 129	Kirby Higbe *	350.00	175.00	35.00
☐ 131	Sid Gordon *	350.00	175.00	35.00
☐ 133	Tommy Holmes *	350.00	175.00	35.00
☐ 136A	Cliff Aberson (full sleeve)	20.00	10.00	2.00
☐ 136B	Cliff Aberson (short sleeve)	200.00	100.00	20.00
☐ 137	Harry Walker *	350.00	175.00	35.00
☐ 138	Larry Doby *	450.00	225.00	45.00
☐ 139	Johnny Hopp	20.00	10.00	2.00
☐ 142	Danny Murtaugh *	350.00	175.00	35.00
☐ 143	Dick Sisler *	350.00	175.00	35.00
☐ 144	Bob Dillinger *	350.00	175.00	35.00
☐ 146	Pete Reiser *	400.00	200.00	40.00
☐ 149	Hank Majeski *	350.00	175.00	35.00
☐ 153	Floyd Baker *	350.00	175.00	35.00
☐ 158	Harry Brecheen *	350.00	175.00	35.00
☐ 159	Mizell Platt	20.00	10.00	2.00
☐ 160	Bob Scheffing *	350.00	175.00	35.00
☐ 161	Vern Stephens *	400.00	200.00	40.00
☐ 163	Fred Hutchinson *	400.00	200.00	40.00
☐ 165	Dale Mitchell *	350.00	175.00	35.00
☐ 168	Phil Cavarretta *	350.00	175.00	35.00

1960 Leaf

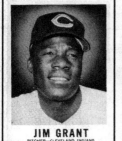

JIM GRANT
PITCHER—CLEVELAND INDIANS

The cards in this 144-card set measure 2 1/2" by 3 1/2". The 1960 Leaf set was issued in a regular gum package style but with a marble instead of gum. The series was a joint production by Sports Novelties, Inc., and Leaf, two Chicago-based companies. Cards 73-144 are more difficult to find than the lower numbers. Photo variations exist (probably proof cards) for the seven cards listed with an asterisk and there is a well-known error card, number 25 showing

Brooks Lawrence (in a Reds uniform) with Jim Grant's name on front, and Grant's biography and record on back. The corrected version with Grant's photo is the more difficult variety.

		NRMT	VG-E	GOOD
COMPLETE SET (145)		900.00	450.00	90.00
COMMON PLAYER (1-72)		1.25	.60	.12
COMMON PLAYER (73-144)		10.00	5.00	1.00
☐ 1	Luis Aparicio *	15.00	3.00	.60
☐ 2	Woodson Held	1.25	.60	.12
☐ 3	Frank Lary	1.25	.60	.12
☐ 4	Camilo Pascual	1.25	.60	.12
☐ 5	Juan Herrera	1.25	.60	.12
☐ 6	Felipe Alou	1.75	.85	.17
☐ 7	Benjamin Daniels	1.25	.60	.12
☐ 8	Roger Craig	3.50	1.75	.35
☐ 9	Edward Kasko	1.25	.60	.12
☐ 10	Robert Anton Grim	1.75	.85	.17
☐ 11	James Busby	1.25	.60	.12
☐ 12	Ken Boyer	3.00	1.50	.30
☐ 13	Robert Boyd	1.25	.60	.12
☐ 14	Samuel Jones	1.25	.60	.12
☐ 15	Lawrence Jackson	1.25	.60	.12
☐ 16	Elroy Face	1.75	.85	.17
☐ 17	Walt Moryn *	1.25	.60	.12
☐ 18	James Gilliam	2.50	1.25	.25
☐ 19	Don Newcombe	1.75	.85	.17
☐ 20	Glen Hobbie	1.25	.60	.12
☐ 21	Pedro Ramos	1.25	.60	.12
☐ 22	Rinold Duren	1.75	.85	.17
☐ 23	Joseph Jay *	1.25	.60	.12
☐ 24	Lou Berberet	1.25	.60	.12
☐ 25A	Jim Grant ERR (photo actually Brooks Lawrence)	10.00	5.00	1.00
☐ 25B	Jim Grant COR	15.00	7.50	1.50
☐ 26	Thomas Borland	1.25	.60	.12
☐ 27	Brooks Robinson	18.00	9.00	1.80
☐ 28	Jerry Adair	1.25	.60	.12
☐ 29	Ronald Jackson	1.25	.60	.12
☐ 30	George Strickland	1.25	.60	.12
☐ 31	Everett Rocky Bridges ...	1.25	.60	.12
☐ 32	William Tuttle	1.25	.60	.12
☐ 33	Kenneth Hunt	1.25	.60	.12
☐ 34	Harold Griggs	1.25	.60	.12
☐ 35	James Coates *	1.25	.60	.12
☐ 36	Brooks Lawrence	1.25	.60	.12
☐ 37	Edwin (Duke) Snider	24.00	12.00	2.40
☐ 38	Albert Spangler	1.25	.60	.12
☐ 39	James Owens	1.25	.60	.12
☐ 40	William Virdon	1.75	.85	.17
☐ 41	Ernest Broglio	1.25	.60	.12
☐ 42	Andre Rodgers	1.25	.60	.12
☐ 43	Julio Becquer	1.25	.60	.12
☐ 44	Antonio(Tony) Taylor	1.25	.60	.12
☐ 45	Gerald Lynch	1.25	.60	.12
☐ 46	Cletis Boyer	1.75	.85	.17
☐ 47	Jerry Lumpe	1.25	.60	.12
☐ 48	Charles Maxwell	1.25	.60	.12
☐ 49	James Perry	1.75	.85	.17
☐ 50	Daniel McDevitt	1.25	.60	.12
☐ 51	Juan Pizarro	1.25	.60	.12
☐ 52	Dallas Green	3.50	1.75	.35
☐ 53	Robert Friend	1.75	.85	.17
☐ 54	Jack Sanford	1.25	.60	.12
☐ 55	Manuel(Jim) Rivera	1.25	.60	.12
☐ 56	Theodore Wills	1.25	.60	.12
☐ 57	Milt Pappas	1.75	.85	.17
☐ 58	Harold Smith *	1.25	.60	.12
☐ 59	Roberto Avila	1.25	.60	.12
☐ 60	Clem Labine	1.75	.85	.17
☐ 61	Norman Rehm *	1.25	.60	.12
☐ 62	John Gabler	1.25	.60	.12
☐ 63	John Tsitouris	1.25	.60	.12
☐ 64	David Sisler	1.25	.60	.12
☐ 65	Vic Power	1.25	.60	.12
☐ 66	Earl Battey	1.25	.60	.12
☐ 67	Robert Purkey	1.25	.60	.12
☐ 68	Myron(Moe) Drabowsky .	1.25	.60	.12
☐ 69	James(Hoyt) Wilhelm	10.00	5.00	1.00
☐ 70	Humberto Robinson	1.25	.60	.12
☐ 71	Dorrel(Whitey) Herzog ..	3.00	1.50	.30
☐ 72	Richard Donovan *	1.25	.60	.12
☐ 73	Gordon Jones	10.00	5.00	1.00
☐ 74	Joe Hicks	10.00	5.00	1.00
☐ 75	Ray Culp	10.00	5.00	1.00
☐ 76	Dick Drott	10.00	5.00	1.00
☐ 77	Bob Duliba	10.00	5.00	1.00
☐ 78	Art Ditmar	10.00	5.00	1.00
☐ 79	Steve Korcheck	10.00	5.00	1.00
☐ 80	Henry Mason	10.00	5.00	1.00
☐ 81	Harry Simpson	10.00	5.00	1.00

			MINT	EXC	G-VG
☐	82	Gene Green	10.00	5.00	1.00
☐	83	Bob Shaw	10.00	5.00	1.00
☐	84	Howard Reed	10.00	5.00	1.00
☐	85	Dick Stigman	10.00	5.00	1.00
☐	86	Rip Repulski	10.00	5.00	1.00
☐	87	Seth Morehead	10.00	5.00	1.00
☐	88	Camilo Carreon	10.00	5.00	1.00
☐	89	John Blanchard	10.00	5.00	1.00
☐	90	Billy Hoeft	10.00	5.00	1.00
☐	91	Fred Hopke	10.00	5.00	1.00
☐	92	Joe Martin	10.00	5.00	1.00
☐	93	Wally Shannon	10.00	5.00	1.00
☐	94	Two Hal Smith's Hal R. Smith Hal W. Smith	15.00	7.50	1.50
☐	95	Al Schroll	10.00	5.00	1.00
☐	96	John Kucks	10.00	5.00	1.00
☐	97	Tom Morgan	10.00	5.00	1.00
☐	98	Willie Jones	10.00	5.00	1.00
☐	99	Marshall Renfroe	10.00	5.00	1.00
☐	100	Willie Tasby	10.00	5.00	1.00
☐	101	Irv Noren	10.00	5.00	1.00
☐	102	Russ Snyder	10.00	5.00	1.00
☐	103	Bob Turley	12.00	6.00	1.20
☐	104	Jim Woods	10.00	5.00	1.00
☐	105	Ronnie Kline	10.00	5.00	1.00
☐	106	Steve Bilko	10.00	5.00	1.00
☐	107	Elmer Valo	10.00	5.00	1.00
☐	108	Tom McAvoy	10.00	5.00	1.00
☐	109	Stan Williams	10.00	5.00	1.00
☐	110	Earl Averill Jr.	10.00	5.00	1.00
☐	111	Lee Walls	10.00	5.00	1.00
☐	112	Paul Richards MG	12.00	6.00	1.20
☐	113	Ed Sadowski	10.00	5.00	1.00
☐	114	Stover McIlwain	10.00	5.00	1.00
☐	115	Chuck Tanner (photo actually Ken Kuhn)	15.00	7.50	1.50
☐	116	Lou Klimchock	10.00	5.00	1.00
☐	117	Neil Chrisley	10.00	5.00	1.00
☐	118	John Callison	12.00	6.00	1.20
☐	119	Hal Smith	10.00	5.00	1.00
☐	120	Carl Sawatski	10.00	5.00	1.00
☐	121	Frank Leja	10.00	5.00	1.00
☐	122	Earl Torgeson	10.00	5.00	1.00
☐	123	Art Schult	10.00	5.00	1.00
☐	124	Jim Brosnan	10.00	5.00	1.00
☐	125	George Anderson	25.00	12.50	2.50
☐	126	Joe Pignatano	10.00	5.00	1.00
☐	127	Rocky Nelson	10.00	5.00	1.00
☐	128	Orlando Cepeda	35.00	17.50	3.50
☐	129	Daryl Spencer	10.00	5.00	1.00
☐	130	Ralph Lumenti	10.00	5.00	1.00
☐	131	Sam Taylor	10.00	5.00	1.00
☐	132	Harry Brecheen	10.00	5.00	1.00
☐	133	Johnny Groth	10.00	5.00	1.00
☐	134	Wayne Terwilliger	10.00	5.00	1.00
☐	135	Kent Hadley	10.00	5.00	1.00
☐	136	Faye Throneberry	10.00	5.00	1.00
☐	137	Jack Meyer	10.00	5.00	1.00
☐	138	Chuck Cottier	10.00	5.00	1.00
☐	139	Joe DeMaestri	10.00	5.00	1.00
☐	140	Gene Freese	10.00	5.00	1.00
☐	141	Curt Flood	20.00	10.00	2.00
☐	142	Gino Cimoli	10.00	5.00	1.00
☐	143	Clay Dalrymple	10.00	5.00	1.00
☐	144	Jim Bunning	40.00	20.00	4.00

1989 Lennox HSE Astros

The 1989 Lennox HSE Astros set contains 26 cards measuring 2 5/8 by 4 1/8 inches. The fronts have color photos with burnt orange and white borders; the backs feature biographical information and career highlights. The set looks very much like the Police Astros sets of the previous years but is not since it was not sponsored by any Police Department and does not have a safety tip anywhere on the card.

			MINT	EXC	G-VG
		COMPLETE SET (26)	6.00	3.00	.60
		COMMON PLAYER (1-26)	.20	.10	.02
☐	1	Billy Hatcher	.20	.10	.02
☐	2	Greg Gross	.20	.10	.02
☐	3	Rick Rhoden	.20	.10	.02
☐	4	Mike Scott	.60	.30	.06
☐	5	Kevin Bass	.30	.15	.03

			MINT	EXC	G-VG
☐	6	Alex Trevino	.20	.10	.02
☐	7	Jim Clancy	.20	.10	.02
☐	8	Bill Doran	.40	.20	.04
☐	9	Dan Schatzeder	.20	.10	.02
☐	10	Bob Knepper	.20	.10	.02
☐	11	Jim Deshaies	.30	.15	.03
☐	12	Eric Yelding	.20	.10	.02
☐	13	Danny Darwin	.20	.10	.02
☐	14	Astros Coaches	.20	.10	.02
☐	15	Craig Reynolds	.20	.10	.02
☐	16	Rafael Ramirez	.20	.10	.02
☐	17	Juan Agosto	.20	.10	.02
☐	18	Larry Andersen	.20	.10	.02
☐	19	Dave Smith	.30	.15	.03
☐	20	Gerald Young	.30	.15	.03
☐	21	Ken Caminiti	.30	.15	.03
☐	22	Terry Puhl	.30	.15	.03
☐	23	Bob Forsch	.30	.15	.03
☐	24	Craig Biggio	.50	.25	.05
☐	25	Art Howe MG	.30	.15	.03
☐	26	Glenn Davis	.60	.30	.06

1989 Marathon Tigers

The 1989 Marathon Tigers set features 28 cards measuring 2 3/4 by 4 1/2 inches. The fronts are blue and white; the horizontally-oriented backs show career stats. The set was given away at the July 15, 1989 Tigers home game. The cards are numbered by the players' uniform numbers.

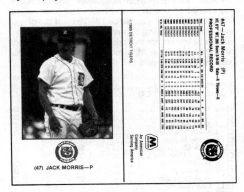

(47) JACK MORRIS—P

			MINT	EXC	G-VG
		COMPLETE SET (28)	7.50	3.75	.75
		COMMON PLAYER	.20	.10	.02
☐	1	Lou Whitaker	.50	.25	.05
☐	3	Alan Trammell	.75	.35	.07
☐	8	Mike Heath	.20	.10	.02
☐	9	Fred Lynn	.40	.20	.04
☐	10	Keith Moreland	.20	.10	.02
☐	11	Sparky Anderson MG	.50	.25	.05
☐	12	Mike Brumley	.20	.10	.02
☐	14	Dave Bergman	.20	.10	.02
☐	15	Pat Sheridan	.20	.10	.02

		NRMT	VG-E	GOOD
☐ 17	Al Pedrique	.20	.10	.02
☐ 18	Ramon Pena	.20	.10	.02
☐ 19	Doyle Alexander	.30	.15	.03
☐ 21	Guillermo Hernandez	.30	.15	.03
☐ 23	Torey Lovullo	.30	.15	.03
☐ 24	Gary Pettis	.30	.15	.03
☐ 25	Ken Williams	.20	.10	.02
☐ 26	Frank Tanana	.30	.15	.03
☐ 27	Charles Hudson	.20	.10	.02
☐ 32	Gary Ward	.20	.10	.02
☐ 33	Matt Nokes	.40	.20	.04
☐ 34	Chet Lemon	.30	.15	.03
☐ 35	Rick Schu	.20	.10	.02
☐ 36	Frank Williams	.20	.10	.02
☐ 39	Mike Henneman	.30	.15	.03
☐ 44	Jeff Robinson	.30	.15	.03
☐ 47	Jack Morris	.50	.25	.05
☐ 48	Paul Gibson	.20	.10	.02
☐ xx	Tiger Coaches	.20	.10	.02
	Billy Consolo			
	Alex Grammas			
	Billy Muffet			
	Vada Pinson			
	Dick Tracewski			

1987 MnM's Star Lineup

The Mars Candy Company is the sponsor of this 24-card set of cards. The cards were printed in perforated pairs. The pairs measure 5" by 3 1/2" whereas the individual cards measure the standard 2 1/2" by 3 1/2". The players are shown without team logos. The cards were designed and produced by MSA, Mike Schechter Associates. The cards are numbered on the front and back. The backs show statistics for every year since 1980 even if the player was not even playing during those earlier years. The values below are for individual players; panels intact would be valued at 25% more than the sum of the two individual players.

		MINT	EXC	G-VG
	COMPLETE SET (24)	12.00	6.00	1.20
	COMMON PLAYER (1-24)	.30	.15	.03
☐ 1	Wally Joyner	.90	.45	.09
☐ 2	Tony Pena	.30	.15	.03
☐ 3	Mike Schmidt	1.25	.60	.12
☐ 4	Ryne Sandberg	.75	.35	.07
☐ 5	Wade Boggs	1.50	.75	.15
☐ 6	Jack Morris	.50	.25	.05
☐ 7	Roger Clemens	1.00	.50	.10
☐ 8	Harold Baines	.40	.20	.04
☐ 9	Dale Murphy	.75	.35	.07
☐ 10	Jose Canseco	2.50	1.25	.25
☐ 11	Don Mattingly	2.50	1.25	.25
☐ 12	Gary Carter	.75	.35	.07
☐ 13	Cal Ripken Jr.	.75	.35	.07
☐ 14	George Brett	.75	.35	.07
☐ 15	Kirby Puckett	1.00	.50	.10
☐ 16	Joe Carter	.50	.25	.05
☐ 17	Mike Witt	.30	.15	.03
☐ 18	Mike Scott	.50	.25	.05
☐ 19	Fernando Valenzuela	.50	.25	.05
☐ 20	Steve Garvey	.75	.35	.07
☐ 21	Steve Sax	.50	.25	.05
☐ 22	Nolan Ryan	1.25	.60	.12
☐ 23	Tony Gwynn	.75	.35	.07
☐ 24	Ozzie Smith	.50	.25	.05

1959 Morrell

The cards in this 12-card set measure 2 1/2" by 3 1/2". The 1959 Morrell Meats set of full color, unnumbered cards features Los Angeles Dodger players only. The photos used are the same as those selected for the Dodger team issue postcards in 1959. The Morrell Meats logo is on the backs of the cards. The Clem Labine card actually features a picture of Stan Williams and the Norm Larker card actually features a picture of Joe Pignatano. The ACC designation is F172-1.

		NRMT	VG-E	GOOD
	COMPLETE SET (12)	1000.00	500.00	100.00
	COMMON PLAYER (1-12)	60.00	30.00	6.00
☐ 1	Don Drysdale	125.00	60.00	12.50
☐ 2	Carl Furillo	75.00	37.50	7.50
☐ 3	Jim Gilliam	75.00	37.50	7.50
☐ 4	Gil Hodges	125.00	60.00	12.50
☐ 5	Sandy Koufax	200.00	100.00	20.00
☐ 6	Clem Labine (photo actually Stan Williams)	60.00	30.00	6.00
☐ 7	Norm Larker (photo actually Joe Pignatano)	60.00	30.00	6.00
☐ 8	Charlie Neal	60.00	30.00	6.00
☐ 9	Johnny Podres	75.00	37.50	7.50
☐ 10	John Roseboro	60.00	30.00	6.00
☐ 11	Duke Snider	200.00	100.00	20.00
☐ 12	Don Zimmer	75.00	37.50	7.50

1960 Morrell

The cards in this 12-card set measure 2 1/2" by 3 1/2". The 1960 Morrell Meats set of full color, unnumbered cards is similar in format to the 1959 Morrell set but can be distinguished from the 1959 set by a red heart which appears in the Morrell logo on the back. The photos used are the same as those selected for the Dodger team issue postcards in 1960. The Furillo, Hodges, and Snider cards received limited distribution and are hence more scarce. The ACC designation is F172-2. The cards were printed in Japan.

		NRMT	VG-E	GOOD
	COMPLETE SET (12)	750.00	375.00	75.00
	COMMON PLAYER (1-12)	20.00	10.00	2.00
☐ 1	Walt Alston MG	40.00	20.00	4.00
☐ 2	Roger Craig	30.00	15.00	3.00
☐ 3	Don Drysdale	50.00	25.00	5.00
☐ 4	Carl Furillo SP	100.00	50.00	10.00
☐ 5	Gil Hodges SP	150.00	75.00	15.00
☐ 6	Sandy Koufax	100.00	50.00	10.00
☐ 7	Wally Moon	20.00	10.00	2.00
☐ 8	Charlie Neal	20.00	10.00	2.00
☐ 9	Johnny Podres	25.00	12.50	2.50
☐ 10	John Roseboro	20.00	10.00	2.00
☐ 11	Larry Sherry	20.00	10.00	2.00
☐ 12	Duke Snider SP	250.00	125.00	25.00

1961 Morrell

The cards in this 6-card set measure 2 1/2" by 3 1/2". The 1961 Morrell Meats set of full color, unnumbered cards features Los Angeles Dodger players only and contains statistical information on the backs of the cards in brown print. The ACC designation is F172-3.

		NRMT	VG-E	GOOD
	COMPLETE SET (6)	200.00	100.00	20.00
	COMMON PLAYER (1-6)	16.00	8.00	1.60
☐ 1	Tommy Davis	20.00	10.00	2.00
☐ 2	Don Drysdale	50.00	25.00	5.00
☐ 3	Frank Howard	20.00	10.00	2.00
☐ 4	Sandy Koufax	100.00	50.00	10.00
☐ 5	Norm Larker	16.00	8.00	1.60
☐ 6	Maury Wills	35.00	17.50	3.50

1983 Mother's Giants

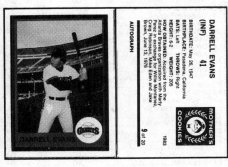

The cards in this 20-card set measure 2 1/2" by 3 1/2". For the first time in 30 years, Mother's Cookies issued a baseball card set. The full color set, produced by hobbyist Barry Colla, features San Francisco Giants players only. Fifteen cards were issued at the Astros vs. Giants game of August 7, 1983. Five of the cards were redeemable by sending in a coupon. The five additional cards received from redemption of the coupon were not guaranteed to be the five needed to complete the set. The fronts feature the player's photo, his name, and the Giants' logo, while the backs feature player biographies and the Mother's Cookies logo. The backs also contain a space in which to obtain the player's autograph.

	MINT	EXC	G-VG
COMPLETE SET (20)	18.00	9.00	1.80
COMMON PLAYER (1-20)	.60	.30	.06

		MINT	EXC	G-VG
☐ 1	Frank Robinson MG	2.00	1.00	.20
☐ 2	Jack Clark	2.50	1.25	.25
☐ 3	Chili Davis	1.50	.75	.15
☐ 4	Johnnie LeMaster	.60	.30	.06
☐ 5	Greg Minton	.75	.35	.07
☐ 6	Bob Brenly	.75	.35	.07
☐ 7	Fred Breining	.60	.30	.06
☐ 8	Jeff Leonard	1.00	.50	.10
☐ 9	Darrell Evans	1.25	.60	.12
☐ 10	Tom O'Malley	.60	.30	.06
☐ 11	Duane Kuiper	.60	.30	.06
☐ 12	Mike Krukow	.75	.35	.07
☐ 13	Atlee Hammaker	.75	.35	.07
☐ 14	Gary Lavelle	.60	.30	.06
☐ 15	Bill Laskey	.60	.30	.06
☐ 16	Max Venable	.60	.30	.06
☐ 17	Joel Youngblood	.60	.30	.06
☐ 18	Dave Bergman	.60	.30	.06
☐ 19	Mike Vail	.60	.30	.06
☐ 20	Andy McGaffigan	.60	.30	.06

1984 Mother's A's

The cards in this 28-card set measure 2 1/2" by 3 1/2". In 1984, the Los Angeles based Mother's Cookies Co. issued five sets of cards featuring players from major league teams. The Oakland A's set features current players depicted by photos. Similar to their 1952 and 1953 issues, the cards have rounded corners. The backs of the cards contain the Mother's Cookies logo. The cards were distributed in partial sets to fans at the respective stadiums of the teams involved. Whereas 20 cards were given to each patron, a redemption card, redeemable for eight more cards, was included. Unfortunately, the eight cards received by redeeming the coupon were not necessarily the eight needed to complete a set.

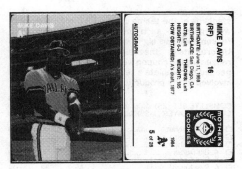

Hobbyist Barry Colla was involved in the production of these sets.

	MINT	EXC	G-VG
COMPLETE SET (28)	15.00	7.50	1.50
COMMON PLAYER (1-28)	.40	.20	.04

		MINT	EXC	G-VG
☐ 1	Steve Boros MG	.40	.20	.04
☐ 2	Rickey Henderson	4.00	2.00	.40
☐ 3	Joe Morgan	2.00	1.00	.20
☐ 4	Dwayne Murphy	.60	.30	.06
☐ 5	Mike Davis	.60	.30	.06
☐ 6	Bruce Bochte	.40	.20	.04
☐ 7	Carney Lansford	1.00	.50	.10
☐ 8	Steve McCatty	.40	.20	.04
☐ 9	Mike Heath	.40	.20	.04
☐ 10	Chris Codiroli	.40	.20	.04
☐ 11	Bill Almon	.40	.20	.04
☐ 12	Bill Caudill	.50	.25	.05
☐ 13	Donnie Hill	.40	.20	.04
☐ 14	Lary Sorensen	.40	.20	.04
☐ 15	Dave Kingman	.80	.40	.08
☐ 16	Garry Hancock	.40	.20	.04
☐ 17	Jeff Burroughs	.50	.25	.05
☐ 18	Tom Burgmeier	.40	.20	.04
☐ 19	Jim Essian	.40	.20	.04
☐ 20	Mike Warren	.40	.20	.04
☐ 21	Davey Lopes	.50	.25	.05
☐ 22	Ray Burris	.50	.25	.05
☐ 23	Tony Phillips	.50	.25	.05
☐ 24	Tim Conroy	.40	.20	.04
☐ 25	Jeff Bettendorf	.40	.20	.04
☐ 26	Keith Atherton	.40	.20	.04
☐ 27	A's Coaches	.40	.20	.04
☐ 28	A's Checklist	.40	.20	.04

1984 Mother's Astros

The cards in this 28-card set measure 2 1/2" by 3 1/2". In 1984, the Los Angeles based Mother's Cookies Co. issued five sets of cards featuring players from major league teams. The Houston Astros set features current players depicted by photos. Similar to their 1952 and 1953 issues, the cards have rounded corners. The backs of the cards contain the Mother's Cookies logo. The cards were distributed in partial sets to fans at the respective stadiums of the teams involved. Whereas 20 cards were given to each patron, a redemption card, redeemable for eight more cards was included. Unfortunately, the eight cards received by redeeming the coupon were not necessarily the eight needed to complete a set. Hobbyist Barry Colla was involved in the production of these sets.

		MINT	EXC	G-VG
COMPLETE SET (28)		13.00	6.50	1.30
COMMON PLAYER (1-28)		.35	.17	.03
☐ 1	Nolan Ryan	4.00	2.00	.40
☐ 2	Joe Niekro	.75	.35	.07
☐ 3	Alan Ashby	.45	.22	.04
☐ 4	Bill Doran	1.00	.50	.10
☐ 5	Phil Garner	.45	.22	.04
☐ 6	Ray Knight	.45	.22	.04
☐ 7	Dickie Thon	.45	.22	.04
☐ 8	Jose Cruz	.60	.30	.06
☐ 9	Jerry Mumphrey	.35	.17	.03
☐ 10	Terry Puhl	.45	.22	.04
☐ 11	Enos Cabell	.35	.17	.03
☐ 12	Harry Spilman	.35	.17	.03
☐ 13	Dave Smith	.60	.30	.06
☐ 14	Mike Scott	1.50	.75	.15
☐ 15	Bob Lillis MG	.35	.17	.03
☐ 16	Bob Knepper	.45	.22	.04
☐ 17	Frank DiPino	.35	.17	.03
☐ 18	Tom Wieghaus	.35	.17	.03
☐ 19	Denny Walling	.35	.17	.03
☐ 20	Tony Scott	.35	.17	.03
☐ 21	Alan Bannister	.35	.17	.03
☐ 22	Bill Dawley	.35	.17	.03
☐ 23	Vern Ruhle	.35	.17	.03
☐ 24	Mike LaCoss	.35	.17	.03
☐ 25	Mike Madden	.35	.17	.03
☐ 26	Craig Reynolds	.45	.22	.04
☐ 27	Astros' Coaches	.35	.17	.03
☐ 28	Astros' Checklist	.35	.17	.03

1984 Mother's Giants

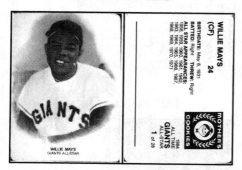

The cards in this 28-card set measure 2 1/2" by 3 1/2". In 1984, the Los Angeles based Mother's Cookies Co. issued five sets of cards featuring players from major league teams. The San Francisco Giants set features previous Giant All-Star selections depicted by drawings. Similar to their 1952 and 1953 issues, the cards have rounded corners. The backs of the cards contain the Mother's Cookies logo. The cards were distributed in partial sets to fans at the respective stadiums of the teams involved. Whereas 20 cards were given to each patron, a redemption card, redeemable for eight more cards was included. Unfortunately, the eight cards received by redeeming the coupon were not necessarily the eight needed to complete a set. Hobbyist Barry Colla was involved in the production of these sets.

	MINT	EXC	G-VG
COMPLETE SET (28)	14.00	7.00	1.40
COMMON PLAYER (1-28)	.40	.20	.04

		MINT	EXC	G-VG
☐ 1	Willie Mays	3.00	1.50	.30
☐ 2	Willie McCovey	2.00	1.00	.20
☐ 3	Juan Marichal	1.50	.75	.15
☐ 4	Gaylord Perry	1.50	.75	.15
☐ 5	Tom Haller	.40	.20	.04
☐ 6	Jim Davenport	.40	.20	.04
☐ 7	Jack Clark	1.25	.60	.12
☐ 8	Greg Minton	.40	.20	.04
☐ 9	Atlee Hammaker	.40	.20	.04
☐ 10	Gary Lavelle	.40	.20	.04
☐ 11	Orlando Cepeda	1.00	.50	.10
☐ 12	Bobby Bonds	.60	.30	.06
☐ 13	John Antonelli	.40	.20	.04
☐ 14	Bob Schmidt (photo actually Wes Westrum)	.40	.20	.04
☐ 15	Sam Jones	.40	.20	.04
☐ 16	Mike McCormick	.40	.20	.04
☐ 17	Ed Bailey	.40	.20	.04
☐ 18	Stu Miller	.40	.20	.04
☐ 19	Felipe Alou	.60	.30	.06
☐ 20	Jim Ray Hart	.40	.20	.04
☐ 21	Dick Dietz	.40	.20	.04
☐ 22	Chris Speier	.40	.20	.04
☐ 23	Bobby Murcer	.60	.30	.06
☐ 24	John Montefusco	.40	.20	.04
☐ 25	Vida Blue	.50	.25	.05
☐ 26	Ed Whitson	.40	.20	.04
☐ 27	Darrell Evans	.75	.35	.07
☐ 28	Checklist Card	.40	.20	.04

1984 Mother's Mariners

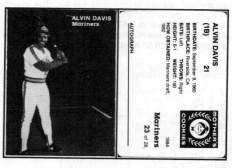

The cards in this 28-card set measure 2 1/2" by 3 1/2". In 1984, The Los Angeles-based Mother's Cookies Co. issued five sets of cards featuring players from major league teams. The Seattle Mariners set features current players depicted by photos. Similar to their 1952 and 1953 issues, the cards have rounded corners. The backs of the cards contain the Mother's Cookies logo. The cards were distributed in partial sets to fans at the respective stadiums of the teams involved. Whereas 20 cards were given to each patron, a redemption card, redeemable for eight more cards was included. Unfortunately, the eight cards received by redeeming the coupon were not necessarily the eight needed to complete a set. Hobbyist Barry Colla was involved in the production of these sets.

		MINT	EXC	G-VG
COMPLETE SET (28)		13.00	6.50	1.30
COMMON PLAYER (1-28)		.40	.20	.04
☐ 1	Del Crandall MG	.50	.25	.05
☐ 2	Barry Bonnell	.40	.20	.04
☐ 3	Dave Henderson	.60	.30	.06
☐ 4	Bob Kearney	.40	.20	.04
☐ 5	Mike Moore	1.00	.50	.10
☐ 6	Spike Owen	.50	.25	.05
☐ 7	Gorman Thomas	.60	.30	.06
☐ 8	Ed VandeBerg	.40	.20	.04
☐ 9	Matt Young	.40	.20	.04
☐ 10	Larry Milbourne	.40	.20	.04
☐ 11	Dave Beard	.40	.20	.04

☐ 12	Jim Beattie	.40	.20	.04
☐ 13	Mark Langston	2.50	1.25	.25
☐ 14	Orlando Mercado	.40	.20	.04
☐ 15	Jack Perconte	.40	.20	.04
☐ 16	Pat Putnam	.40	.20	.04
☐ 17	Paul Mirabella	.40	.20	.04
☐ 18	Domingo Ramos	.40	.20	.04
☐ 19	Al Cowens	.40	.20	.04
☐ 20	Mike Stanton	.40	.20	.04
☐ 21	Steve Henderson	.40	.20	.04
☐ 22	Bob Stoddard	.40	.20	.04
☐ 23	Alvin Davis	2.00	1.00	.20
☐ 24	Phil Bradley	1.00	.50	.10
☐ 25	Roy Thomas	.40	.20	.04
☐ 26	Darnell Coles	.60	.30	.06
☐ 27	Mariners' Coaches	.40	.20	.04
☐ 28	Mariners' Checklist	.40	.20	.04

1984 Mother's Padres

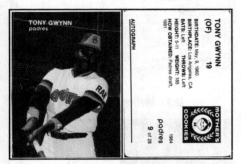

The cards in this 28-card set measure 2 1/2" by 3 1/2". In 1984, the Los Angeles based Mother's Cookies Co. issued five sets of cards featuring current players. The San Diego Padres set features current players depicted by photos. Similar to their 1952 and 1953 issues, the cards have rounded corners. The backs of the cards contain the Mother's Cookies logo. The cards were distributed in partial sets to fans at the respective stadiums of the teams involved. Whereas 20 cards were given to each patron, a redemption card, redeemable for eight more cards was included. Unfortunately, the eight cards received by redeeming the coupon were not necessarily the eight needed to complete a set. Hobbyist Barry Colla was involved in the production of these sets.

		MINT	EXC	G-VG
COMPLETE SET (28)		17.00	8.50	1.70
COMMON PLAYER (1-28)		.50	.25	.05
☐ 1	Dick Williams MG	.60	.30	.06
☐ 2	Rich Gossage	.90	.45	.09
☐ 3	Tim Lollar	.50	.25	.05
☐ 4	Eric Show	.75	.35	.07
☐ 5	Terry Kennedy	.60	.30	.06
☐ 6	Kurt Bevacqua	.50	.25	.05
☐ 7	Steve Garvey	2.00	1.00	.20
☐ 8	Garry Templeton	.60	.30	.06
☐ 9	Tony Gwynn	4.00	2.00	.40
☐ 10	Alan Wiggins	.50	.25	.05
☐ 11	Dave Dravecky	1.00	.50	.10
☐ 12	Tim Flannery	.50	.25	.05
☐ 13	Kevin McReynolds	2.50	1.25	.25
☐ 14	Bobby Brown	.50	.25	.05
☐ 15	Ed Whitson	.60	.30	.06
☐ 16	Doug Gwosdz	.50	.25	.05
☐ 17	Luis DeLeon	.50	.25	.05
☐ 18	Andy Hawkins	.75	.35	.07
☐ 19	Craig Lefferts	.50	.25	.05
☐ 20	Carmelo Martinez	.60	.30	.06
☐ 21	Sid Monge	.50	.25	.05
☐ 22	Graig Nettles	.75	.35	.07
☐ 23	Mario Ramirez	.50	.25	.05
☐ 24	Luis Salazar	.50	.25	.05
☐ 25	Champ Summers	.50	.25	.05

☐ 26	Mark Thurmond	.50	.25	.05
☐ 27	Padres' Coaches	.50	.25	.05
☐ 28	Padres' Checklist	.50	.25	.05

1985 Mother's A's

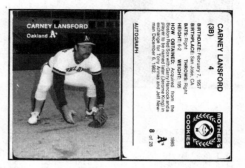

The cards in this 28-card set measure 2 1/2" by 3 1/2". In 1985, the Los Angeles based Mother's Cookies Co. again issued five sets of cards featuring players from major league teams. The Oakland A's set features current players depicted by photos on cards with rounded corners. The backs of the cards contain the Mother's Cookies logo. Cards were passed out at the stadium on July 6.

		MINT	EXC	G-VG
COMPLETE SET (28)		11.00	5.50	1.10
COMMON PLAYER (1-28)		.30	.15	.03
☐ 1	Jackie Moore MG	.30	.15	.03
☐ 2	Dave Kingman	.60	.30	.06
☐ 3	Don Sutton	1.25	.60	.12
☐ 4	Mike Heath	.30	.15	.03
☐ 5	Alfredo Griffin	.50	.25	.05
☐ 6	Dwayne Murphy	.40	.20	.04
☐ 7	Mike Davis	.50	.25	.05
☐ 8	Carney Lansford	.75	.35	.07
☐ 9	Chris Codiroli	.30	.15	.03
☐ 10	Bruce Bochte	.30	.15	.03
☐ 11	Mickey Tettleton	.50	.25	.05
☐ 12	Donnie Hill	.30	.15	.03
☐ 13	Rob Picciolo	.30	.15	.03
☐ 14	Dave Collins	.40	.20	.04
☐ 15	Dusty Baker	.40	.20	.04
☐ 16	Tim Conroy	.30	.15	.03
☐ 17	Keith Atherton	.30	.15	.03
☐ 18	Jay Howell	.50	.25	.05
☐ 19	Mike Warren	.30	.15	.03
☐ 20	Steve McCatty	.30	.15	.03
☐ 21	Bill Krueger	.30	.15	.03
☐ 22	Curt Young	.50	.25	.05
☐ 23	Dan Meyer	.30	.15	.03
☐ 24	Mike Gallego	.30	.15	.03
☐ 25	Jeff Kaiser	.30	.15	.03
☐ 26	Steve Henderson	.30	.15	.03
☐ 27	A's Coaches	.30	.15	.03
☐ 28	A's Checklist	.30	.15	.03

1985 Mother's Astros

The cards in this 28-card set measure 2 1/2" by 3 1/2". In 1985, the Los Angeles-based Mother's Cookies Co. again issued five sets of cards featuring players from major league teams. The Houston Astros set features current players depicted by photos on cards with rounded corners. The backs of the cards contain the Mother's Cookies logo. Cards were passed out at the stadium on July 13. The checklist card features the Astros logo on the obverse.

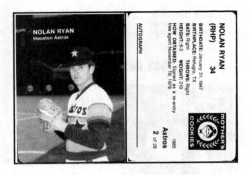

NOLAN RYAN
Houston Astros

AUTOGRAPH

NOLAN RYAN
(RHP)
34

BIRTHDATE: January 31, 1947
BIRTHPLACE: Refugio, TX
BATS: Right   THROWS: Right
HEIGHT: 6-2   WEIGHT: 210
HOW OBTAINED: Signed as a re-entry
free agent November 19, 1979

Astros
1985
2 of 28

		MINT	EXC	G-VG
COMPLETE SET (28)		12.00	6.00	1.20
COMMON PLAYER (1-28)		.35	.17	.03
☐ 1	Bob Lillis MG	.35	.17	.03
☐ 2	Nolan Ryan	3.00	1.50	.30
☐ 3	Phil Garner	.45	.22	.04
☐ 4	Jose Cruz	.60	.30	.06
☐ 5	Denny Walling	.35	.17	.03
☐ 6	Joe Niekro	.75	.35	.07
☐ 7	Terry Puhl	.45	.22	.04
☐ 8	Bill Doran	.75	.35	.07
☐ 9	Dickie Thon	.45	.22	.04
☐ 10	Enos Cabell	.35	.17	.03
☐ 11	Frank DiPino	.35	.17	.03
☐ 12	Julio Solano	.35	.17	.03
☐ 13	Alan Ashby	.45	.22	.04
☐ 14	Craig Reynolds	.35	.17	.03
☐ 15	Jerry Mumphrey	.35	.17	.03
☐ 16	Bill Dawley	.35	.17	.03
☐ 17	Mark Bailey	.35	.17	.03
☐ 18	Mike Scott	1.25	.60	.12
☐ 19	Harry Spilman	.35	.17	.03
☐ 20	Bob Knepper	.45	.22	.04
☐ 21	Dave Smith	.60	.30	.06
☐ 22	Kevin Bass	.60	.30	.06
☐ 23	Tim Tolman	.35	.17	.03
☐ 24	Jeff Calhoun	.35	.17	.03
☐ 25	Jim Pankovits	.35	.17	.03
☐ 26	Ron Mathis	.35	.17	.03
☐ 27	Astros' Coaches	.35	.17	.03
☐ 28	Astros' Checklist	.35	.17	.03

1985 Mother's Giants

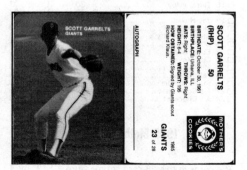

SCOTT GARRELTS
GIANTS

AUTOGRAPH

SCOTT GARRELTS
(RHP)
50

BIRTHDATE: October 30, 1961
BIRTHPLACE: Urbana, ILL
BATS: Right   THROWS: Right
HEIGHT: 6-4   WEIGHT: 195
HOW OBTAINED: Signed by Giants scout
Richard Kilius.

GIANTS
1985
23 of 28

The cards in this 28-card set measure 2 1/2" by 3 1/2". In 1985, the Los Angeles based Mother's Cookies Co. again issued five sets of cards featuring players from major league teams. The San Francisco Giants set features current players depicted by photos on cards with rounded corners. The backs of the cards contain the Mother's Cookies logo. Cards were passed out at the stadium on June 30.

		MINT	EXC	G-VG
COMPLETE SET (28)		10.00	5.00	1.00
COMMON PLAYER (1-28)		.30	.15	.03
☐ 1	Jim Davenport MG	.30	.15	.03
☐ 2	Chili Davis	.75	.35	.07
☐ 3	Dan Gladden	.60	.30	.06
☐ 4	Jeff Leonard	.60	.30	.06
☐ 5	Manny Trillo	.30	.15	.03
☐ 6	Atlee Hammaker	.30	.15	.03
☐ 7	Bob Brenly	.40	.20	.04
☐ 8	Greg Minton	.40	.20	.04
☐ 9	Bill Laskey	.30	.15	.03
☐ 10	Vida Blue	.50	.25	.05
☐ 11	Mike Krukow	.50	.25	.05
☐ 12	Frank Williams	.30	.15	.03
☐ 13	Jose Uribe	.50	.25	.05
☐ 14	Johnnie LeMaster	.30	.15	.03
☐ 15	Scot Thompson	.30	.15	.03
☐ 16	Dave LaPoint	.50	.25	.05
☐ 17	David Green	.30	.15	.03
☐ 18	Chris Brown	.40	.20	.04
☐ 19	Joel Youngblood	.30	.15	.03
☐ 20	Mark Davis	1.50	.75	.15
☐ 21	Jim Gott	.50	.25	.05
☐ 22	Doug Gwosdz	.30	.15	.03
☐ 23	Scott Garrelts	.75	.35	.07
☐ 24	Gary Rajsich	.30	.15	.03
☐ 25	Rob Deer	.75	.35	.07
☐ 26	Brad Wellman	.30	.15	.03
☐ 27	Giants' Coaches	.30	.15	.03
☐ 28	Giants' Checklist	.30	.15	.03

1985 Mother's Mariners

JIM PRESLEY
Seattle Mariners

AUTOGRAPH

JIM PRESLEY
(IN)
17

BIRTHDATE: October 23, 1961
BIRTHPLACE: Pensacola, FL
BATS: Right   THROWS: Right
HEIGHT: 6-1   WEIGHT: 185
HOW OBTAINED: Seattle's 4th round
selection in the regular phase June 1979
free agent draft; signed by scout Rip Tutor.

Mariners
1985
20 of 28

The cards in this 28-card set measure 2 1/2" by 3 1/2". In 1985, the Los Angeles based Mother's Cookies Co. again issued five sets of cards featuring players from major league teams. The Seattle Mariners set features current players depicted by photos on cards with rounded corners. The backs of the cards contain the Mother's Cookies logo. Cards were passed out at the stadium on August 10.

		MINT	EXC	G-VG
COMPLETE SET (28)		12.00	6.00	1.20
COMMON PLAYER (1-28)		.30	.15	.03
☐ 1	Chuck Cottier MG	.30	.15	.03
☐ 2	Alvin Davis	1.50	.75	.15
☐ 3	Mark Langston	2.00	1.00	.20
☐ 4	Dave Henderson	.50	.25	.05
☐ 5	Ed VandeBerg	.30	.15	.03
☐ 6	Al Cowens	.30	.15	.03
☐ 7	Spike Owen	.40	.20	.04
☐ 8	Mike Moore	.75	.35	.07
☐ 9	Gorman Thomas	.50	.25	.05
☐ 10	Barry Bonnell	.30	.15	.03
☐ 11	Jack Perconte	.30	.15	.03
☐ 12	Domingo Ramos	.30	.15	.03
☐ 13	Bob Kearney	.30	.15	.03
☐ 14	Matt Young	.30	.15	.03
☐ 15	Jim Beattie	.30	.15	.03
☐ 16	Mike Stanton	.30	.15	.03
☐ 17	David Valle	.30	.15	.03
☐ 18	Ken Phelps	.50	.25	.05
☐ 19	Salome Barojas	.30	.15	.03
☐ 20	Jim Presley	.90	.45	.09
☐ 21	Phil Bradley	.90	.45	.09

			MINT	EXC	G-VG
☐ 22	Dave Geisel		.30	.15	.03
☐ 23	Harold Reynolds		.90	.45	.09
☐ 24	Ed Nunez		.40	.20	.04
☐ 25	Mike Morgan		.50	.25	.05
☐ 26	Ivan Calderon		.90	.45	.09
☐ 27	Mariners Coaches		.30	.15	.03
☐ 28	Checklist Card		.30	.15	.03

1985 Mother's Padres

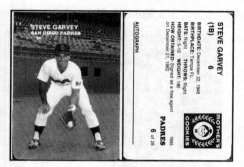

The cards in this 28-card set measure 2 1/2" by 3 1/2". In 1985, the Los Angeles based Mother's Cookies Co. again issued five sets of cards featuring players from major league teams. The San Diego Padres set features current players depicted by photos on cards with rounded corners. The backs of the cards contain the Mother's Cookies logo. Cards were passed out at the stadium on August 11.

			MINT	EXC	G-VG
COMPLETE SET (28)			12.00	6.00	1.20
COMMON PLAYER (1-28)			.30	.15	.03
☐ 1	Dick Williams MG		.40	.20	.04
☐ 2	Tony Gwynn		2.50	1.25	.25
☐ 3	Kevin McReynolds		1.50	.75	.15
☐ 4	Graig Nettles		.75	.35	.07
☐ 5	Rich Gossage		.75	.35	.07
☐ 6	Steve Garvey		1.50	.75	.15
☐ 7	Garry Templeton		.40	.20	.04
☐ 8	Dave Dravecky		.75	.35	.07
☐ 9	Eric Show		.50	.25	.05
☐ 10	Terry Kennedy		.40	.20	.04
☐ 11	Luis DeLeon		.30	.15	.03
☐ 12	Bruce Bochy		.30	.15	.03
☐ 13	Andy Hawkins		.50	.25	.05
☐ 14	Kurt Bevacqua		.30	.15	.03
☐ 15	Craig Lefferts		.40	.20	.04
☐ 16	Mario Ramirez		.30	.15	.03
☐ 17	LaMarr Hoyt		.40	.20	.04
☐ 18	Jerry Royster		.30	.15	.03
☐ 19	Tim Stoddard		.30	.15	.03
☐ 20	Tim Flannery		.30	.15	.03
☐ 21	Mark Thurmond		.30	.15	.03
☐ 22	Greg Booker		.30	.15	.03
☐ 23	Bobby Brown		.30	.15	.03
☐ 24	Carmelo Martinez		.40	.20	.04
☐ 25	Al Bumbry		.30	.15	.03
☐ 26	Jerry Davis		.30	.15	.03
☐ 27	Padres' Coaches		.30	.15	.03
☐ 28	Padres' Checklist		.30	.15	.03

1986 Mother's A's

This set consists of 28 full-color, rounded- corner cards each measuring 2 1/2" by 3 1/2". Starter sets (only 20 cards but also including a certificate for eight more cards) were given out at the ballpark and collectors were encouraged to trade to fill in the rest of their set. The cards were originally given away on July 20th at Oakland Coliseum.

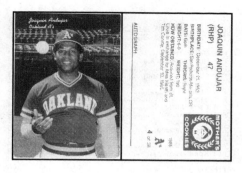

			MINT	EXC	G-VG
COMPLETE SET (28)			24.00	12.00	2.40
COMMON PLAYER (1-28)			.30	.15	.03
☐ 1	Jackie Moore MG		.30	.15	.03
☐ 2	Dave Kingman		.60	.30	.06
☐ 3	Dusty Baker		.40	.20	.04
☐ 4	Joaquin Andujar		.40	.20	.04
☐ 5	Alfredo Griffin		.40	.20	.04
☐ 6	Dwayne Murphy		.40	.20	.04
☐ 7	Mike Davis		.40	.20	.04
☐ 8	Carney Lansford		.75	.35	.07
☐ 9	Jose Canseco		15.00	7.50	1.50
☐ 10	Bruce Bochte		.30	.15	.03
☐ 11	Mickey Tettleton		.50	.25	.05
☐ 12	Donnie Hill		.30	.15	.03
☐ 13	Jose Rijo		.50	.25	.05
☐ 14	Rick Langford		.30	.15	.03
☐ 15	Chris Codiroli		.30	.15	.03
☐ 16	Moose Haas		.30	.15	.03
☐ 17	Keith Atherton		.30	.15	.03
☐ 18	Jay Howell		.40	.20	.04
☐ 19	Tony Phillips		.30	.15	.03
☐ 20	Steve Henderson		.30	.15	.03
☐ 21	Bill Krueger		.30	.15	.03
☐ 22	Steve Ontiveros		.30	.15	.03
☐ 23	Bill Bathe		.30	.15	.03
☐ 24	Ricky Peters		.30	.15	.03
☐ 25	Tim Birtsas		.30	.15	.03
☐ 26	A's Trainers and		.30	.15	.03
	Equipment Managers				
☐ 27	A's Coaches		.30	.15	.03
☐ 28	Checklist Card		.30	.15	.03

1986 Mother's Astros

This set consists of 28 full-color, rounded- corner cards each measuring 2 1/2" by 3 1/2". Starter sets (only 20 cards but also including a certificate for eight more cards) were given out at the ballpark and collectors were encouraged to trade to fill in the rest of their set. Cards were originally given out at the Astrodome on July 10th. Since the 1986 All-Star Game was held in Houston, the set features Astro All-Stars since 1962 as painted by artist Richard Wallich.

		MINT	EXC	G-VG
COMPLETE SET (28)		10.00	5.00	1.00
COMMON PLAYER (1-28)		.30	.15	.03
☐ 1	Dick Farrell	.30	.15	.03
☐ 2	Hal Woodeshick	.30	.15	.03
☐ 3	Joe Morgan	1.50	.75	.15
☐ 4	Claude Raymond	.30	.15	.03
☐ 5	Mike Cuellar	.40	.20	.04
☐ 6	Rusty Staub	.60	.30	.06
☐ 7	Jimmy Wynn	.40	.20	.04
☐ 8	Larry Dierker	.40	.20	.04
☐ 9	Denis Menke	.30	.15	.03
☐ 10	Don Wilson	.30	.15	.03
☐ 11	Cesar Cedeno	.50	.25	.05
☐ 12	Lee May	.40	.20	.04
☐ 13	Bob Watson	.40	.20	.04
☐ 14	Ken Forsch	.30	.15	.03
☐ 15	Joaquin Andujar	.40	.20	.04
☐ 16	Terry Puhl	.40	.20	.04
☐ 17	Joe Niekro	.50	.25	.05
☐ 18	Craig Reynolds	.30	.15	.03
☐ 19	Joe Sambito	.30	.15	.03
☐ 20	Jose Cruz	.50	.25	.05
☐ 21	J.R. Richard	.40	.20	.04
☐ 22	Bob Knepper	.30	.15	.03
☐ 23	Nolan Ryan	2.50	1.25	.25
☐ 24	Ray Knight	.40	.20	.04
☐ 25	Bill Dawley	.30	.15	.03
☐ 26	Dickie Thon	.30	.15	.03
☐ 27	Jerry Mumphrey	.30	.15	.03
☐ 28	Checklist Card	.30	.15	.03

1986 Mother's Giants

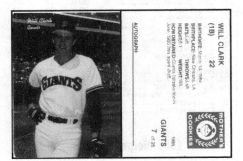

This set consists of 28 full-color, rounded- corner cards each measuring 2 1/2" by 3 1/2". Starter sets (only 20 cards but also including a certificate for eight more cards) were given out at the ballpark and collectors were encouraged to trade to fill in the rest of their set. Cards were originally given out at Candlestick Park on July 13th.

		MINT	EXC	G-VG
COMPLETE SET (28)		20.00	10.00	2.00
COMMON PLAYER (1-28)		.30	.15	.03
☐ 1	Roger Craig MG	.60	.30	.06
☐ 2	Chili Davis	.50	.25	.05
☐ 3	Dan Gladden	.40	.20	.04
☐ 4	Jeff Leonard	.50	.25	.05
☐ 5	Bob Brenly	.30	.15	.03
☐ 6	Atlee Hammaker	.40	.20	.04
☐ 7	Will Clark	12.50	6.25	1.25
☐ 8	Greg Minton	.40	.20	.04
☐ 9	Candy Maldonado	.50	.25	.05
☐ 10	Vida Blue	.50	.25	.05
☐ 11	Mike Krukow	.40	.20	.04
☐ 12	Bob Melvin	.30	.15	.03
☐ 13	Jose Uribe	.40	.20	.04
☐ 14	Dan Driessen	.30	.15	.03
☐ 15	Jeff Robinson	.50	.25	.05
☐ 16	Rob Thompson	.50	.25	.05
☐ 17	Mike LaCoss	.30	.15	.03
☐ 18	Chris Brown	.30	.15	.03
☐ 19	Scott Garrelts	.50	.25	.05

☐ 20	Mark Davis	1.00	.50	.10
☐ 21	Jim Gott	.40	.20	.04
☐ 22	Brad Wellman	.30	.15	.03
☐ 23	Roger Mason	.30	.15	.03
☐ 24	Bill Laskey	.30	.15	.03
☐ 25	Brad Gulden	.30	.15	.03
☐ 26	Joel Youngblood	.30	.15	.03
☐ 27	Juan Berenguer	.30	.15	.03
☐ 28	Checklist Card	.30	.15	.03

1986 Mother's Mariners

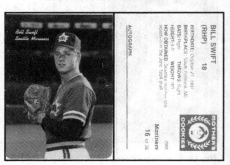

This set consists of 28 full-color, rounded- corner cards each measuring 2 1/2" by 3 1/2". Starter sets (only 20 cards but also including a certificate for eight more cards) were given out at the ballpark and collectors were encouraged to trade to fill in the rest of their set. Cards were originally given out on July 27th at the Seattle Kingdome.

		MINT	EXC	G-VG
COMPLETE SET (28)		10.00	5.00	1.00
COMMON PLAYER (1-28)		.30	.15	.03
☐ 1	Dick Williams MG	.40	.20	.04
☐ 2	Alvin Davis	.75	.35	.07
☐ 3	Mark Langston	1.25	.60	.12
☐ 4	Dave Henderson	.50	.25	.05
☐ 5	Steve Yeager	.30	.15	.03
☐ 6	Al Cowens	.30	.15	.03
☐ 7	Jim Presley	.50	.25	.05
☐ 8	Phil Bradley	.60	.30	.06
☐ 9	Gorman Thomas	.50	.25	.05
☐ 10	Barry Bonnell	.30	.15	.03
☐ 11	Milt Wilcox	.30	.15	.03
☐ 12	Domingo Ramos	.30	.15	.03
☐ 13	Paul Mirabella	.30	.15	.03
☐ 14	Matt Young	.30	.15	.03
☐ 15	Ivan Calderon	.60	.30	.06
☐ 16	Bill Swift	.30	.15	.03
☐ 17	Pete Ladd	.30	.15	.03
☐ 18	Ken Phelps	.40	.20	.04
☐ 19	Karl Best	.30	.15	.03
☐ 20	Spike Owen	.40	.20	.04
☐ 21	Mike Moore	.60	.30	.06
☐ 22	Danny Tartabull	1.50	.75	.15
☐ 23	Bob Kearney	.30	.15	.03
☐ 24	Edwin Nunez	.30	.15	.03
☐ 25	Mike Morgan	.50	.25	.05
☐ 26	Roy Thomas	.30	.15	.03
☐ 27	Jim Beattie	.30	.15	.03
☐ 28	Checklist Card	.30	.15	.03

1987 Mother's Cookies A's

This set consists of 28 full-color, rounded- corner cards each measuring 2 1/2" by 3 1/2". Starter sets (only 20 cards but also including a certificate for eight more cards) were given out at the ballpark and collectors were encouraged to trade to fill in the rest of their set. The cards were originally given away on

BERT CAMPANERIS
(SS) 19

AUTOGRAPH

BIRTHDATE: March 9, 1942
BATTED: Right THREW: Right
ALL STAR PERFORMANCE:

	AB	R	H	RBI	PO	A	E
1968	3	0	0	0	0	0	0
1972	2	0	0	0	0	0	0
1973	3	0	1	0	3	2	0
1974	2	0	0	0	2	3	0
1975	2	0	0	0	0	0	0

ALL TIME
OAKLAND
ATHLETICS
ALLSTAR
1 of 28

1987

MOTHER'S
COOKIES

BERT CAMPANERIS

July 5th at Oakland Coliseum during a game against the Boston Red Sox. This set is actually an All-Time All-Star set including every A's All-Star player since 1968 (when the franchise moved to Oakland). The vintage photos (each shot during the year of All-Star appearance) were taken from the collection of Doug McWilliams. The sets were supposedly given out free to the first 25,000 paid admissions at the game.

		MINT	EXC	G-VG
COMPLETE SET (28)		18.00	9.00	1.80
COMMON PLAYER (1-28)		.30	.15	.03
☐ 1	Bert Campaneris	.30	.15	.03
☐ 2	Rick Monday	.30	.15	.03
☐ 3	John Odom	.30	.15	.03
☐ 4	Sal Bando	.40	.20	.04
☐ 5	Reggie Jackson	1.75	.85	.17
☐ 6	Jim Hunter	1.25	.60	.12
☐ 7	Vida Blue	.40	.20	.04
☐ 8	Dave Duncan	.30	.15	.03
☐ 9	Joe Rudi	.40	.20	.04
☐ 10	Rollie Fingers	1.00	.50	.10
☐ 11	Ken Holtzman	.30	.15	.03
☐ 12	Dick Williams	.40	.20	.04
☐ 13	Alvin Dark	.40	.20	.04
☐ 14	Gene Tenace	.30	.15	.03
☐ 15	Claudell Washington	.40	.20	.04
☐ 16	Phil Garner	.30	.15	.03
☐ 17	Wayne Gross	.30	.15	.03
☐ 18	Matt Keough	.30	.15	.03
☐ 19	Jeff Newman	.30	.15	.03
☐ 20	Rickey Henderson	2.50	1.25	.25
☐ 21	Tony Armas	.40	.20	.04
☐ 22	Mike Norris	.30	.15	.03
☐ 23	Billy Martin	.75	.35	.07
☐ 24	Bill Caudill	.40	.20	.04
☐ 25	Jay Howell	.40	.20	.04
☐ 26	Jose Canseco	4.00	2.00	.40
☐ 27	Jose and Reggie	3.00	1.50	.30
☐ 28	Checklist Card	.30	.15	.03

1987 Mother's Cookies Astros

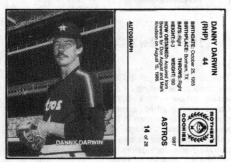

DANNY DARWIN
(RHP) 44

AUTOGRAPH

BIRTHDATE: October 25, 1955
BIRTHPLACE: Bonham, TX
BATS: Right THROWS: Right
HEIGHT:6-3 WEIGHT:190
HOW OBTAINED: Acquired from
Brewers for Don August and Mark
Knudson on August 15, 1986.

ASTROS
14 of 28

1987

MOTHER'S
COOKIES

DANNY DARWIN

This set consists of 28 full-color, rounded-corner cards each measuring 2 1/2" by 3 1/2". Starter sets (only 20 cards but also including a certificate for

eight more cards) were given out at the ballpark and collectors were encouraged to trade to fill in the rest of their set. Cards were originally given out at the Astrodome on July 17th during a game against the Phillies. Photos were taken by Barry Colla. The sets were supposedly given out free to the first 25,000 paid admissions at the game.

		MINT	EXC	G-VG
COMPLETE SET (28)		11.00	5.50	1.10
COMMON PLAYER (1-28)		.30	.15	.03
☐ 1	Hal Lanier MG	.40	.20	.04
☐ 2	Mike Scott	1.00	.50	.10
☐ 3	Jose Cruz	.50	.25	.05
☐ 4	Bill Doran	.75	.35	.07
☐ 5	Bob Knepper	.30	.15	.03
☐ 6	Phil Garner	.40	.20	.04
☐ 7	Terry Puhl	.40	.20	.04
☐ 8	Nolan Ryan	3.50	1.75	.35
☐ 9	Kevin Bass	.40	.20	.04
☐ 10	Glenn Davis	1.00	.50	.10
☐ 11	Alan Ashby	.30	.15	.03
☐ 12	Charlie Kerfeld	.30	.15	.03
☐ 13	Denny Walling	.30	.15	.03
☐ 14	Danny Darwin	.30	.15	.03
☐ 15	Mark Bailey	.30	.15	.03
☐ 16	Davey Lopes	.40	.20	.04
☐ 17	Dave Meads	.30	.15	.03
☐ 18	Aurelio Lopez	.30	.15	.03
☐ 19	Craig Reynolds	.30	.15	.03
☐ 20	Dave Smith	.50	.25	.05
☐ 21	Larry Andersen	.30	.15	.03
☐ 22	Jim Pankovits	.30	.15	.03
☐ 23	Jim Deshaies	.40	.20	.04
☐ 24	Bert Pena	.30	.15	.03
☐ 25	Dickie Thon	.40	.20	.04
☐ 26	Billy Hatcher	.50	.25	.05
☐ 27	Astros' Coaches	.30	.15	.03
☐ 28	Checklist Card	.30	.15	.03

1987 Mother's Cookies Dodgers

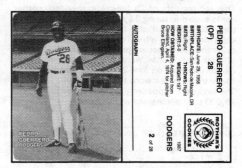

PEDRO GUERRERO
(OF) 28

AUTOGRAPH

BIRTHDATE: June 29, 1956
BIRTHPLACE: San Pedro de Macoris, DR
BATS: Right THROWS: Right
HEIGHT:5-0 WEIGHT: 197
HOW OBTAINED: Acquired from
Cleveland, April 4, 1974 for pitcher
Bruce Ellingsen.

DODGERS
2 of 28

1987

MOTHER'S
COOKIES

PEDRO
GUERRERO
DODGERS

This set consists of 28 full-color, rounded-corner cards each measuring 2 1/2" by 3 1/2". Starter sets (only 20 cards but also including a certificate for eight more cards) were given out at the ballpark and collectors were encouraged to trade to fill in the rest of their set. Cards were originally given out at Dodger Stadium on August 9th. Photos were taken by Barry Colla. The sets were supposedly given out free to all game attendees 14 years of age and under.

		MINT	EXC	G-VG
COMPLETE SET (28)		11.00	5.50	1.10
COMMON PLAYER (1-28)		.30	.15	.03
☐ 1	Tom Lasorda MG	.75	.35	.07
☐ 2	Pedro Guerrero	1.00	.50	.10
☐ 3	Steve Sax	.75	.35	.07
☐ 4	Fernando Valenzuela	1.00	.50	.10
☐ 5	Mike Marshall	.60	.30	.06
☐ 6	Orel Hershiser	2.00	1.00	.20
☐ 7	Mariano Duncan	.40	.20	.04
☐ 8	Bill Madlock	.50	.25	.05
☐ 9	Bob Welch	.50	.25	.05

		MINT	EXC	G-VG
☐ 10	Mike Scioscia	.50	.25	.05
☐ 11	Mike Ramsey	.40	.20	.04
☐ 12	Matt Young	.30	.15	.03
☐ 13	Franklin Stubbs	.40	.20	.04
☐ 14	Tom Niedenfuer	.30	.15	.03
☐ 15	Reggie Williams	.30	.15	.03
☐ 16	Rick Honeycutt	.30	.15	.03
☐ 17	Dave Anderson	.30	.15	.03
☐ 18	Alejandro Pena	.40	.20	.04
☐ 19	Ken Howell	.30	.15	.03
☐ 20	Len Matuszek	.30	.15	.03
☐ 21	Tim Leary	.50	.25	.05
☐ 22	Tracy Woodson	.40	.20	.04
☐ 23	Alex Trevino	.30	.15	.03
☐ 24	Ken Landreaux	.30	.15	.03
☐ 25	Mickey Hatcher	.30	.15	.03
☐ 26	Brian Holton	.40	.20	.04
☐ 27	Dodgers' Coaches	.30	.15	.03
☐ 28	Checklist	.30	.15	.03

1987 Mother's Cookies Giants

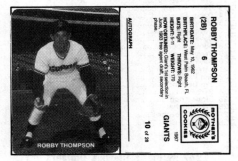

This set consists of 28 full-color, rounded- corner cards each measuring 2 1/2" by 3 1/2". Starter sets (only 20 cards but also including a certificate for eight more cards) were given out at the ballpark and collectors were encouraged to fill in the rest of their set. Cards were originally given out at Candlestick Park on June 27th during a game against the Astros. Photos were taken by Dennis Desprois. The sets were supposedly given out free to the first 25,000 paid admissions at the game.

		MINT	EXC	G-VG
COMPLETE SET (28)		14.00	7.00	1.40
COMMON PLAYER (1-28)		.30	.15	.03
☐ 1	Roger Craig MG	.60	.30	.06
☐ 2	Will Clark	5.00	2.50	.50
☐ 3	Chili Davis	.50	.25	.05
☐ 4	Bob Brenly	.40	.20	.04
☐ 5	Chris Brown	.30	.15	.03
☐ 6	Mike Krukow	.40	.20	.04
☐ 7	Candy Maldonado	.40	.20	.04
☐ 8	Jeffrey Leonard	.50	.25	.05
☐ 9	Greg Minton	.30	.15	.03
☐ 10	Robby Thompson	.40	.20	.04
☐ 11	Scott Garrelts	.50	.25	.05
☐ 12	Bob Melvin	.30	.15	.03
☐ 13	Jose Uribe	.40	.20	.04
☐ 14	Mark Davis	1.00	.50	.10
☐ 15	Eddie Milner	.30	.15	.03
☐ 16	Harry Spilman	.30	.15	.03
☐ 17	Kelly Downs	.40	.20	.04
☐ 18	Chris Speier	.30	.15	.03
☐ 19	Jim Gott	.40	.20	.04
☐ 20	Joel Youngblood	.30	.15	.03
☐ 21	Mike LaCoss	.30	.15	.03
☐ 22	Matt Williams	1.50	.75	.15
☐ 23	Roger Mason	.30	.15	.03
☐ 24	Mike Aldrete	.30	.15	.03
☐ 25	Jeff Robinson	.40	.20	.04
☐ 26	Mark Grant	.30	.15	.03
☐ 27	Giants' Coaches	.30	.15	.03
☐ 28	Checklist Card	.30	.15	.03

1987 Mother's Cookies Mariners

This set consists of 28 full-color, rounded- corner cards each measuring 2 1/2" by 3 1/2". Starter sets (only 20 cards but also including a certificate for eight more cards) were given out at the ballpark and collectors were encouraged to trade to fill in the rest of their set. Cards were originally given out on August 9th at the Seattle Kingdome. Photos were taken by Barry Colla. The sets were supposedly given out free to the first 20,000 paid admissions at the game.

		MINT	EXC	G-VG
COMPLETE SET (28)		10.00	5.00	1.00
COMMON PLAYER (1-28)		.30	.15	.03
☐ 1	Dick Williams MG	.40	.20	.04
☐ 2	Alvin Davis	.75	.35	.07
☐ 3	Mike Moore	.50	.25	.05
☐ 4	Jim Presley	.50	.25	.05
☐ 5	Mark Langston	1.00	.50	.10
☐ 6	Phil Bradley	.50	.25	.05
☐ 7	Ken Phelps	.40	.20	.04
☐ 8	Mike Morgan	.40	.20	.04
☐ 9	David Valle	.30	.15	.03
☐ 10	Harold Reynolds	.60	.30	.06
☐ 11	Edwin Nunez	.40	.20	.04
☐ 12	Bob Kearney	.30	.15	.03
☐ 13	Scott Bankhead	.50	.25	.05
☐ 14	Scott Bradley	.40	.20	.04
☐ 15	Mickey Brantley	.50	.25	.05
☐ 16	Mark Huismann	.30	.15	.03
☐ 17	Mike Kingery	.30	.15	.03
☐ 18	John Moses	.30	.15	.03
☐ 19	Donell Nixon	.30	.15	.03
☐ 20	Rey Quinones	.30	.15	.03
☐ 21	Domingo Ramos	.30	.15	.03
☐ 22	Jerry Reed	.30	.15	.03
☐ 23	Rich Renteria	.40	.20	.04
☐ 24	Rich Monteleone	.40	.20	.04
☐ 25	Mike Trujillo	.30	.15	.03
☐ 26	Bill Wilkinson	.30	.15	.03
☐ 27	John Christensen	.30	.15	.03
☐ 28	Checklist Card	.30	.15	.03

1987 Mother's Cookies McGwire

This set consists of 4 full-color, rounded- corner cards each measuring 2 1/2" by 3 1/2" and showing a different pose of A's slugging rookie Mark McGwire. Cards were originally given out at the national Card Collectors Convention in San Francisco. Later they were available through a mail-in offer involving collectors sending in two proofs-of-purchase from any Mother's Cookies products to get one free card. Photos were taken by Doug McWilliams. The cards are numbered on the back.

		MINT	EXC	G-VG
COMPLETE SET (4)		15.00	7.50	1.50
COMMON PLAYER (1-4)		4.00	2.00	.40

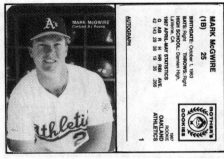

		MINT	EXC	G-VG
☐ 1	Mark McGwire .... close-up shot, head and shoulders	4.00	2.00	.40
☐ 2	Mark McGwire .... waist up, holding bat	4.50	2.25	.45
☐ 3	Mark McGwire .... batting stance, ready to swing	4.50	2.25	.45
☐ 4	Mark McGwire .... home run swing, follow through	5.00	2.50	.50

1987 Mother's Cookies Rangers

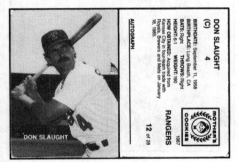

This set consists of 28 full-color, rounded- corner cards each measuring 2 1/2" by 3 1/2". Starter sets (only 20 cards but also including a certificate for eight more cards) were given out at the ballpark and collectors were encouraged to fill in the rest of their set. Cards were originally given out on July 17th during the game against the Yankees. Photos were taken by Barry Colla. The sets were supposedly given out free to the first 25,000 paid admissions at the game.

		MINT	EXC	G-VG
	COMPLETE SET (28)	10.00	5.00	1.00
	COMMON PLAYER (1-28)	.30	.15	.03
☐ 1	Bobby Valentine MG	.50	.25	.05
☐ 2	Pete Incaviglia	.90	.45	.09
☐ 3	Charlie Hough	.40	.20	.04
☐ 4	Oddibe McDowell	.40	.20	.04
☐ 5	Larry Parrish	.30	.15	.03
☐ 6	Scott Fletcher	.40	.20	.04
☐ 7	Steve Buechele	.30	.15	.03
☐ 8	Tom Paciorek	.30	.15	.03
☐ 9	Pete O'Brien	.60	.30	.06
☐ 10	Darrell Porter	.30	.15	.03
☐ 11	Greg Harris	.30	.15	.03
☐ 12	Don Slaught	.30	.15	.03
☐ 13	Ruben Sierra	3.00	1.50	.30
☐ 14	Curtis Wilkerson	.30	.15	.03
☐ 15	Dale Mohorcic	.40	.20	.04
☐ 16	Ron Meredith	.30	.15	.03
☐ 17	Mitch Williams	.60	.30	.06

☐ 18	Bob Brower	.30	.15	.03
☐ 19	Edwin Correa	.30	.15	.03
☐ 20	Geno Petralli	.30	.15	.03
☐ 21	Mike Loynd	.30	.15	.03
☐ 22	Jerry Browne	.30	.15	.03
☐ 23	Jose Guzman	.40	.20	.04
☐ 24	Jeff Kunkel	.30	.15	.03
☐ 25	Bobby Witt	.75	.35	.07
☐ 26	Jeff Russell	.60	.30	.06
☐ 27	Ranger's Trainers	.30	.15	.03
☐ 28	Checklist Card	.30	.15	.03

1988 Mother's Cookies A's

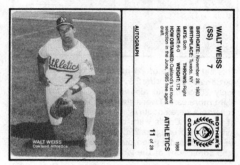

This set consists of 28 full-color, rounded- corner cards each measuring 2 1/2" by 3 1/2". Starter sets (only 20 cards but also including a certificate for eight more cards) were given out at the ballpark and collectors were encouraged to trade to fill in the rest of their set. The cards were originally given away on July 23rd at Oakland Coliseum during a game. Short sets (20 cards plus certificate) were supposedly given out free to the first 35,000 paid admissions at the game.

		MINT	EXC	G-VG
	COMPLETE SET (28)	15.00	7.50	1.50
	COMMON PLAYER (1-28)	.30	.15	.03
☐ 1	Tony LaRussa MG	.50	.25	.05
☐ 2	Mark McGwire	2.50	1.25	.25
☐ 3	Dave Stewart	1.00	.50	.10
☐ 4	Terry Steinbach	.75	.35	.07
☐ 5	Dave Parker	.60	.30	.06
☐ 6	Carney Lansford	.75	.35	.07
☐ 7	Jose Canseco	3.50	1.75	.35
☐ 8	Don Baylor	.50	.25	.05
☐ 9	Bob Welch	.40	.20	.04
☐ 10	Dennis Eckersley	1.00	.50	.10
☐ 11	Walt Weiss	1.00	.50	.10
☐ 12	Tony Phillips	.30	.15	.03
☐ 13	Steve Ontiveros	.30	.15	.03
☐ 14	Dave Henderson	.40	.20	.04
☐ 15	Stan Javier	.30	.15	.03
☐ 16	Ron Hassey	.30	.15	.03
☐ 17	Curt Young	.30	.15	.03
☐ 18	Glenn Hubbard	.30	.15	.03
☐ 19	Storm Davis	.75	.35	.07
☐ 20	Eric Plunk	.40	.20	.04
☐ 21	Matt Young	.30	.15	.03
☐ 22	Mike Gallego	.30	.15	.03
☐ 23	Rick Honeycutt	.30	.15	.03
☐ 24	Doug Jennings	.40	.20	.04
☐ 25	Gene Nelson	.40	.20	.04
☐ 26	Greg Cadaret	.30	.15	.03
☐ 27	Athletics Coaches	.30	.15	.03
☐ 28	Checklist Card	.30	.15	.03

FAMILY FUN: Attend a sports memorabilia show or convention in your area sometime this year. They are both interesting and enjoyable for all members of the family.

1988 Mother's Cookies Astros

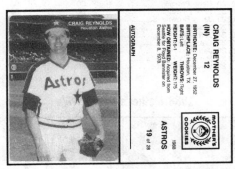

This set consists of 28 full-color, rounded- corner cards each measuring 2 1/2" by 3 1/2". Starter sets (only 20 cards but also including a certificate for eight more cards) were given out at the ballpark and collectors were encouraged to trade to fill in the rest of their set. Cards were originally given out at the Astrodome on August 26th during a game. The sets were supposedly given out free to the first 25,000 paid admissions at the game.

		MINT	EXC	G-VG
COMPLETE SET (28)		10.00	5.00	1.00
COMMON PLAYER (1-28)		.30	.15	.03
☐ 1	Hal Lanier MG	.40	.20	.04
☐ 2	Mike Scott	1.00	.50	.10
☐ 3	Gerald Young	.50	.25	.05
☐ 4	Bill Doran	.50	.25	.05
☐ 5	Bob Knepper	.30	.15	.03
☐ 6	Billy Hatcher	.40	.20	.04
☐ 7	Terry Puhl	.40	.20	.04
☐ 8	Nolan Ryan	2.00	1.00	.20
☐ 9	Kevin Bass	.50	.25	.05
☐ 10	Glenn Davis	1.00	.50	.10
☐ 11	Alan Ashby	.30	.15	.03
☐ 12	Steve Henderson	.30	.15	.03
☐ 13	Denny Walling	.30	.15	.03
☐ 14	Danny Darwin	.30	.15	.03
☐ 15	Mark Bailey	.30	.15	.03
☐ 16	Ernie Camacho	.30	.15	.03
☐ 17	Rafael Ramirez	.30	.15	.03
☐ 18	Jeff Heathcock	.30	.15	.03
☐ 19	Craig Reynolds	.30	.15	.03
☐ 20	Dave Smith	.50	.25	.05
☐ 21	Larry Andersen	.30	.15	.03
☐ 22	Jim Pankovits	.30	.15	.03
☐ 23	Jim Deshaies	.40	.20	.04
☐ 24	Juan Agosto	.30	.15	.03
☐ 25	Chuck Jackson	.30	.15	.03
☐ 26	Joaquin Andujar	.40	.20	.04
☐ 27	Astros' Coaches	.30	.15	.03
☐ 28	Checklist Card	.30	.15	.03

1988 Mother's Cookies Will Clark

This regional set consists of 4 full-color, rounded-corner cards each measuring 2 1/2" by 3 1/2" and showing a different pose of Giants' slugging first baseman Will Clark. Cards were originally found in 18 oz. packages of "Big Bags" of Mother's Cookies at stores in the Northern California area in February and March of 1988. The cards are numbered on the back. Card backs are done in red and purple on white card stock.

		MINT	EXC	G-VG
COMPLETE SET (4)		12.00	6.00	1.20
COMMON PLAYER (1-4)		3.50	1.75	.35
☐ 1	Will Clark	3.50	1.75	.35

		MINT	EXC	G-VG
☐ 2	Will Clark Batting Pose, Waist Up	3.50	1.75	.35
☐ 3	Will Clark Kneeling In On Deck Circle	3.50	1.75	.35
☐ 4	Will Clark Follow Through Swing	3.50	1.75	.35
	Starting Toward First Base			

1988 Mother's Cookies Dodgers

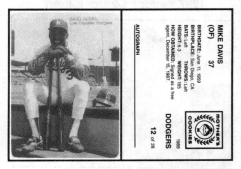

This set consists of 28 full-color, rounded- corner cards each measuring 2 1/2" by 3 1/2". Starter sets (only 20 cards but also including a certificate for eight more cards) were given out at the ballpark and collectors were encouraged to trade to fill in the rest of their set. Cards were originally given out at Dodger Stadium on July 31st. Photos were taken by Barry Colla. The sets were supposedly given out free to the first 25,000 game attendees 14 years of age and under.

		MINT	EXC	G-VG
COMPLETE SET (28)		12.00	6.00	1.20
COMMON PLAYER (1-28)		.30	.15	.03
☐ 1	Tom Lasorda MG	.50	.25	.05
☐ 2	Pedro Guerrero	.75	.35	.07
☐ 3	Steve Sax	.75	.35	.07
☐ 4	Fernando Valenzuela	.75	.35	.07
☐ 5	Mike Marshall	.60	.30	.06
☐ 6	Orel Hershiser	1.50	.75	.15
☐ 7	Alfredo Griffin	.40	.20	.04
☐ 8	Kirk Gibson	1.25	.60	.12
☐ 9	Don Sutton	.75	.35	.07
☐ 10	Mike Scioscia	.40	.20	.04
☐ 11	Franklin Stubbs	.30	.15	.03
☐ 12	Mike Davis	.30	.15	.03
☐ 13	Jesse Orosco	.30	.15	.03
☐ 14	John Shelby	.30	.15	.03
☐ 15	Rick Dempsey	.30	.15	.03
☐ 16	Jay Howell	.50	.25	.05
☐ 17	Dave Anderson	.30	.15	.03
☐ 18	Alejandro Pena	.40	.20	.04

		MINT	EXC	G-VG
☐ 19	Jeff Hamilton	.40	.20	.04
☐ 20	Danny Heep	.30	.15	.03
☐ 21	Tim Leary	.50	.25	.05
☐ 22	Brad Havens	.30	.15	.03
☐ 23	Tim Belcher	.75	.35	.07
☐ 24	Ken Howell	.30	.15	.03
☐ 25	Mickey Hatcher	.30	.15	.03
☐ 26	Brian Holton	.40	.20	.04
☐ 27	Mike Devereaux	.40	.20	.04
☐ 28	Checklist Card	.30	.15	.03

1988 Mother's Cookies Giants

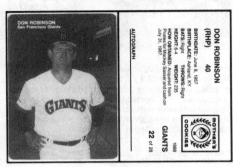

This set consists of 28 full-color, rounded- corner cards each measuring 2 1/2" by 3 1/2". Starter sets (only 20 cards but also including a certificate for eight more cards) were given out at the ballpark and collectors were encouraged to trade to fill in the rest of their set. Cards were originally given out at Candlestick Park on July 30th during a game. Photos were taken by Dennis Desprois. The sets were supposedly given out free to the first 35,000 paid admissions at the game.

		MINT	EXC	G-VG
COMPLETE SET (28)		13.00	6.50	1.30
COMMON PLAYER (1-28)		.30	.15	.03
☐ 1	Roger Craig MG	.50	.25	.05
☐ 2	Will Clark	4.00	2.00	.40
☐ 3	Kevin Mitchell	1.25	.60	.12
☐ 4	Bob Brenly	.30	.15	.03
☐ 5	Mike Aldrete	.30	.15	.03
☐ 6	Mike Krukow	.40	.20	.04
☐ 7	Candy Maldonado	.40	.20	.04
☐ 8	Jeffrey Leonard	.40	.20	.04
☐ 9	Dave Dravecky	.60	.30	.06
☐ 10	Robby Thompson	.40	.20	.04
☐ 11	Scott Garrelts	.50	.25	.05
☐ 12	Bob Melvin	.30	.15	.03
☐ 13	Jose Uribe	.40	.20	.04
☐ 14	Brett Butler	.50	.25	.05
☐ 15	Rick Reuschel	.60	.30	.06
☐ 16	Harry Spilman	.30	.15	.03
☐ 17	Kelly Downs	.40	.20	.04
☐ 18	Chris Speier	.30	.15	.03
☐ 19	Atlee Hammaker	.40	.20	.04
☐ 20	Joel Youngblood	.30	.15	.03
☐ 21	Mike LaCoss	.30	.15	.03
☐ 22	Don Robinson	.30	.15	.03
☐ 23	Mark Wasinger	.40	.20	.04
☐ 24	Craig Lefferts	.40	.20	.04
☐ 25	Phil Garner	.40	.20	.04
☐ 26	Joe Price	.30	.15	.03
☐ 27	Giants' Coaches	.30	.15	.03
☐ 28	Checklist Card	.30	.15	.03

1988 Mother's Cookies Mariners

This set consists of 28 full-color, rounded- corner cards each measuring 2 1/2" by 3 1/2". Starter sets (only 20 cards but also including a certificate for

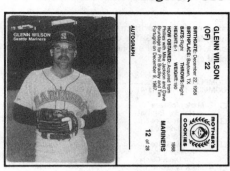

eight more cards) were given out at the ballpark and collectors were encouraged to trade to fill in the rest of their set. Cards were originally given out on August 14th at the Seattle Kingdome. Photos were taken by Barry Colla. The sets were supposedly given out free to the first 20,000 paid admissions at the game.

		MINT	EXC	G-VG
COMPLETE SET (28)		9.00	4.50	.90
COMMON PLAYER (1-28)		.30	.15	.03
☐ 1	Dick Williams MG	.30	.15	.03
☐ 2	Alvin Davis	.75	.35	.07
☐ 3	Mike Moore	.60	.30	.06
☐ 4	Jim Presley	.50	.25	.05
☐ 5	Mark Langston	1.00	.50	.10
☐ 6	Henry Cotto	.30	.15	.03
☐ 7	Ken Phelps	.40	.20	.04
☐ 8	Steve Trout	.30	.15	.03
☐ 9	David Valle	.30	.15	.03
☐ 10	Harold Reynolds	.60	.30	.06
☐ 11	Edwin Nunez	.30	.15	.03
☐ 12	Glenn Wilson	.30	.15	.03
☐ 13	Scott Bankhead	.50	.25	.05
☐ 14	Scott Bradley	.40	.20	.04
☐ 15	Mickey Brantley	.50	.25	.05
☐ 16	Bruce Fields	.30	.15	.03
☐ 17	Mike Kingery	.30	.15	.03
☐ 18	Mike Campbell	.40	.20	.04
☐ 19	Mike Jackson	.40	.20	.04
☐ 20	Rey Quinones	.30	.15	.03
☐ 21	Mario Diaz	.30	.15	.03
☐ 22	Jerry Reed	.30	.15	.03
☐ 23	Rich Renteria	.40	.20	.04
☐ 24	Julio Solano	.30	.15	.03
☐ 25	Bill Swift	.30	.15	.03
☐ 26	Bill Wilkinson	.30	.15	.03
☐ 27	Mariners Coaches	.30	.15	.03
☐ 28	Checklist Card	.30	.15	.03

1988 Mother's Cookies McGwire

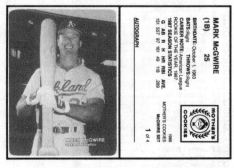

This regional set consists of 4 full-color, rounded-corner cards each measuring 2 1/2" by 3 1/2" and showing a different pose of Athletics' slugging first baseman Mark McGwire. Cards were originally found in 18 oz. packages of "Big Bags" of Mother's Cookies at stores in the Northern California area in February and March of 1988. The cards are numbered on the back. Card backs are done in red and purple on white card stock.

	MINT	EXC	G-VG
COMPLETE SET (4)	12.00	6.00	1.20
COMMON PLAYER (1-4)	4.00	2.00	.40
☐ 1 Mark McGwire .... Holding Big Bat	4.00	2.00	.40
☐ 2 Mark McGwire .... Fielding at First Base	4.00	2.00	.40
☐ 3 Mark McGwire .... Kneeling In On Deck Circle	4.00	2.00	.40
☐ 4 Mark McGwire .... Batting Pose, Waist Up	4.00	2.00	.40

1988 Mother's Cookies Rangers

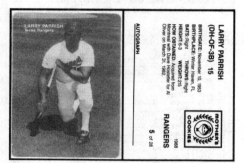

This set consists of 28 full-color, rounded-corner cards each measuring 2 1/2" by 3 1/2". Starter sets (only 20 cards but also including a certificate for eight more cards) were given out at the ballpark and collectors were encouraged to trade to fill in the rest of their set. Cards were originally given out on August 7th. Photos were taken by Barry Colla. The sets were supposedly given out free to the first 25,000 paid admissions at the game.

	MINT	EXC	G-VG
COMPLETE SET (28)	9.00	4.50	.90
COMMON PLAYER (1-28)	.30	.15	.03
☐ 1 Bobby Valentine MG	.50	.25	.05
☐ 2 Pete Incaviglia	.60	.30	.06
☐ 3 Charlie Hough	.50	.25	.05
☐ 4 Oddibe McDowell	.40	.20	.04
☐ 5 Larry Parrish	.30	.15	.03
☐ 6 Scott Fletcher	.30	.15	.03
☐ 7 Steve Buechele	.30	.15	.03
☐ 8 Steve Kemp	.30	.15	.03
☐ 9 Pete O'Brien	.50	.25	.05
☐ 10 Ruben Sierra	1.25	.60	.12
☐ 11 Mike Stanley	.30	.15	.03
☐ 12 Jose Cecena	.30	.15	.03
☐ 13 Cecil Espy	.30	.15	.03
☐ 14 Curtis Wilkerson	.30	.15	.03
☐ 15 Dale Mohorcic	.30	.15	.03
☐ 16 Ray Hayward	.30	.15	.03
☐ 17 Mitch Williams	.50	.25	.05
☐ 18 Bob Brower	.30	.15	.03
☐ 19 Paul Kilgus	.30	.15	.03
☐ 20 Geno Petralli	.30	.15	.03
☐ 21 James Steels	.30	.15	.03
☐ 22 Jerry Browne	.30	.15	.03
☐ 23 Jose Guzman	.40	.20	.04
☐ 24 DeWayne Vaughn	.30	.15	.03
☐ 25 Bobby Witt	.50	.25	.05
☐ 26 Jeff Russell	.50	.25	.05
☐ 27 Rangers Coaches	.30	.15	.03
☐ 28 Checklist Card	.30	.15	.03

1989 Mother's Cookies A's

The 1989 Mother's Cookies Oakland A's set contains 28 standard-size (2 1/2 by 3 1/2 inch) cards with rounded corners. The fronts have borderless color photos, and the horizontally-oriented backs have biographical information. Starter sets containing 20 of these cards were given away at an A's home game during the 1989 season.

	MINT	EXC	G-VG
COMPLETE SET (28)	12.00	6.00	1.20
COMMON PLAYER (1-28)	.30	.15	.03
☐ 1 Tony LaRussa MG	.40	.20	.04
☐ 2 Mark McGwire	1.25	.60	.12
☐ 3 Terry Steinbach	.60	.30	.06
☐ 4 Dave Parker	.60	.30	.06
☐ 5 Carney Lansford	.75	.35	.07
☐ 6 Dave Stewart	.75	.35	.07
☐ 7 Jose Canseco	2.50	1.25	.25
☐ 8 Walt Weiss	.60	.30	.06
☐ 9 Bob Welch	.40	.20	.04
☐ 10 Dennis Eckersley	.75	.35	.07
☐ 11 Tony Phillips	.30	.15	.03
☐ 12 Mike Moore	.60	.30	.06
☐ 13 Dave Henderson	.50	.25	.05
☐ 14 Curt Young	.30	.15	.03
☐ 15 Ron Hassey	.30	.15	.03
☐ 16 Eric Plunk	.30	.15	.03
☐ 17 Luis Polonia	.30	.15	.03
☐ 18 Storm Davis	.50	.25	.05
☐ 19 Glenn Hubbard	.30	.15	.03
☐ 20 Greg Cadaret	.40	.20	.04
☐ 21 Stan Javier	.40	.20	.04
☐ 22 Felix Jose	.40	.20	.04
☐ 23 Mike Gallego	.30	.15	.03
☐ 24 Todd Burns	.40	.20	.04
☐ 25 Rick Honeycutt	.30	.15	.03
☐ 26 Gene Nelson	.30	.15	.03
☐ 27 A's Coaches	.30	.15	.03
☐ 28 Checklist Card	.30	.15	.03

1989 Mothers Cookies A's ROY's

The 1989 Mother's A's ROY's set contains 4 standard-size (2 1/2 by 3 1/2 inch) cards with rounded corners. The fronts have borderless color photos, and the horizontally-oriented backs have biographical information. One card was included in each specially marked box of Mother's Cookies. On the first three cards in the set Rookie of the Year (and year) is mentioned under the player's name.

	MINT	EXC	G-VG
COMPLETE SET (4)	10.00	5.00	1.00
COMMON PLAYER (1-4)	2.50	1.25	.25
☐ 1 Jose Canseco .... 1986 ROY	4.00	2.00	.40
☐ 2 Mark McGwire .... 1987 ROY	3.50	1.75	.35
☐ 3 Walt Weiss .... 1988 ROY	2.50	1.25	.25

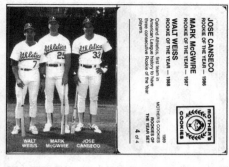

		MINT	EXC	G-VG
☐ 4	Walt Weiss, Mark McGwire, and Jose Canseco	3.00	1.50	.30

1989 Mother's Cookies Astros

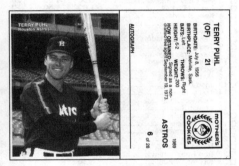

The 1989 Mother's Cookies Houston Astros set contains 28 standard-size (2 1/2 by 3 1/2 inch) cards with rounded corners. The fronts have borderless color photos, and the horizontally-oriented backs have biographical information. Starter sets containing 20 of these cards were given away at an Astros home game during the 1989 season.

		MINT	EXC	G-VG
	COMPLETE SET (28)	9.00	4.50	.90
	COMMON PLAYER (1-28)	.30	.15	.03
☐ 1	Art Howe MG	.30	.15	.03
☐ 2	Mike Scott	1.00	.50	.10
☐ 3	Gerald Young	.40	.20	.04
☐ 4	Bill Doran	.50	.25	.05
☐ 5	Billy Hatcher	.40	.20	.04
☐ 6	Terry Puhl	.40	.20	.04
☐ 7	Bob Knepper	.30	.15	.03
☐ 8	Kevin Bass	.40	.20	.04
☐ 9	Glenn Davis	1.00	.50	.10
☐ 10	Alan Ashby	.30	.15	.03
☐ 11	Bob Forsch	.30	.15	.03
☐ 12	Greg Gross	.30	.15	.03
☐ 13	Danny Darwin	.30	.15	.03
☐ 14	Craig Biggio	1.00	.50	.10
☐ 15	Jim Clancy	.30	.15	.03
☐ 16	Rafael Ramirez	.30	.15	.03
☐ 17	Alex Trevino	.30	.15	.03
☐ 18	Craig Reynolds	.30	.15	.03
☐ 19	Dave Smith	.50	.25	.05
☐ 20	Larry Andersen	.30	.15	.03
☐ 21	Eric Yelding	.40	.20	.04
☐ 22	Jim Deshaies	.40	.20	.04
☐ 23	Juan Agosto	.30	.15	.03
☐ 24	Rick Rhoden	.30	.15	.03
☐ 25	Ken Caminiti	.30	.15	.03
☐ 26	Dave Meads	.30	.15	.03
☐ 27	Astros Coaches	.30	.15	.03
☐ 28	Checklist Card	.30	.15	.03

1989 Mother's Cookies Jose Canseco

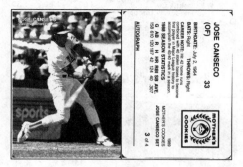

The 1989 Mother's Jose Canseco set contains 4 standard-size (2 1/2 by 3 1/2 inch) cards with rounded corners. The fronts have borderless color photos, and the horizontally-oriented backs have biographical information. One card was included in each specially marked box of Mother's Cookies. Since all four cards picture Jose Canseco, the pose is identified parenthetically in the checklist below in order to distinguish the card fronts.

		MINT	EXC	G-VG
	COMPLETE SET (4)	10.00	5.00	1.00
	COMMON PLAYER (1-4)	3.00	1.50	.30
☐ 1	Jose Canseco (holding ball in hand)	3.00	1.50	.30
☐ 2	Jose Canseco (on one knee with bat)	3.00	1.50	.30
☐ 3	Jose Canseco (swinging at a pitch)	3.00	1.50	.30
☐ 4	Jose Canseco (running toward second)	3.00	1.50	.30

1989 Mother's Cookies Will Clark

The 1989 Mother's Cookies Will Clark set contains 4 standard-size (2 1/2 by 3 1/2 inch) cards with rounded corners. The fronts have borderless color photos, and the horizontally-oriented backs have biographical information. One card was included in each specially marked box of Mother's Cookies. Since all four cards picture Will Clark, the pose is identified parenthetically in the checklist below in order to distinguish the card fronts.

	MINT	EXC	G-VG
COMPLETE SET (4)	10.00	5.00	1.00
COMMON PLAYER (1-4)	3.00	1.50	.30

☐	1	Will Clark	3.00	1.50	.30
		(ball in glove)			
☐	2	Will Clark	3.00	1.50	.30
		(batting stance posed)			
☐	3	Will Clark	3.00	1.50	.30
		(swing follow through)			
☐	4	Will Clark	3.00	1.50	.30
		(starting toward first after hit, still holding bat)			

1989 Mother's Cookies Dodgers

The 1989 Mother's Los Angeles Dodgers set contains 28 standard-size (2 1/2 by 3 1/2 inch) cards with rounded corners. The fronts have borderless color photos, and the horizontally-oriented backs have biographical information. Starter sets containing 20 of these cards were given away at a Dodgers home game during the 1989 season.

			MINT	EXC	G-VG
		COMPLETE SET (28)	9.00	4.50	.90
		COMMON PLAYER (1-28)	.30	.15	.03
☐	1	Tom Lasorda MG	.50	.25	.05
☐	2	Eddie Murray	.75	.35	.07
☐	3	Mike Scioscia	.40	.20	.04
☐	4	Fernando Valenzuela	.75	.35	.07
☐	5	Mike Marshall	.60	.30	.06
☐	6	Orel Hershiser	1.00	.50	.10
☐	7	Alfredo Griffin	.40	.20	.04
☐	8	Kirk Gibson	.75	.35	.07
☐	9	John Tudor	.40	.20	.04
☐	10	Willie Randolph	.40	.20	.04
☐	11	Franklin Stubbs	.30	.15	.03
☐	12	Mike Davis	.30	.15	.03
☐	13	Mike Morgan	.40	.20	.04
☐	14	John Shelby	.30	.15	.03
☐	15	Rick Dempsey	.30	.15	.03
☐	16	Jay Howell	.40	.20	.04
☐	17	Dave Anderson	.30	.15	.03
☐	18	Alejandro Pena	.40	.20	.04
☐	19	Jeff Hamilton	.30	.15	.03
☐	20	Ricky Horton	.30	.15	.03
☐	21	Tim Leary	.50	.25	.05
☐	22	Ray Searage	.30	.15	.03
☐	23	Tim Belcher	.60	.30	.06
☐	24	Tim Crews	.30	.15	.03
☐	25	Mickey Hatcher	.30	.15	.03
☐	26	Mariano Duncan	.30	.15	.03
☐	27	Dodgers Coaches	.30	.15	.03
☐	28	Checklist Card	.30	.15	.03

1989 Mother's Cookies Giants

The 1989 Mother's Cookies San Francisco Giants set contains 28 standard-size (2 1/2 by 3 1/2 inch) cards have borderless color photos, and the horizontally-oriented backs have biographical information.

Starter sets containing 20 of these cards were given away at a Giants home game during the 1989 season.

			MINT	EXC	G-VG
		COMPLETE SET (28)	12.00	6.00	1.20
		COMMON PLAYER (1-28)	.30	.15	.03
☐	1	Roger Craig MG	.50	.25	.05
☐	2	Will Clark	2.50	1.25	.25
☐	3	Kevin Mitchell	1.00	.50	.10
☐	4	Kelly Downs	.40	.20	.04
☐	5	Brett Butler	.40	.20	.04
☐	6	Mike Krukow	.40	.20	.04
☐	7	Candy Maldonado	.40	.20	.04
☐	8	Terry Kennedy	.30	.15	.03
☐	9	Dave Dravecky	.50	.25	.05
☐	10	Robby Thompson	.40	.20	.04
☐	11	Scott Garrelts	.50	.25	.05
☐	12	Matt Williams	1.00	.50	.10
☐	13	Jose Uribe	.30	.15	.03
☐	14	Tracy Jones	.30	.15	.03
☐	15	Rick Reuschel	.50	.25	.05
☐	16	Ernest Riles	.30	.15	.03
☐	17	Jeff Brantley	.40	.20	.04
☐	18	Chris Speier	.30	.15	.03
☐	19	Atlee Hammaker	.30	.15	.03
☐	20	Ed Jurak	.30	.15	.03
☐	21	Mike LaCoss	.30	.15	.03
☐	22	Don Robinson	.30	.15	.03
☐	23	Kirt Manwaring	.30	.15	.03
☐	24	Craig Lefferts	.40	.20	.04
☐	25	Donell Nixon	.30	.15	.03
☐	26	Joe Price	.30	.15	.03
☐	27	Rich Gossage	.50	.25	.05
☐	28	Checklist Card	.30	.15	.03

1989 Mother's Cookies Ken Griffey Jr.

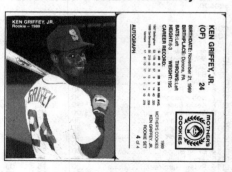

The 1989 Mother's Cookies Ken Griffey Jr. set contains 4 standard-size (2 1/2 by 3 1/2 inch) cards with rounded corners. The fronts have borderless color photos, and the horizontally-oriented backs have biographical information. One card was included in each specially marked box of Mother's Cookies. Since all four cards picture Ken Griffey Jr., the pose is identified parenthetically in the checklist below in order to distinguish the card fronts. Each card back provides a different aspect or background on Ken and his career. The photos were shot by noted sports photographer Barry Colla.

	MINT	EXC	G-VG
COMPLETE SET (4)	12.00	6.00	1.20
COMMON PLAYER (1-4)	4.00	2.00	.40
☐ 1 Ken Griffey Jr. (arms folded)	4.00	2.00	.40
☐ 2 Ken Griffey Jr. (baseball in hand)	4.00	2.00	.40
☐ 3 Ken Griffey Jr. (looking straight ahead with bat)	4.00	2.00	.40
☐ 4 Ken Griffey Jr. (looking over shoulder with bat)	4.00	2.00	.40

1989 Mother's Cookies Mariners

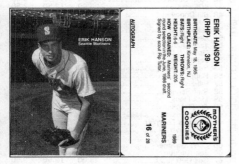

The 1989 Mother's Cookies Seattle Mariners set contains 28 standard-size (2 1/2 by 3 1/2 inch) cards with rounded corners. The fronts have borderless color photos, and the horizontally-oriented backs have biographical information. Starter sets containing 20 of these cards were given away at a Mariners home game during the 1989 season.

	MINT	EXC	G-VG
COMPLETE SET (28)	12.00	6.00	1.20
COMMON PLAYER (1-28)	.30	.15	.03
☐ 1 Jim Lefebvre MG	.30	.15	.03
☐ 2 Alvin Davis	.60	.30	.06
☐ 3 Ken Griffey Jr.	5.00	2.50	.50
☐ 4 Jim Presley	.40	.20	.04
☐ 5 Mark Langston	1.00	.50	.10
☐ 6 Henry Cotto	.30	.15	.03
☐ 7 Mickey Brantley	.40	.20	.04
☐ 8 Jeffrey Leonard	.40	.20	.04
☐ 9 Dave Valle	.30	.15	.03
☐ 10 Harold Reynolds	.50	.25	.05
☐ 11 Edgar Martinez	.30	.15	.03
☐ 12 Tom Niedenfuer	.30	.15	.03
☐ 13 Scott Bankhead	.40	.20	.04
☐ 14 Scott Bradley	.40	.20	.04
☐ 15 Omar Vizquel	.50	.25	.05
☐ 16 Erik Hanson	.40	.20	.04
☐ 17 Bill Swift	.30	.15	.03
☐ 18 Mike Campbell	.30	.15	.03
☐ 19 Mike Jackson	.30	.15	.03
☐ 20 Rich Renteria	.30	.15	.03
☐ 21 Mario Diaz	.30	.15	.03
☐ 22 Jerry Reed	.30	.15	.03
☐ 23 Darnell Coles	.30	.15	.03
☐ 24 Steve Trout	.30	.15	.03
☐ 25 Mike Schooler	.50	.25	.05
☐ 26 Julio Solano	.30	.15	.03
☐ 27 Mariners Coaches	.30	.15	.03
☐ 28 Checklist Card	.30	.15	.03

1989 Mother's Cookies Mark McGwire

The 1989 Mother's Cookies Mark McGwire set contains 4 standard-size (2 1/2 by 3 1/2 inch) cards with rounded corners. The fronts have borderless color photos, and the horizontally-oriented backs have biographical information. One card was included in each specially marked box of Mother's Cookies. Since all four cards picture Mark McGwire, the pose is identified parenthetically in the checklist below in order to distinguish the card fronts.

	MINT	EXC	G-VG
COMPLETE SET (4)	10.00	5.00	1.00
COMMON PLAYER (1-4)	3.00	1.50	.30
☐ 1 Mark McGwire (bat on shoulder)	3.00	1.50	.30
☐ 2 Mark McGwire (batting stance)	3.00	1.50	.30
☐ 3 Mark McGwire (holding bat in front)	3.00	1.50	.30
☐ 4 Mark McGwire (batting follow through)	3.00	1.50	.30

1989 Mother's Cookies Rangers

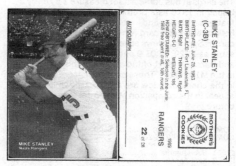

The 1989 Mother's Cookies Texas Rangers set contains 28 standard-size (2 1/2 by 3 1/2 inch) cards with rounded corners. The fronts have borderless color photos, and the horizontally-oriented backs have biographical information. Starter sets containing 20 of these cards were given away at a Rangers home game during the 1989 season.

	MINT	EXC	G-VG
COMPLETE SET (28)	9.00	4.50	.90
COMMON PLAYER (1-28)	.30	.15	.03
☐ 1 Bobby Valentine MG	.40	.20	.04
☐ 2 Nolan Ryan	2.00	1.00	.20
☐ 3 Julio Franco	.75	.35	.07

☐ 4	Charlie Hough	.50	.25	.05
☐ 5	Rafael Palmeiro	.75	.35	.07
☐ 6	Jeff Russell	.50	.25	.05
☐ 7	Ruben Sierra	1.50	.75	.15
☐ 8	Steve Buechele	.30	.15	.03
☐ 9	Buddy Bell	.40	.20	.04
☐ 10	Pete Incaviglia	.50	.25	.05
☐ 11	Geno Petralli	.30	.15	.03
☐ 12	Cecil Espy	.30	.15	.03
☐ 13	Scott Fletcher	.30	.15	.03
☐ 14	Bobby Witt	.40	.20	.04
☐ 15	Brad Arnsberg	.30	.15	.03
☐ 16	Rick Leach	.30	.15	.03
☐ 17	Jamie Moyer	.30	.15	.03
☐ 18	Kevin Brown	.50	.25	.05
☐ 19	Jeff Kunkel	.30	.15	.03
☐ 20	Craig McMurtry	.30	.15	.03
☐ 21	Kenny Rogers	.40	.20	.04
☐ 22	Mike Stanley	.30	.15	.03
☐ 23	Cecilio Guante	.30	.15	.03
☐ 24	Jim Sundberg	.30	.15	.03
☐ 25	Jose Guzman	.30	.15	.03
☐ 26	Jeff Stone	.30	.15	.03
☐ 27	Rangers Coaches	.30	.15	.03
☐ 28	Checklist Card	.30	.15	.03

1916 M101-4 Sporting News

The cards in this 200-card set measure 1 5/8" by 3". Issued in 1916 as a premium offer, the M101-4 set features black and white photos of current ballplayers. Each card is numbered and the reverse carries Sporting News advertising. The fronts are the same as D329, H801-9 and the unclassified Famous and Barr set. Most of the players in this also appear in the M101-5 set. Those cards which are asterisked in the checklist below are those cards which do not appear in the companion M101-5 set issued the year before.

		EX-MT	VG-E	GOOD
COMPLETE SET (200)		11000.00	5500.00	1250.00
COMMON PLAYER (1-200)		25.00	12.50	2.50

☐ 1	Babe Adams	25.00	12.50	2.50
☐ 2	Sam Agnew	25.00	12.50	2.50
☐ 3	Eddie Ainsmith	25.00	12.50	2.50
☐ 4	Grover Alexander	75.00	37.50	7.50
☐ 5	Leon Ames	25.00	12.50	2.50
☐ 6	Jimmy Archer	25.00	12.50	2.50
☐ 7	Jimmy Austin	25.00	12.50	2.50
☐ 8	H.D. Baird *	35.00	17.50	3.50
☐ 9	Frank Baker	60.00	30.00	6.00
☐ 10	Dave Bancroft	50.00	25.00	5.00
☐ 11	Jack Barry	25.00	12.50	2.50
☐ 12	Zinn Beck	25.00	12.50	2.50
☐ 13	Chief Bender *	60.00	30.00	6.00
☐ 14	Joe Benz	25.00	12.50	2.50
☐ 15	Bob Bescher	25.00	12.50	2.50
☐ 16	Al Betzel	25.00	12.50	2.50
☐ 17	Mordecai Brown	50.00	25.00	5.00
☐ 18	Eddie Burns	25.00	12.50	2.50
☐ 19	George Burns *	35.00	17.50	3.50
☐ 20	George J. Burns	25.00	12.50	2.50
☐ 21	Joe Bush	25.00	12.50	2.50
☐ 22	Donie Bush *	35.00	17.50	3.50

☐ 23	Art Butler	25.00	12.50	2.50
☐ 24	Bobbie Byrne	25.00	12.50	2.50
☐ 25	Forrest Cady *	35.00	17.50	3.50
☐ 26	Jim Callahan	25.00	12.50	2.50
☐ 27	Ray Caldwell	25.00	12.50	2.50
☐ 28	Max Carey	50.00	25.00	5.00
☐ 29	George Chalmers	25.00	12.50	2.50
☐ 30	Ray Chapman	35.00	17.50	3.50
☐ 31	Larry Cheney	25.00	12.50	2.50
☐ 32	Ed Cicotte	35.00	17.50	3.50
☐ 33	Tommy Clarke	25.00	12.50	2.50
☐ 34	Eddie Collins	60.00	30.00	6.00
☐ 35	Shano Collins	25.00	12.50	2.50
☐ 36	Charles Comiskey	50.00	25.00	5.00
☐ 37	Joe Connolly	25.00	12.50	2.50
☐ 38	Ty Cobb *	1200.00	600.00	125.00
☐ 39	Harry Coveleskie	25.00	12.50	2.50
☐ 40	Gabby Cravath	35.00	17.50	3.50
☐ 41	Sam Crawford	50.00	25.00	5.00
☐ 42	Jean Dale	25.00	12.50	2.50
☐ 43	Jake Daubert	35.00	17.50	3.50
☐ 44	Charles Deal	25.00	12.50	2.50
☐ 45	Frank Demaree	25.00	12.50	2.50
☐ 46	Josh Devore *	35.00	17.50	3.50
☐ 47	William Doak	25.00	12.50	2.50
☐ 48	Bill Donovan	25.00	12.50	2.50
☐ 49	Red Dooin	25.00	12.50	2.50
☐ 50	Mike Doolan	25.00	12.50	2.50
☐ 51	Larry Doyle	25.00	12.50	2.50
☐ 52	Jean Dubuc	25.00	12.50	2.50
☐ 53	Oscar J. Dugey	25.00	12.50	2.50
☐ 54	John Evers	50.00	25.00	5.00
☐ 55	Red Faber	50.00	25.00	5.00
☐ 56	Happy Felsch	35.00	17.50	3.50
☐ 57	Bill Fischer	25.00	12.50	2.50
☐ 58	Ray Fisher	25.00	12.50	2.50
☐ 59	Max Flack	25.00	12.50	2.50
☐ 60	Art Fletcher	25.00	12.50	2.50
☐ 61	Eddie Foster	25.00	12.50	2.50
☐ 62	Jacques Fournier	25.00	12.50	2.50
☐ 63	Del Gainer	25.00	12.50	2.50
☐ 64	Chick Gandil *	50.00	25.00	5.00
☐ 65	Larry Gardner	25.00	12.50	2.50
☐ 66	Joe Gedeon	25.00	12.50	2.50
☐ 67	Gus Getz	25.00	12.50	2.50
☐ 68	George Gibson	25.00	12.50	2.50
☐ 69	Wilbur Good	25.00	12.50	2.50
☐ 70	Hank Gowdy	25.00	12.50	2.50
☐ 71	Jack Graney	25.00	12.50	2.50
☐ 72	Clark Griffith *	75.00	37.50	7.50
☐ 73	Tommy Griffith	25.00	12.50	2.50
☐ 74	Heine Groh	35.00	17.50	3.50
☐ 75	Earl Hamilton	25.00	12.50	2.50
☐ 76	Bob Harmon	25.00	12.50	2.50
☐ 77	Roy Hartzell	25.00	12.50	2.50
☐ 78	Claude Hendrix	25.00	12.50	2.50
☐ 79	Olaf Henriksen	25.00	12.50	2.50
☐ 80	John Henry	25.00	12.50	2.50
☐ 81	Buck Herzog	25.00	12.50	2.50
☐ 82	Hugh High	25.00	12.50	2.50
☐ 83	Dick Hoblitzell	25.00	12.50	2.50
☐ 84	Harry Hooper	50.00	25.00	5.00
☐ 85	Ivan Howard	25.00	12.50	2.50
☐ 86	Miller Huggins	50.00	25.00	5.00
☐ 87	Joe Jackson	1200.00	600.00	125.00
☐ 88	William James	25.00	12.50	2.50
☐ 89	Harold Janvrin	25.00	12.50	2.50
☐ 90	Hughie Jennings	50.00	25.00	5.00
☐ 91	Walter Johnson	400.00	200.00	40.00
☐ 92	Fielder Jones	25.00	12.50	2.50
☐ 93	Joe Judge *	35.00	17.50	3.50
☐ 94	Benny Kauff	25.00	12.50	2.50
☐ 95	Bill Killifer	25.00	12.50	2.50
☐ 96	Ed Konetchy	25.00	12.50	2.50
☐ 97	Nap Lajoie	200.00	100.00	20.00
☐ 98	Jack Lapp	25.00	12.50	2.50
☐ 99	John Lavan	25.00	12.50	2.50
☐ 100	Jimmy Lavender	25.00	12.50	2.50
☐ 101	Nemo Leibold	25.00	12.50	2.50
☐ 102	Hub Leonard	25.00	12.50	2.50
☐ 103	Duffy Lewis	25.00	12.50	2.50
☐ 104	Hans Lobert	25.00	12.50	2.50
☐ 105	Tom Long	25.00	12.50	2.50
☐ 106	Fred Luderus	25.00	12.50	2.50
☐ 107	Connie Mack	125.00	60.00	12.50
☐ 108	Lee Magee	25.00	12.50	2.50
☐ 109	Sherry Magee *	35.00	17.50	3.50
☐ 110	Al Mamaux	25.00	12.50	2.50
☐ 111	Leslie Mann	25.00	12.50	2.50
☐ 112	Rabbit Maranville	50.00	25.00	5.00
☐ 113	Rube Marquard	50.00	25.00	5.00
☐ 114	J.E. Mayer	25.00	12.50	2.50
☐ 115	George McBride	25.00	12.50	2.50
☐ 116	John McGraw	75.00	37.50	7.50
☐ 117	Jack McInnis	35.00	17.50	3.50

☐ 118	Fred Merkle	35.00	17.50	3.50
☐ 119	Chief Meyers	25.00	12.50	2.50
☐ 120	Clyde Milan *	25.00	12.50	2.50
☐ 121	John Miller *	35.00	17.50	3.50
☐ 122	Otto Miller	25.00	12.50	2.50
☐ 123	Willie Mitchell	25.00	12.50	2.50
☐ 124	Fred Mollwitz	25.00	12.50	2.50
☐ 125	Pat Moran	25.00	12.50	2.50
☐ 126	Ray Morgan	25.00	12.50	2.50
☐ 127	George Moriarty	25.00	12.50	2.50
☐ 128	Guy Morton	25.00	12.50	2.50
☐ 129	Mike Mowrey *	35.00	17.50	3.50
☐ 130	Eddie Murphy	25.00	12.50	2.50
☐ 131	Hy Myers	25.00	12.50	2.50
☐ 132	Bert Niehoff	25.00	12.50	2.50
☐ 133	Rube Oldring	25.00	12.50	2.50
☐ 134	Oliver O'Mara	25.00	12.50	2.50
☐ 135	Steve O'Neill	25.00	12.50	2.50
☐ 136	Dode Paskert	25.00	12.50	2.50
☐ 137	Roger Peckinpaugh	25.00	12.50	2.50
☐ 138	Walter Pipp	35.00	17.50	3.50
☐ 139	Del Pratt	25.00	12.50	2.50
☐ 140	Pat Ragan *	35.00	17.50	3.50
☐ 141	Bill Rariden	25.00	12.50	2.50
☐ 142	Eppa Rixey	50.00	25.00	5.00
☐ 143	Davey Robertson	25.00	12.50	2.50
☐ 144	Wilbert Robinson	75.00	37.50	7.50
☐ 145	Bob Roth	20.00	10.00	2.00
☐ 146	Eddie Roush	60.00	30.00	6.00
☐ 147	Clarence Rowland	25.00	12.50	2.50
☐ 148	Nap Rucker	25.00	12.50	2.50
☐ 149	Dick Rudolph	25.00	12.50	2.50
☐ 150	Reb Russell	25.00	12.50	2.50
☐ 151	Babe Ruth	2250.00	1100.00	250.00
☐ 152	Vic Saier	25.00	12.50	2.50
☐ 153	Slim Sallee	25.00	12.50	2.50
☐ 154	Ray Schalk	50.00	25.00	5.00
☐ 155	Wally Schang	25.00	12.50	2.50
☐ 156	Frank Schulte	25.00	12.50	2.50
☐ 157	Everett Scott	35.00	17.50	3.50
☐ 158	Jim Scott	25.00	12.50	2.50
☐ 159	Tom Seaton	25.00	12.50	2.50
☐ 160	Howard Shanks	25.00	12.50	2.50
☐ 161	Bob Shawkey	35.00	17.50	3.50
☐ 162	Ernie Shore	35.00	17.50	3.50
☐ 163	Bert Shotton	25.00	12.50	2.50
☐ 164	George Sisler	75.00	37.50	7.50
☐ 165	J.C. Smith	25.00	12.50	2.50
☐ 166	Fred Snodgrass	25.00	12.50	2.50
☐ 167	George Stallings	25.00	12.50	2.50
☐ 168	Oscar Stanage	25.00	12.50	2.50
☐ 169	Charles Stengel	400.00	200.00	40.00
☐ 170	Milton Stock	25.00	12.50	2.50
☐ 171	Amos Strunk	25.00	12.50	2.50
☐ 172	Billy Sullivan	35.00	17.50	3.50
☐ 173	Jeff Tesreau	25.00	12.50	2.50
☐ 174	Joe Tinker	50.00	25.00	5.00
☐ 175	Fred Toney	25.00	12.50	2.50
☐ 176	Terry Turner	25.00	12.50	2.50
☐ 177	George Tyler *	35.00	17.50	3.50
☐ 178	Jim Vaughn	25.00	12.50	2.50
☐ 179	Bobby Veach	25.00	12.50	2.50
☐ 180	James Viox	25.00	12.50	2.50
☐ 181	Oscar Vitt	25.00	12.50	2.50
☐ 182	Honus Wagner	400.00	200.00	40.00
☐ 183	Clarence Walker	25.00	12.50	2.50
☐ 184	Ed Walsh	50.00	25.00	5.00
☐ 185	Bill Wambsganss *	35.00	17.50	3.50
☐ 186	Buck Weaver	35.00	17.50	3.50
☐ 187	Carl Weilman	25.00	12.50	2.50
☐ 188	Zack Wheat	50.00	25.00	5.00
☐ 189	George Whitted	25.00	12.50	2.50
☐ 190	Fred Williams	25.00	12.50	2.50
☐ 191	Arthur Wilson	25.00	12.50	2.50
☐ 192	J.O. Wilson	25.00	12.50	2.50
☐ 193	Ivy Wingo	25.00	12.50	2.50
☐ 194	Meldon Wolfgang	25.00	12.50	2.50
☐ 195	Joe Wood	50.00	25.00	5.00
☐ 196	Steve Yerkes	25.00	12.50	2.50
☐ 197	Pep Young * (Detroit Tigers)	35.00	17.50	3.50
☐ 198	Rollie Zeider	25.00	12.50	2.50
☐ 199	Heine Zimmerman	25.00	12.50	2.50
☐ 200	Dutch Zwilling	25.00	12.50	2.50

1915 M101-5 Sporting News

"MEL" WOLFGANG
P.—Chicago White Sox
155

The cards in this 200-card set measure 1 5/8 by 3". The 1915 M101-5 series of black and white, numbered baseball cards is very similar in style to M101-4. The set was offered as a marketing promotion by C.C. Spink and Son, publishers of The Sporting News ("The Baseball Paper of the World"). Most of the players in this also appear in the M101-4 set. Those cards which are asterisked in the checklist below are those cards which do not appear in the companion M101-4 set issued the next year.

			EX-MT	VG-E	GOOD
COMPLETE SET (200)			12500.00	6000.00	1600.00
COMMON PLAYER (1-200)			25.00	12.50	2.50
☐	1	Babe Adams	25.00	12.50	2.50
☐	2	Sam Agnew	25.00	12.50	2.50
☐	3	Ed Ainsmith	25.00	12.50	2.50
☐	4	Grover Alexander	75.00	37.50	7.50
☐	5	Leon Ames	25.00	12.50	2.50
☐	6	Jimmy Archer	25.00	12.50	2.50
☐	7	Jimmy Austin	25.00	12.50	2.50
☐	8	Frank Baker	60.00	30.00	6.00
☐	9	Dave Bancroft	50.00	25.00	5.00
☐	10	Jack Barry	25.00	12.50	2.50
☐	11	Zinn Beck	25.00	12.50	2.50
☐	12	Luke Boone *	35.00	17.50	3.50
☐	13	Joe Benz	25.00	12.50	2.50
☐	14	Bob Bescher	25.00	12.50	2.50
☐	15	Al Betzel	25.00	12.50	2.50
☐	16	Roger Bresnahan *	60.00	30.00	6.00
☐	17	Eddie Burns	25.00	12.50	2.50
☐	18	G.J. Burns	25.00	12.50	2.50
☐	19	Joe Bush	25.00	12.50	2.50
☐	20	Owen Bush *	35.00	17.50	3.50
☐	21	Art Butler	25.00	12.50	2.50
☐	22	Bobby Byrne	25.00	12.50	2.50
☐	23	Mordecai Brown	50.00	25.00	5.00
☐	24	Jimmy Callahan	25.00	12.50	2.50
☐	25	Ray Caldwell	25.00	12.50	2.50
☐	26	Max Carey	50.00	25.00	5.00
☐	27	George Chalmers	25.00	12.50	2.50
☐	28	Frank Chance *	75.00	37.50	7.50
☐	29	Ray Chapman	35.00	17.50	3.50
☐	30	Larry Cheney	25.00	12.50	2.50
☐	31	Ed Cicotte	35.00	17.50	3.50
☐	32	Tommy Clarke	25.00	12.50	2.50
☐	33	Eddie Collins	60.00	30.00	6.00
☐	34	Shano Collins	25.00	12.50	2.50
☐	35	Charles Comiskey	50.00	25.00	5.00
☐	36	Joe Connolly	25.00	12.50	2.50
☐	37	L. Cook *	35.00	17.50	3.50
☐	38	Jack Coombs *	50.00	25.00	5.00
☐	39	Dan Costello *	35.00	17.50	3.50
☐	40	Harry Coveleskie	25.00	12.50	2.50
☐	41	Gavvy Cravath	35.00	17.50	3.50
☐	42	Sam Crawford	50.00	25.00	5.00
☐	43	Jean Dale	25.00	12.50	2.50
☐	44	Jake Daubert	35.00	17.50	3.50
☐	45	G.A. Davis Jr. *	35.00	17.50	3.50
☐	46	Charles Deal	25.00	12.50	2.50
☐	47	Frank Demaree	25.00	12.50	2.50
☐	48	Bill Doak	25.00	12.50	2.50
☐	49	Bill Donovan	25.00	12.50	2.50
☐	50	Red Dooin	25.00	12.50	2.50
☐	51	Mike Doolan	25.00	12.50	2.50

□ 52	Larry Doyle	25.00	12.50	2.50
□ 53	Jean Dubuc	25.00	12.50	2.50
□ 54	Oscar Dugey	25.00	12.50	2.50
□ 55	John Evers	50.00	25.00	5.00
□ 56	Red Faber	50.00	25.00	5.00
□ 57	Happy Felsch	35.00	17.50	3.50
□ 58	Bill Fischer	25.00	12.50	2.50
□ 59	Ray Fisher	25.00	12.50	2.50
□ 60	Max Flack	25.00	12.50	2.50
□ 61	Art Fletcher	25.00	12.50	2.50
□ 62	Eddie Foster	25.00	12.50	2.50
□ 63	Jacques Fournier	25.00	12.50	2.50
□ 64	Del Gainer	25.00	12.50	2.50
□ 65	Larry Gardner	25.00	12.50	2.50
□ 66	Joe Gedeon	25.00	12.50	2.50
□ 67	Gus Getz	25.00	12.50	2.50
□ 68	George Gibson	25.00	12.50	2.50
□ 69	Wilbur Good	25.00	12.50	2.50
□ 70	Hank Gowdy	25.00	12.50	2.50
□ 71	Jack Graney	25.00	12.50	2.50
□ 72	Tommy Griffith	25.00	12.50	2.50
□ 73	Heine Groh	35.00	17.50	3.50
□ 74	Earl Hamilton	25.00	12.50	2.50
□ 75	Bob Harmon	25.00	12.50	2.50
□ 76	Roy Hartzell	25.00	12.50	2.50
□ 77	Claude Hendrix	25.00	12.50	2.50
□ 78	Olaf Henriksen	25.00	12.50	2.50
□ 79	John Henry	25.00	12.50	2.50
□ 80	Buck Herzog	25.00	12.50	2.50
□ 81	Hugh High	25.00	12.50	2.50
□ 82	Dick Hoblitzell	25.00	12.50	2.50
□ 83	Harry Hooper	50.00	25.00	5.00
□ 84	Ivan Howard	25.00	12.50	2.50
□ 85	Miller Huggins	50.00	25.00	5.00
□ 86	Joe Jackson	1200.00	600.00	125.00
□ 87	William James	25.00	12.50	2.50
□ 88	Harold Janvrin	25.00	12.50	2.50
□ 89	Hughie Jennings	50.00	25.00	5.00
□ 90	Walter Johnson	400.00	200.00	40.00
□ 91	Fielder Jones	25.00	12.50	2.50
□ 92	Benny Kauff	25.00	12.50	2.50
□ 93	Bill Killefer	25.00	12.50	2.50
□ 94	Ed Konetchy	25.00	12.50	2.50
□ 95	Napoleon Lajoie	200.00	100.00	20.00
□ 96	Jack Lapp	25.00	12.50	2.50
□ 97	John Lavan	25.00	12.50	2.50
□ 98	Jimmy Lavender	25.00	12.50	2.50
□ 99	Nemo Leibold	25.00	12.50	2.50
□ 100	Hub Leonard	25.00	12.50	2.50
□ 101	Duffy Lewis	25.00	12.50	2.50
□ 102	Hans Lobert	25.00	12.50	2.50
□ 103	Tom Long	25.00	12.50	2.50
□ 104	Fred Luderus	25.00	12.50	2.50
□ 105	Connie Mack	125.00	60.00	12.50
□ 106	Lee Magee	25.00	12.50	2.50
□ 107	Al Mamaux	25.00	12.50	2.50
□ 108	Leslie Mann	25.00	12.50	2.50
□ 109	Rabbit Maranville	50.00	25.00	5.00
□ 110	Rube Marquard	50.00	25.00	5.00
□ 111	Armando Marsans *	35.00	17.50	3.50
□ 112	J.E. Mayer	25.00	12.50	2.50
□ 113	George McBride	25.00	12.50	2.50
□ 114	John McGraw	75.00	37.50	7.50
□ 115	Jack McInnis	35.00	17.50	3.50
□ 116	Fred Merkle	35.00	17.50	3.50
□ 117	Chief Meyers	25.00	12.50	2.50
□ 118	Clyde Milan	25.00	12.50	2.50
□ 119	Otto Miller	25.00	12.50	2.50
□ 120	Willie Mitchell	25.00	12.50	2.50
□ 121	Fred Mollwitz	25.00	12.50	2.50
□ 122	J.H. Moran *	35.00	17.50	3.50
□ 123	Pat Moran	25.00	12.50	2.50
□ 124	Ray Morgan	25.00	12.50	2.50
□ 125	George Moriarty	25.00	12.50	2.50
□ 126	Guy Morton	25.00	12.50	2.50
□ 127	Eddie Murphy	25.00	12.50	2.50
□ 128	Jack Murray *	35.00	17.50	3.50
□ 129	Hy Myers	25.00	12.50	2.50
□ 130	Bert Niehoff	25.00	12.50	2.50
□ 131	Les Nunamaker *	35.00	17.50	3.50
□ 132	Rube Oldring	25.00	12.50	2.50
□ 133	Oliver O'Mara	25.00	12.50	2.50
□ 134	Steve O'Neill	25.00	12.50	2.50
□ 135	Dode Paskert	25.00	12.50	2.50
□ 136	Roger Peckinpaugh	25.00	12.50	2.50
□ 137	E.J. Pfeffer *	35.00	17.50	3.50
□ 138	George Pierce *	35.00	17.50	3.50
□ 139	Walter Pipp	35.00	17.50	3.50
□ 140	Del Pratt	25.00	12.50	2.50
□ 141	Bill Rariden	25.00	12.50	2.50
□ 142	Eppa Rixey	50.00	25.00	5.00
□ 143	Davey Robertson	25.00	12.50	2.50
□ 144	Wilbert Robinson	75.00	37.50	7.50
□ 145	Bob Roth	25.00	12.50	2.50
□ 146	Eddie Roush	60.00	30.00	6.00

□ 147	Clarence Rowland	25.00	12.50	2.50
□ 148	Nap Rucker	25.00	12.50	2.50
□ 149	Dick Rudolph	25.00	12.50	2.50
□ 150	Reb Russell	25.00	12.50	2.50
□ 151	Babe Ruth	3000.00	1500.00	300.00
□ 152	Vic Saier	25.00	12.50	2.50
□ 153	Slim Sallee	25.00	12.50	2.50
□ 154	Germany Schaefer *	35.00	17.50	3.50
□ 155	Ray Schalk	50.00	25.00	5.00
□ 156	Wally Schang	25.00	12.50	2.50
□ 157	Chas. Schmidt *	35.00	17.50	3.50
□ 158	Frank Schulte	25.00	12.50	2.50
□ 159	Jim Scott	25.00	12.50	2.50
□ 160	Everett Scott	35.00	17.50	3.50
□ 161	Tom Seaton	25.00	12.50	2.50
□ 162	Howard Shanks	25.00	12.50	2.50
□ 163	Bob Shawkey	35.00	17.50	3.50
□ 164	Ernie Shore	35.00	17.50	3.50
□ 165	Bert Shotton	25.00	12.50	2.50
□ 166	George Sisler	75.00	37.50	7.50
□ 167	J.C. Smith	25.00	12.50	2.50
□ 168	Fred Snodgrass	25.00	12.50	2.50
□ 169	George Stallings	25.00	12.50	2.50
□ 170	Oscar Stanage	25.00	12.50	2.50
□ 171	Charles Stengel	400.00	200.00	40.00
□ 172	Milton Stock	25.00	12.50	2.50
□ 173	Amos Strunk	25.00	12.50	2.50
□ 174	Billy Sullivan	35.00	17.50	3.50
□ 175	Jeff Tesreau	25.00	12.50	2.50
□ 176	Jim Thorpe *	1500.00	750.00	150.00
□ 177	Joe Tinker	50.00	25.00	5.00
□ 178	Fred Toney	25.00	12.50	2.50
□ 179	Terry Turner	25.00	12.50	2.50
□ 180	Jim Vaughn	25.00	12.50	2.50
□ 181	Bobby Veach	25.00	12.50	2.50
□ 182	James Viox	25.00	12.50	2.50
□ 183	Oscar Vitt	25.00	12.50	2.50
□ 184	Honus Wagner	400.00	200.00	40.00
□ 185	Clarence Walker	25.00	12.50	2.50
□ 186	Zack Wheat	50.00	25.00	5.00
□ 187	Ed Walsh	50.00	25.00	5.00
□ 188	Buck Weaver	35.00	17.50	3.50
□ 189	Carl Weilman	25.00	12.50	2.50
□ 190	George Whitted	25.00	12.50	2.50
□ 191	Fred Williams	25.00	12.50	2.50
□ 192	Arthur Wilson	25.00	12.50	2.50
□ 193	J.O. Wilson	25.00	12.50	2.50
□ 194	Ivy Wingo	25.00	12.50	2.50
□ 195	Meldon Wolfgang	25.00	12.50	2.50
□ 196	Joe Wood	50.00	25.00	5.00
□ 197	Steve Yerkes	25.00	12.50	2.50
□ 198	Rollie Zeider	25.00	12.50	2.50
□ 199	Heinie Zimmerman	25.00	12.50	2.50
□ 200	Dutch Zwilling	25.00	12.50	2.50

1911 M116 Sporting Life

The cards in this 288-card set measure 1 1/2" by 2 5/8". The Sporting Life set was offered as a premium to the publication's subscribers in 1911. Each of the 24 series of 12 cards came in an envelope printed with a list of the players within. Cards marked with an asterisk are also found with a special blue background and are worth double the listed price. McConnell appears with both Boston AL (common) and Chicago White Sox (scarce); McQuillan appears with Phillies (common) and Cincinnati (scarce). Cards are numbered in the checklist below alphabetically within team. Teams are ordered alphabetically within league: Boston AL (1-19), Chicago AL (20-36), Cleveland (37-52), Detroit (53-73), New york AL (74-84), Philadelphia AL (85-105), St. Louis AL (106-120), Washington (121-134), Boston NL (135-147), Brooklyn (148-164), Chicago NL (165-185), Cincinnati (186-203), New york NL (204-223), Philadelphia NL (224-242), Pittsburgh (243-261), and St. Louis (262-279). Cards 280-288 feature minor leaguers and are somewhat more difficult to find since most are from the tougher higher series

		EX-MT	VG-E	GOOD
	COMPLETE SET (290)	17000.00	8500.00	2000.00
	COMMON MAJOR (1-279)	30.00	15.00	3.00
	COMMON MINOR (280-288)	45.00	22.50	4.50
☐ 1	Frank Arellanes	30.00	15.00	3.00
☐ 2	Bill Carrigan	30.00	15.00	3.00
☐ 3	Ed Cicotte	50.00	25.00	5.00
☐ 4	Ray Collins S24	60.00	30.00	6.00
☐ 5	Pat Donahue	30.00	15.00	3.00
☐ 6	Donovan S21	60.00	30.00	6.00
☐ 7	Arthur Engle	30.00	15.00	3.00
☐ 8	Larry Gardner S24	60.00	30.00	6.00
☐ 9	Charles Hall	30.00	15.00	3.00
☐ 10	Harry Hooper S23	150.00	75.00	15.00
☐ 11	Edwin Karger	30.00	15.00	3.00
☐ 12	Harry Lord *	30.00	15.00	3.00
☐ 13	Thomas Madden S24	60.00	30.00	6.00
☐ 14A	Amby McConnell (Boston AL)	30.00	15.00	3.00
☐ 14B	Amby McConnell (Chicago AL)	1500.00	750.00	150.00
☐ 15	Tris Speaker S23	350.00	175.00	35.00
☐ 16	Jake Stahl	40.00	20.00	4.00
☐ 17	John Thoney	30.00	15.00	3.00
☐ 18	Heine Wagner	30.00	15.00	3.00
☐ 19	Joe Wood S23	100.00	50.00	10.00
☐ 20	Blackburn	30.00	15.00	3.00
☐ 21	James J. Block S21	60.00	30.00	6.00
☐ 22	Dougherty	30.00	15.00	3.00
☐ 23	Hugh Duffy	100.00	50.00	10.00
☐ 24	Ed Hahn	30.00	15.00	3.00
☐ 25	Paul Meloan S24	60.00	30.00	6.00
☐ 26	Fred Parent	30.00	15.00	3.00
☐ 27	Frederick Payne S21	60.00	30.00	6.00
☐ 28	William Purtell	30.00	15.00	3.00
☐ 29	James Scott S23	60.00	30.00	6.00
☐ 30	F. Smith	30.00	15.00	3.00
☐ 31	Sullivan	30.00	15.00	3.00
☐ 32	Tannehill	30.00	15.00	3.00
☐ 33	Ed Walsh	75.00	37.50	7.50
☐ 34	Guy (Doc) White	30.00	15.00	3.00
☐ 35	I. Young	30.00	15.00	3.00
☐ 36	Dutch Zwilling S24	60.00	30.00	6.00
☐ 37	Harry Bemis	30.00	15.00	3.00
☐ 38	Charles Berger	30.00	15.00	3.00
☐ 39	Joseph Birmingham	30.00	15.00	3.00
☐ 40	Hugh Bradley	30.00	15.00	3.00
☐ 41	Clarke	30.00	15.00	3.00
☐ 42	Falkenberg	30.00	15.00	3.00
☐ 43	Elmer Flick	100.00	50.00	10.00
☐ 44	Addie Joss	100.00	50.00	10.00
☐ 45	Napoleon Lajoie *	175.00	85.00	18.00
☐ 46	Frederick Linke S20	60.00	30.00	6.00
☐ 47	B. Lord	30.00	15.00	3.00
☐ 48	McGuire	30.00	15.00	3.00
☐ 49	Niles	30.00	15.00	3.00
☐ 50	Stovall	30.00	15.00	3.00
☐ 51	Turner	30.00	15.00	3.00
☐ 52	Cy Young	175.00	85.00	18.00
☐ 53	Beckendorf	30.00	15.00	3.00
☐ 54	Bush	30.00	15.00	3.00
☐ 55	Ty Cobb *	1200.00	600.00	125.00
☐ 56	Sam Crawford *	100.00	50.00	10.00
☐ 57	Jas. Delehanty	40.00	20.00	4.00
☐ 58	W. Donovan	30.00	15.00	3.00
☐ 59	Hugh Jennings *	75.00	37.50	7.50
☐ 60	D. Jones	30.00	15.00	3.00
☐ 61	T. Jones	30.00	15.00	3.00
☐ 62	Lathers S21	60.00	30.00	6.00
☐ 63	McIntyre	30.00	15.00	3.00
☐ 64	Moriarty	30.00	15.00	3.00
☐ 65	Mullin	30.00	15.00	3.00
☐ 66	O'Leary	30.00	15.00	3.00
☐ 67	Pernoll S23	60.00	30.00	6.00
☐ 68	Schmidt	30.00	15.00	3.00
☐ 69	Oscar Stanage	30.00	15.00	3.00
☐ 70	Stroud S21	60.00	30.00	6.00
☐ 71	Summers	30.00	15.00	3.00
☐ 72	Willett	30.00	15.00	3.00
☐ 73	Works	30.00	15.00	3.00
☐ 74	Austin S19	60.00	30.00	6.00
☐ 75	Hal Chase *	60.00	30.00	6.00
☐ 76	Cree	30.00	15.00	3.00
☐ 77	Criger	30.00	15.00	3.00
☐ 78	Ford S23	60.00	30.00	6.00
☐ 79	Gardner S23	60.00	30.00	6.00
☐ 80	Knight S19	60.00	30.00	6.00
☐ 81	LaPorte	30.00	15.00	3.00
☐ 82	Stallings	30.00	15.00	3.00
☐ 83	Sweeney S19	60.00	30.00	6.00
☐ 84	Wolter	30.00	15.00	3.00
☐ 85	Atkins S24	60.00	30.00	6.00
☐ 86	Frank Baker	100.00	50.00	10.00
☐ 87	Jack Barry	30.00	15.00	3.00
☐ 88	Chief Bender *	75.00	37.50	7.50
☐ 89	Eddie Collins *	100.00	50.00	10.00
☐ 90	Jack Coombs	40.00	20.00	4.00
☐ 91	H. Davis *	30.00	15.00	3.00
☐ 92	Dygert	30.00	15.00	3.00
☐ 93	Heitmuller	30.00	15.00	3.00
☐ 94	Hartsel	30.00	15.00	3.00
☐ 95	Krause	30.00	15.00	3.00
☐ 96	Lapp S24	60.00	30.00	6.00
☐ 97	Livingstone	30.00	15.00	3.00
☐ 98	Connie Mack	150.00	75.00	15.00
☐ 99	McInnes S24	60.00	30.00	6.00
☐ 100	Morgan	30.00	15.00	3.00
☐ 101	Murphy	30.00	15.00	3.00
☐ 102	Rube Oldring	30.00	15.00	3.00
☐ 103	Eddie Plank	150.00	75.00	15.00
☐ 104	Amos Strunk S24	60.00	30.00	6.00
☐ 105	Thomas *	30.00	15.00	3.00
☐ 106	Bailey	30.00	15.00	3.00
☐ 107	Criss S19	60.00	30.00	6.00
☐ 108	Graham	30.00	15.00	3.00
☐ 109	Hartzell	30.00	15.00	3.00
☐ 110	Hoffman	30.00	15.00	3.00
☐ 111	Howell	30.00	15.00	3.00
☐ 112	Lake S19	60.00	30.00	6.00
☐ 113	O'Conner	30.00	15.00	3.00
☐ 114	Pelty	30.00	15.00	3.00
☐ 115	Powell	30.00	15.00	3.00
☐ 116	Schweitzer	30.00	15.00	3.00
☐ 117	Stephens	30.00	15.00	3.00
☐ 118	Stone	30.00	15.00	3.00
☐ 119	Rube Waddell	100.00	50.00	10.00
☐ 120	Bobby Wallace	75.00	37.50	7.50
☐ 121	Conroy	30.00	15.00	3.00
☐ 122	Elberfeld	30.00	15.00	3.00
☐ 123	Foster	30.00	15.00	3.00
☐ 124	Gessler	30.00	15.00	3.00
☐ 125	Walter Johnson	400.00	200.00	40.00
☐ 126	Killifer S22	60.00	30.00	6.00
☐ 127	McAleer	30.00	15.00	3.00
☐ 128	McBride S21	60.00	30.00	6.00
☐ 129	Milan	30.00	15.00	3.00
☐ 130	Miller S23	60.00	30.00	6.00
☐ 131	Reisling	30.00	15.00	3.00
☐ 132	Schaefer	30.00	15.00	3.00
☐ 133	Street	30.00	15.00	3.00
☐ 134	Unglaub	30.00	15.00	3.00
☐ 135	Beck	30.00	15.00	3.00
☐ 136	Brown	30.00	15.00	3.00
☐ 137	Curtis S23	60.00	30.00	6.00
☐ 138	Ferguson	30.00	15.00	3.00
☐ 139	Samuel Frock S20	60.00	30.00	6.00
☐ 140	Graham	30.00	15.00	3.00
☐ 141	Buck Herzog	30.00	15.00	3.00
☐ 142	Lake	30.00	15.00	3.00
☐ 143	Bayard Sharpe S23	60.00	30.00	6.00
☐ 144	David Shean S20	60.00	30.00	6.00
☐ 145	C. Smith S22	60.00	30.00	6.00
☐ 146	H. Smith	30.00	15.00	3.00
☐ 147	Sweeney	30.00	15.00	3.00
☐ 148	Barger	30.00	15.00	3.00
☐ 149	Bell	30.00	15.00	3.00
☐ 150	Bergen	30.00	15.00	3.00
☐ 151	Burch	30.00	15.00	3.00
☐ 152	Dahlen	40.00	20.00	4.00
☐ 153	William Davidson S21	60.00	30.00	6.00
☐ 154	Frank Dessau S21	60.00	30.00	6.00
☐ 155	Erwin S20	60.00	30.00	6.00
☐ 156	Hummel	30.00	15.00	3.00
☐ 157	Hunter	30.00	15.00	3.00
☐ 158	Jordan *	30.00	15.00	3.00
☐ 159	Lennox	30.00	15.00	3.00
☐ 160	McElveen	30.00	15.00	3.00
☐ 161	McMillan	30.00	15.00	3.00
☐ 162	Nap Rucker	30.00	15.00	3.00
☐ 163	Scanlon	30.00	15.00	3.00
☐ 164	Wilhelm	30.00	15.00	3.00
☐ 165	Archer S22	60.00	30.00	6.00

☐ 166	Beaumont	30.00	15.00	3.00
☐ 167	Mordecai Brown *	100.00	50.00	10.00
☐ 168	Frank Chance *	125.00	60.00	12.50
☐ 169	Johnny Evers	100.00	50.00	10.00
☐ 170	Hofman	30.00	15.00	3.00
☐ 171	Kane	30.00	15.00	3.00
☐ 172	Kling	30.00	15.00	3.00
☐ 173	Kroh	30.00	15.00	3.00
☐ 174	McIntire	30.00	15.00	3.00
☐ 175	Needham	30.00	15.00	3.00
☐ 176	Overall	30.00	15.00	3.00
☐ 177	Pfeffer S23	60.00	30.00	6.00
☐ 178	Pfiester	30.00	15.00	3.00
☐ 179	Ed Reulbach	30.00	15.00	3.00
☐ 180	L. Richie	30.00	15.00	3.00
☐ 181	Schulte	30.00	15.00	3.00
☐ 182	Scheckard	30.00	15.00	3.00
☐ 183	Harry Steinfeldt	30.00	15.00	3.00
☐ 184	Joe Tinker	100.00	50.00	10.00
☐ 185	Zimmerman S19	60.00	30.00	6.00
☐ 186	Beebe	30.00	15.00	3.00
☐ 187	Bescher	30.00	15.00	3.00
☐ 188	Charles	30.00	15.00	3.00
☐ 189	Tommy Clarke S20	60.00	30.00	6.00
☐ 190	Downey	30.00	15.00	3.00
☐ 191	Doyle	30.00	15.00	3.00
☐ 192	Eagan	30.00	15.00	3.00
☐ 193	Fromme	30.00	15.00	3.00
☐ 194	Gaspar S19	60.00	30.00	6.00
☐ 195	Clark Griffith	75.00	37.50	7.50
☐ 196	Hoblitzel	30.00	15.00	3.00
☐ 197	Hans Lobert	30.00	15.00	3.00
☐ 198	McLean	30.00	15.00	3.00
☐ 199	Mitchell	30.00	15.00	3.00
☐ 200	Phelan S23	60.00	30.00	6.00
☐ 201	Rowan	30.00	15.00	3.00
☐ 202	Space	30.00	15.00	3.00
☐ 203	Suggs	30.00	15.00	3.00
☐ 204	Ames S22	60.00	30.00	6.00
☐ 205	Bridwell	30.00	15.00	3.00
☐ 206	Crandall	30.00	15.00	3.00
☐ 207	Devlin	30.00	15.00	3.00
☐ 208	Devore S19	60.00	30.00	6.00
☐ 209	Doyle *	30.00	15.00	3.00
☐ 210	Fletcher S22	60.00	30.00	6.00
☐ 211	Christy Mathewson	400.00	200.00	40.00
☐ 212	John McGraw	150.00	75.00	15.00
☐ 213	Fred Merkle	40.00	20.00	4.00
☐ 214	Murray	30.00	15.00	3.00
☐ 215	Myers S23	60.00	30.00	6.00
☐ 216	Raymond	30.00	15.00	3.00
☐ 217	Schlei	30.00	15.00	3.00
☐ 218	Seymour	30.00	15.00	3.00
☐ 219	Shafer S19	60.00	30.00	6.00
☐ 220	Fred Snodgrass	30.00	15.00	3.00
☐ 221	Tenney *	30.00	15.00	3.00
☐ 222	Wilson S23	60.00	30.00	6.00
☐ 223	G. Wiltse	30.00	15.00	3.00
☐ 224	Bates	30.00	15.00	3.00
☐ 225	Bransfeld	30.00	15.00	3.00
☐ 226	Dooin *	30.00	15.00	3.00
☐ 227	Doolan	30.00	15.00	3.00
☐ 228	Ewing	30.00	15.00	3.00
☐ 229	Foxen	30.00	15.00	3.00
☐ 230	Grant	30.00	15.00	3.00
☐ 231	Jacklitsch	30.00	15.00	3.00
☐ 232	Knabe	30.00	15.00	3.00
☐ 233	Sherry Magee	30.00	15.00	3.00
☐ 234A	McQuillan * (Philadelphia NL)	30.00	15.00	3.00
☐ 234B	McQuillan (Cincinnati NL)	1500.00	750.00	150.00
☐ 235	Moore	30.00	15.00	3.00
☐ 236	Moran	30.00	15.00	3.00
☐ 237	Moren	30.00	15.00	3.00
☐ 238	Dode Paskert S19	60.00	30.00	6.00
☐ 239	Schettler S20	60.00	30.00	6.00
☐ 240	Sparks	30.00	15.00	3.00
☐ 241	Titus S23	60.00	30.00	6.00
☐ 242A	Jimmy Walsh S20 dark background	100.00	50.00	10.00
☐ 242B	Jimmy Walsh S22 white background	100.00	50.00	10.00
☐ 243	Ed Abbaticchio	30.00	15.00	3.00
☐ 244	Adams	30.00	15.00	3.00
☐ 245	Byrne	30.00	15.00	3.00
☐ 246	Camnitz	30.00	15.00	3.00
☐ 247	Campbell S21	60.00	30.00	6.00
☐ 248	Fred Clarke	100.00	50.00	10.00
☐ 249	Flynn S20	60.00	30.00	6.00
☐ 250	Gibson *	30.00	15.00	3.00
☐ 251	Hyatt	30.00	15.00	3.00
☐ 252	Leach *	30.00	15.00	3.00
☐ 253	Leever	30.00	15.00	3.00
☐ 254	Leifield	30.00	15.00	3.00

☐ 255	Maddox	30.00	15.00	3.00
☐ 256	Miller	30.00	15.00	3.00
☐ 257	O'Conner	30.00	15.00	3.00
☐ 258	Deacon Phillipe	40.00	20.00	4.00
☐ 259	Simon S21	60.00	30.00	6.00
☐ 260	Hans Wagner *	400.00	200.00	40.00
☐ 261	Wilson	30.00	15.00	3.00
☐ 262	Bliss S21	60.00	30.00	6.00
☐ 263	Roger Bresnahan	75.00	37.50	7.50
☐ 264	Bachman	30.00	15.00	3.00
☐ 265	Corridon	30.00	15.00	3.00
☐ 266	Demmitt S22	60.00	30.00	6.00
☐ 267	Ellis	30.00	15.00	3.00
☐ 268	Evans S23	60.00	30.00	6.00
☐ 269	Harmon S20	60.00	30.00	6.00
☐ 270	Miller Huggins	75.00	37.50	7.50
☐ 271	Hulswitt	30.00	15.00	3.00
☐ 272	Konetchy	30.00	15.00	3.00
☐ 273	Lush	30.00	15.00	3.00
☐ 274	Mattern	30.00	15.00	3.00
☐ 275	Mowery S21	60.00	30.00	6.00
☐ 276	Rebel Oakes S24	60.00	30.00	6.00
☐ 277	Phelps	30.00	15.00	3.00
☐ 278	Sallee	30.00	15.00	3.00
☐ 279	Willis	40.00	20.00	4.00
☐ 280	Coveleskie: Louisville S22	90.00	45.00	9.00
☐ 281	Foster: Rochester S19	90.00	45.00	9.00
☐ 282	Frill: Jersey City S20	90.00	45.00	9.00
☐ 283	Hughes: Rochester S23	90.00	45.00	9.00
☐ 284	Krueger: Sacramento S20	90.00	45.00	9.00
☐ 285	Mitchell: Rochester S19	90.00	45.00	9.00
☐ 286	O'Hara: Toronto	45.00	22.50	4.50
☐ 287	Perring: Columbus S20	90.00	45.00	9.00
☐ 288	Ray: Western League S24	90.00	45.00	9.00

N28 Allen and Ginter

This 50-card set of The World's Champions was marketed by Allen and Ginter in 1887. The cards feature color lithographs of champion athletes from seven categories of sport, with baseball, rowing and boxing each having 10 individuals portrayed. Cards numbered 1 to 10 depict baseball players and cards numbered 11 to 20 depict popular boxers of the era. This set is called the first series although no such title appears on the cards. All 50 cards are checklisted on the reverse, and they are unnumbered. An album (ACC: A16) and an advertising banner (ACC: G20) were also issued in conjunction with this set.

	EX-MT	VG-E	GOOD
COMPLETE SET (50)	6000.00	3000.00	600.00
COMMON BASEBALL (1-10)	250.00	125.00	25.00
COMMON BOXERS (11-20)	50.00	20.00	4.00
COMMON OTHERS (21-50)	15.00	7.50	1.50

☐ 1	Adrian C. Anson	1250.00	600.00	150.00
☐ 2	Chas. W. Bennett	250.00	125.00	25.00
☐ 3	R.L. Caruthers	300.00	150.00	30.00
☐ 4	John Clarkson	600.00	300.00	60.00

☐ 5	Charles Comiskey	600.00	300.00	60.00
☐ 6	Capt. Jack Glasscock	300.00	150.00	30.00
☐ 7	Timothy Keefe	600.00	300.00	60.00
☐ 8	Mike Kelly	900.00	450.00	90.00
☐ 9	Joseph Mulvey	250.00	125.00	25.00
☐ 10	John A.H. Ward	600.00	300.00	60.00
☐ 11	Jimmy Carney	50.00	20.00	4.00
☐ 12	Jimmy Carroll	50.00	20.00	4.00
☐ 13	Jack Dempsey	85.00	37.50	7.50
☐ 14	Jake Kilrain	60.00	25.00	5.00
☐ 15	Joe Lannon	50.00	20.00	4.00
☐ 16	Jack McAuliffe	50.00	20.00	4.00
☐ 17	Charlie Mitchell	60.00	25.00	5.00
☐ 18	Jem Smith	50.00	20.00	4.00
☐ 19	John L. Sullivan	125.00	50.00	10.00
☐ 20	Ike Weir	50.00	20.00	4.00
☐ 21	Wm. Beach	15.00	7.50	1.50
☐ 22	Geo. Bubear	15.00	7.50	1.50
☐ 23	Jacob Gaudaur	15.00	7.50	1.50
☐ 24	Albert Hamm	15.00	7.50	1.50
☐ 25	Ed. Hanlan	15.00	7.50	1.50
☐ 26	Geo. H. Hosmer	15.00	7.50	1.50
☐ 27	John McKay	15.00	7.50	1.50
☐ 28	Wallace Ross	15.00	7.50	1.50
☐ 29	John Teemer	15.00	7.50	1.50
☐ 30	E.A. Trickett	15.00	7.50	1.50
☐ 31	Joe Acton	15.00	7.50	1.50
☐ 32	Theo. Bauer	15.00	7.50	1.50
☐ 33	Young Bibby (Geo. Mehling)	15.00	7.50	1.50
☐ 34	J.F. McLaughlin	15.00	7.50	1.50
☐ 35	John McMahon	15.00	7.50	1.50
☐ 36	Wm. Muldoon	15.00	7.50	1.50
☐ 37	Matsada Sorakichi	15.00	7.50	1.50
☐ 38	Capt. A.H. Bogardus	15.00	7.50	1.50
☐ 39	Dr. W.F. Carver	15.00	7.50	1.50
☐ 40	Hon. W.F. Cody (Buffalo Bill)	75.00	37.50	7.50
☐ 41	Miss Annie Oakley	50.00	25.00	5.00
☐ 42	Yank Adams	15.00	7.50	1.50
☐ 43	Maurice Daly	15.00	7.50	1.50
☐ 44	Jos. Dion	15.00	7.50	1.50
☐ 45	J. Schaefer	15.00	7.50	1.50
☐ 46	Wm. Sexton	15.00	7.50	1.50
☐ 47	Geo. F. Slosson	15.00	7.50	1.50
☐ 48	M. Vignaux	15.00	7.50	1.50
☐ 49	Albert Frey	15.00	7.50	1.50
☐ 50	J.L. Malone	15.00	7.50	1.50

COMMON OTHERS (15-50)	25.00	12.50	2.50
☐ 1	Wm. Ewing	1500.00	750.00	150.00
☐ 2	Jas. H. Fogarty	750.00	375.00	75.00
☐ 3	Charles H. Getzin	750.00	375.00	75.00
☐ 4	Geo. F. Miller	750.00	375.00	75.00
☐ 5	John Morrell	750.00	375.00	75.00
☐ 6	James Ryan	750.00	375.00	75.00
☐ 7	Patsey Duffy	100.00	37.50	7.50
☐ 8	Billy Edwards	100.00	37.50	7.50
☐ 9	Jack Havlin	100.00	37.50	7.50
☐ 10	Patsey Kerrigan	100.00	37.50	7.50
☐ 11	Geo. La Blance	100.00	37.50	7.50
☐ 12	Jack McGee	100.00	37.50	7.50
☐ 13	Frank Murphy	100.00	37.50	7.50
☐ 14	Johnny Murphy	100.00	37.50	7.50
☐ 15	Capt. J.C. Daly	25.00	12.50	2.50
☐ 16	M.W. Ford	25.00	12.50	2.50
☐ 17	Duncan C. Ross	25.00	12.50	2.50
☐ 18	W.E. Crist	25.00	12.50	2.50
☐ 19	H.G. Crocken	25.00	12.50	2.50
☐ 20	Willie Harradon	25.00	12.50	2.50
☐ 21	F.F. Ives	25.00	12.50	2.50
☐ 22	Wm. A. Rowe	25.00	12.50	2.50
☐ 23	Percy Stone	25.00	12.50	2.50
☐ 24	Ralph Temple	25.00	12.50	2.50
☐ 25	Fred Wood	25.00	12.50	2.50
☐ 26	Dr. James Dwight	25.00	12.50	2.50
☐ 27	Thomas Pettit	25.00	12.50	2.50
☐ 28	R.D. Sears	25.00	12.50	2.50
☐ 29	H.W. Slocum Jr.	25.00	12.50	2.50
☐ 30	Theobaud Bauer	25.00	12.50	2.50
☐ 31	Edwin Bibby	25.00	12.50	2.50
☐ 32	Hugh McCormack	25.00	12.50	2.50
☐ 33	Axel Paulsen	25.00	12.50	2.50
☐ 34	T. Ray	25.00	12.50	2.50
☐ 35	C.W.V. Clarke	25.00	12.50	2.50
☐ 36	E.D. Lange	25.00	12.50	2.50
☐ 37	E.C. Carter	25.00	12.50	2.50
☐ 38	Wm. Cummings	25.00	12.50	2.50
☐ 39	W.G. George	25.00	12.50	2.50
☐ 40	L.E. Myers	25.00	12.50	2.50
☐ 41	James Albert	25.00	12.50	2.50
☐ 42	Patrick Fitzgerald	25.00	12.50	2.50
☐ 43	W.B. Page	25.00	12.50	2.50
☐ 44	C.A.J. Queckberner	25.00	12.50	2.50
☐ 45	W.J.M. Barry	25.00	12.50	2.50
☐ 46	Wm. G. East	25.00	12.50	2.50
☐ 47	Wm. O'Connor	25.00	12.50	2.50
☐ 48	Gus Hill	25.00	12.50	2.50
☐ 49	Capt. Paul Boyton	25.00	12.50	2.50
☐ 50	Capt. Matthew Webb	25.00	12.50	2.50

N29 Allen and Ginter

The second series of The World's Champions was probably issued in 1888. Like the first series, the cards are backlisted and unnumbered. However, there are 17 distinct categories of sports represented in this set, with only six baseball players portrayed (as opposed to 10 in the first series). Each card has a color lithograph of the individual set against a white background. An album (ACC: A17) and an advertising banner (ACC: G21) were issued in conjunction with the set. The numbering below is alphabetical within sport, e.g., baseball players (1-6), boxers (7-14), and other sports (15-50).

	EX-MT	VG-E	GOOD
COMPLETE SET (50)	6000.00	3000.00	600.00
COMMON BASEBALL (1-6)	750.00	375.00	75.00
COMMON BOXERS (7-14)	100.00	37.50	7.50

N43 Allen and Ginter

The primary designs of this 50-card set are identical to those of N29, but these are placed on a much larger card with extraneous background detail. The set was produced in 1888 by Allen and Ginter as inserts for a larger tobacco package than those in which sets N28 and N29 were marketed. Cards of this set, which is backlisted, are considered to be much scarcer than their counterparts in N29.

	EX-MT	VG-E	GOOD
COMPLETE SET (50)	8000.00	3750.00	800.00
COMMON BASEBALL (1-6)	1000.00	500.00	100.00
COMMON BOXERS (7-14)	125.00	45.00	9.00
COMMON OTHERS (15-50)	30.00	15.00	3.00
☐ 1	William Ewing	2000.00	1000.00	200.00
☐ 2	Jas. J. Fogarty	1000.00	500.00	100.00
☐ 3	Charles Getzein	1000.00	500.00	100.00
☐ 4	Geo. F. Miller	1000.00	500.00	100.00
☐ 5	John Morrell	1000.00	500.00	100.00
☐ 6	James Ryan	1000.00	500.00	100.00
☐ 7	Patsey Duffy	125.00	45.00	9.00
☐ 8	Billy Edwards	125.00	45.00	9.00
☐ 9	Jack Havlin	125.00	45.00	9.00
☐ 10	Patsey Kerrigan	125.00	45.00	9.00
☐ 11	George LaBlanche	125.00	45.00	9.00
☐ 12	Jack McGee	125.00	45.00	9.00
☐ 13	Frank Murphy	125.00	45.00	9.00
☐ 14	Johnny Murphy	125.00	45.00	9.00
☐ 15	James Albert	30.00	15.00	3.00
☐ 16	W.J.M. Barry	30.00	15.00	3.00
☐ 17	Theobaud Bauer	30,00	15.00	3.00
☐ 18	Edwin Bibby	30.00	15.00	3.00

		EX-MT	VG-E	GOOD
COMPLETE SET (50)		7500.00	3750.00	800.00
COMMON BASEBALL (1-8)		450.00	225.00	45.00
COMMON BOXER		65.00	25.00	5.00
COMMON OTHERS		20.00	10.00	2.00
☐ 1	Andrews: Phila.	450.00	225.00	45.00
☐ 2	Anson: Chicago	2000.00	1000.00	200.00
☐ 3	Brouthers: Detroit	900.00	450.00	90.00
☐ 4	Caruthers: Brooklyn	500.00	250.00	50.00
☐ 5	Dunlap: Detroit	450.00	225.00	45.00
☐ 6	Glasscock: Indianapolis	500.00	250.00	50.00
☐ 7	Keefe: New York	900.00	450.00	90.00
☐ 8	Kelly: Boston	1350.00	650.00	150.00
☐ 9	Acton (Wrestler)	20.00	10.00	2.00
☐ 10	Albert (Pedestrian)	20.00	10.00	2.00
☐ 11	Beach (Oarsman)	20.00	10.00	2.00
☐ 12	Beecher (Football)	300.00	150.00	30.00
☐ 13	Beeckman (Lawn Tennis)	20.00	10.00	2.00
☐ 14	Bogardus (Marksman)	20.00	10.00	2.00
☐ 15	Buffalo Bill (Wild West Hunter)	75.00	37.50	7.50
☐ 16	Daly (Billiards)	20.00	10.00	2.00
☐ 17	Dempsey (Pugilist)	125.00	50.00	10.00
☐ 18	D'oro (Pool)	20.00	10.00	2.00
☐ 19	Dwight (Lawn Tennis)	20.00	10.00	2.00
☐ 20	Fitzgerald (Pedestrian)	20.00	10.00	2.00
☐ 21	Garrison (Jockey)	20.00	10.00	2.00
☐ 22	Gaudaur (Oarsman)	20.00	10.00	2.00
☐ 23	Hanlan (Oarsman)	20.00	10.00	2.00
☐ 24	Kilrain (Pugilist)	65.00	25.00	5.00
☐ 25	MacKenzie (Chess)	20.00	10.00	2.00
☐ 26	McLaughlin (Jockey)	20.00	10.00	2.00
☐ 27	Mitchell (Pugilist)	65.00	25.00	5.00
☐ 28	Muldoon (Wrestler)	20.00	10.00	2.00
☐ 29	Murphy (Jockey)	20.00	10.00	2.00
☐ 30	Myers (Runner)	20.00	10.00	2.00
☐ 31	Page (High Jumper)	20.00	10.00	2.00
☐ 32	Prince (Bicyclist)	20.00	10.00	2.00
☐ 33	Ross (Broadswordsman)	20.00	10.00	2.00
☐ 34	Rowe (Bicyclist)	20.00	10.00	2.00
☐ 35	Rowell (Pedestrian)	20.00	10.00	2.00
☐ 36	Schaefer (Billiards)	20.00	10.00	2.00
☐ 37	Sears (Lawn Tennis)	20.00	10.00	2.00
☐ 38	Sexton (Billiards)	20.00	10.00	2.00
☐ 39	Slosson (Billiards)	20.00	10.00	2.00
☐ 40	Smith (Pugilist)	65.00	25.00	5.00
☐ 41	Steinitz (Chess)	20.00	10.00	2.00
☐ 42	Stevens (Bicyclist)	20.00	10.00	2.00
☐ 43	Sullivan (Pugilist)	150.00	60.00	12.50
☐ 44	Taylor (Lawn Tennis)	20.00	10.00	2.00
☐ 45	Teemer (Oarsman)	20.00	10.00	2.00
☐ 46	Vignaux (Billiards)	20.00	10.00	2.00
☐ 47	Voss (Strongest Man in the World)	20.00	10.00	2.00
☐ 48	Wood (Bicyclist)	20.00	10.00	2.00
☐ 49	Wood (Jockey)	20.00	10.00	2.00
☐ 50	Zukertort (Chess)	20.00	10.00	2.00

☐ 19	Capt. Paul Boyton	30.00	15.00	3.00
☐ 20	E.C. Carter	30.00	15.00	3.00
☐ 21	C.W.V. Clarke	30.00	15.00	3.00
☐ 22	W.E. Crist	30.00	15.00	3.00
☐ 23	H.G. Crocker	30.00	15.00	3.00
☐ 24	Wm. Cummings	30.00	15.00	3.00
☐ 25	Capt. J.C. Daly	30.00	15.00	3.00
☐ 26	Dr. James Dwight	30.00	15.00	3.00
☐ 27	Wm. G. East	30.00	15.00	3.00
☐ 28	Patrick Fitzgerald	30.00	15.00	3.00
☐ 29	M.W. Ford	30.00	15.00	3.00
☐ 30	W.G. George	30.00	15.00	3.00
☐ 31	Willie Harradon	30.00	15.00	3.00
☐ 32	Gus Hill	30.00	15.00	3.00
☐ 33	F.F. Ives	30.00	15.00	3.00
☐ 34	E.D. Lange	30.00	15.00	3.00
☐ 35	Hugh McCormack	30.00	15.00	3.00
☐ 36	L.E. Myers	30.00	15.00	3.00
☐ 37	Wm. O'Connor	30.00	15.00	3.00
☐ 38	W.B. Page	30.00	15.00	3.00
☐ 39	Axel. Paulsen	30.00	15.00	3.00
☐ 40	Thomas Pettitt	30.00	15.00	3.00
☐ 41	C.A.J. Queckberner	30.00	15.00	3.00
☐ 42	T. Ray	30.00	15.00	3.00
☐ 43	Duncan C. Ross	30.00	15.00	3.00
☐ 44	Wm. A. Rowe	30.00	15.00	3.00
☐ 45	R.D. Sears	30.00	15.00	3.00
☐ 46	H.W. Slocum Jr.	30.00	15.00	3.00
☐ 47	Percy Stone	30.00	15.00	3.00
☐ 48	Ralph Temple	30.00	15.00	3.00
☐ 49	Capt. Matthew Webb	30.00	15.00	3.00
☐ 50	Fred Wood	30.00	15.00	3.00

N162 Goodwin

This 50-card set issued by Goodwin was one of the major competitors to the N28 and N29 sets marketed by Allen and Ginter. It contains individuals representing 18 sports, with eight baseball players pictured. Each color card is backlisted and bears advertising for "Old Judge" and "Gypsy Queen" cigarettes on the front. The set was released to the public in 1888 and an album (ACC: A36) is associated with it as a premium issue.

N172 Old Judge

The Goodwin Company's baseball series depicts hundreds of ballplayers from more than 40 major and minor league teams as well as boxers and wrestlers. The cards (approximately 1 1/2" by 2 1/2") are actually photographs from the Hall studio in New York which were pasted onto thick

cardboard. The pictures are sepia in color with either a white or pink cast, and the cards are blank backed. They are found either numbered or unnumbered, with or without a copyright date, and with hand printed or machine printed names. All known cards have the name "Goodwin Co., New York" at the base. The cards were marketed during the period 1887-1890 in packs of "Old Judge" and "Gypsy Queen" cigarettes (cards marked with the latter brand are worth double the values listed below). They have been listed alphabetically and assigned numbers in the checklist below for simplicity's sake; the various poses known for some players also have not been listed for the same reason. Some of the players are pictured in horizontal (HOR) poses. In all, more than 2300 different Goodwin cards are known to collectors, with more being discovered every year. Cards from the "Spotted Tie" sub-series are denoted in the checklist below by SPOT.

	EX-MT	VG-E	GOOD
COMPLETE SET	100000.	50000.	12500.
COMMON PLAYER	100.00	50.00	10.00
COMMON PLAYER (DOUBLE)	150.00	75.00	15.00
COMMON BROWNS CHAMP	250.00	125.00	25.00
COMMON PLAYER (PCL)	1000.00	500.00	100.00
COMMON SPOTTED TIE	300.00	150.00	30.00

			EX-MT	VG-E	GOOD
☐	1	Gus Albert: Cleveland-Milwaukee	100.00	50.00	10.00
☐	2	Charles Alcott: St. Louis Whites-Mansfield	100.00	50.00	10.00
☐	3	Alexander: Des Moines	100.00	50.00	10.00
☐	4	Myron Allen: K.C.	100.00	50.00	10.00
☐	5	Bob Allen: Pitts.-Phila. N.L.	100.00	50.00	10.00
☐	6	Uncle Bill Alvord: Toledo-Des Moines	100.00	50.00	10.00
☐	7	Varney Anderson: St.Paul	100.00	50.00	10.00
☐	8	Ed Andrews: Phila.	100.00	50.00	10.00
☐	9	Andrews and Hoover: Philadelphia	150.00	75.00	15.00
☐	10	Wally Andrews: Omaha	100.00	50.00	10.00
☐	11	Bill Annis: Omaha-Worcester	100.00	50.00	10.00
☐	12A	Cap Anson: Chicago (in uniform)	4000.00	2000.00	500.00
☐	12B	Cap Anson: Chicago (not in uniform)	1500.00	250.00	50.00
☐	13	Old Hoss Ardner: Kansas City-St. Joe	100.00	50.00	10.00
☐	14	Tug Arundel: Indianapolis-Whites	100.00	50.00	10.00
☐	15	Bakley: Jersey-Cleve.	100.00	50.00	10.00
☐	16	Clarence Baldwin: Cincinnati	100.00	50.00	10.00
☐	17	Mark (Fido) Baldwin: Chicago-Columbus	100.00	50.00	10.00
☐	18	Lady Baldwin: Detroit	100.00	50.00	10.00
☐	19	James Banning: Wash.	100.00	50.00	10.00
☐	20	Samuel Barkley: Pittsburgh-K.C.	100.00	50.00	10.00
☐	21	John Barnes: Mgr. St. Paul	100.00	50.00	10.00
☐	22	Bald Billy Barnie: Mgr. Baltimore	150.00	75.00	15.00
☐	23	Charles Bassett: Indianapolis-N.Y.	100.00	50.00	10.00
☐	24	Charles Bastian: Phila.-Chicago	100.00	50.00	10.00
☐	25	Bastian and Shriver: Philadelphia	150.00	75.00	15.00
☐	26	Ollie Beard: Cinc.	100.00	50.00	10.00
☐	27	Ebenezer Beatin: Cleve.	100.00	50.00	10.00
☐	28	Jake Beckley: "Eagle Eye" Whites-Pittsburgh	450.00	225.00	45.00
☐	29	Stephen Behel SPOT	400.00	200.00	40.00
☐	30	Charles Bennett: Detroit-Boston	100.00	50.00	10.00
☐	31	Louis Bierbauer: A's	100.00	50.00	10.00
☐	32	Bierbauer and Gamble Athletics	150.00	75.00	15.00
☐	33	Bill Bishop: Pittsburgh-Syracuse	100.00	50.00	10.00
☐	34	William Blair: A's-Hamiltons	100.00	50.00	10.00
☐	35	Ned Bligh: Columbus	100.00	50.00	10.00
☐	36	Bogart: Indianapolis	100.00	50.00	10.00
☐	37	Boyce: Washington	100.00	50.00	10.00
☐	38	Jake Boyd: Maroons	100.00	50.00	10.00
☐	39	Honest John Boyle: St. Louis-Chicago	100.00	50.00	10.00
☐	40	Handsome Henry Boyle . Indianapolis-N.Y.	100.00	50.00	10.00
☐	41	Nick Bradley: K.C.- Worchester	100.00	50.00	10.00
☐	42	George(Grin) Bradley Sioux City	100.00	50.00	10.00
☐	43	Stephen Brady SPOT	400.00	200.00	40.00
☐	44	Breckinridge: Sacramento PCL	1000.00	500.00	100.00
☐	45	Jim Brennan: Kansas City- A's	100.00	50.00	10.00
☐	46	Timothy Brosnan: Minn.-Sioux City	100.00	50.00	10.00
☐	47	Cal Broughton: Detroit-Boston	100.00	50.00	10.00
☐	48	Big Dan Brouthers: Detroit-Boston	400.00	200.00	40.00
☐	49	Thomas Brown: Pittsburgh-Boston	100.00	50.00	10.00
☐	50	Brown: California-N.Y.	100.00	50.00	10.00
☐	51	Pete Browning: "Gladiator" Louisville	150.00	75.00	15.00
☐	52	Charles Brynan: Chicago-Des Moines	100.00	50.00	10.00
☐	53	Al Buckenberger: Mgr. Columbus	100.00	50.00	10.00
☐	54	Dick Buckley: Indianapolis-N.Y.	100.00	50.00	10.00
☐	55	Charles Buffington: Philadelphia	100.00	50.00	10.00
☐	56	Ernest Burch: Brooklyn-Whites	100.00	50.00	10.00
☐	57	Bill Burdick: Omaha-Indianapolis	100.00	50.00	10.00
☐	58	Black Jack Burdock: Boston-Brooklyn	100.00	50.00	10.00
☐	59	Robert Burks: Sioux City	100.00	50.00	10.00
☐	60	George Burnham "Watch" Mgr. Indianapolis	150.00	75.00	15.00
☐	61	Burns: Omaha	100.00	50.00	10.00
☐	62	Jimmy Burns: K.C.	100.00	50.00	10.00
☐	63	Tommy (Oyster) Burns ..	100.00	50.00	10.00

	Baltimore-Brooklyn			
☐ 64	Thomas E. Burns:	100.00	50.00	10.00
	Chicago			
☐ 65A	Doc Bushong: Brook. ...	100.00	50.00	10.00
☐ 65B	Doc Bushong:	250.00	125.00	25.00
	Browns Champ			
☐ 66	Patsy Cahill: Ind.	100.00	50.00	10.00
☐ 67	Count Campau:	100.00	50.00	10.00
	Kansas City-Detroit			
☐ 68	Jimmy Canavan:	100.00	50.00	10.00
	Omaha			
☐ 69	Bart Cantz:	100.00	50.00	10.00
	Whites-Baltimore			
☐ 70	Handsome Jack Carney .	100.00	50.00	10.00
	Washington			
☐ 71	Hick Carpenter	100.00	50.00	10.00
	Cincinnati			
☐ 72	Cliff Carroll: Wash.	100.00	50.00	10.00
☐ 73	Scrappy Carroll:	100.00	50.00	10.00
	St.Paul-Chicago			
☐ 74	Frederick Carroll:	100.00	50.00	10.00
	Pitts.			
☐ 75	Jumbo Cartwright:	100.00	50.00	10.00
	Kansas City-St. Joe			
☐ 76A	Bob Caruthers:	150.00	75.00	15.00
	"Parisian"			
	Brooklyn			
☐ 76B	Bob Caruthers:	300.00	150.00	30.00
	"Parisian"			
	Browns Champs			
☐ 77	Daniel Casey: Phila.	100.00	50.00	10.00
☐ 78	Icebox Chamberlain:	100.00	50.00	10.00
	St. Louis			
☐ 79	Cupid Childs:	100.00	50.00	10.00
	Phila.-Syracuse			
☐ 80	Bob Clark:	100.00	50.00	10.00
	Washington			
☐ 81	Owen Clark:	100.00	50.00	10.00
	Washington			
☐ 82	Clarke and Hughes:	150.00	75.00	15.00
	Brooklyn HOR			
☐ 83	William(Dad) Clarke:	100.00	50.00	10.00
	Chicago-Omaha			
☐ 84	John Clarkson:	400.00	200.00	40.00
	Chicago-Boston			
☐ 85	Jack Clements:	100.00	50.00	10.00
	Philadelphia			
☐ 86	Elmer Cleveland:	100.00	50.00	10.00
	Omaha-New York			
☐ 87	Monk Cline:	100.00	50.00	10.00
	K.C.-Sioux City			
☐ 88	Cody: Des Moines	100.00	50.00	10.00
☐ 89	John Coleman:	100.00	50.00	10.00
	Pittsburgh - A's			
☐ 90	Bill Collins:	100.00	50.00	10.00
	New York-Newark			
☐ 91	Hub Collins:	100.00	50.00	10.00
	Louisville-Brooklyn			
☐ 92A	Charles Comiskey:	750.00	375.00	75.00
	Browns Champs			
☐ 92B	Commy Comiskey:	450.00	225.00	45.00
	St. Louis-Chicago			
☐ 93	Pete Connell:	100.00	50.00	10.00
	Des Moines			
☐ 94A	Roger Connor:	450.00	225.00	45.00
	All-Star			
☐ 94B	Roger Connor:	450.00	225.00	45.00
	New York			
☐ 95	Richard Conway:	100.00	50.00	10.00
	Boston-Worchester			
☐ 96	Peter Conway:	100.00	50.00	10.00
	Det.-Pitts.-Ind.			
☐ 97	James Conway: K.C.	100.00	50.00	10.00
☐ 98	Paul Cook:	100.00	50.00	10.00
	Louisville			
☐ 99	Jimmy Cooney:	100.00	50.00	10.00
	Omaha-Chicago			
☐ 100	Larry Corcoran:	100.00	50.00	10.00
	Indianapolis-London			
☐ 101	Pop Corkhill:	100.00	50.00	10.00
	Cincinnnati-Brooklyn			
☐ 102	Roscoe Coughlin:	100.00	50.00	10.00
	Maroons-Chicago			
☐ 103	Cannon Ball Crane:	100.00	50.00	10.00
	New York			
☐ 104	Samuel Crane: Wash.	100.00	50.00	10.00
☐ 105	Jack Crogan: Maroons ...	100.00	50.00	10.00
☐ 106	John Crooks:	100.00	50.00	10.00
	Whites-Omaha			
☐ 107	Lave Cross:	100.00	50.00	10.00
	Louisville-A's-			
	Phila.			
☐ 108	Bill Crossley: Milw.	100.00	50.00	10.00
☐ 109A	Joe Crotty SPOT	350.00	175.00	35.00
☐ 109B	Joe Crotty:	100.00	50.00	10.00

	Sioux City			
☐ 110	Billy Crowell:	100.00	50.00	10.00
	Cleveland-St. Joe			
☐ 111	Jim Cudworth:	100.00	50.00	10.00
	St. Louis-Worchester			
☐ 112	Bert Cunningham:	100.00	50.00	10.00
	Baltimore-Phila.			
☐ 113	Tacks Curtis:	100.00	50.00	10.00
	St. Joe			
☐ 114A	Ed Cushman SPOT	400.00	200.00	40.00
☐ 114B	Ed Cushman:	100.00	50.00	10.00
	Toledo			
☐ 115	Tony Cusick: Mil.	100.00	50.00	10.00
☐ 116	Dailey: Oakland PCL	1000.00	500.00	100.00
☐ 117	Edward Dailey:	100.00	50.00	10.00
	Phil.-Wash.-			
	Columbus			
☐ 118	Bill Daley: Boston	100.00	50.00	10.00
☐ 119	Con Daley:	100.00	50.00	10.00
	Boston-Indianapolis			
☐ 120	Abner Dalrymple:	100.00	50.00	10.00
	Pittsburgh-Denver			
☐ 121	Tom Daly:	100.00	50.00	10.00
	Chicago-Wash.-Cleve.			
☐ 122	James Daly: Minn.	100.00	50.00	10.00
☐ 123	Law Daniels: K.C.	100.00	50.00	10.00
☐ 124	Dell Darling:	100.00	50.00	10.00
	Chicago			
☐ 125	Wm. Darnbrough:	100.00	50.00	10.00
	Denver			
☐ 126	D. Davin: Milwaukee	100.00	50.00	10.00
☐ 127	Jumbo Davis: K.C.	100.00	50.00	10.00
☐ 128	Pat Dealey: Wash.	100.00	50.00	10.00
☐ 129	Thomas Deasley:	100.00	50.00	10.00
	New York-Washington			
☐ 130	Edward Decker: Phil.	100.00	50.00	10.00
☐ 131	Big Ed Delahanty:	750.00	375.00	75.00
	Philadelphia			
☐ 132	Jeremiah Denny:	100.00	50.00	10.00
	Indianapolis-			
	New York			
☐ 133	James Devlin: St.L.	100.00	50.00	10.00
☐ 134	Thomas Dolan:	100.00	50.00	10.00
	Whites-			
	St. Louis-Denver			
☐ 135	Jack Donahue:	1000.00	500.00	100.00
	San Francisco PCL			
☐ 136A	James Donahue SPOT .	350.00	175.00	35.00
☐ 136B	James Donahue: K.C. ..	100.00	50.00	10.00
☐ 137	James Donnelly:	100.00	50.00	10.00
	Washington			
☐ 138	Dooley: Oakland PCL	1000.00	500.00	100.00
☐ 139	J. Doran: Omaha	100.00	50.00	10.00
☐ 140	Michael Dorgan: N.Y.	100.00	50.00	10.00
☐ 141	Doyle: San Fran. PCL	1000.00	500.00	100.00
☐ 142	Homerun Duffe: St.L.	100.00	50.00	10.00
☐ 143	Hugh Duffy: Chicago	450.00	225.00	45.00
☐ 144	Dan Dugdale:	100.00	50.00	10.00
	Maroons-Minneapolis			
☐ 145	Dugrahm: Maroons	100.00	50.00	10.00
☐ 146	Duck Duke: Minn.	100.00	50.00	10.00
☐ 147	Sure Shot Dunlap:	100.00	50.00	10.00
	Pittsburgh			
☐ 148	J. Dunn: Maroons	100.00	50.00	10.00
☐ 149	Jesse(Cyclone)Duryea ...	100.00	50.00	10.00
	St. Paul-Cinc.			
☐ 150	John Dwyer:	100.00	50.00	10.00
	Chicago-Maroons			
☐ 151	Billy Earle:	100.00	50.00	10.00
	Cincinnati-St.Paul			
☐ 152	Buck Ebright: Wash.	100.00	50.00	10.00
☐ 153	Red Ehret:	100.00	50.00	10.00
	Louisville			
☐ 154	R. Emmerke:	100.00	50.00	10.00
	Des Moines			
☐ 155	Dude Esterbrook:	100.00	50.00	10.00
	Louisville-Ind.-			
	New York-All Star			
☐ 156	Henry Esterday:	100.00	50.00	10.00
	K.C.-Columbus			
☐ 157	Long John Ewing:	100.00	50.00	10.00
	Louisville-N.Y.			
☐ 158	Buck Ewing: New York ...	400.00	200.00	40.00
☐ 159	Ewing and Mascot:	350.00	175.00	35.00
	New York			
☐ 160	Jay Faatz: Cleveland	100.00	50.00	10.00
☐ 161	Clinkgers Fagan:	100.00	50.00	10.00
	Kansas City-Denver			
☐ 162	William Farmer:	100.00	50.00	10.00
	Pittsburgh-St. Paul			
☐ 163	Sidney Farrar:	100.00	50.00	10.00
	Philadelphia			
☐ 164	John(Moose) Farrell:	100.00	50.00	10.00
	Wash.-Baltimore			
☐ 165	Charles(Duke)Farrell	100.00	50.00	10.00

	Chicago			
☐ 166	Frank Fennelly:	100.00	50.00	10.00
	Cincinnati-A's			
☐ 167	Chas. Ferguson:	100.00	50.00	10.00
	Phila.			
☐ 168	Colonel Ferson:	100.00	50.00	10.00
	Washington			
☐ 169	Wallace Fessenden:	150.00	75.00	15.00
	Umpire National			
☐ 170	Jocko Fields: Pitts.	100.00	50.00	10.00
☐ 171	Fischer: Maroons	100.00	50.00	10.00
☐ 172	Thomas Flanigan:	100.00	50.00	10.00
	Cleve.-Sioux City			
☐ 173	Silver Flint:	100.00	50.00	10.00
	Chicago			
☐ 174	Thomas Flood:	100.00	50.00	10.00
	St. Joe			
☐ 175	Flynn: Omaha	100.00	50.00	10.00
☐ 176	James Fogarty:	100.00	50.00	10.00
	Philadelphia			
☐ 177	Frank(Monkey)Foreman .	100.00	50.00	10.00
	Baltimore-Cinc.			
☐ 178	Thomas Forster:	100.00	50.00	10.00
	Milwaukee-Hartford			
☐ 179A	Elmer E. Foster	350.00	175.00	35.00
	SPOT			
☐ 179B	Elmer Foster:	100.00	50.00	10.00
	New York-Chicago			
☐ 180	F.W. Foster SPOT	400.00	200.00	40.00
	T.W. Forster (sic)			
☐ 181A	Scissors Foutz:	250.00	125.00	25.00
	Browns Champ			
☐ 181B	Scissors Foutz:	100.00	50.00	10.00
	Brooklyn			
☐ 182	Julie Freeman:	100.00	50.00	10.00
	St.L.-Milwaukee			
☐ 183	Will Fry: St. Joe	100.00	50.00	10.00
☐ 184	Fudger: Oakland PCL	1000.00	500.00	100.00
☐ 185	William Fuller:	100.00	50.00	10.00
	Milwaukee			
☐ 186	Shorty Fuller:	100.00	50.00	10.00
	St.Louis			
☐ 187	Christopher Fullmer:	100.00	50.00	10.00
	Baltimore			
☐ 188	Fullmer and Tucker:	150.00	75.00	15.00
	Baltimore HOR			
☐ 189	Honest John Gaffney:	150.00	75.00	15.00
	Mgr. Washington			
☐ 190	Pud Galvin: Pitts.	450.00	225.00	45.00
☐ 191	Robert Gamble: A's	100.00	50.00	10.00
☐ 192	Charles Ganzel:	100.00	50.00	10.00
	Detroit-Boston			
☐ 193	Frank (Gid) Gardner:	100.00	50.00	10.00
	Phila.-Washington			
☐ 194	Gardner and Murray:	150.00	75.00	15.00
	Washington HOR			
☐ 195	Ed Gastfield: Omaha	100.00	50.00	10.00
☐ 196	Hank Gastreich:	100.00	50.00	10.00
	Columbus			
☐ 197	Emil Geiss: Chicago	100.00	50.00	10.00
☐ 198	Frenchy Genins:	100.00	50.00	10.00
	Sioux City			
☐ 199	William George: N.Y.	100.00	50.00	10.00
☐ 200	Move Up Joe Gerhardt ..	100.00	50.00	10.00
	All Star-Jersey City			
☐ 201	Pretzels Getzein:	100.00	50.00	10.00
	Detroit-Ind.			
☐ 202	Robert Gilks: Cleve.	100.00	50.00	10.00
☐ 203	Pete Gillespie: N.Y.	100.00	50.00	10.00
☐ 204	Barney Gilligan :	100.00	50.00	10.00
	Washington-Detroit			
☐ 205	Frank Gilmore: Wash.	100.00	50.00	10.00
☐ 206	Lee Gisbon: A's	100.00	50.00	10.00
☐ 207	Pebbly Jack Glasscock ...	150.00	75.00	15.00
	Indianapolis-N.Y.			
☐ 208	Kid Gleason: Phila.	100.00	50.00	10.00
☐ 209A	Brother Bill Gleason	100.00	50.00	10.00
	A's-Louisville			
☐ 209B	William Bill Gleason	250.00	125.00	25.00
	Browns Champs			
☐ 210	Mouse Glenn:	100.00	50.00	10.00
	Sioux City			
☐ 211	Walt Goldsby: Balt.	100.00	50.00	10.00
☐ 212	Michael Goodfellow:	100.00	50.00	10.00
	Cleveland-Detroit			
☐ 213	George Pianolegs Gore ..	100.00	50.00	10.00
	New York			
☐ 214	Frank Graves: Minn.	100.00	50.00	10.00
☐ 215	William Greenwood:	100.00	50.00	10.00
	Baltimore-Columbus			
☐ 216	Michael Greer:	100.00	50.00	10.00
	Cleveland-Brooklyn			
☐ 217	Mike Griffin:	100.00	50.00	10.00
	Baltimore-Phila NL			
☐ 218	Clark Griffith:	500.00	250.00	50.00

	Milwaukee			
☐ 219	Henry Gruber: Cleve.	100.00	50.00	10.00
☐ 220	Addison Gumbert:	100.00	50.00	10.00
	Chicago-Boston			
☐ 221	Thomas Gunning:	100.00	50.00	10.00
	Philadelphia-A's			
☐ 222	Joseph Gunson: K.C.	100.00	50.00	10.00
☐ 223	George Haddock:	100.00	50.00	10.00
	Washington			
☐ 224	William Hafner: K.C.	100.00	50.00	10.00
☐ 225	Willie Hahm:	100.00	50.00	10.00
	Chicago Mascot			
☐ 226	William Hallman:	100.00	50.00	10.00
	Philadelphia			
☐ 227	Charlie Hallstrom:	100.00	50.00	10.00
	Minn.			
☐ 228	Billy Hamilton:	500.00	250.00	50.00
	Kansas City-Phila.			
☐ 229	Hamm and Williamson: ...	150.00	75.00	15.00
☐ 230A	Frank Hankinson:	350.00	175.00	35.00
	SPOT			
☐ 230B	Frank Hankinson:	100.00	50.00	10.00
	Kansas City			
☐ 231	Ned Hanlon:	150.00	75.00	15.00
	Det.-Boston-Pitts.			
☐ 232	William Hanrahan:	100.00	50.00	10.00
	Maroons-Minn.			
☐ 233	Hapeman:	1000.00	500.00	100.00
	Sacramento PCL			
☐ 234	Pa Harkins:	100.00	50.00	10.00
	Brooklyn-Baltimore			
☐ 235	William Hart:	100.00	50.00	10.00
	Cinc.-Des Moines			
☐ 236	Wm. Hasamdear: K.C.	100.00	50.00	10.00
☐ 237	Colonel Hatfield:	100.00	50.00	10.00
	New York			
☐ 238	Egyptian Healey:	100.00	50.00	10.00
	Wash.-Indianapolis			
☐ 239	J.C. Healy:	100.00	50.00	10.00
	Omaha-Denver			
☐ 240	Guy Hecker:	100.00	50.00	10.00
	Louisville			
☐ 241	Tony Hellman:	100.00	50.00	10.00
	Sioux City			
☐ 242	Hardie Henderson:	100.00	50.00	10.00
	Brook.-Pitts.-Balt.			
☐ 243	Henderson and Greer:	150.00	75.00	15.00
	Brooklyn			
☐ 244	Moxie Hengle:	100.00	50.00	10.00
	Maroons-Minneapolis			
☐ 245	John Henry: Phila.	100.00	50.00	10.00
☐ 246	Edward Herr:	100.00	50.00	10.00
	Whites-Milwaukee			
☐ 247	Hunkey Hines: Whites	100.00	50.00	10.00
☐ 248	Paul Hines:	100.00	50.00	10.00
	Wash.-Indianapolis			
☐ 249	Texas Wonder Hoffman: .	100.00	50.00	10.00
	Denver			
☐ 250	Eddie Hogan: Cleve.	100.00	50.00	10.00
☐ 251A	William Holbert	300.00	150.00	30.00
	SPOT			
☐ 251B	William Holbert:	100.00	50.00	10.00
	Brooklyn-Mets-			
	Jersey City			
☐ 252	James(Bugs) Holliday:	100.00	50.00	10.00
	Des Moines-Cinc.			
☐ 253	Charles Hoover:	100.00	50.00	10.00
	Maroons-Chi.-K.C.			
☐ 254	Buster Hoover:	100.00	50.00	10.00
	Phila.-Toronto			
☐ 255	Jack Horner:	100.00	50.00	10.00
	Milwaukee-New Haven			
☐ 256	Horner and Warner:	150.00	75.00	15.00
	Milwaukee			
☐ 257	Michael Horning:	100.00	50.00	10.00
	Boston-Balt.-N.Y.			
☐ 258	Pete Hotaling:	100.00	50.00	10.00
	Cleveland			
☐ 259	William Howes:	100.00	50.00	10.00
	Minn.-St. Paul			
☐ 260	Dummy Hoy:	250.00	125.00	25.00
	Washington			
☐ 261A	Nat Hudson:	250.00	125.00	25.00
	Browns Champ			
☐ 261B	Nat Hudson:	100.00	50.00	10.00
	St. Louis			
☐ 262	Mickey Hughes: Brk.	100.00	50.00	10.00
☐ 263	Hungler: Sioux City	100.00	50.00	10.00
☐ 264	Wild Bill Hutchinson:	100.00	50.00	10.00
	Chicago			
☐ 265	John Irwin:	100.00	50.00	10.00
	Wash.-Wilkes Barre			
☐ 266	Cutrate Irwin:	100.00	50.00	10.00
	Phila.-Boston-Wash.			
☐ 267	A.C. Jantzen: Minn.	100.00	50.00	10.00

☐ 268	Frederick Jevne: .... Minn.-St. Paul	100.00	50.00	10.00
☐ 269	John Johnson: .... K.C.-Columbus	100.00	50.00	10.00
☐ 270	Richard Johnston: .... Boston	100.00	50.00	10.00
☐ 271	Jordan: Minneapolis	100.00	50.00	10.00
☐ 272	Heinie Kappell: .... Columbus-Cincinnati	100.00	50.00	10.00
☐ 273	Keas: Milwaukee	100.00	50.00	10.00
☐ 274	Sir Timothy Keefe: .... New York	400.00	200.00	40.00
☐ 275	Keefe and Richardson .... Stealing 2nd Base New York HOR	350.00	175.00	35.00
☐ 276	George Keefe: Wash.	100.00	50.00	10.00
☐ 277	James Keenan: Cinc.	100.00	50.00	10.00
☐ 278	Mike (King) Kelly "10,000" Chic-Boston	750.00	375.00	75.00
☐ 279	Honest John Kelly: .... Mgr. Louisville	150.00	75.00	15.00
☐ 280	Kelly: (Umpire) .... Western Association	150.00	75.00	15.00
☐ 281	Charles Kelly: .... Philadelphia	100.00	50.00	10.00
☐ 282	Kelly and Powell: .... Umpire and Manager Sioux City	150.00	75.00	15.00
☐ 283A	Rudolph Kemmler: .... Browns Champ	250.00	125.00	25.00
☐ 283B	Rudolph Kemmler: .... St. Paul	100.00	50.00	10.00
☐ 284	Theodore Kennedy: .... Des Moines-Omaha	150.00	75.00	15.00
☐ 285	J.J. Kenyon: .... Whites-Des Moines	100.00	50.00	10.00
☐ 286	John Kerins: .... Louisville	100.00	50.00	10.00
☐ 287	Matthew Kilroy: .... Baltimore-Boston	100.00	50.00	10.00
☐ 288	Charles King: .... St.L.-Chi.	100.00	50.00	10.00
☐ 289	Aug. Kloff: .... Minn.-St.Joe	100.00	50.00	10.00
☐ 290	William Klusman: .... Milwaukee-Denver	100.00	50.00	10.00
☐ 291	Phillip Knell: .... St. Joe-Phila.	100.00	50.00	10.00
☐ 292	Fred Knouf: .... St. Louis	100.00	50.00	10.00
☐ 293	Charles Kremmeyer: ...... Sacramento PCL	1000.00	500.00	100.00
☐ 294	William Krieg: .... Wash.-St. Joe-Minn.	100.00	50.00	10.00
☐ 295	Krieg and Kloff: .... Minneapolis	150.00	75.00	15.00
☐ 296	Gus Krock: Chicago	100.00	50.00	10.00
☐ 297	Willie Kuehne: .... Pittsburgh	100.00	50.00	10.00
☐ 298	Frederick Lange: .... Maroons	100.00	50.00	10.00
☐ 299	Ted Larkin: A's	100.00	50.00	10.00
☐ 300A	Arlie Latham: .... Browns Champ	250.00	125.00	25.00
☐ 300B	Arlie Latham: .... St. Louis-Chicago	150.00	75.00	15.00
☐ 301	John Lauer: .... Pittsburgh	100.00	50.00	10.00
☐ 302	Lawless: Columbus	100.00	50.00	10.00
☐ 303	John Leighton: Omaha ...	100.00	50.00	10.00
☐ 304	Levy: San Fran. PCL	1000.00	500.00	100.00
☐ 305	Tom Loftus MG: .... Whites-Cleveland	100.00	50.00	10.00
☐ 306	Lohbeck: Cleveland	100.00	50.00	10.00
☐ 307	Herman(Germany)Long . Maroons-K.C.	150.00	75.00	15.00
☐ 308	Danny Long: Oak. PCL ...	1000.00	500.00	100.00
☐ 309	Tom Lovett: .... Omaha-Brooklyn	100.00	50.00	10.00
☐ 310	Bobby (Link) Lowe: .... Milwaukee	150.00	75.00	15.00
☐ 311A	Jack Lynch SPOT	400.00	200.00	40.00
☐ 311B	John Lynch: .... All Stars	100.00	50.00	10.00
☐ 312	Dennis Lyons: A's	100.00	50.00	10.00
☐ 313	Harry Lyons: St. L.	100.00	50.00	10.00
☐ 314	Connie Mack: Wash.	1250.00	600.00	150.00
☐ 315	Joe (Reddie) Mack: .... Louisville	100.00	50.00	10.00
☐ 316	James (Little Mack) .... Macullar: Des Moines-Milwaukee	100.00	50.00	10.00
☐ 317	Kid Madden: Boston	100.00	50.00	10.00
☐ 318	Daniel Mahoney:	100.00	50.00	10.00

	St. Joe			
☐ 319	Willard(Grasshopper) ...... Maines: St. Paul	100.00	50.00	10.00
☐ 320	Fred Mann: .... St.Louis-Hartford	100.00	50.00	10.00
☐ 321	Jimmy Manning: K.C.	100.00	50.00	10.00
☐ 322	Charles(Lefty) Marr: ...... Col.-Cinc.	100.00	50.00	10.00
☐ 323	Mascot (Willie .... Breslin): New York	125.00	60.00	12.50
☐ 324	Samuel Maskery: .... Milwaukee-Des Moines	100.00	50.00	10.00
☐ 325	Bobby Mathews: A's	100.00	50.00	10.00
☐ 326	Michael Mattimore: .... New York-A's	100.00	50.00	10.00
☐ 327	Albert Maul: Pitts.	100.00	50.00	10.00
☐ 328A	Albert Mays SPOT	300.00	150.00	30.00
☐ 328B	Albert Mays: .... Columbus	100.00	50.00	10.00
☐ 329	James McAleer: .... Cleveland	100.00	50.00	10.00
☐ 330	Thomas McCarthy: .... Phila.-St. Louis	400.00	200.00	40.00
☐ 331	John McCarthy: K.C.	100.00	50.00	10.00
☐ 332	James McCauley: .... Maroons-Phila.	100.00	50.00	10.00
☐ 333	William McClellan: .... Brooklyn-Denver	100.00	50.00	10.00
☐ 334	John McCormack: .... Whites	100.00	50.00	10.00
☐ 335	Big Jim McCormick: .... Chicago-Pittsburgh	100.00	50.00	10.00
☐ 336	McCreachery: .... Mgr. Indianapolis	150.00	75.00	15.00
☐ 337	Thomas McCullum: .... Minneapolis	100.00	50.00	10.00
☐ 338	James(Chippy)McGarr: .. St. Louis-K.C.	100.00	50.00	10.00
☐ 339	Jack McGeachy: Ind.	100.00	50.00	10.00
☐ 340	John McGlone: .... Cleveland-Detroit	100.00	50.00	10.00
☐ 341	James(Deacon)McGuire . Phila.-Toronto	100.00	50.00	10.00
☐ 342	Bill (Gunner) .... McGunnigle: Mgr. Brooklyn	150.00	75.00	15.00
☐ 343	Ed McKean: Cleveland ...	100.00	50.00	10.00
☐ 344	Alex McKinnon: .... Pittsburgh	100.00	50.00	10.00
☐ 345	Thomas McLaughlin .... SPOT	350.00	175.00	35.00
☐ 346	John (Bid) McPhee: .... Cincinnati	100.00	50.00	10.00
☐ 347	James McQuaid: .... Denver	100.00	50.00	10.00
☐ 348	John McQuaid: .... Umpire Amer. Assoc.	150.00	75.00	15.00
☐ 349	Jame McTamany: .... Brook.-Col.-K.C.	100.00	50.00	10.00
☐ 350	George McVey: .... Mil.-Denver-St. Joe	100.00	50.00	10.00
☐ 351	Meegan: San Fran. .... PCL	1000.00	500.00	100.00
☐ 352	John Messitt: Omaha	100.00	50.00	10.00
☐ 353	George(Doggie)Miller ..... Pittsburgh	100.00	50.00	10.00
☐ 354	Joseph Miller: .... Omaha-Minneapolis	100.00	50.00	10.00
☐ 355	Jocko Milligan: .... St. Louis-Phila.	100.00	50.00	10.00
☐ 356	E.L. Mills: .... Milwaukee	100.00	50.00	10.00
☐ 357	Minnehan: .... Minneapolis	100.00	50.00	10.00
☐ 358	Samuel Moffet: Ind.	100.00	50.00	10.00
☐ 359	Honest Morrill: .... Boston-Washington	100.00	50.00	10.00
☐ 360	Ed(Cannonball)Morris ..... Pittsburgh	100.00	50.00	10.00
☐ 361	Morrisey: St. Paul	100.00	50.00	10.00
☐ 362	Tony(Count) Mullane: ..... Cincinnati	150.00	75.00	15.00
☐ 363	Joseph Mulvey: .... Philadelphia	100.00	50.00	10.00
☐ 364	P.L. Murphy: .... St. Paul	100.00	50.00	10.00
☐ 365	P.J. Murphy: .... New York	100.00	50.00	10.00
☐ 366	Miah Murray: Wash.	100.00	50.00	10.00
☐ 367	James (Truthful) .... Mutrie: Mgr. N.Y.	100.00	50.00	10.00
☐ 368	George Myers: .... Indianapolis-Phila.	100.00	50.00	10.00
☐ 369	Al (Cod) Myers:	100.00	50.00	10.00

	Washington			
☐ 370	Thomas Nagle:	100.00	50.00	10.00
	Omaha-Chi.			
☐ 371	Billy Nash: Boston	100.00	50.00	10.00
☐ 372	Jack(Candy) Nelson:	350.00	175.00	35.00
	SPOT			
☐ 373	Kid Nichols: Omaha	600.00	300.00	60.00
☐ 374	Samuel Nichols:	100.00	50.00	10.00
	Pittsburgh			
☐ 375	J.W. Nicholson	100.00	50.00	10.00
	Maroons-Minn.			
☐ 376	Tom(Parson)Nicholson	100.00	50.00	10.00
	Whites-Cleveland			
☐ 377A	Nicholls Nicol	250.00	125.00	25.00
	Browns Champ			
☐ 377B	Hugh Nicol: Cinc.	100.00	50.00	10.00
☐ 378	Nicol and Reilly	150.00	75.00	15.00
	Cincinnati			
☐ 379	Frederick Nyce	100.00	50.00	10.00
	Whites-Burlington			
☐ 380	Doc Oberlander	100.00	50.00	10.00
	Cleveland-Syracuse			
☐ 381	Jack O'Brien:	100.00	50.00	10.00
	Brooklyn-Baltimore			
☐ 382	William O'Brien:	100.00	50.00	10.00
	Washington			
☐ 383	O'Brien and Irwin:	150.00	75.00	15.00
☐ 384	Darby O'Brien:	100.00	50.00	10.00
	Brooklyn			
☐ 385	John O'Brien: Cleve.	100.00	50.00	10.00
☐ 386	P.J. O'Connell:	100.00	50.00	10.00
	Omaha-Des Moines			
☐ 387	John O'Connor:	100.00	50.00	10.00
	Cincinnati-Columbus			
☐ 388	Hank O'Day:	100.00	50.00	10.00
	Washington-New York			
☐ 389A	James O'Neil:	100.00	50.00	10.00
	St. Louis-Chicago			
☐ 389B	James O'Neil:	250.00	125.00	25.00
	Browns Champs			
☐ 390	O'Neill: Oakland	1000.00	500.00	100.00
	PCL			
☐ 391	Orator O'Rourke:	450.00	225.00	45.00
	New York			
☐ 392	Thomas O'Rourke:	100.00	50.00	10.00
	Boston-Jersey City			
☐ 393A	David Orr SPOT	300.00	150.00	30.00
☐ 393B	David Orr:	100.00	50.00	10.00
	All Star-			
	Brooklyn-Columbus			
☐ 394	Parsons: Minneapolis	100.00	50.00	10.00
☐ 395	Owen Patton:	100.00	50.00	10.00
	Minn.-Des Moines			
☐ 396	James Peeples:	100.00	50.00	10.00
	Brooklyn-Columbus			
☐ 397	Peeples and Henderson	150.00	75.00	15.00
	Brooklyn			
☐ 398	Hip Perrier:	1000.00	500.00	100.00
	San Francisco PCL			
☐ 399	Patrick Pettee:	100.00	50.00	10.00
	Milwaukee-London			
☐ 400	Pettee and Lowe:	150.00	75.00	15.00
	Milwaukee			
☐ 401	Bob Pettit: Chicago	100.00	50.00	10.00
☐ 402	Dandelion Pfeffer:	100.00	50.00	10.00
	Chi.			
☐ 403	Dick Phelan:	100.00	50.00	10.00
	Des Moines			
☐ 404	William Phillips:	100.00	50.00	10.00
	Brooklyn-Kansas City			
☐ 405	Horace Phillips:	100.00	50.00	10.00
	Pittsburgh			
☐ 406	John Pickett:	100.00	50.00	10.00
	St. Paul-K.C.-Phila.			
☐ 407	George Pinkney:	100.00	50.00	10.00
	Brooklyn			
☐ 408	Thomas Poorman:	100.00	50.00	10.00
	A's-Milwaukee			
☐ 409	Henry Porter:	100.00	50.00	10.00
	Brooklyn-Kansas City			
☐ 410	James Powell:	100.00	50.00	10.00
	Sioux City			
☐ 411	Tom Powers:	1000.00	500.00	100.00
	San Francisco PCL			
☐ 412	Bill Blonie Purcell:	100.00	50.00	10.00
	Baltimore-A's			
☐ 413	Thomas Quinn:	100.00	50.00	10.00
	Baltimore			
☐ 414	Joseph Quinn:	100.00	50.00	10.00
	Des Moines-Boston			
☐ 415A	Old Hoss Radbourne:	600.00	300.00	60.00
	Boston (portrait)			
☐ 415B	Old Hoss Radbourne:	450.00	225.00	45.00
	Boston (non-portrait)			
☐ 416	Shorty Radford:	100.00	50.00	10.00

	Brooklyn-Cleveland			
☐ 417	Tom Ramsey:	100.00	50.00	10.00
	Louisville			
☐ 418	Rehse: Minneapolis	100.00	50.00	10.00
☐ 419	Long John Reilly:	100.00	50.00	10.00
	Cincinnati			
☐ 420	Charles Reilly:	100.00	50.00	10.00
	(Princeton) St.Paul			
☐ 421	Charles Reynolds:	100.00	50.00	10.00
	Kansas City			
☐ 422	Hardie Richardson	100.00	50.00	10.00
	Detroit-Boston			
☐ 423	Danny Richardson:	100.00	50.00	10.00
	New York			
☐ 424	Frank Ringo:	100.00	50.00	10.00
	St. Paul			
☐ 425	Charles Ripslager	350.00	175.00	35.00
	SPOT			
☐ 426	John Roach: New York	100.00	50.00	10.00
☐ 427	Wilbert Robinson	500.00	250.00	50.00
	(Uncle Robbie): A's			
☐ 428	M.C. Robinson: Minn.	100.00	50.00	10.00
☐ 429A	Yank Robinson:	100.00	50.00	10.00
	St. Louis			
☐ 429B	Wm.(Yank) Robinson:	250.00	125.00	25.00
	Browns Champs			
☐ 430	George Rooks:	100.00	50.00	10.00
	Maroons-Detroit			
☐ 431	James(Chief) Roseman	350.00	175.00	35.00
	SPOT			
☐ 432	Davis Rowe:	100.00	50.00	10.00
	Mgr. K.C.-Denver			
☐ 433	Jack Rowe: Detroit-	100.00	50.00	10.00
	Pittsburgh			
☐ 434	Amos (Hoosier	600.00	300.00	60.00
	Thunderbolt) Rusie:			
	Ind.-New York			
☐ 435	James Ryan: Chicago	100.00	50.00	10.00
☐ 436	Henry Sage:	100.00	50.00	10.00
	Des Moines-Toledo			
☐ 437	Sage and Van Dyke:	150.00	75.00	15.00
	Des Moines-Toledo			
☐ 438	Frank Salee:	100.00	50.00	10.00
	Omaha-Boston			
☐ 439	Sanders: Omaha	100.00	50.00	10.00
☐ 440	Al (Ben) Sanders:	100.00	50.00	10.00
	Philadelphia			
☐ 441	Frank Scheibeck:	100.00	50.00	10.00
	Detroit			
☐ 442	Albert Schellhase:	100.00	50.00	10.00
	St. Joseph			
☐ 443	William Schenkle:	100.00	50.00	10.00
	Milwaukee			
☐ 444	Bill Schildknecht:	100.00	50.00	10.00
	Des Moines-Milwaukee			
☐ 445	Gus "Pink Whiskers"	100.00	50.00	10.00
	Schmelz			
	Mgr. Cincinnati			
☐ 446	R. F. Schoch: Wash.	100.00	50.00	10.00
☐ 447	Lewis Schoeneck	100.00	50.00	10.00
	(Jumbo):			
	Maroons-Indianapolis			
☐ 448	Pop Schriver: Phila.	100.00	50.00	10.00
☐ 449	John Seery: Ind.	100.00	50.00	10.00
☐ 450	William Serad	100.00	50.00	10.00
	Cincinnnati-Toronto			
☐ 451	Edward Seward: A's	100.00	50.00	10.00
☐ 452	George(Orator)Shafer	100.00	50.00	10.00
	Des Moines			
☐ 453	Frank Shafer:	100.00	50.00	10.00
	St. Paul			
☐ 454	Daniel Shannon:	100.00	50.00	10.00
	Omaha-L'ville-Phila.			
☐ 455	William Sharsig:	150.00	75.00	15.00
	Mgr. Athletics			
☐ 456	Samuel Shaw:	100.00	50.00	10.00
	Baltimore-Newark			
☐ 457	John Shaw:	100.00	50.00	10.00
	Minneapolis			
☐ 458	William Shindle:	100.00	50.00	10.00
	Baltimore-Phila.			
☐ 459	George Shock: Wash.	100.00	50.00	10.00
☐ 460	Otto Shomberg: Ind.	100.00	50.00	10.00
☐ 461	Lev Shreve: Ind.	100.00	50.00	10.00
☐ 462	Ed (Baldy) Silch:	100.00	50.00	10.00
	Brooklyn-Denver			
☐ 463	Michael Slattery:	100.00	50.00	10.00
	New York			
☐ 464	Sam(Skyrocket)Smith:	100.00	50.00	10.00
	Louisville			
☐ 465A	John "Phenomenal"	750.00	375.00	75.00
	Smith: Balt.-A's			
	(portrait)			
☐ 465B	John "Phenomenal"	100.00	50.00	10.00
	Smith: Balt.-A's			

	(non-portrait)			
☐ 466	Elmer Smith: .... Cincinnati	100.00	50.00	10.00
☐ 467	Fred (Sam) Smith: .... Des Moines	100.00	50.00	10.00
☐ 468	George(Germany)Smith . Brooklyn	100.00	50.00	10.00
☐ 469	Pop Smith: .... Pitt.-Bos.-Phila.	100.00	50.00	10.00
☐ 470	Nick Smith: St. Joe	100.00	50.00	10.00
☐ 471	Pop Snyder: Cleve.	100.00	50.00	10.00
☐ 472	P.T. Somers: .... St. Louis	100.00	50.00	10.00
☐ 473	Joe Sommer: Balt.	100.00	50.00	10.00
☐ 474	Pete Sommers: .... Chicago-New York	100.00	50.00	10.00
☐ 475	William Sowders: .... Boston-Pittsburgh	100.00	50.00	10.00
☐ 476	John Sowders: .... St. Paul-Kansas City	100.00	50.00	10.00
☐ 477	Charles Sprague: .... Maroons-Chi.-Cleve.	100.00	50.00	10.00
☐ 478	Edward Sproat: .... Whites	100.00	50.00	10.00
☐ 479	Harry Staley: .... Whites-Pittsburgh	100.00	50.00	10.00
☐ 480	Daniel Stearns: .... Des Moines-K.C.	100.00	50.00	10.00
☐ 481	Billy "Cannonball" .... Stemmyer: Boston-Cleveland	100.00	50.00	10.00
☐ 482	Stengel: Columbus	100.00	50.00	10.00
☐ 483	B.F. Stephens: Milw.	100.00	50.00	10.00
☐ 484	John C. Sterling: .... Minneapolis	100.00	50.00	10.00
☐ 485	Stockwell: S.F. PCL	1000.00	500.00	100.00
☐ 486	Harry Stovey: .... A's-Boston	200.00	100.00	20.00
☐ 487	C. Scott Stratton: .... Louisville	100.00	50.00	10.00
☐ 488	Joseph Straus: .... Omaha-Milwaukee	100.00	50.00	10.00
☐ 489	John (Cub) Stricker: ...... Cleveland	100.00	50.00	10.00
☐ 490	J.O. Struck: Milw.	100.00	50.00	10.00
☐ 491	Marty Sullivan: .... Chicago-Ind.	100.00	50.00	10.00
☐ 492	Michael Sullivan: .... A's	100.00	50.00	10.00
☐ 493	Billy Sunday: .... Chicago-Pittsburgh	400.00	200.00	40.00
☐ 494	Sy Sutcliffe: Cleve.	100.00	50.00	10.00
☐ 495	Ezra Sutton: .... Boston-Milwaukee	100.00	50.00	10.00
☐ 496	Ed Cyrus Swartwood: ..... Brook.-D.Moines-Ham.	100.00	50.00	10.00
☐ 497	Parke Swartzel: K.C.	100.00	50.00	10.00
☐ 498	Peter Sweeney: Wash. ...	100.00	50.00	10.00
☐ 499	Sylvester: Sacra. .... PCL	1000.00	500.00	100.00
☐ 500	Ed (Dimples) Tate: .... Boston-Baltimore	100.00	50.00	10.00
☐ 501	Patsy Tebeau: .... Chi.-Cleve.-Minn.	100.00	50.00	10.00
☐ 502	John Tener: Chicago	125.00	60.00	12.50
☐ 503	Bill (Adonis) Terry: .... Brooklyn	100.00	50.00	10.00
☐ 504	Big Sam Thompson: .... Detroit-Philadelphia	450.00	225.00	45.00
☐ 505	Silent Mike Tiernan: .... New York	100.00	50.00	10.00
☐ 506	Ledell Titcomb: N.Y.	100.00	50.00	10.00
☐ 507	Phillip Tomney: .... Louisville	100.00	50.00	10.00
☐ 508	Stephen Toole: .... Brooklyn-K.C.-Rochester	100.00	50.00	10.00
☐ 509	George Townsend: A's ...	100.00	50.00	10.00
☐ 510	William Traffley: .... Des Moines	100.00	50.00	10.00
☐ 511	George Treadway: .... St. Paul-Denver	100.00	50.00	10.00
☐ 512	Samuel Trott: .... Baltimore-Newark	100.00	50.00	10.00
☐ 513	Trott and Burns: .... Baltimore HOR	150.00	75.00	15.00
☐ 514	Tom(Foghorn) Tucker: ... Baltimore	100.00	50.00	10.00
☐ 515	William Tuckerman: .... St. Paul	100.00	50.00	10.00
☐ 516	Turner: Minneapolis	100.00	50.00	10.00
☐ 517	Lawrence Twitchell: .... Detroit-Cleveland	100.00	50.00	10.00
☐ 518	James Tyng: Phila.	100.00	50.00	10.00
☐ 519	William Van Dyke: .... Des Moines-Toledo	100.00	50.00	10.00
☐ 520	George Rip VanHaltren .. Chicago	100.00	50.00	10.00
☐ 521	Harry Vaughn: .... (Farmer) Louisville-New York	100.00	50.00	10.00
☐ 522	Peek-a-Boo Veach: .... St. Paul	100.00	50.00	10.00
☐ 523	Veach: Sacra. PCL	1000.00	500.00	100.00
☐ 524	Leon Viau: .... Cincinnati	100.00	50.00	10.00
☐ 525	William Vinton: .... Minneapolis	100.00	50.00	10.00
☐ 526	Joseph Visner: .... Brooklyn	100.00	50.00	10.00
☐ 527	Christian VonDer Ahe ..... Owner Browns Champs	350.00	175.00	35.00
☐ 528	Joseph Walsh: Omaha	100.00	50.00	10.00
☐ 529	John (Monte) Ward: .... New York	400.00	200.00	40.00
☐ 530	E.H. Warner: .... Milwaukee	100.00	50.00	10.00
☐ 531	William Watkins: .... Mgr. Detroit-Kansas City	150.00	75.00	15.00
☐ 532	Bill Weaver: .... (Farmer) Louisville	100.00	50.00	10.00
☐ 533	Charles Weber: .... Sioux City	100.00	50.00	10.00
☐ 534	George Weidman .... (Stump): Detroit-New York	100.00	50.00	10.00
☐ 535	William Weidner: .... Columbus	100.00	50.00	10.00
☐ 536A	Curtis Welch: .... Browns Champ	250.00	125.00	25.00
☐ 536B	Curtis Welch: A's	100.00	50.00	10.00
☐ 537	Welch and Gleason: .... Athletics	150.00	75.00	15.00
☐ 538	Smilin'Mickey Welch: ...... All Star-New York	450.00	225.00	45.00
☐ 539	Jake Wells: K.C.	100.00	50.00	10.00
☐ 540	Frank Wells: .... Des Moines-Mil.	150.00	75.00	15.00
☐ 541	Joseph Werrick: .... Louisville-St. Paul	100.00	50.00	10.00
☐ 542	Milton(Buck) West: .... Minneapolis	100.00	50.00	10.00
☐ 543	Gus "Cannonball" .... Weyhing: A's	100.00	50.00	10.00
☐ 544	John Weyhing: .... Athletics-Columbus	100.00	50.00	10.00
☐ 545	Bobby Wheelock: .... Boston-Detroit	100.00	50.00	10.00
☐ 546	Whitacre: A's	100.00	50.00	10.00
☐ 547	Pat Whitaker: Balt.	100.00	50.00	10.00
☐ 548	Deacon White: .... Detroit-Pittsburgh	100.00	50.00	10.00
☐ 549	William White: .... Louisville	100.00	50.00	10.00
☐ 550	Jim "Grasshopper" .... Whitney: Wash.-Indianapolis	100.00	50.00	10.00
☐ 551	Arthur Whitney: .... Pittsburgh-New York	100.00	50.00	10.00
☐ 552	G. Whitney: .... St. Joseph	100.00	50.00	10.00
☐ 553	James Williams: .... Mgr. Cleveland	150.00	75.00	15.00
☐ 554	Ned Williamson: Chi.	150.00	75.00	15.00
☐ 555	Williamson and .... Mascot	150.00	75.00	15.00
☐ 556	C.H. Willis: Omaha	100.00	50.00	10.00
☐ 557	Walt Wilmot: .... Washington-Chicago	100.00	50.00	10.00
☐ 558	George Winkleman: .... Minneapolis-Hartford	100.00	50.00	10.00
☐ 559	Samuel Wise: .... Boston-Washington	100.00	50.00	10.00
☐ 560	William Wolf: .... (Chicken) Louisville	100.00	50.00	10.00
☐ 561	George (Dandy) Wood: ... Philadelphia	100.00	50.00	10.00
☐ 562	Peter Wood: Phila.	100.00	50.00	10.00
☐ 563	Harry Wright: .... Mgr. Philadelphia	1250.00	600.00	150.00
☐ 564	Charles Zimmer .... (Chief) Cleveland	100.00	50.00	10.00
☐ 565	Frank Zinn: .... Athletics	100.00	50.00	10.00

			EX-MT	VG-E	GOOD
☐	49	Clarence Whistler	20.00	10.00	2.00
☐	50	Charles Wood	20.00	10.00	2.00

N184 Kimball's

This set of 50 color pictures of contemporary athletes was Kimball's answer to the sets produced by Allen , Ginter (N28 and N29) and Goodwin (N162). Issued in 1888, the cards are backlisted but are not numbered. The cards are listed below in alphabetical order without regard to sport. There are four baseball players in the set. An album (ACC: A42) was offered as a premium in exchange for coupons found in the tobacco packages. The baseball players are noted in the checklist below by BB after their name.

			EX-MT	VG-E	GOOD
	COMPLETE SET (50)		2800.00	1400.00	300.00
	COMMON BASEBALL		500.00	250.00	50.00
	COMMON BOXER		65.00	25.00	5.00
	COMMON OTHERS		20.00	10.00	2.00
☐	1	Wm. Beach	20.00	10.00	2.00
☐	2	Marve Beardsley	20.00	10.00	2.00
☐	3	Chas. P. Blatt	20.00	10.00	2.00
☐	4	Blondin	20.00	10.00	2.00
☐	5	Paul Boynton	20.00	10.00	2.00
☐	6	E.A.(Ernie) Burch BB	500.00	250.00	50.00
☐	7	Patsy Cardiff	20.00	10.00	2.00
☐	8	Phillip Casey	20.00	10.00	2.00
☐	9	J.C. Cockburn	20.00	10.00	2.00
☐	10	Dell Darling BB	500.00	250.00	50.00
☐	11	Jack Dempsey BOX	125.00	50.00	10.00
☐	12	Della Ferrell	20.00	10.00	2.00
☐	13	Clarence Freeman	20.00	10.00	2.00
☐	14	Louis George	20.00	10.00	2.00
☐	15	W.G. George	20.00	10.00	2.00
☐	16	George W. Hamilton	20.00	10.00	2.00
☐	17	Edward Hanlan	20.00	10.00	2.00
☐	18	C.H. Heins	20.00	10.00	2.00
☐	19	Hardie Henderson BB	500.00	250.00	50.00
☐	20	Thomas H. Hume	20.00	10.00	2.00
☐	21	J.H. Jordon	20.00	10.00	2.00
☐	22	Johnny Kane	20.00	10.00	2.00
☐	23	James McLaughlin	20.00	10.00	2.00
☐	24	John McPherson	20.00	10.00	2.00
☐	25	Joseph Morsler	20.00	10.00	2.00
☐	26	William Muldoon	20.00	10.00	2.00
☐	27	S. Muller	20.00	10.00	2.00
☐	28	Isaac Murphy	20.00	10.00	2.00
☐	29	John Murphy	20.00	10.00	2.00
☐	30	L.E. Myers	20.00	10.00	2.00
☐	31	Annie Oakley	50.00	25.00	5.00
☐	32	Daniel O'Leary	20.00	10.00	2.00
☐	33	James O'Neil BB	600.00	300.00	60.00
☐	34	Wm. Byrd Page	20.00	10.00	2.00
☐	35	Axel Paulsen	20.00	10.00	2.00
☐	36	Master Ray Perry	20.00	10.00	2.00
☐	37	Duncan C. Ross	20.00	10.00	2.00
☐	38	W.A. Rowe	20.00	10.00	2.00
☐	39	Jacob Schaefer	20.00	10.00	2.00
☐	40	M. Schloss	20.00	10.00	2.00
☐	41	Jem Smith	20.00	10.00	2.00
☐	42	Lillian Smith	20.00	10.00	2.00
☐	43	Hattie Stewart	20.00	10.00	2.00
☐	44	John L. Sullivan BOX	125.00	60.00	12.50
☐	45	Arthur Wallace	20.00	10.00	2.00
☐	46	Tommy Warren BOX	65.00	25.00	5.00
☐	47	Ada Webb	20.00	10.00	2.00
☐	48	John Wessels	20.00	10.00	2.00

N284 Buchner

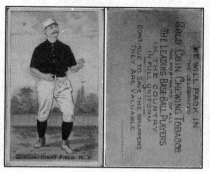

The baseball players found in this Buchner set are a part of a larger group of cards portraying policemen, jockeys and actors, all of which were issued with the tobacco brand "Gold Coin." The set is comprised of three major groupings or types. In the first type, nine players from eight teams, plus three Brooklyn players, are all portrayed in identical poses according to position. In the second type, St. Louis has 14 players depicted in poses which are not repeated. The last group contains 53 additional cards which vary according to pose, team change, spelling, etc. These third type cards are indicated in the checklist below by an asterisk. In all, there are 116 individuals portrayed on 142 cards. The existence of an additional player in the set, McClellan of Brooklyn, has never been verified. The set was issued circa 1887. The cards are numbered below in alphabetical order within team with teams themselves listed in alphabetical order: Baltimore (1-4), Boston (5-13), Brooklyn (14-17), Chicago (18-26), Detroit (27-35), Indianapolis (36-47), LaCrosse (48-51), Milwaukee (52-55), New York Mets (56-63), New York (64-73), Philadelphia (74-83), Pittsburg (84-92), St. Louis (93-106), and Washington (107-117).

			EX-MT	VG-E	GOOD
	COMPLETE SET		15000.00	7500.00	1500.00
	COMMON PLAYERS		75.00	37.50	7.50
	COMMON ST. LOUIS		120.00	60.00	12.00
	COMMON PLAYERS *		120.00	60.00	12.00
☐	1	Burns: Baltimore *	120.00	60.00	12.00
☐	2	Fulmer: Baltimore *	120.00	60.00	12.00
☐	3	Kilroy: Baltimore *	120.00	60.00	12.00
☐	4	Purcell: Baltimore *	120.00	60.00	12.00
☐	5	John Burdock: Boston	75.00	37.50	7.50
☐	6	Bill Daley: Boston	75.00	37.50	7.50
☐	7	Joe Hornung: Boston	75.00	37.50	7.50
☐	8	Johnston: Boston	75.00	37.50	7.50
☐	9A	King Kelly: Boston .... (right field)	250.00	125.00	25.00
☐	9B	King Kelly: Boston .... (catcher) *	350.00	175.00	35.00
☐	10A	Morrill: Boston .... (both hands out-stretched face high)	75.00	37.50	7.50
☐	10B	Morrill: Boston * .... (hands clasped near chin)	120.00	60.00	12.00
☐	11A	Hoss Radbourn: .... Boston	200.00	100.00	20.00
☐	11B	Hoss Radbourn: .... Boston * (hands together above waist)	300.00	150.00	30.00

☐ 12 Sutton: Boston	75.00	37.50	7.50
☐ 13 Wise: Boston	75.00	37.50	7.50
☐ 14 McClellan: Brooklyn (never confirmed)	00.00	.00	.00
☐ 15 Peoples: Brooklyn	75.00	37.50	7.50
☐ 16 Phillips: Brooklyn	75.00	37.50	7.50
☐ 17 Porter: Brooklyn	75.00	37.50	7.50
☐ 18A Adrian Anson: Chicago (both hands outstretched face high)	400.00	200.00	40.00
☐ 18B Adrian Anson: Chicago * (left hand on hip, right hand down)	600.00	300.00	60.00
☐ 19 Burns: Chicago	75.00	37.50	7.50
☐ 20A John Clarkson: Chicago	200.00	100.00	20.00
☐ 20B John Clarkson: Chicago * (right arm extended, left arm near side)	300.00	150.00	30.00
☐ 21 Silver Flint: Chicago	75.00	37.50	7.50
☐ 22 Pfeffer: Chicago	75.00	37.50	7.50
☐ 23 Ryan: Chicago	75.00	37.50	7.50
☐ 24 Billy Sullivan: Chicago	100.00	50.00	10.00
☐ 25 Billy Sunday: Chicago	200.00	100.00	20.00
☐ 26A Williamson: Chicago (shortstop)	75.00	37.50	7.50
☐ 26B Williamson: Chicago (second base) *	120.00	60.00	12.00
☐ 27 Bennett: Detroit	75.00	37.50	7.50
☐ 28A Dan Brouthers: Detroit (fielding)	200.00	100.00	20.00
☐ 28B Dan Brouthers: Detroit * (batting)	300.00	150.00	30.00
☐ 29 Dunlap: Detroit	75.00	37.50	7.50
☐ 30 Getzein: Detroit	75.00	37.50	7.50
☐ 31 Hanlon: Detroit	75.00	37.50	7.50
☐ 32 Manning: Detoit	75.00	37.50	7.50
☐ 33A Richardson: Detroit (hands together in front of chest)	75.00	37.50	7.50
☐ 33B Richardson: Detroit * (right hand holding ball above head)	120.00	60.00	12.00
☐ 34A Sam Thompson: Detroit (looking up with hands at waist)	200.00	100.00	20.00
☐ 34B Sam Thompson: Detroit * (hands chest high)	300.00	150.00	30.00
☐ 35 White: Detroit	75.00	37.50	7.50
☐ 36 Arundel: Indianapolis	75.00	37.50	7.50
☐ 37 Bassett: Indianapolis	75.00	37.50	7.50
☐ 38 Boyle: Indianapolis *	75.00	37.50	7.50
☐ 39 Cahill: Indianapolis *	120.00	60.00	12.00
☐ 40A Denny: Indianapolis (hands on knees, legs bent)	75.00	37.50	7.50
☐ 40B Denny: Indianapolis * (hands on knees, legs not bent)	120.00	60.00	12.00
☐ 41A Jack Glasscock: Indianapolis (crouching, catching a grounder)	100.00	50.00	10.00
☐ 41B Jack Glasscock: Indianapolis * (hands on knees)	150.00	75.00	15.00
☐ 42 Healy: Indianapolis	75.00	37.50	7.50
☐ 43 Meyers: Indianapolis *	120.00	60.00	12.00
☐ 44 McGeachy: Indianapolis	75.00	37.50	7.50
☐ 45 Polhemus: Indianapolis	75.00	37.50	7.50
☐ 46A Seery: Indianapolis (hands together in front of chest)	75.00	37.50	7.50
☐ 46B Seery: Indianapolis *	120.00	60.00	12.00
(hands outstretched head high)			
☐ 47 Shomberg: Indianapolis	75.00	37.50	7.50
☐ 48 Corbett: Lacrosse *	120.00	60.00	12.00
☐ 49 Crowley: Lacrosse *	120.00	60.00	12.00
☐ 50 Kennedy: Lacrosse *	120.00	60.00	12.00
☐ 51 Rooks: Lacrosse *	120.00	60.00	12.00
☐ 52 Forster: Milwaukee *	120.00	60.00	12.00
☐ 53 Hart: Milwaukee *	120.00	60.00	12.00
☐ 54 Morrissy: Milwaukee *	120.00	60.00	12.00
☐ 55 Strauss: Milwaukee *	120.00	60.00	12.00
☐ 56 Cushmann: NY Mets *	120.00	60.00	12.00
☐ 57 Jim Donohue: NY Mets *	120.00	60.00	12.00
☐ 58 Esterbrooke (sic): NY Mets *	120.00	60.00	12.00
☐ 59 Joe Gerhardt: NY Mets *	120.00	60.00	12.00
☐ 60 Frank Hankinson: NY Mets *	120.00	60.00	12.00
☐ 61 Jack Nelson: NY Mets *	120.00	60.00	12.00
☐ 62 Dave Orr: NY Mets *	120.00	60.00	12.00
☐ 63 James Rosemann: NY Mets *	120.00	60.00	12.00
☐ 64A Roger Connor: New York (both hands outstretched face high)	200.00	100.00	20.00
☐ 64B Roger Connor: New York * (hands outstretched, palms up)	300.00	150.00	30.00
☐ 65 Deasley: New York *	120.00	60.00	12.00
☐ 66A Mike Dorgan: New York (fielding)	75.00	37.50	7.50
☐ 66B Mike Dorgan: New York (batting) *	120.00	60.00	12.00
☐ 67A Buck Ewing: New York (ball in left hand, right arm out shoulder high)	200.00	100.00	20.00
☐ 67B Buck Ewing: New York * (appears ready to clap)	300.00	150.00	30.00
☐ 68A Pete Gillespie: New York (fielding)	75.00	37.50	7.50
☐ 68B Pete Gillespie: New York (batting) *	120.00	60.00	12.00
☐ 69 George Gore: New York	75.00	37.50	7.50
☐ 70A Tim Keefe: New York	200.00	100.00	20.00
☐ 70B Tim Keefe: New York * (ball just released from right hand)	300.00	150.00	30.00
☐ 71A Jim O'Rourke: New York (hands cupped in front, thigh high)	200.00	100.00	20.00
☐ 71B Jim O'Rourke: New York * (hands on knees, looking right)	300.00	150.00	30.00
☐ 72A Danny Richardson: New York (third base)	75.00	37.50	7.50
☐ 72B Danny Richardson: New York (second base) *	120.00	60.00	12.00
☐ 73A John M. Ward: New York (crouching, catching a grounder)	200.00	100.00	20.00
☐ 73B John M. Ward: New York * (hands by left knee)	300.00	150.00	30.00
☐ 73C John M. Ward: New York * (hands on knees)	300.00	150.00	30.00
☐ 74A Andrews: Philadelphia (hands together in front of neck)	75.00	37.50	7.50
☐ 74B Andrews: Philadelphia * (catching, hands waist high)	120.00	60.00	12.00
☐ 75 Bastian: Philadelphia	75.00	37.50	7.50
☐ 76 Dan Casey: Philadelphia *	120.00	60.00	12.00

☐ 77	Clements: .... Philadelphia	75.00	37.50	7.50
☐ 78	Sid Farrar: .... Philadelphia	75.00	37.50	7.50
☐ 79	Ferguson: .... Philadelphia	75.00	37.50	7.50
☐ 80	Fogerty: .... Philadelphia	75.00	37.50	7.50
☐ 81	Irwin: Philadelphia	75.00	37.50	7.50
☐ 82A	Mulvey: .... Philadelphia (hands on knees)	75.00	37.50	7.50
☐ 82B	Mulvey: Philadelphia * (hands together above head)	120.00	60.00	12.00
☐ 83A	Pete Wood: Phila- delphia (fielding)	75.00	37.50	7.50
☐ 83B	Pete Wood: Phila- delphia HOR (Stealing a Base) *	120.00	60.00	12.00
☐ 84	Barkley: Pittsburg	75.00	37.50	7.50
☐ 85	Beecher: Pittsburg	75.00	37.50	7.50
☐ 86	Brown: Pittsburg	75.00	37.50	7.50
☐ 87	Carroll: Pittsburg	75.00	37.50	7.50
☐ 88	Coleman: Pittsburg	75.00	37.50	7.50
☐ 89	McCormick: Pittsburg	75.00	37.50	7.50
☐ 90	Miller: Pittsburg	75.00	37.50	7.50
☐ 91	Smith: Pittsburg	75.00	37.50	7.50
☐ 92	Whitney: Pittsburg	75.00	37.50	7.50
☐ 93	Barkley: St. Louis	120.00	60.00	12.00
☐ 94	Bushong: St. Louis	120.00	60.00	12.00
☐ 95	Bob Carruthers .... (sic): St. Louis	150.00	75.00	15.00
☐ 96	Charles Comiskey: .... St. Louis	350.00	175.00	35.00
☐ 97	Dave Foutz: .... St. Louis	120.00	60.00	12.00
☐ 98	William Gleason: .... St. Louis	120.00	60.00	12.00
☐ 99	Arlie Latham: .... St. Louis	120.00	60.00	12.00
☐ 100	McGinnis: St. Louis	120.00	60.00	12.00
☐ 101	Hugh Nicol: .... St. Louis	120.00	60.00	12.00
☐ 102	James O'Neil: .... St. Louis	120.00	60.00	12.00
☐ 103	Robinson: St. Louis	120.00	60.00	12.00
☐ 104	Sullivan: St. Louis	120.00	60.00	12.00
☐ 105	Chris Von Der Ahe: .... St. Louis (actually a photo, rather than drawing)	350.00	175.00	35.00
☐ 106	Curt Welch: .... St. Louis	120.00	60.00	12.00
☐ 107	Carroll: Washington	75.00	37.50	7.50
☐ 108	Craig: Washington *	120.00	60.00	12.00
☐ 109	Crane: Washington *	120.00	60.00	12.00
☐ 110	Dailey: Washington	75.00	37.50	7.50
☐ 111	Donnelly: Washington	75.00	37.50	7.50
☐ 112A	Farrell: .... Washington (ball in left hand, right arm out shoulder high)	75.00	37.50	7.50
☐ 112B	Farrell: .... Washington * (ball in hands near right knee)	120.00	60.00	12.00
☐ 113	Gilligan: Washington	75.00	37.50	7.50
☐ 114A	Hines: Washington .... (fielding)	75.00	37.50	7.50
☐ 114B	Hines: Washington .... (batting) *	120.00	60.00	12.00
☐ 115	Myers: Washington	75.00	37.50	7.50
☐ 116	O'Brien: Washington	75.00	37.50	7.50
☐ 117	Whitney: Washington	75.00	37.50	7.50

N300 Mayo

The Mayo Tobacco Works of Richmond, Va., issued this set of 48 ballplayers about 1895. The cards contain sepia portraits although some pictures appear to be black and white. There are 40 different individuals known in the set; cards 1 to 28 appear in uniform, while the last twelve (29-40) appear in street clothes. Eight of the former also appear with variations in uniform. The player's name appears

within the picture area and a "Mayo's Cut Plug" ad is printed in a panel at the base of the card.

		EX-MT	VG-E	GOOD
COMPLETE SET (48)		17000.00	8500.00	2000.00
COMMON PLAYERS (1-28)		250.00	125.00	25.00
COMMON PLAYERS (29-40)		250.00	125.00	25.00
☐ 1	Cap Anson: Chicago	1350.00	650.00	150.00
☐ 2	Bannon RF: Boston	250.00	125.00	25.00
☐ 3A	Dan Brouthers 1B: .... Baltimore	600.00	300.00	60.00
☐ 3B	Dan Brouthers 1B: .... Louisville	650.00	325.00	65.00
☐ 4	John Clarkson P: .... St. Louis	600.00	300.00	60.00
☐ 5	T.W. Corcoran SS: .... Brooklyn	250.00	125.00	25.00
☐ 6	Cross 2B: .... Philadelphia	250.00	125.00	25.00
☐ 7	Hugh Duffy CF: .... Boston	600.00	300.00	60.00
☐ 8A	Buck Ewing RF: .... Cincinnati	650.00	325.00	65.00
☐ 8B	Buck Ewing RF: .... Cleveland	650.00	325.00	65.00
☐ 9	Dave Foutz 1B: .... Brooklyn	250.00	125.00	25.00
☐ 10	Ganzel C: Boston	250.00	125.00	25.00
☐ 11A	Glasscock SS: .... Pittsburgh	300.00	150.00	30.00
☐ 11B	Glasscock SS: .... Louisville	300.00	150.00	30.00
☐ 12	Griffin CF: .... Brooklyn	250.00	125.00	25.00
☐ 13A	Haddock P: .... Philadelphia	250.00	125.00	25.00
☐ 13B	Haddock P: no team	250.00	125.00	25.00
☐ 14	Joyce CF: Brooklyn	250.00	125.00	25.00
☐ 15	Wm. Kennedy P: .... Brooklyn	250.00	125.00	25.00
☐ 16A	Tom F. Kinslow C: .... Pitts.	250.00	125.00	25.00
☐ 16B	Tom F. Kinslow C: .... no team	250.00	125.00	25.00
☐ 17	Arlie Latham 3B: .... Cincinnati	250.00	125.00	25.00
☐ 18	Long SS: Boston	300.00	150.00	30.00
☐ 19	Lovett P: Boston	250.00	125.00	25.00
☐ 20	Lowe 2B: Boston	300.00	150.00	30.00
☐ 21	McCarthy LF: Boston	600.00	300.00	60.00
☐ 22	Murphy SS: New York	250.00	125.00	25.00
☐ 23	Billy Nash 3B: Boston	250.00	125.00	25.00
☐ 24	Nicols P: Boston	250.00	125.00	25.00
☐ 25A	Pfeffer 2B: .... Louisville	250.00	125.00	25.00
☐ 25B	Pfeffer (retired)	250.00	125.00	25.00
☐ 26A	Amos Rusie P: .... New York	900.00	450.00	90.00
☐ 26B	Amos Russie (sic) P: ...... New York	650.00	325.00	65.00
☐ 27	Tucker 1B: Boston	250.00	125.00	25.00
☐ 28A	John Ward 2B: .... New York	600.00	300.00	60.00
☐ 28B	John Ward (retired)	650.00	325.00	65.00
☐ 29	Chas. S. Abbey CF: .... Washington	250.00	125.00	25.00
☐ 30	E.W. Cartwright FB: .... Washington	250.00	125.00	25.00
☐ 31	W. F. Dahlen SS: .... Chicago	300.00	150.00	30.00
☐ 32	T.P. Daly SB: .... Brooklyn	250.00	125.00	25.00
☐ 33	E.J. Delehanty LF:	800.00	400.00	80.00

	Phila.			
☐ 34	W.W. Hallman SB:	250.00	125.00	25.00
	Phila.			
☐ 35	W.R. Hamilton CF:	600.00	300.00	60.00
	Phila.			
☐ 36	W. Robinson C:	600.00	300.00	60.00
	Baltimore			
☐ 37	James Ryan RF:	250.00	125.00	25.00
	Chicago			
☐ 38	Wm. Shindle TB:	250.00	125.00	25.00
	Brooklyn			
☐ 39	Geo. J. Smith SS:	250.00	125.00	25.00
	Cinc.			
☐ 40	Otis H. Stockdale P:	250.00	125.00	25.00
	Washington			

1986 National Photo Royals

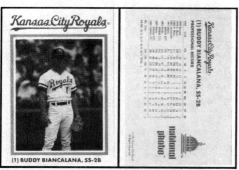

(1) BUDDY BIANCALANA, SS-2B

The set contains 24 cards which are numbered only by uniform number except for the checklist card and discount card, which entitles the bearer to a 40% discount at National Photo. Cards measure 2 7/8" by 4 1/4". Cards were distributed at the stadium on August 14th. The set was supposedly later available for 3.00 directly from the Royals.

		MINT	EXC	G-VG
COMPLETE SET (24)	....	10.00	5.00	1.00
COMMON PLAYER	....	.30	.15	.03
☐ 1	Buddy Biancalana	.30	.15	.03
☐ 3	Jorge Orta	.30	.15	.03
☐ 4	Greg Pryor	.30	.15	.03
☐ 5	George Brett	2.50	1.25	.25
☐ 6	Willie Wilson	.60	.30	.06
☐ 8	Jim Sundberg	.30	.15	.03
☐ 10	Dick Howser MG	.60	.30	.06
☐ 11	Hal McRae	.40	.20	.04
☐ 20	Frank White	.60	.30	.06
☐ 21	Lonnie Smith	.60	.30	.06
☐ 22	Dennis Leonard	.50	.25	.05
☐ 23	Mark Gubicza	1.00	.50	.10
☐ 24	Darryl Motley	.30	.15	.03
☐ 25	Danny Jackson	.60	.30	.06
☐ 26	Steve Farr	.30	.15	.03
☐ 29	Dan Quisenberry	.50	.25	.05
☐ 31	Bret Saberhagen	1.25	.60	.12
☐ 35	Lynn Jones	.30	.15	.03
☐ 37	Charlie Leibrandt	.40	.20	.04
☐ 38	Mark Huismann	.30	.15	.03
☐ 40	Buddy Black	.30	.15	.03
☐ 45	Steve Balboni	.40	.20	.04
☐ xx	Discount card	.30	.15	.03
	(unnumbered)			
☐ xx	Checklist card	.30	.15	.03
	(unnumbered)			

1984 Nestle Dream Team

The cards in this 22-card set measure 2 1/2" by 3 1/2". In conjunction with Topps, the Nestle Company issued this set entitled the Dream Team.

The fronts have the Nestle trademark in the upper frameline, and the backs are identical to the Topps cards of this year except for the number and the Nestle's logo. Cards 1-11 feature stars of the American League while cards 12-22 show National League stars. Each league's "Dream Team" consists of eight position players and three pitchers. The cards were included with the Nestle chocolate bars as a pack of four (three player cards and a checklist header card. This set should not be confused with the Nestle 792-card (same player-number correspondence as 1984 Topps 792) set.

		MINT	EXC	G-VG
COMPLETE SET (22)	....	20.00	10.00	2.00
COMMON PLAYER (1-22)	....	.40	.20	.04
☐ 1	Eddie Murray	1.25	.60	.12
☐ 2	Lou Whitaker	.60	.30	.06
☐ 3	George Brett	2.00	1.00	.20
☐ 4	Cal Ripken	2.00	1.00	.20
☐ 5	Jim Rice	.75	.35	.07
☐ 6	Dave Winfield	1.00	.50	.10
☐ 7	Lloyd Moseby	.40	.20	.04
☐ 8	Lance Parrish	.50	.25	.05
☐ 9	LaMarr Hoyt	.40	.20	.04
☐ 10	Ron Guidry	.60	.30	.06
☐ 11	Dan Quisenberry	.50	.25	.05
☐ 12	Steve Garvey	1.25	.60	.12
☐ 13	Johnny Ray	.40	.20	.04
☐ 14	Mike Schmidt	3.00	1.50	.30
☐ 15	Ozzie Smith	1.00	.50	.10
☐ 16	Andre Dawson	.80	.40	.08
☐ 17	Tim Raines	.80	.40	.08
☐ 18	Dale Murphy	1.50	.75	.15
☐ 19	Tony Pena	.40	.20	.04
☐ 20	John Denny	.40	.20	.04
☐ 21	Steve Carlton	1.00	.50	.10
☐ 22	Al Holland	.40	.20	.04
☐ xx	Checklist card	.40	.20	.04
	(unnumbered)			

1984 Nestle 792

The cards in this 792-card set measure 2 1/2" by 3 1/2" and are extremely similar to the 1984 Topps regular issue (except for the Nestle logo instead of Topps logo on the front). In conjunction with Topps, the Nestle Company issued this set as six sheets available as a premium. The set was (as detailed on the back of the checklist card for the Nestle Dream Team cards) originally available from the Nestle Company in full sheets of 132 cards, 24" by 48", for 4.95 plus five Nestle candy wrappers per sheet. The backs are virtually identical to the Topps cards of this year, i.e., same player-number correspondence. These sheets have been cut up into individual cards and are available from a few dealers around the country. This is one of the few instances in this hobby where the complete uncut sheet is worth

considerably less than the sum of the individual cards due to the expense required in having the sheet cut professionally (and precisely) into individual cards. Supposedly less than 5000 sets were printed. Since the checklist is exactly the same as that of the 1984 Topps, these Nestle cards are generally priced as a multiple of the corresponding Topps card. The list below shows only the two most expensive cards in the set. Cards not listed below are priced at five times the corresponding 1984 Topps price. Beware also on this set to look for fakes and forgeries. Cards billed as Nestle proofs in black and white are fakes. There are even a few counterfeits in color; the two cards listed below are the cards most likely to be reprinted illegally as they are the most valuable in the set.

	MINT	EXC	G-VG
COMPLETE CUT SET (792)	500.00	250.00	50.00
COMMON PLAYER (1-792)	.25	.12	.02
☐ 8 Don Mattingly	200.00	100.00	20.00
☐ 182 Darryl Strawberry	75.00	37.50	7.50

1987 Nestle Dream Team

This 33-card set is, in a sense, three sets: Golden Era (1-11 gold), AL Modern Era (12-22 red), and NL Modern Era (23-33 blue). Cards are 2 1/2" by 3 1/2" and have color coded borders by era. The first 11 card photos are in black and white. The Nestle set was apparently not licensed by Major League Baseball and hence the team logos are not shown in the photos. Six-packs of certain Nestle candy bars contained three cards; cards were also available through a send-in offer.

	MINT	EXC	G-VG
COMPLETE SET (33)	8.00	4.00	.80
COMMON PLAYER (1-33)	.15	.07	.01
☐ 1 Lou Gehrig	.60	.30	.06
☐ 2 Rogers Hornsby	.25	.12	.02

		MINT	EXC	G-VG
☐	3 Pie Traynor	.15	.07	.01
☐	4 Honus Wagner	.35	.17	.03
☐	5 Babe Ruth	1.00	.50	.10
☐	6 Tris Speaker	.25	.12	.02
☐	7 Ty Cobb	.60	.30	.06
☐	8 Mickey Cochrane	.25	.12	.02
☐	9 Walter Johnson	.35	.17	.03
☐	10 Carl Hubbell	.25	.12	.02
☐	11 Jimmy Foxx	.25	.12	.02
☐	12 Rod Carew	.25	.12	.02
☐	13 Nellie Fox	.15	.07	.01
☐	14 Brooks Robinson	.25	.12	.02
☐	15 Luis Aparicio	.15	.07	.01
☐	16 Frank Robinson	.25	.12	.02
☐	17 Mickey Mantle	1.00	.50	.10
☐	18 Ted Williams	.60	.30	.06
☐	19 Yogi Berra	.40	.20	.04
☐	20 Bob Feller	.35	.17	.03
☐	21 Whitey Ford	.30	.15	.03
☐	22 Harmon Killebrew	.25	.12	.02
☐	23 Stan Musial	.35	.17	.03
☐	24 Jackie Robinson	.45	.22	.04
☐	25 Eddie Mathews	.25	.12	.02
☐	26 Ernie Banks	.25	.12	.02
☐	27 Roberto Clemente	.35	.17	.03
☐	28 Willie Mays	.50	.25	.05
☐	29 Hank Aaron	.50	.25	.05
☐	30 Johnny Bench	.35	.17	.03
☐	31 Bob Gibson	.25	.12	.02
☐	32 Warren Spahn	.25	.12	.02
☐	33 Duke Snider	.30	.15	.03

1988 Nestle

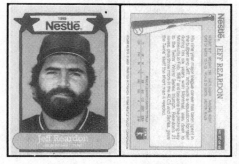

This 44-card set was produced for Nestle by Mike Schechter Associates and was printed in Canada. Cards are 2 1/2" by 3 1/2" and have yellow borders. The Nestle set was apparently not licensed by Major League Baseball and hence the team logos are not shown in the photos. The cards are numbered on the back. The backs are printed in red and blue on white card stock.

		MINT	EXC	G-VG
	COMPLETE SET (44)	20.00	10.00	2.00
	COMMON PLAYER (1-44)	.25	.12	.02
☐	1 Roger Clemens	1.50	.75	.15
☐	2 Dale Murphy	.75	.35	.07
☐	3 Eric Davis	1.25	.60	.12
☐	4 Gary Gaetti	.35	.17	.03
☐	5 Ozzie Smith	.60	.30	.06
☐	6 Mike Schmidt	1.75	.85	.17
☐	7 Ozzie Guillen	.25	.12	.02
☐	8 John Franco	.25	.12	.02
☐	9 Andre Dawson	.50	.25	.05
☐	10 Mark McGwire	1.50	.75	.15
☐	11 Bret Saberhagen	.75	.35	.07
☐	12 Benny Santiago	.50	.25	.05
☐	13 Jose Uribe	.25	.12	.02
☐	14 Will Clark	1.75	.85	.17
☐	15 Don Mattingly	1.75	.85	.17
☐	16 Juan Samuel	.25	.12	.02
☐	17 Jack Clark	.35	.17	.03
☐	18 Darryl Strawberry	1.25	.60	.12
☐	19 Bill Doran	.25	.12	.02
☐	20 Pete Incaviglia	.35	.17	.03
☐	21 Dwight Gooden	1.00	.50	.10

☐ 22	Willie Randolph	.25	.12	.02
☐ 23	Tim Wallach	.25	.12	.02
☐ 24	Pedro Guerrero	.35	.17	.03
☐ 25	Steve Bedrosian	.25	.12	.02
☐ 26	Gary Carter	.45	.22	.04
☐ 27	Jeff Reardon	.25	.12	.02
☐ 28	Dave Righetti	.25	.12	.02
☐ 29	Frank White	.25	.12	.02
☐ 30	Buddy Bell	.25	.12	.02
☐ 31	Tim Raines	.45	.22	.04
☐ 32	Wade Boggs	1.50	.75	.15
☐ 33	Dave Winfield	.60	.30	.06
☐ 34	George Bell	.45	.22	.04
☐ 35	Alan Trammell	.45	.22	.04
☐ 36	Joe Carter	.35	.17	.03
☐ 37	Jose Canseco	2.00	1.00	.20
☐ 38	Carlton Fisk	.60	.30	.06
☐ 39	Kirby Puckett	1.25	.60	.12
☐ 40	Tony Gwynn	.75	.35	.07
☐ 41	Matt Nokes	.35	.17	.03
☐ 42	Keith Hernandez	.35	.17	.03
☐ 43	Nolan Ryan	1.75	.85	.17
☐ 44	Wally Joyner	.50	.25	.05

1954 N.Y. Journal American

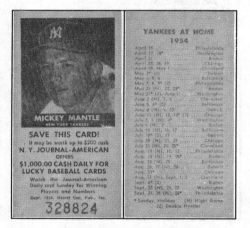

The cards in this 59-card set measure 2" by 4". The 1954 New York Journal American set contains black and white, unnumbered cards issued in conjunction with the newspaper. News stands were given boxes of cards to be distributed with purchases and each card had a serial number for redemption in the contest. The set spotlights New York teams only and carries game schedules on the reverse. The cards have been assigned numbers in the listing below alphabetically within team so that Brooklyn Dodgers are 1- 19, New York Giants are 20-39, and New York Yankees are 40- 59. There is speculation that a 20th Dodger card may exist. The ACC designation for this set is M127.

	NRMT	VG-E	GOOD
COMPLETE SET (59)	1750.00	850.00	200.00
COMMON PLAYER (1-59)	10.00	5.00	1.00

☐ 1	Joe Black	12.00	6.00	1.20
☐ 2	Roy Campanella	100.00	50.00	10.00
☐ 3	Billy Cox	10.00	5.00	1.00
☐ 4	Carl Erskine	14.00	7.00	1.40
☐ 5	Carl Furillo	16.00	8.00	1.60
☐ 6	Junior Gilliam	16.00	8.00	1.60
☐ 7	Gil Hodges	40.00	20.00	4.00
☐ 8	Jim Hughes	10.00	5.00	1.00
☐ 9	Clem Labine	10.00	5.00	1.00
☐ 10	Billy Loes	10.00	5.00	1.00
☐ 11	Russ Meyer	10.00	5.00	1.00
☐ 12	Don Newcombe	16.00	8.00	1.60
☐ 13	Ervin Palica	10.00	5.00	1.00

☐ 14	Pee Wee Reese	50.00	25.00	5.00
☐ 15	Jackie Robinson	125.00	60.00	12.50
☐ 16	Preacher Roe	16.00	8.00	1.60
☐ 17	George Shuba	10.00	5.00	1.00
☐ 18	Duke Snider	100.00	50.00	10.00
☐ 19	Dick Williams	12.00	6.00	1.20
☐ 20	John Antonelli	12.00	6.00	1.20
☐ 21	Alvin Dark	14.00	7.00	1.40
☐ 22	Marv Grissom	10.00	5.00	1.00
☐ 23	Ruben Gomez	10.00	5.00	1.00
☐ 24	Jim Hearn	10.00	5.00	1.00
☐ 25	Bobby Hofman	10.00	5.00	1.00
☐ 26	Monte Irvin	30.00	15.00	3.00
☐ 27	Larry Jansen	10.00	5.00	1.00
☐ 28	Ray Katt	10.00	5.00	1.00
☐ 29	Don Liddle	10.00	5.00	1.00
☐ 30	Whitey Lockman	10.00	5.00	1.00
☐ 31	Sal Maglie	16.00	8.00	1.60
☐ 32	Willie Mays	200.00	100.00	20.00
☐ 33	Don Mueller	12.00	6.00	1.20
☐ 34	Dusty Rhodes	12.00	6.00	1.20
☐ 35	Hank Thompson	12.00	6.00	1.20
☐ 36	Wes Westrum	10.00	5.00	1.00
☐ 37	Hoyt Wilhelm	35.00	17.50	3.50
☐ 38	Davey Williams	10.00	5.00	1.00
☐ 39	Al Worthington	10.00	5.00	1.00
☐ 40	Hank Bauer	16.00	8.00	1.60
☐ 41	Yogi Berra	100.00	50.00	10.00
☐ 42	Harry Byrd	10.00	5.00	1.00
☐ 43	Andy Carey	10.00	5.00	1.00
☐ 44	Jerry Coleman	10.00	5.00	1.00
☐ 45	Joe Collins	10.00	5.00	1.00
☐ 46	Whitey Ford	50.00	25.00	5.00
☐ 47	Steve Kraly	10.00	5.00	1.00
☐ 48	Bob Kuzava	10.00	5.00	1.00
☐ 49	Frank Leja	10.00	5.00	1.00
☐ 50	Ed Lopat	16.00	8.00	1.60
☐ 51	Mickey Mantle	400.00	200.00	40.00
☐ 52	Gil McDougald	16.00	8.00	1.60
☐ 53	Bill Miller	10.00	5.00	1.00
☐ 54	Tom Morgan	10.00	5.00	1.00
☐ 55	Irv Noren	10.00	5.00	1.00
☐ 56	Allie Reynolds	16.00	8.00	1.60
☐ 57	Phil Rizzuto	35.00	17.50	3.50
☐ 58	Eddie Robinson	10.00	5.00	1.00
☐ 59	Gene Woodling	12.00	6.00	1.20

1989 J.J. Nissen

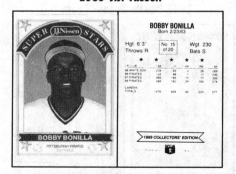

The 1989 J.J. Nissen set contains 20 standard-size (2 1/2 by 3 1/2 inch) cards. The fronts have airbrushed facial photos with white and yellow borders and orange trim. The backs are white and feature career stats. The complete set price below does not include the error version of Mark Grace.

	MINT	EXC	G-VG
COMPLETE SET (20)	12.00	6.00	1.20
COMMON PLAYER (1-20)	.30	.15	.03

☐ 1	Wally Joyner	.50	.25	.05
☐ 2	Wade Boggs	1.00	.50	.10
☐ 3	Ellis Burks	.75	.35	.07
☐ 4	Don Mattingly	1.25	.60	.12
☐ 5	Jose Canseco	1.25	.60	.12
☐ 6	Mike Greenwell	.75	.35	.07
☐ 7	Eric Davis	.75	.35	.07
☐ 8	Kirby Puckett	.75	.35	.07
☐ 9	Kevin Seitzer	.50	.25	.05

		NRMT	VG-E	GOOD
☐ 10	Darryl Strawberry	.75	.35	.07
☐ 11	Gregg Jefferies	.75	.35	.07
☐ 12A	Mark Grace ERR	12.00	4.00	.75
	(photo actually			
	Vance Law)			
☐ 12B	Mark Grace COR	1.25	.60	.12
☐ 13	Matt Nokes	.30	.15	.03
☐ 14	Mark McGwire	.75	.35	.07
☐ 15	Bobby Bonilla	.30	.15	.03
☐ 16	Roger Clemens	.75	.35	.07
☐ 17	Frank Viola	.40	.20	.04
☐ 18	Orel Hershiser	.50	.25	.05
☐ 19	David Cone	.50	.25	.05
☐ 20	Ted Williams	1.25	.60	.12

1960 Nu-Card Hi-Lites

The cards in this 72-card set measure 3 1/4" by 5 3/8". In 1960, the Nu-Card Company introduced its Baseball Hi-Lites set of newspaper style cards. Each card singled out an individual baseball achievement with a picture and story. The reverses contain a baseball quiz. Cards 1-18 are more valuable if found printed totally in black on the front; these are copyrighted CVC as opposed to the NCI designation found on the red and black printed fronts.

		NRMT	VG-E	GOOD
COMPLETE SET (72)		200.00	100.00	20.00
COMMON PLAYER (1-72)		1.50	.75	.15
☐ 1	Babe Hits 3 Homers	10.00	5.00	1.00
	In A Series Game			
☐ 2	Podres Pitching	1.50	.75	.15
	Wins Series			
☐ 3	Bevans Pitches No	1.50	.75	.15
	Hitter, Almost			
☐ 4	Box Score Devised	1.50	.75	.15
	By Reporter			
☐ 5	VanderMeer Pitches	2.00	1.00	.20
	Two No Hitters			
☐ 6	Indians Take Bums	1.50	.75	.15
☐ 7	DiMag Comes Thru	10.00	5.00	1.00
☐ 8	Mathewson Pitches	2.00	1.00	.20
	Three WS Shutouts			
☐ 9	Haddix Pitches 12	1.50	.75	.15
	Perfect Innings			
☐ 10	Thomson's Homer	2.00	1.00	.20
	Sinks Dodgers			
☐ 11	Hubbell Strikes Out	1.50	.75	.15
	Five A.L. Stars			
☐ 12	Pickoff Ends Series	1.50	.75	.15
☐ 13	Cards Take Series	1.50	.75	.15
	From Yanks			
☐ 14	Dizzy And Daffy	3.00	1.50	.30
	Dean Win Series			
☐ 15	Owen Drops 3rd Strike	1.50	.75	.15
☐ 16	Ruth Calls Shot	10.00	5.00	1.00
☐ 17	Merkle Pulls Boner	1.50	.75	.15
☐ 18	Larsen Hurls Perfect	2.00	1.00	.20
	World Series Game			
☐ 19	Bean Ball Ends Career	1.50	.75	.15
	of Mickey Cochrane			
☐ 20	Banks Belts 47 Homers ...	3.50	1.75	.35

	Earns MVP			
☐ 21	Stan Musial Hits Five	4.50	2.25	.45
	Homers in One Day			
☐ 22	Mickey Mantle Hits	12.00	6.00	1.20
	Longest Homer			
☐ 23	Sievers Captures	1.50	.75	.15
	Home Run Title			
☐ 24	Gehrig 2130	6.00	3.00	.60
	Consecutive Game			
	Record Ends			
☐ 25	Red Schoendienst	2.50	1.25	.25
	Key Player			
	Braves Pennant			
☐ 26	Midget Pinch-Hits	2.50	1.25	.25
	For St. Louis			
☐ 27	Willie Mays Makes	6.00	3.00	.60
	Greatest Catch			
☐ 28	Homer by Yogi Berra	4.00	2.00	.40
	Puts Yanks In 1st			
☐ 29	Campy NL MVP	4.00	2.00	.40
☐ 30	Bob Turley Hurls	1.50	.75	.15
	Yankees To			
	WS Champions			
☐ 31	Dodgers Take Series	1.50	.75	.15
	From Sox In Six			
☐ 32	Furillo Hero as	1.50	.75	.15
	Dodgers Beat Chicago			
	in 3rd WS Game			
☐ 33	Adcock Gets 4 Homers	1.50	.75	.15
	And A Double			
☐ 34	Dickey Chosen All-	1.50	.75	.15
	Star Catcher			
☐ 35	Burdette Beats Yanks	1.50	.75	.15
	In Three WS Games			
☐ 36	Umpires Clear	1.50	.75	.15
	White Sox Bench			
☐ 37	Reese Honored As	3.00	1.50	.30
	Greatest Dodger SS			
☐ 38	Joe DiMaggio Hits	10.00	5.00	1.00
	In 56 Straight			
☐ 39	Ted Williams Hits	6.00	3.00	.60
	.406 For Season			
☐ 40	Walter Johnson	2.50	1.25	.25
	Pitches 56 Straight			
☐ 41	Hodges Hits 4 Home	1.50	.75	.15
	Runs In Nite Game			
☐ 42	Greenberg Returns to	1.50	.75	.15
	Tigers From Army			
☐ 43	Ty Cobb Named Best	8.00	4.00	.80
	Player Of All Time			
☐ 44	Robin Roberts Wins	2.00	1.00	.20
	28 Games			
☐ 45	Rizzuto's Two Runs	2.00	1.00	.20
	Save 1st Place			
☐ 46	Tigers Beat Out	1.50	.75	.15
	Senators For Pennant			
☐ 47	Babe Ruth Hits	10.00	5.00	1.00
	60th Home Run			
☐ 48	Cy Young Honored	2.00	1.00	.20
☐ 49	Killebrew Starts	3.00	1.50	.30
	Spring Training			
☐ 50	Mantle Hits Longest	12.00	6.00	1.20
	Homer at Stadium			
☐ 51	Braves Take Pennant	1.50	.75	.15
☐ 52	Ted Williams Hero	5.00	2.50	.50
	Of All-Star Game			
☐ 53	Robinson Saves Dodgers ..	4.50	2.25	.45
	For Play-off Series			
☐ 54	Snodgrass Muffs Fly	1.50	.75	.15
☐ 55	Snider Belts 2 Homers	3.50	1.75	.35
	Ties Homer Record			
☐ 56	Giants Win 26 Straight	1.50	.75	.15
☐ 57	Ted Kluszewski Stars	1.50	.75	.15
	In 1st Series Win			
☐ 58	Ott Walks 5 Times	1.50	.75	.15
	In Single Game			
☐ 59	Harvey Kuenn Takes	1.50	.75	.15
	A.L. Batting Title			
☐ 60	Bob Feller Hurls 3rd	3.50	1.75	.35
	No-Hitter of Career			
☐ 61	Yanks Champs Again	1.50	.75	.15
☐ 62	Aaron's Bat Beats	6.00	3.00	.60
	Yankees In Series			
☐ 63	Warren Spahn Beats	2.50	1.25	.25
	Yanks in W.S.			
☐ 64	Ump's Wrong Call Helps ...	1.50	.75	.15
	Dodgers Beat Yanks			
☐ 65	Kaline Hits 3 Homers	3.00	1.50	.30
	Two In Same Inning			
☐ 66	Bob Allison Named AL	1.50	.75	.15
	Rookie of the Year			
☐ 67	McCovey Blasts Way	3.00	1.50	.30
	Into Giant Lineup			
☐ 68	Colavito Hits Four	1.50	.75	.15
	Homers in One Game			

☐ 69	Erskine Sets Strike Out Record in World Series	1.50	.75	.15
☐ 70	Sal Maglie Pitches No-Hit Game	1.50	.75	.15
☐ 71	Early Wynn Victory Crushes Yanks	1.50	.75	.15
☐ 72	Nellie Fox AL MVP	2.00	1.00	.20

1961 Nu-Card Scoops

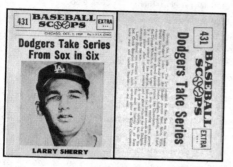

The cards in this 80-card set measure 2 1/2" by 3 1/2". This series depicts great moments in the history of individual ballplayers. Each card is designed as a miniature newspaper front-page, complete with data and picture. Both the number (401-480) and title are printed in red on the obverse, and the story is found on the back. An album was issued to hold the set. The set has been illegally reprinted, which has served to suppress the demand for the originals as well as the reprints.

	NRMT	VG-E	GOOD
COMPLETE SET (80)	100.00	50.00	10.00
COMMON PLAYER (401-480)	.50	.25	.05

☐ 401	Jim Gentile	.50	.25	.05
☐ 402	Warren Spahn (No-hitter)	2.00	1.00	.20
☐ 403	Bill Mazeroski	.75	.35	.07
☐ 404	Willie Mays: (three triples)	5.00	2.50	.50
☐ 405	Woodie Held		.25	.05
☐ 406	Vern Law	.60	.30	.06
☐ 407	Pete Runnels	.50	.25	.05
☐ 408	Lew Burdette (No-hitter)	.60	.30	.06
☐ 409	Dick Stuart	.50	.25	.05
☐ 410	Don Cardwell	.50	.25	.05
☐ 411	Camilo Pascual	.50	.25	.05
☐ 412	Ed Mathews	2.00	1.00	.20
☐ 413	Dick Groat	.75	.35	.07
☐ 414	Gene Autry	2.00	1.00	.20
☐ 415	Bobby Richardson	.75	.35	.07
☐ 416	Roger Maris	5.00	2.50	.50
☐ 417	Fred Merkle	.50	.25	.05
☐ 418	Don Larsen	.60	.30	.06
☐ 419	Mickey Cochrane	.75	.35	.07
☐ 420	Ernie Banks	2.50	1.25	.25
☐ 421	Stan Musial	4.00	2.00	.40
☐ 422	Mickey Mantle (longest homer)	10.00	5.00	1.00
☐ 423	Roy Sievers	.50	.25	.05
☐ 424	Lou Gehrig	5.00	2.50	.50
☐ 425	Red Schoendienst	1.50	.75	.15
☐ 426	Eddie Gaedel	1.50	.75	.15
☐ 427	Willie Mays (greatest catch)	5.00	2.50	.50
☐ 428	Jackie Robinson	4.00	2.00	.40
☐ 429	Roy Campanella	4.00	2.00	.40
☐ 430	Bob Turley	.60	.30	.06
☐ 431	Larry Sherry	.50	.25	.05
☐ 432	Carl Furillo	.60	.30	.06
☐ 433	Joe Adcock	.60	.30	.06
☐ 434	Bill Dickey	.75	.35	.07
☐ 435	Burdette 3 wins	.60	.30	.06
☐ 436	Umpire Clears Bench	.50	.25	.05
☐ 437	Pee Wee Reese	2.50	1.25	.25

☐ 438	Joe DiMaggio (56 Game Hit Streak)	7.50	3.75	.75
☐ 439	Ted Williams Hits .406	5.00	2.50	.50
☐ 440	Walter Johnson	2.50	1.25	.25
☐ 441	Gil Hodges	1.50	.75	.15
☐ 442	Hank Greenberg	1.00	.50	.10
☐ 443	Ty Cobb	6.00	3.00	.60
☐ 444	Robin Roberts	2.00	1.00	.20
☐ 445	Phil Rizzuto	1.50	.75	.15
☐ 446	Hal Newhouser	.75	.35	.07
☐ 447	Babe Ruth 60th Homer	9.00	4.50	.90
☐ 448	Cy Young	2.00	1.00	.20
☐ 449	Harmon Killebrew	2.50	1.25	.25
☐ 450	Mickey Mantle (longest homer)	9.00	4.50	.90
☐ 451	Braves Take Pennant	.50	.25	.05
☐ 452	Ted Williams (All-Star Hero)	5.00	2.50	.50
☐ 453	Yogi Berra	4.00	2.00	.40
☐ 454	Fred Snodgrass	.50	.25	.05
☐ 455	Ruth 3 Homers	9.00	4.50	.90
☐ 456	Giants 26 Game Streak	.50	.25	.05
☐ 457	Ted Kluszewski	.75	.35	.07
☐ 458	Mel Ott	1.50	.75	.15
☐ 459	Harvey Kuenn	.75	.35	.07
☐ 460	Bob Feller	3.00	1.50	.30
☐ 461	Casey Stengel	2.00	1.00	.20
☐ 462	Hank Aaron	5.00	2.50	.50
☐ 463	Spahn Beats Yanks	1.50	.75	.15
☐ 464	Ump's Wrong Call	.50	.25	.05
☐ 465	Al Kaline	3.00	1.50	.30
☐ 466	Bob Allison	.50	.25	.05
☐ 467	Joe DiMaggio (Four Homers)	7.50	3.75	.75
☐ 468	Rocky Colavito	.75	.35	.07
☐ 469	Carl Erskine	.60	.30	.06
☐ 470	Sal Maglie	.60	.30	.06
☐ 471	Early Wynn	1.50	.75	.15
☐ 472	Nellie Fox	1.00	.50	.10
☐ 473	Marty Marion	.75	.35	.07
☐ 474	Johnny Podres	.60	.30	.06
☐ 475	Mickey Owen	.50	.25	.05
☐ 476	Dean Brothers (Dizzy and Daffy)	2.00	1.00	.20
☐ 477	Christy Mathewson	2.50	1.25	.25
☐ 478	Harvey Haddix	.50	.25	.05
☐ 479	Carl Hubbell	.75	.35	.07
☐ 480	Bobby Thomson	.60	.30	.06

1952 Num Num

The cards in this 20-card set measure 3 1/2" by 4 1/2". The 1952 Num Num Potato Chips issue features black and white, numbered cards of the Cleveland Indians. Cards came with and without coupons (tabs). The cards were issued without coupons directly by the Cleveland baseball club. When the complete set was obtained the tabs were cut off and exchanged for an autographed baseball. Card Number 16, Kennedy, is rather scarce. Cards with the tabs still intact are worth approximately 25% more than the values listed below. The ACC designation for this set is F337-2.

	NRMT	VG-E	GOOD
COMPLETE SET (20)	800.00	400.00	80.00
COMMON PLAYER (1-20)	20.00	10.00	2.00
☐ 1 Lou Brissie	20.00	10.00	2.00
☐ 2 Jim Hegan	20.00	10.00	2.00
☐ 3 Birdie Tebbetts	20.00	10.00	2.00
☐ 4 Bob Lemon	60.00	30.00	6.00
☐ 5 Bob Feller	100.00	50.00	10.00
☐ 6 Early Wynn	60.00	30.00	6.00
☐ 7 Mike Garcia	25.00	12.50	2.50
☐ 8 Steve Gromek	20.00	10.00	2.00
☐ 9 Bob Chakales	20.00	10.00	2.00
☐ 10 Al Rosen	40.00	20.00	4.00
☐ 11 Dick Rozek	20.00	10.00	2.00
☐ 12 Luke Easter	25.00	12.50	2.50
☐ 13 Ray Boone	20.00	10.00	2.00
☐ 14 Bobby Avila	20.00	10.00	2.00
☐ 15 Dale Mitchell	25.00	12.50	2.50
☐ 16 Bob Kennedy	400.00	200.00	40.00
☐ 17 Harry Simpson	20.00	10.00	2.00
☐ 18 Larry Doby	40.00	20.00	4.00
☐ 19 Sam Jones	25.00	12.50	2.50
☐ 20 Al Lopez MG	60.00	30.00	6.00

☐ 54 Tom Waddell	.35	.17	.03
☐ xx Coaching Staff	.35	.17	.03
Jack Aker			
Bobby Bonds			
Doc Edwards			
John Goryl			

1988 Pacific Eight Men Out

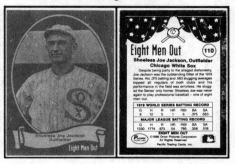

This set was produced by Mike Cramer's Pacific Trading Cards of Edmonds, Washington. The set was released in conjunction with the popular movie of the same name, which told the story of the "fix" of the 1919 World Series between the Cincinnati Reds and the Chicago "Black" Sox. The cards are standard size, 2 1/2" by 3 1/2" and have a raspberry-colored border on the card fronts as well as raspberry-colored print on the white card stock backs. The cards were available either as wax packs or as collated sets. Generally the cards relating to the movie (showing actors) are in full-color whereas the vintage photography showing the actual players involved is in a sepia tone.

	MINT	EXC	G-VG
COMPLETE SET (110)	10.00	5.00	1.00
COMMON PLAYER (1-110)	.10	.05	.01
☐ 1 We're Going To See .... The Sox	.10	.05	.01
☐ 2 White Sox Win .... The Pennant	.10	.05	.01
☐ 3 The Series	.10	.05	.01
☐ 4 1919 Chicago White .... Sox	.10	.05	.01
☐ 5 The Black Sox Scandal ...	.10	.05	.01
☐ 6 Eddie Cicotte 29-7 .... in 1919	.10	.05	.01
☐ 7 "Buck's Their .... Favorite"	.10	.05	.01
☐ 8 Eddie Collins	.20	.10	.02
☐ 9 Michael Rooker as .... Chick Gandil	.10	.05	.01
☐ 10 Charlie Sheen as .... Hap Felsch	.20	.10	.02
☐ 11 James Read as .... Lefty Williams	.10	.05	.01
☐ 12 John Cusak as .... Buck Weaver	.10	.05	.01
☐ 13 D.B. Sweeney as .... Joe Jackson	.15	.07	.01
☐ 14 David Strathairn as .... Eddie Cicotte	.10	.05	.01
☐ 15 Perry Lang as .... Fred McMullin	.10	.05	.01
☐ 16 Don Harvey as .... Swede Risberg	.10	.05	.01
☐ 17 The Gambler Burns .... And Maharg	.10	.05	.01
☐ 18 "Sleepy"Bill Burns	.10	.05	.01
☐ 19 The Key is Cicotte	.10	.05	.01
☐ 20 C'moan Betsy	.10	.05	.01
☐ 21 The Fix	.10	.05	.01
☐ 22 Chick Approaches .... Cicotte	.10	.05	.01
☐ 23 Kid Gleason	.10	.05	.01

1986 Oh Henry Indians

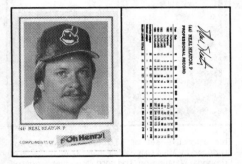

This 30-card set features Cleveland Indians and was distributed at the stadium to fans in attendance on Baseball Card Day. The cards were printed in one folded sheet which was perforated for easy separation into individual cards. The cards have white borders with a blue frame around each photo. The card backs include detailed career year-by-year statistics. The individual cards measure 2 1/4" by 3 1/8" and have full-color fronts.

	MINT	EXC	G-VG
COMPLETE SET (30)	12.00	6.00	1.20
COMMON PLAYER	.35	.17	.03
☐ 2 Brett Butler	.60	.30	.06
☐ 4 Tony Bernazard	.35	.17	.03
☐ 6 Andy Allanson	.35	.17	.03
☐ 7 Pat Corrales MG	.35	.17	.03
☐ 8 Carmen Castillo	.35	.17	.03
☐ 10 Pat Tabler	.60	.30	.06
☐ 13 Ernie Camacho	.45	.22	.04
☐ 14 Julio Franco	1.25	.60	.12
☐ 15 Dan Rohn	.35	.17	.03
☐ 18 Ken Schrom	.35	.17	.03
☐ 20 Otis Nixon	.45	.22	.04
☐ 22 Fran Mullins	.35	.17	.03
☐ 23 Chris Bando	.35	.17	.03
☐ 24 Ed Williams	.45	.22	.04
☐ 26 Brook Jacoby	.60	.30	.06
☐ 27 Mel Hall	.60	.30	.06
☐ 29 Andre Thornton	.75	.35	.07
☐ 30 Joe Carter	1.50	.75	.15
☐ 35 Phil Niekro	1.50	.75	.15
☐ 36 Jamie Easterly	.35	.17	.03
☐ 37 Don Schulze	.35	.17	.03
☐ 42 Rick Yett	.35	.17	.03
☐ 43 Scott Bailes	.45	.22	.04
☐ 44 Neal Heaton	.35	.17	.03
☐ 46 Jim Kern	.35	.17	.03
☐ 48 Dickie Noles	.35	.17	.03
☐ 49 Tom Candiotti	.45	.22	.04
☐ 53 Reggie Ritter	.35	.17	.03

☐	24	Charles Comiskey	.10	.05	.01
		Owner			
☐	25	Chick Gandil	.15	.07	.01
		1st Baseman			
☐	26	Swede Risberg	.10	.05	.01
☐	27	Sport Sullivan	.10	.05	.01
☐	28	Abe Attell And	.10	.05	.01
		Arnold Rothstein			
☐	29	Hugh Fullerton	.10	.05	.01
		Sportswriter			
☐	30	Ring Lardner	.10	.05	.01
		Sportswriter			
☐	31	"Shoeless"Joe His	.20	.10	.02
		Batting Eye			
☐	32	"Shoeless Joe"	.25	.12	.02
☐	33	Buck Can't Sleep	.10	.05	.01
☐	34	George"Buck" Weaver	.10	.05	.01
☐	35	Hugh and Ring	.10	.05	.01
		Confront Kid			
☐	36	Joe Doesn't Want	.10	.05	.01
		To Play			
☐	37	"Shoeless" Joe	.20	.10	.02
		Jackson			
☐	38	"Sore Arm, Cicotte,"	.10	.05	.01
		"Old Man Cicotte"			
☐	39	The Fix Is On	.10	.05	.01
☐	40	Buck Plays To Win	.10	.05	.01
☐	41	Hap Makes A	.10	.05	.01
		Great Catch			
☐	42	Hugh and Ring Suspect	.10	.05	.01
☐	43	Ray Gets Things Going	.10	.05	.01
☐	44	Lefty Loses Game Two	.10	.05	.01
☐	45	Lefty Crosses Up	.10	.05	.01
		Catcher Ray Schalk			
☐	46	Chick's RBI Wins	.10	.05	.01
		Game Three			
☐	47	Dickie Kerr Wins	.10	.05	.01
		Game Three			
☐	48	Chick Leaves Buck	.10	.05	.01
		At Third			
☐	49	Williams Loses	.10	.05	.01
		Game Five			
☐	50	Ray Schalk	.10	.05	.01
☐	51	Schalk Blocks	.10	.05	.01
		The Plate			
☐	52	Schalk Is Thrown Out	.10	.05	.01
☐	53	Chicago Stickball	.10	.05	.01
		Game			
☐	54	I'm Forever Blowing	.10	.05	.01
		Ball Games			
☐	55	Felsch Scores Jackson	.20	.10	.02
☐	56	Kerr Wins Game Six	.10	.05	.01
☐	57	Where's The Money	.10	.05	.01
☐	58	Cicotte Wins Game	.10	.05	.01
		Seven			
☐	59	Kid Watches Eddie	.10	.05	.01
☐	60	Lefty Is Threatened	.10	.05	.01
☐	61	James, Get Your Arm	.10	.05	.01
		Ready, Fast			
☐	62	Shoeless Joe's	.20	.10	.02
		Home Run			
☐	63	Buck Played His Best	.10	.05	.01
☐	64	Hugh Exposes The Fix	.10	.05	.01
☐	65	"Sign The Petition"	.10	.05	.01
☐	66	Baseball Owners Hire	.10	.05	.01
		A Commissioner			
☐	67	Judge Kenesaw	.10	.05	.01
		Mountain Landis			
☐	68	Grand Jury Summoned	.10	.05	.01
☐	69	"Say It Ain't So,	.15	.07	.01
		Joe"			
☐	70	The Swede's A Hard	.10	.05	.01
		Guy			
☐	71	Buck Loves The Game	.10	.05	.01
☐	72	The Trial	.10	.05	.01
☐	73	Kid Gleason Takes	.10	.05	.01
		The Stand			
☐	74	The Verdict	.10	.05	.01
☐	75	Eight Men Out	.10	.05	.01
☐	76	Oscar"Happy" Felsch	.20	.10	.02
☐	77	Who's Joe Jackson	.20	.10	.02
☐	78	Ban Johnson	.10	.05	.01
☐	79	Judge Landis	.10	.05	.01
☐	80	Charles Comiskey	.10	.05	.01
☐	81	Heinie Groth	.10	.05	.01
☐	82	Slim Sallee	.10	.05	.01
☐	83	Dutch Ruether	.10	.05	.01
☐	84	Edd Roush	.25	.12	.02
☐	85	Morrie Rath	.10	.05	.01
☐	86	Bill Rariden	.10	.05	.01
☐	87	Jimmy Ring	.10	.05	.01
☐	88	Greasy Neale	.10	.05	.01
☐	89	Pat Moran	.10	.05	.01
☐	90	Adolfo Luque	.10	.05	.01
☐	91	Larry Kopf	.10	.05	.01

☐	92	Ray Fisher	.10	.05	.01
☐	93	Hod Eller	.10	.05	.01
☐	94	Pat Duncan	.10	.05	.01
☐	95	Jake Daubert	.10	.05	.01
☐	96	Red Faber	.20	.10	.02
☐	97	Dickie Kerr	.10	.05	.01
☐	98	Shano Collins	.10	.05	.01
☐	99	Eddie Collins	.20	.10	.02
☐	100	Ray Schalk	.20	.10	.02
☐	101	Nemo Leibold	.10	.05	.01
☐	102	Kid Gleason	.10	.05	.01
☐	103	Swede Risberg	.10	.05	.01
☐	104	Eddie Cicotte	.10	.05	.01
☐	105	Fred McMullin	.10	.05	.01
☐	106	Chick Gandil	.10	.05	.01
☐	107	Buck Weaver	.10	.05	.01
☐	108	Lefty Williams	.10	.05	.01
☐	109	Happy Felsch	.10	.05	.01
☐	110	Joe Jackson	.30	.15	.03

1988 Pacific Legends

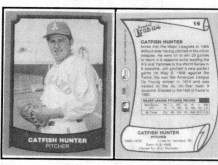

This attractive set of 110 full-color cards was produced by Mike Cramer's Pacific Trading Cards of Edmonds, Washington. The cards are silver bordered and are standard size, 2 1/2" by 3 1/2". Card backs are printed in yellow, black, and gray on white card stock. The cards were available either as wax packs or as collated sets. The players pictured in the set had retired many years before, but most are still well remembered. The statistics on the card backs give the player's career and "best season" statistics. The set was licensed by Major League Baseball Players Alumni.

			MINT	EXC	G-VG
COMPLETE SET (110)			10.00	5.00	1.00
COMMON PLAYER (1-110)			.05	.02	.00
☐	1	Hank Aaron	.75	.35	.07
☐	2	Red Schoendienst	.25	.12	.02
☐	3	Brooks Robinson	.30	.15	.03
☐	4	Luke Appling	.15	.07	.01
☐	5	Gene Woodling	.05	.02	.00
☐	6	Stan Musial	.60	.30	.06
☐	7	Mickey Mantle	1.00	.50	.10
☐	8	Richie Ashburn	.20	.10	.02
☐	9	Ralph Kiner	.25	.12	.02
☐	10	Phil Rizzuto	.15	.07	.01
☐	11	Harvey Haddix	.05	.02	.00
☐	12	Ken Boyer	.10	.05	.01
☐	13	Clete Boyer	.05	.02	.00
☐	14	Ken Harrelson	.10	.05	.01
☐	15	Robin Roberts	.20	.10	.02
☐	16	Catfish Hunter	.20	.10	.02
☐	17	Frank Howard	.10	.05	.01
☐	18	Jim Perry	.05	.02	.00
☐	19A	Elston Howard ERR	.10	.05	.01
		(reversed negative)			
☐	19B	Elston Howard COR	.10	.05	.01
☐	20	Jim Bouton	.10	.05	.01
☐	21	Pee Wee Reese	.25	.12	.02
☐	22A	Mel Stottlemyre ERR	.10	.05	.01
		(spelled Stottlemyer			
		on card front)			
☐	22B	Mel Stottlemyre COR	.10	.05	.01
☐	23	Hank Sauer	.05	.02	.00

☐	24	Willie Mays	.75	.35	.07
☐	25	Tom Tresh	.10	.05	.01
☐	26	Roy Sievers	.05	.02	.00
☐	27	Leo Durocher	.15	.07	.01
☐	28	Al Dark	.05	.02	.00
☐	29	Tony Kubek	.15	.07	.01
☐	30	Johnny VanderMeer	.10	.05	.01
☐	31	Joe Adcock	.05	.02	.00
☐	32	Bob Lemon	.15	.07	.01
☐	33	Don Newcombe	.10	.05	.01
☐	34	Thurman Munson	.30	.15	.03
☐	35	Earl Battey	.05	.02	.00
☐	36	Ernie Banks	.30	.15	.03
☐	37	Matty Alou	.05	.02	.00
☐	38	Dave McNally	.05	.02	.00
☐	39	Mickey Lolich	.10	.05	.01
☐	40	Jackie Robinson	.35	.17	.03
☐	41	Allie Reynolds	.10	.05	.01
☐	42A	Don Larsen ERR	.10	.05	.01
		(misspelled Larson on card front)			
☐	42B	Don Larsen COR	.10	.05	.01
☐	43	Fergie Jenkins	.10	.05	.01
☐	44	Jim Gilliam	.10	.05	.01
☐	45	Bobby Thomson	.10	.05	.01
☐	46	Sparky Anderson	.10	.05	.01
☐	47	Roy Campanella	.35	.17	.03
☐	48	Marv Throneberry	.10	.05	.01
☐	49	Bill Virdon	.05	.02	.00
☐	50	Ted Williams	.50	.25	.05
☐	51	Minnie Minoso	.10	.05	.01
☐	52	Bob Turley	.05	.02	.00
☐	53	Yogi Berra	.35	.17	.03
☐	54	Juan Marichal	.20	.10	.02
☐	55	Duke Snider	.35	.17	.03
☐	56	Harvey Kuenn	.10	.05	.01
☐	57	Nellie Fox	.15	.07	.01
☐	58	Felipe Alou	.05	.02	.00
☐	59	Tony Oliva	.10	.05	.01
☐	60	Bill Mazeroski	.10	.05	.01
☐	61	Bobby Shantz	.05	.02	.00
☐	62	Mark Fidrych	.05	.02	.00
☐	63	Johnny Mize	.20	.10	.02
☐	64	Ralph Terry	.10	.05	.01
☐	65	Gus Bell	.05	.02	.00
☐	66	Jerry Koosman	.10	.05	.01
☐	67	Mike McCormick	.05	.02	.00
☐	68	Lou Burdette	.10	.05	.01
☐	69	George Kell	.20	.10	.02
☐	70	Vic Raschi	.10	.05	.01
☐	71	Chuck Connors	.20	.10	.02
☐	72	Ted Kluszewski	.15	.07	.01
☐	73	Bobby Doerr	.20	.10	.02
☐	74	Bobby Richardson	.15	.07	.01
☐	75	Carl Erskine	.10	.05	.01
☐	76	Hoyt Wilhelm	.20	.10	.02
☐	77	Bob Purkey	.05	.02	.00
☐	78	Bob Friend	.05	.02	.00
☐	79	Monte Irvin	.20	.10	.02
☐	80A	Jim Lonborg ERR	.10	.05	.01
		(misspelled Longborg on card front)			
☐	80B	Jim Lonborg COR	.10	.05	.01
☐	81	Wally Moon	.05	.02	.00
☐	82	Moose Skowron	.10	.05	.01
☐	83	Tommy Davis	.10	.05	.01
☐	84	Enos Slaughter	.20	.10	.02
☐	85	Sal Maglie UER	.10	.05	.01
		(1945-1917 on back)			
☐	86	Harmon Killebrew	.20	.10	.02
☐	87	Gil Hodges	.20	.10	.02
☐	88	Jim Kaat	.10	.05	.01
☐	89	Roger Maris	.40	.20	.04
☐	90	Billy Williams	.20	.10	.02
☐	91	Luis Aparicio	.20	.10	.02
☐	92	Jim Bunning	.15	.07	.01
☐	93	Bill Freehan	.10	.05	.01
☐	94	Orlando Cepeda	.15	.07	.01
☐	95	Early Wynn	.20	.10	.02
☐	96	Tug McGraw	.10	.05	.01
☐	97	Ron Santo	.10	.05	.01
☐	98	Del Crandall	.05	.02	.00
☐	99	Sal Bando	.05	.02	.00
☐	100	Joe DiMaggio	.75	.35	.07
☐	101	Bob Feller	.35	.17	.03
☐	102	Larry Doby	.10	.05	.01
☐	103	Rollie Fingers	.15	.07	.01
☐	104	Al Kaline	.25	.12	.02
☐	105	Johnny Podres	.10	.05	.01
☐	106	Lou Boudreau	.20	.10	.02
☐	107	Zoilo Versalles	.05	.02	.00
☐	108	Dick Groat	.10	.05	.01
☐	109	Warren Spahn	.25	.12	.02
☐	110	Johnny Bench	.35	.17	.03

1989 Pacific Legends II

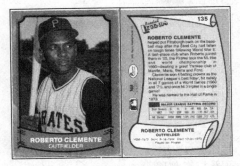

ROBERTO CLEMENTE
OUTFIELDER

The 1989 Pacific Legends Series II set contains 110 standard-size (2 1/2 by 3 1/2 inch) cards. The fronts have vintage color photos with silver borders. The backs are grey and feature career highlights and lifetime statistics. The cards were distributed as sets and in 10- card wax packs.

		MINT	EXC	G-VG
	COMPLETE SET (110)	10.00	5.00	1.00
	COMMON PLAYER (111-220)	.05	.02	.00
☐ 111	Reggie Jackson	.50	.25	.05
☐ 112	Rich Reese	.05	.02	.00
☐ 113	Frankie Frisch	.10	.05	.01
☐ 114	Ed Kranepool	.05	.02	.00
☐ 115	Al Hrabosky	.05	.02	.00
☐ 116	Eddie Mathews	.20	.10	.02
☐ 117	Ty Cobb	.40	.20	.04
☐ 118	Jim Davenport	.05	.02	.00
☐ 119	Buddy Lewis	.05	.02	.00
☐ 120	Virgil Trucks	.05	.02	.00
☐ 121	Del Ennis	.05	.02	.00
☐ 122	Dick Radatz	.05	.02	.00
☐ 123	Andy Pafko	.05	.02	.00
☐ 124	Wilbur Wood	.05	.02	.00
☐ 125	Joe Sewell	.10	.05	.01
☐ 126	Herb Score	.05	.02	.00
☐ 127	Paul Waner	.10	.05	.01
☐ 128	Lloyd Waner	.10	.05	.01
☐ 129	Brooks Robinson	.25	.12	.02
☐ 130	Bo Belinsky	.05	.02	.00
☐ 131	Phil Cavaretta	.05	.02	.00
☐ 132	Claude Osteen	.05	.02	.00
☐ 133	Tito Francona	.05	.02	.00
☐ 134	Billy Pierce	.05	.02	.00
☐ 135	Roberto Clemente	.30	.15	.03
☐ 136	Spud Chandler	.05	.02	.00
☐ 137	Enos Slaughter	.15	.07	.01
☐ 138	Ken Holtzman	.05	.02	.00
☐ 139	John Hopp	.05	.02	.00
☐ 140	Tony LaRussa	.05	.02	.00
☐ 141	Ryne Duren	.05	.02	.00
☐ 142	Glenn Beckert	.05	.02	.00
☐ 143	Ken Keltner	.05	.02	.00
☐ 144	Hank Bauer	.05	.02	.00
☐ 145	Roger Craig	.10	.05	.01
☐ 146	Frank Baker	.10	.05	.01
☐ 147	Jim O'Toole	.05	.02	.00
☐ 148	Rogers Hornsby	.20	.10	.02
☐ 149	Jose Cardenal	.05	.02	.00
☐ 150	Bobby Doerr	.15	.07	.01
☐ 151	Mickey Cochrane	.15	.07	.01
☐ 152	Gaylord Perry	.20	.10	.02
☐ 153	Frank Thomas	.05	.02	.00
☐ 154	Ted Williams	.50	.25	.05
☐ 155	Sam McDowell	.05	.02	.00
☐ 156	Bob Feller	.30	.15	.03
☐ 157	Bert Campaneris	.05	.02	.00
☐ 158	Thornton Lee	.05	.02	.00
☐ 159	Gary Peters	.05	.02	.00
☐ 160	Joe Medwick	.15	.07	.01
☐ 161	Joe Nuxhall	.05	.02	.00
☐ 162	Joe Schultz	.05	.02	.00
☐ 163	Harmon Killebrew	.20	.10	.02
☐ 164	Bucky Walters	.05	.02	.00
☐ 165	Bob Allison	.05	.02	.00
☐ 166	Lou Boudreau	.15	.07	.01
☐ 167	Joe Cronin	.15	.07	.01
☐ 168	Mike Torrez	.05	.02	.00

☐ 169	Rich Rollins	.05	.02	.00
☐ 170	Tony Cuccinello	.05	.02	.00
☐ 171	Hoyt Wilhelm	.20	.10	.02
☐ 172	Ernie Harwell	.05	.02	.00
	(announcer)			
☐ 173	George Foster	.10	.05	.01
☐ 174	Lou Gehrig	.50	.25	.05
☐ 175	Dave Kingman	.10	.05	.01
☐ 176	Babe Ruth	.75	.35	.07
☐ 177	Joe Black	.05	.02	.00
☐ 178	Roy Face	.05	.02	.00
☐ 179	Earl Weaver	.10	.05	.01
☐ 180	Johnny Mize	.15	.07	.01
☐ 181	Roger Cramer	.05	.02	.00
☐ 182	Jim Piersall	.05	.02	.00
☐ 183	Ned Garver	.05	.02	.00
☐ 184	Billy Williams	.15	.07	.01
☐ 185	Lefty Grove	.15	.07	.01
☐ 186	Jim Grant	.05	.02	.00
☐ 187	Elmer Valo	.05	.02	.00
☐ 188	Ewell Blackwell	.05	.02	.00
☐ 189	Mel Ott	.15	.07	.01
☐ 190	Harry Walker	.05	.02	.00
☐ 191	Bill Campbell	.05	.02	.00
☐ 192	Walter Johnson	.20	.10	.02
☐ 193	Catfish Hunter	.20	.10	.02
☐ 194	Charlie Keller	.05	.02	.00
☐ 195	Hank Greenberg	.15	.07	.01
☐ 196	Bobby Murcer	.10	.05	.01
☐ 197	Al Lopez	.15	.07	.01
☐ 198	Vida Blue	.05	.02	.00
☐ 199	Shag Crawford UMP	.05	.02	.00
☐ 200	Arky Vaughan	.15	.07	.01
☐ 201	Smoky Burgess	.05	.02	.00
☐ 202	Rip Sewell	.05	.02	.00
☐ 203	Earl Averill	.10	.05	.01
☐ 204	Milt Pappas	.05	.02	.00
☐ 205	Mel Harder	.05	.02	.00
☐ 206	Sam Jethroe	.05	.02	.00
☐ 207	Randy Hundley	.05	.02	.00
☐ 208	Jesse Haines	.05	.02	.00
☐ 209	Jack Brickhouse	.05	.02	.00
	(announcer)			
☐ 210	Whitey Ford	.25	.12	.02
☐ 211	Honus Wagner	.25	.12	.02
☐ 212	Phil Niekro	.15	.07	.01
☐ 213	Gary Bell	.05	.02	.00
☐ 214	Jon Matlack	.05	.02	.00
☐ 215	Moe Drabowsky	.05	.02	.00
☐ 216	Edd Roush	.15	.07	.01
☐ 217	Joel Horlen	.05	.02	.00
☐ 218	Casey Stengel	.20	.10	.02
☐ 219	Burt Hooton	.05	.02	.00
☐ 220	Joe Jackson	.50	.25	.05

1989-90 Pacific Senior League

Vida Blue
PITCHER

The 1989-90 Pacific Trading Cards Senior League set contains 220 standard-size (2 1/2 by 3 1/2 inch) cards. The fronts feature color photos with silver borders and player names and positions at the bottom. The horizontally-oriented backs are red, white and blue, and show vital statistics and career highlights. The cards were distributed as a boxed set with 15 card-sized logo stickers/puzzle pieces as well as in wax packs. There are several In Action cards in the set, designated by IA in the checklist below.

		MINT	EXC	G-VG
COMPLETE SET (220)		15.00	7.00	1.00
COMMON PLAYER (1-220)		.05	.02	.01

☐ 1	Bobby Tolan	.10	.04	.01
☐ 2	Sergio Ferrer	.05	.02	.01
☐ 3	David Rajsich	.05	.02	.01
☐ 4	Ron LeFlore	.10	.04	.01
☐ 5	Steve Henderson	.05	.02	.01
☐ 6	Jerry Martin	.05	.02	.01
☐ 7	Gary Rajsich	.05	.02	.01
☐ 8	Elias Sosa	.05	.02	.01
☐ 9	Jon Matlock	.10	.04	.01
☐ 10	Steve Kemp	.10	.04	.01
☐ 11	Lenny Randle	.05	.02	.01
☐ 12	Roy Howell	.05	.02	.01
☐ 13	Milt Wilcox	.05	.02	.01
☐ 14	Alan Bannister	.05	.02	.01
☐ 15	Dock Ellis	.05	.02	.01
☐ 16	Mike Williams	.05	.02	.01
☐ 17	Luis Gomez	.05	.02	.01
☐ 18	Joe Sambito	.05	.02	.01
☐ 19	Bake McBride	.05	.02	.01
☐ 20	Pat Zachry	.05	.02	.01
☐ 21	Dwight Lowry	.05	.02	.01
☐ 22	Ozzie Virgil Sr.	.05	.02	.01
☐ 23	Randy Lerch	.05	.02	.01
☐ 24	Butch Benton	.05	.02	.01
☐ 25	Tom Zimmer	.05	.02	.01
☐ 26	Al Holland	.05	.02	.01
☐ 27	Sammy Stewart	.05	.02	.01
☐ 28	Bill Lee	.10	.04	.01
☐ 29	Ferguson Jenkins	.50	.20	.04
☐ 30	Leon Roberts	.05	.02	.01
☐ 31	Rick Wise	.05	.02	.01
☐ 32	Butch Hobson	.05	.02	.01
☐ 33	Pete LaCock	.05	.02	.01
☐ 34	Bill Campbell	.05	.02	.01
☐ 35	Doug Simunic	.05	.02	.01
☐ 36	Mario Guerrero	.05	.02	.01
☐ 37	Jim Willoughby	.05	.02	.01
☐ 38	Joe Pittman	.05	.02	.01
☐ 39	Mark Bomback	.05	.02	.01
☐ 40	Tommy McMillian	.05	.02	.01
☐ 41	Gary Allanson	.05	.02	.01
☐ 42	Cecil Cooper	.10	.04	.01
☐ 43	John LaRosa	.05	.02	.01
☐ 44	Darrell Brandon	.05	.02	.01
☐ 45	Bernie Carbo	.05	.02	.01
☐ 46	Mike Cuellar	.10	.04	.01
☐ 47	Al Bumbry	.05	.02	.01
☐ 48	Gene Richards	.05	.02	.01
☐ 49	Pedro Borbon	.05	.02	.01
☐ 50	Julio Solo	.05	.02	.01
☐ 51	Ed Nottle	.05	.02	.01
☐ 52	Jim Bibby	.05	.02	.01
☐ 53	Doug Griffin	.05	.02	.01
☐ 54	Ed Clements	.05	.02	.01
☐ 55	Dalton Jones	.05	.02	.01
☐ 56	Earl Weaver MG	.50	.20	.04
☐ 57	Jesus De La Rosa	.05	.02	.01
☐ 58	Paul Casanova	.05	.02	.01
☐ 59	Frank Riccelli	.05	.02	.01
☐ 60	Rafael Landestoy	.05	.02	.01
☐ 61	George Hendrick	.10	.04	.01
☐ 62	Cesar Cedeno	.10	.04	.01
☐ 63	Bert Campaneris	.10	.04	.01
☐ 64	Derrell Thomas	.05	.02	.01
☐ 65	Bobby Ramos	.05	.02	.01
☐ 66	Grant Jackson	.05	.02	.01
☐ 67	Steve Whitaker	.05	.02	.01
☐ 68	Pedro Ramos	.05	.02	.01
☐ 69	Joe Hicks	.05	.02	.01
☐ 70	Taylor Duncan	.05	.02	.01
☐ 71	Tom Shopay	.05	.02	.01
☐ 72	Ken Clay	.05	.02	.01
☐ 73	Mike Kekich	.05	.02	.01
☐ 74	Ed Halicki	.05	.02	.01
☐ 75	Ed Figueroa	.05	.02	.01
☐ 76	Paul Blair	.10	.04	.01
☐ 77	Luis Tiant	.25	.09	.01
☐ 78	Stan Bahnsen	.05	.02	.01
☐ 79	Rennie Stennett	.05	.02	.01
☐ 80	Bobby Molinaro	.05	.02	.01
☐ 81	Jim Gideon	.05	.02	.01
☐ 82	Orlando Gonzalez	.05	.02	.01
☐ 83	Amos Otis	.20	.08	.01
☐ 84	Dennis Leonard	.10	.04	.01
☐ 85	Pat Putman	.05	.02	.01
☐ 86	Rick Manning	.05	.02	.01
☐ 87	Pat Dobson	.10	.04	.01
☐ 88	Marty Castillo	.05	.02	.01
☐ 89	Steve McCatty	.05	.02	.01

☐ 90	Doug Bird	.05	.02	.01
☐ 91	Rick Waits	.05	.02	.01
☐ 92	Ron Jackson	.05	.02	.01
☐ 93	Tim Hosley	.05	.02	.01
☐ 94	Steve Luebber	.05	.02	.01
☐ 95	Rich Gale	.05	.02	.01
☐ 96	Champ Summers	.05	.02	.01
☐ 97	Dave LaRoche	.05	.02	.01
☐ 98	Bobby Jones	.05	.02	.01
☐ 99	Kim Allen	.05	.02	.01
☐ 100	Wayne Garland	.05	.02	.01
☐ 101	Tom Spencer	.05	.02	.01
☐ 102	Dan Driessen	.10	.04	.01
☐ 103	Ron Pruitt	.05	.02	.01
☐ 104	Tim Ireland	.05	.02	.01
☐ 105	Dan Driessen IA	.10	.04	.01
☐ 106	Pepe Frias	.05	.02	.01
☐ 107	Eric Rasmussen	.05	.02	.01
☐ 108	Don Hood	.05	.02	.01
☐ 109	Joe Coleman	.05	.02	.01
☐ 110	Jim Slaton	.05	.02	.01
☐ 111	Clint Hurdle	.05	.02	.01
☐ 112	Larry Milbourne	.05	.02	.01
☐ 113	Al Holland	.05	.02	.01
☐ 114	George Foster	.15	.06	.01
☐ 115	Graig Nettles	.15	.06	.01
☐ 116	Oscar Gamble	.05	.02	.01
☐ 117	Ross Grimsley	.05	.02	.01
☐ 118	Bill Travers	.05	.02	.01
☐ 119	Jose Beniquez	.10	.04	.01
☐ 120	Jerry Grote IA	.05	.02	.01
☐ 121	John D'Acquisto	.05	.02	.01
☐ 122	Tom Murphy	.05	.02	.01
☐ 123	Walt Williams	.05	.02	.01
☐ 124	Roy Thomas	.05	.02	.01
☐ 125	Jerry Grote	.05	.02	.01
☐ 126	Jim Nettles	.05	.02	.01
☐ 127	Randy Niemann	.05	.02	.01
☐ 128	Bobby Bonds	.25	.10	.01
☐ 129	Ed Glynn	.05	.02	.01
☐ 130	Ed Hicks	.05	.02	.01
☐ 131	Ivan Murrell	.05	.02	.01
☐ 132	Graig Nettles	.20	.08	.01
☐ 133	Hal McRae	.15	.06	.01
☐ 134	Pat Kelly	.05	.02	.01
☐ 135	Sammy Stewart	.05	.02	.01
☐ 136	Bruce Kison	.05	.02	.01
☐ 137	Jim Morrison	.05	.02	.01
☐ 138	Omar Moreno	.05	.02	.01
☐ 139	Tom Brown	.05	.02	.01
☐ 140	Steve Dillard	.05	.02	.01
☐ 141	Gary Alexander	.05	.02	.01
☐ 142	Al Oliver	.20	.08	.01
☐ 143	Rick Lysander	.05	.02	.01
☐ 144	Tippy Martinez	.10	.05	.01
☐ 145	Al Cowens	.10	.05	.01
☐ 146	Gene Clines	.05	.02	.01
☐ 147	Willie Aikens	.10	.04	.01
☐ 148	Tommy Moore	.05	.02	.01
☐ 149	Clete Boyer	.10	.04	.01
☐ 150	Stan Cliburn	.05	.02	.01
☐ 151	Ken Kravec	.05	.02	.01
☐ 152	Garth Iorg	.05	.02	.01
☐ 153	Rick Peterson	.05	.02	.01
☐ 154	Wayne Nordhagen	.05	.02	.01
☐ 155	Danny Meyer	.05	.02	.01
☐ 156	Wayne Garrett	.05	.02	.01
☐ 157	Wayne Krenchicki	.05	.02	.01
☐ 158	Graig Nettles	.20	.08	.01
☐ 159	Earl Stephenson	.05	.02	.01
☐ 160	Carl Taylor	.05	.02	.01
☐ 161	Rollie Fingers	.50	.20	.01
☐ 162	Toby Harrah	.10	.04	.01
☐ 163	Mickey Rivers	.10	.04	.01
☐ 164	Dave Kingman	.15	.06	.01
☐ 165	Paul Mirabella	.05	.02	.01
☐ 166	Dick Williams	.10	.04	.01
☐ 167	Luis Pujols	.05	.02	.01
☐ 168	Tito Landrum	.10	.04	.01
☐ 169	Tom Underwood	.05	.02	.01
☐ 170	Mark Wagner	.05	.02	.01
☐ 171	Odell Jones	.05	.02	.01
☐ 172	Doug Capilla	.05	.02	.01
☐ 173	Allie Rondon	.05	.02	.01
☐ 174	Lowell Palmer	.05	.02	.01
☐ 175	Juan Eichelberger	.05	.02	.01
☐ 176	Wes Clements	.05	.02	.01
☐ 177	Rodney Scott	.05	.02	.01
☐ 178	Ron Washington	.10	.04	.01
☐ 179	Al Hrabosky	.10	.04	.01
☐ 180	Sid Monge	.05	.02	.01
☐ 181	Randy Johnson	.05	.02	.01
☐ 182	Tim Stoddard	.05	.02	.01
☐ 183	Dick Williams MG	.10	.04	.01
☐ 184	Lee Lacy	.10	.04	.01

☐ 185	Jerry White	.05	.02	.01
☐ 186	Dave Kingman	.15	.06	.01
☐ 187	Checklist 1-110	.05	.02	.01
☐ 188	Jose Cruz	.15	.06	.01
☐ 189	Jamie Easterly	.05	.02	.01
☐ 190	Ike Blessit	.05	.02	.01
☐ 191	Johnny Grubb	.05	.02	.01
☐ 192	Dave Cash	.05	.02	.01
☐ 193	Doug Corbett	.05	.02	.01
☐ 194	Bruce Bochy	.05	.02	.01
☐ 195	Mark Corey	.05	.02	.01
☐ 196	Gil Rondon	.05	.02	.01
☐ 197	Jerry Martin	.05	.02	.01
☐ 198	Gerry Pirtle	.05	.02	.01
☐ 199	Gates Brown	.10	.04	.01
☐ 200	Bob Galasso	.05	.02	.01
☐ 201	Bake McBride	.05	.02	.01
☐ 202	Wayne Granger	.05	.02	.01
☐ 203	Larry Milbourne	.05	.02	.01
☐ 204	Tom Paciorek	.10	.04	.01
☐ 205	U.L. Washington	.05	.02	.01
☐ 206	Larvell Blanks	.05	.02	.01
☐ 207	Bob Shirley	.05	.02	.01
☐ 208	Pete Falcone	.05	.02	.01
☐ 209	Sal Butera	.05	.02	.01
☐ 210	Roy Branch	.05	.02	.01
☐ 211	Dyar Miller	.05	.02	.01
☐ 212	Paul Siebert	.05	.02	.01
☐ 213	Ken Reitz	.05	.02	.01
☐ 214	Bill Madlock	.15	.06	.01
☐ 215	Vida Blue	.10	.04	.01
☐ 216	Dave Hilton	.05	.02	.01
☐ 217	Ramos and Bren	.05	.02	.01
☐ 218	Checklist 111-220	.05	.02	.01
☐ 219	Dobson and Weaver	.15	.06	.01
☐ 220	Curt Flood	.20	.08	.01

1988 Pepsi Tigers

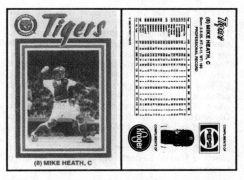

(8) MIKE HEATH, C

This set of 25 cards features members of the Detroit Tigers and was sponsored by Pepsi Cola and Kroger. The cards are in full color on the fronts and measure approximately 2 7/8" by 4 1/4". The card backs contain complete Major and Minor League season-by-season statistics. The cards are unnumbered so they are listed below by uniform number, which is given on the card.

		MINT	EXC	G-VG
COMPLETE SET (25)		8.00	4.00	.80
COMMON PLAYER		.20	.10	.02
☐ 1	Lou Whitaker	.60	.30	.06
☐ 2	Alan Trammell	.75	.35	.07
☐ 8	Mike Heath	.20	.10	.02
☐ 11	Sparky Anderson MG	.40	.20	.04
☐ 12	Luis Salazar	.20	.10	.02
☐ 14	Dave Bergman	.20	.10	.02
☐ 15	Pat Sheridan	.20	.10	.02
☐ 16	Tom Brookens	.20	.10	.02
☐ 19	Doyle Alexander	.30	.15	.03
☐ 21	Guillermo Hernandez	.30	.15	.03
☐ 22	Ray Knight	.30	.15	.03
☐ 24	Gary Pettis	.30	.15	.03
☐ 25	Eric King	.20	.10	.02
☐ 26	Frank Tanana	.30	.15	.03
☐ 31	Larry Herndon	.20	.10	.02

☐ 32	Jim Walewander	.20	.10	.02
☐ 33	Matt Nokes	.40	.20	.04
☐ 34	Chet Lemon	.30	.15	.03
☐ 35	Walt Terrell	.30	.15	.03
☐ 39	Mike Henneman	.30	.15	.03
☐ 41	Darrell Evans	.40	.20	.04
☐ 44	Jeff Robinson	.40	.20	.04
☐ 47	Jack Morris	.50	.25	.05
☐ 48	Paul Gibson	.20	.10	.02
☐ xx	Tigers Coaches	.20	.10	.02

Billy Consolo
Alex Grammas
Billy Muffett
Vada Pinson
Dick Tracewski

1989 Pepsi McGwire

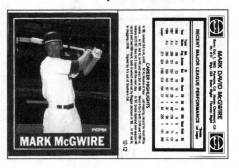

This set includes 12 cards each depicting Mark McGwire. The cards are standard size, 2 1/2" by 3 1/2" and are printed on rather thin card stock. The cards have a distinctive blue outer border. The cards are numbered on the back in the lower right corner. The Pepsi logo is shown on the front and back of each card. All the pictures used in the set are posed showing McGwire in a generic uniform with a Pepsi patch on his upper arm and his number 25 on his chest; in each case his cap or batting helmet is in the Oakland colors but without their logo. The card backs all contain exactly the same statistical and biographical information, only the card number is different. Supposedly cards were distributed inside specially marked 12-packs of Pepsi in the Northern California area.

		MINT	EXC	G-VG
	COMPLETE SET (12)	15.00	7.50	1.50
	COMMON PLAYER (1-12)	1.50	.75	.15
☐ 1	Mark McGwire (batting stance with left foot lifted)	1.50	.75	.15
☐ 2	Mark McGwire (fielding position at first base)	1.50	.75	.15
☐ 3	Mark McGwire (reaching out with glove for ball)	1.50	.75	.15
☐ 4	Mark McGwire (batting stance in empty stadium)	1.50	.75	.15
☐ 5	Mark McGwire (on one knee with bat)	1.50	.75	.15
☐ 6	Mark McGwire (stretching for ball at first base)	1.50	.75	.15
☐ 7	Mark McGwire (smiling with bat on shoulder facing camera)	1.50	.75	.15
☐ 8	Mark McGwire (holding bat in green windbreaker)	1.50	.75	.15
☐ 9	Mark McGwire (Rawlings bat on left shoulder)	1.50	.75	.15
☐ 10	Mark McGwire	1.50	.75	.15

	(holding bat parallel to ground in green windbreaker)			
☐ 11	Mark McGwire (holding bat parallel to ground in uniform, toothy smile)	1.50	.75	.15
☐ 12	Mark McGwire (serious looking follow through)	1.50	.75	.15

1939 Playball

The cards in this 162-card set measure 2 1/2" by 3 1/8". Gum Incorporated introduced a brief (war-shortened) but innovative era of baseball card production with its set of 1939. The combination of actual player photos (black and white), large card size, and extensive biography proved extremely popular. Player names are found either entirely capitalized or with initial caps only, and a "sample card" overprint is not uncommon. Card number 126 was never issued, and cards 116-162 were produced in lesser quantities than 1-115. The ACC designation for this set is R334.

		EX-MT	VG-E	GOOD
	COMPLETE SET	9500.00	4500.00	1100.00
	COMMON PLAYER (1-115)	10.00	5.00	1.00
	COMMON PLAYER (116-162)	100.00	50.00	10.00
☐ 1	Jake Powell	75.00	7.50	1.50
☐ 2	Lee Grissom	10.00	5.00	1.00
☐ 3	Red Ruffing	75.00	37.50	7.50
☐ 4	Eldon Auker	10.00	5.00	1.00
☐ 5	Luke Sewell	15.00	7.50	1.50
☐ 6	Leo Durocher	50.00	25.00	5.00
☐ 7	Bobby Doerr	75.00	37.50	7.50
☐ 8	Henry Pippen	10.00	5.00	1.00
☐ 9	James Tobin	10.00	5.00	1.00
☐ 10	James DeShong	10.00	5.00	1.00
☐ 11	Johnny Rizzo	10.00	5.00	1.00
☐ 12	Hershel Martin	10.00	5.00	1.00
☐ 13	Luke Hamlin	10.00	5.00	1.00
☐ 14	Jim Tabor	10.00	5.00	1.00
☐ 15	Paul Derringer	15.00	7.50	1.50
☐ 16	John Peacock	10.00	5.00	1.00
☐ 17	Emerson Dickman	10.00	5.00	1.00
☐ 18	Harry Danning	10.00	5.00	1.00
☐ 19	Paul Dean	20.00	10.00	2.00
☐ 20	Joe Heving	10.00	5.00	1.00
☐ 21	Dutch Leonard	10.00	5.00	1.00
☐ 22	Bucky Walters	15.00	7.50	1.50
☐ 23	Burgess Whitehead	10.00	5.00	1.00
☐ 24	Richard Coffman	10.00	5.00	1.00
☐ 25	George Selkirk	20.00	10.00	2.00
☐ 26	Joe DiMaggio	1500.00	750.00	150.00
☐ 27	Fred Ostermueller	10.00	5.00	1.00
☐ 28	Sylvester Johnson	10.00	5.00	1.00
☐ 29	John (Jack) Wilson	10.00	5.00	1.00
☐ 30	Bill Dickey	125.00	60.00	12.50
☐ 31	Sam West	10.00	5.00	1.00
☐ 32	Bob Seeds	10.00	5.00	1.00
☐ 33	Del Young	10.00	5.00	1.00
☐ 34	Frank Demaree	10.00	5.00	1.00
☐ 35	Bill Jurges	10.00	5.00	1.00
☐ 36	Frank McCormick	10.00	5.00	1.00
☐ 37	Virgil Davis	10.00	5.00	1.00

☐ 38	Billy Myers	10.00	5.00	1.00
☐ 39	Rick Ferrell	60.00	30.00	6.00
☐ 40	James Bagby Jr.	10.00	5.00	1.00
☐ 41	Lon Warneke	10.00	5.00	1.00
☐ 42	Arndt Jorgens	10.00	5.00	1.00
☐ 43	Melo Almada	10.00	5.00	1.00
☐ 44	Don Heffner	10.00	5.00	1.00
☐ 45	Merrill May	10.00	5.00	1.00
☐ 46	Morris Arnovich	10.00	5.00	1.00
☐ 47	Buddy Lewis	10.00	5.00	1.00
☐ 48	Lefty Gomez	100.00	50.00	10.00
☐ 49	Eddie Miller	10.00	5.00	1.00
☐ 50	Charlie Gehringer	100.00	50.00	10.00
☐ 51	Mel Ott	125.00	60.00	12.50
☐ 52	Tommy Henrich	25.00	12.50	2.50
☐ 53	Carl Hubbell	100.00	50.00	10.00
☐ 54	Harry Gumpert	10.00	5.00	1.00
☐ 55	Arky Vaughan	60.00	30.00	6.00
☐ 56	Hank Greenberg	125.00	60.00	12.50
☐ 57	Buddy Hassett	10.00	5.00	1.00
☐ 58	Lou Chiozza	10.00	5.00	1.00
☐ 59	Ken Chase	10.00	5.00	1.00
☐ 60	Schoolboy Rowe	15.00	7.50	1.50
☐ 61	Tony Cuccinello	10.00	5.00	1.00
☐ 62	Tom Carey	10.00	5.00	1.00
☐ 63	Emmett Mueller	10.00	5.00	1.00
☐ 64	Wally Moses	10.00	5.00	1.00
☐ 65	Harry Craft	10.00	5.00	1.00
☐ 66	Jimmy Ripple	10.00	5.00	1.00
☐ 67	Ed Joost	10.00	5.00	1.00
☐ 68	Fred Sington	10.00	5.00	1.00
☐ 69	Elbie Fletcher	10.00	5.00	1.00
☐ 70	Fred Frankhouse	10.00	5.00	1.00
☐ 71	Monte Pearson	10.00	5.00	1.00
☐ 72	Debs Garms	10.00	5.00	1.00
☐ 73	Hal Schumacher	10.00	5.00	1.00
☐ 74	Cookie Lavagetto	10.00	5.00	1.00
☐ 75	Stan Bordagaray	10.00	5.00	1.00
☐ 76	Goody Rosen	10.00	5.00	1.00
☐ 77	Lew Riggs	10.00	5.00	1.00
☐ 78	Julius Solters	10.00	5.00	1.00
☐ 79	Jo Jo Moore	10.00	5.00	1.00
☐ 80	Pete Fox	10.00	5.00	1.00
☐ 81	Babe Dahlgren	10.00	5.00	1.00
☐ 82	Chuck Klein	100.00	50.00	10.00
☐ 83	Gus Suhr	10.00	5.00	1.00
☐ 84	Skeeter Newsom	10.00	5.00	1.00
☐ 85	Johnny Cooney	10.00	5.00	1.00
☐ 86	Dolph Camilli	10.00	5.00	1.00
☐ 87	Milburn Shoffner	10.00	5.00	1.00
☐ 88	Charlie Keller	20.00	10.00	2.00
☐ 89	Lloyd Waner	60.00	30.00	6.00
☐ 90	Robert Klinger	10.00	5.00	1.00
☐ 91	John Knott	10.00	5.00	1.00
☐ 92	Ted Williams	1500.00	750.00	150.00
☐ 93	Charles Gelbert	10.00	5.00	1.00
☐ 94	Heinie Manush	60.00	30.00	6.00
☐ 95	Whit Wyatt	10.00	5.00	1.00
☐ 96	Babe Phelps	10.00	5.00	1.00
☐ 97	Bob Johnson	15.00	7.50	1.50
☐ 98	Pinky Whitney	10.00	5.00	1.00
☐ 99	Wally Berger	10.00	5.00	1.00
☐ 100	Charles Myer	10.00	5.00	1.00
☐ 101	Roger Cramer	15.00	7.50	1.50
☐ 102	Lem Young	10.00	5.00	1.00
☐ 103	Moe Berg	25.00	12.50	2.50
☐ 104	Tom Bridges	15.00	7.50	1.50
☐ 105	Rabbit McNair	10.00	5.00	1.00
☐ 106	Dolly Stark	10.00	5.00	1.00
☐ 107	Joe Vosmik	10.00	5.00	1.00
☐ 108	Frank Hayes	10.00	5.00	1.00
☐ 109	Myril Hoag	10.00	5.00	1.00
☐ 110	Fred Fitzsimmons	10.00	5.00	1.00
☐ 111	Van Lingle Mungo	10.00	5.00	1.00
☐ 112	Paul Waner	60.00	30.00	6.00
☐ 113	Al Schacht	15.00	7.50	1.50
☐ 114	Cecil Travis	10.00	5.00	1.00
☐ 115	Ralph Kress	10.00	5.00	1.00
☐ 116	Gene Desautels	100.00	50.00	10.00
☐ 117	Wayne Ambler	100.00	50.00	10.00
☐ 118	Lynn Nelson	100.00	50.00	10.00
☐ 119	Will Hershberger	100.00	50.00	10.00
☐ 120	Rabbit Warstler	100.00	50.00	10.00
☐ 121	Bill Posedel	100.00	50.00	10.00
☐ 122	George McQuinn	100.00	50.00	10.00
☐ 123	Ray T. Davis	100.00	50.00	10.00
☐ 124	Walter Brown	100.00	50.00	10.00
☐ 125	Cliff Melton	100.00	50.00	10.00
☐ 126	Not issued	00.00	00.00	00.00
☐ 127	Gil Brack	100.00	50.00	10.00
☐ 128	Joe Bowman	100.00	50.00	10.00
☐ 129	Bill Swift	100.00	50.00	10.00
☐ 130	Bill Brubaker	100.00	50.00	10.00
☐ 131	Mort Cooper	125.00	60.00	12.50
☐ 132	Jim Brown	100.00	50.00	10.00

☐ 133	Lynn Myers	100.00	50.00	10.00
☐ 134	Tot Presnell	100.00	50.00	10.00
☐ 135	Mickey Owen	125.00	60.00	12.50
☐ 136	Roy Bell	100.00	50.00	10.00
☐ 137	Pete Appleton	100.00	50.00	10.00
☐ 138	George Case	100.00	50.00	10.00
☐ 139	Vito Tamulis	100.00	50.00	10.00
☐ 140	Ray Hayworth	100.00	50.00	10.00
☐ 141	Pete Coscarart	100.00	50.00	10.00
☐ 142	Ira Hutchinson	100.00	50.00	10.00
☐ 143	Earl Averill	300.00	150.00	30.00
☐ 144	Zeke Bonura	100.00	50.00	10.00
☐ 145	Hugh Mulcahy	100.00	50.00	10.00
☐ 146	Tom Sunkel	100.00	50.00	10.00
☐ 147	George Coffman	100.00	50.00	10.00
☐ 148	Bill Trotter	100.00	50.00	10.00
☐ 149	Max West	100.00	50.00	10.00
☐ 150	James Walkup	100.00	50.00	10.00
☐ 151	Hugh Casey	125.00	60.00	12.50
☐ 152	Roy Weatherly	100.00	50.00	10.00
☐ 153	Paul Trout	125.00	60.00	12.50
☐ 154	Johnny Hudson	100.00	50.00	10.00
☐ 155	Jimmy Outlaw	100.00	50.00	10.00
☐ 156	Ray Berres	100.00	50.00	10.00
☐ 157	Don Padgett	100.00	50.00	10.00
☐ 158	Bud Thomas	100.00	50.00	10.00
☐ 159	Red Evans	100.00	50.00	10.00
☐ 160	Gene Moore	100.00	50.00	10.00
☐ 161	Lonnie Frey	100.00	50.00	10.00
☐ 162	Whitey Moore	125.00	60.00	12.50

1940 Playball

The cards in this 240-card series measure 2 1/2" by 3 1/8". Gum Inc. improved upon its 1939 design by enclosing the 1940 black and white player photo with a frame line and printing the player's name in a panel below the picture (often using a nickname). The set included many Hall of Famers and Old Timers. Cards 181-240 are scarcer than cards 1-180. The backs contain an extensive biography and a dated copyright line. The ACC catalog number is R335.

		EX-MT	VG-E	GOOD
COMPLETE SET (240)		13500.00	6500.00	1700.00
COMMON PLAYER (1-120)		12.50	6.25	1.25
COMMON PLAYER (121-180)		15.00	7.50	1.50
COMMON PLAYER (181-240)		60.00	30.00	6.00

☐ 1	Joe DiMaggio	1800.00	600.00	150.00
☐ 2	Art Jorgens	12.50	6.25	1.25
☐ 3	Babe Dahlgren	15.00	7.50	1.50
☐ 4	Tommy Henrich	25.00	12.50	2.50
☐ 5	Monte Pearson	15.00	7.50	1.50
☐ 6	Lefty Gomez	150.00	75.00	15.00
☐ 7	Bill Dickey	175.00	85.00	18.00
☐ 8	George Selkirk	20.00	10.00	2.00
☐ 9	Charlie Keller	25.00	12.50	2.50
☐ 10	Red Ruffing	75.00	37.50	7.50
☐ 11	Jake Powell	12.50	6.25	1.25
☐ 12	Johnny Schulte	12.50	6.25	1.25
☐ 13	Jack Knott	12.50	6.25	1.25
☐ 14	Rabbit McNair	12.50	6.25	1.25
☐ 15	George Case	12.50	6.25	1.25
☐ 16	Cecil Travis	12.50	6.25	1.25
☐ 17	Buddy Myer	12.50	6.25	1.25
☐ 18	Charlie Gelbert	12.50	6.25	1.25
☐ 19	Ken Chase	12.50	6.25	1.25
☐ 20	Buddy Lewis	12.50	6.25	1.25
☐ 21	Rick Ferrell	60.00	30.00	6.00

22	Sammy West	12.50	6.25	1.25
23	Dutch Leonard	15.00	7.50	1.50
24	Frank Hayes	12.50	6.25	1.25
25	Bob Johnson	15.00	7.50	1.50
26	Wally Moses	15.00	7.50	1.50
27	Ted Williams	1000.00	500.00	100.00
28	Gene Desautels	12.50	6.25	1.25
29	Doc Cramer	15.00	7.50	1.50
30	Moe Berg	25.00	12.50	2.50
31	Jack Wilson	12.50	6.25	1.25
32	Jim Bagby	12.50	6.25	1.25
33	Fritz Ostermueller	12.50	6.25	1.25
34	John Peacock	12.50	6.25	1.25
35	Joe Heving	12.50	6.25	1.25
36	Jim Tabor	12.50	6.25	1.25
37	Emerson Dickman	12.50	6.25	1.25
38	Bobby Doerr	60.00	30.00	6.00
39	Tom Carey	12.50	6.25	1.25
40	Hank Greenberg	150.00	75.00	15.00
41	Charley Gehringer	125.00	60.00	12.50
42	Bud Thomas	12.50	6.25	1.25
43	Pete Fox	12.50	6.25	1.25
44	Dizzy Trout	15.00	7.50	1.50
45	Red Kress	12.50	6.25	1.25
46	Earl Averill	75.00	37.50	7.50
47	Ol' Os Vitt	12.50	6.25	1.25
48	Luke Sewell	15.00	7.50	1.50
49	Stormy Weatherly	12.50	6.25	1.25
50	Hal Trosky	15.00	7.50	1.50
51	Don Heffner	12.50	6.25	1.25
52	Myril Hoag	12.50	6.25	1.25
53	Mac McQuinn	12.50	6.25	1.25
54	Bill Trotter	12.50	6.25	1.25
55	Slick Coffman	12.50	6.25	1.25
56	Eddie Miller	12.50	6.25	1.25
57	Max West	12.50	6.25	1.25
58	Bill Posedel	12.50	6.25	1.25
59	Rabbit Warstler	12.50	6.25	1.25
60	John Cooney	12.50	6.25	1.25
61	Tony Cuccinello	12.50	6.25	1.25
62	Buddy Hassett	12.50	6.25	1.25
63	Pete Coscarart	12.50	6.25	1.25
64	Van Lingle Mungo	15.00	7.50	1.50
65	Fitz Fitzsimmons	12.50	6.25	1.25
66	Babe Phelps	12.50	6.25	1.25
67	Whit Wyatt	15.00	7.50	1.50
68	Dolph Camilli	12.50	6.25	1.25
69	Cookie Lavagetto	15.00	7.50	1.50
70	Hot Potato Hamlin	12.50	6.25	1.25
71	Mel Almada	12.50	6.25	1.25
72	Chuck Dressen	15.00	7.50	1.50
73	Bucky Walters	15.00	7.50	1.50
74	Duke Derringer	20.00	10.00	2.00
75	Buck McCormick	15.00	7.50	1.50
76	Lonny Frey	12.50	6.25	1.25
77	Bill Hershberger	12.50	6.25	1.25
78	Lew Riggs	12.50	6.25	1.25
79	Harry Wildfire Craft	12.50	6.25	1.25
80	Billy Myers	12.50	6.25	1.25
81	Wally Berger	15.00	7.50	1.50
82	Hank Gowdy	12.50	6.25	1.25
83	Cliff Melton	12.50	6.25	1.25
84	Jo Jo Moore	12.50	6.25	1.25
85	Hal Schumacher	15.00	7.50	1.50
86	Harry Gumbert	12.50	6.25	1.25
87	Carl Hubbell	125.00	60.00	12.50
88	Mel Ott	150.00	75.00	15.00
89	Bill Jurges	12.50	6.25	1.25
90	Frank Demaree	12.50	6.25	1.25
91	Suitcase Seeds	12.50	6.25	1.25
92	Whitey Whitehead	12.50	6.25	1.25
93	Harry Danning	12.50	6.25	1.25
94	Gus Suhr	12.50	6.25	1.25
95	Mul Mulcahy	12.50	6.25	1.25
96	Heinie Mueller	12.50	6.25	1.25
97	Morry Arnovich	12.50	6.25	1.25
98	Pinky May	12.50	6.25	1.25
99	Syl Johnson	12.50	6.25	1.25
100	Hersh Martin	12.50	6.25	1.25
101	Del Young	12.50	6.25	1.25
102	Chuck Klein	100.00	50.00	10.00
103	Elbie Fletcher	12.50	6.25	1.25
104	Big Poison Waner	75.00	37.50	7.50
105	Little Poison Waner	75.00	37.50	7.50
106	Pep Young	12.50	6.25	1.25
107	Arky Vaughan	60.00	30.00	6.00
108	Johnny Rizzo	12.50	6.25	1.25
109	Don Padgett	12.50	6.25	1.25
110	Tom Sunkel	12.50	6.25	1.25
111	Mickey Owen	15.00	7.50	1.50
112	Jimmy Brown	12.50	6.25	1.25
113	Mort Cooper	15.00	7.50	1.50
114	Lon Warneke	12.50	6.25	1.25
115	Mike Gonzales	12.50	6.25	1.25
116	Al Schacht	15.00	7.50	1.50
117	Dolly Stark	15.00	7.50	1.50
118	Schoolboy Hoyt	75.00	37.50	7.50
119	Ol Pete Alexander	125.00	60.00	12.50
120	Walter Johnson	200.00	100.00	20.00
121	Atley Donald	15.00	7.50	1.50
122	Sandy Sundra	15.00	7.50	1.50
123	Hildy Hildebrand	15.00	7.50	1.50
124	Colonel Earle Combs	100.00	50.00	10.00
125	Art Fletcher	15.00	7.50	1.50
126	Jake Solters	15.00	7.50	1.50
127	Muddy Ruel	15.00	7.50	1.50
128	Pete Appleton	15.00	7.50	1.50
129	Bucky Harris	60.00	30.00	6.00
130	Deerfoot Milan	15.00	7.50	1.50
131	Zeke Bonura	15.00	7.50	1.50
132	Connie Mack	125.00	60.00	12.50
133	Jimmie Foxx	200.00	100.00	20.00
134	Joe Cronin	125.00	60.00	12.50
135	Line Drive Nelson	15.00	7.50	1.50
136	Cotton Pippen	15.00	7.50	1.50
137	Bing Miller	15.00	7.50	1.50
138	Beau Bell	15.00	7.50	1.50
139	Elden Auker	15.00	7.50	1.50
140	Dick Coffman	15.00	7.50	1.50
141	Casey Stengel	175.00	85.00	18.00
142	Highpockets Kelly	75.00	37.50	7.50
143	Gene Moore	15.00	7.50	1.50
144	Joe Vosmik	15.00	7.50	1.50
145	Vito Tamulis	15.00	7.50	1.50
146	Tot Pressnell	15.00	7.50	1.50
147	Johnny Hudson	15.00	7.50	1.50
148	Hugh Casey	15.00	7.50	1.50
149	Pinky Shoffner	15.00	7.50	1.50
150	Whitey Moore	15.00	7.50	1.50
151	Edwin Joost	15.00	7.50	1.50
152	Jimmy Wilson	15.00	7.50	1.50
153	Bill McKechnie	75.00	37.50	7.50
154	Jumbo Brown	15.00	7.50	1.50
155	Ray Hayworth	15.00	7.50	1.50
156	Daffy Dean	25.00	12.50	2.50
157	Lou Chiozza	15.00	7.50	1.50
158	Travis Jackson	75.00	37.50	7.50
159	Pancho Snyder	15.00	7.50	1.50
160	Hans Lobert	15.00	7.50	1.50
161	Debs Garms	15.00	7.50	1.50
162	Joe Bowman	15.00	7.50	1.50
163	Spud Davis	15.00	7.50	1.50
164	Ray Berres	15.00	7.50	1.50
165	Bob Klinger	15.00	7.50	1.50
166	Bill Brubaker	15.00	7.50	1.50
167	Frankie Frisch	100.00	50.00	10.00
168	Honus Wagner	200.00	100.00	20.00
169	Gabby Street	15.00	7.50	1.50
170	Tris Speaker	175.00	85.00	18.00
171	Harry Heilmann	100.00	50.00	10.00
172	Chief Bender	75.00	37.50	7.50
173	Larry Lajoie	175.00	85.00	18.00
174	Johnny Evers	75.00	37.50	7.50
175	Christy Mathewson	200.00	100.00	20.00
176	Heinie Manush	75.00	37.50	7.50
177	Homerun Baker	100.00	50.00	10.00
178	Max Carey	75.00	37.50	7.50
179	George Sisler	100.00	50.00	10.00
180	Mickey Cochrane	150.00	75.00	15.00
181	Spud Chandler	75.00	37.50	7.50
182	Knick Knickerbocker	60.00	30.00	6.00
183	Marvin Breuer	60.00	30.00	6.00
184	Mule Haas	60.00	30.00	6.00
185	Joe Kuhel	60.00	30.00	6.00
186	Taft Wright	60.00	30.00	6.00
187	Jimmy Dykes	75.00	37.50	7.50
188	Joe Krakauskas	60.00	30.00	6.00
189	Jim Bloodworth	60.00	30.00	6.00
190	Charley Berry	60.00	30.00	6.00
191	John Babich	60.00	30.00	6.00
192	Dick Siebert	60.00	30.00	6.00
193	Chubby Dean	60.00	30.00	6.00
194	Sam Chapman	60.00	30.00	6.00
195	Dee Miles	60.00	30.00	6.00
196	Nonny Nonnenkamp	60.00	30.00	6.00
197	Lou Finney	60.00	30.00	6.00
198	Denny Galehouse	60.00	30.00	6.00
199	Pinky Higgins	60.00	30.00	6.00
200	Soup Campbell	60.00	30.00	6.00
201	Barney McCosky	60.00	30.00	6.00
202	Al Milnar	60.00	30.00	6.00
203	Bad News Hale	60.00	30.00	6.00
204	Harry Eisenstat	60.00	30.00	6.00
205	Rollie Hemsley	60.00	30.00	6.00
206	Chet Laabs	60.00	30.00	6.00
207	Gus Mancuso	60.00	30.00	6.00
208	Lee Gamble	60.00	30.00	6.00
209	Hy Vandenberg	60.00	30.00	6.00
210	Bill Lohrman	60.00	30.00	6.00
211	Pop Joiner	60.00	30.00	6.00

		EX-MT	VG-E	GOOD
□ 212	Babe Young	60.00	30.00	6.00
□ 213	John Rucker	60.00	30.00	6.00
□ 214	Ken O'Dea	60.00	30.00	6.00
□ 215	Johnnie McCarthy	60.00	30.00	6.00
□ 216	Joe Marty	60.00	30.00	6.00
□ 217	Walter Beck	60.00	30.00	6.00
□ 218	Wally Millies	60.00	30.00	6.00
□ 219	Russ Bauers	60.00	30.00	6.00
□ 220	Mace Brown	60.00	30.00	6.00
□ 221	Lee Handley	60.00	30.00	6.00
□ 222	Max Butcher	60.00	30.00	6.00
□ 223	Hugh Jennings	125.00	60.00	12.50
□ 224	Pie Traynor	150.00	75.00	15.00
□ 225	Shoeless Joe Jackson	1200.00	600.00	125.00
□ 226	Harry Hooper	125.00	60.00	12.50
□ 227	Pop Haines	125.00	60.00	12.50
□ 228	Charley Grimm	75.00	37.50	7.50
□ 229	Buck Herzog	60.00	30.00	6.00
□ 230	Red Faber	125.00	60.00	12.50
□ 231	Dolf Luque	60.00	30.00	6.00
□ 232	Goose Goslin	125.00	60.00	12.50
□ 233	Moose Earnshaw	60.00	30.00	6.00
□ 234	Frank(Husk) Chance	125.00	60.00	12.50
□ 235	John J. McGraw	175.00	85.00	18.00
□ 236	Jim Bottomley	125.00	60.00	12.50
□ 237	Wee Willie Keeler	150.00	75.00	15.00
□ 238	Tony Lazzeri	100.00	50.00	10.00
□ 239	George Uhle	60.00	30.00	6.00
□ 240	Bill Atwood	75.00	37.50	7.50

1941 Playball

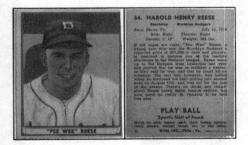

The cards in this 72-card set measure 2 1/2" by 3 1/8". Many of the cards in the 1941 Play Ball series are simply color versions of pictures appearing in the 1940 set. This was the only color baseball card set produced by Gum, Inc., and it carries the ACC designation R336. Card numbers 49-72 are slightly more difficult to obtain as they were not issued until 1942. In 1942, numbers 1-48 were also reissued but without the copyright date. The cards were also printed on paper without a cardboard backing; these are generally encountered in sheets or strips.

		EX-MT	VG-E	GOOD
COMPLETE SET		8500.00	4200.00	1000.00
COMMON PLAYER (1-48)		35.00	17.50	3.50
COMMON PLAYER (49-72)		60.00	30.00	6.00
□ 1	Eddie Miller	100.00	20.00	4.00
□ 2	Max West	35.00	17.50	3.50
□ 3	Bucky Walters	45.00	22.50	4.50
□ 4	Paul Derringer	35.00	17.50	3.50
□ 5	Buck McCormick	45.00	22.50	4.50
□ 6	Carl Hubbell	150.00	75.00	15.00
□ 7	Harry Danning	35.00	17.50	3.50
□ 8	Mel Ott	200.00	100.00	20.00
□ 9	Pinky May	35.00	17.50	3.50
□ 10	Arky Vaughan	80.00	40.00	8.00
□ 11	Debs Garms	35.00	17.50	3.50
□ 12	Jimmy Brown	35.00	17.50	3.50
□ 13	Jimmy Foxx	300.00	150.00	30.00
□ 14	Ted Williams	1000.00	500.00	100.00
□ 15	Joe Cronin	100.00	50.00	10.00
□ 16	Hal Trosky	45.00	22.50	4.50
□ 17	Roy Weatherly	35.00	17.50	3.50
□ 18	Hank Greenberg	175.00	85.00	18.00
□ 19	Charlie Gehringer	150.00	75.00	15.00
□ 20	Red Ruffing	100.00	50.00	10.00
□ 21	Charlie Keller	60.00	30.00	6.00
□ 22	Indian Bob Johnson	45.00	22.50	4.50
□ 23	George McQuinn	35.00	17.50	3.50
□ 24	Dutch Leonard	45.00	22.50	4.50
□ 25	Gene Moore	35.00	17.50	3.50
□ 26	Harry Gumpert	35.00	17.50	3.50
□ 27	Babe Young	35.00	17.50	3.50
□ 28	Joe Marty	35.00	17.50	3.50
□ 29	Jack Wilson	35.00	17.50	3.50
□ 30	Lou Finney	35.00	17.50	3.50
□ 31	Joe Kuhel	35.00	17.50	3.50
□ 32	Taft Wright	35.00	17.50	3.50
□ 33	Al Milnar	35.00	17.50	3.50
□ 34	Rollie Hemsley	35.00	17.50	3.50
□ 35	Pinky Higgins	35.00	17.50	3.50
□ 36	Barney McCosky	35.00	17.50	3.50
□ 37	Bruce Campbell	35.00	17.50	3.50
□ 38	Atley Donald	35.00	17.50	3.50
□ 39	Tom Henrich	60.00	30.00	6.00
□ 40	John Babich	35.00	17.50	3.50
□ 41	Frank "Blimp" Hayes	35.00	17.50	3.50
□ 42	Wally Moses	45.00	22.50	4.50
□ 43	Al Brancato	35.00	17.50	3.50
□ 44	Sam Chapman	35.00	17.50	3.50
□ 45	Eldon Auker	35.00	17.50	3.50
□ 46	Sid Hudson	35.00	17.50	3.50
□ 47	Buddy Lewis	35.00	17.50	3.50
□ 48	Cecil Travis	35.00	17.50	3.50
□ 49	Babe Dahlgren	75.00	37.50	7.50
□ 50	Johnny Cooney	60.00	30.00	6.00
□ 51	Dolph Camilli	75.00	37.50	7.50
□ 52	Kirby Higbe	60.00	30.00	6.00
□ 53	Luke Hamlin	60.00	30.00	6.00
□ 54	Pee Wee Reese	500.00	250.00	50.00
□ 55	Whit Wyatt	75.00	37.50	7.50
□ 56	Johnny VanderMeer	100.00	50.00	10.00
□ 57	Moe Arnovich	60.00	30.00	6.00
□ 58	Frank Demaree	60.00	30.00	6.00
□ 59	Bill Jurges	60.00	30.00	6.00
□ 60	Chuck Klein	150.00	75.00	15.00
□ 61	Vince DiMaggio	200.00	100.00	20.00
□ 62	Elbie Fletcher	60.00	30.00	6.00
□ 63	Dom DiMaggio	200.00	100.00	20.00
□ 64	Bobby Doerr	150.00	75.00	15.00
□ 65	Tommy Bridges	75.00	37.50	7.50
□ 66	Harland Clift	60.00	30.00	6.00
□ 67	Walt Judnich	60.00	30.00	6.00
□ 68	John Knott	60.00	30.00	6.00
□ 69	George Case	60.00	30.00	6.00
□ 70	Bill Dickey	400.00	200.00	40.00
□ 71	Joe DiMaggio	2000.00	1000.00	200.00
□ 72	Lefty Gomez	300.00	150.00	30.00

1985 Polaroid Indians

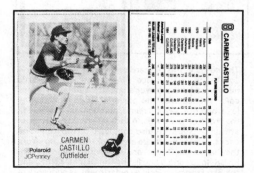

This 32-card set features cards (each measuring 2 13/16" by 4 1/8") of the Cleveland Indians. The cards are unnumbered except for uniform number, as they are listed below. The set was also sponsored by J.C. Penney and was distributed at the stadium to fans in attendance on Baseball Card Day.

		MINT	EXC	G-VG
COMPLETE SET (32)		15.00	7.50	1.50
COMMON PLAYER		.35	.17	.03
□ 2	Brett Butler	.75	.35	.07
□ 4	Tony Bernazard	.45	.22	.04

☐ 8	Carmen Castillo	.35	.17	.03
☐ 10	Pat Tabler	.45	.22	.04
☐ 12	Benny Ayala	.35	.17	.03
☐ 13	Ernie Camacho	.35	.17	.03
☐ 14	Julio Franco	1.25	.60	.12
☐ 16	Jerry Willard	.35	.17	.03
☐ 18	Pat Corrales MG	.35	.17	.03
☐ 20	Otis Nixon	.35	.17	.03
☐ 21	Mike Hargrove	.45	.22	.04
☐ 22	Mike Fischlin	.35	.17	.03
☐ 23	Chris Bando	.35	.17	.03
☐ 24	George Vukovich	.35	.17	.03
☐ 26	Brook Jacoby	.60	.30	.06
☐ 27	Mel Hall	.75	.35	.07
☐ 28	Bert Blyleven	1.00	.50	.10
☐ 29	Andre Thornton	.60	.30	.06
☐ 30	Joe Carter	1.25	.60	.12
☐ 32	Rick Behenna	.35	.17	.03
☐ 33	Roy Smith	.35	.17	.03
☐ 35	Jerry Reed	.35	.17	.03
☐ 36	Jamie Easterly	.35	.17	.03
☐ 38	Dave Von Ohlen	.35	.17	.03
☐ 41	Rich Thompson	.35	.17	.03
☐ 43	Bryan Clark	.35	.17	.03
☐ 44	Neal Heaton	.45	.22	.04
☐ 48	Vern Ruhle	.35	.17	.03
☐ 49	Jeff Barkley	.35	.17	.03
☐ 50	Ramon Romero	.35	.17	.03
☐ 54	Tom Waddell	.35	.17	.03
☐ xx	Coaching Staff	.35	.17	.03
	Bobby Bonds			
	John Goryl			
	Don McMahon			
	Ed Napolean			
	Dennis Sommers			

1979 Police Giants

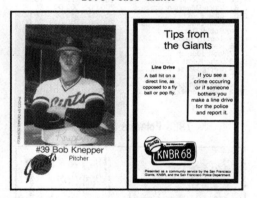

#39 Bob Knepper
Pitcher

Tips from the Giants

Line Drive
A ball hit on a direct line, as opposed to a fly ball or pop fly.

If you see a crime occuring or if someone bothers you make a line drive for the police and report it.

KNBR 68

Presented as a community service by the San Francisco Giants, KNBR, and the San Francisco Police Department

The cards in this 30-card set measure 2 5/8" by 4 1/8". The 1979 Police Giants set features cards numbered by the player's uniform number. This full color set features the player's photo, the Giants' logo, and the player's name, number and position on the front of the cards. A facsimile autograph in an attractive blue ink is also contained on the front. The backs, printed in orange and black, feature Tips from the Giants, the Giants' and sponsoring radio station, KNBR, logos and a line listing the Giants, KNBR, and the San Francisco Police Department as sponsors of the set. The 15 cards which are shown with an asterisk below were available only from the Police. The other 15 cards were given away at the ballpark on June 17, 1979. These cards look very similar to the Giants police set issued in 1980, the following year. Both sets credit Dennis Desprois photographically on each card but this (1979) set seems to have a fuzzier focus on the pictures. The sets can be distinguished on the front since this set's cards have a number sign (#) before the player's uniform number on the front. Also on the card backs

the KNBR logo is usually left justified for the cards in the 1979 set whereas the 1980 set has the KNBR logo centered on the card back.

		NRMT	VG-E	GOOD
	COMPLETE SET (30)	16.00	8.00	1.60
	COMMON PLAYER	.35	.17	.03
☐ 1	Dave Bristol MG	.35	.17	.03
☐ 2	Marc Hill	.35	.17	.03
☐ 3	Mike Sadek *	.45	.22	.04
☐ 5	Tom Haller	.35	.17	.03
☐ 6	Joe Altobelli CO *	.45	.22	.04
☐ 8	Larry Shepard CO *	.45	.22	.04
☐ 9	Heity Cruz	.35	.17	.03
☐ 10	Johnnie LeMaster	.35	.17	.03
☐ 12	Jim Davenport	.45	.22	.04
☐ 14	Vida Blue	.45	.22	.04
☐ 15	Mike Ivie	.35	.17	.03
☐ 16	Roger Metzger	.35	.17	.03
☐ 17	Randy Moffitt	.35	.17	.03
☐ 18	Bill Madlock	.75	.35	.07
☐ 21	Rob Andrews *	.45	.22	.04
☐ 22	Jack Clark *	2.50	1.25	.25
☐ 25	Dave Roberts	.35	.17	.03
☐ 26	John Montefusco	.45	.22	.04
☐ 28	Ed Halicki *	.45	.22	.04
☐ 30	John Tamargo	.35	.17	.03
☐ 31	Larry Herndon	.45	.22	.04
☐ 36	Bill North *	.45	.22	.04
☐ 39	Bob Knepper *	.60	.30	.06
☐ 40	John Curtis *	.45	.22	.04
☐ 41	Darrell Evans *	1.25	.60	.12
☐ 43	Tom Griffin *	.45	.22	.04
☐ 44	Willie McCovey *	3.50	1.75	.35
☐ 45	Terry Whitfield *	.45	.22	.04
☐ 46	Gary Lavelle *	.45	.22	.04
☐ 49	Max Venable *	.45	.22	.04

1980 Police Dodgers

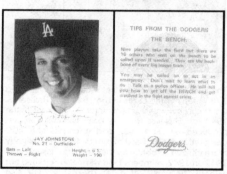

JAY JOHNSTONE
No. 21 — Outfielder
Bats — Left   Height — 6'1"
Throws — Right   Weight — 190

TIPS FROM THE DODGERS
THE BENCH.

Dodgers

The cards in this 30-card set measure 2 13/16" by 4 1/8". The full color 1980 Police Los Angeles Dodgers set features the player's name, uniform number, position, and biographical data on the fronts in addition to the photo. The backs feature Tips from the Dodgers, the LAPD logo, and the Dodgers' logo. The cards are listed below according to uniform number.

		MINT	EXC	G-VG
	COMPLETE SET (30)	11.00	5.50	1.10
	COMMON PLAYER	.25	.12	.02
☐ 5	Johnny Oates	.25	.12	.02
☐ 6	Steve Garvey	1.25	.60	.12
☐ 7	Steve Yeager	.35	.17	.03
☐ 8	Reggie Smith	.45	.22	.04
☐ 9	Gary Thomasson	.25	.12	.02
☐ 10	Ron Cey	.45	.22	.04
☐ 12	Dusty Baker	.35	.17	.03
☐ 13	Joe Ferguson	.25	.12	.02
☐ 15	Davey Lopes	.35	.17	.03
☐ 16	Rick Monday	.35	.17	.03
☐ 18	Bill Russell	.35	.17	.03
☐ 20	Don Sutton	1.00	.50	.10

☐21	Jay Johnstone	.35	.17	.03
☐23	Teddy Martinez	.25	.12	.02
☐27	Joe Beckwith	.25	.12	.02
☐28	Pedro Guerrero	1.25	.60	.12
☐29	Don Stanhouse	.25	.12	.02
☐30	Derrel Thomas	.25	.12	.02
☐31	Doug Rau	.25	.12	.02
☐34	Ken Brett	.25	.12	.02
☐35	Bob Welch	.45	.22	.04
☐37	Robert Castillo	.25	.12	.02
☐38	Dave Goltz	.25	.12	.02
☐41	Jerry Reuss	.35	.17	.03
☐43	Rick Sutcliffe	.75	.35	.07
☐44	Mickey Hatcher	.25	.12	.02
☐46	Burt Hooton	.25	.12	.02
☐49	Charlie Hough	.45	.22	.04
☐xx	Team Card	.25	.12	.02
	(unnumbered)			

1980 Police Giants

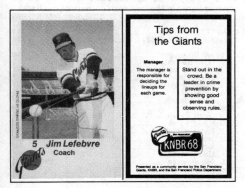

5 Jim Lefebvre
Coach

Tips from the Giants

Manager
The manager is responsible for deciding the lineups for each game.

Stand out in the crowd. Be a leader in crime prevention by showing good sense and observing rules.

KNBR 68

Presented as a community service by the San Francisco Giants, KNBR, and the San Francisco Police Department.

The cards in this 31-card set measure 2 5/8" by 4 1/8". The 1980 Police San Francisco Giants set features cards numbered by the player's uniform number. This full color set features the player's photo, the Giants' logo, and the player's name, number and position on the front of the cards. A facsimile autograph in an attractive blue ink is also contained on the front. The backs, printed in orange and black, feature Tips from the Giants, the Giants' and sponsoring radio station, KNBR, logos and a line listing the Giants, KNBR, and the San Francisco Police Department as sponsors of the set. The sets were given away at the ballpark on May 31, 1980.

		MINT	EXC	G-VG
COMPLETE SET (31)		11.00	5.50	1.10
COMMON PLAYER		.25	.12	.02
☐ 1	Dave Bristol MG	.25	.12	.02
☐ 2	Marc Hill	.25	.12	.02
☐ 3	Mike Sadek	.25	.12	.02
☐ 5	Jim Lefebvre	.45	.22	.04
☐ 6	Rennie Stennett	.25	.12	.02
☐ 7	Milt May	.25	.12	.02
☐ 8	Vern Benson CO	.25	.12	.02
☐ 9	Jim Wohlford	.25	.12	.02
☐10	Johnnie LeMaster	.25	.12	.02
☐12	Jim Davenport	.35	.17	.03
☐14	Vida Blue	.45	.22	.04
☐15	Mike Ivie	.25	.12	.02
☐16	Roger Metzger	.25	.12	.02
☐17	Randy Moffitt	.25	.12	.02
☐19	Al Holland	.25	.12	.02
☐20	Joe Strain	.25	.12	.02
☐22	Jack Clark	2.00	1.00	.20
☐26	John Montefusco	.35	.17	.03
☐28	Ed Halicki	.25	.12	.02
☐31	Larry Herndon	.25	.12	.02
☐32	Ed Whitson	.35	.17	.03
☐36	Bill North	.25	.12	.02
☐38	Greg Minton	.35	.17	.03
☐39	Bob Knepper	.35	.17	.03
☐41	Darrell Evans	1.00	.50	.10

☐42	John Van Ornum	.25	.12	.02
☐43	Tom Griffin	.25	.12	.02
☐44	Willie McCovey	2.50	1.25	.25
☐45	Terry Whitfield	.25	.12	.02
☐46	Gary Lavelle	.35	.17	.03
☐47	Don McMahon CO	.25	.12	.02

1981 Police Braves

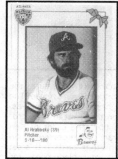

AL HRABOSKY
Born July 21, 1949
The colorful relief specialist is nick-named "The Mad Hungarian" in reference to his ethnic background and flashy mound antics.
Tips from The BRAVES
If your friends are doing something you know is wrong—don't join in just to be part of the group.

Al Hrabosky (39)
Pitcher
5-18---'80

Printed by Williams Printing Company

The cards in this 27-card set measure 2 5/8" by 4 1/8". This first Atlanta Police set features full color cards sponsored by the Braves, the Atlanta Police Department, Coca-Cola and Hostess. The cards are numbered by uniform number, which is contained on the front along with an Atlanta Police Athletic League logo, a black and white Braves logo, and a green bow in the upper right corner of the frameline. The backs feature brief player biographies, logos of Coke and Hostess, and Tips from the Braves. It is reported that 33,000 of these sets were printed. The Terry Harper card is supposed to be more difficult to obtain than other cards in the set.

		MINT	EXC	G-VG
COMPLETE SET (27)		10.00	5.00	1.00
COMMON PLAYER		.30	.15	.03
☐ 1	Jerry Royster	.30	.15	.03
☐ 3	Dale Murphy	3.00	1.50	.30
☐ 4	Biff Pocoroba	.30	.15	.03
☐ 5	Bob Horner	.90	.45	.09
☐ 6	Bobby Cox MG	.30	.15	.03
☐ 9	Luis Gomez	.30	.15	.03
☐10	Chris Chambliss	.40	.20	.04
☐15	Bill Nahorodny	.30	.15	.03
☐16	Rafael Ramirez	.30	.15	.03
☐17	Glenn Hubbard	.30	.15	.03
☐18	Claudell Washington	.50	.25	.05
☐19	Terry Harper	.75	.35	.07
☐20	Bruce Benedict	.30	.15	.03
☐24	John Montefusco	.40	.20	.04
☐25	Rufino Linares	.30	.15	.03
☐26	Gene Garber	.40	.20	.04
☐30	Brian Asselstine	.30	.15	.03
☐34	Larry Bradford	.30	.15	.03
☐35	Phil Niekro	1.75	.85	.17
☐37	Rick Camp	.30	.15	.03
☐39	Al Hrabosky	.50	.25	.05
☐40	Tommy Boggs	.30	.15	.03
☐42	Rick Mahler	.40	.20	.04
☐44	Hank Aaron CO	2.50	1.25	.25
☐45	Ed Miller	.30	.15	.03
☐46	Gaylord Perry	1.50	.75	.15
☐49	Preston Hanna	.30	.15	.03

1981 Police Dodgers

The cards in this 32-card set measure 2 13/16" by 4 1/8". The full color set of 1981 Los Angeles Dodgers features the player's name, number,

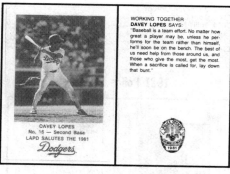

WORKING TOGETHER
DAVEY LOPES SAYS:
"Baseball is a team effort. No matter how great a player may be, unless he performs for the team rather than himself, he'll soon be on the bench. The best of us need help from those around us, and those who give the most, get the most. When a sacrifice is called for, lay down that bunt."

CAVEY LOPES
No. 15 — Second Base
LAPD SALUTES THE 1981
Dodgers

SHANE RAWLEY Pitcher

Seattle Mariners

TIPS from the MARINERS

ERROR

All big leaguers make errors. Don't get discouraged when it happens to you. Bounce back and be ready for the next play.

Don't let another person's error mislead you. Always use good common sense.

COURTESY OF THE FOLLOWING SPONSORS AND YOUR LOCAL LAW ENFORCEMENT AGENCY

Washington State Crime Prevention Association   RIGHTSTART Hand-In-Hand With Youth

Coca-Cola   ERNST home centers

position and a line stating that the LAPD salutes the 1981 Dodgers, in addition to the player's photo. The backs feature the LAPD logo and short narratives, attributable to the player on the front of the card, revealing police associated tips. The cards of Ken Landreaux and Dave Stewart are reported to be more difficult to obtain than other cards in this set due to the fact that they are replacements for Stanhouse (released 4/17/81) and Hatcher (traded for Landreaux 3/30/81). The complete set price below refers to all 32 cards, i.e., including the variations.

	MINT	EXC	G-VG
COMPLETE SET (32)	12.00	6.00	1.20
COMMON PLAYER	.25	.12	.02
☐ 2 Tom Lasorda MG	.50	.25	.05
☐ 3 Rudy Law	.25	.12	.02
☐ 6 Steve Garvey	1.25	.60	.12
☐ 7 Steve Yeager	.35	.17	.03
☐ 8 Reggie Smith	.45	.22	.04
☐ 10 Ron Cey	.45	.22	.04
☐ 12 Dusty Baker	.35	.17	.03
☐ 13 Joe Ferguson	.25	.12	.02
☐ 14 Mike Scioscia	.35	.17	.03
☐ 15 Davey Lopes	.35	.17	.03
☐ 16 Rick Monday	.35	.17	.03
☐ 18 Bill Russell	.35	.17	.03
☐ 21 Jay Johnstone	.35	.17	.03
☐ 26 Don Stanhouse	.50	.25	.05
☐ 27 Joe Beckwith	.25	.12	.02
☐ 28 Pedro Guerrero	1.00	.50	.10
☐ 30 Derrel Thomas	.25	.12	.02
☐ 34 Fernando Valenzuela	2.00	1.00	.20
☐ 35 Bob Welch	.45	.22	.04
☐ 36 Pepe Frias	.25	.12	.02
☐ 37 Robert Castillo	.25	.12	.02
☐ 38 Dave Goltz	.25	.12	.02
☐ 41 Jerry Reuss	.35	.17	.03
☐ 43 Rick Sutcliffe	.75	.35	.07
☐ 44A Mickey Hatcher	.50	.25	.05
☐ 44B Ken Landreaux	1.25	.60	.12
☐ 46 Burt Hooton	.25	.12	.02
☐ 48 Dave Stewart	2.50	1.25	.25
☐ 51 Terry Forster	.35	.17	.03
☐ 57 Steve Howe	.25	.12	.02
☐ xx Team Photo (Checklist) (unnumbered)	.25	.12	.02
☐ xx Coaching Staff (unnumbered)	.25	.12	.02

1981 Police Mariners

The cards in this 16-card set measure 2 5/8" by 4 1/8". The full color Seattle Mariners Police set of this year was sponsored by the Washington State Crime Prevention Association, the Kiwanis Club, Coca-Cola and Ernst Home Centers. The fronts feature the player's name, his position, and the Seattle Mariners name in addition to the player's photo. The backs, in red and blue, feature Tips from the Mariners and

the logos of the four sponsors of the set. The cards are numbered in the lower left corners of the backs.

	MINT	EXC	G-VG
COMPLETE SET (16)	5.00	2.50	.50
COMMON PLAYER (1-16)	.30	.15	.03
☐ 1 Jeff Burroughs	.40	.20	.04
☐ 2 Floyd Bannister	.40	.20	.04
☐ 3 Glenn Abbott	.30	.15	.03
☐ 4 Jim Anderson	.30	.15	.03
☐ 5 Danny Meyer	.30	.15	.03
☐ 6 Julio Cruz	.40	.20	.04
☐ 7 Dave Edler	.30	.15	.03
☐ 8 Kenny Clay	.30	.15	.03
☐ 9 Lenny Randle	.30	.15	.03
☐ 10 Mike Parrott	.30	.15	.03
☐ 11 Tom Paciorek	.40	.20	.04
☐ 12 Jerry Narron	.30	.15	.03
☐ 13 Richie Zisk	.40	.20	.04
☐ 14 Maury Wills MG	.75	.35	.07
☐ 15 Joe Simpson	.30	.15	.03
☐ 16 Shane Rawley	.40	.20	.04

1981 Police Royals

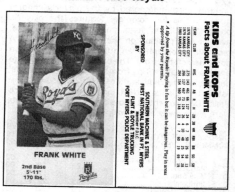

FRANK WHITE
2nd Base
5'-11"
170 lbs.

KIDS and KOPS
Facts about FRANK WHITE

SPONSORED BY

SOUTHERN MACHINE & STEEL
FIRST NATIONAL BANK IN FT. MYERS
FLINT & DOYLE TRUCKING
FORT MYERS POLICE DEPARTMENT

The cards in this 10-card set measure 2 1/2" by 4 1/8". The 1981 Police Kansas City Royals set features full color cards of Royals players. The fronts feature the player's name, position, height and weight, and the Royals' logo in addition to the photo and facsimile autograph of the player. The backs feature player statistics, Tips from the Royals, and identification of the sponsoring organizations.

	MINT	EXC	G-VG
COMPLETE SET (10)	40.00	20.00	4.00
COMMON PLAYER (1-10)	2.00	1.00	.20
☐ 1 Willie Aikens	2.00	1.00	.20
☐ 2 George Brett	20.00	10.00	2.00
☐ 3 Rich Gale	2.00	1.00	.20
☐ 4 Clint Hurdle	2.00	1.00	.20

			MINT	EXC	G-VG
☐	5	Dennis Leonard	2.50	1.25	.25
☐	6	Hal McRae	2.50	1.25	.25
☐	7	Amos Otis	2.50	1.25	.25
☐	8	U.L. Washington	2.00	1.00	.20
☐	9	Frank White	4.00	2.00	.40
☐	10	Willie Wilson	4.00	2.00	.40

1982 Police Braves

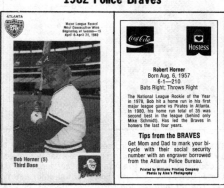

ATLANTA

Major League Record
Most Consecutive Wins
Beginning of Season—15
April 6-April 21, 1982

Coca Cola

Hostess

Robert Horner
Born Aug. 6, 1957
6-1—210
Bats Right; Throws Right

The National League Rookie of the Year
in 1978, Bob hit a home run in his first
major league game vs Pirates in Atlanta.
In 1980, his home run total of 35 was
second best in the league (behind only
Mike Schmidt). Has led the Braves in
homers the last four years.

Tips from the BRAVES
Get Mom and Dad to mark your bi-
cycle with their social security
number with an engraver borrowed
from the Atlanta Police Bureau.

Bob Horner (5)
Third Base

Printed by Williams Printing Company
Photos by Alex's Photography

The cards in this 30-card set measure 2 5/8" by 4 1/8". The Atlanta Police Department followed up on their successful 1981 safety set by publishing a new Braves set for 1982. Featured in excellent color photos are manager Joe Torre, 24 players, and 5 coaches. The cards are numbered, by uniform number, on the front only, while the backs contain a short biography of the individual and a Tips from the Braves section. The logos for the Atlanta PAL and the Braves appear on the front; those of Coca-Cola and Hostess are found on the back. A line commemorating Atlanta's record-shattering, season-beginning win streak is located in the upper right corner on every card obverse. The player list on the reverse of the Torre card is a roster list and not a checklist for the set. There were 8,000 sets reportedly printed. The Bob Watson card is supposedly more difficult to obtain than others in this set.

			MINT	EXC	G-VG
		COMPLETE SET (30)	16.00	8.00	1.60
		COMMON PLAYER	.35	.17	.03
☐	1	Jerry Royster	.35	.17	.03
☐	3	Dale Murphy	5.00	2.50	.50
☐	4	Biff Pocoroba	.35	.17	.03
☐	5	Bob Horner	1.00	.50	.10
☐	6	Randy Johnson	.35	.17	.03
☐	8	Bob Watson	1.50	.75	.15
☐	9	Joe Torre MG	.75	.35	.07
☐	10	Chris Chambliss	.50	.25	.05
☐	15	Claudell Washington	.50	.25	.05
☐	16	Rafael Ramirez	.35	.17	.03
☐	17	Glenn Hubbard	.35	.17	.03
☐	20	Bruce Benedict	.35	.17	.03
☐	22	Brett Butler	1.00	.50	.10
☐	23	Tommy Aaron CO	.35	.17	.03
☐	25	Rufino Linares	.35	.17	.03
☐	26	Gene Garber	.35	.17	.03
☐	27	Larry McWilliams	.35	.17	.03
☐	28	Larry Whisenton	.35	.17	.03
☐	32	Steve Bedrosian	1.00	.50	.10
☐	35	Phil Niekro	2.50	1.25	.25
☐	37	Rick Camp	.35	.17	.03
☐	38	Joe Cowley	.35	.17	.03
☐	39	Al Hrabosky	.50	.25	.05
☐	42	Rick Mahler	.35	.17	.03
☐	43	Bob Walk	.50	.25	.05
☐	45	Bob Gibson CO	1.50	.75	.15
☐	49	Preston Hanna	.35	.17	.03
☐	52	Joe Pignatano CO	.35	.17	.03
☐	53	Dal Maxvill CO	.35	.17	.03
☐	54	Rube Walker CO	.35	.17	.03

1982 Police Brewers

ROBIN YOUNT
No. 19 — Shortstop
Milwaukee Police Department
Salutes The 1982
Milwaukee Brewers

The cards in this 30-card set measure 2 13/16" by 4 1/8". The 1982 series of 30 Milwaukee Brewers baseball cards is noted for its excellent color photographs set upon a simple white background. The set was initially distributed at the stadium on May 5th, but was also handed out by several local police departments, and credit lines for the Wisconsin State Fair Park Police (no shield design on reverse), Milwaukee, Brookfield, and Wauwatosa PD's have already been found. The reverses feature advice concerning safety measures, social situations, and crime prevention (Romero card in both Spanish and English). The team card carries a checklist which lists the Brewer's coaches separately although they all appear on a single card; VP/GM Harry Dalton is not mentioned on this list but is included in the set. The prices below are for the basic set without regard to the Police Department listed on the backs. Cards from the more obscure corners and small towns of Wisconsin (where fewer cards were produced) will be valued higher.

			MINT	EXC	G-VG
		COMPLETE SET (30)	12.00	6.00	1.20
		COMMON PLAYER	.25	.12	.02
☐	4	Paul Molitor	1.50	.75	.15
☐	5	Ned Yost	.25	.12	.02
☐	7	Don Money	.35	.17	.03
☐	9	Larry Hisle	.35	.17	.03
☐	10	Bob McClure	.25	.12	.02
☐	11	Ed Romero	.25	.12	.02
☐	13	Roy Howell	.25	.12	.02
☐	15	Cecil Cooper	.50	.25	.05
☐	17	Jim Gantner	.50	.25	.05
☐	19	Robin Yount	3.00	1.50	.30
☐	20	Gorman Thomas	.50	.25	.05
☐	22	Charlie Moore	.25	.12	.02
☐	23	Ted Simmons	.60	.30	.06
☐	24	Ben Oglivie	.35	.17	.03
☐	26	Kevin Bass	.50	.25	.05
☐	28	Jamie Easterly	.25	.12	.02
☐	29	Mark Brouhard	.25	.12	.02
☐	30	Moose Haas	.35	.17	.03
☐	34	Rollie Fingers	1.00	.50	.10
☐	35	Randy Lerch	.25	.12	.02
☐	41	Jim Slaton	.35	.17	.03
☐	45	Doug Jones	.35	.17	.03
☐	46	Jerry Augustine	.25	.12	.02
☐	47	Dwight Bernard	.25	.12	.02
☐	48	Mike Caldwell	.35	.17	.03
☐	50	Pete Vuckovich	.35	.17	.03
☐	xx	Team Card (unnumbered)	.25	.12	.02

☐ xx	Harry Dalton GM .... (unnumbered)	.25	.12	.02
☐ xx	Buck Rodgers MG .... (unnumbered)	.25	.12	.02
☐ xx	Brewer Coaches .... (unnumbered)	.25	.12	.02

1982 Police Dodgers

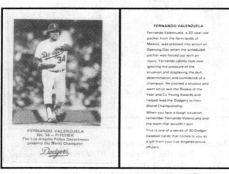

The cards in this 30-card set measure 2 13/16" by 4 1/8". The 1982 Los Angeles Dodgers police set depicts the players and events of the 1981 season. There is a World Series trophy card, three cards commemorating the Division, League, and World Series wins, one manager card, and 25 player cards. The obverses have brilliant color photos set on white, and the player cards are numbered according to the uniform number of the individual. The reverses contain biographical material, information about stadium events, and a safety feature emphasizing "the team that wouldn't quit."

		MINT	EXC	G-VG
	COMPLETE SET (30)	8.00	4.00	.80
	COMMON PLAYER	.15	.07	.01
☐ 2	Tom Lasorda MG	.35	.17	.03
☐ 6	Steve Garvey	1.00	.50	.10
☐ 7	Steve Yeager	.25	.12	.02
☐ 8	Mark Belanger	.25	.12	.02
☐ 10	Ron Cey	.35	.17	.03
☐ 12	Dusty Baker	.25	.12	.02
☐ 14	Mike Scioscia	.25	.12	.02
☐ 16	Rick Monday	.25	.12	.02
☐ 18	Bill Russell	.25	.12	.02
☐ 21	Jay Johnstone	.25	.12	.02
☐ 26	Alejandro Pena	.35	.17	.03
☐ 28	Pedro Guerrero	1.00	.50	.10
☐ 30	Derrel Thomas	.15	.07	.01
☐ 31	Jorge Orta	.15	.07	.01
☐ 34	Fernando Valenzuela	1.00	.50	.10
☐ 35	Bob Welch	.35	.17	.03
☐ 38	Dave Goltz	.15	.07	.01
☐ 40	Ron Roenicke	.15	.07	.01
☐ 41	Jerry Reuss	.25	.12	.02
☐ 44	Ken Landreaux	.15	.07	.01
☐ 46	Burt Hooton	.15	.07	.01
☐ 48	Dave Stewart	.75	.35	.07
☐ 49	Tom Niedenfuer	.25	.12	.02
☐ 51	Terry Forster	.35	.17	.03
☐ 52	Steve Sax	1.00	.50	.10
☐ 57	Steve Howe	.15	.07	.01
☐ xx	World Series Trophy .... (checklist back) (unnumbered)	.15	.07	.01
☐ xx	World Series Commemorative (unnumbered)	.15	.07	.01
☐ xx	NL Champions .... (unnumbered)	.15	.07	.01
☐ xx	Division Champs .... (unnumbered)	.15	.07	.01

1983 Police Braves

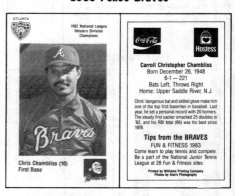

The cards in this 30-card set measure 2 5/8" by 4 1/8". For the third year in a row, the Atlanta Braves, in cooperation with the Atlanta Police Department, Coca-Cola, and Hostess, issued a full color safety set. The set features Joe Torre, five coaches, and 24 of the Atlanta Braves. Numbered only by uniform number, the statement that the Braves were the 1982 National League Western Division Champions is included on the fronts along with the Braves and Police Athletic biographies, a short narrative on the player, Tips from the Braves, and the Coke and Hostess logos.

		MINT	EXC	G-VG
	COMPLETE SET (30)	11.00	5.50	1.10
	COMMON PLAYER	.35	.17	.03
☐ 1	Jerry Royster	.35	.17	.03
☐ 3	Dale Murphy	3.50	1.75	.35
☐ 4	Biff Pocoroba	.35	.17	.03
☐ 5	Bob Horner	.90	.45	.09
☐ 6	Randy Johnson	.35	.17	.03
☐ 8	Bob Watson	.50	.25	.05
☐ 9	Joe Torre MG	.60	.30	.06
☐ 10	Chris Chambliss	.50	.25	.05
☐ 11	Ken Smith	.35	.17	.03
☐ 15	Claudell Washington	.50	.25	.05
☐ 16	Rafael Ramirez	.35	.17	.03
☐ 17	Glenn Hubbard	.35	.17	.03
☐ 19	Terry Harper	.35	.17	.03
☐ 20	Bruce Benedict	.35	.17	.03
☐ 22	Brett Butler	.75	.35	.07
☐ 24	Larry Owen	.35	.17	.03
☐ 26	Gene Garber	.35	.17	.03
☐ 27	Pascual Perez	.75	.35	.07
☐ 29	Craig McMurtry	.35	.17	.03
☐ 32	Steve Bedrosian	.75	.35	.07
☐ 33	Pete Falcone	.35	.17	.03
☐ 35	Phil Niekro	1.50	.75	.15
☐ 36	Sonny Jackson CO	.35	.17	.03
☐ 37	Rick Camp	.35	.17	.03
☐ 45	Bob Gibson CO	1.50	.75	.15
☐ 49	Rick Behenna	.35	.17	.03
☐ 51	Terry Forster	.50	.25	.05
☐ 52	Joe Pignatano CO	.35	.17	.03
☐ 53	Dal Maxvill CO	.35	.17	.03
☐ 54	Rube Walker CO	.35	.17	.03

1983 Police Brewers

The cards in this 30-card set measure 2 13/16" by 4 1/8". The 1983 Police Milwaukee Brewers set contains full color cards issued by the Milwaukee Police Department in conjunction with the Brewers. The cards are numbered on the fronts by the player uniform number and contain the line, "The Milwaukee Police Department Presents the 1983

34 ROLLIE FINGERS — P
The Milwaukee Police Department
Presents The 1982
Milwaukee Brewers

DAVE STEWART 46
Dodgers
1983

Milwaukee Braves." The backs contain a brief narrative attributable to the player on the front, the Milwaukee Police logo, and a Milwaukee Brewers logo stating that they were the 1982 American League Champions. In all, 28 variations of these Police sets have been found to date. Prices below are for the basic set without regard to the Police Department listed on the backs of the cards; cards from the more obscure corners and small towns of Wisconsin (whose cards were produced in lesser quantities) will be valued higher.

		MINT	EXC	G-VG
COMPLETE SET (30)		9.00	4.50	.90
COMMON PLAYER		.20	.10	.02
☐ 4	Paul Molitor	1.00	.50	.10
☐ 5	Ned Yost	.20	.10	.02
☐ 7	Don Money	.30	.15	.03
☐ 8	Rob Picciolo	.20	.10	.02
☐ 10	Bob McClure	.20	.10	.02
☐ 11	Ed Romero	.20	.10	.02
☐ 12	Larry Haney CO	.20	.10	.02
☐ 13	Roy Howell	.20	.10	.02
☐ 15	Cecil Cooper	.50	.25	.05
☐ 16	Marshall Edwards	.20	.10	.02
☐ 17	Jim Gantner	.40	.20	.04
☐ 18	Ron Hansen CO	.20	.10	.02
☐ 19	Robin Yount	2.00	1.00	.20
☐ 20	Gorman Thomas	.40	.20	.04
☐ 21	Don Sutton	1.00	.50	.10
☐ 22	Charlie Moore	.20	.10	.02
☐ 23	Ted Simmons	.60	.30	.06
☐ 24	Ben Oglivie	.30	.15	.03
☐ 26	Bob Skube	.20	.10	.02
☐ 27	Pete Ladd	.20	.10	.02
☐ 28	Jamie Easterly	.20	.10	.02
☐ 30	Moose Haas	.30	.15	.03
☐ 32	Harvey Kuenn MG	.50	.25	.05
☐ 34	Rollie Fingers	1.00	.50	.10
☐ 40	Bob L. Gibson	.20	.10	.02
☐ 41	Jim Slaton	.20	.10	.02
☐ 42	Tom Tellmann	.20	.10	.02
☐ 45	Pat Dobson CO	.30	.15	.03
☐ 46	Jerry Augustine	.20	.10	.02
☐ 48	Mike Caldwell	.30	.15	.03
☐ 50	Pete Vuckovich	.30	.15	.03
☐ xx	Dave Garcia CO	.20	.10	.02
☐ xx	Team Photo	.20	.10	.02
	(Checklist back)			
	(unnumbered)			

1983 Police Dodgers

The cards in this 30-card set measure 2 13/16" by 4 1/8". The full color Police Los Angeles Dodgers set of 1983 features the player's name and uniform number on the front along with the Dodger's logo, the year, and the player's photo. The backs feature a small insert portrait picture of the player, player biographies, and career statistics. The logo of the Los Angeles Police Department, the sponsor of the set, is found on the backs of the cards.

		MINT	EXC	G-VG
COMPLETE SET (30)		7.00	3.50	.70
COMMON PLAYER		.15	.07	.01
☐ 2	Tom Lasorda MG	.35	.17	.03
☐ 3	Steve Sax	.75	.35	.07
☐ 5	Mike Marshall	.60	.30	.06
☐ 7	Steve Yeager	.25	.12	.02
☐ 12	Dusty Baker	.25	.12	.02
☐ 14	Mike Scioscia	.25	.12	.02
☐ 16	Rick Monday	.25	.12	.02
☐ 17	Greg Brock	.25	.12	.02
☐ 18	Bill Russell	.25	.12	.02
☐ 20	Candy Maldonado	.25	.12	.02
☐ 21	Ricky Wright	.15	.07	.01
☐ 22	Mark Bradley	.15	.07	.01
☐ 23	Dave Sax	.15	.07	.01
☐ 26	Alejandro Pena	.25	.12	.02
☐ 27	Joe Beckwith	.15	.07	.01
☐ 28	Pedro Guerrero	.75	.35	.07
☐ 30	Derrel Thomas	.15	.07	.01
☐ 34	Fernando Valenzuela	.75	.35	.07
☐ 35	Bob Welch	.35	.17	.03
☐ 38	Pat Zachry	.15	.07	.01
☐ 40	Ron Roenicke	.15	.07	.01
☐ 41	Jerry Reuss	.25	.12	.02
☐ 43	Jose Morales	.15	.07	.01
☐ 44	Ken Landreaux	.15	.07	.01
☐ 46	Burt Hooton	.15	.07	.01
☐ 47	Larry White	.15	.07	.01
☐ 48	Dave Stewart	.60	.30	.06
☐ 49	Tom Niedenfuer	.25	.12	.02
☐ 57	Steve Howe	.15	.07	.01
☐ xx	Coaching Staff	.15	.07	.01
	(unnumbered)			

1983 Police Royals

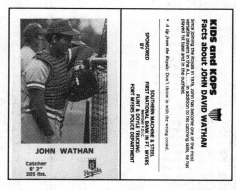

JOHN WATHAN
Catcher
6' 2"
205 lbs.

The cards in this 10-card set measure 2 1/2" by 4 1/8". The 1983 Police Kansas City Royals set features full color cards of Royals players. The fronts feature the player's name, height and weight, and the Royals' logo in addition to the player's photo and a facsimile autograph. The backs feature Kids and Cops Facts about the players, Tips from the Royals, and identification of the sponsors of the set. The cards are unnumbered.

	MINT	EXC	G-VG
COMPLETE SET (10)	35.00	17.50	3.50
COMMON PLAYER (1-10)	1.75	.85	.17
☐ 1 Willie Aikens	1.75	.85	.17
☐ 2 George Brett	16.00	8.00	1.60
☐ 3 Dennis Leonard	2.50	1.25	.25
☐ 4 Hal McRae	2.50	1.25	.25
☐ 5 Amos Otis	2.50	1.25	.25
☐ 6 Dan Quisenberry	3.50	1.75	.35
☐ 7 U.L. Washington	1.75	.85	.17
☐ 8 John Wathan	2.50	1.25	.25
☐ 9 Frank White	4.00	2.00	.40
☐ 10 Willie Wilson	4.00	2.00	.40

1984 Police Braves

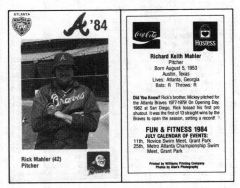

The cards in this 30-card set measure 2 5/8" by 4 1/8". For the fourth straight year, the Atlanta Police Department issued a full color set of Atlanta Braves. The cards were given out two per week by Atlanta police officers. In addition to the police department, the set was sponsored by Coke and Hostess. The backs of the cards of Perez and Ramirez are in Spanish. The Joe Torre card contains the checklist.

	MINT	EXC	G-VG
COMPLETE SET (30)	10.00	5.00	1.00
COMMON PLAYER	.30	.15	.03
☐ 1 Jerry Royster	.30	.15	.03
☐ 3 Dale Murphy	3.00	1.50	.30
☐ 5 Bob Horner	.75	.35	.07
☐ 6 Randy Johnson	.30	.15	.03
☐ 8 Bob Watson	.40	.20	.04
☐ 9 Joe Torre MG	.50	.25	.05
(checklist back)			
☐ 10 Chris Chambliss	.40	.20	.04
☐ 11 Mike Jorgensen	.30	.15	.03
☐ 15 Claudell Washington	.40	.20	.04
☐ 16 Rafael Ramirez	.30	.15	.03
☐ 17 Glenn Hubbard	.30	.15	.03
☐ 19 Terry Harper	.30	.15	.03
☐ 20 Bruce Benedict	.30	.15	.03
☐ 25 Alex Trevino	.30	.15	.03
☐ 26 Gene Garber	.30	.15	.03
☐ 27 Pascual Perez	.60	.30	.06
☐ 28 Gerald Perry	.75	.35	.07
☐ 29 Craig McMurtry	.30	.15	.03
☐ 31 Donnie Moore	.30	.15	.03
☐ 32 Steve Bedrosian	.75	.35	.07
☐ 33 Pete Falcone	.30	.15	.03
☐ 37 Rick Camp	.30	.15	.03
☐ 39 Len Barker	.30	.15	.03
☐ 42 Rick Mahler	.30	.15	.03
☐ 45 Bob Gibson CO	1.00	.50	.10
☐ 51 Terry Forster	.40	.20	.04
☐ 52 Joe Pignatano CO	.30	.15	.03
☐ 53 Dal Maxvill CO	.30	.15	.03
☐ 54 Rube Walker CO	.30	.15	.03
☐ 55 Luke Appling CO	.50	.25	.05

1984 Police Brewers

The cards in this 30-card set measure 2 13/16" by 4 1/8". Again this year, the police departments in and around Milwaukee issued sets of the Milwaukee Brewers. Although each set contained the same players and numbers, the individual police departments placed their own name on the fronts of cards to show that they were the particular jurisdiction issuing the set. The backs contain the Brewers logo, a safety tip, and in some cases, a badge of the jurisdiction. To date, 59 variations of this set have been found. Prices below are for the basic set without regard to the Police Department issuing the cards; cards from the more obscure corners and small towns of Wisconsin will be valued higher. Cards are numbered by uniform number.

	MINT	EXC	G-VG
COMPLETE SET (30)	7.00	3.50	.70
COMMON PLAYER	.15	.07	.01
☐ 2 Randy Ready	.25	.12	.02
☐ 4 Paul Molitor	.75	.35	.07
☐ 8 Jim Sundberg	.25	.12	.02
☐ 9 Rene Lachemann MG	.15	.07	.01
☐ 10 Bob McClure	.15	.07	.01
☐ 11 Ed Romero	.15	.07	.01
☐ 13 Roy Howell	.15	.07	.01
☐ 14 Dion James	.25	.12	.02
☐ 15 Cecil Cooper	.45	.22	.04
☐ 17 Jim Gantner	.35	.17	.03
☐ 19 Robin Yount	1.75	.85	.17
☐ 20 Don Sutton	.75	.35	.07
☐ 21 Bill Schroeder	.15	.07	.01
☐ 22 Charlie Moore	.15	.07	.01
☐ 23 Ted Simmons	.45	.22	.04
☐ 24 Ben Oglivie	.25	.12	.02
☐ 25 Bob Clark	.15	.07	.01
☐ 27 Pete Ladd	.15	.07	.01
☐ 28 Rick Manning	.15	.07	.01
☐ 29 Mark Brouhard	.15	.07	.01
☐ 30 Moose Haas	.15	.07	.01
☐ 34 Rollie Fingers	.75	.35	.07
☐ 42 Tom Tellmann	.15	.07	.01
☐ 43 Chuck Porter	.15	.07	.01
☐ 46 Jerry Augustine	.15	.07	.01
☐ 47 Jaime Cocanower	.15	.07	.01
☐ 48 Mike Caldwell	.25	.12	.02
☐ 50 Pete Vuckovich	.25	.12	.02
☐ xx Coaches Card	.15	.07	.01
(unnumbered)			
☐ xx Team Photo	.15	.07	.01
(Checklist back)			
(unnumbered)			

1984 Police Dodgers

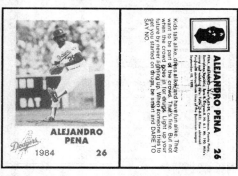

The cards in this 30-card set measure 2 13/16" by 4 1/8". For the fifth straight year, the Los Angeles Police Department sponsored a set of Dodger baseball cards. The set is numbered by player uniform number, which is featured on both the fronts and backs of the cards. The Dodgers' logo appears on the front, and the LAPD logo is superimposed on the backs of the cards. The backs are printed in Dodger blue ink and contain a small photo of the player on the front. Player biographical data and "Dare to Say No" antidrug information are featured on the back.

		MINT	EXC	G-VG
COMPLETE SET (30)		7.00	3.50	.70
COMMON PLAYER		.15	.07	.01
☐ 2	Tom Lasorda MG	.35	.17	.03
☐ 3	Steve Sax	.75	.35	.07
☐ 5	Mike Marshall	.60	.30	.06
☐ 7	Steve Yeager	.25	.12	.02
☐ 9	Greg Brock	.25	.12	.02
☐ 10	Dave Anderson	.15	.07	.01
☐ 14	Mike Scioscia	.25	.12	.02
☐ 16	Rick Monday	.25	.12	.02
☐ 17	Rafael Landestoy	.15	.07	.01
☐ 18	Bill Russell	.25	.12	.02
☐ 20	Candy Maldonado	.25	.12	.02
☐ 21	Bob Bailor	.15	.07	.01
☐ 25	German Rivera	.15	.07	.01
☐ 26	Alejandro Pena	.25	.12	.02
☐ 27	Carlos Diaz	.15	.07	.01
☐ 28	Pedro Guerrero	.75	.35	.07
☐ 31	Jack Fimple	.15	.07	.01
☐ 34	Fernando Valenzuela	.75	.35	.07
☐ 35	Bob Welch	.35	.17	.03
☐ 38	Pat Zachry	.15	.07	.01
☐ 40	Rick Honeycutt	.15	.07	.01
☐ 41	Jerry Reuss	.25	.12	.02
☐ 43	Jose Morales	.15	.07	.01
☐ 44	Ken Landreaux	.15	.07	.01
☐ 45	Terry Whitfield	.15	.07	.01
☐ 46	Burt Hooton	.15	.07	.01
☐ 49	Tom Niedenfuer	.25	.12	.02
☐ 55	Orel Hershiser	2.00	1.00	.20
☐ 56	Richard Rodas	.15	.07	.01
☐ xx	Coaching Staff (unnumbered)	.15	.07	.01

1985 Police Braves

The cards in this 30-card set measure 2 5/8" by 4 1/8". For the fifth straight year, the Atlanta Police Department issued a full color set of Atlanta Braves. The set was also sponsored by Coca Cola and Hostess. In the upper right of the obverse is a logo commemorating the 20th anniversary of the Braves in Atlanta. Cards are numbered by uniform number.

Cards feature a safety tip on the back. Each card except for Manager Haas has an interesting "Did You Know" fact about the player.

		MINT	EXC	G-VG
COMPLETE SET (30)		10.00	5.00	1.00
COMMON PLAYER		.30	.15	.03
☐ 2	Albert Hall	.40	.20	.04
☐ 3	Dale Murphy	3.00	1.50	.30
☐ 5	Rick Cerone	.30	.15	.03
☐ 7	Bobby Wine CO	.30	.15	.03
☐ 10	Chris Chambliss	.40	.20	.04
☐ 11	Bob Horner	.75	.35	.07
☐ 12	Paul Runge	.30	.15	.03
☐ 15	Claudell Washington	.40	.20	.04
☐ 16	Rafael Ramirez	.30	.15	.03
☐ 17	Glenn Hubbard	.30	.15	.03
☐ 18	Paul Zuvella	.30	.15	.03
☐ 19	Terry Harper	.30	.15	.03
☐ 20	Bruce Benedict	.30	.15	.03
☐ 22	Eddie Haas MG	.30	.15	.03
☐ 24	Ken Oberkfell	.30	.15	.03
☐ 26	Gene Garber	.30	.15	.03
☐ 27	Pascual Perez	.60	.30	.06
☐ 28	Gerald Perry	.60	.30	.06
☐ 29	Craig McMurtry	.30	.15	.03
☐ 32	Steve Bedrosian	.60	.30	.06
☐ 33	Johnny Sain CO	.50	.25	.05
☐ 34	Zane Smith	.50	.25	.05
☐ 36	Brad Komminsk	.40	.20	.04
☐ 37	Rick Camp	.30	.15	.03
☐ 39	Len Barker	.30	.15	.03
☐ 40	Bruce Sutter	.50	.25	.05
☐ 42	Rick Mahler	.30	.15	.03
☐ 51	Terry Forster	.40	.20	.04
☐ 52	Leo Mazzone CO	.30	.15	.03
☐ 53	Bobby Dews CO	.30	.15	.03

1985 Police Brewers

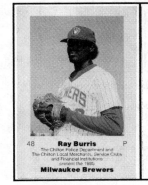

The cards in this 30-card set measure 2 3/4" by 4 1/8". Again this year, the police departments in and around Milwaukee issued sets of the Milwaukee

Brewers. The backs contain the Brewers logo, a safety tip, and in some cases, a badge of the jurisdiction. Prices below are for the basic set without regard to the Police Department issuing the cards; cards from the more obscure corners and small towns of Wisconsin (smaller production) will be valued higher. Cards are numbered by uniform number.

	MINT	EXC	G-VG
COMPLETE SET (30)	7.00	3.50	.70
COMMON PLAYER	.15	.07	.01

		MINT	EXC	G-VG
☐ 2	Randy Ready	.25	.12	.02
☐ 4	Paul Molitor	.75	.35	.07
☐ 5	Doug Loman	.25	.12	.02
☐ 7	Paul Householder	.15	.07	.01
☐ 10	Bob McClure	.15	.07	.01
☐ 11	Ed Romero	.15	.07	.01
☐ 14	Dion James	.25	.12	.02
☐ 15	Cecil Cooper	.45	.22	.04
☐ 17	Jim Gantner	.35	.17	.03
☐ 18	Danny Darwin	.15	.07	.01
☐ 19	Robin Yount	1.75	.85	.17
☐ 21	Bill Schroeder	.15	.07	.01
☐ 22	Charlie Moore	.15	.07	.01
☐ 23	Ted Simmons	.45	.22	.04
☐ 24	Ben Oglivie	.25	.12	.02
☐ 26	Brian Giles	.15	.07	.01
☐ 27	Pete Ladd	.15	.07	.01
☐ 28	Rick Manning	.15	.07	.01
☐ 29	Mark Brouhard	.15	.07	.01
☐ 30	Moose Haas	.15	.07	.01
☐ 31	George Bamberger MG	.15	.07	.01
☐ 34	Rollie Fingers	.75	.35	.07
☐ 40	Bob L. Gibson	.15	.07	.01
☐ 41	Ray Searage	.15	.07	.01
☐ 47	Jaime Cocanower	.15	.07	.01
☐ 48	Ray Burris	.15	.07	.01
☐ 49	Ted Higuera	.75	.35	.07
☐ 50	Pete Vuckovich	.25	.12	.02
☐ xx	Team Roster (unnumbered)	.15	.07	.01
☐ xx	Coaches (unnumbered)	.15	.07	.01
☐ xx	Newspaper Carrier (unnumbered)	.15	.07	.01

1986 Police Astros

This 26-card safety set was also sponsored by Kool-Aid. The backs contain a biographical paragraph above a "Tip from the Dugout". The front features a full- color photo of the player, his name, and uniform number. The cards are numbered on the back and measure 2 5/8" by 4 1/8". The backs are printed in orange and blue on white card stock. Sets were distributed at the Astrodome on June 14th as well as given away throughout the summer by the Houston Police.

	MINT	EXC	G-VG
COMPLETE SET (26)	7.00	3.50	.70
COMMON PLAYER (1-26)	.15	.07	.01

		MINT	EXC	G-VG
☐ 1	Jim Pankovits	.15	.07	.01
☐ 2	Nolan Ryan	2.00	1.00	.20
☐ 3	Mike Scott	.75	.35	.07
☐ 4	Kevin Bass	.40	.20	.04
☐ 5	Bill Doran	.40	.20	.04
☐ 6	Hal Lanier MG	.25	.12	.02
☐ 7	Denny Walling	.15	.07	.01
☐ 8	Alan Ashby	.15	.07	.01
☐ 9	Phil Garner	.15	.07	.01
☐ 10	Charlie Kerfeld	.15	.07	.01
☐ 11	Dave Smith	.35	.17	.03
☐ 12	Jose Cruz	.45	.22	.04
☐ 13	Craig Reynolds	.15	.07	.01
☐ 14	Mark Bailey	.15	.07	.01
☐ 15	Bob Knepper	.25	.12	.02
☐ 16	Julio Solano	.15	.07	.01
☐ 17	Dickie Thon	.25	.12	.02
☐ 18	Mike Madden	.15	.07	.01
☐ 19	Jeff Calhoun	.15	.07	.01
☐ 20	Tony Walker	.15	.07	.01
☐ 21	Terry Puhl	.25	.12	.02
☐ 22	Glenn Davis	1.00	.50	.10
☐ 23	Billy Hatcher	.25	.12	.02
☐ 24	Jim Deshaies	.25	.12	.02
☐ 25	Frank DiPino	.15	.07	.01
☐ 26	Coaching Staff	.15	.07	.01

1986 Police Braves

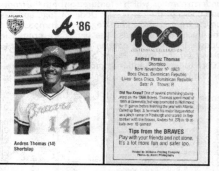

Andres Thomas (14)
Shortstop

This 30-card safety set was also sponsored by Coca-Cola. The backs contain the usual biographical info and safety tip. The front features a full-color photo of the player, his name, and uniform number. The cards measure 2 5/8" by 4 1/8". Cards were freely distributed throughout the summer by the Police Departments in the Atlanta area. Cards are numbered below by uniform number.

	MINT	EXC	G-VG
COMPLETE SET (30)	10.00	5.00	1.00
COMMON PLAYER	.25	.12	.02

		MINT	EXC	G-VG
☐ 2	Russ Nixon COA	.25	.12	.02
☐ 3	Dale Murphy	2.50	1.25	.25
☐ 4	Bob Skinner COA	.35	.17	.03
☐ 5	Billy Sample	.25	.12	.02
☐ 7	Chuck Tanner MG	.35	.17	.03
☐ 8	Willie Stargell COA	1.00	.50	.10
☐ 9	Ozzie Virgil	.25	.12	.02
☐ 10	Chris Chambliss	.35	.17	.03
☐ 11	Bob Horner	.65	.30	.06
☐ 14	Andres Thomas	.45	.22	.04
☐ 15	Claudell Washington	.35	.17	.03
☐ 16	Rafael Ramirez	.25	.12	.02
☐ 17	Glenn Hubbard	.25	.12	.02
☐ 18	Omar Moreno	.25	.12	.02
☐ 19	Terry Harper	.25	.12	.02
☐ 20	Bruce Benedict	.25	.12	.02
☐ 23	Ted Simmons	.45	.22	.04
☐ 24	Ken Oberkfell	.25	.12	.02
☐ 26	Gene Garber	.25	.12	.02
☐ 29	Craig McMurtry	.25	.12	.02
☐ 30	Paul Assenmacher	.25	.12	.02
☐ 33	Johnny Sain COA	.45	.22	.04
☐ 34	Zane Smith	.45	.22	.04
☐ 38	Joe Johnson	.25	.12	.02
☐ 40	Bruce Sutter	.45	.22	.04
☐ 42	Rick Mahler	.35	.17	.03

☐	46	David Palmer	.35	.17	.03
☐	48	Duane Ward	.35	.17	.03
☐	49	Jeff Dedmon	.25	.12	.02
☐	52	Al Monchak COA	.25	.12	.02

1986 Police Brewers

16   **Mike Felder**   OF
The Glendale Police Department
presents the 1986
Milwaukee Brewers

This 32-card safety set was also sponsored by WTMJ Radio and Kinney Shoes. The backs contain the usual biographical info and safety tip. The front features a full-color photo of the player, his name, position, and uniform number. The cards measure 2 5/8" by 4 1/8". Cards were freely distributed throughout the summer by the Police Departments in the Milwaukee area. Cards are numbered below by uniform number.

			MINT	EXC	G-VG
		COMPLETE SET (32)	6.00	3.00	.60
		COMMON PLAYER	.10	.05	.01
☐	1	Ernest Riles	.20	.10	.02
☐	2	Randy Ready	.15	.07	.01
☐	3	Juan Castillo	.15	.07	.01
☐	4	Paul Molitor	.65	.30	.06
☐	7	Paul Householder	.10	.05	.01
☐	8	Andy Etchebarren CO	.10	.05	.01
☐	10	Bob McClure	.10	.05	.01
☐	11	Rick Cerone	.10	.05	.01
☐	12	Larry Haney CO	.10	.05	.01
☐	13	Billy Jo Robidoux	.15	.07	.01
☐	15	Cecil Cooper	.35	.17	.03
☐	16	Mike Felder	.20	.10	.02
☐	17	Jim Gantner	.25	.12	.02
☐	18	Danny Darwin	.10	.05	.01
☐	19	Robin Yount	1.50	.75	.15
☐	20	Juan Nieves	.20	.10	.02
☐	21	Bill Schroeder	.10	.05	.01
☐	22	Charlie Moore	.10	.05	.01
☐	24	Ben Oglivie	.20	.10	.02
☐	25	Mark Clear	.10	.05	.01
☐	28	Rick Manning	.10	.05	.01
☐	31	George Bamberger MG	.15	.07	.01
☐	33	Frank Howard CO	.15	.07	.01
☐	35	Tony Muser CO	.10	.05	.01
☐	37	Dan Plesac	.35	.17	.03
☐	38	Herm Starrette CO	.10	.05	.01
☐	39	Tim Leary	.25	.12	.02
☐	42	Tom Trebelhorn CO	.20	.10	.02
☐	45	Rob Deer	.35	.17	.03
☐	46	Bill Wegman	.15	.07	.01
☐	47	Jaime Cocanower	.10	.05	.01
☐	49	Teddy Higuera	.60	.30	.06

1986 Police Dodgers

This 30-card set features full-color cards each measuring 2 13/16" by 4 1/8". The cards are unnumbered except for uniform numbers. The backs give a safety tip as well as a short capsule biography. The sets were given away at Dodger Stadium on May 18th.

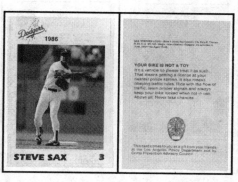

STEVE SAX   3

			MINT	EXC	G-VG
		COMPLETE SET (30)	6.00	3.00	.60
		COMMON PLAYER	.10	.05	.01
☐	2	Tom Lasorda MG	.25	.12	.02
☐	3	Steve Sax	.60	.30	.06
☐	5	Mike Marshall	.50	.25	.05
☐	9	Greg Brock	.20	.10	.02
☐	10	Dave Anderson	.10	.05	.01
☐	12	Bill Madlock	.20	.10	.02
☐	14	Mike Scioscia	.20	.10	.02
☐	17	Len Matuszek	.10	.05	.01
☐	18	Bill Russell	.20	.10	.02
☐	22	Franklin Stubbs	.20	.10	.02
☐	23	Enos Cabell	.10	.05	.01
☐	25	Mariano Duncan	.10	.05	.01
☐	26	Alejandro Pena	.20	.10	.02
☐	27	Carlos Diaz	.10	.05	.01
☐	28	Pedro Guerrero	.75	.35	.07
☐	29	Alex Trevino	.10	.05	.01
☐	31	Ed VandeBerg	.10	.05	.01
☐	34	Fernando Valenzuela	.75	.35	.07
☐	35	Bob Welch	.25	.12	.02
☐	40	Rick Honeycutt	.10	.05	.01
☐	41	Jerry Reuss	.15	.07	.01
☐	43	Ken Howell	.10	.05	.01
☐	44	Ken Landreaux	.10	.05	.01
☐	45	Terry Whitfield	.10	.05	.01
☐	48	Dennis Powell	.10	.05	.01
☐	49	Tom Niedenfuer	.15	.07	.01
☐	51	Reggie Williams	.10	.05	.01
☐	55	Orel Hershiser	1.25	.60	.12
☐	xx	Coaching Staff	.10	.05	.01
		(unnumbered)		
		Don McMahon		
		Mark Cresse		
		Ben Hines		
		Ron Perranoski		
		Monty Basgall		
		Manny Mota		
		Joe Amalfitano		
☐	xx	Team Photo	.10	.05	.01
		(unnumbered)		
		(checklist back)		

1987 Police Astros

This 26-card safety set was sponsored by the Astros, Deer Park Hospital, and Sportsmedia Presentations. The backs contain a biographical paragraph above a "Tip from the Dugout". The front features a full-color photo of the player, his name, position, and uniform number. The cards are numbered on the back and measure 2 5/8" by 4 1/8". The first twelve cards were distributed at the Astrodome on July 14th and the rest were given away later in the summer by the Deer Park Hospital.

			MINT	EXC	G-VG
		COMPLETE SET (26)	6.00	3.00	.60
		COMMON PLAYER (1-26)	.15	.07	.01
☐	1	Larry Andersen	.15	.07	.01
☐	2	Mark Bailey	.15	.07	.01

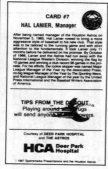

☐	3	Jose Cruz	.35	.17	.03
☐	4	Danny Darwin	.15	.07	.01
☐	5	Bill Doran	.45	.22	.04
☐	6	Billy Hatcher	.25	.12	.02
☐	7	Hal Lanier MG	.25	.12	.02
☐	8	Davey Lopes	.25	.12	.02
☐	9	Dave Meads	.15	.07	.01
☐	10	Craig Reynolds	.15	.07	.01
☐	11	Mike Scott	.75	.35	.07
☐	12	Denny Walling	.15	.07	.01
☐	13	Aurelio Lopez	.15	.07	.01
☐	14	Dickie Thon	.25	.12	.02
☐	15	Terry Puhl	.25	.12	.02
☐	16	Nolan Ryan	2.00	1.00	.20
☐	17	Dave Smith	.35	.17	.03
☐	18	Julio Solano	.15	.07	.01
☐	19	Jim Deshaies	.25	.12	.02
☐	20	Bob Knepper	.15	.07	.01
☐	21	Alan Ashby	.15	.07	.01
☐	22	Kevin Bass	.35	.17	.03
☐	23	Glenn Davis	.75	.35	.07
☐	24	Phil Garner	.25	.12	.02
☐	25	Jim Pankovits	.15	.07	.01
☐	26	Coaching Staff	.15	.07	.01

1987 Police Brewers

Juan Nieves says:

"Baseball players are constantly tempted by drug dealers. They love to hang around celebrities and try to get us to join them at parties. We learn to just to say no. We tell them to get lost or we'll call the police.

Call it what you want, pot, grass, speed, angel dust, or coke. It's dangerous stuff that can hurt you or even kill. If you're approached, just say no, and then call your local police or tell your parents."

KINNEY THE GREAT AMERICAN SHOE STORE

WTMJ Radio 62

Listen to **WTMJ Radio** in Milwaukee or your local Brewers network station to learn who will be the 2 players featured on next weeks baseball cards.

20 Juan Nieves P
The Milwaukee Police Department Kinney Shoes and WTMJ Radio present the 1987 Milwaukee Brewers

This 30-card safety set was also sponsored by WTMJ Radio and Kinney Shoes. The backs contain the usual biographical info and safety tip. The front features a full-color photo of the player, his name, position, and uniform number. The cards measure 2 5/8" by 4 1/8". Cards were freely distributed throughout the summer by the Police Departments in the Milwaukee area and throughout other parts of Wisconsin. Cards are numbered below by uniform number.

			MINT	EXC	G-VG
COMPLETE SET (30)			6.00	3.00	.60
COMMON PLAYER			.15	.07	.01
☐	1	Ernest Riles	.25	.12	.02
☐	2	Edgar Diaz	.25	.12	.02

☐	3	Juan Castillo	.15	.07	.01
☐	4	Paul Molitor	.75	.35	.07
☐	5	B.J. Surhoff	.60	.30	.06
☐	7	Dale Sveum	.25	.12	.02
☐	9	Greg Brock	.25	.12	.02
☐	13	Billy Jo Robidoux	.15	.07	.01
☐	14	Jim Paciorek	.15	.07	.01
☐	15	Cecil Cooper	.35	.17	.03
☐	16	Mike Felder	.15	.07	.01
☐	17	Jim Gantner	.35	.17	.03
☐	19	Robin Yount	1.50	.75	.15
☐	20	Juan Nieves	.25	.12	.02
☐	21	Bill Schroeder	.15	.07	.01
☐	25	Mark Clear	.15	.07	.01
☐	26	Glenn Braggs	.35	.17	.03
☐	28	Rick Manning	.15	.07	.01
☐	29	Chris Bosio	.35	.17	.03
☐	32	Chuck Crim	.15	.07	.01
☐	34	Mark Ciardi	.15	.07	.01
☐	37	Dan Plesac	.35	.17	.03
☐	38	John Henry Johnson	.15	.07	.01
☐	40	Mike Birkbeck	.25	.12	.02
☐	42	Tom Trebelhorn MG	.25	.12	.02
☐	45	Rob Deer	.35	.17	.03
☐	46	Bill Wegman	.15	.07	.01
☐	49	Teddy Higuera	.45	.22	.04
☐	xx	Coaching Staff	.15	.07	.01
☐	xx	Brewers Team	.15	.07	.01
		(Checklist on back)			

1987 Police Dodgers

This 30-card set features full-color cards each measuring 2 13/16" by 4 1/8". The cards are unnumbered except for uniform numbers. The backs give a safety tip as well as a short capsule biography. Cards were given away at Dodger Stadium on April 24th and later during the summer by LAPD officers at a rate of two cards per week.

			MINT	EXC	G-VG
COMPLETE SET (30)			5.00	2.50	.50
COMMON PLAYER (1-30)			.15	.07	.01
☐	1	Tom Lasorda MG 2	.35	.17	.03
☐	2	Steve Sax 3	.60	.30	.06
☐	3	Mike Marshall 5	.50	.25	.05
☐	4	Dave Anderson 10	.15	.07	.01
☐	5	Bill Madlock 12	.25	.12	.02
☐	6	Mike Scioscia 14	.25	.12	.02
☐	7	Gilberto Reyes 15	.15	.07	.01
☐	8	Len Matuszek 17	.15	.07	.01
☐	9	Reggie Williams 21	.15	.07	.01
☐	10	Franklin Stubbs 22	.15	.07	.01
☐	11	Tim Leary 23	.35	.17	.03
☐	12	Mariano Duncan 25	.15	.07	.01
☐	13	Alejandro Pena 26	.25	.12	.02
☐	14	Pedro Guerrero 28	.75	.35	.07
☐	15	Alex Trevino 29	.15	.07	.01
☐	16	Jeff Hamilton 33	.25	.12	.02
☐	17	Fernando Valenzuela 34	.75	.35	.07
☐	18	Bob Welch 35	.35	.17	.03
☐	19	Matt Young 36	.15	.07	.01
☐	20	Rick Honeycutt 40	.15	.07	.01
☐	21	Jerry Reuss 41	.25	.12	.02
☐	22	Ken Howell 43	.15	.07	.01
☐	23	Ken Landreaux 44	.15	.07	.01
☐	24	Ralph Bryant 46	.15	.07	.01

			MINT	EXC	G-VG
☐ 25	Jose Gonzalez 47		.25	.12	.02
☐ 26	Tom Niedenfuer 49		.15	.07	.01
☐ 27	Brian Holton 51		.15	.07	.01
☐ 28	Orel Hershiser 55		1.00	.50	.10
☐ 29	Coaching Staff		.15	.07	.01
☐ 30	Dodgers Stadium (25th Anniversary)		.15	.07	.01

1988 Police Astros

This 26-card safety set was sponsored by the Astros, Deer Park Hospital, and Sportsmedia Presentations. The backs contain a biographical paragraph above "Tips from the Dugout". The front features a full-color photo of the player, his name, position, and uniform number. The cards are numbered on the back and measure 2 5/8" by 4 1/8". The sets were supposedly distributed to the first 15,000 youngsters attending the New York Mets game against the Astros at the Astrodome on July 9th.

			MINT	EXC	G-VG
COMPLETE SET (26)			7.00	3.50	.70
COMMON PLAYER (1-26)			.25	.12	.02
☐ 1	Juan Agosto		.25	.12	.02
☐ 2	Larry Andersen		.25	.12	.02
☐ 3	Joaquin Andujar		.35	.17	.03
☐ 4	Alan Ashby		.25	.12	.02
☐ 5	Mark Bailey		.25	.12	.02
☐ 6	Kevin Bass		.45	.22	.04
☐ 7	Danny Darwin		.25	.12	.02
☐ 8	Glenn Davis		.75	.35	.07
☐ 9	Jim Deshaies		.35	.17	.03
☐ 10	Bill Doran		.45	.22	.04
☐ 11	Billy Hatcher		.35	.17	.03
☐ 12	Jeff Heathcock		.25	.12	.02
☐ 13	Steve Henderson		.25	.12	.02
☐ 14	Chuck Jackson		.25	.12	.02
☐ 15	Bob Knepper		.25	.12	.02
☐ 16	Jim Pankovits		.25	.12	.02
☐ 17	Terry Puhl		.35	.17	.03
☐ 18	Rafael Ramirez		.25	.12	.02
☐ 19	Craig Reynolds		.25	.12	.02
☐ 20	Nolan Ryan		2.00	1.00	.20
☐ 21	Mike Scott		.75	.35	.07
☐ 22	Dave Smith		.35	.17	.03
☐ 23	Denny Walling		.25	.12	.02
☐ 24	Gerald Young		.35	.17	.03
☐ 25	Hal Lanier MG		.25	.12	.02
☐ 26	Coaching Staff		.25	.12	.02

1988 Police Brewers

This 30-card safety set was also sponsored by WTMJ Radio and Stadia Athletic Shoes. The backs contain the usual biographical info and safety tip. The front features a full-color photo of the player, his name, position, and uniform number. The cards measure approximately 2 7/8" by 4 1/8". Cards were freely

distributed throughout the summer by the Police Departments in the Milwaukee area and throughout other parts of Wisconsin. Cards are numbered below by uniform number.

			MINT	EXC	G-VG
COMPLETE SET (30)			6.00	3.00	.60
COMMON PLAYER			.15	.07	.01
☐ 1	Ernest Riles		.15	.07	.01
☐ 3	Juan Castillo		.15	.07	.01
☐ 4	Paul Molitor		.60	.30	.06
☐ 5	B.J. Surhoff		.35	.17	.03
☐ 7	Dale Sveum		.25	.12	.02
☐ 9	Greg Brock		.25	.12	.02
☐ 11	Charlie O'Brien		.15	.07	.01
☐ 14	Jim Adduci		.25	.12	.02
☐ 16	Mike Felder		.15	.07	.01
☐ 17	Jim Gantner		.35	.17	.03
☐ 19	Robin Yount		1.50	.75	.15
☐ 20	Juan Nieves		.25	.12	.02
☐ 21	Bill Schroeder		.15	.07	.01
☐ 23	Joey Meyer		.25	.12	.02
☐ 25	Mark Clear		.15	.07	.01
☐ 26	Glenn Braggs		.35	.17	.03
☐ 28	Odell Jones		.15	.07	.01
☐ 29	Chris Bosio		.25	.12	.02
☐ 30	Steve Kiefer		.15	.07	.01
☐ 32	Chuck Crim		.15	.07	.01
☐ 33	Jay Aldrich		.15	.07	.01
☐ 37	Dan Plesac		.35	.17	.03
☐ 40	Mike Birkbeck		.25	.12	.02
☐ 42	Tom Trebelhorn MG		.15	.07	.01
☐ 43	Dave Stapleton		.15	.07	.01
☐ 45	Rob Deer		.35	.17	.03
☐ 46	Bill Wegman		.15	.07	.01
☐ 49	Ted Higuera		.45	.22	.04
☐ x	Team Photo HOR (unnumbered)		.15	.07	.01
☐ x	Manager and Coaches HOR (unnumbered)		.15	.07	.01

1988 Police Dodgers

This 30-card set features full-color cards each measuring approximately 2 13/16" by 4 1/8". The cards are unnumbered except for uniform numbers. The backs give a safety tip as well as a short capsule biography. Cards were given during the summer by LAPD officers. The set is very similar to the 1987 set, the 1988 set is distinguished by the fact that it does not have the 25th anniversary (of Dodger Stadium) logo on the card front.

			MINT	EXC	G-VG
COMPLETE SET (30)			6.00	3.00	.60
COMMON PLAYER			.15	.07	.01
☐ 2	Tom Lasorda MG		.35	.17	.03
☐ 3	Steve Sax		.60	.30	.06
☐ 5	Mike Marshall		.40	.20	.04
☐ 7	Alfredo Griffin		.25	.12	.02
☐ 9	Mickey Hatcher		.15	.07	.01

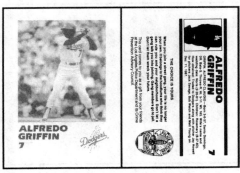

ALFREDO
GRIFFIN
7

			MINT	EXC	G-VG
☐	10	Dave Anderson	.15	.07	.01
☐	12	Danny Heep	.15	.07	.01
☐	14	Mike Scioscia	.25	.12	.02
☐	20	Don Sutton	.60	.30	.06
☐	21	Tito Landrum and	.15	.07	.01
		17 Len Matuszak			
☐	22	Franklin Stubbs	.15	.07	.01
☐	23	Kirk Gibson	.75	.35	.07
☐	25	Mariano Duncan	.15	.07	.01
☐	26	Alejandro Pena	.25	.12	.02
☐	27	Mike Sharperson and	.15	.07	.01
		52 Tim Crews			
☐	28	Pedro Guerrero	.60	.30	.06
☐	29	Alex Trevino	.15	.07	.01
☐	31	John Shelby	.15	.07	.01
☐	33	Jeff Hamilton	.25	.12	.02
☐	34	Fernando Valenzuela	.60	.30	.06
☐	37	Mike Davis	.15	.07	.01
☐	41	Brad Havens	.15	.07	.01
☐	43	Ken Howell	.15	.07	.01
☐	47	Jesse Orosco	.15	.07	.01
☐	49	Tim Belcher and	.35	.17	.03
		57 Shawn Hillegas			
☐	50	Jay Howell	.25	.12	.02
☐	51	Brian Holton	.15	.07	.01
☐	54	Tim Leary	.35	.17	.03
☐	55	Orel Hershiser	1.00	.50	.10
☐	x	Tom Lasorda MG	.35	.17	.03
		and Coaches			
		(unnumbered)			

1988 Police Tigers

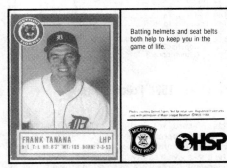

Batting helmets and seat belts both help to keep you in the game of life.

FRANK TANANA   LHP

This set was sponsored by the Michigan State Police and the Detroit Tigers organization. There are 14 blue-bordered cards in the set; each card measures approximately 2 1/2" by 3 1/2". The cards are completely unnumbered as there is not even any reference to uniform numbers on the cards; the cards are listed below in alphabetical order.

		MINT	EXC	G-VG
COMPLETE SET (14)		30.00	15.00	3.00
COMMON PLAYER (1-14)		1.00	.50	.10
☐ 1	Doyle Alexander	2.00	1.00	.20
☐ 2	Sparky Anderson MG	3.00	1.50	.30

			MINT	EXC	G-VG
☐	3	Dave Bergman	1.50	.75	.15
☐	4	Tom Brookens	1.50	.75	.15
☐	5	Darrell Evans	2.00	1.00	.20
☐	6	Larry Herndon	1.50	.75	.15
☐	7	Chet Lemon	2.00	1.00	.20
☐	8	Jack Morris	3.50	1.75	.35
☐	9	Matt Nokes	3.00	1.50	.30
☐	10	Jeff Robinson	3.00	1.50	.30
☐	11	Frank Tanana	2.00	1.00	.20
☐	12	Walt Terrell	1.50	.75	.15
☐	13	Alan Trammell	4.50	2.25	.45
☐	14	Lou Whitaker	4.00	2.00	.40

1989 Police Brewers

Paul Molitor   1F

The Waukesha Police Department and
Fan Appreciation, 200 W. Main St., Waukesha
present the 1989
Milwaukee Brewers

The 1989 Police Milwaukee Brewers set contains 30 cards measuring 2 3/4 by 4 1/4 inches. The fronts have color photos with white borders; the backs feature safety tips. The unnumbered cards were given away by various local Wisconsin police departments. The cards are numbered below by uniform number.

			MINT	EXC	G-VG
COMPLETE SET (30)			6.00	3.00	.60
COMMON PLAYER			.10	.05	.01
☐	1	Gary Sheffield	.75	.35	.07
☐	4	Paul Molitor	.60	.30	.06
☐	5	B.J. Surhoff	.30	.15	.03
☐	6	Bill Spiers	.50	.25	.05
☐	7	Dale Sveum	.15	.07	.01
☐	9	Greg Brock	.15	.07	.01
☐	14	Gus Polidor	.10	.05	.01
☐	16	Mike Felder	.10	.05	.01
☐	17	Jim Gantner	.20	.10	.02
☐	19	Robin Yount	1.25	.60	.12
☐	20	Juan Nieves	.15	.07	.01
☐	22	Charlie O'Brien	.10	.05	.01
☐	23	Joey Meyer	.15	.07	.01
☐	25	Dave Engle	.10	.05	.01
☐	26	Glenn Braggs	.25	.12	.02
☐	27	Paul Mirabella	.10	.05	.01
☐	29	Chris Bosio	.20	.10	.02
☐	30	Terry Francona	.10	.05	.01
☐	32	Chuck Crim	.10	.05	.01
☐	37	Dan Plesac	.30	.15	.03
☐	38	Don August	.15	.07	.01
☐	40	Mike Birkbeck	.10	.05	.01
☐	41	Mark Knudson	.10	.05	.01
☐	42	Tom Trebelhorn MG	.10	.05	.01
☐	45	Rob Deer	.20	.10	.02
☐	46	Bill Wegman	.10	.05	.01
☐	48	Bryan Clutterbuck	.10	.05	.01
☐	49	Teddy Higuera	.30	.15	.03
☐	xx	Team Card	.10	.05	.01
		(checklist on back)			
☐	xx	Coaches Card	.10	.05	.01

1989 Police Dodgers

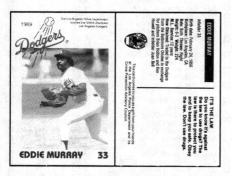

The 1989 Police Los Angeles Dodgers set contains 30 cards measuring 2 5/8 by 4 1/4 inches. The fronts have color photos with white borders; the backs feature safety tips and biographical information. The unnumbered cards were given away by various Los Angeles-area police departments.

		MINT	EXC	G-VG
COMPLETE SET (30)		5.00	2.50	.50
COMMON PLAYER		.10	.05	.01
☐ 1	Dodger Coaches	.10	.05	.01
☐ 2	Tom Lasorda MG	.25	.12	.02
☐ 3	Jeff Hamilton	.20	.10	.02
☐ 4	Mike Marshall	.40	.20	.04
☐ 5	Alfredo Griffin	.20	.10	.02
☐ 6	Mickey Hatcher	.10	.05	.01
☐ 7	Dave Anderson	.10	.05	.01
☐ 8	Willie Randolph	.20	.10	.02
☐ 9	Mike Scioscia	.20	.10	.02
☐ 10	Rick Dempsey	.10	.05	.01
☐ 11	Mike Davis	.10	.05	.01
☐ 12	Tracy Woodson	.20	.10	.02
☐ 13	Franklin Stubbs	.10	.05	.01
☐ 14	Kirk Gibson	.50	.25	.05
☐ 15	Mariano Duncan	.10	.05	.01
☐ 16	Alejandro Pena	.15	.07	.01
☐ 17	Mike Sharperson	.10	.05	.01
☐ 18	Ricky Horton	.10	.05	.01
☐ 19	John Tudor	.20	.10	.02
☐ 20	John Shelby	.10	.05	.01
☐ 21	Eddie Murray	.45	.22	.04
☐ 22	Fernando Valenzuela	.50	.25	.05
☐ 23	Mike Morgan	.20	.10	.02
☐ 24	Ramon Martinez	.40	.20	.04
☐ 25	Tim Belcher	.25	.12	.02
☐ 26	Jay Howell	.20	.10	.02
☐ 27	Tim Crews	.10	.05	.01
☐ 28	Tim Leary	.20	.10	.02
☐ 29	Orel Hershiser	.75	.35	.07
☐ 30	Ray Searage	.10	.05	.01

1989 Police Tigers

The 1989 Police Detroit Tigers set contains 14 standard-size (2 1/2 by 3 1/2 inch) cards. The fronts have color photos with blue and orange borders; the backs feature safety tips. These unnumbered cards were given away by the Michigan state police. The cards are numbered below according to uniform number.

		MINT	EXC	G-VG
COMPLETE SET (14)		7.50	3.75	.75
COMMON PLAYER		.30	.15	.03
☐ 1	Lou Whitaker	.75	.35	.07
☐ 3	Alan Trammell	1.00	.50	.10
☐ 9	Fred Lynn	.50	.25	.05

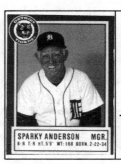

Protective headgear is worn by every player who steps up to bat. Don't be caught without your protective gear while riding in an automobile. **WEAR YOUR SAFETY BELT.**

☐ 14	Dave Bergman	.30	.15	.03
☐ 15	Pat Sheridan	.30	.15	.03
☐ 19	Doyle Alexander	.40	.20	.04
☐ 21	Guillermo Hernandez	.40	.20	.04
☐ 26	Frank Tanana	.40	.20	.04
☐ 33	Matt Nokes	.40	.20	.04
☐ 34	Chet Lemon	.40	.20	.04
☐ 39	Mike Henneman	.40	.20	.04
☐ 44	Jeff Robinson	.40	.20	.04
☐ 47	Jack Morris	.50	.25	.05
☐ xx	Sparky Anderson MG	.50	.25	.05

1961 Post Cereal

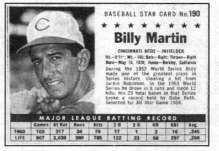

The cards in this 200-card set measure 2 1/2" by 3 1/2". The 1961 Post set was this company's first major set. The cards were available on thick cardbox stock, singly or in various panel sizes from cereal boxes (BOX), or in team sheets, printed on thinner cardboard stock, directly from the Post Cereal Company (COM). Many variations exist and are noted in the checklist below. There are many cards which were produced in lesser quantities; the prices below reflect the relative scarcity of the cards. Cards 10, 23, 70, 73, 94, 113, 135, 163, and 183 are examples of cards printed in limited quantities and hence commanding premium prices. The cards are numbered essentially in team groups, i.e., New York Yankees (1-18), Chicago White Sox (19-34), Detroit (35-46), Boston (47-56), Cleveland (57-67), Baltimore (68-80), Kansas City (81-90), Minnesota (91-100), Milwaukee (101-114), Philadelphia (115-124), Pittsburgh (125-140), San Francisco (141-155), Los Angeles Dodgers (156-170), St. Louis (171-180), Cincinnati (181-190), and Chicago Cubs (191-200). The catalog number is F278-33. The complete set prices refer to both ways of collecting the set, all variations (357) or one of each player (200).

	NRMT	VG-E	GOOD
COMPLETE SET (357)	2000.00	900.00	200.00
COMPLETE SET (200)	1300.00	600.00	150.00
COMMON PLAYER (1-200)	1.50	.75	.15

☐ 1A Yogi Berra COM	20.00	10.00	2.00
☐ 1B Yogi Berra BOX	20.00	10.00	2.00
☐ 2A Elston Howard COM	2.50	1.25	.25
☐ 2B Elston Howard BOX	3.50	1.75	.35
☐ 3A Bill Skowron COM	2.50	1.25	.25
☐ 3B Bill Skowron BOX	2.00	1.00	.20
☐ 4A Mickey Mantle COM	100.00	50.00	10.00
☐ 4B Mickey Mantle BOX	100.00	50.00	10.00
☐ 5 Bob Turley COM only	12.00	6.00	1.20
☐ 6A Whitey Ford COM	7.50	3.75	.75
☐ 6B Whitey Ford BOX	7.50	3.75	.75
☐ 7A Roger Maris COM	20.00	10.00	2.00
☐ 7B Roger Maris BOX	20.00	10.00	2.00
☐ 8A B.Richardson COM	2.50	1.25	.25
☐ 8B B.Richardson BOX	2.00	1.00	.20
☐ 9A Tony Kubek COM	2.50	1.25	.25
☐ 9B Tony Kubek BOX	2.00	1.00	.20
☐ 10 G.McDougald BOX only	30.00	15.00	3.00
☐ 11 Cletis Boyer BOX only	1.50	.75	.15
☐ 12A Hector Lopes COM	1.50	.75	.15
☐ 12B Hector Lopes BOX	1.50	.75	.15
☐ 13 Bob Cerv BOX only	1.50	.75	.15
☐ 14 Ryne Duren BOX only	1.50	.75	.15
☐ 15 Bobby Shantz BOX only	1.50	.75	.15
☐ 16 Art Ditmar BOX only	1.50	.75	.15
☐ 17 Jim Coates BOX only	1.50	.75	.15
☐ 18 J.Blanchard BOX only	1.50	.75	.15
☐ 19A Luis Aparicio COM	5.00	2.50	.50
☐ 19B Luis Aparicio BOX	5.00	2.50	.50
☐ 20A Nelson Fox COM	4.00	2.00	.40
☐ 20B Nelson Fox BOX	4.00	2.00	.40
☐ 21A Bill Pierce COM	3.00	1.50	.30
☐ 21B Bill Pierce BOX	5.00	2.50	.50
☐ 22A Early Wynn COM	7.50	3.75	.75
☐ 22B Early Wynn BOX	10.00	5.00	1.00
☐ 23 Bob Shaw BOX only	75.00	37.50	7.50
☐ 24A Al Smith COM	1.50	.75	.15
☐ 24B Al Smith BOX	2.50	1.25	.25
☐ 25A Minnie Minoso COM	2.50	1.25	.25
☐ 25B Minnie Minoso BOX	2.50	1.25	.25
☐ 26A Roy Sievers COM	1.50	.75	.15
☐ 26B Roy Sievers BOX	1.50	.75	.15
☐ 27A Jim Landis COM	2.50	1.25	.25
☐ 27B Jim Landis BOX	2.50	1.25	.25
☐ 28A Sherm Lollar COM	2.50	1.25	.25
☐ 28B Sherm Lollar BOX	2.50	1.25	.25
☐ 29 Gerry Staley BOX only	1.50	.75	.15
☐ 30A Gene Freese COM (Reds)	5.00	2.50	.50
☐ 30B Gene Freese BOX (White Sox)	1.50	.75	.15
☐ 31 Ted Kluszewski BOX only	2.00	1.00	.20
☐ 32 Turk Lown BOX only	1.50	.75	.15
☐ 33A Jim Rivera COM	1.50	.75	.15
☐ 33B Jim Rivera BOX	1.50	.75	.15
☐ 34 F.Baumann BOX only	1.50	.75	.15
☐ 35A Al Kaline COM	15.00	7.50	1.50
☐ 35B Al Kaline BOX	15.00	7.50	1.50
☐ 36A Rocky Colavito COM	4.00	2.00	.40
☐ 36B Rocky Colavito BOX	4.00	2.00	.40
☐ 37A C.Maxwell COM	1.50	.75	.15
☐ 37B C.Maxwell BOX	2.50	1.25	.25
☐ 38A Frank Lary COM	1.50	.75	.15
☐ 38B Frank Lary BOX	1.50	.75	.15
☐ 39A Jim Bunning COM	3.00	1.50	.30
☐ 39B Jim Bunning BOX	3.00	1.50	.30
☐ 40A Norm Cash COM	2.00	1.00	.20
☐ 40B Norm Cash BOX	1.50	.75	.15
☐ 41B Frank Bolling COM (Braves)	4.00	2.00	.40
☐ 41A Frank Bolling BOX (Tigers)	6.00	3.00	.60
☐ 42A Don Mossi COM	1.50	.75	.15
☐ 42B Don Mossi BOX	1.50	.75	.15
☐ 43A Lou Berberet COM	1.50	.75	.15
☐ 43B Lou Berberet BOX	1.50	.75	.15
☐ 44 Dave Sisler BOX only	1.50	.75	.15
☐ 45 Ed Yost BOX only	1.50	.75	.15
☐ 46 Pete Burnside BOX only	1.50	.75	.15
☐ 47A Pete Runnels COM	2.00	1.00	.20
☐ 47B Pete Runnels BOX	3.00	1.50	.30
☐ 48A Frank Malzone COM	1.50	.75	.15
☐ 48B Frank Malzone BOX	1.50	.75	.15
☐ 49A Vic Wertz COM	4.00	2.00	.40
☐ 49B Vic Wertz BOX	4.00	2.00	.40
☐ 50A Tom Brewer COM	1.50	.75	.15
☐ 50B Tom Brewer BOX	2.00	1.00	.20
☐ 51A Willie Tasby COM (Sold to Wash.)	5.00	2.50	.50
☐ 51B Willie Tasby BOX	1.50	.75	.15

(no sale mention)			
☐ 52A Russ Nixon COM	2.00	1.00	.20
☐ 52B Russ Nixon BOX	2.00	1.00	.20
☐ 53A Don Buddin COM	1.50	.75	.15
☐ 53B Don Buddin BOX	1.50	.75	.15
☐ 54A B.Monbouquette COM	1.50	.75	.15
☐ 54B B.Monbouquette BOX	1.50	.75	.15
☐ 55A Frank Sullivan COM (Phillies)	6.00	3.00	.60
☐ 55B Frank Sullivan BOX (Red Sox)	1.50	.75	.15
☐ 56A H.Sullivan COM	1.50	.75	.15
☐ 56B H.Sullivan BOX	1.50	.75	.15
☐ 57A Harvey Kuenn COM (Giants)	5.00	2.50	.50
☐ 57B Harvey Kuenn BOX (Indians)	3.00	1.50	.30
☐ 58A Gary Bell COM	3.00	1.50	.30
☐ 58B Gary Bell BOX	4.00	2.00	.40
☐ 59A Jim Perry COM	1.50	.75	.15
☐ 59B Jim Perry BOX	1.50	.75	.15
☐ 60A Jim Grant COM	2.00	1.00	.20
☐ 60B Jim Grant BOX	3.00	1.50	.30
☐ 61A Johnny Temple COM	1.50	.75	.15
☐ 61B Johnny Temple BOX	1.50	.75	.15
☐ 62A Paul Foytack COM	1.50	.75	.15
☐ 62B Paul Foytack BOX	1.50	.75	.15
☐ 63A Vic Power COM	1.50	.75	.15
☐ 63B Vic Power BOX	1.50	.75	.15
☐ 64A Tito Francona COM	1.50	.75	.15
☐ 64B Tito Francona BOX	1.50	.75	.15
☐ 65A Ken Aspromonte COM (Sold to L.A.)	6.00	3.00	.60
☐ 65B Ken Aspromonte BOX (no sale mention)	6.00	3.00	.60
☐ 66 Bob Wilson BOX only	1.50	.75	.15
☐ 67A John Romano COM	1.50	.75	.15
☐ 67B John Romano BOX	1.50	.75	.15
☐ 68A Jim Gentile COM	2.00	1.00	.20
☐ 68B Jim Gentile BOX	2.00	1.00	.20
☐ 69A Gus Triandos COM	2.00	1.00	.20
☐ 69B Gus Triandos BOX	3.00	1.50	.30
☐ 70 G.Woodling BOX only	30.00	15.00	3.00
☐ 71A Milt Pappas COM	3.00	1.50	.30
☐ 71B Milt Pappas BOX	3.00	1.50	.30
☐ 72A Ron Hansen COM	2.00	1.00	.20
☐ 72B Ron Hansen BOX	2.00	1.00	.20
☐ 73 Chuck Estrada COM only	75.00	37.50	7.50
☐ 74A Steve Barber COM	2.00	1.00	.20
☐ 74B Steve Barber BOX	2.00	1.00	.20
☐ 75A B.Robinson COM	15.00	7.50	1.50
☐ 75B B.Robinson BOX	15.00	7.50	1.50
☐ 76A Jackie Brandt COM	1.50	.75	.15
☐ 76B Jackie Brandt BOX	1.50	.75	.15
☐ 77A Marv Breeding COM	1.50	.75	.15
☐ 77B Marv Breeding BOX	1.50	.75	.15
☐ 78 Hal Brown BOX only	1.50	.75	.15
☐ 79 Billy Klaus BOX only	1.50	.75	.15
☐ 80A Hoyt Wilhelm COM	7.50	3.75	.75
☐ 80B Hoyt Wilhelm BOX	5.00	2.50	.50
☐ 81A Jerry Lumpe COM	4.00	2.00	.40
☐ 81B Jerry Lumpe BOX	4.00	2.00	.40
☐ 82A Norm Siebern COM	1.50	.75	.15
☐ 82B Norm Siebern BOX	1.50	.75	.15
☐ 83A Bud Daley COM	3.00	1.50	.30
☐ 83B Bud Daley BOX	2.00	1.00	.20
☐ 84A Bill Tuttle COM	1.50	.75	.15
☐ 84B Bill Tuttle BOX	2.00	1.00	.20
☐ 85A M.Throneberry COM	2.00	1.00	.20
☐ 85B M.Throneberry BOX	2.00	1.00	.20
☐ 86A Dick Williams COM	1.50	.75	.15
☐ 86B Dick Williams BOX	1.50	.75	.15
☐ 87A Ray Herbert COM	1.50	.75	.15
☐ 87B Ray Herbert BOX	1.50	.75	.15
☐ 88A Whitey Herzog COM	1.50	.75	.15
☐ 88B Whitey Herzog BOX	1.50	.75	.15
☐ 89A Ken Hamlin COM (Sold to L.A.)	10.00	5.00	1.00
☐ 89B Ken Hamlin BOX (no sale mention)	1.50	.75	.15
☐ 90A Hank Bauer COM	1.50	.75	.15
☐ 90B Hank Bauer BOX	1.50	.75	.15
☐ 91A Bob Allison COM (Minnesota)	4.00	2.00	.40
☐ 91B Bob Allison BOX (Minneapolis)	4.00	2.00	.40
☐ 92A Harmon Killebrew (Minnesota) COM	20.00	10.00	2.00
☐ 92B Harmon Killebrew (Minneapolis) BOX	20.00	10.00	2.00
☐ 93A Jim Lemon COM (Minnesota)	15.00	7.50	1.50
☐ 93B Jim Lemon BOX (Minneapolis)	30.00	15.00	3.00

☐ 94A	Chuck Stobbs .... (Minnesota) COM only	125.00	60.00	12.50
☐ 95A	Reno Bertoia COM .... (Minnesota)	4.00	2.00	.40
☐ 95B	Reno Bertoia BOX .... (Minneapolis)	1.50	.75	.15
☐ 96A	Billy Gardner COM .... (Minnesota)	4.00	2.00	.40
☐ 96B	Billy Gardner BOX .... (Minneapolis)	1.50	.75	.15
☐ 97A	Earl Battey COM .... (Minnesota)	4.00	2.00	.40
☐ 97B	Earl Battey BOX .... (Minneapolis)	1.50	.75	.15
☐ 98A	Pedro Ramos COM ...... (Minnesota)	4.00	2.00	.40
☐ 98B	Pedro Ramos BOX .... (Minneapolis)	1.50	.75	.15
☐ 99A	Camilo Pascual COM .... (Minnesota)	4.00	2.00	.40
☐ 99B	Camilo Pascual BOX .... (Minneapolis)	1.50	.75	.15
☐ 100A	Billy Consolo COM ...... (Minnesota)	4.00	2.00	.40
☐ 100B	Billy Consolo BOX ...... (Minneapolis)	1.50	.75	.15
☐ 101A	Warren Spahn COM	15.00	7.50	1.50
☐ 101B	Warren Spahn BOX	15.00	7.50	1.50
☐ 102A	Lew Burdette COM	2.50	1.25	.25
☐ 102B	Lew Burdette BOX	2.50	1.25	.25
☐ 103A	Bob Buhl COM	1.50	.75	.15
☐ 103B	Bob Buhl BOX	1.50	.75	.15
☐ 104A	Joe Adcock COM	3.00	1.50	.30
☐ 104B	Joe Adcock BOX	3.00	1.50	.30
☐ 105A	John Logan COM	3.00	1.50	.30
☐ 105B	John Logan BOX	3.00	1.50	.30
☐ 106	Ed Mathews COM only ...	25.00	12.50	2.50
☐ 107A	Hank Aaron COM	20.00	10.00	2.00
☐ 107B	Hank Aaron BOX	20.00	10.00	2.00
☐ 108A	Wes Covington COM	1.50	.75	.15
☐ 108B	Wes Covington BOX	1.50	.75	.15
☐ 109A	Bill Bruton COM .... (Tigers)	5.00	2.50	.50
☐ 109B	Bill Bruton BOX .... (Braves)	5.00	2.50	.50
☐ 110A	Del Crandall COM	3.00	1.50	.30
☐ 110B	Del Crandall BOX	3.00	1.50	.30
☐ 111	Red Schoendienst .... BOX only	2.50	1.25	.25
☐ 112	Juan Pizarro	1.50	.75	.15
☐ 113	Chuck Cottier .... BOX only	10.00	5.00	1.00
☐ 114	Al Spangler BOX only	1.50	.75	.15
☐ 115A	Dick Farrell COM	4.00	2.00	.40
☐ 115B	Dick Farrell BOX	4.00	2.00	.40
☐ 116A	Jim Owens COM	4.00	2.00	.40
☐ 116B	Jim Owens BOX	4.00	2.00	.40
☐ 117A	Robin Roberts COM	7.50	3.75	.75
☐ 117B	Robin Roberts BOX	5.00	2.50	.50
☐ 118A	Tony Taylor COM	1.50	.75	.15
☐ 118B	Tony Taylor BOX	1.50	.75	.15
☐ 119A	Lee Walls COM	1.50	.75	.15
☐ 119B	Lee Walls BOX	1.50	.75	.15
☐ 120A	Tony Curry COM	1.50	.75	.15
☐ 120B	Tony Curry BOX	1.50	.75	.15
☐ 121A	Pancho Herrera COM ...	1.50	.75	.15
☐ 121B	Pancho Herrera BOX	1.50	.75	.15
☐ 122A	Ken Walters COM	1.50	.75	.15
☐ 122B	Ken Walters BOX	1.50	.75	.15
☐ 123A	John Callison COM	1.50	.75	.15
☐ 123B	John Callison BOX	1.50	.75	.15
☐ 124A	Gene Conley COM .... (Red Sox)	8.00	4.00	.80
☐ 124B	Gene Conley BOX .... (Phillies)	1.50	.75	.15
☐ 125A	Bob Friend COM	3.00	1.50	.30
☐ 125B	Bob Friend BOX	3.00	1.50	.30
☐ 126A	Vernon Law COM	3.00	1.50	.30
☐ 126B	Vernon Law BOX	3.00	1.50	.30
☐ 127A	Dick Stuart COM	1.50	.75	.15
☐ 127B	Dick Stuart BOX	1.50	.75	.15
☐ 128A	Bill Mazeroski COM	2.00	1.00	.20
☐ 128B	Bill Mazeroski BOX	1.50	.75	.15
☐ 129A	Dick Groat COM	2.00	1.00	.20
☐ 129B	Dick Groat BOX	2.00	1.00	.20
☐ 130A	Don Hoak COM	1.50	.75	.15
☐ 130B	Don Hoak BOX	1.50	.75	.15
☐ 131A	Bob Skinner COM	1.50	.75	.15
☐ 131B	Bob Skinner BOX	1.50	.75	.15
☐ 132A	Bob Clemente COM	25.00	12.50	2.50
☐ 132B	Bob Clemente BOX	25.00	12.50	2.50
☐ 133	Roy Face BOX only	2.50	1.25	.25
☐ 134	H.Haddix BOX only	1.50	.75	.15
☐ 135	Bill Virdon BOX only	30.00	15.00	3.00
☐ 136A	Gino Cimoli COM	1.50	.75	.15
☐ 136B	Gino Cimoli BOX	1.50	.75	.15
☐ 137	Rocky Nelson .... BOX only	1.50	.75	.15
☐ 138A	Smoky Burgess COM	1.50	.75	.15
☐ 138B	Smoky Burgess BOX	1.50	.75	.15
☐ 139	Hal Smith BOX only	1.50	.75	.15
☐ 140	Wilmer Mizell .... BOX only	1.50	.75	.15
☐ 141A	M.McCormick COM	1.50	.75	.15
☐ 141B	M.McCormick BOX	1.50	.75	.15
☐ 142A	John Antonelli COM ...... (Cleveland)	4.00	2.00	.40
☐ 142B	John Antonelli BOX ...... (San Francisco)	3.00	1.50	.30
☐ 143A	Sam Jones COM	3.00	1.50	.30
☐ 143B	Sam Jones BOX	4.00	2.00	.40
☐ 144A	Orlando Cepeda COM ..	5.00	2.50	.50
☐ 144B	Orlando Cepeda BOX ..	5.00	2.50	.50
☐ 145A	Willie Mays COM	20.00	10.00	2.00
☐ 145B	Willie Mays BOX	20.00	10.00	2.00
☐ 146A	Willie Kirkland .... (Cleve.) COM	3.50	1.75	.35
☐ 146B	Willie Kirkland .... (San Fran.) BOX	3.00	1.50	.30
☐ 147A	Willie McCovey COM	9.00	4.50	.90
☐ 147B	Willie McCovey BOX	6.00	3.00	.60
☐ 148A	Don Blasingame COM ..	1.50	.75	.15
☐ 148B	Don Blasingame BOX ..	1.50	.75	.15
☐ 149A	Jim Davenport COM	1.50	.75	.15
☐ 149B	Jim Davenport BOX	1.50	.75	.15
☐ 150A	Hobie Landrith COM	1.50	.75	.15
☐ 150B	Hobie Landrith BOX	1.50	.75	.15
☐ 151	Bob Schmidt BOX only ...	1.50	.75	.15
☐ 152A	Ed Bressoud COM	1.50	.75	.15
☐ 152B	Ed Bressoud BOX	1.50	.75	.15
☐ 153A	Andre Rodgers .... (no trade mention) BOX only	12.00	6.00	1.20
☐ 153B	Andre Rodgers .... (Traded to Milw.) BOX only	2.50	1.25	.25
☐ 154	Jack Sanford .... BOX only	1.50	.75	.15
☐ 155	Billy O'Dell .... BOX only	1.50	.75	.15
☐ 156A	Norm Larker COM	2.00	1.00	.20
☐ 156B	Norm Larker BOX	2.00	1.00	.20
☐ 157A	Charlie Neal COM	1.50	.75	.15
☐ 157B	Charlie Neal BOX	1.50	.75	.15
☐ 158A	Jim Gilliam COM	3.00	1.50	.30
☐ 158B	Jim Gilliam BOX	3.00	1.50	.30
☐ 159A	Wally Moon COM	1.50	.75	.15
☐ 159B	Wally Moon BOX	1.50	.75	.15
☐ 160A	Don Drysdale COM	7.50	3.75	.75
☐ 160B	Don Drysdale BOX	7.50	3.75	.75
☐ 161A	Larry Sherry COM	1.50	.75	.15
☐ 161B	Larry Sherry BOX	1.50	.75	.15
☐ 162	Stan Williams .... BOX only	5.00	2.50	.50
☐ 163	Mel Roach BOX only	60.00	30.00	6.00
☐ 164A	Maury Wills COM	3.50	1.75	.35
☐ 164B	Maury Wills BOX	3.00	1.50	.30
☐ 165	Tommy Davis BOX only ..	1.50	.75	.15
☐ 166A	John Roseboro COM	1.50	.75	.15
☐ 166B	John Roseboro BOX	1.50	.75	.15
☐ 167A	Duke Snider COM	9.00	4.50	.90
☐ 167B	Duke Snider BOX	5.00	2.50	.50
☐ 168A	Gil Hodges COM	7.50	3.75	.75
☐ 168B	Gil Hodges BOX	5.00	2.50	.50
☐ 169	John Podres BOX only ...	1.50	.75	.15
☐ 170	Ed Roebuck BOX only ...	1.50	.75	.15
☐ 171A	Ken Boyer COM	6.00	3.00	.60
☐ 171B	Ken Boyer BOX	6.00	3.00	.60
☐ 172A	J.Cunningham COM	2.00	1.00	.20
☐ 172B	J.Cunningham BOX	2.00	1.00	.20
☐ 173A	Daryl Spencer COM	1.50	.75	.15
☐ 173B	Daryl Spencer BOX	1.50	.75	.15
☐ 174A	Larry Jackson COM	2.00	1.00	.20
☐ 174B	Larry Jackson BOX	2.00	1.00	.20
☐ 175A	Lindy McDaniel COM	1.50	.75	.15
☐ 175B	Lindy McDaniel BOX	1.50	.75	.15
☐ 176A	Bill White COM	2.50	1.25	.25
☐ 176B	Bill White BOX	1.50	.75	.15
☐ 177A	Alex Grammas COM	1.50	.75	.15
☐ 177B	Alex Grammas BOX	1.50	.75	.15
☐ 178A	Curt Flood COM	2.50	1.25	.25
☐ 178B	Curt Flood BOX	1.50	.75	.15
☐ 179A	Ernie Broglio COM	1.50	.75	.15
☐ 179B	Ernie Broglio BOX	1.50	.75	.15
☐ 180A	Hal Smith COM	1.50	.75	.15
☐ 180B	Hal Smith BOX	1.50	.75	.15
☐ 181A	Vada Pinson COM	2.50	1.25	.25
☐ 181B	Vada Pinson BOX	1.50	.75	.15

		NRMT	VG-E	GOOD
☐ 182A	Frank Robinson COM ...	25.00	12.50	2.50
☐ 182B	Frank Robinson BOX	25.00	12.50	2.50
☐ 183	Roy McMillan	60.00	30.00	6.00
	BOX only			
☐ 184A	Bob Purkey COM	1.50	.75	.15
☐ 184B	Bob Purkey BOX	1.50	.75	.15
☐ 185A	Ed Kasko COM	1.50	.75	.15
☐ 185B	Ed Kasko BOX	1.50	.75	.15
☐ 186A	Gus Bell COM	2.00	1.00	.20
☐ 186B	Gus Bell BOX	2.00	1.00	.20
☐ 187A	Jerry Lynch COM	1.50	.75	.15
☐ 187B	Jerry Lynch BOX	1.50	.75	.15
☐ 188A	Ed Bailey COM	1.50	.75	.15
☐ 188B	Ed Bailey BOX	1.50	.75	.15
☐ 189A	Jim O'Toole COM	1.50	.75	.15
☐ 189B	Jim O'Toole BOX	1.50	.75	.15
☐ 190A	Billy Martin COM	6.00	3.00	.60
	(Sold to Milw.)			
☐ 190B	Billy Martin BOX	2.50	1.25	.25
	(no sale mention)			
☐ 191A	Ernie Banks COM	15.00	7.50	1.50
☐ 191B	Ernie Banks BOX	15.00	7.50	1.50
☐ 192A	Richie Ashburn COM	3.00	1.50	.30
☐ 192B	Richie Ashburn BOX	3.00	1.50	.30
☐ 193A	Frank Thomas COM	10.00	5.00	1.00
☐ 193B	Frank Thomas BOX	20.00	10.00	2.00
☐ 194A	Don Cardwell COM	2.00	1.00	.20
☐ 194B	Don Cardwell BOX	2.00	1.00	.20
☐ 195A	George Altman COM	1.50	.75	.15
☐ 195B	George Altman BOX	1.50	.75	.15
☐ 196A	Ron Santo COM	2.50	1.25	.25
☐ 196B	Ron Santo BOX	1.50	.75	.15
☐ 197A	Glen Hobbie COM	1.50	.75	.15
☐ 197B	Glen Hobbie BOX	1.50	.75	.15
☐ 198A	Sam Taylor COM	1.50	.75	.15
☐ 198B	Sam Taylor BOX	1.50	.75	.15
☐ 199A	Jerry Kindall COM	1.50	.75	.15
☐ 199B	Jerry Kindall BOX	1.50	.75	.15
☐ 200A	Don Elston COM	1.50	.75	.15
☐ 200B	Don Elston BOX	1.50	.75	.15

1962 Post Cereal

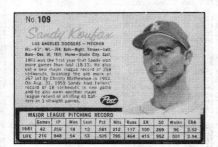

The cards in this 200-card series measure 2 1/2" by 3 1/2". The 1962 Post set is the easiest of the Post sets to complete. The cards are grouped numerically by team, for example, New York Yankees (1-13), Detroit (14-26), Baltimore (27-36), Cleveland (37-45), Chicago White Sox (46- 55), Boston (56-64), Washington (65-73), Los Angeles Angels (74-82), Minnesota (83-91), Kansas City (92-100), Los Angeles Dodgers (101-115), Cincinnati (116-130), San Francisco (131-144), Milwaukee (145-157), St. Louis (158- 168), Pittsburgh (169-181), Chicago Cubs (182-191), and Philadelphia (192-200). Cards 5B and 6B were printed on thin stock in a two card panel and distributed in a magazine promotion. The scarce cards are 55, 92, 101, 116, 121, and 140. The checklist for this set is the same as that of 1962 Jello and 1962 Post Canadian, but those sets are considered separate issues. The catalog number for this set is F278- 37.

	NRMT	VG-E	GOOD
COMPLETE SET (208)	1250.00	600.00	150.00
COMMON PLAYER (1-200)	1.25	.60	.12

☐ 1	Bill Skowron	2.00	1.00	.20
☐ 2	Bobby Richardson	2.00	1.00	.20
☐ 3	Cletis Boyer	1.25	.60	.12
☐ 4	Tony Kubek	2.00	1.00	.20
☐ 5A	Mickey Mantle	75.00	37.50	7.50
☐ 5B	Mickey Mantle AD	75.00	37.50	7.50
☐ 6A	Roger Maris	20.00	10.00	2.00
☐ 6B	Roger Maris AD	20.00	10.00	2.00
☐ 7	Yogi Berra	15.00	7.50	1.50
☐ 8	Elston Howard	2.00	1.00	.20
☐ 9	Whitey Ford	7.50	3.75	.75
☐ 10	Ralph Terry	1.25	.60	.12
☐ 11	John Blanchard	1.25	.60	.12
☐ 12	Luis Arroyo	1.25	.60	.12
☐ 13	Bill Stafford	1.25	.60	.12
☐ 14	Norm Cash	1.25	.60	.12
☐ 15	Jake Wood	1.25	.60	.12
☐ 16	Steve Boros	1.25	.60	.12
☐ 17	Chico Fernandez	1.25	.60	.12
☐ 18	Bill Bruton	1.25	.60	.12
☐ 19	Rocky Colavito	2.00	1.00	.20
☐ 20	Al Kaline	10.00	5.00	1.00
☐ 21	Dick Brown	1.25	.60	.12
☐ 22	Frank Lary	1.25	.60	.12
☐ 23	Don Mossi	1.25	.60	.12
☐ 24	Phil Regan	1.25	.60	.12
☐ 25	Charley Maxwell	1.25	.60	.12
☐ 26	Jim Bunning	3.50	1.75	.35
☐ 27A	Jim Gentile	2.00	1.00	.20
	Home: Baltimore			
☐ 27B	Jim Gentile	12.00	6.00	1.20
	Home: San Lorenzo			
☐ 28	Marv Breeding	1.25	.60	.12
☐ 29	Brooks Robinson	10.00	5.00	1.00
☐ 30	Ron Hansen	1.25	.60	.12
☐ 31	Jackie Brandt	1.25	.60	.12
☐ 32	Dick Williams	1.25	.60	.12
☐ 33	Gus Triandos	1.25	.60	.12
☐ 34	Milt Pappas	1.25	.60	.12
☐ 35	Hoyt Wilhelm	6.00	3.00	.60
☐ 36	Chuck Estrada	5.00	2.50	.50
☐ 37	Vic Power	1.25	.60	.12
☐ 38	Johnny Temple	1.25	.60	.12
☐ 39	Bubba Phillips	1.25	.60	.12
☐ 40	Tito Francona	1.25	.60	.12
☐ 41	Willie Kirkland	1.25	.60	.12
☐ 42	John Romano	1.25	.60	.12
☐ 43	Jim Perry	1.25	.60	.12
☐ 44	Woodie Held	1.25	.60	.12
☐ 45	Chuck Essegian	1.25	.60	.12
☐ 46	Roy Sievers	1.25	.60	.12
☐ 47	Nellie Fox	2.50	1.25	.25
☐ 48	Al Smith	1.25	.60	.12
☐ 49	Luis Aparicio	3.00	1.50	.30
☐ 50	Jim Landis	1.25	.60	.12
☐ 51	Minnie Minoso	2.00	1.00	.20
☐ 52	Andy Carey	1.25	.60	.12
☐ 53	Sherman Lollar	1.25	.60	.12
☐ 54	Bill Pierce	2.00	1.00	.20
☐ 55	Early Wynn	25.00	12.50	2.50
☐ 56	Chuck Schilling	1.25	.60	.12
☐ 57	Pete Runnels	1.25	.60	.12
☐ 58	Frank Malzone	1.25	.60	.12
☐ 59	Don Buddin	1.25	.60	.12
☐ 60	Gary Geiger	1.25	.60	.12
☐ 61	Carl Yastrzemski	35.00	17.50	3.50
☐ 62	Jackie Jensen	1.25	.60	.12
☐ 63	Jim Pagliaroni	1.25	.60	.12
☐ 64	Don Schwall	1.25	.60	.12
☐ 65	Dale Long	1.25	.60	.12
☐ 66	Chuck Cottier	1.25	.60	.12
☐ 67	Billy Klaus	1.25	.60	.12
☐ 68	Coot Veal	1.25	.60	.12
☐ 69	Marty Keough	30.00	15.00	3.00
☐ 70	Willie Tasby	1.25	.60	.12
☐ 71	Gene Woodling	1.25	.60	.12
☐ 72	Gene Green	1.25	.60	.12
☐ 73	Dick Donovan	1.25	.60	.12
☐ 74	Steve Bilko	1.25	.60	.12
☐ 75	Rocky Bridges	1.25	.60	.12
☐ 76	Eddie Yost	1.25	.60	.12
☐ 77	Leon Wagner	1.25	.60	.12
☐ 78	Albie Pearson	1.25	.60	.12
☐ 79	Ken Hunt	1.25	.60	.12
☐ 80	Earl Averill Jr.	1.25	.60	.12
☐ 81	Ryne Duren	1.25	.60	.12
☐ 82	Ted Kluszewski	2.00	1.00	.20
☐ 83	Bob Allison	20.00	10.00	2.00
☐ 84	Billy Martin	2.00	1.00	.20
☐ 85	Harmon Killebrew	7.50	3.75	.75
☐ 86	Zoilo Versalles	1.25	.60	.12
☐ 87	Lenny Green	1.25	.60	.12
☐ 88	Bill Tuttle	1.25	.60	.12
☐ 89	Jim Lemon	1.25	.60	.12
☐ 90	Earl Battey	1.25	.60	.12

		NRMT	VG-E	GOOD
☐ 91	Camilo Pascual	1.25	.60	.12
☐ 92	Norm Sieburn	50.00	25.00	5.00
☐ 93	Jerry Lumpe	1.25	.60	.12
☐ 94	Dick Howser	2.00	1.00	.20
☐ 95A	Gene Stephens	2.00	1.00	.20
	Born: Jan. 5			
☐ 95B	Gene Stephens	12.00	6.00	1.20
	Born: Jan. 20			
☐ 96	Leo Posada	1.25	.60	.12
☐ 97	Joe Pignatano	1.25	.60	.12
☐ 98	Jim Archer	1.25	.60	.12
☐ 99	Haywood Sullivan	1.25	.60	.12
☐ 100	Art Ditmar	1.25	.60	.12
☐ 101	Gil Hodges	60.00	30.00	6.00
☐ 102	Charlie Neal	1.25	.60	.12
☐ 103	Daryl Spencer	20.00	10.00	2.00
☐ 104	Maury Wills	3.50	1.75	.35
☐ 105	Tommy Davis	2.00	1.00	.20
☐ 106	Willie Davis	1.25	.60	.12
☐ 107	John Roseboro	1.25	.60	.12
☐ 108	John Podres	2.00	1.00	.20
☐ 109A	Sandy Koufax	20.00	10.00	2.00
☐ 109B	Sandy Koufax	50.00	25.00	5.00
	(with blue lines)			
☐ 110	Don Drysdale	7.50	3.75	.75
☐ 111	Larry Sherry	3.00	1.50	.30
☐ 112	Jim Gilliam	2.00	1.00	.20
☐ 113	Norm Larker	30.00	15.00	3.00
☐ 114	Duke Snider	6.00	3.00	.60
☐ 115	Stan Williams	1.25	.60	.12
☐ 116	Gordy Coleman	60.00	30.00	6.00
☐ 117	Don Blasingame	1.25	.60	.12
☐ 118	Gene Freese	1.25	.60	.12
☐ 119	Ed Kasko	1.25	.60	.12
☐ 120	Gus Bell	1.25	.60	.12
☐ 121	Vada Pinson	2.00	1.00	.20
☐ 122	Frank Robinson	20.00	10.00	2.00
☐ 123	Bob Purkey	1.25	.60	.12
☐ 124A	Joey Jay	2.00	1.00	.20
☐ 124B	Joey Jay	12.00	6.00	1.20
	(with blue lines)			
☐ 125	Jim Brosnan	25.00	12.50	2.50
☐ 126	Jim O'Toole	1.25	.60	.12
☐ 127	Jerry Lynch	50.00	25.00	5.00
☐ 128	Wally Post	1.25	.60	.12
☐ 129	Ken Hunt	1.25	.60	.12
☐ 130	Jerry Zimmerman	1.25	.60	.12
☐ 131	Willie McCovey	60.00	30.00	6.00
☐ 132	Jose Pagan	1.25	.60	.12
☐ 133	Felipe Alou	1.25	.60	.12
☐ 134	Jim Davenport	1.25	.60	.12
☐ 135	Harvey Kuenn	2.00	1.00	.20
☐ 136	Orlando Cepeda	3.00	1.50	.30
☐ 137	Ed Bailey	1.25	.60	.12
☐ 138	Sam Jones	1.25	.60	.12
☐ 139	Mike McCormick	1.25	.60	.12
☐ 140	Juan Marichal	75.00	37.50	7.50
☐ 141	Jack Sanford	1.25	.60	.12
☐ 142	Willie Mays	25.00	12.50	2.50
☐ 143	Stu Miller	5.00	2.50	.50
☐ 144	Joe Amalfitano	12.00	6.00	1.20
☐ 145A	Joe Adcock	2.00	1.00	.20
☐ 145B	Joe Adock (sic) ERR	40.00	20.00	4.00
☐ 146	Frank Bolling	1.25	.60	.12
☐ 147	Ed Mathews	7.50	3.75	.75
☐ 148	Roy McMillan	1.25	.60	.12
☐ 149	Hank Aaron	25.00	12.50	2.50
☐ 150	Gino Cimoli	1.25	.60	.12
☐ 151	Frank Thomas	1.25	.60	.12
☐ 152	Joe Torre	2.00	1.00	.20
☐ 153	Lew Burdette	2.00	1.00	.20
☐ 154	Bob Buhl	1.25	.60	.12
☐ 155	Carlton Willey	1.25	.60	.12
☐ 156	Lee Maye	1.25	.60	.12
☐ 157	Al Spangler	1.25	.60	.12
☐ 158	Bill White	30.00	15.00	3.00
☐ 159	Ken Boyer	2.50	1.25	.25
☐ 160	Joe Cunningham	1.25	.60	.12
☐ 161	Carl Warwick	1.25	.60	.12
☐ 162	Carl Sawatski	1.25	.60	.12
☐ 163	Lindy McDaniel	1.25	.60	.12
☐ 164	Ernie Broglio	1.25	.60	.12
☐ 165	Larry Jackson	1.25	.60	.12
☐ 166	Curt Flood	2.00	1.00	.20
☐ 167	Curt Simmons	1.25	.60	.12
☐ 168	Alex Grammas	1.25	.60	.12
☐ 169	Dick Stuart	1.25	.60	.12
☐ 170	Bill Mazeroski	2.00	1.00	.20
☐ 171	Don Hoak	1.25	.60	.12
☐ 172	Dick Groat	2.00	1.00	.20
☐ 173A	Roberto Clemente	20.00	10.00	2.00
☐ 173B	Roberto Clemente	50.00	25.00	5.00
	(with blue lines)			
☐ 174	Bob Skinner	1.25	.60	.12
☐ 175	Bill Virdon	1.25	.60	.12

☐ 176	Smoky Burgess	1.25	.60	.12
☐ 177	Elroy Face	2.00	1.00	.20
☐ 178	Bob Friend	1.25	.60	.12
☐ 179	Vernon Law	1.25	.60	.12
☐ 180	Harvey Haddix	1.25	.60	.12
☐ 181	Hal Smith	1.25	.60	.12
☐ 182	Ed Bouchee	1.25	.60	.12
☐ 183	Don Zimmer	1.25	.60	.12
☐ 184	Ron Santo	2.00	1.00	.20
☐ 185	Andre Rodgers	1.25	.60	.12
☐ 186	Richie Ashburn	2.50	1.25	.25
☐ 187	George Altman	1.50	.75	.15
☐ 188	Ernie Banks	10.00	5.00	1.00
☐ 189	Sam Taylor	3.00	1.50	.30
☐ 190	Don Elston	1.25	.60	.12
☐ 191	Jerry Kindall	1.25	.60	.12
☐ 192	Pancho Herrera	1.25	.60	.12
☐ 193	Tony Taylor	1.25	.60	.12
☐ 194	Ruben Amaro	1.25	.60	.12
☐ 195	Don Demeter	1.25	.60	.12
☐ 196	Bobby Gene Smith	1.25	.60	.12
☐ 197	Clay Dalrymple	1.25	.60	.12
☐ 198	Robin Roberts	5.00	2.50	.50
☐ 199	Art Mahaffey	1.25	.60	.12
☐ 200	John Buzhardt	1.25	.60	.12

1963 Post Cereal

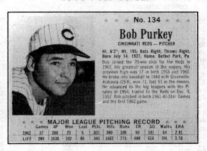

The cards in this 200-card set measure 2 1/2" by 3 1/2". The players are grouped by team with American Leaguers comprising 1-100 and National Leaguers 101-200. The ordering of teams is as follows: Minnesota (1- 11), New York Yankees, Los Angeles Angels (24-34), Chicago White Sox (35-45), Detroit (46-56), Baltimore (57-66), Cleveland (67-76), Boston (77-84), Kansas City (85-92), Washington (93-100), San Francisco (101-112), Los Angeles Dodgers (113-124), Cincinnati (125-136), Pittsburgh (137- 147), Milwaukee (148-157), St. Louis (158-168), Chicago Cubs (169-176), Philadelphia (177-184), Houston (185-192), and New York Mets (193-200). In contrast to the 1962 issue, the 1963 Post baseball card series is very difficult to complete. There are many card scarcities reflected in the price list below. Cards of the Post set are easily confused with those of the 1963 Jello set, which are 1/4" narrower (a difference which is often eliminated by bad cutting). The catalog designation is F278-38.

		NRMT	VG-E	GOOD
COMPLETE SET (205)		3300.00	1600.00	350.00
COMMON PLAYER (1-200)		2.00	1.00	.20
☐ 1	Vic Power	2.00	1.00	.20
☐ 2	Bernie Allen	2.00	1.00	.20
☐ 3	Zoilo Versalles	2.00	1.00	.20
☐ 4	Rich Rollins	2.00	1.00	.20
☐ 5	Harmon Killebrew	15.00	7.50	1.50
☐ 6	Lenny Green	35.00	17.50	3.50
☐ 7	Bob Allison	2.00	1.00	.20
☐ 8	Earl Battey	2.00	1.00	.20
☐ 9	Camilo Pascual	2.00	1.00	.20
☐ 10	Jim Kaat	3.00	1.50	.30
☐ 11	Jack Kralick	2.00	1.00	.20
☐ 12	Bill Skowron	2.00	1.00	.20

13	Bobby Richardson	3.00	1.50	.30
14	Cletis Boyer	2.00	1.00	.20
15	Mickey Mantle	250.00	125.00	25.00
16	Roger Maris	150.00	75.00	15.00
17	Yogi Berra	15.00	7.50	1.50
18	Elston Howard	3.00	1.50	.30
19	Whitey Ford	9.00	4.50	.90
20	Ralph Terry	2.00	1.00	.20
21	John Blanchard	2.00	1.00	.20
22	Bill Stafford	2.00	1.00	.20
23	Tom Tresh	2.00	1.00	.20
24	Steve Bilko	2.00	1.00	.20
25	Bill Moran	2.00	1.00	.20
26A	Joe Koppe BA: .277	2.00	1.00	.20
26B	Joe Koppe BA: .227	12.00	6.00	1.20
27	Felix Torres	2.00	1.00	.20
28A	Leon Wagner BA: .278	2.00	1.00	.20
28B	Leon Wagner BA: .272	12.00	6.00	1.20
29	Albie Pearson	2.00	1.00	.20
30	Lee Thomas (photo actually George Thomas)	75.00	37.50	7.50
31	Bob Rodgers	2.00	1.00	.20
32	Dean Chance	2.00	1.00	.20
33	Ken McBride	2.00	1.00	.20
34	George Thomas (photo actually Lee Thomas)	2.00	1.00	.20
35	Joe Cunningham	2.00	1.00	.20
36	Nelson Fox	3.00	1.50	.30
37	Luis Aparicio	4.00	2.00	.40
38	Al Smith	30.00	15.00	3.00
39	Floyd Robinson	90.00	45.00	9.00
40	Jim Landis	2.00	1.00	.20
41	Charlie Maxwell	2.00	1.00	.20
42	Sherman Lollar	2.00	1.00	.20
43	Early Wynn	5.00	2.50	.50
44	Juan Pizarro	2.00	1.00	.20
45	Ray Herbert	2.00	1.00	.20
46	Norm Cash	2.00	1.00	.20
47	Steve Boros	2.00	1.00	.20
48	Dick McAuliffe	20.00	10.00	2.00
49	Bill Bruton	3.00	1.50	.30
50	Rocky Colavito	3.00	1.50	.30
51	Al Kaline	15.00	7.50	1.50
52	Dick Brown	2.00	1.00	.20
53	Jim Bunning	125.00	60.00	12.50
54	Hank Aguirre	2.00	1.00	.20
55	Frank Lary	2.00	1.00	.20
56	Don Mossi	2.00	1.00	.20
57	Jim Gentile	2.00	1.00	.20
58	Jackie Brandt	2.00	1.00	.20
59	Brooks Robinson	15.00	7.50	1.50
60	Ron Hansen	3.00	1.50	.30
61	Jerry Adair	150.00	75.00	15.00
62	John (Boog) Powell	3.00	1.50	.30
63	Russ Snyder	2.00	1.00	.20
64	Steve Barber	2.00	1.00	.20
65	Milt Pappas	2.00	1.00	.20
66	Robin Roberts	5.00	2.50	.50
67	Tito Francona	2.00	1.00	.20
68	Jerry Kindall	2.00	1.00	.20
69	Woody Held	2.00	1.00	.20
70	Bubba Phillips	12.00	6.00	1.20
71	Chuck Essegian	2.00	1.00	.20
72	Willie Kirkland	2.00	1.00	.20
73	Al Luplow	2.00	1.00	.20
74	Ty Cline	2.00	1.00	.20
75	Dick Donovan	2.00	1.00	.20
76	John Romano	2.00	1.00	.20
77	Pete Runnels	2.00	1.00	.20
78	Ed Bressoud	2.00	1.00	.20
79	Frank Malzone	2.00	1.00	.20
80	Carl Yastrzemski	300.00	150.00	30.00
81	Gary Geiger	2.00	1.00	.20
82	Lou Clinton	2.00	1.00	.20
83	Earl Wilson	2.00	1.00	.20
84	Bill Monbouquette	2.00	1.00	.20
85	Norm Sieburn	2.00	1.00	.20
86	Jerry Lumpe	90.00	45.00	9.00
87	Manny Jimenez	90.00	45.00	9.00
88	Gino Cimoli	2.00	1.00	.20
89	Ed Charles	2.00	1.00	.20
90	Ed Rakow	2.00	1.00	.20
91	Bob Del Greco	2.00	1.00	.20
92	Haywood Sullivan	2.00	1.00	.20
93	Chuck Hinton	2.00	1.00	.20
94	Ken Retzer	2.00	1.00	.20
95	Harry Bright	2.00	1.00	.20
96	Bob Johnson	2.00	1.00	.20
97	Dave Stenhouse	12.00	6.00	1.20
98	Chuck Cottier	20.00	10.00	2.00
99	Tom Cheney	2.00	1.00	.20
100	Claude Osteen	12.00	6.00	1.20
101	Orlando Cepeda	3.00	1.50	.30
102	Charley Hiller	2.00	1.00	.20
103	Jose Pagan	2.00	1.00	.20
104	Jim Davenport	2.00	1.00	.20
105	Harvey Kuenn	3.00	1.50	.30
106	Willie Mays	35.00	17.50	3.50
107	Felipe Alou	2.00	1.00	.20
108	Tom Haller	90.00	45.00	9.00
109	Juan Marichal	5.00	2.50	.50
110	Jack Sanford	2.00	1.00	.20
111	Bill O'Dell	2.00	1.00	.20
112	Willie McCovey	6.00	3.00	.60
113	Lee Walls	2.00	1.00	.20
114	Jim Gilliam	2.00	1.00	.20
115	Maury Wills	3.00	1.50	.30
116	Ron Fairly	2.00	1.00	.20
117	Tommy Davis	2.00	1.00	.20
118	Duke Snider	7.50	3.75	.75
119	Willie Davis	150.00	75.00	15.00
120	John Roseboro	2.00	1.00	.20
121	Sandy Koufax	20.00	10.00	2.00
122	Stan Williams	2.00	1.00	.20
123	Don Drysdale	6.00	3.00	.60
124	Daryl Spencer	2.00	1.00	.20
125	Gordy Coleman	2.00	1.00	.20
126	Don Blasingame	2.00	1.00	.20
127	Leo Cardenas	2.00	1.00	.20
128	Eddie Kasko	150.00	75.00	15.00
129	Jerry Lynch	12.00	6.00	1.20
130	Vada Pinson	2.00	1.00	.20
131A	Frank Robinson (no stripes)	12.00	6.00	1.20
131B	Frank Robinson (stripes on hat)	25.00	12.50	2.50
132	John Edwards	2.00	1.00	.20
133	Joey Jay	2.00	1.00	.20
134	Bob Purkey	2.00	1.00	.20
135	Marty Keough	20.00	10.00	2.00
136	Jim O'Toole	2.00	1.00	.20
137	Dick Stuart	2.00	1.00	.20
138	Bill Mazeroski	2.00	1.00	.20
139	Dick Groat	2.00	1.00	.20
140	Don Hoak	25.00	12.50	2.50
141	Bob Skinner	12.00	6.00	1.20
142	Bill Virdon	2.00	1.00	.20
143	Roberto Clemente	20.00	10.00	2.00
144	Smoky Burgess	2.00	1.00	.20
145	Bob Friend	2.00	1.00	.20
146	Al McBean	2.00	1.00	.20
147	Elroy Face	2.00	1.00	.20
148	Joe Adcock	2.00	1.00	.20
149	Frank Bolling	2.00	1.00	.20
150	Roy McMillan	2.00	1.00	.20
151	Eddie Mathews	10.00	5.00	1.00
152	Hank Aaron	100.00	50.00	10.00
153	Del Crandall	30.00	15.00	3.00
154A	Bob Shaw COR	2.00	1.00	.20
154B	Bob Shaw ERR (two "in 1959" in same sentence)	12.00	6.00	1.20
155	Lew Burdette	2.00	1.00	.20
156	Joe Torre	2.00	1.00	.20
157	Bill Cloninger	2.00	1.00	.20
158	Bill White	3.00	1.50	.30
159	Julian Javier	2.00	1.00	.20
160	Ken Boyer	3.00	1.50	.30
161	Julio Gotay	2.00	1.00	.20
162	Curt Flood	100.00	50.00	10.00
163	Charlie James	3.00	1.50	.30
164	Gene Oliver	2.00	1.00	.20
165	Ernie Broglio	2.00	1.00	.20
166	Bob Gibson	6.00	3.00	.60
167A	Lindy McDaniel (no asterisk)	5.00	2.50	.50
167B	Lindy McDaniel (asterisk traded line)	5.00	2.50	.50
168	Ray Washburn	2.00	1.00	.20
169	Ernie Banks	9.00	4.50	.90
170	Ron Santo	2.00	1.00	.20
171	George Altman	2.00	1.00	.20
172	Billy Williams	125.00	60.00	12.50
173	Andre Rodgers	10.00	5.00	1.00
174	Ken Hubbs	20.00	10.00	2.00
175	Don Landrum	2.00	1.00	.20
176	Dick Bertell	15.00	7.50	1.50
177	Roy Sievers	2.00	1.00	.20
178	Tony Taylor	2.00	1.00	.20
179	John Callison	2.00	1.00	.20
180	Don Demeter	2.00	1.00	.20
181	Tony Gonzalez	10.00	5.00	1.00
182	Wes Covington	20.00	10.00	2.00
183	Art Mahaffey	2.00	1.00	.20

☐ 184	Clay Dalrymple	2.00	1.00	.20
☐ 185	Al Spangler	3.00	1.50	.30
☐ 186	Roman Mejias	2.00	1.00	.20
☐ 187	Bob Aspromonte	300.00	150.00	30.00
☐ 188	Norm Larker	30.00	15.00	3.00
☐ 189	Johnny Temple	2.00	1.00	.20
☐ 190	Carl Warwick	2.00	1.00	.20
☐ 191	Bob Lillis	2.00	1.00	.20
☐ 192	Dick Farrell	2.00	1.00	.20
☐ 193	Gil Hodges	6.00	3.00	.60
☐ 194	Marv Throneberry	2.00	1.00	.20
☐ 195	Charlie Neal	7.50	3.75	.75
☐ 196	Frank Thomas	150.00	75.00	15.00
☐ 197	Richie Ashburn	20.00	10.00	2.00
☐ 198	Felix Mantilla	2.00	1.00	.20
☐ 199	Rod Kanehl	15.00	7.50	1.50
☐ 200	Roger Craig	3.00	1.50	.30

☐ 34	Offer Card for the complete set (unnumbered)	.03	.01	.00

1986 Quaker Granola

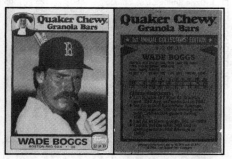

This set of 33 cards was available in packages of Quaker Oats Chewy Granola, three player cards plus a complete set offer card in each package. The set was also available through a mail-in offer where anyone sending in four UPC seals from Chewy Granola (before 12/31/86) would receive a complete set. The cards were produced by Topps for Quaker Oats and are 2 1/2" by 3 1/2". Card backs are printed in red and blue on gray card stock. The cards are numbered on the front and the back.

	MINT	EXC	G-VG
COMPLETE SET (33)	7.00	3.50	.70
COMMON PLAYER (1-33)	.10	.05	.01

☐ 1	Willie McGee	.20	.10	.02
☐ 2	Dwight Gooden	.60	.30	.06
☐ 3	Vince Coleman	.30	.15	.03
☐ 4	Gary Carter	.30	.15	.03
☐ 5	Jack Clark	.20	.10	.02
☐ 6	Steve Garvey	.40	.20	.04
☐ 7	Tony Gwynn	.50	.25	.05
☐ 8	Dale Murphy	.40	.20	.04
☐ 9	Dave Parker	.20	.10	.02
☐ 10	Tim Raines	.25	.12	.02
☐ 11	Pete Rose	.60	.30	.06
☐ 12	Nolan Ryan	1.00	.50	.10
☐ 13	Ryne Sandberg	.35	.17	.03
☐ 14	Mike Schmidt	.75	.35	.07
☐ 15	Ozzie Smith	.30	.15	.03
☐ 16	Darryl Strawberry	.50	.25	.05
☐ 17	Fernando Valenzuela	.25	.12	.02
☐ 18	Don Mattingly	1.00	.50	.10
☐ 19	Bret Saberhagen	.35	.17	.03
☐ 20	Ozzie Guillen	.10	.05	.01
☐ 21	Bert Blyleven	.15	.07	.01
☐ 22	Wade Boggs	.75	.35	.07
☐ 23	George Brett	.45	.22	.04
☐ 24	Darrell Evans	.10	.05	.01
☐ 25	Rickey Henderson	.60	.30	.06
☐ 26	Reggie Jackson	.50	.25	.05
☐ 27	Eddie Murray	.35	.17	.03
☐ 28	Phil Niekro	.20	.10	.02
☐ 29	Dan Quisenberry	.15	.07	.01
☐ 30	Jim Rice	.25	.12	.02
☐ 31	Cal Ripken	.30	.15	.03
☐ 32	Tom Seaver	.30	.15	.03
☐ 33	Dave Winfield	.25	.12	.02

1984 Ralston Purina

The cards in this 33-card set measure 2 1/2" by 3 1/2". In 1984 the Ralston Purina Company issued what it has entitled "The First Annual Collectors Edition of Baseball Cards." The cards feature portrait photos of the players rather than batting action shots. The Topps logo appears along with the Ralston logo on the front of the card. The backs are completely different from the Topps cards of this year; in fact, they contain neither a Topps logo nor a Topps copyright. Large quantities of these cards were obtained by card dealers for direct distribution into the organized hobby, hence the relatively low price of the set.

	MINT	EXC	G-VG
COMPLETE SET (33)	4.00	2.00	.40
COMMON PLAYER (1-33)	.05	.02	.00

☐ 1	Eddie Murray	.25	.12	.02
☐ 2	Ozzie Smith	.15	.07	.01
☐ 3	Ted Simmons	.05	.02	.00
☐ 4	Pete Rose	.50	.25	.05
☐ 5	Greg Luzinski	.05	.02	.00
☐ 6	Andre Dawson	.20	.10	.02
☐ 7	Dave Winfield	.20	.10	.02
☐ 8	Tom Seaver	.25	.12	.02
☐ 9	Jim Rice	.15	.07	.01
☐ 10	Fernando Valenzuela	.15	.07	.01
☐ 11	Wade Boggs	.50	.25	.05
☐ 12	Dale Murphy	.35	.17	.03
☐ 13	George Brett	.35	.17	.03
☐ 14	Nolan Ryan	.75	.35	.07
☐ 15	Rickey Henderson	.40	.20	.04
☐ 16	Steve Carlton	.25	.12	.02
☐ 17	Rod Carew	.25	.12	.02
☐ 18	Steve Garvey	.25	.12	.02
☐ 19	Reggie Jackson	.35	.17	.03
☐ 20	Dave Concepcion	.05	.02	.00
☐ 21	Robin Yount	.35	.17	.03
☐ 22	Mike Schmidt	.60	.30	.06
☐ 23	Jim Palmer	.25	.12	.02
☐ 24	Bruce Sutter	.10	.05	.01
☐ 25	Dan Quisenberry	.10	.05	.01
☐ 26	Bill Madlock	.05	.02	.00
☐ 27	Cecil Cooper	.05	.02	.00
☐ 28	Gary Carter	.20	.10	.02
☐ 29	Fred Lynn	.10	.05	.01
☐ 30	Pedro Guerrero	.15	.07	.01
☐ 31	Ron Guidry	.10	.05	.01
☐ 32	Keith Hernandez	.15	.07	.01
☐ 33	Carlton Fisk	.20	.10	.02

1987 Ralston Purina

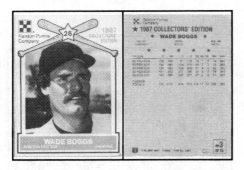

The Ralston Purina Company issued a set of 15 cards picturing players without their respective team logos. The cards measure approximately 2 1/2" by 3 3/8" and are in full-color on the front. The cards are numbered on the back in the lower right hand corner; the player's uniform number is prominently displayed on the front. The cards were distributed as inserts inside packages of certain flavors of Ralston Purina's breakfast cereals. Three cards and a contest card were packaged in cellophane and inserted within the cereal box. The set was also available as an uncut sheet through a mail-in offer. Since the uncut sheets are relatively common, the value of the sheet is essentially the same as the value of the sum of the individual cards. In fact there were two uncut sheets issued, one had "Honey Graham Chex" printed at the top and the other had "Cookie Crisp" printed at the top. Also cards were issued with and without the words "1987 Collectors Edition" printed in blue on the front. Supposedly 100,000 of the uncut sheets were given away free via instant win certificates inserted in with the cereal or collectors could send in two non-winning contest cards plus 1.00 for each uncut sheet.

	MINT	EXC	G-VG
COMPLETE SET (15)	10.00	5.00	1.00
COMMON PLAYER (1-15)	.35	.17	.03
☐ 1 Nolan Ryan	1.75	.85	.17
☐ 2 Steve Garvey	.60	.30	.06
☐ 3 Wade Boggs	1.25	.60	.12
☐ 4 Dave Winfield	.45	.22	.04
☐ 5 Don Mattingly	1.75	.85	.17
☐ 6 Don Sutton	.35	.17	.03
☐ 7 Dave Parker	.35	.17	.03
☐ 8 Eddie Murray	.45	.22	.04
☐ 9 Gary Carter	.45	.22	.04
☐ 10 Roger Clemens	1.00	.50	.10
☐ 11 Fernando Valenzuela	.60	.30	.06
☐ 12 Cal Ripken	.60	.30	.06
☐ 13 Ozzie Smith	.60	.30	.06
☐ 14 Mike Schmidt	1.25	.60	.12
☐ 15 Ryne Sandberg	.60	.30	.06

1989 Ralston Purina Superstars

The 1989 Ralston Purina Superstars set contains 12 cards measuring 2 1/2 by 3 1/2 inches. The fronts have white borders and mugshots with airbrushed logos. The vertically-oriented backs show career statistics. Two cards were included in each specially-marked Ralston Purina cereal box.

	MINT	EXC	G-VG
COMPLETE SET (12)	7.50	3.75	.75

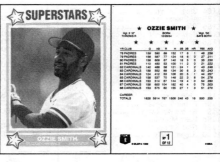

	MINT	EXC	G-VG
COMMON PLAYER (1-12)	.40	.20	.04
☐ 1 Ozzie Smith	.50	.25	.05
☐ 2 Andre Dawson	.50	.25	.05
☐ 3 Darryl Strawberry	.75	.35	.07
☐ 4 Mike Schmidt	1.00	.50	.10
☐ 5 Orel Hershiser	.60	.30	.06
☐ 6 Tim Raines	.40	.20	.04
☐ 7 Roger Clemens	.75	.35	.07
☐ 8 Kirby Puckett	.75	.35	.07
☐ 9 George Brett	.60	.30	.06
☐ 10 Alan Trammell	.40	.20	.04
☐ 11 Don Mattingly	1.00	.50	.10
☐ 12 Jose Canseco	1.00	.50	.10

1983 Rangers Affiliated Food

The cards in this 28-card set measure 2 3/8" by 3 1/2". The Affiliated Food Stores chain of Arlington, Texas, produced this set of Texas Rangers late during the 1983 baseball season. Complete sets were given to children 13 and under at the September 3, 1983, Rangers game. The cards are numbered by uniform number and feature the player's name, card number, and the words "1983 Rangers" on the bottom front. The backs contain biographical data, career totals, a small black and white insert picture of the player, and the Affiliated Food Stores' logo. The coaches card is unnumbered.

	MINT	EXC	G-VG
COMPLETE SET (28)	6.00	3.00	.60
COMMON PLAYER	.15	.07	.01
☐ 1 Bill Stein	.15	.07	.01
☐ 2 Mike Richardt	.15	.07	.01
☐ 3 Wayne Tolleson	.15	.07	.01
☐ 5 Billy Sample	.15	.07	.01
☐ 6 Bobby Jones	.15	.07	.01
☐ 7 Bucky Dent	.50	.25	.05
☐ 8 Bobby Johnson	.15	.07	.01
☐ 9 Pete O'Brien	.75	.35	.07
☐ 10 Jim Sundberg	.25	.12	.02
☐ 11 Doug Rader MG	.35	.17	.03
☐ 12 Dave Hostetler	.15	.07	.01
☐ 14 Larry Biittner	.15	.07	.01

		MINT	EXC	G-VG
☐ 15	Larry Parrish	.25	.12	.02
☐ 17	Mickey Rivers	.25	.12	.02
☐ 21	Odell Jones	.15	.07	.01
☐ 24	Dave Schmidt	.25	.12	.02
☐ 25	Buddy Bell	.50	.25	.05
☐ 26	George Wright	.15	.07	.01
☐ 28	Frank Tanana	.25	.12	.02
☐ 29	John Butcher	.15	.07	.01
☐ 32	John Matlack	.25	.12	.02
☐ 40	Rick Honeycutt	.15	.07	.01
☐ 41	Dave Tobik	.15	.07	.01
☐ 44	Danny Darwin	.15	.07	.01
☐ 46	Jim Anderson	.15	.07	.01
☐ 48	Mike Smithson	.15	.07	.01
☐ 49	Charlie Hough	.35	.17	.03
☐ xx	Rangers Coaches:	.15	.07	.01

(unnumbered)
Wayne Terwilliger 42
Merv Rettenmund 22
Dick Such 52
Glenn Ezell 18
Rich Donnelly 37

1984 Rangers Jarvis Press

PETE O'BRIEN   1B

The cards in this 30-card set measure 2 1/2" by 3 1/2". The Jarvis Press of Dallas issued this full-color regional set of Texas Rangers. Cards are numbered on the front by the players uniform number. The cards were issued on an uncut sheet. Twenty-seven player cards, a manager card, a trainer card (unnumbered) and a coaches card (unnumbered) comprise this set. The backs are black and white and contain biographical information, statistics, and an additional photo of the player.

		MINT	EXC	G-VG
COMPLETE SET (30)		6.00	3.00	.60
COMMON PLAYER		.15	.07	.01
☐ 1	Bill Stein	.15	.07	.01
☐ 2	Alan Bannister	.15	.07	.01
☐ 3	Wayne Tolleson	.15	.07	.01
☐ 5	Billy Sample	.15	.07	.01
☐ 6	Bobby Jones	.15	.07	.01
☐ 7	Ned Yost	.15	.07	.01
☐ 9	Pete O'Brien	.60	.30	.06
☐ 11	Doug Rader MG	.35	.17	.03
☐ 13	Tommy Dunbar	.15	.07	.01
☐ 14	Jim Anderson	.15	.07	.01
☐ 15	Larry Parrish	.25	.12	.02
☐ 16	Mike Mason	.15	.07	.01
☐ 17	Mickey Rivers	.25	.12	.02
☐ 19	Curtis Wilkerson	.15	.07	.01
☐ 20	Jeff Kunkel	.35	.17	.03
☐ 21	Odell Jones	.15	.07	.01
☐ 24	Dave Schmidt	.25	.12	.02
☐ 25	Buddy Bell	.60	.30	.06
☐ 26	George Wright	.15	.07	.01
☐ 28	Frank Tanana	.25	.12	.02
☐ 30	Marv Foley	.15	.07	.01
☐ 31	Dave Stewart	.75	.35	.07
☐ 32	Gary Ward	.15	.07	.01
☐ 36	Dickie Noles	.15	.07	.01
☐ 43	Donnie Scott	.15	.07	.01
☐ 44	Danny Darwin	.15	.07	.01
☐ 49	Charlie Hough	.35	.17	.03
☐ 53	Joey McLaughlin	.15	.07	.01

		MINT	EXC	G-VG
☐ xx	Bill Ziegler (Trainer)	.15	.07	.01

(unnumbered)

☐ xx	Rangers Coaches:	.15	.07	.01

(unnumbered)
Merv Rettenmund 22
Rich Donnelly 37
Glenn Ezell 18
Dick Such 52
Wayne Terwilliger 42

1985 Rangers Performance

BUDDY BELL   IF

The cards in this 28-card set measure 2 3/8" by 3 1/2". Performance Printing sponsored this full-color regional set of Texas Rangers. Cards are numbered on the back by the players uniform number. The cards were also issued on an uncut sheet. Twenty-five player cards, a manager card, a trainer card (unnumbered) and a coaches card (unnumbered) comprise this set. The backs are black and white and contain biographical information, statistics, and an additional photo of the player.

		MINT	EXC	G-VG
COMPLETE SET (28)		6.00	3.00	.60
COMMON PLAYER		.15	.07	.01
☐ 0	Oddibe McDowell	.50	.25	.05
☐ 1	Bill Stein	.15	.07	.01
☐ 2	Bobby Valentine MG	.35	.17	.03
☐ 3	Wayne Tolleson	.15	.07	.01
☐ 4	Don Slaught	.15	.07	.01
☐ 5	Alan Bannister	.15	.07	.01
☐ 6	Bobby Jones	.15	.07	.01
☐ 7	Glenn Brummer	.15	.07	.01
☐ 8	Luis Pujols	.15	.07	.01
☐ 9	Pete O'Brien	.60	.30	.06
☐ 11	Toby Harrah	.25	.12	.02
☐ 13	Tommy Dunbar	.15	.07	.01
☐ 15	Larry Parrish	.25	.12	.02
☐ 16	Mike Mason	.15	.07	.01
☐ 19	Curtis Wilkerson	.15	.07	.01
☐ 24	Dave Schmidt	.25	.12	.02
☐ 25	Buddy Bell	.50	.25	.05
☐ 27	Greg Harris	.15	.07	.01
☐ 30	Dave Rozema	.15	.07	.01
☐ 32	Gary Ward	.15	.07	.01
☐ 36	Dickie Noles	.15	.07	.01
☐ 41	Chris Welsh	.15	.07	.01
☐ 44	Cliff Johnson	.15	.07	.01
☐ 46	Burt Hooton	.15	.07	.01
☐ 48	Dave Stewart	.75	.35	.07
☐ 49	Charlie Hough	.35	.17	.03
☐ xx	Trainers: Bill Ziegler	.15	.07	.01

Danny Wheat
(unnumbered)

☐ xx	Rangers Coaches:	.15	.07	.01

(unnumbered)
Art Howe 10
Rich Donnelly 37
Glenn Ezell 18
Tom House 35
Wayne Terwilliger 42

FAMILY FUN: Take along a family member with you to a sports show.

1986 Rangers Performance

Performance Printing of Dallas produced a 28-card set of Texas Rangers which were given out at the stadium on August 23rd. Cards measure 2 3/8" by 3 1/2" and are in full color. The cards are unnumbered except for uniform number which is given on the card back. Card backs feature black printing on white card stock with a small picture of the player's head in the upper left corner. The set seems to be more desirable than the previous Ranger sets due to the Rangers' 1986 success which was directly related to their outstanding rookie crop.

		MINT	EXC	G-VG
COMPLETE SET (28)		9.00	4.50	.90
COMMON PLAYER		.10	.05	.01
□ 0	Oddibe McDowell	.30	.15	.03
□ 1	Scott Fletcher	.20	.10	.02
□ 2	Bobby Valentine MG	.25	.12	.02
□ 3	Ruben Sierra	3.00	1.50	.30
□ 4	Don Slaught	.15	.07	.01
□ 9	Pete O'Brien	.50	.25	.05
□ 11	Toby Harrah	.20	.10	.02
□ 12	Geno Petralli	.10	.05	.01
□ 15	Larry Parrish	.15	.07	.01
□ 16	Mike Mason	.10	.05	.01
□ 17	Darrell Porter	.10	.05	.01
□ 18	Edwin Correa	.25	.12	.02
□ 19	Curtis Wilkerson	.10	.05	.01
□ 22	Steve Buechele	.20	.10	.02
□ 23	Jose Guzman	.25	.12	.02
□ 24	Ricky Wright	.10	.05	.01
□ 27	Greg Harris	.10	.05	.01
□ 28	Mitch Williams	.50	.25	.05
□ 29	Pete Incaviglia	1.00	.50	.10
□ 32	Gary Ward	.10	.05	.01
□ 34	Dale Mohorcic	.15	.07	.01
□ 40	Jeff Russell	.30	.15	.03
□ 44	Tom Paciorek	.10	.05	.01
□ 46	Mike Loynd	.20	.10	.02
□ 48	Bobby Witt	.40	.20	.04
□ 49	Charlie Hough	.30	.15	.03
□ xx	Coaching Staff: (unnumbered) Art Howe 10 Joe Ferguson 13 Tim Foli 14 Tom Robson 31 Tom House 35	.10	.05	.01
□ xx	Trainers: (unnumbered) Bill Zeigler Danny Wheat	.10	.05	.01

1954 Red Heart

The cards in this 33-card set measure 2 5/8" by 3 3/4". The 1954 Red Heart baseball series was marketed by Red Heart dog food, which, incidentally, was a subsidiary of Morrell Meats. The set consists of three series of eleven unnumbered cards each of

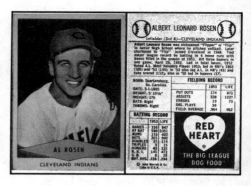

which could be ordered from the company via an offer (two can labels plus ten cents for each series) on the can label. Each series has a specific color background (red, green or blue) behind the color player photo. Cards with red backgrounds are considered scarcer and are marked with an asterisk in the checklist (which has been alphabetized and numbered for reference). The ACC designation is F156.

		NRMT	VG-E	GOOD
COMPLETE SET (33)		1800.00	900.00	200.00
COMMON PLAYER (1-33)		25.00	12.50	2.50
COMMON * (RED) PLAYER		35.00	17.50	3.50
□ 1	Richie Ashburn *	55.00	27.50	5.50
□ 2	Frank Baumholtz *	35.00	17.50	3.50
□ 3	Gus Bell	25.00	12.50	2.50
□ 4	Billy Cox	25.00	12.50	2.50
□ 5	Alvin Dark	30.00	15.00	3.00
□ 6	Carl Erskine *	45.00	22.50	4.50
□ 7	Ferris Fain	25.00	12.50	2.50
□ 8	Dee Fondy	25.00	12.50	2.50
□ 9	Nelson Fox	45.00	22.50	4.50
□ 10	Jim Gilliam	35.00	17.50	3.50
□ 11	Jim Hegan *	35.00	17.50	3.50
□ 12	George Kell	55.00	27.50	5.50
□ 13	Ralph Kiner *	75.00	37.50	7.50
□ 14	Ted Kluszewski *	55.00	27.50	5.50
□ 15	Harvey Kuenn	35.00	17.50	3.50
□ 16	Bob Lemon *	65.00	32.50	6.50
□ 17	Sherman Lollar	25.00	12.50	2.50
□ 18	Mickey Mantle	400.00	200.00	40.00
□ 19	Billy Martin	55.00	27.50	5.50
□ 20	Gil McDougald *	45.00	22.50	4.50
□ 21	Roy McMillan	25.00	12.50	2.50
□ 22	Minnie Minoso	35.00	17.50	3.50
□ 23	Stan Musial *	250.00	125.00	25.00
□ 24	Billy Pierce	30.00	15.00	3.00
□ 25	Al Rosen *	45.00	22.50	4.50
□ 26	Hank Sauer	25.00	12.50	2.50
□ 27	Red Schoendienst *	65.00	32.50	6.50
□ 28	Enos Slaughter	65.00	32.50	6.50
□ 29	Duke Snider	100.00	50.00	10.00
□ 30	Warren Spahn	55.00	27.50	5.50
□ 31	Sammy White	25.00	12.50	2.50
□ 32	Eddie Yost	25.00	12.50	2.50
□ 33	Gus Zernial	25.00	12.50	2.50

1952 Red Man

The cards in this 52-card set measure 3 1/2" by 4" (or 3 1/2" by 3 5/8" without the tab). This Red Man issue was the first nationally available tobacco issue since the T cards of the teens early in this century. This 52 card set contains 26 top players from each league. Cards that have the tab (coupon) attached are generally worth two and a half times the price of cards with the tab removed. Card numbers are located on the tabs. The prices listed below refer to cards without tabs.

	NRMT	VG-E	GOOD
COMPLETE SET (52)	650.00	300.00	60.00
COMMON PLAYER	6.00	3.00	.60

	NRMT	VG-E	GOOD
☐ AL1 Casey Stengel MG	20.00	10.00	2.00
☐ AL2 Roberto Avila	6.00	3.00	.60
☐ AL3 Yogi Berra	30.00	15.00	3.00
☐ AL4 Gil Coan	6.00	3.00	.60
☐ AL5 Dom DiMaggio	9.00	4.50	.90
☐ AL6 Larry Doby	7.50	3.75	.75
☐ AL7 Ferris Fain	6.00	3.00	.60
☐ AL8 Bob Feller	30.00	15.00	3.00
☐ AL9 Nelson Fox	12.00	6.00	1.20
☐ AL10 Johnny Groth	6.00	3.00	.60
☐ AL11 Jim Hegan	6.00	3.00	.60
☐ AL12 Eddie Joost	6.00	3.00	.60
☐ AL13 George Kell	16.00	8.00	1.60
☐ AL14 Gil McDougald	9.00	4.50	.90
☐ AL15 Minnie Minoso	9.00	4.50	.90
☐ AL16 Billy Pierce	7.50	3.75	.75
☐ AL17 Bob Porterfield	6.00	3.00	.60
☐ AL18 Eddie Robinson	6.00	3.00	.60
☐ AL19 Saul Rogovin	6.00	3.00	.60
☐ AL20 Bobby Shantz	7.50	3.75	.75
☐ AL21 Vern Stephens	6.00	3.00	.60
☐ AL22 Vic Wertz	6.00	3.00	.60
☐ AL23 Ted Williams	90.00	45.00	9.00
☐ AL24 Early Wynn	16.00	8.00	1.60
☐ AL25 Eddie Yost	6.00	3.00	.60
☐ AL26 Gus Zernial	6.00	3.00	.60
☐ NL1 Leo Durocher MG	16.00	8.00	1.60
☐ NL2 Richie Ashburn	13.50	6.00	1.20
☐ NL3 Ewell Blackwell	7.50	3.75	.75
☐ NL4 Cliff Chambers	6.00	3.00	.60
☐ NL5 Murray Dickson	6.00	3.00	.60
☐ NL6 Sid Gordon	6.00	3.00	.60
☐ NL7 Granny Hamner	6.00	3.00	.60
☐ NL8 Jim Hearn	6.00	3.00	.60
☐ NL9 Monte Irvin	13.50	6.00	1.20
☐ NL10 Larry Jansen	6.00	3.00	.60
☐ NL11 Willie Jones	6.00	3.00	.60
☐ NL12 Ralph Kiner	18.00	9.00	1.80
☐ NL13 Whitey Lockman	6.00	3.00	.60
☐ NL14 Sal Maglie	9.00	4.50	.90
☐ NL15 Willie Mays	75.00	37.50	7.50
☐ NL16 Stan Musial	60.00	30.00	6.00
☐ NL17 Pee Wee Reese	25.00	12.50	2.50
☐ NL18 Robin Roberts	18.00	9.00	1.80
☐ NL19 Al Schoendienst	16.00	8.00	1.60
☐ NL20 Enos Slaughter	18.00	9.00	1.80
☐ NL21 Duke Snider	45.00	22.50	4.50
☐ NL22 Warren Spahn	18.00	9.00	1.80
☐ NL23 Ed Stanky	7.50	3.75	.75
☐ NL24 Bobby Thomson	9.00	4.50	.90
☐ NL25 Earl Torgeson	6.00	3.00	.60
☐ NL26 Wes Westrum	6.00	3.00	.60

	NRMT	VG-E	GOOD
COMPLETE SET (52)	600.00	300.00	60.00
COMMON PLAYER	6.00	3.00	.60

	NRMT	VG-E	GOOD
☐ AL1 Casey Stengel MG	20.00	10.00	2.00
☐ AL2 Hank Bauer	9.00	4.50	.90
☐ AL3 Yogi Berra	30.00	15.00	3.00
☐ AL4 Walt Dropo	6.00	3.00	.60
☐ AL5 Nelson Fox	12.00	6.00	1.20
☐ AL6 Jackie Jensen	9.00	4.50	.90
☐ AL7 Eddie Joost	6.00	3.00	.60
☐ AL8 George Kell	16.00	8.00	1.60
☐ AL9 Dale Mitchell	6.00	3.00	.60
☐ AL10 Phil Rizzuto	16.00	8.00	1.60
☐ AL11 Eddie Robinson	6.00	3.00	.60
☐ AL12 Gene Woodling	7.50	3.75	.75
☐ AL13 Gus Zernial	6.00	3.00	.60
☐ AL14 Early Wynn	16.00	8.00	1.60
☐ AL15 Joe Dobson	6.00	3.00	.60
☐ AL16 Billy Pierce	7.50	3.75	.75
☐ AL17 Bob Lemon	16.00	8.00	1.60
☐ AL18 Johnny Mize	18.00	9.00	1.80
☐ AL19 Bob Porterfield	6.00	3.00	.60
☐ AL20 Bobby Shantz	7.50	3.75	.75
☐ AL21 Mickey Vernon	7.50	3.75	.75
☐ AL22 Dom DiMaggio	9.00	4.50	.90
☐ AL23 Gil McDougald	9.00	4.50	.90
☐ AL24 Al Rosen	9.00	4.50	.90
☐ AL25 Mel Parnell	7.50	3.75	.75
☐ AL26 Bobby Avila	6.00	3.00	.60
☐ NL1 Charlie Dressen MG	7.50	3.75	.75
☐ NL2 Bobby Adams	6.00	3.00	.60
☐ NL3 Richie Ashburn	13.50	6.00	1.20
☐ NL4 Joe Black	7.50	3.75	.75
☐ NL5 Roy Campanella	45.00	22.50	4.50
☐ NL6 Ted Kluszewski	9.00	4.50	.90
☐ NL7 Whitey Lockman	6.00	3.00	.60
☐ NL8 Sal Maglie	9.00	4.50	.90
☐ NL9 Andy Pafko	6.00	3.00	.60
☐ NL10 Pee Wee Reese	25.00	12.50	2.50
☐ NL11 Robin Roberts	18.00	9.00	1.80
☐ NL12 Al Schoendienst	16.00	8.00	1.60
☐ NL13 Enos Slaughter	18.00	9.00	1.80
☐ NL14 Duke Snider	45.00	22.50	4.50
☐ NL15 Ralph Kiner	18.00	9.00	1.80
☐ NL16 Hank Sauer	6.00	3.00	.60
☐ NL17 Del Ennis	6.00	3.00	.60
☐ NL18 Granny Hamner	6.00	3.00	.60
☐ NL19 Warren Spahn	18.00	9.00	1.80
☐ NL20 Wes Westrum	6.00	3.00	.60
☐ NL21 Hoyt Wilhelm	16.00	8.00	1.60
☐ NL22 Murray Dickson	6.00	3.00	.60
☐ NL23 Warren Hacker	6.00	3.00	.60
☐ NL24 Gerry Staley	6.00	3.00	.60
☐ NL25 Bobby Thomson	9.00	4.50	.90
☐ NL26 Stan Musial	60.00	30.00	6.00

1953 Red Man

The cards in this 52-card set measure 3 1/2" by 4"
(or 3 1/2" by 3 5/8" without the tab). The 1953 Red
Man set contains 26 National League stars and 26
American League stars. Card numbers are located
both on the write-up of the player and on the tab.
Cards that have the tab (coupon) attached are
generally worth two and a half times the price of
cards with the tab removed. The prices listed below
refer to cards without tabs.

1954 Red Man

The cards in this 50-card set measure 3 1/2" by 4"
(or 3 1/2" by 3 5/8" without the tab). The 1954 Red
Man set witnessed a reduction to 25 players from
each league. George Kell, Sam Mele, and Dave
Philley are known to exist with two different teams.
Card number 19 of the National League exists as
Enos Slaughter and as Gus Bell. Card numbers are
on the write-ups of the players. Cards that have the

tab (coupon) attached are generally worth two and a half times the price of cards with the tab removed. The prices listed below refer to cards without tabs. The complete set price below refers to all 54 cards including the four variations.

	NRMT	VG-E	GOOD
COMPLETE SET (54)	750.00	300.00	60.00
COMMON PLAYERS	6.00	3.00	.60
☐ AL1 Bobby Avila	6.00	3.00	.60
☐ AL2 Jim Busby	6.00	3.00	.60
☐ AL3 Nelson Fox	12.00	6.00	1.20
☐ AL4A George Kell	20.00	10.00	2.00
(Boston)			
☐ AL4B George Kell	40.00	20.00	4.00
(Chicago)			
☐ AL5 Sherman Lollar	6.00	3.00	.60
☐ AL6A Sam Mele	10.00	5.00	1.00
(Baltimore)			
☐ AL6B Sam Mele	30.00	15.00	3.00
(Chicago)			
☐ AL7 Minnie Minoso	9.00	4.50	.90
☐ AL8 Mel Parnell	7.50	3.75	.75
☐ AL9A Dave Philley	10.00	5.00	1.00
(Cleveland)			
☐ AL9B Dave Philley	30.00	15.00	3.00
(Philadelphia)			
☐ AL10 Billy Pierce	7.50	3.75	.75
☐ AL11 Jim Piersall	9.00	4.50	.90
☐ AL12 Al Rosen	9.00	4.50	.90
☐ AL13 Mickey Vernon	7.50	3.75	.75
☐ AL14 Sammy White	6.00	3.00	.60
☐ AL15 Gene Woodling	7.50	3.75	.75
☐ AL16 Whitey Ford	25.00	12.50	2.50
☐ AL17 Phil Rizzuto	16.00	8.00	1.60
☐ AL18 Bob Porterfield	6.00	3.00	.60
☐ AL19 Chico Carrasquel	6.00	3.00	.60
☐ AL20 Yogi Berra	30.00	15.00	3.00
☐ AL21 Bob Lemon	16.00	8.00	1.60
☐ AL22 Ferris Fain	6.00	3.00	.60
☐ AL23 Hank Bauer	9.00	4.50	.90
☐ AL24 Jim Delsing	6.00	3.00	.60
☐ AL25 Gil McDougald	9.00	4.50	.90
☐ NL1 Richie Ashburn	13.50	6.00	1.20
☐ NL2 Billy Cox	6.00	3.00	.60
☐ NL3 Del Crandall	6.00	3.00	.60
☐ NL4 Carl Erskine	7.50	3.75	.75
☐ NL5 Monte Irvin	13.50	6.00	1.20
☐ NL6 Ted Kluszewski	9.00	4.50	.90
☐ NL7 Don Mueller	6.00	3.00	.60
☐ NL8 Andy Pafko	6.00	3.00	.60
☐ NL9 Del Rice	6.00	3.00	.60
☐ NL10 Al Schoendienst	16.00	8.00	1.60
☐ NL11 Warren Spahn	18.00	9.00	1.80
☐ NL12 Curt Simmons	7.50	3.75	.75
☐ NL13 Roy Campanella	45.00	22.50	4.50
☐ NL14 Jim Gilliam	9.00	4.50	.90
☐ NL15 Pee Wee Reese	25.00	12.50	2.50
☐ NL16 Duke Snider	45.00	22.50	4.50
☐ NL17 Rip Repulski	6.00	3.00	.60
☐ NL18 Robin Roberts	18.00	9.00	1.80
☐ NL19A Enos Slaughter	50.00	25.00	5.00
☐ NL19B Gus Bell	30.00	15.00	3.00
☐ NL20 Johnny Logan	6.00	3.00	.60
☐ NL21 John Antonelli	7.50	3.75	.75
☐ NL22 Gil Hodges	20.00	10.00	2.00
☐ NL23 Eddie Mathews	18.00	9.00	1.80
☐ NL24 Lew Burdette	7.50	3.75	.75
☐ NL25 Willie Mays	75.00	37.50	7.50

1955 Red Man

The cards in this 50-card set measure 3 1/2" by 4" (or 3 1/2" by 3 5/8" without the tab). The 1955 Red Man set contains 25 players from each league. Card numbers are on the write-ups of the players. Cards that have the tab (coupon) attached are generally worth two and a half times the price of cards with the tab removed. The prices listed below refer to cards without tabs.

	NRMT	VG-E	GOOD
COMPLETE SET (50)	550.00	250.00	60.00
COMMON PLAYER	6.00	3.00	.60
☐ AL1 Ray Boone	6.00	3.00	.60
☐ AL2 Jim Busby	6.00	3.00	.60
☐ AL3 Whitey Ford	25.00	12.50	2.50
☐ AL4 Nelson Fox	12.00	6.00	1.20
☐ AL5 Bob Grim	6.00	3.00	.60
☐ AL6 Jack Harshman	6.00	3.00	.60
☐ AL7 Jim Hegan	6.00	3.00	.60
☐ AL8 Bob Lemon	16.00	8.00	1.60
☐ AL9 Irv Noren	6.00	3.00	.60
☐ AL10 Bob Porterfield	6.00	3.00	.60
☐ AL11 Al Rosen	9.00	4.50	.90
☐ AL12 Mickey Vernon	7.50	3.75	.75
☐ AL13 Vic Wertz	6.00	3.00	.60
☐ AL14 Early Wynn	16.00	8.00	1.60
☐ AL15 Bobby Avila	6.00	3.00	.60
☐ AL16 Yogi Berra	30.00	15.00	3.00
☐ AL17 Joe Coleman	6.00	3.00	.60
☐ AL18 Larry Doby	7.50	3.75	.75
☐ AL19 Jackie Jensen	7.50	3.75	.75
☐ AL20 Pete Runnels	6.00	3.00	.60
☐ AL21 Jim Piersall	9.00	4.50	.90
☐ AL22 Hank Bauer	9.00	4.50	.90
☐ AL23 Chico Carrasquel	6.00	3.00	.60
☐ AL24 Minnie Minoso	9.00	4.50	.90
☐ AL25 Sandy Consuegra	6.00	3.00	.60
☐ NL1 Richie Ashburn	13.50	6.00	1.20
☐ NL2 Del Crandall	6.00	3.00	.60
☐ NL3 Gil Hodges	20.00	10.00	2.00
☐ NL4 Brooks Lawrence	6.00	3.00	.60
☐ NL5 Johnny Logan	6.00	3.00	.60
☐ NL6 Sal Maglie	6.00	3.00	.60
☐ NL7 Willie Mays	75.00	37.50	7.50
☐ NL8 Don Mueller	6.00	3.00	.60
☐ NL9 Bill Sarni	6.00	3.00	.60
☐ NL10 Warren Spahn	18.00	9.00	1.80
☐ NL11 Hank Thompson	6.00	3.00	.60
☐ NL12 Hoyt Wilhelm	16.00	8.00	1.60
☐ NL13 John Antonelli	7.50	3.75	.75
☐ NL14 Carl Erskine	7.50	3.75	.75
☐ NL15 Granny Hamner	6.00	3.00	.60
☐ NL16 Ted Kluszewski	9.00	4.50	.90
☐ NL17 Pee Wee Reese	25.00	12.50	2.50
☐ NL18 Al Schoendienst	16.00	8.00	1.60
☐ NL19 Duke Snider	45.00	22.50	4.50
☐ NL20 Frank Thomas	6.00	3.00	.60
☐ NL21 Ray Jablonski	6.00	3.00	.60
☐ NL22 Dusty Rhodes	6.00	3.00	.60
☐ NL23 Gus Bell	6.00	3.00	.60
☐ NL24 Curt Simmons	6.00	3.00	.60
☐ NL25 Marv Grissom	6.00	3.00	.60

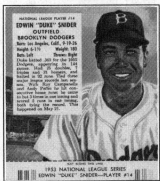

1955 Rodeo Meats

Hector Lopez

The cards in this 47-card set measure 2 1/2" by 3 1/2". The 1955 Rodeo Meats set contains unnumbered, color cards of the first Kansas City A's team. There are many background color variations noted in the checklist, and the card reverses carry a scrapbook offer. The Grimes and Kryhoski cards listed in the scrapbook album were apparently never issued. The ACC catalog number is F152-1. The cards have been arranged in alphabetical order and assigned numbers for reference.

		NRMT	VG-E	GOOD
COMPLETE SET (47)		4400.00	2200.00	500.00
COMMON PLAYER (1-47)		75.00	37.50	7.50
□	1 Joe Astroth	75.00	37.50	7.50
□	2 Harold Bevan	100.00	50.00	10.00
□	3 Charles Bishop	100.00	50.00	10.00
□	4 Don Bollweg	100.00	50.00	10.00
□	5 Lou Boudreau	225.00	110.00	22.00
□	6 Cloyd Boyer (salmon)	75.00	37.50	7.50
□	7 Cloyd Boyer (light blue)	100.00	50.00	10.00
□	8 Ed Burtschy	150.00	75.00	15.00
□	9 Art Ceccarelli	100.00	50.00	10.00
□	10 Joe DeMaestri (yellow)	75.00	37.50	7.50
□	11 Joe DeMaestri (green)	75.00	37.50	7.50
□	12 Art Ditmar	75.00	37.50	7.50
□	13 John Dixon	100.00	50.00	10.00
□	14 Jim Finigan	75.00	37.50	7.50
□	15 Marion Fricano	100.00	50.00	10.00
□	16 Tom Gorman	75.00	37.50	7.50
□	17 John Gray	100.00	50.00	10.00
□	18 Ray Herbert	75.00	37.50	7.50
□	19 Forest Jacobs	150.00	75.00	15.00
□	20 Alex Kellner	75.00	37.50	7.50
□	21 Harry Kraft	75.00	37.50	7.50
□	22 Jack Littrell	75.00	37.50	7.50
□	23 Hector Lopez	75.00	37.50	7.50
□	24 Oscar Melillo	75.00	37.50	7.50
□	25 Arnold Portocarrero (purple)	100.00	50.00	10.00
□	26 Arnold Portocarrero (gray)	75.00	37.50	7.50
□	27 Vic Power (yellow)	75.00	37.50	7.50
□	28 Vic Power (pink)	100.00	50.00	10.00
□	29 Vic Raschi	100.00	50.00	10.00
□	30 Bill Renna (lavender)	75.00	37.50	7.50
□	31 Bill Renna (dark pink)	100.00	50.00	10.00
□	32 Al Robertson	100.00	50.00	10.00
□	33 Johnny Sain	150.00	75.00	15.00
□	35 Bobby Schantz ERR (misspelling)	200.00	100.00	20.00
□	34 Bobby Shantz COR	150.00	75.00	15.00
□	36 Wilmer Shantz (orange)	75.00	37.50	7.50
□	37 Wilmer Shantz (lavender)	75.00	37.50	7.50
□	38 Harry Simpson	75.00	37.50	7.50
□	39 Enos Slaughter	250.00	125.00	25.00
□	40 Lou Sleator	75.00	37.50	7.50
□	41 George Susce	100.00	50.00	10.00
□	42 Bob Trice	100.00	50.00	10.00
□	43 Elmer Valo (yellow)	100.00	50.00	10.00
□	44 Elmer Valo (green sky)	75.00	37.50	7.50
□	45 Bill Wilson (yellow)	100.00	50.00	10.00
□	46 Bill Wilson (lavender sky)	75.00	37.50	7.50
□	47 Gus Zernial	75.00	37.50	7.50

1956 Rodeo Meats

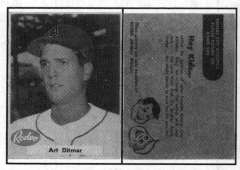

Art Ditmar

The cards in this 12-card set measure 2 1/2" by 3 1/2". The unnumbered, color cards of the 1956 Rodeo baseball series are easily distinguished from their 1955 counterparts by the absence of the scrapbook offer on the reverse. They were available only in packages of Rodeo All- Meat Wieners. The ACC designation is F152-2, and the cards have been assigned numbers in alphabetical order in the checklist below.

		NRMT	VG-E	GOOD
COMPLETE SET (12)		1200.00	550.00	125.00
COMMON PLAYER (1-12)		75.00	37.50	7.50
□	1 Joe Astroth	75.00	37.50	7.50
□	2 Lou Boudreau	225.00	110.00	22.00
□	3 Joe DeMaestri	75.00	37.50	7.50
□	4 Art Ditmar	75.00	37.50	7.50
□	5 Jim Finigan	75.00	37.50	7.50
□	6 Hector Lopez	75.00	37.50	7.50
□	7 Vic Power	75.00	37.50	7.50
□	8 Bobby Shantz	125.00	60.00	12.50
□	9 Harry Simpson	75.00	37.50	7.50
□	10 Enos Slaughter	250.00	125.00	25.00
□	11 Elmer Valo	75.00	37.50	7.50
□	12 Gus Zernial	75.00	37.50	7.50

1958 S.F. Call-Bulletin

The cards in this 25-card set measure 2" by 4". The 1958 San Francisco Call-Bulletin set of unnumbered cards features black print on orange paper. These cards were given away as inserts in the San Francisco Call-Bulletin newspaper. The backs of the cards list the Giants home schedule and a radio station ad. The cards are entitled "Giant Payoff" and feature San Francisco Giant players only. The bottom part of the card (tab) could be detached as a ticket stub; hence, cards with the tab intact are worth approximately double the prices listed below. The ACC designation is M126. The Tom Bowers card was issued in very short supply; also Bressoud, Jablonski, and Kirkland are somewhat tougher to find than the others. All of

these tougher cards are asterisked in the checklist below.

		NRMT	VG-E	GOOD
	COMPLETE SET (25)	650.00	325.00	65.00
	COMMON PLAYER (1-25)	6.00	3.00	.60
☐ 1	John Antonelli	7.50	3.75	.75
☐ 2	Curt Barclay	6.00	3.00	.60
☐ 3	Tom Bowers *	300.00	150.00	30.00
☐ 4	Ed Bressoud *	30.00	15.00	3.00
☐ 5	Orlando Cepeda	35.00	17.50	3.50
☐ 6	Ray Crone	6.00	3.00	.60
☐ 7	Jim Davenport	7.50	3.75	.75
☐ 8	Paul Giel	6.00	3.00	.60
☐ 9	Ruben Gomez	6.00	3.00	.60
☐ 10	Marv Grissom	6.00	3.00	.60
☐ 11	Ray Jablonski *	12.00	6.00	1.20
☐ 12	Willie Kirkland *	40.00	20.00	4.00
☐ 13	Whitey Lockman	6.00	3.00	.60
☐ 14	Willie Mays	175.00	85.00	18.00
☐ 15	Mike McCormick	7.50	3.75	.75
☐ 16	Stu Miller	7.50	3.75	.75
☐ 17	Ray Monzant	6.00	3.00	.60
☐ 18	Danny O'Connell	6.00	3.00	.60
☐ 19	Bill Rigney	7.50	3.75	.75
☐ 20	Hank Sauer	7.50	3.75	.75
☐ 21	Bob Schmidt	6.00	3.00	.60
☐ 22	Daryl Spencer	6.00	3.00	.60
☐ 23	Valmy Thomas	6.00	3.00	.60
☐ 24	Bobby Thomson	9.00	4.50	.90
☐ 25	Al Worthington	6.00	3.00	.60

1987-88 Score Test Samples

Late in 1987 near the end of the season, Score prepared some samples to show prospective dealers and buyers of the new Score cards what they would look like. These sample cards are distinguished by

the fact that there is a row of zeroes for the 1987 season statistics since the season was not over when these sample cards were being printed. The cards are standard size, 2 1/2" by 3 1/2" and are virtually indistinguishable from the regular 1988 Score cards of the same players except for border color variations in a few instances.

		MINT	EXC	G-VG
	COMPLETE SET (6)	10.00	5.00	1.00
	COMMON PLAYER	1.50	.75	.15
☐ 30	Mark Langston	3.00	1.50	.30
☐ 48	Tony Pena	1.50	.75	.15
☐ 71	Keith Moreland	1.50	.75	.15
☐ 72	Barry Larkin	3.00	1.50	.30
☐ 121	Dennis Boyd	1.50	.75	.15
☐ 145	Denny Walling	1.50	.75	.15

1988 Score

This 660-card set was distributed by Major League Marketing. Cards measure 2 1/2" by 3 1/2" and feature six distinctive border colors on the front. Highlights (652- 660) and Rookie Prospects (623-647) are included in the set. Reggie Jackson's career is honored with a 5-card subset on cards 500-504. The set is distinguished by the fact that each card back shows a full-color picture of the player. The company also produced a very limited "glossy" set which is valued at eight times the value of the regular (non-glossy) set. Although exact production quantities of this glossy set are not known, it is generally accepted that the number of Score glossy sets produced in 1988 was much smaller (estimated only 10% to 15% as many) than the number of Topps Tiffany or Fleer Tin sets.is

		MINT	EXC	G-VG
	COMPLETE SET (660)	25.00	12.50	2.50
	COMMON PLAYER (1-660)	.03	.01	.00
☐ 1	Don Mattingly	1.50	.40	.08
☐ 2	Wade Boggs	.75	.35	.07
☐ 3	Tim Raines	.15	.07	.01
☐ 4	Andre Dawson	.15	.07	.01
☐ 5	Mark McGwire	1.25	.60	.12
☐ 6	Kevin Seitzer	.65	.30	.06
☐ 7	Wally Joyner	.35	.17	.03
☐ 8	Jesse Barfield	.10	.05	.01
☐ 9	Pedro Guerrero	.12	.06	.01
☐ 10	Eric Davis	.60	.30	.06
☐ 11	George Brett	.25	.12	.02
☐ 12	Ozzie Smith	.15	.07	.01
☐ 13	Rickey Henderson	.25	.12	.02
☐ 14	Jim Rice	.12	.06	.01
☐ 15	Matt Nokes	.35	.17	.03
☐ 16	Mike Schmidt	.25	.12	.02
☐ 17	Dave Parker	.10	.05	.01
☐ 18	Eddie Murray	.15	.07	.01
☐ 19	Andres Galarraga	.15	.07	.01
☐ 20	Tony Fernandez	.10	.05	.01
☐ 21	Kevin McReynolds	.12	.06	.01

□	#	Name			
□	22	B.J. Surhoff	.10	.05	.01
□	23	Pat Tabler	.06	.03	.00
□	24	Kirby Puckett	.40	.20	.04
□	25	Benny Santiago	.40	.20	.04
□	26	Ryne Sandberg	.20	.10	.02
□	27	Kelly Downs	.08	.04	.01
		(Will Clark in back-ground, out of focus)			
□	28	Jose Cruz	.06	.03	.00
□	29	Pete O'Brien	.06	.03	.00
□	30	Mark Langston	.12	.06	.01
□	31	Lee Smith	.06	.03	.00
□	32	Juan Samuel	.08	.04	.01
□	33	Kevin Bass	.06	.03	.00
□	34	R.J. Reynolds	.03	.01	.00
□	35	Steve Sax	.12	.06	.01
□	36	John Kruk	.08	.04	.01
□	37	Alan Trammell	.12	.06	.01
□	38	Chris Bosio	.06	.03	.00
□	39	Brook Jacoby	.06	.03	.00
□	40	Willie McGee	.08	.04	.01
□	41	Dave Magadan	.12	.06	.01
□	42	Fred Lynn	.10	.05	.01
□	43	Kent Hrbek	.12	.06	.01
□	44	Brian Downing	.03	.01	.00
□	45	Jose Canseco	1.25	.60	.12
□	46	Jim Presley	.06	.03	.00
□	47	Mike Stanley	.06	.03	.00
□	48	Tony Pena	.06	.03	.00
□	49	David Cone	.75	.35	.07
□	50	Rick Sutcliffe	.08	.04	.01
□	51	Doug Drabek	.06	.03	.00
□	52	Bill Doran	.06	.03	.00
□	53	Mike Scioscia	.03	.01	.00
□	54	Candy Maldonado	.06	.03	.00
□	55	Dave Winfield	.18	.09	.01
□	56	Lou Whitaker	.10	.05	.01
□	57	Tom Henke	.06	.03	.00
□	58	Ken Gerhart	.06	.03	.00
□	59	Glenn Braggs	.08	.04	.01
□	60	Julio Franco	.10	.05	.01
□	61	Charlie Leibrandt	.03	.01	.00
□	62	Gary Gaetti	.10	.05	.01
□	63	Bob Boone	.08	.04	.01
□	64	Luis Polonia	.20	.10	.02
□	65	Dwight Evans	.10	.05	.01
□	66	Phil Bradley	.08	.04	.01
□	67	Mike Boddicker	.03	.01	.00
□	68	Vince Coleman	.15	.07	.01
□	69	Howard Johnson	.15	.07	.01
□	70	Tim Wallach	.08	.04	.01
□	71	Keith Moreland	.03	.01	.00
□	72	Barry Larkin	.25	.12	.02
□	73	Alan Ashby	.03	.01	.00
□	74	Rick Rhoden	.03	.01	.00
□	75	Darrell Evans	.06	.03	.00
□	76	Dave Stieb	.08	.04	.01
□	77	Dan Plesac	.06	.03	.00
□	78	Will Clark	1.50	.75	.15
□	79	Frank White	.06	.03	.00
□	80	Joe Carter	.15	.07	.01
□	81	Mike Witt	.06	.03	.00
□	82	Terry Steinbach	.20	.10	.02
□	83	Alvin Davis	.10	.05	.01
□	84	Tommy Herr	.08	.04	.01
		(Will Clark shown sliding into second)			
□	85	Vance Law	.03	.01	.00
□	86	Kal Daniels	.12	.06	.01
□	87	Rick Honeycutt UER	.03	.01	.00
		(wrong years for stats on back)			
□	88	Alfredo Griffin	.06	.03	.00
□	89	Bret Saberhagen	.20	.10	.02
□	90	Bert Blyleven	.10	.05	.01
□	91	Jeff Reardon	.08	.04	.01
□	92	Cory Snyder	.12	.06	.01
□	93A	Greg Walker ERR	3.00	1.00	.30
		(93 of 66)			
□	93B	Greg Walker COR	.10	.04	.01
		(93 of 660)			
□	94	Joe Magrane	.50	.25	.05
□	95	Rob Deer	.08	.04	.01
□	96	Ray Knight	.06	.03	.00
□	97	Casey Candaele	.03	.01	.00
□	98	John Cerutti	.03	.01	.00
□	99	Buddy Bell	.06	.03	.00
□	100	Jack Clark	.12	.06	.01
□	101	Eric Bell	.03	.01	.00
□	102	Willie Wilson	.06	.03	.00
□	103	Dave Schmidt	.03	.01	.00
□	104	Dennis Eckersley	.10	.05	.01
□	105	Don Sutton	.12	.06	.01
□	106	Danny Tartabull	.18	.09	.01
□	107	Fred McGriff	1.00	.50	.10

□	#	Name			
□	108	Les Straker	.08	.04	.01
□	109	Lloyd Moseby	.06	.03	.00
□	110	Roger Clemens	.50	.25	.05
□	111	Glenn Hubbard	.03	.01	.00
□	112	Ken Williams	.18	.09	.01
□	113	Ruben Sierra	.35	.17	.03
□	114	Stan Jefferson	.12	.06	.01
□	115	Milt Thompson	.03	.01	.00
□	116	Bobby Bonilla	.15	.07	.01
□	117	Wayne Tolleson	.03	.01	.00
□	118	Matt Williams	.75	.35	.07
□	119	Chet Lemon	.03	.01	.00
□	120	Dale Sveum	.03	.01	.00
□	121	Dennis Boyd	.06	.03	.00
□	122	Brett Butler	.06	.03	.00
□	123	Terry Kennedy	.03	.01	.00
□	124	Jack Howell	.03	.01	.00
□	125	Curt Young	.03	.01	.00
□	126A	Dave Valle ERR	.25	.12	.02
		(misspelled Dale on card front)			
□	126B	Dave Valle COR	.10	.05	.01
□	127	Curt Wilkerson	.03	.01	.00
□	128	Tim Teufel	.03	.01	.00
□	129	Ozzie Virgil	.03	.01	.00
□	130	Brian Fisher	.03	.01	.00
□	131	Lance Parrish	.08	.04	.01
□	132	Tom Browning	.08	.04	.01
□	133A	Larry Andersen ERR	.20	.10	.02
		(misspelled Anderson on card front)			
□	133B	Larry Andersen COR	.06	.03	.00
□	134A	Bob Brenly ERR	.20	.10	.02
		(misspelled Brenley on card front)			
□	134B	Bob Brenly COR	.06	.03	.00
□	135	Mike Marshall	.08	.04	.01
□	136	Gerald Perry	.06	.03	.00
□	137	Bobby Meacham	.03	.01	.00
□	138	Larry Herndon	.03	.01	.00
□	139	Fred Manrique	.10	.05	.01
□	140	Charlie Hough	.03	.01	.00
□	141	Ron Darling	.08	.04	.01
□	142	Herm Winningham	.03	.01	.00
□	143	Mike Diaz	.03	.01	.00
□	144	Mike Jackson	.12	.06	.01
□	145	Denny Walling	.03	.01	.00
□	146	Robby Thompson	.03	.01	.00
□	147	Franklin Stubbs	.03	.01	.00
□	148	Albert Hall	.03	.01	.00
□	149	Bobby Witt	.06	.03	.00
□	150	Lance McCullers	.06	.03	.00
□	151	Scott Bradley	.03	.01	.00
□	152	Mark McLemore	.03	.01	.00
□	153	Tim Laudner	.03	.01	.00
□	154	Greg Swindell	.12	.06	.01
□	155	Marty Barrett	.06	.03	.00
□	156	Mike Heath	.03	.01	.00
□	157	Gary Ward	.03	.01	.00
□	158A	Lee Mazzilli ERR	.20	.10	.02
		(misspelled Mazilli on card front)			
□	158B	Lee Mazzilli COR	.06	.03	.00
□	159	Tom Foley	.03	.01	.00
□	160	Robin Yount	.25	.12	.02
□	161	Steve Bedrosian	.08	.04	.01
□	162	Bob Walk	.03	.01	.00
□	163	Nick Esasky	.08	.04	.01
□	164	Ken Caminiti	.20	.10	.02
□	165	Jose Uribe	.03	.01	.00
□	166	Dave Anderson	.03	.01	.00
□	167	Ed Whitson	.03	.01	.00
□	168	Ernie Whitt	.03	.01	.00
□	169	Cecil Cooper	.08	.04	.01
□	170	Mike Pagliarulo	.06	.03	.00
□	171	Pat Sheridan	.03	.01	.00
□	172	Chris Bando	.03	.01	.00
□	173	Lee Lacy	.03	.01	.00
□	174	Steve Lombardozzi	.03	.01	.00
□	175	Mike Greenwell	1.25	.60	.12
□	176	Greg Minton	.03	.01	.00
□	177	Moose Haas	.03	.01	.00
□	178	Mike Kingery	.03	.01	.00
□	179	Greg Harris	.03	.01	.00
□	180	Bo Jackson	1.25	.60	.12
□	181	Carmelo Martinez	.03	.01	.00
□	182	Alex Trevino	.03	.01	.00
□	183	Ron Oester	.03	.01	.00
□	184	Danny Darwin	.03	.01	.00
□	185	Mike Krukow	.03	.01	.00
□	186	Rafael Palmeiro	.50	.25	.05
□	187	Tim Burke	.03	.01	.00
□	188	Roger McDowell	.06	.03	.00
□	189	Garry Templeton	.06	.03	.00
□	190	Terry Pendleton	.03	.01	.00

☐ 191	Larry Parrish	.03	.01	.00	☐ 281	Terry McGriff	.08	.04	.01
☐ 192	Rey Quinones	.03	.01	.00	☐ 282	Terry Puhl	.03	.01	.00
☐ 193	Joaquin Andujar	.06	.03	.00	☐ 283	Mark Wasinger	.15	.07	.01
☐ 194	Tom Brunansky	.10	.05	.01	☐ 284	Luis Salazar	.03	.01	.00
☐ 195	Donnie Moore	.03	.01	.00	☐ 285	Ted Simmons	.08	.04	.01
☐ 196	Dan Pasqua	.03	.01	.00	☐ 286	John Shelby	.03	.01	.00
☐ 197	Jim Gantner	.03	.01	.00	☐ 287	John Smiley	.25	.12	.02
☐ 198	Mark Eichhorn	.03	.01	.00	☐ 288	Curt Ford	.03	.01	.00
☐ 199	John Grubb	.03	.01	.00	☐ 289	Steve Crawford	.03	.01	.00
☐ 200	Bill Ripken	.15	.07	.01	☐ 290	Dan Quisenberry	.08	.04	.01
☐ 201	Sam Horn	.15	.07	.01	☐ 291	Alan Wiggins	.03	.01	.00
☐ 202	Todd Worrell	.10	.05	.01	☐ 292	Randy Bush	.03	.01	.00
☐ 203	Terry Leach	.06	.03	.00	☐ 293	John Candelaria	.06	.03	.00
☐ 204	Garth Iorg	.03	.01	.00	☐ 294	Tony Phillips	.03	.01	.00
☐ 205	Brian Dayett	.03	.01	.00	☐ 295	Mike Morgan	.06	.03	.00
☐ 206	Bo Diaz	.03	.01	.00	☐ 296	Bill Wegman	.03	.01	.00
☐ 207	Craig Reynolds	.03	.01	.00	☐ 297A	Terry Francona ERR	.20	.10	.02
☐ 208	Brian Holton	.08	.04	.01		(misspelled Franciona			
☐ 209	Marvell Wynne UER	.06	.03	.00		on card front)			
	(misspelled Marvelle				☐ 297B	Terry Francona COR	.06	.03	.00
	on card front)				☐ 298	Mickey Hatcher	.03	.01	.00
☐ 210	Dave Concepcion	.06	.03	.00	☐ 299	Andres Thomas	.03	.01	.00
☐ 211	Mike Davis	.03	.01	.00	☐ 300	Bob Stanley	.03	.01	.00
☐ 212	Devon White	.12	.06	.01	☐ 301	Al Pedrique	.08	.04	.01
☐ 213	Mickey Brantley	.06	.03	.00	☐ 302	Jim Lindeman	.06	.03	.00
☐ 214	Greg Gagne	.03	.01	.00	☐ 303	Wally Backman	.03	.01	.00
☐ 215	Oddibe McDowell	.06	.03	.00	☐ 304	Paul O'Neill	.10	.05	.01
☐ 216	Jimmy Key	.06	.03	.00	☐ 305	Hubie Brooks	.08	.04	.01
☐ 217	Dave Bergman	.03	.01	.00	☐ 306	Steve Buechele	.03	.01	.00
☐ 218	Calvin Schiraldi	.03	.01	.00	☐ 307	Bobby Thigpen	.06	.03	.00
☐ 219	Larry Sheets	.06	.03	.00	☐ 308	George Hendrick	.03	.01	.00
☐ 220	Mike Easler	.03	.01	.00	☐ 309	John Moses	.03	.01	.00
☐ 221	Kurt Stillwell	.03	.01	.00	☐ 310	Ron Guidry	.08	.04	.01
☐ 222	Chuck Jackson	.08	.04	.01	☐ 311	Bill Schroeder	.03	.01	.00
☐ 223	Dave Martinez	.06	.03	.00	☐ 312	Jose Nunez	.12	.06	.01
☐ 224	Tim Leary	.08	.04	.01	☐ 313	Bud Black	.03	.01	.00
☐ 225	Steve Garvey	.20	.10	.02	☐ 314	Joe Sambito	.03	.01	.00
☐ 226	Greg Mathews	.03	.01	.00	☐ 315	Scott McGregor	.03	.01	.00
☐ 227	Doug Sisk	.03	.01	.00	☐ 316	Rafael Santana	.03	.01	.00
☐ 228	Dave Henderson	.06	.03	.00	☐ 317	Frank Williams	.03	.01	.00
☐ 229	Jimmy Dwyer	.03	.01	.00	☐ 318	Mike Fitzgerald	.03	.01	.00
☐ 230	Larry Owen	.03	.01	.00	☐ 319	Rick Mahler	.03	.01	.00
☐ 231	Andre Thornton	.03	.01	.00	☐ 320	Jim Gott	.03	.01	.00
☐ 232	Mark Salas	.03	.01	.00	☐ 321	Mariano Duncan	.03	.01	.00
☐ 233	Tom Brookens	.03	.01	.00	☐ 322	Jose Guzman	.03	.01	.00
☐ 234	Greg Brock	.03	.01	.00	☐ 323	Lee Guetterman	.03	.01	.00
☐ 235	Rance Mulliniks	.03	.01	.00	☐ 324	Dan Gladden	.06	.03	.00
☐ 236	Bob Brower	.06	.03	.00	☐ 325	Gary Carter	.15	.07	.01
☐ 237	Joe Niekro	.06	.03	.00	☐ 326	Tracy Jones	.06	.03	.00
☐ 238	Scott Bankhead	.06	.03	.00	☐ 327	Floyd Youmans	.03	.01	.00
☐ 239	Doug DeCinces	.03	.01	.00	☐ 328	Bill Dawley	.03	.01	.00
☐ 240	Tommy John	.10	.05	.01	☐ 329	Paul Noce	.08	.04	.01
☐ 241	Rich Gedman	.03	.01	.00	☐ 330	Angel Salazar	.03	.01	.00
☐ 242	Ted Power	.03	.01	.00	☐ 331	Goose Gossage	.08	.04	.01
☐ 243	Dave Meads	.08	.04	.01	☐ 332	George Frazier	.03	.01	.00
☐ 244	Jim Sundberg	.03	.01	.00	☐ 333	Ruppert Jones	.03	.01	.00
☐ 245	Ken Oberkfell	.03	.01	.00	☐ 334	Billy Jo Robidoux	.03	.01	.00
☐ 246	Jimmy Jones	.10	.05	.01	☐ 335	Mike Scott	.12	.06	.01
☐ 247	Ken Landreaux	.03	.01	.00	☐ 336	Randy Myers	.15	.07	.01
☐ 248	Jose Oquendo	.03	.01	.00	☐ 337	Bob Sebra	.03	.01	.00
☐ 249	John Mitchell	.10	.05	.01	☐ 338	Eric Show	.03	.01	.00
☐ 250	Don Baylor	.08	.04	.01	☐ 339	Mitch Williams	.08	.04	.01
☐ 251	Scott Fletcher	.03	.01	.00	☐ 340	Paul Molitor	.10	.05	.01
☐ 252	Al Newman	.03	.01	.00	☐ 341	Gus Polidor	.03	.01	.00
☐ 253	Carney Lansford	.08	.04	.01	☐ 342	Steve Trout	.03	.01	.00
☐ 254	Johnny Ray	.06	.03	.00	☐ 343	Jerry Don Gleaton	.03	.01	.00
☐ 255	Gary Pettis	.03	.01	.00	☐ 344	Bob Knepper	.03	.01	.00
☐ 256	Ken Phelps	.06	.03	.00	☐ 345	Mitch Webster	.03	.01	.00
☐ 257	Rick Leach	.03	.01	.00	☐ 346	John Morris	.03	.01	.00
☐ 258	Tim Stoddard	.03	.01	.00	☐ 347	Andy Hawkins	.03	.01	.00
☐ 259	Ed Romero	.03	.01	.00	☐ 348	Dave Leiper	.03	.01	.00
☐ 260	Sid Bream	.03	.01	.00	☐ 349	Ernest Riles	.03	.01	.00
☐ 261A	Tom Niedenfuer ERR	.20	.10	.02	☐ 350	Dwight Gooden	.40	.20	.04
	(misspelled Neidenfuer				☐ 351	Dave Righetti	.08	.04	.01
	on card front)				☐ 352	Pat Dodson	.08	.04	.01
☐ 261B	Tom Niedenfuer COR	.06	.03	.00	☐ 353	John Habyan	.06	.03	.00
☐ 262	Rick Dempsey	.03	.01	.00	☐ 354	Jim Deshaies	.03	.01	.00
☐ 263	Lonnie Smith	.08	.04	.01	☐ 355	Butch Wynegar	.03	.01	.00
☐ 264	Bob Forsch	.03	.01	.00	☐ 356	Bryn Smith	.06	.03	.00
☐ 265	Barry Bonds	.15	.07	.01	☐ 357	Matt Young	.03	.01	.00
☐ 266	Willie Randolph	.06	.03	.00	☐ 358	Tom Pagnozzi	.10	.05	.01
☐ 267	Mike Ramsey	.10	.05	.01	☐ 359	Floyd Rayford	.03	.01	.00
☐ 268	Don Slaught	.03	.01	.00	☐ 360	Darryl Strawberry	.40	.20	.04
☐ 269	Mickey Tettleton	.08	.04	.01	☐ 361	Sal Butera	.03	.01	.00
☐ 270	Jerry Reuss	.03	.01	.00	☐ 362	Domingo Ramos	.03	.01	.00
☐ 271	Marc Sullivan	.03	.01	.00	☐ 363	Chris Brown	.03	.01	.00
☐ 272	Jim Morrison	.03	.01	.00	☐ 364	Jose Gonzalez	.08	.04	.01
☐ 273	Steve Balboni	.03	.01	.00	☐ 365	Dave Smith	.03	.01	.00
☐ 274	Dick Schofield	.03	.01	.00	☐ 366	Andy McGaffigan	.03	.01	.00
☐ 275	John Tudor	.08	.04	.01	☐ 367	Stan Javier	.03	.01	.00
☐ 276	Gene Larkin	.20	.10	.02	☐ 368	Henry Cotto	.03	.01	.00
☐ 277	Harold Reynolds	.06	.03	.00	☐ 369	Mike Birkbeck	.08	.04	.01
☐ 278	Jerry Browne	.06	.03	.00	☐ 370	Len Dykstra	.06	.03	.00
☐ 279	Willie Upshaw	.03	.01	.00	☐ 371	Dave Collins	.03	.01	.00
☐ 280	Ted Higuera	.08	.04	.01	☐ 372	Spike Owen	.03	.01	.00

☐ 373	Geno Petralli	.03	.01	.00		☐ 464	Mike Moore	.06	.03	.00
☐ 374	Ron Karkovice	.03	.01	.00		☐ 465	Mike LaCoss	.03	.01	.00
☐ 375	Shane Rawley	.03	.01	.00		☐ 466	Steve Farr	.03	.01	.00
☐ 376	DeWayne Buice	.08	.04	.01		☐ 467	Jerry Mumphrey	.03	.01	.00
☐ 377	Bill Pecota	.08	.04	.01		☐ 468	Kevin Gross	.03	.01	.00
☐ 378	Leon Durham	.03	.01	.00		☐ 469	Bruce Bochy	.03	.01	.00
☐ 379	Ed Olwine	.03	.01	.00		☐ 470	Orel Hershiser	.20	.10	.02
☐ 380	Bruce Hurst	.10	.05	.01		☐ 471	Eric King	.03	.01	.00
☐ 381	Bob McClure	.03	.01	.00		☐ 472	Ellis Burks	1.00	.50	.10
☐ 382	Mark Thurmond	.03	.01	.00		☐ 473	Darren Daulton	.03	.01	.00
☐ 383	Buddy Biancalana	.03	.01	.00		☐ 474	Mookie Wilson	.06	.03	.00
☐ 384	Tim Conroy	.03	.01	.00		☐ 475	Frank Viola	.12	.06	.01
☐ 385	Tony Gwynn	.30	.15	.03		☐ 476	Ron Robinson	.03	.01	.00
☐ 386	Greg Gross	.03	.01	.00		☐ 477	Bob Melvin	.03	.01	.00
☐ 387	Barry Lyons	.20	.10	.02		☐ 478	Jeff Musselman	.08	.04	.01
☐ 388	Mike Felder	.03	.01	.00		☐ 479	Charlie Kerfeld	.03	.01	.00
☐ 389	Pat Clements	.03	.01	.00		☐ 480	Richard Dotson	.03	.01	.00
☐ 390	Ken Griffey	.08	.04	.01		☐ 481	Kevin Mitchell	.45	.22	.04
☐ 391	Mark Davis	.12	.06	.01		☐ 482	Gary Roenicke	.03	.01	.00
☐ 392	Jose Rijo	.06	.03	.00		☐ 483	Tim Flannery	.03	.01	.00
☐ 393	Mike Young	.03	.01	.00		☐ 484	Rich Yett	.03	.01	.00
☐ 394	Willie Fraser	.03	.01	.00		☐ 485	Pete Incaviglia	.12	.06	.01
☐ 395	Dion James	.03	.01	.00		☐ 486	Rick Cerone	.03	.01	.00
☐ 396	Steve Shields	.03	.01	.00		☐ 487	Tony Armas	.06	.03	.00
☐ 397	Randy St.Claire	.03	.01	.00		☐ 488	Jerry Reed	.03	.01	.00
☐ 398	Danny Jackson	.08	.04	.01		☐ 489	Dave Lopes	.06	.03	.00
☐ 399	Cecil Fielder	.03	.01	.00		☐ 490	Frank Tanana	.03	.01	.00
☐ 400	Keith Hernandez	.12	.06	.01		☐ 491	Mike Loynd	.06	.03	.00
☐ 401	Don Carman	.03	.01	.00		☐ 492	Bruce Ruffin	.03	.01	.00
☐ 402	Chuck Crim	.08	.04	.01		☐ 493	Chris Speier	.03	.01	.00
☐ 403	Rob Woodward	.03	.01	.00		☐ 494	Tom Hume	.03	.01	.00
☐ 404	Junior Ortiz	.03	.01	.00		☐ 495	Jesse Orosco	.03	.01	.00
☐ 405	Glenn Wilson	.03	.01	.00		☐ 496	Robbie Wine UER	.12	.06	.01
☐ 406	Ken Howell	.03	.01	.00			(misspelled Robby			
☐ 407	Jeff Kunkel	.03	.01	.00			on card front)			
☐ 408	Jeff Reed	.03	.01	.00		☐ 497	Jeff Montgomery	.35	.17	.03
☐ 409	Chris James	.10	.05	.01		☐ 498	Jeff Dedmon	.03	.01	.00
☐ 410	Zane Smith	.03	.01	.00		☐ 499	Luis Aguayo	.03	.01	.00
☐ 411	Ken Dixon	.03	.01	.00		☐ 500	Reggie Jackson	.20	.10	.02
☐ 412	Ricky Horton	.03	.01	.00			(Oakland A's)			
☐ 413	Frank DiPino	.03	.01	.00		☐ 501	Reggie Jackson	.20	.10	.02
☐ 414	Shane Mack	.08	.04	.01			(Baltimore Orioles)			
☐ 415	Danny Cox	.03	.01	.00		☐ 502	Reggie Jackson	.20	.10	.02
☐ 416	Andy Van Slyke	.12	.06	.01			(New York Yankees)			
☐ 417	Danny Heep	.03	.01	.00		☐ 503	Reggie Jackson	.20	.10	.02
☐ 418	John Cangelosi	.03	.01	.00			(California Angels)			
☐ 419A	John Christensen ERR	.20	.10	.02		☐ 504	Reggie Jackson	.20	.10	.02
	(Christiansen						(Oakland A's)			
	on card front)					☐ 505	Billy Hatcher	.03	.01	.00
☐ 419B	John Christensen COR	.06	.03	.00		☐ 506	Ed Lynch	.03	.01	.00
☐ 420	Joey Cora	.10	.05	.01		☐ 507	Willie Hernandez	.06	.03	.00
☐ 421	Mike LaValliere	.03	.01	.00		☐ 508	Jose DeLeon	.06	.03	.00
☐ 422	Kelly Gruber	.06	.03	.00		☐ 509	Joel Youngblood	.03	.01	.00
☐ 423	Bruce Benedict	.03	.01	.00		☐ 510	Bob Welch	.06	.03	.00
☐ 424	Len Matuszek	.03	.01	.00		☐ 511	Steve Ontiveros	.03	.01	.00
☐ 425	Kent Tekulve	.03	.01	.00		☐ 512	Randy Ready	.03	.01	.00
☐ 426	Rafael Ramirez	.03	.01	.00		☐ 513	Juan Nieves	.03	.01	.00
☐ 427	Mike Flanagan	.06	.03	.00		☐ 514	Jeff Russell	.06	.03	.00
☐ 428	Mike Gallego	.03	.01	.00		☐ 515	Von Hayes	.08	.04	.01
☐ 429	Juan Castillo	.06	.03	.00		☐ 516	Mark Gubicza	.10	.05	.01
☐ 430	Neal Heaton	.03	.01	.00		☐ 517	Ken Dayley	.03	.01	.00
☐ 431	Phil Garner	.03	.01	.00		☐ 518	Don Aase	.03	.01	.00
☐ 432	Mike Dunne	.08	.04	.01		☐ 519	Rick Reuschel	.08	.04	.01
☐ 433	Wallace Johnson	.03	.01	.00		☐ 520	Mike Henneman	.20	.10	.02
☐ 434	Jack O'Connor	.03	.01	.00		☐ 521	Rick Aguilera	.03	.01	.00
☐ 435	Steve Jeltz	.03	.01	.00		☐ 522	Jay Howell	.06	.03	.00
☐ 436	Donnell Nixon	.10	.05	.01		☐ 523	Ed Correa	.03	.01	.00
☐ 437	Jack Lazorko	.03	.01	.00		☐ 524	Manny Trillo	.03	.01	.00
☐ 438	Keith Comstock	.08	.04	.01		☐ 525	Kirk Gibson	.18	.09	.01
☐ 439	Jeff Robinson	.06	.03	.00		☐ 526	Wally Ritchie	.08	.04	.01
	(Pirates pitcher)					☐ 527	Al Nipper	.03	.01	.00
☐ 440	Graig Nettles	.08	.04	.01		☐ 528	Atlee Hammaker	.03	.01	.00
☐ 441	Mel Hall	.06	.03	.00		☐ 529	Shawon Dunston	.08	.04	.01
☐ 442	Gerald Young	.25	.12	.02		☐ 530	Jim Clancy	.03	.01	.00
☐ 443	Gary Redus	.03	.01	.00		☐ 531	Tom Paciorek	.03	.01	.00
☐ 444	Charlie Moore	.03	.01	.00		☐ 532	Joel Skinner	.03	.01	.00
☐ 445	Bill Madlock	.06	.03	.00		☐ 533	Scott Garrelts	.06	.03	.00
☐ 446	Mark Clear	.03	.01	.00		☐ 534	Tom O'Malley	.03	.01	.00
☐ 447	Greg Booker	.03	.01	.00		☐ 535	John Franco	.08	.04	.01
☐ 448	Rick Schu	.03	.01	.00		☐ 536	Paul Kilgus	.12	.06	.01
☐ 449	Ron Kittle	.08	.04	.01		☐ 537	Darrell Porter	.03	.01	.00
☐ 450	Dale Murphy	.20	.10	.02		☐ 538	Walt Terrell	.03	.01	.00
☐ 451	Bob Dernier	.03	.01	.00		☐ 539	Bill Long	.08	.04	.01
☐ 452	Dale Mohorcic	.03	.01	.00		☐ 540	George Bell	.15	.07	.01
☐ 453	Rafael Belliard	.03	.01	.00		☐ 541	Jeff Sellers	.03	.01	.00
☐ 454	Charlie Puleo	.03	.01	.00		☐ 542	Joe Boever	.15	.07	.01
☐ 455	Dwayne Murphy	.03	.01	.00		☐ 543	Steve Howe	.03	.01	.00
☐ 456	Jim Eisenreich	.03	.01	.00		☐ 544	Scott Sanderson	.03	.01	.00
☐ 457	David Palmer	.03	.01	.00		☐ 545	Jack Morris	.10	.05	.01
☐ 458	Dave Stewart	.10	.05	.01		☐ 546	Todd Benzinger	.25	.12	.02
☐ 459	Pascual Perez	.08	.04	.01		☐ 547	Steve Henderson	.03	.01	.00
☐ 460	Glenn Davis	.15	.07	.01		☐ 548	Eddie Milner	.03	.01	.00
☐ 461	Dan Petry	.03	.01	.00		☐ 549	Jeff Robinson	.25	.12	.02
☐ 462	Jim Winn	.03	.01	.00			(Tigers pitcher)			
☐ 463	Darrell Miller	.03	.01	.00		☐ 550	Cal Ripken	.20	.10	.02

□ 551	Jody Davis	.03	.01	.00
□ 552	Kirk McCaskill	.03	.01	.00
□ 553	Craig Lefferts	.06	.03	.00
□ 554	Darnell Coles	.03	.01	.00
□ 555	Phil Niekro	.12	.06	.01
□ 556	Mike Aldrete	.03	.01	.00
□ 557	Pat Perry	.03	.01	.00
□ 558	Juan Agosto	.03	.01	.00
□ 559	Rob Murphy	.03	.01	.00
□ 560	Dennis Rasmussen	.06	.03	.00
□ 561	Manny Lee	.03	.01	.00
□ 562	Jeff Blauser	.20	.10	.02
□ 563	Bob Ojeda	.06	.03	.00
□ 564	Dave Dravecky	.08	.04	.01
□ 565	Gene Garber	.03	.01	.00
□ 566	Ron Roenicke	.03	.01	.00
□ 567	Tommy Hinzo	.08	.04	.01
□ 568	Eric Nolte	.08	.04	.01
□ 569	Ed Hearn	.03	.01	.00
□ 570	Mark Davidson	.08	.04	.01
□ 571	Jim Walewander	.12	.06	.01
□ 572	Donnie Hill	.03	.01	.00
□ 573	Jamie Moyer	.03	.01	.00
□ 574	Ken Schrom	.03	.01	.00
□ 575	Nolan Ryan	.35	.17	.03
□ 576	Jim Acker	.03	.01	.00
□ 577	Jamie Quirk	.03	.01	.00
□ 578	Jay Aldrich	.08	.04	.01
□ 579	Claudell Washington	.06	.03	.00
□ 580	Jeff Leonard	.06	.03	.00
□ 581	Carmen Castillo	.03	.01	.00
□ 582	Daryl Boston	.03	.01	.00
□ 583	Jeff DeWillis	.08	.04	.01
□ 584	John Marzano	.08	.04	.01
□ 585	Bill Gullickson	.03	.01	.00
□ 586	Andy Allanson	.03	.01	.00
□ 587	Lee Tunnell	.03	.01	.00
□ 588	Gene Nelson	.03	.01	.00
□ 589	Dave LaPoint	.03	.01	.00
□ 590	Harold Baines	.08	.04	.01
□ 591	Bill Buckner	.08	.04	.01
□ 592	Carlton Fisk	.10	.05	.01
□ 593	Rick Manning	.03	.01	.00
□ 594	Doug Jones	.25	.12	.02
□ 595	Tom Candiotti	.03	.01	.00
□ 596	Steve Lake	.03	.01	.00
□ 597	Jose Lind	.20	.10	.02
□ 598	Ross Jones	.08	.04	.01
□ 599	Gary Matthews	.03	.01	.00
□ 600	Fernando Valenzuela	.12	.06	.01
□ 601	Dennis Martinez	.03	.01	.00
□ 602	Les Lancaster	.12	.06	.01
□ 603	Ozzie Guillen	.06	.03	.00
□ 604	Tony Bernazard	.03	.01	.00
□ 605	Chili Davis	.06	.03	.00
□ 606	Roy Smalley	.03	.01	.00
□ 607	Ivan Calderon	.06	.03	.00
□ 608	Jay Tibbs	.03	.01	.00
□ 609	Guy Hoffman	.03	.01	.00
□ 610	Doyle Alexander	.03	.01	.00
□ 611	Mike Bielecki	.06	.03	.00
□ 612	Shawn Hillegas	.15	.07	.01
□ 613	Keith Atherton	.03	.01	.00
□ 614	Eric Plunk	.03	.01	.00
□ 615	Sid Fernandez	.08	.04	.01
□ 616	Dennis Lamp	.03	.01	.00
□ 617	Dave Engle	.03	.01	.00
□ 618	Harry Spilman	.03	.01	.00
□ 619	Don Robinson	.03	.01	.00
□ 620	John Farrell	.20	.10	.02
□ 621	Nelson Liriano	.15	.07	.01
□ 622	Floyd Bannister	.03	.01	.00
□ 623	Randy Milligan	.30	.15	.03
□ 624	Kevin Elster	.20	.10	.02
□ 625	Jody Reed	.35	.17	.03
□ 626	Shawn Abner	.15	.07	.01
□ 627	Kurt Manwaring	.20	.10	.02
□ 628	Pete Stanicek	.18	.09	.01
□ 629	Rob Ducey	.20	.10	.02
□ 630	Steve Kiefer	.03	.01	.00
□ 631	Gary Thurman	.18	.09	.01
□ 632	Darrel Akerfelds	.12	.06	.01
□ 633	Dave Clark	.12	.06	.01
□ 634	Roberto Kelly	.60	.30	.06
□ 635	Keith Hughes	.15	.07	.01
□ 636	John Davis	.12	.06	.01
□ 637	Mike Devereaux	.25	.12	.02
□ 638	Tom Glavine	.30	.15	.03
□ 639	Keith Miller (New York Mets)	.20	.10	.02
□ 640	Chris Gwynn UER (wrong batting and throwing on back)	.25	.12	.02
□ 641	Tim Crews	.08	.04	.01
□ 642	Mackey Sasser	.25	.12	.02

□ 643	Vicente Palacios	.10	.05	.01
□ 644	Kevin Romine	.08	.04	.01
□ 645	Gregg Jefferies	2.50	1.25	.25
□ 646	Jeff Treadway	.25	.12	.02
□ 647	Ron Gant	.35	.17	.03
□ 648	Mark McGwire and Matt Nokes (Rookie Sluggers)	.25	.12	.02
□ 649	Eric Davis and Tim Raines (Speed and Power)	.18	.09	.01
□ 650	Don Mattingly and Jack Clark	.40	.20	.04
□ 651	Tony Fernandez, Alan Trammell, and Cal Ripken	.10	.05	.01
□ 652	Vince Coleman HL 100 Stolen Bases	.10	.05	.01
□ 653	Kirby Puckett HL 10 Hits in a Row	.15	.07	.01
□ 654	Benito Santiago HL Hitting Streak	.12	.06	.01
□ 655	Juan Nieves HL No Hitter	.06	.03	.00
□ 656	Steve Bedrosian HL Saves Record	.06	.03	.00
□ 657	Mike Schmidt HL 500 Homers	.15	.07	.01
□ 658	Don Mattingly HL Home Run Streak	.40	.20	.04
□ 659	Mark McGwire HL Rookie HR Record	.30	.15	.03
□ 660	Paul Molitor HL Hitting Streak	.10	.05	.01

1988 Score Box Bottoms

There are six different wax box bottom panels each featuring three players and a trivia (related to a particular stadium for a given year) question. The players and trivia question cards are individually numbered. The trivia are numbered below with the prefix T in order to avoid confusion. The trivia cards are very unpopular with collectors since they do not picture any players. When panels of four are cut into individuals, the cards are standard size, 2/1/2" by 3 1/2". The card backs of the players feature the respective League logos most prominently.

		MINT	EXC	G-VG
COMPLETE SET (24)		2.00	1.00	.20
COMMON PLAYER (1-18)		.06	.03	.00
COMMON TRIVIA (T1-T6)		.03	.01	.00

□ 1	Terry Kennedy	.06	.03	.00
□ 2	Don Mattingly	.50	.25	.05
□ 3	Willie Randolph	.10	.05	.01
□ 4	Wade Boggs	.35	.17	.03
□ 5	Cal Ripken	.20	.10	.02
□ 6	George Bell	.12	.06	.01
□ 7	Rickey Henderson	.25	.12	.02
□ 8	Dave Winfield	.20	.10	.02
□ 9	Bret Saberhagen	.25	.12	.02
□ 10	Gary Carter	.20	.10	.02
□ 11	Jack Clark	.12	.06	.01
□ 12	Ryne Sandberg	.20	.10	.02
□ 13	Mike Schmidt	.35	.17	.03

		MINT	EXC	G-VG
☐ 14	Ozzie Smith	.15	.07	.01
☐ 15	Eric Davis	.25	.12	.02
☐ 16	Andre Dawson	.15	.07	.01
☐ 17	Darryl Strawberry	.35	.17	.03
☐ 18	Mike Scott	.10	.05	.01
☐ T1	Fenway Park '60 Ted (Williams) Hits To The End	.06	.03	.00
☐ T2	Comiskey Park '83 Grand Slam (Fred Lynn) Breaks Jinx	.03	.01	.00
☐ T3	Anaheim Stadium '87 Old Rookie Record Falls (Mark McGwire)	.06	.03	.00
☐ T4	Wrigley Field '38 Gabby (Hartnett) Gets Pennant Homer	.03	.01	.00
☐ T5	Comiskey Park '50 Red (Schoendienst) Rips Winning HR	.03	.01	.00
☐ T6	County Stadium '87 Rookie (John Farrell) Stops Hit Streak (Paul Molitor)	.03	.01	.00

☐ 27	Wally Joyner	.50	.25	.05
☐ 28	Robby Thompson	.15	.07	.01
☐ 29	Ken Caminiti	.15	.07	.01
☐ 30	Jose Canseco	1.25	.60	.12
☐ 31	Todd Benzinger	.25	.12	.02
☐ 32	Pete Incaviglia	.30	.15	.03
☐ 33	John Farrell	.15	.07	.01
☐ 34	Casey Candaele	.10	.05	.01
☐ 35	Mike Aldrete	.10	.05	.01
☐ 36	Ruben Sierra	.50	.25	.05
☐ 37	Ellis Burks	.50	.25	.05
☐ 38	Tracy Jones	.20	.10	.02
☐ 39	Kal Daniels	.25	.12	.02
☐ 40	Cory Snyder	.25	.12	.02

1988 Score Young Superstars II

This attractive high-gloss 40-card set of "Young Superstars" was distributed in a small purple box which had the checklist of the set on a side panel of the box. The cards are in full color on the front and also have a full-color small portrait on the card back. The cards are standard size, 2 1/2" by 3 1/2". The cards in this series are distinguishable from the cards in Series I by the fact that this series has a blue and pink border on the card front instead of the (Series I) blue and green border.

1988 Score Young Superstars I

This attractive high-gloss 40-card set of "Young Superstars" was distributed in a small blue box which had the checklist of the set on a side panel of the box. The cards are in full color on the front and also have a full-color small portrait on the card back. The cards are standard size, 2 1/2" by 3 1/2". The cards in this series are distinguishable from the cards in Series II by the fact that this series has a blue and green border on the card front instead of the (Series II) blue and pink border.

		MINT	EXC	G-VG
COMPLETE SET (40)		9.00	4.50	.90
COMMON PLAYER (1-40)		.10	.05	.01
☐ 1	Mark McGwire	1.00	.50	.10
☐ 2	Benito Santiago	.50	.25	.05
☐ 3	Sam Horn	.15	.07	.01
☐ 4	Chris Bosio	.20	.10	.02
☐ 5	Matt Nokes	.25	.12	.02
☐ 6	Ken Williams	.15	.07	.01
☐ 7	Dion James	.10	.05	.01
☐ 8	B.J. Surhoff	.20	.10	.02
☐ 9	Joe Magrane	.25	.12	.02
☐ 10	Kevin Seitzer	.50	.25	.05
☐ 11	Stanley Jefferson	.15	.07	.01
☐ 12	Devon White	.25	.12	.02
☐ 13	Nelson Liriano	.10	.05	.01
☐ 14	Chris James	.20	.10	.02
☐ 15	Mike Henneman	.20	.10	.02
☐ 16	Terry Steinbach	.25	.12	.02
☐ 17	John Kruk	.25	.12	.02
☐ 18	Matt Williams	1.00	.50	.10
☐ 19	Kelly Downs	.15	.07	.01
☐ 20	Bill Ripken	.15	.07	.01
☐ 21	Ozzie Guillen	.15	.07	.01
☐ 22	Luis Polonia	.15	.07	.01
☐ 23	Dave Magadan	.20	.10	.02
☐ 24	Mike Greenwell	1.00	.50	.10
☐ 25	Will Clark	1.25	.60	.12
☐ 26	Mike Dunn	.10	.05	.01

		MINT	EXC	G-VG
COMPLETE SET (40)		7.50	3.75	.75
COMMON PLAYER (1-40)		.10	.05	.01
☐ 1	Eric Davis	1.00	.50	.10
☐ 2	Glenn Braggs	.20	.10	.02
☐ 3	Dwight Gooden	.60	.30	.06
☐ 4	Jose Lind	.15	.07	.01
☐ 5	Danny Tartabull	.35	.17	.03
☐ 6	Tony Fernandez	.25	.12	.02
☐ 7	Julio Franco	.20	.10	.02
☐ 8	Andres Galarraga	.35	.17	.03
☐ 9	Bobby Bonilla	.25	.12	.02
☐ 10	Rob Mallicoat	.10	.05	.01
☐ 11	Gerald Young	.20	.10	.02
☐ 12	Barry Bonds	.25	.12	.02
☐ 13	Jerry Browne	.15	.07	.01
☐ 14	Jeff Blauser	.20	.10	.02
☐ 15	Mickey Brantley	.15	.07	.01
☐ 16	Floyd Youmans	.10	.05	.01
☐ 17	Bret Saberhagen	.35	.17	.03
☐ 18	Shawon Dunston	.15	.07	.01
☐ 19	Len Dykstra	.15	.07	.01
☐ 20	Darryl Strawberry	.60	.30	.06
☐ 21	Rick Aguilera	.15	.07	.01
☐ 22	Ivan Calderon	.15	.07	.01
☐ 23	Roger Clemens	.60	.30	.06
☐ 24	Vince Coleman	.30	.15	.03
☐ 25	Gary Thurman	.20	.10	.02
☐ 26	Jeff Treadway	.15	.07	.01
☐ 27	Oddibe McDowell	.15	.07	.01
☐ 28	Fred McGriff	.60	.30	.06
☐ 29	Mark McLemore	.10	.05	.01
☐ 30	Jeff Musselman	.10	.05	.01
☐ 31	Matt Williams	1.00	.50	.10
☐ 32	Dan Plesac	.15	.07	.01
☐ 33	Juan Nieves	.15	.07	.01
☐ 34	Barry Larkin	.35	.17	.03
☐ 35	Greg Matthews	.20	.10	.02
☐ 36	Shane Mack	.15	.07	.01

		MINT	EXC	G-VG
☐ 37	Scott Bankhead	.20	.10	.02
☐ 38	Eric Bell	.10	.05	.01
☐ 39	Greg Swindell	.25	.12	.02
☐ 40	Kevin Elster	.20	.10	.02

1988 Score Traded

This 110-card set featured traded players (1-65) and rookies (66-110) for the 1988 season. The cards are distinguishable from the regular Score set by the orange borders and by the fact that the numbering on the back has a T suffix. The cards are standard size, 2 1/2" by 3 1/2", and were distributed by Score as a collated set in a special collector box along with some trivia cards.

	MINT	EXC	G-VG
COMPLETE SET (110)	36.00	16.00	3.50
COMMON PLAYER (1-65)	.07	.03	.01
COMMON PLAYER (66-110)	.07	.03	.01

☐ 1T	Jack Clark	.25	.12	.02
☐ 2T	Danny Jackson	.15	.07	.01
☐ 3T	Brett Butler	.10	.05	.01
☐ 4T	Kurt Stillwell	.07	.03	.01
☐ 5T	Tom Brunansky	.15	.07	.01
☐ 6T	Dennis Lamp	.07	.03	.01
☐ 7T	Jose DeLeon	.10	.05	.01
☐ 8T	Tom Herr	.10	.05	.01
☐ 9T	Keith Moreland	.07	.03	.01
☐ 10T	Kirk Gibson	.25	.12	.02
☐ 11T	Bud Black	.07	.03	.01
☐ 12T	Rafael Ramirez	.07	.03	.01
☐ 13T	Luis Salazar	.07	.03	.01
☐ 14T	Goose Gossage	.15	.07	.01
☐ 15T	Bob Welch	.10	.05	.01
☐ 16T	Vance Law	.07	.03	.01
☐ 17T	Ray Knight	.07	.03	.01
☐ 18T	Dan Quisenberry	.10	.05	.01
☐ 19T	Don Slaught	.07	.03	.01
☐ 20T	Lee Smith	.10	.05	.01
☐ 21T	Rick Cerone	.07	.03	.01
☐ 22T	Pat Tabler	.07	.03	.01
☐ 23T	Larry McWilliams	.07	.03	.01
☐ 24T	Ricky Horton	.07	.03	.01
☐ 25T	Graig Nettles	.15	.07	.01
☐ 26T	Dan Petry	.07	.03	.01
☐ 27T	Jose Rijo	.10	.05	.01
☐ 28T	Chili Davis	.10	.05	.01
☐ 29T	Dickie Thon	.07	.03	.01
☐ 30T	Mackey Sasser	.15	.07	.01
☐ 31T	Mickey Tettleton	.15	.07	.01
☐ 32T	Rick Dempsey	.07	.03	.01
☐ 33T	Ron Hassey	.07	.03	.01
☐ 34T	Phil Bradley	.10	.05	.01
☐ 35T	Jay Howell	.10	.05	.01
☐ 36T	Bill Buckner	.10	.05	.01
☐ 37T	Alfredo Griffin	.10	.05	.01
☐ 38T	Gary Pettis	.07	.03	.01
☐ 39T	Calvin Schiraldi	.07	.03	.01
☐ 40T	John Candelaria	.10	.05	.01
☐ 41T	Joe Orsulak	.07	.03	.01
☐ 42T	Willie Upshaw	.07	.03	.01
☐ 43T	Herm Winningham	.07	.03	.01
☐ 44T	Ron Kittle	.15	.07	.01
☐ 45T	Bob Dernier	.07	.03	.01
☐ 46T	Steve Balboni	.07	.03	.01
☐ 47T	Steve Shields	.07	.03	.01

☐ 48T	Henry Cotto	.07	.03	.01
☐ 49T	Dave Henderson	.10	.05	.01
☐ 50T	Dave Parker	.15	.07	.01
☐ 51T	Mike Young	.07	.03	.01
☐ 52T	Mark Salas	.07	.03	.01
☐ 53T	Mike Davis	.07	.03	.01
☐ 54T	Rafael Santana	.07	.03	.01
☐ 55T	Don Baylor	.15	.07	.01
☐ 56T	Dan Pasqua	.10	.05	.01
☐ 57T	Ernest Riles	.07	.03	.01
☐ 58T	Glenn Hubbard	.07	.03	.01
☐ 59T	Mike Smithson	.07	.03	.01
☐ 60T	Richard Dotson	.07	.03	.01
☐ 61T	Jerry Reuss	.07	.03	.01
☐ 62T	Mike Jackson	.10	.05	.01
☐ 63T	Floyd Bannister	.07	.03	.01
☐ 64T	Jesse Orosco	.07	.03	.01
☐ 65T	Larry Parrish	.07	.03	.01
☐ 66T	Jeff Bittiger	.15	.07	.01
☐ 67T	Ray Hayward	.12	.06	.01
☐ 68T	Ricky Jordan	4.50	2.25	.45
☐ 69T	Tommy Gregg	.25	.12	.02
☐ 70T	Brady Anderson	.35	.17	.03
☐ 71T	Jeff Montgomery	.20	.10	.02
☐ 72T	Darryl Hamilton	.25	.12	.02
☐ 73T	Cecil Espy	.20	.10	.02
☐ 74T	Gregg Briley	2.50	1.25	.25
☐ 75T	Joey Meyer	.18	.09	.01
☐ 76T	Mike MacFarlane	.20	.10	.02
☐ 77T	Oswald Peraza	.15	.07	.01
☐ 78T	Jack Armstrong	.35	.17	.03
☐ 79T	Don Heinkel	.15	.07	.01
☐ 80T	Mark Grace	9.00	4.50	.90
☐ 81T	Steve Curry	.15	.07	.01
☐ 82T	Damon Berryhill	.75	.35	.07
☐ 83T	Steve Ellsworth	.15	.07	.01
☐ 84T	Pete Smith	.15	.07	.01
☐ 85T	Jack McDowell	.15	.07	.01
☐ 86T	Rob Dibble	.65	.30	.06
☐ 87T	Bryan Harvey	.35	.17	.03
☐ 88T	John Dopson	.30	.15	.03
☐ 89T	Dave Gallagher	.60	.30	.06
☐ 90T	Todd Stottlemyre	.25	.12	.02
☐ 91T	Mike Schooler	.50	.25	.05
☐ 92T	Don Gordon	.15	.07	.01
☐ 93T	Sil Campusano	.25	.12	.02
☐ 94T	Jeff Pico	.20	.10	.02
☐ 95T	Jay Buhner	.35	.17	.03
☐ 96T	Nelson Santovenia	.35	.17	.03
☐ 97T	Al Leiter	.25	.12	.02
☐ 98T	Luis Alicea	.15	.07	.01
☐ 99T	Pat Borders	.15	.07	.01
☐ 100T	Chris Sabo	1.75	.85	.17
☐ 101T	Tim Belcher	.50	.25	.05
☐ 102T	Walt Weiss	1.75	.85	.17
☐ 103T	Craig Biggio	2.25	1.10	.22
☐ 104T	Don August	.20	.10	.02
☐ 105T	Roberto Alomar	.75	.35	.07
☐ 106T	Todd Burns	.45	.22	.04
☐ 107T	John Costello	.20	.10	.02
☐ 108T	Melido Perez	.25	.12	.02
☐ 109T	Darrin Jackson	.20	.10	.02
☐ 110T	Orestes Destrade	.20	.10	.02

1989 Score

This 660-card set was distributed by Major League Marketing. Cards measure 2 1/2" by 3 1/2" and feature six distinctive inner border (inside a white outer border) colors on the front. Highlights (652-

660) and Rookie Prospects (621-651) are included in the set. The set is distinguished by the fact that each card back shows a full- color picture (portrait) of the player. Score "missed" many of the mid-season and later trades; there are numerous examples of inconsistency with regard to the treatment of these players. Study as examples of this inconsistency on handling of late trades, cards #49, 71, 77, 83, 106, 126, 139, 145, 173, 177, 242, 348, 384, 420, 439, 488, 494, and 525.

	MINT	EXC	G-VG
COMPLETE SET (660)	25.00	12.50	2.50
COMMON PLAYER (1-660)	.03	.01	.00

		MINT	EXC	G-VG
☐ 1	Jose Canseco	1.00	.25	.05
☐ 2	Andre Dawson	.12	.06	.01
☐ 3	Mark McGwire UER	.50	.25	.05
	(bio says 116 RBI's, should be 118)			
☐ 4	Benny Santiago	.12	.06	.01
☐ 5	Rick Reuschel	.06	.03	.00
☐ 6	Fred McGriff	.15	.07	.01
☐ 7	Kal Daniels	.08	.04	.01
☐ 8	Gary Gaetti	.08	.04	.01
☐ 9	Ellis Burks	.25	.12	.02
☐ 10	Darryl Strawberry	.30	.15	.03
☐ 11	Julio Franco	.08	.04	.01
☐ 12	Lloyd Moseby	.06	.03	.00
☐ 13	Jeff Pico	.10	.05	.01
☐ 14	Johnny Ray	.06	.03	.00
☐ 15	Cal Ripken Jr.	.15	.07	.01
☐ 16	Dick Schofield	.03	.01	.00
☐ 17	Mel Hall	.06	.03	.00
☐ 18	Bill Ripken	.03	.01	.00
☐ 19	Brook Jacoby	.06	.03	.00
☐ 20	Kirby Puckett	.25	.12	.02
☐ 21	Bill Doran	.06	.03	.00
☐ 22	Pete O'Brien	.06	.03	.00
☐ 23	Matt Nokes	.08	.04	.01
☐ 24	Brian Fisher	.03	.01	.00
☐ 25	Jack Clark	.10	.05	.01
☐ 26	Gary Pettis	.03	.01	.00
☐ 27	Dave Valle	.03	.01	.00
☐ 28	Willie Wilson	.06	.03	.00
☐ 29	Curt Young	.03	.01	.00
☐ 30	Dale Murphy	.15	.07	.01
☐ 31	Barry Larkin	.12	.06	.01
☐ 32	Dave Stewart	.10	.05	.01
☐ 33	Mike LaValliere	.03	.01	.00
☐ 34	Glenn Hubbard	.03	.01	.00
☐ 35	Ryne Sandberg	.15	.07	.01
☐ 36	Tony Pena	.06	.03	.00
☐ 37	Greg Walker	.03	.01	.00
☐ 38	Von Hayes	.08	.04	.01
☐ 39	Kevin Mitchell	.25	.12	.02
☐ 40	Tim Raines	.12	.06	.01
☐ 41	Keith Hernandez	.10	.05	.01
☐ 42	Keith Moreland	.03	.01	.00
☐ 43	Ruben Sierra	.20	.10	.02
☐ 44	Chet Lemon	.03	.01	.00
☐ 45	Willie Randolph	.06	.03	.00
☐ 46	Andy Allanson	.03	.01	.00
☐ 47	Candy Maldonado	.03	.01	.00
☐ 48	Sid Bream	.03	.01	.00
☐ 49	Denny Walling	.03	.01	.00
☐ 50	Dave Winfield	.15	.07	.01
☐ 51	Alvin Davis	.08	.04	.01
☐ 52	Cory Snyder	.08	.04	.01
☐ 53	Hubie Brooks	.06	.03	.00
☐ 54	Chili Davis	.06	.03	.00
☐ 55	Kevin Seitzer	.12	.06	.01
☐ 56	Jose Uribe	.03	.01	.00
☐ 57	Tony Fernandez	.08	.04	.01
☐ 58	Tim Teufel	.03	.01	.00
☐ 59	Oddibe McDowell	.06	.03	.00
☐ 60	Les Lancaster	.03	.01	.00
☐ 61	Billy Hatcher	.03	.01	.00
☐ 62	Dan Gladden	.03	.01	.00
☐ 63	Marty Barrett	.03	.01	.00
☐ 64	Nick Esasky	.06	.03	.00
☐ 65	Wally Joyner	.15	.07	.01
☐ 66	Mike Greenwell	.50	.25	.05
☐ 67	Ken Williams	.03	.01	.00
☐ 68	Bob Horner	.08	.04	.01
☐ 69	Steve Sax	.10	.05	.01
☐ 70	Rickey Henderson	.20	.10	.02
☐ 71	Mitch Webster	.03	.01	.00
☐ 72	Rob Deer	.06	.03	.00
☐ 73	Jim Presley	.03	.01	.00
☐ 74	Albert Hall	.03	.01	.00
☐ 75A	George Brett ERR	1.00	.50	.10

		MINT	EXC	G-VG
	(at age 33)			
☐ 75B	George Brett COR	.30	.15	.03
	(at age 35)			
☐ 76	Brian Downing	.03	.01	.00
☐ 77	Dave Martinez	.03	.01	.00
☐ 78	Scott Fletcher	.03	.01	.00
☐ 79	Phil Bradley	.06	.03	.00
☐ 80	Ozzie Smith	.10	.05	.01
☐ 81	Larry Sheets	.03	.01	.00
☐ 82	Mike Aldrete	.03	.01	.00
☐ 83	Darnell Coles	.03	.01	.00
☐ 84	Len Dykstra	.06	.03	.00
☐ 85	Jim Rice	.10	.05	.01
☐ 86	Jeff Treadway	.03	.01	.00
☐ 87	Jose Lind	.03	.01	.00
☐ 88	Willie McGee	.08	.04	.01
☐ 89	Mickey Brantley	.06	.03	.00
☐ 90	Tony Gwynn	.15	.07	.01
☐ 91	R.J. Reynolds	.03	.01	.00
☐ 92	Milt Thompson	.03	.01	.00
☐ 93	Kevin McReynolds	.10	.05	.01
☐ 94	Eddie Murray UER	.12	.06	.01
	('86 batting .025, should be .305)			
☐ 95	Lance Parrish	.08	.04	.01
☐ 96	Ron Kittle	.08	.04	.01
☐ 97	Gerald Young	.03	.01	.00
☐ 98	Ernie Whitt	.03	.01	.00
☐ 99	Jeff Reed	.03	.01	.00
☐ 100	Don Mattingly	.75	.35	.07
☐ 101	Gerald Perry	.06	.03	.00
☐ 102	Vance Law	.03	.01	.00
☐ 103	John Shelby	.03	.01	.00
☐ 104	Chris Sabo	.35	.17	.03
☐ 105	Danny Tartabull	.10	.05	.01
☐ 106	Glenn Wilson	.03	.01	.00
☐ 107	Mark Davidson	.03	.01	.00
☐ 108	Dave Parker	.08	.04	.01
☐ 109	Eric Davis	.25	.12	.02
☐ 110	Alan Trammell	.12	.06	.01
☐ 111	Ozzie Virgil	.03	.01	.00
☐ 112	Frank Tanana	.03	.01	.00
☐ 113	Rafael Ramirez	.03	.01	.00
☐ 114	Dennis Martinez	.03	.01	.00
☐ 115	Jose DeLeon	.06	.03	.00
☐ 116	Bob Ojeda	.06	.03	.00
☐ 117	Doug Drabek	.06	.03	.00
☐ 118	Andy Hawkins	.03	.01	.00
☐ 119	Greg Maddux	.15	.07	.01
☐ 120	Cecil Fielder UER	.06	.03	.00
	(photo on back reversed)			
☐ 121	Mike Scioscia	.03	.01	.00
☐ 122	Dan Petry	.03	.01	.00
☐ 123	Terry Kennedy	.03	.01	.00
☐ 124	Kelly Downs	.03	.01	.00
☐ 125	Greg Gross UER	.03	.01	.00
	(Gregg on back)			
☐ 126	Fred Lynn	.08	.04	.01
☐ 127	Barry Bonds	.08	.04	.01
☐ 128	Harold Baines	.08	.04	.01
☐ 129	Doyle Alexander	.03	.01	.00
☐ 130	Kevin Elster	.06	.03	.00
☐ 131	Mike Heath	.03	.01	.00
☐ 132	Teddy Higuera	.06	.03	.00
☐ 133	Charlie Leibrandt	.03	.01	.00
☐ 134	Tim Laudner	.03	.01	.00
☐ 135A	Ray Knight ERR	1.00	.50	.10
	(reverse negative)			
☐ 135B	Ray Knight COR	.10	.05	.01
☐ 136	Howard Johnson	.12	.06	.01
☐ 137	Terry Pendleton	.03	.01	.00
☐ 138	Andy McGaffigan	.03	.01	.00
☐ 139	Ken Oberkfell	.03	.01	.00
☐ 140	Butch Wynegar	.03	.01	.00
☐ 141	Rob Murphy	.03	.01	.00
☐ 142	Rich Renteria	.10	.05	.01
☐ 143	Jose Guzman	.03	.01	.00
☐ 144	Andres Galarraga	.10	.05	.01
☐ 145	Ricky Horton	.03	.01	.00
☐ 146	Frank DiPino	.03	.01	.00
☐ 147	Glenn Braggs	.06	.03	.00
☐ 148	John Kruk	.06	.03	.00
☐ 149	Mike Schmidt	.25	.12	.02
☐ 150	Lee Smith	.06	.03	.00
☐ 151	Robin Yount	.15	.07	.01
☐ 152	Mark Eichhorn	.03	.01	.00
☐ 153	DeWayne Buice	.03	.01	.00
☐ 154	B.J. Surhoff	.06	.03	.00
☐ 155	Vince Coleman	.10	.05	.01
☐ 156	Tony Phillips	.03	.01	.00
☐ 157	Willie Fraser	.03	.01	.00
☐ 158	Lance McCullers	.03	.01	.00
☐ 159	Greg Gagne	.03	.01	.00
☐ 160	Jesse Barfield	.08	.04	.01

☐ 161 Mark Langston	.12	.06	.01
☐ 162 Kurt Stillwell	.03	.01	.00
☐ 163 Dion James	.03	.01	.00
☐ 164 Glenn Davis	.10	.05	.01
☐ 165 Walt Weiss	.30	.15	.03
☐ 166 Dave Concepcion	.06	.03	.00
☐ 167 Alfredo Griffin	.03	.01	.00
☐ 168 Don Heinkel	.08	.04	.01
☐ 169 Luis Rivera	.03	.01	.00
☐ 170 Shane Rawley	.03	.01	.00
☐ 171 Darrell Evans	.06	.03	.00
☐ 172 Robby Thompson	.03	.01	.00
☐ 173 Jody Davis	.06	.03	.00
☐ 174 Andy Van Slyke	.08	.04	.01
☐ 175 Wade Boggs UER	.50	.25	.05
(bio says .364, should be .356)			
☐ 176 Garry Templeton	.06	.03	.00
('85 stats off-centered)			
☐ 177 Gary Redus	.03	.01	.00
☐ 178 Craig Lefferts	.06	.03	.00
☐ 179 Carney Lansford	.08	.04	.01
☐ 180 Ron Darling	.08	.04	.01
☐ 181 Kirk McCaskill	.03	.01	.00
☐ 182 Tony Armas	.06	.03	.00
☐ 183 Steve Farr	.03	.01	.00
☐ 184 Tom Brunansky	.08	.04	.01
☐ 185 Bryan Harvey UER	.20	.10	.02
('87 games 47, should be 3)			
☐ 186 Mike Marshall	.08	.04	.01
☐ 187 Bo Diaz	.03	.01	.00
☐ 188 Willie Upshaw	.03	.01	.00
☐ 189 Mike Pagliarulo	.06	.03	.00
☐ 190 Mike Krukow	.03	.01	.00
☐ 191 Tommy Herr	.03	.01	.00
☐ 192 Jim Pankovits	.03	.01	.00
☐ 193 Dwight Evans	.08	.04	.01
☐ 194 Kelly Gruber	.06	.03	.00
☐ 195 Bobby Bonilla	.10	.05	.01
☐ 196 Wallace Johnson	.03	.01	.00
☐ 197 Dave Stieb	.08	.04	.01
☐ 198 Pat Borders	.12	.06	.01
☐ 199 Rafael Palmeiro	.10	.05	.01
☐ 200 Dwight Gooden	.25	.12	.02
☐ 201 Pete Incaviglia	.08	.04	.01
☐ 202 Chris James	.06	.03	.00
☐ 203 Marvell Wynne	.03	.01	.00
☐ 204 Pat Sheridan	.03	.01	.00
☐ 205 Don Baylor	.08	.04	.01
☐ 206 Paul O'Neill	.08	.04	.01
☐ 207 Pete Smith	.10	.05	.01
☐ 208 Mark McLemore	.03	.01	.00
☐ 209 Henry Cotto	.03	.01	.00
☐ 210 Kirk Gibson	.12	.06	.01
☐ 211 Claudell Washington	.06	.03	.00
☐ 212 Randy Bush	.03	.01	.00
☐ 213 Joe Carter	.12	.06	.01
☐ 214 Bill Buckner	.06	.03	.00
☐ 215 Bert Blyleven UER	.08	.04	.01
(wrong birth year)			
☐ 216 Brett Butler	.06	.03	.00
☐ 217 Lee Mazzilli	.03	.01	.00
☐ 218 Spike Owen	.03	.01	.00
☐ 219 Bill Swift	.03	.01	.00
☐ 220 Tim Wallach	.06	.03	.00
☐ 221 David Cone	.15	.07	.01
☐ 222 Don Carman	.03	.01	.00
☐ 223 Rich Gossage	.08	.04	.01
☐ 224 Bob Walk	.03	.01	.00
☐ 225 Dave Righetti	.08	.04	.01
☐ 226 Kevin Bass	.06	.03	.00
☐ 227 Kevin Gross	.03	.01	.00
☐ 228 Tim Burke	.06	.03	.00
☐ 229 Rick Mahler	.03	.01	.00
☐ 230 Lou Whitaker UER	.08	.04	.01
(252 games in '85, should be 152)			
☐ 231 Luis Alicea	.08	.04	.01
☐ 232 Roberto Alomar	.30	.15	.03
☐ 233 Bob Boone	.08	.04	.01
☐ 234 Dickie Thon	.03	.01	.00
☐ 235 Shawon Dunston	.08	.04	.01
☐ 236 Pete Stanicek	.03	.01	.00
☐ 237 Craig Biggio	.40	.20	.04
(inconsistent design, portrait on front)			
☐ 238 Dennis Boyd	.06	.03	.00
☐ 239 Tom Candiotti	.03	.01	.00
☐ 240 Gary Carter	.12	.06	.01
☐ 241 Mike Stanley	.03	.01	.00
☐ 242 Ken Phelps	.06	.03	.00
☐ 243 Chris Bosio	.06	.03	.00
☐ 244 Les Straker	.03	.01	.00
☐ 245 Dave Smith	.03	.01	.00

☐ 246 John Candelaria	.06	.03	.00
☐ 247 Joe Orsulak	.03	.01	.00
☐ 248 Storm Davis	.06	.03	.00
☐ 249 Floyd Bannister UER	.03	.01	.00
(ML Batting Record)			
☐ 250 Jack Morris	.08	.04	.01
☐ 251 Bret Saberhagen	.15	.07	.01
☐ 252 Tom Niedenfuer	.03	.01	.00
☐ 253 Neal Heaton	.03	.01	.00
☐ 254 Eric Show	.03	.01	.00
☐ 255 Juan Samuel	.08	.04	.01
☐ 256 Dale Sveum	.03	.01	.00
☐ 257 Jim Gott	.03	.01	.00
☐ 258 Scott Garrelts	.03	.01	.00
☐ 259 Larry McWilliams	.03	.01	.00
☐ 260 Steve Bedrosian	.08	.04	.01
☐ 261 Jack Howell	.03	.01	.00
☐ 262 Jay Tibbs	.03	.01	.00
☐ 263 Jamie Moyer	.03	.01	.00
☐ 264 Doug Sisk	.03	.01	.00
☐ 265 Todd Worrell	.08	.04	.01
☐ 266 John Farrell	.03	.01	.00
☐ 267 Dave Collins	.03	.01	.00
☐ 268 Sid Fernandez	.08	.04	.01
☐ 269 Tom Brookens	.03	.01	.00
☐ 270 Shane Mack	.06	.03	.00
☐ 271 Paul Kilgus	.03	.01	.00
☐ 272 Chuck Crim	.03	.01	.00
☐ 273 Bob Knepper	.03	.01	.00
☐ 274 Mike Moore	.06	.03	.00
☐ 275 Guillermo Hernandez	.06	.03	.00
☐ 276 Dennis Eckersley	.10	.05	.01
☐ 277 Graig Nettles	.08	.04	.01
☐ 278 Rich Dotson	.03	.01	.00
☐ 279 Larry Herndon	.03	.01	.00
☐ 280 Gene Larkin	.03	.01	.00
☐ 281 Roger McDowell	.06	.03	.00
☐ 282 Greg Swindell	.08	.04	.01
☐ 283 Juan Agosto	.03	.01	.00
☐ 284 Jeff Robinson	.06	.03	.00
Detroit Tigers			
☐ 285 Mike Dunne	.06	.03	.00
☐ 286 Greg Mathews	.03	.01	.00
☐ 287 Kent Tekulve	.03	.01	.00
☐ 288 Jerry Mumphrey	.03	.01	.00
☐ 289 Jack McDowell	.10	.05	.01
☐ 290 Frank Viola	.12	.06	.01
☐ 291 Mark Gubicza	.08	.04	.01
☐ 292 Dave Schmidt	.03	.01	.00
☐ 293 Mike Henneman	.03	.01	.00
☐ 294 Jimmy Jones	.03	.01	.00
☐ 295 Charlie Hough	.03	.01	.00
☐ 296 Rafael Santana	.03	.01	.00
☐ 297 Chris Speier	.03	.01	.00
☐ 298 Mike Witt	.06	.03	.00
☐ 299 Pascual Perez	.08	.04	.01
☐ 300 Nolan Ryan	.30	.15	.03
☐ 301 Mitch Williams	.08	.04	.01
☐ 302 Mookie Wilson	.06	.03	.00
☐ 303 Mackey Sasser	.08	.04	.01
☐ 304 John Cerutti	.03	.01	.00
☐ 305 Jeff Reardon	.08	.04	.01
☐ 306 Randy Myers	.06	.03	.00
(6 hits in '87, should be 61)			
☐ 307 Greg Brock	.03	.01	.00
☐ 308 Bob Welch	.06	.03	.00
☐ 309 Jeff Robinson	.06	.03	.00
Pittsburgh Pirates			
☐ 310 Harold Reynolds	.06	.03	.00
☐ 311 Jim Walewander	.03	.01	.00
☐ 312 Dave Magadan	.08	.04	.01
☐ 313 Jim Gantner	.03	.01	.00
☐ 314 Walt Terrell	.03	.01	.00
☐ 315 Wally Backman	.03	.01	.00
☐ 316 Luis Salazar	.03	.01	.00
☐ 317 Rick Rhoden	.03	.01	.00
☐ 318 Tom Henke	.06	.03	.00
☐ 319 Mike Macfarlane	.12	.06	.01
☐ 320 Dan Plesac	.06	.03	.00
☐ 321 Calvin Schiraldi	.03	.01	.00
☐ 322 Stan Javier	.03	.01	.00
☐ 323 Devon White	.10	.05	.01
☐ 324 Scott Bradley	.03	.01	.00
☐ 325 Bruce Hurst	.08	.04	.01
☐ 326 Manny Lee	.03	.01	.00
☐ 327 Rick Aguilera	.03	.01	.00
☐ 328 Bruce Ruffin	.03	.01	.00
☐ 329 Ed Whitson	.03	.01	.00
☐ 330 Bo Jackson	.50	.25	.05
☐ 331 Ivan Calderon	.06	.03	.00
☐ 332 Mickey Hatcher	.03	.01	.00
☐ 333 Barry Jones	.03	.01	.00
☐ 334 Ron Hassey	.03	.01	.00
☐ 335 Bill Wegman	.03	.01	.00

□ 336	Damon Berryhill	.20	.10	.02
□ 337	Steve Ontiveros	.03	.01	.00
□ 338	Dan Pasqua	.03	.01	.00
□ 339	Bill Pecota	.03	.01	.00
□ 340	Greg Cadaret	.10	.05	.01
□ 341	Scott Bankhead	.06	.03	.00
□ 342	Ron Guidry	.08	.04	.01
□ 343	Danny Heep	.03	.01	.00
□ 344	Bob Brower	.03	.01	.00
□ 345	Rich Gedman	.03	.01	.00
□ 346	Nelson Santovenia	.15	.07	.01
□ 347	George Bell	.12	.06	.01
□ 348	Ted Power	.03	.01	.00
□ 349	Mark Grant	.03	.01	.00
□ 350A	Roger Clemens ERR (778 career wins)	4.00	2.00	.40
□ 350B	Roger Clemens COR (78 career wins)	.60	.30	.06
□ 351	Bill Long	.03	.01	.00
□ 352	Jay Bell	.08	.04	.01
□ 353	Steve Balboni	.03	.01	.00
□ 354	Bob Kipper	.03	.01	.00
□ 355	Steve Jeltz	.03	.01	.00
□ 356	Jesse Orosco	.03	.01	.00
□ 357	Bob Dernier	.03	.01	.00
□ 358	Mickey Tettleton	.08	.04	.01
□ 359	Duane Ward	.03	.01	.00
□ 360	Darrin Jackson	.10	.05	.01
□ 361	Rey Quinones	.03	.01	.00
□ 362	Mark Grace	2.00	1.00	.20
□ 363	Steve Lake	.03	.01	.00
□ 364	Pat Perry	.03	.01	.00
□ 365	Terry Steinbach	.08	.04	.01
□ 366	Alan Ashby	.03	.01	.00
□ 367	Jeff Montgomery	.08	.04	.01
□ 368	Steve Buechele	.03	.01	.00
□ 369	Chris Brown	.03	.01	.00
□ 370	Orel Hershiser	.20	.10	.02
□ 371	Todd Benzinger	.03	.01	.00
□ 372	Ron Gant	.10	.05	.01
□ 373	Paul Assenmacher	.03	.01	.00
□ 374	Joey Meyer	.08	.04	.01
□ 375	Neil Allen	.03	.01	.00
□ 376	Mike Davis	.03	.01	.00
□ 377	Jeff Parrett	.08	.04	.01
□ 378	Jay Howell	.06	.03	.00
□ 379	Rafael Belliard	.03	.01	.00
□ 380	Luis Polonia UER (2 triples in '87, should be 10)	.03	.01	.00
□ 381	Keith Atherton	.03	.01	.00
□ 382	Kent Hrbek	.10	.05	.01
□ 383	Bob Stanley	.03	.01	.00
□ 384	Dave LaPoint	.03	.01	.00
□ 385	Rance Mulliniks	.03	.01	.00
□ 386	Melido Perez	.10	.05	.01
□ 387	Doug Jones	.06	.03	.00
□ 388	Steve Lyons	.03	.01	.00
□ 389	Alejandro Pena	.03	.01	.00
□ 390	Frank White	.06	.03	.00
□ 391	Pat Tabler	.06	.03	.00
□ 392	Eric Plunk	.03	.01	.00
□ 393	Mike Maddux	.03	.01	.00
□ 394	Allan Anderson	.06	.03	.00
□ 395	Bob Brenly	.03	.01	.00
□ 396	Rick Cerone	.03	.01	.00
□ 397	Scott Terry	.03	.01	.00
□ 398	Mike Jackson	.03	.01	.00
□ 399	Bobby Thigpen UER (bio says 37 saves in '88, should be 34)	.06	.03	.00
□ 400	Don Sutton	.10	.05	.01
□ 401	Cecil Espy	.08	.04	.01
□ 402	Junior Ortiz	.03	.01	.00
□ 403	Mike Smithson	.03	.01	.00
□ 404	Bud Black	.03	.01	.00
□ 405	Tom Foley	.03	.01	.00
□ 406	Andres Thomas	.03	.01	.00
□ 407	Rick Sutcliffe	.08	.04	.01
□ 408	Brian Harper	.03	.01	.00
□ 409	John Smiley	.06	.03	.00
□ 410	Juan Nieves	.03	.01	.00
□ 411	Shawn Abner	.06	.03	.00
□ 412	Wes Gardner	.08	.04	.01
□ 413	Darren Daulton	.03	.01	.00
□ 414	Juan Berenguer	.03	.01	.00
□ 415	Charles Hudson	.03	.01	.00
□ 416	Rick Honeycutt	.03	.01	.00
□ 417	Greg Booker	.03	.01	.00
□ 418	Tim Belcher	.20	.10	.02
□ 419	Don August	.06	.03	.00
□ 420	Dale Mohorcic	.03	.01	.00
□ 421	Steve Lombardozzi	.03	.01	.00
□ 422	Atlee Hammaker	.03	.01	.00
□ 423	Jerry Don Gleaton	.03	.01	.00
□ 424	Scott Bailes	.03	.01	.00
□ 425	Bruce Sutter	.08	.04	.01
□ 426	Randy Ready	.03	.01	.00
□ 427	Jerry Reed	.03	.01	.00
□ 428	Bryn Smith	.06	.03	.00
□ 429	Tim Leary	.06	.03	.00
□ 430	Mark Clear	.03	.01	.00
□ 431	Terry Leach	.06	.03	.00
□ 432	John Moses	.03	.01	.00
□ 433	Ozzie Guillen	.06	.03	.00
□ 434	Gene Nelson	.03	.01	.00
□ 435	Gary Ward	.03	.01	.00
□ 436	Luis Aguayo	.03	.01	.00
□ 437	Fernando Valenzuela	.10	.05	.01
□ 438	Jeff Russell	.06	.03	.00
□ 439	Cecilio Guante	.03	.01	.00
□ 440	Don Robinson	.03	.01	.00
□ 441	Rick Anderson	.03	.01	.00
□ 442	Tom Glavine	.06	.03	.00
□ 443	Daryl Boston	.03	.01	.00
□ 444	Joe Price	.03	.01	.00
□ 445	Stewart Cliburn	.03	.01	.00
□ 446	Manny Trillo	.03	.01	.00
□ 447	Joel Skinner	.03	.01	.00
□ 448	Charlie Puleo	.03	.01	.00
□ 449	Carlton Fisk	.10	.05	.01
□ 450	Will Clark	.60	.30	.06
□ 451	Otis Nixon	.03	.01	.00
□ 452	Rick Schu	.03	.01	.00
□ 453	Todd Stottlemyre UER (ML Batting Record)	.15	.07	.01
□ 454	Tim Birtsas	.03	.01	.00
□ 455	Dave Gallagher	.15	.07	.01
□ 456	Barry Lyons	.03	.01	.00
□ 457	Fred Manrique	.03	.01	.00
□ 458	Ernest Riles	.03	.01	.00
□ 459	Doug Jennings	.18	.09	.01
□ 460	Joe Magrane	.08	.04	.01
□ 461	Jamie Quirk	.03	.01	.00
□ 462	Jack Armstrong	.25	.12	.02
□ 463	Bobby Witt	.06	.03	.00
□ 464	Keith Miller New York Mets	.03	.01	.00
□ 465	Todd Burns	.30	.15	.03
□ 466	John Dopson	.15	.07	.01
□ 467	Rich Yett	.03	.01	.00
□ 468	Craig Reynolds	.03	.01	.00
□ 469	Dave Bergman	.03	.01	.00
□ 470	Rex Hudler	.03	.01	.00
□ 471	Eric King	.03	.01	.00
□ 472	Joaquin Andujar	.06	.03	.00
□ 473	Sil Campusano	.20	.10	.02
□ 474	Terry Mulholland	.03	.01	.00
□ 475	Mike Flanagan	.03	.01	.00
□ 476	Greg Harris Philadelphia Phillies	.03	.01	.00
□ 477	Tommy John	.08	.04	.01
□ 478	Dave Anderson	.03	.01	.00
□ 479	Fred Toliver	.03	.01	.00
□ 480	Jimmy Key	.06	.03	.00
□ 481	Donell Nixon	.03	.01	.00
□ 482	Mark Portugal	.03	.01	.00
□ 483	Tom Pagnozzi	.03	.01	.00
□ 484	Jeff Kunkel	.03	.01	.00
□ 485	Frank Williams	.03	.01	.00
□ 486	Jody Reed	.06	.03	.00
□ 487	Roberto Kelly	.15	.07	.01
□ 488	Shawn Hillegas UER (165 innings in '87, should be 165.2)	.03	.01	.00
□ 489	Jerry Reuss	.03	.01	.00
□ 490	Mark Davis	.12	.06	.01
□ 491	Jeff Sellers	.03	.01	.00
□ 492	Zane Smith	.03	.01	.00
□ 493	Al Newman	.03	.01	.00
□ 494	Mike Young	.03	.01	.00
□ 495	Larry Parrish	.03	.01	.00
□ 496	Herm Winningham	.03	.01	.00
□ 497	Carmen Castillo	.03	.01	.00
□ 498	Joe Hesketh	.03	.01	.00
□ 499	Darrell Miller	.03	.01	.00
□ 500	Mike LaCoss	.03	.01	.00
□ 501	Charlie Lea	.03	.01	.00
□ 502	Bruce Benedict	.03	.01	.00
□ 503	Chuck Finley	.06	.03	.00
□ 504	Brad Wellman	.03	.01	.00
□ 505	Tim Crews	.03	.01	.00
□ 506	Ken Gerhart	.03	.01	.00
□ 507	Brian Holton UER (born 1/25/65 Denver, should be 11/29/59 in McKeesport)	.10	.05	.01
□ 508	Dennis Lamp	.03	.01	.00
□ 509	Bobby Meacham UER ('84 games 099)	.10	.05	.01

☐ 510	Tracy Jones	.03	.01	.00
☐ 511	Mike Fitzgerald	.03	.01	.00
	Montreal Expos			
☐ 512	Jeff Bittiger	.12	.06	.01
☐ 513	Tim Flannery	.03	.01	.00
☐ 514	Ray Hayward	.06	.03	.00
☐ 515	Dave Leiper	.03	.01	.00
☐ 516	Rod Scurry	.03	.01	.00
☐ 517	Carmelo Martinez	.03	.01	.00
☐ 518	Curtis Wilkerson	.03	.01	.00
☐ 519	Stan Jefferson	.06	.03	.00
☐ 520	Dan Quisenberry	.08	.04	.01
☐ 521	Lloyd McClendon	.08	.04	.01
☐ 522	Steve Trout	.03	.01	.00
☐ 523	Larry Andersen	.03	.01	.00
☐ 524	Don Aase	.03	.01	.00
☐ 525	Bob Forsch	.03	.01	.00
☐ 526	Geno Petralli	.03	.01	.00
☐ 527	Angel Salazar	.03	.01	.00
☐ 528	Mike Schooler	.25	.12	.02
☐ 529	Jose Oquendo	.03	.01	.00
☐ 530	Jay Buhner	.15	.07	.01
☐ 531	Tom Bolton	.08	.04	.01
☐ 532	Al Nipper	.03	.01	.00
☐ 533	Dave Henderson	.06	.03	.00
☐ 534	John Costello	.10	.05	.01
☐ 535	Donnie Moore	.03	.01	.00
☐ 536	Mike Laga	.03	.01	.00
☐ 537	Mike Gallego	.03	.01	.00
☐ 538	Jim Clancy	.03	.01	.00
☐ 539	Joel Youngblood	.03	.01	.00
☐ 540	Rick Leach	.03	.01	.00
☐ 541	Kevin Romine	.03	.01	.00
☐ 542	Mark Salas	.03	.01	.00
☐ 543	Greg Minton	.03	.01	.00
☐ 544	Dave Palmer	.03	.01	.00
☐ 545	Dwayne Murphy UER	.03	.01	.00
	(game-sinning)			
☐ 546	Jim Deshaies	.03	.01	.00
☐ 547	Don Gordon	.08	.04	.01
☐ 548	Ricky Jordan	1.50	.75	.15
☐ 549	Mike Boddicker	.03	.01	.00
☐ 550	Mike Scott	.10	.05	.01
☐ 551	Jeff Ballard	.18	.09	.01
☐ 552A	Jose Rijo ERR	1.00	.50	.10
	(uniform listed as 27 on back)			
☐ 552B	Jose Rijo COR	.15	.07	.01
	(uniform listed as 24 on back)			
☐ 553	Danny Darwin	.03	.01	.00
☐ 554	Tom Browning	.08	.04	.01
☐ 555	Danny Jackson	.08	.04	.01
☐ 556	Rick Dempsey	.03	.01	.00
☐ 557	Jeffrey Leonard	.06	.03	.00
☐ 558	Jeff Musselman	.03	.01	.00
☐ 559	Ron Robinson	.03	.01	.00
☐ 560	John Tudor	.08	.04	.01
☐ 561	Don Slaught	.03	.01	.00
☐ 562	Dennis Rasmussen	.06	.03	.00
☐ 563	Brady Anderson	.20	.10	.02
☐ 564	Pedro Guerrero	.10	.05	.01
☐ 565	Paul Molitor	.10	.05	.01
☐ 566	Terry Clark	.10	.05	.01
☐ 567	Terry Puhl	.03	.01	.00
☐ 568	Mike Campbell	.10	.05	.01
☐ 569	Paul Mirabella	.03	.01	.00
☐ 570	Jeff Hamilton	.03	.01	.00
☐ 571	Oswald Peraza	.08	.04	.01
☐ 572	Bob McClure	.03	.01	.00
☐ 573	Jose Bautista	.08	.04	.01
☐ 574	Alex Trevino	.03	.01	.00
☐ 575	John Franco	.06	.03	.00
☐ 576	Mark Parent	.10	.05	.01
☐ 577	Nelson Liriano	.03	.01	.00
☐ 578	Steve Shields	.03	.01	.00
☐ 579	Odell Jones	.03	.01	.00
☐ 580	Al Leiter	.10	.05	.01
☐ 581	Dave Stapleton	.08	.04	.01
☐ 582	World Series '88	.15	.07	.01
	Orel Hershiser			
	Jose Canseco			
	Kirk Gibson			
	Dave Stewart			
☐ 583	Donnie Hill	.03	.01	.00
☐ 584	Chuck Jackson	.03	.01	.00
☐ 585	Rene Gonzales	.08	.04	.01
☐ 586	Tracy Woodson	.08	.04	.01
☐ 587	Jim Adduci	.03	.01	.00
☐ 588	Mario Soto	.03	.01	.00
☐ 589	Jeff Blauser	.03	.01	.00
☐ 590	Jim Traber	.03	.01	.00
☐ 591	Jon Perlman	.08	.04	.01
☐ 592	Mark Williamson	.08	.04	.01
☐ 593	Dave Meads	.03	.01	.00

☐ 594	Jim Eisenreich	.03	.01	.00
☐ 595A	Paul Gibson P1	2.00	1.00	.20
☐ 595B	Paul Gibson P2	.15	.07	.01
	(airbrushed leg on player in background)			
☐ 596	Mike Birkbeck	.03	.01	.00
☐ 597	Terry Francona	.03	.01	.00
☐ 598	Paul Zuvella	.03	.01	.00
☐ 599	Franklin Stubbs	.03	.01	.00
☐ 600	Gregg Jefferies	1.00	.50	.10
☐ 601	John Cangelosi	.03	.01	.00
☐ 602	Mike Sharperson	.03	.01	.00
☐ 603	Mike Diaz	.03	.01	.00
☐ 604	Gary Varsho	.12	.06	.01
☐ 605	Terry Blocker	.12	.06	.01
☐ 606	Charlie O'Brien	.08	.04	.01
☐ 607	Jim Eppard	.08	.04	.01
☐ 608	John Davis	.03	.01	.00
☐ 609	Ken Griffey Sr.	.08	.04	.01
☐ 610	Buddy Bell	.06	.03	.00
☐ 611	Ted Simmons UER	.08	.04	.01
	('78 stats Cardinal)			
☐ 612	Matt Williams	.15	.07	.01
☐ 613	Danny Cox	.03	.01	.00
☐ 614	Al Pedrique	.03	.01	.00
☐ 615	Ron Oester	.03	.01	.00
☐ 616	John Smoltz	.35	.17	.03
☐ 617	Bob Melvin	.03	.01	.00
☐ 618	Rob Dibble	.20	.10	.02
☐ 619	Kirt Manwaring	.03	.01	.00
☐ 620	Felix Fermin	.08	.04	.01
☐ 621	Doug Dascenzo	.15	.07	.01
☐ 622	Bill Brennan	.15	.07	.01
☐ 623	Carlos Quintana	.25	.12	.02
☐ 624	Mike Harkey UER	.30	.15	.03
	(13 and 31 walks in '88, should be 35 and 33)			
☐ 625	Gary Sheffield	1.00	.50	.10
☐ 626	Tom Prince	.08	.04	.01
☐ 627	Steve Searcy	.18	.09	.01
☐ 628	Charlie Hayes	.15	.07	.01
	(listed as outfielder)			
☐ 629	Felix Jose	.25	.12	.02
☐ 630	Sandy Alomar	.75	.35	.07
☐ 631	Derek Lilliquist	.20	.10	.02
☐ 632	Geronimo Berroa	.10	.05	.01
☐ 633	Luis Medina	.25	.12	.02
☐ 634	Tom Gordon UER	1.00	.50	.10
	(height 6'0")			
☐ 635	Ramon Martinez	.35	.17	.03
☐ 636	Craig Worthington	.35	.17	.03
☐ 637	Edgar Martinez	.10	.05	.01
☐ 638	Chad Kreuter	.15	.07	.01
☐ 639	Ron Jones	.25	.12	.02
☐ 640	Van Snider	.20	.10	.02
☐ 641	Lance Blankenship	.20	.10	.02
☐ 642	Dwight Smith UER	2.00	1.00	.20
	(10 HR's in '87, should be 18)			
☐ 643	Cameron Drew	.18	.09	.01
☐ 644	Jerald Clark	.18	.09	.01
☐ 645	Randy Johnson	.20	.10	.02
☐ 646	Norm Charlton	.15	.07	.01
☐ 647	Todd Frohwirth UER	.10	.05	.01
	(southpaw on back)			
☐ 648	Luis De Los Santos	.20	.10	.02
☐ 649	Tim Jones	.10	.05	.01
☐ 650	Dave West UER	.25	.12	.02
	(ML hits 3, should be 6)			
☐ 651	Bob Milacki	.25	.12	.02
☐ 652	Wrigley Field HL	.03	.01	.00
	(Let There Be Lights)			
☐ 653	Orel Hershiser HL	.15	.07	.01
	(The Streak)			
☐ 654A	Wade Boggs HL ERR	3.50	1.75	.35
	(Wade Whacks 'Em) ("seaason" on back)			
☐ 654B	Wade Boggs HL COR	.50	.25	.05
	(Wade Whacks 'Em)			
☐ 655	Jose Canseco HL	.40	.20	.04
	(One of a Kind)			
☐ 656	Doug Jones HL	.06	.03	.00
	(Doug Sets Saves)			
☐ 657	Rickey Henderson HL	.20	.10	.02
	(Rickey Rocks 'Em)			
☐ 658	Tom Browning HL	.06	.03	.00
	(Tom Perfect Pitches)			
☐ 659	Mike Greenwell HL	.20	.10	.02
	(Greenwell Gamers)			
☐ 660	Boston Red Sox HL	.06	.03	.00
	(Joe Morgan MG, Sox Sock 'Em)			

1989 Score Hottest 100 Rookies

CARLOS QUINTANA

This set was distributed by Publications International in January 1989 through many retail stores and chains; the card set was packaged along with a colorful 48- page book for a suggested retail price of 12.95. Supposedly 225,000 sets were produced. The cards measure the standard 2 1/2" by 3 1/2" and show full color on both sides of the card. The cards were produced by Score as indicated on the card backs. The set is subtitled "Rising Star" on the reverse. The first six cards (#1-#6) of a 12-card set of Score's trivia cards, subtitled "Rookies to Remember" is included along with each set. The cards are numbered on the back. This set is distinguished by the sharp blue borders and the player's first initial inside a yellow triangle in the lower left corner of the obverse.

	MINT	EXC	G-VG
COMPLETE SET (100)	12.50	6.25	1.25
COMMON PLAYER (1-100)	.05	.02	.00
☐ 1 Gregg Jefferies	1.00	.50	.10
☐ 2 Vicente Palacios	.05	.02	.00
☐ 3 Cameron Drew	.15	.07	.01
☐ 4 Doug Dascenzo	.15	.07	.01
☐ 5 Luis Medina	.20	.10	.02
☐ 6 Craig Worthington	.25	.12	.02
☐ 7 Rob Ducey	.10	.05	.01
☐ 8 Hal Morris	.20	.10	.02
☐ 9 Bill Brennan	.15	.07	.01
☐ 10 Gary Sheffield	.90	.45	.09
☐ 11 Mike Devereaux	.15	.07	.01
☐ 12 Hensley Meulens	.60	.30	.06
☐ 13 Carlos Quintana	.25	.12	.02
☐ 14 Todd Frohwirth	.05	.02	.00
☐ 15 Scott Lusader	.05	.02	.00
☐ 16 Mark Carreon	.10	.05	.01
☐ 17 Torey Lovullo	.10	.05	.01
☐ 18 Randy Velarde	.05	.02	.00
☐ 19 Billy Bean	.05	.02	.00
☐ 20 Lance Blankenship	.15	.07	.01
☐ 21 Chris Gwynn	.15	.07	.01
☐ 22 Felix Jose	.20	.10	.02
☐ 23 Derek Lilliquist	.05	.02	.00
☐ 24 Gary Thurman	.10	.05	.01
☐ 25 Ron Jones	.15	.07	.01
☐ 26 Dave Justice	.10	.05	.01
☐ 27 Johnny Paredes	.05	.02	.00
☐ 28 Tim Jones	.10	.05	.01
☐ 29 Jose Gonzales	.10	.05	.01
☐ 30 Geronimo Berroa	.10	.05	.01
☐ 31 Trevor Wilson	.10	.05	.01
☐ 32 Morris Madden	.05	.02	.00
☐ 33 Lance Johnson	.10	.05	.01
☐ 34 Marvin Freeman	.05	.02	.00
☐ 35 Jose Cecena	.05	.02	.00
☐ 36 Jim Corsi	.10	.05	.01
☐ 37 Rolando Roomes	.15	.07	.01
☐ 38 Scott Medvin	.05	.02	.00
☐ 39 Charlie Hayes	.10	.05	.01
☐ 40 Edgar Martinez	.15	.07	.01
☐ 41 Van Snider	.15	.07	.01
☐ 42 John Fishel	.10	.05	.01
☐ 43 Bruce Fields	.05	.02	.00
☐ 44 Darryl Hamilton	.15	.07	.01
☐ 45 Tom Prince	.10	.05	.01
☐ 46 Kirt Manwaring	.15	.07	.01
☐ 47 Steve Searcy	.20	.10	.02
☐ 48 Mike Harkey	.25	.12	.02
☐ 49 German Gonzalez	.05	.02	.00
☐ 50 Tony Perezchica	.10	.05	.01
☐ 51 Chad Kreuter	.10	.05	.01
☐ 52 Luis De los Santos	.20	.10	.02
☐ 53 Steve Curry	.10	.05	.01
☐ 54 Greg Briley	.35	.17	.03
☐ 55 Ramon Martinez	.35	.17	.03
☐ 56 Ron Tingley	.10	.05	.01
☐ 57 Randy Kramer	.05	.02	.00
☐ 58 Alex Madrid	.10	.05	.01
☐ 59 Kevin Reimer	.05	.02	.00
☐ 60 Dave Otto	.10	.05	.01
☐ 61 Ken Patterson	.05	.02	.00
☐ 62 Keith Miller	.10	.05	.01
☐ 63 Randy Johnson	.15	.07	.01
☐ 64 Dwight Smith	.60	.30	.06
☐ 65 Eric Yelding	.10	.05	.01
☐ 66 Bob Geren	.15	.07	.01
☐ 67 Shane Turner	.15	.07	.01
☐ 68 Tom Gordon	.50	.25	.05
☐ 69 Jeff Huson	.10	.05	.01
☐ 70 Marty Brown	.15	.07	.01
☐ 71 Nelson Santovenia	.15	.07	.01
☐ 72 Roberto Alomar	.25	.12	.02
☐ 73 Mike Schooler	.20	.10	.02
☐ 74 Pete Smith	.10	.05	.01
☐ 75 John Costello	.15	.07	.01
☐ 76 Chris Sabo	.30	.15	.03
☐ 77 Damon Berryhill	.30	.15	.03
☐ 78 Mark Grace	1.00	.50	.10
☐ 79 Melido Perez	.15	.07	.01
☐ 80 Al Leiter	.15	.07	.01
☐ 81 Todd Stottlemyre	.15	.07	.01
☐ 82 Mackey Sasser	.15	.07	.01
☐ 83 Don August	.10	.05	.01
☐ 84 Jeff Treadway	.10	.05	.01
☐ 85 Jody Reed	.10	.05	.01
☐ 86 Mike Campbell	.10	.05	.01
☐ 87 Ron Gant	.25	.12	.02
☐ 88 Ricky Jordan	1.00	.50	.10
☐ 89 Terry Clark	.10	.05	.01
☐ 90 Roberto Kelly	.35	.17	.03
☐ 91 Pat Borders	.10	.05	.01
☐ 92 Bryan Harvey	.15	.07	.01
☐ 93 Joey Meyer	.10	.05	.01
☐ 94 Tim Belcher	.20	.10	.02
☐ 95 Walt Weiss	.35	.17	.03
☐ 96 Dave Gallagher	.15	.07	.01
☐ 97 Mike Macfarlane	.10	.05	.01
☐ 98 Craig Biggio	.50	.25	.05
☐ 99 Jack Armstrong	.20	.10	.02
☐ 100 Todd Burns	.15	.07	.01

1989 Score Hottest 100 Stars

DANNY JACKSON

This set was distributed by Publications International in January 1989 through many retail stores and chains; the card set was packaged along with a colorful 48- page book for a suggested retail price of 12.95. Supposedly 225,000 sets were produced. The cards measure the standard 2 1/2" by 3 1/2" and show full color on both sides of the card. The cards were produced by Score as indicated on the card backs. The set is subtitled "Superstar" on the reverse. The last six cards (#7-#12) of a 12-card set of Score's trivia cards, subtitled "Rookies to Remember" is included along with each set. The cards are numbered on the back. This set is distinguished by the sharp red borders and the player's first initial inside a yellow triangle in the upper left corner of the obverse.

		MINT	EXC	G-VG
COMPLETE SET (100)		12.50	6.25	1.25
COMMON PLAYER (1-100)		.05	.02	.00
☐	1 Jose Canseco	1.25	.60	.12
☐	2 David Cone	.25	.12	.02
☐	3 Dave Winfield	.25	.12	.02
☐	4 George Brett	.35	.17	.03
☐	5 Frank Viola	.20	.10	.02
☐	6 Cory Snyder	.20	.10	.02
☐	7 Alan Trammell	.20	.10	.02
☐	8 Dwight Evans	.15	.07	.01
☐	9 Tim Leary	.10	.05	.01
☐	10 Don Mattingly	1.00	.50	.10
☐	11 Kirby Puckett	.90	.45	.09
☐	12 Carney Lansford	.20	.10	.02
☐	13 Dennis Martinez	.05	.02	.00
☐	14 Kent Hrbek	.20	.10	.02
☐	15 Doc Gooden	.40	.20	.04
☐	16 Dennis Eckersley	.20	.10	.02
☐	17 Kevin Seitzer	.30	.15	.03
☐	18 Lee Smith	.05	.02	.00
☐	19 Danny Tartabull	.20	.10	.02
☐	20 Gerald Perry	.05	.02	.00
☐	21 Gary Gaetti	.15	.07	.01
☐	22 Rick Reuschel	.10	.05	.01
☐	23 Keith Hernandez	.20	.10	.02
☐	24 Jeff Reardon	.10	.05	.01
☐	25 Mark McGwire	.90	.45	.09
☐	26 Juan Samuel	.10	.05	.01
☐	27 Jack Clark	.15	.07	.01
☐	28 Robin Yount	.45	.22	.04
☐	29 Steve Bedrosian	.10	.05	.01
☐	30 Kirk Gibson	.30	.15	.03
☐	31 Barry Bonds	.25	.12	.02
☐	32 Dan Plesac	.10	.05	.01
☐	33 Steve Sax	.20	.10	.02
☐	34 Jeff Robinson	.10	.05	.01
☐	35 Orel Hershiser	.65	.30	.06
☐	36 Julio Franco	.15	.07	.01
☐	37 Dave Righetti	.10	.05	.01
☐	38 Bob Knepper	.05	.02	.00
☐	39 Carlton Fisk	.20	.10	.02
☐	40 Tony Gwynn	.35	.17	.03
☐	41 Doug Jones	.05	.02	.00
☐	42 Bobby Bonilla	.25	.12	.02
☐	43 Ellis Burks	.35	.17	.03
☐	44 Pedro Guerrero	.20	.10	.02
☐	45 Rickey Henderson	.40	.20	.04
☐	46 Glenn Davis	.25	.12	.02
☐	47 Benny Santiago	.25	.12	.02
☐	48 Greg Maddux	.15	.07	.01
☐	49 Teddy Higuera	.10	.05	.01
☐	50 Darryl Strawberry	.60	.30	.06
☐	51 Ozzie Guillen	.10	.05	.01
☐	52 Barry Larkin	.25	.12	.02
☐	53 Tony Fernandez	.15	.07	.01
☐	54 Ryne Sandberg	.30	.15	.03
☐	55 Joe Carter	.20	.10	.02
☐	56 Rafael Palmeiro	.15	.07	.01
☐	57 Paul Molitor	.15	.07	.01
☐	58 Eric Davis	.75	.35	.07
☐	59 Mike Henneman	.10	.05	.01
☐	60 Mike Scott	.15	.07	.01
☐	61 Tom Browning	.10	.05	.01
☐	62 Mark Davis	.20	.10	.02
☐	63 Tom Henke	.05	.02	.00
☐	64 Nolan Ryan	1.00	.50	.10
☐	65 Fred McGriff	.50	.25	.05
☐	66 Dale Murphy	.40	.20	.04
☐	67 Mark Langston	.10	.05	.01
☐	68 Bobby Thigpen	.10	.05	.01
☐	69 Mark Gubicza	.15	.07	.01
☐	70 Mike Greenwell	1.00	.50	.10
☐	71 Ron Darling	.15	.07	.01
☐	72 Gerald Young	.10	.05	.01
☐	73 Wally Joyner	.30	.15	.03
☐	74 Andres Galarraga	.20	.10	.02
☐	75 Danny Jackson	.10	.05	.01
☐	76 Mike Schmidt	.75	.35	.07
☐	77 Cal Ripken Jr.	.25	.12	.02
☐	78 Alvin Davis	.10	.05	.01
☐	79 Bruce Hurst	.15	.07	.01
☐	80 Andre Dawson	.20	.10	.02
☐	81 Bob Boone	.15	.07	.01
☐	82 Harold Reynolds	.10	.05	.01
☐	83 Eddie Murray	.25	.12	.02
☐	84 Robby Thompson	.10	.05	.01
☐	85 Will Clark	1.25	.60	.12
☐	86 Vince Coleman	.20	.10	.02
☐	87 Doug Drabek	.10	.05	.01
☐	88 Ozzie Smith	.25	.12	.02
☐	89 Bob Welch	.05	.02	.00
☐	90 Roger Clemens	.60	.30	.06
☐	91 George Bell	.20	.10	.02
☐	92 Andy Van Slyke	.15	.07	.01
☐	93 Willie McGee	.15	.07	.01
☐	94 Todd Worrell	.15	.07	.01
☐	95 Tim Raines	.25	.12	.02
☐	96 Kevin McReynolds	.25	.12	.02
☐	97 John Franco	.10	.05	.01
☐	98 Jim Gott	.05	.02	.00
☐	99 Johnny Ray	.05	.02	.00
☐	100 Wade Boggs	1.00	.50	.10

1989 Score Young Superstars I

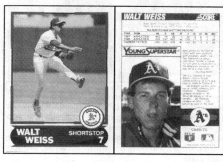

The 1989 Score Young Superstars set I contains 42 standard-size (2 1/2 by 3 1/2 inch) cards. The fronts are pink, white and blue. The vertically-oriented backs have color facial shots, 1988 and career stats, and biographical information. One card was included in each 1989 Score rack pack, and the cards were also distributed as a boxed set with five Magic Motion trivia cards.

		MINT	EXC	G-VG
COMPLETE SET (42)		7.50	3.75	.75
COMMON PLAYER (1-42)		.10	.05	.01
☐	1 Gregg Jefferies	.75	.35	.07
☐	2 Jody Reed	.10	.05	.01
☐	3 Mark Grace	1.00	.50	.10
☐	4 Dave Gallagher	.20	.10	.02
☐	5 Bo Jackson	1.00	.50	.10
☐	6 Jay Buhner	.20	.10	.02
☐	7 Melido Perez	.10	.05	.01
☐	8 Bobby Witt	.15	.07	.01
☐	9 David Cone	.25	.12	.02
☐	10 Chris Sabo	.25	.12	.02
☐	11 Pat Borders	.15	.07	.01
☐	12 Mark Grant	.10	.05	.01
☐	13 Mike Macfarlane	.15	.07	.01
☐	14 Mike Jackson	.10	.05	.01
☐	15 Ricky Jordan	.75	.35	.07
☐	16 Ron Gant	.20	.10	.02
☐	17 Al Leiter	.15	.07	.01
☐	18 Jeff Parrett	.10	.05	.01
☐	19 Pete Smith	.10	.05	.01
☐	20 Walt Weiss	.25	.12	.02
☐	21 Doug Drabek	.10	.05	.01
☐	22 Kirt Manwaring	.15	.07	.01
☐	23 Keith Miller	.10	.05	.01
☐	24 Damon Berryhill	.30	.15	.03
☐	25 Gary Sheffield	.75	.35	.07
☐	26 Brady Anderson	.20	.10	.02
☐	27 Mitch Williams	.20	.10	.02
☐	28 Roberto Alomar	.25	.12	.02
☐	29 Bobby Thigpen	.20	.10	.02
☐	30 Bryan Harvey UER (47 games in '87)	.20	.10	.02
☐	31 Jose Rijo	.15	.07	.01
☐	32 Dave West	.25	.12	.02

		MINT	EXC	G-VG
☐ 33	Joey Meyer	.15	.07	.01
☐ 34	Allan Anderson	.15	.07	.01
☐ 35	Rafael Palmeiro	.25	.12	.02
☐ 36	Tim Belcher	.20	.10	.02
☐ 37	John Smiley	.15	.07	.01
☐ 38	Mackey Sasser	.15	.07	.01
☐ 39	Greg Maddux	.20	.10	.02
☐ 40	Ramon Martinez	.35	.17	.03
☐ 41	Randy Myers	.15	.07	.01
☐ 42	Scott Bankhead	.15	.07	.01

1989 Score Young Superstars II

The 1989 Score Young Superstars II set contains 42 standard-size (2 1/2 by 3 1/2 inch) cards. The fronts are orange, white and purple. The vertically-oriented backs have color facial shots, 1988 and career stats, and biographical information. The cards were distributed as a boxed set with five Magic Motion trivia cards.

		MINT	EXC	G-VG
	COMPLETE SET (42)	6.00	3.00	.60
	COMMON PLAYER (1-42)	.10	.05	.01
☐ 1	Sandy Alomar Jr.	.75	.35	.07
☐ 2	Tom Gordon	.60	.30	.06
☐ 3	Ron Jones	.20	.10	.02
☐ 4	Todd Burns	.15	.07	.01
☐ 5	Paul O'Neill	.20	.10	.02
☐ 6	Gene Larkin	.15	.07	.01
☐ 7	Eric King	.10	.05	.01
☐ 8	Jeff Robinson	.15	.07	.01
☐ 9	Bill Wegman	.10	.05	.01
☐ 10	Cecil Espy	.10	.05	.01
☐ 11	Jose Guzman	.10	.05	.01
☐ 12	Kelly Gruber	.15	.07	.01
☐ 13	Duane Ward	.10	.05	.01
☐ 14	Mark Gubicza	.15	.07	.01
☐ 15	Norm Charlton	.10	.05	.01
☐ 16	Jose Oquendo	.10	.05	.01
☐ 17	Geronimo Berroa	.10	.05	.01
☐ 18	Ken Griffey Jr.	1.25	.60	.12
☐ 19	Lance McCullers	.15	.07	.01
☐ 20	Todd Stottlemyre	.15	.07	.01
☐ 21	Craig Worthington	.20	.10	.02
☐ 22	Mike Devereaux	.15	.07	.01
☐ 23	Tom Glavine	.20	.10	.02
☐ 24	Dale Sveum	.10	.05	.01
☐ 25	Roberto Kelly	.40	.20	.04
☐ 26	Luis Medina	.20	.10	.02
☐ 27	Steve Searcy	.20	.10	.02
☐ 28	Don August	.10	.05	.01
☐ 29	Shawn Hillegas	.15	.07	.01
☐ 30	Mike Campbell	.15	.07	.01
☐ 31	Mike Harkey	.25	.12	.02
☐ 32	Randy Johnson	.15	.07	.01
☐ 33	Craig Biggio	.40	.20	.04
☐ 34	Mike Schooler	.25	.12	.02
☐ 35	Andres Thomas	.15	.07	.01
☐ 36	Jerome Walton	1.00	.50	.10
☐ 37	Cris Carpenter	.15	.07	.01
☐ 38	Kevin Mitchell	.60	.30	.06
☐ 39	Eddie Williams	.15	.07	.01
☐ 40	Chad Kreuter	.15	.07	.01
☐ 41	Danny Jackson	.15	.07	.01
☐ 42	Kurt Stillwell	.15	.07	.01

1989 Score Scoremasters

The 1989 Score Scoremasters set contains 42 standard-size (2 1/2 by 3 1/2 inch) cards. The fronts are "pure" with attractively-drawn action portraits. The backs feature write-ups of the players' careers. The cards were distributed as a boxed set.

		MINT	EXC	G-VG
	COMPLETE SET (42)	10.00	5.00	1.00
	COMMON PLAYER (1-42)	.10	.05	.01
☐ 1	Bo Jackson	1.00	.50	.10
☐ 2	Jerome Walton	1.00	.50	.10
☐ 3	Cal Ripken Jr.	.30	.15	.03
☐ 4	Mike Scott	.20	.10	.02
☐ 5	Nolan Ryan	1.00	.50	.10
☐ 6	Don Mattingly	1.00	.50	.10
☐ 7	Tom Gordon	.50	.25	.05
☐ 8	Jack Morris	.10	.05	.01
☐ 9	Carlton Fisk	.30	.15	.03
☐ 10	Will Clark	1.00	.50	.10
☐ 11	George Brett	.50	.25	.05
☐ 12	Kevin Mitchell	.50	.25	.05
☐ 13	Mark Langston	.30	.15	.03
☐ 14	Dave Stewart	.20	.10	.02
☐ 15	Dale Murphy	.40	.20	.04
☐ 16	Gary Gaetti	.20	.10	.02
☐ 17	Wade Boggs	1.00	.50	.10
☐ 18	Eric Davis	.75	.35	.07
☐ 19	Kirby Puckett	.90	.45	.09
☐ 20	Roger Clemens	.75	.35	.07
☐ 21	Orel Hershiser	.50	.25	.05
☐ 22	Mark Grace	1.00	.50	.10
☐ 23	Ryne Sandberg	.25	.12	.02
☐ 24	Barry Larkin	.25	.12	.02
☐ 25	Ellis Burks	.35	.17	.03
☐ 26	Dwight Gooden	.40	.20	.04
☐ 27	Ozzie Smith	.20	.10	.02
☐ 28	Andre Dawson	.20	.10	.02
☐ 29	Julio Franco	.10	.05	.01
☐ 30	Ken Griffey Jr.	1.00	.50	.10
☐ 31	Ruben Sierra	.50	.25	.05
☐ 32	Mark McGwire	.75	.35	.07
☐ 33	Andres Galarraga	.20	.10	.02
☐ 34	Joe Carter	.20	.10	.02
☐ 35	Vince Coleman	.25	.12	.02
☐ 36	Mike Greenwell	.75	.35	.07
☐ 37	Tony Gwynn	.60	.30	.06
☐ 38	Andy Van Slyke	.15	.07	.01
☐ 39	Gregg Jefferies	.75	.35	.07
☐ 40	Jose Canseco	1.00	.50	.10
☐ 41	Dave Winfield	.25	.12	.02
☐ 42	Darryl Strawberry	.60	.30	.06

1989 Score Nat West Yankees

The 1989 Score Nat West New York Yankees set features 33 standard-size (2 1/2 by 3 1/2 inch) cards. The fronts and backs are navy; the backs have color mug shots, 1988 and career stats. The set was given away at a 1989 Yankees' home game.

	MINT	EXC	G-VG
COMPLETE SET (33)	12.50	6.25	1.25
COMMON PLAYER (1-33)	.20	.10	.02

		MINT	EXC	G-VG
COMPLETE SET (110)		13.50	6.00	1.00
COMMON PLAYER (1-80)		.05	.02	.00
COMMON PLAYER (81-110)		.06	.03	.00
☐	1 Rafael Palmeiro	.12	.02	.01
☐	2 Nolan Ryan	1.25	.60	.12
☐	3 Jack Clark	.10	.05	.01
☐	4 Dave LaPoint	.05	.02	.00
☐	5 Mike Moore	.10	.05	.01
☐	6 Pete O'Brien	.10	.05	.01
☐	7 Jeffrey Leonard	.10	.05	.01
☐	8 Rob Murphy	.05	.02	.00
☐	9 Tom Herr	.05	.02	.00
☐	10 Claudell Washington	.10	.05	.01
☐	11 Mike Pagliarulo	.05	.02	.00
☐	12 Steve Lake	.05	.02	.00
☐	13 Spike Owen	.05	.02	.00
☐	14 Andy Hawkins	.10	.05	.01
☐	15 Todd Benzinger	.05	.02	.00
☐	16 Mookie Wilson	.10	.05	.01
☐	17 Bert Blyleven	.15	.07	.01
☐	18 Jeff Treadway	.05	.02	.00
☐	19 Bruce Hurst	.10	.05	.01
☐	20 Steve Sax	.15	.07	.01
☐	21 Juan Samuel	.15	.07	.01
☐	22 Jesse Barfield	.15	.07	.01
☐	23 Carmen Castillo	.05	.02	.00
☐	24 Terry Leach	.05	.02	.00
☐	25 Mark Langston	.20	.10	.02
☐	26 Eric King	.05	.02	.00
☐	27 Steve Balboni	.05	.02	.00
☐	28 Len Dykstra	.10	.05	.01
☐	29 Keith Moreland	.05	.02	.00
☐	30 Terry Kennedy	.05	.02	.00
☐	31 Eddie Murray	.12	.06	.01
☐	32 Mitch Williams	.20	.10	.02
☐	33 Jeff Parrett	.10	.05	.01
☐	34 Wally Backman	.05	.02	.00
☐	35 Julio Franco	.15	.07	.01
☐	36 Lance Parrish	.15	.07	.01
☐	37 Nick Esasky	.15	.07	.01
☐	38 Luis Polonia	.05	.02	.00
☐	39 Kevin Gross	.05	.02	.00
☐	40 John Dopson	.10	.05	.01
☐	41 Willie Randolph	.10	.05	.01
☐	42 Jim Clancy	.05	.02	.00
☐	43 Tracy Jones	.10	.05	.01
☐	44 Phil Bradley	.10	.05	.01
☐	45 Milt Thompson	.05	.02	.00
☐	46 Chris James	.10	.05	.01
☐	47 Scott Fletcher	.05	.02	.00
☐	48 Kal Daniels	.10	.05	.01
☐	49 Steve Bedrosian	.10	.05	.01
☐	50 Rickey Henderson	.50	.25	.05
☐	51 Dion James	.05	.02	.00
☐	52 Tim Leary	.10	.05	.01
☐	53 Roger McDowell	.10	.05	.01
☐	54 Mel Hall	.10	.05	.01
☐	55 Dickie Thon	.05	.02	.00
☐	56 Zane Smith	.05	.02	.00
☐	57 Danny Heep	.05	.02	.00
☐	58 Bob McClure	.05	.02	.00
☐	59 Brian Holton	.05	.02	.00
☐	60 Randy Ready	.05	.02	.00
☐	61 Bob Melvin	.05	.02	.00
☐	62 Harold Baines	.15	.07	.01
☐	63 Lance McCullers	.05	.02	.00
☐	64 Jody Davis	.05	.02	.00
☐	65 Darrell Evans	.10	.05	.01
☐	66 Joel Youngblood	.05	.02	.00
☐	67 Frank Viola	.15	.07	.01
☐	68 Mike Aldrete	.05	.02	.00
☐	69 Greg Cadaret	.10	.05	.01
☐	70 John Kruk	.10	.05	.01
☐	71 Pat Sheridan	.05	.02	.00
☐	72 Oddibe McDowell	.10	.05	.01
☐	73 Tom Brookens	.05	.02	.00
☐	74 Bob Boone	.15	.07	.01
☐	75 Walt Terrell	.05	.02	.00
☐	76 Joel Skinner	.05	.02	.00
☐	77 Randy Johnson	.15	.07	.01
☐	78 Felix Fermin	.05	.02	.00
☐	79 Rick Mahler	.05	.02	.00
☐	80 Richard Dotson	.05	.02	.00
☐	81 Cris Carpenter	.15	.07	.01
☐	82 Bill Spiers	.35	.17	.03
☐	83 Junior Felix	.90	.45	.09
☐	84 Joe Girardi	.30	.15	.03
☐	85 Jerome Walton	3.50	1.75	.35
☐	86 Greg Litton	.30	.15	.03
☐	87 Greg W. Harris	.20	.10	.02
☐	88 Jim Abbott	2.50	1.25	.25

☐	1 Don Mattingly	2.50	1.25	.25
☐	2 Steve Sax	.75	.35	.07
☐	3 Alvaro Espinoza	.20	.10	.02
☐	4 Luis Polonia	.30	.15	.03
☐	5 Jesse Barfield	.40	.20	.04
☐	6 Dave Righetti	.40	.20	.04
☐	7 Dave Winfield	.75	.35	.07
☐	8 John Candelaria	.20	.10	.02
☐	9 Wayne Tolleson	.20	.10	.02
☐	10 Ken Phelps	.20	.10	.02
☐	11 Rafael Santana	.20	.10	.02
☐	12 Don Slaught	.20	.10	.02
☐	13 Mike Pagliarulo	.30	.15	.03
☐	14 Lance McCullers	.20	.10	.02
☐	15 Dave LaPoint	.20	.10	.02
☐	16 Dale Mohorcic	.20	.10	.02
☐	17 Steve Balboni	.20	.10	.02
☐	18 Roberto Kelly	.50	.25	.05
☐	19 Andy Hawkins	.30	.15	.03
☐	20 Mel Hall	.40	.20	.04
☐	21 Tom Brookens	.30	.15	.03
☐	22 Deion Sanders	1.25	.60	.12
☐	23 Richard Dotson	.20	.10	.02
☐	24 Lee Guetterman	.20	.10	.02
☐	25 Bob Geren	.30	.15	.03
☐	26 Jimmy Jones	.20	.10	.02
☐	27 Chuck Cary	.30	.15	.03
☐	28 Ron Guidry	.50	.25	.05
☐	29 Hal Morris	.30	.15	.03
☐	30 Clay Parker	.30	.15	.03
☐	31 Dallas Green MG	.30	.15	.03
☐	32 Thurman Munson	2.00	1.00	.20
☐	33 Yankees Team Card	.50	.25	.05

1989 Score Traded

The 1989 Score Traded set contains 110 standard-size (2 1/2 by 3 1/2 inch) cards. The fronts have coral green borders with pink diamonds at the bottom. The vertically-oriented backs have color facial shots, career stats, and biographical information. Cards 1-80 feature traded players; cards 81-110 feature 1989 rookies. The set was distributed in a blue box with 10 Magic Motion trivia cards.

			MINT	EXC	G-VG
☐	89	Kevin Brown	.20	.10	.02
☐	90	John Wetteland	.40	.20	.04
☐	91	Gary Wayne	.20	.10	.02
☐	92	Rich Monteleone	.20	.10	.02
☐	93	Bob Geren	.30	.15	.03
☐	94	Clay Parker	.20	.10	.02
☐	95	Steve Finley	.20	.10	.02
☐	96	Gregg Olson	1.25	.60	.12
☐	97	Ken Patterson	.15	.07	.01
☐	98	Ken Hill	.20	.10	.02
☐	99	Scott Scudder	.30	.15	.03
☐	100	Ken Griffey Jr.	2.50	1.25	.25
☐	101	Jeff Brantley	.20	.10	.02
☐	102	Donn Pall	.15	.07	.01
☐	103	Carlos Martinez	.20	.10	.02
☐	104	Joe Oliver	.30	.15	.03
☐	105	Omar Vizquel	.30	.15	.03
☐	106	Joey Belle	1.00	.50	.10
☐	107	Kenny Rogers	.20	.10	.02
☐	108	Mark Carreon	.15	.07	.01
☐	109	Rolando Roomes	.20	.10	.02
☐	110	Pete Harnisch	.20	.10	.02

1990 Score

The 1990 Score set contains 704 standard- size (2 1/2 by 3 1/2 inch) cards. The front borders are red, blue, green or white. The vertically-oriented backs are white with borders that match the fronts, and feature color mugshots. Cards numbered 661-682 contain the first round draft picks subset noted as DC for "draft choice" in the checklist below. Cards numbered 683-695 contain the "Dream Team" subset noted by DT in the checklist below.

			MINT	EXC	G-VG
	COMPLETE SET (704)		24.00	12.00	2.40
	COMMON PLAYER (1-704)		.03	.01	.00
☐	1	Don Mattingly	.60	.20	.04
☐	2	Cal Ripken	.12	.06	.01
☐	3	Dwight Evans	.08	.04	.01
☐	4	Barry Bonds	.08	.04	.01
☐	5	Kevin McReynolds	.08	.04	.01
☐	6	Ozzie Guillen	.06	.03	.00
☐	7	Terry Kennedy	.03	.01	.00
☐	8	Bryan Harvey	.03	.01	.00
☐	9	Alan Trammell	.08	.04	.01
☐	10	Cory Snyder	.08	.04	.01
☐	11	Jody Reed	.03	.01	.00
☐	12	Roberto Alomar	.08	.04	.01
☐	13	Pedro Guerrero	.08	.04	.01
☐	14	Gary Redus	.03	.01	.00
☐	15	Marty Barrett	.03	.01	.00
☐	16	Ricky Jordan	.20	.10	.02
☐	17	Joe Magrane	.08	.04	.01
☐	18	Sid Fernandez	.08	.04	.01
☐	19	Richard Dotson	.03	.01	.00
☐	20	Jack Clark	.08	.04	.01
☐	21	Bob Walk	.03	.01	.00
☐	22	Ron Karkovice	.03	.01	.00
☐	23	Lenny Harris	.08	.04	.01
☐	24	Phil Bradley	.06	.03	.00
☐	25	Andres Galarraga	.08	.04	.01
☐	26	Brian Downing	.03	.01	.00
☐	27	Dave Martinez	.03	.01	.00
☐	28	Eric King	.03	.01	.00
☐	29	Barry Lyons	.03	.01	.00

			MINT	EXC	G-VG
☐	30	Dave Schmidt	.03	.01	.00
☐	31	Mike Boddicker	.03	.01	.00
☐	32	Tom Foley	.03	.01	.00
☐	33	Brady Anderson	.03	.01	.00
☐	34	Jim Presley	.03	.01	.00
☐	35	Lance Parrish	.08	.04	.01
☐	36	Von Hayes	.08	.04	.01
☐	37	Lee Smith	.06	.03	.00
☐	38	Herm Winningham	.03	.01	.00
☐	39	Alejandro Pena	.03	.01	.00
☐	40	Mike Scott	.08	.04	.01
☐	41	Joe Orsulak	.03	.01	.00
☐	42	Rafael Ramirez	.03	.01	.00
☐	43	Gerald Young	.03	.01	.00
☐	44	Dick Schofield	.03	.01	.00
☐	45	Dave Smith	.03	.01	.00
☐	46	Dave Magadan	.06	.03	.00
☐	47	Dennis Martinez	.03	.01	.00
☐	48	Greg Minton	.03	.01	.00
☐	49	Milt Thompson	.03	.01	.00
☐	50	Orel Hershiser	.10	.05	.01
☐	51	Bip Roberts	.03	.01	.00
☐	52	Jerry Browne	.03	.01	.00
☐	53	Bob Ojeda	.06	.03	.00
☐	54	Fernando Valenzuela	.08	.04	.01
☐	55	Matt Nokes	.06	.03	.00
☐	56	Brook Jacoby	.06	.03	.00
☐	57	Frank Tanana	.03	.01	.00
☐	58	Scott Fletcher	.03	.01	.00
☐	59	Ron Oester	.03	.01	.00
☐	60	Bob Boone	.06	.03	.00
☐	61	Dan Gladden	.03	.01	.00
☐	62	Darnell Coles	.03	.01	.00
☐	63	Gregg Olson	.30	.15	.03
☐	64	Todd Burns	.06	.03	.00
☐	65	Todd Benzinger	.03	.01	.00
☐	66	Dale Murphy	.12	.06	.01
☐	67	Mike Flanagan	.03	.01	.00
☐	68	Jose Oquendo	.03	.01	.00
☐	69	Cecil Espy	.03	.01	.00
☐	70	Chris Sabo	.06	.03	.00
☐	71	Shane Rawley	.03	.01	.00
☐	72	Tom Brunansky	.08	.04	.01
☐	73	Vance Law	.03	.01	.00
☐	74	B.J. Surhoff	.06	.03	.00
☐	75	Lou Whitaker	.08	.04	.01
☐	76	Ken Caminiti	.03	.01	.00
☐	77	Nelson Liriano	.03	.01	.00
☐	78	Tommy Gregg	.06	.03	.00
☐	79	Don Slaught	.03	.01	.00
☐	80	Eddie Murray	.10	.05	.01
☐	81	Joe Boever	.03	.01	.00
☐	82	Charlie Leibrandt	.03	.01	.00
☐	83	Jose Lind	.03	.01	.00
☐	84	Tony Phillips	.03	.01	.00
☐	85	Mitch Webster	.03	.01	.00
☐	86	Dan Plesac	.06	.03	.00
☐	87	Rick Mahler	.03	.01	.00
☐	88	Steve Lyons	.03	.01	.00
☐	89	Tony Fernandez	.08	.04	.01
☐	90	Ryne Sandberg	.12	.06	.01
☐	91	Nick Esasky	.06	.03	.00
☐	92	Luis Salazar	.03	.01	.00
☐	93	Pete Incaviglia	.06	.03	.00
☐	94	Ivan Calderon	.06	.03	.00
☐	95	Jeff Treadway	.03	.01	.00
☐	96	Kurt Stillwell	.03	.01	.00
☐	97	Gary Sheffield	.30	.15	.03
☐	98	Jeffrey Leonard	.06	.03	.00
☐	99	Andres Thomas	.03	.01	.00
☐	100	Roberto Kelly	.08	.04	.01
☐	101	Alvaro Espinoza	.03	.01	.00
☐	102	Greg Gagne	.03	.01	.00
☐	103	John Farrell	.03	.01	.00
☐	104	Willie Wilson	.06	.03	.00
☐	105	Glenn Braggs	.06	.03	.00
☐	106	Chet Lemon	.03	.01	.00
☐	107	Jamie Moyer	.03	.01	.00
☐	108	Chuck Crim	.03	.01	.00
☐	109	Dave Valle	.03	.01	.00
☐	110	Walt Weiss	.08	.04	.01
☐	111	Larry Sheets	.03	.01	.00
☐	112	Don Robinson	.03	.01	.00
☐	113	Danny Heep	.03	.01	.00
☐	114	Carmelo Martinez	.03	.01	.00
☐	115	Dave Gallagher	.03	.01	.00
☐	116	Mike LaValliere	.03	.01	.00
☐	117	Bob McClure	.03	.01	.00
☐	118	Rene Gonzales	.03	.01	.00
☐	119	Mark Parent	.03	.01	.00
☐	120	Wally Joyner	.08	.04	.01
☐	121	Mark Gubicza	.08	.04	.01
☐	122	Tony Pena	.06	.03	.00
☐	123	Carmen Castillo	.03	.01	.00
☐	124	Howard Johnson	.10	.05	.01

☐ 125	Steve Sax	.08	.04	.01
☐ 126	Tim Belcher	.06	.03	.00
☐ 127	Tim Burke	.06	.03	.00
☐ 128	Al Newman	.03	.01	.00
☐ 129	Dennis Rasmussen	.03	.01	.00
☐ 130	Doug Jones	.06	.03	.00
☐ 131	Fred Lynn	.06	.03	.00
☐ 132	Jeff Hamilton	.03	.01	.00
☐ 133	German Gonzalez	.03	.01	.00
☐ 134	John Morris	.03	.01	.00
☐ 135	Dave Parker	.08	.04	.01
☐ 136	Gary Pettis	.03	.01	.00
☐ 137	Dennis Boyd	.03	.01	.00
☐ 138	Candy Maldonado	.03	.01	.00
☐ 139	Rick Cerone	.03	.01	.00
☐ 140	George Brett	.12	.06	.01
☐ 141	Dave Clark	.03	.01	.00
☐ 142	Dickie Thon	.03	.01	.00
☐ 143	Junior Ortiz	.03	.01	.00
☐ 144	Don August	.03	.01	.00
☐ 145	Gary Gaetti	.08	.04	.01
☐ 146	Kirt Manwaring	.03	.01	.00
☐ 147	Jeff Reed	.03	.01	.00
☐ 148	Jose Alvarez	.03	.01	.00
☐ 149	Mike Schooler	.06	.03	.00
☐ 150	Mark Grace	.35	.17	.03
☐ 151	Geronimo Berroa	.03	.01	.00
☐ 152	Barry Jones	.03	.01	.00
☐ 153	Geno Petralli	.03	.01	.00
☐ 154	Jim Deshaies	.03	.01	.00
☐ 155	Barry Larkin	.08	.04	.01
☐ 156	Alfredo Griffin	.03	.01	.00
☐ 157	Tom Henke	.06	.03	.00
☐ 158	Mike Jeffcoat	.03	.01	.00
☐ 159	Bob Welch	.06	.03	.00
☐ 160	Julio Franco	.06	.03	.00
☐ 161	Henry Cotto	.03	.01	.00
☐ 162	Terry Steinbach	.06	.03	.00
☐ 163	Damon Berryhill	.08	.04	.01
☐ 164	Tim Crews	.03	.01	.00
☐ 165	Tom Browning	.06	.03	.00
☐ 166	Fred Manrique	.03	.01	.00
☐ 167	Harold Reynolds	.06	.03	.00
☐ 168	Ron Hassey	.03	.01	.00
☐ 169	Shawon Dunston	.06	.03	.00
☐ 170	Bobby Bonilla	.08	.04	.01
☐ 171	Tommy Herr	.03	.01	.00
☐ 172	Mike Heath	.03	.01	.00
☐ 173	Rich Gedman	.03	.01	.00
☐ 174	Bill Ripken	.03	.01	.00
☐ 175	Pete O'Brien	.06	.03	.00
☐ 176A	Lloyd McClendon ERR (uniform number on back listed as 1)	1.00	.50	.10
☐ 176B	Lloyd McClendon COR (uniform number on back listed as 10)	.08	.04	.01
☐ 177	Brian Holton	.03	.01	.00
☐ 178	Jeff Blauser	.03	.01	.00
☐ 179	Jim Eisenreich	.03	.01	.00
☐ 180	Bert Blyleven	.08	.04	.01
☐ 181	Rob Murphy	.03	.01	.00
☐ 182	Bill Doran	.06	.03	.00
☐ 183	Curt Ford	.03	.01	.00
☐ 184	Mike Henneman	.03	.01	.00
☐ 185	Eric Davis	.20	.10	.02
☐ 186	Lance McCullers	.03	.01	.00
☐ 187	Steve Davis	.12	.06	.01
☐ 188	Bill Wegman	.03	.01	.00
☐ 189	Brian Harper	.03	.01	.00
☐ 190	Mike Moore	.06	.03	.00
☐ 191	Dale Mohorcic	.03	.01	.00
☐ 192	Tim Wallach	.06	.03	.00
☐ 193	Keith Hernandez	.08	.04	.01
☐ 194	Dave Righetti	.08	.04	.01
☐ 195	Bret Saberhagen	.10	.05	.01
☐ 196	Paul Kilgus	.03	.01	.00
☐ 197	Bud Black	.03	.01	.00
☐ 198	Juan Samuel	.06	.03	.00
☐ 199	Kevin Seitzer	.08	.04	.01
☐ 200	Darryl Strawberry	.25	.12	.02
☐ 201	Dave Stieb	.08	.04	.01
☐ 202	Charlie Hough	.03	.01	.00
☐ 203	Jack Morris	.08	.04	.01
☐ 204	Rance Mulliniks	.03	.01	.00
☐ 205	Alvin Davis	.08	.04	.01
☐ 206	Jack Howell	.03	.01	.00
☐ 207	Ken Patterson	.08	.04	.01
☐ 208	Terry Pendleton	.03	.01	.00
☐ 209	Craig Lefferts	.03	.01	.00
☐ 210	Kevin Brown	.10	.05	.01
☐ 211	Dan Petry	.03	.01	.00
☐ 212	Dave Leiper	.03	.01	.00
☐ 213	Daryl Boston	.03	.01	.00
☐ 214	Kevin Hickey	.03	.01	.00
☐ 215	Mike Krukow	.03	.01	.00
☐ 216	Terry Francona	.03	.01	.00
☐ 217	Kirk McCaskill	.03	.01	.00
☐ 218	Scott Bailes	.03	.01	.00
☐ 219	Bob Forsch	.03	.01	.00
☐ 220	Mike Aldrete	.03	.01	.00
☐ 221	Steve Buechele	.03	.01	.00
☐ 222	Jesse Barfield	.08	.04	.01
☐ 223	Juan Berenguer	.03	.01	.00
☐ 224	Andy McGaffigan	.03	.01	.00
☐ 225	Pete Smith	.03	.01	.00
☐ 226	Mike Witt	.06	.03	.00
☐ 227	Jay Howell	.03	.01	.00
☐ 228	Scott Bradley	.03	.01	.00
☐ 229	Jerome Walton	1.00	.50	.10
☐ 230	Greg Swindell	.08	.04	.01
☐ 231	Atlee Hammaker	.03	.01	.00
☐ 232	Mike Devereaux	.03	.01	.00
☐ 233	Ken Hill	.08	.04	.01
☐ 234	Craig Worthington	.08	.04	.01
☐ 235	Scott Terry	.03	.01	.00
☐ 236	Brett Butler	.06	.03	.00
☐ 237	Doyle Alexander	.03	.01	.00
☐ 238	Dave Anderson	.03	.01	.00
☐ 239	Bob Milacki	.03	.01	.00
☐ 240	Dwight Smith	.35	.17	.03
☐ 241	Otis Nixon	.03	.01	.00
☐ 242	Pat Tabler	.03	.01	.00
☐ 243	Derek Lilliquist	.06	.03	.00
☐ 244	Danny Tartabull	.08	.04	.01
☐ 245	Wade Boggs	.25	.12	.02
☐ 246	Scott Garrelts	.06	.03	.00
☐ 247	Spike Owen	.03	.01	.00
☐ 248	Norm Charlton	.03	.01	.00
☐ 249	Gerald Perry	.06	.03	.00
☐ 250	Nolan Ryan	.25	.12	.02
☐ 251	Kevin Gross	.03	.01	.00
☐ 252	Randy Milligan	.03	.01	.00
☐ 253	Mike LaCoss	.03	.01	.00
☐ 254	Dave Bergman	.03	.01	.00
☐ 255	Tony Gwynn	.15	.07	.01
☐ 256	Felix Fermin	.03	.01	.00
☐ 257	Greg Harris	.10	.05	.01
☐ 258	Junior Felix	.30	.15	.03
☐ 259	Mark Davis	.08	.04	.01
☐ 260	Vince Coleman	.08	.04	.01
☐ 261	Paul Gibson	.03	.01	.00
☐ 262	Mitch Williams	.06	.03	.00
☐ 263	Jeff Russell	.06	.03	.00
☐ 264	Omar Vizquel	.12	.06	.01
☐ 265	Andre Dawson	.10	.05	.01
☐ 266	Storm Davis	.06	.03	.00
☐ 267	Guillermo Hernandez	.06	.03	.00
☐ 268	Mike Felder	.03	.01	.00
☐ 269	Tom Candiotti	.03	.01	.00
☐ 270	Bruce Hurst	.06	.03	.00
☐ 271	Fred McGriff	.12	.06	.01
☐ 272	Glenn Davis	.10	.05	.01
☐ 273	John Franco	.06	.03	.00
☐ 274	Rich Yett	.03	.01	.00
☐ 275	Craig Biggio	.08	.04	.01
☐ 276	Gene Larkin	.03	.01	.00
☐ 277	Rob Dibble	.06	.03	.00
☐ 278	Randy Bush	.03	.01	.00
☐ 279	Kevin Bass	.06	.03	.00
☐ 280	Bo Jackson	.50	.25	.05
☐ 281	Wally Backman	.03	.01	.00
☐ 282	Larry Andersen	.03	.01	.00
☐ 283	Chris Bosio	.06	.03	.00
☐ 284	Juan Agosto	.03	.01	.00
☐ 285	Ozzie Smith	.08	.04	.01
☐ 286	George Bell	.08	.04	.01
☐ 287	Rex Hudler	.03	.01	.00
☐ 288	Pat Borders	.03	.01	.00
☐ 289	Danny Jackson	.06	.03	.00
☐ 290	Carlton Fisk	.10	.05	.01
☐ 291	Tracy Jones	.03	.01	.00
☐ 292	Allan Anderson	.06	.03	.00
☐ 293	Johnny Ray	.06	.03	.00
☐ 294	Lee Guetterman	.03	.01	.00
☐ 295	Paul O'Neill	.08	.04	.01
☐ 296	Carney Lansford	.08	.04	.01
☐ 297	Tom Brookens	.03	.01	.00
☐ 298	Claudell Washington	.06	.03	.00
☐ 299	Hubie Brooks	.06	.03	.00
☐ 300	Will Clark	.50	.25	.05
☐ 301	Kenny Rogers	.12	.06	.01
☐ 302	Darrell Evans	.06	.03	.00
☐ 303	Greg Briley	.20	.10	.02
☐ 304	Donn Pall	.08	.04	.01
☐ 305	Teddy Higuera	.06	.03	.00
☐ 306	Dan Pasqua	.03	.01	.00
☐ 307	Dave Winfield	.10	.05	.01
☐ 308	Dennis Powell	.03	.01	.00
☐ 309	Jose DeLeon	.06	.03	.00

☐ 310	Roger Clemens	.20	.10	.02
☐ 311	Melido Perez	.06	.03	.00
☐ 312	Devon White	.08	.04	.01
☐ 313	Dwight Gooden	.20	.10	.02
☐ 314	Carlos Martinez	.20	.10	.02
☐ 315	Dennis Eckersley	.10	.05	.01
☐ 316	Clay Parker	.03	.01	.00
☐ 317	Rick Honeycutt	.03	.01	.00
☐ 318	Tim Laudner	.03	.01	.00
☐ 319	Joe Carter	.10	.05	.01
☐ 320	Robin Yount	.25	.12	.02
☐ 321	Felix Jose	.03	.01	.00
☐ 322	Mickey Tettleton	.06	.03	.00
☐ 323	Mike Gallego	.03	.01	.00
☐ 324	Edgar Martinez	.03	.01	.00
☐ 325	Dave Henderson	.03	.01	.00
☐ 326	Chili Davis	.06	.03	.00
☐ 327	Steve Balboni	.03	.01	.00
☐ 328	Jody Davis	.03	.01	.00
☐ 329	Shawn Hillegas	.03	.01	.00
☐ 330	Jim Abbott	.75	.35	.07
☐ 331	John Dopson	.03	.01	.00
☐ 332	Mark Williamson	.03	.01	.00
☐ 333	Jeff Robinson	.06	.03	.00
☐ 334	John Smiley	.06	.03	.00
☐ 335	Bobby Thigpen	.06	.03	.00
☐ 336	Garry Templeton	.06	.03	.00
☐ 337	Marvell Wynne	.03	.01	.00
☐ 338A	Ken Griffey Sr. ERR (uniform number on back listed as 25)	1.00	.50	.10
☐ 338B	Ken Griffey Sr. COR (uniform number on back listed as 30)	.08	.04	.01
☐ 339	Steve Finley	.12	.06	.01
☐ 340	Ellis Burks	.15	.07	.01
☐ 341	Frank Williams	.03	.01	.00
☐ 342	Mike Morgan	.03	.01	.00
☐ 343	Kevin Mitchell	.15	.07	.01
☐ 344	Joel Youngblood	.03	.01	.00
☐ 345	Mike Greenwell	.20	.10	.02
☐ 346	Glenn Wilson	.03	.01	.00
☐ 347	John Costello	.03	.01	.00
☐ 348	Wes Gardner	.03	.01	.00
☐ 349	Jeff Ballard	.06	.03	.00
☐ 350	Mark Thurmond	.03	.01	.00
☐ 351	Randy Myers	.06	.03	.00
☐ 352	Shawn Abner	.03	.01	.00
☐ 353	Jesse Orosco	.03	.01	.00
☐ 354	Greg Walker	.03	.01	.00
☐ 355	Pete Harnisch	.06	.03	.00
☐ 356	Steve Farr	.03	.01	.00
☐ 357	Dave LaPoint	.03	.01	.00
☐ 358	Willie Fraser	.03	.01	.00
☐ 359	Mickey Hatcher	.03	.01	.00
☐ 360	Rickey Henderson	.25	.12	.02
☐ 361	Mike Fitzgerald	.03	.01	.00
☐ 362	Bill Schroeder	.03	.01	.00
☐ 363	Mark Carreon	.06	.03	.00
☐ 364	Ron Jones	.06	.03	.00
☐ 365	Jeff Montgomery	.06	.03	.00
☐ 366	Bill Krueger	.03	.01	.00
☐ 367	John Cangelosi	.03	.01	.00
☐ 368	Jose Gonzalez	.03	.01	.00
☐ 369	Greg Hibbard	.12	.06	.01
☐ 370	John Smoltz	.08	.04	.01
☐ 371	Jeff Brantley	.15	.07	.01
☐ 372	Frank White	.06	.03	.00
☐ 373	Ed Whitson	.03	.01	.00
☐ 374	Willie McGee	.08	.04	.01
☐ 375	Jose Canseco	.50	.25	.05
☐ 376	Randy Ready	.03	.01	.00
☐ 377	Don Aase	.03	.01	.00
☐ 378	Tony Armas	.06	.03	.00
☐ 379	Steve Bedrosian	.06	.03	.00
☐ 380	Chuck Finley	.06	.03	.00
☐ 381	Kent Hrbek	.08	.04	.01
☐ 382	Jim Gantner	.03	.01	.00
☐ 383	Mel Hall	.06	.03	.00
☐ 384	Mike Marshall	.08	.04	.01
☐ 385	Mark McGwire	.25	.12	.02
☐ 386	Wayne Tolleson	.03	.01	.00
☐ 387	Brian Holman	.08	.04	.01
☐ 388	John Wetteland	.20	.10	.02
☐ 389	Darren Daulton	.03	.01	.00
☐ 390	Rob Deer	.06	.03	.00
☐ 391	John Moses	.03	.01	.00
☐ 392	Todd Worrell	.08	.04	.01
☐ 393	Chuck Cary	.06	.03	.00
☐ 394	Stan Javier	.03	.01	.00
☐ 395	Willie Randolph	.06	.03	.00
☐ 396	Bill Buckner	.06	.03	.00
☐ 397	Robby Thompson	.03	.01	.00
☐ 398	Mike Scioscia	.03	.01	.00
☐ 399	Lonnie Smith	.06	.03	.00
☐ 400	Kirby Puckett	.25	.12	.02
☐ 401	Mark Langston	.08	.04	.01
☐ 402	Danny Darwin	.03	.01	.00
☐ 403	Greg Maddux	.06	.03	.00
☐ 404	Lloyd Moseby	.06	.03	.00
☐ 405	Rafael Palmeiro	.06	.03	.00
☐ 406	Chad Kreuter	.03	.01	.00
☐ 407	Jimmy Key	.06	.03	.00
☐ 408	Tim Birtsas	.03	.01	.00
☐ 409	Tim Raines	.10	.05	.01
☐ 410	Dave Stewart	.08	.04	.01
☐ 411	Eric Yelding	.10	.05	.01
☐ 412	Kent Anderson	.10	.05	.01
☐ 413	Les Lancaster	.03	.01	.00
☐ 414	Rick Dempsey	.03	.01	.00
☐ 415	Randy Johnson	.03	.01	.00
☐ 416	Gary Carter	.08	.04	.01
☐ 417	Rolando Roomes	.08	.04	.01
☐ 418	Dan Schatzeder	.03	.01	.00
☐ 419	Bryn Smith	.06	.03	.00
☐ 420	Ruben Sierra	.20	.10	.02
☐ 421	Steve Jeltz	.03	.01	.00
☐ 422	Ken Oberkfell	.03	.01	.00
☐ 423	Sid Bream	.03	.01	.00
☐ 424	Jim Clancy	.03	.01	.00
☐ 425	Kelly Gruber	.06	.03	.00
☐ 426	Rick Leach	.03	.01	.00
☐ 427	Len Dykstra	.06	.03	.00
☐ 428	Jeff Pico	.03	.01	.00
☐ 429	John Cerutti	.03	.01	.00
☐ 430	David Cone	.10	.05	.01
☐ 431	Jeff Kunkel	.03	.01	.00
☐ 432	Luis Aquino	.03	.01	.00
☐ 433	Ernie Whitt	.03	.01	.00
☐ 434	Bo Diaz	.03	.01	.00
☐ 435	Steve Lake	.03	.01	.00
☐ 436	Pat Perry	.03	.01	.00
☐ 437	Mike Davis	.03	.01	.00
☐ 438	Cecilio Guante	.03	.01	.00
☐ 439	Duane Ward	.03	.01	.00
☐ 440	Andy Van Slyke	.08	.04	.01
☐ 441	Gene Nelson	.03	.01	.00
☐ 442	Luis Polonia	.03	.01	.00
☐ 443	Kevin Elster	.06	.03	.00
☐ 444	Keith Moreland	.03	.01	.00
☐ 445	Roger McDowell	.06	.03	.00
☐ 446	Ron Darling	.08	.04	.01
☐ 447	Ernest Riles	.03	.01	.00
☐ 448	Mookie Wilson	.06	.03	.00
☐ 449A	Billy Spiers ERR (no birth year)	2.00	1.00	.20
☐ 449B	Billy Spiers COR (born in 1966)	.40	.20	.04
☐ 450	Rick Sutcliffe	.06	.03	.00
☐ 451	Nelson Santovenia	.03	.01	.00
☐ 452	Andy Allanson	.03	.01	.00
☐ 453	Bob Melvin	.03	.01	.00
☐ 454	Benito Santiago	.08	.04	.01
☐ 455	Jose Uribe	.03	.01	.00
☐ 456	Bill Landrum	.03	.01	.00
☐ 457	Bobby Witt	.06	.03	.00
☐ 458	Kevin Romine	.03	.01	.00
☐ 459	Lee Mazzilli	.03	.01	.00
☐ 460	Paul Molitor	.08	.04	.01
☐ 461	Ramon Martinez	.08	.04	.01
☐ 462	Frank DiPino	.03	.01	.00
☐ 463	Walt Terrell	.03	.01	.00
☐ 464	Bob Geren	.15	.07	.01
☐ 465	Rick Reuschel	.06	.03	.00
☐ 466	Mark Grant	.03	.01	.00
☐ 467	John Kruk	.06	.03	.00
☐ 468	Gregg Jefferies	.35	.17	.03
☐ 469	R.J. Reynolds	.03	.01	.00
☐ 470	Harold Baines	.08	.04	.01
☐ 471	Dennis Lamp	.03	.01	.00
☐ 472	Tom Gordon	.35	.17	.03
☐ 473	Terry Puhl	.03	.01	.00
☐ 474	Curt Wilkerson	.03	.01	.00
☐ 475	Dan Quisenberry	.06	.03	.00
☐ 476	Oddibe McDowell	.06	.03	.00
☐ 477	Zane Smith	.03	.01	.00
☐ 478	Franklin Stubbs	.03	.01	.00
☐ 479	Wallace Johnson	.03	.01	.00
☐ 480	Jay Tibbs	.03	.01	.00
☐ 481	Tom Glavine	.06	.03	.00
☐ 482	Manny Lee	.03	.01	.00
☐ 483	Joe Hesketh	.03	.01	.00
☐ 484	Mike Bielecki	.06	.03	.00
☐ 485	Greg Brock	.03	.01	.00
☐ 486	Pascual Perez	.06	.03	.00
☐ 487	Kirk Gibson	.08	.04	.01
☐ 488	Scott Sanderson	.03	.01	.00
☐ 489	Domingo Ramos	.03	.01	.00
☐ 490	Kal Daniels	.08	.04	.01
☐ 491A	David Wells ERR	2.50	1.00	.20

(reverse negative photo on card back)			
☐ 491B David Wells COR	.10	.04	.01
☐ 492 Jerry Reed	.03	.01	.00
☐ 493 Eric Show	.03	.01	.00
☐ 494 Mike Pagliarulo	.06	.03	.00
☐ 495 Ron Robinson	.03	.01	.00
☐ 496 Brad Komminsk	.03	.01	.00
☐ 497 Greg Litton	.20	.10	.02
☐ 498 Chris James	.06	.03	.00
☐ 499 Luis Quinones	.03	.01	.00
☐ 500 Frank Viola	.08	.04	.01
☐ 501 Tim Teufel	.03	.01	.00
☐ 502 Terry Leach	.03	.01	.00
☐ 503 Matt Williams	.12	.06	.01
☐ 504 Tim Leary	.06	.03	.00
☐ 505 Doug Drabek	.06	.03	.00
☐ 506 Mariano Duncan	.03	.01	.00
☐ 507 Charlie Hayes	.06	.03	.00
☐ 508 Joey Belle	.50	.25	.05
☐ 509 Pat Sheridan	.03	.01	.00
☐ 510 Mackey Sasser	.06	.03	.00
☐ 511 Jose Rijo	.03	.01	.00
☐ 512 Mike Smithson	.03	.01	.00
☐ 513 Gary Ward	.03	.01	.00
☐ 514 Dion James	.03	.01	.00
☐ 515 Jim Gott	.03	.01	.00
☐ 516 Drew Hall	.03	.01	.00
☐ 517 Doug Bair	.03	.01	.00
☐ 518 Scott Scudder	.15	.07	.01
☐ 519 Rick Aguilera	.03	.01	.00
☐ 520 Rafael Belliard	.03	.01	.00
☐ 521 Jay Buhner	.06	.03	.00
☐ 522 Jeff Reardon	.06	.03	.00
☐ 523 Steve Rosenberg	.08	.04	.01
☐ 524 Randy Velarde	.06	.03	.00
☐ 525 Jeff Musselman	.03	.01	.00
☐ 526 Bill Long	.03	.01	.00
☐ 527 Gary Wayne	.10	.05	.01
☐ 528 Dave Johnson (P)	.12	.06	.01
☐ 529 Ron Kittle	.06	.03	.00
☐ 530 Erik Hanson	.10	.05	.01
☐ 531 Steve Wilson	.08	.04	.01
☐ 532 Joey Meyer	.06	.03	.00
☐ 533 Curt Young	.03	.01	.00
☐ 534 Kelly Downs	.03	.01	.00
☐ 535 Joe Girardi	.12	.06	.01
☐ 536 Lance Blankenship	.03	.01	.00
☐ 537 Greg Mathews	.03	.01	.00
☐ 538 Donell Nixon	.03	.01	.00
☐ 539 Mark Knudson	.08	.04	.01
☐ 540 Jeff Wetherby	.12	.06	.01
☐ 541 Darrin Jackson	.03	.01	.00
☐ 542 Terry Mulholland	.03	.01	.00
☐ 543 Eric Hetzel	.08	.04	.01
☐ 544 Rick Reed	.12	.06	.01
☐ 545 Dennis Cook	.10	.05	.01
☐ 546 Mike Jackson	.03	.01	.00
☐ 547 Brian Fisher	.03	.01	.00
☐ 548 Gene Harris	.15	.07	.01
☐ 549 Jeff King	.10	.05	.01
☐ 550 Dave Dravecky	.08	.04	.01
☐ 551 Randy Kutcher	.03	.01	.00
☐ 552 Mark Portugal	.03	.01	.00
☐ 553 Jim Corsi	.08	.04	.01
☐ 554 Todd Stottlemyre	.06	.03	.00
☐ 555 Scott Bankhead	.06	.03	.00
☐ 556 Ken Dayley	.03	.01	.00
☐ 557 Rick Wrona	.15	.07	.01
☐ 558 Sammy Sosa	.40	.20	.04
☐ 559 Keith Miller	.03	.01	.00
☐ 560 Ken Griffey Jr.	1.00	.50	.10
☐ 561A Ryne Sandberg HL ERR	16.00	8.00	1.60
(position on front listed as 3B)			
☐ 561B Ryne Sandberg HL COR	.50	.25	.05
☐ 562 Billy Hatcher	.03	.01	.00
☐ 563 Jay Bell	.03	.01	.00
☐ 564 Jack Daugherty	.10	.05	.01
☐ 565 Rich Monteleone	.10	.05	.01
☐ 566 Bo Jackson AS-MVP	.35	.17	.03
☐ 567 Tony Fossas	.10	.05	.01
☐ 568 Roy Smith	.03	.01	.00
☐ 569 Jaime Navarro	.20	.10	.02
☐ 570 Lance Johnson	.10	.05	.01
☐ 571 Mike Dyer	.15	.07	.01
☐ 572 Kevin Ritz	.15	.07	.01
☐ 573 Dave West	.06	.03	.00
☐ 574 Gary Mielke	.10	.05	.01
☐ 575 Scott Lusader	.03	.01	.00
☐ 576 Joe Oliver	.15	.07	.01
☐ 577 Sandy Alomar Jr.	.25	.12	.02
☐ 578 Andy Benes	.35	.17	.03
☐ 579 Tim Jones	.03	.01	.00
☐ 580 Randy McCament	.12	.06	.01
☐ 581 Curt Schilling	.08	.04	.01
☐ 582 John Orton	.15	.07	.01
☐ 583A Milt Cuyler ERR (989 games)	2.00	1.00	.20
☐ 583B Milt Cuyler COR (98 games)	.40	.20	.04
☐ 584 Eric Anthony	1.50	.75	.15
☐ 585 Greg Vaughn	1.25	.60	.12
☐ 586 Deion Sanders	.50	.25	.05
☐ 587 Jose DeJesus	.03	.01	.00
☐ 588 Chip Hale	.15	.07	.01
☐ 589 John Olerud	2.50	1.00	.20
☐ 590 Steve Olin	.12	.06	.01
☐ 591 Marquis Grissom	.50	.25	.05
☐ 592 Moises Alou	.25	.12	.02
☐ 593 Mark Lemke	.08	.04	.01
☐ 594 Dean Palmer	.25	.12	.02
☐ 595 Robin Ventura	.50	.25	.05
☐ 596 Tino Martinez	.35	.17	.03
☐ 597 Mike Huff	.20	.10	.02
☐ 598 Scott Hemond	.20	.10	.02
☐ 599 Wally Whitehurst	.10	.05	.01
☐ 600 Todd Zeile	1.25	.60	.12
☐ 601 Glenallen Hill	.20	.10	.02
☐ 602 Hal Morris	.15	.07	.01
☐ 603 Juan Bell	.20	.10	.02
☐ 604 Bobby Rose	.20	.10	.02
☐ 605 Matt Merullo	.12	.06	.01
☐ 606 Kevin Maas	.25	.12	.02
☐ 607 Randy Nosek	.15	.07	.01
☐ 608 Billy Bates	.12	.06	.01
☐ 609 Mike Stanton	.20	.10	.02
☐ 610 Mauro Gozzo	.20	.10	.02
☐ 611 Charles Nagy	.20	.10	.02
☐ 612 Scott Coolbaugh	.25	.12	.02
☐ 613 Jose Vizcaino	.20	.10	.02
☐ 614 Greg Smith	.15	.07	.01
☐ 615 Jeff Huson	.12	.06	.01
☐ 616 Mickey Weston	.10	.05	.01
☐ 617 John Pawlowski	.08	.04	.01
☐ 618 Joe Skalski	.12	.06	.01
☐ 619 Bernie Williams	.45	.22	.04
☐ 620 Shawn Holman	.12	.06	.01
☐ 621 Gary Eave	.12	.06	.01
☐ 622 Darrin Fletcher	.12	.06	.01
☐ 623 Pat Combs	.30	.15	.03
☐ 624 Mike Blowers	.20	.10	.02
☐ 625 Kevin Appier	.12	.06	.01
☐ 626 Pat Austin	.12	.06	.01
☐ 627 Kelly Mann	.12	.06	.01
☐ 628 Matt Kinzer	.10	.05	.01
☐ 629 Chris Hammond	.15	.07	.01
☐ 630 Dean Wilkins	.12	.06	.01
☐ 631 Larry Walker	.20	.10	.02
☐ 632 Blaine Beatty	.15	.07	.01
☐ 633 Tommy Barrett	.08	.04	.01
☐ 634 Stan Belinda	.10	.05	.01
☐ 635 Mike (Tex) Smith	.10	.05	.01
☐ 636 Hensley Meulens	.20	.10	.02
☐ 637 Juan Gonzalez	.60	.30	.06
☐ 638 Lenny Webster	.12	.06	.01
☐ 639 Mark Gardner	.12	.06	.01
☐ 640 Tommy Greene	.40	.20	.04
☐ 641 Mike Hartley	.10	.05	.01
☐ 642 Phil Stephenson	.10	.05	.01
☐ 643 Kevin Mmahat	.20	.10	.02
☐ 644 Ed Whited	.20	.10	.02
☐ 645 Delino DeShields	.30	.15	.03
☐ 646 Kevin Blankenship	.08	.04	.01
☐ 647 Paul Sorrento	.15	.07	.01
☐ 648 Mike Roesler	.12	.06	.01
☐ 649 Jason Grimsley	.15	.07	.01
☐ 650 Dave Justice	.20	.10	.02
☐ 651 Scott Cooper	.20	.10	.02
☐ 652 Dave Eiland	.08	.04	.01
☐ 653 Mike Munoz	.12	.06	.01
☐ 654 Jeff Fischer	.10	.05	.01
☐ 655 Terry Jorgenson	.12	.06	.01
☐ 656 George Canale	.15	.07	.01
☐ 657 Brian Dubois	.12	.06	.01
☐ 658 Carlos Quintana	.06	.03	.00
☐ 659 Luis De Los Santos	.03	.01	.00
☐ 660 Jerald Clark	.03	.01	.00
☐ 661 Donald Harris DC	.30	.15	.03
☐ 662 Paul Coleman DC	.30	.15	.03
☐ 663 Frank Thomas DC	.30	.15	.03
☐ 664 Brent Mayne DC	.20	.10	.02
☐ 665 Eddie Zosky DC	.20	.10	.02
☐ 666 Steve Hosey DC	.20	.10	.02
☐ 667 Scott Bryant DC	.20	.10	.02
☐ 668 Tom Goodwin DC	.40	.20	.04
☐ 669 Cal Eldred DC	.20	.10	.02
☐ 670 Earl Cunningham DC	.40	.20	.04
☐ 671 Alan Zinter DC	.20	.10	.02
☐ 672 Chuck Knoblauch DC	.20	.10	.02

			MINT	EXC	G-VG
☐ 673	Kyle Abbott DC		.20	.10	.02
☐ 674	Roger Salkeld DC		.20	.10	.02
☐ 675	Maurice Vaughn DC		.30	.15	.03
☐ 676	Keith (Kiki) Jones DC		.40	.20	.04
☐ 677	Tyler Houston DC		.40	.20	.04
☐ 678	Jeff Jackson DC		.25	.12	.02
☐ 679	Greg Gohr DC		.20	.10	.02
☐ 680	Ben McDonald DC		1.75	.85	.17
☐ 681	Greg Blosser DC		.20	.10	.02
☐ 682	Willie Green DC		.20	.10	.02
☐ 683	Wade Boggs DT		.20	.10	.02
☐ 684	Will Clark DT		.35	.17	.03
☐ 685	Tony Gwynn DT		.15	.07	.01
☐ 686	Rickey Henderson DT		.20	.10	.02
☐ 687	Bo Jackson DT		.35	.17	.03
☐ 688	Mark Langston DT		.10	.05	.01
☐ 689	Barry Larkin DT		.10	.05	.01
☐ 690	Kirby Puckett DT		.20	.10	.02
☐ 691	Ryne Sandberg DT		.12	.06	.01
☐ 692	Mike Scott DT		.08	.04	.01
☐ 693	Terry Steinbach DT		.06	.03	.00
☐ 694	Bobby Thigpen DT		.06	.03	.00
☐ 695	Mitch Williams DT		.06	.03	.00
☐ 696	Nolan Ryan HL		.25	.12	.02
☐ 697	Bo Jackson FB/BB		1.50	.50	.10
☐ 698	Rickey Henderson ALCS-MVP		.20	.10	.02
☐ 699	Will Clark NLCS-MVP		.30	.15	.03
☐ 700	WS Games 1/2		.06	.03	.00
☐ 701	Candlestick		.06	.03	.00
☐ 702	WS Game 3		.06	.03	.00
☐ 703	WS Wrap-up		.06	.03	.00
☐ 704	Wade Boggs		.15	.07	.01

1990 Score 100 Rising Stars

The 1990 Score Rising Stars set contains 100 standard size (2 1/2 by 3 1/2 inch) cards. The fronts are green, blue and white. The vertically-oriented backs feature a large color facial shot and career highlights. The cards were distributed as a set in a blister pack, which also included a full color booklet with more information about each player.

		MINT	EXC	G-VG
COMPLETE SET (100)		12.50	6.25	1.25
COMMON PLAYER (1-100)		.05	.02	.00
☐ 1	Tom Gordon	.50	.25	.05
☐ 2	Jerome Walton	1.00	.50	.10
☐ 3	Ken Griffey Jr.	1.00	.50	.10
☐ 4	Dwight Smith	.50	.25	.05
☐ 5	Jim Abbott	1.00	.50	.10
☐ 6	Todd Zeile	1.00	.50	.10
☐ 7	Donn Pall	.10	.05	.01
☐ 8	Rick Reed	.10	.05	.01
☐ 9	Joey Belle	.50	.25	.05
☐ 10	Gregg Jefferies	.60	.30	.06
☐ 11	Kevin Ritz	.15	.07	.01
☐ 12	Charlie Hayes	.10	.05	.01
☐ 13	Kevin Appier	.10	.05	.01
☐ 14	Jeff Huson	.10	.05	.01
☐ 15	Gary Wayne	.10	.05	.01
☐ 16	Eric Yelding	.10	.05	.01
☐ 17	Clay Parker	.10	.05	.01
☐ 18	Junior Felix	.30	.15	.03
☐ 19	Derek Lilliquist	.15	.07	.01
☐ 20	Gary Sheffield	.50	.25	.05

☐ 21	Craig Worthington	.20	.10	.02
☐ 22	Jeff Brantley	.15	.07	.01
☐ 23	Eric Hetzel	.15	.07	.01
☐ 24	Greg W.Harris	.10	.05	.01
☐ 25	John Wetteland	.25	.12	.02
☐ 26	Joe Oliver	.20	.10	.02
☐ 27	Kevin Maas	.25	.12	.02
☐ 28	Kevin Brown	.20	.10	.02
☐ 29	Mike Stanton	.20	.10	.02
☐ 30	Greg Vaughn	.75	.35	.07
☐ 31	Ron Jones	.20	.10	.02
☐ 32	Gregg Olson	.50	.25	.05
☐ 33	Joe Girardi	.20	.10	.02
☐ 34	Ken Hill	.15	.07	.01
☐ 35	Sammy Sosa	.35	.17	.03
☐ 36	Geronimo Berroa	.10	.05	.01
☐ 37	Omar Vizquel	.15	.07	.01
☐ 38	Dean Palmer	.25	.12	.02
☐ 39	John Olerud	1.50	.75	.15
☐ 40	Deion Sanders	.75	.35	.07
☐ 41	Randy Kramer	.10	.05	.01
☐ 42	Scott Lusader	.10	.05	.01
☐ 43	Dave Johnson (P)	.15	.07	.01
☐ 44	Jeff Wetherby	.15	.07	.01
☐ 45	Eric Anthony	1.00	.50	.10
☐ 46	Kenny Rogers	.15	.07	.01
☐ 47	Matt Winters	.20	.10	.02
☐ 48	Mauro Gozzo	.20	.10	.02
☐ 49	Carlos Quintana	.20	.10	.02
☐ 50	Bob Geren	.15	.07	.01
☐ 51	Chad Kreuter	.15	.07	.01
☐ 52	Randy Johnson	.15	.07	.01
☐ 53	Hensley Meulens	.40	.20	.04
☐ 54	Gene Harris	.15	.07	.01
☐ 55	Bill Spiers	.25	.12	.02
☐ 56	Kelly Mann	.20	.10	.02
☐ 57	Tom McCarthy	.15	.07	.01
☐ 58	Steve Finley	.15	.07	.01
☐ 59	Ramon Martinez	.30	.15	.03
☐ 60	Greg Briley	.30	.15	.03
☐ 61	Jack Daugherty	.10	.05	.01
☐ 62	Tim Jones	.10	.05	.01
☐ 63	Doug Strange	.10	.05	.01
☐ 64	John Orton	.15	.07	.01
☐ 65	Scott Scudder	.15	.07	.01
☐ 66	Mark Gardner	.10	.05	.01
☐ 67	Mark Carreon	.10	.05	.01
☐ 68	Bob Milacki	.10	.05	.01
☐ 69	Andy Benes	.75	.35	.07
☐ 70	Carlos Martinez	.20	.10	.02
☐ 71	Jeff King	.15	.07	.01
☐ 72	Brad Arnsberg	.10	.05	.01
☐ 73	Rick Wrona	.20	.10	.02
☐ 74	Cris Carpenter	.10	.05	.01
☐ 75	Dennis Cook	.10	.05	.01
☐ 76	Pete Harnisch	.05	.02	.00
☐ 77	Greg Hibbard	.10	.05	.01
☐ 78	Ed Whited	.20	.10	.02
☐ 79	Scott Coolbaugh	.25	.12	.02
☐ 80	Billy Bates	.15	.07	.01
☐ 81	German Gonzalez	.05	.02	.00
☐ 82	Lance Blankenship	.10	.05	.01
☐ 83	Lenny Harris	.15	.07	.01
☐ 84	Milt Cuyler	.15	.07	.01
☐ 85	Erik Hanson	.10	.05	.01
☐ 86	Kent Anderson	.10	.05	.01
☐ 87	Hal Morris	.20	.10	.02
☐ 88	Mike Brumley	.10	.05	.01
☐ 89	Ken Patterson	.10	.05	.01
☐ 90	Mike Devereaux	.10	.05	.01
☐ 91	Greg Litton	.20	.10	.02
☐ 92	Rolando Roomes	.15	.07	.01
☐ 93	Ben McDonald	1.00	.50	.10
☐ 94	Curt Schilling	.10	.05	.01
☐ 95	Jose DeJesus	.10	.05	.01
☐ 96	Robin Ventura	.50	.25	.05
☐ 97	Steve Searcy	.20	.10	.02
☐ 98	Chip Hale	.15	.07	.01
☐ 99	Marquis Grissom	.50	.25	.05
☐ 100	Luis de los Santos	.15	.07	.01

1990 Score 100 Superstars

The 1990 Score Superstars set contains 100 standard size (2 1/2 by 3 1/2 inch) cards. The fronts are red, white, blue and purple. The vertically-oriented backs feature a large color facial shot and career highlights. The cards were distributed as a set

in a blister pack, which also included a full color booklet with more information about each player.

		MINT	EXC	G-VG
COMPLETE SET (100)		12.50	6.25	1.25
COMMON PLAYER (1-100)		.05	.02	.00

			MINT	EXC	G-VG
☐	1	Kirby Puckett	.50	.25	.05
☐	2	Steve Sax	.20	.10	.02
☐	3	Tony Gwynn	.30	.15	.03
☐	4	Willie Randolph	.10	.05	.01
☐	5	Jose Canseco	1.00	.50	.10
☐	6	Ozzie Smith	.20	.10	.02
☐	7	Rick Reuschel	.10	.05	.01
☐	8	Bill Doran	.10	.05	.01
☐	9	Mickey Tettleton	.10	.05	.01
☐	10	Don Mattingly	1.00	.50	.10
☐	11	Greg Swindell	.15	.07	.01
☐	12	Bert Blyleven	.15	.07	.01
☐	13	Dave Stewart	.15	.07	.01
☐	14	Andres Galarraga	.20	.10	.02
☐	15	Darryl Strawberry	.50	.25	.05
☐	16	Ellis Burks	.35	.17	.03
☐	17	Paul O'Neill	.20	.10	.02
☐	18	Bruce Hurst	.10	.05	.01
☐	19	Dave Smith	.05	.02	.00
☐	20	Carney Lansford	.15	.07	.01
☐	21	Robby Thompson	.10	.05	.01
☐	22	Gary Gaetti	.10	.05	.01
☐	23	Jeff Russell	.10	.05	.01
☐	24	Chuck Finley	.10	.05	.01
☐	25	Mark McGwire	.75	.35	.07
☐	26	Alvin Davis	.10	.05	.01
☐	27	George Bell	.15	.07	.01
☐	28	Cory Snyder	.15	.07	.01
☐	29	Keith Hernandez	.15	.07	.01
☐	30	Will Clark	1.00	.50	.10
☐	31	Steve Bedrosian	.10	.05	.01
☐	32	Ryne Sandberg	.25	.12	.02
☐	33	Tom Browning	.10	.05	.01
☐	34	Tim Burke	.10	.05	.01
☐	35	John Smoltz	.20	.10	.02
☐	36	Phil Bradley	.10	.05	.01
☐	37	Bobby Bonilla	.15	.07	.01
☐	38	Kirk McCaskill	.05	.02	.00
☐	39	Dave Righetti	.15	.07	.01
☐	40	Bo Jackson	1.00	.50	.10
☐	41	Alan Trammell	.15	.07	.01
☐	42	Mike Moore	.10	.05	.01
☐	43	Harold Reynolds	.10	.05	.01
☐	44	Nolan Ryan	1.00	.50	.10
☐	45	Fred McGriff	.40	.20	.04
☐	46	Brian Downing	.05	.02	.00
☐	47	Brett Butler	.10	.05	.01
☐	48	Mike Scioscia	.05	.02	.00
☐	49	John Franco	.10	.05	.01
☐	50	Kevin Mitchell	.50	.25	.05
☐	51	Mark Davis	.20	.10	.02
☐	52	Glenn Davis	.20	.10	.02
☐	53	Barry Bonds	.15	.07	.01
☐	54	Dwight Evans	.15	.07	.01
☐	55	Terry Steinbach	.10	.05	.01
☐	56	Dave Gallagher	.10	.05	.01
☐	57	Roberto Kelly	.30	.15	.03
☐	58	Rafael Palmeiro	.20	.10	.02
☐	59	Joe Carter	.20	.10	.02
☐	60	Mark Grace	1.00	.50	.10
☐	61	Pedro Guerrero	.15	.07	.01
☐	62	Von Hayes	.10	.05	.01
☐	63	Benito Santiago	.30	.15	.03
☐	64	Dale Murphy	.40	.20	.04
☐	65	John Smiley	.10	.05	.01
☐	66	Cal Ripken Jr.	.30	.15	.03
☐	67	Mike Greenwell	.50	.25	.05
☐	68	Devon White	.15	.07	.01
☐	69	Ed Whitson	.05	.02	.00
☐	70	Carlton Fisk	.20	.10	.02
☐	71	Lou Whitaker	.15	.07	.01
☐	72	Danny Tartabull	.20	.10	.02
☐	73	Vince Coleman	.20	.10	.02
☐	74	Andre Dawson	.20	.10	.02
☐	75	Tim Raines	.20	.10	.02
☐	76	George Brett	.30	.15	.03
☐	77	Tom Herr	.05	.02	.00
☐	78	Andy Van Slyke	.10	.05	.01
☐	79	Roger Clemens	.50	.25	.05
☐	80	Wade Boggs	.60	.30	.06
☐	81	Wally Joyner	.35	.17	.03
☐	82	Lonnie Smith	.10	.05	.01
☐	83	Howard Johnson	.20	.10	.02
☐	84	Julio Franco	.15	.07	.01
☐	85	Ruben Sierra	.50	.25	.05
☐	86	Dan Plesac	.10	.05	.01
☐	87	Bobby Thigpen	.10	.05	.01
☐	88	Kevin Seitzer	.30	.15	.03
☐	89	Dave Stieb	.15	.07	.01
☐	90	Rickey Henderson	.50	.25	.05
☐	91	Jeffrey Leonard	.10	.05	.01
☐	92	Robin Yount	.50	.25	.05
☐	93	Mitch Williams	.15	.07	.01
☐	94	Orel Hershiser	.40	.20	.04
☐	95	Eric Davis	.50	.25	.05
☐	96	Mark Langston	.20	.10	.02
☐	97	Mike Scott	.15	.07	.01
☐	98	Paul Molitor	.10	.05	.01
☐	99	Dwight Gooden	.35	.17	.03
☐	100	Kevin Bass	.10	.05	.01

1985 7-Eleven Twins

This 13-card set of Minnesota Twins was produced and distributed by the Twins in conjunction with the 7-Eleven stores and the Fire Marshall's Association. The cards measure approximately 2 1/2" by 3 1/2" and are in full color. Supposedly 20,000 sets of cards were distributed during the promotion which began on June 2nd and lasted throughout the month of July. The card backs have some statistics and a fire safety tip.

		MINT	EXC	G-VG
COMPLETE SET (13)		8.00	4.00	.80
COMMON PLAYER (1-13)		.25	.12	.02

			MINT	EXC	G-VG
☐	1	Kirby Puckett	4.00	2.00	.40
☐	2	Frank Viola	1.00	.50	.10
☐	3	Mickey Hatcher	.25	.12	.02
☐	4	Kent Hrbek	1.00	.50	.10
☐	5	John Butcher	.25	.12	.02
☐	6	Roy Smalley	.25	.12	.02
☐	7	Tom Brunansky	.50	.25	.05
☐	8	Ron Davis	.25	.12	.02
☐	9	Gary Gaetti	1.00	.50	.10
☐	10	Tim Teufel	.25	.12	.02
☐	11	Mike Smithson	.25	.12	.02
☐	12	Tim Laudner	.35	.17	.03
☐	xx	Checklist Card	.25	.12	.02

1984 Smokey Angels

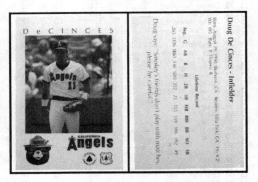

1984 Smokey Dodgers

The cards in this 32-card set measure 2 1/2" by 3 3/4" and feature the California Angels in full color. Sets were given out to persons 15 and under attending the June 16th game against the Indians. Unlike the Padres set of this year, Smokey the Bear is not featured on these cards. The player's photo, the Angels' logo, and the Smokey the Bear logo appear on the front, in addition to the California Department of Forestry and the U.S. Forest Service logos. The abbreviated backs contain short biographical data, career statistics, and an anti-wildfire hint from the player on the front. Since the cards are unnumbered, they are ordered and numbered below alphabetically by the player's name.

	MINT	EXC	G-VG
COMPLETE SET (32)	8.00	4.00	.80
COMMON PLAYER (1-32)	.20	.10	.02
☐ 1 Don Aase	.20	.10	.02
☐ 2 Juan Beniquez	.20	.10	.02
☐ 3 Bob Boone	.50	.25	.05
☐ 4 Rick Burleson	.30	.15	.03
☐ 5 Rod Carew	1.00	.50	.10
☐ 6 John Curtis	.20	.10	.02
☐ 7 Doug DeCinces	.30	.15	.03
☐ 8 Brian Downing	.40	.20	.04
☐ 9 Ken Forsch	.20	.10	.02
☐ 10 Bobby Grich	.30	.15	.03
☐ 11 Reggie Jackson	1.50	.75	.15
☐ 12 Ron Jackson	.20	.10	.02
☐ 13 Tommy John	.60	.30	.06
☐ 14 Curt Kaufman	.20	.10	.02
☐ 15 Bruce Kison	.20	.10	.02
☐ 16 Frank LaCorte	.20	.10	.02
☐ 17 Logo Card (Forestry Dept.)	.20	.10	.02
☐ 18 Fred Lynn	.40	.20	.04
☐ 19 John McNamara MG	.30	.15	.03
☐ 20 Jerry Narron	.20	.10	.02
☐ 21 Gary Pettis	.40	.20	.04
☐ 22 Rob Picciolo	.20	.10	.02
☐ 23 Ron Romanick	.20	.10	.02
☐ 24 Luis Sanchez	.20	.10	.02
☐ 25 Dick Schofield	.30	.15	.03
☐ 26 Daryl Sconiers	.20	.10	.02
☐ 27 Jim Slaton	.20	.10	.02
☐ 28 Smokey the Bear	.20	.10	.02
☐ 29 Ellis Valentine	.20	.10	.02
☐ 30 Rob Wilfong	.20	.10	.02
☐ 31 Mike Witt	.40	.20	.04
☐ 32 Geoff Zahn	.20	.10	.02

This four-card set was not widely distributed and has not proven to be very popular with collectors. Cards were supposedly distributed by fire agencies in Southern California at fairs, mall displays, and special events. Cards are approximately 5" by 7" and feature a color picture of Smokey the Bear with a Dodger. The cards were printed on relatively thin card stock; printing on the back is black on white.

	MINT	EXC	G-VG
COMPLETE SET (4)	12.00	6.00	1.20
COMMON PLAYER (1-4)	1.50	.75	.15
☐ 1 Ken Landreaux with Smokey	2.50	1.25	.25
☐ 2 Tom Niedenfuer with Smokey	2.50	1.25	.25
☐ 3 Steve Sax with Smokey	7.50	3.75	.75
☐ 4 Smokey the Bear (batting pose)	1.50	.75	.15

1984 Smokey Padres

The cards in this 29-card set measure 2 1/2" by 3 3/4". This unnumbered, full color set features the Fire Prevention Bear and a Padres player, coach, manager, or associate on each card. The set was given out at the ballpark at the May 14th game against the Expos. Logos of the California Department of Forestry and the U.S. Forest Service appear in conjunction with a Smokey the Bear logo on the obverse. The set commemorates the 40th birthday of Smokey the Bear. The backs contain short biographical data, statistics and a fire prevention hint from the player pictured on the front.

	MINT	EXC	G-VG
COMPLETE SET (29)	9.00	4.50	.90
COMMON PLAYER (1-29)	.25	.12	.02
☐ 1 Kurt Bevacqua	.25	.12	.02
☐ 2 Bobby Brown	.25	.12	.02
☐ 3 Dave Campbell	.25	.12	.02
(Broadcast Team)			
☐ 4 The Chicken (Mascot)	.35	.17	.03
☐ 5 Jerry Coleman	.25	.12	.02
(Broadcast Team)			
☐ 6 Luis DeLeon	.25	.12	.02
☐ 7 Dave Dravecky	.75	.35	.07
☐ 8 Harry Dunlop CO	.25	.12	.02
☐ 9 Tim Flannery	.25	.12	.02
☐ 10 Steve Garvey	1.25	.60	.12
☐ 11 Doug Gwosdz	.25	.12	.02
☐ 12 Tony Gwynn	1.75	.85	.17
☐ 13 Harold (Doug) Harvey	.25	.12	.02
(ex-UMP)			
☐ 14 Terry Kennedy	.25	.12	.02
☐ 15 Jack Krol CO	.25	.12	.02
☐ 16 Tim Lollar	.25	.12	.02
☐ 17 Jack McKeon (VP for	.50	.25	.05
Baseball Operations)			
☐ 18 Kevin McReynolds	1.25	.60	.12
☐ 19 Sid Monge	.25	.12	.02
☐ 20 Luis Salazar	.35	.17	.03
☐ 21 Norm Sherry CO	.25	.12	.02
☐ 22 Eric Show	.35	.17	.03
☐ 23 Smokey the Bear	.25	.12	.02
☐ 24 Garry Templeton	.35	.17	.03
☐ 25 Mark Thurmond	.25	.12	.02
☐ 26 Ozzie Virgil CO	.25	.12	.02
☐ 27 Ed Whitson	.35	.17	.03
☐ 28 Alan Wiggins	.25	.12	.02
☐ 29 Dick Williams MG	.35	.17	.03

☐ 19 Ruppert Jones	.20	.10	.02
☐ 20 Rob Wilfong	.20	.10	.02
☐ 21 Donnie Moore	.20	.10	.02
☐ 22 Pat Clements	.20	.10	.02
☐ 23 Tommy John	.50	.25	.05
☐ 24 Gene Mauch MG	.20	.10	.02

1986 Smokey Angels

The Forestry Service (in conjunction with the California Angels) produced this large, attractive 24-card set. The cards feature Smokey the Bear pictured in the upper right corner of the card. The card backs give a fire safety tip. The set was given out free at Anaheim Stadium on August 9th. The cards measure 4 1/4" by 6" and are subtitled "Wildfire Prevention" on the front.

	MINT	EXC	G-VG
COMPLETE SET (24)	8.00	4.00	.80
COMMON PLAYER (1-24)	.20	.10	.02
☐ 1 Mike Witt	.40	.20	.04
☐ 2 Reggie Jackson	1.00	.50	.10
☐ 3 Bob Boone	.50	.25	.05
☐ 4 Don Sutton	.65	.30	.06
☐ 5 Kirk McCaskill	.30	.15	.03
☐ 6 Doug DeCinces	.30	.15	.03
☐ 7 Brian Downing	.30	.15	.03
☐ 8 Doug Corbett	.20	.10	.02
☐ 9 Gary Pettis	.30	.15	.03
☐ 10 Jerry Narron	.20	.10	.02
☐ 11 Ron Romanick	.20	.10	.02
☐ 12 Bobby Grich	.30	.15	.03
☐ 13 Dick Schofield	.30	.15	.03
☐ 14 George Hendrick	.20	.10	.02
☐ 15 Rick Burleson	.20	.10	.02
☐ 16 John Candelaria	.30	.15	.03
☐ 17 Jim Slaton	.20	.10	.02
☐ 18 Darrell Miller	.20	.10	.02
☐ 19 Ruppert Jones	.20	.10	.02
☐ 20 Rob Wilfong	.20	.10	.02
☐ 21 Donnie Moore	.20	.10	.02
☐ 22 Wally Joyner	1.50	.75	.15
☐ 23 Terry Forster	.20	.10	.02
☐ 24 Gene Mauch MG	.20	.10	.02

1985 Smokey Angels

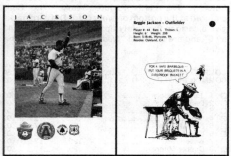

The cards in this 24-card set measure 4 1/4" by 6" and feature the California Angels in full color. The player's photo, the Angels' logo, and the Smokey the Bear logo appear on the front, in addition to the California Department of Forestry and the U.S. Forest Service logos. The abbreviated backs contain short biographical data and an anti-wildfire hint.

	MINT	EXC	G-VG
COMPLETE SET (24)	7.00	3.50	.70
COMMON PLAYER (1-24)	.20	.10	.02
☐ 1 Mike Witt	.40	.20	.04
☐ 2 Reggie Jackson	1.25	.60	.12
☐ 3 Bob Boone	.50	.25	.05
☐ 4 Mike Brown	.20	.10	.02
☐ 5 Rod Carew	1.00	.50	.10
☐ 6 Doug DeCinces	.30	.15	.03
☐ 7 Brian Downing	.40	.20	.04
☐ 8 Ken Forsch	.20	.10	.02
☐ 9 Gary Pettis	.30	.15	.03
☐ 10 Jerry Narron	.20	.10	.02
☐ 11 Ron Romanick	.20	.10	.02
☐ 12 Bobby Grich	.30	.15	.03
☐ 13 Dick Schofield	.30	.15	.03
☐ 14 Juan Beniquez	.20	.10	.02
☐ 15 Geoff Zahn	.20	.10	.02
☐ 16 Luis Sanchez	.20	.10	.02
☐ 17 Jim Slaton	.20	.10	.02
☐ 18 Doug Corbett	.20	.10	.02

1987 Smokey A's Colorgrams

These cards are actually pages of a booklet featuring members of the Oakland A's and Smokey's fire safety tips. The booklet has 12 pages each containing a black and white photo card (approximately 2 1/2" by 3 3/4") and a black and white player caricature (oversized head) postcard (approximately 3 3/4" by 5 5/8"). The cards are unnumbered but they have biographical information and a fire-prevention cartoon on the back of the card.

	MINT	EXC	G-VG
COMPLETE SET (12)	8.00	4.00	.80
COMMON PLAYER (1-12)	.50	.25	.05

☐ 10	Larry Sheets	....	.25	.12	.02
☐ 11	Mike Moore	....	.35	.17	.03
☐ 12	Charlie Hough	....	.25	.12	.02
☐ 13	National Smokey	....	.25	.12	.02
	Bear Day 1987				
☐ 14	Tom Henke	....	.25	.12	.02
☐ 15	Jim Gantner	....	.25	.12	.02
☐ 16	American League		.25	.12	.02
	Smokey Bear Day 1987				

1987 Smokey Angels

The U.S. Forestry Service (in conjunction with the California Angels) produced this large, attractive 24-card set to commemorate the 43rd birthday of Smokey. The cards feature Smokey the Bear pictured at the bottom of every card. The card backs give a cartoon fire safety tip. The cards measure 4" by 6" and are subtitled "Wildfire Prevention" on the front.

			MINT	EXC	G-VG
COMPLETE SET (24)	....		8.00	4.00	.80
COMMON PLAYER (1-24)	....		.25	.12	.02
☐ 1	John Candelaria	....	.35	.17	.03
☐ 2	Don Sutton	....	.75	.35	.07
☐ 3	Mike Witt	....	.50	.25	.05
☐ 4	Gary Lucas	....	.25	.12	.02
☐ 5	Kirk McCaskill	....	.35	.17	.03
☐ 6	Chuck Finley	....	.50	.25	.05
☐ 7	Willie Fraser	....	.25	.12	.02
☐ 8	Donnie Moore	....	.25	.12	.02
☐ 9	Urbano Lugo	....	.25	.12	.02
☐ 10	Butch Wynegar	....	.25	.12	.02
☐ 11	Darrell Miller	....	.25	.12	.02
☐ 12	Wally Joyner	....	1.25	.60	.12
☐ 13	Mark McLemore	....	.25	.12	.02
☐ 14	Mark Ryal	....	.25	.12	.02
☐ 15	Dick Schofield	....	.35	.17	.03
☐ 16	Jack Howell	....	.35	.17	.03
☐ 17	Doug DeCinces	....	.35	.17	.03
☐ 18	Gus Polidor	....	.25	.12	.02
☐ 19	Brian Downing	....	.35	.17	.03
☐ 20	Gary Pettis	....	.35	.17	.03
☐ 21	Ruppert Jones	....	.25	.12	.02
☐ 22	George Hendrick	....	.25	.12	.02
☐ 23	Devon White	....	1.00	.50	.10
☐ 24	Checklist Card	....	.25	.12	.02

1987 Smokey Braves

The U.S. Forestry Service (in conjunction with the Atlanta Braves) produced this large, attractive 27-card set to commemorate the 43rd birthday of Smokey. The cards feature Smokey the Bear pictured in the top right corner of every card. The card backs give a cartoon fire safety tip. The cards measure 4" by 6" and are subtitled "Wildfire

☐ 1	Joaquin Andujar	....	.50	.25	.05
☐ 2	Jose Canseco	....	2.50	1.25	.25
☐ 3	Mike Davis	....	.50	.25	.05
☐ 4	Alfredo Griffin	....	.60	.30	.06
☐ 5	Moose Haas	....	.50	.25	.05
☐ 6	Jay Howell	....	.75	.35	.07
☐ 7	Reggie Jackson	....	1.50	.75	.15
☐ 8	Carney Lansford	....	1.00	.50	.10
☐ 9	Dwayne Murphy	....	.60	.30	.06
☐ 10	Tony Phillips	....	.60	.30	.06
☐ 11	Dave Stewart	....	1.25	.60	.12
☐ 12	Curt Young	....	.50	.25	.05

1987 Smokey AL

The U.S. Forestry Service (in conjunction with Major League Baseball) produced this large, attractive 14 player card set to commemorate the 43rd birthday of Smokey. The cards feature Smokey the Bear pictured on every card with the player. The card backs give a fire safety tip. The cards measure 4" by 6" and are subtitled "National Smokey Bear Day 1987" on the front. The cards were printed on an uncut (but perforated) sheet that measured 18" by 24".

			MINT	EXC	G-VG
COMPLETE SET (16)	....		6.00	3.00	.60
COMMON PLAYER (1-16)	....		.25	.12	.02
☐ 1	Jose Canseco	....	2.00	1.00	.20
☐ 2	Dennis Oil Can Boyd	....	.25	.12	.02
☐ 3	John Candelaria	....	.25	.12	.02
☐ 4	Harold Baines	....	.35	.17	.03
☐ 5	Joe Carter	....	.50	.25	.05
☐ 6	Jack Morris	....	.35	.17	.03
☐ 7	Buddy Biancalana	....	.25	.12	.02
☐ 8	Kirby Puckett	....	1.25	.60	.12
☐ 9	Mike Pagliarulo	....	.25	.12	.02

Prevention" on the front. Distribution of the cards was gradual at the stadium throughout the summer. These large cards are numbered on the back.

		MINT	EXC	G-VG
COMPLETE SET (27)		15.00	7.50	1.50
COMMON PLAYER (1-26)		.40	.20	.04
☐ 1	Zane Smith	.60	.30	.06
☐ 2	Charlie Puleo	.40	.20	.04
☐ 3	Randy O'Neal	.40	.20	.04
☐ 4	David Palmer	.50	.25	.05
☐ 5	Rick Mahler	.50	.25	.05
☐ 6	Ed Olwine	.40	.20	.04
☐ 7	Jeff Dedmon	.40	.20	.04
☐ 8	Paul Assenmacher	.40	.20	.04
☐ 9	Gene Garber	.40	.20	.04
☐ 10	Jim Acker	.40	.20	.04
☐ 11	Bruce Benedict	.40	.20	.04
☐ 12	Ozzie Virgil	.40	.20	.04
☐ 13	Ted Simmons	.80	.40	.08
☐ 14	Dale Murphy	2.00	1.00	.20
☐ 15	Graig Nettles	.60	.30	.06
☐ 16	Ken Oberkfell	.40	.20	.04
☐ 17	Gerald Perry	.60	.30	.06
☐ 18	Rafael Ramirez	.40	.20	.04
☐ 19	Ken Griffey	.60	.30	.06
☐ 20	Andres Thomas	.50	.25	.05
☐ 21	Glenn Hubbard	.40	.20	.04
☐ 22	Damaso Garcia	.40	.20	.04
☐ 23	Gary Roenicke	.40	.20	.04
☐ 24	Dion James	.40	.20	.04
☐ 25	Albert Hall	.40	.20	.04
☐ 26	Chuck Tanner MG	.40	.20	.04
☐ xx	Smokey/Checklist (unnumbered)	.40	.20	.04

1987 Smokey Cardinals

The U.S. Forestry Service (in conjunction with the St. Louis Cardinals) produced this large, attractive 25-card set to commemorate the 43rd birthday of Smokey. The cards feature Smokey the Bear pictured in the top right corner of every card. The

card backs give a cartoon fire safety tip. The cards measure 4" by 6" and are subtitled "Wildfire Prevention" on the front. Sets were supposedly available from the Cardinals team for 3.50 postpaid. Also a limited number of 8 1/2" by 12" full-color team photos were available from the team to those who sent in a large SASE. The large team photo is not considered part of the complete set.

		MINT	EXC	G-VG
COMPLETE SET (25)		10.00	5.00	1.00
COMMON PLAYER (1-25)		.30	.15	.03
☐ 1	Ray Soff	.30	.15	.03
☐ 2	Todd Worrell	.50	.25	.05
☐ 3	John Tudor	.40	.20	.04
☐ 4	Pat Perry	.30	.15	.03
☐ 5	Rick Horton	.30	.15	.03
☐ 6	Danny Cox	.40	.20	.04
☐ 7	Bob Forsch	.30	.15	.03
☐ 8	Greg Matthews	.40	.20	.04
☐ 9	Bill Dawley	.30	.15	.03
☐ 10	Steve Lake	.30	.15	.03
☐ 11	Tony Pena	.40	.20	.04
☐ 12	Tom Pagnozzi	.30	.15	.03
☐ 13	Jack Clark	.75	.35	.07
☐ 14	Jim Lindeman	.30	.15	.03
☐ 15	Mike Laga	.30	.15	.03
☐ 16	Terry Pendleton	.40	.20	.04
☐ 17	Ozzie Smith	1.00	.50	.10
☐ 18	Jose Oquendo	.40	.20	.04
☐ 19	Tom Lawless	.30	.15	.03
☐ 20	Tom Herr	.40	.20	.04
☐ 21	Curt Ford	.30	.15	.03
☐ 22	Willie McGee	.50	.25	.05
☐ 23	Tito Landrum	.30	.15	.03
☐ 24	Vince Coleman	.75	.35	.07
☐ 25	Whitey Herzog MG	.40	.20	.04
☐ xx	Team Photo (large)	1.00	.50	.10

1987 Smokey Dodger All-Stars

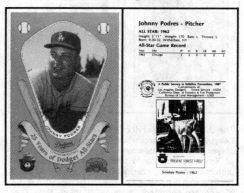

This 40-card set was issued by the U.S. Forestry Service to commemorate the Los Angeles Dodgers selected for the All-Star game over the past 25 years. The cards measure 2 1/2" by 3 3/4" and have full-color fronts. The card fronts are distinguished by their thick silver borders and the bats, balls, and stadium design layout. The 25th anniversary logo for Dodger Stadium is in the lower right corner of each card.

		MINT	EXC	G-VG
COMPLETE SET (40)		8.00	4.00	.80
COMMON PLAYER (1-40)		.15	.07	.01
☐ 1	Walt Alston MG	.50	.25	.05
☐ 2	Dusty Baker	.15	.07	.01
☐ 3	Jim Brewer	.15	.07	.01
☐ 4	Ron Cey	.25	.12	.02
☐ 5	Tommy Davis	.25	.12	.02
☐ 6	Willie Davis	.25	.12	.02
☐ 7	Don Drysdale	.75	.35	.07

				MINT	EXC	G-VG
☐	8	Steve Garvey		.75	.35	.07
☐	9	Bill Grabarkewitz		.15	.07	.01
☐	10	Pedro Guerrero		.75	.35	.07
☐	11	Tom Haller		.15	.07	.01
☐	12	Orel Hershiser		1.00	.50	.10
☐	13	Burt Hooton		.15	.07	.01
☐	14	Steve Howe		.15	.07	.01
☐	15	Tommy John		.35	.17	.03
☐	16	Sandy Koufax		1.00	.50	.10
☐	17	Tom Lasorda MG		.35	.17	.03
☐	18	Jim Lefebvre		.25	.12	.02
☐	19	Davey Lopes		.25	.12	.02
☐	20	Mike Marshall (pitcher)		.25	.12	.02
☐	21	Mike Marshall (outfielder)		.35	.17	.03
☐	22	Andy Messersmith		.15	.07	.01
☐	23	Rick Monday		.15	.07	.01
☐	24	Manny Mota		.25	.12	.02
☐	25	Claude Osteen		.15	.07	.01
☐	26	Johnny Podres		.25	.12	.02
☐	27	Phil Regan		.15	.07	.01
☐	28	Jerry Reuss		.15	.07	.01
☐	29	Rick Rhoden		.15	.07	.01
☐	30	John Roseboro		.15	.07	.01
☐	31	Bill Russell		.25	.12	.02
☐	32	Steve Sax		.50	.25	.05
☐	33	Bill Singer		.15	.07	.01
☐	34	Reggie Smith		.25	.12	.02
☐	35	Don Sutton		.60	.30	.06
☐	36	Fernando Valenzuela		.60	.30	.06
☐	37	Bob Welch		.35	.17	.03
☐	38	Maury Wills		.35	.17	.03
☐	39	Jim Wynn		.15	.07	.01
☐	40	Checklist Card		.15	.07	.01

1987 Smokey National League

The U.S. Forestry Service (in conjunction with Major League Baseball) produced this large, attractive 14 player card set to commemorate the 43rd birthday of Smokey. The cards feature Smokey the Bear pictured on every card with the player. The card backs give a fire safety tip. The cards measure 4" by 6" and are subtitled "National Smokey Bear Day 1987" on the front. The set price below does not include the more difficult variation cards.

			MINT	EXC	G-VG
	COMPLETE SET (15)		6.00	3.00	.60
	COMMON PLAYER (1-15)		.25	.12	.02
☐	1	Steve Sax	.50	.25	.05
☐	2A	Dale Murphy (holding bat)	1.50	.75	.15
☐	2B	Dale Murphy (no bat, arm around Smokey)	12.50	6.25	1.25
☐	3A	Jody Davis (kneeling with Smokey)	.35	.17	.03
☐	3B	Jody Davis (standing, shaking Smokey's hand)	8.00	4.00	.80
☐	4	Bill Gullickson	.25	.12	.02
☐	5	Mike Scott	.60	.30	.06
☐	6	Roger McDowell	.35	.17	.03
☐	7	Steve Bedrosian	.50	.25	.05

				MINT	EXC	G-VG
☐	8	Johnny Ray		.35	.17	.03
☐	9	Ozzie Smith		.75	.35	.07
☐	10	Steve Garvey		.75	.35	.07
☐	11	National Smokey Bear Day		.25	.12	.02
☐	12	Mike Krukow		.25	.12	.02
☐	13	Smokey the Bear		.25	.12	.02
☐	14	Mike Fitzgerald		.25	.12	.02
☐	15	National League Logo		.25	.12	.02

1987 Smokey Rangers

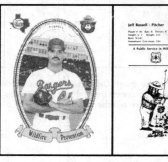

The U.S. Forestry Service (in conjunction with the Texas Rangers) produced this large, attractive 32-card set. The cards feature Smokey the Bear pictured in the upper-right corner of every player's card. The card backs give a cartoon fire safety tip. The cards measure approximately 4 1/4" by 6" and are subtitled "Wildfire Prevention" on the front. These large cards are numbered on the back. Cards 4 Mike Mason and 14 Tom Paciorek were withdrawn and were never formally released as part of the set and hence are quite scarce.

				MINT	EXC	G-VG
	COMPLETE SET (32)			75.00	37.50	7.50
	COMMON PLAYER (1-32)			.35	.17	.03
☐	1	Charlie Hough		.60	.30	.06
☐	2	Greg Harris		.35	.17	.03
☐	3	Jose Guzman		.50	.25	.05
☐	4	Mike Mason SP		30.00	15.00	3.00
☐	5	Dale Mohorcic		.50	.25	.05
☐	6	Bobby Witt		.75	.35	.07
☐	7	Mitch Williams		.75	.35	.07
☐	8	Geno Petralli		.35	.17	.03
☐	9	Don Slaught		.35	.17	.03
☐	10	Darrell Porter		.35	.17	.03
☐	11	Steve Buechele		.50	.25	.05
☐	12	Pete O'Brien		.60	.30	.06
☐	13	Scott Fletcher		.50	.25	.05
☐	14	Tom Paciorek		30.00	15.00	3.00
☐	15	Pete Incaviglia		.90	.45	.09
☐	16	Oddibe McDowell		.50	.25	.05
☐	17	Ruben Sierra		2.00	1.00	.20
☐	18	Larry Parrish		.50	.25	.05
☐	19	Bobby Valentine MG		.60	.30	.06
☐	20	Tom House CO		.35	.17	.03
☐	21	Tom Robson CO		.35	.17	.03
☐	22	Edwin Correa		.35	.17	.03
☐	23	Mike Stanley		.50	.25	.05
☐	24	Joe Ferguson CO		.35	.17	.03
☐	25	Art Howe CO		.50	.25	.05
☐	26	Bob Brower		.50	.25	.05
☐	27	Mike Loynd		.35	.17	.03
☐	28	Curtis Wilkerson		.35	.17	.03
☐	29	Tim Foli CO		.35	.17	.03
☐	30	Dave Oliver		.35	.17	.03
☐	31	Jerry Browne		.50	.25	.05
☐	32	Jeff Russell		.60	.30	.06

1988 Smokey Angels

The U.S. Forestry Service (in conjunction with the California Angels) produced this attractive 25-card set. The cards feature Smokey the Bear pictured at the bottom of every card. The card backs give a cartoon fire safety tip. The cards measure approximately 2 1/2" by 3 1/2" and are in full color. The cards are numbered on the back. They were distributed during promotions on August 28, September 4, and September 18.

		MINT	EXC	G-VG
	COMPLETE SET (25)	10.00	5.00	1.00
	COMMON PLAYER (1-24)	.30	.15	.03
☐ 1	Cookie Rojas MG	.30	.15	.03
☐ 2	Johnny Ray	.50	.25	.05
☐ 3	Jack Howell	.40	.20	.04
☐ 4	Mike Witt	.50	.25	.05
☐ 5	Tony Armas	.40	.20	.04
☐ 6	Gus Polidor	.30	.15	.03
☐ 7	DeWayne Buice	.40	.20	.04
☐ 8	Dan Petry	.30	.15	.03
☐ 9	Bob Boone	.60	.30	.06
☐ 10	Chili Davis	.50	.25	.05
☐ 11	Greg Minton	.40	.20	.04
☐ 12	Kirk McCaskill	.40	.20	.04
☐ 13	Devon White	.75	.35	.07
☐ 14	Willie Fraser	.30	.15	.03
☐ 15	Chuck Finley	.50	.25	.05
☐ 16	Dick Schofield	.40	.20	.04
☐ 17	Wally Joyner	1.00	.50	.10
☐ 18	Brian Downing	.40	.20	.04
☐ 19	Stewart Cliburn	.30	.15	.03
☐ 20	Donnie Moore	.30	.15	.03
☐ 21	Bryan Harvey	.50	.25	.05
☐ 22	Mark McLemore	.30	.15	.03
☐ 23	Butch Wynegar	.30	.15	.03
☐ 24	George Hendrick	.30	.15	.03
☐ xx	Checklist/Logo Card	.30	.15	.03

1988 Smokey Cardinals

The U.S. Forestry Service (in conjunction with the St. Louis Cardinals) produced this attractive 25- card set. The cards feature Smokey the Bear pictured in the lower right corner of every card. The card backs give a cartoon fire safety tip. The cards measure approximately 3" by 5" and are in full color. The cards are numbered on the backs. The sets were distributed on July 19th during the Cardinals' game against the Los Angeles Dodgers to fans 15 years of age and under.

		MINT	EXC	G-VG
	COMPLETE SET (25)	12.00	6.00	1.20
	COMMON PLAYER (1-25)	.35	.17	.03
☐ 1	Whitey Herzog MG	.45	.22	.04
☐ 2	Danny Cox	.45	.22	.04
☐ 3	Ken Dayley	.35	.17	.03

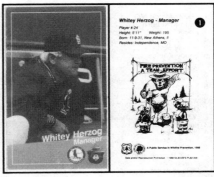

☐ 4	Jose DeLeon	.60	.30	.06
☐ 5	Bob Forsch	.45	.22	.04
☐ 6	Joe Magrane	.75	.35	.07
☐ 7	Greg Mathews	.45	.22	.04
☐ 8	Scott Terry	.45	.22	.04
☐ 9	John Tudor	.60	.30	.06
☐ 10	Todd Worrell	.60	.30	.06
☐ 11	Steve Lake	.35	.17	.03
☐ 12	Tom Pagnozzi	.35	.17	.03
☐ 13	Tony Pena	.45	.22	.04
☐ 14	Bob Horner	.60	.30	.06
☐ 15	Tom Lawless	.35	.17	.03
☐ 16	Jose Oquendo	.45	.22	.04
☐ 17	Terry Pendleton	.45	.22	.04
☐ 18	Ozzie Smith	.90	.45	.09
☐ 19	Vince Coleman	.75	.35	.07
☐ 20	Curt Ford	.35	.17	.03
☐ 21	Willie McGee	.60	.30	.06
☐ 22	Larry McWilliams	.35	.17	.03
☐ 23	Steve Peters	.45	.22	.04
☐ 24	Luis Alicea	.45	.22	.04
☐ 25	Tom Brunansky	.60	.30	.06

1988 Smokey Dodgers

This 32-card set was issued by the U.S. Forestry Service as a perforated sheet that could be separated into individual cards. The set commemorates Los Angeles Dodgers who hold various team and league records, i.e., "L.A. Dodgers Record-Breakers." The cards measure approximately 2 1/2" by 4" and have full-color fronts. The card fronts are distinguished by their thick light blue borders and the bats, balls, and stadium design layout. The sheets of cards were distributed at the Dodgers' Smokey Bear Day game on September 9th.

		MINT	EXC	G-VG
	COMPLETE SET (32)	10.00	5.00	1.00
	COMMON PLAYER (1-32)	.20	.10	.02

			MINT	EXC	G-VG
☐	1	Walter Alston MG	.50	.25	.05
☐	2	John Roseboro	.20	.10	.02
☐	3	Frank Howard	.30	.15	.03
☐	4	Sandy Koufax	.75	.35	.07
☐	5	Manny Mota	.30	.15	.03
☐	6	Sandy Koufax, Jerry Reuss, and Bill Singer	.30	.15	.03
☐	7	Maury Wills	.40	.20	.04
☐	8	Tommy Davis	.30	.15	.03
☐	9	Phil Regan	.20	.10	.02
☐	10	Wes Parker	.20	.10	.02
☐	11	Don Drysdale	.50	.25	.05
☐	12	Willie Davis	.30	.15	.03
☐	13	Bill Russell	.30	.15	.03
☐	14	Jim Brewer	.20	.10	.02
☐	15	Steve Garvey, Davey Lopes, Bill Russell, and Ron Cey	.30	.15	.03
☐	16	Mike Marshall	.30	.15	.03
☐	17	Steve Garvey	.50	.25	.05
☐	18	Davey Lopes	.30	.15	.03
☐	19	Burt Hooton	.20	.10	.02
☐	20	Jim Wynn	.20	.10	.02
☐	21	Dusty Baker, Ron Cey, Steve Garvey, and Reggie Smith	.30	.15	.03
☐	22	Dusty Baker	.20	.10	.02
☐	23	Tommy Lasorda MG	.50	.25	.05
☐	24	Fernando Valenzuela	.50	.25	.05
☐	25	Steve Sax	.40	.20	.04
☐	26	Dodger Stadium	.20	.10	.02
☐	27	Ron Cey	.30	.15	.03
☐	28	Pedro Guerrero	.50	.25	.05
☐	29	Mike Marshall	.30	.15	.03
☐	30	Don Sutton	.40	.20	.04
☐	xx	Checklist Card (unnumbered)	.20	.10	.02
☐	xx	Smokey Bear (unnumbered)	.20	.10	.02

			MINT	EXC	G-VG
		COMPLETE SET (31)	15.00	7.50	1.50
		COMMON PLAYER (1-31)	.40	.20	.04
☐	1	Shawn Abner	.50	.25	.05
☐	2	Roberto Alomar	1.00	.50	.10
☐	3	Sandy Alomar CO	.40	.20	.04
☐	4	Greg Booker	.40	.20	.04
☐	5	Chris Brown	.40	.20	.04
☐	6	Mark Davis	1.00	.50	.10
☐	7	Pat Dobson CO	.40	.20	.04
☐	8	Tim Flannery	.40	.20	.04
☐	9	Mark Grant	.40	.20	.04
☐	10	Tony Gwynn	1.25	.60	.12
☐	11	Andy Hawkins	.50	.25	.05
☐	12	Stan Jefferson	.50	.25	.05
☐	13	Jimmy Jones	.50	.25	.05
☐	14	John Kruk	.60	.30	.06
☐	15	Dave Leiper	.40	.20	.04
☐	16	Shane Mack	.50	.25	.05
☐	17	Carmelo Martinez	.40	.20	.04
☐	18	Lance McCullers	.50	.25	.05
☐	19	Keith Moreland	.40	.20	.04
☐	20	Eric Nolte	.40	.20	.04
☐	21	Amos Otis CO	.50	.25	.05
☐	22	Mark Parent	.40	.20	.04
☐	23	Randy Ready	.40	.20	.04
☐	24	Greg Riddoch	.40	.20	.04
☐	25	Benito Santiago	1.00	.50	.10
☐	26	Eric Show	.50	.25	.05
☐	27	Denny Sommers CO	.40	.20	.04
☐	28	Gary Templeton	.50	.25	.05
☐	29	Dickie Thon	.50	.25	.05
☐	30	Ed Whitson	.50	.25	.05
☐	31	Marvell Wynne	.40	.20	.04

1988 Smokey Rangers

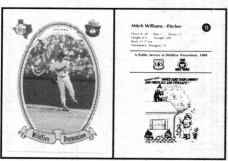

The cards in this 21-card set measure approximately 3 1/2" by 5". This numbered, full color set features the Fire Prevention Bear, Smokey, and a Rangers player (or manager) on each card. The set was given out at Arlington Stadium to fans during the Smokey Bear Day game promotion on August 7th. The logos of the Texas Forest Service and the U.S. Forestry Service appear on the reverse in conjunction with a Smokey the Bear logo on the obverse. The backs contain short biographical data and a fire prevention hint from Smokey.

			MINT	EXC	G-VG
		COMPLETE SET (21)	12.00	6.00	1.20
		COMMON PLAYER (1-21)	.40	.20	.04
☐	1	Tom O'Malley	.40	.20	.04
☐	2	Pete O'Brien	.60	.30	.06
☐	3	Geno Petralli	.40	.20	.04
☐	4	Pete Incaviglia	.75	.35	.07
☐	5	Oddibe McDowell	.50	.25	.05
☐	6	Dal Mohorcic	.40	.20	.04
☐	7	Bobby Witt	.60	.30	.06
☐	8	Bobby Valentine MG	.60	.30	.06
☐	9	Ruben Sierra	2.00	1.00	.20
☐	10	Scott Fletcher	.50	.25	.05
☐	11	Mike Stanley	.40	.20	.04
☐	12	Steve Buechele	.40	.20	.04

1988 Smokey Padres

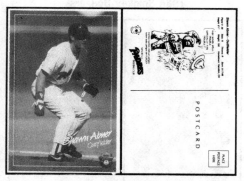

The cards in this 31-card set measure approximately 3 3/4" by 5 3/4". This unnumbered, full color set features the Fire Prevention Bear, Smokey, and a Padres player, coach, manager, or associate on each card. The set was given out at Jack Murphy Stadium to fans under the age of 14 during the Smokey Bear Day game promotion. The logo of the California Department of Forestry appears on the reverse in conjunction with a Smokey the Bear logo on the obverse. The backs contain short biographical data and a fire prevention hint from Smokey. The set is numbered below in alphabetical order. The card backs are actually postcards that can be addressed and mailed. Cards of Larry Bowa and Candy Sierra were printed but were not officially released since they were no longer members of the Padres by the time the cards were to be distributed.

		MINT	EXC	G-VG
☐ 13	Charlie Hough	.50	.25	.05
☐ 14	Larry Parrish	.40	.20	.04
☐ 15	Jerry Browne	.40	.20	.04
☐ 16	Bob Brower	.40	.20	.04
☐ 17	Jeff Russell	.50	.25	.05
☐ 18	Edwin Correa	.40	.20	.04
☐ 19	Mitch Williams	.60	.30	.06
☐ 20	Jose Guzman	.50	.25	.05
☐ 21	Curtis Wilkerson	.40	.20	.04

1988 Smokey Royals

This set of 28 cards features caricatures of the Kansas City Royals players. The cards are nunmbered on the back except for the unnumbered title/checklist card. The card set was distributed as a giveaway item at the stadium on August 14th to kids age 14 and under. The cards are approximately 3" by 5" and are in full color on the card fronts. The Smokey logo is in the upper right corner of every obverse.

		MINT	EXC	G-VG
COMPLETE SET (28)		10.00	5.00	1.00
COMMON PLAYER (1-27)		.30	.15	.03
☐ 1	John Wathan MG	.40	.20	.04
☐ 2	Royals Coaches	.30	.15	.03
☐ 3	Willie Wilson	.50	.25	.05
☐ 4	Danny Tartabull	.75	.35	.07
☐ 5	Bo Jackson	2.00	1.00	.20
☐ 6	Gary Thurman	.40	.20	.04
☐ 7	Jerry Don Gleaton	.30	.15	.03
☐ 8	Floyd Bannister	.30	.15	.03
☐ 9	Buddy Black	.40	.20	.04
☐ 10	Steve Farr	.30	.15	.03
☐ 11	Gene Garber	.30	.15	.03
☐ 12	Mark Gubicza	.75	.35	.07
☐ 13	Charlie Liebrandt	.50	.25	.05
☐ 14	Ted Power	.30	.15	.03
☐ 15	Dan Quisenberry	.50	.25	.05
☐ 16	Bret Saberhagen	1.00	.50	.10
☐ 17	Mike Macfarlane	.40	.20	.04
☐ 18	Scotti Madison	.30	.15	.03
☐ 19	Jamie Quirk	.30	.15	.03
☐ 20	George Brett	1.00	.50	.10
☐ 21	Kevin Seitzer	.75	.35	.07
☐ 22	Bill Pecota	.30	.15	.03
☐ 23	Kurt Stillwell	.40	.20	.04
☐ 24	Brad Wellman	.30	.15	.03
☐ 25	Frank White	.50	.25	.05
☐ 26	Jim Eisenreich	.40	.20	.04
☐ 27	Smokey Bear	.30	.15	.03
☐ xx	Checklist Card	.30	.15	.03

AD INDEX: Our advertisers are listed at the end of the Table of Contents. Check out your favorite dealer and tell him you saw his ad in this price guide.

1988 Smokey Twins Colorgrams

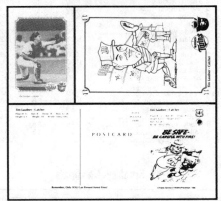

These cards are actually pages of a booklet featuring members of the Minnesota Twins and Smokey's fire safety tips. The booklet has 12 pages each containing a black and white photo card (approximately 2 1/2" by 3 3/4") and a black and white player caricature (oversized head) postcard (approximately 3 3/4" by 5 5/8"). The cards are unnumbered but they have biographical information and a fire-prevention cartoon on the back of the card.

		MINT	EXC	G-VG
COMPLETE SET (12)		10.00	5.00	1.00
COMMON PLAYER (1-12)		.50	.25	.05
☐ 1	Frank Viola	1.00	.50	.10
☐ 2	Gary Gaetti	1.00	.50	.10
☐ 3	Kent Hrbek	1.25	.60	.12
☐ 4	Jeff Reardon	.75	.35	.07
☐ 5	Gene Larkin	.60	.30	.06
☐ 6	Bert Blyleven	1.00	.50	.10
☐ 7	Tim Laudner	.60	.30	.06
☐ 8	Greg Gagne	.50	.25	.05
☐ 9	Randy Bush	.50	.25	.05
☐ 10	Dan Gladden	.60	.30	.06
☐ 11	Al Newman	.50	.25	.05
☐ 12	Kirby Puckett	2.00	1.00	.20

1989 Smokey Angels All-Stars

The 1989 Smokey Angels All-Stars set contains 20 standard-size (2 1/2 by 3 1/2 inch) cards. The fronts have red and white borders. The backs are blue and red and feature career highlights. This set, which depicts current and former Angels who appeared in the All-Star game, was given away at the June 25, 1989 Angels home game.

		MINT	EXC	G-VG
COMPLETE SET (20)		6.00	3.00	.60
COMMON PLAYER (1-20)		.20	.10	.02

			MINT	EXC	G-VG
☐	1	Bill Rigney	.20	.10	.02
☐	2	Dean Chance	.30	.15	.03
☐	3	Jim Fregosi	.30	.15	.03
☐	4	Bobby Knoop	.20	.10	.02
☐	5	Don Mincher	.20	.10	.02
☐	6	Clyde Wright	.20	.10	.02
☐	7	Nolan Ryan	1.25	.60	.12
☐	8	Frank Robinson	.75	.35	.07
☐	9	Frank Tanana	.30	.15	.03
☐	10	Rod Carew	1.00	.50	.10
☐	11	Bobby Grich	.30	.15	.03
☐	12	Brian Downing	.30	.15	.03
☐	13	Don Baylor	.30	.15	.03
☐	14	Fred Lynn	.40	.20	.04
☐	15	Reggie Jackson	1.00	.50	.10
☐	16	Doug DeCinces	.30	.15	.03
☐	17	Bob Boone	.40	.20	.04
☐	18	Wally Joyner	.75	.35	.07
☐	19	Mike Witt	.30	.15	.03
☐	20	Johnny Ray	.20	.10	.02

1989 Smokey Cardinals

The 1989 Smokey Cardinals set contains 24 cards measuring 4 by 6 inches. The fronts have color photos with white and red borders. The backs feature biographical information.

		MINT	EXC	G-VG
COMPLETE SET (24)		7.00	3.50	.70
COMMON PLAYER (1-24)		.20	.10	.02

			MINT	EXC	G-VG
☐	1	Tom Brunansky	.40	.20	.04
☐	2	Vince Coleman	.50	.25	.05
☐	3	John Costello	.30	.15	.03
☐	4	Ken Dayley	.20	.10	.02
☐	5	Jose DeLeon	.40	.20	.04
☐	6	Frank DiPino	.20	.10	.02
☐	7	Pedro Guerrero	.75	.35	.07
☐	8	Whitey Herzog MG	.30	.15	.03
☐	9	Ken Hill	.30	.15	.03
☐	10	Tim Jones	.20	.10	.02
☐	11	Jim Lindeman	.20	.10	.02
☐	12	Joe Magrane	.40	.20	.04
☐	13	Willie McGee	.40	.20	.04
☐	14	John Morris	.20	.10	.02
☐	15	Jose Oquendo	.30	.15	.03
☐	16	Tom Pagnozzi	.20	.10	.02
☐	17	Tony Pena	.30	.15	.03
☐	18	Terry Pendleton	.30	.15	.03
☐	19	Dan Quisenberry	.40	.20	.04
☐	20	Ozzie Smith	.75	.35	.07
☐	21	Scott Terry	.20	.10	.02
☐	22	Milt Thompson	.30	.15	.03
☐	23	Denny Walling	.20	.10	.02
☐	24	Todd Worrell	.40	.20	.04

1989 Smokey Colt .45s

The 1989 Smokey Houston Colt .45s set contains 29 standard-size (2 1/2 by 3 1/2 inch) cards. The fronts have black and white photos with white and light blue borders. This set depicts old Houston Colt .45s' players.

		MINT	EXC	G-VG
COMPLETE SET (29)		6.00	3.00	.60
COMMON PLAYER (1-29)		.20	.10	.02

			MINT	EXC	G-VG
☐	1	Bob Bruce	.20	.10	.02
☐	2	Al Cicotte	.20	.10	.02
☐	3	Dave Giusti	.40	.20	.04
☐	4	Jim Golden	.20	.10	.02
☐	5	Ken Johnson	.20	.10	.02
☐	6	Tom Borland	.20	.10	.02
☐	7	Bobby Shantz	.50	.25	.05
☐	8	Dick Farrell	.40	.20	.04
☐	9	Jim Umbricht	.20	.10	.02
☐	10	Hal Woodeshick	.20	.10	.02
☐	11	Merritt Ranew	.20	.10	.02
☐	12	Hal Smith	.20	.10	.02
☐	13	Jim Campbell	.20	.10	.02
☐	14	Norm Larker	.20	.10	.02
☐	15	Joe Amalfitano	.20	.10	.02
☐	16	Bob Aspromonte	.20	.10	.02
☐	17	Bob Lillis	.30	.15	.03
☐	18	Dick Gernert	.20	.10	.02
☐	19	Don Buddin	.20	.10	.02
☐	20	Pidge Browne	.20	.10	.02
☐	21	Von McDaniel	.20	.10	.02
☐	22	Don Taussig	.20	.10	.02
☐	23	Al Spangler	.20	.10	.02
☐	24	Al Heist	.20	.10	.02
☐	25	Jim Pendleton	.20	.10	.02
☐	26	Johnny Weekly	.20	.10	.02
☐	27	Harry Craft	.20	.10	.02
☐	28	Colt Coaches	.20	.10	.02
☐	29	1962 Houston Colt 45s	.20	.10	.02

1989 Smokey Dodger Greats

The 1989 Smokey Dodger Greats set contains 104 standard-size (2 1/2 by 3 1/2 inch) cards. The fronts and backs have white and blue borders. The backs are vertically-oriented and feature career totals and fire prevention cartoons. The set depicts notable Dodgers of all eras, and was distributed in perforated sheet format.

		MINT	EXC	G-VG
COMPLETE SET (104)		12.00	6.00	1.20
COMMON PLAYER (1-104)		.10	.05	.01

			MINT	EXC	G-VG
☐	1	Walter Alston	.20	.10	.02
☐	2	David Bancroft	.20	.10	.02
☐	3	Dan Brouthers	.20	.10	.02
☐	4	Roy Campanella	.30	.15	.03
☐	5	Max Carey	.20	.10	.02
☐	6	Hazen "KiKi" Cuyler	.20	.10	.02
☐	7	Don Drysdale	.30	.15	.03
☐	8	Burleigh Grimes	.20	.10	.02

☐	84	Mike G. Marshall	.10	.05	.01
☐	85	Andy Messersmith	.10	.05	.01
☐	86	Jimmy Wynn	.10	.05	.01
☐	87	Rick Rhoden	.10	.05	.01
☐	88	Reggie Smith	.15	.07	.01
☐	89	Jay Howell	.15	.07	.01
☐	90	Rick Monday	.10	.05	.01
☐	91	Tommy John	.20	.10	.02
☐	92	Bob Welch	.15	.07	.01
☐	93	Dusty Baker	.15	.07	.01
☐	94	Pedro Guerrero	.20	.10	.02
☐	95	Burt Hooton	.10	.05	.01
☐	96	Davey Lopes	.15	.07	.01
☐	97	Fernando Valenzuela	.20	.10	.02
☐	98	Steve Howe	.10	.05	.01
☐	99	Steve Sax	.20	.10	.02
☐	100	Orel Hershiser	.30	.15	.03
☐	101	Mike A. Marshall	.20	.10	.02
☐	102	Ernie Lombardi	.20	.10	.02
☐	103	Fred Lindstrom	.20	.10	.02
☐	104	Wilbert Robinson	.20	.10	.02

☐	9	Billy Herman	.20	.10	.02
☐	10	Waite Hoyt	.20	.10	.02
☐	11	Hughie Jennings	.20	.10	.02
☐	12	Willie Keeler	.20	.10	.02
☐	13	Joseph Kelley	.20	.10	.02
☐	14	George Kelly	.20	.10	.02
☐	15	Sandy Koufax	.30	.15	.03
☐	16	Henry"Heinie" Manush	.20	.10	.02
☐	17	Juan Marichal	.20	.10	.02
☐	18	Rabbit Maranville	.20	.10	.02
☐	19	Rube Marquard	.20	.10	.02
☐	20	Thomas McCarthy	.20	.10	.02
☐	21	Joseph McGinnity	.20	.10	.02
☐	22	Joe Medwick	.20	.10	.02
☐	23	Pee Wee Reese	.30	.15	.03
☐	24	Frank Robinson	.30	.15	.03
☐	25	Jackie Robinson	.50	.25	.05
☐	26	George"Babe" Ruth	.50	.25	.05
☐	27	Duke Snider	.30	.15	.03
☐	28	Casey Stengel	.30	.15	.03
☐	29	Dazzy Vance	.20	.10	.02
☐	30	Arky Vaughan	.20	.10	.02
☐	31	Mike Scioscia	.10	.05	.01
☐	32	Lloyd Waner	.20	.10	.02
☐	33	John"Monte" Ward	.20	.10	.02
☐	34	Zack Wheat	.20	.10	.02
☐	35	Hoyt Wilhelm	.20	.10	.02
☐	36	Hack Wilson	.20	.10	.02
☐	37	Tony Cuccinello	.10	.05	.01
☐	38	Al Lopez	.20	.10	.02
☐	39	Leo Durocher	.20	.10	.02
☐	40	Cookie Lavagetto	.10	.05	.01
☐	41	Babe Phelps	.10	.05	.01
☐	42	Dolph Camilli	.10	.05	.01
☐	43	Whitlow Wyatt	.10	.05	.01
☐	44	Mickey Owen	.10	.05	.01
☐	45	Van Mungo	.10	.05	.01
☐	46	Pete Coscarart	.10	.05	.01
☐	47	Pete Reiser	.10	.05	.01
☐	48	Augie Galan	.10	.05	.01
☐	49	Dixie Walker	.10	.05	.01
☐	50	Kirby Higbe	.10	.05	.01
☐	51	Ralph Branca	.20	.10	.02
☐	52	Bruce Edwards	.10	.05	.01
☐	53	Eddie Stanky	.10	.05	.01
☐	54	Gil Hodges	.20	.10	.02
☐	55	Don Newcombe	.20	.10	.02
☐	56	Preacher Roe	.20	.10	.02
☐	57	Willie Randolph	.10	.05	.01
☐	58	Carl Furillo	.20	.10	.02
☐	59	Charlie Dressen	.10	.05	.01
☐	60	Carl Erskine	.20	.10	.02
☐	61	Clem Labine	.10	.05	.01
☐	62	Gino Cimoli	.10	.05	.01
☐	63	Johnny Podres	.20	.10	.02
☐	64	Johnny Roseboro	.10	.05	.01
☐	65	Wally Moon	.10	.05	.01
☐	66	Charlie Neal	.10	.05	.01
☐	67	Norm Larker	.10	.05	.01
☐	68	Stan Williams	.10	.05	.01
☐	69	Maury Wills	.20	.10	.02
☐	70	Tommy Davis	.20	.10	.02
☐	71	Jim Lefebvre	.20	.10	.02
☐	72	Phil Regan	.10	.05	.01
☐	73	Claude Osteen	.10	.05	.01
☐	74	Tom Haller	.10	.05	.01
☐	75	Bill Singer	.10	.05	.01
☐	76	Bill Grabarkewitz	.10	.05	.01
☐	77	Willie Davis	.10	.05	.01
☐	78	Don Sutton	.10	.05	.01
☐	79	Jim Brewer	.10	.05	.01
☐	80	Manny Mota	.15	.07	.01
☐	81	Bill Russell	.15	.07	.01
☐	82	Ron Cey	.15	.07	.01
☐	83	Steve Garvey	.30	.15	.03

1985-86 Sportflics Prototypes

The 1985-86 Sportflics Proof set contains four standard-size (2 1/2 by 3 1/2 inch) unnumbered cards, one mini (1 5/16 by 1 5/16 inch) Joe DiMaggio card, and one trivia card (1 3/4 by 2 inches). The standard-size cards resemble regular 1986 Sportflics cards, but have different photos and stats only through 1984. One of the Winfield cards has a bio only; unfortunately the biographical statements on the back are incorrect in several instances. The DiMaggio card has black and white photos on the front, and career totals on the back. The trivia card is the same as those distributed with 1986 Sportflics, except it shows the major league baseball logo on the front. These test cards were apparently produced in limited quantity to show Major League Baseball and the Major League Baseball Players Association what Sportflics was proposing in order to be a new licensee for producing cards. These cards are very difficult to find. These cards are considerably rarer than the Sportflics Test cards which were given out after the Sportflics license had been granted.

	MINT	EXC	G-VG
COMPLETE SET (5)	75.00	37.50	7.50
COMMON PLAYER (1-5)	10.00	5.00	1.00
☐ 1 Joe DiMaggio (small size)	25.00	12.50	2.50
☐ 2 Mike Schmidt (stats on back)	30.00	15.00	3.00
☐ 3 Bruce Sutter (stats on back)	10.00	5.00	1.00
☐ 4 Dave Winfield (biographical back)	15.00	7.50	1.50
☐ 5 Dave Winfield (stats on back)	25.00	12.50	2.50

1985-86 Sportflics Test

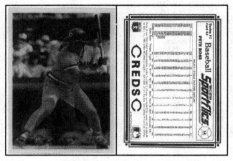

This three card pack was a test, distributed freely by salesmen to potential buyers to show them what the new Sportflics product would look like. The set is sometimes referred to as the Vendor Sample Kit. Some of these packs even found their way to the retail counters. They are not rare although they are obviously much less common than the regular issue of Sportflics. The cards show statistics only up through 1984. The copyright date on the card backs shows 1986. The cards are standard size, 2 1/2" by 3 1/2".

	MINT	EXC	G-VG
COMPLETE SET (3)	18.00	9.00	1.80
COMMON PLAYER	5.00	2.50	.50
☐ 1 RBI Sluggers Mike Schmidt Dale Murphy Jim Rice	5.00	2.50	.50
☐ 43 Pete Rose (pictured with batting helmet; Pete is #50 in regular 1986 set)	10.00	5.00	1.00
☐ 45 Tom Seaver (Tom is #25 in regular 1986 set)	7.00	3.50	.70

1986 Sportflics

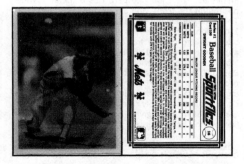

This 200-card set was marketed with 133 small trivia cards. This inaugural set for Sportflics was initially fairly well received by the public. Sportflics was distributed by Major League Marketing; the company is also affiliated with Wrigley and Amurol. The set features 139 single player "magic motion" cards (which can be tilted to show three different pictures of the same player), 50 "Tri- Stars" (which show three different players), 10 "Big Six" cards (which show six players who share similar achievements),

and one World Champs card featuring 12 members of the victorious Kansas City Royals. All cards measure 2 1/2" by 3 1/2". Some of the cards also have (limited production and rarely seen) proof versions with some player selection differences; a proof version of #178 includes Jim Wilson instead of Mark Funderburk. Also a proof of #179 with Karl Best, Mark Funderburk, Andres Galarraga, Dwayne Henry, Pete Incaviglia, and Todd Worrell was produced.

		MINT	EXC	G-VG
COMPLETE SET (200)		40.00	20.00	4.00
COMMON PLAYER (1-200)		.12	.06	.01
☐	1 George Brett	1.25	.60	.12
☐	2 Don Mattingly	4.00	2.00	.40
☐	3 Wade Boggs	2.50	1.25	.25
☐	4 Eddie Murray	.75	.35	.07
☐	5 Dale Murphy	.90	.45	.09
☐	6 Rickey Henderson	1.00	.50	.10
☐	7 Harold Baines	.30	.15	.03
☐	8 Cal Ripken	1.00	.50	.10
☐	9 Orel Hershiser	1.00	.50	.10
☐	10 Bret Saberhagen	.75	.35	.07
☐	11 Tim Raines	.50	.25	.05
☐	12 Fernando Valenzuela	.40	.20	.04
☐	13 Tony Gwynn	.90	.45	.09
☐	14 Pedro Guerrero	.35	.17	.03
☐	15 Keith Hernandez	.35	.17	.03
☐	16 Ernie Riles	.20	.10	.02
☐	17 Jim Rice	.40	.20	.04
☐	18 Ron Guidry	.30	.15	.03
☐	19 Willie McGee	.35	.17	.03
☐	20 Ryne Sandberg	1.00	.50	.10
☐	21 Kirk Gibson	.60	.30	.06
☐	22 Ozzie Guillen	.40	.20	.04
☐	23 Dave Parker	.30	.15	.03
☐	24 Vince Coleman	1.25	.60	.12
☐	25 Tom Seaver	.75	.35	.07
☐	26 Brett Butler	.20	.10	.02
☐	27 Steve Carlton	.60	.30	.06
☐	28 Gary Carter	.50	.25	.05
☐	29 Cecil Cooper	.20	.10	.02
☐	30 Jose Cruz	.12	.06	.01
☐	31 Alvin Davis	.20	.10	.02
☐	32 Dwight Evans	.25	.12	.02
☐	33 Julio Franco	.25	.12	.02
☐	34 Damaso Garcia	.12	.06	.01
☐	35 Steve Garvey	.75	.35	.07
☐	36 Kent Hrbek	.40	.20	.04
☐	37 Reggie Jackson	1.00	.50	.10
☐	38 Fred Lynn	.30	.15	.03
☐	39 Paul Molitor	.40	.20	.04
☐	40 Jim Presley	.20	.10	.02
☐	41 Dave Righetti	.30	.15	.03
☐	42 Robin Yount	.75	.35	.07
☐	43 Nolan Ryan	1.50	.75	.15
☐	44 Mike Schmidt	1.50	.75	.15
☐	45 Lee Smith	.12	.06	.01
☐	46 Rick Sutcliffe	.20	.10	.02
☐	47 Bruce Sutter	.20	.10	.02
☐	48 Lou Whitaker	.25	.12	.02
☐	49 Dave Winfield	.65	.30	.06
☐	50 Pete Rose	1.50	.75	.15
☐	51 NL MVP's Ryne Sandberg Steve Garvey Pete Rose	.75	.35	.07
☐	52 Slugging Stars George Brett Harold Baines Jim Rice	.40	.20	.04
☐	53 No-Hitters Phil Niekro Jerry Reuss Mike Witt	.20	.10	.02
☐	54 Big Hitters Don Mattingly Cal Ripken Robin Yount	1.00	.50	.10
☐	55 Bullpen Aces Dan Quisenberry Goose Gossage Lee Smith	.20	.10	.02
☐	56 Rookies of The Year Darryl Strawberry Steve Sax Pete Rose	1.00	.50	.10
☐	57 AL MVP's Cal Ripken Don Baylor	.50	.25	.05

	Reggie Jackson			
☐ 58	Repeat Batting Champs .	.75	.35	.07
	Dave Parker			
	Bill Madlock			
	Pete Rose			
☐ 59	Cy Young Winners	.12	.06	.01
	LaMarr Hoyt			
	Mike Flanagan			
	Ron Guidry			
☐ 60	Double Award Winners ...	.30	.15	.03
	Fernando Valenzuela			
	Rick Sutcliffe			
	Tom Seaver			
☐ 61	Home Run Champs	.65	.30	.06
	Reggie Jackson			
	Jim Rice			
	Tony Armas			
☐ 62	NL MVP's	.75	.35	.07
	Keith Hernandez			
	Dale Murphy			
	Mike Schmidt			
☐ 63	AL MVP's	.60	.30	.06
	Robin Yount			
	George Brett			
	Fred Lynn			
☐ 64	Comeback Players	.12	.06	.01
	Bert Blyleven			
	Jerry Koosman			
	John Denny			
☐ 65	Cy Young Relievers	.20	.10	.02
	Willie Hernandez			
	Rollie Fingers			
	Bruce Sutter			
☐ 66	Rookies of The Year	.20	.10	.02
	Bob Horner			
	Andre Dawson			
	Gary Matthews			
☐ 67	Rookies of The Year	.35	.17	.03
	Ron Kittle			
	Carlton Fisk			
	Tom Seaver			
☐ 68	Home Run Champs	.35	.17	.03
	Mike Schmidt			
	George Foster			
	Dave Kingman			
☐ 69	Double Award Winners ...	1.00	.50	.10
	Cal Ripken			
	Rod Carew			
	Pete Rose			
☐ 70	Cy Young Winners	.40	.20	.04
	Rick Sutcliffe			
	Steve Carlton			
	Tom Seaver			
☐ 71	Top Sluggers	.50	.25	.05
	Reggie Jackson			
	Fred Lynn			
	Robin Yount			
☐ 72	Rookies of The Year	.25	.12	.02
	Dave Righetti			
	Fernando Valenzuela			
	Rick Sutcliffe			
☐ 73	Rookies of The Year	.50	.25	.05
	Fred Lynn			
	Eddie Murray			
	Cal Ripken			
☐ 74	Rookies of The Year	.25	.12	.02
	Alvin Davis			
	Lou Whitaker			
	Rod Carew			
☐ 75	Batting Champs	1.25	.60	.12
	Don Mattingly			
	Wade Boggs			
	Carney Lansford			
☐ 76	Jesse Barfield	.30	.15	.03
☐ 77	Phil Bradley	.25	.12	.02
☐ 78	Chris Brown	.20	.10	.02
☐ 79	Tom Browning	.30	.15	.03
☐ 80	Tom Brunansky	.25	.12	.02
☐ 81	Bill Buckner	.20	.10	.02
☐ 82	Chili Davis	.20	.10	.02
☐ 83	Mike Davis	.12	.06	.01
☐ 84	Rich Gedman	.12	.06	.01
☐ 85	Willie Hernandez	.20	.10	.02
☐ 86	Ron Kittle	.20	.10	.02
☐ 87	Lee Lacy	.12	.06	.01
☐ 88	Bill Madlock	.20	.10	.02
☐ 89	Mike Marshall	.20	.10	.02
☐ 90	Keith Moreland	.12	.06	.01
☐ 91	Graig Nettles	.20	.10	.02
☐ 92	Lance Parrish	.30	.15	.03
☐ 93	Kirby Puckett	1.25	.60	.12
☐ 94	Juan Samuel	.30	.15	.03
☐ 95	Steve Sax	.35	.17	.03
☐ 96	Dave Stieb	.20	.10	.02
☐ 97	Darryl Strawberry	1.25	.60	.12

☐ 98	Willie Upshaw	.12	.06	.01
☐ 99	Frank Viola	.30	.15	.03
☐ 100	Dwight Gooden	1.25	.60	.12
☐ 101	Joaquin Andujar	.12	.06	.01
☐ 102	George Bell	.40	.20	.04
☐ 103	Bert Blyleven	.25	.12	.02
☐ 104	Mike Boddicker	.12	.06	.01
☐ 105	Britt Burns	.12	.06	.01
☐ 106	Rod Carew	.75	.35	.07
☐ 107	Jack Clark	.35	.17	.03
☐ 108	Danny Cox	.20	.10	.02
☐ 109	Ron Darling	.35	.17	.03
☐ 110	Andre Dawson	.50	.25	.05
☐ 111	Leon Durham	.12	.06	.01
☐ 112	Tony Fernandez	.25	.12	.02
☐ 113	Tommy Herr	.12	.06	.01
☐ 114	Teddy Higuera	.35	.17	.03
☐ 115	Bob Horner	.20	.10	.02
☐ 116	Dave Kingman	.20	.10	.02
☐ 117	Jack Morris	.25	.12	.02
☐ 118	Dan Quisenberry	.20	.10	.02
☐ 119	Jeff Reardon	.20	.10	.02
☐ 120	Bryn Smith	.20	.10	.02
☐ 121	Ozzie Smith	.50	.25	.05
☐ 122	John Tudor	.20	.10	.02
☐ 123	Tim Wallach	.12	.06	.01
☐ 124	Willie Wilson	.20	.10	.02
☐ 125	Carlton Fisk	.30	.15	.03
☐ 126	RBI Sluggers	.20	.10	.02
	Gary Carter			
	Al Oliver			
	George Foster			
☐ 127	Run Scorers	.40	.20	.04
	Tim Raines			
	Ryne Sandberg			
	Keith Hernandez			
☐ 128	Run Scorers	.35	.17	.03
	Paul Molitor			
	Cal Ripken			
	Willie Wilson			
☐ 129	No-Hitters	.12	.06	.01
	John Candelaria			
	Dennis Eckersley			
	Bob Forsch			
☐ 130	World Series MVP's	.60	.30	.06
	Pete Rose			
	Ron Cey			
	Rollie Fingers			
☐ 131	All-Star Game MVP's	.12	.06	.01
	Dave Concepcion			
	George Foster			
	Bill Madlock			
☐ 132	Cy Young Winners	.12	.06	.01
	John Denny			
	Fernando Valenzuela			
	Vida Blue			
☐ 133	Comeback Players	.12	.06	.01
	Rich Dotson			
	Joaquin Andujar			
	Doyle Alexander			
☐ 134	Big Winners	.35	.17	.03
	Rick Sutcliffe			
	Tom Seaver			
	John Denny			
☐ 135	Veteran Pitchers	.50	.25	.05
	Tom Seaver			
	Phil Niekro			
	Don Sutton			
☐ 136	Rookies of The Year	.75	.35	.07
	Dwight Gooden			
	Vince Coleman			
	Alfredo Griffin			
☐ 137	All-Star Game MVP's	.40	.20	.04
	Gary Carter			
	Fred Lynn			
	Steve Garvey			
☐ 138	Veteran Hitters	.60	.30	.06
	Tony Perez			
	Rusty Staub			
	Pete Rose			
☐ 139	Power Hitters	.50	.25	.05
	Mike Schmidt			
	Jim Rice			
	George Foster			
☐ 140	Batting Champs	.25	.12	.02
	Tony Gwynn			
	Al Oliver			
	Bill Buckner			
☐ 141	No-Hitters	.50	.25	.05
	Nolan Ryan			
	Jack Morris			
	Dave Righetti			
☐ 142	No-Hitters	.30	.15	.03
	Tom Seaver			
	Bert Blyleven			

	Vida Blue				
☐ 143	Strikeout Kings	1.00	.50	.10
	Nolan Ryan			
	Fernando Valenzuela			
	Dwight Gooden			
☐ 144	Base Stealers	.20	.10	.02
	Tim Raines			
	Willie Wilson			
	Davey Lopes			
☐ 145	RBI Sluggers	.20	.10	.02
	Tony Armas			
	Cecil Cooper			
	Eddie Murray			
☐ 146	AL MVP's	.40	.20	.04
	Rod Carew			
	Jim Rice			
	Rollie Fingers			
☐ 147	World Series MVP's	.35	.17	.03
	Alan Trammell			
	Rick Dempsey			
	Reggie Jackson			
☐ 148	World Series MVP's	.40	.20	.04
	Darrell Porter			
	Pedro Guerrero			
	Mike Schmidt			
☐ 149	ERA Leaders	.12	.06	.01
	Mike Boddicker			
	Rick Sutcliffe			
	Ron Guidry			
☐ 150	Comeback Players	.35	.17	.03
	Reggie Jackson			
	Dave Kingman			
	Fred Lynn			
☐ 151	Buddy Bell	.20	.10	.02
☐ 152	Dennis Boyd	.12	.06	.01
☐ 153	Dave Concepcion	.20	.10	.02
☐ 154	Brian Downing	.12	.06	.01
☐ 155	Shawon Dunston	.30	.15	.03
☐ 156	John Franco	.35	.17	.03
☐ 157	Scott Garrelts	.20	.10	.02
☐ 158	Bob James	.12	.06	.01
☐ 159	Charlie Leibrandt	.12	.06	.01
☐ 160	Oddibe McDowell	.25	.12	.02
☐ 161	Roger McDowell	.30	.15	.03
☐ 162	Mike Moore	.30	.15	.03
☐ 163	Phil Niekro	.50	.25	.05
☐ 164	Al Oliver	.20	.10	.02
☐ 165	Tony Pena	.20	.10	.02
☐ 166	Ted Power	.12	.06	.01
☐ 167	Mike Scioscia	.12	.06	.01
☐ 168	Mario Soto	.12	.06	.01
☐ 169	Bob Stanley	.12	.06	.01
☐ 170	Gary Templeton	.12	.06	.01
☐ 171	Andre Thornton	.12	.06	.01
☐ 172	Alan Trammell	.45	.22	.04
☐ 173	Doug DeCinces	.20	.10	.02
☐ 174	Greg Walker	.12	.06	.01
☐ 175	Don Sutton	.40	.20	.04
☐ 176	1985 Award Winners	.90	.45	.09
	Ozzie Guillen			
	Bret Saberhagen			
	Don Mattingly			
	Vince Coleman			
	Dwight Gooden			
	Willie McGee			
☐ 177	1985 Hot Rookies	.30	.15	.03
	Stew Cliburn			
	Brian Fisher			
	Joe Hesketh			
	Joe Orsulak			
	Mark Salas			
	Larry Sheets			
☐ 178	1986 Rookies To Watch	18.00	9.00	1.80
	Jose Canseco			
	Mark Funderburk			
	Mike Greenwell			
	Steve Lombardozzi			
	Billy Joe Robidoux			
	Danny Tartabull			
☐ 179	1985 Gold Glovers	.75	.35	.07
	George Brett			
	Ron Guidry			
	Keith Hernandez			
	Don Mattingly			
	Willie McGee			
	Dale Murphy			
☐ 180	Active Lifetime .300	.75	.35	.07
	Wade Boggs			
	George Brett			
	Rod Carew			
	Cecil Cooper			
	Don Mattingly			
	Willie Wilson			
☐ 181	Active Lifetime .300	.60	.30	.06
	Tony Gwynn			

	Bill Madlock				
	Pedro Guerrero			
	Dave Parker			
	Pete Rose			
	Keith Hernandez			
☐ 182	1985 Milestones	.75	.35	.07
	Rod Carew			
	Phil Niekro			
	Pete Rose			
	Nolan Ryan			
	Tom Seaver			
	Matt Tallman (fan)			
☐ 183	1985 Triple Crown	.75	.35	.07
	Wade Boggs			
	Darrell Evans			
	Don Mattingly			
	Willie McGee			
	Dale Murphy			
	Dave Parker			
☐ 184	1985 Highlights	.75	.35	.07
	Wade Boggs			
	Dwight Gooden			
	Rickey Henderson			
	Don Mattingly			
	Willie McGee			
	John Tudor			
☐ 185	1985 20 Game Winners	.75	.35	.07
	Dwight Gooden			
	Ron Guidry			
	John Tudor			
	Joaquin Andujar			
	Bret Saberhagen			
	Tom Browning			
☐ 186	World Series Champs	.35	.17	.03
	L. Smith, Dane Iorg			
	W. Wilson, Leibrandt			
	G. Brett, Saberhagen			
	Motley, Quisenberry			
	D. Jackson, Sundberg			
	S. Balboni, F. White			
☐ 187	Hubie Brooks	.20	.10	.02
☐ 188	Glenn Davis	.75	.35	.07
☐ 189	Darrell Evans	.20	.10	.02
☐ 190	Rich Gossage	.25	.12	.02
☐ 191	Andy Hawkins	.20	.10	.02
☐ 192	Jay Howell	.12	.06	.01
☐ 193	LaMarr Hoyt	.12	.06	.01
☐ 194	Davey Lopes	.12	.06	.01
☐ 195	Mike Scott	.50	.25	.05
☐ 196	Ted Simmons	.20	.10	.02
☐ 197	Gary Ward	.12	.06	.01
☐ 198	Bob Welch	.20	.10	.02
☐ 199	Mike Young	.12	.06	.01
☐ 200	Buddy Biancalana	.12	.06	.01

1986 Sportflics Decade Greats

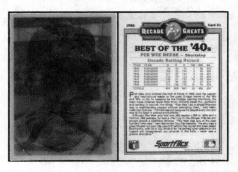

This set of 75 three-phase "animated" cards was produced by Sportflics and manufactured by Opti-Graphics of Arlington, Texas. Cards are standard size, 2 1/2" by 3 1/2", and feature both sepia (players of the '30s and '40s) and full color cards. The concept of the set was that the best players at each position for each decade (from the '30s to the '80s) were chosen. The bios were written by Les Woodcock. Also included with the set in the specially designed collector box are 51 trivia cards with historical questions about the six decades of All-Star games.

	MINT	EXC	G-VG
COMPLETE SET (75)	15.00	7.50	1.50
COMMON PLAYER (1-75)	.15	.07	.01

		MINT	EXC	G-VG
☐ 1	Babe Ruth	3.00	1.50	.30
☐ 2	Jimmie Foxx	.35	.17	.03
☐ 3	Lefty Grove	.35	.17	.03
☐ 4	Hank Greenberg	.35	.17	.03
☐ 5	Al Simmons	.25	.12	.02
☐ 6	Carl Hubbell	.25	.12	.02
☐ 7	Joe Cronin	.25	.12	.02
☐ 8	Mel Ott	.35	.17	.03
☐ 9	Lefty Gomez	.25	.12	.02
☐ 10	Lou Gehrig	1.00	.50	.10
	(Best '30s Player)			
☐ 11	Pie Traynor	.25	.12	.02
☐ 12	Charlie Gehringer	.25	.12	.02
☐ 13	Best '30s Catchers	.25	.12	.02
	Bill Dickey			
	Mickey Cochrane			
	Gabby Hartnett			
☐ 14	Best '30s Pitchers	.25	.12	.02
	Dizzy Dean			
	Red Ruffing			
	Paul Derringer			
☐ 15	Best '30s Outfielders	.15	.07	.01
	Paul Waner			
	Joe Medwick			
	Earl Averill			
☐ 16	Bob Feller	.75	.35	.07
☐ 17	Lou Boudreau	.25	.12	.02
☐ 18	Enos Slaughter	.35	.17	.03
☐ 19	Hal Newhouser	.15	.07	.01
☐ 20	Joe DiMaggio	1.50	.75	.15
☐ 21	Pee Wee Reese	.45	.22	.04
☐ 22	Phil Rizzuto	.35	.17	.03
☐ 23	Ernie Lombardi	.15	.07	.01
☐ 24	Best '40s Infielders	.25	.12	.02
	Johnny Mize			
	Joe Gordon			
	George Kell			
☐ 25	Ted Williams	1.00	.50	.10
	(Best '40s Player)			
☐ 26	Mickey Mantle	3.00	1.50	.30
☐ 27	Warren Spahn	.35	.17	.03
☐ 28	Jackie Robinson	.75	.35	.07
☐ 29	Ernie Banks	.35	.17	.03
☐ 30	Stan Musial	.75	.35	.07
	(Best '50s Player)			
☐ 31	Yogi Berra	.75	.35	.07
☐ 32	Duke Snider	.75	.35	.07
☐ 33	Roy Campanella	.75	.35	.07
☐ 34	Eddie Mathews	.35	.17	.03
☐ 35	Ralph Kiner	.25	.12	.02
☐ 36	Early Wynn	.25	.12	.02
☐ 37	Double Play Duo	.25	.12	.02
	Nellie Fox			
	Luis Aparicio			
☐ 38	Best '50s First Base	.15	.07	.01
	Gil Hodges			
	Ted Kluszewski			
	Mickey Vernon			
☐ 39	Best '50s Pitchers	.15	.07	.01
	Bob Lemon			
	Don Newcombe			
	Robin Roberts			
☐ 40	Henry Aaron	1.00	.50	.10
☐ 41	Frank Robinson	.35	.17	.03
☐ 42	Bob Gibson	.35	.17	.03
☐ 43	Roberto Clemente	1.00	.50	.10
☐ 44	Whitey Ford	.45	.22	.04
☐ 45	Brooks Robinson	.50	.25	.05
☐ 46	Juan Marichal	.25	.12	.02
☐ 47	Carl Yastrzemski	1.00	.50	.10
☐ 48	Best '60s First Base	.25	.12	.02
	Willie McCovey			
	Harmon Killebrew			
	Orlando Cepeda			
☐ 49	Best '60s Catchers	.15	.07	.01
	Joe Torre			
	Elston Howard			
	Bill Freehan			
☐ 50	Willie Mays	1.00	.50	.10
	(Best '50s Player)			
☐ 51	Best '60s Outfielders	.25	.12	.02
	Al Kaline			
	Tony Oliva			
	Billy Williams			
☐ 52	Tom Seaver	.75	.35	.07
☐ 53	Reggie Jackson	1.00	.50	.10
☐ 54	Steve Carlton	.75	.35	.07

		MINT	EXC	G-VG
☐ 55	Mike Schmidt	1.25	.60	.12
☐ 56	Joe Morgan	.45	.22	.04
☐ 57	Jim Rice	.25	.12	.02
☐ 58	Jim Palmer	.45	.22	.04
☐ 59	Lou Brock	.35	.17	.03
☐ 60	Pete Rose	1.25	.60	.12
	(Best '70s Player)			
☐ 61	Steve Garvey	.50	.25	.05
☐ 62	Best '70s Catchers	.25	.12	.02
	Thurman Munson			
	Carlton Fisk			
	Ted Simmons			
☐ 63	Best '70s Pitchers	.35	.17	.03
	Vida Blue			
	Catfish Hunter			
	Nolan Ryan			
☐ 64	George Brett	1.00	.50	.10
☐ 65	Don Mattingly	1.50	.75	.15
☐ 66	Fernando Valenzuela	.25	.12	.02
☐ 67	Dale Murphy	.75	.35	.07
☐ 68	Wade Boggs	1.25	.60	.12
☐ 69	Rickey Henderson	1.00	.50	.10
☐ 70	Eddie Murray	.50	.25	.05
	(Best '80s Player)			
☐ 71	Ron Guidry	.15	.07	.01
☐ 72	Best '80s Catchers	.25	.12	.02
	Gary Carter			
	Lance Parrish			
	Tony Pena			
☐ 73	Best '80s Infielders	.25	.12	.02
	Cal Ripken			
	Lou Whitaker			
	Robin Yount			
☐ 74	Best '80s Outfielders	.25	.12	.02
	Pedro Guerrero			
	Tim Raines			
	Dave Winfield			
☐ 75	Dwight Gooden	.75	.35	.07

1986 Sportflics Rookies

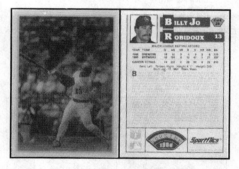

This set of 50 three-phase "animated" cards features top rookies of 1986 as well as a few outstanding rookies from the past. These "Magic Motion" cards are standard size, 2 1/2" by 3 1/2", and feature a distinctive light blue border on the front of the card. Cards were distributed in a light blue box, which also contained 34 trivia cards, each measuring 1 3/4" by 2". There are 47 single player cards along with two Tri-Stars and one Big Six.

	MINT	EXC	G-VG
COMPLETE SET (50)	18.00	9.00	1.80
COMMON PLAYER (1-50)	.10	.05	.01

		MINT	EXC	G-VG
☐ 1	John Kruk	.30	.15	.03
☐ 2	Edwin Correa	.15	.07	.01
☐ 3	Pete Incaviglia	.75	.35	.07
☐ 4	Dale Sveum	.15	.07	.01
☐ 5	Juan Nieves	.15	.07	.01
☐ 6	Will Clark	4.50	2.25	.45
☐ 7	Wally Joyner	2.00	1.00	.20
☐ 8	Lance McCullers	.15	.07	.01
☐ 9	Scott Bailes	.15	.07	.01
☐ 10	Dan Plesac	.20	.10	.02
☐ 11	Jose Canseco	4.50	2.25	.45
☐ 12	Bobby Witt	.20	.10	.02
☐ 13	Barry Bonds	.75	.35	.07

☐ 14	Andres Thomas	.20	.10	.02
☐ 15	Jim Deshaies	.20	.10	.02
☐ 16	Ruben Sierra	2.50	1.25	.25
☐ 17	Steve Lombardozzi	.10	.05	.01
☐ 18	Cory Snyder	1.00	.50	.10
☐ 19	Reggie Williams	.10	.05	.01
☐ 20	Mitch Williams	.25	.12	.02
☐ 21	Glenn Braggs	.25	.12	.02
☐ 22	Danny Tartabull	.75	.35	.07
☐ 23	Charlie Kerfeld	.10	.05	.01
☐ 24	Paul Assenmacher	.10	.05	.01
☐ 25	Robby Thompson	.25	.12	.02
☐ 26	Bobby Bonilla	.75	.35	.07
☐ 27	Andres Galarraga	.75	.35	.07
☐ 28	Billy Jo Robidoux	.15	.07	.01
☐ 29	Bruce Ruffin	.15	.07	.01
☐ 30	Greg Swindell	.50	.25	.05
☐ 31	John Cangelosi	.10	.05	.01
☐ 32	Jim Traber	.10	.05	.01
☐ 33	Russ Morman	.15	.07	.01
☐ 34	Barry Larkin	1.50	.75	.15
☐ 35	Todd Worrell	.50	.25	.05
☐ 36	John Cerutti	.15	.07	.01
☐ 37	Mike Kingery	.10	.05	.01
☐ 38	Mark Eichhorn	.10	.05	.01
☐ 39	Scott Bankhead	.20	.10	.02
☐ 40	Bo Jackson	3.50	1.75	.35
☐ 41	Greg Mathews	.15	.07	.01
☐ 42	Eric King	.15	.07	.01
☐ 43	Kal Daniels	.75	.35	.07
☐ 44	Calvin Schiraldi	.15	.07	.01
☐ 45	Mickey Brantley	.20	.10	.02
☐ 46	Tri-Stars Willie Mays Pete Rose Fred Lynn	.50	.25	.05
☐ 47	Tri-Stars Tom Seaver Fern. Valenzuela Dwight Gooden	.50	.25	.05
☐ 48	Big Six Eddie Murray Lou Whitaker Dave Righetti Steve Sax Cal Ripken Jr. Darryl Strawberry	.50	.25	.05
☐ 49	Kevin Mitchell	2.00	1.00	.20
☐ 50	Mike Diaz	.15	.07	.01

1987 Sportflics

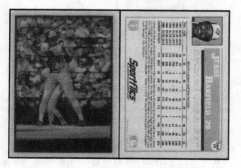

This 200-card set was produced by Sportflics and again features three sequence action pictures on each card. Cards measure 2 1/2" by 3 1/2" and are in full color. Also included with the cards were 136 small team logo and trivia cards. There are 165 individual players, 20 Tri-Stars (the top three players in each league at each position), and 15 other miscellaneous multi-player cards. The cards feature a red border on the front. A full-color face shot of the player is printed on the back of the card. Cards are numbered on the back in the upper right corner. The cards in the factory-collated sets are copyrighted 1986, while the cards in the wax packs are copyrighted 1987 or show no copyright year on the

back. Cards from wax packs with 1987 copyright are 1-35, 41-75, 81-115, 121-155, and 161-195; the rest of the numbers (when taken from wax packs) are found without a copyright year.

			MINT	EXC	G-VG
		COMPLETE SET (200)	35.00	17.50	3.50
		COMMON PLAYER (1-200)	.12	.06	.01
☐	1	Don Mattingly	3.00	1.50	.30
☐	2	Wade Boggs	1.50	.75	.15
☐	3	Dale Murphy	.90	.45	.09
☐	4	Rickey Henderson	.90	.45	.09
☐	5	George Brett	.75	.35	.07
☐	6	Eddie Murray	.60	.30	.06
☐	7	Kirby Puckett	.90	.45	.09
☐	8	Ryne Sandberg	.50	.25	.05
☐	9	Cal Ripken	.50	.25	.05
☐	10	Roger Clemens	1.25	.60	.12
☐	11	Ted Higuera	.25	.12	.02
☐	12	Steve Sax	.25	.12	.02
☐	13	Chris Brown	.12	.06	.01
☐	14	Jesse Barfield	.25	.12	.02
☐	15	Kent Hrbek	.30	.15	.03
☐	16	Robin Yount	.75	.35	.07
☐	17	Glenn Davis	.50	.25	.05
☐	18	Hubie Brooks	.12	.06	.01
☐	19	Mike Scott	.30	.15	.03
☐	20	Darryl Strawberry	.90	.45	.09
☐	21	Alvin Davis	.20	.10	.02
☐	22	Eric Davis	1.25	.60	.12
☐	23	Danny Tartabull	.45	.22	.04
☐	24A	Cory Snyder ERR '86 (photo on front is Pat Tabler)	3.00	1.50	.30
☐	24B	Cory Snyder ERR '87 (photos on front and back are Pat Tabler)	2.00	1.00	.20
☐	24C	Cory Snyder COR '86	2.00	1.00	.20
☐	25	Pete Rose	1.00	.50	.10
☐	26	Wally Joyner	1.00	.50	.10
☐	27	Pedro Guerrero	.25	.12	.02
☐	28	Tom Seaver	.60	.30	.06
☐	29	Bob Knepper	.15	.07	.01
☐	30	Mike Schmidt	1.00	.50	.10
☐	31	Tony Gwynn	.75	.35	.07
☐	32	Don Slaught	.12	.06	.01
☐	33	Todd Worrell	.30	.15	.03
☐	34	Tim Raines	.30	.15	.03
☐	35	Dave Parker	.25	.12	.02
☐	36	Bob Ojeda	.12	.06	.01
☐	37	Pete Incaviglia	.50	.25	.05
☐	38	Bruce Hurst	.20	.10	.02
☐	39	Bobby Witt	.20	.10	.02
☐	40	Steve Garvey	.60	.30	.06
☐	41	Dave Winfield	.40	.20	.04
☐	42	Jose Cruz	.12	.06	.01
☐	43	Orel Hershiser	.75	.35	.07
☐	44	Reggie Jackson	.90	.45	.09
☐	45	Chili Davis	.12	.06	.01
☐	46	Robby Thompson	.12	.06	.01
☐	47	Dennis Boyd	.12	.06	.01
☐	48	Kirk Gibson	.40	.20	.04
☐	49	Fred Lynn	.20	.10	.02
☐	50	Gary Carter	.40	.20	.04
☐	51	George Bell	.30	.15	.03
☐	52	Pete O'Brien	.12	.06	.01
☐	53	Ron Darling	.20	.10	.02
☐	54	Paul Molitor	.30	.15	.03
☐	55	Mike Pagliarulo	.12	.06	.01
☐	56	Mike Boddicker	.12	.06	.01
☐	57	Dave Righetti	.20	.10	.02
☐	58	Len Dykstra	.20	.10	.02
☐	59	Mike Witt	.20	.10	.02
☐	60	Tony Bernazard	.12	.06	.01
☐	61	John Kruk	.25	.12	.02
☐	62	Mike Krukow	.12	.06	.01
☐	63	Sid Fernandez	.25	.12	.02
☐	64	Gary Gaetti	.25	.12	.02
☐	65	Vince Coleman	.50	.25	.05
☐	66	Pat Tabler	.12	.06	.01
☐	67	Mike Scioscia	.12	.06	.01
☐	68	Scott Garrelts	.12	.06	.01
☐	69	Brett Butler	.12	.06	.01
☐	70	Bill Buckner	.20	.10	.02
☐	71A	Dennis Rasmussen ERR '86 copyright (photo on back is John Montefusco)	1.00	.50	.10
☐	71B	Dennis Rasmussen COR '87 copyright (photo with mustache)	.50	.25	.05
☐	72	Tim Wallach	.12	.06	.01
☐	73	Bob Horner	.20	.10	.02

☐ 74	Willie McGee	.25	.12	.02
☐ 75	Tri-Stars	1.00	.50	.10
	Don Mattingly			
	Wally Joyner			
	Eddie Murray			
☐ 76A	Jesse Orosco COR	.12	.06	.01
	'86 copyright			
☐ 76B	Jesse Orosco ERR	.12	.06	.01
	'87 copyright			
	(number on back is 96)			
☐ 77	Tri-Stars	.12	.06	.01
	Todd Worrell			
	Jeff Reardon			
	Lee Smith			
☐ 78	Candy Maldonado	.12	.06	.01
☐ 79	Tri-Stars	.20	.10	.02
	Ozzie Smith			
	Hubie Brooks			
	Shawon Dunston			
☐ 80	Tri-Stars	1.00	.50	.10
	George Bell			
	Jose Canseco			
	Jim Rice			
☐ 81	Bert Blyleven	.25	.12	.02
☐ 82	Mike Marshall	.20	.10	.02
☐ 83	Ron Guidry	.20	.10	.02
☐ 84	Julio Franco	.20	.10	.02
☐ 85	Willie Wilson	.20	.10	.02
☐ 86	Lee Lacy	.12	.06	.01
☐ 87	Jack Morris	.25	.12	.02
☐ 88	Ray Knight	.12	.06	.01
☐ 89	Phil Bradley	.12	.06	.01
☐ 90	Jose Canseco	2.50	1.25	.25
☐ 91	Gary Ward	.12	.06	.01
☐ 92	Mike Easler	.12	.06	.01
☐ 93	Tony Pena	.12	.06	.01
☐ 94	Dave Smith	.12	.06	.01
☐ 95	Will Clark	2.50	1.25	.25
☐ 96	Lloyd Moseby	.12	.06	.01
	(see also #76B)			
☐ 97	Jim Rice	.30	.15	.03
☐ 98	Shawon Dunston	.25	.12	.02
☐ 99	Don Sutton	.35	.17	.03
☐ 100	Dwight Gooden	.90	.45	.09
☐ 101	Lance Parrish	.25	.12	.02
☐ 102	Mark Langston	.35	.17	.03
☐ 103	Floyd Youmans	.12	.06	.01
☐ 104	Lee Smith	.12	.06	.01
☐ 105	Willie Hernandez	.20	.10	.02
☐ 106	Doug DeCinces	.12	.06	.01
☐ 107	Ken Schrom	.12	.06	.01
☐ 108	Don Carman	.12	.06	.01
☐ 109	Brook Jacoby	.20	.10	.02
☐ 110	Steve Bedrosian	.25	.12	.02
☐ 111	Tri-Stars	.50	.25	.05
	Roger Clemens			
	Jack Morris			
	Ted Higuera			
☐ 112	Tri-Stars	.12	.06	.01
	Marty Barrett			
	Tony Bernazard			
	Lou Whitaker			
☐ 113	Tri-Stars	.25	.12	.02
	Cal Ripken			
	Scott Fletcher			
	Tony Fernandez			
☐ 114	Tri-Stars	.75	.35	.07
	Wade Boggs			
	George Brett			
	Gary Gaetti			
☐ 115	Tri-Stars	.50	.25	.05
	Mike Schmidt			
	Chris Brown			
	Tim Wallach			
☐ 116	Tri-Stars	.25	.12	.02
	Ryne Sandberg			
	Johnny Ray			
	Bill Doran			
☐ 117	Tri-Stars	.25	.12	.02
	Dave Parker			
	Tony Gwynn			
	Kevin Bass			
☐ 118	Big Six Rookies	1.50	.75	.15
	Ty Gainey			
	Terry Steinbach			
	Dave Clark			
	Pat Dodson			
	Phil Lombardi			
	Benito Santiago			
☐ 119	Hi-Lite Tri-Stars	.25	.12	.02
	Dave Righetti			
	Fernando Valenzuela			
	Mike Scott			
☐ 120	Tri-Stars	.50	.25	.05
	Fernando Valenzuela			
	Mike Scott			
	Dwight Gooden			
☐ 121	Johnny Ray	.12	.06	.01
☐ 122	Keith Moreland	.12	.06	.01
☐ 123	Juan Samuel	.20	.10	.02
☐ 124	Wally Backman	.12	.06	.01
☐ 125	Nolan Ryan	1.25	.60	.12
☐ 126	Greg Harris	.12	.06	.01
☐ 127	Kirk McCaskill	.12	.06	.01
☐ 128	Dwight Evans	.25	.12	.02
☐ 129	Rick Rhoden	.12	.06	.01
☐ 130	Bill Madlock	.12	.06	.01
☐ 131	Oddibe McDowell	.20	.10	.02
☐ 132	Darrell Evans	.20	.10	.02
☐ 133	Keith Hernandez	.30	.15	.03
☐ 134	Tom Brunansky	.20	.10	.02
☐ 135	Kevin McReynolds	.50	.25	.05
☐ 136	Scott Fletcher	.12	.06	.01
☐ 137	Lou Whitaker	.20	.10	.02
☐ 138	Carney Lansford	.25	.12	.02
☐ 139	Andre Dawson	.35	.17	.03
☐ 140	Carlton Fisk	.30	.15	.03
☐ 141	Buddy Bell	.20	.10	.02
☐ 142	Ozzie Smith	.50	.25	.05
☐ 143	Dan Pasqua	.12	.06	.01
☐ 144	Kevin Mitchell	.75	.35	.07
☐ 145	Bret Saberhagen	.50	.25	.05
☐ 146	Charlie Kerfeld	.12	.06	.01
☐ 147	Phil Niekro	.35	.17	.03
☐ 148	John Candelaria	.12	.06	.01
☐ 149	Rich Gedman	.12	.06	.01
☐ 150	Fernando Valenzuela	.35	.17	.03
☐ 151	Tri-Stars	.20	.10	.02
	Gary Carter			
	Mike Scioscia			
	Tony Pena			
☐ 152	Tri-Stars	.30	.15	.03
	Tim Raines			
	Jose Cruz			
	Vince Coleman			
☐ 153	Tri-Stars	.25	.12	.02
	Jesse Barfield			
	Harold Baines			
	Dave Winfield			
☐ 154	Tri-Stars	.12	.06	.01
	Lance Parrish			
	Don Slaught			
	Rich Gedman			
☐ 155	Tri-Stars	.75	.35	.07
	Dale Murphy			
	Kevin McReynolds			
	Eric Davis			
☐ 156	Hi-Lite Tri-Stars	.45	.22	.04
	Don Sutton			
	Mike Schmidt			
	Jim Deshaies			
☐ 157	Speedburners	.30	.15	.03
	Rickey Henderson			
	John Cangelosi			
	Gary Pettis			
☐ 158	Big Six Rookies	2.00	1.00	.20
	Randy Asadoor			
	Casey Candaele			
	Kevin Seitzer			
	Rafael Palmeiro			
	Tim Pyznarski			
	Dave Cochrane			
☐ 159	Big Six	1.50	.75	.15
	Don Mattingly			
	Rickey Henderson			
	Roger Clemens			
	Dale Murphy			
	Eddie Murray			
	Dwight Gooden			
☐ 160	Roger McDowell	.20	.10	.02
☐ 161	Brian Downing	.12	.06	.01
☐ 162	Bill Doran	.20	.10	.02
☐ 163	Don Baylor	.20	.10	.02
☐ 164A	Alfredo Griffin ERR	.25	.12	.02
	(no uniform number on card back) '87			
☐ 164B	Alfredo Griffin COR '86	.25	.12	.02
☐ 165	Don Aase	.12	.06	.01
☐ 166	Glenn Wilson	.12	.06	.01
☐ 167	Dan Quisenberry	.20	.10	.02
☐ 168	Frank White	.12	.06	.01
☐ 169	Cecil Cooper	.12	.06	.01
☐ 170	Jody Davis	.12	.06	.01
☐ 171	Harold Baines	.25	.12	.02
☐ 172	Rob Deer	.20	.10	.02
☐ 173	John Tudor	.20	.10	.02
☐ 174	Larry Parrish	.12	.06	.01
☐ 175	Kevin Bass	.20	.10	.02
☐ 176	Joe Carter	.40	.20	.04

☐ 177	Mitch Webster	.12	.06	.01
☐ 178	Dave Kingman	.20	.10	.02
☐ 179	Jim Presley	.12	.06	.01
☐ 180	Mel Hall	.20	.10	.02
☐ 181	Shane Rawley	.12	.06	.01
☐ 182	Marty Barrett	.20	.10	.02
☐ 183	Damaso Garcia	.12	.06	.01
☐ 184	Bobby Grich	.20	.10	.02
☐ 185	Leon Durham	.12	.06	.01
☐ 186	Ozzie Guillen	.20	.10	.02
☐ 187	Tony Fernandez	.25	.12	.02
☐ 188	Alan Trammell	.35	.17	.03
☐ 189	Jim Clancy	.12	.06	.01
☐ 190	Bo Jackson	2.00	1.00	.20
☐ 191	Bob Forsch	.12	.06	.01
☐ 192	John Franco	.20	.10	.02
☐ 193	Von Hayes	.20	.10	.02
☐ 194	Tri-Stars	.12	.06	.01
	Don Aase			
	Dave Righetti			
	Mark Eichhorn			
☐ 195	Tri-Stars	.60	.30	.06
	Keith Hernandez			
	Will Clark			
	Glenn Davis			
☐ 196	Hi-Lite Tri-Stars	.45	.22	.04
	Roger Clemens			
	Joe Cowley			
	Bob Horner			
☐ 197	Big Six	.75	.35	.07
	George Brett			
	Hubie Brooks			
	Tony Gwynn			
	Ryne Sandberg			
	Tim Raines			
	Wade Boggs			
☐ 198	Tri-Stars	.50	.25	.05
	Kirby Puckett			
	Rickey Henderson			
	Fred Lynn			
☐ 199	Speedburners	.60	.30	.06
	Tim Raines			
	Vince Coleman			
	Eric Davis			
☐ 200	Steve Carlton	.40	.20	.04

1987 Sportflics Dealer Panels

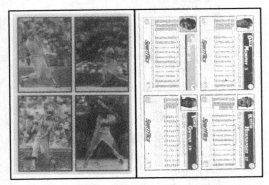

These "Magic Motion" card panels of four were issued only to dealers who were ordering other Sportflics product in quantity. If cut into individual cards, the interior white borders will be slightly narrower than the regular issue Sportflics since the panels of four measure a shade under 4 7/8" by 6 7/8". The cards have a 1986 copyright on the back same as the factory collated sets. Other than the slight difference in size, these cards are essentially styled the same as the regular issue of 1987 Sportflics. This set of sixteen top players was accompanied by the inclusion of four smaller panels of four team logo/team fact cards. The 16 small team cards correspond directly to the 16 players in the sets. The checklist below prices the panels and gives the card number for each player, which is the same as the player's card number in the Sportflics regular set.

		MINT	EXC	G-VG
COMPLETE SET (4)		12.00	6.00	1.20
COMMON PANEL (1-4)		3.00	1.50	.30
☐ 1	Don Mattingly 1	5.00	2.50	.50
	Roger Clemens 10			
	Mike Schmidt 30			
	Tim Raines 34			
☐ 2	Wade Boggs 2	3.50	1.75	.35
	Eddie Murray 6			
	Wally Joyner 26			
	Fern.Valenzuela 150			
☐ 3	Dale Murphy 3	3.00	1.50	.30
	Tony Gwynn 31			
	Jim Rice 97			
	Keith Hernandez 133			
☐ 4	Rickey Henderson 4	3.00	1.50	.30
	George Brett 5			
	Cal Ripken 9			
	Dwight Gooden 100			

1987 Sportflics Team Preview

This 26-card set features a card for each Major League team. Each card shows 12 different players on that team via four "Magic Motion" trios. The cards are numbered on the backs. The narrative on the back gives Outlook, Newcomers to Watch, and Summary for each team. The list of players appearing on the front is given at the bottom of the reverse of each card. Cards are standard size, 2 1/2" by 3 1/2". The was distributed as a complete set in its own box along with 26 team logo trivia cards measuring 1 3/4" by 2".

		MINT	EXC	G-VG
COMPLETE SET (26)		6.00	3.00	.60
COMMON PLAYER (1-26)		.30	.15	.03
☐ 1	Texas Rangers	.30	.15	.03
☐ 2	New York Mets	.40	.20	.04
☐ 3	Cleveland Indians	.30	.15	.03
☐ 4	Cincinnati Reds	.40	.20	.04
☐ 5	Toronto Blue Jays	.30	.15	.03
☐ 6	Philadelphia Phillies	.30	.15	.03
☐ 7	New York Yankees	.40	.20	.04
☐ 8	Houston Astros	.30	.15	.03
☐ 9	Boston Red Sox	.40	.20	.04
☐ 10	San Francisco Giants	.30	.15	.03
☐ 11	California Angels	.30	.15	.03
☐ 12	St. Louis Cardinals	.40	.20	.04
☐ 13	Kansas City Royals	.40	.20	.04
☐ 14	Los Angeles Dodgers	.40	.20	.04
☐ 15	Detroit Tigers	.40	.20	.04
☐ 16	San Diego Padres	.30	.15	.03
☐ 17	Minnesota Twins	.40	.20	.04
☐ 18	Pittsburgh Pirates	.30	.15	.03
☐ 19	Milwaukee Brewers	.30	.15	.03
☐ 20	Montreal Expos	.30	.15	.03
☐ 21	Baltimore Orioles	.40	.20	.04
☐ 22	Chicago Cubs	.30	.15	.03
☐ 23	Oakland Athletics	.40	.20	.04
☐ 24	Atlanta Braves	.30	.15	.03
☐ 25	Seattle Mariners	.30	.15	.03

☐ 26 Chicago White Sox .... .30 .15 .03

1987 Sportflics Rookie Packs

This two pack set consists of 10 "rookie" players and 2 trivia cards. Each of the two different packs had half the set and the outside of the wrapper told which cards were inside. The cards are all 2 1/2" by 3 1/2". The set includes the first major league baseball cards ever of Alonzo Powell, John Smiley, and Brick Smith. Dealers received one rookie pack with every Team Preview set they ordered. The card backs also feature a full-color small photo of the player.

	MINT	EXC	G-VG
COMPLETE SET (10)	8.00	4.00	.80
COMMON PLAYER (1-10)	.40	.20	.04
☐ 1 Terry Steinbach .... (pack two)	1.50	.75	.15
☐ 2 Rafael Palmeiro .... (pack one)	1.50	.75	.15
☐ 3 Dave Magadan .... (pack two)	.80	.40	.08
☐ 4 Marvin Freeman .... (pack two)	.40	.20	.04
☐ 5 Brick Smith .... (pack two)	.40	.20	.04
☐ 6 B.J. Surhoff .... (pack one)	.80	.40	.08
☐ 7 John Smiley .... (pack one)	.80	.40	.08
☐ 8 Alonzo Powell .... (pack two)	.40	.20	.04
☐ 9 Benny Santiago .... (pack one)	2.50	1.25	.25
☐ 10 Devon White .... (pack one)	1.50	.75	.15

1987 Sportflics Rookies I

These "Magic Motion" cards were issued as a series of 25 cards packaged in its own complete set box, along with 17 trivia cards. Cards are 2 1/2" by 3 1/2." The three front photos show the player in two action poses and one portrait pose. The card backs also provide a full-color photo (1 3/8" by 2 1/4") of the player as well as the usual statistics and biographical notes. The front photos are framed by a wide, round-cornered, red border and have the player's name and uniform number at the bottom.

	MINT	EXC	G-VG
COMPLETE SET (25)	8.00	4.00	.80
COMMON PLAYER (1-25)	.12	.06	.01
☐ 1 Eric Bell	.12	.06	.01
☐ 2 Chris Bosio	.25	.12	.02
☐ 3 Bob Brower	.12	.06	.01
☐ 4 Jerry Browne	.20	.10	.02

☐ 5 Ellis Burks	1.25	.60	.12
☐ 6 Casey Candaele	.12	.06	.01
☐ 7 Ken Gerhart	.12	.06	.01
☐ 8 Mike Greenwell	2.00	1.00	.20
☐ 9 Stan Jefferson	.25	.12	.02
☐ 10 Dave Magadan	.35	.17	.03
☐ 11 Joe Magrane	.50	.25	.05
☐ 12 Fred McGriff	1.25	.60	.12
☐ 13 Mark McGwire	1.75	.85	.17
☐ 14 Mark McLemore	.12	.06	.01
☐ 15 Jeff Musselman	.12	.06	.01
☐ 16 Matt Nokes	.45	.22	.04
☐ 17 Paul O'Neill	.35	.17	.03
☐ 18 Luis Polonia	.25	.12	.02
☐ 19 Benny Santiago	1.00	.50	.10
☐ 20 Kevin Seitzer	1.25	.60	.12
☐ 21 John Smiley	.30	.15	.03
☐ 22 Terry Steinbach	.50	.25	.05
☐ 23 B.J. Surhoff	.35	.17	.03
☐ 24 Devon White	.50	.25	.05
☐ 25 Matt Williams	1.50	.75	.15

1987 Sportflics Rookies II

These "Magic Motion" cards were issued as a series of 25 cards packaged in its own complete set box, along with 17 trivia cards. Cards are 2 1/2" by 3 1/2." In this second set the card numbering begins with number 26. The three front photos show the player in two action poses and one portrait pose. The card backs also provide a full-color photo (1 3/8" by 2 1/4") of the player as well as the usual statistics and biographical notes. The front photos are framed by a wide, round-cornered, red border and have the player's name and uniform number at the bottom.

	MINT	EXC	G-VG
COMPLETE SET (25)	6.00	3.00	.60
COMMON PLAYER (26-50)	.12	.06	.01
☐ 26 DeWayne Buice	.12	.06	.01
☐ 27 Willie Fraser	.12	.06	.01
☐ 28 Billy Ripken	.20	.10	.02
☐ 29 Mike Henneman	.20	.10	.02
☐ 30 Shawn Hillegas	.12	.06	.01
☐ 31 Shane Mack	.20	.10	.02
☐ 32 Rafael Palmeiro	.60	.30	.06

☐ 33	Mike Jackson		.12	.06	.01
☐ 34	Gene Larkin		.20	.10	.02
☐ 35	Jimmy Jones		.12	.06	.01
☐ 36	Gerald Young		.25	.12	.02
☐ 37	Ken Caminiti		.20	.10	.02
☐ 38	Sam Horn		.20	.10	.02
☐ 39	David Cone		1.00	.50	.10
☐ 40	Mike Dunne		.12	.06	.01
☐ 41	Ken Williams		.20	.10	.02
☐ 42	John Morris		.12	.06	.01
☐ 43	Jim Lindeman		.12	.06	.01
☐ 44	Todd Benzinger		.25	.12	.02
☐ 45	Mike Stanley		.12	.06	.01
☐ 46	Les Straker		.12	.06	.01
☐ 47	Jeff Robinson		.30	.15	.03
☐ 48	Jeff Blauser		.25	.12	.02
☐ 49	John Marzano		.20	.10	.02
☐ 50	Keith Miller		.25	.12	.02

1988 Sportflics

This 225-card set was produced by Sportflics and again features three sequence action pictures on each card. Cards measure 2 1/2" by 3 1/2" and are in full color. There are 219 individual players, 3 Highlights trios, and 3 Rookie Prospect trio cards. The cards feature a red border on the front. A full-color action picture of the player is printed on the back of the card. Cards are numbered on the back in the lower right corner.

			MINT	EXC	G-VG
	COMPLETE SET (225)		40.00	20.00	4.00
	COMMON PLAYER (1-225)		.12	.06	.01
☐	1	Don Mattingly	2.50	1.25	.25
☐	2	Tim Raines	.40	.20	.04
☐	3	Andre Dawson	.40	.20	.04
☐	4	George Bell	.35	.17	.03
☐	5	Joe Carter	.30	.15	.03
☐	6	Matt Nokes	.40	.20	.04
☐	7	Dave Winfield	.40	.20	.04
☐	8	Kirby Puckett	.90	.45	.09
☐	9	Will Clark	1.50	.75	.15
☐	10	Eric Davis	.90	.45	.09
☐	11	Rickey Henderson	.75	.35	.07
☐	12	Ryne Sandberg	.45	.22	.04
☐	13	Jesse Barfield UER (misspelled Jessie on card back)	.30	.15	.03
☐	14	Ozzie Guillen	.20	.10	.02
☐	15	Bret Saberhagen	.35	.17	.03
☐	16	Tony Gwynn	.50	.25	.05
☐	17	Kevin Seitzer	.75	.35	.07
☐	18	Jack Clark	.30	.15	.03
☐	19	Danny Tartabull	.40	.20	.04
☐	20	Ted Higuera	.25	.12	.02
☐	21	Charlie Leibrandt UER (misspelled Liebrandt on card front)	.15	.07	.01
☐	22	Benny Santiago	.75	.35	.07
☐	23	Fred Lynn	.25	.12	.02
☐	24	Rob Thompson	.15	.07	.01
☐	25	Alan Trammell	.35	.17	.03
☐	26	Tony Fernandez	.25	.12	.02
☐	27	Rick Sutcliffe	.20	.10	.02
☐	28	Gary Carter	.35	.17	.03
☐	29	Cory Snyder	.35	.17	.03

☐	30	Lou Whitaker	.20	.10	.02
☐	31	Keith Hernandez	.30	.15	.03
☐	32	Mike Witt	.20	.10	.02
☐	33	Harold Baines	.20	.10	.02
☐	34	Robin Yount	.75	.35	.07
☐	35	Mike Schmidt	1.00	.50	.10
☐	36	Dion James	.12	.06	.01
☐	37	Tom Candiotti	.12	.06	.01
☐	38	Tracy Jones	.20	.10	.02
☐	39	Nolan Ryan	1.25	.60	.12
☐	40	Fernando Valenzuela	.35	.17	.03
☐	41	Vance Law	.12	.06	.01
☐	42	Roger McDowell	.20	.10	.02
☐	43	Carlton Fisk	.30	.15	.03
☐	44	Scott Garrelts	.20	.10	.02
☐	45	Lee Guetterman	.12	.06	.01
☐	46	Mark Langston	.30	.15	.03
☐	47	Willie Randolph	.20	.10	.02
☐	48	Bill Doran	.20	.10	.02
☐	49	Larry Parrish	.12	.06	.01
☐	50	Wade Boggs	1.25	.60	.12
☐	51	Shane Rawley	.12	.06	.01
☐	52	Alvin Davis	.20	.10	.02
☐	53	Jeff Reardon	.20	.10	.02
☐	54	Jim Presley	.12	.06	.01
☐	55	Kevin Bass	.12	.06	.01
☐	56	Kevin McReynolds	.40	.20	.04
☐	57	B.J. Surhoff	.20	.10	.02
☐	58	Julio Franco	.20	.10	.02
☐	59	Eddie Murray	.45	.22	.04
☐	60	Jody Davis	.12	.06	.01
☐	61	Todd Worrell	.20	.10	.02
☐	62	Von Hayes	.20	.10	.02
☐	63	Billy Hatcher	.12	.06	.01
☐	64	John Kruk	.20	.10	.02
☐	65	Tom Henke	.12	.06	.01
☐	66	Mike Scott	.30	.15	.03
☐	67	Vince Coleman	.35	.17	.03
☐	68	Ozzie Smith	.35	.17	.03
☐	69	Ken Williams	.20	.10	.02
☐	70	Steve Bedrosian	.20	.10	.02
☐	71	Luis Polonia	.20	.10	.02
☐	72	Brook Jacoby	.12	.06	.01
☐	73	Ron Darling	.20	.10	.02
☐	74	Lloyd Moseby	.12	.06	.01
☐	75	Wally Joyner	.45	.22	.04
☐	76	Dan Quisenberry	.20	.10	.02
☐	77	Scott Fletcher	.12	.06	.01
☐	78	Kirk McCaskill	.12	.06	.01
☐	79	Paul Molitor	.30	.15	.03
☐	80	Mike Aldrete	.12	.06	.01
☐	81	Neal Heaton	.12	.06	.01
☐	82	Jeffrey Leonard	.12	.06	.01
☐	83	Dave Magadan	.20	.10	.02
☐	84	Danny Cox	.12	.06	.01
☐	85	Lance McCullers	.12	.06	.01
☐	86	Jay Howell	.12	.06	.01
☐	87	Charlie Hough	.12	.06	.01
☐	88	Gene Garber	.12	.06	.01
☐	89	Jesse Orosco	.12	.06	.01
☐	90	Don Robinson	.12	.06	.01
☐	91	Willie McGee	.25	.12	.02
☐	92	Bert Blyleven	.25	.12	.02
☐	93	Phil Bradley	.20	.10	.02
☐	94	Terry Kennedy	.12	.06	.01
☐	95	Kent Hrbek	.30	.15	.03
☐	96	Juan Samuel	.25	.12	.02
☐	97	Pedro Guerrero	.30	.15	.03
☐	98	Sid Bream	.12	.06	.01
☐	99	Devon White	.30	.15	.03
☐ 100		Mark McGwire	1.00	.50	.10
☐ 101		Dave Parker	.25	.12	.02
☐ 102		Glenn Davis	.35	.17	.03
☐ 103		Greg Walker	.12	.06	.01
☐ 104		Rick Rhoden	.12	.06	.01
☐ 105		Mitch Webster	.12	.06	.01
☐ 106		Lenny Dykstra	.20	.10	.02
☐ 107		Gene Larkin	.12	.06	.01
☐ 108		Floyd Youmans	.12	.06	.01
☐ 109		Andy Van Slyke	.25	.12	.02
☐ 110		Mike Scioscia	.12	.06	.01
☐ 111		Kirk Gibson	.40	.20	.04
☐ 112		Kal Daniels	.30	.15	.03
☐ 113		Ruben Sierra	.75	.35	.07
☐ 114		Sam Horn	.20	.10	.02
☐ 115		Ray Knight	.12	.06	.01
☐ 116		Jimmy Key	.12	.06	.01
☐ 117		Bo Diaz	.12	.06	.01
☐ 118		Mike Greenwell	1.25	.60	.12
☐ 119		Barry Bonds	.30	.15	.03
☐ 120		Reggie Jackson UER (463 lifetime homers)	.75	.35	.07
☐ 121		Mike Pagliarulo	.12	.06	.01
☐ 122		Tommy John	.25	.12	.02
☐ 123		Bill Madlock	.12	.06	.01

☐ 124	Ken Caminiti	.20	.10	.02
☐ 125	Gary Ward	.12	.06	.01
☐ 126	Candy Maldonado	.12	.06	.01
☐ 127	Harold Reynolds	.12	.06	.01
☐ 128	Joe Magrane	.40	.20	.04
☐ 129	Mike Henneman	.20	.10	.02
☐ 130	Jim Gantner	.12	.06	.01
☐ 131	Bobby Bonilla	.35	.17	.03
☐ 132	John Farrell	.25	.12	.02
☐ 133	Frank Tanana	.12	.06	.01
☐ 134	Zane Smith	.12	.06	.01
☐ 135	Dave Righetti	.20	.10	.02
☐ 136	Rick Reuschel	.20	.10	.02
☐ 137	Dwight Evans	.25	.12	.02
☐ 138	Howard Johnson	.35	.17	.03
☐ 139	Terry Leach	.12	.06	.01
☐ 140	Casey Candaele	.12	.06	.01
☐ 141	Tom Herr	.12	.06	.01
☐ 142	Tony Pena	.20	.10	.02
☐ 143	Lance Parrish	.25	.12	.02
☐ 144	Ellis Burks	1.25	.60	.12
☐ 145	Pete O'Brien	.20	.10	.02
☐ 146	Mike Boddicker	.12	.06	.01
☐ 147	Buddy Bell	.12	.06	.01
☐ 148	Bo Jackson	1.50	.75	.15
☐ 149	Frank White	.20	.10	.02
☐ 150	George Brett	.50	.25	.05
☐ 151	Tim Wallach	.12	.06	.01
☐ 152	Cal Ripken Jr.	.40	.20	.04
☐ 153	Brett Butler	.12	.06	.01
☐ 154	Gary Gaetti	.25	.12	.02
☐ 155	Darryl Strawberry	.75	.35	.07
☐ 156	Alredo Griffin	.12	.06	.01
☐ 157	Marty Barrett	.12	.06	.01
☐ 158	Jim Rice	.30	.15	.03
☐ 159	Terry Pendleton	.12	.06	.01
☐ 160	Orel Hershiser	.65	.30	.06
☐ 161	Larry Sheets	.12	.06	.01
☐ 162	Dave Stewart UER	.50	.25	.05
	(Braves logo)			
☐ 163	Shawon Dunston	.20	.10	.02
☐ 164	Keith Moreland	.12	.06	.01
☐ 165	Ken Oberkfell	.12	.06	.01
☐ 166	Ivan Calderon	.20	.10	.02
☐ 167	Bob Welch	.20	.10	.02
☐ 168	Fred McGriff	.50	.25	.05
☐ 169	Pete Incaviglia	.30	.15	.03
☐ 170	Dale Murphy	.60	.30	.06
☐ 171	Mike Dunne	.12	.06	.01
☐ 172	Chili Davis	.20	.10	.02
☐ 173	Milt Thompson	.12	.06	.01
☐ 174	Terry Steinbach	.25	.12	.02
☐ 175	Oddibe McDowell	.20	.10	.02
☐ 176	Jack Morris	.25	.12	.02
☐ 177	Sid Fernandez	.20	.10	.02
☐ 178	Ken Griffey	.20	.10	.02
☐ 179	Lee Smith	.12	.06	.01
☐ 180	Highlights 1987	.45	.22	.04
	Kirby Puckett			
	Juan Nieves			
	Mike Schmidt			
☐ 181	Brian Downing	.12	.06	.01
☐ 182	Andres Galarraga	.35	.17	.03
☐ 183	Rob Deer	.20	.10	.02
☐ 184	Greg Brock	.12	.06	.01
☐ 185	Doug DeCinces	.12	.06	.01
☐ 186	Johnny Ray	.12	.06	.01
☐ 187	Hubie Brooks	.12	.06	.01
☐ 188	Darrell Evans	.12	.06	.01
☐ 189	Mel Hall	.12	.06	.01
☐ 190	Jim Deshaies	.12	.06	.01
☐ 191	Dan Plesac	.20	.10	.02
☐ 192	Willie Wilson	.20	.10	.02
☐ 193	Mike LaValliere	.12	.06	.01
☐ 194	Tom Brunansky	.25	.12	.02
☐ 195	John Franco	.20	.10	.02
☐ 196	Frank Viola	.30	.15	.03
☐ 197	Bruce Hurst	.20	.10	.02
☐ 198	John Tudor	.20	.10	.02
☐ 199	Bob Forsch	.12	.06	.01
☐ 200	Dwight Gooden	.75	.35	.07
☐ 201	Jose Canseco	1.50	.75	.15
☐ 202	Carney Lansford	.25	.12	.02
☐ 203	Kelly Downs	.12	.06	.01
☐ 204	Glenn Wilson	.12	.06	.01
☐ 205	Pat Tabler	.12	.06	.01
☐ 206	Mike Davis	.12	.06	.01
☐ 207	Roger Clemens	.90	.45	.09
☐ 208	Dave Smith	.12	.06	.01
☐ 209	Curt Young	.12	.06	.01
☐ 210	Mark Eichhorn	.12	.06	.01
☐ 211	Juan Nieves	.12	.06	.01
☐ 212	Bob Boone	.20	.10	.02
☐ 213	Don Sutton	.35	.17	.03
☐ 214	Willie Upshaw	.12	.06	.01

☐ 215	Jim Clancy	.12	.06	.01
☐ 216	Bill Ripken	.20	.10	.02
☐ 217	Ozzie Virgil	.12	.06	.01
☐ 218	Dave Concepcion	.20	.10	.02
☐ 219	Alan Ashby	.12	.06	.01
☐ 220	Mike Marshall	.20	.10	.02
☐ 221	Highlights 1987	.60	.30	.06
	Mark McGwire			
	Paul Molitor			
	Vince Coleman			
☐ 222	Highlights 1987	.75	.35	.07
	Benito Santiago			
	Steve Bedrosian			
	Don Mattingly			
☐ 223	Rookie Prospects	.45	.22	.04
	Shawn Abner			
	Jay Buhner			
	Gary Thurman			
☐ 224	Rookie Prospects	.30	.15	.03
	Tim Crews			
	Vincente Palacios			
	John Davis			
☐ 225	Rookie Prospects	.45	.22	.04
	Jody Reed			
	Jeff Treadway			
	Keith Miller			

1988 Sportflics Gamewinners

This 25-card set of "Gamewinners" was distributed in a green and yellow box along with 17 trivia cards by Weiser Card Company of New Jersey. The 25 players selected for the set show a strong New York preference. The set was ostensibly produced for use as a youth organizational fund raiser. The cards are the standard size, 2 1/2" by 3 1/2" and are done in the typical Sportflics' Magic Motion (three picture) style. The cards are numbered on the back.

		MINT	EXC	G-VG
COMPLETE SET (25)		10.00	5.00	1.00
COMMON PLAYER (1-25)		.20	.10	.02
☐ 1	Don Mattingly	1.25	.60	.12
☐ 2	Mark McGwire	.90	.45	.09
☐ 3	Wade Boggs	1.00	.50	.10
☐ 4	Will Clark	1.25	.60	.12
☐ 5	Eric Davis	.90	.45	.09
☐ 6	Willie Randolph	.20	.10	.02
☐ 7	Dave Winfield	.40	.20	.04
☐ 8	Rickey Henderson	.75	.35	.07
☐ 9	Dwight Gooden	.50	.25	.05
☐ 10	Benny Santiago	.50	.25	.05
☐ 11	Keith Hernandez	.40	.20	.04
☐ 12	Juan Samuel	.30	.15	.03
☐ 13	Kevin Seitzer	.40	.20	.04
☐ 14	Gary Carter	.40	.20	.04
☐ 15	Darryl Strawberry	.90	.45	.09
☐ 16	Rick Rhoden	.20	.10	.02
☐ 17	Howard Johnson	.50	.25	.05
☐ 18	Matt Nokes	.30	.15	.03
☐ 19	Dave Righetti	.30	.15	.03
☐ 20	Roger Clemens	.75	.35	.07
☐ 21	Mike Schmidt	1.00	.50	.10
☐ 22	Kevin McReynolds	.40	.20	.04
☐ 23	Mike Pagliarulo	.20	.10	.02
☐ 24	Kevin Elster	.30	.15	.03
☐ 25	Jack Clark	.30	.15	.03

1989 Sportflics

This 225-card set was produced by Sportflics (distributed by Major League Marketing) and again features three sequence action pictures on each card. Cards measure 2 1/2" by 3 1/2" and are in full color. There are 219 individual players, 2 Highlights trios, and 3 Rookie Prospect trio cards. The cards feature a white border on the front with red and blue inner trim colors. A full-color action picture of the player is printed on the back of the card. Cards are numbered on the back in the lower right corner.

	MINT	EXC	G-VG
COMPLETE SET (225)	40.00	20.00	4.00
COMMON PLAYER (1-225)	.10	.05	.01

		MINT	EXC	G-VG
☐	1 Jose Canseco	1.50	.75	.15
☐	2 Wally Joyner	.40	.20	.04
☐	3 Roger Clemens	.75	.35	.07
☐	4 Greg Swindell	.30	.15	.03
☐	5 Jack Morris	.20	.10	.02
☐	6 Mickey Brantley	.15	.07	.01
☐	7 Jim Presley	.10	.05	.01
☐	8 Pete O'Brien	.15	.07	.01
☐	9 Jesse Barfield	.25	.12	.02
☐	10 Frank Viola	.20	.10	.02
☐	11 Kevin Bass	.10	.05	.01
☐	12 Glenn Wilson	.10	.05	.01
☐	13 Chris Sabo	.35	.17	.03
☐	14 Fred McGriff	.50	.25	.05
☐	15 Mark Grace	1.00	.50	.10
☐	16 Devon White	.20	.10	.02
☐	17 Juan Samuel	.15	.07	.01
☐	18 Lou Whitaker	.15	.07	.01
☐	19 Greg Walker	.10	.05	.01
☐	20 Roberto Alomar	.35	.17	.03
☐	21 Mike Schmidt	1.00	.50	.10
☐	22 Benny Santiago	.50	.25	.05
☐	23 Dave Stewart	.25	.12	.02
☐	24 Dave Winfield	.40	.20	.04
☐	25 George Bell	.20	.10	.02
☐	26 Jack Clark	.20	.10	.02
☐	27 Doug Drabek	.10	.05	.01
☐	28 Ron Gant	.20	.10	.02
☐	29 Glenn Braggs	.15	.07	.01
☐	30 Rafael Palmeiro	.30	.15	.03
☐	31 Brett Butler	.15	.07	.01
☐	32 Ron Darling	.20	.10	.02
☐	33 Alvin Davis	.15	.07	.01
☐	34 Bob Walk	.10	.05	.01
☐	35 Dave Stieb	.15	.07	.01
☐	36 Orel Hershiser	.75	.35	.07
☐	37 John Farrell	.15	.07	.01
☐	38 Doug Jones	.15	.07	.01
☐	39 Kelly Downs	.15	.07	.01
☐	40 Bob Boone	.20	.10	.02
☐	41 Gary Sheffield	1.00	.50	.10
☐	42 Doug Dascenzo	.20	.10	.02
☐	43 Chad Kreuter	.20	.10	.02
☐	44 Ricky Jordan	1.00	.50	.10
☐	45 Dave West	.30	.15	.03
☐	46 Danny Tartabull	.25	.12	.02
☐	47 Teddy Higuera	.15	.07	.01
☐	48 Gary Gaetti	.15	.07	.01
☐	49 Dave Parker	.20	.10	.02
☐	50 Don Mattingly	1.25	.60	.12
☐	51 David Cone	.50	.25	.05
☐	52 Kal Daniels	.25	.12	.02
☐	53 Carney Lansford	.20	.10	.02
☐	54 Mike Marshall	.20	.10	.02
☐	55 Kevin Seitzer	.30	.15	.03
☐	56 Mike Henneman	.15	.07	.01
☐	57 Bill Doran	.15	.07	.01
☐	58 Steve Sax	.20	.10	.02
☐	59 Lance Parrish	.15	.07	.01
☐	60 Keith Hernandez	.20	.10	.02
☐	61 Jose Uribe	.10	.05	.01
☐	62 Jose Lind	.10	.05	.01
☐	63 Steve Bedrosian	.15	.07	.01
☐	64 George Brett	.30	.15	.03
☐	65 Kirk Gibson	.30	.15	.03
☐	66 Cal Ripken Jr.	.25	.12	.02
☐	67 Mitch Webster	.10	.05	.01
☐	68 Fred Lynn	.20	.10	.02
☐	69 Eric Davis	.75	.35	.07
☐	70 Bo Jackson	1.25	.60	.12
☐	71 Kevin Elster	.20	.10	.02
☐	72 Rick Reuschel	.15	.07	.01
☐	73 Tim Burke	.10	.05	.01
☐	74 Mark Davis	.25	.12	.02
☐	75 Claudell Washington	.15	.07	.01
☐	76 Lance McCullers	.10	.05	.01
☐	77 Mike Moore	.15	.07	.01
☐	78 Robby Thompson	.15	.07	.01
☐	79 Roger McDowell	.15	.07	.01
☐	80 Danny Jackson	.15	.07	.01
☐	81 Tim Leary	.15	.07	.01
☐	82 Bobby Witt	.15	.07	.01
☐	83 Jim Gott	.10	.05	.01
☐	84 Andy Hawkins	.15	.07	.01
☐	85 Ozzie Guillen	.15	.07	.01
☐	86 John Tudor	.15	.07	.01
☐	87 Todd Burns	.20	.10	.02
☐	88 Dave Gallagher	.15	.07	.01
☐	89 Jay Buhner	.20	.10	.02
☐	90 Gregg Jefferies	1.00	.50	.10
☐	91 Bob Welch	.15	.07	.01
☐	92 Charlie Hough	.10	.05	.01
☐	93 Tony Fernandez	.20	.10	.02
☐	94 Ozzie Virgil	.10	.05	.01
☐	95 Andre Dawson	.25	.12	.02
☐	96 Hubie Brooks	.15	.07	.01
☐	97 Kevin McReynolds	.30	.15	.03
☐	98 Mike LaValliere	.10	.05	.01
☐	99 Terry Pendleton	.15	.07	.01
☐	100 Wade Boggs	1.00	.50	.10
☐	101 Dennis Eckersley	.20	.10	.02
☐	102 Mark Gubicza	.20	.10	.02
☐	103 Frank Tanana	.15	.07	.01
☐	104 Joe Carter	.25	.12	.02
☐	105 Ozzie Smith	.25	.12	.02
☐	106 Dennis Martinez	.10	.05	.01
☐	107 Jeff Treadway	.15	.07	.01
☐	108 Greg Maddux	.25	.12	.02
☐	109 Bret Saberhagen	.35	.17	.03
☐	110 Dale Murphy	.35	.17	.03
☐	111 Rob Deer	.15	.07	.01
☐	112 Pete Incaviglia	.25	.12	.02
☐	113 Vince Coleman	.25	.12	.02
☐	114 Tim Wallach	.15	.07	.01
☐	115 Nolan Ryan	1.00	.50	.10
☐	116 Walt Weiss	.35	.17	.03
☐	117 Brian Downing	.10	.05	.01
☐	118 Melido Perez	.15	.07	.01
☐	119 Terry Steinbach	.20	.10	.02
☐	120 Mike Scott	.25	.12	.02
☐	121 Tim Belcher	.20	.10	.02
☐	122 Mike Boddicker	.10	.05	.01
☐	123 Len Dykstra	.15	.07	.01
☐	124 Fernando Valenzuela	.25	.12	.02
☐	125 Gerald Young	.20	.10	.02
☐	126 Tom Henke	.10	.05	.01
☐	127 Dave Henderson	.10	.05	.01
☐	128 Dan Plesac	.15	.07	.01
☐	129 Chili Davis	.15	.07	.01
☐	130 Bryan Harvey	.15	.07	.01
☐	131 Don August	.10	.05	.01
☐	132 Mike Harkey	.25	.12	.02
☐	133 Luis Polonia	.15	.07	.01
☐	134 Craig Worthington	.25	.12	.02
☐	135 Joey Meyer	.15	.07	.01
☐	136 Barry Larkin	.30	.15	.03
☐	137 Glenn Davis	.25	.12	.02
☐	138 Mike Scioscia	.10	.05	.01
☐	139 Andres Galarraga	.20	.10	.02
☐	140 Dwight Gooden	.50	.25	.05
☐	141 Keith Moreland	.10	.05	.01
☐	142 Kevin Mitchell	.50	.25	.05
☐	143 Mike Greenwell	1.00	.50	.10
☐	144 Mel Hall	.15	.07	.01
☐	145 Rickey Henderson	.60	.30	.06

☐ 146	Barry Bonds	.25	.12	.02
☐ 147	Eddie Murray	.40	.20	.04
☐ 148	Lee Smith	.15	.07	.01
☐ 149	Julio Franco	.20	.10	.02
☐ 150	Tim Raines	.20	.10	.02
☐ 151	Mitch Williams	.20	.10	.02
☐ 152	Tim Laudner	.10	.05	.01
☐ 153	Mike Pagliarulo	.10	.05	.01
☐ 154	Floyd Bannister	.10	.05	.01
☐ 155	Gary Carter	.25	.12	.02
☐ 156	Kirby Puckett	.75	.35	.07
☐ 157	Harold Baines	.15	.07	.01
☐ 158	Dave Righetti	.15	.07	.01
☐ 159	Mark Langston	.20	.10	.02
☐ 160	Tony Gwynn	.35	.17	.03
☐ 161	Tom Brunansky	.15	.07	.01
☐ 162	Vance Law	.10	.05	.01
☐ 163	Kelly Gruber	.15	.07	.01
☐ 164	Gerald Perry	.15	.07	.01
☐ 165	Harold Reynolds	.15	.07	.01
☐ 166	Andy Van Slyke	.20	.10	.02
☐ 167	Jimmy Key	.10	.05	.01
☐ 168	Jeff Reardon	.15	.07	.01
☐ 169	Milt Thompson	.10	.05	.01
☐ 170	Will Clark	1.25	.60	.12
☐ 171	Chet Lemon	.10	.05	.01
☐ 172	Pat Tabler	.10	.05	.01
☐ 173	Jim Rice	.20	.10	.02
☐ 174	Billy Hatcher	.10	.05	.01
☐ 175	Bruce Hurst	.15	.07	.01
☐ 176	John Franco	.15	.07	.01
☐ 177	Van Snider	.20	.10	.02
☐ 178	Ron Jones	.20	.10	.02
☐ 179	Jerald Clark	.20	.10	.02
☐ 180	Tom Browning	.20	.10	.02
☐ 181	Von Hayes	.15	.07	.01
☐ 182	Bobby Bonilla	.25	.12	.02
☐ 183	Todd Worrell	.15	.07	.01
☐ 184	John Kruk	.15	.07	.01
☐ 185	Scott Fletcher	.10	.05	.01
☐ 186	Willie Wilson	.15	.07	.01
☐ 187	Jody Davis	.10	.05	.01
☐ 188	Kent Hrbek	.20	.10	.02
☐ 189	Ruben Sierra	.60	.30	.06
☐ 190	Shawon Dunston	.15	.07	.01
☐ 191	Ellis Burks	.30	.15	.03
☐ 192	Brook Jacoby	.15	.07	.01
☐ 193	Jeff Robinson Detroit Tigers	.15	.07	.01
☐ 194	Rich Dotson	.10	.05	.01
☐ 195	Johnny Ray	.10	.05	.01
☐ 196	Cory Snyder	.20	.10	.02
☐ 197	Mike Witt	.15	.07	.01
☐ 198	Marty Barrett	.10	.05	.01
☐ 199	Robin Yount	.50	.25	.05
☐ 200	Mark McGwire	.75	.35	.07
☐ 201	Ryne Sandberg	.30	.15	.03
☐ 202	John Candelaria	.15	.07	.01
☐ 203	Matt Nokes	.20	.10	.02
☐ 204	Dwight Evans	.20	.10	.02
☐ 205	Darryl Strawberry	.75	.35	.07
☐ 206	Willie McGee	.20	.10	.02
☐ 207	Bobby Thigpen	.15	.07	.01
☐ 208	B.J. Surhoff	.15	.07	.01
☐ 209	Paul Molitor	.20	.10	.02
☐ 210	Jody Reed	.15	.07	.01
☐ 211	Doyle Alexander	.10	.05	.01
☐ 212	Dennis Rasmussen	.10	.05	.01
☐ 213	Kevin Gross	.10	.05	.01
☐ 214	Kirk McCaskill	.10	.05	.01
☐ 215	Alan Trammell	.25	.12	.02
☐ 216	Damon Berryhill	.20	.10	.02
☐ 217	Rick Sutcliffe	.15	.07	.01
☐ 218	Don Slaught	.10	.05	.01
☐ 219	Carlton Fisk	.25	.12	.02
☐ 220	Allan Anderson	.20	.10	.02
☐ 221	Jose Canseco Wade Boggs Mike Greenwell	1.25	.60	.12
☐ 222	Orel Hershiser Dennis Eckersley Tom Browning	.40	.20	.04
☐ 223	Gary Sheffield Gregg Jefferies Sandy Alomar Jr.	2.50	1.25	.25
☐ 224	Bob Milacki Randy Johnson Ramon Martinez	.30	.15	.03
☐ 225	Cameron Drew Geronimo Berroa Ron Jones	.30	.15	.03

1990 Sportflics

The 1990 Sportflics set contains 225 standard-size (2 1/2 by 3 1/2 inch) cards. On the fronts, the black, white, orange and yellow borders surround two photos which can each be seen depending on the angle. The set is considered an improvement over the previous years' versions by many collectors due to the increased clarity of the fronts caused by having two images rather than three. The backs are dominated by large color photos.

		MINT	EXC	G-VG
	COMPLETE SET (225)	40.00	20.00	4.00
	COMMON PLAYER (1-225)	.10	.05	.01
☐	1 Kevin Mitchell	.50	.25	.05
☐	2 Wade Boggs	1.00	.50	.10
☐	3 Cory Snyder	.20	.10	.02
☐	4 Paul O'Neill	.20	.10	.02
☐	5 Will Clark	1.25	.60	.12
☐	6 Tony Fernandez	.20	.10	.02
☐	7 Ken Griffey Jr.	1.25	.60	.12
☐	8 Nolan Ryan	1.00	.50	.10
☐	9 Rafael Palmeiro	.20	.10	.02
☐	10 Jesse Barfield	.20	.10	.02
☐	11 Kirby Puckett	.50	.25	.05
☐	12 Steve Sax	.20	.10	.02
☐	13 Fred McGriff	.30	.15	.03
☐	14 Gregg Jefferies	.50	.25	.05
☐	15 Mark Grace	.75	.35	.07
☐	16 Ozzie Smith	.20	.10	.02
☐	17 George Bell	.20	.10	.02
☐	18 Robin Yount	.40	.20	.04
☐	19 Glenn Davis	.25	.12	.02
☐	20 Jeffrey Leonard	.10	.05	.01
☐	21 Chili Davis	.10	.05	.01
☐	22 Craig Biggio	.30	.15	.03
☐	23 Jose Canseco	1.00	.50	.10
☐	24 Derek Lilliquist	.15	.07	.01
☐	25 Chris Bosio	.15	.07	.01
☐	26 Dave Stieb	.15	.07	.01
☐	27 Bobby Thigpen	.10	.05	.01
☐	28 Jack Clark	.20	.10	.02
☐	29 Kevin Ritz	.20	.10	.02
☐	30 Tom Gordon	.40	.20	.04
☐	31 Bryan Harvey	.20	.10	.02
☐	32 Jim Deshaies	.10	.05	.01
☐	33 Terry Steinbach	.20	.10	.02
☐	34 Tom Glavine	.10	.05	.01
☐	35 Bob Welch	.15	.07	.01
☐	36 Charlie Hayes	.15	.07	.01
☐	37 Jeff Reardon	.15	.07	.01
☐	38 Joe Orsulak	.10	.05	.01
☐	39 Scott Garrelts	.15	.07	.01
☐	40 Bob Boone	.20	.10	.02
☐	41 Scott Bankhead	.15	.07	.01
☐	42 Tom Henke	.10	.05	.01
☐	43 Greg Briley	.30	.15	.03
☐	44 Teddy Higuera	.20	.10	.02
☐	45 Pat Borders	.15	.07	.01
☐	46 Kevin Seitzer	.30	.15	.03
☐	47 Bruce Hurst	.15	.07	.01
☐	48 Ozzie Guillen	.15	.07	.01
☐	49 Wally Joyner	.30	.15	.03
☐	50 Mike Greenwell	.75	.35	.07
☐	51 Gary Gaetti	.20	.10	.02
☐	52 Gary Sheffield	.50	.25	.05
☐	53 Dennis Martinez	.10	.05	.01
☐	54 Ryne Sandberg	.30	.15	.03

☐ 55	Mike Scott	.20	.10	.02
☐ 56	Todd Benzinger	.20	.10	.02
☐ 57	Kelly Gruber	.15	.07	.01
☐ 58	Jose Lind	.10	.05	.01
☐ 59	Allan Anderson	.15	.07	.01
☐ 60	Robby Thompson	.10	.05	.01
☐ 61	John Smoltz	.30	.15	.03
☐ 62	Mark Davis	.25	.12	.02
☐ 63	Tom Herr	.10	.05	.01
☐ 64	Randy Johnson	.15	.07	.01
☐ 65	Lonnie Smith	.15	.07	.01
☐ 66	Pedro Guerrero	.20	.10	.02
☐ 67	Jerome Walton	1.00	.50	.10
☐ 68	Ramon Martinez	.30	.15	.03
☐ 69	Tim Raines	.20	.10	.02
☐ 70	Matt Williams	.75	.35	.07
☐ 71	Joe Oliver	.20	.10	.02
☐ 72	Nick Esasky	.20	.10	.02
☐ 73	Kevin Brown	.20	.10	.02
☐ 74	Walt Weiss	.30	.15	.03
☐ 75	Roger McDowell	.15	.07	.01
☐ 76	Jose DeLeon	.15	.07	.01
☐ 77	Brian Downing	.10	.05	.01
☐ 78	Jay Howell	.10	.05	.01
☐ 79	Jose Uribe	.10	.05	.01
☐ 80	Ellis Burks	.50	.25	.05
☐ 81	Sammy Sosa	.40	.20	.04
☐ 82	Johnny Ray	.10	.05	.01
☐ 83	Danny Darwin	.10	.05	.01
☐ 84	Carney Lansford	.15	.07	.01
☐ 85	Jose Oquendo	.10	.05	.01
☐ 86	John Cerutti	.10	.05	.01
☐ 87	Dave Winfield	.25	.12	.02
☐ 88	Dave Righetti	.15	.07	.01
☐ 89	Danny Jackson	.15	.07	.01
☐ 90	Andy Benes	.60	.30	.06
☐ 91	Tom Browning	.15	.07	.01
☐ 92	Pete O'Brien	.15	.07	.01
☐ 93	Roberto Alomar	.25	.12	.02
☐ 94	Bret Saberhagen	.30	.15	.03
☐ 95	Phil Bradley	.15	.07	.01
☐ 96	Doug Jones	.15	.07	.01
☐ 97	Eric Davis	.60	.30	.06
☐ 98	Tony Gwynn	.45	.22	.04
☐ 99	Jim Abbott	1.00	.50	.10
☐ 100	Cal Ripken	.40	.20	.04
☐ 101	Andy Van Slyke	.20	.10	.02
☐ 102	Dan Plesac	.15	.07	.01
☐ 103	Lou Whitaker	.20	.10	.02
☐ 104	Steve Bedrosian	.15	.07	.01
☐ 105	Dave Gallagher	.15	.07	.01
☐ 106	Keith Hernandez	.20	.10	.02
☐ 107	Duane Ward	.10	.05	.01
☐ 108	Andre Dawson	.20	.10	.02
☐ 109	Howard Johnson	.30	.15	.03
☐ 110	Mark Langston	.25	.12	.02
☐ 111	Jerry Browne	.15	.07	.01
☐ 112	Alvin Davis	.15	.07	.01
☐ 113	Sid Fernandez	.15	.07	.01
☐ 114	Mike Devereaux	.15	.07	.01
☐ 115	Benito Santiago	.25	.12	.02
☐ 116	Bip Roberts	.10	.05	.01
☐ 117	Craig Worthington	.20	.10	.02
☐ 118	Kevin Elster	.15	.07	.01
☐ 119	Harold Reynolds	.15	.07	.01
☐ 120	Joe Carter	.20	.10	.02
☐ 121	Brian Harper	.10	.05	.01
☐ 122	Frank Viola	.20	.10	.02
☐ 123	Jeff Ballard	.20	.10	.02
☐ 124	John Kruk	.20	.10	.02
☐ 125	Harold Baines	.20	.10	.02
☐ 126	Tom Candiotti	.10	.05	.01
☐ 127	Kevin McReynolds	.20	.10	.02
☐ 128	Mookie Wilson	.15	.07	.01
☐ 129	Danny Tartabull	.20	.10	.02
☐ 130	Craig Lefferts	.10	.05	.01
☐ 131	Jose DeJesus	.10	.05	.01
☐ 132	John Orton	.15	.07	.01
☐ 133	Curt Schilling	.10	.05	.01
☐ 134	Marquis Grissom	.45	.22	.04
☐ 135	Greg Vaughn	1.00	.50	.10
☐ 136	Brett Butler	.15	.07	.01
☐ 137	Rob Deer	.15	.07	.01
☐ 138	John Franco	.15	.07	.01
☐ 139	Keith Moreland	.10	.05	.01
☐ 140	Dave Smith	.10	.05	.01
☐ 141	Mark McGwire	.75	.35	.07
☐ 142	Vince Coleman	.35	.17	.03
☐ 143	Barry Bonds	.20	.10	.02
☐ 144	Mike Henneman	.10	.05	.01
☐ 145	Dwight Gooden	.45	.22	.04
☐ 146	Darryl Strawberry	.60	.30	.06
☐ 147	Von Hayes	.20	.10	.02
☐ 148	Andres Galarraga	.20	.10	.02
☐ 149	Roger Clemens	.50	.25	.05

☐ 150	Don Mattingly	1.00	.50	.10
☐ 151	Joe Magrane	.25	.12	.02
☐ 152	Dwight Smith	.60	.30	.06
☐ 153	Ricky Jordan	.75	.35	.07
☐ 154	Alan Trammell	.20	.10	.02
☐ 155	Brook Jacoby	.15	.07	.01
☐ 156	Len Dykstra	.15	.07	.01
☐ 157	Mike LaValliere	.10	.05	.01
☐ 158	Julio Franco	.15	.07	.01
☐ 159	Joey Belle	.45	.22	.04
☐ 160	Barry Larkin	.25	.12	.02
☐ 161	Rick Reuschel	.15	.07	.01
☐ 162	Nelson Santovenia	.15	.07	.01
☐ 163	Mike Scioscia	.10	.05	.01
☐ 164	Damon Berryhill	.20	.10	.02
☐ 165	Todd Worrell	.20	.10	.02
☐ 166	Jim Eisenreich	.15	.07	.01
☐ 167	Ivan Calderon	.15	.07	.01
☐ 168	Mauro Gozzo	.20	.10	.02
☐ 169	Kirk McCaskill	.10	.05	.01
☐ 170	Dennis Eckersley	.20	.10	.02
☐ 171	Mickey Tettleton	.20	.10	.02
☐ 172	Chuck Finley	.15	.07	.01
☐ 173	Dave Magadan	.15	.07	.01
☐ 174	Terry Pendleton	.10	.05	.01
☐ 175	Willie Randolph	.15	.07	.01
☐ 176	Jeff Huson	.15	.07	.01
☐ 177	Todd Zeile	1.00	.50	.10
☐ 178	Steve Olin	.15	.07	.01
☐ 179	Eric Anthony	1.00	.50	.10
☐ 180	Scott Coolbaugh	.30	.15	.03
☐ 181	Rick Sutcliffe	.20	.10	.02
☐ 182	Tim Wallach	.15	.07	.01
☐ 183	Paul Molitor	.20	.10	.02
☐ 184	Roberto Kelly	.30	.15	.03
☐ 185	Mike Moore	.15	.07	.01
☐ 186	Junior Felix	.30	.15	.03
☐ 187	Mike Schooler	.20	.10	.02
☐ 188	Ruben Sierra	.60	.30	.06
☐ 189	Dale Murphy	.35	.17	.03
☐ 190	Dan Gladden	.10	.05	.01
☐ 191	John Smiley	.15	.07	.01
☐ 192	Jeff Russell	.15	.07	.01
☐ 193	Bert Blyleven	.20	.10	.02
☐ 194	Dave Stewart	.30	.15	.03
☐ 195	Bobby Bonilla	.20	.10	.02
☐ 196	Mitch Williams	.20	.10	.02
☐ 197	Orel Hershiser	.40	.20	.04
☐ 198	Kevin Bass	.10	.05	.01
☐ 199	Tim Burke	.10	.05	.01
☐ 200	Bo Jackson	1.25	.60	.12
☐ 201	David Cone	.25	.12	.02
☐ 202	Gary Pettis	.10	.05	.01
☐ 203	Kent Hrbek	.20	.10	.02
☐ 204	Carlton Fisk	.20	.10	.02
☐ 205	Bob Geren	.20	.10	.02
☐ 206	Bill Spiers	.25	.12	.02
☐ 207	Oddibe McDowell	.10	.05	.01
☐ 208	Rickey Henderson	.50	.25	.05
☐ 209	Ken Caminiti	.15	.07	.01
☐ 210	Devon White	.15	.07	.01
☐ 211	Greg Maddux	.15	.07	.01
☐ 212	Ed Whitson	.10	.05	.01
☐ 213	Carlos Martinez	.20	.10	.02
☐ 214	George Brett	.30	.15	.03
☐ 215	Gregg Olson	.50	.25	.05
☐ 216	Kenny Rogers	.15	.07	.01
☐ 217	Dwight Evans	.15	.07	.01
☐ 218	Pat Tabler	.15	.07	.01
☐ 219	Jeff Treadway	.10	.05	.01
☐ 220	Scott Fletcher	.10	.05	.01
☐ 221	Deion Sanders	.75	.35	.07
☐ 222	Robin Ventura	.50	.25	.05
☐ 223	Chip Hale	.20	.10	.02
☐ 224	Tommy Greene	.35	.17	.03
☐ 225	Dean Palmer	.35	.17	.03

1981 Squirt

The cards in this 22-panel set consist of 33 different individual cards, each measuring 2 1/2" by 3 1/2" while the panels measure 2 1/2" by 10 1/2"as the 1981 Squirt cards were issued individually as well as in two card panels. Cards numbered 1-11 appear twice, whereas cards 12- 33 appear only once in the 22-panel set. The pattern for pairings was 1/12 and 1/23, 2/13 and 2/24, 3/14 and 3/25, and so forth

on up to 11/22 and 11/33. Two card panels have a value equal to the sum of the individual cards on the panel. Supposedly panels 4/15, 4/26, 5/27, and 6/28 are more difficult to find than the other panels and are marked as SP in the checklist below.

		MINT	EXC	G-VG
	COMPLETE PANEL SET	20.00	10.00	2.00
	COMPLETE IND. SET	10.00	5.00	1.00
	COMMON PANEL	.40	.20	.04
	COMMON PLAYER (1-11) DP	.20	.10	.02
	COMMON PLAYER (12-33)	.20	.10	.02
☐ 1	George Brett DP	.50	.25	.05
☐ 2	George Foster DP	.20	.10	.02
☐ 3	Ben Oglivie DP	.20	.10	.02
☐ 4	Steve Garvey DP	.75	.35	.07
☐ 5	Reggie Jackson DP	.75	.35	.07
☐ 6	Bill Buckner DP	.20	.10	.02
☐ 7	Jim Rice DP	.25	.12	.02
☐ 8	Mike Schmidt DP	.75	.35	.07
☐ 9	Rod Carew DP	.50	.25	.05
☐ 10	Dave Parker DP	.25	.12	.02
☐ 11	Pete Rose DP	.90	.45	.09
☐ 12	Garry Templeton	.20	.10	.02
☐ 13	Rick Burleson	.20	.10	.02
☐ 14	Dave Kingman	.20	.10	.02
☐ 15	Eddie Murray SP	3.50	1.75	.35
☐ 16	Don Sutton	.60	.30	.06
☐ 17	Dusty Baker	.20	.10	.02
☐ 18	Jack Clark	.50	.25	.05
☐ 19	Dave Winfield	1.00	.50	.10
☐ 20	Johnny Bench	1.25	.60	.12
☐ 21	Lee Mazzilli	.20	.10	.02
☐ 22	Al Oliver	.20	.10	.02
☐ 23	Jerry Mumphrey	.20	.10	.02
☐ 24	Tony Armas	.20	.10	.02
☐ 25	Fred Lynn	.30	.15	.03
☐ 26	Ron LeFlore SP	1.00	.50	.10
☐ 27	Steve Kemp SP	1.00	.50	.10
☐ 28	Rickey Henderson SP	5.00	2.50	.50
☐ 29	John Castino	.20	.10	.02
☐ 30	Cecil Cooper	.20	.10	.02
☐ 31	Bruce Bochte	.20	.10	.02
☐ 32	Joe Charboneau	.20	.10	.02
☐ 33	Chet Lemon	.20	.10	.02

1982 Squirt

The cards in this 22-card set measure 2 1/2" by 3 1/2". Although the 1982 "Exclusive Limited Edition" was prepared for Squirt by Topps, the format and pictures are completely different from the regular Topps cards of this year. Each color picture is obliquely cut and the word Squirt is printed in red in the top left corner. The cards are numbered 1 through 22 and the reverses are yellow and black on white. The cards were issued on four types of panels: (1) yellow attachment card at top with picture card in center and scratch-off game at bottom; (2) yellow attachment card at top with scratch-off game in center and picture card at bottom; (3) white attachment card at top with "Collect all 22" panel

in center and picture card at bottom; (4) two card panel with attachment card at top. The two card panels have parallel cards; that is, numbers 1 and 12 together, numbers 2 and 13 together, etc. Two card panels have a value equal to the sum of the individual cards on the panel. The two types (1 and 2) with the scratch-off games are more slightly difficult to obtain than the other two types and hence command prices double those below.

		MINT	EXC	G-VG
	COMPLETE SET (22)	6.00	3.00	.60
	COMMON PLAYER (1-22)	.15	.07	.01
☐ 1	Cecil Cooper	.20	.10	.02
☐ 2	Jerry Remy	.15	.07	.01
☐ 3	George Brett	.75	.35	.07
☐ 4	Alan Trammell	.35	.17	.03
☐ 5	Reggie Jackson	.90	.45	.09
☐ 6	Kirk Gibson	.45	.22	.04
☐ 7	Dave Winfield	.45	.22	.04
☐ 8	Carlton Fisk	.35	.17	.03
☐ 9	Ron Guidry	.20	.10	.02
☐ 10	Dennis Leonard	.15	.07	.01
☐ 11	Rollie Fingers	.30	.15	.03
☐ 12	Pete Rose	1.00	.50	.10
☐ 13	Phil Garner	.15	.07	.01
☐ 14	Mike Schmidt	1.00	.50	.10
☐ 15	Dave Concepcion	.20	.10	.02
☐ 16	George Hendrick	.15	.07	.01
☐ 17	Andre Dawson	.35	.17	.03
☐ 18	George Foster	.20	.10	.02
☐ 19	Gary Carter	.40	.20	.04
☐ 20	Fernando Valenzuela	.30	.15	.03
☐ 21	Tom Seaver	.55	.27	.05
☐ 22	Bruce Sutter	.20	.10	.02

1976 SSPC

The cards in this 630-card set measure 2 1/2" by 3 1/2". The 1976 "Pure Card" set issued by TCMA derives its name from the lack of borders, logos, signatures, etc., which often clutter up the picture areas of some baseball sets. It differs from other sets produced by this company in that it cannot be reissued due to an agreement entered into by the manufacturer. Thus, while not technically a legitimate issue, it is significant because it cannot be reprinted, unlike other collector issues. There are no scarcities known. The cards are numbered in team groups, i.e., Atlanta (1-21), Cincinnati (22-46), Houston (47-65), Los Angeles (66-91), San Francisco (92-113), San Diego (114-133), Chicago White Sox (134-158), Kansas City (159-195), California (186-204), Minnesota (205-225), Milwaukee (226-251), Texas (252-273), St. Louis (274-300), Chicago Cubs (301-321), Montreal (322-351), Detroit (352- 373), Baltimore (374-401), Boston (402-424), New York Yankees (425-455), Philadelphia (456-477), Oakland (478- 503), Cleveland (504-532), New York Mets (533-560), and Pittsburgh (561-586). The rest of the numbers are filled in with checklists (589-595), miscellaneous players, and a heavy dose of coaches.

	NRMT	VG-E	GOOD
COMPLETE SET (630)	70.00	35.00	7.00
COMMON PLAYER (1-630)	.10	.05	.01

		NRMT	VG-E	GOOD
☐	1 Buzz Capra	.10	.05	.01
☐	2 Tom House	.15	.07	.01
☐	3 Max Leon	.10	.05	.01
☐	4 Carl Morton	.10	.05	.01
☐	5 Phil Niekro	2.00	1.00	.20
☐	6 Mike Thompson	.10	.05	.01
☐	7 Elias Sosa	.10	.05	.01
☐	8 Larvell Blanks	.10	.05	.01
☐	9 Darrell Evans	.35	.17	.03
☐	10 Rod Gilbreath	.10	.05	.01
☐	11 Mike Lum	.10	.05	.01
☐	12 Craig Robinson	.10	.05	.01
☐	13 Earl Williams	.10	.05	.01
☐	14 Vic Correll	.10	.05	.01
☐	15 Biff Pocoroba	.10	.05	.01
☐	16 Dusty Baker	.20	.10	.02
☐	17 Ralph Garr	.15	.07	.01
☐	18 Cito Gaston	.25	.12	.02
☐	19 Dave May	.10	.05	.01
☐	20 Rowland Office	.10	.05	.01
☐	21 Bob Beall	.10	.05	.01
☐	22 Sparky Anderson MG	.35	.17	.03
☐	23 Jack Billingham	.10	.05	.01
☐	24 Pedro Borbon	.10	.05	.01
☐	25 Clay Carroll	.10	.05	.01
☐	26 Pat Darcy	.10	.05	.01
☐	27 Don Gullett	.15	.07	.01
☐	28 Clay Kirby	.10	.05	.01
☐	29 Gary Nolan	.10	.05	.01
☐	30 Fred Norman	.10	.05	.01
☐	31 Johnny Bench	6.00	3.00	.60
☐	32 Bill Plummer	.10	.05	.01
☐	33 Darrel Chaney	.10	.05	.01
☐	34 Dave Concepcion	.25	.12	.02
☐	35 Terry Crowley	.10	.05	.01
☐	36 Dan Driessen	.15	.07	.01
☐	37 Doug Flynn	.10	.05	.01
☐	38 Joe Morgan	3.00	1.50	.30
☐	39 Tony Perez	.90	.45	.09
☐	40 Ken Griffey	.35	.17	.03
☐	41 Pete Rose	10.00	5.00	1.00
☐	42 Ed Armbrister	.10	.05	.01
☐	43 John Vukovich	.10	.05	.01
☐	44 George Foster	.90	.45	.09
☐	45 Cesar Geronimo	.10	.05	.01
☐	46 Merv Rettenmund	.10	.05	.01
☐	47 Jim Crawford	.10	.05	.01
☐	48 Ken Forsch	.10	.05	.01
☐	49 Doug Konieczny	.10	.05	.01
☐	50 Joe Niekro	.30	.15	.03
☐	51 Cliff Johnson	.10	.05	.01
☐	52 Skip Jutze	.10	.05	.01
☐	53 Milt May	.10	.05	.01
☐	54 Rob Andrews	.10	.05	.01
☐	55 Ken Boswell	.10	.05	.01
☐	56 Tommy Helms	.15	.07	.01
☐	57 Roger Metzger	.10	.05	.01
☐	58 Larry Milbourne	.10	.05	.01
☐	59 Doug Rader	.20	.10	.02
☐	60 Bob Watson	.20	.10	.02
☐	61 Enos Cabell	.10	.05	.01
☐	62 Jose Cruz	.30	.15	.03
☐	63 Cesar Cedeno	.20	.10	.02
☐	64 Greg Gross	.10	.05	.01
☐	65 Wilbur Howard	.10	.05	.01
☐	66 Al Downing	.10	.05	.01
☐	67 Burt Hooton	.10	.05	.01
☐	68 Charlie Hough	.20	.10	.02
☐	69 Tommy John	.75	.35	.07
☐	70 Andy Messersmith	.15	.07	.01
☐	71 Doug Rau	.10	.05	.01
☐	72 Rick Rhoden	.20	.10	.02
☐	73 Don Sutton	1.25	.60	.12
☐	74 Rick Auerbach	.10	.05	.01
☐	75 Ron Cey	.40	.20	.04
☐	76 Ivan DeJesus	.10	.05	.01
☐	77 Steve Garvey	4.00	2.00	.40
☐	78 Lee Lacy	.10	.05	.01
☐	79 Dave Lopes	.20	.10	.02
☐	80 Ken McMullen	.10	.05	.01
☐	81 Joe Ferguson	.10	.05	.01
☐	82 Paul Powell	.10	.05	.01
☐	83 Steve Yeager	.10	.05	.01
☐	84 Willie Crawford	.10	.05	.01
☐	85 Henry Cruz	.10	.05	.01
☐	86 Charlie Manuel	.10	.05	.01
☐	87 Manny Mota	.15	.07	.01
☐	88 Tom Paciorek	.10	.05	.01
☐	89 Jim Wynn	.15	.07	.01
☐	90 Walt Alston MG	.75	.35	.07
☐	91 Bill Buckner	.40	.20	.04
☐	92 Jim Barr	.10	.05	.01
☐	93 Mike Caldwell	.15	.07	.01
☐	94 John D'Acquisto	.10	.05	.01
☐	95 Dave Heaverlo	.10	.05	.01
☐	96 Gary Lavelle	.10	.05	.01
☐	97 John Montefusco	.15	.07	.01
☐	98 Charlie Williams	.10	.05	.01
☐	99 Chris Arnold	.10	.05	.01
☐	100 Marc Hill	.10	.05	.01
☐	101 Dave Rader	.10	.05	.01
☐	102 Bruce Miller	.10	.05	.01
☐	103 Willie Montanez	.10	.05	.01
☐	104 Steve Ontiveros	.10	.05	.01
☐	105 Chris Speier	.10	.05	.01
☐	106 Derrel Thomas	.10	.05	.01
☐	107 Gary Thomasson	.10	.05	.01
☐	108 Glenn Adams	.10	.05	.01
☐	109 Von Joshua	.10	.05	.01
☐	110 Gary Matthews	.20	.10	.02
☐	111 Bobby Murcer	.40	.20	.04
☐	112 Horace Speed	.10	.05	.01
☐	113 Wes Westrum MG	.10	.05	.01
☐	114 Rich Folkers	.10	.05	.01
☐	115 Alan Foster	.10	.05	.01
☐	116 Dave Freisleben	.10	.05	.01
☐	117 Dan Frisella	.10	.05	.01
☐	118 Randy Jones	.15	.07	.01
☐	119 Dan Spillner	.10	.05	.01
☐	120 Larry Hardy	.10	.05	.01
☐	121 Randy Hundley	.10	.05	.01
☐	122 Fred Kendall	.10	.05	.01
☐	123 John McNamara MG	.15	.07	.01
☐	124 Tito Fuentes	.10	.05	.01
☐	125 Enzo Hernandez	.10	.05	.01
☐	126 Steve Huntz	.10	.05	.01
☐	127 Mike Ivie	.10	.05	.01
☐	128 Hector Torres	.10	.05	.01
☐	129 Ted Kubiak	.10	.05	.01
☐	130 John Grubb	.10	.05	.01
☐	131 John Scott	.10	.05	.01
☐	132 Bob Tolan	.10	.05	.01
☐	133 Dave Winfield	3.50	1.75	.35
☐	134 Bill Gogolewski	.10	.05	.01
☐	135 Dan Osborn	.10	.05	.01
☐	136 Jim Kaat	.60	.30	.06
☐	137 Claude Osteen	.15	.07	.01
☐	138 Cecil Upshaw	.10	.05	.01
☐	139 Wilbur Wood	.15	.07	.01
☐	140 Lloyd Allen	.10	.05	.01
☐	141 Brian Downing	.25	.12	.02
☐	142 Jim Essian	.10	.05	.01
☐	143 Bucky Dent	.40	.20	.04
☐	144 Jorge Orta	.10	.05	.01
☐	145 Lee Richard	.10	.05	.01
☐	146 Bill Stein	.10	.05	.01
☐	147 Ken Henderson	.10	.05	.01
☐	148 Carlos May	.10	.05	.01
☐	149 Nyls Nyman	.10	.05	.01
☐	150 Bob Coluccio	.10	.05	.01
☐	151 Chuck Tanner MG	.15	.07	.01
☐	152 Pat Kelly	.10	.05	.01
☐	153 Jerry Hairston	.10	.05	.01
☐	154 Pete Varney	.10	.05	.01
☐	155 Bill Melton	.10	.05	.01
☐	156 Rich Gossage	.90	.45	.09
☐	157 Terry Forster	.15	.07	.01
☐	158 Rich Hinton	.10	.05	.01
☐	159 Nelson Briles	.10	.05	.01
☐	160 Al Fitzmorris	.10	.05	.01
☐	161 Steve Mingori	.10	.05	.01

☐ 162	Marty Pattin	.10	.05	.01
☐ 163	Paul Splittorff	.15	.07	.01
☐ 164	Dennis Leonard	.20	.10	.02
☐ 165	Buck Martinez	.10	.05	.01
☐ 166	Bob Stinson	.10	.05	.01
☐ 167	George Brett	8.00	4.00	.80
☐ 168	Harmon Killebrew	2.50	1.25	.25
☐ 169	John Mayberry	.15	.07	.01
☐ 170	Fred Patek	.10	.05	.01
☐ 171	Cookie Rojas	.10	.05	.01
☐ 172	Rodney Scott	.10	.05	.01
☐ 173	Tony Solaita	.10	.05	.01
☐ 174	Frank White	.25	.12	.02
☐ 175	Al Cowens	.10	.05	.01
☐ 176	Hal McRae	.20	.10	.02
☐ 177	Amos Otis	.25	.12	.02
☐ 178	Vada Pinson	.35	.17	.03
☐ 179	Jim Wohlford	.10	.05	.01
☐ 180	Doug Bird	.10	.05	.01
☐ 181	Mark Littell	.10	.05	.01
☐ 182	Bob McClure	.10	.05	.01
☐ 183	Steve Busby	.15	.07	.01
☐ 184	Fran Healy	.10	.05	.01
☐ 185	Whitey Herzog MG	.25	.12	.02
☐ 186	Andy Hassler	.10	.05	.01
☐ 187	Nolan Ryan	9.00	4.50	.90
☐ 188	Bill Singer	.10	.05	.01
☐ 189	Frank Tanana	.15	.07	.01
☐ 190	Ed Figueroa	.10	.05	.01
☐ 191	Dave Collins	.15	.07	.01
☐ 192	Dick Williams	.15	.07	.01
☐ 193	Ellie Rodriguez	.10	.05	.01
☐ 194	Dave Chalk	.10	.05	.01
☐ 195	Winston Llenas	.10	.05	.01
☐ 196	Rudy Meoli	.10	.05	.01
☐ 197	Orlando Ramirez	.10	.05	.01
☐ 198	Jerry Remy	.10	.05	.01
☐ 199	Billy Smith	.10	.05	.01
☐ 200	Bruce Bochte	.10	.05	.01
☐ 201	Joe Lahoud	.10	.05	.01
☐ 202	Morris Nettles	.10	.05	.01
☐ 203	Mickey Rivers	.20	.10	.02
☐ 204	Leroy Stanton	.10	.05	.01
☐ 205	Vic Albury	.10	.05	.01
☐ 206	Tom Burgmeier	.10	.05	.01
☐ 207	Bill Butler	.10	.05	.01
☐ 208	Bill Campbell	.10	.05	.01
☐ 209	Ray Corbin	.10	.05	.01
☐ 210	Joe Decker	.10	.05	.01
☐ 211	Jim Hughes	.10	.05	.01
☐ 212	Ed Bane (photo actually Mike Pazik)	.10	.05	.01
☐ 213	Glenn Borgman	.10	.05	.01
☐ 214	Rod Carew	4.50	2.25	.45
☐ 215	Steve Brye	.10	.05	.01
☐ 216	Dan Ford	.10	.05	.01
☐ 217	Tony Oliva	.90	.45	.09
☐ 218	Dave Goltz	.10	.05	.01
☐ 219	Bert Blyleven	.75	.35	.07
☐ 220	Larry Hisle	.10	.05	.01
☐ 221	Steve Braun	.10	.05	.01
☐ 222	Jerry Terrell	.10	.05	.01
☐ 223	Eric Soderholm	.10	.05	.01
☐ 224	Phil Roof	.10	.05	.01
☐ 225	Danny Thompson	.10	.05	.01
☐ 226	Jim Colborn	.10	.05	.01
☐ 227	Tom Murphy	.10	.05	.01
☐ 228	Ed Rodriguez	.10	.05	.01
☐ 229	Jim Slaton	.10	.05	.01
☐ 230	Ed Sprague	.10	.05	.01
☐ 231	Charlie Moore	.10	.05	.01
☐ 232	Darrell Porter	.10	.05	.01
☐ 233	Kurt Bevacqua	.10	.05	.01
☐ 234	Pedro Garcia	.10	.05	.01
☐ 235	Mike Hegan	.10	.05	.01
☐ 236	Don Money	.10	.05	.01
☐ 237	George Scott	.15	.07	.01
☐ 238	Robin Yount	9.00	4.50	.90
☐ 239	Hank Aaron	7.50	3.75	.75
☐ 240	Rob Ellis	.10	.05	.01
☐ 241	Sixto Lezcano	.10	.05	.01
☐ 242	Bob Mitchell	.10	.05	.01
☐ 243	Gorman Thomas	.30	.15	.03
☐ 244	Bill Travers	.10	.05	.01
☐ 245	Pete Broberg	.10	.05	.01
☐ 246	Bill Sharp	.10	.05	.01
☐ 247	Bobby Darwin	.10	.05	.01
☐ 248	Rick Austin (photo actually Larry Anderson)	.10	.05	.01
☐ 249	Larry Anderson (photo actually Rick Austin)	.10	.05	.01
☐ 250	Tom Bianco	.10	.05	.01
☐ 251	L. Currence	.10	.05	.01
☐ 252	Steve Foucault	.10	.05	.01
☐ 253	Bill Hands	.10	.05	.01
☐ 254	Steve Hargan	.10	.05	.01
☐ 255	Fergie Jenkins	.75	.35	.07
☐ 256	Bob Sheldon	.10	.05	.01
☐ 257	Jim Umbarger	.10	.05	.01
☐ 258	Clyde Wright	.10	.05	.01
☐ 259	Bill Fahey	.10	.05	.01
☐ 260	Jim Sundberg	.15	.07	.01
☐ 261	Leo Cardenas	.10	.05	.01
☐ 262	Jim Fregosi	.20	.10	.02
☐ 263	Mike Hargrove	.15	.07	.01
☐ 264	Toby Harrah	.20	.10	.02
☐ 265	Roy Howell	.10	.05	.01
☐ 266	Lenny Randle	.10	.05	.01
☐ 267	Roy Smalley	.15	.07	.01
☐ 268	Jim Spencer	.10	.05	.01
☐ 269	Jeff Burroughs	.15	.07	.01
☐ 270	Tom Grieve	.20	.10	.02
☐ 271	Joe Lovitto	.10	.05	.01
☐ 272	Frank Lucchesi MG	.10	.05	.01
☐ 273	Dave Nelson	.10	.05	.01
☐ 274	Ted Simmons	.60	.30	.06
☐ 275	Lou Brock	3.50	1.75	.35
☐ 276	Ron Fairly	.10	.05	.01
☐ 277	Bake McBride	.10	.05	.01
☐ 278	Reggie Smith	.25	.12	.02
☐ 279	Willie Davis	.15	.07	.01
☐ 280	Ken Reitz	.10	.05	.01
☐ 281	Buddy Bradford	.10	.05	.01
☐ 282	Luis Melendez	.10	.05	.01
☐ 283	Mike Tyson	.10	.05	.01
☐ 284	Ted Sizemore	.10	.05	.01
☐ 285	Mario Guerrero	.10	.05	.01
☐ 286	Larry Lintz	.10	.05	.01
☐ 287	Ken Rudolph	.10	.05	.01
☐ 288	Dick Billings	.10	.05	.01
☐ 289	Jerry Mumphrey	.10	.05	.01
☐ 290	Mike Wallace	.10	.05	.01
☐ 291	Al Hrabosky	.15	.07	.01
☐ 292	Ken Reynolds	.10	.05	.01
☐ 293	Mike Garman	.10	.05	.01
☐ 294	Bob Forsch	.15	.07	.01
☐ 295	John Denny	.20	.10	.02
☐ 296	Harry Rasmussen	.10	.05	.01
☐ 297	Lynn McGlothen	.10	.05	.01
☐ 298	Mike Barlow	.10	.05	.01
☐ 299	Greg Terlecky	.10	.05	.01
☐ 300	Red Schoendienst MG	.50	.25	.05
☐ 301	Rick Reuschel	.40	.20	.04
☐ 302	Steve Stone	.20	.10	.02
☐ 303	Bill Bonham	.10	.05	.01
☐ 304	Oscar Zamora	.10	.05	.01
☐ 305	Ken Frailing	.10	.05	.01
☐ 306	Milt Wilcox	.10	.05	.01
☐ 307	Darold Knowles	.10	.05	.01
☐ 308	Jim Marshall	.10	.05	.01
☐ 309	Bill Madlock	.75	.35	.07
☐ 310	Jose Cardenal	.10	.05	.01
☐ 311	Rick Monday	.15	.07	.01
☐ 312	Jerry Morales	.10	.05	.01
☐ 313	Tim Hosley	.10	.05	.01
☐ 314	Gene Hiser	.10	.05	.01
☐ 315	Don Kessinger	.20	.10	.02
☐ 316	Manny Trillo	.10	.05	.01
☐ 317	Pete LaCock	.10	.05	.01
☐ 318	George Mitterwald	.10	.05	.01
☐ 319	Steve Swisher	.10	.05	.01
☐ 320	Rob Sperring	.10	.05	.01
☐ 321	Vic Harris	.10	.05	.01
☐ 322	Ron Dunn	.10	.05	.01
☐ 323	Jose Morales	.10	.05	.01
☐ 324	Pete Mackanin	.10	.05	.01
☐ 325	Jim Cox	.10	.05	.01
☐ 326	Larry Parrish	.35	.17	.03
☐ 327	Mike Jorgensen	.10	.05	.01
☐ 328	Tim Foli	.10	.05	.01
☐ 329	Hal Breeden	.10	.05	.01
☐ 330	Nate Colbert	.10	.05	.01
☐ 331	Pepe Frias	.10	.05	.01
☐ 332	Pat Scanlon	.10	.05	.01
☐ 333	Bob Bailey	.10	.05	.01
☐ 334	Gary Carter	4.00	2.00	.40
☐ 335	Pepe Mangual	.10	.05	.01
☐ 336	Larry Biittner	.10	.05	.01
☐ 337	Jim Lyttle	.10	.05	.01
☐ 338	Gary Roenicke	.10	.05	.01
☐ 339	Tony Scott	.10	.05	.01
☐ 340	Jerry White	.10	.05	.01
☐ 341	Jim Dwyer	.10	.05	.01
☐ 342	Ellis Valentine	.10	.05	.01
☐ 343	Fred Scherman	.10	.05	.01
☐ 344	Dennis Blair	.10	.05	.01
☐ 345	Woodie Fryman	.10	.05	.01

☐ 346 Chuck Taylor	.10	.05	.01
☐ 347 Dan Warthen	.10	.05	.01
☐ 348 Dan Carrithers	.10	.05	.01
☐ 349 Steve Rogers	.15	.07	.01
☐ 350 Dale Murray	.10	.05	.01
☐ 351 Duke Snider CO	2.00	1.00	.20
☐ 352 Ralph Houk MG	.20	.10	.02
☐ 353 John Hiller	.15	.07	.01
☐ 354 Mickey Lolich	.35	.17	.03
☐ 355 Dave Lemancyzk	.10	.05	.01
☐ 356 Lerrin LaGrow	.10	.05	.01
☐ 357 Fred Arroyo	.10	.05	.01
☐ 358 Joe Coleman	.10	.05	.01
☐ 359 Ben Oglivie	.20	.10	.02
☐ 360 Willie Horton	.15	.07	.01
☐ 361 John Knox	.10	.05	.01
☐ 362 Leon Roberts	.10	.05	.01
☐ 363 Ron LeFlore	.15	.07	.01
☐ 364 G. Sutherland	.10	.05	.01
☐ 365 Dan Meyer	.10	.05	.01
☐ 366 Aurelio Rodriguez	.10	.05	.01
☐ 367 Tom Veryzer	.10	.05	.01
☐ 368 Jack Pierce	.10	.05	.01
☐ 369 Gene Michael	.15	.07	.01
☐ 370 Billy Baldwin	.10	.05	.01
☐ 371 Gates Brown	.15	.07	.01
☐ 372 Mickey Stanley	.15	.07	.01
☐ 373 Terry Humphrey	.10	.05	.01
☐ 374 Doyle Alexander	.20	.10	.02
☐ 375 Mike Cuellar	.15	.07	.01
☐ 376 Wayne Garland	.10	.05	.01
☐ 377 Ross Grimsley	.10	.05	.01
☐ 378 Grant Jackson	.10	.05	.01
☐ 379 Dyar Miller	.10	.05	.01
☐ 380 Jim Palmer	4.00	2.00	.40
☐ 381 Mike Torrez	.15	.07	.01
☐ 382 Mike Willis	.10	.05	.01
☐ 383 Dave Duncan	.10	.05	.01
☐ 384 Ellie Hendricks	.10	.05	.01
☐ 385 Jim Hutto	.10	.05	.01
☐ 386 Bob Bailor	.10	.05	.01
☐ 387 Doug DeCinces	.35	.17	.03
☐ 388 Bob Grich	.30	.15	.03
☐ 389 Lee May	.20	.10	.02
☐ 390 Tony Muser	.10	.05	.01
☐ 391 Tim Nordbrook	.10	.05	.01
☐ 392 Brooks Robinson	3.50	1.75	.35
☐ 393 Royle Stillman	.10	.05	.01
☐ 394 Don Baylor	.35	.17	.03
☐ 395 Paul Blair	.15	.07	.01
☐ 396 Al Bumbry	.10	.05	.01
☐ 397 Larry Harlow	.10	.05	.01
☐ 398 Tommy Davis	.20	.10	.02
☐ 399 Jim Northrup	.15	.07	.01
☐ 400 Ken Singleton	.30	.15	.03
☐ 401 Tom Shopay	.10	.05	.01
☐ 402 Fred Lynn	.90	.45	.09
☐ 403 Carlton Fisk	2.00	1.00	.20
☐ 404 Cecil Cooper	.50	.25	.05
☐ 405 Jim Rice	3.00	1.50	.30
☐ 406 Juan Beniquez	.15	.07	.01
☐ 407 Denny Doyle	.10	.05	.01
☐ 408 Dwight Evans	1.00	.50	.10
☐ 409 Carl Yastrzemski	8.00	4.00	.80
☐ 410 Rick Burleson	.15	.07	.01
☐ 411 Bernie Carbo	.10	.05	.01
☐ 412 Doug Griffin	.10	.05	.01
☐ 413 Rico Petrocelli	.15	.07	.01
☐ 414 Bob Montgomery	.10	.05	.01
☐ 415 Tim Blackwell	.10	.05	.01
☐ 416 Rick Miller	.10	.05	.01
☐ 417 Darrell Johnson	.10	.05	.01
☐ 418 Jim Burton	.10	.05	.01
☐ 419 Jim Willoughby	.10	.05	.01
☐ 420 Rogelio Moret	.10	.05	.01
☐ 421 Bill Lee	.15	.07	.01
☐ 422 Dick Drago	.10	.05	.01
☐ 423 Diego Segui	.10	.05	.01
☐ 424 Luis Tiant	.30	.15	.03
☐ 425 Jim Hunter	2.00	1.00	.20
☐ 426 Rick Sawyer	.10	.05	.01
☐ 427 Rudy May	.10	.05	.01
☐ 428 Dick Tidrow	.10	.05	.01
☐ 429 Sparky Lyle	.35	.17	.03
☐ 430 Doc Medich	.10	.05	.01
☐ 431 Pat Dobson	.15	.07	.01
☐ 432 Dave Pagan	.10	.05	.01
☐ 433 Thurman Munson	3.50	1.75	.35
☐ 434 Chris Chambliss	.20	.10	.02
☐ 435 Roy White	.15	.07	.01
☐ 436 Walt Williams	.10	.05	.01
☐ 437 Graig Nettles	.75	.35	.07
☐ 438 Rick Dempsey	.15	.07	.01
☐ 439 Bobby Bonds	.35	.17	.03
☐ 440 Ed Herrmann	.10	.05	.01

☐ 441 Sandy Alomar	.15	.07	.01
☐ 442 Fred Stanley	.10	.05	.01
☐ 443 Terry Whitfield	.10	.05	.01
☐ 444 Rich Bladt	.10	.05	.01
☐ 445 Lou Piniella	.40	.20	.04
☐ 446 Rich Coggins	.10	.05	.01
☐ 447 Ed Brinkman	.10	.05	.01
☐ 448 Jim Mason	.10	.05	.01
☐ 449 Larry Murray	.10	.05	.01
☐ 450 Ron Blomberg	.10	.05	.01
☐ 451 Elliott Maddox	.10	.05	.01
☐ 452 Kerry Dineen	.10	.05	.01
☐ 453 Billy Martin MG	1.00	.50	.10
☐ 454 Dave Bergman	.10	.05	.01
☐ 455 Otto Velez	.10	.05	.01
☐ 456 Joe Hoerner	.10	.05	.01
☐ 457 Tug McGraw	.40	.20	.04
☐ 458 Gene Garber	.15	.07	.01
☐ 459 Steve Carlton	3.50	1.75	.35
☐ 460 Larry Christenson	.10	.05	.01
☐ 461 Tom Underwood	.10	.05	.01
☐ 462 Jim Lonborg	.15	.07	.01
☐ 463 Jay Johnstone	.15	.07	.01
☐ 464 Larry Bowa	.35	.17	.03
☐ 465 Dave Cash	.10	.05	.01
☐ 466 Ollie Brown	.10	.05	.01
☐ 467 Greg Luzinski	.25	.12	.02
☐ 468 Johnny Oates	.10	.05	.01
☐ 469 Mike Anderson	.10	.05	.01
☐ 470 Mike Schmidt	9.00	4.50	.90
☐ 471 Bob Boone	.50	.25	.05
☐ 472 Tom Hutton	.10	.05	.01
☐ 473 Rich Allen	.40	.20	.04
☐ 474 Tony Taylor	.10	.05	.01
☐ 475 Jerry Martin	.10	.05	.01
☐ 476 Danny Ozark MG	.10	.05	.01
☐ 477 Dick Ruthven	.10	.05	.01
☐ 478 Jim Todd	.10	.05	.01
☐ 479 Paul Lindblad	.10	.05	.01
☐ 480 Rollie Fingers	1.50	.75	.15
☐ 481 Vida Blue	.25	.12	.02
☐ 482 Ken Holtzman	.15	.07	.01
☐ 483 Dick Bosman	.10	.05	.01
☐ 484 Sonny Siebert	.10	.05	.01
☐ 485 Glenn Abbott	.10	.05	.01
☐ 486 Stan Bahnsen	.10	.05	.01
☐ 487 Mike Norris	.15	.07	.01
☐ 488 Alvin Dark MG	.15	.07	.01
☐ 489 Claudell Washington	.25	.12	.02
☐ 490 Joe Rudi	.15	.07	.01
☐ 491 Bill North	.10	.05	.01
☐ 492 Bert Campaneris	.20	.10	.02
☐ 493 Gene Tenace	.15	.07	.01
☐ 494 Reggie Jackson	7.00	3.50	.70
☐ 495 Phil Garner	.15	.07	.01
☐ 496 Billy Williams	2.00	1.00	.20
☐ 497 Sal Bando	.20	.10	.02
☐ 498 Jim Holt	.10	.05	.01
☐ 499 Ted Martinez	.10	.05	.01
☐ 500 Ray Fosse	.10	.05	.01
☐ 501 Matt Alexander	.10	.05	.01
☐ 502 Larry Haney	.10	.05	.01
☐ 503 Angel Mangual	.10	.05	.01
☐ 504 Fred Beene	.10	.05	.01
☐ 505 Tom Buskey	.10	.05	.01
☐ 506 Dennis Eckersley	2.00	1.00	.20
☐ 507 Roric Harrison	.10	.05	.01
☐ 508 Don Hood	.10	.05	.01
☐ 509 Jim Kern	.10	.05	.01
☐ 510 Dave LaRoche	.10	.05	.01
☐ 511 Fritz Peterson	.10	.05	.01
☐ 512 Jim Strickland	.10	.05	.01
☐ 513 Rick Waits	.10	.05	.01
☐ 514 Alan Ashby	.10	.05	.01
☐ 515 John Ellis	.10	.05	.01
☐ 516 Rick Cerone	.10	.05	.01
☐ 517 Buddy Bell	.40	.20	.04
☐ 518 Jack Brohamer	.10	.05	.01
☐ 519 Rico Carty	.15	.07	.01
☐ 520 Ed Crosby	.10	.05	.01
☐ 521 Frank Duffy	.10	.05	.01
☐ 522 Duane Kuiper (photo actually Rick Manning)	.10	.05	.01
☐ 523 Joe Lis	.10	.05	.01
☐ 524 Boog Powell	.60	.30	.06
☐ 525 Frank Robinson	2.50	1.25	.25
☐ 526 Oscar Gamble	.15	.07	.01
☐ 527 George Hendrick	.15	.07	.01
☐ 528 John Lowenstein	.10	.05	.01
☐ 529 Rick Manning (photo actually Duane Kuiper)	.10	.05	.01
☐ 530 Tommy Smith	.10	.05	.01
☐ 531 Charlie Spikes	.10	.05	.01

☐ 532	Steve Kline	.10	.05	.01
☐ 533	Ed Kranepool	.15	.07	.01
☐ 534	Mike Vail	.10	.05	.01
☐ 535	Del Unser	.10	.05	.01
☐ 536	Felix Millan	.10	.05	.01
☐ 537	Rusty Staub	.35	.17	.03
☐ 538	Jesus Alou	.10	.05	.01
☐ 539	Wayne Garrett	.10	.05	.01
☐ 540	Mike Phillips	.10	.05	.01
☐ 541	Joe Torre	.40	.20	.04
☐ 542	Dave Kingman	.70	.35	.07
☐ 543	Gene Clines	.10	.05	.01
☐ 544	Jack Heidemann	.10	.05	.01
☐ 545	Bud Harrelson	.15	.07	.01
☐ 546	John Stearns	.15	.07	.01
☐ 547	John Milner	.10	.05	.01
☐ 548	Bob Apodaca	.10	.05	.01
☐ 549	Skip Lockwood	.10	.05	.01
☐ 550	Ken Sanders	.10	.05	.01
☐ 551	Tom Seaver	4.50	2.25	.45
☐ 552	Rick Baldwin	.10	.05	.01
☐ 553	Hank Webb	.10	.05	.01
☐ 554	Jon Matlack	.15	.07	.01
☐ 555	Randy Tate	.10	.05	.01
☐ 556	Tom Hall	.10	.05	.01
☐ 557	George Stone	.10	.05	.01
☐ 558	Craig Swan	.15	.07	.01
☐ 559	Jerry Cram	.10	.05	.01
☐ 560	Roy Staiger	.10	.05	.01
☐ 561	Kent Tekulve	.20	.10	.02
☐ 562	Jerry Reuss	.15	.07	.01
☐ 563	John Candelaria	.25	.12	.02
☐ 564	Larry Demery	.10	.05	.01
☐ 565	Dave Giusti	.15	.07	.01
☐ 566	Jim Rooker	.10	.05	.01
☐ 567	Ramon Hernandez	.10	.05	.01
☐ 568	Bruce Kison	.10	.05	.01
☐ 569	Ken Brett	.10	.05	.01
☐ 570	Bob Moose	.15	.07	.01
☐ 571	Manny Sanguillen	.20	.10	.02
☐ 572	Dave Parker	2.00	1.00	.20
☐ 573	Willie Stargell	3.00	1.50	.30
☐ 574	Richie Zisk	.15	.07	.01
☐ 575	Rennie Stennett	.10	.05	.01
☐ 576	Al Oliver	.70	.35	.07
☐ 577	Bill Robinson	.20	.10	.02
☐ 578	Bob Robertson	.10	.05	.01
☐ 579	Rich Hebner	.10	.05	.01
☐ 580	Ed Kirkpatrick	.10	.05	.01
☐ 581	Duffy Dyer	.10	.05	.01
☐ 582	Craig Reynolds	.10	.05	.01
☐ 583	Frank Taveras	.10	.05	.01
☐ 584	Willie Randolph	1.00	.50	.10
☐ 585	Art Howe	.20	.10	.02
☐ 586	Danny Murtaugh MG	.10	.05	.01
☐ 587	Rick McKinney	.10	.05	.01
☐ 588	Ed Goodson	.10	.05	.01
☐ 589	Checklist 1 George Brett Al Cowens	1.00	.50	.10
☐ 590	Checklist 2 Keith Hernandez Lou Brock	1.00	.50	.10
☐ 591	Checklist 3 Jerry Koosman Duke Snider	.50	.25	.05
☐ 592	Checklist 4 Maury Wills John Knox	.25	.12	.02
☐ 593A	Checklist 5 ERR Jim Hunter Nolan Ryan (Noland on front)	75.00	37.50	7.50
☐ 593B	Checklist 5 COR Jim Hunter Nolan Ryan	3.50	1.75	.35
☐ 594	Checklist 6 Ralph Branca Carl Erskine Pee Wee Reese	.30	.15	.03
☐ 595	Checklist 7 Willie Mays Herb Score	.75	.35	.07
☐ 596	Larry Cox	.10	.05	.01
☐ 597	Gene Mauch MG	.15	.07	.01
☐ 598	Whitey Wietelmann	.10	.05	.01
☐ 599	Wayne Simpson	.10	.05	.01
☐ 600	Mel Thomason	.10	.05	.01
☐ 601	Ike Hampton	.10	.05	.01
☐ 602	Ken Crosby	.10	.05	.01
☐ 603	Ralph Rowe	.10	.05	.01
☐ 604	Jim Tyrone	.10	.05	.01
☐ 605	Mick Kelleher	.10	.05	.01
☐ 606	Mario Mendoza	.10	.05	.01
☐ 607	Mike Rogodzinski	.10	.05	.01

☐ 608	Bob Gallagher	.10	.05	.01
☐ 609	Jerry Koosman	.20	.10	.02
☐ 610	Joe Frazier	.10	.05	.01
☐ 611	Karl Kuehl	.10	.05	.01
☐ 612	Frank LaCorte	.10	.05	.01
☐ 613	Ray Bare	.10	.05	.01
☐ 614	Billy Muffett	.10	.05	.01
☐ 615	Bill Laxton	.10	.05	.01
☐ 616	Willie Mays	6.00	3.00	.60
☐ 617	Phil Cavarretta CO	.15	.07	.01
☐ 618	Ted Kluszewski CO	.35	.17	.03
☐ 619	Elston Howard CO	.35	.17	.03
☐ 620	Alex Grammas CO	.10	.05	.01
☐ 621	Mickey Vernon CO	.15	.07	.01
☐ 622	Dick Sisler CO	.10	.05	.01
☐ 623	Harvey Haddix CO	.15	.07	.01
☐ 624	Bobby Winkles CO	.10	.05	.01
☐ 625	John Pesky CO	.10	.05	.01
☐ 626	Jim Davenport CO	.15	.07	.01
☐ 627	Dave Tomlin	.10	.05	.01
☐ 628	Roger Craig CO	.35	.17	.03
☐ 629	Joe Amalfitano CO	.10	.05	.01
☐ 630	Jim Reese CO	.15	.07	.01

1953 Stahl Meyer

The cards in this 9-card set measure 3 1/4" by 4 1/2". The 1953 Stahl Meyer set of full color, unnumbered cards includes three players from each of the three New York teams. The cards have white borders. The Lockman card is the most plentiful of any card in the set. Some batting and fielding statistics and short biography are included on the back. The cards are ordered in the checklist below by alphabetical order without regard to team affiliation.

		NRMT	VG-E	GOOD
COMPLETE SET		3500.00	1750.00	350.00
COMMON PLAYER (1-9)		125.00	60.00	12.50
☐ 1	Hank Bauer	150.00	75.00	15.00
☐ 2	Roy Campanella	600.00	300.00	60.00
☐ 3	Gil Hodges	300.00	150.00	30.00
☐ 4	Monte Irvin	200.00	100.00	20.00
☐ 5	Whitey Lockman	125.00	60.00	12.50
☐ 6	Mickey Mantle	2000.00	1000.00	200.00
☐ 7	Phil Rizzuto	300.00	150.00	30.00
☐ 8	Duke Snider	600.00	300.00	60.00
☐ 9	Bobby Thomson	150.00	75.00	15.00

1954 Stahl Meyer

The cards in this 12-card set measure 3 1/4" by 4 1/2". The 1954 Stahl Meyer set of full color, unnumbered cards includes four players from each of the three New York teams. The cards have yellow borders and the backs, oriented horizontally, include an ad for a baseball kit and the player's statistics. No player biography is included on the back. The cards are ordered in the checklist below by alphabetical order without regard to team affiliation.

		NRMT	VG-E	GOOD
COMPLETE SET		5500.00	2750.00	600.00
COMMON PLAYER (1-12)		150.00	75.00	15.00
☐ 1	Hank Bauer	175.00	85.00	18.00
☐ 2	Carl Erskine	175.00	85.00	18.00
☐ 3	Gil Hodges	300.00	150.00	30.00
☐ 4	Monte Irvin	250.00	125.00	25.00
☐ 5	Whitey Lockman	150.00	75.00	15.00
☐ 6	Mickey Mantle	2500.00	1250.00	300.00
☐ 7	Willie Mays	1250.00	600.00	150.00
☐ 8	Gil McDougald	175.00	85.00	18.00
☐ 9	Don Mueller	150.00	75.00	15.00
☐ 10	Don Newcombe	175.00	85.00	18.00
☐ 11	Phil Rizzuto	300.00	150.00	30.00
☐ 12	Duke Snider	600.00	300.00	60.00

1955 Stahl Meyer

The cards in this 12 card set measure 3 1/4" by 4 1/2". The 1955 Stahl Meyer set of full color, unnumbered cards contains four players each from the three New York teams. As in the 1954 set, the cards have yellow borders; however, the back of the cards contain a sketch of Mickey Mantle with an ad for a baseball cap or a pennant. The cards are ordered in the checklist below by alphabetical order without regard to team affiliation.

			NRMT	VG-E	GOOD
	COMPLETE SET		4250.00	2100.00	500.00
	COMMON PLAYER (1-12)		150.00	75.00	15.00
☐	1	Hank Bauer	175.00	85.00	18.00
☐	2	Carl Erskine	175.00	85.00	18.00
☐	3	Gil Hodges	300.00	150.00	30.00
☐	4	Monte Irvin	250.00	125.00	25.00
☐	5	Whitey Lockman	150.00	75.00	15.00
☐	6	Mickey Mantle	2500.00	1250.00	300.00
☐	7	Gil McDougald	175.00	85.00	18.00
☐	8	Don Mueller	150.00	75.00	15.00
☐	9	Don Newcombe	175.00	85.00	18.00
☐	10	Dusty Rhodes	150.00	75.00	15.00
☐	11	Phil Rizzuto	300.00	150.00	30.00
☐	12	Duke Snider	600.00	300.00	60.00

1962 Sugardale

The cards in this 22-card set measure 3 3/4" by 5 1/8". The 1962 Sugardale Meats set of black and white, numbered and lettered cards features the Cleveland Indians and the Pittsburgh Pirates. The Indians are numbered while the Pirates are lettered. The backs, in red print, give player tips. The Bob Nieman card was just recently discovered and is quite scarce. The catalog designation is F174-1.

			NRMT	VG-E	GOOD
	COMPLETE SET (22)		1800.00	900.00	200.00
	COMMON PLAYER (1-19)		45.00	22.50	4.50
	COMMON PLAYER (A-D)		75.00	37.50	7.50
☐	1	Barry Latman	45.00	22.50	4.50
☐	2	Gary Bell	45.00	22.50	4.50
☐	3	Dick Donovan	45.00	22.50	4.50
☐	4	Frank Funk	45.00	22.50	4.50
☐	5	Jim Perry	75.00	37.50	7.50
☐	6	not issued	00.00	00.00	0.00
☐	7	John Romano	45.00	22.50	4.50
☐	8	Ty Cline	45.00	22.50	4.50
☐	9	Tito Francona	45.00	22.50	4.50
☐	10	Bob Nieman	250.00	125.00	25.00
☐	11	Willie Kirkland	45.00	22.50	4.50
☐	12	Woody Held	45.00	22.50	4.50
☐	13	Jerry Kindall	45.00	22.50	4.50
☐	14	Bubba Phillips	45.00	22.50	4.50
☐	15	Mel Harder	45.00	22.50	4.50
☐	16	Salty Parker	45.00	22.50	4.50
☐	17	Ray Katt	45.00	22.50	4.50
☐	18	Mel McGaha	45.00	22.50	4.50
☐	19	Pedro Ramos	45.00	22.50	4.50
☐	A	Dick Groat	90.00	45.00	9.00
☐	B	Robert Clemente	750.00	375.00	75.00
☐	C	Don Hoak	75.00	37.50	7.50
☐	D	Dick Stuart	90.00	45.00	9.00

DON'T MISS OUT. Consult the Picture Gallery on page 693 for the 1962 Sugardale photo.

1963 Sugardale

The cards in this 31-card set measure 3 3/4" by 5 1/8". The 1963 Sugardale Meats set of 31 black and white, numbered cards features the Cleveland Indians and Pittsburgh Pirates. The backs are printed in red and give player tips. The 1963 Sugardale set can be distinguished from the 1962 Sugardale set by examining the biographies on the card for mention of the 1962 season. The Perry and Skinner cards were withdrawn after June trades and are difficult to obtain.

			NRMT	VG-E	GOOD
	COMPLETE SET (31)		1800.00	900.00	200.00
	COMMON PLAYER (1-33)		45.00	22.50	4.50
	COMMON PLAYER (34-38)		75.00	37.50	7.50
☐	1	Barry Latman	45.00	22.50	4.50
☐	2	Gary Bell	45.00	22.50	4.50
☐	3	Dick Donovan	45.00	22.50	4.50
☐	4	Joe Adcock	75.00	37.50	7.50
☐	5	Jim Perry	175.00	85.00	18.00
☐	6	Not issued	00.00	00.00	0.00
☐	7	John Romano	45.00	22.50	4.50
☐	8	Mike de la Hoz	45.00	22.50	4.50
☐	9	Tito Francona	45.00	22.50	4.50
☐	10	Gene Green	45.00	22.50	4.50
☐	11	Willie Kirkland	45.00	22.50	4.50
☐	12	Woody Held	45.00	22.50	4.50
☐	13	Jerry Kindall	45.00	22.50	4.50
☐	14	Max Alvis	45.00	22.50	4.50
☐	15	Mel Harder	45.00	22.50	4.50
☐	16	George Strickland	45.00	22.50	4.50
☐	17	Elmer Valo	45.00	22.50	4.50
☐	18	Birdie Tebbetts	45.00	22.50	4.50
☐	19	Pedro Ramos	45.00	22.50	4.50
☐	20	Al Luplow	45.00	22.50	4.50
☐	21	Not issued	00.00	00.00	0.00
☐	22	Not issued	00.00	00.00	0.00
☐	23	Jim Grant	45.00	22.50	4.50
☐	24	Victor Davalillo	45.00	22.50	4.50
☐	25	Jerry Walker	45.00	22.50	4.50
☐	26	Sam McDowell	75.00	37.50	7.50
☐	27	Fred Whitfield	45.00	22.50	4.50
☐	28	Jack Kralick	45.00	22.50	4.50
☐	29	Not issued	00.00	00.00	0.00
☐	30	Not issued	00.00	00.00	0.00
☐	31	Not issued	00.00	00.00	0.00
☐	32	Not issued	00.00	00.00	0.00
☐	33	Bob Allen	45.00	22.50	4.50
☐	34	Don Cardwell	75.00	37.50	7.50
☐	35	Bob Skinner	250.00	125.00	25.00
☐	36	Don Schwall	75.00	37.50	7.50
☐	37	Jim Pagliaroni	75.00	37.50	7.50
☐	38	Dick Schofield	75.00	37.50	7.50

1948 Swell Sport Thrills

The cards in this 20-card set measure 2 1/2" by 3". The 1948 Swell Gum Sports Thrills set of black and white, numbered cards highlights events from baseball history. The cards have picture framed borders with the title "Sports Thrills Highlights in the World of Sport" on the front. The backs of the cards give the story of the event pictured on the front. Cards numbered 9, 11, 16, and 20 are more difficult to obtain than the other cards in this set. The ACC designation is R448.

			NRMT	VG-E	GOOD
	COMPLETE SET (20)		850.00	400.00	90.00
	COMMON PLAYER (1-20)		15.00	7.50	1.50
☐	1	Greatest Single Inning Athletics' 10 Run Rally	15.00	7.50	1.50
☐	2	Amazing Record: Reiser's Debut With Dodgers	15.00	7.50	1.50
☐	3	Dramatic Debut:	125.00	60.00	12.50

Jackie Robinson ROY

			MINT	EXC	G-VG

☐ 4 Greatest Pitcher of 50.00 25.00 5.00
Them All: W.Johnson
☐ 5 Three Strikes Not Out: 15.00 7.50 1.50
Lost Third Strike
Changes Tide of 1941
World Series
☐ 6 Home Run Wins Series: 25.00 12.50 2.50
Bill Dickey's Last
Home Run
☐ 7 Never Say Die Pitcher: 15.00 7.50 1.50
Schumacher Pitching
☐ 8 Five Strikeouts: 25.00 12.50 2.50
Nationals Lose All
Star Game (Hubbell)
☐ 9 Greatest Catch: Al 25.00 12.50 2.50
Gionfriddo's Catch
☐ 10 No Hits No Runs: 25.00 12.50 2.50
VanderMeer Comes
Back
☐ 11 Bases Loaded: 40.00 20.00 4.00
Alexander The Great
☐ 12 Most Dramatic Homer: 150.00 75.00 15.00
Babe Ruth Points
☐ 13 Winning Run: Bridges' 15.00 7.50 1.50
Pitching and Goslin's
Single Wins 1935
World Series
☐ 14 Great Slugging: Lou 100.00 50.00 10.00
Gehrig's Four
Homers
☐ 15 Four Men To Stop Him: 40.00 20.00 4.00
DiMaggio's Bat
Streak
☐ 16 Three Run Homer in 125.00 60.00 12.50
Ninth: Williams'
Homer
☐ 17 Football Block: 15.00 7.50 1.50
Lindell's Football
Block Paves Way For
Yank's Series Victory
☐ 18 Home Run To Fame: 40.00 20.00 4.00
Reese's Grand Slam
☐ 19 Strikeout Record: 40.00 20.00 4.00
Feller Whiffs Five
☐ 20 Rifle Arm: Furillo 40.00 20.00 4.00

1989 Swell Baseball Greats

The 1989 Swell Baseball Greats set contains 135 standard-size (2 1/2 by 3 1/2 inch) cards. The fronts have vintage color photos with beige, red and white borders. The horizontally-oriented backs are white and scarlet, and feature career highlights and lifetime stats. The set was produced by Philadelphia Chewing Gum Corporation.

	MINT	EXC	G-VG
COMPLETE SET (135)	10.00	5.00	1.00
COMMON PLAYER (1-135)	.05	.02	.00

☐ 1 Babe Ruth .... .75 .35 .07
☐ 2 Ty Cobb .... .50 .25 .05
☐ 3 Walter Johnson .... .30 .15 .03

☐ 4 Honus Wagner .... .30 .15 .03
☐ 5 Cy Young .... .20 .10 .02
☐ 6 Joe Adcock .... .05 .02 .00
☐ 7 Jim Bunning .... .10 .05 .01
☐ 8 Orlando Cepeda .... .10 .05 .01
☐ 9 Harvey Kuenn .... .05 .02 .00
☐ 10 Jim Hunter .... .20 .10 .02
☐ 11 Johnny VanderMeer .... .10 .05 .01
☐ 12 Tony Oliva .... .10 .05 .01
☐ 13 Harvey Haddix UER .... .10 .05 .01
(reverse negative)
☐ 14 Dick McAuliffe .... .05 .02 .00
☐ 15 Lefty Grove .... .20 .10 .02
☐ 16 Bo Belinsky .... .05 .02 .00
☐ 17 Claude Osteen .... .05 .02 .00
☐ 18 Doc Medich .... .05 .02 .00
☐ 19 Del Ennis .... .05 .02 .00
☐ 20 Rogers Hornsby .... .20 .10 .02
☐ 21 Bob Buhl .... .05 .02 .00
☐ 22 Phil Niekro .... .20 .10 .02
☐ 23 Don Zimmer .... .10 .05 .01
☐ 24 Greg Luzinski .... .05 .02 .00
☐ 25 Lou Gehrig .... .50 .25 .05
☐ 26 Ken Singleton .... .10 .05 .01
☐ 27 Bob Allison .... .05 .02 .00
☐ 28 Ed Kranepool .... .05 .02 .00
☐ 29 Manny Sanguillen .... .05 .02 .00
☐ 30 Luke Appling .... .15 .07 .01
☐ 31 Ralph Terry .... .05 .02 .00
☐ 32 Smoky Burgess .... .05 .02 .00
☐ 33 Gil Hodges .... .20 .10 .02
☐ 34 Harry Walker .... .05 .02 .00
☐ 35 Edd Roush .... .15 .07 .01
☐ 36 Ron Santo .... .10 .05 .01
☐ 37 Jim Perry .... .05 .02 .00
☐ 38 Jose Morales .... .05 .02 .00
☐ 39 Stan Bahnsen .... .05 .02 .00
☐ 40 Al Kaline .... .25 .12 .02
☐ 41 Mel Harder .... .05 .02 .00
☐ 42 Ralph Houk .... .05 .02 .00
☐ 43 Jack Billingham .... .05 .02 .00
☐ 44 Carl Erskine .... .10 .05 .01
☐ 45 Hoyt Wilhelm .... .20 .10 .02
☐ 46 Dick Radatz .... .05 .02 .00
☐ 47 Roy Sievers .... .05 .02 .00
☐ 48 Jim Lonborg .... .05 .02 .00
☐ 49 Bobby Richardson .... .10 .05 .01
☐ 50 Whitey Ford .... .25 .12 .02
☐ 51 Roy Face .... .10 .05 .01
☐ 52 Tom Tresh .... .05 .02 .00
☐ 53 Joe Nuxhall .... .05 .02 .00
☐ 54 Mickey Vernon .... .05 .02 .00
☐ 55 Johnny Mize .... .20 .10 .02
☐ 56 Scott McGregor .... .05 .02 .00
☐ 57 Billy Pierce .... .10 .05 .01
☐ 58 Dave Giusti .... .05 .02 .00
☐ 59 Minnie Minoso .... .10 .05 .01
☐ 60 Early Wynn .... .15 .07 .01
☐ 61 Jose Cardenal .... .05 .02 .00
☐ 62 Sam Jethroe .... .05 .02 .00
☐ 63 Sal Bando .... .05 .02 .00
☐ 64 Elrod Hendricks .... .05 .02 .00
☐ 65 Enos Slaughter .... .15 .07 .01
☐ 66 Jim Bouton .... .05 .02 .00
☐ 67 Bill Mazeroski .... .10 .05 .01
☐ 68 Tony Kubek .... .10 .05 .01
☐ 69 Joe Black .... .05 .02 .00
☐ 70 Harmon Killebrew .... .20 .10 .02
☐ 71 Sam McDowell .... .05 .02 .00
☐ 72 Bucky Dent .... .10 .05 .01
☐ 73 Virgil Trucks .... .05 .02 .00
☐ 74 Andy Pafko .... .05 .02 .00
☐ 75 Bob Feller .... .25 .12 .02
☐ 76 Tito Francona .... .05 .02 .00
☐ 77 Al Dark .... .05 .02 .00

☐ 78	Larry Dierker	.05	.02	.00
☐ 79	Nellie Briles	.05	.02	.00
☐ 80	Lou Boudreau	.15	.07	.01
☐ 81	Wally Moon	.05	.02	.00
☐ 82	Hank Bauer	.05	.02	.00
☐ 83	Jim Piersall	.05	.02	.00
☐ 84	Jim Grant	.05	.02	.00
☐ 85	Richie Ashburn	.15	.07	.01
☐ 86	Bob Friend	.05	.02	.00
☐ 87	Ken Keltner	.05	.02	.00
☐ 88	Jim Kaat	.10	.05	.01
☐ 89	Dean Chance	.05	.02	.00
☐ 90	Al Lopez	.15	.07	.01
☐ 91	Dick Groat	.10	.05	.01
☐ 92	Johnny Blanchard	.05	.02	.00
☐ 93	Chuck Hinton	.05	.02	.00
☐ 94	Clete Boyer	.05	.02	.00
☐ 95	Steve Carlton	.20	.10	.02
☐ 96	Tug McGraw	.10	.05	.01
☐ 97	Mickey Lolich	.10	.05	.01
☐ 98	Earl Weaver	.10	.05	.01
☐ 99	Sal Maglie	.10	.05	.01
☐ 100	Ted Williams	.50	.25	.05
☐ 101	Allie Reynolds UER (photo actually Marius Russo)	.20	.10	.02
☐ 102	Gene Woodling UER (photo actually Irv Noren)	.20	.10	.02
☐ 103	Moe Drabowsky	.05	.02	.00
☐ 104	Mickey Stanley	.05	.02	.00
☐ 105	Jim Palmer	.25	.12	.02
☐ 106	Bill Freehan	.05	.02	.00
☐ 107	Bob Robertson	.05	.02	.00
☐ 108	Walt Dropo	.05	.02	.00
☐ 109	Jerry Koosman	.10	.05	.01
☐ 110	Bobby Doerr	.20	.10	.02
☐ 111	Phil Rizzuto	.20	.10	.02
☐ 112	Don Kessinger	.10	.05	.01
☐ 113	Milt Pappas	.10	.05	.01
☐ 114	Herb Score	.10	.05	.01
☐ 115	Larry Doby	.10	.05	.01
☐ 116	Glenn Beckert	.05	.02	.00
☐ 117	Andre Thornton	.05	.02	.00
☐ 118	Gary Matthews	.05	.02	.00
☐ 119	Bill Virdon	.10	.05	.01
☐ 120	Billy Williams	.20	.10	.02
☐ 121	Johnny Sain	.10	.05	.01
☐ 122	Don Newcombe	.10	.05	.01
☐ 123	Rico Petrocelli	.05	.02	.00
☐ 124	Dick Bosman	.05	.02	.00
☐ 125	Roberto Clemente	.40	.20	.04
☐ 126	Rocky Colavito	.10	.05	.01
☐ 127	Wilbur Wood	.05	.02	.00
☐ 128	Duke Sims	.05	.02	.00
☐ 129	Ken Holtzman	.05	.02	.00
☐ 130	Casey Stengel	.20	.10	.02
☐ 131	Bobby Shantz	.10	.05	.01
☐ 132	Del Crandall	.10	.05	.01
☐ 133	Bobby Thomson	.10	.05	.01
☐ 134	Brooks Robinson	.30	.15	.03
☐ 135	Checklist Card	.05	.02	.00

1957 Swifts Franks

The cards in this 18-card set measure 3 1/2" by 4". These full color, numbered cards issued in 1957 by the Swift Company are die-cut. Each card consists of several pieces which can be punched out and assembled to form a stand-up model of the player. The cards and a game board were available directly from the company. The ACC designation is F162.

		NRMT	VG-E	GOOD
COMPLETE SET (18)		1600.00	800.00	200.00
COMMON PLAYER (1-18)		45.00	22.50	4.50
☐ 1	John Podres	60.00	30.00	6.00
☐ 2	Gus Triandos	45.00	22.50	4.50
☐ 3	Dale Long	45.00	22.50	4.50
☐ 4	Billy Pierce	60.00	30.00	6.00
☐ 5	Ed Bailey	45.00	22.50	4.50
☐ 6	Vic Wertz	45.00	22.50	4.50
☐ 7	Nelson Fox	100.00	50.00	10.00
☐ 8	Ken Boyer	90.00	45.00	9.00
☐ 9	Gil McDougald	75.00	37.50	7.50
☐ 10	Junior Gilliam	75.00	37.50	7.50
☐ 11	Eddie Yost	45.00	22.50	4.50

☐ 12	Johnny Logan	45.00	22.50	4.50
☐ 13	Hank Aaron	500.00	250.00	50.00
☐ 14	Bill Tuttle	45.00	22.50	4.50
☐ 15	Jackie Jensen	75.00	37.50	7.50
☐ 16	Frank Robinson	150.00	75.00	15.00
☐ 17	Richie Ashburn	125.00	60.00	12.50
☐ 18	Rocky Colavito	90.00	45.00	9.00

1986 Texas Gold Reds

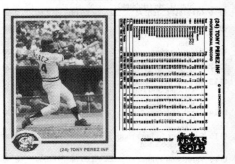

Texas Gold Ice Cream is the sponsor of this 28-card set of Cincinnati Reds. The cards are 2 1/2" by 3 1/2" and feature player photos in full color with a red and white border on the front of the card. The set was distributed to fans attending the Reds game at Riverfront Stadium on September 19th. The card backs contain the player's career statistics, uniform number, name, position, and the Texas Gold logo.

		MINT	EXC	G-VG
COMPLETE SET (28)		25.00	12.50	2.50
COMMON PLAYER		.30	.15	.03
☐ 6	Bo Diaz	.30	.15	.03
☐ 9	Max Venable	.30	.15	.03
☐ 11	Kurt Stillwell	.50	.25	.05
☐ 12	Nick Esasky	.50	.25	.05
☐ 13	Dave Concepcion	.50	.25	.05
☐ 14A	Pete Rose INF	2.50	1.25	.25
☐ 14B	Pete Rose MG	2.50	1.25	.25
☐ 14C	Pete Rose (commemorative)	2.50	1.25	.25
☐ 16	Ron Oester	.30	.15	.03
☐ 20	Eddie Milner	.30	.15	.03
☐ 22	Sal Butera	.30	.15	.03
☐ 24	Tony Perez	.75	.35	.07
☐ 25	Buddy Bell	.50	.25	.05
☐ 28	Kal Daniels	1.50	.75	.15
☐ 29	Tracy Jones	.50	.25	.05
☐ 31	John Franco	.75	.35	.07
☐ 32	Tom Browning	.75	.35	.07
☐ 33	Ron Robinson	.40	.20	.04
☐ 34	Bill Gullickson	.40	.20	.04

☐ 36	Mario Soto	.40	.20	.04
☐ 39	Dave Parker	.75	.35	.07
☐ 40	John Denny	.40	.20	.04
☐ 44	Eric Davis	7.50	3.75	.75
☐ 45	Chris Welsh	.30	.15	.03
☐ 48	Ted Power	.30	.15	.03
☐ 49	Joe Price	.30	.15	.03
☐ xx	Reds Coaches	.30	.15	.03
	George Scherger			
	Bruce Kimm			
	Billy DeMars			
	Tommy Helms			
	Scott Breeden			
	Jim Lett			
☐ xx	Preferred Customer Card .	.30	.15	.03
	(Discount Coupon)			

1947 Tip Top

GEORGE KELL
Third Base, Detroit, A.L.

Umpire Housewife declares TIP-TOP "safe" at the home plate. TIP - TOP "scores" with everybody

Look for the stars on the TIP TOP wrapper and the stars on the diamond

Enriched
TIP-TOP is Better Bread.

There are 15 photos of your favorite baseball players in this club group Should you get duplicate photos (two or more of same player) trade cards until you have the complete set. Root for your home team and for TIP-TOP BREAD Compliments of TIP-TOP Bakers

The cards in this 163-card set measure 2 1/4" by 3". The 1947 Tip Top Bread issue contains unnumbered cards with black and white player photos. The set is of interest to baseball historians in that it contains cards of many players not appearing in any other card sets. The cards were issued locally for the eleven following teams: Red Sox (1-15), White Sox (16-30), Tigers (31-45), Yankees (46-60), Browns (61-75), Braves (76-90), Dodgers (91-104), Cubs (105-119), Giants (120-135), Pirates (136-149), and Cardinals (150-164). Players of the Red Sox, Tigers, White Sox, Braves, and the Cubs are scarcer than those of the other teams; players from these tougher teams are marked by SP below to indicate their scarcity. The ACC designation is D323.

		NRMT	VG-E	GOOD
COMPLETE SET (163)		10000.00	5000.00	1000.00
COMMON PLAYER (1-164)		25.00	12.50	2.50
☐ 1	Leon Culberson SP	75.00	37.50	7.50
☐ 2	Dom DiMaggio SP	125.00	60.00	12.50
☐ 3	Joe Dobson SP	75.00	37.50	7.50
☐ 4	Bob Doerr SP	250.00	125.00	25.00
☐ 5	Dave(Boo) Ferris SP	75.00	37.50	7.50
☐ 6	Mickey Harris SP	75.00	37.50	7.50
☐ 7	Frank Hayes SP	75.00	37.50	7.50
☐ 8	Cecil Hughson SP	75.00	37.50	7.50
☐ 9	Earl Johnson SP	75.00	37.50	7.50
☐ 10	Roy Partee SP	75.00	37.50	7.50
☐ 11	Johnny Pesky SP	90.00	45.00	9.00
☐ 12	Rip Russell SP	75.00	37.50	7.50
☐ 13	Hal Wagner SP	75.00	37.50	7.50
☐ 14	Rudy York SP	90.00	45.00	9.00
☐ 15	Bill Zuber SP	75.00	37.50	7.50
☐ 16	Floyd Baker SP	75.00	37.50	7.50
☐ 17	Earl Caldwell SP	75.00	37.50	7.50
☐ 18	Lloyd Christopher SP	75.00	37.50	7.50
☐ 19	George Dickey SP	75.00	37.50	7.50
☐ 20	Ralph Hodgin SP	75.00	37.50	7.50
☐ 21	Bob Kennedy SP	75.00	37.50	7.50
☐ 22	Joe Kuhel SP	75.00	37.50	7.50
☐ 23	Thornton Lee SP	75.00	37.50	7.50
☐ 24	Ed Lopat SP	125.00	60.00	12.50
☐ 25	Cass Michaels SP	75.00	37.50	7.50

☐ 26	John Rigney SP	75.00	37.50	7.50
☐ 27	Mike Tresh SP	75.00	37.50	7.50
☐ 28	Thurman Tucker SP	75.00	37.50	7.50
☐ 29	Jack Wallasca SP	75.00	37.50	7.50
☐ 30	Taft Wright SP	75.00	37.50	7.50
☐ 31	Walter(Hoot)Evers SP	75.00	37.50	7.50
☐ 32	John Gorsica SP	75.00	37.50	7.50
☐ 33	Fred Hutchinson SP	90.00	45.00	9.00
☐ 34	George Kell SP	350.00	175.00	35.00
☐ 35	Eddie Lake SP	75.00	37.50	7.50
☐ 36	Ed Mayo SP	75.00	37.50	7.50
☐ 37	Arthur Mills SP	75.00	37.50	7.50
☐ 38	Pat Mullin SP	75.00	37.50	7.50
☐ 39	James Outlaw SP	75.00	37.50	7.50
☐ 40	Frank Overmire SP	75.00	37.50	7.50
☐ 41	Bob Swift SP	75.00	37.50	7.50
☐ 42	Birdie Tebbetts SP	75.00	37.50	7.50
☐ 43	Paul(Diz) Trout SP	90.00	45.00	9.00
☐ 44	Virgil Trucks SP	90.00	45.00	9.00
☐ 45	Dick Wakefield SP	75.00	37.50	7.50
☐ 46	Larry Berra	350.00	175.00	35.00
☐ 47	Floyd(Bill) Bevans	25.00	12.50	2.50
☐ 48	Bobby Brown	45.00	22.50	4.50
☐ 49	Thomas Byrne	25.00	12.50	2.50
☐ 50	Frank Crosetti	40.00	20.00	4.00
☐ 51	Tom Henrich	40.00	20.00	4.00
☐ 52	Charlie Keller	35.00	17.50	3.50
☐ 53	Johnny Lindell	25.00	12.50	2.50
☐ 54	Joe Page	25.00	12.50	2.50
☐ 55	Mel Queen	25.00	12.50	2.50
☐ 56	Allie Reynolds	45.00	22.50	4.50
☐ 57	Phil Rizzuto	125.00	60.00	12.50
☐ 58	Aaron Robinson	25.00	12.50	2.50
☐ 59	George Stirnweiss	25.00	12.50	2.50
☐ 60	Charles Wensloff	25.00	12.50	2.50
☐ 61	John Berardino	25.00	12.50	2.50
☐ 62	Clifford Fannin	25.00	12.50	2.50
☐ 63	Dennis Galehouse	25.00	12.50	2.50
☐ 64	Jeff Heath	25.00	12.50	2.50
☐ 65	Walter Judnich	25.00	12.50	2.50
☐ 66	Jack Kramer	25.00	12.50	2.50
☐ 67	Paul Lehner	25.00	12.50	2.50
☐ 68	Lester Moss	25.00	12.50	2.50
☐ 69	Bob Muncrief	25.00	12.50	2.50
☐ 70	Nelson Potter	25.00	12.50	2.50
☐ 71	Fred Sanford	25.00	12.50	2.50
☐ 72	Joe Schultz	25.00	12.50	2.50
☐ 73	Vern Stephens	35.00	17.50	3.50
☐ 74	Jerry Witte	25.00	12.50	2.50
☐ 75	Al Zarilla	25.00	12.50	2.50
☐ 76	Charles Barrett SP	75.00	37.50	7.50
☐ 77	Hank Camelli SP	75.00	37.50	7.50
☐ 78	Dick Culler SP	75.00	37.50	7.50
☐ 79	Nanny Fernandez SP	75.00	37.50	7.50
☐ 80	Si Johnson SP	75.00	37.50	7.50
☐ 81	Danny Litwhiler SP	75.00	37.50	7.50
☐ 82	Phil Masi SP	75.00	37.50	7.50
☐ 83	Carvel Rowell SP	75.00	37.50	7.50
☐ 84	Connie Ryan SP	75.00	37.50	7.50
☐ 85	John Sain SP	125.00	60.00	12.50
☐ 86	Ray Sanders SP	75.00	37.50	7.50
☐ 87	Sibby Sisti SP	75.00	37.50	7.50
☐ 88	Billy Southworth SP	75.00	37.50	7.50
☐ 89	Warren Spahn SP	400.00	200.00	40.00
☐ 90	Ed Wright SP	75.00	37.50	7.50
☐ 91	Bob Bragan	25.00	12.50	2.50
☐ 92	Ralph Branca	35.00	17.50	3.50
☐ 93	Hugh Casey	25.00	12.50	2.50
☐ 94	Bruce Edwards	25.00	12.50	2.50
☐ 95	Hal Gregg	25.00	12.50	2.50
☐ 96	Joe Hatten	25.00	12.50	2.50
☐ 97	Gene Hermanski	25.00	12.50	2.50
☐ 98	John Jorgensen	25.00	12.50	2.50
☐ 99	Harry Lavagetto	25.00	12.50	2.50
☐ 100	Vic Lombardi	25.00	12.50	2.50
☐ 101	Frank Melton	25.00	12.50	2.50
☐ 102	Ed Miksis	25.00	12.50	2.50
☐ 103	Marv Rackley	25.00	12.50	2.50
☐ 104	Ed Stevens	25.00	12.50	2.50
☐ 105	Phil Cavarretta SP	125.00	60.00	12.50
☐ 106	Bob Chipman SP	75.00	37.50	7.50
☐ 107	Stanley Hack SP	90.00	45.00	9.00
☐ 108	Don Johnson SP	75.00	37.50	7.50
☐ 109	Emil Kush SP	75.00	37.50	7.50
☐ 110	Bill Lee SP	75.00	37.50	7.50
☐ 111	Mickey Livingston SP	75.00	37.50	7.50
☐ 112	Harry Lowrey SP	75.00	37.50	7.50
☐ 113	Clyde McCullough SP	75.00	37.50	7.50
☐ 114	Andy Pafko SP	90.00	45.00	9.00
☐ 115	Marv Rickert SP	75.00	37.50	7.50
☐ 116	John Schmitz SP	75.00	37.50	7.50
☐ 117	Bobby Sturgeon SP	75.00	37.50	7.50
☐ 118	Ed Waitkus SP	75.00	37.50	7.50
☐ 119	Henry Wyse SP	75.00	37.50	7.50
☐ 120	Bill Ayers	25.00	12.50	2.50

		MINT	EXC	G-VG
☐ 121	Robert Blattner	25.00	12.50	2.50
☐ 122	Mike Budnick	25.00	12.50	2.50
☐ 123	Sid Gordon	25.00	12.50	2.50
☐ 124	Clinton Hartung	25.00	12.50	2.50
☐ 125	Monte Kennedy	25.00	12.50	2.50
☐ 126	Dave Koslo	25.00	12.50	2.50
☐ 127	Carroll Lockman	25.00	12.50	2.50
☐ 128	Jack Lohrke	25.00	12.50	2.50
☐ 129	Ernie Lombardi	75.00	37.50	7.50
☐ 130	Willard Marshall	25.00	12.50	2.50
☐ 131	John Mize	100.00	50.00	10.00
☐ 132	Eugene Thompson (does not exist)	0.00	.00	.00
☐ 133	Ken Trinkle	25.00	12.50	2.50
☐ 134	Bill Voiselle	25.00	12.50	2.50
☐ 135	Mickey Witek	25.00	12.50	2.50
☐ 136	Eddie Basinski	25.00	12.50	2.50
☐ 137	Ernie Bonham	25.00	12.50	2.50
☐ 138	Billy Cox	35.00	17.50	3.50
☐ 139	Elbie Fletcher	25.00	12.50	2.50
☐ 140	Frank Gustine	25.00	12.50	2.50
☐ 141	Kirby Higbe	25.00	12.50	2.50
☐ 142	Leroy Jarvis	25.00	12.50	2.50
☐ 143	Ralph Kiner	100.00	50.00	10.00
☐ 144	Fred Ostermueller	25.00	12.50	2.50
☐ 145	Preacher Roe	45.00	22.50	4.50
☐ 146	Jim Russell	25.00	12.50	2.50
☐ 147	Rip Sewell	25.00	12.50	2.50
☐ 148	Nick Strincevich	25.00	12.50	2.50
☐ 149	Honus Wagner	125.00	60.00	12.50
☐ 150	Alpha Brazle	25.00	12.50	2.50
☐ 151	Ken Burkhart	25.00	12.50	2.50
☐ 152	Bernard Creger	25.00	12.50	2.50
☐ 153	Joffre Cross	25.00	12.50	2.50
☐ 154	Charles E. Diering	25.00	12.50	2.50
☐ 155	Ervin Dusak	25.00	12.50	2.50
☐ 156	Joe Garagiola	100.00	50.00	10.00
☐ 157	Tony Kaufmann	25.00	12.50	2.50
☐ 158	George Kurowski	25.00	12.50	2.50
☐ 159	Marty Marion	50.00	25.00	5.00
☐ 160	George Munger	25.00	12.50	2.50
☐ 161	Del Rice	25.00	12.50	2.50
☐ 162	Dick Sisler	25.00	12.50	2.50
☐ 163	Enos Slaughter	100.00	50.00	10.00
☐ 164	Ted Wilks	25.00	12.50	2.50

1989-90 T/M Senior League

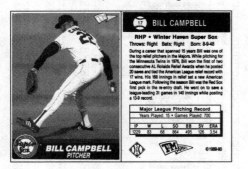

The 1989-90 T/M Senior League set contains 120 standard-size (2 1/2 by 3 1/2 inch) cards depicting members of the new Senior League. The fronts are borderless, with full color photos and black bands at the bottom with player names and positions. The vertically-oriented backs are gray and red, and show career major league totals and highlights. The cards were distributed as a boxed set with a checklist card and eight card-sized puzzle pieces.

		MINT	EXC	G-VG
	COMPLETE SET (120)	12.00	5.00	1.00
	COMMON PLAYER (1-120)	.10	.05	.01
☐ 1	Curt Flood (commissioner)	.30	.12	.01
☐ 2	Willie Aikens	.20	.08	.01
☐ 3	Gary Allenson	.10	.05	.01
☐ 4	Stan Bahnsen	.10	.05	.01
☐ 5	Alan Bannister	.10	.05	.01
☐ 6	Juan Beniquez	.10	.05	.01
☐ 7	Jim Bibby	.10	.05	.01
☐ 8	Paul Blair	.20	.08	.01
☐ 9	Vida Blue	.20	.08	.01
☐ 10	Bobby Bonds	.30	.12	.01
☐ 11	Pedro Borbon	.10	.05	.01
☐ 12	Clete Boyer	.20	.08	.01
☐ 13	Gates Brown	.20	.08	.01
☐ 14	Al Bumbry	.10	.05	.01
☐ 15	Sal Butera	.10	.05	.01
☐ 16	Bert Campaneris	.20	.08	.01
☐ 17	Bill Campbell	.10	.05	.01
☐ 18	Bernie Carbo	.10	.05	.01
☐ 19	Dave Cash	.10	.05	.01
☐ 20	Cesar Cedeno	.20	.08	.01
☐ 21	Gene Clines	.10	.05	.01
☐ 22	Dave Collins	.20	.08	.01
☐ 23	Cecil Cooper	.20	.08	.01
☐ 24	Doug Corbett	.10	.05	.01
☐ 25	Al Cowens	.20	.08	.01
☐ 26	Jose Cruz	.20	.08	.01
☐ 27	Mike Cuellar	.20	.08	.01
☐ 28	Pat Dobson	.20	.08	.01
☐ 29	Dick Drago	.10	.05	.01
☐ 30	Dan Driessen	.20	.08	.01
☐ 31	Jamie Easterly	.10	.05	.01
☐ 32	Juan Eichelberger	.10	.05	.01
☐ 33	Dock Ellis	.20	.08	.01
☐ 34	Ed Figueroa	.10	.05	.01
☐ 35	Rollie Fingers	.50	.15	.01
☐ 36	George Foster	.30	.12	.01
☐ 37	Oscar Gamble	.20	.08	.01
☐ 38	Wayne Garland	.10	.05	.01
☐ 39	Wayne Garrett	.10	.05	.01
☐ 40	Ross Grimsley	.10	.05	.01
☐ 41	Jerry Grote	.10	.05	.01
☐ 42	Johnny Grubb	.10	.05	.01
☐ 43	Mario Guerrero	.10	.05	.01
☐ 44	Toby Harrah	.20	.08	.01
☐ 45	Steve Henderson	.10	.05	.01
☐ 46	George Hendrick	.20	.08	.01
☐ 47	Butch Hobson	.10	.05	.01
☐ 48	Roy Howell	.10	.05	.01
☐ 49	Al Hrabosky	.20	.08	.01
☐ 50	Clint Hurdle	.10	.05	.01
☐ 51	Garth Iorg	.10	.05	.01
☐ 52	Tim Ireland	.10	.05	.01
☐ 53	Grant Jackson	.10	.05	.01
☐ 54	Ron Jackson	.10	.05	.01
☐ 55	Ferguson Jenkins	.40	.15	.01
☐ 56	Odell Jones	.10	.05	.01
☐ 57	Mike Kekich	.10	.05	.01
☐ 58	Steve Kemp	.20	.08	.01
☐ 59	Dave Kingman	.30	.12	.01
☐ 60	Bruce Kison	.10	.05	.01
☐ 61	Lee Lacy	.20	.08	.01
☐ 62	Rafael Landestoy	.10	.05	.01
☐ 63	Ken Landreaux	.20	.08	.01
☐ 64	Tito Landrum	.10	.05	.01
☐ 65	Dave LaRoche	.10	.05	.01
☐ 66	Bill Lee	.20	.08	.01
☐ 67	Ron LeFlore	.20	.08	.01
☐ 68	Dennis Leonard	.20	.08	.01
☐ 69	Bill Madlock	.20	.08	.01
☐ 70	Mickey Mahler	.10	.05	.01
☐ 71	Rich Manning	.10	.05	.01
☐ 72	Tippy Martinez	.20	.08	.01
☐ 73	Jon Matlack	.20	.08	.01
☐ 74	Bake McBride	.10	.05	.01
☐ 75	Steve McCatty	.10	.05	.01
☐ 76	Hal McRae	.20	.08	.01
☐ 77	Dan Meyer	.10	.05	.01
☐ 78	Felix Millan	.10	.05	.01
☐ 79	Paul Mirabella	.10	.05	.01
☐ 80	Omar Moreno	.10	.05	.01
☐ 81	Jim Morrison	.10	.05	.01
☐ 82	Graig Nettles	.20	.08	.01
☐ 83	Al Oliver	.20	.08	.01
☐ 84	Amos Otis	.20	.08	.01
☐ 85	Tom Paciorek	.10	.05	.01
☐ 86	Lowell Palmer	.10	.05	.01
☐ 87	Pat Putnam	.10	.05	.01
☐ 88	Lenny Randle	.10	.05	.01
☐ 89	Ken Reitz	.10	.05	.01
☐ 90	Gene Richards	.10	.05	.01
☐ 91	Mickey Rivers	.20	.08	.01
☐ 92	Leon Roberts	.10	.05	.01
☐ 93	Joe Sambito	.10	.05	.01
☐ 94	Rodney Scott	.10	.05	.01
☐ 95	Bob Shirley	.10	.05	.01
☐ 96	Jim Slaton	.10	.05	.01
☐ 97	Elias Sosa	.10	.05	.01
☐ 98	Fred Stanley	.10	.05	.01
☐ 99	Bill Stein	.10	.05	.01
☐ 100	Rennie Stennett	.10	.05	.01

		NRMT	VG-E	GOOD
☐ 101	Sammy Stewart	.10	.05	.01
☐ 102	Tim Stoddard	.10	.05	.01
☐ 103	Champ Summers	.10	.05	.01
☐ 104	Derrel Thomas	.10	.05	.01
☐ 105	Luis Tiant	.30	.12	.01
☐ 106	Bobby Tolan	.20	.08	.01
☐ 107	Bill Travers	.10	.05	.01
☐ 108	Tom Underwood	.10	.05	.01
☐ 109	Ricks Waits	.10	.05	.01
☐ 110	Ron Washington	.10	.05	.01
☐ 111	U.L. Washington	.10	.05	.01
☐ 112	Earl Weaver MG	.30	.12	.01
☐ 113	Jerry White	.10	.05	.01
☐ 114	Milt Wilcox	.10	.05	.01
☐ 115	Dick Williams MG	.20	.08	.01
☐ 116	Walt Williams	.10	.05	.01
☐ 117	Rick Wise	.10	.05	.01
☐ 118	Favorite Suns	.15	.07	.01
	Luis Tiant			
	Cesar Cedeno			
☐ 119	Home Run Legends	.15	.07	.01
	George Foster			
	Bobby Bonds			
☐ 120	Sunshine Skippers	.10	.05	.01
	Earl Weaver			
	Dick Williams			
☐ 121	Checklist 1-120	.10	.02	.01
	(unnumbered)			

		NRMT	VG-E	GOOD
☐ 22	Bob Kuzava	25.00	12.50	2.50
☐ 23	Dizzy Trout	25.00	12.50	2.50
☐ 24	Sherman Lollar	25.00	12.50	2.50
☐ 25	Sam Mele	25.00	12.50	2.50
☐ 26	Chico Carrasquel	25.00	12.50	2.50
☐ 27	Andy Pafko	25.00	12.50	2.50
☐ 28	Harry Brecheen	25.00	12.50	2.50
☐ 29	Granville Hamner	25.00	12.50	2.50
☐ 30	Enos Slaughter	90.00	45.00	9.00
☐ 31	Lou Brissie	25.00	12.50	2.50
☐ 32	Bob Elliott	30.00	15.00	3.00
☐ 33	Don Lenhardt	25.00	12.50	2.50
☐ 34	Earl Torgeson	25.00	12.50	2.50
☐ 35	Tommy Byrne	25.00	12.50	2.50
☐ 36	Cliff Fannin	25.00	12.50	2.50
☐ 37	Bobby Doerr	75.00	37.50	7.50
☐ 38	Irv Noren	25.00	12.50	2.50
☐ 39	Ed Lopat	40.00	20.00	4.00
☐ 40	Vic Wertz	30.00	15.00	3.00
☐ 41	Johnny Schmitz	25.00	12.50	2.50
☐ 42	Bruce Edwards	25.00	12.50	2.50
☐ 43	Willie Jones	25.00	12.50	2.50
☐ 44	Johnny Wyrostek	25.00	12.50	2.50
☐ 45	Billy Pierce	35.00	17.50	3.50
☐ 46	Gerry Priddy	25.00	12.50	2.50
☐ 47	Herman Wehmeier	25.00	12.50	2.50
☐ 48	Billy Cox	30.00	15.00	3.00
☐ 49	Henry Sauer	30.00	15.00	3.00
☐ 50	Johnny Mize	100.00	50.00	10.00
☐ 51	Eddie Waitkus	25.00	12.50	2.50
☐ 52	Sam Chapman	25.00	12.50	2.50

1951 Topps Blue Backs

The cards in this 52-card set measure 2" by 2 5/8". The 1951 Topps series of blue backed baseball cards could be used to play a baseball game by shuffling the cards and drawing them from a pile. These cards were marketed with a piece of caramel candy, which often melted or was squashed in such a way as to damage the card and wrapper (despite the fact that a paper shield was inserted between candy and card). Blue Backs are more difficult to obtain than the similarly styled Red Backs. The set is denoted on the cards as "Set B" and the Red Back set is correspondingly Set A. Appropriately leading off the set is Eddie Yost.

		NRMT	VG-E	GOOD
COMPLETE SET (52)		1650.00	800.00	200.00
COMMON PLAYER (1-52)		25.00	12.50	2.50
☐ 1	Eddie Yost	25.00	12.50	2.50
☐ 2	Hank Majeski	25.00	12.50	2.50
☐ 3	Richie Ashburn	65.00	32.50	6.50
☐ 4	Del Ennis	25.00	12.50	2.50
☐ 5	Johnny Pesky	25.00	12.50	2.50
☐ 6	Al Schoendienst	75.00	37.50	7.50
☐ 7	Gerry Staley	25.00	12.50	2.50
☐ 8	Dick Sisler	25.00	12.50	2.50
☐ 9	Johnny Sain	35.00	17.50	3.50
☐ 10	Joe Page	30.00	15.00	3.00
☐ 11	Johnny Groth	25.00	12.50	2.50
☐ 12	Sam Jethroe	25.00	12.50	2.50
☐ 13	Mickey Vernon	30.00	15.00	3.00
☐ 14	Red Munger	25.00	12.50	2.50
☐ 15	Eddie Joost	25.00	12.50	2.50
☐ 16	Murry Dickson	25.00	12.50	2.50
☐ 17	Roy Smalley	25.00	12.50	2.50
☐ 18	Ned Garver	25.00	12.50	2.50
☐ 19	Phil Masi	25.00	12.50	2.50
☐ 20	Ralph Branca	35.00	17.50	3.50
☐ 21	Billy Johnson	25.00	12.50	2.50

1951 Topps Red Backs

The cards in this 52-card set measure 2" by 2 5/8". The 1951 Topps Red Back set is identical in style to the Blue Back set of the same year. The cards have rounded corners and were designed to be used as a baseball game. Zernial, number 36, is listed with either the White Sox or Athletics, and Holmes, number 52, with either the Braves or Hartford. The set is denoted on the cards as "Set A" and the Blue Back set is correspondingly Set B.

		NRMT	VG-E	GOOD
COMPLETE SET (54)		550.00	250.00	50.00
COMMON PLAYER (1-52)		5.00	2.50	.50
☐ 1	Yogi Berra	75.00	20.00	4.00
☐ 2	Sid Gordon	5.00	2.50	.50
☐ 3	Ferris Fain	6.00	3.00	.60
☐ 4	Vern Stephens	6.00	3.00	.60
☐ 5	Phil Rizzuto	20.00	10.00	2.00
☐ 6	Allie Reynolds	9.00	4.50	.90
☐ 7	Howie Pollet	5.00	2.50	.50
☐ 8	Early Wynn	15.00	7.50	1.50
☐ 9	Roy Sievers	6.00	3.00	.60
☐ 10	Mel Parnell	6.00	3.00	.60
☐ 11	Gene Hermanski	5.00	2.50	.50
☐ 12	Jim Hegan	5.00	2.50	.50
☐ 13	Dale Mitchell	5.00	2.50	.50
☐ 14	Wayne Terwilliger	5.00	2.50	.50
☐ 15	Ralph Kiner	20.00	10.00	2.00
☐ 16	Preacher Roe	7.50	3.75	.75
☐ 17	Dave (Gus) Bell	7.50	3.75	.75
☐ 18	Gerry Coleman	7.50	3.75	.75
☐ 19	Dick Kokos	5.00	2.50	.50
☐ 20	Dom DiMaggio	7.50	3.75	.75
☐ 21	Larry Jansen	5.00	2.50	.50
☐ 22	Bob Feller	30.00	15.00	3.00
☐ 23	Ray Boone	6.00	3.00	.60

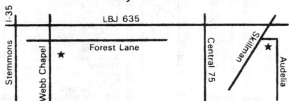

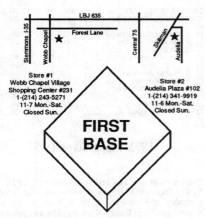

Store #1
Webb Chapel Village
Shopping Center #231
1-(214) 243-5271
11-7 Mon.-Sat.
Closed Sun.

Store #2
Audelia Plaza #102
1-(214) 341-9919
11-6 Mon.-Sat.
Closed Sun.

FIRST BASE

BASEBALL CARD LOTS
Our Choice - No Superstars

1959 Topps 10 diff (f-vg)	$10.00
1960 Topps 10 diff (f-vg)	7.50
1961 Topps 10 diff (f-vg)	7.50
1962 Topps 10 diff (f-vg)	7.00
1963 Topps 10 diff (f-vg)	6.50
1964 Topps 10 diff (f-vg)	5.00
1965 Topps 10 diff (f-vg)	5.00
1966 Topps 10 diff (f-vg)	3.50
1967 Topps 10 diff (f-vg)	3.50
1968 Topps 10 diff (f-vg)	3.00
1969 Topps 25 diff (f-vg)	5.95
1970 Topps 25 diff (f-vg)	3.95
1971 Topps 25 diff (f-vg)	3.95
1972 Topps 25 diff (f-vg)	3.95
1973 Topps 25 diff (f-vg)	3.95
1974 Topps 25 diff (f-vg)	3.95
1975 Topps 25 diff (f-vg)	3.95
1976 Topps 25 diff (f-vg)	2.95
1977 Topps 25 diff (f-vg)	2.95
1978 Topps 50 diff (f-vg)	3.95
1979 Topps 50 diff (f-vg)	2.95
1980 Topps 50 diff (f-vg)	2.95
1981 Donruss 50 diff (ex-m)	2.50
1981 Fleer 50 diff (ex-m)	2.50
1982 Fleer 50 diff (ex-m)	2.50

FOOTBALL CARD LOTS
Our Choice - No Superstars

1969 Topps 25 diff (f-vg)	$6.95
1970 Topps 25 diff (f-vg)	5.95
1971 Topps 25 diff (f-vg)	4.95
1972 Topps 25 diff (f-vg)	4.95
1973 Topps 25 diff (f-vg)	4.95
1974 Topps 25 diff (f-vg)	2.50
1975 Topps 25 diff (f-vg)	2.50
1976 Topps 25 diff (f-vg)	2.50
1977 Topps 25 diff (f-vg)	2.00
1978 Topps 50 diff (f-vg)	3.00
1979 Topps 50 diff (f-vg)	3.00
1980 Topps 50 diff (f-vg)	2.50

ORDERING INSTRUCTIONS

Offers expire March 1991 while supply lasts.
Please include $3.00 per order for postage
and handling.

Send orders to:

FIRST BASE
231 Webb Chapel Village
Dallas, Texas 75229
(214) 243-5271

Our current price lists sent free with orders.
To receive price lists without ordering send
$1.00 or a **large** self addressed stamped (65¢
in stamps) envelope to the above address.

SPECIAL OFFERS

#1: Type Set: One card from each year of
Topps baseball 1952 through 1989, our
choice of cards, Good to EX, 38 cards for
$39.95.

#2: 1987 Fleer Baseball Record Setters -
Complete Set of 44 cards — $4.00.

#3: Robert Redford Poster as "The Natural" -
$6.95.

#4: 1983 Affiliated Foods Texas Rangers -
Complete Set of 28 — $5.00.
Uncut Poster (All 28 cards) — $7.50

#5: 1982 Topps Baseball Stickers (48 Diff.)
— $2.50.

#6: 1989 Score "A Year to Remember" Trivia
Cards. Complete Set of 56 — $3.95.

#7: 1985 Circle K All-Time Home Run
Kings. Complete Set of 33 — $7.95.

#8: 1982 K-Mart Baseball Set of 33 — $2.50.

#9: 50 Diff. Basketball cards - our choice —
$5.00.

#10: Super Bowl XX Game Program —
$8.00.

#11: 1986 McDonalds Dallas Cowboys
Football Card Set of 25 with Herschel
Walker — $9.95.

#12: 1986 McDonalds NFL All-Stars
Football Card Set of 24 — $3.95.

#13: Dallas Cowboys Police/Safety Sets:
1979 (15) — $14.95, 1980 (14) — $9.95,
1981 (14) — $9.95, 1983 (28) — $9.95.

#14: Dallas Cowboys Media Guides (not
issued to the public) 1989 edition $5.00,
1988 edition $5.00, 1987 edition $5.00,
1986 edition $7.50, 1985 edition $7.50.

#15: 1987 Texas Rangers Surf Book (shows
pictures of all Rangers cards) — $7.95.

		NRMT	VG-E	GOOD
☐ 24	Hank Bauer	9.00	4.50	.90
☐ 25	Cliff Chambers	5.00	2.50	.50
☐ 26	Luke Easter	5.00	2.50	.50
☐ 27	Wally Westlake	5.00	2.50	.50
☐ 28	Elmer Valo	5.00	2.50	.50
☐ 29	Bob Kennedy	5.00	2.50	.50
☐ 30	Warren Spahn	25.00	12.50	2.50
☐ 31	Gil Hodges	20.00	10.00	2.00
☐ 32	Henry Thompson	6.00	3.00	.60
☐ 33	William Werle	5.00	2.50	.50
☐ 34	Grady Hatton	5.00	2.50	.50
☐ 35	Al Rosen	9.00	4.50	.90
☐ 36A	Gus Zernial (Chicago)	20.00	10.00	2.00
☐ 36B	Gus Zernial (Philadelphia)	15.00	7.50	1.50
☐ 37	Wes Westrum	5.00	2.50	.50
☐ 38	Duke Snider	50.00	25.00	5.00
☐ 39	Ted Kluszewski	9.00	4.50	.90
☐ 40	Mike Garcia	6.00	3.00	.60
☐ 41	Whitey Lockman	6.00	3.00	.60
☐ 42	Ray Scarborough	5.00	2.50	.50
☐ 43	Maurice McDermott	5.00	2.50	.50
☐ 44	Sid Hudson	5.00	2.50	.50
☐ 45	Andy Seminick	5.00	2.50	.50
☐ 46	Billy Goodman	6.00	3.00	.60
☐ 47	Tommy Glaviano	5.00	2.50	.50
☐ 48	Eddie Stanky	7.50	3.75	.75
☐ 49	Al Zarilla	5.00	2.50	.50
☐ 50	Monte Irvin	30.00	15.00	3.00
☐ 51	Eddie Robinson	5.00	2.50	.50
☐ 52A	Tommy Holmes (Boston)	20.00	10.00	2.00
☐ 52B	Tommy Holmes (Hartford)	15.00	7.50	1.50

1951 Topps Teams

The cards in this 9-card set measure 2 1/16" by 5 1/4". These unnumbered team cards issued by Topps in 1951 carry black and white photographs framed by a yellow border. They are found with or without "1950" printed in the name panel before the team name (no difference in value for either variety). These cards were issued in the same 5 cent wrapper as the Connie Mack and Current All Stars. They have been assigned reference numbers in the checklist alphabetically by team city and name.

		NRMT	VG-E	GOOD
COMPLETE SET (9)		1500.00	700.00	175.00
COMMON TEAM (1-9)		125.00	60.00	12.50
☐ 1	Boston Red Sox	250.00	125.00	25.00
☐ 2	Brooklyn Dodgers	200.00	100.00	20.00
☐ 3	Chicago White Sox	175.00	85.00	18.00
☐ 4	Cincinnati Reds	150.00	75.00	15.00
☐ 5	New York Giants	175.00	85.00	18.00
☐ 6	Philadelphia Athletics	125.00	60.00	12.50
☐ 7	Philadelphia Phillies	150.00	75.00	15.00
☐ 8	St. Louis Cardinals	250.00	125.00	25.00
☐ 9	Washington Senators	125.00	60.00	12.50

1951 Topps Connie Mack

The cards in this 11-card set measure 2 1/16" by 5 1/4". The series of die-cut cards which comprise the set entitled Connie Mack All-Stars was one of Topps' most distinctive and fragile card designs. Printed on thin cardboard, these elegant cards were protected in the wrapper by panels of accompanying Red Backs, but once removed were easily damaged (after all, they were intended to be folded and used as toy figures). Cards without tops have a value less than one-half of that listed below. The cards are unnumbered and are listed below in alphabetical order.

		NRMT	VG-E	GOOD
COMPLETE SET (11)		4500.00	2250.00	500.00
COMMON PLAYER (1-11)		125.00	60.00	12.50
☐ 1	Grover C. Alexander	350.00	175.00	35.00
☐ 2	Mickey Cochrane	250.00	125.00	25.00
☐ 3	Ed Collins	125.00	60.00	12.50
☐ 4	Jimmy Collins	125.00	60.00	12.50
☐ 5	Lou Gehrig	1000.00	500.00	100.00
☐ 6	Walter Johnson	500.00	250.00	50.00
☐ 7	Connie Mack	250.00	125.00	25.00
☐ 8	Christy Mathewson	250.00	125.00	25.00
☐ 9	Babe Ruth	1500.00	750.00	150.00
☐ 10	Tris Speaker	125.00	60.00	12.50
☐ 11	Honus Wagner	250.00	125.00	25.00

1951 Topps Current AS

The cards in this 11-card set measure 2 1/16" by 5 1/4". The 1951 Topps Current All-Star series is probably the rarest of all legitimate, nationally issued, post war baseball issues. The set price listed below does not include the prices for the cards of Konstanty, Roberts and Stanky, which likely never were released to the public in gum packs. These three cards (SP in the checklist below) were probably obtained directly from the company and exist in extremely limited numbers. As with the Connie Mack set, cards without the die-cut background are worth half of the value listed below. The cards are unnumbered and are listed below in alphabetical order.

		NRMT	VG-E	GOOD
COMPLETE SET (8)		3300.00	1650.00	400.00
COMMON PLAYER (1-11)		150.00	75.00	15.00
☐ 1	Yogi Berra	900.00	450.00	90.00
☐ 2	Larry Doby	200.00	100.00	20.00
☐ 3	Walt Dropo	250.00	125.00	25.00
☐ 4	Hoot Evers	150.00	75.00	15.00
☐ 5	George Kell	450.00	225.00	45.00
☐ 6	Ralph Kiner	500.00	250.00	50.00
☐ 7	Jim Konstanty SP	10000.00	5000.00	1000.00
☐ 8	Bob Lemon	450.00	225.00	45.00
☐ 9	Phil Rizzuto	450.00	225.00	45.00
☐ 10	Robin Roberts SP	12000.00	6000.00	1200.00
☐ 11	Eddie Stanky SP	10000.00	5000.00	1000.00

1952 Topps

The cards in this 407-card set measure 2 5/8" by 3 3/4". The 1952 Topps set is Topps' first truly major set. Card numbers 1 to 80 were issued with red or black backs, both of which are less plentiful than card numbers 81 to 250. In fact the first series is considered the most difficult with respect to finding Mint condition cards. Card number 48 (Joe Page)

and number 49 (Johnny Sain) can be found with each other's write-up on their back. Card numbers 251 to 310 are somewhat scarce and numbers 311 to 407 are quite scarce. Cards 281-300 were single printed compared to the other cards in the next to last series. Cards 311-313 were double printed on the last high number printing sheet. The key card in the set is obviously Mickey Mantle #311, Mickey's first of many Topps cards. Although rarely seen, there exists a salesman's sample panel of three cards containing the fronts of Bob Mahoney, Robin Roberts, and Sid Hudson with ad information on the back.

		NRMT	VG-E	GOOD
	COMPLETE SET (407)	42000.	18000.	6000.
	COMMON PLAYER (1-80)	50.00	25.00	5.00
	COMMON PLAYER (81-250)	25.00	12.50	2.50
	COMMON PLAYER (251-280)	40.00	20.00	4.00
	COMMON PLAYER (281-300)	50.00	25.00	5.00
	COMMON PLAYER (301-310)	40.00	20.00	4.00
	COMMON PLAYER (311-407)	150.00	75.00	15.00
☐ 1	Andy Pafko	1200.00	75.00	10.00
☐ 2	Pete Runnels	55.00	27.50	5.50
☐ 3	Hank Thompson	55.00	27.50	5.50
☐ 4	Don Lenhardt	50.00	25.00	5.00
☐ 5	Larry Jansen	50.00	25.00	5.00
☐ 6	Grady Hatton	50.00	25.00	5.00
☐ 7	Wayne Terwilliger	50.00	25.00	5.00
☐ 8	Fred Marsh	50.00	25.00	5.00
☐ 9	Robert Hogue	50.00	25.00	5.00
☐ 10	Al Rosen	70.00	35.00	7.00
☐ 11	Phil Rizzuto	150.00	75.00	15.00
☐ 12	Romanus Basgall	50.00	25.00	5.00
☐ 13	Johnny Wyrostek	50.00	25.00	5.00
☐ 14	Bob Elliott	55.00	27.50	5.50
☐ 15	Johnny Pesky	55.00	27.50	5.50
☐ 16	Gene Hermanski	50.00	25.00	5.00
☐ 17	Jim Hegan	55.00	27.50	5.50
☐ 18	Merrill Combs	50.00	25.00	5.00
☐ 19	Johnny Bucha	50.00	25.00	5.00
☐ 20	Billy Loes	90.00	45.00	9.00
☐ 21	Ferris Fain	55.00	27.50	5.50
☐ 22	Dom DiMaggio	75.00	37.50	7.50
☐ 23	Billy Goodman	55.00	27.50	5.50
☐ 24	Luke Easter	55.00	27.50	5.50
☐ 25	Johnny Groth	50.00	25.00	5.00
☐ 26	Monte Irvin	100.00	50.00	10.00
☐ 27	Sam Jethroe	50.00	25.00	5.00
☐ 28	Jerry Priddy	50.00	25.00	5.00
☐ 29	Ted Kluszewski	70.00	35.00	7.00
☐ 30	Mel Parnell	55.00	27.50	5.50
☐ 31	Gus Zernial	60.00	30.00	6.00
☐ 32	Eddie Robinson	50.00	25.00	5.00
☐ 33	Warren Spahn	175.00	85.00	18.00
☐ 34	Elmer Valo	50.00	25.00	5.00
☐ 35	Hank Sauer	65.00	32.50	6.50
☐ 36	Gil Hodges	125.00	60.00	12.50
☐ 37	Duke Snider	250.00	125.00	25.00
☐ 38	Wally Westlake	50.00	25.00	5.00
☐ 39	Dizzy Trout	55.00	27.50	5.50
☐ 40	Irv Noren	50.00	25.00	5.00
☐ 41	Bob Wellman	50.00	25.00	5.00
☐ 42	Lou Kretlow	50.00	25.00	5.00
☐ 43	Ray Scarborough	50.00	25.00	5.00
☐ 44	Con Dempsey	50.00	25.00	5.00
☐ 45	Eddie Joost	50.00	25.00	5.00
☐ 46	Gordon Goldsberry	50.00	25.00	5.00
☐ 47	Willie Jones	50.00	25.00	5.00
☐ 48A	Joe Page COR	65.00	32.50	6.50
☐ 48B	Joe Page ERR	300.00	150.00	30.00
	(bio for Sain)			
☐ 49A	Johnny Sain COR	80.00	40.00	8.00
☐ 49B	Johnny Sain ERR	300.00	150.00	30.00
	(bio for Page)			
☐ 50	Marv Rickert	50.00	25.00	5.00
☐ 51	Jim Russell	50.00	25.00	5.00
☐ 52	Don Mueller	60.00	30.00	6.00
☐ 53	Chris Van Cuyk	50.00	25.00	5.00
☐ 54	Leo Kiely	50.00	25.00	5.00
☐ 55	Ray Boone	55.00	27.50	5.50
☐ 56	Tommy Glaviano	50.00	25.00	5.00
☐ 57	Ed Lopat	90.00	45.00	9.00
☐ 58	Bob Mahoney	50.00	25.00	5.00
☐ 59	Robin Roberts	125.00	60.00	12.50
☐ 60	Sid Hudson	50.00	25.00	5.00
☐ 61	Tookie Gilbert	50.00	25.00	5.00
☐ 62	Chuck Stobbs	50.00	25.00	5.00
☐ 63	Howie Pollet	50.00	25.00	5.00
☐ 64	Roy Sievers	55.00	27.50	5.50
☐ 65	Enos Slaughter	125.00	60.00	12.50
☐ 66	Preacher Roe	90.00	45.00	9.00
☐ 67	Allie Reynolds	90.00	45.00	9.00
☐ 68	Cliff Chambers	50.00	25.00	5.00
☐ 69	Virgil Stallcup	50.00	25.00	5.00
☐ 70	Al Zarilla	50.00	25.00	5.00
☐ 71	Tom Upton	50.00	25.00	5.00
☐ 72	Karl Olson	50.00	25.00	5.00
☐ 73	Bill Werle	50.00	25.00	5.00
☐ 74	Andy Hansen	50.00	25.00	5.00
☐ 75	Wes Westrum	50.00	25.00	5.00
☐ 76	Eddie Stanky	60.00	30.00	6.00
☐ 77	Bob Kennedy	55.00	27.50	5.50
☐ 78	Ellis Kinder	50.00	25.00	5.00
☐ 79	Jerald Staley	50.00	25.00	5.00
☐ 80	Herman Wehmeier	50.00	25.00	5.00
☐ 81	Vernon Law	30.00	15.00	3.00
☐ 82	Duane Pillette	25.00	12.50	2.50
☐ 83	Billy Johnson	25.00	12.50	2.50
☐ 84	Vern Stephens	30.00	15.00	3.00
☐ 85	Bob Kuzava	25.00	12.50	2.50
☐ 86	Ted Gray	25.00	12.50	2.50
☐ 87	Dale Coogan	25.00	12.50	2.50
☐ 88	Bob Feller	125.00	60.00	12.50
☐ 89	Johnny Lipon	25.00	12.50	2.50
☐ 90	Mickey Grasso	25.00	12.50	2.50
☐ 91	Red Schoendienst	65.00	32.50	6.50
☐ 92	Dale Mitchell	30.00	15.00	3.00
☐ 93	Al Sima	25.00	12.50	2.50
☐ 94	Sam Mele	25.00	12.50	2.50
☐ 95	Ken Holcombe	25.00	12.50	2.50
☐ 96	Willard Marshall	25.00	12.50	2.50
☐ 97	Earl Torgeson	25.00	12.50	2.50
☐ 98	Billy Pierce	30.00	15.00	3.00
☐ 99	Gene Woodling	45.00	22.50	4.50
☐ 100	Del Rice	25.00	12.50	2.50
☐ 101	Max Lanier	25.00	12.50	2.50
☐ 102	Bill Kennedy	25.00	12.50	2.50
☐ 103	Cliff Mapes	25.00	12.50	2.50
☐ 104	Don Kolloway	25.00	12.50	2.50
☐ 105	Johnny Pramesa	25.00	12.50	2.50
☐ 106	Mickey Vernon	30.00	15.00	3.00
☐ 107	Connie Ryan	25.00	12.50	2.50
☐ 108	Jim Konstanty	30.00	15.00	3.00
☐ 109	Ted Wilks	25.00	12.50	2.50
☐ 110	Dutch Leonard	25.00	12.50	2.50
☐ 111	Peanuts Lowrey	25.00	12.50	2.50
☐ 112	Hank Majeski	25.00	12.50	2.50
☐ 113	Dick Sisler	25.00	12.50	2.50
☐ 114	Willard Ramsdell	25.00	12.50	2.50
☐ 115	Red Munger	25.00	12.50	2.50
☐ 116	Carl Scheib	25.00	12.50	2.50
☐ 117	Sherm Lollar	30.00	15.00	3.00
☐ 118	Ken Raffensberger	25.00	12.50	2.50
☐ 119	Mickey McDermott	25.00	12.50	2.50
☐ 120	Bob Chakales	25.00	12.50	2.50
☐ 121	Gus Niarhos	25.00	12.50	2.50
☐ 122	Jackie Jensen	65.00	32.50	6.50
☐ 123	Eddie Yost	25.00	12.50	2.50
☐ 124	Monte Kennedy	25.00	12.50	2.50
☐ 125	Bill Rigney	25.00	12.50	2.50
☐ 126	Fred Hutchinson	30.00	15.00	3.00
☐ 127	Paul Minner	25.00	12.50	2.50
☐ 128	Don Bollweg	25.00	12.50	2.50
☐ 129	Johnny Mize	75.00	37.50	7.50
☐ 130	Sheldon Jones	25.00	12.50	2.50
☐ 131	Morrie Martin	25.00	12.50	2.50
☐ 132	Clyde Klutz	25.00	12.50	2.50
☐ 133	Al Widmar	25.00	12.50	2.50
☐ 134	Joe Tipton	25.00	12.50	2.50
☐ 135	Dixie Howell	25.00	12.50	2.50
☐ 136	Johnny Schmitz	25.00	12.50	2.50
☐ 137	Roy McMillan	25.00	12.50	2.50
☐ 138	Bill MacDonald	25.00	12.50	2.50
☐ 139	Ken Wood	25.00	12.50	2.50
☐ 140	Johnny Antonelli	30.00	15.00	3.00
☐ 141	Clint Hartung	25.00	12.50	2.50
☐ 142	Harry Perkowski	25.00	12.50	2.50
☐ 143	Les Moss	25.00	12.50	2.50
☐ 144	Ed Blake	25.00	12.50	2.50
☐ 145	Joe Haynes	25.00	12.50	2.50
☐ 146	Frank House	25.00	12.50	2.50
☐ 147	Bob Young	25.00	12.50	2.50
☐ 148	Johnny Klippstein	25.00	12.50	2.50
☐ 149	Dick Kryhoski	25.00	12.50	2.50
☐ 150	Ted Beard	25.00	12.50	2.50
☐ 151	Wally Post	30.00	15.00	3.00
☐ 152	Al Evans	25.00	12.50	2.50
☐ 153	Bob Rush	25.00	12.50	2.50
☐ 154	Joe Muir	25.00	12.50	2.50
☐ 155	Frank Overmire	25.00	12.50	2.50
☐ 156	Frank Hiller	25.00	12.50	2.50
☐ 157	Bob Usher	25.00	12.50	2.50
☐ 158	Eddie Waitkus	25.00	12.50	2.50
☐ 159	Saul Rogovin	25.00	12.50	2.50

☐ 160	Owen Friend	25.00	12.50	2.50	☐ 255	Clyde Vollmer	40.00	20.00	4.00
☐ 161	Bud Byerly	25.00	12.50	2.50	☐ 256	Pete Suder	40.00	20.00	4.00
☐ 162	Del Crandall	30.00	15.00	3.00	☐ 257	Bobby Avila	45.00	22.50	4.50
☐ 163	Stan Rojek	25.00	12.50	2.50	☐ 258	Steve Gromek	40.00	20.00	4.00
☐ 164	Walt Dubiel	25.00	12.50	2.50	☐ 259	Bob Addis	40.00	20.00	4.00
☐ 165	Eddie Kazak	25.00	12.50	2.50	☐ 260	Pete Castiglione	40.00	20.00	4.00
☐ 166	Paul LaPalme	25.00	12.50	2.50	☐ 261	Willie Mays	1100.00	450.00	100.00
☐ 167	Bill Howerton	25.00	12.50	2.50	☐ 262	Virgil Trucks	45.00	22.50	4.50
☐ 168	Charlie Silvera	30.00	15.00	3.00	☐ 263	Harry Brecheen	45.00	22.50	4.50
☐ 169	Howie Judson	25.00	12.50	2.50	☐ 264	Roy Hartsfield	40.00	20.00	4.00
☐ 170	Gus Bell	30.00	15.00	3.00	☐ 265	Chuck Diering	40.00	20.00	4.00
☐ 171	Ed Erautt	25.00	12.50	2.50	☐ 266	Murry Dickson	40.00	20.00	4.00
☐ 172	Eddie Miksis	25.00	12.50	2.50	☐ 267	Sid Gordon	40.00	20.00	4.00
☐ 173	Roy Smalley	25.00	12.50	2.50	☐ 268	Bob Lemon	150.00	75.00	15.00
☐ 174	Clarence Marshall	25.00	12.50	2.50	☐ 269	Willard Nixon	40.00	20.00	4.00
☐ 175	Billy Martin	300.00	150.00	30.00	☐ 270	Lou Brissie	40.00	20.00	4.00
☐ 176	Hank Edwards	25.00	12.50	2.50	☐ 271	Jim Delsing	40.00	20.00	4.00
☐ 177	Bill Wight	25.00	12.50	2.50	☐ 272	Mike Garcia	50.00	25.00	5.00
☐ 178	Cass Michaels	25.00	12.50	2.50	☐ 273	Erv Palica	40.00	20.00	4.00
☐ 179	Frank Smith	25.00	12.50	2.50	☐ 274	Ralph Branca	75.00	37.50	7.50
☐ 180	Charley Maxwell	30.00	15.00	3.00	☐ 275	Pat Mullin	40.00	20.00	4.00
☐ 181	Bob Swift	25.00	12.50	2.50	☐ 276	Jim Wilson	40.00	20.00	4.00
☐ 182	Billy Hitchcock	25.00	12.50	2.50	☐ 277	Early Wynn	150.00	75.00	15.00
☐ 183	Erv Dusak	25.00	12.50	2.50	☐ 278	Allie Clark	40.00	20.00	4.00
☐ 184	Bob Ramazotti	25.00	12.50	2.50	☐ 279	Eddie Stewart	40.00	20.00	4.00
☐ 185	Bill Nicholson	25.00	12.50	2.50	☐ 280	Cloyd Boyer	45.00	22.50	4.50
☐ 186	Walt Masterson	25.00	12.50	2.50	☐ 281	Tommy Brown SP	50.00	25.00	5.00
☐ 187	Bob Miller	25.00	12.50	2.50	☐ 282	Birdie Tebbetts SP	55.00	27.50	5.50
☐ 188	Clarence Podbielan	25.00	12.50	2.50	☐ 283	Phil Masi SP	50.00	25.00	5.00
☐ 189	Pete Reiser	35.00	17.50	3.50	☐ 284	Hank Arft SP	50.00	25.00	5.00
☐ 190	Don Johnson	25.00	12.50	2.50	☐ 285	Cliff Fannin SP	50.00	25.00	5.00
☐ 191	Yogi Berra	350.00	175.00	35.00	☐ 286	Joe DeMaestri SP	50.00	25.00	5.00
☐ 192	Myron Ginsberg	25.00	12.50	2.50	☐ 287	Steve Bilko SP	50.00	25.00	5.00
☐ 193	Harry Simpson	25.00	12.50	2.50	☐ 288	Chet Nichols SP	50.00	25.00	5.00
☐ 194	Joe Hatton	25.00	12.50	2.50	☐ 289	Tommy Holmes SP	60.00	30.00	6.00
☐ 195	Minnie Minoso	60.00	30.00	6.00	☐ 290	Joe Astroth SP	50.00	25.00	5.00
☐ 196	Solly Hemus	25.00	12.50	2.50	☐ 291	Gil Coan SP	50.00	25.00	5.00
☐ 197	George Strickland	25.00	12.50	2.50	☐ 292	Floyd Baker SP	50.00	25.00	5.00
☐ 198	Phil Haugstad	25.00	12.50	2.50	☐ 293	Sibby Sisti SP	50.00	25.00	5.00
☐ 199	George Zuverink	25.00	12.50	2.50	☐ 294	Walker Cooper SP	50.00	25.00	5.00
☐ 200	Ralph Houk	60.00	30.00	6.00	☐ 295	Phil Cavarretta SP	60.00	30.00	6.00
☐ 201	Alex Kellner	25.00	12.50	2.50	☐ 296	Red Rolfe SP	60.00	30.00	6.00
☐ 202	Joe Collins	35.00	17.50	3.50	☐ 297	Andy Seminick SP	50.00	25.00	5.00
☐ 203	Curt Simmons	30.00	15.00	3.00	☐ 298	Bob Ross SP	50.00	25.00	5.00
☐ 204	Ron Northey	25.00	12.50	2.50	☐ 299	Ray Murray SP	50.00	25.00	5.00
☐ 205	Clyde King	25.00	12.50	2.50	☐ 300	Barney McCosky SP	55.00	27.50	5.50
☐ 206	Joe Ostrowski	25.00	12.50	2.50	☐ 301	Bob Porterfield	40.00	20.00	4.00
☐ 207	Mickey Harris	25.00	12.50	2.50	☐ 302	Max Surkont	40.00	20.00	4.00
☐ 208	Marlin Stuart	25.00	12.50	2.50	☐ 303	Harry Dorish	40.00	20.00	4.00
☐ 209	Howie Fox	25.00	12.50	2.50	☐ 304	Sam Dente	40.00	20.00	4.00
☐ 210	Dick Fowler	25.00	12.50	2.50	☐ 305	Paul Richards	50.00	25.00	5.00
☐ 211	Ray Coleman	25.00	12.50	2.50	☐ 306	Lou Sleater	40.00	20.00	4.00
☐ 212	Ned Garver	25.00	12.50	2.50	☐ 307	Frank Campos	40.00	20.00	4.00
☐ 213	Nippy Jones	25.00	12.50	2.50	☐ 308	Luis Aloma	40.00	20.00	4.00
☐ 214	Johnny Hopp	30.00	15.00	3.00	☐ 309	Jim Busby	40.00	20.00	4.00
☐ 215	Hank Bauer	40.00	20.00	4.00	☐ 310	George Metkovich	60.00	30.00	6.00
☐ 216	Richie Ashburn	80.00	40.00	8.00	☐ 311	Mickey Mantle DP	6600.00	2500.00	600.00
☐ 217	Snuffy Stirnweiss	30.00	15.00	3.00	☐ 312	Jackie Robinson DP	850.00	425.00	85.00
☐ 218	Clyde McCullough	25.00	12.50	2.50	☐ 313	Bobby Thomson DP	175.00	85.00	18.00
☐ 219	Bobby Shantz	35.00	17.50	3.50	☐ 314	Roy Campanella	1250.00	500.00	150.00
☐ 220	Joe Presko	25.00	12.50	2.50	☐ 315	Leo Durocher	275.00	135.00	27.00
☐ 221	Granny Hamner	25.00	12.50	2.50	☐ 316	Dave Williams	175.00	85.00	18.00
☐ 222	Hoot Evers	25.00	12.50	2.50	☐ 317	Conrado Marrero	150.00	75.00	15.00
☐ 223	Del Ennis	30.00	15.00	3.00	☐ 318	Harold Gregg	150.00	75.00	15.00
☐ 224	Bruce Edwards	25.00	12.50	2.50	☐ 319	Al Walker	150.00	75.00	15.00
☐ 225	Frank Baumholtz	25.00	12.50	2.50	☐ 320	John Rutherford	150.00	75.00	15.00
☐ 226	Dave Philley	25.00	12.50	2.50	☐ 321	Joe Black	225.00	110.00	22.00
☐ 227	Joe Garagiola	80.00	40.00	8.00	☐ 322	Randy Jackson	150.00	75.00	15.00
☐ 228	Al Brazle	25.00	12.50	2.50	☐ 323	Bubba Church	150.00	75.00	15.00
☐ 229	Gene Bearden	25.00	12.50	2.50	☐ 324	Warren Hacker	150.00	75.00	15.00
☐ 230	Matt Batts	25.00	12.50	2.50	☐ 325	Bill Serena	150.00	75.00	15.00
☐ 231	Sam Zoldak	25.00	12.50	2.50	☐ 326	George Shuba	175.00	85.00	18.00
☐ 232	Billy Cox	30.00	15.00	3.00	☐ 327	Al Wilson	150.00	75.00	15.00
☐ 233	Bob Friend	30.00	15.00	3.00	☐ 328	Bob Borkowski	150.00	75.00	15.00
☐ 234	Steve Souchock	25.00	12.50	2.50	☐ 329	Ike Delock	150.00	75.00	15.00
☐ 235	Walt Dropo	30.00	15.00	3.00	☐ 330	Turk Lown	150.00	75.00	15.00
☐ 236	Ed Fitzgerald	25.00	12.50	2.50	☐ 331	Tom Morgan	150.00	75.00	15.00
☐ 237	Jerry Coleman	30.00	15.00	3.00	☐ 332	Anthony Bartirome	150.00	75.00	15.00
☐ 238	Art Houtteman	25.00	12.50	2.50	☐ 333	Pee Wee Reese	650.00	325.00	65.00
☐ 239	Rocky Bridges	25.00	12.50	2.50	☐ 334	Wilmer Mizell	150.00	75.00	15.00
☐ 240	Jack Phillips	25.00	12.50	2.50	☐ 335	Ted Lepcio	150.00	75.00	15.00
☐ 241	Tommy Byrne	25.00	12.50	2.50	☐ 336	Dave Koslo	150.00	75.00	15.00
☐ 242	Tom Poholsky	25.00	12.50	2.50	☐ 337	Jim Hearn	150.00	75.00	15.00
☐ 243	Larry Doby	40.00	20.00	4.00	☐ 338	Sal Yvars	150.00	75.00	15.00
☐ 244	Vic Wertz	30.00	15.00	3.00	☐ 339	Russ Meyer	150.00	75.00	15.00
☐ 245	Sherry Robertson	25.00	12.50	2.50	☐ 340	Bob Hooper	150.00	75.00	15.00
☐ 246	George Kell	65.00	32.50	6.50	☐ 341	Hal Jeffcoat	150.00	75.00	15.00
☐ 247	Randy Gumpert	25.00	12.50	2.50	☐ 342	Clem Labine	175.00	85.00	18.00
☐ 248	Frank Shea	25.00	12.50	2.50	☐ 343	Dick Gernert	150.00	75.00	15.00
☐ 249	Bobby Adams	25.00	12.50	2.50	☐ 344	Ewell Blackwell	175.00	85.00	18.00
☐ 250	Carl Erskine	50.00	25.00	5.00	☐ 345	Sammy White	150.00	75.00	15.00
☐ 251	Chico Carrasquel	40.00	20.00	4.00	☐ 346	George Spencer	150.00	75.00	15.00
☐ 252	Vern Bickford	40.00	20.00	4.00	☐ 347	Joe Adcock	200.00	100.00	20.00
☐ 253	Johnny Berardino	45.00	22.50	4.50	☐ 348	Robert Kelly	150.00	75.00	15.00
☐ 254	Joe Dobson	40.00	20.00	4.00	☐ 349	Bob Cain	150.00	75.00	15.00

		NRMT	VG-E	GOOD
☐ 350	Cal Abrams	150.00	75.00	15.00
☐ 351	Alvin Dark	200.00	100.00	20.00
☐ 352	Karl Drews	150.00	75.00	15.00
☐ 353	Bobby Del Greco	150.00	75.00	15.00
☐ 354	Fred Hatfield	150.00	75.00	15.00
☐ 355	Bobby Morgan	150.00	75.00	15.00
☐ 356	Toby Atwell	150.00	75.00	15.00
☐ 357	Smoky Burgess	175.00	85.00	18.00
☐ 358	John Kucab	150.00	75.00	15.00
☐ 359	Dee Fondy	150.00	75.00	15.00
☐ 360	George Crowe	150.00	75.00	15.00
☐ 361	William Posedel	150.00	75.00	15.00
☐ 362	Ken Heintzelman	150.00	75.00	15.00
☐ 363	Dick Rozek	150.00	75.00	15.00
☐ 364	Clyde Sukeforth	150.00	75.00	15.00
☐ 365	Cookie Lavagetto	150.00	75.00	15.00
☐ 366	Dave Madison	150.00	75.00	15.00
☐ 367	Ben Thorpe	150.00	75.00	15.00
☐ 368	Ed Wright	150.00	75.00	15.00
☐ 369	Dick Groat	250.00	125.00	25.00
☐ 370	Billy Hoeft	150.00	75.00	15.00
☐ 371	Bobby Hofman	150.00	75.00	15.00
☐ 372	Gil McDougald	275.00	135.00	27.00
☐ 373	Jim Turner CO	175.00	85.00	18.00
☐ 374	John Benton	150.00	75.00	15.00
☐ 375	John Merson	150.00	75.00	15.00
☐ 376	Faye Throneberry	150.00	75.00	15.00
☐ 377	Chuck Dressen MG	175.00	85.00	18.00
☐ 378	Leroy Fusselman	150.00	75.00	15.00
☐ 379	Joe Rossi	150.00	75.00	15.00
☐ 380	Clem Koshorek	150.00	75.00	15.00
☐ 381	Milton Stock	150.00	75.00	15.00
☐ 382	Sam Jones	175.00	85.00	18.00
☐ 383	Del Wilber	150.00	75.00	15.00
☐ 384	Frank Crosetti CO	250.00	125.00	25.00
☐ 385	Herman Franks	175.00	85.00	18.00
☐ 386	John Yuhas	150.00	75.00	15.00
☐ 387	Billy Meyer	150.00	75.00	15.00
☐ 388	Bob Chipman	150.00	75.00	15.00
☐ 389	Ben Wade	150.00	75.00	15.00
☐ 390	Glenn Nelson	150.00	75.00	15.00
☐ 391	Ben Chapman	150.00	75.00	15.00
	(photo actually Sam Chapman)			
☐ 392	Hoyt Wilhelm	500.00	250.00	50.00
☐ 393	Ebba St.Claire	150.00	75.00	15.00
☐ 394	Billy Herman CO	250.00	125.00	25.00
☐ 395	Jake Pitler CO	150.00	75.00	15.00
☐ 396	Dick Williams	250.00	125.00	25.00
☐ 397	Forrest Main	150.00	75.00	15.00
☐ 398	Hal Rice	150.00	75.00	15.00
☐ 399	Jim Fridley	150.00	75.00	15.00
☐ 400	Bill Dickey CO	500.00	250.00	50.00
☐ 401	Bob Schultz	150.00	75.00	15.00
☐ 402	Earl Harrist	150.00	75.00	15.00
☐ 403	Bill Miller	150.00	75.00	15.00
☐ 404	Dick Brodowski	150.00	75.00	15.00
☐ 405	Eddie Pellagrini	150.00	75.00	15.00
☐ 406	Joe Nuxhall	200.00	100.00	20.00
☐ 407	Eddie Mathews	1600.00	500.00	100.00

1953 Topps

The cards in this 274-card set measure 2 5/8" by 3 3/4". Although the last card is numbered 280, there are only 274 cards in the set since numbers 253, 261, 267, 268, 271, and 275 were never issued. The 1953 Topps series contains line drawings of players in full color. The name and team panel at the card base is easily damaged, making it very difficult to

complete a mint set. The high number series, 221 to 280, was produced in shorter supply late in the year and hence is more difficult to complete than the lower numbers. The key cards in the set are Mickey Mantle #82 and Willie Mays #244. There are a number of double-printed cards (actually not double but 50% more of each of these numbers were printed compared to the other cards in the series) indicated by DP in the checklist below. In addition there are five numbers which were printed in with the more plentiful series 166-220; these cards (94, 107, 131, 145, and 156) are also indicated by DP in the checklist below. There were some three-card advertising panels produced by Topps; the players include Johnny Mize, Clem Koshorek, and Toby Atwell and Mickey Mantle, Johnny Wyrostek, and Sal Yvars. When cut apart, these advertising cards are distinguished by the non-standard card back, i.e., part of an advertisement for the 1953 Topps set instead of the typical statistics and biographical information about the player pictured.

		NRMT	VG-E	GOOD
COMPLETE SET (274)		12500.00	6000.00	1750.00
COMMON PLAYER (1-165)		22.00	11.00	2.20
COMMON DP (1-165)		16.00	8.00	1.60
COMMON PLAYER (166-220)		16.00	8.00	1.60
COMMON PLAYER (221-280)		80.00	40.00	8.00
COMMON DP (221-280)		40.00	20.00	4.00

		NRMT	VG-E	GOOD
☐ 1	Jackie Robinson DP	550.00	150.00	30.00
☐ 2	Luke Easter DP	16.00	8.00	1.60
☐ 3	George Crowe	22.00	11.00	2.20
☐ 4	Ben Wade	22.00	11.00	2.20
☐ 5	Joe Dobson	22.00	11.00	2.20
☐ 6	Sam Jones	22.00	11.00	2.20
☐ 7	Bob Borkowski DP	16.00	8.00	1.60
☐ 8	Clem Koshorek DP	16.00	8.00	1.60
☐ 9	Joe Collins	30.00	15.00	3.00
☐ 10	Smoky Burgess	25.00	12.50	2.50
☐ 11	Sal Yvars	22.00	11.00	2.20
☐ 12	Howie Judson DP	16.00	8.00	1.60
☐ 13	Conrado Marrero DP	16.00	8.00	1.60
☐ 14	Clem Labine DP	22.00	11.00	2.20
☐ 15	Bobo Newsom DP	20.00	10.00	2.00
☐ 16	Peanuts Lowrey DP	16.00	8.00	1.60
☐ 17	Billy Hitchcock	22.00	11.00	2.20
☐ 18	Ted Lepcio DP	16.00	8.00	1.60
☐ 19	Mel Parnell DP	22.00	11.00	2.20
☐ 20	Hank Thompson	25.00	12.50	2.50
☐ 21	Billy Johnson	22.00	11.00	2.20
☐ 22	Howie Fox	22.00	11.00	2.20
☐ 23	Toby Atwell DP	16.00	8.00	1.60
☐ 24	Ferris Fain	25.00	12.50	2.50
☐ 25	Ray Boone	25.00	12.50	2.50
☐ 26	Dale Mitchell DP	18.00	9.00	1.80
☐ 27	Roy Campanella DP	200.00	100.00	20.00
☐ 28	Eddie Pellagrini	22.00	11.00	2.20
☐ 29	Hal Jeffcoat	22.00	11.00	2.20
☐ 30	Willard Nixon	22.00	11.00	2.20
☐ 31	Ewell Blackwell	35.00	17.50	3.50
☐ 32	Clyde Vollmer	22.00	11.00	2.20
☐ 33	Bob Kennedy DP	16.00	8.00	1.60
☐ 34	George Shuba	25.00	12.50	2.50
☐ 35	Irv Noren DP	16.00	8.00	1.60
☐ 36	Johnny Groth DP	16.00	8.00	1.60
☐ 37	Eddie Mathews DP	80.00	40.00	8.00
☐ 38	Jim Hearn DP	16.00	8.00	1.60
☐ 39	Eddie Miksis	22.00	11.00	2.20
☐ 40	John Lipon	22.00	11.00	2.20
☐ 41	Enos Slaughter	65.00	32.50	6.50
☐ 42	Gus Zernial DP	16.00	8.00	1.60
☐ 43	Gil McDougald	35.00	17.50	3.50
☐ 44	Ellis Kinder	22.00	11.00	2.20
☐ 45	Grady Hatton DP	16.00	8.00	1.60
☐ 46	Johnny Klippstein DP	16.00	8.00	1.60
☐ 47	Bubba Church DP	16.00	8.00	1.60
☐ 48	Bob Del Greco DP	16.00	8.00	1.60
☐ 49	Faye Throneberry DP	16.00	8.00	1.60
☐ 50	Chuck Dressen MG DP	20.00	10.00	2.00
☐ 51	Frank Campos DP	16.00	8.00	1.60
☐ 52	Ted Gray DP	16.00	8.00	1.60
☐ 53	Sherm Lollar DP	18.00	9.00	1.80
☐ 54	Bob Feller DP	90.00	45.00	9.00
☐ 55	Maurice McDermott DP	16.00	8.00	1.60
☐ 56	Jerry Staley DP	16.00	8.00	1.60
☐ 57	Carl Scheib	22.00	11.00	2.20
☐ 58	George Metkovich	22.00	11.00	2.20

☐	59	Karl Drews DP	16.00	8.00	1.60
☐	60	Cloyd Boyer DP	16.00	8.00	1.60
☐	61	Early Wynn	65.00	32.50	6.50
☐	62	Monte Irvin DP	40.00	20.00	4.00
☐	63	Gus Niarhos DP	16.00	8.00	1.60
☐	64	Dave Philley	22.00	11.00	2.20
☐	65	Earl Harrist	22.00	11.00	2.20
☐	66	Minnie Minoso	35.00	17.50	3.50
☐	67	Roy Sievers DP	18.00	9.00	1.80
☐	68	Del Rice	22.00	11.00	2.20
☐	69	Dick Brodowski	22.00	11.00	2.20
☐	70	Ed Yuhas	22.00	11.00	2.20
☐	71	Tony Bartirome	22.00	11.00	2.20
☐	72	Fred Hutchinson	25.00	12.50	2.50
☐	73	Eddie Robinson	22.00	11.00	2.20
☐	74	Joe Rossi	22.00	11.00	2.20
☐	75	Mike Garcia	25.00	12.50	2.50
☐	76	Pee Wee Reese	90.00	45.00	9.00
☐	77	Johnny Mize DP	55.00	27.50	5.50
☐	78	Al(Red) Schoendienst	50.00	25.00	5.00
☐	79	Johnny Wyrostek	22.00	11.00	2.20
☐	80	Jim Hegan	25.00	12.50	2.50
☐	81	Joe Black	45.00	22.50	4.50
☐	82	Mickey Mantle	1750.00	600.00	150.00
☐	83	Howie Pollet	22.00	11.00	2.20
☐	84	Bob Hooper DP	16.00	8.00	1.60
☐	85	Bobby Morgan DP	16.00	8.00	1.60
☐	86	Billy Martin	90.00	45.00	9.00
☐	87	Ed Lopat	35.00	17.50	3.50
☐	88	Willie Jones DP	16.00	8.00	1.60
☐	89	Chuck Stobbs DP	16.00	8.00	1.60
☐	90	Hank Edwards DP	16.00	8.00	1.60
☐	91	Ebba St.Claire DP	16.00	8.00	1.60
☐	92	Paul Minner DP	16.00	8.00	1.60
☐	93	Hal Rice DP	16.00	8.00	1.60
☐	94	Bill Kennedy DP	16.00	8.00	1.60
☐	95	Willard Marshall DP	16.00	8.00	1.60
☐	96	Virgil Trucks	25.00	12.50	2.50
☐	97	Don Kolloway DP	16.00	8.00	1.60
☐	98	Cal Abrams DP	16.00	8.00	1.60
☐	99	Dave Madison	22.00	11.00	2.20
☐	100	Bill Miller	22.00	11.00	2.20
☐	101	Ted Wilks	22.00	11.00	2.20
☐	102	Connie Ryan DP	16.00	8.00	1.60
☐	103	Joe Astroth DP	16.00	8.00	1.60
☐	104	Yogi Berra	180.00	90.00	18.00
☐	105	Joe Nuxhall DP	18.00	9.00	1.80
☐	106	Johnny Antonelli	25.00	12.50	2.50
☐	107	Danny O'Connell DP	16.00	8.00	1.60
☐	108	Bob Porterfield DP	16.00	8.00	1.60
☐	109	Alvin Dark	27.00	13.50	2.70
☐	110	Herman Wehmeier DP	16.00	8.00	1.60
☐	111	Hank Sauer DP	18.00	9.00	1.80
☐	112	Ned Garver DP	16.00	8.00	1.60
☐	113	Jerry Priddy	22.00	11.00	2.20
☐	114	Phil Rizzuto	75.00	37.50	7.50
☐	115	George Spencer	22.00	11.00	2.20
☐	116	Frank Smith DP	16.00	8.00	1.60
☐	117	Sid Gordon DP	16.00	8.00	1.60
☐	118	Gus Bell DP	18.00	9.00	1.80
☐	119	Johnny Sain	35.00	17.50	3.50
☐	120	Davey Williams	30.00	15.00	3.00
☐	121	Walt Dropo	25.00	12.50	2.50
☐	122	Elmer Valo	22.00	11.00	2.20
☐	123	Tommy Byrne DP	18.00	9.00	1.80
☐	124	Sibby Sisti DP	16.00	8.00	1.60
☐	125	Dick Williams DP	20.00	10.00	2.00
☐	126	Bill Connelly DP	16.00	8.00	1.60
☐	127	Clint Courtney DP	16.00	8.00	1.60
☐	128	Wilmer Mizell DP	16.00	8.00	1.60
☐	129	Keith Thomas	22.00	11.00	2.20
☐	130	Turk Lown DP	16.00	8.00	1.60
☐	131	Harry Byrd DP	16.00	8.00	1.60
☐	132	Tom Morgan	22.00	11.00	2.20
☐	133	Gil Coan	22.00	11.00	2.20
☐	134	Rube Walker	25.00	12.50	2.50
☐	135	Al Rosen DP	30.00	15.00	3.00
☐	136	Ken Heintzelman DP	16.00	8.00	1.60
☐	137	John Rutherford DP	16.00	8.00	1.60
☐	138	George Kell	45.00	22.50	4.50
☐	139	Sammy White	22.00	11.00	2.20
☐	140	Tommy Glaviano	22.00	11.00	2.20
☐	141	Allie Reynolds DP	30.00	15.00	3.00
☐	142	Vic Wertz	25.00	12.50	2.50
☐	143	Billy Pierce	30.00	15.00	3.00
☐	144	Bob Schultz DP	16.00	8.00	1.60
☐	145	Harry Dorish DP	16.00	8.00	1.60
☐	146	Granny Hamner	22.00	11.00	2.20
☐	147	Warren Spahn	90.00	45.00	9.00
☐	148	Mickey Grasso	22.00	11.00	2.20
☐	149	Dom DiMaggio DP	30.00	15.00	3.00
☐	150	Harry Simpson DP	16.00	8.00	1.60
☐	151	Hoyt Wilhelm	55.00	27.50	5.50
☐	152	Bob Adams DP	16.00	8.00	1.60
☐	153	Andy Seminick DP	16.00	8.00	1.60
☐	154	Dick Groat	30.00	15.00	3.00
☐	155	Dutch Leonard	22.00	11.00	2.20
☐	156	Jim Rivera DP	16.00	8.00	1.60
☐	157	Bob Addis DP	16.00	8.00	1.60
☐	158	Johnny Logan	25.00	12.50	2.50
☐	159	Wayne Terwilliger DP	16.00	8.00	1.60
☐	160	Bob Young	22.00	11.00	2.20
☐	161	Vern Bickford DP	16.00	8.00	1.60
☐	162	Ted Kluszewski	35.00	17.50	3.50
☐	163	Fred Hatfield DP	16.00	8.00	1.60
☐	164	Frank Shea DP	16.00	8.00	1.60
☐	165	Billy Hoeft	22.00	11.00	2.20
☐	166	Billy Hunter	16.00	8.00	1.60
☐	167	Art Schult	16.00	8.00	1.60
☐	168	Willard Schmidt	16.00	8.00	1.60
☐	169	Dizzy Trout	16.00	8.00	1.60
☐	170	Bill Werle	16.00	8.00	1.60
☐	171	Bill Glynn	16.00	8.00	1.60
☐	172	Rip Repulski	16.00	8.00	1.60
☐	173	Preston Ward	16.00	8.00	1.60
☐	174	Billy Loes	18.00	9.00	1.80
☐	175	Ron Kline	16.00	8.00	1.60
☐	176	Don Hoak	20.00	10.00	2.00
☐	177	Jim Dyck	16.00	8.00	1.60
☐	178	Jim Waugh	16.00	8.00	1.60
☐	179	Gene Hermanski	16.00	8.00	1.60
☐	180	Virgil Stallcup	16.00	8.00	1.60
☐	181	Al Zarilla	16.00	8.00	1.60
☐	182	Bobby Hofman	16.00	8.00	1.60
☐	183	Stu Miller	16.00	8.00	1.60
☐	184	Hal Brown	16.00	8.00	1.60
☐	185	Jim Pendleton	16.00	8.00	1.60
☐	186	Charlie Bishop	16.00	8.00	1.60
☐	187	Jim Fridley	16.00	8.00	1.60
☐	188	Andy Carey	20.00	10.00	2.00
☐	189	Ray Jablonski	16.00	8.00	1.60
☐	190	Dixie Walker	16.00	8.00	1.60
☐	191	Ralph Kiner	45.00	22.50	4.50
☐	192	Wally Westlake	16.00	8.00	1.60
☐	193	Mike Clark	16.00	8.00	1.60
☐	194	Eddie Kazak	16.00	8.00	1.60
☐	195	Ed McGhee	16.00	8.00	1.60
☐	196	Bob Keegan	18.00	9.00	1.80
☐	197	Del Crandall	16.00	8.00	1.60
☐	198	Forrest Main	16.00	8.00	1.60
☐	199	Marion Fricano	16.00	8.00	1.60
☐	200	Gordon Goldsberry	16.00	8.00	1.60
☐	201	Paul LaPalme	16.00	8.00	1.60
☐	202	Carl Sawatski	16.00	8.00	1.60
☐	203	Cliff Fannin	16.00	8.00	1.60
☐	204	Dick Bokelman	16.00	8.00	1.60
☐	205	Vern Benson	16.00	8.00	1.60
☐	206	Ed Bailey	18.00	9.00	1.80
☐	207	Whitey Ford	110.00	55.00	11.00
☐	208	Jim Wilson	16.00	8.00	1.60
☐	209	Jim Greengrass	16.00	8.00	1.60
☐	210	Bob Cerv	20.00	10.00	2.00
☐	211	J.W. Porter	16.00	8.00	1.60
☐	212	Jack Dittmer	16.00	8.00	1.60
☐	213	Ray Scarborough	16.00	8.00	1.60
☐	214	Bill Bruton	18.00	9.00	1.80
☐	215	Gene Conley	18.00	9.00	1.80
☐	216	Jim Hughes	16.00	8.00	1.60
☐	217	Murray Wall	16.00	8.00	1.60
☐	218	Les Fusselman	16.00	8.00	1.60
☐	219	Pete Runnels (photo actually Don Johnson)	18.00	9.00	1.80
☐	220	Satchel Paige UER (misspelled Satchell on card front)	350.00	175.00	35.00
☐	221	Bob Milliken	80.00	40.00	8.00
☐	222	Vic Janowicz DP	45.00	22.50	4.50
☐	223	Johnny O'Brien DP	45.00	22.50	4.50
☐	224	Lou Sleater DP	40.00	20.00	4.00
☐	225	Bobby Shantz	90.00	45.00	9.00
☐	226	Ed Erautt	80.00	40.00	8.00
☐	227	Morrie Martin	80.00	40.00	8.00
☐	228	Hal Newhouser	100.00	50.00	10.00
☐	229	Rockey Krsnich	80.00	40.00	8.00
☐	230	Johnny Lindell DP	40.00	20.00	4.00
☐	231	Solly Hemus DP	40.00	20.00	4.00
☐	232	Dick Kokos	80.00	40.00	8.00
☐	233	Al Aber	80.00	40.00	8.00
☐	234	Ray Murray DP	40.00	20.00	4.00
☐	235	John Hetki DP	40.00	20.00	4.00
☐	236	Harry Perkowski DP	40.00	20.00	4.00
☐	237	Bud Podbielan DP	40.00	20.00	4.00
☐	238	Cal Hogue DP	40.00	20.00	4.00
☐	239	Jim Delsing	80.00	40.00	8.00
☐	240	Fred Marsh	80.00	40.00	8.00
☐	241	Al Sima DP	40.00	20.00	4.00
☐	242	Charlie Silvera	80.00	40.00	8.00
☐	243	Carlos Bernier DP	40.00	20.00	4.00
☐	244	Willie Mays	1400.00	500.00	125.00

		NRMT	VG-E	GOOD
☐ 245	Bill Norman	80.00	40.00	8.00
☐ 246	Roy Face DP	80.00	40.00	8.00
☐ 247	Mike Sandlock DP	40.00	20.00	4.00
☐ 248	Gene Stephens DP	40.00	20.00	4.00
☐ 249	Eddie O'Brien	80.00	40.00	8.00
☐ 250	Bob Wilson	80.00	40.00	8.00
☐ 251	Sid Hudson	80.00	40.00	8.00
☐ 252	Hank Foiles	80.00	40.00	8.00
☐ 253	Does not exist	00.00	00.00	0.00
☐ 254	Preacher Roe DP	80.00	40.00	8.00
☐ 255	Dixie Howell	80.00	40.00	8.00
☐ 256	Les Peden	80.00	40.00	8.00
☐ 257	Bob Boyd	80.00	40.00	8.00
☐ 258	Jim Gilliam	275.00	135.00	27.00
☐ 259	Roy McMillan DP	40.00	20.00	4.00
☐ 260	Sam Calderone	80.00	40.00	8.00
☐ 261	Does not exist	00.00	00.00	0.00
☐ 262	Bob Oldis	80.00	40.00	8.00
☐ 263	Johnny Podres	250.00	125.00	25.00
☐ 264	Gene Woodling DP	60.00	30.00	6.00
☐ 265	Jackie Jensen	100.00	50.00	10.00
☐ 266	Bob Cain	80.00	40.00	8.00
☐ 267	Does not exist	00.00	00.00	0.00
☐ 268	Does not exist	00.00	00.00	0.00
☐ 269	Duane Pillette	80.00	40.00	8.00
☐ 270	Vern Stephens	90.00	45.00	9.00
☐ 271	Does not exist	00.00	00.00	0.00
☐ 272	Bill Antonello	80.00	40.00	8.00
☐ 273	Harvey Haddix	100.00	50.00	10.00
☐ 274	John Riddle	80.00	40.00	8.00
☐ 275	Does not exist	00.00	00.00	0.00
☐ 276	Ken Raffensberger	80.00	40.00	8.00
☐ 277	Don Lund	80.00	40.00	8.00
☐ 278	Willie Miranda	80.00	40.00	8.00
☐ 279	Joe Coleman DP	40.00	20.00	4.00
☐ 280	Milt Bolling	300.00	50.00	50.00

1954 Topps

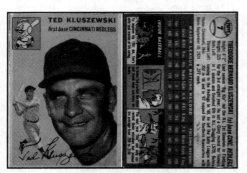

The cards in this 250-card set measure 2 5/8" by 3 3/4". Each of the cards in the 1954 Topps set contains a large "head" shot of the player in color plus a smaller full-length photo in black and white set against a color background. This series contains the rookie cards of Hank Aaron, Ernie Banks, and Al Kaline and two separate cards of Ted Williams (number 1 and number 250). Conspicuous by his absence is Mickey Mantle who apparently was the exclusive property of Bowman during 1954 (and 1955).

	NRMT	VG-E	GOOD
COMPLETE SET (250)	7000.00	3500.00	900.00
COMMON PLAYER (1-50)	8.00	4.00	.80
COMMON PLAYER (51-75)	22.00	10.00	2.00
COMMON PLAYER (76-125)	9.00	4.50	.90
COMMON PLAYER (126-250)	10.00	5.00	1.00

		NRMT	VG-E	GOOD
☐ 1	Ted Williams	500.00	150.00	30.00
☐ 2	Gus Zernial	8.00	4.00	.80
☐ 3	Monte Irvin	25.00	12.50	2.50
☐ 4	Hank Sauer	9.00	4.50	.90
☐ 5	Ed Lopat	16.00	8.00	1.60
☐ 6	Pete Runnels	9.00	4.50	.90
☐ 7	Ted Kluszewski	16.00	8.00	1.60
☐ 8	Bob Young	8.00	4.00	.80
☐ 9	Harvey Haddix	10.00	5.00	1.00
☐ 10	Jackie Robinson	200.00	100.00	20.00

		NRMT	VG-E	GOOD
☐ 11	Paul Leslie Smith	8.00	4.00	.80
☐ 12	Del Crandall	9.00	4.50	.90
☐ 13	Billy Martin	60.00	30.00	6.00
☐ 14	Preacher Roe	16.00	8.00	1.60
☐ 15	Al Rosen	14.00	7.00	1.40
☐ 16	Vic Janowicz	9.00	4.50	.90
☐ 17	Phil Rizzuto	55.00	27.50	5.50
☐ 18	Walt Dropo	9.00	4.50	.90
☐ 19	Johnny Lipon	8.00	4.00	.80
☐ 20	Warren Spahn	70.00	35.00	7.00
☐ 21	Bobby Shantz	10.00	5.00	1.00
☐ 22	Jim Greengrass	8.00	4.00	.80
☐ 23	Luke Easter	9.00	4.50	.90
☐ 24	Granny Hamner	8.00	4.00	.80
☐ 25	Harvey Kuenn	25.00	12.50	2.50
☐ 26	Ray Jablonski	8.00	4.00	.80
☐ 27	Ferris Fain	9.00	4.50	.90
☐ 28	Paul Minner	8.00	4.00	.80
☐ 29	Jim Hegan	9.00	4.50	.90
☐ 30	Eddie Mathews	65.00	32.50	6.50
☐ 31	Johnny Klippstein	8.00	4.00	.80
☐ 32	Duke Snider	100.00	50.00	10.00
☐ 33	Johnny Schmitz	8.00	4.00	.80
☐ 34	Jim Rivera	8.00	4.00	.80
☐ 35	Jim Gilliam	15.00	7.50	1.50
☐ 36	Hoyt Wilhelm	30.00	15.00	3.00
☐ 37	Whitey Ford	70.00	35.00	7.00
☐ 38	Eddie Stanky	9.00	4.50	.90
☐ 39	Sherm Lollar	9.00	4.50	.90
☐ 40	Mel Parnell	9.00	4.50	.90
☐ 41	Willie Jones	8.00	4.00	.80
☐ 42	Don Mueller	9.00	4.50	.90
☐ 43	Dick Groat	10.00	5.00	1.00
☐ 44	Ned Garver	8.00	4.00	.80
☐ 45	Richie Ashburn	27.00	13.50	2.70
☐ 46	Ken Raffensberger	8.00	4.00	.80
☐ 47	Ellis Kinder	8.00	4.00	.80
☐ 48	Billy Hunter	8.00	4.00	.80
☐ 49	Ray Murray	8.00	4.00	.80
☐ 50	Yogi Berra	180.00	90.00	18.00
☐ 51	Johnny Lindell	22.00	10.00	2.00
☐ 52	Vic Power	22.00	10.00	2.00
☐ 53	Jack Dittmer	22.00	10.00	2.00
☐ 54	Vern Stephens	27.00	12.50	2.50
☐ 55	Phil Cavarretta	27.00	12.50	2.50
☐ 56	Willie Miranda	22.00	10.00	2.00
☐ 57	Luis Aloma	22.00	10.00	2.00
☐ 58	Bob Wilson	22.00	10.00	2.00
☐ 59	Gene Conley	27.00	12.50	2.50
☐ 60	Frank Baumholtz	22.00	10.00	2.00
☐ 61	Bob Cain	22.00	10.00	2.00
☐ 62	Eddie Robinson	27.00	12.50	2.50
☐ 63	Johnny Pesky	27.00	12.50	2.50
☐ 64	Hank Thompson	27.00	12.50	2.50
☐ 65	Bob Swift	22.00	10.00	2.00
☐ 66	Ted Lepcio	22.00	10.00	2.00
☐ 67	Jim Willis	22.00	10.00	2.00
☐ 68	Sam Calderone	22.00	10.00	2.00
☐ 69	Bud Podbielan	22.00	10.00	2.00
☐ 70	Larry Doby	40.00	20.00	4.00
☐ 71	Frank Smith	22.00	10.00	2.00
☐ 72	Preston Ward	22.00	10.00	2.00
☐ 73	Wayne Terwilliger	22.00	10.00	2.00
☐ 74	Bill Taylor	22.00	10.00	2.00
☐ 75	Fred Haney	22.00	10.00	2.00
☐ 76	Bob Scheffing	9.00	4.50	.90
☐ 77	Ray Boone	10.00	5.00	1.00
☐ 78	Ted Kazanski	9.00	4.50	.90
☐ 79	Andy Pafko	10.00	5.00	1.00
☐ 80	Jackie Jensen	14.00	7.00	1.40
☐ 81	Dave Hoskins	9.00	4.50	.90
☐ 82	Milt Bolling	9.00	4.50	.90
☐ 83	Joe Collins	12.00	6.00	1.20
☐ 84	Dick Cole	9.00	4.50	.90
☐ 85	Bob Turley	20.00	10.00	2.00
☐ 86	Billy Herman	18.00	9.00	1.80
☐ 87	Roy Face	12.00	6.00	1.20
☐ 88	Matt Batts	9.00	4.50	.90
☐ 89	Howie Pollet	9.00	4.50	.90
☐ 90	Willie Mays	325.00	160.00	32.00
☐ 91	Bob Oldis	9.00	4.50	.90
☐ 92	Wally Westlake	9.00	4.50	.90
☐ 93	Sid Hudson	9.00	4.50	.90
☐ 94	Ernie Banks	600.00	300.00	60.00
☐ 95	Hal Rice	9.00	4.50	.90
☐ 96	Charlie Silvera	9.00	4.50	.90
☐ 97	Jerald Hal Lane	9.00	4.50	.90
☐ 98	Joe Black	12.00	6.00	1.20
☐ 99	Bobby Hofman	9.00	4.50	.90
☐ 100	Bob Keegan	9.00	4.50	.90
☐ 101	Gene Woodling	12.00	6.00	1.20
☐ 102	Gil Hodges	65.00	32.50	6.50
☐ 103	Jim Lemon	10.00	5.00	1.00
☐ 104	Mike Sandlock	9.00	4.50	.90
☐ 105	Andy Carey	12.00	6.00	1.20

☐ 106	Dick Kokos	9.00	4.50	.90
☐ 107	Duane Pillette	9.00	4.50	.90
☐ 108	Thornton Kipper	9.00	4.50	.90
☐ 109	Bill Bruton	10.00	5.00	1.00
☐ 110	Harry Dorish	9.00	4.50	.90
☐ 111	Jim Delsing	9.00	4.50	.90
☐ 112	Bill Renna	9.00	4.50	.90
☐ 113	Bob Boyd	9.00	4.50	.90
☐ 114	Dean Stone	9.00	4.50	.90
☐ 115	Rip Repulski	9.00	4.50	.90
☐ 116	Steve Bilko	9.00	4.50	.90
☐ 117	Solly Hemus	9.00	4.50	.90
☐ 118	Carl Scheib	9.00	4.50	.90
☐ 119	Johnny Antonelli	12.00	6.00	1.20
☐ 120	Roy McMillan	9.00	4.50	.90
☐ 121	Clem Labine	12.00	6.00	1.20
☐ 122	Johnny Logan	10.00	5.00	1.00
☐ 123	Bobby Adams	9.00	4.50	.90
☐ 124	Marion Fricano	9.00	4.50	.90
☐ 125	Harry Perkowski	9.00	4.50	.90
☐ 126	Ben Wade	10.00	5.00	1.00
☐ 127	Steve O'Neill	10.00	5.00	1.00
☐ 128	Hank Aaron	1100.00	450.00	125.00
☐ 129	Forrest Jacobs	10.00	5.00	1.00
☐ 130	Hank Bauer	20.00	10.00	2.00
☐ 131	Reno Bertoia	10.00	5.00	1.00
☐ 132	Tom Lasorda	150.00	75.00	15.00
☐ 133	Dave Baker	10.00	5.00	1.00
☐ 134	Cal Hogue	10.00	5.00	1.00
☐ 135	Joe Presko	10.00	5.00	1.00
☐ 136	Connie Ryan	10.00	5.00	1.00
☐ 137	Wally Moon	18.00	9.00	1.80
☐ 138	Bob Borkowski	10.00	5.00	1.00
☐ 139	The O'Briens	21.00	10.50	2.10
	Johnny O'Brien			
	Eddie O'Brien			
☐ 140	Tom Wright	10.00	5.00	1.00
☐ 141	Joey Jay	12.00	6.00	1.20
☐ 142	Tom Poholsky	10.00	5.00	1.00
☐ 143	Ralston Hemsley	10.00	5.00	1.00
☐ 144	Bill Werle	10.00	5.00	1.00
☐ 145	Elmer Valo	10.00	5.00	1.00
☐ 146	Don Johnson	10.00	5.00	1.00
☐ 147	Johnny Riddle	10.00	5.00	1.00
☐ 148	Bob Trice	10.00	5.00	1.00
☐ 149	Al Robertson	10.00	5.00	1.00
☐ 150	Dick Kryhoski	10.00	5.00	1.00
☐ 151	Alex Grammas	10.00	5.00	1.00
☐ 152	Michael Blyzka	10.00	5.00	1.00
☐ 153	Al Walker	12.00	6.00	1.20
☐ 154	Mike Fornieles	10.00	5.00	1.00
☐ 155	Bob Kennedy	12.00	6.00	1.20
☐ 156	Joe Coleman	10.00	5.00	1.00
☐ 157	Don Lenhardt	10.00	5.00	1.00
☐ 158	Peanuts Lowrey	10.00	5.00	1.00
☐ 159	Dave Philley	10.00	5.00	1.00
☐ 160	Ralph Kress	10.00	5.00	1.00
☐ 161	John Hetki	10.00	5.00	1.00
☐ 162	Herman Wehmeier	10.00	5.00	1.00
☐ 163	Frank House	10.00	5.00	1.00
☐ 164	Stu Miller	12.00	6.00	1.20
☐ 165	Jim Pendleton	10.00	5.00	1.00
☐ 166	Johnny Podres	21.00	10.50	2.10
☐ 167	Don Lund	10.00	5.00	1.00
☐ 168	Morrie Martin	10.00	5.00	1.00
☐ 169	Jim Hughes	10.00	5.00	1.00
☐ 170	James(Dusty) Rhodes	14.00	7.00	1.40
☐ 171	Leo Kiely	10.00	5.00	1.00
☐ 172	Harold Brown	10.00	5.00	1.00
☐ 173	Jack Harshman	10.00	5.00	1.00
☐ 174	Tom Qualters	10.00	5.00	1.00
☐ 175	Frank Leja	12.00	6.00	1.20
☐ 176	Robert Keeley	10.00	5.00	1.00
☐ 177	Bob Milliken	10.00	5.00	1.00
☐ 178	Bill Glynn	10.00	5.00	1.00
☐ 179	Gair Allie	10.00	5.00	1.00
☐ 180	Wes Westrum	12.00	6.00	1.20
☐ 181	Mel Roach	10.00	5.00	1.00
☐ 182	Chuck Harmon	10.00	5.00	1.00
☐ 183	Earle Combs CO	18.00	9.00	1.80
☐ 184	Ed Bailey	10.00	5.00	1.00
☐ 185	Chuck Stobbs	10.00	5.00	1.00
☐ 186	Karl Olson	10.00	5.00	1.00
☐ 187	Henry Manush CO	18.00	9.00	1.80
☐ 188	Dave Jolly	10.00	5.00	1.00
☐ 189	Floyd Ross	10.00	5.00	1.00
☐ 190	Ray Herbert	10.00	5.00	1.00
☐ 191	John(Dick) Schofield	12.00	6.00	1.20
☐ 192	Ellis Deal	10.00	5.00	1.00
☐ 193	Johnny Hopp	12.00	6.00	1.20
☐ 194	Bill Sarni	10.00	5.00	1.00
☐ 195	Billy Consolo	10.00	5.00	1.00
☐ 196	Stan Jok	10.00	5.00	1.00
☐ 197	Lynwood Rowe	12.00	6.00	1.20
☐ 198	Carl Sawatski	10.00	5.00	1.00

☐ 199	Glenn(Rocky) Nelson	10.00	5.00	1.00
☐ 200	Larry Jansen	12.00	6.00	1.20
☐ 201	Al Kaline	600.00	300.00	60.00
☐ 202	Bob Purkey	10.00	5.00	1.00
☐ 203	Harry Brecheen	12.00	6.00	1.20
☐ 204	Angel Scull	10.00	5.00	1.00
☐ 205	Johnny Sain	21.00	10.50	2.10
☐ 206	Ray Crone	10.00	5.00	1.00
☐ 207	Tom Oliver	10.00	5.00	1.00
☐ 208	Grady Hatton	10.00	5.00	1.00
☐ 209	Chuck Thompson	10.00	5.00	1.00
☐ 210	Bob Buhl	12.00	6.00	1.20
☐ 211	Don Hoak	12.00	6.00	1.20
☐ 212	Bob Micelotta	10.00	5.00	1.00
☐ 213	Johnny Fitzpatrick	10.00	5.00	1.00
☐ 214	Arnie Portocarrero	10.00	5.00	1.00
☐ 215	Warren McGhee	10.00	5.00	1.00
☐ 216	Al Sima	10.00	5.00	1.00
☐ 217	Paul Schreiber	10.00	5.00	1.00
☐ 218	Fred Marsh	10.00	5.00	1.00
☐ 219	Chuck Kress	10.00	5.00	1.00
☐ 220	Ruben Gomez	10.00	5.00	1.00
☐ 221	Dick Brodowski	10.00	5.00	1.00
☐ 222	Bill Wilson	10.00	5.00	1.00
☐ 223	Joe Haynes	10.00	5.00	1.00
☐ 224	Dick Weik	10.00	5.00	1.00
☐ 225	Don Liddle	10.00	5.00	1.00
☐ 226	Jehosie Heard	10.00	5.00	1.00
☐ 227	Colonel Mills	10.00	5.00	1.00
☐ 228	Gene Hermanski	10.00	5.00	1.00
☐ 229	Bob Talbot	10.00	5.00	1.00
☐ 230	Bob Kuzava	12.00	6.00	1.20
☐ 231	Roy Smalley	10.00	5.00	1.00
☐ 232	Lou Limmer	10.00	5.00	1.00
☐ 233	Augie Galan	10.00	5.00	1.00
☐ 234	Jerry Lynch	12.00	6.00	1.20
☐ 235	Vernon Law	12.00	6.00	1.20
☐ 236	Paul Penson	10.00	5.00	1.00
☐ 237	Dominic Ryba	10.00	5.00	1.00
☐ 238	Al Aber	10.00	5.00	1.00
☐ 239	Bill Skowron	45.00	22.50	4.50
☐ 240	Sam Mele	10.00	5.00	1.00
☐ 241	Robert Miller	10.00	5.00	1.00
☐ 242	Curt Roberts	10.00	5.00	1.00
☐ 243	Ray Blades	10.00	5.00	1.00
☐ 244	Leroy Wheat	10.00	5.00	1.00
☐ 245	Roy Sievers	12.00	6.00	1.20
☐ 246	Howie Fox	10.00	5.00	1.00
☐ 247	Ed Mayo	10.00	5.00	1.00
☐ 248	Al Smith	12.00	6.00	1.20
☐ 249	Wilmer Mizell	12.00	6.00	1.20
☐ 250	Ted Williams	550.00	150.00	30.00

1955 Topps

The cards in this 206-card set measure 2 5/8" by 3 3/4". Both the large "head" shot and the smaller full-length photos used on each card of the 1955 Topps set are in color. The card fronts were designed horizontally for the first time in Topps' history. The first card features Dusty Rhodes, hitting star for the Giants' 1954 World Series sweep over the Indians. A "high" series, 161 to 210, is more difficult to find than cards 1 to 160. Numbers 175, 186, 203, and 209 were never issued. To fill in for the four cards not issued in the high number series, Topps double

printed four players, those appearing on cards 170, 172, 184, and 188.

	NRMT	VG-E	GOOD
COMPLETE SET (206)	5600.00	2700.00	700.00
COMMON PLAYER (1-150)	6.00	3.00	.60
COMMON PLAYER (151-160)	12.00	6.00	1.20
COMMON PLAYER (161-210)	15.00	7.50	1.50

		NRMT	VG-E	GOOD
☐	1 Dusty Rhodes	30.00	5.00	1.00
☐	2 Ted Williams	300.00	150.00	30.00
☐	3 Art Fowler	6.00	3.00	.60
☐	4 Al Kaline	125.00	60.00	12.50
☐	5 Jim Gilliam	11.00	5.50	1.10
☐	6 Stan Hack	6.00	3.00	.60
☐	7 Jim Hegan	6.00	3.00	.60
☐	8 Harold Smith	6.00	3.00	.60
☐	9 Robert Miller	6.00	3.00	.60
☐	10 Bob Keegan	6.00	3.00	.60
☐	11 Ferris Fain	6.00	3.00	.60
☐	12 Vernon Thies	6.00	3.00	.60
☐	13 Fred Marsh	6.00	3.00	.60
☐	14 Jim Finigan	6.00	3.00	.60
☐	15 Jim Pendleton	6.00	3.00	.60
☐	16 Roy Sievers	7.00	3.50	.70
☐	17 Bobby Hofman	6.00	3.00	.60
☐	18 Russ Kemmerer	6.00	3.00	.60
☐	19 Billy Herman	10.00	5.00	1.00
☐	20 Andy Carey	8.00	4.00	.80
☐	21 Alex Grammas	6.00	3.00	.60
☐	22 Bill Skowron	12.00	6.00	1.20
☐	23 Jack Parks	6.00	3.00	.60
☐	24 Hal Newhouser	10.00	5.00	1.00
☐	25 Johnny Podres	12.00	6.00	1.20
☐	26 Dick Groat	8.00	4.00	.80
☐	27 Billy Gardner	7.00	3.50	.70
☐	28 Ernie Banks	110.00	55.00	11.00
☐	29 Herman Wehmeier	6.00	3.00	.60
☐	30 Vic Power	6.00	3.00	.60
☐	31 Warren Spahn	60.00	30.00	6.00
☐	32 Warren McGhee	6.00	3.00	.60
☐	33 Tom Qualters	6.00	3.00	.60
☐	34 Wayne Terwilliger	6.00	3.00	.60
☐	35 Dave Jolly	6.00	3.00	.60
☐	36 Leo Kiely	6.00	3.00	.60
☐	37 Joe Cunningham	7.00	3.50	.70
☐	38 Bob Turley	10.00	5.00	1.00
☐	39 Bill Glynn	6.00	3.00	.60
☐	40 Don Hoak	6.00	3.00	.60
☐	41 Chuck Stobbs	6.00	3.00	.60
☐	42 John(Windy) McCall	6.00	3.00	.60
☐	43 Harvey Haddix	7.00	3.50	.70
☐	44 Harold Valentine	6.00	3.00	.60
☐	45 Hank Sauer	7.00	3.50	.70
☐	46 Ted Kazanski	6.00	3.00	.60
☐	47 Hank Aaron	250.00	125.00	25.00
☐	48 Bob Kennedy	6.00	3.00	.60
☐	49 J.W. Porter	6.00	3.00	.60
☐	50 Jackie Robinson	175.00	85.00	18.00
☐	51 Jim Hughes	6.00	3.00	.60
☐	52 Bill Tremel	6.00	3.00	.60
☐	53 Bill Taylor	6.00	3.00	.60
☐	54 Lou Limmer	6.00	3.00	.60
☐	55 Rip Repulski	6.00	3.00	.60
☐	56 Ray Jablonski	6.00	3.00	.60
☐	57 Billy O'Dell	6.00	3.00	.60
☐	58 Jim Rivera	6.00	3.00	.60
☐	59 Gair Allie	6.00	3.00	.60
☐	60 Dean Stone	6.00	3.00	.60
☐	61 Forrest Jacobs	6.00	3.00	.60
☐	62 Thornton Kipper	6.00	3.00	.60
☐	63 Joe Collins	8.00	4.00	.80
☐	64 Gus Triandos	7.00	3.50	.70
☐	65 Ray Boone	6.00	3.00	.60
☐	66 Ron Jackson	6.00	3.00	.60
☐	67 Wally Moon	7.00	3.50	.70
☐	68 Jim Davis	6.00	3.00	.60
☐	69 Ed Bailey	6.00	3.00	.60
☐	70 Al Rosen	9.00	4.50	.90
☐	71 Ruben Gomez	6.00	3.00	.60
☐	72 Karl Olson	6.00	3.00	.60
☐	73 Jack Shepard	6.00	3.00	.60
☐	74 Bob Borkowski	6.00	3.00	.60
☐	75 Sandy Amoros	9.00	4.50	.90
☐	76 Howie Pollet	6.00	3.00	.60
☐	77 Arnie Portocarrero	6.00	3.00	.60
☐	78 Gordon Jones	6.00	3.00	.60
☐	79 Clyde Schell	6.00	3.00	.60
☐	80 Bob Grim	9.00	4.50	.90
☐	81 Gene Conley	6.00	3.00	.60
☐	82 Chuck Harmon	6.00	3.00	.60
☐	83 Tom Brewer	6.00	3.00	.60
☐	84 Camilo Pascual	8.00	4.00	.80
☐	85 Don Mossi	8.00	4.00	.80
☐	86 Bill Wilson	6.00	3.00	.60
☐	87 Frank House	6.00	3.00	.60
☐	88 Bob Skinner	7.00	3.50	.70
☐	89 Joe Frazier	6.00	3.00	.60
☐	90 Karl Spooner	7.00	3.50	.70
☐	91 Milt Bolling	6.00	3.00	.60
☐	92 Don Zimmer	21.00	10.50	2.10
☐	93 Steve Bilko	6.00	3.00	.60
☐	94 Reno Bertoia	6.00	3.00	.60
☐	95 Preston Ward	6.00	3.00	.60
☐	96 Chuck Bishop	6.00	3.00	.60
☐	97 Carlos Paula	6.00	3.00	.60
☐	98 John Riddle	6.00	3.00	.60
☐	99 Frank Leja	6.00	3.00	.60
☐	100 Monte Irvin	21.00	10.50	2.10
☐	101 Johnny Gray	6.00	3.00	.60
☐	102 Wally Westlake	6.00	3.00	.60
☐	103 Chuck White	6.00	3.00	.60
☐	104 Jack Harshman	6.00	3.00	.60
☐	105 Chuck Diering	6.00	3.00	.60
☐	106 Frank Sullivan	6.00	3.00	.60
☐	107 Curt Roberts	6.00	3.00	.60
☐	108 Al Walker	6.00	3.00	.60
☐	109 Ed Lopat	11.00	5.50	1.10
☐	110 Gus Zernial	7.00	3.50	.70
☐	111 Bob Milliken	6.00	3.00	.60
☐	112 Nelson King	6.00	3.00	.60
☐	113 Harry Brecheen	6.00	3.00	.60
☐	114 Louis Ortiz	6.00	3.00	.60
☐	115 Ellis Kinder	6.00	3.00	.60
☐	116 Tom Hurd	6.00	3.00	.60
☐	117 Mel Roach	6.00	3.00	.60
☐	118 Bob Purkey	6.00	3.00	.60
☐	119 Bob Lennon	6.00	3.00	.60
☐	120 Ted Kluszewski	11.00	5.50	1.10
☐	121 Bill Renna	6.00	3.00	.60
☐	122 Carl Sawatski	6.00	3.00	.60
☐	123 Sandy Koufax	650.00	325.00	65.00
☐	124 Harmon Killebrew	250.00	125.00	25.00
☐	125 Ken Boyer	40.00	20.00	4.00
☐	126 Dick Hall	6.00	3.00	.60
☐	127 Dale Long	7.00	3.50	.70
☐	128 Ted Lepcio	6.00	3.00	.60
☐	129 Elvin Tappe	6.00	3.00	.60
☐	130 Mayo Smith MG	6.00	3.00	.60
☐	131 Grady Hatton	6.00	3.00	.60
☐	132 Bob Trice	6.00	3.00	.60
☐	133 Dave Hoskins	6.00	3.00	.60
☐	134 Joey Jay	6.00	3.00	.60
☐	135 Johnny O'Brien	6.00	3.00	.60
☐	136 Vernon Stewart	6.00	3.00	.60
☐	137 Harry Elliott	6.00	3.00	.60
☐	138 Ray Herbert	6.00	3.00	.60
☐	139 Steve Kraly	6.00	3.00	.60
☐	140 Mel Parnell	8.00	4.00	.80
☐	141 Tom Wright	6.00	3.00	.60
☐	142 Jerry Lynch	6.00	3.00	.60
☐	143 John(Dick) Schofield	6.00	3.00	.60
☐	144 John(Joe) Amalfitano	6.00	3.00	.60
☐	145 Elmer Valo	6.00	3.00	.60
☐	146 Dick Donovan	6.00	3.00	.60
☐	147 Hugh Pepper	6.00	3.00	.60
☐	148 Hector Brown	6.00	3.00	.60
☐	149 Ray Crone	6.00	3.00	.60
☐	150 Mike Higgins	6.00	3.00	.60
☐	151 Ralph Kress	12.00	6.00	1.20
☐	152 Harry Agganis	60.00	30.00	6.00
☐	153 Bud Podbielan	12.00	6.00	1.20
☐	154 Willie Miranda	12.00	6.00	1.20
☐	155 Eddie Mathews	80.00	40.00	8.00
☐	156 Joe Black	16.00	8.00	1.60
☐	157 Robert Miller	12.00	6.00	1.20
☐	158 Tommy Carroll	14.00	7.00	1.40
☐	159 Johnny Schmitz	12.00	6.00	1.20
☐	160 Ray Narleski	14.00	7.00	1.40
☐	161 Chuck Tanner	27.00	13.50	2.70
☐	162 Joe Coleman	15.00	7.50	1.50
☐	163 Faye Throneberry	15.00	7.50	1.50
☐	164 Roberto Clemente	950.00	475.00	95.00
☐	165 Don Johnson	15.00	7.50	1.50
☐	166 Hank Bauer	30.00	15.00	3.00
☐	167 Thomas Casagrande	15.00	7.50	1.50
☐	168 Duane Pillette	15.00	7.50	1.50
☐	169 Bob Oldis	15.00	7.50	1.50
☐	170 Jim Pearce DP	9.00	4.50	.90
☐	171 Dick Brodowski	15.00	7.50	1.50
☐	172 Frank Baumholtz DP	9.00	4.50	.90
☐	173 Johnny Kline	15.00	7.50	1.50
☐	174 Rudy Minarcin	15.00	7.50	1.50
☐	175 Does not exist	0.00	0.00	0.00
☐	176 Norm Zauchin	15.00	7.50	1.50
☐	177 Al Robertson	15.00	7.50	1.50
☐	178 Bobby Adams	15.00	7.50	1.50
☐	179 Jim Bolger	15.00	7.50	1.50
☐	180 Clem Labine	20.00	10.00	2.00

☐ 181	Roy McMillan	15.00	7.50	1.50
☐ 182	Humberto Robinson	15.00	7.50	1.50
☐ 183	Anthony Jacobs	15.00	7.50	1.50
☐ 184	Harry Perkowski DP	9.00	4.50	.90
☐ 185	Don Ferrarese	15.00	7.50	1.50
☐ 186	Does not exist	0.00	0.00	0.00
☐ 187	Gil Hodges	120.00	60.00	12.00
☐ 188	Charlie Silvera DP	9.00	4.50	.90
☐ 189	Phil Rizzuto	120.00	60.00	12.00
☐ 190	Gene Woodling	20.00	10.00	2.00
☐ 191	Eddie Stanky	20.00	10.00	2.00
☐ 192	Jim Delsing	15.00	7.50	1.50
☐ 193	Johnny Sain	27.00	13.50	2.70
☐ 194	Willie Mays	400.00	200.00	40.00
☐ 195	Ed Roebuck	20.00	10.00	2.00
☐ 196	Gale Wade	15.00	7.50	1.50
☐ 197	Al Smith	18.00	9.00	1.80
☐ 198	Yogi Berra	200.00	100.00	20.00
☐ 199	Odbert Hamric	15.00	7.50	1.50
☐ 200	Jackie Jensen	45.00	22.50	4.50
☐ 201	Sherm Lollar	18.00	9.00	1.80
☐ 202	Jim Owens	15.00	7.50	1.50
☐ 203	Does not exist	0.00	0.00	0.00
☐ 204	Frank Smith	15.00	7.50	1.50
☐ 205	Gene Freese	15.00	7.50	1.50
☐ 206	Pete Daley	15.00	7.50	1.50
☐ 207	Billy Consolo	15.00	7.50	1.50
☐ 208	Ray Moore	15.00	7.50	1.50
☐ 209	Does not exist	0.00	0.00	0.00
☐ 210	Duke Snider	400.00	100.00	25.00

1955 Topps Double Header

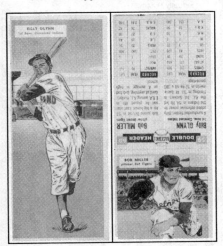

The cards in ths 66-card set measure 2 1/16" by 4 7/8". Borrowing a design from the T201 Mecca series, Topps issued a 132-player "Double Header" set in a separate wrapper in 1955. Each player is numbered in the biographical section on the reverse. When open, with perforated flap up, one player is revealed; when the flap is lowered, or closed, the player design on top incorporates a portion of the inside player artwork. When the cards are placed side by side, a continuous ballpark background is formed. Some cards have been found without perforations, and all players pictured appear in the low series of the 1955 regular issue.

		NRMT	VG-E	GOOD
COMPLETE SET (66)		2500.00	1250.00	300.00
COMMON PAIR (1-132)		25.00	12.50	2.50
☐ 1	Al Rosen and	30.00	15.00	3.00
	2 Chuck Diering			
☐ 3	Monte Irvin and	35.00	17.50	3.50
	4 Russ Kemmerer			
☐ 5	Ted Kazanski and	25.00	12.50	2.50
	6 Gordon Jones			
☐ 7	Bill Taylor and	25.00	12.50	2.50
	8 Billy O'Dell			
☐ 9	J.W. Porter and	25.00	12.50	2.50
	10 Thornton Kipper			
☐ 11	Curt Roberts and	25.00	12.50	2.50
	12 Arnie Portocarrero			
☐ 13	Wally Westlake and	25.00	12.50	2.50
	14 Frank House			
☐ 15	Rube Walker and	25.00	12.50	2.50
	16 Lou Limmer			
☐ 17	Dean Stone and	25.00	12.50	2.50
	18 Charlie White			
☐ 19	Karl Spooner and	25.00	12.50	2.50
	20 Jim Hughes			
☐ 21	Bill Skowron and	30.00	15.00	3.00
	22 Frank Sullivan			
☐ 23	Jack Shepard and	25.00	12.50	2.50
	24 Stan Hack			
☐ 25	Jackie Robinson and	150.00	75.00	15.00
	26 Don Hoak			
☐ 27	Dusty Rhodes and	25.00	12.50	2.50
	28 Jim Davis			
☐ 29	Vic Power and	25.00	12.50	2.50
	30 Ed Bailey			
☐ 31	Howie Pollet and	125.00	60.00	12.50
	32 Ernie Banks			
☐ 33	Jim Pendleton and	25.00	12.50	2.50
	34 Gene Conley			
☐ 35	Karl Olson and	25.00	12.50	2.50
	36 Andy Carey			
☐ 37	Wally Moon and	25.00	12.50	2.50
	38 Joe Cunningham			
☐ 39	Freddie Marsh and	25.00	12.50	2.50
	40 Vernon Thies			
☐ 41	Eddie Lopat and	30.00	15.00	3.00
	42 Harvey Haddix			
☐ 43	Leo Kiely and	25.00	12.50	2.50
	44 Chuck Stobbs			
☐ 45	Al Kaline and	150.00	75.00	15.00
	46 Harold Valentine			
☐ 47	Forrest Jacobs and	25.00	12.50	2.50
	48 Johnny Gray			
☐ 49	Ron Jackson and	25.00	12.50	2.50
	50 Jim Finigan			
☐ 51	Ray Jablonski and	25.00	12.50	2.50
	52 Bob Keegan			
☐ 53	Billy Herman and	35.00	17.50	3.50
	54 Sandy Amoros			
☐ 55	Chuck Harmon and	25.00	12.50	2.50
	56 Bob Skinner			
☐ 57	Dick Hall and	25.00	12.50	2.50
	58 Bob Grim			
☐ 59	Billy Glynn and	25.00	12.50	2.50
	60 Bob Miller			
☐ 61	Billy Gardner and	25.00	12.50	2.50
	62 John Hetki			
☐ 63	Bob Borkowski and	30.00	15.00	3.00
	64 Bob Turley			
☐ 65	Joe Collins and	25.00	12.50	2.50
	66 Jack Harshman			
☐ 67	Jim Hegan and	25.00	12.50	2.50
	68 Jack Parks			
☐ 69	Ted Williams and	250.00	125.00	25.00
	70 Mayo Smith			
☐ 71	Gair Allie and	25.00	12.50	2.50
	72 Grady Hatton			
☐ 73	Jerry Lynch and	25.00	12.50	2.50
	74 Harry Brecheen			
☐ 75	Tom Wright and	25.00	12.50	2.50
	76 Vernon Stewart			
☐ 77	Dave Hoskins and	25.00	12.50	2.50
	78 Warren McGhee			
☐ 79	Roy Sievers and	25.00	12.50	2.50
	80 Art Fowler			
☐ 81	Danny Schell and	25.00	12.50	2.50
	82 Gus Triandos			
☐ 83	Joe Frazier and	25.00	12.50	2.50
	84 Don Mossi			
☐ 85	Elmer Valo and	25.00	12.50	2.50
	86 Hector Brown			
☐ 87	Bob Kennedy and	25.00	12.50	2.50
	88 Windy McCall			
☐ 89	Ruben Gomez and	25.00	12.50	2.50
	90 Jim Rivera			
☐ 91	Louis Ortiz and	25.00	12.50	2.50
	92 Milt Bolling			
☐ 93	Carl Sawatski and	25.00	12.50	2.50
	94 El Tappe			
☐ 95	Dave Jolly and	25.00	12.50	2.50
	96 Bobby Hofman			
☐ 97	Preston Ward and	30.00	15.00	3.00
	98 Don Zimmer			
☐ 99	Bill Renna and	30.00	15.00	3.00
	100 Dick Groat			

		NRMT	VG-E	GOOD
☐ 101	Bill Wilson and .... 102 Bill Tremel	25.00	12.50	2.50
☐ 103	Hank Sauer and .... 104 Camilo Pascual	30.00	15.00	3.00
☐ 105	Hank Aaron and .... 106 Ray Herbert	300.00	150.00	30.00
☐ 107	Alex Grammas and .... 108 Tom Qualters	25.00	12.50	2.50
☐ 109	Hal Newhouser and .... 110 Chuck Bishop	30.00	15.00	3.00
☐ 111	Harmon Killebrew .... 112 John Podres	125.00	60.00	12.50
☐ 113	Ray Boone and .... 114 Bob Purkey	25.00	12.50	2.50
☐ 115	Dale Long and .... 116 Ferris Fain	25.00	12.50	2.50
☐ 117	Steve Bilko and .... 118 Bob Milliken	25.00	12.50	2.50
☐ 119	Mel Parnell and .... 120 Tom Hurd	25.00	12.50	2.50
☐ 121	Ted Kluszewski and .... 122 Jim Owens	30.00	15.00	3.00
☐ 123	Gus Zernial and .... 124 Bob Trice	25.00	12.50	2.50
☐ 125	Rip Repulski and .... 126 Ted Lepcio	25.00	12.50	2.50
☐ 127	Warren Spahn and .... 128 Tom Brewer	100.00	50.00	10.00
☐ 129	Jim Gilliam and .... 130 Ellis Kinder	30.00	15.00	3.00
☐ 131	Herm Wehmeier and ...... 132 Wayne Terwilliger	25.00	12.50	2.50

1956 Topps

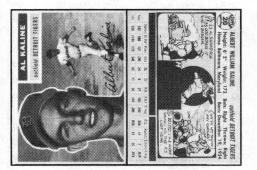

The cards in this 340-card set measure 2 5/8" by 3 3/4". Following up with another horizontally oriented card in 1956, Topps improved the format by layering the color "head" shot onto an actual action sequence involving the player. Cards 1 to 180 come with either white or gray backs: in the 1 to 100 sequence, gray backs are less common (worth about 10% more) and in the 101 to 180 sequence, white backs are less common (worth 30% more). The team cards, used for the first time in a regular set by Topps, are found dated 1955, or undated, with the team name appearing on either side. The dated team cards in the first series were not printed on the gray stock. The two unnumbered checklist cards are highly prized (must be unmarked to qualify as excellent or mint). The complete set price below does not include the unnumbered checklist cards or any of the variations.

	NRMT	VG-E	GOOD
COMPLETE SET (340)	6000.00	3000.00	700.00
COMMON PLAYER (1-100)	5.00	2.50	.50
COMMON PLAYER (101-180)	6.00	3.00	.60
COMMON PLAYER (181-260)	11.00	5.00	1.00
COMMON PLAYER (261-340)	7.00	3.50	.70

☐ 1	William Harridge .... (AL President)	100.00	10.00	2.00
☐ 2	Warren Giles DP .... (NL President)	12.00	6.00	1.20
☐ 3	Elmer Valo	5.00	2.50	.50
☐ 4	Carlos Paula	5.00	2.50	.50
☐ 5	Ted Williams	200.00	100.00	20.00
☐ 6	Ray Boone	5.00	2.50	.50
☐ 7	Ron Negray	5.00	2.50	.50
☐ 8	Walter Alston MG	25.00	11.00	2.25
☐ 9	Ruben Gomez	5.00	2.50	.50
☐ 10	Warren Spahn DP	45.00	22.50	4.50
☐ 11A	Chicago Cubs .... (centered)	15.00	7.50	1.50
☐ 11B	Cubs Team .... (dated 1955)	40.00	20.00	4.00
☐ 11C	Cubs Team .... (name at far left)	15.00	7.50	1.50
☐ 12	Andy Carey	6.00	3.00	.60
☐ 13	Roy Face	7.00	3.50	.70
☐ 14	Ken Boyer	10.00	5.00	1.00
☐ 15	Ernie Banks DP	55.00	27.50	5.50
☐ 16	Hector Lopez	5.00	2.50	.50
☐ 17	Gene Conley	5.00	2.50	.50
☐ 18	Dick Donovan	5.00	2.50	.50
☐ 19	Chuck Diering	5.00	2.50	.50
☐ 20	Al Kaline	65.00	32.50	6.50
☐ 21	Joe Collins	6.00	3.00	.60
☐ 22	Jim Finigan	5.00	2.50	.50
☐ 23	Fred Marsh	5.00	2.50	.50
☐ 24	Dick Groat	7.00	3.50	.70
☐ 25	Ted Kluszewski	12.00	6.00	1.20
☐ 26	Grady Hatton	5.00	2.50	.50
☐ 27	Nelson Burbrink	5.00	2.50	.50
☐ 28	Bobby Hofman	5.00	2.50	.50
☐ 29	Jack Harshman	5.00	2.50	.50
☐ 30	Jackie Robinson DP	125.00	60.00	12.50
☐ 31	Hank Aaron DP .... (small photo actually W.Mays)	160.00	80.00	16.00
☐ 32	Frank House	5.00	2.50	.50
☐ 33	Roberto Clemente	250.00	125.00	25.00
☐ 34	Tom Brewer	5.00	2.50	.50
☐ 35	Al Rosen DP	8.00	4.00	.80
☐ 36	Rudy Minarcin	5.00	2.50	.50
☐ 37	Alex Grammas	5.00	2.50	.50
☐ 38	Bob Kennedy	5.00	2.50	.50
☐ 39	Don Mossi	6.00	3.00	.60
☐ 40	Bob Turley	8.00	4.00	.80
☐ 41	Hank Sauer	6.00	3.00	.60
☐ 42	Sandy Amoros	7.00	3.50	.70
☐ 43	Ray Moore	5.00	2.50	.50
☐ 44	Windy McCall	5.00	2.50	.50
☐ 45	Gus Zernial	5.00	2.50	.50
☐ 46	Gene Freese	5.00	2.50	.50
☐ 47	Art Fowler	5.00	2.50	.50
☐ 48	Jim Hegan	5.00	2.50	.50
☐ 49	Pedro Ramos	5.00	2.50	.50
☐ 50	Dusty Rhodes	6.00	3.00	.60
☐ 51	Ernie Oravetz	5.00	2.50	.50
☐ 52	Bob Grim	6.00	3.00	.60
☐ 53	Arnie Portocarrero	5.00	2.50	.50
☐ 54	Bob Keegan	5.00	2.50	.50
☐ 55	Wally Moon	7.00	3.50	.70
☐ 56	Dale Long	6.00	3.00	.60
☐ 57	Duke Maas	5.00	2.50	.50
☐ 58	Ed Roebuck	6.00	3.00	.60
☐ 59	Jose Santiago	5.00	2.50	.50
☐ 60	Mayo Smith MG	5.00	2.50	.50
☐ 61	Bill Skowron	10.00	5.00	1.00
☐ 62	Hal Smith	5.00	2.50	.50
☐ 63	Roger Craig	18.00	9.00	1.80
☐ 64	Luis Arroyo	6.00	3.00	.60
☐ 65	Johnny O'Brien	5.00	2.50	.50
☐ 66	Bob Speake	5.00	2.50	.50
☐ 67	Vic Power	5.00	2.50	.50
☐ 68	Chuck Stobbs	5.00	2.50	.50
☐ 69	Chuck Tanner	7.00	3.50	.70
☐ 70	Jim Rivera	5.00	2.50	.50
☐ 71	Frank Sullivan	5.00	2.50	.50
☐ 72A	Phillies Team DP .... (centered)	15.00	7.50	1.50
☐ 72B	Phillies Team .... (dated 1955)	40.00	20.00	4.00
☐ 72C	Phillies Team .... (name at far left)	15.00	7.50	1.50
☐ 73	Wayne Terwilliger	5.00	2.50	.50
☐ 74	Jim King	5.00	2.50	.50
☐ 75	Roy Sievers	6.00	3.00	.60
☐ 76	Ray Crone	5.00	2.50	.50
☐ 77	Harvey Haddix	6.00	3.00	.60
☐ 78	Herman Wehmeier	5.00	2.50	.50
☐ 79	Sandy Koufax	225.00	110.00	22.00
☐ 80	Gus Triandos	6.00	3.00	.60
☐ 81	Wally Westlake	5.00	2.50	.50
☐ 82	Bill Renna	5.00	2.50	.50
☐ 83	Karl Spooner	6.00	3.00	.60
☐ 84	Babe Birrer	5.00	2.50	.50

☐ 85A	Cleveland Indians (centered)	15.00	7.50	1.50
☐ 85B	Indians Team (dated 1955)	40.00	20.00	4.00
☐ 85C	Indians Team (name at far left)	15.00	7.50	1.50
☐ 86	Ray Jablonski	5.00	2.50	.50
☐ 87	Dean Stone	5.00	2.50	.50
☐ 88	Johnny Kucks	6.00	3.00	.60
☐ 89	Norm Zauchin	5.00	2.50	.50
☐ 90A	Cincinnati Redlegs Team (centered)	15.00	7.50	1.50
☐ 90B	Reds Team (dated 1955)	40.00	20.00	4.00
☐ 90C	Reds Team (name at far left)	15.00	7.50	1.50
☐ 91	Gail Harris	5.00	2.50	.50
☐ 92	Bob(Red) Wilson	5.00	2.50	.50
☐ 93	George Susce	5.00	2.50	.50
☐ 94	Ron Kline	5.00	2.50	.50
☐ 95A	Milwaukee Braves Team (centered)	15.00	7.50	1.50
☐ 95B	Braves Team (dated 1955)	40.00	20.00	4.00
☐ 95C	Braves Team (name at far left)	15.00	7.50	1.50
☐ 96	Bill Tremel	5.00	2.50	.50
☐ 97	Jerry Lynch	5.00	2.50	.50
☐ 98	Camilo Pascual	6.00	3.00	.60
☐ 99	Don Zimmer	12.00	6.00	1.20
☐ 100A	Baltimore Orioles Team (centered)	15.00	7.50	1.50
☐ 100B	Orioles Team (dated 1955)	40.00	20.00	4.00
☐ 100C	Orioles Team (name at far left)	15.00	7.50	1.50
☐ 101	Roy Campanella	110.00	55.00	11.00
☐ 102	Jim Davis	6.00	3.00	.60
☐ 103	Willie Miranda	6.00	3.00	.60
☐ 104	Bob Lennon	6.00	3.00	.60
☐ 105	Al Smith	6.00	3.00	.60
☐ 106	Joe Astroth	6.00	3.00	.60
☐ 107	Eddie Mathews	45.00	22.50	4.50
☐ 108	Laurin Pepper	6.00	3.00	.60
☐ 109	Enos Slaughter	22.00	11.00	2.20
☐ 110	Yogi Berra	110.00	55.00	11.00
☐ 111	Boston Red Sox Team Card	15.00	7.50	1.50
☐ 112	Dee Fondy	6.00	3.00	.60
☐ 113	Phil Rizzuto	35.00	17.50	3.50
☐ 114	Jim Owens	6.00	3.00	.60
☐ 115	Jackie Jensen	10.00	5.00	1.00
☐ 116	Eddie O'Brien	6.00	3.00	.60
☐ 117	Virgil Trucks	7.00	3.50	.70
☐ 118	Nellie Fox	18.00	9.00	1.80
☐ 119	Larry Jackson	6.00	3.00	.60
☐ 120	Richie Ashburn	20.00	10.00	2.00
☐ 121	Pittsburgh Pirates Team Card	15.00	7.50	1.50
☐ 122	Willard Nixon	6.00	3.00	.60
☐ 123	Roy McMillan	6.00	3.00	.60
☐ 124	Don Kaiser	6.00	3.00	.60
☐ 125	Minnie Minoso	12.00	6.00	1.20
☐ 126	Jim Brady	6.00	3.00	.60
☐ 127	Willie Jones	6.00	3.00	.60
☐ 128	Eddie Yost	6.00	3.00	.60
☐ 129	Jake Martin	6.00	3.00	.60
☐ 130	Willie Mays	225.00	110.00	22.00
☐ 131	Bob Roselli	6.00	3.00	.60
☐ 132	Bobby Avila	7.00	3.50	.70
☐ 133	Ray Narleski	6.00	3.00	.60
☐ 134	St. Louis Cardinals Team Card	15.00	7.50	1.50
☐ 135	Mickey Mantle	750.00	375.00	75.00
☐ 136	Johnny Logan	7.00	3.50	.70
☐ 137	Al Silvera	6.00	3.00	.60
☐ 138	Johnny Antonelli	8.00	4.00	.80
☐ 139	Tommy Carroll	7.00	3.50	.70
☐ 140	Herb Score	16.00	8.00	1.60
☐ 141	Joe Frazier	6.00	3.00	.60
☐ 142	Gene Baker	6.00	3.00	.60
☐ 143	Jim Piersall	9.00	4.50	.90
☐ 144	Leroy Powell	6.00	3.00	.60
☐ 145	Gil Hodges	32.00	16.00	3.20
☐ 146	Washington Nationals Team Card	15.00	7.50	1.50
☐ 147	Earl Torgeson	6.00	3.00	.60
☐ 148	Alvin Dark	8.00	4.00	.80
☐ 149	Dixie Howell	6.00	3.00	.60
☐ 150	Duke Snider	100.00	50.00	10.00
☐ 151	Spook Jacobs	6.00	3.00	.60
☐ 152	Billy Hoeft	6.00	3.00	.60
☐ 153	Frank Thomas	7.00	3.50	.70
☐ 154	Dave Pope	6.00	3.00	.60
☐ 155	Harvey Kuenn	8.00	4.00	.80
☐ 156	Wes Westrum	6.00	3.00	.60
☐ 157	Dick Brodowski	6.00	3.00	.60
☐ 158	Wally Post	7.00	3.50	.70
☐ 159	Clint Courtney	6.00	3.00	.60
☐ 160	Billy Pierce	8.00	4.00	.80
☐ 161	Joe DeMaestri	6.00	3.00	.60
☐ 162	Dave(Gus) Bell	7.00	3.50	.70
☐ 163	Gene Woodling	8.00	4.00	.80
☐ 164	Harmon Killebrew	75.00	37.50	7.50
☐ 165	Red Schoendienst	24.00	12.00	2.40
☐ 166	Brooklyn Dodgers Team Card	150.00	75.00	15.00
☐ 167	Harry Dorish	6.00	3.00	.60
☐ 168	Sammy White	6.00	3.00	.60
☐ 169	Bob Nelson	6.00	3.00	.60
☐ 170	Bill Virdon	10.00	5.00	1.00
☐ 171	Jim Wilson	6.00	3.00	.60
☐ 172	Frank Torre	7.00	3.50	.70
☐ 173	Johnny Podres	12.00	6.00	1.20
☐ 174	Glen Gorbous	6.00	3.00	.60
☐ 175	Del Crandall	7.00	3.50	.70
☐ 176	Alex Kellner	6.00	3.00	.60
☐ 177	Hank Bauer	12.00	6.00	1.20
☐ 178	Joe Black	8.00	4.00	.80
☐ 179	Harry Chiti	6.00	3.00	.60
☐ 180	Robin Roberts	24.00	12.00	2.40
☐ 181	Billy Martin	60.00	30.00	6.00
☐ 182	Paul Minner	11.00	5.00	1.00
☐ 183	Stan Lopata	11.00	5.00	1.00
☐ 184	Don Bessent	11.00	5.00	1.00
☐ 185	Bill Bruton	11.00	5.00	1.00
☐ 186	Ron Jackson	11.00	5.00	1.00
☐ 187	Early Wynn	30.00	15.00	3.00
☐ 188	Chicago White Sox Team Card	24.00	12.00	2.40
☐ 189	Ned Garver	11.00	5.00	1.00
☐ 190	Carl Furillo	18.00	9.00	1.80
☐ 191	Frank Lary	12.50	6.00	1.20
☐ 192	Smoky Burgess	12.50	6.00	1.20
☐ 193	Wilmer Mizell	11.00	5.00	1.00
☐ 194	Monte Irvin	25.00	12.50	2.50
☐ 195	George Kell	25.00	12.50	2.50
☐ 196	Tom Poholsky	11.00	5.00	1.00
☐ 197	Granny Hamner	11.00	5.00	1.00
☐ 198	Ed Fitzgerald	11.00	5.00	1.00
☐ 199	Hank Thompson	12.50	6.00	1.20
☐ 200	Bob Feller	80.00	40.00	8.00
☐ 201	Rip Repulski	11.00	5.00	1.00
☐ 202	Jim Hearn	11.00	5.00	1.00
☐ 203	Bill Tuttle	11.00	5.00	1.00
☐ 204	Art Swanson	11.00	5.00	1.00
☐ 205	Whitey Lockman	12.50	6.00	1.20
☐ 206	Erv Palica	11.00	5.00	1.00
☐ 207	Jim Small	11.00	5.00	1.00
☐ 208	Elston Howard	30.00	15.00	3.00
☐ 209	Max Surkont	11.00	5.00	1.00
☐ 210	Mike Garcia	12.50	6.00	1.20
☐ 211	Murry Dickson	11.00	5.00	1.00
☐ 212	Johnny Temple	12.50	6.00	1.20
☐ 213	Detroit Tigers Team Card	30.00	15.00	3.00
☐ 214	Bob Rush	11.00	5.00	1.00
☐ 215	Tommy Byrne	12.50	6.00	1.20
☐ 216	Jerry Schoonmaker	11.00	5.00	1.00
☐ 217	Billy Klaus	11.00	5.00	1.00
☐ 218	Joe Nuxall (sic, Nuxhall)	12.50	6.00	1.20
☐ 219	Lew Burdette	16.00	8.00	1.60
☐ 220	Del Ennis	12.50	6.00	1.20
☐ 221	Bob Friend	12.50	6.00	1.20
☐ 222	Dave Philley	11.00	5.00	1.00
☐ 223	Randy Jackson	11.00	5.00	1.00
☐ 224	Bud Podbielan	11.00	5.00	1.00
☐ 225	Gil McDougald	18.00	9.00	1.80
☐ 226	New York Giants Team Card	50.00	25.00	5.00
☐ 227	Russ Meyer	11.00	5.00	1.00
☐ 228	Mickey Vernon	14.00	7.00	1.40
☐ 229	Harry Brecheen	12.50	6.00	1.20
☐ 230	Chico Carrasquel	11.00	5.00	1.00
☐ 231	Bob Hale	11.00	5.00	1.00
☐ 232	Toby Atwell	11.00	5.00	1.00
☐ 233	Carl Erskine	16.00	8.00	1.60
☐ 234	Pete Runnels	12.50	6.00	1.20
☐ 235	Don Newcombe	30.00	15.00	3.00
☐ 236	Kansas City Athletics Team Card	20.00	10.00	2.00
☐ 237	Jose Valdivielso	11.00	5.00	1.00
☐ 238	Walt Dropo	12.50	6.00	1.20
☐ 239	Harry Simpson	11.00	5.00	1.00
☐ 240	Whitey Ford	85.00	42.50	8.50
☐ 241	Don Mueller UER (6" tall)	14.00	7.00	1.40
☐ 242	Hershell Freeman	11.00	5.00	1.00
☐ 243	Sherm Lollar	12.50	6.00	1.20

☐ 244	Bob Buhl	11.00	5.00	1.00
☐ 245	Billy Goodman	12.50	6.00	1.20
☐ 246	Tom Gorman	11.00	5.00	1.00
☐ 247	Bill Sarni	11.00	5.00	1.00
☐ 248	Bob Porterfield	11.00	5.00	1.00
☐ 249	Johnny Klippstein	11.00	5.00	1.00
☐ 250	Larry Doby	15.00	7.50	1.50
☐ 251	New York Yankees Team Card	150.00	75.00	15.00
☐ 252	Vern Law	12.50	6.00	1.20
☐ 253	Irv Noren	12.50	6.00	1.20
☐ 254	George Crowe	11.00	5.00	1.00
☐ 255	Bob Lemon	30.00	15.00	3.00
☐ 256	Tom Hurd	11.00	5.00	1.00
☐ 257	Bobby Thomson	14.00	7.00	1.40
☐ 258	Art Ditmar	12.50	6.00	1.20
☐ 259	Sam Jones	12.50	6.00	1.20
☐ 260	Pee Wee Reese	100.00	50.00	10.00
☐ 261	Bobby Shantz	10.00	5.00	1.00
☐ 262	Howie Pollet	7.00	3.50	.70
☐ 263	Bob Miller	7.00	3.50	.70
☐ 264	Ray Monzant	7.00	3.50	.70
☐ 265	Sandy Consuegra	7.00	3.50	.70
☐ 266	Don Ferrarese	7.00	3.50	.70
☐ 267	Bob Nieman	7.00	3.50	.70
☐ 268	Dale Mitchell	8.00	4.00	.80
☐ 269	Jack Meyer	7.00	3.50	.70
☐ 270	Billy Loes	8.00	4.00	.80
☐ 271	Foster Castleman	7.00	3.50	.70
☐ 272	Danny O'Connell	7.00	3.50	.70
☐ 273	Walker Cooper	7.00	3.50	.70
☐ 274	Frank Baumholtz	7.00	3.50	.70
☐ 275	Jim Greengrass	7.00	3.50	.70
☐ 276	George Zuverink	7.00	3.50	.70
☐ 277	Daryl Spencer	7.00	3.50	.70
☐ 278	Chet Nichols	7.00	3.50	.70
☐ 279	Johnny Groth	7.00	3.50	.70
☐ 280	Jim Gilliam	12.00	6.00	1.20
☐ 281	Art Houtteman	7.00	3.50	.70
☐ 282	Warren Hacker	7.00	3.50	.70
☐ 283	Hal Smith	7.00	3.50	.70
☐ 284	Ike Delock	7.00	3.50	.70
☐ 285	Eddie Miksis	7.00	3.50	.70
☐ 286	Bill Wight	7.00	3.50	.70
☐ 287	Bobby Adams	7.00	3.50	.70
☐ 288	Bob Cerv	11.00	5.50	1.10
☐ 289	Hal Jeffcoat	7.00	3.50	.70
☐ 290	Curt Simmons	9.00	4.50	.90
☐ 291	Frank Kellert	7.00	3.50	.70
☐ 292	Luis Aparicio	100.00	50.00	10.00
☐ 293	Stu Miller	8.00	4.00	.80
☐ 294	Ernie Johnson	8.00	4.00	.80
☐ 295	Clem Labine	9.00	4.50	.90
☐ 296	Andy Seminick	7.00	3.50	.70
☐ 297	Bob Skinner	8.00	4.00	.80
☐ 298	Johnny Schmitz	7.00	3.50	.70
☐ 299	Charlie Neal	14.00	7.00	1.40
☐ 300	Vic Wertz	8.00	4.00	.80
☐ 301	Marv Grissom	7.00	3.50	.70
☐ 302	Eddie Robinson	7.00	3.50	.70
☐ 303	Jim Dyck	7.00	3.50	.70
☐ 304	Frank Malzone	14.00	7.00	1.40
☐ 305	Brooks Lawrence	7.00	3.50	.70
☐ 306	Curt Roberts	7.00	3.50	.70
☐ 307	Hoyt Wilhelm	25.00	12.50	2.50
☐ 308	Chuck Harmon	7.00	3.50	.70
☐ 309	Don Blasingame	7.00	3.50	.70
☐ 310	Steve Gromek	7.00	3.50	.70
☐ 311	Hal Naragon	7.00	3.50	.70
☐ 312	Andy Pafko	8.00	4.00	.80
☐ 313	Gene Stephens	7.00	3.50	.70
☐ 314	Hobie Landrith	7.00	3.50	.70
☐ 315	Milt Bolling	7.00	3.50	.70
☐ 316	Jerry Coleman	9.00	4.50	.90
☐ 317	Al Aber	7.00	3.50	.70
☐ 318	Fred Hatfield	7.00	3.50	.70
☐ 319	Jack Crimian	7.00	3.50	.70
☐ 320	Joe Adcock	9.00	4.50	.90
☐ 321	Jim Konstanty	8.00	4.00	.80
☐ 322	Karl Olson	7.00	3.50	.70
☐ 323	Willard Schmidt	7.00	3.50	.70
☐ 324	Rocky Bridges	7.00	3.50	.70
☐ 325	Don Liddle	7.00	3.50	.70
☐ 326	Connie Johnson	7.00	3.50	.70
☐ 327	Bob Wiesler	7.00	3.50	.70
☐ 328	Preston Ward	7.00	3.50	.70
☐ 329	Lou Berberet	7.00	3.50	.70
☐ 330	Jim Busby	7.00	3.50	.70
☐ 331	Dick Hall	7.00	3.50	.70
☐ 332	Don Larsen	21.00	10.50	2.10
☐ 333	Rube Walker	8.00	4.00	.80
☐ 334	Bob Miller	7.00	3.50	.70
☐ 335	Don Hoak	8.00	4.00	.80
☐ 336	Ellis Kinder	7.00	3.50	.70
☐ 337	Bobby Morgan	7.00	3.50	.70
☐ 338	Jim Delsing	7.00	3.50	.70
☐ 339	Rance Pless	7.00	3.50	.70
☐ 340	Mickey McDermott	20.00	4.00	.80
☐ 341	Checklist 1/3 (unnumbered)	225.00	25.00	5.00
☐ 342	Checklist 2/4 (unnumbered)	225.00	25.00	5.00

1957 Topps

The cards in this 407-card set measure 2 1/2" by 3 1/2". In 1957, Topps returned to the vertical obverse, adopted what we now call the standard card size, and used a large, uncluttered color photo for the first time since 1952. Cards in the series 265 to 352 and the unnumbered checklist cards are scarcer than other cards in the set. However within this scarce series (265-352) there are 22 cards which were printed in double the quantity of the other cards in the series; these 22 double prints are indicated by DP in the checklist below. The first star combination cards, #400 and #407, are quite popular with collectors. They feature the big stars of the previous season's World Series teams, the Dodgers (Furillo, Hodges, Campanella, and Snider) and Yankees (Berra and Mantle). The complete set price below does not include the unnumbered checklist cards.

	NRMT	VG-E	GOOD
COMPLETE SET (407)	6900.00	3300.00	850.00
COMMON PLAYER (1-88)	5.00	2.50	.50
COMMON PLAYER (89-176)	4.00	2.00	.40
COMMON PLAYER (177-264)	3.00	1.50	.30
COMMON PLAYER (265-352)	15.00	7.50	1.50
COMMON DP (265-352)	10.00	5.00	1.00
COMMON PLAYER (353-407)	4.00	2.00	.40

☐ 1	Ted Williams	400.00	100.00	20.00
☐ 2	Yogi Berra	125.00	60.00	12.50
☐ 3	Dale Long	6.00	3.00	.60
☐ 4	Johnny Logan	6.00	3.00	.60
☐ 5	Sal Maglie	8.00	4.00	.80
☐ 6	Hector Lopez	5.00	2.50	.50
☐ 7	Luis Aparicio	25.00	12.50	2.50
☐ 8	Don Mossi	6.00	3.00	.60
☐ 9	Johnny Temple	6.00	3.00	.60
☐ 10	Willie Mays	180.00	90.00	18.00
☐ 11	George Zuverink	5.00	2.50	.50
☐ 12	Dick Groat	8.00	4.00	.80
☐ 13	Wally Burnette	5.00	2.50	.50
☐ 14	Bob Nieman	5.00	2.50	.50
☐ 15	Robin Roberts	20.00	10.00	2.00
☐ 16	Walt Moryn	5.00	2.50	.50
☐ 17	Billy Gardner	6.00	3.00	.60
☐ 18	Don Drysdale	175.00	85.00	18.00
☐ 19	Bob Wilson	5.00	2.50	.50
☐ 20	Hank Aaron (reverse negative photo on front)	200.00	100.00	20.00
☐ 21	Frank Sullivan	5.00	2.50	.50
☐ 22	Jerry Snyder (photo actually Ed Fitzgerald)	5.00	2.50	.50
☐ 23	Sherm Lollar	6.00	3.00	.60

☐	24	Bill Mazeroski	25.00	12.50	2.50
☐	25	Whitey Ford	50.00	25.00	5.00
☐	26	Bob Boyd	5.00	2.50	.50
☐	27	Ted Kazanski	5.00	2.50	.50
☐	28	Gene Conley	5.00	2.50	.50
☐	29	Whitey Herzog	20.00	10.00	2.00
☐	30	Pee Wee Reese	45.00	22.50	4.50
☐	31	Ron Northey	5.00	2.50	.50
☐	32	Hershell Freeman	5.00	2.50	.50
☐	33	Jim Small	5.00	2.50	.50
☐	34	Tom Sturdivant	5.00	2.50	.50
☐	35	Frank Robinson	200.00	100.00	20.00
☐	36	Bob Grim	6.00	3.00	.60
☐	37	Frank Torre	5.00	2.50	.50
☐	38	Nellie Fox	13.00	6.50	1.30
☐	39	Al Worthington	5.00	2.50	.50
☐	40	Early Wynn	18.00	9.00	1.80
☐	41	Hal W. Smith	5.00	2.50	.50
☐	42	Dee Fondy	5.00	2.50	.50
☐	43	Connie Johnson	5.00	2.50	.50
☐	44	Joe DeMaestri	5.00	2.50	.50
☐	45	Carl Furillo	9.00	4.50	.90
☐	46	Robert J. Miller	5.00	2.50	.50
☐	47	Don Blasingame	5.00	2.50	.50
☐	48	Bill Bruton	6.00	3.00	.60
☐	49	Daryl Spencer	5.00	2.50	.50
☐	50	Herb Score	8.00	4.00	.80
☐	51	Clint Courtney	5.00	2.50	.50
☐	52	Lee Walls	5.00	2.50	.50
☐	53	Clem Labine	6.00	3.00	.60
☐	54	Elmer Valo	5.00	2.50	.50
☐	55	Ernie Banks	65.00	32.50	6.50
☐	56	Dave Sisler	5.00	2.50	.50
☐	57	Jim Lemon	6.00	3.00	.60
☐	58	Ruben Gomez	5.00	2.50	.50
☐	59	Dick Williams	6.00	3.00	.60
☐	60	Billy Hoeft	5.00	2.50	.50
☐	61	James "Dusty" Rhodes	6.00	3.00	.60
☐	62	Billy Martin	40.00	20.00	4.00
☐	63	Ike Delock	5.00	2.50	.50
☐	64	Pete Runnels	6.00	3.00	.60
☐	65	Wally Moon	6.00	3.00	.60
☐	66	Brooks Lawrence	5.00	2.50	.50
☐	67	Chico Carrasquel	5.00	2.50	.50
☐	68	Ray Crone	5.00	2.50	.50
☐	69	Roy McMillan	5.00	2.50	.50
☐	70	Richie Ashburn	15.00	7.50	1.50
☐	71	Murry Dickson	5.00	2.50	.50
☐	72	Bill Tuttle	5.00	2.50	.50
☐	73	George Crowe	5.00	2.50	.50
☐	74	Vito Valentinetti	5.00	2.50	.50
☐	75	Jim Piersall	8.00	4.00	.80
☐	76	Roberto Clemente	160.00	80.00	16.00
☐	77	Paul Foytack	5.00	2.50	.50
☐	78	Vic Wertz	6.00	3.00	.60
☐	79	Lindy McDaniel	6.00	3.00	.60
☐	80	Gil Hodges	32.00	16.00	3.20
☐	81	Herman Wehmeier	5.00	2.50	.50
☐	82	Elston Howard	10.00	5.00	1.00
☐	83	Lou Skizas	5.00	2.50	.50
☐	84	Moe Drabowsky	5.00	2.50	.50
☐	85	Larry Doby	8.00	4.00	.80
☐	86	Bill Sarni	5.00	2.50	.50
☐	87	Tom Gorman	5.00	2.50	.50
☐	88	Harvey Kuenn	8.00	4.00	.80
☐	89	Roy Sievers	5.00	2.50	.50
☐	90	Warren Spahn	45.00	22.50	4.50
☐	91	Mack Burk	4.00	2.00	.40
☐	92	Mickey Vernon	5.00	2.50	.50
☐	93	Hal Jeffcoat	4.00	2.00	.40
☐	94	Bobby Del Greco	4.00	2.00	.40
☐	95	Mickey Mantle	750.00	375.00	75.00
☐	96	Hank Aguirre	4.00	2.00	.40
☐	97	New York Yankees Team Card	33.00	15.00	3.00
☐	98	Alvin Dark	6.00	3.00	.60
☐	99	Bob Keegan	4.00	2.00	.40
☐	100	Giles and Harridge League Presidents	6.00	3.00	.60
☐	101	Chuck Stobbs	4.00	2.00	.40
☐	102	Ray Boone	5.00	2.50	.50
☐	103	Joe Nuxhall	5.00	2.50	.50
☐	104	Hank Foiles	4.00	2.00	.40
☐	105	Johnny Antonelli	5.00	2.50	.50
☐	106	Ray Moore	4.00	2.00	.40
☐	107	Jim Rivera	4.00	2.00	.40
☐	108	Tommy Byrne	5.00	2.50	.50
☐	109	Hank Thompson	5.00	2.50	.50
☐	110	Bill Virdon	6.00	3.00	.60
☐	111	Hal R. Smith	4.00	2.00	.40
☐	112	Tom Brewer	4.00	2.00	.40
☐	113	Wilmer Mizell	4.00	2.00	.40
☐	114	Milwaukee Braves Team Card	9.00	4.50	.90
☐	115	Jim Gilliam	8.00	4.00	.80
☐	116	Mike Fornieles	4.00	2.00	.40
☐	117	Joe Adcock	6.00	3.00	.60
☐	118	Bob Porterfield	4.00	2.00	.40
☐	119	Stan Lopata	4.00	2.00	.40
☐	120	Bob Lemon	16.00	8.00	1.60
☐	121	Clete Boyer	12.00	6.00	1.20
☐	122	Ken Boyer	8.00	4.00	.80
☐	123	Steve Ridzik	4.00	2.00	.40
☐	124	Dave Philley	4.00	2.00	.40
☐	125	Al Kaline	65.00	32.50	6.50
☐	126	Bob Wiesler	4.00	2.00	.40
☐	127	Bob Buhl	4.00	2.00	.40
☐	128	Ed Bailey	5.00	2.50	.50
☐	129	Saul Rogovin	4.00	2.00	.40
☐	130	Don Newcombe	8.00	4.00	.80
☐	131	Milt Bolling	4.00	2.00	.40
☐	132	Art Ditmar	5.00	2.50	.50
☐	133	Del Crandall	5.00	2.50	.50
☐	134	Don Kaiser	4.00	2.00	.40
☐	135	Bill Skowron	10.00	5.00	1.00
☐	136	Jim Hegan	5.00	2.50	.50
☐	137	Bob Rush	4.00	2.00	.40
☐	138	Minnie Minoso	8.00	4.00	.80
☐	139	Lou Kretlow	4.00	2.00	.40
☐	140	Frank Thomas	5.00	2.50	.50
☐	141	Al Aber	4.00	2.00	.40
☐	142	Charley Thompson	4.00	2.00	.40
☐	143	Andy Pafko	5.00	2.50	.50
☐	144	Ray Narleski	4.00	2.00	.40
☐	145	Al Smith	4.00	2.00	.40
☐	146	Don Ferrarese	4.00	2.00	.40
☐	147	Al Walker	4.00	2.00	.40
☐	148	Don Mueller	5.00	2.50	.50
☐	149	Bob Kennedy	4.00	2.00	.40
☐	150	Bob Friend	5.00	2.50	.50
☐	151	Willie Miranda	4.00	2.00	.40
☐	152	Jack Harshman	4.00	2.00	.40
☐	153	Karl Olson	4.00	2.00	.40
☐	154	Red Schoendienst	18.50	9.00	2.00
☐	155	Jim Brosnan	5.00	2.50	.50
☐	156	Gus Triandos	5.00	2.50	.50
☐	157	Wally Post	5.00	2.50	.50
☐	158	Curt Simmons	5.00	2.50	.50
☐	159	Solly Drake	4.00	2.00	.40
☐	160	Billy Pierce	6.00	3.00	.60
☐	161	Pittsburgh Pirates Team Card	8.00	4.00	.80
☐	162	Jack Meyer	4.00	2.00	.40
☐	163	Sammy White	4.00	2.00	.40
☐	164	Tommy Carroll	4.00	2.00	.40
☐	165	Ted Kluszewski	12.00	6.00	1.20
☐	166	Roy Face	6.00	3.00	.60
☐	167	Vic Power	5.00	2.50	.50
☐	168	Frank Lary	5.00	2.50	.50
☐	169	Herb Plews	4.00	2.00	.40
☐	170	Duke Snider	80.00	40.00	8.00
☐	171	Boston Red Sox Team Card	9.00	4.50	.90
☐	172	Gene Woodling	6.00	3.00	.60
☐	173	Roger Craig	9.00	4.50	.90
☐	174	Willie Jones	4.00	2.00	.40
☐	175	Don Larsen	10.00	5.00	1.00
☐	176	Gene Baker	4.00	2.00	.40
☐	177	Eddie Yost	3.00	1.50	.30
☐	178	Don Bessent	3.00	1.50	.30
☐	179	Ernie Oravetz	3.00	1.50	.30
☐	180	Dave (Gus) Bell	4.00	2.00	.40
☐	181	Dick Donovan	3.00	1.50	.30
☐	182	Hobie Landrith	3.00	1.50	.30
☐	183	Chicago Cubs Team Card	7.00	3.50	.70
☐	184	Tito Francona	4.00	2.00	.40
☐	185	Johnny Kucks	4.00	2.00	.40
☐	186	Jim King	3.00	1.50	.30
☐	187	Virgil Trucks	4.00	2.00	.40
☐	188	Felix Mantilla	3.00	1.50	.30
☐	189	Willard Nixon	3.00	1.50	.30
☐	190	Randy Jackson	3.00	1.50	.30
☐	191	Joe Margoneri	3.00	1.50	.30
☐	192	Jerry Coleman	4.00	2.00	.40
☐	193	Del Rice	3.00	1.50	.30
☐	194	Hal Brown	3.00	1.50	.30
☐	195	Bobby Avila	3.00	1.50	.30
☐	196	Larry Jackson	3.00	1.50	.30
☐	197	Hank Sauer	4.00	2.00	.40
☐	198	Detroit Tigers Team Card	9.00	4.50	.90
☐	199	Vern Law	4.00	2.00	.40
☐	200	Gil McDougald	8.00	4.00	.80
☐	201	Sandy Amoros	4.00	2.00	.40
☐	202	Dick Gernert	3.00	1.50	.30
☐	203	Hoyt Wilhelm	16.00	8.00	1.60
☐	204	Kansas City Athletics Team Card	7.00	3.50	.70
☐	205	Charlie Maxwell	3.00	1.50	.30

☐ 206	Willard Schmidt	3.00	1.50	.30
☐ 207	Gordon(Billy) Hunter	3.00	1.50	.30
☐ 208	Lou Burdette	5.00	2.50	.50
☐ 209	Bob Skinner	4.00	2.00	.40
☐ 210	Roy Campanella	80.00	40.00	8.00
☐ 211	Camilo Pascual	4.00	2.00	.40
☐ 212	Rocco Colavito	40.00	20.00	4.00
☐ 213	Les Moss	3.00	1.50	.30
☐ 214	Philadelphia Phillies Team Card	7.00	3.50	.70
☐ 215	Enos Slaughter	18.00	9.00	1.80
☐ 216	Marv Grissom	3.00	1.50	.30
☐ 217	Gene Stephens	3.00	1.50	.30
☐ 218	Ray Jablonski	3.00	1.50	.30
☐ 219	Tom Acker	3.00	1.50	.30
☐ 220	Jackie Jensen	7.00	3.50	.70
☐ 221	Dixie Howell	3.00	1.50	.30
☐ 222	Alex Grammas	3.00	1.50	.30
☐ 223	Frank House	3.00	1.50	.30
☐ 224	Marv Blaylock	3.00	1.50	.30
☐ 225	Harry Simpson	3.00	1.50	.30
☐ 226	Preston Ward	3.00	1.50	.30
☐ 227	Jerry Staley	3.00	1.50	.30
☐ 228	Smoky Burgess	4.00	2.00	.40
☐ 229	George Susce	3.00	1.50	.30
☐ 230	George Kell	15.00	7.50	1.50
☐ 231	Solly Hemus	3.00	1.50	.30
☐ 232	Whitey Lockman	4.00	2.00	.40
☐ 233	Art Fowler	3.00	1.50	.30
☐ 234	Dick Cole	3.00	1.50	.30
☐ 235	Tom Poholsky	3.00	1.50	.30
☐ 236	Joe Ginsberg	3.00	1.50	.30
☐ 237	Foster Castleman	3.00	1.50	.30
☐ 238	Eddie Robinson	3.00	1.50	.30
☐ 239	Tom Morgan	3.00	1.50	.30
☐ 240	Hank Bauer	8.00	4.00	.80
☐ 241	Joe Lonnett	3.00	1.50	.30
☐ 242	Charlie Neal	4.00	2.00	.40
☐ 243	St. Louis Cardinals Team Card	9.00	4.50	.90
☐ 244	Billy Loes	4.00	2.00	.40
☐ 245	Rip Repulski	3.00	1.50	.30
☐ 246	Jose Valdivielso	3.00	1.50	.30
☐ 247	Turk Lown	3.00	1.50	.30
☐ 248	Jim Finigan	3.00	1.50	.30
☐ 249	Dave Pope	3.00	1.50	.30
☐ 250	Eddie Mathews	25.00	12.50	2.50
☐ 251	Baltimore Orioles Team Card	8.00	4.00	.80
☐ 252	Carl Erskine	7.00	3.50	.70
☐ 253	Gus Zernial	4.00	2.00	.40
☐ 254	Ron Negray	3.00	1.50	.30
☐ 255	Charlie Silvera	3.00	1.50	.30
☐ 256	Ron Kline	3.00	1.50	.30
☐ 257	Walt Dropo	3.00	1.50	.30
☐ 258	Steve Gromek	3.00	1.50	.30
☐ 259	Eddie O'Brien	3.00	1.50	.30
☐ 260	Del Ennis	4.00	2.00	.40
☐ 261	Bob Chakales	3.00	1.50	.30
☐ 262	Bobby Thomson	7.00	3.50	.70
☐ 263	George Strickland	3.00	1.50	.30
☐ 264	Bob Turley	8.00	4.00	.80
☐ 265	Harvey Haddix DP	15.00	7.50	1.50
☐ 266	Ken Kuhn DP	10.00	5.00	1.00
☐ 267	Danny Kravitz	15.00	7.50	1.50
☐ 268	Jack Collum	15.00	7.50	1.50
☐ 269	Bob Cerv	18.00	9.00	1.80
☐ 270	Washington Senators Team Card	30.00	15.00	3.00
☐ 271	Danny O'Connell DP	10.00	5.00	1.00
☐ 272	Bobby Shantz	22.00	11.00	2.20
☐ 273	Jim Davis	15.00	7.50	1.50
☐ 274	Don Hoak	18.00	9.00	1.80
☐ 275	Cleveland Indians Team Card	30.00	15.00	3.00
☐ 276	Jim Pyburn	15.00	7.50	1.50
☐ 277	Johnny Podres DP	45.00	20.00	4.00
☐ 278	Fred Hatfield DP	10.00	5.00	1.00
☐ 279	Bob Thurman	15.00	7.50	1.50
☐ 280	Alex Kellner	15.00	7.50	1.50
☐ 281	Gail Harris	15.00	7.50	1.50
☐ 282	Jack Dittmer DP	10.00	5.00	1.00
☐ 283	Wes Covington DP	12.00	6.00	1.20
☐ 284	Don Zimmer	22.00	11.00	2.20
☐ 285	Ned Garver	15.00	7.50	1.50
☐ 286	Bobby Richardson	90.00	45.00	9.00
☐ 287	Sam Jones	18.00	9.00	1.80
☐ 288	Ted Lepcio	15.00	7.50	1.50
☐ 289	Jim Bolger DP	10.00	5.00	1.00
☐ 290	Andy Carey DP	15.00	7.50	1.50
☐ 291	Windy McCall	15.00	7.50	1.50
☐ 292	Billy Klaus	15.00	7.50	1.50
☐ 293	Ted Abernathy	15.00	7.50	1.50
☐ 294	Rocky Bridges DP	10.00	5.00	1.00
☐ 295	Joe Collins DP	15.00	7.50	1.50
☐ 296	Johnny Klippstein	15.00	7.50	1.50
☐ 297	Jack Crimian	15.00	7.50	1.50
☐ 298	Irv Noren DP	10.00	5.00	1.00
☐ 299	Chuck Harmon	15.00	7.50	1.50
☐ 300	Mike Garcia	18.00	9.00	1.80
☐ 301	Sammy Esposito DP	10.00	5.00	1.00
☐ 302	Sandy Koufax DP	300.00	125.00	30.00
☐ 303	Billy Goodman	18.00	9.00	1.80
☐ 304	Joe Cunningham	18.00	9.00	1.80
☐ 305	Chico Fernandez	15.00	7.50	1.50
☐ 306	Darrell Johnson DP	15.00	7.50	1.50
☐ 307	Jack D. Phillips DP	10.00	5.00	1.00
☐ 308	Dick Hall	15.00	7.50	1.50
☐ 309	Jim Busby DP	10.00	5.00	1.00
☐ 310	Max Surkont DP	10.00	5.00	1.00
☐ 311	Al Pilarcik DP	10.00	5.00	1.00
☐ 312	Tony Kubek DP	100.00	45.00	9.00
☐ 313	Mel Parnell	18.00	9.00	1.80
☐ 314	Ed Bouchee DP	10.00	5.00	1.00
☐ 315	Lou Berberet DP	10.00	5.00	1.00
☐ 316	Billy O'Dell	15.00	7.50	1.50
☐ 317	New York Giants Team Card	50.00	25.00	5.00
☐ 318	Mickey McDermott	15.00	7.50	1.50
☐ 319	Gino Cimoli	18.00	9.00	1.80
☐ 320	Neil Chrisley	15.00	7.50	1.50
☐ 321	John (Red) Murff	15.00	7.50	1.50
☐ 322	Cincinnati Reds Team Card	50.00	25.00	5.00
☐ 323	Wes Westrum	18.00	9.00	1.80
☐ 324	Brooklyn Dodgers Team Card	100.00	50.00	10.00
☐ 325	Frank Bolling	15.00	7.50	1.50
☐ 326	Pedro Ramos	15.00	7.50	1.50
☐ 327	Jim Pendleton	15.00	7.50	1.50
☐ 328	Brooks Robinson	350.00	175.00	35.00
☐ 329	Chicago White Sox Team Card	30.00	15.00	3.00
☐ 330	Jim Wilson	15.00	7.50	1.50
☐ 331	Ray Katt	15.00	7.50	1.50
☐ 332	Bob Bowman	15.00	7.50	1.50
☐ 333	Ernie Johnson	18.00	9.00	1.80
☐ 334	Jerry Schoonmaker	15.00	7.50	1.50
☐ 335	Granny Hamner	15.00	7.50	1.50
☐ 336	Haywood Sullivan	18.00	9.00	1.80
☐ 337	Rene Valdes	15.00	7.50	1.50
☐ 338	Jim Bunning	100.00	50.00	10.00
☐ 339	Bob Speake	15.00	7.50	1.50
☐ 340	Bill Wight	15.00	7.50	1.50
☐ 341	Don Gross	15.00	7.50	1.50
☐ 342	Gene Mauch	18.00	9.00	1.80
☐ 343	Taylor Phillips	15.00	7.50	1.50
☐ 344	Paul LaPalme	15.00	7.50	1.50
☐ 345	Paul Smith	15.00	7.50	1.50
☐ 346	Dick Littlefield	15.00	7.50	1.50
☐ 347	Hal Naragon	15.00	7.50	1.50
☐ 348	Jim Hearn	15.00	7.50	1.50
☐ 349	Nellie King	15.00	7.50	1.50
☐ 350	Eddie Miksis	15.00	7.50	1.50
☐ 351	Dave Hillman	15.00	7.50	1.50
☐ 352	Ellis Kinder	15.00	7.50	1.50
☐ 353	Cal Neeman	4.00	2.00	.40
☐ 354	W. (Rip) Coleman	4.00	2.00	.40
☐ 355	Frank Malzone	5.00	2.50	.50
☐ 356	Faye Throneberry	4.00	2.00	.40
☐ 357	Earl Torgeson	4.00	2.00	.40
☐ 358	Jerry Lynch	4.00	2.00	.40
☐ 359	Tom Cheney	4.00	2.00	.40
☐ 360	Johnny Groth	4.00	2.00	.40
☐ 361	Curt Barclay	4.00	2.00	.40
☐ 362	Roman Mejias	4.00	2.00	.40
☐ 363	Eddie Kasko	4.00	2.00	.40
☐ 364	Cal McLish	4.00	2.00	.40
☐ 365	Ozzie Virgil	4.00	2.00	.40
☐ 366	Ken Lehman	4.00	2.00	.40
☐ 367	Ed Fitzgerald	4.00	2.00	.40
☐ 368	Bob Purkey	4.00	2.00	.40
☐ 369	Milt Graff	4.00	2.00	.40
☐ 370	Warren Hacker	4.00	2.00	.40
☐ 371	Bob Lennon	4.00	2.00	.40
☐ 372	Norm Zauchin	4.00	2.00	.40
☐ 373	Pete Whisenant	4.00	2.00	.40
☐ 374	Don Cardwell	4.00	2.00	.40
☐ 375	Jim Landis	4.00	2.00	.40
☐ 376	Don Elston	4.00	2.00	.40
☐ 377	Andre Rodgers	4.00	2.00	.40
☐ 378	Elmer Singleton	4.00	2.00	.40
☐ 379	Don Lee	4.00	2.00	.40
☐ 380	Walker Cooper	4.00	2.00	.40
☐ 381	Dean Stone	4.00	2.00	.40
☐ 382	Jim Brideweser	4.00	2.00	.40
☐ 383	Juan Pizarro	4.00	2.00	.40
☐ 384	Bobby G. Smith	4.00	2.00	.40
☐ 385	Art Houtteman	4.00	2.00	.40
☐ 386	Lyle Luttrell	4.00	2.00	.40

		NRMT	VG-E	GOOD
☐ 387	Jack Sanford	7.00	3.50	.70
☐ 388	Pete Daley	4.00	2.00	.40
☐ 389	Dave Jolly	4.00	2.00	.40
☐ 390	Reno Bertoia	4.00	2.00	.40
☐ 391	Ralph Terry	8.00	4.00	.80
☐ 392	Chuck Tanner	6.00	3.00	.60
☐ 393	Raul Sanchez	4.00	2.00	.40
☐ 394	Luis Arroyo	5.00	2.50	.50
☐ 395	J.M.(Bubba) Phillips	4.00	2.00	.40
☐ 396	K. (Casey) Wise	4.00	2.00	.40
☐ 397	Roy Smalley	4.00	2.00	.40
☐ 398	Al Cicotte	5.00	2.50	.50
☐ 399	Billy Consolo	4.00	2.00	.40
☐ 400	Dodgers' Sluggers	150.00	75.00	15.00
	Carl Furillo			
	Gil Hodges			
	Roy Campanella			
	Duke Snider			
☐ 401	Earl Battey	5.00	2.50	.50
☐ 402	Jim Pisoni	4.00	2.00	.40
☐ 403	Dick Hyde	4.00	2.00	.40
☐ 404	Harry Anderson	4.00	2.00	.40
☐ 405	Duke Maas	4.00	2.00	.40
☐ 406	Bob Hale	4.00	2.00	.40
☐ 407	Yankee Power Hitters	300.00	100.00	20.00
	Mickey Mantle			
	Yogi Berra			
☐ 408	Checklist 1/2	100.00	10.00	2.00
	(unnumbered)			
☐ 409	Checklist 2/3	250.00	25.00	5.00
	(unnumbered)			
☐ 410	Checklist 3/4	300.00	30.00	6.00
	(unnumbered)			
☐ 411	Checklist 4/5	500.00	50.00	10.00
	(unnumbered)			

1958 Topps

The cards in this 494-card set measure 2 1/2" by 3 1/2". Although the last card is numbered 495, number 145 was not issued, bringing the set total to 494 cards. The 1958 Topps set contains the first Sport Magazine All-Star Selection series (475-495) and expanded use of combination cards. The team cards carried series checklists on back (Milwaukee, Detroit, Baltimore, and Cincinnati are also found with players listed alphabetically. Cards with the scarce yellow name (YL) or team (YT) lettering, as opposed to the common white lettering, are noted in the checklist. In the last series cards of Stan Musial and Mickey Mantle were triple printed; the cards they replaced (443, 446, 450, and 462) on the printing sheet were hence printed in shorter supply than other cards in the last series and are marked with an SP in the list below.

	NRMT	VG-E	GOOD
COMPLETE SET (494)	4000.00	2000.00	500.00
COMMON PLAYER (1-110)	4.00	2.00	.40
COMMON PLAYER (111-198)	3.00	1.50	.30
COMMON PLAYER (199-352)	2.50	1.25	.25
COMMON PLAYER (353-440)	2.25	1.10	.22
COMMON PLAYER (441-474)	2.00	1.00	.20
COMMON PLAYER (475-495)	2.50	1.25	.25

		NRMT	VG-E	GOOD
☐ 1	Ted Williams	325.00	100.00	20.00
☐ 2A	Bob Lemon	15.00	7.50	1.50
☐ 2B	Bob Lemon YT	35.00	17.50	3.50
☐ 3	Alex Kellner	4.00	2.00	.40
☐ 4	Hank Foiles	4.00	2.00	.40
☐ 5	Willie Mays	135.00	65.00	13.50
☐ 6	George Zuverink	4.00	2.00	.40
☐ 7	Dale Long	5.00	2.50	.50
☐ 8A	Eddie Kasko	4.00	2.00	.40
☐ 8B	Eddie Kasko YL	21.00	10.50	2.10
☐ 9	Hank Bauer	7.00	3.50	.70
☐ 10	Lou Burdette	6.00	3.00	.60
☐ 11A	Jim Rivera	4.00	2.00	.40
☐ 11B	Jim Rivera YT	16.00	8.00	1.60
☐ 12	George Crowe	4.00	2.00	.40
☐ 13A	Billy Hoeft	4.00	2.00	.40
☐ 13B	Billy Hoeft YL	21.00	10.50	2.10
☐ 14	Rip Repulski	4.00	2.00	.40
☐ 15	Jim Lemon	5.00	2.50	.50
☐ 16	Charlie Neal	5.00	2.50	.50
☐ 17	Felix Mantilla	4.00	2.00	.40
☐ 18	Frank Sullivan	4.00	2.00	.40
☐ 19	New York Giants	15.00	4.00	.80
	Team Card			
	(checklist on back)			
☐ 20A	Gil McDougald	8.00	4.00	.80
☐ 20B	Gil McDougald YL	25.00	12.50	2.50
☐ 21	Curt Barclay	4.00	2.00	.40
☐ 22	Hal Naragon	4.00	2.00	.40
☐ 23A	Bill Tuttle	4.00	2.00	.40
☐ 23B	Bill Tuttle YL	21.00	10.50	2.10
☐ 24A	Hobie Landrith	4.00	2.00	.40
☐ 24B	Hobie Landrith YL	21.00	10.50	2.10
☐ 25	Don Drysdale	40.00	20.00	4.00
☐ 26	Ron Jackson	4.00	2.00	.40
☐ 27	Bud Freeman	4.00	2.00	.40
☐ 28	Jim Busby	4.00	2.00	.40
☐ 29	Ted Lepcio	4.00	2.00	.40
☐ 30A	Hank Aaron	135.00	65.00	13.50
☐ 30B	Hank Aaron YL	275.00	125.00	25.00
☐ 31	Tex Clevenger	4.00	2.00	.40
☐ 32A	J.W. Porter	4.00	2.00	.40
☐ 32B	J.W. Porter YL	21.00	10.50	2.10
☐ 33A	Cal Neeman	4.00	2.00	.40
☐ 33B	Cal Neeman YT	16.00	8.00	1.60
☐ 34	Bob Thurman	4.00	2.00	.40
☐ 35A	Don Mossi	5.00	2.50	.50
☐ 35B	Don Mossi YT	16.00	8.00	1.60
☐ 36	Ted Kazanski	4.00	2.00	.40
☐ 37	Mike McCormick	6.00	3.00	.60
	(photo actually			
	Ray Monzant)			
☐ 38	Dick Gernert	4.00	2.00	.40
☐ 39	Bob Martyn	4.00	2.00	.40
☐ 40	George Kell	12.50	6.25	1.25
☐ 41	Dave Hillman	4.00	2.00	.40
☐ 42	John Roseboro	7.00	3.50	.70
☐ 43	Sal Maglie	7.00	3.50	.70
☐ 44	Washington Senators	7.50	2.50	.50
	Team Card			
	(checklist on back)			
☐ 45	Dick Groat	6.00	3.00	.60
☐ 46A	Lou Sleater	4.00	2.00	.40
☐ 46B	Lou Sleater YL	21.00	10.50	2.10
☐ 47	Roger Maris	300.00	150.00	30.00
☐ 48	Chuck Harmon	4.00	2.00	.40
☐ 49	Smoky Burgess	5.00	2.50	.50
☐ 50A	Billy Pierce	6.00	3.00	.60
☐ 50B	Billy Pierce YT	21.00	10.50	2.10
☐ 51	Del Rice	4.00	2.00	.40
☐ 52A	Bob Clemente	90.00	45.00	9.00
☐ 52B	Bob Clemente YT	160.00	80.00	16.00
☐ 53A	Morrie Martin	4.00	2.00	.40
☐ 53B	Morrie Martin YL	21.00	10.50	2.10
☐ 54	Norm Siebern	4.00	2.00	.40
☐ 55	Chico Carrasquel	4.00	2.00	.40
☐ 56	Bill Fischer	4.00	2.00	.40
☐ 57A	Tim Thompson	4.00	2.00	.40
☐ 57B	Tim Thompson YL	21.00	10.50	2.10
☐ 58A	Art Schult	4.00	2.00	.40
☐ 58B	Art Schult YT	16.00	8.00	1.60
☐ 59	Dave Sisler	4.00	2.00	.40
☐ 60A	Del Ennis	5.00	2.50	.50
☐ 60B	Del Ennis YL	21.00	10.50	2.10
☐ 61A	Darrell Johnson	5.00	2.50	.50
☐ 61B	Darrell Johnson YL	21.00	10.50	2.10
☐ 62	Joe DeMaestri	4.00	2.00	.40
☐ 63	Joe Nuxhall	5.00	2.50	.50
☐ 64	Joe Lonnett	4.00	2.00	.40
☐ 65A	Von McDaniel	4.00	2.00	.40
☐ 65B	Von McDaniel YL	21.00	10.50	2.10
☐ 66	Lee Walls	4.00	2.00	.40
☐ 67	Joe Ginsberg	4.00	2.00	.40
☐ 68	Daryl Spencer	4.00	2.00	.40
☐ 69	Wally Burnette	4.00	2.00	.40

☐ 70A	Al Kaline	55.00	27.50	5.50		☐ 149	Tom Acker	3.00	1.50	.30
☐ 70B	Al Kaline YL	110.00	55.00	11.00		☐ 150	Mickey Mantle	500.00	250.00	50.00
☐ 71	Dodgers Team	20.00	6.00	1.25		☐ 151	Buddy Pritchard	3.00	1.50	.30
	(checklist on back)					☐ 152	Johnny Antonelli	4.00	2.00	.40
☐ 72	Bud Byerly	4.00	2.00	.40		☐ 153	Les Moss	3.00	1.50	.30
☐ 73	Pete Daley	4.00	2.00	.40		☐ 154	Harry Byrd	3.00	1.50	.30
☐ 74	Roy Face	6.00	3.00	.60		☐ 155	Hector Lopez	3.00	1.50	.30
☐ 75	Gus Bell	5.00	2.50	.50		☐ 156	Dick Hyde	3.00	1.50	.30
☐ 76A	Dick Farrell	5.00	2.50	.50		☐ 157	Dee Fondy	3.00	1.50	.30
☐ 76B	Dick Farrell YT	21.00	10.50	2.10		☐ 158	Cleveland Indians	7.50	2.50	.50
☐ 77A	Don Zimmer	7.00	3.50	.70			Team Card			
☐ 77B	Don Zimmer YT	21.00	10.50	2.10			(checklist on back)			
☐ 78A	Ernie Johnson	5.00	2.50	.50		☐ 159	Taylor Phillips	3.00	1.50	.30
☐ 78B	Ernie Johnson YL	21.00	10.50	2.10		☐ 160	Don Hoak	4.00	2.00	.40
☐ 79A	Dick Williams	5.00	2.50	.50		☐ 161	Don Larsen	7.00	3.50	.70
☐ 79B	Dick Williams YT	21.00	10.50	2.10		☐ 162	Gil Hodges	18.00	9.00	1.80
☐ 80	Dick Drott	4.00	2.00	.40		☐ 163	Jim Wilson	3.00	1.50	.30
☐ 81A	Steve Boros	5.00	2.50	.50		☐ 164	Bob Taylor	3.00	1.50	.30
☐ 81B	Steve Boros YT	21.00	10.50	2.10		☐ 165	Bob Nieman	3.00	1.50	.30
☐ 82	Ron Kline	4.00	2.00	.40		☐ 166	Danny O'Connell	3.00	1.50	.30
☐ 83	Bob Hazle	5.00	2.50	.50		☐ 167	Frank Baumann	3.00	1.50	.30
☐ 84	Billy O'Dell	4.00	2.00	.40		☐ 168	Joe Cunningham	4.00	2.00	.40
☐ 85A	Luis Aparicio	16.00	8.00	1.60		☐ 169	Ralph Terry	5.00	2.50	.50
☐ 85B	Luis Aparicio YT	32.00	16.00	3.20		☐ 170	Vic Wertz	4.00	2.00	.40
☐ 86	Valmy Thomas	4.00	2.00	.40		☐ 171	Harry Anderson	3.00	1.50	.30
☐ 87	Johnny Kucks	4.00	2.00	.40		☐ 172	Don Gross	3.00	1.50	.30
☐ 88	Duke Snider	50.00	25.00	5.00		☐ 173	Eddie Yost	3.00	1.50	.30
☐ 89	Billy Klaus	4.00	2.00	.40		☐ 174	Athletics Team	7.50	2.50	.50
☐ 90	Robin Roberts	13.00	6.50	1.30			(checklist on back)			
☐ 91	Chuck Tanner	5.00	2.50	.50		☐ 175	Marv Throneberry	7.00	3.50	.70
☐ 92A	Clint Courtney	4.00	2.00	.40		☐ 176	Bob Buhl	3.00	1.50	.30
☐ 92B	Clint Courtney YL	20.00	10.00	2.00		☐ 177	Al Smith	3.00	1.50	.30
☐ 93	Sandy Amoros	5.00	2.50	.50		☐ 178	Ted Kluszewski	7.00	3.50	.70
☐ 94	Bob Skinner	4.00	2.00	.40		☐ 179	Willie Miranda	3.00	1.50	.30
☐ 95	Frank Bolling	4.00	2.00	.40		☐ 180	Lindy McDaniel	4.00	2.00	.40
☐ 96	Joe Durham	4.00	2.00	.40		☐ 181	Willie Jones	3.00	1.50	.30
☐ 97A	Larry Jackson	4.00	2.00	.40		☐ 182	Joe Caffie	3.00	1.50	.30
☐ 97B	Larry Jackson YL	21.00	10.50	2.10		☐ 183	Dave Jolly	3.00	1.50	.30
☐ 98A	Billy Hunter	4.00	2.00	.40		☐ 184	Elvin Tappe	3.00	1.50	.30
☐ 98B	Billy Hunter YL	21.00	10.50	2.10		☐ 185	Ray Boone	4.00	2.00	.40
☐ 99	Bobby Adams	4.00	2.00	.40		☐ 186	Jack Meyer	3.00	1.50	.30
☐ 100A	Early Wynn	13.00	6.50	1.30		☐ 187	Sandy Koufax	100.00	50.00	10.00
☐ 100B	Early Wynn YL	30.00	15.00	3.00		☐ 188	Milt Bolling	3.00	1.50	.30
☐ 101A	Bobby Richardson	10.00	5.00	1.00			(photo actually			
☐ 101B	Bobby Richardson YL	30.00	15.00	3.00			Lou Berberet)			
☐ 102	George Strickland	4.00	2.00	.40		☐ 189	George Susce	3.00	1.50	.30
☐ 103	Jerry Lynch	4.00	2.00	.40		☐ 190	Red Schoendienst	14.00	7.00	1.40
☐ 104	Jim Pendleton	4.00	2.00	.40		☐ 191	Art Ceccarelli	3.00	1.50	.30
☐ 105	Billy Gardner	5.00	2.50	.50		☐ 192	Milt Graff	3.00	1.50	.30
☐ 106	Dick Schofield	4.00	2.00	.40		☐ 193	Jerry Lumpe	3.00	1.50	.30
☐ 107	Ossie Virgil	4.00	2.00	.40		☐ 194	Roger Craig	7.00	3.50	.70
☐ 108A	Jim Landis	4.00	2.00	.40		☐ 195	Whitey Lockman	4.00	2.00	.40
☐ 108B	Jim Landis YT	16.00	8.00	1.60		☐ 196	Mike Garcia	4.00	2.00	.40
☐ 109	Herb Plews	4.00	2.00	.40		☐ 197	Haywood Sullivan	4.00	2.00	.40
☐ 110	Johnny Logan	5.00	2.50	.50		☐ 198	Bill Virdon	4.00	2.00	.40
☐ 111	Stu Miller	3.00	1.50	.30		☐ 199	Don Blasingame	2.50	1.25	.25
☐ 112	Gus Zernial	4.00	2.00	.40		☐ 200	Bob Keegan	2.50	1.25	.25
☐ 113	Jerry Walker	3.00	1.50	.30		☐ 201	Jim Bolger	2.50	1.25	.25
☐ 114	Irv Noren	3.00	1.50	.30		☐ 202	Woody Held	2.50	1.25	.25
☐ 115	Jim Bunning	12.00	6.00	1.20		☐ 203	Al Walker	2.50	1.25	.25
☐ 116	Dave Philley	3.00	1.50	.30		☐ 204	Leo Kiely	2.50	1.25	.25
☐ 117	Frank Torre	3.00	1.50	.30		☐ 205	Johnny Temple	3.00	1.50	.30
☐ 118	Harvey Haddix	4.00	2.00	.40		☐ 206	Bob Shaw	3.00	1.50	.30
☐ 119	Harry Chiti	3.00	1.50	.30		☐ 207	Solly Hemus	2.50	1.25	.25
☐ 120	Johnny Podres	7.00	3.50	.70		☐ 208	Cal McLish	2.50	1.25	.25
☐ 121	Eddie Miksis	3.00	1.50	.30		☐ 209	Bob Anderson	2.50	1.25	.25
☐ 122	Walt Moryn	3.00	1.50	.30		☐ 210	Wally Moon	3.50	1.75	.35
☐ 123	Dick Tomanek	3.00	1.50	.30		☐ 211	Pete Burnside	2.50	1.25	.25
☐ 124	Bobby Usher	3.00	1.50	.30		☐ 212	Bubba Phillips	2.50	1.25	.25
☐ 125	Alvin Dark	4.00	2.00	.40		☐ 213	Red Wilson	2.50	1.25	.25
☐ 126	Stan Palys	3.00	1.50	.30		☐ 214	Willard Schmidt	2.50	1.25	.25
☐ 127	Tom Sturdivant	4.00	2.00	.40		☐ 215	Jim Gilliam	7.00	3.50	.70
☐ 128	Willie Kirkland	4.00	2.00	.40		☐ 216	St. Louis Cardinals	9.00	2.50	.50
☐ 129	Jim Derrington	3.00	1.50	.30			Team Card			
☐ 130	Jackie Jensen	7.00	3.50	.70			(checklist on back)			
☐ 131	Bob Henrich	3.00	1.50	.30		☐ 217	Jack Harshman	2.50	1.25	.25
☐ 132	Vern Law	4.00	2.00	.40		☐ 218	Dick Rand	2.50	1.25	.25
☐ 133	Russ Nixon	5.00	2.50	.50		☐ 219	Camilo Pascual	3.00	1.50	.30
☐ 134	Philadelphia Phillies	7.50	2.50	.50		☐ 220	Tom Brewer	2.50	1.25	.25
	Team Card					☐ 221	Jerry Kindall	3.00	1.50	.30
	(checklist on back)					☐ 222	Bud Daley	2.50	1.25	.25
☐ 135	Mike(Moe) Drabowsky	4.00	2.00	.40		☐ 223	Andy Pafko	3.00	1.50	.30
☐ 136	Jim Finigan	3.00	1.50	.30		☐ 224	Bob Grim	3.00	1.50	.30
☐ 137	Russ Kemmerer	3.00	1.50	.30		☐ 225	Billy Goodman	3.00	1.50	.30
☐ 138	Earl Torgeson	3.00	1.50	.30		☐ 226	Bob Smith	2.50	1.25	.25
☐ 139	George Brunet	3.00	1.50	.30		☐ 227	Gene Stephens	2.50	1.25	.25
☐ 140	Wes Covington	4.00	2.00	.40		☐ 228	Duke Maas	2.50	1.25	.25
☐ 141	Ken Lehman	3.00	1.50	.30		☐ 229	Frank Zupo	2.50	1.25	.25
☐ 142	Enos Slaughter	16.00	8.00	1.60		☐ 230	Richie Ashburn	10.00	5.00	1.00
☐ 143	Billy Muffett	3.00	1.50	.30		☐ 231	Lloyd Merritt	2.50	1.25	.25
☐ 144	Bobby Morgan	3.00	1.50	.30		☐ 232	Reno Bertoia	2.50	1.25	.25
☐ 145	Never issued	0.00	.00	.00		☐ 233	Mickey Vernon	3.50	1.75	.35
☐ 146	Dick Gray	3.00	1.50	.30		☐ 234	Carl Sawatski	2.50	1.25	.25
☐ 147	Don McMahon	4.00	2.00	.40		☐ 235	Tom Gorman	2.50	1.25	.25
☐ 148	Billy Consolo	3.00	1.50	.30		☐ 236	Ed Fitzgerald	2.50	1.25	.25

FREE ILLUSTRATED CATALOGUE

Our 64-page Illustrated Catalogues are sent six times a year to over 25,000 collectors. Each sale offers Star Cards, Rookie Cards, Complete Sets, 1930s Cards, Investors Specials, Unopened Cases and Gum Packs, Tobacco Cards, Rare and Unusual Cards, Special Topps Issues, and other Premium Cards. **To receive our current catalogue (and future ones), please send (4) 25¢ stamps.**

KIT YOUNG

Dept. C
8310 NW 13th Ct.
Vancouver, WA 98665
(206) 573-8383

"Serving Collectors Since 1976"

BUYING CARDS — We have been buying cards through the mail since 1976, and now make hundreds of purchases each year. If you have cards (including Complete Collections, Star Cards, Complete Sets, or 1950s, '60s or '70s Cards), please send a listing of your cards or send (4) 25¢ stamps for our current buying list. All transactions are guaranteed to your satisfaction.

HAWAII TRADE CONVENTION AND BASEBALL CARD SHOW

Each year we host the annual **Hawaiian Sports Collectors Show.** Our sixth annual show is scheduled for mid-February 1991. The show offers one of the strongest rosters of dealers of any show in the country, drawing dealers from about 20 states. Please write if you would like information about the show. **This is a great way to combine your favorite hobby with a midwinter vacation in Hawaii!**

DEALERS/SHOP OWNERS/COLLECTORS — Our card show is part of the hobby's only 6-day trade convention. The forum features social activities, roundtable discussions and seminars. Plus, special Hawaiian activities for you and your spouse. We have room for more participants in this year's show (you may participate without having tables at the card show). This is a great opportunity to learn more about our hobby plus ways to improve your business, including new trends, problems, and new developments in the industry. Plus, share a vacation in the 80-degree winter weather in paradise — please write **Kit Young** for information (see address in above ad).

☐ 237	Bill Wight	2.50	1.25	.25
☐ 238	Bill Mazeroski	8.00	4.00	.80
☐ 239	Chuck Stobbs	2.50	1.25	.25
☐ 240	Bill Skowron	8.00	4.00	.80
☐ 241	Dick Littlefield	2.50	1.25	.25
☐ 242	Johnny Klippstein	2.50	1.25	.25
☐ 243	Larry Raines	2.50	1.25	.25
☐ 244	Don Demeter	2.50	1.25	.25
☐ 245	Frank Lary	3.50	1.75	.35
☐ 246	New York Yankees Team Card (checklist on back)	33.00	8.00	2.00
☐ 247	Casey Wise	2.50	1.25	.25
☐ 248	Herman Wehmeier	2.50	1.25	.25
☐ 249	Ray Moore	2.50	1.25	.25
☐ 250	Roy Sievers	3.50	1.75	.35
☐ 251	Warren Hacker	2.50	1.25	.25
☐ 252	Bob Trowbridge	2.50	1.25	.25
☐ 253	Don Mueller	3.00	1.50	.30
☐ 254	Alex Grammas	2.50	1.25	.25
☐ 255	Bob Turley	7.00	3.50	.70
☐ 256	Chicago White Sox Team Card (checklist on back)	7.50	2.50	.50
☐ 257	Hal Smith	2.50	1.25	.25
☐ 258	Carl Erskine	5.50	2.75	.55
☐ 259	Al Pilarcik	2.50	1.25	.25
☐ 260	Frank Malzone	3.50	1.75	.35
☐ 261	Turk Lown	2.50	1.25	.25
☐ 262	Johnny Groth	2.50	1.25	.25
☐ 263	Eddie Bressoud	2.50	1.25	.25
☐ 264	Jack Sanford	3.00	1.50	.30
☐ 265	Pete Runnels	3.00	1.50	.30
☐ 266	Connie Johnson	2.50	1.25	.25
☐ 267	Sherm Lollar	3.00	1.50	.30
☐ 268	Granny Hamner	2.50	1.25	.25
☐ 269	Paul Smith	2.50	1.25	.25
☐ 270	Warren Spahn	32.00	16.00	3.20
☐ 271	Billy Martin	14.00	7.00	1.40
☐ 272	Ray Crone	2.50	1.25	.25
☐ 273	Hal Smith	2.50	1.25	.25
☐ 274	Rocky Bridges	2.50	1.25	.25
☐ 275	Elston Howard	8.00	4.00	.80
☐ 276	Bobby Avila	3.00	1.50	.30
☐ 277	Virgil Trucks	3.00	1.50	.30
☐ 278	Mack Burk	2.50	1.25	.25
☐ 279	Bob Boyd	2.50	1.25	.25
☐ 280	Jim Piersall	6.00	3.00	.60
☐ 281	Sammy Taylor	2.50	1.25	.25
☐ 282	Paul Foytack	2.50	1.25	.25
☐ 283	Ray Shearer	2.50	1.25	.25
☐ 284	Ray Katt	2.50	1.25	.25
☐ 285	Frank Robinson	55.00	27.50	5.50
☐ 286	Gino Cimoli	3.00	1.50	.30
☐ 287	Sam Jones	3.00	1.50	.30
☐ 288	Harmon Killebrew	45.00	22.50	4.50
☐ 289	Series Hurling Rivals Lou Burdette Bobby Shantz	4.00	2.00	.40
☐ 290	Dick Donovan	2.50	1.25	.25
☐ 291	Don Landrum	2.50	1.25	.25
☐ 292	Ned Garver	2.50	1.25	.25
☐ 293	Gene Freese	2.50	1.25	.25
☐ 294	Hal Jeffcoat	2.50	1.25	.25
☐ 295	Minnie Minoso	7.00	3.50	.70
☐ 296	Ryne Duren	7.00	3.50	.70
☐ 297	Don Buddin	2.50	1.25	.25
☐ 298	Jim Hearn	2.50	1.25	.25
☐ 299	Harry Simpson	2.50	1.25	.25
☐ 300	Harridge and Giles League Presidents	6.00	3.00	.60
☐ 301	Randy Jackson	2.50	1.25	.25
☐ 302	Mike Baxes	2.50	1.25	.25
☐ 303	Neil Chrisley	2.50	1.25	.25
☐ 304	Tigers' Big Bats Harvey Kuenn Al Kaline	9.00	4.50	.90
☐ 305	Clem Labine	3.50	1.75	.35
☐ 306	Whammy Douglas	2.50	1.25	.25
☐ 307	Brooks Robinson	60.00	30.00	6.00
☐ 308	Paul Giel	2.50	1.25	.25
☐ 309	Gail Harris	2.50	1.25	.25
☐ 310	Ernie Banks	50.00	25.00	5.00
☐ 311	Bob Purkey	2.50	1.25	.25
☐ 312	Boston Red Sox Team Card (checklist on back)	9.00	2.50	.50
☐ 313	Bob Rush	2.50	1.25	.25
☐ 314	Dodgers' Boss and Power: Duke Snider Walt Alston	15.00	7.50	1.50
☐ 315	Bob Friend	3.50	1.75	.35
☐ 316	Tito Francona	2.50	1.25	.25
☐ 317	Albie Pearson	3.50	1.75	.35
☐ 318	Frank House	2.50	1.25	.25
☐ 319	Lou Skizas	2.50	1.25	.25
☐ 320	Whitey Ford	35.00	17.50	3.50
☐ 321	Sluggers Supreme Ted Kluszewski Ted Williams	25.00	12.50	2.50
☐ 322	Harding Peterson	3.00	1.50	.30
☐ 323	Elmer Valo	2.50	1.25	.25
☐ 324	Hoyt Wilhelm	13.00	6.50	1.30
☐ 325	Joe Adcock	3.50	1.75	.35
☐ 326	Bob Miller	2.50	1.25	.25
☐ 327	Chicago Cubs Team Card (checklist on back)	9.00	2.50	.50
☐ 328	Ike Delock	2.50	1.25	.25
☐ 329	Bob Cerv	3.00	1.50	.30
☐ 330	Ed Bailey	3.00	1.50	.30
☐ 331	Pedro Ramos	2.50	1.25	.25
☐ 332	Jim King	2.50	1.25	.25
☐ 333	Andy Carey	3.50	1.75	.35
☐ 334	Mound Aces Bob Friend Billy Pierce	4.00	2.00	.40
☐ 335	Ruben Gomez	2.50	1.25	.25
☐ 336	Bert Hamric	2.50	1.25	.25
☐ 337	Hank Aguirre	2.50	1.25	.25
☐ 338	Walt Dropo	2.50	1.25	.25
☐ 339	Fred Hatfield	2.50	1.25	.25
☐ 340	Don Newcombe	6.00	3.00	.60
☐ 341	Pittsburgh Pirates Team Card (checklist on back)	7.50	2.50	.50
☐ 342	Jim Brosnan	3.00	1.50	.30
☐ 343	Orlando Cepeda	45.00	22.50	4.50
☐ 344	Bob Porterfield	2.50	1.25	.25
☐ 345	Jim Hegan	3.00	1.50	.30
☐ 346	Steve Bilko	2.50	1.25	.25
☐ 347	Don Rudolph	2.50	1.25	.25
☐ 348	Chico Fernandez	2.50	1.25	.25
☐ 349	Murry Dickson	2.50	1.25	.25
☐ 350	Ken Boyer	6.00	3.00	.60
☐ 351	Braves Fence Busters Del Crandall Eddie Mathews Hank Aaron Joe Adcock	18.00	9.00	1.80
☐ 352	Herb Score	5.00	2.50	.50
☐ 353	Stan Lopata	2.50	1.25	.25
☐ 354	Art Ditmar	3.00	1.50	.30
☐ 355	Bill Bruton	3.00	1.50	.30
☐ 356	Bob Malkmus	2.50	1.25	.25
☐ 357	Danny McDevitt	2.50	1.25	.25
☐ 358	Gene Baker	2.50	1.25	.25
☐ 359	Billy Loes	2.50	1.25	.25
☐ 360	Roy McMillan	2.50	1.25	.25
☐ 361	Mike Fornieles	2.50	1.25	.25
☐ 362	Ray Jablonski	2.50	1.25	.25
☐ 363	Don Elston	2.50	1.25	.25
☐ 364	Earl Battey	3.00	1.50	.30
☐ 365	Tom Morgan	2.50	1.25	.25
☐ 366	Gene Green	2.50	1.25	.25
☐ 367	Jack Urban	2.50	1.25	.25
☐ 368	Rocky Colavito	10.00	5.00	1.00
☐ 369	Ralph Lumenti	2.50	1.25	.25
☐ 370	Yogi Berra	65.00	32.50	6.50
☐ 371	Marty Keough	2.50	1.25	.25
☐ 372	Don Cardwell	2.50	1.25	.25
☐ 373	Joe Pignatano	2.50	1.25	.25
☐ 374	Brooks Lawrence	2.50	1.25	.25
☐ 375	Pee Wee Reese	35.00	17.50	3.50
☐ 376	Charley Rabe	2.50	1.25	.25
☐ 377A	Milwaukee Braves Team Card (alphabetical)	7.50	3.50	.70
☐ 377B	Milwaukee Team numerical checklist	60.00	10.00	2.00
☐ 378	Hank Sauer	3.50	1.75	.35
☐ 379	Ray Herbert	2.50	1.25	.25
☐ 380	Charley Maxwell	3.00	1.50	.30
☐ 381	Hal Brown	2.50	1.25	.25
☐ 382	Al Cicotte	3.00	1.50	.30
☐ 383	Lou Berberet	2.50	1.25	.25
☐ 384	John Goryl	2.50	1.25	.25
☐ 385	Wilmer Mizell	2.50	1.25	.25
☐ 386	Birdie's Sluggers Ed Bailey Birdie Tebbetts Frank Robinson	6.00	3.00	.60
☐ 387	Wally Post	3.00	1.50	.30
☐ 388	Billy Moran	2.50	1.25	.25
☐ 389	Bill Taylor	2.50	1.25	.25
☐ 390	Del Crandall	3.00	1.50	.30
☐ 391	Dave Melton	2.50	1.25	.25
☐ 392	Bennie Daniels	2.50	1.25	.25
☐ 393	Tony Kubek	12.50	6.25	1.25
☐ 394	Jim Grant	3.00	1.50	.30

		NRMT	VG-E	GOOD
☐ 395	Willard Nixon	2.50	1.25	.25
☐ 396	Dutch Dotterer	2.50	1.25	.25
☐ 397A	Detroit Tigers Team Card (alphabetical)	7.50	3.50	.70
☐ 397B	Detroit Team numerical checklist	60.00	10.00	2.00
☐ 398	Gene Woodling	3.50	1.75	.35
☐ 399	Marv Grissom	2.50	1.25	.25
☐ 400	Nellie Fox	9.00	4.50	.90
☐ 401	Don Bessent	3.00	1.50	.30
☐ 402	Bobby Gene Smith	2.50	1.25	.25
☐ 403	Steve Korcheck	2.50	1.25	.25
☐ 404	Curt Simmons	3.50	1.75	.35
☐ 405	Ken Aspromonte	2.50	1.25	.25
☐ 406	Vic Power	3.00	1.50	.30
☐ 407	Carlton Willey	2.50	1.25	.25
☐ 408A	Baltimore Orioles Team Card (alphabetical)	7.50	3.50	.70
☐ 408B	Baltimore Team numerical checklist	60.00	10.00	2.00
☐ 409	Frank Thomas	3.00	1.50	.30
☐ 410	Murray Wall	2.50	1.25	.25
☐ 411	Tony Taylor	2.50	1.25	.25
☐ 412	Jerry Staley	2.50	1.25	.25
☐ 413	Jim Davenport	3.00	1.50	.30
☐ 414	Sammy White	2.50	1.25	.25
☐ 415	Bob Bowman	2.50	1.25	.25
☐ 416	Foster Castleman	2.50	1.25	.25
☐ 417	Carl Furillo	6.00	3.00	.60
☐ 418	World Series Batting Foes: Mickey Mantle Hank Aaron	125.00	60.00	12.50
☐ 419	Bobby Shantz	5.00	2.50	.50
☐ 420	Vada Pinson	16.00	8.00	1.60
☐ 421	Dixie Howell	2.50	1.25	.25
☐ 422	Norm Zauchin	2.50	1.25	.25
☐ 423	Phil Clark	2.50	1.25	.25
☐ 424	Larry Doby	5.00	2.50	.50
☐ 425	Sammy Esposito	2.50	1.25	.25
☐ 426	Johnny O'Brien	2.50	1.25	.25
☐ 427	Al Worthington	2.50	1.25	.25
☐ 428A	Cincinnati Reds Team Card (alphabetical)	7.50	3.50	.70
☐ 428B	Cincinnati Team numerical checklist	60.00	10.00	2.00
☐ 429	Gus Triandos	3.00	1.50	.30
☐ 430	Bobby Thomson	4.00	2.00	.40
☐ 431	Gene Conley	3.00	1.50	.30
☐ 432	John Powers	2.50	1.25	.25
☐ 433A	Pancho Herrer ERR	500.00	250.00	50.00
☐ 433B	Pancho Herrera COR	2.50	1.25	.25
☐ 434	Harvey Kuenn	5.00	2.50	.50
☐ 435	Ed Roebuck	3.00	1.50	.30
☐ 436	Rival Fence Busters Willie Mays Duke Snider	45.00	22.50	4.50
☐ 437	Bob Speake	2.50	1.25	.25
☐ 438	Whitey Herzog	5.00	2.50	.50
☐ 439	Ray Narleski	2.50	1.25	.25
☐ 440	Eddie Mathews	27.00	13.50	2.70
☐ 441	Jim Marshall	2.00	1.00	.20
☐ 442	Phil Paine	2.00	1.00	.20
☐ 443	Billy Harrell SP	8.00	4.00	.80
☐ 444	Danny Kravitz	2.00	1.00	.20
☐ 445	Bob Smith	2.00	1.00	.20
☐ 446	Carroll Hardy SP	8.00	4.00	.80
☐ 447	Ray Monzant	2.00	1.00	.20
☐ 448	Charlie Lau	5.00	2.50	.50
☐ 449	Gene Fodge	2.00	1.00	.20
☐ 450	Preston Ward SP	8.00	4.00	.80
☐ 451	Joe Taylor	2.00	1.00	.20
☐ 452	Roman Mejias	2.00	1.00	.20
☐ 453	Tom Qualters	2.00	1.00	.20
☐ 454	Harry Hanebrink	2.00	1.00	.20
☐ 455	Hal Griggs	2.00	1.00	.20
☐ 456	Dick Brown	2.00	1.00	.20
☐ 457	Milt Pappas	5.00	2.50	.50
☐ 458	Julio Becquer	2.00	1.00	.20
☐ 459	Ron Blackburn	2.00	1.00	.20
☐ 460	Chuck Essegian	2.00	1.00	.20
☐ 461	Ed Mayer	2.00	1.00	.20
☐ 462	Gary Geiger SP	8.00	4.00	.80
☐ 463	Vito Valentinetti	2.00	1.00	.20
☐ 464	Curt Flood	11.00	5.50	1.10
☐ 465	Arnie Portocarrero	2.00	1.00	.20
☐ 466	Pete Whisenant	2.00	1.00	.20
☐ 467	Glen Hobbie	2.00	1.00	.20
☐ 468	Bob Schmidt	2.00	1.00	.20
☐ 469	Don Ferrarese	2.00	1.00	.20
☐ 470	R.C. Stevens	2.00	1.00	.20
☐ 471	Lenny Green	2.00	1.00	.20
☐ 472	Joey Jay	2.50	1.25	.25

		NRMT	VG-E	GOOD
☐ 473	Bill Renna	2.00	1.00	.20
☐ 474	Roman Semproch	2.00	1.00	.20
☐ 475	Haney/Stengel AS (checklist back)	13.50	5.00	1.00
☐ 476	Stan Musial AS TP	25.00	12.50	2.50
☐ 477	Bill Skowron AS	4.00	2.00	.40
☐ 478	Johnny Temple AS	2.50	1.25	.25
☐ 479	Nellie Fox AS	6.00	3.00	.60
☐ 480	Eddie Mathews AS	11.00	5.50	1.10
☐ 481	Frank Malzone AS	2.50	1.25	.25
☐ 482	Ernie Banks AS	12.50	6.25	1.25
☐ 483	Luis Aparicio AS	8.00	4.00	.80
☐ 484	Frank Robinson AS	12.50	6.25	1.25
☐ 485	Ted Williams AS	45.00	22.50	4.50
☐ 486	Willie Mays AS	32.00	16.00	3.20
☐ 487	Mickey Mantle AS TP	65.00	32.50	6.50
☐ 488	Hank Aaron AS	32.00	16.00	3.20
☐ 489	Jackie Jensen AS	3.50	1.75	.35
☐ 490	Ed Bailey AS	2.50	1.25	.25
☐ 491	Sherm Lollar AS	2.50	1.25	.25
☐ 492	Bob Friend AS	2.50	1.25	.25
☐ 493	Bob Turley AS	3.00	1.50	.30
☐ 494	Warren Spahn AS	12.50	6.25	1.25
☐ 495	Herb Score AS	5.00	1.50	.30

1959 Topps

The cards in this 572-card set measure 2 1/2" by 3 1/2". The 1959 Topps set contains bust pictures of the players in a colored circle. Card numbers 551 to 572 are Sporting News All-Star Selections. High numbers 507 to 572 have the card number in a black background on the reverse rather than a green background as in the lower numbers. The high numbers are more difficult to obtain. Several cards in the 300s exist with or without an extra traded or option line on the back of the card. Cards 199 to 286 exist with either white or gray backs. Cards 461 to 470 contain "Highlights" while cards 116 to 146 give an alphabetically ordered listing of "Rookie Prospects." These Rookie Prospects (RP) were Topps' first organized inclusion of untested "Rookie" cards. Card 440 features Lew Burdette erroneously posing as a left-handed pitcher. There were some three-card advertising panels produced by Topps; the players included are from the first series; one panel shows Don McMahon, Red Wilson, and Bob Boyd on the front with Ted Kluszewski's reverse on one of the backs. When cut apart, these advertising cards are distinguished by the non- standard card back, i.e., part of an advertisement for the 1959 Topps set instead of the typical statistics and biographical information about the player pictured.

	NRMT	VG-E	GOOD
COMPLETE SET (572)	4000.00	2000.00	500.00
COMMON PLAYER (1-110)	3.00	1.50	.30
COMMON PLAYER (111-506)	2.00	1.00	.20
COMMON PLAYER (507-550)	8.50	4.25	.85
COMMON PLAYER (551-572)	10.00	5.00	1.00
☐ 1 Ford Frick	40.00	6.00	1.25

☐ 2	Eddie Yost	3.00	1.50	.30
☐ 3	Don McMahon	3.00	1.50	.30
☐ 4	Albie Pearson	3.00	1.50	.30
☐ 5	Dick Donovan	3.00	1.50	.30
☐ 6	Alex Grammas	3.00	1.50	.30
☐ 7	Al Pilarcik	3.00	1.50	.30
☐ 8	Phillies Team	7.50	2.50	.50
	(checklist on back)			
☐ 9	Paul Giel	3.00	1.50	.30
☐ 10	Mickey Mantle	300.00	150.00	30.00
☐ 11	Billy Hunter	3.00	1.50	.30
☐ 12	Vern Law	4.00	2.00	.40
☐ 13	Dick Gernert	3.00	1.50	.30
☐ 14	Pete Whisenant	3.00	1.50	.30
☐ 15	Dick Drott	3.00	1.50	.30
☐ 16	Joe Pignatano	3.00	1.50	.30
☐ 17	Danny's Stars	4.00	2.00	.40
	Frank Thomas			
	Danny Murtaugh			
	Ted Kluszewski			
☐ 18	Jack Urban	3.00	1.50	.30
☐ 19	Eddie Bressoud	3.00	1.50	.30
☐ 20	Duke Snider	42.00	20.00	4.00
☐ 21	Connie Johnson	3.00	1.50	.30
☐ 22	Al Smith	3.00	1.50	.30
☐ 23	Murry Dickson	3.00	1.50	.30
☐ 24	Red Wilson	3.00	1.50	.30
☐ 25	Don Hoak	3.00	1.50	.30
☐ 26	Chuck Stobbs	3.00	1.50	.30
☐ 27	Andy Pafko	3.00	1.50	.30
☐ 28	Al Worthington	3.00	1.50	.30
☐ 29	Jim Bolger	3.00	1.50	.30
☐ 30	Nellie Fox	8.00	4.00	.80
☐ 31	Ken Lehman	3.00	1.50	.30
☐ 32	Don Buddin	3.00	1.50	.30
☐ 33	Ed Fitzgerald	3.00	1.50	.30
☐ 34	Pitchers Beware	7.00	3.50	.70
	Al Kaline			
	Charley Maxwell			
☐ 35	Ted Kluszewski	6.00	3.00	.60
☐ 36	Hank Aguirre	3.00	1.50	.30
☐ 37	Gene Green	3.00	1.50	.30
☐ 38	Morrie Martin	3.00	1.50	.30
☐ 39	Ed Bouchee	3.00	1.50	.30
☐ 40	Warren Spahn	32.00	16.00	3.20
☐ 41	Bob Martyn	3.00	1.50	.30
☐ 42	Murray Wall	3.00	1.50	.30
☐ 43	Steve Bilko	3.00	1.50	.30
☐ 44	Vito Valentinetti	3.00	1.50	.30
☐ 45	Andy Carey	4.00	2.00	.40
☐ 46	Bill R. Henry	3.00	1.50	.30
☐ 47	Jim Finigan	3.00	1.50	.30
☐ 48	Orioles Team	7.50	2.50	.50
	(checklist on back)			
☐ 49	Bill Hall	3.00	1.50	.30
☐ 50	Willie Mays	110.00	55.00	11.00
☐ 51	Rip Coleman	3.00	1.50	.30
☐ 52	Coot Veal	3.00	1.50	.30
☐ 53	Stan Williams	3.00	1.50	.30
☐ 54	Mel Roach	3.00	1.50	.30
☐ 55	Tom Brewer	3.00	1.50	.30
☐ 56	Carl Sawatski	3.00	1.50	.30
☐ 57	Al Cicotte	3.00	1.50	.30
☐ 58	Eddie Miksis	3.00	1.50	.30
☐ 59	Irv Noren	3.00	1.50	.30
☐ 60	Bob Turley	6.00	3.00	.60
☐ 61	Dick Brown	3.00	1.50	.30
☐ 62	Tony Taylor	3.00	1.50	.30
☐ 63	Jim Hearn	3.00	1.50	.30
☐ 64	Joe DeMaestri	3.00	1.50	.30
☐ 65	Frank Torre	3.00	1.50	.30
☐ 66	Joe Ginsberg	3.00	1.50	.30
☐ 67	Brooks Lawrence	3.00	1.50	.30
☐ 68	Dick Schofield	3.00	1.50	.30
☐ 69	Giants Team	7.50	2.50	.50
	(checklist on back)			
☐ 70	Harvey Kuenn	5.00	2.50	.50
☐ 71	Don Bessent	3.00	1.50	.30
☐ 72	Bill Renna	3.00	1.50	.30
☐ 73	Ron Jackson	3.00	1.50	.30
☐ 74	Directing Power	4.00	2.00	.40
	Jim Lemon			
	Cookie Lavagetto			
	Roy Sievers			
☐ 75	Sam Jones	4.00	2.00	.40
☐ 76	Bobby Richardson	8.00	4.00	.80
☐ 77	John Goryl	3.00	1.50	.30
☐ 78	Pedro Ramos	3.00	1.50	.30
☐ 79	Harry Chiti	3.00	1.50	.30
☐ 80	Minnie Minoso	6.00	3.00	.60
☐ 81	Hal Jeffcoat	3.00	1.50	.30
☐ 82	Bob Boyd	3.00	1.50	.30
☐ 83	Bob Smith	3.00	1.50	.30
☐ 84	Reno Bertoia	3.00	1.50	.30
☐ 85	Harry Anderson	3.00	1.50	.30

☐ 86	Bob Keegan	3.00	1.50	.30
☐ 87	Danny O'Connell	3.00	1.50	.30
☐ 88	Herb Score	5.00	2.50	.50
☐ 89	Billy Gardner	4.00	2.00	.40
☐ 90	Bill Skowron	7.00	3.50	.70
☐ 91	Herb Moford	3.00	1.50	.30
☐ 92	Dave Philley	3.00	1.50	.30
☐ 93	Julio Becquer	3.00	1.50	.30
☐ 94	White Sox Team	7.50	2.50	.50
	(checklist on back)			
☐ 95	Carl Willey	3.00	1.50	.30
☐ 96	Lou Berberet	3.00	1.50	.30
☐ 97	Jerry Lynch	3.00	1.50	.30
☐ 98	Arnie Portocarrero	3.00	1.50	.30
☐ 99	Ted Kazanski	3.00	1.50	.30
☐ 100	Bob Cerv	4.00	2.00	.40
☐ 101	Alex Kellner	3.00	1.50	.30
☐ 102	Felipe Alou	7.00	3.50	.70
☐ 103	Billy Goodman	4.00	2.00	.40
☐ 104	Del Rice	3.00	1.50	.30
☐ 105	Lee Walls	3.00	1.50	.30
☐ 106	Hal Woodeshick	3.00	1.50	.30
☐ 107	Norm Larker	4.00	2.00	.40
☐ 108	Zack Monroe	3.00	1.50	.30
☐ 109	Bob Schmidt	3.00	1.50	.30
☐ 110	George Witt	3.00	1.50	.30
☐ 111	Redlegs Team	7.50	2.50	.50
	(checklist on back)			
☐ 112	Billy Consolo	2.00	1.00	.20
☐ 113	Taylor Phillips	2.00	1.00	.20
☐ 114	Earl Battey	2.00	1.00	.20
☐ 115	Mickey Vernon	3.00	1.50	.30
☐ 116	Bob Allison RP	5.00	2.50	.50
☐ 117	John Blanchard RP	3.00	1.50	.30
☐ 118	John Buzhardt RP	2.00	1.00	.20
☐ 119	John Callison RP	4.00	2.00	.40
☐ 120	Chuck Coles RP	2.00	1.00	.20
☐ 121	Bob Conley RP	2.00	1.00	.20
☐ 122	Bennie Daniels RP	2.00	1.00	.20
☐ 123	Don Dillard RP	2.00	1.00	.20
☐ 124	Dan Dobbek RP	2.00	1.00	.20
☐ 125	Ron Fairly RP	4.00	2.00	.40
☐ 126	Ed Haas RP	2.50	1.25	.25
☐ 127	Kent Hadley RP	2.00	1.00	.20
☐ 128	Bob Hartman RP	2.00	1.00	.20
☐ 129	Frank Herrera RP	2.00	1.00	.20
☐ 130	Lou Jackson RP	2.00	1.00	.20
☐ 131	Deron Johnson RP	3.00	1.50	.30
☐ 132	Don Lee RP	2.00	1.00	.20
☐ 133	Bob Lillis RP	3.00	1.50	.30
☐ 134	Jim McDaniel RP	2.00	1.00	.20
☐ 135	Gene Oliver RP	2.00	1.00	.20
☐ 136	Jim O'Toole RP	3.00	1.50	.30
☐ 137	Dick Ricketts RP	2.00	1.00	.20
☐ 138	John Romano RP	2.50	1.25	.25
☐ 139	Ed Sadowski RP	2.00	1.00	.20
☐ 140	Charlie Secrest RP	2.00	1.00	.20
☐ 141	Joe Shipley RP	2.00	1.00	.20
☐ 142	Dick Stigman RP	2.00	1.00	.20
☐ 143	Willie Tasby RP	2.00	1.00	.20
☐ 144	Jerry Walker RP	2.00	1.00	.20
☐ 145	Dom Zanni RP	2.00	1.00	.20
☐ 146	Jerry Zimmerman RP	2.00	1.00	.20
☐ 147	Cubs Clubbers	7.00	3.50	.70
	Dale Long			
	Ernie Banks			
	Walt Moryn			
☐ 148	Mike McCormick	3.00	1.50	.30
☐ 149	Jim Bunning	8.00	4.00	.80
☐ 150	Stan Musial	110.00	55.00	11.00
☐ 151	Bob Malkmus	2.00	1.00	.20
☐ 152	Johnny Klippstein	2.00	1.00	.20
☐ 153	Jim Marshall	2.00	1.00	.20
☐ 154	Ray Herbert	2.00	1.00	.20
☐ 155	Enos Slaughter	12.50	6.25	1.25
☐ 156	Ace Hurlers	4.00	2.00	.40
	Billy Pierce			
	Robin Roberts			
☐ 157	Felix Mantilla	2.00	1.00	.20
☐ 158	Walt Dropo	2.00	1.00	.20
☐ 159	Bob Shaw	2.00	1.00	.20
☐ 160	Dick Groat	4.00	2.00	.40
☐ 161	Frank Baumann	2.00	1.00	.20
☐ 162	Bobby G. Smith	2.00	1.00	.20
☐ 163	Sandy Koufax	100.00	50.00	10.00
☐ 164	Johnny Groth	2.00	1.00	.20
☐ 165	Bill Bruton	2.50	1.25	.25
☐ 166	Destruction Crew	5.00	2.50	.50
	Minnie Minoso			
	Rocky Colavito			
	(misspelled Colovito			
	on card back)			
	Larry Doby			
☐ 167	Duke Maas	2.00	1.00	.20
☐ 168	Carroll Hardy	2.00	1.00	.20

☐ 169	Ted Abernathy	2.00	1.00	.20
☐ 170	Gene Woodling	3.00	1.50	.30
☐ 171	Willard Schmidt	2.00	1.00	.20
☐ 172	Athletics Team	7.50	2.50	.50
	(checklist on back)			
☐ 173	Bill Monbouquette	2.00	1.00	.20
☐ 174	Jim Pendleton	2.00	1.00	.20
☐ 175	Dick Farrell	2.00	1.00	.20
☐ 176	Preston Ward	2.00	1.00	.20
☐ 177	John Briggs	2.00	1.00	.20
☐ 178	Ruben Amaro	2.00	1.00	.20
☐ 179	Don Rudolph	2.00	1.00	.20
☐ 180	Yogi Berra	50.00	25.00	5.00
☐ 181	Bob Porterfield	2.00	1.00	.20
☐ 182	Milt Graff	2.00	1.00	.20
☐ 183	Stu Miller	2.50	1.25	.25
☐ 184	Harvey Haddix	3.00	1.50	.30
☐ 185	Jim Busby	2.00	1.00	.20
☐ 186	Mudcat Grant	2.00	1.00	.20
☐ 187	Bubba Phillips	2.00	1.00	.20
☐ 188	Juan Pizarro	2.00	1.00	.20
☐ 189	Neil Chrisley	2.00	1.00	.20
☐ 190	Bill Virdon	3.50	1.75	.35
☐ 191	Russ Kemmerer	2.00	1.00	.20
☐ 192	Charlie Beamon	2.00	1.00	.20
☐ 193	Sammy Taylor	2.00	1.00	.20
☐ 194	Jim Brosnan	2.50	1.25	.25
☐ 195	Rip Repulski	2.00	1.00	.20
☐ 196	Billy Moran	2.00	1.00	.20
☐ 197	Ray Semproch	2.00	1.00	.20
☐ 198	Jim Davenport	2.50	1.25	.25
☐ 199	Leo Kiely	2.00	1.00	.20
☐ 200	Warren Giles	4.00	2.00	.40
	(NL President)			
☐ 201	Tom Acker	2.00	1.00	.20
☐ 202	Roger Maris	100.00	50.00	10.00
☐ 203	Ossie Virgil	2.00	1.00	.20
☐ 204	Casey Wise	2.00	1.00	.20
☐ 205	Don Larsen	4.00	2.00	.40
☐ 206	Carl Furillo	5.00	2.50	.50
☐ 207	George Strickland	2.00	1.00	.20
☐ 208	Willie Jones	2.00	1.00	.20
☐ 209	Lenny Green	2.00	1.00	.20
☐ 210	Ed Bailey	2.50	1.25	.25
☐ 211	Bob Blaylock	2.00	1.00	.20
☐ 212	Fence Busters	25.00	11.00	2.20
	Hank Aaron			
	Eddie Mathews			
☐ 213	Jim Rivera	2.00	1.00	.20
☐ 214	Marcelino Solis	2.00	1.00	.20
☐ 215	Jim Lemon	2.50	1.25	.25
☐ 216	Andre Rodgers	2.00	1.00	.20
☐ 217	Carl Erskine	3.50	1.75	.35
☐ 218	Roman Mejias	2.00	1.00	.20
☐ 219	George Zuverink	2.00	1.00	.20
☐ 220	Frank Malzone	2.50	1.25	.25
☐ 221	Bob Bowman	2.00	1.00	.20
☐ 222	Bobby Shantz	3.00	1.50	.30
☐ 223	Cardinals Team	7.50	2.50	.50
	(checklist on back)			
☐ 224	Claude Osteen	3.50	1.75	.35
☐ 225	Johnny Logan	2.50	1.25	.25
☐ 226	Art Ceccarelli	2.00	1.00	.20
☐ 227	Hal W. Smith	2.00	1.00	.20
☐ 228	Don Gross	2.00	1.00	.20
☐ 229	Vic Power	2.50	1.25	.25
☐ 230	Bill Fischer	2.00	1.00	.20
☐ 231	Ellis Burton	2.00	1.00	.20
☐ 232	Eddie Kasko	2.00	1.00	.20
☐ 233	Paul Foytack	2.00	1.00	.20
☐ 234	Chuck Tanner	3.00	1.50	.30
☐ 235	Valmy Thomas	2.00	1.00	.20
☐ 236	Ted Bowsfield	2.00	1.00	.20
☐ 237	Run Preventers	5.00	2.50	.50
	Gil McDougald			
	Bob Turley			
	Bobby Richardson			
☐ 238	Gene Baker	2.00	1.00	.20
☐ 239	Bob Trowbridge	2.00	1.00	.20
☐ 240	Hank Bauer	4.50	2.25	.45
☐ 241	Billy Muffett	2.00	1.00	.20
☐ 242	Ron Samford	2.00	1.00	.20
☐ 243	Marv Grissom	2.00	1.00	.20
☐ 244	Ted Gray	2.00	1.00	.20
☐ 245	Ned Garver	2.00	1.00	.20
☐ 246	J.W. Porter	2.00	1.00	.20
☐ 247	Don Ferrarese	2.00	1.00	.20
☐ 248	Red Sox Team	9.00	2.50	.50
	(checklist on back)			
☐ 249	Bobby Adams	2.00	1.00	.20
☐ 250	Billy O'Dell	2.00	1.00	.20
☐ 251	Clete Boyer	3.50	1.75	.35
☐ 252	Ray Boone	2.50	1.25	.25
☐ 253	Seth Morehead	2.00	1.00	.20
☐ 254	Zeke Bella	2.00	1.00	.20
☐ 255	Del Ennis	2.50	1.25	.25
☐ 256	Jerry Davie	2.00	1.00	.20
☐ 257	Leon Wagner	2.00	1.00	.20
☐ 258	Fred Kipp	2.00	1.00	.20
☐ 259	Jim Pisoni	2.00	1.00	.20
☐ 260	Early Wynn	12.00	6.00	1.20
☐ 261	Gene Stephens	2.00	1.00	.20
☐ 262	Hitters' Foes	4.50	2.25	.45
	Johnny Podres			
	Clem Labine			
	Don Drysdale			
☐ 263	Bud Daley	2.00	1.00	.20
☐ 264	Chico Carrasquel	2.00	1.00	.20
☐ 265	Ron Kline	2.00	1.00	.20
☐ 266	Woody Held	2.00	1.00	.20
☐ 267	John Romonosky	2.00	1.00	.20
☐ 268	Tito Francona	2.50	1.25	.25
☐ 269	Jack Meyer	2.00	1.00	.20
☐ 270	Gil Hodges	12.50	6.25	1.25
☐ 271	Orlando Pena	2.00	1.00	.20
☐ 272	Jerry Lumpe	2.00	1.00	.20
☐ 273	Joey Jay	2.00	1.00	.20
☐ 274	Jerry Kindall	2.50	1.25	.25
☐ 275	Jack Sanford	2.50	1.25	.25
☐ 276	Pete Daley	2.00	1.00	.20
☐ 277	Turk Lown	2.00	1.00	.20
☐ 278	Chuck Essegian	2.50	1.25	.25
☐ 279	Ernie Johnson	2.50	1.25	.25
☐ 280	Frank Bolling	2.00	1.00	.20
☐ 281	Walt Craddock	2.00	1.00	.20
☐ 282	R.C. Stevens	2.00	1.00	.20
☐ 283	Russ Heman	2.00	1.00	.20
☐ 284	Steve Korcheck	2.00	1.00	.20
☐ 285	Joe Cunningham	2.50	1.25	.25
☐ 286	Dean Stone	2.00	1.00	.20
☐ 287	Don Zimmer	4.00	2.00	.40
☐ 288	Dutch Dotterer	2.00	1.00	.20
☐ 289	Johnny Kucks	2.50	1.25	.25
☐ 290	Wes Covington	2.50	1.25	.25
☐ 291	Pitching Partners	2.50	1.25	.25
	Pedro Ramos			
	Camilo Pascual			
☐ 292	Dick Williams	3.00	1.50	.30
☐ 293	Ray Moore	2.00	1.00	.20
☐ 294	Hank Foiles	2.00	1.00	.20
☐ 295	Billy Martin	9.00	4.50	.90
☐ 296	Ernie Broglio	3.00	1.50	.30
☐ 297	Jackie Brandt	2.00	1.00	.20
☐ 298	Tex Clevenger	2.00	1.00	.20
☐ 299	Billy Klaus	2.00	1.00	.20
☐ 300	Richie Ashburn	9.00	4.50	.90
☐ 301	Earl Averill	2.00	1.00	.20
☐ 302	Don Mossi	2.50	1.25	.25
☐ 303	Marty Keough	2.00	1.00	.20
☐ 304	Cubs Team	8.00	2.50	.50
	(checklist on back)			
☐ 305	Curt Raydon	2.00	1.00	.20
☐ 306	Jim Gilliam	5.00	2.50	.50
☐ 307	Curt Barclay	2.00	1.00	.20
☐ 308	Norm Siebern	2.00	1.00	.20
☐ 309	Sal Maglie	4.00	2.00	.40
☐ 310	Luis Aparicio	12.00	6.00	1.20
☐ 311	Norm Zauchin	2.00	1.00	.20
☐ 312	Don Newcombe	3.50	1.75	.35
☐ 313	Frank House	2.00	1.00	.20
☐ 314	Don Cardwell	2.00	1.00	.20
☐ 315	Joe Adcock	3.00	1.50	.30
☐ 316A	Ralph Lumenti	2.00	1.00	.20
	(option)			
	(photo actually			
	Camilo Pascual)			
☐ 316B	Ralph Lumenti	80.00	40.00	8.00
	(no option)			
	(photo actually			
	Camilo Pascual)			
☐ 317	Hitting Kings	15.00	7.50	1.50
	Willie Mays			
	Richie Ashburn			
☐ 318	Rocky Bridges	2.00	1.00	.20
☐ 319	Dave Hillman	2.00	1.00	.20
☐ 320	Bob Skinner	2.50	1.25	.25
☐ 321A	Bob Giallombardo	2.00	1.00	.20
	(option)			
☐ 321B	Bob Giallombardo	80.00	40.00	8.00
	(no option)			
☐ 322A	Harry Hanebrink	2.00	1.00	.20
	(traded)			
☐ 322B	Harry Hanebrink	80.00	40.00	8.00
	(no trade)			
☐ 323	Frank Sullivan	2.00	1.00	.20
☐ 324	Don Demeter	2.00	1.00	.20
☐ 325	Ken Boyer	4.50	2.25	.45
☐ 326	Marv Throneberry	3.00	1.50	.30
☐ 327	Gary Bell	2.00	1.00	.20
☐ 328	Lou Skizas	2.00	1.00	.20

329	Tigers Team (checklist on back)	9.00	2.50	.50
330	Gus Triandos	2.50	1.25	.25
331	Steve Boros	2.50	1.25	.25
332	Ray Monzant	2.00	1.00	.20
333	Harry Simpson	2.00	1.00	.20
334	Glen Hobbie	2.00	1.00	.20
335	Johnny Temple	2.50	1.25	.25
336A	Billy Loes (with traded line)	2.00	1.00	.20
336B	Billy Loes (no trade)	80.00	40.00	8.00
337	George Crowe	2.00	1.00	.20
338	Sparky Anderson	16.00	8.00	1.60
339	Roy Face	4.00	2.00	.40
340	Roy Sievers	2.50	1.25	.25
341	Tom Qualters	2.00	1.00	.20
342	Ray Jablonski	2.00	1.00	.20
343	Billy Hoeft	2.00	1.00	.20
344	Russ Nixon	2.50	1.25	.25
345	Gil McDougald	5.00	2.50	.50
346	Batter Bafflers Dave Sisler Tom Brewer	2.50	1.25	.25
347	Bob Buhl	2.00	1.00	.20
348	Ted Lepcio	2.00	1.00	.20
349	Hoyt Wilhelm	12.00	6.00	1.20
350	Ernie Banks	45.00	22.50	4.50
351	Earl Torgeson	2.00	1.00	.20
352	Robin Roberts	12.50	6.25	1.25
353	Curt Flood	4.00	2.00	.40
354	Pete Burnside	2.00	1.00	.20
355	Jim Piersall	3.50	1.75	.35
356	Bob Mabe	2.00	1.00	.20
357	Dick Stuart	3.00	1.50	.30
358	Ralph Terry	3.00	1.50	.30
359	Bill White	15.00	7.50	1.50
360	Al Kaline	45.00	22.50	4.50
361	Willard Nixon	2.00	1.00	.20
362A	Dolan Nichols (with option line)	2.00	1.00	.20
362B	Dolan Nichols (no option)	80.00	40.00	8.00
363	Bobby Avila	2.50	1.25	.25
364	Danny McDevitt	2.00	1.00	.20
365	Gus Bell	2.50	1.25	.25
366	Humberto Robinson	2.00	1.00	.20
367	Cal Neeman	2.00	1.00	.20
368	Don Mueller	2.50	1.25	.25
369	Dick Tomanek	2.00	1.00	.20
370	Pete Runnels	2.50	1.25	.25
371	Dick Brodowski	2.00	1.00	.20
372	Jim Hegan	2.50	1.25	.25
373	Herb Plews	2.00	1.00	.20
374	Art Ditmar	2.50	1.25	.25
375	Bob Nieman	2.00	1.00	.20
376	Hal Naragon	2.00	1.00	.20
377	John Antonelli	2.50	1.25	.25
378	Gail Harris	2.00	1.00	.20
379	Bob Miller	2.00	1.00	.20
380	Hank Aaron	90.00	45.00	9.00
381	Mike Baxes	2.00	1.00	.20
382	Curt Simmons	2.50	1.25	.25
383	Words of Wisdom Don Larsen Casey Stengel	6.00	3.00	.60
384	Dave Sisler	2.00	1.00	.20
385	Sherm Lollar	2.50	1.25	.25
386	Jim Delsing	2.00	1.00	.20
387	Don Drysdale	25.00	12.50	2.50
388	Bob Will	2.00	1.00	.20
389	Joe Nuxhall	2.50	1.25	.25
390	Orlando Cepeda	8.00	4.00	.80
391	Milt Pappas	3.00	1.50	.30
392	Whitey Herzog	4.00	2.00	.40
393	Frank Lary	2.50	1.25	.25
394	Randy Jackson	2.00	1.00	.20
395	Elston Howard	5.00	2.50	.50
396	Bob Rush	2.00	1.00	.20
397	Senators Team (checklist on back)	7.50	2.50	.50
398	Wally Post	2.50	1.25	.25
399	Larry Jackson	2.00	1.00	.20
400	Jackie Jensen	4.00	2.00	.40
401	Ron Blackburn	2.00	1.00	.20
402	Hector Lopez	2.00	1.00	.20
403	Clem Labine	2.50	1.25	.25
404	Hank Sauer	2.50	1.25	.25
405	Roy McMillan	2.00	1.00	.20
406	Solly Drake	2.00	1.00	.20
407	Moe Drabowsky	2.00	1.00	.20
408	Keystone Combo Nellie Fox Luis Aparicio	6.00	3.00	.60
409	Gus Zernial	2.50	1.25	.25
410	Billy Pierce	3.00	1.50	.30
411	Whitey Lockman	2.50	1.25	.25
412	Stan Lopata	2.00	1.00	.20
413	Camilo Pascual UER (listed as Camillo on front and Pasqual on back)	2.50	1.25	.25
414	Dale Long	2.50	1.25	.25
415	Bill Mazeroski	4.50	2.25	.45
416	Haywood Sullivan	2.50	1.25	.25
417	Virgil Trucks	2.50	1.25	.25
418	Gino Cimoli	2.00	1.00	.20
419	Braves Team (checklist on back)	7.50	2.50	.50
420	Rocky Colavito	5.00	2.50	.50
421	Herman Wehmeier	2.00	1.00	.20
422	Hobie Landrith	2.00	1.00	.20
423	Bob Grim	2.50	1.25	.25
424	Ken Aspromonte	2.00	1.00	.20
425	Del Crandall	2.50	1.25	.25
426	Jerry Staley	2.00	1.00	.20
427	Charlie Neal	2.50	1.25	.25
428	Buc Hill Aces Ron Kline Bob Friend Vernon Law Roy Face	3.00	1.50	.30
429	Bobby Thomson	3.00	1.50	.30
430	Whitey Ford	30.00	15.00	3.00
431	Whammy Douglas	2.00	1.00	.20
432	Smoky Burgess	2.50	1.25	.25
433	Billy Harrell	2.00	1.00	.20
434	Hal Griggs	2.00	1.00	.20
435	Frank Robinson	30.00	15.00	3.00
436	Granny Hamner	2.00	1.00	.20
437	Ike Delock	2.00	1.00	.20
438	Sammy Esposito	2.00	1.00	.20
439	Brooks Robinson	35.00	17.50	3.50
440	Lou Burdette (posing as if lefthanded)	6.00	3.00	.60
441	John Roseboro	3.00	1.50	.30
442	Ray Narleski	2.00	1.00	.20
443	Daryl Spencer	2.00	1.00	.20
444	Ron Hansen	2.50	1.25	.25
445	Cal McLish	2.00	1.00	.20
446	Rocky Nelson	2.00	1.00	.20
447	Bob Anderson	2.00	1.00	.20
448	Vada Pinson	4.00	2.00	.40
449	Tom Gorman	2.00	1.00	.20
450	Eddie Mathews	22.00	11.00	2.20
451	Jimmy Constable	2.00	1.00	.20
452	Chico Fernandez	2.00	1.00	.20
453	Les Moss	2.00	1.00	.20
454	Phil Clark	2.00	1.00	.20
455	Larry Doby	4.00	2.00	.40
456	Jerry Casale	2.00	1.00	.20
457	Dodgers Team (checklist on back)	12.50	3.50	.75
458	Gordon Jones	2.00	1.00	.20
459	Bill Tuttle	2.00	1.00	.20
460	Bob Friend	2.50	1.25	.25
461	Mantle Hits Homer	30.00	15.00	3.00
462	Colavito's Catch	3.50	1.75	.35
463	Kaline Batting Champ	8.00	4.00	.80
464	Mays' Series Catch	15.00	7.50	1.50
465	Sievers Sets Mark	3.00	1.50	.30
466	Pierce All-Star	3.00	1.50	.30
467	Aaron Clubs Homer	15.00	7.50	1.50
468	Snider's Play	8.00	4.00	.80
469	Hustler Banks	8.00	4.00	.80
470	Musial's 3000 Hit	12.00	6.00	1.20
471	Tom Sturdivant	2.00	1.00	.20
472	Gene Freese	2.00	1.00	.20
473	Mike Fornieles	2.00	1.00	.20
474	Moe Thacker	2.00	1.00	.20
475	Jack Harshman	2.00	1.00	.20
476	Indians Team (checklist on back)	7.50	2.50	.50
477	Barry Latman	2.00	1.00	.20
478	Bob Clemente	70.00	35.00	7.00
479	Lindy McDaniel	2.50	1.25	.25
480	Red Schoendienst	11.00	5.50	1.10
481	Charlie Maxwell	2.00	1.00	.20
482	Russ Meyer	2.00	1.00	.20
483	Clint Courtney	2.00	1.00	.20
484	Willie Kirkland	2.00	1.00	.20
485	Ryne Duren	3.00	1.50	.30
486	Sammy White	2.00	1.00	.20
487	Hal Brown	2.00	1.00	.20
488	Walt Moryn	2.00	1.00	.20
489	John Powers	2.00	1.00	.20
490	Frank Thomas	2.50	1.25	.25
491	Don Blasingame	2.00	1.00	.20
492	Gene Conley	2.00	1.00	.20

□ 493	Jim Landis	2.00	1.00	.20
□ 494	Don Pavletich	2.00	1.00	.20
□ 495	Johnny Podres	4.00	2.00	.40
□ 496	Wayne Terwilliger	2.00	1.00	.20
□ 497	Hal R. Smith	2.00	1.00	.20
□ 498	Dick Hyde	2.00	1.00	.20
□ 499	Johnny O'Brien	2.00	1.00	.20
□ 500	Vic Wertz	2.50	1.25	.25
□ 501	Bob Tiefenauer	2.00	1.00	.20
□ 502	Alvin Dark	3.00	1.50	.30
□ 503	Jim Owens	2.00	1.00	.20
□ 504	Ossie Alvarez	2.00	1.00	.20
□ 505	Tony Kubek	8.00	4.00	.80
□ 506	Bob Purkey	2.00	1.00	.20
□ 507	Bob Hale	8.50	4.25	.85
□ 508	Art Fowler	8.50	4.25	.85
□ 509	Norm Cash	25.00	12.50	2.50
□ 510	Yankees Team	40.00	10.00	2.00
	(checklist on back)			
□ 511	George Susce	8.50	4.25	.85
□ 512	George Altman	8.50	4.25	.85
□ 513	Tommy Carroll	8.50	4.25	.85
□ 514	Bob Gibson	300.00	150.00	30.00
□ 515	Harmon Killebrew	85.00	42.50	8.50
□ 516	Mike Garcia	10.00	5.00	1.00
□ 517	Joe Koppe	8.50	4.25	.85
□ 518	Mike Cueller	15.00	7.50	1.50
	(sic, Cuellar)			
□ 519	Infield Power	12.00	6.00	1.20
	Pete Runnels			
	Dick Gernert			
	Frank Malzone			
□ 520	Don Elston	8.50	4.25	.85
□ 521	Gary Geiger	8.50	4.25	.85
□ 522	Gene Snyder	8.50	4.25	.85
□ 523	Harry Bright	8.50	4.25	.85
□ 524	Larry Osborne	8.50	4.25	.85
□ 525	Jim Coates	8.50	4.25	.85
□ 526	Bob Speake	8.50	4.25	.85
□ 527	Solly Hemus	8.50	4.25	.85
□ 528	Pirates Team	22.00	7.00	1.50
	(checklist on back)			
□ 529	George Bamberger	12.00	6.00	1.20
□ 530	Wally Moon	10.00	5.00	1.00
□ 531	Ray Webster	8.50	4.25	.85
□ 532	Mark Freeman	8.50	4.25	.85
□ 533	Darrell Johnson	10.00	5.00	1.00
□ 534	Faye Throneberry	8.50	4.25	.85
□ 535	Ruben Gomez	8.50	4.25	.85
□ 536	Danny Kravitz	8.50	4.25	.85
□ 537	Rudolph Arias	8.50	4.25	.85
□ 538	Chick King	8.50	4.25	.85
□ 539	Gary Blaylock	8.50	4.25	.85
□ 540	Willie Miranda	8.50	4.25	.85
□ 541	Bob Thurman	8.50	4.25	.85
□ 542	Jim Perry	15.00	7.50	1.50
□ 543	Corsair Trio	50.00	25.00	5.00
	Bob Skinner			
	Bill Virdon			
	Roberto Clemente			
□ 544	Lee Tate	8.50	4.25	.85
□ 545	Tom Morgan	8.50	4.25	.85
□ 546	Al Schroll	8.50	4.25	.85
□ 547	Jim Baxes	8.50	4.25	.85
□ 548	Elmer Singleton	8.50	4.25	.85
□ 549	Howie Nunn	8.50	4.25	.85
□ 550	Roy Campanella	100.00	50.00	10.00
	(Symbol of Courage)			
□ 551	Fred Haney MG AS	10.00	5.00	1.00
□ 552	Casey Stengel MG AS	25.00	12.50	2.50
□ 553	Orlando Cepeda AS	12.50	6.25	1.25
□ 554	Bill Skowron AS	11.00	5.50	1.10
□ 555	Bill Mazeroski AS	11.00	5.50	1.10
□ 556	Nellie Fox AS	14.00	7.00	1.40
□ 557	Ken Boyer AS	12.50	6.25	1.25
□ 558	Frank Malzone AS	10.00	5.00	1.00
□ 559	Ernie Banks AS	30.00	15.00	3.00
□ 560	Luis Aparicio AS	17.00	8.50	1.70
□ 561	Hank Aaron AS	80.00	40.00	8.00
□ 562	Al Kaline AS	30.00	15.00	3.00
□ 563	Willie Mays AS	80.00	40.00	8.00
□ 564	Mickey Mantle AS	175.00	85.00	18.00
□ 565	Wes Covington AS	10.00	5.00	1.00
□ 566	Roy Sievers AS	10.00	5.00	1.00
□ 567	Del Crandall AS	10.00	5.00	1.00
□ 568	Gus Triandos AS	10.00	5.00	1.00
□ 569	Bob Friend AS	10.00	5.00	1.00
□ 570	Bob Turley AS	11.00	5.50	1.10
□ 571	Warren Spahn AS	30.00	15.00	3.00
□ 572	Billy Pierce AS	14.00	5.00	1.00

1960 Topps

The cards in this 572-card set measure 2 1/2" by 3 1/2". The 1960 Topps set is the only Topps standard size issue to use a horizontally oriented front. World Series cards appeared for the first time (385 to 391), and there is a Rookie Prospect (RP) series (117-148), the most famous of which is Carl Yastrzemski, and a Sport Magazine All-Star Selection (AS) series (553-572). There are 16 manager cards listed alphabetically from 212 through 227. The coaching staff of each team was also afforded their own card in a 16-card subset (455-470). Cards 375 to 440 come with either gray or white backs, and the high series (507- 572) were printed on a more limited basis than the rest of the set. The team cards have series checklists on the reverse.

		NRMT	VG-E	GOOD
COMPLETE SET (572)		3500.00	1600.00	400.00
COMMON PLAYER (1-110)		1.25	.60	.12
COMMON PLAYER (111-198)		1.25	.60	.12
COMMON PLAYER (199-286)		1.50	.75	.15
COMMON PLAYER (287-440)		1.75	.85	.17
COMMON PLAYER (441-506)		3.00	1.50	.30
COMMON PLAYER (507-552)		8.00	4.00	.80
COMMON PLAYER (553-572)		10.00	5.00	1.00
□	1 Early Wynn	30.00	15.00	3.00
□	2 Roman Mejias	1.25	.60	.12
□	3 Joe Adcock	1.75	.85	.17
□	4 Bob Purkey	1.25	.60	.12
□	5 Wally Moon	1.75	.85	.17
□	6 Lou Berberet	1.25	.60	.12
□	7 Master and Mentor	10.00	5.00	1.00
	Willie Mays			
	Bill Rigney			
□	8 Bud Daley	1.25	.60	.12
□	9 Faye Throneberry	1.25	.60	.12
□	10 Ernie Banks	30.00	13.50	2.70
□	11 Norm Siebern	1.25	.60	.12
□	12 Milt Pappas	1.75	.85	.17
□	13 Wally Post	1.25	.60	.12
□	14 Jim Grant	1.25	.60	.12
□	15 Pete Runnels	1.75	.85	.17
□	16 Ernie Broglio	1.75	.85	.17
□	17 Johnny Callison	1.75	.85	.17
□	18 Dodgers Team	10.00	3.00	.50
	(checklist on back)			
□	19 Felix Mantilla	1.25	.60	.12
□	20 Roy Face	2.50	1.25	.25
□	21 Dutch Dotterer	1.25	.60	.12
□	22 Rocky Bridges	1.25	.60	.12
□	23 Eddie Fisher	1.25	.60	.12
□	24 Dick Gray	1.25	.60	.12
□	25 Roy Sievers	1.75	.85	.17
□	26 Wayne Terwilliger	1.25	.60	.12
□	27 Dick Drott	1.25	.60	.12
□	28 Brooks Robinson	32.00	16.00	3.20
□	29 Clem Labine	1.75	.85	.17
□	30 Tito Francona	1.75	.85	.17
□	31 Sammy Esposito	1.25	.60	.12
□	32 Sophomore Stalwarts	1.75	.85	.17
	Jim O'Toole			
	Vada Pinson			
□	33 Tom Morgan	1.25	.60	.12
□	34 George Anderson	3.50	1.75	.35
□	35 Whitey Ford	27.00	13.50	2.70

☐ 36	Russ Nixon	1.75	.85	.17
☐ 37	Bill Bruton	1.25	.60	.12
☐ 38	Jerry Casale	1.25	.60	.12
☐ 39	Earl Averill	1.25	.60	.12
☐ 40	Joe Cunningham	1.75	.85	.17
☐ 41	Barry Latman	1.25	.60	.12
☐ 42	Hobie Landrith	1.25	.60	.12
☐ 43	Senators Team	5.00	2.00	.40
	(checklist on back)			
☐ 44	Bobby Locke	1.25	.60	.12
☐ 45	Roy McMillan	1.25	.60	.12
☐ 46	Jerry Fisher	1.25	.60	.12
☐ 47	Don Zimmer	3.00	1.50	.30
☐ 48	Hal W. Smith	1.25	.60	.12
☐ 49	Curt Raydon	1.25	.60	.12
☐ 50	Al Kaline	27.00	13.50	2.70
☐ 51	Jim Coates	1.25	.60	.12
☐ 52	Dave Philley	1.25	.60	.12
☐ 53	Jackie Brandt	1.25	.60	.12
☐ 54	Mike Fornieles	1.25	.60	.12
☐ 55	Bill Mazeroski	3.00	1.50	.30
☐ 56	Steve Korcheck	1.25	.60	.12
☐ 57	Win Savers	1.75	.85	.17
	Turk Lown			
	Jerry Staley			
☐ 58	Gino Cimoli	1.25	.60	.12
☐ 59	Juan Pizarro	1.25	.60	.12
☐ 60	Gus Triandos	1.75	.85	.17
☐ 61	Eddie Kasko	1.25	.60	.12
☐ 62	Roger Craig	3.50	1.75	.35
☐ 63	George Strickland	1.25	.60	.12
☐ 64	Jack Meyer	1.25	.60	.12
☐ 65	Elston Howard	4.00	2.00	.40
☐ 66	Bob Trowbridge	1.25	.60	.12
☐ 67	Jose Pagan	1.25	.60	.12
☐ 68	Dave Hillman	1.25	.60	.12
☐ 69	Billy Goodman	1.75	.85	.17
☐ 70	Lew Burdette	2.50	1.25	.25
☐ 71	Marty Keough	1.25	.60	.12
☐ 72	Tigers Team	7.50	2.50	.50
	(checklist on back)			
☐ 73	Bob Gibson	32.00	16.00	3.20
☐ 74	Walt Moryn	1.25	.60	.12
☐ 75	Vic Power	1.25	.60	.12
☐ 76	Bill Fischer	1.25	.60	.12
☐ 77	Hank Foiles	1.25	.60	.12
☐ 78	Bob Grim	1.25	.60	.12
☐ 79	Walt Dropo	1.25	.60	.12
☐ 80	Johnny Antonelli	1.75	.85	.17
☐ 81	Russ Snyder	1.25	.60	.12
☐ 82	Ruben Gomez	1.25	.60	.12
☐ 83	Tony Kubek	4.50	2.25	.45
☐ 84	Hal R. Smith	1.25	.60	.12
☐ 85	Frank Lary	1.75	.85	.17
☐ 86	Dick Gernert	1.25	.60	.12
☐ 87	John Romonosky	1.25	.60	.12
☐ 88	John Roseboro	1.75	.85	.17
☐ 89	Hal Brown	1.25	.60	.12
☐ 90	Bobby Avila	1.25	.60	.12
☐ 91	Bennie Daniels	1.25	.60	.12
☐ 92	Whitey Herzog	3.50	1.75	.35
☐ 93	Art Schult	1.25	.60	.12
☐ 94	Leo Kiely	1.25	.60	.12
☐ 95	Frank Thomas	1.75	.85	.17
☐ 96	Ralph Terry	2.50	1.25	.25
☐ 97	Ted Lepcio	1.25	.60	.12
☐ 91	Gordon Jones	1.25	.60	.12
☐ 99	Lenny Green	1.25	.60	.12
☐ 100	Nellie Fox	5.00	2.50	.50
☐ 101	Bob Miller	1.25	.60	.12
☐ 102	Kent Hadley	1.25	.60	.12
☐ 103	Dick Farrell	1.25	.60	.12
☐ 104	Dick Schofield	1.25	.60	.12
☐ 105	Larry Sherry	2.50	1.25	.25
☐ 106	Billy Gardner	1.75	.85	.17
☐ 107	Carlton Willey	1.25	.60	.12
☐ 108	Pete Daley	1.25	.60	.12
☐ 109	Clete Boyer	2.50	1.25	.25
☐ 110	Cal McLish	1.25	.60	.12
☐ 111	Vic Wertz	1.75	.85	.17
☐ 112	Jack Harshman	1.25	.60	.12
☐ 113	Bob Skinner	1.75	.85	.17
☐ 114	Ken Aspromonte	1.25	.60	.12
☐ 115	Fork and Knuckler	4.00	2.00	.40
	Roy Face			
	Hoyt Wilhelm			
☐ 116	Jim Rivera	1.25	.60	.12
☐ 117	Tom Borland RP	1.25	.60	.12
☐ 118	Bob Bruce RP	1.25	.60	.12
☐ 119	Chico Cardenas RP	1.75	.85	.17
☐ 120	Duke Carmel RP	1.25	.60	.12
☐ 121	Camilo Carreon RP	1.75	.85	.17
☐ 122	Don Dillard RP	1.25	.60	.12
☐ 123	Dan Dobbek RP	1.25	.60	.12
☐ 124	Jim Donohue RP	1.25	.60	.12
☐ 125	Dick Ellsworth RP	2.50	1.25	.25
☐ 126	Chuck Estrada RP	2.50	1.25	.25
☐ 127	Ron Hansen RP	1.75	.85	.17
☐ 128	Bill Harris RP	1.25	.60	.12
☐ 129	Bob Hartman RP	1.25	.60	.12
☐ 130	Frank Herrera RP	1.25	.60	.12
☐ 131	Ed Hobaugh RP	1.25	.60	.12
☐ 132	Frank Howard RP	10.00	5.00	1.00
☐ 133	Manuel Javier RP	2.50	1.25	.25
	(sic, Julian)			
☐ 134	Deron Johnson RP	1.75	.85	.17
☐ 135	Ken Johnson RP	1.25	.60	.12
☐ 136	Jim Kaat RP	21.00	10.50	2.10
☐ 137	Lou Klimchock RP	1.25	.60	.12
☐ 138	Art Mahaffey RP	1.75	.85	.17
☐ 139	Carl Mathias RP	1.25	.60	.12
☐ 140	Julio Navarro RP	1.75	.85	.17
☐ 141	Jim Proctor RP	1.25	.60	.12
☐ 142	Bill Short RP	1.75	.85	.17
☐ 143	Al Spangler RP	1.25	.60	.12
☐ 144	Al Stieglitz RP	1.25	.60	.12
☐ 145	Jim Umbricht RP	1.25	.60	.12
☐ 146	Ted Wieand RP	1.25	.60	.12
☐ 147	Bob Will RP	1.25	.60	.12
☐ 148	Carl Yastrzemski RP	350.00	175.00	35.00
☐ 149	Bob Nieman	1.25	.60	.12
☐ 150	Billy Pierce	2.50	1.25	.25
☐ 151	Giants Team	6.00	2.00	.40
	(checklist on back)			
☐ 152	Gail Harris	1.25	.60	.12
☐ 153	Bobby Thomson	2.50	1.25	.25
☐ 154	Jim Davenport	1.75	.85	.17
☐ 155	Charlie Neal	1.75	.85	.17
☐ 156	Art Ceccarelli	1.25	.60	.12
☐ 157	Rocky Nelson	1.25	.60	.12
☐ 158	Wes Covington	1.75	.85	.17
☐ 159	Jim Piersall	2.50	1.25	.25
☐ 160	Rival All-Stars	30.00	15.00	3.00
	Mickey Mantle			
	Ken Boyer			
☐ 161	Ray Narleski	1.25	.60	.12
☐ 162	Sammy Taylor	1.25	.60	.12
☐ 163	Hector Lopez	1.25	.60	.12
☐ 164	Reds Team	6.00	2.00	.40
	(checklist on back)			
☐ 165	Jack Sanford	1.75	.85	.17
☐ 166	Chuck Essegian	1.25	.60	.12
☐ 167	Valmy Thomas	1.25	.60	.12
☐ 168	Alex Grammas	1.25	.60	.12
☐ 169	Jake Striker	1.25	.60	.12
☐ 170	Del Crandall	1.75	.85	.17
☐ 171	Johnny Groth	1.25	.60	.12
☐ 172	Willie Kirkland	1.25	.60	.12
☐ 173	Billy Martin	7.00	3.50	.70
☐ 174	Indians Team	5.00	2.00	.40
	(checklist on back)			
☐ 175	Pedro Ramos	1.25	.60	.12
☐ 176	Vada Pinson	3.00	1.50	.30
☐ 177	Johnny Kucks	1.25	.60	.12
☐ 178	Woody Held	1.25	.60	.12
☐ 179	Rip Coleman	1.25	.60	.12
☐ 180	Harry Simpson	1.25	.60	.12
☐ 181	Billy Loes	1.25	.60	.12
☐ 182	Glen Hobbie	1.25	.60	.12
☐ 183	Eli Grba	1.25	.60	.12
☐ 184	Gary Geiger	1.25	.60	.12
☐ 185	Jim Owens	1.25	.60	.12
☐ 186	Dave Sisler	1.25	.60	.12
☐ 187	Jay Hook	1.25	.60	.12
☐ 188	Dick Williams	2.50	1.25	.25
☐ 189	Don McMahon	1.25	.60	.12
☐ 190	Gene Woodling	1.75	.85	.17
☐ 191	Johnny Klippstein	1.25	.60	.12
☐ 192	Danny O'Connell	1.25	.60	.12
☐ 193	Dick Hyde	1.25	.60	.12
☐ 194	Bobby Gene Smith	1.25	.60	.12
☐ 195	Lindy McDaniel	1.75	.85	.17
☐ 196	Andy Carey	1.75	.85	.17
☐ 197	Ron Kline	1.25	.60	.12
☐ 198	Jerry Lynch	1.25	.60	.12
☐ 199	Dick Donovan	1.50	.75	.15
☐ 200	Willie Mays	80.00	40.00	8.00
☐ 201	Larry Osborne	1.50	.75	.15
☐ 202	Fred Kipp	1.50	.75	.15
☐ 203	Sammy White	1.50	.75	.15
☐ 204	Ryne Duren	2.50	1.25	.25
☐ 205	Johnny Logan	2.00	1.00	.20
☐ 206	Claude Osteen	2.00	1.00	.20
☐ 207	Bob Boyd	1.50	.75	.15
☐ 208	White Sox Team	5.00	2.00	.40
	(checklist on back)			
☐ 209	Ron Blackburn	1.50	.75	.15
☐ 210	Harmon Killebrew	21.00	10.50	2.10
☐ 211	Taylor Phillips	1.50	.75	.15
☐ 212	Walt Alston MG	8.00	4.00	.80

☐ 213	Chuck Dressen MG	2.00	1.00	.20
☐ 214	Jimmy Dykes MG	2.00	1.00	.20
☐ 215	Bob Elliott MG	2.00	1.00	.20
☐ 216	Joe Gordon MG	2.00	1.00	.20
☐ 217	Charlie Grimm MG	2.00	1.00	.20
☐ 218	Solly Hemus MG	2.00	1.00	.20
☐ 219	Fred Hutchinson MG	2.00	1.00	.20
☐ 220	Billy Jurges MG	2.00	1.00	.20
☐ 221	Cookie Lavagetto MG	2.00	1.00	.20
☐ 222	Al Lopez MG	6.00	3.00	.60
☐ 223	Danny Murtaugh MG	2.00	1.00	.20
☐ 224	Paul Richards MG	2.00	1.00	.20
☐ 225	Bill Rigney MG	2.00	1.00	.20
☐ 226	Eddie Sawyer MG	2.00	1.00	.20
☐ 227	Casey Stengel MG	15.00	7.50	1.50
☐ 228	Ernie Johnson	2.00	1.00	.20
☐ 229	Joe M. Morgan	5.00	2.50	.50
☐ 230	Mound Magicians	5.00	2.50	.50
	Lou Burdette			
	Warren Spahn			
	Bob Buhl			
☐ 231	Hal Naragon	1.50	.75	.15
☐ 232	Jim Busby	1.50	.75	.15
☐ 233	Don Elston	1.50	.75	.15
☐ 234	Don Demeter	1.50	.75	.15
☐ 235	Gus Bell	2.00	1.00	.20
☐ 236	Dick Ricketts	1.50	.75	.15
☐ 237	Elmer Valo	1.50	.75	.15
☐ 238	Danny Kravitz	1.50	.75	.15
☐ 239	Joe Shipley	1.50	.75	.15
☐ 240	Luis Aparicio	10.00	5.00	1.00
☐ 241	Albie Pearson	1.50	.75	.15
☐ 242	Cardinals Team	6.00	2.00	.40
	(checklist on back)			
☐ 243	Bubba Phillips	1.50	.75	.15
☐ 244	Hal Griggs	1.50	.75	.15
☐ 245	Eddie Yost	1.50	.75	.15
☐ 246	Lee Maye	1.50	.75	.15
☐ 247	Gil McDougald	3.50	1.75	.35
☐ 248	Del Rice	1.50	.75	.15
☐ 249	Earl Wilson	2.00	1.00	.20
☐ 250	Stan Musial	80.00	40.00	8.00
☐ 251	Bob Malkmus	1.50	.75	.15
☐ 252	Ray Herbert	1.50	.75	.15
☐ 253	Eddie Bressoud	1.50	.75	.15
☐ 254	Arnie Portocarrero	1.50	.75	.15
☐ 255	Jim Gilliam	3.50	1.75	.35
☐ 256	Dick Brown	1.50	.75	.15
☐ 257	Gordy Coleman	2.00	1.00	.20
☐ 258	Dick Groat	3.50	1.75	.35
☐ 259	George Altman	1.50	.75	.15
☐ 260	Power Plus	2.00	1.00	.20
	Rocky Colavito			
	Tito Francona			
☐ 261	Pete Burnside	1.50	.75	.15
☐ 262	Hank Bauer	2.50	1.25	.25
☐ 263	Darrell Johnson	2.00	1.00	.20
☐ 264	Robin Roberts	11.00	5.50	1.10
☐ 265	Rip Repulski	1.50	.75	.15
☐ 266	Joey Jay	1.50	.75	.15
☐ 267	Jim Marshall	1.50	.75	.15
☐ 268	Al Worthington	1.50	.75	.15
☐ 269	Gene Green	1.50	.75	.15
☐ 270	Bob Turley	2.50	1.25	.25
☐ 271	Julio Becquer	1.50	.75	.15
☐ 272	Fred Green	1.50	.75	.15
☐ 273	Neil Chrisley	1.50	.75	.15
☐ 274	Tom Acker	1.50	.75	.15
☐ 275	Curt Flood	2.50	1.25	.25
☐ 276	Ken McBride	1.50	.75	.15
☐ 277	Harry Bright	1.50	.75	.15
☐ 278	Stan Williams	1.50	.75	.15
☐ 279	Chuck Tanner	2.00	1.00	.20
☐ 280	Frank Sullivan	1.50	.75	.15
☐ 281	Ray Boone	2.00	1.00	.20
☐ 282	Joe Nuxhall	2.00	1.00	.20
☐ 283	John Blanchard	2.00	1.00	.20
☐ 284	Don Gross	1.50	.75	.15
☐ 285	Harry Anderson	1.50	.75	.15
☐ 286	Ray Semproch	1.50	.75	.15
☐ 287	Felipe Alou	2.50	1.25	.25
☐ 288	Bob Mabe	1.75	.85	.17
☐ 289	Willie Jones	1.75	.85	.17
☐ 290	Jerry Lumpe	1.75	.85	.17
☐ 291	Bob Keegan	1.75	.85	.17
☐ 292	Dodger Backstops	2.50	1.25	.25
	Joe Pignatano			
	John Roseboro			
☐ 293	Gene Conley	1.75	.85	.17
☐ 294	Tony Taylor	1.75	.85	.17
☐ 295	Gil Hodges	11.00	5.50	1.10
☐ 296	Nelson Chittum	1.75	.85	.17
☐ 297	Reno Bertoia	1.75	.85	.17
☐ 298	George Witt	1.75	.85	.17
☐ 299	Earl Torgeson	1.75	.85	.17
☐ 300	Hank Aaron	80.00	40.00	8.00
☐ 301	Jerry Davie	1.75	.85	.17
☐ 302	Phillies Team	5.00	2.00	.40
	(checklist on back)			
☐ 303	Billy O'Dell	1.75	.85	.17
☐ 304	Joe Ginsberg	1.75	.85	.17
☐ 305	Richie Ashburn	7.00	3.50	.70
☐ 306	Frank Baumann	1.75	.85	.17
☐ 307	Gene Oliver	1.75	.85	.17
☐ 308	Dick Hall	1.75	.85	.17
☐ 309	Bob Hale	1.75	.85	.17
☐ 310	Frank Malzone	2.50	1.25	.25
☐ 311	Raul Sanchez	1.75	.85	.17
☐ 312	Charley Lau	2.50	1.25	.25
☐ 313	Turk Lown	1.75	.85	.17
☐ 314	Chico Fernandez	1.75	.85	.17
☐ 315	Bobby Shantz	3.00	1.50	.30
☐ 316	Willie McCovey	135.00	65.00	13.50
☐ 317	Pumpsie Green	1.75	.85	.17
☐ 318	Jim Baxes	1.75	.85	.17
☐ 319	Joe Koppe	1.75	.85	.17
☐ 320	Bob Allison	3.00	1.50	.30
☐ 321	Ron Fairly	2.50	1.25	.25
☐ 322	Willie Tasby	1.75	.85	.17
☐ 323	John Romano	1.75	.85	.17
☐ 324	Jim Perry	3.00	1.50	.30
☐ 325	Jim O'Toole	2.50	1.25	.25
☐ 326	Bob Clemente	75.00	37.50	7.50
☐ 327	Ray Sadecki	1.75	.85	.17
☐ 328	Earl Battey	1.75	.85	.17
☐ 329	Zack Monroe	1.75	.85	.17
☐ 330	Harvey Kuenn	3.50	1.75	.35
☐ 331	Henry Mason	1.75	.85	.17
☐ 332	Yankees Team	20.00	5.00	1.00
	(checklist on back)			
☐ 333	Danny McDevitt	1.75	.85	.17
☐ 334	Ted Abernathy	1.75	.85	.17
☐ 335	Red Schoendienst	10.00	5.00	1.00
☐ 336	Ike Delock	1.75	.85	.17
☐ 337	Cal Neeman	1.75	.85	.17
☐ 338	Ray Monzant	1.75	.85	.17
☐ 339	Harry Chiti	1.75	.85	.17
☐ 340	Harvey Haddix	2.50	1.25	.25
☐ 341	Carroll Hardy	1.75	.85	.17
☐ 342	Casey Wise	1.75	.85	.17
☐ 343	Sandy Koufax	80.00	40.00	8.00
☐ 344	Clint Courtney	1.75	.85	.17
☐ 345	Don Newcombe	3.00	1.50	.30
☐ 346	J.C. Martin	1.75	.85	.17
	(face actually			
	Gary Peters)			
☐ 347	Ed Bouchee	1.75	.85	.17
☐ 348	Barry Shetrone	1.75	.85	.17
☐ 349	Moe Drabowsky	1.75	.85	.17
☐ 350	Mickey Mantle	300.00	150.00	30.00
☐ 351	Don Nottebart	1.75	.85	.17
☐ 352	Cincy Clouters	4.00	2.00	.40
	Gus Bell			
	Frank Robinson			
	Jerry Lynch			
☐ 353	Don Larsen	3.00	1.50	.30
☐ 354	Bob Lillis	2.50	1.25	.25
☐ 355	Bill White	4.00	2.00	.40
☐ 356	Joe Amalfitano	1.75	.85	.17
☐ 357	Al Schroll	1.75	.85	.17
☐ 358	Joe DeMaestri	1.75	.85	.17
☐ 359	Buddy Gilbert	1.75	.85	.17
☐ 360	Herb Score	2.50	1.25	.25
☐ 361	Bob Oldis	1.75	.85	.17
☐ 362	Russ Kemmerer	1.75	.85	.17
☐ 363	Gene Stephens	1.75	.85	.17
☐ 364	Paul Foytack	1.75	.85	.17
☐ 365	Minnie Minoso	3.50	1.75	.35
☐ 366	Dallas Green	7.50	3.75	.75
☐ 367	Bill Tuttle	1.75	.85	.17
☐ 368	Daryl Spencer	1.75	.85	.17
☐ 369	Billy Hoeft	1.75	.85	.17
☐ 370	Bill Skowron	5.00	2.50	.50
☐ 371	Bud Byerly	1.75	.85	.17
☐ 372	Frank House	1.75	.85	.17
☐ 373	Don Hoak	1.75	.85	.17
☐ 374	Bob Buhl	1.75	.85	.17
☐ 375	Dale Long	2.50	1.25	.25
☐ 376	John Briggs	1.75	.85	.17
☐ 377	Roger Maris	85.00	42.50	8.50
☐ 378	Stu Miller	1.75	.85	.17
☐ 379	Red Wilson	1.75	.85	.17
☐ 380	Bob Shaw	1.75	.85	.17
☐ 381	Braves Team	5.00	2.00	.40
	(checklist on back)			
☐ 382	Ted Bowsfield	1.75	.85	.17
☐ 383	Leon Wagner	1.75	.85	.17
☐ 384	Don Cardwell	1.75	.85	.17
☐ 385	World Series Game 1	3.50	1.75	.35
	Neal Steals Second			

☐ 386	World Series Game 2 ..... Neal Belts 2nd Homer	3.50	1.75	.35
☐ 387	World Series Game 3 ..... Furillo Breaks Game	4.00	2.00	.40
☐ 388	World Series Game 4 ..... Hodges' Homer	5.00	2.50	.50
☐ 389	World Series Game 5 ..... Luis Swipes Base	5.00	2.50	.50
☐ 390	World Series Game 6 ..... Scrambling After Ball	3.50	1.75	.35
☐ 391	World Series Summary .. The Champs Celebrate	3.50	1.75	.35
☐ 392	Tex Clevenger	1.75	.85	.17
☐ 393	Smoky Burgess	2.50	1.25	.25
☐ 394	Norm Larker	1.75	.85	.17
☐ 395	Hoyt Wilhelm	11.00	5.50	1.10
☐ 396	Steve Bilko	1.75	.85	.17
☐ 397	Don Blasingame	1.75	.85	.17
☐ 398	Mike Cuellar	2.50	1.25	.25
☐ 399	Young Hill Stars Milt Pappas Jack Fisher Jerry Walker	2.50	1.25	.25
☐ 400	Rocky Colavito	4.50	2.25	.45
☐ 401	Bob Duliba	1.75	.85	.17
☐ 402	Dick Stuart	2.50	1.25	.25
☐ 403	Ed Sadowski	1.75	.85	.17
☐ 404	Bob Rush	1.75	.85	.17
☐ 405	Bobby Richardson	4.50	2.25	.45
☐ 406	Billy Klaus	1.75	.85	.17
☐ 407	Gary Peters (face actually J.C. Martin)	2.50	1.25	.25
☐ 408	Carl Furillo	4.00	2.00	.40
☐ 409	Ron Samford	1.75	.85	.17
☐ 410	Sam Jones	1.75	.85	.17
☐ 411	Ed Bailey	1.75	.85	.17
☐ 412	Bob Anderson	1.75	.85	.17
☐ 413	Athletics Team (checklist on back)	5.00	2.00	.40
☐ 414	Don Williams	1.75	.85	.17
☐ 415	Bob Cerv	2.50	1.25	.25
☐ 416	Humberto Robinson	1.75	.85	.17
☐ 417	Chuck Cottier	2.50	1.25	.25
☐ 418	Don Mossi	2.50	1.25	.25
☐ 419	George Crowe	1.75	.85	.17
☐ 420	Eddie Mathews	21.00	10.50	2.10
☐ 421	Duke Maas	1.75	.85	.17
☐ 422	John Powers	1.75	.85	.17
☐ 423	Ed Fitzgerald	1.75	.85	.17
☐ 424	Pete Whisenant	1.75	.85	.17
☐ 425	Johnny Podres	3.50	1.75	.35
☐ 426	Ron Jackson	1.75	.85	.17
☐ 427	Al Grunwald	1.75	.85	.17
☐ 428	Al Smith	1.75	.85	.17
☐ 429	AL Kings Nellie Fox Harvey Kuenn	3.50	1.75	.35
☐ 430	Art Ditmar	1.75	.85	.17
☐ 431	Andre Rodgers	1.75	.85	.17
☐ 432	Chuck Stobbs	1.75	.85	.17
☐ 433	Irv Noren	1.75	.85	.17
☐ 434	Brooks Lawrence	1.75	.85	.17
☐ 435	Gene Freese	1.75	.85	.17
☐ 436	Marv Throneberry	2.50	1.25	.25
☐ 437	Bob Friend	2.50	1.25	.25
☐ 438	Jim Coker	1.75	.85	.17
☐ 439	Tom Brewer	1.75	.85	.17
☐ 440	Jim Lemon	2.50	1.25	.25
☐ 441	Gary Bell	3.00	1.50	.30
☐ 442	Joe Pignatano	3.00	1.50	.30
☐ 443	Charley Maxwell	3.00	1.50	.30
☐ 444	Jerry Kindall	3.00	1.50	.30
☐ 445	Warren Spahn	27.00	13.50	2.70
☐ 446	Ellis Burton	3.00	1.50	.30
☐ 447	Ray Moore	3.00	1.50	.30
☐ 448	Jim Gentile	4.50	2.25	.45
☐ 449	Jim Brosnan	3.50	1.75	.35
☐ 450	Orlando Cepeda	7.50	3.75	.75
☐ 451	Curt Simmons	4.00	2.00	.40
☐ 452	Ray Webster	3.00	1.50	.30
☐ 453	Vern Law	4.00	2.00	.40
☐ 454	Hal Woodeshick	3.00	1.50	.30
☐ 455	Baltimore Coaches Eddie Robinson Harry Brecheen Luman Harris	4.00	2.00	.40
☐ 456	Red Sox Coaches Rudy York Billy Herman Sal Maglie Del Baker	5.00	2.50	.50
☐ 457	Cubs Coaches Charlie Root Lou Klein Elvin Tappe	4.00	2.00	.40
☐ 458	White Sox Coaches Johnny Cooney Don Gutteridge Tony Cuccinello Ray Berres	4.00	2.00	.40
☐ 459	Reds Coaches Reggie Otero Cot Deal Wally Moses	4.00	2.00	.40
☐ 460	Indians Coaches Mel Harder Jo-Jo White Bob Lemon Ralph(Red) Kress	5.00	2.50	.50
☐ 461	Tigers Coaches Tom Ferrick Luke Appling Billy Hitchcock	5.00	2.50	.50
☐ 462	Athletics Coaches Fred Fitzsimmons Don Heffner Walker Cooper	4.00	2.00	.40
☐ 463	Dodgers Coaches Bobby Bragan Pete Reiser Joe Becker Greg Mulleavy	5.00	2.50	.50
☐ 464	Braves Coaches Bob Scheffing Whitlow Wyatt Andy Pafko George Myatt	4.00	2.00	.40
☐ 465	Yankees Coaches Bill Dickey Ralph Houk Frank Crosetti Ed Lopat	9.00	4.50	.90
☐ 466	Phillies Coaches Ken Silvestri Dick Carter Andy Cohen	4.00	2.00	.40
☐ 467	Pirates Coaches Mickey Vernon Frank Oceak Sam Narron Bill Burwell	4.00	2.00	.40
☐ 468	Cardinals Coaches Johnny Keane Howie Pollet Ray Katt Harry Walker	4.00	2.00	.40
☐ 469	Giants Coaches Wes Westrum Salty Parker Bill Posedel	4.00	2.00	.40
☐ 470	Senators Coaches Bob Swift Ellis Clary Sam Mele	4.00	2.00	.40
☐ 471	Ned Garver	3.00	1.50	.30
☐ 472	Alvin Dark	4.00	2.00	.40
☐ 473	Al Cicotte	3.00	1.50	.30
☐ 474	Haywood Sullivan	3.50	1.75	.35
☐ 475	Don Drysdale	27.00	13.50	2.70
☐ 476	Lou Johnson	3.50	1.75	.35
☐ 477	Don Ferrarese	3.00	1.50	.30
☐ 478	Frank Torre	3.00	1.50	.30
☐ 479	Georges Maranda	3.00	1.50	.30
☐ 480	Yogi Berra	50.00	25.00	5.00
☐ 481	Wes Stock	3.00	1.50	.30
☐ 482	Frank Bolling	3.00	1.50	.30
☐ 483	Camilo Pascual	3.50	1.75	.35
☐ 484	Pirates Team (checklist on back)	12.50	4.00	.80
☐ 485	Ken Boyer	5.00	2.50	.50
☐ 486	Bobby Del Greco	3.00	1.50	.30
☐ 487	Tom Sturdivant	3.00	1.50	.30
☐ 488	Norm Cash	4.50	2.25	.45
☐ 489	Steve Ridzik	3.00	1.50	.30
☐ 490	Frank Robinson	35.00	17.50	3.50
☐ 491	Mel Roach	3.00	1.50	.30
☐ 492	Larry Jackson	3.00	1.50	.30
☐ 493	Duke Snider	40.00	20.00	4.00
☐ 494	Orioles Team (checklist on back)	7.50	2.50	.50
☐ 495	Sherm Lollar	3.50	1.75	.35
☐ 496	Bill Virdon	4.50	2.25	.45
☐ 497	John Tsitouris	3.00	1.50	.30
☐ 498	Al Pilarcik	3.00	1.50	.30
☐ 499	Johnny James	3.00	1.50	.30
☐ 500	Johnny Temple	3.50	1.75	.35
☐ 501	Bob Schmidt	3.00	1.50	.30
☐ 502	Jim Bunning	7.50	3.75	.75
☐ 503	Don Lee	3.00	1.50	.30

□ 504	Seth Morehead	3.00	1.50	.30
□ 505	Ted Kluszewski	4.50	2.25	.45
□ 506	Lee Walls	3.00	1.50	.30
□ 507	Dick Stigman	8.00	4.00	.80
□ 508	Billy Consolo	8.00	4.00	.80
□ 509	Tommy Davis	15.00	7.50	1.50
□ 510	Jerry Staley	8.00	4.00	.80
□ 511	Ken Walters	8.00	4.00	.80
□ 512	Joe Gibbon	8.00	4.00	.80
□ 513	Chicago Cubs	24.00	7.00	1.50
	Team Card			
	(checklist on back)			
□ 514	Steve Barber	8.00	4.00	.80
□ 515	Stan Lopata	8.00	4.00	.80
□ 516	Marty Kutyna	8.00	4.00	.80
□ 517	Charlie James	8.00	4.00	.80
□ 518	Tony Gonzalez	8.00	4.00	.80
□ 519	Ed Roebuck	8.00	4.00	.80
□ 520	Don Buddin	8.00	4.00	.80
□ 521	Mike Lee	8.00	4.00	.80
□ 522	Ken Hunt	8.00	4.00	.80
□ 523	Clay Dalrymple	8.00	4.00	.80
□ 524	Bill Henry	8.00	4.00	.80
□ 525	Marv Breeding	8.00	4.00	.80
□ 526	Paul Giel	8.00	4.00	.80
□ 527	Jose Valdivielso	8.00	4.00	.80
□ 528	Ben Johnson	8.00	4.00	.80
□ 529	Norm Sherry	9.00	4.50	.90
□ 530	Mike McCormick	9.00	4.50	.90
□ 531	Sandy Amoros	9.00	4.50	.90
□ 532	Mike Garcia	10.00	5.00	1.00
□ 533	Lu Clinton	8.00	4.00	.80
□ 534	Ken MacKenzie	8.00	4.00	.80
□ 535	Whitey Lockman	9.00	4.50	.90
□ 536	Wynn Hawkins	8.00	4.00	.80
□ 537	Boston Red Sox	24.00	11.00	2.20
	Team Card			
	(checklist on back)			
□ 538	Frank Barnes	8.00	4.00	.80
□ 539	Gene Baker	8.00	4.00	.80
□ 540	Jerry Walker	8.00	4.00	.80
□ 541	Tony Curry	8.00	4.00	.80
□ 542	Ken Hamlin	8.00	4.00	.80
□ 543	Elio Chacon	8.00	4.00	.80
□ 544	Bill Monbouquette	9.00	4.50	.90
□ 545	Carl Sawatski	8.00	4.00	.80
□ 546	Hank Aguirre	8.00	4.00	.80
□ 547	Bob Aspromonte	8.00	4.00	.80
□ 548	Don Mincher	9.00	4.50	.90
□ 549	John Buzhardt	8.00	4.00	.80
□ 550	Jim Landis	8.00	4.00	.80
□ 551	Ed Rakow	8.00	4.00	.80
□ 552	Walt Bond	8.00	4.00	.80
□ 553	Bill Skowron AS	11.00	5.50	1.10
□ 554	Willie McCovey AS	33.00	15.00	3.00
□ 555	Nellie Fox AS	12.50	6.25	1.25
□ 556	Charlie Neal AS	10.00	5.00	1.00
□ 557	Frank Malzone AS	10.00	5.00	1.00
□ 558	Eddie Mathews AS	22.00	11.00	2.20
□ 559	Luis Aparicio AS	17.00	8.50	1.70
□ 560	Ernie Banks AS	30.00	15.00	3.00
□ 561	Al Kaline AS	30.00	15.00	3.00
□ 562	Joe Cunningham AS	10.00	5.00	1.00
□ 563	Mickey Mantle AS	175.00	85.00	18.00
□ 564	Willie Mays AS	80.00	40.00	8.00
□ 565	Roger Maris AS	60.00	30.00	6.00
□ 566	Hank Aaron AS	80.00	40.00	8.00
□ 567	Sherm Lollar AS	10.00	5.00	1.00
□ 568	Del Crandall AS	10.00	5.00	1.00
□ 569	Camilo Pascual AS	10.00	5.00	1.00
□ 570	Don Drysdale AS	20.00	10.00	2.00
□ 571	Billy Pierce AS	11.00	5.50	1.10
□ 572	Johnny Antonelli AS	12.00	6.00	1.20

1961 Topps

The cards in this 587-card set measure 2 1/2" by 3 1/2". In 1961, Topps returned to the vertical obverse format. Introduced for the first time were "League Leaders" (41 to 50) and separate, numbered checklist cards. Two number 463's exist: the Braves team card carrying that number was meant to be number 426. There are three versions of the second series checklist card #98; the variations are distinguished by the color of the "CHECKLIST" headline on the front of the card, the color of the printing of the card number on the

ROGER MARIS
Outfield

bottom of the reverse, and the presence of the copyright notice running vertically on the card back. There are two groups of managers (131-139 and 219-226) as well as separate series of World Series cards (306-313), Baseball Thrills (401 to 410), previous MVP's (AL 471-478 and NL 479-486) and Sporting News All-Stars (566 to 589). The usual last series scarcity (523 to 589) exists. The set actually totals 587 cards since numbers 587 and 588 were never issued.

		NRMT	VG-E	GOOD
COMPLETE SET (587)		4800.00	2400.00	600.00
COMMON PLAYER (1-110)		1.00	.50	.10
COMMON PLAYER (111-370)		1.25	.60	.12
COMMON PLAYER (371-446)		1.75	.85	.17
COMMON PLAYER (447-522)		2.25	1.10	.22
COMMON PLAYER (523-565)		20.00	10.00	2.00
COMMON PLAYER (566-589)		21.00	10.50	2.10
□	1 Dick Groat	12.00	6.00	1.20
□	2 Roger Maris	100.00	50.00	10.00
□	3 John Buzhardt	1.00	.50	.10
□	4 Lenny Green	1.00	.50	.10
□	5 John Romano	1.00	.50	.10
□	6 Ed Roebuck	1.00	.50	.10
□	7 White Sox Team	3.00	1.50	.30
□	8 Dick Williams	1.50	.75	.15
□	9 Bob Purkey	1.00	.50	.10
□	10 Brooks Robinson	25.00	12.50	2.50
□	11 Curt Simmons	1.50	.75	.15
□	12 Moe Thacker	1.00	.50	.10
□	13 Chuck Cottier	1.00	.50	.10
□	14 Don Mossi	1.50	.75	.15
□	15 Willie Kirkland	1.00	.50	.10
□	16 Billy Muffett	1.00	.50	.10
□	17 Checklist 1	6.00	1.00	.20
□	18 Jim Grant	1.00	.50	.10
□	19 Clete Boyer	1.50	.75	.15
□	20 Robin Roberts	10.00	5.00	1.00
□	21 Zorro Versalles	1.00	.50	.10
□	22 Clem Labine	1.50	.75	.15
□	23 Don Demeter	1.00	.50	.10
□	24 Ken Johnson	1.00	.50	.10
□	25 Reds' Heavy Artillery	4.00	2.00	.40
	Vada Pinson			
	Gus Bell			
	Frank Robinson			
□	26 Wes Stock	1.00	.50	.10
□	27 Jerry Kindall	1.00	.50	.10
□	28 Hector Lopez	1.00	.50	.10
□	29 Don Nottebart	1.00	.50	.10
□	30 Nellie Fox	5.00	2.50	.50
□	31 Bob Schmidt	1.00	.50	.10
□	32 Ray Sadecki	1.00	.50	.10
□	33 Gary Geiger	1.00	.50	.10
□	34 Wynn Hawkins	1.00	.50	.10
□	35 Ron Santo	12.00	6.00	1.20
□	36 Jack Kralick	1.00	.50	.10
□	37 Charley Maxwell	1.00	.50	.10
□	38 Bob Lillis	1.00	.50	.10
□	39 Leo Posada	1.00	.50	.10
□	40 Bob Turley	2.50	1.25	.25
□	41 NL Batting Leaders	5.00		
	Dick Groat			
	Norm Larker			
	Willie Mays			
	Roberto Clemente			
□	42 AL Batting Leaders	2.00	1.00	.20
	Pete Runnels			
	Al Smith			

	Minnie Minoso			
	Bill Skowron			
☐ 43	NL Home Run Leaders ...	7.00	3.50	.70
	Ernie Banks			
	Hank Aaron			
	Ed Mathews			
	Ken Boyer			
☐ 44	AL Home Run Leaders ...	15.00	7.50	1.50
	Mickey Mantle			
	Roger Maris			
	Jim Lemon			
	Rocky Colavito			
☐ 45	NL ERA Leaders	2.00	1.00	.20
	Mike McCormick			
	Ernie Broglio			
	Don Drysdale			
	Bob Friend			
	Stan Williams			
☐ 46	AL ERA Leaders	2.00	1.00	.20
	Frank Baumann			
	Jim Bunning			
	Art Ditmar			
	H. Brown			
☐ 47	NL Pitching Leaders	2.00	1.00	.20
	Ernie Broglio			
	Warren Spahn			
	Vern Law			
	Lou Burdette			
☐ 48	AL Pitching Leaders	2.00	1.00	.20
	Chuck Estrada			
	Jim Perry			
	Bud Daley			
	Art Ditmar			
	Frank Lary			
	Milt Pappas			
☐ 49	NL Strikeout Leaders	4.00	2.00	.40
	Don Drysdale			
	Sandy Koufax			
	Sam Jones			
	Ernie Broglio			
☐ 50	AL Strikeout Leaders	2.00	1.00	.20
	Jim Bunning			
	Pedro Ramos			
	Early Wynn			
	Frank Lary			
☐ 51	Detroit Tigers	3.00	1.50	.30
	Team Card			
☐ 52	George Crowe	1.00	.50	.10
☐ 53	Russ Nixon	1.50	.75	.15
☐ 54	Earl Francis	1.00	.50	.10
☐ 55	Jim Davenport	1.50	.75	.15
☐ 56	Russ Kemmerer	1.00	.50	.10
☐ 57	Marv Throneberry	1.50	.75	.15
☐ 58	Joe Schaffernoth	1.00	.50	.10
☐ 59	Jim Woods	1.00	.50	.10
☐ 60	Woody Held	1.00	.50	.10
☐ 61	Ron Piche	1.00	.50	.10
☐ 62	Al Pilarcik	1.00	.50	.10
☐ 63	Jim Kaat	6.50	3.25	.65
☐ 64	Alex Grammas	1.00	.50	.10
☐ 65	Ted Kluszewski	3.50	1.75	.35
☐ 66	Billy Henry	1.00	.50	.10
☐ 67	Ossie Virgil	1.00	.50	.10
☐ 68	Deron Johnson	1.50	.75	.15
☐ 69	Earl Wilson	1.00	.50	.10
☐ 70	Bill Virdon	2.00	1.00	.20
☐ 71	Jerry Adair	1.00	.50	.10
☐ 72	Stu Miller	1.00	.50	.10
☐ 73	Al Spangler	1.00	.50	.10
☐ 74	Joe Pignatano	1.00	.50	.10
☐ 75	Lindy Shows Larry	1.50	.75	.15
	Lindy McDaniel			
	Larry Jackson			
☐ 76	Harry Anderson	1.00	.50	.10
☐ 77	Dick Stigman	1.00	.50	.10
☐ 78	Lee Walls	1.00	.50	.10
☐ 79	Joe Ginsberg	1.00	.50	.10
☐ 80	Harmon Killebrew	18.00	9.00	1.80
☐ 81	Tracy Stallard	1.00	.50	.10
☐ 82	Joe Christopher	1.00	.50	.10
☐ 83	Bob Bruce	1.00	.50	.10
☐ 84	Lee Maye	1.00	.50	.10
☐ 85	Jerry Walker	1.00	.50	.10
☐ 86	Los Angeles Dodgers	4.00	2.00	.40
	Team Card			
☐ 87	Joe Amalfitano	1.00	.50	.10
☐ 88	Richie Ashburn	6.00	3.00	.60
☐ 89	Billy Martin	6.00	3.00	.60
☐ 90	Jerry Staley	1.00	.50	.10
☐ 91	Walt Moryn	1.00	.50	.10
☐ 92	Hal Naragon	1.00	.50	.10
☐ 93	Tony Gonzalez	1.00	.50	.10
☐ 94	Johnny Kucks	1.00	.50	.10
☐ 95	Norm Cash	2.50	1.25	.25
☐ 96	Billy O'Dell	1.00	.50	.10

☐ 97	Jerry Lynch	1.00	.50	.10
☐ 98A	Checklist 2	6.00	1.00	.20
	(red "Checklist",			
	98 black on white)			
☐ 98B	Checklist 2	6.00		.20
	(yellow "Checklist",			
	98 black on white)			
☐ 98C	Checklist 2	6.00	1.00	.20
	(yellow "Checklist",			
	98 white on black,			
	no copyright)			
☐ 99	Don Buddin UER	1.00	.50	.10
	(66 HR's)			
☐ 100	Harvey Haddix	2.00	1.00	.20
☐ 101	Bubba Phillips	1.00	.50	.10
☐ 102	Gene Stephens	1.00	.50	.10
☐ 103	Ruben Amaro	1.00	.50	.10
☐ 104	John Blanchard	1.50	.75	.15
☐ 105	Carl Willey	1.00	.50	.10
☐ 106	Whitey Herzog	3.00	1.50	.30
☐ 107	Seth Morehead	1.00	.50	.10
☐ 108	Dan Dobbek	1.00	.50	.10
☐ 109	Johnny Podres	2.50	1.25	.25
☐ 110	Vada Pinson	2.50	1.25	.25
☐ 111	Jack Meyer	1.25	.60	.12
☐ 112	Chico Fernandez	1.25	.60	.12
☐ 113	Mike Fornieles	1.25	.60	.12
☐ 114	Hobie Landrith	1.25	.60	.12
☐ 115	Johnny Antonelli	1.75	.85	.17
☐ 116	Joe DeMaestri	1.25	.60	.12
☐ 117	Dale Long	1.75	.85	.17
☐ 118	Chris Cannizzaro	1.25	.60	.12
☐ 119	A's Big Armor	1.75	.85	.17
	Norm Siebern			
	Hank Bauer			
	Jerry Lumpe			
☐ 120	Eddie Mathews	18.00	9.00	1.80
☐ 121	Eli Grba	1.25	.60	.12
☐ 122	Chicago Cubs	3.00	1.50	.30
	Team Card			
☐ 123	Billy Gardner	1.75	.85	.17
☐ 124	J.C. Martin	1.25	.60	.12
☐ 125	Steve Barber	1.25	.60	.12
☐ 126	Dick Stuart	1.75	.85	.17
☐ 127	Ron Kline	1.25	.60	.12
☐ 128	Rip Repulski	1.25	.60	.12
☐ 129	Ed Hobaugh	1.25	.60	.12
☐ 130	Norm Larker	1.25	.60	.12
☐ 131	Paul Richards MG	1.75	.85	.17
☐ 132	Al Lopez MG	4.00	2.00	.40
☐ 133	Ralph Houk MG	3.00	1.50	.30
☐ 134	Mickey Vernon MG	1.75	.85	.17
☐ 135	Fred Hutchinson MG	1.75	.85	.17
☐ 136	Walt Alston MG	5.00	2.50	.50
☐ 137	Chuck Dressen MG	1.75	.85	.17
☐ 138	Danny Murtaugh MG	1.75	.85	.17
☐ 139	Solly Hemus MG	1.75	.85	.17
☐ 140	Gus Triandos	1.75	.85	.17
☐ 141	Billy Williams	75.00	37.50	7.50
☐ 142	Luis Arroyo	1.75	.85	.17
☐ 143	Russ Snyder	1.25	.60	.12
☐ 144	Jim Coker	1.25	.60	.12
☐ 145	Bob Buhl	1.25	.60	.12
☐ 146	Marty Keough	1.25	.60	.12
☐ 147	Ed Rakow	1.25	.60	.12
☐ 148	Julian Javier	1.25	.60	.12
☐ 149	Bob Oldis	1.25	.60	.12
☐ 150	Willie Mays	80.00	40.00	8.00
☐ 151	Jim Donohue	1.25	.60	.12
☐ 152	Earl Torgeson	1.25	.60	.12
☐ 153	Don Lee	1.25	.60	.12
☐ 154	Bobby Del Greco	1.25	.60	.12
☐ 155	Johnny Temple	1.25	.60	.12
☐ 156	Ken Hunt	1.25	.60	.12
☐ 157	Cal McLish	1.25	.60	.12
☐ 158	Pete Daley	1.25	.60	.12
☐ 159	Orioles Team	3.00	1.50	.30
☐ 160	Whitey Ford	25.00	12.50	2.50
☐ 161	Sherman Jones	1.25	.60	.12
	(photo actually			
	Eddie Fisher)			
☐ 162	Jay Hook	1.25	.60	.12
☐ 163	Ed Sadowski	1.25	.60	.12
☐ 164	Felix Mantilla	1.25	.60	.12
☐ 165	Gino Cimoli	1.25	.60	.12
☐ 166	Danny Kravitz	1.25	.60	.12
☐ 167	San Francisco Giants	3.00	1.50	.30
	Team Card			
☐ 168	Tommy Davis	2.50	1.25	.25
☐ 169	Don Elston	1.25	.60	.12
☐ 170	Al Smith	1.25	.60	.12
☐ 171	Paul Foytack	1.25	.60	.12
☐ 172	Don Dillard	1.25	.60	.12
☐ 173	Beantown Bombers	1.75	.85	.17
	Frank Malzone			

Vic Wertz
Jackie Jensen

☐ 174	Ray Semproch	1.25	.60	.12
☐ 175	Gene Freese	1.25	.60	.12
☐ 176	Ken Aspromonte	1.25	.60	.12
☐ 177	Don Larsen	2.50	1.25	.25
☐ 178	Bob Nieman	1.25	.60	.12
☐ 179	Joe Koppe	1.25	.60	.12
☐ 180	Bobby Richardson	4.00	2.00	.40
☐ 181	Fred Green	1.25	.60	.12
☐ 182	Dave Nicholson	1.25	.60	.12
☐ 183	Andre Rodgers	1.25	.60	.12
☐ 184	Steve Bilko	1.25	.60	.12
☐ 185	Herb Score	1.75	.85	.17
☐ 186	Elmer Valo	1.25	.60	.12
☐ 187	Billy Klaus	1.25	.60	.12
☐ 188	Jim Marshall	1.25	.60	.12
☐ 189A	Checklist 3	7.50	1.25	.20

(copyright symbol
almost adjacent to
#263 Ken Hamlin)

☐ 189B	Checklist 3	7.50	1.25	.20

(copyright symbol
adjacent to
#264 Glen Hobbie)

☐ 190	Stan Williams	1.25	.60	.12
☐ 191	Mike De La Hoz	1.25	.60	.12
☐ 192	Dick Brown	1.25	.60	.12
☐ 193	Gene Conley	1.25	.60	.12
☐ 194	Gordy Coleman	1.25	.60	.12
☐ 195	Jerry Casale	1.25	.60	.12
☐ 196	Ed Bouchee	1.25	.60	.12
☐ 197	Dick Hall	1.25	.60	.12
☐ 198	Carl Sawatski	1.25	.60	.12
☐ 199	Bob Boyd	1.25	.60	.12
☐ 200	Warren Spahn	22.00	11.00	2.20
☐ 201	Pete Whisenant	1.25	.60	.12
☐ 202	Al Neiger	1.25	.60	.12
☐ 203	Eddie Bressoud	1.25	.60	.12
☐ 204	Bob Skinner	1.25	.60	.12
☐ 205	Billy Pierce	1.75	.85	.17
☐ 206	Gene Green	1.25	.60	.12
☐ 207	Dodger Southpaws	15.00	7.50	1.50

Sandy Koufax
Johnny Podres

☐ 208	Larry Osborne	1.25	.60	.12
☐ 209	Ken McBride	1.25	.60	.12
☐ 210	Pete Runnels	1.75	.85	.17
☐ 211	Bob Gibson	22.00	11.00	2.20
☐ 212	Haywood Sullivan	1.75	.85	.17
☐ 213	Bill Stafford	1.25	.60	.12
☐ 214	Danny Murphy	1.25	.60	.12
☐ 215	Gus Bell	1.75	.85	.17
☐ 216	Ted Bowsfield	1.25	.60	.12
☐ 217	Mel Roach	1.25	.60	.12
☐ 218	Hal Brown	1.25	.60	.12
☐ 219	Gene Mauch MG	1.75	.85	.17
☐ 220	Alvin Dark MG	1.75	.85	.17
☐ 221	Mike Higgins MG	1.75	.85	.17
☐ 222	Jimmy Dykes MG	1.75	.85	.17
☐ 223	Bob Scheffing MG	1.75	.85	.17
☐ 224	Joe Gordon MG	1.75	.85	.17
☐ 225	Bill Rigney MG	1.75	.85	.17
☐ 226	Harry Lavagetto MG	1.75	.85	.17
☐ 227	Juan Pizarro	1.25	.60	.12
☐ 228	New York Yankees	15.00	7.50	1.50

Team Card

☐ 229	Rudy Hernandez	1.25	.60	.12
☐ 230	Don Hoak	1.25	.60	.12
☐ 231	Dick Drott	1.25	.60	.12
☐ 232	Bill White	3.50	1.75	.35
☐ 233	Joey Jay	1.25	.60	.12
☐ 234	Ted Lepcio	1.25	.60	.12
☐ 235	Camilo Pascual	1.25	.60	.12
☐ 236	Don Gile	1.25	.60	.12
☐ 237	Billy Loes	1.25	.60	.12
☐ 238	Jim Gilliam	2.50	1.25	.25
☐ 239	Dave Sisler	1.25	.60	.12
☐ 240	Ron Hansen	1.25	.60	.12
☐ 241	Al Cicotte	1.25	.60	.12
☐ 242	Hal Smith	1.25	.60	.12
☐ 243	Frank Lary	1.75	.85	.17
☐ 244	Chico Cardenas	1.25	.60	.12
☐ 245	Joe Adcock	1.75	.85	.17
☐ 246	Bob Davis	1.25	.60	.12
☐ 247	Billy Goodman	1.75	.85	.17
☐ 248	Ed Keegan	1.25	.60	.12
☐ 249	Cincinnati Reds	3.50	1.75	.35

Team Card

☐ 250	Buc Hill Aces	1.75	.85	.17

Vern Law
Roy Face

☐ 251	Bill Bruton	1.25	.60	.12
☐ 252	Bill Short	1.25	.60	.12
☐ 253	Sammy Taylor	1.25	.60	.12

☐ 254	Ted Sadowski	1.25	.60	.12
☐ 255	Vic Power	1.25	.60	.12
☐ 256	Billy Hoeft	1.25	.60	.12
☐ 257	Carroll Hardy	1.25	.60	.12
☐ 258	Jack Sanford	1.75	.85	.17
☐ 259	John Schaive	1.25	.60	.12
☐ 260	Don Drysdale	18.00	9.00	1.80
☐ 261	Charlie Lau	1.75	.85	.17
☐ 262	Tony Curry	1.25	.60	.12
☐ 263	Ken Hamlin	1.25	.60	.12
☐ 264	Glen Hobbie	1.25	.60	.12
☐ 265	Tony Kubek	5.00	2.50	.50
☐ 266	Lindy McDaniel	1.25	.60	.12
☐ 267	Norm Siebern	1.25	.60	.12
☐ 268	Ike Delock	1.25	.60	.12
☐ 269	Harry Chiti	1.25	.60	.12
☐ 270	Bob Friend	1.75	.85	.17
☐ 271	Jim Landis	1.25	.60	.12
☐ 272	Tom Morgan	1.25	.60	.12
☐ 273A	Checklist 4	12.00	1.50	.30

(copyright symbol
adjacent to
#336 Don Mincher)

☐ 273A	Checklist 4	6.00	1.00	.20

(copyright symbol
adjacent to
#339 Gene Baker)

☐ 274	Gary Bell	1.25	.60	.12
☐ 275	Gene Woodling	1.75	.85	.17
☐ 276	Ray Rippelmeyer	1.25	.60	.12
☐ 277	Hank Foiles	1.25	.60	.12
☐ 278	Don McMahon	1.25	.60	.12
☐ 279	Jose Pagan	1.25	.60	.12
☐ 280	Frank Howard	3.00	1.50	.30
☐ 281	Frank Sullivan	1.25	.60	.12
☐ 282	Faye Throneberry	1.25	.60	.12
☐ 283	Bob Anderson	1.25	.60	.12
☐ 284	Dick Gernert	1.25	.60	.12
☐ 285	Sherm Lollar	1.75	.85	.17
☐ 286	George Witt	1.25	.60	.12
☐ 287	Carl Yastrzemski	150.00	75.00	15.00
☐ 288	Albie Pearson	1.25	.60	.12
☐ 289	Ray Moore	1.25	.60	.12
☐ 290	Stan Musial	75.00	37.50	7.50
☐ 291	Tex Clevenger	1.25	.60	.12
☐ 292	Jim Baumer	1.25	.60	.12
☐ 293	Tom Sturdivant	1.25	.60	.12
☐ 294	Don Blasingame	1.25	.60	.12
☐ 295	Milt Pappas	1.75	.85	.17
☐ 296	Wes Covington	1.25	.60	.12
☐ 297	Athletics Team	2.50	1.25	.25
☐ 298	Jim Golden	1.25	.60	.12
☐ 299	Clay Dalrymple	1.25	.60	.12
☐ 300	Mickey Mantle	300.00	150.00	30.00
☐ 301	Chet Nichols	1.25	.60	.12
☐ 302	Al Heist	1.25	.60	.12
☐ 303	Gary Peters	1.25	.60	.12
☐ 304	Rocky Nelson	1.25	.60	.12
☐ 305	Mike McCormick	1.25	.60	.12
☐ 306	World Series Game 1	3.50	1.75	.35

Virdon Saves Game

☐ 307	World Series Game 2	25.00	12.50	2.50

Mantle 2 Homers

☐ 308	World Series Game 3	5.00	2.50	.50

Richardson is Hero

☐ 309	World Series Game 4	3.50	1.75	.35

Cimoli Safe

☐ 310	World Series Game 5	3.50	1.75	.35

Face Saves the Day

☐ 311	World Series Game 6	6.00	3.00	.60

Ford Second Shutout

☐ 312	World Series Game 7	5.00	2.50	.50

Mazeroski's Homer

☐ 313	World Series Summary	3.50	1.75	.35

Pirates Celebrate

☐ 314	Bob Miller	1.25	.60	.12
☐ 315	Earl Battey	1.25	.60	.12
☐ 316	Bobby Gene Smith	1.25	.60	.12
☐ 317	Jim Brewer	1.25	.60	.12
☐ 318	Danny O'Connell	1.25	.60	.12
☐ 319	Valmy Thomas	1.25	.60	.12
☐ 320	Lou Burdette	2.50	1.25	.25
☐ 321	Marv Breeding	1.25	.60	.12
☐ 322	Bill Kunkel	1.75	.85	.17
☐ 323	Sammy Esposito	1.25	.60	.12
☐ 324	Hank Aguirre	1.25	.60	.12
☐ 325	Wally Moon	1.75	.85	.17
☐ 326	Dave Hillman	1.25	.60	.12
☐ 327	Matty Alou	4.00	2.00	.40
☐ 328	Jim O'Toole	1.25	.60	.12
☐ 329	Julio Becquer	1.25	.60	.12
☐ 330	Rocky Colavito	4.00	2.00	.40
☐ 331	Ned Garver	1.25	.60	.12
☐ 332	Dutch Dotterer	1.25	.60	.12

(photo actually

Tommy Dotterer, Dutch's brother)			
☐ 333 Fritz Brickell	1.25	.60	.12
☐ 334 Walt Bond	1.25	.60	.12
☐ 335 Frank Bolling	1.25	.60	.12
☐ 336 Don Mincher	1.25	.60	.12
☐ 337 Al's Aces	4.00	2.00	.40
Early Wynn			
Al Lopez			
Herb Score			
☐ 338 Don Landrum	1.25	.60	.12
☐ 339 Gene Baker	1.25	.60	.12
☐ 340 Vic Wertz	1.75	.85	.17
☐ 341 Jim Owens	1.25	.60	.12
☐ 342 Clint Courtney	1.25	.60	.12
☐ 343 Earl Robinson	1.25	.60	.12
☐ 344 Sandy Koufax	80.00	40.00	8.00
☐ 345 Jim Piersall	2.50	1.25	.25
☐ 346 Howie Nunn	1.25	.60	.12
☐ 347 St. Louis Cardinals	3.00	1.50	.30
Team Card			
☐ 348 Steve Boros	1.75	.85	.17
☐ 349 Danny McDevitt	1.25	.60	.12
☐ 350 Ernie Banks	27.00	13.50	2.70
☐ 351 Jim King	1.25	.60	.12
☐ 352 Bob Shaw	1.25	.60	.12
☐ 353 Howie Bedell	1.25	.60	.12
☐ 354 Billy Harrell	1.25	.60	.12
☐ 355 Bob Allison	1.75	.85	.17
☐ 356 Ryne Duren	1.75	.85	.17
☐ 357 Daryl Spencer	1.25	.60	.12
☐ 358 Earl Averill	1.25	.60	.12
☐ 359 Dallas Green	3.50	1.75	.35
☐ 360 Frank Robinson	30.00	15.00	3.00
☐ 361A Checklist 5	6.00	1.00	.20
(no ad on back)			
☐ 361B Checklist 5	12.00	2.00	.40
(Special Feature ad on back)			
☐ 362 Frank Funk	1.25	.60	.12
☐ 363 John Roseboro	1.75	.85	.17
☐ 364 Moe Drabowsky	1.25	.60	.12
☐ 365 Jerry Lumpe	1.25	.60	.12
☐ 366 Eddie Fisher	1.25	.60	.12
☐ 367 Jim Rivera	1.25	.60	.12
☐ 368 Bennie Daniels	1.25	.60	.12
☐ 369 Dave Philley	1.25	.60	.12
☐ 370 Roy Face	2.50	1.25	.25
☐ 371 Bill Skowron SP	14.00	7.00	1.40
☐ 372 Bob Hendley	1.75	.85	.17
☐ 373 Boston Red Sox	3.50	1.75	.35
Team Card			
☐ 374 Paul Giel	1.75	.85	.17
☐ 375 Ken Boyer	4.00	2.00	.40
☐ 376 Mike Roarke	1.75	.85	.17
☐ 377 Ruben Gomez	1.75	.85	.17
☐ 378 Wally Post	1.75	.85	.17
☐ 379 Bobby Shantz	3.00	1.50	.30
☐ 380 Minnie Minoso	3.00	1.50	.30
☐ 381 Dave Wickersham	1.75	.85	.17
☐ 382 Frank Thomas	2.25	1.10	.22
☐ 383 Frisco First Liners	2.25	1.10	.22
Mike McCormick			
Jack Sanford			
Billy O'Dell			
☐ 384 Chuck Essegian	2.25	1.10	.22
☐ 385 Jim Perry	3.00	1.50	.30
☐ 386 Joe Hicks	1.75	.85	.17
☐ 387 Duke Maas	1.75	.85	.17
☐ 388 Bob Clemente	70.00	35.00	7.00
☐ 389 Ralph Terry	3.00	1.50	.30
☐ 390 Del Crandall	2.25	1.10	.22
☐ 391 Winston Brown	1.75	.85	.17
☐ 392 Reno Bertoia	1.75	.85	.17
☐ 393 Batter Bafflers	2.25	1.10	.22
Don Cardwell			
Glen Hobbie			
☐ 394 Ken Walters	1.75	.85	.17
☐ 395 Chuck Estrada	2.25	1.10	.22
☐ 396 Bob Aspromonte	1.75	.85	.17
☐ 397 Hal Woodeshick	1.75	.85	.17
☐ 398 Hank Bauer	2.25	1.10	.22
☐ 399 Cliff Cook	1.75	.85	.17
☐ 400 Vern Law	2.25	1.10	.22
☐ 401 Ruth 60th Homer	15.00	7.50	1.50
☐ 402 Perfect Game	7.50	3.75	.75
(Don Larsen)			
☐ 403 26 Inning Tie	3.50	1.75	.35
☐ 404 Hornsby .424 Average	4.00	2.00	.40
☐ 405 Gehrig's Streak	10.00	5.00	1.00
☐ 406 Mantle 565 Ft. Homer	35.00	17.50	3.50
☐ 407 Chesbro Wins 41	3.50	1.75	.35
☐ 408 Mathewson Fans 267	4.00	2.00	.40
☐ 409 Johnson Shutouts	4.00	2.00	.40
☐ 410 Haddix 12 Perfect	3.50	1.75	.35
Innings			
☐ 411 Tony Taylor	1.75	.85	.17
☐ 412 Larry Sherry	2.25	1.10	.22
☐ 413 Eddie Yost	1.75	.85	.17
☐ 414 Dick Donovan	1.75	.85	.17
☐ 415 Hank Aaron	85.00	42.50	8.50
☐ 416 Dick Howser	7.00	3.50	.70
☐ 417 Juan Marichal	80.00	40.00	8.00
☐ 418 Ed Bailey	1.75	.85	.17
☐ 419 Tom Borland	1.75	.85	.17
☐ 420 Ernie Broglio	2.25	1.10	.22
☐ 421 Ty Cline	1.75	.85	.17
☐ 422 Bud Daley	1.75	.85	.17
☐ 423 Charlie Neal SP	4.00	2.00	.40
☐ 424 Turk Lown	1.75	.85	.17
☐ 425 Yogi Berra	55.00	27.50	5.50
☐ 426 Milwaukee Braves	6.50	3.25	.65
Team Card			
(back numbered 463)			
☐ 427 Dick Ellsworth	2.25	1.10	.22
☐ 428 Ray Barker SP	3.50	1.75	.35
☐ 429 Al Kaline	33.00	15.00	3.00
☐ 430 Bill Mazeroski SP	9.00	4.50	.90
☐ 431 Chuck Stobbs	1.75	.85	.17
☐ 432 Coot Veal	1.75	.85	.17
☐ 433 Art Mahaffey	1.75	.85	.17
☐ 434 Tom Brewer	1.75	.85	.17
☐ 435 Orlando Cepeda	6.00	3.00	.60
☐ 436 Jim Maloney	6.00	3.00	.60
☐ 437A Checklist 6	9.00	1.50	.30
440 Louis Aparicio			
☐ 437B Checklist 6	9.00	1.50	.30
440 Luis Aparicio			
☐ 438 Curt Flood	3.00	1.50	.30
☐ 439 Phil Regan	2.25	1.10	.22
☐ 440 Luis Aparicio	11.00	5.50	1.10
☐ 441 Dick Bertell	1.75	.85	.17
☐ 442 Gordon Jones	1.75	.85	.17
☐ 443 Duke Snider	35.00	17.50	3.50
☐ 444 Joe Nuxhall	2.25	1.10	.22
☐ 445 Frank Malzone	2.25	1.10	.22
☐ 446 Bob Taylor	1.75	.85	.17
☐ 447 Harry Bright	2.25	1.10	.22
☐ 448 Del Rice	2.25	1.10	.22
☐ 449 Bob Bolin	2.25	1.10	.22
☐ 450 Jim Lemon	3.00	1.50	.30
☐ 451 Power for Ernie	3.00	1.50	.30
Daryl Spencer			
Bill White			
Ernie Broglio			
☐ 452 Bob Allen	2.25	1.10	.22
☐ 453 Dick Schofield	2.25	1.10	.22
☐ 454 Pumpsie Green	2.25	1.10	.22
☐ 455 Early Wynn	10.00	5.00	1.00
☐ 456 Hal Bevan	2.25	1.10	.22
☐ 457 John James	2.25	1.10	.22
☐ 458 Willie Tasby	2.25	1.10	.22
☐ 459 Terry Fox	2.25	1.10	.22
☐ 460 Gil Hodges	11.00	5.50	1.10
☐ 461 Smoky Burgess	3.00	1.50	.30
☐ 462 Lou Klimchock	2.25	1.10	.22
☐ 463 Jack Fisher	3.00	1.50	.30
(See also 426)			
☐ 464 Lee Thomas	4.50	2.25	.45
☐ 465 Roy McMillan	2.25	1.10	.22
☐ 466 Ron Moeller	2.25	1.10	.22
☐ 467 Cleveland Indians	4.50	2.25	.45
Team Card			
☐ 468 John Callison	3.00	1.50	.30
☐ 469 Ralph Lumenti	2.25	1.10	.22
☐ 470 Roy Sievers	3.00	1.50	.30
☐ 471 Phil Rizzuto MVP	10.00	5.00	1.00
☐ 472 Yogi Berra MVP	30.00	15.00	3.00
☐ 473 Bob Shantz MVP	3.00	1.50	.30
☐ 474 Al Rosen MVP	3.50	1.75	.35
☐ 475 Mickey Mantle MVP	80.00	40.00	8.00
☐ 476 Jackie Jensen MVP	3.50	1.75	.35
☐ 477 Nellie Fox MVP	4.00	2.00	.40
☐ 478 Roger Maris MVP	30.00	15.00	3.00
☐ 479 Jim Konstanty MVP	3.00	1.50	.30
☐ 480 Roy Campanella MVP	22.00	11.00	2.20
☐ 481 Hank Sauer MVP	3.00	1.50	.30
☐ 482 Willie Mays MVP	32.00	16.00	3.20
☐ 483 Don Newcombe MVP	3.00	1.50	.30
☐ 484 Hank Aaron MVP	32.00	16.00	3.20
☐ 485 Ernie Banks MVP	15.00	7.50	1.50
☐ 486 Dick Groat MVP	3.00	1.50	.30
☐ 487 Gene Oliver	2.25	1.10	.22
☐ 488 Joe McClain	2.25	1.10	.22
☐ 489 Walt Dropo	2.25	1.10	.22
☐ 490 Jim Bunning	7.50	3.75	.75
☐ 491 Philadelphia Phillies	4.50	2.25	.45
Team Card			
☐ 492 Ron Fairly	3.00	1.50	.30
☐ 493 Don Zimmer UER	4.00	2.00	.40

(Brooklyn A.L.)

☐ 494	Tom Cheney	2.25	1.10	.22
☐ 495	Elston Howard	4.50	2.25	.45
☐ 496	Ken MacKenzie	2.25	1.10	.22
☐ 497	Willie Jones	2.25	1.10	.22
☐ 498	Ray Herbert	2.25	1.10	.22
☐ 499	Chuck Schilling	2.25	1.10	.22
☐ 500	Harvey Kuenn	4.00	2.00	.40
☐ 501	John DeMerit	2.25	1.10	.22
☐ 502	Clarence Coleman	2.25	1.10	.22
☐ 503	Tito Francona	3.00	1.50	.30
☐ 504	Billy Consolo	2.25	1.10	.22
☐ 505	Red Schoendienst	12.00	6.00	1.20
☐ 506	Willie Davis	7.00	3.50	.70
☐ 507	Pete Burnside	2.25	1.10	.22
☐ 508	Rocky Bridges	2.25	1.10	.22
☐ 509	Camilo Carreon	2.25	1.10	.22
☐ 510	Art Ditmar	2.25	1.10	.22
☐ 511	Joe M. Morgan	3.50	1.75	.35
☐ 512	Bob Will	2.25	1.10	.22
☐ 513	Jim Brosnan	3.00	1.50	.30
☐ 514	Jake Wood	2.25	1.10	.22
☐ 515	Jackie Brandt	2.25	1.10	.22
☐ 516	Checklist 7	9.00	1.50	.30
☐ 517	Willie McCovey	45.00	22.50	4.50
☐ 518	Andy Carey	3.00	1.50	.30
☐ 519	Jim Pagliaroni	2.25	1.10	.22
☐ 520	Joe Cunningham	3.00	1.50	.30
☐ 521	Brother Battery	3.00	1.50	.30
	Norm Sherry			
	Larry Sherry			
☐ 522	Dick Farrell	3.00	1.50	.30
☐ 523	Joe Gibbon	20.00	10.00	2.00
☐ 524	Johnny Logan	22.00	11.00	2.20
☐ 525	Ron Perranoski	22.00	11.00	2.20
☐ 526	R.C. Stevens	20.00	10.00	2.00
☐ 527	Gene Leek	20.00	10.00	2.00
☐ 528	Pedro Ramos	20.00	10.00	2.00
☐ 529	Bob Roselli	20.00	10.00	2.00
☐ 530	Bob Malkmus	20.00	10.00	2.00
☐ 531	Jim Coates	20.00	10.00	2.00
☐ 532	Bob Hale	20.00	10.00	2.00
☐ 533	Jack Curtis	20.00	10.00	2.00
☐ 534	Eddie Kasko	20.00	10.00	2.00
☐ 535	Larry Jackson	20.00	10.00	2.00
☐ 536	Bill Tuttle	20.00	10.00	2.00
☐ 537	Bobby Locke	20.00	10.00	2.00
☐ 538	Chuck Hiller	20.00	10.00	2.00
☐ 539	Johnny Klippstein	20.00	10.00	2.00
☐ 540	Jackie Jensen	30.00	15.00	3.00
☐ 541	Roland Sheldon	20.00	10.00	2.00
☐ 542	Minnesota Twins	42.00	18.00	4.00
	Team Card			
☐ 543	Roger Craig	30.00	15.00	3.00
☐ 544	George Thomas	20.00	10.00	2.00
☐ 545	Hoyt Wilhelm	55.00	27.50	5.50
☐ 546	Marty Kutyna	20.00	10.00	2.00
☐ 547	Leon Wagner	20.00	10.00	2.00
☐ 548	Ted Wills	20.00	10.00	2.00
☐ 549	Hal R. Smith	20.00	10.00	2.00
☐ 550	Frank Baumann	20.00	10.00	2.00
☐ 551	George Altman	20.00	10.00	2.00
☐ 552	Jim Archer	20.00	10.00	2.00
☐ 553	Bill Fischer	20.00	10.00	2.00
☐ 554	Pittsburgh Pirates	38.00	18.00	3.50
	Team Card			
☐ 555	Sam Jones	22.00	11.00	2.20
☐ 556	Ken R. Hunt	20.00	10.00	2.00
☐ 557	Jose Valdivielso	20.00	10.00	2.00
☐ 558	Don Ferrarese	20.00	10.00	2.00
☐ 559	Jim Gentile	22.00	11.00	2.20
☐ 560	Barry Latman	20.00	10.00	2.00
☐ 561	Charley James	20.00	10.00	2.00
☐ 562	Bill Monbouquette	22.00	11.00	2.20
☐ 563	Bob Cerv	22.00	11.00	2.20
☐ 564	Don Cardwell	20.00	10.00	2.00
☐ 565	Felipe Alou	22.00	11.00	2.20
☐ 566	Paul Richards MG AS	21.00	10.50	2.10
☐ 567	Danny Murtaugh MG AS	21.00	10.50	2.10
☐ 568	Bill Skowron AS	22.00	11.00	2.20
☐ 569	Frank Herrera AS	21.00	10.50	2.10
☐ 570	Nellie Fox AS	30.00	15.00	3.00
☐ 571	Bill Mazeroski AS	22.00	11.00	2.20
☐ 572	Brooks Robinson AS	75.00	37.50	7.50
☐ 573	Ken Boyer AS	24.00	12.00	2.40
☐ 574	Luis Aparicio AS	40.00	20.00	4.00
☐ 575	Ernie Banks AS	75.00	37.50	7.50
☐ 576	Roger Maris AS	100.00	50.00	10.00
☐ 577	Hank Aaron AS	135.00	65.00	13.50
☐ 578	Mickey Mantle AS	300.00	150.00	30.00
☐ 579	Willie Mays AS	135.00	65.00	13.50
☐ 580	Al Kaline AS	75.00	37.50	7.50
☐ 581	Frank Robinson AS	75.00	37.50	7.50
☐ 582	Earl Battey AS	21.00	10.50	2.10
☐ 583	Del Crandall AS	21.00	10.50	2.10
☐ 584	Jim Perry AS	21.00	10.50	2.10
☐ 585	Bob Friend AS	21.00	10.50	2.10
☐ 586	Whitey Ford AS	75.00	37.50	7.50
☐ 587	Does not exist	00.00	00.00	0.00
☐ 588	Does not exist	00.00	00.00	0.00
☐ 589	Warren Spahn AS	125.00	40.00	8.00

1962 Topps

The cards in this 598-card set measure 2 1/2" by 3 1/2". The 1962 Topps set contains a mini-series spotlighting Babe Ruth (135 to 144). Other subsets in the set include League Leaders (51-60), World Series cards (232-237), In Action cards (311-319), NL All Stars (390-399), AL All Stars (466-475), and Rookie Prospects (591-598). The All-Star selections were again provided by Sport Magazine as in 1958 and 1960. The second series had two distinct printings which are distinguishable by numerous color and pose variations. Card number 139 exists as A: Babe Ruth Special card, B: Hal Reniff with arms over head, or C: Hal Reniff in the same pose as card number 159. In addition, two poses exist for players depicted on card numbers 129, 132, 134, 147, 174, 176, and 190. The high number series, 523 to 598, is somewhat more difficult to obtain than other cards in the set. Within the last series (523-598) there are 43 cards which were printed in lesser quantities; these are marked SP in the checklist below. The set price listed does not include the pose variations (see checklist below for individual values).

		NRMT	VG-E	GOOD
COMPLETE SET		4000.00	2000.00	500.00
COMMON PLAYER (1-109)		1.00	.50	.10
COMMON PLAYER (110-196)		1.00	.50	.10
COMMON PLAYER (197-283)		1.25	.60	.12
COMMON PLAYER (284-370)		1.25	.60	.12
COMMON PLAYER (371-446)		2.00	1.00	.20
COMMON PLAYER (447-522)		3.00	1.50	.30
COMMON PLAYER (523-590)		9.00	4.50	.90
COMMON SP (523-590)		18.00	9.00	1.80
COMMON PLAYER (591-598)		18.00	9.00	1.80
☐	1 Roger Maris	150.00	40.00	8.00
☐	2 Jim Brosnan	1.00	.50	.10
☐	3 Pete Runnels	1.00	.50	.10
☐	4 John DeMerit	1.00	.50	.10
☐	5 Sandy Koufax	80.00	40.00	8.00
☐	6 Marv Breeding	1.00	.50	.10
☐	7 Frank Thomas	1.00	.50	.10
☐	8 Ray Herbert	1.00	.50	.10
☐	9 Jim Davenport	1.00	.50	.10
☐	10 Bob Clemente	70.00	35.00	7.00
☐	11 Tom Morgan	1.00	.50	.10
☐	12 Harry Craft MG	1.00	.50	.10
☐	13 Dick Howser	2.00	1.00	.20
☐	14 Bill White	2.50	1.25	.25
☐	15 Dick Donovan	1.00	.50	.10
☐	16 Darrell Johnson	1.00	.50	.10
☐	17 John Callison	1.50	.75	.15
☐	18 Managers' Dream	100.00	50.00	10.00
	Mickey Mantle			
	Willie Mays			

☐	19 Ray Washburn	1.00	.50	.10
☐	20 Rocky Colavito	3.00	1.50	.30
☐	21 Jim Kaat	4.00	2.00	.40
☐	22A Checklist 1 COR	5.00	1.00	.20
☐	22B Checklist 1 ERR	6.00	1.00	.20
	(121-176 on back)			
☐	23 Norm Larker	1.00	.50	.10
☐	24 Tigers Team	3.00	1.50	.30
☐	25 Ernie Banks	25.00	12.50	2.50
☐	26 Chris Cannizzaro	1.00	.50	.10
☐	27 Chuck Cottier	1.00	.50	.10
☐	28 Minnie Minoso	2.00	1.00	.20
☐	29 Casey Stengel MG	12.50	6.25	1.25
☐	30 Eddie Mathews	18.00	9.00	1.80
☐	31 Tom Tresh	8.00	4.00	.80
☐	32 John Roseboro	1.50	.75	.15
☐	33 Don Larsen	2.00	1.00	.20
☐	34 Johnny Temple	1.00	.50	.10
☐	35 Don Schwall	1.00	.50	.10
☐	36 Don Leppert	1.00	.50	.10
☐	37 Tribe Hill Trio	1.50	.75	.15
	Barry Latman			
	Dick Stigman			
	Jim Perry			
☐	38 Gene Stephens	1.00	.50	.10
☐	39 Joe Koppe	1.00	.50	.10
☐	40 Orlando Cepeda	4.00	2.00	.40
☐	41 Cliff Cook	1.00	.50	.10
☐	42 Jim King	1.00	.50	.10
☐	43 Los Angeles Dodgers	3.50	1.75	.35
	Team Card			
☐	44 Don Taussig	1.00	.50	.10
☐	45 Brooks Robinson	25.00	12.50	2.50
☐	46 Jack Baldschun	1.00	.50	.10
☐	47 Bob Will	1.00	.50	.10
☐	48 Ralph Terry	1.50	.75	.15
☐	49 Hal Jones	1.00	.50	.10
☐	50 Stan Musial	70.00	35.00	7.00
☐	51 AL Batting Leaders	2.00	1.00	.20
	Norm Cash			
	Jim Piersall			
	Al Kaline			
	Elston Howard			
☐	52 NL Batting Leaders	4.00	2.00	.40
	Bob Clemente			
	Vada Pinson			
	Ken Boyer			
	Wally Moon			
☐	53 AL Home Run Leaders	25.00	12.50	2.50
	Roger Maris			
	Mickey Mantle			
	Jim Gentile			
	Harmon Killebrew			
☐	54 NL Home Run Leaders	4.00	2.00	.40
	Orlando Cepeda			
	Willie Mays			
	Frank Robinson			
☐	55 AL ERA Leaders	2.00	1.00	.20
	Dick Donovan			
	Bill Stafford			
	Don Mossi			
	Milt Pappas			
☐	56 NL ERA Leaders	3.00	1.50	.30
	Warren Spahn			
	Jim O'Toole			
	Curt Simmons			
	Mike McCormick			
☐	57 AL Wins Leaders	3.00	1.50	.30
	Whitey Ford			
	Frank Lary			
	Steve Barber			
	Jim Bunning			
☐	58 NL Wins Leaders	3.00	1.50	.30
	Warren Spahn			
	Joe Jay			
	Jim O'Toole			
☐	59 AL Strikeout Leaders	2.00	1.00	.20
	Camilo Pascual			
	Whitey Ford			
	Jim Bunning			
	Juan Pizzaro			
☐	60 NL Strikeout Leaders	4.00	2.00	.40
	Sandy Koufax			
	Stan Williams			
	Don Drysdale			
	Jim O'Toole			
☐	61 Cardinals Team	3.00	1.50	.30
☐	62 Steve Boros	1.50	.75	.15
☐	63 Tony Cloninger	1.00	.50	.10
☐	64 Russ Snyder	1.00	.50	.10
☐	65 Bobby Richardson	4.50	2.25	.45
☐	66 Cuno Barragon	1.00	.50	.10
☐	67 Harvey Haddix	1.50	.75	.15
☐	68 Ken Hunt	1.00	.50	.10
☐	69 Phil Ortega	1.00	.50	.10

☐	70 Harmon Killebrew	18.00	9.00	1.80
☐	71 Dick LeMay	1.00	.50	.10
☐	72 Bob's Pupils	1.00	.50	.10
	Steve Boros			
	Bob Scheffing			
	Jake Wood			
☐	73 Nellie Fox	4.50	2.25	.45
☐	74 Bob Lillis	1.00	.50	.10
☐	75 Milt Pappas	1.50	.75	.15
☐	76 Howie Bedell	1.00	.50	.10
☐	77 Tony Taylor	1.00	.50	.10
☐	78 Gene Green	1.00	.50	.10
☐	79 Ed Hobaugh	1.00	.50	.10
☐	80 Vada Pinson	2.50	1.25	.25
☐	81 Jim Pagliaroni	1.00	.50	.10
☐	82 Deron Johnson	1.00	.50	.10
☐	83 Larry Jackson	1.00	.50	.10
☐	84 Lenny Green	1.00	.50	.10
☐	85 Gil Hodges	10.00	5.00	1.00
☐	86 Donn Clendenon	1.50	.75	.15
☐	87 Mike Roarke	1.00	.50	.10
☐	88 Ralph Houk MG	2.50	1.25	.25
	(Berra in background)			
☐	89 Barney Schultz	1.00	.50	.10
☐	90 Jim Piersall	2.00	1.00	.20
☐	91 J.C. Martin	1.00	.50	.10
☐	92 Sam Jones	1.00	.50	.10
☐	93 John Blanchard	1.50	.75	.15
☐	94 Jay Hook	1.00	.50	.10
☐	95 Don Hoak	1.00	.50	.10
☐	96 Eli Grba	1.00	.50	.10
☐	97 Tito Francona	1.00	.50	.10
☐	98 Checklist 2	5.00	1.00	.20
☐	99 John (Boog) Powell	10.00	5.00	1.00
☐	100 Warren Spahn	25.00	12.50	2.50
☐	101 Carroll Hardy	1.00	.50	.10
☐	102 Al Schroll	1.00	.50	.10
☐	103 Don Blasingame	1.00	.50	.10
☐	104 Ted Savage	1.00	.50	.10
☐	105 Don Mossi	1.50	.75	.15
☐	106 Carl Sawatski	1.00	.50	.10
☐	107 Mike McCormick	1.50	.75	.15
☐	108 Willie Davis	2.00	1.00	.20
☐	109 Bob Shaw	1.00	.50	.10
☐	110 Bill Skowron	3.50	1.75	.35
☐	111 Dallas Green	3.50	1.75	.35
☐	112 Hank Foiles	1.00	.50	.10
☐	113 Chicago White Sox	3.00	1.50	.30
	Team Card			
☐	114 Howie Koplitz	1.00	.50	.10
☐	115 Bob Skinner	1.00	.50	.10
☐	116 Herb Score	1.50	.75	.15
☐	117 Gary Geiger	1.00	.50	.10
☐	118 Julian Javier	1.00	.50	.10
☐	119 Danny Murphy	1.00	.50	.10
☐	120 Bob Purkey	1.00	.50	.10
☐	121 Billy Hitchcock MG	1.00	.50	.10
☐	122 Norm Bass	1.00	.50	.10
☐	123 Mike De La Hoz	1.00	.50	.10
☐	124 Bill Pleis	1.00	.50	.10
☐	125 Gene Woodling	1.50	.75	.15
☐	126 Al Cicotte	1.00	.50	.10
☐	127 Pride of A's	1.50	.75	.15
	Norm Siebern			
	Hank Bauer			
	Jerry Lumpe			
☐	128 Art Fowler	1.00	.50	.10
☐	129A Lee Walls	1.00	.50	.10
	(facing right)			
☐	129B Lee Walls	12.50	6.25	1.25
	(face left)			
☐	130 Frank Bolling	1.00	.50	.10
☐	131 Pete Richert	1.00	.50	.10
☐	132A Angels Team	3.00	1.50	.30
	(without photo)			
☐	132B Angels Team	12.50	6.25	1.25
	(with photo)			
☐	133 Felipe Alou	2.00	1.00	.20
☐	134A Billy Hoeft	1.00	.50	.10
	(facing right)			
☐	134B Billy Hoeft	12.50	6.25	1.25
	(facing straight)			
☐	135 Babe Ruth Special 1	6.50	3.25	.65
	Babe as a Boy			
☐	136 Babe Ruth Special 2	6.50	3.25	.65
	Babe Joins Yanks			
☐	137 Babe Ruth Special 3	6.50	3.25	.65
	Babe with Huggins			
☐	138 Babe Ruth Special 4	6.50	3.25	.65
	Famous Slugger			
☐	139A Babe Ruth Special 5	10.00	5.00	1.00
☐	139B Hal Reniff PORT	10.00	5.00	1.00
☐	139C Hal Reniff	45.00	22.50	4.50
	(pitching)			
☐	140 Babe Ruth Special 6	10.00	5.00	1.00

	Gehrig and Ruth			
☐ 141	Babe Ruth Special 7	6.50	3.25	.65
	Twilight Years			
☐ 142	Babe Ruth Special 8	6.50	3.25	.65
	Coaching Dodgers			
☐ 143	Babe Ruth Special 9	6.50	3.25	.65
	Greatest Sports Hero			
☐ 144	Babe Ruth Special 10	6.50	3.25	.65
	Farewell Speech			
☐ 145	Barry Latman	1.00	.50	.10
☐ 146	Don Demeter	1.00	.50	.10
☐ 147A	Bill Kunkel PORT	1.00	.50	.10
☐ 147B	Bill Kunkel	12.50	6.25	1.25
	(pitching pose)			
☐ 148	Wally Post	1.00	.50	.10
☐ 149	Bob Duliba	1.00	.50	.10
☐ 150	Al Kaline	24.00	12.00	2.40
☐ 151	Johnny Klippstein	1.00	.50	.10
☐ 152	Mickey Vernon	1.50	.75	.15
☐ 153	Pumpsie Green	1.00	.50	.10
☐ 154	Lee Thomas	2.00	1.00	.20
☐ 155	Stu Miller	1.00	.50	.10
☐ 156	Merritt Ranew	1.00	.50	.10
☐ 157	Wes Covington	1.00	.50	.10
☐ 158	Braves Team	3.00	1.50	.30
☐ 159	Hal Reniff	1.50	.75	.15
☐ 160	Dick Stuart	1.50	.75	.15
☐ 161	Frank Baumann	1.00	.50	.10
☐ 162	Sammy Drake	1.00	.50	.10
☐ 163	Hot Corner Guard	1.50	.75	.15
	Billy Gardner			
	Cletis Boyer			
☐ 164	Hal Naragon	1.00	.50	.10
☐ 165	Jackie Brandt	1.00	.50	.10
☐ 166	Don Lee	1.00	.50	.10
☐ 167	Tim McCarver	15.00	7.50	1.50
☐ 168	Leo Posada	1.00	.50	.10
☐ 169	Bob Cerv	1.50	.75	.15
☐ 170	Ron Santo	3.50	1.75	.35
☐ 171	Dave Sisler	1.00	.50	.10
☐ 172	Fred Hutchinson MG	1.50	.75	.15
☐ 173	Chico Fernandez	1.00	.50	.10
☐ 174A	Carl Willey	1.00	.50	.10
	(capless)			
☐ 174B	Carl Willey	12.50	6.25	1.25
	(with cap)			
☐ 175	Frank Howard	2.00	1.00	.20
☐ 176A	Eddie Yost PORT	1.00	.50	.10
☐ 176B	Eddie Yost BATTING	12.50	6.25	1.25
☐ 177	Bobby Shantz	2.00	1.00	.20
☐ 178	Camilo Carreon	1.00	.50	.10
☐ 179	Tom Sturdivant	1.00	.50	.10
☐ 180	Bob Allison	1.50	.75	.15
☐ 181	Paul Brown	1.00	.50	.10
☐ 182	Bob Nieman	1.00	.50	.10
☐ 183	Roger Craig	2.50	1.25	.25
☐ 184	Haywood Sullivan	1.50	.75	.15
☐ 185	Roland Sheldon	1.00	.50	.10
☐ 186	Mack Jones	1.00	.50	.10
☐ 187	Gene Conley	1.00	.50	.10
☐ 188	Chuck Hiller	1.00	.50	.10
☐ 189	Dick Hall	1.00	.50	.10
☐ 190A	Wally Moon PORT	1.50	.75	.15
☐ 190B	Wally Moon BATTING	12.50	6.25	1.25
☐ 191	Jim Brewer	1.00	.50	.10
☐ 192A	Checklist 3	5.00	1.00	.20
	(without comma)			
☐ 192B	Checklist 3	7.50	1.25	.30
	(comma after			
	Checklist)			
☐ 193	Eddie Kasko	1.00	.50	.10
☐ 194	Dean Chance	2.00	1.00	.20
☐ 195	Joe Cunningham	1.50	.75	.15
☐ 196	Terry Fox	1.00	.50	.10
☐ 197	Daryl Spencer	1.25	.60	.12
☐ 198	Johnny Keane MG	1.75	.85	.17
☐ 199	Gaylord Perry	100.00	45.00	9.00
☐ 200	Mickey Mantle	350.00	175.00	35.00
☐ 201	Ike Delock	1.25	.60	.12
☐ 202	Carl Warwick	1.25	.60	.12
☐ 203	Jack Fisher	1.25	.60	.12
☐ 204	Johnny Weekly	1.25	.60	.12
☐ 205	Gene Freese	1.25	.60	.12
☐ 206	Senators Team	3.00	1.50	.30
☐ 207	Pete Burnside	1.25	.60	.12
☐ 208	Billy Martin	6.00	3.00	.60
☐ 209	Jim Fregosi	5.00	2.50	.50
☐ 210	Roy Face	2.00	1.00	.20
☐ 211	Midway Masters	1.25	.60	.12
	Frank Bolling			
	Roy McMillan			
☐ 212	Jim Owens	1.25	.60	.12
☐ 213	Richie Ashburn	5.00	2.50	.50
☐ 214	Dom Zanni	1.25	.60	.12
☐ 215	Woody Held	1.25	.60	.12

☐ 216	Ron Kline	1.25	.60	.12
☐ 217	Walt Alston MG	4.50	2.25	.45
☐ 218	Joe Torre	10.00	5.00	1.00
☐ 219	Al Downing	3.00	1.50	.30
☐ 220	Roy Sievers	1.75	.85	.17
☐ 221	Bill Short	1.25	.60	.12
☐ 222	Jerry Zimmerman	1.25	.60	.12
☐ 223	Alex Grammas	1.25	.60	.12
☐ 224	Don Rudolph	1.25	.60	.12
☐ 225	Frank Malzone	1.75	.85	.17
☐ 226	San Francisco Giants	3.00	1.50	.30
	Team Card			
☐ 227	Bob Tiefenauer	1.25	.60	.12
☐ 228	Dale Long	1.75	.85	.17
☐ 229	Jesus McFarlane	1.25	.60	.12
☐ 230	Camilo Pascual	1.75	.85	.17
☐ 231	Ernie Bowman	1.25	.60	.12
☐ 232	World Series Game 1	3.00	1.50	.30
	Yanks win opener			
☐ 233	World Series Game 2	3.00	1.50	.30
	Jay ties it up			
☐ 234	World Series Game 3	9.00	4.50	.90
	Maris wins in 9th			
☐ 235	World Series Game 4	5.00	2.50	.50
	Ford sets new mark			
☐ 236	World Series Game 5	3.00	1.50	.30
	Yanks crush Reds			
☐ 237	World Series Summary	3.00	1.50	.30
	Yanks celebrate			
☐ 238	Norm Sherry	1.25	.60	.12
☐ 239	Cecil Butler	1.25	.60	.12
☐ 240	George Altman	1.25	.60	.12
☐ 241	Johnny Kucks	1.25	.60	.12
☐ 242	Mel McGaha	1.25	.60	.12
☐ 243	Robin Roberts	10.00	5.00	1.00
☐ 244	Don Gile	1.25	.60	.12
☐ 245	Ron Hansen	1.25	.60	.12
☐ 246	Art Ditmar	1.25	.60	.12
☐ 247	Joe Pignatano	1.25	.60	.12
☐ 248	Bob Aspromonte	1.25	.60	.12
☐ 249	Ed Keegan	1.25	.60	.12
☐ 250	Norm Cash	2.50	1.25	.25
☐ 251	New York Yankees	12.50	6.25	1.25
	Team Card			
☐ 252	Earl Francis	1.25	.60	.12
☐ 253	Harry Chiti	1.25	.60	.12
☐ 254	Gordon Windhorn	1.25	.60	.12
☐ 255	Juan Pizarro	1.25	.60	.12
☐ 256	Elio Chacon	1.25	.60	.12
☐ 257	Jack Spring	1.25	.60	.12
☐ 258	Marty Keough	1.25	.60	.12
☐ 259	Lou Klimchock	1.25	.60	.12
☐ 260	Billy Pierce	1.75	.85	.17
☐ 261	George Alusik	1.25	.60	.12
☐ 262	Bob Schmidt	1.25	.60	.12
☐ 263	The Right Pitch	1.25	.60	.12
	Bob Purkey			
	Jim Turner			
	Joe Jay			
☐ 264	Dick Ellsworth	1.25	.60	.12
☐ 265	Joe Adcock	1.75	.85	.17
☐ 266	John Anderson	1.25	.60	.12
☐ 267	Dan Dobbek	1.25	.60	.12
☐ 268	Ken McBride	1.25	.60	.12
☐ 269	Bob Oldis	1.25	.60	.12
☐ 270	Dick Groat	2.50	1.25	.25
☐ 271	Ray Rippelmeyer	1.25	.60	.12
☐ 272	Earl Robinson	1.25	.60	.12
☐ 273	Gary Bell	1.25	.60	.12
☐ 274	Sammy Taylor	1.25	.60	.12
☐ 275	Norm Siebern	1.25	.60	.12
☐ 276	Hal Kolstad	1.25	.60	.12
☐ 277	Checklist 4	5.00	1.00	.20
☐ 278	Ken Johnson	1.25	.60	.12
☐ 279	Hobie Landrith UER	1.25	.60	.12
	(wrong birthdate)			
☐ 280	Johnny Podres	2.50	1.25	.25
☐ 281	Jake Gibbs	1.25	.60	.12
☐ 282	Dave Hillman	1.25	.60	.12
☐ 283	Charlie Smith	1.25	.60	.12
☐ 284	Ruben Amaro	1.25	.60	.12
☐ 285	Curt Simmons	1.75	.85	.17
☐ 286	Al Lopez MG	3.00	1.50	.30
☐ 287	George Witt	1.25	.60	.12
☐ 288	Billy Williams	25.00	10.00	2.00
☐ 289	Mike Krsnich	1.25	.60	.12
☐ 290	Jim Gentile	1.75	.85	.17
☐ 291	Hal Stowe	1.25	.60	.12
☐ 292	Jerry Kindall	1.25	.60	.12
☐ 293	Bob Miller	1.25	.60	.12
☐ 294	Phillies Team	3.00	1.50	.30
☐ 295	Vern Law	1.75	.85	.17
☐ 296	Ken Hamlin	1.25	.60	.12
☐ 297	Ron Perranoski	1.75	.85	.17
☐ 298	Bill Tuttle	1.25	.60	.12

☐ 299	Don Wert	1.25	.60	.12
☐ 300	Willie Mays	100.00	50.00	10.00
☐ 301	Galen Cisco	1.25	.60	.12
☐ 302	Johnny Edwards	1.25	.60	.12
☐ 303	Frank Torre	1.25	.60	.12
☐ 304	Dick Farrell	1.25	.60	.12
☐ 305	Jerry Lumpe	1.25	.60	.12
☐ 306	Redbird Rippers	1.75	.85	.17
	Lindy McDaniel			
	Larry Jackson			
☐ 307	Jim Grant	1.25	.60	.12
☐ 308	Neil Chrisley	1.25	.60	.12
☐ 309	Moe Morhardt	1.25	.60	.12
☐ 310	Whitey Ford	25.00	12.50	2.50
☐ 311	Tony Kubek IA	2.50	1.25	.25
☐ 312	Warren Spahn IA	6.00	3.00	.60
☐ 313	Roger Maris IA	12.50	6.25	1.25
☐ 314	Rocky Colavito IA	2.50	1.25	.25
☐ 315	Whitey Ford IA	6.00	3.00	.60
☐ 316	Harmon Killebrew IA	5.00	2.50	.50
☐ 317	Stan Musial IA	10.00	5.00	1.00
☐ 318	Mickey Mantle IA	40.00	20.00	4.00
☐ 319	Mike McCormick IA	1.75	.85	.17
☐ 320	Hank Aaron	100.00	50.00	10.00
☐ 321	Lee Stange	1.25	.60	.12
☐ 322	Alvin Dark	1.75	.85	.17
☐ 323	Don Landrum	1.25	.60	.12
☐ 324	Joe McClain	1.25	.60	.12
☐ 325	Luis Aparicio	10.00	5.00	1.00
☐ 326	Tom Parsons	1.25	.60	.12
☐ 327	Ozzie Virgil	1.25	.60	.12
☐ 328	Ken Walters	1.25	.60	.12
☐ 329	Bob Bolin	1.25	.60	.12
☐ 330	John Romano	1.25	.60	.12
☐ 331	Moe Drabowsky	1.25	.60	.12
☐ 332	Don Buddin	1.25	.60	.12
☐ 333	Frank Cipriani	1.25	.60	.12
☐ 334	Boston Red Sox	3.00	1.50	.30
	Team Card			
☐ 335	Bill Bruton	1.75	.85	.17
☐ 336	Billy Muffett	1.25	.60	.12
☐ 337	Jim Marshall	1.25	.60	.12
☐ 338	Billy Gardner	1.75	.85	.17
☐ 339	Jose Valdivielso	1.25	.60	.12
☐ 340	Don Drysdale	24.00	12.00	2.40
☐ 341	Mike Hershberger	1.25	.60	.12
☐ 342	Ed Rakow	1.25	.60	.12
☐ 343	Albie Pearson	1.25	.60	.12
☐ 344	Ed Bauta	1.25	.60	.12
☐ 345	Chuck Schilling	1.25	.60	.12
☐ 346	Jack Kralick	1.25	.60	.12
☐ 347	Chuck Hinton	1.25	.60	.12
☐ 348	Larry Burright	1.25	.60	.12
☐ 349	Paul Foytack	1.25	.60	.12
☐ 350	Frank Robinson	25.00	12.50	2.50
☐ 351	Braves' Backstops	1.75	.85	.17
	Joe Torre			
	Del Crandall			
☐ 352	Frank Sullivan	1.25	.60	.12
☐ 353	Bill Mazeroski	3.00	1.50	.30
☐ 354	Roman Mejias	1.25	.60	.12
☐ 355	Steve Barber	1.25	.60	.12
☐ 356	Tom Haller	1.75	.85	.17
☐ 357	Jerry Walker	1.25	.60	.12
☐ 358	Tommy Davis	2.50	1.25	.25
☐ 359	Bobby Locke	1.25	.60	.12
☐ 360	Yogi Berra	45.00	22.50	4.50
☐ 361	Bob Hendley	1.25	.60	.12
☐ 362	Ty Cline	1.25	.60	.12
☐ 363	Bob Roselli	1.25	.60	.12
☐ 364	Ken Hunt	1.25	.60	.12
☐ 365	Charlie Neal	1.75	.85	.17
☐ 366	Phil Regan	1.75	.85	.17
☐ 367	Checklist 5	5.00	1.00	.20
☐ 368	Bob Tillman	1.25	.60	.12
☐ 369	Ted Bowsfield	1.25	.60	.12
☐ 370	Ken Boyer	3.50	1.75	.35
☐ 371	Earl Battey	2.00	1.00	.20
☐ 372	Jack Curtis	2.00	1.00	.20
☐ 373	Al Heist	2.00	1.00	.20
☐ 374	Gene Mauch	2.50	1.25	.25
☐ 375	Ron Fairly	2.50	1.25	.25
☐ 376	Bud Daley	2.00	1.00	.20
☐ 377	John Orsino	2.00	1.00	.20
☐ 378	Bennie Daniels	2.00	1.00	.20
☐ 379	Chuck Essegian	2.00	1.00	.20
☐ 380	Lou Burdette	3.00	1.50	.30
☐ 381	Chico Cardenas	2.00	1.00	.20
☐ 382	Dick Williams	2.50	1.25	.25
☐ 383	Ray Sadecki	2.00	1.00	.20
☐ 384	K.C. Athletics	4.00	2.00	.40
	Team Card			
☐ 385	Early Wynn	10.00	5.00	1.00
☐ 386	Don Mincher	2.50	1.25	.25
☐ 387	Lou Brock	100.00	50.00	10.00
☐ 388	Ryne Duren	2.50	1.25	.25
☐ 389	Smoky Burgess	2.50	1.25	.25
☐ 390	Orlando Cepeda AS	3.50	1.75	.35
☐ 391	Bill Mazeroski AS	3.00	1.50	.30
☐ 392	Ken Boyer AS	3.00	1.50	.30
☐ 393	Roy McMillan AS	2.50	1.25	.25
☐ 394	Hank Aaron AS	25.00	12.50	2.50
☐ 395	Willie Mays AS	25.00	12.50	2.50
☐ 396	Frank Robinson AS	9.00	4.50	.90
☐ 397	John Roseboro AS	2.50	1.25	.25
☐ 398	Don Drysdale AS	7.50	3.75	.75
☐ 399	Warren Spahn AS	8.50	4.25	.85
☐ 400	Elston Howard	5.00	2.50	.50
☐ 401	AL/NL Homer Kings	25.00	12.00	2.40
	Roger Maris			
	Orlando Cepeda			
☐ 402	Gino Cimoli	2.00	1.00	.20
☐ 403	Chet Nichols	2.00	1.00	.20
☐ 404	Tim Harkness	2.00	1.00	.20
☐ 405	Jim Perry	2.50	1.25	.25
☐ 406	Bob Taylor	2.00	1.00	.20
☐ 407	Hank Aguirre	2.00	1.00	.20
☐ 408	Gus Bell	2.50	1.25	.25
☐ 409	Pittsburgh Pirates	4.00	2.00	.40
	Team Card			
☐ 410	Al Smith	2.00	1.00	.20
☐ 411	Danny O'Connell	2.00	1.00	.20
☐ 412	Charlie James	2.00	1.00	.20
☐ 413	Matty Alou	3.00	1.50	.30
☐ 414	Joe Gaines	2.00	1.00	.20
☐ 415	Bill Virdon	3.00	1.50	.30
☐ 416	Bob Scheffing MG	2.00	1.00	.20
☐ 417	Joe Azcue	2.00	1.00	.20
☐ 418	Andy Carey	2.00	1.00	.20
☐ 419	Bob Bruce	2.00	1.00	.20
☐ 420	Gus Triandos	2.50	1.25	.25
☐ 421	Ken MacKenzie	2.00	1.00	.20
☐ 422	Steve Bilko	2.00	1.00	.20
☐ 423	Rival League	4.00	2.00	.40
	Relief Aces:			
	Roy Face			
	Hoyt Wilhelm			
☐ 424	Al McBean	2.00	1.00	.20
☐ 425	Carl Yastrzemski	150.00	75.00	15.00
☐ 426	Bob Farley	2.00	1.00	.20
☐ 427	Jake Wood	2.00	1.00	.20
☐ 428	Joe Hicks	2.00	1.00	.20
☐ 429	Billy O'Dell	2.00	1.00	.20
☐ 430	Tony Kubek	7.00	3.50	.70
☐ 431	Bob Rodgers	4.00	2.00	.40
☐ 432	Jim Pendleton	2.00	1.00	.20
☐ 433	Jim Archer	2.00	1.00	.20
☐ 434	Clay Dalrymple	2.00	1.00	.20
☐ 435	Larry Sherry	2.50	1.25	.25
☐ 436	Felix Mantilla	2.00	1.00	.20
☐ 437	Ray Moore	2.00	1.00	.20
☐ 438	Dick Brown	2.00	1.00	.20
☐ 439	Jerry Buchek	2.00	1.00	.20
☐ 440	Joey Jay	2.00	1.00	.20
☐ 441	Checklist 6	6.00	1.00	.20
☐ 442	Wes Stock	2.50	1.25	.25
☐ 443	Del Crandall	2.50	1.25	.25
☐ 444	Ted Wills	2.00	1.00	.20
☐ 445	Vic Power	2.00	1.00	.20
☐ 446	Don Elston	2.00	1.00	.20
☐ 447	Willie Kirkland	3.00	1.50	.30
☐ 448	Joe Gibbon	3.00	1.50	.30
☐ 449	Jerry Adair	3.00	1.50	.30
☐ 450	Jim O'Toole	3.00	1.50	.30
☐ 451	Jose Tartabull	3.00	1.50	.30
☐ 452	Earl Averill	3.00	1.50	.30
☐ 453	Cal McLish	3.00	1.50	.30
☐ 454	Floyd Robinson	3.00	1.50	.30
☐ 455	Luis Arroyo	3.00	1.50	.30
☐ 456	Joe Amalfitano	3.00	1.50	.30
☐ 457	Lou Clinton	3.00	1.50	.30
☐ 458A	Bob Buhl	3.00	1.50	.30
	(Braves cap emblem)			
☐ 458B	Bob Buhl	40.00	20.00	4.00
	(no emblem on cap)			
☐ 459	Ed Bailey	3.00	1.50	.30
☐ 460	Jim Bunning	7.50	3.75	.75
☐ 461	Ken Hubbs	7.50	3.75	.75
☐ 462A	Willie Tasby	3.00	1.50	.30
	(Senators cap emblem)			
☐ 462B	Willie Tasby	40.00	20.00	4.00
	(no emblem on cap)			
☐ 463	Hank Bauer	4.00	2.00	.40
☐ 464	Al Jackson	3.00	1.50	.30
☐ 465	Reds Team	6.00	3.00	.60
☐ 466	Norm Cash AS	3.50	1.75	.35
☐ 467	Chuck Schilling AS	3.00	1.50	.30
☐ 468	Brooks Robinson AS	11.00	5.50	1.10
☐ 469	Luis Aparicio AS	6.50	3.25	.65
☐ 470	Al Kaline AS	11.00	5.50	1.10

		NRMT	VG-E	GOOD
☐ 471	Mickey Mantle AS	80.00	40.00	8.00
☐ 472	Rocky Colavito AS	3.50	1.75	.35
☐ 473	Elston Howard AS	3.50	1.75	.35
☐ 474	Frank Lary AS	3.00	1.50	.30
☐ 475	Whitey Ford AS	10.00	5.00	1.00
☐ 476	Orioles Team	6.00	3.00	.60
☐ 477	Andre Rodgers	3.00	1.50	.30
☐ 478	Don Zimmer	4.50	2.25	.45
☐ 479	Joel Horlen	3.00	1.50	.30
☐ 480	Harvey Kuenn	4.50	2.25	.45
☐ 481	Vic Wertz	3.50	1.75	.35
☐ 482	Sam Mele MG	3.00	1.50	.30
☐ 483	Don McMahon	3.00	1.50	.30
☐ 484	Dick Schofield	3.00	1.50	.30
☐ 485	Pedro Ramos	3.00	1.50	.30
☐ 486	Jim Gilliam	5.00	2.50	.50
☐ 487	Jerry Lynch	3.00	1.50	.30
☐ 488	Hal Brown	3.00	1.50	.30
☐ 489	Julio Gotay	3.00	1.50	.30
☐ 490	Clete Boyer	3.50	1.75	.35
☐ 491	Leon Wagner	3.00	1.50	.30
☐ 492	Hal W. Smith	3.00	1.50	.30
☐ 493	Danny McDevitt	3.00	1.50	.30
☐ 494	Sammy White	3.00	1.50	.30
☐ 495	Don Cardwell	3.00	1.50	.30
☐ 496	Wayne Causey	3.00	1.50	.30
☐ 497	Ed Bouchee	3.00	1.50	.30
☐ 498	Jim Donohue	3.00	1.50	.30
☐ 499	Zoilo Versalles	3.00	1.50	.30
☐ 500	Duke Snider	35.00	17.50	3.50
☐ 501	Claude Osteen	3.50	1.75	.35
☐ 502	Hector Lopez	3.00	1.50	.30
☐ 503	Danny Murtaugh MG	3.00	1.50	.30
☐ 504	Eddie Bressoud	3.00	1.50	.30
☐ 505	Juan Marichal	30.00	15.00	3.00
☐ 506	Charlie Maxwell	3.00	1.50	.30
☐ 507	Ernie Broglio	3.00	1.50	.30
☐ 508	Gordy Coleman	3.50	1.75	.35
☐ 509	Dave Giusti	3.50	1.75	.35
☐ 510	Jim Lemon	3.50	1.75	.35
☐ 511	Bubba Phillips	3.00	1.50	.30
☐ 512	Mike Fornieles	3.00	1.50	.30
☐ 513	Whitey Herzog	4.50	2.25	.45
☐ 514	Sherm Lollar	3.50	1.75	.35
☐ 515	Stan Williams	3.00	1.50	.30
☐ 516	Checklist 7	9.00	1.25	.30
☐ 517	Dave Wickersham	3.00	1.50	.30
☐ 518	Lee Maye	3.00	1.50	.30
☐ 519	Bob Johnson	3.00	1.50	.30
☐ 520	Bob Friend	3.50	1.75	.35
☐ 521	Jacke Davis	3.00	1.50	.30
☐ 522	Lindy McDaniel	3.50	1.75	.35
☐ 523	Russ Nixon SP	18.00	9.00	1.80
☐ 524	Howie Nunn SP	18.00	9.00	1.80
☐ 525	George Thomas	9.00	4.50	.90
☐ 526	Hal Woodeshick SP	18.00	9.00	1.80
☐ 527	Dick McAuliffe	12.00	6.00	1.20
☐ 528	Turk Lown	9.00	4.50	.90
☐ 529	John Schaive SP	18.00	9.00	1.80
☐ 530	Bob Gibson SP	100.00	50.00	10.00
☐ 531	Bobby G. Smith	9.00	4.50	.90
☐ 532	Dick Stigman	9.00	4.50	.90
☐ 533	Charley Lau SP	18.00	9.00	1.80
☐ 534	Tony Gonzalez SP	18.00	9.00	1.80
☐ 535	Ed Roebuck	9.00	4.50	.90
☐ 536	Dick Gernert	9.00	4.50	.90
☐ 537	Cleveland Indians Team Card	18.00	9.00	1.80
☐ 538	Jack Sanford SP	18.00	9.00	1.80
☐ 539	Billy Moran	9.00	4.50	.90
☐ 540	Jim Landis SP	18.00	9.00	1.80
☐ 541	Don Nottebart SP	18.00	9.00	1.80
☐ 542	Dave Philley	9.00	4.50	.90
☐ 543	Bob Allen SP	18.00	9.00	1.80
☐ 544	Willie McCovey SP	100.00	50.00	10.00
☐ 545	Hoyt Wilhelm SP	50.00	25.00	5.00
☐ 546	Moe Thacker SP	18.00	9.00	1.80
☐ 547	Don Ferrarese	9.00	4.50	.90
☐ 548	Bobby Del Greco	9.00	4.50	.90
☐ 549	Bill Rigney MG SP	18.00	9.00	1.80
☐ 550	Art Mahaffey SP	18.00	9.00	1.80
☐ 551	Harry Bright	9.00	4.50	.90
☐ 552	Chicago Cubs SP Team Card	30.00	15.00	3.00
☐ 553	Jim Coates	18.00	9.00	1.80
☐ 554	Bubba Morton SP	18.00	9.00	1.80
☐ 555	John Buzhardt SP	18.00	9.00	1.80
☐ 556	Al Spangler	9.00	4.50	.90
☐ 557	Bob Anderson	9.00	4.50	.90
☐ 558	John Goryl	9.00	4.50	.90
☐ 559	Mike Higgins MG	9.00	4.50	.90
☐ 560	Chuck Estrada SP	18.00	9.00	1.80
☐ 561	Gene Oliver SP	18.00	9.00	1.80
☐ 562	Bill Henry	9.00	4.50	.90
☐ 563	Ken Aspromonte	9.00	4.50	.90
☐ 564	Bob Grim	9.00	4.50	.90
☐ 565	Jose Pagan	9.00	4.50	.90
☐ 566	Marty Kutyna SP	18.00	9.00	1.80
☐ 567	Tracy Stallard SP	18.00	9.00	1.80
☐ 568	Jim Golden	9.00	4.50	.90
☐ 569	Ed Sadowski SP	18.00	9.00	1.80
☐ 570	Bill Stafford SP	18.00	9.00	1.80
☐ 571	Billy Klaus SP	18.00	9.00	1.80
☐ 572	Bob G. Miller SP	18.00	9.00	1.80
☐ 573	Johnny Logan	12.00	6.00	1.20
☐ 574	Dean Stone	9.00	4.50	.90
☐ 575	Red Schoendienst SP	40.00	20.00	4.00
☐ 576	Russ Kemmerer SP	18.00	9.00	1.80
☐ 577	Dave Nicholson SP	18.00	9.00	1.80
☐ 578	Jim Duffalo	9.00	4.50	.90
☐ 579	Jim Schaffer SP	18.00	9.00	1.80
☐ 580	Bill Monbouquette	9.00	4.50	.90
☐ 581	Mel Roach	9.00	4.50	.90
☐ 582	Ron Piche	9.00	4.50	.90
☐ 583	Larry Osborne	9.00	4.50	.90
☐ 584	Minnesota Twins SP Team Card	30.00	15.00	3.00
☐ 585	Glen Hobbie	9.00	4.50	.90
☐ 586	Sammy Esposito SP	18.00	9.00	1.80
☐ 587	Frank Funk SP	18.00	9.00	1.80
☐ 588	Birdie Tebbetts MG	9.00	4.50	.90
☐ 589	Bob Turley	15.00	6.00	1.20
☐ 590	Curt Flood	15.00	6.00	1.20
☐ 591	Rookie Pitchers SP Sam McDowell Ron Taylor Ron Nischwitz Art Quirk Dick Radatz	30.00	15.00	3.00
☐ 592	Rookie Pitchers SP Dan Pfister Bo Belinsky Dave Stenhouse Jim Bouton Joe Bonikowski	40.00	20.00	4.00
☐ 593	Rookie Pitchers SP Jack Lamabe Craig Anderson Jack Hamilton Bob Moorhead Bob Veale	20.00	10.00	2.00
☐ 594	Rookie Catchers SP Doc Edwards Ken Retzer Bob Uecker Doug Camilli Don Pavletich	125.00	50.00	10.00
☐ 595	Rookie Infielders SP Bob Sadowski Felix Torres Marlan Coughtry Ed Charles	18.00	9.00	1.80
☐ 596	Rookie Infielders SP Bernie Allen Joe Pepitone Phil Linz Rich Rollins	30.00	15.00	3.00
☐ 597	Rookie Infielders SP Jim McKnight Rod Kanehl Amado Samuel Denis Menke	18.00	9.00	1.80
☐ 598	Rookie Outfielders SP Al Luplow Manny Jimenez Howie Goss Jim Hickman Ed Olivares	40.00	15.00	3.00

1963 Topps

The cards in this 576-card set measure 2 1/2" by 3 1/2". The sharp color photographs of the 1963 set are a vivid contrast to the drab pictures of 1962. In addition to the "League Leaders" series (1-10) and World Series cards (142-148), the seventh and last series of cards (523-576) contains seven rookie cards (each depicting four players). This set has gained special prominence in recent years since it contains the rookie card of Pete Rose, #537.

	NRMT	VG-E	GOOD
COMPLETE SET (576)	4000.00	2000.00	500.00
COMMON PLAYER (1-109)	.75	.35	.07
COMMON PLAYER (110-196)	.85	.40	.08

COMMON PLAYER (197-283) .... 1.00 .50 .10
COMMON PLAYER (284-446) .... 1.50 .75 .15
COMMON PLAYER (447-522) .... 7.00 3.50 .70
COMMON PLAYER (523-576) .... 5.00 2.50 .50

☐	1 NL Batting Leaders	20.00	5.00	1.00
	Tommy Davis			
	Frank Robinson			
	Stan Musial			
	Hank Aaron			
	Bill White			
☐	2 AL Batting Leaders	10.00	5.00	1.00
	Pete Runnels			
	Mickey Mantle			
	Floyd Robinson			
	Norm Siebern			
	Chuck Hinton			
☐	3 NL Home Run Leaders ...	10.00	5.00	1.00
	Willie Mays			
	Hank Aaron			
	Frank Robinson			
	Orlando Cepeda			
	Ernie Banks			
☐	4 AL Home Run Leaders ...	3.00	1.50	.30
	Harmon Killebrew			
	Norm Cash			
	Rocky Colavito			
	Roger Maris			
	Jim Gentile			
	Leon Wagner			
☐	5 NL ERA Leaders	3.00	1.50	.30
	Sandy Koufax			
	Bob Shaw			
	Bob Purkey			
	Bob Gibson			
	Don Drysdale			
☐	6 AL ERA Leaders	2.50	1.25	.25
	Hank Aguirre			
	Robin Roberts			
	Whitey Ford			
	Eddie Fisher			
	Dean Chance			
☐	7 AL Pitching Leaders	2.00	1.00	.20
	Don Drysdale			
	Jack Sanford			
	Bob Purkey			
	Billy O'Dell			
	Art Mahaffey			
	Joe Jay			
☐	8 AL Pitching Leaders	1.50	.75	.15
	Ralph Terry			
	Dick Donovan			
	Ray Herbert			
	Jim Bunning			
	Camilo Pascual			
☐	9 NL Strikeout Leaders	3.50	1.75	.35
	Don Drysdale			
	Sandy Koufax			
	Bob Gibson			
	Billy O'Dell			
	Dick Farrell			
☐	10 AL Strikeout Leaders	1.50	.75	.15
	Camilo Pascual			
	Jim Bunning			
	Ralph Terry			
	Juan Pizarro			
	Jim Kaat			
☐	11 Lee Walls	.75	.35	.07
☐	12 Steve Barber	.75	.35	.07
☐	13 Philadelphia Phillies	1.75	.85	.17
	Team Card			
☐	14 Pedro Ramos	.75	.35	.07
☐	15 Ken Hubbs	1.75	.85	.17
☐	16 Al Smith	.75	.35	.07
☐	17 Ryne Duren	1.00	.50	.10
☐	18 Buc Blasters	7.50	3.75	.75
	Smoky Burgess			
	Dick Stuart			
	Bob Clemente			
	Bob Skinner			
☐	19 Pete Burnside	.75	.35	.07
☐	20 Tony Kubek	3.00	1.50	.30
☐	21 Marty Keough	.75	.35	.07
☐	22 Curt Simmons	1.00	.50	.10
☐	23 Ed Lopat MG	1.50	.75	.15
☐	24 Bob Bruce	.75	.35	.07
☐	25 Al Kaline	24.00	12.00	2.40
☐	26 Ray Moore	.75	.35	.07
☐	27 Choo Choo Coleman	.75	.35	.07
☐	28 Mike Fornieles	.75	.35	.07
☐	29A 1962 Rookie Stars	4.00	2.00	.40
	Sammy Ellis			
	Ray Culp			
	John Boozer			
	Jesse Gonder			
☐	29B 1963 Rookie Stars	1.50	.75	.15
	Sammy Ellis			
	Ray Culp			
	John Boozer			
	Jesse Gonder			
☐	30 Harvey Kuenn	1.50	.75	.15
☐	31 Cal Koonce	.75	.35	.07
☐	32 Tony Gonzalez	.75	.35	.07
☐	33 Bo Belinsky	1.00	.50	.10
☐	34 Dick Schofield	.75	.35	.07
☐	35 John Buzhardt	.75	.35	.07
☐	36 Jerry Kindall	.75	.35	.07
☐	37 Jerry Lynch	.75	.35	.07
☐	38 Bud Daley	.75	.35	.07
☐	39 Angels Team	1.75	.85	.17
☐	40 Vic Power	.75	.35	.07
☐	41 Charley Lau	1.00	.50	.10
☐	42 Stan Williams	.75	.35	.07
☐	43 Veteran Masters	3.50	1.75	.35
	Casey Stengel			
	Gene Woodling			
☐	44 Terry Fox	.75	.35	.07
☐	45 Bob Aspromonte	.75	.35	.07
☐	46 Tommy Aaron	1.00	.50	.10
☐	47 Don Lock	.75	.35	.07
☐	48 Birdie Tebbetts MG	.75	.35	.07
☐	49 Dal Maxvill	.75	.35	.07
☐	50 Billy Pierce	1.00	.50	.10
☐	51 George Alusik	.75	.35	.07
☐	52 Chuck Schilling	.75	.35	.07
☐	53 Joe Moeller	.75	.35	.07
☐	54A 1962 Rookie Stars	7.50	3.75	.75
	Nelson Mathews			
	Harry Fanok			
	Jack Cullen			
	Dave DeBusschere			
☐	54B 1963 Rookie Stars	3.50	1.75	.35
	Nelson Mathews			
	Harry Fanok			
	Jack Cullen			
	Dave DeBusschere			
☐	55 Bill Virdon	1.50	.75	.15
☐	56 Dennis Bennett	.75	.35	.07
☐	57 Billy Moran	.75	.35	.07
☐	58 Bob Will	.75	.35	.07
☐	59 Craig Anderson	.75	.35	.07
☐	60 Elston Howard	4.00	2.00	.40
☐	61 Ernie Bowman	.75	.35	.07
☐	62 Bob Hendley	.75	.35	.07
☐	63 Reds Team	1.75	.85	.17
☐	64 Dick McAuliffe	.75	.35	.07
☐	65 Jackie Brandt	.75	.35	.07
☐	66 Mike Joyce	.75	.35	.07
☐	67 Ed Charles	.75	.35	.07
☐	68 Friendly Foes	7.50	3.75	.75
	Duke Snider			
	Gil Hodges			
☐	69 Bud Zipfel	.75	.35	.07
☐	70 Jim O'Toole	.75	.35	.07
☐	71 Bobby Wine	.75	.35	.07
☐	72 Johnny Romano	.75	.35	.07
☐	73 Bobby Bragan MG	.75	.35	.07
☐	74 Denny Lemaster	.75	.35	.07
☐	75 Bob Allison	1.00	.50	.10
☐	76 Earl Wilson	.75	.35	.07
☐	77 Al Spangler	.75	.35	.07
☐	78 Marv Throneberry	1.00	.50	.10
☐	79 Checklist 1	4.00	.75	.15
☐	80 Jim Gilliam	2.00	1.00	.20
☐	81 Jim Schaffer	.75	.35	.07
☐	82 Ed Rakow	.75	.35	.07
☐	83 Charley James	.75	.35	.07

☐ 84	Ron Kline	.75	.35	.07
☐ 85	Tom Haller	.75	.35	.07
☐ 86	Charley Maxwell	.75	.35	.07
☐ 87	Bob Veale	.75	.35	.07
☐ 88	Ron Hansen	.75	.35	.07
☐ 89	Dick Stigman	.75	.35	.07
☐ 90	Gordy Coleman	.75	.35	.07
☐ 91	Dallas Green	2.00	1.00	.20
☐ 92	Hector Lopez	.75	.35	.07
☐ 93	Galen Cisco	.75	.35	.07
☐ 94	Bob Schmidt	.75	.35	.07
☐ 95	Larry Jackson	.75	.35	.07
☐ 96	Lou Clinton	.75	.35	.07
☐ 97	Bob Duliba	.75	.35	.07
☐ 98	George Thomas	.75	.35	.07
☐ 99	Jim Umbricht	.75	.35	.07
☐ 100	Joe Cunningham	1.00	.50	.10
☐ 101	Joe Gibbon	.75	.35	.07
☐ 102A	Checklist 2 (red on yellow)	5.00	1.00	.20
☐ 102B	Checklist 2 (white on red)	7.00	1.25	.25
☐ 103	Chuck Essegian	.75	.35	.07
☐ 104	Lew Krausse	.75	.35	.07
☐ 105	Ron Fairly	1.00	.50	.10
☐ 106	Bobby Bolin	.75	.35	.07
☐ 107	Jim Hickman	.75	.35	.07
☐ 108	Hoyt Wilhelm	7.50	3.75	.75
☐ 109	Lee Maye	.75	.35	.07
☐ 110	Rich Rollins	.85	.40	.08
☐ 111	Al Jackson	.85	.40	.08
☐ 112	Dick Brown	.85	.40	.08
☐ 113	Don Landrum UER (photo actually Ron Santo)	1.25	.60	.12
☐ 114	Dan Osinski	.85	.40	.08
☐ 115	Carl Yastrzemski	75.00	37.50	7.50
☐ 116	Jim Brosnan	.85	.40	.08
☐ 117	Jacke Davis	.85	.40	.08
☐ 118	Sherm Lollar	.85	.40	.08
☐ 119	Bob Lillis	.85	.40	.08
☐ 120	Roger Maris	45.00	22.50	4.50
☐ 121	Jim Hannan	.85	.40	.08
☐ 122	Julio Gotay	.85	.40	.08
☐ 123	Frank Howard	2.00	1.00	.20
☐ 124	Dick Howser	1.50	.75	.15
☐ 125	Robin Roberts	9.00	4.50	.90
☐ 126	Bob Uecker	25.00	12.50	2.50
☐ 127	Bill Tuttle	.85	.40	.08
☐ 128	Matty Alou	1.25	.60	.12
☐ 129	Gary Bell	.85	.40	.08
☐ 130	Dick Groat	1.50	.75	.15
☐ 131	Washington Senators Team Card	1.75	.85	.17
☐ 132	Jack Hamilton	.85	.40	.08
☐ 133	Gene Freese	.85	.40	.08
☐ 134	Bob Scheffing MG	.85	.40	.08
☐ 135	Richie Ashburn	4.50	2.25	.45
☐ 136	Ike Delock	.85	.40	.08
☐ 137	Mack Jones	.85	.40	.08
☐ 138	Pride of NL Willie Mays Stan Musial	25.00	12.50	2.50
☐ 139	Earl Averill	.85	.40	.08
☐ 140	Frank Lary	1.25	.60	.12
☐ 141	Manny Mota	5.00	2.50	.50
☐ 142	World Series Game 1 Ford wins series opener	4.50	2.25	.45
☐ 143	World Series Game 2 Sanford flashes shutout magic	3.00	1.50	.30
☐ 144	World Series Game 3 Maris sparks Yankee rally	7.50	3.75	.75
☐ 145	World Series Game 4 Hiller blasts grand slammer	3.00	1.50	.30
☐ 146	World Series Game 5 Tresh's homer defeats Giants	3.00	1.50	.30
☐ 147	World Series Game 6 Pierce stars in 3 hit victory	3.00	1.50	.30
☐ 148	World Series Game 7 Yanks celebrate as Terry wins	3.00	1.50	.30
☐ 149	Marv Breeding	.85	.40	.08
☐ 150	Johnny Podres	2.00	1.00	.20
☐ 151	Pirates Team	1.75	.85	.17
☐ 152	Ron Nischwitz	.85	.40	.08
☐ 153	Hal Smith	.85	.40	.08
☐ 154	Walt Alston MG	3.50	1.75	.35
☐ 155	Bill Stafford	.85	.40	.08
☐ 156	Roy McMillan	.85	.40	.08
☐ 157	Diego Segui	.85	.40	.08
☐ 158	Rookie Stars Rogelio Alvares Dave Roberts Tommy Harper Bob Saverine	1.25	.60	.12
☐ 159	Jim Pagliaroni	.85	.40	.08
☐ 160	Juan Pizarro	.85	.40	.08
☐ 161	Frank Torre	.85	.40	.08
☐ 162	Twins Team	1.75	.85	.17
☐ 163	Don Larsen	1.75	.85	.17
☐ 164	Bubba Morton	.85	.40	.08
☐ 165	Jim Kaat	3.50	1.75	.35
☐ 166	Johnny Keane MG	1.25	.60	.12
☐ 167	Jim Fregosi	1.75	.85	.17
☐ 168	Russ Nixon	1.25	.60	.12
☐ 169	Rookie Stars Dick Egan Julio Navarro Tommie Sisk Gaylord Perry	18.00	9.00	1.80
☐ 170	Joe Adcock	1.25	.60	.12
☐ 171	Steve Hamilton	.85	.40	.08
☐ 172	Gene Oliver	.85	.40	.08
☐ 173	Bombers' Best Tom Tresh Mickey Mantle Bobby Richardson	40.00	20.00	4.00
☐ 174	Larry Burright	.85	.40	.08
☐ 175	Bob Buhl	.85	.40	.08
☐ 176	Jim King	.85	.40	.08
☐ 177	Bubba Phillips	.85	.40	.08
☐ 178	Johnny Edwards	.85	.40	.08
☐ 179	Ron Piche	.85	.40	.08
☐ 180	Bill Skowron	1.75	.85	.17
☐ 181	Sammy Esposito	.85	.40	.08
☐ 182	Albie Pearson	.85	.40	.08
☐ 183	Joe Pepitone	2.50	1.25	.25
☐ 184	Vern Law	1.25	.60	.12
☐ 185	Chuck Hiller	.85	.40	.08
☐ 186	Jerry Zimmerman	.85	.40	.08
☐ 187	Willie Kirkland	.85	.40	.08
☐ 188	Eddie Bressoud	.85	.40	.08
☐ 189	Dave Giusti	1.25	.60	.12
☐ 190	Minnie Minoso	2.00	1.00	.20
☐ 191	Checklist 3	4.50	.75	.15
☐ 192	Clay Dalrymple	.85	.40	.08
☐ 193	Andre Rodgers	.85	.40	.08
☐ 194	Joe Nuxhall	1.25	.60	.12
☐ 195	Manny Jimenez	.85	.40	.08
☐ 196	Doug Camilli	.85	.40	.08
☐ 197	Roger Craig	2.50	1.25	.25
☐ 198	Lenny Green	1.00	.50	.10
☐ 199	Joe Amalfitano	1.00	.50	.10
☐ 200	Mickey Mantle	300.00	150.00	30.00
☐ 201	Cecil Butler	1.00	.50	.10
☐ 202	Boston Red Sox Team Card	2.50	1.25	.25
☐ 203	Chico Cardenas	1.00	.50	.10
☐ 204	Don Nottebart	1.00	.50	.10
☐ 205	Luis Aparicio	11.00	5.50	1.10
☐ 206	Ray Washburn	1.00	.50	.10
☐ 207	Ken Hunt	1.00	.50	.10
☐ 208	Rookie Stars Ron Herbel John Miller Wally Wolf Ron Taylor	1.00	.50	.10
☐ 209	Hobie Landrith	1.00	.50	.10
☐ 210	Sandy Koufax	110.00	55.00	11.00
☐ 211	Fred Whitfield	1.00	.50	.10
☐ 212	Glen Hobbie	1.00	.50	.10
☐ 213	Billy Hitchcock MG	1.00	.50	.10
☐ 214	Orlando Pena	1.00	.50	.10
☐ 215	Bob Skinner	1.00	.50	.10
☐ 216	Gene Conley	1.00	.50	.10
☐ 217	Joe Christopher	1.00	.50	.10
☐ 218	Tiger Twirlers Frank Lary Don Mossi Jim Bunning	1.50	.75	.15
☐ 219	Chuck Cottier	1.00	.50	.10
☐ 220	Camilo Pascual	1.00	.50	.10
☐ 221	Cookie Rojas	2.00	1.00	.20
☐ 222	Cubs Team	2.50	1.25	.25
☐ 223	Eddie Fisher	1.00	.50	.10
☐ 224	Mike Roarke	1.00	.50	.10
☐ 225	Joey Jay	1.00	.50	.10
☐ 226	Julian Javier	1.00	.50	.10
☐ 227	Jim Grant	1.00	.50	.10
☐ 228	Rookie Stars Max Alvis Bob Bailey Pedro Oliva Ed Kranepool	30.00	15.00	3.00

☐ 229	Willie Davis	1.50	.75	.15	☐ 309	Jim Brewer	1.50	.75	.15
☐ 230	Pete Runnels	1.00	.50	.10	☐ 310	Tommy Davis	2.50	1.25	.25
☐ 231	Eli Grba	1.00	.50	.10	☐ 311	Joe McClain	1.50	.75	.15
	(large photo is				☐ 312	Houston Colts	8.00	4.00	.80
	Ryne Duren)					Team Card			
☐ 232	Frank Malzone	1.00	.50	.10	☐ 313	Ernie Broglio	1.50	.75	.15
☐ 233	Casey Stengel MG	12.00	6.00	1.20	☐ 314	John Goryl	1.50	.75	.15
☐ 234	Dave Nicholson	1.00	.50	.10	☐ 315	Ralph Terry	2.00	1.00	.20
☐ 235	Billy O'Dell	1.00	.50	.10	☐ 316	Norm Sherry	1.50	.75	.15
☐ 236	Bill Bryan	1.00	.50	.10	☐ 317	Sam McDowell	2.50	1.25	.25
☐ 237	Jim Coates	1.00	.50	.10	☐ 318	Gene Mauch MG	2.00	1.00	.20
☐ 238	Lou Johnson	1.00	.50	.10	☐ 319	Joe Gaines	1.50	.75	.15
☐ 239	Harvey Haddix	1.50	.75	.15	☐ 320	Warren Spahn	24.00	12.00	2.40
☐ 240	Rocky Colavito	3.00	1.50	.30	☐ 321	Gino Cimoli	1.50	.75	.15
☐ 241	Bob Smith	1.00	.50	.10	☐ 322	Bob Turley	2.50	1.25	.25
☐ 242	Power Plus	18.00	9.00	1.80	☐ 323	Bill Mazeroski	2.50	1.25	.25
	Ernie Banks				☐ 324	Rookie Stars	2.50	1.25	.25
	Hank Aaron					George Williams			
☐ 243	Don Leppert	1.00	.50	.10		Pete Ward			
☐ 244	John Tsitouris	1.00	.50	.10		Phil Ward			
☐ 245	Gil Hodges	11.00	5.50	1.10		Vic Davalillo			
☐ 246	Lee Stange	1.00	.50	.10	☐ 325	Jack Sanford	2.00	1.00	.20
☐ 247	Yankees Team	10.00	5.00	1.00	☐ 326	Hank Foiles	1.50	.75	.15
☐ 248	Tito Francona	1.00	.50	.10	☐ 327	Paul Foytack	1.50	.75	.15
☐ 249	Leo Burke	1.00	.50	.10	☐ 328	Dick Williams	2.00	1.00	.20
☐ 250	Stan Musial	80.00	40.00	8.00	☐ 329	Lindy McDaniel	2.00	1.00	.20
☐ 251	Jack Lamabe	1.00	.50	.10	☐ 330	Chuck Hinton	1.50	.75	.15
☐ 252	Ron Santo	2.50	1.25	.25	☐ 331	Series Foes	2.00	1.00	.20
☐ 253	Rookie Stars	1.00	.50	.10		Bill Stafford			
	Len Gabrielson					Bill Pierce			
	Pete Jernigan				☐ 332	Joel Horlen	1.50	.75	.15
	John Wojcik				☐ 333	Carl Warwick	1.50	.75	.15
	Deacon Jones				☐ 334	Wynn Hawkins	1.50	.75	.15
☐ 254	Mike Hershberger	1.00	.50	.10	☐ 335	Leon Wagner	1.50	.75	.15
☐ 255	Bob Shaw	1.00	.50	.10	☐ 336	Ed Bauta	1.50	.75	.15
☐ 256	Jerry Lumpe	1.00	.50	.10	☐ 337	Dodgers Team	8.00	4.00	.80
☐ 257	Hank Aguirre	1.00	.50	.10	☐ 338	Russ Kemmerer	1.50	.75	.15
☐ 258	Alvin Dark MG	1.50	.75	.15	☐ 339	Ted Bowsfield	1.50	.75	.15
☐ 259	Johnny Logan	1.50	.75	.15	☐ 340	Yogi Berra	60.00	27.50	5.50
☐ 260	Jim Gentile	1.50	.75	.15	☐ 341	Jack Baldschun	1.50	.75	.15
☐ 261	Bob Miller	1.00	.50	.10	☐ 342	Gene Woodling	2.00	1.00	.20
☐ 262	Ellis Burton	1.00	.50	.10	☐ 343	Johnny Pesky MG	2.00	1.00	.20
☐ 263	Dave Stenhouse	1.00	.50	.10	☐ 344	Don Schwall	2.00	1.00	.20
☐ 264	Phil Linz	1.50	.75	.15	☐ 345	Brooks Robinson	35.00	17.50	3.50
☐ 265	Vada Pinson	2.50	1.25	.25	☐ 346	Billy Hoeft	1.50	.75	.15
☐ 266	Bob Allen	1.00	.50	.10	☐ 347	Joe Torre	3.50	1.75	.35
☐ 267	Carl Sawatski	1.00	.50	.10	☐ 348	Vic Wertz	1.50	.75	.15
☐ 268	Don Demeter	1.00	.50	.10	☐ 349	Zoilo Versalles	1.50	.75	.15
☐ 269	Don Mincher	1.00	.50	.10	☐ 350	Bob Purkey	1.50	.75	.15
☐ 270	Felipe Alou	1.50	.75	.15	☐ 351	Al Luplow	1.50	.75	.15
☐ 271	Dean Stone	1.00	.50	.10	☐ 352	Ken Johnson	1.50	.75	.15
☐ 272	Danny Murphy	1.00	.50	.10	☐ 353	Billy Williams	18.00	9.00	1.80
☐ 273	Sammy Taylor	1.00	.50	.10	☐ 354	Dom Zanni	1.50	.75	.15
☐ 274	Checklist 4	4.50	.75	.15	☐ 355	Dean Chance	2.00	1.00	.20
☐ 275	Eddie Mathews	16.00	8.00	1.60	☐ 356	John Schaive	1.50	.75	.15
☐ 276	Barry Shetrone	1.00	.50	.10	☐ 357	George Altman	1.50	.75	.15
☐ 277	Dick Farrell	1.00	.50	.10	☐ 358	Milt Pappas	2.00	1.00	.20
☐ 278	Chico Fernandez	1.00	.50	.10	☐ 359	Haywood Sullivan	2.00	1.00	.20
☐ 279	Wally Moon	1.50	.75	.15	☐ 360	Don Drysdale	18.00	9.00	1.80
☐ 280	Bob Rodgers	1.50	.75	.15	☐ 361	Clete Boyer	2.50	1.25	.25
☐ 281	Tom Sturdivant	1.00	.50	.10	☐ 362	Checklist 5	5.00	1.00	.20
☐ 282	Bobby Del Greco	1.00	.50	.10	☐ 363	Dick Radatz	2.50	1.25	.25
☐ 283	Roy Sievers	1.50	.75	.15	☐ 364	Howie Goss	1.50	.75	.15
☐ 284	Dave Sisler	1.50	.75	.15	☐ 365	Jim Bunning	6.00	3.00	.60
☐ 285	Dick Stuart	2.00	1.00	.20	☐ 366	Tony Taylor	1.50	.75	.15
☐ 286	Stu Miller	1.50	.75	.15	☐ 367	Tony Cloninger	1.50	.75	.15
☐ 287	Dick Bertell	1.50	.75	.15	☐ 368	Ed Bailey	1.50	.75	.15
☐ 288	Chicago White Sox	3.00	1.50	.30	☐ 369	Jim Lemon MG	2.00	1.00	.20
	Team Card				☐ 370	Dick Donovan	1.50	.75	.15
☐ 289	Hal Brown	1.50	.75	.15	☐ 371	Rod Kanehl	1.50	.75	.15
☐ 290	Bill White	2.50	1.25	.25	☐ 372	Don Lee	1.50	.75	.15
☐ 291	Don Rudolph	1.50	.75	.15	☐ 373	Jim Campbell	1.50	.75	.15
☐ 292	Pumpsie Green	1.50	.75	.15	☐ 374	Claude Osteen	2.00	1.00	.20
☐ 293	Bill Pleis	1.50	.75	.15	☐ 375	Ken Boyer	3.50	1.75	.35
☐ 294	Bill Rigney MG	1.50	.75	.15	☐ 376	John Wyatt	1.50	.75	.15
☐ 295	Ed Roebuck	1.50	.75	.15	☐ 377	Baltimore Orioles	3.00	1.50	.30
☐ 296	Doc Edwards	2.00	1.00	.20		Team Card			
☐ 297	Jim Golden	1.50	.75	.15	☐ 378	Bill Henry	1.50	.75	.15
☐ 298	Don Dillard	1.50	.75	.15	☐ 379	Bob Anderson	1.50	.75	.15
☐ 299	Rookie Stars	1.50	.75	.15	☐ 380	Ernie Banks	36.00	18.00	3.60
	Dave Morehead				☐ 381	Frank Baumann	1.50	.75	.15
	Bob Dustal				☐ 382	Ralph Houk MG	2.50	1.25	.25
	Tom Butters				☐ 383	Pete Richert	1.50	.75	.15
	Dan Schneider				☐ 384	Bob Tillman	1.50	.75	.15
☐ 300	Willie Mays	100.00	50.00	10.00	☐ 385	Art Mahaffey	1.50	.75	.15
☐ 301	Bill Fischer	1.50	.75	.15	☐ 386	Rookie Stars	2.00	1.00	.20
☐ 302	Whitey Herzog	2.50	1.25	.25		Ed Kirkpatrick			
☐ 303	Earl Francis	1.50	.75	.15		John Bateman			
☐ 304	Harry Bright	1.50	.75	.15		Larry Bearnarth			
☐ 305	Don Hoak	1.50	.75	.15		Garry Roggenburk			
☐ 306	Star Receivers	2.50	1.25	.25	☐ 387	Al McBean	1.50		.15
	Earl Battey				☐ 388	Jim Davenport	2.00	1.00	.20
	Elston Howard				☐ 389	Frank Sullivan	1.50	.75	.15
☐ 307	Chet Nichols	1.50	.75	.15	☐ 390	Hank Aaron	100.00	50.00	10.00
☐ 308	Camilo Carreon	1.50	.75	.15	☐ 391	Bill Dailey	1.50	.75	.15

☐ 392	Tribe Thumpers	2.00	1.00	.20
	Johnny Romano			
	Tito Francona			
☐ 393	Ken MacKenzie	1.50	.75	.15
☐ 394	Tim McCarver	6.00	3.00	.60
☐ 395	Don McMahon	1.50	.75	.15
☐ 396	Joe Koppe	1.50	.75	.15
☐ 397	Kansas City Athletics	3.00	1.50	.30
	Team Card			
☐ 398	Boog Powell	7.50	3.75	.75
☐ 399	Dick Ellsworth	2.00	1.00	.20
☐ 400	Frank Robinson	32.00	16.00	3.20
☐ 401	Jim Bouton	3.50	1.75	.35
☐ 402	Mickey Vernon	2.00	1.00	.20
☐ 403	Ron Perranoski	2.00	1.00	.20
☐ 404	Bob Oldis	1.50	.75	.15
☐ 405	Floyd Robinson	1.50	.75	.15
☐ 406	Howie Koplitz	1.50	.75	.15
☐ 407	Rookie Stars	1.50	.75	.15
	Frank Kostro			
	Chico Ruiz			
	Larry Elliot			
	Dick Simpson			
☐ 408	Billy Gardner	1.50	.75	.15
☐ 409	Roy Face	2.50	1.25	.25
☐ 410	Earl Battey	1.50	.75	.15
☐ 411	Jim Constable	1.50	.75	.15
☐ 412	Dodger Big Three	25.00	12.50	2.50
	Johnny Podres			
	Don Drysdale			
	Sandy Koufax			
☐ 413	Jerry Walker	1.50	.75	.15
☐ 414	Ty Cline	1.50	.75	.15
☐ 415	Bob Gibson	27.00	13.50	2.70
☐ 416	Alex Grammas	1.50	.75	.15
☐ 417	Giants Team	3.00	1.50	.30
☐ 418	John Orsino	1.50	.75	.15
☐ 419	Tracy Stallard	1.50	.75	.15
☐ 420	Bobby Richardson	5.00	2.50	.50
☐ 421	Tom Morgan	1.50	.75	.15
☐ 422	Fred Hutchinson MG	2.00	1.00	.20
☐ 423	Ed Hobaugh	1.50	.75	.15
☐ 424	Charlie Smith	1.50	.75	.15
☐ 425	Smoky Burgess	2.00	1.00	.20
☐ 426	Barry Latman	1.50	.75	.15
☐ 427	Bernie Allen	1.50	.75	.15
☐ 428	Carl Boles	1.50	.75	.15
☐ 429	Lou Burdette	2.50	1.25	.25
☐ 430	Norm Siebern	1.50	.75	.15
☐ 431A	Checklist 6	5.00	1.00	.20
	(white on red)			
☐ 431B	Checklist 6	10.00	2.00	.40
	(black on orange)			
☐ 432	Roman Mejias	1.50	.75	.15
☐ 433	Denis Menke	1.50	.75	.15
☐ 434	John Callison	2.00	1.00	.20
☐ 435	Woody Held	1.50	.75	.15
☐ 436	Tim Harkness	1.50	.75	.15
☐ 437	Bill Bruton	1.50	.75	.15
☐ 438	Wes Stock	1.50	.75	.15
☐ 439	Don Zimmer	2.50	1.25	.25
☐ 440	Juan Marichal	18.00	9.00	1.80
☐ 441	Lee Thomas	2.50	1.25	.25
☐ 442	J.C. Hartman	1.50	.75	.15
☐ 443	Jim Piersall	2.50	1.25	.25
☐ 444	Jim Maloney	2.50	1.25	.25
☐ 445	Norm Cash	3.00	1.50	.30
☐ 446	Whitey Ford	32.00	16.00	3.20
☐ 447	Felix Mantilla	7.00	3.50	.70
☐ 448	Jack Kralick	7.00	3.50	.70
☐ 449	Jose Tartabull	7.00	3.50	.70
☐ 450	Bob Friend	8.00	4.00	.80
☐ 451	Indians Team	12.50	6.25	1.25
☐ 452	Buddy Schultz	7.00	3.50	.70
☐ 453	Jake Wood	7.00	3.50	.70
☐ 454A	Art Fowler	7.00	3.50	.70
	(card number on			
	white background)			
☐ 454B	Art Fowler	15.00	7.50	1.50
	(card number on			
	orange background)			
☐ 455	Ruben Amaro	7.00	3.50	.70
☐ 456	Jim Coker	7.00	3.50	.70
☐ 457	Tex Clevenger	7.00	3.50	.70
☐ 458	Al Lopez MG	12.00	6.00	1.20
☐ 459	Dick LeMay	7.00	3.50	.70
☐ 460	Del Crandall	8.00	4.00	.80
☐ 461	Norm Bass	7.00	3.50	.70
☐ 462	Wally Post	7.00	3.50	.70
☐ 463	Joe Schaffernoth	7.00	3.50	.70
☐ 464	Ken Aspromonte	7.00	3.50	.70
☐ 465	Chuck Estrada	8.00	4.00	.80
☐ 466	Rookie Stars SP	24.00	12.00	2.40
	Nate Oliver			
	Tony Martinez			

	Bill Freehan			
	Jerry Robinson			
☐ 467	Phil Ortega	7.00	3.50	.70
☐ 468	Carroll Hardy	7.00	3.50	.70
☐ 469	Jay Hook	7.00	3.50	.70
☐ 470	Tom Tresh SP	24.00	12.00	2.40
☐ 471	Ken Retzer	7.00	3.50	.70
☐ 472	Lou Brock	100.00	45.00	9.00
☐ 473	New York Mets	40.00	17.50	3.50
	Team Card			
☐ 474	Jack Fisher	7.00	3.50	.70
☐ 475	Gus Triandos	8.00	4.00	.80
☐ 476	Frank Funk	7.00	3.50	.70
☐ 477	Donn Clendenon	8.00	4.00	.80
☐ 478	Paul Brown	7.00	3.50	.70
☐ 479	Ed Brinkman	7.00	3.50	.70
☐ 480	Bill Monbouquette	7.00	3.50	.70
☐ 481	Bill Taylor	7.00	3.50	.70
☐ 482	Felix Torres	7.00	3.50	.70
☐ 483	Jim Owens	7.00	3.50	.70
☐ 484	Dale Long	8.00	4.00	.80
☐ 485	Jim Landis	7.00	3.50	.70
☐ 486	Ray Sadecki	7.00	3.50	.70
☐ 487	John Roseboro	8.00	4.00	.80
☐ 488	Jerry Adair	7.00	3.50	.70
☐ 489	Paul Toth	7.00	3.50	.70
☐ 490	Willie McCovey	80.00	40.00	8.00
☐ 491	Harry Craft MG	7.00	3.50	.70
☐ 492	Dave Wickersham	7.00	3.50	.70
☐ 493	Walt Bond	7.00	3.50	.70
☐ 494	Phil Regan	8.00	4.00	.80
☐ 495	Frank Thomas	8.00	4.00	.80
☐ 496	Rookie Stars	8.00	4.00	.80
	Steve Dalkowski			
	Fred Newman			
	Jack Smith			
	Carl Bouldin			
☐ 497	Bennie Daniels	7.00	3.50	.70
☐ 498	Eddie Kasko	7.00	3.50	.70
☐ 499	J.C. Martin	7.00	3.50	.70
☐ 500	Harmon Killebrew	60.00	30.00	6.00
☐ 501	Joe Azcue	7.00	3.50	.70
☐ 502	Daryl Spencer	7.00	3.50	.70
☐ 503	Braves Team	12.50	6.25	1.25
☐ 504	Bob Johnson	7.00	3.50	.70
☐ 505	Curt Flood	14.00	7.00	1.40
☐ 506	Gene Green	7.00	3.50	.70
☐ 507	Roland Sheldon	7.00	3.50	.70
☐ 508	Ted Savage	7.00	3.50	.70
☐ 509A	Checklist 7	15.00	3.00	.40
	(copyright centered)			
☐ 509B	Checklist 7	15.00	3.00	.40
	(copyright to right)			
☐ 510	Ken McBride	7.00	3.50	.70
☐ 511	Charlie Neal	7.00	3.50	.70
☐ 512	Cal McLish	7.00	3.50	.70
☐ 513	Gary Geiger	7.00	3.50	.70
☐ 514	Larry Osborne	7.00	3.50	.70
☐ 515	Don Elston	7.00	3.50	.70
☐ 516	Purnell Goldy	7.00	3.50	.70
☐ 517	Hal Woodeshick	7.00	3.50	.70
☐ 518	Don Blasingame	7.00	3.50	.70
☐ 519	Claude Raymond	7.00	3.50	.70
☐ 520	Orlando Cepeda	15.00	7.00	1.40
☐ 521	Dan Pfister	7.00	3.50	.70
☐ 522	Rookie Stars	7.00	3.50	.70
	Mel Nelson			
	Gary Peters			
	Jim Roland			
	Art Quirk			
☐ 523	Bill Kunkel	5.00	2.50	.50
☐ 524	Cardinals Team	12.00	6.00	1.20
☐ 525	Nellie Fox	12.00	6.00	1.20
☐ 526	Dick Hall	5.00	2.50	.50
☐ 527	Ed Sadowski	5.00	2.50	.50
☐ 528	Carl Willey	5.00	2.50	.50
☐ 529	Wes Covington	6.00	3.00	.60
☐ 530	Don Mossi	6.00	3.00	.60
☐ 531	Sam Mele MG	5.00	2.50	.50
☐ 532	Steve Boros	6.00	3.00	.60
☐ 533	Bobby Shantz	7.00	3.50	.70
☐ 534	Ken Walters	5.00	2.50	.50
☐ 535	Jim Perry	7.00	3.50	.70
☐ 536	Norm Larker	5.00	2.50	.50
☐ 537	Rookie Stars	650.00	325.00	65.00
	Pedro Gonzales			
	Ken McMullen			
	Al Weis			
	Pete Rose			
☐ 538	George Brunet	5.00	2.50	.50
☐ 539	Wayne Causey	5.00	2.50	.50
☐ 540	Bob Clemente	150.00	75.00	15.00
☐ 541	Ron Moeller	5.00	2.50	.50
☐ 542	Lou Klimchock	5.00	2.50	.50
☐ 543	Russ Snyder	5.00	2.50	.50

			NRMT	VG-E	GOOD
	COMPLETE SET (587)		2500.00	1200.00	300.00
	COMMON PLAYER (1-196)		.75	.35	.07
	COMMON PLAYER (197-370)		.85	.40	.08
	COMMON PLAYER (371-522)		1.50	.75	.15
	COMMON PLAYER (523-587)		5.00	2.50	.50

□ 544	Rookie Stars	27.00	13.50	2.70
	Duke Carmel			
	Bill Haas			
	Rusty Staub			
	Dick Phillips			
□ 545	Jose Pagan	5.00	2.50	.50
□ 546	Hal Reniff	5.00	2.50	.50
□ 547	Gus Bell	6.00	3.00	.60
□ 548	Tom Satriano	5.00	2.50	.50
□ 549	Rookie Stars	5.00	2.50	.50
	Marcelino Lopez			
	Pete Lovrich			
	Paul Ratliff			
	Elmo Plaskett			
□ 550	Duke Snider	65.00	32.50	6.50
□ 551	Billy Klaus	5.00	2.50	.50
□ 552	Detroit Tigers	20.00	10.00	2.00
	Team Card			
□ 553	Rookie Stars	200.00	100.00	20.00
	Brock Davis			
	Jim Gosger			
	Willie Stargell			
	John Herrnstein			
□ 554	Hank Fischer	5.00	2.50	.50
□ 555	John Blanchard	6.00	3.00	.60
□ 556	Al Worthington	5.00	2.50	.50
□ 557	Cuno Barragan	5.00	2.50	.50
□ 558	Rookie Stars	5.00	2.50	.50
	Bill Faul			
	Ron Hunt			
	Al Moran			
	Bob Lipski			
□ 559	Danny Murtaugh MG	5.00	2.50	.50
□ 560	Ray Herbert	5.00	2.50	.50
□ 561	Mike De La Hoz	5.00	2.50	.50
□ 562	Rookie Stars	9.00	4.50	.90
	Randy Cardinal			
	Dave McNally			
	Ken Rowe			
	Don Rowe			
□ 563	Mike McCormick	6.00	3.00	.60
□ 564	George Banks	5.00	2.50	.50
□ 565	Larry Sherry	6.00	3.00	.60
□ 566	Cliff Cook	5.00	2.50	.50
□ 567	Jim Duffalo	5.00	2.50	.50
□ 568	Bob Sadowski	5.00	2.50	.50
□ 569	Luis Arroyo	6.00	3.00	.60
□ 570	Frank Bolling	5.00	2.50	.50
□ 571	Johnny Klippstein	5.00	2.50	.50
□ 572	Jack Spring	5.00	2.50	.50
□ 573	Coot Veal	5.00	2.50	.50
□ 574	Hal Kolstad	5.00	2.50	.50
□ 575	Don Cardwell	5.00	2.50	.50
□ 576	Johnny Temple	7.50	2.50	.50

1964 Topps

The cards in this 587-card set measure 2 1/2" by 3 1/2". Players in the 1964 Topps baseball series were easy to sort by team due to the giant block lettering found at the top of each card. The name and position of the player are found underneath the picture, and the card is numbered in a ball design on the orange-colored back. The usual last series scarcity holds for this set (523 to 587). Subsets within this set include League Leaders (1-12) and World Series cards (136-140).

□ 1	NL ERA Leaders	10.00	2.50	.50
	Sandy Koufax			
	Dick Ellsworth			
	Bob Friend			
□ 2	AL ERA Leaders	1.50	.75	.15
	Gary Peters			
	Juan Pizarro			
	Camilo Pascual			
□ 3	NL Pitching Leaders	6.00	3.00	.60
	Sandy Koufax			
	Juan Marichal			
	Warren Spahn			
	Jim Maloney			
□ 4	AL Pitching Leaders	2.00	1.00	.20
	Whitey Ford			
	Camilo Pascual			
	Jim Bouton			
□ 5	NL Strikeout Leaders	5.00	2.50	.50
	Sandy Koufax			
	Jim Maloney			
	Don Drysdale			
□ 6	AL Strikeout Leaders	1.50	.75	.15
	Camilo Pascual			
	Jim Bunning			
	Dick Stigman			
□ 7	NL Batting Leaders	3.50	1.75	.35
	Tommy Davis			
	Bob Clemente			
	Dick Groat			
	Hank Aaron			
□ 8	AL Batting Leaders	5.00	2.50	.50
	Carl Yastrzemski			
	Al Kaline			
	Rich Rollins			
□ 9	NL Home Run Leaders	9.00	4.50	.90
	Hank Aaron			
	Willie McCovey			
	Willie Mays			
	Orlando Cepeda			
□ 10	AL Home Run Leaders	1.50	.75	.15
	Harmon Killebrew			
	Dick Stuart			
	Bob Allison			
□ 11	NL RBI Leaders	3.00	1.50	.30
	Hank Aaron			
	Ken Boyer			
	Bill White			
□ 12	AL RBI Leaders	2.00	1.00	.20
	Dick Stuart			
	Al Kaline			
	Harmon Killebrew			
□ 13	Hoyt Wilhelm	7.50	3.75	.75
□ 14	Dodgers Rookies	.75	.35	.07
	Dick Nen			
	Nick Willhite			
□ 15	Zoilo Versalles	.75	.35	.07
□ 16	John Boozer	.75	.35	.07
□ 17	Willie Kirkland	.75	.35	.07
□ 18	Billy O'Dell	.75	.35	.07
□ 19	Don Wert	.75	.35	.07
□ 20	Bob Friend	1.00	.50	.10
□ 21	Yogi Berra	30.00	15.00	3.00
□ 22	Jerry Adair	.75	.35	.07
□ 23	Chris Zachary	.75	.35	.07
□ 24	Carl Sawatski	.75	.35	.07
□ 25	Bill Monbouquette	.75	.35	.07
□ 26	Gino Cimoli	.75	.35	.07
□ 27	New York Mets	3.00	1.50	.30
	Team Card			
□ 28	Claude Osteen	1.00	.50	.10
□ 29	Lou Brock	25.00	12.50	2.50
□ 30	Ron Perranoski	1.00	.50	.10
□ 31	Dave Nicholson	.75	.35	.07
□ 32	Dean Chance	1.25	.60	.12
□ 33	Reds Rookies	1.00	.50	.10
	Sammy Ellis			
	Mel Queen			
□ 34	Jim Perry	1.25	.60	.12
□ 35	Eddie Mathews	12.00	6.00	1.20
□ 36	Hal Reniff	.75	.35	.07
□ 37	Smoky Burgess	1.00	.50	.10
□ 38	Jim Wynn	2.00	1.00	.20
□ 39	Hank Aguirre	.75	.35	.07
□ 40	Dick Groat	1.25	.60	.12
□ 41	Friendly Foes	3.00	1.50	.30
	Willie McCovey			

		Leon Wagner			
☐	42	Moe Drabowsky	.75	.35	.07
☐	43	Roy Sievers	1.00	.50	.10
☐	44	Duke Carmel	.75	.35	.07
☐	45	Milt Pappas	1.00	.50	.10
☐	46	Ed Brinkman	.75	.35	.07
☐	47	Giants Rookies	1.00	.50	.10
		Jesus Alou			
		Ron Herbel			
☐	48	Bob Perry	.75	.35	.07
☐	49	Bill Henry	.75	.35	.07
☐	50	Mickey Mantle	200.00	100.00	20.00
☐	51	Pete Richert	.75	.35	.07
☐	52	Chuck Hinton	.75	.35	.07
☐	53	Denis Menke	.75	.35	.07
☐	54	Sam Mele MG	.75	.35	.07
☐	55	Ernie Banks	22.00	11.00	2.20
☐	56	Hal Brown	.75	.35	.07
☐	57	Tim Harkness	.75	.35	.07
☐	58	Don Demeter	.75	.35	.07
☐	59	Ernie Broglio	.75	.35	.07
☐	60	Frank Malzone	1.00	.50	.10
☐	61	Angel Backstops	1.00	.50	.10
		Bob Rodgers			
		Ed Sadowski			
☐	62	Ted Savage	.75	.35	.07
☐	63	John Orsino	.75	.35	.07
☐	64	Ted Abernathy	.75	.35	.07
☐	65	Felipe Alou	1.25	.60	.12
☐	66	Eddie Fisher	.75	.35	.07
☐	67	Tigers Team	2.00	1.00	.20
☐	68	Willie Davis	1.25	.60	.12
☐	69	Clete Boyer	1.00	.50	.10
☐	70	Joe Torre	2.00	1.00	.20
☐	71	Jack Spring	.75	.35	.07
☐	72	Chico Cardenas	.75	.35	.07
☐	73	Jimmie Hall	1.00	.50	.10
☐	74	Pirates Rookies	.75	.35	.07
		Bob Priddy			
		Tom Butters			
☐	75	Wayne Causey	.75	.35	.07
☐	76	Checklist 1	4.00	.75	.15
☐	77	Jerry Walker	.75	.35	.07
☐	78	Merritt Ranew	.75	.35	.07
☐	79	Bob Heffner	.75	.35	.07
☐	80	Vada Pinson	2.00	1.00	.20
☐	81	All-Star Vets	5.00	2.50	.50
		Nellie Fox			
		Harmon Killebrew			
☐	82	Jim Davenport	1.00	.50	.10
☐	83	Gus Triandos	1.00	.50	.10
☐	84	Carl Willey	.75	.35	.07
☐	85	Pete Ward	.75	.35	.07
☐	86	Al Downing	.75	.35	.07
☐	87	St. Louis Cardinals	2.00	1.00	.20
		Team Card			
☐	88	John Roseboro	1.00	.50	.10
☐	89	Boog Powell	2.50	1.25	.25
☐	90	Earl Battey	.75	.35	.07
☐	91	Bob Bailey	.75	.35	.07
☐	92	Steve Ridzik	.75	.35	.07
☐	93	Gary Geiger	.75	.35	.07
☐	94	Braves Rookies	.75	.35	.07
		Jim Britton			
		Larry Maxie			
☐	95	George Altman	.75	.35	.07
☐	96	Bob Buhl	.75	.35	.07
☐	97	Jim Fregosi	1.25	.60	.12
☐	98	Bill Bruton	.75	.35	.07
☐	99	Al Stanek	.75	.35	.07
☐	100	Elston Howard	2.50	1.25	.25
☐	101	Walt Alston MG	3.00	1.50	.30
☐	102	Checklist 2	4.00	.75	.15
☐	103	Curt Flood	1.75	.85	.17
☐	104	Art Mahaffey	.75	.35	.07
☐	105	Woody Held	.75	.35	.07
☐	106	Joe Nuxhall	1.00	.50	.10
☐	107	White Sox Rookies	.75	.35	.07
		Bruce Howard			
		Frank Kreutzer			
☐	108	John Wyatt	.75	.35	.07
☐	109	Rusty Staub	5.00	2.50	.50
☐	110	Albie Pearson	.75	.35	.07
☐	111	Don Elston	.75	.35	.07
☐	112	Bob Tillman	.75	.35	.07
☐	113	Grover Powell	.75	.35	.07
☐	114	Don Lock	.75	.35	.07
☐	115	Frank Bolling	.75	.35	.07
☐	116	Twins Rookies	8.00	3.75	.75
		Jay Ward			
		Tony Oliva			
☐	117	Earl Francis	.75	.35	.07
☐	118	John Blanchard	.75	.35	.07
☐	119	Gary Kolb	.75	.35	.07
☐	120	Don Drysdale	12.50	6.25	1.25
☐	121	Pete Runnels	.75	.35	.07
☐	122	Don McMahon	.75	.35	.07
☐	123	Jose Pagan	.75	.35	.07
☐	124	Orlando Pena	.75	.35	.07
☐	125	Pete Rose	175.00	85.00	18.00
☐	126	Russ Snyder	.75	.35	.07
☐	127	Angels Rookies	.75	.35	.07
		Aubrey Gatewood			
		Dick Simpson			
☐	128	Mickey Lolich	10.00	5.00	1.00
☐	129	Amado Samuel	.75	.35	.07
☐	130	Gary Peters	.75	.35	.07
☐	131	Steve Boros	.75	.35	.07
☐	132	Braves Team	2.00	1.00	.20
☐	133	Jim Grant	.75	.35	.07
☐	134	Don Zimmer	1.50	.75	.15
☐	135	Johnny Callison	1.00	.50	.10
☐	136	World Series Game 1	8.00	4.00	.80
		Koufax strikes out 15			
☐	137	World Series Game 2	2.50	1.25	.25
		Davis sparks rally			
☐	138	World Series Game 3	2.50	1.25	.25
		LA 3 straight			
☐	139	World Series Game 4	2.50	1.25	.25
		Sealing Yanks doom			
☐	140	World Series Summary	2.50	1.25	.25
		Dodgers celebrate			
☐	141	Danny Murtaugh MG	.75	.35	.07
☐	142	John Bateman	.75	.35	.07
☐	143	Bubba Phillips	.75	.35	.07
☐	144	Al Worthington	.75	.35	.07
☐	145	Norm Siebern	.75	.35	.07
☐	146	Indians Rookies	45.00	22.50	4.50
		Tommy John			
		Bob Chance			
☐	147	Ray Sadecki	.75	.35	.07
☐	148	J.C. Martin	.75	.35	.07
☐	149	Paul Foytack	.75	.35	.07
☐	150	Willie Mays	65.00	32.50	6.50
☐	151	Athletics Team	1.75	.85	.17
☐	152	Denny Lemaster	.75	.35	.07
☐	153	Dick Williams	1.00	.50	.10
☐	154	Dick Tracewski	.75	.35	.07
☐	155	Duke Snider	20.00	10.00	2.00
☐	156	Bill Dailey	.75	.35	.07
☐	157	Gene Mauch MG	1.00	.50	.10
☐	158	Ken Johnson	.75	.35	.07
☐	159	Charlie Dees	.75	.35	.07
☐	160	Ken Boyer	4.00	2.00	.40
☐	161	Dave McNally	1.50	.75	.15
☐	162	Hitting Area	1.00	.50	.10
		Dick Sisler			
		Vada Pinson			
☐	163	Donn Clendenon	1.00	.50	.10
☐	164	Bud Daley	.75	.35	.07
☐	165	Jerry Lumpe	.75	.35	.07
☐	166	Marty Keough	.75	.35	.07
☐	167	Senators Rookies	20.00	10.00	2.00
		Mike Brumley			
		Lou Piniella			
☐	168	Al Weis	.75	.35	.07
☐	169	Del Crandall	1.00	.50	.10
☐	170	Dick Radatz	1.25	.60	.12
☐	171	Ty Cline	.75	.35	.07
☐	172	Indians Team	1.75	.85	.17
☐	173	Ryne Duren	1.00	.50	.10
☐	174	Doc Edwards	1.50	.75	.15
☐	175	Billy Williams	11.00	5.50	1.10
☐	176	Tracy Stallard	.75	.35	.07
☐	177	Harmon Killebrew	12.50	6.25	1.25
☐	178	Hank Bauer MG	1.25	.60	.12
☐	179	Carl Warwick	.75	.35	.07
☐	180	Tommy Davis	1.50	.75	.15
☐	181	Dave Wickersham	.75	.35	.07
☐	182	Sox Sockers	8.00	4.00	.80
		Carl Yastrzemski			
		Chuck Schilling			
☐	183	Ron Taylor	.75	.35	.07
☐	184	Al Luplow	.75	.35	.07
☐	185	Jim O'Toole	.75	.35	.07
☐	186	Roman Mejias	.75	.35	.07
☐	187	Ed Roebuck	.75	.35	.07
☐	188	Checklist 3	4.00	.75	.15
☐	189	Bob Hendley	.75	.35	.07
☐	190	Bobby Richardson	3.50	1.75	.35
☐	191	Clay Dalrymple	.75	.35	.07
☐	192	Cubs Rookies	.75	.35	.07
		John Boccabella			
		Billy Cowan			
☐	193	Jerry Lynch	.75	.35	.07
☐	194	John Goryl	.75	.35	.07
☐	195	Floyd Robinson	.75	.35	.07
☐	196	Jim Gentile	1.00	.50	.10
☐	197	Frank Lary	1.25	.60	.12
☐	198	Len Gabrielson	.85	.40	.08

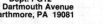

☐ 199	Joe Azcue	.85	.40	.08
☐ 200	Sandy Koufax	65.00	32.50	6.50
☐ 201	Orioles Rookies	1.25	.60	.12
	Sam Bowens			
	Wally Bunker			
☐ 202	Galen Cisco	.85	.40	.08
☐ 203	John Kennedy	.85	.40	.08
☐ 204	Matty Alou	1.25	.60	.12
☐ 205	Nellie Fox	3.50	1.75	.35
☐ 206	Steve Hamilton	.85	.40	.08
☐ 207	Fred Hutchinson MG	1.25	.60	.12
☐ 208	Wes Covington	.85	.40	.08
☐ 209	Bob Allen	.85	.40	.08
☐ 210	Carl Yastrzemski	70.00	35.00	7.00
☐ 211	Jim Coker	.85	.40	.08
☐ 212	Pete Lovrich	.85	.40	.08
☐ 213	Angels Team	1.75	.85	.17
☐ 214	Ken McMullen	.85	.40	.08
☐ 215	Ray Herbert	.85	.40	.08
☐ 216	Mike De La Hoz	.85	.40	.08
☐ 217	Jim King	.85	.40	.08
☐ 218	Hank Fischer	.85	.40	.08
☐ 219	Young Aces	2.00	1.00	.20
	Al Downing			
	Jim Bouton			
☐ 220	Dick Ellsworth	1.25	.60	.12
☐ 221	Bob Saverine	.85	.40	.08
☐ 222	Billy Pierce	1.25	.60	.12
☐ 223	George Banks	.85	.40	.08
☐ 224	Tommie Sisk	.85	.40	.08
☐ 225	Roger Maris	40.00	20.00	4.00
☐ 226	Colts Rookies	1.25	.60	.12
	Gerald Grote			
	Larry Yellen			
☐ 227	Barry Latman	.85	.40	.08
☐ 228	Felix Mantilla	.85	.40	.08
☐ 229	Charley Lau	1.25	.60	.12
☐ 230	Brooks Robinson	24.00	12.00	2.40
☐ 231	Dick Calmus	.85	.40	.08
☐ 232	Al Lopez MG	2.50	1.25	.25
☐ 233	Hal Smith	.85	.40	.08
☐ 234	Gary Bell	.85	.40	.08
☐ 235	Ron Hunt	.85	.40	.08
☐ 236	Bill Faul	.85	.40	.08
☐ 237	Cubs Team	2.00	1.00	.20
☐ 238	Roy McMillan	.85	.40	.08
☐ 239	Herm Starrette	.85	.40	.08
☐ 240	Bill White	2.00	1.00	.20
☐ 241	Jim Owens	.85	.40	.08
☐ 242	Harvey Kuenn	1.50	.75	.15
☐ 243	Phillies Rookies	10.00	5.00	1.00
	Richie Allen			
	John Herrnstein			
☐ 244	Tony LaRussa	8.00	4.00	.80
☐ 245	Dick Stigman	.85	.40	.08
☐ 246	Manny Mota	1.25	.60	.12
☐ 247	Dave DeBusschere	2.50	1.25	.25
☐ 248	Johnny Pesky MG	1.25	.60	.12
☐ 249	Doug Camilli	.85	.40	.08
☐ 250	Al Kaline	21.00	10.50	2.10
☐ 251	Choo Choo Coleman	.85	.40	.08
☐ 252	Ken Aspromonte	.85	.40	.08
☐ 253	Wally Post	.85	.40	.08
☐ 254	Don Hoak	.85	.40	.08
☐ 255	Lee Thomas	1.25	.60	.12
☐ 256	Johnny Weekly	.85	.40	.08
☐ 257	San Francisco Giants	2.00	1.00	.20
	Team Card			
☐ 258	Garry Roggenburk	.85	.40	.08
☐ 259	Harry Bright	.85	.40	.08
☐ 260	Frank Robinson	15.00	7.50	1.50
☐ 261	Jim Hannan	.85	.40	.08
☐ 262	Cards Rookies	4.00	2.00	.40
	Mike Shannon			
	Harry Fanok			
☐ 263	Chuck Estrada	1.25	.60	.12
☐ 264	Jim Landis	.85	.40	.08
☐ 265	Jim Bunning	4.00	2.00	.40
☐ 266	Gene Freese	.85	.40	.08
☐ 267	Wilbur Wood	1.25	.60	.12
☐ 268	Bill's Got It	1.25	.60	.12
	Danny Murtaugh			
	Bill Virdon			
☐ 269	Ellis Burton	.85	.40	.08
☐ 270	Rich Rollins	1.25	.60	.12
☐ 271	Bob Sadowski	.85	.40	.08
☐ 272	Jake Wood	.85	.40	.08
☐ 273	Mel Nelson	.85	.40	.08
☐ 274	Checklist 4	4.00	.75	.15
☐ 275	John Tsitouris	.85	.40	.08
☐ 276	Jose Tartabull	.85	.40	.08
☐ 277	Ken Retzer	.85	.40	.08
☐ 278	Bobby Shantz	1.50	.75	.15
☐ 279	Joe Koppe (glove on wrong hand)	1.25	.60	.12
☐ 280	Juan Marichal	9.00	4.50	.90
☐ 281	Yankees Rookies	1.25	.60	.12
	Jake Gibbs			
	Tom Metcalf			
☐ 282	Bob Bruce	.85	.40	.08
☐ 283	Tom McCraw	.85	.40	.08
☐ 284	Dick Schofield	.85	.40	.08
☐ 285	Robin Roberts	8.00	4.00	.80
☐ 286	Don Landrum	.85	.40	.08
☐ 287	Red Sox Rookies	10.00	5.00	1.00
	Tony Conigliaro			
	Bill Spanswick			
☐ 288	Al Moran	.85	.40	.08
☐ 289	Frank Funk	.85	.40	.08
☐ 290	Bob Allison	1.25	.60	.12
☐ 291	Phil Ortega	.85	.40	.08
☐ 292	Mike Roarke	.85	.40	.08
☐ 293	Phillies Team	2.00	1.00	.20
☐ 294	Ken L. Hunt	.85	.40	.08
☐ 295	Roger Craig	1.75	.85	.17
☐ 296	Ed Kirkpatrick	.85	.40	.08
☐ 297	Ken MacKenzie	.85	.40	.08
☐ 298	Harry Craft MG	.85	.40	.08
☐ 299	Bill Stafford	.85	.40	.08
☐ 300	Hank Aaron	70.00	35.00	7.00
☐ 301	Larry Brown	.85	.40	.08
☐ 302	Dan Pfister	.85	.40	.08
☐ 303	Jim Campbell	.85	.40	.08
☐ 304	Bob Johnson	.85	.40	.08
☐ 305	Jack Lamabe	.85	.40	.08
☐ 306	Giant Gunners	15.00	7.50	1.50
	Willie Mays			
	Orlando Cepeda			
☐ 307	Joe Gibbon	.85	.40	.08
☐ 308	Gene Stephens	.85	.40	.08
☐ 309	Paul Toth	.85	.40	.08
☐ 310	Jim Gilliam	2.25	1.10	.22
☐ 311	Tom Brown	.85	.40	.08
☐ 312	Tigers Rookies	.85	.40	.08
	Fritz Fisher			
	Fred Gladding			
☐ 313	Chuck Hiller	.85	.40	.08
☐ 314	Jerry Buchek	.85	.40	.08
☐ 315	Bo Belinsky	1.25	.60	.12
☐ 316	Gene Oliver	.85	.40	.08
☐ 317	Al Smith	.85	.40	.08
☐ 318	Minnesota Twins	2.00	1.00	.20
	Team Card			
☐ 319	Paul Brown	.85	.40	.08
☐ 320	Rocky Colavito	2.50	1.10	.22
☐ 321	Bob Lillis	.85	.40	.08
☐ 322	George Brunet	.85	.40	.08
☐ 323	John Buzhardt	.85	.40	.08
☐ 324	Casey Stengel MG	10.00	5.00	1.00
☐ 325	Hector Lopez	.85	.40	.08
☐ 326	Ron Brand	.85	.40	.08
☐ 327	Don Blasingame	.85	.40	.08
☐ 328	Bob Shaw	.85	.40	.08
☐ 329	Russ Nixon	1.25	.60	.12
☐ 330	Tommy Harper	1.25	.60	.12
☐ 331	AL Bombers	60.00	30.00	6.00
	Roger Maris			
	Norm Cash			
	Mickey Mantle			
	Al Kaline			
☐ 332	Ray Washburn	.85	.40	.08
☐ 333	Billy Moran	.85	.40	.08
☐ 334	Lew Krausse	.85	.40	.08
☐ 335	Don Mossi	.85	.40	.08
☐ 336	Andre Rodgers	.85	.40	.08
☐ 337	Dodgers Rookies	2.50	1.25	.25
	Al Ferrara			
	Jeff Torborg			
☐ 338	Jack Kralick	.85	.40	.08
☐ 339	Walt Bond	.85	.40	.08
☐ 340	Joe Cunningham	1.25	.60	.12
☐ 341	Jim Roland	.85	.40	.08
☐ 342	Willie Stargell	36.00	18.00	3.60
☐ 343	Senators Team	1.75	.85	.17
☐ 344	Phil Linz	1.25	.60	.12
☐ 345	Frank Thomas	1.25	.60	.12
☐ 346	Joey Jay	.85	.40	.08
☐ 347	Bobby Wine	.85	.40	.08
☐ 348	Ed Lopat MG	1.50	.75	.15
☐ 349	Art Fowler	.85	.40	.08
☐ 350	Willie McCovey	17.00	8.50	1.70
☐ 351	Dan Schneider	.85	.40	.08
☐ 352	Eddie Bressoud	.85	.40	.08
☐ 353	Wally Moon	1.25	.60	.12
☐ 354	Dave Giusti	1.25	.60	.12
☐ 355	Vic Power	.85	.40	.08
☐ 356	Reds Rookies	1.25	.60	.12
	Bill McCool			
	Chico Ruiz			
☐ 357	Charley James	.85	.40	.08

☐ 358	Ron Kline	.85	.40	.08	☐ 435	Vic Davalillo	1.50	.75	.15
☐ 359	Jim Schaffer	.85	.40	.08	☐ 436	Charlie Neal	1.50	.75	.15
☐ 360	Joe Pepitone	1.75	.85	.17	☐ 437	Ed Bailey	1.50	.75	.15
☐ 361	Jay Hook	.85	.40	.08	☐ 438	Checklist 6	5.00	1.00	.20
☐ 362	Checklist 5	4.00	1.00	.20	☐ 439	Harvey Haddix	2.00	1.00	.20
☐ 363	Dick McAuliffe	1.25	.60	.12	☐ 440	Bob Clemente	65.00	32.50	6.50
☐ 364	Joe Gaines	.85	.40	.08	☐ 441	Bob Duliba	1.50	.75	.15
☐ 365	Cal McLish	.85	.40	.08	☐ 442	Pumpsie Green	1.50	.75	.15
☐ 366	Nelson Mathews	.85	.40	.08	☐ 443	Chuck Dressen MG	2.00	1.00	.20
☐ 367	Fred Whitfield	.85	.40	.08	☐ 444	Larry Jackson	1.50	.75	.15
☐ 368	White Sox Rookies	1.50	.75	.15	☐ 445	Bill Skowron	2.50	1.25	.25
	Fritz Ackley				☐ 446	Julian Javier	1.50	.75	.15
	Don Buford				☐ 447	Ted Bowsfield	1.50	.75	.15
☐ 369	Jerry Zimmerman	.85	.40	.08	☐ 448	Cookie Rojas	2.00	1.00	.20
☐ 370	Hal Woodeshick	.85	.40	.08	☐ 449	Deron Johnson	2.00	1.00	.20
☐ 371	Frank Howard	2.00	1.00	.20	☐ 450	Steve Barber	1.50	.75	.15
☐ 372	Howie Koplitz	1.50	.75	.15	☐ 451	Joe Amalfitano	1.50	.75	.15
☐ 373	Pirates Team	3.00	1.50	.30	☐ 452	Giants Rookies	2.50	1.25	.25
☐ 374	Bobby Bolin	1.50	.75	.15		Gil Garrido			
☐ 375	Ron Santo	2.50	1.25	.25		Jim Ray Hart			
☐ 376	Dave Morehead	1.50	.75	.15	☐ 453	Frank Baumann	1.50	.75	.15
☐ 377	Bob Skinner	1.50	.75	.15	☐ 454	Tommie Aaron	2.00	1.00	.20
☐ 378	Braves Rookies	2.50	1.25	.25	☐ 455	Bernie Allen	1.50	.75	.15
	Woody Woodward				☐ 456	Dodgers Rookies	2.50	1.25	.25
	Jack Smith					Wes Parker			
☐ 379	Tony Gonzalez	1.50	.75	.15		John Werhas			
☐ 380	Whitey Ford	20.00	10.00	2.00	☐ 457	Jesse Gonder	1.50	.75	.15
☐ 381	Bob Taylor	1.50	.75	.15	☐ 458	Ralph Terry	2.00	1.00	.20
☐ 382	Wes Stock	1.50	.75	.15	☐ 459	Red Sox Rookies	1.50	.75	.15
☐ 383	Bill Rigney MG	1.50	.75	.15		Pete Charton			
☐ 384	Ron Hansen	1.50	.75	.15		Dalton Jones			
☐ 385	Curt Simmons	2.00	1.00	.20	☐ 460	Bob Gibson	22.00	11.00	2.20
☐ 386	Lenny Green	1.50	.75	.15	☐ 461	George Thomas	1.50	.75	.15
☐ 387	Terry Fox	1.50	.75	.15	☐ 462	Birdie Tebbetts MG	1.50	.75	.15
☐ 388	A's Rookies	1.50	.75	.15	☐ 463	Don Leppert	1.50	.75	.15
	John O'Donoghue				☐ 464	Dallas Green	2.50	1.25	.25
	George Williams				☐ 465	Mike Hershberger	1.50	.75	.15
☐ 389	Jim Umbricht	1.50	.75	.15	☐ 466	A's Rookies	1.50	.75	.15
☐ 390	Orlando Cepeda	5.50	2.75	.55		Dick Green			
☐ 391	Sam McDowell	2.50	1.25	.25		Aurelio Monteagudo			
☐ 392	Jim Pagliaroni	1.50	.75	.15	☐ 467	Bob Aspromonte	1.50	.75	.15
☐ 393	Casey Teaches	4.00	2.00	.40	☐ 468	Gaylord Perry	22.00	11.00	2.20
	Casey Stengel				☐ 469	Cubs Rookies	1.50	.75	.15
	Ed Kranepool					Fred Norman			
☐ 394	Bob Miller	1.50	.75	.15		Sterling Slaughter			
☐ 395	Tom Tresh	2.50	1.25	.25	☐ 470	Jim Bouton	3.00	1.50	.30
☐ 396	Dennis Bennett	1.50	.75	.15	☐ 471	Gates Brown	2.50	1.25	.25
☐ 397	Chuck Cottier	1.50	.75	.15	☐ 472	Vern Law	2.00	1.00	.20
☐ 398	Mets Rookies	1.50	.75	.15	☐ 473	Baltimore Orioles	3.00	1.50	.30
	Bill Haas					Team Card			
	Dick Smith				☐ 474	Larry Sherry	2.00	1.00	.20
☐ 399	Jackie Brandt	1.50	.75	.15	☐ 475	Ed Charles	1.50	.75	.15
☐ 400	Warren Spahn	21.00	10.50	2.10	☐ 476	Braves Rookies	5.00	2.50	.50
☐ 401	Charlie Maxwell	1.50	.75	.15		Rico Carty			
☐ 402	Tom Sturdivant	1.50	.75	.15		Dick Kelley			
☐ 403	Reds Team	3.00	1.50	.30	☐ 477	Mike Joyce	1.50	.75	.15
☐ 404	Tony Martinez	1.50	.75	.15	☐ 478	Dick Howser	2.50	1.25	.25
☐ 405	Ken McBride	1.50	.75	.15	☐ 479	Cardinals Rookies	1.50	.75	.15
☐ 406	Al Spangler	1.50	.75	.15		Dave Bakenhaster			
☐ 407	Bill Freehan	3.00	1.50	.30		Johnny Lewis			
☐ 408	Cubs Rookies	1.50	.75	.15	☐ 480	Bob Purkey	1.50	.75	.15
	Jim Stewart				☐ 481	Chuck Schilling	1.50	.75	.15
	Fred Burdette				☐ 482	Phillies Rookies	2.00	1.00	.20
☐ 409	Bill Fischer	1.50	.75	.15		John Briggs			
☐ 410	Dick Stuart	2.00	1.00	.20		Danny Cater			
☐ 411	Lee Walls	1.50	.75	.15	☐ 483	Fred Valentine	1.50	.75	.15
☐ 412	Ray Culp	1.50	.75	.15	☐ 484	Bill Pleis	1.50	.75	.15
☐ 413	Johnny Keane MG	2.00	1.00	.20	☐ 485	Tom Haller	1.50	.75	.15
☐ 414	Jack Sanford	2.00	1.00	.20	☐ 486	Bob Kennedy MG	1.50	.75	.15
☐ 415	Tony Kubek	5.00	2.50	.50	☐ 487	Mike McCormick	2.00	1.00	.20
☐ 416	Lee Maye	1.50	.75	.15	☐ 488	Yankees Rookies	1.50	.75	.15
☐ 417	Don Cardwell	1.50	.75	.15		Pete Mikkelsen			
☐ 418	Orioles Rookies	2.00	1.00	.20		Bob Meyer			
	Darold Knowles				☐ 489	Julio Navarro	1.50	.75	.15
	Les Narum				☐ 490	Ron Fairly	2.00	1.00	.20
☐ 419	Ken Harrelson	4.50	2.25	.45	☐ 491	Ed Rakow	1.50	.75	.15
☐ 420	Jim Maloney	2.50	1.25	.25	☐ 492	Colts Rookies	1.50	.75	.15
☐ 421	Camilo Carreon	1.50	.75	.15		Jim Beauchamp			
☐ 422	Jack Fisher	1.50	.75	.15		Mike White			
☐ 423	Tops in NL	60.00	27.50	5.50	☐ 493	Don Lee	1.50	.75	.15
	Hank Aaron				☐ 494	Al Jackson	1.50	.75	.15
	Willie Mays				☐ 495	Bill Virdon	2.50	1.25	.25
☐ 424	Dick Bertell	1.50	.75	.15	☐ 496	White Sox Team	3.00	1.50	.30
☐ 425	Norm Cash	2.50	1.25	.25	☐ 497	Jeoff Long	1.50	.75	.15
☐ 426	Bob Rodgers	2.00	1.00	.20	☐ 498	Dave Stenhouse	1.50	.75	.15
☐ 427	Don Rudolph	1.50	.75	.15	☐ 499	Indians Rookies	1.50	.75	.15
☐ 428	Red Sox Rookies	1.50	.75	.15		Chico Salmon			
	Archie Skeen					Gordon Seyfried			
	Pete Smith				☐ 500	Camilo Pascual	2.00	1.00	.20
☐ 429	Tim McCarver	5.00	2.50	.50	☐ 501	Bob Veale	1.50	.75	.15
☐ 430	Juan Pizarro	1.50	.75	.15	☐ 502	Angels Rookies	2.00	1.00	.20
☐ 431	George Alusik	1.50	.75	.15		Bobby Knoop			
☐ 432	Ruben Amaro	1.50	.75	.15		Bob Lee			
☐ 433	Yankees Team	10.00	5.00	1.00	☐ 503	Earl Wilson	1.50	.75	.15
☐ 434	Don Nottebart	1.50	.75	.15	☐ 504	Claude Raymond	1.50	.75	.15

☐ 505	Stan Williams	1.50	.75	.15
☐ 506	Bobby Bragan MG	1.50	.75	.15
☐ 507	Johnny Edwards	1.50	.75	.15
☐ 508	Diego Segui	1.50	.75	.15
☐ 509	Pirates Rookies	2.50	1.25	.25
	Gene Alley			
	Orlando McFarlane			
☐ 510	Lindy McDaniel	2.00	1.00	.20
☐ 511	Lou Jackson	1.50	.75	.15
☐ 512	Tigers Rookies	5.00	2.50	.50
	Willie Horton			
	Joe Sparma			
☐ 513	Don Larsen	2.50	1.25	.25
☐ 514	Jim Hickman	1.50	.75	.15
☐ 515	Johnny Romano	1.50	.75	.15
☐ 516	Twins Rookies	1.50	.75	.15
	Jerry Arrigo			
	Dwight Siebler			
☐ 517A	Checklist 7 ERR	10.00	2.00	.40
	(incorrect numbering			
	sequence on back)			
☐ 517B	Checklist 7 COR	6.00	1.00	.20
	(correct numbering			
	on back)			
☐ 518	Carl Bouldin	1.50	.75	.15
☐ 519	Charlie Smith	1.50	.75	.15
☐ 520	Jack Baldschun	1.50	.75	.15
☐ 521	Tom Satriano	1.50	.75	.15
☐ 522	Bob Tiefenauer	1.50	.75	.15
☐ 523	Lou Burdette UER	7.00	3.50	.70
	(pitching lefty)			
☐ 524	Reds Rookies	5.00	2.50	.50
	Jim Dickson			
	Bobby Klaus			
☐ 525	Al McBean	5.00	2.50	.50
☐ 526	Lou Clinton	5.00	2.50	.50
☐ 527	Larry Bearnarth	5.00	2.50	.50
☐ 528	A's Rookies	6.00	3.00	.60
	Dave Duncan			
	Tommie Reynolds			
☐ 529	Alvin Dark MG	6.00	3.00	.60
☐ 530	Leon Wagner	5.00	2.50	.50
☐ 531	Los Angeles Dodgers	10.00	5.00	1.00
	Team Card			
☐ 532	Twins Rookies	5.00	2.50	.50
	Bud Bloomfield			
	(Bloomfield photo			
	actually Jay Ward)			
	Joe Nossek			
☐ 533	Johnny Klippstein	5.00	2.50	.50
☐ 534	Gus Bell	6.00	3.00	.60
☐ 535	Phil Regan	6.00	3.00	.60
☐ 536	Mets Rookies	5.00	2.50	.50
	Larry Elliot			
	John Stephenson			
☐ 537	Dan Osinski	5.00	2.50	.50
☐ 538	Minnie Minoso	7.00	3.50	.70
☐ 539	Roy Face	6.00	3.00	.60
☐ 540	Luis Aparicio	12.50	6.25	1.25
☐ 541	Braves Rookies	125.00	60.00	12.50
	Phil Roof			
	Phil Niekro			
☐ 542	Don Mincher	6.00	3.00	.60
☐ 543	Bob Uecker	45.00	22.50	4.50
☐ 544	Colts Rookies	5.00	2.50	.50
	Steve Hertz			
	Joe Hoerner			
☐ 545	Max Alvis	5.00	2.50	.50
☐ 546	Joe Christopher	5.00	2.50	.50
☐ 547	Gil Hodges	11.00	5.50	1.10
☐ 548	NL Rookies	5.00	2.50	.50
	Wayne Schurr			
	Paul Speckenbach			
☐ 549	Joe Moeller	5.00	2.50	.50
☐ 550	Ken Hubbs	10.00	5.00	1.00
	(in memoriam)			
☐ 551	Billy Hoeft	5.00	2.50	.50
☐ 552	Indians Rookies	6.00	3.00	.60
	Tom Kelley			
	Sonny Siebert			
☐ 553	Jim Brewer	5.00	2.50	.50
☐ 554	Hank Foiles	5.00	2.50	.50
☐ 555	Lee Stange	5.00	2.50	.50
☐ 556	Mets Rookies	5.00	2.50	.50
	Steve Dillon			
	Ron Locke			
☐ 557	Leo Burke	5.00	2.50	.50
☐ 558	Don Schwall	5.00	2.50	.50
☐ 559	Dick Phillips	5.00	2.50	.50
☐ 560	Dick Farrell	5.00	2.50	.50
☐ 561	Phillies Rookies	6.00	3.00	.60
	Dave Bennett			
	(19 ... is 18)			
	Rick Wise			
☐ 562	Pedro Ramos	5.00	2.50	.50

☐ 563	Dal Maxvill	5.00	2.50	.50
☐ 564	AL Rookies	5.00	2.50	.50
	Joe McCabe			
	Jerry McNertney			
☐ 565	Stu Miller	5.00	2.50	.50
☐ 566	Ed Kranepool	6.00	3.00	.60
☐ 567	Jim Kaat	9.00	4.50	.90
☐ 568	NL Rookies	5.00	2.50	.50
	Phil Gagliano			
	Cap Peterson			
☐ 569	Fred Newman	5.00	2.50	.50
☐ 570	Bill Mazeroski	7.00	3.50	.70
☐ 571	Gene Conley	5.00	2.50	.50
☐ 572	AL Rookies	5.00	2.50	.50
	Dave Gray			
	Dick Egan			
☐ 573	Jim Duffalo	5.00	2.50	.50
☐ 574	Manny Jimenez	5.00	2.50	.50
☐ 575	Tony Cloninger	5.00	2.50	.50
☐ 576	Mets Rookies	5.00	2.50	.50
	Jerry Hinsley			
	Bill Wakefield			
☐ 577	Gordy Coleman	5.00	2.50	.50
☐ 578	Glen Hobbie	5.00	2.50	.50
☐ 579	Red Sox Team	10.00	5.00	1.00
☐ 580	Johnny Podres	7.00	3.50	.70
☐ 581	Yankees Rookies	5.00	2.50	.50
	Pedro Gonzalez			
	Archie Moore			
☐ 582	Rod Kanehl	5.00	2.50	.50
☐ 583	Tito Francona	5.00	2.50	.50
☐ 584	Joel Horlen	5.00	2.50	.50
☐ 585	Tony Taylor	5.00	2.50	.50
☐ 586	Jim Piersall	6.00	3.00	.60
☐ 587	Bennie Daniels	5.00	2.50	.50

1964 Topps Giants

The cards in this 60-card set measure 3 1/8" by 5 1/4". The 1964 Topps Giants are postcard size cards containing color player photographs. They are numbered on the backs, which also contain biographical information presented in a newspaper format. These "giant size" cards were distributed in both cellophane and waxed gum packs apart from the Topps regular issue of 1964. Cards 3, 28, 42, 45, 47, 51 and 60 slightly more difficult to find and are indicated by SP in the checklist below.

		NRMT	VG-E	GOOD
	COMPLETE SET (60)	80.00	40.00	8.00
	COMMON PLAYER (1-60)	.12	.05	.01
☐ 1	Gary Peters	.12	.05	.01
☐ 2	Ken Johnson	.12	.05	.01
☐ 3	Sandy Koufax SP	15.00	7.50	1.50
☐ 4	Bob Bailey	.12	.05	.01
☐ 5	Milt Pappas	.12	.05	.01
☐ 6	Ron Hunt	.12	.05	.01
☐ 7	Whitey Ford	2.00	1.00	.20
☐ 8	Roy McMillan	.12	.05	.01
☐ 9	Rocky Colavito	.30	.15	.03
☐ 10	Jim Bunning	.50	.25	.05
☐ 11	Bob Clemente	4.00	2.00	.40

☐ 12	Al Kaline	2.50	1.25	.25
☐ 13	Nellie Fox	.50	.25	.05
☐ 14	Tony Gonzalez	.12	.05	.01
☐ 15	Jim Gentile	.12	.05	.01
☐ 16	Dean Chance	.12	.05	.01
☐ 17	Dick Ellsworth	.12	.05	.01
☐ 18	Jim Fregosi	.15	.07	.01
☐ 19	Dick Groat	.15	.07	.01
☐ 20	Chuck Hinton	.12	.05	.01
☐ 21	Elston Howard	.30	.15	.03
☐ 22	Dick Farrell	.12	.05	.01
☐ 23	Albie Pearson	.12	.05	.01
☐ 24	Frank Howard	.20	.10	.02
☐ 25	Mickey Mantle	10.00	5.00	1.00
☐ 26	Joe Torre	.25	.12	.02
☐ 27	Eddie Brinkman	.12	.05	.01
☐ 28	Bob Friend SP	5.00	2.50	.50
☐ 29	Frank Robinson	2.00	1.00	.20
☐ 30	Bill Freehan	.15	.07	.01
☐ 31	Warren Spahn	1.50	.75	.15
☐ 32	Camilo Pascual	.12	.05	.01
☐ 33	Pete Ward	.12	.05	.01
☐ 34	Jim Maloney	.12	.05	.01
☐ 35	Dave Wickersham	.12	.05	.01
☐ 36	Johnny Callison	.12	.05	.01
☐ 37	Juan Marichal	1.50	.75	.15
☐ 38	Harmon Killebrew	1.50	.75	.15
☐ 39	Luis Aparicio	1.50	.75	.15
☐ 40	Dick Radatz	.12	.05	.01
☐ 41	Bob Gibson	1.50	.75	.15
☐ 42	Dick Stuart SP	5.00	2.50	.50
☐ 43	Tommy Davis	.15	.07	.01
☐ 44	Tony Oliva	.30	.15	.03
☐ 45	Wayne Causey SP	5.00	2.50	.50
☐ 46	Max Alvis	.12	.05	.01
☐ 47	Galen Cisco SP	5.00	2.50	.50
☐ 48	Carl Yastrzemski	4.00	2.00	.40
☐ 49	Hank Aaron	4.00	2.00	.40
☐ 50	Brooks Robinson	3.00	1.50	.30
☐ 51	Willie Mays SP	15.00	7.50	1.50
☐ 52	Billy Williams	1.50	.75	.15
☐ 53	Juan Pizarro	.12	.05	.01
☐ 54	Leon Wagner	.12	.05	.01
☐ 55	Orlando Cepeda	.50	.25	.05
☐ 56	Vada Pinson	.20	.10	.02
☐ 57	Ken Boyer	.20	.10	.02
☐ 58	Ron Santo	.20	.10	.02
☐ 59	John Romano	.12	.05	.01
☐ 60	Bill Skowron SP	5.00	2.50	.50

1964 Topps Stand Ups

BOOG POWELL
BALT. ORIOLES   OUTFIELD

In 1964 Topps produced a die-cut "Stand-Up" card design for the first time since their Connie Mack and Current All Stars of 1951. The cards have full-length, color player photos set against a green and yellow background. Of the 77 cards in the set, 22 were single printed and these are marked in the checklist below with an SP. These unnumbered cards are standard-size (2 1/2" by 3 1/2"), blank backed, and have been numbered for reference in alphabetical order of players.

	NRMT	VG-E	GOOD
COMPLETE SET (77)	2000.00	1000.00	250.00
COMMON PLAYER (1-77)	4.00	2.00	.40

COMMON PLAYER SP		20.00	10.00	2.00
☐ 1	Hank Aaron	100.00	50.00	10.00
☐ 2	Hank Aguirre	4.00	2.00	.40
☐ 3	George Altman	4.00	2.00	.40
☐ 4	Max Alvis	4.00	2.00	.40
☐ 5	Bob Aspromonte	4.00	2.00	.40
☐ 6	Jack Baldschun SP	20.00	10.00	2.00
☐ 7	Ernie Banks	40.00	20.00	4.00
☐ 8	Steve Barber	4.00	2.00	.40
☐ 9	Earl Battey	4.00	2.00	.40
☐ 10	Ken Boyer	5.00	2.50	.50
☐ 11	Ernie Broglio	4.00	2.00	.40
☐ 12	John Callison	4.00	2.00	.40
☐ 13	Norm Cash SP	25.00	12.50	2.50
☐ 14	Wayne Causey	4.00	2.00	.40
☐ 15	Orlando Cepeda	6.00	3.00	.60
☐ 16	Ed Charles	4.00	2.00	.40
☐ 17	Bob Clemente	75.00	37.50	7.50
☐ 18	Donn Clendenon SP	20.00	10.00	2.00
☐ 19	Rocky Colavito	5.00	2.50	.50
☐ 20	Ray Culp SP	20.00	10.00	2.00
☐ 21	Tommy Davis	5.00	2.50	.50
☐ 22	Don Drysdale SP	75.00	37.50	7.50
☐ 23	Dick Ellsworth	4.00	2.00	.40
☐ 24	Dick Farrell	4.00	2.00	.40
☐ 25	Jim Fregosi	5.00	2.50	.50
☐ 26	Bob Friend	4.00	2.00	.40
☐ 27	Jim Gentile	4.00	2.00	.40
☐ 28	Jesse Gonder SP	20.00	10.00	2.00
☐ 29	Tony Gonzalez SP	20.00	10.00	2.00
☐ 30	Dick Groat	4.00	2.00	.40
☐ 31	Woody Held	4.00	2.00	.40
☐ 32	Chuck Hinton	4.00	2.00	.40
☐ 33	Elston Howard	5.00	2.50	.50
☐ 34	Frank Howard SP	25.00	12.50	2.50
☐ 35	Ron Hunt	4.00	2.00	.40
☐ 36	Al Jackson	4.00	2.00	.40
☐ 37	Ken Johnson	4.00	2.00	.40
☐ 38	Al Kaline	50.00	25.00	5.00
☐ 39	Harmon Killebrew	30.00	15.00	3.00
☐ 40	Sandy Koufax	75.00	37.50	7.50
☐ 41	Don Lock SP	20.00	10.00	2.00
☐ 42	Jerry Lumpe SP	20.00	10.00	2.00
☐ 43	Jim Maloney	5.00	2.50	.50
☐ 44	Frank Malzone	5.00	2.50	.50
☐ 45	Mickey Mantle	400.00	200.00	40.00
☐ 46	Juan Marichal SP	75.00	37.50	7.50
☐ 47	Eddie Mathews SP	90.00	45.00	9.00
☐ 48	Willie Mays	90.00	45.00	9.00
☐ 49	Bill Mazeroski	5.00	2.50	.50
☐ 50	Ken McBride	4.00	2.00	.40
☐ 51	Willie McCovey SP	90.00	45.00	9.00
☐ 52	Claude Osteen	4.00	2.00	.40
☐ 53	Jim O'Toole	4.00	2.00	.40
☐ 54	Camilo Pascual	4.00	2.00	.40
☐ 55	Albie Pearson SP	20.00	10.00	2.00
☐ 56	Gary Peters	4.00	2.00	.40
☐ 57	Vada Pinson	5.00	2.50	.50
☐ 58	Juan Pizarro	4.00	2.00	.40
☐ 59	Boog Powell	6.00	3.00	.60
☐ 60	Bobby Richardson	6.00	3.00	.60
☐ 61	Brooks Robinson	45.00	22.50	4.50
☐ 62	Floyd Robinson	4.00	2.00	.40
☐ 63	Frank Robinson	35.00	17.50	3.50
☐ 64	Ed Roebuck SP	20.00	10.00	2.00
☐ 65	Rich Rollins	4.00	2.00	.40
☐ 66	John Romano	4.00	2.00	.40
☐ 67	Ron Santo SP	25.00	12.50	2.50
☐ 68	Norm Siebern	4.00	2.00	.40
☐ 69	Warren Spahn SP	90.00	45.00	9.00
☐ 70	Dick Stuart SP	20.00	10.00	2.00
☐ 71	Lee Thomas	5.00	2.50	.50
☐ 72	Joe Torre	6.00	3.00	.60
☐ 73	Pete Ward	4.00	2.00	.40
☐ 74	Bill White	25.00	12.50	2.50
☐ 75	Billy Williams SP	75.00	37.50	7.50
☐ 76	Hal Woodeshick SP	20.00	10.00	2.00
☐ 77	Carl Yastrzemski SP	350.00	175.00	35.00

1965 Topps

The cards in this 598-card set measure 2 1/2" by 3 1/2". The cards comprising the 1965 Topps set have team names located within a distinctive pennant design below the picture. The cards have blue borders on the reverse and were issued by series. Cards 523 to 598 are more difficult to obtain than

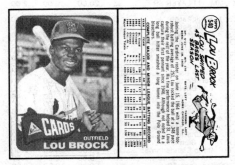

all other series. Within this last series there are 44 cards which were printed in lesser quantities than the other cards in that series; these shorter-printed cards are marked by SP in the checklist below. In addition, the sixth series (447-522) is more difficult to obtain than series one through five. Featured subsets within this set include League Leaders (1-12) and World Series cards (132-139). Key cards in this set include Steve Carlton's rookie, Mickey Mantle, and Pete Rose.

	NRMT	VG-E	GOOD
COMPLETE SET (598)	2700.00	1300.00	350.00
COMMON PLAYER (1-196)	.75	.35	.07
COMMON PLAYER (197-283)	.85	.40	.08
COMMON PLAYER (284-370)	1.00	.50	.10
COMMON PLAYER (371-446)	1.25	.60	.12
COMMON PLAYER (447-522)	3.00	1.50	.30
COMMON PLAYER (523-598)	3.50	1.75	.35
COMMON SP (523-598)	7.00	3.50	.70

☐	1 AL Batting Leaders .... Tony Oliva Elston Howard Brooks Robinson	9.00	1.50	.30
☐	2 NL Batting Leaders .... Bob Clemente Hank Aaron Rico Carty	5.00	2.50	.50
☐	3 AL Home Run Leaders ... Harmon Killebrew Mickey Mantle Boog Powell	8.00	4.00	.80
☐	4 NL Home Run Leaders ... Willie Mays Billy Williams Jim Ray Hart Orlando Cepeda Johnny Callison	5.00	2.50	.50
☐	5 AL RBI Leaders .... Brooks Robinson Harmon Killebrew Mickey Mantle Dick Stuart	8.00	4.00	.80
☐	6 NL RBI Leaders .... Ken Boyer Willie Mays Ron Santo	2.50	1.25	.25
☐	7 AL ERA Leaders .... Dean Chance Joel Horlen	1.50	.75	.15
☐	8 NL ERA Leaders .... Sandy Koufax Don Drysdale	6.00	3.00	.60
☐	9 AL Pitching Leaders .... Dean Chance Gary Peters Dave Wickersham Juan Pizarro Wally Bunker	1.50	.75	.15
☐	10 NL Pitching Leaders .... Larry Jackson Ray Sadecki Juan Marichal	1.50	.75	.15
☐	11 AL Strikeout Leaders ..... Al Downing Dean Chance Camilo Pascual	1.50	.75	.15
☐	12 NL Strikeout Leaders ..... Bob Veale Don Drysdale	2.50	1.25	.25

	Bob Gibson			
☐	13 Pedro Ramos	.75	.35	.07
☐	14 Len Gabrielson	.75	.35	.07
☐	15 Robin Roberts	7.00	3.50	.70
☐	16 Houston Rookies .... Joe Morgan Sonny Jackson	110.00	55.00	11.00
☐	17 Johnny Romano	.75	.35	.07
☐	18 Bill McCool	.75	.35	.07
☐	19 Gates Brown	1.00	.50	.10
☐	20 Jim Bunning	3.50	1.75	.35
☐	21 Don Blasingame	.75	.35	.07
☐	22 Charlie Smith	.75	.35	.07
☐	23 Bob Tiefenauer	.75	.35	.07
☐	24 Minnesota Twins .... Team Card	2.50	1.25	.25
☐	25 Al McBean	.75	.35	.07
☐	26 Bobby Knoop	.75	.35	.07
☐	27 Dick Bertell	.75	.35	.07
☐	28 Barney Schultz	.75	.35	.07
☐	29 Felix Mantilla	.75	.35	.07
☐	30 Jim Bouton	1.50	.75	.15
☐	31 Mike White	.75	.35	.07
☐	32 Herman Franks MG	.75	.35	.07
☐	33 Jackie Brandt	.75	.35	.07
☐	34 Cal Koonce	.75	.35	.07
☐	35 Ed Charles	.75	.35	.07
☐	36 Bobby Wine	.75	.35	.07
☐	37 Fred Gladding	.75	.35	.07
☐	38 Jim King	.75	.35	.07
☐	39 Gerry Arrigo	.75	.35	.07
☐	40 Frank Howard	1.50	.75	.15
☐	41 White Sox Rookies .... Bruce Howard Marv Staehle	.75	.35	.07
☐	42 Earl Wilson	.75	.35	.07
☐	43 Mike Shannon	1.25	.60	.12
☐	44 Wade Blasingame	.75	.35	.07
☐	45 Roy McMillan	.75	.35	.07
☐	46 Bob Lee	.75	.35	.07
☐	47 Tommy Harper	1.00	.50	.10
☐	48 Claude Raymond	.75	.35	.07
☐	49 Orioles Rookies .... Curt Blefary John Miller	1.25	.60	.12
☐	50 Juan Marichal	7.50	3.75	.75
☐	51 Bill Bryan	.75	.35	.07
☐	52 Ed Roebuck	.75	.35	.07
☐	53 Dick McAuliffe	1.00	.50	.10
☐	54 Joe Gibbon	.75	.35	.07
☐	55 Tony Conigliaro	3.50	1.75	.35
☐	56 Ron Kline	.75	.35	.07
☐	57 Cardinals Team	1.75	.85	.17
☐	58 Fred Talbot	.75	.35	.07
☐	59 Nate Oliver	.75	.35	.07
☐	60 Jim O'Toole	.75	.35	.07
☐	61 Chris Cannizzaro	.75	.35	.07
☐	62 Jim Katt (sic, Kaat)	4.00	2.00	.40
☐	63 Ty Cline	.75	.35	.07
☐	64 Lou Burdette	1.50	.75	.15
☐	65 Tony Kubek	3.00	1.50	.30
☐	66 Bill Rigney MG	.75	.35	.07
☐	67 Harvey Haddix	1.00	.50	.10
☐	68 Del Crandall	1.00	.50	.10
☐	69 Bill Virdon	1.25	.60	.12
☐	70 Bill Skowron	1.50	.75	.15
☐	71 John O'Donoghue	.75	.35	.07
☐	72 Tony Gonzalez	.75	.35	.07
☐	73 Dennis Ribant	.75	.35	.07
☐	74 Red Sox Rookies .... Rico Petrocelli Jerry Stephenson	3.50	1.75	.35
☐	75 Deron Johnson	1.00	.50	.10
☐	76 Sam McDowell	1.00	.50	.10
☐	77 Doug Camilli	.75	.35	.07
☐	78 Dal Maxvill	.75	.35	.07
☐	79 Checklist 1	4.00	.75	.15
☐	80 Turk Farrell	.75	.35	.07
☐	81 Don Buford	.75	.35	.07
☐	82 Braves Rookies .... Santos Alomar John Braun	1.25	.60	.12
☐	83 George Thomas	.75	.35	.07
☐	84 Ron Herbel	.75	.35	.07
☐	85 Willie Smith	.75	.35	.07
☐	86 Les Narum	.75	.35	.07
☐	87 Nelson Mathews	.75	.35	.07
☐	88 Jack Lamabe	.75	.35	.07
☐	89 Mike Hershberger	.75	.35	.07
☐	90 Rich Rollins	1.00	.50	.10
☐	91 Cubs Team	1.75	.85	.17
☐	92 Dick Howser	1.50	.75	.15
☐	93 Jack Fisher	.75	.35	.07
☐	94 Charlie Lau	1.00	.50	.10
☐	95 Bill Mazeroski	1.50	.75	.15

□	#	Player		Price1	Price2	Price3
□	96	Sonny Siebert	....	1.00	.50	.10
□	97	Pedro Gonzalez	....	.75	.35	.07
□	98	Bob Miller	....	.75	.35	.07
□	99	Gil Hodges MG	....	5.50	2.75	.55
□	100	Ken Boyer	....	2.50	1.25	.25
□	101	Fred Newman	....	.75	.35	.07
□	102	Steve Boros	....	1.00	.50	.10
□	103	Harvey Kuenn	....	1.50	.75	.15
□	104	Checklist 2	....	4.00	.75	.15
□	105	Chico Salmon	....	.75	.35	.07
□	106	Gene Oliver	....	.75	.35	.07
□	107	Phillies Rookies	....	1.50	.75	.15
		Pat Corrales				
		Costen Shockley				
□	108	Don Mincher	....	.75	.35	.07
□	109	Walt Bond	....	.75	.35	.07
□	110	Ron Santo	....	1.75	.85	.17
□	111	Lee Thomas	....	1.25	.60	.12
□	112	Derrell Griffith	....	.75	.35	.07
□	113	Steve Barber	....	.75	.35	.07
□	114	Jim Hickman	....	.75	.35	.07
□	115	Bobby Richardson	....	2.50	1.25	.25
□	116	Cardinals Rookies	....	1.25	.60	.12
		Dave Dowling				
		Bob Tolan				
□	117	Wes Stock	....	.75	.35	.07
□	118	Hal Lanier	....	1.50	.75	.15
□	119	John Kennedy	....	.75	.35	.07
□	120	Frank Robinson	....	15.00	7.50	1.50
□	121	Gene Alley	....	1.00	.50	.10
□	122	Bill Pleis	....	.75	.35	.07
□	123	Frank Thomas	....	1.00	.50	.10
□	124	Tom Satriano	....	.75	.35	.07
□	125	Juan Pizarro	....	.75	.35	.07
□	126	Dodgers Team	....	3.50	1.75	.35
□	127	Frank Lary	....	1.00	.50	.10
□	128	Vic Davalillo	....	.75	.35	.07
□	129	Bennie Daniels	....	.75	.35	.07
□	130	Al Kaline	....	18.00	9.00	1.80
□	131	Johnny Keane MG	....	1.00	.50	.10
□	132	World Series Game 1	.....	2.25	1.10	.22
		Cards take opener				
□	133	World Series Game 2	.....	2.25	1.10	.22
		Stottlemyre wins				
□	134	World Series Game 3	.....	25.00	12.50	2.50
		Mantle's homer				
□	135	World Series Game 4	.....	3.00	1.50	.30
		Boyer's grand-slam				
□	136	World Series Game 5	.....	2.25	1.10	.22
		10th inning triumph				
□	137	World Series Game 6	.....	3.00	1.50	.30
		Bouton wins again				
□	138	World Series Game 7	.....	5.00	2.50	.50
		Gibson wins finale				
□	139	World Series Summary	..	2.25	1.10	.22
		Cards celebrate				
□	140	Dean Chance	....	1.00	.50	.10
□	141	Charlie James	....	.75	.35	.07
□	142	Bill Monbouquette	....	.75	.35	.07
□	143	Pirates Rookies	....	.75	.35	.07
		John Gelnar				
		Jerry May				
□	144	Ed Kranepool	....	1.25	.60	.12
□	145	Luis Tiant	....	7.50	3.75	.75
□	146	Ron Hansen	....	.75	.35	.07
□	147	Dennis Bennett	....	.75	.35	.07
□	148	Willie Kirkland	....	.75	.35	.07
□	149	Wayne Schurr	....	.75	.35	.07
□	150	Brooks Robinson	....	18.00	9.00	1.80
□	151	Athletics Team	....	1.75	.85	.17
□	152	Phil Ortega	....	.75	.35	.07
□	153	Norm Cash	....	1.50	.75	.15
□	154	Bob Humphreys	....	.75	.35	.07
□	155	Roger Maris	....	40.00	20.00	4.00
□	156	Bob Sadowski	....	.75	.35	.07
□	157	Zoilo Versalles	....	.75	.35	.07
□	158	Dick Sisler	....	.75	.35	.07
□	159	Jim Duffalo	....	.75	.35	.07
□	160	Bob Clemente	....	55.00	27.50	5.50
□	161	Frank Baumann	....	.75	.35	.07
□	162	Russ Nixon	....	1.00	.50	.10
□	163	Johnny Briggs	....	.75	.35	.07
□	164	Al Spangler	....	.75	.35	.07
□	165	Dick Ellsworth	....	1.00	.50	.10
□	166	Indians Rookies	....	1.25	.60	.12
		George Culver				
		Tommie Agee				
□	167	Bill Wakefield	....	.75	.35	.07
□	168	Dick Green	....	.75	.35	.07
□	169	Dave Vineyard	....	.75	.35	.07
□	170	Hank Aaron	....	60.00	30.00	6.00
□	171	Jim Roland	....	.75	.35	.07
□	172	Jim Piersall	....	1.25	.60	.12
□	173	Detroit Tigers	....	1.75	.85	.17
		Team Card				

□	#	Player		Price1	Price2	Price3
□	174	Joey Jay	....	.75	.35	.07
□	175	Bob Aspromonte	....	.75	.35	.07
□	176	Willie McCovey	....	12.00	6.00	1.20
□	177	Pete Mikkelsen	....	.75	.35	.07
□	178	Dalton Jones	....	.75	.35	.07
□	179	Hal Woodeshick	....	.75	.35	.07
□	180	Bob Allison	....	1.00	.50	.10
□	181	Senators Rookies	....	.75	.35	.07
		Don Loun				
		Joe McCabe				
□	182	Mike De La Hoz	....	.75	.35	.07
□	183	Dave Nicholson	....	.75	.35	.07
□	184	John Boozer	....	.75	.35	.07
□	185	Max Alvis	....	.75	.35	.07
□	186	Billy Cowan	....	.75	.35	.07
□	187	Casey Stengel MG	....	10.00	5.00	1.00
□	188	Sam Bowens	....	.75	.35	.07
□	189	Checklist 3	....	4.00	.75	.15
□	190	Bill White	....	1.50	.75	.15
□	191	Phil Regan	....	1.00	.50	.10
□	192	Jim Coker	....	.75	.35	.07
□	193	Gaylord Perry	....	10.00	5.00	1.00
□	194	Rookie Stars	....	1.00	.50	.10
		Bill Kelso				
		Rick Reichardt				
□	195	Bob Veale	....	.75	.35	.07
□	196	Ron Fairly	....	1.00	.50	.10
□	197	Diego Segui	....	.85	.40	.08
□	198	Smoky Burgess	....	1.00	.50	.10
□	199	Bob Heffner	....	.85	.40	.08
□	200	Joe Torre	....	1.75	.85	.17
□	201	Twins Rookies	....	1.25	.60	.12
		Sandy Valdespino				
		Cesar Tovar				
□	202	Leo Burke	....	.85	.40	.08
□	203	Dallas Green	....	2.00	1.00	.20
□	204	Russ Snyder	....	.85	.40	.08
□	205	Warren Spahn	....	15.00	7.50	1.50
□	206	Willie Horton	....	1.50	.75	.15
□	207	Pete Rose	....	150.00	75.00	15.00
□	208	Tommy John	....	10.00	5.00	1.00
□	209	Pirates Team	....	1.75	.85	.17
□	210	Jim Fregosi	....	1.50	.75	.15
□	211	Steve Ridzik	....	.85	.40	.08
□	212	Ron Brand	....	.85	.40	.08
□	213	Jim Davenport	....	1.25	.60	.12
□	214	Bob Purkey	....	.85	.40	.08
□	215	Pete Ward	....	.85	.40	.08
□	216	Al Worthington	....	.85	.40	.08
□	217	Walt Alston MG	....	3.50	1.75	.35
□	218	Dick Schofield	....	.85	.40	.08
□	219	Bob Meyer	....	.85	.40	.08
□	220	Billy Williams	....	8.00	4.00	.80
□	221	John Tsitouris	....	.85	.40	.08
□	222	Bob Tillman	....	.85	.40	.08
□	223	Dan Osinski	....	.85	.40	.08
□	224	Bob Chance	....	.85	.40	.08
□	225	Bo Belinsky	....	1.25	.60	.12
□	226	Yankees Rookies	....	1.25	.60	.12
		Elvio Jimenez				
		Jake Gibbs				
□	227	Bobby Klaus	....	.85	.40	.08
□	228	Jack Sanford	....	1.25	.60	.12
□	229	Lou Clinton	....	.85	.40	.08
□	230	Ray Sadecki	....	.85	.40	.08
□	231	Jerry Adair	....	.85	.40	.08
□	232	Steve Blass	....	1.50	.75	.15
□	233	Don Zimmer	....	1.50	.75	.15
□	234	White Sox Team	....	1.75	.85	.17
□	235	Chuck Hinton	....	.85	.40	.08
□	236	Denny McLain	....	12.00	6.00	1.20
□	237	Bernie Allen	....	.85	.40	.08
□	238	Joe Moeller	....	.85	.40	.08
□	239	Doc Edwards	....	1.50	.75	.15
□	240	Bob Bruce	....	.85	.40	.08
□	241	Mack Jones	....	.85	.40	.08
□	242	George Brunet	....	.85	.40	.08
□	243	Reds Rookies	....	2.00	1.00	.20
		Ted Davidson				
		Tommy Helms				
□	244	Lindy McDaniel	....	1.25	.60	.12
□	245	Joe Pepitone	....	1.75	.85	.17
□	246	Tom Butters	....	.85	.40	.08
□	247	Wally Moon	....	1.25	.60	.12
□	248	Gus Triandos	....	1.25	.60	.12
□	249	Dave McNally	....	1.50	.75	.15
□	250	Willie Mays	....	75.00	37.50	7.50
□	251	Billy Herman MG	....	2.00	1.00	.20
□	252	Pete Richert	....	.85	.40	.08
□	253	Danny Cater	....	1.25	.60	.12
□	254	Roland Sheldon	....	.85	.40	.08
□	255	Camilo Pascual	....	1.25	.60	.12
□	256	Tito Francona	....	1.25	.60	.12
□	257	Jim Wynn	....	1.75	.85	.17
□	258	Larry Bearnarth	....	.85	.40	.08

☐ 259	Tigers Rookies Jim Northrup Ray Oyler	2.00	1.00	.20
☐ 260	Don Drysdale	12.50	6.25	1.25
☐ 261	Duke Carmel	.85	.40	.08
☐ 262	Bud Daley	.85	.40	.08
☐ 263	Marty Keough	.85	.40	.08
☐ 264	Bob Buhl	.85	.40	.08
☐ 265	Jim Pagliaroni	.85	.40	.08
☐ 266	Bert Campaneris	3.50	1.75	.35
☐ 267	Senators Team	1.75	.85	.17
☐ 268	Ken McBride	.85	.40	.08
☐ 269	Frank Bolling	.85	.40	.08
☐ 270	Milt Pappas	1.25	.60	.12
☐ 271	Don Wert	.85	.40	.08
☐ 272	Chuck Schilling	.85	.40	.08
☐ 273	Checklist 4	4.00	.75	.15
☐ 274	Lum Harris MG	.85	.40	.08
☐ 275	Dick Groat	1.50	.75	.15
☐ 276	Hoyt Wilhelm	7.50	3.75	.75
☐ 277	Johnny Lewis	.85	.40	.08
☐ 278	Ken Retzer	.85	.40	.08
☐ 279	Dick Tracewski	.85	.40	.08
☐ 280	Dick Stuart	1.25	.60	.12
☐ 281	Bill Stafford	.85	.40	.08
☐ 282	Giants Rookies Dick Estelle Masanori Murakami	1.25	.60	.12
☐ 283	Fred Whitfield	.85	.40	.08
☐ 284	Nick Willhite	1.00	.50	.10
☐ 285	Ron Hunt	1.00	.50	.10
☐ 286	Athletics Rookies Jim Dickson Aurelio Monteagudo	1.00	.50	.10
☐ 287	Gary Kolb	1.00	.50	.10
☐ 288	Jack Hamilton	1.00	.50	.10
☐ 289	Gordy Coleman	1.25	.60	.12
☐ 290	Wally Bunker	1.25	.60	.12
☐ 291	Jerry Lynch	1.00	.50	.10
☐ 292	Larry Yellen	1.00	.50	.10
☐ 293	Angels Team	2.00	1.00	.20
☐ 294	Tim McCarver	2.50	1.25	.25
☐ 295	Dick Radatz	1.50	.75	.15
☐ 296	Tony Taylor	1.00	.50	.10
☐ 297	Dave Debusschere	2.50	1.25	.25
☐ 298	Jim Stewart	1.00	.50	.10
☐ 299	Jerry Zimmerman	1.00	.50	.10
☐ 300	Sandy Koufax	75.00	37.50	7.50
☐ 301	Birdie Tebbetts MG	1.00	.50	.10
☐ 302	Al Stanek	1.00	.50	.10
☐ 303	John Orsino	1.00	.50	.10
☐ 304	Dave Stenhouse	1.00	.50	.10
☐ 305	Rico Carty	1.50	.75	.15
☐ 306	Bubba Phillips	1.00	.50	.10
☐ 307	Barry Latman	1.00	.50	.10
☐ 308	Mets Rookies Cleon Jones Tom Parsons	1.50	.75	.15
☐ 309	Steve Hamilton	1.00	.50	.10
☐ 310	Johnny Callison	1.50	.75	.15
☐ 311	Orlando Pena	1.00	.50	.10
☐ 312	Joe Nuxhall	1.50	.75	.15
☐ 313	Jim Schaffer	1.00	.50	.10
☐ 314	Sterling Slaughter	1.00	.50	.10
☐ 315	Frank Malzone	1.50	.75	.15
☐ 316	Reds Team	2.50	1.25	.25
☐ 317	Don McMahon	1.00	.50	.10
☐ 318	Matty Alou	1.50	.75	.15
☐ 319	Ken McMullen	1.00	.50	.10
☐ 320	Bob Gibson	18.00	9.00	1.80
☐ 321	Rusty Staub	3.00	1.50	.30
☐ 322	Rick Wise	1.50	.75	.15
☐ 323	Hank Bauer MG	1.50	.75	.15
☐ 324	Bobby Locke	1.00	.50	.10
☐ 325	Donn Clendenon	1.50	.75	.15
☐ 326	Dwight Siebler	1.00	.50	.10
☐ 327	Denis Menke	1.00	.50	.10
☐ 328	Eddie Fisher	1.00	.50	.10
☐ 329	Hawk Taylor	1.00	.50	.10
☐ 330	Whitey Ford	18.00	9.00	1.80
☐ 331	Dodgers Rookies Al Ferrara John Purdin	1.00	.50	.10
☐ 332	Ted Abernathy	1.00	.50	.10
☐ 333	Tom Reynolds	1.00	.50	.10
☐ 334	Vic Roznovsky	1.00	.50	.10
☐ 335	Mickey Lolich	3.00	1.50	.30
☐ 336	Woody Held	1.00	.50	.10
☐ 337	Mike Cuellar	1.50	.75	.15
☐ 338	Philadelphia Phillies Team Card	2.00	1.00	.20
☐ 339	Ryne Duren	1.50	.75	.15
☐ 340	Tony Oliva	4.50	2.00	.40
☐ 341	Bob Bolin	1.00	.50	.10
☐ 342	Bob Rodgers	1.50	.75	.15
☐ 343	Mike McCormick	1.50	.75	.15
☐ 344	Wes Parker	1.50	.75	.15
☐ 345	Floyd Robinson	1.00	.50	.10
☐ 346	Bobby Bragan MG	1.00	.50	.10
☐ 347	Roy Face	2.00	1.00	.20
☐ 348	George Banks	1.00	.50	.10
☐ 349	Larry Miller	1.00	.50	.10
☐ 350	Mickey Mantle	375.00	175.00	37.00
☐ 351	Jim Perry	1.50	.75	.15
☐ 352	Alex Johnson	1.50	.75	.15
☐ 353	Jerry Lumpe	1.00	.50	.10
☐ 354	Cubs Rookies Billy Ott Jack Warner	1.00	.50	.10
☐ 355	Vada Pinson	1.50	.75	.15
☐ 356	Bill Spanswick	1.00	.50	.10
☐ 357	Carl Warwick	1.00	.50	.10
☐ 358	Albie Pearson	1.00	.50	.10
☐ 359	Ken Johnson	1.00	.50	.10
☐ 360	Orlando Cepeda	4.00	2.00	.40
☐ 361	Checklist 5	4.00	.75	.15
☐ 362	Don Schwall	1.00	.50	.10
☐ 363	Bob Johnson	1.00	.50	.10
☐ 364	Galen Cisco	1.00	.50	.10
☐ 365	Jim Gentile	1.50	.75	.15
☐ 366	Dan Schneider	1.00	.50	.10
☐ 367	Leon Wagner	1.00	.50	.10
☐ 368	White Sox Rookies Ken Berry Joel Gibson	1.50	.75	.15
☐ 369	Phil Linz	1.50	.75	.15
☐ 370	Tommy Davis	1.50	.75	.15
☐ 371	Frank Kreutzer	1.25	.60	.12
☐ 372	Clay Dalrymple	1.25	.60	.12
☐ 373	Curt Simmons	1.50	.75	.15
☐ 374	Angels Rookies Jose Cardenal Dick Simpson	1.50	.75	.15
☐ 375	Dave Wickersham	1.25	.60	.12
☐ 376	Jim Landis	1.25	.60	.12
☐ 377	Willie Stargell	21.00	10.50	2.10
☐ 378	Chuck Estrada	1.25	.60	.12
☐ 379	Giants Team	2.50	1.25	.25
☐ 380	Rocky Colavito	2.25	1.10	.22
☐ 381	Al Jackson	1.25	.60	.12
☐ 382	J.C. Martin	1.25	.60	.12
☐ 383	Felipe Alou	1.50	.75	.15
☐ 384	Johnny Klippstein	1.25	.60	.12
☐ 385	Carl Yastrzemski	80.00	40.00	8.00
☐ 386	Cubs Rookies Paul Jaeckel Fred Norman	1.50	.75	.15
☐ 387	Johnny Podres	1.75	.85	.17
☐ 388	John Blanchard	1.75	.75	.15
☐ 389	Don Larsen	1.75	.85	.17
☐ 390	Bill Freehan	2.50	1.25	.25
☐ 391	Mel McGaha MG	1.25	.60	.12
☐ 392	Bob Friend	1.50	.75	.15
☐ 393	Ed Kirkpatrick	1.25	.60	.12
☐ 394	Jim Hannan	1.25	.60	.12
☐ 395	Jim Ray Hart	1.50	.75	.15
☐ 396	Frank Bertaina	1.25	.60	.12
☐ 397	Jerry Buchek	1.25	.60	.12
☐ 398	Reds Rookies Dan Neville Art Shamsky	1.50	.75	.15
☐ 399	Ray Herbert	1.25	.60	.12
☐ 400	Harmon Killebrew	15.00	7.50	1.50
☐ 401	Carl Willey	1.25	.60	.12
☐ 402	Joe Amalfitano	1.25	.60	.12
☐ 403	Boston Red Sox Team Card	2.50	1.25	.25
☐ 404	Stan Williams	1.50	.75	.15
☐ 405	John Roseboro	1.50	.75	.15
☐ 406	Ralph Terry	1.50	.75	.15
☐ 407	Lee Maye	1.25	.60	.12
☐ 408	Larry Sherry	1.50	.75	.15
☐ 409	Astros Rookies Jim Beauchamp Larry Dierker	1.75	.85	.17
☐ 410	Luis Aparicio	7.50	3.75	.75
☐ 411	Roger Craig	2.50	1.25	.25
☐ 412	Bob Bailey	1.25	.60	.12
☐ 413	Hal Reniff	1.25	.60	.12
☐ 414	Al Lopez MG	2.50	1.25	.25
☐ 415	Curt Flood	2.50	1.25	.25
☐ 416	Jim Brewer	1.25	.60	.12
☐ 417	Ed Brinkman	1.25	.60	.12
☐ 418	Johnny Edwards	1.25	.60	.12
☐ 419	Ruben Amaro	1.25	.60	.12
☐ 420	Larry Jackson	1.25	.60	.12
☐ 421	Twins Rookies Gary Dotter Jay Ward	1.25	.60	.12
☐ 422	Aubrey Gatewood	1.25	.60	.12

□ 423 Jesse Gonder	1.25	.60	.12
□ 424 Gary Bell	1.25	.60	.12
□ 425 Wayne Causey	1.25	.60	.12
□ 426 Braves Team	2.50	1.25	.25
□ 427 Bob Saverine	1.25	.60	.12
□ 428 Bob Shaw	1.25	.60	.12
□ 429 Don Demeter	1.25	.60	.12
□ 430 Gary Peters	1.50	.75	.15
□ 431 Cards Rookies	2.00	1.00	.20
Nelson Briles			
Wayne Spiezio			
□ 432 Jim Grant	1.25	.60	.12
□ 433 John Bateman	1.25	.60	.12
□ 434 Dave Morehead	1.25	.60	.12
□ 435 Willie Davis	1.75	.85	.17
□ 436 Don Elston	1.25	.60	.12
□ 437 Chico Cardenas	1.25	.60	.12
□ 438 Harry Walker MG	1.25	.60	.12
□ 439 Moe Drabowsky	1.25	.60	.12
□ 440 Tom Tresh	1.75	.85	.17
□ 441 Denny Lemaster	1.25	.60	.12
□ 442 Vic Power	1.25	.60	.12
□ 443 Checklist 6	4.50	.75	.15
□ 444 Bob Hendley	1.25	.60	.12
□ 445 Don Lock	1.25	.60	.12
□ 446 Art Mahaffey	1.25	.60	.12
□ 447 Julian Javier	3.00	1.50	.30
□ 448 Lee Stange	3.00	1.50	.30
□ 449 Mets Rookies	3.00	1.50	.30
Jerry Hinsley			
Gary Kroll			
□ 450 Elston Howard	4.50	2.25	.45
□ 451 Jim Owens	3.00	1.50	.30
□ 452 Gary Geiger	3.00	1.50	.30
□ 453 Dodgers Rookies	3.50	1.75	.35
Willie Crawford			
John Werhas			
□ 454 Ed Rakow	3.00	1.50	.30
□ 455 Norm Siebern	3.00	1.50	.30
□ 456 Bill Henry	3.00	1.50	.30
□ 457 Bob Kennedy MG	3.00	1.50	.30
□ 458 John Buzhardt	3.00	1.50	.30
□ 459 Frank Kostro	3.00	1.50	.30
□ 460 Richie Allen	5.00	2.50	.50
□ 461 Braves Rookies	35.00	17.50	3.50
Clay Carroll			
Phil Niekro			
□ 462 Lew Krausse	3.00	1.50	.30
(photo actually			
Pete Lovrich)			
□ 463 Manny Mota	3.50	1.75	.35
□ 464 Ron Piche	3.00	1.50	.30
□ 465 Tom Haller	3.00	1.50	.30
□ 466 Senators Rookies	3.00	1.50	.30
Pete Craig			
Dick Nen			
□ 467 Ray Washburn	3.00	1.50	.30
□ 468 Larry Brown	3.00	1.50	.30
□ 469 Don Nottebart	3.00	1.50	.30
□ 470 Yogi Berra MG	45.00	22.50	4.50
□ 471 Billy Hoeft	3.00	1.50	.30
□ 472 Don Pavletich	3.00	1.50	.30
□ 473 Orioles Rookies	10.00	5.00	1.00
Paul Blair			
Dave Johnson			
□ 474 Cookie Rojas	3.50	1.75	.35
□ 475 Clete Boyer	3.50	1.75	.35
□ 476 Billy O'Dell	3.00	1.50	.30
□ 477 Cards Rookies	250.00	110.00	22.00
Fritz Ackley			
Steve Carlton			
□ 478 Wilbur Wood	3.50	1.75	.35
□ 479 Ken Harrelson	4.00	2.00	.40
□ 480 Joel Horlen	3.00	1.50	.30
□ 481 Cleveland Indians	6.00	3.00	.60
Team Card			
□ 482 Bob Priddy	3.00	1.50	.30
□ 483 George Smith	3.00	1.50	.30
□ 484 Ron Perranoski	3.50	1.75	.35
□ 485 Nellie Fox	6.00	3.00	.60
□ 486 Angels Rookies	3.00	1.50	.30
Tom Egan			
Pat Rogan			
□ 487 Woody Woodward	3.50	1.75	.35
□ 488 Ted Wills	3.00	1.50	.30
□ 489 Gene Mauch MG	3.50	1.75	.35
□ 490 Earl Battey	3.00	1.50	.30
□ 491 Tracy Stallard	3.00	1.50	.30
□ 492 Gene Freese	3.00	1.50	.30
□ 493 Tigers Rookies	3.00	1.50	.30
Bill Roman			
Bruce Brubaker			
□ 494 Jay Ritchie	3.00	1.50	.30
□ 495 Joe Christopher	3.00	1.50	.30
□ 496 Joe Cunningham	3.50	1.75	.35

□ 497 Giants Rookies	3.50	1.75	.35
Ken Henderson			
Jack Hiatt			
□ 498 Gene Stephens	3.00	1.50	.30
□ 499 Stu Miller	3.00	1.50	.30
□ 500 Eddie Mathews	22.00	11.00	2.20
□ 501 Indians Rookies	3.00	1.50	.30
Ralph Gagliano			
Jim Rittwage			
□ 502 Don Cardwell	3.00	1.50	.30
□ 503 Phil Gagliano	3.00	1.50	.30
□ 504 Jerry Grote	3.00	1.50	.30
□ 505 Ray Culp	3.00	1.50	.30
□ 506 Sam Mele MG	3.00	1.50	.30
□ 507 Sammy Ellis	3.00	1.50	.30
□ 508 Checklist 7	7.00	1.00	.20
□ 509 Red Sox Rookies	3.00	1.50	.30
Bob Guindon			
Gerry Vezendy			
□ 510 Ernie Banks	45.00	22.50	4.50
□ 511 Ron Locke	3.00	1.50	.30
□ 512 Cap Peterson	3.00	1.50	.30
□ 513 New York Yankees	10.00	5.00	1.00
Team Card			
□ 514 Joe Azcue	3.00	1.50	.30
□ 515 Vern Law	3.50	1.75	.35
□ 516 Al Weis	3.00	1.50	.30
□ 517 Angels Rookies	3.00	1.50	.30
Paul Schaal			
Jack Warner			
□ 518 Ken Rowe	3.00	1.50	.30
□ 519 Bob Uecker	40.00	20.00	4.00
□ 520 Tony Cloninger	3.00	1.50	.30
□ 521 Phillies Rookies	3.00	1.50	.30
Dave Bennett			
Morrie Stevens			
□ 522 Hank Aguirre	3.00	1.50	.30
□ 523 Mike Brumley SP	7.00	3.50	.70
□ 524 Dave Giusti SP	7.00	3.50	.70
□ 525 Eddie Bressoud	3.50	1.75	.35
□ 526 Athletics Rookies SP	100.00	45.00	9.00
Rene Lachemann			
Johnny Odom			
Jim Hunter ERR			
("Tim" on back)			
Skip Lockwood			
□ 527 Jeff Torborg SP	9.00	4.50	.70
□ 528 George Altman	3.50	1.75	.35
□ 529 Jerry Fosnow SP	7.00	3.50	.70
□ 530 Jim Maloney	5.00	2.25	.45
□ 531 Chuck Hiller	3.50	1.75	.35
□ 532 Hector Lopez	4.00	1.75	.35
□ 533 Mets Rookies SP	20.00	9.00	1.75
Dan Napoleon			
Ron Swoboda			
Tug McGraw			
Jim Bethke			
□ 534 John Herrnstein	3.50	1.75	.35
□ 535 Jack Kralick SP	7.00	3.50	.70
□ 536 Andre Rodgers SP	7.00	3.50	.70
□ 537 Angels Rookies	4.00	1.75	.35
Marcelino Lopes			
Phil Roof			
Rudy May			
□ 538 Chuck Dressen MG SP	7.00	3.50	.70
□ 539 Herm Starrette	3.50	1.75	.35
□ 540 Lou Brock SP	45.00	20.00	4.00
□ 541 White Sox Rookies	3.50	1.75	.35
Greg Bollo			
Bob Locker			
□ 542 Lou Klimchock	3.50	1.75	.35
□ 543 Ed Connolly SP	7.00	3.50	.70
□ 544 Howie Reed	3.50	1.75	.35
□ 545 Jesus Alou SP	7.00	3.50	.70
□ 546 Indians Rookies	3.50	1.75	.35
Bill Davis			
Mike Hedlund			
Ray Barker			
Floyd Weaver			
□ 547 Jake Wood SP	7.00	3.50	.70
□ 548 Dick Stigman	3.50	1.75	.35
□ 549 Cubs Rookies SP	10.00	4.50	.90
Roberto Pena			
Glenn Beckert			
□ 550 Mel Stottlemyre SP	20.00	9.00	1.70
□ 551 New York Mets SP	15.00	6.50	1.20
Team Card			
□ 552 Julio Gotay	3.50	1.75	.35
□ 553 Astros Rookies	3.50	1.75	.35
Dan Coombs			
Gene Ratliff			
Jack McClure			
□ 554 Chico Ruiz SP	7.00	3.50	.70
□ 555 Jack Baldschun SP	7.00	3.50	.70
□ 556 Red Schoendienst	15.00	6.50	1.20

MG SP
☐ 557	Jose Santiago		3.50	1.75	.35
☐ 558	Tommie Sisk		3.50	1.75	.35
☐ 559	Ed Bailey SP		7.00	3.50	.70
☐ 560	Boog Powell SP		10.00	4.50	.90
☐ 561	Dodgers Rookies		10.00	4.50	.90
	Dennis Daboll				
	Mike Kekich				
	Hector Valle				
	Jim Lefebvre				
☐ 562	Billy Moran		3.50	1.75	.35
☐ 563	Julio Navarro		3.50	1.75	.35
☐ 564	Mel Nelson		3.50	1.75	.35
☐ 565	Ernie Broglio SP		7.00	3.50	.70
☐ 566	Yankees Rookies SP		7.00	3.50	.70
	Gil Blanco				
	Ross Moschitto				
	Art Lopez				
☐ 567	Tommie Aaron		4.00	1.75	.35
☐ 568	Ron Taylor SP		7.00	3.50	.70
☐ 569	Gino Cimoli SP		7.00	3.50	.70
☐ 570	Claude Osteen SP		7.00	3.50	.70
☐ 571	Ossie Virgil SP		7.00	3.50	.70
☐ 572	Baltimore Orioles SP		10.00	4.50	.90
	Team Card				
☐ 573	Red Sox Rookies SP		15.00	6.50	1.20
	Jim Lonborg				
	Gerry Moses				
	Bill Schlesinger				
	Mike Ryan				
☐ 574	Roy Sievers		4.00	1.75	.35
☐ 575	Jose Pagan		3.50	1.75	.35
☐ 576	Terry Fox SP		7.00	3.50	.70
☐ 577	AL Rookie Stars SP		8.00	3.50	.70
	Darold Knowles				
	Don Buschhorn				
	Richie Scheinblum				
☐ 578	Camilo Carreon SP		7.00	3.50	.70
☐ 579	Dick Smith SP		7.00	3.50	.70
☐ 580	Jimmie Hall SP		8.00	3.50	.70
☐ 581	NL Rookie Stars SP		80.00	35.00	6.50
	Tony Perez				
	Dave Ricketts				
	Kevin Collins				
☐ 582	Bob Schmidt SP		7.00	3.50	.70
☐ 583	Wes Covington SP		7.00	3.50	.70
☐ 584	Harry Bright		3.50	1.75	.35
☐ 585	Hank Fischer		3.50	1.75	.35
☐ 586	Tom McCraw SP		7.00	3.50	.70
☐ 587	Joe Sparma		3.50	1.75	.35
☐ 588	Lenny Green		3.50	1.75	.35
☐ 589	Giants Rookies SP		7.00	3.50	.70
	Frank Linzy				
	Bob Schroder				
☐ 590	John Wyatt		3.50	1.75	.35
☐ 591	Bob Skinner SP		7.00	3.50	.70
☐ 592	Frank Bork SP		7.00	3.50	.70
☐ 593	Tigers Rookies SP		7.00	3.50	.70
	Jackie Moore				
	John Sullivan				
☐ 594	Joe Gaines		3.50	1.75	.35
☐ 595	Don Lee		3.50	1.75	.35
☐ 596	Don Landrum SP		7.00	3.50	.70
☐ 597	Twins Rookies		3.50	1.75	.35
	Joe Nossek				
	John Sevcik				
	Dick Reese				
☐ 598	Al Downing SP		10.00	3.50	.70

1966 Topps

The cards in this 598-card set measure 2 1/2" by 3 1/2". There are the same number of cards as in the 1965 set. Once again, the seventh series cards (523 to 598) are considered more difficult to obtain than the cards of any other series in the set. Within this last series there are 43 cards which were printed in lesser quantities than the other cards in that series; these shorter-printed cards are marked by SP in the checklist below. The only featured subset within this set is League Leaders (215-226). Noteworthy rookie cards in the set include Jim Palmer (126) and Don Sutton (288). Palmer is described in the bio (on his card back) as a lefthander.

	NRMT	VG-E	GOOD
COMPLETE SET (598)	3600.00	1800.00	450.00
COMMON PLAYER (1-109)	.75	.35	.07

COMMON PLAYER (110-283)	.85	.40	.08
COMMON PLAYER (284-370)	1.00	.50	.10
COMMON PLAYER (371-446)	1.50	.75	.15
COMMON PLAYER (447-522)	3.50	1.75	.35
COMMON PLAYER (523-598)	12.00	6.00	1.20
COMMON SP (523-598)	25.00	12.50	2.50

☐	1	Willie Mays	125.00	30.00	6.00
☐	2	Ted Abernathy	.75	.35	.07
☐	3	Sam Mele MG	.75	.35	.07
☐	4	Ray Culp	.75	.35	.07
☐	5	Jim Fregosi	1.00	.50	.10
☐	6	Chuck Schilling	.75	.35	.07
☐	7	Tracy Stallard	.75	.35	.07
☐	8	Floyd Robinson	.75	.35	.07
☐	9	Clete Boyer	1.00	.50	.10
☐	10	Tony Cloninger	.75	.35	.07
☐	11	Senators Rookies	.75	.35	.07
		Brant Alyea			
		Pete Craig			
☐	12	John Tsitouris	.75	.35	.07
☐	13	Lou Johnson	.75	.35	.07
☐	14	Norm Siebern	.75	.35	.07
☐	15	Vern Law	1.00	.50	.10
☐	16	Larry Brown	.75	.35	.07
☐	17	John Stephenson	.75	.35	.07
☐	18	Roland Sheldon	.75	.35	.07
☐	19	San Francisco Giants	1.75	.85	.17
		Team Card			
☐	20	Willie Horton	1.00	.50	.10
☐	21	Don Nottebart	.75	.35	.07
☐	22	Joe Nossek	.75	.35	.07
☐	23	Jack Sanford	.75	.35	.07
☐	24	Don Kessinger	2.00	1.00	.20
☐	25	Pete Ward	.75	.35	.07
☐	26	Ray Sadecki	.75	.35	.07
☐	27	Orioles Rookies	1.00	.50	.10
		Darold Knowles			
		Andy Etchebarren			
☐	28	Phil Niekro	12.00	6.00	1.20
☐	29	Mike Brumley	.75	.35	.07
☐	30	Pete Rose	65.00	32.50	6.50
☐	31	Jack Cullen	.75	.35	.07
☐	32	Adolfo Phillips	.75	.35	.07
☐	33	Jim Pagliaroni	.75	.35	.07
☐	34	Checklist 1	3.50	.50	.10
☐	35	Ron Swoboda	1.00	.50	.10
☐	36	Jim Hunter	25.00	12.50	2.50
☐	37	Billy Herman MG	1.50	.75	.15
☐	38	Ron Nischwitz	.75	.35	.07
☐	39	Ken Henderson	.75	.35	.07
☐	40	Jim Grant	.75	.35	.07
☐	41	Don LeJohn	.75	.35	.07
☐	42	Aubrey Gatewood	.75	.35	.07
☐	43	Don Landrum	.75	.35	.07
☐	44	Indians Rookies	.75	.35	.07
		Bill Davis			
		Tom Kelley			
☐	45	Jim Gentile	1.00	.50	.10
☐	46	Howie Koplitz	.75	.35	.07
☐	47	J.C. Martin	.75	.35	.07
☐	48	Paul Blair	1.00	.50	.10
☐	49	Woody Woodward	1.00	.50	.10
☐	50	Mickey Mantle	175.00	85.00	18.00
☐	51	Gordon Richardson	.75	.35	.07
☐	52	Power Plus	1.00	.50	.10
		Wes Covington			
		Johnny Callison			
☐	53	Bob Duliba	.75	.35	.07
☐	54	Jose Pagan	.75	.35	.07
☐	55	Ken Harrelson	1.25	.60	.12
☐	56	Sandy Valdespino	.75	.35	.07
☐	57	Jim Lefebvre	1.25	.60	.12

☐ 58 Dave Wickersham	.75	.35	.07
☐ 59 Reds Team	1.75	.85	.17
☐ 60 Curt Flood	1.25	.60	.12
☐ 61 Bob Bolin	.75	.35	.07
☐ 62A Merritt Ranew	.75	.35	.07
(with sold line)			
☐ 62B Merritt Ranew	30.00	12.50	2.50
(without sold line)			
☐ 63 Jim Stewart	.75	.35	.07
☐ 64 Bob Bruce	.75	.35	.07
☐ 65 Leon Wagner	.75	.35	.07
☐ 66 Al Weis	.75	.35	.07
☐ 67 Mets Rookies	1.00	.50	.10
Cleon Jones			
Dick Selma			
☐ 68 Hal Reniff	.75	.35	.07
☐ 69 Ken Hamlin	.75	.35	.07
☐ 70 Carl Yastrzemski	50.00	25.00	5.00
☐ 71 Frank Carpin	.75	.35	.07
☐ 72 Tony Perez	12.00	6.00	1.20
☐ 73 Jerry Zimmerman	.75	.35	.07
☐ 74 Don Mossi	1.00	.50	.10
☐ 75 Tommy Davis	1.25	.60	.12
☐ 76 Red Schoendienst MG	4.00	2.00	.40
☐ 77 John Orsino	.75	.35	.07
☐ 78 Frank Linzy	.75	.35	.07
☐ 79 Joe Pepitone	1.50	.75	.15
☐ 80 Richie Allen	2.00	1.00	.20
☐ 81 Ray Oyler	.75	.35	.07
☐ 82 Bob Hendley	.75	.35	.07
☐ 83 Albie Pearson	.75	.35	.07
☐ 84 Braves Rookies	.75	.35	.07
Jim Beauchamp			
Dick Kelley			
☐ 85 Eddie Fisher	.75	.35	.07
☐ 86 John Bateman	.75	.35	.07
☐ 87 Dan Napoleon	.75	.35	.07
☐ 88 Fred Whitfield	.75	.35	.07
☐ 89 Ted Davidson	.75	.35	.07
☐ 90 Luis Aparicio	6.50	3.25	.65
☐ 91A Bob Uecker	15.00	7.50	1.50
(with traded line)			
☐ 91B Bob Uecker	60.00	30.00	6.00
(no traded line)			
☐ 92 Yankees Team	3.50	1.75	.35
☐ 93 Jim Lonborg	1.50	.75	.15
☐ 94 Matty Alou	1.00	.50	.10
☐ 95 Pete Richert	.75	.35	.07
☐ 96 Felipe Alou	1.00	.50	.10
☐ 97 Jim Merritt	.75	.35	.07
☐ 98 Don Demeter	.75	.35	.07
☐ 99 Buc Belters	3.50	1.75	.35
Willie Stargell			
Donn Clendenon			
☐ 100 Sandy Koufax	65.00	32.50	6.50
☐ 101A Checklist 2	5.00	1.00	.20
(115 Bill Henry)			
☐ 101B Checklist 2	10.00	2.00	.40
(115 W. Spahn)			
☐ 102 Ed Kirkpatrick	.75	.35	.07
☐ 103A Dick Groat	1.25	.60	.12
(with traded line)			
☐ 103B Dick Groat	30.00	12.50	2.50
(no traded line)			
☐ 104A Alex Johnson	1.00	.50	.10
(with traded line)			
☐ 104B Alex Johnson	30.00	12.50	2.50
(no traded line)			
☐ 105 Milt Pappas	1.00	.50	.10
☐ 106 Rusty Staub	1.75	.85	.17
☐ 107 A's Rookies	.75	.35	.07
Larry Stahl			
Ron Tompkins			
☐ 108 Bobby Klaus	.75	.35	.07
☐ 109 Ralph Terry	1.00	.50	.10
☐ 110 Ernie Banks	15.00	7.50	1.50
☐ 111 Gary Peters	.85	.40	.08
☐ 112 Manny Mota	1.25	.60	.12
☐ 113 Hank Aguirre	.85	.40	.08
☐ 114 Jim Gosger	.85	.40	.08
☐ 115 Bill Henry	.85	.40	.08
☐ 116 Walt Alston MG	3.00	1.50	.30
☐ 117 Jake Gibbs	.85	.40	.08
☐ 118 Mike McCormick	.85	.40	.08
☐ 119 Art Shamsky	.85	.40	.08
☐ 120 Harmon Killebrew	12.50	6.25	1.25
☐ 121 Ray Herbert	.85	.40	.08
☐ 122 Joe Gaines	.85	.40	.08
☐ 123 Pirates Rookies	.85	.40	.08
Frank Bork			
Jerry May			
☐ 124 Tug McGraw	2.50	1.25	.25
☐ 125 Lou Brock	12.00	6.00	1.20
☐ 126 Jim Palmer	150.00	75.00	15.00
☐ 127 Ken Berry	.85	.40	.08

☐ 128 Jim Landis	.85	.40	.08
☐ 129 Jack Kralick	.85	.40	.08
☐ 130 Joe Torre	1.50	.75	.15
☐ 131 Angels Team	1.75	.85	.17
☐ 132 Orlando Cepeda	3.50	1.75	.35
☐ 133 Don McMahon	.85	.40	.08
☐ 134 Wes Parker	1.25	.60	.12
☐ 135 Dave Morehead	.85	.40	.08
☐ 136 Woody Held	.85	.40	.08
☐ 137 Pat Corrales	1.25	.60	.12
☐ 138 Roger Repoz	.85	.40	.08
☐ 139 Cubs Rookies	.85	.40	.08
Byron Browne			
Don Young			
☐ 140 Jim Maloney	1.25	.60	.12
☐ 141 Tom McCraw	.85	.40	.08
☐ 142 Don Dennis	.85	.40	.08
☐ 143 Jose Tartabull	.85	.40	.08
☐ 144 Don Schwall	.85	.40	.08
☐ 145 Bill Freehan	1.50	.75	.15
☐ 146 George Altman	.85	.40	.08
☐ 147 Lum Harris MG	.85	.40	.08
☐ 148 Bob Johnson	.85	.40	.08
☐ 149 Dick Nen	.85	.40	.08
☐ 150 Rocky Colavito	1.50	.75	.15
☐ 151 Gary Wagner	.85	.40	.08
☐ 152 Frank Malzone	1.25	.60	.12
☐ 153 Rico Carty	1.50	.75	.15
☐ 154 Chuck Hiller	.85	.40	.08
☐ 155 Marcelino Lopez	.85	.40	.08
☐ 156 Double Play Combo	1.25	.60	.12
Dick Schofield			
Hal Lanier			
☐ 157 Rene Lachemann	1.50	.75	.15
☐ 158 Jim Brewer	.85	.40	.08
☐ 159 Chico Ruiz	.85	.40	.08
☐ 160 Whitey Ford	13.00	6.50	1.30
☐ 161 Jerry Lumpe	.85	.40	.08
☐ 162 Lee Maye	.85	.40	.08
☐ 163 Tito Francona	.85	.40	.08
☐ 164 White Sox Rookies	1.25	.60	.12
Tommie Agee			
Marv Staehle			
☐ 165 Don Lock	.85	.40	.08
☐ 166 Chris Krug	.85	.40	.08
☐ 167 Boog Powell	2.00	1.00	.20
☐ 168 Dan Osinski	.85	.40	.08
☐ 169 Duke Sims	.85	.40	.08
☐ 170 Cookie Rojas	.85	.40	.08
☐ 171 Nick Willhite	.85	.40	.08
☐ 172 Mets Team	2.00	1.00	.20
☐ 173 Al Spangler	.85	.40	.08
☐ 174 Ron Taylor	.85	.40	.08
☐ 175 Bert Campaneris	1.25	.60	.12
☐ 176 Jim Davenport	1.25	.60	.12
☐ 177 Hector Lopez	.85	.40	.08
☐ 178 Bob Tillman	.85	.40	.08
☐ 179 Cards Rookies	1.25	.60	.12
Dennis Aust			
Bob Tolan			
☐ 180 Vada Pinson	1.50	.75	.15
☐ 181 Al Worthington	.85	.40	.08
☐ 182 Jerry Lynch	.85	.40	.08
☐ 183 Checklist 3	3.50	.50	.10
☐ 184 Denis Menke	.85	.40	.08
☐ 185 Bob Buhl	.85	.40	.08
☐ 186 Ruben Amaro	.85	.40	.08
☐ 187 Chuck Dressen MG	.85	.40	.08
☐ 188 Al Luplow	.85	.40	.08
☐ 189 John Roseboro	.85	.40	.08
☐ 190 Jimmie Hall	.85	.40	.08
☐ 191 Darrell Sutherland	.85	.40	.08
☐ 192 Vic Power	.85	.40	.08
☐ 193 Dave McNally	1.25	.60	.12
☐ 194 Senators Team	1.75	.85	.17
☐ 195 Joe Morgan	32.00	16.00	3.20
☐ 196 Don Pavletich	.85	.40	.08
☐ 197 Sonny Siebert	.85	.40	.08
☐ 198 Mickey Stanley	1.25	.60	.12
☐ 199 Chisox Clubbers	1.25	.60	.12
Bill Skowron			
Johnny Romano			
Floyd Robinson			
☐ 200 Eddie Mathews	9.00	4.50	.90
☐ 201 Jim Dickson	.85	.40	.08
☐ 202 Clay Dalrymple	.85	.40	.08
☐ 203 Jose Santiago	.85	.40	.08
☐ 204 Cubs Team	1.75	.85	.17
☐ 205 Tom Tresh	1.50	.75	.15
☐ 206 Al Jackson	.85	.40	.08
☐ 207 Frank Quilici	.85	.40	.08
☐ 208 Bob Miller	.85	.40	.08
☐ 209 Tigers Rookies	1.50	.75	.15
Fritz Fisher			
John Hiller			

☐ 210	Bill Mazeroski	1.50	.75	.15
☐ 211	Frank Kreutzer	.85	.40	.08
☐ 212	Ed Kranepool	1.25	.60	.12
☐ 213	Fred Newman	.85	.40	.08
☐ 214	Tommy Harper	1.25	.60	.12
☐ 215	NL Batting Leaders	12.00	6.00	1.20
	Bob Clemente			
	Hank Aaron			
	Willie Mays			
☐ 216	AL Batting Leaders	3.00	1.50	.30
	Tony Oliva			
	Carl Yastrzemski			
	Vic Davalillo			
☐ 217	NL Home Run Leaders	9.00	4.50	.90
	Willie Mays			
	Willie McCovey			
	Billy Williams			
☐ 218	AL Home Run Leaders	2.00	1.00	.20
	Tony Conigliaro			
	Norm Cash			
	Willie Horton			
☐ 219	NL RBI Leaders	3.00	1.50	.30
	Deron Johnson			
	Frank Robinson			
	Willie Mays			
☐ 220	AL RBI Leaders	1.50	.75	.15
	Rocky Colavito			
	Willie Horton			
	Tony Oliva			
☐ 221	NL ERA Leaders	3.00	1.50	.30
	Sandy Koufax			
	Juan Marichal			
	Vern Law			
☐ 222	AL ERA Leaders	1.50	.75	.15
	Sam McDowell			
	Eddie Fisher			
	Sonny Siebert			
☐ 223	NL Pitching Leaders	3.00	1.50	.30
	Sandy Koufax			
	Tony Cloninger			
	Don Drysdale			
☐ 224	AL Pitching Leaders	1.50	.75	.15
	Jim Grant			
	Mel Stottlemyre			
	Jim Kaat			
☐ 225	NL Strikeout Leaders	3.00	1.50	.30
	Sandy Koufax			
	Bob Veale			
	Bob Gibson			
☐ 226	AL Strikeout Leaders	1.50	.75	.15
	Sam McDowell			
	Mickey Lolich			
	Dennis McLain			
	Sonny Siebert			
☐ 227	Russ Nixon	1.25	.60	.12
☐ 228	Larry Dierker	1.25	.60	.12
☐ 229	Hank Bauer MG	1.25	.60	.12
☐ 230	Johnny Callison	1.25	.60	.12
☐ 231	Floyd Weaver	.85	.40	.08
☐ 232	Glenn Beckert	1.25	.60	.12
☐ 233	Dom Zanni	.85	.40	.08
☐ 234	Yankees Rookies	3.50	1.75	.35
	Rich Beck			
	Roy White			
☐ 235	Don Cardwell	.85	.40	.08
☐ 236	Mike Hershberger	.85	.40	.08
☐ 237	Billy O'Dell	.85	.40	.08
☐ 238	Dodgers Team	2.25	1.10	.22
☐ 239	Orlando Pena	.85	.40	.08
☐ 240	Earl Battey	.85	.40	.08
☐ 241	Dennis Ribant	.85	.40	.08
☐ 242	Jesus Alou	.85	.40	.08
☐ 243	Nelson Briles	1.25	.60	.12
☐ 244	Astros Rookies	.85	.40	.08
	Chuck Harrison			
	Sonny Jackson			
☐ 245	John Buzhardt	.85	.40	.08
☐ 246	Ed Bailey	.85	.40	.08
☐ 247	Carl Warwick	.85	.40	.08
☐ 248	Pete Mikkelsen	.85	.40	.08
☐ 249	Bill Rigney MG	.85	.40	.08
☐ 250	Sammy Ellis	.85	.40	.08
☐ 251	Ed Brinkman	.85	.40	.08
☐ 252	Denny Lemaster	.85	.40	.08
☐ 253	Don Wert	.85	.40	.08
☐ 254	Phillies Rookies	33.00	15.00	3.00
	Ferguson Jenkins			
	Bill Sorrell			
☐ 255	Willie Stargell	15.00	7.50	1.50
☐ 256	Lew Krausse	.85	.40	.08
☐ 257	Jeff Torborg	1.50	.75	.15
☐ 258	Dave Giusti	1.25	.60	.12
☐ 259	Boston Red Sox	2.00	1.00	.20
	Team Card			
☐ 260	Bob Shaw	.85	.40	.08

☐ 261	Ron Hansen	.85	.40	.08
☐ 262	Jack Hamilton	.85	.40	.08
☐ 263	Tom Egan	.85	.40	.08
☐ 264	Twins Rookies	.85	.40	.08
	Andy Kosco			
	Ted Uhlaender			
☐ 265	Stu Miller	.85	.40	.08
☐ 266	Pedro Gonzalez	.85	.40	.08
	(misspelled Gonzales			
	on card back)			
☐ 267	Joe Sparma	.85	.40	.08
☐ 268	John Blanchard	.85	.40	.08
☐ 269	Don Heffner MG	.85	.40	.08
☐ 270	Claude Osteen	1.25	.60	.12
☐ 271	Hal Lanier	1.25	.60	.12
☐ 272	Jack Baldschun	.85	.40	.08
☐ 273	Astro Aces	1.25	.60	.12
	Bob Aspromonte			
	Rusty Staub			
☐ 274	Buster Narum	.85	.40	.08
☐ 275	Tim McCarver	2.00	1.00	.20
☐ 276	Jim Bouton	1.50	.75	.15
☐ 277	George Thomas	.85	.40	.08
☐ 278	Cal Koonce	.85	.40	.08
☐ 279	Checklist 4	3.50	.50	.10
☐ 280	Bobby Knoop	.85	.40	.08
☐ 281	Bruce Howard	.85	.40	.08
☐ 282	Johnny Lewis	.85	.40	.08
☐ 283	Jim Perry	1.25	.60	.12
☐ 284	Bobby Wine	1.00	.50	.10
☐ 285	Luis Tiant	2.00	1.00	.20
☐ 286	Gary Geiger	1.00	.50	.10
☐ 287	Jack Aker	1.00	.50	.10
☐ 288	Dodgers Rookies	90.00	45.00	9.00
	Bill Singer			
	Don Sutton			
☐ 289	Larry Sherry	1.25	.60	.12
☐ 290	Ron Santo	1.75	.85	.17
☐ 291	Moe Drabowsky	1.00	.50	.10
☐ 292	Jim Coker	1.00	.50	.10
☐ 293	Mike Shannon	1.50	.75	.15
☐ 294	Steve Ridzik	1.00	.50	.10
☐ 295	Jim Ray Hart	1.25	.60	.12
☐ 296	Johnny Keane MG	1.25	.60	.12
☐ 297	Jim Owens	1.00	.50	.10
☐ 298	Rico Petrocelli	1.50	.75	.15
☐ 299	Lou Burdette	1.75	.85	.17
☐ 300	Bob Clemente	65.00	32.50	6.50
☐ 301	Greg Bollo	1.00	.50	.10
☐ 302	Ernie Bowman	1.00	.50	.10
☐ 303	Cleveland Indians	2.00	1.00	.20
	Team Card			
☐ 304	John Herrnstein	1.00	.50	.10
☐ 305	Camilo Pascual	1.25	.60	.12
☐ 306	Ty Cline	1.00	.50	.10
☐ 307	Clay Carroll	1.00	.50	.10
☐ 308	Tom Haller	1.25	.60	.12
☐ 309	Diego Segui	1.00	.50	.10
☐ 310	Frank Robinson	24.00	12.00	2.40
☐ 311	Reds Rookies	1.25	.60	.12
	Tommy Helms			
	Dick Simpson			
☐ 312	Bob Saverine	1.00	.50	.10
☐ 313	Chris Zachary	1.00	.50	.10
☐ 314	Hector Valle	1.00	.50	.10
☐ 315	Norm Cash	1.75	.85	.17
☐ 316	Jack Fisher	1.00	.50	.10
☐ 317	Dalton Jones	1.00	.50	.10
☐ 318	Harry Walker MG	1.00	.50	.10
☐ 319	Gene Freese	1.00	.50	.10
☐ 320	Bob Gibson	14.00	7.00	1.40
☐ 321	Rick Reichardt	1.00	.50	.10
☐ 322	Bill Faul	1.00	.50	.10
☐ 323	Ray Barker	1.00	.50	.10
☐ 324	John Boozer	1.00	.50	.10
☐ 325	Vic Davalillo	1.00	.50	.10
☐ 326	Braves Team	2.00	1.00	.20
☐ 327	Bernie Allen	1.00	.50	.10
☐ 328	Jerry Grote	1.00	.50	.10
☐ 329	Pete Charton	1.00	.50	.10
☐ 330	Ron Fairly	1.25	.60	.12
☐ 331	Ron Herbel	1.00	.50	.10
☐ 332	Bill Bryan	1.00	.50	.10
☐ 333	Senators Rookies	1.00	.50	.10
	Joe Coleman			
	Jim French			
☐ 334	Marty Keough	1.00	.50	.10
☐ 335	Juan Pizarro	1.00	.50	.10
☐ 336	Gene Alley	1.25	.60	.12
☐ 337	Fred Gladding	1.00	.50	.10
☐ 338	Dal Maxvill	1.00	.50	.10
☐ 339	Del Crandall	1.25	.60	.12
☐ 340	Dean Chance	1.25	.60	.12
☐ 341	Wes Westrum MG	1.00	.50	.10
☐ 342	Bob Humphreys	1.00	.50	.10

☐ 343	Joe Christopher	1.00	.50	.10
☐ 344	Steve Blass	1.25	.60	.12
☐ 345	Bob Allison	1.25	.60	.12
☐ 346	Mike De La Hoz	1.00	.50	.10
☐ 347	Phil Regan	1.25	.60	.12
☐ 348	Orioles Team	2.00	1.00	.20
☐ 349	Cap Peterson	1.00	.50	.10
☐ 350	Mel Stottlemyre	2.50	1.25	.25
☐ 351	Fred Valentine	1.00	.50	.10
☐ 352	Bob Aspromonte	1.00	.50	.10
☐ 353	Al McBean	1.00	.50	.10
☐ 354	Smoky Burgess	1.25	.60	.12
☐ 355	Wade Blasingame	1.00	.50	.10
☐ 356	Red Sox Rookies	1.00	.50	.10
	Owen Johnson			
	Ken Sanders			
☐ 357	Gerry Arrigo	1.00	.50	.10
☐ 358	Charlie Smith	1.00	.50	.10
☐ 359	Johnny Briggs	1.00	.50	.10
☐ 360	Ron Hunt	1.00	.50	.10
☐ 361	Tom Satriano	1.00	.50	.10
☐ 362	Gates Brown	1.25	.60	.12
☐ 363	Checklist 5	3.50	.50	.10
☐ 364	Nate Oliver	1.00	.50	.10
☐ 365	Roger Maris	40.00	20.00	4.00
☐ 366	Wayne Causey	1.00	.50	.10
☐ 367	Mel Nelson	1.00	.50	.10
☐ 368	Charlie Lau	1.25	.60	.12
☐ 369	Jim King	1.00	.50	.10
☐ 370	Chico Cardenas	1.00	.50	.10
☐ 371	Lee Stange	1.50	.75	.15
☐ 372	Harvey Kuenn	2.50	1.25	.25
☐ 373	Giants Rookies	1.50	.75	.15
	Jack Hiatt			
	Dick Estelle			
☐ 374	Bob Locker	1.50	.75	.15
☐ 375	Donn Clendenon	2.00	1.00	.20
☐ 376	Paul Schaal	1.50	.75	.15
☐ 377	Turk Farrell	1.50	.75	.15
☐ 378	Dick Tracewski	1.50	.75	.15
☐ 379	Cardinal Team	3.00	1.50	.30
☐ 380	Tony Conigliaro	3.50	1.75	.35
☐ 381	Hank Fischer	1.50	.75	.15
☐ 382	Phil Roof	1.50	.75	.15
☐ 383	Jackie Brandt	1.50	.75	.15
☐ 384	Al Downing	2.00	1.00	.20
☐ 385	Ken Boyer	2.50	1.25	.25
☐ 386	Gil Hodges MG	4.50	2.25	.45
☐ 387	Howie Reed	1.50	.75	.15
☐ 388	Don Mincher	1.50	.75	.15
☐ 389	Jim O'Toole	1.50	.75	.15
☐ 390	Brooks Robinson	17.00	8.50	1.70
☐ 391	Chuck Hinton	1.50	.75	.15
☐ 392	Cubs Rookies	1.75	.85	.17
	Bill Hands			
	Randy Hundley			
☐ 393	George Brunet	1.50	.75	.15
☐ 394	Ron Brand	1.50	.75	.15
☐ 395	Len Gabrielson	1.50	.75	.15
☐ 396	Jerry Stephenson	1.50	.75	.15
☐ 397	Bill White	2.00	1.00	.20
☐ 398	Danny Cater	1.50	.75	.15
☐ 399	Ray Washburn	1.50	.75	.15
☐ 400	Zoilo Versalles	1.50	.75	.15
☐ 401	Ken McMullen	1.50	.75	.15
☐ 402	Jim Hickman	1.50	.75	.15
☐ 403	Fred Talbot	1.50	.75	.15
☐ 404	Pittsburgh Pirates	3.00	1.50	.30
	Team Card			
☐ 405	Elston Howard	3.00	1.50	.30
☐ 406	Joey Jay	1.50	.75	.15
☐ 407	John Kennedy	1.50	.75	.15
☐ 408	Lee Thomas	2.00	1.00	.20
☐ 409	Billy Hoeft	1.50	.75	.15
☐ 410	Al Kaline	18.00	9.00	1.80
☐ 411	Gene Mauch MG	2.00	1.00	.20
☐ 412	Sam Bowens	1.50	.75	.15
☐ 413	Johnny Romano	1.50	.75	.15
☐ 414	Dan Coombs	1.50	.75	.15
☐ 415	Max Alvis	1.50	.75	.15
☐ 416	Phil Ortega	1.50	.75	.15
☐ 417	Angels Rookies	1.50	.75	.15
	Jim McGlothlin			
	Ed Sukla			
☐ 418	Phil Gagliano	1.50	.75	.15
☐ 419	Mike Ryan	1.50	.75	.15
☐ 420	Juan Marichal	7.50	3.75	.75
☐ 421	Roy McMillan	1.50	.75	.15
☐ 422	Ed Charles	1.50	.75	.15
☐ 423	Ernie Broglio	1.50	.75	.15
☐ 424	Reds Rookies	3.50	1.75	.35
	Lee May			
	Darrell Osteen			
☐ 425	Bob Veale	1.50	.75	.15
☐ 426	White Sox Team	3.00	1.50	.30
☐ 427	John Miller	1.50	.75	.15
☐ 428	Sandy Alomar	2.00	1.00	.20
☐ 429	Bill Monbouquette	1.50	.75	.15
☐ 430	Don Drysdale	12.00	6.00	1.20
☐ 431	Walt Bond	1.50	.75	.15
☐ 432	Bob Heffner	1.50	.75	.15
☐ 433	Alvin Dark MG	2.00	1.00	.20
☐ 434	Willie Kirkland	1.50	.75	.15
☐ 435	Jim Bunning	4.50	2.25	.45
☐ 436	Julian Javier	1.50	.75	.15
☐ 437	Al Stanek	1.50	.75	.15
☐ 438	Willie Smith	1.50	.75	.15
☐ 439	Pedro Ramos	1.50	.75	.15
☐ 440	Deron Johnson	1.50	.75	.15
☐ 441	Tommie Sisk	1.50	.75	.15
☐ 442	Orioles Rookies	1.50	.75	.15
	Ed Barnowski			
	Eddie Watt			
☐ 443	Bill Wakefield	1.50	.75	.15
☐ 444	Checklist 6	5.00	1.00	.20
☐ 445	Jim Kaat	5.00	2.50	.50
☐ 446	Mack Jones	1.50	.75	.15
☐ 447	Dick Ellsworth	4.50	2.25	.45
	(photo actually			
	Ken Hubbs)			
☐ 448	Eddie Stanky MG	4.50	2.25	.45
☐ 449	Joe Moeller	3.50	1.75	.35
☐ 450	Tony Oliva	6.50	3.00	.60
☐ 451	Barry Latman	3.50	1.75	.35
☐ 452	Joe Azcue	3.50	1.75	.35
☐ 453	Ron Kline	3.50	1.75	.35
☐ 454	Jerry Buchek	3.50	1.75	.35
☐ 455	Mickey Lolich	5.00	2.50	.50
☐ 456	Red Sox Rookies	3.50	1.75	.35
	Darrell Brandon			
	Joe Foy			
☐ 457	Joe Gibbon	3.50	1.75	.35
☐ 458	Manny Jiminez	3.50	1.75	.35
☐ 459	Bill McCool	3.50	1.75	.35
☐ 460	Curt Blefary	3.50	1.75	.35
☐ 461	Roy Face	4.50	2.25	.45
☐ 462	Bob Rodgers	4.50	2.25	.45
☐ 463	Philadelphia Phillies	7.00	3.50	.70
	Team Card			
☐ 464	Larry Bearnarth	3.50	1.75	.35
☐ 465	Don Buford	4.50	2.25	.45
☐ 466	Ken Johnson	3.50	1.75	.35
☐ 467	Vic Roznovsky	3.50	1.75	.35
☐ 468	Johnny Podres	5.00	2.50	.50
☐ 469	Yankees Rookies	9.00	4.50	.90
	Bobby Murcer			
	Dooley Womack			
☐ 470	Sam McDowell	4.50	2.25	.45
☐ 471	Bob Skinner	3.50	1.75	.35
☐ 472	Terry Fox	3.50	1.75	.35
☐ 473	Rich Rollins	3.50	1.75	.35
☐ 474	Dick Schofield	3.50	1.75	.35
☐ 475	Dick Radatz	4.50	2.25	.45
☐ 476	Bobby Bragan MG	3.50	1.75	.35
☐ 477	Steve Barber	3.50	1.75	.35
☐ 478	Tony Gonzalez	3.50	1.75	.35
☐ 479	Jim Hannan	3.50	1.75	.35
☐ 480	Dick Stuart	4.50	2.25	.45
☐ 481	Bob Lee	3.50	1.75	.35
☐ 482	Cubs Rookies	3.50	1.75	.35
	John Boccabella			
	Dave Dowling			
☐ 483	Joe Nuxhall	4.50	2.25	.45
☐ 484	Wes Covington	3.50	1.75	.35
☐ 485	Bob Bailey	3.50	1.75	.35
☐ 486	Tommy John	8.00	4.00	.80
☐ 487	Al Ferrara	3.50	1.75	.35
☐ 488	George Banks	3.50	1.75	.35
☐ 489	Curt Simmons	4.50	2.25	.45
☐ 490	Bobby Richardson	8.00	4.00	.80
☐ 491	Dennis Bennett	3.50	1.75	.35
☐ 492	Athletics Team	7.00	3.50	.70
☐ 493	Johnny Klippstein	3.50	1.75	.35
☐ 494	Gordy Coleman	3.50	1.75	.35
☐ 495	Dick McAuliffe	3.50	1.75	.35
☐ 496	Lindy McDaniel	3.50	1.75	.35
☐ 497	Chris Cannizzaro	3.50	1.75	.35
☐ 498	Pirates Rookies	4.50	2.25	.45
	Luke Walker			
	Woody Fryman			
☐ 499	Wally Bunker	3.50	1.75	.35
☐ 500	Hank Aaron	75.00	37.50	7.50
☐ 501	John O'Donoghue	3.50	1.75	.35
☐ 502	Lenny Green	3.50	1.75	.35
☐ 503	Steve Hamilton	3.50	1.75	.35
☐ 504	Grady Hatton MG	3.50	1.75	.35
☐ 505	Jose Cardenal	3.50	1.75	.35
☐ 506	Bo Belinsky	3.50	1.75	.35
☐ 507	Johnny Edwards	3.50	1.75	.35
☐ 508	Steve Hargan	3.50	1.75	.35

☐ 509	Jake Wood	3.50	1.75	.35
☐ 510	Hoyt Wilhelm	11.00	5.50	1.10
☐ 511	Giants Rookies	3.50	1.75	.35
	Bob Barton			
	Tito Fuentes			
☐ 512	Dick Stigman	3.50	1.75	.35
☐ 513	Camilo Carreon	3.50	1.75	.35
☐ 514	Hal Woodeshick	3.50	1.75	.35
☐ 515	Frank Howard	4.50	2.25	.45
☐ 516	Eddie Bressoud	3.50	1.75	.35
☐ 517A	Checklist 7	10.00	1.50	.30
	529 White Sox Rookies			
	544 Cardinals Rookies			
☐ 517B	Checklist 7	10.00	1.50	.30
	529 W. Sox Rookies			
	544 Cards Rookies			
☐ 518	Braves Rookies	3.50	1.75	.35
	Herb Hippauf			
	Arnie Umbach			
☐ 519	Bob Friend	4.50	2.25	.45
☐ 520	Jim Wynn	4.50	2.25	.45
☐ 521	John Wyatt	3.50	1.75	.35
☐ 522	Phil Linz	4.50	2.25	.45
☐ 523	Bob Sadowski	12.00	6.00	1.20
☐ 524	Giants Rookies SP	25.00	12.50	2.50
	Ollie Brown			
	Don Mason			
☐ 525	Gary Bell SP	25.00	12.50	2.50
☐ 526	Twins Team SP	50.00	22.50	4.50
☐ 527	Julio Navarro	12.00	6.00	1.20
☐ 528	Jesse Gonder SP	25.00	12.50	2.50
☐ 529	White Sox Rookies	16.00	8.00	1.60
	Lee Elia			
	Dennis Higgins			
	Bill Voss			
☐ 530	Robin Roberts	35.00	17.50	3.50
☐ 531	Joe Cunningham	12.00	6.00	1.20
☐ 532	Aurelio Monteagudo SP	25.00	12.50	2.50
☐ 533	Jerry Adair SP	25.00	12.50	2.50
☐ 534	Mets Rookies	12.00	6.00	1.20
	Dave Eilers			
	Rob Gardner			
☐ 535	Willie Davis SP	30.00	15.00	3.00
☐ 536	Dick Egan	12.00	6.00	1.20
☐ 537	Herman Franks MG	12.00	6.00	1.20
☐ 538	Bob Allen SP	25.00	12.50	2.50
☐ 539	Astros Rookies	12.00	6.00	1.20
	Bill Heath			
	Carroll Sembera			
☐ 540	Denny McLain SP	50.00	22.50	4.50
☐ 541	Gene Oliver SP	25.00	12.50	2.50
☐ 542	George Smith	12.00	6.00	1.20
☐ 543	Roger Craig SP	30.00	15.00	3.00
☐ 544	Cardinals Rookies SP	25.00	12.50	2.50
	Joe Hoerner			
	George Kernek			
	Jimmy Williams			
☐ 545	Dick Green SP	25.00	12.50	2.50
☐ 546	Dwight Siebler	12.00	6.00	1.20
☐ 547	Horace Clarke SP	35.00	15.00	3.00
☐ 548	Gary Kroll SP	25.00	12.50	2.50
☐ 549	Senators Rookies	12.00	6.00	1.20
	Al Closter			
	Casey Cox			
☐ 550	Willie McCovey SP	100.00	45.00	9.00
☐ 551	Bob Purkey SP	25.00	12.50	2.50
☐ 552	Birdie Tebbetts	25.00	12.50	2.50
	MG SP			
☐ 553	Rookie Stars	12.00	6.00	1.20
	Pat Garrett			
	Jackie Warner			
☐ 554	Jim Northrup SP	30.00	15.00	3.00
☐ 555	Ron Perranoski SP	30.00	15.00	3.00
☐ 556	Mel Queen SP	25.00	12.50	2.50
☐ 557	Felix Mantilla SP	25.00	12.50	2.50
☐ 558	Red Sox Rookies	18.00	9.00	1.80
	Guido Grilli			
	Pete Magrini			
	George Scott			
☐ 559	Roberto Pena SP	25.00	12.50	2.50
☐ 560	Joel Horlen	12.00	6.00	1.20
☐ 561	ChooChoo Coleman SP	30.00	15.00	3.00
☐ 562	Russ Snyder	12.00	6.00	1.20
☐ 563	Twins Rookies	12.00	6.00	1.20
	Pete Cimino			
	Cesar Tovar			
☐ 564	Bob Chance SP	25.00	12.50	2.50
☐ 565	Jim Piersall SP	30.00	15.00	3.00
☐ 566	Mike Cuellar SP	30.00	15.00	3.00
☐ 567	Dick Howser SP	30.00	15.00	3.00
☐ 568	Athletics Rookies	12.00	6.00	1.20
	Paul Lindblad			
	Rod Stone			
☐ 569	Orlando McFarlane SP	25.00	12.50	2.50
☐ 570	Art Mahaffey SP	25.00	12.50	2.50

☐ 571	Dave Roberts SP	25.00	12.50	2.50
☐ 572	Bob Priddy	12.00	6.00	1.20
☐ 573	Derrell Griffith	12.00	6.00	1.20
☐ 574	Mets Rookies	12.00	6.00	1.20
	Bill Hepler			
	Bill Murphy			
☐ 575	Earl Wilson	12.00	6.00	1.20
☐ 576	Dave Nicholson SP	25.00	12.50	2.50
☐ 577	Jack Lamabe SP	25.00	12.50	2.50
☐ 578	Chi Chi Olivo SP	25.00	12.50	2.50
☐ 579	Orioles Rookies	18.00	9.00	1.80
	Frank Bertaina			
	Gene Brabender			
	Dave Johnson			
☐ 580	Billy Williams SP	75.00	35.00	6.00
☐ 581	Tony Martinez	12.00	6.00	1.20
☐ 582	Garry Roggenburk	12.00	6.00	1.20
☐ 583	Tigers Team SP	90.00	42.50	8.50
☐ 584	Yankees Rookies	12.00	6.00	1.20
	Frank Fernandez			
	Fritz Peterson			
☐ 585	Tony Taylor	12.00	6.00	1.20
☐ 586	Claude Raymond SP	25.00	12.50	2.50
☐ 587	Dick Bertell	12.00	6.00	1.20
☐ 588	Athletics Rookies	12.00	6.00	1.20
	Chuck Dobson			
	Ken Suarez			
☐ 589	Lou Klimchock SP	25.00	12.50	2.50
☐ 590	Bill Skowron SP	35.00	17.50	3.50
☐ 591	NL Rookies SP	30.00	15.00	3.00
	Bart Shirley			
	Grant Jackson			
☐ 592	Andre Rodgers	12.00	6.00	1.20
☐ 593	Doug Camilli SP	25.00	12.50	2.50
☐ 594	Chico Salmon	12.00	6.00	1.20
☐ 595	Larry Jackson	12.00	6.00	1.20
☐ 596	Astros Rookies SP	25.00	12.50	2.50
	Nate Colbert			
	Greg Sims			
☐ 597	John Sullivan	12.00	6.00	1.20
☐ 598	Gaylord Perry SP	200.00	50.00	10.00

1967 Topps

The cards in this 609-card set measure 2 1/2" by 3 1/2". The 1967 Topps series is considered by some collectors to be one of the company's finest accomplishments in baseball card production. Excellent color photographs are combined with easy-to-read backs. Cards 458 to 533 are slightly harder to find than numbers 1 to 457, and the inevitable (difficult to find) high series (534 to 609) exists. Each checklist card features a small circular picture of a popular player included in that series. Printing discrepancies resulted in some high series cards being in shorter supply. The checklist below identifies (by DP) 22 double-printed high numbers; of the 76 cards in the last series, 54 cards were short printed and the other 22 cards are much more plentiful. Featured subsets within this set include World Series cards (151-155) and League Leaders (233-244). Although there are several relatively expensive cards in this popular set, the key cards in the set are undoubtedly the Tom Seaver rookie card

(581) and the Rod Carew rookie card (569). Although rarely seen, there exists a salesman's sample panel of three cards which pictures Earl Battey, Manny Mota, and Gene Brabender with ad information on the back about the "new" Topps cards.

	NRMT	VG-E	GOOD
COMPLETE SET (609)	4000.00	2000.00	500.00
COMMON PLAYER (1-109)	.75	.35	.07
COMMON PLAYER (110-370)	.85	.40	.08
COMMON PLAYER (371-457)	1.50	.75	.15
COMMON PLAYER (458-533)	4.00	2.00	.40
COMMON PLAYER (534-609)	15.00	7.50	1.50
COMMON DP (534-609)	6.00	3.00	.60

			NRMT	VG-E	GOOD
☐	1	The Champs	10.00	1.25	.25
		Frank Robinson			
		Hank Bauer			
		Brooks Robinson			
☐	2	Jack Hamilton	.75	.35	.07
☐	3	Duke Sims	.75	.35	.07
☐	4	Hal Lanier	1.00	.50	.10
☐	5	Whitey Ford UER	13.00	6.00	1.20
		(1953 listed as			
		1933 in stats on back)			
☐	6	Dick Simpson	.75	.35	.07
☐	7	Don McMahon	.75	.35	.07
☐	8	Chuck Harrison	.75	.35	.07
☐	9	Ron Hansen	.75	.35	.07
☐	10	Matty Alou	1.00	.50	.10
☐	11	Barry Moore	.75	.35	.07
☐	12	Dodgers Rookies	1.00	.50	.10
		Jim Campanis			
		Bill Singer			
☐	13	Joe Sparma	.75	.35	.07
☐	14	Phil Linz	1.00	.50	.10
☐	15	Earl Battey	.75	.35	.07
☐	16	Bill Hands	.75	.35	.07
☐	17	Jim Gosger	.75	.35	.07
☐	18	Gene Oliver	.75	.35	.07
☐	19	Jim McGlothlin	.75	.35	.07
☐	20	Orlando Cepeda	5.00	2.50	.50
☐	21	Dave Bristol MG	.75	.35	.07
☐	22	Gene Brabender	.75	.35	.07
☐	23	Larry Elliot	.75	.35	.07
☐	24	Bob Allen	.75	.35	.07
☐	25	Elston Howard	2.50	1.25	.25
☐	26A	Bob Priddy	.75	.35	.07
		(with traded line)			
☐	26B	Bob Priddy	25.00	12.50	2.50
		(no traded line)			
☐	27	Bob Saverine	.75	.35	.07
☐	28	Barry Latman	.75	.35	.07
☐	29	Tom McCraw	.75	.35	.07
☐	30	Al Kaline	14.00	6.00	1.20
☐	31	Jim Brewer	.75	.35	.07
☐	32	Bob Bailey	.75	.35	.07
☐	33	Athletic Rookies	2.00	1.00	.20
		Sal Bando			
		Randy Schwartz			
☐	34	Pete Cimino	.75	.35	.07
☐	35	Rico Carty	1.00	.50	.10
☐	36	Bob Tillman	.75	.35	.07
☐	37	Rick Wise	1.00	.50	.10
☐	38	Bob Johnson	.75	.35	.07
☐	39	Curt Simmons	1.00	.50	.10
☐	40	Rick Reichardt	.75	.35	.07
☐	41	Joe Hoerner	.75	.35	.07
☐	42	Mets Team	2.00	1.00	.20
☐	43	Chico Salmon	.75	.35	.07
☐	44	Joe Nuxhall	1.00	.50	.10
☐	45	Roger Maris	30.00	15.00	3.00
☐	46	Lindy McDaniel	1.00	.50	.10
☐	47	Ken McMullen	.75	.35	.07
☐	48	Bill Freehan	1.50	.75	.15
☐	49	Roy Face	1.25	.60	.12
☐	50	Tony Oliva	3.50	1.50	.30
☐	51	Astros Rookies	.75	.35	.07
		Dave Adlesh			
		Wes Bales			
☐	52	Dennis Higgins	.75	.35	.07
☐	53	Clay Dalrymple	.75	.35	.07
☐	54	Dick Green	.75	.35	.07
☐	55	Don Drysdale	9.00	4.50	.90
☐	56	Jose Tartabull	.75	.35	.07
☐	57	Pat Jarvis	.75	.35	.07
☐	58	Paul Schaal	.75	.35	.07
☐	59	Ralph Terry	1.00	.50	.10
☐	60	Luis Aparicio	6.00	3.00	.60
☐	61	Gordy Coleman	.75	.35	.07
☐	62	Checklist 1	3.00	.40	.10
		Frank Robinson			
☐	63	Cards' Clubbers	5.00	2.50	.50
		Lou Brock			
		Curt Flood			
☐	64	Fred Valentine	.75	.35	.07
☐	65	Tom Haller	.75	.35	.07
☐	66	Manny Mota	1.00	.50	.10
☐	67	Ken Berry	.75	.35	.07
☐	68	Bob Buhl	.75	.35	.07
☐	69	Vic Davalillo	.75	.35	.07
☐	70	Ron Santo	1.50	.75	.15
☐	71	Camilo Pascual	1.00	.50	.10
☐	72	Tigers Rookies	.75	.35	.07
		George Korince			
		(Photo actually			
		James Murray Brown)			
		John (Tom) Matchick			
☐	73	Rusty Staub	1.50	.75	.15
☐	74	Wes Stock	.75	.35	.07
☐	75	George Scott	1.25	.60	.12
☐	76	Jim Barbieri	.75	.35	.07
☐	77	Dooley Womack	.75	.35	.07
☐	78	Pat Corrales	1.00	.50	.10
☐	79	Bubba Morton	.75	.35	.07
☐	80	Jim Maloney	1.00	.50	.10
☐	81	Eddie Stanky MG	1.00	.50	.10
☐	82	Steve Barber	.75	.35	.07
☐	83	Ollie Brown	.75	.35	.07
☐	84	Tommie Sisk	.75	.35	.07
☐	85	Johnny Callison	1.00	.50	.10
☐	86A	Mike McCormick	1.00	.50	.10
		(with traded line)			
☐	86B	Mike McCormick	25.00	12.50	2.50
		(no traded line)			
☐	87	George Altman	.75	.35	.07
☐	88	Mickey Lolich	2.00	1.00	.20
☐	89	Felix Millan	.75	.35	.07
☐	90	Jim Nash	.75	.35	.07
☐	91	Johnny Lewis	.75	.35	.07
☐	92	Ray Washburn	.75	.35	.07
☐	93	Yankees Rookies	2.50	1.25	.25
		Stan Bahnsen			
		Bobby Murcer			
☐	94	Ron Fairly	1.00	.50	.10
☐	95	Sonny Siebert	.75	.35	.07
☐	96	Art Shamsky	.75	.35	.07
☐	97	Mike Cuellar	1.00	.50	.10
☐	98	Rich Rollins	1.00	.50	.10
☐	99	Lee Stange	.75	.35	.07
☐	100	Frank Robinson	13.00	6.00	1.20
☐	101	Ken Johnson	.75	.35	.07
☐	102	Philadelphia Phillies	1.75	.85	.17
		Team Card			
☐	103	Checklist 2	6.00	1.00	.20
		Mickey Mantle			
☐	104	Minnie Rojas	.75	.35	.07
☐	105	Ken Boyer	1.50	.75	.15
☐	106	Randy Hundley	.75	.35	.07
☐	107	Joel Horlen	.75	.35	.07
☐	108	Alex Johnson	.75	.35	.07
☐	109	Tribe Thumpers	1.00	.50	.10
		Rocky Colavito			
		Leon Wagner			
☐	110	Jack Aker	.85	.40	.08
☐	111	John Kennedy	.85	.40	.08
☐	112	Dave Wickersham	.85	.40	.08
☐	113	Dave Nicholson	.85	.40	.08
☐	114	Jack Baldschun	.85	.40	.08
☐	115	Paul Casanova	.85	.40	.08
☐	116	Herman Franks MG	.85	.40	.08
☐	117	Darrell Brandon	.85	.40	.08
☐	118	Bernie Allen	.85	.40	.08
☐	119	Wade Blasingame	.85	.40	.08
☐	120	Floyd Robinson	.85	.40	.08
☐	121	Eddie Bressoud	.85	.40	.08
☐	122	George Brunet	.85	.40	.08
☐	123	Pirates Rookies	.85	.40	.08
		Jim Price			
		Luke Walker			
☐	124	Jim Stewart	.85	.40	.08
☐	125	Moe Drabowsky	.85	.40	.08
☐	126	Tony Taylor	.85	.40	.08
☐	127	John O'Donoghue	.85	.40	.08
☐	128	Ed Spiezio	.85	.40	.08
☐	129	Phil Roof	.85	.40	.08
☐	130	Phil Regan	1.25	.60	.12
☐	131	Yankees Team	3.00	1.50	.30
☐	132	Ozzie Virgil	.85	.40	.08
☐	133	Ron Kline	.85	.40	.08
☐	134	Gates Brown	1.25	.60	.12
☐	135	Deron Johnson	1.25	.60	.12
☐	136	Carroll Sembera	.85	.40	.08
☐	137	Twins Rookies	.85	.40	.08
		Ron Clark			
		Jim Ollum			
☐	138	Dick Kelley	.85	.40	.08
☐	139	Dalton Jones	.85	.40	.08

☐ 140	Willie Stargell	14.00	7.00	1.40
☐ 141	John Miller	.85	.40	.08
☐ 142	Jackie Brandt	.85	.40	.08
☐ 143	Sox Sockers	.85	.40	.08
	Pete Ward			
	Don Buford			
☐ 144	Bill Hepler	.85	.40	.08
☐ 145	Larry Brown	.85	.40	.08
☐ 146	Steve Carlton	60.00	30.00	6.00
☐ 147	Tom Egan	.85	.40	.08
☐ 148	Adolfo Phillips	.85	.40	.08
☐ 149	Joe Moeller	.85	.40	.08
☐ 150	Mickey Mantle	200.00	100.00	20.00
☐ 151	World Series Game 1	2.00	1.00	.20
	Moe mows down 11			
☐ 152	World Series Game 2	4.00	2.00	.40
	Palmer blanks Dodgers			
☐ 153	World Series Game 3	2.00	1.00	.20
	Blair's homer			
	defeats L.A.			
☐ 154	World Series Game 4	2.00	1.00	.20
	Orioles 4 straight			
☐ 155	World Series Summary	2.00	1.00	.20
	Winners celebrate			
☐ 156	Ron Herbel	.85	.40	.08
☐ 157	Danny Cater	.85	.40	.08
☐ 158	Jimmie Coker	.85	.40	.08
☐ 159	Bruce Howard	.85	.40	.08
☐ 160	Willie Davis	1.25	.60	.12
☐ 161	Dick Williams MG	1.25	.60	.12
☐ 162	Billy O'Dell	.85	.40	.08
☐ 163	Vic Roznovsky	.85	.40	.08
☐ 164	Dwight Siebler	.85	.40	.08
☐ 165	Cleon Jones	.85	.40	.08
☐ 166	Eddie Mathews	9.00	4.50	.90
☐ 167	Senators Rookies	.85	.40	.08
	Joe Coleman			
	Tim Cullen			
☐ 168	Ray Culp	.85	.40	.08
☐ 169	Horace Clarke	.85	.40	.08
☐ 170	Dick McAuliffe	.85	.40	.08
☐ 171	Cal Koonce	.85	.40	.08
☐ 172	Bill Heath	.85	.40	.08
☐ 173	St. Louis Cardinals	1.75	.85	.17
	Team Card			
☐ 174	Dick Radatz	1.25	.60	.12
☐ 175	Bobby Knoop	.85	.40	.08
☐ 176	Sammy Ellis	.85	.40	.08
☐ 177	Tito Fuentes	.85	.40	.08
☐ 178	John Buzhardt	.85	.40	.08
☐ 179	Braves Rookies	.85	.40	.08
	Charles Vaughan			
	Cecil Upshaw			
☐ 180	Curt Blefary	.85	.40	.08
☐ 181	Terry Fox	.85	.40	.08
☐ 182	Ed Charles	.85	.40	.08
☐ 183	Jim Pagliaroni	.85	.40	.08
☐ 184	George Thomas	.85	.40	.08
☐ 185	Ken Holtzman	1.50	.75	.15
☐ 186	Mets Maulers	1.25	.60	.12
	Ed Kranepool			
	Ron Swoboda			
☐ 187	Pedro Ramos	.85	.40	.08
☐ 188	Ken Harrelson	1.50	.75	.15
☐ 189	Chuck Hinton	.85	.40	.08
☐ 190	Turk Farrell	.85	.40	.08
☐ 191A	Checklist 3	4.00	.40	.10
	(214 Tom Kelley)			
	(Willie Mays)			
☐ 191B	Checklist 3	8.00	.80	.15
	(214 Dick Kelley)			
	(Willie Mays)			
☐ 192	Fred Gladding	.85	.40	.08
☐ 193	Jose Cardenal	.85	.40	.08
☐ 194	Bob Allison	1.25	.60	.12
☐ 195	Al Jackson	.85	.40	.08
☐ 196	Johnny Romano	.85	.40	.08
☐ 197	Ron Perranoski	1.25	.60	.12
☐ 198	Chuck Hiller	.85	.40	.08
☐ 199	Billy Hitchcock MG	.85	.40	.08
☐ 200	Willie Mays	60.00	27.50	5.50
☐ 201	Hal Reniff	.85	.40	.08
☐ 202	Johnny Edwards	.85	.40	.08
☐ 203	Al McBean	.85	.40	.08
☐ 204	Orioles Rookies	1.25	.60	.12
	Mike Epstein			
	Tom Phoebus			
☐ 205	Dick Groat	1.50	.75	.15
☐ 206	Dennis Bennett	.85	.40	.08
☐ 207	John Orsino	.85	.40	.08
☐ 208	Jack Lamabe	.85	.40	.08
☐ 209	Joe Nossek	.85	.40	.08
☐ 210	Bob Gibson	14.00	6.50	1.30
☐ 211	Twins Team	1.75	.85	.17
☐ 212	Chris Zachary	.85	.40	.08

☐ 213	Jay Johnstone	1.50	.75	.15
☐ 214	Dick Kelley	.85	.40	.08
☐ 215	Ernie Banks	14.00	6.50	1.30
☐ 216	Bengal Belters	4.00	2.00	.40
	Norm Cash			
	Al Kaline			
☐ 217	Rob Gardner	.85	.40	.08
☐ 218	Wes Parker	1.25	.60	.12
☐ 219	Clay Carroll	.85	.40	.08
☐ 220	Jim Ray Hart	1.25	.60	.12
☐ 221	Woodie Fryman	.85	.40	.08
☐ 222	Reds Rookies	1.50	.75	.15
	Darrell Osteen			
	Lee May			
☐ 223	Mike Ryan	.85	.40	.08
☐ 224	Walt Bond	.85	.40	.08
☐ 225	Mel Stottlemyre	1.75	.85	.17
☐ 226	Julian Javier	.85	.40	.08
☐ 227	Paul Lindblad	.85	.40	.08
☐ 228	Gil Hodges MG	4.00	2.00	.40
☐ 229	Larry Jackson	.85	.40	.08
☐ 230	Boog Powell	2.00	1.00	.20
☐ 231	John Bateman	.85	.40	.08
☐ 232	Don Buford	.85	.40	.08
☐ 233	AL ERA Leaders	1.50	.75	.15
	Gary Peters			
	Joel Horlen			
	Steve Hargan			
☐ 234	NL ERA Leaders	4.50	2.25	.45
	Sandy Koufax			
	Mike Cuellar			
	Juan Marichal			
☐ 235	AL Pitching Leaders	1.50	.75	.15
	Jim Kaat			
	Denny McLain			
	Earl Wilson			
☐ 236	NL Pitching Leaders	9.00	4.50	.90
	Sandy Koufax			
	Juan Marichal			
	Bob Gibson			
	Gaylord Perry			
☐ 237	AL Strikeout Leaders	1.50	.75	.15
	Sam McDowell			
	Jim Kaat			
	Earl Wilson			
☐ 238	NL Strikeout Leaders	3.00	1.50	.30
	Sandy Koufax			
	Jim Bunning			
	Bob Veale			
☐ 239	AL Batting Leaders	4.00	2.00	.40
	Frank Robinson			
	Tony Oliva			
	Al Kaline			
☐ 240	NL Batting Leaders	1.50	.75	.15
	Matty Alou			
	Felipe Alou			
	Rico Carty			
☐ 241	AL RBI Leaders	3.00	1.50	.30
	Frank Robinson			
	Harmon Killebrew			
	Boog Powell			
☐ 242	NL RBI Leaders	5.00	2.50	.50
	Hank Aaron			
	Bob Clemente			
	Richie Allen			
☐ 243	AL Home Run Leaders	3.00	1.50	.30
	Frank Robinson			
	Harmon Killebrew			
	Boog Powell			
☐ 244	NL Home Run Leaders	5.00	2.50	.50
	Hank Aaron			
	Richie Allen			
	Willie Mays			
☐ 245	Curt Flood	1.25	.60	.12
☐ 246	Jim Perry	1.25	.60	.12
☐ 247	Jerry Lumpe	.85	.40	.08
☐ 248	Gene Mauch MG	1.25	.60	.12
☐ 249	Nick Willhite	.85	.40	.08
☐ 250	Hank Aaron	60.00	30.00	6.00
☐ 251	Woody Held	.85	.40	.08
☐ 252	Bob Bolin	.85	.40	.08
☐ 253	Indians Rookies	.85	.40	.08
	Bill Davis			
	Gus Gil			
☐ 254	Milt Pappas	1.25	.60	.12
☐ 255	Frank Howard	1.50	.75	.15
☐ 256	Bob Hendley	.85	.40	.08
☐ 257	Charlie Smith	.85	.40	.08
☐ 258	Lee Maye	.85	.40	.08
☐ 259	Don Dennis	.85	.40	.08
☐ 260	Jim Lefebvre	1.50	.75	.15
☐ 261	John Wyatt	.85	.40	.08
☐ 262	Athletics Team	1.75	.85	.17
☐ 263	Hank Aguirre	.85	.40	.08
☐ 264	Ron Swoboda	1.25	.60	.12

☐ 265	Lou Burdette	1.75	.85	.17	☐ 344	Ossie Chavarria	.85	.40	.08
☐ 266	Pitt Power	3.50	1.75	.35	☐ 345	Stu Miller	.85	.40	.08
	Willie Stargell				☐ 346	Jim Hickman	.85	.40	.08
	Donn Clendenon				☐ 347	Grady Hatton MG	.85	.40	.08
☐ 267	Don Schwall	.85	.40	.08	☐ 348	Tug McGraw	1.50	.75	.15
☐ 268	Johnny Briggs	.85	.40	.08	☐ 349	Bob Chance	.85	.40	.08
☐ 269	Don Nottebart	.85	.40	.08	☐ 350	Joe Torre	1.50	.75	.15
☐ 270	Zoilo Versalles	.85	.40	.08	☐ 351	Vern Law	1.25	.60	.12
☐ 271	Eddie Watt	.85	.40	.08	☐ 352	Ray Oyler	.85	.40	.08
☐ 272	Cubs Rookies	.85	.40	.08	☐ 353	Bill McCool	.85	.40	.08
	Bill Connors				☐ 354	Cubs Team	1.75	.85	.17
	Dave Dowling				☐ 355	Carl Yastrzemski	90.00	45.00	9.00
☐ 273	Dick Lines	.85	.40	.08	☐ 356	Larry Jaster	.85	.40	.08
☐ 274	Bob Aspromonte	.85	.40	.08	☐ 357	Bill Skowron	1.50	.75	.15
☐ 275	Fred Whitfield	.85	.40	.08	☐ 358	Ruben Amaro	.85	.40	.08
☐ 276	Bruce Brubaker	.85	.40	.08	☐ 359	Dick Ellsworth	1.25	.60	.12
☐ 277	Steve Whitaker	.85	.40	.08	☐ 360	Leon Wagner	.85	.40	.08
☐ 278	Checklist 4	3.00	.40	.10	☐ 361	Checklist 5	4.00	.40	.10
	Jim Kaat					Roberto Clemente			
☐ 279	Frank Linzy	.85	.40	.08	☐ 362	Darold Knowles	.85	.40	.08
☐ 280	Tony Conigliaro	2.50	1.25	.25	☐ 363	Dave Johnson	2.00	1.00	.20
☐ 281	Bob Rodgers	1.25	.60	.12	☐ 364	Claude Raymond	.85	.40	.08
☐ 282	John Odom	.85	.40	.08	☐ 365	John Roseboro	1.25	.60	.12
☐ 283	Gene Alley	1.25	.60	.12	☐ 366	Andy Kosco	.85	.40	.08
☐ 284	Johnny Podres	1.75	.85	.17	☐ 367	Angels Rookies	.85	.40	.08
☐ 285	Lou Brock	13.00	6.50	1.30		Bill Kelso			
☐ 286	Wayne Causey	.85	.40	.08		Don Wallace			
☐ 287	Mets Rookies	.85	.40	.08	☐ 368	Jack Hiatt	.85	.40	.08
	Greg Goossen				☐ 369	Jim Hunter	12.00	6.00	1.20
	Bart Shirley				☐ 370	Tommy Davis	1.25	.60	.12
☐ 288	Denny Lemaster	.85	.40	.08	☐ 371	Jim Lonborg	2.50	1.25	.25
☐ 289	Tom Tresh	1.50	.75	.15	☐ 372	Mike De La Hoz	1.50	.75	.15
☐ 290	Bill White	1.50	.75	.15	☐ 373	White Sox Rookies	1.50	.75	.15
☐ 291	Jim Hannan	.85	.40	.08		Duane Josephson			
☐ 292	Don Pavletich	.85	.40	.08		Fred Klages			
☐ 293	Ed Kirkpatrick	.85	.40	.08	☐ 374	Mel Queen	1.50	.75	.15
☐ 294	Walt Alston MG	2.50	1.25	.25	☐ 375	Jake Gibbs	1.50	.75	.15
☐ 295	Sam McDowell	1.25	.60	.12	☐ 376	Don Lock	1.50	.75	.15
☐ 296	Glenn Beckert	1.25	.60	.12	☐ 377	Luis Tiant	2.50	1.25	.25
☐ 297	Dave Morehead	.85	.40	.08	☐ 378	Detroit Tigers	3.50	1.75	.35
☐ 298	Ron Davis	.85	.40	.08		Team Card			
☐ 299	Norm Siebern	.85	.40	.08	☐ 379	Jerry May	1.50	.75	.15
☐ 300	Jim Kaat	3.50	1.75	.35	☐ 380	Dean Chance	2.00	1.00	.20
☐ 301	Jesse Gonder	.85	.40	.08	☐ 381	Dick Schofield	1.50	.75	.15
☐ 302	Orioles Team	1.75	.85	.17	☐ 382	Dave McNally	2.00	1.00	.20
☐ 303	Gil Blanco	.85	.40	.08	☐ 383	Ken Henderson	1.50	.75	.15
☐ 304	Phil Gagliano	.85	.40	.08	☐ 384	Cardinals Rookies	1.50	.75	.15
☐ 305	Earl Wilson	.85	.40	.08		Jim Cosman			
☐ 306	Bud Harrelson	1.25	.60	.12		Dick Hughes			
☐ 307	Jim Beauchamp	.85	.40	.08	☐ 385	Jim Fregosi	2.00	1.00	.20
☐ 308	Al Downing	1.25	.60	.12		(batting wrong)			
☐ 309	Hurlers Beware	1.25	.60	.12	☐ 386	Dick Selma	1.50	.75	.15
	Johnny Callison				☐ 387	Cap Peterson	1.50	.75	.15
	Richie Allen				☐ 388	Arnold Earley	1.50	.75	.15
☐ 310	Gary Peters	.85	.40	.08	☐ 389	Alvin Dark MG	2.00	1.00	.20
☐ 311	Ed Brinkman	.85	.40	.08	☐ 390	Jim Wynn	2.00	1.00	.20
☐ 312	Don Mincher	.85	.40	.08	☐ 391	Wilbur Wood	2.00	1.00	.20
☐ 313	Bob Lee	.85	.40	.08	☐ 392	Tommy Harper	2.00	1.00	.20
☐ 314	Red Sox Rookies	3.00	1.50	.30	☐ 393	Jim Bouton	2.50	1.25	.25
	Mike Andrews				☐ 394	Jake Wood	1.50	.75	.15
	Reggie Smith				☐ 395	Chris Short	1.50	.75	.15
☐ 315	Billy Williams	7.50	3.75	.75	☐ 396	Atlanta Aces	1.50	.75	.15
☐ 316	Jack Kralick	.85	.40	.08		Denis Menke			
☐ 317	Cesar Tovar	.85	.40	.08		Tony Cloninger			
☐ 318	Dave Giusti	.85	.40	.08	☐ 397	Willie Smith	1.50	.75	.15
☐ 319	Paul Blair	.85	.40	.08	☐ 398	Jeff Torborg	2.00	1.00	.20
☐ 320	Gaylord Perry	7.00	3.50	.70	☐ 399	Al Worthington	1.50	.75	.15
☐ 321	Mayo Smith MG	.85	.40	.08	☐ 400	Bob Clemente	55.00	27.50	5.50
☐ 322	Jose Pagan	.85	.40	.08	☐ 401	Jim Coates	1.50	.75	.15
☐ 323	Mike Hershberger	.85	.40	.08	☐ 402	Phillies Rookies	1.50	.75	.15
☐ 324	Hal Woodeshick	.85	.40	.08		Grant Jackson			
☐ 325	Chico Cardenas	.85	.40	.08		Billy Wilson			
☐ 326	Bob Uecker	15.00	7.50	1.50	☐ 403	Dick Nen	1.50	.75	.15
☐ 327	California Angels	1.75	.85	.17	☐ 404	Nelson Briles	1.50	.75	.15
	Team Card				☐ 405	Russ Snyder	1.50	.75	.15
☐ 328	Clete Boyer	1.25	.60	.12	☐ 406	Lee Elia	2.00	1.00	.20
☐ 329	Charlie Lau	1.25	.60	.12	☐ 407	Reds Team	3.00	1.50	.30
☐ 330	Claude Osteen	1.25	.60	.12	☐ 408	Jim Northrup	2.00	1.00	.20
☐ 331	Joe Foy	.85	.40	.08	☐ 409	Ray Sadecki	1.50	.75	.15
☐ 332	Jesus Alou	.85	.40	.08	☐ 410	Lou Johnson	1.50	.75	.15
☐ 333	Fergie Jenkins	6.50	3.25	.65	☐ 411	Dick Howser	2.50	1.25	.25
☐ 334	Twin Terrors	3.50	1.75	.35	☐ 412	Astros Rookies	2.50	1.25	.25
	Bob Allison					Norm Miller			
	Harmon Killebrew					Doug Rader			
☐ 335	Bob Veale	.85	.40	.08	☐ 413	Jerry Grote	1.50	.75	.15
☐ 336	Joe Azcue	.85	.40	.08	☐ 414	Casey Cox	1.50	.75	.15
☐ 337	Joe Morgan	14.00	7.00	1.40	☐ 415	Sonny Jackson	1.50	.75	.15
☐ 338	Bob Locker	.85	.40	.08	☐ 416	Roger Repoz	1.50	.75	.15
☐ 339	Chico Ruiz	.85	.40	.08	☐ 417A	Bob Bruce ERR	25.00	10.00	2.00
☐ 340	Joe Pepitone	1.50	.75	.15		(RBAVES on back)			
☐ 341	Giants Rookies	.85	.40	.08	☐ 417B	Bob Bruce COR	2.00	1.00	.20
	Dick Dietz				☐ 418	Sam Mele MG	1.50	.75	.15
	Bill Sorrell				☐ 419	Don Kessinger	2.00	1.00	.20
☐ 342	Hank Fischer	.85	.40	.08	☐ 420	Denny McLain	3.50	1.75	.35
☐ 343	Tom Satriano	.85	.40	.08	☐ 421	Dal Maxvill	1.50	.75	.15

☐ 422	Hoyt Wilhelm	7.50	3.75	.75
☐ 423	Fence Busters	12.50	6.25	1.25
	Willie Mays			
	Willie McCovey			
☐ 424	Pedro Gonzalez	1.50	.75	.15
☐ 425	Pete Mikkelsen	1.50	.75	.15
☐ 426	Lou Clinton	1.50	.75	.15
☐ 427	Ruben Gomez	1.50	.75	.15
☐ 428	Dodgers Rookies	2.00	1.00	.20
	Tom Hutton			
	Gene Michael			
☐ 429	Garry Roggenburk	1.50	.75	.15
☐ 430	Pete Rose	75.00	37.50	7.50
☐ 431	Ted Uhlaender	1.50	.75	.15
☐ 432	Jimmie Hall	1.50	.75	.15
☐ 433	Al Luplow	1.50	.75	.15
☐ 434	Eddie Fisher	1.50	.75	.15
☐ 435	Mack Jones	1.50	.75	.15
☐ 436	Pete Ward	1.50	.75	.15
☐ 437	Senators Team	3.00	1.50	.30
☐ 438	Chuck Dobson	1.50	.75	.15
☐ 439	Byron Browne	1.50	.75	.15
☐ 440	Steve Hargan	1.50	.75	.15
☐ 441	Jim Davenport	2.00	1.00	.20
☐ 442	Yankees Rookies	2.00	1.00	.20
	Bill Robinson			
	Joe Verbanic			
☐ 443	Tito Francona	1.50	.75	.15
☐ 444	George Smith	1.50	.75	.15
☐ 445	Don Sutton	18.00	9.00	1.80
☐ 446	Russ Nixon	2.00	1.00	.20
☐ 447	Bo Belinsky	2.00	1.00	.20
☐ 448	Harry Walker MG	1.50	.75	.15
☐ 449	Orlando Pena	1.50	.75	.15
☐ 450	Richie Allen	3.00	1.50	.30
☐ 451	Fred Newman	1.50	.75	.15
☐ 452	Ed Kranepool	2.00	1.00	.20
☐ 453	Aurelio Monteagudo	1.50	.75	.15
☐ 454A	Checklist 6	4.00	.40	.10
	Juan Marichal			
	(missing left ear)			
☐ 454B	Checklist 6	8.00	.75	.15
	Juan Marichal			
	(left ear showing)			
☐ 455	Tommy Agee	2.00	1.00	.20
☐ 456	Phil Niekro	9.00	4.50	.90
☐ 457	Andy Etchebarren	1.50	.75	.15
☐ 458	Lee Thomas	5.00	2.50	.50
☐ 459	Senators Rookies	4.00	2.00	.40
	Dick Bosman			
	Pete Craig			
☐ 460	Harmon Killebrew	35.00	15.00	3.00
☐ 461	Bob Miller	4.00	2.00	.40
☐ 462	Bob Barton	4.00	2.00	.40
☐ 463	Hill Aces	5.00	2.50	.50
	Sam McDowell			
	Sonny Siebert			
☐ 464	Dan Coombs	4.00	2.00	.40
☐ 465	Willie Horton	5.00	2.50	.50
☐ 466	Bobby Wine	4.00	2.00	.40
☐ 467	Jim O'Toole	4.00	2.00	.40
☐ 468	Ralph Houk MG	5.00	2.50	.50
☐ 469	Len Gabrielson	4.00	2.00	.40
☐ 470	Bob Shaw	4.00	2.00	.40
☐ 471	Rene Lachemann	5.00	2.50	.50
☐ 472	Rookies Pirates	4.00	2.00	.40
	John Gelnar			
	George Spriggs			
☐ 473	Jose Santiago	4.00	2.00	.40
☐ 474	Bob Tolan	5.00	2.50	.50
☐ 475	Jim Palmer	65.00	30.00	6.00
☐ 476	Tony Perez SP	50.00	25.00	5.00
☐ 477	Braves Team	8.00	4.00	.80
☐ 478	Bob Humphreys	4.00	2.00	.40
☐ 479	Gary Bell	4.00	2.00	.40
☐ 480	Willie McCovey	20.00	10.00	2.00
☐ 481	Leo Durocher MG	6.00	3.00	.60
☐ 482	Bill Monbouquette	4.00	2.00	.40
☐ 483	Jim Landis	4.00	2.00	.40
☐ 484	Jerry Adair	4.00	2.00	.40
☐ 485	Tim McCarver	8.00	4.00	.80
☐ 486	Twins Rookies	4.00	2.00	.40
	Rich Reese			
	Bill Whitby			
☐ 487	Tommie Reynolds	4.00	2.00	.40
☐ 488	Gerry Arrigo	4.00	2.00	.40
☐ 489	Doug Clemens	4.00	2.00	.40
☐ 490	Tony Cloninger	4.00	2.00	.40
☐ 491	Sam Bowens	4.00	2.00	.40
☐ 492	Pittsburgh Pirates	8.00	4.00	.80
	Team Card			
☐ 493	Phil Ortega	4.00	2.00	.40
☐ 494	Bill Rigney MG	4.00	2.00	.40
☐ 495	Fritz Peterson	4.00	2.00	.40
☐ 496	Orlando McFarlane	4.00	2.00	.40
☐ 497	Ron Campbell	4.00	2.00	.40
☐ 498	Larry Dierker	4.00	2.00	.40
☐ 499	Indians Rookies	4.00	2.00	.40
	George Culver			
	Jose Vidal			
☐ 500	Juan Marichal	14.00	7.00	1.40
☐ 501	Jerry Zimmerman	4.00	2.00	.40
☐ 502	Derrell Griffith	4.00	2.00	.40
☐ 503	Los Angeles Dodgers	8.00	4.00	.80
	Team Card			
☐ 504	Orlando Martinez	4.00	2.00	.40
☐ 505	Tommy Helms	5.00	2.50	.50
☐ 506	Smoky Burgess	5.00	2.50	.50
☐ 507	Orioles Rookies	4.00	2.00	.40
	Ed Barnowski			
	Larry Haney			
☐ 508	Dick Hall	4.00	2.00	.40
☐ 509	Jim King	4.00	2.00	.40
☐ 510	Bill Mazeroski	6.00	3.00	.60
☐ 511	Don Wert	4.00	2.00	.40
☐ 512	Red Schoendienst MG	8.00	4.00	.80
☐ 513	Marcelino Lopez	4.00	2.00	.40
☐ 514	John Werhas	4.00	2.00	.40
☐ 515	Bert Campaneris	5.00	2.50	.50
☐ 516	Giants Team	8.00	4.00	.80
☐ 517	Fred Talbot	4.00	2.00	.40
☐ 518	Denis Menke	4.00	2.00	.40
☐ 519	Ted Davidson	4.00	2.00	.40
☐ 520	Max Alvis	4.00	2.00	.40
☐ 521	Bird Bombers	5.00	2.50	.50
	Boog Powell			
	Curt Blefary			
☐ 522	John Stephenson	4.00	2.00	.40
☐ 523	Jim Merritt	4.00	2.00	.40
☐ 524	Felix Mantilla	4.00	2.00	.40
☐ 525	Ron Hunt	4.00	2.00	.40
☐ 526	Tigers Rookies	5.50	2.75	.55
	Pat Dobson			
	George Korince			
	(See 67T-72)			
☐ 527	Dennis Ribant	4.00	2.00	.40
☐ 528	Rico Petrocelli	5.00	2.50	.50
☐ 529	Gary Wagner	4.00	2.00	.40
☐ 530	Felipe Alou	5.00	2.50	.50
☐ 531	Checklist 7	8.00	.75	.15
	Brooks Robinson			
☐ 532	Jim Hicks	4.00	2.00	.40
☐ 533	Jack Fisher	4.00	2.00	.40
☐ 534	Hank Bauer MG DP	7.50	3.50	.75
☐ 535	Donn Clendenon	20.00	10.00	2.00
☐ 536	Cubs Rookies	30.00	12.50	2.50
	Joe Niekro			
	Paul Popovich			
☐ 537	Chuck Estrada DP	6.00	3.00	.60
☐ 538	J.C. Martin	15.00	7.50	1.50
☐ 539	Dick Egan DP	6.00	3.00	.60
☐ 540	Norm Cash	30.00	15.00	3.00
☐ 541	Joe Gibbon	15.00	7.50	1.50
☐ 542	Athletics Rookies DP	10.00	5.00	1.00
	Rick Monday			
	Tony Pierce			
☐ 543	Dan Schneider	15.00	7.50	1.50
☐ 544	Cleveland Indians	30.00	10.00	2.00
	Team Card			
☐ 545	Jim Grant	15.00	7.50	1.50
☐ 546	Woody Woodward	15.00	7.50	1.50
☐ 547	Red Sox Rookies DP	6.00	3.00	.60
	Russ Gibson			
	Bill Rohr			
☐ 548	Tony Gonzalez DP	6.00	3.00	.60
☐ 549	Jack Sanford	15.00	7.50	1.50
☐ 550	Vada Pinson DP	9.00	4.50	.90
☐ 551	Doug Camilli DP	6.00	3.00	.60
☐ 552	Ted Savage	15.00	7.50	1.50
☐ 553	Yankees Rookies	25.00	12.50	2.50
	Mike Hegan			
	Thad Tillotson			
☐ 554	Andre Rodgers DP	6.00	3.00	.60
☐ 555	Don Cardwell	15.00	7.50	1.50
☐ 556	Al Weis DP	6.00	3.00	.60
☐ 557	Al Ferrara	15.00	7.50	1.50
☐ 558	Orioles Rookies	35.00	17.50	3.50
	Mark Belanger			
	Bill Dillman			
☐ 559	Dick Tracewski DP	6.00	3.00	.60
☐ 560	Jim Bunning	40.00	18.00	3.60
☐ 561	Sandy Alomar	15.00	7.50	1.50
☐ 562	Steve Blass DP	6.00	3.00	.60
☐ 563	Joe Adcock	20.00	10.00	2.00
☐ 564	Astros Rookies DP	6.00	3.00	.60
	Alonzo Harris			
	Aaron Pointer			
☐ 565	Lew Krausse	15.00	7.50	1.50
☐ 566	Gary Geiger DP	6.00	3.00	.60
☐ 567	Steve Hamilton	15.00	7.50	1.50

		NRMT	VG-E	GOOD
☐ 568	John Sullivan	15.00	7.50	1.50
☐ 569	AL Rookies DP	300.00	135.00	27.00
	Rod Carew			
	Hank Allen			
☐ 570	Maury Wills	80.00	37.50	7.50
☐ 571	Larry Sherry	15.00	7.50	1.50
☐ 572	Don Demeter	15.00	7.50	1.50
☐ 573	Chicago White Sox	30.00	15.00	3.00
	Team Card UER			
	(Indians team			
	stats on back)			
☐ 574	Jerry Buchek	15.00	7.50	1.50
☐ 575	Dave Boswell	15.00	7.50	1.50
☐ 576	NL Rookies	20.00	10.00	2.00
	Ramon Hernandez			
	Norm Gigon			
☐ 577	Bill Short	15.00	7.50	1.50
☐ 578	John Boccabella	15.00	7.50	1.50
☐ 579	Bill Henry	15.00	7.50	1.50
☐ 580	Rocky Colavito	35.00	15.00	3.00
☐ 581	Mets Rookies	950.00	400.00	75.00
	Bill Denehy			
	Tom Seaver			
☐ 582	Jim Owens DP	6.00	3.00	.60
☐ 583	Ray Barker	15.00	7.50	1.50
☐ 584	Jim Piersall	22.00	10.00	2.00
☐ 585	Wally Bunker	15.00	7.50	1.50
☐ 586	Manny Jimenez	15.00	7.50	1.50
☐ 587	NL Rookies	20.00	10.00	2.00
	Don Shaw			
	Gary Sutherland			
☐ 588	Johnny Klippstein DP	6.00	3.00	.60
☐ 589	Dave Ricketts DP	6.00	3.00	.60
☐ 590	Pete Richert	15.00	7.50	1.50
☐ 591	Ty Cline	15.00	7.50	1.50
☐ 592	NL Rookies	20.00	10.00	2.00
	Jim Shellenback			
	Ron Willis			
☐ 593	Wes Westrum MG	20.00	10.00	2.00
☐ 594	Dan Osinski	15.00	7.50	1.50
☐ 595	Cookie Rojas	20.00	10.00	2.00
☐ 596	Galen Cisco DP	6.00	3.00	.60
☐ 597	Ted Abernathy	15.00	7.50	1.50
☐ 598	White Sox Rookies	20.00	10.00	2.00
	Walt Williams			
	Ed Stroud			
☐ 599	Bob Duliba DP	6.00	3.00	.60
☐ 600	Brooks Robinson	200.00	100.00	20.00
☐ 601	Bill Bryan DP	6.00	3.00	.60
☐ 602	Juan Pizarro	15.00	7.50	1.50
☐ 603	Athletics Rookies	15.00	7.50	1.50
	Tim Talton			
	Ramon Webster			
☐ 604	Red Sox Team	100.00	50.00	10.00
☐ 605	Mike Shannon	40.00	20.00	4.00
☐ 606	Ron Taylor	15.00	7.50	1.50
☐ 607	Mickey Stanley	30.00	15.00	3.00
☐ 608	Cubs Rookies DP	6.00	3.00	.60
	Rich Nye			
	John Upham			
☐ 609	Tommy John	100.00	25.00	5.00

1968 Topps

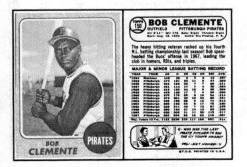

The cards in this 598-card set measure 2 1/2" by 3 1/2". The 1968 Topps set includes Sporting News All-Star Selections as card numbers 361 to 380. Other subsets in the set include League Leaders (1-12) and World Series cards (151-158). The front of

each checklist card features a picture of a popular player inside a circle. High numbers 534 to 598 are slightly more difficult to obtain. The first series looks different from the other series, as it has a lighter, wider mesh background on the card front. The later series all had a much darker, finer mesh pattern. Key cards in the set are the rookie cards of Johnny Bench (247) and Nolan Ryan (177).

		NRMT	VG-E	GOOD
COMPLETE SET (598)		2500.00	1200.00	300.00
COMMON PLAYER (1-109)		.65	.30	.06
COMMON PLAYER (110-196)		.65	.30	.06
COMMON PLAYER (197-457)		.65	.30	.06
COMMON PLAYER (458-533)		.80	.40	.08
COMMON PLAYER (534-598)		.80	.40	.08
☐ 1	NL Batting Leaders	7.00	1.50	.30
	Bob Clemente			
	Tony Gonzales			
	Matty Alou			
☐ 2	AL Batting Leaders	6.00	3.00	.60
	Carl Yastrzemski			
	Frank Robinson			
	Al Kaline			
☐ 3	NL RBI Leaders	4.00	2.00	.40
	Orlando Cepeda			
	Bob Clemente			
	Hank Aaron			
☐ 4	AL RBI Leaders	6.00	3.00	.60
	Carl Yastrzemski			
	Harmon Killebrew			
	Frank Robinson			
☐ 5	NL Home Run Leaders ...	3.00	1.50	.30
	Hank Aaron			
	Jim Wynn			
	Ron Santo			
	Willie McCovey			
☐ 6	NL Home Run Leaders ...	4.00	2.00	.40
	Carl Yastrzemski			
	Harmon Killebrew			
	Frank Howard			
☐ 7	NL ERA Leaders	1.50	.75	.15
	Phil Niekro			
	Jim Bunning			
	Chris Short			
☐ 8	AL ERA Leaders	1.25	.60	.12
	Joel Horlen			
	Gary Peters			
	Sonny Siebert			
☐ 9	NL Pitching Leaders	1.25	.60	.12
	Mike McCormick			
	Ferguson Jenkins			
	Jim Bunning			
	Claude Osteen			
☐ 10	AL Pitching Leaders	1.25	.60	.12
	Jim Lonborg			
	Earl Wilson			
	Dean Chance			
☐ 11	NL Strikeout Leaders	1.50	.75	.15
	Jim Bunning			
	Ferguson Jenkins			
	Gaylord Perry			
☐ 12	AL Strikeout Leaders	1.25	.60	.12
	Jim Lonborg UER			
	(misspelled Longberg			
	on card back)			
	Sam McDowell			
	Dean Chance			
☐ 13	Chuck Hartenstein	.65	.30	.06
☐ 14	Jerry McNertney	.65	.30	.06
☐ 15	Ron Hunt	.65	.30	.06
☐ 16	Indians Rookies	2.00	1.00	.20
	Lou Piniella			
	Richie Scheinblum			
☐ 17	Dick Hall	.65	.30	.06
☐ 18	Mike Hershberger	.65	.30	.06
☐ 19	Juan Pizarro	.65	.30	.06
☐ 20	Brooks Robinson	13.00	6.00	1.20
☐ 21	Ron Davis	.65	.30	.06
☐ 22	Pat Dobson	.65	.30	.06
☐ 23	Chico Cardenas	.65	.30	.06
☐ 24	Bobby Locke	.65	.30	.06
☐ 25	Julian Javier	.65	.30	.06
☐ 26	Darrell Brandon	.65	.30	.06
☐ 27	Gil Hodges MG	3.50	1.75	.35
☐ 28	Ted Uhlaender	.65	.30	.06
☐ 29	Joe Verbanic	.65	.30	.06
☐ 30	Joe Torre	1.25	.60	.12
☐ 31	Ed Stroud	.65	.30	.06
☐ 32	Joe Gibbon	.65	.30	.06
☐ 33	Pete Ward	.65	.30	.06

☐ 34	Al Ferrara	.65	.30	.06
☐ 35	Steve Hargan	.65	.30	.06
☐ 36	Pirates Rookies	1.00	.50	.10
	Bob Moose			
	Bob Robertson			
☐ 37	Billy Williams	6.50	3.25	.65
☐ 38	Tony Pierce	.65	.30	.06
☐ 39	Cookie Rojas	.65	.30	.06
☐ 40	Denny McLain	4.00	2.00	.40
☐ 41	Julio Gotay	.65	.30	.06
☐ 42	Larry Haney	.65	.30	.06
☐ 43	Gary Bell	.65	.30	.06
☐ 44	Frank Kostro	.65	.30	.06
☐ 45	Tom Seaver	125.00	60.00	12.50
☐ 46	Dave Ricketts	.65	.30	.06
☐ 47	Ralph Houk MG	1.00	.50	.10
☐ 48	Ted Davidson	.65	.30	.06
☐ 49A	Eddie Brinkman	.65	.30	.06
	(white team name)			
☐ 49B	Eddie Brinkman	40.00	20.00	4.00
	(yellow team name)			
☐ 50	Willie Mays	50.00	22.50	4.50
☐ 51	Bob Locker	.65	.30	.06
☐ 52	Hawk Taylor	.65	.30	.06
☐ 53	Gene Alley	.65	.30	.06
☐ 54	Stan Williams	.65	.30	.06
☐ 55	Felipe Alou	1.00	.50	.10
☐ 56	Orioles Rookies	.65	.30	.06
	Dave Leonhard			
	Dave May			
☐ 57	Dan Schneider	.65	.30	.06
☐ 58	Eddie Mathews	7.00	3.50	.70
☐ 59	Don Lock	.65	.30	.06
☐ 60	Ken Holtzman	1.00	.50	.10
☐ 61	Reggie Smith	1.25	.60	.12
☐ 62	Chuck Dobson	.65	.30	.06
☐ 63	Dick Kenworthy	.65	.30	.06
☐ 64	Jim Merritt	.65	.30	.06
☐ 65	John Roseboro	.65	.30	.06
☐ 66A	Casey Cox	.65	.30	.06
	(white team name)			
☐ 66B	Casey Cox	40.00	20.00	4.00
	(yellow team name)			
☐ 67	Checklist 1	3.00	.40	.10
	Jim Kaat			
☐ 68	Ron Willis	.65	.30	.06
☐ 69	Tom Tresh	1.00	.50	.10
☐ 70	Bob Veale	.65	.30	.06
☐ 71	Vern Fuller	.65	.30	.06
☐ 72	Tommy John	4.00	2.00	.40
☐ 73	Jim Ray Hart	.65	.30	.06
☐ 74	Milt Pappas	.65	.30	.06
☐ 75	Don Mincher	.65	.30	.06
☐ 76	Braves Rookies	.65	.30	.06
	Jim Britton			
	Ron Reed			
☐ 77	Don Wilson	.65	.30	.06
☐ 78	Jim Northrup	1.00	.50	.10
☐ 79	Ted Kubiak	.65	.30	.06
☐ 80	Rod Carew	80.00	37.50	7.50
☐ 81	Larry Jackson	.65	.30	.06
☐ 82	Sam Bowens	.65	.30	.06
☐ 83	John Stephenson	.65	.30	.06
☐ 84	Bob Tolan	.65	.30	.06
☐ 85	Gaylord Perry	6.00	3.00	.60
☐ 86	Willie Stargell	8.00	4.00	.80
☐ 87	Dick Williams MG	1.00	.50	.10
☐ 88	Phil Regan	.65	.30	.06
☐ 89	Jake Gibbs	.65	.30	.06
☐ 90	Vada Pinson	1.00	.50	.10
☐ 91	Jim Ollom	.65	.30	.06
☐ 92	Ed Kranepool	1.00	.50	.10
☐ 93	Tony Cloninger	.65	.30	.06
☐ 94	Lee Maye	.65	.30	.06
☐ 95	Bob Aspromonte	.65	.30	.06
☐ 96	Senator Rookies	.65	.30	.06
	Frank Coggins			
	Dick Nold			
☐ 97	Tom Phoebus	.65	.30	.06
☐ 98	Gary Sutherland	.65	.30	.06
☐ 99	Rocky Colavito	1.50	.75	.15
☐ 100	Bob Gibson	13.50	6.00	1.25
☐ 101	Glenn Beckert	.65	.30	.06
☐ 102	Jose Cardenal	.65	.30	.06
☐ 103	Don Sutton	6.50	3.25	.65
☐ 104	Dick Dietz	.65	.30	.06
☐ 105	Al Downing	.65	.30	.06
☐ 106	Dalton Jones	.65	.30	.06
☐ 107A	Checklist 2	3.00	.35	.10
	Juan Marichal			
	(tan wide mesh)			
☐ 107B	Checklist 2	3.00	.35	.10
	Juan Marichal			
	(brown fine mesh)			
☐ 108	Don Pavletich	.65	.30	.06
☐ 109	Bert Campaneris	1.00	.50	.10
☐ 110	Hank Aaron	50.00	22.50	4.50
☐ 111	Rich Reese	.65	.30	.06
☐ 112	Woodie Fryman	.65	.30	.06
☐ 113	Tigers Rookies	.65	.30	.06
	Tom Matchick			
	Daryl Patterson			
☐ 114	Ron Swoboda	1.00	.50	.10
☐ 115	Sam McDowell	1.00	.50	.10
☐ 116	Ken McMullen	.65	.30	.06
☐ 117	Larry Jaster	.65	.30	.06
☐ 118	Mark Belanger	1.00	.50	.10
☐ 119	Ted Savage	.65	.30	.06
☐ 120	Mel Stottlemyre	1.25	.60	.12
☐ 121	Jimmie Hall	.65	.30	.06
☐ 122	Gene Mauch MG	1.00	.50	.10
☐ 123	Jose Santiago	.65	.30	.06
☐ 124	Nate Oliver	.65	.30	.06
☐ 125	Joel Horlen	.65	.30	.06
☐ 126	Bobby Etheridge	.65	.30	.06
☐ 127	Paul Lindblad	.65	.30	.06
☐ 128	Astros Rookies	.65	.30	.06
	Tom Dukes			
	Alonzo Harris			
☐ 129	Mickey Stanley	1.00	.50	.10
☐ 130	Tony Perez	6.00	3.00	.60
☐ 131	Frank Bertaina	.65	.30	.06
☐ 132	Bud Harrelson	.65	.30	.06
☐ 133	Fred Whitfield	.65	.30	.06
☐ 134	Pat Jarvis	.65	.30	.06
☐ 135	Paul Blair	.65	.30	.06
☐ 136	Randy Hundley	.65	.30	.06
☐ 137	Twins Team	1.50	.75	.15
☐ 138	Ruben Amaro	.65	.30	.06
☐ 139	Chris Short	.65	.30	.06
☐ 140	Tony Conigliaro	1.50	.75	.15
☐ 141	Dal Maxvill	.65	.30	.06
☐ 142	White Sox Rookies	.65	.30	.06
	Buddy Bradford			
	Bill Voss			
☐ 143	Pete Cimino	.65	.30	.06
☐ 144	Joe Morgan	10.00	5.00	1.00
☐ 145	Don Drysdale	7.50	3.75	.75
☐ 146	Sal Bando	1.00	.50	.10
☐ 147	Frank Linzy	.65	.30	.06
☐ 148	Dave Bristol MG	.65	.30	.06
☐ 149	Bob Saverine	.65	.30	.06
☐ 150	Bob Clemente	40.00	17.50	3.50
☐ 151	World Series Game 1	4.00	2.00	.40
	Brock socks 4 hits			
	in opener			
☐ 152	World Series Game 2	6.00	3.00	.60
	Yaz smashes 2 homers			
☐ 153	World Series Game 3	2.00	1.00	.20
	Briles cools Boston			
☐ 154	World Series Game 4	4.00	2.00	.40
	Gibson hurls shutout			
☐ 155	World Series Game 5	2.00	1.00	.20
	Lonborg wins again			
☐ 156	World Series Game 6	2.00	1.00	.20
	Petrocelli 2 homers			
☐ 157	World Series Game 7	2.00	1.00	.20
	St. Louis wins it			
☐ 158	World Series Summary	2.00	1.00	.20
	Cardinals celebrate			
☐ 159	Don Kessinger	.65	.30	.06
☐ 160	Earl Wilson	.65	.30	.06
☐ 161	Norm Miller	.65	.30	.06
☐ 162	Cards Rookies	1.00	.50	.10
	Hal Gilson			
	Mike Torrez			
☐ 163	Gene Brabender	.65	.30	.06
☐ 164	Ramon Webster	.65	.30	.06
☐ 165	Tony Oliva	3.00	1.50	.30
☐ 166	Claude Raymond	.65	.30	.06
☐ 167	Elston Howard	2.25	1.10	.22
☐ 168	Dodgers Team	1.50	.75	.15
☐ 169	Bob Bolin	.65	.30	.06
☐ 170	Jim Fregosi	1.00	.50	.10
☐ 171	Don Nottebart	.65	.30	.06
☐ 172	Walt Williams	.65	.30	.06
☐ 173	John Boozer	.65	.30	.06
☐ 174	Bob Tillman	.65	.30	.06
☐ 175	Maury Wills	3.50	1.75	.35
☐ 176	Bob Allen	.65	.30	.06
☐ 177	Mets Rookies	950.00	475.00	95.00
	Jerry Koosman			
	Nolan Ryan			
☐ 178	Don Wert	.65	.30	.06
☐ 179	Bill Stoneman	.65	.30	.06
☐ 180	Curt Flood	1.00	.50	.10
☐ 181	Jerry Zimmerman	.65	.30	.06
☐ 182	Dave Giusti	.65	.30	.06
☐ 183	Bob Kennedy MG	.65	.30	.06
☐ 184	Lou Johnson	.65	.30	.06

185	Tom Haller	.65	.30	.06
186	Eddie Watt	.65	.30	.06
187	Sonny Jackson	.65	.30	.06
188	Cap Peterson	.65	.30	.06
189	Bill Landis	.65	.30	.06
190	Bill White	1.25	.60	.12
191	Dan Frisella	.65	.30	.06
192	Checklist 3	3.50	.40	.10
	Carl Yastrzemski			
193	Jack Hamilton	.65	.30	.06
194	Don Buford	.65	.30	.06
195	Joe Pepitone	1.25	.60	.12
196	Gary Nolan	.65	.30	.06
197	Larry Brown	.65	.30	.06
198	Roy Face	1.25	.60	.12
199	A's Rookies	.65	.30	.06
	Roberto Rodriquez			
	Darrell Osteen			
200	Orlando Cepeda	3.00	1.50	.30
201	Mike Marshall	1.25	.60	.12
202	Adolfo Phillips	.65	.30	.06
203	Dick Kelley	.65	.30	.06
204	Andy Etchebarren	.65	.30	.06
205	Juan Marichal	5.50	2.75	.55
206	Cal Ermer MG	.65	.30	.06
207	Carroll Sembera	.65	.30	.06
208	Willie Davis	1.00	.50	.10
209	Tim Cullen	.65	.30	.06
210	Gary Peters	.65	.30	.06
211	J.C. Martin	.65	.30	.06
212	Dave Morehead	.65	.30	.06
213	Chico Ruiz	.65	.30	.06
214	Yankees Rookies	1.00	.50	.10
	Stan Bahnsen			
	Frank Fernandez			
215	Jim Bunning	3.00	1.50	.30
216	Bubba Morton	.65	.30	.06
217	Turk Farrell	.65	.30	.06
218	Ken Suarez	.65	.30	.06
219	Rob Gardner	.65	.30	.06
220	Harmon Killebrew	11.00	5.00	1.00
221	Braves Team	1.50	.75	.15
222	Jim Hardin	.65	.30	.06
223	Ollie Brown	.65	.30	.06
224	Jack Aker	.65	.30	.06
225	Richie Allen	1.50	.75	.15
226	Jimmie Price	.65	.30	.06
227	Joe Hoerner	.65	.30	.06
228	Dodgers Rookies	.65	.30	.06
	Jack Billingham			
	Jim Fairey			
229	Fred Klages	.65	.30	.06
230	Pete Rose	50.00	25.00	5.00
231	Dave Baldwin	.65	.30	.06
232	Denis Menke	.65	.30	.06
233	George Scott	1.00	.50	.10
234	Bill Monbouquette	.65	.30	.06
235	Ron Santo	1.25	.60	.12
236	Tug McGraw	1.25	.60	.12
237	Alvin Dark MG	1.00	.50	.10
238	Tom Satriano	.65	.30	.06
239	Bill Henry	.65	.30	.06
240	Al Kaline	14.00	7.00	1.40
241	Felix Millan	.65	.30	.06
242	Moe Drabowsky	.65	.30	.06
243	Rich Rollins	.65	.30	.06
244	John Donaldson	.65	.30	.06
245	Tony Gonzalez	.65	.30	.06
246	Fritz Peterson	.65	.30	.06
247	Reds Rookies	375.00	175.00	37.00
	Johnny Bench			
	Ron Tompkins			
248	Fred Valentine	.65	.30	.06
249	Bill Singer	.65	.30	.06
250	Carl Yastrzemski	33.00	15.00	3.00
251	Manny Sanguillen	2.00	1.00	.20
252	Angels Team	1.50	.75	.15
253	Dick Hughes	.65	.30	.06
254	Cleon Jones	.65	.30	.06
255	Dean Chance	1.00	.50	.10
256	Norm Cash	2.00	1.00	.20
257	Phil Niekro	5.00	2.50	.50
258	Cubs Rookies	.65	.30	.06
	Jose Arcia			
	Bill Schlesinger			
259	Ken Boyer	1.25	.60	.12
260	Jim Wynn	1.00	.50	.10
261	Dave Duncan	.65	.30	.06
262	Rick Wise	.65	.30	.06
263	Horace Clarke	.65	.30	.06
264	Ted Abernathy	.65	.30	.06
265	Tommy Davis	1.00	.50	.10
266	Paul Popovich	.65	.30	.06
267	Herman Franks MG	.65	.30	.06
268	Bob Humphreys	.65	.30	.06
269	Bob Tiefenauer	.65	.30	.06
270	Matty Alou	1.00	.50	.10
271	Bobby Knoop	.65	.30	.06
272	Ray Culp	.65	.30	.06
273	Dave Johnson	1.25	.60	.12
274	Mike Cuellar	1.00	.50	.10
275	Tim McCarver	1.50	.75	.15
276	Jim Roland	.65	.30	.06
277	Jerry Buchek	.65	.30	.06
278	Checklist 4	3.00	.30	.10
	Orlando Cepeda			
279	Bill Hands	.65	.30	.06
280	Mickey Mantle	175.00	85.00	18.00
281	Jim Campanis	.65	.30	.06
282	Rick Monday	1.00	.50	.10
283	Mel Queen	.65	.30	.06
284	Johnny Briggs	.65	.30	.06
285	Dick McAuliffe	.65	.30	.06
286	Cecil Upshaw	.65	.30	.06
287	White Sox Rookies	.65	.30	.06
	Mickey Abarbanel			
	Cisco Carlos			
288	Dave Wickersham	.65	.30	.06
289	Woody Held	.65	.30	.06
290	Willie McCovey	7.50	3.75	.75
291	Dick Lines	.65	.30	.06
292	Art Shamsky	.65	.30	.06
293	Bruce Howard	.65	.30	.06
294	Red Schoendienst MG	3.00	1.50	.30
295	Sonny Siebert	.65	.30	.06
296	Byron Browne	.65	.30	.06
297	Russ Gibson	.65	.30	.06
298	Jim Brewer	.65	.30	.06
299	Gene Michael	1.00	.50	.10
300	Rusty Staub	1.25	.60	.12
301	Twins Rookies	.65	.30	.06
	George Mitterwald			
	Rick Renick			
302	Gerry Arrigo	.65	.30	.06
303	Dick Green	.65	.30	.06
304	Sandy Valdespino	.65	.30	.06
305	Minnie Rojas	.65	.30	.06
306	Mike Ryan	.65	.30	.06
307	John Hiller	1.00	.50	.10
308	Pirates Team	1.50	.75	.15
309	Ken Henderson	.65	.30	.06
310	Luis Aparicio	5.00	2.50	.50
311	Jack Lamabe	.65	.30	.06
312	Curt Blefary	.65	.30	.06
313	Al Weis	.65	.30	.06
314	Red Sox Rookies	.65	.30	.06
	Bill Rohr			
	George Spriggs			
315	Zoilo Versalles	.65	.30	.06
316	Steve Barber	.65	.30	.06
317	Ron Brand	.65	.30	.06
318	Chico Salmon	.65	.30	.06
319	George Culver	.65	.30	.06
320	Frank Howard	1.25	.60	.12
321	Leo Durocher MG	1.50	.75	.15
322	Dave Boswell	.65	.30	.06
323	Deron Johnson	.65	.30	.06
324	Jim Nash	.65	.30	.06
325	Manny Mota	1.00	.50	.10
326	Dennis Ribant	.65	.30	.06
327	Tony Taylor	.65	.30	.06
328	Angels Rookies	.65	.30	.06
	Chuck Vinson			
	Jim Weaver			
329	Duane Josephson	.65	.30	.06
330	Roger Maris	24.00	12.00	2.40
331	Dan Osinski	.65	.30	.06
332	Doug Rader	1.00	.50	.10
333	Ron Herbel	.65	.30	.06
334	Orioles Team	1.50	.75	.15
335	Bob Allison	1.00	.50	.10
336	John Purdin	.65	.30	.06
337	Bill Robinson	1.00	.50	.10
338	Bob Johnson	.65	.30	.06
339	Rich Nye	.65	.30	.06
340	Max Alvis	.65	.30	.06
341	Jim Lemon MG	.65	.30	.06
342	Ken Johnson	.65	.30	.06
343	Jim Gosger	.65	.30	.06
344	Donn Clendenon	1.00	.50	.10
345	Bob Hendley	.65	.30	.06
346	Jerry Adair	.65	.30	.06
347	George Brunet	.65	.30	.06
348	Phillies Rookies	.65	.30	.06
	Larry Colton			
	Dick Thoenen			
349	Ed Spiezio	.65	.30	.06
350	Hoyt Wilhelm	5.50	2.75	.55
351	Bob Barton	.65	.30	.06
352	Jackie Hernandez	.65	.30	.06

☐ 353	Mack Jones	.65	.30	.06	
☐ 354	Pete Richert	.65	.30	.06	
☐ 355	Ernie Banks	11.00	5.50	1.10	
☐ 356A	Checklist 5	3.00	.30	.10	
	Ken Holtzman				
	(head centered				
	within circle)				
☐ 356B	Checklist 5	3.00	.30	.10	
	Ken Holtzman				
	(head shifted right				
	within circle)				
☐ 357	Len Gabrielson	.65	.30	.06	
☐ 358	Mike Epstein	.65	.30	.06	
☐ 359	Joe Moeller	.65	.30	.06	
☐ 360	Willie Horton	1.00	.50	.10	
☐ 361	Harmon Killebrew AS	4.50	2.25	.45	
☐ 362	Orlando Cepeda AS	1.50	.75	.15	
☐ 363	Rod Carew AS	9.00	4.50	.90	
☐ 364	Joe Morgan AS	5.00	2.25	.45	
☐ 365	Brooks Robinson AS	5.00	2.50	.50	
☐ 366	Ron Santo AS	1.00	.50	.10	
☐ 367	Jim Fregosi AS	1.00	.50	.10	
☐ 368	Gene Alley AS	.65	.30	.06	
☐ 369	Carl Yastrzemski AS	10.00	5.00	1.00	
☐ 370	Hank Aaron AS	10.00	5.00	1.00	
☐ 371	Tony Oliva AS	1.25	.60	.12	
☐ 372	Lou Brock AS	5.00	2.50	.50	
☐ 373	Frank Robinson AS	5.00	2.50	.50	
☐ 374	Bob Clemente AS	9.00	4.50	.90	
☐ 375	Bill Freehan AS	1.00	.50	.10	
☐ 376	Tim McCarver AS	1.00	.50	.10	
☐ 377	Joel Horlen AS	.65	.30	.06	
☐ 378	Bob Gibson AS	4.50	2.25	.45	
☐ 379	Gary Peters AS	.65	.30	.06	
☐ 380	Ken Holtzman AS	.65	.30	.06	
☐ 381	Boog Powell	1.50	.75	.15	
☐ 382	Ramon Hernandez	.65	.30	.06	
☐ 383	Steve Whitaker	.65	.30	.06	
☐ 384	Reds Rookies	4.50	2.25	.45	
	Bill Henry				
	Hal McRae				
☐ 385	Jim Hunter	8.50	4.25	.85	
☐ 386	Greg Goossen	.65	.30	.06	
☐ 387	Joe Foy	.65	.30	.06	
☐ 388	Ray Washburn	.65	.30	.06	
☐ 389	Jay Johnstone	1.00	.50	.10	
☐ 390	Bill Mazeroski	1.25	.60	.12	
☐ 391	Bob Priddy	.65	.30	.06	
☐ 392	Grady Hatton MG	.65	.30	.06	
☐ 393	Jim Perry	1.00	.50	.10	
☐ 394	Tommie Aaron	1.00	.50	.10	
☐ 395	Camilo Pascual	.65	.30	.06	
☐ 396	Bobby Wine	.65	.30	.06	
☐ 397	Vic Davalillo	.65	.30	.06	
☐ 398	Jim Grant	.65	.30	.06	
☐ 399	Ray Oyler	.65	.30	.06	
☐ 400A	Mike McCormick	.65	.30	.06	
	(yellow letters)				
☐ 400B	Mike McCormick	40.00	20.00	4.00	
	(team name in				
	white letters)				
☐ 401	Mets Team	1.75	.85	.17	
☐ 402	Mike Hegan	.65	.30	.06	
☐ 403	John Buzhardt	.65	.30	.06	
☐ 404	Floyd Robinson	.65	.30	.06	
☐ 405	Tommy Helms	.65	.30	.06	
☐ 406	Dick Ellsworth	.65	.30	.06	
☐ 407	Gary Kolb	.65	.30	.06	
☐ 408	Steve Carlton	33.00	15.00	3.00	
☐ 409	Orioles Rookies	.65	.30	.06	
	Frank Peters				
	Don Stone				
☐ 410	Fergie Jenkins	4.00	2.00	.40	
☐ 411	Ron Hansen	.65	.30	.06	
☐ 412	Clay Carroll	.65	.30	.06	
☐ 413	Tom McCraw	.65	.30	.06	
☐ 414	Mickey Lolich	2.25	1.10	.22	
☐ 415	Johnny Callison	1.00	.50	.10	
☐ 416	Bill Rigney MG	.65	.30	.06	
☐ 417	Willie Crawford	.65	.30	.06	
☐ 418	Eddie Fisher	.65	.30	.06	
☐ 419	Jack Hiatt	.65	.30	.06	
☐ 420	Cesar Tovar	.65	.30	.06	
☐ 421	Ron Taylor	.65	.30	.06	
☐ 422	Rene Lachemann	1.00	.50	.10	
☐ 423	Fred Gladding	.65	.30	.06	
☐ 424	Chicago White Sox	1.50	.75	.15	
	Team Card				
☐ 425	Jim Maloney	1.00	.50	.10	
☐ 426	Hank Allen	.65	.30	.06	
☐ 427	Dick Calmus	.65	.30	.06	
☐ 428	Vic Roznovsky	.65	.30	.06	
☐ 429	Tommie Sisk	.65	.30	.06	
☐ 430	Rico Petrocelli	1.00	.50	.10	
☐ 431	Dooley Womack	.65	.30	.06	
☐ 432	Indians Rookies	.65	.30	.06	
	Bill Davis				
	Jose Vidal				
☐ 433	Bob Rodgers	1.00	.50	.10	
☐ 434	Ricardo Joseph	.65	.30	.06	
☐ 435	Ron Perranoski	1.00	.50	.10	
☐ 436	Hal Lanier	1.00	.50	.10	
☐ 437	Don Cardwell	.65	.30	.06	
☐ 438	Lee Thomas	1.00	.50	.10	
☐ 439	Lum Harris MG	.65	.30	.06	
☐ 440	Claude Osteen	.65	.30	.06	
☐ 441	Alex Johnson	.65	.30	.06	
☐ 442	Dick Bosman	.65	.30	.06	
☐ 443	Joe Azcue	.65	.30	.06	
☐ 444	Jack Fisher	.65	.30	.06	
☐ 445	Mike Shannon	1.00	.50	.10	
☐ 446	Ron Kline	.65	.30	.06	
☐ 447	Tigers Rookies	.65	.30	.06	
	George Korince				
	Fred Lasher				
☐ 448	Gary Wagner	.65	.30	.06	
☐ 449	Gene Oliver	.65	.30	.06	
☐ 450	Jim Kaat	3.00	1.50	.30	
☐ 451	Al Spangler	.65	.30	.06	
☐ 452	Jesus Alou	.65	.30	.06	
☐ 453	Sammy Ellis	.65	.30	.06	
☐ 454A	Checklist 6	3.00	.30	.10	
	Frank Robinson				
	(cap complete				
	within circle)				
☐ 454B	Checklist 6	3.00	.30	.10	
	Frank Robinson				
	(cap partially				
	within circle)				
☐ 455	Rico Carty	1.00	.50	.10	
☐ 456	John O'Donoghue	.65	.30	.06	
☐ 457	Jim Lefebvre	1.25	.60	.12	
☐ 458	Lew Krausse	.80	.40	.08	
☐ 459	Dick Simpson	.80	.40	.08	
☐ 460	Jim Lonborg	1.50	.75	.15	
☐ 461	Chuck Hiller	.80	.40	.08	
☐ 462	Barry Moore	.80	.40	.08	
☐ 463	Jim Schaffer	.80	.40	.08	
☐ 464	Don McMahon	.80	.40	.08	
☐ 465	Tommie Agee	1.00	.50	.10	
☐ 466	Bill Dillman	.80	.40	.08	
☐ 467	Dick Howser	1.25	.60	.12	
☐ 468	Larry Sherry	1.00	.50	.10	
☐ 469	Ty Cline	.80	.40	.08	
☐ 470	Bill Freehan	1.50	.75	.15	
☐ 471	Orlando Pena	.80	.40	.08	
☐ 472	Walt Alston MG	2.00	1.00	.20	
☐ 473	Al Worthington	.80	.40	.08	
☐ 474	Paul Schaal	.80	.40	.08	
☐ 475	Joe Niekro	1.50	.75	.15	
☐ 476	Woody Woodward	1.00	.50	.10	
☐ 477	Philadelphia Phillies	1.75	.85	.17	
	Team Card				
☐ 478	Dave McNally	1.25	.60	.12	
☐ 479	Phil Gagliano	.80	.40	.08	
☐ 480	Manager's Dream	15.00	7.50	1.50	
	Tony Oliva				
	Chico Cardenas				
	Bob Clemente				
☐ 481	John Wyatt	.80	.40	.08	
☐ 482	Jose Pagan	.80	.40	.08	
☐ 483	Darold Knowles	.80	.40	.08	
☐ 484	Phil Roof	.80	.40	.08	
☐ 485	Ken Berry	.80	.40	.08	
☐ 486	Cal Koonce	.80	.40	.08	
☐ 487	Lee May	1.25	.60	.12	
☐ 488	Dick Tracewski	.80	.40	.08	
☐ 489	Wally Bunker	.80	.40	.08	
☐ 490	Super Stars	45.00	22.50	4.50	
	Harmon Killebrew				
	Willie Mays				
	Mickey Mantle				
☐ 491	Denny Lemaster	.80	.40	.08	
☐ 492	Jeff Torborg	1.25	.60	.12	
☐ 493	Jim McGlothlin	.80	.40	.08	
☐ 494	Ray Sadecki	.80	.40	.08	
☐ 495	Leon Wagner	.80	.40	.08	
☐ 496	Steve Hamilton	.80	.40	.08	
☐ 497	Cards Team	1.75	.85	.17	
☐ 498	Bill Bryan	.80	.40	.08	
☐ 499	Steve Blass	1.00	.50	.10	
☐ 500	Frank Robinson	12.00	6.00	1.20	
☐ 501	John Odom	.80	.40	.08	
☐ 502	Mike Andrews	.80	.40	.08	
☐ 503	Al Jackson	.80	.40	.08	
☐ 504	Russ Snyder	.80	.40	.08	
☐ 505	Joe Sparma	.80	.40	.08	
☐ 506	Clarence Jones	.80	.40	.08	
☐ 507	Wade Blasingame	.80	.40	.08	
☐ 508	Duke Sims	.80	.40	.08	

☐ 509	Dennis Higgins	.80	.40	.08
☐ 510	Ron Fairly	1.00	.50	.10
☐ 511	Bill Kelso	.80	.40	.08
☐ 512	Grant Jackson	.80	.40	.08
☐ 513	Hank Bauer MG	1.25	.60	.12
☐ 514	Al McBean	.80	.40	.08
☐ 515	Russ Nixon	1.00	.50	.10
☐ 516	Pete Mikkelsen	.80	.40	.08
☐ 517	Diego Segui	.80	.40	.08
☐ 518A	Checklist 7	4.00	.40	.10
	(539 ML Rookies)			
	(Clete Boyer)			
☐ 518B	Checklist 7	8.00	.60	.15
	(539 AL Rookies)			
	(Clete Boyer)			
☐ 519	Jerry Stephenson	.80	.40	.08
☐ 520	Lou Brock	13.00	6.00	1.20
☐ 521	Don Shaw	.80	.40	.08
☐ 522	Wayne Causey	.80	.40	.08
☐ 523	John Tsitouris	.80	.40	.08
☐ 524	Andy Kosco	.80	.40	.08
☐ 525	Jim Davenport	1.00	.50	.10
☐ 526	Bill Denehy	.80	.40	.08
☐ 527	Tito Francona	.80	.40	.08
☐ 528	Tigers Team	15.00	6.00	1.20
☐ 529	Bruce Von Hoff	.80	.40	.08
☐ 530	Bird Belters	6.00	3.00	.60
	Brooks Robinson			
	Frank Robinson			
☐ 531	Chuck Hinton	.80	.40	.08
☐ 532	Luis Tiant	1.50	.75	.15
☐ 533	Wes Parker	1.00	.50	.10
☐ 534	Bob Miller	.80	.40	.08
☐ 535	Danny Cater	.80	.40	.08
☐ 536	Bill Short	.80	.40	.08
☐ 537	Norm Siebern	.80	.40	.08
☐ 538	Manny Jimenez	.80	.40	.08
☐ 539	Major League Rookies	1.25	.60	.12
	Jim Ray			
	Mike Ferraro			
☐ 540	Nelson Briles	1.00	.50	.10
☐ 541	Sandy Alomar	1.00	.50	.10
☐ 542	John Boccabella	.80	.40	.08
☐ 543	Bob Lee	.80	.40	.08
☐ 544	Mayo Smith MG	.80	.40	.08
☐ 545	Lindy McDaniel	1.00	.50	.10
☐ 546	Roy White	1.25	.60	.12
☐ 547	Dan Coombs	.80	.40	.08
☐ 548	Bernie Allen	.80	.40	.08
☐ 549	Orioles Rookies	.80	.40	.08
	Curt Motton			
	Roger Nelson			
☐ 550	Clete Boyer	1.25	.60	.12
☐ 551	Darrell Sutherland	.80	.40	.08
☐ 552	Ed Kirkpatrick	.80	.40	.08
☐ 553	Hank Aguirre	.80	.40	.08
☐ 554	A's Team	2.00	1.00	.20
☐ 555	Jose Tartabull	.80	.40	.08
☐ 556	Dick Selma	.80	.40	.08
☐ 557	Frank Quilici	.80	.40	.08
☐ 558	Johnny Edwards	.80	.40	.08
☐ 559	Pirates Rookies	1.00	.50	.10
	Carl Taylor			
	Luke Walker			
☐ 560	Paul Casanova	.80	.40	.08
☐ 561	Lee Elia	1.25	.60	.12
☐ 562	Jim Bouton	1.50	.75	.15
☐ 563	Ed Charles	.80	.40	.08
☐ 564	Eddie Stanky MG	1.00	.50	.10
☐ 565	Larry Dierker	1.00	.50	.10
☐ 566	Ken Harrelson	1.50	.75	.15
☐ 567	Clay Dalrymple	.80	.40	.08
☐ 568	Willie Smith	.80	.40	.08
☐ 569	NL Rookies	.80	.40	.08
	Ivan Murrell			
	Les Rohr			
☐ 570	Rick Reichardt	.80	.40	.08
☐ 571	Tony LaRussa	2.00	1.00	.20
☐ 572	Don Bosch	.80	.40	.08
☐ 573	Joe Coleman	.80	.40	.08
☐ 574	Cincinnati Reds	2.00	1.00	.20
	Team Card			
☐ 575	Jim Palmer	25.00	12.50	2.50
☐ 576	Dave Adlesh	.80	.40	.08
☐ 577	Fred Talbot	.80	.40	.08
☐ 578	Orlando Martinez	.80	.40	.08
☐ 579	NL Rookies	1.00	.50	.10
	Larry Hisle			
	Mike Lum			
☐ 580	Bob Bailey	.80	.40	.08
☐ 581	Garry Roggenburk	.80	.40	.08
☐ 582	Jerry Grote	.80	.40	.08
☐ 583	Gates Brown	1.00	.50	.10
☐ 584	Larry Shepard MG	.80	.40	.08
☐ 585	Wilbur Wood	1.00	.50	.10

☐ 586	Jim Pagliaroni	.80	.40	.08
☐ 587	Roger Repoz	.80	.40	.08
☐ 588	Dick Schofield	.80	.40	.08
☐ 589	Twins Rookies	.80	.40	.08
	Ron Clark			
	Moe Ogier			
☐ 590	Tommy Harper	1.00	.50	.10
☐ 591	Dick Nen	.80	.40	.08
☐ 592	John Bateman	.80	.40	.08
☐ 593	Lee Stange	.80	.40	.08
☐ 594	Phil Linz	1.00	.50	.10
☐ 595	Phil Ortega	.80	.40	.08
☐ 596	Charlie Smith	.80	.40	.08
☐ 597	Bill McCool	.80	.40	.08
☐ 598	Jerry May	1.50	.50	.10

1968 Topps Game

The cards in this 33-card set measure 2 1/4" by 3 1/4". This "Game" card set of players, issued as inserts with the regular 1968 Topps baseball series, was patterned directly after the Red Back and Blue Back sets of 1951. Each card has a color player photo set upon a pure white background, with a facsimile autograph underneath the picture. The cards have blue backs, and were also sold in boxed sets on a limited basis.

			NRMT	VG-E	GOOD
	COMPLETE SET (33)		60.00	30.00	6.00
	COMMON PLAYER (1-33)		.30	.15	.03
☐ 1	Matty Alou		.30	.15	.03
☐ 2	Mickey Mantle		15.00	7.50	1.50
☐ 3	Carl Yastrzemski		9.00	4.50	.90
☐ 4	Hank Aaron		6.00	3.00	.60
☐ 5	Harmon Killebrew		2.00	1.00	.20
☐ 6	Roberto Clemente		5.00	2.50	.50
☐ 7	Frank Robinson		3.00	1.50	.30
☐ 8	Willie Mays		6.00	3.00	.60
☐ 9	Brooks Robinson		3.50	1.75	.35
☐ 10	Tommy Davis		.30	.15	.03
☐ 11	Bill Freehan		.40	.20	.04
☐ 12	Claude Osteen		.30	.15	.03
☐ 13	Gary Peters		.30	.15	.03
☐ 14	Jim Lonborg		.30	.15	.03
☐ 15	Steve Hargan		.30	.15	.03
☐ 16	Dean Chance		.30	.15	.03
☐ 17	Mike McCormick		.30	.15	.03
☐ 18	Tim McCarver		.60	.30	.06
☐ 19	Ron Santo		.50	.25	.05
☐ 20	Tony Gonzalez		.30	.15	.03
☐ 21	Frank Howard		.40	.20	.04
☐ 22	George Scott		.30	.15	.03
☐ 23	Rich Allen		.40	.20	.04
☐ 24	Jim Wynn		.30	.15	.03
☐ 25	Gene Alley		.30	.15	.03
☐ 26	Rick Monday		.30	.15	.03
☐ 27	Al Kaline		3.50	1.75	.35
☐ 28	Rusty Staub		.50	.25	.05
☐ 29	Rod Carew		4.00	2.00	.40
☐ 30	Pete Rose		9.00	4.50	.90
☐ 31	Joe Torre		.50	.25	.05
☐ 32	Orlando Cepeda		.50	.25	.05
☐ 33	Jim Fregosi		.40	.20	.04

1969 Topps

The cards in this 664-card set measure 2 1/2" by 3 1/2". The 1969 Topps set includes Sporting News All-Star Selections as card numbers 416 to 435. Other popular subsets within this set include League Leaders (1-12) and World Series cards (162-169). The fifth series contains several variations; the more difficult variety consists of cards with the player's first name, last name, and/or position in white letters instead of lettering in some other color. These are designated in the checklist below by WL (white letters). Each checklist card features a different popular player's picture inside a circle on the front of the checklist card. Two different poses of Clay Dalrymple and Donn Clendenon exist as indicated in the checklist.

		NRMT	VG-E	GOOD
COMPLETE SET (664)		2000.00	1000.00	250.00
COMMON PLAYER (1-218)		.50	.25	.05
COMMON PLAYER (219-327)		.80	.40	.08
COMMON PLAYER (328-512)		.50	.25	.05
COMMON PLAYER (513-588)		.60	.30	.06
COMMON PLAYER (589-664)		.80	.40	.08

			NRMT	VG-E	GOOD
☐	1	AL Batting Leaders	7.50	1.50	.30
		Carl Yastrzemski			
		Danny Cater			
		Tony Oliva			
☐	2	NL Batting Leaders	3.50	1.75	.35
		Pete Rose			
		Matty Alou			
		Felipe Alou			
☐	3	AL RBI Leaders	1.50	.75	.15
		Ken Harrelson			
		Frank Howard			
		Jim Northrup			
☐	4	NL RBI Leaders	2.50	1.25	.25
		Willie McCovey			
		Ron Santo			
		Billy Williams			
☐	5	AL Home Run Leaders	1.50	.75	.15
		Frank Howard			
		Willie Horton			
		Ken Harrelson			
☐	6	NL Home Run Leaders	2.50	1.25	.25
		Willie McCovey			
		Richie Allen			
		Ernie Banks			
☐	7	AL ERA Leaders	1.50	.75	.15
		Luis Tiant			
		Sam McDowell			
		Dave McNally			
☐	8	NL ERA Leaders	1.50	.75	.15
		Bob Gibson			
		Bobby Bolin			
		Bob Veale			
☐	9	AL Pitching Leaders	1.50	.75	.15
		Denny McLain			
		Dave McNally			
		Luis Tiant			
		Mel Stottlemyre			
☐	10	NL Pitching Leaders	2.50	1.25	.25
		Juan Marichal			
		Bob Gibson			
		Fergie Jenkins			
☐	11	AL Strikeout Leaders	1.50	.75	.15

			NRMT	VG-E	GOOD
		Sam McDowell			
		Denny McLain			
		Luis Tiant			
☐	12	NL Strikeout Leaders	1.50	.75	.15
		Bob Gibson			
		Fergie Jenkins			
		Bill Singer			
☐	13	Mickey Stanley	.75	.35	.07
☐	14	Al McBean	.50	.25	.05
☐	15	Boog Powell	1.50	.75	.15
☐	16	Giants Rookies	.50	.25	.05
		Cesar Gutierrez			
		Rich Robertson			
☐	17	Mike Marshall	.75	.35	.07
☐	18	Dick Schofield	.50	.25	.05
☐	19	Ken Suarez	.50	.25	.05
☐	20	Ernie Banks	10.00	5.00	1.00
☐	21	Jose Santiago	.50	.25	.05
☐	22	Jesus Alou	.50	.25	.05
☐	23	Lew Krausse	.50	.25	.05
☐	24	Walt Alston MG	1.75	.85	.17
☐	25	Roy White	.75	.35	.07
☐	26	Clay Carroll	.50	.25	.05
☐	27	Bernie Allen	.50	.25	.05
☐	28	Mike Ryan	.50	.25	.05
☐	29	Dave Morehead	.50	.25	.05
☐	30	Bob Allison	.75	.35	.07
☐	31	Mets Rookies	1.50	.75	.15
		Gary Gentry			
		Amos Otis			
☐	32	Sammy Ellis	.50	.25	.05
☐	33	Wayne Causey	.50	.25	.05
☐	34	Gary Peters	.75	.35	.07
☐	35	Joe Morgan	8.00	4.00	.80
☐	36	Luke Walker	.50	.25	.05
☐	37	Curt Motton	.50	.25	.05
☐	38	Zoilo Versalles	.50	.25	.05
☐	39	Dick Hughes	.50	.25	.05
☐	40	Mayo Smith MG	.50	.25	.05
☐	41	Bob Barton	.50	.25	.05
☐	42	Tommy Harper	.75	.35	.07
☐	43	Joe Niekro	1.00	.50	.10
☐	44	Danny Cater	.50	.25	.05
☐	45	Maury Wills	2.00	1.00	.20
☐	46	Fritz Peterson	.50	.25	.05
☐	47A	Paul Popovich	.50	.25	.05
		(no helmet emblem)			
☐	47B	Paul Popovich	15.00	7.50	1.50
		(C emblem on helmet)			
☐	48	Brant Alyea	.50	.25	.05
☐	49A	Royals Rookies	.50	.25	.05
		Steve Jones			
		E. Rodriguez "g"			
☐	49B	Royals Rookies	15.00	7.50	1.50
		Steve Jones			
		E. Rodriquez "q"			
☐	50	Bob Clemente UER	35.00	15.00	3.00
		(Bats Right			
		listed twice)			
☐	51	Woodie Fryman	.50	.25	.05
☐	52	Mike Andrews	.50	.25	.05
☐	53	Sonny Jackson	.50	.25	.05
☐	54	Cisco Carlos	.50	.25	.05
☐	55	Jerry Grote	.50	.25	.05
☐	56	Rich Reese	.50	.25	.05
☐	57	Checklist 1	2.50	.30	.10
		Denny McLain			
☐	58	Fred Gladding	.50	.25	.05
☐	59	Jay Johnstone	.75	.35	.07
☐	60	Nelson Briles	.50	.25	.05
☐	61	Jimmie Hall	.50	.25	.05
☐	62	Chico Salmon	.50	.25	.05
☐	63	Jim Hickman	.50	.25	.05
☐	64	Bill Monbouquette	.50	.25	.05
☐	65	Willie Davis	.75	.35	.07
☐	66	Orioles Rookies	.75	.35	.07
		Mike Adamson			
		Merv Rettenmund			
☐	67	Bill Stoneman	.50	.25	.05
☐	68	Dave Duncan	.50	.25	.05
☐	69	Steve Hamilton	.50	.25	.05
☐	70	Tommy Helms	.75	.35	.07
☐	71	Steve Whitaker	.50	.25	.05
☐	72	Ron Taylor	.50	.25	.05
☐	73	Johnny Briggs	.50	.25	.05
☐	74	Preston Gomez MG	.50	.25	.05
☐	75	Luis Aparicio	5.00	2.50	.50
☐	76	Norm Miller	.50	.25	.05
☐	77A	Ron Perranoski	.75	.35	.07
		(no emblem on cap)			
☐	77B	Ron Perranoski	15.00	7.50	1.50
		(LA on cap)			
☐	78	Tom Satriano	.50	.25	.05
☐	79	Milt Pappas	.75	.35	.07
☐	80	Norm Cash	1.25	.60	.12

☐ 81	Mel Queen	.50	.25	.05
☐ 82	Pirates Rookies	8.00	4.00	.80
	Rich Hebner			
	Al Oliver			
☐ 83	Mike Ferraro	.75	.35	.07
☐ 84	Bob Humphreys	.50	.25	.05
☐ 85	Lou Brock	10.00	5.00	1.00
☐ 86	Pete Richert	.50	.25	.05
☐ 87	Horace Clarke	.50	.25	.05
☐ 88	Rich Nye	.50	.25	.05
☐ 89	Russ Gibson	.50	.25	.05
☐ 90	Jerry Koosman	2.00	1.00	.20
☐ 91	Alvin Dark MG	.75	.35	.07
☐ 92	Jack Billingham	.50	.25	.05
☐ 93	Joe Foy	.50	.25	.05
☐ 94	Hank Aguirre	.50	.25	.05
☐ 95	Johnny Bench	125.00	60.00	12.50
☐ 96	Denny Lemaster	.50	.25	.05
☐ 97	Buddy Bradford	.50	.25	.05
☐ 98	Dave Giusti	.75	.35	.07
☐ 99A	Twins Rookies	15.00	7.50	1.50
	Danny Morris			
	Graig Nettles			
	(no loop)			
☐ 99B	Twins Rookies	30.00	15.00	3.00
	(errant loop in			
	upper left corner			
	of obverse)			
☐ 100	Hank Aaron	40.00	17.50	3.50
☐ 101	Daryl Patterson	.50	.25	.05
☐ 102	Jim Davenport	.75	.35	.07
☐ 103	Roger Repoz	.50	.25	.05
☐ 104	Steve Blass	.75	.35	.07
☐ 105	Rick Monday	.75	.35	.07
☐ 106	Jim Hannan	.50	.25	.05
☐ 107A	Checklist 2	2.50	.30	.10
	(161 Jim Purdin)			
	(Bob Gibson)			
☐ 107B	Checklist 2	6.00	.75	.15
	(161 John Purdin)			
	(Bob Gibson)			
☐ 108	Tony Taylor	.50	.25	.05
☐ 109	Jim Lonborg	1.00	.50	.10
☐ 110	Mike Shannon	.75	.35	.07
☐ 111	Johnny Morris	.50	.25	.05
☐ 112	J.C. Martin	.50	.25	.05
☐ 113	Dave May	.50	.25	.05
☐ 114	Yankees Rookies	.50	.25	.05
	Alan Closter			
	John Cumberland			
☐ 115	Bill Hands	.50	.25	.05
☐ 116	Chuck Harrison	.50	.25	.05
☐ 117	Jim Fairey	.50	.25	.05
☐ 118	Stan Williams	.50	.25	.05
☐ 119	Doug Rader	.75	.35	.07
☐ 120	Pete Rose	35.00	17.50	3.50
☐ 121	Joe Grzenda	.50	.25	.05
☐ 122	Ron Fairly	.75	.35	.07
☐ 123	Wilbur Wood	.75	.35	.07
☐ 124	Hank Bauer MG	.75	.35	.07
☐ 125	Ray Sadecki	.50	.25	.05
☐ 126	Dick Tracewski	.50	.25	.05
☐ 127	Kevin Collins	.50	.25	.05
☐ 128	Tommie Aaron	.75	.35	.07
☐ 129	Bill McCool	.50	.25	.05
☐ 130	Carl Yastrzemski	28.00	13.50	2.70
☐ 131	Chris Cannizzaro	.50	.25	.05
☐ 132	Dave Baldwin	.50	.25	.05
☐ 133	Johnny Callison	.75	.35	.07
☐ 134	Jim Weaver	.50	.25	.05
☐ 135	Tommy Davis	1.00	.50	.10
☐ 136	Cards Rookies	.75	.35	.07
	Steve Huntz			
	Mike Torrez			
☐ 137	Wally Bunker	.50	.25	.05
☐ 138	John Bateman	.50	.25	.05
☐ 139	Andy Kosco	.50	.25	.05
☐ 140	Jim Lefebvre	1.00	.50	.10
☐ 141	Bill Dillman	.50	.25	.05
☐ 142	Woody Woodward	.75	.35	.07
☐ 143	Joe Nossek	.50	.25	.05
☐ 144	Bob Hendley	.50	.25	.05
☐ 145	Max Alvis	.50	.25	.05
☐ 146	Jim Perry	.75	.35	.07
☐ 147	Leo Durocher MG	1.25	.60	.12
☐ 148	Lee Stange	.50	.25	.05
☐ 149	Ollie Brown	.50	.25	.05
☐ 150	Denny McLain	2.50	1.25	.25
☐ 151A	Clay Dalrymple	.50	.25	.05
	(Portrait, Orioles)			
☐ 151B	Clay Dalrymple	15.00	7.50	1.50
	(Catching, Phillies)			
☐ 152	Tommie Sisk	.50	.25	.05
☐ 153	Ed Brinkman	.50	.25	.05
☐ 154	Jim Britton	.50	.25	.05
☐ 155	Pete Ward	.50	.25	.05
☐ 156	Houston Rookies	.50	.25	.05
	Hal Gilson			
	Leon McFadden			
☐ 157	Bob Rodgers	.75	.35	.07
☐ 158	Joe Gibbon	.50	.25	.05
☐ 159	Jerry Adair	.50	.25	.05
☐ 160	Vada Pinson	1.00	.50	.10
☐ 161	John Purdin	.50	.25	.05
☐ 162	World Series Game 1	3.50	1.75	.35
	Gibson fans 17			
☐ 163	World Series Game 2	2.00	1.00	.20
	Tiger homers			
	deck the Cards			
☐ 164	World Series Game 3	2.50	1.25	.25
	McCarver's homer			
☐ 165	World Series Game 4	3.50	1.75	.35
	Brock lead-off homer			
☐ 166	World Series Game 5	4.50	2.25	.45
	Kaline's key hit			
☐ 167	World Series Game 6	2.00	1.00	.20
	Northrup grandslam			
☐ 168	World Series Game 7	3.50	1.75	.35
	Lolich outduels			
	Bob Gibson			
☐ 169	World Series Summary	2.00	1.00	.20
	Tigers celebrate			
☐ 170	Frank Howard	1.00	.50	.10
☐ 171	Glenn Beckert	.75	.35	.07
☐ 172	Jerry Stephenson	.50	.25	.05
☐ 173	White Sox Rookies	.50	.25	.05
	Bob Christian			
	Gerry Nyman			
☐ 174	Grant Jackson	.50	.25	.05
☐ 175	Jim Bunning	2.50	1.25	.25
☐ 176	Joe Azcue	.50	.25	.05
☐ 177	Ron Reed	.50	.25	.05
☐ 178	Ray Oyler	.50	.25	.05
☐ 179	Don Pavletich	.50	.25	.05
☐ 180	Willie Horton	.75	.35	.07
☐ 181	Mel Nelson	.50	.25	.05
☐ 182	Bill Rigney MG	.50	.25	.05
☐ 183	Don Shaw	.50	.25	.05
☐ 184	Roberto Pena	.50	.25	.05
☐ 185	Tom Phoebus	.50	.25	.05
☐ 186	Johnny Edwards	.50	.25	.05
☐ 187	Leon Wagner	.50	.25	.05
☐ 188	Rick Wise	.75	.35	.07
☐ 189	Red Sox Rookies	.50	.25	.05
	Joe Lahoud			
	John Thibodeau			
☐ 190	Willie Mays	40.00	17.50	3.50
☐ 191	Lindy McDaniel	.75	.35	.07
☐ 192	Jose Pagan	.50	.25	.05
☐ 193	Don Cardwell	.50	.25	.05
☐ 194	Ted Uhlaender	.50	.25	.05
☐ 195	John Odom	.50	.25	.05
☐ 196	Lum Harris MG	.50	.25	.05
☐ 197	Dick Selma	.50	.25	.05
☐ 198	Willie Smith	.50	.25	.05
☐ 199	Jim French	.50	.25	.05
☐ 200	Bob Gibson	9.00	4.50	.90
☐ 201	Russ Snyder	.50	.25	.05
☐ 202	Don Wilson	.50	.25	.05
☐ 203	Dave Johnson	1.00	.50	.10
☐ 204	Jack Hiatt	.50	.25	.05
☐ 205	Rick Reichardt	.50	.25	.05
☐ 206	Phillies Rookies	.75	.35	.07
	Larry Hisle			
	Barry Lersch			
☐ 207	Roy Face	.75	.35	.07
☐ 208A	Donn Clendenon	.75	.35	.07
	(Houston)			
☐ 208B	Donn Clendenon	15.00	7.50	1.50
	(Expos)			
☐ 209	Larry Haney	.50	.25	.05
	(reverse negative)			
☐ 210	Felix Millan	.50	.25	.05
☐ 211	Galen Cisco	.50	.25	.05
☐ 212	Tom Tresh	.75	.35	.07
☐ 213	Gerry Arrigo	.50	.25	.05
☐ 214	Checklist 3	2.50	.30	.10
	With 69T deckle CL			
	on back (no player)			
☐ 215	Rico Petrocelli	.75	.35	.07
☐ 216	Don Sutton	5.00	2.50	.50
☐ 217	John Donaldson	.50	.25	.05
☐ 218	John Roseboro	.75	.35	.07
☐ 219	Freddie Patek	1.25	.60	.12
☐ 220	Sam McDowell	1.25	.60	.12
☐ 221	Art Shamsky	.85	.40	.08
☐ 222	Duane Josephson	.85	.40	.08
☐ 223	Tom Dukes	.85	.40	.08
☐ 224	Angels Rookies	.85	.40	.08
	Bill Harrelson			

	Steve Kealey			
225	Don Kessinger	1.25	.60	.12
226	Bruce Howard	.85	.40	.08
227	Frank Johnson	.85	.40	.08
228	Dave Leonhard	.85	.40	.08
229	Don Lock	.85	.40	.08
230	Rusty Staub	1.75	.85	.17
231	Pat Dobson	1.25	.60	.12
232	Dave Ricketts	.85	.40	.08
233	Steve Barber	.85	.40	.08
234	Dave Bristol MG	.85	.40	.08
235	Jim Hunter	9.00	4.50	.90
236	Manny Mota	1.25	.60	.12
237	Bobby Cox	1.25	.60	.12
238	Ken Johnson	.85	.40	.08
239	Bob Taylor	.85	.40	.08
240	Ken Harrelson	1.50	.75	.15
241	Jim Brewer	.85	.40	.08
242	Frank Kostro	.85	.40	.08
243	Ron Kline	.85	.40	.08
244	Indians Rookies	1.25	.60	.12
	Ray Fosse			
	George Woodson			
245	Ed Charles	.85	.40	.08
246	Joe Coleman	.85	.40	.08
247	Gene Oliver	.85	.40	.08
248	Bob Priddy	.85	.40	.08
249	Ed Spiezio	.85	.40	.08
250	Frank Robinson	15.00	7.50	1.50
251	Ron Herbel	.85	.40	.08
252	Chuck Cottier	.85	.40	.08
253	Jerry Johnson	.85	.40	.08
254	Joe Schultz	.85	.40	.08
255	Steve Carlton	30.00	15.00	3.00
256	Gates Brown	1.25	.60	.12
257	Jim Ray	.85	.40	.08
258	Jackie Hernandez	.85	.40	.08
259	Bill Short	.85	.40	.08
260	Reggie Jackson	350.00	175.00	35.00
261	Bob Johnson	.85	.40	.08
262	Mike Kekich	.85	.40	.08
263	Jerry May	.85	.40	.08
264	Bill Landis	.85	.40	.08
265	Chico Cardenas	.85	.40	.08
266	Dodger Rookies	.85	.40	.08
	Tom Hutton			
	Alan Foster			
267	Vicente Romo	.85	.40	.08
268	Al Spangler	.85	.40	.08
269	Al Weis	.85	.40	.08
270	Mickey Lolich	1.75	.85	.17
271	Larry Stahl	.85	.40	.08
272	Ed Stroud	.85	.40	.08
273	Ron Willis	.85	.40	.08
274	Clyde King MG	.85	.40	.08
275	Vic Davalillo	.85	.40	.08
276	Gary Wagner	.85	.40	.08
277	Elrod Hendricks	.85	.40	.08
278	Gary Geiger	1.25	.60	.12
	(Batting wrong)			
279	Roger Nelson	.85	.40	.08
280	Alex Johnson	1.25	.60	.12
281	Ted Kubiak	.85	.40	.08
282	Pat Jarvis	.85	.40	.08
283	Sandy Alomar	.85	.40	.08
284	Expos Rookies	.85	.40	.08
	Jerry Robertson			
	Mike Wegener			
285	Don Mincher	.85	.40	.08
286	Dock Ellis	1.25	.60	.12
287	Jose Tartabull	.85	.40	.08
288	Ken Holtzman	1.25	.60	.12
289	Bart Shirley	.85	.40	.08
290	Jim Kaat	3.50	1.75	.35
291	Vern Fuller	.85	.40	.08
292	Al Downing	1.25	.60	.12
293	Dick Dietz	.85	.40	.08
294	Jim Lemon MG	1.25	.60	.12
295	Tony Perez	6.00	3.00	.60
296	Andy Messersmith	1.50	.75	.15
297	Deron Johnson	1.25	.60	.12
298	Dave Nicholson	.85	.40	.08
299	Mark Belanger	1.25	.60	.12
300	Felipe Alou	1.25	.60	.12
301	Darrell Brandon	.85	.40	.08
302	Jim Pagliaroni	.85	.40	.08
303	Cal Koonce	.85	.40	.08
304	Padres Rookies	2.00	1.00	.20
	Bill Davis			
	Clarence Gaston			
305	Dick McAuliffe	1.25	.60	.12
306	Jim Grant	.85	.40	.08
307	Gary Kolb	.85	.40	.08
308	Wade Blasingame	.85	.40	.08
309	Walt Williams	.85	.40	.08
310	Tom Haller	.85	.40	.08
311	Sparky Lyle	6.00	3.00	.60
312	Lee Elia	1.25	.60	.12
313	Bill Robinson	1.25	.60	.12
314	Checklist 4	3.00	.30	.10
	Don Drysdale			
315	Eddie Fisher	.85	.40	.08
316	Hal Lanier	1.25	.60	.12
317	Bruce Look	.85	.40	.08
318	Jack Fisher	.85	.40	.08
319	Ken McMullen	.85	.40	.08
320	Dal Maxvill	.85	.40	.08
321	Jim McAndrew	.85	.40	.08
322	Jose Vidal	.85	.40	.08
323	Larry Miller	.85	.40	.08
324	Tiger Rookies	.85	.40	.08
	Les Cain			
	Dave Campbell			
325	Jose Cardenal	.85	.40	.08
326	Gary Sutherland	.85	.40	.08
327	Willie Crawford	.85	.40	.08
328	Joel Horlen	.50	.25	.05
329	Rick Joseph	.50	.25	.05
330	Tony Conigliaro	1.50	.75	.15
331	Braves Rookies	.75	.35	.07
	Gil Garrido			
	Tom House			
332	Fred Talbot	.50	.25	.05
333	Ivan Murrell	.50	.25	.05
334	Phil Roof	.50	.25	.05
335	Bill Mazeroski	1.00	.50	.10
336	Jim Roland	.50	.25	.05
337	Marty Martinez	.50	.25	.05
338	Del Unser	.50	.25	.05
339	Reds Rookies	.50	.25	.05
	Steve Mingori			
	Jose Pena			
340	Dave McNally	.75	.35	.07
341	Dave Adlesh	.50	.25	.05
342	Bubba Morton	.50	.25	.05
343	Dan Frisella	.50	.25	.05
344	Tom Matchick	.50	.25	.05
345	Frank Linzy	.50	.25	.05
346	Wayne Comer	.50	.25	.05
347	Randy Hundley	.75	.35	.07
348	Steve Hargan	.50	.25	.05
349	Dick Williams MG	.75	.35	.07
350	Richie Allen	1.25	.60	.12
351	Carroll Sembera	.50	.25	.05
352	Paul Schaal	.50	.25	.05
353	Jeff Torborg	.75	.35	.07
354	Nate Oliver	.50	.25	.05
355	Phil Niekro	4.00	2.00	.40
356	Frank Quilici MG	.50	.25	.05
357	Carl Taylor	.50	.25	.05
358	Athletics Rookies	.50	.25	.05
	George Lauzerique			
	Roberto Rodriguez			
359	Dick Kelley	.50	.25	.05
360	Jim Wynn	.75	.35	.07
361	Gary Holman	.50	.25	.05
362	Jim Maloney	.75	.35	.07
363	Russ Nixon	.75	.35	.07
364	Tommie Agee	.75	.35	.07
365	Jim Fregosi	.75	.35	.07
366	Bo Belinsky	.75	.35	.07
367	Lou Johnson	.50	.25	.05
368	Vic Roznovsky	.50	.25	.05
369	Bob Skinner	.50	.25	.05
370	Juan Marichal	4.50	2.25	.45
371	Sal Bando	.75	.35	.07
372	Adolfo Phillips	.50	.25	.05
373	Fred Lasher	.50	.25	.05
374	Bob Tillman	.50	.25	.05
375	Harmon Killebrew	12.00	5.50	1.10
376	Royals Rookies	.75	.35	.07
	Mike Fiore			
	Jim Rooker			
377	Gary Bell	.50	.25	.05
378	Jose Herrera	.50	.25	.05
379	Ken Boyer	1.00	.50	.10
380	Stan Bahnsen	.50	.25	.05
381	Ed Kranepool	.75	.35	.07
382	Pat Corrales	.75	.35	.07
383	Casey Cox	.50	.25	.05
384	Larry Shepard MG	.50	.25	.05
385	Orlando Cepeda	2.50	1.25	.25
386	Jim McGlothlin	.50	.25	.05
387	Bobby Klaus	.50	.25	.05
388	Tom McCraw	.50	.25	.05
389	Dan Coombs	.50	.25	.05
390	Bill Freehan	1.00	.50	.10
391	Ray Culp	.50	.25	.05
392	Bob Burda	.50	.25	.05
393	Gene Brabender	.50	.25	.05

☐ 394	Pilots Rookies	3.00	1.50	.30
	Lou Piniella			
	Marv Staehle			
☐ 395	Chris Short	.50	.25	.05
☐ 396	Jim Campanis	.50	.25	.05
☐ 397	Chuck Dobson	.50	.25	.05
☐ 398	Tito Francona	.75	.35	.07
☐ 399	Bob Bailey	.50	.25	.05
☐ 400	Don Drysdale	7.00	3.50	.70
☐ 401	Jake Gibbs	.50	.25	.05
☐ 402	Ken Boswell	.50	.25	.05
☐ 403	Bob Miller	.50	.25	.05
☐ 404	Cubs Rookies	.50	.25	.05
	Vic LaRose			
	Gary Ross			
☐ 405	Lee May	.75	.35	.07
☐ 406	Phil Ortega	.50	.25	.05
☐ 407	Tom Egan	.50	.25	.05
☐ 408	Nate Colbert	.50	.25	.05
☐ 409	Bob Moose	.50	.25	.05
☐ 410	Al Kaline	10.00	5.00	1.00
☐ 411	Larry Dierker	.75	.35	.07
☐ 412	Checklist 5	6.00	1.00	.20
	Mickey Mantle			
☐ 413	Roland Sheldon	.50	.25	.05
☐ 414	Duke Sims	.50	.25	.05
☐ 415	Ray Washburn	.50	.25	.05
☐ 416	Willie McCovey AS	4.50	2.25	.45
☐ 417	Ken Harrelson AS	.75	.35	.07
☐ 418	Tommy Helms AS	.75	.35	.07
☐ 419	Rod Carew AS	6.00	3.00	.60
☐ 420	Ron Santo AS	.75	.35	.07
☐ 421	Brooks Robinson AS	4.50	2.25	.45
☐ 422	Don Kessinger AS	.75	.35	.07
☐ 423	Bert Campaneris AS	.75	.35	.07
☐ 424	Pete Rose AS	10.00	5.00	1.00
☐ 425	Carl Yastrzemski AS	9.00	4.50	.90
☐ 426	Curt Flood AS	.75	.35	.07
☐ 427	Tony Oliva AS	1.00	.50	.10
☐ 428	Lou Brock AS	4.50	2.25	.45
☐ 429	Willie Horton AS	.75	.35	.07
☐ 430	Johnny Bench AS	12.00	6.00	1.20
☐ 431	Bill Freehan AS	.75	.35	.07
☐ 432	Bob Gibson AS	4.00	2.00	.40
☐ 433	Denny McLain AS	.75	.35	.07
☐ 434	Jerry Koosman AS	.75	.35	.07
☐ 435	Sam McDowell AS	.75	.35	.07
☐ 436	Gene Alley	.75	.35	.07
☐ 437	Luis Alcaraz	.50	.25	.05
☐ 438	Gary Waslewski	.50	.25	.05
☐ 439	White Sox Rookies	.50	.25	.05
	Ed Herrmann			
	Dan Lazar			
☐ 440A	Willie McCovey	15.00	7.50	1.50
☐ 440B	Willie McCovey WL	80.00	40.00	8.00
	(McCovey white)			
☐ 441A	Dennis Higgins	.50	.25	.05
☐ 441B	Dennis Higgins WL	15.00	7.50	1.50
	(Higgins white)			
☐ 442	Ty Cline	.50	.25	.05
☐ 443	Don Wert	.50	.25	.05
☐ 444A	Joe Moeller	.50	.25	.05
☐ 444B	Joe Moeller WL	15.00	7.50	1.50
	(Moeller white)			
☐ 445	Bobby Knoop	.50	.25	.05
☐ 446	Claude Raymond	.50	.25	.05
☐ 447A	Ralph Houk MG	.75	.35	.07
☐ 447B	Ralph Houk WL MG	15.00	7.50	1.50
	(Houk white)			
☐ 448	Bob Tolan	.75	.35	.07
☐ 449	Paul Lindblad	.50	.25	.05
☐ 450	Billy Williams	6.00	3.00	.60
☐ 451A	Rich Rollins	.75	.35	.07
☐ 451B	Rich Rollins WL	15.00	7.50	1.50
	(Rich and 3B white)			
☐ 452A	Al Ferrara	.50	.25	.05
☐ 452B	Al Ferrara WL	15.00	7.50	1.50
	(Al and OF white)			
☐ 453	Mike Cuellar	1.00	.50	.10
☐ 454A	Phillies Rookies	.75	.35	.07
	Larry Colton			
	Don Money			
☐ 454B	Phillies Rookies WL	15.00	7.50	1.50
	Larry Colton			
	Don Money			
	(names in white)			
☐ 455	Sonny Siebert	.75	.35	.07
☐ 456	Bud Harrelson	.75	.35	.07
☐ 457	Dalton Jones	.50	.25	.05
☐ 458	Curt Blefary	.50	.25	.05
☐ 459	Dave Boswell	.50	.25	.05
☐ 460	Joe Torre	1.00	.50	.10
☐ 461A	Mike Epstein	.50	.25	.05
☐ 461B	Mike Epstein WL	15.00	7.50	1.50
	(Epstein white)			

☐ 462	Red Schoendienst MG	2.50	1.25	.25
☐ 463	Dennis Ribant	.50	.25	.05
☐ 464A	Dave Marshall	.50	.25	.05
☐ 464B	Dave Marshall WL	15.00	7.50	1.50
	(Marshall white)			
☐ 465	Tommy John	3.50	1.75	.35
☐ 466	John Boccabella	.50	.25	.05
☐ 467	Tommie Reynolds	.50	.25	.05
☐ 468A	Pirates Rookies	.50	.25	.05
	Bruce Dal Canton			
	Bob Robertson			
☐ 468B	Pirates Rookies WL	15.00	7.50	1.50
	Bruce Dal Canton			
	Bob Robertson			
	(names in white)			
☐ 469	Chico Ruiz	.50	.25	.05
☐ 470A	Mel Stottlemyre	1.25	.60	.12
☐ 470B	Mel Stottlemyre WL	18.00	9.00	1.80
	(Stottlemyre white)			
☐ 471A	Ted Savage	.50	.25	.05
☐ 471B	Ted Savage WL	15.00	7.50	1.50
	(Savage white)			
☐ 472	Jim Price	.50	.25	.05
☐ 473A	Jose Arcia	.50	.25	.05
☐ 473B	Jose Arcia WL	15.00	7.50	1.50
	(Jose and 2B white)			
☐ 474	Tom Murphy	.50	.25	.05
☐ 475	Tim McCarver	1.50	.75	.15
☐ 476A	Boston Rookies	.75	.35	.07
	Ken Brett			
	Gerry Moses			
☐ 476B	Boston Rookies WL	15.00	7.50	1.50
	Ken Brett			
	Gerry Moses			
	(names in white)			
☐ 477	Jeff James	.50	.25	.05
☐ 478	Don Buford	.75	.35	.07
☐ 479	Richie Scheinblum	.50	.25	.05
☐ 480	Tom Seaver	80.00	40.00	8.00
☐ 481	Bill Melton	.50	.25	.05
☐ 482A	Jim Gosger	.50	.25	.05
☐ 482B	Jim Gosger WL	15.00	7.50	1.50
	(Jim and OF white)			
☐ 483	Ted Abernathy	.50	.25	.05
☐ 484	Joe Gordon MG	.75	.35	.07
☐ 485A	Gaylord Perry	6.00	3.00	.60
☐ 485B	Gaylord Perry WL	60.00	30.00	6.00
	(Perry white)			
☐ 486A	Paul Casanova	.50	.25	.05
☐ 486B	Paul Casanova WL	15.00	7.50	1.50
	(Casanova white)			
☐ 487	Denis Menke	.50	.25	.05
☐ 488	Joe Sparma	.50	.25	.05
☐ 489	Clete Boyer	.75	.35	.07
☐ 490	Matty Alou	.75	.35	.07
☐ 491A	Twins Rookies	.50	.25	.05
	Jerry Crider			
	George Mitterwald			
☐ 491B	Twins Rookies WL	15.00	7.50	1.50
	Jerry Crider			
	George Mitterwald			
	(names in white)			
☐ 492	Tony Cloninger	.50	.25	.05
☐ 493A	Wes Parker	.75	.35	.07
☐ 493B	Wes Parker WL	15.00	7.50	1.50
	(Parker white)			
☐ 494	Ken Berry	.50	.25	.05
☐ 495	Bert Campaneris	.75	.35	.07
☐ 496	Larry Jaster	.50	.25	.05
☐ 497	Julian Javier	.50	.25	.05
☐ 498	Juan Pizarro	.50	.25	.05
☐ 499	Astro Rookies	.50	.25	.05
	Don Bryant			
	Steve Shea			
☐ 500A	Mickey Mantle	175.00	85.00	18.00
☐ 500B	Mickey Mantle WL	500.00	250.00	50.00
	(Mantle white)			
☐ 501A	Tony Gonzalez	.50	.25	.05
☐ 501B	Tony Gonzalez WL	15.00	7.50	1.50
	(Tony and OF white)			
☐ 502	Minnie Rojas	.50	.25	.05
☐ 503	Larry Brown	.50	.25	.05
☐ 504	Checklist 6	3.00	.30	.10
	Brooks Robinson			
☐ 505A	Bobby Bolin	.50	.25	.05
☐ 505B	Bobby Bolin WL	15.00	7.50	1.50
	(Bolin white)			
☐ 506	Paul Blair	.75	.35	.07
☐ 507	Cookie Rojas	.75	.35	.07
☐ 508	Moe Drabowsky	.50	.25	.05
☐ 509	Manny Sanguillen	1.00	.50	.10
☐ 510	Rod Carew	45.00	20.00	4.00
☐ 511A	Diego Segui	.50	.25	.05
☐ 511B	Diego Segui WL	15.00	7.50	1.50
	(Diego and P white)			

☐ 512	Cleon Jones	.50	.25	.05
☐ 513	Camilo Pascual	.85	.40	.08
☐ 514	Mike Lum	.60	.30	.06
☐ 515	Dick Green	.60	.30	.06
☐ 516	Earl Weaver MG	5.00	2.50	.50
☐ 517	Mike McCormick	.85	.40	.08
☐ 518	Fred Whitfield	.60	.30	.06
☐ 519	Yankees Rookies	.60	.30	.06
	Gerry Kenney			
	Len Boehmer			
☐ 520	Bob Veale	.85	.40	.08
☐ 521	George Thomas	.60	.30	.06
☐ 522	Joe Hoerner	.60	.30	.06
☐ 523	Bob Chance	.60	.30	.06
☐ 524	Expos Rookies	.60	.30	.06
	Jose Laboy			
	Floyd Wicker			
☐ 525	Earl Wilson	.60	.30	.06
☐ 526	Hector Torres	.60	.30	.06
☐ 527	Al Lopez MG	2.50	1.25	.25
☐ 528	Claude Osteen	.85	.40	.08
☐ 529	Ed Kirkpatrick	.60	.30	.06
☐ 530	Cesar Tovar	.60	.30	.06
☐ 531	Dick Farrell	.60	.30	.06
☐ 532	Bird Hill Aces	.85	.40	.08
	Tom Phoebus			
	Jim Hardin			
	Dave McNally			
	Mike Cuellar			
☐ 533	Nolan Ryan	225.00	110.00	22.00
☐ 534	Jerry McNertney	.60	.30	.06
☐ 535	Phil Regan	.85	.40	.08
☐ 536	Padres Rookies	.60	.30	.06
	Danny Breeden			
	Dave Roberts			
☐ 537	Mike Paul	.60	.30	.06
☐ 538	Charlie Smith	.60	.30	.06
☐ 539	Ted Shows How	4.00	2.00	.40
	Mike Epstein			
	Ted Williams			
☐ 540	Curt Flood	1.00	.50	.10
☐ 541	Joe Verbanic	.60	.30	.06
☐ 542	Bob Aspromonte	.60	.30	.06
☐ 543	Fred Newman	.60	.30	.06
☐ 544	Tigers Rookies	.60	.30	.06
	Mike Kilkenny			
	Ron Woods			
☐ 545	Willie Stargell	10.00	5.00	1.00
☐ 546	Jim Nash	.60	.30	.06
☐ 547	Billy Martin MG	3.00	1.50	.30
☐ 548	Bob Locker	.60	.30	.06
☐ 549	Ron Brand	.60	.30	.06
☐ 550	Brooks Robinson	12.00	5.50	1.10
☐ 551	Wayne Granger	.60	.30	.06
☐ 552	Dodgers Rookies	.85	.40	.08
	Ted Sizemore			
	Bill Sudakis			
☐ 553	Ron Davis	.60	.30	.06
☐ 554	Frank Bertaina	.60	.30	.06
☐ 555	Jim Ray Hart	.85	.40	.08
☐ 556	A's Stars	.85	.40	.08
	Sal Bando			
	Bert Campaneris			
	Danny Cater			
☐ 557	Frank Fernandez	.60	.30	.06
☐ 558	Tom Burgmeier	.85	.40	.08
☐ 559	Cardinals Rookies	.60	.30	.06
	Joe Hague			
	Jim Hicks			
☐ 560	Luis Tiant	1.25	.60	.12
☐ 561	Ron Clark	.60	.30	.06
☐ 562	Bob Watson	2.50	1.25	.25
☐ 563	Marty Pattin	.60	.30	.06
☐ 564	Gil Hodges MG	6.00	3.00	.60
☐ 565	Hoyt Wilhelm	5.50	2.75	.55
☐ 566	Ron Hansen	.60	.30	.06
☐ 567	Pirates Rookies	.60	.30	.06
	Elvio Jimenez			
	Jim Shellenback			
☐ 568	Cecil Upshaw	.60	.30	.06
☐ 569	Billy Harris	.60	.30	.06
☐ 570	Ron Santo	1.50	.75	.15
☐ 571	Cap Peterson	.60	.30	.06
☐ 572	Giants Heroes	7.00	3.50	.70
	Willie McCovey			
	Juan Marichal			
☐ 573	Jim Palmer	20.00	10.00	2.00
☐ 574	George Scott	.85	.40	.08
☐ 575	Bill Singer	.85	.40	.08
☐ 576	Phillies Rookies	.60	.30	.06
	Ron Stone			
	Bill Wilson			
☐ 577	Mike Hegan	.60	.30	.06
☐ 578	Don Bosch	.60	.30	.06
☐ 579	Dave Nelson	.85	.40	.08

☐ 580	Jim Northrup	.85	.40	.08
☐ 581	Gary Nolan	.60	.30	.06
☐ 582A	Checklist 7	3.00	.30	.10
	(white circle on back)			
	(Tony Oliva)			
☐ 582B	Checklist 7	5.00	.50	.10
	(red circle on back)			
	(Tony Oliva)			
☐ 583	Clyde Wright	.60	.30	.06
☐ 584	Don Mason	.60	.30	.06
☐ 585	Ron Swoboda	.85	.40	.08
☐ 586	Tim Cullen	.60	.30	.06
☐ 587	Joe Rudi	2.00	1.00	.20
☐ 588	Bill White	1.50	.75	.15
☐ 589	Joe Pepitone	1.25	.60	.12
☐ 590	Rico Carty	1.25	.60	.12
☐ 591	Mike Hedlund	.80	.40	.08
☐ 592	Padres Rookies	.80	.40	.08
	Rafael Robles			
	Al Santorini			
☐ 593	Don Nottebart	.80	.40	.08
☐ 594	Dooley Womack	.80	.40	.08
☐ 595	Lee Maye	.80	.40	.08
☐ 596	Chuck Hartenstein	.80	.40	.08
☐ 597	A.L. Rookies	40.00	20.00	4.00
	Bob Floyd			
	Larry Burchart			
	Rollie Fingers			
☐ 598	Ruben Amaro	.80	.40	.08
☐ 599	John Boozer	.80	.40	.08
☐ 600	Tony Oliva	3.00	1.50	.30
☐ 601	Tug McGraw	1.50	.75	.15
☐ 602	Cubs Rookies	.80	.40	.08
	Alec Distaso			
	Don Young			
	Jim Qualls			
☐ 603	Joe Keough	.80	.40	.08
☐ 604	Bobby Etheridge	.80	.40	.08
☐ 605	Dick Ellsworth	1.25	.60	.12
☐ 606	Gene Mauch MG	1.25	.60	.12
☐ 607	Dick Bosman	.80	.40	.08
☐ 608	Dick Simpson	.80	.40	.08
☐ 609	Phil Gagliano	.80	.40	.08
☐ 610	Jim Hardin	.80	.40	.08
☐ 611	Braves Rookies	1.25	.60	.12
	Bob Didier			
	Walt Hriniak			
	Gary Neibauer			
☐ 612	Jack Aker	.80	.40	.08
☐ 613	Jim Beauchamp	.80	.40	.08
☐ 614	Houston Rookies	.80	.40	.08
	Tom Griffin			
	Skip Guinn			
☐ 615	Len Gabrielson	.80	.40	.08
☐ 616	Don McMahon	.80	.40	.08
☐ 617	Jesse Gonder	.80	.40	.08
☐ 618	Ramon Webster	.80	.40	.08
☐ 619	Royals Rookies	1.25	.60	.12
	Bill Butler			
	Pat Kelly			
	Juan Rios			
☐ 620	Dean Chance	1.25	.60	.12
☐ 621	Bill Voss	.80	.40	.08
☐ 622	Dan Osinski	.80	.40	.08
☐ 623	Hank Allen	.80	.40	.08
☐ 624	NL Rookies	.80	.40	.08
	Darrel Chaney			
	Duffy Dyer			
	Terry Harmon			
☐ 625	Mack Jones	.80	.40	.08
	(Batting wrong)			
☐ 626	Gene Michael	1.25	.60	.12
☐ 627	George Stone	.80	.40	.08
☐ 628	Red Sox Rookies	1.25	.60	.12
	Bill Conigliaro			
	Syd O'Brien			
	Fred Wenz			
☐ 629	Jack Hamilton	.80	.40	.08
☐ 630	Bobby Bonds	10.00	5.00	1.00
☐ 631	John Kennedy	.80	.40	.08
☐ 632	Jon Warden	.80	.40	.08
☐ 633	Harry Walker MG	.80	.40	.08
☐ 634	Andy Etchebarren	.80	.40	.08
☐ 635	George Culver	.80	.40	.08
☐ 636	Woody Held	.80	.40	.08
☐ 637	Padres Rookies	.80	.40	.08
	Jerry DaVanon			
	Frank Reberger			
	Clay Kirby			
☐ 638	Ed Sprague	.80	.40	.08
☐ 639	Barry Moore	.80	.40	.08
☐ 640	Fergie Jenkins	4.00	2.00	.40
☐ 641	NL Rookies	.80	.40	.08
	Bobby Darwin			
	John Miller			

	Tommy Dean			
☐ 642	John Hiller	1.25	.60	.12
☐ 643	Billy Cowan	.80	.40	.08
☐ 644	Chuck Hinton	.80	.40	.08
☐ 645	George Brunet	.80	.40	.08
☐ 646	Expos Rookies	.80	.40	.08
	Dan McGinn			
	Carl Morton			
☐ 647	Dave Wickersham	.80	.40	.08
☐ 648	Bobby Wine	.80	.40	.08
☐ 649	Al Jackson	.80	.40	.08
☐ 650	Ted Williams MG	8.00	4.00	.80
☐ 651	Gus Gil	.80	.40	.08
☐ 652	Eddie Watt	.80	.40	.08
☐ 653	Aurelio Rodriguez	1.50	.75	.15
	(photo actually			
	Angels' batboy)			
☐ 654	White Sox Rookies	1.25	.60	.12
	Carlos May			
	Don Secrist			
	Rich Morales			
☐ 655	Mike Hershberger	.80	.40	.08
☐ 656	Dan Schneider	.80	.40	.08
☐ 657	Bobby Murcer	1.50	.75	.15
☐ 658	AL Rookies	.80	.40	.08
	Tom Hall			
	Bill Burbach			
	Jim Miles			
☐ 659	Johnny Podres	1.50	.75	.15
☐ 660	Reggie Smith	1.50	.75	.15
☐ 661	Jim Merritt	.80	.40	.08
☐ 662	Royals Rookies	1.25	.60	.12
	Dick Drago			
	George Spriggs			
	Bob Oliver			
☐ 663	Dick Radatz	1.25	.60	.12
☐ 664	Ron Hunt	1.25	.60	.12

1969 Topps Deckle

The cards in this 33-card set measure 2 1/4" by 3 1/4". This unusual black and white insert set derives its name from the serrated border, or edge, of the cards. The cards were included as inserts in the regularly issued Topps baseball series of 1969. Card number 11 is found with either Hoyt Wilhelm or Jim Wynn, and number 22 with either Rusty Staub or Joe Foy. The set price below does include all variations.

		NRMT	VG-E	GOOD
	COMPLETE SET (35)	60.00	30.00	6.00
	COMMON PLAYER (1-33)	.30	.15	.03
☐ 1	Brooks Robinson	3.50	1.50	.30
☐ 2	Boog Powell	.50	.25	.05
☐ 3	Ken Harrelson	.40	.20	.04
☐ 4	Carl Yastrzemski	6.00	2.50	.50
☐ 5	Jim Fregosi	.40	.20	.04
☐ 6	Luis Aparicio	1.25	.60	.12
☐ 7	Luis Tiant	.40	.20	.04
☐ 8	Denny McLain	.40	.20	.04
☐ 9	Willie Horton	.30	.15	.03
☐ 10	Bill Freehan	.30	.15	.03
☐ 11A	Hoyt Wilhelm	5.00	2.50	.50
☐ 11B	Jim Wynn	6.00	3.00	.60
☐ 12	Rod Carew	4.00	2.00	.40
☐ 13	Mel Stottlemyre	.30	.15	.03

☐ 14	Rick Monday	.30	.15	.03
☐ 15	Tommy Davis	.30	.15	.03
☐ 16	Frank Howard	.40	.20	.04
☐ 17	Felipe Alou	.30	.15	.03
☐ 18	Don Kessinger	.30	.15	.03
☐ 19	Ron Santo	.40	.20	.04
☐ 20	Tommy Helms	.30	.15	.03
☐ 21	Pete Rose	8.00	4.00	.80
☐ 22A	Rusty Staub	2.50	1.25	.25
☐ 22B	Joe Foy	6.00	3.00	.60
☐ 23	Tom Haller	.30	.15	.03
☐ 24	Maury Wills	.60	.30	.06
☐ 25	Jerry Koosman	.40	.20	.04
☐ 26	Richie Allen	.40	.20	.04
☐ 27	Bob Clemente	5.00	2.00	.40
☐ 28	Curt Flood	.40	.20	.04
☐ 29	Bob Gibson	2.00	1.00	.20
☐ 30	Al Ferrara	.30	.15	.03
☐ 31	Willie McCovey	2.50	1.25	.25
☐ 32	Juan Marichal	2.00	1.00	.20
☐ 33	Willie Mays	6.00	2.50	.50

1969 Topps Super

The cards in this 66-card set measure 2 1/4" by 3 1/4". This beautiful Topps set was released independently of the regular baseball series of 1969. It is referred to as "Super Baseball" on the back of the card, a title which was also used for the postcard-size cards issued in 1970 and 1971. Complete sheets, and cards with square corners cut from these sheets, are sometimes encountered.

		NRMT	VG-E	GOOD
	COMPLETE SET (66)	3750.00	1750.00	400.00
	COMMON PLAYER (1-66)	8.00	4.00	.80
☐ 1	Dave McNally	10.00	5.00	1.00
☐ 2	Frank Robinson	150.00	75.00	15.00
☐ 3	Brooks Robinson	200.00	100.00	20.00
☐ 4	Ken Harrelson	10.00	5.00	1.00
☐ 5	Carl Yastrzemski	400.00	200.00	40.00
☐ 6	Ray Culp	8.00	4.00	.80
☐ 7	Jim Fregosi	10.00	5.00	1.00
☐ 8	Rick Reichardt	8.00	4.00	.80
☐ 9	Vic Davalillo	8.00	4.00	.80
☐ 10	Luis Aparicio	75.00	37.50	7.50
☐ 11	Pete Ward	8.00	4.00	.80
☐ 12	Joe Horlen	8.00	4.00	.80
☐ 13	Luis Tiant	12.00	6.00	1.20
☐ 14	Sam McDowell	10.00	5.00	1.00
☐ 15	Jose Cardenal	8.00	4.00	.80
☐ 16	Willie Horton	10.00	5.00	1.00
☐ 17	Denny McLain	12.00	6.00	1.20
☐ 18	Bill Freehan	10.00	5.00	1.00
☐ 19	Harmon Killebrew	100.00	50.00	10.00
☐ 20	Tony Oliva	15.00	7.50	1.50
☐ 21	Dean Chance	8.00	4.00	.80
☐ 22	Joe Foy	8.00	4.00	.80
☐ 23	Roger Nelson	8.00	4.00	.80
☐ 24	Mickey Mantle	750.00	375.00	75.00
☐ 25	Mel Stottlemyre	12.00	6.00	1.20
☐ 26	Roy White	10.00	5.00	1.00
☐ 27	Rick Monday	10.00	5.00	1.00
☐ 28	Reggie Jackson	500.00	250.00	50.00
☐ 29	Bert Campaneris	8.00	4.00	.80
☐ 30	Frank Howard	10.00	5.00	1.00

☐ 31	Camilo Pascual	8.00	4.00	.80
☐ 32	Tommy Davis	10.00	5.00	1.00
☐ 33	Don Mincher	8.00	4.00	.80
☐ 34	Hank Aaron	350.00	175.00	35.00
☐ 35	Felipe Alou	8.00	4.00	.80
☐ 36	Joe Torre	12.00	6.00	1.20
☐ 37	Fergie Jenkins	20.00	10.00	2.00
☐ 38	Ron Santo	12.00	6.00	1.20
☐ 39	Billy Williams	75.00	37.50	7.50
☐ 40	Tommy Helms	8.00	4.00	.80
☐ 41	Pete Rose	500.00	250.00	50.00
☐ 42	Joe Morgan	100.00	50.00	10.00
☐ 43	Jim Wynn	8.00	4.00	.80
☐ 44	Curt Blefary	8.00	4.00	.80
☐ 45	Willie Davis	10.00	5.00	1.00
☐ 46	Don Drysdale	75.00	37.50	7.50
☐ 47	Tom Haller	8.00	4.00	.80
☐ 48	Rusty Staub	12.00	6.00	1.20
☐ 49	Maury Wills	15.00	7.50	1.50
☐ 50	Cleon Jones	8.00	4.00	.80
☐ 51	Jerry Koosman	10.00	5.00	1.00
☐ 52	Tom Seaver	250.00	125.00	25.00
☐ 53	Richie Allen	12.00	6.00	1.20
☐ 54	Chris Short	8.00	4.00	.80
☐ 55	Cookie Rojas	8.00	4.00	.80
☐ 56	Matty Alou	8.00	4.00	.80
☐ 57	Steve Blass	8.00	4.00	.80
☐ 58	Bob Clemente	250.00	125.00	25.00
☐ 59	Curt Flood	15.00	7.50	1.50
☐ 60	Bob Gibson	100.00	50.00	10.00
☐ 61	Tim McCarver	15.00	7.50	1.50
☐ 62	Dick Selma	8.00	4.00	.80
☐ 63	Ollie Brown	8.00	4.00	.80
☐ 64	Juan Marichal	100.00	50.00	10.00
☐ 65	Willie Mays	350.00	175.00	35.00
☐ 66	Willie McCovey	125.00	60.00	12.50

1970 Topps

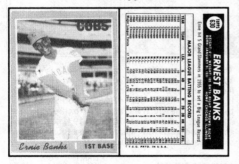

Ernie Banks — 1ST BASE

The cards in this 720-card set measure 2 1/2" by 3 1/2". The Topps set for 1970 has color photos surrounded by white frame lines and gray borders. The backs have a blue biographical section and a yellow record section. All-Star selections are featured on cards 450 to 469. Other topical subsets within this set include League Leaders (61-72), Playoffs cards (195-202), and World Series cards (305-310). There are graduations of scarcity, terminating in the high series (634-720), which are outlined in the value summary.

	NRMT	VG-E	GOOD
COMPLETE SET (720)	1650.00	800.00	200.00
COMMON PLAYER (1-132)	.30	.15	.03
COMMON PLAYER (133-263)	.35	.17	.03
COMMON PLAYER (264-459)	.40	.20	.04
COMMON PLAYER (460-546)	.55	.27	.05
COMMON PLAYER (547-633)	1.00	.50	.10
COMMON PLAYER (634-720)	2.25	1.10	.22

☐ 1	New York Mets Team Card	6.00	1.00	.20
☐ 2	Diego Segui	.30	.15	.03
☐ 3	Darrel Chaney	.30	.15	.03
☐ 4	Tom Egan	.30	.15	.03
☐ 5	Wes Parker	.50	.25	.05
☐ 6	Grant Jackson	.30	.15	.03

☐ 7	Indians Rookies Gary Boyd Russ Nagelson	.30	.15	.03
☐ 8	Jose Martinez	.30	.15	.03
☐ 9	Checklist 1	2.00	.20	.04
☐ 10	Carl Yastrzemski	27.00	12.50	2.50
☐ 11	Nate Colbert	.30	.15	.03
☐ 12	John Hiller	.50	.25	.05
☐ 13	Jack Hiatt	.30	.15	.03
☐ 14	Hank Allen	.30	.15	.03
☐ 15	Larry Dierker	.50	.25	.05
☐ 16	Charlie Metro MG	.30	.15	.03
☐ 17	Hoyt Wilhelm	3.50	1.75	.35
☐ 18	Carlos May	.30	.15	.03
☐ 19	John Boccabella	.30	.15	.03
☐ 20	Dave McNally	.50	.25	.05
☐ 21	A's Rookies Vida Blue Gene Tenace	2.50	1.25	.25
☐ 22	Ray Washburn	.30	.15	.03
☐ 23	Bill Robinson	.50	.25	.05
☐ 24	Dick Selma	.30	.15	.03
☐ 25	Cesar Tovar	.30	.15	.03
☐ 26	Tug McGraw	1.00	.50	.10
☐ 27	Chuck Hinton	.30	.15	.03
☐ 28	Billy Wilson	.30	.15	.03
☐ 29	Sandy Alomar	.30	.15	.03
☐ 30	Matty Alou	.50	.25	.05
☐ 31	Marty Pattin	.30	.15	.03
☐ 32	Harry Walker MG	.30	.15	.03
☐ 33	Don Wert	.30	.15	.03
☐ 34	Willie Crawford	.30	.15	.03
☐ 35	Joel Horlen	.30	.15	.03
☐ 36	Red Rookies Danny Breeden Bernie Carbo	.50	.25	.05
☐ 37	Dick Drago	.30	.15	.03
☐ 38	Mack Jones	.30	.15	.03
☐ 39	Mike Nagy	.30	.15	.03
☐ 40	Rich Allen	1.00	.50	.10
☐ 41	George Lauzerique	.30	.15	.03
☐ 42	Tito Fuentes	.30	.15	.03
☐ 43	Jack Aker	.30	.15	.03
☐ 44	Roberto Pena	.30	.15	.03
☐ 45	Dave Johnson	.75	.35	.07
☐ 46	Ken Rudolph	.30	.15	.03
☐ 47	Bob Miller	.30	.15	.03
☐ 48	Gil Garrido	.30	.15	.03
☐ 49	Tim Cullen	.30	.15	.03
☐ 50	Tommie Agee	.50	.25	.05
☐ 51	Bob Christian	.30	.15	.03
☐ 52	Bruce Dal Canton	.30	.15	.03
☐ 53	John Kennedy	.30	.15	.03
☐ 54	Jeff Torborg	.50	.25	.05
☐ 55	John Odom	.30	.15	.03
☐ 56	Phillies Rookies Joe Lis Scott Reid	.30	.15	.03
☐ 57	Pat Kelly	.30	.15	.03
☐ 58	Dave Marshall	.30	.15	.03
☐ 59	Dick Ellsworth	.50	.25	.05
☐ 60	Jim Wynn	.50	.25	.05
☐ 61	NL Batting Leaders Pete Rose Bob Clemente Cleon Jones	3.50	1.75	.35
☐ 62	AL Batting Leaders Rod Carew Reggie Smith Tony Oliva	1.50	.75	.15
☐ 63	NL RBI Leaders Willie McCovey Ron Santo Tony Perez	1.50	.75	.15
☐ 64	AL RBI Leaders Harmon Killebrew Boog Powell Reggie Jackson	2.50	1.25	.25
☐ 65	NL Home Run Leaders Willie McCovey Hank Aaron Lee May	2.50	1.25	.25
☐ 66	AL Home Run Leaders Harmon Killebrew Frank Howard Reggie Jackson	2.50	1.25	.25
☐ 67	NL ERA Leaders Juan Marichal Steve Carlton Bob Gibson	3.50	1.75	.35
☐ 68	AL ERA Leaders Dick Bosman Jim Palmer Mike Cuellar	1.50	.75	.15
☐ 69	NL Pitching Leaders	2.50	1.25	.25

	Tom Seaver			
	Phil Niekro			
	Fergie Jenkins			
	Juan Marichal			
☐ 70	AL Pitching Leaders	1.50	.75	.15
	Dennis McLain			
	Mike Cuellar			
	Dave Boswell			
	Dave McNally			
	Jim Perry			
	Mel Stottlemyre			
☐ 71	NL Strikeout Leaders	1.50	.75	.15
	Fergie Jenkins			
	Bob Gibson			
	Bill Singer			
☐ 72	AL Strikeout Leaders	1.50	.75	.15
	Sam McDowell			
	Mickey Lolich			
	Andy Messersmith			
☐ 73	Wayne Granger	.30	.15	.03
☐ 74	Angels Rookies	.30	.15	.03
	Greg Washburn			
	Wally Wolf			
☐ 75	Jim Kaat	2.00	1.00	.20
☐ 76	Carl Taylor	.30	.15	.03
☐ 77	Frank Linzy	.30	.15	.03
☐ 78	Joe Lahoud	.30	.15	.03
☐ 79	Clay Kirby	.30	.15	.03
☐ 80	Don Kessinger	.50	.25	.05
☐ 81	Dave May	.30	.15	.03
☐ 82	Frank Fernandez	.30	.15	.03
☐ 83	Don Cardwell	.30	.15	.03
☐ 84	Paul Casanova	.30	.15	.03
☐ 85	Max Alvis	.30	.15	.03
☐ 86	Lum Harris MG	.30	.15	.03
☐ 87	Steve Renko	.30	.15	.03
☐ 88	Pilots Rookies	.30	.15	.03
	Miguel Fuentes			
	Dick Baney			
☐ 89	Juan Rios	.30	.15	.03
☐ 90	Tim McCarver	1.00	.50	.10
☐ 91	Rich Morales	.30	.15	.03
☐ 92	George Culver	.30	.15	.03
☐ 93	Rick Renick	.30	.15	.03
☐ 94	Freddie Patek	.50	.25	.05
☐ 95	Earl Wilson	.30	.15	.03
☐ 96	Cardinals Rookies	2.00	1.00	.20
	Leron Lee			
	Jerry Reuss			
☐ 97	Joe Moeller	.30	.15	.03
☐ 98	Gates Brown	.50	.25	.05
☐ 99	Bobby Pfeil	.30	.15	.03
☐ 100	Mel Stottlemyre	1.00	.50	.10
☐ 101	Bobby Floyd	.30	.15	.03
☐ 102	Joe Rudi	.75	.35	.07
☐ 103	Frank Reberger	.30	.15	.03
☐ 104	Gerry Moses	.30	.15	.03
☐ 105	Tony Gonzalez	.30	.15	.03
☐ 106	Darold Knowles	.30	.15	.03
☐ 107	Bobby Etheridge	.30	.15	.03
☐ 108	Tom Burgmeier	.30	.15	.03
☐ 109	Expos Rookies	.50	.25	.05
	Garry Jestadt			
	Carl Morton			
☐ 110	Bob Moose	.30	.15	.03
☐ 111	Mike Hegan	.30	.15	.03
☐ 112	Dave Nelson	.30	.15	.03
☐ 113	Jim Ray	.30	.15	.03
☐ 114	Gene Michael	.50	.25	.05
☐ 115	Alex Johnson	.50	.25	.05
☐ 116	Sparky Lyle	1.00	.50	.10
☐ 117	Don Young	.30	.15	.03
☐ 118	George Mitterwald	.30	.15	.03
☐ 119	Chuck Taylor	.30	.15	.03
☐ 120	Sal Bando	.75	.35	.07
☐ 121	Orioles Rookies	.50	.25	.05
	Fred Beene			
	Terry Crowley			
☐ 122	George Stone	.30	.15	.03
☐ 123	Don Gutteridge	.30	.15	.03
☐ 124	Larry Jaster	.30	.15	.03
☐ 125	Deron Johnson	.30	.15	.03
☐ 126	Marty Martinez	.30	.15	.03
☐ 127	Joe Coleman	.30	.15	.03
☐ 128	Checklist 2	2.00	.20	.04
☐ 129	Jimmie Price	.30	.15	.03
☐ 130	Ollie Brown	.30	.15	.03
☐ 131	Dodgers Rookies	.30	.15	.03
	Ray Lamb			
	Bob Stinson			
☐ 132	Jim McGlothlin	.30	.15	.03
☐ 133	Clay Carroll	.35	.17	.03
☐ 134	Danny Walton	.35	.17	.03
☐ 135	Dick Dietz	.35	.17	.03
☐ 136	Steve Hargan	.35	.17	.03

☐ 137	Art Shamsky	.35	.17	.03
☐ 138	Joe Foy	.35	.17	.03
☐ 139	Rich Nye	.35	.17	.03
☐ 140	Reggie Jackson	75.00	37.50	7.50
☐ 141	Pirates Rookies	.50	.25	.05
	Dave Cash			
	Johnny Jeter			
☐ 142	Fritz Peterson	.35	.17	.03
☐ 143	Phil Gagliano	.35	.17	.03
☐ 144	Ray Culp	.35	.17	.03
☐ 145	Rico Carty	.75	.35	.07
☐ 146	Danny Murphy	.35	.17	.03
☐ 147	Angel Hermoso	.35	.17	.03
☐ 148	Earl Weaver MG	1.00	.50	.10
☐ 149	Billy Champion	.35	.17	.03
☐ 150	Harmon Killebrew	5.00	2.50	.50
☐ 151	Dave Roberts	.35	.17	.03
☐ 152	Ike Brown	.35	.17	.03
☐ 153	Gary Gentry	.35	.17	.03
☐ 154	Senators Rookies	.35	.17	.03
	Jim Miles			
	Jan Dukes			
☐ 155	Denis Menke	.35	.17	.03
☐ 156	Eddie Fisher	.35	.17	.03
☐ 157	Manny Mota	.50	.25	.05
☐ 158	Jerry McNertney	.35	.17	.03
☐ 159	Tommy Helms	.50	.25	.05
☐ 160	Phil Niekro	3.50	1.75	.35
☐ 161	Richie Scheinblum	.35	.17	.03
☐ 162	Jerry Johnson	.35	.17	.03
☐ 163	Syd O'Brien	.35	.17	.03
☐ 164	Ty Cline	.35	.17	.03
☐ 165	Ed Kirkpatrick	.35	.17	.03
☐ 166	Al Oliver	2.00	1.00	.20
☐ 167	Bill Burbach	.35	.17	.03
☐ 168	Dave Watkins	.35	.17	.03
☐ 169	Tom Hall	.35	.17	.03
☐ 170	Billy Williams	4.00	2.00	.40
☐ 171	Jim Nash	.35	.17	.03
☐ 172	Braves Rookies	1.00	.50	.10
	Garry Hill			
	Ralph Garr			
☐ 173	Jim Hicks	.35	.17	.03
☐ 174	Ted Sizemore	.50	.25	.05
☐ 175	Dick Bosman	.35	.17	.03
☐ 176	Jim Ray Hart	.50	.25	.05
☐ 177	Jim Northrup	.50	.25	.05
☐ 178	Denny Lemaster	.35	.17	.03
☐ 179	Ivan Murrell	.35	.17	.03
☐ 180	Tommy John	2.50	1.25	.25
☐ 181	Sparky Anderson MG	1.00	.50	.10
☐ 182	Dick Hall	.35	.17	.03
☐ 183	Jerry Grote	.35	.17	.03
☐ 184	Ray Fosse	.35	.17	.03
☐ 185	Don Mincher	.50	.25	.05
☐ 186	Rick Joseph	.35	.17	.03
☐ 187	Mike Hedlund	.35	.17	.03
☐ 188	Manny Sanguillen	.75	.35	.07
☐ 189	Yankees Rookies	60.00	30.00	6.00
	Thurman Munson			
	Dave McDonald			
☐ 190	Joe Torre	1.00	.50	.10
☐ 191	Vicente Romo	.35	.17	.03
☐ 192	Jim Qualls	.35	.17	.03
☐ 193	Mike Wegener	.35	.17	.03
☐ 194	Chuck Manuel	.35	.17	.03
☐ 195	NL Playoff Game 1	3.50	1.75	.35
	Seaver wins opener			
☐ 196	NL Playoff Game 2	1.50	.75	.15
	Mets show muscle			
☐ 197	NL Playoff Game 3	4.00	2.00	.40
	Ryan saves the day			
☐ 198	NL Playoff Summary	1.50	.75	.15
	Mets celebrate			
☐ 199	AL Playoff Game 1	1.50	.75	.15
	Orioles win			
	squeaker (Cuellar)			
☐ 200	AL Playoff Game 2	1.50	.75	.15
	Powell scores			
	winning run			
☐ 201	AL Playoff Game 3	1.50	.75	.15
	Birds wrap it up			
☐ 202	AL Playoff Summary	1.50	.75	.15
	Orioles celebrate			
☐ 203	Rudy May	.35	.17	.03
☐ 204	Len Gabrielson	.35	.17	.03
☐ 205	Bert Campaneris	.50	.25	.05
☐ 206	Clete Boyer	.50	.25	.05
☐ 207	Tigers Rookies	.35	.17	.03
	Norman McRae			
	Bob Reed			
☐ 208	Fred Gladding	.35	.17	.03
☐ 209	Ken Suarez	.35	.17	.03
☐ 210	Juan Marichal	4.50	2.25	.45
☐ 211	Ted Williams MG	6.00	3.00	.60

☐ 212	Al Santorini	.35	.17	.03
☐ 213	Andy Etchebarren	.35	.17	.03
☐ 214	Ken Boswell	.35	.17	.03
☐ 215	Reggie Smith	1.00	.50	.10
☐ 216	Chuck Hartenstein	.35	.17	.03
☐ 217	Ron Hansen	.35	.17	.03
☐ 218	Ron Stone	.35	.17	.03
☐ 219	Jerry Kenney	.35	.17	.03
☐ 220	Steve Carlton	14.00	6.00	1.25
☐ 221	Ron Brand	.35	.17	.03
☐ 222	Jim Rooker	.35	.17	.03
☐ 223	Nate Oliver	.35	.17	.03
☐ 224	Steve Barber	.35	.17	.03
☐ 225	Lee May	.50	.25	.05
☐ 226	Ron Perranoski	.50	.25	.05
☐ 227	Astros Rookies	1.00	.50	.10
	John Mayberry			
	Bob Watkins			
☐ 228	Aurelio Rodriguez	.35	.17	.03
☐ 229	Rich Robertson	.35	.17	.03
☐ 230	Brooks Robinson	8.00	4.00	.80
☐ 231	Luis Tiant	1.00	.50	.10
☐ 232	Bob Didier	.35	.17	.03
☐ 233	Lew Krausse	.35	.17	.03
☐ 234	Tommy Dean	.35	.17	.03
☐ 235	Mike Epstein	.35	.17	.03
☐ 236	Bob Veale	.50	.25	.05
☐ 237	Russ Gibson	.35	.17	.03
☐ 238	Jose Laboy	.35	.17	.03
☐ 239	Ken Berry	.35	.17	.03
☐ 240	Fergie Jenkins	3.00	1.50	.30
☐ 241	Royals Rookies	.35	.17	.03
	Al Fitzmorris			
	Scott Northey			
☐ 242	Walter Alston MG	1.50	.75	.15
☐ 243	Joe Sparma	.35	.17	.03
☐ 244A	Checklist 3	2.50	.25	.05
	(red bat on front)			
☐ 244B	Checklist 3	3.00	.25	.05
	(brown bat on front)			
☐ 245	Leo Cardenas	.35	.17	.03
☐ 246	Jim McAndrew	.35	.17	.03
☐ 247	Lou Klimchock	.35	.17	.03
☐ 248	Jesus Alou	.35	.17	.03
☐ 249	Bob Locker	.35	.17	.03
☐ 250	Willie McCovey	6.50	3.25	.65
☐ 251	Dick Schofield	.35	.17	.03
☐ 252	Lowell Palmer	.35	.17	.03
☐ 253	Ron Woods	.35	.17	.03
☐ 254	Camilo Pascual	.50	.25	.05
☐ 255	Jim Spencer	.35	.17	.03
☐ 256	Vic Davalillo	.35	.17	.03
☐ 257	Dennis Higgins	.35	.17	.03
☐ 258	Paul Popovich	.35	.17	.03
☐ 259	Tommie Reynolds	.35	.17	.03
☐ 260	Claude Osteen	.50	.25	.05
☐ 261	Curt Motton	.35	.17	.03
☐ 262	Padres Rookies	.50	.25	.05
	Jerry Morales			
	Jim Williams			
☐ 263	Duane Josephson	.35	.17	.03
☐ 264	Rich Hebner	.75	.35	.07
☐ 265	Randy Hundley	.50	.25	.05
☐ 266	Wally Bunker	.40	.20	.04
☐ 267	Twins Rookies	.40	.20	.04
	Herman Hill			
	Paul Ratliff			
☐ 268	Claude Raymond	.40	.20	.04
☐ 269	Cesar Gutierrez	.40	.20	.04
☐ 270	Chris Short	.40	.20	.04
☐ 271	Greg Goossen	.40	.20	.04
☐ 272	Hector Torres	.40	.20	.04
☐ 273	Ralph Houk MG	.50	.25	.05
☐ 274	Gerry Arrigo	.40	.20	.04
☐ 275	Duke Sims	.40	.20	.04
☐ 276	Ron Hunt	.40	.20	.04
☐ 277	Paul Doyle	.40	.20	.04
☐ 278	Tommie Aaron	.50	.25	.05
☐ 279	Bill Lee	.75	.35	.07
☐ 280	Donn Clendenon	.50	.25	.05
☐ 281	Casey Cox	.40	.20	.04
☐ 282	Steve Huntz	.40	.20	.04
☐ 283	Angel Bravo	.40	.20	.04
☐ 284	Jack Baldschun	.40	.20	.04
☐ 285	Paul Blair	.50	.25	.05
☐ 286	Dodgers Rookies	6.00	3.00	.60
	Jack Jenkins			
	Bill Buckner			
☐ 287	Fred Talbot	.40	.20	.04
☐ 288	Larry Hisle	.50	.25	.05
☐ 289	Gene Brabender	.40	.20	.04
☐ 290	Rod Carew	18.00	8.50	1.70
☐ 291	Leo Durocher MG	1.25	.60	.12
☐ 292	Eddie Leon	.40	.20	.04
☐ 293	Bob Bailey	.40	.20	.04
☐ 294	Jose Azcue	.40	.20	.04
☐ 295	Cecil Upshaw	.40	.20	.04
☐ 296	Woody Woodward	.50	.25	.05
☐ 297	Curt Blefary	.40	.20	.04
☐ 298	Ken Henderson	.40	.20	.04
☐ 299	Buddy Bradford	.40	.20	.04
☐ 300	Tom Seaver	45.00	22.50	4.50
☐ 301	Chico Salmon	.40	.20	.04
☐ 302	Jeff James	.40	.20	.04
☐ 303	Brant Alyea	.40	.20	.04
☐ 304	Bill Russell	1.50	.75	.15
☐ 305	World Series Game 1	1.50	.75	.15
	Buford leadoff homer			
☐ 306	World Series Game 2	1.50	.75	.15
	Clendenon's homer			
	breaks ice			
☐ 307	World Series Game 3	1.50	.75	.15
	Agee's catch			
	saves the day			
☐ 308	World Series Game 4	1.50	.75	.15
	Martin's bunt			
	ends deadlock			
☐ 309	World Series Game 5	1.50	.75	.15
	Koosman shuts door			
☐ 310	World Series Summary	1.50	.75	.15
	Mets whoop it up			
☐ 311	Dick Green	.40	.20	.04
☐ 312	Mike Torrez	.50	.25	.05
☐ 313	Mayo Smith MG	.40	.20	.04
☐ 314	Bill McCool	.40	.20	.04
☐ 315	Luis Aparicio	3.50	1.75	.35
☐ 316	Skip Guinn	.40	.20	.04
☐ 317	Red Sox Rookies	.50	.25	.05
	Billy Conigliaro			
	Luis Alvarado			
☐ 318	Willie Smith	.40	.20	.04
☐ 319	Clay Dalrymple	.40	.20	.04
☐ 320	Jim Maloney	.50	.25	.05
☐ 321	Lou Piniella	1.25	.60	.12
☐ 322	Luke Walker	.40	.20	.04
☐ 323	Wayne Comer	.40	.20	.04
☐ 324	Tony Taylor	.40	.20	.04
☐ 325	Dave Boswell	.40	.20	.04
☐ 326	Bill Voss	.40	.20	.04
☐ 327	Hal King	.40	.20	.04
☐ 328	George Brunet	.40	.20	.04
☐ 329	Chris Cannizzaro	.40	.20	.04
☐ 330	Lou Brock	6.00	3.00	.60
☐ 331	Chuck Dobson	.40	.20	.04
☐ 332	Bobby Wine	.40	.20	.04
☐ 333	Bobby Murcer	1.00	.50	.10
☐ 334	Phil Regan	.50	.25	.05
☐ 335	Bill Freehan	.75	.35	.07
☐ 336	Del Unser	.40	.20	.04
☐ 337	Mike McCormick	.50	.25	.05
☐ 338	Paul Schaal	.40	.20	.04
☐ 339	Johnny Edwards	.40	.20	.04
☐ 340	Tony Conigliaro	1.00	.50	.10
☐ 341	Bill Sudakis	.40	.20	.04
☐ 342	Wilbur Wood	.50	.25	.05
☐ 343A	Checklist 4	2.50	.25	.05
	(red bat on front)			
☐ 343B	Checklist 4	3.00	.25	.05
	(brown bat on front)			
☐ 344	Marcelino Lopez	.40	.20	.04
☐ 345	Al Ferrara	.40	.20	.04
☐ 346	Red Schoendienst MG	1.75	.85	.17
☐ 347	Russ Snyder	.40	.20	.04
☐ 348	Mets Rookies	.50	.25	.05
	Mike Jorgensen			
	Jesse Hudson			
☐ 349	Steve Hamilton	.40	.20	.04
☐ 350	Roberto Clemente	35.00	16.00	3.20
☐ 351	Tom Murphy	.40	.20	.04
☐ 352	Bob Barton	.40	.20	.04
☐ 353	Stan Williams	.50	.25	.05
☐ 354	Amos Otis	1.00	.50	.10
☐ 355	Doug Rader	.75	.35	.07
☐ 356	Fred Lasher	.40	.20	.04
☐ 357	Bob Burda	.40	.20	.04
☐ 358	Pedro Borbon	.40	.20	.04
☐ 359	Phil Roof	.40	.20	.04
☐ 360	Curt Flood	1.00	.50	.10
☐ 361	Ray Jarvis	.40	.20	.04
☐ 362	Joe Hague	.40	.20	.04
☐ 363	Tom Shopay	.40	.20	.04
☐ 364	Dan McGinn	.40	.20	.04
☐ 365	Zoilo Versalles	.40	.20	.04
☐ 366	Barry Moore	.40	.20	.04
☐ 367	Mike Lum	.40	.20	.04
☐ 368	Ed Herrmann	.40	.20	.04
☐ 369	Alan Foster	.40	.20	.04
☐ 370	Tommy Harper	.50	.25	.05
☐ 371	Rod Gaspar	.40	.20	.04
☐ 372	Dave Giusti	.50	.25	.05

☐ 373	Roy White	.75	.35	.07
☐ 374	Tommie Sisk	.40	.20	.04
☐ 375	Johnny Callison	.50	.25	.05
☐ 376	Lefty Phillips MG	.40	.20	.04
☐ 377	Bill Butler	.40	.20	.04
☐ 378	Jim Davenport	.50	.25	.05
☐ 379	Tom Tischinski	.40	.20	.04
☐ 380	Tony Perez	3.50	1.75	.35
☐ 381	Athletics Rookies	.40	.20	.04
	Bobby Brooks			
	Mike Olivo			
☐ 382	Jack DiLauro	.40	.20	.04
☐ 383	Mickey Stanley	.75	.35	.07
☐ 384	Gary Neibauer	.40	.20	.04
☐ 385	George Scott	.75	.35	.07
☐ 386	Bill Dillman	.40	.20	.04
☐ 387	Baltimore Orioles	1.25	.60	.12
	Team Card			
☐ 388	Byron Browne	.40	.20	.04
☐ 389	Jim Shellenback	.40	.20	.04
☐ 390	Willie Davis	.75	.35	.07
☐ 391	Larry Brown	.40	.20	.04
☐ 392	Walt Hriniak	.50	.25	.05
☐ 393	John Gelnar	.40	.20	.04
☐ 394	Gil Hodges MG	3.50	1.75	.35
☐ 395	Walt Williams	.40	.20	.04
☐ 396	Steve Blass	.50	.25	.05
☐ 397	Roger Repoz	.40	.20	.04
☐ 398	Bill Stoneman	.40	.20	.04
☐ 399	New York Yankees	1.50	.75	.15
	Team Card			
☐ 400	Denny McLain	1.00	.50	.10
☐ 401	Giants Rookies	.40	.20	.04
	John Harrell			
	Bernie Williams			
☐ 402	Ellie Rodriguez	.40	.20	.04
☐ 403	Jim Bunning	2.50	1.25	.25
☐ 404	Rich Reese	.50	.25	.05
☐ 405	Bill Hands	.40	.20	.04
☐ 406	Mike Andrews	.40	.20	.04
☐ 407	Bob Watson	.75	.35	.07
☐ 408	Paul Lindblad	.40	.20	.04
☐ 409	Bob Tolan	.50	.25	.05
☐ 410	Boog Powell	2.50	1.25	.25
☐ 411	Los Angeles Dodgers	1.50	.75	.15
	Team Card			
☐ 412	Larry Burchart	.40	.20	.04
☐ 413	Sonny Jackson	.40	.20	.04
☐ 414	Paul Edmondson	.40	.20	.04
☐ 415	Julian Javier	.50	.25	.05
☐ 416	Joe Verbanic	.40	.20	.04
☐ 417	John Bateman	.40	.20	.04
☐ 418	John Donaldson	.40	.20	.04
☐ 419	Ron Taylor	.40	.20	.04
☐ 420	Ken McMullen	.40	.20	.04
☐ 421	Pat Dobson	.50	.25	.05
☐ 422	Royals Team	1.00	.50	.10
☐ 423	Jerry May	.40	.20	.04
☐ 424	Mike Kilkenny	.40	.20	.04
	(inconsistent design,			
	card # in white circle)			
☐ 425	Bobby Bonds	2.25	1.10	.22
☐ 426	Bill Rigney MG	.40	.20	.04
☐ 427	Fred Norman	.40	.20	.04
☐ 428	Don Buford	.50	.25	.05
☐ 429	Cubs Rookies	.40	.20	.04
	Randy Bobb			
	Jim Cosman			
☐ 430	Andy Messersmith	.50	.25	.05
☐ 431	Ron Swoboda	.50	.25	.05
☐ 432A	Checklist 5	2.50	.25	.05
	("Baseball" in			
	yellow letters)			
☐ 432B	Checklist 5	3.00	.25	.05
	("Baseball" in			
	white letters)			
☐ 433	Ron Bryant	.40	.20	.04
☐ 434	Felipe Alou	.50	.25	.05
☐ 435	Nelson Briles	.50	.25	.05
☐ 436	Philadelphia Phillies	1.00	.50	.10
	Team Card			
☐ 437	Danny Cater	.40	.20	.04
☐ 438	Pat Jarvis	.40	.20	.04
☐ 439	Lee Maye	.40	.20	.04
☐ 440	Bill Mazeroski	1.00	.50	.10
☐ 441	John O'Donoghue	.40	.20	.04
☐ 442	Gene Mauch MG	.50	.25	.05
☐ 443	Al Jackson	.40	.20	.04
☐ 444	White Sox Rookies	.40	.20	.04
	Billy Farmer			
	John Matias			
☐ 445	Vada Pinson	1.00	.50	.10
☐ 446	Billy Grabarkewitz	.40	.20	.04
☐ 447	Lee Stange	.40	.20	.04
☐ 448	Houston Astros	1.00	.50	.10
	Team Card			
☐ 449	Jim Palmer	12.00	6.00	1.20
☐ 450	Willie McCovey AS	3.50	1.75	.35
☐ 451	Boog Powell AS	.75	.35	.07
☐ 452	Felix Millan AS	.50	.25	.05
☐ 453	Rod Carew AS	4.50	2.25	.45
☐ 454	Ron Santo AS	.50	.25	.05
☐ 455	Brooks Robinson AS	4.00	2.00	.40
☐ 456	Don Kessinger AS	.50	.25	.05
☐ 457	Rico Petrocelli AS	.50	.25	.05
☐ 458	Pete Rose AS	10.00	5.00	1.00
☐ 459	Reggie Jackson AS	10.00	5.00	1.00
☐ 460	Matty Alou AS	.75	.35	.07
☐ 461	Carl Yastrzemski AS	8.00	4.00	.80
☐ 462	Hank Aaron AS	8.00	4.00	.80
☐ 463	Frank Robinson AS	4.00	2.00	.40
☐ 464	Johnny Bench AS	8.00	4.00	.80
☐ 465	Bill Freehan AS	.75	.35	.07
☐ 466	Juan Marichal AS	3.00	1.50	.30
☐ 467	Denny McLain AS	.75	.35	.07
☐ 468	Jerry Koosman AS	.75	.35	.07
☐ 469	Sam McDowell AS	.75	.35	.07
☐ 470	Willie Stargell	6.50	3.25	.65
☐ 471	Chris Zachary	.60	.30	.06
☐ 472	Braves Team	1.25	.60	.12
☐ 473	Don Bryant	.60	.30	.06
☐ 474	Dick Kelley	.60	.30	.06
☐ 475	Dick McAuliffe	.75	.35	.07
☐ 476	Don Shaw	.60	.30	.06
☐ 477	Orioles Rookies	.60	.30	.06
	Al Severinsen			
	Roger Freed			
☐ 478	Bobby Heise	.60	.30	.06
☐ 479	Dick Woodson	.60	.30	.06
☐ 480	Glenn Beckert	.75	.35	.07
☐ 481	Jose Tartabull	.60	.30	.06
☐ 482	Tom Hilgendorf	.60	.30	.06
☐ 483	Gail Hopkins	.60	.30	.06
☐ 484	Gary Nolan	.60	.30	.06
☐ 485	Jay Johnstone	.75	.35	.07
☐ 486	Terry Harmon	.60	.30	.06
☐ 487	Cisco Carlos	.60	.30	.06
☐ 488	J.C. Martin	.60	.30	.06
☐ 489	Eddie Kasko MG	.60	.30	.06
☐ 490	Bill Singer	.75	.35	.07
☐ 491	Graig Nettles	4.00	2.00	.40
☐ 492	Astros Rookies	.60	.30	.06
	Keith Lampard			
	Scipio Spinks			
☐ 493	Lindy McDaniel	.75	.35	.07
☐ 494	Larry Stahl	.60	.30	.06
☐ 495	Dave Morehead	.60	.30	.06
☐ 496	Steve Whitaker	.60	.30	.06
☐ 497	Eddie Watt	.60	.30	.06
☐ 498	Al Weis	.60	.30	.06
☐ 499	Skip Lockwood	.60	.30	.06
☐ 500	Hank Aaron	30.00	13.50	2.70
☐ 501	Chicago White Sox	1.25	.60	.12
	Team Card			
☐ 502	Rollie Fingers	7.00	3.50	.70
☐ 503	Dal Maxvill	.60	.30	.06
☐ 504	Don Pavletich	.60	.30	.06
☐ 505	Ken Holtzman	.75	.35	.07
☐ 506	Ed Stroud	.60	.30	.06
☐ 507	Pat Corrales	.75	.35	.07
☐ 508	Joe Niekro	1.00	.50	.10
☐ 509	Montreal Expos	1.50	.75	.15
	Team Card			
☐ 510	Tony Oliva	1.50	.75	.15
☐ 511	Joe Hoerner	.60	.30	.06
☐ 512	Billy Harris	.60	.30	.06
☐ 513	Preston Gomez MG	.60	.30	.06
☐ 514	Steve Hovley	.60	.30	.06
☐ 515	Don Wilson	.60	.30	.06
☐ 516	Yankees Rookies	.60	.30	.06
	John Ellis			
	Jim Lyttle			
☐ 517	Joe Gibbon	.60	.30	.06
☐ 518	Bill Melton	.60	.30	.06
☐ 519	Don McMahon	.60	.30	.06
☐ 520	Willie Horton	.75	.35	.07
☐ 521	Cal Koonce	.60	.30	.06
☐ 522	Angels Team	1.25	.60	.12
☐ 523	Jose Pena	.60	.30	.06
☐ 524	Alvin Dark MG	.75	.35	.07
☐ 525	Jerry Adair	.60	.30	.06
☐ 526	Ron Herbel	.60	.30	.06
☐ 527	Don Bosch	.60	.30	.06
☐ 528	Elrod Hendricks	.60	.30	.06
☐ 529	Bob Aspromonte	.60	.30	.06
☐ 530	Bob Gibson	8.00	4.00	.80
☐ 531	Ron Clark	.60	.30	.06
☐ 532	Danny Murtaugh MG	.60	.30	.06
☐ 533	Buzz Stephen	.60	.30	.06
☐ 534	Twins Team	1.25	.60	.12

☐ 535	Andy Kosco	.60	.30	.06
☐ 536	Mike Kekich	.60	.30	.06
☐ 537	Joe Morgan	6.50	3.25	.65
☐ 538	Bob Humphreys	.60	.30	.06
☐ 539	Phillies Rookies	4.00	2.00	.40
	Dennis Doyle			
	Larry Bowa			
☐ 540	Gary Peters	.60	.30	.06
☐ 541	Bill Heath	.60	.30	.06
☐ 542	Checklist 6	3.00	.25	.05
☐ 543	Clyde Wright	.60	.30	.06
☐ 544	Cincinnati Reds	1.50	.75	.15
	Team Card			
☐ 545	Ken Harrelson	1.25	.60	.12
☐ 546	Ron Reed	.60	.30	.06
☐ 547	Rick Monday	1.50	.75	.15
☐ 548	Howie Reed	1.00	.50	.10
☐ 549	Cardinals Team	2.00	1.00	.20
☐ 550	Frank Howard	1.50	.75	.15
☐ 551	Dock Ellis	1.00	.50	.10
☐ 552	Royals Rookies	1.00	.50	.10
	Don O'Riley			
	Dennis Paepke			
	Fred Rico			
☐ 553	Jim Lefebvre	1.50	.75	.15
☐ 554	Tom Timmermann	1.00	.50	.10
☐ 555	Orlando Cepeda	3.00	1.50	.30
☐ 556	Dave Bristol MG	1.00	.50	.10
☐ 557	Ed Kranepool	1.50	.75	.15
☐ 558	Vern Fuller	1.00	.50	.10
☐ 559	Tommy Davis	1.50	.75	.15
☐ 560	Gaylord Perry	6.00	3.00	.60
☐ 561	Tom McCraw	1.00	.50	.10
☐ 562	Ted Abernathy	1.00	.50	.10
☐ 563	Boston Red Sox	2.00	1.00	.20
	Team Card			
☐ 564	Johnny Briggs	1.00	.50	.10
☐ 565	Jim Hunter	7.00	3.50	.70
☐ 566	Gene Alley	1.00	.50	.10
☐ 567	Bob Oliver	1.00	.50	.10
☐ 568	Stan Bahnsen	1.00	.50	.10
☐ 569	Cookie Rojas	1.00	.50	.10
☐ 570	Jim Fregosi	1.50	.75	.15
☐ 571	Jim Brewer	1.00	.50	.10
☐ 572	Frank Quilici MG	1.00	.50	.10
☐ 573	Padres Rookies	1.00	.50	.10
	Mike Corkins			
	Rafael Robles			
	Ron Slocum			
☐ 574	Bobby Bolin	1.00	.50	.10
☐ 575	Cleon Jones	1.00	.50	.10
☐ 576	Milt Pappas	1.50	.75	.15
☐ 577	Bernie Allen	1.00	.50	.10
☐ 578	Tom Griffin	1.00	.50	.10
☐ 579	Detroit Tigers	2.50	1.25	.25
	Team Card			
☐ 580	Pete Rose	75.00	37.50	7.50
☐ 581	Tom Satriano	1.00	.50	.10
☐ 582	Mike Paul	1.00	.50	.10
☐ 583	Hal Lanier	1.50	.75	.15
☐ 584	Al Downing	1.50	.75	.15
☐ 585	Rusty Staub	1.75	.85	.17
☐ 586	Rickey Clark	1.00	.50	.10
☐ 587	Jose Arcia	1.00	.50	.10
☐ 588A	Checklist 7	3.50	.25	.05
	(666 Adolpho)			
☐ 588B	Checklist 7	6.50	.50	.10
	(666 Adolfo)			
☐ 589	Joe Keough	1.00	.50	.10
☐ 590	Mike Cuellar	1.50	.75	.15
☐ 591	Mike Ryan	1.00	.50	.10
☐ 592	Daryl Patterson	1.00	.50	.10
☐ 593	Chicago Cubs	2.00	1.00	.20
	Team Card			
☐ 594	Jake Gibbs	1.00	.50	.10
☐ 595	Maury Wills	2.50	1.25	.25
☐ 596	Mike Hershberger	1.00	.50	.10
☐ 597	Sonny Siebert	1.00	.50	.10
☐ 598	Joe Pepitone	1.50	.75	.15
☐ 599	Senators Rookies	1.00	.50	.10
	Dick Stelmaszek			
	Gene Martin			
	Dick Such			
☐ 600	Willie Mays	45.00	20.00	4.00
☐ 601	Pete Richert	1.00	.50	.10
☐ 602	Ted Savage	1.00	.50	.10
☐ 603	Ray Oyler	1.00	.50	.10
☐ 604	Clarence Gaston	1.50	.75	.15
☐ 605	Rick Wise	1.50	.75	.15
☐ 606	Chico Ruiz	1.00	.50	.10
☐ 607	Gary Waslewski	1.00	.50	.10
☐ 608	Pittsburgh Pirates	2.00	1.00	.20
	Team Card			
☐ 609	Buck Martinez	1.00	.50	.10
	(inconsistent design,			

	card # in white circle)			
☐ 610	Jerry Koosman	1.50	.75	.15
☐ 611	Norm Cash	1.50	.75	.15
☐ 612	Jim Hickman	1.00	.50	.10
☐ 613	Dave Baldwin	1.00	.50	.10
☐ 614	Mike Shannon	1.50	.75	.15
☐ 615	Mark Belanger	1.50	.75	.15
☐ 616	Jim Merritt	1.00	.50	.10
☐ 617	Jim French	1.00	.50	.10
☐ 618	Billy Wynne	1.00	.50	.10
☐ 619	Norm Miller	1.00	.50	.10
☐ 620	Jim Perry	1.50	.75	.15
☐ 621	Braves Rookies	14.00	6.25	1.25
	Mike McQueen			
	Darrell Evans			
	Rick Kester			
☐ 622	Don Sutton	6.50	3.25	.65
☐ 623	Horace Clarke	1.00	.50	.10
☐ 624	Clyde King MG	1.00	.50	.10
☐ 625	Dean Chance	1.50	.75	.15
☐ 626	Dave Ricketts	1.00	.50	.10
☐ 627	Gary Wagner	1.00	.50	.10
☐ 628	Wayne Garrett	1.00	.50	.10
☐ 629	Merv Rettenmund	1.00	.50	.10
☐ 630	Ernie Banks	17.00	8.00	1.60
☐ 631	Oakland Athletics	2.50	1.25	.25
	Team Card			
☐ 632	Gary Sutherland	1.00	.50	.10
☐ 633	Roger Nelson	1.00	.50	.10
☐ 634	Bud Harrelson	3.00	1.50	.30
☐ 635	Bob Allison	3.00	1.50	.30
☐ 636	Jim Stewart	2.25	1.10	.22
☐ 637	Cleveland Indians	4.50	2.25	.45
	Team Card			
☐ 638	Frank Bertaina	2.25	1.10	.22
☐ 639	Dave Campbell	2.25	1.10	.22
☐ 640	Al Kaline	33.00	15.00	3.00
☐ 641	Al McBean	2.25	1.10	.22
☐ 642	Angels Rookies	2.25	1.10	.22
	Greg Garrett			
	Gordon Lund			
	Jarvis Tatum			
☐ 643	Jose Pagan	2.25	1.10	.22
☐ 644	Gerry Nyman	2.25	1.10	.22
☐ 645	Don Money	2.25	1.10	.22
☐ 646	Jim Britton	2.25	1.10	.22
☐ 647	Tom Matchick	2.25	1.10	.22
☐ 648	Larry Haney	2.25	1.10	.22
☐ 649	Jimmie Hall	2.25	1.10	.22
☐ 650	Sam McDowell	3.00	1.50	.30
☐ 651	Jim Gosger	2.25	1.10	.22
☐ 652	Rich Rollins	2.25	1.10	.22
☐ 653	Moe Drabowsky	2.25	1.10	.22
☐ 654	NL Rookies	3.50	1.75	.35
	Oscar Gamble			
	Boots Day			
	Angel Mangual			
☐ 655	John Roseboro	2.25	1.10	.22
☐ 656	Jim Hardin	2.25	1.10	.22
☐ 657	San Diego Padres	4.50	2.25	.45
	Team Card			
☐ 658	Ken Tatum	2.25	1.10	.22
☐ 659	Pete Ward	2.25	1.10	.22
☐ 660	Johnny Bench	135.00	65.00	13.50
☐ 661	Jerry Robertson	2.25	1.10	.22
☐ 662	Frank Lucchesi MG	2.25	1.10	.22
☐ 663	Tito Francona	2.25	1.10	.22
☐ 664	Bob Robertson	2.25	1.10	.22
☐ 665	Jim Lonborg	3.00	1.50	.30
☐ 666	Adolpho Phillips	2.25	1.10	.22
☐ 667	Bob Meyer	2.25	1.10	.22
☐ 668	Bob Tillman	2.25	1.10	.22
☐ 669	White Sox Rookies	2.25	1.10	.22
	Bart Johnson			
	Dan Lazar			
	Mickey Scott			
☐ 670	Ron Santo	4.00	2.00	.40
☐ 671	Jim Campanis	2.25	1.10	.22
☐ 672	Leon McFadden	2.25	1.10	.22
☐ 673	Ted Uhlaender	2.25	1.10	.22
☐ 674	Dave Leonhard	2.25	1.10	.22
☐ 675	Jose Cardenal	2.25	1.10	.22
☐ 676	Senators Team	4.50	2.25	.45
☐ 677	Woodie Fryman	2.25	1.10	.22
☐ 678	Dave Duncan	2.25	1.10	.22
☐ 679	Ray Sadecki	2.25	1.10	.22
☐ 680	Rico Petrocelli	3.00	1.50	.30
☐ 681	Bob Garibaldi	2.25	1.10	.22
☐ 682	Dalton Jones	2.25	1.10	.22
☐ 683	Reds Rookies	4.00	2.00	.40
	Vern Geishert			
	Hal McRae			
	Wayne Simpson			
☐ 684	Jack Fisher	2.25	1.10	.22
☐ 685	Tom Haller	2.25	1.10	.22

□ 686	Jackie Hernandez	2.25	1.10	.22
□ 687	Bob Priddy	2.25	1.10	.22
□ 688	Ted Kubiak	2.25	1.10	.22
□ 689	Frank Tepedino	2.25	1.10	.22
□ 690	Ron Fairly	2.25	1.10	.22
□ 691	Joe Grzenda	2.25	1.10	.22
□ 692	Duffy Dyer	2.25	1.10	.22
□ 693	Bob Johnson	2.25	1.10	.22
□ 694	Gary Ross	2.25	1.10	.22
□ 695	Bobby Knoop	2.25	1.10	.22
□ 696	San Francisco Giants Team Card	4.50	2.25	.45
□ 697	Jim Hannan	2.25	1.10	.22
□ 698	Tom Tresh	4.00	2.00	.40
□ 699	Hank Aguirre	2.25	1.10	.22
□ 700	Frank Robinson	33.00	15.00	3.00
□ 701	Jack Billingham	2.25	1.10	.22
□ 702	AL Rookies Bob Johnson Ron Klimkowski Bill Zepp	2.25	1.10	.22
□ 703	Lou Marone	2.25	1.10	.22
□ 704	Frank Baker	2.25	1.10	.22
□ 705	Tony Cloninger	2.25	1.10	.22
□ 706	John McNamara MG	6.00	3.00	.60
□ 707	Kevin Collins	2.25	1.10	.22
□ 708	Jose Santiago	2.25	1.10	.22
□ 709	Mike Fiore	2.25	1.10	.22
□ 710	Felix Millan	2.25	1.10	.22
□ 711	Ed Brinkman	2.25	1.10	.22
□ 712	Nolan Ryan	225.00	110.00	22.00
□ 713	Pilots Team	12.00	6.00	1.20
□ 714	Al Spangler	2.25	1.10	.22
□ 715	Mickey Lolich	4.50	2.25	.45
□ 716	Cardinals Rookies Sal Campisi Reggie Cleveland Santiago Guzman	2.25	1.10	.22
□ 717	Tom Phoebus	2.25	1.10	.22
□ 718	Ed Spiezio	2.25	1.10	.22
□ 719	Jim Roland	2.25	1.10	.22
□ 720	Rick Reichardt	3.00	1.50	.30

1971 Topps

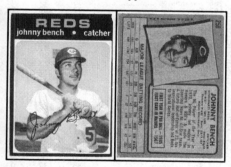

The cards in this 752-card set measure 2 1/2" by 3 1/2". The 1971 Topps set is a challenge to complete in strict mint condition because the black obverse border is easily scratched and damaged. An unusual feature of this set is that the player is also pictured in black and white on the back of the card. Featured subsets within this set include League Leaders (61-72), Playoffs cards (195-202), and World Series cards (327-332). Cards 524-643 and the last series (644-752) are somewhat scarce. The last series was printed in two sheets of 132. On the printing sheets 44 cards were printed in 50% greater quantity than the other 66 cards. These 66 (slightly) shorter-printed numbers are identified in the checklist below by SP.

	NRMT	VG-E	GOOD
COMPLETE SET (752)	1600.00	750.00	200.00
COMMON PLAYER (1-263)	.35	.17	.03
COMMON PLAYER (264-393)	.40	.20	.04
COMMON PLAYER (394-523)	.60	.30	.06

		NRMT	VG-E	GOOD
COMMON PLAYER (524-643)		1.00	.50	.10
COMMON PLAYER (644-752)		2.50	1.10	.22
COMMON SP (644-752)		3.50	1.50	.30
□ 1	Baltimore Orioles Team Card	6.00	1.00	.20
□ 2	Dock Ellis	.35	.17	.03
□ 3	Dick McAuliffe	.35	.17	.03
□ 4	Vic Davalillo	.35	.17	.03
□ 5	Thurman Munson	21.00	10.50	2.10
□ 6	Ed Spiezio	.35	.17	.03
□ 7	Jim Holt	.35	.17	.03
□ 8	Mike McQueen	.35	.17	.03
□ 9	George Scott	.50	.25	.05
□ 10	Claude Osteen	.50	.25	.05
□ 11	Elliott Maddox	.35	.17	.03
□ 12	Johnny Callison	.50	.25	.05
□ 13	White Sox Rookies Charlie Brinkman Dick Moloney	.35	.17	.03
□ 14	Dave Concepcion	6.00	3.00	.60
□ 15	Andy Messersmith	.50	.25	.05
□ 16	Ken Singleton	2.00	1.00	.20
□ 17	Billy Sorrell	.35	.17	.03
□ 18	Norm Miller	.35	.17	.03
□ 19	Skip Pitlock	.35	.17	.03
□ 20	Reggie Jackson	36.00	16.00	3.50
□ 21	Dan McGinn	.35	.17	.03
□ 22	Phil Roof	.35	.17	.03
□ 23	Oscar Gamble	.50	.25	.05
□ 24	Rich Hand	.35	.17	.03
□ 25	Clarence Gaston	.75	.35	.07
□ 26	Bert Blyleven	30.00	15.00	3.00
□ 27	Pirates Rookies Fred Cambria Gene Clines	.35	.17	.03
□ 28	Ron Klimkowski	.35	.17	.03
□ 29	Don Buford	.50	.25	.05
□ 30	Phil Niekro	3.50	1.75	.35
□ 31	Eddie Kasko MG	.35	.17	.03
□ 32	Jerry DaVanon	.35	.17	.03
□ 33	Del Unser	.35	.17	.03
□ 34	Sandy Vance	.35	.17	.03
□ 35	Lou Piniella	1.00	.50	.10
□ 36	Dean Chance	.50	.25	.05
□ 37	Rich McKinney	.35	.17	.03
□ 38	Jim Colborn	.35	.17	.03
□ 39	Tiger Rookies Lerrin LaGrow Gene Lamont	.35	.17	.03
□ 40	Lee May	.50	.25	.05
□ 41	Rick Austin	.35	.17	.03
□ 42	Boots Day	.35	.17	.03
□ 43	Steve Kealey	.35	.17	.03
□ 44	Johnny Edwards	.35	.17	.03
□ 45	Jim Hunter	4.50	2.25	.45
□ 46	Dave Campbell	.35	.17	.03
□ 47	Johnny Jeter	.35	.17	.03
□ 48	Dave Baldwin	.35	.17	.03
□ 49	Don Money	.35	.17	.03
□ 50	Willie McCovey	6.00	3.00	.60
□ 51	Steve Kline	.35	.17	.03
□ 52	Braves Rookies Oscar Brown Earl Williams	.50	.25	.05
□ 53	Paul Blair	.50	.25	.05
□ 54	Checklist 1	2.00	.20	.04
□ 55	Steve Carlton	14.00	6.50	1.25
□ 56	Duane Josephson	.35	.17	.03
□ 57	Von Joshua	.35	.17	.03
□ 58	Bill Lee	.50	.25	.05
□ 59	Gene Mauch MG	.50	.25	.05
□ 60	Dick Bosman	.35	.17	.03
□ 61	AL Batting Leaders Alex Johnson Carl Yastrzemski Tony Oliva	2.00	1.00	.20
□ 62	NL Batting Leaders Rico Carty Joe Torre Manny Sanguillen	1.25	.60	.12
□ 63	AL RBI Leaders Frank Howard Tony Conigliaro Boog Powell	1.25	.60	.12
□ 64	NL RBI Leaders Johnny Bench Tony Perez Billy Williams	2.00	1.00	.20
□ 65	AL HR Leaders Frank Howard Harmon Killebrew Carl Yastrzemski	2.00	1.00	.20
□ 66	NL HR Leaders Johnny Bench	2.00	1.00	.20

	Billy Williams			
	Tony Perez			
☐ 67	AL ERA Leaders	1.25	.60	.12
	Diego Segui			
	Jim Palmer			
	Clyde Wright			
☐ 68	NL ERA Leaders	1.25	.60	.12
	Tom Seaver			
	Wayne Simpson			
	Luke Walker			
☐ 69	AL Pitching Leaders	1.25	.60	.12
	Mike Cuellar			
	Dave McNally			
	Jim Perry			
☐ 70	NL Pitching Leaders	2.00	1.00	.20
	Bob Gibson			
	Gaylord Perry			
	Fergie Jenkins			
☐ 71	AL Strikeout Leaders	1.25	.60	.12
	Sam McDowell			
	Mickey Lolich			
	Bob Johnson			
☐ 72	NL Strikeout Leaders	2.00	1.00	.20
	Tom Seaver			
	Bob Gibson			
	Fergie Jenkins			
☐ 73	George Brunet	.35	.17	.03
☐ 74	Twins Rookies	.35	.17	.03
	Pete Hamm			
	Jim Nettles			
☐ 75	Gary Nolan	.35	.17	.03
☐ 76	Ted Savage	.35	.17	.03
☐ 77	Mike Compton	.35	.17	.03
☐ 78	Jim Spencer	.35	.17	.03
☐ 79	Wade Blasingame	.35	.17	.03
☐ 80	Bill Melton	.35	.17	.03
☐ 81	Felix Millan	.35	.17	.03
☐ 82	Casey Cox	.35	.17	.03
☐ 83	Met Rookies	.50	.25	.05
	Tim Foli			
	Randy Bobb			
☐ 84	Marcel Lachemann	.50	.25	.05
☐ 85	Billy Grabarkewitz	.35	.17	.03
☐ 86	Mike Kilkenny	.35	.17	.03
☐ 87	Jack Heidemann	.35	.17	.03
☐ 88	Hal King	.35	.17	.03
☐ 89	Ken Brett	.50	.25	.05
☐ 90	Joe Pepitone	.75	.35	.07
☐ 91	Bob Lemon MG	1.50	.75	.15
☐ 92	Fred Wenz	.35	.17	.03
☐ 93	Senators Rookies	.35	.17	.03
	Norm McRae			
	Denny Riddleberger			
☐ 94	Don Hahn	.35	.17	.03
☐ 95	Luis Tiant	.75	.35	.07
☐ 96	Joe Hague	.35	.17	.03
☐ 97	Floyd Wicker	.35	.17	.03
☐ 98	Joe Decker	.35	.17	.03
☐ 99	Mark Belanger	.50	.25	.05
☐ 100	Pete Rose	45.00	22.50	4.50
☐ 101	Les Cain	.35	.17	.03
☐ 102	Astros Rookies	1.00	.50	.10
	Ken Forsch			
	Larry Howard			
☐ 103	Rich Severson	.35	.17	.03
☐ 104	Dan Frisella	.35	.17	.03
☐ 105	Tony Conigliaro	1.00	.50	.10
☐ 106	Tom Dukes	.35	.17	.03
☐ 107	Roy Foster	.35	.17	.03
☐ 108	John Cumberland	.35	.17	.03
☐ 109	Steve Hovley	.35	.17	.03
☐ 110	Bill Mazeroski	.75	.35	.07
☐ 111	Yankee Rookies	.35	.17	.03
	Loyd Colson			
	Bobby Mitchell			
☐ 112	Manny Mota	.50	.25	.05
☐ 113	Jerry Crider	.35	.17	.03
☐ 114	Billy Conigliaro	.50	.25	.05
☐ 115	Donn Clendenon	.50	.25	.05
☐ 116	Ken Sanders	.35	.17	.03
☐ 117	Ted Simmons	8.00	4.00	.80
☐ 118	Cookie Rojas	.50	.25	.05
☐ 119	Frank Lucchesi MG	.35	.17	.03
☐ 120	Willie Horton	.50	.25	.05
☐ 121	Cubs Rookies	.35	.17	.03
	Jim Dunegan			
	Roe Skidmore			
☐ 122	Eddie Watt	.35	.17	.03
☐ 123A	Checklist 2	2.50	.25	.05
	(card number			
	at bottom right)			
☐ 123B	Checklist 2	3.00	.25	.05
	(card number			
	centered)			
☐ 124	Don Gullett	.75	.35	.07

☐ 125	Ray Fosse	.35	.17	.03
☐ 126	Danny Coombs	.35	.17	.03
☐ 127	Danny Thompson	.35	.17	.03
☐ 128	Frank Johnson	.35	.17	.03
☐ 129	Aurelio Monteagudo	.35	.17	.03
☐ 130	Denis Menke	.35	.17	.03
☐ 131	Curt Blefary	.35	.17	.03
☐ 132	Jose Laboy	.35	.17	.03
☐ 133	Mickey Lolich	1.00	.50	.10
☐ 134	Jose Arcia	.35	.17	.03
☐ 135	Rick Monday	.50	.25	.05
☐ 136	Duffy Dyer	.35	.17	.03
☐ 137	Marcelino Lopez	.35	.17	.03
☐ 138	Phillies Rookies	.50	.25	.05
	Joe Lis			
	Willie Montanez			
☐ 139	Paul Casanova	.35	.17	.03
☐ 140	Gaylord Perry	3.50	1.75	.35
☐ 141	Frank Quilici	.35	.17	.03
☐ 142	Mack Jones	.35	.17	.03
☐ 143	Steve Blass	.50	.25	.05
☐ 144	Jackie Hernandez	.35	.17	.03
☐ 145	Bill Singer	.50	.25	.05
☐ 146	Ralph Houk MG	.50	.25	.05
☐ 147	Bob Priddy	.35	.17	.03
☐ 148	John Mayberry	.50	.25	.05
☐ 149	Mike Hershberger	.35	.17	.03
☐ 150	Sam McDowell	.50	.25	.05
☐ 151	Tommy Davis	.50	.25	.05
☐ 152	Angels Rookies	.35	.17	.03
	Lloyd Allen			
	Winston Llenas			
☐ 153	Gary Ross	.35	.17	.03
☐ 154	Cesar Gutierrez	.35	.17	.03
☐ 155	Ken Henderson	.35	.17	.03
☐ 156	Bart Johnson	.35	.17	.03
☐ 157	Bob Bailey	.35	.17	.03
☐ 158	Jerry Reuss	.75	.35	.07
☐ 159	Jarvis Tatum	.35	.17	.03
☐ 160	Tom Seaver	30.00	15.00	3.00
☐ 161	Coin Checklist	2.00	.20	.04
☐ 162	Jack Billingham	.35	.17	.03
☐ 163	Buck Martinez	.35	.17	.03
☐ 164	Reds Rookies	.50	.25	.05
	Frank Duffy			
	Milt Wilcox			
☐ 165	Cesar Tovar	.35	.17	.03
☐ 166	Joe Hoerner	.35	.17	.03
☐ 167	Tom Grieve	1.00	.50	.10
☐ 168	Bruce Dal Canton	.35	.17	.03
☐ 169	Ed Herrmann	.35	.17	.03
☐ 170	Mike Cuellar	.50	.25	.05
☐ 171	Bobby Wine	.35	.17	.03
☐ 172	Duke Sims	.35	.17	.03
☐ 173	Gil Garrido	.35	.17	.03
☐ 174	Dave LaRoche	.35	.17	.03
☐ 175	Jim Hickman	.35	.17	.03
☐ 176	Red Sox Rookies	.35	.17	.03
	Bob Montgomery			
	Doug Griffin			
☐ 177	Hal McRae	.75	.35	.07
☐ 178	Dave Duncan	.35	.17	.03
☐ 179	Mike Corkins	.35	.17	.03
☐ 180	Al Kaline UER	12.00	5.00	1.00
	(Home instead of Birth)			
☐ 181	Hal Lanier	.50	.25	.05
☐ 182	Al Downing	.50	.25	.05
☐ 183	Gil Hodges MG	3.00	1.50	.30
☐ 184	Stan Bahnsen	.35	.17	.03
☐ 185	Julian Javier	.35	.17	.03
☐ 186	Bob Spence	.35	.17	.03
☐ 187	Ted Abernathy	.35	.17	.03
☐ 188	Dodgers Rookies	2.00	1.00	.20
	Bob Valentine			
	Mike Strahler			
☐ 189	George Mitterwald	.35	.17	.03
☐ 190	Bob Tolan	.50	.25	.05
☐ 191	Mike Andrews	.35	.17	.03
☐ 192	Billy Wilson	.35	.17	.03
☐ 193	Bob Grich	2.25	1.10	.22
☐ 194	Mike Lum	.35	.17	.03
☐ 195	AL Playoff Game 1	1.50	.75	.15
	Powell muscles Twins			
☐ 196	AL Playoff Game 2	1.50	.75	.15
	McNally makes it			
	two straight			
☐ 197	AL Playoff Game 3	2.50	1.25	.25
	Palmer mows'em down			
☐ 198	AL Playoff Summary	1.50	.75	.15
	Orioles celebrate			
☐ 199	NL Playoff Game 1	1.50	.75	.15
	Cline pinch-triple			
	decides it			
☐ 200	NL Playoff Game 2	1.50	.75	.15
	Tolan scores for			

	third time			
☐ 201	NL Playoff Game 3	1.50	.75	.15
	Cline scores			
	winning run			
☐ 202	NL Playoff Summary	1.50	.75	.15
	Reds celebrate			
☐ 203	Larry Gura	.75	.35	.07
☐ 204	Brewers Rookies	.35	.17	.03
	Bernie Smith			
	George Kopacz			
☐ 205	Gerry Moses	.35	.17	.03
☐ 206	Checklist 3	2.00	.20	.04
☐ 207	Alan Foster	.35	.17	.03
☐ 208	Billy Martin MG	2.50	1.25	.25
☐ 209	Steve Renko	.35	.17	.03
☐ 210	Rod Carew	18.00	8.50	1.70
☐ 211	Phil Hennigan	.35	.17	.03
☐ 212	Rich Hebner	.50	.25	.05
☐ 213	Frank Baker	.35	.17	.03
☐ 214	Al Ferrara	.35	.17	.03
☐ 215	Diego Segui	.35	.17	.03
☐ 216	Cards Rookies	.35	.17	.03
	Reggie Cleveland			
	Luis Melendez			
☐ 217	Ed Stroud	.35	.17	.03
☐ 218	Tony Cloninger	.35	.17	.03
☐ 219	Elrod Hendricks	.35	.17	.03
☐ 220	Ron Santo	1.00	.50	.10
☐ 221	Dave Morehead	.35	.17	.03
☐ 222	Bob Watson	.50	.25	.05
☐ 223	Cecil Upshaw	.35	.17	.03
☐ 224	Alan Gallagher	.35	.17	.03
☐ 225	Gary Peters	.35	.17	.03
☐ 226	Bill Russell	.75	.35	.07
☐ 227	Floyd Weaver	.35	.17	.03
☐ 228	Wayne Garrett	.35	.17	.03
☐ 229	Jim Hannan	.35	.17	.03
☐ 230	Willie Stargell	6.50	3.25	.65
☐ 231	Indians Rookies	.50	.25	.05
	Vince Colbert			
	John Lowenstein			
☐ 232	John Strohmayer	.35	.17	.03
☐ 233	Larry Bowa	1.75	.85	.17
☐ 234	Jim Lyttle	.35	.17	.03
☐ 235	Nate Colbert	.35	.17	.03
☐ 236	Bob Humphreys	.35	.17	.03
☐ 237	Cesar Cedeno	1.50	.75	.15
☐ 238	Chuck Dobson	.35	.17	.03
☐ 239	Red Schoendienst MG	1.25	.60	.12
☐ 240	Clyde Wright	.35	.17	.03
☐ 241	Dave Nelson	.35	.17	.03
☐ 242	Jim Ray	.35	.17	.03
☐ 243	Carlos May	.35	.17	.03
☐ 244	Bob Tillman	.35	.17	.03
☐ 245	Jim Kaat	2.00	1.00	.20
☐ 246	Tony Taylor	.35	.17	.03
☐ 247	Royals Rookies	.75	.35	.07
	Jerry Cram			
	Paul Splittorff			
☐ 248	Hoyt Wilhelm	3.50	1.75	.35
☐ 249	Chico Salmon	.35	.17	.03
☐ 250	Johnny Bench	36.00	16.00	3.50
☐ 251	Frank Reberger	.35	.17	.03
☐ 252	Eddie Leon	.35	.17	.03
☐ 253	Bill Sudakis	.35	.17	.03
☐ 254	Cal Koonce	.35	.17	.03
☐ 255	Bob Robertson	.35	.17	.03
☐ 256	Tony Gonzalez	.35	.17	.03
☐ 257	Nelson Briles	.35	.17	.03
☐ 258	Dick Green	.35	.17	.03
☐ 259	Dave Marshall	.35	.17	.03
☐ 260	Tommy Harper	.50	.25	.05
☐ 261	Darold Knowles	.35	.17	.03
☐ 262	Padres Rookies	.35	.17	.03
	Jim Williams			
	Dave Robinson			
☐ 263	John Ellis	.35	.17	.03
☐ 264	Joe Morgan	6.00	3.00	.60
☐ 265	Jim Northrup	.50	.25	.05
☐ 266	Bill Stoneman	.40	.20	.04
☐ 267	Rich Morales	.40	.20	.04
☐ 268	Phillies Team	1.00	.50	.10
☐ 269	Gail Hopkins	.40	.20	.04
☐ 270	Rico Carty	.75	.35	.07
☐ 271	Bill Zepp	.40	.20	.04
☐ 272	Tommy Helms	.50	.25	.05
☐ 273	Pete Richert	.40	.20	.04
☐ 274	Ron Slocum	.40	.20	.04
☐ 275	Vada Pinson	1.00	.50	.10
☐ 276	Giants Rookies	5.00	2.50	.50
	Mike Davison			
	George Foster			
☐ 277	Gary Waslewski	.40	.20	.04
☐ 278	Jerry Grote	.40	.20	.04
☐ 279	Lefty Phillips MG	.40	.20	.04

☐ 280	Fergie Jenkins	3.00	1.50	.30
☐ 281	Danny Walton	.40	.20	.04
☐ 282	Jose Pagan	.40	.20	.04
☐ 283	Dick Such	.40	.20	.04
☐ 284	Jim Gosger	.40	.20	.04
☐ 285	Sal Bando	.75	.35	.07
☐ 286	Jerry McNertney	.40	.20	.04
☐ 287	Mike Fiore	.40	.20	.04
☐ 288	Joe Moeller	.40	.20	.04
☐ 289	White Sox Team	1.00	.50	.10
☐ 290	Tony Oliva	2.00	1.00	.20
☐ 291	George Culver	.40	.20	.04
☐ 292	Jay Johnstone	.75	.35	.07
☐ 293	Pat Corrales	.50	.25	.05
☐ 294	Steve Dunning	.40	.20	.04
☐ 295	Bobby Bonds	1.50	.75	.15
☐ 296	Tom Timmermann	.40	.20	.04
☐ 297	Johnny Briggs	.40	.20	.04
☐ 298	Jim Nelson	.40	.20	.04
☐ 299	Ed Kirkpatrick	.40	.20	.04
☐ 300	Brooks Robinson	9.00	4.50	.90
☐ 301	Earl Wilson	.40	.20	.04
☐ 302	Phil Gagliano	.40	.20	.04
☐ 303	Lindy McDaniel	.50	.25	.05
☐ 304	Ron Brand	.40	.20	.04
☐ 305	Reggie Smith	.75	.35	.07
☐ 306	Jim Nash	.40	.20	.04
☐ 307	Don Wert	.40	.20	.04
☐ 308	St. Louis Cardinals	1.00	.50	.10
	Team Card			
☐ 309	Dick Ellsworth	.50	.25	.05
☐ 310	Tommie Agee	.50	.25	.05
☐ 311	Lee Stange	.40	.20	.04
☐ 312	Harry Walker MG	.40	.20	.04
☐ 313	Tom Hall	.40	.20	.04
☐ 314	Jeff Torborg	.50	.25	.05
☐ 315	Ron Fairly	.50	.25	.05
☐ 316	Fred Scherman	.40	.20	.04
☐ 317	Athletic Rookies	.40	.20	.04
	Jim Driscoll			
	Angel Mangual			
☐ 318	Rudy May	.40	.20	.04
☐ 319	Ty Cline	.40	.20	.04
☐ 320	Dave McNally	.50	.25	.05
☐ 321	Tom Matchick	.40	.20	.04
☐ 322	Jim Beauchamp	.40	.20	.04
☐ 323	Billy Champion	.40	.20	.04
☐ 324	Graig Nettles	2.25	1.10	.22
☐ 325	Juan Marichal	4.50	2.25	.45
☐ 326	Richie Scheinblum	.40	.20	.04
☐ 327	World Series Game 1	1.50	.75	.15
	Powell homers to			
	opposite field			
☐ 328	World Series Game 2	1.50	.75	.15
	Don Buford			
☐ 329	World Series Game 3	2.00	1.00	.20
	Frank Robinson			
	shows muscle			
☐ 330	World Series Game 4	1.50	.75	.15
	Reds stay alive			
☐ 331	World Series Game 5	2.00	1.00	.20
	Brooks Robinson			
	commits robbery			
☐ 332	World Series Summary	1.50	.75	.15
	Orioles celebrate			
☐ 333	Clay Kirby	.40	.20	.04
☐ 334	Roberto Pena	.40	.20	.04
☐ 335	Jerry Koosman	.75	.35	.07
☐ 336	Detroit Tigers	1.00	.50	.10
	Team Card			
☐ 337	Jesus Alou	.40	.20	.04
☐ 338	Gene Tenace	.75	.35	.07
☐ 339	Wayne Simpson	.40	.20	.04
☐ 340	Rico Petrocelli	.50	.25	.05
☐ 341	Steve Garvey	75.00	37.50	7.50
☐ 342	Frank Tepedino	.40	.20	.04
☐ 343	Pirates Rookies	.40	.20	.04
	Ed Acosta			
	Milt May			
☐ 344	Ellie Rodriguez	.40	.20	.04
☐ 345	Joel Horlen	.40	.20	.04
☐ 346	Lum Harris MG	.40	.20	.04
☐ 347	Ted Uhlaender	.40	.20	.04
☐ 348	Fred Norman	.40	.20	.04
☐ 349	Rich Reese	.40	.20	.04
☐ 350	Billy Williams	4.00	2.00	.40
☐ 351	Jim Shellenback	.40	.20	.04
☐ 352	Denny Doyle	.40	.20	.04
☐ 353	Carl Taylor	.40	.20	.04
☐ 354	Don McMahon	.40	.20	.04
☐ 355	Bud Harrelson	.50	.25	.05
☐ 356	Bob Locker	.40	.20	.04
☐ 357	Reds Team	1.00	.50	.10
☐ 358	Danny Cater	.40	.20	.04
☐ 359	Ron Reed	.40	.20	.04

☐ 360	Jim Fregosi	.75	.35	.07
☐ 361	Don Sutton	3.50	1.75	.35
☐ 362	Orioles Rookies	.40	.20	.04
	Mike Adamson			
	Roger Freed			
☐ 363	Mike Nagy	.40	.20	.04
☐ 364	Tommy Dean	.40	.20	.04
☐ 365	Bob Johnson	.40	.20	.04
☐ 366	Ron Stone	.40	.20	.04
☐ 367	Dalton Jones	.40	.20	.04
☐ 368	Bob Veale	.50	.25	.05
☐ 369	Checklist 4	2.00	.20	.04
☐ 370	Joe Torre	2.00	1.00	.20
☐ 371	Jack Hiatt	.40	.20	.04
☐ 372	Lew Krausse	.40	.20	.04
☐ 373	Tom McCraw	.40	.20	.04
☐ 374	Clete Boyer	.50	.25	.05
☐ 375	Steve Hargan	.40	.20	.04
☐ 376	Expos Rookies	.40	.20	.04
	Clyde Mashore			
	Ernie McAnally			
☐ 377	Greg Garrett	.40	.20	.04
☐ 378	Tito Fuentes	.40	.20	.04
☐ 379	Wayne Granger	.40	.20	.04
☐ 380	Ted Williams MG	5.00	2.50	.50
☐ 381	Fred Gladding	.40	.20	.04
☐ 382	Jake Gibbs	.40	.20	.04
☐ 383	Rod Gaspar	.40	.20	.04
☐ 384	Rollie Fingers	4.00	2.00	.40
☐ 385	Maury Wills	1.50	.75	.15
☐ 386	Red Sox Team	1.00	.50	.10
☐ 387	Ron Herbel	.40	.20	.04
☐ 388	Al Oliver	1.75	.85	.17
☐ 389	Ed Brinkman	.40	.20	.04
☐ 390	Glenn Beckert	.50	.25	.05
☐ 391	Twins Rookies	.50	.25	.05
	Steve Brye			
	Cotton Nash			
☐ 392	Grant Jackson	.40	.20	.04
☐ 393	Merv Rettenmund	.40	.20	.04
☐ 394	Clay Carroll	.60	.30	.06
☐ 395	Roy White	.75	.35	.07
☐ 396	Dick Schofield	.60	.30	.06
☐ 397	Alvin Dark MG	.75	.35	.07
☐ 398	Howie Reed	.60	.30	.06
☐ 399	Jim French	.60	.30	.06
☐ 400	Hank Aaron	30.00	14.00	2.80
☐ 401	Tom Murphy	.60	.30	.06
☐ 402	Dodgers Team	1.25	.60	.12
☐ 403	Joe Coleman	.60	.30	.06
☐ 404	Astros Rookies	.60	.30	.06
	Buddy Harris			
	Roger Metzger			
☐ 405	Leo Cardenas	.60	.30	.06
☐ 406	Ray Sadecki	.60	.30	.06
☐ 407	Joe Rudi	.75	.35	.07
☐ 408	Rafael Robles	.60	.30	.06
☐ 409	Don Pavletich	.60	.30	.06
☐ 410	Ken Holtzman	.75	.35	.07
☐ 411	George Spriggs	.60	.30	.06
☐ 412	Jerry Johnson	.60	.30	.06
☐ 413	Pat Kelly	.60	.30	.06
☐ 414	Woodie Fryman	.60	.30	.06
☐ 415	Mike Hegan	.60	.30	.06
☐ 416	Gene Alley	.75	.35	.07
☐ 417	Dick Hall	.60	.30	.06
☐ 418	Adolfo Phillips	.60	.30	.06
☐ 419	Ron Hansen	.60	.30	.06
☐ 420	Jim Merritt	.60	.30	.06
☐ 421	John Stephenson	.60	.30	.06
☐ 422	Frank Bertaina	.60	.30	.06
☐ 423	Tigers Rookies	.60	.30	.06
	Dennis Saunders			
	Tim Marting			
☐ 424	R. Rodriguez	.60	.30	.06
☐ 425	Doug Rader	1.00	.50	.10
☐ 426	Chris Cannizzaro	.60	.30	.06
☐ 427	Bernie Allen	.60	.30	.06
☐ 428	Jim McAndrew	.60	.30	.06
☐ 429	Chuck Hinton	.60	.30	.06
☐ 430	Wes Parker	.75	.35	.07
☐ 431	Tom Burgmeier	.60	.30	.06
☐ 432	Bob Didier	.60	.30	.06
☐ 433	Skip Lockwood	.60	.30	.06
☐ 434	Gary Sutherland	.60	.30	.06
☐ 435	Jose Cardenal	.60	.30	.06
☐ 436	Wilbur Wood	.75	.35	.07
☐ 437	Danny Murtaugh MG	.60	.30	.06
☐ 438	Mike McCormick	.75	.35	.07
☐ 439	Phillies Rookies	2.25	1.10	.22
	Greg Luzinski			
	Scott Reid			
☐ 440	Bert Campaneris	.75	.35	.07
☐ 441	Milt Pappas	.75	.35	.07
☐ 442	California Angels	1.25	.60	.12

	Team Card			
☐ 443	Rich Robertson	.60	.30	.06
☐ 444	Jimmie Price	.60	.30	.06
☐ 445	Art Shamsky	.60	.30	.06
☐ 446	Bobby Bolin	.60	.30	.06
☐ 447	Cesar Geronimo	.60	.30	.06
☐ 448	Dave Roberts	.60	.30	.06
☐ 449	Brant Alyea	.60	.30	.06
☐ 450	Bob Gibson	7.50	3.75	.75
☐ 451	Joe Keough	.60	.30	.06
☐ 452	John Boccabella	.60	.30	.06
☐ 453	Terry Crowley	.60	.30	.06
☐ 454	Mike Paul	.60	.30	.06
☐ 455	Don Kessinger	.75	.35	.07
☐ 456	Bob Meyer	.60	.30	.06
☐ 457	Willie Smith	.60	.30	.06
☐ 458	White Sox Rookies	.60	.30	.06
	Ron Lolich			
	Dave Lemonds			
☐ 459	Jim Lefebvre	1.00	.50	.10
☐ 460	Fritz Peterson	.60	.30	.06
☐ 461	Jim Ray Hart	.75	.35	.07
☐ 462	Senators Team	1.25	.60	.12
☐ 463	Tom Kelley	.60	.30	.06
☐ 464	Aurelio Rodriguez	.60	.30	.06
☐ 465	Tim McCarver	1.25	.60	.12
☐ 466	Ken Berry	.60	.30	.06
☐ 467	Al Santorini	.60	.30	.06
☐ 468	Frank Fernandez	.60	.30	.06
☐ 469	Bob Aspromonte	.60	.30	.06
☐ 470	Bob Oliver	.60	.30	.06
☐ 471	Tom Griffin	.60	.30	.06
☐ 472	Ken Rudolph	.60	.30	.06
☐ 473	Gary Wagner	.60	.30	.06
☐ 474	Jim Fairey	.60	.30	.06
☐ 475	Ron Perranoski	.75	.35	.07
☐ 476	Dal Maxvill	.60	.30	.06
☐ 477	Earl Weaver MG	1.00	.50	.10
☐ 478	Bernie Carbo	.60	.30	.06
☐ 479	Dennis Higgins	.60	.30	.06
☐ 480	Manny Sanguillen	1.00	.50	.10
☐ 481	Daryl Patterson	.60	.30	.06
☐ 482	Padres Team	1.25	.60	.12
☐ 483	Gene Michael	.75	.35	.07
☐ 484	Don Wilson	.60	.30	.06
☐ 485	Ken McMullen	.60	.30	.06
☐ 486	Steve Huntz	.60	.30	.06
☐ 487	Paul Schaal	.60	.30	.06
☐ 488	Jerry Stephenson	.60	.30	.06
☐ 489	Luis Alvarado	.60	.30	.06
☐ 490	Deron Johnson	.75	.35	.07
☐ 491	Jim Hardin	.60	.30	.06
☐ 492	Ken Boswell	.60	.30	.06
☐ 493	Dave May	.60	.30	.06
☐ 494	Braves Rookies	.75	.35	.07
	Ralph Garr			
	Rick Kester			
☐ 495	Felipe Alou	.75	.35	.07
☐ 496	Woody Woodward	.75	.35	.07
☐ 497	Horacio Pina	.60	.30	.06
☐ 498	John Kennedy	.60	.30	.06
☐ 499	Checklist 5	2.00	.20	.04
☐ 500	Jim Perry	1.00	.50	.10
☐ 501	Andy Etchebarren	.60	.30	.06
☐ 502	Cubs Team	1.25	.60	.12
☐ 503	Gates Brown	.75	.35	.07
☐ 504	Ken Wright	.60	.30	.06
☐ 505	Ollie Brown	.60	.30	.06
☐ 506	Bobby Knoop	.60	.30	.06
☐ 507	George Stone	.60	.30	.06
☐ 508	Roger Repoz	.60	.30	.06
☐ 509	Jim Grant	.60	.30	.06
☐ 510	Ken Harrelson	1.00	.50	.10
☐ 511	Chris Short	.60	.30	.06
☐ 512	Red Sox Rookies	.60	.30	.06
	Dick Mills			
	Mike Garman			
☐ 513	Nolan Ryan	90.00	37.50	7.50
☐ 514	Ron Woods	.60	.30	.06
☐ 515	Carl Morton	.60	.30	.06
☐ 516	Ted Kubiak	.60	.30	.06
☐ 517	Charlie Fox MG	.60	.30	.06
☐ 518	Joe Grzenda	.60	.30	.06
☐ 519	Willie Crawford	.60	.30	.06
☐ 520	Tommy John	2.50	1.25	.25
☐ 521	Leron Lee	.60	.30	.06
☐ 522	Twins Team	1.25	.60	.12
☐ 523	John Odom	.60	.30	.06
☐ 524	Mickey Stanley	1.50	.75	.15
☐ 525	Ernie Banks	17.00	7.50	1.50
☐ 526	Ray Jarvis	1.00	.50	.10
☐ 527	Cleon Jones	1.00	.50	.10
☐ 528	Wally Bunker	1.00	.50	.10
☐ 529	NL Rookie Infielders	3.50	1.75	.35
	Enzo Hernandez			

	Bill Buckner			
	Marty Perez			
☐ 530	Carl Yastrzemski	35.00	17.50	3.50
☐ 531	Mike Torrez	1.00	.50	.10
☐ 532	Bill Rigney MG	1.00	.50	.10
☐ 533	Mike Ryan	1.00	.50	.10
☐ 534	Luke Walker	1.00	.50	.10
☐ 535	Curt Flood	1.50	.75	.15
☐ 536	Claude Raymond	1.00	.50	.10
☐ 537	Tom Egan	1.00	.50	.10
☐ 538	Angel Bravo	1.00	.50	.10
☐ 539	Larry Brown	1.00	.50	.10
☐ 540	Larry Dierker	1.00	.50	.10
☐ 541	Bob Burda	1.00	.50	.10
☐ 542	Bob Miller	1.00	.50	.10
☐ 543	New York Yankees	2.50	1.25	.25
	Team Card			
☐ 544	Vida Blue	3.00	1.50	.30
☐ 545	Dick Dietz	1.00	.50	.10
☐ 546	John Matias	1.00	.50	.10
☐ 547	Pat Dobson	1.00	.50	.10
☐ 548	Don Mason	1.00	.50	.10
☐ 549	Jim Brewer	1.00	.50	.10
☐ 550	Harmon Killebrew	12.00	6.00	1.20
☐ 551	Frank Linzy	1.00	.50	.10
☐ 552	Buddy Bradford	1.00	.50	.10
☐ 553	Kevin Collins	1.00	.50	.10
☐ 554	Lowell Palmer	1.00	.50	.10
☐ 555	Walt Williams	1.00	.50	.10
☐ 556	Jim McGlothlin	1.00	.50	.10
☐ 557	Tom Satriano	1.00	.50	.10
☐ 558	Hector Torres	1.00	.50	.10
☐ 559	AL Rookie Pitchers	1.00	.50	.10
	Terry Cox			
	Bill Gogolewski			
	Gary Jones			
☐ 560	Rusty Staub	2.00	1.00	.20
☐ 561	Syd O'Brien	1.00	.50	.10
☐ 562	Dave Giusti	1.00	.50	.10
☐ 563	Giants Team	2.00	1.00	.20
☐ 564	Al Fitzmorris	1.00	.50	.10
☐ 565	Jim Wynn	1.50	.75	.15
☐ 566	Tim Cullen	1.00	.50	.10
☐ 567	Walt Alston MG	2.50	1.25	.25
☐ 568	Sal Campisi	1.00	.50	.10
☐ 569	Ivan Murrell	1.00	.50	.10
☐ 570	Jim Palmer	14.00	6.00	1.20
☐ 571	Ted Sizemore	1.00	.50	.10
☐ 572	Jerry Kenney	1.00	.50	.10
☐ 573	Ed Kranepool	1.50	.75	.15
☐ 574	Jim Bunning	2.50	1.25	.25
☐ 575	Bill Freehan	1.50	.75	.15
☐ 576	Cubs Rookies	1.00	.50	.10
	Adrian Garrett			
	Brock Davis			
	Garry Jestadt			
☐ 577	Jim Lonborg	1.50	.75	.15
☐ 578	Ron Hunt	1.00	.50	.10
☐ 579	Marty Pattin	1.00	.50	.10
☐ 580	Tony Perez	4.00	2.00	.40
☐ 581	Roger Nelson	1.00	.50	.10
☐ 582	Dave Cash	1.00	.50	.10
☐ 583	Ron Cook	1.00	.50	.10
☐ 584	Indians Team	2.00	1.00	.20
☐ 585	Willie Davis	1.50	.75	.15
☐ 586	Dick Woodson	1.00	.50	.10
☐ 587	Sonny Jackson	1.00	.50	.10
☐ 588	Tom Bradley	1.00	.50	.10
☐ 589	Bob Barton	1.00	.50	.10
☐ 590	Alex Johnson	1.00	.50	.10
☐ 591	Jackie Brown	1.00	.50	.10
☐ 592	Randy Hundley	1.00	.50	.10
☐ 593	Jack Aker	1.00	.50	.10
☐ 594	Cards Rookies	2.00	1.00	.20
	Bob Chlupsa			
	Bob Stinson			
	Al Hrabosky			
☐ 595	Dave Johnson	2.00	1.00	.20
☐ 596	Mike Jorgensen	1.00	.50	.10
☐ 597	Ken Suarez	1.00	.50	.10
☐ 598	Rick Wise	1.50	.75	.15
☐ 599	Norm Cash	2.00	1.00	.20
☐ 600	Willie Mays	50.00	20.00	4.00
☐ 601	Ken Tatum	1.00	.50	.10
☐ 602	Marty Martinez	1.00	.50	.10
☐ 603	Pirates Team	2.00	1.00	.20
☐ 604	John Gelnar	1.00	.50	.10
☐ 605	Orlando Cepeda	3.50	1.75	.35
☐ 606	Chuck Taylor	1.00	.50	.10
☐ 607	Paul Ratliff	1.00	.50	.10
☐ 608	Mike Wegener	1.00	.50	.10
☐ 609	Leo Durocher MG	2.00	1.00	.20
☐ 610	Amos Otis	1.50	.75	.15
☐ 611	Tom Phoebus	1.00	.50	.10
☐ 612	Indians Rookies	1.00	.50	.10

	Lou Camilli			
	Ted Ford			
	Steve Mingori			
☐ 613	Pedro Borbon	1.00	.50	.10
☐ 614	Billy Cowan	1.00	.50	.10
☐ 615	Mel Stottlemyre	2.00	1.00	.20
☐ 616	Larry Hisle	1.00	.50	.10
☐ 617	Clay Dalrymple	1.00	.50	.10
☐ 618	Tug McGraw	2.00	1.00	.20
☐ 619A	Checklist 6	3.00	.25	.05
	(copyright on back)			
☐ 619B	Checklist 6	4.00	.25	.05
	(no copyright)			
☐ 620	Frank Howard	2.00	1.00	.20
☐ 621	Ron Bryant	1.00	.50	.10
☐ 622	Joe Lahoud	1.00	.50	.10
☐ 623	Pat Jarvis	1.00	.50	.10
☐ 624	Athletics Team	2.00	1.00	.20
☐ 625	Lou Brock	12.00	6.00	1.20
☐ 626	Freddie Patek	1.50	.75	.15
☐ 627	Steve Hamilton	1.00	.50	.10
☐ 628	John Bateman	1.00	.50	.10
☐ 629	John Hiller	1.50	.75	.15
☐ 630	Roberto Clemente	35.00	15.00	3.00
☐ 631	Eddie Fisher	1.00	.50	.10
☐ 632	Darrel Chaney	1.00	.50	.10
☐ 633	AL Rookie Outfielders	1.00	.50	.10
	Bobby Brooks			
	Pete Koegel			
	Scott Northey			
☐ 634	Phil Regan	1.50	.75	.15
☐ 635	Bobby Murcer	2.00	1.00	.20
☐ 636	Denny Lemaster	1.00	.50	.10
☐ 637	Dave Bristol MG	1.00	.50	.10
☐ 638	Stan Williams	1.00	.50	.10
☐ 639	Tom Haller	1.00	.50	.10
☐ 640	Frank Robinson	18.00	8.00	1.60
☐ 641	New York Mets	3.00	1.50	.30
	Team Card			
☐ 642	Jim Roland	1.00	.50	.10
☐ 643	Rick Reichardt	1.00	.50	.10
☐ 644	Jim Stewart SP	3.50	1.50	.30
☐ 645	Jim Maloney SP	3.50	1.50	.30
☐ 646	Bobby Floyd SP	3.50	1.50	.30
☐ 647	Juan Pizarro	2.50	1.10	.22
☐ 648	Mets Rookies SP	4.50	2.00	.40
	Rich Folkers			
	Ted Martinez			
	John Matlack			
☐ 649	Sparky Lyle SP	4.50	2.00	.40
☐ 650	Rich Allen SP	8.00	3.75	.75
☐ 651	Jerry Robertson SP	3.50	1.50	.30
☐ 652	Braves Team	5.00	2.25	.45
☐ 653	Russ Snyder SP	3.50	1.50	.30
☐ 654	Don Shaw SP	3.50	1.50	.30
☐ 655	Mike Epstein SP	3.50	1.50	.30
☐ 656	Gerry Nyman SP	3.50	1.50	.30
☐ 657	Jose Azcue	2.50	1.10	.22
☐ 658	Paul Lindblad SP	3.50	1.50	.30
☐ 659	Byron Browne SP	3.50	1.50	.30
☐ 660	Ray Culp	2.50	1.10	.22
☐ 661	Chuck Tanner MG SP	4.00	1.75	.35
☐ 662	Mike Hedlund SP	3.50	1.50	.30
☐ 663	Marv Staehle	2.50	1.10	.22
☐ 664	Rookie Pitchers SP	3.50	1.50	.30
	Archie Reynolds			
	Bob Reynolds			
	Ken Reynolds			
☐ 665	Ron Swoboda SP	3.50	1.50	.30
☐ 666	Gene Brabender SP	3.50	1.50	.30
☐ 667	Pete Ward	2.50	1.10	.22
☐ 668	Gary Neibauer	2.50	1.10	.22
☐ 669	Ike Brown SP	3.50	1.50	.30
☐ 670	Bill Hands	2.50	1.10	.22
☐ 671	Bill Voss SP	3.50	1.50	.30
☐ 672	Ed Crosby SP	3.50	1.50	.30
☐ 673	Gerry Janeski SP	3.50	1.50	.30
☐ 674	Montreal Expos	5.00	2.25	.45
	Team Card			
☐ 675	Dave Boswell	2.50	1.10	.22
☐ 676	Tommie Reynolds	2.50	1.10	.22
☐ 677	Jack DiLauro SP	3.50	1.50	.30
☐ 678	George Thomas	2.50	1.10	.22
☐ 679	Don O'Riley	2.50	1.10	.22
☐ 680	Don Mincher SP	3.50	1.50	.30
☐ 681	Bill Butler	2.50	1.10	.22
☐ 682	Terry Harmon	2.50	1.10	.22
☐ 683	Bill Burbach SP	3.50	1.50	.30
☐ 684	Curt Motton	2.50	1.10	.22
☐ 685	Moe Drabowsky	2.50	1.10	.22
☐ 686	Chico Ruiz SP	3.50	1.50	.30
☐ 687	Ron Taylor SP	3.50	1.50	.30
☐ 688	Sparky Anderson MG SP	6.50	3.00	.60
☐ 689	Frank Baker	2.50	1.10	.22
☐ 690	Bob Moose	2.50	1.10	.22

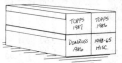

SAN ◈ DIEGO
◈ SPORTS·COLLECTIBLES ◈

"The West Coast's Largest Baseball Card Store"

COMPLETE MINT BASEBALL SETS

	1981	1982	1983	1984	1985	1986	1987	1988	1989	1990*
TOPPS	99.00	99.00	115.50	115.50	129.95	38.50	44.95	25.95	24.95	24.95*
DONRUSS	49.95	49.95	90.00	285.00	175.00	149.00	129.95	34.50	34.95	29.95*
FLEER	34.50	45.00	90.00	175.00	135.00	135.00	129.95	44.95	34.95	29.95*
TOPPS TRADED	39.50	39.50	129.95	119.95	29.95	39.95	16.95	34.50	17.95	—

Early Bird Special - Spring Delivery - Order all 3 Topps, Fleer and Donruss for special price of $79.95
SATISFACTION GUARANTEED OR YOUR MONEY BACK   **PRICES SUBJECT TO CHANGE WITHOUT NOTICE**

☎ ORDER TOLL-FREE 1-800-227-0483 ☎

OTHER COMPLETE SETS

1990 Score	$24.95*
1989 Score	25.95
1988 Score	27.95
1989 Fleer Update	24.95
1988 Fleer Update	19.95
1987 Fleer Update	19.95
1986 Fleer Update	39.95
1985 Fleer Update	19.95
1989 Upper Deck (800)	125.00
1989 Upper Deck (Traded)	39.95

1989 Donruss Traded	$ 9.95
1987 Donruss Highlights	9.95
1986 Donruss Highlights	11.95
1989 Donruss MVPs	8.95
1988 Donruss MVPs	9.95
1987 Donruss All Stars	12.95
1986 Donruss All Stars	12.95
1985 Donruss All Stars	15.95
1988 Topps Glossy Rookies	19.95
1987 Topps Glossy Rookies	22.95
1989 Fleer World Series	5.95
1988 Fleer World Series	9.95
1987 Fleer World Series	15.95

1989 Official Padres Set	$ 14.95
1989 Topps N.F.L.	25.95
1988 Topps N.F.L.	39.95
1987 Topps N.F.L.	39.95
1989 Umpire Set	12.95
1988 Umpire Set	14.95
1987 Fleer Minis	11.95
1986 Fleer Minis	15.95
1980 Topps	179.00
1979 Topps	179.00
1978 Topps	245.00
1977 Topps	325.00
1976 Topps	325.00

CLASSIC REPRINT SETS

1880 Old Judge	$ 5.95
1887 Lone Jack	5.95
1888 Allen & Ginter	5.95
1895 Mayo Cut Plug	5.00
1910 T-206	49.95
1911 Mecca T-201	14.95

1913 T-200 Team Cards	$ 6.95
1915 Cracker Jack	39.95
1933 Sport Kings	7.00
1933 Goudey	39.95
1933 Goudey Babe Ruth Card	3.00
1933 Goudey Lou Gehrig Card	2.00
1934 Goudey	10.95
1935 Diamond Stars	10.00
1935 Goudey	5.00
1936 Goudey	5.95
1937 Diamond Stars	3.00
1938 Goudey	7.00
1940 Play Ball	27.50

1941 Play Ball	$ 9.95
1941 Goudey	8.95
1948 Bowman	6.95
1948 Sport Thrills	6.95
1949 Bowman	29.95
1949 Bowman P.C.L.	6.95
1951 Bowman	39.95
1952 Red Man Tobacco	19.95
1954 Dan Dee	9.95
1954 Red Heart	11.95
1959 Home Run Derby	5.95
1960 Maris & Mantle (both)	3.95
1989 Legends—Minor Leagues	4.95

ORDER TOLL-FREE
1-800-227-0483
7 a.m.-7 p.m. Pacific Time

ORDERING INSTRUCTIONS
Mail Payment To:
**SAN DIEGO
SPORTS COLLECTIBLES**
9530 Chesapeake Dr.
No. 503 - Dept. B-12
San Diego, CA 92123

Please add $2.95 per item for postage. California residents add 7¼% sales tax. There is a $1.00 credit card fee and a $4.00 C.O.D. fee. Prices subject to change. 100% Guarantee. 30 day return privilege.

30-DAY MONEY-BACK GUARANTEE
YOU MUST BE SATISFIED OR RETURN ANY PURCHASE IN 30 DAYS FOR FULL REFUND.

1990
BBC **SCD** BCN
C U S T O M E R
S E R V I C E
A W A R D

SEND FOR HOBBY'S FINEST AND MOST COMPLETE 72-PAGE ILLUSTRATED CATALOGUE! LISTS THOUSANDS OF OLD BASEBALL CARDS AND SETS. TO RECEIVE THE NEXT 3 ISSUES PLEASE SEND NAME AND ADDRESS WITH $1.00 OR FIVE STAMPS.

☐ 691	Bobby Heise	2.50	1.10	.22
☐ 692	AL Rookie Pitchers SP	3.50	1.50	.30
	Hal Haydel			
	Rogelio Moret			
	Wayne Twitchell			
☐ 693	Jose Pena SP	3.50	1.50	.30
☐ 694	Rick Renick SP	3.50	1.50	.30
☐ 695	Joe Niekro	4.00	2.00	.40
☐ 696	Jerry Morales	2.50	1.10	.22
☐ 697	Rickey Clark SP	3.50	1.50	.30
☐ 698	Milwaukee Brewers SP	7.00	3.00	.60
	Team Card			
☐ 699	Jim Britton	2.50	1.10	.22
☐ 700	Boog Powell SP	6.50	3.00	.60
☐ 701	Bob Garibaldi	2.50	1.10	.22
☐ 702	Milt Ramirez	2.50	1.10	.22
☐ 703	Mike Kekich	2.50	1.10	.22
☐ 704	J.C. Martin SP	3.50	1.50	.30
☐ 705	Dick Selma SP	3.50	1.50	.30
☐ 706	Joe Foy SP	3.50	1.50	.30
☐ 707	Fred Lasher	2.50	1.10	.22
☐ 708	Russ Nagelson SP	3.50	1.50	.30
☐ 709	Rookie Outfielders SP	25.00	12.50	2.50
	Dusty Baker			
	Don Baylor			
	Tom Paciorek			
☐ 710	Sonny Siebert	2.50	1.10	.22
☐ 711	Larry Stahl SP	3.50	1.50	.30
☐ 712	Jose Martinez	2.50	1.10	.22
☐ 713	Mike Marshall SP	4.00	1.75	.35
☐ 714	Dick Williams MG SP	4.00	1.75	.35
☐ 715	Horace Clarke SP	4.00	1.50	.30
☐ 716	Dave Leonhard	2.50	1.10	.22
☐ 717	Tommie Aaron SP	4.00	1.75	.35
☐ 718	Billy Wynne	2.50	1.10	.22
☐ 719	Jerry May SP	3.50	1.50	.30
☐ 720	Matty Alou	3.50	1.50	.30
☐ 721	John Morris	2.50	1.10	.22
☐ 722	Houston Astros SP	7.00	3.00	.60
	Team Card			
☐ 723	Vicente Romo SP	3.50	1.50	.30
☐ 724	Tom Tischinski SP	3.50	1.50	.30
☐ 725	Gary Gentry SP	3.50	1.50	.30
☐ 726	Paul Popovich	2.50	1.10	.22
☐ 727	Ray Lamb SP	3.50	1.50	.30
☐ 728	NL Rookie Outfielders	2.50	1.10	.22
	Wayne Redmond			
	Keith Lampard			
	Bernie Williams			
☐ 729	Dick Billings	2.50	1.10	.22
☐ 730	Jim Rooker	2.50	1.10	.22
☐ 731	Jim Qualls SP	3.50	1.50	.30
☐ 732	Bob Reed	2.50	1.10	.22
☐ 733	Lee Maye SP	3.50	1.50	.30
☐ 734	Rob Gardner SP	3.50	1.50	.30
☐ 735	Mike Shannon SP	4.50	2.00	.40
☐ 736	Mel Queen SP	3.50	1.50	.30
☐ 737	Preston Gomez MG SP	3.50	1.50	.30
☐ 738	Russ Gibson SP	3.50	1.50	.30
☐ 739	Barry Lersch SP	3.50	1.50	.30
☐ 740	Luis Aparicio SP	12.50	6.00	1.20
☐ 741	Skip Guinn	2.50	1.10	.22
☐ 742	Kansas City Royals	5.00	2.25	.45
	Team Card			
☐ 743	John O'Donoghue SP	3.50	1.50	.30
☐ 744	Chuck Manuel SP	3.50	1.50	.30
☐ 745	Sandy Alomar SP	3.50	1.50	.30
☐ 746	Andy Kosco	2.50	1.10	.22
☐ 747	NL Rookie Pitchers	2.50	1.10	.22
	Al Severinsen			
	Scipio Spinks			
	Balor Moore			
☐ 748	John Purdin SP	3.50	1.50	.30
☐ 749	Ken Szotkiewicz	2.50	1.10	.22
☐ 750	Denny McLain SP	6.00	2.50	.50
☐ 751	Al Weis SP	4.00	1.50	.30
☐ 752	Dick Drago	3.50	1.50	.30

1972 Topps

The cards in this 787-card set measure 2 1/2" by 3 1/2". The 1972 Topps set contained the most cards ever for a Topps set to that point in time. Features appearing for the first time were "Boyhood Photos" (KP: 341-348 and 491-498), Awards and Trophy cards (621-626), "In Action" (distributed throughout the set) and "Traded Cards" (TR: 751-757). Other subsets included League Leaders (85-96), Playoffs

JOSE CRUZ

cards (221-222), and World Series cards (223-230). The curved lines of the color picture are a departure from the rectangular designs of other years. There is a series of intermediate scarcity (526-656) and the usual high numbers (657-787).

	NRMT	VG-E	GOOD
COMPLETE SET (787)	1500.00	750.00	200.00
COMMON PLAYER (1-132)	.30	.15	.03
COMMON PLAYER (133-263)	.35	.17	.03
COMMON PLAYER (264-394)	.40	.20	.04
COMMON PLAYER (395-525)	.60	.30	.06
COMMON PLAYER (526-656)	1.00	.50	.10
COMMON PLAYER (657-787)	2.25	1.10	.22

☐	1	Pittsburgh Pirates	4.00	.75	.15
		Team Card			
☐	2	Ray Culp	.30	.15	.03
☐	3	Bob Tolan	.30	.15	.03
☐	4	Checklist 1	1.50	.20	.04
☐	5	John Bateman	.30	.15	.03
☐	6	Fred Scherman	.30	.15	.03
☐	7	Enzo Hernandez	.30	.15	.03
☐	8	Ron Swoboda	.30	.15	.03
☐	9	Stan Williams	.30	.15	.03
☐	10	Amos Otis	.50	.25	.05
☐	11	Bobby Valentine	.75	.35	.07
☐	12	Jose Cardenal	.30	.15	.03
☐	13	Joe Grzenda	.30	.15	.03
☐	14	Phillies Rookies	.30	.15	.03
		Pete Koegel			
		Mike Anderson			
		Wayne Twitchell			
☐	15	Walt Williams	.30	.15	.03
☐	16	Mike Jorgensen	.30	.15	.03
☐	17	Dave Duncan	.30	.15	.03
☐	18A	Juan Pizarro	.30	.15	.03
		(yellow underline			
		C and S of Cubs)			
☐	18B	Juan Pizarro	5.00	2.50	.50
		(green underline			
		C and S of Cubs)			
☐	19	Billy Cowan	.30	.15	.03
☐	20	Don Wilson	.30	.15	.03
☐	21	Braves Team	.75	.35	.07
☐	22	Rob Gardner	.30	.15	.03
☐	23	Ted Kubiak	.30	.15	.03
☐	24	Ted Ford	.30	.15	.03
☐	25	Bill Singer	.50	.25	.05
☐	26	Andy Etchebarren	.30	.15	.03
☐	27	Bob Johnson	.30	.15	.03
☐	28	Twins Rookies	.30	.15	.03
		Bob Gebhard			
		Steve Brye			
		Hal Haydel			
☐	29A	Bill Bonham	.30	.15	.03
		(yellow underline			
		C and S of Cubs)			
☐	29B	Bill Bonham	5.00	2.50	.50
		(green underline			
		C and S of Cubs)			
☐	30	Rico Petrocelli	.50	.25	.05
☐	31	Cleon Jones	.30	.15	.03
☐	32	Jones In Action	.30	.15	.03
☐	33	Billy Martin MG	2.50	1.25	.25
☐	34	Martin In Action	1.00	.50	.10
☐	35	Jerry Johnson	.30	.15	.03
☐	36	Johnson In Action	.30	.15	.03
☐	37	Carl Yastrzemski	16.00	8.00	1.60
☐	38	Yastrzemski In Action	6.50	3.25	.65
☐	39	Bob Barton	.30	.15	.03
☐	40	Barton In Action	.30	.15	.03
☐	41	Tommy Davis	.50	.25	.05

☐ 42	Davis In Action	.30	.15	.03
☐ 43	Rick Wise	.30	.15	.03
☐ 44	Wise In Action	.30	.15	.03
☐ 45A	Glenn Beckert	.50	.25	.05
	(yellow underline C and S of Cubs)			
☐ 45B	Glenn Beckert	5.00	2.50	.50
	(green underline C and S of Cubs)			
☐ 46	Beckert In Action	.30	.15	.03
☐ 47	John Ellis	.30	.15	.03
☐ 48	Ellis In Action	.30	.15	.03
☐ 49	Willie Mays	20.00	9.00	1.80
☐ 50	Mays In Action	7.50	3.50	.70
☐ 51	Harmon Killebrew	4.00	2.00	.40
☐ 52	Killebrew In Action	1.50	.75	.15
☐ 53	Bud Harrelson	.50	.25	.05
☐ 54	Harrelson In Action	.30	.15	.03
☐ 55	Clyde Wright	.30	.15	.03
☐ 56	Rich Chiles	.30	.15	.03
☐ 57	Bob Oliver	.30	.15	.03
☐ 58	Ernie McAnally	.30	.15	.03
☐ 59	Fred Stanley	.30	.15	.03
☐ 60	Manny Sanguillen	.50	.25	.05
☐ 61	Cubs Rookies	.75	.35	.07
	Burt Hooton Gene Hiser Earl Stephenson			
☐ 62	Angel Mangual	.30	.15	.03
☐ 63	Duke Sims	.30	.15	.03
☐ 64	Pete Broberg	.30	.15	.03
☐ 65	Cesar Cedeno	.75	.35	.07
☐ 66	Ray Corbin	.30	.15	.03
☐ 67	Red Schoendienst MG	1.25	.60	.12
☐ 68	Jim York	.30	.15	.03
☐ 69	Roger Freed	.30	.15	.03
☐ 70	Mike Cuellar	.50	.25	.05
☐ 71	Angels Team	.75	.35	.07
☐ 72	Bruce Kison	.75	.35	.07
☐ 73	Steve Huntz	.30	.15	.03
☐ 74	Cecil Upshaw	.30	.15	.03
☐ 75	Bert Campaneris	.50	.25	.05
☐ 76	Don Carrithers	.30	.15	.03
☐ 77	Ron Theobald	.30	.15	.03
☐ 78	Steve Arlin	.30	.15	.03
☐ 79	Red Sox Rookies	60.00	30.00	6.00
	Mike Garman Cecil Cooper Carlton Fisk			
☐ 80	Tony Perez	2.50	1.25	.25
☐ 81	Mike Hedlund	.30	.15	.03
☐ 82	Ron Woods	.30	.15	.03
☐ 83	Dalton Jones	.30	.15	.03
☐ 84	Vince Colbert	.30	.15	.03
☐ 85	NL Batting Leaders	1.00	.50	.10
	Joe Torre Ralph Garr Glenn Beckert			
☐ 86	AL Batting Leaders	1.00	.50	.10
	Tony Oliva Bobby Murcer Merv Rettenmund			
☐ 87	NL RBI Leaders	2.00	1.00	.20
	Joe Torre Willie Stargell Hank Aaron			
☐ 88	AL RBI Leaders	1.50	.75	.15
	Harmon Killebrew Frank Robinson Reggie Smith			
☐ 89	NL Home Run Leaders	2.00	1.00	.20
	Willie Stargell Hank Aaron Lee May			
☐ 90	AL Home Run Leaders	1.50	.75	.15
	Bill Melton Norm Cash Reggie Jackson			
☐ 91	NL ERA Leaders	1.50	.75	.15
	Tom Seaver Dave Roberts (photo actually Danny Coombs) Don Wilson			
☐ 92	AL ERA Leaders	1.00	.50	.10
	Vida Blue Wilbur Wood Jim Palmer			
☐ 93	NL Pitching Leaders	1.50	.75	.15
	Fergie Jenkins Steve Carlton Al Downing Tom Seaver			
☐ 94	AL Pitching Leaders	1.00	.50	.10
	Mickey Lolich Vida Blue Wilbur Wood			
☐ 95	NL Strikeout Leaders	1.50	.75	.15
	Tom Seaver Fergie Jenkins Bill Stoneman			
☐ 96	AL Strikeout Leaders	1.00	.50	.10
	Mickey Lolich Vida Blue Joe Coleman			
☐ 97	Tom Kelley	.30	.15	.03
☐ 98	Chuck Tanner MG	.50	.25	.05
☐ 99	Ross Grimsley	.30	.15	.03
☐ 100	Frank Robinson	4.50	2.25	.45
☐ 101	Astros Rookies	1.50	.75	.15
	Bill Greif J.R. Richard Ray Busse			
☐ 102	Lloyd Allen	.30	.15	.03
☐ 103	Checklist 2	1.50	.20	.04
☐ 104	Toby Harrah	1.25	.60	.12
☐ 105	Gary Gentry	.30	.15	.03
☐ 106	Brewers Team	.75	.35	.07
☐ 107	Jose Cruz	1.50	.75	.15
☐ 108	Gary Waslewski	.30	.15	.03
☐ 109	Jerry May	.30	.15	.03
☐ 110	Ron Hunt	.30	.15	.03
☐ 111	Jim Grant	.30	.15	.03
☐ 112	Greg Luzinski	1.00	.50	.10
☐ 113	Rogelio Moret	.30	.15	.03
☐ 114	Bill Buckner	1.50	.75	.15
☐ 115	Jim Fregosi	.50	.25	.05
☐ 116	Ed Farmer	.30	.15	.03
☐ 117A	Cleo James	.30	.15	.03
	(yellow underline C and S of Cubs)			
☐ 117B	Cleo James	5.00	2.50	.50
	(green underline C and S of Cubs)			
☐ 118	Skip Lockwood	.30	.15	.03
☐ 119	Marty Perez	.30	.15	.03
☐ 120	Bill Freehan	.75	.35	.07
☐ 121	Ed Sprague	.30	.15	.03
☐ 122	Larry Biittner	.30	.15	.03
☐ 123	Ed Acosta	.30	.15	.03
☐ 124	Yankees Rookies	.30	.15	.03
	Alan Closter Rusty Torres Roger Hambright			
☐ 125	Dave Cash	.30	.15	.03
☐ 126	Bart Johnson	.30	.15	.03
☐ 127	Duffy Dyer	.30	.15	.03
☐ 128	Eddie Watt	.30	.15	.03
☐ 129	Charlie Fox MG	.30	.15	.03
☐ 130	Bob Gibson	4.50	2.25	.45
☐ 131	Jim Nettles	.30	.15	.03
☐ 132	Joe Morgan	4.50	2.25	.45
☐ 133	Joe Keough	.35	.17	.03
☐ 134	Carl Morton	.35	.17	.03
☐ 135	Vada Pinson	.75	.35	.07
☐ 136	Darrell Chaney	.35	.17	.03
☐ 137	Dick Williams MG	.50	.25	.05
☐ 138	Mike Kekich	.35	.17	.03
☐ 139	Tim McCarver	.75	.35	.07
☐ 140	Pat Dobson	.50	.25	.05
☐ 141	Mets Rookies	.50	.25	.05
	Buzz Capra Leroy Stanton Jon Matlack			
☐ 142	Chris Chambliss	1.50	.75	.15
☐ 143	Garry Jestadt	.35	.17	.03
☐ 144	Marty Pattin	.35	.17	.03
☐ 145	Don Kessinger	.50	.25	.05
☐ 146	Steve Kealey	.35	.17	.03
☐ 147	Dave Kingman	5.00	2.50	.50
☐ 148	Dick Billings	.35	.17	.03
☐ 149	Gary Neibauer	.35	.17	.03
☐ 150	Norm Cash	1.00	.50	.10
☐ 151	Jim Brewer	.35	.17	.03
☐ 152	Gene Clines	.35	.17	.03
☐ 153	Rick Auerbach	.35	.17	.03
☐ 154	Ted Simmons	1.50	.75	.15
☐ 155	Larry Dierker	.50	.25	.05
☐ 156	Minnesota Twins Team Card	.75	.35	.07
☐ 157	Don Gullett	.50	.25	.05
☐ 158	Jerry Kenney	.35	.17	.03
☐ 159	John Boccabella	.35	.17	.03
☐ 160	Andy Messersmith	.50	.25	.05
☐ 161	Brock Davis	.35	.17	.03
☐ 162	Brewers Rookies UER	.75	.35	.07
	Jerry Bell Darrell Porter Bob Reynolds (Porter and Bell			

photos switched)

☐ 163	Tug McGraw	.75	.35	.07
☐ 164	McGraw In Action	.50	.25	.05
☐ 165	Chris Speier	.50	.25	.05
☐ 166	Speier In Action	.35	.17	.03
☐ 167	Deron Johnson	.35	.17	.03
☐ 168	Johnson In Action	.35	.17	.03
☐ 169	Vida Blue	.75	.35	.07
☐ 170	Blue In Action	.50	.25	.05
☐ 171	Darrell Evans	1.50	.75	.15
☐ 172	Evans In Action	.50	.25	.05
☐ 173	Clay Kirby	.35	.17	.03
☐ 174	Kirby In Action	.35	.17	.03
☐ 175	Tom Haller	.35	.17	.03
☐ 176	Haller In Action	.35	.17	.03
☐ 177	Paul Schaal	.35	.17	.03
☐ 178	Schaal In Action	.35	.17	.03
☐ 179	Dock Ellis	.35	.17	.03
☐ 180	Ellis In Action	.35	.17	.03
☐ 181	Ed Kranepool	.50	.25	.05
☐ 182	Kranepool In Action	.35	.17	.03
☐ 183	Bill Melton	.35	.17	.03
☐ 184	Melton In Action	.35	.17	.03
☐ 185	Ron Bryant	.35	.17	.03
☐ 186	Bryant In Action	.35	.17	.03
☐ 187	Gates Brown	.50	.25	.05
☐ 188	Frank Lucchesi MG	.35	.17	.03
☐ 189	Gene Tenace	.50	.25	.05
☐ 190	Dave Giusti	.50	.25	.05
☐ 191	Jeff Burroughs	.75	.35	.07
☐ 192	Cubs Team	.75	.35	.07
☐ 193	Kurt Bevacqua	.35	.17	.03
☐ 194	Fred Norman	.35	.17	.03
☐ 195	Orlando Cepeda	1.75	.85	.17
☐ 196	Mel Queen	.35	.17	.03
☐ 197	Johnny Briggs	.35	.17	.03
☐ 198	Dodgers Rookies	1.75	.85	.17
	Charlie Hough			
	Bob O'Brien			
	Mike Strahler			
☐ 199	Mike Fiore	.35	.17	.03
☐ 200	Lou Brock	4.50	2.25	.45
☐ 201	Phil Roof	.35	.17	.03
☐ 202	Scipio Spinks	.35	.17	.03
☐ 203	Ron Blomberg	.35	.17	.03
☐ 204	Tommy Helms	.50	.25	.05
☐ 205	Dick Drago	.35	.17	.03
☐ 206	Dal Maxvill	.35	.17	.03
☐ 207	Tom Egan	.35	.17	.03
☐ 208	Milt Pappas	.50	.25	.05
☐ 209	Joe Rudi	.50	.25	.05
☐ 210	Denny McLain	1.00	.50	.10
☐ 211	Gary Sutherland	.35	.17	.03
☐ 212	Grant Jackson	.35	.17	.03
☐ 213	Angels Rookies	.35	.17	.03
	Billy Parker			
	Art Kusnyer			
	Tom Silverio			
☐ 214	Mike McQueen	.35	.17	.03
☐ 215	Alex Johnson	.50	.25	.05
☐ 216	Joe Niekro	.75	.35	.07
☐ 217	Roger Metzger	.35	.17	.03
☐ 218	Eddie Kasko MG	.35	.17	.03
☐ 219	Rennie Stennett	.50	.25	.05
☐ 220	Jim Perry	.75	.35	.07
☐ 221	NL Playoffs	1.00	.50	.10
	Bucs champs			
☐ 222	AL Playoffs	1.50	.75	.15
	Orioles champs			
	(Brooks Robinson)			
☐ 223	World Series Game 1	1.00	.50	.10
	(McNally pitching)			
☐ 224	World Series Game 2	1.00	.50	.10
	(Dave Johnson and			
	Mark Belanger)			
☐ 225	World Series Game 3	1.00	.50	.10
	(Sanguillen scoring)			
☐ 226	World Series Game 4	2.25	1.10	.22
	(Clemente on 2nd)			
☐ 227	World Series Game 5	1.00	.50	.10
	(Briles pitching)			
☐ 228	World Series Game 6	1.25	.60	.12
	(Frank Robinson and			
	Manny Sanguillen)			
☐ 229	World Series Game 7	1.00	.50	.10
	(Blass pitching)			
☐ 230	World Series Summary	1.00	.50	.10
	Pirates celebrate			
☐ 231	Casey Cox	.35	.17	.03
☐ 232	Giants Rookies	.35	.17	.03
	Chris Arnold			
	Jim Barr			
	Dave Rader			
☐ 233	Jay Johnstone	.50	.25	.05
☐ 234	Ron Taylor	.35	.17	.03
☐ 235	Merv Rettenmund	.35	.17	.03
☐ 236	Jim McGlothlin	.35	.17	.03
☐ 237	Yankees Team	1.00	.50	.10
☐ 238	Leron Lee	.35	.17	.03
☐ 239	Tom Timmermann	.35	.17	.03
☐ 240	Rich Allen	1.75	.85	.17
☐ 241	Rollie Fingers	3.00	1.50	.30
☐ 242	Don Mincher	.35	.17	.03
☐ 243	Frank Linzy	.35	.17	.03
☐ 244	Steve Braun	.35	.17	.03
☐ 245	Tommie Agee	.50	.25	.05
☐ 246	Tom Burgmeier	.35	.17	.03
☐ 247	Milt May	.35	.17	.03
☐ 248	Tom Bradley	.35	.17	.03
☐ 249	Harry Walker MG	.35	.17	.03
☐ 250	Boog Powell	1.00	.50	.10
☐ 251	Checklist 3	1.50	.20	.04
☐ 252	Ken Reynolds	.35	.17	.03
☐ 253	Sandy Alomar	.50	.25	.05
☐ 254	Boots Day	.35	.17	.03
☐ 255	Jim Lonborg	.75	.35	.07
☐ 256	George Foster	1.50	.75	.15
☐ 257	Tigers Rookies	.35	.17	.03
	Jim Foor			
	Tim Hosley			
	Paul Jata			
☐ 258	Randy Hundley	.50	.25	.05
☐ 259	Sparky Lyle	.75	.35	.07
☐ 260	Ralph Garr	.50	.25	.05
☐ 261	Steve Mingori	.35	.17	.03
☐ 262	San Diego Padres	1.00	.50	.10
	Team Card			
☐ 263	Felipe Alou	.50	.25	.05
☐ 264	Tommy John	2.00	1.00	.20
☐ 265	Wes Parker	.50	.25	.05
☐ 266	Bobby Bolin	.40	.20	.04
☐ 267	Dave Concepcion	1.50	.75	.15
☐ 268	A's Rookies	.40	.20	.04
	Dwain Anderson			
	Chris Floethe			
☐ 269	Don Hahn	.40	.20	.04
☐ 270	Jim Palmer	7.00	3.50	.70
☐ 271	Ken Rudolph	.40	.20	.04
☐ 272	Mickey Rivers	1.00	.50	.10
☐ 273	Bobby Floyd	.40	.20	.04
☐ 274	Al Severinsen	.40	.20	.04
☐ 275	Cesar Tovar	.40	.20	.04
☐ 276	Gene Mauch MG	.50	.25	.05
☐ 277	Elliott Maddox	.40	.20	.04
☐ 278	Dennis Higgins	.40	.20	.04
☐ 279	Larry Brown	.40	.20	.04
☐ 280	Willie McCovey	4.50	2.25	.45
☐ 281	Bill Parsons	.40	.20	.04
☐ 282	Astros Team	1.00	.50	.10
☐ 283	Darrell Brandon	.40	.20	.04
☐ 284	Ike Brown	.40	.20	.04
☐ 285	Gaylord Perry	4.50	2.25	.45
☐ 286	Gene Alley	.50	.25	.05
☐ 287	Jim Hardin	.40	.20	.04
☐ 288	Johnny Jeter	.40	.20	.04
☐ 289	Syd O'Brien	.40	.20	.04
☐ 290	Sonny Siebert	.50	.25	.05
☐ 291	Hal McRae	.75	.35	.07
☐ 292	McRae In Action	.50	.25	.05
☐ 293	Dan Frisella	.40	.20	.04
☐ 294	Frisella In Action	.40	.20	.04
☐ 295	Dick Dietz	.40	.20	.04
☐ 296	Dietz In Action	.40	.20	.04
☐ 297	Claude Osteen	.50	.25	.05
☐ 298	Osteen In Action	.40	.20	.04
☐ 299	Hank Aaron	20.00	9.00	1.80
☐ 300	Aaron in Action	7.50	3.50	.70
☐ 301	George Mitterwald	.40	.20	.04
☐ 302	Mitterwald In Action	.40	.20	.04
☐ 303	Joe Pepitone	.75	.35	.07
☐ 304	Pepitone In Action	.50	.25	.05
☐ 305	Ken Boswell	.40	.20	.04
☐ 306	Boswell In Action	.40	.20	.04
☐ 307	Steve Renko	.40	.20	.04
☐ 308	Renko In Action	.40	.20	.04
☐ 309	Roberto Clemente	17.00	8.00	1.60
☐ 310	Clemente In Action	6.00	3.00	.60
☐ 311	Clay Carroll	.40	.20	.04
☐ 312	Carroll In Action	.40	.20	.04
☐ 313	Luis Aparicio	3.00	1.50	.30
☐ 314	Aparicio In Action	1.25	.60	.12
☐ 315	Paul Splittorff	.50	.25	.05
☐ 316	Cardinals Rookies	.50	.25	.05
	Jim Bibby			
	Jorge Roque			
	Santiago Guzman			
☐ 317	Rich Hand	.40	.20	.04
☐ 318	Sonny Jackson	.40	.20	.04
☐ 319	Aurelio Rodriguez	.40	.20	.04
☐ 320	Steve Blass	.50	.25	.05

☐ 321	Joe Lahoud	.40	.20	.04	☐ 403	John Cumberland	.60	.30	.06
☐ 322	Jose Pena	.40	.20	.04	☐ 404	Jeff Torborg	.75	.35	.07
☐ 323	Earl Weaver MG	.75	.35	.07	☐ 405	Ron Fairly	.75	.35	.07
☐ 324	Mike Ryan	.40	.20	.04	☐ 406	George Hendrick	1.00	.50	.10
☐ 325	Mel Stottlemyre	.75	.35	.07	☐ 407	Chuck Taylor	.60	.30	.06
☐ 326	Pat Kelly	.40	.20	.04	☐ 408	Jim Northrup	.75	.35	.07
☐ 327	Steve Stone	.75	.35	.07	☐ 409	Frank Baker	.60	.30	.06
☐ 328	Red Sox Team	1.00	.50	.10	☐ 410	Fergie Jenkins	2.00	1.00	.20
☐ 329	Roy Foster	.40	.20	.04	☐ 411	Bob Montgomery	.60	.30	.06
☐ 330	Jim Hunter	3.00	1.50	.30	☐ 412	Dick Kelley	.60	.30	.06
☐ 331	Stan Swanson	.40	.20	.04	☐ 413	White Sox Rookies	.60	.30	.06
☐ 332	Buck Martinez	.40	.20	.04		Don Eddy			
☐ 333	Steve Barber	.40	.20	.04		Dave Lemonds			
☐ 334	Rangers Rookies	.40	.20	.04	☐ 414	Bob Miller	.60	.30	.06
	Bill Fahey				☐ 415	Cookie Rojas	.60	.30	.06
	Jim Mason				☐ 416	Johnny Edwards	.60	.30	.06
	Tom Ragland				☐ 417	Tom Hall	.60	.30	.06
☐ 335	Bill Hands	.40	.20	.04	☐ 418	Tom Shopay	.60	.30	.06
☐ 336	Marty Martinez	.40	.20	.04	☐ 419	Jim Spencer	.60	.30	.06
☐ 337	Mike Kilkenny	.40	.20	.04	☐ 420	Steve Carlton	15.00	7.00	1.40
☐ 338	Bob Grich	.75	.35	.07	☐ 421	Ellie Rodriguez	.60	.30	.06
☐ 339	Ron Cook	.40	.20	.04	☐ 422	Ray Lamb	.60	.30	.06
☐ 340	Roy White	.50	.25	.05	☐ 423	Oscar Gamble	.75	.35	.07
☐ 341	KP: Joe Torre	.50	.25	.05	☐ 424	Bill Gogolewski	.60	.30	.06
☐ 342	KP: Wilbur Wood	.40	.20	.04	☐ 425	Ken Singleton	1.00	.50	.10
☐ 343	KP: Willie Stargell	1.00	.50	.10	☐ 426	Singleton In Action	.75	.35	.07
☐ 344	KP: Dave McNally	.40	.20	.04	☐ 427	Tito Fuentes	.60	.30	.06
☐ 345	KP: Rick Wise	.40	.20	.04	☐ 428	Fuentes In Action	.60	.30	.06
☐ 346	KP: Jim Fregosi	.50	.25	.05	☐ 429	Bob Robertson	.60	.30	.06
☐ 347	KP: Tom Seaver	1.50	.75	.15	☐ 430	Robertson In Action	.60	.30	.06
☐ 348	KP: Sal Bando	.40	.20	.04	☐ 431	Clarence Gaston	1.00	.50	.10
☐ 349	Al Fitzmorris	.40	.20	.04	☐ 432	Gaston In Action	.75	.35	.07
☐ 350	Frank Howard	.75	.35	.07	☐ 433	Johnny Bench	30.00	14.00	2.80
☐ 351	Braves Rookies	.50	.25	.05	☐ 434	Bench In Action	10.00	5.00	1.00
	Tom House				☐ 435	Reggie Jackson	27.00	12.50	2.50
	Rick Kester				☐ 436	Jackson In Action	9.00	4.50	.90
	Jimmy Britton				☐ 437	Maury Wills	1.25	.60	.12
☐ 352	Dave LaRoche	.40	.20	.04	☐ 438	Wills In Action	.75	.35	.07
☐ 353	Art Shamsky	.40	.20	.04	☐ 439	Billy Williams	3.00	1.50	.30
☐ 354	Tom Murphy	.40	.20	.04	☐ 440	Williams In Action	1.25	.60	.12
☐ 355	Bob Watson	.50	.25	.05	☐ 441	Thurman Munson	13.00	6.50	1.30
☐ 356	Gerry Moses	.40	.20	.04	☐ 442	Munson In Action	5.00	2.50	.50
☐ 357	Woodie Fryman	.40	.20	.04	☐ 443	Ken Henderson	.60	.30	.06
☐ 358	Sparky Anderson MG	1.00	.50	.10	☐ 444	Henderson In Action	.60	.30	.06
☐ 359	Don Pavletich	.40	.20	.04	☐ 445	Tom Seaver	18.00	9.00	1.80
☐ 360	Dave Roberts	.40	.20	.04	☐ 446	Seaver In Action	7.00	3.50	.70
☐ 361	Mike Andrews	.40	.20	.04	☐ 447	Willie Stargell	5.00	2.50	.50
☐ 362	New York Mets	1.00	.50	.10	☐ 448	Stargell In Action	2.00	1.00	.20
	Team Card				☐ 449	Bob Lemon MG	1.00	.50	.10
☐ 363	Ron Klimkowski	.40	.20	.04	☐ 450	Mickey Lolich	1.00	.50	.10
☐ 364	Johnny Callison	.50	.25	.05	☐ 451	Tony LaRussa	1.00	.50	.10
☐ 365	Dick Bosman	.40	.20	.04	☐ 452	Ed Herrmann	.60	.30	.06
☐ 366	Jimmy Rosario	.40	.20	.04	☐ 453	Barry Lersch	.60	.30	.06
☐ 367	Ron Perranoski	.50	.25	.05	☐ 454	Oakland A's	1.25	.60	.12
☐ 368	Danny Thompson	.40	.20	.04		Team Card			
☐ 369	Jim Lefebvre	.75	.35	.07	☐ 455	Tommy Harper	.75	.35	.07
☐ 370	Don Buford	.50	.25	.05	☐ 456	Mark Belanger	.75	.35	.07
☐ 371	Denny Lemaster	.40	.20	.04	☐ 457	Padres Rookies	.60	.30	.06
☐ 372	Royals Rookies	.40	.20	.04		Darcy Fast			
	Lance Clemons					Derrel Thomas			
	Monty Montgomery					Mike Ivie			
☐ 373	John Mayberry	.50	.25	.05	☐ 458	Aurelio Monteagudo	.60	.30	.06
☐ 374	Jack Heidemann	.40	.20	.04	☐ 459	Rick Renick	.60	.30	.06
☐ 375	Reggie Cleveland	.40	.20	.04	☐ 460	Al Downing	.75	.35	.07
☐ 376	Andy Kosco	.40	.20	.04	☐ 461	Tim Cullen	.60	.30	.06
☐ 377	Terry Harmon	.40	.20	.04	☐ 462	Rickey Clark	.60	.30	.06
☐ 378	Checklist 4	1.50	.20	.04	☐ 463	Bernie Carbo	.60	.30	.06
☐ 379	Ken Berry	.40	.20	.04	☐ 464	Jim Roland	.60	.30	.06
☐ 380	Earl Williams	.40	.20	.04	☐ 465	Gil Hodges MG	2.50	1.25	.25
☐ 381	Chicago White Sox	1.00	.50	.10	☐ 466	Norm Miller	.60	.30	.06
	Team Card				☐ 467	Steve Kline	.60	.30	.06
☐ 382	Joe Gibbon	.40	.20	.04	☐ 468	Richie Scheinblum	.60	.30	.06
☐ 383	Brant Alyea	.40	.20	.04	☐ 469	Ron Herbel	.60	.30	.06
☐ 384	Dave Campbell	.40	.20	.04	☐ 470	Ray Fosse	.75	.35	.07
☐ 385	Mickey Stanley	.50	.25	.05	☐ 471	Luke Walker	.60	.30	.06
☐ 386	Jim Colborn	.40	.20	.04	☐ 472	Phil Gagliano	.60	.30	.06
☐ 387	Horace Clarke	.40	.20	.04	☐ 473	Dan McGinn	.60	.30	.06
☐ 388	Charlie Williams	.40	.20	.04	☐ 474	Orioles Rookies	2.00	1.00	.20
☐ 389	Bill Rigney MG	.40	.20	.04		Don Baylor			
☐ 390	Willie Davis	.50	.25	.05		Roric Harrison			
☐ 391	Ken Sanders	.40	.20	.04		Johnny Oates			
☐ 392	Pirates Rookies	.75	.35	.07	☐ 475	Gary Nolan	.60	.30	.06
	Fred Cambria				☐ 476	Lee Richard	.60	.30	.06
	Richie Zisk				☐ 477	Tom Phoebus	.60	.30	.06
☐ 393	Curt Motton	.40	.20	.04	☐ 478	Checklist 5	1.50	.20	.04
☐ 394	Ken Forsch	.50	.25	.05	☐ 479	Don Shaw	.60	.30	.06
☐ 395	Matty Alou	.75	.35	.07	☐ 480	Lee May	.75	.35	.07
☐ 396	Paul Lindblad	.60	.30	.06	☐ 481	Billy Conigliaro	.60	.30	.06
☐ 397	Philadelphia Phillies	1.25	.60	.12	☐ 482	Joe Hoerner	.60	.30	.06
	Team Card				☐ 483	Ken Suarez	.60	.30	.06
☐ 398	Larry Hisle	.75	.35	.07	☐ 484	Lum Harris MG	.60	.30	.06
☐ 399	Milt Wilcox	.60	.30	.06	☐ 485	Phil Regan	.75	.35	.07
☐ 400	Tony Oliva	1.50	.75	.15	☐ 486	John Lowenstein	.60	.30	.06
☐ 401	Jim Nash	.60	.30	.06	☐ 487	Tigers Team	1.25	.60	.12
☐ 402	Bobby Heise	.60	.30	.06	☐ 488	Mike Nagy	.60	.30	.06

☐ 489	Expos Rookies	.60	.30	.06	☐ 577	Mike Paul	1.00	.50	.10
	Terry Humphrey				☐ 578	Billy Grabarkewitz	1.00	.50	.10
	Keith Lampard				☐ 579	Doyle Alexander	3.00	1.50	.30
☐ 490	Dave McNally	.75	.35	.07	☐ 580	Lou Piniella	2.50	1.25	.25
☐ 491	KP: Lou Piniella	.75	.35	.07	☐ 581	Wade Blasingame	1.00	.50	.10
☐ 492	KP: Mel Stottlemyre	.75	.35	.07	☐ 582	Montreal Expos	2.00	1.00	.20
☐ 493	KP: Bob Bailey	.60	.30	.06		Team Card			
☐ 494	KP: Willie Horton	.60	.30	.06	☐ 583	Darold Knowles	1.00	.50	.10
☐ 495	KP: Bill Melton	.60	.30	.06	☐ 584	Jerry McNertney	1.00	.50	.10
☐ 496	KP: Bud Harrelson	.60	.30	.06	☐ 585	George Scott	1.50	.75	.15
☐ 497	KP: Jim Perry	.60	.30	.06	☐ 586	Denis Menke	1.00	.50	.10
☐ 498	KP: Brooks Robinson	1.50	.75	.15	☐ 587	Billy Wilson	1.00	.50	.10
☐ 499	Vicente Romo	.60	.30	.06	☐ 588	Jim Holt	1.00	.50	.10
☐ 500	Joe Torre	1.00	.50	.10	☐ 589	Hal Lanier	1.50	.75	.15
☐ 501	Pete Hamm	.60	.30	.06	☐ 590	Graig Nettles	2.50	1.25	.25
☐ 502	Jackie Hernandez	.60	.30	.06	☐ 591	Paul Casanova	1.00	.50	.10
☐ 503	Gary Peters	.60	.30	.06	☐ 592	Lew Krausse	1.00	.50	.10
☐ 504	Ed Spiezio	.60	.30	.06	☐ 593	Rich Morales	1.00	.50	.10
☐ 505	Mike Marshall	.75	.35	.07	☐ 594	Jim Beauchamp	1.00	.50	.10
☐ 506	Indians Rookies	.75	.35	.07	☐ 595	Nolan Ryan	65.00	30.00	6.00
	Terry Ley				☐ 596	Manny Mota	1.50	.75	.15
	Jim Moyer				☐ 597	Jim Magnuson	1.00	.50	.10
	Dick Tidrow				☐ 598	Hal King	1.00	.50	.10
☐ 507	Fred Gladding	.60	.30	.06	☐ 599	Billy Champion	1.00	.50	.10
☐ 508	Elrod Hendricks	.60	.30	.06	☐ 600	Al Kaline	15.00	6.00	1.25
☐ 509	Don McMahon	.60	.30	.06	☐ 601	George Stone	1.00	.50	.10
☐ 510	Ted Williams MG	6.00	3.00	.60	☐ 602	Dave Bristol MG	1.00	.50	.10
☐ 511	Tony Taylor	.60	.30	.06	☐ 603	Jim Ray	1.00	.50	.10
☐ 512	Paul Popovich	.60	.30	.06	☐ 604A	Checklist 6	4.00	.40	.10
☐ 513	Lindy McDaniel	.75	.35	.07		(copyright on back			
☐ 514	Ted Sizemore	.75	.35	.07		bottom right)			
☐ 515	Bert Blyleven	7.00	3.50	.70	☐ 604B	Checklist 6	6.00		.10
☐ 516	Oscar Brown	.60	.30	.06		(copyright on back			
☐ 517	Ken Brett	.60	.30	.06		bottom left)			
☐ 518	Wayne Garrett	.60	.30	.06	☐ 605	Nelson Briles	1.00	.50	.10
☐ 519	Ted Abernathy	.60	.30	.06	☐ 606	Luis Melendez	1.00	.50	.10
☐ 520	Larry Bowa	1.50	.75	.15	☐ 607	Frank Duffy	1.00	.50	.10
☐ 521	Alan Foster	.60	.30	.06	☐ 608	Mike Corkins	1.00	.50	.10
☐ 522	Dodgers Team	1.25	.60	.12	☐ 609	Tom Grieve	1.50	.75	.15
☐ 523	Chuck Dobson	.60	.30	.06	☐ 610	Bill Stoneman	1.00	.50	.10
☐ 524	Reds Rookies	.60	.30	.06	☐ 611	Rich Reese	1.00	.50	.10
	Ed Armbrister				☐ 612	Joe Decker	1.00	.50	.10
	Mel Behney				☐ 613	Mike Ferraro	1.00	.50	.10
☐ 525	Carlos May	.60	.30	.06	☐ 614	Ted Uhlaender	1.00	.50	.10
☐ 526	Bob Bailey	1.00	.50	.10	☐ 615	Steve Hargan	1.00	.50	.10
☐ 527	Dave Leonhard	1.00	.50	.10	☐ 616	Joe Ferguson	1.00	.50	.10
☐ 528	Ron Stone	1.00	.50	.10	☐ 617	Kansas City Royals	2.00	1.00	.20
☐ 529	Dave Nelson	1.00	.50	.10		Team Card			
☐ 530	Don Sutton	4.00	2.00	.40	☐ 618	Rich Robertson	1.00	.50	.10
☐ 531	Freddie Patek	1.50	.75	.15	☐ 619	Rich McKinney	1.00	.50	.10
☐ 532	Fred Kendall	1.00	.50	.10	☐ 620	Phil Niekro	4.00	2.00	.40
☐ 533	Ralph Houk MG	1.50	.75	.15	☐ 621	Commissioners Award	1.00	.50	.10
☐ 534	Jim Hickman	1.00	.50	.10	☐ 622	MVP Award	1.00	.50	.10
☐ 535	Ed Brinkman	1.00	.50	.10	☐ 623	Cy Young Award	1.00	.50	.10
☐ 536	Doug Rader	1.50	.75	.15	☐ 624	Minor League Player	1.00	.50	.10
☐ 537	Bob Locker	1.00	.50	.10	☐ 625	Rookie of the Year	1.00	.50	.10
☐ 538	Charlie Sands	1.00	.50	.10	☐ 626	Babe Ruth Award	1.50	.75	.15
☐ 539	Terry Forster	1.50	.75	.15	☐ 627	Moe Drabowsky	1.00	.50	.10
☐ 540	Felix Millan	1.00	.50	.10	☐ 628	Terry Crowley	1.00	.50	.10
☐ 541	Roger Repoz	1.00	.50	.10	☐ 629	Paul Doyle	1.00	.50	.10
☐ 542	Jack Billingham	1.00	.50	.10	☐ 630	Rich Hebner	1.00	.50	.10
☐ 543	Duane Josephson	1.00	.50	.10	☐ 631	John Strohmayer	1.00	.50	.10
☐ 544	Ted Martinez	1.00	.50	.10	☐ 632	Mike Hegan	1.00	.50	.10
☐ 545	Wayne Granger	1.00	.50	.10	☐ 633	Jack Hiatt	1.00	.50	.10
☐ 546	Joe Hague	1.00	.50	.10	☐ 634	Dick Woodson	1.00	.50	.10
☐ 547	Indians Team	2.00	1.00	.20	☐ 635	Don Money	1.00	.50	.10
☐ 548	Frank Reberger	1.00	.50	.10	☐ 636	Bill Lee	1.50	.75	.15
☐ 549	Dave May	1.00	.50	.10	☐ 637	Preston Gomez MG	1.00	.50	.10
☐ 550	Brooks Robinson	14.00	6.00	1.25	☐ 638	Ken Wright	1.00	.50	.10
☐ 551	Ollie Brown	1.00	.50	.10	☐ 639	J.C. Martin	1.00	.50	.10
☐ 552	Brown In Action	1.00	.50	.10	☐ 640	Joe Coleman	1.00	.50	.10
☐ 553	Wilbur Wood	1.00	.50	.10	☐ 641	Mike Lum	1.00	.50	.10
☐ 554	Wood In Action	1.00	.50	.10	☐ 642	Dennis Riddleberger	1.00	.50	.10
☐ 555	Ron Santo	2.00	1.00	.20	☐ 643	Russ Gibson	1.00	.50	.10
☐ 556	Santo In Action	1.50	.75	.15	☐ 644	Bernie Allen	1.00	.50	.10
☐ 557	John Odom	1.00	.50	.10	☐ 645	Jim Maloney	1.50	.75	.15
☐ 558	Odom In Action	1.00	.50	.10	☐ 646	Chico Salmon	1.00	.50	.10
☐ 559	Pete Rose	60.00	30.00	6.00	☐ 647	Bob Moose	1.00	.50	.10
☐ 560	Rose In Action	20.00	10.00	2.00	☐ 648	Jim Lyttle	1.00	.50	.10
☐ 561	Leo Cardenas	1.00	.50	.10	☐ 649	Pete Richert	1.00	.50	.10
☐ 562	Cardenas In Action	1.00	.50	.10	☐ 650	Sal Bando	1.50	.75	.15
☐ 563	Ray Sadecki	1.00	.50	.10	☐ 651	Cincinnati Reds	2.00	1.00	.20
☐ 564	Sadecki In Action	1.00	.50	.10		Team Card			
☐ 565	Reggie Smith	1.50	.75	.15	☐ 652	Marcelino Lopez	1.00	.50	.10
☐ 566	Smith In Action	1.00	.50	.10	☐ 653	Jim Fairey	1.00	.50	.10
☐ 567	Juan Marichal	5.00	2.50	.50	☐ 654	Horacio Pina	1.00	.50	.10
☐ 568	Marichal In Action	2.00	1.00	.20	☐ 655	Jerry Grote	1.00	.50	.10
☐ 569	Ed Kirkpatrick	1.00	.50	.10	☐ 656	Rudy May	1.00	.50	.10
☐ 570	Kirkpatrick In Action	1.00	.50	.10	☐ 657	Bobby Wine	2.25	1.10	.22
☐ 571	Nate Colbert	1.00	.50	.10	☐ 658	Steve Dunning	2.25	1.10	.22
☐ 572	Colbert In Action	1.00	.50	.10	☐ 659	Bob Aspromonte	2.25	1.10	.22
☐ 573	Fritz Peterson	1.00	.50	.10	☐ 660	Paul Blair	3.00	1.50	.30
☐ 574	Peterson In Action	1.00	.50	.10	☐ 661	Bill Virdon	3.50	1.75	.35
☐ 575	Al Oliver	1.75	.85	.17	☐ 662	Stan Bahnsen	2.25	1.10	.22
☐ 576	Leo Durocher MG	1.50	.75	.15	☐ 663	Fran Healy	2.25	1.10	.22

☐ 664	Bobby Knoop	2.25	1.10	.22
☐ 665	Chris Short	2.25	1.10	.22
☐ 666	Hector Torres	2.25	1.10	.22
☐ 667	Ray Newman	2.25	1.10	.22
☐ 668	Texas Rangers Team Card	5.00	2.50	.50
☐ 669	Willie Crawford	2.25	1.10	.22
☐ 670	Ken Holtzman	3.00	1.50	.30
☐ 671	Donn Clendenon	3.00	1.50	.30
☐ 672	Archie Reynolds	2.25	1.10	.22
☐ 673	Dave Marshall	2.25	1.10	.22
☐ 674	John Kennedy	2.25	1.10	.22
☐ 675	Pat Jarvis	2.25	1.10	.22
☐ 676	Danny Cater	2.25	1.10	.22
☐ 677	Ivan Murrell	2.25	1.10	.22
☐ 678	Steve Luebber	2.25	1.10	.22
☐ 679	Astros Rookies Bob Fenwick Bob Stinson	2.25	1.10	.22
☐ 680	Dave Johnson	4.00	2.00	.40
☐ 681	Bobby Pfeil	2.25	1.10	.22
☐ 682	Mike McCormick	3.00	1.50	.30
☐ 683	Steve Hovley	2.25	1.10	.22
☐ 684	Hal Breeden	2.25	1.10	.22
☐ 685	Joel Horlen	2.25	1.10	.22
☐ 686	Steve Garvey	75.00	37.50	7.50
☐ 687	Del Unser	2.25	1.10	.22
☐ 688	St. Louis Cardinals Team Card	4.50	2.25	.45
☐ 689	Eddie Fisher	2.25	1.10	.22
☐ 690	Willie Montanez	2.25	1.10	.22
☐ 691	Curt Blefary	2.25	1.10	.22
☐ 692	Blefary In Action	2.25	1.10	.22
☐ 693	Alan Gallagher	2.25	1.10	.22
☐ 694	Gallagher In Action	2.25	1.10	.22
☐ 695	Rod Carew	70.00	35.00	7.00
☐ 696	Carew In Action	25.00	12.50	2.50
☐ 697	Jerry Koosman	5.00	2.50	.50
☐ 698	Koosman In Action	3.00	1.50	.30
☐ 699	Bobby Murcer	5.00	2.50	.50
☐ 700	Murcer In Action	3.00	1.50	.30
☐ 701	Jose Pagan	2.25	1.10	.22
☐ 702	Pagan In Action	2.25	1.10	.22
☐ 703	Doug Griffin	2.25	1.10	.22
☐ 704	Griffin In Action	2.25	1.10	.22
☐ 705	Pat Corrales	3.00	1.50	.30
☐ 706	Corrales In Action	2.25	1.10	.22
☐ 707	Tim Foli	2.25	1.10	.22
☐ 708	Foli In Action	2.25	1.10	.22
☐ 709	Jim Kaat	7.50	3.75	.75
☐ 710	Kaat In Action	3.50	1.75	.35
☐ 711	Bobby Bonds	6.00	3.00	.60
☐ 712	Bonds In Action	3.50	1.75	.35
☐ 713	Gene Michael	3.00	1.50	.30
☐ 714	Michael In Action	2.25	1.10	.22
☐ 715	Mike Epstein	2.25	1.10	.22
☐ 716	Jesus Alou	2.25	1.10	.22
☐ 717	Bruce Dal Canton	2.25	1.10	.22
☐ 718	Del Rice MG	2.25	1.10	.22
☐ 719	Cesar Geronimo	2.25	1.10	.22
☐ 720	Sam McDowell	3.00	1.50	.30
☐ 721	Eddie Leon	2.25	1.10	.22
☐ 722	Bill Sudakis	2.25	1.10	.22
☐ 723	Al Santorini	2.25	1.10	.22
☐ 724	AL Rookie Pitchers John Curtis Rich Hinton Mickey Scott	3.00	1.50	.30
☐ 725	Dick McAuliffe	2.25	1.10	.22
☐ 726	Dick Selma	2.25	1.10	.22
☐ 727	Jose LaBoy	2.25	1.10	.22
☐ 728	Gail Hopkins	2.25	1.10	.22
☐ 729	Bob Veale	2.25	1.10	.22
☐ 730	Rick Monday	3.00	1.50	.30
☐ 731	Baltimore Orioles Team Card	4.50	2.25	.45
☐ 732	George Culver	2.25	1.10	.22
☐ 733	Jim Ray Hart	2.25	1.10	.22
☐ 734	Bob Burda	2.25	1.10	.22
☐ 735	Diego Segui	2.25	1.10	.22
☐ 736	Bill Russell	3.50	1.75	.35
☐ 737	Len Randle	2.25	1.10	.22
☐ 738	Jim Merritt	2.25	1.10	.22
☐ 739	Don Mason	2.25	1.10	.22
☐ 740	Rico Carty	3.00	1.50	.30
☐ 741	Rookie First Basemen Tom Hutton John Milner Rick Miller	3.00	1.50	.30
☐ 742	Jim Rooker	2.25	1.10	.22
☐ 743	Cesar Gutierrez	2.25	1.10	.22
☐ 744	Jim Slaton	2.25	1.10	.22
☐ 745	Julian Javier	2.25	1.10	.22
☐ 746	Lowell Palmer	2.25	1.10	.22
☐ 747	Jim Stewart	2.25	1.10	.22
☐ 748	Phil Hennigan	2.25	1.10	.22
☐ 749	Walter Alston MG	5.00	2.50	.50
☐ 750	Willie Horton	3.00	1.50	.30
☐ 751	Steve Carlton TR	36.00	18.00	3.60
☐ 752	Joe Morgan TR	28.00	14.00	2.80
☐ 753	Denny McLain TR	5.00	2.50	.50
☐ 754	Frank Robinson TR	22.00	11.00	2.20
☐ 755	Jim Fregosi TR	3.50	1.75	.35
☐ 756	Rick Wise TR	3.00	1.50	.30
☐ 757	Jose Cardenal TR	3.00	1.50	.30
☐ 758	Gil Garrido	2.25	1.10	.22
☐ 759	Chris Cannizzaro	2.25	1.10	.22
☐ 760	Bill Mazeroski	4.00	2.00	.40
☐ 761	Rookie Outfielders Ben Oglivie Ron Cey Bernie Williams	11.00	5.50	1.10
☐ 762	Wayne Simpson	2.25	1.10	.22
☐ 763	Ron Hansen	2.25	1.10	.22
☐ 764	Dusty Baker	4.00	2.00	.40
☐ 765	Ken McMullen	2.25	1.10	.22
☐ 766	Steve Hamilton	2.25	1.10	.22
☐ 767	Tom McCraw	2.25	1.10	.22
☐ 768	Denny Doyle	2.25	1.10	.22
☐ 769	Jack Aker	2.25	1.10	.22
☐ 770	Jim Wynn	3.00	1.50	.30
☐ 771	San Francisco Giants Team Card	4.50	2.25	.45
☐ 772	Ken Tatum	2.25	1.10	.22
☐ 773	Ron Brand	2.25	1.10	.22
☐ 774	Luis Alvarado	2.25	1.10	.22
☐ 775	Jerry Reuss	3.00	1.50	.30
☐ 776	Bill Voss	2.25	1.10	.22
☐ 777	Hoyt Wilhelm	10.00	5.00	1.00
☐ 778	Twins Rookies Vic Albury Rick Dempsey Jim Strickland	4.00	2.00	.40
☐ 779	Tony Cloninger	2.25	1.10	.22
☐ 780	Dick Green	2.25	1.10	.22
☐ 781	Jim McAndrew	2.25	1.10	.22
☐ 782	Larry Stahl	2.25	1.10	.22
☐ 783	Les Cain	2.25	1.10	.22
☐ 784	Ken Aspromonte	2.25	1.10	.22
☐ 785	Vic Davalillo	2.25	1.10	.22
☐ 786	Chuck Brinkman	2.25	1.10	.22
☐ 787	Ron Reed	3.00	1.50	.30

1973 Topps

The cards in this 660-card set measure 2 1/2" by 3 1/2". The 1973 Topps set marked the last year in which Topps marketed baseball cards in consecutive series. The last series (529-660) is more difficult to obtain. Beginning in 1974, all Topps cards were printed at the same time, thus eliminating the "high number" factor. The set features team leader cards featuring small individual pictures of the coaching staff members with a larger picture of the manager. The "background" variations below with respect to these leader cards are subtle and are best understood after a side-by-side comparison of the two varieties. An "All-Time Leaders" series (471-478) appeared for the first time in this set. Kid Pictures appeared again for the second year in a row (341-346). Other topical subsets within the set included League Leaders (61-68), Playoffs cards (201-202), World Series cards (203-210), and Rookie Prospects (601-616).

		NRMT	VG-E	GOOD
	COMPLETE SET (660)	900.00	350.00	90.00
	COMMON PLAYER (1-264)	.25	.12	.02
	COMMON PLAYER (265-396)	.30	.15	.03
	COMMON PLAYER (397-528)	.50	.25	.05
	COMMON PLAYER (529-660)	1.50	.75	.15
☐ 1	All-Time HR Leaders	15.00	4.00	.75
	Babe Ruth 714			
	Hank Aaron 673			
	Willie Mays 654			
☐ 2	Rich Hebner	.25	.12	.02
☐ 3	Jim Lonborg	.50	.25	.05
☐ 4	John Milner	.25	.12	.02
☐ 5	Ed Brinkman	.25	.12	.02
☐ 6	Mac Scarce	.25	.12	.02
☐ 7	Texas Rangers Team	.60	.30	.06
☐ 8	Tom Hall	.25	.12	.02
☐ 9	Johnny Oates	.25	.12	.02
☐ 10	Don Sutton	2.25	1.10	.22
☐ 11	Chris Chambliss	.50	.25	.05
☐ 12A	Padres Leaders	.50	.25	.05
	Don Zimmer MG			
	Dave Garcia CO			
	Johnny Podres CO			
	Bob Skinner CO			
	Whitey Wietelmann CO			
	(Podres no right ear)			
☐ 12B	Padres Leaders	1.00	.50	.10
	(Podres has right ear)			
☐ 13	George Hendrick	.50	.25	.05
☐ 14	Sonny Siebert	.25	.12	.02
☐ 15	Ralph Garr	.25	.12	.02
☐ 16	Steve Braun	.25	.12	.02
☐ 17	Fred Gladding	.25	.12	.02
☐ 18	Leroy Stanton	.25	.12	.02
☐ 19	Tim Foli	.25	.12	.02
☐ 20	Stan Bahnsen	.25	.12	.02
☐ 21	Randy Hundley	.25	.12	.02
☐ 22	Ted Abernathy	.25	.12	.02
☐ 23	Dave Kingman	1.50	.75	.15
☐ 24	Al Santorini	.25	.12	.02
☐ 25	Roy White	.50	.25	.05
☐ 26	Pittsburgh Pirates	.60	.30	.06
	Team Card			
☐ 27	Bill Gogolewski	.25	.12	.02
☐ 28	Hal McRae	.50	.25	.05
☐ 29	Tony Taylor	.25	.12	.02
☐ 30	Tug McGraw	.75	.35	.07
☐ 31	Buddy Bell	4.00	2.00	.40
☐ 32	Fred Norman	.25	.12	.02
☐ 33	Jim Breazeale	.25	.12	.02
☐ 34	Pat Dobson	.25	.12	.02
☐ 35	Willie Davis	.50	.25	.05
☐ 36	Steve Barber	.25	.12	.02
☐ 37	Bill Robinson	.50	.25	.05
☐ 38	Mike Epstein	.25	.12	.02
☐ 39	Dave Roberts	.25	.12	.02
☐ 40	Reggie Smith	.60	.30	.06
☐ 41	Tom Walker	.25	.12	.02
☐ 42	Mike Andrews	.25	.12	.02
☐ 43	Randy Moffitt	.25	.12	.02
☐ 44	Rick Monday	.50	.25	.05
☐ 45	Ellie Rodriguez	.25	.12	.02
	(photo actually			
	John Felske)			
☐ 46	Lindy McDaniel	.25	.12	.02
☐ 47	Luis Melendez	.25	.12	.02
☐ 48	Paul Splittorff	.25	.12	.02
☐ 49A	Twins Leaders	.50	.25	.05
	Frank Quilici MG			
	Vern Morgan CO			
	Bob Rodgers CO			
	Ralph Rowe CO			
	Al Worthington CO			
	(solid backgrounds)			
☐ 49B	Twins Leaders	1.00	.50	.10
	(natural backgrounds)			
☐ 50	Roberto Clemente	20.00	10.00	2.00
☐ 51	Chuck Seelbach	.25	.12	.02
☐ 52	Denis Menke	.25	.12	.02
☐ 53	Steve Dunning	.25	.12	.02
☐ 54	Checklist 1	1.50	.20	.04
☐ 55	Jon Matlack	.25	.12	.02
☐ 56	Merv Rettenmund	.25	.12	.02
☐ 57	Derrel Thomas	.25	.12	.02
☐ 58	Mike Paul	.25	.12	.02
☐ 59	Steve Yeager	.60	.30	.06
☐ 60	Ken Holtzman	.50	.25	.05
☐ 61	Batting Leaders	1.50	.75	.15

	Billy Williams			
	Rod Carew			
☐ 62	Home Run Leaders	1.50	.75	.15
	Johnny Bench			
	Dick Allen			
☐ 63	RBI Leaders	1.50	.75	.15
	Johnny Bench			
	Dick Allen			
☐ 64	Stolen Base Leaders	1.00	.50	.10
	Lou Brock			
	Bert Campaneris			
☐ 65	ERA Leaders	1.00	.50	.10
	Steve Carlton			
	Luis Tiant			
☐ 66	Victory Leaders	1.00	.50	.10
	Steve Carlton			
	Gaylord Perry			
	Wilbur Wood			
☐ 67	Strikeout Leaders	4.00	2.00	.40
	Steve Carlton			
	Nolan Ryan			
☐ 68	Leading Firemen	.75	.35	.07
	Clay Carroll			
	Sparky Lyle			
☐ 69	Phil Gagliano	.25	.12	.02
☐ 70	Milt Pappas	.50	.25	.05
☐ 71	Johnny Briggs	.25	.12	.02
☐ 72	Ron Reed	.25	.12	.02
☐ 73	Ed Herrmann	.25	.12	.02
☐ 74	Billy Champion	.25	.12	.02
☐ 75	Vada Pinson	.60	.30	.06
☐ 76	Doug Rader	.50	.25	.05
☐ 77	Mike Torrez	.25	.12	.02
☐ 78	Richie Scheinblum	.25	.12	.02
☐ 79	Jim Willoughby	.25	.12	.02
☐ 80	Tony Oliva UER	1.00	.50	.10
	(Minnseota on front)			
☐ 81A	Cubs Leaders	.50	.25	.05
	Whitey Lockman MG			
	Hank Aguirre CO			
	Ernie Banks CO			
	Larry Jansen CO			
	Pete Reiser CO			
	(solid backgrounds)			
☐ 81B	Cubs Leaders	1.00	.50	.10
	(natural backgrounds)			
☐ 82	Fritz Peterson	.25	.12	.02
☐ 83	Leron Lee	.25	.12	.02
☐ 84	Rollie Fingers	2.25	1.10	.22
☐ 85	Ted Simmons	1.00	.50	.10
☐ 86	Tom McCraw	.25	.12	.02
☐ 87	Ken Boswell	.25	.12	.02
☐ 88	Mickey Stanley	.50	.25	.05
☐ 89	Jack Billingham	.25	.12	.02
☐ 90	Brooks Robinson	4.00	2.00	.40
☐ 91	Dodgers Team	.75	.35	.07
☐ 92	Jerry Bell	.25	.12	.02
☐ 93	Jesus Alou	.25	.12	.02
☐ 94	Dick Billings	.25	.12	.02
☐ 95	Steve Blass	.50	.25	.05
☐ 96	Doug Griffin	.25	.12	.02
☐ 97	Willie Montanez	.25	.12	.02
☐ 98	Dick Woodson	.25	.12	.02
☐ 99	Carl Taylor	.25	.12	.02
☐ 100	Hank Aaron	16.00	8.00	1.60
☐ 101	Ken Henderson	.25	.12	.02
☐ 102	Rudy May	.25	.12	.02
☐ 103	Celerino Sanchez	.25	.12	.02
☐ 104	Reggie Cleveland	.25	.12	.02
☐ 105	Carlos May	.25	.12	.02
☐ 106	Terry Humphrey	.25	.12	.02
☐ 107	Phil Hennigan	.25	.12	.02
☐ 108	Bill Russell	.50	.25	.05
☐ 109	Doyle Alexander	.75	.35	.07
☐ 110	Bob Watson	.50	.25	.05
☐ 111	Dave Nelson	.25	.12	.02
☐ 112	Gary Ross	.25	.12	.02
☐ 113	Jerry Grote	.25	.12	.02
☐ 114	Lynn McGlothen	.25	.12	.02
☐ 115	Ron Santo	.75	.35	.07
☐ 116A	Yankees Leaders	.60	.30	.06
	Ralph Houk MG			
	Jim Hegan CO			
	Elston Howard CO			
	Dick Howser CO			
	Jim Turner CO			
	(solid backgrounds)			
☐ 116B	Yankees Leaders	1.00	.50	.10
	(natural backgrounds)			
☐ 117	Ramon Hernandez	.25	.12	.02
☐ 118	John Mayberry	.50	.25	.05
☐ 119	Larry Bowa	.75	.35	.07
☐ 120	Joe Coleman	.25	.12	.02
☐ 121	Dave Rader	.25	.12	.02
☐ 122	Jim Strickland	.25	.12	.02

☐ 123 Sandy Alomar	.25	.12	.02
☐ 124 Jim Hardin	.25	.12	.02
☐ 125 Ron Fairly	.25	.12	.02
☐ 126 Jim Brewer	.25	.12	.02
☐ 127 Brewers Team	.60	.30	.06
☐ 128 Ted Sizemore	.25	.12	.02
☐ 129 Terry Forster	.50	.25	.05
☐ 130 Pete Rose	20.00	10.00	2.00
☐ 131A Red Sox Leaders	.50	.25	.05
Eddie Kasko MG			
Doug Camilli CO			
Don Lenhardt CO			
Eddie Popowski CO			
(no right ear)			
Lee Stange CO			
☐ 131B Red Sox Leaders	1.00	.50	.10
(Popowski has right			
ear showing)			
☐ 132 Matty Alou	.50	.25	.05
☐ 133 Dave Roberts	.25	.12	.02
☐ 134 Milt Wilcox	.25	.12	.02
☐ 135 Lee May UER	.50	.25	.05
(career average .000)			
☐ 136A Orioles Leaders	.75	.35	.07
Earl Weaver MG			
George Bamberger CO			
Jim Frey CO			
Billy Hunter CO			
George Staller CO			
(orange backgrounds)			
☐ 136B Orioles Leaders	1.00	.50	.10
(dark pale			
backgrounds)			
☐ 137 Jim Beauchamp	.25	.12	.02
☐ 138 Horacio Pina	.25	.12	.02
☐ 139 Carmen Fanzone	.25	.12	.02
☐ 140 Lou Piniella	.75	.35	.07
☐ 141 Bruce Kison	.25	.12	.02
☐ 142 Thurman Munson	7.50	3.75	.75
☐ 143 John Curtis	.25	.12	.02
☐ 144 Marty Perez	.25	.12	.02
☐ 145 Bobby Bonds	.75	.35	.07
☐ 146 Woodie Fryman	.25	.12	.02
☐ 147 Mike Anderson	.25	.12	.02
☐ 148 Dave Goltz	.25	.12	.02
☐ 149 Ron Hunt	.25	.12	.02
☐ 150 Wilbur Wood	.25	.12	.02
☐ 151 Wes Parker	.50	.25	.05
☐ 152 Dave May	.25	.12	.02
☐ 153 Al Hrabosky	.50	.25	.05
☐ 154 Jeff Torborg	.50	.25	.05
☐ 155 Sal Bando	.50	.25	.05
☐ 156 Cesar Geronimo	.25	.12	.02
☐ 157 Denny Riddleberger	.25	.12	.02
☐ 158 Astros Team	.60	.30	.06
☐ 159 Clarence Gaston	.60	.30	.06
☐ 160 Jim Palmer	5.50	2.75	.55
☐ 161 Ted Martinez	.25	.12	.02
☐ 162 Pete Broberg	.25	.12	.02
☐ 163 Vic Davalillo	.25	.12	.02
☐ 164 Monty Montgomery	.25	.12	.02
☐ 165 Luis Aparicio	2.50	1.25	.25
☐ 166 Terry Harmon	.25	.12	.02
☐ 167 Steve Stone	.50	.25	.05
☐ 168 Jim Northrup	.50	.25	.05
☐ 169 Ron Schueler	.25	.12	.02
☐ 170 Harmon Killebrew	3.50	1.75	.35
☐ 171 Bernie Carbo	.25	.12	.02
☐ 172 Steve Kline	.25	.12	.02
☐ 173 Hal Breeden	.25	.12	.02
☐ 174 Rich Gossage	7.50	3.75	.75
☐ 175 Frank Robinson	3.50	1.75	.35
☐ 176 Chuck Taylor	.25	.12	.02
☐ 177 Bill Plummer	.25	.12	.02
☐ 178 Don Rose	.25	.12	.02
☐ 179A A's Leaders	.50	.25	.05
Dick Williams MG			
Jerry Adair CO			
Vern Hoscheit CO			
Irv Noren CO			
Wes Stock CO			
(orange backgrounds)			
☐ 179B A's Leaders	1.00	.50	.10
(dark pale			
backgrounds)			
☐ 180 Fergie Jenkins	1.50	.75	.15
☐ 181 Jack Brohamer	.25	.12	.02
☐ 182 Mike Caldwell	.50	.25	.05
☐ 183 Don Buford	.25	.12	.02
☐ 184 Jerry Koosman	.75	.35	.07
☐ 185 Jim Wynn	.50	.25	.05
☐ 186 Bill Fahey	.25	.12	.02
☐ 187 Luke Walker	.25	.12	.02
☐ 188 Cookie Rojas	.25	.12	.02
☐ 189 Greg Luzinski	.75	.35	.07
☐ 190 Bob Gibson	3.50	1.75	.35
☐ 191 Tigers Team	.75	.35	.07
☐ 192 Pat Jarvis	.25	.12	.02
☐ 193 Carlton Fisk	12.00	5.00	1.00
☐ 194 Jorge Orta	.25	.12	.02
☐ 195 Clay Carroll	.25	.12	.02
☐ 196 Ken McMullen	.25	.12	.02
☐ 197 Ed Goodson	.25	.12	.02
☐ 198 Horace Clarke	.25	.12	.02
☐ 199 Bert Blyleven	3.50	1.75	.35
☐ 200 Billy Williams	3.00	1.50	.30
☐ 201 A.L. Playoffs	.75	.35	.07
A's over Tigers;			
Hendrick scores			
winning run			
☐ 202 N.L. Playoffs	.75	.35	.07
Reds over Pirates			
Foster's run decides			
☐ 203 World Series Game 1	.75	.35	.07
Tenace the Menace			
☐ 204 World Series Game 2	.75	.35	.07
A's two straight			
☐ 205 World Series Game 3	.75	.35	.07
Reds win squeeker			
☐ 206 World Series Game 4	.75	.35	.07
Tenace singles			
in ninth			
☐ 207 World Series Game 5	.75	.35	.07
Odom out at plate			
☐ 208 World Series Game 6	.75	.35	.07
Red's slugging			
ties series			
☐ 209 World Series Game 7	.75	.35	.07
Campy stars			
winning rally			
☐ 210 World Series Summary	.75	.35	.07
World champions:			
A's Win			
☐ 211 Balor Moore	.25	.12	.02
☐ 212 Joe Lahoud	.25	.12	.02
☐ 213 Steve Garvey	13.00	6.50	1.30
☐ 214 Steve Hamilton	.25	.12	.02
☐ 215 Dusty Baker	.60	.30	.06
☐ 216 Toby Harrah	.50	.25	.05
☐ 217 Don Wilson	.25	.12	.02
☐ 218 Aurelio Rodriguez	.25	.12	.02
☐ 219 Cardinals Team	.60	.30	.06
☐ 220 Nolan Ryan	30.00	15.00	3.00
☐ 221 Fred Kendall	.25	.12	.02
☐ 222 Rob Gardner	.25	.12	.02
☐ 223 Bud Harrelson	.25	.12	.02
☐ 224 Bill Lee	.25	.12	.02
☐ 225 Al Oliver	1.00	.50	.10
☐ 226 Ray Fosse	.25	.12	.02
☐ 227 Wayne Twitchell	.25	.12	.02
☐ 228 Bobby Darwin	.25	.12	.02
☐ 229 Roric Harrison	.25	.12	.02
☐ 230 Joe Morgan	4.50	2.25	.45
☐ 231 Bill Parsons	.25	.12	.02
☐ 232 Ken Singleton	.50	.25	.05
☐ 233 Ed Kirkpatrick	.25	.12	.02
☐ 234 Bill North	.25	.12	.02
☐ 235 Jim Hunter	3.00	1.50	.30
☐ 236 Tito Fuentes	.25	.12	.02
☐ 237A Braves Leaders	1.00	.50	.10
Eddie Mathews MG			
Lew Burdette CO			
Jim Busby CO			
Roy Hartsfield CO			
Ken Silvestri CO			
(orange backgrounds)			
☐ 237B Braves Leaders	1.50	.75	.15
(dark pale			
backgrounds)			
☐ 238 Tony Muser	.25	.12	.02
☐ 239 Pete Richert	.25	.12	.02
☐ 240 Bobby Murcer	.60	.30	.06
☐ 241 Dwain Anderson	.25	.12	.02
☐ 242 George Culver	.25	.12	.02
☐ 243 Angels Team	.60	.30	.06
☐ 244 Ed Acosta	.25	.12	.02
☐ 245 Carl Yastrzemski	13.00	6.50	1.30
☐ 246 Ken Sanders	.25	.12	.02
☐ 247 Del Unser	.25	.12	.02
☐ 248 Jerry Johnson	.25	.12	.02
☐ 249 Larry Biittner	.25	.12	.02
☐ 250 Manny Sanguillen	.50	.25	.05
☐ 251 Roger Nelson	.25	.12	.02
☐ 252A Giants Leaders	.50	.25	.05
Charlie Fox MG			
Joe Amalfitano CO			
Andy Gilbert CO			
Don McMahon CO			
John McNamara CO			
(orange backgrounds)			

☐ 252B	Giants Leaders .... (dark pale backgrounds)	1.00	.50	.10
☐ 253	Mark Belanger	.50	.25	.05
☐ 254	Bill Stoneman	.25	.12	.02
☐ 255	Reggie Jackson	17.00	8.50	1.70
☐ 256	Chris Zachary	.25	.12	.02
☐ 257A	Mets Leaders .... Yogi Berra MG Roy McMillan CO Joe Pignatano CO Rube Walker CO Eddie Yost CO (orange backgrounds)	1.50	.75	.15
☐ 257B	Mets Leaders .... (dark pale backgrounds)	2.00	1.00	.20
☐ 258	Tommy John	1.50	.75	.15
☐ 259	Jim Holt	.25	.12	.02
☐ 260	Gary Nolan	.25	.12	.02
☐ 261	Pat Kelly	.25	.12	.02
☐ 262	Jack Aker	.25	.12	.02
☐ 263	George Scott	.50	.25	.05
☐ 264	Checklist 2	1.50	.20	.04
☐ 265	Gene Michael	.50	.25	.05
☐ 266	Mike Lum	.30	.15	.03
☐ 267	Lloyd Allen	.30	.15	.03
☐ 268	Jerry Morales	.30	.15	.03
☐ 269	Tim McCarver	.75	.35	.07
☐ 270	Luis Tiant	.75	.35	.07
☐ 271	Tom Hutton	.30	.15	.03
☐ 272	Ed Farmer	.30	.15	.03
☐ 273	Chris Speier	.30	.15	.03
☐ 274	Darold Knowles	.30	.15	.03
☐ 275	Tony Perez	1.50	.75	.15
☐ 276	Joe Lovitto	.30	.15	.03
☐ 277	Bob Miller	.30	.15	.03
☐ 278	Baltimore Orioles .... Team Card	.75	.35	.07
☐ 279	Mike Strahler	.30	.15	.03
☐ 280	Al Kaline	5.00	2.50	.50
☐ 281	Mike Jorgensen	.30	.15	.03
☐ 282	Steve Hovley	.30	.15	.03
☐ 283	Ray Sadecki	.30	.15	.03
☐ 284	Glenn Borgmann	.30	.15	.03
☐ 285	Don Kessinger	.50	.25	.05
☐ 286	Frank Linzy	.30	.15	.03
☐ 287	Eddie Leon	.30	.15	.03
☐ 288	Gary Gentry	.30	.15	.03
☐ 289	Bob Oliver	.30	.15	.03
☐ 290	Cesar Cedeno	.60	.30	.06
☐ 291	Rogelio Moret	.30	.15	.03
☐ 292	Jose Cruz	.60	.30	.06
☐ 293	Bernie Allen	.30	.15	.03
☐ 294	Steve Arlin	.30	.15	.03
☐ 295	Bert Campaneris	.50	.25	.05
☐ 296	Reds Leaders .... Sparky Anderson MG Alex Grammas CO Ted Kluszewski CO George Scherger CO Larry Shepard CO	.75	.35	.07
☐ 297	Walt Williams	.30	.15	.03
☐ 298	Ron Bryant	.30	.15	.03
☐ 299	Ted Ford	.30	.15	.03
☐ 300	Steve Carlton	8.00	4.00	.80
☐ 301	Billy Grabarkewitz	.30	.15	.03
☐ 302	Terry Crowley	.30	.15	.03
☐ 303	Nelson Briles	.30	.15	.03
☐ 304	Duke Sims	.30	.15	.03
☐ 305	Willie Mays	20.00	10.00	2.00
☐ 306	Tom Burgmeier	.30	.15	.03
☐ 307	Boots Day	.30	.15	.03
☐ 308	Skip Lockwood	.30	.15	.03
☐ 309	Paul Popovich	.30	.15	.03
☐ 310	Dick Allen	.60	.30	.06
☐ 311	Joe Decker	.30	.15	.03
☐ 312	Oscar Brown	.30	.15	.03
☐ 313	Jim Ray	.30	.15	.03
☐ 314	Ron Swoboda	.30	.15	.03
☐ 315	John Odom	.30	.15	.03
☐ 316	San Diego Padres .... Team Card	.75	.35	.07
☐ 317	Danny Cater	.30	.15	.03
☐ 318	Jim McGlothlin	.30	.15	.03
☐ 319	Jim Spencer	.30	.15	.03
☐ 320	Lou Brock	4.00	2.00	.40
☐ 321	Rich Hinton	.30	.15	.03
☐ 322	Garry Maddox	.60	.30	.06
☐ 323	Tigers Leaders .... Billy Martin MG Art Fowler CO Charlie Silvera CO Dick Tracewski CO	1.00	.50	.10
☐ 324	Al Downing	.30	.15	.03

☐ 325	Boog Powell	.75	.35	.07
☐ 326	Darrell Brandon	.30	.15	.03
☐ 327	John Lowenstein	.30	.15	.03
☐ 328	Bill Bonham	.30	.15	.03
☐ 329	Ed Kranepool	.50	.25	.05
☐ 330	Rod Carew	9.00	4.00	.80
☐ 331	Carl Morton	.30	.15	.03
☐ 332	John Felske	.30	.15	.03
☐ 333	Gene Clines	.30	.15	.03
☐ 334	Freddie Patek	.30	.15	.03
☐ 335	Bob Tolan	.30	.15	.03
☐ 336	Tom Bradley	.30	.15	.03
☐ 337	Dave Duncan	.30	.15	.03
☐ 338	Checklist 3	1.50	.20	.04
☐ 339	Dick Tidrow	.30	.15	.03
☐ 340	Nate Colbert	.30	.15	.03
☐ 341	KP: Jim Palmer	1.25	.60	.12
☐ 342	KP: Sam McDowell	.30	.15	.03
☐ 343	KP: Bobby Murcer	.40	.20	.04
☐ 344	KP: Jim Hunter	.75	.35	.07
☐ 345	KP: Chris Speier	.30	.15	.03
☐ 346	KP: Gaylord Perry	.75	.35	.07
☐ 347	Kansas City Royals .... Team Card	.75	.35	.07
☐ 348	Rennie Stennett	.30	.15	.03
☐ 349	Dick McAuliffe	.30	.15	.03
☐ 350	Tom Seaver	14.00	6.50	1.30
☐ 351	Jimmy Stewart	.30	.15	.03
☐ 352	Don Stanhouse	.30	.15	.03
☐ 353	Steve Brye	.30	.15	.03
☐ 354	Billy Parker	.30	.15	.03
☐ 355	Mike Marshall	.50	.25	.05
☐ 356	White Sox Leaders .... Chuck Tanner MG Joe Lonnett CO Jim Mahoney CO Al Monchak CO Johnny Sain CO	.50	.25	.05
☐ 357	Ross Grimsley	.30	.15	.03
☐ 358	Jim Nettles	.30	.15	.03
☐ 359	Cecil Upshaw	.30	.15	.03
☐ 360	Joe Rudi .... (photo actually Gene Tenace)	.50	.25	.05
☐ 361	Fran Healy	.30	.15	.03
☐ 362	Eddie Watt	.30	.15	.03
☐ 363	Jackie Hernandez	.30	.15	.03
☐ 364	Rick Wise	.50	.25	.05
☐ 365	Rico Petrocelli	.50	.25	.05
☐ 366	Brock Davis	.30	.15	.03
☐ 367	Burt Hooton	.50	.25	.05
☐ 368	Bill Buckner	.75	.35	.07
☐ 369	Lerrin LaGrow	.30	.15	.03
☐ 370	Willie Stargell	3.50	1.75	.35
☐ 371	Mike Kekich	.30	.15	.03
☐ 372	Oscar Gamble	.50	.25	.05
☐ 373	Clyde Wright	.30	.15	.03
☐ 374	Darrell Evans	.75	.35	.07
☐ 375	Larry Dierker	.50	.25	.05
☐ 376	Frank Duffy	.30	.15	.03
☐ 377	Expos Leaders .... Gene Mauch MG Dave Bristol CO Larry Doby CO Cal McLish CO Jerry Zimmerman CO	.50	.25	.05
☐ 378	Len Randle	.30	.15	.03
☐ 379	Cy Acosta	.30	.15	.03
☐ 380	Johnny Bench	16.00	7.50	1.50
☐ 381	Vicente Romo	.30	.15	.03
☐ 382	Mike Hegan	.30	.15	.03
☐ 383	Diego Segui	.30	.15	.03
☐ 384	Don Baylor	1.00	.50	.10
☐ 385	Jim Perry	.50	.25	.05
☐ 386	Don Money	.30	.15	.03
☐ 387	Jim Barr	.30	.15	.03
☐ 388	Ben Oglivie	.50	.25	.05
☐ 389	New York Mets .... Team Card	1.50	.75	.15
☐ 390	Mickey Lolich	.75	.35	.07
☐ 391	Lee Lacy	.50	.25	.05
☐ 392	Dick Drago	.30	.15	.03
☐ 393	Jose Cardenal	.30	.15	.03
☐ 394	Sparky Lyle	.60	.30	.06
☐ 395	Roger Metzger	.30	.15	.03
☐ 396	Grant Jackson	.30	.15	.03
☐ 397	Dave Cash	.50	.25	.05
☐ 398	Rich Hand	.50	.25	.05
☐ 399	George Foster	1.50	.75	.15
☐ 400	Gaylord Perry	2.50	1.25	.25
☐ 401	Clyde Mashore	.50	.25	.05
☐ 402	Jack Hiatt	.50	.25	.05
☐ 403	Sonny Jackson	.50	.25	.05
☐ 404	Chuck Brinkman	.50	.25	.05
☐ 405	Cesar Tovar	.50	.25	.05

☐ 406	Paul Lindblad	.50	.25	.05
☐ 407	Felix Millan	.50	.25	.05
☐ 408	Jim Colborn	.50	.25	.05
☐ 409	Ivan Murrell	.50	.25	.05
☐ 410	Willie McCovey	3.50	1.75	.35
	(Bench behind plate)			
☐ 411	Ray Corbin	.50	.25	.05
☐ 412	Manny Mota	.75	.35	.07
☐ 413	Tom Timmermann	.50	.25	.05
☐ 414	Ken Rudolph	.50	.25	.05
☐ 415	Marty Pattin	.50	.25	.05
☐ 416	Paul Schaal	.50	.25	.05
☐ 417	Scipio Spinks	.50	.25	.05
☐ 418	Bob Grich	.75	.35	.07
☐ 419	Casey Cox	.50	.25	.05
☐ 420	Tommie Agee	.50	.25	.05
☐ 421A	Angels Leaders	.75	.35	.07
	Bobby Winkles MG			
	Tom Morgan CO			
	Salty Parker CO			
	Jimmie Reese CO			
	John Roseboro CO			
	(orange backgrounds)			
☐ 421B	Angels Leaders	1.00	.50	.10
	(dark pale			
	backgrounds)			
☐ 422	Bob Robertson	.50	.25	.05
☐ 423	Johnny Jeter	.50	.25	.05
☐ 424	Denny Doyle	.50	.25	.05
☐ 425	Alex Johnson	.50	.25	.05
☐ 426	Dave LaRoche	.50	.25	.05
☐ 427	Rick Auerbach	.50	.25	.05
☐ 428	Wayne Simpson	.50	.25	.05
☐ 429	Jim Fairey	.50	.25	.05
☐ 430	Vida Blue	.75	.35	.07
☐ 431	Gerry Moses	.50	.25	.05
☐ 432	Dan Frisella	.50	.25	.05
☐ 433	Willie Horton	.75	.35	.07
☐ 434	San Francisco Giants	1.25	.60	.12
	Team Card			
☐ 435	Rico Carty	.75	.35	.07
☐ 436	Jim McAndrew	.50	.25	.05
☐ 437	John Kennedy	.50	.25	.05
☐ 438	Enzo Hernandez	.50	.25	.05
☐ 439	Eddie Fisher	.50	.25	.05
☐ 440	Glenn Beckert	.75	.35	.07
☐ 441	Gail Hopkins	.50	.25	.05
☐ 442	Dick Dietz	.50	.25	.05
☐ 443	Danny Thompson	.50	.25	.05
☐ 444	Ken Brett	.50	.25	.05
☐ 445	Ken Berry	.50	.25	.05
☐ 446	Jerry Reuss	.75	.35	.07
☐ 447	Joe Hague	.50	.25	.05
☐ 448	John Hiller	.75	.35	.07
☐ 449A	Indians Leaders	.75	.35	.07
	Ken Aspromonte MG			
	Rocky Colavito CO			
	Joe Lutz CO			
	Warren Spahn CO			
	(Spahn's right			
	ear pointed)			
☐ 449B	Indians Leaders	1.00	.50	.10
	(Spahn's right			
	ear round)			
☐ 450	Joe Torre	1.00	.50	.10
☐ 451	John Vukovich	.50	.25	.05
☐ 452	Paul Casanova	.50	.25	.05
☐ 453	Checklist 4	1.50	.20	.04
☐ 454	Tom Haller	.50	.25	.05
☐ 455	Bill Melton	.50	.25	.05
☐ 456	Dick Green	.50	.25	.05
☐ 457	John Strohmayer	.50	.25	.05
☐ 458	Jim Mason	.50	.25	.05
☐ 459	Jimmy Howarth	.50	.25	.05
☐ 460	Bill Freehan	1.00	.50	.10
☐ 461	Mike Corkins	.50	.25	.05
☐ 462	Ron Blomberg	.50	.25	.05
☐ 463	Ken Tatum	.50	.25	.05
☐ 464	Chicago Cubs	1.25	.60	.12
	Team Card			
☐ 465	Dave Giusti	.75	.35	.07
☐ 466	Jose Arcia	.50	.25	.05
☐ 467	Mike Ryan	.50	.25	.05
☐ 468	Tom Griffin	.50	.25	.05
☐ 469	Dan Monzon	.50	.25	.05
☐ 470	Mike Cuellar	.75	.35	.07
☐ 471	Hits Leaders	3.00	1.50	.30
	Ty Cobb 4191			
☐ 472	Grand Slam Leaders	3.00	1.50	.30
	Lou Gehrig 23			
☐ 473	Total Bases Leaders	3.00	1.50	.30
	Hank Aaron 6172			
☐ 474	RBI Leaders	5.00	2.50	.50
	Babe Ruth 2209			
☐ 475	Batting Leaders	3.00	1.50	.30
	Ty Cobb .367			
☐ 476	Shutout Leaders	1.50	.75	.15
	Walter Johnson 113			
☐ 477	Victory Leaders	1.50	.75	.15
	Cy Young 511			
☐ 478	Strikeout Leaders	1.50	.75	.15
	Walter Johnson 3508			
☐ 479	Hal Lanier	.75	.35	.07
☐ 480	Juan Marichal	3.50	1.75	.35
☐ 481	Chicago White Sox	1.25	.60	.12
	Team Card			
☐ 482	Rick Reuschel	6.00	3.00	.60
☐ 483	Dal Maxvill	.50	.25	.05
☐ 484	Ernie McAnally	.50	.25	.05
☐ 485	Norm Cash	1.00	.50	.10
☐ 486A	Phillies Leaders	.75	.35	.07
	Danny Ozark MG			
	Carroll Beringer CO			
	Billy DeMars CO			
	Ray Rippelmeyer CO			
	Bobby Wine CO			
	(orange backgrounds)			
☐ 486B	Phillies Leaders	1.00	.50	.10
	(dark pale			
	backgrounds)			
☐ 487	Bruce Dal Canton	.50	.25	.05
☐ 488	Dave Campbell	.50	.25	.05
☐ 489	Jeff Burroughs	.75	.35	.07
☐ 490	Claude Osteen	.75	.35	.07
☐ 491	Bob Montgomery	.50	.25	.05
☐ 492	Pedro Borbon	.50	.25	.05
☐ 493	Duffy Dyer	.50	.25	.05
☐ 494	Rich Morales	.50	.25	.05
☐ 495	Tommy Helms	.75	.35	.07
☐ 496	Ray Lamb	.50	.25	.05
☐ 497A	Cardinals Leaders	1.00	.50	.10
	Red Schoendienst MG			
	Vern Benson CO			
	George Kissell CO			
	Barney Schultz CO			
	(orange backgrounds)			
☐ 497B	Cardinals Leaders	1.50	.75	.15
	(dark pale			
	backgrounds)			
☐ 498	Graig Nettles	2.25	1.10	.22
☐ 499	Bob Moose	.50	.25	.05
☐ 500	Oakland A's Team	1.25	.60	.12
☐ 501	Larry Gura	.75	.35	.07
☐ 502	Bobby Valentine	1.00	.50	.10
☐ 503	Phil Niekro	3.50	1.75	.35
☐ 504	Earl Williams	.50	.25	.05
☐ 505	Bob Bailey	.50	.25	.05
☐ 506	Bart Johnson	.50	.25	.05
☐ 507	Darrel Chaney	.50	.25	.05
☐ 508	Gates Brown	.75	.35	.07
☐ 509	Jim Nash	.50	.25	.05
☐ 510	Amos Otis	1.00	.50	.10
☐ 511	Sam McDowell	.75	.35	.07
☐ 512	Dalton Jones	.50	.25	.05
☐ 513	Dave Marshall	.50	.25	.05
☐ 514	Jerry Kenney	.50	.25	.05
☐ 515	Andy Messersmith	.75	.35	.07
☐ 516	Danny Walton	.50	.25	.05
☐ 517A	Pirates Leaders	.75	.35	.07
	Bill Virdon MG			
	Don Leppert CO			
	Bill Mazeroski CO			
	Dave Ricketts CO			
	Mel Wright CO			
	(Mazeroski has			
	no right ear)			
☐ 517B	Pirates Leaders	1.00	.50	.10
	(Mazeroski has			
	right ear)			
☐ 518	Bob Veale	.75	.35	.07
☐ 519	Johnny Edwards	.50	.25	.05
☐ 520	Mel Stottlemyre	1.00	.50	.10
☐ 521	Atlanta Braves	1.25	.60	.12
	Team Card			
☐ 522	Leo Cardenas	.50	.25	.05
☐ 523	Wayne Granger	.50	.25	.05
☐ 524	Gene Tenace	.75	.35	.07
☐ 525	Jim Fregosi	.75	.35	.07
☐ 526	Ollie Brown	.50	.25	.05
☐ 527	Dan McGinn	.50	.25	.05
☐ 528	Paul Blair	.75	.35	.07
☐ 529	Milt May	1.50	.75	.15
☐ 530	Jim Kaat	3.50	1.75	.35
☐ 531	Ron Woods	1.50	.75	.15
☐ 532	Steve Mingori	1.50	.75	.15
☐ 533	Larry Stahl	1.50	.75	.15
☐ 534	Dave Lemonds	1.50	.75	.15
☐ 535	Johnny Callison	2.00	1.00	.20
☐ 536	Philadelphia Phillies	3.00	1.50	.30
	Team Card			

☐ 537 Bill Slayback	1.50	.75	.15
☐ 538 Jim Ray Hart	2.00	1.00	.20
☐ 539 Tom Murphy	1.50	.75	.15
☐ 540 Cleon Jones	2.00	1.00	.20
☐ 541 Bob Bolin	1.50	.75	.15
☐ 542 Pat Corrales	2.00	1.00	.20
☐ 543 Alan Foster	1.50	.75	.15
☐ 544 Von Joshua	1.50	.75	.15
☐ 545 Orlando Cepeda	3.00	1.50	.30
☐ 546 Jim York	1.50	.75	.15
☐ 547 Bobby Heise	1.50	.75	.15
☐ 548 Don Durham	1.50	.75	.15
☐ 549 Rangers Leaders	2.50	1.25	.25
Whitey Herzog MG			
Chuck Estrada CO			
Chuck Hiller CO			
Jackie Moore CO			
☐ 550 Dave Johnson	2.50	1.25	.25
☐ 551 Mike Kilkenny	1.50	.75	.15
☐ 552 J.C. Martin	1.50	.75	.15
☐ 553 Mickey Scott	1.50	.75	.15
☐ 554 Dave Concepcion	3.00	1.50	.30
☐ 555 Bill Hands	1.50	.75	.15
☐ 556 New York Yankees	3.50	1.75	.35
Team Card			
☐ 557 Bernie Williams	1.50	.75	.15
☐ 558 Jerry May	1.50	.75	.15
☐ 559 Barry Lersch	1.50	.75	.15
☐ 560 Frank Howard	2.50	1.25	.25
☐ 561 Jim Geddes	1.50	.75	.15
☐ 562 Wayne Garrett	1.50	.75	.15
☐ 563 Larry Haney	1.50	.75	.15
☐ 564 Mike Thompson	1.50	.75	.15
☐ 565 Jim Hickman	1.50	.75	.15
☐ 566 Lew Krausse	1.50	.75	.15
☐ 567 Bob Fenwick	1.50	.75	.15
☐ 568 Ray Newman	1.50	.75	.15
☐ 569 Dodgers Leaders	3.00	1.50	.30
Walt Alston MG			
Red Adams CO			
Monty Basgall CO			
Jim Gilliam CO			
Tom Lasorda CO			
☐ 570 Bill Singer	2.00	1.00	.20
☐ 571 Rusty Torres	1.50	.75	.15
☐ 572 Gary Sutherland	1.50	.75	.15
☐ 573 Fred Beene	1.50	.75	.15
☐ 574 Bob Didier	1.50	.75	.15
☐ 575 Dock Ellis	1.50	.75	.15
☐ 576 Montreal Expos	3.00	1.50	.30
Team Card			
☐ 577 Eric Soderholm	1.50	.75	.15
☐ 578 Ken Wright	1.50	.75	.15
☐ 579 Tom Grieve	2.00	1.00	.20
☐ 580 Joe Pepitone	2.00	1.00	.20
☐ 581 Steve Kealey	1.50	.75	.15
☐ 582 Darrell Porter	1.50	.75	.15
☐ 583 Bill Grief	1.50	.75	.15
☐ 584 Chris Arnold	1.50	.75	.15
☐ 585 Joe Niekro	2.50	1.25	.25
☐ 586 Bill Sudakis	1.50	.75	.15
☐ 587 Rich McKinney	1.50	.75	.15
☐ 588 Checklist 5	12.00	1.50	.30
☐ 589 Ken Forsch	2.00	1.00	.20
☐ 590 Deron Johnson	1.50	.75	.15
☐ 591 Mike Hedlund	1.50	.75	.15
☐ 592 John Boccabella	1.50	.75	.15
☐ 593 Royals Leaders	2.50	1.25	.25
Jack McKeon MG			
Galen Cisco CO			
Harry Dunlop CO			
Charlie Lau CO			
☐ 594 Vic Harris	1.50	.75	.15
☐ 595 Don Gullett	2.00	1.00	.20
☐ 596 Red Sox Team	3.00	1.50	.30
☐ 597 Mickey Rivers	2.00	1.00	.20
☐ 598 Phil Roof	1.50	.75	.15
☐ 599 Ed Crosby	1.50	.75	.15
☐ 600 Dave McNally	2.00	1.00	.20
☐ 601 Rookie Catchers	1.50	.75	.15
Sergio Robles			
George Pena			
Rick Stelmaszek			
☐ 602 Rookie Pitchers	1.50	.75	.15
Mel Behney			
Ralph Garcia			
Doug Rau			
☐ 603 Rookie 3rd Basemen	1.50	.75	.15
Terry Hughes			
Bill McNulty			
Ken Reitz			
☐ 604 Rookie Pitchers	1.50	.75	.15
Jesse Jefferson			
Dennis O'Toole			
Bob Strampe			

☐ 605 Rookie 1st Basemen	1.50	.75	.15
Enos Cabell			
Pat Bourque			
Gonzalo Marquez			
☐ 606 Rookie Outfielders	2.50	1.25	.25
Gary Matthews			
Tom Paciorek			
Jorge Roque			
☐ 607 Rookie Shortstops	1.50	.75	.15
Pepe Frias			
Ray Busse			
Mario Guerrero			
☐ 608 Rookie Pitchers	1.50	.75	.15
Steve Busby			
Dick Colpaert			
George Medich			
☐ 609 Rookie 2nd Basemen	3.00	1.50	.30
Larvell Blanks			
Pedro Garcia			
Dave Lopes			
☐ 610 Rookie Pitchers	2.00	1.00	.20
Jimmy Freeman			
Charlie Hough			
Hank Webb			
☐ 611 Rookie Outfielders	1.50	.75	.15
Rich Coggins			
Jim Wohlford			
Richie Zisk			
☐ 612 Rookie Pitchers	1.50	.75	.15
Steve Lawson			
Bob Reynolds			
Brent Strom			
☐ 613 Rookie Catchers	20.00	10.00	2.00
Bob Boone			
Skip Jutze			
Mike Ivie			
☐ 614 Rookie Outfielders	50.00	25.00	5.00
Alonza Bumbry			
Dwight Evans			
Charlie Spikes			
☐ 615 Rookie 3rd Basemen	325.00	160.00	32.00
Ron Cey			
John Hilton			
Mike Schmidt			
☐ 616 Rookie Pitchers	1.50	.75	.15
Norm Angelini			
Steve Blateric			
Mike Garman			
☐ 617 Rich Chiles	1.50	.75	.15
☐ 618 Andy Etchebarren	1.50	.75	.15
☐ 619 Billy Wilson	1.50	.75	.15
☐ 620 Tommy Harper	2.00	1.00	.20
☐ 621 Joe Ferguson	1.50	.75	.15
☐ 622 Larry Hisle	1.50	.75	.15
☐ 623 Steve Renko	1.50	.75	.15
☐ 624 Astros Leaders	2.50	1.25	.25
Leo Durocher MG			
Preston Gomez CO			
Grady Hatton CO			
Hub Kittle CO			
Jim Owens CO			
☐ 625 Angel Mangual	1.50	.75	.15
☐ 626 Bob Barton	1.50	.75	.15
☐ 627 Luis Alvarado	1.50	.75	.15
☐ 628 Jim Slaton	1.50	.75	.15
☐ 629 Indians Team	3.00	1.50	.30
☐ 630 Denny McLain	3.00	1.50	.30
☐ 631 Tom Matchick	1.50	.75	.15
☐ 632 Dick Selma	1.50	.75	.15
☐ 633 Ike Brown	1.50	.75	.15
☐ 634 Alan Closter	1.50	.75	.15
☐ 635 Gene Alley	1.50	.75	.15
☐ 636 Rickey Clark	1.50	.75	.15
☐ 637 Norm Miller	1.50	.75	.15
☐ 638 Ken Reynolds	1.50	.75	.15
☐ 639 Willie Crawford	1.50	.75	.15
☐ 640 Dick Bosman	1.50	.75	.15
☐ 641 Cincinnati Reds	3.00	1.50	.30
Team Card			
☐ 642 Jose LaBoy	1.50	.75	.15
☐ 643 Al Fitzmorris	1.50	.75	.15
☐ 644 Jack Heidemann	1.50	.75	.15
☐ 645 Bob Locker	1.50	.75	.15
☐ 646 Brewers Leaders	2.00	1.00	.20
Del Crandall MG			
Harvey Kuenn CO			
Joe Nossek CO			
Bob Shaw CO			
Jim Walton CO			
☐ 647 George Stone	1.50	.75	.15
☐ 648 Tom Egan	1.50	.75	.15
☐ 649 Rich Folkers	1.50	.75	.15
☐ 650 Felipe Alou	2.00	1.00	.20
☐ 651 Don Carrithers	1.50	.75	.15
☐ 652 Ted Kubiak	1.50	.75	.15

		NRMT	VG-E	GOOD
☐ 653	Joe Hoerner	1.50	.75	.15
☐ 654	Twins Team	3.00	1.50	.30
☐ 655	Clay Kirby	1.50	.75	.15
☐ 656	John Ellis	1.50	.75	.15
☐ 657	Bob Johnson	1.50	.75	.15
☐ 658	Elliott Maddox	1.50	.75	.15
☐ 659	Jose Pagan	1.50	.75	.15
☐ 660	Fred Scherman	2.50	1.25	.25

1974 Topps

The cards in this 660-card set measure 2 1/2" by 3 1/2". This year marked the first time Topps issued all the cards of its baseball set at the same time rather than in series. Some interesting variations were created by the rumored move of the San Diego Padres to Washington. Fifteen cards (13 players, the team card, and the rookie card #599) of the Padres were printed either as "San Diego" (SD) or "Washington." The latter are the scarcer variety and are denoted in the checklist below by WAS. Each team's manager and his coaches again have a combined card with small pictures of each coach below the larger photo of the team's manager. The first six cards in the set (1-6) feature Hank Aaron and his illustrious career. Other topical subsets included in the set are League Leaders (201-208), All-Star selections (331-339), Playoffs cards (470-471), World Series cards (472-479), and Rookie Prospects (596-608).

		NRMT	VG-E	GOOD
	COMPLETE SET (660)	450.00	200.00	40.00
	COMMON PLAYER (1-660)	.25	.12	.02
☐ 1	Hank Aaron	20.00	5.00	1.00
	Complete ML record			
☐ 2	Aaron Special 54-57	3.50	1.75	.35
	Records on back			
☐ 3	Aaron Special 58-61	3.50	1.75	.35
	Memorable homers			
☐ 4	Aaron Special 62-65	3.50	1.75	.35
	Life in ML's 1954-63			
☐ 5	Aaron Special 66-69	3.50	1.75	.35
	Life in ML's 1964-73			
☐ 6	Aaron Special 70-73	3.50	1.75	.35
	Milestone homers			
☐ 7	Jim Hunter	3.00	1.50	.30
☐ 8	George Theodore	.25	.12	.02
☐ 9	Mickey Lolich	.60	.30	.06
☐ 10	Johnny Bench	11.00	5.50	1.10
☐ 11	Jim Bibby	.25	.12	.02
☐ 12	Dave May	.25	.12	.02
☐ 13	Tom Hilgendorf	.25	.12	.02
☐ 14	Paul Popovich	.25	.12	.02
☐ 15	Joe Torre	.60	.30	.06
☐ 16	Baltimore Orioles	.60	.30	.06
	Team Card			
☐ 17	Doug Bird	.25	.12	.02
☐ 18	Gary Thomasson	.25	.12	.02
☐ 19	Gerry Moses	.25	.12	.02
☐ 20	Nolan Ryan	24.00	12.00	2.40
☐ 21	Bob Gallagher	.25	.12	.02
☐ 22	Cy Acosta	.25	.12	.02
☐ 23	Craig Robinson	.25	.12	.02

		NRMT	VG-E	GOOD
☐ 24	John Hiller	.40	.20	.04
☐ 25	Ken Singleton	.50	.25	.05
☐ 26	Bill Campbell	.25	.12	.02
☐ 27	George Scott	.40	.20	.04
☐ 28	Manny Sanguillen	.40	.20	.04
☐ 29	Phil Niekro	2.00	1.00	.20
☐ 30	Bobby Bonds	.60	.30	.06
☐ 31	Astros Leaders	.40	.20	.04
	Preston Gomez MG			
	Roger Craig CO			
	Hub Kittle CO			
	Grady Hatton CO			
	Bob Lillis CO			
☐ 32A	Johnny Grubb SD	.25	.12	.02
☐ 32B	Johnny Grubb WAS	4.00	2.00	.40
☐ 33	Don Newhauser	.25	.12	.02
☐ 34	Andy Kosco	.25	.12	.02
☐ 35	Gaylord Perry	2.25	1.10	.22
☐ 36	St. Louis Cardinals	.60	.30	.06
	Team Card			
☐ 37	Dave Sells	.25	.12	.02
☐ 38	Don Kessinger	.40	.20	.04
☐ 39	Ken Suarez	.25	.12	.02
☐ 40	Jim Palmer	5.00	2.50	.50
☐ 41	Bobby Floyd	.25	.12	.02
☐ 42	Claude Osteen	.25	.12	.02
☐ 43	Jim Wynn	.50	.25	.05
☐ 44	Mel Stottlemyre	.60	.30	.06
☐ 45	Dave Johnson	.60	.30	.06
☐ 46	Pat Kelly	.25	.12	.02
☐ 47	Dick Ruthven	.25	.12	.02
☐ 48	Dick Sharon	.25	.12	.02
☐ 49	Steve Renko	.25	.12	.02
☐ 50	Rod Carew	6.50	3.25	.65
☐ 51	Bobby Heise	.25	.12	.02
☐ 52	Al Oliver	.75	.35	.07
☐ 53A	Fred Kendall SD	.25	.12	.02
☐ 53B	Fred Kendall WAS	4.00	2.00	.40
☐ 54	Elias Sosa	.25	.12	.02
☐ 55	Frank Robinson	3.50	1.75	.35
☐ 56	New York Mets Team	.75	.35	.07
☐ 57	Darold Knowles	.25	.12	.02
☐ 58	Charlie Spikes	.25	.12	.02
☐ 59	Ross Grimsley	.25	.12	.02
☐ 60	Lou Brock	3.50	1.75	.35
☐ 61	Luis Aparicio	2.00	1.00	.20
☐ 62	Bob Locker	.25	.12	.02
☐ 63	Bill Sudakis	.25	.12	.02
☐ 64	Doug Rau	.25	.12	.02
☐ 65	Amos Otis	.50	.25	.05
☐ 66	Sparky Lyle	.50	.25	.05
☐ 67	Tommy Helms	.40	.20	.04
☐ 68	Grant Jackson	.25	.12	.02
☐ 69	Del Unser	.25	.12	.02
☐ 70	Dick Allen	.60	.30	.06
☐ 71	Dan Frisella	.25	.12	.02
☐ 72	Aurelio Rodriguez	.25	.12	.02
☐ 73	Mike Marshall	.40	.20	.04
☐ 74	Twins Team	.60	.30	.06
☐ 75	Jim Colborn	.25	.12	.02
☐ 76	Mickey Rivers	.40	.20	.04
☐ 77A	Rich Troedson SD	.25	.12	.02
☐ 77B	Rich Troedson WAS	4.00	2.00	.40
☐ 78	Giants Leaders	.40	.20	.04
	Charlie Fox MG			
	John McNamara CO			
	Joe Amalfitano CO			
	Andy Gilbert CO			
	Don McMahon CO			
☐ 79	Gene Tenace	.40	.20	.04
☐ 80	Tom Seaver	8.00	4.00	.80
☐ 81	Frank Duffy	.25	.12	.02
☐ 82	Dave Giusti	.25	.12	.02
☐ 83	Orlando Cepeda	1.00	.50	.10
☐ 84	Rick Wise	.25	.12	.02
☐ 85	Joe Morgan	3.50	1.75	.35
☐ 86	Joe Ferguson	.25	.12	.02
☐ 87	Fergie Jenkins	1.25	.60	.12
☐ 88	Freddie Patek	.25	.12	.02
☐ 89	Jackie Brown	.25	.12	.02
☐ 90	Bobby Murcer	.60	.30	.06
☐ 91	Ken Forsch	.25	.12	.02
☐ 92	Paul Blair	.25	.12	.02
☐ 93	Rod Gilbreath	.25	.12	.02
☐ 94	Tigers Team	.60	.30	.06
☐ 95	Steve Carlton	6.00	3.00	.60
☐ 96	Jerry Hairston	.25	.12	.02
☐ 97	Bob Bailey	.25	.12	.02
☐ 98	Bert Blyleven	2.00	1.00	.20
☐ 99	Brewers Leaders	.40	.20	.04
	Del Crandall MG			
	Harvey Kuenn CO			
	Joe Nossek CO			
	Jim Walton CO			
	Al Widmar CO			

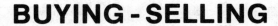

☐ 100	Willie Stargell	3.00	1.50	.30
☐ 101	Bobby Valentine	.50	.25	.05
☐ 102A	Bill Greif SD	.25	.12	.02
☐ 102B	Bill Greif WAS	4.00	2.00	.40
☐ 103	Sal Bando	.50	.25	.05
☐ 104	Ron Bryant	.25	.12	.02
☐ 105	Carlton Fisk	6.00	3.00	.60
☐ 106	Harry Parker	.25	.12	.02
☐ 107	Alex Johnson	.25	.12	.02
☐ 108	Al Hrabosky	.25	.12	.02
☐ 109	Bob Grich	.50	.25	.05
☐ 110	Billy Williams	2.75	1.35	.27
☐ 111	Clay Carroll	.25	.12	.02
☐ 112	Dave Lopes	.50	.25	.05
☐ 113	Dick Drago	.25	.12	.02
☐ 114	Angels Team	.60	.30	.06
☐ 115	Willie Horton	.40	.20	.04
☐ 116	Jerry Reuss	.40	.20	.04
☐ 117	Ron Blomberg	.25	.12	.02
☐ 118	Bill Lee	.25	.12	.02
☐ 119	Phillies Leaders	.40	.20	.04
	Danny Ozark MG			
	Ray Ripplemeyer CO			
	Bobby Wine CO			
	Carroll Beringer CO			
	Billy DeMars CO			
☐ 120	Wilbur Wood	.25	.12	.02
☐ 121	Larry Lintz	.25	.12	.02
☐ 122	Jim Holt	.25	.12	.02
☐ 123	Nelson Briles	.25	.12	.02
☐ 124	Bobby Coluccio	.25	.12	.02
☐ 125A	Nate Colbert SD	.25	.12	.02
☐ 125B	Nate Colbert WAS	4.00	2.00	.40
☐ 126	Checklist 1	1.25	.15	.03
☐ 127	Tom Paciorek	.25	.12	.02
☐ 128	John Ellis	.25	.12	.02
☐ 129	Chris Speier	.25	.12	.02
☐ 130	Reggie Jackson	11.00	5.50	1.10
☐ 131	Bob Boone	2.25	1.10	.22
☐ 132	Felix Millan	.25	.12	.02
☐ 133	David Clyde	.25	.12	.02
☐ 134	Denis Menke	.25	.12	.02
☐ 135	Roy White	.40	.20	.04
☐ 136	Rick Reuschel	1.75	.85	.17
☐ 137	Al Bumbry	.25	.12	.02
☐ 138	Eddie Brinkman	.25	.12	.02
☐ 139	Aurelio Monteagudo	.25	.12	.02
☐ 140	Darrell Evans	.60	.30	.06
☐ 141	Pat Bourque	.25	.12	.02
☐ 142	Pedro Garcia	.25	.12	.02
☐ 143	Dick Woodson	.25	.12	.02
☐ 144	Dodgers Leaders	1.00	.50	.10
	Walter Alston MG			
	Tom Lasorda CO			
	Jim Gilliam CO			
	Red Adams CO			
	Monty Basgall CO			
☐ 145	Dock Ellis	.25	.12	.02
☐ 146	Ron Fairly	.25	.12	.02
☐ 147	Bart Johnson	.25	.12	.02
☐ 148A	Dave Hilton SD	.25	.12	.02
☐ 148B	Dave Hilton WAS	4.00	2.00	.40
☐ 149	Mac Scarce	.25	.12	.02
☐ 150	John Mayberry	.40	.20	.04
☐ 151	Diego Segui	.25	.12	.02
☐ 152	Oscar Gamble	.40	.20	.04
☐ 153	Jon Matlack	.25	.12	.02
☐ 154	Astros Team	.60	.30	.06
☐ 155	Bert Campaneris	.40	.20	.04
☐ 156	Randy Moffitt	.25	.12	.02
☐ 157	Vic Harris	.25	.12	.02
☐ 158	Jack Billingham	.25	.12	.02
☐ 159	Jim Ray Hart	.25	.12	.02
☐ 160	Brooks Robinson	4.00	2.00	.40
☐ 161	Ray Burris	.50	.25	.05
☐ 162	Bill Freehan	.50	.25	.05
☐ 163	Ken Berry	.25	.12	.02
☐ 164	Tom House	.25	.12	.02
☐ 165	Willie Davis	.40	.20	.04
☐ 166	Royals Leaders	.40	.20	.04
	Jack McKeon MG			
	Charlie Lau CO			
	Harry Dunlop CO			
	Galen Cisco CO			
☐ 167	Luis Tiant	.60	.30	.06
☐ 168	Danny Thompson	.25	.12	.02
☐ 169	Steve Rogers	.50	.25	.05
☐ 170	Bill Melton	.25	.12	.02
☐ 171	Eduardo Rodriguez	.25	.12	.02
☐ 172	Gene Clines	.25	.12	.02
☐ 173A	Randy Jones SD	.60	.30	.06
☐ 173B	Randy Jones WAS	4.00	2.00	.40
☐ 174	Bill Robinson	.40	.20	.04
☐ 175	Reggie Cleveland	.25	.12	.02
☐ 176	John Lowenstein	.25	.12	.02
☐ 177	Dave Roberts	.25	.12	.02
☐ 178	Garry Maddox	.40	.20	.04
☐ 179	Mets Leaders	1.25	.60	.12
	Yogi Berra MG			
	Rube Walker CO			
	Eddie Yost CO			
	Roy McMillan CO			
	Joe Pignatano CO			
☐ 180	Ken Holtzman	.40	.20	.04
☐ 181	Cesar Geronimo	.25	.12	.02
☐ 182	Lindy McDaniel	.25	.12	.02
☐ 183	Johnny Oates	.25	.12	.02
☐ 184	Texas Rangers	.60	.30	.06
	Team Card			
☐ 185	Jose Cardenal	.25	.12	.02
☐ 186	Fred Scherman	.25	.12	.02
☐ 187	Don Baylor	1.00	.50	.10
☐ 188	Rudy Meoli	.25	.12	.02
☐ 189	Jim Brewer	.25	.12	.02
☐ 190	Tony Oliva	1.00	.50	.10
☐ 191	Al Fitzmorris	.25	.12	.02
☐ 192	Mario Guerrero	.25	.12	.02
☐ 193	Tom Walker	.25	.12	.02
☐ 194	Darrell Porter	.25	.12	.02
☐ 195	Carlos May	.25	.12	.02
☐ 196	Jim Fregosi	.40	.20	.04
☐ 197A	Vicente Romo SD	.25	.12	.02
☐ 197B	Vicente Romo WAS	4.00	2.00	.40
☐ 198	Dave Cash	.25	.12	.02
☐ 199	Mike Kekich	.25	.12	.02
☐ 200	Cesar Cedeno	.40	.20	.04
☐ 201	Batting Leaders	3.50	1.75	.35
	Rod Carew			
	Pete Rose			
☐ 202	Home Run Leaders	2.00	1.00	.20
	Reggie Jackson			
	Willie Stargell			
☐ 203	RBI Leaders	2.00	1.00	.20
	Reggie Jackson			
	Willie Stargell			
☐ 204	Stolen Base Leaders	.75	.35	.07
	Tommy Harper			
	Lou Brock			
☐ 205	Victory Leaders	.60	.30	.06
	Wilbur Wood			
	Ron Bryant			
☐ 206	ERA Leaders	2.50	1.25	.25
	Jim Palmer			
	Tom Seaver			
☐ 207	Strikeout Leaders	3.00	1.50	.30
	Nolan Ryan			
	Tom Seaver			
☐ 208	Leading Firemen	.60	.30	.06
	John Hiller			
	Mike Marshall			
☐ 209	Ted Sizemore	.25	.12	.02
☐ 210	Bill Singer	.25	.12	.02
☐ 211	Chicago Cubs Team	.60	.30	.06
☐ 212	Rollie Fingers	2.25	1.10	.22
☐ 213	Dave Rader	.25	.12	.02
☐ 214	Billy Grabarkewitz	.25	.12	.02
☐ 215	Al Kaline	4.50	2.25	.45
☐ 216	Ray Sadecki	.25	.12	.02
☐ 217	Tim Foli	.25	.12	.02
☐ 218	Johnny Briggs	.25	.12	.02
☐ 219	Doug Griffin	.25	.12	.02
☐ 220	Don Sutton	2.00	1.00	.20
☐ 221	White Sox Leaders	.40	.20	.04
	Chuck Tanner MG			
	Jim Mahoney CO			
	Alex Monchak CO			
	Johnny Sain CO			
	Joe Lonnett CO			
☐ 222	Ramon Hernandez	.25	.12	.02
☐ 223	Jeff Burroughs	.50	.25	.05
☐ 224	Roger Metzger	.25	.12	.02
☐ 225	Paul Splittorff	.25	.12	.02
☐ 226A	Padres Team SD	1.00	.50	.10
☐ 226B	Padres Team WAS	5.00	2.50	.50
☐ 227	Mike Lum	.25	.12	.02
☐ 228	Ted Kubiak	.25	.12	.02
☐ 229	Fritz Peterson	.25	.12	.02
☐ 230	Tony Perez	1.50	.75	.15
☐ 231	Dick Tidrow	.25	.12	.02
☐ 232	Steve Brye	.25	.12	.02
☐ 233	Jim Barr	.25	.12	.02
☐ 234	John Milner	.25	.12	.02
☐ 235	Dave McNally	.40	.20	.04
☐ 236	Cardinals Leaders	.60	.30	.06
	Red Schoendienst MG			
	Barney Schultz CO			
	George Kissell CO			
	Johnny Lewis CO			
	Vern Benson CO			
☐ 237	Ken Brett	.25	.12	.02

☐ 238	Fran Healy HOR (Munson sliding in background)	.40	.20	.04
☐ 239	Bill Russell	.40	.20	.04
☐ 240	Joe Coleman	.25	.12	.02
☐ 241A	Glenn Beckert SD	.40	.20	.04
☐ 241B	Glenn Beckert WAS	4.00	2.00	.40
☐ 242	Bill Gogolewski	.25	.12	.02
☐ 243	Bob Oliver	.25	.12	.02
☐ 244	Carl Morton	.25	.12	.02
☐ 245	Cleon Jones	.25	.12	.02
☐ 246	Athletics Team	.60	.30	.06
☐ 247	Rick Miller	.25	.12	.02
☐ 248	Tom Hall	.25	.12	.02
☐ 249	George Mitterwald	.25	.12	.02
☐ 250A	Willie McCovey SD	4.00	2.00	.40
☐ 250B	Willie McCovey WAS	25.00	12.50	2.50
☐ 251	Graig Nettles	1.50	.75	.15
☐ 252	Dave Parker	25.00	12.50	2.50
☐ 253	John Boccabella	.25	.12	.02
☐ 254	Stan Bahnsen	.25	.12	.02
☐ 255	Larry Bowa	.60	.30	.06
☐ 256	Tom Griffin	.25	.12	.02
☐ 257	Buddy Bell	1.00	.50	.10
☐ 258	Jerry Morales	.25	.12	.02
☐ 259	Bob Reynolds	.25	.12	.02
☐ 260	Ted Simmons	1.00	.50	.10
☐ 261	Jerry Bell	.25	.12	.02
☐ 262	Ed Kirkpatrick	.25	.12	.02
☐ 263	Checklist 2	1.25	.15	.03
☐ 264	Joe Rudi	.40	.20	.04
☐ 265	Tug McGraw	.60	.30	.06
☐ 266	Jim Northrup	.40	.20	.04
☐ 267	Andy Messersmith	.40	.20	.04
☐ 268	Tom Grieve	.40	.20	.04
☐ 269	Bob Johnson	.25	.12	.02
☐ 270	Ron Santo	.60	.30	.06
☐ 271	Bill Hands	.25	.12	.02
☐ 272	Paul Casanova	.25	.12	.02
☐ 273	Checklist 3	1.25	.15	.03
☐ 274	Fred Beene	.25	.12	.02
☐ 275	Ron Hunt	.25	.12	.02
☐ 276	Angels Leaders Bobby Winkles MG John Roseboro CO Tom Morgan CO Jimmie Reese CO Salty Parker CO	.40	.20	.04
☐ 277	Gary Nolan	.25	.12	.02
☐ 278	Cookie Rojas	.25	.12	.02
☐ 279	Jim Crawford	.25	.12	.02
☐ 280	Carl Yastrzemski	11.00	5.50	1.10
☐ 281	Giants Team	.60	.30	.06
☐ 282	Doyle Alexander	.50	.25	.05
☐ 283	Mike Schmidt	65.00	32.50	6.50
☐ 284	Dave Duncan	.25	.12	.02
☐ 285	Reggie Smith	.50	.25	.05
☐ 286	Tony Muser	.25	.12	.02
☐ 287	Clay Kirby	.25	.12	.02
☐ 288	Gorman Thomas	1.75	.85	.17
☐ 289	Rick Auerbach	.25	.12	.02
☐ 290	Vida Blue	.50	.25	.05
☐ 291	Don Hahn	.25	.12	.02
☐ 292	Chuck Seelbach	.25	.12	.02
☐ 293	Milt May	.25	.12	.02
☐ 294	Steve Foucault	.25	.12	.02
☐ 295	Rick Monday	.40	.20	.04
☐ 296	Ray Corbin	.25	.12	.02
☐ 297	Hal Breeden	.25	.12	.02
☐ 298	Roric Harrison	.25	.12	.02
☐ 299	Gene Michael	.40	.20	.04
☐ 300	Pete Rose	16.00	8.00	1.60
☐ 301	Bob Montgomery	.25	.12	.02
☐ 302	Rudy May	.25	.12	.02
☐ 303	George Hendrick	.40	.20	.04
☐ 304	Don Wilson	.25	.12	.02
☐ 305	Tito Fuentes	.25	.12	.02
☐ 306	Orioles Leaders Earl Weaver MG Jim Frey CO George Bamberger CO Billy Hunter CO George Staller CO	.75	.35	.07
☐ 307	Luis Melendez	.25	.12	.02
☐ 308	Bruce Dal Canton	.25	.12	.02
☐ 309A	Dave Roberts SD	.25	.12	.02
☐ 309B	Dave Roberts WAS	5.00	2.50	.50
☐ 310	Terry Forster	.40	.20	.04
☐ 311	Jerry Grote	.25	.12	.02
☐ 312	Deron Johnson	.25	.12	.02
☐ 313	Barry Lersch	.25	.12	.02
☐ 314	Milwaukee Brewers Team Card	.60	.30	.06
☐ 315	Ron Cey	1.00	.50	.10
☐ 316	Jim Perry	.40	.20	.04
☐ 317	Richie Zisk	.25	.12	.02
☐ 318	Jim Merritt	.25	.12	.02
☐ 319	Randy Hundley	.25	.12	.02
☐ 320	Dusty Baker	.50	.25	.05
☐ 321	Steve Braun	.25	.12	.02
☐ 322	Ernie McAnally	.25	.12	.02
☐ 323	Richie Scheinblum	.25	.12	.02
☐ 324	Steve Kline	.25	.12	.02
☐ 325	Tommy Harper	.40	.20	.04
☐ 326	Reds Leaders Sparky Anderson MG Larry Shephard CO George Scherger CO Alex Grammas CO Ted Kluszewski CO	.75	.35	.07
☐ 327	Tom Timmermann	.25	.12	.02
☐ 328	Skip Jutze	.25	.12	.02
☐ 329	Mark Belanger	.40	.20	.04
☐ 330	Juan Marichal	2.50	1.25	.25
☐ 331	All-Star Catchers Carlton Fisk Johnny Bench	2.00	1.00	.20
☐ 332	All-Star 1B Dick Allen Hank Aaron	1.75	.85	.17
☐ 333	All-Star 2B Rod Carew Joe Morgan	2.00	1.00	.20
☐ 334	All-Star 3B Brooks Robinson Ron Santo	1.00	.50	.10
☐ 335	All-Star SS Bert Campaneris Chris Speier	.40	.20	.04
☐ 336	All-Star LF Bobby Murcer Pete Rose	2.50	1.25	.25
☐ 337	All-Star CF Amos Otis Cesar Cedeno	.40	.20	.04
☐ 338	All-Star RF Reggie Jackson Billy Williams	2.50	1.25	.25
☐ 339	All-Star Pitchers Jim Hunter Rick Wise	.50	.25	.05
☐ 340	Thurman Munson	5.00	2.50	.50
☐ 341	Dan Driessen	.75	.35	.07
☐ 342	Jim Lonborg	.40	.20	.04
☐ 343	Royals Team	.60	.30	.06
☐ 344	Mike Caldwell	.40	.20	.04
☐ 345	Bill North	.25	.12	.02
☐ 346	Ron Reed	.25	.12	.02
☐ 347	Sandy Alomar	.25	.12	.02
☐ 348	Pete Richert	.25	.12	.02
☐ 349	John Vukovich	.25	.12	.02
☐ 350	Bob Gibson	3.00	1.50	.30
☐ 351	Dwight Evans	7.50	3.75	.75
☐ 352	Bill Stoneman	.25	.12	.02
☐ 353	Rich Coggins	.25	.12	.02
☐ 354	Cubs Leaders Whitey Lockman MG J.C. Martin CO Hank Aguirre CO Al Spangler CO Jim Marshall CO	.40	.20	.04
☐ 355	Dave Nelson	.25	.12	.02
☐ 356	Jerry Koosman	.60	.30	.06
☐ 357	Buddy Bradford	.25	.12	.02
☐ 358	Dal Maxvill	.25	.12	.02
☐ 359	Brent Strom	.25	.12	.02
☐ 360	Greg Luzinski	.75	.35	.07
☐ 361	Don Carrithers	.25	.12	.02
☐ 362	Hal King	.25	.12	.02
☐ 363	Yankees Team	.60	.30	.06
☐ 364A	Cito Gaston SD	.50	.25	.05
☐ 364B	Cito Gaston WAS	5.00	2.50	.50
☐ 365	Steve Busby	.40	.20	.04
☐ 366	Larry Hisle	.40	.20	.04
☐ 367	Norm Cash	.75	.35	.07
☐ 368	Manny Mota	.40	.20	.04
☐ 369	Paul Lindblad	.25	.12	.02
☐ 370	Bob Watson	.40	.20	.04
☐ 371	Jim Slaton	.25	.12	.02
☐ 372	Ken Reitz	.25	.12	.02
☐ 373	John Curtis	.25	.12	.02
☐ 374	Marty Perez	.25	.12	.02
☐ 375	Earl Williams	.25	.12	.02
☐ 376	Jorge Orta	.25	.12	.02
☐ 377	Ron Woods	.25	.12	.02
☐ 378	Burt Hooton	.40	.20	.04
☐ 379	Rangers Leaders Billy Martin MG Frank Lucchesi CO Art Fowler CO	1.00	.50	.10

	Charlie Silvera CO			
	Jackie Moore CO			
☐ 380	Bud Harrelson	.40	.20	.04
☐ 381	Charlie Sands	.25	.12	.02
☐ 382	Bob Moose	.25	.12	.02
☐ 383	Phillies Team	.60	.30	.06
☐ 384	Chris Chambliss	.50	.25	.05
☐ 385	Don Gullett	.40	.20	.04
☐ 386	Gary Matthews	.50	.25	.05
☐ 387A	Rich Morales SD	.25	.12	.02
☐ 387B	Rich Morales WAS	5.00	2.50	.50
☐ 388	Phil Roof	.25	.12	.02
☐ 389	Gates Brown	.40	.20	.04
☐ 390	Lou Piniella	.60	.30	.06
☐ 391	Billy Champion	.25	.12	.02
☐ 392	Dick Green	.25	.12	.02
☐ 393	Orlando Pena	.25	.12	.02
☐ 394	Ken Henderson	.25	.12	.02
☐ 395	Doug Rader	.40	.20	.04
☐ 396	Tommy Davis	.40	.20	.04
☐ 397	George Stone	.25	.12	.02
☐ 398	Duke Sims	.25	.12	.02
☐ 399	Mike Paul	.25	.12	.02
☐ 400	Harmon Killebrew	3.00	1.50	.30
☐ 401	Elliott Maddox	.25	.12	.02
☐ 402	Jim Rooker	.25	.12	.02
☐ 403	Red Sox Leaders	.40	.20	.04
	Darrell Johnson MG			
	Eddie Popowski CO			
	Lee Stange CO			
	Don Zimmer CO			
	Don Bryant CO			
☐ 404	Jim Howarth	.25	.12	.02
☐ 405	Ellie Rodriguez	.25	.12	.02
☐ 406	Steve Arlin	.25	.12	.02
☐ 407	Jim Wohlford	.25	.12	.02
☐ 408	Charlie Hough	.50	.25	.05
☐ 409	Ike Brown	.25	.12	.02
☐ 410	Pedro Borbon	.25	.12	.02
☐ 411	Frank Baker	.25	.12	.02
☐ 412	Chuck Taylor	.25	.12	.02
☐ 413	Don Money	.25	.12	.02
☐ 414	Checklist 4	1.25	.15	.03
☐ 415	Gary Gentry	.25	.12	.02
☐ 416	White Sox Team	.60	.30	.06
☐ 417	Rich Folkers	.25	.12	.02
☐ 418	Walt Williams	.25	.12	.02
☐ 419	Wayne Twitchell	.25	.12	.02
☐ 420	Ray Fosse	.25	.12	.02
☐ 421	Dan Fife	.25	.12	.02
☐ 422	Gonzalo Marquez	.25	.12	.02
☐ 423	Fred Stanley	.25	.12	.02
☐ 424	Jim Beauchamp	.25	.12	.02
☐ 425	Pete Broberg	.25	.12	.02
☐ 426	Rennie Stennett	.25	.12	.02
☐ 427	Bobby Bolin	.25	.12	.02
☐ 428	Gary Sutherland	.25	.12	.02
☐ 429	Dick Lange	.25	.12	.02
☐ 430	Matty Alou	.40	.20	.04
☐ 431	Gene Garber	.40	.20	.04
☐ 432	Chris Arnold	.25	.12	.02
☐ 433	Lerrin LaGrow	.25	.12	.02
☐ 434	Ken McMullen	.25	.12	.02
☐ 435	Dave Concepcion	.75	.35	.07
☐ 436	Don Hood	.25	.12	.02
☐ 437	Jim Lyttle	.25	.12	.02
☐ 438	Ed Herrmann	.25	.12	.02
☐ 439	Norm Miller	.25	.12	.02
☐ 440	Jim Kaat	1.00	.50	.10
☐ 441	Tom Ragland	.25	.12	.02
☐ 442	Alan Foster	.25	.12	.02
☐ 443	Tom Hutton	.25	.12	.02
☐ 444	Vic Davalillo	.25	.12	.02
☐ 445	George Medich	.25	.12	.02
☐ 446	Len Randle	.25	.12	.02
☐ 447	Twins Leaders	.40	.20	.04
	Frank Quilici MG			
	Ralph Rowe CO			
	Bob Rodgers CO			
	Vern Morgan CO			
☐ 448	Ron Hodges	.25	.12	.02
☐ 449	Tom McCraw	.25	.12	.02
☐ 450	Rich Hebner	.25	.12	.02
☐ 451	Tommy John	1.50	.75	.15
☐ 452	Gene Hiser	.25	.12	.02
☐ 453	Balor Moore	.25	.12	.02
☐ 454	Kurt Bevacqua	.25	.12	.02
☐ 455	Tom Bradley	.25	.12	.02
☐ 456	Dave Winfield	40.00	20.00	4.00
☐ 457	Chuck Goggin	.25	.12	.02
☐ 458	Jim Ray	.25	.12	.02
☐ 459	Cincinnati Reds	.60	.30	.06
	Team Card			
☐ 460	Boog Powell	.60	.30	.06
☐ 461	John Odom	.25	.12	.02

☐ 462	Luis Alvarado	.25	.12	.02
☐ 463	Pat Dobson	.25	.12	.02
☐ 464	Jose Cruz	.50	.25	.05
☐ 465	Dick Bosman	.25	.12	.02
☐ 466	Dick Billings	.25	.12	.02
☐ 467	Winston Llenas	.25	.12	.02
☐ 468	Pepe Frias	.25	.12	.02
☐ 469	Joe Decker	.25	.12	.02
☐ 470	AL Playoffs	2.50	1.25	.25
	A's over Orioles			
	(Reggie Jackson)			
☐ 471	NL Playoffs	.75	.35	.07
	Mets over Reds			
	(Matlack pitching)			
☐ 472	World Series Game 1	.75	.35	.07
	(Knowles pitching)			
☐ 473	World Series Game 2	2.50	1.25	.25
	(Willie Mays batting)			
☐ 474	World Series Game 3	.75	.35	.07
	(Campaneris stealing)			
☐ 475	World Series Game 4	.75	.35	.07
	(Staub batting)			
☐ 476	World Series Game 5	.75	.35	.07
	Cleon Jones scoring)			
☐ 477	World Series Game 6	2.50	1.25	.25
	(Reggie Jackson)			
☐ 478	World Series Game 7	.75	.35	.07
	(Campaneris batting)			
☐ 479	World Series Summary	.75	.35	.07
	A's celebrate; win			
	2nd consecutive			
	championship			
☐ 480	Willie Crawford	.25	.12	.02
☐ 481	Jerry Terrell	.25	.12	.02
☐ 482	Bob Didier	.25	.12	.02
☐ 483	Atlanta Braves	.60	.30	.06
	Team Card			
☐ 484	Carmen Fanzone	.25	.12	.02
☐ 485	Felipe Alou	.40	.20	.04
☐ 486	Steve Stone	.40	.20	.04
☐ 487	Ted Martinez	.25	.12	.02
☐ 488	Andy Etchebarren	.25	.12	.02
☐ 489	Pirates Leaders	.40	.20	.04
	Danny Murtaugh MG			
	Don Osborn CO			
	Don Leppert CO			
	Bill Mazeroski CO			
	Bob Skinner CO			
☐ 490	Vada Pinson	.60	.30	.06
☐ 491	Roger Nelson	.25	.12	.02
☐ 492	Mike Rogodzinski	.25	.12	.02
☐ 493	Joe Hoerner	.25	.12	.02
☐ 494	Ed Goodson	.25	.12	.02
☐ 495	Dick McAuliffe	.25	.12	.02
☐ 496	Tom Murphy	.25	.12	.02
☐ 497	Bobby Mitchell	.25	.12	.02
☐ 498	Pat Corrales	.40	.20	.04
☐ 499	Rusty Torres	.25	.12	.02
☐ 500	Lee May	.40	.20	.04
☐ 501	Eddie Leon	.25	.12	.02
☐ 502	Dave LaRoche	.25	.12	.02
☐ 503	Eric Soderholm	.25	.12	.02
☐ 504	Joe Niekro	.50	.25	.05
☐ 505	Bill Buckner	.60	.30	.06
☐ 506	Ed Farmer	.25	.12	.02
☐ 507	Larry Stahl	.25	.12	.02
☐ 508	Expos Team	.60	.30	.06
☐ 509	Jesse Jefferson	.25	.12	.02
☐ 510	Wayne Garrett	.25	.12	.02
☐ 511	Toby Harrah	.40	.20	.04
☐ 512	Joe Lahoud	.25	.12	.02
☐ 513	Jim Campanis	.25	.12	.02
☐ 514	Paul Schaal	.25	.12	.02
☐ 515	Willie Montanez	.25	.12	.02
☐ 516	Horacio Pina	.25	.12	.02
☐ 517	Mike Hegan	.25	.12	.02
☐ 518	Derrel Thomas	.25	.12	.02
☐ 519	Bill Sharp	.25	.12	.02
☐ 520	Tim McCarver	.60	.30	.06
☐ 521	Indians Leaders	.40	.20	.04
	Ken Aspromonte MG			
	Clay Bryant CO			
	Tony Pacheco CO			
☐ 522	J.R. Richard	.50	.25	.05
☐ 523	Cecil Cooper	1.75	.85	.17
☐ 524	Bill Plummer	.25	.12	.02
☐ 525	Clyde Wright	.25	.12	.02
☐ 526	Frank Tepedino	.25	.12	.02
☐ 527	Bobby Darwin	.25	.12	.02
☐ 528	Bill Bonham	.25	.12	.02
☐ 529	Horace Clarke	.25	.12	.02
☐ 530	Mickey Stanley	.40	.20	.04
☐ 531	Expos Leaders	.40	.20	.04
	Gene Mauch MG			
	Dave Bristol CO			

Cal McLish CO
Larry Doby CO
Jerry Zimmerman CO

☐ 532	Skip Lockwood	.25	.12	.02
☐ 533	Mike Phillips	.25	.12	.02
☐ 534	Eddie Watt	.25	.12	.02
☐ 535	Bob Tolan	.25	.12	.02
☐ 536	Duffy Dyer	.25	.12	.02
☐ 537	Steve Mingori	.25	.12	.02
☐ 538	Cesar Tovar	.25	.12	.02
☐ 539	Lloyd Allen	.25	.12	.02
☐ 540	Bob Robertson	.25	.12	.02
☐ 541	Cleveland Indians Team Card	.60	.30	.06
☐ 542	Rich Gossage	1.75	.85	.17
☐ 543	Danny Cater	.25	.12	.02
☐ 544	Ron Schueler	.25	.12	.02
☐ 545	Billy Conigliaro	.25	.12	.02
☐ 546	Mike Corkins	.25	.12	.02
☐ 547	Glenn Borgmann	.25	.12	.02
☐ 548	Sonny Siebert	.25	.12	.02
☐ 549	Mike Jorgensen	.25	.12	.02
☐ 550	Sam McDowell	.40	.20	.04
☐ 551	Von Joshua	.25	.12	.02
☐ 552	Denny Doyle	.25	.12	.02
☐ 553	Jim Willoughby	.25	.12	.02
☐ 554	Tim Johnson	.25	.12	.02
☐ 555	Woodie Fryman	.25	.12	.02
☐ 556	Dave Campbell	.25	.12	.02
☐ 557	Jim McGlothlin	.25	.12	.02
☐ 558	Bill Fahey	.25	.12	.02
☐ 559	Darrell Chaney	.25	.12	.02
☐ 560	Mike Cuellar	.40	.20	.04
☐ 561	Ed Kranepool	.40	.20	.04
☐ 562	Jack Aker	.25	.12	.02
☐ 563	Hal McRae	.40	.20	.04
☐ 564	Mike Ryan	.25	.12	.02
☐ 565	Milt Wilcox	.25	.12	.02
☐ 566	Jackie Hernandez	.25	.12	.02
☐ 567	Red Sox Team	.60	.30	.06
☐ 568	Mike Torrez	.40	.20	.04
☐ 569	Rick Dempsey	.40	.20	.04
☐ 570	Ralph Garr	.40	.20	.04
☐ 571	Rich Hand	.25	.12	.02
☐ 572	Enzo Hernandez	.25	.12	.02
☐ 573	Mike Adams	.25	.12	.02
☐ 574	Bill Parsons	.25	.12	.02
☐ 575	Steve Garvey	11.00	5.50	1.10
☐ 576	Scipio Spinks	.25	.12	.02
☐ 577	Mike Sadek	.25	.12	.02
☐ 578	Ralph Houk MG	.40	.20	.04
☐ 579	Cecil Upshaw	.25	.12	.02
☐ 580	Jim Spencer	.25	.12	.02
☐ 581	Fred Norman	.25	.12	.02
☐ 582	Bucky Dent	1.50	.75	.15
☐ 583	Marty Pattin	.25	.12	.02
☐ 584	Ken Rudolph	.25	.12	.02
☐ 585	Merv Rettenmund	.25	.12	.02
☐ 586	Jack Brohamer	.25	.12	.02
☐ 587	Larry Christenson	.25	.12	.02
☐ 588	Hal Lanier	.40	.20	.04
☐ 589	Boots Day	.25	.12	.02
☐ 590	Roger Moret	.25	.12	.02
☐ 591	Sonny Jackson	.25	.12	.02
☐ 592	Ed Bane	.25	.12	.02
☐ 593	Steve Yeager	.40	.20	.04
☐ 594	Leroy Stanton	.25	.12	.02
☐ 595	Steve Blass	.40	.20	.04
☐ 596	Rookie Pitchers	.40	.20	.04
	Wayne Garland			
	Fred Holdsworth			
	Mark Littell			
	Dick Pole			
☐ 597	Rookie Shortstops	.60	.30	.06
	Dave Chalk			
	John Gamble			
	Pete MacKanin			
	Manny Trillo			
☐ 598	Rookie Outfielders	4.50	2.25	.45
	Dave Augustine			
	Ken Griffey			
	Steve Ontiveros			
	Jim Tyrone			
☐ 599A	Rookie Pitchers WAS	.60	.30	.06
	Ron Diorio			
	Dave Freisleben			
	Frank Riccelli			
	Greg Shanahan			
☐ 599B	Rookie Pitchers SD (SD in large print)	3.00	1.50	.30
☐ 599C	Rookie Pitchers SD (SD in small print)	4.50	2.25	.45
☐ 600	Rookie Infielders	5.00	2.50	.50
	Ron Cash			
	Jim Cox			

Bill Madlock
Reggie Sanders

☐ 601	Rookie Outfielders	2.50	1.25	.25
	Ed Armbrister			
	Rich Bladt			
	Brian Downing			
	Bake McBride			
☐ 602	Rookie Pitchers	.50	.25	.05
	Glen Abbott			
	Rick Henninger			
	Craig Swan			
	Dan Vossler			
☐ 603	Rookie Catchers	.50	.25	.05
	Barry Foote			
	Tom Lundstedt			
	Charlie Moore			
	Sergio Robles			
☐ 604	Rookie Infielders	3.50	1.75	.35
	Terry Hughes			
	John Knox			
	Andy Thornton			
	Frank White			
☐ 605	Rookie Pitchers	2.00	1.00	.20
	Vic Albury			
	Ken Frailing			
	Kevin Kobel			
	Frank Tanana			
☐ 606	Rookie Outfielders	.40	.20	.04
	Jim Fuller			
	Wilbur Howard			
	Tommy Smith			
	Otto Velez			
☐ 607	Rookie Shortstops	.40	.20	.04
	Leo Foster			
	Tom Heintzelman			
	Dave Rosello			
	Frank Taveras			
☐ 608A	Rookie Pitchers: ERR	...	1.00	.20
	Bob Apodaco (sic)			
	Dick Baney			
	John D'Acquisto			
	Mike Wallace			
☐ 608B	Rookie Pitchers: COR	.40	.20	.04
	Bob Apodaca			
	Dick Baney			
	John D'Acquisto			
	Mike Wallace			
☐ 609	Rico Petrocelli	.40	.20	.04
☐ 610	Dave Kingman	1.00	.50	.10
☐ 611	Rich Stelmaszek	.25	.12	.02
☐ 612	Luke Walker	.25	.12	.02
☐ 613	Dan Monzon	.25	.12	.02
☐ 614	Adrian Devine	.25	.12	.02
☐ 615	Johnny Jeter	.25	.12	.02
☐ 616	Larry Gura	.40	.20	.04
☐ 617	Ted Ford	.25	.12	.02
☐ 618	Jim Mason	.25	.12	.02
☐ 619	Mike Anderson	.25	.12	.02
☐ 620	Al Downing	.40	.20	.04
☐ 621	Bernie Carbo	.25	.12	.02
☐ 622	Phil Gagliano	.25	.12	.02
☐ 623	Celerino Sanchez	.25	.12	.02
☐ 624	Bob Miller	.25	.12	.02
☐ 625	Ollie Brown	.25	.12	.02
☐ 626	Pittsburgh Pirates Team Card	.60	.30	.06
☐ 627	Carl Taylor	.25	.12	.02
☐ 628	Ivan Murrell	.25	.12	.02
☐ 629	Rusty Staub	.60	.30	.06
☐ 630	Tommy Agee	.40	.20	.04
☐ 631	Steve Barber	.25	.12	.02
☐ 632	George Culver	.25	.12	.02
☐ 633	Dave Hamilton	.25	.12	.02
☐ 634	Braves Leaders	1.00	.50	.10
	Eddie Mathews MG			
	Herm Starrette CO			
	Connie Ryan CO			
	Jim Busby CO			
	Ken Silvestri CO			
☐ 635	Johnny Edwards	.25	.12	.02
☐ 636	Dave Goltz	.25	.12	.02
☐ 637	Checklist 5	1.25	.15	.03
☐ 638	Ken Sanders	.25	.12	.02
☐ 639	Joe Lovitto	.25	.12	.02
☐ 640	Milt Pappas	.40	.20	.04
☐ 641	Chuck Brinkman	.25	.12	.02
☐ 642	Terry Harmon	.25	.12	.02
☐ 643	Dodgers Team	.75	.35	.07
☐ 644	Wayne Granger	.25	.12	.02
☐ 645	Ken Boswell	.25	.12	.02
☐ 646	George Foster	1.25	.60	.12
☐ 647	Juan Beniquez	.60	.30	.06
☐ 648	Terry Crowley	.25	.12	.02
☐ 649	Fernando Gonzalez	.25	.12	.02
☐ 650	Mike Epstein	.25	.12	.02

		NRMT	VG-E	GOOD
☐ 651	Leron Lee	.25	.12	.02
☐ 652	Gail Hopkins	.25	.12	.02
☐ 653	Bob Stinson	.25	.12	.02
☐ 654A	Jesus Alou ERR (no position)	6.00	3.00	.60
☐ 654B	Jesus Alou COR (outfield)	.40	.20	.04
☐ 655	Mike Tyson	.25	.12	.02
☐ 656	Adrian Garrett	.25	.12	.02
☐ 657	Jim Shellenback	.25	.12	.02
☐ 658	Lee Lacy	.25	.12	.02
☐ 659	Joe Lis	.25	.12	.02
☐ 660	Larry Dierker	.50	.25	.05

1974 Topps Traded

The cards in this 44-card set measure 2 1/2" by 3 1/2". The 1974 Topps Traded set contains 43 player cards and one unnumbered checklist card. The obverses have the word "traded" in block letters and the backs are designed in newspaper style. Card numbers are the same as in the regular set except they are followed by a "T." No known scarcities exist for this set.

		NRMT	VG-E	GOOD
COMPLETE SET (44)		7.00	3.25	.65
COMMON PLAYER		.12	.06	.01
☐ 23T	Craig Robinson	.12	.06	.01
☐ 42T	Claude Osteen	.20	.10	.02
☐ 43T	Jim Wynn	.20	.10	.02
☐ 51T	Bobby Heise	.12	.06	.01
☐ 59T	Ross Grimsley	.12	.06	.01
☐ 62T	Bob Locker	.12	.06	.01
☐ 63T	Bill Sudakis	.12	.06	.01
☐ 73T	Mike Marshall	.30	.15	.03
☐ 123T	Nelson Briles	.20	.10	.02
☐ 139T	Aurelio Monteagudo	.12	.06	.01
☐ 151T	Diego Segui	.12	.06	.01
☐ 165T	Willie Davis	.25	.12	.02
☐ 175T	Reggie Cleveland	.12	.06	.01
☐ 182T	Lindy McDaniel	.20	.10	.02
☐ 186T	Fred Scherman	.12	.06	.01
☐ 249T	George Mitterwald	.12	.06	.01
☐ 262T	Ed Kirkpatrick	.12	.06	.01
☐ 269T	Bob Johnson	.12	.06	.01
☐ 270T	Ron Santo	.40	.20	.04
☐ 313T	Barry Lersch	.12	.06	.01
☐ 319T	Randy Hundley	.20	.10	.02
☐ 330T	Juan Marichal	1.50	.75	.15
☐ 348T	Pete Richert	.12	.06	.01
☐ 373T	John Curtis	.12	.06	.01
☐ 390T	Lou Piniella	.35	.17	.03
☐ 428T	Gary Sutherland	.12	.06	.01
☐ 454T	Kurt Bevacqua	.12	.06	.01
☐ 458T	Jim Ray	.12	.06	.01
☐ 485T	Felipe Alou	.20	.10	.02
☐ 486T	Steve Stone	.20	.10	.02
☐ 496T	Tom Murphy	.12	.06	.01
☐ 516T	Horacio Pina	.12	.06	.01
☐ 534T	Eddie Watt	.12	.06	.01
☐ 538T	Cesar Tovar	.12	.06	.01
☐ 544T	Ron Schueler	.12	.06	.01
☐ 579T	Cecil Upshaw	.12	.06	.01
☐ 585T	Merv Rettenmund	.12	.06	.01
☐ 612T	Luke Walker	.12	.06	.01
☐ 616T	Larry Gura	.20	.10	.02

		NRMT	VG-E	GOOD
☐ 618T	Jim Mason	.12	.06	.01
☐ 630T	Tommie Agee	.15	.07	.01
☐ 648T	Terry Crowley	.12	.06	.01
☐ 649T	Fernando Gonzalez	.12	.06	.01
☐ xxxT	Traded Checklist (unnumbered)	.50	.25	.05

1975 Topps

The cards in the 1975 Topps set were issued in two different sizes: a regular standard size (2 1/2" by 3 1/2") and a mini size (2 1/2" by 3 1/8") which was issued as a test in certain areas of the country. The 660-card Topps baseball set for 1975 was radically different in appearance from sets of the preceding years. The most prominent change was the use of a two-color frame surrounding the picture area rather than a single, subdued color. A facsimile autograph appears on the picture, and the backs are printed in red and green on gray. Cards 189-212 depict the MVP's of both leagues from 1951 through 1974. The first seven cards (1-7) feature players breaking records or achieving milestones during the previous season. Cards 306-313 picture league leaders in various statistical categories. Cards 459-466 depict the results of post-season action. Team cards feature a checklist back for players on that team and show a small inset photo of the manager on the front. The Phillies Team card #46 erroneously lists Terry Harmon as #339 instead of #399. This set is quite popular with collectors, at least in part due to the fact that the rookie cards of Robin Yount, George Brett, Jim Rice, Gary Carter, Fred Lynn, and Keith Hernandez are all in the set. Topps minis have the same checklist and are worth approximately double the prices listed below.

		NRMT	VG-E	GOOD
COMPLETE SET (660)		650.00	300.00	65.00
COMMON PLAYER (1-132)		.25	.12	.02
COMMON PLAYER (133-660)		.25	.12	.02
☐ 1	RB: Hank Aaron Sets Homer Mark	15.00	4.00	.75
☐ 2	RB: Lou Brock 118 Stolen Bases	2.25	1.10	.22
☐ 3	RB: Bob Gibson 3000th Strikeout	2.25	1.10	.22
☐ 4	RB: Al Kaline 3000 Hit Club	2.25	1.10	.22
☐ 5	RB: Nolan Ryan Fans 300 for 3rd Year in a Row	4.50	2.25	.45
☐ 6	RB: Mike Marshall Hurls 106 Games	.50	.25	.05
☐ 7	No Hitters Steve Busby Dick Bosman Nolan Ryan	1.00	.50	.10
☐ 8	Rogelio Moret	.25	.12	.02
☐ 9	Frank Tepedino	.25	.12	.02
☐ 10	Willie Davis	.40	.20	.04

☐ 11	Bill Melton	.25	.12	.02
☐ 12	David Clyde	.25	.12	.02
☐ 13	Gene Locklear	.25	.12	.02
☐ 14	Milt Wilcox	.25	.12	.02
☐ 15	Jose Cardenal	.25	.12	.02
☐ 16	Frank Tanana	.60	.30	.06
☐ 17	Dave Concepcion	.60	.30	.06
☐ 18	Tigers: Team/Mgr.	.75	.35	.07
	Ralph Houk			
	(checklist back)			
☐ 19	Jerry Koosman	.60	.30	.06
☐ 20	Thurman Munson	4.00	2.00	.40
☐ 21	Rollie Fingers	1.75	.85	.17
☐ 22	Dave Cash	.25	.12	.02
☐ 23	Bill Russell	.40	.20	.04
☐ 24	Al Fitzmorris	.25	.12	.02
☐ 25	Lee May	.40	.20	.04
☐ 26	Dave McNally	.40	.20	.04
☐ 27	Ken Reitz	.25	.12	.02
☐ 28	Tom Murphy	.25	.12	.02
☐ 29	Dave Parker	8.00	4.00	.80
☐ 30	Bert Blyleven	1.75	.85	.17
☐ 31	Dave Rader	.25	.12	.02
☐ 32	Reggie Cleveland	.25	.12	.02
☐ 33	Dusty Baker	.40	.20	.04
☐ 34	Steve Renko	.25	.12	.02
☐ 35	Ron Santo	.50	.25	.05
☐ 36	Joe Lovitto	.25	.12	.02
☐ 37	Dave Freisleben	.25	.12	.02
☐ 38	Buddy Bell	.75	.35	.07
☐ 39	Andre Thornton	.50	.25	.05
☐ 40	Bill Singer	.25	.12	.02
☐ 41	Cesar Geronimo	.25	.12	.02
☐ 42	Joe Coleman	.25	.12	.02
☐ 43	Cleon Jones	.25	.12	.02
☐ 44	Pat Dobson	.25	.12	.02
☐ 45	Joe Rudi	.40	.20	.04
☐ 46	Phillies: Team/Mgr.	.75	.35	.07
	Danny Ozark			
	(checklist back)			
☐ 47	Tommy John	1.25	.60	.12
☐ 48	Freddie Patek	.25	.12	.02
☐ 49	Larry Dierker	.25	.12	.02
☐ 50	Brooks Robinson	3.50	1.75	.35
☐ 51	Bob Forsch	1.00	.50	.10
☐ 52	Darrell Porter	.25	.12	.02
☐ 53	Dave Giusti	.25	.12	.02
☐ 54	Eric Soderholm	.25	.12	.02
☐ 55	Bobby Bonds	.50	.25	.05
☐ 56	Rick Wise	.25	.12	.02
☐ 57	Dave Johnson	.50	.25	.05
☐ 58	Chuck Taylor	.25	.12	.02
☐ 59	Ken Henderson	.25	.12	.02
☐ 60	Fergie Jenkins	1.25	.60	.12
☐ 61	Dave Winfield	12.00	6.00	1.20
☐ 62	Fritz Peterson	.25	.12	.02
☐ 63	Steve Swisher	.25	.12	.02
☐ 64	Dave Chalk	.25	.12	.02
☐ 65	Don Gullett	.40	.20	.04
☐ 66	Willie Horton	.40	.20	.04
☐ 67	Tug McGraw	.50	.25	.05
☐ 68	Ron Blomberg	.25	.12	.02
☐ 69	John Odom	.25	.12	.02
☐ 70	Mike Schmidt	36.00	18.00	3.60
☐ 71	Charlie Hough	.50	.25	.05
☐ 72	Royals: Team/Mgr.	.75	.35	.07
	Jack McKeon			
	(checklist back)			
☐ 73	J.R. Richard	.40	.20	.04
☐ 74	Mark Belanger	.40	.20	.04
☐ 75	Ted Simmons	.75	.35	.07
☐ 76	Ed Sprague	.25	.12	.02
☐ 77	Richie Zisk	.25	.12	.02
☐ 78	Ray Corbin	.25	.12	.02
☐ 79	Gary Matthews	.40	.20	.04
☐ 80	Carlton Fisk	4.00	2.00	.40
☐ 81	Ron Reed	.25	.12	.02
☐ 82	Pat Kelly	.25	.12	.02
☐ 83	Jim Merritt	.25	.12	.02
☐ 84	Enzo Hernandez	.25	.12	.02
☐ 85	Bill Bonham	.25	.12	.02
☐ 86	Joe Lis	.25	.12	.02
☐ 87	George Foster	1.25	.60	.12
☐ 88	Tom Egan	.25	.12	.02
☐ 89	Jim Ray	.25	.12	.02
☐ 90	Rusty Staub	.50	.25	.05
☐ 91	Dick Green	.25	.12	.02
☐ 92	Cecil Upshaw	.25	.12	.02
☐ 93	Dave Lopes	.50	.25	.05
☐ 94	Jim Lonborg	.40	.20	.04
☐ 95	John Mayberry	.40	.20	.04
☐ 96	Mike Cosgrove	.25	.12	.02
☐ 97	Earl Williams	.25	.12	.02
☐ 98	Rich Folkers	.25	.12	.02
☐ 99	Mike Hegan	.25	.12	.02
☐ 100	Willie Stargell	3.00	1.50	.30
☐ 101	Expos: Team/Mgr.	.75	.35	.07
	Gene Mauch			
	(checklist back)			
☐ 102	Joe Decker	.25	.12	.02
☐ 103	Rick Miller	.25	.12	.02
☐ 104	Bill Madlock	1.25	.60	.12
☐ 105	Buzz Capra	.25	.12	.02
☐ 106	Mike Hargrove	.75	.35	.07
☐ 107	Jim Barr	.25	.12	.02
☐ 108	Tom Hall	.25	.12	.02
☐ 109	George Hendrick	.40	.20	.04
☐ 110	Wilbur Wood	.25	.12	.02
☐ 111	Wayne Garrett	.25	.12	.02
☐ 112	Larry Hardy	.25	.12	.02
☐ 113	Elliott Maddox	.25	.12	.02
☐ 114	Dick Lange	.25	.12	.02
☐ 115	Joe Ferguson	.25	.12	.02
☐ 116	Lerrin LaGrow	.25	.12	.02
☐ 117	Orioles: Team/Mgr.	.75	.35	.07
	Earl Weaver			
	(checklist back)			
☐ 118	Mike Anderson	.25	.12	.02
☐ 119	Tommy Helms	.40	.20	.04
☐ 120	Steve Busby	.25	.12	.02
	(photo actually			
	Fran Healy)			
☐ 121	Bill North	.25	.12	.02
☐ 122	Al Hrabosky	.25	.12	.02
☐ 123	Johnny Briggs	.25	.12	.02
☐ 124	Jerry Reuss	.40	.20	.04
☐ 125	Ken Singleton	.40	.20	.04
☐ 126	Checklist 1-132	1.00	.10	.02
☐ 127	Glenn Borgmann	.25	.12	.02
☐ 128	Bill Lee	.40	.20	.04
☐ 129	Rick Monday	.40	.20	.04
☐ 130	Phil Niekro	2.25	1.10	.22
☐ 131	Toby Harrah	.40	.20	.04
☐ 132	Randy Moffitt	.25	.12	.02
☐ 133	Dan Driessen	.40	.20	.04
☐ 134	Ron Hodges	.25	.12	.02
☐ 135	Charlie Spikes	.25	.12	.02
☐ 136	Jim Mason	.25	.12	.02
☐ 137	Terry Forster	.40	.20	.04
☐ 138	Del Unser	.25	.12	.02
☐ 139	Horacio Pina	.25	.12	.02
☐ 140	Steve Garvey	6.50	3.25	.65
☐ 141	Mickey Stanley	.40	.20	.04
☐ 142	Bob Reynolds	.25	.12	.02
☐ 143	Cliff Johnson	.25	.12	.02
☐ 144	Jim Wohlford	.25	.12	.02
☐ 145	Ken Holtzman	.40	.20	.04
☐ 146	Padres: Team/Mgr.	.75	.35	.07
	John McNamara			
	(checklist back)			
☐ 147	Pedro Garcia	.25	.12	.02
☐ 148	Jim Rooker	.25	.12	.02
☐ 149	Tim Foli	.25	.12	.02
☐ 150	Bob Gibson	3.00	1.50	.30
☐ 151	Steve Brye	.25	.12	.02
☐ 152	Mario Guerrero	.25	.12	.02
☐ 153	Rick Reuschel	.75	.35	.07
☐ 154	Mike Lum	.25	.12	.02
☐ 155	Jim Bibby	.40	.20	.04
☐ 156	Dave Kingman	1.00	.50	.10
☐ 157	Pedro Borbon	.25	.12	.02
☐ 158	Jerry Grote	.25	.12	.02
☐ 159	Steve Arlin	.25	.12	.02
☐ 160	Graig Nettles	1.25	.60	.12
☐ 161	Stan Bahnsen	.25	.12	.02
☐ 162	Willie Montanez	.25	.12	.02
☐ 163	Jim Brewer	.25	.12	.02
☐ 164	Mickey Rivers	.40	.20	.04
☐ 165	Doug Rader	.40	.20	.04
☐ 166	Woodie Fryman	.25	.12	.02
☐ 167	Rich Coggins	.25	.12	.02
☐ 168	Bill Greif	.25	.12	.02
☐ 169	Cookie Rojas	.25	.12	.02
☐ 170	Bert Campaneris	.40	.20	.04
☐ 171	Ed Kirkpatrick	.25	.12	.02
☐ 172	Red Sox: Team/Mgr.	.75	.35	.07
	Darrell Johnson			
	(checklist back)			
☐ 173	Steve Rogers	.40	.20	.04
☐ 174	Bake McBride	.40	.20	.04
☐ 175	Don Money	.25	.12	.02
☐ 176	Burt Hooton	.25	.12	.02
☐ 177	Vic Correll	.25	.12	.02
☐ 178	Cesar Tovar	.25	.12	.02
☐ 179	Tom Bradley	.25	.12	.02
☐ 180	Joe Morgan	5.00	2.50	.50
☐ 181	Fred Beene	.25	.12	.02
☐ 182	Don Hahn	.25	.12	.02
☐ 183	Mel Stottlemyre	.50	.25	.05
☐ 184	Jorge Orta	.25	.12	.02

☐ 185	Steve Carlton	5.50	2.75	.55
☐ 186	Willie Crawford	.25	.12	.02
☐ 187	Denny Doyle	.25	.12	.02
☐ 188	Tom Griffin	.25	.12	.02
☐ 189	1951 MVP's	1.50	.75	.15
	Larry (Yogi) Berra			
	Roy Campanella			
	(Campy never issued)			
☐ 190	1952 MVP's	.50	.25	.05
	Bobby Shantz			
	Hank Sauer			
☐ 191	1953 MVP's	.75	.35	.07
	Al Rosen			
	Roy Campanella			
☐ 192	1954 MVP's	1.50	.75	.15
	Yogi Berra			
	Willie Mays			
☐ 193	1955 MVP's	1.50	.75	.15
	Yogi Berra			
	Roy Campanella			
	(Campy never issued)			
☐ 194	1956 MVP's	4.00	2.00	.40
	Mickey Mantle			
	Don Newcombe			
☐ 195	1957 MVP's	5.00	2.50	.50
	Mickey Mantle			
	Hank Aaron			
☐ 196	1958 MVP's	.60	.30	.06
	Jackie Jensen			
	Ernie Banks			
☐ 197	1959 MVP's	.60	.30	.06
	Nellie Fox			
	Ernie Banks			
☐ 198	1960 MVP's	.75	.35	.07
	Roger Maris			
	Dick Groat			
☐ 199	1961 MVP's	1.00	.50	.10
	Roger Maris			
	Frank Robinson			
☐ 200	1962 MVP's	4.00	2.00	.40
	Mickey Mantle			
	Maury Wills			
	(Wills never issued)			
☐ 201	1963 MVP's	.75	.35	.07
	Elston Howard			
	Sandy Koufax			
☐ 202	1964 MVP's	.60	.30	.06
	Brooks Robinson			
	Ken Boyer			
☐ 203	1965 MVP's	.75	.35	.07
	Zoilo Versalles			
	Willie Mays			
☐ 204	1966 MVP's	1.00	.50	.10
	Frank Robinson			
	Bob Clemente			
☐ 205	1967 MVP's	1.00	.50	.10
	Carl Yastrzemski			
	Orlando Cepeda			
☐ 206	1968 MVP's	.60	.30	.06
	Denny McLain			
	Bob Gibson			
☐ 207	1969 MVP's	.75	.35	.07
	Harmon Killebrew			
	Willie McCovey			
☐ 208	1970 MVP's	.75	.35	.07
	Boog Powell			
	Johnny Bench			
☐ 209	1971 MVP's	.50	.25	.05
	Vida Blue			
	Joe Torre			
☐ 210	1972 MVP's	.75	.35	.07
	Rich Allen			
	Johnny Bench			
☐ 211	1973 MVP's	3.00	1.50	.30
	Reggie Jackson			
	Pete Rose			
☐ 212	1974 MVP's	.60	.30	.06
	Jeff Burroughs			
	Steve Garvey			
☐ 213	Oscar Gamble	.40	.20	.04
☐ 214	Harry Parker	.25	.12	.02
☐ 215	Bobby Valentine	.50	.25	.05
☐ 216	Giants: Team/Mgr.	.75	.35	.07
	Wes Westrum			
	(checklist back)			
☐ 217	Lou Piniella	.60	.30	.06
☐ 218	Jerry Johnson	.25	.12	.02
☐ 219	Ed Herrmann	.25	.12	.02
☐ 220	Don Sutton	2.00	1.00	.20
☐ 221	Aurelio Rodriguez	.25	.12	.02
☐ 222	Dan Spillner	.25	.12	.02
☐ 223	Robin Yount	110.00	55.00	11.00
☐ 224	Ramon Hernandez	.25	.12	.02
☐ 225	Bob Grich	.40	.20	.04
☐ 226	Bill Campbell	.25	.12	.02
☐ 227	Bob Watson	.40	.20	.04
☐ 228	George Brett	90.00	45.00	9.00
☐ 229	Barry Foote	.25	.12	.02
☐ 230	Jim Hunter	2.25	1.10	.22
☐ 231	Mike Tyson	.25	.12	.02
☐ 232	Diego Segui	.25	.12	.02
☐ 233	Billy Grabarkewitz	.25	.12	.02
☐ 234	Tom Grieve	.40	.20	.04
☐ 235	Jack Billingham	.25	.12	.02
☐ 236	Angels: Team/Mgr.	.75	.35	.07
	Dick Williams			
	(checklist back)			
☐ 237	Carl Morton	.25	.12	.02
☐ 238	Dave Duncan	.25	.12	.02
☐ 239	George Stone	.25	.12	.02
☐ 240	Garry Maddox	.40	.20	.04
☐ 241	Dick Tidrow	.25	.12	.02
☐ 242	Jay Johnstone	.40	.20	.04
☐ 243	Jim Kaat	1.00	.50	.10
☐ 244	Bill Buckner	.50	.25	.05
☐ 245	Mickey Lolich	.50	.25	.05
☐ 246	Cardinals: Team/Mgr.	.75	.35	.07
	Red Schoendienst			
	(checklist back)			
☐ 247	Enos Cabell	.25	.12	.02
☐ 248	Randy Jones	.40	.20	.04
☐ 249	Danny Thompson	.25	.12	.02
☐ 250	Ken Brett	.25	.12	.02
☐ 251	Fran Healy	.25	.12	.02
☐ 252	Fred Scherman	.25	.12	.02
☐ 253	Jesus Alou	.25	.12	.02
☐ 254	Mike Torrez	.25	.12	.02
☐ 255	Dwight Evans	3.00	1.50	.30
☐ 256	Billy Champion	.25	.12	.02
☐ 257	Checklist: 133-264	1.00	.10	.02
☐ 258	Dave LaRoche	.25	.12	.02
☐ 259	Len Randle	.25	.12	.02
☐ 260	Johnny Bench	8.50	4.25	.85
☐ 261	Andy Hassler	.25	.12	.02
☐ 262	Rowland Office	.25	.12	.02
☐ 263	Jim Perry	.40	.20	.04
☐ 264	John Milner	.25	.12	.02
☐ 265	Ron Bryant	.25	.12	.02
☐ 266	Sandy Alomar	.25	.12	.02
☐ 267	Dick Ruthven	.25	.12	.02
☐ 268	Hal McRae	.40	.20	.04
☐ 269	Doug Rau	.25	.12	.02
☐ 270	Ron Fairly	.25	.12	.02
☐ 271	Gerry Moses	.25	.12	.02
☐ 272	Lynn McGlothen	.25	.12	.02
☐ 273	Steve Braun	.25	.12	.02
☐ 274	Vicente Romo	.25	.12	.02
☐ 275	Paul Blair	.25	.12	.02
☐ 276	White Sox Team/Mgr.	.75	.35	.07
	Chuck Tanner			
	(checklist back)			
☐ 277	Frank Taveras	.25	.12	.02
☐ 278	Paul Lindblad	.25	.12	.02
☐ 279	Milt May	.25	.12	.02
☐ 280	Carl Yastrzemski	8.50	4.25	.85
☐ 281	Jim Slaton	.25	.12	.02
☐ 282	Jerry Morales	.25	.12	.02
☐ 283	Steve Foucault	.25	.12	.02
☐ 284	Ken Griffey	.75	.35	.07
☐ 285	Ellie Rodriguez	.25	.12	.02
☐ 286	Mike Jorgensen	.25	.12	.02
☐ 287	Roric Harrison	.25	.12	.02
☐ 288	Bruce Ellingsen	.25	.12	.02
☐ 289	Ken Rudolph	.25	.12	.02
☐ 290	Jon Matlack	.40	.20	.04
☐ 291	Bill Sudakis	.25	.12	.02
☐ 292	Ron Schueler	.25	.12	.02
☐ 293	Dick Sharon	.25	.12	.02
☐ 294	Geoff Zahn	.25	.12	.02
☐ 295	Vada Pinson	.50	.25	.05
☐ 296	Alan Foster	.25	.12	.02
☐ 297	Craig Kusick	.25	.12	.02
☐ 298	Johnny Grubb	.25	.12	.02
☐ 299	Bucky Dent	.75	.35	.07
☐ 300	Reggie Jackson	10.00	5.00	1.00
☐ 301	Dave Roberts	.25	.12	.02
☐ 302	Rick Burleson	.50	.25	.05
☐ 303	Grant Jackson	.25	.12	.02
☐ 304	Pirates: Team/Mgr.	.75	.35	.07
	Danny Murtaugh			
	(checklist back)			
☐ 305	Jim Colborn	.25	.12	.02
☐ 306	Batting Leaders	.75	.35	.07
	Rod Carew			
	Ralph Garr			
☐ 307	Home Run Leaders	1.00	.50	.10
	Dick Allen			
	Mike Schmidt			
☐ 308	RBI Leaders	.75	.35	.07
	Jeff Burroughs			

	Johnny Bench			
☐ 309	Stolen Base Leaders	.75	.35	.07
	Bill North			
	Lou Brock			
☐ 310	Victory Leaders	.75	.35	.07
	Jim Hunter			
	Fergie Jenkins			
	Andy Messersmith			
	Phil Niekro			
☐ 311	ERA Leaders	.75	.35	.07
	Jim Hunter			
	Buzz Capra			
☐ 312	Strikeout Leaders	3.00	1.50	.30
	Nolan Ryan			
	Steve Carlton			
☐ 313	Leading Firemen	.60	.30	.06
	Terry Forster			
	Mike Marshall			
☐ 314	Buck Martinez	.25	.12	.02
☐ 315	Don Kessinger	.40	.20	.04
☐ 316	Jackie Brown	.25	.12	.02
☐ 317	Joe Lahoud	.25	.12	.02
☐ 318	Ernie McAnally	.25	.12	.02
☐ 319	Johnny Oates	.25	.12	.02
☐ 320	Pete Rose	15.00	7.50	1.50
☐ 321	Rudy May	.25	.12	.02
☐ 322	Ed Goodson	.25	.12	.02
☐ 323	Fred Holdsworth	.25	.12	.02
☐ 324	Ed Kranepool	.40	.20	.04
☐ 325	Tony Oliva	.75	.35	.07
☐ 326	Wayne Twitchell	.25	.12	.02
☐ 327	Jerry Hairston	.25	.12	.02
☐ 328	Sonny Siebert	.25	.12	.02
☐ 329	Ted Kubiak	.25	.12	.02
☐ 330	Mike Marshall	.40	.20	.04
☐ 331	Indians: Team/Mgr.	.75	.35	.07
	Frank Robinson			
	(checklist back)			
☐ 332	Fred Kendall	.25	.12	.02
☐ 333	Dick Drago	.25	.12	.02
☐ 334	Greg Gross	.25	.12	.02
☐ 335	Jim Palmer	4.50	2.25	.45
☐ 336	Rennie Stennett	.25	.12	.02
☐ 337	Kevin Kobel	.25	.12	.02
☐ 338	Rich Stelmaszek	.25	.12	.02
☐ 339	Jim Fregosi	.40	.20	.04
☐ 340	Paul Splittorff	.25	.12	.02
☐ 341	Hal Breeden	.25	.12	.02
☐ 342	Leroy Stanton	.25	.12	.02
☐ 343	Danny Frisella	.25	.12	.02
☐ 344	Ben Oglivie	.40	.20	.04
☐ 345	Clay Carroll	.25	.12	.02
☐ 346	Bobby Darwin	.25	.12	.02
☐ 347	Mike Caldwell	.25	.12	.02
☐ 348	Tony Muser	.25	.12	.02
☐ 349	Ray Sadecki	.25	.12	.02
☐ 350	Bobby Murcer	.50	.25	.05
☐ 351	Bob Boone	1.00	.50	.10
☐ 352	Darold Knowles	.25	.12	.02
☐ 353	Luis Melendez	.25	.12	.02
☐ 354	Dick Bosman	.25	.12	.02
☐ 355	Chris Cannizzaro	.25	.12	.02
☐ 356	Rico Petrocelli	.40	.20	.04
☐ 357	Ken Forsch	.25	.12	.02
☐ 358	Al Bumbry	.25	.12	.02
☐ 359	Paul Popovich	.25	.12	.02
☐ 360	George Scott	.40	.20	.04
☐ 361	Dodgers: Team/Mgr.	1.00	.50	.10
	Walter Alston			
	(checklist back)			
☐ 362	Steve Hargan	.25	.12	.02
☐ 363	Carmen Fanzone	.25	.12	.02
☐ 364	Doug Bird	.25	.12	.02
☐ 365	Bob Bailey	.25	.12	.02
☐ 366	Ken Sanders	.25	.12	.02
☐ 367	Craig Robinson	.25	.12	.02
☐ 368	Vic Albury	.25	.12	.02
☐ 369	Merv Rettenmund	.25	.12	.02
☐ 370	Tom Seaver	7.00	3.50	.70
☐ 371	Gates Brown	.40	.20	.04
☐ 372	John D'Acquisto	.25	.12	.02
☐ 373	Bill Sharp	.25	.12	.02
☐ 374	Eddie Watt	.25	.12	.02
☐ 375	Roy White	.40	.20	.04
☐ 376	Steve Yeager	.40	.20	.04
☐ 377	Tom Hilgendorf	.25	.12	.02
☐ 378	Derrel Thomas	.25	.12	.02
☐ 379	Bernie Carbo	.25	.12	.02
☐ 380	Sal Bando	.40	.20	.04
☐ 381	John Curtis	.25	.12	.02
☐ 382	Don Baylor	.75	.35	.07
☐ 383	Jim York	.25	.12	.02
☐ 384	Brewers: Team/Mgr.	.75	.35	.07
	Del Crandall			
	(checklist back)			

☐ 385	Dock Ellis	.25	.12	.02
☐ 386	Checklist: 265-396	1.00	.10	.02
☐ 387	Jim Spencer	.25	.12	.02
☐ 388	Steve Stone	.40	.20	.04
☐ 389	Tony Solaita	.25	.12	.02
☐ 390	Ron Cey	.60	.30	.06
☐ 391	Don DeMola	.25	.12	.02
☐ 392	Bruce Bochte	.40	.20	.04
☐ 393	Gary Gentry	.25	.12	.02
☐ 394	Larvell Blanks	.25	.12	.02
☐ 395	Bud Harrelson	.40	.20	.04
☐ 396	Fred Norman	.25	.12	.02
☐ 397	Bill Freehan	.50	.25	.05
☐ 398	Elias Sosa	.25	.12	.02
☐ 399	Terry Harmon	.25	.12	.02
☐ 400	Dick Allen	.50	.25	.05
☐ 401	Mike Wallace	.25	.12	.02
☐ 402	Bob Tolan	.25	.12	.02
☐ 403	Tom Buskey	.25	.12	.02
☐ 404	Ted Sizemore	.25	.12	.02
☐ 405	John Montague	.25	.12	.02
☐ 406	Bob Gallagher	.25	.12	.02
☐ 407	Herb Washington	.25	.12	.02
☐ 408	Clyde Wright	.25	.12	.02
☐ 409	Bob Robertson	.25	.12	.02
☐ 410	Mike Cueller	.40	.20	.04
	(sic, Cuellar)			
☐ 411	George Mitterwald	.25	.12	.02
☐ 412	Bill Hands	.25	.12	.02
☐ 413	Marty Pattin	.25	.12	.02
☐ 414	Manny Mota	.40	.20	.04
☐ 415	John Hiller	.40	.20	.04
☐ 416	Larry Lintz	.25	.12	.02
☐ 417	Skip Lockwood	.25	.12	.02
☐ 418	Leo Foster	.25	.12	.02
☐ 419	Dave Goltz	.25	.12	.02
☐ 420	Larry Bowa	.50	.25	.05
☐ 421	Mets: Team/Mgr.	1.00	.50	.10
	Yogi Berra			
	(checklist back)			
☐ 422	Brian Downing	.50	.25	.05
☐ 423	Clay Kirby	.25	.12	.02
☐ 424	John Lowenstein	.25	.12	.02
☐ 425	Tito Fuentes	.25	.12	.02
☐ 426	George Medich	.25	.12	.02
☐ 427	Clarence Gaston	.50	.25	.05
☐ 428	Dave Hamilton	.25	.12	.02
☐ 429	Jim Dwyer	.25	.12	.02
☐ 430	Luis Tiant	.50	.25	.05
☐ 431	Rod Gilbreath	.25	.12	.02
☐ 432	Ken Berry	.25	.12	.02
☐ 433	Larry Demery	.25	.12	.02
☐ 434	Bob Locker	.25	.12	.02
☐ 435	Dave Nelson	.25	.12	.02
☐ 436	Ken Frailing	.25	.12	.02
☐ 437	Al Cowens	.40	.20	.04
☐ 438	Don Carrithers	.25	.12	.02
☐ 439	Ed Brinkman	.25	.12	.02
☐ 440	Andy Messersmith	.40	.20	.04
☐ 441	Bobby Heise	.25	.12	.02
☐ 442	Maximino Leon	.25	.12	.02
☐ 443	Twins: Team/Mgr.	.75	.35	.07
	Frank Quilici			
	(checklist back)			
☐ 444	Gene Garber	.25	.12	.02
☐ 445	Felix Millan	.25	.12	.02
☐ 446	Bart Johnson	.25	.12	.02
☐ 447	Terry Crowley	.25	.12	.02
☐ 448	Frank Duffy	.25	.12	.02
☐ 449	Charlie Williams	.25	.12	.02
☐ 450	Willie McCovey	3.00	1.50	.30
☐ 451	Rick Dempsey	.40	.20	.04
☐ 452	Angel Mangual	.25	.12	.02
☐ 453	Claude Osteen	.40	.20	.04
☐ 454	Doug Griffin	.25	.12	.02
☐ 455	Don Wilson	.25	.12	.02
☐ 456	Bob Coluccio	.25	.12	.02
☐ 457	Mario Mendoza	.25	.12	.02
☐ 458	Ross Grimsley	.25	.12	.02
☐ 459	1974 AL Champs	.60	.30	.06
	A's over Orioles			
	(2B action pictured)			
☐ 460	1974 NL Champs	.75	.35	.07
	Dodgers over Pirates			
	(Taveras/Garvey at 2B)			
☐ 461	World Series Game 1	2.00	1.00	.20
	(Reggie Jackson)			
☐ 462	World Series Game 2	.60	.30	.06
	(Dodger dugout)			
☐ 463	World Series Game 3	.75	.35	.07
	(Fingers pitching)			
☐ 464	World Series Game 4	.60	.30	.06
	(A's batter)			
☐ 465	World Series Game 5	.60	.30	.06
	(Rudi rounding third)			

☐ 466	World Series Summary .. A's do it again; win third straight (A's group picture)	.60	.30	.06
☐ 467	Ed Halicki	.25	.12	.02
☐ 468	Bobby Mitchell	.25	.12	.02
☐ 469	Tom Dettore	.25	.12	.02
☐ 470	Jeff Burroughs	.40	.20	.04
☐ 471	Bob Stinson	.25	.12	.02
☐ 472	Bruce Dal Canton	.25	.12	.02
☐ 473	Ken McMullen	.25	.12	.02
☐ 474	Luke Walker	.25	.12	.02
☐ 475	Darrell Evans	.60	.30	.06
☐ 476	Ed Figueroa	.25	.12	.02
☐ 477	Tom Hutton	.25	.12	.02
☐ 478	Tom Burgmeier	.25	.12	.02
☐ 479	Ken Boswell	.25	.12	.02
☐ 480	Carlos May	.25	.12	.02
☐ 481	Will McEnaney	.25	.12	.02
☐ 482	Tom McCraw	.25	.12	.02
☐ 483	Steve Ontiveros	.25	.12	.02
☐ 484	Glenn Beckert	.40	.20	.04
☐ 485	Sparky Lyle	.50	.25	.05
☐ 486	Ray Fosse	.25	.12	.02
☐ 487	Astros: Team/Mgr. Preston Gomez (checklist back)	.75	.35	.07
☐ 488	Bill Travers	.25	.12	.02
☐ 489	Cecil Cooper	1.00	.50	.10
☐ 490	Reggie Smith	.50	.25	.05
☐ 491	Doyle Alexander	.50	.25	.05
☐ 492	Rich Hebner	.25	.12	.02
☐ 493	Don Stanhouse	.25	.12	.02
☐ 494	Pete LaCock	.25	.12	.02
☐ 495	Nelson Briles	.25	.12	.02
☐ 496	Pepe Frias	.25	.12	.02
☐ 497	Jim Nettles	.25	.12	.02
☐ 498	Al Downing	.25	.12	.02
☐ 499	Marty Perez	.25	.12	.02
☐ 500	Nolan Ryan	22.00	11.00	2.20
☐ 501	Bill Robinson	.40	.20	.04
☐ 502	Pat Bourque	.25	.12	.02
☐ 503	Fred Stanley	.25	.12	.02
☐ 504	Buddy Bradford	.25	.12	.02
☐ 505	Chris Speier	.25	.12	.02
☐ 506	Leron Lee	.25	.12	.02
☐ 507	Tom Carroll	.25	.12	.02
☐ 508	Bob Hansen	.25	.12	.02
☐ 509	Dave Hilton	.25	.12	.02
☐ 510	Vida Blue	.50	.25	.05
☐ 511	Rangers: Team/Mgr. Billy Martin (checklist back)	1.00	.50	.10
☐ 512	Larry Milbourne	.25	.12	.02
☐ 513	Dick Pole	.25	.12	.02
☐ 514	Jose Cruz	.40	.20	.04
☐ 515	Manny Sanguillen	.40	.20	.04
☐ 516	Don Hood	.25	.12	.02
☐ 517	Checklist: 397-528	1.00	.10	.02
☐ 518	Leo Cardenas	.25	.12	.02
☐ 519	Jim Todd	.25	.12	.02
☐ 520	Amos Otis	.40	.20	.04
☐ 521	Dennis Blair	.25	.12	.02
☐ 522	Gary Sutherland	.25	.12	.02
☐ 523	Tom Paciorek	.25	.12	.02
☐ 524	John Doherty	.25	.12	.02
☐ 525	Tom House	.25	.12	.02
☐ 526	Larry Hisle	.25	.12	.02
☐ 527	Mac Scarce	.25	.12	.02
☐ 528	Eddie Leon	.25	.12	.02
☐ 529	Gary Thomasson	.25	.12	.02
☐ 530	Gaylord Perry	2.25	1.10	.22
☐ 531	Reds: Team/Mgr. Sparky Anderson (checklist back)	1.00	.50	.10
☐ 532	Gorman Thomas	.60	.30	.06
☐ 533	Rudy Meoli	.25	.12	.02
☐ 534	Alex Johnson	.25	.12	.02
☐ 535	Gene Tenace	.40	.20	.04
☐ 536	Bob Moose	.25	.12	.02
☐ 537	Tommy Harper	.40	.20	.04
☐ 538	Duffy Dyer	.25	.12	.02
☐ 539	Jesse Jefferson	.25	.12	.02
☐ 540	Lou Brock	3.00	1.50	.30
☐ 541	Roger Metzger	.25	.12	.02
☐ 542	Pete Broberg	.25	.12	.02
☐ 543	Larry Biittner	.25	.12	.02
☐ 544	Steve Mingori	.25	.12	.02
☐ 545	Billy Williams	2.50	1.25	.25
☐ 546	John Knox	.25	.12	.02
☐ 547	Von Joshua	.25	.12	.02
☐ 548	Charlie Sands	.25	.12	.02
☐ 549	Bill Butler	.25	.12	.02
☐ 550	Ralph Garr	.25	.12	.02
☐ 551	Larry Christenson	.25	.12	.02
☐ 552	Jack Brohamer	.25	.12	.02
☐ 553	John Boccabella	.25	.12	.02
☐ 554	Rich Gossage	1.25	.60	.12
☐ 555	Al Oliver	.75	.35	.07
☐ 556	Tim Johnson	.25	.12	.02
☐ 557	Larry Gura	.40	.20	.04
☐ 558	Dave Roberts	.25	.12	.02
☐ 559	Bob Montgomery	.25	.12	.02
☐ 560	Tony Perez	1.25	.60	.12
☐ 561	A's: Team/Mgr. Alvin Dark (checklist back)	.75	.35	.07
☐ 562	Gary Nolan	.25	.12	.02
☐ 563	Wilbur Howard	.25	.12	.02
☐ 564	Tommy Davis	.40	.20	.04
☐ 565	Joe Torre	.60	.30	.06
☐ 566	Ray Burris	.25	.12	.02
☐ 567	Jim Sundberg	.60	.30	.06
☐ 568	Dale Murray	.25	.12	.02
☐ 569	Frank White	.75	.35	.07
☐ 570	Jim Wynn	.40	.20	.04
☐ 571	Dave Lemanczyk	.25	.12	.02
☐ 572	Roger Nelson	.25	.12	.02
☐ 573	Orlando Pena	.25	.12	.02
☐ 574	Tony Taylor	.25	.12	.02
☐ 575	Gene Clines	.25	.12	.02
☐ 576	Phil Roof	.25	.12	.02
☐ 577	John Morris	.25	.12	.02
☐ 578	Dave Tomlin	.25	.12	.02
☐ 579	Skip Pitlock	.25	.12	.02
☐ 580	Frank Robinson	3.00	1.50	.30
☐ 581	Darrel Chaney	.25	.12	.02
☐ 582	Eduardo Rodriguez	.25	.12	.02
☐ 583	Andy Etchebarren	.25	.12	.02
☐ 584	Mike Garman	.25	.12	.02
☐ 585	Chris Chambliss	.50	.25	.05
☐ 586	Tim McCarver	.50	.25	.05
☐ 587	Chris Ward	.25	.12	.02
☐ 588	Rick Auerbach	.25	.12	.02
☐ 589	Braves: Team/Mgr. Clyde King (checklist back)	.75	.35	.07
☐ 590	Cesar Cedeno	.40	.20	.04
☐ 591	Glenn Abbott	.25	.12	.02
☐ 592	Balor Moore	.25	.12	.02
☐ 593	Gene Lamont	.25	.12	.02
☐ 594	Jim Fuller	.25	.12	.02
☐ 595	Joe Niekro	.50	.25	.05
☐ 596	Ollie Brown	.25	.12	.02
☐ 597	Winston Llenas	.25	.12	.02
☐ 598	Bruce Kison	.25	.12	.02
☐ 599	Nate Colbert	.25	.12	.02
☐ 600	Rod Carew	5.00	2.50	.50
☐ 601	Juan Beniquez	.40	.20	.04
☐ 602	John Vukovich	.25	.12	.02
☐ 603	Lew Krausse	.25	.12	.02
☐ 604	Oscar Zamora	.25	.12	.02
☐ 605	John Ellis	.25	.12	.02
☐ 606	Bruce Miller	.25	.12	.02
☐ 607	Jim Holt	.25	.12	.02
☐ 608	Gene Michael	.40	.20	.04
☐ 609	Elrod Hendricks	.25	.12	.02
☐ 610	Ron Hunt	.25	.12	.02
☐ 611	Yankees: Team/Mgr. Bill Virdon (checklist back)	1.00	.50	.10
☐ 612	Terry Hughes	.25	.12	.02
☐ 613	Bill Parsons	.25	.12	.02
☐ 614	Rookie Pitchers Jack Kucek Dyar Miller Vern Ruhle Paul Siebert	.40	.20	.04
☐ 615	Rookie Pitchers Pat Darcy Dennis Leonard Tom Underwood Hank Webb	1.00	.50	.10
☐ 616	Rookie Outfielders Dave Augustine Pepe Mangual Jim Rice John Scott	30.00	15.00	3.00
☐ 617	Rookie Infielders Mike Cubbage Doug DeCinces Reggie Sanders Manny Trillo	1.75	.85	.17
☐ 618	Rookie Pitchers Jamie Easterly Tom Johnson Scott McGregor Rick Rhoden	2.50	1.25	.25
☐ 619	Rookie Outfielders Benny Ayala	.40	.20	.04

Nyls Nyman
Tommy Smith
Jerry Turner
- [ ] 620 Rookie Catcher/OF 35.00 17.50 3.50
Gary Carter
Marc Hill
Danny Meyer
Leon Roberts
- [ ] 621 Rookie Pitchers .... .75 .35 .07
John Denny
Rawly Eastwick
Jim Kern
Juan Veintidos
- [ ] 622 Rookie Outfielders 12.00 6.00 1.20
Ed Armbrister
Fred Lynn
Tom Poquette
Terry Whitfield
- [ ] 623 Rookie Infielders 24.00 12.00 2.40
Phil Garner
Keith Hernandez
(sic, bats right)
Bob Sheldon
Tom Veryzer
- [ ] 624 Rookie Pitchers .... .40 .20 .04
Doug Konieczny
Gary Lavelle
Jim Otten
Eddie Solomon
- [ ] 625 Boog Powell .... .50 .25 .05
- [ ] 626 Larry Haney .... .25 .12 .02
(photo actually
Dave Duncan)
- [ ] 627 Tom Walker .... .25 .12 .02
- [ ] 628 Ron LeFlore .... .50 .25 .05
- [ ] 629 Joe Hoerner .... .25 .12 .02
- [ ] 630 Greg Luzinski .... .60 .30 .06
- [ ] 631 Lee Lacy .... .25 .12 .02
- [ ] 632 Morris Nettles .... .25 .12 .02
- [ ] 633 Paul Casanova .... .25 .12 .02
- [ ] 634 Cy Acosta .... .25 .12 .02
- [ ] 635 Chuck Dobson .... .25 .12 .02
- [ ] 636 Charlie Moore .... .25 .12 .02
- [ ] 637 Ted Martinez .... .25 .12 .02
- [ ] 638 Cubs: Team/Mgr. .... .75 .35 .07
Jim Marshall
(checklist back)
- [ ] 639 Steve Kline .... .25 .12 .02
- [ ] 640 Harmon Killebrew .... 3.00 1.50 .30
- [ ] 641 Jim Northrup .... .40 .20 .04
- [ ] 642 Mike Phillips .... .25 .12 .02
- [ ] 643 Brent Strom .... .25 .12 .02
- [ ] 644 Bill Fahey .... .25 .12 .02
- [ ] 645 Danny Cater .... .25 .12 .02
- [ ] 646 Checklist: 529-660 .... 1.00 .10 .02
- [ ] 647 Claudell Washington .... 2.50 1.25 .25
- [ ] 648 Dave Pagan .... .25 .12 .02
- [ ] 649 Jack Heidemann .... .25 .12 .02
- [ ] 650 Dave May .... .25 .12 .02
- [ ] 651 John Morlan .... .25 .12 .02
- [ ] 652 Lindy McDaniel .... .25 .12 .02
- [ ] 653 Lee Richard .... .25 .12 .02
- [ ] 654 Jerry Terrell .... .25 .12 .02
- [ ] 655 Rico Carty .... .40 .20 .04
- [ ] 656 Bill Plummer .... .25 .12 .02
- [ ] 657 Bob Oliver .... .25 .12 .02
- [ ] 658 Vic Harris .... .25 .12 .02
- [ ] 659 Bob Apodaca .... .25 .12 .02
- [ ] 660 Hank Aaron .... 16.00 4.00 .75

1976 Topps

The 1976 Topps set of 660 cards (measuring 2 1/2"
by 3 1/2") is known for its sharp color photographs
and interesting presentation of subjects. Team cards
feature a checklist back for players on that team and
show a small inset photo of the manager on the front.
A "Father and Son" series (66-70) spotlights five
Major Leaguers whose fathers also made the "Big
Show." Other subseries include "All Time All Stars"
(341-350), "Record Breakers" from the previous
season (1-6), League Leaders (191-205), Post-
season cards (461-462), and Rookie Prospects (589-
599).

	NRMT	VG-E	GOOD
COMPLETE SET (660)	325.00	150.00	30.00
COMMON PLAYER (1-660)	.20	.10	.02

HANK AARON
BREWERS
DES. HITTER
550

- [ ] 1 RB: Hank Aaron .... 10.00 2.50 .50
Most RBI's, 2262
- [ ] 2 RB: Bobby Bonds .... .40 .20 .04
Most leadoff HR's 32;
plus three seasons
30 homers/30 steals
- [ ] 3 RB: Mickey Lolich .... .40 .20 .04
Lefthander, Most
Strikeouts, 2679
- [ ] 4 RB: Dave Lopes .... .30 .15 .03
Most Consecutive
SB attempts, 38
- [ ] 5 RB: Tom Seaver .... 1.75 .85 .17
Most Cons. seasons
with 200 SO's, 8
- [ ] 6 RB: Rennie Stennett ...... .30 .15 .03
Most Hits in a 9
inning game, 7
- [ ] 7 Jim Umbarger .... .20 .10 .02
- [ ] 8 Tito Fuentes .... .20 .10 .02
- [ ] 9 Paul Lindblad .... .20 .10 .02
- [ ] 10 Lou Brock .... 2.50 1.25 .25
- [ ] 11 Jim Hughes .... .20 .10 .02
- [ ] 12 Richie Zisk .... .30 .15 .03
- [ ] 13 John Wockenfuss .... .20 .10 .02
- [ ] 14 Gene Garber .... .20 .10 .02
- [ ] 15 George Scott .... .30 .15 .03
- [ ] 16 Bob Apodaca .... .20 .10 .02
- [ ] 17 New York Yankees .... 1.00 .50 .10
Team Card
(checklist back)
- [ ] 18 Dale Murray .... .20 .10 .02
- [ ] 19 George Brett 22.00 11.00 2.20
- [ ] 20 Bob Watson .... .30 .15 .03
- [ ] 21 Dave LaRoche .... .20 .10 .02
- [ ] 22 Bill Russell .... .30 .15 .03
- [ ] 23 Brian Downing .... .40 .20 .04
- [ ] 24 Cesar Geronimo .... .20 .10 .02
- [ ] 25 Mike Torrez .... .20 .10 .02
- [ ] 26 Andre Thornton .... .30 .15 .03
- [ ] 27 Ed Figueroa .... .20 .10 .02
- [ ] 28 Dusty Baker .... .40 .20 .04
- [ ] 29 Rick Burleson .... .30 .15 .03
- [ ] 30 John Montefusco .... .30 .15 .03
- [ ] 31 Len Randle .... .20 .10 .02
- [ ] 32 Danny Frisella .... .20 .10 .02
- [ ] 33 Bill North .... .20 .10 .02
- [ ] 34 Mike Garman .... .20 .10 .02
- [ ] 35 Tony Oliva .... .75 .35 .07
- [ ] 36 Frank Taveras .... .20 .10 .02
- [ ] 37 John Hiller .... .30 .15 .03
- [ ] 38 Garry Maddox .... .30 .15 .03
- [ ] 39 Pete Broberg .... .20 .10 .02
- [ ] 40 Dave Kingman .... .75 .35 .07
- [ ] 41 Tippy Martinez .... .30 .15 .03
- [ ] 42 Barry Foote .... .20 .10 .02
- [ ] 43 Paul Splittorff .... .20 .10 .02
- [ ] 44 Doug Rader .... .30 .15 .03
- [ ] 45 Boog Powell .... .50 .25 .05
- [ ] 46 Dodgers Team .... .75 .35 .07
(checklist back)
- [ ] 47 Jesse Jefferson .... .20 .10 .02
- [ ] 48 Dave Concepcion .... .50 .25 .05
- [ ] 49 Dave Duncan .... .20 .10 .02
- [ ] 50 Fred Lynn .... 2.25 1.10 .22
- [ ] 51 Ray Burris .... .20 .10 .02
- [ ] 52 Dave Chalk .... .20 .10 .02
- [ ] 53 Mike Beard .... .20 .10 .02
- [ ] 54 Dave Rader .... .20 .10 .02
- [ ] 55 Gaylord Perry .... 1.75 .85 .17
- [ ] 56 Bob Tolan .... .20 .10 .02
- [ ] 57 Phil Garner .... .30 .15 .03

☐ 58	Ron Reed	.20	.10	.02
☐ 59	Larry Hisle	.30	.15	.03
☐ 60	Jerry Reuss	.30	.15	.03
☐ 61	Ron LeFlore	.30	.15	.03
☐ 62	Johnny Oates	.20	.10	.02
☐ 63	Bobby Darwin	.20	.10	.02
☐ 64	Jerry Koosman	.50	.25	.05
☐ 65	Chris Chambliss	.40	.20	.04
☐ 66	Father and Son Gus Bell Buddy Bell	.40	.20	.04
☐ 67	Father and Son Ray Boone Bob Boone	.40	.20	.04
☐ 68	Father and Son Joe Coleman Joe Coleman Jr.	.25	.12	.02
☐ 69	Father and Son Jim Hegan Mike Hegan	.25	.12	.02
☐ 70	Father and Son Roy Smalley Roy Smalley Jr.	.25	.12	.02
☐ 71	Steve Rogers	.30	.15	.03
☐ 72	Hal McRae	.40	.20	.04
☐ 73	Baltimore Orioles Team Card (checklist back)	.75	.35	.07
☐ 74	Oscar Gamble	.30	.15	.03
☐ 75	Larry Dierker	.30	.15	.03
☐ 76	Willie Crawford	.20	.10	.02
☐ 77	Pedro Borbon	.20	.10	.02
☐ 78	Cecil Cooper	.90	.45	.09
☐ 79	Jerry Morales	.20	.10	.02
☐ 80	Jim Kaat	.75	.35	.07
☐ 81	Darrell Evans	.60	.30	.06
☐ 82	Von Joshua	.20	.10	.02
☐ 83	Jim Spencer	.20	.10	.02
☐ 84	Brent Strom	.20	.10	.02
☐ 85	Mickey Rivers	.30	.15	.03
☐ 86	Mike Tyson	.20	.10	.02
☐ 87	Tom Burgmeier	.20	.10	.02
☐ 88	Duffy Dyer	.20	.10	.02
☐ 89	Vern Ruhle	.20	.10	.02
☐ 90	Sal Bando	.40	.20	.04
☐ 91	Tom Hutton	.20	.10	.02
☐ 92	Eduardo Rodriguez	.20	.10	.02
☐ 93	Mike Phillips	.20	.10	.02
☐ 94	Jim Dwyer	.20	.10	.02
☐ 95	Brooks Robinson	2.50	1.25	.25
☐ 96	Doug Bird	.20	.10	.02
☐ 97	Wilbur Howard	.20	.10	.02
☐ 98	Dennis Eckersley	5.00	2.50	.50
☐ 99	Lee Lacy	.20	.10	.02
☐ 100	Jim Hunter	2.25	1.10	.22
☐ 101	Pete LaCock	.20	.10	.02
☐ 102	Jim Willoughby	.20	.10	.02
☐ 103	Biff Pocoroba	.20	.10	.02
☐ 104	Reds Team (checklist back)	.75	.35	.07
☐ 105	Gary Lavelle	.20	.10	.02
☐ 106	Tom Grieve	.30	.15	.03
☐ 107	Dave Roberts	.20	.10	.02
☐ 108	Don Kirkwood	.20	.10	.02
☐ 109	Larry Lintz	.20	.10	.02
☐ 110	Carlos May	.20	.10	.02
☐ 111	Danny Thompson	.20	.10	.02
☐ 112	Kent Tekulve	1.00	.50	.10
☐ 113	Gary Sutherland	.20	.10	.02
☐ 114	Jay Johnstone	.30	.15	.03
☐ 115	Ken Holtzman	.30	.15	.03
☐ 116	Charlie Moore	.20	.10	.02
☐ 117	Mike Jorgensen	.20	.10	.02
☐ 118	Red Sox Team (checklist back)	.75	.35	.07
☐ 119	Checklist 1-132	.90	.10	.02
☐ 120	Rusty Staub	.50	.25	.05
☐ 121	Tony Solaita	.20	.10	.02
☐ 122	Mike Cosgrove	.20	.10	.02
☐ 123	Walt Williams	.20	.10	.02
☐ 124	Doug Rau	.20	.10	.02
☐ 125	Don Baylor	.60	.30	.06
☐ 126	Tom Dettore	.20	.10	.02
☐ 127	Larvell Blanks	.20	.10	.02
☐ 128	Ken Griffey	.50	.25	.05
☐ 129	Andy Etchebarren	.20	.10	.02
☐ 130	Luis Tiant	.50	.25	.05
☐ 131	Bill Stein	.20	.10	.02
☐ 132	Don Hood	.20	.10	.02
☐ 133	Gary Matthews	.30	.15	.03
☐ 134	Mike Ivie	.20	.10	.02
☐ 135	Bake McBride	.30	.15	.03
☐ 136	Dave Goltz	.20	.10	.02
☐ 137	Bill Robinson	.30	.15	.03
☐ 138	Lerrin LaGrow	.20	.10	.02

☐ 139	Gorman Thomas	.50	.25	.05
☐ 140	Vida Blue	.40	.20	.04
☐ 141	Larry Parrish	.90	.45	.09
☐ 142	Dick Drago	.20	.10	.02
☐ 143	Jerry Grote	.20	.10	.02
☐ 144	Al Fitzmorris	.20	.10	.02
☐ 145	Larry Bowa	.50	.25	.05
☐ 146	George Medich	.20	.10	.02
☐ 147	Astros Team (checklist back)	.75	.35	.07
☐ 148	Stan Thomas	.20	.10	.02
☐ 149	Tommy Davis	.30	.15	.03
☐ 150	Steve Garvey	5.00	2.50	.50
☐ 151	Bill Bonham	.20	.10	.02
☐ 152	Leroy Stanton	.20	.10	.02
☐ 153	Buzz Capra	.20	.10	.02
☐ 154	Bucky Dent	.50	.25	.05
☐ 155	Jack Billingham	.20	.10	.02
☐ 156	Rico Carty	.30	.15	.03
☐ 157	Mike Caldwell	.30	.15	.03
☐ 158	Ken Reitz	.20	.10	.02
☐ 159	Jerry Terrell	.20	.10	.02
☐ 160	Dave Winfield	6.00	3.00	.60
☐ 161	Bruce Kison	.20	.10	.02
☐ 162	Jack Pierce	.20	.10	.02
☐ 163	Jim Slaton	.20	.10	.02
☐ 164	Pepe Mangual	.20	.10	.02
☐ 165	Gene Tenace	.30	.15	.03
☐ 166	Skip Lockwood	.20	.10	.02
☐ 167	Freddie Patek	.20	.10	.02
☐ 168	Tom Hilgendorf	.20	.10	.02
☐ 169	Graig Nettles	1.00	.50	.10
☐ 170	Rick Wise	.30	.15	.03
☐ 171	Greg Gross	.20	.10	.02
☐ 172	Rangers Team (checklist back)	.75	.35	.07
☐ 173	Steve Swisher	.20	.10	.02
☐ 174	Charlie Hough	.40	.20	.04
☐ 175	Ken Singleton	.40	.20	.04
☐ 176	Dick Lange	.20	.10	.02
☐ 177	Marty Perez	.20	.10	.02
☐ 178	Tom Buskey	.20	.10	.02
☐ 179	George Foster	1.00	.50	.10
☐ 180	Rich Gossage	1.25	.60	.12
☐ 181	Willie Montanez	.20	.10	.02
☐ 182	Harry Rasmussen	.20	.10	.02
☐ 183	Steve Braun	.20	.10	.02
☐ 184	Bill Greif	.20	.10	.02
☐ 185	Dave Parker	4.00	2.00	.40
☐ 186	Tom Walker	.20	.10	.02
☐ 187	Pedro Garcia	.20	.10	.02
☐ 188	Fred Scherman	.20	.10	.02
☐ 189	Claudell Washington	.50	.25	.05
☐ 190	Jon Matlack	.30	.15	.03
☐ 191	NL Batting Leaders Bill Madlock Ted Simmons Manny Sanguillen	.40	.20	.04
☐ 192	AL Batting Leaders Rod Carew Fred Lynn Thurman Munson	1.50	.75	.15
☐ 193	NL Home Run Leaders Mike Schmidt Dave Kingman Greg Luzinski	.75	.35	.07
☐ 194	AL Home Run Leaders Reggie Jackson George Scott John Mayberry	.75	.35	.07
☐ 195	NL RBI Leaders Greg Luzinski Johnny Bench Tony Perez	.60	.30	.06
☐ 196	AL RBI Leaders George Scott John Mayberry Fred Lynn	.40	.20	.04
☐ 197	NL Steals Leaders Dave Lopes Joe Morgan Lou Brock	.75	.35	.07
☐ 198	AL Steals Leaders Mickey Rivers Claudell Washington Amos Otis	.40	.20	.04
☐ 199	NL Victory Leaders Tom Seaver Randy Jones Andy Messersmith	.60	.30	.06
☐ 200	AL Victory Leaders Jim Hunter Jim Palmer Vida Blue	1.00	.50	.10
☐ 201	NL ERA Leaders	.50	.25	.05

	Randy Jones			
	Andy Messersmith			
	Tom Seaver			
☐ 202	AL ERA Leaders	1.50	.75	.15
	Jim Palmer			
	Jim Hunter			
	Dennis Eckersley			
☐ 203	NL Strikeout Leaders	.60	.30	.06
	Tom Seaver			
	John Montefusco			
	Andy Messersmith			
☐ 204	AL Strikeout Leaders	.50	.25	.05
	Frank Tanana			
	Bert Blyleven			
	Gaylord Perry			
☐ 205	Leading Firemen	.40	.20	.04
	Al Hrabosky			
	Rich Gossage			
☐ 206	Manny Trillo	.20	.10	.02
☐ 207	Andy Hassler	.20	.10	.02
☐ 208	Mike Lum	.20	.10	.02
☐ 209	Alan Ashby	.30	.15	.03
☐ 210	Lee May	.30	.15	.03
☐ 211	Clay Carroll	.20	.10	.02
☐ 212	Pat Kelly	.20	.10	.02
☐ 213	Dave Heaverlo	.20	.10	.02
☐ 214	Eric Soderholm	.20	.10	.02
☐ 215	Reggie Smith	.40	.20	.04
☐ 216	Expos Team	.65	.30	.06
	(checklist back)			
☐ 217	Dave Freisleben	.20	.10	.02
☐ 218	John Knox	.20	.10	.02
☐ 219	Tom Murphy	.20	.10	.02
☐ 220	Manny Sanguillen	.30	.15	.03
☐ 221	Jim Todd	.20	.10	.02
☐ 222	Wayne Garrett	.20	.10	.02
☐ 223	Ollie Brown	.20	.10	.02
☐ 224	Jim York	.20	.10	.02
☐ 225	Roy White	.30	.15	.03
☐ 226	Jim Sundberg	.30	.15	.03
☐ 227	Oscar Zamora	.20	.10	.02
☐ 228	John Hale	.20	.10	.02
☐ 229	Jerry Remy	.30	.15	.03
☐ 230	Carl Yastrzemski	7.50	3.75	.75
☐ 231	Tom House	.30	.15	.03
☐ 232	Frank Duffy	.20	.10	.02
☐ 233	Grant Jackson	.20	.10	.02
☐ 234	Mike Sadek	.20	.10	.02
☐ 235	Bert Blyleven	1.50	.75	.15
☐ 236	Kansas City Royals	.75	.35	.07
	Team Card			
	(checklist back)			
☐ 237	Dave Hamilton	.20	.10	.02
☐ 238	Larry Biittner	.20	.10	.02
☐ 239	John Curtis	.20	.10	.02
☐ 240	Pete Rose	15.00	7.50	1.50
☐ 241	Hector Torres	.20	.10	.02
☐ 242	Dan Meyer	.20	.10	.02
☐ 243	Jim Rooker	.20	.10	.02
☐ 244	Bill Sharp	.20	.10	.02
☐ 245	Felix Millan	.20	.10	.02
☐ 246	Cesar Tovar	.20	.10	.02
☐ 247	Terry Harmon	.20	.10	.02
☐ 248	Dick Tidrow	.20	.10	.02
☐ 249	Cliff Johnson	.20	.10	.02
☐ 250	Fergie Jenkins	.75	.35	.07
☐ 251	Rick Monday	.30	.15	.03
☐ 252	Tim Nordbrook	.20	.10	.02
☐ 253	Bill Buckner	.40	.20	.04
☐ 254	Rudy Meoli	.20	.10	.02
☐ 255	Fritz Peterson	.20	.10	.02
☐ 256	Rowland Office	.20	.10	.02
☐ 257	Ross Grimsley	.20	.10	.02
☐ 258	Nyls Nyman	.20	.10	.02
☐ 259	Darrel Chaney	.20	.10	.02
☐ 260	Steve Busby	.30	.15	.03
☐ 261	Gary Thomasson	.20	.10	.02
☐ 262	Checklist 133-264	.90	.10	.02
☐ 263	Lyman Bostock	.50	.25	.05
☐ 264	Steve Renko	.20	.10	.02
☐ 265	Willie Davis	.30	.15	.03
☐ 266	Alan Foster	.20	.10	.02
☐ 267	Aurelio Rodriguez	.20	.10	.02
☐ 268	Del Unser	.20	.10	.02
☐ 269	Rick Austin	.20	.10	.02
☐ 270	Willie Stargell	3.00	1.50	.30
☐ 271	Jim Lonborg	.30	.15	.03
☐ 272	Rick Dempsey	.30	.15	.03
☐ 273	Joe Niekro	.40	.20	.04
☐ 274	Tommy Harper	.30	.15	.03
☐ 275	Rick Manning	.20	.10	.02
☐ 276	Mickey Scott	.20	.10	.02
☐ 277	Cubs Team	.75	.35	.07
	(checklist back)			
☐ 278	Bernie Carbo	.20	.10	.02
☐ 279	Roy Howell	.20	.10	.02
☐ 280	Burt Hooton	.30	.15	.03
☐ 281	Dave May	.20	.10	.02
☐ 282	Dan Osborn	.20	.10	.02
☐ 283	Merv Rettenmund	.20	.10	.02
☐ 284	Steve Ontiveros	.20	.10	.02
☐ 285	Mike Cuellar	.30	.15	.03
☐ 286	Jim Wohlford	.20	.10	.02
☐ 287	Pete Mackanin	.20	.10	.02
☐ 288	Bill Campbell	.20	.10	.02
☐ 289	Enzo Hernandez	.20	.10	.02
☐ 290	Ted Simmons	.75	.35	.07
☐ 291	Ken Sanders	.20	.10	.02
☐ 292	Leon Roberts	.20	.10	.02
☐ 293	Bill Castro	.20	.10	.02
☐ 294	Ed Kirkpatrick	.20	.10	.02
☐ 295	Dave Cash	.20	.10	.02
☐ 296	Pat Dobson	.30	.15	.03
☐ 297	Roger Metzger	.20	.10	.02
☐ 298	Dick Bosman	.20	.10	.02
☐ 299	Champ Summers	.20	.10	.02
☐ 300	Johnny Bench	6.50	3.25	.65
☐ 301	Jackie Brown	.20	.10	.02
☐ 302	Rick Miller	.20	.10	.02
☐ 303	Steve Foucault	.20	.10	.02
☐ 304	Angels Team	.75	.35	.07
	(checklist back)			
☐ 305	Andy Messersmith	.30	.15	.03
☐ 306	Rod Gilbreath	.20	.10	.02
☐ 307	Al Bumbry	.20	.10	.02
☐ 308	Jim Barr	.20	.10	.02
☐ 309	Bill Melton	.20	.10	.02
☐ 310	Randy Jones	.30	.15	.03
☐ 311	Cookie Rojas	.20	.10	.02
☐ 312	Don Carrithers	.20	.10	.02
☐ 313	Dan Ford	.20	.10	.02
☐ 314	Ed Kranepool	.30	.15	.03
☐ 315	Al Hrabosky	.30	.15	.03
☐ 316	Robin Yount	28.00	14.00	2.80
☐ 317	John Candelaria	2.00	1.00	.20
☐ 318	Bob Boone	.75	.35	.07
☐ 319	Larry Dierker	.30	.15	.03
☐ 320	Willie Horton	.30	.15	.03
☐ 321	Jose Cruz	.40	.20	.04
☐ 322	Glenn Abbott	.20	.10	.02
☐ 323	Rob Sperring	.20	.10	.02
☐ 324	Jim Bibby	.20	.10	.02
☐ 325	Tony Perez	.90	.45	.09
☐ 326	Dick Pole	.20	.10	.02
☐ 327	Dave Moates	.20	.10	.02
☐ 328	Carl Morton	.20	.10	.02
☐ 329	Joe Ferguson	.20	.10	.02
☐ 330	Nolan Ryan	16.00	8.00	1.60
☐ 331	San Diego Padres	.75	.35	.07
	Team Card			
	(checklist back)			
☐ 332	Charlie Williams	.20	.10	.02
☐ 333	Bob Coluccio	.20	.10	.02
☐ 334	Dennis Leonard	.30	.15	.03
☐ 335	Bob Grich	.40	.20	.04
☐ 336	Vic Albury	.20	.10	.02
☐ 337	Bud Harrelson	.30	.15	.03
☐ 338	Bob Bailey	.20	.10	.02
☐ 339	John Denny	.30	.15	.03
☐ 340	Jim Rice	7.50	3.75	.75
☐ 341	All-Time 1B	3.00	1.50	.30
	Lou Gehrig			
☐ 342	All-Time 2B	1.50	.75	.15
	Rogers Hornsby			
☐ 343	All-Time 3B	.75	.35	.07
	Pie Traynor			
☐ 344	All-Time SS	1.50	.75	.15
	Honus Wagner			
☐ 345	All-Time OF	5.00	2.50	.50
	Babe Ruth			
☐ 346	All-Time OF	3.00	1.50	.30
	Ty Cobb			
☐ 347	All-Time OF	3.00	1.50	.30
	Ted Williams			
☐ 348	All-Time C	.75	.35	.07
	Mickey Cochrane			
☐ 349	All-Time RHP	1.50	.75	.15
	Walter Johnson			
☐ 350	All-Time LHP	1.25	.60	.12
	Lefty Grove			
☐ 351	Randy Hundley	.20	.10	.02
☐ 352	Dave Giusti	.20	.10	.02
☐ 353	Sixto Lezcano	.20	.10	.02
☐ 354	Ron Blomberg	.20	.10	.02
☐ 355	Steve Carlton	4.50	2.25	.45
☐ 356	Ted Martinez	.20	.10	.02
☐ 357	Ken Forsch	.20	.10	.02
☐ 358	Buddy Bell	.50	.25	.05
☐ 359	Rick Reuschel	.60	.30	.06
☐ 360	Jeff Burroughs	.30	.15	.03

☐ 361	Detroit Tigers Team Card (checklist back)	.75	.35	.07
☐ 362	Will McEnaney	.20	.10	.02
☐ 363	Dave Collins	.60	.30	.06
☐ 364	Elias Sosa	.20	.10	.02
☐ 365	Carlton Fisk	2.50	1.25	.25
☐ 366	Bobby Valentine	.40	.20	.04
☐ 367	Bruce Miller	.20	.10	.02
☐ 368	Wilbur Wood	.20	.10	.02
☐ 369	Frank White	.40	.20	.04
☐ 370	Ron Cey	.50	.25	.05
☐ 371	Elrod Hendricks	.20	.10	.02
☐ 372	Rick Baldwin	.20	.10	.02
☐ 373	Johnny Briggs	.20	.10	.02
☐ 374	Dan Warthen	.20	.10	.02
☐ 375	Ron Fairly	.30	.15	.03
☐ 376	Rich Hebner	.20	.10	.02
☐ 377	Mike Hegan	.20	.10	.02
☐ 378	Steve Stone	.30	.15	.03
☐ 379	Ken Boswell	.20	.10	.02
☐ 380	Bobby Bonds	.40	.20	.04
☐ 381	Denny Doyle	.20	.10	.02
☐ 382	Matt Alexander	.20	.10	.02
☐ 383	John Ellis	.20	.10	.02
☐ 384	Phillies Team (checklist back)	.75	.35	.07
☐ 385	Mickey Lolich	.40	.20	.04
☐ 386	Ed Goodson	.20	.10	.02
☐ 387	Mike Miley	.20	.10	.02
☐ 388	Stan Perzanowski	.20	.10	.02
☐ 389	Glenn Adams	.20	.10	.02
☐ 390	Don Gullett	.30	.15	.03
☐ 391	Jerry Hairston	.20	.10	.02
☐ 392	Checklist 265-396	.90	.10	.02
☐ 393	Paul Mitchell	.20	.10	.02
☐ 394	Fran Healy	.20	.10	.02
☐ 395	Jim Wynn	.30	.15	.03
☐ 396	Bill Lee	.30	.15	.03
☐ 397	Tim Foli	.20	.10	.02
☐ 398	Dave Tomlin	.20	.10	.02
☐ 399	Luis Melendez	.20	.10	.02
☐ 400	Rod Carew	4.50	2.00	.40
☐ 401	Ken Brett	.20	.10	.02
☐ 402	Don Money	.20	.10	.02
☐ 403	Geoff Zahn	.20	.10	.02
☐ 404	Enos Cabell	.20	.10	.02
☐ 405	Rollie Fingers	1.25	.60	.12
☐ 406	Ed Herrmann	.20	.10	.02
☐ 407	Tom Underwood	.20	.10	.02
☐ 408	Charlie Spikes	.20	.10	.02
☐ 409	Dave Lemanczyk	.20	.10	.02
☐ 410	Ralph Garr	.30	.15	.03
☐ 411	Bill Singer	.20	.10	.02
☐ 412	Toby Harrah	.30	.15	.03
☐ 413	Pete Varney	.20	.10	.02
☐ 414	Wayne Garland	.20	.10	.02
☐ 415	Vada Pinson	.40	.20	.04
☐ 416	Tommy John	1.00	.50	.10
☐ 417	Gene Clines	.20	.10	.02
☐ 418	Jose Morales	.20	.10	.02
☐ 419	Reggie Cleveland	.20	.10	.02
☐ 420	Joe Morgan	4.50	2.25	.45
☐ 421	A's Team (checklist back)	.75	.35	.07
☐ 422	Johnny Grubb	.20	.10	.02
☐ 423	Ed Halicki	.20	.10	.02
☐ 424	Phil Roof	.20	.10	.02
☐ 425	Rennie Stennett	.20	.10	.02
☐ 426	Bob Forsch	.20	.10	.02
☐ 427	Kurt Bevacqua	.20	.10	.02
☐ 428	Jim Crawford	.20	.10	.02
☐ 429	Fred Stanley	.20	.10	.02
☐ 430	Jose Cardenal	.20	.10	.02
☐ 431	Dick Ruthven	.20	.10	.02
☐ 432	Tom Veryzer	.20	.10	.02
☐ 433	Rick Waits	.20	.10	.02
☐ 434	Morris Nettles	.20	.10	.02
☐ 435	Phil Niekro	1.75	.85	.17
☐ 436	Bill Fahey	.20	.10	.02
☐ 437	Terry Forster	.30	.15	.03
☐ 438	Doug DeCinces	.60	.30	.06
☐ 439	Rick Rhoden	.60	.30	.06
☐ 440	John Mayberry	.30	.15	.03
☐ 441	Gary Carter	9.00	4.50	.90
☐ 442	Hank Webb	.20	.10	.02
☐ 443	Giants Team (checklist back)	.75	.35	.07
☐ 444	Gary Nolan	.20	.10	.02
☐ 445	Rico Petrocelli	.30	.15	.03
☐ 446	Larry Haney	.20	.10	.02
☐ 447	Gene Locklear	.20	.10	.02
☐ 448	Tom Johnson	.20	.10	.02
☐ 449	Bob Robertson	.20	.10	.02
☐ 450	Jim Palmer	4.50	2.25	.45
☐ 451	Buddy Bradford	.20	.10	.02
☐ 452	Tom Hausman	.20	.10	.02
☐ 453	Lou Piniella	.40	.20	.04
☐ 454	Tom Griffin	.20	.10	.02
☐ 455	Dick Allen	.40	.20	.04
☐ 456	Joe Coleman	.20	.10	.02
☐ 457	Ed Crosby	.20	.10	.02
☐ 458	Earl Williams	.20	.10	.02
☐ 459	Jim Brewer	.20	.10	.02
☐ 460	Cesar Cedeno	.30	.15	.03
☐ 461	NL and AL Champs Reds sweep Bucs, Bosox surprise A's	.40	.20	.04
☐ 462	'75 World Series Reds Champs	.40	.20	.04
☐ 463	Steve Hargan	.20	.10	.02
☐ 464	Ken Henderson	.20	.10	.02
☐ 465	Mike Marshall	.30	.15	.03
☐ 466	Bob Stinson	.20	.10	.02
☐ 467	Woodie Fryman	.20	.10	.02
☐ 468	Jesus Alou	.20	.10	.02
☐ 469	Rawly Eastwick	.20	.10	.02
☐ 470	Bobby Murcer	.40	.20	.04
☐ 471	Jim Burton	.20	.10	.02
☐ 472	Bob Davis	.20	.10	.02
☐ 473	Paul Blair	.30	.15	.03
☐ 474	Ray Corbin	.20	.10	.02
☐ 475	Joe Rudi	.30	.15	.03
☐ 476	Bob Moose	.20	.10	.02
☐ 477	Indians Team (checklist back)	.75	.35	.07
☐ 478	Lynn McGlothen	.20	.10	.02
☐ 479	Bobby Mitchell	.20	.10	.02
☐ 480	Mike Schmidt	20.00	10.00	2.00
☐ 481	Rudy May	.20	.10	.02
☐ 482	Tim Hosley	.20	.10	.02
☐ 483	Mickey Stanley	.30	.15	.03
☐ 484	Eric Raich	.20	.10	.02
☐ 485	Mike Hargrove	.30	.15	.03
☐ 486	Bruce Dal Canton	.20	.10	.02
☐ 487	Leron Lee	.20	.10	.02
☐ 488	Claude Osteen	.30	.15	.03
☐ 489	Skip Jutze	.20	.10	.02
☐ 490	Frank Tanana	.40	.20	.04
☐ 491	Terry Crowley	.20	.10	.02
☐ 492	Marty Pattin	.20	.10	.02
☐ 493	Derrel Thomas	.20	.10	.02
☐ 494	Craig Swan	.30	.15	.03
☐ 495	Nate Colbert	.20	.10	.02
☐ 496	Juan Beniquez	.20	.10	.02
☐ 497	Joe McIntosh	.20	.10	.02
☐ 498	Glenn Borgmann	.20	.10	.02
☐ 499	Mario Guerrero	.20	.10	.02
☐ 500	Reggie Jackson	8.00	4.00	.80
☐ 501	Billy Champion	.20	.10	.02
☐ 502	Tim McCarver	.40	.20	.04
☐ 503	Elliott Maddox	.20	.10	.02
☐ 504	Pirates Team (checklist back)	.75	.35	.07
☐ 505	Mark Belanger	.30	.15	.03
☐ 506	George Mitterwald	.20	.10	.02
☐ 507	Ray Bare	.20	.10	.02
☐ 508	Duane Kuiper	.20	.10	.02
☐ 509	Bill Hands	.20	.10	.02
☐ 510	Amos Otis	.40	.20	.04
☐ 511	Jamie Easterley	.20	.10	.02
☐ 512	Ellie Rodriguez	.20	.10	.02
☐ 513	Bart Johnson	.20	.10	.02
☐ 514	Dan Driessen	.30	.15	.03
☐ 515	Steve Yeager	.20	.10	.02
☐ 516	Wayne Granger	.20	.10	.02
☐ 517	John Milner	.20	.10	.02
☐ 518	Doug Flynn	.20	.10	.02
☐ 519	Steve Brye	.20	.10	.02
☐ 520	Willie McCovey	2.50	1.25	.25
☐ 521	Jim Colborn	.20	.10	.02
☐ 522	Ted Sizemore	.20	.10	.02
☐ 523	Bob Montgomery	.20	.10	.02
☐ 524	Pete Falcone	.20	.10	.02
☐ 525	Billy Williams	1.75	.85	.17
☐ 526	Checklist 397-528	.90	.10	.02
☐ 527	Mike Anderson	.20	.10	.02
☐ 528	Dock Ellis	.20	.10	.02
☐ 529	Deron Johnson	.20	.10	.02
☐ 530	Don Sutton	1.50	.75	.15
☐ 531	New York Mets Team Card (checklist back)	.90	.45	.09
☐ 532	Milt May	.20	.10	.02
☐ 533	Lee Richard	.20	.10	.02
☐ 534	Stan Bahnsen	.20	.10	.02
☐ 535	Dave Nelson	.20	.10	.02
☐ 536	Mike Thompson	.20	.10	.02
☐ 537	Tony Muser	.20	.10	.02
☐ 538	Pat Darcy	.20	.10	.02

☐ 539 John Balaz	.20	.10	.02
☐ 540 Bill Freehan	.40	.20	.04
☐ 541 Steve Mingori	.20	.10	.02
☐ 542 Keith Hernandez	6.00	3.00	.60
☐ 543 Wayne Twitchell	.20	.10	.02
☐ 544 Pepe Frias	.20	.10	.02
☐ 545 Sparky Lyle	.40	.20	.04
☐ 546 Dave Rosello	.20	.10	.02
☐ 547 Roric Harrison	.20	.10	.02
☐ 548 Manny Mota	.30	.15	.03
☐ 549 Randy Tate	.20	.10	.02
☐ 550 Hank Aaron	11.00	5.50	1.10
☐ 551 Jerry DaVanon	.20	.10	.02
☐ 552 Terry Humphrey	.20	.10	.02
☐ 553 Randy Moffitt	.20	.10	.02
☐ 554 Ray Fosse	.20	.10	.02
☐ 555 Dyar Miller	.20	.10	.02
☐ 556 Twins Team	.75	.35	.07
(checklist back)			
☐ 557 Dan Spillner	.20	.10	.02
☐ 558 Clarence Gaston	.40	.20	.04
☐ 559 Clyde Wright	.20	.10	.02
☐ 560 Jorge Orta	.20	.10	.02
☐ 561 Tom Carroll	.20	.10	.02
☐ 562 Adrian Garrett	.20	.10	.02
☐ 563 Larry Demery	.20	.10	.02
☐ 564 Bubble Gum Champ	.20	.10	.02
Kurt Bevacqua			
☐ 565 Tug McGraw	.40	.20	.04
☐ 566 Ken McMullen	.20	.10	.02
☐ 567 George Stone	.20	.10	.02
☐ 568 Rob Andrews	.20	.10	.02
☐ 569 Nelson Briles	.20	.10	.02
☐ 570 George Hendrick	.30	.15	.03
☐ 571 Don DeMola	.20	.10	.02
☐ 572 Rich Coggins	.20	.10	.02
☐ 573 Bill Travers	.20	.10	.02
☐ 574 Don Kessinger	.30	.15	.03
☐ 575 Dwight Evans	2.00	1.00	.20
☐ 576 Maximino Leon	.20	.10	.02
☐ 577 Marc Hill	.20	.10	.02
☐ 578 Ted Kubiak	.20	.10	.02
☐ 579 Clay Kirby	.20	.10	.02
☐ 580 Bert Campaneris	.30	.15	.03
☐ 581 Cardinals Team	.75	.35	.07
(checklist back)			
☐ 582 Mike Kekich	.20	.10	.02
☐ 583 Tommy Helms	.30	.15	.03
☐ 584 Stan Wall	.20	.10	.02
☐ 585 Joe Torre	.50	.25	.05
☐ 586 Ron Schueler	.20	.10	.02
☐ 587 Leo Cardenas	.20	.10	.02
☐ 588 Kevin Kobel	.20	.10	.02
☐ 589 Rookie Pitchers	2.00	1.00	.20
Santo Alcala			
Mike Flanagan			
Joe Pactwa			
Pablo Torrealba			
☐ 590 Rookie Outfielders	1.00	.50	.10
Henry Cruz			
Chet Lemon			
Ellis Valentine			
Terry Whitfield			
☐ 591 Rookie Pitchers	.30	.15	.03
Steve Grilli			
Craig Mitchell			
Jose Sosa			
George Throop			
☐ 592 Rookie Infielders	5.00	2.50	.50
Willie Randolph			
Dave McKay			
Jerry Royster			
Roy Staiger			
☐ 593 Rookie Pitchers	.40	.20	.04
Larry Anderson			
Ken Crosby			
Mark Littell			
Butch Metzger			
☐ 594 Rookie Catchers/OF	.40	.20	.04
Andy Merchant			
Ed Ott			
Royle Stillman			
Jerry White			
☐ 595 Rookie Pitchers	.40	.20	.04
Art DeFillipis			
Randy Lerch			
Sid Monge			
Steve Barr			
☐ 596 Rookie Infielders	.50	.25	.05
Craig Reynolds			
Lamar Johnson			
Johnnie LeMaster			
Jerry Manuel			
☐ 597 Rookie Pitchers	.60	.30	.06
Don Aase			

Jack Kucek			
Frank LaCorte			
Mike Pazik			
☐ 598 Rookie Outfielders	.30	.15	.03
Hector Cruz			
Jamie Quirk			
Jerry Turner			
Joe Wallis			
☐ 599 Rookie Pitchers	10.00	5.00	1.00
Rob Dressler			
Ron Guidry			
Bob McClure			
Pat Zachry			
☐ 600 Tom Seaver	6.00	2.75	.55
☐ 601 Ken Rudolph	.20	.10	.02
☐ 602 Doug Konieczny	.20	.10	.02
☐ 603 Jim Holt	.20	.10	.02
☐ 604 Joe Lovitto	.20	.10	.02
☐ 605 Al Downing	.30	.15	.03
☐ 606 Milwaukee Brewers	.75	.35	.07
Team Card			
(checklist back)			
☐ 607 Rich Hinton	.20	.10	.02
☐ 608 Vic Correll	.20	.10	.02
☐ 609 Fred Norman	.20	.10	.02
☐ 610 Greg Luzinski	.50	.25	.05
☐ 611 Rich Folkers	.20	.10	.02
☐ 612 Joe Lahoud	.20	.10	.02
☐ 613 Tim Johnson	.20	.10	.02
☐ 614 Fernando Arroyo	.20	.10	.02
☐ 615 Mike Cubbage	.20	.10	.02
☐ 616 Buck Martinez	.20	.10	.02
☐ 617 Darold Knowles	.20	.10	.02
☐ 618 Jack Brohamer	.20	.10	.02
☐ 619 Bill Butler	.20	.10	.02
☐ 620 Al Oliver	.50	.25	.05
☐ 621 Tom Hall	.20	.10	.02
☐ 622 Rick Auerbach	.20	.10	.02
☐ 623 Bob Allietta	.20	.10	.02
☐ 624 Tony Taylor	.20	.10	.02
☐ 625 J.R. Richard	.30	.15	.03
☐ 626 Bob Sheldon	.20	.10	.02
☐ 627 Bill Plummer	.20	.10	.02
☐ 628 John D'Acquisto	.20	.10	.02
☐ 629 Sandy Alomar	.20	.10	.02
☐ 630 Chris Speier	.20	.10	.02
☐ 631 Braves Team	.75	.35	.07
(checklist back)			
☐ 632 Rogelio Moret	.20	.10	.02
☐ 633 John Stearns	.30	.15	.03
☐ 634 Larry Christenson	.20	.10	.02
☐ 635 Jim Fregosi	.30	.15	.03
☐ 636 Joe Decker	.20	.10	.02
☐ 637 Bruce Bochte	.20	.10	.02
☐ 638 Doyle Alexander	.30	.15	.03
☐ 639 Fred Kendall	.20	.10	.02
☐ 640 Bill Madlock	.75	.35	.07
☐ 641 Tom Paciorek	.20	.10	.02
☐ 642 Dennis Blair	.20	.10	.02
☐ 643 Checklist 529-660	.90	.10	.02
☐ 644 Tom Bradley	.20	.10	.02
☐ 645 Darrell Porter	.20	.10	.02
☐ 646 John Lowenstein	.20	.10	.02
☐ 647 Ramon Hernandez	.20	.10	.02
☐ 648 Al Cowens	.30	.15	.03
☐ 649 Dave Roberts	.20	.10	.02
☐ 650 Thurman Munson	5.50	2.75	.55
☐ 651 John Odom	.20	.10	.02
☐ 652 Ed Armbrister	.20	.10	.02
☐ 653 Mike Norris	.30	.15	.03
☐ 654 Doug Griffin	.20	.10	.02
☐ 655 Mike Vail	.20	.10	.02
☐ 656 Chicago White Sox	.75	.35	.07
Team Card			
(checklist back)			
☐ 657 Roy Smalley	.50	.25	.05
☐ 658 Jerry Johnson	.20	.10	.02
☐ 659 Ben Oglivie	.40	.20	.04
☐ 660 Dave Lopes	.65	.15	.03

1976 Topps Traded

The cards in this 44-card set measure 2 1/2" by 3 1/2". The 1976 Topps Traded set contains 43 players and one unnumbered checklist card. The individuals pictured were traded after the Topps regular set was printed. A "Sports Extra" heading design is found on each picture and is also used to

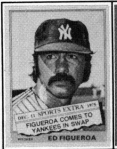

introduce the biographical section of the reverse. Each card is numbered according to the player's regular 1976 card with the addition of "T" to indicate his new status.

	NRMT	VG-E	GOOD
COMPLETE SET (44)	7.00	3.25	.65
COMMON PLAYER	.12	.06	.01
☐ 27T Ed Figueroa	.12	.06	.01
☐ 28T Dusty Baker	.30	.15	.03
☐ 44T Doug Rader	.20	.10	.02
☐ 58T Ron Reed	.15	.07	.01
☐ 74T Oscar Gamble	.20	.10	.02
☐ 80T Jim Kaat	.75	.35	.07
☐ 83T Jim Spencer	.12	.06	.01
☐ 85T Mickey Rivers	.15	.07	.01
☐ 99T Lee Lacy	.15	.07	.01
☐ 120T Rusty Staub	.40	.20	.04
☐ 127T Larvell Blanks	.12	.06	.01
☐ 146T George Medich	.12	.06	.01
☐ 158T Ken Reitz	.12	.06	.01
☐ 208T Mike Lum	.12	.06	.01
☐ 211T Clay Carroll	.12	.06	.01
☐ 231T Tom House	.15	.07	.01
☐ 250T Fergie Jenkins	.75	.35	.07
☐ 259T Darrel Chaney	.12	.06	.01
☐ 292T Leon Roberts	.12	.06	.01
☐ 296T Pat Dobson	.15	.07	.01
☐ 309T Bill Melton	.12	.06	.01
☐ 338T Bob Bailey	.12	.06	.01
☐ 380T Bobby Bonds	.30	.15	.03
☐ 383T John Ellis	.12	.06	.01
☐ 385T Mickey Lolich	.30	.15	.03
☐ 401T Ken Brett	.12	.06	.01
☐ 410T Ralph Garr	.15	.07	.01
☐ 411T Bill Singer	.12	.06	.01
☐ 428T Jim Crawford	.12	.06	.01
☐ 434T Morris Nettles	.12	.06	.01
☐ 464T Ken Henderson	.12	.06	.01
☐ 497T Joe McIntosh	.12	.06	.01
☐ 524T Pete Falcone	.12	.06	.01
☐ 527T Mike Anderson	.12	.06	.01
☐ 528T Dock Ellis	.12	.06	.01
☐ 532T Milt May	.12	.06	.01
☐ 554T Ray Fosse	.12	.06	.01
☐ 579T Clay Kirby	.12	.06	.01
☐ 583T Tommy Helms	.15	.07	.01
☐ 592T Willie Randolph	.90	.45	.09
☐ 618T Jack Brohamer	.12	.06	.01
☐ 632T Rogelio Moret	.12	.06	.01
☐ 649T Dave Roberts	.12	.06	.01
☐ xxxT Traded Checklist (unnumbered)	.50	.25	.05

1977 Topps

The cards in this 660-card set measure 2 1/2" by 3 1/2". In 1977 for the fifth consecutive year, Topps produced a 660-card baseball set. The player's name, team affiliation, and his position are compactly arranged over the picture area and a facsimile autograph appears on the photo. Team cards feature a checklist of that team's players in the set and a small picture of the manager on the front

of the card. Appearing for the first time are the series "Brothers" (631-634) and "Turn Back The Clock" (433-437). Other subseries in the set are League Leaders (1-8), Record Breakers (231-234), Playoffs cards (276-277), World Series cards (411-413), and Rookie Prospects (472-479 and 487-494). The key card in the set is the rookie card of Dale Murphy (#476). Cards numbered 23 or lower which feature Yankees and do not follow the numbering checklisted below are not necessarily error cards. They are probably Burger King cards, a separate set with its own pricing and mass distribution. Burger King cards are indistinguishable from the corresponding Topps cards except for the card numbering difference and the fact that Burger King cards do not have a printing sheet designation (such as A through F like the regular Topps) anywhere on the card back in very small print. There was an aluminum version of the Dale Murphy rookie card #476 produced (legally) in the early '80s; proceeds from the sales (originally priced at 10.00) of this "card" went to the Huntington's Disease Foundation.

			NRMT	VG-E	GOOD
		COMPLETE SET (660)	325.00	150.00	30.00
		COMMON PLAYER (1-660)	.16	.08	.01
☐	1	Batting Leaders George Brett Bill Madlock	2.00	.30	.06
☐	2	Home Run Leaders Graig Nettles Mike Schmidt	.75	.35	.07
☐	3	RBI Leaders Lee May George Foster	.30	.15	.03
☐	4	Stolen Base Leaders Bill North Dave Lopes	.30	.15	.03
☐	5	Victory Leaders Jim Palmer Randy Jones	.40	.20	.04
☐	6	Strikeout Leaders Nolan Ryan Tom Seaver	2.50	1.25	.25
☐	7	ERA Leaders Mark Fidrych John Denny	.30	.15	.03
☐	8	Leading Firemen Bill Campbell Rawly Eastwick	.30	.15	.03
☐	9	Doug Rader	.25	.12	.02
☐	10	Reggie Jackson	7.00	3.50	.70
☐	11	Rob Dressler	.16	.08	.01
☐	12	Larry Haney	.16	.08	.01
☐	13	Luis Gomez	.16	.08	.01
☐	14	Tommy Smith	.16	.08	.01
☐	15	Don Gullett	.25	.12	.02
☐	16	Bob Jones	.16	.08	.01
☐	17	Steve Stone	.25	.12	.02
☐	18	Indians Team/Mgr. Frank Robinson (checklist back)	.65	.30	.06
☐	19	John D'Acquisto	.16	.08	.01
☐	20	Graig Nettles	.75	.35	.07
☐	21	Ken Forsch	.16	.08	.01
☐	22	Bill Freehan	.25	.12	.02

☐ 23 Dan Driessen	.25	.12	.02
☐ 24 Carl Morton	.16	.08	.01
☐ 25 Dwight Evans	1.75	.85	.17
☐ 26 Ray Sadecki	.16	.08	.01
☐ 27 Bill Buckner	.35	.17	.03
☐ 28 Woodie Fryman	.16	.08	.01
☐ 29 Bucky Dent	.35	.17	.03
☐ 30 Greg Luzinski	.35	.17	.03
☐ 31 Jim Todd	.16	.08	.01
☐ 32 Checklist 1	.80	.10	.02
☐ 33 Wayne Garland	.16	.08	.01
☐ 34 Angels Team/Mgr.	.65	.30	.06
Norm Sherry			
(checklist back)			
☐ 35 Rennie Stennett	.16	.08	.01
☐ 36 John Ellis	.16	.08	.01
☐ 37 Steve Hargan	.16	.08	.01
☐ 38 Craig Kusick	.16	.08	.01
☐ 39 Tom Griffin	.16	.08	.01
☐ 40 Bobby Murcer	.35	.17	.03
☐ 41 Jim Kern	.16	.08	.01
☐ 42 Jose Cruz	.25	.12	.02
☐ 43 Ray Bare	.16	.08	.01
☐ 44 Bud Harrelson	.25	.12	.02
☐ 45 Rawly Eastwick	.16	.08	.01
☐ 46 Buck Martinez	.16	.08	.01
☐ 47 Lynn McGlothen	.16	.08	.01
☐ 48 Tom Paciorek	.16	.08	.01
☐ 49 Grant Jackson	.16	.08	.01
☐ 50 Ron Cey	.35	.17	.03
☐ 51 Brewers Team/Mgr.	.65	.30	.06
Alex Grammas			
(checklist back)			
☐ 52 Ellis Valentine	.16	.08	.01
☐ 53 Paul Mitchell	.16	.08	.01
☐ 54 Sandy Alomar	.16	.08	.01
☐ 55 Jeff Burroughs	.25	.12	.02
☐ 56 Rudy May	.16	.08	.01
☐ 57 Marc Hill	.16	.08	.01
☐ 58 Chet Lemon	.25	.12	.02
☐ 59 Larry Christenson	.16	.08	.01
☐ 60 Jim Rice	4.00	2.00	.40
☐ 61 Manny Sanguillen	.25	.12	.02
☐ 62 Eric Raich	.16	.08	.01
☐ 63 Tito Fuentes	.16	.08	.01
☐ 64 Larry Biittner	.16	.08	.01
☐ 65 Skip Lockwood	.16	.08	.01
☐ 66 Roy Smalley	.25	.12	.02
☐ 67 Joaquin Andujar	.75	.35	.07
☐ 68 Bruce Bochte	.16	.08	.01
☐ 69 Jim Crawford	.16	.08	.01
☐ 70 Johnny Bench	5.50	2.75	.55
☐ 71 Dock Ellis	.16	.08	.01
☐ 72 Mike Anderson	.16	.08	.01
☐ 73 Charlie Williams	.16	.08	.01
☐ 74 A's Team/Mgr.	.65	.30	.06
Jack McKeon			
(checklist back)			
☐ 75 Dennis Leonard	.25	.12	.02
☐ 76 Tim Foli	.16	.08	.01
☐ 77 Dyar Miller	.16	.08	.01
☐ 78 Bob Davis	.16	.08	.01
☐ 79 Don Money	.16	.08	.01
☐ 80 Andy Messersmith	.25	.12	.02
☐ 81 Juan Beniquez	.16	.08	.01
☐ 82 Jim Rooker	.16	.08	.01
☐ 83 Kevin Bell	.16	.08	.01
☐ 84 Ollie Brown	.16	.08	.01
☐ 85 Duane Kuiper	.16	.08	.01
☐ 86 Pat Zachry	.16	.08	.01
☐ 87 Glenn Borgmann	.16	.08	.01
☐ 88 Stan Wall	.16	.08	.01
☐ 89 Butch Hobson	.16	.08	.01
☐ 90 Cesar Cedeno	.25	.12	.02
☐ 91 John Verhoeven	.16	.08	.01
☐ 92 Dave Rosello	.16	.08	.01
☐ 93 Tom Poquette	.16	.08	.01
☐ 94 Craig Swan	.16	.08	.01
☐ 95 Keith Hernandez	3.00	1.50	.30
☐ 96 Lou Piniella	.35	.17	.03
☐ 97 Dave Heaverlo	.16	.08	.01
☐ 98 Milt May	.16	.08	.01
☐ 99 Tom Hausman	.16	.08	.01
☐ 100 Joe Morgan	2.00	1.00	.20
☐ 101 Dick Bosman	.16	.08	.01
☐ 102 Jose Morales	.16	.08	.01
☐ 103 Mike Bacsik	.16	.08	.01
☐ 104 Omar Moreno	.25	.12	.02
☐ 105 Steve Yeager	.25	.12	.02
☐ 106 Mike Flanagan	.35	.17	.03
☐ 107 Bill Melton	.16	.08	.01
☐ 108 Alan Foster	.16	.08	.01
☐ 109 Jorge Orta	.16	.08	.01
☐ 110 Steve Carlton	4.50	2.00	.40
☐ 111 Rico Petrocelli	.25	.12	.02

☐ 112 Bill Greif	.16	.08	.01
☐ 113 Blue Jays Leaders	.50	.25	.05
Roy Hartsfield MG			
Don Leppert CO			
Bob Miller CO			
Jackie Moore CO			
Harry Warner CO			
(checklist back)			
☐ 114 Bruce Dal Canton	.16	.08	.01
☐ 115 Rick Manning	.16	.08	.01
☐ 116 Joe Niekro	.35	.17	.03
☐ 117 Frank White	.35	.17	.03
☐ 118 Rick Jones	.16	.08	.01
☐ 119 John Stearns	.16	.08	.01
☐ 120 Rod Carew	4.50	2.00	.40
☐ 121 Gary Nolan	.16	.08	.01
☐ 122 Ben Oglivie	.25	.12	.02
☐ 123 Fred Stanley	.16	.08	.01
☐ 124 George Mitterwald	.16	.08	.01
☐ 125 Bill Travers	.16	.08	.01
☐ 126 Rod Gilbreath	.16	.08	.01
☐ 127 Ron Fairly	.16	.08	.01
☐ 128 Tommy John	1.00	.50	.10
☐ 129 Mike Sadek	.16	.08	.01
☐ 130 Al Oliver	.40	.20	.04
☐ 131 Orlando Ramirez	.16	.08	.01
☐ 132 Chip Lang	.16	.08	.01
☐ 133 Ralph Garr	.25	.12	.02
☐ 134 Padres Team/Mgr.	.65	.30	.06
John McNamara			
(checklist back)			
☐ 135 Mark Belanger	.25	.12	.02
☐ 136 Jerry Mumphrey	.35	.17	.03
☐ 137 Jeff Terpko	.16	.08	.01
☐ 138 Bob Stinson	.16	.08	.01
☐ 139 Fred Norman	.16	.08	.01
☐ 140 Mike Schmidt	14.00	7.00	1.40
☐ 141 Mark Littell	.16	.08	.01
☐ 142 Steve Dillard	.16	.08	.01
☐ 143 Ed Herrmann	.16	.08	.01
☐ 144 Bruce Sutter	2.50	1.25	.25
☐ 145 Tom Veryzer	.16	.08	.01
☐ 146 Dusty Baker	.25	.12	.02
☐ 147 Jackie Brown	.16	.08	.01
☐ 148 Fran Healy	.16	.08	.01
☐ 149 Mike Cubbage	.16	.08	.01
☐ 150 Tom Seaver	5.00	2.25	.45
☐ 151 Johnny LeMaster	.16	.08	.01
☐ 152 Gaylord Perry	1.75	.85	.17
☐ 153 Ron Jackson	.16	.08	.01
☐ 154 Dave Giusti	.16	.08	.01
☐ 155 Joe Rudi	.25	.12	.02
☐ 156 Pete Mackanin	.16	.08	.01
☐ 157 Ken Brett	.16	.08	.01
☐ 158 Ted Kubiak	.16	.08	.01
☐ 159 Bernie Carbo	.16	.08	.01
☐ 160 Will McEnaney	.16	.08	.01
☐ 161 Garry Templeton	1.00	.50	.10
☐ 162 Mike Cuellar	.25	.12	.02
☐ 163 Dave Hilton	.16	.08	.01
☐ 164 Tug McGraw	.35	.17	.03
☐ 165 Jim Wynn	.25	.12	.02
☐ 166 Bill Campbell	.16	.08	.01
☐ 167 Rich Hebner	.16	.08	.01
☐ 168 Charlie Spikes	.16	.08	.01
☐ 169 Darold Knowles	.16	.08	.01
☐ 170 Thurman Munson	4.00	2.00	.40
☐ 171 Ken Sanders	.16	.08	.01
☐ 172 John Milner	.16	.08	.01
☐ 173 Chuck Scrivener	.16	.08	.01
☐ 174 Nelson Briles	.16	.08	.01
☐ 175 Butch Wynegar	.50	.25	.05
☐ 176 Bob Robertson	.16	.08	.01
☐ 177 Bart Johnson	.16	.08	.01
☐ 178 Bombo Rivera	.16	.08	.01
☐ 179 Paul Hartzell	.16	.08	.01
☐ 180 Dave Lopes	.25	.12	.02
☐ 181 Ken McMullen	.16	.08	.01
☐ 182 Dan Spillner	.16	.08	.01
☐ 183 Cardinals Team/Mgr.	.65	.30	.06
Vern Rapp			
(checklist back)			
☐ 184 Bo McLaughlin	.16	.08	.01
☐ 185 Sixto Lezcano	.16	.08	.01
☐ 186 Doug Flynn	.16	.08	.01
☐ 187 Dick Pole	.16	.08	.01
☐ 188 Bob Tolan	.16	.08	.01
☐ 189 Rick Dempsey	.25	.12	.02
☐ 190 Ray Burris	.16	.08	.01
☐ 191 Doug Griffin	.16	.08	.01
☐ 192 Clarence Gaston	.35	.17	.03
☐ 193 Larry Gura	.25	.12	.02
☐ 194 Gary Matthews	.25	.12	.02
☐ 195 Ed Figueroa	.16	.08	.01
☐ 196 Len Randle	.16	.08	.01

☐ 197 Ed Ott	.16	.08	.01
☐ 198 Wilbur Wood	.25	.12	.02
☐ 199 Pepe Frias	.16	.08	.01
☐ 200 Frank Tanana	.35	.17	.03
☐ 201 Ed Kranepool	.25	.12	.02
☐ 202 Tom Johnson	.16	.08	.01
☐ 203 Ed Armbrister	.16	.08	.01
☐ 204 Jeff Newman	.16	.08	.01
☐ 205 Pete Falcone	.16	.08	.01
☐ 206 Boog Powell	.40	.20	.04
☐ 207 Glenn Abbott	.16	.08	.01
☐ 208 Checklist 2	.80	.10	.02
☐ 209 Rob Andrews	.16	.08	.01
☐ 210 Fred Lynn	1.50	.75	.15
☐ 211 Giants Team/Mgr.	.65	.30	.06
Joe Altobelli			
(checklist back)			
☐ 212 Jim Mason	.16	.08	.01
☐ 213 Maximino Leon	.16	.08	.01
☐ 214 Darrell Porter	.16	.08	.01
☐ 215 Butch Metzger	.16	.08	.01
☐ 216 Doug DeCinces	.25	.12	.02
☐ 217 Tom Underwood	.16	.08	.01
☐ 218 John Wathan	1.50	.75	.15
☐ 219 Joe Coleman	.16	.08	.01
☐ 220 Chris Chambliss	.35	.17	.03
☐ 221 Bob Bailey	.16	.08	.01
☐ 222 Francisco Barrios	.16	.08	.01
☐ 223 Earl Williams	.16	.08	.01
☐ 224 Rusty Torres	.16	.08	.01
☐ 225 Bob Apodaca	.16	.08	.01
☐ 226 Leroy Stanton	.16	.08	.01
☐ 227 Joe Sambito	.25	.12	.02
☐ 228 Twins Team/Mgr.	.65	.30	.06
Gene Mauch			
(checklist back)			
☐ 229 Don Kessinger	.25	.12	.02
☐ 230 Vida Blue	.35	.17	.03
☐ 231 RB: George Brett	2.00	1.00	.20
Most cons. games			
with 3 or more hits			
☐ 232 RB: Minnie Minoso	.25	.12	.02
Oldest to hit safely			
☐ 233 RB: Jose Morales, Most	.25	.12	.02
pinch-hits, season			
☐ 234 RB: Nolan Ryan	3.00	1.50	.30
Most seasons, 300			
or more strikeouts			
☐ 235 Cecil Cooper	.50	.25	.05
☐ 236 Tom Buskey	.16	.08	.01
☐ 237 Gene Clines	.16	.08	.01
☐ 238 Tippy Martinez	.25	.12	.02
☐ 239 Bill Plummer	.16	.08	.01
☐ 240 Ron LeFlore	.25	.12	.02
☐ 241 Dave Tomlin	.16	.08	.01
☐ 242 Ken Henderson	.16	.08	.01
☐ 243 Ron Reed	.16	.08	.01
☐ 244 John Mayberry	.35	.17	.03
(cartoon mentions			
T206 Wagner)			
☐ 245 Rick Rhoden	.25	.12	.02
☐ 246 Mike Vail	.16	.08	.01
☐ 247 Chris Knapp	.16	.08	.01
☐ 248 Wilbur Howard	.16	.08	.01
☐ 249 Pete Redfern	.16	.08	.01
☐ 250 Bill Madlock	.50	.25	.05
☐ 251 Tony Muser	.16	.08	.01
☐ 252 Dale Murray	.16	.08	.01
☐ 253 John Hale	.16	.08	.01
☐ 254 Doyle Alexander	.25	.12	.02
☐ 255 George Scott	.25	.12	.02
☐ 256 Joe Hoerner	.16	.08	.01
☐ 257 Mike Miley	.16	.08	.01
☐ 258 Luis Tiant	.35	.17	.03
☐ 259 Mets Team/Mgr.	.75	.35	.07
Joe Frazier			
(checklist back)			
☐ 260 J.R. Richard	.25	.12	.02
☐ 261 Phil Garner	.25	.12	.02
☐ 262 Al Cowens	.25	.12	.02
☐ 263 Mike Marshall	.25	.12	.02
☐ 264 Tom Hutton	.16	.08	.01
☐ 265 Mark Fidrych	.50	.25	.05
☐ 266 Derrel Thomas	.16	.08	.01
☐ 267 Ray Fosse	.16	.08	.01
☐ 268 Rick Sawyer	.16	.08	.01
☐ 269 Joe Lis	.16	.08	.01
☐ 270 Dave Parker	2.75	1.35	.27
☐ 271 Terry Forster	.25	.12	.02
☐ 272 Lee Lacy	.16	.08	.01
☐ 273 Eric Soderholm	.16	.08	.01
☐ 274 Don Stanhouse	.16	.08	.01
☐ 275 Mike Hargrove	.25	.12	.02
☐ 276 AL Champs	.35	.17	.03
Chambliss' homer			

decides it			
☐ 277 NL Champs	.35	.17	.03
Reds sweep Phillies			
☐ 278 Danny Frisella	.16	.08	.01
☐ 279 Joe Wallis	.16	.08	.01
☐ 280 Jim Hunter	2.00	1.00	.20
☐ 281 Roy Staiger	.16	.08	.01
☐ 282 Sid Monge	.16	.08	.01
☐ 283 Jerry DaVanon	.16	.08	.01
☐ 284 Mike Norris	.16	.08	.01
☐ 285 Brooks Robinson	2.50	1.25	.25
☐ 286 Johnny Grubb	.16	.08	.01
☐ 287 Reds Team/Mgr.	.75	.35	.07
Sparky Anderson			
(checklist back)			
☐ 288 Bob Montgomery	.16	.08	.01
☐ 289 Gene Garber	.16	.08	.01
☐ 290 Amos Otis	.35	.17	.03
☐ 291 Jason Thompson	.25	.12	.02
☐ 292 Rogelio Moret	.16	.08	.01
☐ 293 Jack Brohamer	.16	.08	.01
☐ 294 George Medich	.16	.08	.01
☐ 295 Gary Carter	5.00	2.50	.50
☐ 296 Don Hood	.16	.08	.01
☐ 297 Ken Reitz	.16	.08	.01
☐ 298 Charlie Hough	.25	.12	.02
☐ 299 Otto Velez	.16	.08	.01
☐ 300 Jerry Koosman	.35	.17	.03
☐ 301 Toby Harrah	.25	.12	.02
☐ 302 Mike Garman	.16	.08	.01
☐ 303 Gene Tenace	.25	.12	.02
☐ 304 Jim Hughes	.16	.08	.01
☐ 305 Mickey Rivers	.25	.12	.02
☐ 306 Rick Waits	.16	.08	.01
☐ 307 Gary Sutherland	.16	.08	.01
☐ 308 Gene Pentz	.16	.08	.01
☐ 309 Red Sox Team/Mgr.	.65	.30	.06
Don Zimmer			
(checklist back)			
☐ 310 Larry Bowa	.40	.20	.04
☐ 311 Vern Ruhle	.16	.08	.01
☐ 312 Rob Belloir	.16	.08	.01
☐ 313 Paul Blair	.25	.12	.02
☐ 314 Steve Mingori	.16	.08	.01
☐ 315 Dave Chalk	.16	.08	.01
☐ 316 Steve Rogers	.25	.12	.02
☐ 317 Kurt Bevacqua	.16	.08	.01
☐ 318 Duffy Dyer	.16	.08	.01
☐ 319 Rich Gossage	.75	.35	.07
☐ 320 Ken Griffey	.35	.17	.03
☐ 321 Dave Goltz	.16	.08	.01
☐ 322 Bill Russell	.25	.12	.02
☐ 323 Larry Lintz	.16	.08	.01
☐ 324 John Curtis	.16	.08	.01
☐ 325 Mike Ivie	.16	.08	.01
☐ 326 Jesse Jefferson	.16	.08	.01
☐ 327 Astros Team/Mgr.	.65	.30	.06
Bill Virdon			
(checklist back)			
☐ 328 Tommy Boggs	.16	.08	.01
☐ 329 Ron Hodges	.16	.08	.01
☐ 330 George Hendrick	.25	.12	.02
☐ 331 Jim Colborn	.16	.08	.01
☐ 332 Elliott Maddox	.16	.08	.01
☐ 333 Paul Reuschel	.16	.08	.01
☐ 334 Bill Stein	.16	.08	.01
☐ 335 Bill Robinson	.25	.12	.02
☐ 336 Denny Doyle	.16	.08	.01
☐ 337 Ron Schueler	.16	.08	.01
☐ 338 Dave Duncan	.16	.08	.01
☐ 339 Adrian Devine	.16	.08	.01
☐ 340 Hal McRae	.25	.12	.02
☐ 341 Joe Kerrigan	.16	.08	.01
☐ 342 Jerry Remy	.16	.08	.01
☐ 343 Ed Halicki	.16	.08	.01
☐ 344 Brian Downing	.25	.12	.02
☐ 345 Reggie Smith	.35	.17	.03
☐ 346 Bill Singer	.16	.08	.01
☐ 347 George Foster	1.25	.60	.12
☐ 348 Brent Strom	.16	.08	.01
☐ 349 Jim Holt	.16	.08	.01
☐ 350 Larry Dierker	.16	.08	.01
☐ 351 Jim Sundberg	.25	.12	.02
☐ 352 Mike Phillips	.16	.08	.01
☐ 353 Stan Thomas	.16	.08	.01
☐ 354 Pirates Team/Mgr.	.65	.30	.06
Chuck Tanner			
(checklist back)			
☐ 355 Lou Brock	2.50	1.25	.25
☐ 356 Checklist 3	.80	.10	.02
☐ 357 Tim McCarver	.35	.17	.03
☐ 358 Tom Hoso	.25	.12	.02
☐ 359 Willie Randolph	.90	.45	.09
☐ 360 Rick Monday	.25	.12	.02
☐ 361 Eduardo Rodriguez	.16	.08	.01

☐ 362 Tommy Davis	.35	.17	.03
☐ 363 Dave Roberts	.16	.08	.01
☐ 364 Vic Correll	.16	.08	.01
☐ 365 Mike Torrez	.25	.12	.02
☐ 366 Ted Sizemore	.16	.08	.01
☐ 367 Dave Hamilton	.16	.08	.01
☐ 368 Mike Jorgensen	.16	.08	.01
☐ 369 Terry Humphrey	.16	.08	.01
☐ 370 John Montefusco	.25	.12	.02
☐ 371 Royals Team/Mgr.	.65	.30	.06
Whitey Herzog			
(checklist back)			
☐ 372 Rich Folkers	.16	.08	.01
☐ 373 Bert Campaneris	.25	.12	.02
☐ 374 Kent Tekulve	.25	.12	.02
☐ 375 Larry Hisle	.25	.12	.02
☐ 376 Nino Espinosa	.16	.08	.01
☐ 377 Dave McKay	.16	.08	.01
☐ 378 Jim Umbarger	.16	.08	.01
☐ 379 Larry Cox	.16	.08	.01
☐ 380 Lee May	.25	.12	.02
☐ 381 Bob Forsch	.25	.12	.02
☐ 382 Charlie Moore	.16	.08	.01
☐ 383 Stan Bahnsen	.16	.08	.01
☐ 384 Darrel Chaney	.16	.08	.01
☐ 385 Dave LaRoche	.16	.08	.01
☐ 386 Manny Mota	.25	.12	.02
☐ 387 Yankees Team	.75	.35	.07
(checklist back)			
☐ 388 Terry Harmon	.16	.08	.01
☐ 389 Ken Kravec	.16	.08	.01
☐ 390 Dave Winfield	4.00	2.00	.40
☐ 391 Dan Warthen	.16	.08	.01
☐ 392 Phil Roof	.16	.08	.01
☐ 393 John Lowenstein	.16	.08	.01
☐ 394 Bill Laxton	.16	.08	.01
☐ 395 Manny Trillo	.16	.08	.01
☐ 396 Tom Murphy	.16	.08	.01
☐ 397 Larry Herndon	.25	.12	.02
☐ 398 Tom Burgmeier	.16	.08	.01
☐ 399 Bruce Boisclair	.16	.08	.01
☐ 400 Steve Garvey	3.50	1.75	.35
☐ 401 Mickey Scott	.16	.08	.01
☐ 402 Tommy Helms	.25	.12	.02
☐ 403 Tom Grieve	.25	.12	.02
☐ 404 Eric Rasmussen	.16	.08	.01
☐ 405 Claudell Washington	.35	.17	.03
☐ 406 Tim Johnson	.16	.08	.01
☐ 407 Dave Freisleben	.16	.08	.01
☐ 408 Cesar Tovar	.16	.08	.01
☐ 409 Pete Broberg	.16	.08	.01
☐ 410 Willie Montanez	.16	.08	.01
☐ 411 W.S. Games 1 and 2	.60	.30	.06
Morgan homers opener;			
Bench stars as			
Reds take 2nd game			
☐ 412 W.S. Games 3 and 4	.60	.30	.06
Reds stop Yankees;			
Bench's two homers			
wrap it up			
☐ 413 World Series Summary	.50	.25	.05
Cincy wins 2nd			
straight series			
☐ 414 Tommy Harper	.25	.12	.02
☐ 415 Jay Johnstone	.25	.12	.02
☐ 416 Chuck Hartenstein	.16	.08	.01
☐ 417 Wayne Garrett	.16	.08	.01
☐ 418 White Sox Team/Mgr.	.65	.30	.06
Bob Lemon			
(checklist back)			
☐ 419 Steve Swisher	.16	.08	.01
☐ 420 Rusty Staub	.35	.17	.03
☐ 421 Doug Rau	.16	.08	.01
☐ 422 Freddie Patek	.16	.08	.01
☐ 423 Gary Lavelle	.16	.08	.01
☐ 424 Steve Brye	.16	.08	.01
☐ 425 Joe Torre	.35	.17	.03
☐ 426 Dick Drago	.16	.08	.01
☐ 427 Dave Rader	.16	.08	.01
☐ 428 Rangers Team/Mgr.	.65	.30	.06
Frank Lucchesi			
(checklist back)			
☐ 429 Ken Boswell	.16	.08	.01
☐ 430 Fergie Jenkins	.75	.35	.07
☐ 431 Dave Collins	.25	.12	.02
(photo actually			
Bobby Jones)			
☐ 432 Buzz Capra	.16	.08	.01
☐ 433 Turn back clock 1972	.25	.12	.02
Nate Colbert			
☐ 434 Turn back clock 1967	2.00	1.00	.20
Yaz Triple Crown			
☐ 435 Turn back clock 1962	.35	.17	.03
Wills 104 steals			
☐ 436 Turn back clock 1957	.25	.12	.02

Keegan hurls Majors'			
only no-hitter			
☐ 437 Turn back clock 1952	.40	.20	.04
Kiner leads NL HR's			
7th straight year			
☐ 438 Marty Perez	.16	.08	.01
☐ 439 Gorman Thomas	.35	.17	.03
☐ 440 Jon Matlack	.25	.12	.02
☐ 441 Larvell Blanks	.16	.08	.01
☐ 442 Braves Team/Mgr.	.65	.30	.06
Dave Bristol			
(checklist back)			
☐ 443 Lamar Johnson	.16	.08	.01
☐ 444 Wayne Twitchell	.16	.08	.01
☐ 445 Ken Singleton	.25	.12	.02
☐ 446 Bill Bonham	.16	.08	.01
☐ 447 Jerry Turner	.16	.08	.01
☐ 448 Ellie Rodriguez	.16	.08	.01
☐ 449 Al Fitzmorris	.16	.08	.01
☐ 450 Pete Rose	9.00	4.50	.90
☐ 451 Checklist 4	.80	.10	.02
☐ 452 Mike Caldwell	.16	.08	.01
☐ 453 Pedro Garcia	.16	.08	.01
☐ 454 Andy Etchebarren	.16	.08	.01
☐ 455 Rick Wise	.16	.08	.01
☐ 456 Leon Roberts	.16	.08	.01
☐ 457 Steve Luebber	.16	.08	.01
☐ 458 Leo Foster	.16	.08	.01
☐ 459 Steve Foucault	.16	.08	.01
☐ 460 Willie Stargell	2.50	1.25	.25
☐ 461 Dick Tidrow	.16	.08	.01
☐ 462 Don Baylor	.60	.30	.06
☐ 463 Jamie Quirk	.16	.08	.01
☐ 464 Randy Moffitt	.16	.08	.01
☐ 465 Rico Carty	.25	.12	.02
☐ 466 Fred Holdsworth	.16	.08	.01
☐ 467 Phillies Team/Mgr.	.65	.30	.06
Danny Ozark			
(checklist back)			
☐ 468 Ramon Hernandez	.16	.08	.01
☐ 469 Pat Kelly	.16	.08	.01
☐ 470 Ted Simmons	.50	.25	.05
☐ 471 Del Unser	.16	.08	.01
☐ 472 Rookie Pitchers	.35	.17	.03
Don Aase			
Bob McClure			
Gil Patterson			
Dave Wehrmeister			
☐ 473 Rookie Outfielders	32.00	16.00	3.20
Andre Dawson			
Gene Richards			
John Scott			
Denny Walling			
☐ 474 Rookie Shortstops	.25	.12	.02
Bob Bailor			
Kiko Garcia			
Craig Reynolds			
Alex Taveras			
☐ 475 Rookie Pitchers	.40	.20	.04
Chris Batton			
Rick Camp			
Scott McGregor			
Manny Sarmiento			
☐ 476 Rookie Catchers	50.00	25.00	5.00
Gary Alexander			
Rick Cerone			
Dale Murphy			
Kevin Pasley			
☐ 477 Rookie Infielders	.25	.12	.02
Doug Ault			
Rich Dauer			
Orlando Gonzalez			
Phil Mankowski			
☐ 478 Rookie Pitchers	.25	.12	.02
Jim Gideon			
Leon Hooten			
Dave Johnson			
Mark Lemongello			
☐ 479 Rookie Outfielders	.25	.12	.02
Brian Asselstine			
Wayne Gross			
Sam Mejias			
Alvis Woods			
☐ 480 Carl Yastrzemski	5.50	2.75	.55
☐ 481 Roger Metzger	.16	.08	.01
☐ 482 Tony Solaita	.16	.08	.01
☐ 483 Richie Zisk	.16	.08	.01
☐ 484 Burt Hooton	.16	.08	.01
☐ 485 Roy White	.25	.12	.02
☐ 486 Ed Bane	.16	.08	.01
☐ 487 Rookie Pitchers	.25	.12	.02
Larry Anderson			
Ed Glynn			
Joe Henderson			
Greg Terlecky			

□ 488	Rookie Outfielders	18.00	9.00	1.80
	Jack Clark			
	Ruppert Jones			
	Lee Mazzilli			
	Dan Thomas			
□ 489	Rookie Pitchers	.35	.17	.03
	Len Barker			
	Randy Lerch			
	Greg Minton			
	Mike Overy			
□ 490	Rookie Shortstops	.25	.12	.02
	Billy Almon			
	Mickey Klutts			
	Tommy McMillan			
	Mark Wagner			
□ 491	Rookie Pitchers	2.00	1.00	.20
	Mike Dupree			
	Denny Martinez			
	Craig Mitchell			
	Bob Sykes			
□ 492	Rookie Outfielders	1.00	.50	.10
	Tony Armas			
	Steve Kemp			
	Carlos Lopez			
	Gary Woods			
□ 493	Rookie Pitchers	.75	.35	.07
	Mike Krukow			
	Jim Otten			
	Gary Wheelock			
	Mike Willis			
□ 494	Rookie Infielders	.50	.25	.05
	Juan Bernhardt			
	Mike Champion			
	Jim Gantner			
	Bump Wills			
□ 495	Al Hrabosky	.25	.12	.02
□ 496	Gary Thomasson	.16	.08	.01
□ 497	Clay Carroll	.16	.08	.01
□ 498	Sal Bando	.25	.12	.02
□ 499	Pablo Torrealba	.16	.08	.01
□ 500	Dave Kingman	.50	.25	.05
□ 501	Jim Bibby	.16	.08	.01
□ 502	Randy Hundley	.16	.08	.01
□ 503	Bill Lee	.25	.12	.02
□ 504	Dodgers Team/Mgr.	.75	.35	.07
	Tom Lasorda			
	(checklist back)			
□ 505	Oscar Gamble	.25	.12	.02
□ 506	Steve Grilli	.16	.08	.01
□ 507	Mike Hegan	.16	.08	.01
□ 508	Dave Pagan	.16	.08	.01
□ 509	Cookie Rojas	.25	.12	.02
□ 510	John Candelaria	.60	.30	.06
□ 511	Bill Fahey	.16	.08	.01
□ 512	Jack Billingham	.16	.08	.01
□ 513	Jerry Terrell	.16	.08	.01
□ 514	Cliff Johnson	.16	.08	.01
□ 515	Chris Speier	.16	.08	.01
□ 516	Bake McBride	.16	.08	.01
□ 517	Pete Vuckovich	.50	.25	.05
□ 518	Cubs Team/Mgr.	.65	.30	.06
	Herman Franks			
	(checklist back)			
□ 519	Don Kirkwood	.16	.08	.01
□ 520	Garry Maddox	.25	.12	.02
□ 521	Bob Grich	.25	.12	.02
□ 522	Enzo Hernandez	.16	.08	.01
□ 523	Rollie Fingers	1.00	.50	.10
□ 524	Rowland Office	.16	.08	.01
□ 525	Dennis Eckersley	1.50	.75	.15
□ 526	Larry Parrish	.25	.12	.02
□ 527	Dan Meyer	.16	.08	.01
□ 528	Bill Castro	.16	.08	.01
□ 529	Jim Essian	.16	.08	.01
□ 530	Rick Reuschel	.50	.25	.05
□ 531	Lyman Bostock	.25	.12	.02
□ 532	Jim Willoughby	.16	.08	.01
□ 533	Mickey Stanley	.25	.12	.02
□ 534	Paul Splittorff	.16	.08	.01
□ 535	Cesar Geronimo	.16	.08	.01
□ 536	Vic Albury	.16	.08	.01
□ 537	Dave Roberts	.16	.08	.01
□ 538	Frank Taveras	.16	.08	.01
□ 539	Mike Wallace	.16	.08	.01
□ 540	Bob Watson	.25	.12	.02
□ 541	John Denny	.25	.12	.02
□ 542	Frank Duffy	.16	.08	.01
□ 543	Ron Blomberg	.16	.08	.01
□ 544	Gary Ross	.16	.08	.01
□ 545	Bob Boone	.50	.25	.05
□ 546	Orioles Team/Mgr.	.75	.35	.07
	Earl Weaver			
	(checklist back)			
□ 547	Willie McCovey	2.25	1.10	.22
□ 548	Joel Youngblood	.16	.08	.01
□ 549	Jerry Royster	.16	.08	.01
□ 550	Randy Jones	.16	.08	.01
□ 551	Bill North	.16	.08	.01
□ 552	Pepe Mangual	.16	.08	.01
□ 553	Jack Heidemann	.16	.08	.01
□ 554	Bruce Kimm	.16	.08	.01
□ 555	Dan Ford	.16	.08	.01
□ 556	Doug Bird	.16	.08	.01
□ 557	Jerry White	.16	.08	.01
□ 558	Elias Sosa	.16	.08	.01
□ 559	Alan Bannister	.16	.08	.01
□ 560	Dave Concepcion	.35	.17	.03
□ 561	Pete LaCock	.16	.08	.01
□ 562	Checklist 5	.80	.10	.02
□ 563	Bruce Kison	.16	.08	.01
□ 564	Alan Ashby	.25	.12	.02
□ 565	Mickey Lolich	.35	.17	.03
□ 566	Rick Miller	.16	.08	.01
□ 567	Enos Cabell	.16	.08	.01
□ 568	Carlos May	.16	.08	.01
□ 569	Jim Lonborg	.25	.12	.02
□ 570	Bobby Bonds	.35	.17	.03
□ 571	Darrell Evans	.50	.25	.05
□ 572	Ross Grimsley	.16	.08	.01
□ 573	Joe Ferguson	.16	.08	.01
□ 574	Aurelio Rodriguez	.16	.08	.01
□ 575	Dick Ruthven	.16	.08	.01
□ 576	Fred Kendall	.16	.08	.01
□ 577	Jerry Augustine	.16	.08	.01
□ 578	Bob Randall	.16	.08	.01
□ 579	Don Carrithers	.16	.08	.01
□ 580	George Brett	11.00	5.50	1.10
□ 581	Pedro Borbon	.16	.08	.01
□ 582	Ed Kirkpatrick	.16	.08	.01
□ 583	Paul Lindblad	.16	.08	.01
□ 584	Ed Goodson	.16	.08	.01
□ 585	Rick Burleson	.25	.12	.02
□ 586	Steve Renko	.16	.08	.01
□ 587	Rick Baldwin	.16	.08	.01
□ 588	Dave Moates	.16	.08	.01
□ 589	Mike Cosgrove	.16	.08	.01
□ 590	Buddy Bell	.40	.20	.04
□ 591	Chris Arnold	.16	.08	.01
□ 592	Dan Briggs	.16	.08	.01
□ 593	Dennis Blair	.16	.08	.01
□ 594	Biff Pocoroba	.16	.08	.01
□ 595	John Hiller	.25	.12	.02
□ 596	Jerry Martin	.16	.08	.01
□ 597	Mariners Leaders	.50	.25	.05
	Darrell Johnson MG			
	Don Bryant CO			
	Jim Busby CO			
	Vada Pinson CO			
	Wes Stock CO			
	(checklist back)			
□ 598	Sparky Lyle	.50	.25	.05
□ 599	Mike Tyson	.16	.08	.01
□ 600	Jim Palmer	2.50	1.25	.25
□ 601	Mike Lum	.16	.08	.01
□ 602	Andy Hassler	.16	.08	.01
□ 603	Willie Davis	.25	.12	.02
□ 604	Jim Slaton	.16	.08	.01
□ 605	Felix Millan	.16	.08	.01
□ 606	Steve Braun	.16	.08	.01
□ 607	Larry Demery	.16	.08	.01
□ 608	Roy Howell	.16	.08	.01
□ 609	Jim Barr	.16	.08	.01
□ 610	Jose Cardenal	.16	.08	.01
□ 611	Dave Lemanczyk	.16	.08	.01
□ 612	Barry Foote	.16	.08	.01
□ 613	Reggie Cleveland	.16	.08	.01
□ 614	Greg Gross	.16	.08	.01
□ 615	Phil Niekro	1.50	.75	.15
□ 616	Tommy Sandt	.16	.08	.01
□ 617	Bobby Darwin	.16	.08	.01
□ 618	Pat Dobson	.25	.12	.02
□ 619	Johnny Oates	.16	.08	.01
□ 620	Don Sutton	1.50	.75	.15
□ 621	Tigers Team/Mgr.	.75	.35	.07
	Ralph Houk			
	(checklist back)			
□ 622	Jim Wohlford	.16	.08	.01
□ 623	Jack Kucek	.16	.08	.01
□ 624	Hector Cruz	.16	.08	.01
□ 625	Ken Holtzman	.25	.12	.02
□ 626	Al Bumbry	.16	.08	.01
□ 627	Bob Myrick	.16	.08	.01
□ 628	Mario Guerrero	.16	.08	.01
□ 629	Bobby Valentine	.35	.17	.03
□ 630	Bert Blyleven	.90	.45	.09
□ 631	Big League Brothers	1.50	.75	.15
	George Brett			
	Ken Brett			
□ 632	Big League Brothers	.25	.12	.02
	Bob Forsch			

	Ken Forsch			
☐ 633	Big League Brothers	.25	.12	.02
	Lee May			
	Carlos May			
☐ 634	Big League Brothers	.25	.12	.02
	Paul Reuschel			
	Rick Reuschel			
	(photos switched)			
☐ 635	Robin Yount	14.00	7.00	1.40
☐ 636	Santo Alcala	.16	.08	.01
☐ 637	Alex Johnson	.16	.08	.01
☐ 638	Jim Kaat	.60	.30	.06
☐ 639	Jerry Morales	.16	.08	.01
☐ 640	Carlton Fisk	2.00	1.00	.20
☐ 641	Dan Larson	.16	.08	.01
☐ 642	Willie Crawford	.16	.08	.01
☐ 643	Mike Pazik	.16	.08	.01
☐ 644	Matt Alexander	.16	.08	.01
☐ 645	Jerry Reuss	.25	.12	.02
☐ 646	Andres Mora	.16	.08	.01
☐ 647	Expos Team/Mgr.	.65	.30	.06
	Dick Williams			
	(checklist back)			
☐ 648	Jim Spencer	.16	.08	.01
☐ 649	Dave Cash	.16	.08	.01
☐ 650	Nolan Ryan	13.00	6.50	1.30
☐ 651	Von Joshua	.16	.08	.01
☐ 652	Tom Walker	.16	.08	.01
☐ 653	Diego Segui	.16	.08	.01
☐ 654	Ron Pruitt	.16	.08	.01
☐ 655	Tony Perez	.75	.35	.07
☐ 656	Ron Guidry	2.75	1.35	.27
☐ 657	Mick Kelleher	.16	.08	.01
☐ 658	Marty Pattin	.16	.08	.01
☐ 659	Merv Rettenmund	.16	.08	.01
☐ 660	Willie Horton	.25	.12	.02

1978 Topps

KEITH HERNANDEZ

The cards in this 726-card set measure 2 1/2" by 3 1/2". The 1978 Topps set experienced an increase in number of cards from the previous five regular issue sets of 660. Cards 1 through 7 feature Record Breakers (RB) of the 1977 season. Other subsets within this set include League Leaders (201-208), Post-season cards (411-413), and Rookie Prospects (701-711). While no scarcities exist, 66 of the cards are more abundant in supply as they were "double printed." These 66 double-printed cards are noted in the checklist by DP. Team cards again feature a checklist of that team's players in the set on the back. Cards numbered 23 or lower which feature Astros, Rangers, Tigers, or Yankees and do not follow the numbering checklisted below are not necessarily error cards. They are probably Burger King cards, a separate set with its own pricing and mass distribution. Burger King cards are indistinguishable from the corresponding Topps cards except for the card numbering difference and the fact that Burger King cards do not have a printing sheet designation (such as A through F like the regular Topps) anywhere on the card back in very small print.

			NRMT	VG-E	GOOD
	COMPLETE SET (726)		225.00	90.00	25.00
	COMMON PLAYER (1-726)		.12	.06	.01
	COMMON DP's (1-726)		.06	.03	.00
☐	1	RB: Lou Brock	2.00	.50	.10
		Most steals, lifetime			
☐	2	RB: Sparky Lyle	.20	.10	.02
		Most games, pure			
		relief, lifetime			
☐	3	RB: Willie McCovey	1.00	.50	.10
		Most times, 2 HR's			
		in inning, lifetime			
☐	4	RB: Brooks Robinson	1.00	.50	.10
		Most consecutive			
		seasons with one club			
☐	5	RB: Pete Rose	2.25	1.10	.22
		Most hits, switch			
		hitter, lifetime			
☐	6	RB: Nolan Ryan	2.50	1.25	.25
		Most games with			
		10 or more			
		strikeouts, lifetime			
☐	7	RB: Reggie Jackson	2.25	1.10	.22
		Most homers,			
		one World Series			
☐	8	Mike Sadek	.12	.06	.01
☐	9	Doug DeCinces	.20	.10	.02
☐	10	Phil Niekro	1.25	.60	.12
☐	11	Rick Manning	.12	.06	.01
☐	12	Don Aase	.20	.10	.02
☐	13	Art Howe	.40	.20	.04
☐	14	Lerrin LaGrow	.12	.06	.01
☐	15	Tony Perez DP	.30	.15	.03
☐	16	Roy White	.20	.10	.02
☐	17	Mike Krukow	.20	.10	.02
☐	18	Bob Grich	.20	.10	.02
☐	19	Darrell Porter	.12	.06	.01
☐	20	Pete Rose DP	4.00	2.00	.40
☐	21	Steve Kemp	.20	.10	.02
☐	22	Charlie Hough	.20	.10	.02
☐	23	Bump Wills	.12	.06	.01
☐	24	Don Money DP	.06	.03	.00
☐	25	Jon Matlack	.20	.10	.02
☐	26	Rich Hebner	.12	.06	.01
☐	27	Geoff Zahn	.12	.06	.01
☐	28	Ed Ott	.12	.06	.01
☐	29	Bob Lacey	.12	.06	.01
☐	30	George Hendrick	.20	.10	.02
☐	31	Glenn Abbott	.12	.06	.01
☐	32	Garry Templeton	.20	.10	.02
☐	33	Dave Lemanczyk	.12	.06	.01
☐	34	Willie McCovey	2.00	1.00	.20
☐	35	Sparky Lyle	.30	.15	.03
☐	36	Eddie Murray	35.00	17.50	3.50
☐	37	Rick Waits	.12	.06	.01
☐	38	Willie Montanez	.12	.06	.01
☐	39	Floyd Bannister	.90	.45	.09
☐	40	Carl Yastrzemski	3.75	1.85	.37
☐	41	Burt Hooton	.12	.06	.01
☐	42	Jorge Orta	.12	.06	.01
☐	43	Bill Atkinson	.12	.06	.01
☐	44	Toby Harrah	.20	.10	.02
☐	45	Mark Fidrych	.30	.15	.03
☐	46	Al Cowens	.12	.06	.01
☐	47	Jack Billingham	.12	.06	.01
☐	48	Don Baylor	.50	.25	.05
☐	49	Ed Kranepool	.20	.10	.02
☐	50	Rick Reuschel	.45	.20	.04
☐	51	Charlie Moore DP	.06	.03	.00
☐	52	Jim Lonborg	.20	.10	.02
☐	53	Phil Garner DP	.06	.03	.00
☐	54	Tom Johnson	.12	.06	.01
☐	55	Mitchell Page	.12	.06	.01
☐	56	Randy Jones	.12	.06	.01
☐	57	Dan Meyer	.12	.06	.01
☐	58	Bob Forsch	.20	.10	.02
☐	59	Otto Velez	.12	.06	.01
☐	60	Thurman Munson	2.75	1.35	.27
☐	61	Larvell Blanks	.12	.06	.01
☐	62	Jim Barr	.12	.06	.01
☐	63	Don Zimmer	.20	.10	.02
☐	64	Gene Pentz	.12	.06	.01
☐	65	Ken Singleton	.20	.10	.02
☐	66	White Sox Team	.50	.25	.05
		(checklist back)			
☐	67	Claudell Washington	.20	.10	.02
☐	68	Steve Foucault DP	.06	.03	.00
☐	69	Mike Vail	.12	.06	.01
☐	70	Rich Gossage	.75	.35	.07
☐	71	Terry Humphrey	.12	.06	.01
☐	72	Andre Dawson	6.50	3.25	.65
☐	73	Andy Hassler	.12	.06	.01

74	Checklist 1	.50	.05	.01
75	Dick Ruthven	.12	.06	.01
76	Steve Ontiveros	.12	.06	.01
77	Ed Kirkpatrick	.12	.06	.01
78	Pablo Torrealba	.12	.06	.01
79	Darrell Johnson DP	.06	.03	.00
80	Ken Griffey	.30	.15	.03
81	Pete Redfern	.12	.06	.01
82	Giants Team	.50	.25	.05
	(checklist back)			
83	Bob Montgomery	.12	.06	.01
84	Kent Tekulve	.20	.10	.02
85	Ron Fairly	.12	.06	.01
86	Dave Tomlin	.12	.06	.01
87	John Lowenstein	.12	.06	.01
88	Mike Phillips	.12	.06	.01
89	Ken Clay	.12	.06	.01
90	Larry Bowa	.30	.15	.03
91	Oscar Zamora	.12	.06	.01
92	Adrian Devine	.12	.06	.01
93	Bobby Cox DP	.06	.03	.00
94	Chuck Scrivener	.12	.06	.01
95	Jamie Quirk	.12	.06	.01
96	Orioles Team	.50	.25	.05
	(checklist back)			
97	Stan Bahnsen	.12	.06	.01
98	Jim Essian	.12	.06	.01
99	Willie Hernandez	.90	.45	.09
100	George Brett	5.00	2.50	.50
101	Sid Monge	.12	.06	.01
102	Matt Alexander	.12	.06	.01
103	Tom Murphy	.12	.06	.01
104	Lee Lacy	.12	.06	.01
105	Reggie Cleveland	.12	.06	.01
106	Bill Plummer	.12	.06	.01
107	Ed Halicki	.12	.06	.01
108	Von Joshua	.12	.06	.01
109	Joe Torre	.30	.15	.03
110	Richie Zisk	.12	.06	.01
111	Mike Tyson	.12	.06	.01
112	Astros Team	.50	.25	.05
	(checklist back)			
113	Don Carrithers	.12	.06	.01
114	Paul Blair	.12	.06	.01
115	Gary Nolan	.12	.06	.01
116	Tucker Ashford	.12	.06	.01
117	John Montague	.12	.06	.01
118	Terry Harmon	.12	.06	.01
119	Denny Martinez	.30	.15	.03
120	Gary Carter	3.00	1.50	.30
121	Alvis Woods	.12	.06	.01
122	Dennis Eckersley	1.00	.50	.10
123	Manny Trillo	.12	.06	.01
124	Dave Rozema	.12	.06	.01
125	George Scott	.20	.10	.02
126	Paul Moskau	.12	.06	.01
127	Chet Lemon	.20	.10	.02
128	Bill Russell	.20	.10	.02
129	Jim Colborn	.12	.06	.01
130	Jeff Burroughs	.20	.10	.02
131	Bert Blyleven	.75	.35	.07
132	Enos Cabell	.12	.06	.01
133	Jerry Augustine	.12	.06	.01
134	Steve Henderson	.12	.06	.01
135	Ron Guidry DP	.60	.30	.06
136	Ted Sizemore	.12	.06	.01
137	Craig Kusick	.12	.06	.01
138	Larry Demery	.12	.06	.01
139	Wayne Gross	.12	.06	.01
140	Rollie Fingers	.75	.35	.07
141	Ruppert Jones	.12	.06	.01
142	John Montefusco	.20	.10	.02
143	Keith Hernandez	2.50	1.25	.25
144	Jesse Jefferson	.12	.06	.01
145	Rick Monday	.20	.10	.02
146	Doyle Alexander	.20	.10	.02
147	Lee Mazzilli	.12	.06	.01
148	Andre Thornton	.20	.10	.02
149	Dale Murray	.12	.06	.01
150	Bobby Bonds	.30	.15	.03
151	Milt Wilcox	.12	.06	.01
152	Ivan DeJesus	.12	.06	.01
153	Steve Stone	.20	.10	.02
154	Cecil Cooper DP	.20	.10	.02
155	Butch Hobson	.12	.06	.01
156	Andy Messersmith	.20	.10	.02
157	Pete LaCock DP	.06	.03	.00
158	Joaquin Andujar	.30	.15	.03
159	Lou Piniella	.30	.15	.03
160	Jim Palmer	2.50	1.25	.25
161	Bob Boone	.45	.20	.04
162	Paul Thormodsgard	.12	.06	.01
163	Bill North	.12	.06	.01
164	Bob Owchinko	.12	.06	.01
165	Rennie Stennett	.12	.06	.01
166	Carlos Lopez	.12	.06	.01
167	Tim Foli	.12	.06	.01
168	Reggie Smith	.30	.15	.03
169	Jerry Johnson	.12	.06	.01
170	Lou Brock	2.00	1.00	.20
171	Pat Zachry	.12	.06	.01
172	Mike Hargrove	.20	.10	.02
173	Robin Yount	7.50	3.75	.75
174	Wayne Garland	.12	.06	.01
175	Jerry Morales	.12	.06	.01
176	Milt May	.12	.06	.01
177	Gene Garber DP	.06	.03	.00
178	Dave Chalk	.12	.06	.01
179	Dick Tidrow	.12	.06	.01
180	Dave Concepcion	.30	.15	.03
181	Ken Forsch	.12	.06	.01
182	Jim Spencer	.12	.06	.01
183	Doug Bird	.12	.06	.01
184	Checklist 2	.50	.05	.01
185	Ellis Valentine	.12	.06	.01
186	Bob Stanley DP	.30	.15	.03
187	Jerry Royster DP	.06	.03	.00
188	Al Bumbry	.12	.06	.01
189	Tom Lasorda MG	.30	.15	.03
190	John Candelaria	.30	.15	.03
191	Rodney Scott	.12	.06	.01
192	Padres Team	.50	.25	.05
	(checklist back)			
193	Rich Chiles	.12	.06	.01
194	Derrel Thomas	.12	.06	.01
195	Larry Dierker	.12	.06	.01
196	Bob Bailor	.12	.06	.01
197	Nino Espinosa	.12	.06	.01
198	Ron Pruitt	.12	.06	.01
199	Craig Reynolds	.12	.06	.01
200	Reggie Jackson	4.00	2.00	.40
201	Batting Leaders	.60	.30	.06
	Dave Parker			
	Rod Carew			
202	Home Run Leaders DP	.12	.06	.01
	George Foster			
	Jim Rice			
203	RBI Leaders	.20	.10	.02
	George Foster			
	Larry Hisle			
204	Steals Leaders DP	.12	.06	.01
	Frank Taveras			
	Freddie Patek			
205	Victory Leaders	.50	.25	.05
	Steve Carlton			
	Dave Goltz			
	Dennis Leonard			
	Jim Palmer			
206	Strikeout Leaders DP	.30	.15	.03
	Phil Niekro			
	Nolan Ryan			
207	ERA Leaders DP	.12	.06	.01
	John Candelaria			
	Frank Tanana			
208	Top Firemen	.20	.10	.02
	Rollie Fingers			
	Bill Campbell			
209	Dock Ellis	.12	.06	.01
210	Jose Cardenal	.12	.06	.01
211	Earl Weaver MG DP	.12	.06	.01
212	Mike Caldwell	.12	.06	.01
213	Alan Bannister	.12	.06	.01
214	Angels Team	.50	.25	.05
	(checklist back)			
215	Darrell Evans	.40	.20	.04
216	Mike Paxton	.12	.06	.01
217	Rod Gilbreath	.12	.06	.01
218	Marty Pattin	.12	.06	.01
219	Mike Cubbage	.12	.06	.01
220	Pedro Borbon	.12	.06	.01
221	Chris Speier	.12	.06	.01
222	Jerry Martin	.12	.06	.01
223	Bruce Kison	.12	.06	.01
224	Jerry Tabb	.12	.06	.01
225	Don Gullett DP	.12	.06	.01
226	Joe Ferguson	.12	.06	.01
227	Al Fitzmorris	.12	.06	.01
228	Manny Mota DP	.12	.06	.01
229	Leo Foster	.12	.06	.01
230	Al Hrabosky	.12	.06	.01
231	Wayne Nordhagen	.12	.06	.01
232	Mickey Stanley	.20	.10	.02
233	Dick Pole	.12	.06	.01
234	Herman Franks MG	.12	.06	.01
235	Tim McCarver	.30	.15	.03
236	Terry Whitfield	.12	.06	.01
237	Rich Dauer	.12	.06	.01
238	Juan Beniquez	.12	.06	.01
239	Dyar Miller	.12	.06	.01
240	Gene Tenace	.20	.10	.02

☐ 241	Pete Vuckovich	.20	.10	.02
☐ 242	Barry Bonnell DP	.12	.06	.01
☐ 243	Bob McClure	.12	.06	.01
☐ 244	Expos Team DP	.20	.10	.02
	(checklist back)			
☐ 245	Rick Burleson	.20	.10	.02
☐ 246	Dan Driessen	.12	.06	.01
☐ 247	Larry Christenson	.12	.06	.01
☐ 248	Frank White DP	.12	.06	.01
☐ 249	Dave Goltz DP	.06	.03	.00
☐ 250	Graig Nettles DP	.20	.10	.02
☐ 251	Don Kirkwood	.12	.06	.01
☐ 252	Steve Swisher DP	.06	.03	.00
☐ 253	Jim Kern	.12	.06	.01
☐ 254	Dave Collins	.12	.06	.01
☐ 255	Jerry Reuss	.20	.10	.02
☐ 256	Joe Altobelli MG	.12	.06	.01
☐ 257	Hector Cruz	.12	.06	.01
☐ 258	John Hiller	.20	.10	.02
☐ 259	Dodgers Team	.50	.25	.05
	(checklist back)			
☐ 260	Bert Campaneris	.20	.10	.02
☐ 261	Tim Hosley	.12	.06	.01
☐ 262	Rudy May	.12	.06	.01
☐ 263	Danny Walton	.12	.06	.01
☐ 264	Jamie Easterly	.12	.06	.01
☐ 265	Sal Bando DP	.12	.06	.01
☐ 266	Bob Shirley	.12	.06	.01
☐ 267	Doug Ault	.12	.06	.01
☐ 268	Gil Flores	.12	.06	.01
☐ 269	Wayne Twitchell	.12	.06	.01
☐ 270	Carlton Fisk	1.50	.75	.15
☐ 271	Randy Lerch DP	.06	.03	.00
☐ 272	Royle Stillman	.12	.06	.01
☐ 273	Fred Norman	.12	.06	.01
☐ 274	Freddie Patek	.12	.06	.01
☐ 275	Dan Ford	.12	.06	.01
☐ 276	Bill Bonham DP	.06	.03	.00
☐ 277	Bruce Boisclair	.12	.06	.01
☐ 278	Enrique Romo	.12	.06	.01
☐ 279	Bill Virdon MG	.20	.10	.02
☐ 280	Buddy Bell	.30	.15	.03
☐ 281	Eric Rasmussen DP	.06	.03	.00
☐ 282	Yankees Team	.60	.30	.06
	(checklist back)			
☐ 283	Omar Moreno	.12	.06	.01
☐ 284	Randy Moffitt	.12	.06	.01
☐ 285	Steve Yeager DP	.12	.06	.01
☐ 286	Ben Oglivie	.20	.10	.02
☐ 287	Kiko Garcia	.12	.06	.01
☐ 288	Dave Hamilton	.12	.06	.01
☐ 289	Checklist 3	.50	.05	.01
☐ 290	Willie Horton	.20	.10	.02
☐ 291	Gary Ross	.12	.06	.01
☐ 292	Gene Richards	.12	.06	.01
☐ 293	Mike Willis	.12	.06	.01
☐ 294	Larry Parrish	.20	.10	.02
☐ 295	Bill Lee	.20	.10	.02
☐ 296	Biff Pocoroba	.12	.06	.01
☐ 297	Warren Brusstar DP	.06	.03	.00
☐ 298	Tony Armas	.20	.10	.02
☐ 299	Whitey Herzog MG	.20	.10	.02
☐ 300	Joe Morgan	1.75	.85	.17
☐ 301	Buddy Schultz	.12	.06	.01
☐ 302	Cubs Team	.50	.25	.05
	(checklist back)			
☐ 303	Sam Hinds	.12	.06	.01
☐ 304	John Milner	.12	.06	.01
☐ 305	Rico Carty	.20	.10	.02
☐ 306	Joe Niekro	.30	.15	.03
☐ 307	Glenn Borgmann	.12	.06	.01
☐ 308	Jim Rooker	.12	.06	.01
☐ 309	Cliff Johnson	.12	.06	.01
☐ 310	Don Sutton	1.25	.60	.12
☐ 311	Jose Baez DP	.06	.03	.00
☐ 312	Greg Minton	.12	.06	.01
☐ 313	Andy Etchebarren	.12	.06	.01
☐ 314	Paul Lindblad	.12	.06	.01
☐ 315	Mark Belanger	.20	.10	.02
☐ 316	Henry Cruz DP	.06	.03	.00
☐ 317	Dave Johnson	.30	.15	.03
☐ 318	Tom Griffin	.12	.06	.01
☐ 319	Alan Ashby	.12	.06	.01
☐ 320	Fred Lynn	.75	.35	.07
☐ 321	Santo Alcala	.12	.06	.01
☐ 322	Tom Paciorek	.12	.06	.01
☐ 323	Jim Fregosi DP	.12	.06	.01
☐ 324	Vern Rapp MG	.12	.06	.01
☐ 325	Bruce Sutter	.60	.30	.06
☐ 326	Mike Lum DP	.06	.03	.00
☐ 327	Rick Langford DP	.06	.03	.00
☐ 328	Milwaukee Brewers Team Card	.50	.25	.05
	(checklist back)			
☐ 329	John Verhoeven	.12	.06	.01
☐ 330	Bob Watson	.20	.10	.02
☐ 331	Mark Littell	.12	.06	.01
☐ 332	Duane Kuiper	.12	.06	.01
☐ 333	Jim Todd	.12	.06	.01
☐ 334	John Stearns	.12	.06	.01
☐ 335	Bucky Dent	.30	.15	.03
☐ 336	Steve Busby	.12	.06	.01
☐ 337	Tom Grieve	.20	.10	.02
☐ 338	Dave Heaverlo	.12	.06	.01
☐ 339	Mario Guerrero	.12	.06	.01
☐ 340	Bake McBride	.12	.06	.01
☐ 341	Mike Flanagan	.30	.15	.03
☐ 342	Aurelio Rodriguez	.12	.06	.01
☐ 343	John Wathan DP	.12	.06	.01
☐ 344	Sam Ewing	.12	.06	.01
☐ 345	Luis Tiant	.30	.15	.03
☐ 346	Larry Biittner	.12	.06	.01
☐ 347	Terry Forster	.20	.10	.02
☐ 348	Del Unser	.12	.06	.01
☐ 349	Rick Camp DP	.06	.03	.00
☐ 350	Steve Garvey	3.00	1.50	.30
☐ 351	Jeff Torborg	.20	.10	.02
☐ 352	Tony Scott	.12	.06	.01
☐ 353	Doug Bair	.12	.06	.01
☐ 354	Cesar Geronimo	.12	.06	.01
☐ 355	Bill Travers	.12	.06	.01
☐ 356	New York Mets Team Card	.50	.25	.05
	(checklist back)			
☐ 357	Tom Poquette	.12	.06	.01
☐ 358	Mark Lemongello	.12	.06	.01
☐ 359	Marc Hill	.12	.06	.01
☐ 360	Mike Schmidt	7.50	3.75	.75
☐ 361	Chris Knapp	.12	.06	.01
☐ 362	Dave May	.12	.06	.01
☐ 363	Bob Randall	.12	.06	.01
☐ 364	Jerry Turner	.12	.06	.01
☐ 365	Ed Figueroa	.12	.06	.01
☐ 366	Larry Milbourne DP	.06	.03	.00
☐ 367	Rick Dempsey	.12	.06	.01
☐ 368	Balor Moore	.12	.06	.01
☐ 369	Tim Nordbrook	.12	.06	.01
☐ 370	Rusty Staub	.30	.15	.03
☐ 371	Ray Burris	.12	.06	.01
☐ 372	Brian Asselstine	.12	.06	.01
☐ 373	Jim Willoughby	.12	.06	.01
☐ 374	Jose Morales	.12	.06	.01
☐ 375	Tommy John	.75	.35	.07
☐ 376	Jim Wohlford	.12	.06	.01
☐ 377	Manny Sarmiento	.12	.06	.01
☐ 378	Bobby Winkles MG	.12	.06	.01
☐ 379	Skip Lockwood	.12	.06	.01
☐ 380	Ted Simmons	.40	.20	.04
☐ 381	Phillies Team	.50	.25	.05
	(checklist back)			
☐ 382	Joe Lahoud	.12	.06	.01
☐ 383	Mario Mendoza	.12	.06	.01
☐ 384	Jack Clark	4.00	2.00	.40
☐ 385	Tito Fuentes	.12	.06	.01
☐ 386	Bob Gorinski	.12	.06	.01
☐ 387	Ken Holtzman	.20	.10	.02
☐ 388	Bill Fahey DP	.06	.03	.00
☐ 389	Julio Gonzalez	.12	.06	.01
☐ 390	Oscar Gamble	.12	.06	.01
☐ 391	Larry Haney	.12	.06	.01
☐ 392	Billy Almon	.12	.06	.01
☐ 393	Tippy Martinez	.12	.06	.01
☐ 394	Roy Howell DP	.06	.03	.00
☐ 395	Jim Hughes	.12	.06	.01
☐ 396	Bob Stinson DP	.06	.03	.00
☐ 397	Greg Gross	.12	.06	.01
☐ 398	Don Hood	.12	.06	.01
☐ 399	Pete Mackanin	.12	.06	.01
☐ 400	Nolan Ryan	9.00	4.50	.90
☐ 401	Sparky Anderson MG	.20	.10	.02
☐ 402	Dave Campbell	.12	.06	.01
☐ 403	Bud Harrelson	.12	.06	.01
☐ 404	Tigers Team	.50	.25	.05
	(checklist back)			
☐ 405	Rawly Eastwick	.12	.06	.01
☐ 406	Mike Jorgensen	.12	.06	.01
☐ 407	Odell Jones	.12	.06	.01
☐ 408	Joe Zdeb	.12	.06	.01
☐ 409	Ron Schueler	.12	.06	.01
☐ 410	Bill Madlock	.50	.25	.05
☐ 411	AL Champs Yankees rally to defeat Royals	.50	.25	.05
☐ 412	NL Champs Dodgers overpower Phillies in four	.50	.25	.05
☐ 413	World Series Reggie and Yankees reign supreme	1.50	.75	.15
☐ 414	Darold Knowles DP	.06	.03	.00

☐ 415	Ray Fosse	.12	.06	.01
☐ 416	Jack Brohamer	.12	.06	.01
☐ 417	Mike Garman DP	.06	.03	.00
☐ 418	Tony Muser	.12	.06	.01
☐ 419	Jerry Garvin	.12	.06	.01
☐ 420	Greg Luzinski	.30	.15	.03
☐ 421	Junior Moore	.12	.06	.01
☐ 422	Steve Braun	.12	.06	.01
☐ 423	Dave Rosello	.12	.06	.01
☐ 424	Boston Red Sox	.50	.25	.05
	Team Card			
	(checklist back)			
☐ 425	Steve Rogers DP	.12	.06	.01
☐ 426	Fred Kendall	.12	.06	.01
☐ 427	Mario Soto	.60	.30	.06
☐ 428	Joel Youngblood	.12	.06	.01
☐ 429	Mike Barlow	.12	.06	.01
☐ 430	Al Oliver	.30	.15	.03
☐ 431	Butch Metzger	.12	.06	.01
☐ 432	Terry Bulling	.12	.06	.01
☐ 433	Fernando Gonzalez	.12	.06	.01
☐ 434	Mike Norris	.12	.06	.01
☐ 435	Checklist 4	.50	.05	.01
☐ 436	Vic Harris DP	.06	.03	.00
☐ 437	Bo McLaughlin	.12	.06	.01
☐ 438	John Ellis	.12	.06	.01
☐ 439	Ken Kravec	.12	.06	.01
☐ 440	Dave Lopes	.20	.10	.02
☐ 441	Larry Gura	.12	.06	.01
☐ 442	Elliott Maddox	.12	.06	.01
☐ 443	Darrel Chaney	.12	.06	.01
☐ 444	Roy Hartsfield MG	.12	.06	.01
☐ 445	Mike Ivie	.12	.06	.01
☐ 446	Tug McGraw	.30	.15	.03
☐ 447	Leroy Stanton	.12	.06	.01
☐ 448	Bill Castro	.12	.06	.01
☐ 449	Tim Blackwell DP	.06	.03	.00
☐ 450	Tom Seaver	3.50	1.60	.32
☐ 451	Minnesota Twins	.50	.25	.05
	Team Card			
	(checklist back)			
☐ 452	Jerry Mumphrey	.12	.06	.01
☐ 453	Doug Flynn	.12	.06	.01
☐ 454	Dave LaRoche	.12	.06	.01
☐ 455	Bill Robinson	.20	.10	.02
☐ 456	Vern Ruhle	.12	.06	.01
☐ 457	Bob Bailey	.12	.06	.01
☐ 458	Jeff Newman	.12	.06	.01
☐ 459	Charlie Spikes	.12	.06	.01
☐ 460	Jim Hunter	1.50	.75	.15
☐ 461	Rob Andrews DP	.06	.03	.00
☐ 462	Rogelio Moret	.12	.06	.01
☐ 463	Kevin Bell	.12	.06	.01
☐ 464	Jerry Grote	.12	.06	.01
☐ 465	Hal McRae	.20	.10	.02
☐ 466	Dennis Blair	.12	.06	.01
☐ 467	Alvin Dark MG	.12	.06	.01
☐ 468	Warren Cromartie	.30	.15	.03
☐ 469	Rick Cerone	.20	.10	.02
☐ 470	J.R. Richard	.20	.10	.02
☐ 471	Roy Smalley	.12	.06	.01
☐ 472	Ron Reed	.12	.06	.01
☐ 473	Bill Buckner	.30	.15	.03
☐ 474	Jim Slaton	.12	.06	.01
☐ 475	Gary Matthews	.20	.10	.02
☐ 476	Bill Stein	.12	.06	.01
☐ 477	Doug Capilla	.12	.06	.01
☐ 478	Jerry Remy	.12	.06	.01
☐ 479	Cardinals Team	.50	.25	.05
	(checklist back)			
☐ 480	Ron LeFlore	.12	.06	.01
☐ 481	Jackson Todd	.12	.06	.01
☐ 482	Rick Miller	.12	.06	.01
☐ 483	Ken Macha	.12	.06	.01
☐ 484	Jim Norris	.12	.06	.01
☐ 485	Chris Chambliss	.20	.10	.02
☐ 486	John Curtis	.12	.06	.01
☐ 487	Jim Tyrone	.12	.06	.01
☐ 488	Dan Spillner	.12	.06	.01
☐ 489	Rudy Meoli	.12	.06	.01
☐ 490	Amos Otis	.20	.10	.02
☐ 491	Scott McGregor	.20	.10	.02
☐ 492	Jim Sundberg	.12	.06	.01
☐ 493	Steve Renko	.12	.06	.01
☐ 494	Chuck Tanner MG	.12	.06	.01
☐ 495	Dave Cash	.12	.06	.01
☐ 496	Jim Clancy DP	.20	.10	.02
☐ 497	Glenn Adams	.12	.06	.01
☐ 498	Joe Sambito	.12	.06	.01
☐ 499	Seattle Mariners	.50	.25	.05
	Team Card			
	(checklist back)			
☐ 500	George Foster	.60	.30	.06
☐ 501	Dave Roberts	.12	.06	.01
☐ 502	Pat Rockett	.12	.06	.01
☐ 503	Ike Hampton	.12	.06	.01
☐ 504	Roger Freed	.12	.06	.01
☐ 505	Felix Millan	.12	.06	.01
☐ 506	Ron Blomberg	.12	.06	.01
☐ 507	Willie Crawford	.12	.06	.01
☐ 508	Johnny Oates	.12	.06	.01
☐ 509	Brent Strom	.12	.06	.01
☐ 510	Willie Stargell	2.00	1.00	.20
☐ 511	Frank Duffy	.12	.06	.01
☐ 512	Larry Herndon	.12	.06	.01
☐ 513	Barry Foote	.12	.06	.01
☐ 514	Rob Sperring	.12	.06	.01
☐ 515	Tim Corcoran	.12	.06	.01
☐ 516	Gary Beare	.12	.06	.01
☐ 517	Andres Mora	.12	.06	.01
☐ 518	Tommy Boggs DP	.06	.03	.00
☐ 519	Brian Downing	.20	.10	.02
☐ 520	Larry Hisle	.12	.06	.01
☐ 521	Steve Staggs	.12	.06	.01
☐ 522	Dick Williams MG	.12	.06	.01
☐ 523	Donnie Moore	.20	.10	.02
☐ 524	Bernie Carbo	.12	.06	.01
☐ 525	Jerry Terrell	.12	.06	.01
☐ 526	Reds Team	.50	.25	.05
	(checklist back)			
☐ 527	Vic Correll	.12	.06	.01
☐ 528	Rob Picciolo	.12	.06	.01
☐ 529	Paul Hartzell	.12	.06	.01
☐ 530	Dave Winfield	2.50	1.25	.25
☐ 531	Tom Underwood	.12	.06	.01
☐ 532	Skip Jutze	.12	.06	.01
☐ 533	Sandy Alomar	.12	.06	.01
☐ 534	Wilbur Howard	.12	.06	.01
☐ 535	Checklist 5	.50	.05	.01
☐ 536	Roric Harrison	.12	.06	.01
☐ 537	Bruce Bochte	.12	.06	.01
☐ 538	Johnny LeMaster	.12	.06	.01
☐ 539	Vic Davalillo DP	.06	.03	.00
☐ 540	Steve Carlton	2.75	1.35	.27
☐ 541	Larry Cox	.12	.06	.01
☐ 542	Tim Johnson	.12	.06	.01
☐ 543	Larry Harlow DP	.06	.03	.00
☐ 544	Len Randle DP	.06	.03	.00
☐ 545	Bill Campbell	.12	.06	.01
☐ 546	Ted Martinez	.12	.06	.01
☐ 547	John Scott	.12	.06	.01
☐ 548	Billy Hunter MG DP	.06	.03	.00
☐ 549	Joe Kerrigan	.12	.06	.01
☐ 550	John Mayberry	.20	.10	.02
☐ 551	Atlanta Braves	.50	.25	.05
	Team Card			
	(checklist back)			
☐ 552	Francisco Barrios	.12	.06	.01
☐ 553	Terry Puhl	.40	.20	.04
☐ 554	Joe Coleman	.12	.06	.01
☐ 555	Butch Wynegar	.12	.06	.01
☐ 556	Ed Armbrister	.12	.06	.01
☐ 557	Tony Solaita	.12	.06	.01
☐ 558	Paul Mitchell	.12	.06	.01
☐ 559	Phil Mankowski	.12	.06	.01
☐ 560	Dave Parker	2.25	1.10	.22
☐ 561	Charlie Williams	.12	.06	.01
☐ 562	Glenn Burke	.12	.06	.01
☐ 563	Dave Rader	.12	.06	.01
☐ 564	Mick Kelleher	.12	.06	.01
☐ 565	Jerry Koosman	.30	.15	.03
☐ 566	Merv Rettenmund	.12	.06	.01
☐ 567	Dick Drago	.12	.06	.01
☐ 568	Tom Hutton	.12	.06	.01
☐ 569	Lary Sorensen	.12	.06	.01
☐ 570	Dave Kingman	.50	.25	.05
☐ 571	Buck Martinez	.12	.06	.01
☐ 572	Rick Wise	.12	.06	.01
☐ 573	Luis Gomez	.12	.06	.01
☐ 574	Bob Lemon MG	.30	.15	.03
☐ 575	Pat Dobson	.20	.10	.02
☐ 576	Sam Mejias	.12	.06	.01
☐ 577	Oakland A's	.50	.25	.05
	Team Card			
	(checklist back)			
☐ 578	Buzz Capra	.12	.06	.01
☐ 579	Rance Mulliniks	.30	.15	.03
☐ 580	Rod Carew	2.50	1.25	.25
☐ 581	Lynn McGlothen	.12	.06	.01
☐ 582	Fran Healy	.12	.06	.01
☐ 583	George Medich	.12	.06	.01
☐ 584	John Hale	.12	.06	.01
☐ 585	Woodie Fryman DP	.06	.03	.00
☐ 586	Ed Goodson	.12	.06	.01
☐ 587	John Urrea	.12	.06	.01
☐ 588	Jim Mason	.12	.06	.01
☐ 589	Bob Knepper	1.25	.60	.12
☐ 590	Bobby Murcer	.30	.15	.03
☐ 591	George Zeber	.12	.06	.01
☐ 592	Bob Apodaca	.12	.06	.01

☐ 593	Dave Skaggs	.12	.06	.01
☐ 594	Dave Freisleben	.12	.06	.01
☐ 595	Sixto Lezcano	.12	.06	.01
☐ 596	Gary Wheelock	.12	.06	.01
☐ 597	Steve Dillard	.12	.06	.01
☐ 598	Eddie Solomon	.12	.06	.01
☐ 599	Gary Woods	.12	.06	.01
☐ 600	Frank Tanana	.20	.10	.02
☐ 601	Gene Mauch MG	.12	.06	.01
☐ 602	Eric Soderholm	.12	.06	.01
☐ 603	Will McEnaney	.12	.06	.01
☐ 604	Earl Williams	.12	.06	.01
☐ 605	Rick Rhoden	.20	.10	.02
☐ 606	Pirates Team	.50	.25	.05
	(checklist back)			
☐ 607	Fernando Arroyo	.12	.06	.01
☐ 608	Johnny Grubb	.12	.06	.01
☐ 609	John Denny	.20	.10	.02
☐ 610	Garry Maddox	.20	.10	.02
☐ 611	Pat Scanlon	.12	.06	.01
☐ 612	Ken Henderson	.12	.06	.01
☐ 613	Marty Perez	.12	.06	.01
☐ 614	Joe Wallis	.12	.06	.01
☐ 615	Clay Carroll	.12	.06	.01
☐ 616	Pat Kelly	.12	.06	.01
☐ 617	Joe Nolan	.12	.06	.01
☐ 618	Tommy Helms	.20	.10	.02
☐ 619	Thad Bosley DP	.12	.06	.01
☐ 620	Willie Randolph	.40	.20	.04
☐ 621	Craig Swan DP	.12	.06	.01
☐ 622	Champ Summers	.12	.06	.01
☐ 623	Eduardo Rodriguez	.12	.06	.01
☐ 624	Gary Alexander DP	.06	.03	.00
☐ 625	Jose Cruz	.20	.10	.02
☐ 626	Blue Jays Team DP	.20	.10	.02
	(checklist back)			
☐ 627	David Johnson	.12	.06	.01
☐ 628	Ralph Garr	.12	.06	.01
☐ 629	Don Stanhouse	.12	.06	.01
☐ 630	Ron Cey	.30	.15	.03
☐ 631	Danny Ozark MG	.12	.06	.01
☐ 632	Rowland Office	.12	.06	.01
☐ 633	Tom Veryzer	.12	.06	.01
☐ 634	Len Barker	.12	.06	.01
☐ 635	Joe Rudi	.20	.10	.02
☐ 636	Jim Bibby	.12	.06	.01
☐ 637	Duffy Dyer	.12	.06	.01
☐ 638	Paul Splittorff	.12	.06	.01
☐ 639	Gene Clines	.12	.06	.01
☐ 640	Lee May DP	.12	.06	.01
☐ 641	Doug Rau	.12	.06	.01
☐ 642	Denny Doyle	.12	.06	.01
☐ 643	Tom House	.12	.06	.01
☐ 644	Jim Dwyer	.12	.06	.01
☐ 645	Mike Torrez	.12	.06	.01
☐ 646	Rick Auerbach DP	.06	.03	.00
☐ 647	Steve Dunning	.12	.06	.01
☐ 648	Gary Thomasson	.12	.06	.01
☐ 649	Moose Haas	.20	.10	.02
☐ 650	Cesar Cedeno	.20	.10	.02
☐ 651	Doug Rader	.20	.10	.02
☐ 652	Checklist 6	.50	.05	.01
☐ 653	Ron Hodges DP	.06	.03	.00
☐ 654	Pepe Frias	.12	.06	.01
☐ 655	Lyman Bostock	.20	.10	.02
☐ 656	Dave Garcia MG	.12	.06	.01
☐ 657	Bombo Rivera	.12	.06	.01
☐ 658	Manny Sanguillen	.20	.10	.02
☐ 659	Rangers Team	.50	.25	.05
	(checklist back)			
☐ 660	Jason Thompson	.20	.10	.02
☐ 661	Grant Jackson	.12	.06	.01
☐ 662	Paul Dade	.12	.06	.01
☐ 663	Paul Reuschel	.12	.06	.01
☐ 664	Fred Stanley	.12	.06	.01
☐ 665	Dennis Leonard	.20	.10	.02
☐ 666	Billy Smith	.12	.06	.01
☐ 667	Jeff Byrd	.12	.06	.01
☐ 668	Dusty Baker	.20	.10	.02
☐ 669	Pete Falcone	.12	.06	.01
☐ 670	Jim Rice	3.50	1.75	.35
☐ 671	Gary Lavelle	.12	.06	.01
☐ 672	Don Kessinger	.20	.10	.02
☐ 673	Steve Brye	.12	.06	.01
☐ 674	Ray Knight	1.25	.60	.12
☐ 675	Jay Johnstone	.20	.10	.02
☐ 676	Bob Myrick	.12	.06	.01
☐ 677	Ed Herrmann	.12	.06	.01
☐ 678	Tom Burgmeier	.12	.06	.01
☐ 679	Wayne Garrett	.12	.06	.01
☐ 680	Vida Blue	.20	.10	.02
☐ 681	Rob Belloir	.12	.06	.01
☐ 682	Ken Brett	.12	.06	.01
☐ 683	Mike Champion	.12	.06	.01
☐ 684	Ralph Houk MG	.20	.10	.02

☐ 685	Frank Taveras	.12	.06	.01
☐ 686	Gaylord Perry	1.75	.85	.17
☐ 687	Julio Cruz	.20	.10	.02
☐ 688	George Mitterwald	.12	.06	.01
☐ 689	Indians Team	.50	.25	.05
	(checklist back)			
☐ 690	Mickey Rivers	.20	.10	.02
☐ 691	Ross Grimsley	.12	.06	.01
☐ 692	Ken Reitz	.12	.06	.01
☐ 693	Lamar Johnson	.12	.06	.01
☐ 694	Elias Sosa	.12	.06	.01
☐ 695	Dwight Evans	1.25	.60	.12
☐ 696	Steve Mingori	.12	.06	.01
☐ 697	Roger Metzger	.12	.06	.01
☐ 698	Juan Bernhardt	.12	.06	.01
☐ 699	Jackie Brown	.12	.06	.01
☐ 700	Johnny Bench	3.75	1.85	.37
☐ 701	Rookie Pitchers	.30	.15	.03
	Tom Hume			
	Larry Landreth			
	Steve McCatty			
	Bruce Taylor			
☐ 702	Rookie Catchers	.20	.10	.02
	Bill Nahordony			
	Kevin Pasley			
	Rick Sweet			
	Don Werner			
☐ 703	Rookie Pitchers DP	6.00	3.00	.60
	Larry Andersen			
	Tim Jones			
	Mickey Mahler			
	Jack Morris			
☐ 704	Rookie 2nd Basemen	12.00	6.00	1.20
	Garth Iorg			
	Dave Oliver			
	Sam Perlozzo			
	Lou Whitaker			
☐ 705	Rookie Outfielders	.40	.20	.04
	Dave Bergman			
	Miguel Dilone			
	Clint Hurdle			
	Willie Norwood			
☐ 706	Rookie 1st Basemen	.20	.10	.02
	Wayne Cage			
	Ted Cox			
	Pat Putnam			
	Dave Revering			
☐ 707	Rookie Shortstops	42.00	20.00	4.00
	Mickey Klutts			
	Paul Molitor			
	Alan Trammell			
	U.L. Washington			
☐ 708	Rookie Catchers	24.00	12.00	2.40
	Bo Diaz			
	Dale Murphy			
	Lance Parrish			
	Ernie Whitt			
☐ 709	Rookie Pitchers	.40	.20	.04
	Steve Burke			
	Matt Keough			
	Lance Rautzhan			
	Dan Schatzeder			
☐ 710	Rookie Outfielders	.60	.30	.06
	Dell Alston			
	Rick Bosetti			
	Mike Easler			
	Keith Smith			
☐ 711	Rookie Pitchers DP	.12	.06	.01
	Cardell Camper			
	Dennis Lamp			
	Craig Mitchell			
	Roy Thomas			
☐ 712	Bobby Valentine	.30	.15	.03
☐ 713	Bob Davis	.12	.06	.01
☐ 714	Mike Anderson	.12	.06	.01
☐ 715	Jim Kaat	.50	.25	.05
☐ 716	Clarence Gaston	.30	.15	.03
☐ 717	Nelson Briles	.12	.06	.01
☐ 718	Ron Jackson	.12	.06	.01
☐ 719	Randy Elliott	.12	.06	.01
☐ 720	Fergie Jenkins	.60	.30	.06
☐ 721	Billy Martin MG	.60	.30	.06
☐ 722	Pete Broberg	.12	.06	.01
☐ 723	John Wockenfuss	.12	.06	.01
☐ 724	Kansas City Royals	.50	.25	.05
	Team Card			
	(checklist back)			
☐ 725	Kurt Bevacqua	.12	.06	.01
☐ 726	Wilbur Wood	.20	.10	.02

BUY A SUB: Subscribing to a hobby periodical extends your collecting fun.

1979 Topps

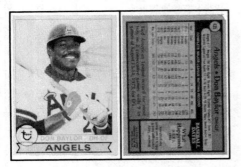

The cards in this 726-card set measure 2 1/2" by 3 1/2". Topps continued with the same number of cards as in 1978. Various series spotlight League Leaders (1-8), "Season and Career Record Holders" (411-418), "Record Breakers of 1978" (201-206) and one "Prospects" card for each team (701-726). Team cards feature a checklist on back of that team's players in the set and a small picture of the manager on the front of the card. There are 66 cards that were double printed and these are noted in the checklist by the abbreviation DP. Bump Wills was initially depicted in a Ranger uniform but with a Blue Jays affiliation; later printings correctly labeled him with Texas. The set price listed does not include the scarcer Wills (Rangers) card. Cards numbered 23 or lower which feature Phillies or Yankees and do not follow the numbering checklisted below are not necessarily error cards. They are probably Burger King cards, a separate set with its own pricing and mass distribution. Burger King cards are indistinguishable from the corresponding Topps cards except for the card numbering difference and the fact that Burger King cards do not have a printing sheet designation (such as A through F like the regular Topps) anywhere on the card back in very small print.

	NRMT	VG-E	GOOD
COMPLETE SET (726)	175.00	75.00	15.00
COMMON PLAYER (1-726)	.10	.05	.01
COMMON DP's (1-726)	.05	.02	.00

			NRMT	VG-E	GOOD
☐	1	Batting Leaders Rod Carew Dave Parker	1.50	.30	.06
☐	2	Home Run Leaders Jim Rice George Foster	.30	.15	.03
☐	3	RBI Leaders Jim Rice George Foster	.30	.15	.03
☐	4	Stolen Base Leaders Ron LeFlore Omar Moreno	.20	.10	.02
☐	5	Victory Leaders Ron Guidry Gaylord Perry	.30	.15	.03
☐	6	Strikeout Leaders Nolan Ryan J.R. Richard	1.00	.50	.10
☐	7	ERA Leaders Ron Guidry Craig Swan	.20	.10	.02
☐	8	Leading Firemen Rich Gossage Rollie Fingers	.30	.15	.03
☐	9	Dave Campbell	.10	.05	.01
☐	10	Lee May	.20	.10	.02
☐	11	Marc Hill	.10	.05	.01
☐	12	Dick Drago	.10	.05	.01
☐	13	Paul Dade	.10	.05	.01
☐	14	Rafael Landestoy	.10	.05	.01
☐	15	Ross Grimsley	.10	.05	.01
☐	16	Fred Stanley	.10	.05	.01
☐	17	Donnie Moore	.10	.05	.01
☐	18	Tony Solaita	.10	.05	.01
☐	19	Larry Gura DP	.10	.05	.01
☐	20	Joe Morgan DP	.60	.30	.06
☐	21	Kevin Kobel	.10	.05	.01
☐	22	Mike Jorgensen	.10	.05	.01
☐	23	Terry Forster	.20	.10	.02
☐	24	Paul Molitor	4.00	2.00	.40
☐	25	Steve Carlton	2.25	1.10	.22
☐	26	Jamie Quirk	.10	.05	.01
☐	27	Dave Goltz	.10	.05	.01
☐	28	Steve Brye	.10	.05	.01
☐	29	Rick Langford	.10	.05	.01
☐	30	Dave Winfield	2.50	1.25	.25
☐	31	Tom House DP	.10	.05	.01
☐	32	Jerry Mumphrey	.10	.05	.01
☐	33	Dave Rozema	.10	.05	.01
☐	34	Rob Andrews	.10	.05	.01
☐	35	Ed Figueroa	.10	.05	.01
☐	36	Alan Ashby	.10	.05	.01
☐	37	Joe Kerrigan DP	.05	.02	.00
☐	38	Bernie Carbo	.10	.05	.01
☐	39	Dale Murphy	7.50	3.75	.75
☐	40	Dennis Eckersley	.75	.35	.07
☐	41	Twins Team/Mgr. Gene Mauch (checklist back)	.40	.20	.04
☐	42	Ron Blomberg	.10	.05	.01
☐	43	Wayne Twitchell	.10	.05	.01
☐	44	Kurt Bevacqua	.10	.05	.01
☐	45	Al Hrabosky	.10	.05	.01
☐	46	Ron Hodges	.10	.05	.01
☐	47	Fred Norman	.10	.05	.01
☐	48	Merv Rettenmund	.10	.05	.01
☐	49	Vern Ruhle	.10	.05	.01
☐	50	Steve Garvey DP	1.25	.60	.12
☐	51	Ray Fosse DP	.05	.02	.00
☐	52	Randy Lerch	.10	.05	.01
☐	53	Mick Kelleher	.10	.05	.01
☐	54	Dell Alston DP	.05	.02	.00
☐	55	Willie Stargell	2.00	1.00	.20
☐	56	John Hale	.10	.05	.01
☐	57	Eric Rasmussen	.10	.05	.01
☐	58	Bob Randall DP	.05	.02	.00
☐	59	John Denny DP	.10	.05	.01
☐	60	Mickey Rivers	.20	.10	.02
☐	61	Bo Diaz	.20	.10	.02
☐	62	Randy Moffitt	.10	.05	.01
☐	63	Jack Brohamer	.10	.05	.01
☐	64	Tom Underwood	.10	.05	.01
☐	65	Mark Belanger	.20	.10	.02
☐	66	Tigers Team/Mgr. Les Moss (checklist back)	.40	.20	.04
☐	67	Jim Mason DP	.05	.02	.00
☐	68	Joe Niekro DP	.10	.05	.01
☐	69	Elliott Maddox	.10	.05	.01
☐	70	John Candelaria	.30	.15	.03
☐	71	Brian Downing	.20	.10	.02
☐	72	Steve Mingori	.10	.05	.01
☐	73	Ken Henderson	.10	.05	.01
☐	74	Shane Rawley	.90	.45	.09
☐	75	Steve Yeager	.10	.05	.01
☐	76	Warren Cromartie	.10	.05	.01
☐	77	Dan Briggs DP	.05	.02	.00
☐	78	Elias Sosa	.10	.05	.01
☐	79	Ted Cox	.10	.05	.01
☐	80	Jason Thompson	.10	.05	.01
☐	81	Roger Erickson	.10	.05	.01
☐	82	Mets Team/Mgr. Joe Torre (checklist back)	.40	.20	.04
☐	83	Fred Kendall	.10	.05	.01
☐	84	Greg Minton	.10	.05	.01
☐	85	Gary Matthews	.20	.10	.02
☐	86	Rodney Scott	.10	.05	.01
☐	87	Pete Falcone	.10	.05	.01
☐	88	Bob Molinaro	.10	.05	.01
☐	89	Dick Tidrow	.10	.05	.01
☐	90	Bob Boone	.40	.20	.04
☐	91	Terry Crowley	.10	.05	.01
☐	92	Jim Bibby	.10	.05	.01
☐	93	Phil Mankowski	.10	.05	.01
☐	94	Len Barker	.10	.05	.01
☐	95	Robin Yount	6.00	3.00	.60
☐	96	Indians Team/Mgr. Jeff Torborg (checklist back)	.40	.20	.04
☐	97	Sam Mejias	.10	.05	.01
☐	98	Ray Burris	.10	.05	.01
☐	99	John Wathan	.30	.15	.03
☐	100	Tom Seaver DP	1.50	.75	.15
☐	101	Roy Howell	.10	.05	.01

☐ 102	Mike Anderson	.10	.05	.01
☐ 103	Jim Todd	.10	.05	.01
☐ 104	Johnny Oates DP	.05	.02	.00
☐ 105	Rick Camp DP	.05	.02	.00
☐ 106	Frank Duffy	.10	.05	.01
☐ 107	Jesus Alou DP	.05	.02	.00
☐ 108	Eduardo Rodriguez	.10	.05	.01
☐ 109	Joel Youngblood	.10	.05	.01
☐ 110	Vida Blue	.20	.10	.02
☐ 111	Roger Freed	.10	.05	.01
☐ 112	Phillies Team/Mgr.	.40	.20	.04
	Danny Ozark			
	(checklist back)			
☐ 113	Pete Redfern	.10	.05	.01
☐ 114	Cliff Johnson	.10	.05	.01
☐ 115	Nolan Ryan	7.00	3.50	.70
☐ 116	Ozzie Smith	30.00	14.00	2.80
☐ 117	Grant Jackson	.10	.05	.01
☐ 118	Bud Harrelson	.10	.05	.01
☐ 119	Don Stanhouse	.10	.05	.01
☐ 120	Jim Sundberg	.10	.05	.01
☐ 121	Checklist 1 DP	.10	.02	.00
☐ 122	Mike Paxton	.10	.05	.01
☐ 123	Lou Whitaker	3.00	1.50	.30
☐ 124	Dan Schatzeder	.10	.05	.01
☐ 125	Rick Burleson	.20	.10	.02
☐ 126	Doug Bair	.10	.05	.01
☐ 127	Thad Bosley	.10	.05	.01
☐ 128	Ted Martinez	.10	.05	.01
☐ 129	Marty Pattin DP	.05	.02	.00
☐ 130	Bob Watson DP	.10	.05	.01
☐ 131	Jim Clancy	.10	.05	.01
☐ 132	Rowland Office	.10	.05	.01
☐ 133	Bill Castro	.10	.05	.01
☐ 134	Alan Bannister	.10	.05	.01
☐ 135	Bobby Murcer	.30	.15	.03
☐ 136	Jim Kaat	.40	.20	.04
☐ 137	Larry Wolfe DP	.05	.02	.00
☐ 138	Mark Lee	.10	.05	.01
☐ 139	Luis Pujols	.10	.05	.01
☐ 140	Don Gullett	.20	.10	.02
☐ 141	Tom Paciorek	.10	.05	.01
☐ 142	Charlie Williams	.10	.05	.01
☐ 143	Tony Scott	.10	.05	.01
☐ 144	Sandy Alomar	.10	.05	.01
☐ 145	Rick Rhoden	.20	.10	.02
☐ 146	Duane Kuiper	.10	.05	.01
☐ 147	Dave Hamilton	.10	.05	.01
☐ 148	Bruce Boisclair	.10	.05	.01
☐ 149	Manny Sarmiento	.10	.05	.01
☐ 150	Wayne Cage	.10	.05	.01
☐ 151	John Hiller	.20	.10	.02
☐ 152	Rick Cerone	.20	.10	.02
☐ 153	Dennis Lamp	.10	.05	.01
☐ 154	Jim Gantner DP	.10	.05	.01
☐ 155	Dwight Evans	1.00	.50	.10
☐ 156	Buddy Solomon	.10	.05	.01
☐ 157	U.L. Washington UER	.10	.05	.01
	(sic, bats left,			
	should be right)			
☐ 158	Joe Sambito	.10	.05	.01
☐ 159	Roy White	.20	.10	.02
☐ 160	Mike Flanagan	.30	.15	.03
☐ 161	Barry Foote	.10	.05	.01
☐ 162	Tom Johnson	.10	.05	.01
☐ 163	Glenn Burke	.10	.05	.01
☐ 164	Mickey Lolich	.30	.15	.03
☐ 165	Frank Taveras	.10	.05	.01
☐ 166	Leon Roberts	.10	.05	.01
☐ 167	Roger Metzger DP	.05	.02	.00
☐ 168	Dave Freisleben	.10	.05	.01
☐ 169	Bill Nahorodny	.10	.05	.01
☐ 170	Don Sutton	1.25	.60	.12
☐ 171	Gene Clines	.10	.05	.01
☐ 172	Mike Bruhert	.10	.05	.01
☐ 173	John Lowenstein	.10	.05	.01
☐ 174	Rick Auerbach	.10	.05	.01
☐ 175	George Hendrick	.20	.10	.02
☐ 176	Aurelio Rodriguez	.10	.05	.01
☐ 177	Ron Reed	.10	.05	.01
☐ 178	Alvis Woods	.10	.05	.01
☐ 179	Jim Beattie DP	.10	.05	.01
☐ 180	Larry Hisle	.10	.05	.01
☐ 181	Mike Garman	.10	.05	.01
☐ 182	Tim Johnson	.10	.05	.01
☐ 183	Paul Splittorff	.10	.05	.01
☐ 184	Darrel Chaney	.10	.05	.01
☐ 185	Mike Torrez	.10	.05	.01
☐ 186	Eric Soderholm	.10	.05	.01
☐ 187	Mark Lemongello	.10	.05	.01
☐ 188	Pat Kelly	.10	.05	.01
☐ 189	Eddie Whitson	.90	.45	.09
☐ 190	Ron Cey	.30	.15	.03
☐ 191	Mike Norris	.10	.05	.01
☐ 192	Cardinals Team/Mgr.	.40	.20	.04

	Ken Boyer			
	(checklist back)			
☐ 193	Glenn Adams	.10	.05	.01
☐ 194	Randy Jones	.10	.05	.01
☐ 195	Bill Madlock	.40	.20	.04
☐ 196	Steve Kemp DP	.10	.05	.01
☐ 197	Bob Apodaca	.10	.05	.01
☐ 198	Johnny Grubb	.10	.05	.01
☐ 199	Larry Milbourne	.10	.05	.01
☐ 200	Johnny Bench DP	1.50	.75	.15
☐ 201	RB: Mike Edwards	.10	.05	.01
	Most unassisted DP's,			
	second basemen			
☐ 202	RB: Ron Guidry, Most	.30	.15	.03
	strikeouts, lefthander,			
	nine inning game			
☐ 203	RB: J.R. Richard	.20	.10	.02
	Most strikeouts,			
	season, righthander			
☐ 204	RB: Pete Rose	1.50	.75	.15
	Most consecutive			
	games batting safely			
☐ 205	RB: John Stearns	.10	.05	.01
	Most SB's by			
	catcher, season			
☐ 206	RB: Sammy Stewart	.10	.05	.01
	7 straight SO's,			
	first ML game			
☐ 207	Dave Lemanczyk	.10	.05	.01
☐ 208	Clarence Gaston	.20	.10	.02
☐ 209	Reggie Cleveland	.10	.05	.01
☐ 210	Larry Bowa	.30	.15	.03
☐ 211	Denny Martinez	.30	.15	.03
☐ 212	Carney Lansford	5.00	2.50	.50
☐ 213	Bill Travers	.10	.05	.01
☐ 214	Red Sox Team/Mgr.	.40	.20	.04
	Don Zimmer			
	(checklist back)			
☐ 215	Willie McCovey	1.50	.75	.15
☐ 216	Wilbur Wood	.20	.10	.02
☐ 217	Steve Dillard	.10	.05	.01
☐ 218	Dennis Leonard	.20	.10	.02
☐ 219	Roy Smalley	.10	.05	.01
☐ 220	Cesar Geronimo	.10	.05	.01
☐ 221	Jesse Jefferson	.10	.05	.01
☐ 222	Bob Beall	.10	.05	.01
☐ 223	Kent Tekulve	.20	.10	.02
☐ 224	Dave Revering	.10	.05	.01
☐ 225	Rich Gossage	.50	.25	.05
☐ 226	Ron Pruitt	.10	.05	.01
☐ 227	Steve Stone	.20	.10	.02
☐ 228	Vic Davalillo	.10	.05	.01
☐ 229	Doug Flynn	.10	.05	.01
☐ 230	Bob Forsch	.10	.05	.01
☐ 231	John Wockenfuss	.10	.05	.01
☐ 232	Jimmy Sexton	.10	.05	.01
☐ 233	Paul Mitchell	.10	.05	.01
☐ 234	Toby Harrah	.20	.10	.02
☐ 235	Steve Rogers	.10	.05	.01
☐ 236	Jim Dwyer	.10	.05	.01
☐ 237	Billy Smith	.10	.05	.01
☐ 238	Balor Moore	.10	.05	.01
☐ 239	Willie Horton	.20	.10	.02
☐ 240	Rick Reuschel	.40	.20	.04
☐ 241	Checklist 2 DP	.10	.02	.00
☐ 242	Pablo Torrealba	.10	.05	.01
☐ 243	Buck Martinez DP	.05	.02	.00
☐ 244	Pirates Team/Mgr.	.40	.20	.04
	Chuck Tanner			
	(checklist back)			
☐ 245	Jeff Burroughs	.20	.10	.02
☐ 246	Darrell Jackson	.10	.05	.01
☐ 247	Tucker Ashford DP	.05	.02	.00
☐ 248	Pete LaCock	.10	.05	.01
☐ 249	Paul Thormodsgard	.10	.05	.01
☐ 250	Willie Randolph	.30	.15	.03
☐ 251	Jack Morris	2.50	1.25	.25
☐ 252	Bob Stinson	.10	.05	.01
☐ 253	Rick Wise	.20	.10	.02
☐ 254	Luis Gomez	.10	.05	.01
☐ 255	Tommy John	.60	.30	.06
☐ 256	Mike Sadek	.10	.05	.01
☐ 257	Adrian Devine	.10	.05	.01
☐ 258	Mike Phillips	.10	.05	.01
☐ 259	Reds Team/Mgr.	.40	.20	.04
	Sparky Anderson			
	(checklist back)			
☐ 260	Richie Zisk	.10	.05	.01
☐ 261	Mario Guerrero	.10	.05	.01
☐ 262	Nelson Briles	.10	.05	.01
☐ 263	Oscar Gamble	.10	.05	.01
☐ 264	Don Robinson	.75	.35	.07
☐ 265	Don Money	.10	.05	.01
☐ 266	Jim Willoughby	.10	.05	.01
☐ 267	Joe Rudi	.20	.10	.02

☐ 268	Julio Gonzalez	.10	.05	.01
☐ 269	Woodie Fryman	.10	.05	.01
☐ 270	Butch Hobson	.10	.05	.01
☐ 271	Rawly Eastwick	.10	.05	.01
☐ 272	Tim Corcoran	.10	.05	.01
☐ 273	Jerry Terrell	.10	.05	.01
☐ 274	Willie Norwood	.10	.05	.01
☐ 275	Junior Moore	.10	.05	.01
☐ 276	Jim Colborn	.10	.05	.01
☐ 277	Tom Grieve	.20	.10	.02
☐ 278	Andy Messersmith	.20	.10	.02
☐ 279	Jerry Grote DP	.05	.02	.00
☐ 280	Andre Thornton	.20	.10	.02
☐ 281	Vic Correll DP	.05	.02	.00
☐ 282	Blue Jays Team/Mgr. Roy Hartsfield (checklist back)	.30	.15	.03
☐ 283	Ken Kravec	.10	.05	.01
☐ 284	Johnnie LeMaster	.10	.05	.01
☐ 285	Bobby Bonds	.30	.15	.03
☐ 286	Duffy Dyer	.10	.05	.01
☐ 287	Andres Mora	.10	.05	.01
☐ 288	Milt Wilcox	.10	.05	.01
☐ 289	Jose Cruz	.20	.10	.02
☐ 290	Dave Lopes	.20	.10	.02
☐ 291	Tom Griffin	.10	.05	.01
☐ 292	Don Reynolds	.10	.05	.01
☐ 293	Jerry Garvin	.10	.05	.01
☐ 294	Pepe Frias	.10	.05	.01
☐ 295	Mitchell Page	.10	.05	.01
☐ 296	Preston Hanna	.10	.05	.01
☐ 297	Ted Sizemore	.10	.05	.01
☐ 298	Rich Gale	.10	.05	.01
☐ 299	Steve Ontiveros	.10	.05	.01
☐ 300	Rod Carew	2.25	1.10	.22
☐ 301	Tom Hume	.10	.05	.01
☐ 302	Braves Team/Mgr. Bobby Cox (checklist back)	.40	.20	.04
☐ 303	Lary Sorensen	.10	.05	.01
☐ 304	Steve Swisher	.10	.05	.01
☐ 305	Willie Montanez	.10	.05	.01
☐ 306	Floyd Bannister	.20	.10	.02
☐ 307	Larvell Blanks	.10	.05	.01
☐ 308	Bert Blyleven	.60	.30	.06
☐ 309	Ralph Garr	.20	.10	.02
☐ 310	Thurman Munson	2.00	1.00	.20
☐ 311	Gary Lavelle	.10	.05	.01
☐ 312	Bob Robertson	.10	.05	.01
☐ 313	Dyar Miller	.10	.05	.01
☐ 314	Larry Harlow	.10	.05	.01
☐ 315	Jon Matlack	.10	.05	.01
☐ 316	Milt May	.10	.05	.01
☐ 317	Jose Cardenal	.10	.05	.01
☐ 318	Bob Welch	3.00	1.50	.30
☐ 319	Wayne Garrett	.10	.05	.01
☐ 320	Carl Yastrzemski	3.00	1.50	.30
☐ 321	Gaylord Perry	1.50	.75	.15
☐ 322	Danny Goodwin	.10	.05	.01
☐ 323	Lynn McGlothen	.10	.05	.01
☐ 324	Mike Tyson	.10	.05	.01
☐ 325	Cecil Cooper	.40	.20	.04
☐ 326	Pedro Borbon	.10	.05	.01
☐ 327	Art Howe	.20	.10	.02
☐ 328	Oakland A's Team/Mgr. Jack McKeon (checklist back)	.40	.20	.04
☐ 329	Joe Coleman	.10	.05	.01
☐ 330	George Brett	4.00	2.00	.40
☐ 331	Mickey Mahler	.10	.05	.01
☐ 332	Gary Alexander	.10	.05	.01
☐ 333	Chet Lemon	.20	.10	.02
☐ 334	Craig Swan	.10	.05	.01
☐ 335	Chris Chambliss	.20	.10	.02
☐ 336	Bobby Thompson	.10	.05	.01
☐ 337	John Montague	.10	.05	.01
☐ 338	Vic Harris	.10	.05	.01
☐ 339	Ron Jackson	.10	.05	.01
☐ 340	Jim Palmer	2.00	1.00	.20
☐ 341	Willie Upshaw	.50	.25	.05
☐ 342	Dave Roberts	.10	.05	.01
☐ 343	Ed Glynn	.10	.05	.01
☐ 344	Jerry Royster	.10	.05	.01
☐ 345	Tug McGraw	.30	.15	.03
☐ 346	Bill Buckner	.30	.15	.03
☐ 347	Doug Rau	.10	.05	.01
☐ 348	Andre Dawson	5.00	2.50	.50
☐ 349	Jim Wright	.10	.05	.01
☐ 350	Garry Templeton	.20	.10	.02
☐ 351	Wayne Nordhagen	.10	.05	.01
☐ 352	Steve Renko	.10	.05	.01
☐ 353	Checklist 3	.40	.05	.01
☐ 354	Bill Bonham	.10	.05	.01
☐ 355	Lee Mazzilli	.10	.05	.01
☐ 356	Giants Team/Mgr.	.40	.20	.04

	Joe Altobelli (checklist back)			
☐ 357	Jerry Augustine	.10	.05	.01
☐ 358	Alan Trammell	6.00	3.00	.60
☐ 359	Dan Spillner DP	.05	.02	.00
☐ 360	Amos Otis	.20	.10	.02
☐ 361	Tom Dixon	.10	.05	.01
☐ 362	Mike Cubbage	.10	.05	.01
☐ 363	Craig Skok	.10	.05	.01
☐ 364	Gene Richards	.10	.05	.01
☐ 365	Sparky Lyle	.30	.15	.03
☐ 366	Juan Bernhardt	.10	.05	.01
☐ 367	Dave Skaggs	.10	.05	.01
☐ 368	Don Aase	.10	.05	.01
☐ 369A	Bump Wills ERR (Blue Jays)	3.00	1.50	.30
☐ 369B	Bump Wills COR (Rangers)	3.50	1.75	.35
☐ 370	Dave Kingman	.40	.20	.04
☐ 371	Jeff Holly	.10	.05	.01
☐ 372	Lamar Johnson	.10	.05	.01
☐ 373	Lance Rautzhan	.10	.05	.01
☐ 374	Ed Herrmann	.10	.05	.01
☐ 375	Bill Campbell	.10	.05	.01
☐ 376	Gorman Thomas	.30	.15	.03
☐ 377	Paul Moskau	.10	.05	.01
☐ 378	Rob Picciolo DP	.05	.02	.00
☐ 379	Dale Murray	.10	.05	.01
☐ 380	John Mayberry	.20	.10	.02
☐ 381	Astros Team/Mgr. Bill Virdon (checklist back)	.40	.20	.04
☐ 382	Jerry Martin	.10	.05	.01
☐ 383	Phil Garner	.10	.05	.01
☐ 384	Tommy Boggs	.10	.05	.01
☐ 385	Dan Ford	.10	.05	.01
☐ 386	Francisco Barrios	.10	.05	.01
☐ 387	Gary Thomasson	.10	.05	.01
☐ 388	Jack Billingham	.10	.05	.01
☐ 389	Joe Zdeb	.10	.05	.01
☐ 390	Rollie Fingers	.75	.35	.07
☐ 391	Al Oliver	.30	.15	.03
☐ 392	Doug Ault	.10	.05	.01
☐ 393	Scott McGregor	.20	.10	.02
☐ 394	Randy Stein	.10	.05	.01
☐ 395	Dave Cash	.10	.05	.01
☐ 396	Bill Plummer	.10	.05	.01
☐ 397	Sergio Ferrer	.10	.05	.01
☐ 398	Ivan DeJesus	.10	.05	.01
☐ 399	David Clyde	.10	.05	.01
☐ 400	Jim Rice	2.50	1.25	.25
☐ 401	Ray Knight	.30	.15	.03
☐ 402	Paul Hartzell	.10	.05	.01
☐ 403	Tim Foli	.10	.05	.01
☐ 404	White Sox Team/Mgr Don Kessinger (checklist back)	.40	.20	.04
☐ 405	Butch Wynegar DP	.05	.02	.00
☐ 406	Joe Wallis DP	.05	.02	.00
☐ 407	Pete Vuckovich	.10	.05	.01
☐ 408	Charlie Moore DP	.05	.02	.00
☐ 409	Willie Wilson	1.50	.75	.15
☐ 410	Darrell Evans	.30	.15	.03
☐ 411	Hits Record Season: G.Sisler Career: Ty Cobb	.40	.20	.04
☐ 412	RBI Record Season: Hack Wilson Career: Hank Aaron	.40	.20	.04
☐ 413	Home Run Record Season: Roger Maris Career: Hank Aaron	.60	.30	.06
☐ 414	Batting Record Season: R.Hornsby Career: Ty Cobb	.40	.20	.04
☐ 415	Steals Record Season: Lou Brock Career: Lou Brock	.40	.20	.04
☐ 416	Wins Record Season: Jack Chesbro Career: Cy Young	.20	.10	.02
☐ 417	Strikeout Record DP Season: Nolan Ryan Career: W.Johnson	.20	.10	.02
☐ 418	ERA Record DP Season: Dutch Leonard Career: W.Johnson	.10	.05	.01
☐ 419	Dick Ruthven	.10	.05	.01
☐ 420	Ken Griffey	.30	.15	.03
☐ 421	Doug DeCinces	.20	.10	.02
☐ 422	Ruppert Jones	.10	.05	.01
☐ 423	Bob Montgomery	.10	.05	.01
☐ 424	Angels Team/Mgr. Jim Fregosi (checklist back)	.40	.20	.04

☐ 425	Rick Manning	.10	.05	.01
☐ 426	Chris Speier	.10	.05	.01
☐ 427	Andy Replogle	.10	.05	.01
☐ 428	Bobby Valentine	.20	.10	.02
☐ 429	John Urrea DP	.05	.02	.00
☐ 430	Dave Parker	1.25	.60	.12
☐ 431	Glenn Borgmann	.10	.05	.01
☐ 432	Dave Heaverlo	.10	.05	.01
☐ 433	Larry Biittner	.10	.05	.01
☐ 434	Ken Clay	.10	.05	.01
☐ 435	Gene Tenace	.10	.05	.01
☐ 436	Hector Cruz	.10	.05	.01
☐ 437	Rick Williams	.10	.05	.01
☐ 438	Horace Speed	.10	.05	.01
☐ 439	Frank White	.20	.10	.02
☐ 440	Rusty Staub	.30	.15	.03
☐ 441	Lee Lacy	.10	.05	.01
☐ 442	Doyle Alexander	.20	.10	.02
☐ 443	Bruce Bochte	.10	.05	.01
☐ 444	Aurelio Lopez	.20	.10	.02
☐ 445	Steve Henderson	.10	.05	.01
☐ 446	Jim Lonborg	.20	.10	.02
☐ 447	Manny Sanguillen	.20	.10	.02
☐ 448	Moose Haas	.10	.05	.01
☐ 449	Bombo Rivera	.10	.05	.01
☐ 450	Dave Concepcion	.20	.10	.02
☐ 451	Royals Team/Mgr. Whitey Herzog (checklist back)	.40	.20	.04
☐ 452	Jerry Morales	.10	.05	.01
☐ 453	Chris Knapp	.10	.05	.01
☐ 454	Len Randle	.10	.05	.01
☐ 455	Bill Lee DP	.10	.05	.01
☐ 456	Chuck Baker	.10	.05	.01
☐ 457	Bruce Sutter	.60	.30	.06
☐ 458	Jim Essian	.10	.05	.01
☐ 459	Sid Monge	.10	.05	.01
☐ 460	Graig Nettles	.40	.20	.04
☐ 461	Jim Barr DP	.05	.02	.00
☐ 462	Otto Velez	.10	.05	.01
☐ 463	Steve Comer	.10	.05	.01
☐ 464	Joe Nolan	.10	.05	.01
☐ 465	Reggie Smith	.20	.10	.02
☐ 466	Mark Littell	.10	.05	.01
☐ 467	Don Kessinger DP	.10	.05	.01
☐ 468	Stan Bahnsen DP	.05	.02	.00
☐ 469	Lance Parrish	3.00	1.50	.30
☐ 470	Garry Maddox DP	.10	.05	.01
☐ 471	Joaquin Andujar	.20	.10	.02
☐ 472	Craig Kusick	.10	.05	.01
☐ 473	Dave Roberts	.10	.05	.01
☐ 474	Dick Davis	.10	.05	.01
☐ 475	Dan Driessen	.10	.05	.01
☐ 476	Tom Poquette	.10	.05	.01
☐ 477	Bob Grich	.20	.10	.02
☐ 478	Juan Beniquez	.10	.05	.01
☐ 479	Padres Team/Mgr. Roger Craig (checklist back)	.40	.20	.04
☐ 480	Fred Lynn	.75	.35	.07
☐ 481	Skip Lockwood	.10	.05	.01
☐ 482	Craig Reynolds	.10	.05	.01
☐ 483	Checklist 4 DP	.10	.02	.00
☐ 484	Rick Waits	.10	.05	.01
☐ 485	Bucky Dent	.30	.15	.03
☐ 486	Bob Knepper	.20	.10	.02
☐ 487	Miguel Dilone	.10	.05	.01
☐ 488	Bob Owchinko	.10	.05	.01
☐ 489	Larry Cox UER (photo actually Dave Rader)	.10	.05	.01
☐ 490	Al Cowens	.10	.05	.01
☐ 491	Tippy Martinez	.10	.05	.01
☐ 492	Bob Bailor	.10	.05	.01
☐ 493	Larry Christenson	.10	.05	.01
☐ 494	Jerry White	.10	.05	.01
☐ 495	Tony Perez	.50	.25	.05
☐ 496	Barry Bonnell DP	.05	.02	.00
☐ 497	Glenn Abbott	.10	.05	.01
☐ 498	Rich Chiles	.10	.05	.01
☐ 499	Rangers Team/Mgr. Pat Corrales (checklist back)	.40	.20	.04
☐ 500	Ron Guidry	1.00	.50	.10
☐ 501	Junior Kennedy	.10	.05	.01
☐ 502	Steve Braun	.10	.05	.01
☐ 503	Terry Humphrey	.10	.05	.01
☐ 504	Larry McWilliams	.30	.15	.03
☐ 505	Ed Kranepool	.10	.05	.01
☐ 506	John D'Acquisto	.10	.05	.01
☐ 507	Tony Armas	.20	.10	.02
☐ 508	Charlie Hough	.20	.10	.02
☐ 509	Mario Mendoza	.10	.05	.01
☐ 510	Ted Simmons	.40	.20	.04
☐ 511	Paul Reuschel DP	.05	.02	.00
☐ 512	Jack Clark	2.25	1.10	.22
☐ 513	Dave Johnson	.20	.10	.02
☐ 514	Mike Proly	.10	.05	.01
☐ 515	Enos Cabell	.10	.05	.01
☐ 516	Champ Summers DP	.05	.02	.00
☐ 517	Al Bumbry	.10	.05	.01
☐ 518	Jim Umbarger	.10	.05	.01
☐ 519	Ben Oglivie	.20	.10	.02
☐ 520	Gary Carter	2.50	1.25	.25
☐ 521	Sam Ewing	.10	.05	.01
☐ 522	Ken Holtzman	.20	.10	.02
☐ 523	John Milner	.10	.05	.01
☐ 524	Tom Burgmeier	.10	.05	.01
☐ 525	Freddie Patek	.10	.05	.01
☐ 526	Dodgers Team/Mgr. Tom Lasorda (checklist back)	.50	.25	.05
☐ 527	Lerrin LaGrow	.10	.05	.01
☐ 528	Wayne Gross DP	.05	.02	.00
☐ 529	Brian Asselstine	.10	.05	.01
☐ 530	Frank Tanana	.20	.10	.02
☐ 531	Fernando Gonzalez	.10	.05	.01
☐ 532	Buddy Schultz	.10	.05	.01
☐ 533	Leroy Stanton	.10	.05	.01
☐ 534	Ken Forsch	.10	.05	.01
☐ 535	Ellis Valentine	.10	.05	.01
☐ 536	Jerry Reuss	.20	.10	.02
☐ 537	Tom Veryzer	.10	.05	.01
☐ 538	Mike Ivie DP	.05	.02	.00
☐ 539	John Ellis	.10	.05	.01
☐ 540	Greg Luzinski	.30	.15	.03
☐ 541	Jim Slaton	.10	.05	.01
☐ 542	Rick Bosetti	.10	.05	.01
☐ 543	Kiko Garcia	.10	.05	.01
☐ 544	Fergie Jenkins	.60	.30	.06
☐ 545	John Stearns	.10	.05	.01
☐ 546	Bill Russell	.20	.10	.02
☐ 547	Clint Hurdle	.10	.05	.01
☐ 548	Enrique Romo	.10	.05	.01
☐ 549	Bob Bailey	.10	.05	.01
☐ 550	Sal Bando	.20	.10	.02
☐ 551	Cubs Team/Mgr. Herman Franks (checklist back)	.40	.20	.04
☐ 552	Jose Morales	.10	.05	.01
☐ 553	Denny Walling	.10	.05	.01
☐ 554	Matt Keough	.10	.05	.01
☐ 555	Biff Pocoroba	.10	.05	.01
☐ 556	Mike Lum	.10	.05	.01
☐ 557	Ken Brett	.10	.05	.01
☐ 558	Jay Johnstone	.20	.10	.02
☐ 559	Greg Pryor	.10	.05	.01
☐ 560	John Montefusco	.20	.10	.02
☐ 561	Ed Ott	.10	.05	.01
☐ 562	Dusty Baker	.30	.15	.03
☐ 563	Roy Thomas	.10	.05	.01
☐ 564	Jerry Turner	.10	.05	.01
☐ 565	Rico Carty	.20	.10	.02
☐ 566	Nino Espinosa	.10	.05	.01
☐ 567	Richie Hebner	.10	.05	.01
☐ 568	Carlos Lopez	.10	.05	.01
☐ 569	Bob Sykes	.10	.05	.01
☐ 570	Cesar Cedeno	.20	.10	.02
☐ 571	Darrell Porter	.10	.05	.01
☐ 572	Rod Gilbreath	.10	.05	.01
☐ 573	Jim Kern	.10	.05	.01
☐ 574	Claudell Washington	.20	.10	.02
☐ 575	Luis Tiant	.30	.15	.03
☐ 576	Mike Parrott	.10	.05	.01
☐ 577	Brewers Team/Mgr. George Bamberger (checklist back)	.40	.20	.04
☐ 578	Pete Broberg	.10	.05	.01
☐ 579	Greg Gross	.10	.05	.01
☐ 580	Ron Fairly	.10	.05	.01
☐ 581	Darold Knowles	.10	.05	.01
☐ 582	Paul Blair	.10	.05	.01
☐ 583	Julio Cruz	.10	.05	.01
☐ 584	Jim Rooker	.10	.05	.01
☐ 585	Hal McRae	.20	.10	.02
☐ 586	Bob Horner	1.50	.75	.15
☐ 587	Ken Reitz	.10	.05	.01
☐ 588	Tom Murphy	.10	.05	.01
☐ 589	Terry Whitfield	.10	.05	.01
☐ 590	J.R. Richard	.20	.10	.02
☐ 591	Mike Hargrove	.20	.10	.02
☐ 592	Mike Krukow	.20	.10	.02
☐ 593	Rick Dempsey	.20	.10	.02
☐ 594	Bob Shirley	.10	.05	.01
☐ 595	Phil Niekro	1.25	.60	.12
☐ 596	Jim Wohlford	.10	.05	.01
☐ 597	Bob Stanley	.10	.05	.01
☐ 598	Mark Wagner	.10	.05	.01
☐ 599	Jim Spencer	.10	.05	.01
☐ 600	George Foster	.60	.30	.06

☐ 601	Dave LaRoche	.10	.05	.01
☐ 602	Checklist 5	.40	.05	.01
☐ 603	Rudy May	.10	.05	.01
☐ 604	Jeff Newman	.10	.05	.01
☐ 605	Rick Monday DP	.10	.05	.01
☐ 606	Expos Team/Mgr. Dick Williams (checklist back)	.40	.20	.04
☐ 607	Omar Moreno	.10	.05	.01
☐ 608	Dave McKay	.10	.05	.01
☐ 609	Silvio Martinez	.10	.05	.01
☐ 610	Mike Schmidt	5.00	2.50	.50
☐ 611	Jim Norris	.10	.05	.01
☐ 612	Rick Honeycutt	.50	.25	.05
☐ 613	Mike Edwards	.10	.05	.01
☐ 614	Willie Hernandez	.40	.20	.04
☐ 615	Ken Singleton	.20	.10	.02
☐ 616	Billy Almon	.10	.05	.01
☐ 617	Terry Puhl	.10	.05	.01
☐ 618	Jerry Remy	.10	.05	.01
☐ 619	Ken Landreaux	.30	.15	.03
☐ 620	Bert Campaneris	.20	.10	.02
☐ 621	Pat Zachry	.10	.05	.01
☐ 622	Dave Collins	.10	.05	.01
☐ 623	Bob McClure	.10	.05	.01
☐ 624	Larry Herndon	.10	.05	.01
☐ 625	Mark Fidrych	.20	.10	.02
☐ 626	Yankees Team/Mgr. Bob Lemon (checklist back)	.50	.25	.05
☐ 627	Gary Serum	.10	.05	.01
☐ 628	Del Unser	.10	.05	.01
☐ 629	Gene Garber	.10	.05	.01
☐ 630	Bake McBride	.10	.05	.01
☐ 631	Jorge Orta	.10	.05	.01
☐ 632	Don Kirkwood	.10	.05	.01
☐ 633	Rob Wilfong DP	.05	.02	.00
☐ 634	Paul Lindblad	.10	.05	.01
☐ 635	Don Baylor	.75	.35	.07
☐ 636	Wayne Garland	.10	.05	.01
☐ 637	Bill Robinson	.20	.10	.02
☐ 638	Al Fitzmorris	.10	.05	.01
☐ 639	Manny Trillo	.10	.05	.01
☐ 640	Eddie Murray	5.00	2.50	.50
☐ 641	Bobby Castillo	.10	.05	.01
☐ 642	Wilbur Howard DP	.05	.02	.00
☐ 643	Tom Hausman	.10	.05	.01
☐ 644	Manny Mota	.20	.10	.02
☐ 645	George Scott DP	.10	.05	.01
☐ 646	Rick Sweet	.10	.05	.01
☐ 647	Bob Lacey	.10	.05	.01
☐ 648	Lou Piniella	.30	.15	.03
☐ 649	John Curtis	.10	.05	.01
☐ 650	Pete Rose	4.50	2.25	.45
☐ 651	Mike Caldwell	.10	.05	.01
☐ 652	Stan Papi	.10	.05	.01
☐ 653	Warren Brusstar DP	.05	.02	.00
☐ 654	Rick Miller	.10	.05	.01
☐ 655	Jerry Koosman	.30	.15	.03
☐ 656	Hosken Powell	.10	.05	.01
☐ 657	George Medich	.10	.05	.01
☐ 658	Taylor Duncan	.10	.05	.01
☐ 659	Mariners Team/Mgr. Darrell Johnson (checklist back)	.40	.20	.04
☐ 660	Ron LeFlore DP	.10	.05	.01
☐ 661	Bruce Kison	.10	.05	.01
☐ 662	Kevin Bell	.10	.05	.01
☐ 663	Mike Vail	.10	.05	.01
☐ 664	Doug Bird	.10	.05	.01
☐ 665	Lou Brock	1.50	.75	.15
☐ 666	Rich Dauer	.10	.05	.01
☐ 667	Don Hood	.10	.05	.01
☐ 668	Bill North	.10	.05	.01
☐ 669	Checklist 6	.40	.05	.01
☐ 670	Jim Hunter DP	.60	.30	.06
☐ 671	Joe Ferguson DP	.05	.02	.00
☐ 672	Ed Halicki	.10	.05	.01
☐ 673	Tom Hutton	.10	.05	.01
☐ 674	Dave Tomlin	.10	.05	.01
☐ 675	Tim McCarver	.30	.15	.03
☐ 676	Johnny Sutton	.10	.05	.01
☐ 677	Larry Parrish	.20	.10	.02
☐ 678	Geoff Zahn	.10	.05	.01
☐ 679	Derrel Thomas	.10	.05	.01
☐ 680	Carlton Fisk	1.25	.60	.12
☐ 681	John Henry Johnson	.10	.05	.01
☐ 682	Dave Chalk	.10	.05	.01
☐ 683	Dan Meyer DP	.05	.02	.00
☐ 684	Jamie Easterly DP	.05	.02	.00
☐ 685	Sixto Lezcano	.10	.05	.01
☐ 686	Ron Schueler DP	.05	.02	.00
☐ 687	Rennie Stennett	.10	.05	.01
☐ 688	Mike Willis	.10	.05	.01
☐ 689	Orioles Team/Mgr. Earl Weaver (checklist back)	.50	.25	.05
☐ 690	Buddy Bell DP	.10	.05	.01
☐ 691	Dock Ellis DP	.05	.02	.00
☐ 692	Mickey Stanley	.10	.05	.01
☐ 693	Dave Rader	.10	.05	.01
☐ 694	Burt Hooton	.10	.05	.01
☐ 695	Keith Hernandez	2.25	1.10	.22
☐ 696	Andy Hassler	.10	.05	.01
☐ 697	Dave Bergman	.10	.05	.01
☐ 698	Bill Stein	.10	.05	.01
☐ 699	Hal Dues	.10	.05	.01
☐ 700	Reggie Jackson DP	1.75	.85	.17
☐ 701	Orioles Prospects Mark Corey John Flinn Sammy Stewart	.20	.10	.02
☐ 702	Red Sox Prospects Joel Finch Garry Hancock Allen Ripley	.20	.10	.02
☐ 703	Angels Prospects Jim Anderson Dave Frost Bob Slater	.10	.05	.01
☐ 704	White Sox Prospects Ross Baumgarten Mike Colbern Mike Squires	.10	.05	.01
☐ 705	Indians Prospects Alfredo Griffin Tim Norrid Dave Oliver	1.00	.50	.10
☐ 706	Tigers Prospects Dave Stegman Dave Tobik Kip Young	.10	.05	.01
☐ 707	Royals Prospects Randy Bass Jim Gaudet Randy McGilberry	.30	.15	.03
☐ 708	Brewers Prospects Kevin Bass Eddie Romero Ned Yost	1.25	.60	.12
☐ 709	Twins Prospects Sam Perlozzo Rick Sofield Kevin Stanfield	.10	.05	.01
☐ 710	Yankees Prospects Brian Doyle Mike Heath Dave Rajsich	.30	.15	.03
☐ 711	A's Prospects Dwayne Murphy Bruce Robinson Alan Wirth	.30	.15	.03
☐ 712	Mariners Prospects Bud Anderson Greg Biercevicz Byron McLaughlin	.10	.05	.01
☐ 713	Rangers Prospects Danny Darwin Pat Putnam Billy Sample	.40	.20	.04
☐ 714	Blue Jays Prospects Victor Cruz Pat Kelly Ernie Whitt	.40	.20	.04
☐ 715	Braves Prospects Bruce Benedict Glenn Hubbard Larry Whisenton	.30	.15	.03
☐ 716	Cubs Prospects Dave Geisel Karl Pagel Scot Thompson	.10	.05	.01
☐ 717	Reds Prospects Mike LaCoss Ron Oester Harry Spilman	.40	.20	.04
☐ 718	Astros Prospects Bruce Bochy Mike Fischlin Don Pisker	.10	.05	.01
☐ 719	Dodgers Prospects Pedro Guerrero Rudy Law Joe Simpson	10.00	5.00	1.00
☐ 720	Expos Prospects Jerry Fry Jerry Pirtle Scott Sanderson	.30	.15	.03
☐ 721	Mets Prospects Juan Berenguer	.30	.15	.03

			MINT	EXC	G-VG
		Dwight Bernard			
		Dan Norman			
☐	722	Phillies Prospects	2.50	1.10	.22
		Jim Morrison			
		Lonnie Smith			
		Jim Wright			
☐	723	Pirates Prospects	.30	.15	.03
		Dale Berra			
		Eugenio Cotes			
		Ben Wiltbank			
☐	724	Cardinals Prospects	.40	.20	.04
		Tom Bruno			
		George Frazier			
		Terry Kennedy			
☐	725	Padres Prospects	.10	.05	.01
		Jim Beswick			
		Steve Mura			
		Broderick Perkins			
☐	726	Giants Prospects	.20	.10	.02
		Greg Johnston			
		Joe Strain			
		John Tamargo			

1980 Topps

The cards in this 726-card set measure 2 1/2" by 3 1/2". In 1980 Topps released another set of the same size and number of cards as the previous two years. As with those sets, Topps again has produced 66 double-printed cards in the set; they are noted by DP in the checklist below. The player's name appears over the picture and his position and team are found in pennant design. Every card carries a facsimile autograph. Team cards feature a team checklist of players in the set on the back and the manager's name on the front. Cards 1-6 show Highlights (HL) of the 1979 season, cards 201-207 are League Leaders, and cards 661-686 feature American and National League rookie "Future Stars," one card for each team showing three young prospects.

			MINT	EXC	G-VG
		COMPLETE SET (726)	165.00	75.00	15.00
		COMMON PLAYER (1-726)	.10	.05	.01
		COMMON DP's (1-726)	.05	.02	.00
☐	1	HL: Brock and Yaz, ... Enter 3000 hit circle	1.50	.35	.07
☐	2	HL: Willie McCovey, ... 512th homer sets new mark for NL lefties	.75	.35	.07
☐	3	HL: Manny Mota, All- ...... time pinch-hits, 145	.20	.10	.02
☐	4	HL: Pete Rose, Career ... Record 10th season with 200 or more hits	2.00	1.00	.20
☐	5	HL: Garry Templeton, ... First with 100 hits from each side of plate	.20	.10	.02
☐	6	HL: Del Unser, 3rd .... cons. pinch homer sets new ML standard	.10	.05	.01
☐	7	Mike Lum	.10	.05	.01
☐	8	Craig Swan	.10	.05	.01
☐	9	Steve Braun	.10	.05	.01
☐	10	Denny Martinez	.20	.10	.02

☐	11	Jimmy Sexton	.10	.05	.01
☐	12	John Curtis DP	.05	.02	.00
☐	13	Ron Pruitt	.10	.05	.01
☐	14	Dave Cash	.10	.05	.01
☐	15	Bill Campbell	.10	.05	.01
☐	16	Jerry Narron	.10	.05	.01
☐	17	Bruce Sutter	.40	.20	.04
☐	18	Ron Jackson	.10	.05	.01
☐	19	Balor Moore	.10	.05	.01
☐	20	Dan Ford	.10	.05	.01
☐	21	Manny Sarmiento	.10	.05	.01
☐	22	Pat Putnam	.10	.05	.01
☐	23	Derrel Thomas	.10	.05	.01
☐	24	Jim Slaton	.10	.05	.01
☐	25	Lee Mazzilli	.10	.05	.01
☐	26	Marty Pattin	.10	.05	.01
☐	27	Del Unser	.10	.05	.01
☐	28	Bruce Kison	.10	.05	.01
☐	29	Mark Wagner	.10	.05	.01
☐	30	Vida Blue	.20	.10	.02
☐	31	Jay Johnstone	.20	.10	.02
☐	32	Julio Cruz DP	.10	.05	.01
☐	33	Tony Scott	.10	.05	.01
☐	34	Jeff Newman DP	.05	.02	.00
☐	35	Luis Tiant	.20	.10	.02
☐	36	Rusty Torres	.10	.05	.01
☐	37	Kiko Garcia	.10	.05	.01
☐	38	Dan Spillner DP	.05	.02	.00
☐	39	Rowland Office	.10	.05	.01
☐	40	Carlton Fisk	1.25	.60	.12
☐	41	Rangers Team/Mgr. .... Pat Corrales (checklist back)	.35	.17	.03
☐	42	David Palmer	.35	.17	.03
☐	43	Bombo Rivera	.10	.05	.01
☐	44	Bill Fahey	.10	.05	.01
☐	45	Frank White	.30	.15	.03
☐	46	Rico Carty	.20	.10	.02
☐	47	Bill Bonham DP	.05	.02	.00
☐	48	Rick Miller	.10	.05	.01
☐	49	Mario Guerrero	.10	.05	.01
☐	50	J.R. Richard	.20	.10	.02
☐	51	Joe Ferguson DP	.05	.02	.00
☐	52	Warren Brusstar	.10	.05	.01
☐	53	Ben Oglivie	.20	.10	.02
☐	54	Dennis Lamp	.10	.05	.01
☐	55	Bill Madlock	.30	.15	.03
☐	56	Bobby Valentine	.20	.10	.02
☐	57	Pete Vuckovich	.10	.05	.01
☐	58	Doug Flynn	.10	.05	.01
☐	59	Eddy Putman	.10	.05	.01
☐	60	Bucky Dent	.30	.15	.03
☐	61	Gary Serum	.10	.05	.01
☐	62	Mike Ivie	.10	.05	.01
☐	63	Bob Stanley	.10	.05	.01
☐	64	Joe Nolan	.10	.05	.01
☐	65	Al Bumbry	.10	.05	.01
☐	66	Royals Team/Mgr. .... Jim Frey (checklist back)	.35	.17	.03
☐	67	Doyle Alexander	.20	.10	.02
☐	68	Larry Harlow	.10	.05	.01
☐	69	Rick Williams	.10	.05	.01
☐	70	Gary Carter	2.00	1.00	.20
☐	71	John Milner DP	.05	.02	.00
☐	72	Fred Howard DP	.05	.02	.00
☐	73	Dave Collins	.10	.05	.01
☐	74	Sid Monge	.10	.05	.01
☐	75	Bill Russell	.20	.10	.02
☐	76	John Stearns	.10	.05	.01
☐	77	Dave Stieb	4.00	2.00	.40
☐	78	Ruppert Jones	.10	.05	.01
☐	79	Bob Owchinko	.10	.05	.01
☐	80	Ron LeFlore	.10	.05	.01
☐	81	Ted Sizemore	.10	.05	.01
☐	82	Astros Team/Mgr. .... Bill Virdon (checklist back)	.35	.17	.03
☐	83	Steve Trout	.30	.15	.03
☐	84	Gary Lavelle	.10	.05	.01
☐	85	Ted Simmons	.40	.20	.04
☐	86	Dave Hamilton	.10	.05	.01
☐	87	Pepe Frias	.10	.05	.01
☐	88	Ken Landreaux	.10	.05	.01
☐	89	Don Hood	.10	.05	.01
☐	90	Manny Trillo	.10	.05	.01
☐	91	Rick Dempsey	.10	.05	.01
☐	92	Rick Rhoden	.20	.10	.02
☐	93	Dave Roberts DP	.05	.02	.00
☐	94	Neil Allen	.40	.20	.04
☐	95	Cecil Cooper	.30	.15	.03
☐	96	A's Team/Mgr. .... Jim Marshall (checklist back)	.35	.17	.03
☐	97	Bill Lee	.10	.05	.01

☐ 98	Jerry Terrell	.10	.05	.01
☐ 99	Victor Cruz	.10	.05	.01
☐ 100	Johnny Bench	2.75	1.35	.27
☐ 101	Aurelio Lopez	.10	.05	.01
☐ 102	Rich Dauer	.10	.05	.01
☐ 103	Bill Caudill	.30	.15	.03
☐ 104	Manny Mota	.20	.10	.02
☐ 105	Frank Tanana	.20	.10	.02
☐ 106	Jeff Leonard	1.50	.75	.15
☐ 107	Francisco Barrios	.10	.05	.01
☐ 108	Bob Horner	.75	.35	.07
☐ 109	Bill Travers	.10	.05	.01
☐ 110	Fred Lynn DP	.35	.17	.03
☐ 111	Bob Knepper	.20	.10	.02
☐ 112	White Sox Team/Mgr. ... Tony LaRussa (checklist back)	.35	.17	.03
☐ 113	Geoff Zahn	.10	.05	.01
☐ 114	Juan Beniquez	.10	.05	.01
☐ 115	Sparky Lyle	.20	.10	.02
☐ 116	Larry Cox	.10	.05	.01
☐ 117	Dock Ellis	.10	.05	.01
☐ 118	Phil Garner	.10	.05	.01
☐ 119	Sammy Stewart	.10	.05	.01
☐ 120	Greg Luzinski	.20	.10	.02
☐ 121	Checklist 1	.30	.04	.01
☐ 122	Dave Rosello DP	.05	.02	.00
☐ 123	Lynn Jones	.10	.05	.01
☐ 124	Dave Lemanczyk	.10	.05	.01
☐ 125	Tony Perez	.50	.25	.05
☐ 126	Dave Tomlin	.10	.05	.01
☐ 127	Gary Thomasson	.10	.05	.01
☐ 128	Tom Burgmeier	.10	.05	.01
☐ 129	Craig Reynolds	.10	.05	.01
☐ 130	Amos Otis	.20	.10	.02
☐ 131	Paul Mitchell	.10	.05	.01
☐ 132	Biff Pocoroba	.10	.05	.01
☐ 133	Jerry Turner	.10	.05	.01
☐ 134	Matt Keough	.10	.05	.01
☐ 135	Bill Buckner	.30	.15	.03
☐ 136	Dick Ruthven	.10	.05	.01
☐ 137	John Castino	.10	.05	.01
☐ 138	Ross Baumgarten	.10	.05	.01
☐ 139	Dane Iorg	.20	.10	.02
☐ 140	Rich Gossage	.50	.25	.05
☐ 141	Gary Alexander	.10	.05	.01
☐ 142	Phil Huffman	.10	.05	.01
☐ 143	Bruce Bochte DP	.10	.05	.01
☐ 144	Steve Comer	.10	.05	.01
☐ 145	Darrell Evans	.30	.15	.03
☐ 146	Bob Welch	.60	.30	.06
☐ 147	Terry Puhl	.10	.05	.01
☐ 148	Manny Sanguillen	.20	.10	.02
☐ 149	Tom Hume	.10	.05	.01
☐ 150	Jason Thompson	.10	.05	.01
☐ 151	Tom Hausman DP	.05	.02	.00
☐ 152	John Fulgham	.10	.05	.01
☐ 153	Tim Blackwell	.10	.05	.01
☐ 154	Lary Sorensen	.10	.05	.01
☐ 155	Jerry Remy	.10	.05	.01
☐ 156	Tony Brizzolara	.10	.05	.01
☐ 157	Willie Wilson DP	.20	.10	.02
☐ 158	Rob Picciolo DP	.05	.02	.00
☐ 159	Ken Clay	.10	.05	.01
☐ 160	Eddie Murray	3.50	1.75	.35
☐ 161	Larry Christenson	.10	.05	.01
☐ 162	Bob Randall	.10	.05	.01
☐ 163	Steve Swisher	.10	.05	.01
☐ 164	Greg Pryor	.10	.05	.01
☐ 165	Omar Moreno	.10	.05	.01
☐ 166	Glenn Abbott	.10	.05	.01
☐ 167	Jack Clark	2.00	1.00	.20
☐ 168	Rick Waits	.10	.05	.01
☐ 169	Luis Gomez	.10	.05	.01
☐ 170	Burt Hooton	.10	.05	.01
☐ 171	Fernando Gonzalez	.10	.05	.01
☐ 172	Ron Hodges	.10	.05	.01
☐ 173	John Henry Johnson	.10	.05	.01
☐ 174	Ray Knight	.20	.10	.02
☐ 175	Rick Reuschel	.35	.15	.03
☐ 176	Champ Summers	.10	.05	.01
☐ 177	Dave Heaverlo	.10	.05	.01
☐ 178	Tim McCarver	.30	.15	.03
☐ 179	Ron Davis	.20	.10	.02
☐ 180	Warren Cromartie	.10	.05	.01
☐ 181	Moose Haas	.10	.05	.01
☐ 182	Ken Reitz	.10	.05	.01
☐ 183	Jim Anderson DP	.05	.02	.00
☐ 184	Steve Renko DP	.05	.02	.00
☐ 185	Hal McRae	.20	.10	.02
☐ 186	Junior Moore	.10	.05	.01
☐ 187	Alan Ashby	.10	.05	.01
☐ 188	Terry Crowley	.10	.05	.01
☐ 189	Kevin Kobel	.10	.05	.01
☐ 190	Buddy Bell	.30	.15	.03

☐ 191	Ted Martinez	.10	.05	.01
☐ 192	Braves Team/Mgr. .... Bobby Cox (checklist back)	.35	.17	.03
☐ 193	Dave Goltz	.10	.05	.01
☐ 194	Mike Easler	.20	.10	.02
☐ 195	John Montefusco	.20	.10	.02
☐ 196	Lance Parrish	1.50	.75	.15
☐ 197	Byron McLaughlin	.10	.05	.01
☐ 198	Dell Alston DP	.05	.02	.00
☐ 199	Mike LaCoss	.20	.10	.02
☐ 200	Jim Rice	1.50	.75	.15
☐ 201	Batting Leaders Keith Hernandez Fred Lynn	.30	.15	.03
☐ 202	Home Run Leaders .... Dave Kingman Gorman Thomas	.20	.10	.02
☐ 203	RBI Leaders Dave Winfield Don Baylor	.30	.15	.03
☐ 204	Stolen Base Leaders ...... Omar Moreno Willie Wilson	.20	.10	.02
☐ 205	Victory Leaders Joe Niekro Phil Niekro Mike Flanagan	.20	.10	.02
☐ 206	Strikeout Leaders .... J.R. Richard Nolan Ryan	1.00	.50	.10
☐ 207	ERA Leaders J.R. Richard Ron Guidry	.20	.10	.02
☐ 208	Wayne Cage	.10	.05	.01
☐ 209	Von Joshua	.10	.05	.01
☐ 210	Steve Carlton	2.25	1.10	.22
☐ 211	Dave Skaggs DP	.05	.02	.00
☐ 212	Dave Roberts	.10	.05	.01
☐ 213	Mike Jorgensen DP	.05	.02	.00
☐ 214	Angels Team/Mgr. .... Jim Fregosi (checklist back)	.35	.17	.03
☐ 215	Sixto Lezcano	.10	.05	.01
☐ 216	Phil Mankowski	.10	.05	.01
☐ 217	Ed Halicki	.10	.05	.01
☐ 218	Jose Morales	.10	.05	.01
☐ 219	Steve Mingori	.10	.05	.01
☐ 220	Dave Concepcion	.30	.15	.03
☐ 221	Joe Cannon	.10	.05	.01
☐ 222	Ron Hassey	.30	.15	.03
☐ 223	Bob Sykes	.10	.05	.01
☐ 224	Willie Montanez	.10	.05	.01
☐ 225	Lou Piniella	.30	.15	.03
☐ 226	Bill Stein	.10	.05	.01
☐ 227	Len Barker	.10	.05	.01
☐ 228	Johnny Oates	.10	.05	.01
☐ 229	Jim Bibby	.10	.05	.01
☐ 230	Dave Winfield	2.00	1.00	.20
☐ 231	Steve McCatty	.10	.05	.01
☐ 232	Alan Trammell	2.50	1.25	.25
☐ 233	LaRue Washington	.10	.05	.01
☐ 234	Vern Ruhle	.10	.05	.01
☐ 235	Andre Dawson	2.50	1.25	.25
☐ 236	Marc Hill	.10	.05	.01
☐ 237	Scott McGregor	.20	.10	.02
☐ 238	Rob Wilfong	.10	.05	.01
☐ 239	Don Aase	.10	.05	.01
☐ 240	Dave Kingman	.30	.15	.03
☐ 241	Checklist 2	.30	.04	.01
☐ 242	Lamar Johnson	.10	.05	.01
☐ 243	Jerry Augustine	.10	.05	.01
☐ 244	Cardinals Team/Mgr. ...... Ken Boyer (checklist back)	.35	.17	.03
☐ 245	Phil Niekro	.90	.45	.09
☐ 246	Tim Foli DP	.05	.02	.00
☐ 247	Frank Riccelli	.10	.05	.01
☐ 248	Jamie Quirk	.10	.05	.01
☐ 249	Jim Clancy	.10	.05	.01
☐ 250	Jim Kaat	.40	.20	.04
☐ 251	Kip Young	.10	.05	.01
☐ 252	Ted Cox	.10	.05	.01
☐ 253	John Montague	.10	.05	.01
☐ 254	Paul Dade DP	.05	.02	.00
☐ 255	Dusty Baker DP	.10	.05	.01
☐ 256	Roger Erickson	.10	.05	.01
☐ 257	Larry Herndon	.10	.05	.01
☐ 258	Paul Moskau	.10	.05	.01
☐ 259	Mets Team/Mgr. .... Joe Torre (checklist back)	.40	.20	.04
☐ 260	Al Oliver	.30	.15	.03
☐ 261	Dave Chalk	.10	.05	.01
☐ 262	Benny Ayala	.10	.05	.01

☐ 263	Dave LaRoche DP	.05	.02	.00
☐ 264	Bill Robinson	.20	.10	.02
☐ 265	Robin Yount	4.00	2.00	.40
☐ 266	Bernie Carbo	.10	.05	.01
☐ 267	Dan Schatzeder	.10	.05	.01
☐ 268	Rafael Landestoy	.10	.05	.01
☐ 269	Dave Tobik	.10	.05	.01
☐ 270	Mike Schmidt DP	2.00	1.00	.20
☐ 271	Dick Drago DP	.05	.02	.00
☐ 272	Ralph Garr	.10	.05	.01
☐ 273	Eduardo Rodriguez	.10	.05	.01
☐ 274	Dale Murphy	6.00	3.00	.60
☐ 275	Jerry Koosman	.30	.15	.03
☐ 276	Tom Veryzer	.10	.05	.01
☐ 277	Rick Bosetti	.10	.05	.01
☐ 278	Jim Spencer	.10	.05	.01
☐ 279	Rob Andrews	.10	.05	.01
☐ 280	Gaylord Perry	1.00	.50	.10
☐ 281	Paul Blair	.10	.05	.01
☐ 282	Mariners Team/Mgr. Darrell Johnson (checklist back)	.35	.17	.03
☐ 283	John Ellis	.10	.05	.01
☐ 284	Larry Murray DP	.05	.02	.00
☐ 285	Don Baylor	.40	.20	.04
☐ 286	Darold Knowles DP	.05	.02	.00
☐ 287	John Lowenstein	.10	.05	.01
☐ 288	Dave Rozema	.10	.05	.01
☐ 289	Bruce Bochy	.10	.05	.01
☐ 290	Steve Garvey	2.00	1.00	.20
☐ 291	Randy Scarberry	.10	.05	.01
☐ 292	Dale Berra	.10	.05	.01
☐ 293	Elias Sosa	.10	.05	.01
☐ 294	Charlie Spikes	.10	.05	.01
☐ 295	Larry Gura	.10	.05	.01
☐ 296	Dave Rader	.10	.05	.01
☐ 297	Tim Johnson	.10	.05	.01
☐ 298	Ken Holtzman	.20	.10	.02
☐ 299	Steve Henderson	.10	.05	.01
☐ 300	Ron Guidry	.75	.35	.07
☐ 301	Mike Edwards	.10	.05	.01
☐ 302	Dodgers Team/Mgr. Tom Lasorda (checklist back)	.45	.22	.04
☐ 303	Bill Castro	.10	.05	.01
☐ 304	Butch Wynegar	.10	.05	.01
☐ 305	Randy Jones	.10	.05	.01
☐ 306	Denny Walling	.10	.05	.01
☐ 307	Rick Honeycutt	.10	.05	.01
☐ 308	Mike Hargrove	.20	.10	.02
☐ 309	Larry McWilliams	.10	.05	.01
☐ 310	Dave Parker	1.25	.60	.12
☐ 311	Roger Metzger	.10	.05	.01
☐ 312	Mike Barlow	.10	.05	.01
☐ 313	Johnny Grubb	.10	.05	.01
☐ 314	Tim Stoddard	.20	.10	.02
☐ 315	Steve Kemp	.20	.10	.02
☐ 316	Bob Lacey	.10	.05	.01
☐ 317	Mike Anderson DP	.05	.02	.00
☐ 318	Jerry Reuss	.20	.10	.02
☐ 319	Chris Speier	.10	.05	.01
☐ 320	Dennis Eckersley	.50	.25	.05
☐ 321	Keith Hernandez	1.50	.75	.15
☐ 322	Claudell Washington	.20	.10	.02
☐ 323	Mick Kelleher	.10	.05	.01
☐ 324	Tom Underwood	.10	.05	.01
☐ 325	Dan Driessen	.10	.05	.01
☐ 326	Bo McLaughlin	.10	.05	.01
☐ 327	Ray Fosse DP	.05	.02	.00
☐ 328	Twins Team/Mgr. Gene Mauch (checklist back)	.35	.17	.03
☐ 329	Bert Roberge	.10	.05	.01
☐ 330	Al Cowens	.10	.05	.01
☐ 331	Richie Hebner	.10	.05	.01
☐ 332	Enrique Romo	.10	.05	.01
☐ 333	Jim Norris DP	.05	.02	.00
☐ 334	Jim Beattie	.10	.05	.01
☐ 335	Willie McCovey	1.50	.75	.15
☐ 336	George Medich	.10	.05	.01
☐ 337	Carney Lansford	1.50	.75	.15
☐ 338	John Wockenfuss	.10	.05	.01
☐ 339	John D'Acquisto	.10	.05	.01
☐ 340	Ken Singleton	.20	.10	.02
☐ 341	Jim Essian	.10	.05	.01
☐ 342	Odell Jones	.10	.05	.01
☐ 343	Mike Vail	.10	.05	.01
☐ 344	Randy Lerch	.10	.05	.01
☐ 345	Larry Parrish	.20	.10	.02
☐ 346	Buddy Solomon	.10	.05	.01
☐ 347	Harry Chappas	.10	.05	.01
☐ 348	Checklist 3	.30	.04	.01
☐ 349	Jack Brohamer	.10	.05	.01
☐ 350	George Hendrick	.20	.10	.02
☐ 351	Bob Davis	.10	.05	.01
☐ 352	Dan Briggs	.10	.05	.01
☐ 353	Andy Hassler	.10	.05	.01
☐ 354	Rick Auerbach	.10	.05	.01
☐ 355	Gary Matthews	.20	.10	.02
☐ 356	Padres Team/Mgr. Jerry Coleman (checklist back)	.35	.17	.03
☐ 357	Bob McClure	.10	.05	.01
☐ 358	Lou Whitaker	1.50	.75	.15
☐ 359	Randy Moffitt	.10	.05	.01
☐ 360	Darrell Porter DP	.10	.05	.01
☐ 361	Wayne Garland	.10	.05	.01
☐ 362	Danny Goodwin	.10	.05	.01
☐ 363	Wayne Gross	.10	.05	.01
☐ 364	Ray Burris	.10	.05	.01
☐ 365	Bobby Murcer	.30	.15	.03
☐ 366	Rob Dressler	.10	.05	.01
☐ 367	Billy Smith	.10	.05	.01
☐ 368	Willie Aikens	.25	.12	.02
☐ 369	Jim Kern	.10	.05	.01
☐ 370	Cesar Cedeno	.20	.10	.02
☐ 371	Jack Morris	1.25	.60	.12
☐ 372	Joel Youngblood	.10	.05	.01
☐ 373	Dan Petry DP	.40	.20	.04
☐ 374	Jim Gantner	.20	.10	.02
☐ 375	Ross Grimsley	.10	.05	.01
☐ 376	Gary Allenson	.10	.05	.01
☐ 377	Junior Kennedy	.10	.05	.01
☐ 378	Jerry Mumphrey	.10	.05	.01
☐ 379	Kevin Bell	.10	.05	.01
☐ 380	Garry Maddox	.20	.10	.02
☐ 381	Cubs Team/Mgr. Preston Gomez (checklist back)	.35	.17	.03
☐ 382	Dave Freisleben	.10	.05	.01
☐ 383	Ed Ott	.10	.05	.01
☐ 384	Joey McLaughlin	.10	.05	.01
☐ 385	Enos Cabell	.10	.05	.01
☐ 386	Darrell Jackson	.10	.05	.01
☐ 387A	Fred Stanley (yellow name on front)	1.00	.50	.10
☐ 387B	Fred Stanley (red name on front)	.10	.05	.01
☐ 388	Mike Paxton	.10	.05	.01
☐ 389	Pete LaCock	.10	.05	.01
☐ 390	Fergie Jenkins	.40	.20	.04
☐ 391	Tony Armas DP	.10	.05	.01
☐ 392	Milt Wilcox	.10	.05	.01
☐ 393	Ozzie Smith	4.50	2.25	.45
☐ 394	Reggie Cleveland	.10	.05	.01
☐ 395	Ellis Valentine	.10	.05	.01
☐ 396	Dan Meyer	.10	.05	.01
☐ 397	Roy Thomas DP	.05	.02	.00
☐ 398	Barry Foote	.10	.05	.01
☐ 399	Mike Proly DP	.05	.02	.00
☐ 400	George Foster	.50	.25	.05
☐ 401	Pete Falcone	.10	.05	.01
☐ 402	Merv Rettenmund	.10	.05	.01
☐ 403	Pete Redfern DP	.05	.02	.00
☐ 404	Orioles Team/Mgr. Earl Weaver (checklist back)	.40	.20	.04
☐ 405	Dwight Evans	.80	.40	.08
☐ 406	Paul Molitor	1.50	.75	.15
☐ 407	Tony Solaita	.10	.05	.01
☐ 408	Bill North	.10	.05	.01
☐ 409	Paul Splittorff	.10	.05	.01
☐ 410	Bobby Bonds	.30	.15	.03
☐ 411	Frank LaCorte	.10	.05	.01
☐ 412	Thad Bosley	.10	.05	.01
☐ 413	Allen Ripley	.10	.05	.01
☐ 414	George Scott	.10	.05	.01
☐ 415	Bill Atkinson	.10	.05	.01
☐ 416	Tom Brookens	.10	.05	.01
☐ 417	Craig Chamberlain DP	.05	.02	.00
☐ 418	Roger Freed DP	.05	.02	.00
☐ 419	Vic Correll	.10	.05	.01
☐ 420	Butch Hobson	.10	.05	.01
☐ 421	Doug Bird	.10	.05	.01
☐ 422	Larry Milbourne	.10	.05	.01
☐ 423	Dave Frost	.10	.05	.01
☐ 424	Yankees Team/Mgr. Dick Howser (checklist back)	.40	.20	.04
☐ 425	Mark Belanger	.20	.10	.02
☐ 426	Grant Jackson	.10	.05	.01
☐ 427	Tom Hutton DP	.05	.02	.00
☐ 428	Pat Zachry	.10	.05	.01
☐ 429	Duane Kuiper	.10	.05	.01
☐ 430	Larry Hisle DP	.10	.05	.01
☐ 431	Mike Krukow	.20	.10	.02
☐ 432	Willie Norwood	.10	.05	.01
☐ 433	Rich Gale	.10	.05	.01
☐ 434	Johnnie LeMaster	.10	.05	.01
☐ 435	Don Gullett	.20	.10	.02

☐ 436 Billy Almon	.10	.05	.01
☐ 437 Joe Niekro	.30	.15	.03
☐ 438 Dave Revering	.10	.05	.01
☐ 439 Mike Phillips	.10	.05	.01
☐ 440 Don Sutton	1.00	.50	.10
☐ 441 Eric Soderholm	.10	.05	.01
☐ 442 Jorge Orta	.10	.05	.01
☐ 443 Mike Parrott	.10	.05	.01
☐ 444 Alvis Woods	.10	.05	.01
☐ 445 Mark Fidrych	.20	.10	.02
☐ 446 Duffy Dyer	.10	.05	.01
☐ 447 Nino Espinosa	.10	.05	.01
☐ 448 Jim Wohlford	.10	.05	.01
☐ 449 Doug Bair	.10	.05	.01
☐ 450 George Brett	4.00	2.00	.40
☐ 451 Indians Team/Mgr.	.35	.17	.03
Dave Garcia (checklist back)			
☐ 452 Steve Dillard	.10	.05	.01
☐ 453 Mike Bacsik	.10	.05	.01
☐ 454 Tom Donohue	.10	.05	.01
☐ 455 Mike Torrez	.10	.05	.01
☐ 456 Frank Taveras	.10	.05	.01
☐ 457 Bert Blyleven	.50	.25	.05
☐ 458 Billy Sample	.10	.05	.01
☐ 459 Mickey Lolich DP	.10	.05	.01
☐ 460 Willie Randolph	.30	.15	.03
☐ 461 Dwayne Murphy	.10	.05	.01
☐ 462 Mike Sadek DP	.05	.02	.00
☐ 463 Jerry Royster	.10	.05	.01
☐ 464 John Denny	.20	.10	.02
☐ 465 Rick Monday	.20	.10	.02
☐ 466 Mike Squires	.10	.05	.01
☐ 467 Jesse Jefferson	.10	.05	.01
☐ 468 Aurelio Rodriguez	.10	.05	.01
☐ 469 Randy Niemann DP	.05	.02	.00
☐ 470 Bob Boone	.40	.20	.04
☐ 471 Hosken Powell DP	.05	.02	.00
☐ 472 Willie Hernandez	.30	.15	.03
☐ 473 Bump Wills	.10	.05	.01
☐ 474 Steve Busby	.10	.05	.01
☐ 475 Cesar Geronimo	.10	.05	.01
☐ 476 Bob Shirley	.10	.05	.01
☐ 477 Buck Martinez	.10	.05	.01
☐ 478 Gil Flores	.10	.05	.01
☐ 479 Expos Team/Mgr.	.30	.15	.03
Dick Williams (checklist back)			
☐ 480 Bob Watson	.20	.10	.02
☐ 481 Tom Paciorek	.10	.05	.01
☐ 482 Rickey Henderson	60.00	24.00	6.00
☐ 483 Bo Diaz	.10	.05	.01
☐ 484 Checklist 4	.30	.04	.01
☐ 485 Mickey Rivers	.20	.10	.02
☐ 486 Mike Tyson DP	.05	.02	.00
☐ 487 Wayne Nordhagen	.10	.05	.01
☐ 488 Roy Howell	.10	.05	.01
☐ 489 Preston Hanna DP	.05	.02	.00
☐ 490 Lee May	.10	.05	.01
☐ 491 Steve Mura DP	.05	.02	.00
☐ 492 Todd Cruz	.10	.05	.01
☐ 493 Jerry Martin	.10	.05	.01
☐ 494 Craig Minetto	.10	.05	.01
☐ 495 Bake McBride	.10	.05	.01
☐ 496 Silvio Martinez	.10	.05	.01
☐ 497 Jim Mason	.10	.05	.01
☐ 498 Danny Darwin	.10	.05	.01
☐ 499 Giants Team/Mgr.	.35	.17	.03
Dave Bristol (checklist back)			
☐ 500 Tom Seaver	2.00	1.00	.20
☐ 501 Rennie Stennett	.10	.05	.01
☐ 502 Rich Wortham DP	.05	.02	.00
☐ 503 Mike Cubbage	.10	.05	.01
☐ 504 Gene Garber	.10	.05	.01
☐ 505 Bert Campaneris	.20	.10	.02
☐ 506 Tom Buskey	.10	.05	.01
☐ 507 Leon Roberts	.10	.05	.01
☐ 508 U.L. Washington	.10	.05	.01
☐ 509 Ed Glynn	.10	.05	.01
☐ 510 Ron Cey	.30	.15	.03
☐ 511 Eric Wilkins	.10	.05	.01
☐ 512 Jose Cardenal	.10	.05	.01
☐ 513 Tom Dixon DP	.05	.02	.00
☐ 514 Steve Ontiveros	.10	.05	.01
☐ 515 Mike Caldwell	.10	.05	.01
☐ 516 Hector Cruz	.10	.05	.01
☐ 517 Don Stanhouse	.10	.05	.01
☐ 518 Nelson Norman	.10	.05	.01
☐ 519 Steve Nicosia	.10	.05	.01
☐ 520 Steve Rogers	.10	.05	.01
☐ 521 Ken Brett	.10	.05	.01
☐ 522 Jim Morrison	.10	.05	.01
☐ 523 Ken Henderson	.10	.05	.01
☐ 524 Jim Wright DP	.05	.02	.00
☐ 525 Clint Hurdle	.10	.05	.01
☐ 526 Phillies Team/Mgr.	.40	.20	.04
Dallas Green (checklist back)			
☐ 527 Doug Rau DP	.05	.02	.00
☐ 528 Adrian Devine	.10	.05	.01
☐ 529 Jim Barr	.10	.05	.01
☐ 530 Jim Sundberg DP	.10	.05	.01
☐ 531 Eric Rasmussen	.10	.05	.01
☐ 532 Willie Horton	.20	.10	.02
☐ 533 Checklist 5	.30	.04	.01
☐ 534 Andre Thornton	.20	.10	.02
☐ 535 Bob Forsch	.10	.05	.01
☐ 536 Lee Lacy	.10	.05	.01
☐ 537 Alex Trevino	.20	.10	.02
☐ 538 Joe Strain	.10	.05	.01
☐ 539 Rudy May	.10	.05	.01
☐ 540 Pete Rose	4.00	2.00	.40
☐ 541 Miguel Dilone	.10	.05	.01
☐ 542 Joe Coleman	.10	.05	.01
☐ 543 Pat Kelly	.10	.05	.01
☐ 544 Rick Sutcliffe	3.50	1.75	.35
☐ 545 Jeff Burroughs	.10	.05	.01
☐ 546 Rick Langford	.10	.05	.01
☐ 547 John Wathan	.20	.10	.02
☐ 548 Dave Rajsich	.10	.05	.01
☐ 549 Larry Wolfe	.10	.05	.01
☐ 550 Ken Griffey	.30	.15	.03
☐ 551 Pirates Team/Mgr.	.35	.17	.03
Chuck Tanner (checklist back)			
☐ 552 Bill Nahorodny	.10	.05	.01
☐ 553 Dick Davis	.10	.05	.01
☐ 554 Art Howe	.20	.10	.02
☐ 555 Ed Figueroa	.10	.05	.01
☐ 556 Joe Rudi	.20	.10	.02
☐ 557 Mark Lee	.10	.05	.01
☐ 558 Alfredo Griffin	.20	.10	.02
☐ 559 Dale Murray	.10	.05	.01
☐ 560 Dave Lopes	.20	.10	.02
☐ 561 Eddie Whitson	.20	.10	.02
☐ 562 Joe Wallis	.10	.05	.01
☐ 563 Will McEnaney	.10	.05	.01
☐ 564 Rick Manning	.10	.05	.01
☐ 565 Dennis Leonard	.20	.10	.02
☐ 566 Bud Harrelson	.10	.05	.01
☐ 567 Skip Lockwood	.10	.05	.01
☐ 568 Gary Roenicke	.20	.10	.02
☐ 569 Terry Kennedy	.20	.10	.02
☐ 570 Roy Smalley	.10	.05	.01
☐ 571 Joe Sambito	.10	.05	.01
☐ 572 Jerry Morales DP	.05	.02	.00
☐ 573 Kent Tekulve	.20	.10	.02
☐ 574 Scot Thompson	.10	.05	.01
☐ 575 Ken Kravec	.10	.05	.01
☐ 576 Jim Dwyer	.10	.05	.01
☐ 577 Blue Jays Team/Mgr.	.30	.15	.03
Bobby Mattick (checklist back)			
☐ 578 Scott Sanderson	.20	.10	.02
☐ 579 Charlie Moore	.10	.05	.01
☐ 580 Nolan Ryan	5.00	2.50	.50
☐ 581 Bob Bailor	.10	.05	.01
☐ 582 Brian Doyle	.10	.05	.01
☐ 583 Bob Stinson	.10	.05	.01
☐ 584 Kurt Bevacqua	.10	.05	.01
☐ 585 Al Hrabosky	.20	.10	.02
☐ 586 Mitchell Page	.10	.05	.01
☐ 587 Garry Templeton	.20	.10	.02
☐ 588 Greg Minton	.10	.05	.01
☐ 589 Chet Lemon	.10	.05	.01
☐ 590 Jim Palmer	1.75	.85	.17
☐ 591 Rick Cerone	.10	.05	.01
☐ 592 Jon Matlack	.10	.05	.01
☐ 593 Jesus Alou	.10	.05	.01
☐ 594 Dick Tidrow	.10	.05	.01
☐ 595 Don Money	.10	.05	.01
☐ 596 Rick Matula	.10	.05	.01
☐ 597 Tom Poquette	.10	.05	.01
☐ 598 Fred Kendall DP	.05	.02	.00
☐ 599 Mike Norris	.10	.05	.01
☐ 600 Reggie Jackson	2.50	1.25	.25
☐ 601 Buddy Schultz	.10	.05	.01
☐ 602 Brian Downing	.20	.10	.02
☐ 603 Jack Billingham DP	.05	.02	.00
☐ 604 Glenn Adams	.10	.05	.01
☐ 605 Terry Forster	.20	.10	.02
☐ 606 Reds Team/Mgr.	.35	.17	.03
John McNamara (checklist back)			
☐ 607 Woodie Fryman	.10	.05	.01
☐ 608 Alan Bannister	.10	.05	.01
☐ 609 Ron Reed	.10	.05	.01
☐ 610 Willie Stargell	1.50	.75	.15
☐ 611 Jerry Garvin DP	.05	.02	.00

☐ 612 Cliff Johnson	.10	.05	.01
☐ 613 Randy Stein	.10	.05	.01
☐ 614 John Hiller	.20	.10	.02
☐ 615 Doug DeCinces	.20	.10	.02
☐ 616 Gene Richards	.10	.05	.01
☐ 617 Joaquin Andujar	.20	.10	.02
☐ 618 Bob Montgomery DP	.05	.02	.00
☐ 619 Sergio Ferrer	.10	.05	.01
☐ 620 Richie Zisk	.10	.05	.01
☐ 621 Bob Grich	.20	.10	.02
☐ 622 Mario Soto	.20	.10	.02
☐ 623 Gorman Thomas	.20	.10	.02
☐ 624 Lerrin LaGrow	.10	.05	.01
☐ 625 Chris Chambliss	.20	.10	.02
☐ 626 Tigers Team/Mgr.	.40	.20	.04
Sparky Anderson			
(checklist back)			
☐ 627 Pedro Borbon	.10	.05	.01
☐ 628 Doug Capilla	.10	.05	.01
☐ 629 Jim Todd	.10	.05	.01
☐ 630 Larry Bowa	.30	.15	.03
☐ 631 Mark Littell	.10	.05	.01
☐ 632 Barry Bonnell	.10	.05	.01
☐ 633 Bob Apodaca	.10	.05	.01
☐ 634 Glenn Borgmann DP	.05	.02	.00
☐ 635 John Candelaria	.30	.15	.03
☐ 636 Toby Harrah	.20	.10	.02
☐ 637 Joe Simpson	.10	.05	.01
☐ 638 Mark Clear	.20	.10	.02
☐ 639 Larry Biittner	.10	.05	.01
☐ 640 Mike Flanagan	.20	.10	.02
☐ 641 Ed Kranepool	.10	.05	.01
☐ 642 Ken Forsch DP	.10	.05	.01
☐ 643 John Mayberry	.20	.10	.02
☐ 644 Charlie Hough	.20	.10	.02
☐ 645 Rick Burleson	.20	.10	.02
☐ 646 Checklist 6	.30	.04	.01
☐ 647 Milt May	.10	.05	.01
☐ 648 Roy White	.20	.10	.02
☐ 649 Tom Griffin	.10	.05	.01
☐ 650 Joe Morgan	1.50	.75	.15
☐ 651 Rollie Fingers	.60	.30	.06
☐ 652 Mario Mendoza	.10	.05	.01
☐ 653 Stan Bahnsen	.10	.05	.01
☐ 654 Bruce Boisclair DP	.05	.02	.00
☐ 655 Tug McGraw	.30	.15	.03
☐ 656 Larvell Blanks	.10	.05	.01
☐ 657 Dave Edwards	.10	.05	.01
☐ 658 Chris Knapp	.10	.05	.01
☐ 659 Brewers Team/Mgr.	.35	.17	.03
George Bamberger			
(checklist back)			
☐ 660 Rusty Staub	.30	.15	.03
☐ 661 Orioles Rookies	.20	.10	.02
Mark Corey			
Dave Ford			
Wayne Krenchicki			
☐ 662 Red Sox Rookies	.20	.10	.02
Joel Finch			
Mike O'Berry			
Chuck Rainey			
☐ 663 Angels Rookies	.60	.30	.06
Ralph Botting			
Bob Clark			
Dickie Thon			
☐ 664 White Sox Rookies	.20	.10	.02
Mike Colbern			
Guy Hoffman			
Dewey Robinson			
☐ 665 Indians Rookies	.30	.15	.03
Larry Andersen			
Bobby Cuellar			
Sandy Wihtol			
☐ 666 Tigers Rookies	.20	.10	.02
Mike Chris			
Al Greene			
Bruce Robbins			
☐ 667 Royals Rookies	1.50	.75	.15
Renie Martin			
Bill Paschall			
Dan Quisenberry			
☐ 668 Brewers Rookies	.20	.10	.02
Danny Boitano			
Willie Mueller			
Lenn Sakata			
☐ 669 Twins Rookies	.40	.20	.04
Dan Graham			
Rick Sofield			
Gary Ward			
☐ 670 Yankees Rookies	.20	.10	.02
Bobby Brown			
Brad Gulden			
Darryl Jones			
☐ 671 A's Rookies	1.00	.50	.10
Derek Bryant			
Brian Kingman			
Mike Morgan			
☐ 672 Mariners Rookies	.20	.10	.02
Charlie Beamon			
Rodney Craig			
Rafael Vasquez			
☐ 673 Rangers Rookies	.20	.10	.02
Brian Allard			
Jerry Don Gleaton			
Greg Mahlberg			
☐ 674 Blue Jays Rookies	.20	.10	.02
Butch Edge			
Pat Kelly			
Ted Wilborn			
☐ 675 Braves Rookies	.20	.10	.02
Bruce Benedict			
Larry Bradford			
Eddie Miller			
☐ 676 Cubs Rookies	.20	.10	.02
Dave Geisel			
Steve Macko			
Karl Pagel			
☐ 677 Reds Rookies	.20	.10	.02
Art DeFreites			
Frank Pastore			
Harry Spilman			
☐ 678 Astros Rookies	.20	.10	.02
Reggie Baldwin			
Alan Knicely			
Pete Ladd			
☐ 679 Dodgers Rookies	.50	.25	.05
Joe Beckwith			
Mickey Hatcher			
Dave Patterson			
☐ 680 Expos Rookies	.35	.17	.03
Tony Bernazard			
Randy Miller			
John Tamargo			
☐ 681 Mets Rookies	10.00	5.00	1.00
Dan Norman			
Jesse Orosco			
Mike Scott			
☐ 682 Phillies Rookies	.30	.15	.03
Ramon Aviles			
Dickie Noles			
Kevin Saucier			
☐ 683 Pirates Rookies	.20	.10	.02
Dorian Boyland			
Alberto Lois			
Harry Saferight			
☐ 684 Cardinals Rookies	.75	.35	.07
George Frazier			
Tom Herr			
Dan O'Brien			
☐ 685 Padres Rookies	.30	.15	.03
Tim Flannery			
Brian Greer			
Jim Wilhelm			
☐ 686 Giants Rookies	.20	.10	.02
Greg Johnston			
Dennis Littlejohn			
Phil Nastu			
☐ 687 Mike Heath DP	.05	.02	.00
☐ 688 Steve Stone	.20	.10	.02
☐ 689 Red Sox Team/Mgr.	.35	.17	.03
Don Zimmer			
(checklist back)			
☐ 690 Tommy John	.50	.25	.05
☐ 691 Ivan DeJesus	.10	.05	.01
☐ 692 Rawly Eastwick DP	.05	.02	.00
☐ 693 Craig Kusick	.10	.05	.01
☐ 694 Jim Rooker	.10	.05	.01
☐ 695 Reggie Smith	.20	.10	.02
☐ 696 Julio Gonzalez	.10	.05	.01
☐ 697 David Clyde	.10	.05	.01
☐ 698 Oscar Gamble	.10	.05	.01
☐ 699 Floyd Bannister	.10	.05	.01
☐ 700 Rod Carew DP	1.25	.60	.12
☐ 701 Ken Oberkfell	.30	.15	.03
☐ 702 Ed Farmer	.10	.05	.01
☐ 703 Otto Velez	.10	.05	.01
☐ 704 Gene Tenace	.20	.10	.02
☐ 705 Freddie Patek	.10	.05	.01
☐ 706 Tippy Martinez	.10	.05	.01
☐ 707 Elliott Maddox	.10	.05	.01
☐ 708 Bob Tolan	.10	.05	.01
☐ 709 Pat Underwood	.10	.05	.01
☐ 710 Graig Nettles	.30	.15	.03
☐ 711 Bob Galasso	.10	.05	.01
☐ 712 Rodney Scott	.10	.05	.01
☐ 713 Terry Whitfield	.10	.05	.01
☐ 714 Fred Norman	.10	.05	.01
☐ 715 Sal Bando	.20	.10	.02
☐ 716 Lynn McGlothen	.10	.05	.01
☐ 717 Mickey Klutts DP	.05	.02	.00

		MINT	EXC	G-VG
☐ 718	Greg Gross	.10	.05	.01
☐ 719	Don Robinson	.20	.10	.02
☐ 720	Carl Yastrzemski DP	1.75	.85	.17
☐ 721	Paul Hartzell	.10	.05	.01
☐ 722	Jose Cruz	.20	.10	.02
☐ 723	Shane Rawley	.20	.10	.02
☐ 724	Jerry White	.10	.05	.01
☐ 725	Rick Wise	.10	.05	.01
☐ 726	Steve Yeager	.20	.10	.02

1981 Topps

The cards in this 726-card set measure 2 1/2" by 3 1/2". League Leaders (1-8), Record Breakers (201-208), and Post-season cards (401-404) are topical subsets found in this set marketed by Topps in 1981. The team cards are all grouped together (661-686) and feature team checklist backs and a very small photo of the team's manager in the upper right corner of the obverse. The obverses carry the player's position and team in a baseball cap design, and the company name is printed in a small baseball. The backs are red and gray. The 66 double-printed cards are noted in the checklist by DP. The set is quite popular with collectors partly due to the presence of rookie cards of Fernando Valenzuela, Tim Raines, Kirk Gibson, Harold Baines, John Tudor, Lloyd Moseby, Hubie Brooks, Mike Boddicker, and Tony Pena.

	MINT	EXC	G-VG
COMPLETE SET (726)	90.00	45.00	9.00
COMMON PLAYER (1-726)	.08	.04	.01
COMMON DP's (1-726)	.04	.02	.00

			MINT	EXC	G-VG
☐	1	Batting Leaders George Brett Bill Buckner	.65	.15	.03
☐	2	Home Run Leaders Reggie Jackson Ben Oglivie Mike Schmidt	.35	.17	.03
☐	3	RBI Leaders Cecil Cooper Mike Schmidt	.20	.10	.02
☐	4	Stolen Base Leaders Rickey Henderson Ron LeFlore	.18	.09	.01
☐	5	Victory Leaders Steve Stone Steve Carlton	.15	.07	.01
☐	6	Strikeout Leaders Len Barker Steve Carlton	.15	.07	.01
☐	7	ERA Leaders Rudy May Don Sutton	.12	.06	.01
☐	8	Leading Firemen Dan Quisenberry Rollie Fingers Tom Hume	.12	.06	.01
☐	9	Pete LaCock DP	.04	.02	.00
☐	10	Mike Flanagan	.12	.06	.01
☐	11	Jim Wohlford DP	.04	.02	.00
☐	12	Mark Clear	.08	.04	.01
☐	13	Joe Charboneau	.12	.06	.01
☐	14	John Tudor	1.50	.75	.15
☐	15	Larry Parrish	.12	.06	.01
☐	16	Ron Davis	.08	.04	.01
☐	17	Cliff Johnson	.08	.04	.01
☐	18	Glenn Adams	.08	.04	.01
☐	19	Jim Clancy	.08	.04	.01
☐	20	Jeff Burroughs	.12	.06	.01
☐	21	Ron Oester	.12	.06	.01
☐	22	Danny Darwin	.08	.04	.01
☐	23	Alex Trevino	.08	.04	.01
☐	24	Don Stanhouse	.08	.04	.01
☐	25	Sixto Lezcano	.08	.04	.01
☐	26	U.L. Washington	.08	.04	.01
☐	27	Champ Summers DP	.04	.02	.00
☐	28	Enrique Romo	.08	.04	.01
☐	29	Gene Tenace	.12	.06	.01
☐	30	Jack Clark	.65	.30	.06
☐	31	Checklist 1-121 DP	.08	.01	.00
☐	32	Ken Oberkfell	.08	.04	.01
☐	33	Rick Honeycutt	.08	.04	.01
☐	34	Aurelio Rodriguez	.08	.04	.01
☐	35	Mitchell Page	.08	.04	.01
☐	36	Ed Farmer	.08	.04	.01
☐	37	Gary Roenicke	.08	.04	.01
☐	38	Win Remmerswaal	.08	.04	.01
☐	39	Tom Veryzer	.08	.04	.01
☐	40	Tug McGraw	.15	.07	.01
☐	41	Ranger Rookies Bob Babcock John Butcher Jerry Don Gleaton	.12	.06	.01
☐	42	Jerry White DP	.04	.02	.00
☐	43	Jose Morales	.08	.04	.01
☐	44	Larry McWilliams	.08	.04	.01
☐	45	Enos Cabell	.08	.04	.01
☐	46	Rick Bosetti	.08	.04	.01
☐	47	Ken Brett	.08	.04	.01
☐	48	Dave Skaggs	.08	.04	.01
☐	49	Bob Shirley	.08	.04	.01
☐	50	Dave Lopes	.15	.07	.01
☐	51	Bill Robinson DP	.04	.02	.00
☐	52	Hector Cruz	.08	.04	.01
☐	53	Kevin Saucier	.08	.04	.01
☐	54	Ivan DeJesus	.08	.04	.01
☐	55	Mike Norris	.08	.04	.01
☐	56	Buck Martinez	.08	.04	.01
☐	57	Dave Roberts	.08	.04	.01
☐	58	Joel Youngblood	.08	.04	.01
☐	59	Dan Petry	.12	.06	.01
☐	60	Willie Randolph	.15	.07	.01
☐	61	Butch Wynegar	.08	.04	.01
☐	62	Joe Pettini	.08	.04	.01
☐	63	Steve Renko DP	.04	.02	.00
☐	64	Brian Asselstine	.08	.04	.01
☐	65	Scott McGregor	.12	.06	.01
☐	66	Royals Rookies Manny Castillo Tim Ireland Mike Jones	.12	.06	.01
☐	67	Ken Kravec	.08	.04	.01
☐	68	Matt Alexander DP	.04	.02	.00
☐	69	Ed Halicki	.08	.04	.01
☐	70	Al Oliver DP	.12	.06	.01
☐	71	Hal Dues	.08	.04	.01
☐	72	Barry Evans DP	.04	.02	.00
☐	73	Doug Bair	.08	.04	.01
☐	74	Mike Hargrove	.12	.06	.01
☐	75	Reggie Smith	.15	.07	.01
☐	76	Mario Mendoza	.08	.04	.01
☐	77	Mike Barlow	.08	.04	.01
☐	78	Steve Dillard	.08	.04	.01
☐	79	Bruce Robbins	.08	.04	.01
☐	80	Rusty Staub	.20	.10	.02
☐	81	Dave Stapleton	.12	.06	.01
☐	82	Astros Rookies DP Danny Heep Alan Knicely Bobby Sprowl	.12	.06	.01
☐	83	Mike Proly	.08	.04	.01
☐	84	Johnnie LeMaster	.08	.04	.01
☐	85	Mike Caldwell	.08	.04	.01
☐	86	Wayne Gross	.08	.04	.01
☐	87	Rick Camp	.08	.04	.01
☐	88	Joe Lefebvre	.12	.06	.01
☐	89	Darrell Jackson	.08	.04	.01
☐	90	Bake McBride	.08	.04	.01
☐	91	Tim Stoddard DP	.08	.04	.01
☐	92	Mike Easler	.12	.06	.01
☐	93	Ed Glynn DP	.04	.02	.00
☐	94	Harry Spilman DP	.04	.02	.00
☐	95	Jim Sundberg	.12	.06	.01
☐	96	A's Rookies Dave Beard Ernie Camacho	.15	.07	.01

	Pat Dempsey				
☐ 97	Chris Speier	.08	.04	.01
☐ 98	Clint Hurdle	.08	.04	.01
☐ 99	Eric Wilkins	.08	.04	.01
☐ 100	Rod Carew	1.25	.60	.12
☐ 101	Benny Ayala	.08	.04	.01
☐ 102	Dave Tobik	.08	.04	.01
☐ 103	Jerry Martin	.08	.04	.01
☐ 104	Terry Forster	.12	.06	.01
☐ 105	Jose Cruz	.15	.07	.01
☐ 106	Don Money	.08	.04	.01
☐ 107	Rich Wortham	.08	.04	.01
☐ 108	Bruce Benedict	.08	.04	.01
☐ 109	Mike Scott	1.75	.85	.17
☐ 110	Carl Yastrzemski	1.75	.85	.17
☐ 111	Greg Minton	.08	.04	.01
☐ 112	White Sox Rookies	.12	.06	.01
	Rusty Kuntz			
	Fran Mullin			
	Leo Sutherland			
☐ 113	Mike Phillips	.08	.04	.01
☐ 114	Tom Underwood	.08	.04	.01
☐ 115	Roy Smalley	.08	.04	.01
☐ 116	Joe Simpson	.08	.04	.01
☐ 117	Pete Falcone	.08	.04	.01
☐ 118	Kurt Bevacqua	.08	.04	.01
☐ 119	Tippy Martinez	.08	.04	.01
☐ 120	Larry Bowa	.15	.07	.01
☐ 121	Larry Harlow	.08	.04	.01
☐ 122	John Denny	.12	.06	.01
☐ 123	Al Cowens	.08	.04	.01
☐ 124	Jerry Garvin	.08	.04	.01
☐ 125	Andre Dawson	1.00	.50	.10
☐ 126	Charlie Leibrandt	.40	.20	.04
☐ 127	Rudy Law	.08	.04	.01
☐ 128	Gary Allenson DP	.04	.02	.00
☐ 129	Art Howe	.15	.07	.01
☐ 130	Larry Gura	.12	.06	.01
☐ 131	Keith Moreland	.40	.20	.04
☐ 132	Tommy Boggs	.08	.04	.01
☐ 133	Jeff Cox	.08	.04	.01
☐ 134	Steve Mura	.08	.04	.01
☐ 135	Gorman Thomas	.20	.10	.02
☐ 136	Doug Capilla	.08	.04	.01
☐ 137	Hosken Powell	.08	.04	.01
☐ 138	Rich Dotson DP	.25	.12	.02
☐ 139	Oscar Gamble	.12	.06	.01
☐ 140	Bob Forsch	.08	.04	.01
☐ 141	Miguel Dilone	.08	.04	.01
☐ 142	Jackson Todd	.08	.04	.01
☐ 143	Dan Meyer	.08	.04	.01
☐ 144	Allen Ripley	.08	.04	.01
☐ 145	Mickey Rivers	.12	.06	.01
☐ 146	Bobby Castillo	.08	.04	.01
☐ 147	Dale Berra	.08	.04	.01
☐ 148	Randy Niemann	.08	.04	.01
☐ 149	Joe Nolan	.08	.04	.01
☐ 150	Mark Fidrych	.15	.07	.01
☐ 151	Claudell Washington	.15	.07	.01
☐ 152	John Urrea	.08	.04	.01
☐ 153	Tom Poquette	.08	.04	.01
☐ 154	Rick Langford	.08	.04	.01
☐ 155	Chris Chambliss	.15	.07	.01
☐ 156	Bob McClure	.08	.04	.01
☐ 157	John Wathan	.15	.07	.01
☐ 158	Fergie Jenkins	.30	.15	.03
☐ 159	Brian Doyle	.08	.04	.01
☐ 160	Garry Maddox	.12	.06	.01
☐ 161	Dan Graham	.08	.04	.01
☐ 162	Doug Corbett	.12	.06	.01
☐ 163	Bill Almon	.08	.04	.01
☐ 164	LaMarr Hoyt	.25	.12	.02
☐ 165	Tony Scott	.08	.04	.01
☐ 166	Floyd Bannister	.12	.06	.01
☐ 167	Terry Whitfield	.08	.04	.01
☐ 168	Don Robinson DP	.04	.02	.00
☐ 169	John Mayberry	.12	.06	.01
☐ 170	Ross Grimsley	.08	.04	.01
☐ 171	Gene Richards	.08	.04	.01
☐ 172	Gary Woods	.08	.04	.01
☐ 173	Bump Wills	.08	.04	.01
☐ 174	Doug Rau	.08	.04	.01
☐ 175	Dave Collins	.08	.04	.01
☐ 176	Mike Krukow	.12	.06	.01
☐ 177	Rick Peters	.08	.04	.01
☐ 178	Jim Essian DP	.04	.02	.00
☐ 179	Rudy May	.08	.04	.01
☐ 180	Pete Rose	3.50	1.75	.35
☐ 181	Elias Sosa	.08	.04	.01
☐ 182	Bob Grich	.15	.07	.01
☐ 183	Dick Davis DP	.04	.02	.00
☐ 184	Jim Dwyer	.08	.04	.01
☐ 185	Dennis Leonard	.12	.06	.01
☐ 186	Wayne Nordhagen	.08	.04	.01
☐ 187	Mike Parrott	.08	.04	.01
☐ 188	Doug DeCinces	.15	.07	.01
☐ 189	Craig Swan	.12	.06	.01
☐ 190	Cesar Cedeno	.15	.07	.01
☐ 191	Rick Sutcliffe	.60	.30	.06
☐ 192	Braves Rookies	.30	.15	.03
	Terry Harper			
	Ed Miller			
	Rafael Ramirez			
☐ 193	Pete Vuckovich	.12	.06	.01
☐ 194	Rod Scurry	.08	.04	.01
☐ 195	Rich Murray	.08	.04	.01
☐ 196	Duffy Dyer	.08	.04	.01
☐ 197	Jim Kern	.08	.04	.01
☐ 198	Jerry Dybzinski	.08	.04	.01
☐ 199	Chuck Rainey	.08	.04	.01
☐ 200	George Foster	.25	.12	.02
☐ 201	RB: Johnny Bench	.40	.20	.04
	Most homers,			
	lifetime, catcher			
☐ 202	RB: Steve Carlton	.35	.17	.03
	Most strikeouts,			
	lefthander, lifetime			
☐ 203	RB: Bill Gullickson	.12	.06	.01
	Most strikeouts,			
	game, rookie			
☐ 204	RB: Ron LeFlore and	.12	.06	.01
	Rodney Scott			
	Most stolen bases,			
	teammates, season			
☐ 205	RB: Pete Rose	.75	.35	.07
	Most cons. seasons			
	600 or more at-bats			
☐ 206	RB: Mike Schmidt	.50	.25	.05
	Most homers, third			
	baseman, season			
☐ 207	RB: Ozzie Smith	.15	.07	.01
	Most assists			
	season, shortstop			
☐ 208	RB: Willie Wilson	.12	.06	.01
	Most at-bats, season			
☐ 209	Dickie Thon DP	.12	.06	.01
☐ 210	Jim Palmer	1.25	.60	.12
☐ 211	Derrel Thomas	.08	.04	.01
☐ 212	Steve Nicosia	.08	.04	.01
☐ 213	Al Holland	.12	.06	.01
☐ 214	Angels Rookies	.12	.06	.01
	Ralph Botting			
	Jim Dorsey			
	John Harris			
☐ 215	Larry Hisle	.12	.06	.01
☐ 216	John Henry Johnson	.08	.04	.01
☐ 217	Rich Hebner	.08	.04	.01
☐ 218	Paul Splittorff	.08	.04	.01
☐ 219	Ken Landreaux	.08	.04	.01
☐ 220	Tom Seaver	1.25	.60	.12
☐ 221	Bob Davis	.08	.04	.01
☐ 222	Jorge Orta	.08	.04	.01
☐ 223	Roy Lee Jackson	.08	.04	.01
☐ 224	Pat Zachry	.08	.04	.01
☐ 225	Ruppert Jones	.08	.04	.01
☐ 226	Manny Sanguillen DP	.08	.04	.01
☐ 227	Fred Martinez	.08	.04	.01
☐ 228	Tom Paciorek	.08	.04	.01
☐ 229	Rollie Fingers	.60	.30	.06
☐ 230	George Hendrick	.12	.06	.01
☐ 231	Joe Beckwith	.08	.04	.01
☐ 232	Mickey Klutts	.08	.04	.01
☐ 233	Skip Lockwood	.08	.04	.01
☐ 234	Lou Whitaker	.50	.25	.05
☐ 235	Scott Sanderson	.12	.06	.01
☐ 236	Mike Ivie	.08	.04	.01
☐ 237	Charlie Moore	.08	.04	.01
☐ 238	Willie Hernandez	.25	.12	.02
☐ 239	Rick Miller DP	.04	.02	.00
☐ 240	Nolan Ryan	2.75	1.35	.27
☐ 241	Checklist 122-242 DP	.08	.01	.00
☐ 242	Chet Lemon	.12	.06	.01
☐ 243	Sal Butera	.08	.04	.01
☐ 244	Cardinals Rookies	.15	.07	.01
	Tito Landrum			
	Al Olmsted			
	Andy Rincon			
☐ 245	Ed Figueroa	.08	.04	.01
☐ 246	Ed Ott DP	.04	.02	.00
☐ 247	Glenn Hubbard DP	.04	.02	.00
☐ 248	Joey McLaughlin	.08	.04	.01
☐ 249	Larry Cox	.08	.04	.01
☐ 250	Ron Guidry	.50	.25	.05
☐ 251	Tom Brookens	.08	.04	.01
☐ 252	Victor Cruz	.08	.04	.01
☐ 253	Dave Bergman	.08	.04	.01
☐ 254	Ozzie Smith	2.00	1.00	.20
☐ 255	Mark Littell	.08	.04	.01
☐ 256	Bombo Rivera	.08	.04	.01
☐ 257	Rennie Stennett	.08	.04	.01

☐ 258	Joe Price	.12	.06	.01
☐ 259	Mets Rookies	2.00	1.00	.20
	Juan Berenguer			
	Hubie Brooks			
	Mookie Wilson			
☐ 260	Ron Cey	.25	.12	.02
☐ 261	Rickey Henderson	6.50	3.25	.65
☐ 262	Sammy Stewart	.08	.04	.01
☐ 263	Brian Downing	.12	.06	.01
☐ 264	Jim Norris	.08	.04	.01
☐ 265	John Candelaria	.15	.07	.01
☐ 266	Tom Herr	.20	.10	.02
☐ 267	Stan Bahnsen	.08	.04	.01
☐ 268	Jerry Royster	.08	.04	.01
☐ 269	Ken Forsch	.08	.04	.01
☐ 270	Greg Luzinski	.20	.10	.02
☐ 271	Bill Castro	.08	.04	.01
☐ 272	Bruce Kimm	.08	.04	.01
☐ 273	Stan Papi	.08	.04	.01
☐ 274	Craig Chamberlain	.08	.04	.01
☐ 275	Dwight Evans	.40	.20	.04
☐ 276	Dan Spillner	.08	.04	.01
☐ 277	Alfredo Griffin	.15	.07	.01
☐ 278	Rick Sofield	.08	.04	.01
☐ 279	Bob Knepper	.15	.07	.01
☐ 280	Ken Griffey	.20	.10	.02
☐ 281	Fred Stanley	.08	.04	.01
☐ 282	Mariners Rookies	.12	.06	.01
	Rick Anderson			
	Greg Biercevicz			
	Rodney Craig			
☐ 283	Billy Sample	.08	.04	.01
☐ 284	Brian Kingman	.08	.04	.01
☐ 285	Jerry Turner	.08	.04	.01
☐ 286	Dave Frost	.08	.04	.01
☐ 287	Lenn Sakata	.08	.04	.01
☐ 288	Bob Clark	.08	.04	.01
☐ 289	Mickey Hatcher	.12	.06	.01
☐ 290	Bob Boone DP	.12	.06	.01
☐ 291	Aurelio Lopez	.08	.04	.01
☐ 292	Mike Squires	.08	.04	.01
☐ 293	Charlie Lea	.20	.10	.02
☐ 294	Mike Tyson DP	.04	.02	.00
☐ 295	Hal McRae	.12	.06	.01
☐ 296	Bill Nahorodny DP	.04	.02	.00
☐ 297	Bob Bailor	.08	.04	.01
☐ 298	Buddy Solomon	.08	.04	.01
☐ 299	Elliott Maddox	.08	.04	.01
☐ 300	Paul Molitor	.50	.25	.05
☐ 301	Matt Keough	.08	.04	.01
☐ 302	Dodgers Rookies	6.00	3.00	.60
	Jack Perconte			
	Mike Scioscia			
	Fernando Valenzuela			
☐ 303	Johnny Oates	.08	.04	.01
☐ 304	John Castino	.08	.04	.01
☐ 305	Ken Clay	.08	.04	.01
☐ 306	Juan Beniquez DP	.04	.02	.00
☐ 307	Gene Garber	.08	.04	.01
☐ 308	Rick Manning	.08	.04	.01
☐ 309	Luis Salazar	.20	.10	.02
☐ 310	Vida Blue DP	.12	.06	.01
☐ 311	Freddie Patek	.08	.04	.01
☐ 312	Rick Rhoden	.12	.06	.01
☐ 313	Luis Pujols	.08	.04	.01
☐ 314	Rich Dauer	.08	.04	.01
☐ 315	Kirk Gibson	7.00	3.50	.70
☐ 316	Craig Minetto	.08	.04	.01
☐ 317	Lonnie Smith	.20	.10	.02
☐ 318	Steve Yeager	.08	.04	.01
☐ 319	Rowland Office	.08	.04	.01
☐ 320	Tom Burgmeier	.08	.04	.01
☐ 321	Leon Durham	.40	.20	.04
☐ 322	Neil Allen	.12	.06	.01
☐ 323	Jim Morrison DP	.08	.04	.01
☐ 324	Mike Willis	.08	.04	.01
☐ 325	Ray Knight	.20	.10	.02
☐ 326	Biff Pocoroba	.08	.04	.01
☐ 327	Moose Haas	.12	.06	.01
☐ 328	Twins Rookies	.20	.10	.02
	Dave Engle			
	Greg Johnston			
	Gary Ward			
☐ 329	Joaquin Andujar	.15	.07	.01
☐ 330	Frank White	.15	.07	.01
☐ 331	Dennis Lamp	.08	.04	.01
☐ 332	Lee Lacy DP	.08	.04	.01
☐ 333	Sid Monge	.08	.04	.01
☐ 334	Dane Iorg	.08	.04	.01
☐ 335	Rick Cerone	.12	.06	.01
☐ 336	Eddie Whitson	.12	.06	.01
☐ 337	Lynn Jones	.08	.04	.01
☐ 338	Checklist 243-363	.20	.03	.01
☐ 339	John Ellis	.08	.04	.01
☐ 340	Bruce Kison	.08	.04	.01

☐ 341	Dwayne Murphy	.08	.04	.01
☐ 342	Eric Rasmussen DP	.04	.02	.00
☐ 343	Frank Taveras	.08	.04	.01
☐ 344	Byron McLaughlin	.08	.04	.01
☐ 345	Warren Cromartie	.08	.04	.01
☐ 346	Larry Christenson DP	.04	.02	.00
☐ 347	Harold Baines	3.75	1.85	.37
☐ 348	Bob Sykes	.08	.04	.01
☐ 349	Glenn Hoffman	.08	.04	.01
☐ 350	J.R. Richard	.15	.07	.01
☐ 351	Otto Velez	.08	.04	.01
☐ 352	Dick Tidrow DP	.04	.02	.00
☐ 353	Terry Kennedy	.12	.06	.01
☐ 354	Mario Soto	.15	.07	.01
☐ 355	Bob Horner	.25	.12	.02
☐ 356	Padres Rookies	.12	.06	.01
	George Stablein			
	Craig Stimac			
	Tom Tellmann			
☐ 357	Jim Slaton	.08	.04	.01
☐ 358	Mark Wagner	.08	.04	.01
☐ 359	Tom Hausman	.08	.04	.01
☐ 360	Willie Wilson	.25	.12	.02
☐ 361	Joe Strain	.08	.04	.01
☐ 362	Bo Diaz	.12	.06	.01
☐ 363	Geoff Zahn	.08	.04	.01
☐ 364	Mike Davis	.35	.17	.03
☐ 365	Graig Nettles DP	.12	.06	.01
☐ 366	Mike Ramsey	.08	.04	.01
☐ 367	Dennis Martinez	.15	.07	.01
☐ 368	Leon Roberts	.08	.04	.01
☐ 369	Frank Tanana	.15	.07	.01
☐ 370	Dave Winfield	1.25	.60	.12
☐ 371	Charlie Hough	.15	.07	.01
☐ 372	Jay Johnstone	.15	.07	.01
☐ 373	Pat Underwood	.08	.04	.01
☐ 374	Tommy Hutton	.08	.04	.01
☐ 375	Dave Concepcion	.15	.07	.01
☐ 376	Ron Reed	.08	.04	.01
☐ 377	Jerry Morales	.08	.04	.01
☐ 378	Dave Rader	.08	.04	.01
☐ 379	Lary Sorensen	.08	.04	.01
☐ 380	Willie Stargell	1.00	.50	.10
☐ 381	Cubs Rookies	.12	.06	.01
	Carlos Lezcano			
	Steve Macko			
	Randy Martz			
☐ 382	Paul Mirabella	.08	.04	.01
☐ 383	Eric Soderholm DP	.04	.02	.00
☐ 384	Mike Sadek	.08	.04	.01
☐ 385	Joe Sambito	.08	.04	.01
☐ 386	Dave Edwards	.08	.04	.01
☐ 387	Phil Niekro	.70	.35	.07
☐ 388	Andre Thornton	.12	.06	.01
☐ 389	Marty Pattin	.08	.04	.01
☐ 390	Cesar Geronimo	.08	.04	.01
☐ 391	Dave Lemanczyk DP	.04	.02	.00
☐ 392	Lance Parrish	.60	.30	.06
☐ 393	Broderick Perkins	.08	.04	.01
☐ 394	Woodie Fryman	.08	.04	.01
☐ 395	Scot Thompson	.08	.04	.01
☐ 396	Bill Campbell	.08	.04	.01
☐ 397	Julio Cruz	.08	.04	.01
☐ 398	Ross Baumgarten	.08	.04	.01
☐ 399	Orioles Rookies	1.50	.75	.15
	Mike Boddicker			
	Mark Corey			
	Floyd Rayford			
☐ 400	Reggie Jackson	1.75	.85	.17
☐ 401	AL Champs	.50	.25	.05
	Royals sweep Yanks			
	(Brett swinging)			
☐ 402	NL Champs	.20	.10	.02
	Phillies squeak			
	past Astros			
☐ 403	1980 World Series	.20	.10	.02
	Phillies beat			
	Royals in six			
☐ 404	1980 World Series	.20	.10	.02
	Phillies win first			
	World Series			
☐ 405	Nino Espinosa	.08	.04	.01
☐ 406	Dickie Noles	.08	.04	.01
☐ 407	Ernie Whitt	.15	.07	.01
☐ 408	Fernando Arroyo	.08	.04	.01
☐ 409	Larry Herndon	.08	.04	.01
☐ 410	Bert Campaneris	.12	.06	.01
☐ 411	Terry Puhl	.12	.06	.01
☐ 412	Britt Burns	.25	.12	.02
☐ 413	Tony Bernazard	.12	.06	.01
☐ 414	John Pacella DP	.04	.02	.00
☐ 415	Ben Oglivie	.12	.06	.01
☐ 416	Gary Alexander	.08	.04	.01
☐ 417	Dan Schatzeder	.08	.04	.01
☐ 418	Bobby Brown	.08	.04	.01

	Mike Rowland		
☐ 419 Tom Hume	.08	.04	.01
☐ 420 Keith Hernandez	.75	.35	.07
☐ 421 Bob Stanley	.08	.04	.01
☐ 422 Dan Ford	.08	.04	.01
☐ 423 Shane Rawley	.12	.06	.01
☐ 424 Yankees Rookies	.12	.06	.01
Tim Lollar			
Bruce Robinson			
Dennis Werth			
☐ 425 Al Bumbry	.08	.04	.01
☐ 426 Warren Brusstar	.08	.04	.01
☐ 427 John D'Acquisto	.08	.04	.01
☐ 428 John Stearns	.08	.04	.01
☐ 429 Mick Kelleher	.08	.04	.01
☐ 430 Jim Bibby	.08	.04	.01
☐ 431 Dave Roberts	.08	.04	.01
☐ 432 Len Barker	.08	.04	.01
☐ 433 Rance Mulliniks	.08	.04	.01
☐ 434 Roger Erickson	.08	.04	.01
☐ 435 Jim Spencer	.08	.04	.01
☐ 436 Gary Lucas	.12	.06	.01
☐ 437 Mike Heath DP	.04	.02	.00
☐ 438 John Montefusco	.12	.06	.01
☐ 439 Denny Walling	.08	.04	.01
☐ 440 Jerry Reuss	.15	.07	.01
☐ 441 Ken Reitz	.08	.04	.01
☐ 442 Ron Pruitt	.08	.04	.01
☐ 443 Jim Beattie DP	.04	.02	.00
☐ 444 Garth Iorg	.08	.04	.01
☐ 445 Ellis Valentine	.08	.04	.01
☐ 446 Checklist 364-484	.20	.03	.01
☐ 447 Junior Kennedy DP	.04	.02	.00
☐ 448 Tim Corcoran	.08	.04	.01
☐ 449 Paul Mitchell	.08	.04	.01
☐ 450 Dave Kingman DP	.12	.06	.01
☐ 451 Indians Rookies	.12	.06	.01
Chris Bando			
Tom Brennan			
Sandy Wihtol			
☐ 452 Renie Martin	.08	.04	.01
☐ 453 Rob Wilfong DP	.04	.02	.00
☐ 454 Andy Hassler	.08	.04	.01
☐ 455 Rick Burleson	.12	.06	.01
☐ 456 Jeff Reardon	1.25	.60	.12
☐ 457 Mike Lum	.08	.04	.01
☐ 458 Randy Jones	.08	.04	.01
☐ 459 Greg Gross	.08	.04	.01
☐ 460 Rich Gossage	.35	.17	.03
☐ 461 Dave McKay	.08	.04	.01
☐ 462 Jack Brohamer	.08	.04	.01
☐ 463 Milt May	.08	.04	.01
☐ 464 Adrian Devine	.08	.04	.01
☐ 465 Bill Russell	.12	.06	.01
☐ 466 Bob Molinaro	.08	.04	.01
☐ 467 Dave Stieb	.60	.30	.06
☐ 468 John Wockenfuss	.08	.04	.01
☐ 469 Jeff Leonard	.25	.12	.02
☐ 470 Manny Trillo	.08	.04	.01
☐ 471 Mike Vail	.08	.04	.01
☐ 472 Dyar Miller DP	.04	.02	.00
☐ 473 Jose Cardenal	.08	.04	.01
☐ 474 Mike LaCoss	.08	.04	.01
☐ 475 Buddy Bell	.20	.10	.02
☐ 476 Jerry Koosman	.15	.07	.01
☐ 477 Luis Gomez	.08	.04	.01
☐ 478 Juan Eichelberger	.08	.04	.01
☐ 479 Expos Rookies	8.50	4.25	.85
Tim Raines			
Roberto Ramos			
Bobby Pate			
☐ 480 Carlton Fisk	.65	.30	.06
☐ 481 Bob Lacey DP	.04	.02	.00
☐ 482 Jim Gantner	.08	.04	.01
☐ 483 Mike Griffin	.08	.04	.01
☐ 484 Max Venable DP	.04	.02	.00
☐ 485 Garry Templeton	.15	.07	.01
☐ 486 Marc Hill	.08	.04	.01
☐ 487 Dewey Robinson	.08	.04	.01
☐ 488 Damaso Garcia	.15	.07	.01
☐ 489 Jim Littlefield	.08	.04	.01
☐ 490 Eddie Murray	1.50	.75	.15
☐ 491 Gordy Pladson	.08	.04	.01
☐ 492 Barry Foote	.08	.04	.01
☐ 493 Dan Quisenberry	.25	.12	.02
☐ 494 Bob Walk	.35	.17	.03
☐ 495 Dusty Baker	.12	.06	.01
☐ 496 Paul Dade	.08	.04	.01
☐ 497 Fred Norman	.08	.04	.01
☐ 498 Pat Putnam	.08	.04	.01
☐ 499 Frank Pastore	.08	.04	.01
☐ 500 Jim Rice	.75	.35	.07
☐ 501 Tim Foli DP	.04	.02	.00
☐ 502 Giants Rookies	.12	.06	.01
Chris Bourjos			
Al Hargesheimer			

☐ 503 Steve McCatty	.08	.04	.01
☐ 504 Dale Murphy	2.25	1.10	.22
☐ 505 Jason Thompson	.08	.04	.01
☐ 506 Phil Huffman	.08	.04	.01
☐ 507 Jamie Quirk	.08	.04	.01
☐ 508 Rob Dressler	.08	.04	.01
☐ 509 Pete Mackanin	.08	.04	.01
☐ 510 Lee Mazzilli	.08	.04	.01
☐ 511 Wayne Garland	.08	.04	.01
☐ 512 Gary Thomasson	.08	.04	.01
☐ 513 Frank LaCorte	.08	.04	.01
☐ 514 George Riley	.08	.04	.01
☐ 515 Robin Yount	2.25	1.10	.22
☐ 516 Doug Bird	.08	.04	.01
☐ 517 Richie Zisk	.12	.06	.01
☐ 518 Grant Jackson	.08	.04	.01
☐ 519 John Tamargo DP	.04	.02	.00
☐ 520 Steve Stone	.12	.06	.01
☐ 521 Sam Mejias	.08	.04	.01
☐ 522 Mike Colbern	.08	.04	.01
☐ 523 John Fulgham	.08	.04	.01
☐ 524 Willie Aikens	.12	.06	.01
☐ 525 Mike Torrez	.08	.04	.01
☐ 526 Phillies Rookies	.15	.07	.01
Marty Bystrom			
Jay Loviglio			
Jim Wright			
☐ 527 Danny Goodwin	.08	.04	.01
☐ 528 Gary Matthews	.12	.06	.01
☐ 529 Dave LaRoche	.08	.04	.01
☐ 530 Steve Garvey	1.25	.60	.12
☐ 531 John Curtis	.08	.04	.01
☐ 532 Bill Stein	.08	.04	.01
☐ 533 Jesus Figueroa	.08	.04	.01
☐ 534 Dave Smith	.45	.22	.04
☐ 535 Omar Moreno	.08	.04	.01
☐ 536 Bob Owchinko DP	.04	.02	.00
☐ 537 Ron Hodges	.08	.04	.01
☐ 538 Tom Griffin	.08	.04	.01
☐ 539 Rodney Scott	.08	.04	.01
☐ 540 Mike Schmidt DP	1.50	.75	.15
☐ 541 Steve Swisher	.08	.04	.01
☐ 542 Larry Bradford DP	.04	.02	.00
☐ 543 Terry Crowley	.08	.04	.01
☐ 544 Rich Gale	.08	.04	.01
☐ 545 Johnny Grubb	.08	.04	.01
☐ 546 Paul Moskau	.08	.04	.01
☐ 547 Mario Guerrero	.08	.04	.01
☐ 548 Dave Goltz	.08	.04	.01
☐ 549 Jerry Remy	.08	.04	.01
☐ 550 Tommy John	.35	.17	.03
☐ 551 Pirates Rookies	2.00	1.00	.20
Vance Law			
Tony Pena			
Pascual Perez			
☐ 552 Steve Trout	.12	.06	.01
☐ 553 Tim Blackwell	.08	.04	.01
☐ 554 Bert Blyleven	.35	.17	.03
☐ 555 Cecil Cooper	.25	.12	.02
☐ 556 Jerry Mumphrey	.08	.04	.01
☐ 557 Chris Knapp	.08	.04	.01
☐ 558 Barry Bonnell	.08	.04	.01
☐ 559 Willie Montanez	.08	.04	.01
☐ 560 Joe Morgan	.65	.30	.06
☐ 561 Dennis Littlejohn	.08	.04	.01
☐ 562 Checklist 485-605	.20	.03	.01
☐ 563 Jim Kaat	.25	.12	.02
☐ 564 Ron Hassey DP	.08	.04	.01
☐ 565 Burt Hooton	.08	.04	.01
☐ 566 Del Unser	.08	.04	.01
☐ 567 Mark Bomback	.08	.04	.01
☐ 568 Dave Revering	.08	.04	.01
☐ 569 Al Williams DP	.04	.02	.00
☐ 570 Ken Singleton	.15	.07	.01
☐ 571 Todd Cruz	.08	.04	.01
☐ 572 Jack Morris	.50	.25	.05
☐ 573 Phil Garner	.08	.04	.01
☐ 574 Bill Caudill	.08	.04	.01
☐ 575 Tony Perez	.30	.15	.03
☐ 576 Reggie Cleveland	.08	.04	.01
☐ 577 Blue Jays Rookies	.15	.07	.01
Luis Leal			
Brian Milner			
Ken Schrom			
☐ 578 Bill Gullickson	.30	.15	.03
☐ 579 Tim Flannery	.08	.04	.01
☐ 580 Don Baylor	.25	.12	.02
☐ 581 Roy Howell	.08	.04	.01
☐ 582 Gaylord Perry	.50	.25	.05
☐ 583 Larry Milbourne	.08	.04	.01
☐ 584 Randy Lerch	.08	.04	.01
☐ 585 Amos Otis	.15	.07	.01
☐ 586 Silvio Martinez	.08	.04	.01
☐ 587 Jeff Newman	.08	.04	.01

☐ 588 Gary Lavelle	.08	.04	.01
☐ 589 Lamar Johnson	.08	.04	.01
☐ 590 Bruce Sutter	.25	.12	.02
☐ 591 John Lowenstein	.08	.04	.01
☐ 592 Steve Comer	.08	.04	.01
☐ 593 Steve Kemp	.12	.06	.01
☐ 594 Preston Hanna DP	.04	.02	.00
☐ 595 Butch Hobson	.08	.04	.01
☐ 596 Jerry Augustine	.08	.04	.01
☐ 597 Rafael Landestoy	.08	.04	.01
☐ 598 George Vukovich DP	.04	.02	.00
☐ 599 Dennis Kinney	.08	.04	.01
☐ 600 Johnny Bench	1.50	.75	.15
☐ 601 Don Aase	.08	.04	.01
☐ 602 Bobby Murcer	.15	.07	.01
☐ 603 John Verhoeven	.08	.04	.01
☐ 604 Rob Picciolo	.08	.04	.01
☐ 605 Don Sutton	.60	.30	.06
☐ 606 Reds Rookies DP	.08	.04	.01
Bruce Berenyi			
Geoff Combe			
Paul Householder			
☐ 607 David Palmer	.12	.06	.01
☐ 608 Greg Pryor	.08	.04	.01
☐ 609 Lynn McGlothen	.08	.04	.01
☐ 610 Darrell Porter	.08	.04	.01
☐ 611 Rick Matula DP	.04	.02	.00
☐ 612 Duane Kuiper	.08	.04	.01
☐ 613 Jim Anderson	.08	.04	.01
☐ 614 Dave Rozema	.08	.04	.01
☐ 615 Rick Dempsey	.08	.04	.01
☐ 616 Rick Wise	.08	.04	.01
☐ 617 Craig Reynolds	.08	.04	.01
☐ 618 John Milner	.08	.04	.01
☐ 619 Steve Henderson	.08	.04	.01
☐ 620 Dennis Eckersley	.35	.17	.03
☐ 621 Tom Donohue	.08	.04	.01
☐ 622 Randy Moffitt	.08	.04	.01
☐ 623 Sal Bando	.12	.06	.01
☐ 624 Bob Welch	.20	.10	.02
☐ 625 Bill Buckner	.20	.10	.02
☐ 626 Tigers Rookies	.12	.06	.01
Dave Steffen			
Jerry Ujdur			
Roger Weaver			
☐ 627 Luis Tiant	.15	.07	.01
☐ 628 Vic Correll	.08	.04	.01
☐ 629 Tony Armas	.15	.07	.01
☐ 630 Steve Carlton	1.25	.50	.10
☐ 631 Ron Jackson	.08	.04	.01
☐ 632 Alan Bannister	.08	.04	.01
☐ 633 Bill Lee	.12	.06	.01
☐ 634 Doug Flynn	.08	.04	.01
☐ 635 Bobby Bonds	.15	.07	.01
☐ 636 Al Hrabosky	.12	.06	.01
☐ 637 Jerry Narron	.08	.04	.01
☐ 638 Checklist 606-726	.20	.03	.01
☐ 639 Carney Lansford	.45	.22	.04
☐ 640 Dave Parker	.50	.25	.05
☐ 641 Mark Belanger	.12	.06	.01
☐ 642 Vern Ruhle	.08	.04	.01
☐ 643 Lloyd Moseby	1.00	.50	.10
☐ 644 Ramon Aviles DP	.04	.02	.00
☐ 645 Rick Reuschel	.25	.12	.02
☐ 646 Marvis Foley	.08	.04	.01
☐ 647 Dick Drago	.08	.04	.01
☐ 648 Darrell Evans	.25	.12	.02
☐ 649 Manny Sarmiento	.08	.04	.01
☐ 650 Bucky Dent	.20	.10	.02
☐ 651 Pedro Guerrero	2.25	1.10	.22
☐ 652 John Montague	.08	.04	.01
☐ 653 Bill Fahey	.08	.04	.01
☐ 654 Ray Burris	.08	.04	.01
☐ 655 Dan Driessen	.08	.04	.01
☐ 656 Jon Matlack	.08	.04	.01
☐ 657 Mike Cubbage DP	.04	.02	.00
☐ 658 Milt Wilcox	.08	.04	.01
☐ 659 Brewers Rookies	.12	.06	.01
John Flinn			
Ed Romero			
Ned Yost			
☐ 660 Gary Carter	1.50	.75	.15
☐ 661 Orioles Team/Mgr.	.25	.12	.02
Earl Weaver			
(checklist back)			
☐ 662 Red Sox Team/Mgr.	.20	.10	.02
Ralph Houk			
(checklist back)			
☐ 663 Angels Team/Mgr.	.20	.10	.02
Jim Fregosi			
(checklist back)			
☐ 664 White Sox Team/Mgr. ...	.20	.10	.02
Tony LaRussa			
(checklist back)			
☐ 665 Indians Team/Mgr.	.20	.10	.02

Dave Garcia			
(checklist back)			
☐ 666 Tigers Team/Mgr.	.25	.12	.02
Sparky Anderson			
(checklist back)			
☐ 667 Royals Team/Mgr.	.20	.10	.02
Jim Frey			
(checklist back)			
☐ 668 Brewers Team/Mgr.	.20	.10	.02
Bob Rodgers			
(checklist back)			
☐ 669 Twins Team/Mgr.	.20	.10	.02
John Goryl			
(checklist back)			
☐ 670 Yankees Team/Mgr.	.25	.12	.02
Gene Michael			
(checklist back)			
☐ 671 A's Team/Mgr.	.25	.12	.02
Billy Martin			
(checklist back)			
☐ 672 Mariners Team/Mgr.	.20	.10	.02
Maury Wills			
(checklist back)			
☐ 673 Rangers Team/Mgr.	.20	.10	.02
Don Zimmer			
(checklist back)			
☐ 674 Blue Jays Team/Mgr.	.20	.10	.02
Bobby Mattick			
(checklist back)			
☐ 675 Braves Team/Mgr.	.20	.10	.02
Bobby Cox			
(checklist back)			
☐ 676 Cubs Team/Mgr.	.20	.10	.02
Joe Amalfitano			
(checklist back)			
☐ 677 Reds Team/Mgr.	.20	.10	.02
John McNamara			
(checklist back)			
☐ 678 Astros Team/Mgr.	.20	.10	.02
Bill Virdon			
(checklist back)			
☐ 679 Dodgers Team/Mgr.	.25	.12	.02
Tom Lasorda			
(checklist back)			
☐ 680 Expos Team/Mgr.	.20	.10	.02
Dick Williams			
(checklist back)			
☐ 681 Mets Team/Mgr.	.25	.12	.02
Joe Torre			
(checklist back)			
☐ 682 Phillies Team/Mgr.	.20	.10	.02
Dallas Green			
(checklist back)			
☐ 683 Pirates Team/Mgr.	.20	.10	.02
Chuck Tanner			
(checklist back)			
☐ 684 Cardinals Team/Mgr.	.20	.10	.02
Whitey Herzog			
(checklist back)			
☐ 685 Padres Team/Mgr.	.20	.10	.02
Frank Howard			
(checklist back)			
☐ 686 Giants Team/Mgr.	.20	.10	.02
Dave Bristol			
(checklist back)			
☐ 687 Jeff Jones	.08	.04	.01
☐ 688 Kiko Garcia	.08	.04	.01
☐ 689 Red Sox Rookies	2.50	1.25	.25
Bruce Hurst			
Keith MacWhorter			
Reid Nichols			
☐ 690 Bob Watson	.12	.06	.01
☐ 691 Dick Ruthven	.08	.04	.01
☐ 692 Lenny Randle	.08	.04	.01
☐ 693 Steve Howe	.12	.06	.01
☐ 694 Bud Harrelson DP	.04	.02	.00
☐ 695 Kent Tekulve	.12	.06	.01
☐ 696 Alan Ashby	.08	.04	.01
☐ 697 Rick Waits	.08	.04	.01
☐ 698 Mike Jorgensen	.08	.04	.01
☐ 699 Glenn Abbott	.08	.04	.01
☐ 700 George Brett	2.25	1.10	.22
☐ 701 Joe Rudi	.12	.06	.01
☐ 702 George Medich	.08	.04	.01
☐ 703 Alvis Woods	.08	.04	.01
☐ 704 Bill Travers DP	.04	.02	.00
☐ 705 Ted Simmons	.25	.12	.02
☐ 706 Dave Ford	.08	.04	.01
☐ 707 Dave Cash	.08	.04	.01
☐ 708 Doyle Alexander	.12	.06	.01
☐ 709 Alan Trammell DP	.30	.15	.03
☐ 710 Ron LeFlore DP	.08	.04	.01
☐ 711 Joe Ferguson	.08	.04	.01
☐ 712 Bill Bonham	.08	.04	.01
☐ 713 Bill North	.08	.04	.01

		MINT	EXC	G-VG
☐ 714	Pete Redfern	.08	.04	.01
☐ 715	Bill Madlock	.15	.07	.01
☐ 716	Glenn Borgmann	.08	.04	.01
☐ 717	Jim Barr DP	.04	.02	.00
☐ 718	Larry Biittner	.08	.04	.01
☐ 719	Sparky Lyle	.15	.07	.01
☐ 720	Fred Lynn	.30	.15	.03
☐ 721	Toby Harrah	.12	.06	.01
☐ 722	Joe Niekro	.15	.07	.01
☐ 723	Bruce Bochte	.08	.04	.01
☐ 724	Lou Piniella	.15	.07	.01
☐ 725	Steve Rogers	.12	.06	.01
☐ 726	Rick Monday	.20	.10	.02

1981 Topps Traded

The cards in this 132-card set measure 2 1/2" by 3 1/2". For the first time since 1976, Topps issued a "traded" set in 1981. Unlike the small traded sets of 1974 and 1976, this set contains a larger number of cards and was sequentially numbered, alphabetically, from 727 to 858. Thus, this set gives the impression it is a continuation of their regular issue of this year. The sets were issued only through hobby card dealers and were boxed in complete sets of 132 cards.

		MINT	EXC	G-VG
COMPLETE SET (132)		25.00	12.50	2.50
COMMON PLAYER (727-858)		.08	.04	.01

		MINT	EXC	G-VG
☐ 727	Danny Ainge	.75	.35	.07
☐ 728	Doyle Alexander	.20	.10	.02
☐ 729	Gary Alexander	.08	.04	.01
☐ 730	Bill Almon	.08	.04	.01
☐ 731	Joaquin Andujar	.15	.07	.01
☐ 732	Bob Bailor	.08	.04	.01
☐ 733	Juan Beniquez	.08	.04	.01
☐ 734	Dave Bergman	.08	.04	.01
☐ 735	Tony Bernazard	.08	.04	.01
☐ 736	Larry Biittner	.08	.04	.01
☐ 737	Doug Bird	.08	.04	.01
☐ 738	Bert Blyleven	.75	.35	.07
☐ 739	Mark Bomback	.08	.04	.01
☐ 740	Bobby Bonds	.25	.12	.02
☐ 741	Rick Bosetti	.08	.04	.01
☐ 742	Hubie Brooks	1.50	.75	.15
☐ 743	Rick Burleson	.15	.07	.01
☐ 744	Ray Burris	.08	.04	.01
☐ 745	Jeff Burroughs	.15	.07	.01
☐ 746	Enos Cabell	.08	.04	.01
☐ 747	Ken Clay	.08	.04	.01
☐ 748	Mark Clear	.08	.04	.01
☐ 749	Larry Cox	.08	.04	.01
☐ 750	Hector Cruz	.08	.04	.01
☐ 751	Victor Cruz	.08	.04	.01
☐ 752	Mike Cubbage	.08	.04	.01
☐ 753	Dick Davis	.08	.04	.01
☐ 754	Brian Doyle	.08	.04	.01
☐ 755	Dick Drago	.08	.04	.01
☐ 756	Leon Durham	.40	.20	.04
☐ 757	Jim Dwyer	.08	.04	.01
☐ 758	Dave Edwards	.08	.04	.01
☐ 759	Jim Essian	.08	.04	.01
☐ 760	Bill Fahey	.08	.04	.01
☐ 761	Rollie Fingers	1.00	.50	.10
☐ 762	Carlton Fisk	1.50	.75	.15
☐ 763	Barry Foote	.08	.04	.01

		MINT	EXC	G-VG
☐ 764	Ken Forsch	.08	.04	.01
☐ 765	Kiko Garcia	.08	.04	.01
☐ 766	Cesar Geronimo	.08	.04	.01
☐ 767	Gary Gray	.08	.04	.01
☐ 768	Mickey Hatcher	.20	.10	.02
☐ 769	Steve Henderson	.08	.04	.01
☐ 770	Marc Hill	.08	.04	.01
☐ 771	Butch Hobson	.08	.04	.01
☐ 772	Rick Honeycutt	.08	.04	.01
☐ 773	Roy Howell	.08	.04	.01
☐ 774	Mike Ivie	.08	.04	.01
☐ 775	Roy Lee Jackson	.08	.04	.01
☐ 776	Cliff Johnson	.08	.04	.01
☐ 777	Randy Jones	.15	.07	.01
☐ 778	Ruppert Jones	.08	.04	.01
☐ 779	Mick Kelleher	.08	.04	.01
☐ 780	Terry Kennedy	.15	.07	.01
☐ 781	Dave Kingman	.35	.17	.03
☐ 782	Bob Knepper	.15	.07	.01
☐ 783	Ken Kravec	.08	.04	.01
☐ 784	Bob Lacey	.08	.04	.01
☐ 785	Dennis Lamp	.08	.04	.01
☐ 786	Rafael Landestoy	.08	.04	.01
☐ 787	Ken Landreaux	.15	.07	.01
☐ 788	Carney Lansford	1.00	.50	.10
☐ 789	Dave LaRoche	.08	.04	.01
☐ 790	Joe Lefebvre	.08	.04	.01
☐ 791	Ron LeFlore	.15	.07	.01
☐ 792	Randy Lerch	.08	.04	.01
☐ 793	Sixto Lezcano	.08	.04	.01
☐ 794	John Littlefield	.08	.04	.01
☐ 795	Mike Lum	.08	.04	.01
☐ 796	Greg Luzinski	.25	.12	.02
☐ 797	Fred Lynn	.50	.25	.05
☐ 798	Jerry Martin	.08	.04	.01
☐ 799	Buck Martinez	.08	.04	.01
☐ 800	Gary Matthews	.15	.07	.01
☐ 801	Mario Mendoza	.08	.04	.01
☐ 802	Larry Milbourne	.08	.04	.01
☐ 803	Rick Miller	.08	.04	.01
☐ 804	John Montefusco	.15	.07	.01
☐ 805	Jerry Morales	.08	.04	.01
☐ 806	Jose Morales	.08	.04	.01
☐ 807	Joe Morgan	1.50	.75	.15
☐ 808	Jerry Mumphrey	.08	.04	.01
☐ 809	Gene Nelson	.40	.20	.04
☐ 810	Ed Ott	.08	.04	.01
☐ 811	Bob Owchinko	.08	.04	.01
☐ 812	Gaylord Perry	1.25	.60	.12
☐ 813	Mike Phillips	.08	.04	.01
☐ 814	Darrell Porter	.15	.07	.01
☐ 815	Mike Proly	.08	.04	.01
☐ 816	Tim Raines	8.00	3.75	.75
☐ 817	Lenny Randle	.08	.04	.01
☐ 818	Doug Rau	.08	.04	.01
☐ 819	Jeff Reardon	.75	.35	.07
☐ 820	Ken Reitz	.08	.04	.01
☐ 821	Steve Renko	.08	.04	.01
☐ 822	Rick Reuschel	.40	.20	.04
☐ 823	Dave Revering	.08	.04	.01
☐ 824	Dave Roberts	.08	.04	.01
☐ 825	Leon Roberts	.08	.04	.01
☐ 826	Joe Rudi	.15	.07	.01
☐ 827	Kevin Saucier	.08	.04	.01
☐ 828	Tony Scott	.08	.04	.01
☐ 829	Bob Shirley	.08	.04	.01
☐ 830	Ted Simmons	.50	.25	.05
☐ 831	Lary Sorensen	.08	.04	.01
☐ 832	Jim Spencer	.08	.04	.01
☐ 833	Harry Spilman	.08	.04	.01
☐ 834	Fred Stanley	.08	.04	.01
☐ 835	Rusty Staub	.25	.12	.02
☐ 836	Bill Stein	.08	.04	.01
☐ 837	Joe Strain	.08	.04	.01
☐ 838	Bruce Sutter	.40	.20	.04
☐ 839	Don Sutton	1.25	.60	.12
☐ 840	Steve Swisher	.08	.04	.01
☐ 841	Frank Tanana	.20	.10	.02
☐ 842	Gene Tenace	.15	.07	.01
☐ 843	Jason Thompson	.35	.17	.03
☐ 844	Dickie Thon	.35	.17	.03
☐ 845	Bill Travers	.08	.04	.01
☐ 846	Tom Underwood	.08	.04	.01
☐ 847	John Urrea	.08	.04	.01
☐ 848	Mike Vail	.08	.04	.01
☐ 849	Ellis Valentine	.15	.07	.01
☐ 850	Fernando Valenzuela	4.50	2.25	.45
☐ 851	Pete Vuckovich	.15	.07	.01
☐ 852	Mark Wagner	.08	.04	.01
☐ 853	Bob Walk	.25	.12	.02
☐ 854	Claudell Washington	.20	.10	.02
☐ 855	Dave Winfield	2.50	1.25	.25
☐ 856	Geoff Zahn	.08	.04	.01
☐ 857	Richie Zisk	.15	.07	.01
☐ 858	Checklist 727-858	.08	.01	.00

1982 Topps

CUBS
JODY DAVIS

The cards in this 792-card set measure 2 1/2" by 3 1/2". The 1982 baseball series is the largest set Topps has ever issued at one printing. The 66-card increase from the previous year's total eliminated the "double print" practice which had occurred in every regular issue since 1978. Cards 1-6 depict Highlights (HL) of the 1981 season, cards 161-168 picture League Leaders, and there are mini-series of AL (547-557) and NL (337-347) All-Stars (AS). The abbreviation "SA" in the checklist is given for the 40 "Super Action" cards introduced in this set. The team cards are actually Team Leader (TL) cards picturing the batting and pitching leader for that team with a checklist back.

	MINT	EXC	G-VG
COMPLETE SET (792)	90.00	45.00	9.00
COMMON PLAYER (1-792)	.06	.03	.00

☐	1	HL: Steve Carlton Sets new NL strikeout record	.45	.10	.02
☐	2	HL: Ron Davis Fans 8 straight in relief	.10	.05	.01
☐	3	HL: Tim Raines Swipes 71 bases as rookie	.25	.12	.02
☐	4	HL: Pete Rose Sets NL career hits mark	.75	.35	.07
☐	5	HL: Nolan Ryan Pitches fifth career no-hitter	.75	.35	.07
☐	6	HL: Fern. Valenzuela 8 shutouts as rookie	.20	.10	.02
☐	7	Scott Sanderson	.06	.03	.00
☐	8	Rich Dauer	.06	.03	.00
☐	9	Ron Guidry	.30	.15	.03
☐	10	SA: Ron Guidry	.15	.07	.01
☐	11	Gary Alexander	.06	.03	.00
☐	12	Moose Haas	.06	.03	.00
☐	13	Lamar Johnson	.06	.03	.00
☐	14	Steve Howe	.06	.03	.00
☐	15	Ellis Valentine	.06	.03	.00
☐	16	Steve Comer	.06	.03	.00
☐	17	Darrell Evans	.15	.07	.01
☐	18	Fernando Arroyo	.06	.03	.00
☐	19	Ernie Whitt	.10	.05	.01
☐	20	Garry Maddox	.10	.05	.01
☐	21	Orioles Rookies Bob Bonner Cal Ripken Jeff Schneider	12.50	6.25	1.25
☐	22	Jim Beattie	.06	.03	.00
☐	23	Willie Hernandez	.20	.10	.02
☐	24	Dave Frost	.06	.03	.00
☐	25	Jerry Remy	.06	.03	.00
☐	26	Jorge Orta	.06	.03	.00
☐	27	Tom Herr	.15	.07	.01
☐	28	John Urrea	.06	.03	.00
☐	29	Dwayne Murphy	.06	.03	.00
☐	30	Tom Seaver	.75	.35	.07
☐	31	SA: Tom Seaver	.35	.17	.03
☐	32	Gene Garber	.06	.03	.00
☐	33	Jerry Morales	.06	.03	.00
☐	34	Joe Sambito	.06	.03	.00
☐	35	Willie Aikens	.06	.03	.00
☐	36	Rangers TL Mgr. Don Zimmer Batting: Al Oliver Pitching: Doc Medich	.15	.07	.01
☐	37	Dan Graham	.06	.03	.00
☐	38	Charlie Lea	.06	.03	.00
☐	39	Lou Whitaker	.35	.17	.03
☐	40	Dave Parker	.30	.15	.03
☐	41	SA: Dave Parker	.15	.07	.01
☐	42	Rick Sofield	.06	.03	.00
☐	43	Mike Cubbage	.06	.03	.00
☐	44	Britt Burns	.06	.03	.00
☐	45	Rick Cerone	.06	.03	.00
☐	46	Jerry Augustine	.06	.03	.00
☐	47	Jeff Leonard	.10	.05	.01
☐	48	Bobby Castillo	.06	.03	.00
☐	49	Alvis Woods	.06	.03	.00
☐	50	Buddy Bell	.15	.07	.01
☐	51	Cubs Rookies Jay Howell Carlos Lezcano Ty Waller	.45	.22	.04
☐	52	Larry Andersen	.06	.03	.00
☐	53	Greg Gross	.06	.03	.00
☐	54	Ron Hassey	.06	.03	.00
☐	55	Rick Burleson	.10	.05	.01
☐	56	Mark Littell	.06	.03	.00
☐	57	Craig Reynolds	.06	.03	.00
☐	58	John D'Acquisto	.06	.03	.00
☐	59	Rich Gedman	.50	.25	.05
☐	60	Tony Armas	.10	.05	.01
☐	61	Tommy Boggs	.06	.03	.00
☐	62	Mike Tyson	.06	.03	.00
☐	63	Mario Soto	.10	.05	.01
☐	64	Lynn Jones	.06	.03	.00
☐	65	Terry Kennedy	.06	.03	.00
☐	66	Astros TL Mgr. Bill Virdon Batting: Art Howe Pitching: Nolan Ryan	.20	.10	.02
☐	67	Rich Gale	.06	.03	.00
☐	68	Roy Howell	.06	.03	.00
☐	69	Al Williams	.06	.03	.00
☐	70	Tim Raines	2.00	1.00	.20
☐	71	Roy Lee Jackson	.06	.03	.00
☐	72	Rick Auerbach	.06	.03	.00
☐	73	Buddy Solomon	.06	.03	.00
☐	74	Bob Clark	.06	.03	.00
☐	75	Tommy John	.25	.12	.02
☐	76	Greg Pryor	.06	.03	.00
☐	77	Miguel Dilone	.06	.03	.00
☐	78	George Medich	.06	.03	.00
☐	79	Bob Bailor	.06	.03	.00
☐	80	Jim Palmer	.75	.35	.07
☐	81	SA: Jim Palmer	.35	.17	.03
☐	82	Bob Welch	.15	.07	.01
☐	83	Yankees Rookies Steve Balboni Andy McGaffigan Andre Robertson	.35	.17	.03
☐	84	Rennie Stennett	.06	.03	.00
☐	85	Lynn McGlothen	.06	.03	.00
☐	86	Dane Iorg	.06	.03	.00
☐	87	Matt Keough	.06	.03	.00
☐	88	Biff Pocoroba	.06	.03	.00
☐	89	Steve Henderson	.06	.03	.00
☐	90	Nolan Ryan	2.00	1.00	.20
☐	91	Carney Lansford	.30	.12	.02
☐	92	Brad Havens	.06	.03	.00
☐	93	Larry Hisle	.06	.03	.00
☐	94	Andy Hassler	.06	.03	.00
☐	95	Ozzie Smith	.75	.35	.07
☐	96	Royals TL Mgr. Jim Frey Batting: George Brett Pitching: Larry Gura	.20	.10	.02
☐	97	Paul Moskau	.06	.03	.00
☐	98	Terry Bulling	.06	.03	.00
☐	99	Barry Bonnell	.06	.03	.00
☐	100	Mike Schmidt	1.75	.85	.17
☐	101	SA: Mike Schmidt	.75	.35	.07
☐	102	Dan Briggs	.06	.03	.00
☐	103	Bob Lacey	.06	.03	.00
☐	104	Rance Mulliniks	.06	.03	.00
☐	105	Kirk Gibson	1.25	.60	.12
☐	106	Enrique Romo	.06	.03	.00
☐	107	Wayne Krenchicki	.06	.03	.00
☐	108	Bob Sykes	.06	.03	.00
☐	109	Dave Revering	.06	.03	.00
☐	110	Carlton Fisk	.45	.22	.04

☐ 111	SA: Carlton Fisk	.35	.17	.03
☐ 112	Billy Sample	.06	.03	.00
☐ 113	Steve McCatty	.06	.03	.00
☐ 114	Ken Landreaux	.06	.03	.00
☐ 115	Gaylord Perry	.35	.17	.03
☐ 116	Jim Wohlford	.06	.03	.00
☐ 117	Rawly Eastwick	.06	.03	.00
☐ 118	Expos Rookies	.65	.30	.06
	Terry Francona			
	Brad Mills			
	Bryn Smith			
☐ 119	Joe Pittman	.06	.03	.00
☐ 120	Gary Lucas	.06	.03	.00
☐ 121	Ed Lynch	.10	.05	.01
☐ 122	Jamie Easterly UER	.06	.03	.00
	(photo actually			
	Reggie Cleveland)			
☐ 123	Danny Goodwin	.06	.03	.00
☐ 124	Reid Nichols	.06	.03	.00
☐ 125	Danny Ainge	.25	.12	.02
☐ 126	Braves TL	.15	.07	.01
	Mgr. Bobby Cox			
	Batting: C.Washington			
	Pitching: Rick Mahler			
☐ 127	Lonnie Smith	.15	.07	.01
☐ 128	Frank Pastore	.06	.03	.00
☐ 129	Checklist 1-132	.10	.01	.00
☐ 130	Julio Cruz	.06	.03	.00
☐ 131	Stan Bahnsen	.06	.03	.00
☐ 132	Lee May	.10	.05	.01
☐ 133	Pat Underwood	.06	.03	.00
☐ 134	Dan Ford	.06	.03	.00
☐ 135	Andy Rincon	.06	.03	.00
☐ 136	Lenn Sakata	.06	.03	.00
☐ 137	George Cappuzzello	.06	.03	.00
☐ 138	Tony Pena	.25	.12	.02
☐ 139	Jeff Jones	.06	.03	.00
☐ 140	Ron LeFlore	.10	.05	.01
☐ 141	Indians Rookies	1.50	.75	.15
	Chris Bando			
	Tom Brennan			
	Von Hayes			
☐ 142	Dave LaRoche	.06	.03	.00
☐ 143	Mookie Wilson	.20	.10	.02
☐ 144	Fred Breining	.06	.03	.00
☐ 145	Bob Horner	.20	.10	.02
☐ 146	Mike Griffin	.06	.03	.00
☐ 147	Denny Walling	.06	.03	.00
☐ 148	Mickey Klutts	.06	.03	.00
☐ 149	Pat Putnam	.06	.03	.00
☐ 150	Ted Simmons	.20	.10	.02
☐ 151	Dave Edwards	.06	.03	.00
☐ 152	Ramon Aviles	.06	.03	.00
☐ 153	Roger Erickson	.06	.03	.00
☐ 154	Dennis Werth	.06	.03	.00
☐ 155	Otto Velez	.06	.03	.00
☐ 156	Oakland A's TL	.25	.12	.02
	Mgr. Billy Martin			
	Batting: R.Henderson			
	Pitching: S. McCatty			
☐ 157	Steve Crawford	.06	.03	.00
☐ 158	Brian Downing	.10	.05	.01
☐ 159	Larry Biittner	.06	.03	.00
☐ 160	Luis Tiant	.15	.07	.01
☐ 161	Batting Leaders	.15	.07	.01
	Bill Madlock			
	Carney Lansford			
☐ 162	Home Run Leaders	.20	.10	.02
	Mike Schmidt			
	Tony Armas			
	Dwight Evans			
	Bobby Grich			
	Eddie Murray			
☐ 163	RBI Leaders	.35	.17	.03
	Mike Schmidt			
	Eddie Murray			
☐ 164	Stolen Base Leaders	.35	.17	.03
	Tim Raines			
	Rickey Henderson			
☐ 165	Victory Leaders	.15	.07	.01
	Tom Seaver			
	Denny Martinez			
	Steve McCatty			
	Jack Morris			
	Pete Vuckovich			
☐ 166	Strikeout Leaders	.15	.07	.01
	Fernando Valenzuela			
	Len Barker			
☐ 167	ERA Leaders	.35	.17	.03
	Nolan Ryan			
	Steve McCatty			
☐ 168	Leading Firemen	.15	.07	.01
	Bruce Sutter			
	Rollie Fingers			
☐ 169	Charlie Leibrandt	.06	.03	.00

☐ 170	Jim Bibby	.06	.03	.00
☐ 171	Giants Rookies	1.00	.50	.10
	Bob Brenly			
	Chili Davis			
	Bob Tufts			
☐ 172	Bill Gullickson	.06	.03	.00
☐ 173	Jamie Quirk	.06	.03	.00
☐ 174	Dave Ford	.06	.03	.00
☐ 175	Jerry Mumphrey	.06	.03	.00
☐ 176	Dewey Robinson	.06	.03	.00
☐ 177	John Ellis	.06	.03	.00
☐ 178	Dyar Miller	.06	.03	.00
☐ 179	Steve Garvey	.85	.40	.08
☐ 180	SA: Steve Garvey	.35	.17	.03
☐ 181	Silvio Martinez	.06	.03	.00
☐ 182	Larry Herndon	.06	.03	.00
☐ 183	Mike Proly	.06	.03	.00
☐ 184	Mick Kelleher	.06	.03	.00
☐ 185	Phil Niekro	.45	.22	.04
☐ 186	Cardinals TL	.15	.07	.01
	Mgr. Whitey Herzog			
	Batting K. Hernandez			
	Pitching Bob Forsch			
☐ 187	Jeff Newman	.06	.03	.00
☐ 188	Randy Martz	.06	.03	.00
☐ 189	Glenn Hoffman	.06	.03	.00
☐ 190	J.R. Richard	.10	.05	.01
☐ 191	Tim Wallach	1.50	.75	.15
☐ 192	Broderick Perkins	.06	.03	.00
☐ 193	Darrell Jackson	.06	.03	.00
☐ 194	Mike Vail	.06	.03	.00
☐ 195	Paul Molitor	.35	.17	.03
☐ 196	Willie Upshaw	.06	.03	.00
☐ 197	Shane Rawley	.06	.03	.00
☐ 198	Chris Speier	.06	.03	.00
☐ 199	Don Aase	.06	.03	.00
☐ 200	George Brett	1.50	.75	.15
☐ 201	SA: George Brett	.60	.30	.06
☐ 202	Rick Manning	.06	.03	.00
☐ 203	Blue Jays Rookies	3.50	1.75	.35
	Jesse Barfield			
	Brian Milner			
	Boomer Wells			
☐ 204	Gary Roenicke	.06	.03	.00
☐ 205	Neil Allen	.10	.05	.01
☐ 206	Tony Bernazard	.06	.03	.00
☐ 207	Rod Scurry	.06	.03	.00
☐ 208	Bobby Murcer	.15	.07	.01
☐ 209	Gary Lavelle	.06	.03	.00
☐ 210	Keith Hernandez	.50	.25	.05
☐ 211	Dan Petry	.06	.03	.00
☐ 212	Mario Mendoza	.06	.03	.00
☐ 213	Dave Stewart	5.00	2.50	.50
☐ 214	Brian Asselstine	.06	.03	.00
☐ 215	Mike Krukow	.10	.05	.01
☐ 216	White Sox TL	.15	.07	.01
	Mgr. Tony LaRussa			
	Batting: Chet Lemon			
	Pitching: Dennis Lamp			
☐ 217	Bo McLaughlin	.06	.03	.00
☐ 218	Dave Roberts	.06	.03	.00
☐ 219	John Curtis	.06	.03	.00
☐ 220	Manny Trillo	.06	.03	.00
☐ 221	Jim Slaton	.06	.03	.00
☐ 222	Butch Wynegar	.06	.03	.00
☐ 223	Lloyd Moseby	.20	.10	.02
☐ 224	Bruce Bochte	.06	.03	.00
☐ 225	Mike Torrez	.06	.03	.00
☐ 226	Checklist 133-264	.10	.01	.00
☐ 227	Ray Burris	.06	.03	.00
☐ 228	Sam Mejias	.06	.03	.00
☐ 229	Geoff Zahn	.06	.03	.00
☐ 230	Willie Wilson	.20	.10	.02
☐ 231	Phillies Rookies	1.50	.75	.15
	Mark Davis			
	Bob Dernier			
	Ozzie Virgil			
☐ 232	Terry Crowley	.06	.03	.00
☐ 233	Duane Kuiper	.06	.03	.00
☐ 234	Ron Hodges	.06	.03	.00
☐ 235	Mike Easler	.10	.05	.01
☐ 236	John Martin	.06	.03	.00
☐ 237	Rusty Kuntz	.06	.03	.00
☐ 238	Kevin Saucier	.06	.03	.00
☐ 239	Jon Matlack	.06	.03	.00
☐ 240	Bucky Dent	.15	.07	.01
☐ 241	SA: Bucky Dent	.10	.05	.01
☐ 242	Milt May	.06	.03	.00
☐ 243	Bob Owchinko	.06	.03	.00
☐ 244	Rufino Linares	.06	.03	.00
☐ 245	Ken Reitz	.06	.03	.00
☐ 246	New York Mets TL	.20	.10	.02
	Mgr. Joe Torre			
	Batting: Hubie Brooks			
	Pitching: Mike Scott			

☐ 247	Pedro Guerrero	1.00	.50	.10
☐ 248	Frank LaCorte	.06	.03	.00
☐ 249	Tim Flannery	.06	.03	.00
☐ 250	Tug McGraw	.15	.07	.01
☐ 251	Fred Lynn	.30	.15	.03
☐ 252	SA: Fred Lynn	.15	.07	.01
☐ 253	Chuck Baker	.06	.03	.00
☐ 254	Jorge Bell	8.00	4.00	.80
☐ 255	Tony Perez	.25	.12	.02
☐ 256	SA: Tony Perez	.10	.05	.01
☐ 257	Larry Harlow	.06	.03	.00
☐ 258	Bo Diaz	.06	.03	.00
☐ 259	Rodney Scott	.06	.03	.00
☐ 260	Bruce Sutter	.20	.10	.02
☐ 261	Tigers Rookies	.10	.05	.01
	Howard Bailey			
	Marty Castillo			
	Dave Rucker			
☐ 262	Doug Bair	.06	.03	.00
☐ 263	Victor Cruz	.06	.03	.00
☐ 264	Dan Quisenberry	.20	.10	.02
☐ 265	Al Bumbry	.06	.03	.00
☐ 266	Rick Leach	.06	.03	.00
☐ 267	Kurt Bevacqua	.06	.03	.00
☐ 268	Rickey Keeton	.06	.03	.00
☐ 269	Jim Essian	.06	.03	.00
☐ 270	Rusty Staub	.15	.07	.01
☐ 271	Larry Bradford	.06	.03	.00
☐ 272	Bump Wills	.06	.03	.00
☐ 273	Doug Bird	.06	.03	.00
☐ 274	Bob Ojeda	.75	.35	.07
☐ 275	Bob Watson	.10	.05	.01
☐ 276	Angels TL	.20	.10	.02
	Mgr. Gene Mauch			
	Batting: Rod Carew			
	Pitching: Ken Forsch			
☐ 277	Terry Puhl	.06	.03	.00
☐ 278	John Littlefield	.06	.03	.00
☐ 279	Bill Russell	.10	.05	.01
☐ 280	Ben Oglivie	.10	.05	.01
☐ 281	John Verhoeven	.06	.03	.00
☐ 282	Ken Macha	.06	.03	.00
☐ 283	Brian Allard	.06	.03	.00
☐ 284	Bob Grich	.10	.05	.01
☐ 285	Sparky Lyle	.15	.07	.01
☐ 286	Bill Fahey	.06	.03	.00
☐ 287	Alan Bannister	.06	.03	.00
☐ 288	Garry Templeton	.10	.05	.01
☐ 289	Bob Stanley	.06	.03	.00
☐ 290	Ken Singleton	.10	.05	.01
☐ 291	Pirates Rookies	1.25	.60	.12
	Vance Law			
	Bob Long			
	Johnny Ray			
☐ 292	David Palmer	.06	.03	.00
☐ 293	Rob Picciolo	.06	.03	.00
☐ 294	Mike LaCoss	.06	.03	.00
☐ 295	Jason Thompson	.06	.03	.00
☐ 296	Bob Walk	.10	.05	.01
☐ 297	Clint Hurdle	.06	.03	.00
☐ 298	Danny Darwin	.06	.03	.00
☐ 299	Steve Trout	.06	.03	.00
☐ 300	Reggie Jackson	1.25	.60	.12
☐ 301	SA: Reggie Jackson	.60	.30	.06
☐ 302	Doug Flynn	.06	.03	.00
☐ 303	Bill Caudill	.06	.03	.00
☐ 304	Johnnie LeMaster	.06	.03	.00
☐ 305	Don Sutton	.50	.25	.05
☐ 306	SA: Don Sutton	.20	.10	.02
☐ 307	Randy Bass	.10	.05	.01
☐ 308	Charlie Moore	.06	.03	.00
☐ 309	Pete Redfern	.06	.03	.00
☐ 310	Mike Hargrove	.10	.05	.01
☐ 311	Dodgers TL	.15	.07	.01
	Mgr. Tom Lasorda			
	Batting: Dusty Baker			
	Pitching: Burt Hooton			
☐ 312	Lenny Randle	.06	.03	.00
☐ 313	John Harris	.06	.03	.00
☐ 314	Buck Martinez	.06	.03	.00
☐ 315	Burt Hooton	.06	.03	.00
☐ 316	Steve Braun	.06	.03	.00
☐ 317	Dick Ruthven	.06	.03	.00
☐ 318	Mike Heath	.06	.03	.00
☐ 319	Dave Rozema	.06	.03	.00
☐ 320	Chris Chambliss	.10	.05	.01
☐ 321	SA: Chris Chambliss	.06	.03	.00
☐ 322	Garry Hancock	.06	.03	.00
☐ 323	Bill Lee	.10	.05	.01
☐ 324	Steve Dillard	.06	.03	.00
☐ 325	Jose Cruz	.10	.05	.01
☐ 326	Pete Falcone	.06	.03	.00
☐ 327	Joe Nolan	.06	.03	.00
☐ 328	Ed Farmer	.06	.03	.00
☐ 329	U.L. Washington	.06	.03	.00

☐ 330	Rick Wise	.06	.03	.00
☐ 331	Benny Ayala	.06	.03	.00
☐ 332	Don Robinson	.06	.03	.00
☐ 333	Brewers Rookies	.10	.05	.01
	Frank DiPino			
	Marshall Edwards			
	Chuck Porter			
☐ 334	Aurelio Rodriguez	.06	.03	.00
☐ 335	Jim Sundberg	.10	.05	.01
☐ 336	Mariners TL	.10	.05	.01
	Mgr. Rene Lachemann			
	Batting: Tom Paciorek			
	Pitching: Glenn Abbott			
☐ 337	Pete Rose AS	.75	.35	.07
☐ 338	Dave Lopes AS	.10	.05	.01
☐ 339	Mike Schmidt AS	.40	.20	.04
☐ 340	Dave Concepcion AS	.10	.05	.01
☐ 341	Andre Dawson AS	.20	.10	.02
☐ 342A	George Foster AS	.25	.12	.02
	(with autograph)			
☐ 342B	George Foster AS	1.75	.85	.17
	(w/o autograph)			
☐ 343	Dave Parker AS	.15	.07	.01
☐ 344	Gary Carter AS	.25	.12	.02
☐ 345	Fern. Valenzuela AS	.15	.07	.01
☐ 346A	Tom Seaver AS ERR	1.00	.50	.10
	("t ed")			
☐ 346B	Tom Seaver AS COR	.30	.15	.03
	("tied")			
☐ 347	Bruce Sutter AS	.10	.05	.01
☐ 348	Derrel Thomas	.06	.03	.00
☐ 349	George Frazier	.06	.03	.00
☐ 350	Thad Bosley	.06	.03	.00
☐ 351	Reds Rookies	.10	.05	.01
	Scott Brown			
	Geoff Coumbe			
	Paul Householder			
☐ 352	Dick Davis	.06	.03	.00
☐ 353	Jack O'Connor	.06	.03	.00
☐ 354	Roberto Ramos	.06	.03	.00
☐ 355	Dwight Evans	.25	.12	.02
☐ 356	Denny Lewallyn	.06	.03	.00
☐ 357	Butch Hobson	.06	.03	.00
☐ 358	Mike Parrott	.06	.03	.00
☐ 359	Jim Dwyer	.06	.03	.00
☐ 360	Len Barker	.06	.03	.00
☐ 361	Rafael Landestoy	.06	.03	.00
☐ 362	Jim Wright	.06	.03	.00
☐ 363	Bob Molinaro	.06	.03	.00
☐ 364	Doyle Alexander	.10	.05	.01
☐ 365	Bill Madlock	.15	.07	.01
☐ 366	Padres TL	.10	.05	.01
	Mgr. Frank Howard			
	Batting: Luis Salazar			
	Pitching: Eichelberger			
☐ 367	Jim Kaat	.15	.07	.01
☐ 368	Alex Trevino	.06	.03	.00
☐ 369	Champ Summers	.06	.03	.00
☐ 370	Mike Norris	.06	.03	.00
☐ 371	Jerry Don Gleaton	.06	.03	.00
☐ 372	Luis Gomez	.06	.03	.00
☐ 373	Gene Nelson	.15	.07	.01
☐ 374	Tim Blackwell	.06	.03	.00
☐ 375	Dusty Baker	.10	.05	.01
☐ 376	Chris Welsh	.06	.03	.00
☐ 377	Kiko Garcia	.06	.03	.00
☐ 378	Mike Caldwell	.06	.03	.00
☐ 379	Rob Wilfong	.06	.03	.00
☐ 380	Dave Stieb	.20	.10	.02
☐ 381	Red Sox Rookies	.75	.35	.07
	Bruce Hurst			
	Dave Schmidt			
	Julio Valdez			
☐ 382	Joe Simpson	.06	.03	.00
☐ 383A	Pascual Perez ERR	30.00	15.00	3.00
	(no position			
	on front)			
☐ 383B	Pascual Perez COR	.25	.12	.02
☐ 384	Keith Moreland	.06	.03	.00
☐ 385	Ken Forsch	.06	.03	.00
☐ 386	Jerry White	.06	.03	.00
☐ 387	Tom Veryzer	.06	.03	.00
☐ 388	Joe Rudi	.10	.05	.01
☐ 389	George Vukovich	.06	.03	.00
☐ 390	Eddie Murray	1.25	.60	.12
☐ 391	Dave Tobik	.06	.03	.00
☐ 392	Rick Bosetti	.06	.03	.00
☐ 393	Al Hrabosky	.10	.05	.01
☐ 394	Checklist 265-396	.10	.01	.00
☐ 395	Omar Moreno	.06	.03	.00
☐ 396	Twins TL	.10	.05	.01
	Mgr. Billy Gardner			
	Batting: John Castino			
	Pitching: F. Arroyo			
☐ 397	Ken Brett	.06	.03	.00

☐ 398	Mike Squires	.06	.03	.00
☐ 399	Pat Zachry	.06	.03	.00
☐ 400	Johnny Bench	1.00	.50	.10
☐ 401	SA: Johnny Bench	.40	.20	.04
☐ 402	Bill Stein	.06	.03	.00
☐ 403	Jim Tracy	.06	.03	.00
☐ 404	Dickie Thon	.10	.05	.01
☐ 405	Rick Reuschel	.20	.10	.02
☐ 406	Al Holland	.06	.03	.00
☐ 407	Danny Boone	.06	.03	.00
☐ 408	Ed Romero	.06	.03	.00
☐ 409	Don Cooper	.06	.03	.00
☐ 410	Ron Cey	.15	.07	.01
☐ 411	SA: Ron Cey	.10	.05	.01
☐ 412	Luis Leal	.06	.03	.00
☐ 413	Dan Meyer	.06	.03	.00
☐ 414	Elias Sosa	.06	.03	.00
☐ 415	Don Baylor	.15	.07	.01
☐ 416	Marty Bystrom	.06	.03	.00
☐ 417	Pat Kelly	.06	.03	.00
☐ 418	Rangers Rookies	.30	.15	.03
	John Butcher			
	Bobby Johnson			
	Dave Schmidt			
☐ 419	Steve Stone	.10	.05	.01
☐ 420	George Hendrick	.10	.05	.01
☐ 421	Mark Clear	.06	.03	.00
☐ 422	Cliff Johnson	.06	.03	.00
☐ 423	Stan Papi	.06	.03	.00
☐ 424	Bruce Benedict	.06	.03	.00
☐ 425	John Candelaria	.10	.05	.01
☐ 426	Orioles TL	.20	.10	.02
	Mgr. Earl Weaver			
	Batting: Eddie Murray			
	Pitching: Sam Stewart			
☐ 427	Ron Oester	.06	.03	.00
☐ 428	LaMarr Hoyt	.10	.05	.01
☐ 429	John Wathan	.10	.05	.01
☐ 430	Vida Blue	.10	.05	.01
☐ 431	SA: Vida Blue	.06	.03	.00
☐ 432	Mike Scott	.75	.35	.07
☐ 433	Alan Ashby	.06	.03	.00
☐ 434	Joe Lefebvre	.06	.03	.00
☐ 435	Robin Yount	1.75	.85	.17
☐ 436	Joe Strain	.06	.03	.00
☐ 437	Juan Berenguer	.06	.03	.00
☐ 438	Pete Mackanin	.06	.03	.00
☐ 439	Dave Righetti	2.00	1.00	.20
☐ 440	Jeff Burroughs	.10	.05	.01
☐ 441	Astros Rookies	.10	.05	.01
	Danny Heep			
	Billy Smith			
	Bobby Sprowl			
☐ 442	Bruce Kison	.06	.03	.00
☐ 443	Mark Wagner	.06	.03	.00
☐ 444	Terry Forster	.10	.05	.01
☐ 445	Larry Parrish	.10	.05	.01
☐ 446	Wayne Garland	.06	.03	.00
☐ 447	Darrell Porter	.06	.03	.00
☐ 448	SA: Darrell Porter	.06	.03	.00
☐ 449	Luis Aguayo	.06	.03	.00
☐ 450	Jack Morris	.45	.22	.04
☐ 451	Ed Miller	.06	.03	.00
☐ 452	Lee Smith	.80	.40	.08
☐ 453	Art Howe	.10	.05	.01
☐ 454	Rick Langford	.06	.03	.00
☐ 455	Tom Burgmeier	.06	.03	.00
☐ 456	Chicago Cubs TL	.10	.05	.01
	Mgr. Joe Amalfitano			
	Batting: Bill Buckner			
	Pitching: Randy Martz			
☐ 457	Tim Stoddard	.06	.03	.00
☐ 458	Willie Montanez	.06	.03	.00
☐ 459	Bruce Berenyi	.06	.03	.00
☐ 460	Jack Clark	.40	.20	.04
☐ 461	Rich Dotson	.10	.05	.01
☐ 462	Dave Chalk	.06	.03	.00
☐ 463	Jim Kern	.06	.03	.00
☐ 464	Juan Bonilla	.06	.03	.00
☐ 465	Lee Mazzilli	.06	.03	.00
☐ 466	Randy Lerch	.06	.03	.00
☐ 467	Mickey Hatcher	.10	.05	.01
☐ 468	Floyd Bannister	.06	.03	.00
☐ 469	Ed Ott	.06	.03	.00
☐ 470	John Mayberry	.10	.05	.01
☐ 471	Royals Rookies	.20	.10	.02
	Atlee Hammaker			
	Mike Jones			
	Darryl Motley			
☐ 472	Oscar Gamble	.06	.03	.00
☐ 473	Mike Stanton	.06	.03	.00
☐ 474	Ken Oberkfell	.06	.03	.00
☐ 475	Alan Trammell	.50	.25	.05
☐ 476	Brian Kingman	.06	.03	.00
☐ 477	Steve Yeager	.06	.03	.00

☐ 478	Ray Searage	.06	.03	.00
☐ 479	Rowland Office	.06	.03	.00
☐ 480	Steve Carlton	.90	.45	.09
☐ 481	SA: Steve Carlton	.40	.20	.04
☐ 482	Glenn Hubbard	.06	.03	.00
☐ 483	Gary Woods	.06	.03	.00
☐ 484	Ivan DeJesus	.06	.03	.00
☐ 485	Kent Tekulve	.10	.05	.01
☐ 486	Yankees TL	.15	.07	.01
	Mgr. Bob Lemon			
	Batting: J. Mumphrey			
	Pitching: Tommy John			
☐ 487	Bob McClure	.06	.03	.00
☐ 488	Ron Jackson	.06	.03	.00
☐ 489	Rick Dempsey	.06	.03	.00
☐ 490	Dennis Eckersley	.25	.12	.02
☐ 491	Checklist 397-528	.10	.01	.00
☐ 492	Joe Price	.06	.03	.00
☐ 493	Chet Lemon	.10	.05	.01
☐ 494	Hubie Brooks	.25	.12	.02
☐ 495	Dennis Leonard	.10	.05	.01
☐ 496	Johnny Grubb	.06	.03	.00
☐ 497	Jim Anderson	.06	.03	.00
☐ 498	Dave Bergman	.06	.03	.00
☐ 499	Paul Mirabella	.06	.03	.00
☐ 500	Rod Carew	.85	.40	.08
☐ 501	SA: Rod Carew	.40	.20	.04
☐ 502	Braves Rookies	2.00	1.00	.20
	Steve Bedrosian			
	Brett Butler			
	Larry Owen			
☐ 503	Julio Gonzalez	.06	.03	.00
☐ 504	Rick Peters	.06	.03	.00
☐ 505	Graig Nettles	.20	.10	.02
☐ 506	SA: Graig Nettles	.10	.05	.01
☐ 507	Terry Harper	.06	.03	.00
☐ 508	Jody Davis	.50	.25	.05
☐ 509	Harry Spilman	.06	.03	.00
☐ 510	Fernando Valenzuela	1.25	.60	.12
☐ 511	Ruppert Jones	.06	.03	.00
☐ 512	Jerry Dybzinski	.06	.03	.00
☐ 513	Rick Rhoden	.10	.05	.01
☐ 514	Joe Ferguson	.06	.03	.00
☐ 515	Larry Bowa	.15	.07	.01
☐ 516	SA: Larry Bowa	.06	.03	.00
☐ 517	Mark Brouhard	.06	.03	.00
☐ 518	Garth Iorg	.06	.03	.00
☐ 519	Glenn Adams	.06	.03	.00
☐ 520	Mike Flanagan	.10	.05	.01
☐ 521	Bill Almon	.06	.03	.00
☐ 522	Chuck Rainey	.06	.03	.00
☐ 523	Gary Gray	.06	.03	.00
☐ 524	Tom Hausman	.06	.03	.00
☐ 525	Ray Knight	.10	.05	.01
☐ 526	Expos TL	.10	.05	.01
	Mgr. Jim Fanning			
	Batting: W.Cromartie			
	Pitching: B.Gullickson			
☐ 527	John Henry Johnson	.06	.03	.00
☐ 528	Matt Alexander	.06	.03	.00
☐ 529	Allen Ripley	.06	.03	.00
☐ 530	Dickie Noles	.06	.03	.00
☐ 531	A's Rookies	.10	.05	.01
	Rich Bordi			
	Mark Budaska			
	Kelvin Moore			
☐ 532	Toby Harrah	.10	.05	.01
☐ 533	Joaquin Andujar	.10	.05	.01
☐ 534	Dave McKay	.06	.03	.00
☐ 535	Lance Parrish	.30	.15	.03
☐ 536	Rafael Ramirez	.06	.03	.00
☐ 537	Doug Capilla	.06	.03	.00
☐ 538	Lou Piniella	.15	.07	.01
☐ 539	Vern Ruhle	.06	.03	.00
☐ 540	Andre Dawson	.50	.25	.05
☐ 541	Barry Evans	.06	.03	.00
☐ 542	Ned Yost	.06	.03	.00
☐ 543	Bill Robinson	.10	.05	.01
☐ 544	Larry Christenson	.06	.03	.00
☐ 545	Reggie Smith	.10	.05	.01
☐ 546	SA: Reggie Smith	.06	.03	.00
☐ 547	Rod Carew AS	.25	.12	.02
☐ 548	Willie Randolph AS	.10	.05	.01
☐ 549	George Brett AS	.45	.22	.04
☐ 550	Bucky Dent AS	.10	.05	.01
☐ 551	Reggie Jackson AS	.40	.20	.04
☐ 552	Ken Singleton AS	.06	.03	.00
☐ 553	Dave Winfield AS	.30	.15	.03
☐ 554	Carlton Fisk AS	.15	.07	.01
☐ 555	Scott McGregor AS	.06	.03	.00
☐ 556	Jack Morris AS	.10	.05	.01
☐ 557	Rich Gossage AS	.10	.05	.01
☐ 558	John Tudor AS	.30	.15	.03
☐ 559	Indians TL	.10	.05	.01
	Mgr. Dave Garcia			

Batting: Mike Hargrove
Pitching: Bert Blyleven

☐ 560	Doug Corbett	.06	.03	.00
☐ 561	Cardinals Rookies	.10	.05	.01
	Glenn Brummer			
	Luis DeLeon			
	Gene Roof			
☐ 562	Mike O'Berry	.06	.03	.00
☐ 563	Ross Baumgarten	.06	.03	.00
☐ 564	Doug DeCinces	.10	.05	.01
☐ 565	Jackson Todd	.06	.03	.00
☐ 566	Mike Jorgensen	.06	.03	.00
☐ 567	Bob Babcock	.06	.03	.00
☐ 568	Joe Pettini	.06	.03	.00
☐ 569	Willie Randolph	.10	.05	.01
☐ 570	SA: Willie Randolph	.06	.03	.00
☐ 571	Glenn Abbott	.06	.03	.00
☐ 572	Juan Beniquez	.06	.03	.00
☐ 573	Rick Waits	.06	.03	.00
☐ 574	Mike Ramsey	.06	.03	.00
☐ 575	Al Cowens	.06	.03	.00
☐ 576	Giants TL	.10	.05	.01
	Mgr. Frank Robinson			
	Batting: Milt May			
	Pitching: Vida Blue			
☐ 577	Rick Monday	.10	.05	.01
☐ 578	Shooty Babitt	.06	.03	.00
☐ 579	Rick Mahler	.30	.15	.03
☐ 580	Bobby Bonds	.15	.07	.01
☐ 581	Ron Reed	.06	.03	.00
☐ 582	Luis Pujols	.06	.03	.00
☐ 583	Tippy Martinez	.06	.03	.00
☐ 584	Hosken Powell	.06	.03	.00
☐ 585	Rollie Fingers	.25	.12	.02
☐ 586	SA: Rollie Fingers	.15	.07	.01
☐ 587	Tim Lollar	.06	.03	.00
☐ 588	Dale Berra	.06	.03	.00
☐ 589	Dave Stapleton	.06	.03	.00
☐ 590	Al Oliver	.15	.07	.01
☐ 591	SA: Al Oliver	.06	.03	.00
☐ 592	Craig Swan	.06	.03	.00
☐ 593	Billy Smith	.06	.03	.00
☐ 594	Renie Martin	.06	.03	.00
☐ 595	Dave Collins	.06	.03	.00
☐ 596	Damaso Garcia	.10	.05	.01
☐ 597	Wayne Nordhagen	.06	.03	.00
☐ 598	Bob Galasso	.06	.03	.00
☐ 599	White Sox Rookies	.10	.05	.01
	Jay Loviglio			
	Reggie Patterson			
	Leo Sutherland			
☐ 600	Dave Winfield	.75	.35	.07
☐ 601	Sid Monge	.06	.03	.00
☐ 602	Freddie Patek	.06	.03	.00
☐ 603	Rich Hebner	.06	.03	.00
☐ 604	Orlando Sanchez	.06	.03	.00
☐ 605	Steve Rogers	.06	.03	.00
☐ 606	Blue Jays TL	.10	.05	.01
	Mgr. Bobby Mattick			
	Batting: J.Mayberry			
	Pitching: Dave Stieb			
☐ 607	Leon Durham	.10	.05	.01
☐ 608	Jerry Royster	.06	.03	.00
☐ 609	Rick Sutcliffe	.25	.12	.02
☐ 610	Rickey Henderson	3.25	1.60	.32
☐ 611	Joe Niekro	.15	.07	.01
☐ 612	Gary Ward	.10	.05	.01
☐ 613	Jim Gantner	.06	.03	.00
☐ 614	Juan Eichelberger	.06	.03	.00
☐ 615	Bob Boone	.15	.07	.01
☐ 616	SA: Bob Boone	.10	.05	.01
☐ 617	Scott McGregor	.10	.05	.01
☐ 618	Tim Foli	.06	.03	.00
☐ 619	Bill Campbell	.06	.03	.00
☐ 620	Ken Griffey	.15	.07	.01
☐ 621	SA: Ken Griffey	.10	.05	.01
☐ 622	Dennis Lamp	.06	.03	.00
☐ 623	Mets Rookies	1.00	.50	.10
	Ron Gardenhire			
	Terry Leach			
	Tim Leary			
☐ 624	Fergie Jenkins	.20	.10	.02
☐ 625	Hal McRae	.10	.05	.01
☐ 626	Randy Jones	.06	.03	.00
☐ 627	Enos Cabell	.06	.03	.00
☐ 628	Bill Travers	.06	.03	.00
☐ 629	John Wockenfuss	.06	.03	.00
☐ 630	Joe Charboneau	.10	.05	.01
☐ 631	Gene Tenace	.06	.03	.00
☐ 632	Bryan Clark	.06	.03	.00
☐ 633	Mitchell Page	.06	.03	.00
☐ 634	Checklist 529-660	.10	.01	.00
☐ 635	Ron Davis	.06	.03	.00
☐ 636	Phillies TL	.35	.17	.03
	Mgr. Dallas Green			

Batting: Pete Rose
Pitching: S.Carlton

☐ 637	Rick Camp	.06	.03	.00
☐ 638	John Milner	.06	.03	.00
☐ 639	Ken Kravec	.06	.03	.00
☐ 640	Cesar Cedeno	.10	.05	.01
☐ 641	Steve Mura	.06	.03	.00
☐ 642	Mike Scioscia	.10	.05	.01
☐ 643	Pete Vuckovich	.10	.05	.01
☐ 644	John Castino	.06	.03	.00
☐ 645	Frank White	.10	.05	.01
☐ 646	SA: Frank White	.06	.03	.00
☐ 647	Warren Brusstar	.06	.03	.00
☐ 648	Jose Morales	.06	.03	.00
☐ 649	Ken Clay	.06	.03	.00
☐ 650	Carl Yastrzemski	1.50	.75	.15
☐ 651	SA: Carl Yastrzemski	.60	.30	.06
☐ 652	Steve Nicosia	.06	.03	.00
☐ 653	Angels Rookies	2.00	1.00	.20
	Tom Brunansky			
	Luis Sanchez			
	Daryl Sconiers			
☐ 654	Jim Morrison	.06	.03	.00
☐ 655	Joel Youngblood	.06	.03	.00
☐ 656	Eddie Whitson	.10	.05	.01
☐ 657	Tom Poquette	.06	.03	.00
☐ 658	Tito Landrum	.06	.03	.00
☐ 659	Fred Martinez	.06	.03	.00
☐ 660	Dave Concepcion	.15	.07	.01
☐ 661	SA: Dave Concepcion	.10	.05	.01
☐ 662	Luis Salazar	.10	.05	.01
☐ 663	Hector Cruz	.06	.03	.00
☐ 664	Dan Spillner	.06	.03	.00
☐ 665	Jim Clancy	.06	.03	.00
☐ 666	Tigers TL	.10	.05	.01
	Mgr. Sparky Anderson			
	Batting: Steve Kemp			
	Pitching: Dan Petry			
☐ 667	Jeff Reardon	.25	.10	.02
☐ 668	Dale Murphy	2.00	1.00	.20
☐ 669	Larry Milbourne	.06	.03	.00
☐ 670	Steve Kemp	.10	.05	.01
☐ 671	Mike Davis	.10	.05	.01
☐ 672	Bob Knepper	.10	.05	.01
☐ 673	Keith Drumwright	.06	.03	.00
☐ 674	Dave Goltz	.06	.03	.00
☐ 675	Cecil Cooper	.20	.10	.02
☐ 676	Sal Butera	.06	.03	.00
☐ 677	Alfredo Griffin	.10	.05	.01
☐ 678	Tom Paciorek	.06	.03	.00
☐ 679	Sammy Stewart	.06	.03	.00
☐ 680	Gary Matthews	.10	.05	.01
☐ 681	Dodgers Rookies	4.00	2.00	.40
	Mike Marshall			
	Ron Roenicke			
	Steve Sax			
☐ 682	Jesse Jefferson	.06	.03	.00
☐ 683	Phil Garner	.06	.03	.00
☐ 684	Harold Baines	.75	.35	.07
☐ 685	Bert Blyleven	.25	.12	.02
☐ 686	Gary Allenson	.06	.03	.00
☐ 687	Greg Minton	.06	.03	.00
☐ 688	Leon Roberts	.06	.03	.00
☐ 689	Lary Sorensen	.06	.03	.00
☐ 690	Dave Kingman	.20	.10	.02
☐ 691	Dan Schatzeder	.06	.03	.00
☐ 692	Wayne Gross	.06	.03	.00
☐ 693	Cesar Geronimo	.06	.03	.00
☐ 694	Dave Wehrmeister	.06	.03	.00
☐ 695	Warren Cromartie	.06	.03	.00
☐ 696	Pirates TL	.10	.05	.01
	Mgr. Chuck Tanner			
	Batting: Bill Madlock			
	Pitching:Eddie Solomon			
☐ 697	John Montefusco	.10	.05	.01
☐ 698	Tony Scott	.06	.03	.00
☐ 699	Dick Tidrow	.06	.03	.00
☐ 700	George Foster	.25	.12	.02
☐ 701	SA: George Foster	.10	.05	.01
☐ 702	Steve Renko	.06	.03	.00
☐ 703	Brewers TL	.10	.05	.01
	Mgr. Bob Rodgers			
	Batting: Cecil Cooper			
	Pitching: P.Vuckovich			
☐ 704	Mickey Rivers	.10	.05	.01
☐ 705	SA: Mickey Rivers	.06	.03	.00
☐ 706	Barry Foote	.06	.03	.00
☐ 707	Mark Bomback	.06	.03	.00
☐ 708	Gene Richards	.06	.03	.00
☐ 709	Don Money	.06	.03	.00
☐ 710	Jerry Reuss	.10	.05	.01
☐ 711	Mariners Rookies	1.00	.50	.10
	Dave Edler			
	Dave Henderson			
	Reggie Walton			

☐ 712	Dennis Martinez	.10	.05	.01
☐ 713	Del Unser	.06	.03	.00
☐ 714	Jerry Koosman	.15	.07	.01
☐ 715	Willie Stargell	.60	.30	.06
☐ 716	SA: Willie Stargell	.25	.12	.02
☐ 717	Rick Miller	.06	.03	.00
☐ 718	Charlie Hough	.10	.05	.01
☐ 719	Jerry Narron	.06	.03	.00
☐ 720	Greg Luzinski	.15	.07	.01
☐ 721	SA: Greg Luzinski	.10	.05	.01
☐ 722	Jerry Martin	.06	.03	.00
☐ 723	Junior Kennedy	.06	.03	.00
☐ 724	Dave Rosello	.06	.03	.00
☐ 725	Amos Otis	.10	.05	.01
☐ 726	SA: Amos Otis	.06	.03	.00
☐ 727	Sixto Lezcano	.06	.03	.00
☐ 728	Aurelio Lopez	.06	.03	.00
☐ 729	Jim Spencer	.06	.03	.00
☐ 730	Gary Carter	.75	.35	.07
☐ 731	Padres Rookies	.10	.05	.01
	Mike Armstrong			
	Doug Gwosdz			
	Fred Kuhaulua			
☐ 732	Mike Lum	.06	.03	.00
☐ 733	Larry McWilliams	.06	.03	.00
☐ 734	Mike Ivie	.06	.03	.00
☐ 735	Rudy May	.06	.03	.00
☐ 736	Jerry Turner	.06	.03	.00
☐ 737	Reggie Cleveland	.06	.03	.00
☐ 738	Dave Engle	.06	.03	.00
☐ 739	Joey McLaughlin	.06	.03	.00
☐ 740	Dave Lopes	.10	.05	.01
☐ 741	SA: Dave Lopes	.06	.03	.00
☐ 742	Dick Drago	.06	.03	.00
☐ 743	John Stearns	.06	.03	.00
☐ 744	Mike Witt	.90	.45	.09
☐ 745	Bake McBride	.06	.03	.00
☐ 746	Andre Thornton	.10	.05	.01
☐ 747	John Lowenstein	.06	.03	.00
☐ 748	Marc Hill	.06	.03	.00
☐ 749	Bob Shirley	.06	.03	.00
☐ 750	Jim Rice	.60	.30	.06
☐ 751	Rick Honeycutt	.06	.03	.00
☐ 752	Lee Lacy	.06	.03	.00
☐ 753	Tom Brookens	.06	.03	.00
☐ 754	Joe Morgan	.50	.25	.05
☐ 755	SA: Joe Morgan	.20	.10	.02
☐ 756	Reds TL	.20	.10	.02
	Mgr. John McNamara			
	Batting: Ken Griffey			
	Pitching: Tom Seaver			
☐ 757	Tom Underwood	.06	.03	.00
☐ 758	Claudell Washington	.10	.05	.01
☐ 759	Paul Splittorff	.06	.03	.00
☐ 760	Bill Buckner	.15	.07	.01
☐ 761	Dave Smith	.10	.05	.01
☐ 762	Mike Phillips	.06	.03	.00
☐ 763	Tom Hume	.06	.03	.00
☐ 764	Steve Swisher	.06	.03	.00
☐ 765	Gorman Thomas	.15	.07	.01
☐ 766	Twins Rookies	4.50	2.25	.45
	Lenny Faedo			
	Kent Hrbek			
	Tim Laudner			
☐ 767	Roy Smalley	.06	.03	.00
☐ 768	Jerry Garvin	.06	.03	.00
☐ 769	Richie Zisk	.10	.05	.01
☐ 770	Rich Gossage	.25	.12	.02
☐ 771	SA: Rich Gossage	.10	.05	.01
☐ 772	Bert Campaneris	.10	.05	.01
☐ 773	John Denny	.10	.05	.01
☐ 774	Jay Johnstone	.10	.05	.01
☐ 775	Bob Forsch	.06	.03	.00
☐ 776	Mark Belanger	.10	.05	.01
☐ 777	Tom Griffin	.06	.03	.00
☐ 778	Kevin Hickey	.06	.03	.00
☐ 779	Grant Jackson	.06	.03	.00
☐ 780	Pete Rose	2.25	1.10	.22
☐ 781	SA: Pete Rose	.75	.35	.07
☐ 782	Frank Taveras	.06	.03	.00
☐ 783	Greg Harris	.20	.10	.02
☐ 784	Milt Wilcox	.06	.03	.00
☐ 785	Dan Driessen	.06	.03	.00
☐ 786	Red Sox TL	.10	.05	.01
	Mgr. Ralph Houk			
	Batting: C.Lansford			
	Pitching: Mike Torrez			
☐ 787	Fred Stanley	.06	.03	.00
☐ 788	Woodie Fryman	.06	.03	.00
☐ 789	Checklist 661-792	.10	.01	.00
☐ 790	Larry Gura	.06	.03	.00
☐ 791	Bobby Brown	.06	.03	.00
☐ 792	Frank Tanana	.15	.07	.01

1982 Topps Traded

The cards in this 132-card set measure 2 1/2" by 3 1/2". The 1982 Topps Traded or extended series is distinguished by a "T" printed after the number (located on the reverse). Of the total cards, 70 players represent the American League and 61 represent the National League, with the remaining card a numbered checklist (132T). The Cubs lead the pack with 12 changes, while the Red Sox are the only team in either league to have no new additions. All 131 player photos used in the set are completely new. Of this total, 112 individuals are seen in the uniform of their new team, 11 others have been elevated to single card status from "Future Stars" cards, and eight more are entirely new to the 1982 Topps lineup. The backs are almost completely red in color with black print.

		MINT	EXC	G-VG
COMPLETE SET (132)		30.00	15.00	3.00
COMMON PLAYER (1-132)		.08	.04	.01
☐	1T Doyle Alexander	.15	.07	.01
☐	2T Jesse Barfield	2.00	1.00	.20
☐	3T Ross Baumgarten	.08	.04	.01
☐	4T Steve Bedrosian	.75	.35	.07
☐	5T Mark Belanger	.15	.07	.01
☐	6T Kurt Bevacqua	.08	.04	.01
☐	7T Tim Blackwell	.08	.04	.01
☐	8T Vida Blue	.15	.07	.01
☐	9T Bob Boone	.35	.17	.03
☐	10T Larry Bowa	.20	.10	.02
☐	11T Dan Briggs	.08	.04	.01
☐	12T Bobby Brown	.08	.04	.01
☐	13T Tom Brunansky	1.50	.75	.15
☐	14T Jeff Burroughs	.15	.07	.01
☐	15T Enos Cabell	.08	.04	.01
☐	16T Bill Campbell	.08	.04	.01
☐	17T Bobby Castillo	.08	.04	.01
☐	18T Bill Caudill	.08	.04	.01
☐	19T Cesar Cedeno	.20	.10	.02
☐	20T Dave Collins	.08	.04	.01
☐	21T Doug Corbett	.08	.04	.01
☐	22T Al Cowens	.08	.04	.01
☐	23T Chili Davis	1.25	.60	.12
☐	24T Dick Davis	.08	.04	.01
☐	25T Ron Davis	.08	.04	.01
☐	26T Doug DeCinces	.20	.10	.02
☐	27T Ivan DeJesus	.08	.04	.01
☐	28T Bob Dernier	.15	.07	.01
☐	29T Bo Diaz	.15	.07	.01
☐	30T Roger Erickson	.08	.04	.01
☐	31T Jim Essian	.08	.04	.01
☐	32T Ed Farmer	.08	.04	.01
☐	33T Doug Flynn	.08	.04	.01
☐	34T Tim Foli	.08	.04	.01
☐	35T Dan Ford	.08	.04	.01
☐	36T George Foster	.40	.20	.04
☐	37T Dave Frost	.08	.04	.01
☐	38T Rich Gale	.08	.04	.01
☐	39T Ron Gardenhire	.15	.07	.01
☐	40T Ken Griffey	.25	.12	.02
☐	41T Greg Harris	.15	.07	.01
☐	42T Von Hayes	1.25	.60	.12
☐	43T Larry Herndon	.08	.04	.01
☐	44T Kent Hrbek	5.00	2.50	.50

☐ 45T	Mike Ivie	.08	.04	.01
☐ 46T	Grant Jackson	.08	.04	.01
☐ 47T	Reggie Jackson	3.00	1.50	.30
☐ 48T	Ron Jackson	.08	.04	.01
☐ 49T	Fergie Jenkins	.40	.20	.04
☐ 50T	Lamar Johnson	.08	.04	.01
☐ 51T	Randy Johnson	.08	.04	.01
☐ 52T	Jay Johnstone	.20	.10	.02
☐ 53T	Mick Kelleher	.08	.04	.01
☐ 54T	Steve Kemp	.15	.07	.01
☐ 55T	Junior Kennedy	.08	.04	.01
☐ 56T	Jim Kern	.08	.04	.01
☐ 57T	Ray Knight	.25	.12	.02
☐ 58T	Wayne Krenchicki	.08	.04	.01
☐ 59T	Mike Krukow	.15	.07	.01
☐ 60T	Duane Kuiper	.08	.04	.01
☐ 61T	Mike LaCoss	.08	.04	.01
☐ 62T	Chet Lemon	.15	.07	.01
☐ 63T	Sixto Lezcano	.08	.04	.01
☐ 64T	Dave Lopes	.20	.10	.02
☐ 65T	Jerry Martin	.08	.04	.01
☐ 66T	Renie Martin	.08	.04	.01
☐ 67T	John Mayberry	.15	.07	.01
☐ 68T	Lee Mazzilli	.08	.04	.01
☐ 69T	Bake McBride	.08	.04	.01
☐ 70T	Dan Meyer	.08	.04	.01
☐ 71T	Larry Milbourne	.08	.04	.01
☐ 72T	Eddie Milner	.15	.07	.01
☐ 73T	Sid Monge	.08	.04	.01
☐ 74T	John Montefusco	.15	.07	.01
☐ 75T	Jose Morales	.08	.04	.01
☐ 76T	Keith Moreland	.15	.07	.01
☐ 77T	Jim Morrison	.08	.04	.01
☐ 78T	Rance Mulliniks	.08	.04	.01
☐ 79T	Steve Mura	.08	.04	.01
☐ 80T	Gene Nelson	.15	.07	.01
☐ 81T	Joe Nolan	.08	.04	.01
☐ 82T	Dickie Noles	.08	.04	.01
☐ 83T	Al Oliver	.20	.10	.02
☐ 84T	Jorge Orta	.08	.04	.01
☐ 85T	Tom Paciorek	.08	.04	.01
☐ 86T	Larry Parrish	.15	.07	.01
☐ 87T	Jack Perconte	.08	.04	.01
☐ 88T	Gaylord Perry	1.00	.50	.10
☐ 89T	Rob Picciolo	.08	.04	.01
☐ 90T	Joe Pittman	.08	.04	.01
☐ 91T	Hosken Powell	.08	.04	.01
☐ 92T	Mike Proly	.08	.04	.01
☐ 93T	Greg Pryor	.08	.04	.01
☐ 94T	Charlie Puleo	.15	.07	.01
☐ 95T	Shane Rawley	.15	.07	.01
☐ 96T	Johnny Ray	1.00	.50	.10
☐ 97T	Dave Revering	.08	.04	.01
☐ 98T	Cal Ripken	11.00	5.50	1.10
☐ 99T	Allen Ripley	.08	.04	.01
☐ 100T	Bill Robinson	.15	.07	.01
☐ 101T	Aurelio Rodriguez	.08	.04	.01
☐ 102T	Joe Rudi	.15	.07	.01
☐ 103T	Steve Sax	4.00	2.00	.40
☐ 104T	Dan Schatzeder	.08	.04	.01
☐ 105T	Bob Shirley	.08	.04	.01
☐ 106T	Eric Show	1.00	.50	.10
☐ 107T	Roy Smalley	.15	.07	.01
☐ 108T	Lonnie Smith	.25	.12	.02
☐ 109T	Ozzie Smith	4.50	2.25	.45
☐ 110T	Reggie Smith	.20	.10	.02
☐ 111T	Lary Sorensen	.08	.04	.01
☐ 112T	Elias Sosa	.08	.04	.01
☐ 113T	Mike Stanton	.08	.04	.01
☐ 114T	Steve Strougher	.08	.04	.01
☐ 115T	Champ Summers	.08	.04	.01
☐ 116T	Rick Sutcliffe	.45	.22	.04
☐ 117T	Frank Tanana	.15	.07	.01
☐ 118T	Frank Taveras	.08	.04	.01
☐ 119T	Garry Templeton	.15	.07	.01
☐ 120T	Alex Trevino	.08	.04	.01
☐ 121T	Jerry Turner	.08	.04	.01
☐ 122T	Ed VandeBerg	.15	.07	.01
☐ 123T	Tom Veryzer	.08	.04	.01
☐ 124T	Ron Washington	.15	.07	.01
☐ 125T	Bob Watson	.15	.07	.01
☐ 126T	Dennis Werth	.08	.04	.01
☐ 127T	Eddie Whitson	.15	.07	.01
☐ 128T	Rob Wilfong	.08	.04	.01
☐ 129T	Bump Wills	.08	.04	.01
☐ 130T	Gary Woods	.08	.04	.01
☐ 131T	Butch Wynegar	.15	.07	.01
☐ 132T	Checklist: 1-132	.08	.01	.00

1983 Topps

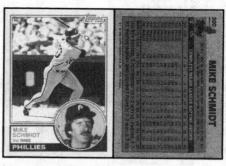

The cards in this 792-card set measure 2 1/2" by 3 1/2". Each regular card of the Topps set for 1983 features a large action shot of a player with a small cameo portrait at bottom right. There are special series for AL and NL All Stars (386-407), League Leaders (701-708) and Record Breakers (1-6). In addition, there are 34 "Super Veteran" (SV) cards and six numbered checklist cards. The Super Veteran cards are oriented horizontally and show two pictures of the featured player, a recent picture and a picture showing the player as a rookie when he broke in. The cards are numbered on the reverse at the upper left corner. The team cards are actually Team Leader (TL) cards picturing the batting and pitching leader for that team with a checklist back.

		MINT	EXC	G-VG
COMPLETE SET (792)		100.00	50.00	10.00
COMMON PLAYER (1-792)		.06	.03	.00
☐ 1	RB: Tony Armas 11 putouts by rightfielder	.12	.03	.01
☐ 2	RB: Rickey Henderson Sets modern record for steals, season	.35	.17	.03
☐ 3	RB: Greg Minton 269 1/3 homerless innings streak	.10	.05	.01
☐ 4	RB: Lance Parrish Threw out three baserunners in All-Star game	.15	.07	.01
☐ 5	RB: Manny Trillo 479 consecutive errorless chances, second baseman	.10	.05	.01
☐ 6	RB: John Wathan ML steals record for catchers, 31	.10	.05	.01
☐ 7	Gene Richards	.06	.03	.00
☐ 8	Steve Balboni	.10	.05	.01
☐ 9	Joey McLaughlin	.06	.03	.00
☐ 10	Gorman Thomas	.15	.07	.01
☐ 11	Billy Gardner MG	.06	.03	.00
☐ 12	Paul Mirabella	.06	.03	.00
☐ 13	Larry Herndon	.06	.03	.00
☐ 14	Frank LaCorte	.06	.03	.00
☐ 15	Ron Cey	.15	.07	.01
☐ 16	George Vukovich	.06	.03	.00
☐ 17	Kent Tekulve	.10	.05	.01
☐ 18	SV: Kent Tekulve	.06	.03	.00
☐ 19	Oscar Gamble	.06	.03	.00
☐ 20	Carlton Fisk	.35	.17	.03
☐ 21	Baltimore Orioles TL BA: Eddie Murray ERA: Jim Palmer	.30	.15	.03
☐ 22	Randy Martz	.06	.03	.00
☐ 23	Mike Heath	.06	.03	.00
☐ 24	Steve Mura	.06	.03	.00
☐ 25	Hal McRae	.10	.05	.01
☐ 26	Jerry Royster	.06	.03	.00
☐ 27	Doug Corbett	.06	.03	.00
☐ 28	Bruce Bochte	.06	.03	.00
☐ 29	Randy Jones	.06	.03	.00
☐ 30	Jim Rice	.35	.17	.03

☐	31	Bill Gullickson	.10	.05	.01	☐ 119	Tom Brookens	.06	.03	.00
☐	32	Dave Bergman	.06	.03	.00	☐ 120	Len Barker	.06	.03	.00
☐	33	Jack O'Connor	.06	.03	.00	☐ 121	Mickey Hatcher	.10	.05	.01
☐	34	Paul Householder	.06	.03	.00	☐ 122	Jimmy Smith	.06	.03	.00
☐	35	Rollie Fingers	.30	.15	.03	☐ 123	George Frazier	.06	.03	.00
☐	36	SV: Rollie Fingers	.15	.07	.01	☐ 124	Marc Hill	.06	.03	.00
☐	37	Darrell Johnson MG	.06	.03	.00	☐ 125	Leon Durham	.10	.05	.01
☐	38	Tim Flannery	.06	.03	.00	☐ 126	Joe Torre MG	.10	.05	.01
☐	39	Terry Puhl	.06	.03	.00	☐ 127	Preston Hanna	.06	.03	.00
☐	40	Fernando Valenzuela	.45	.22	.04	☐ 128	Mike Ramsey	.06	.03	.00
☐	41	Jerry Turner	.06	.03	.00	☐ 129	Checklist: 1-132	.10	.01	.00
☐	42	Dale Murray	.06	.03	.00	☐ 130	Dave Stieb	.20	.10	.02
☐	43	Bob Dernier	.06	.03	.00	☐ 131	Ed Ott	.06	.03	.00
☐	44	Don Robinson	.06	.03	.00	☐ 132	Todd Cruz	.06	.03	.00
☐	45	John Mayberry	.10	.05	.01	☐ 133	Jim Barr	.06	.03	.00
☐	46	Richard Dotson	.10	.05	.01	☐ 134	Hubie Brooks	.15	.07	.01
☐	47	Dave McKay	.06	.03	.00	☐ 135	Dwight Evans	.20	.10	.02
☐	48	Lary Sorensen	.06	.03	.00	☐ 136	Willie Aikens	.06	.03	.00
☐	49	Willie McGee	1.75	.85	.17	☐ 137	Woodie Fryman	.06	.03	.00
☐	50	Bob Horner	.20	.10	.02	☐ 138	Rick Dempsey	.06	.03	.00
		('82 RBI total 7)				☐ 139	Bruce Berenyi	.06	.03	.00
☐	51	Chicago Cubs TL	.15	.07	.01	☐ 140	Willie Randolph	.10	.05	.01
		BA: Leon Durham				☐ 141	Indians TL	.10	.05	.01
		ERA: Fergie Jenkins					BA: Toby Harrah			
☐	52	Onix Concepcion	.06	.03	.00		ERA: Rick Sutcliffe			
☐	53	Mike Witt	.20	.10	.02	☐ 142	Mike Caldwell	.06	.03	.00
☐	54	Jim Maler	.06	.03	.00	☐ 143	Joe Pettini	.06	.03	.00
☐	55	Mookie Wilson	.15	.07	.01	☐ 144	Mark Wagner	.06	.03	.00
☐	56	Chuck Rainey	.06	.03	.00	☐ 145	Don Sutton	.40	.20	.04
☐	57	Tim Blackwell	.06	.03	.00	☐ 146	SV: Don Sutton	.20	.10	.02
☐	58	Al Holland	.06	.03	.00	☐ 147	Rick Leach	.06	.03	.00
☐	59	Benny Ayala	.06	.03	.00	☐ 148	Dave Roberts	.06	.03	.00
☐	60	Johnny Bench	.75	.35	.07	☐ 149	Johnny Ray	.15	.07	.01
☐	61	SV: Johnny Bench	.35	.17	.03	☐ 150	Bruce Sutter	.15	.07	.01
☐	62	Bob McClure	.06	.03	.00	☐ 151	SV: Bruce Sutter	.10	.05	.01
☐	63	Rick Monday	.10	.05	.01	☐ 152	Jay Johnstone	.10	.05	.01
☐	64	Bill Stein	.06	.03	.00	☐ 153	Jerry Koosman	.10	.05	.01
☐	65	Jack Morris	.30	.15	.03	☐ 154	Johnnie LeMaster	.06	.03	.00
☐	66	Bob Lillis MG	.06	.03	.00	☐ 155	Dan Quisenberry	.15	.07	.01
☐	67	Sal Butera	.06	.03	.00	☐ 156	Billy Martin MG	.15	.07	.01
☐	68	Eric Show	.40	.20	.04	☐ 157	Steve Bedrosian	.25	.12	.02
☐	69	Lee Lacy	.06	.03	.00	☐ 158	Rob Wilfong	.06	.03	.00
☐	70	Steve Carlton	.55	.27	.05	☐ 159	Mike Stanton	.06	.03	.00
☐	71	SV: Steve Carlton	.25	.12	.02	☐ 160	Dave Kingman	.15	.07	.01
☐	72	Tom Paciorek	.06	.03	.00	☐ 161	SV: Dave Kingman	.10	.05	.01
☐	73	Allen Ripley	.06	.03	.00	☐ 162	Mark Clear	.06	.03	.00
☐	74	Julio Gonzalez	.06	.03	.00	☐ 163	Cal Ripken	2.50	1.25	.25
☐	75	Amos Otis	.10	.05	.01	☐ 164	David Palmer	.06	.03	.00
☐	76	Rick Mahler	.06	.03	.00	☐ 165	Dan Driessen	.06	.03	.00
☐	77	Hosken Powell	.06	.03	.00	☐ 166	John Pacella	.06	.03	.00
☐	78	Bill Caudill	.06	.03	.00	☐ 167	Mark Brouhard	.06	.03	.00
☐	79	Mick Kelleher	.06	.03	.00	☐ 168	Juan Eichelberger	.06	.03	.00
☐	80	George Foster	.20	.10	.02	☐ 169	Doug Flynn	.06	.03	.00
☐	81	Yankees TL	.15	.07	.01	☐ 170	Steve Howe	.06	.03	.00
		BA: Jerry Mumphrey				☐ 171	Giants TL	.15	.07	.01
		ERA: Dave Righetti					BA: Joe Morgan			
☐	82	Bruce Hurst	.35	.17	.03		ERA: Bill Laskey			
☐	83	Ryne Sandberg	11.00	5.00	1.00	☐ 172	Vern Ruhle	.06	.03	.00
☐	84	Milt May	.06	.03	.00	☐ 173	Jim Morrison	.06	.03	.00
☐	85	Ken Singleton	.10	.05	.01	☐ 174	Jerry Ujdur	.06	.03	.00
☐	86	Tom Hume	.06	.03	.00	☐ 175	Bo Diaz	.06	.03	.00
☐	87	Joe Rudi	.10	.05	.01	☐ 176	Dave Righetti	.35	.17	.03
☐	88	Jim Gantner	.06	.03	.00	☐ 177	Harold Baines	.35	.17	.03
☐	89	Leon Roberts	.06	.03	.00	☐ 178	Luis Tiant	.10	.05	.01
☐	90	Jerry Reuss	.10	.05	.01	☐ 179	SV: Luis Tiant	.06	.03	.00
☐	91	Larry Milbourne	.06	.03	.00	☐ 180	Rickey Henderson	1.75	.85	.17
☐	92	Mike LaCoss	.06	.03	.00	☐ 181	Terry Felton	.06	.03	.00
☐	93	John Castino	.06	.03	.00	☐ 182	Mike Fischlin	.06	.03	.00
☐	94	Dave Edwards	.06	.03	.00	☐ 183	Ed VandeBerg	.10	.05	.01
☐	95	Alan Trammell	.40	.20	.04	☐ 184	Bob Clark	.06	.03	.00
☐	96	Dick Howser MG	.10	.05	.01	☐ 185	Tim Lollar	.06	.03	.00
☐	97	Ross Baumgarten	.06	.03	.00	☐ 186	Whitey Herzog MG	.06	.03	.00
☐	98	Vance Law	.15	.07	.01	☐ 187	Terry Leach	.15	.07	.01
☐	99	Dickie Noles	.06	.03	.00	☐ 188	Rick Miller	.06	.03	.00
☐	100	Pete Rose	2.00	1.00	.20	☐ 189	Dan Schatzeder	.06	.03	.00
☐	101	SV: Pete Rose	.75	.35	.07	☐ 190	Cecil Cooper	.15	.07	.01
☐	102	Dave Beard	.06	.03	.00	☐ 191	Joe Price	.06	.03	.00
☐	103	Darrell Porter	.06	.03	.00	☐ 192	Floyd Rayford	.06	.03	.00
☐	104	Bob Walk	.10	.05	.01	☐ 193	Harry Spilman	.06	.03	.00
☐	105	Don Baylor	.15	.07	.01	☐ 194	Cesar Geronimo	.06	.03	.00
☐	106	Gene Nelson	.06	.03	.00	☐ 195	Bob Stoddard	.06	.03	.00
☐	107	Mike Jorgensen	.06	.03	.00	☐ 196	Bill Fahey	.06	.03	.00
☐	108	Glenn Hoffman	.06	.03	.00	☐ 197	Jim Eisenreich	.75	.35	.07
☐	109	Luis Leal	.06	.03	.00	☐ 198	Kiko Garcia	.06	.03	.00
☐	110	Ken Griffey	.15	.07	.01	☐ 199	Marty Bystrom	.06	.03	.00
☐	111	Montreal Expos TL	.10	.05	.01	☐ 200	Rod Carew	.75	.30	.06
		BA: Al Oliver				☐ 201	SV: Rod Carew	.25	.12	.02
		ERA: Steve Rogers				☐ 202	Blue Jays TL	.10	.05	.01
☐	112	Bob Shirley	.06	.03	.00		BA: Damaso Garcia			
☐	113	Ron Roenicke	.06	.03	.00		ERA: Dave Stieb			
☐	114	Jim Slaton	.06	.03	.00	☐ 203	Mike Morgan	.10	.05	.01
☐	115	Chili Davis	.15	.07	.01	☐ 204	Junior Kennedy	.06	.03	.00
☐	116	Dave Schmidt	.10	.05	.01	☐ 205	Dave Parker	.25	.12	.02
☐	117	Alan Knicely	.06	.03	.00	☐ 206	Ken Oberkfell	.06	.03	.00
☐	118	Chris Welsh	.06	.03	.00	☐ 207	Rick Camp	.06	.03	.00

☐ 208	Dan Meyer	.06	.03	.00
☐ 209	Mike Moore	2.00	1.00	.20
☐ 210	Jack Clark	.35	.17	.03
☐ 211	John Denny	.10	.05	.01
☐ 212	John Stearns	.06	.03	.00
☐ 213	Tom Burgmeier	.06	.03	.00
☐ 214	Jerry White	.06	.03	.00
☐ 215	Mario Soto	.10	.05	.01
☐ 216	Tony LaRussa MG	.10	.05	.01
☐ 217	Tim Stoddard	.06	.03	.00
☐ 218	Roy Howell	.06	.03	.00
☐ 219	Mike Armstrong	.06	.03	.00
☐ 220	Dusty Baker	.10	.05	.01
☐ 221	Joe Niekro	.10	.05	.01
☐ 222	Damaso Garcia	.06	.03	.00
☐ 223	John Montefusco	.06	.03	.00
☐ 224	Mickey Rivers	.10	.05	.01
☐ 225	Enos Cabell	.06	.03	.00
☐ 226	Enrique Romo	.06	.03	.00
☐ 227	Chris Bando	.06	.03	.00
☐ 228	Joaquin Andujar	.10	.05	.01
☐ 229	Phillies TL BA: Bo Diaz ERA: Steve Carlton	.15	.07	.01
☐ 230	Fergie Jenkins	.15	.07	.01
☐ 231	SV: Fergie Jenkins	.10	.05	.01
☐ 232	Tom Brunansky	.40	.20	.04
☐ 233	Wayne Gross	.06	.03	.00
☐ 234	Larry Andersen	.06	.03	.00
☐ 235	Claudell Washington	.10	.05	.01
☐ 236	Steve Renko	.06	.03	.00
☐ 237	Dan Norman	.06	.03	.00
☐ 238	Bud Black	.25	.12	.02
☐ 239	Dave Stapleton	.06	.03	.00
☐ 240	Rich Gossage	.25	.12	.02
☐ 241	SV: Rich Gossage	.10	.05	.01
☐ 242	Joe Nolan	.06	.03	.00
☐ 243	Duane Walker	.06	.03	.00
☐ 244	Dwight Bernard	.06	.03	.00
☐ 245	Steve Sax	.65	.30	.06
☐ 246	George Bamberger MG	.06	.03	.00
☐ 247	Dave Smith	.10	.05	.01
☐ 248	Bake McBride	.06	.03	.00
☐ 249	Checklist: 133-264	.10	.01	.00
☐ 250	Bill Buckner	.15	.07	.01
☐ 251	Alan Wiggins	.15	.07	.01
☐ 252	Luis Aguayo	.06	.03	.00
☐ 253	Larry McWilliams	.06	.03	.00
☐ 254	Rick Cerone	.06	.03	.00
☐ 255	Gene Garber	.06	.03	.00
☐ 256	SV: Gene Garber	.06	.03	.00
☐ 257	Jesse Barfield	.60	.30	.06
☐ 258	Manny Castillo	.06	.03	.00
☐ 259	Jeff Jones	.06	.03	.00
☐ 260	Steve Kemp	.10	.05	.01
☐ 261	Tigers TL BA: Larry Herndon ERA: Dan Petry	.10	.05	.01
☐ 262	Ron Jackson	.06	.03	.00
☐ 263	Renie Martin	.06	.03	.00
☐ 264	Jamie Quirk	.06	.03	.00
☐ 265	Joel Youngblood	.06	.03	.00
☐ 266	Paul Boris	.06	.03	.00
☐ 267	Terry Francona	.06	.03	.00
☐ 268	Storm Davis	1.00	.50	.10
☐ 269	Ron Oester	.06	.03	.00
☐ 270	Dennis Eckersley	.25	.12	.02
☐ 271	Ed Romero	.06	.03	.00
☐ 272	Frank Tanana	.10	.05	.01
☐ 273	Mark Belanger	.10	.05	.01
☐ 274	Terry Kennedy	.06	.03	.00
☐ 275	Ray Knight	.10	.05	.01
☐ 276	Gene Mauch MG	.06	.03	.00
☐ 277	Rance Mulliniks	.06	.03	.00
☐ 278	Kevin Hickey	.06	.03	.00
☐ 279	Greg Gross	.06	.03	.00
☐ 280	Bert Blyleven	.20	.10	.02
☐ 281	Andre Robertson	.06	.03	.00
☐ 282	Reggie Smith (Ryne Sandberg ducking back)	.15	.07	.01
☐ 283	SV: Reggie Smith	.06	.03	.00
☐ 284	Jeff Lahti	.06	.03	.00
☐ 285	Lance Parrish	.30	.15	.03
☐ 286	Rick Langford	.06	.03	.00
☐ 287	Bobby Brown	.06	.03	.00
☐ 288	Joe Cowley	.10	.05	.01
☐ 289	Jerry Dybzinski	.06	.03	.00
☐ 290	Jeff Reardon	.20	.10	.02
☐ 291	Pirates TL BA: Bill Madlock ERA: John Candelaria	.10	.05	.01
☐ 292	Craig Swan	.06	.03	.00
☐ 293	Glenn Gulliver	.06	.03	.00
☐ 294	Dave Engle	.06	.03	.00
☐ 295	Jerry Remy	.06	.03	.00
☐ 296	Greg Harris	.06	.03	.00
☐ 297	Ned Yost	.06	.03	.00
☐ 298	Floyd Chiffer	.06	.03	.00
☐ 299	George Wright	.06	.03	.00
☐ 300	Mike Schmidt	1.50	.75	.15
☐ 301	SV: Mike Schmidt	.60	.30	.06
☐ 302	Ernie Whitt	.10	.05	.01
☐ 303	Miguel Dilone	.06	.03	.00
☐ 304	Dave Rucker	.06	.03	.00
☐ 305	Larry Bowa	.10	.05	.01
☐ 306	Tom Lasorda MG	.10	.05	.01
☐ 307	Lou Piniella	.10	.05	.01
☐ 308	Jesus Vega	.06	.03	.00
☐ 309	Jeff Leonard	.10	.05	.01
☐ 310	Greg Luzinski	.10	.05	.01
☐ 311	Glenn Brummer	.06	.03	.00
☐ 312	Brian Kingman	.06	.03	.00
☐ 313	Gary Gray	.06	.03	.00
☐ 314	Ken Dayley	.10	.05	.01
☐ 315	Rick Burleson	.10	.05	.01
☐ 316	Paul Splittorff	.06	.03	.00
☐ 317	Gary Rajsich	.06	.03	.00
☐ 318	John Tudor	.30	.15	.03
☐ 319	Lenn Sakata	.06	.03	.00
☐ 320	Steve Rogers	.06	.03	.00
☐ 321	Brewers TL BA: Robin Yount ERA: Pete Vuckovich	.15	.07	.01
☐ 322	Dave Van Gorder	.06	.03	.00
☐ 323	Luis DeLeon	.06	.03	.00
☐ 324	Mike Marshall	.30	.15	.03
☐ 325	Von Hayes	.30	.15	.03
☐ 326	Garth Iorg	.06	.03	.00
☐ 327	Bobby Castillo	.06	.03	.00
☐ 328	Craig Reynolds	.06	.03	.00
☐ 329	Randy Niemann	.06	.03	.00
☐ 330	Buddy Bell	.15	.07	.01
☐ 331	Mike Krukow	.10	.05	.01
☐ 332	Glenn Wilson	.45	.22	.04
☐ 333	Dave LaRoche	.06	.03	.00
☐ 334	SV: Dave LaRoche	.06	.03	.00
☐ 335	Steve Henderson	.06	.03	.00
☐ 336	Rene Lachemann MG	.06	.03	.00
☐ 337	Tito Landrum	.06	.03	.00
☐ 338	Bob Owchinko	.06	.03	.00
☐ 339	Terry Harper	.06	.03	.00
☐ 340	Larry Gura	.06	.03	.00
☐ 341	Doug DeCinces	.10	.05	.01
☐ 342	Atlee Hammaker	.10	.05	.01
☐ 343	Bob Bailor	.06	.03	.00
☐ 344	Roger LaFrancois	.06	.03	.00
☐ 345	Jim Clancy	.06	.03	.00
☐ 346	Joe Pittman	.06	.03	.00
☐ 347	Sammy Stewart	.06	.03	.00
☐ 348	Alan Bannister	.06	.03	.00
☐ 349	Checklist: 265-396	.10	.01	.00
☐ 350	Robin Yount	1.00	.50	.10
☐ 351	Reds TL BA: Cesar Cedeno ERA: Mario Soto	.10	.05	.01
☐ 352	Mike Scioscia	.10	.05	.01
☐ 353	Steve Comer	.06	.03	.00
☐ 354	Randy Johnson	.06	.03	.00
☐ 355	Jim Bibby	.06	.03	.00
☐ 356	Gary Woods	.06	.03	.00
☐ 357	Len Matuszek	.06	.03	.00
☐ 358	Jerry Garvin	.06	.03	.00
☐ 359	Dave Collins	.06	.03	.00
☐ 360	Nolan Ryan	2.00	1.00	.20
☐ 361	SV: Nolan Ryan	.75	.35	.07
☐ 362	Bill Almon	.06	.03	.00
☐ 363	John Stuper	.06	.03	.00
☐ 364	Brett Butler	.10	.05	.01
☐ 365	Dave Lopes	.10	.05	.01
☐ 366	Dick Williams MG	.06	.03	.00
☐ 367	Bud Anderson	.06	.03	.00
☐ 368	Richie Zisk	.06	.03	.00
☐ 369	Jesse Orosco	.06	.03	.00
☐ 370	Gary Carter	.50	.25	.05
☐ 371	Mike Richardt	.06	.03	.00
☐ 372	Terry Crowley	.06	.03	.00
☐ 373	Kevin Saucier	.06	.03	.00
☐ 374	Wayne Krenchicki	.06	.03	.00
☐ 375	Pete Vuckovich	.10	.05	.01
☐ 376	Ken Landreaux	.06	.03	.00
☐ 377	Lee May	.10	.05	.01
☐ 378	SV: Lee May	.06	.03	.00
☐ 379	Guy Sularz	.06	.03	.00
☐ 380	Ron Davis	.06	.03	.00
☐ 381	Red Sox TL BA: Jim Rice ERA: Bob Stanley	.15	.07	.01
☐ 382	Bob Knepper	.10	.05	.01
☐ 383	Ozzie Virgil	.06	.03	.00

□ 384	Dave Dravecky	1.00	.50	.10
□ 385	Mike Easler	.10	.05	.01
□ 386	Rod Carew AS	.20	.10	.02
□ 387	Bob Grich AS	.10	.05	.01
□ 388	George Brett AS	.30	.15	.03
□ 389	Robin Yount AS	.30	.15	.03
□ 390	Reggie Jackson AS	.30	.15	.03
□ 391	Rickey Henderson AS	.40	.20	.04
□ 392	Fred Lynn AS	.10	.05	.01
□ 393	Carlton Fisk AS	.15	.07	.01
□ 394	Pete Vuckovich AS	.06	.03	.00
□ 395	Larry Gura AS	.06	.03	.00
□ 396	Dan Quisenberry AS	.10	.05	.01
□ 397	Pete Rose AS	.50	.25	.05
□ 398	Manny Trillo AS	.06	.03	.00
□ 399	Mike Schmidt AS	.40	.20	.04
□ 400	Dave Concepcion AS	.06	.03	.00
□ 401	Dale Murphy AS	.35	.17	.03
□ 402	Andre Dawson AS	.20	.10	.02
□ 403	Tim Raines AS	.20	.10	.02
□ 404	Gary Carter AS	.20	.10	.02
□ 405	Steve Rogers AS	.06	.03	.00
□ 406	Steve Carlton AS	.20	.10	.02
□ 407	Bruce Sutter AS	.10	.05	.01
□ 408	Rudy May	.06	.03	.00
□ 409	Marvis Foley	.06	.03	.00
□ 410	Phil Niekro	.35	.17	.03
□ 411	SV: Phil Niekro	.15	.07	.01
□ 412	Rangers TL	.10	.05	.01
	BA: Buddy Bell			
	ERA: Charlie Hough			
□ 413	Matt Keough	.06	.03	.00
□ 414	Julio Cruz	.06	.03	.00
□ 415	Bob Forsch	.06	.03	.00
□ 416	Joe Ferguson	.06	.03	.00
□ 417	Tom Hausman	.06	.03	.00
□ 418	Greg Pryor	.06	.03	.00
□ 419	Steve Crawford	.06	.03	.00
□ 420	Al Oliver	.10	.05	.01
□ 421	SV: Al Oliver	.06	.03	.00
□ 422	George Cappuzzello	.06	.03	.00
□ 423	Tom Lawless	.10	.05	.01
□ 424	Jerry Augustine	.06	.03	.00
□ 425	Pedro Guerrero	.50	.25	.05
□ 426	Earl Weaver MG	.10	.05	.01
□ 427	Roy Lee Jackson	.06	.03	.00
□ 428	Champ Summers	.06	.03	.00
□ 429	Eddie Whitson	.06	.03	.00
□ 430	Kirk Gibson	.50	.25	.05
□ 431	Gary Gaetti	4.50	2.25	.45
□ 432	Porfirio Altamirano	.06	.03	.00
□ 433	Dale Berra	.06	.03	.00
□ 434	Dennis Lamp	.06	.03	.00
□ 435	Tony Armas	.10	.05	.01
□ 436	Bill Campbell	.06	.03	.00
□ 437	Rick Sweet	.06	.03	.00
□ 438	Dave LaPoint	.45	.22	.04
□ 439	Rafael Ramirez	.06	.03	.00
□ 440	Ron Guidry	.20	.10	.02
□ 441	Astros TL	.10	.05	.01
	BA: Ray Knight			
	ERA: Joe Niekro			
□ 442	Brian Downing	.10	.05	.01
□ 443	Don Hood	.06	.03	.00
□ 444	Wally Backman	.20	.10	.02
□ 445	Mike Flanagan	.10	.05	.01
□ 446	Reid Nichols	.06	.03	.00
□ 447	Bryn Smith	.15	.07	.01
□ 448	Darrell Evans	.15	.07	.01
□ 449	Eddie Milner	.10	.05	.01
□ 450	Ted Simmons	.15	.07	.01
□ 451	SV: Ted Simmons	.10	.05	.01
□ 452	Lloyd Moseby	.10	.05	.01
□ 453	Lamar Johnson	.06	.03	.00
□ 454	Bob Welch	.10	.05	.01
□ 455	Sixto Lezcano	.06	.03	.00
□ 456	Lee Elia MG	.06	.03	.00
□ 457	Milt Wilcox	.06	.03	.00
□ 458	Ron Washington	.06	.03	.00
□ 459	Ed Farmer	.06	.03	.00
□ 460	Roy Smalley	.06	.03	.00
□ 461	Steve Trout	.06	.03	.00
□ 462	Steve Nicosia	.06	.03	.00
□ 463	Gaylord Perry	.30	.15	.03
□ 464	SV: Gaylord Perry	.15	.07	.01
□ 465	Lonnie Smith	.15	.07	.01
□ 466	Tom Underwood	.06	.03	.00
□ 467	Rufino Linares	.06	.03	.00
□ 468	Dave Goltz	.06	.03	.00
□ 469	Ron Gardenhire	.06	.03	.00
□ 470	Greg Minton	.06	.03	.00
□ 471	K.C. Royals TL	.10	.05	.01
	BA: Willie Wilson			
	ERA: Vida Blue			
□ 472	Gary Allenson	.06	.03	.00

□ 473	John Lowenstein	.06	.03	.00
□ 474	Ray Burris	.06	.03	.00
□ 475	Cesar Cedeno	.10	.05	.01
□ 476	Rob Picciolo	.06	.03	.00
□ 477	Tom Niedenfuer	.10	.05	.01
□ 478	Phil Garner	.06	.03	.00
□ 479	Charlie Hough	.10	.05	.01
□ 480	Toby Harrah	.10	.05	.01
□ 481	Scot Thompson	.06	.03	.00
□ 482	Tony Gwynn	20.00	10.00	2.00
□ 483	Lynn Jones	.06	.03	.00
□ 484	Dick Ruthven	.06	.03	.00
□ 485	Omar Moreno	.06	.03	.00
□ 486	Clyde King MG	.06	.03	.00
□ 487	Jerry Hairston	.06	.03	.00
□ 488	Alfredo Griffin	.10	.05	.01
□ 489	Tom Herr	.10	.05	.01
□ 490	Jim Palmer	.50	.25	.05
□ 491	SV: Jim Palmer	.20	.10	.02
□ 492	Paul Serna	.06	.03	.00
□ 493	Steve McCatty	.06	.03	.00
□ 494	Bob Brenly	.06	.03	.00
□ 495	Warren Cromartie	.06	.03	.00
□ 496	Tom Veryzer	.06	.03	.00
□ 497	Rick Sutcliffe	.20	.10	.02
□ 498	Wade Boggs	35.00	17.50	3.50
□ 499	Jeff Little	.06	.03	.00
□ 500	Reggie Jackson	1.00	.50	.10
□ 501	SV: Reggie Jackson	.40	.20	.04
□ 502	Atlanta Braves TL	.25	.12	.02
	BA: Dale Murphy			
	ERA: Phil Niekro			
□ 503	Moose Haas	.06	.03	.00
□ 504	Don Werner	.06	.03	.00
□ 505	Garry Templeton	.10	.05	.01
□ 506	Jim Gott	.35	.17	.03
□ 507	Tony Scott	.06	.03	.00
□ 508	Tom Filer	.15	.07	.01
□ 509	Lou Whitaker	.30	.15	.03
□ 510	Tug McGraw	.15	.07	.01
□ 511	SV: Tug McGraw	.10	.05	.01
□ 512	Doyle Alexander	.10	.05	.01
□ 513	Fred Stanley	.06	.03	.00
□ 514	Rudy Law	.06	.03	.00
□ 515	Gene Tenace	.06	.03	.00
□ 516	Bill Virdon MG	.06	.03	.00
□ 517	Gary Ward	.10	.05	.01
□ 518	Bill Laskey	.06	.03	.00
□ 519	Terry Bulling	.06	.03	.00
□ 520	Fred Lynn	.25	.12	.02
□ 521	Bruce Benedict	.06	.03	.00
□ 522	Pat Zachry	.06	.03	.00
□ 523	Carney Lansford	.25	.10	.02
□ 524	Tom Brennan	.06	.03	.00
□ 525	Frank White	.10	.05	.01
□ 526	Checklist: 397-528	.10	.01	.00
□ 527	Larry Biittner	.06	.03	.00
□ 528	Jamie Easterly	.06	.03	.00
□ 529	Tim Laudner	.06	.03	.00
□ 530	Eddie Murray	.75	.35	.07
□ 531	Oakland A's TL	.20	.10	.02
	BA: Rickey Henderson			
	ERA: Rick Langford			
□ 532	Dave Stewart	.75	.35	.07
□ 533	Luis Salazar	.10	.05	.01
□ 534	John Butcher	.06	.03	.00
□ 535	Manny Trillo	.06	.03	.00
□ 536	John Wockenfuss	.06	.03	.00
□ 537	Rod Scurry	.06	.03	.00
□ 538	Danny Heep	.06	.03	.00
□ 539	Roger Erickson	.06	.03	.00
□ 540	Ozzie Smith	.60	.30	.06
□ 541	Britt Burns	.06	.03	.00
□ 542	Jody Davis	.10	.05	.01
□ 543	Alan Fowlkes	.06	.03	.00
□ 544	Larry Whisenton	.06	.03	.00
□ 545	Floyd Bannister	.06	.03	.00
□ 546	Dave Garcia MG	.06	.03	.00
□ 547	Geoff Zahn	.06	.03	.00
□ 548	Brian Giles	.06	.03	.00
□ 549	Charlie Puleo	.06	.03	.00
□ 550	Carl Yastrzemski	1.00	.50	.10
□ 551	SV: Carl Yastrzemski	.40	.20	.04
□ 552	Tim Wallach	.25	.12	.02
□ 553	Dennis Martinez	.10	.05	.01
□ 554	Mike Vail	.06	.03	.00
□ 555	Steve Yeager	.06	.03	.00
□ 556	Willie Upshaw	.06	.03	.00
□ 557	Rick Honeycutt	.06	.03	.00
□ 558	Dickie Thon	.10	.05	.01
□ 559	Pete Redfern	.06	.03	.00
□ 560	Ron LeFlore	.10	.05	.01
□ 561	Cardinals TL	.10	.05	.01
	BA: Lonnie Smith			
	ERA: Joaquin Andujar			

562	Dave Rozema	.06	.03	.00
563	Juan Bonilla	.06	.03	.00
564	Sid Monge	.06	.03	.00
565	Bucky Dent	.15	.07	.01
566	Manny Sarmiento	.06	.03	.00
567	Joe Simpson	.06	.03	.00
568	Willie Hernandez	.10	.05	.01
569	Jack Perconte	.06	.03	.00
570	Vida Blue	.10	.05	.01
571	Mickey Klutts	.06	.03	.00
572	Bob Watson	.10	.05	.01
573	Andy Hassler	.06	.03	.00
574	Glenn Adams	.06	.03	.00
575	Neil Allen	.06	.03	.00
576	Frank Robinson MG	.15	.07	.01
577	Luis Aponte	.06	.03	.00
578	David Green	.06	.03	.00
579	Rich Dauer	.06	.03	.00
580	Tom Seaver	.75	.35	.07
581	SV: Tom Seaver	.35	.17	.03
582	Marshall Edwards	.06	.03	.00
583	Terry Forster	.10	.05	.01
584	Dave Hostetler	.06	.03	.00
585	Jose Cruz	.10	.05	.01
586	Frank Viola	6.00	3.00	.60
587	Ivan DeJesus	.06	.03	.00
588	Pat Underwood	.06	.03	.00
589	Alvis Woods	.06	.03	.00
590	Tony Pena	.20	.10	.02
591	White Sox TL BA: Greg Luzinski ERA: LaMarr Hoyt	.10	.05	.01
592	Shane Rawley	.10	.05	.01
593	Broderick Perkins	.06	.03	.00
594	Eric Rasmussen	.06	.03	.00
595	Tim Raines	.80	.40	.08
596	Randy Johnson	.06	.03	.00
597	Mike Proly	.06	.03	.00
598	Dwayne Murphy	.06	.03	.00
599	Don Aase	.06	.03	.00
600	George Brett	1.00	.50	.10
601	Ed Lynch	.06	.03	.00
602	Rich Gedman	.10	.05	.01
603	Joe Morgan	.40	.20	.04
604	SV: Joe Morgan	.15	.07	.01
605	Gary Roenicke	.06	.03	.00
606	Bobby Cox MG	.06	.03	.00
607	Charlie Leibrandt	.06	.03	.00
608	Don Money	.06	.03	.00
609	Danny Darwin	.06	.03	.00
610	Steve Garvey	.70	.35	.07
611	Bert Roberge	.06	.03	.00
612	Steve Swisher	.06	.03	.00
613	Mike Ivie	.06	.03	.00
614	Ed Glynn	.06	.03	.00
615	Garry Maddox	.06	.03	.00
616	Bill Nahorodny	.06	.03	.00
617	Butch Wynegar	.06	.03	.00
618	LaMarr Hoyt	.10	.05	.01
619	Keith Moreland	.06	.03	.00
620	Mike Norris	.06	.03	.00
621	New York Mets TL BA: Mookie Wilson ERA: Craig Swan	.10	.05	.01
622	Dave Edler	.06	.03	.00
623	Luis Sanchez	.06	.03	.00
624	Glenn Hubbard	.06	.03	.00
625	Ken Forsch	.06	.03	.00
626	Jerry Martin	.06	.03	.00
627	Doug Bair	.06	.03	.00
628	Julio Valdez	.06	.03	.00
629	Charlie Lea	.06	.03	.00
630	Paul Molitor	.25	.12	.02
631	Tippy Martinez	.06	.03	.00
632	Alex Trevino	.06	.03	.00
633	Vicente Romo	.06	.03	.00
634	Max Venable	.06	.03	.00
635	Graig Nettles	.15	.07	.01
636	SV: Graig Nettles	.10	.05	.01
637	Pat Corrales MG	.06	.03	.00
638	Dan Petry	.06	.03	.00
639	Art Howe	.10	.05	.01
640	Andre Thornton	.10	.05	.01
641	Billy Sample	.06	.03	.00
642	Checklist: 529-660	.10	.01	.00
643	Bump Wills	.06	.03	.00
644	Joe Lefebvre	.06	.03	.00
645	Bill Madlock	.10	.05	.01
646	Jim Essian	.06	.03	.00
647	Bobby Mitchell	.06	.03	.00
648	Jeff Burroughs	.10	.05	.01
649	Tommy Boggs	.06	.03	.00
650	George Hendrick	.10	.05	.01
651	Angels TL BA: Rod Carew ERA: Mike Witt	.20	.10	.02
652	Butch Hobson	.06	.03	.00
653	Ellis Valentine	.06	.03	.00
654	Bob Ojeda	.15	.07	.01
655	Al Bumbry	.06	.03	.00
656	Dave Frost	.06	.03	.00
657	Mike Gates	.06	.03	.00
658	Frank Pastore	.06	.03	.00
659	Charlie Moore	.06	.03	.00
660	Mike Hargrove	.10	.05	.01
661	Bill Russell	.10	.05	.01
662	Joe Sambito	.06	.03	.00
663	Tom O'Malley	.06	.03	.00
664	Bob Molinaro	.06	.03	.00
665	Jim Sundberg	.06	.03	.00
666	Sparky Anderson MG	.10	.05	.01
667	Dick Davis	.06	.03	.00
668	Larry Christenson	.06	.03	.00
669	Mike Squires	.06	.03	.00
670	Jerry Mumphrey	.06	.03	.00
671	Lenny Faedo	.06	.03	.00
672	Jim Kaat	.15	.07	.01
673	SV: Jim Kaat	.10	.05	.01
674	Kurt Bevacqua	.06	.03	.00
675	Jim Beattie	.06	.03	.00
676	Biff Pocoroba	.06	.03	.00
677	Dave Revering	.06	.03	.00
678	Juan Beniquez	.06	.03	.00
679	Mike Scott	.45	.22	.04
680	Andre Dawson	.45	.22	.04
681	Dodgers Leaders BA: Pedro Guerrero ERA: Fern.Valenzuela	.25	.12	.02
682	Bob Stanley	.06	.03	.00
683	Dan Ford	.06	.03	.00
684	Rafael Landestoy	.06	.03	.00
685	Lee Mazzilli	.06	.03	.00
686	Randy Lerch	.06	.03	.00
687	U.L. Washington	.06	.03	.00
688	Jim Wohlford	.06	.03	.00
689	Ron Hassey	.06	.03	.00
690	Kent Hrbek	.75	.35	.07
691	Dave Tobik	.06	.03	.00
692	Denny Walling	.06	.03	.00
693	Sparky Lyle	.10	.05	.01
694	SV: Sparky Lyle	.06	.03	.00
695	Ruppert Jones	.06	.03	.00
696	Chuck Tanner MG	.06	.03	.00
697	Barry Foote	.06	.03	.00
698	Tony Bernazard	.06	.03	.00
699	Lee Smith	.15	.07	.01
700	Keith Hernandez	.45	.22	.04
701	Batting Leaders AL: Willie Wilson NL: Al Oliver	.10	.05	.01
702	Home Run Leaders AL: Reggie Jackson AL: Gorman Thomas NL: Dave Kingman	.15	.07	.01
703	RBI Leaders AL: Hal McRae NL: Dale Murphy NL: Al Oliver	.15	.07	.01
704	SB Leaders AL: Rickey Henderson NL: Tim Raines	.25	.12	.02
705	Victory Leaders AL: LaMarr Hoyt NL: Steve Carlton	.12	.06	.01
706	Strikeout Leaders AL: Floyd Bannister NL: Steve Carlton	.12	.06	.01
707	ERA Leaders AL: Rick Sutcliffe NL: Steve Rogers	.10	.05	.01
708	Leading Firemen AL: Dan Quisenberry NL: Bruce Sutter	.10	.05	.01
709	Jimmy Sexton	.06	.03	.00
710	Willie Wilson	.15	.07	.01
711	Mariners TL BA: Bruce Bochte ERA: Jim Beattie	.10	.05	.01
712	Bruce Kison	.06	.03	.00
713	Ron Hodges	.06	.03	.00
714	Wayne Nordhagen	.06	.03	.00
715	Tony Perez	.20	.10	.02
716	SV: Tony Perez	.10	.05	.01
717	Scott Sanderson	.06	.03	.00
718	Jim Dwyer	.06	.03	.00
719	Rich Gale	.06	.03	.00
720	Dave Concepcion	.15	.07	.01
721	John Martin	.06	.03	.00
722	Jorge Orta	.06	.03	.00
723	Randy Moffitt	.06	.03	.00

☐ 724 Johnny Grubb	.06	.03	.00
☐ 725 Dan Spillner	.06	.03	.00
☐ 726 Harvey Kuenn MG	.06	.03	.00
☐ 727 Chet Lemon	.10	.05	.01
☐ 728 Ron Reed	.06	.03	.00
☐ 729 Jerry Morales	.06	.03	.00
☐ 730 Jason Thompson	.06	.03	.00
☐ 731 Al Williams	.06	.03	.00
☐ 732 Dave Henderson	.15	.07	.01
☐ 733 Buck Martinez	.06	.03	.00
☐ 734 Steve Braun	.06	.03	.00
☐ 735 Tommy John	.20	.10	.02
☐ 736 SV: Tommy John	.10	.05	.01
☐ 737 Mitchell Page	.06	.03	.00
☐ 738 Tim Foli	.06	.03	.00
☐ 739 Rick Ownbey	.06	.03	.00
☐ 740 Rusty Staub	.15	.07	.01
☐ 741 SV: Rusty Staub	.10	.05	.01
☐ 742 Padres TL	.10	.05	.01
BA: Terry Kennedy			
ERA: Tim Lollar			
☐ 743 Mike Torrez	.06	.03	.00
☐ 744 Brad Mills	.06	.03	.00
☐ 745 Scott McGregor	.10	.05	.01
☐ 746 John Wathan	.10	.05	.01
☐ 747 Fred Breining	.06	.03	.00
☐ 748 Derrel Thomas	.06	.03	.00
☐ 749 Jon Matlack	.06	.03	.00
☐ 750 Ben Oglivie	.10	.05	.01
☐ 751 Brad Havens	.06	.03	.00
☐ 752 Luis Pujols	.06	.03	.00
☐ 753 Elias Sosa	.06	.03	.00
☐ 754 Bill Robinson	.10	.05	.01
☐ 755 John Candelaria	.10	.05	.01
☐ 756 Russ Nixon MG	.06	.03	.00
☐ 757 Rick Manning	.06	.03	.00
☐ 758 Aurelio Rodriguez	.06	.03	.00
☐ 759 Doug Bird	.06	.03	.00
☐ 760 Dale Murphy	1.50	.75	.15
☐ 761 Gary Lucas	.06	.03	.00
☐ 762 Cliff Johnson	.06	.03	.00
☐ 763 Al Cowens	.06	.03	.00
☐ 764 Pete Falcone	.06	.03	.00
☐ 765 Bob Boone	.20	.10	.02
☐ 766 Barry Bonnell	.06	.03	.00
☐ 767 Duane Kuiper	.06	.03	.00
☐ 768 Chris Speier	.06	.03	.00
☐ 769 Checklist: 661-792	.10	.01	.00
☐ 770 Dave Winfield	.60	.30	.06
☐ 771 Twins TL	.10	.05	.01
BA: Kent Hrbek			
ERA: Bobby Castillo			
☐ 772 Jim Kern	.06	.03	.00
☐ 773 Larry Hisle	.06	.03	.00
☐ 774 Alan Ashby	.06	.03	.00
☐ 775 Burt Hooton	.06	.03	.00
☐ 776 Larry Parrish	.10	.05	.01
☐ 777 John Curtis	.06	.03	.00
☐ 778 Rich Hebner	.06	.03	.00
☐ 779 Rick Waits	.06	.03	.00
☐ 780 Gary Matthews	.10	.05	.01
☐ 781 Rick Rhoden	.10	.05	.01
☐ 782 Bobby Murcer	.10	.05	.01
☐ 783 SV: Bobby Murcer	.06	.03	.00
☐ 784 Jeff Newman	.06	.03	.00
☐ 785 Dennis Leonard	.10	.05	.01
☐ 786 Ralph Houk MG	.06	.03	.00
☐ 787 Dick Tidrow	.06	.03	.00
☐ 788 Dane Iorg	.06	.03	.00
☐ 789 Bryan Clark	.06	.03	.00
☐ 790 Bob Grich	.10	.05	.01
☐ 791 Gary Lavelle	.06	.03	.00
☐ 792 Chris Chambliss	.15	.07	.01

1983 Topps Traded

The cards in this 132-card set measure 2 1/2" by 3 1/2". For the third year in a row, Topps issued a 132-card Traded (or extended) set featuring some of the year's top rookies and players who had changed teams during the year, but were featured with their old team in the Topps regular issue of 1983. The cards were available only through hobby dealers and were printed in Ireland by the Topps affiliate in that country. The set is numbered alphabetically by the last name of the player of the card. The Darryl Strawberry card #108 can be found with either one or two asterisks (in the lower left corner of the reverse).

		MINT	EXC	G-VG
COMPLETE SET (132)		90.00	45.00	9.00
COMMON PLAYER (1-132)		.08	.04	.01
☐	1T Neil Allen	.15	.07	.01
☐	2T Bill Almon	.08	.04	.01
☐	3T Joe Altobelli MG	.08	.04	.01
☐	4T Tony Armas	.15	.07	.01
☐	5T Doug Bair	.08	.04	.01
☐	6T Steve Baker	.08	.04	.01
☐	7T Floyd Bannister	.15	.07	.01
☐	8T Don Baylor	.25	.12	.02
☐	9T Tony Bernazard	.08	.04	.01
☐	10T Larry Biittner	.08	.04	.01
☐	11T Dann Bilardello	.08	.04	.01
☐	12T Doug Bird	.08	.04	.01
☐	13T Steve Boros MG	.08	.04	.01
☐	14T Greg Brock	.35	.17	.03
☐	15T Mike Brown	.15	.07	.01
☐	(Red Sox pitcher)			
☐	16T Tom Burgmeier	.08	.04	.01
☐	17T Randy Bush	.35	.17	.03
☐	18T Bert Campaneris	.15	.07	.01
☐	19T Ron Cey	.20	.10	.02
☐	20T Chris Codiroli	.15	.07	.01
☐	21T Dave Collins	.08	.04	.01
☐	22T Terry Crowley	.08	.04	.01
☐	23T Julio Cruz	.08	.04	.01
☐	24T Mike Davis	.15	.07	.01
☐	25T Frank DiPino	.08	.04	.01
☐	26T Bill Doran	1.25	.60	.12
☐	27T Jerry Dybzinski	.08	.04	.01
☐	28T Jamie Easterly	.08	.04	.01
☐	29T Juan Eichelberger	.08	.04	.01
☐	30T Jim Essian	.08	.04	.01
☐	31T Pete Falcone	.08	.04	.01
☐	32T Mike Ferraro MG	.08	.04	.01
☐	33T Terry Forster	.15	.07	.01
☐	34T Julio Franco	3.50	1.75	.35
☐	35T Rich Gale	.08	.04	.01
☐	36T Kiko Garcia	.08	.04	.01
☐	37T Steve Garvey	1.50	.75	.15
☐	38T Johnny Grubb	.08	.04	.01
☐	39T Mel Hall	1.25	.60	.12
☐	40T Von Hayes	1.00	.50	.10
☐	41T Danny Heep	.15	.07	.01
☐	42T Steve Henderson	.08	.04	.01
☐	43T Keith Hernandez	1.00	.50	.10
☐	44T Leo Hernandez	.15	.07	.01
☐	45T Willie Hernandez	.25	.12	.02
☐	46T Al Holland	.08	.04	.01
☐	47T Frank Howard MG	.15	.07	.01
☐	48T Bobby Johnson	.08	.04	.01
☐	49T Cliff Johnson	.08	.04	.01
☐	50T Odell Jones	.08	.04	.01
☐	51T Mike Jorgensen	.08	.04	.01
☐	52T Bob Kearney	.08	.04	.01
☐	53T Steve Kemp	.15	.07	.01
☐	54T Matt Keough	.08	.04	.01
☐	55T Ron Kittle	.75	.35	.07
☐	56T Mickey Klutts	.08	.04	.01
☐	57T Alan Knicely	.08	.04	.01
☐	58T Mike Krukow	.15	.07	.01
☐	59T Rafael Landestoy	.08	.04	.01
☐	60T Carney Lansford	.40	.17	.03
☐	61T Joe Lefebvre	.08	.04	.01
☐	62T Bryan Little	.08	.04	.01
☐	63T Aurelio Lopez	.08	.04	.01
☐	64T Mike Madden	.08	.04	.01
☐	65T Rick Manning	.08	.04	.01
☐	66T Billy Martin MG	.30	.15	.03

☐ 67T	Lee Mazzilli	.08	.04	.01
☐ 68T	Andy McGaffigan	.08	.04	.01
☐ 69T	Craig McMurtry	.15	.07	.01
☐ 70T	John McNamara MG	.15	.07	.01
☐ 71T	Orlando Mercado	.15	.07	.01
☐ 72T	Larry Milbourne	.08	.04	.01
☐ 73T	Randy Moffitt	.08	.04	.01
☐ 74T	Sid Monge	.08	.04	.01
☐ 75T	Jose Morales	.08	.04	.01
☐ 76T	Omar Moreno	.08	.04	.01
☐ 77T	Joe Morgan	1.50	.75	.15
☐ 78T	Mike Morgan	.20	.10	.02
☐ 79T	Dale Murray	.08	.04	.01
☐ 80T	Jeff Newman	.08	.04	.01
☐ 81T	Pete O'Brien	1.75	.85	.17
☐ 82T	Jorge Orta	.08	.04	.01
☐ 83T	Alejandro Pena	.60	.30	.06
☐ 84T	Pascual Perez	.30	.15	.03
☐ 85T	Tony Perez	.60	.30	.06
☐ 86T	Broderick Perkins	.08	.04	.01
☐ 87T	Tony Phillips	.40	.20	.04
☐ 88T	Charlie Puleo	.08	.04	.01
☐ 89T	Pat Putnam	.08	.04	.01
☐ 90T	Jamie Quirk	.08	.04	.01
☐ 91T	Doug Rader MG	.15	.07	.01
☐ 92T	Chuck Rainey	.08	.04	.01
☐ 93T	Bobby Ramos	.08	.04	.01
☐ 94T	Gary Redus	.45	.22	.04
☐ 95T	Steve Renko	.08	.04	.01
☐ 96T	Leon Roberts	.08	.04	.01
☐ 97T	Aurelio Rodriguez	.08	.04	.01
☐ 98T	Dick Ruthven	.08	.04	.01
☐ 99T	Daryl Sconiers	.08	.04	.01
☐ 100T	Mike Scott	1.50	.75	.15
☐ 101T	Tom Seaver	2.00	1.00	.20
☐ 102T	John Shelby	.45	.22	.04
☐ 103T	Bob Shirley	.08	.04	.01
☐ 104T	Joe Simpson	.08	.04	.01
☐ 105T	Doug Sisk	.15	.07	.01
☐ 106T	Mike Smithson	.15	.07	.01
☐ 107T	Elias Sosa	.08	.04	.01
☐ 108T	Darryl Strawberry	65.00	32.50	6.50
☐ 109T	Tom Tellmann	.08	.04	.01
☐ 110T	Gene Tenace	.15	.07	.01
☐ 111T	Gorman Thomas	.20	.10	.02
☐ 112T	Dick Tidrow	.08	.04	.01
☐ 113T	Dave Tobik	.08	.04	.01
☐ 114T	Wayne Tolleson	.15	.07	.01
☐ 115T	Mike Torrez	.08	.04	.01
☐ 116T	Manny Trillo	.08	.04	.01
☐ 117T	Steve Trout	.08	.04	.01
☐ 118T	Lee Tunnell	.15	.07	.01
☐ 119T	Mike Vail	.08	.04	.01
☐ 120T	Ellis Valentine	.08	.04	.01
☐ 121T	Tom Veryzer	.08	.04	.01
☐ 122T	George Vukovich	.08	.04	.01
☐ 123T	Rick Waits	.08	.04	.01
☐ 124T	Greg Walker	.60	.30	.06
☐ 125T	Chris Welsh	.08	.04	.01
☐ 126T	Len Whitehouse	.08	.04	.01
☐ 127T	Eddie Whitson	.08	.04	.01
☐ 128T	Jim Wohlford	.08	.04	.01
☐ 129T	Matt Young	.15	.07	.01
☐ 130T	Joel Youngblood	.08	.04	.01
☐ 131T	Pat Zachry	.08	.04	.01
☐ 132T	Checklist 1T-132T	.08	.01	.00

☐ 5	Robin Yount	1.00	.50	.10
☐ 6	Terry Kennedy	.15	.07	.01
☐ 7	Dave Winfield	.50	.25	.05
☐ 8	Mike Schmidt	1.25	.60	.12
☐ 9	Buddy Bell	.20	.10	.02
☐ 10	Fernando Valenzuela	.35	.17	.03
☐ 11	Rich Gossage	.20	.10	.02
☐ 12	Bob Horner	.20	.10	.02
☐ 13	Toby Harrah	.15	.07	.01
☐ 14	Pete Rose	1.25	.60	.12
☐ 15	Cecil Cooper	.20	.10	.02
☐ 16	Dale Murphy	1.00	.50	.10
☐ 17	Carlton Fisk	.35	.17	.03
☐ 18	Ray Knight	.15	.07	.01
☐ 19	Jim Palmer	.60	.30	.06
☐ 20	Gary Carter	.50	.25	.05
☐ 21	Richie Zisk	.15	.07	.01
☐ 22	Dusty Baker	.15	.07	.01
☐ 23	Willie Wilson	.20	.10	.02
☐ 24	Bill Buckner	.15	.07	.01
☐ 25	Dave Stieb	.20	.10	.02
☐ 26	Bill Madlock	.15	.07	.01
☐ 27	Lance Parrish	.25	.12	.02
☐ 28	Nolan Ryan	1.25	.60	.12
☐ 29	Rod Carew	.75	.35	.07
☐ 30	Al Oliver	.25	.12	.02
☐ 31	George Brett	1.00	.50	.10
☐ 32	Jack Clark	.30	.15	.03
☐ 33	Ricky Henderson	1.00	.50	.10
☐ 34	Dave Concepcion	.20	.10	.02
☐ 35	Kent Hrbek	.45	.22	.04
☐ 36	Steve Carlton	.60	.30	.06
☐ 37	Eddie Murray	.75	.35	.07
☐ 38	Ruppert Jones	.15	.07	.01
☐ 39	Reggie Jackson	1.00	.50	.10
☐ 40	Bruce Sutter	.20	.10	.02

1983 Topps Glossy 40

The cards in this 40-card set measure 2 1/2" by 3 1/2". The 1983 Topps "Collector's Edition" or "All-Star Set" (popularly known as "Glossies") consists of color ballplayer picture cards with shiny, glazed surfaces. The player's name appears in small print outside the frame line at bottom left. The backs contain no biography or record and list only the set titles, the player's name, team, position, and the card number.

		MINT	EXC	G-VG
COMPLETE SET (40)		12.50	6.25	1.25
COMMON PLAYER (1-40)		.15	.07	.01
☐ 1	Carl Yastrzemski	1.25	.60	.12
☐ 2	Mookie Wilson	.20	.10	.02
☐ 3	Andre Thornton	.15	.07	.01
☐ 4	Keith Hernandez	.35	.17	.03

1984 Topps

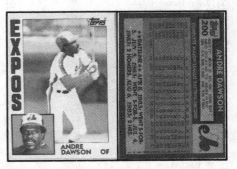

The cards in this 792-card set measure 2 1/2" by 3 1/2". For the second year in a row, Topps utilized a dual picture on the front of the card. A portrait is shown in a square insert and an action shot is featured in the main photo. Card numbers 1-6 feature 1983 Highlights (HL), cards 131-138 depict League Leaders, card numbers 386-407 feature All-Stars and card numbers 701-718 feature active

Major League career leaders in various statistical categories. Each team leader (TL) card features the team's leading hitter and pitcher pictured on the front with a team checklist back. There are six numerical checklist cards in the set. The player cards feature team logos in the upper right corner of the reverse. Topps also produced a specially boxed "glossy" edition frequently referred to as the Topps Tiffany set. There were supposedly only 10,000 sets of the Tiffany cards produced; they were marketed to hobby dealers. The checklist of cards (792 regular and 132 Traded) is identical to that of the normal non-glossy cards. There are two primary distinguishing features of the Tiffany cards, white card stock reverses and high gloss obverses. These Tiffany cards are valued at approximately five times the values listed below.

		MINT	EXC	G-VG
COMPLETE SET (792)		100.00	50.00	10.00
COMMON PLAYER (1-792)		.05	.02	.00
☐	1 HL: Steve Carlton 300th win and all-time SO king	.30	.07	.01
☐	2 HL: Rickey Henderson 100 stolen bases, three times	.30	.15	.03
☐	3 HL: Dan Quisenberry Sets save record	.10	.05	.01
☐	4 HL: Nolan Ryan, Steve Carlton, and Gaylord Perry (All surpass Johnson)	.30	.15	.03
☐	5 HL: Dave Righetti, Bob Forsch, and Mike Warren (All pitch no-hitters)	.10	.05	.01
☐	6 HL: Johnny Bench Gaylord Perry, and Carl Yastrzemski (Superstars retire)	.30	.15	.03
☐	7 Gary Lucas	.05	.02	.00
☐	8 Don Mattingly	27.00	10.00	2.00
☐	9 Jim Gott	.10	.05	.01
☐	10 Robin Yount	.75	.35	.07
☐	11 Minnesota Twins TL Kent Hrbek Ken Schrom	.10	.05	.01
☐	12 Billy Sample	.05	.02	.00
☐	13 Scott Holman	.05	.02	.00
☐	14 Tom Brookens	.05	.02	.00
☐	15 Burt Hooton	.05	.02	.00
☐	16 Omar Moreno	.05	.02	.00
☐	17 John Denny	.08	.04	.01
☐	18 Dale Berra	.05	.02	.00
☐	19 Ray Fontenot	.08	.04	.01
☐	20 Greg Luzinski	.10	.05	.01
☐	21 Joe Altobelli MG	.05	.02	.00
☐	22 Bryan Clark	.05	.02	.00
☐	23 Keith Moreland	.05	.02	.00
☐	24 John Martin	.05	.02	.00
☐	25 Glenn Hubbard	.05	.02	.00
☐	26 Bud Black	.05	.02	.00
☐	27 Daryl Sconiers	.05	.02	.00
☐	28 Frank Viola	.80	.40	.08
☐	29 Danny Heep	.05	.02	.00
☐	30 Wade Boggs	7.00	3.50	.70
☐	31 Andy McGaffigan	.05	.02	.00
☐	32 Bobby Ramos	.05	.02	.00
☐	33 Tom Burgmeier	.05	.02	.00
☐	34 Eddie Milner	.05	.02	.00
☐	35 Don Sutton	.30	.15	.03
☐	36 Denny Walling	.05	.02	.00
☐	37 Texas Rangers TL Buddy Bell Rick Honeycutt	.10	.05	.01
☐	38 Luis DeLeon	.05	.02	.00
☐	39 Garth Iorg	.05	.02	.00
☐	40 Dusty Baker	.08	.04	.01
☐	41 Tony Bernazard	.05	.02	.00
☐	42 Johnny Grubb	.05	.02	.00
☐	43 Ron Reed	.05	.02	.00
☐	44 Jim Morrison	.05	.02	.00
☐	45 Jerry Mumphrey	.05	.02	.00
☐	46 Ray Smith	.05	.02	.00
☐	47 Rudy Law	.05	.02	.00
☐	48 Julio Franco	1.50	.75	.15
☐	49 John Stuper	.05	.02	.00
☐	50 Chris Chambliss	.10	.05	.01
☐	51 Jim Frey MG	.05	.02	.00
☐	52 Paul Splittorff	.05	.02	.00
☐	53 Juan Beniquez	.05	.02	.00
☐	54 Jesse Orosco	.05	.02	.00
☐	55 Dave Concepcion	.10	.05	.01
☐	56 Gary Allenson	.05	.02	.00
☐	57 Dan Schatzeder	.05	.02	.00
☐	58 Max Venable	.05	.02	.00
☐	59 Sammy Stewart	.05	.02	.00
☐	60 Paul Molitor	.20	.10	.02
☐	61 Chris Codiroli	.08	.04	.01
☐	62 Dave Hostetler	.05	.02	.00
☐	63 Ed VandeBerg	.05	.02	.00
☐	64 Mike Scioscia	.08	.04	.01
☐	65 Kirk Gibson	.35	.17	.03
☐	66 Houston Astros TL Jose Cruz Nolan Ryan	.20	.10	.02
☐	67 Gary Ward	.08	.04	.01
☐	68 Luis Salazar	.05	.02	.00
☐	69 Rod Scurry	.05	.02	.00
☐	70 Gary Matthews	.08	.04	.01
☐	71 Leo Hernandez	.05	.02	.00
☐	72 Mike Squires	.05	.02	.00
☐	73 Jody Davis	.08	.04	.01
☐	74 Jerry Martin	.05	.02	.00
☐	75 Bob Forsch	.05	.02	.00
☐	76 Alfredo Griffin	.08	.04	.01
☐	77 Brett Butler	.10	.05	.01
☐	78 Mike Torrez	.05	.02	.00
☐	79 Rob Wilfong	.05	.02	.00
☐	80 Steve Rogers	.05	.02	.00
☐	81 Billy Martin MG	.15	.07	.01
☐	82 Doug Bird	.05	.02	.00
☐	83 Richie Zisk	.05	.02	.00
☐	84 Lenny Faedo	.05	.02	.00
☐	85 Atlee Hammaker	.05	.02	.00
☐	86 John Shelby	.25	.12	.02
☐	87 Frank Pastore	.05	.02	.00
☐	88 Rob Picciolo	.05	.02	.00
☐	89 Mike Smithson	.08	.04	.01
☐	90 Pedro Guerrero	.35	.17	.03
☐	91 Dan Spillner	.05	.02	.00
☐	92 Lloyd Moseby	.12	.06	.01
☐	93 Bob Knepper	.08	.04	.01
☐	94 Mario Ramirez	.05	.02	.00
☐	95 Aurelio Lopez	.05	.02	.00
☐	96 K.C. Royals TL Hal McRae Larry Gura	.10	.05	.01
☐	97 LaMarr Hoyt	.08	.04	.01
☐	98 Steve Nicosia	.05	.02	.00
☐	99 Craig Lefferts	.25	.12	.02
☐	100 Reggie Jackson	.75	.35	.07
☐	101 Porfirio Altamirano	.05	.02	.00
☐	102 Ken Oberkfell	.05	.02	.00
☐	103 Dwayne Murphy	.05	.02	.00
☐	104 Ken Dayley	.05	.02	.00
☐	105 Tony Armas	.08	.04	.01
☐	106 Tim Stoddard	.05	.02	.00
☐	107 Ned Yost	.05	.02	.00
☐	108 Randy Moffitt	.05	.02	.00
☐	109 Brad Wellman	.05	.02	.00
☐	110 Ron Guidry	.25	.12	.02
☐	111 Bill Virdon MG	.05	.02	.00
☐	112 Tom Niedenfuer	.08	.04	.01
☐	113 Kelly Paris	.08	.04	.01
☐	114 Checklist 1-132	.08	.01	.00
☐	115 Andre Thornton	.08	.04	.01
☐	116 George Bjorkman	.05	.02	.00
☐	117 Tom Veryzer	.05	.02	.00
☐	118 Charlie Hough	.08	.04	.01
☐	119 John Wockenfuss	.05	.02	.00
☐	120 Keith Hernandez	.35	.17	.03
☐	121 Pat Sheridan	.20	.10	.02
☐	122 Cecilio Guante	.08	.04	.01
☐	123 Butch Wynegar	.05	.02	.00
☐	124 Damaso Garcia	.05	.02	.00
☐	125 Britt Burns	.05	.02	.00
☐	126 Atlanta Braves TL Dale Murphy Craig McMurtry	.15	.07	.01
☐	127 Mike Madden	.05	.02	.00
☐	128 Rick Manning	.05	.02	.00
☐	129 Bill Laskey	.05	.02	.00
☐	130 Ozzie Smith	.40	.20	.04
☐	131 Batting Leaders Bill Madlock Wade Boggs	.25	.12	.02
☐	132 Home Run Leaders Mike Schmidt Jim Rice	.25	.12	.02
☐	133 RBI Leaders Dale Murphy	.20	.10	.02

Cecil Cooper
Jim Rice

134	Stolen Base Leaders	.25	.12	.02
	Tim Raines			
	Rickey Henderson			
135	Victory Leaders	.08	.04	.01
	John Denny			
	LaMarr Hoyt			
136	Strikeout Leaders	.15	.07	.01
	Steve Carlton			
	Jack Morris			
137	ERA Leaders	.08	.04	.01
	Atlee Hammaker			
	Rick Honeycutt			
138	Leading Firemen	.08	.04	.01
	Al Holland			
	Dan Quisenberry			
139	Bert Campaneris	.08	.04	.01
140	Storm Davis	.12	.06	.01
141	Pat Corrales MG	.05	.02	.00
142	Rich Gale	.05	.02	.00
143	Jose Morales	.05	.02	.00
144	Brian Harper	.25	.12	.02
145	Gary Lavelle	.05	.02	.00
146	Ed Romero	.05	.02	.00
147	Dan Petry	.05	.02	.00
148	Joe Lefebvre	.05	.02	.00
149	Jon Matlack	.05	.02	.00
150	Dale Murphy	1.00	.50	.10
151	Steve Trout	.05	.02	.00
152	Glenn Brummer	.05	.02	.00
153	Dick Tidrow	.05	.02	.00
154	Dave Henderson	.15	.07	.01
155	Frank White	.10	.05	.01
156	Oakland A's TL	.15	.07	.01
	Rickey Henderson			
	Tim Conroy			
157	Gary Gaetti	.75	.35	.07
158	John Curtis	.05	.02	.00
159	Darryl Cias	.05	.02	.00
160	Mario Soto	.05	.02	.00
161	Junior Ortiz	.05	.02	.00
162	Bob Ojeda	.10	.05	.01
163	Lorenzo Gray	.05	.02	.00
164	Scott Sanderson	.05	.02	.00
165	Ken Singleton	.10	.05	.01
166	Jamie Nelson	.05	.02	.00
167	Marshall Edwards	.05	.02	.00
168	Juan Bonilla	.05	.02	.00
169	Larry Parrish	.08	.04	.01
170	Jerry Reuss	.08	.04	.01
171	Frank Robinson MG	.12	.06	.01
172	Frank DiPino	.05	.02	.00
173	Marvell Wynne	.10	.05	.01
174	Juan Berenguer	.05	.02	.00
175	Graig Nettles	.15	.07	.01
176	Lee Smith	.10	.05	.01
177	Jerry Hairston	.05	.02	.00
178	Bill Krueger	.05	.02	.00
179	Buck Martinez	.05	.02	.00
180	Manny Trillo	.05	.02	.00
181	Roy Thomas	.05	.02	.00
182	Darryl Strawberry	15.00	7.50	1.50
183	Al Williams	.05	.02	.00
184	Mike O'Berry	.05	.02	.00
185	Sixto Lezcano	.05	.02	.00
186	Cardinal TL	.10	.05	.01
	Lonnie Smith			
	John Stuper			
187	Luis Aponte	.05	.02	.00
188	Bryan Little	.05	.02	.00
189	Tim Conroy	.08	.04	.01
190	Ben Oglivie	.08	.04	.01
191	Mike Boddicker	.10	.05	.01
192	Nick Esasky	2.25	1.10	.22
193	Darrell Brown	.05	.02	.00
194	Domingo Ramos	.05	.02	.00
195	Jack Morris	.20	.10	.02
196	Don Slaught	.15	.07	.01
197	Garry Hancock	.05	.02	.00
198	Bill Doran	.75	.35	.07
199	Willie Hernandez	.20	.10	.02
200	Andre Dawson	.40	.20	.04
201	Bruce Kison	.05	.02	.00
202	Bobby Cox MG	.05	.02	.00
203	Matt Keough	.05	.02	.00
204	Bobby Meacham	.10	.05	.01
205	Greg Minton	.05	.02	.00
206	Andy Van Slyke	2.50	1.25	.25
207	Donnie Moore	.05	.02	.00
208	Jose Oquendo	.50	.25	.05
209	Manny Sarmiento	.05	.02	.00
210	Joe Morgan	.35	.17	.03
211	Rick Sweet	.05	.02	.00
212	Broderick Perkins	.05	.02	.00
213	Bruce Hurst	.20	.10	.02
214	Paul Householder	.05	.02	.00
215	Tippy Martinez	.05	.02	.00
216	White Sox TL	.12	.06	.01
	Carlton Fisk			
	Richard Dotson			
217	Alan Ashby	.05	.02	.00
218	Rick Waits	.05	.02	.00
219	Joe Simpson	.05	.02	.00
220	Fernando Valenzuela	.30	.15	.03
221	Cliff Johnson	.05	.02	.00
222	Rick Honeycutt	.05	.02	.00
223	Wayne Krenchicki	.05	.02	.00
224	Sid Monge	.05	.02	.00
225	Lee Mazzilli	.05	.02	.00
226	Juan Eichelberger	.05	.02	.00
227	Steve Braun	.05	.02	.00
228	John Rabb	.05	.02	.00
229	Paul Owens MG	.05	.02	.00
230	Rickey Henderson	1.25	.60	.12
231	Gary Woods	.05	.02	.00
232	Tim Wallach	.15	.07	.01
233	Checklist 133-264	.08	.01	.00
234	Rafael Ramirez	.05	.02	.00
235	Matt Young	.08	.04	.01
236	Ellis Valentine	.05	.02	.00
237	John Castino	.05	.02	.00
238	Reid Nichols	.05	.02	.00
239	Jay Howell	.10	.05	.01
240	Eddie Murray	.55	.27	.05
241	Bill Almon	.05	.02	.00
242	Alex Trevino	.05	.02	.00
243	Pete Ladd	.05	.02	.00
244	Candy Maldonado	.25	.12	.02
245	Rick Sutcliffe	.25	.12	.02
246	New York Mets TL	.15	.07	.01
	Mookie Wilson			
	Tom Seaver			
247	Onix Concepcion	.05	.02	.00
248	Bill Dawley	.10	.05	.01
249	Jay Johnstone	.08	.04	.01
250	Bill Madlock	.10	.05	.01
251	Tony Gwynn	3.00	1.50	.30
252	Larry Christenson	.05	.02	.00
253	Jim Wohlford	.05	.02	.00
254	Shane Rawley	.08	.04	.01
255	Bruce Benedict	.05	.02	.00
256	Dave Geisel	.05	.02	.00
257	Julio Cruz	.05	.02	.00
258	Luis Sanchez	.05	.02	.00
259	Sparky Anderson MG	.08	.04	.01
260	Scott McGregor	.08	.04	.01
261	Bobby Brown	.05	.02	.00
262	Tom Candiotti	.30	.15	.03
263	Jack Fimple	.05	.02	.00
264	Doug Frobel	.05	.02	.00
265	Donnie Hill	.08	.04	.01
266	Steve Lubratich	.05	.02	.00
267	Carmelo Martinez	.25	.12	.02
268	Jack O'Connor	.05	.02	.00
269	Aurelio Rodriguez	.05	.02	.00
270	Jeff Russell	.50	.25	.05
271	Moose Haas	.05	.02	.00
272	Rick Dempsey	.05	.02	.00
273	Charlie Puleo	.05	.02	.00
274	Rick Monday	.08	.04	.01
275	Len Matuszek	.05	.02	.00
276	Angels TL	.15	.07	.01
	Rod Carew			
	Geoff Zahn			
277	Eddie Whitson	.08	.04	.01
278	Jorge Bell	1.25	.60	.12
279	Ivan DeJesus	.05	.02	.00
280	Floyd Bannister	.05	.02	.00
281	Larry Milbourne	.05	.02	.00
282	Jim Barr	.05	.02	.00
283	Larry Biittner	.05	.02	.00
284	Howard Bailey	.05	.02	.00
285	Darrell Porter	.05	.02	.00
286	Lary Sorensen	.05	.02	.00
287	Warren Cromartie	.05	.02	.00
288	Jim Beattie	.05	.02	.00
289	Randy Johnson	.05	.02	.00
290	Dave Dravecky	.20	.10	.02
291	Chuck Tanner MG	.05	.02	.00
292	Tony Scott	.05	.02	.00
293	Ed Lynch	.05	.02	.00
294	U.L. Washington	.05	.02	.00
295	Mike Flanagan	.08	.04	.01
296	Jeff Newman	.05	.02	.00
297	Bruce Berenyi	.05	.02	.00
298	Jim Gantner	.05	.02	.00
299	John Butcher	.05	.02	.00
300	Pete Rose	1.25	.60	.12
301	Frank LaCorte	.05	.02	.00

☐ 302	Barry Bonnell	.05	.02	.00
☐ 303	Marty Castillo	.05	.02	.00
☐ 304	Warren Brusstar	.05	.02	.00
☐ 305	Roy Smalley	.05	.02	.00
☐ 306	Dodgers TL	.10	.05	.01
	Pedro Guerrero			
	Bob Welch			
☐ 307	Bobby Mitchell	.05	.02	.00
☐ 308	Ron Hassey	.08	.04	.01
☐ 309	Tony Phillips	.25	.12	.02
☐ 310	Willie McGee	.30	.15	.03
☐ 311	Jerry Koosman	.10	.05	.01
☐ 312	Jorge Orta	.05	.02	.00
☐ 313	Mike Jorgensen	.05	.02	.00
☐ 314	Orlando Mercado	.05	.02	.00
☐ 315	Bob Grich	.08	.04	.01
☐ 316	Mark Bradley	.05	.02	.00
☐ 317	Greg Pryor	.05	.02	.00
☐ 318	Bill Gullickson	.05	.02	.00
☐ 319	Al Bumbry	.05	.02	.00
☐ 320	Bob Stanley	.05	.02	.00
☐ 321	Harvey Kuenn MG	.05	.02	.00
☐ 322	Ken Schrom	.05	.02	.00
☐ 323	Alan Knicely	.05	.02	.00
☐ 324	Alejandro Pena	.25	.12	.02
☐ 325	Darrell Evans	.15	.07	.01
☐ 326	Bob Kearney	.05	.02	.00
☐ 327	Ruppert Jones	.05	.02	.00
☐ 328	Vern Ruhle	.05	.02	.00
☐ 329	Pat Tabler	.20	.10	.02
☐ 330	John Candelaria	.10	.05	.01
☐ 331	Bucky Dent	.12	.06	.01
☐ 332	Kevin Gross	.35	.17	.03
☐ 333	Larry Herndon	.05	.02	.00
☐ 334	Chuck Rainey	.05	.02	.00
☐ 335	Don Baylor	.12	.06	.01
☐ 336	Seattle Mariners TL	.10	.05	.01
	Pat Putnam			
	Matt Young			
☐ 337	Kevin Hagen	.05	.02	.00
☐ 338	Mike Warren	.08	.04	.01
☐ 339	Roy Lee Jackson	.05	.02	.00
☐ 340	Hal McRae	.08	.04	.01
☐ 341	Dave Tobik	.05	.02	.00
☐ 342	Tim Foli	.05	.02	.00
☐ 343	Mark Davis	.25	.12	.02
☐ 344	Rick Miller	.05	.02	.00
☐ 345	Kent Hrbek	.45	.22	.04
☐ 346	Kurt Bevacqua	.05	.02	.00
☐ 347	Allan Ramirez	.05	.02	.00
☐ 348	Toby Harrah	.05	.02	.00
☐ 349	Bob L. Gibson	.08	.04	.01
	(Brewers Pitcher)			
☐ 350	George Foster	.20	.10	.02
☐ 351	Russ Nixon MG	.05	.02	.00
☐ 352	Dave Stewart	.60	.30	.06
☐ 353	Jim Anderson	.05	.02	.00
☐ 354	Jeff Burroughs	.05	.02	.00
☐ 355	Jason Thompson	.05	.02	.00
☐ 356	Glenn Abbott	.05	.02	.00
☐ 357	Ron Cey	.10	.05	.01
☐ 358	Bob Dernier	.05	.02	.00
☐ 359	Jim Acker	.08	.04	.01
☐ 360	Willie Randolph	.10	.05	.01
☐ 361	Dave Smith	.08	.04	.01
☐ 362	David Green	.05	.02	.00
☐ 363	Tim Laudner	.05	.02	.00
☐ 364	Scott Fletcher	.20	.10	.02
☐ 365	Steve Bedrosian	.15	.07	.01
☐ 366	Padres TL	.10	.05	.01
	Terry Kennedy			
	Dave Dravecky			
☐ 367	Jamie Easterly	.05	.02	.00
☐ 368	Hubie Brooks	.10	.05	.01
☐ 369	Steve McCatty	.05	.02	.00
☐ 370	Tim Raines	.50	.25	.05
☐ 371	Dave Gumpert	.05	.02	.00
☐ 372	Gary Roenicke	.05	.02	.00
☐ 373	Bill Scherrer	.05	.02	.00
☐ 374	Don Money	.05	.02	.00
☐ 375	Dennis Leonard	.08	.04	.01
☐ 376	Dave Anderson	.15	.07	.01
☐ 377	Danny Darwin	.05	.02	.00
☐ 378	Bob Brenly	.05	.02	.00
☐ 379	Checklist 265-396	.08	.01	.00
☐ 380	Steve Garvey	.50	.25	.05
☐ 381	Ralph Houk MG	.05	.02	.00
☐ 382	Chris Nyman	.05	.02	.00
☐ 383	Terry Puhl	.05	.02	.00
☐ 384	Lee Tunnell	.10	.05	.01
☐ 385	Tony Perez	.20	.10	.02
☐ 386	George Hendrick AS	.08	.04	.01
☐ 387	Johnny Ray AS	.08	.04	.01
☐ 388	Mike Schmidt AS	.35	.17	.03
☐ 389	Ozzie Smith AS	.15	.07	.01
☐ 390	Tim Raines AS	.15	.07	.01
☐ 391	Dale Murphy AS	.30	.15	.03
☐ 392	Andre Dawson AS	.15	.07	.01
☐ 393	Gary Carter AS	.15	.07	.01
☐ 394	Steve Rogers AS	.08	.04	.01
☐ 395	Steve Carlton AS	.20	.10	.02
☐ 396	Jesse Orosco AS	.08	.04	.01
☐ 397	Eddie Murray AS	.15	.07	.01
☐ 398	Lou Whitaker AS	.10	.05	.01
☐ 399	George Brett AS	.25	.12	.02
☐ 400	Cal Ripken AS	.20	.10	.02
☐ 401	Jim Rice AS	.15	.07	.01
☐ 402	Dave Winfield AS	.15	.07	.01
☐ 403	Lloyd Moseby AS	.08	.04	.01
☐ 404	Ted Simmons AS	.08	.04	.01
☐ 405	LaMarr Hoyt AS	.08	.04	.01
☐ 406	Ron Guidry AS	.10	.05	.01
☐ 407	Dan Quisenberry AS	.08	.04	.01
☐ 408	Lou Piniella	.10	.05	.01
☐ 409	Juan Agosto	.15	.07	.01
☐ 410	Claudell Washington	.08	.04	.01
☐ 411	Houston Jimenez	.08	.04	.01
☐ 412	Doug Rader MG	.05	.02	.00
☐ 413	Spike Owen	.20	.10	.02
☐ 414	Mitchell Page	.05	.02	.00
☐ 415	Tommy John	.20	.10	.02
☐ 416	Dane Iorg	.05	.02	.00
☐ 417	Mike Armstrong	.05	.02	.00
☐ 418	Ron Hodges	.05	.02	.00
☐ 419	John Henry Johnson	.05	.02	.00
☐ 420	Cecil Cooper	.12	.06	.01
☐ 421	Charlie Lea	.05	.02	.00
☐ 422	Jose Cruz	.10	.05	.01
☐ 423	Mike Morgan	.10	.05	.01
☐ 424	Dann Bilardello	.05	.02	.00
☐ 425	Steve Howe	.05	.02	.00
☐ 426	Orioles TL	.15	.07	.01
	Cal Ripken			
	Mike Boddicker			
☐ 427	Rick Leach	.05	.02	.00
☐ 428	Fred Breining	.05	.02	.00
☐ 429	Randy Bush	.25	.12	.02
☐ 430	Rusty Staub	.10	.05	.01
☐ 431	Chris Bando	.05	.02	.00
☐ 432	Charles Hudson	.20	.10	.02
☐ 433	Rich Hebner	.05	.02	.00
☐ 434	Harold Baines	.30	.15	.03
☐ 435	Neil Allen	.05	.02	.00
☐ 436	Rick Peters	.05	.02	.00
☐ 437	Mike Proly	.05	.02	.00
☐ 438	Biff Pocoroba	.05	.02	.00
☐ 439	Bob Stoddard	.05	.02	.00
☐ 440	Steve Kemp	.08	.04	.01
☐ 441	Bob Lillis MG	.05	.02	.00
☐ 442	Byron McLaughlin	.05	.02	.00
☐ 443	Benny Ayala	.05	.02	.00
☐ 444	Steve Renko	.05	.02	.00
☐ 445	Jerry Remy	.05	.02	.00
☐ 446	Luis Pujols	.05	.02	.00
☐ 447	Tom Brunansky	.30	.15	.03
☐ 448	Ben Hayes	.05	.02	.00
☐ 449	Joe Pettini	.05	.02	.00
☐ 450	Gary Carter	.40	.20	.04
☐ 451	Bob Jones	.05	.02	.00
☐ 452	Chuck Porter	.05	.02	.00
☐ 453	Willie Upshaw	.05	.02	.00
☐ 454	Joe Beckwith	.05	.02	.00
☐ 455	Terry Kennedy	.05	.02	.00
☐ 456	Chicago Cubs TL	.10	.05	.01
	Keith Moreland			
	Fergie Jenkins			
☐ 457	Dave Rozema	.05	.02	.00
☐ 458	Kiko Garcia	.05	.02	.00
☐ 459	Kevin Hickey	.05	.02	.00
☐ 460	Dave Winfield	.45	.22	.04
☐ 461	Jim Maler	.05	.02	.00
☐ 462	Lee Lacy	.05	.02	.00
☐ 463	Dave Engle	.05	.02	.00
☐ 464	Jeff A. Jones	.05	.02	.00
	(A's Pitcher)			
☐ 465	Mookie Wilson	.10	.05	.01
☐ 466	Gene Garber	.05	.02	.00
☐ 467	Mike Ramsey	.05	.02	.00
☐ 468	Geoff Zahn	.05	.02	.00
☐ 469	Tom O'Malley	.05	.02	.00
☐ 470	Nolan Ryan	1.75	.85	.17
☐ 471	Dick Howser MG	.08	.04	.01
☐ 472	Mike Brown	.08	.04	.01
	(Red Sox Pitcher)			
☐ 473	Jim Dwyer	.05	.02	.00
☐ 474	Greg Bargar	.05	.02	.00
☐ 475	Gary Redus	.25	.12	.02
☐ 476	Tom Tellmann	.05	.02	.00
☐ 477	Rafael Landestoy	.05	.02	.00
☐ 478	Alan Bannister	.05	.02	.00

☐ 479 Frank Tanana	.08	.04	.01
☐ 480 Ron Kittle	.25	.12	.02
☐ 481 Mark Thurmond	.10	.05	.01
☐ 482 Enos Cabell	.05	.02	.00
☐ 483 Fergie Jenkins	.20	.10	.02
☐ 484 Ozzie Virgil	.05	.02	.00
☐ 485 Rick Rhoden	.08	.04	.01
☐ 486 N.Y. Yankees TL	.10	.05	.01
Don Baylor			
Ron Guidry			
☐ 487 Ricky Adams	.05	.02	.00
☐ 488 Jesse Barfield	.30	.15	.03
☐ 489 Dave Von Ohlen	.05	.02	.00
☐ 490 Cal Ripken	.90	.45	.09
☐ 491 Bobby Castillo	.05	.02	.00
☐ 492 Tucker Ashford	.05	.02	.00
☐ 493 Mike Norris	.05	.02	.00
☐ 494 Chili Davis	.15	.07	.01
☐ 495 Rollie Fingers	.20	.10	.02
☐ 496 Terry Francona	.05	.02	.00
☐ 497 Bud Anderson	.05	.02	.00
☐ 498 Rich Gedman	.08	.04	.01
☐ 499 Mike Witt	.10	.05	.01
☐ 500 George Brett	.75	.35	.07
☐ 501 Steve Henderson	.05	.02	.00
☐ 502 Joe Torre MG	.08	.04	.01
☐ 503 Elias Sosa	.05	.02	.00
☐ 504 Mickey Rivers	.08	.04	.01
☐ 505 Pete Vuckovich	.08	.04	.01
☐ 506 Ernie Whitt	.08	.04	.01
☐ 507 Mike LaCoss	.05	.02	.00
☐ 508 Mel Hall	.45	.22	.04
☐ 509 Brad Havens	.05	.02	.00
☐ 510 Alan Trammell	.35	.17	.03
☐ 511 Marty Bystrom	.05	.02	.00
☐ 512 Oscar Gamble	.05	.02	.00
☐ 513 Dave Beard	.05	.02	.00
☐ 514 Floyd Rayford	.05	.02	.00
☐ 515 Gorman Thomas	.10	.05	.01
☐ 516 Montreal Expos TL	.10	.05	.01
Al Oliver			
Charlie Lea			
☐ 517 John Moses	.08	.04	.01
☐ 518 Greg Walker	.40	.20	.04
☐ 519 Ron Davis	.05	.02	.00
☐ 520 Bob Boone	.15	.07	.01
☐ 521 Pete Falcone	.05	.02	.00
☐ 522 Dave Bergman	.05	.02	.00
☐ 523 Glenn Hoffman	.05	.02	.00
☐ 524 Carlos Diaz	.05	.02	.00
☐ 525 Willie Wilson	.12	.06	.01
☐ 526 Ron Oester	.05	.02	.00
☐ 527 Checklist 397-528	.08	.01	.00
☐ 528 Mark Brouhard	.05	.02	.00
☐ 529 Keith Atherton	.05	.02	.00
☐ 530 Dan Ford	.05	.02	.00
☐ 531 Steve Boros MG	.05	.02	.00
☐ 532 Eric Show	.08	.04	.01
☐ 533 Ken Landreaux	.05	.02	.00
☐ 534 Pete O'Brien	.90	.45	.09
☐ 535 Bo Diaz	.05	.02	.00
☐ 536 Doug Bair	.05	.02	.00
☐ 537 Johnny Ray	.12	.06	.01
☐ 538 Kevin Bass	.10	.05	.01
☐ 539 George Frazier	.05	.02	.00
☐ 540 George Hendrick	.08	.04	.01
☐ 541 Dennis Lamp	.05	.02	.00
☐ 542 Duane Kuiper	.05	.02	.00
☐ 543 Craig McMurtry	.08	.04	.01
☐ 544 Cesar Geronimo	.05	.02	.00
☐ 545 Bill Buckner	.10	.05	.01
☐ 546 Indians TL	.10	.05	.01
Mike Hargrove			
Lary Sorensen			
☐ 547 Mike Moore	.25	.12	.02
☐ 548 Ron Jackson	.05	.02	.00
☐ 549 Walt Terrell	.45	.22	.04
☐ 550 Jim Rice	.30	.15	.03
☐ 551 Scott Ullger	.05	.02	.00
☐ 552 Ray Burris	.05	.02	.00
☐ 553 Joe Nolan	.05	.02	.00
☐ 554 Ted Power	.05	.02	.00
☐ 555 Greg Brock	.15	.07	.01
☐ 556 Joey McLaughlin	.05	.02	.00
☐ 557 Wayne Tolleson	.08	.04	.01
☐ 558 Mike Davis	.08	.04	.01
☐ 559 Mike Scott	.35	.17	.03
☐ 560 Carlton Fisk	.35	.17	.03
☐ 561 Whitey Herzog MG	.05	.02	.00
☐ 562 Manny Castillo	.05	.02	.00
☐ 563 Glenn Wilson	.08	.04	.01
☐ 564 Al Holland	.05	.02	.00
☐ 565 Leon Durham	.08	.04	.01
☐ 566 Jim Bibby	.05	.02	.00
☐ 567 Mike Heath	.05	.02	.00

☐ 568 Pete Filson	.05	.02	.00
☐ 569 Bake McBride	.05	.02	.00
☐ 570 Dan Quisenberry	.12	.06	.01
☐ 571 Bruce Bochy	.05	.02	.00
☐ 572 Jerry Royster	.05	.02	.00
☐ 573 Dave Kingman	.15	.07	.01
☐ 574 Brian Downing	.08	.04	.01
☐ 575 Jim Clancy	.05	.02	.00
☐ 576 Giants TL	.10	.05	.01
Jeff Leonard			
Atlee Hammaker			
☐ 577 Mark Clear	.05	.02	.00
☐ 578 Lenn Sakata	.05	.02	.00
☐ 579 Bob James	.20	.10	.02
☐ 580 Lonnie Smith	.12	.06	.01
☐ 581 Jose DeLeon	.45	.22	.04
☐ 582 Bob McClure	.05	.02	.00
☐ 583 Derrel Thomas	.05	.02	.00
☐ 584 Dave Schmidt	.08	.04	.01
☐ 585 Dan Driessen	.05	.02	.00
☐ 586 Joe Niekro	.10	.05	.01
☐ 587 Von Hayes	.18	.09	.01
☐ 588 Milt Wilcox	.05	.02	.00
☐ 589 Mike Easler	.08	.04	.01
☐ 590 Dave Stieb	.18	.09	.01
☐ 591 Tony LaRussa MG	.05	.02	.00
☐ 592 Andre Robertson	.05	.02	.00
☐ 593 Jeff Lahti	.05	.02	.00
☐ 594 Gene Richards	.05	.02	.00
☐ 595 Jeff Reardon	.15	.07	.01
☐ 596 Ryne Sandberg	1.50	.75	.15
☐ 597 Rick Camp	.05	.02	.00
☐ 598 Rusty Kuntz	.05	.02	.00
☐ 599 Doug Sisk	.08	.04	.01
☐ 600 Rod Carew	.50	.22	.04
☐ 601 John Tudor	.15	.07	.01
☐ 602 John Wathan	.08	.04	.01
☐ 603 Renie Martin	.05	.02	.00
☐ 604 John Lowenstein	.05	.02	.00
☐ 605 Mike Caldwell	.05	.02	.00
☐ 606 Blue Jays TL	.10	.05	.01
Lloyd Moseby			
Dave Stieb			
☐ 607 Tom Hume	.05	.02	.00
☐ 608 Bobby Johnson	.05	.02	.00
☐ 609 Dan Meyer	.05	.02	.00
☐ 610 Steve Sax	.30	.15	.03
☐ 611 Chet Lemon	.08	.04	.01
☐ 612 Harry Spilman	.05	.02	.00
☐ 613 Greg Gross	.05	.02	.00
☐ 614 Len Barker	.05	.02	.00
☐ 615 Garry Templeton	.08	.04	.01
☐ 616 Don Robinson	.05	.02	.00
☐ 617 Rick Cerone	.05	.02	.00
☐ 618 Dickie Noles	.05	.02	.00
☐ 619 Jerry Dybzinski	.05	.02	.00
☐ 620 Al Oliver	.10	.05	.01
☐ 621 Frank Howard MG	.05	.02	.00
☐ 622 Al Cowens	.05	.02	.00
☐ 623 Ron Washington	.05	.02	.00
☐ 624 Terry Harper	.05	.02	.00
☐ 625 Larry Gura	.05	.02	.00
☐ 626 Bob Clark	.05	.02	.00
☐ 627 Dave LaPoint	.08	.04	.01
☐ 628 Ed Jurak	.05	.02	.00
☐ 629 Rick Langford	.05	.02	.00
☐ 630 Ted Simmons	.12	.06	.01
☐ 631 Dennis Martinez	.08	.04	.01
☐ 632 Tom Foley	.05	.02	.00
☐ 633 Mike Krukow	.08	.04	.01
☐ 634 Mike Marshall	.18	.09	.01
☐ 635 Dave Righetti	.18	.09	.01
☐ 636 Pat Putnam	.05	.02	.00
☐ 637 Phillies TL	.10	.05	.01
Gary Matthews			
John Denny			
☐ 638 George Vukovich	.05	.02	.00
☐ 639 Rick Lysander	.05	.02	.00
☐ 640 Lance Parrish	.25	.12	.02
☐ 641 Mike Richardt	.05	.02	.00
☐ 642 Tom Underwood	.05	.02	.00
☐ 643 Mike Brown	.08	.04	.01
(Angels OF)			
☐ 644 Tim Lollar	.05	.02	.00
☐ 645 Tony Pena	.15	.07	.01
☐ 646 Checklist 529-660	.08	.01	.00
☐ 647 Ron Roenicke	.05	.02	.00
☐ 648 Len Whitehouse	.05	.02	.00
☐ 649 Tom Herr	.10	.05	.01
☐ 650 Phil Niekro	.20	.10	.02
☐ 651 John McNamara MG	.05	.02	.00
☐ 652 Rudy May	.05	.02	.00
☐ 653 Dave Stapleton	.05	.02	.00
☐ 654 Bob Bailor	.05	.02	.00
☐ 655 Amos Otis	.10	.05	.01

☐ 656 Bryn Smith	.12	.06	.01
☐ 657 Thad Bosley	.05	.02	.00
☐ 658 Jerry Augustine	.05	.02	.00
☐ 659 Duane Walker	.05	.02	.00
☐ 660 Ray Knight	.10	.05	.01
☐ 661 Steve Yeager	.05	.02	.00
☐ 662 Tom Brennan	.05	.02	.00
☐ 663 Johnnie LeMaster	.05	.02	.00
☐ 664 Dave Stegman	.05	.02	.00
☐ 665 Buddy Bell	.12	.06	.01
☐ 666 Detroit Tigers TL	.15	.07	.01
Lou Whitaker			
Jack Morris			
☐ 667 Vance Law	.08	.04	.01
☐ 668 Larry McWilliams	.05	.02	.01
☐ 669 Dave Lopes	.08	.04	.01
☐ 670 Rich Gossage	.18	.09	.01
☐ 671 Jamie Quirk	.05	.02	.00
☐ 672 Ricky Nelson	.05	.02	.00
☐ 673 Mike Walters	.05	.02	.00
☐ 674 Tim Flannery	.05	.02	.00
☐ 675 Pascual Perez	.15	.07	.01
☐ 676 Brian Giles	.05	.02	.00
☐ 677 Doyle Alexander	.08	.04	.01
☐ 678 Chris Speier	.05	.02	.00
☐ 679 Art Howe	.08	.04	.01
☐ 680 Fred Lynn	.20	.10	.02
☐ 681 Tom Lasorda MG	.08	.04	.01
☐ 682 Dan Morogiello	.05	.02	.00
☐ 683 Marty Barrett	1.50	.75	.15
☐ 684 Bob Shirley	.05	.02	.00
☐ 685 Willie Aikens	.05	.02	.00
☐ 686 Joe Price	.05	.02	.00
☐ 687 Roy Howell	.05	.02	.00
☐ 688 George Wright	.05	.02	.00
☐ 689 Mike Fischlin	.05	.02	.00
☐ 690 Jack Clark	.25	.12	.02
☐ 691 Steve Lake	.05	.02	.00
☐ 692 Dickie Thon	.08	.04	.01
☐ 693 Alan Wiggins	.05	.02	.00
☐ 694 Mike Stanton	.05	.02	.00
☐ 695 Lou Whitaker	.25	.12	.02
☐ 696 Pirates TL	.10	.05	.01
Bill Madlock			
Rick Rhoden			
☐ 697 Dale Murray	.05	.02	.00
☐ 698 Marc Hill	.05	.02	.00
☐ 699 Dave Rucker	.05	.02	.00
☐ 700 Mike Schmidt	1.00	.50	.10
☐ 701 NL Active Batting	.20	.10	.02
Bill Madlock			
Pete Rose			
Dave Parker			
☐ 702 NL Active Hits	.20	.10	.02
Pete Rose			
Rusty Staub			
Tony Perez			
☐ 703 NL Active Home Run	.15	.07	.01
Mike Schmidt			
Tony Perez			
Dave Kingman			
☐ 704 NL Active RBI	.10	.05	.01
Tony Perez			
Rusty Staub			
Al Oliver			
☐ 705 NL Active Steals	.10	.05	.01
Joe Morgan			
Cesar Cedeno			
Larry Bowa			
☐ 706 NL Active Victory	.20	.10	.02
Steve Carlton			
Fergie Jenkins			
Tom Seaver			
☐ 707 NL Active Strikeout	.25	.12	.02
Steve Carlton			
Nolan Ryan			
Tom Seaver			
☐ 708 NL Active ERA	.18	.09	.01
Tom Seaver			
Steve Carlton			
Steve Rogers			
☐ 709 NL Active Save	.10	.05	.01
Bruce Sutter			
Tug McGraw			
Gene Garber			
☐ 710 AL Active Batting	.20	.10	.02
Rod Carew			
George Brett			
Cecil Cooper			
☐ 711 AL Active Hits	.18	.09	.01
Rod Carew			
Bert Campaneris			
Reggie Jackson			
☐ 712 AL Active Home Run	.15	.07	.01
Reggie Jackson			
Graig Nettles			
Greg Luzinski			
☐ 713 AL Active RBI	.15	.07	.01
Reggie Jackson			
Ted Simmons			
Graig Nettles			
☐ 714 AL Active Steals	.08	.04	.01
Bert Campaneris			
Dave Lopes			
Omar Moreno			
☐ 715 AL Active Victory	.18	.09	.01
Jim Palmer			
Don Sutton			
Tommy John			
☐ 716 AL Active Strikeout	.08	.04	.01
Don Sutton			
Bert Blyleven			
Jerry Koosman			
☐ 717 AL Active ERA	.15	.07	.01
Jim Palmer			
Rollie Fingers			
Ron Guidry			
☐ 718 AL Active Save	.12	.06	.01
Rollie Fingers			
Rich Gossage			
Dan Quisenberry			
☐ 719 Andy Hassler	.05	.02	.00
☐ 720 Dwight Evans	.18	.09	.01
☐ 721 Del Crandall MG	.05	.02	.00
☐ 722 Bob Welch	.08	.04	.01
☐ 723 Rich Dauer	.05	.02	.00
☐ 724 Eric Rasmussen	.05	.02	.00
☐ 725 Cesar Cedeno	.08	.04	.01
☐ 726 Brewers TL	.10	.05	.01
Ted Simmons			
Moose Haas			
☐ 727 Joel Youngblood	.05	.02	.00
☐ 728 Tug McGraw	.10	.05	.01
☐ 729 Gene Tenace	.05	.02	.00
☐ 730 Bruce Sutter	.12	.06	.01
☐ 731 Lynn Jones	.05	.02	.00
☐ 732 Terry Crowley	.05	.02	.00
☐ 733 Dave Collins	.05	.02	.00
☐ 734 Odell Jones	.05	.02	.00
☐ 735 Rick Burleson	.08	.04	.01
☐ 736 Dick Ruthven	.05	.02	.00
☐ 737 Jim Essian	.05	.02	.00
☐ 738 Bill Schroeder	.10	.05	.01
☐ 739 Bob Watson	.08	.04	.01
☐ 740 Tom Seaver	.50	.25	.05
☐ 741 Wayne Gross	.05	.02	.00
☐ 742 Dick Williams MG	.05	.02	.00
☐ 743 Don Hood	.05	.02	.00
☐ 744 Jamie Allen	.05	.02	.00
☐ 745 Dennis Eckersley	.25	.10	.02
☐ 746 Mickey Hatcher	.08	.04	.01
☐ 747 Pat Zachry	.05	.02	.00
☐ 748 Jeff Leonard	.10	.05	.01
☐ 749 Doug Flynn	.05	.02	.00
☐ 750 Jim Palmer	.45	.22	.04
☐ 751 Charlie Moore	.05	.02	.00
☐ 752 Phil Garner	.05	.02	.00
☐ 753 Doug Gwosdz	.05	.02	.00
☐ 754 Kent Tekulve	.08	.04	.01
☐ 755 Garry Maddox	.08	.04	.01
☐ 756 Reds TL	.10	.05	.01
Ron Oester			
Mario Soto			
☐ 757 Larry Bowa	.10	.05	.01
☐ 758 Bill Stein	.05	.02	.00
☐ 759 Richard Dotson	.08	.04	.00
☐ 760 Bob Horner	.15	.07	.01
☐ 761 John Montefusco	.05	.02	.00
☐ 762 Rance Mulliniks	.05	.02	.00
☐ 763 Craig Swan	.05	.02	.00
☐ 764 Mike Hargrove	.08	.04	.01
☐ 765 Ken Forsch	.05	.02	.00
☐ 766 Mike Vail	.05	.02	.00
☐ 767 Carney Lansford	.15	.07	.01
☐ 768 Champ Summers	.05	.02	.00
☐ 769 Bill Caudill	.05	.02	.00
☐ 770 Ken Griffey	.12	.06	.01
☐ 771 Billy Gardner MG	.05	.02	.00
☐ 772 Jim Slaton	.05	.02	.00
☐ 773 Todd Cruz	.05	.02	.00
☐ 774 Tom Gorman	.08	.04	.01
☐ 775 Dave Parker	.20	.10	.02
☐ 776 Craig Reynolds	.05	.02	.00
☐ 777 Tom Paciorek	.05	.02	.00
☐ 778 Andy Hawkins	.60	.30	.06
☐ 779 Jim Sundberg	.05	.02	.00
☐ 780 Steve Carlton	.35	.17	.03
☐ 781 Checklist 661-792	.08	.01	.00
☐ 782 Steve Balboni	.08	.04	.01
☐ 783 Luis Leal	.05	.02	.00

☐ 784	Leon Roberts	.05	.02	.00
☐ 785	Joaquin Andujar	.10	.05	.01
☐ 786	Red Sox TL	.25	.12	.02
	Wade Boggs			
	Bob Ojeda			
☐ 787	Bill Campbell	.05	.02	.00
☐ 788	Milt May	.05	.02	.00
☐ 789	Bert Blyleven	.20	.07	.01
☐ 790	Doug DeCinces	.08	.04	.01
☐ 791	Terry Forster	.08	.04	.01
☐ 792	Bill Russell	.15	.07	.01

1984 Topps Traded

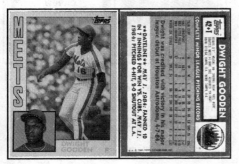

The cards in this 132-card set measure 2 1/2" by 3 1/2". In its now standard procedure, Topps issued its Traded (or extended) set for the fourth year in a row. Because all photos and statistics of its regular set for the year were developed during the fall and winter months of the preceding year, players who changed teams during the fall, winter, and spring months are portrayed with the teams they were with in 1983. The Traded set amends the shortcomings of the regular set by presenting the players with their proper teams for the current year. Rookies not contained in the regular set are also picked up in the Traded set. Again this year, the Topps affiliate in Ireland printed the cards, and the cards were available through hobby channels only. Topps also produced a specially boxed "glossy" edition frequently referred to as the Topps Traded Tiffany set. There were supposedly only 10,000 sets of the Tiffany cards produced; they were marketed to hobby dealers. The checklist of cards is identical to that of the normal non-glossy cards. There are two primary distinguishing features of the Tiffany cards, white card stock reverses and high gloss obverses. These Tiffany cards are valued at approximately five times the values listed below.

		MINT	EXC	G-VG
COMPLETE SET (132)		100.00	50.00	10.00
COMMON PLAYER (1-132)		.10	.05	.01

☐ 1T	Willie Aikens	.20	.10	.02
☐ 2T	Luis Aponte	.10	.05	.01
☐ 3T	Mike Armstrong	.10	.05	.01
☐ 4T	Bob Bailor	.10	.05	.01
☐ 5T	Dusty Baker	.20	.10	.02
☐ 6T	Steve Balboni	.20	.10	.02
☐ 7T	Alan Bannister	.10	.05	.01
☐ 8T	Dave Beard	.10	.05	.01
☐ 9T	Joe Beckwith	.10	.05	.01
☐ 10T	Bruce Berenyi	.10	.05	.01
☐ 11T	Dave Bergman	.10	.05	.01
☐ 12T	Tony Bernazard	.10	.05	.01
☐ 13T	Yogi Berra MG	.40	.20	.04
☐ 14T	Barry Bonnell	.10	.05	.01
☐ 15T	Phil Bradley	2.00	1.00	.20
☐ 16T	Fred Breining	.10	.05	.01
☐ 17T	Bill Buckner	.30	.15	.03
☐ 18T	Ray Burris	.10	.05	.01
☐ 19T	John Butcher	.10	.05	.01

☐ 20T	Brett Butler	.30	.15	.03
☐ 21T	Enos Cabell	.10	.05	.01
☐ 22T	Bill Campbell	.10	.05	.01
☐ 23T	Bill Caudill	.10	.05	.01
☐ 24T	Bob Clark	.10	.05	.01
☐ 25T	Bryan Clark	.10	.05	.01
☐ 26T	Jaime Cocanower	.20	.10	.02
☐ 27T	Ron Darling	5.00	2.50	.50
☐ 28T	Alvin Davis	7.00	3.50	.70
☐ 29T	Ken Dayley	.20	.10	.02
☐ 30T	Jeff Dedmon	.20	.10	.02
☐ 31T	Bob Dernier	.20	.10	.02
☐ 32T	Carlos Diaz	.10	.05	.01
☐ 33T	Mike Easler	.10	.05	.01
☐ 34T	Dennis Eckersley	.60	.30	.06
☐ 35T	Jim Essian	.10	.05	.01
☐ 36T	Darrell Evans	.30	.15	.03
☐ 37T	Mike Fitzgerald	.20	.10	.02
☐ 38T	Tim Foli	.10	.05	.01
☐ 39T	George Frazier	.10	.05	.01
☐ 40T	Rich Gale	.10	.05	.01
☐ 41T	Barbaro Garbey	.20	.10	.02
☐ 42T	Dwight Gooden	42.00	18.00	4.00
☐ 43T	Rich Gossage	.35	.17	.03
☐ 44T	Wayne Gross	.10	.05	.01
☐ 45T	Mark Gubicza	5.00	2.50	.50
☐ 46T	Jackie Gutierrez	.20	.10	.02
☐ 47T	Mel Hall	.40	.20	.04
☐ 48T	Toby Harrah	.20	.10	.02
☐ 49T	Ron Hassey	.20	.10	.02
☐ 50T	Rich Hebner	.10	.05	.01
☐ 51T	Willie Hernandez	.30	.15	.03
☐ 52T	Ricky Horton	.35	.17	.03
☐ 53T	Art Howe	.20	.10	.02
☐ 54T	Dane Iorg	.10	.05	.01
☐ 55T	Brook Jacoby	1.25	.60	.12
☐ 56T	Mike Jeffcoat	.20	.10	.02
☐ 57T	Dave Johnson MG	.30	.15	.03
☐ 58T	Lynn Jones	.10	.05	.01
☐ 59T	Ruppert Jones	.10	.05	.01
☐ 60T	Mike Jorgensen	.10	.05	.01
☐ 61T	Bob Kearney	.10	.05	.01
☐ 62T	Jimmy Key	3.00	1.50	.30
☐ 63T	Dave Kingman	.30	.15	.03
☐ 64T	Jerry Koosman	.30	.15	.03
☐ 65T	Wayne Krenchicki	.10	.05	.01
☐ 66T	Rusty Kuntz	.10	.05	.01
☐ 67T	Rene Lachemann MG	.10	.05	.01
☐ 68T	Frank LaCorte	.10	.05	.01
☐ 69T	Dennis Lamp	.10	.05	.01
☐ 70T	Mark Langston	18.00	9.00	1.80
☐ 71T	Rick Leach	.10	.05	.01
☐ 72T	Craig Lefferts	.30	.15	.03
☐ 73T	Gary Lucas	.10	.05	.01
☐ 74T	Jerry Martin	.10	.05	.01
☐ 75T	Carmelo Martinez	.20	.10	.02
☐ 76T	Mike Mason	.20	.10	.02
☐ 77T	Gary Matthews	.20	.10	.02
☐ 78T	Andy McGaffigan	.10	.05	.01
☐ 79T	Larry Milbourne	.10	.05	.01
☐ 80T	Sid Monge	.10	.05	.01
☐ 81T	Jackie Moore MG	.10	.05	.01
☐ 82T	Joe Morgan	2.00	1.00	.20
☐ 83T	Graig Nettles	.40	.20	.04
☐ 84T	Phil Niekro	1.00	.50	.10
☐ 85T	Ken Oberkfell	.10	.05	.01
☐ 86T	Mike O'Berry	.10	.05	.01
☐ 87T	Al Oliver	.30	.15	.03
☐ 88T	Jorge Orta	.10	.05	.01
☐ 89T	Amos Otis	.20	.10	.02
☐ 90T	Dave Parker	1.00	.50	.10
☐ 91T	Tony Perez	.60	.30	.06
☐ 92T	Gerald Perry	1.00	.50	.10
☐ 93T	Gary Pettis	.40	.20	.04
☐ 94T	Rob Picciolo	.10	.05	.01
☐ 95T	Vern Rapp MG	.10	.05	.01
☐ 96T	Floyd Rayford	.10	.05	.01
☐ 97T	Randy Ready	.35	.17	.03
☐ 98T	Ron Reed	.10	.05	.01
☐ 99T	Gene Richards	.10	.05	.01
☐ 100T	Jose Rijo	1.50	.75	.15
☐ 101T	Jeff Robinson	.75	.35	.07
	(Giants pitcher)			
☐ 102T	Ron Romanick	.20	.10	.02
☐ 103T	Pete Rose	7.50	3.75	.75
☐ 104T	Bret Saberhagen	21.00	10.50	2.10
☐ 105T	Juan Samuel	3.00	1.50	.30
☐ 106T	Scott Sanderson	.20	.10	.02
☐ 107T	Dick Schofield	.45	.22	.04
☐ 108T	Tom Seaver	3.00	1.50	.30
☐ 109T	Jim Slaton	.10	.05	.01
☐ 110T	Mike Smithson	.10	.05	.01
☐ 111T	Lary Sorensen	.10	.05	.01
☐ 112T	Tim Stoddard	.10	.05	.01
☐ 113T	Champ Summers	.10	.05	.01

			MINT	EXC	G-VG
☐ 114T	Jim Sundberg		.10	.05	.01
☐ 115T	Rick Sutcliffe		.50	.25	.05
☐ 116T	Craig Swan		.10	.05	.01
☐ 117T	Tim Teufel		.35	.17	.03
☐ 118T	Derrel Thomas		.10	.05	.01
☐ 119T	Gorman Thomas		.30	.15	.03
☐ 120T	Alex Trevino		.10	.05	.01
☐ 121T	Manny Trillo		.10	.05	.01
☐ 122T	John Tudor		.30	.15	.03
☐ 123T	Tom Underwood		.10	.05	.01
☐ 124T	Mike Vail		.10	.05	.01
☐ 125T	Tom Waddell		.20	.10	.02
☐ 126T	Gary Ward		.20	.10	.02
☐ 127T	Curt Wilkerson		.20	.10	.02
☐ 128T	Frank Williams		.30	.15	.03
☐ 129T	Glenn Wilson		.20	.10	.02
☐ 130T	John Wockenfuss		.10	.05	.01
☐ 131T	Ned Yost		.10	.05	.01
☐ 132T	Checklist 1-132		.10	.01	.00

1984 Topps Glossy 22

The cards in this 22-card set measure 2 1/2" by 3 1/2". Unlike the 1983 Topps Glossy set which was not distributed with its regular baseball cards, the 1984 Topps Glossy set was distributed as inserts in Topps Rak-Paks. The set features the nine American and National League All-Stars who started in the 1983 All Star game in Chicago. The managers and team captains (Yastrzemski and Bench) complete the set. The cards are numbered on the back and are ordered by position in league (AL: 1-11 and NL: 12-22).

			MINT	EXC	G-VG
COMPLETE SET (22)			4.00	2.00	.40
COMMON PLAYER (1-22)			.10	.05	.01
☐ 1	Harvey Kuenn MG		.10	.05	.01
☐ 2	Rod Carew		.40	.20	.04
☐ 3	Manny Trillo		.10	.05	.01
☐ 4	George Brett		.60	.30	.06
☐ 5	Robin Yount		.60	.30	.06
☐ 6	Jim Rice		.25	.12	.02
☐ 7	Fred Lynn		.20	.10	.02
☐ 8	Dave Winfield		.30	.15	.03
☐ 9	Ted Simmons		.15	.07	.01
☐ 10	Dave Stieb		.15	.07	.01
☐ 11	Carl Yastrzemski CAPT		.50	.25	.05
☐ 12	Whitey Herzog MG		.10	.05	.01
☐ 13	Al Oliver		.15	.07	.01
☐ 14	Steve Sax		.25	.12	.02
☐ 15	Mike Schmidt		.90	.45	.09
☐ 16	Ozzie Smith		.35	.17	.03
☐ 17	Tim Raines		.35	.17	.03
☐ 18	Andre Dawson		.35	.17	.03
☐ 19	Dale Murphy		.65	.30	.06
☐ 20	Gary Carter		.30	.15	.03
☐ 21	Mario Soto		.10	.05	.01
☐ 22	Johnny Bench CAPT		.30	.15	.03

BUY A SUB: Subscribing to a hobby periodical extends your collecting fun.

1984 Topps Glossy 40

The cards in this 40-card set measure 2 1/2" by 3 1/2". Similar to last year's glossy set, this set was issued as a bonus prize to Topps All-Star Baseball Game cards found in wax packs. Twenty-five bonus runs from the game cards were necessary to obtain a five card subset of the series. There were eight different subsets of five cards. The cards are numbered and contain 20 stars from each league.

			MINT	EXC	G-VG
COMPLETE SET (40)			12.50	6.25	1.25
COMMON PLAYER (1-40)			.15	.07	.01
☐ 1	Pete Rose		1.25	.60	.12
☐ 2	Lance Parrish		.25	.12	.02
☐ 3	Steve Rogers		.15	.07	.01
☐ 4	Eddie Murray		.75	.35	.07
☐ 5	Johnny Ray		.20	.10	.02
☐ 6	Rickey Henderson		1.00	.50	.10
☐ 7	Atlee Hammaker		.15	.07	.01
☐ 8	Wade Boggs		1.50	.75	.15
☐ 9	Gary Carter		.40	.20	.04
☐ 10	Jack Morris		.25	.12	.02
☐ 11	Darrell Evans		.20	.10	.02
☐ 12	George Brett		1.00	.50	.10
☐ 13	Bob Horner		.25	.12	.02
☐ 14	Ron Guidry		.25	.12	.02
☐ 15	Nolan Ryan		1.25	.60	.12
☐ 16	Dave Winfield		.50	.25	.05
☐ 17	Ozzie Smith		.30	.15	.03
☐ 18	Ted Simmons		.20	.10	.02
☐ 19	Bill Madlock		.15	.07	.01
☐ 20	Tony Armas		.15	.07	.01
☐ 21	Al Oliver		.20	.10	.02
☐ 22	Jim Rice		.30	.15	.03
☐ 23	George Hendrick		.15	.07	.01
☐ 24	Dave Stieb		.15	.07	.01
☐ 25	Pedro Guerrero		.35	.17	.03
☐ 26	Rod Carew		.60	.30	.06
☐ 27	Steve Carlton		.60	.30	.06
☐ 28	Dave Righetti		.20	.10	.02
☐ 29	Darryl Strawberry		1.50	.75	.15
☐ 30	Lou Whitaker		.25	.12	.02
☐ 31	Dale Murphy		1.00	.50	.10
☐ 32	LaMarr Hoyt		.15	.07	.01
☐ 33	Jesse Orosco		.15	.07	.01
☐ 34	Cecil Cooper		.20	.10	.02
☐ 35	Andre Dawson		.35	.17	.03
☐ 36	Robin Yount		.75	.35	.07
☐ 37	Tim Raines		.35	.17	.03
☐ 38	Dan Quisenberry		.20	.10	.02
☐ 39	Mike Schmidt		1.25	.60	.12
☐ 40	Carlton Fisk		.35	.17	.03

1984 Topps Cereal

The cards in this 33 card-set measure 2 1/2" by 3 1/2". The cards are numbered both on the front and the back. The 1984 Topps Cereal Series is exactly the same as the Ralston-Purina issue of this year except for a Topps logo and the words "Cereal Series" on

the tops of the fronts of the cards in place of the Ralston checkerboard background. The checkerboard background is absent from the reverse, and a Topps logo is on the reverse of the cereal cards. These cards were distributed in unmarked boxes of Ralston-Purina cereal with a pack of four cards (three players and a checklist) being inside random cereal boxes. The back of the checklist details an offer to obtain any twelve cards direct from the issuer for only 1.50.

		MINT	EXC	G-VG
COMPLETE SET (34)		12.00	6.00	1.20
COMMON PLAYER (1-33)		.20	.10	.02
☐ 1	Eddie Murray	.75	.35	.07
☐ 2	Ozzie Smith	.35	.17	.03
☐ 3	Ted Simmons	.25	.12	.02
☐ 4	Pete Rose	1.25	.60	.12
☐ 5	Greg Luzinski	.20	.10	.02
☐ 6	Andre Dawson	.35	.17	.03
☐ 7	Dave Winfield	.45	.22	.04
☐ 8	Tom Seaver	.60	.30	.06
☐ 9	Jim Rice	.35	.17	.03
☐ 10	Fernando Valenzuela	.35	.17	.03
☐ 11	Wade Boggs	1.50	.75	.15
☐ 12	Dale Murphy	1.00	.50	.10
☐ 13	George Brett	1.00	.50	.10
☐ 14	Nolan Ryan	1.25	.60	.12
☐ 15	Rickey Henderson	1.00	.50	.10
☐ 16	Steve Carlton	.60	.30	.06
☐ 17	Rod Carew	.60	.30	.06
☐ 18	Steve Garvey	.60	.30	.06
☐ 19	Reggie Jackson	1.00	.50	.10
☐ 20	Dave Concepcion	.20	.10	.02
☐ 21	Robin Yount	1.00	.50	.10
☐ 22	Mike Schmidt	1.25	.60	.12
☐ 23	Jim Palmer	.50	.25	.05
☐ 24	Bruce Sutter	.25	.12	.02
☐ 25	Dan Quisenberry	.25	.12	.02
☐ 26	Bill Madlock	.20	.10	.02
☐ 27	Cecil Cooper	.20	.10	.02
☐ 28	Gary Carter	.50	.25	.05
☐ 29	Fred Lynn	.25	.12	.02
☐ 30	Pedro Guerrero	.35	.17	.03
☐ 31	Ron Guidry	.25	.12	.02
☐ 32	Keith Hernandez	.35	.17	.03
☐ 33	Carlton Fisk	.35	.17	.03
☐ 34	Checklist card colors	.25	.12	.02
	(unnumbered)			

1985 Topps

The cards in this 792-card set measure 2 1/2" by 3 1/2". The 1985 Topps set contains full color cards. The fronts feature both the Topps and team logos along with the team name, player's name, and his position. The backs feature player statistics with ink colors of light green and maroon on a gray stock. A trivia quiz is included on the lower portion of the backs. The first ten cards (1- 10) are Record Breakers (RB), cards 131-143 are Father and Son (FS) cards, and cards 701 to 722 portray All-Star

selections (AS). Cards 271 to 282 represent "First Draft Picks" still active in the Major Leagues and cards 389-404 feature the coach and players on the 1984 U.S. Olympic Baseball Team. The manager cards in the set are important in that they contain the checklist of that team's players on the back. Topps also produced a specially boxed "glossy" edition frequently referred to as the Topps Tiffany set. There were supposedly only 5,000 sets of the Tiffany cards produced; they were marketed to hobby dealers. The checklist of cards (792 regular and 132 Traded) is identical to that of the normal non-glossy cards. There are two primary distinguishing features of the Tiffany cards, white card stock reverses and high gloss obverses. These Tiffany cards are valued at approximately five times the values listed below.

		MINT	EXC	G-VG
COMPLETE SET (792)		100.00	50.00	10.00
COMMON PLAYER (1-792)		.04	.02	.00
☐ 1	Carlton Fisk RB	.20	.04	.01
	Longest game by catcher			
☐ 2	Steve Garvey RB	.20	.10	.02
	Consecutive error-less games, 1B			
☐ 3	Dwight Gooden RB	.75	.35	.07
	Most strikeouts, rookie, season			
☐ 4	Cliff Johnson RB	.04	.02	.00
	Most pinch homers, lifetime			
☐ 5	Joe Morgan RB	.12	.06	.01
	Most homers, 2B, lifetime			
☐ 6	Pete Rose RB	.50	.25	.05
	Most singles, lifetime			
☐ 7	Nolan Ryan RB	.50	.25	.05
	Most strikeouts, lifetime			
☐ 8	Juan Samuel RB	.12	.06	.01
	Most stolen bases, rookie, season			
☐ 9	Bruce Sutter RB	.07	.03	.01
	Most saves, season, NL			
☐ 10	Don Sutton RB	.10	.05	.01
	Most seasons, 100 or more K's			
☐ 11	Ralph Houk MG	.07	.03	.01
	(checklist back)			
☐ 12	Dave Lopes	.07	.03	.01
☐ 13	Tim Lollar	.04	.02	.00
☐ 14	Chris Bando	.04	.02	.00
☐ 15	Jerry Koosman	.07	.03	.01
☐ 16	Bobby Meacham	.04	.02	.00
☐ 17	Mike Scott	.30	.15	.03
☐ 18	Mickey Hatcher	.04	.02	.00
☐ 19	George Frazier	.04	.02	.00
☐ 20	Chet Lemon	.07	.03	.01
☐ 21	Lee Tunnell	.04	.02	.00
☐ 22	Duane Kuiper	.04	.02	.00
☐ 23	Bret Saberhagen	5.50	2.75	.55
☐ 24	Jesse Barfield	.25	.12	.02
☐ 25	Steve Bedrosian	.15	.07	.01
☐ 26	Roy Smalley	.04	.02	.00

☐ 27	Bruce Berenyi	.04	.02	.00
☐ 28	Dann Bilardello	.04	.02	.00
☐ 29	Odell Jones	.04	.02	.00
☐ 30	Cal Ripken	.50	.25	.05
☐ 31	Terry Whitfield	.04	.02	.00
☐ 32	Chuck Porter	.04	.02	.00
☐ 33	Tito Landrum	.04	.02	.00
☐ 34	Ed Nunez	.07	.03	.01
☐ 35	Graig Nettles	.10	.05	.01
☐ 36	Fred Breining	.04	.02	.00
☐ 37	Reid Nichols	.04	.02	.00
☐ 38	Jackie Moore MG	.07	.03	.01
	(checklist back)			
☐ 39	John Wockenfuss	.04	.02	.00
☐ 40	Phil Niekro	.18	.09	.01
☐ 41	Mike Fischlin	.04	.02	.00
☐ 42	Luis Sanchez	.04	.02	.00
☐ 43	Andre David	.04	.02	.00
☐ 44	Dickie Thon	.04	.02	.00
☐ 45	Greg Minton	.04	.02	.00
☐ 46	Gary Woods	.04	.02	.00
☐ 47	Dave Rozema	.04	.02	.00
☐ 48	Tony Fernandez	1.50	.75	.15
☐ 49	Butch Davis	.04	.02	.00
☐ 50	John Candelaria	.07	.03	.01
☐ 51	Bob Watson	.07	.03	.01
☐ 52	Jerry Dybzinski	.04	.02	.00
☐ 53	Tom Gorman	.04	.02	.00
☐ 54	Cesar Cedeno	.07	.03	.01
☐ 55	Frank Tanana	.07	.03	.01
☐ 56	Jim Dwyer	.04	.02	.00
☐ 57	Pat Zachry	.04	.02	.00
☐ 58	Orlando Mercado	.04	.02	.00
☐ 59	Rick Waits	.04	.02	.00
☐ 60	George Hendrick	.07	.03	.01
☐ 61	Curt Kaufman	.04	.02	.00
☐ 62	Mike Ramsey	.04	.02	.00
☐ 63	Steve McCatty	.04	.02	.00
☐ 64	Mark Bailey	.04	.02	.00
☐ 65	Bill Buckner	.10	.05	.01
☐ 66	Dick Williams MG	.07	.03	.01
	(checklist back)			
☐ 67	Rafael Santana	.25	.12	.02
☐ 68	Von Hayes	.15	.07	.01
☐ 69	Jim Winn	.04	.02	.00
☐ 70	Don Baylor	.10	.05	.01
☐ 71	Tim Laudner	.04	.02	.00
☐ 72	Rick Sutcliffe	.12	.06	.01
☐ 73	Rusty Kuntz	.04	.02	.00
☐ 74	Mike Krukow	.04	.02	.00
☐ 75	Willie Upshaw	.04	.02	.00
☐ 76	Alan Bannister	.04	.02	.00
☐ 77	Joe Beckwith	.04	.02	.00
☐ 78	Scott Fletcher	.07	.03	.01
☐ 79	Rick Mahler	.04	.02	.00
☐ 80	Keith Hernandez	.30	.15	.03
☐ 81	Lenn Sakata	.04	.02	.00
☐ 82	Joe Price	.04	.02	.00
☐ 83	Charlie Moore	.04	.02	.00
☐ 84	Spike Owen	.04	.02	.00
☐ 85	Mike Marshall	.12	.06	.01
☐ 86	Don Aase	.04	.02	.00
☐ 87	David Green	.04	.02	.00
☐ 88	Bryn Smith	.07	.03	.01
☐ 89	Jackie Gutierrez	.07	.03	.01
☐ 90	Rich Gossage	.12	.06	.01
☐ 91	Jeff Burroughs	.04	.02	.00
☐ 92	Paul Owens MG	.07	.03	.01
	(checklist back)			
☐ 93	Don Schulze	.04	.02	.00
☐ 94	Toby Harrah	.04	.02	.00
☐ 95	Jose Cruz	.10	.05	.01
☐ 96	Johnny Ray	.10	.05	.01
☐ 97	Pete Filson	.04	.02	.00
☐ 98	Steve Lake	.04	.02	.00
☐ 99	Milt Wilcox	.04	.02	.00
☐ 100	George Brett	.50	.25	.05
☐ 101	Jim Acker	.04	.02	.00
☐ 102	Tommy Dunbar	.04	.02	.00
☐ 103	Randy Lerch	.04	.02	.00
☐ 104	Mike Fitzgerald	.04	.02	.00
☐ 105	Ron Kittle	.12	.06	.01
☐ 106	Pascual Perez	.10	.05	.01
☐ 107	Tom Foley	.04	.02	.00
☐ 108	Darnell Coles	.10	.05	.01
☐ 109	Gary Roenicke	.04	.02	.00
☐ 110	Alejandro Pena	.07	.03	.01
☐ 111	Doug DeCinces	.07	.03	.01
☐ 112	Tom Tellmann	.04	.02	.00
☐ 113	Tom Herr	.07	.03	.01
☐ 114	Bob James	.04	.02	.00
☐ 115	Rickey Henderson	.60	.30	.06
☐ 116	Dennis Boyd	.20	.10	.02
☐ 117	Greg Gross	.04	.02	.00
☐ 118	Eric Show	.07	.03	.01
☐ 119	Pat Corrales MG	.07	.03	.01
	(checklist back)			
☐ 120	Steve Kemp	.07	.03	.01
☐ 121	Checklist: 1-132	.07	.01	.00
☐ 122	Tom Brunansky	.18	.09	.01
☐ 123	Dave Smith	.07	.03	.01
☐ 124	Rich Hebner	.04	.02	.00
☐ 125	Kent Tekulve	.07	.03	.01
☐ 126	Ruppert Jones	.04	.02	.00
☐ 127	Mark Gubicza	1.25	.60	.12
☐ 128	Ernie Whitt	.07	.03	.01
☐ 129	Gene Garber	.04	.02	.00
☐ 130	Al Oliver	.10	.05	.01
☐ 131	Buddy/Gus Bell FS	.07	.03	.01
☐ 132	Dale/Yogi Berra FS	.15	.07	.01
☐ 133	Bob/Ray Boone FS	.07	.03	.01
☐ 134	Terry/Tito Francona FS	.07	.03	.01
☐ 135	Terry/Bob Kennedy FS	.07	.03	.01
☐ 136	Jeff/Jim Kunkel FS	.07	.03	.01
☐ 137	Vance/Vern Law FS	.07	.03	.01
☐ 138	Dick/Dick Schofield FS	.07	.03	.01
☐ 139	Joel/Bob Skinner FS	.07	.03	.01
☐ 140	Roy/Roy Smalley FS	.07	.03	.01
☐ 141	Mike/D.Stenhouse FS	.07	.03	.01
☐ 142	Steve/Dizzy Trout FS	.07	.03	.01
☐ 143	Ozzie/Ozzie Virgil FS	.07	.03	.01
☐ 144	Ron Gardenhire	.04	.02	.00
☐ 145	Alvin Davis	2.00	1.00	.20
☐ 146	Gary Redus	.04	.02	.00
☐ 147	Bill Swaggerty	.04	.02	.00
☐ 148	Steve Yeager	.04	.02	.00
☐ 149	Dickie Noles	.04	.02	.00
☐ 150	Jim Rice	.25	.12	.02
☐ 151	Moose Haas	.04	.02	.00
☐ 152	Steve Braun	.04	.02	.00
☐ 153	Frank LaCorte	.04	.02	.00
☐ 154	Argenis Salazar	.04	.02	.00
☐ 155	Yogi Berra MG	.15	.07	.01
	(checklist back)			
☐ 156	Craig Reynolds	.04	.02	.00
☐ 157	Tug McGraw	.10	.05	.01
☐ 158	Pat Tabler	.07	.03	.01
☐ 159	Carlos Diaz	.04	.02	.00
☐ 160	Lance Parrish	.18	.09	.01
☐ 161	Ken Schrom	.04	.02	.00
☐ 162	Benny Distefano	.10	.05	.01
☐ 163	Dennis Eckersley	.15	.07	.01
☐ 164	Jorge Orta	.04	.02	.00
☐ 165	Dusty Baker	.07	.03	.01
☐ 166	Keith Atherton	.04	.02	.00
☐ 167	Rufino Linares	.04	.02	.00
☐ 168	Garth Iorg	.04	.02	.00
☐ 169	Dan Spillner	.04	.02	.00
☐ 170	George Foster	.10	.05	.01
☐ 171	Bill Stein	.04	.02	.00
☐ 172	Jack Perconte	.04	.02	.00
☐ 173	Mike Young	.10	.05	.01
☐ 174	Rick Honeycutt	.04	.02	.00
☐ 175	Dave Parker	.18	.09	.01
☐ 176	Bill Schroeder	.04	.02	.00
☐ 177	Dave Von Ohlen	.04	.02	.00
☐ 178	Miguel Dilone	.04	.02	.00
☐ 179	Tommy John	.15	.07	.01
☐ 180	Dave Winfield	.35	.17	.03
☐ 181	Roger Clemens	10.00	5.00	1.00
☐ 182	Tim Flannery	.04	.02	.00
☐ 183	Larry McWilliams	.04	.02	.00
☐ 184	Carmen Castillo	.04	.02	.00
☐ 185	Al Holland	.04	.02	.00
☐ 186	Bob Lillis MG	.07	.03	.01
	(checklist back)			
☐ 187	Mike Walters	.04	.02	.00
☐ 188	Greg Pryor	.04	.02	.00
☐ 189	Warren Brusstar	.04	.02	.00
☐ 190	Rusty Staub	.10	.05	.01
☐ 191	Steve Nicosia	.04	.02	.00
☐ 192	Howard Johnson	4.00	2.00	.40
☐ 193	Jimmy Key	1.00	.50	.10
☐ 194	Dave Stegman	.04	.02	.00
☐ 195	Glenn Hubbard	.04	.02	.00
☐ 196	Pete O'Brien	.10	.05	.01
☐ 197	Mike Warren	.04	.02	.00
☐ 198	Eddie Milner	.04	.02	.00
☐ 199	Dennis Martinez	.07	.03	.01
☐ 200	Reggie Jackson	.45	.22	.04
☐ 201	Burt Hooton	.04	.02	.00
☐ 202	Gorman Thomas	.10	.05	.01
☐ 203	Bob McClure	.04	.02	.00
☐ 204	Art Howe	.07	.03	.01
☐ 205	Steve Rogers	.04	.02	.00
☐ 206	Phil Garner	.04	.02	.00
☐ 207	Mark Clear	.04	.02	.00
☐ 208	Champ Summers	.04	.02	.00
☐ 209	Bill Campbell	.04	.02	.00
☐ 210	Gary Matthews	.07	.03	.01

☐ 211	Clay Christiansen	.04	.02	.00
☐ 212	George Vukovich	.04	.02	.00
☐ 213	Billy Gardner MG	.07	.03	.01
	(checklist back)			
☐ 214	John Tudor	.15	.07	.01
☐ 215	Bob Brenly	.04	.02	.00
☐ 216	Jerry Don Gleaton	.04	.02	.00
☐ 217	Leon Roberts	.04	.02	.00
☐ 218	Doyle Alexander	.07	.03	.01
☐ 219	Gerald Perry	.30	.15	.03
☐ 220	Fred Lynn	.15	.07	.01
☐ 221	Ron Reed	.04	.02	.00
☐ 222	Hubie Brooks	.12	.06	.01
☐ 223	Tom Hume	.04	.02	.00
☐ 224	Al Cowens	.04	.02	.00
☐ 225	Mike Boddicker	.10	.05	.01
☐ 226	Juan Beniquez	.04	.02	.00
☐ 227	Danny Darwin	.04	.02	.00
☐ 228	Dion James	.15	.07	.01
☐ 229	Dave LaPoint	.07	.03	.01
☐ 230	Gary Carter	.30	.15	.03
☐ 231	Dwayne Murphy	.04	.02	.00
☐ 232	Dave Beard	.04	.02	.00
☐ 233	Ed Jurak	.04	.02	.00
☐ 234	Jerry Narron	.04	.02	.00
☐ 235	Garry Maddox	.04	.02	.00
☐ 236	Mark Thurmond	.04	.02	.00
☐ 237	Julio Franco	.40	.20	.04
☐ 238	Jose Rijo	.45	.22	.04
☐ 239	Tim Teufel	.12	.06	.01
☐ 240	Dave Stieb	.12	.06	.01
☐ 241	Jim Frey MG	.07	.03	.01
	(checklist back)			
☐ 242	Greg Harris	.04	.02	.00
☐ 243	Barbaro Garbey	.04	.02	.00
☐ 244	Mike Jones	.04	.02	.00
☐ 245	Chili Davis	.10	.05	.01
☐ 246	Mike Norris	.04	.02	.00
☐ 247	Wayne Tolleson	.04	.02	.00
☐ 248	Terry Forster	.07	.03	.01
☐ 249	Harold Baines	.15	.07	.01
☐ 250	Jesse Orosco	.04	.02	.00
☐ 251	Brad Gulden	.04	.02	.00
☐ 252	Dan Ford	.04	.02	.00
☐ 253	Sid Bream	.30	.15	.03
☐ 254	Pete Vuckovich	.04	.02	.00
☐ 255	Lonnie Smith	.07	.03	.01
☐ 256	Mike Stanton	.04	.02	.00
☐ 257	Bryan Little	.04	.02	.00
☐ 258	Mike Brown	.04	.02	.00
	(Angels OF)			
☐ 259	Gary Allenson	.04	.02	.00
☐ 260	Dave Righetti	.12	.06	.01
☐ 261	Checklist: 133-264	.07	.01	.00
☐ 262	Greg Booker	.04	.02	.00
☐ 263	Mel Hall	.10	.05	.01
☐ 264	Joe Sambito	.04	.02	.00
☐ 265	Juan Samuel	.60	.30	.06
☐ 266	Frank Viola	.30	.15	.03
☐ 267	Henry Cotto	.15	.07	.01
☐ 268	Chuck Tanner MG	.07	.03	.01
	(checklist back)			
☐ 269	Doug Baker	.04	.02	.00
☐ 270	Dan Quisenberry	.12	.06	.01
☐ 271	Tim Foli FDP68	.04	.02	.00
☐ 272	Jeff Burroughs FDP69	.04	.02	.00
☐ 273	Bill Almon FDP74	.04	.02	.00
☐ 274	Floyd Bannister FDP76	.04	.02	.00
☐ 275	Harold Baines FDP77	.12	.06	.01
☐ 276	Bob Horner FDP78	.12	.06	.01
☐ 277	Al Chambers FDP79	.04	.02	.00
☐ 278	D.Strawberry FDP80	1.00	.50	.10
☐ 279	Mike Moore FDP81	.10	.05	.01
☐ 280	Sh.Dunston FDP82	1.50	.75	.15
☐ 281	Tim Belcher FDP83	1.50	.75	.15
☐ 282	Shawn Abner FDP84	.35	.17	.03
☐ 283	Fran Mullins	.04	.02	.00
☐ 284	Marty Bystrom	.04	.02	.00
☐ 285	Dan Driessen	.04	.02	.00
☐ 286	Rudy Law	.04	.02	.00
☐ 287	Walt Terrell	.04	.02	.00
☐ 288	Jeff Kunkel	.07	.03	.01
☐ 289	Tom Underwood	.04	.02	.00
☐ 290	Cecil Cooper	.10	.05	.01
☐ 291	Bob Welch	.07	.03	.01
☐ 292	Brad Komminsk	.04	.02	.00
☐ 293	Curt Young	.25	.12	.02
☐ 294	Tom Nieto	.04	.02	.00
☐ 295	Joe Niekro	.07	.03	.01
☐ 296	Ricky Nelson	.04	.02	.00
☐ 297	Gary Lucas	.04	.02	.00
☐ 298	Marty Barrett	.12	.06	.01
☐ 299	Andy Hawkins	.10	.05	.01
☐ 300	Rod Carew	.35	.17	.03
☐ 301	John Montefusco	.04	.02	.00
☐ 302	Tim Corcoran	.04	.02	.00
☐ 303	Mike Jeffcoat	.04	.02	.00
☐ 304	Gary Gaetti	.30	.15	.03
☐ 305	Dale Berra	.04	.02	.00
☐ 306	Rick Reuschel	.12	.06	.01
☐ 307	Sparky Anderson MG	.07	.03	.01
	(checklist back)			
☐ 308	John Wathan	.04	.02	.00
☐ 309	Mike Witt	.10	.05	.01
☐ 310	Manny Trillo	.04	.02	.00
☐ 311	Jim Gott	.04	.02	.00
☐ 312	Marc Hill	.04	.02	.00
☐ 313	Dave Schmidt	.07	.03	.01
☐ 314	Ron Oester	.04	.02	.00
☐ 315	Doug Sisk	.04	.02	.00
☐ 316	John Lowenstein	.04	.02	.00
☐ 317	Jack Lazorko	.04	.02	.00
☐ 318	Ted Simmons	.10	.05	.01
☐ 319	Jeff Jones	.04	.02	.00
☐ 320	Dale Murphy	.60	.30	.06
☐ 321	Ricky Horton	.20	.10	.02
☐ 322	Dave Stapleton	.04	.02	.00
☐ 323	Andy McGaffigan	.04	.02	.00
☐ 324	Bruce Bochy	.04	.02	.00
☐ 325	John Denny	.07	.03	.01
☐ 326	Kevin Bass	.10	.05	.01
☐ 327	Brook Jacoby	.25	.12	.02
☐ 328	Bob Shirley	.04	.02	.00
☐ 329	Ron Washington	.04	.02	.00
☐ 330	Leon Durham	.07	.03	.01
☐ 331	Bill Laskey	.04	.02	.00
☐ 332	Brian Harper	.04	.02	.00
☐ 333	Willie Hernandez	.10	.05	.01
☐ 334	Dick Howser MG	.07	.03	.01
	(checklist back)			
☐ 335	Bruce Benedict	.04	.02	.00
☐ 336	Rance Mulliniks	.04	.02	.00
☐ 337	Billy Sample	.04	.02	.00
☐ 338	Britt Burns	.04	.02	.00
☐ 339	Danny Heep	.04	.02	.00
☐ 340	Robin Yount	.50	.25	.05
☐ 341	Floyd Rayford	.04	.02	.00
☐ 342	Ted Power	.04	.02	.00
☐ 343	Bill Russell	.07	.03	.01
☐ 344	Dave Henderson	.10	.05	.01
☐ 345	Charlie Lea	.04	.02	.00
☐ 346	Terry Pendleton	.45	.22	.04
☐ 347	Rick Langford	.04	.02	.00
☐ 348	Bob Boone	.12	.06	.01
☐ 349	Domingo Ramos	.04	.02	.00
☐ 350	Wade Boggs	3.50	1.75	.35
☐ 351	Juan Agosto	.04	.02	.00
☐ 352	Joe Morgan	.20	.10	.02
☐ 353	Julio Solano	.04	.02	.00
☐ 354	Andre Robertson	.04	.02	.00
☐ 355	Bert Blyleven	.15	.07	.01
☐ 356	Dave Meier	.04	.02	.00
☐ 357	Rich Bordi	.04	.02	.00
☐ 358	Tony Pena	.10	.05	.01
☐ 359	Pat Sheridan	.04	.02	.00
☐ 360	Steve Carlton	.30	.15	.03
☐ 361	Alfredo Griffin	.07	.03	.01
☐ 362	Craig McMurtry	.04	.02	.00
☐ 363	Ron Hodges	.04	.02	.00
☐ 364	Richard Dotson	.07	.03	.01
☐ 365	Danny Ozark MG	.07	.03	.01
	(checklist back)			
☐ 366	Todd Cruz	.04	.02	.00
☐ 367	Keefe Cato	.04	.02	.00
☐ 368	Dave Bergman	.04	.02	.00
☐ 369	R.J. Reynolds	.20	.10	.02
☐ 370	Bruce Sutter	.10	.05	.01
☐ 371	Mickey Rivers	.07	.03	.01
☐ 372	Roy Howell	.04	.02	.00
☐ 373	Mike Moore	.10	.05	.01
☐ 374	Brian Downing	.07	.03	.01
☐ 375	Jeff Reardon	.10	.05	.01
☐ 376	Jeff Newman	.04	.02	.00
☐ 377	Checklist: 265-396	.07	.01	.00
☐ 378	Alan Wiggins	.04	.02	.00
☐ 379	Charles Hudson	.04	.02	.00
☐ 380	Ken Griffey	.10	.05	.01
☐ 381	Roy Smith	.04	.02	.00
☐ 382	Denny Walling	.04	.02	.00
☐ 383	Rick Lysander	.04	.02	.00
☐ 384	Jody Davis	.07	.03	.01
☐ 385	Jose DeLeon	.07	.03	.01
☐ 386	Dan Gladden	.35	.17	.03
☐ 387	Buddy Biancalana	.07	.03	.01
☐ 388	Bert Roberge	.04	.02	.00
☐ 389	Rod Dedeaux OLY CO	.04	.02	.00
☐ 390	Sid Akins OLY	.07	.03	.01
☐ 391	Flavio Alfaro OLY	.04	.02	.00
☐ 392	Don August OLY	.35	.17	.03
☐ 393	Scott Bankhead OLY	.75	.35	.07

☐ 394	Bob Caffrey OLY	.07	.03	.01
☐ 395	Mike Dunne OLY	.35	.17	.03
☐ 396	Gary Green OLY	.12	.06	.01
☐ 397	John Hoover OLY	.12	.06	.01
☐ 398	Shane Mack OLY	.35	.17	.03
☐ 399	John Marzano OLY	.25	.12	.02
☐ 400	Oddibe McDowell OLY	.65	.30	.06
☐ 401	Mark McGwire OLY	18.00	9.00	1.80
☐ 402	Pat Pacillo OLY	.15	.07	.01
☐ 403	Cory Snyder OLY	4.00	2.00	.40
☐ 404	Billy Swift OLY	.20	.10	.02
☐ 405	Tom Veryzer	.04	.02	.00
☐ 406	Len Whitehouse	.04	.02	.00
☐ 407	Bobby Ramos	.04	.02	.00
☐ 408	Sid Monge	.04	.02	.00
☐ 409	Brad Wellman	.04	.02	.00
☐ 410	Bob Horner	.12	.06	.01
☐ 411	Bobby Cox MG (checklist back)	.07	.03	.01
☐ 412	Bud Black	.04	.02	.00
☐ 413	Vance Law	.07	.03	.01
☐ 414	Gary Ward	.07	.03	.01
☐ 415	Ron Darling UER (no trivia answer)	1.00	.50	.10
☐ 416	Wayne Gross	.04	.02	.00
☐ 417	John Franco	1.25	.60	.12
☐ 418	Ken Landreaux	.04	.02	.00
☐ 419	Mike Caldwell	.04	.02	.00
☐ 420	Andre Dawson	.30	.15	.03
☐ 421	Dave Rucker	.04	.02	.00
☐ 422	Carney Lansford	.12	.06	.01
☐ 423	Barry Bonnell	.04	.02	.00
☐ 424	Al Nipper	.10	.05	.01
☐ 425	Mike Hargrove	.04	.02	.00
☐ 426	Vern Ruhle	.04	.02	.00
☐ 427	Mario Ramirez	.04	.02	.00
☐ 428	Larry Andersen	.04	.02	.00
☐ 429	Rick Cerone	.04	.02	.00
☐ 430	Ron Davis	.04	.02	.00
☐ 431	U.L. Washington	.04	.02	.00
☐ 432	Thad Bosley	.04	.02	.00
☐ 433	Jim Morrison	.04	.02	.00
☐ 434	Gene Richards	.04	.02	.00
☐ 435	Dan Petry	.04	.02	.00
☐ 436	Willie Aikens	.04	.02	.00
☐ 437	Al Jones	.04	.02	.00
☐ 438	Joe Torre MG (checklist back)	.07	.03	.01
☐ 439	Junior Ortiz	.04	.02	.00
☐ 440	Fernando Valenzuela	.25	.12	.02
☐ 441	Duane Walker	.04	.02	.00
☐ 442	Ken Forsch	.04	.02	.00
☐ 443	George Wright	.04	.02	.00
☐ 444	Tony Phillips	.04	.02	.00
☐ 445	Tippy Martinez	.04	.02	.00
☐ 446	Jim Sundberg	.04	.02	.00
☐ 447	Jeff Lahti	.04	.02	.00
☐ 448	Derrel Thomas	.04	.02	.00
☐ 449	Phil Bradley	.65	.30	.06
☐ 450	Steve Garvey	.40	.20	.04
☐ 451	Bruce Hurst	.15	.07	.01
☐ 452	John Castino	.04	.02	.00
☐ 453	Tom Waddell	.07	.03	.01
☐ 454	Glenn Wilson	.07	.03	.01
☐ 455	Bob Knepper	.07	.03	.01
☐ 456	Tim Foli	.04	.02	.00
☐ 457	Cecilio Guante	.04	.02	.00
☐ 458	Randy Johnson	.04	.02	.00
☐ 459	Charlie Leibrandt	.04	.02	.00
☐ 460	Ryne Sandberg	.45	.22	.04
☐ 461	Marty Castillo	.04	.02	.00
☐ 462	Gary Lavelle	.04	.02	.00
☐ 463	Dave Collins	.04	.02	.00
☐ 464	Mike Mason	.07	.03	.01
☐ 465	Bob Grich	.07	.03	.01
☐ 466	Tony LaRussa MG (checklist back)	.07	.03	.01
☐ 467	Ed Lynch	.04	.02	.00
☐ 468	Wayne Krenchicki	.04	.02	.00
☐ 469	Sammy Stewart	.04	.02	.00
☐ 470	Steve Sax	.25	.12	.02
☐ 471	Pete Ladd	.04	.02	.00
☐ 472	Jim Essian	.04	.02	.00
☐ 473	Tim Wallach	.10	.05	.01
☐ 474	Kurt Kepshire	.07	.03	.01
☐ 475	Andre Thornton	.07	.03	.01
☐ 476	Jeff Stone	.10	.05	.01
☐ 477	Bob Ojeda	.10	.05	.01
☐ 478	Kurt Bevacqua	.04	.02	.00
☐ 479	Mike Madden	.04	.02	.00
☐ 480	Lou Whitaker	.18	.09	.01
☐ 481	Dale Murray	.04	.02	.00
☐ 482	Harry Spilman	.04	.02	.00
☐ 483	Mike Smithson	.04	.02	.00
☐ 484	Larry Bowa	.10	.05	.01
☐ 485	Matt Young	.04	.02	.00
☐ 486	Steve Balboni	.04	.02	.00
☐ 487	Frank Williams	.12	.06	.01
☐ 488	Joel Skinner	.07	.03	.01
☐ 489	Bryan Clark	.04	.02	.00
☐ 490	Jason Thompson	.04	.02	.00
☐ 491	Rick Camp	.04	.02	.00
☐ 492	Dave Johnson MG (checklist back)	.07	.03	.01
☐ 493	Orel Hershiser	7.00	3.50	.70
☐ 494	Rich Dauer	.04	.02	.00
☐ 495	Mario Soto	.04	.02	.00
☐ 496	Donnie Scott	.04	.02	.00
☐ 497	Gary Pettis UER (photo actually Gary's little brother, Lynn)	.25	.12	.02
☐ 498	Ed Romero	.04	.02	.00
☐ 499	Danny Cox	.20	.10	.02
☐ 500	Mike Schmidt	.60	.30	.06
☐ 501	Dan Schatzeder	.04	.02	.00
☐ 502	Rick Miller	.04	.02	.00
☐ 503	Tim Conroy	.04	.02	.00
☐ 504	Jerry Willard	.04	.02	.00
☐ 505	Jim Beattie	.04	.02	.00
☐ 506	Franklin Stubbs	.25	.12	.02
☐ 507	Ray Fontenot	.04	.02	.00
☐ 508	John Shelby	.04	.02	.00
☐ 509	Milt May	.04	.02	.00
☐ 510	Kent Hrbek	.30	.15	.03
☐ 511	Lee Smith	.07	.03	.01
☐ 512	Tom Brookens	.04	.02	.00
☐ 513	Lynn Jones	.04	.02	.00
☐ 514	Jeff Cornell	.04	.02	.00
☐ 515	Dave Concepcion	.07	.03	.01
☐ 516	Roy Lee Jackson	.04	.02	.00
☐ 517	Jerry Martin	.04	.02	.00
☐ 518	Chris Chambliss	.07	.03	.01
☐ 519	Doug Rader MG (checklist back)	.07	.03	.01
☐ 520	LaMarr Hoyt	.07	.03	.01
☐ 521	Rick Dempsey	.04	.02	.00
☐ 522	Paul Molitor	.15	.07	.01
☐ 523	Candy Maldonado	.10	.05	.01
☐ 524	Rob Wilfong	.04	.02	.00
☐ 525	Darrell Porter	.04	.02	.00
☐ 526	David Palmer	.04	.02	.00
☐ 527	Checklist: 397-528	.07	.01	.00
☐ 528	Bill Krueger	.04	.02	.00
☐ 529	Rich Gedman	.07	.03	.01
☐ 530	Dave Dravecky	.12	.06	.01
☐ 531	Joe Lefebvre	.04	.02	.00
☐ 532	Frank DiPino	.04	.02	.00
☐ 533	Tony Bernazard	.04	.02	.00
☐ 534	Brian Dayett	.04	.02	.00
☐ 535	Pat Putnam	.04	.02	.00
☐ 536	Kirby Puckett	12.00	6.00	1.20
☐ 537	Don Robinson	.04	.02	.00
☐ 538	Keith Moreland	.04	.02	.00
☐ 539	Aurelio Lopez	.04	.02	.00
☐ 540	Claudell Washington	.07	.03	.01
☐ 541	Mark Davis	.15	.07	.01
☐ 542	Don Slaught	.04	.02	.00
☐ 543	Mike Squires	.04	.02	.00
☐ 544	Bruce Kison	.04	.02	.00
☐ 545	Lloyd Moseby	.10	.05	.01
☐ 546	Brent Gaff	.04	.02	.00
☐ 547	Pete Rose MG (checklist back)	.45	.22	.04
☐ 548	Larry Parrish	.04	.02	.00
☐ 549	Mike Scioscia	.07	.03	.01
☐ 550	Scott McGregor	.07	.03	.01
☐ 551	Andy Van Slyke	.35	.17	.03
☐ 552	Chris Codiroli	.04	.02	.00
☐ 553	Bob Clark	.04	.02	.00
☐ 554	Doug Flynn	.04	.02	.00
☐ 555	Bob Stanley	.04	.02	.00
☐ 556	Sixto Lezcano	.04	.02	.00
☐ 557	Len Barker	.04	.02	.00
☐ 558	Carmelo Martinez	.04	.02	.00
☐ 559	Jay Howell	.07	.03	.01
☐ 560	Bill Madlock	.07	.03	.01
☐ 561	Darryl Motley	.04	.02	.00
☐ 562	Houston Jimenez	.04	.02	.00
☐ 563	Dick Ruthven	.04	.02	.00
☐ 564	Alan Ashby	.04	.02	.00
☐ 565	Kirk Gibson	.30	.15	.03
☐ 566	Ed VandeBerg	.04	.02	.00
☐ 567	Joel Youngblood	.04	.02	.00
☐ 568	Cliff Johnson	.04	.02	.00
☐ 569	Ken Oberkfell	.04	.02	.00
☐ 570	Darryl Strawberry	3.00	1.50	.30
☐ 571	Charlie Hough	.07	.03	.01
☐ 572	Tom Paciorek	.04	.02	.00
☐ 573	Jay Tibbs	.10	.05	.01

□ 574 Joe Altobelli MG (checklist back)	.07	.03	.01
□ 575 Pedro Guerrero	.25	.12	.02
□ 576 Jaime Cocanower	.04	.02	.00
□ 577 Chris Speier	.04	.02	.00
□ 578 Terry Francona	.04	.02	.00
□ 579 Ron Romanick	.04	.02	.00
□ 580 Dwight Evans	.12	.06	.01
□ 581 Mark Wagner	.04	.02	.00
□ 582 Ken Phelps	.25	.12	.02
□ 583 Bobby Brown	.04	.02	.00
□ 584 Kevin Gross	.04	.02	.00
□ 585 Butch Wynegar	.04	.02	.00
□ 586 Bill Scherrer	.04	.02	.00
□ 587 Doug Frobel	.04	.02	.00
□ 588 Bobby Castillo	.04	.02	.00
□ 589 Bob Dernier	.04	.02	.00
□ 590 Ray Knight	.07	.03	.01
□ 591 Larry Herndon	.04	.02	.00
□ 592 Jeff Robinson (Giants pitcher)	.30	.15	.03
□ 593 Rick Leach	.04	.02	.00
□ 594 Curt Wilkerson	.04	.02	.00
□ 595 Larry Gura	.04	.02	.00
□ 596 Jerry Hairston	.04	.02	.00
□ 597 Brad Lesley	.04	.02	.00
□ 598 Jose Oquendo	.07	.03	.01
□ 599 Storm Davis	.10	.05	.01
□ 600 Pete Rose	1.00	.50	.10
□ 601 Tom Lasorda MG (checklist back)	.07	.03	.01
□ 602 Jeff Dedmon	.04	.02	.00
□ 603 Rick Manning	.04	.02	.00
□ 604 Daryl Sconiers	.04	.02	.00
□ 605 Ozzie Smith	.25	.12	.02
□ 606 Rich Gale	.04	.02	.00
□ 607 Bill Almon	.04	.02	.00
□ 608 Craig Lefferts	.07	.03	.01
□ 609 Broderick Perkins	.04	.02	.00
□ 610 Jack Morris	.15	.07	.01
□ 611 Ozzie Virgil	.04	.02	.00
□ 612 Mike Armstrong	.04	.02	.00
□ 613 Terry Puhl	.04	.02	.00
□ 614 Al Williams	.04	.02	.00
□ 615 Marvell Wynne	.04	.02	.00
□ 616 Scott Sanderson	.04	.02	.00
□ 617 Willie Wilson	.10	.05	.01
□ 618 Pete Falcone	.04	.02	.00
□ 619 Jeff Leonard	.07	.03	.01
□ 620 Dwight Gooden	9.00	4.50	.90
□ 621 Marvis Foley	.04	.02	.00
□ 622 Luis Leal	.04	.02	.00
□ 623 Greg Walker	.07	.03	.01
□ 624 Benny Ayala	.04	.02	.00
□ 625 Mark Langston	3.25	1.60	.32
□ 626 German Rivera	.07	.03	.01
□ 627 Eric Davis	13.50	6.00	1.25
□ 628 Rene Lachemann MG (checklist back)	.07	.03	.01
□ 629 Dick Schofield	.12	.06	.01
□ 630 Tim Raines	.35	.17	.03
□ 631 Bob Forsch	.04	.02	.00
□ 632 Bruce Bochte	.04	.02	.00
□ 633 Glenn Hoffman	.04	.02	.00
□ 634 Bill Dawley	.04	.02	.00
□ 635 Terry Kennedy	.04	.02	.00
□ 636 Shane Rawley	.04	.02	.00
□ 637 Brett Butler	.07	.03	.01
□ 638 Mike Pagliarulo	.65	.30	.06
□ 639 Ed Hodge	.04	.02	.00
□ 640 Steve Henderson	.10	.05	.01
□ 641 Rod Scurry	.04	.02	.00
□ 642 Dave Owen	.04	.02	.00
□ 643 Johnny Grubb	.04	.02	.00
□ 644 Mark Huismann	.04	.02	.00
□ 645 Damaso Garcia	.04	.02	.00
□ 646 Scot Thompson	.04	.02	.00
□ 647 Rafael Ramirez	.04	.02	.00
□ 648 Bob Jones	.04	.02	.00
□ 649 Sid Fernandez	.85	.40	.08
□ 650 Greg Luzinski	.10	.05	.01
□ 651 Jeff Russell	.12	.06	.01
□ 652 Joe Nolan	.04	.02	.00
□ 653 Mark Brouhard	.04	.02	.00
□ 654 Dave Anderson	.04	.02	.00
□ 655 Joaquin Andujar	.10	.05	.01
□ 656 Chuck Cottier MG (checklist back)	.07	.03	.01
□ 657 Jim Slaton	.04	.02	.00
□ 658 Mike Stenhouse	.07	.03	.01
□ 659 Checklist: 529-660	.07	.01	.00
□ 660 Tony Gwynn	1.25	.60	.12
□ 661 Steve Crawford	.04	.02	.00
□ 662 Mike Heath	.04	.02	.00
□ 663 Luis Aguayo	.04	.02	.00
□ 664 Steve Farr	.25	.12	.02
□ 665 Don Mattingly	9.00	4.50	.90
□ 666 Mike LaCoss	.04	.02	.00
□ 667 Dave Engle	.04	.02	.00
□ 668 Steve Trout	.04	.02	.00
□ 669 Lee Lacy	.04	.02	.00
□ 670 Tom Seaver	.30	.15	.03
□ 671 Dane Iorg	.04	.02	.00
□ 672 Juan Berenguer	.04	.02	.00
□ 673 Buck Martinez	.04	.02	.00
□ 674 Atlee Hammaker	.04	.02	.00
□ 675 Tony Perez	.15	.07	.01
□ 676 Albert Hall	.10	.05	.01
□ 677 Wally Backman	.04	.02	.00
□ 678 Joey McLaughlin	.04	.02	.00
□ 679 Bob Kearney	.04	.02	.00
□ 680 Jerry Reuss	.07	.03	.01
□ 681 Ben Oglivie	.07	.03	.01
□ 682 Doug Corbett	.04	.02	.00
□ 683 Whitey Herzog MG (checklist back)	.07	.03	.01
□ 684 Bill Doran	.10	.05	.01
□ 685 Bill Caudill	.04	.02	.00
□ 686 Mike Easler	.04	.02	.00
□ 687 Bill Gullickson	.04	.02	.00
□ 688 Len Matuszek	.04	.02	.00
□ 689 Luis DeLeon	.04	.02	.00
□ 690 Alan Trammell	.30	.15	.03
□ 691 Dennis Rasmussen	.25	.12	.02
□ 692 Randy Bush	.04	.02	.00
□ 693 Tim Stoddard	.04	.02	.00
□ 694 Joe Carter	2.50	1.25	.25
□ 695 Rick Rhoden	.07	.03	.01
□ 696 John Rabb	.04	.02	.00
□ 697 Onix Concepcion	.04	.02	.00
□ 698 Jorge Bell	.50	.25	.05
□ 699 Donnie Moore	.04	.02	.00
□ 700 Eddie Murray	.45	.22	.04
□ 701 Eddie Murray AS	.15	.07	.01
□ 702 Damaso Garcia AS	.04	.02	.00
□ 703 George Brett AS	.25	.12	.02
□ 704 Cal Ripken AS	.20	.10	.02
□ 705 Dave Winfield AS	.15	.07	.01
□ 706 Rickey Henderson AS	.30	.15	.03
□ 707 Tony Armas AS	.07	.03	.01
□ 708 Lance Parrish AS	.10	.05	.01
□ 709 Mike Boddicker AS	.07	.03	.01
□ 710 Frank Viola AS	.10	.05	.01
□ 711 Dan Quisenberry AS	.07	.03	.01
□ 712 Keith Hernandez AS	.15	.07	.01
□ 713 Ryne Sandberg AS	.20	.10	.02
□ 714 Mike Schmidt AS	.35	.17	.03
□ 715 Ozzie Smith AS	.15	.07	.01
□ 716 Dale Murphy AS	.25	.12	.02
□ 717 Tony Gwynn AS	.30	.15	.03
□ 718 Jeff Leonard AS	.07	.03	.01
□ 719 Gary Carter AS	.15	.07	.01
□ 720 Rick Sutcliffe AS	.07	.03	.01
□ 721 Bob Knepper AS	.07	.03	.01
□ 722 Bruce Sutter AS	.07	.03	.01
□ 723 Dave Stewart	.25	.12	.02
□ 724 Oscar Gamble	.04	.02	.00
□ 725 Floyd Bannister	.04	.02	.00
□ 726 Al Bumbry	.04	.02	.00
□ 727 Frank Pastore	.04	.02	.00
□ 728 Bob Bailor	.04	.02	.00
□ 729 Don Sutton	.25	.12	.02
□ 730 Dave Kingman	.10	.05	.01
□ 731 Neil Allen	.04	.02	.00
□ 732 John McNamara MG (checklist back)	.07	.03	.01
□ 733 Tony Scott	.04	.02	.00
□ 734 John Henry Johnson	.04	.02	.00
□ 735 Garry Templeton	.07	.03	.01
□ 736 Jerry Mumphrey	.04	.02	.00
□ 737 Bo Diaz	.04	.02	.00
□ 738 Omar Moreno	.04	.02	.00
□ 739 Ernie Camacho	.04	.02	.00
□ 740 Jack Clark	.25	.12	.02
□ 741 John Butcher	.04	.02	.00
□ 742 Ron Hassey	.04	.02	.00
□ 743 Frank White	.07	.03	.01
□ 744 Doug Bair	.04	.02	.00
□ 745 Buddy Bell	.10	.05	.01
□ 746 Jim Clancy	.04	.02	.00
□ 747 Alex Trevino	.04	.02	.00
□ 748 Lee Mazzilli	.04	.02	.00
□ 749 Julio Cruz	.04	.02	.00
□ 750 Rollie Fingers	.15	.07	.01
□ 751 Kelvin Chapman	.04	.02	.00
□ 752 Bob Owchinko	.04	.02	.00
□ 753 Greg Brock	.04	.02	.00
□ 754 Larry Milbourne	.04	.02	.00
□ 755 Ken Singleton	.07	.03	.01
□ 756 Rob Picciolo	.04	.02	.00

☐ 757	Willie McGee	.25	.12	.02
☐ 758	Ray Burris	.04	.02	.00
☐ 759	Jim Fanning MG	.07	.03	.01
	(checklist back)			
☐ 760	Nolan Ryan	1.00	.50	.10
☐ 761	Jerry Remy	.04	.02	.00
☐ 762	Eddie Whitson	.04	.02	.00
☐ 763	Kiko Garcia	.04	.02	.00
☐ 764	Jamie Easterly	.04	.02	.00
☐ 765	Willie Randolph	.07	.03	.01
☐ 766	Paul Mirabella	.04	.02	.00
☐ 767	Darrell Brown	.04	.02	.00
☐ 768	Ron Cey	.10	.05	.01
☐ 769	Joe Cowley	.04	.02	.00
☐ 770	Carlton Fisk	.25	.12	.02
☐ 771	Geoff Zahn	.04	.02	.00
☐ 772	Johnnie LeMaster	.04	.02	.00
☐ 773	Hal McRae	.07	.03	.01
☐ 774	Dennis Lamp	.04	.02	.00
☐ 775	Mookie Wilson	.10	.05	.01
☐ 776	Jerry Royster	.04	.02	.00
☐ 777	Ned Yost	.04	.02	.00
☐ 778	Mike Davis	.07	.03	.01
☐ 779	Nick Esasky	.25	.10	.02
☐ 780	Mike Flanagan	.07	.03	.01
☐ 781	Jim Gantner	.04	.02	.00
☐ 782	Tom Niedenfuer	.04	.02	.00
☐ 783	Mike Jorgensen	.04	.02	.00
☐ 784	Checklist: 661-792	.07	.01	.00
☐ 785	Tony Armas	.07	.03	.01
☐ 786	Enos Cabell	.04	.02	.00
☐ 787	Jim Wohlford	.04	.02	.00
☐ 788	Steve Comer	.04	.02	.00
☐ 789	Luis Salazar	.07	.03	.01
☐ 790	Ron Guidry	.15	.07	.01
☐ 791	Ivan DeJesus	.04	.02	.00
☐ 792	Darrell Evans	.15	.07	.01

1985 Topps Glossy 22

The cards in this 22-card set measure 2 1/2" by 3 1/2". Similar in design, both front and back, to last year's Glossy set, this edition features the managers, starting nine players and honorary captains of the National and American League teams in the 1984 All-Star game. The set is numbered on the reverse with plyers essentially ordered by position within league, NL: 1-11 and AL: 12-22.

		MINT	EXC	G-VG
COMPLETE SET (22)		4.00	2.00	.40
COMMON PLAYER (1-22)		.10	.05	.01
☐ 1	Paul Owens MG	.10	.05	.01
☐ 2	Steve Garvey	.40	.20	.04
☐ 3	Ryne Sandberg	.45	.22	.04
☐ 4	Mike Schmidt	.75	.35	.07
☐ 5	Ozzie Smith	.25	.12	.02
☐ 6	Tony Gwynn	.50	.25	.05
☐ 7	Dale Murphy	.60	.30	.06
☐ 8	Darryl Strawberry	.75	.35	.07
☐ 9	Gary Carter	.25	.12	.02
☐ 10	Charlie Lea	.10	.05	.01
☐ 11	Willie McCovey CAPT	.20	.10	.02
☐ 12	Joe Altobelli MG	.10	.05	.01
☐ 13	Rod Carew	.40	.20	.04
☐ 14	Lou Whitaker	.15	.07	.01
☐ 15	George Brett	.60	.30	.06

☐ 16	Cal Ripken	.40	.20	.04
☐ 17	Dave Winfield	.30	.15	.03
☐ 18	Chet Lemon	.10	.05	.01
☐ 19	Reggie Jackson	.60	.30	.06
☐ 20	Lance Parrish	.20	.10	.02
☐ 21	Dave Stieb	.15	.07	.01
☐ 22	Hank Greenberg CAPT	.15	.07	.01

1985 Topps Glossy 40

The cards in this 40-card set measure 2 1/2" by 3 1/2". Similar to last year's glossy set, this set was issued as a bonus prize to Topps All-Star Baseball Game cards found in wax packs. The set could be obtained by sending in the "Bonus Runs" from the "Winning Pitch" game insert cards. For 25 runs and 75 cents, a collector could send in for one of the eight different five card series plus automatically be entered in the Grand Prize Sweepstakes for a chance at a free trip to the All-Star game. The cards are numbered and contain 20 stars from each league.

		MINT	EXC	G-VG
COMPLETE SET (40)		12.50	6.25	1.25
COMMON PLAYER (1-40)		.15	.07	.01
☐ 1	Dale Murphy	1.00	.50	.10
☐ 2	Jesse Orosco	.15	.07	.01
☐ 3	Bob Brenly	.15	.07	.01
☐ 4	Mike Boddicker	.15	.07	.01
☐ 5	Dave Kingman	.20	.10	.02
☐ 6	Jim Rice	.30	.15	.03
☐ 7	Frank Viola	.40	.20	.04
☐ 8	Alvin Davis	.30	.15	.03
☐ 9	Rick Sutcliffe	.25	.12	.02
☐ 10	Pete Rose	1.25	.60	.12
☐ 11	Leon Durham	.15	.07	.01
☐ 12	Joaquin Andujar	.15	.07	.01
☐ 13	Keith Hernandez	.35	.17	.03
☐ 14	Dave Winfield	.45	.22	.04
☐ 15	Reggie Jackson	1.00	.50	.10
☐ 16	Alan Trammell	.35	.17	.03
☐ 17	Bert Blyleven	.25	.12	.02
☐ 18	Tony Armas	.15	.07	.01
☐ 19	Rich Gossage	.20	.10	.02
☐ 20	Jose Cruz	.15	.07	.01
☐ 21	Ryne Sandberg	.45	.22	.04
☐ 22	Bruce Sutter	.20	.10	.02
☐ 23	Mike Schmidt	1.25	.60	.12
☐ 24	Cal Ripken	.90	.45	.09
☐ 25	Dan Petry	.15	.07	.01
☐ 26	Jack Morris	.20	.10	.02
☐ 27	Don Mattingly	2.50	1.25	.25
☐ 28	Eddie Murray	.65	.30	.06
☐ 29	Tony Gwynn	.75	.35	.07
☐ 30	Charlie Lea	.15	.07	.01
☐ 31	Juan Samuel	.25	.12	.02
☐ 32	Phil Niekro	.35	.17	.03
☐ 33	Alejandro Pena	.15	.07	.01
☐ 34	Harold Baines	.25	.12	.02
☐ 35	Dan Quisenberry	.20	.10	.02
☐ 36	Gary Carter	.45	.22	.04
☐ 37	Mario Soto	.15	.07	.01
☐ 38	Dwight Gooden	1.25	.60	.12
☐ 39	Tom Brunansky	.20	.10	.02
☐ 40	Dave Stieb	.20	.10	.02

1985 Topps Traded

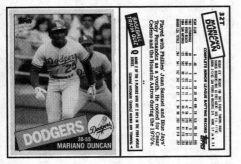

The cards in this 132-card set measure 2 1/2" by 3 1/2". In its now standard procedure, Topps issued its Traded (or extended) set for the fifth year in a row. Because photos and statistics of its regular set for the year were developed during the fall and winter months of the preceding year, players who changed teams during the fall, winter, and spring months are portrayed in the 1985 regular issue set with the teams they were with in 1984. The Traded set amends the shortcomings of the regular set by presenting the players with their proper teams for the current year. Rookies not contained in the regular set are also picked up in the Traded set. Again this year, the Topps affiliate in Ireland printed the cards, and the cards were available through hobby channels only. Topps also produced a specially boxed "glossy" edition frequently referred to as the Topps Traded Tiffany set. There were supposedly only 5,000 sets of the Tiffany cards produced; they were marketed to hobby dealers. The checklist of cards is identical to that of the normal non-glossy cards. There are two primary distinguishing features of the Tiffany cards, white card stock reverses and high gloss obverses. These Tiffany cards are valued at approximately five times the values listed below.

	MINT	EXC	G-VG
COMPLETE SET (132)	15.00	7.50	1.50
COMMON PLAYER (1-132)	.06	.03	.00

		MINT	EXC	G-VG
☐	1T Don Aase	.10	.05	.01
☐	2T Bill Almon	.06	.03	.00
☐	3T Benny Ayala	.06	.03	.00
☐	4T Dusty Baker	.10	.05	.01
☐	5T G.Bamberger MG	.10	.05	.01
☐	6T Dale Berra	.06	.03	.00
☐	7T Rich Bordi	.06	.03	.00
☐	8T Daryl Boston	.10	.05	.01
☐	9T Hubie Brooks	.25	.12	.02
☐	10T Chris Brown	.20	.10	.02
☐	11T Tom Browning	1.25	.60	.12
☐	12T Al Bumbry	.06	.03	.00
☐	13T Ray Burris	.06	.03	.00
☐	14T Jeff Burroughs	.10	.05	.01
☐	15T Bill Campbell	.06	.03	.00
☐	16T Don Carman	.25	.12	.02
☐	17T Gary Carter	.70	.35	.07
☐	18T Bobby Castillo	.06	.03	.00
☐	19T Bill Caudill	.06	.03	.00
☐	20T Rick Cerone	.10	.05	.01
☐	21T Bryan Clark	.06	.03	.00
☐	22T Jack Clark	.35	.17	.03
☐	23T Pat Clements	.10	.05	.01
☐	24T Vince Coleman	4.50	2.25	.45
☐	25T Dave Collins	.06	.03	.00
☐	26T Danny Darwin	.06	.03	.00
☐	27T Jim Davenport MG	.06	.03	.00
☐	28T Jerry Davis	.10	.05	.01
☐	29T Brian Dayett	.06	.03	.00
☐	30T Ivan DeJesus	.06	.03	.00
☐	31T Ken Dixon	.12	.06	.01
☐	32T Mariano Duncan	.20	.10	.02
☐	33T John Felske MG	.06	.03	.00
☐	34T Mike Fitzgerald	.06	.03	.00
☐	35T Ray Fontenot	.06	.03	.00
☐	36T Greg Gagne	.30	.15	.03
☐	37T Oscar Gamble	.06	.03	.00
☐	38T Scott Garrelts	.50	.25	.05
☐	39T Bob L. Gibson	.06	.03	.00
☐	40T Jim Gott	.10	.05	.01
☐	41T David Green	.06	.03	.00
☐	42T Alfredo Griffin	.10	.05	.01
☐	43T Ozzie Guillen	1.25	.60	.12
☐	44T Eddie Haas MG	.06	.03	.00
☐	45T Terry Harper	.06	.03	.00
☐	46T Toby Harrah	.10	.05	.01
☐	47T Greg Harris	.06	.03	.00
☐	48T Ron Hassey	.06	.03	.00
☐	49T Rickey Henderson	1.75	.85	.17
☐	50T Steve Henderson	.06	.03	.00
☐	51T George Hendrick	.10	.05	.01
☐	52T Joe Hesketh	.15	.07	.01
☐	53T Teddy Higuera	2.00	1.00	.20
☐	54T Donnie Hill	.10	.05	.01
☐	55T Al Holland	.06	.03	.00
☐	56T Burt Hooton	.06	.03	.00
☐	57T Jay Howell	.15	.07	.01
☐	58T Ken Howell	.20	.10	.02
☐	59T LaMarr Hoyt	.10	.05	.01
☐	60T Tim Hulett	.10	.05	.01
☐	61T Bob James	.10	.05	.01
☐	62T Steve Jeltz	.10	.05	.01
☐	63T Cliff Johnson	.06	.03	.00
☐	64T Howard Johnson	2.25	1.10	.22
☐	65T Ruppert Jones	.06	.03	.00
☐	66T Steve Kemp	.10	.05	.01
☐	67T Bruce Kison	.06	.03	.00
☐	68T Alan Knicely	.06	.03	.00
☐	69T Mike LaCoss	.06	.03	.00
☐	70T Lee Lacy	.06	.03	.00
☐	71T Dave LaPoint	.10	.05	.01
☐	72T Gary Lavelle	.06	.03	.00
☐	73T Vance Law	.10	.05	.01
☐	74T Johnnie LeMaster	.06	.03	.00
☐	75T Sixto Lezcano	.06	.03	.00
☐	76T Tim Lollar	.06	.03	.00
☐	77T Fred Lynn	.25	.12	.02
☐	78T Billy Martin MG	.20	.10	.02
☐	79T Ron Mathis	.10	.05	.01
☐	80T Len Matuszek	.06	.03	.00
☐	81T Gene Mauch MG	.06	.03	.00
☐	82T Oddibe McDowell	.50	.25	.05
☐	83T Roger McDowell	.80	.40	.08
☐	84T John McNamara MG	.10	.05	.01
☐	85T Donnie Moore	.06	.03	.00
☐	86T Gene Nelson	.06	.03	.00
☐	87T Steve Nicosia	.06	.03	.00
☐	88T Al Oliver	.15	.07	.01
☐	89T Joe Orsulak	.20	.10	.02
☐	90T Rob Picciolo	.06	.03	.00
☐	91T Chris Pittaro	.10	.05	.01
☐	92T Jim Presley	.70	.35	.07
☐	93T Rick Reuschel	.20	.10	.02
☐	94T Bert Roberge	.06	.03	.00
☐	95T Bob Rodgers MG	.06	.03	.00
☐	96T Jerry Royster	.06	.03	.00
☐	97T Dave Rozema	.06	.03	.00
☐	98T Dave Rucker	.06	.03	.00
☐	99T Vern Ruhle	.06	.03	.00
☐	100T Paul Runge	.10	.05	.01
☐	101T Mark Salas	.12	.06	.01
☐	102T Luis Salazar	.06	.03	.00
☐	103T Joe Sambito	.06	.03	.00
☐	104T Rick Schu	.12	.06	.01
☐	105T Donnie Scott	.06	.03	.00
☐	106T Larry Sheets	.25	.12	.02
☐	107T Don Slaught	.06	.03	.00
☐	108T Roy Smalley	.06	.03	.00
☐	109T Lonnie Smith	.15	.07	.01
☐	110T Nate Snell UER (headings on back for a batter)	.12	.06	.01
☐	111T Chris Speier	.06	.03	.00
☐	112T Mike Stenhouse	.10	.05	.01
☐	113T Tim Stoddard	.06	.03	.00
☐	114T Jim Sundberg	.06	.03	.00
☐	115T Bruce Sutter	.20	.10	.02
☐	116T Don Sutton	.50	.25	.05
☐	117T Kent Tekulve	.10	.05	.01
☐	118T Tom Tellmann	.06	.03	.00
☐	119T Walt Terrell	.10	.05	.01
☐	120T Mickey Tettleton	1.00	.50	.10
☐	121T Derrel Thomas	.06	.03	.00
☐	122T Rich Thompson	.10	.05	.01
☐	123T Alex Trevino	.06	.03	.00
☐	124T John Tudor	.25	.12	.02
☐	125T Jose Uribe	.30	.15	.03

		MINT	EXC	G-VG
☐ 126T	Bobby Valentine MG	.10	.05	.01
☐ 127T	Dave Von Ohlen	.06	.03	.00
☐ 128T	U.L. Washington	.06	.03	.00
☐ 129T	Earl Weaver MG	.10	.05	.01
☐ 130T	Eddie Whitson	.10	.05	.01
☐ 131T	Herm Winningham	.15	.07	.01
☐ 132T	Checklist 1-132	.06	.01	.00

1986 Topps

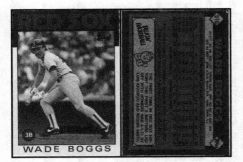

WADE BOGGS

The cards in this 792-card set are standard- size (2 1/2" by 3 1/2"). The first seven cards are a tribute to Pete Rose and his career. Cards 2-7 show small photos of Pete's Topps cards of the given years on the front with biographical information pertaining to those years on the back. The team leader cards were done differently with a simple player action shot on a white background; the player pictured is dubbed the "Dean" of that team, i.e., the player with the longest continuous service with that team. Topps again features a "Turn Back The Clock" series (401-405). Record breakers of the previous year are acknowledged on cards 201 to 207. Cards 701-722 feature All-Star selections from each league. Manager cards feature the team checklist on the reverse. Ryne Sandberg (#690) is the only player card in the set without a Topps logo on the front of the card; this omission was never corrected by Topps. There are two other uncorrected errors involving misnumbered cards; see card numbers 51, 57, 141, and 171 in the checklist below. The backs of all the cards have a distinctive red background. Topps also produced a specially boxed "glossy" edition frequently referred to as the Topps Tiffany set. There were supposedly only 5,000 sets of the Tiffany cards produced; they were marketed to hobby dealers. The checklist of cards (792 regular and 132 Traded) is identical to that of the normal non-glossy cards. There are two primary distinguishing features of the Tiffany cards, white card stock reverses and high gloss obverses. These Tiffany cards are valued at approximately five times the values listed below.

		MINT	EXC	G-VG
COMPLETE SET (792)	....	35.00	17.50	3.50
COMMON PLAYER (1-792)	....	.03	.01	.00
☐ 1	Pete Rose	1.00	.20	.04
☐ 2	Rose Special: '63-'66	.30	.15	.03
☐ 3	Rose Special: '67-'70	.30	.15	.03
☐ 4	Rose Special: '71-'74	.30	.15	.03
☐ 5	Rose Special: '75-'78	.30	.15	.03
☐ 6	Rose Special: '79-'82	.30	.15	.03
☐ 7	Rose Special: '83-'85	.30	.15	.03
☐ 8	Dwayne Murphy	.03	.01	.00
☐ 9	Roy Smith	.03	.01	.00
☐ 10	Tony Gwynn	.60	.30	.06
☐ 11	Bob Ojeda	.06	.03	.00
☐ 12	Jose Uribe	.25	.12	.02

		MINT	EXC	G-VG
☐ 13	Bob Kearney	.03	.01	.00
☐ 14	Julio Cruz	.03	.01	.00
☐ 15	Eddie Whitson	.03	.01	.00
☐ 16	Rick Schu	.06	.03	.00
☐ 17	Mike Stenhouse	.03	.01	.00
☐ 18	Brent Gaff	.03	.01	.00
☐ 19	Rich Hebner	.03	.01	.00
☐ 20	Lou Whitaker	.12	.06	.01
☐ 21	G.Bamberger MG	.06	.03	.00
	(checklist back)			
☐ 22	Duane Walker	.03	.01	.00
☐ 23	Manny Lee	.10	.05	.01
☐ 24	Len Barker	.03	.01	.00
☐ 25	Willie Wilson	.10	.05	.01
☐ 26	Frank DiPino	.03	.01	.00
☐ 27	Ray Knight	.06	.03	.00
☐ 28	Eric Davis	2.50	1.25	.25
☐ 29	Tony Phillips	.03	.01	.00
☐ 30	Eddie Murray	.30	.15	.03
☐ 31	Jamie Easterly	.03	.01	.00
☐ 32	Steve Yeager	.03	.01	.00
☐ 33	Jeff Lahti	.03	.01	.00
☐ 34	Ken Phelps	.06	.03	.00
☐ 35	Jeff Reardon	.08	.04	.01
☐ 36	Tigers Leaders	.08	.04	.01
	Lance Parrish			
☐ 37	Mark Thurmond	.03	.01	.00
☐ 38	Glenn Hoffman	.03	.01	.00
☐ 39	Dave Rucker	.03	.01	.00
☐ 40	Ken Griffey	.08	.04	.01
☐ 41	Brad Wellman	.03	.01	.00
☐ 42	Geoff Zahn	.03	.01	.00
☐ 43	Dave Engle	.03	.01	.00
☐ 44	Lance McCullers	.25	.12	.02
☐ 45	Damaso Garcia	.03	.01	.00
☐ 46	Billy Hatcher	.08	.04	.01
☐ 47	Juan Berenguer	.03	.01	.00
☐ 48	Bill Almon	.03	.01	.00
☐ 49	Rick Manning	.03	.01	.00
☐ 50	Dan Quisenberry	.10	.05	.01
☐ 51	Bobby Wine MG ERR	.08	.04	.01
	(checklist back)			
	(number of card on			
	back is actually 57)			
☐ 52	Chris Welsh	.03	.01	.00
☐ 53	Len Dykstra	.60	.30	.06
☐ 54	John Franco	.12	.06	.01
☐ 55	Fred Lynn	.12	.06	.01
☐ 56	Tom Niedenfuer	.03	.01	.00
☐ 57	Bill Doran	.08	.04	.01
	(see also 51)			
☐ 58	Bill Krueger	.03	.01	.00
☐ 59	Andre Thornton	.06	.03	.00
☐ 60	Dwight Evans	.12	.06	.01
☐ 61	Karl Best	.10	.05	.01
☐ 62	Bob Boone	.08	.04	.01
☐ 63	Ron Roenicke	.03	.01	.00
☐ 64	Floyd Bannister	.03	.01	.00
☐ 65	Dan Driessen	.03	.01	.00
☐ 66	Cardinals Leaders	.03	.01	.00
	Bob Forsch			
☐ 67	Carmelo Martinez	.03	.01	.00
☐ 68	Ed Lynch	.03	.01	.00
☐ 69	Luis Aguayo	.03	.01	.00
☐ 70	Dave Winfield	.25	.12	.02
☐ 71	Ken Schrom	.03	.01	.00
☐ 72	Shawon Dunston	.20	.10	.02
☐ 73	Randy O'Neal	.03	.01	.00
☐ 74	Rance Mulliniks	.03	.01	.00
☐ 75	Jose DeLeon	.06	.03	.00
☐ 76	Dion James	.03	.01	.00
☐ 77	Charlie Leibrandt	.03	.01	.00
☐ 78	Bruce Benedict	.03	.01	.00
☐ 79	Dave Schmidt	.03	.01	.00
☐ 80	Darryl Strawberry	1.00	.50	.10
☐ 81	Gene Mauch MG	.06	.03	.00
	(checklist back)			
☐ 82	Tippy Martinez	.03	.01	.00
☐ 83	Phil Garner	.03	.01	.00
☐ 84	Curt Young	.03	.01	.00
☐ 85	Tony Perez	.20	.10	.02
	(Eric Davis also			
	shown on card)			
☐ 86	Tom Waddell	.03	.01	.00
☐ 87	Candy Maldonado	.06	.03	.00
☐ 88	Tom Nieto	.03	.01	.00
☐ 89	Randy St.Claire	.03	.01	.00
☐ 90	Garry Templeton	.06	.03	.00
☐ 91	Steve Crawford	.03	.01	.00
☐ 92	Al Cowens	.03	.01	.00
☐ 93	Scot Thompson	.03	.01	.00
☐ 94	Rich Bordi	.03	.01	.00
☐ 95	Ozzie Virgil	.03	.01	.00
☐ 96	Blue Jays Leaders	.03	.01	.00
	Jim Clancy			

☐ 97	Gary Gaetti	.10	.05	.01
☐ 98	Dick Ruthven	.03	.01	.00
☐ 99	Buddy Biancalana	.03	.01	.00
☐ 100	Nolan Ryan	.60	.30	.06
☐ 101	Dave Bergman	.03	.01	.00
☐ 102	Joe Orsulak	.10	.05	.01
☐ 103	Luis Salazar	.03	.01	.00
☐ 104	Sid Fernandez	.12	.06	.01
☐ 105	Gary Ward	.03	.01	.00
☐ 106	Ray Burris	.03	.01	.00
☐ 107	Rafael Ramirez	.03	.01	.00
☐ 108	Ted Power	.03	.01	.00
☐ 109	Len Matuszek	.03	.01	.00
☐ 110	Scott McGregor	.06	.03	.00
☐ 111	Roger Craig MG	.06	.03	.00
	(checklist back)			
☐ 112	Bill Campbell	.03	.01	.00
☐ 113	U.L. Washington	.03	.01	.00
☐ 114	Mike Brown	.03	.01	.00
	(Pirates OF)			
☐ 115	Jay Howell	.06	.03	.00
☐ 116	Brook Jacoby	.06	.03	.00
☐ 117	Bruce Kison	.03	.01	.00
☐ 118	Jerry Royster	.03	.01	.00
☐ 119	Barry Bonnell	.03	.01	.00
☐ 120	Steve Carlton	.20	.10	.02
☐ 121	Nelson Simmons	.06	.03	.00
☐ 122	Pete Filson	.03	.01	.00
☐ 123	Greg Walker	.06	.03	.00
☐ 124	Luis Sanchez	.03	.01	.00
☐ 125	Dave Lopes	.06	.03	.00
☐ 126	Mets Leaders	.06	.03	.00
	Mookie Wilson			
☐ 127	Jack Howell	.30	.15	.03
☐ 128	John Wathan	.03	.01	.00
☐ 129	Jeff Dedmon	.03	.01	.00
☐ 130	Alan Trammell	.20	.10	.02
☐ 131	Checklist: 1-132	.06	.01	.00
☐ 132	Razor Shines	.06	.03	.00
☐ 133	Andy McGaffigan	.03	.01	.00
☐ 134	Carney Lansford	.08	.04	.01
☐ 135	Joe Niekro	.08	.04	.01
☐ 136	Mike Hargrove	.06	.03	.00
☐ 137	Charlie Moore	.03	.01	.00
☐ 138	Mark Davis	.15	.07	.01
☐ 139	Daryl Boston	.06	.03	.00
☐ 140	John Candelaria	.06	.03	.00
☐ 141	Chuck Cottier MG	.08	.04	.01
	(checklist back)			
	(see also 171)			
☐ 142	Bob Jones	.03	.01	.00
☐ 143	Dave Van Gorder	.03	.01	.00
☐ 144	Doug Sisk	.03	.01	.00
☐ 145	Pedro Guerrero	.15	.07	.01
☐ 146	Jack Perconte	.03	.01	.00
☐ 147	Larry Sheets	.08	.04	.01
☐ 148	Mike Heath	.03	.01	.00
☐ 149	Brett Butler	.06	.03	.00
☐ 150	Joaquin Andujar	.06	.03	.00
☐ 151	Dave Stapleton	.03	.01	.00
☐ 152	Mike Morgan	.06	.03	.00
☐ 153	Ricky Adams	.03	.01	.00
☐ 154	Bert Roberge	.03	.01	.00
☐ 155	Bob Grich	.06	.03	.00
☐ 156	White Sox Leaders	.03	.01	.00
	Richard Dotson			
☐ 157	Ron Hassey	.03	.01	.00
☐ 158	Derrel Thomas	.03	.01	.00
☐ 159	Orel Hershiser UER	1.25	.60	.12
	(82 Alburquerque)			
☐ 160	Chet Lemon	.06	.03	.00
☐ 161	Lee Tunnell	.03	.01	.00
☐ 162	Greg Gagne	.08	.04	.01
☐ 163	Pete Ladd	.03	.01	.00
☐ 164	Steve Balboni	.03	.01	.00
☐ 165	Mike Davis	.03	.01	.00
☐ 166	Dickie Thon	.03	.01	.00
☐ 167	Zane Smith	.10	.05	.01
☐ 168	Jeff Burroughs	.03	.01	.00
☐ 169	George Wright	.03	.01	.00
☐ 170	Gary Carter	.25	.12	.02
☐ 171	Bob Rodgers MG ERR	.08	.04	.01
	(checklist back)			
	(number of card on			
	back actually 141)			
☐ 172	Jerry Reed	.03	.01	.00
☐ 173	Wayne Gross	.03	.01	.00
☐ 174	Brian Snyder	.03	.01	.00
☐ 175	Steve Sax	.15	.07	.01
☐ 176	Jay Tibbs	.03	.01	.00
☐ 177	Joel Youngblood	.03	.01	.00
☐ 178	Ivan DeJesus	.03	.01	.00
☐ 179	Stu Cliburn	.08	.04	.01
☐ 180	Don Mattingly	3.00	1.50	.30
☐ 181	Al Nipper	.03	.01	.00
☐ 182	Bobby Brown	.03	.01	.00
☐ 183	Larry Andersen	.03	.01	.00
☐ 184	Tim Laudner	.03	.01	.00
☐ 185	Rollie Fingers	.12	.06	.01
☐ 186	Astros Leaders	.03	.01	.00
	Jose Cruz			
☐ 187	Scott Fletcher	.03	.01	.00
☐ 188	Bob Dernier	.03	.01	.00
☐ 189	Mike Mason	.03	.01	.00
☐ 190	George Hendrick	.06	.03	.00
☐ 191	Wally Backman	.03	.01	.00
☐ 192	Milt Wilcox	.03	.01	.00
☐ 193	Daryl Sconiers	.03	.01	.00
☐ 194	Craig McMurtry	.03	.01	.00
☐ 195	Dave Concepcion	.06	.03	.00
☐ 196	Doyle Alexander	.06	.03	.00
☐ 197	Enos Cabell	.03	.01	.00
☐ 198	Ken Dixon	.03	.01	.00
☐ 199	Dick Howser MG	.06	.03	.00
	(checklist back)			
☐ 200	Mike Schmidt	.50	.25	.05
☐ 201	RB: Vince Coleman	.20	.10	.02
	Most stolen bases,			
	season, rookie			
☐ 202	RB: Dwight Gooden	.30	.15	.03
	Youngest 20 game			
	winner			
☐ 203	RB: Keith Hernandez	.12	.06	.01
	Most game-winning			
	RBI's			
☐ 204	RB: Phil Niekro	.10	.05	.01
	Oldest shutout			
	pitcher			
☐ 205	RB: Tony Perez	.10	.05	.01
	Oldest grand slammer			
☐ 206	RB: Pete Rose	.35	.17	.03
	Most hits, lifetime			
☐ 207	RB: Fern.Valenzuela	.12	.06	.01
	Most cons. innings,			
	start of season,			
	no earned runs			
☐ 208	Ramon Romero	.03	.01	.00
☐ 209	Randy Ready	.08	.04	.01
☐ 210	Calvin Schiraldi	.06	.03	.00
☐ 211	Ed Wojna	.06	.03	.00
☐ 212	Chris Speier	.03	.01	.00
☐ 213	Bob Shirley	.03	.01	.00
☐ 214	Randy Bush	.03	.01	.00
☐ 215	Frank White	.06	.03	.00
☐ 216	A's Leaders	.03	.01	.00
	Dwayne Murphy			
☐ 217	Bill Scherrer	.03	.01	.00
☐ 218	Randy Hunt	.03	.01	.00
☐ 219	Dennis Lamp	.03	.01	.00
☐ 220	Bob Horner	.10	.05	.01
☐ 221	Dave Henderson	.06	.03	.00
☐ 222	Craig Gerber	.03	.01	.00
☐ 223	Atlee Hammaker	.03	.01	.00
☐ 224	Cesar Cedeno	.06	.03	.00
☐ 225	Ron Darling	.15	.07	.01
☐ 226	Lee Lacy	.03	.01	.00
☐ 227	Al Jones	.03	.01	.00
☐ 228	Tom Lawless	.03	.01	.00
☐ 229	Bill Gullickson	.03	.01	.00
☐ 230	Terry Kennedy	.03	.01	.00
☐ 231	Jim Frey MG	.06	.03	.00
	(checklist back)			
☐ 232	Rick Rhoden	.06	.03	.00
☐ 233	Steve Lyons	.06	.03	.00
☐ 234	Doug Corbett	.03	.01	.00
☐ 235	Butch Wynegar	.03	.01	.00
☐ 236	Frank Eufemia	.03	.01	.00
☐ 237	Ted Simmons	.08	.04	.01
☐ 238	Larry Parrish	.03	.01	.00
☐ 239	Joel Skinner	.03	.01	.00
☐ 240	Tommy John	.12	.06	.01
☐ 241	Tony Fernandez	.20	.10	.02
☐ 242	Rich Thompson	.03	.01	.00
☐ 243	Johnny Grubb	.03	.01	.00
☐ 244	Craig Lefferts	.06	.03	.00
☐ 245	Jim Sundberg	.03	.01	.00
☐ 246	Phillies Leaders	.12	.06	.01
	Steve Carlton			
☐ 247	Terry Harper	.03	.01	.00
☐ 248	Spike Owen	.03	.01	.00
☐ 249	Rob Deer	.40	.20	.04
☐ 250	Dwight Gooden	1.75	.85	.17
☐ 251	Rich Dauer	.03	.01	.00
☐ 252	Bobby Castillo	.03	.01	.00
☐ 253	Dann Bilardello	.03	.01	.00
☐ 254	Ozzie Guillen	.40	.20	.04
☐ 255	Tony Armas	.06	.03	.00
☐ 256	Kurt Kepshire	.03	.01	.00
☐ 257	Doug DeCinces	.06	.03	.00
☐ 258	Tim Burke	.25	.12	.02

259	Dan Pasqua	.12	.06	.01
260	Tony Pena	.08	.04	.01
261	Bobby Valentine MG (checklist back)	.06	.03	.00
262	Mario Ramirez	.03	.01	.00
263	Checklist: 133-264	.06	.01	.00
264	Darren Daulton	.12	.06	.01
265	Ron Davis	.03	.01	.00
266	Keith Moreland	.03	.01	.00
267	Paul Molitor	.12	.06	.01
268	Mike Scott	.30	.15	.03
269	Dane Iorg	.03	.01	.00
270	Jack Morris	.12	.06	.01
271	Dave Collins	.03	.01	.00
272	Tim Tolman	.03	.01	.00
273	Jerry Willard	.03	.01	.00
274	Ron Gardenhire	.03	.01	.00
275	Charlie Hough	.06	.03	.00
276	Yankees Leaders Willie Randolph	.03	.01	.00
277	Jaime Cocanower	.03	.01	.00
278	Sixto Lezcano	.03	.01	.00
279	Al Pardo	.03	.01	.00
280	Tim Raines	.25	.12	.02
281	Steve Mura	.03	.01	.00
282	Jerry Mumphrey	.03	.01	.00
283	Mike Fischlin	.03	.01	.00
284	Brian Dayett	.03	.01	.00
285	Buddy Bell	.06	.03	.00
286	Luis DeLeon	.03	.01	.00
287	John Christensen	.03	.01	.00
288	Don Aase	.03	.01	.00
289	Johnnie LeMaster	.03	.01	.00
290	Carlton Fisk	.20	.10	.02
291	Tom Lasorda MG (checklist back)	.10	.05	.01
292	Chuck Porter	.03	.01	.00
293	Chris Chambliss	.06	.03	.00
294	Danny Cox	.06	.03	.00
295	Kirk Gibson	.25	.12	.02
296	Geno Petralli	.03	.01	.00
297	Tim Lollar	.03	.01	.00
298	Craig Reynolds	.03	.01	.00
299	Bryn Smith	.06	.03	.00
300	George Brett	.40	.20	.04
301	Dennis Rasmussen	.06	.03	.00
302	Greg Gross	.03	.01	.00
303	Curt Wardle	.03	.01	.00
304	Mike Gallego	.03	.01	.00
305	Phil Bradley	.06	.03	.00
306	Padres Leaders Terry Kennedy	.03	.01	.00
307	Dave Sax	.03	.01	.00
308	Ray Fontenot	.03	.01	.00
309	John Shelby	.03	.01	.00
310	Greg Minton	.03	.01	.00
311	Dick Schofield	.03	.01	.00
312	Tom Filer	.03	.01	.00
313	Joe DeSa	.03	.01	.00
314	Frank Pastore	.03	.01	.00
315	Mookie Wilson	.08	.04	.01
316	Sammy Khalifa	.08	.04	.01
317	Ed Romero	.03	.01	.00
318	Terry Whitfield	.03	.01	.00
319	Rick Camp	.03	.01	.00
320	Jim Rice	.18	.09	.01
321	Earl Weaver MG (checklist back)	.06	.03	.00
322	Bob Forsch	.03	.01	.00
323	Jerry Davis	.03	.01	.00
324	Dan Schatzeder	.03	.01	.00
325	Juan Beniquez	.03	.01	.00
326	Kent Tekulve	.08	.04	.01
327	Mike Pagliarulo	.08	.04	.01
328	Pete O'Brien	.08	.04	.01
329	Kirby Puckett	2.50	1.25	.25
330	Rick Sutcliffe	.10	.05	.01
331	Alan Ashby	.03	.01	.00
332	Darryl Motley	.03	.01	.00
333	Tom Henke	.15	.07	.01
334	Ken Oberkfell	.03	.01	.00
335	Don Sutton	.15	.07	.01
336	Indians Leaders Andre Thornton	.03	.01	.00
337	Darnell Coles	.03	.01	.00
338	Jorge Bell	.20	.10	.02
339	Bruce Berenyi	.03	.01	.00
340	Cal Ripken	.30	.15	.03
341	Frank Williams	.03	.01	.00
342	Gary Redus	.03	.01	.00
343	Carlos Diaz	.03	.01	.00
344	Jim Wohlford	.03	.01	.00
345	Donnie Moore	.03	.01	.00
346	Bryan Little	.03	.01	.00
347	Teddy Higuera	1.00	.50	.10
348	Cliff Johnson	.03	.01	.00
349	Mark Clear	.03	.01	.00
350	Jack Clark	.20	.10	.02
351	Chuck Tanner MG (checklist back)	.06	.03	.00
352	Harry Spilman	.03	.01	.00
353	Keith Atherton	.03	.01	.00
354	Tony Bernazard	.03	.01	.00
355	Lee Smith	.06	.03	.00
356	Mickey Hatcher	.03	.01	.00
357	Ed VandeBerg	.03	.01	.00
358	Rick Dempsey	.03	.01	.00
359	Mike LaCoss	.03	.01	.00
360	Lloyd Moseby	.08	.04	.01
361	Shane Rawley	.03	.01	.00
362	Tom Paciorek	.03	.01	.00
363	Terry Forster	.06	.03	.00
364	Reid Nichols	.03	.01	.00
365	Mike Flanagan	.06	.03	.00
366	Reds Leaders Dave Concepcion	.03	.01	.00
367	Aurelio Lopez	.03	.01	.00
368	Greg Brock	.03	.01	.00
369	Al Holland	.03	.01	.00
370	Vince Coleman	1.50	.75	.15
371	Bill Stein	.03	.01	.00
372	Ben Oglivie	.06	.03	.00
373	Urbano Lugo	.03	.01	.00
374	Terry Francona	.03	.01	.00
375	Rich Gedman	.03	.01	.00
376	Bill Dawley	.03	.01	.00
377	Joe Carter	.35	.17	.03
378	Bruce Bochte	.03	.01	.00
379	Bobby Meacham	.03	.01	.00
380	LaMarr Hoyt	.06	.03	.00
381	Ray Miller MG (checklist back)	.06	.03	.00
382	Ivan Calderon	.50	.25	.05
383	Chris Brown	.15	.07	.01
384	Steve Trout	.03	.01	.00
385	Cecil Cooper	.08	.04	.01
386	Cecil Fielder	.15	.07	.01
387	Steve Kemp	.03	.01	.00
388	Dickie Noles	.03	.01	.00
389	Glenn Davis	2.25	1.10	.22
390	Tom Seaver	.30	.15	.03
391	Julio Franco	.20	.10	.02
392	John Russell	.03	.01	.00
393	Chris Pittaro	.03	.01	.00
394	Checklist: 265-396	.06	.01	.00
395	Scott Garrelts	.25	.12	.02
396	Red Sox Leaders Dwight Evans	.08	.04	.01
397	Steve Buechele	.20	.10	.02
398	Earnie Riles	.20	.10	.02
399	Bill Swift	.06	.03	.00
400	Rod Carew	.30	.15	.03
401	Turn Back 5 Years Fern.Valenzuela '81	.10	.05	.01
402	Turn Back 10 Years Tom Seaver '76	.15	.07	.01
403	Turn Back 15 Years Willie Mays '71	.15	.07	.01
404	Turn Back 20 Years Frank Robinson '66	.10	.05	.01
405	Turn Back 25 Years Roger Maris '61	.15	.07	.01
406	Scott Sanderson	.03	.01	.00
407	Sal Butera	.03	.01	.00
408	Dave Smith	.06	.03	.00
409	Paul Runge	.03	.01	.00
410	Dave Kingman	.08	.04	.01
411	Sparky Anderson MG (checklist back)	.06	.03	.00
412	Jim Clancy	.03	.01	.00
413	Tim Flannery	.03	.01	.00
414	Tom Gorman	.03	.01	.00
415	Hal McRae	.06	.03	.00
416	Dennis Martinez	.06	.03	.00
417	R.J. Reynolds	.03	.01	.00
418	Alan Knicely	.03	.01	.00
419	Frank Wills	.03	.01	.00
420	Von Hayes	.08	.04	.01
421	David Palmer	.03	.01	.00
422	Mike Jorgensen	.03	.01	.00
423	Dan Spillner	.03	.01	.00
424	Rick Miller	.03	.01	.00
425	Larry McWilliams	.03	.01	.00
426	Brewers Leaders Charlie Moore	.03	.01	.00
427	Joe Cowley	.03	.01	.00
428	Max Venable	.03	.01	.00
429	Greg Booker	.03	.01	.00
430	Kent Hrbek	.15	.07	.01
431	George Frazier	.03	.01	.00

☐ 432	Mark Bailey	.03	.01	.00
☐ 433	Chris Codiroli	.03	.01	.00
☐ 434	Curt Wilkerson	.03	.01	.00
☐ 435	Bill Caudill	.03	.01	.00
☐ 436	Doug Flynn	.03	.01	.00
☐ 437	Rick Mahler	.03	.01	.00
☐ 438	Clint Hurdle	.03	.01	.00
☐ 439	Rick Honeycutt	.03	.01	.00
☐ 440	Alvin Davis	.18	.09	.01
☐ 441	Whitey Herzog MG (checklist back)	.06	.03	.00
☐ 442	Ron Robinson	.08	.04	.01
☐ 443	Bill Buckner	.06	.03	.00
☐ 444	Alex Trevino	.03	.01	.00
☐ 445	Bert Blyleven	.10	.05	.01
☐ 446	Lenn Sakata	.03	.01	.00
☐ 447	Jerry Don Gleaton	.03	.01	.00
☐ 448	Herm Winningham	.10	.05	.01
☐ 449	Rod Scurry	.03	.01	.00
☐ 450	Graig Nettles	.10	.05	.01
☐ 451	Mark Brown	.06	.03	.00
☐ 452	Bob Clark	.03	.01	.00
☐ 453	Steve Jeltz	.03	.01	.00
☐ 454	Burt Hooton	.03	.01	.00
☐ 455	Willie Randolph	.08	.04	.01
☐ 456	Braves Leaders Dale Murphy	.12	.06	.01
☐ 457	Mickey Tettleton	.45	.22	.04
☐ 458	Kevin Bass	.08	.04	.01
☐ 459	Luis Leal	.03	.01	.00
☐ 460	Leon Durham	.06	.03	.00
☐ 461	Walt Terrell	.03	.01	.00
☐ 462	Domingo Ramos	.03	.01	.00
☐ 463	Jim Gott	.06	.03	.00
☐ 464	Ruppert Jones	.03	.01	.00
☐ 465	Jesse Orosco	.03	.01	.00
☐ 466	Tom Foley	.03	.01	.00
☐ 467	Bob James	.03	.01	.00
☐ 468	Mike Scioscia	.06	.03	.00
☐ 469	Storm Davis	.08	.04	.01
☐ 470	Bill Madlock	.08	.04	.01
☐ 471	Bobby Cox MG (checklist back)	.06	.03	.00
☐ 472	Joe Hesketh	.06	.03	.00
☐ 473	Mark Brouhard	.03	.01	.00
☐ 474	John Tudor	.10	.05	.01
☐ 475	Juan Samuel	.12	.06	.01
☐ 476	Ron Mathis	.06	.03	.00
☐ 477	Mike Easler	.03	.01	.00
☐ 478	Andy Hawkins	.08	.04	.01
☐ 479	Bob Melvin	.10	.05	.01
☐ 480	Oddibe McDowell	.12	.06	.01
☐ 481	Scott Bradley	.08	.04	.01
☐ 482	Rick Lysander	.03	.01	.00
☐ 483	George Vukovich	.03	.01	.00
☐ 484	Donnie Hill	.03	.01	.00
☐ 485	Gary Matthews	.06	.03	.00
☐ 486	Angels Leaders Bobby Grich	.03	.01	.00
☐ 487	Bret Saberhagen	.75	.35	.07
☐ 488	Lou Thornton	.08	.04	.01
☐ 489	Jim Winn	.03	.01	.00
☐ 490	Jeff Leonard	.08	.04	.01
☐ 491	Pascual Perez	.08	.04	.01
☐ 492	Kelvin Chapman	.03	.01	.00
☐ 493	Gene Nelson	.03	.01	.00
☐ 494	Gary Roenicke	.03	.01	.00
☐ 495	Mark Langston	.50	.25	.05
☐ 496	Jay Johnstone	.06	.03	.00
☐ 497	John Stuper	.03	.01	.00
☐ 498	Tito Landrum	.03	.01	.00
☐ 499	Bob L. Gibson	.03	.01	.00
☐ 500	Rickey Henderson	.45	.22	.04
☐ 501	Dave Johnson MG (checklist back)	.06	.03	.00
☐ 502	Glen Cook	.06	.03	.00
☐ 503	Mike Fitzgerald	.03	.01	.00
☐ 504	Denny Walling	.03	.01	.00
☐ 505	Jerry Koosman	.08	.04	.01
☐ 506	Bill Russell	.06	.03	.00
☐ 507	Steve Ontiveros	.08	.04	.01
☐ 508	Alan Wiggins	.03	.01	.00
☐ 509	Ernie Camacho	.03	.01	.00
☐ 510	Wade Boggs	2.00	1.00	.20
☐ 511	Ed Nunez	.03	.01	.00
☐ 512	Thad Bosley	.03	.01	.00
☐ 513	Ron Washington	.03	.01	.00
☐ 514	Mike Jones	.03	.01	.00
☐ 515	Darrell Evans	.08	.04	.01
☐ 516	Giants Leaders Greg Minton	.03	.01	.00
☐ 517	Milt Thompson	.25	.12	.02
☐ 518	Buck Martinez	.03	.01	.00
☐ 519	Danny Darwin	.03	.01	.00
☐ 520	Keith Hernandez	.25	.12	.02
☐ 521	Nate Snell	.06	.03	.00
☐ 522	Bob Bailor	.03	.01	.00
☐ 523	Joe Price	.03	.01	.00
☐ 524	Darrell Miller	.06	.03	.00
☐ 525	Marvell Wynne	.03	.01	.00
☐ 526	Charlie Lea	.03	.01	.00
☐ 527	Checklist: 397-528	.06	.01	.00
☐ 528	Terry Pendleton	.06	.03	.00
☐ 529	Marc Sullivan	.03	.01	.00
☐ 530	Rich Gossage	.10	.05	.01
☐ 531	Tony LaRussa MG (checklist back)	.06	.03	.00
☐ 532	Don Carman	.20	.10	.02
☐ 533	Billy Sample	.03	.01	.00
☐ 534	Jeff Calhoun	.03	.01	.00
☐ 535	Toby Harrah	.03	.01	.00
☐ 536	Jose Rijo	.08	.04	.01
☐ 537	Mark Salas	.03	.01	.00
☐ 538	Dennis Eckersley	.12	.06	.01
☐ 539	Glenn Hubbard	.03	.01	.00
☐ 540	Dan Petry	.03	.01	.00
☐ 541	Jorge Orta	.03	.01	.00
☐ 542	Don Schulze	.03	.01	.00
☐ 543	Jerry Narron	.03	.01	.00
☐ 544	Eddie Milner	.03	.01	.00
☐ 545	Jimmy Key	.10	.05	.01
☐ 546	Mariners Leaders Dave Henderson	.03	.01	.00
☐ 547	Roger McDowell	.35	.17	.03
☐ 548	Mike Young	.06	.03	.00
☐ 549	Bob Welch	.06	.03	.00
☐ 550	Tom Herr	.06	.03	.00
☐ 551	Dave LaPoint	.06	.03	.00
☐ 552	Marc Hill	.03	.01	.00
☐ 553	Jim Morrison	.03	.01	.00
☐ 554	Paul Householder	.03	.01	.00
☐ 555	Hubie Brooks	.08	.04	.01
☐ 556	John Denny	.06	.03	.00
☐ 557	Gerald Perry	.10	.05	.01
☐ 558	Tim Stoddard	.03	.01	.00
☐ 559	Tommy Dunbar	.03	.01	.00
☐ 560	Dave Righetti	.10	.05	.01
☐ 561	Bob Lillis MG (checklist back)	.06	.03	.00
☐ 562	Joe Beckwith	.03	.01	.00
☐ 563	Alejandro Sanchez	.03	.01	.00
☐ 564	Warren Brusstar	.03	.01	.00
☐ 565	Tom Brunansky	.12	.06	.01
☐ 566	Alfredo Griffin	.06	.03	.00
☐ 567	Jeff Barkley	.03	.01	.00
☐ 568	Donnie Scott	.03	.01	.00
☐ 569	Jim Acker	.03	.01	.00
☐ 570	Rusty Staub	.08	.04	.01
☐ 571	Mike Jeffcoat	.03	.01	.00
☐ 572	Paul Zuvella	.03	.01	.00
☐ 573	Tom Hume	.03	.01	.00
☐ 574	Ron Kittle	.10	.05	.01
☐ 575	Mike Boddicker	.08	.04	.01
☐ 576	Expos Leaders Andre Dawson	.10	.05	.01
☐ 577	Jerry Reuss	.06	.03	.00
☐ 578	Lee Mazzilli	.03	.01	.00
☐ 579	Jim Slaton	.03	.01	.00
☐ 580	Willie McGee	.12	.06	.01
☐ 581	Bruce Hurst	.12	.06	.01
☐ 582	Jim Gantner	.03	.01	.00
☐ 583	Al Bumbry	.03	.01	.00
☐ 584	Brian Fisher	.18	.09	.01
☐ 585	Garry Maddox	.03	.01	.00
☐ 586	Greg Harris	.03	.01	.00
☐ 587	Rafael Santana	.03	.01	.00
☐ 588	Steve Lake	.03	.01	.00
☐ 589	Sid Bream	.03	.01	.00
☐ 590	Bob Knepper	.06	.03	.00
☐ 591	Jackie Moore MG (checklist back)	.06	.03	.00
☐ 592	Frank Tanana	.06	.03	.00
☐ 593	Jesse Barfield	.18	.09	.01
☐ 594	Chris Bando	.03	.01	.00
☐ 595	Dave Parker	.15	.07	.01
☐ 596	Onix Concepcion	.03	.01	.00
☐ 597	Sammy Stewart	.03	.01	.00
☐ 598	Jim Presley	.15	.07	.01
☐ 599	Rick Aguilera	.25	.12	.02
☐ 600	Dale Murphy	.35	.17	.03
☐ 601	Gary Lucas	.03	.01	.00
☐ 602	Mariano Duncan	.15	.07	.01
☐ 603	Bill Laskey	.03	.01	.00
☐ 604	Gary Pettis	.06	.03	.00
☐ 605	Dennis Boyd	.08	.04	.01
☐ 606	Royals Leaders Hal McRae	.03	.01	.00
☐ 607	Ken Dayley	.03	.01	.00
☐ 608	Bruce Bochy	.03	.01	.00
☐ 609	Barbaro Garbey	.03	.01	.00

☐ 610 Ron Guidry	.10	.05	.01		
☐ 611 Gary Woods	.03	.01	.00		
☐ 612 Richard Dotson	.06	.03	.00		
☐ 613 Roy Smalley	.03	.01	.00		
☐ 614 Rick Waits	.03	.01	.00		
☐ 615 Johnny Ray	.08	.04	.01		
☐ 616 Glenn Brummer	.03	.01	.00		
☐ 617 Lonnie Smith	.08	.04	.01		
☐ 618 Jim Pankovits	.03	.01	.00		
☐ 619 Danny Heep	.03	.01	.00		
☐ 620 Bruce Sutter	.10	.05	.01		
☐ 621 John Felske MG	.06	.03	.00		
(checklist back)					
☐ 622 Gary Lavelle	.03	.01	.00		
☐ 623 Floyd Rayford	.03	.01	.00		
☐ 624 Steve McCatty	.03	.01	.00		
☐ 625 Bob Brenly	.03	.01	.00		
☐ 626 Roy Thomas	.03	.01	.00		
☐ 627 Ron Oester	.03	.01	.00		
☐ 628 Kirk McCaskill	.45	.22	.04		
☐ 629 Mitch Webster	.25	.12	.02		
☐ 630 Fernando Valenzuela	.20	.10	.02		
☐ 631 Steve Braun	.03	.01	.00		
☐ 632 Dave Von Ohlen	.03	.01	.00		
☐ 633 Jackie Gutierrez	.03	.01	.00		
☐ 634 Roy Lee Jackson	.03	.01	.00		
☐ 635 Jason Thompson	.03	.01	.00		
☐ 636 Cubs Leaders	.03	.01	.00		
Lee Smith					
☐ 637 Rudy Law	.03	.01	.00		
☐ 638 John Butcher	.03	.01	.00		
☐ 639 Bo Diaz	.03	.01	.00		
☐ 640 Jose Cruz	.08	.04	.01		
☐ 641 Wayne Tolleson	.03	.01	.00		
☐ 642 Ray Searage	.03	.01	.00		
☐ 643 Tom Brookens	.03	.01	.00		
☐ 644 Mark Gubicza	.20	.07	.01		
☐ 645 Dusty Baker	.06	.03	.00		
☐ 646 Mike Moore	.08	.04	.01		
☐ 647 Mel Hall	.08	.04	.01		
☐ 648 Steve Bedrosian	.10	.05	.01		
☐ 649 Ronn Reynolds	.03	.01	.00		
☐ 650 Dave Stieb	.10	.05	.01		
☐ 651 Billy Martin MG	.12	.06	.01		
(checklist back)					
☐ 652 Tom Browning	.25	.12	.02		
☐ 653 Jim Dwyer	.03	.01	.00		
☐ 654 Ken Howell	.08	.04	.01		
☐ 655 Manny Trillo	.03	.01	.00		
☐ 656 Brian Harper	.03	.01	.00		
☐ 657 Juan Agosto	.03	.01	.00		
☐ 658 Rob Wilfong	.03	.01	.00		
☐ 659 Checklist: 529-660	.06	.01	.00		
☐ 660 Steve Garvey	.35	.17	.03		
☐ 661 Roger Clemens	2.00	1.00	.20		
☐ 662 Bill Schroeder	.03	.01	.00		
☐ 663 Neil Allen	.03	.01	.00		
☐ 664 Tim Corcoran	.03	.01	.00		
☐ 665 Alejandro Pena	.06	.03	.00		
☐ 666 Rangers Leaders	.03	.01	.00		
Charlie Hough					
☐ 667 Tim Teufel	.03	.01	.00		
☐ 668 Cecilio Guante	.03	.01	.00		
☐ 669 Ron Cey	.06	.03	.00		
☐ 670 Willie Hernandez	.08	.04	.01		
☐ 671 Lynn Jones	.03	.01	.00		
☐ 672 Rob Picciolo	.03	.01	.00		
☐ 673 Ernie Whitt	.03	.01	.00		
☐ 674 Pat Tabler	.08	.04	.01		
☐ 675 Claudell Washington	.06	.03	.00		
☐ 676 Matt Young	.03	.01	.00		
☐ 677 Nick Esasky	.12	.06	.01		
☐ 678 Dan Gladden	.06	.03	.00		
☐ 679 Britt Burns	.03	.01	.00		
☐ 680 George Foster	.10	.05	.01		
☐ 681 Dick Williams MG	.06	.03	.00		
(checklist back)					
☐ 682 Junior Ortiz	.03	.01	.00		
☐ 683 Andy Van Slyke	.20	.10	.02		
☐ 684 Bob McClure	.03	.01	.00		
☐ 685 Tim Wallach	.08	.04	.01		
☐ 686 Jeff Stone	.03	.01	.00		
☐ 687 Mike Trujillo	.03	.01	.00		
☐ 688 Larry Herndon	.03	.01	.00		
☐ 689 Dave Stewart	.25	.12	.02		
☐ 690 Ryne Sandberg	.35	.17	.03		
(no Topps logo on front)					
☐ 691 Mike Madden	.03	.01	.00		
☐ 692 Dale Berra	.03	.01	.00		
☐ 693 Tom Tellmann	.03	.01	.00		
☐ 694 Garth Iorg	.03	.01	.00		
☐ 695 Mike Smithson	.03	.01	.00		
☐ 696 Dodgers Leaders	.03	.01	.00		
Bill Russell					

☐ 697 Bud Black	.03	.01	.00
☐ 698 Brad Komminsk	.03	.01	.00
☐ 699 Pat Corrales MG	.06	.03	.00
(checklist back)			
☐ 700 Reggie Jackson	.35	.17	.03
☐ 701 Keith Hernandez AS	.12	.06	.01
☐ 702 Tom Herr AS	.06	.03	.00
☐ 703 Tim Wallach AS	.06	.03	.00
☐ 704 Ozzie Smith AS	.10	.05	.01
☐ 705 Dale Murphy AS	.20	.10	.02
☐ 706 Pedro Guerrero AS	.10	.05	.01
☐ 707 Willie McGee AS	.08	.04	.01
☐ 708 Gary Carter AS	.15	.07	.01
☐ 709 Dwight Gooden AS	.30	.15	.03
☐ 710 John Tudor AS	.06	.03	.00
☐ 711 Jeff Reardon AS	.06	.03	.00
☐ 712 Don Mattingly AS	.75	.35	.07
☐ 713 Damaso Garcia AS	.06	.03	.00
☐ 714 George Brett AS	.25	.12	.02
☐ 715 Cal Ripken AS	.20	.10	.02
☐ 716 Rickey Henderson AS	.25	.12	.02
☐ 717 Dave Winfield AS	.15	.07	.01
☐ 718 George Bell AS	.10	.05	.01
☐ 719 Carlton Fisk AS	.12	.06	.01
☐ 720 Bret Saberhagen AS	.12	.06	.01
☐ 721 Ron Guidry AS	.06	.03	.00
☐ 722 Dan Quisenberry AS	.06	.03	.00
☐ 723 Marty Bystrom	.03	.01	.00
☐ 724 Tim Hulett	.03	.01	.00
☐ 725 Mario Soto	.03	.01	.00
☐ 726 Orioles Leaders	.03	.01	.00
Rick Dempsey			
☐ 727 David Green	.03	.01	.00
☐ 728 Mike Marshall	.10	.05	.01
☐ 729 Jim Beattie	.03	.01	.00
☐ 730 Ozzie Smith	.18	.09	.01
☐ 731 Don Robinson	.03	.01	.00
☐ 732 Floyd Youmans	.25	.12	.02
☐ 733 Ron Romanick	.03	.01	.00
☐ 734 Marty Barrett	.08	.04	.01
☐ 735 Dave Dravecky	.08	.04	.01
☐ 736 Glenn Wilson	.03	.01	.00
☐ 737 Pete Vuckovich	.06	.03	.00
☐ 738 Andre Robertson	.03	.01	.00
☐ 739 Dave Rozema	.03	.01	.00
☐ 740 Lance Parrish	.12	.06	.01
☐ 741 Pete Rose MG	.35	.17	.03
(checklist back)			
☐ 742 Frank Viola	.25	.12	.02
☐ 743 Pat Sheridan	.03	.01	.00
☐ 744 Lary Sorensen	.03	.01	.00
☐ 745 Willie Upshaw	.03	.01	.00
☐ 746 Denny Gonzalez	.03	.01	.00
☐ 747 Rick Cerone	.03	.01	.00
☐ 748 Steve Henderson	.03	.01	.00
☐ 749 Ed Jurak	.03	.01	.00
☐ 750 Gorman Thomas	.06	.03	.00
☐ 751 Howard Johnson	.30	.15	.03
☐ 752 Mike Krukow	.03	.01	.00
☐ 753 Dan Ford	.03	.01	.00
☐ 754 Pat Clements	.08	.04	.01
☐ 755 Harold Baines	.10	.05	.01
☐ 756 Pirates Leaders	.03	.01	.00
Rick Rhoden			
☐ 757 Darrell Porter	.03	.01	.00
☐ 758 Dave Anderson	.03	.01	.00
☐ 759 Moose Haas	.03	.01	.00
☐ 760 Andre Dawson	.25	.12	.02
☐ 761 Don Slaught	.03	.01	.00
☐ 762 Eric Show	.06	.03	.00
☐ 763 Terry Puhl	.03	.01	.00
☐ 764 Kevin Gross	.03	.01	.00
☐ 765 Don Baylor	.10	.05	.01
☐ 766 Rick Langford	.03	.01	.00
☐ 767 Jody Davis	.06	.03	.00
☐ 768 Vern Ruhle	.03	.01	.00
☐ 769 Harold Reynolds	.60	.30	.06
☐ 770 Vida Blue	.06	.03	.00
☐ 771 John McNamara MG	.06	.03	.00
(checklist back)			
☐ 772 Brian Downing	.06	.03	.00
☐ 773 Greg Pryor	.03	.01	.00
☐ 774 Terry Leach	.08	.04	.01
☐ 775 Al Oliver	.08	.04	.01
☐ 776 Gene Garber	.03	.01	.00
☐ 777 Wayne Krenchicki	.03	.01	.00
☐ 778 Jerry Hairston	.03	.01	.00
☐ 779 Rick Reuschel	.10	.05	.01
☐ 780 Robin Yount	.35	.17	.03
☐ 781 Joe Nolan	.03	.01	.00
☐ 782 Ken Landreaux	.03	.01	.00
☐ 783 Ricky Horton	.03	.01	.00
☐ 784 Alan Bannister	.03	.01	.00
☐ 785 Bob Stanley	.03	.01	.00
☐ 786 Twins Leaders	.03	.01	.00

Mickey Hatcher
☐ 787	Vance Law	.03	.01	.00
☐ 788	Marty Castillo	.03	.01	.00
☐ 789	Kurt Bevacqua	.03	.01	.00
☐ 790	Phil Niekro	.15	.07	.01
☐ 791	Checklist: 661-792	.06	.01	.00
☐ 792	Charles Hudson	.06	.03	.00

1986 Topps Wax Box Cards

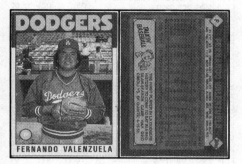

Topps printed cards (each measuring the standard 2 1/2" by 3 1/2") on the bottoms of their wax pack boxes for their regular issue cards; there are four different boxes, each with four cards. These sixteen cards ("numbered" A through P) are listed below; they are not considered an integral part of the regular set but are considered a separate set. They are styled almost exactly like the 1986 Topps regular issue cards.

		MINT	EXC	G-VG
COMPLETE SET (16)	....	6.00	3.00	.60
COMMON PLAYER (A-P)	....	.10	.05	.01
☐ A	Jorge Bell	.25	.12	.02
☐ B	Wade Boggs	1.00	.50	.10
☐ C	George Brett	.50	.25	.05
☐ D	Vince Coleman	1.00	.50	.10
☐ E	Carlton Fisk	.25	.12	.02
☐ F	Dwight Gooden	.75	.35	.07
☐ G	Pedro Guerrero	.20	.10	.02
☐ H	Ron Guidry	.15	.07	.01
☐ I	Reggie Jackson	.50	.25	.05
☐ J	Don Mattingly	1.50	.75	.15
☐ K	Oddibe McDowell	.15	.07	.01
☐ L	Willie McGee	.20	.10	.02
☐ M	Dale Murphy	.60	.30	.06
☐ N	Pete Rose	1.00	.50	.10
☐ O	Bret Saberhagen	.50	.25	.05
☐ P	Fernando Valenzuela	.15	.07	.01

1986 Topps Glossy 22

This 22-card set was distributed as an insert, one card per rak pack. The players featured are the starting lineups of the 1985 All-Star Game played in Minnesota. Cards are very colorful with a high gloss finish and are standard-size, 2 1/2" by 3 1/2". Cards are numbered on the back.

		MINT	EXC	G-VG
COMPLETE SET (22)	....	4.00	2.00	.40
COMMON PLAYER (1-22)	....	.10	.05	.01
☐ 1	Sparky Anderson MG	.10	.05	.01
☐ 2	Eddie Murray	.25	.12	.02
☐ 3	Lou Whitaker	.15	.07	.01
☐ 4	George Brett	.40	.20	.04
☐ 5	Cal Ripken	.35	.17	.03
☐ 6	Jim Rice	.25	.12	.02
☐ 7	Rickey Henderson	.45	.22	.04

			MINT	EXC	G-VG
☐	8	Dave Winfield	.30	.15	.03
☐	9	Carlton Fisk	.25	.12	.02
☐	10	Jack Morris	.15	.07	.01
☐	11	AL Team Photo	.10	.05	.01
☐	12	Dick Williams MG	.10	.05	.01
☐	13	Steve Garvey	.30	.15	.03
☐	14	Tom Herr	.10	.05	.01
☐	15	Graig Nettles	.15	.07	.01
☐	16	Ozzie Smith	.25	.12	.02
☐	17	Tony Gwynn	.45	.22	.04
☐	18	Dale Murphy	.45	.22	.04
☐	19	Darryl Strawberry	.50	.25	.05
☐	20	Terry Kennedy	.10	.05	.01
☐	21	LaMarr Hoyt	.10	.05	.01
☐	22	NL Team Photo	.10	.05	.01

1986 Topps Glossy 60

This 60-card glossy set was produced by Topps and distributed ten cards at a time based on the offer found on the wax packs. Cards measure the standard 2 1/2" by 3 1/2". Each series of ten cards was available by sending in 1.00 plus six "special offer" cards inserted one per wax pack. The card backs are printed in red and blue on white card stock. The card fronts feature a white border and a green frame surrounding a full-color photo of the player.

			MINT	EXC	G-VG
COMPLETE SET (60)		....	12.50	6.25	1.25
COMMON PLAYER (1-60)		....	.10	.05	.01
☐	1	Oddibe McDowell	.15	.07	.01
☐	2	Reggie Jackson	.50	.25	.05
☐	3	Fernando Valenzuela	.25	.12	.02
☐	4	Jack Clark	.20	.10	.02
☐	5	Rickey Henderson	.50	.25	.05
☐	6	Steve Balboni	.10	.05	.01
☐	7	Keith Hernandez	.25	.12	.02
☐	8	Lance Parrish	.20	.10	.02
☐	9	Willie McGee	.20	.10	.02
☐	10	Chris Brown	.10	.05	.01
☐	11	Darryl Strawberry	.75	.35	.07
☐	12	Ron Guidry	.20	.10	.02
☐	13	Dave Parker	.20	.10	.02
☐	14	Cal Ripken	.30	.15	.03
☐	15	Tim Raines	.25	.12	.02

		MINT	EXC	G-VG
☐ 16	Rod Carew	.35	.17	.03
☐ 17	Mike Schmidt	.75	.35	.07
☐ 18	George Brett	.60	.30	.06
☐ 19	Joe Hesketh	.10	.05	.01
☐ 20	Dan Pasqua	.10	.05	.01
☐ 21	Vince Coleman	.50	.25	.05
☐ 22	Tom Seaver	.35	.17	.03
☐ 23	Gary Carter	.25	.12	.02
☐ 24	Orel Hershiser	.75	.35	.07
☐ 25	Pedro Guerrero	.25	.12	.02
☐ 26	Wade Boggs	1.00	.50	.10
☐ 27	Bret Saberhagen	.40	.20	.04
☐ 28	Carlton Fisk	.25	.12	.02
☐ 29	Kirk Gibson	.35	.17	.03
☐ 30	Brian Fisher	.10	.05	.01
☐ 31	Don Mattingly	2.00	1.00	.20
☐ 32	Tom Herr	.10	.05	.01
☐ 33	Eddie Murray	.35	.17	.03
☐ 34	Ryne Sandberg	.35	.17	.03
☐ 35	Dan Quisenberry	.15	.07	.01
☐ 36	Jim Rice	.25	.12	.02
☐ 37	Dale Murphy	.50	.25	.05
☐ 38	Steve Garvey	.40	.20	.04
☐ 39	Roger McDowell	.10	.05	.01
☐ 40	Earnie Riles	.10	.05	.01
☐ 41	Dwight Gooden	.90	.45	.09
☐ 42	Dave Winfield	.30	.15	.03
☐ 43	Dave Stieb	.15	.07	.01
☐ 44	Bob Horner	.15	.07	.01
☐ 45	Nolan Ryan	1.25	.60	.12
☐ 46	Ozzie Smith	.25	.12	.02
☐ 47	Jorge Bell	.20	.10	.02
☐ 48	Gorman Thomas	.15	.07	.01
☐ 49	Tom Browning	.20	.10	.02
☐ 50	Larry Sheets	.15	.07	.01
☐ 51	Pete Rose	1.00	.50	.10
☐ 52	Brett Butler	.15	.07	.01
☐ 53	John Tudor	.15	.07	.01
☐ 54	Phil Bradley	.15	.07	.01
☐ 55	Jeff Reardon	.15	.07	.01
☐ 56	Rich Gossage	.15	.07	.01
☐ 57	Tony Gwynn	.50	.25	.05
☐ 58	Ozzie Guillen	.15	.07	.01
☐ 59	Glenn Davis	.40	.20	.04
☐ 60	Darrell Evans	.15	.07	.01

		MINT	EXC	G-VG
☐ 11	Carlton Fisk	.15	.07	.01
☐ 12	Brett Butler	.10	.05	.01
☐ 13	Darrell Evans	.10	.05	.01
☐ 14	Jack Morris	.15	.07	.01
☐ 15	Lance Parrish	.15	.07	.01
☐ 16	Walt Terrell	.05	.02	.00
☐ 17	Steve Balboni	.05	.02	.00
☐ 18	George Brett	.25	.12	.02
☐ 19	Charlie Leibrandt	.05	.02	.00
☐ 20	Bret Saberhagen	.25	.12	.02
☐ 21	Lonnie Smith	.10	.05	.01
☐ 22	Willie Wilson	.10	.05	.01
☐ 23	Bert Blyleven	.15	.07	.01
☐ 24	Mike Smithson	.05	.02	.00
☐ 25	Frank Viola	.20	.10	.02
☐ 26	Ron Guidry	.10	.05	.01
☐ 27	Rickey Henderson	.30	.15	.03
☐ 28	Don Mattingly	1.00	.50	.10
☐ 29	Dave Winfield	.25	.12	.02
☐ 30	Mike Moore	.10	.05	.01
☐ 31	Gorman Thomas	.10	.05	.01
☐ 32	Toby Harrah	.05	.02	.00
☐ 33	Charlie Hough	.05	.02	.00
☐ 34	Doyle Alexander	.10	.05	.01
☐ 35	Jimmy Key	.05	.02	.00
☐ 36	Dave Stieb	.10	.05	.01
☐ 37	Dale Murphy	.25	.12	.02
☐ 38	Keith Moreland	.05	.02	.00
☐ 39	Ryne Sandberg	.20	.10	.02
☐ 40	Tom Browning	.05	.02	.00
☐ 41	Dave Parker	.15	.07	.01
☐ 42	Mario Soto	.05	.02	.00
☐ 43	Nolan Ryan	.75	.35	.07
☐ 44	Pedro Guerrero	.15	.07	.01
☐ 45	Orel Hershiser	.45	.22	.04
☐ 46	Mike Scioscia	.05	.02	.00
☐ 47	Fernando Valenzuela	.20	.10	.02
☐ 48	Bob Welch	.10	.05	.01
☐ 49	Tim Raines	.20	.10	.02
☐ 50	Gary Carter	.20	.10	.02
☐ 51	Sid Fernandez	.10	.05	.01
☐ 52	Dwight Gooden	.50	.25	.05
☐ 53	Keith Hernandez	.20	.10	.02
☐ 54	Juan Samuel	.15	.07	.01
☐ 55	Mike Schmidt	.75	.35	.07
☐ 56	Glenn Wilson	.05	.02	.00
☐ 57	Rick Reuschel	.10	.05	.01
☐ 58	Joaquin Andujar	.05	.02	.00
☐ 59	Jack Clark	.20	.10	.02
☐ 60	Vince Coleman	.30	.15	.03
☐ 61	Danny Cox	.05	.02	.00
☐ 62	Tom Herr	.05	.02	.00
☐ 63	Willie McGee	.15	.07	.01
☐ 64	John Tudor	.10	.05	.01
☐ 65	Tony Gwynn	.35	.17	.03
☐ 66	Checklist Card	.05	.02	.00

1986 Topps Mini Leaders

The 1986 Topps Mini set of Major League Leaders features 66 cards of leaders of the various statistical categories for the 1985 season. The cards are numbered on the back and measure 2 1/8" by 2 15/16". They are very similar in design to the Team Leader "Dean" cards in the 1986 Topps regular issue.

		MINT	EXC	G-VG
COMPLETE SET (66)		7.00	3.50	.70
COMMON PLAYER (1-66)		.05	.02	.00
☐ 1	Eddie Murray	.25	.12	.02
☐ 2	Cal Ripken	.25	.12	.02
☐ 3	Wade Boggs	.60	.30	.06
☐ 4	Dennis Boyd	.05	.02	.00
☐ 5	Dwight Evans	.15	.07	.01
☐ 6	Bruce Hurst	.10	.05	.01
☐ 7	Gary Pettis	.05	.02	.00
☐ 8	Harold Baines	.10	.05	.01
☐ 9	Floyd Bannister	.05	.02	.00
☐ 10	Britt Burns	.05	.02	.00

1986 Topps Traded

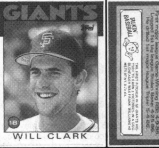

This 132-card Traded or extended set was distributed by Topps to dealers in a special red and white box as a complete set. The card fronts are identical in style to the Topps regular issue and are also 2 1/2" by 3 1/2". The backs are printed in red and black on white card stock. Cards are numbered (with a T suffix) alphabetically according to the name of the player. Topps also produced a specially boxed "glossy" edition frequently referred to as the Topps

Traded Tiffany set. There were supposedly only 5,000 sets of the Tiffany cards produced; they were marketed to hobby dealers. The checklist of cards is identical to that of the normal non-glossy cards. There are two primary distinguishing features of the Tiffany cards, white card stock reverses and high gloss obverses. These Tiffany cards are valued at approximately five times the values listed below.

		MINT	EXC	G-VG
	COMPLETE SET (132)	30.00	15.00	3.00
	COMMON PLAYER (1-132)	.05	.02	.00
☐	1T Andy Allanson	.15	.04	.01
☐	2T Neil Allen	.05	.02	.00
☐	3T Joaquin Andujar	.10	.05	.01
☐	4T Paul Assenmacher	.15	.07	.01
☐	5T Scott Bailes	.15	.07	.01
☐	6T Don Baylor	.10	.05	.01
☐	7T Steve Bedrosian	.15	.07	.01
☐	8T Juan Beniquez	.05	.02	.00
☐	9T Juan Berenguer	.05	.02	.00
☐	10T Mike Bielecki	.35	.17	.03
☐	11T Barry Bonds	1.00	.50	.10
☐	12T Bobby Bonilla	1.00	.50	.10
☐	13T Juan Bonilla	.05	.02	.00
☐	14T Rich Bordi	.05	.02	.00
☐	15T Steve Boros MG	.05	.02	.00
☐	16T Rick Burleson	.10	.05	.01
☐	17T Bill Campbell	.05	.02	.00
☐	18T Tom Candiotti	.10	.05	.01
☐	19T John Cangelosi	.15	.07	.01
☐	20T Jose Canseco	8.50	4.25	.85
☐	21T Carmen Castillo	.05	.02	.00
☐	22T Rick Cerone	.05	.02	.00
☐	23T John Cerutti	.25	.12	.02
☐	24T Will Clark	10.00	5.00	1.00
☐	25T Mark Clear	.05	.02	.00
☐	26T Darnell Coles	.10	.05	.01
☐	27T Dave Collins	.05	.02	.00
☐	28T Tim Conroy	.05	.02	.00
☐	29T Joe Cowley	.05	.02	.00
☐	30T Joel Davis	.15	.07	.01
☐	31T Rob Deer	.15	.07	.01
☐	32T John Denny	.10	.05	.01
☐	33T Mike Easler	.05	.02	.00
☐	34T Mark Eichhorn	.10	.05	.01
☐	35T Steve Farr	.05	.02	.00
☐	36T Scott Fletcher	.10	.05	.01
☐	37T Terry Forster	.10	.05	.01
☐	38T Terry Francona	.05	.02	.00
☐	39T Jim Fregosi MG	.05	.02	.00
☐	40T Andres Galarraga	1.50	.75	.15
☐	41T Ken Griffey	.15	.07	.01
☐	42T Bill Gullickson	.05	.02	.00
☐	43T Jose Guzman	.20	.10	.02
☐	44T Moose Haas	.05	.02	.00
☐	45T Billy Hatcher	.10	.05	.01
☐	46T Mike Heath	.05	.02	.00
☐	47T Tom Hume	.05	.02	.00
☐	48T Pete Incaviglia	.70	.35	.07
☐	49T Dane Iorg	.05	.02	.00
☐	50T Bo Jackson	9.00	4.50	.90
☐	51T Wally Joyner	2.00	1.00	.20
☐	52T Charlie Kerfeld	.10	.05	.01
☐	53T Eric King	.15	.07	.01
☐	54T Bob Kipper	.05	.02	.00
☐	55T Wayne Krenchicki	.05	.02	.00
☐	56T John Kruk	.35	.17	.03
☐	57T Mike LaCoss	.05	.02	.00
☐	58T Pete Ladd	.05	.02	.00
☐	59T Mike Laga	.10	.05	.01
☐	60T Hal Lanier MG	.05	.02	.00
☐	61T Dave LaPoint	.10	.05	.01
☐	62T Rudy Law	.05	.02	.00
☐	63T Rick Leach	.05	.02	.00
☐	64T Tim Leary	.20	.10	.02
☐	65T Dennis Leonard	.10	.05	.01
☐	66T Jim Leyland MG	.05	.02	.00
☐	67T Steve Lyons	.05	.02	.00
☐	68T Mickey Mahler	.05	.02	.00
☐	69T Candy Maldonado	.10	.05	.01
☐	70T Roger Mason	.10	.05	.01
☐	71T Bob McClure	.05	.02	.00
☐	72T Andy McGaffigan	.05	.02	.00
☐	73T Gene Michael MG	.05	.02	.00
☐	74T Kevin Mitchell	5.00	2.50	.50
☐	75T Omar Moreno	.05	.02	.00
☐	76T Jerry Mumphrey	.05	.02	.00
☐	77T Phil Niekro	.30	.15	.03
☐	78T Randy Niemann	.05	.02	.00
☐	79T Juan Nieves	.15	.07	.01
☐	80T Otis Nixon	.15	.07	.01
☐	81T Bob Ojeda	.10	.05	.01
☐	82T Jose Oquendo	.10	.05	.01
☐	83T Tom Paciorek	.05	.02	.00
☐	84T David Palmer	.05	.02	.00
☐	85T Frank Pastore	.05	.02	.00
☐	86T Lou Piniella MG	.10	.05	.01
☐	87T Dan Plesac	.30	.15	.03
☐	88T Darrell Porter	.05	.02	.00
☐	89T Rey Quinones	.20	.10	.02
☐	90T Gary Redus	.05	.02	.00
☐	91T Bip Roberts	.20	.10	.02
☐	92T Billy Jo Robidoux	.10	.05	.01
☐	93T Jeff Robinson (Giants pitcher)	.20	.10	.02
☐	94T Gary Roenicke	.05	.02	.00
☐	95T Ed Romero	.05	.02	.00
☐	96T Argenis Salazar	.05	.02	.00
☐	97T Joe Sambito	.05	.02	.00
☐	98T Billy Sample	.05	.02	.00
☐	99T Dave Schmidt	.10	.05	.01
☐	100T Ken Schrom	.05	.02	.00
☐	101T Tom Seaver	.50	.25	.05
☐	102T Ted Simmons	.15	.07	.01
☐	103T Sammy Stewart	.05	.02	.00
☐	104T Kurt Stillwell	.25	.12	.02
☐	105T Franklin Stubbs	.05	.02	.00
☐	106T Dale Sveum	.20	.10	.02
☐	107T Chuck Tanner MG	.05	.02	.00
☐	108T Danny Tartabull	.75	.35	.07
☐	109T Tim Teufel	.05	.02	.00
☐	110T Bob Tewksbury	.15	.07	.01
☐	111T Andres Thomas	.20	.10	.02
☐	112T Milt Thompson	.10	.05	.01
☐	113T Robby Thompson	.35	.17	.03
☐	114T Jay Tibbs	.05	.02	.00
☐	115T Wayne Tolleson	.05	.02	.00
☐	116T Alex Trevino	.05	.02	.00
☐	117T Manny Trillo	.05	.02	.00
☐	118T Ed VandeBerg	.05	.02	.00
☐	119T Ozzie Virgil	.05	.02	.00
☐	120T Bob Walk	.05	.02	.00
☐	121T Gene Walter	.10	.05	.01
☐	122T Claudell Washington	.10	.05	.01
☐	123T Bill Wegman	.10	.05	.01
☐	124T Dick Williams MG	.05	.02	.00
☐	125T Mitch Williams	.40	.20	.04
☐	126T Bobby Witt	.35	.17	.03
☐	127T Todd Worrell	.50	.25	.05
☐	128T George Wright	.05	.02	.00
☐	129T Ricky Wright	.05	.02	.00
☐	130T Steve Yeager	.05	.02	.00
☐	131T Paul Zuvella	.05	.02	.00
☐	132T Checklist 1-132	.05	.01	.00

1987 Topps

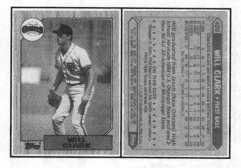

This 792-card set is reminiscent of the 1962 Topps baseball cards with their simulated wood grain borders. The backs are printed in yellow and blue on gray card stock. The manager cards contain a checklist of the respective team's players on the back. Subsets in the set include Record Breakers (1-7), Turn Back The Clock (311-315), and All-Star selections (595-616). The Team Leader cards typically show players conferring on the mound inside a white cloud. The wax pack wrapper gives details of "Spring Fever Baseball" where a lucky collector can win a trip for four to Spring Training. Topps also produced a specially boxed "glossy" edition frequently referred to as the Topps Tiffany set. This year Topps did not disclose the number of sets they produced or sold. It is apparent from the availability that there were many more sets produced this year compared to the 1984-86 Tiffany sets, perhaps more than three times as many. The checklist of cards (792 regular and 132 Traded) is identical to that of the normal non-glossy cards. There are two primary distinguishing features of the Tiffany cards, white card stock reverses and high gloss obverses. These Tiffany cards are valued at approximately four times the values listed below.

		MINT	EXC	G-VG
COMPLETE SET (792)		35.00	17.50	3.50
COMMON PLAYER (1-792)		.03	.01	.00

		MINT	EXC	G-VG
☐ 1	RB: Roger Clemens Most strikeouts, nine inning game	.40	.10	.02
☐ 2	RB: Jim Deshaies Most cons. K's, start of game	.06	.03	.00
☐ 3	RB: Dwight Evans Earliest home run, season	.08	.04	.01
☐ 4	RB: Davey Lopes Most steals, season, 40-year-old	.06	.03	.00
☐ 5	RB: Dave Righetti Most saves, season	.08	.04	.01
☐ 6	RB: Ruben Sierra Youngest player to switch hit homers in game	.25	.12	.02
☐ 7	RB: Todd Worrell Most saves, season, rookie	.08	.04	.01
☐ 8	Terry Pendleton	.03	.01	.00
☐ 9	Jay Tibbs	.03	.01	.00
☐ 10	Cecil Cooper	.08	.04	.01
☐ 11	Indians Team (mound conference)	.03	.01	.00
☐ 12	Jeff Sellers	.10	.05	.01
☐ 13	Nick Esasky	.10	.05	.01
☐ 14	Dave Stewart	.15	.07	.01
☐ 15	Claudell Washington	.06	.03	.00
☐ 16	Pat Clements	.03	.01	.00
☐ 17	Pete O'Brien	.08	.04	.01
☐ 18	Dick Howser MG (checklist back)	.06	.03	.00
☐ 19	Matt Young	.03	.01	.00
☐ 20	Gary Carter	.18	.09	.01
☐ 21	Mark Davis	.12	.06	.01
☐ 22	Doug DeCinces	.06	.03	.00
☐ 23	Lee Smith	.06	.03	.00
☐ 24	Tony Walker	.08	.04	.01
☐ 25	Bert Blyleven	.10	.05	.01
☐ 26	Greg Brock	.03	.01	.00
☐ 27	Joe Cowley	.03	.01	.00
☐ 28	Rick Dempsey	.03	.01	.00
☐ 29	Jimmy Key	.08	.04	.01
☐ 30	Tim Raines	.15	.07	.01
☐ 31	Braves Team (Hubbard/Ramirez)	.03	.01	.00
☐ 32	Tim Leary	.06	.03	.00
☐ 33	Andy Van Slyke	.15	.07	.01
☐ 34	Jose Rijo	.06	.03	.00
☐ 35	Sid Bream	.03	.01	.00
☐ 36	Eric King	.12	.06	.01
☐ 37	Marvell Wynne	.03	.01	.00
☐ 38	Dennis Leonard	.03	.01	.00
☐ 39	Marty Barrett	.06	.03	.00
☐ 40	Dave Righetti	.10	.05	.01
☐ 41	Bo Diaz	.03	.01	.00
☐ 42	Gary Redus	.03	.01	.00
☐ 43	Gene Michael MG (checklist back)	.06	.03	.00
☐ 44	Greg Harris	.03	.01	.00
☐ 45	Jim Presley	.06	.03	.00
☐ 46	Dan Gladden	.06	.03	.00
☐ 47	Dennis Powell	.03	.01	.00
☐ 48	Wally Backman	.03	.01	.00
☐ 49	Terry Harper	.03	.01	.00
☐ 50	Dave Smith	.03	.01	.00
☐ 51	Mel Hall	.06	.03	.00
☐ 52	Keith Atherton	.03	.01	.00

		MINT	EXC	G-VG
☐ 53	Ruppert Jones	.03	.01	.00
☐ 54	Bill Dawley	.03	.01	.00
☐ 55	Tim Wallach	.08	.04	.01
☐ 56	Brewers Team (mound conference)	.03	.01	.00
☐ 57	Scott Nielsen	.12	.06	.01
☐ 58	Thad Bosley	.03	.01	.00
☐ 59	Ken Dayley	.03	.01	.00
☐ 60	Tony Pena	.08	.04	.01
☐ 61	Bobby Thigpen	.25	.12	.02
☐ 62	Bobby Meacham	.03	.01	.00
☐ 63	Fred Toliver	.03	.01	.00
☐ 64	Harry Spilman	.03	.01	.00
☐ 65	Tom Browning	.10	.05	.01
☐ 66	Marc Sullivan	.03	.01	.00
☐ 67	Bill Swift	.03	.01	.00
☐ 68	Tony LaRussa MG (checklist back)	.06	.03	.00
☐ 69	Lonnie Smith	.08	.04	.01
☐ 70	Charlie Hough	.06	.03	.00
☐ 71	Mike Aldrete	.15	.07	.01
☐ 72	Walt Terrell	.03	.01	.00
☐ 73	Dave Anderson	.03	.01	.00
☐ 74	Dan Pasqua	.06	.03	.00
☐ 75	Ron Darling	.15	.07	.01
☐ 76	Rafael Ramirez	.03	.01	.00
☐ 77	Bryan Oelkers	.03	.01	.00
☐ 78	Tom Foley	.03	.01	.00
☐ 79	Juan Nieves	.08	.04	.01
☐ 80	Wally Joyner	1.25	.60	.12
☐ 81	Padres Team (Hawkins/Kennedy)	.03	.01	.00
☐ 82	Rob Murphy	.20	.10	.02
☐ 83	Mike Davis	.03	.01	.00
☐ 84	Steve Lake	.03	.01	.00
☐ 85	Kevin Bass	.06	.03	.00
☐ 86	Nate Snell	.03	.01	.00
☐ 87	Mark Salas	.03	.01	.00
☐ 88	Ed Wojna	.03	.01	.00
☐ 89	Ozzie Guillen	.08	.04	.01
☐ 90	Dave Stieb	.10	.05	.01
☐ 91	Harold Reynolds	.06	.03	.00
☐ 92A	Urbano Lugo ERR (no trademark)	.25	.12	.02
☐ 92B	Urbano Lugo COR	.06	.03	.00
☐ 93	Jim Leyland MG (checklist back)	.06	.03	.00
☐ 94	Calvin Schiraldi	.06	.03	.00
☐ 95	Oddibe McDowell	.08	.04	.01
☐ 96	Frank Williams	.03	.01	.00
☐ 97	Glenn Wilson	.03	.01	.00
☐ 98	Bill Scherrer	.03	.01	.00
☐ 99	Darryl Motley	.03	.01	.00
☐ 100	Steve Garvey	.20	.10	.02
☐ 101	Carl Willis	.06	.03	.00
☐ 102	Paul Zuvella	.03	.01	.00
☐ 103	Rick Aguilera	.03	.01	.00
☐ 104	Billy Sample	.03	.01	.00
☐ 105	Floyd Youmans	.06	.03	.00
☐ 106	Blue Jays Team (Bell/Barfield)	.12	.06	.01
☐ 107	John Butcher	.03	.01	.00
☐ 108	Jim Gantner UER (Brewers logo reversed)	.06	.03	.00
☐ 109	R.J. Reynolds	.03	.01	.00
☐ 110	John Tudor	.10	.05	.01
☐ 111	Alfredo Griffin	.06	.03	.00
☐ 112	Alan Ashby	.03	.01	.00
☐ 113	Neil Allen	.03	.01	.00
☐ 114	Billy Beane	.06	.03	.00
☐ 115	Donnie Moore	.03	.01	.00
☐ 116	Bill Russell	.03	.01	.00
☐ 117	Jim Beattie	.03	.01	.00
☐ 118	Bobby Valentine MG (checklist back)	.06	.03	.00
☐ 119	Ron Robinson	.03	.01	.00
☐ 120	Eddie Murray	.18	.09	.01
☐ 121	Kevin Romine	.10	.05	.01
☐ 122	Jim Clancy	.03	.01	.00
☐ 123	John Kruk	.30	.15	.03
☐ 124	Ray Fontenot	.03	.01	.00
☐ 125	Bob Brenly	.03	.01	.00
☐ 126	Mike Loynd	.06	.03	.00
☐ 127	Vance Law	.03	.01	.00
☐ 128	Checklist 1-132	.06	.01	.00
☐ 129	Rick Cerone	.03	.01	.00
☐ 130	Dwight Gooden	.65	.30	.06
☐ 131	Pirates Team (Bream/Pena)	.03	.01	.00
☐ 132	Paul Assenmacher	.06	.03	.00
☐ 133	Jose Oquendo	.03	.01	.00
☐ 134	Rich Yett	.03	.01	.00
☐ 135	Mike Easler	.03	.01	.00
☐ 136	Ron Romanick	.03	.01	.00

☐ 137	Jerry Willard	.03	.01	.00
☐ 138	Roy Lee Jackson	.03	.01	.00
☐ 139	Devon White	1.00	.50	.10
☐ 140	Bret Saberhagen	.25	.12	.02
☐ 141	Herm Winningham	.03	.01	.00
☐ 142	Rick Sutcliffe	.10	.05	.01
☐ 143	Steve Boros MG	.06	.03	.00
	(checklist back)			
☐ 144	Mike Scioscia	.03	.01	.00
☐ 145	Charlie Kerfeld	.03	.01	.00
☐ 146	Tracy Jones	.15	.07	.01
☐ 147	Randy Niemann	.03	.01	.00
☐ 148	Dave Collins	.03	.01	.00
☐ 149	Ray Searage	.03	.01	.00
☐ 150	Wade Boggs	1.25	.60	.12
☐ 151	Mike LaCoss	.03	.01	.00
☐ 152	Toby Harrah	.03	.01	.00
☐ 153	Duane Ward	.15	.07	.01
☐ 154	Tom O'Malley	.03	.01	.00
☐ 155	Eddie Whitson	.03	.01	.00
☐ 156	Mariners Team	.03	.01	.00
	(mound conference)			
☐ 157	Danny Darwin	.03	.01	.00
☐ 158	Tim Teufel	.03	.01	.00
☐ 159	Ed Olwine	.06	.03	.00
☐ 160	Julio Franco	.12	.06	.01
☐ 161	Steve Ontiveros	.03	.01	.00
☐ 162	Mike LaValliere	.15	.07	.01
☐ 163	Kevin Gross	.03	.01	.00
☐ 164	Sammy Khalifa	.03	.01	.00
☐ 165	Jeff Reardon	.08	.04	.01
☐ 166	Bob Boone	.08	.04	.01
☐ 167	Jim Deshaies	.20	.10	.02
☐ 168	Lou Piniella MG	.08	.04	.01
	(checklist back)			
☐ 169	Ron Washington	.03	.01	.00
☐ 170	Bo Jackson	3.50	1.75	.35
☐ 171	Chuck Cary	.20	.10	.02
☐ 172	Ron Oester	.03	.01	.00
☐ 173	Alex Trevino	.03	.01	.00
☐ 174	Henry Cotto	.03	.01	.00
☐ 175	Bob Stanley	.03	.01	.00
☐ 176	Steve Buechele	.03	.01	.00
☐ 177	Keith Moreland	.03	.01	.00
☐ 178	Cecil Fielder	.06	.03	.00
☐ 179	Bill Wegman	.06	.03	.00
☐ 180	Chris Brown	.03	.01	.00
☐ 181	Cardinals Team	.03	.01	.00
	(mound conference)			
☐ 182	Lee Lacy	.03	.01	.00
☐ 183	Andy Hawkins	.06	.03	.00
☐ 184	Bobby Bonilla	.75	.35	.07
☐ 185	Roger McDowell	.06	.03	.00
☐ 186	Bruce Benedict	.03	.01	.00
☐ 187	Mark Huismann	.03	.01	.00
☐ 188	Tony Phillips	.03	.01	.00
☐ 189	Joe Hesketh	.03	.01	.00
☐ 190	Jim Sundberg	.03	.01	.00
☐ 191	Charles Hudson	.03	.01	.00
☐ 192	Cory Snyder	.40	.20	.04
☐ 193	Roger Craig MG	.06	.03	.00
	(checklist back)			
☐ 194	Kirk McCaskill	.03	.01	.00
☐ 195	Mike Pagliarulo	.06	.03	.00
☐ 196	Randy O'Neal UER	.03	.01	.00
	(wrong ML career			
	W-L totals)			
☐ 197	Mark Bailey	.03	.01	.00
☐ 198	Lee Mazzilli	.03	.01	.00
☐ 199	Mariano Duncan	.03	.01	.00
☐ 200	Pete Rose	.45	.22	.04
☐ 201	John Cangelosi	.08	.04	.01
☐ 202	Ricky Wright	.03	.01	.00
☐ 203	Mike Kingery	.08	.04	.01
☐ 204	Sammy Stewart	.03	.01	.00
☐ 205	Graig Nettles	.08	.04	.01
☐ 206	Twins Team	.06	.03	.00
	(Frank Viola and			
	Tim Laudner)			
☐ 207	George Frazier	.03	.01	.00
☐ 208	John Shelby	.03	.01	.00
☐ 209	Rick Schu	.03	.01	.00
☐ 210	Lloyd Moseby	.06	.03	.00
☐ 211	John Morris	.03	.01	.00
☐ 212	Mike Fitzgerald	.03	.01	.00
☐ 213	Randy Myers	.45	.22	.04
☐ 214	Omar Moreno	.03	.01	.00
☐ 215	Mark Langston	.25	.12	.02
☐ 216	B.J. Surhoff	.35	.17	.03
☐ 217	Chris Codiroli	.03	.01	.00
☐ 218	Sparky Anderson MG	.06	.03	.00
	(checklist back)			
☐ 219	Cecilio Guante	.03	.01	.00
☐ 220	Joe Carter	.25	.12	.02
☐ 221	Vern Ruhle	.03	.01	.00
☐ 222	Denny Walling	.03	.01	.00
☐ 223	Charlie Leibrandt	.03	.01	.00
☐ 224	Wayne Tolleson	.03	.01	.00
☐ 225	Mike Smithson	.03	.01	.00
☐ 226	Max Venable	.03	.01	.00
☐ 227	Jamie Moyer	.15	.07	.01
☐ 228	Curt Wilkerson	.03	.01	.00
☐ 229	Mike Birkbeck	.10	.05	.01
☐ 230	Don Baylor	.08	.04	.01
☐ 231	Giants Team	.03	.01	.00
	(Bob Brenly and			
	Jim Gott)			
☐ 232	Reggie Williams	.06	.03	.00
☐ 233	Russ Morman	.10	.05	.01
☐ 234	Pat Sheridan	.03	.01	.00
☐ 235	Alvin Davis	.10	.05	.01
☐ 236	Tommy John	.10	.05	.01
☐ 237	Jim Morrison	.03	.01	.00
☐ 238	Bill Krueger	.03	.01	.00
☐ 239	Juan Espino	.03	.01	.00
☐ 240	Steve Balboni	.03	.01	.00
☐ 241	Danny Heep	.03	.01	.00
☐ 242	Rick Mahler	.03	.01	.00
☐ 243	Whitey Herzog MG	.06	.03	.00
	(checklist back)			
☐ 244	Dickie Noles	.03	.01	.00
☐ 245	Willie Upshaw	.03	.01	.00
☐ 246	Jim Dwyer	.03	.01	.00
☐ 247	Jeff Reed	.03	.01	.00
☐ 248	Gene Walter	.03	.01	.00
☐ 249	Jim Pankovits	.03	.01	.00
☐ 250	Teddy Higuera	.15	.07	.01
☐ 251	Rob Wilfong	.03	.01	.00
☐ 252	Dennis Martinez	.06	.03	.00
☐ 253	Eddie Milner	.03	.01	.00
☐ 254	Bob Tewksbury	.10	.05	.01
☐ 255	Juan Samuel	.10	.05	.01
☐ 256	Royals Team	.10	.05	.01
	(Brett/F.White)			
☐ 257	Bob Forsch	.03	.01	.00
☐ 258	Steve Yeager	.03	.01	.00
☐ 259	Mike Greenwell	4.00	2.00	.40
☐ 260	Vida Blue	.06	.03	.00
☐ 261	Ruben Sierra	2.50	1.25	.25
☐ 262	Jim Winn	.03	.01	.00
☐ 263	Stan Javier	.06	.03	.00
☐ 264	Checklist 133-264	.06	.01	.00
☐ 265	Darrell Evans	.08	.04	.01
☐ 266	Jeff Hamilton	.15	.07	.01
☐ 267	Howard Johnson	.20	.10	.02
☐ 268	Pat Corrales MG	.06	.03	.00
	(checklist back)			
☐ 269	Cliff Speck	.06	.03	.00
☐ 270	Jody Davis	.03	.01	.00
☐ 271	Mike Brown	.03	.01	.00
	(Mariners pitcher)			
☐ 272	Andres Galarraga	.90	.45	.09
☐ 273	Gene Nelson	.03	.01	.00
☐ 274	Jeff Hearron	.10	.05	.01
	(duplicate 1986			
	stat line on back)			
☐ 275	LaMarr Hoyt	.06	.03	.00
☐ 276	Jackie Gutierrez	.03	.01	.00
☐ 277	Juan Agosto	.03	.01	.00
☐ 278	Gary Pettis	.03	.01	.00
☐ 279	Dan Plesac	.25	.12	.02
☐ 280	Jeff Leonard	.06	.03	.00
☐ 281	Reds Team	.10	.05	.01
	(Pete Rose, Bo Diaz,			
	and Bill Gullickson)			
☐ 282	Jeff Calhoun	.03	.01	.00
☐ 283	Doug Drabek	.30	.15	.03
☐ 284	John Moses	.03	.01	.00
☐ 285	Dennis Boyd	.06	.03	.00
☐ 286	Mike Woodard	.03	.01	.00
☐ 287	Dave Von Ohlen	.03	.01	.00
☐ 288	Tito Landrum	.03	.01	.00
☐ 289	Bob Kipper	.03	.01	.00
☐ 290	Leon Durham	.06	.03	.00
☐ 291	Mitch Williams	.30	.15	.03
☐ 292	Franklin Stubbs	.03	.01	.00
☐ 293	Bob Rodgers MG	.06	.03	.00
	(checklist back)			
☐ 294	Steve Jeltz	.03	.01	.00
☐ 295	Len Dykstra	.08	.04	.01
☐ 296	Andres Thomas	.12	.06	.01
☐ 297	Don Schulze	.03	.01	.00
☐ 298	Larry Herndon	.03	.01	.00
☐ 299	Joel Davis	.03	.01	.00
☐ 300	Reggie Jackson	.30	.15	.03
☐ 301	Luis Aquino	.06	.03	.00
	UER (no trademark,			
	never corrected)			
☐ 302	Bill Schroeder	.03	.01	.00
☐ 303	Juan Berenguer	.03	.01	.00

☐ 304	Phil Garner	.03	.01	.00
☐ 305	John Franco	.08	.04	.01
☐ 306	Red Sox Team	.08	.04	.01
	(Tom Seaver, John McNamara, and Rich Gedman)			
☐ 307	Lee Guetterman	.12	.06	.01
☐ 308	Don Slaught	.03	.01	.00
☐ 309	Mike Young	.03	.01	.00
☐ 310	Frank Viola	.15	.07	.01
☐ 311	Turn Back 1982	.12	.06	.01
	Rickey Henderson			
☐ 312	Turn Back 1977	.12	.06	.01
	Reggie Jackson			
☐ 313	Turn Back 1972	.12	.06	.01
	Roberto Clemente			
☐ 314	Turn Back 1967 UER	.12	.06	.01
	Carl Yastrzemski (sic, 112 RBI's on back)			
☐ 315	Turn Back 1962	.06	.03	.00
	Maury Wills			
☐ 316	Brian Fisher	.03	.01	.00
☐ 317	Clint Hurdle	.03	.01	.00
☐ 318	Jim Fregosi MG	.06	.03	.00
	(checklist back)			
☐ 319	Greg Swindell	1.00	.50	.10
☐ 320	Barry Bonds	.75	.35	.07
☐ 321	Mike Laga	.03	.01	.00
☐ 322	Chris Bando	.03	.01	.00
☐ 323	Al Newman	.06	.03	.00
☐ 324	David Palmer	.03	.01	.00
☐ 325	Garry Templeton	.06	.03	.00
☐ 326	Mark Gubicza	.12	.06	.01
☐ 327	Dale Sveum	.15	.07	.01
☐ 328	Bob Welch	.06	.03	.00
☐ 329	Ron Roenicke	.03	.01	.00
☐ 330	Mike Scott	.20	.10	.02
☐ 331	Mets Team	.15	.07	.01
	(Gary Carter and Darryl Strawberry)			
☐ 332	Joe Price	.03	.01	.00
☐ 333	Ken Phelps	.06	.03	.00
☐ 334	Ed Correa	.10	.05	.01
☐ 335	Candy Maldonado	.06	.03	.00
☐ 336	Allan Anderson	.25	.12	.02
☐ 337	Darrell Miller	.03	.01	.00
☐ 338	Tim Conroy	.03	.01	.00
☐ 339	Donnie Hill	.03	.01	.00
☐ 340	Roger Clemens	1.00	.50	.10
☐ 341	Mike Brown	.03	.01	.00
	(Pirates OF)			
☐ 342	Bob James	.03	.01	.00
☐ 343	Hal Lanier MG	.06	.03	.00
	(checklist back)			
☐ 344A	Joe Niekro	.10	.05	.01
	(copyright inside righthand border)			
☐ 344B	Joe Niekro	.50	.25	.05
	(copyright outside righthand border)			
☐ 345	Andre Dawson	.25	.12	.02
☐ 346	Shawon Dunston	.12	.06	.01
☐ 347	Mickey Brantley	.12	.06	.01
☐ 348	Carmelo Martinez	.03	.01	.00
☐ 349	Storm Davis	.08	.04	.01
☐ 350	Keith Hernandez	.18	.09	.01
☐ 351	Gene Garber	.03	.01	.00
☐ 352	Mike Felder	.06	.03	.00
☐ 353	Ernie Camacho	.03	.01	.00
☐ 354	Jamie Quirk	.03	.01	.00
☐ 355	Don Carman	.03	.01	.00
☐ 356	White Sox Team	.03	.01	.00
	(mound conference)			
☐ 357	Steve Fireovid	.06	.03	.00
☐ 358	Sal Butera	.03	.01	.00
☐ 359	Doug Corbett	.03	.01	.00
☐ 360	Pedro Guerrero	.12	.06	.01
☐ 361	Mark Thurmond	.03	.01	.00
☐ 362	Luis Quinones	.08	.04	.01
☐ 363	Jose Guzman	.08	.04	.01
☐ 364	Randy Bush	.03	.01	.00
☐ 365	Rick Rhoden	.06	.03	.00
☐ 366	Mark McGwire	3.00	1.50	.30
☐ 367	Jeff Lahti	.03	.01	.00
☐ 368	John McNamara MG	.06	.03	.00
	(checklist back)			
☐ 369	Brian Dayett	.03	.01	.00
☐ 370	Fred Lynn	.10	.05	.01
☐ 371	Mark Eichhorn	.08	.04	.01
☐ 372	Jerry Mumphrey	.03	.01	.00
☐ 373	Jeff Dedmon	.03	.01	.00
☐ 374	Glenn Hoffman	.03	.01	.00
☐ 375	Ron Guidry	.10	.05	.01
☐ 376	Scott Bradley	.03	.01	.00
☐ 377	John Henry Johnson	.03	.01	.00
☐ 378	Rafael Santana	.03	.01	.00
☐ 379	John Russell	.03	.01	.00
☐ 380	Rich Gossage	.08	.04	.01
☐ 381	Expos Team	.03	.01	.00
	(mound conference)			
☐ 382	Rudy Law	.03	.01	.00
☐ 383	Ron Davis	.03	.01	.00
☐ 384	Johnny Grubb	.03	.01	.00
☐ 385	Orel Hershiser	.30	.15	.03
☐ 386	Dickie Thon	.03	.01	.00
☐ 387	T.R. Bryden	.06	.03	.00
☐ 388	Geno Petralli	.03	.01	.00
☐ 389	Jeff Robinson	.08	.04	.01
	(Giants pitcher)			
☐ 390	Gary Matthews	.03	.01	.00
☐ 391	Jay Howell	.06	.03	.00
☐ 392	Checklist 265-396	.06	.01	.00
☐ 393	Pete Rose MG	.35	.17	.03
	(checklist back)			
☐ 394	Mike Bielecki	.15	.07	.01
☐ 395	Damaso Garcia	.03	.01	.00
☐ 396	Tim Lollar	.03	.01	.00
☐ 397	Greg Walker	.06	.03	.00
☐ 398	Brad Havens	.03	.01	.00
☐ 399	Curt Ford	.06	.03	.00
☐ 400	George Brett	.30	.15	.03
☐ 401	Billy Jo Robidoux	.06	.03	.00
☐ 402	Mike Trujillo	.03	.01	.00
☐ 403	Jerry Royster	.03	.01	.00
☐ 404	Doug Sisk	.03	.01	.00
☐ 405	Brook Jacoby	.06	.03	.00
☐ 406	Yankees Team	.25	.12	.02
	(Henderson/Mattingly)			
☐ 407	Jim Acker	.03	.01	.00
☐ 408	John Mizerock	.03	.01	.00
☐ 409	Milt Thompson	.06	.03	.00
☐ 410	Fernando Valenzuela	.15	.07	.01
☐ 411	Darnell Coles	.03	.01	.00
☐ 412	Eric Davis	.90	.45	.09
☐ 413	Moose Haas	.03	.01	.00
☐ 414	Joe Orsulak	.03	.01	.00
☐ 415	Bobby Witt	.25	.12	.02
☐ 416	Tom Nieto	.03	.01	.00
☐ 417	Pat Perry	.03	.01	.00
☐ 418	Dick Williams MG	.06	.03	.00
	(checklist back)			
☐ 419	Mark Portugal	.15	.07	.01
☐ 420	Will Clark	5.00	2.50	.50
☐ 421	Jose DeLeon	.06	.03	.00
☐ 422	Jack Howell	.03	.01	.00
☐ 423	Jaime Cocanower	.03	.01	.00
☐ 424	Chris Speier	.03	.01	.00
☐ 425	Tom Seaver	.25	.12	.02
☐ 426	Floyd Rayford	.03	.01	.00
☐ 427	Edwin Nunez	.03	.01	.00
☐ 428	Bruce Bochy	.03	.01	.00
☐ 429	Tim Pyznarski	.08	.04	.01
☐ 430	Mike Schmidt	.35	.17	.03
☐ 431	Dodgers Team	.06	.03	.00
	(mound conference)			
☐ 432	Jim Slaton	.03	.01	.00
☐ 433	Ed Hearn	.06	.03	.00
☐ 434	Mike Fischlin	.03	.01	.00
☐ 435	Bruce Sutter	.08	.04	.01
☐ 436	Andy Allanson	.06	.03	.00
☐ 437	Ted Power	.03	.01	.00
☐ 438	Kelly Downs	.25	.12	.02
☐ 439	Karl Best	.03	.01	.00
☐ 440	Willie McGee	.10	.05	.01
☐ 441	Dave Leiper	.06	.03	.00
☐ 442	Mitch Webster	.03	.01	.00
☐ 443	John Felske MG	.06	.03	.00
	(checklist back)			
☐ 444	Jeff Russell	.06	.03	.00
☐ 445	Dave Lopes	.06	.03	.00
☐ 446	Chuck Finley	.35	.17	.03
☐ 447	Bill Almon	.03	.01	.00
☐ 448	Chris Bosio	.30	.15	.03
☐ 449	Pat Dodson	.10	.05	.01
☐ 450	Kirby Puckett	.60	.30	.06
☐ 451	Joe Sambito	.03	.01	.00
☐ 452	Dave Henderson	.06	.03	.00
☐ 453	Scott Terry	.25	.12	.02
☐ 454	Luis Salazar	.03	.01	.00
☐ 455	Mike Boddicker	.06	.03	.00
☐ 456	A's Team	.03	.01	.00
	(mound conference)			
☐ 457	Len Matuszek	.03	.01	.00
☐ 458	Kelly Gruber	.08	.04	.01
☐ 459	Dennis Eckersley	.12	.06	.01
☐ 460	Darryl Strawberry	.50	.25	.05
☐ 461	Craig McMurtry	.03	.01	.00
☐ 462	Scott Fletcher	.03	.01	.00
☐ 463	Tom Candiotti	.03	.01	.00
☐ 464	Butch Wynegar	.03	.01	.00

□ 465 Todd Worrell	.20	.10	.02
□ 466 Kal Daniels	.60	.30	.06
□ 467 Randy St.Claire	.03	.01	.00
□ 468 George Bamberger MG (checklist back)	.06	.03	.00
□ 469 Mike Diaz	.10	.05	.01
□ 470 Dave Dravecky	.08	.04	.01
□ 471 Ronn Reynolds	.03	.01	.00
□ 472 Bill Doran	.08	.04	.01
□ 473 Steve Farr	.03	.01	.00
□ 474 Jerry Narron	.03	.01	.00
□ 475 Scott Garrelts	.06	.03	.00
□ 476 Danny Tartabull	.75	.35	.07
□ 477 Ken Howell	.03	.01	.00
□ 478 Tim Laudner	.03	.01	.00
□ 479 Bob Sebra	.08	.04	.01
□ 480 Jim Rice	.15	.07	.01
□ 481 Phillies Team (Glenn Wilson, Juan Samuel, and Von Hayes)	.06	.03	.00
□ 482 Daryl Boston	.03	.01	.00
□ 483 Dwight Lowry	.08	.04	.01
□ 484 Jim Traber	.03	.01	.00
□ 485 Tony Fernandez	.12	.06	.01
□ 486 Otis Nixon	.08	.04	.01
□ 487 Dave Gumpert	.03	.01	.00
□ 488 Ray Knight	.06	.03	.00
□ 489 Bill Gullickson	.03	.01	.00
□ 490 Dale Murphy	.30	.15	.03
□ 491 Ron Karkovice	.06	.03	.00
□ 492 Mike Heath	.03	.01	.00
□ 493 Tom Lasorda MG (checklist back)	.08	.04	.01
□ 494 Barry Jones	.10	.05	.01
□ 495 Gorman Thomas	.08	.04	.01
□ 496 Bruce Bochte	.03	.01	.00
□ 497 Dale Mohorcic	.12	.06	.01
□ 498 Bob Kearney	.03	.01	.00
□ 499 Bruce Ruffin	.12	.06	.01
□ 500 Don Mattingly	1.25	.60	.12
□ 501 Craig Lefferts	.06	.03	.00
□ 502 Dick Schofield	.03	.01	.00
□ 503 Larry Andersen	.03	.01	.00
□ 504 Mickey Hatcher	.03	.01	.00
□ 505 Bryn Smith	.06	.03	.00
□ 506 Orioles Team (mound conference)	.03	.01	.00
□ 507 Dave Stapleton (infielder)	.03	.01	.00
□ 508 Scott Bankhead	.08	.04	.01
□ 509 Enos Cabell	.03	.01	.00
□ 510 Tom Henke	.08	.04	.01
□ 511 Steve Lyons	.03	.01	.00
□ 512 Dave Magadan	.40	.20	.04
□ 513 Carmen Castillo	.03	.01	.00
□ 514 Orlando Mercado	.03	.01	.00
□ 515 Willie Hernandez	.08	.04	.01
□ 516 Ted Simmons	.08	.04	.01
□ 517 Mario Soto	.03	.01	.00
□ 518 Gene Mauch MG (checklist back)	.06	.03	.00
□ 519 Curt Young	.03	.01	.00
□ 520 Jack Clark	.18	.09	.01
□ 521 Rick Reuschel	.08	.04	.01
□ 522 Checklist 397-528	.06	.01	.00
□ 523 Earnie Riles	.03	.01	.00
□ 524 Bob Shirley	.03	.01	.00
□ 525 Phil Bradley	.08	.04	.01
□ 526 Roger Mason	.03	.01	.00
□ 527 Jim Wohlford	.03	.01	.00
□ 528 Ken Dixon	.03	.01	.00
□ 529 Alvaro Espinoza	.03	.01	.00
□ 530 Tony Gwynn	.40	.20	.04
□ 531 Astros Team (Y.Berra conference)	.10	.05	.01
□ 532 Jeff Stone	.03	.01	.00
□ 533 Argenis Salazar	.03	.01	.00
□ 534 Scott Sanderson	.03	.01	.00
□ 535 Tony Armas	.06	.03	.00
□ 536 Terry Mulholland	.08	.04	.01
□ 537 Rance Mulliniks	.03	.01	.00
□ 538 Tom Niedenfuer	.03	.01	.00
□ 539 Reid Nichols	.03	.01	.00
□ 540 Terry Kennedy	.03	.01	.00
□ 541 Rafael Belliard	.06	.03	.00
□ 542 Ricky Horton	.03	.01	.00
□ 543 Dave Johnson MG (checklist back)	.08	.04	.01
□ 544 Zane Smith	.06	.03	.00
□ 545 Buddy Bell	.08	.04	.01
□ 546 Mike Morgan	.06	.03	.00
□ 547 Rob Deer	.15	.07	.01
□ 548 Bill Mooneyham	.06	.03	.00
□ 549 Bob Melvin	.03	.01	.00

□ 550 Pete Incaviglia	.60	.30	.06
□ 551 Frank Wills	.03	.01	.00
□ 552 Larry Sheets	.06	.03	.00
□ 553 Mike Maddux	.12	.06	.01
□ 554 Buddy Biancalana	.03	.01	.00
□ 555 Dennis Rasmussen	.06	.03	.00
□ 556 Angels Team (Lachemann, Witt, and Boone)	.06	.03	.00
□ 557 John Cerutti	.15	.07	.01
□ 558 Greg Gagne	.03	.01	.00
□ 559 Lance McCullers	.06	.03	.00
□ 560 Glenn Davis	.25	.12	.02
□ 561 Rey Quinones	.15	.07	.01
□ 562 Bryan Clutterbuck	.06	.03	.00
□ 563 John Stefero	.03	.01	.00
□ 564 Larry McWilliams	.03	.01	.00
□ 565 Dusty Baker	.06	.03	.00
□ 566 Tim Hulett	.03	.01	.00
□ 567 Greg Mathews	.20	.10	.02
□ 568 Earl Weaver MG (checklist back)	.08	.04	.01
□ 569 Wade Rowdon	.06	.03	.00
□ 570 Sid Fernandez	.12	.06	.01
□ 571 Ozzie Virgil	.03	.01	.00
□ 572 Pete Ladd	.03	.01	.00
□ 573 Hal McRae	.06	.03	.00
□ 574 Manny Lee	.03	.01	.00
□ 575 Pat Tabler	.06	.03	.00
□ 576 Frank Pastore	.03	.01	.00
□ 577 Dann Bilardello	.03	.01	.00
□ 578 Billy Hatcher	.06	.03	.00
□ 579 Rick Burleson	.06	.03	.00
□ 580 Mike Krukow	.03	.01	.00
□ 581 Cubs Team (Cey/Trout)	.03	.01	.00
□ 582 Bruce Berenyi	.03	.01	.00
□ 583 Junior Ortiz	.03	.01	.00
□ 584 Ron Kittle	.08	.04	.01
□ 585 Scott Bailes	.10	.05	.01
□ 586 Ben Oglivie	.06	.03	.00
□ 587 Eric Plunk	.06	.03	.00
□ 588 Wallace Johnson	.06	.03	.00
□ 589 Steve Crawford	.03	.01	.00
□ 590 Vince Coleman	.20	.10	.02
□ 591 Spike Owen	.03	.01	.00
□ 592 Chris Welsh	.03	.01	.00
□ 593 Chuck Tanner MG (checklist back)	.06	.03	.00
□ 594 Rick Anderson	.08	.04	.01
□ 595 Keith Hernandez AS	.10	.05	.01
□ 596 Steve Sax AS	.08	.04	.01
□ 597 Mike Schmidt AS	.25	.12	.02
□ 598 Ozzie Smith AS	.10	.05	.01
□ 599 Tony Gwynn AS	.20	.10	.02
□ 600 Dave Parker AS	.08	.04	.01
□ 601 Darryl Strawberry AS	.20	.10	.02
□ 602 Gary Carter AS	.12	.06	.01
□ 603A Dwight Gooden AS ERR (no trademark)	1.00	.50	.10
□ 603B Dwight Gooden AS COR	.30	.15	.03
□ 604 Fern. Valenzuela AS	.10	.05	.01
□ 605 Todd Worrell AS	.08	.04	.01
□ 606A Don Mattingly AS ERR (no trademark)	2.00	1.00	.20
□ 606B Don Mattingly AS COR	.65	.30	.06
□ 607 Tony Bernazard AS	.06	.03	.00
□ 608 Wade Boggs AS	.35	.17	.03
□ 609 Cal Ripken AS	.15	.07	.01
□ 610 Jim Rice AS	.10	.05	.01
□ 611 Kirby Puckett AS	.25	.12	.02
□ 612 George Bell AS	.10	.05	.01
□ 613 Lance Parrish AS UER (Pitcher heading on back)	.08	.04	.01
□ 614 Roger Clemens AS	.20	.10	.02
□ 615 Teddy Higuera AS	.06	.03	.00
□ 616 Dave Righetti AS	.08	.04	.01
□ 617 Al Nipper	.03	.01	.00
□ 618 Tom Kelly MG (checklist back)	.08	.04	.01
□ 619 Jerry Reed	.03	.01	.00
□ 620 Jose Canseco	4.00	2.00	.40
□ 621 Danny Cox	.06	.03	.00
□ 622 Glenn Braggs	.45	.22	.04
□ 623 Kurt Stillwell	.20	.10	.02
□ 624 Tim Burke	.06	.03	.00
□ 625 Mookie Wilson	.06	.03	.00
□ 626 Joel Skinner	.03	.01	.00
□ 627 Ken Oberkfell	.03	.01	.00
□ 628 Bob Walk	.03	.01	.00
□ 629 Larry Parrish	.03	.01	.00
□ 630 John Candelaria	.06	.03	.00
□ 631 Tigers Team (mound conference)	.03	.01	.00

☐ 632	Rob Woodward	.06	.03	.00
☐ 633	Jose Uribe	.03	.01	.00
☐ 634	Rafael Palmeiro	.75	.35	.07
☐ 635	Ken Schrom	.03	.01	.00
☐ 636	Darren Daulton	.03	.01	.00
☐ 637	Bip Roberts	.12	.06	.01
☐ 638	Rich Bordi	.03	.01	.00
☐ 639	Gerald Perry	.08	.04	.01
☐ 640	Mark Clear	.03	.01	.00
☐ 641	Domingo Ramos	.03	.01	.00
☐ 642	Al Pulido	.06	.03	.00
☐ 643	Ron Shepherd	.06	.03	.00
☐ 644	John Denny	.06	.03	.00
☐ 645	Dwight Evans	.10	.05	.01
☐ 646	Mike Mason	.03	.01	.00
☐ 647	Tom Lawless	.03	.01	.00
☐ 648	Barry Larkin	1.25	.60	.12
☐ 649	Mickey Tettleton	.10	.05	.01
☐ 650	Hubie Brooks	.08	.04	.01
☐ 651	Benny Distefano	.06	.03	.00
☐ 652	Terry Forster	.06	.03	.00
☐ 653	Kevin Mitchell	3.00	1.50	.30
☐ 654	Checklist 529-660	.06	.01	.00
☐ 655	Jesse Barfield	.15	.07	.01
☐ 656	Rangers Team (Valentine/R.Wright)	.03	.01	.00
☐ 657	Tom Waddell	.03	.01	.00
☐ 658	Robby Thompson	.20	.10	.02
☐ 659	Aurelio Lopez	.03	.01	.00
☐ 660	Bob Horner	.10	.05	.01
☐ 661	Lou Whitaker	.12	.06	.01
☐ 662	Frank DiPino	.03	.01	.00
☐ 663	Cliff Johnson	.03	.01	.00
☐ 664	Mike Marshall	.10	.05	.01
☐ 665	Rod Scurry	.03	.01	.00
☐ 666	Von Hayes	.08	.04	.01
☐ 667	Ron Hassey	.03	.01	.00
☐ 668	Juan Bonilla	.03	.01	.00
☐ 669	Bud Black	.03	.01	.00
☐ 670	Jose Cruz	.06	.03	.00
☐ 671A	Ray Soff ERR (no D* before copyright line)	.08	.04	.01
☐ 671B	Ray Soff COR (D* before copyright line)	.08	.04	.01
☐ 672	Chili Davis	.08	.04	.01
☐ 673	Don Sutton	.12	.06	.01
☐ 674	Bill Campbell	.03	.01	.00
☐ 675	Ed Romero	.03	.01	.00
☐ 676	Charlie Moore	.03	.01	.00
☐ 677	Bob Grich	.06	.03	.00
☐ 678	Carney Lansford	.10	.05	.01
☐ 679	Kent Hrbek	.15	.07	.01
☐ 680	Ryne Sandberg	.20	.10	.02
☐ 681	George Bell	.20	.10	.02
☐ 682	Jerry Reuss	.03	.01	.00
☐ 683	Gary Roenicke	.03	.01	.00
☐ 684	Kent Tekulve	.03	.01	.00
☐ 685	Jerry Hairston	.03	.01	.00
☐ 686	Doyle Alexander	.03	.01	.00
☐ 687	Alan Trammell	.15	.07	.01
☐ 688	Juan Beniquez	.03	.01	.00
☐ 689	Darrell Porter	.03	.01	.00
☐ 690	Dane Iorg	.03	.01	.00
☐ 691	Dave Parker	.12	.06	.01
☐ 692	Frank White	.06	.03	.00
☐ 693	Terry Puhl	.03	.01	.00
☐ 694	Phil Niekro	.12	.06	.01
☐ 695	Chico Walker	.08	.04	.01
☐ 696	Gary Lucas	.03	.01	.00
☐ 697	Ed Lynch	.03	.01	.00
☐ 698	Ernie Whitt	.03	.01	.00
☐ 699	Ken Landreaux	.03	.01	.00
☐ 700	Dave Bergman	.06	.03	.00
☐ 701	Willie Randolph	.03	.01	.00
☐ 702	Greg Gross	.03	.01	.00
☐ 703	Dave Schmidt	.06	.03	.00
☐ 704	Jesse Orosco	.03	.01	.00
☐ 705	Bruce Hurst	.10	.05	.01
☐ 706	Rick Manning	.03	.01	.00
☐ 707	Bob McClure	.03	.01	.00
☐ 708	Scott McGregor	.06	.03	.00
☐ 709	Dave Kingman	.08	.04	.01
☐ 710	Gary Gaetti	.10	.05	.01
☐ 711	Ken Griffey	.08	.04	.01
☐ 712	Don Robinson	.03	.01	.00
☐ 713	Tom Brookens	.03	.01	.00
☐ 714	Dan Quisenberry	.08	.04	.01
☐ 715	Bob Dernier	.03	.01	.00
☐ 716	Rick Leach	.03	.01	.00
☐ 717	Ed VandeBerg	.03	.01	.00
☐ 718	Steve Carlton	.20	.10	.02
☐ 719	Tom Hume	.03	.01	.00
☐ 720	Richard Dotson	.06	.03	.00
☐ 721	Tom Herr	.06	.03	.00
☐ 722	Bob Knepper	.06	.03	.00
☐ 723	Brett Butler	.06	.03	.00
☐ 724	Greg Minton	.03	.01	.00
☐ 725	George Hendrick	.03	.01	.00
☐ 726	Frank Tanana	.06	.03	.00
☐ 727	Mike Moore	.08	.04	.01
☐ 728	Tippy Martinez	.03	.01	.00
☐ 729	Tom Paciorek	.03	.01	.00
☐ 730	Eric Show	.06	.03	.00
☐ 731	Dave Concepcion	.06	.03	.00
☐ 732	Manny Trillo	.03	.01	.00
☐ 733	Bill Caudill	.03	.01	.00
☐ 734	Bill Madlock	.08	.04	.01
☐ 735	Rickey Henderson	.30	.15	.03
☐ 736	Steve Bedrosian	.10	.05	.01
☐ 737	Floyd Bannister	.03	.01	.00
☐ 738	Jorge Orta	.03	.01	.00
☐ 739	Chet Lemon	.03	.01	.00
☐ 740	Rich Gedman	.03	.01	.00
☐ 741	Paul Molitor	.10	.05	.01
☐ 742	Andy McGaffigan	.03	.01	.00
☐ 743	Dwayne Murphy	.03	.01	.00
☐ 744	Roy Smalley	.03	.01	.00
☐ 745	Glenn Hubbard	.03	.01	.00
☐ 746	Bob Ojeda	.06	.03	.00
☐ 747	Johnny Ray	.06	.03	.00
☐ 748	Mike Flanagan	.06	.03	.00
☐ 749	Ozzie Smith	.15	.07	.01
☐ 750	Steve Trout	.03	.01	.00
☐ 751	Garth Iorg	.03	.01	.00
☐ 752	Dan Petry	.03	.01	.00
☐ 753	Rick Honeycutt	.03	.01	.00
☐ 754	Dave LaPoint	.06	.03	.00
☐ 755	Luis Aguayo	.03	.01	.00
☐ 756	Carlton Fisk	.15	.07	.01
☐ 757	Nolan Ryan	.35	.17	.03
☐ 758	Tony Bernazard	.03	.01	.00
☐ 759	Joel Youngblood	.03	.01	.00
☐ 760	Mike Witt	.06	.03	.00
☐ 761	Greg Pryor	.03	.01	.00
☐ 762	Gary Ward	.03	.01	.00
☐ 763	Tim Flannery	.03	.01	.00
☐ 764	Bill Buckner	.06	.03	.00
☐ 765	Kirk Gibson	.15	.07	.01
☐ 766	Don Aase	.03	.01	.00
☐ 767	Ron Cey	.06	.03	.00
☐ 768	Dennis Lamp	.03	.01	.00
☐ 769	Steve Sax	.12	.06	.01
☐ 770	Dave Winfield	.20	.10	.02
☐ 771	Shane Rawley	.06	.03	.00
☐ 772	Harold Baines	.10	.05	.01
☐ 773	Robin Yount	.25	.12	.02
☐ 774	Wayne Krenchicki	.03	.01	.00
☐ 775	Joaquin Andujar	.06	.03	.00
☐ 776	Tom Brunansky	.10	.05	.01
☐ 777	Chris Chambliss	.06	.03	.00
☐ 778	Jack Morris	.10	.05	.01
☐ 779	Craig Reynolds	.03	.01	.00
☐ 780	Andre Thornton	.06	.03	.00
☐ 781	Atlee Hammaker	.03	.01	.00
☐ 782	Brian Downing	.06	.03	.00
☐ 783	Willie Wilson	.08	.04	.01
☐ 784	Cal Ripken	.20	.10	.02
☐ 785	Terry Francona	.03	.01	.00
☐ 786	Jimy Williams MG (checklist back)	.06	.03	.00
☐ 787	Alejandro Pena	.03	.01	.00
☐ 788	Tim Stoddard	.03	.01	.00
☐ 789	Dan Schatzeder	.03	.01	.00
☐ 790	Julio Cruz	.03	.01	.00
☐ 791	Lance Parrish UER (no trademark, never corrected)	.15	.07	.01
☐ 792	Checklist 661-792	.06	.01	.00

1987 Topps Wax Box Cards

This set of 8 cards is really four different sets of two smaller (2 1/8" by 3") cards which were printed on the side of the wax pack box; these eight cards are lettered A through H and are very similar in design to the Topps regular issue cards. The card backs are done in a newspaper headline style describing something about that player that happened the previous season. The card backs feature blue and yellow ink on gray card stock.

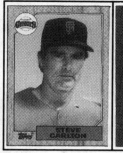

1987 Topps Jumbo Glossy Rookies

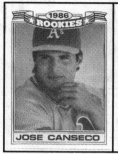

Inserted in each supermarket jumbo pack is a card from this series of 22 of 1986's best rookies as determined by Topps. Jumbo packs consisted of 100 (regular issue 1987 Topps baseball) cards with a stick of gum plus the insert "Rookie" card. The card fronts are in full color and measure 2 1/2" by 3 1/2". The card backs are printed in red and blue on white card stock and are numbered at the bottom essentially by alphabetical order.

			MINT	EXC	G-VG
	COMPLETE SET (22)		12.00	6.00	1.20
	COMMON PLAYER (1-22)		.20	.10	.02
☐	1	Andy Allanson	.20	.10	.02
☐	2	John Cangelosi	.20	.10	.02
☐	3	Jose Canseco	2.50	1.25	.25
☐	4	Will Clark	3.00	1.50	.30
☐	5	Mark Eichhorn	.20	.10	.02
☐	6	Pete Incaviglia	.60	.30	.06
☐	7	Wally Joyner	1.25	.60	.12
☐	8	Eric King	.20	.10	.02
☐	9	Dave Magadan	.40	.20	.04
☐	10	John Morris	.20	.10	.02
☐	11	Juan Nieves	.20	.10	.02
☐	12	Rafael Palmeiro	.50	.25	.05
☐	13	Billy Jo Robidoux	.20	.10	.02
☐	14	Bruce Ruffin	.20	.10	.02
☐	15	Ruben Sierra	2.00	1.00	.20
☐	16	Cory Snyder	1.00	.50	.10
☐	17	Kurt Stillwell	.40	.20	.04
☐	18	Dale Sveum	.30	.15	.03
☐	19	Danny Tartabull	.90	.45	.09
☐	20	Andres Thomas	.30	.15	.03
☐	21	Robby Thompson	.30	.15	.03
☐	22	Todd Worrell	.60	.30	.06

1987 Topps Glossy All-Stars 22

This set of 22 glossy cards was inserted one per rack pack. Players selected for the set are the starting players (plus manager and two pitchers) in the 1986 All-Star Game in Houston. Cards measure standard size, 2 1/2" by 3 1/2" and the backs feature red and blue printing on a white card stock.

			MINT	EXC	G-VG
	COMPLETE SET (22)		4.00	2.00	.40
	COMMON PLAYER (1-22)		.10	.05	.01
☐	1	Whitey Herzog MG	.10	.05	.01
☐	2	Keith Hernandez	.20	.10	.02
☐	3	Ryne Sandberg	.25	.12	.02
☐	4	Mike Schmidt	.50	.25	.05
☐	5	Ozzie Smith	.25	.12	.02
☐	6	Tony Gwynn	.35	.17	.03
☐	7	Dale Murphy	.45	.22	.04
☐	8	Darryl Strawberry	.50	.25	.05
☐	9	Gary Carter	.25	.12	.02
☐	10	Dwight Gooden	.45	.22	.04
☐	11	Fernando Valenzuela	.25	.12	.02
☐	12	Dick Howser MG	.10	.05	.01
☐	13	Wally Joyner	.60	.30	.06
☐	14	Lou Whitaker	.15	.07	.01
☐	15	Wade Boggs	.75	.35	.07
☐	16	Cal Ripken	.25	.12	.02
☐	17	Dave Winfield	.25	.12	.02
☐	18	Rickey Henderson	.40	.20	.04
☐	19	Kirby Puckett	.50	.25	.05
☐	20	Lance Parrish	.20	.10	.02
☐	21	Roger Clemens	.50	.25	.05

1987 Topps Glossy 60

Topps issued this set through a mail-in offer explained and advertised on the wax packs. This 60-card set features glossy fronts with each card measuring 2 1/2" by 3 1/2". The offer provided your choice of any one of the six 10-card subsets (1-10, 11-20, etc.) for 1.00 plus six of the Special Offer ("Spring Fever Baseball") insert cards, which were found one per wax pack. The last two players (numerically) in each ten-card subset are actually "Hot Prospects."

			MINT	EXC	G-VG
	COMPLETE SET (60)		12.50	6.25	1.25
	COMMON PLAYER (1-60)		.10	.05	.01
☐	1	Don Mattingly	1.50	.75	.15
☐	2	Tony Gwynn	.60	.30	.06

			MINT	EXC	G-VG
	COMPLETE SET (8)		1.25	.60	.12
	COMMON PLAYER (A-H)		.10	.05	.01
☐	A	Don Baylor	.15	.07	.01
☐	B	Steve Carlton	.30	.15	.03
☐	C	Ron Cey	.10	.05	.01
☐	D	Cecil Cooper	.10	.05	.01
☐	E	Rickey Henderson	.50	.25	.05
☐	F	Jim Rice	.20	.10	.02
☐	G	Don Sutton	.20	.10	.02
☐	H	Dave Winfield	.30	.15	.03

☐	3	Gary Gaetti	.25	.12	.02
☐	4	Glenn Davis	.30	.15	.03
☐	5	Roger Clemens	.90	.45	.09
☐	6	Dale Murphy	.60	.30	.06
☐	7	Lou Whitaker	.20	.10	.02
☐	8	Roger McDowell	.10	.05	.01
☐	9	Cory Snyder	.40	.20	.04
☐	10	Todd Worrell	.25	.12	.02
☐	11	Gary Carter	.25	.12	.02
☐	12	Eddie Murray	.30	.15	.03
☐	13	Bob Knepper	.10	.05	.01
☐	14	Harold Baines	.15	.07	.01
☐	15	Jeff Reardon	.10	.05	.01
☐	16	Joe Carter	.25	.12	.02
☐	17	Dave Parker	.20	.10	.02
☐	18	Wade Boggs	1.25	.60	.12
☐	19	Danny Tartabull	.45	.22	.04
☐	20	Jim Deshaies	.15	.07	.01
☐	21	Rickey Henderson	.60	.30	.06
☐	22	Rob Deer	.15	.07	.01
☐	23	Ozzie Smith	.25	.12	.02
☐	24	Dave Righetti	.20	.10	.02
☐	25	Kent Hrbek	.25	.12	.02
☐	26	Keith Hernandez	.25	.12	.02
☐	27	Don Baylor	.15	.07	.01
☐	28	Mike Schmidt	1.00	.50	.10
☐	29	Pete Incaviglia	.45	.22	.04
☐	30	Barry Bonds	.45	.22	.04
☐	31	George Brett	.60	.30	.06
☐	32	Darryl Strawberry	.90	.45	.09
☐	33	Mike Witt	.10	.05	.01
☐	34	Kevin Bass	.10	.05	.01
☐	35	Jesse Barfield	.20	.10	.02
☐	36	Bob Ojeda	.10	.05	.01
☐	37	Cal Ripken	.30	.15	.03
☐	38	Vince Coleman	.30	.15	.03
☐	39	Wally Joyner	.75	.35	.07
☐	40	Robby Thompson	.15	.07	.01
☐	41	Pete Rose	.75	.35	.07
☐	42	Jim Rice	.25	.12	.02
☐	43	Tony Bernazard	.10	.05	.01
☐	44	Eric Davis	1.00	.50	.10
☐	45	George Bell	.25	.12	.02
☐	46	Hubie Brooks	.15	.07	.01
☐	47	Jack Morris	.20	.10	.02
☐	48	Tim Raines	.25	.12	.02
☐	49	Mark Eichhorn	.10	.05	.01
☐	50	Kevin Mitchell	.15	.07	.01
☐	51	Dwight Gooden	.65	.30	.06
☐	52	Doug DeCinces	.10	.05	.01
☐	53	Fernando Valenzuela	.25	.12	.02
☐	54	Reggie Jackson	.50	.25	.05
☐	55	Johnny Ray	.10	.05	.01
☐	56	Mike Pagliarulo	.10	.05	.01
☐	57	Kirby Puckett	.75	.35	.07
☐	58	Lance Parrish	.20	.10	.02
☐	59	Jose Canseco	2.00	1.00	.20
☐	60	Greg Mathews	.20	.10	.02

1987 Topps Mini Leaders

The 1987 Topps Mini set of Major League Leaders features 77 cards of leaders of the various statistical categories for the 1986 season. The cards are numbered on the back and measure 2 5/32" by 3". The card backs are printed in orange and brown on white card stock. They are very similar in design to the Team Leader cards in the 1987 Topps regular issue. The cards were distributed as a separate issue in wax packs of seven for 30 cents. Eleven of the cards were double printed and are hence more plentiful; they are marked DP in the checklist below.

			MINT	EXC	G-VG
COMPLETE SET (77)			7.00	3.50	.70
COMMON PLAYER (1-77)			.06	.03	.00
COMMON PLAYER DP			.03	.01	.00
☐	1	Bob Horner DP	.06	.03	.00
☐	2	Dale Murphy	.35	.17	.03
☐	3	Lee Smith	.06	.03	.00
☐	4	Eric Davis	.65	.30	.06
☐	5	John Franco	.06	.03	.00
☐	6	Dave Parker	.10	.05	.01
☐	7	Kevin Bass	.06	.03	.00
☐	8	Glenn Davis DP	.10	.05	.01
☐	9	Bill Doran DP	.06	.03	.00
☐	10	Bob Knepper DP	.03	.01	.00
☐	11	Mike Scott	.15	.07	.01
☐	12	Dave Smith	.06	.03	.00
☐	13	Mariano Duncan	.06	.03	.00
☐	14	Orel Hershiser	.40	.20	.04
☐	15	Steve Sax DP	.10	.05	.01
☐	16	Fernando Valenzuela	.20	.10	.02
☐	17	Tim Raines	.20	.10	.02
☐	18	Jeff Reardon	.06	.03	.00
☐	19	Floyd Youmans	.06	.03	.00
☐	20	Gary Carter DP	.15	.07	.01
☐	21	Ron Darling	.10	.05	.01
☐	22	Sid Fernandez	.10	.05	.01
☐	23	Dwight Gooden	.50	.25	.05
☐	24	Keith Hernandez	.20	.10	.02
☐	25	Bob Ojeda	.10	.05	.01
☐	26	Darryl Strawberry	.60	.30	.06
☐	27	Steve Bedrosian	.10	.05	.01
☐	28	Von Hayes DP	.06	.03	.00
☐	29	Juan Samuel	.10	.05	.01
☐	30	Mike Schmidt	.75	.35	.07
☐	31	Rick Rhoden	.06	.03	.00
☐	32	Vince Coleman	.20	.10	.02
☐	33	Danny Cox	.06	.03	.00
☐	34	Todd Worrell	.20	.10	.02
☐	35	Tony Gwynn	.45	.22	.04
☐	36	Mike Krukow	.06	.03	.00
☐	37	Candy Maldonado	.06	.03	.00
☐	38	Don Aase	.06	.03	.00
☐	39	Eddie Murray	.25	.12	.02
☐	40	Cal Ripken	.35	.17	.03
☐	41	Wade Boggs	.75	.35	.07
☐	42	Roger Clemens	.50	.25	.05
☐	43	Bruce Hurst	.10	.05	.01
☐	44	Jim Rice	.20	.10	.02
☐	45	Wally Joyner	.35	.17	.03
☐	46	Donnie Moore	.06	.03	.00
☐	47	Gary Pettis	.06	.03	.00
☐	48	Mike Witt	.06	.03	.00
☐	49	John Cangelosi	.06	.03	.00
☐	50	Tom Candiotti	.06	.03	.00
☐	51	Joe Carter	.15	.07	.01
☐	52	Pat Tabler	.06	.03	.00
☐	53	Kirk Gibson DP	.10	.05	.01
☐	54	Willie Hernandez	.10	.05	.01
☐	55	Jack Morris	.15	.07	.01
☐	56	Alan Trammell DP	.10	.05	.01
☐	57	George Brett	.45	.22	.04
☐	58	Willie Wilson	.10	.05	.01
☐	59	Rob Deer	.10	.05	.01
☐	60	Teddy Higuera	.10	.05	.01
☐	61	Bert Blyleven DP	.06	.03	.00
☐	62	Gary Gaetti DP	.06	.03	.00
☐	63	Kirby Puckett	.50	.25	.05

		MINT	EXC	G-VG
☐ 64	Rickey Henderson	.50	.25	.05
☐ 65	Don Mattingly	1.00	.50	.10
☐ 66	Dennis Rasmussen	.10	.05	.01
☐ 67	Dave Righetti	.10	.05	.01
☐ 68	Jose Canseco	1.25	.60	.12
☐ 69	Dave Kingman	.10	.05	.01
☐ 70	Phil Bradley	.10	.05	.01
☐ 71	Mark Langston	.20	.10	.02
☐ 72	Pete O'Brien	.10	.05	.01
☐ 73	Jesse Barfield	.15	.07	.01
☐ 74	George Bell	.20	.10	.02
☐ 75	Tony Fernandez	.15	.07	.01
☐ 76	Tom Henke	.10	.05	.01
☐ 77	Checklist Card	.06	.03	.00

1987 Topps Traded

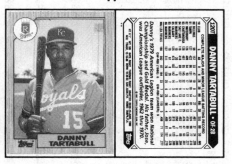

This 132-card Traded or extended set was distributed by Topps to dealers in a special green and white box as a complete set. The card fronts are identical in style to the Topps regular issue and are also 2 1/2" by 3 1/2". The backs are printed in yellow and blue on white card stock. Cards are numbered (with a T suffix) alphabetically according to the name of the player. Topps also produced a specially boxed "glossy" edition frequently referred to as the Topps Traded Tiffany set. This year Topps did not disclose the number of sets they produced or sold. It is apparent from the availability that there were many more sets produced this year compared to the 1984-86 Tiffany sets, perhaps more than three times as many. The checklist of cards is identical to that of the normal non-glossy cards. There are two primary distinguishing features of the Tiffany cards, white card stock reverses and high gloss obverses. These Tiffany cards are valued at approximately four times the values listed below.

		MINT	EXC	G-VG
COMPLETE SET (132)		15.00	7.00	1.40
COMMON PLAYER (1-132)		.05	.02	.00
☐ 1T	Bill Almon	.05	.02	.00
☐ 2T	Scott Bankhead	.10	.05	.01
☐ 3T	Eric Bell	.10	.05	.01
☐ 4T	Juan Beniquez	.05	.02	.00
☐ 5T	Juan Berenguer	.05	.02	.00
☐ 6T	Greg Booker	.05	.02	.00
☐ 7T	Thad Bosley	.05	.02	.00
☐ 8T	Larry Bowa MG	.10	.05	.01
☐ 9T	Greg Brock	.10	.05	.01
☐ 10T	Bob Brower	.12	.06	.01
☐ 11T	Jerry Browne	.25	.12	.02
☐ 12T	Ralph Bryant	.10	.05	.01
☐ 13T	DeWayne Buice	.10	.05	.01
☐ 14T	Ellis Burks	2.00	1.00	.20
☐ 15T	Ivan Calderon	.20	.10	.02
☐ 16T	Jeff Calhoun	.05	.02	.00
☐ 17T	Casey Candaele	.10	.05	.01
☐ 18T	John Cangelosi	.10	.05	.01
☐ 19T	Steve Carlton	.25	.12	.02
☐ 20T	Juan Castillo	.10	.05	.01
☐ 21T	Rick Cerone	.05	.02	.00
☐ 22T	Ron Cey	.10	.05	.01

		MINT	EXC	G-VG
☐ 23T	John Christensen	.05	.02	.00
☐ 24T	David Cone	1.75	.85	.17
☐ 25T	Chuck Crim	.10	.05	.01
☐ 26T	Storm Davis	.15	.07	.01
☐ 27T	Andre Dawson	.35	.17	.03
☐ 28T	Rick Dempsey	.10	.05	.01
☐ 29T	Doug Drabek	.15	.07	.01
☐ 30T	Mike Dunne	.10	.05	.01
☐ 31T	Dennis Eckersley	.25	.12	.02
☐ 32T	Lee Elia MG	.05	.02	.00
☐ 33T	Brian Fisher	.10	.05	.01
☐ 34T	Terry Francona	.05	.02	.00
☐ 35T	Willie Fraser	.10	.05	.01
☐ 36T	Billy Gardner MG	.05	.02	.00
☐ 37T	Ken Gerhart	.10	.05	.01
☐ 38T	Dan Gladden	.10	.05	.01
☐ 39T	Jim Gott	.10	.05	.01
☐ 40T	Cecilio Guante	.05	.02	.00
☐ 41T	Albert Hall	.10	.05	.01
☐ 42T	Terry Harper	.05	.02	.00
☐ 43T	Mickey Hatcher	.05	.02	.00
☐ 44T	Brad Havens	.05	.02	.00
☐ 45T	Neal Heaton	.05	.02	.00
☐ 46T	Mike Henneman	.30	.15	.03
☐ 47T	Donnie Hill	.05	.02	.00
☐ 48T	Guy Hoffman	.05	.02	.00
☐ 49T	Brian Holton	.15	.07	.01
☐ 50T	Charles Hudson	.05	.02	.00
☐ 51T	Danny Jackson	.15	.07	.01
☐ 52T	Reggie Jackson	.50	.25	.05
☐ 53T	Chris James	.45	.22	.04
☐ 54T	Dion James	.10	.05	.01
☐ 55T	Stan Jefferson	.20	.10	.02
☐ 56T	Joe Johnson	.10	.05	.01
☐ 57T	Terry Kennedy	.05	.02	.00
☐ 58T	Mike Kingery	.10	.05	.01
☐ 59T	Ray Knight	.10	.05	.01
☐ 60T	Gene Larkin	.30	.15	.03
☐ 61T	Mike LaValliere	.10	.05	.01
☐ 62T	Jack Lazorko	.05	.02	.00
☐ 63T	Terry Leach	.12	.06	.01
☐ 64T	Tim Leary	.20	.10	.02
☐ 65T	Jim Lindeman	.10	.05	.01
☐ 66T	Steve Lombardozzi	.10	.05	.01
☐ 67T	Bill Long	.12	.06	.01
☐ 68T	Barry Lyons	.35	.17	.03
☐ 69T	Shane Mack	.12	.06	.01
☐ 70T	Greg Maddux	.75	.35	.07
☐ 71T	Bill Madlock	.10	.05	.01
☐ 72T	Joe Magrane	1.25	.60	.12
☐ 73T	Dave Martinez	.20	.10	.02
☐ 74T	Fred McGriff	2.00	1.00	.20
☐ 75T	Mark McLemore	.05	.02	.00
☐ 76T	Kevin McReynolds	.20	.10	.02
☐ 77T	Dave Meads	.10	.05	.01
☐ 78T	Eddie Milner	.05	.02	.00
☐ 79T	Greg Minton	.05	.02	.00
☐ 80T	John Mitchell	.15	.07	.01
☐ 81T	Kevin Mitchell	1.25	.60	.12
☐ 82T	Charlie Moore	.05	.02	.00
☐ 83T	Jeff Musselman	.15	.07	.01
☐ 84T	Gene Nelson	.05	.02	.00
☐ 85T	Graig Nettles	.15	.07	.01
☐ 86T	Al Newman	.05	.02	.00
☐ 87T	Reid Nichols	.05	.02	.00
☐ 88T	Tom Niedenfuer	.05	.02	.00
☐ 89T	Joe Niekro	.10	.05	.01
☐ 90T	Tom Nieto	.05	.02	.00
☐ 91T	Matt Nokes	.45	.22	.04
☐ 92T	Dickie Noles	.05	.02	.00
☐ 93T	Pat Pacillo	.10	.05	.01
☐ 94T	Lance Parrish	.15	.07	.01
☐ 95T	Tony Pena	.15	.07	.01
☐ 96T	Luis Polonia	.25	.12	.02
☐ 97T	Randy Ready	.10	.05	.01
☐ 98T	Jeff Reardon	.15	.07	.01
☐ 99T	Gary Redus	.05	.02	.00
☐ 100T	Jeff Reed	.05	.02	.00
☐ 101T	Rick Rhoden	.10	.05	.01
☐ 102T	Cal Ripken Sr. MG	.05	.02	.00
☐ 103T	Wally Ritchie	.10	.05	.01
☐ 104T	Jeff Robinson	.35	.17	.03
	(Tigers pitcher)			
☐ 105T	Gary Roenicke	.05	.02	.00
☐ 106T	Jerry Royster	.05	.02	.00
☐ 107T	Mark Salas	.05	.02	.00
☐ 108T	Luis Salazar	.05	.02	.00
☐ 109T	Benny Santiago	1.00	.50	.10
☐ 110T	Dave Schmidt	.10	.05	.01
☐ 111T	Kevin Seitzer	1.00	.50	.10
☐ 112T	John Shelby	.05	.02	.00
☐ 113T	Steve Shields	.10	.05	.01
☐ 114T	John Smiley	.35	.17	.03
☐ 115T	Chris Speier	.05	.02	.00
☐ 116T	Mike Stanley	.15	.07	.01

		MINT	EXC	G-VG
☐ 117T	Terry Steinbach	.50	.25	.05
☐ 118T	Les Straker	.12	.06	.01
☐ 119T	Jim Sundberg	.05	.02	.00
☐ 120T	Danny Tartabull	.30	.15	.03
☐ 121T	Tom Trebelhorn MG	.05	.02	.00
☐ 122T	Dave Valle	.05	.02	.00
☐ 123T	Ed VandeBerg	.05	.02	.00
☐ 124T	Andy Van Slyke	.20	.10	.02
☐ 125T	Gary Ward	.05	.02	.00
☐ 126T	Alan Wiggins	.05	.02	.00
☐ 127T	Bill Wilkinson	.12	.06	.01
☐ 128T	Frank Williams	.05	.02	.00
☐ 129T	Matt Williams	2.00	1.00	.20
☐ 130T	Jim Winn	.05	.02	.00
☐ 131T	Matt Young	.05	.02	.00
☐ 132T	Checklist	.05	.01	.00

1988 Topps

This 792-card set features backs which are printed in orange and black on white card stock. The manager cards contain a checklist of the respective team's players on the back. Subsets in the set include Record Breakers (1-7), Turn Back The Clock (661-665), and All-Star selections (386-407). The Team Leader cards typically show two players together inside a white cloud. Topps also produced a specially boxed "glossy" edition frequently referred to as the Topps Tiffany set. This year, again, Topps did not disclose the number of Tiffany sets they produced or sold. It is apparent from the availability that there were many more sets produced this year compared to the 1984-86 Tiffany sets, perhaps more than three times as many similar to the 1987 Tiffany cards. The checklist of cards (792 regular and 132 Traded) is identical to that of the normal non-glossy cards. There are two primary distinguishing features of the Tiffany cards, white card stock reverses and high gloss obverses. These Tiffany cards are valued at approximately four times the values listed below.

		MINT	EXC	G-VG
	COMPLETE SET (792)	25.00	12.50	2.50
	COMMON PLAYER (1-792)	.03	.01	.00
☐ 1	Vince Coleman RB .... 100 Steals for Third Cons. Season	.20	.04	.01
☐ 2	Don Mattingly RB .... Six Grand Slams	.30	.15	.03
☐ 3A	Mark McGwire RB .... Rookie Homer Record (white spot behind left foot)	1.00	.50	.10
☐ 3B	Mark McGwire RB .... Rookie Homer Record (no white spot)	.30	.15	.03
☐ 4A	Eddie Murray RB .... Switch Home Runs, Two Straight Games (caption in box on card front)	1.00	.50	.10
☐ 4B	Eddie Murray RB	.20	.10	.02
	Switch Home Runs, Two Straight Games (no caption on front)			
☐ 5	Phil/Joe Niekro RB .... Brothers Win Record	.06	.03	.00
☐ 6	Nolan Ryan RB .... 11th Season with 200 Strikeouts	.20	.10	.02
☐ 7	Benito Santiago RB .... 34-Game Hitting Streak, Rookie Record	.10	.05	.01
☐ 8	Kevin Elster	.15	.07	.01
☐ 9	Andy Hawkins	.03	.01	.00
☐ 10	Ryne Sandberg	.15	.07	.01
☐ 11	Mike Young	.03	.01	.00
☐ 12	Bill Schroeder	.03	.01	.00
☐ 13	Andres Thomas	.03	.01	.00
☐ 14	Sparky Anderson MG ..... (checklist back)	.06	.03	.00
☐ 15	Chili Davis	.06	.03	.00
☐ 16	Kirk McCaskill	.03	.01	.00
☐ 17	Ron Oester	.03	.01	.00
☐ 18A	Al Leiter ERR .... (photo actually Steve George, right ear visible)	.90	.45	.09
☐ 18B	Al Leiter COR .... (left ear visible)	.60	.30	.06
☐ 19	Mark Davidson	.10	.05	.01
☐ 20	Kevin Gross	.03	.01	.00
☐ 21	Red Sox TL .... Wade Boggs and Spike Owen	.12	.06	.01
☐ 22	Greg Swindell	.12	.06	.01
☐ 23	Ken Landreaux	.03	.01	.00
☐ 24	Jim Deshaies	.03	.01	.00
☐ 25	Andres Galarraga	.15	.07	.01
☐ 26	Mitch Williams	.06	.03	.00
☐ 27	R.J. Reynolds	.03	.01	.00
☐ 28	Jose Nunez	.10	.05	.01
☐ 29	Argenis Salazar	.03	.01	.00
☐ 30	Sid Fernandez	.08	.04	.01
☐ 31	Bruce Bochy	.03	.01	.00
☐ 32	Mike Morgan	.06	.03	.00
☐ 33	Rob Deer	.06	.03	.00
☐ 34	Ricky Horton	.03	.01	.00
☐ 35	Harold Baines	.08	.04	.01
☐ 36	Jamie Moyer	.03	.01	.00
☐ 37	Ed Romero	.03	.01	.00
☐ 38	Jeff Calhoun	.03	.01	.00
☐ 39	Gerald Perry	.06	.03	.00
☐ 40	Orel Hershiser	.20	.10	.02
☐ 41	Bob Melvin	.03	.01	.00
☐ 42	Bill Landrum	.20	.10	.02
☐ 43	Dick Schofield	.03	.01	.00
☐ 44	Lou Piniella MG .... (checklist back)	.06	.03	.00
☐ 45	Kent Hrbek	.12	.06	.01
☐ 46	Darnell Coles	.03	.01	.00
☐ 47	Joaquin Andujar	.06	.03	.00
☐ 48	Alan Ashby	.03	.01	.00
☐ 49	Dave Clark	.10	.05	.01
☐ 50	Hubie Brooks	.08	.04	.01
☐ 51	Orioles TL .... Eddie Murray and Cal Ripken	.15	.07	.01
☐ 52	Don Robinson	.03	.01	.00
☐ 53	Curt Wilkerson	.03	.01	.00
☐ 54	Jim Clancy	.03	.01	.00
☐ 55	Phil Bradley	.06	.03	.00
☐ 56	Ed Hearn	.03	.01	.00
☐ 57	Tim Crews	.08	.04	.01
☐ 58	Dave Magadan	.10	.05	.01
☐ 59	Danny Cox	.06	.03	.00
☐ 60	Rickey Henderson	.25	.12	.02
☐ 61	Mark Knudson	.10	.05	.01
☐ 62	Jeff Hamilton	.06	.03	.00
☐ 63	Jimmy Jones	.10	.05	.01
☐ 64	Ken Caminiti	.18	.09	.01
☐ 65	Leon Durham	.03	.01	.00
☐ 66	Shane Rawley	.03	.01	.00
☐ 67	Ken Oberkfell	.03	.01	.00
☐ 68	Dave Dravecky	.08	.04	.01
☐ 69	Mike Hart	.06	.03	.00
☐ 70	Roger Clemens	.50	.25	.05
☐ 71	Gary Pettis	.03	.01	.00
☐ 72	Dennis Eckersley	.10	.05	.00
☐ 73	Randy Bush	.03	.01	.00
☐ 74	Tom Lasorda MG .... (checklist back)	.08	.04	.01
☐ 75	Joe Carter	.12	.06	.01
☐ 76	Dennis Martinez	.03	.01	.00
☐ 77	Tom O'Malley	.03	.01	.00
☐ 78	Dan Petry	.03	.01	.00
☐ 79	Ernie Whitt	.03	.01	.00

☐ 80	Mark Langston	.12	.06	.01
☐ 81	Reds TL	.03	.01	.00
	Ron Robinson			
	and John Franco			
☐ 82	Darrel Akerfelds	.08	.04	.01
☐ 83	Jose Oquendo	.03	.01	.00
☐ 84	Cecilio Guante	.03	.01	.00
☐ 85	Howard Johnson	.12	.06	.01
☐ 86	Ron Karkovice	.03	.01	.00
☐ 87	Mike Mason	.03	.01	.00
☐ 88	Earnie Riles	.03	.01	.00
☐ 89	Gary Thurman	.18	.09	.01
☐ 90	Dale Murphy	.20	.10	.02
☐ 91	Joey Cora	.12	.06	.01
☐ 92	Len Matuszek	.03	.01	.00
☐ 93	Bob Sebra	.03	.01	.00
☐ 94	Chuck Jackson	.08	.04	.01
☐ 95	Lance Parrish	.08	.04	.01
☐ 96	Todd Benzinger	.20	.10	.02
☐ 97	Scott Garrelts	.06	.03	.00
☐ 98	Rene Gonzales	.10	.05	.01
☐ 99	Chuck Finley	.06	.03	.00
☐ 100	Jack Clark	.12	.06	.01
☐ 101	Allan Anderson	.06	.03	.00
☐ 102	Barry Larkin	.18	.09	.01
☐ 103	Curt Young	.03	.01	.00
☐ 104	Dick Williams MG	.06	.03	.00
	(checklist back)			
☐ 105	Jesse Orosco	.03	.01	.00
☐ 106	Jim Walewander	.10	.05	.01
☐ 107	Scott Bailes	.03	.01	.00
☐ 108	Steve Lyons	.03	.01	.00
☐ 109	Joel Skinner	.03	.01	.00
☐ 110	Teddy Higuera	.08	.04	.01
☐ 111	Expos TL	.03	.01	.00
	Hubie Brooks and			
	Vance Law			
☐ 112	Les Lancaster	.12	.06	.01
☐ 113	Kelly Gruber	.06	.03	.00
☐ 114	Jeff Russell	.06	.03	.00
☐ 115	Johnny Ray	.06	.03	.00
☐ 116	Jerry Don Gleaton	.03	.01	.00
☐ 117	James Steels	.06	.03	.00
☐ 118	Bob Welch	.06	.03	.00
☐ 119	Robbie Wine	.08	.04	.01
☐ 120	Kirby Puckett	.40	.20	.04
☐ 121	Checklist 1-132	.06	.01	.00
☐ 122	Tony Bernazard	.03	.01	.00
☐ 123	Tom Candiotti	.03	.01	.00
☐ 124	Ray Knight	.06	.03	.00
☐ 125	Bruce Hurst	.10	.05	.01
☐ 126	Steve Jeltz	.03	.01	.00
☐ 127	Jim Gott	.03	.01	.00
☐ 128	Johnny Grubb	.03	.01	.00
☐ 129	Greg Minton	.03	.01	.00
☐ 130	Buddy Bell	.06	.03	.00
☐ 131	Don Schulze	.03	.01	.00
☐ 132	Donnie Hill	.03	.01	.00
☐ 133	Greg Mathews	.03	.01	.00
☐ 134	Chuck Tanner MG	.06	.03	.00
	(checklist back)			
☐ 135	Dennis Rasmussen	.06	.03	.00
☐ 136	Brian Dayett	.03	.01	.00
☐ 137	Chris Bosio	.06	.03	.00
☐ 138	Mitch Webster	.03	.01	.00
☐ 139	Jerry Browne	.10	.05	.01
☐ 140	Jesse Barfield	.10	.05	.01
☐ 141	Royals TL	.15	.07	.01
	George Brett and			
	Bret Saberhagen			
☐ 142	Andy Van Slyke	.12	.06	.01
☐ 143	Mickey Tettleton	.08	.04	.01
☐ 144	Don Gordon	.08	.04	.01
☐ 145	Bill Madlock	.06	.03	.00
☐ 146	Donnell Nixon	.10	.05	.01
☐ 147	Bill Buckner	.06	.03	.00
☐ 148	Carmelo Martinez	.03	.01	.00
☐ 149	Ken Howell	.03	.01	.00
☐ 150	Eric Davis	.40	.20	.04
☐ 151	Bob Knepper	.03	.01	.00
☐ 152	Jody Reed	.30	.15	.03
☐ 153	John Habyan	.03	.01	.00
☐ 154	Jeff Stone	.03	.01	.00
☐ 155	Bruce Sutter	.08	.04	.01
☐ 156	Gary Matthews	.03	.01	.00
☐ 157	Atlee Hammaker	.03	.01	.00
☐ 158	Tim Hulett	.03	.01	.00
☐ 159	Brad Arnsberg	.10	.05	.01
☐ 160	Willie McGee	.08	.04	.01
☐ 161	Bryn Smith	.06	.03	.00
☐ 162	Mark McLemore	.03	.01	.00
☐ 163	Dale Mohorcic	.03	.01	.00
☐ 164	Dave Johnson MG	.06	.03	.00
	(checklist back)			
☐ 165	Robin Yount	.20	.10	.02

☐ 166	Rick Rodriquez	.10	.05	.01
☐ 167	Rance Mulliniks	.03	.01	.00
☐ 168	Barry Jones	.03	.01	.00
☐ 169	Ross Jones	.08	.04	.01
☐ 170	Rich Gossage	.08	.04	.01
☐ 171	Cubs TL	.03	.01	.00
	Shawon Dunston			
	and Manny Trillo			
☐ 172	Lloyd McClendon	.15	.07	.01
☐ 173	Eric Plunk	.03	.01	.00
☐ 174	Phil Garner	.03	.01	.00
☐ 175	Kevin Bass	.06	.03	.00
☐ 176	Jeff Reed	.03	.01	.00
☐ 177	Frank Tanana	.03	.01	.00
☐ 178	Dwayne Henry	.06	.03	.00
☐ 179	Charlie Puleo	.03	.01	.00
☐ 180	Terry Kennedy	.03	.01	.00
☐ 181	David Cone	.80	.40	.08
☐ 182	Ken Phelps	.06	.03	.00
☐ 183	Tom Lawless	.03	.01	.00
☐ 184	Ivan Calderon	.06	.03	.00
☐ 185	Rick Rhoden	.03	.01	.00
☐ 186	Rafael Palmeiro	.20	.10	.02
☐ 187	Steve Kiefer	.03	.01	.00
☐ 188	John Russell	.03	.01	.00
☐ 189	Wes Gardner	.15	.07	.01
☐ 190	Candy Maldonado	.03	.01	.00
☐ 191	John Cerutti	.03	.01	.00
☐ 192	Devon White	.12	.06	.01
☐ 193	Brian Fisher	.03	.01	.00
☐ 194	Tom Kelly MG	.06	.03	.00
	(checklist back)			
☐ 195	Dan Quisenberry	.08	.04	.01
☐ 196	Dave Engle	.03	.01	.00
☐ 197	Lance McCullers	.06	.03	.00
☐ 198	Franklin Stubbs	.03	.01	.00
☐ 199	Dave Meads	.08	.04	.01
☐ 200	Wade Boggs	.65	.30	.06
☐ 201	Rangers TL	.06	.03	.00
	Bobby Valentine,			
	Pete O'Brien,			
	Pete Incaviglia, and			
	Steve Buechele			
☐ 202	Glenn Hoffman	.03	.01	.00
☐ 203	Fred Toliver	.03	.01	.00
☐ 204	Paul O'Neill	.15	.07	.01
☐ 205	Nelson Liriano	.15	.07	.01
☐ 206	Domingo Ramos	.03	.01	.00
☐ 207	John Mitchell	.12	.06	.01
☐ 208	Steve Lake	.03	.01	.00
☐ 209	Richard Dotson	.03	.01	.00
☐ 210	Willie Randolph	.06	.03	.00
☐ 211	Frank DiPino	.03	.01	.00
☐ 212	Greg Brock	.03	.01	.00
☐ 213	Albert Hall	.03	.01	.00
☐ 214	Dave Schmidt	.03	.01	.00
☐ 215	Von Hayes	.08	.04	.01
☐ 216	Jerry Reuss	.03	.01	.00
☐ 217	Harry Spilman	.03	.01	.00
☐ 218	Dan Schatzeder	.03	.01	.00
☐ 219	Mike Stanley	.06	.03	.00
☐ 220	Tom Henke	.06	.03	.00
☐ 221	Rafael Belliard	.03	.01	.00
☐ 222	Steve Farr	.03	.01	.00
☐ 223	Stan Jefferson	.08	.04	.01
☐ 224	Tom Trebelhorn MG	.06	.03	.00
	(checklist back)			
☐ 225	Mike Scioscia	.03	.01	.00
☐ 226	Dave Lopes	.06	.03	.00
☐ 227	Ed Correa	.03	.01	.00
☐ 228	Wallace Johnson	.03	.01	.00
☐ 229	Jeff Musselman	.08	.04	.01
☐ 230	Pat Tabler	.06	.03	.00
☐ 231	Pirates TL	.10	.05	.01
	Barry Bonds and			
	Bobby Bonilla			
☐ 232	Bob James	.03	.01	.00
☐ 233	Rafael Santana	.03	.01	.00
☐ 234	Ken Dayley	.03	.01	.00
☐ 235	Gary Ward	.03	.01	.00
☐ 236	Ted Power	.03	.01	.00
☐ 237	Mike Heath	.03	.01	.00
☐ 238	Luis Polonia	.20	.10	.02
☐ 239	Roy Smalley	.03	.01	.00
☐ 240	Lee Smith	.06	.03	.00
☐ 241	Damaso Garcia	.03	.01	.00
☐ 242	Tom Niedenfuer	.03	.01	.00
☐ 243	Mark Ryal	.08	.04	.01
☐ 244	Jeff D. Robinson	.06	.03	.00
	(Pirates pitcher)			
☐ 245	Rich Gedman	.03	.01	.00
☐ 246	Mike Campbell	.15	.07	.01
☐ 247	Thad Bosley	.03	.01	.00
☐ 248	Storm Davis	.06	.03	.00
☐ 249	Mike Marshall	.08	.04	.01

☐ 250	Nolan Ryan	.30	.15	.03
☐ 251	Tom Foley	.03	.01	.00
☐ 252	Bob Brower	.08	.04	.01
☐ 253	Checklist 133-264	.06	.01	.00
☐ 254	Lee Elia MG (checklist back)	.06	.03	.00
☐ 255	Mookie Wilson	.06	.03	.00
☐ 256	Ken Schrom	.03	.01	.00
☐ 257	Jerry Royster	.03	.01	.00
☐ 258	Ed Nunez	.03	.01	.00
☐ 259	Ron Kittle	.08	.04	.01
☐ 260	Vince Coleman	.12	.06	.01
☐ 261	Giants TL (five players)	.03	.01	.00
☐ 262	Drew Hall	.10	.05	.01
☐ 263	Glenn Braggs	.06	.03	.00
☐ 264	Les Straker	.08	.04	.01
☐ 265	Bo Diaz	.03	.01	.00
☐ 266	Paul Assenmacher	.03	.01	.00
☐ 267	Billy Bean	.15	.07	.01
☐ 268	Bruce Ruffin	.03	.01	.00
☐ 269	Ellis Burks	1.00	.50	.10
☐ 270	Mike Witt	.06	.03	.00
☐ 271	Ken Gerhart	.06	.03	.00
☐ 272	Steve Ontiveros	.03	.01	.00
☐ 273	Garth Iorg	.03	.01	.00
☐ 274	Junior Ortiz	.03	.01	.00
☐ 275	Kevin Seitzer	.65	.30	.06
☐ 276	Luis Salazar	.03	.01	.00
☐ 277	Alejandro Pena	.06	.03	.00
☐ 278	Jose Cruz	.06	.03	.00
☐ 279	Randy St.Claire	.03	.01	.00
☐ 280	Pete Incaviglia	.12	.06	.01
☐ 281	Jerry Hairston	.03	.01	.00
☐ 282	Pat Perry	.03	.01	.00
☐ 283	Phil Lombardi	.08	.04	.01
☐ 284	Larry Bowa MG (checklist back)	.06	.03	.00
☐ 285	Jim Presley	.06	.03	.00
☐ 286	Chuck Crim	.08	.04	.01
☐ 287	Manny Trillo	.03	.01	.00
☐ 288	Pat Pacillo (Chris Sabo in background of photo)	.06	.03	.00
☐ 289	Dave Bergman	.03	.01	.00
☐ 290	Tony Fernandez	.10	.05	.01
☐ 291	Astros TL Billy Hatcher and Kevin Bass	.06	.03	.00
☐ 292	Carney Lansford	.08	.04	.01
☐ 293	Doug Jones	.25	.12	.02
☐ 294	Al Pedrique	.08	.04	.01
☐ 295	Bert Blyleven	.08	.04	.01
☐ 296	Floyd Rayford	.03	.01	.00
☐ 297	Zane Smith	.03	.01	.00
☐ 298	Milt Thompson	.03	.01	.00
☐ 299	Steve Crawford	.03	.01	.00
☐ 300	Don Mattingly	1.25	.60	.12
☐ 301	Bud Black	.03	.01	.00
☐ 302	Jose Uribe	.03	.01	.00
☐ 303	Eric Show	.03	.01	.00
☐ 304	George Hendrick	.03	.01	.00
☐ 305	Steve Sax	.10	.05	.01
☐ 306	Billy Hatcher	.03	.01	.00
☐ 307	Mike Trujillo	.03	.01	.00
☐ 308	Lee Mazzilli	.03	.01	.00
☐ 309	Bill Long	.08	.04	.01
☐ 310	Tom Herr	.03	.01	.00
☐ 311	Scott Sanderson	.03	.01	.00
☐ 312	Joey Meyer	.10	.05	.01
☐ 313	Bob McClure	.03	.01	.00
☐ 314	Jimy Williams MG (checklist back)	.06	.03	.00
☐ 315	Dave Parker	.10	.05	.01
☐ 316	Jose Rijo	.03	.01	.00
☐ 317	Tom Nieto	.03	.01	.00
☐ 318	Mel Hall	.06	.03	.00
☐ 319	Mike Loynd	.03	.01	.00
☐ 320	Alan Trammell	.12	.06	.01
☐ 321	White Sox TL Harold Baines and Carlton Fisk	.10	.05	.01
☐ 322	Vicente Palacios	.10	.05	.01
☐ 323	Rick Leach	.03	.01	.00
☐ 324	Danny Jackson	.08	.04	.01
☐ 325	Glenn Hubbard	.03	.01	.00
☐ 326	Al Nipper	.03	.01	.00
☐ 327	Larry Sheets	.06	.03	.00
☐ 328	Greg Cadaret	.15	.07	.01
☐ 329	Chris Speier	.03	.01	.00
☐ 330	Eddie Whitson	.03	.01	.00
☐ 331	Brian Downing	.03	.01	.00
☐ 332	Jerry Reed	.03	.01	.00
☐ 333	Wally Backman	.03	.01	.00
☐ 334	Dave LaPoint	.03	.01	.00
☐ 335	Claudell Washington	.06	.03	.00
☐ 336	Ed Lynch	.03	.01	.00
☐ 337	Jim Gantner	.03	.01	.00
☐ 338	Brian Holton	.08	.04	.01
☐ 339	Kurt Stillwell	.03	.01	.00
☐ 340	Jack Morris	.10	.05	.01
☐ 341	Carmen Castillo	.03	.01	.00
☐ 342	Larry Andersen	.03	.01	.00
☐ 343	Greg Gagne	.03	.01	.00
☐ 344	Tony LaRussa MG (checklist back)	.06	.03	.00
☐ 345	Scott Fletcher	.03	.01	.00
☐ 346	Vance Law	.03	.01	.00
☐ 347	Joe Johnson	.03	.01	.00
☐ 348	Jim Eisenreich	.03	.01	.00
☐ 349	Bob Walk	.03	.01	.00
☐ 350	Will Clark	1.00	.50	.10
☐ 351	Cardinals TL Red Schoendienst and Tony Pena	.06	.03	.00
☐ 352	Billy Ripken	.15	.07	.01
☐ 353	Ed Olwine	.03	.01	.00
☐ 354	Marc Sullivan	.03	.01	.00
☐ 355	Roger McDowell	.06	.03	.00
☐ 356	Luis Aguayo	.03	.01	.00
☐ 357	Floyd Bannister	.03	.01	.00
☐ 358	Rey Quinones	.03	.01	.00
☐ 359	Tim Stoddard	.03	.01	.00
☐ 360	Tony Gwynn	.30	.15	.03
☐ 361	Greg Maddux	.35	.17	.03
☐ 362	Juan Castillo	.08	.04	.01
☐ 363	Willie Fraser	.03	.01	.00
☐ 364	Nick Esasky	.08	.04	.01
☐ 365	Floyd Youmans	.03	.01	.00
☐ 366	Chet Lemon	.03	.01	.00
☐ 367	Tim Leary	.06	.03	.00
☐ 368	Gerald Young	.25	.12	.02
☐ 369	Greg Harris	.03	.01	.00
☐ 370	Jose Canseco	1.25	.60	.12
☐ 371	Joe Hesketh	.03	.01	.00
☐ 372	Matt Williams	1.00	.50	.10
☐ 373	Checklist 265-396	.06	.01	.00
☐ 374	Doc Edwards MG (checklist back)	.06	.03	.00
☐ 375	Tom Brunansky	.08	.04	.01
☐ 376	Bill Wilkinson	.10	.05	.01
☐ 377	Sam Horn	.12	.06	.01
☐ 378	Todd Frohwirth	.08	.04	.01
☐ 379	Rafael Ramirez	.03	.01	.00
☐ 380	Joe Magrane	.45	.22	.04
☐ 381	Angels TL Wally Joyner and Jack Howell	.10	.05	.01
☐ 382	Keith Miller (New York Mets)	.20	.10	.02
☐ 383	Eric Bell	.03	.01	.00
☐ 384	Neil Allen	.03	.01	.00
☐ 385	Carlton Fisk	.10	.05	.01
☐ 386	Don Mattingly AS	.40	.20	.04
☐ 387	Willie Randolph AS	.06	.03	.00
☐ 388	Wade Boggs AS	.25	.12	.02
☐ 389	Alan Trammell AS	.08	.04	.01
☐ 390	George Bell AS	.10	.05	.01
☐ 391	Kirby Puckett AS	.15	.07	.01
☐ 392	Dave Winfield AS	.10	.05	.01
☐ 393	Matt Nokes AS	.10	.05	.01
☐ 394	Roger Clemens AS	.20	.10	.02
☐ 395	Jimmy Key AS	.06	.03	.00
☐ 396	Tom Henke AS	.06	.03	.00
☐ 397	Jack Clark AS	.08	.04	.01
☐ 398	Juan Samuel AS	.06	.03	.00
☐ 399	Tim Wallach AS	.06	.03	.00
☐ 400	Ozzie Smith AS	.10	.05	.01
☐ 401	Andre Dawson AS	.12	.06	.01
☐ 402	Tony Gwynn AS	.20	.10	.02
☐ 403	Tim Raines AS	.10	.05	.01
☐ 404	Benny Santiago AS	.12	.06	.01
☐ 405	Dwight Gooden AS	.20	.10	.02
☐ 406	Shane Rawley AS	.06	.03	.00
☐ 407	Steve Bedrosian AS	.06	.03	.00
☐ 408	Dion James	.03	.01	.00
☐ 409	Joel McKeon	.03	.01	.00
☐ 410	Tony Pena	.06	.03	.00
☐ 411	Wayne Tolleson	.03	.01	.00
☐ 412	Randy Myers	.08	.04	.01
☐ 413	John Christensen	.03	.01	.00
☐ 414	John McNamara MG (checklist back)	.06	.03	.00
☐ 415	Don Carman	.03	.01	.00
☐ 416	Keith Moreland	.03	.01	.00
☐ 417	Mark Ciardi	.08	.04	.01
☐ 418	Joel Youngblood	.03	.01	.00
☐ 419	Scott McGregor	.03	.01	.00
☐ 420	Wally Joyner	.30	.15	.03
☐ 421	Ed VandeBerg	.03	.01	.00

□	Card					□	Card				
□	422	Dave Concepcion	.06	.03	.00	□	506	John Cangelosi	.03	.01	.00
□	423	John Smiley	.25	.12	.02	□	507	Mark Gubicza	.10	.05	.01
□	424	Dwayne Murphy	.03	.01	.00	□	508	Tim Teufel	.03	.01	.00
□	425	Jeff Reardon	.06	.03	.00	□	509	Bill Dawley	.03	.01	.00
□	426	Randy Ready	.03	.01	.00	□	510	Dave Winfield	.15	.07	.01
□	427	Paul Kilgus	.10	.05	.01	□	511	Joel Davis	.03	.01	.00
□	428	John Shelby	.03	.01	.00	□	512	Alex Trevino	.03	.01	.00
□	429	Tigers TL Alan Trammell and Kirk Gibson	.15	.07	.01	□	513	Tim Flannery	.03	.01	.00
						□	514	Pat Sheridan	.03	.01	.00
□	430	Glenn Davis	.12	.06	.01	□	515	Juan Nieves	.03	.01	.00
□	431	Casey Candaele	.03	.01	.00	□	516	Jim Sundberg	.03	.01	.00
□	432	Mike Moore	.06	.03	.00	□	517	Ron Robinson	.03	.01	.00
□	433	Bill Pecota	.10	.05	.01	□	518	Greg Gross	.03	.01	.00
□	434	Rick Aguilera	.03	.01	.00	□	519	Mariners TL Harold Reynolds and Phil Bradley	.06	.03	.00
□	435	Mike Pagliarulo	.06	.03	.00						
□	436	Mike Bielecki	.06	.03	.00	□	520	Dave Smith	.03	.01	.00
□	437	Fred Manrique	.10	.05	.01	□	521	Jim Dwyer	.03	.01	.00
□	438	Rob Ducey	.15	.07	.01	□	522	Bob Patterson	.08	.04	.01
□	439	Dave Martinez	.08	.04	.01	□	523	Gary Roenicke	.03	.01	.00
□	440	Steve Bedrosian	.08	.04	.01	□	524	Gary Lucas	.03	.01	.00
□	441	Rick Manning	.03	.01	.00	□	525	Marty Barrett	.06	.03	.00
□	442	Tom Bolton	.10	.05	.01	□	526	Juan Berenguer	.03	.01	.00
□	443	Ken Griffey	.08	.04	.01	□	527	Steve Henderson	.03	.01	.00
□	444	Cal Ripken, Sr. MG (checklist back) UER (two copyrights)	.06	.03	.00	□	528A	Checklist 397-528 ERR (455 S. Carlton)	.75	.05	.01
						□	528B	Checklist 397-528 COR (455 S. Hillegas)	.08	.01	.00
□	445	Mike Krukow	.03	.01	.00						
□	446	Doug DeCinces	.03	.01	.00	□	529	Tim Burke	.03	.01	.00
□	447	Jeff Montgomery	.25	.12	.02	□	530	Gary Carter	.15	.07	.01
□	448	Mike Davis	.03	.01	.00	□	531	Rich Yett	.03	.01	.00
□	449	Jeff M. Robinson (Tigers pitcher)	.25	.12	.02	□	532	Mike Kingery	.03	.01	.00
						□	533	John Farrell	.20	.10	.02
□	450	Barry Bonds	.15	.07	.01	□	534	John Wathan MG (checklist back)	.06	.03	.00
□	451	Keith Atherton	.03	.01	.00						
□	452	Willie Wilson	.06	.03	.00	□	535	Ron Guidry	.08	.04	.01
□	453	Dennis Powell	.03	.01	.00	□	536	John Morris	.03	.01	.00
□	454	Marvell Wynne	.03	.01	.00	□	537	Steve Buechele	.03	.01	.00
□	455	Shawn Hillegas	.15	.07	.01	□	538	Bill Wegman	.03	.01	.00
□	456	Dave Anderson	.03	.01	.00	□	539	Mike LaValliere	.03	.01	.00
□	457	Terry Leach	.06	.03	.00	□	540	Bret Saberhagen	.15	.07	.01
□	458	Ron Hassey	.03	.01	.00	□	541	Juan Beniquez	.03	.01	.00
□	459	Yankees TL Dave Winfield and Willie Randolph	.10	.05	.01	□	542	Paul Noce	.08	.04	.01
						□	543	Kent Tekulve	.03	.01	.00
□	460	Ozzie Smith	.12	.06	.01	□	544	Jim Traber	.03	.01	.00
□	461	Danny Darwin	.03	.01	.00	□	545	Don Baylor	.08	.04	.01
□	462	Don Slaught	.03	.01	.00	□	546	John Candelaria	.06	.03	.00
□	463	Fred McGriff	1.00	.50	.10	□	547	Felix Fermin	.08	.04	.01
□	464	Jay Tibbs	.03	.01	.00	□	548	Shane Mack	.08	.04	.01
□	465	Paul Molitor	.10	.05	.01	□	549	Braves TL Albert Hall, Dale Murphy, Ken Griffey, and Dion James	.06	.03	.00
□	466	Jerry Mumphrey	.03	.01	.00						
□	467	Don Aase	.03	.01	.00						
□	468	Darren Daulton	.03	.01	.00						
□	469	Jeff Dedmon	.03	.01	.00						
□	470	Dwight Evans	.10	.05	.01	□	550	Pedro Guerrero	.10	.05	.01
□	471	Donnie Moore	.03	.01	.00	□	551	Terry Steinbach	.20	.10	.02
□	472	Robby Thompson	.03	.01	.00	□	552	Mark Thurmond	.03	.01	.00
□	473	Joe Niekro	.06	.03	.00	□	553	Tracy Jones	.03	.01	.00
□	474	Tom Brookens	.03	.01	.00	□	554	Mike Smithson	.03	.01	.00
□	475	Pete Rose MG (checklist back)	.30	.15	.03	□	555	Brook Jacoby	.06	.03	.00
						□	556	Stan Clarke	.06	.03	.00
□	476	Dave Stewart	.12	.06	.01	□	557	Craig Reynolds	.03	.01	.00
□	477	Jamie Quirk	.03	.01	.00	□	558	Bob Ojeda	.06	.03	.00
□	478	Sid Bream	.03	.01	.00	□	559	Ken Williams	.15	.07	.01
□	479	Brett Butler	.06	.03	.00	□	560	Tim Wallach	.06	.03	.00
□	480	Dwight Gooden	.40	.20	.04	□	561	Rick Cerone	.03	.01	.00
□	481	Mariano Duncan	.03	.01	.00	□	562	Jim Lindeman	.06	.03	.00
□	482	Mark Davis	.12	.06	.01	□	563	Jose Guzman	.03	.01	.00
□	483	Rod Booker	.10	.05	.01	□	564	Frank Lucchesi MG (checklist back)	.06	.03	.00
□	484	Pat Clements	.03	.01	.00						
□	485	Harold Reynolds	.06	.03	.00	□	565	Lloyd Moseby	.06	.03	.00
□	486	Pat Keedy	.08	.04	.01	□	566	Charlie O'Brien	.08	.04	.01
□	487	Jim Pankovits	.03	.01	.00	□	567	Mike Diaz	.03	.01	.00
□	488	Andy McGaffigan	.03	.01	.00	□	568	Chris Brown	.03	.01	.00
□	489	Dodgers TL Pedro Guerrero and Fernando Valenzuela	.12	.06	.01	□	569	Charlie Leibrandt	.03	.01	.00
						□	570	Jeffrey Leonard	.06	.03	.00
□	490	Larry Parrish	.03	.01	.00	□	571	Mark Williamson	.08	.04	.01
□	491	B.J. Surhoff	.08	.04	.01	□	572	Chris James	.15	.07	.01
□	492	Doyle Alexander	.03	.01	.00	□	573	Bob Stanley	.03	.01	.00
□	493	Mike Greenwell	1.25	.60	.12	□	574	Graig Nettles	.08	.04	.01
□	494	Wally Ritchie	.08	.04	.01	□	575	Don Sutton	.10	.05	.01
□	495	Eddie Murray	.15	.07	.01	□	576	Tommy Hinzo	.08	.04	.01
□	496	Guy Hoffman	.03	.01	.00	□	577	Tom Browning	.08	.04	.01
□	497	Kevin Mitchell	.35	.17	.03	□	578	Gary Gaetti	.10	.05	.01
□	498	Bob Boone	.08	.04	.01	□	579	Mets TL Gary Carter and Kevin McReynolds	.15	.07	.01
□	499	Eric King	.03	.01	.00						
□	500	Andre Dawson	.15	.07	.01	□	580	Mark McGwire	1.00	.50	.10
□	501	Tim Birtsas	.03	.01	.00	□	581	Tito Landrum	.03	.01	.00
□	502	Dan Gladden	.06	.03	.00	□	582	Mike Henneman	.20	.10	.02
□	503	Junior Noboa	.08	.04	.01	□	583	Dave Valle	.06	.03	.00
□	504	Bob Rodgers MG (checklist back)	.06	.03	.00	□	584	Steve Trout	.03	.01	.00
						□	585	Ozzie Guillen	.06	.03	.00
□	505	Willie Upshaw	.03	.01	.00	□	586	Bob Forsch	.03	.01	.00
						□	587	Terry Puhl	.03	.01	.00

☐ 588 Jeff Parrett	.15	.07	.01
☐ 589 Geno Petralli	.03	.01	.00
☐ 590 George Bell	.15	.07	.01
☐ 591 Doug Drabek	.06	.03	.00
☐ 592 Dale Sveum	.03	.01	.00
☐ 593 Bob Tewksbury	.03	.01	.00
☐ 594 Bobby Valentine MG	.06	.03	.00
(checklist back)			
☐ 595 Frank White	.06	.03	.00
☐ 596 John Kruk	.08	.04	.01
☐ 597 Gene Garber	.03	.01	.00
☐ 598 Lee Lacy	.03	.01	.00
☐ 599 Calvin Schiraldi	.03	.01	.00
☐ 600 Mike Schmidt	.30	.15	.03
☐ 601 Jack Lazorko	.03	.01	.00
☐ 602 Mike Aldrete	.03	.01	.00
☐ 603 Rob Murphy	.03	.01	.00
☐ 604 Chris Bando	.03	.01	.00
☐ 605 Kirk Gibson	.15	.07	.01
☐ 606 Moose Haas	.03	.01	.00
☐ 607 Mickey Hatcher	.03	.01	.00
☐ 608 Charlie Kerfeld	.03	.01	.00
☐ 609 Twins TL	.10	.05	.01
Gary Gaetti and			
Kent Hrbek			
☐ 610 Keith Hernandez	.12	.06	.01
☐ 611 Tommy John	.08	.04	.01
☐ 612 Curt Ford	.03	.01	.00
☐ 613 Bobby Thigpen	.08	.04	.01
☐ 614 Herm Winningham	.03	.01	.00
☐ 615 Jody Davis	.03	.01	.00
☐ 616 Jay Aldrich	.08	.04	.01
☐ 617 Oddibe McDowell	.06	.03	.00
☐ 618 Cecil Fielder	.03	.01	.00
☐ 619 Mike Dunne	.08	.04	.01
(inconsistent design,			
black name on front)			
☐ 620 Cory Snyder	.12	.06	.01
☐ 621 Gene Nelson	.03	.01	.00
☐ 622 Kal Daniels	.12	.06	.01
☐ 623 Mike Flanagan	.06	.03	.00
☐ 624 Jim Leyland MG	.06	.03	.00
(checklist back)			
☐ 625 Frank Viola	.15	.07	.01
☐ 626 Glenn Wilson	.03	.01	.00
☐ 627 Joe Boever	.10	.05	.01
☐ 628 Dave Henderson	.06	.03	.00
☐ 629 Kelly Downs	.06	.03	.00
☐ 630 Darrell Evans	.06	.03	.00
☐ 631 Jack Howell	.03	.01	.00
☐ 632 Steve Shields	.03	.01	.00
☐ 633 Barry Lyons	.15	.07	.01
☐ 634 Jose DeLeon	.06	.03	.00
☐ 635 Terry Pendleton	.03	.01	.00
☐ 636 Charles Hudson	.03	.01	.00
☐ 637 Jay Bell	.15	.07	.01
☐ 638 Steve Balboni	.03	.01	.00
☐ 639 Brewers TL	.03	.01	.00
Glenn Braggs			
and Tony Muser CO			
☐ 640 Garry Templeton	.06	.03	.00
(inconsistent design,			
green border)			
☐ 641 Rick Honeycutt	.03	.01	.00
☐ 642 Bob Dernier	.03	.01	.00
☐ 643 Rocky Childress	.08	.04	.01
☐ 644 Terry McGriff	.08	.04	.01
☐ 645 Matt Nokes	.35	.17	.03
☐ 646 Checklist 529-660	.06	.01	.00
☐ 647 Pascual Perez	.08	.04	.01
☐ 648 Al Newman	.03	.01	.00
☐ 649 DeWayne Buice	.08	.04	.01
☐ 650 Cal Ripken	.18	.09	.01
☐ 651 Mike Jackson	.15	.07	.01
☐ 652 Bruce Benedict	.03	.01	.00
☐ 653 Jeff Sellers	.03	.01	.00
☐ 654 Roger Craig MG	.06	.03	.00
(checklist back)			
☐ 655 Len Dykstra	.08	.04	.01
☐ 656 Lee Guetterman	.03	.01	.00
☐ 657 Gary Redus	.03	.01	.00
☐ 658 Tim Conroy	.03	.01	.00
(inconsistent design,			
name in white)			
☐ 659 Bobby Meacham	.03	.01	.00
☐ 660 Rick Reuschel	.08	.04	.01
☐ 661 Turn Back Clock 1983	.20	.10	.02
Nolan Ryan			
☐ 662 Turn Back Clock 1978	.08	.04	.01
Jim Rice			
☐ 663 Turn Back Clock 1973	.03	.01	.00
Ron Blomberg			
☐ 664 Turn Back Clock 1968	.10	.05	.01
Bob Gibson			
☐ 665 Turn Back Clock 1963	.15	.07	.01
Stan Musial			
☐ 666 Mario Soto	.03	.01	.00
☐ 667 Luis Quinones	.03	.01	.00
☐ 668 Walt Terrell	.03	.01	.00
☐ 669 Phillies TL	.06	.03	.00
Lance Parrish			
and Mike Ryan CO			
☐ 670 Dan Plesac	.06	.03	.00
☐ 671 Tim Laudner	.03	.01	.00
☐ 672 John Davis	.12	.06	.01
☐ 673 Tony Phillips	.03	.01	.00
☐ 674 Mike Fitzgerald	.03	.01	.00
☐ 675 Jim Rice	.12	.06	.01
☐ 676 Ken Dixon	.03	.01	.00
☐ 677 Eddie Milner	.03	.01	.00
☐ 678 Jim Acker	.03	.01	.00
☐ 679 Darrell Miller	.03	.01	.00
☐ 680 Charlie Hough	.03	.01	.00
☐ 681 Bobby Bonilla	.12	.06	.01
☐ 682 Jimmy Key	.06	.03	.00
☐ 683 Julio Franco	.10	.05	.01
☐ 684 Hal Lanier MG	.06	.03	.00
(checklist back)			
☐ 685 Ron Darling	.08	.04	.01
☐ 686 Terry Francona	.03	.01	.00
☐ 687 Mickey Brantley	.06	.03	.00
☐ 688 Jim Winn	.03	.01	.00
☐ 689 Tom Pagnozzi	.08	.04	.01
☐ 690 Jay Howell	.03	.01	.00
☐ 691 Dan Pasqua	.03	.01	.00
☐ 692 Mike Birkbeck	.03	.01	.00
☐ 693 Benny Santiago	.45	.22	.04
☐ 694 Eric Nolte	.10	.05	.01
☐ 695 Shawon Dunston	.08	.04	.01
☐ 696 Duane Ward	.03	.01	.00
☐ 697 Steve Lombardozzi	.03	.01	.00
☐ 698 Brad Havens	.03	.01	.00
☐ 699 Padres TL	.20	.10	.02
Benito Santiago			
and Tony Gwynn			
☐ 700 George Brett	.25	.12	.02
☐ 701 Sammy Stewart	.03	.01	.00
☐ 702 Mike Gallego	.03	.01	.00
☐ 703 Bob Brenly	.03	.01	.00
☐ 704 Dennis Boyd	.06	.03	.00
☐ 705 Juan Samuel	.08	.04	.01
☐ 706 Rick Mahler	.03	.01	.00
☐ 707 Fred Lynn	.10	.05	.01
☐ 708 Gus Polidor	.06	.03	.00
☐ 709 George Frazier	.03	.01	.00
☐ 710 Darryl Strawberry	.35	.17	.03
☐ 711 Bill Gullickson	.03	.01	.00
☐ 712 John Moses	.03	.01	.00
☐ 713 Willie Hernandez	.06	.03	.00
☐ 714 Jim Fregosi MG	.06	.03	.00
(checklist back)			
☐ 715 Todd Worrell	.10	.05	.01
☐ 716 Lenn Sakata	.03	.01	.00
☐ 717 Jay Baller	.03	.01	.00
☐ 718 Mike Felder	.03	.01	.00
☐ 719 Denny Walling	.03	.01	.00
☐ 720 Tim Raines	.15	.07	.01
☐ 721 Pete O'Brien	.06	.03	.00
☐ 722 Manny Lee	.03	.01	.00
☐ 723 Bob Kipper	.03	.01	.00
☐ 724 Danny Tartabull	.15	.07	.01
☐ 725 Mike Boddicker	.03	.01	.00
☐ 726 Alfredo Griffin	.03	.01	.00
☐ 727 Greg Booker	.03	.01	.00
☐ 728 Andy Allanson	.03	.01	.00
☐ 729 Blue Jays TL	.12	.06	.01
George Bell and			
Fred McGriff			
☐ 730 John Franco	.08	.04	.01
☐ 731 Rick Schu	.03	.01	.00
☐ 732 David Palmer	.03	.01	.00
☐ 733 Spike Owen	.03	.01	.00
☐ 734 Craig Lefferts	.06	.03	.00
☐ 735 Kevin McReynolds	.15	.07	.01
☐ 736 Matt Young	.03	.01	.00
☐ 737 Butch Wynegar	.03	.01	.00
☐ 738 Scott Bankhead	.06	.03	.00
☐ 739 Daryl Boston	.03	.01	.00
☐ 740 Rick Sutcliffe	.08	.04	.01
☐ 741 Mike Easler	.03	.01	.00
☐ 742 Mark Clear	.03	.01	.00
☐ 743 Larry Herndon	.03	.01	.00
☐ 744 Whitey Herzog MG	.06	.03	.00
(checklist back)			
☐ 745 Bill Doran	.06	.03	.00
☐ 746 Gene Larkin	.20	.10	.00
☐ 747 Bobby Witt	.06	.03	.00
☐ 748 Reid Nichols	.03	.01	.00
☐ 749 Mark Eichhorn	.03	.01	.00
☐ 750 Bo Jackson	.90	.45	.09

			MINT	EXC	G-VG

☐ 751	Jim Morrison	.03	.01	.00
☐ 752	Mark Grant	.03	.01	.00
☐ 753	Danny Heep	.03	.01	.00
☐ 754	Mike LaCoss	.03	.01	.00
☐ 755	Ozzie Virgil	.03	.01	.00
☐ 756	Mike Maddux	.03	.01	.00
☐ 757	John Marzano	.08	.04	.01
☐ 758	Eddie Williams	.15	.07	.01
☐ 759	A's TL	.35	.17	.03
	Mark McGwire and Jose Canseco			
☐ 760	Mike Scott	.12	.06	.01
☐ 761	Tony Armas	.06	.03	.00
☐ 762	Scott Bradley	.03	.01	.00
☐ 763	Doug Sisk	.03	.01	.00
☐ 764	Greg Walker	.06	.03	.00
☐ 765	Neal Heaton	.03	.01	.00
☐ 766	Henry Cotto	.03	.01	.00
☐ 767	Jose Lind	.18	.09	.01
☐ 768	Dickie Noles	.03	.01	.00
☐ 769	Cecil Cooper	.08	.04	.01
☐ 770	Lou Whitaker	.08	.04	.01
☐ 771	Ruben Sierra	.35	.17	.03
☐ 772	Sal Butera	.03	.01	.00
☐ 773	Frank Williams	.03	.01	.00
☐ 774	Gene Mauch MG	.06	.03	.00
	(checklist back)			
☐ 775	Dave Stieb	.08	.04	.01
☐ 776	Checklist 661-792	.06	.01	.00
☐ 777	Lonnie Smith	.06	.03	.00
☐ 778A	Keith Comstock ERR	7.50	3.75	.75
	(white "Padres")			
☐ 778B	Keith Comstock COR	.15	.07	.01
	(blue "Padres")			
☐ 779	Tom Glavine	.30	.15	.03
☐ 780	Fernando Valenzuela	.12	.06	.01
☐ 781	Keith Hughes	.15	.07	.01
☐ 782	Jeff Ballard	.35	.17	.03
☐ 783	Ron Roenicke	.03	.01	.00
☐ 784	Joe Sambito	.03	.01	.00
☐ 785	Alvin Davis	.08	.04	.01
☐ 786	Joe Price	.03	.01	.00
	(inconsistent design, orange team name)			
☐ 787	Bill Almon	.03	.01	.00
☐ 788	Ray Searage	.03	.01	.00
☐ 789	Indians' TL	.10	.05	.01
	Joe Carter and Cory Snyder			
☐ 790	Dave Righetti	.08	.04	.01
☐ 791	Ted Simmons	.08	.04	.01
☐ 792	John Tudor	.10	.05	.01

1988 Topps Wax Box Cards

The cards in this 16-card set measure the standard 2 1/2" by 3 1/2". Cards have essentially the same design as the 1988 Topps regular issue set. The cards were printed on the bottoms of the regular issue wax pack boxes. These 16 cards, "lettered" A through P, are considered a separate set in their own right and are not typically included in a complete set of the regular issue 1988 Topps cards. The value of the panels uncut is slightly greater, perhaps by 25% greater, than the value of the individual cards cut up carefully.

			MINT	EXC	G-VG
COMPLETE SET (16)			3.00	1.50	.30
COMMON PLAYER (A-P)			.05	.02	.00
☐ A	Don Baylor		.10	.05	.01
☐ B	Steve Bedrosian		.10	.05	.01
☐ C	Juan Beniquez		.05	.02	.00
☐ D	Bob Boone		.15	.07	.01
☐ E	Darrell Evans		.10	.05	.01
☐ F	Tony Gwynn		.35	.17	.03
☐ G	John Kruk		.15	.07	.01
☐ H	Marvell Wynne		.05	.02	.00
☐ I	Joe Carter		.20	.10	.02
☐ J	Eric Davis		.50	.25	.05
☐ K	Howard Johnson		.20	.10	.02
☐ L	Darryl Strawberry		.50	.25	.05
☐ M	Rickey Henderson		.40	.20	.04
☐ N	Nolan Ryan		.60	.30	.06
☐ O	Mike Schmidt		.60	.30	.06
☐ P	Kent Tekulve		.05	.02	.00

1988 Topps Glossy All-Stars 22

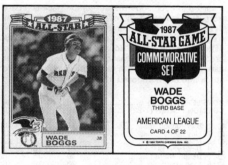

This set of 22 glossy cards was inserted one per rack pack. Players selected for the set are the starting players (plus manager and honorary captain) in the 1987 All- Star Game in Oakland. Cards measure standard size, 2 1/2" by 3 1/2" and the backs feature red and blue printing on a white card stock.

		MINT	EXC	G-VG
COMPLETE SET (22)		4.00	2.00	.40
COMMON PLAYER (1-22)		.10	.05	.01
☐ 1	John McNamara MG	.10	.05	.01
☐ 2	Don Mattingly	.60	.30	.06
☐ 3	Willie Randolph	.10	.05	.01
☐ 4	Wade Boggs	.50	.25	.05
☐ 5	Cal Ripken	.25	.12	.02
☐ 6	George Bell	.20	.10	.02
☐ 7	Rickey Henderson	.35	.17	.03
☐ 8	Dave Winfield	.25	.12	.02
☐ 9	Terry Kennedy	.10	.05	.01
☐ 10	Bret Saberhagen	.20	.10	.02
☐ 11	Jim Hunter CAPT	.15	.07	.01
☐ 12	Dave Johnson MG	.10	.05	.01
☐ 13	Jack Clark	.15	.07	.01
☐ 14	Ryne Sandberg	.25	.12	.02
☐ 15	Mike Schmidt	.50	.25	.05
☐ 16	Ozzie Smith	.20	.10	.02
☐ 17	Eric Davis	.45	.22	.04
☐ 18	Andre Dawson	.25	.12	.02
☐ 19	Darryl Strawberry	.45	.22	.04
☐ 20	Gary Carter	.20	.10	.02
☐ 21	Mike Scott	.15	.07	.01
☐ 22	Billy Williams CAPT	.15	.07	.01

1988 Topps Jumbo Rookies

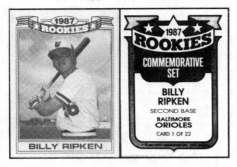

Inserted in each supermarket jumbo pack is a card from this series of 22 of 1987's best rookies as determined by Topps. Jumbo packs consisted of 100 (regular issue 1988 Topps baseball) cards with a stick of gum plus the insert "Rookie" card. The card fronts are in full color and measure 2 1/2" by 3 1/2". The card backs are printed in red and blue on white card stock and are numbered at the bottom.

		MINT	EXC	G-VG
	COMPLETE SET (22)	10.00	5.00	1.00
	COMMON PLAYER (1-22)	.20	.10	.02
☐ 1	Billy Ripken	.30	.15	.03
☐ 2	Ellis Burks	1.25	.60	.12
☐ 3	Mike Greenwell	1.75	.85	.17
☐ 4	DeWayne Buice	.20	.10	.02
☐ 5	Devon White	.50	.25	.05
☐ 6	Fred Manrique	.20	.10	.02
☐ 7	Mike Henneman	.30	.15	.03
☐ 8	Matt Nokes	.50	.25	.05
☐ 9	Kevin Seitzer	.75	.35	.07
☐ 10	B.J. Surhoff	.40	.20	.04
☐ 11	Casey Candaele	.20	.10	.02
☐ 12	Randy Myers	.40	.20	.04
☐ 13	Mark McGwire	1.50	.75	.15
☐ 14	Luis Polonia	.30	.15	.03
☐ 15	Terry Steinbach	.50	.25	.05
☐ 16	Mike Dunne	.30	.15	.03
☐ 17	Al Pedrique	.20	.10	.02
☐ 18	Benny Santiago	.90	.45	.09
☐ 19	Kelly Downs	.30	.15	.03
☐ 20	Joe Magrane	.50	.25	.05
☐ 21	Jerry Browne	.30	.15	.03
☐ 22	Jeff Musselman	.20	.10	.02

1988 Topps Revco League Leaders

Topps produced this 33-card boxed set for Revco stores subtitled "League Leaders". The cards measure 2 1/2" by 3 1/2" and feature a high-gloss, full-color photo of the player inside a white border.

The card backs are printed in red and black on white card stock. The cards are numbered on the back. The statistics provided on the card backs cover only two lines, last season and Major League totals.

		MINT	EXC	G-VG
	COMPLETE SET (33)	4.50	2.25	.45
	COMMON PLAYER (1-33)	.10	.05	.01
☐ 1	Tony Gwynn	.35	.17	.03
☐ 2	Andre Dawson	.20	.10	.02
☐ 3	Vince Coleman	.20	.10	.02
☐ 4	Jack Clark	.20	.10	.02
☐ 5	Tim Raines	.20	.10	.02
☐ 6	Tim Wallach	.10	.05	.01
☐ 7	Juan Samuel	.15	.07	.01
☐ 8	Nolan Ryan	.50	.25	.05
☐ 9	Rick Sutcliffe	.15	.07	.01
☐ 10	Kent Tekulve	.10	.05	.01
☐ 11	Steve Bedrosian	.15	.07	.01
☐ 12	Orel Hershiser	.35	.17	.03
☐ 13	Rick Reuschel	.10	.05	.01
☐ 14	Fernando Valenzuela	.20	.10	.02
☐ 15	Bob Welch	.10	.05	.01
☐ 16	Wade Boggs	.50	.25	.05
☐ 17	Mark McGwire	.40	.20	.04
☐ 18	George Bell	.20	.10	.02
☐ 19	Harold Reynolds	.10	.05	.01
☐ 20	Paul Molitor	.20	.10	.02
☐ 21	Kirby Puckett	.45	.22	.04
☐ 22	Kevin Seitzer	.30	.15	.03
☐ 23	Brian Downing	.10	.05	.01
☐ 24	Dwight Evans	.15	.07	.01
☐ 25	Willie Wilson	.10	.05	.01
☐ 26	Danny Tartabull	.20	.10	.02
☐ 27	Jimmy Key	.10	.05	.01
☐ 28	Roger Clemens	.40	.20	.04
☐ 29	Dave Stewart	.25	.12	.02
☐ 30	Mark Eichhorn	.10	.05	.01
☐ 31	Tom Henke	.10	.05	.01
☐ 32	Charlie Hough	.10	.05	.01
☐ 33	Mark Langston	.20	.10	.02

1988 Topps Rite-Aid Team MVP's

Topps produced this 33-card boxed set for Rite Aid Drug and Discount Stores subtitled "Team MVP's". The Rite Aid logo is at the top of every obverse. The cards measure 2 1/2" by 3 1/2" and feature a high-gloss, full- color photo of the player inside a red, white, and blue border. The card backs are printed in blue and black on white card stock. The cards are numbered on the back and the checklist for the set is found on the back panel of the small collector box. The statistics provided on the card backs cover only two lines, last season and Major League totals.

		MINT	EXC	G-VG
	COMPLETE SET (33)	4.50	2.25	.45
	COMMON PLAYER (1-33)	.10	.05	.01
☐ 1	Dale Murphy	.30	.15	.03
☐ 2	Andre Dawson	.20	.10	.02
☐ 3	Eric Davis	.40	.20	.04
☐ 4	Mike Scott	.15	.07	.01
☐ 5	Pedro Guerrero	.20	.10	.02

		MINT	EXC	G-VG
☐ 6	Tim Raines	.20	.10	.02
☐ 7	Darryl Strawberry	.50	.25	.05
☐ 8	Mike Schmidt	.50	.25	.05
☐ 9	Mike Dunne	.10	.05	.01
☐ 10	Jack Clark	.20	.10	.02
☐ 11	Tony Gwynn	.30	.15	.03
☐ 12	Will Clark	.60	.30	.06
☐ 13	Cal Ripken	.25	.12	.02
☐ 14	Wade Boggs	.50	.25	.05
☐ 15	Wally Joyner	.25	.12	.02
☐ 16	Harold Baines	.15	.07	.01
☐ 17	Joe Carter	.20	.10	.02
☐ 18	Alan Trammell	.20	.10	.02
☐ 19	Kevin Seitzer	.25	.12	.02
☐ 20	Paul Molitor	.20	.10	.02
☐ 21	Kirby Puckett	.45	.22	.04
☐ 22	Don Mattingly	.60	.30	.06
☐ 23	Mark McGwire	.40	.20	.04
☐ 24	Alvin Davis	.15	.07	.01
☐ 25	Ruben Sierra	.45	.22	.04
☐ 26	George Bell	.20	.10	.02
☐ 27	Jack Morris	.15	.07	.01
☐ 28	Jeff Reardon	.10	.05	.01
☐ 29	John Tudor	.15	.07	.01
☐ 30	Rick Reuschel	.10	.05	.01
☐ 31	Gary Gaetti	.15	.07	.01
☐ 32	Jeffrey Leonard	.10	.05	.01
☐ 33	Frank Viola	.20	.10	.02

1988 Topps UK Minis

JOSE CANSECO   Outfield

The 1988 Topps UK (United Kingdom) Mini set of "American Baseball" features 88 cards. The cards are numbered on the back and measure approximately 2 1/8" by 3". The card backs are printed in blue, red, and yellow on white card stock. The cards were distributed as a separate issue in packs. A custom black and yellow small set box was also available for holding a complete set; the box has a complete checklist on the back panel. The set player numbering is according to alphabetical order. Topps also produced a specially boxed "glossy" edition frequently referred to as the Topps UK Tiffany set. Topps did not disclose the number of UK Tiffany sets they produced or sold. The checklist of Tiffany cards is identical to that of the normal UK non-glossy cards. These Tiffany cards are valued at approximately double the values listed below.

	MINT	EXC	G-VG
COMPLETE SET (88)	8.00	4.00	.80
COMMON PLAYER (1-88)	.05	.02	.00

☐ 1	Harold Baines	.10	.05	.01
☐ 2	Steve Bedrosian	.10	.05	.01
☐ 3	Goerge Bell	.15	.07	.01
☐ 4	Wade Boggs	.65	.30	.06
☐ 5	Barry Bonds	.15	.07	.01
☐ 6	Bob Boone	.15	.07	.01
☐ 7	George Brett	.35	.17	.03
☐ 8	Hubie Brooks	.10	.05	.01
☐ 9	Ivan Calderon	.10	.05	.01
☐ 10	Jose Canseco	1.00	.50	.10
☐ 11	Gary Carter	.20	.10	.02
☐ 12	Joe Carter	.20	.10	.02
☐ 13	Jack Clark	.20	.10	.02
☐ 14	Will Clark	1.00	.50	.10
☐ 15	Roger Clemens	.50	.25	.05
☐ 16	Vince Coleman	.20	.10	.02
☐ 17	Alvin Davis	.10	.05	.01
☐ 18	Eric Davis	.50	.25	.05
☐ 19	Glenn Davis	.20	.10	.02
☐ 20	Andre Dawson	.20	.10	.02
☐ 21	Mike Dunne	.05	.02	.00
☐ 22	Dwight Evans	.15	.07	.01
☐ 23	Tony Fernandez	.15	.07	.01
☐ 24	John Franco	.10	.05	.01
☐ 25	Gary Gaetti	.10	.05	.01
☐ 26	Kirk Gibson	.25	.12	.02
☐ 27	Dwight Gooden	.45	.22	.04
☐ 28	Pedro Guerrero	.15	.07	.01
☐ 29	Tony Gwynn	.35	.17	.03
☐ 30	Billy Hatcher	.05	.02	.00
☐ 31	Rickey Henderson	.40	.20	.04
☐ 32	Tom Henke	.05	.02	.00
☐ 33	Keith Hernandez	.20	.10	.02
☐ 34	Orel Hershiser	.40	.20	.04
☐ 35	Teddy Higuera	.10	.05	.01
☐ 36	Charlie Hough	.05	.02	.00
☐ 37	Kent Hrbek	.15	.07	.01
☐ 38	Brook Jacoby	.10	.05	.01
☐ 39	Dion James	.05	.02	.00
☐ 40	Wally Joyner	.25	.12	.02
☐ 41	John Kruk	.10	.05	.01
☐ 42	Mark Langston	.20	.10	.02
☐ 43	Jeffrey Leonard	.05	.02	.00
☐ 44	Candy Maldonado	.05	.02	.00
☐ 45	Don Mattingly	1.00	.50	.10
☐ 46	Willie McGee	.10	.05	.01
☐ 47	Mark McGwire	.60	.30	.06
☐ 48	Kevin Mitchell	.10	.05	.01
☐ 49	Paul Molitor	.15	.07	.01
☐ 50	Jack Morris	.15	.07	.01
☐ 51	Lloyd Moseby	.10	.05	.01
☐ 52	Dale Murphy	.35	.17	.03
☐ 53	Eddie Murray	.25	.12	.02
☐ 54	Matt Nokes	.20	.10	.02
☐ 55	Dave Parker	.15	.07	.01
☐ 56	Larry Parrish	.05	.02	.00
☐ 57	Kirby Puckett	.50	.25	.05
☐ 58	Tim Raines	.20	.10	.02
☐ 59	Willie Randolph	.10	.05	.01
☐ 60	Harold Reynolds	.10	.05	.01
☐ 61	Cal Ripken	.30	.15	.03
☐ 62	Nolan Ryan	1.00	.50	.10
☐ 63	Bret Saberhagen	.35	.17	.03
☐ 64	Juan Samuel	.10	.05	.01
☐ 65	Ryne Sandberg	.25	.12	.02
☐ 66	Benny Santiago	.30	.15	.03
☐ 67	Mike Schmidt	.75	.35	.07
☐ 68	Mike Scott	.15	.07	.01
☐ 69	Kevin Seitzer	.25	.12	.02
☐ 70	Larry Sheets	.05	.02	.00
☐ 71	Ruben Sierra	.50	.25	.05
☐ 72	Ozzie Smith	.25	.12	.02
☐ 73	Zane Smith	.05	.02	.00
☐ 74	Cory Snyder	.20	.10	.02
☐ 75	Dave Stewart	.20	.10	.02
☐ 76	Darryl Strawberry	.50	.25	.05
☐ 77	Rick Sutcliffe	.10	.05	.01
☐ 78	Danny Tartabull	.20	.10	.02
☐ 79	Alan Trammell	.20	.10	.02
☐ 80	Fernando Valenzuela	.15	.07	.01
☐ 81	Andy Van Slyke	.15	.07	.01
☐ 82	Frank Viola	.20	.10	.02
☐ 83	Greg Walker	.05	.02	.00
☐ 84	Tim Wallach	.10	.05	.01
☐ 85	Dave Winfield	.25	.12	.02
☐ 86	Mike Witt	.05	.02	.00
☐ 87	Robin Yount	.50	.25	.05
☐ 88	Checklist Card	.05	.02	.00

1988 Topps Send-In Glossy 60

Topps issued this set through a mail-in offer explained and advertised on the wax packs. This 60-card set features glossy fronts with each card measuring 2 1/2" by 3 1/2". The offer provided your choice of any one of the six 10-card subsets (1-10, 11-20, etc.) for 1.25 plus six of the Special Offer ("Spring Fever Baseball") insert cards, which were found one per wax pack. The last two players (numerically) in each ten-card subset are actually "Hot Prospects."

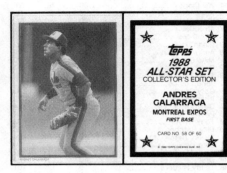

1988 Topps Big Cards

	MINT	EXC	G-VG
COMPLETE SET (60)	12.50	6.25	1.25
COMMON PLAYER (1-60)	.10	.05	.01

		MINT	EXC	G-VG
☐	1 Andre Dawson	.20	.10	.02
☐	2 Jesse Barfield	.15	.07	.01
☐	3 Mike Schmidt	.50	.25	.05
☐	4 Ruben Sierra	.40	.20	.04
☐	5 Mike Scott	.15	.07	.01
☐	6 Cal Ripken	.25	.12	.02
☐	7 Gary Carter	.25	.12	.02
☐	8 Kent Hrbek	.20	.10	.02
☐	9 Kevin Seitzer	.25	.12	.02
☐	10 Mike Henneman	.15	.07	.01
☐	11 Don Mattingly	1.00	.50	.10
☐	12 Tim Raines	.25	.12	.02
☐	13 Roger Clemens	.75	.35	.07
☐	14 Ryne Sandberg	.25	.12	.02
☐	15 Tony Fernandez	.15	.07	.01
☐	16 Eric Davis	.60	.30	.06
☐	17 Jack Morris	.20	.10	.02
☐	18 Tim Wallach	.10	.05	.01
☐	19 Mike Dunne	.10	.05	.01
☐	20 Mike Greenwell	1.00	.50	.10
☐	21 Dwight Evans	.15	.07	.01
☐	22 Darryl Strawberry	.75	.35	.07
☐	23 Cory Snyder	.20	.10	.02
☐	24 Pedro Guerrero	.20	.10	.02
☐	25 Rickey Henderson	.45	.22	.04
☐	26 Dale Murphy	.40	.20	.04
☐	27 Kirby Puckett	.50	.25	.05
☐	28 Steve Bedrosian	.15	.07	.01
☐	29 Devon White	.20	.10	.02
☐	30 Benny Santiago	.30	.15	.03
☐	31 George Bell	.20	.10	.02
☐	32 Keith Hernandez	.20	.10	.02
☐	33 Dave Stewart	.20	.10	.02
☐	34 Dave Parker	.20	.10	.02
☐	35 Tom Henke	.10	.05	.01
☐	36 Willie McGee	.15	.07	.01
☐	37 Alan Trammell	.20	.10	.02
☐	38 Tony Gwynn	.35	.17	.03
☐	39 Mark McGwire	.50	.25	.05
☐	40 Joe Magrane	.25	.12	.02
☐	41 Jack Clark	.20	.10	.02
☐	42 Willie Randolph	.15	.07	.01
☐	43 Juan Samuel	.15	.07	.01
☐	44 Joe Carter	.20	.10	.02
☐	45 Shane Rawley	.10	.05	.01
☐	46 Dave Winfield	.30	.15	.03
☐	47 Ozzie Smith	.25	.12	.02
☐	48 Wally Joyner	.25	.12	.02
☐	49 B.J. Surhoff	.15	.07	.01
☐	50 Ellis Burks	.75	.35	.07
☐	51 Wade Boggs	.75	.35	.07
☐	52 Howard Johnson	.25	.12	.02
☐	53 George Brett	.40	.20	.04
☐	54 Dwight Gooden	.50	.25	.05
☐	55 Jose Canseco	1.25	.60	.12
☐	56 Lee Smith	.10	.05	.01
☐	57 Paul Molitor	.20	.10	.02
☐	58 Andres Galarraga	.25	.12	.02
☐	59 Matt Nokes	.25	.12	.02
☐	60 Casey Candaele	.10	.05	.01

This set of 264 cards was issued as three separately distributed series of 88 cards each. Cards were distributed in wax packs with seven cards for a suggested retail of 40 cents. These cards are very reminiscent in style of the 1956 Topps card set and are popular with collectors perhaps for that reason. The cards measure approximately 2 5/8" by 3 3/4" and are oriented horizontally.

	MINT	EXC	G-VG
COMPLETE SET (264)	27.00	13.50	2.70
COMMON PLAYER (1-88)	.05	.02	.00
COMMON PLAYER (89-176)	.05	.02	.00
COMMON PLAYER (177-264)	.05	.02	.00

		MINT	EXC	G-VG
☐	1 Paul Molitor	.12	.06	.01
☐	2 Milt Thompson	.05	.02	.00
☐	3 Billy Hatcher	.05	.02	.00
☐	4 Mike Witt	.05	.02	.00
☐	5 Vince Coleman	.12	.06	.01
☐	6 Dwight Evans	.12	.06	.01
☐	7 Tim Wallach	.08	.04	.01
☐	8 Alan Trammell	.15	.07	.01
☐	9 Will Clark	1.25	.60	.12
☐	10 Jeff Reardon	.08	.04	.01
☐	11 Dwight Gooden	.50	.25	.05
☐	12 Benny Santiago	.15	.07	.01
☐	13 Jose Canseco	1.25	.60	.12
☐	14 Dale Murphy	.35	.17	.03
☐	15 George Bell	.20	.10	.02
☐	16 Ryne Sandberg	.20	.10	.02
☐	17 Brook Jacoby	.08	.04	.01
☐	18 Fernando Valenzuela	.12	.06	.01
☐	19 Scott Fletcher	.05	.02	.00
☐	20 Eric Davis	.75	.35	.07
☐	21 Willie Wilson	.10	.05	.01
☐	22 B.J. Surhoff	.10	.05	.01
☐	23 Steve Bedrosian	.10	.05	.01
☐	24 Dave Winfield	.30	.15	.03
☐	25 Bobby Bonilla	.15	.07	.01
☐	26 Larry Sheets	.05	.02	.00
☐	27 Ozzie Guillen	.08	.04	.01
☐	28 Checklist 1-88	.05	.02	.00
☐	29 Nolan Ryan	1.00	.50	.10
☐	30 Bob Boone	.12	.06	.01
☐	31 Tom Herr	.08	.04	.01
☐	32 Wade Boggs	1.00	.50	.10
☐	33 Neal Heaton	.05	.02	.00
☐	34 Doyle Alexander	.05	.02	.00
☐	35 Candy Maldonado	.05	.02	.00
☐	36 Kirby Puckett	.50	.25	.05
☐	37 Gary Carter	.20	.10	.02
☐	38 Lance McCullers	.08	.04	.01
☐	39A Terry Steinbach	.15	.07	.01
	(Topps logo in black)			
☐	39B Terry Steinbach	.15	.07	.01
	(Topps logo in white)			
☐	40 Gerald Perry	.08	.04	.01
☐	41 Tom Henke	.05	.02	.00
☐	42 Leon Durham	.05	.02	.00
☐	43 Cory Snyder	.15	.07	.01
☐	44 Dale Sveum	.05	.02	.00
☐	45 Lance Parrish	.12	.06	.01
☐	46 Steve Sax	.15	.07	.01
☐	47 Charlie Hough	.05	.02	.00
☐	48 Kal Daniels	.15	.07	.01
☐	49 Bo Jackson	1.25	.60	.12

	#	Player					#	Player			
☐	50	Ron Guidry	.12	.06	.01	☐	145	Devon White	.10	.05	.01
☐	51	Bill Doran	.08	.04	.01	☐	146	Jeff Stone	.05	.02	.00
☐	52	Wally Joyner	.35	.17	.03	☐	147	Chet Lemon	.05	.02	.00
☐	53	Terry Pendleton	.05	.02	.00	☐	148	Ozzie Virgil	.05	.02	.00
☐	54	Marty Barrett	.05	.02	.00	☐	149	Todd Worrell	.12	.06	.01
☐	55	Andres Galarraga	.15	.07	.01	☐	150	Mitch Webster	.05	.02	.00
☐	56	Larry Herndon	.05	.02	.00	☐	151	Rob Deer	.08	.04	.01
☐	57	Kevin Mitchell	.50	.25	.05	☐	152	Rich Gedman	.05	.02	.00
☐	58	Greg Gagne	.05	.02	.00	☐	153	Andre Dawson	.20	.10	.02
☐	59	Keith Hernandez	.20	.10	.02	☐	154	Mike Davis	.05	.02	.00
☐	60	John Kruk	.10	.05	.01	☐	155	Nelson Liriano	.05	.02	.00
☐	61	Mike LaValliere	.05	.02	.00	☐	156	Greg Swindell	.12	.06	.01
☐	62	Cal Ripken	.30	.15	.03	☐	157	George Brett	.35	.17	.03
☐	63	Ivan Calderon	.10	.05	.01	☐	158	Kevin McReynolds	.20	.10	.02
☐	64	Alvin Davis	.10	.05	.01	☐	159	Brian Fisher	.05	.02	.00
☐	65	Luis Polonia	.08	.04	.01	☐	160	Mike Kingery	.05	.02	.00
☐	66	Robin Yount	.50	.25	.05	☐	161	Tony Gwynn	.35	.17	.03
☐	67	Juan Samuel	.10	.05	.01	☐	162	Don Baylor	.10	.05	.01
☐	68	Andres Thomas	.08	.04	.01	☐	163	Jerry Browne	.08	.04	.01
☐	69	Jeff Musselman	.05	.02	.00	☐	164	Dan Pasqua	.05	.02	.00
☐	70	Jerry Mumphrey	.05	.02	.00	☐	165	Rickey Henderson	.45	.22	.04
☐	71	Joe Carter	.15	.07	.01	☐	166	Brett Butler	.10	.05	.01
☐	72	Mike Scioscia	.05	.02	.00	☐	167	Nick Esasky	.12	.06	.01
☐	73	Pete Incaviglia	.20	.10	.02	☐	168	Kirk McCaskill	.08	.04	.01
☐	74	Barry Larkin	.25	.12	.02	☐	169	Fred Lynn	.12	.06	.01
☐	75	Frank White	.08	.04	.01	☐	170	Jack Morris	.12	.06	.01
☐	76	Willie Randolph	.08	.04	.01	☐	171	Pedro Guerrero	.15	.07	.01
☐	77	Kevin Bass	.08	.04	.01	☐	172	Dave Stieb	.10	.05	.01
☐	78	Brian Downing	.05	.02	.00	☐	173	Pat Tabler	.05	.02	.00
☐	79	Willie McGee	.12	.06	.01	☐	174	Floyd Bannister	.05	.02	.00
☐	80	Ellis Burks	.50	.25	.05	☐	175	Rafael Belliard	.05	.02	.00
☐	81	Hubie Brooks	.08	.04	.01	☐	176	Mark Langston	.15	.07	.01
☐	82	Darrell Evans	.08	.04	.01	☐	177	Greg Mathews	.08	.04	.01
☐	83	Robby Thompson	.05	.02	.00	☐	178	Claudell Washington	.08	.04	.01
☐	84	Kent Hrbek	.15	.07	.01	☐	179	Mark McGwire	1.00	.50	.10
☐	85	Ron Darling	.10	.05	.01	☐	180	Bert Blyleven	.12	.06	.01
☐	86	Stan Jefferson	.08	.04	.01	☐	181	Jim Rice	.15	.07	.01
☐	87	Teddy Higuera	.08	.04	.01	☐	182	Mookie Wilson	.08	.04	.01
☐	88	Mike Schmidt	.75	.35	.07	☐	183	Willie Fraser	.05	.02	.00
☐	89	Barry Bonds	.15	.07	.01	☐	184	Andy Van Slyke	.12	.06	.01
☐	90	Jim Presley	.08	.04	.01	☐	185	Matt Nokes	.15	.07	.01
☐	91	Orel Hershiser	.60	.30	.06	☐	186	Eddie Whitson	.05	.02	.00
☐	92	Jesse Barfield	.15	.07	.01	☐	187	Tony Fernandez	.10	.05	.01
☐	93	Tom Candiotti	.05	.02	.00	☐	188	Rick Reuschel	.10	.05	.01
☐	94	Bret Saberhagen	.25	.12	.02	☐	189	Ken Phelps	.08	.04	.01
☐	95	Jose Uribe	.05	.02	.00	☐	190	Juan Nieves	.05	.02	.00
☐	96	Tom Browning	.12	.06	.01	☐	191	Kirk Gibson	.25	.12	.02
☐	97	Johnny Ray	.08	.04	.01	☐	192	Glenn Davis	.25	.12	.02
☐	98	Mike Morgan	.08	.04	.01	☐	193	Zane Smith	.05	.02	.00
☐	99	Lou Whitaker	.12	.06	.01	☐	194	Jose DeLeon	.08	.04	.01
☐	100	Jim Sundberg	.05	.02	.00	☐	195	Gary Ward	.05	.02	.00
☐	101	Roger McDowell	.05	.02	.00	☐	196	Pascual Perez	.10	.05	.01
☐	102	Randy Ready	.05	.02	.00	☐	197	Carlton Fisk	.20	.10	.02
☐	103	Mike Gallego	.05	.02	.00	☐	198	Oddibe McDowell	.08	.04	.01
☐	104	Steve Buechele	.05	.02	.00	☐	199	Mark Gubicza	.12	.06	.01
☐	105	Greg Walker	.05	.02	.00	☐	200	Glenn Hubbard	.05	.02	.00
☐	106	Jose Lind	.08	.04	.01	☐	201	Frank Viola	.15	.07	.01
☐	107	Steve Trout	.05	.02	.00	☐	202	Jody Reed	.08	.04	.01
☐	108	Rick Rhoden	.05	.02	.00	☐	203	Len Dykstra	.08	.04	.01
☐	109	Jim Pankovits	.05	.02	.00	☐	204	Dick Schofield	.05	.02	.00
☐	110	Ken Griffey Sr.	.10	.05	.01	☐	205	Sid Bream	.05	.02	.00
☐	111	Danny Cox	.08	.04	.01	☐	206	Guillermo Hernandez	.08	.04	.01
☐	112	Franklin Stubbs	.05	.02	.00	☐	207	Keith Moreland	.05	.02	.00
☐	113	Lloyd Moseby	.08	.04	.01	☐	208	Mark Eichhorn	.05	.02	.00
☐	114	Mel Hall	.08	.04	.01	☐	209	Rene Gonzalez	.08	.04	.01
☐	115	Kevin Seitzer	.30	.15	.03	☐	210	Dave Valle	.05	.02	.00
☐	116	Tim Raines	.25	.12	.02	☐	211	Tom Brunansky	.10	.05	.01
☐	117	Juan Castillo	.05	.02	.00	☐	212	Charles Hudson	.05	.02	.00
☐	118	Roger Clemens	.75	.35	.07	☐	213	John Farrell	.08	.04	.01
☐	119	Mike Aldrete	.05	.02	.00	☐	214	Jeff Treadway	.08	.04	.01
☐	120	Mario Soto	.05	.02	.00	☐	215	Eddie Murray	.25	.12	.02
☐	121	Jack Howell	.05	.02	.00	☐	216	Checklist 177-264	.05	.02	.00
☐	122	Rick Schu	.05	.02	.00	☐	217	Greg Brock	.05	.02	.00
☐	123	Jeff Robinson	.08	.04	.01	☐	218	John Shelby	.05	.02	.00
☐	124	Doug Drabek	.05	.02	.00	☐	219	Craig Reynolds	.05	.02	.00
☐	125	Henry Cotto	.05	.02	.00	☐	220	Dion James	.05	.02	.00
☐	126	Checklist 89-176	.05	.02	.00	☐	221	Carney Lansford	.12	.06	.01
☐	127	Gary Gaetti	.12	.06	.01	☐	222	Juan Berenguer	.05	.02	.00
☐	128	Rick Sutcliffe	.10	.05	.01	☐	223	Luis Rivera	.05	.02	.00
☐	129	Howard Johnson	.15	.07	.01	☐	224	Harold Baines	.12	.06	.01
☐	130	Chris Brown	.05	.02	.00	☐	225	Shawon Dunston	.12	.06	.01
☐	131	Dave Henderson	.05	.02	.00	☐	226	Luis Aguayo	.05	.02	.00
☐	132	Curt Wilkerson	.05	.02	.00	☐	227	Pete O'Brien	.08	.04	.01
☐	133	Mike Marshall	.10	.05	.01	☐	228	Ozzie Smith	.15	.07	.01
☐	134	Kelly Gruber	.08	.04	.01	☐	229	Don Mattingly	1.25	.60	.12
☐	135	Julio Franco	.12	.06	.01	☐	230	Danny Tartabull	.25	.12	.02
☐	136	Kurt Stillwell	.08	.04	.01	☐	231	Andy Allanson	.05	.02	.00
☐	137	Donnie Hill	.05	.02	.00	☐	232	John Franco	.08	.04	.01
☐	138	Mike Pagliarulo	.08	.04	.01	☐	233	Mike Greenwell	1.00	.50	.10
☐	139	Von Hayes	.10	.05	.01	☐	234	Bob Ojeda	.08	.04	.01
☐	140	Mike Scott	.15	.07	.01	☐	235	Chili Davis	.08	.04	.01
☐	141	Bob Kipper	.05	.02	.00	☐	236	Mike Dunne	.05	.02	.00
☐	142	Harold Reynolds	.08	.04	.01	☐	237	Jim Morrison	.05	.02	.00
☐	143	Bob Brenley	.05	.02	.00	☐	238	Carmelo Martinez	.05	.02	.00
☐	144	Dave Concepcion	.10	.05	.01	☐	239	Ernie Whitt	.05	.02	.00

☐ 240	Scott Garrelts	.08	.04	.01
☐ 241	Mike Moore	.10	.05	.01
☐ 242	Dave Parker	.12	.06	.01
☐ 243	Tim Laudner	.05	.02	.00
☐ 244	Bill Wegman	.05	.02	.00
☐ 245	Bob Horner	.10	.05	.01
☐ 246	Rafael Santana	.05	.02	.00
☐ 247	Alfredo Griffin	.05	.02	.00
☐ 248	Mark Bailey	.05	.02	.00
☐ 249	Ron Gant	.15	.07	.01
☐ 250	Bryn Smith	.08	.04	.01
☐ 251	Lance Johnson	.08	.04	.01
☐ 252	Sam Horn	.08	.04	.01
☐ 253	Darryl Strawberry	.75	.35	.07
☐ 254	Chuck Finley	.08	.04	.01
☐ 255	Darnell Coles	.05	.02	.00
☐ 256	Mike Henneman	.08	.04	.01
☐ 257	Andy Hawkins	.05	.02	.00
☐ 258	Jim Clancy	.05	.02	.00
☐ 259	Atlee Hammaker	.05	.02	.00
☐ 260	Glenn Wilson	.05	.02	.00
☐ 261	Larry McWilliams	.05	.02	.00
☐ 262	Jack Clark	.15	.07	.01
☐ 263	Walt Weiss	.30	.15	.03
☐ 264	Gene Larkin	.10	.05	.01

☐ 31	Mark McGwire	.75	.35	.07
☐ 32	Dave Stewart	.15	.07	.01
☐ 33	Phil Bradley	.08	.04	.01
☐ 34	Mark Langston	.15	.07	.01
☐ 35	Harold Reynolds	.08	.04	.01
☐ 36	Charlie Hough	.05	.02	.00
☐ 37	George Bell	.15	.07	.01
☐ 38	Tom Henke	.05	.02	.00
☐ 39	Jimmy Key	.05	.02	.00
☐ 40	Dion James	.05	.02	.00
☐ 41	Dale Murphy	.30	.15	.03
☐ 42	Zane Smith	.05	.02	.00
☐ 43	Andre Dawson	.20	.10	.02
☐ 44	Lee Smith	.05	.02	.00
☐ 45	Rick Sutcliffe	.10	.05	.01
☐ 46	Eric Davis	.45	.22	.04
☐ 47	John Franco	.08	.04	.01
☐ 48	Dave Parker	.12	.06	.01
☐ 49	Billy Hatcher	.05	.02	.00
☐ 50	Nolan Ryan	.75	.35	.07
☐ 51	Mike Scott	.15	.07	.01
☐ 52	Pedro Guerrero	.15	.07	.01
☐ 53	Orel Hershiser	.35	.17	.03
☐ 54	Fernando Valenzuela	.15	.07	.01
☐ 55	Bob Welch	.08	.04	.01
☐ 56	Andres Galarraga	.20	.10	.02
☐ 57	Tim Raines	.20	.10	.02
☐ 58	Tim Wallach	.08	.04	.01
☐ 59	Len Dykstra	.08	.04	.01
☐ 60	Dwight Gooden	.40	.20	.04
☐ 61	Howard Johnson	.15	.07	.01
☐ 62	Roger McDowell	.05	.02	.00
☐ 63	Darryl Strawberry	.50	.25	.05
☐ 64	Steve Bedrosian	.08	.04	.01
☐ 65	Shane Rawley	.05	.02	.00
☐ 66	Juan Samuel	.08	.04	.01
☐ 67	Mike Schmidt	.60	.30	.06
☐ 68	Mike Dunne	.05	.02	.00
☐ 69	Jack Clark	.15	.07	.01
☐ 70	Vince Coleman	.20	.10	.02
☐ 71	Willie McGee	.12	.06	.01
☐ 72	Ozzie Smith	.15	.07	.01
☐ 73	Todd Worrell	.12	.06	.01
☐ 74	Tony Gwynn	.35	.17	.03
☐ 75	John Kruk	.10	.05	.01
☐ 76	Rick Reuschel	.10	.05	.01
☐ 77	Checklist Card	.05	.02	.00

1988 Topps Mini Leaders

MARK McGWIRE

The 1988 Topps Mini set of Major League Leaders features 77 cards of leaders of the various statistical categories for the 1987 season. The cards are numbered on the back and measure approximately 2 1/8" by 3". The card backs are printed in blue, red, and yellow on white card stock. The cards were distributed as a separate issue in wax packs.

		MINT	EXC	G-VG
	COMPLETE SET (77)	7.00	3.50	.70
	COMMON PLAYER (1-77)	.05	.02	.00
☐ 1	Wade Boggs	.60	.30	.06
☐ 2	Roger Clemens	.45	.22	.04
☐ 3	Dwight Evans	.10	.05	.01
☐ 4	DeWayne Buice	.05	.02	.00
☐ 5	Brian Downing	.05	.02	.00
☐ 6	Wally Joyner	.25	.12	.02
☐ 7	Ivan Calderon	.10	.05	.01
☐ 8	Carlton Fisk	.15	.07	.01
☐ 9	Gary Redus	.05	.02	.00
☐ 10	Darrell Evans	.10	.05	.01
☐ 11	Jack Morris	.12	.06	.01
☐ 12	Alan Trammell	.15	.07	.01
☐ 13	Lou Whitaker	.12	.06	.01
☐ 14	Bret Saberhagen	.20	.10	.02
☐ 15	Kevin Seitzer	.25	.12	.02
☐ 16	Danny Tartabull	.15	.07	.01
☐ 17	Willie Wilson	.10	.05	.01
☐ 18	Teddy Higuera	.10	.05	.01
☐ 19	Paul Molitor	.12	.06	.01
☐ 20	Dan Plesac	.08	.04	.01
☐ 21	Robin Yount	.45	.22	.04
☐ 22	Kent Hrbek	.15	.07	.01
☐ 23	Kirby Puckett	.45	.22	.04
☐ 24	Jeff Reardon	.08	.04	.01
☐ 25	Frank Viola	.15	.07	.01
☐ 26	Rickey Henderson	.45	.22	.04
☐ 27	Don Mattingly	1.00	.50	.10
☐ 28	Willie Randolph	.08	.04	.01
☐ 29	Dave Righetti	.10	.05	.01
☐ 30	Jose Canseco	1.00	.50	.10

1988 Topps Traded

SCOTT SERVAIS

This 132-card Traded or extended set was distributed by Topps to dealers in a special blue and white box as a complete set. The card fronts are identical in style to the Topps regular issue and are also 2 1/2" by 3 1/2". The backs are printed in orange and black on white card stock. Cards are numbered (with a T suffix) alphabetically according to the name of the player. This set has generated additional interest due to the inclusion of the 1988 U.S. Olympic Baseball team members. These Olympians are indicated in the checklist below by OLY. Topps also produced a specially boxed "glossy" edition frequently referred to as the Topps Traded Tiffany set. This year, again, Topps did not disclose the number of Tiffany sets they produced or sold. It is apparent from the availability that there were

many more sets produced this year compared to the 1984-86 Tiffany sets, perhaps more than three times as many similar to the 1987 Tiffany cards. The checklist of cards is identical to that of the normal non-glossy cards. There are two primary distinguishing features of the Tiffany cards, white card stock reverses and high gloss obverses. These Tiffany cards are valued at approximately four times the values listed below.

		MINT	EXC	G-VG
COMPLETE SET (132)		27.00	13.50	2.70
COMMON PLAYER (1-132)		.06	.03	.00
☐	1T Jim Abbott OLY	10.00	5.00	1.00
☐	2T Juan Agosto	.06	.03	.00
☐	3T Luis Alicea	.10	.05	.01
☐	4T Roberto Alomar	.60	.30	.06
☐	5T Brady Anderson	.35	.17	.03
☐	6T Jack Armstrong	.25	.12	.02
☐	7T Don August	.10	.05	.01
☐	8T Floyd Bannister	.06	.03	.00
☐	9T Bret Barberie OLY	.25	.12	.02
☐	10T Jose Bautista	.12	.06	.01
☐	11T Don Baylor	.10	.05	.01
☐	12T Tim Belcher	.20	.10	.02
☐	13T Buddy Bell	.10	.05	.01
☐	14T Andy Benes OLY	3.00	1.50	.30
☐	15T Damon Berryhill	.35	.17	.03
☐	16T Bud Black	.06	.03	.00
☐	17T Pat Borders	.15	.07	.01
☐	18T Phil Bradley	.10	.05	.01
☐	19T Jeff Branson OLY	.25	.12	.02
☐	20T Tom Brunansky	.15	.07	.01
☐	21T Jay Buhner	.35	.17	.03
☐	22T Brett Butler	.10	.05	.01
☐	23T Jim Campanis OLY	.25	.12	.02
☐	24T Sil Campusano	.20	.10	.02
☐	25T John Candelaria	.10	.05	.01
☐	26T Jose Cecena	.10	.05	.01
☐	27T Rick Cerone	.06	.03	.00
☐	28T Jack Clark	.15	.07	.01
☐	29T Kevin Coffman	.10	.05	.01
☐	30T Pat Combs OLY	1.50	.75	.15
☐	31T Henry Cotto	.06	.03	.00
☐	32T Chili Davis	.10	.05	.01
☐	33T Mike Davis	.06	.03	.00
☐	34T Jose DeLeon	.10	.05	.01
☐	35T Richard Dotson	.06	.03	.00
☐	36T Cecil Espy	.15	.07	.01
☐	37T Tom Filer	.06	.03	.00
☐	38T Mike Fiore OLY	.30	.15	.03
☐	39T Ron Gant	.45	.22	.04
☐	40T Kirk Gibson	.15	.07	.01
☐	41T Rich Gossage	.15	.07	.01
☐	42T Mark Grace	3.50	1.75	.35
☐	43T Alfredo Griffin	.10	.05	.01
☐	44T Ty Griffin OLY	1.25	.60	.12
☐	45T Bryan Harvey	.30	.15	.03
☐	46T Ron Hassey	.06	.03	.00
☐	47T Ray Hayward	.10	.05	.01
☐	48T Dave Henderson	.10	.05	.01
☐	49T Tom Herr	.10	.05	.01
☐	50T Bob Horner	.10	.05	.01
☐	51T Ricky Horton	.06	.03	.00
☐	52T Jay Howell	.10	.05	.01
☐	53T Glenn Hubbard	.06	.03	.00
☐	54T Jeff Innis	.20	.10	.02
☐	55T Danny Jackson	.15	.07	.01
☐	56T Darrin Jackson	.15	.07	.01
☐	57T Roberto Kelly	.65	.30	.06
☐	58T Ron Kittle	.15	.07	.01
☐	59T Ray Knight	.10	.05	.01
☐	60T Vance Law	.06	.03	.00
☐	61T Jeffrey Leonard	.10	.05	.01
☐	62T Mike Macfarlane	.20	.10	.02
☐	63T Scotti Madison	.15	.07	.01
☐	64T Kirt Manwaring	.15	.07	.01
☐	65T Mark Marquess OLY	.06	.03	.00
☐	66T Tino Martinez OLY	1.25	.60	.12
☐	67T Billy Masse OLY	.25	.12	.02
☐	68T Jack McDowell	.15	.07	.01
☐	69T Jack McKeon MG	.06	.03	.00
☐	70T Larry McWilliams	.06	.03	.00
☐	71T Mickey Morandini OLY	.35	.17	.03
☐	72T Keith Moreland	.06	.03	.00
☐	73T Mike Morgan	.10	.05	.01
☐	74T Charles Nagy OLY	.25	.12	.02
☐	75T Al Nipper	.06	.03	.00
☐	76T Russ Nixon MG	.06	.03	.00
☐	77T Jesse Orosco	.06	.03	.00
☐	78T Joe Orsulak	.06	.03	.00
☐	79T Dave Palmer	.06	.03	.00
☐	80T Mark Parent	.20	.10	.02
☐	81T Dave Parker	.15	.07	.01
☐	82T Dan Pasqua	.10	.05	.01
☐	83T Melido Perez	.25	.12	.02
☐	84T Steve Peters	.15	.07	.01
☐	85T Dan Petry	.06	.03	.00
☐	86T Gary Pettis	.06	.03	.00
☐	87T Jeff Pico	.15	.07	.01
☐	88T Jim Poole OLY	.25	.12	.02
☐	89T Ted Power	.06	.03	.00
☐	90T Rafael Ramirez	.06	.03	.00
☐	91T Dennis Rasmussen	.10	.05	.01
☐	92T Jose Rijo	.10	.05	.01
☐	93T Ernie Riles	.06	.03	.00
☐	94T Luis Rivera	.10	.05	.01
☐	95T Doug Robbins OLY	.25	.12	.02
☐	96T Frank Robinson MG	.15	.07	.01
☐	97T Cookie Rojas MG	.06	.03	.00
☐	98T Chris Sabo	1.00	.50	.10
☐	99T Mark Salas	.06	.03	.00
☐	100T Luis Salazar	.06	.03	.00
☐	101T Rafael Santana	.06	.03	.00
☐	102T Nelson Santovenia	.25	.12	.02
☐	103T Mackey Sasser	.15	.07	.01
☐	104T Calvin Schiraldi	.06	.03	.00
☐	105T Mike Schooler	.30	.15	.03
☐	106T Scott Servais OLY	.25	.12	.02
☐	107T Dave Silvestri OLY	.25	.12	.02
☐	108T Don Slaught	.06	.03	.00
☐	109T Joe Slusarski OLY	.25	.12	.02
☐	110T Lee Smith	.10	.05	.01
☐	111T Pete Smith	.15	.07	.01
☐	112T Jim Snyder MG	.06	.03	.00
☐	113T Ed Sprague OLY	.35	.17	.03
☐	114T Pete Stanicek	.15	.07	.01
☐	115T Kurt Stillwell	.10	.05	.01
☐	116T Todd Stottlemyre	.25	.12	.02
☐	117T Bill Swift	.15	.07	.01
☐	118T Pat Tabler	.10	.05	.01
☐	119T Scott Terry	.06	.03	.00
☐	120T Mickey Tettleton	.15	.07	.01
☐	121T Dickie Thon	.06	.03	.00
☐	122T Jeff Treadway	.25	.12	.02
☐	123T Willie Upshaw	.06	.03	.00
☐	124T Robin Ventura OLY	2.00	1.00	.20
☐	125T Ron Washington	.06	.03	.00
☐	126T Walt Weiss	.90	.45	.09
☐	127T Bob Welch	.15	.07	.01
☐	128T David Wells	.15	.07	.01
☐	129T Glenn Wilson	.06	.03	.00
☐	130T Ted Wood OLY	.35	.17	.03
☐	131T Don Zimmer MG	.10	.05	.01
☐	132T Checklist 1T-132T	.06	.01	.00

1989 Topps

This 792-card set features backs which are printed in pink and black on gray card stock. The manager cards contain a checklist of the respective team's players on the back. Subsets in the set include Record Breakers (1- 7), Turn Back the Clock (661-665), and All-Star selections (386-407). The bonus cards distributed throughout the set that are indicated on the Topps checklist cards are actually Team Leader (TL) cards. Also sprinkled throughout the set are Future Stars (FS) and First Draft Picks

(FDP). There are subtle variations found in the Future Stars cards with respect to the placement of photo and type on the card; in fact each card has at least two varieties but they are difficult to detect (requiring precise measurement) as well as difficult to explain. Topps also produced a specially boxed "glossy" edition frequently referred to as the Topps Tiffany set. This year, again, Topps did not disclose the number of Tiffany sets they produced or sold but it seems that production quantities were roughly similar (or slightly smaller) to the previous two years. The checklist of cards (792 regular and 132 Traded) is identical to that of the normal non-glossy cards. There are two primary distinguishing features of the Tiffany cards, white card stock reverses and high gloss obverses. These Tiffany cards are valued at approximately four times the values listed below.

	MINT	EXC	G-VG
COMPLETE SET (792)	25.00	12.50	2.50
COMMON PLAYER (1-792)	.03	.01	.00

		MINT	EXC	G-VG
☐ 1	George Bell RB Slams 3 HR on Opening Day	.12	.02	.01
☐ 2	Wade Boggs RB Gets 200 Hits 6th Straight Season	.15	.07	.01
☐ 3	Gary Carter RB Sets Record for Career Putouts	.08	.04	.01
☐ 4	Andre Dawson RB Logs Double Figures in HR and SB	.08	.04	.01
☐ 5	Orel Hershiser RB Pitches 59 Scoreless Innings	.12	.06	.01
☐ 6	Doug Jones RB Earns His 15th Straight Save (photo actually Chris Codiroli)	.06	.03	.00
☐ 7	Kevin McReynolds RB Steals 21 Without Being Caught	.08	.04	.01
☐ 8	Dave Eiland	.12	.06	.01
☐ 9	Tim Teufel	.03	.01	.00
☐ 10	Andre Dawson	.10	.05	.01
☐ 11	Bruce Sutter	.08	.04	.01
☐ 12	Dale Sveum	.03	.01	.00
☐ 13	Doug Sisk	.03	.01	.00
☐ 14	Tom Kelly MG (team checklist back)	.06	.03	.00
☐ 15	Robby Thompson	.03	.01	.00
☐ 16	Ron Robinson	.03	.01	.00
☐ 17	Brian Downing	.03	.01	.00
☐ 18	Rick Rhoden	.03	.01	.00
☐ 19	Greg Gagne	.03	.01	.00
☐ 20	Steve Bedrosian	.08	.04	.01
☐ 21	Chicago White Sox TL Greg Walker	.03	.01	.00
☐ 22	Tim Crews	.03	.01	.00
☐ 23	Mike Fitzgerald Montreal Expos	.03	.01	.00
☐ 24	Larry Andersen	.03	.01	.00
☐ 25	Frank White	.06	.03	.00
☐ 26	Dale Mohorcic	.03	.01	.00
☐ 27A	Orestes Destrade (F* next to copyright)	.20	.10	.02
☐ 27B	Orestes Destrade (E*F* next to copyright)	.20	.10	.02
☐ 28	Mike Moore	.06	.03	.00
☐ 29	Kelly Gruber	.06	.03	.00
☐ 30	Dwight Gooden	.25	.12	.02
☐ 31	Terry Francona	.03	.01	.00
☐ 32	Dennis Rasmussen	.06	.03	.00
☐ 33	B.J. Surhoff	.06	.03	.00
☐ 34	Ken Williams	.03	.01	.00
☐ 35	John Tudor UER ('84 Pirates record, should be Red Sox)	.08	.04	.01
☐ 36	Mitch Webster	.03	.01	.00
☐ 37	Bob Stanley	.03	.01	.00
☐ 38	Paul Runge	.03	.01	.00
☐ 39	Mike Maddux	.03	.01	.00
☐ 40	Steve Sax	.10	.05	.01
☐ 41	Terry Mulholland	.03	.01	.00
☐ 42	Jim Eppard	.08	.04	.01
☐ 43	Guillermo Hernandez	.06	.03	.00
☐ 44	Jim Snyder MG (team checklist back)	.06	.03	.00
☐ 45	Kal Daniels	.08	.04	.01
☐ 46	Mark Portugal	.03	.01	.00
☐ 47	Carney Lansford	.08	.04	.01
☐ 48	Tim Burke	.06	.03	.00
☐ 49	Craig Biggio	.35	.17	.03
☐ 50	George Bell	.10	.05	.01
☐ 51	California Angels TL Mark McLemore	.03	.01	.00
☐ 52	Bob Brenly	.03	.01	.00
☐ 53	Ruben Sierra	.18	.09	.01
☐ 54	Steve Trout	.03	.01	.00
☐ 55	Julio Franco	.08	.04	.01
☐ 56	Pat Tabler	.06	.03	.00
☐ 57	Alejandro Pena	.03	.01	.00
☐ 58	Lee Mazzilli	.03	.01	.00
☐ 59	Mark Davis	.12	.06	.01
☐ 60	Tom Brunansky	.08	.04	.01
☐ 61	Neil Allen	.03	.01	.00
☐ 62	Alfredo Griffin	.03	.01	.00
☐ 63	Mark Clear	.03	.01	.00
☐ 64	Alex Trevino	.03	.01	.00
☐ 65	Rick Reuschel	.06	.03	.00
☐ 66	Manny Trillo	.03	.01	.00
☐ 67	Dave Palmer	.03	.01	.00
☐ 68	Darrell Miller	.03	.01	.00
☐ 69	Jeff Ballard	.08	.04	.01
☐ 70	Mark McGwire	.50	.25	.05
☐ 71	Mike Boddicker	.03	.01	.00
☐ 72	John Moses	.03	.01	.00
☐ 73	Pascual Perez	.08	.04	.01
☐ 74	Nick Leyva MG (team checklist back)	.06	.03	.00
☐ 75	Tom Henke	.06	.03	.00
☐ 76	Terry Blocker	.12	.06	.01
☐ 77	Doyle Alexander	.03	.01	.00
☐ 78	Jim Sundberg	.03	.01	.00
☐ 79	Scott Bankhead	.03	.01	.00
☐ 80	Cory Snyder	.08	.04	.01
☐ 81	Montreal Expos TL Tim Raines	.08	.04	.01
☐ 82	Dave Leiper	.03	.01	.00
☐ 83	Jeff Blauser	.12	.06	.01
☐ 84	Bill Bene FDP	.12	.06	.01
☐ 85	Kevin McReynolds	.10	.05	.01
☐ 86	Al Nipper	.03	.01	.00
☐ 87	Larry Owen	.03	.01	.00
☐ 88	Darryl Hamilton	.15	.07	.01
☐ 89	Dave LaPoint	.03	.01	.00
☐ 90	Vince Coleman UER (wrong birth year)	.10	.05	.01
☐ 91	Floyd Youmans	.03	.01	.00
☐ 92	Jeff Kunkel	.03	.01	.00
☐ 93	Ken Howell	.03	.01	.00
☐ 94	Chris Speier	.03	.01	.00
☐ 95	Gerald Young	.06	.03	.00
☐ 96	Rick Cerone (Ellis Burks in background of photo)	.06	.03	.00
☐ 97	Greg Mathews	.03	.01	.00
☐ 98	Larry Sheets	.03	.01	.00
☐ 99	Sherman Corbett	.08	.04	.01
☐ 100	Mike Schmidt	.20	.10	.02
☐ 101	Les Straker	.03	.01	.00
☐ 102	Mike Gallego	.03	.01	.00
☐ 103	Tim Birtsas	.03	.01	.00
☐ 104	Dallas Green MG (team checklist back)	.06	.03	.00
☐ 105	Ron Darling	.08	.04	.01
☐ 106	Willie Upshaw	.03	.01	.00
☐ 107	Jose DeLeon	.06	.03	.00
☐ 108	Fred Manrique	.03	.01	.00
☐ 109	Hipolito Pena	.08	.04	.01
☐ 110	Paul Molitor	.10	.05	.01
☐ 111	Cincinnati Reds TL Eric Davis (swinging bat)	.10	.05	.01
☐ 112	Jim Presley	.03	.01	.00
☐ 113	Lloyd Moseby	.06	.03	.00
☐ 114	Bob Kipper	.03	.01	.00
☐ 115	Jody Davis	.03	.01	.00
☐ 116	Jeff Montgomery	.06	.03	.00
☐ 117	Dave Anderson	.03	.01	.00
☐ 118	Checklist 1-132	.06	.01	.00
☐ 119	Terry Puhl	.03	.01	.00
☐ 120	Frank Viola	.12	.06	.01
☐ 121	Garry Templeton	.06	.03	.00
☐ 122	Lance Johnson	.08	.04	.00
☐ 123	Spike Owen	.03	.01	.00
☐ 124	Jim Traber	.03	.01	.00
☐ 125	Mike Krukow	.03	.01	.00
☐ 126	Sid Bream	.03	.01	.00
☐ 127	Walt Terrell	.03	.01	.00
☐ 128	Milt Thompson	.03	.01	.00

☐ 129	Terry Clark	.10	.05	.01
☐ 130	Gerald Perry	.06	.03	.00
☐ 131	Dave Otto	.08	.04	.01
☐ 132	Curt Ford	.03	.01	.00
☐ 133	Bill Long	.03	.01	.00
☐ 134	Don Zimmer MG	.06	.03	.00
	(team checklist back)			
☐ 135	Jose Rijo	.03	.01	.00
☐ 136	Joey Meyer	.06	.03	.00
☐ 137	Geno Petralli	.03	.01	.00
☐ 138	Wallace Johnson	.03	.01	.00
☐ 139	Mike Flanagan	.03	.01	.00
☐ 140	Shawon Dunston	.06	.03	.00
☐ 141	Cleveland Indians TL	.06	.03	.00
	Brook Jacoby			
☐ 142	Mike Diaz	.03	.01	.00
☐ 143	Mike Campbell	.03	.01	.00
☐ 144	Jay Bell	.03	.01	.00
☐ 145	Dave Stewart	.10	.05	.01
☐ 146	Gary Pettis	.03	.01	.00
☐ 147	DeWayne Buice	.03	.01	.00
☐ 148	Bill Pecota	.03	.01	.00
☐ 149	Doug Dascenzo	.15	.07	.01
☐ 150	Fernando Valenzuela	.10	.05	.01
☐ 151	Terry McGriff	.03	.01	.00
☐ 152	Mark Thurmond	.03	.01	.00
☐ 153	Jim Pankovits	.03	.01	.00
☐ 154	Don Carman	.03	.01	.00
☐ 155	Marty Barrett	.03	.01	.00
☐ 156	Dave Gallagher	.15	.07	.01
☐ 157	Tom Glavine	.06	.03	.00
☐ 158	Mike Aldrete	.03	.01	.00
☐ 159	Pat Clements	.03	.01	.00
☐ 160	Jeffrey Leonard	.06	.03	.00
☐ 161	Gregg Olson FDP	.65	.30	.06
	(born Scribner, NE, should be Omaha, NE)			
☐ 162	John Davis	.03	.01	.00
☐ 163	Bob Forsch	.03	.01	.00
☐ 164	Hal Lanier MG	.06	.03	.00
	(team checklist back)			
☐ 165	Mike Dunne	.03	.01	.00
☐ 166	Doug Jennings	.15	.07	.01
☐ 167	Steve Searcy FS	.18	.09	.01
☐ 168	Willie Wilson	.06	.03	.00
☐ 169	Mike Jackson	.03	.01	.00
☐ 170	Tony Fernandez	.08	.04	.01
☐ 171	Atlanta Braves TL	.03	.01	.00
	Andres Thomas			
☐ 172	Frank Williams	.03	.01	.00
☐ 173	Mel Hall	.06	.03	.00
☐ 174	Todd Burns	.20	.10	.02
☐ 175	John Shelby	.03	.01	.00
☐ 176	Jeff Parrett	.03	.01	.00
☐ 177	Monty Fariss FDP	.25	.12	.02
☐ 178	Mark Grant	.03	.01	.00
☐ 179	Ozzie Virgil	.03	.01	.00
☐ 180	Mike Scott	.10	.05	.01
☐ 181	Craig Worthington	.35	.17	.03
☐ 182	Bob McClure	.03	.01	.00
☐ 183	Oddibe McDowell	.06	.03	.00
☐ 184	John Costello	.10	.05	.01
☐ 185	Claudell Washington	.06	.03	.00
☐ 186	Pat Perry	.03	.01	.00
☐ 187	Darren Daulton	.03	.01	.00
☐ 188	Dennis Lamp	.03	.01	.00
☐ 189	Kevin Mitchell	.30	.15	.03
☐ 190	Mike Witt	.06	.03	.00
☐ 191	Sil Campusano	.20	.10	.02
☐ 192	Paul Mirabella	.03	.01	.00
☐ 193	Sparky Anderson MG	.06	.03	.00
	(team checklist back) UER (553 Salazer)			
☐ 194	Greg W. Harris	.20	.10	.02
	San Diego Padres			
☐ 195	Ozzie Guillen	.06	.03	.00
☐ 196	Denny Walling	.03	.01	.00
☐ 197	Neal Heaton	.03	.01	.00
☐ 198	Danny Heep	.03	.01	.00
☐ 199	Mike Schooler	.25	.12	.02
☐ 200	George Brett	.20	.10	.02
☐ 201	Blue Jays TL	.06	.03	.00
	Kelly Gruber			
☐ 202	Brad Moore	.12	.06	.01
☐ 203	Rob Ducey	.06	.03	.00
☐ 204	Brad Havens	.03	.01	.00
☐ 205	Dwight Evans	.08	.04	.01
☐ 206	Roberto Alomar	.25	.12	.02
☐ 207	Terry Leach	.06	.03	.00
☐ 208	Tom Pagnozzi	.03	.01	.00
☐ 209	Jeff Bittiger	.10	.05	.01
☐ 210	Dale Murphy	.15	.07	.01
☐ 211	Mike Pagliarulo	.06	.03	.00
☐ 212	Scott Sanderson	.03	.01	.00
☐ 213	Rene Gonzales	.03	.01	.00
☐ 214	Charlie O'Brien	.03	.01	.00
☐ 215	Kevin Gross	.03	.01	.00
☐ 216	Jack Howell	.03	.01	.00
☐ 217	Joe Price	.03	.01	.00
☐ 218	Mike LaValliere	.03	.01	.00
☐ 219	Jim Clancy	.03	.01	.00
☐ 220	Gary Gaetti	.08	.04	.01
☐ 221	Cecil Espy	.08	.04	.01
☐ 222	Mark Lewis FDP	.30	.15	.03
☐ 223	Jay Buhner	.12	.06	.01
☐ 224	Tony LaRussa MG	.06	.03	.00
	(team checklist back)			
☐ 225	Ramon Martinez	.30	.15	.03
☐ 226	Bill Doran	.06	.03	.00
☐ 227	John Farrell	.03	.01	.00
☐ 228	Nelson Santovenia	.12	.06	.01
☐ 229	Jimmy Key	.06	.03	.00
☐ 230	Ozzie Smith	.10	.05	.01
☐ 231	San Diego Padres TL	.10	.05	.01
	Roberto Alomar (G.Carter at plate)			
☐ 232	Ricky Horton	.03	.01	.00
☐ 233	Gregg Jefferies FS	1.75	.85	.17
☐ 234	Tom Browning	.08	.04	.01
☐ 235	John Kruk	.06	.03	.00
☐ 236	Charles Hudson	.03	.01	.00
☐ 237	Glenn Hubbard	.03	.01	.00
☐ 238	Eric King	.03	.01	.00
☐ 239	Tim Laudner	.03	.01	.00
☐ 240	Greg Maddux	.08	.04	.01
☐ 241	Brett Butler	.06	.03	.00
☐ 242	Ed Vandeberg	.03	.01	.00
☐ 243	Bob Boone	.08	.04	.01
☐ 244	Jim Acker	.03	.01	.00
☐ 245	Jim Rice	.10	.05	.01
☐ 246	Rey Quinones	.03	.01	.00
☐ 247	Shawn Hillegas	.03	.01	.00
☐ 248	Tony Phillips	.03	.01	.00
☐ 249	Tim Leary	.06	.03	.00
☐ 250	Cal Ripken	.15	.07	.01
☐ 251	John Dopson	.15	.07	.01
☐ 252	Billy Hatcher	.03	.01	.00
☐ 253	Jose Alvarez	.08	.04	.01
☐ 254	Tom Lasorda MG	.06	.03	.00
	(team checklist back)			
☐ 255	Ron Guidry	.08	.04	.01
☐ 256	Benny Santiago	.10	.05	.01
☐ 257	Rick Aguilera	.03	.01	.00
☐ 258	Checklist 133-264	.06	.01	.00
☐ 259	Larry McWilliams	.03	.01	.00
☐ 260	Dave Winfield	.12	.06	.01
☐ 261	St.Louis Cardinals TL	.06	.03	.00
	Tom Brunansky (with Luis Alicea)			
☐ 262	Jeff Pico	.10	.05	.01
☐ 263	Mike Felder	.03	.01	.00
☐ 264	Rob Dibble	.20	.10	.02
☐ 265	Kent Hrbek	.10	.05	.01
☐ 266	Luis Aquino	.03	.01	.00
☐ 267	Jeff Robinson	.06	.03	.00
	Detroit Tigers			
☐ 268	Keith Miller	.15	.07	.01
	Philadelphia Phillies			
☐ 269	Tom Bolton	.03	.01	.00
☐ 270	Wally Joyner	.12	.06	.01
☐ 271	Jay Tibbs	.03	.01	.00
☐ 272	Ron Hassey	.03	.01	.00
☐ 273	Jose Lind	.03	.01	.00
☐ 274	Mark Eichhorn	.03	.01	.00
☐ 275	Danny Tartabull UER	.08	.04	.01
	(Born San Juan, PR should be Miami, FL)			
☐ 276	Paul Kilgus	.03	.01	.00
☐ 277	Mike Davis	.03	.01	.00
☐ 278	Andy McGaffigan	.03	.01	.00
☐ 279	Scott Bradley	.03	.01	.00
☐ 280	Bob Knepper	.03	.01	.00
☐ 281	Gary Redus	.03	.01	.00
☐ 282	Cris Carpenter	.15	.07	.01
☐ 283	Andy Allanson	.03	.01	.00
☐ 284	Jim Leyland MG	.06	.03	.00
	(team checklist back)			
☐ 285	John Candelaria	.06	.03	.00
☐ 286	Darrin Jackson	.10	.05	.01
☐ 287	Juan Nieves	.03	.01	.00
☐ 288	Pat Sheridan	.03	.01	.00
☐ 289	Ernie Whitt	.03	.01	.00
☐ 290	John Franco	.06	.03	.00
☐ 291	New York Mets TL	.12	.06	.01
	Darryl Strawberry (with K.Hernandez and K.McReynolds)			
☐ 292	Jim Corsi	.12	.06	.01
☐ 293	Glenn Wilson	.03	.01	.00
☐ 294	Juan Berenguer	.03	.01	.00

☐ 295	Scott Fletcher	.03	.01	.00
☐ 296	Ron Gant	.15	.07	.01
☐ 297	Oswald Peraza	.08	.04	.01
☐ 298	Chris James	.06	.03	.00
☐ 299	Steve Ellsworth	.12	.06	.01
☐ 300	Darryl Strawberry	.30	.15	.03
☐ 301	Charlie Leibrandt	.03	.01	.00
☐ 302	Gary Ward	.03	.01	.00
☐ 303	Felix Fermin	.03	.01	.00
☐ 304	Joel Youngblood	.03	.01	.00
☐ 305	Dave Smith	.03	.01	.00
☐ 306	Tracy Woodson	.10	.05	.01
☐ 307	Lance McCullers	.03	.01	.00
☐ 308	Ron Karkovice	.03	.01	.00
☐ 309	Mario Diaz	.08	.04	.01
☐ 310	Rafael Palmeiro	.10	.05	.01
☐ 311	Chris Bosio	.06	.03	.00
☐ 312	Tom Lawless	.03	.01	.00
☐ 313	Dennis Martinez	.06	.03	.00
☐ 314	Bobby Valentine MG (team checklist back)	.06	.03	.00
☐ 315	Greg Swindell	.08	.04	.01
☐ 316	Walt Weiss	.30	.15	.03
☐ 317	Jack Armstrong	.20	.10	.02
☐ 318	Gene Larkin	.03	.01	.00
☐ 319	Greg Booker	.03	.01	.00
☐ 320	Lou Whitaker	.08	.04	.01
☐ 321	Boston Red Sox TL Jody Reed	.08	.04	.01
☐ 322	John Smiley	.06	.03	.00
☐ 323	Gary Thurman	.03	.01	.00
☐ 324	Bob Milacki	.20	.10	.02
☐ 325	Jesse Barfield	.08	.04	.01
☐ 326	Dennis Boyd	.06	.03	.00
☐ 327	Mark Lemke	.10	.05	.01
☐ 328	Rick Honeycutt	.03	.01	.00
☐ 329	Bob Melvin	.03	.01	.00
☐ 330	Eric Davis	.25	.12	.02
☐ 331	Curt Wilkerson	.03	.01	.00
☐ 332	Tony Armas	.06	.03	.00
☐ 333	Bob Ojeda	.06	.03	.00
☐ 334	Steve Lyons	.03	.01	.00
☐ 335	Dave Righetti	.08	.04	.01
☐ 336	Steve Balboni	.03	.01	.00
☐ 337	Calvin Schiraldi	.03	.01	.00
☐ 338	Jim Adduci	.03	.01	.00
☐ 339	Scott Bailes	.03	.01	.00
☐ 340	Kirk Gibson	.12	.06	.01
☐ 341	Jim Deshaies	.03	.01	.00
☐ 342	Tom Brookens	.03	.01	.00
☐ 343	Gary Sheffield FS	1.25	.60	.12
☐ 344	Tom Trebelhorn MG (team checklist back)	.06	.03	.00
☐ 345	Charlie Hough	.03	.01	.00
☐ 346	Rex Hudler	.03	.01	.00
☐ 347	John Cerutti	.03	.01	.00
☐ 348	Ed Hearn	.03	.01	.00
☐ 349	Ron Jones	.25	.12	.02
☐ 350	Andy Van Slyke	.08	.04	.01
☐ 351	San Fran. Giants TL Bob Melvin (with Bill Fahey CO)	.03	.01	.00
☐ 352	Rick Schu	.03	.01	.00
☐ 353	Marvell Wynne	.03	.01	.00
☐ 354	Larry Parrish	.03	.01	.00
☐ 355	Mark Langston	.12	.06	.01
☐ 356	Kevin Elster	.06	.03	.00
☐ 357	Jerry Reuss	.03	.01	.00
☐ 358	Ricky Jordan	1.25	.60	.12
☐ 359	Tommy John	.08	.04	.01
☐ 360	Ryne Sandberg	.15	.07	.01
☐ 361	Kelly Downs	.03	.01	.00
☐ 362	Jack Lazorko	.03	.01	.00
☐ 363	Rich Yett	.03	.01	.00
☐ 364	Rob Deer	.06	.03	.00
☐ 365	Mike Henneman	.03	.01	.00
☐ 366	Herm Winningham	.03	.01	.00
☐ 367	Johnny Paredes	.10	.05	.01
☐ 368	Brian Holton	.03	.01	.00
☐ 369	Ken Caminiti	.03	.01	.00
☐ 370	Dennis Eckersley	.08	.04	.01
☐ 371	Manny Lee	.03	.01	.00
☐ 372	Craig Lefferts	.06	.03	.00
☐ 373	Tracy Jones	.03	.01	.00
☐ 374	John Wathan MG (team checklist back)	.06	.03	.00
☐ 375	Terry Pendleton	.03	.01	.00
☐ 376	Steve Lombardozzi	.03	.01	.00
☐ 377	Mike Smithson	.03	.01	.00
☐ 378	Checklist 265-396	.06	.01	.00
☐ 379	Tim Flannery	.03	.01	.00
☐ 380	Rickey Henderson	.25	.12	.02
☐ 381	Baltimore Orioles TL Larry Sheets	.03	.01	.00
☐ 382	John Smoltz	.35	.17	.03

☐ 383	Howard Johnson	.12	.06	.01
☐ 384	Mark Salas	.03	.01	.00
☐ 385	Von Hayes	.08	.04	.01
☐ 386	Andres Galarraga AS	.08	.04	.01
☐ 387	Ryne Sandberg AS	.10	.05	.01
☐ 388	Bobby Bonilla AS	.08	.04	.01
☐ 389	Ozzie Smith AS	.08	.04	.01
☐ 390	Darryl Strawberry AS	.15	.07	.01
☐ 391	Andre Dawson AS	.10	.05	.01
☐ 392	Andy Van Slyke AS	.08	.04	.01
☐ 393	Gary Carter AS	.10	.05	.01
☐ 394	Orel Hershiser AS	.10	.05	.01
☐ 395	Danny Jackson AS	.06	.03	.00
☐ 396	Kirk Gibson AS	.10	.05	.01
☐ 397	Don Mattingly AS	.30	.15	.03
☐ 398	Julio Franco AS	.08	.04	.01
☐ 399	Wade Boggs AS	.25	.12	.02
☐ 400	Alan Trammell AS	.08	.04	.01
☐ 401	Jose Canseco AS	.30	.15	.03
☐ 402	Mike Greenwell AS	.20	.10	.02
☐ 403	Kirby Puckett AS	.15	.07	.01
☐ 404	Bob Boone AS	.08	.04	.01
☐ 405	Roger Clemens AS	.15	.07	.01
☐ 406	Frank Viola AS	.08	.04	.01
☐ 407	Dave Winfield AS	.10	.05	.01
☐ 408	Greg Walker	.03	.01	.00
☐ 409	Ken Dayley	.03	.01	.00
☐ 410	Jack Clark	.08	.04	.01
☐ 411	Mitch Williams	.08	.04	.01
☐ 412	Barry Lyons	.03	.01	.00
☐ 413	Mike Kingery	.03	.01	.00
☐ 414	Jim Fregosi MG (team checklist back)	.06	.03	.00
☐ 415	Rich Gossage	.08	.04	.01
☐ 416	Fred Lynn	.08	.04	.01
☐ 417	Mike LaCoss	.03	.01	.00
☐ 418	Bob Dernier	.03	.01	.00
☐ 419	Tom Filer	.03	.01	.00
☐ 420	Joe Carter	.10	.05	.01
☐ 421	Kirk McCaskill	.03	.01	.00
☐ 422	Bo Diaz	.03	.01	.00
☐ 423	Brian Fisher	.03	.01	.00
☐ 424	Luis Polonia UER (wrong birthdate)	.03	.01	.00
☐ 425	Jay Howell	.06	.03	.00
☐ 426	Dan Gladden	.03	.01	.00
☐ 427	Eric Show	.03	.01	.00
☐ 428	Craig Reynolds	.03	.01	.00
☐ 429	Minnesota Twins TL Greg Gagne (taking throw at 2nd)	.03	.01	.00
☐ 430	Mark Gubicza	.08	.04	.01
☐ 431	Luis Rivera	.03	.01	.00
☐ 432	Chad Kreuter	.10	.05	.01
☐ 433	Albert Hall	.03	.01	.00
☐ 434	Ken Patterson	.08	.04	.01
☐ 435	Len Dykstra	.06	.03	.00
☐ 436	Bobby Meacham	.03	.01	.00
☐ 437	Andy Benes FDP	.75	.35	.07
☐ 438	Greg Gross	.03	.01	.00
☐ 439	Frank DiPino	.03	.01	.00
☐ 440	Bobby Bonilla	.08	.04	.01
☐ 441	Jerry Reed	.03	.01	.00
☐ 442	Jose Oquendo	.03	.01	.00
☐ 443	Rod Nichols	.10	.05	.01
☐ 444	Moose Stubing MG (team checklist back)	.06	.03	.00
☐ 445	Matt Nokes	.08	.04	.01
☐ 446	Rob Murphy	.03	.01	.00
☐ 447	Donell Nixon	.03	.01	.00
☐ 448	Eric Plunk	.03	.01	.00
☐ 449	Carmelo Martinez	.03	.01	.00
☐ 450	Roger Clemens	.25	.12	.02
☐ 451	Mark Davidson	.03	.01	.00
☐ 452	Israel Sanchez	.10	.05	.01
☐ 453	Tom Prince	.08	.04	.01
☐ 454	Paul Assenmacher	.03	.01	.00
☐ 455	Johnny Ray	.06	.03	.00
☐ 456	Tim Belcher	.08	.04	.01
☐ 457	Mackey Sasser	.08	.04	.01
☐ 458	Donn Pall	.08	.04	.01
☐ 459	Seattle Mariners TL Dave Valle	.03	.01	.00
☐ 460	Dave Stieb	.08	.04	.01
☐ 461	Buddy Bell	.06	.03	.00
☐ 462	Jose Guzman	.03	.01	.00
☐ 463	Steve Lake	.03	.01	.00
☐ 464	Bryn Smith	.06	.03	.00
☐ 465	Mark Grace	2.50	1.25	.25
☐ 466	Chuck Crim	.03	.01	.00
☐ 467	Jim Walewander	.03	.01	.00
☐ 468	Henry Cotto	.03	.01	.00
☐ 469	Jose Bautista	.10	.05	.01
☐ 470	Lance Parrish	.08	.04	.01
☐ 471	Steve Curry	.10	.05	.01

☐ 472	Brian Harper	.03	.01	.00
☐ 473	Don Robinson	.03	.01	.00
☐ 474	Bob Rodgers MG	.06	.03	.00
	(team checklist back)			
☐ 475	Dave Parker	.08	.04	.01
☐ 476	Jon Perlman	.08	.04	.01
☐ 477	Dick Schofield	.03	.01	.00
☐ 478	Doug Drabek	.06	.03	.00
☐ 479	Mike Macfarlane	.12	.06	.01
☐ 480	Keith Hernandez	.10	.05	.01
☐ 481	Chris Brown	.03	.01	.00
☐ 482	Steve Peters	.10	.05	.01
☐ 483	Mickey Hatcher	.03	.01	.00
☐ 484	Steve Shields	.03	.01	.00
☐ 485	Hubie Brooks	.06	.03	.00
☐ 486	Jack McDowell	.10	.05	.01
☐ 487	Scott Lusader	.08	.04	.01
☐ 488	Kevin Coffman	.08	.04	.01
	("Now with Cubs")			
☐ 489	Phila. Phillies TL	.12	.06	.01
	Mike Schmidt			
☐ 490	Chris Sabo	.40	.20	.04
☐ 491	Mike Birkbeck	.03	.01	.00
☐ 492	Alan Ashby	.03	.01	.00
☐ 493	Todd Benzinger	.03	.01	.00
☐ 494	Shane Rawley	.03	.01	.00
☐ 495	Candy Maldonado	.03	.01	.00
☐ 496	Dwayne Henry	.03	.01	.00
☐ 497	Pete Stanicek	.08	.04	.01
☐ 498	Dave Valle	.03	.01	.00
☐ 499	Don Heinkel	.08	.04	.01
☐ 500	Jose Canseco	.80	.40	.08
☐ 501	Vance Law	.03	.01	.00
☐ 502	Duane Ward	.03	.01	.00
☐ 503	Al Newman	.03	.01	.00
☐ 504	Bob Walk	.03	.01	.00
☐ 505	Pete Rose MG	.25	.12	.02
	(team checklist back)			
☐ 506	Kirt Manwaring	.08	.04	.01
☐ 507	Steve Farr	.03	.01	.00
☐ 508	Wally Backman	.03	.01	.00
☐ 509	Bud Black	.03	.01	.00
☐ 510	Bob Horner	.08	.04	.01
☐ 511	Richard Dotson	.03	.01	.00
☐ 512	Donnie Hill	.03	.01	.00
☐ 513	Jesse Orosco	.03	.01	.00
☐ 514	Chet Lemon	.03	.01	.00
☐ 515	Barry Larkin	.10	.05	.01
☐ 516	Eddie Whitson	.03	.01	.00
☐ 517	Greg Brock	.03	.01	.00
☐ 518	Bruce Ruffin	.03	.01	.00
☐ 519	New York Yankees TL	.06	.03	.00
	Willie Randolph			
☐ 520	Rick Sutcliffe	.08	.04	.01
☐ 521	Mickey Tettleton	.08	.04	.01
☐ 522	Randy Kramer	.10	.05	.01
☐ 523	Andres Thomas	.03	.01	.00
☐ 524	Checklist 397-528	.06	.01	.00
☐ 525	Chili Davis	.06	.03	.00
☐ 526	Wes Gardner	.03	.01	.00
☐ 527	Dave Henderson	.06	.03	.00
☐ 528	Luis Medina	.25	.12	.02
	(lower left front			
	has white triangle)			
☐ 529	Tom Foley	.03	.01	.00
☐ 530	Nolan Ryan	.25	.12	.02
☐ 531	Dave Hengel	.10	.05	.01
☐ 532	Jerry Browne	.03	.01	.00
☐ 533	Andy Hawkins	.03	.01	.00
☐ 534	Doc Edwards MG	.06	.03	.00
	(team checklist back)			
☐ 535	Todd Worrell UER	.08	.04	.01
	(4 wins in '88,			
	should be 5)			
☐ 536	Joel Skinner	.03	.01	.00
☐ 537	Pete Smith	.10	.05	.01
☐ 538	Juan Castillo	.03	.01	.00
☐ 539	Barry Jones	.03	.01	.00
☐ 540	Bo Jackson	.50	.25	.05
☐ 541	Cecil Fielder	.03	.01	.00
☐ 542	Todd Frohwirth	.03	.01	.00
☐ 543	Damon Berryhill	.30	.15	.03
☐ 544	Jeff Sellers	.03	.01	.00
☐ 545	Mookie Wilson	.06	.03	.00
☐ 546	Mark Williamson	.03	.01	.00
☐ 547	Mark McLemore	.03	.01	.00
☐ 548	Bobby Witt	.06	.03	.00
☐ 549	Chicago Cubs TL	.03	.01	.00
	Jamie Moyer			
	(pitching)			
☐ 550	Orel Hershiser	.20	.10	.02
☐ 551	Randy Ready	.03	.01	.00
☐ 552	Greg Cadaret	.03	.01	.00
☐ 553	Luis Salazar	.03	.01	.00
☐ 554	Nick Esasky	.06	.03	.00
☐ 555	Bert Blyleven	.08	.04	.01
☐ 556	Bruce Fields	.03	.01	.00
☐ 557	Keith Miller	.03	.01	.00
	New York Mets			
☐ 558	Dan Pasqua	.03	.01	.00
☐ 559	Juan Agosto	.03	.01	.00
☐ 560	Tim Raines	.12	.06	.01
☐ 561	Luis Aguayo	.03	.01	.00
☐ 562	Danny Cox	.03	.01	.00
☐ 563	Bill Schroeder	.03	.01	.00
☐ 564	Russ Nixon MG	.06	.03	.00
	(team checklist back)			
☐ 565	Jeff Russell	.06	.03	.00
☐ 566	Al Pedrique	.03	.01	.00
☐ 567	David Wells UER	.08	.04	.01
	(Complete Pitching			
	Recor)			
☐ 568	Mickey Brantley	.06	.03	.00
☐ 569	German Jimenez	.08	.04	.01
☐ 570	Tony Gwynn UER	.15	.07	.01
	('88 average should			
	be italicized as			
	league leader)			
☐ 571	Billy Ripken	.03	.01	.00
☐ 572	Atlee Hammaker	.03	.01	.00
☐ 573	Jim Abbott FDP	2.00	1.00	.20
☐ 574	Dave Clark	.06	.03	.00
☐ 575	Juan Samuel	.08	.04	.01
☐ 576	Greg Minton	.03	.01	.00
☐ 577	Randy Bush	.03	.01	.00
☐ 578	John Morris	.03	.01	.00
☐ 579	Houston Astros TL	.06	.03	.00
	Glenn Davis			
	(batting stance)			
☐ 580	Harold Reynolds	.06	.03	.00
☐ 581	Gene Nelson	.03	.01	.00
☐ 582	Mike Marshall	.08	.04	.01
☐ 583	Paul Gibson	.10	.05	.01
☐ 584	Randy Velarde UER	.08	.04	.01
	(signed 1935,			
	should be 1985)			
☐ 585	Harold Baines	.08	.04	.01
☐ 586	Joe Boever	.03	.01	.00
☐ 587	Mike Stanley	.03	.01	.00
☐ 588	Luis Alicea	.10	.05	.01
☐ 589	Dave Meads	.03	.01	.00
☐ 590	Andres Galarraga	.10	.05	.01
☐ 591	Jeff Musselman	.03	.01	.00
☐ 592	John Cangelosi	.03	.01	.00
☐ 593	Drew Hall	.03	.01	.00
☐ 594	Jimy Williams MG	.06	.03	.00
	(team checklist back)			
☐ 595	Teddy Higuera	.06	.03	.00
☐ 596	Kurt Stillwell	.03	.01	.00
☐ 597	Terry Taylor	.12	.06	.01
☐ 598	Ken Gerhart	.03	.01	.00
☐ 599	Tom Candiotti	.03	.01	.00
☐ 600	Wade Boggs	.50	.25	.05
☐ 601	Dave Dravecky	.08	.04	.01
☐ 602	Devon White	.08	.04	.01
☐ 603	Frank Tanana	.03	.01	.00
☐ 604	Paul O'Neill	.03	.01	.00
☐ 605A	Bob Welch ERR	4.00	2.00	.40
	(missing line on back,			
	"Complete M.L.			
	Pitching Record")			
☐ 605B	Bob Welch COR	.15	.07	.01
☐ 606	Rick Dempsey	.03	.01	.00
☐ 607	Willie Ansley FDP	.35	.17	.03
☐ 608	Phil Bradley	.06	.03	.00
☐ 609	Detroit Tigers TL	.06	.03	.00
	Frank Tanana			
	(with Alan Trammell			
	and Mike Heath)			
☐ 610	Randy Myers	.06	.03	.00
☐ 611	Don Slaught	.03	.01	.00
☐ 612	Dan Quisenberry	.08	.04	.01
☐ 613	Gary Varsho	.10	.05	.01
☐ 614	Joe Hesketh	.03	.01	.00
☐ 615	Robin Yount	.15	.07	.01
☐ 616	Steve Rosenberg	.10	.05	.01
☐ 617	Mark Parent	.10	.05	.01
☐ 618	Rance Mulliniks	.03	.01	.00
☐ 619	Checklist 529-660	.06	.01	.00
☐ 620	Barry Bonds	.08	.04	.01
☐ 621	Rick Mahler	.03	.01	.00
☐ 622	Stan Javier	.03	.01	.00
☐ 623	Fred Toliver	.03	.01	.00
☐ 624	Jack McKeon MG	.06	.03	.00
	(team checklist back)			
☐ 625	Eddie Murray	.12	.06	.01
☐ 626	Jeff Reed	.03	.01	.00
☐ 627	Greg Harris	.03	.01	.00
	Philadelphia Phillies			
☐ 628	Matt Williams	.15	.07	.01

629	Pete O'Brien	.06	.03	.00
630	Mike Greenwell	.45	.22	.04
631	Dave Bergman	.03	.01	.00
632	Bryan Harvey	.18	.09	.01
633	Daryl Boston	.03	.01	.00
634	Marvin Freeman	.03	.01	.00
635	Willie Randolph	.06	.03	.00
636	Bill Wilkinson	.03	.01	.00
637	Carmen Castillo	.03	.01	.00
638	Floyd Bannister	.03	.01	.00
639	Oakland A's TL Walt Weiss	.10	.05	.01
640	Willie McGee	.08	.04	.01
641	Curt Young	.03	.01	.00
642	Argenis Salazar	.03	.01	.00
643	Louie Meadows	.08	.04	.01
644	Lloyd McClendon	.03	.01	.00
645	Jack Morris	.08	.04	.01
646	Kevin Bass	.06	.03	.00
647	Randy Johnson	.18	.09	.01
648	Sandy Alomar FS	.90	.45	.09
649	Stewart Cliburn	.03	.01	.00
650	Kirby Puckett	.25	.12	.02
651	Tom Niedenfuer	.03	.01	.00
652	Rich Gedman	.03	.01	.00
653	Tommy Barrett	.10	.05	.01
654	Whitey Herzog MG (team checklist back)	.06	.03	.00
655	Dave Magadan	.08	.04	.01
656	Ivan Calderon	.06	.03	.00
657	Joe Magrane	.08	.04	.01
658	R.J. Reynolds	.03	.01	.00
659	Al Leiter	.08	.04	.01
660	Will Clark	.50	.25	.05
661	Dwight Gooden TBC84	.12	.06	.01
662	Lou Brock TBC79	.08	.04	.01
663	Hank Aaron TBC74	.10	.05	.01
664	Gil Hodges TBC69	.08	.04	.01
665A	Tony Oliva TBC64 ERR (fabricated card) (Topps copyright missing)	2.00	1.00	.20
665B	Tony Oliva TBC64 COR (fabricated card)	.10	.05	.01
666	Randy St.Claire	.03	.01	.00
667	Dwayne Murphy	.03	.01	.00
668	Mike Bielecki	.06	.03	.00
669	L.A. Dodgers TL Orel Hershiser (mound conference with Mike Scioscia)	.15	.07	.01
670	Kevin Seitzer	.12	.06	.01
671	Jim Gantner	.03	.01	.00
672	Allan Anderson	.06	.03	.00
673	Don Baylor	.06	.03	.00
674	Otis Nixon	.03	.01	.00
675	Bruce Hurst	.08	.04	.01
676	Ernie Riles	.03	.01	.00
677	Dave Schmidt	.03	.01	.00
678	Dion James	.03	.01	.00
679	Willie Fraser	.03	.01	.00
680	Gary Carter	.12	.06	.01
681	Jeff Robinson Pittsburgh Pirates	.06	.03	.00
682	Rick Leach	.03	.01	.00
683	Jose Cecena	.08	.04	.01
684	Dave Johnson MG (team checklist back)	.06	.03	.00
685	Jeff Treadway	.10	.05	.01
686	Scott Terry	.03	.01	.00
687	Alvin Davis	.08	.04	.01
688	Zane Smith	.03	.01	.00
689A	Stan Jefferson (pink triangle on front bottom left)	.10	.05	.01
689B	Stan Jefferson (violet triangle on front bottom left)	.10	.05	.01
690	Doug Jones	.06	.03	.00
691	Roberto Kelly UER (83 Oneonita)	.25	.12	.02
692	Steve Ontiveros	.03	.01	.00
693	Pat Borders	.15	.07	.01
694	Les Lancaster	.03	.01	.00
695	Carlton Fisk	.10	.05	.01
696	Don August	.06	.03	.00
697A	Franklin Stubbs (team name on front in white)	.10	.05	.01
697B	Franklin Stubbs (team name on front in gray)	.10	.05	.01
698	Keith Atherton	.03	.01	.00
699	Pittsburgh Pirates TL Al Pedrique	.08	.04	.01

	(Tony Gwynn sliding)			
700	Don Mattingly	.75	.35	.07
701	Storm Davis	.06	.03	.00
702	Jamie Quirk	.03	.01	.00
703	Scott Garrelts	.06	.03	.00
704	Carlos Quintana	.25	.12	.02
705	Terry Kennedy	.03	.01	.00
706	Pete Incaviglia	.08	.04	.01
707	Steve Jeltz	.03	.01	.00
708	Chuck Finley	.06	.03	.00
709	Tom Herr	.03	.01	.00
710	David Cone	.15	.07	.01
711	Candy Sierra	.10	.05	.01
712	Bill Swift	.03	.01	.00
713	Ty Griffin FDP	.75	.35	.07
714	Joe Morgan MG (team checklist back)	.06	.03	.00
715	Tony Pena	.06	.03	.00
716	Wayne Tolleson	.03	.01	.00
717	Jamie Moyer	.03	.01	.00
718	Glenn Braggs	.03	.01	.00
719	Danny Darwin	.03	.01	.00
720	Tim Wallach	.06	.03	.00
721	Ron Tingley	.08	.04	.01
722	Todd Stottlemyre	.12	.06	.01
723	Rafael Belliard	.03	.01	.00
724	Jerry Don Gleaton	.03	.01	.00
725	Terry Steinbach	.08	.04	.01
726	Dickie Thon	.03	.01	.00
727	Joe Orsulak	.03	.01	.00
728	Charlie Puleo	.03	.01	.00
729	Texas Rangers TL Steve Buechele (inconsistent design, team name on front surrounded by black, should be white)	.03	.01	.00
730	Danny Jackson	.08	.04	.01
731	Mike Young	.03	.01	.00
732	Steve Buechele	.03	.01	.00
733	Randy Bockus	.08	.04	.01
734	Jody Reed	.06	.03	.00
735	Roger McDowell	.06	.03	.00
736	Jeff Hamilton	.03	.01	.00
737	Norm Charlton	.12	.06	.01
738	Darnell Coles	.03	.01	.00
739	Brook Jacoby	.06	.03	.00
740	Dan Plesac	.06	.03	.00
741	Ken Phelps	.06	.03	.00
742	Mike Harkey FS	.25	.12	.02
743	Mike Heath	.03	.01	.00
744	Roger Craig MG (team checklist back)	.06	.03	.00
745	Fred McGriff	.15	.07	.01
746	German Gonzalez UER (wrong birthdate)	.10	.05	.01
747	Will Tejada	.03	.01	.00
748	Jimmy Jones	.06	.03	.00
749	Rafael Ramirez	.03	.01	.00
750	Bret Saberhagen	.12	.06	.01
751	Ken Oberkfell	.03	.01	.00
752	Jim Gott	.03	.01	.00
753	Jose Uribe	.03	.01	.00
754	Bob Brower	.03	.01	.00
755	Mike Scioscia	.03	.01	.00
756	Scott Medvin	.10	.05	.01
757	Brady Anderson	.20	.10	.02
758	Gene Walter	.03	.01	.00
759	Milwaukee Brewers TL Rob Deer	.06	.03	.00
760	Lee Smith	.06	.03	.00
761	Dante Bichette	.18	.09	.01
762	Bobby Thigpen	.06	.03	.00
763	Dave Martinez	.03	.01	.00
764	Robin Ventura FDP	1.00	.50	.10
765	Glenn Davis	.10	.05	.01
766	Cecilio Guante	.03	.01	.00
767	Mike Capel	.12	.06	.01
768	Bill Wegman	.03	.01	.00
769	Junior Ortiz	.03	.01	.00
770	Alan Trammell	.12	.06	.01
771	Ron Kittle	.06	.03	.00
772	Ron Oester	.03	.01	.00
773	Keith Moreland	.03	.01	.00
774	Frank Robinson MG (team checklist back)	.10	.05	.01
775	Jeff Reardon	.06	.03	.00
776	Nelson Liriano	.03	.01	.00
777	Ted Power	.03	.01	.00
778	Bruce Benedict	.03	.01	.00
779	Craig McMurtry	.03	.01	.00
780	Pedro Guerrero	.10	.05	.01
781	Greg Briley	.60	.30	.06
782	Checklist 661-792	.06	.01	.00
783	Trevor Wilson	.12	.06	.01

		MINT	EXC	G-VG
☐ 784	Steve Avery FDP	.50	.25	.05
☐ 785	Ellis Burks	.25	.12	.02
☐ 786	Melido Perez	.12	.06	.01
☐ 787	Dave West	.35	.17	.03
☐ 788	Mike Morgan	.06	.03	.00
☐ 789	Kansas City Royals TL ... Bo Jackson (throwing)	.15	.07	.01
☐ 790	Sid Fernandez	.08	.04	.01
☐ 791	Jim Lindeman	.03	.01	.00
☐ 792	Rafael Santana	.06	.03	.00

1989 Topps Wax Box Cards

The cards in this 16-card set measure the standard 2 1/2" by 3 1/2". Cards have essentially the same design as the 1989 Topps regular issue set. The cards were printed on the bottoms of the regular issue wax pack boxes. These 16 cards, "lettered" A through P, are considered a separate set in their own right and are not typically included in a complete set of the regular issue 1989 Topps cards. The value of the panels uncut is slightly greater, perhaps by 25% greater, than the value of the individual cards cut up carefully. The sixteen cards in this set honor players (and one manager) who reached career milestones during the 1988 season.

		MINT	EXC	G-VG
	COMPLETE SET (16)	3.00	1.50	.30
	COMMON PLAYER (A-P)	.05	.02	.00
☐ A	George Brett 475th Double	.35	.17	.03
☐ B	Bill Buckner 2600th Hit	.10	.05	.01
☐ C	Darrell Evans 400th Home Run	.10	.05	.01
☐ D	Rich Gossage 300th Save	.10	.05	.01
☐ E	Greg Gross 125th Pinch Hit	.05	.02	.00
☐ F	Rickey Henderson 775th Stolen Base	.40	.20	.04
☐ G	Keith Hernandez 125th Game-Winning RBI	.15	.07	.01
☐ H	Tom Lasorda 1000th Managerial Win	.10	.05	.01
☐ I	Jim Rice 1400th Run Batted In	.20	.10	.02
☐ J	Cal Ripken 1000th Cons. Game	.30	.15	.03
☐ K	Nolan Ryan 4700th Strikeout	.50	.25	.05
☐ L	Mike Schmidt 1000th Long Hit	.50	.25	.05
☐ M	Bruce Sutter 300th Save	.10	.05	.01
☐ N	Don Sutton 750th Game Started	.20	.10	.02
☐ O	Kent Tekulve 1000th Appearance	.05	.02	.00
☐ P	Dave Winfield 1400th Run Batted In	.25	.12	.02

1989 Topps Glossy All-Stars 22

These glossy cards were inserted with Topps rack packs and honor the starting line-ups, managers, and honorary captains of the 1988 National and American League All-Star teams. The cards are standard size, 2 1/2" by 3 1/2" and very similar to the design Topps has used since 1984. The backs are printed in red and blue on white card stock.

		MINT	EXC	G-VG
	COMPLETE SET (22)	4.00	2.00	.40
	COMMON PLAYER (1-22)	.10	.05	.01
☐ 1	Tom Kelly MG	.10	.05	.01
☐ 2	Mark McGwire	.40	.20	.04
☐ 3	Paul Molitor	.20	.10	.02
☐ 4	Wade Boggs	.50	.25	.05
☐ 5	Cal Ripken Jr.	.25	.12	.02
☐ 6	Jose Canseco	.75	.35	.07
☐ 7	Rickey Henderson	.35	.17	.03
☐ 8	Dave Winfield	.25	.12	.02
☐ 9	Terry Steinbach	.15	.07	.01
☐ 10	Frank Viola	.15	.07	.01
☐ 11	Bobby Doerr CAPT	.15	.07	.01
☐ 12	Whitey Herzog MG	.10	.05	.01
☐ 13	Will Clark	.75	.35	.07
☐ 14	Ryne Sandberg	.25	.12	.02
☐ 15	Bobby Bonilla	.20	.10	.02
☐ 16	Ozzie Smith	.20	.10	.02
☐ 17	Vince Coleman	.20	.10	.02
☐ 18	Andre Dawson	.20	.10	.02
☐ 19	Darryl Strawberry	.40	.20	.04
☐ 20	Gary Carter	.25	.12	.02
☐ 21	Doc Gooden	.30	.15	.03
☐ 22	Willie Stargell CAPT	.20	.10	.02

1989 Topps Jumbo Rookies

Inserted in each supermarket jumbo pack is a card from this series of 22 of 1988's best rookies as determined by Topps. Jumbo packs consisted of 100 (regular issue 1989 Topps baseball) cards with a stick of gum plus the insert "Rookie" card. The card fronts are in full color and measure 2 1/2" by 3 1/2". The card backs are printed in red and blue on white card stock and are numbered at the bottom.

		MINT	EXC	G-VG
	COMPLETE SET (22)	10.00	5.00	1.00
	COMMON PLAYER (1-22)	.20	.10	.02
☐ 1	Roberto Alomar	.60	.30	.06
☐ 2	Brady Anderson	.35	.17	.03
☐ 3	Tim Belcher	.35	.17	.03
☐ 4	Damon Berryhill	.40	.20	.04
☐ 5	Jay Buhner	.40	.20	.04
☐ 6	Kevin Elster	.25	.12	.02
☐ 7	Cecil Espy	.20	.10	.02
☐ 8	Dave Gallagher	.30	.15	.03
☐ 9	Ron Gant	.35	.17	.03
☐ 10	Paul Gibson	.20	.10	.02
☐ 11	Mark Grace	1.50	.75	.15
☐ 12	Darrin Jackson	.30	.15	.03
☐ 13	Gregg Jefferies	1.50	.75	.15
☐ 14	Ricky Jordan	1.00	.50	.10
☐ 15	Al Leiter	.30	.15	.03
☐ 16	Melido Perez	.30	.15	.03
☐ 17	Chris Sabo	.60	.30	.06
☐ 18	Nelson Santovenia	.35	.17	.03
☐ 19	Mackey Sasser	.30	.15	.03
☐ 20	Gary Sheffield	.90	.45	.09
☐ 21	Walt Weiss	.60	.30	.06
☐ 22	David Wells	.25	.12	.02

☐ 26	Kevin McReynolds	.20	.10	.02
☐ 27	George Bell	.20	.10	.02
☐ 28	Bruce Hurst	.15	.07	.01
☐ 29	Mark Grace	1.00	.50	.10
☐ 30	Tim Belcher	.20	.10	.02
☐ 31	Mike Greenwell	.75	.35	.07
☐ 32	Glenn Davis	.20	.10	.02
☐ 33	Gary Gaetti	.15	.07	.01
☐ 34	Ryne Sandberg	.25	.12	.02
☐ 35	Rickey Henderson	.40	.20	.04
☐ 36	Dwight Evans	.15	.07	.01
☐ 37	Dwight Gooden	.40	.20	.04
☐ 38	Robin Yount	.50	.25	.05
☐ 39	Damon Berryhill	.30	.15	.03
☐ 40	Chris Sabo	.25	.12	.02
☐ 41	Mark McGwire	.60	.30	.06
☐ 42	Ozzie Smith	.25	.12	.02
☐ 43	Paul Molitor	.20	.10	.02
☐ 44	Andres Galarraga	.20	.10	.02
☐ 45	Dave Stewart	.20	.10	.02
☐ 46	Tom Browning	.15	.07	.01
☐ 47	Cal Ripken	.30	.15	.03
☐ 48	Orel Hershiser	.35	.17	.03
☐ 49	Dave Gallagher	.20	.10	.02
☐ 50	Walt Weiss	.30	.15	.03
☐ 51	Don Mattingly	1.00	.50	.10
☐ 52	Tony Fernandez	.15	.07	.01
☐ 53	Tim Raines	.20	.10	.02
☐ 54	Jeff Reardon	.10	.05	.01
☐ 55	Kirk Gibson	.25	.12	.02
☐ 56	Jack Clark	.20	.10	.02
☐ 57	Danny Jackson	.10	.05	.01
☐ 58	Tony Gwynn	.35	.17	.03
☐ 59	Cecil Espy	.10	.05	.01
☐ 60	Jody Reed	.10	.05	.01

1989 Topps Glossy Send-In 60

The 1989 Topps Glossy Send-In set contains 60 standard-size (2 1/2 by 3 1/2 inch) cards. The fronts have color photos with white borders; the backs are light blue. The cards were distributed through the mail by Topps in six groups of 10 cards.

		MINT	EXC	G-VG
	COMPLETE SET (60)	9.00	4.50	.90
	COMMON PLAYER (1-60)	.10	.05	.01
☐ 1	Kirby Puckett	.50	.25	.05
☐ 2	Eric Davis	.50	.25	.05
☐ 3	Joe Carter	.20	.10	.02
☐ 4	Andy Van Slyke	.15	.07	.01
☐ 5	Wade Boggs	.60	.30	.06
☐ 6	David Cone	.30	.15	.03
☐ 7	Kent Hrbek	.20	.10	.02
☐ 8	Darryl Strawberry	.50	.25	.05
☐ 9	Jay Buhner	.20	.10	.02
☐ 10	Ron Gant	.20	.10	.02
☐ 11	Will Clark	1.00	.50	.10
☐ 12	Jose Canseco	1.00	.50	.10
☐ 13	Juan Samuel	.15	.07	.01
☐ 14	George Brett	.40	.20	.04
☐ 15	Benito Santiago	.30	.15	.03
☐ 16	Dennis Eckersley	.20	.10	.02
☐ 17	Gary Carter	.25	.12	.02
☐ 18	Frank Viola	.15	.07	.01
☐ 19	Roberto Alomar	.20	.10	.02
☐ 20	Paul Gibson	.10	.05	.01
☐ 21	Dave Winfield	.25	.12	.02
☐ 22	Howard Johnson	.20	.10	.02
☐ 23	Roger Clemens	.40	.20	.04
☐ 24	Bobby Bonilla	.20	.10	.02
☐ 25	Alan Trammell	.20	.10	.02

1989 Topps Big Baseball

The 1989 Topps Big Baseball set contains 330 glossy cards measuring 2 1/2 by 3 3/4 inches. The fronts feature mug shots superimposed on action photos. The horizontally-oriented backs have color cartoons, 1988 and career stats. The set was released in three series of 110 cards. The cards were distributed in seven-card cello packs marked with the series number.

		MINT	EXC	G-VG
	COMPLETE SET (330)	30.00	15.00	3.00
	COMMON PLAYER (1-110)	.05	.02	.00
	COMMON PLAYER (111-220)	.05	.02	.00
	COMMON PLAYER (221-330)	.06	.02	.00
☐ 1	Orel Hershiser	.35	.17	.03
☐ 2	Harold Reynolds	.10	.05	.01
☐ 3	Jody Davis	.05	.02	.00
☐ 4	Greg Walker	.05	.02	.00
☐ 5	Barry Bonds	.12	.06	.01
☐ 6	Bret Saberhagen	.20	.10	.02
☐ 7	Johnny Ray	.08	.04	.01
☐ 8	Mike Fiore	.12	.06	.01
☐ 9	Juan Castillo	.05	.02	.00
☐ 10	Todd Burns	.08	.04	.01
☐ 11	Carmelo Martinez	.05	.02	.00
☐ 12	Geno Petralli	.05	.02	.00
☐ 13	Mel Hall	.08	.04	.01
☐ 14	Tom Browning	.08	.04	.01

15	Fred McGriff	.20	.10	.02
16	Kevin Elster	.12	.06	.01
17	Tim Leary	.08	.04	.01
18	Jim Rice	.20	.10	.02
19	Bret Barberie	.20	.10	.02
20	Jay Buhner	.10	.05	.01
21	Atlee Hammaker	.05	.02	.00
22	Lou Whitaker	.12	.06	.01
23	Paul Runge	.08	.04	.01
24	Carlton Fisk	.20	.10	.02
25	Jose Lind	.05	.02	.00
26	Mark Gubicza	.10	.05	.01
27	Billy Ripken	.08	.04	.01
28	Mike Pagliarulo	.05	.02	.00
29	Jim Deshaies	.05	.02	.00
30	Mark McLemore	.05	.02	.00
31	Scott Terry	.05	.02	.00
32	Franklin Stubbs	.05	.02	.00
33	Don August	.05	.02	.00
34	Mark McGwire	.60	.30	.06
35	Eric Show	.05	.02	.00
36	Cecil Espy	.08	.04	.01
37	Ron Tingley	.05	.02	.00
38	Mickey Brantley	.08	.04	.01
39	Paul O'Neill	.10	.05	.01
40	Ed Sprague	.15	.07	.01
41	Len Dykstra	.08	.04	.01
42	Roger Clemens	.40	.20	.04
43	Ron Gant	.10	.05	.01
44	Dan Pasqua	.05	.02	.00
45	Jeff Robinson	.08	.04	.01
46	George Brett	.35	.17	.03
47	Bryn Smith	.08	.04	.01
48	Mike Marshall	.10	.05	.01
49	Doug Robbins	.10	.05	.01
50	Don Mattingly	.75	.35	.07
51	Mike Scott	.15	.07	.01
52	Steve Jeltz	.05	.02	.00
53	Dick Schofield	.05	.02	.00
54	Tom Brunansky	.10	.05	.01
55	Gary Sheffield	.50	.25	.05
56	Dave Valle	.05	.02	.00
57	Carney Lansford	.12	.06	.01
58	Tony Gwynn	.30	.15	.03
59	Checklist 1-110	.05	.02	.00
60	Damon Berryhill	.12	.06	.01
61	Jack Morris	.12	.06	.01
62	Brett Butler	.08	.04	.01
63	Mickey Hatcher	.05	.02	.00
64	Bruce Sutter	.08	.04	.01
65	Robin Ventura	.40	.20	.04
66	Junior Ortiz	.05	.02	.00
67	Pat Tabler	.05	.02	.00
68	Greg Swindell	.10	.05	.01
69	Jeff Branson	.10	.05	.01
70	Manny Lee	.05	.02	.00
71	Dave Magadan	.10	.05	.01
72	Rich Gedman	.05	.02	.00
73	Tim Raines	.15	.07	.01
74	Mike Maddux	.05	.02	.00
75	Jim Presley	.05	.02	.00
76	Chuck Finley	.08	.04	.01
77	Jose Oquendo	.08	.04	.01
78	Rob Deer	.08	.04	.01
79	Jay Howell	.08	.04	.01
80	Terry Steinbach	.10	.05	.01
81	Ed Whitson	.05	.02	.00
82	Ruben Sierra	.40	.20	.04
83	Bruce Benedict	.05	.02	.00
84	Fred Manrique	.05	.02	.00
85	John Smiley	.08	.04	.01
86	Mike Macfarlane	.08	.04	.01
87	Rene Gonzales	.05	.02	.00
88	Charles Hudson	.05	.02	.00
89	Glenn Davis	.15	.07	.01
90	Les Straker	.05	.02	.00
91	Carmen Castillo	.05	.02	.00
92	Tracy Woodson	.05	.02	.00
93	Tino Martinez	.50	.25	.05
94	Herm Winningham	.05	.02	.00
95	Kelly Gruber	.08	.04	.01
96	Terry Leach	.05	.02	.00
97	Jody Reed	.08	.04	.01
98	Nelson Santovenia	.08	.04	.01
99	Tony Armas	.05	.02	.00
100	Greg Brock	.05	.02	.00
101	Dave Stewart	.12	.06	.01
102	Roberto Alomar	.20	.10	.02
103	Jim Sundberg	.05	.02	.00
104	Albert Hall	.05	.02	.00
105	Steve Lyons	.05	.02	.00
106	Sid Bream	.05	.02	.00
107	Danny Tartabull	.12	.06	.01
108	Rick Dempsey	.05	.02	.00
109	Rich Renteria	.05	.02	.00
110	Ozzie Smith	.20	.10	.02
111	Steve Sax	.15	.07	.01
112	Kelly Downs	.08	.04	.01
113	Larry Sheets	.05	.02	.00
114	Andy Benes	.50	.25	.05
115	Pete O'Brien	.08	.04	.01
116	Kevin McReynolds	.12	.06	.01
117	Juan Berenguer	.05	.02	.00
118	Billy Hatcher	.05	.02	.00
119	Rick Cerone	.05	.02	.00
120	Andre Dawson	.20	.10	.02
121	Storm Davis	.08	.04	.01
122	Devon White	.10	.05	.01
123	Alan Trammell	.15	.07	.01
124	Vince Coleman	.15	.07	.01
125	Al Leiter	.08	.04	.01
126	Dale Sveum	.05	.02	.00
127	Pete Incaviglia	.12	.06	.01
128	Dave Stieb	.12	.06	.01
129	Kevin Mitchell	.40	.20	.04
130	Dave Schmidt	.05	.02	.00
131	Gary Redus	.05	.02	.00
132	Ron Robinson	.05	.02	.00
133	Darnell Coles	.05	.02	.00
134	Benito Santiago	.20	.10	.02
135	John Farrell	.08	.04	.01
136	Willie Wilson	.10	.05	.01
137	Steve Bedrosian	.10	.05	.01
138	Don Slaught	.05	.02	.00
139	Darryl Strawberry	.50	.25	.05
140	Frank Viola	.15	.07	.01
141	Dave Silvestri	.12	.06	.01
142	Carlos Quintana	.12	.06	.01
143	Vance Law	.05	.02	.00
144	Dave Parker	.15	.07	.01
145	Tim Belcher	.15	.07	.01
146	Will Clark	1.00	.50	.10
147	Mark Williamson	.05	.02	.00
148	Ozzie Guillen	.08	.04	.01
149	Kirk McCaskill	.08	.04	.01
150	Pat Sheridan	.05	.02	.00
151	Terry Pendleton	.05	.02	.00
152	Roberto Kelly	.20	.10	.02
153	Joey Meyer	.08	.04	.01
154	Mark Grant	.05	.02	.00
155	Joe Carter	.15	.07	.01
156	Steve Buechele	.05	.02	.00
157	Tony Fernandez	.10	.05	.01
158	Jeff Reed	.05	.02	.00
159	Bobby Bonilla	.12	.06	.01
160	Henry Cotto	.05	.02	.00
161	Kurt Stillwell	.08	.04	.01
162	Mickey Morandini	.20	.10	.02
163	Robby Thompson	.05	.02	.00
164	Rick Schu	.05	.02	.00
165	Stan Jefferson	.05	.02	.00
166	Ron Darling	.10	.05	.01
167	Kirby Puckett	.40	.20	.04
168	Bill Doran	.08	.04	.01
169	Dennis Lamp	.05	.02	.00
170	Ty Griffin	.60	.30	.06
171	Ron Hassey	.05	.02	.00
172	Dale Murphy	.30	.15	.03
173	Andres Galarraga	.15	.07	.01
174	Tim Flannery	.05	.02	.00
175	Cory Snyder	.15	.07	.01
176	Checklist 111-220	.05	.02	.00
177	Tommy Barrett	.08	.04	.01
178	Dan Petry	.05	.02	.00
179	Billy Masse	.12	.06	.01
180	Terry Kennedy	.05	.02	.00
181	Joe Orsulak	.05	.02	.00
182	Doyle Alexander	.05	.02	.00
183	Willie McGee	.10	.05	.01
184	Jim Gantner	.05	.02	.00
185	Keith Hernandez	.15	.07	.01
186	Greg Gagne	.05	.02	.00
187	Kevin Bass	.08	.04	.01
188	Mark Eichhorn	.05	.02	.00
189	Mark Grace	.75	.35	.07
190	Jose Canseco	.75	.35	.07
191	Bobby Witt	.08	.04	.01
192	Rafael Santana	.05	.02	.00
193	Dwight Evans	.10	.05	.01
194	Greg Booker	.05	.02	.00
195	Brook Jacoby	.08	.04	.01
196	Rafael Belliard	.05	.02	.00
197	Candy Maldonado	.05	.02	.00
198	Mickey Tettleton	.10	.05	.01
199	Barry Larkin	.15	.07	.01
200	Frank White	.08	.04	.01
201	Wally Joyner	.15	.07	.01
202	Chet Lemon	.05	.02	.00
203	Joe Magrane	.10	.05	.01
204	Glenn Braggs	.10	.05	.01

☐ 205 Scott Fletcher	.05	.02	.00
☐ 206 Gary Ward	.05	.02	.00
☐ 207 Nelson Liriano	.05	.02	.00
☐ 208 Howard Johnson	.15	.07	.01
☐ 209 Kent Hrbek	.15	.07	.01
☐ 210 Ken Caminiti	.08	.04	.01
☐ 211 Mike Greenwell	.60	.30	.06
☐ 212 Ryne Sandberg	.25	.12	.02
☐ 213 Joe Slusarski	.15	.07	.01
☐ 214 Donell Nixon	.05	.02	.00
☐ 215 Tim Wallach	.08	.04	.01
☐ 216 John Kruk	.10	.05	.01
☐ 217 Charles Nagy	.20	.10	.02
☐ 218 Alvin Davis	.10	.05	.01
☐ 219 Oswald Peraza	.08	.04	.01
☐ 220 Mike Schmidt	.75	.35	.07
☐ 221 Spike Owen	.06	.02	.00
☐ 222 Mike Smithson	.06	.02	.00
☐ 223 Dion James	.06	.02	.00
☐ 224 Ernie Whitt	.06	.02	.00
☐ 225 Mike Davis	.06	.02	.00
☐ 226 Gene Larkin	.06	.02	.00
☐ 227 Pat Combs	.75	.35	.07
☐ 228 Jack Howell	.06	.02	.00
☐ 229 Ron Oester	.06	.02	.00
☐ 230 Paul Gibson	.06	.02	.00
☐ 231 Mookie Wilson	.08	.04	.01
☐ 232 Glenn Hubbard	.06	.02	.00
☐ 233 Shawon Dunston	.10	.05	.01
☐ 234 Otis Nixon	.06	.02	.00
☐ 235 Melido Perez	.08	.04	.01
☐ 236 Jerry Browne	.08	.04	.01
☐ 237 Rick Rhoden	.06	.02	.00
☐ 238 Bo Jackson	1.00	.50	.10
☐ 239 Randy Velarde	.06	.02	.00
☐ 240 Jack Clark	.12	.06	.01
☐ 241 Wade Boggs	.60	.30	.06
☐ 242 Lonnie Smith	.10	.05	.01
☐ 243 Mike Flanagan	.08	.04	.01
☐ 244 Willie Randolph	.08	.04	.01
☐ 245 Oddibe McDowell	.08	.04	.01
☐ 246 Ricky Jordan	.50	.25	.05
☐ 247 Greg Briley	.25	.12	.02
☐ 248 Rex Hudler	.08	.04	.01
☐ 249 Robin Yount	.40	.20	.04
☐ 250 Lance Parrish	.12	.06	.01
☐ 251 Chris Sabo	.20	.10	.02
☐ 252 Mike Henneman	.08	.04	.01
☐ 253 Gregg Jefferies	.75	.35	.07
☐ 254 Curt Young	.06	.02	.00
☐ 255 Andy Van Slyke	.12	.06	.01
☐ 256 Rod Booker	.06	.02	.00
☐ 257 Rafael Palmeiro	.15	.07	.01
☐ 258 Jose Uribe	.06	.02	.00
☐ 259 Ellis Burks	.35	.17	.03
☐ 260 John Smoltz	.25	.12	.02
☐ 261 Tom Foley	.06	.02	.00
☐ 262 Lloyd Moseby	.08	.04	.01
☐ 263 Jim Poole	.12	.06	.01
☐ 264 Gary Gaetti	.10	.05	.01
☐ 265 Bob Dernier	.06	.02	.00
☐ 266 Harold Baines	.12	.06	.01
☐ 267 Tom Candiotti	.08	.04	.01
☐ 268 Rafael Ramirez	.06	.02	.00
☐ 269 Bob Boone	.10	.05	.01
☐ 270 Buddy Bell	.08	.04	.01
☐ 271 Rickey Henderson	.40	.20	.04
☐ 272 Willie Fraser	.06	.02	.00
☐ 273 Eric Davis	.50	.25	.05
☐ 274 Jeff Robinson	.08	.04	.01
☐ 275 Damaso Garcia	.06	.02	.00
☐ 276 Sid Fernandez	.10	.05	.01
☐ 277 Stan Javier	.08	.04	.01
☐ 278 Marty Barrett	.06	.02	.00
☐ 279 Gerald Perry	.08	.04	.01
☐ 280 Rob Ducey	.08	.04	.01
☐ 281 Mike Scioscia	.06	.02	.00
☐ 282 Randy Bush	.06	.02	.00
☐ 283 Tom Herr	.06	.02	.00
☐ 284 Glenn Wilson	.06	.02	.00
☐ 285 Pedro Guerrero	.15	.07	.01
☐ 286 Cal Ripken	.25	.12	.02
☐ 287 Randy Johnson	.10	.05	.01
☐ 288 Julio Franco	.12	.06	.01
☐ 289 Ivan Calderon	.10	.05	.01
☐ 290 Rich Yett	.06	.02	.00
☐ 291 Scott Servais	.15	.07	.01
☐ 292 Bill Pecota	.06	.02	.00
☐ 293 Ken Phelps	.06	.02	.00
☐ 294 Chili Davis	.08	.04	.01
☐ 295 Manny Trillo	.06	.02	.00
☐ 296 Mike Boddicker	.06	.02	.00
☐ 297 Geronimo Berroa	.06	.02	.00
☐ 298 Todd Stottlemyre	.08	.04	.01
☐ 299 Kirk Gibson	.15	.07	.01

☐ 300 Wally Backman	.06	.02	.00
☐ 301 Hubie Brooks	.08	.04	.01
☐ 302 Von Hayes	.10	.05	.01
☐ 303 Matt Nokes	.12	.06	.01
☐ 304 Dwight Gooden	.30	.15	.03
☐ 305 Walt Weiss	.20	.10	.02
☐ 306 Mike LaValliere	.06	.02	.00
☐ 307 Cris Carpenter	.08	.04	.01
☐ 308 Ted Wood	.25	.12	.02
☐ 309 Jeff Russell	.08	.04	.01
☐ 310 Dave Gallagher	.08	.04	.01
☐ 311 Andy Allanson	.06	.02	.00
☐ 312 Craig Reynolds	.06	.02	.00
☐ 313 Kevin Seitzer	.20	.10	.02
☐ 314 Dave Winfield	.20	.10	.02
☐ 315 Andy McGaffigan	.06	.02	.00
☐ 316 Nick Esasky	.10	.05	.01
☐ 317 Jeff Blauser	.08	.04	.01
☐ 318 George Bell	.15	.07	.01
☐ 319 Eddie Murray	.20	.10	.02
☐ 320 Mark Davidson	.06	.02	.00
☐ 321 Juan Samuel	.10	.05	.01
☐ 322 Jim Abbott	1.00	.50	.10
☐ 323 Kal Daniels	.10	.05	.01
☐ 324 Mike Brumley	.08	.04	.01
☐ 325 Gary Carter	.15	.07	.01
☐ 326 Dave Henderson	.08	.04	.01
☐ 327 Checklist 221-330	.06	.02	.00
☐ 328 Garry Templeton	.08	.04	.01
☐ 329 Pat Perry	.06	.02	.00
☐ 330 Paul Molitor	.12	.06	.01

1989 Topps Mini Leaders

The 1989 Topps Mini League Leaders set contains 77 cards measuring 2 1/8 by 3 inches. The fronts have color photos with large white borders. The backs are yellow and feature 1988 and career stats. The cards were distributed in seven-card cello packs.

	MINT	EXC	G-VG
COMPLETE SET (77)	7.00	3.50	.70
COMMON PLAYER (1-77)	.05	.02	.00

☐ 1 Dale Murphy	.25	.12	.02
☐ 2 Gerald Perry	.05	.02	.00
☐ 3 Andre Dawson	.15	.07	.01
☐ 4 Greg Maddux	.10	.05	.01
☐ 5 Rafael Palmeiro	.10	.05	.01
☐ 6 Tom Browning	.10	.05	.01
☐ 7 Kal Daniels	.10	.05	.01
☐ 8 Eric Davis	.40	.20	.04
☐ 9 John Franco	.10	.05	.01
☐ 10 Danny Jackson	.05	.02	.00
☐ 11 Barry Larkin	.15	.07	.01
☐ 12 Jose Rijo	.05	.02	.00
☐ 13 Chris Sabo	.15	.07	.01
☐ 14 Mike Scott	.10	.05	.01
☐ 15 Nolan Ryan	.50	.25	.05
☐ 16 Gerald Young	.10	.05	.01
☐ 17 Kirk Gibson	.15	.07	.01
☐ 18 Orel Hershiser	.25	.12	.02
☐ 19 Steve Sax	.15	.07	.01
☐ 20 John Tudor	.10	.05	.01
☐ 21 Hubie Brooks	.05	.02	.00
☐ 22 Andres Galarraga	.15	.07	.01
☐ 23 Otis Nixon	.05	.02	.00
☐ 24 David Cone	.20	.10	.02
☐ 25 Sid Fernandez	.10	.05	.01
☐ 26 Dwight Gooden	.35	.17	.03

☐ 27 Kevin McReynolds	.15	.07	.01
☐ 28 Darryl Strawberry	.50	.25	.05
☐ 29 Juan Samuel	.10	.05	.01
☐ 30 Bobby Bonilla	.10	.05	.01
☐ 31 Sid Bream	.05	.02	.00
☐ 32 Andy Van Slyke	.10	.05	.01
☐ 33 Vince Coleman	.15	.07	.01
☐ 34 Jose DeLeon	.05	.02	.00
☐ 35 Joe Magrane	.10	.05	.01
☐ 36 Ozzie Smith	.15	.07	.01
☐ 37 Todd Worrell	.10	.05	.01
☐ 38 Tony Gwynn	.30	.15	.03
☐ 39 Brett Butler	.05	.02	.00
☐ 40 Will Clark	.75	.35	.07
☐ 41 Jim Gott	.05	.02	.00
☐ 42 Rick Reuschel	.10	.05	.01
☐ 43 Checklist Card	.05	.02	.00
☐ 44 Eddie Murray	.20	.10	.02
☐ 45 Wade Boggs	.45	.22	.04
☐ 46 Roger Clemens	.35	.17	.03
☐ 47 Dwight Evans	.10	.05	.01
☐ 48 Mike Greenwell	.40	.20	.04
☐ 49 Bruce Hurst	.10	.05	.01
☐ 50 Johnny Ray	.05	.02	.00
☐ 51 Doug Jones	.10	.05	.01
☐ 52 Greg Swindell	.10	.05	.01
☐ 53 Gary Pettis	.05	.02	.00
☐ 54 George Brett	.30	.15	.03
☐ 55 Mark Gubicza	.10	.05	.01
☐ 56 Willie Wilson	.10	.05	.01
☐ 57 Teddy Higuera	.10	.05	.01
☐ 58 Paul Molitor	.10	.05	.01
☐ 59 Robin Yount	.40	.20	.04
☐ 60 Allan Anderson	.10	.05	.01
☐ 61 Gary Gaetti	.10	.05	.01
☐ 62 Kirby Puckett	.40	.20	.04
☐ 63 Jeff Reardon	.10	.05	.01
☐ 64 Frank Viola	.15	.07	.01
☐ 65 Jack Clark	.15	.07	.01
☐ 66 Rickey Henderson	.40	.20	.04
☐ 67 Dave Winfield	.20	.10	.02
☐ 68 Jose Canseco	.75	.35	.07
☐ 69 Dennis Eckersley	.15	.07	.01
☐ 70 Mark McGwire	.50	.25	.05
☐ 71 Dave Stewart	.20	.10	.02
☐ 72 Alvin Davis	.15	.07	.01
☐ 73 Mark Langston	.20	.10	.02
☐ 74 Harold Reynolds	.05	.02	.00
☐ 75 George Bell	.15	.07	.01
☐ 76 Tony Fernandez	.10	.05	.01
☐ 77 Fred McGriff	.20	.10	.02

☐ 4 Wade Boggs	.50	.25	.05
☐ 5 Barry Bonds	.10	.05	.01
☐ 6 Bobby Bonilla	.10	.05	.01
☐ 7 George Brett	.30	.15	.03
☐ 8 Hubie Brooks	.05	.02	.00
☐ 9 Tom Brunansky	.10	.05	.01
☐ 10 Jay Buhner	.10	.05	.01
☐ 11 Brett Butler	.05	.02	.00
☐ 12 Jose Canseco	.75	.35	.07
☐ 13 Joe Carter	.15	.07	.01
☐ 14 Jack Clark	.15	.07	.01
☐ 15 Will Clark	.75	.35	.07
☐ 16 Roger Clemens	.40	.20	.04
☐ 17 David Cone	.25	.12	.02
☐ 18 Alvin Davis	.10	.05	.01
☐ 19 Eric Davis	.40	.20	.04
☐ 20 Glenn Davis	.20	.10	.02
☐ 21 Andre Dawson	.20	.10	.02
☐ 22 Bill Doran	.10	.05	.01
☐ 23 Dennis Eckersley	.15	.07	.01
☐ 24 Dwight Evans	.10	.05	.01
☐ 25 Tony Fernandez	.10	.05	.01
☐ 26 Carlton Fisk	.20	.10	.02
☐ 27 John Franco	.10	.05	.01
☐ 28 Andres Galarraga	.15	.07	.01
☐ 29 Ron Gant	.15	.07	.01
☐ 30 Kirk Gibson	.20	.10	.02
☐ 31 Dwight Gooden	.30	.15	.03
☐ 32 Mike Greenwell	.50	.25	.05
☐ 33 Mark Gubicza	.10	.05	.01
☐ 34 Pedro Guerrero	.15	.07	.01
☐ 35 Ozzie Guillen	.10	.05	.01
☐ 36 Tony Gwynn	.30	.15	.03
☐ 37 Rickey Henderson	.40	.20	.04
☐ 38 Orel Hershiser	.30	.15	.03
☐ 39 Teddy Higuera	.10	.05	.01
☐ 40 Charlie Hough	.05	.02	.00
☐ 41 Kent Hrbek	.15	.07	.01
☐ 42 Bruce Hurst	.10	.05	.01
☐ 43 Bo Jackson	.75	.35	.07
☐ 44 Gregg Jefferies	.60	.30	.06
☐ 45 Ricky Jordan	.50	.25	.05
☐ 46 Wally Joyner	.25	.12	.02
☐ 47 Mark Langston	.15	.07	.01
☐ 48 Mike Marshall	.10	.05	.01
☐ 49 Don Mattingly	.75	.35	.07
☐ 50 Fred McGriff	.25	.12	.02
☐ 51 Mark McGwire	.50	.25	.05
☐ 52 Kevin McReynolds	.15	.07	.01
☐ 53 Paul Molitor	.10	.05	.01
☐ 54 Jack Morris	.10	.05	.01
☐ 55 Dale Murphy	.25	.12	.02
☐ 56 Eddie Murray	.20	.10	.02
☐ 57 Pete O'Brien	.10	.05	.01
☐ 58 Rafael Palmeiro	.15	.07	.01
☐ 59 Gerald Perry	.05	.02	.00
☐ 60 Kirby Puckett	.50	.25	.05
☐ 61 Tim Raines	.20	.10	.02
☐ 62 Johnny Ray	.05	.02	.00
☐ 63 Rick Reuschel	.10	.05	.01
☐ 64 Cal Ripken	.25	.12	.02
☐ 65 Chris Sabo	.20	.10	.02
☐ 66 Juan Samuel	.10	.05	.01
☐ 67 Ryne Sandberg	.25	.12	.02
☐ 68 Benito Santiago	.20	.10	.02
☐ 69 Steve Sax	.15	.07	.01
☐ 70 Mike Schmidt	.75	.35	.07
☐ 71 Ruben Sierra	.50	.25	.05
☐ 72 Ozzie Smith	.25	.12	.02
☐ 73 Cory Snyder	.15	.07	.01
☐ 74 Dave Stewart	.15	.07	.01
☐ 75 Darryl Strawberry	.50	.25	.05
☐ 76 Greg Swindell	.15	.07	.01
☐ 77 Alan Trammell	.15	.07	.01
☐ 78 Fernando Valenzuela	.15	.07	.01
☐ 79 Andy Van Slyke	.10	.05	.01
☐ 80 Frank Viola	.15	.07	.01
☐ 81 Claudell Washington	.05	.02	.00
☐ 82 Walt Weiss	.20	.10	.02
☐ 83 Lou Whitaker	.15	.07	.01
☐ 84 Dave Winfield	.20	.10	.02
☐ 85 Mike Witt	.05	.02	.00
☐ 86 Gerald Young	.10	.05	.01
☐ 87 Robin Yount	.40	.20	.04
☐ 88 Checklist Card	.05	.02	.00

1989 Topps UK Mini

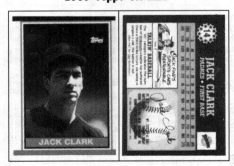

The 1989 Topps UK Mini baseball set contains 88 cards measuring 2 1/8 by 3 inches. The fronts are red, white and blue. The backs are yellow and red, and feature 1988 and career stats. The cards were distributed in five- card poly packs. The card set numbering is essentially in alphabetical order by player's name.

	MINT	EXC	G-VG
COMPLETE SET (88)	7.50	3.75	.75
COMMON PLAYER (1-88)	.05	.02	.00
☐ 1 Brady Anderson	.15	.07	.01
☐ 2 Harold Baines	.10	.05	.01
☐ 3 George Bell	.15	.07	.01

1989 Topps Ames 20/20 Club

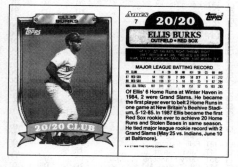

The 1989 (Topps) Ames 20/20 Club set contains 33 standard-size (2 1/2 by 3 1/2 inch) glossy cards. The fronts resemble plaques with gold and silver trim. The vertically-oriented backs show career stats. The cards were distributed at Ames department stores as a boxed set. The set was produced by Topps for Ames; the Topps logo is also on the front of each card.

			MINT	EXC	G-VG
COMPLETE SET (33)			4.00	2.00	.40
COMMON PLAYER (1-33)			.10	.05	.01
☐	1	Jesse Barfield	.10	.05	.01
☐	2	Kevin Bass	.10	.05	.01
☐	3	Don Baylor	.10	.05	.01
☐	4	George Bell	.15	.07	.01
☐	5	Barry Bonds	.10	.05	.01
☐	6	Phil Bradley	.10	.05	.01
☐	7	Ellis Burks	.25	.12	.02
☐	8	Jose Canseco	.75	.35	.07
☐	9	Joe Carter	.15	.07	.01
☐	10	Kal Daniels	.10	.05	.01
☐	11	Eric Davis	.25	.12	.02
☐	12	Mike Davis	.10	.05	.01
☐	13	Andre Dawson	.15	.07	.01
☐	14	Kirk Gibson	.15	.07	.01
☐	15	Pedro Guerrero	.15	.07	.01
☐	16	Rickey Henderson	.25	.12	.02
☐	17	Bo Jackson	.75	.35	.07
☐	18	Howard Johnson	.15	.07	.01
☐	19	Jeffrey Leonard	.10	.05	.01
☐	20	Kevin McReynolds	.10	.05	.01
☐	21	Dale Murphy	.15	.07	.01
☐	22	Dwayne Murphy	.10	.05	.01
☐	23	Dave Parker	.10	.05	.01
☐	24	Kirby Puckett	.25	.12	.02
☐	25	Juan Samuel	.10	.05	.01
☐	26	Ryne Sandberg	.20	.10	.02
☐	27	Mike Schmidt	.35	.17	.03
☐	28	Darryl Strawberry	.30	.15	.03
☐	29	Alan Trammell	.15	.07	.01
☐	30	Andy Van Slyke	.10	.05	.01
☐	31	Devon White	.10	.05	.01
☐	32	Dave Winfield	.15	.07	.01
☐	33	Robin Yount	.25	.12	.02

1989 Topps Cap'n Crunch

The 1989 Topps Cap'n Crunch set contains 22 standard-size (2 1/2 by 3 1/2 inch) cards. The fronts have red, white and blue borders surrounding "mugshot" photos. The backs are horizontally-oriented and show lifetime stats. The set was produced by Topps, but has team logos airbrushed out. Two cards were included (in a cellophane wrapper with a piece of gum) in each specially-marked Cap'n Crunch cereal box. The set was not available as a complete set as part of any mail-in offer. The set was produced by Topps.

			MINT	EXC	G-VG
COMPLETE SET (22)			16.00	8.00	1.60
COMMON PLAYER (1-22)			.50	.25	.05
☐	1	Jose Canseco	1.00	.50	.10
☐	2	Kirk Gibson	.60	.30	.06
☐	3	Orel Hershiser	.75	.35	.07
☐	4	Frank Viola	.60	.30	.06
☐	5	Tony Gwynn	.75	.35	.07
☐	6	Cal Ripken	.60	.30	.06
☐	7	Darryl Strawberry	.90	.45	.09
☐	8	Don Mattingly	1.00	.50	.10
☐	9	George Brett	.75	.35	.07
☐	10	Andre Dawson	.50	.25	.05
☐	11	Dale Murphy	.60	.30	.06
☐	12	Alan Trammell	.50	.25	.05
☐	13	Eric Davis	.75	.35	.07
☐	14	Jack Clark	.50	.25	.05
☐	15	Eddie Murray	.50	.25	.05
☐	16	Mike Schmidt	1.00	.50	.10
☐	17	Dwight Gooden	.75	.35	.07
☐	18	Roger Clemens	.75	.35	.07
☐	19	Will Clark	1.00	.50	.10
☐	20	Kirby Puckett	.90	.45	.09
☐	21	Robin Yount	.75	.35	.07
☐	22	Mark McGwire	.90	.45	.09

1989 Topps Hills Team MVP's

The 1989 Topps Hills Team MVP's set contains 33 glossy standard-size (2 1/2 by 3 1/2 inch) cards. The fronts and backs are yellow, red, white and navy. The horizontally-oriented backs are green. The cards were distributed through Hills stores as a boxed set. The set was produced by Topps although it was printed in Ireland.

			MINT	EXC	G-VG
COMPLETE SET (33)			4.50	2.25	.45
COMMON PLAYER (1-33)			.10	.05	.01
☐	1	Harold Baines	.15	.07	.01
☐	2	Wade Boggs	.40	.20	.04
☐	3	George Brett	.30	.15	.03
☐	4	Tom Brunansky	.15	.07	.01
☐	5	Jose Canseco	.75	.35	.07

		MINT	EXC	G-VG
☐ 6	Joe Carter	.15	.07	.01
☐ 7	Will Clark	.75	.35	.07
☐ 8	Roger Clemens	.35	.17	.03
☐ 9	David Cone	.20	.10	.02
☐ 10	Glenn Davis	.20	.10	.02
☐ 11	Andre Dawson	.20	.10	.02
☐ 12	Dennis Eckersley	.15	.07	.01
☐ 13	Andres Galarraga	.15	.07	.01
☐ 14	Kirk Gibson	.15	.07	.01
☐ 15	Mike Greenwell	.50	.25	.05
☐ 16	Tony Gwynn	.35	.17	.03
☐ 17	Orel Hershiser	.30	.15	.03
☐ 18	Danny Jackson	.10	.05	.01
☐ 19	Mark Langston	.15	.07	.01
☐ 20	Fred McGriff	.20	.10	.02
☐ 21	Dale Murphy	.30	.15	.03
☐ 22	Eddie Murray	.25	.12	.02
☐ 23	Kirby Puckett	.40	.20	.04
☐ 24	Johnny Ray	.10	.05	.01
☐ 25	Juan Samuel	.15	.07	.01
☐ 26	Ruben Sierra	.40	.20	.04
☐ 27	Dave Stewart	.20	.10	.02
☐ 28	Darryl Strawberry	.40	.20	.04
☐ 29	Alan Trammell	.15	.07	.01
☐ 30	Andy Van Slyke	.15	.07	.01
☐ 31	Frank Viola	.15	.07	.01
☐ 32	Dave Winfield	.20	.10	.02
☐ 33	Robin Yount	.40	.20	.04

1989 Topps Traded

The 1989 Topps Traded set contains 132 standard-size (2 1/2 by 3 1/2 inch) cards. The fronts have white borders; the horizontally-oriented backs are red and pink. From the front the cards' style is indistinguishable from the 1989 Topps regular issue. The cards were distributed as a boxed set. Topps also produced a specially boxed "glossy" edition frequently referred to as the Topps Traded Tiffany set. This year, again, Topps did not disclose the number of Tiffany sets they produced or sold but it seems that production quantities were roughly similar (or slightly smaller) to the previous two years. The checklist of cards is identical to that of the normal non-glossy cards. There are two primary distinguishing features of the Tiffany cards, white card stock reverses and high gloss obverses. These Tiffany cards are valued at approximately four times the values listed below.

		MINT	EXC	G-VG
COMPLETE SET (132)		12.50	6.25	1.25
COMMON PLAYER (1-132)		.05	.02	.00
☐ 1T	Don Aase	.10	.02	.01
☐ 2T	Jim Abbott	1.50	.75	.15
☐ 3T	Kent Anderson	.20	.10	.02
☐ 4T	Keith Atherton	.05	.02	.00
☐ 5T	Wally Backman	.05	.02	.00
☐ 6T	Steve Balboni	.05	.02	.00
☐ 7T	Jesse Barfield	.10	.05	.01
☐ 8T	Steve Bedrosian	.10	.05	.01
☐ 9T	Todd Benzinger	.10	.05	.01
☐ 10T	Geronimo Berroa	.10	.05	.01
☐ 11T	Bert Blyleven	.15	.07	.01
☐ 12T	Bob Boone	.15	.07	.01
☐ 13T	Phil Bradley	.10	.05	.01
☐ 14T	Jeff Brantley	.20	.10	.02
☐ 15T	Kevin Brown	.20	.10	.02
☐ 16T	Jerry Browne	.10	.05	.01
☐ 17T	Chuck Cary	.10	.05	.01
☐ 18T	Carmen Castillo	.05	.02	.00
☐ 19T	Jim Clancy	.05	.02	.00
☐ 20T	Jack Clark	.12	.06	.01
☐ 21T	Bryan Clutterbuck	.05	.02	.00
☐ 22T	Jody Davis	.05	.02	.00
☐ 23T	Mike Devereaux	.15	.07	.01
☐ 24T	Frank DiPino	.05	.02	.00
☐ 25T	Benny Distefano	.05	.02	.00
☐ 26T	John Dopson	.10	.05	.01
☐ 27T	Len Dykstra	.10	.05	.01
☐ 28T	Jim Eisenreich	.10	.05	.01
☐ 29T	Nick Esasky	.15	.07	.01
☐ 30T	Alvaro Espinoza	.10	.05	.01
☐ 31T	Darrell Evans	.10	.05	.01
☐ 32T	Junior Felix	1.00	.50	.10
☐ 33T	Felix Fermin	.05	.02	.00
☐ 34T	Julio Franco	.15	.07	.01
☐ 35T	Terry Francona	.05	.02	.00
☐ 36T	Cito Gaston MG	.10	.05	.01
☐ 37T	Bob Geren UER (photo actually Mike Fennell)	.60	.30	.06
☐ 38T	Tom Gordon	1.00	.50	.10
☐ 39T	Tommy Gregg	.10	.05	.01
☐ 40T	Ken Griffey Sr.	.15	.07	.01
☐ 41T	Ken Griffey Jr.	3.00	1.50	.30
☐ 42T	Kevin Gross	.05	.02	.00
☐ 43T	Lee Guetterman	.05	.02	.00
☐ 44T	Mel Hall	.10	.05	.01
☐ 45T	Erik Hanson	.20	.10	.02
☐ 46T	Gene Harris	.30	.15	.03
☐ 47T	Andy Hawkins	.10	.05	.01
☐ 48T	Rickey Henderson	.35	.17	.03
☐ 49T	Tom Herr	.10	.05	.01
☐ 50T	Ken Hill	.20	.10	.02
☐ 51T	Brian Holman	.20	.10	.02
☐ 52T	Brian Holton	.10	.05	.01
☐ 53T	Art Howe MG	.05	.02	.00
☐ 54T	Ken Howell	.05	.02	.00
☐ 55T	Bruce Hurst	.10	.05	.01
☐ 56T	Chris James	.10	.05	.01
☐ 57T	Randy Johnson	.15	.07	.01
☐ 58T	Jimmy Jones	.05	.02	.00
☐ 59T	Terry Kennedy	.05	.02	.00
☐ 60T	Paul Kilgus	.05	.02	.00
☐ 61T	Eric King	.05	.02	.00
☐ 62T	Ron Kittle	.10	.05	.01
☐ 63T	John Kruk	.10	.05	.01
☐ 64T	Randy Kutcher	.05	.02	.00
☐ 65T	Steve Lake	.05	.02	.00
☐ 66T	Mark Langston	.25	.12	.02
☐ 67T	Dave LaPoint	.05	.02	.00
☐ 68T	Rick Leach	.05	.02	.00
☐ 69T	Terry Leach	.10	.05	.01
☐ 70T	Jim Lefebvre MG	.05	.02	.00
☐ 71T	Al Leiter	.10	.05	.01
☐ 72T	Jeffrey Leonard	.10	.05	.01
☐ 73T	Derek Lilliquist	.20	.10	.02
☐ 74T	Rick Mahler	.05	.02	.00
☐ 75T	Tom McCarthy	.15	.07	.01
☐ 76T	Lloyd McClendon	.10	.05	.01
☐ 77T	Lance McCullers	.10	.05	.01
☐ 78T	Oddibe McDowell	.10	.05	.01
☐ 79T	Roger McDowell	.10	.05	.01
☐ 80T	Larry McWilliams	.05	.02	.00
☐ 81T	Randy Milligan	.10	.05	.01
☐ 82T	Mike Moore	.10	.05	.01
☐ 83T	Keith Moreland	.05	.02	.00
☐ 84T	Mike Morgan	.10	.05	.01
☐ 85T	Jamie Moyer	.05	.02	.00
☐ 86T	Rob Murphy	.05	.02	.00
☐ 87T	Eddie Murray	.12	.06	.01
☐ 88T	Pete O'Brien	.10	.05	.01
☐ 89T	Gregg Olson	.75	.35	.07
☐ 90T	Steve Ontiveros	.05	.02	.00
☐ 91T	Jesse Orosco	.05	.02	.00
☐ 92T	Spike Owen	.05	.02	.00
☐ 93T	Rafael Palmeiro	.12	.06	.01
☐ 94T	Clay Parker	.25	.12	.02
☐ 95T	Jeff Parrett	.10	.05	.01
☐ 96T	Lance Parrish	.10	.05	.01
☐ 97T	Dennis Powell	.05	.02	.00
☐ 98T	Rey Quinones	.05	.02	.00
☐ 99T	Doug Rader MG	.05	.02	.00
☐ 100T	Willie Randolph	.10	.05	.01
☐ 101T	Shane Rawley	.05	.02	.00
☐ 102T	Randy Ready	.05	.02	.00
☐ 103T	Bip Roberts	.10	.05	.01
☐ 104T	Kenny Rogers	.20	.10	.02

		MINT	EXC	G-VG
☐ 105T	Ed Romero	.05	.02	.00
☐ 106T	Nolan Ryan	1.25	.60	.12
☐ 107T	Luis Salazar	.05	.02	.00
☐ 108T	Juan Samuel	.15	.07	.01
☐ 109T	Alex Sanchez	.25	.12	.02
☐ 110T	Deion Sanders	1.00	.50	.10
☐ 111T	Steve Sax	.12	.06	.01
☐ 112T	Rick Schu	.05	.02	.00
☐ 113T	Dwight Smith	1.50	.75	.15
☐ 114T	Lonnie Smith	.15	.07	.01
☐ 115T	Billy Spiers	.35	.17	.03
☐ 116T	Kent Tekulve	.05	.02	.00
☐ 117T	Walt Terrell	.05	.02	.00
☐ 118T	Milt Thompson	.05	.02	.00
☐ 119T	Dickie Thon	.05	.02	.00
☐ 120T	Jeff Torborg MG	.05	.02	.00
☐ 121T	Jeff Treadway	.05	.02	.00
☐ 122T	Omar Vizquel	.25	.12	.02
☐ 123T	Jerome Walton	3.50	1.75	.35
☐ 124T	Gary Ward	.05	.02	.00
☐ 125T	Claudell Washington	.10	.05	.01
☐ 126T	Curt Wilkerson	.05	.02	.00
☐ 127T	Eddie Williams	.05	.02	.00
☐ 128T	Frank Williams	.05	.02	.00
☐ 129T	Ken Williams	.10	.05	.01
☐ 130T	Mitch Williams	.20	.10	.02
☐ 131T	Steve Wilson	.15	.07	.01
☐ 132T	Checklist 1T-132T	.05	.01	.00

1990 Topps

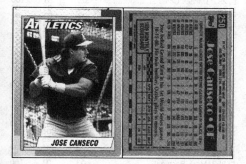

JOSE CANSECO

The 1990 Topps set contains 792 standard- size (2 1/2 by 3 1/2 inch) cards. The front borders are various colors. The horizontally-oriented backs are yellowish green. Cards 385-407 contain the All-Stars. Cards 661-665 contain the Turn Back the Clock cards. The manager cards this year contain information that had been on the backs of the Team Leader cards in the past few years; the Team Leader cards were discontinued, apparently in order to allow better individual player card selection. Topps really concentrated on individual player cards in this set with 725, the most ever in a baseball card set. The checklist cards are oriented alphabetically by team name and player name.

		MINT	EXC	G-VG
COMPLETE SET (792)		24.00	12.00	2.40
COMMON PLAYER (1-792)		.03	.01	.00
☐ 1	Nolan Ryan	.30	.10	.02
☐ 2	Nolan Ryan Salute New York Mets	.12	.06	.01
☐ 3	Nolan Ryan Salute California Angels	.12	.06	.01
☐ 4	Nolan Ryan Salute Houston Astros	.12	.06	.01
☐ 5	Nolan Ryan Salute Texas Rangers	.12	.06	.01
☐ 6	Vince Coleman RB (50 consecutive stolen bases)	.08	.04	.01
☐ 7	Rickey Henderson RB (40 career leadoff home runs)	.10	.05	.01
☐ 8	Cal Ripken RB (20 or more homers for 8 consecutive years, record for shortstops)	.08	.04	.01

		MINT	EXC	G-VG
☐ 9	Eric Plunk	.03	.01	.00
☐ 10	Barry Larkin	.08	.04	.01
☐ 11	Paul Gibson	.03	.01	.00
☐ 12	Joe Girardi	.10	.05	.01
☐ 13	Mark Williamson	.03	.01	.00
☐ 14	Mike Fetters	.15	.07	.01
☐ 15	Teddy Higuera	.06	.03	.00
☐ 16	Kent Anderson	.10	.05	.01
☐ 17	Kelly Downs	.03	.01	.00
☐ 18	Carlos Quintana	.06	.03	.00
☐ 19	Al Newman	.03	.01	.00
☐ 20	Mark Gubicza	.06	.03	.00
☐ 21	Jeff Torborg MG	.03	.01	.00
☐ 22	Bruce Ruffin	.03	.01	.00
☐ 23	Randy Velarde	.03	.01	.00
☐ 24	Joe Hesketh	.03	.01	.00
☐ 25	Willie Randolph	.06	.03	.00
☐ 26	Don Slaught	.03	.01	.00
☐ 27	Rick Leach	.03	.01	.00
☐ 28	Duane Ward	.03	.01	.00
☐ 29	John Cangelosi	.03	.01	.00
☐ 30	David Cone	.10	.05	.01
☐ 31	Henry Cotto	.03	.01	.00
☐ 32	John Farrell	.03	.01	.00
☐ 33	Greg Walker	.03	.01	.00
☐ 34	Tony Fossas	.10	.05	.01
☐ 35	Benito Santiago	.10	.05	.01
☐ 36	John Costello	.03	.01	.00
☐ 37	Domingo Ramos	.03	.01	.00
☐ 38	Wes Gardner	.03	.01	.00
☐ 39	Curt Ford	.03	.01	.00
☐ 40	Jay Howell	.03	.01	.00
☐ 41	Matt Williams	.10	.05	.01
☐ 42	Jeff Robinson	.06	.03	.00
☐ 43	Dante Bichette	.03	.01	.00
☐ 44	Roger Salkeld FDP	.20	.10	.02
☐ 45	Dave Parker	.08	.04	.01
☐ 46	Rob Dibble	.06	.03	.00
☐ 47	Brian Harper	.03	.01	.00
☐ 48	Zane Smith	.03	.01	.00
☐ 49	Tom Lawless	.03	.01	.00
☐ 50	Glenn Davis	.08	.04	.01
☐ 51	Doug Rader MG	.03	.01	.00
☐ 52	Jack Daugherty	.12	.06	.01
☐ 53	Mike LaCoss	.03	.01	.00
☐ 54	Joel Skinner	.03	.01	.00
☐ 55	Darrell Evans	.06	.03	.00
☐ 56	Franklin Stubbs	.03	.01	.00
☐ 57	Greg Vaughn	1.25	.60	.12
☐ 58	Keith Miller	.03	.01	.00
☐ 59	Ted Power	.03	.01	.00
☐ 60	George Brett	.12	.06	.01
☐ 61	Deion Sanders	.40	.20	.04
☐ 62	Ramon Martinez	.08	.04	.01
☐ 63	Mike Pagliarulo	.06	.03	.00
☐ 64	Danny Darwin	.03	.01	.00
☐ 65	Devon White	.08	.04	.01
☐ 66	Greg Litton	.20	.10	.02
☐ 67	Scott Sanderson	.03	.01	.00
☐ 68	Dave Henderson	.03	.01	.00
☐ 69	Todd Frohwirth	.03	.01	.00
☐ 70	Mike Greenwell	.20	.10	.02
☐ 71	Allan Anderson	.06	.03	.00
☐ 72	Jeff Huson	.12	.06	.01
☐ 73	Bob Milacki	.06	.03	.00
☐ 74	Jeff Jackson FDP	.25	.12	.02
☐ 75	Doug Jones	.06	.03	.00
☐ 76	Dave Valle	.03	.01	.00
☐ 77	Dave Bergman	.03	.01	.00
☐ 78	Mike Flanagan	.03	.01	.00
☐ 79	Ron Kittle	.06	.03	.00
☐ 80	Jeff Russell	.06	.03	.00
☐ 81	Bob Rodgers MG	.03	.01	.00
☐ 82	Scott Terry	.03	.01	.00
☐ 83	Hensley Meulens	.20	.10	.02
☐ 84	Ray Searage	.03	.01	.00
☐ 85	Juan Samuel	.06	.03	.00
☐ 86	Paul Kilgus	.03	.01	.00
☐ 87	Rick Luecken	.12	.06	.01
☐ 88	Glenn Braggs	.06	.03	.00
☐ 89	Clint Zavaras	.12	.06	.01
☐ 90	Jack Clark	.08	.04	.01
☐ 91	Steve Frey	.12	.06	.01
☐ 92	Mike Stanley	.03	.01	.00
☐ 93	Shawn Hillegas	.03	.01	.00
☐ 94	Herm Winningham	.03	.01	.00
☐ 95	Todd Worrell	.08	.04	.01
☐ 96	Jody Reed	.03	.01	.00
☐ 97	Curt Schilling	.08	.04	.01
☐ 98	Jose Gonzalez	.06	.03	.00
☐ 99	Rich Monteleone	.10	.05	.01
☐ 100	Will Clark	.50	.25	.05
☐ 101	Shane Rawley	.03	.01	.00
☐ 102	Stan Javier	.03	.01	.00
☐ 103	Marvin Freeman	.03	.01	.00

☐ 104 Bob Knepper	.03	.01	.00	
☐ 105 Randy Myers	.06	.03	.00	
☐ 106 Charlie O'Brien	.03	.01	.00	
☐ 107 Fred Lynn	.06	.03	.00	
☐ 108 Rod Nichols	.03	.01	.00	
☐ 109 Roberto Kelly	.08	.04	.01	
☐ 110 Tommy Helms MG	.03	.01	.00	
☐ 111 Ed Whited	.15	.07	.01	
☐ 112 Glenn Wilson	.03	.01	.00	
☐ 113 Manny Lee	.03	.01	.00	
☐ 114 Mike Bielecki	.06	.03	.00	
☐ 115 Tony Pena	.06	.03	.00	
☐ 116 Floyd Bannister	.03	.01	.00	
☐ 117 Mike Sharperson	.03	.01	.00	
☐ 118 Erik Hanson	.10	.05	.01	
☐ 119 Billy Hatcher	.03	.01	.00	
☐ 120 John Franco	.06	.03	.00	
☐ 121 Robin Ventura	.25	.12	.02	
☐ 122 Shawn Abner	.03	.01	.00	
☐ 123 Rich Gedman	.03	.01	.00	
☐ 124 Dave Dravecky	.06	.03	.00	
☐ 125 Kent Hrbek	.08	.04	.01	
☐ 126 Randy Kramer	.03	.01	.00	
☐ 127 Mike Devereaux	.06	.03	.00	
☐ 128 Checklist 1	.06	.01	.00	
☐ 129 Ron Jones	.06	.03	.00	
☐ 130 Bert Blyleven	.08	.04	.01	
☐ 131 Matt Nokes	.06	.03	.00	
☐ 132 Lance Blankenship	.08	.04	.01	
☐ 133 Ricky Horton	.03	.01	.00	
☐ 134 Earl Cunningham FDP	.35	.17	.03	
☐ 135 Dave Magadan	.06	.03	.00	
☐ 136 Kevin Brown	.10	.05	.01	
☐ 137 Marty Pevey	.10	.05	.01	
☐ 138 Al Leiter	.06	.03	.00	
☐ 139 Greg Brock	.03	.01	.00	
☐ 140 Andre Dawson	.08	.04	.01	
☐ 141 John Hart MG	.03	.01	.00	
☐ 142 Jeff Wetherby	.12	.06	.01	
☐ 143 Rafael Belliard	.03	.01	.00	
☐ 144 Bud Black	.03	.01	.00	
☐ 145 Terry Steinbach	.06	.03	.00	
☐ 146 Rob Richie	.15	.07	.01	
☐ 147 Chuck Finley	.06	.03	.00	
☐ 148 Edgar Martinez	.03	.01	.00	
☐ 149 Steve Farr	.03	.01	.00	
☐ 150 Kirk Gibson	.08	.04	.01	
☐ 151 Rick Mahler	.03	.01	.00	
☐ 152 Lonnie Smith	.06	.03	.00	
☐ 153 Randy Milligan	.06	.03	.00	
☐ 154 Mike Maddux	.03	.01	.00	
☐ 155 Ellis Burks	.15	.07	.01	
☐ 156 Ken Patterson	.03	.01	.00	
☐ 157 Craig Biggio	.08	.04	.01	
☐ 158 Craig Lefferts	.03	.01	.00	
☐ 159 Mike Felder	.03	.01	.00	
☐ 160 Dave Righetti	.08	.04	.01	
☐ 161 Harold Reynolds	.06	.03	.00	
☐ 162 Todd Zeile	1.25	.60	.12	
☐ 163 Phil Bradley	.06	.03	.00	
☐ 164 Jeff Juden FDP	.25	.12	.02	
☐ 165 Walt Weiss	.08	.04	.01	
☐ 166 Bobby Witt	.06	.03	.00	
☐ 167 Kevin Appier	.12	.06	.01	
☐ 168 Jose Lind	.03	.01	.00	
☐ 169 Richard Dotson	.03	.01	.00	
☐ 170 George Bell	.08	.04	.01	
☐ 171 Russ Nixon MG	.03	.01	.00	
☐ 172 Tom Lampkin	.06	.03	.00	
☐ 173 Tim Belcher	.06	.03	.00	
☐ 174 Jeff Kunkel	.03	.01	.00	
☐ 175 Mike Moore	.06	.03	.00	
☐ 176 Luis Quinones	.03	.01	.00	
☐ 177 Mike Henneman	.03	.01	.00	
☐ 178 Chris James	.06	.03	.00	
☐ 179 Brian Holton	.03	.01	.00	
☐ 180 Tim Raines	.10	.05	.01	
☐ 181 Juan Agosto	.03	.01	.00	
☐ 182 Mookie Wilson	.06	.03	.00	
☐ 183 Steve Lake	.03	.01	.00	
☐ 184 Danny Cox	.03	.01	.00	
☐ 185 Ruben Sierra	.20	.10	.02	
☐ 186 Dave LaPoint	.03	.01	.00	
☐ 187 Rick Wrona	.15	.07	.01	
☐ 188 Mike Smithson	.03	.01	.00	
☐ 189 Dick Schofield	.03	.01	.00	
☐ 190 Rick Reuschel	.06	.03	.00	
☐ 191 Pat Borders	.03	.01	.00	
☐ 192 Don August	.03	.01	.00	
☐ 193 Andy Benes	.30	.15	.03	
☐ 194 Glenallen Hill	.20	.10	.02	
☐ 195 Tim Burke	.06	.03	.00	
☐ 196 Gerald Young	.03	.01	.00	
☐ 197 Doug Drabek	.03	.01	.00	
☐ 198 Mike Marshall	.08	.04	.01	
☐ 199 Sergio Valdez	.12	.06	.01	
☐ 200 Don Mattingly	.50	.25	.05	
☐ 201 Cito Gaston MG	.06	.03	.00	
☐ 202 Mike Macfarlane	.03	.01	.00	
☐ 203 Mike Roesler	.10	.05	.01	
☐ 204 Bob Dernier	.03	.01	.00	
☐ 205 Mark Davis	.08	.04	.01	
☐ 206 Nick Esasky	.06	.03	.00	
☐ 207 Bob Ojeda	.06	.03	.00	
☐ 208 Brook Jacoby	.06	.03	.00	
☐ 209 Greg Mathews	.03	.01	.00	
☐ 210 Ryne Sandberg	.10	.05	.01	
☐ 211 John Cerutti	.03	.01	.00	
☐ 212 Joe Orsulak	.03	.01	.00	
☐ 213 Scott Bankhead	.06	.03	.00	
☐ 214 Terry Francona	.03	.01	.00	
☐ 215 Kirk McCaskill	.03	.01	.00	
☐ 216 Ricky Jordan	.20	.10	.02	
☐ 217 Don Robinson	.03	.01	.00	
☐ 218 Wally Backman	.03	.01	.00	
☐ 219 Donn Pall	.03	.01	.00	
☐ 220 Barry Bonds	.08	.04	.01	
☐ 221 Gary Mielke	.10	.05	.01	
☐ 222 Kurt Stillwell	.03	.01	.00	
☐ 223 Tommy Gregg	.08	.04	.01	
☐ 224 Delino DeShields	.30	.15	.03	
☐ 225 Jim Deshaies	.03	.01	.00	
☐ 226 Mickey Hatcher	.03	.01	.00	
☐ 227 Kevin Tapani	.15	.07	.01	
☐ 228 Dave Martinez	.03	.01	.00	
☐ 229 David Wells	.03	.01	.00	
☐ 230 Keith Hernandez	.08	.04	.01	
☐ 231 Jack McKeon MG	.03	.01	.00	
☐ 232 Darnell Coles	.03	.01	.00	
☐ 233 Ken Hill	.06	.03	.00	
☐ 234 Mariano Duncan	.03	.01	.00	
☐ 235 Jeff Reardon	.06	.03	.00	
☐ 236 Hal Morris	.08	.04	.01	
☐ 237 Kevin Ritz	.15	.07	.01	
☐ 238 Felix Jose	.08	.04	.01	
☐ 239 Eric Show	.03	.01	.00	
☐ 240 Mark Grace	.30	.15	.03	
☐ 241 Mike Krukow	.03	.01	.00	
☐ 242 Fred Manrique	.03	.01	.00	
☐ 243 Barry Jones	.03	.01	.00	
☐ 244 Bill Schroeder	.03	.01	.00	
☐ 245 Roger Clemens	.20	.10	.02	
☐ 246 Jim Eisenreich	.03	.01	.00	
☐ 247 Jerry Reed	.03	.01	.00	
☐ 248 Dave Anderson	.03	.01	.00	
☐ 249 Mike Smith	.12	.06	.01	
☐ 250 Jose Canseco	.50	.25	.05	
☐ 251 Jeff Blauser	.03	.01	.00	
☐ 252 Otis Nixon	.03	.01	.00	
☐ 253 Mark Portugal	.03	.01	.00	
☐ 254 Francisco Cabrera	.15	.07	.01	
☐ 255 Bobby Thigpen	.06	.03	.00	
☐ 256 Marvell Wynne	.03	.01	.00	
☐ 257 Jose DeLeon	.06	.03	.00	
☐ 258 Barry Lyons	.03	.01	.00	
☐ 259 Lance McCullers	.03	.01	.00	
☐ 260 Eric Davis	.20	.10	.02	
☐ 261 Whitey Herzog MG	.03	.01	.00	
☐ 262 Checklist 2	.06	.01	.00	
☐ 263 Mel Stottlemyre Jr.	.10	.05	.01	
☐ 264 Bryan Clutterbuck	.03	.01	.00	
☐ 265 Pete O'Brien	.06	.03	.00	
☐ 266 German Gonzalez	.03	.01	.00	
☐ 267 Mark Davidson	.03	.01	.00	
☐ 268 Rob Murphy	.03	.01	.00	
☐ 269 Dickie Thon	.03	.01	.00	
☐ 270 Dave Stewart	.08	.04	.01	
☐ 271 Chet Lemon	.03	.01	.00	
☐ 272 Bryan Harvey	.03	.01	.00	
☐ 273 Bobby Bonilla	.08	.04	.01	
☐ 274 Mauro Gozzo	.15	.07	.01	
☐ 275 Mickey Tettleton	.06	.03	.00	
☐ 276 Gary Thurman	.03	.01	.00	
☐ 277 Lenny Harris	.08	.04	.01	
☐ 278 Pascual Perez	.06	.03	.00	
☐ 279 Steve Buechele	.03	.01	.00	
☐ 280 Lou Whitaker	.08	.04	.01	
☐ 281 Kevin Bass	.06	.03	.00	
☐ 282 Derek Lilliquist	.08	.04	.01	
☐ 283 Joey Belle	.50	.25	.05	
☐ 284 Mark Gardner	.12	.06	.01	
☐ 285 Willie McGee	.08	.04	.01	
☐ 286 Lee Guetterman	.03	.01	.00	
☐ 287 Vance Law	.03	.01	.00	
☐ 288 Greg Briley	.15	.07	.01	
☐ 289 Norm Charlton	.03	.01	.00	
☐ 290 Robin Yount	.25	.12	.02	
☐ 291 Dave Johnson MG	.03	.01	.00	
☐ 292 Jim Gott	.03	.01	.00	
☐ 293 Mike Gallego	.03	.01	.00	

RETAIL STORE OWNERS

Write on your letterhead or call to find out how you can increase your profits by carrying MARVEL COMICS. MARVEL COMICS are released every week, are high profit sales and are bought primarily by males between the ages of 10 to 25. Act now to get comics into your store.

COMICS UNLIMITED LTD.
6833-BB Amboy Road
Staten Island, NY 10309
(718) 948-2223

☐ 294 Craig McMurtry	.03	.01	.00
☐ 295 Fred McGriff	.10	.05	.01
☐ 296 Jeff Ballard	.06	.03	.00
☐ 297 Tommy Herr	.03	.01	.00
☐ 298 Dan Gladden	.03	.01	.00
☐ 299 Adam Peterson	.06	.03	.00
☐ 300 Bo Jackson	.40	.20	.04
☐ 301 Don Aase	.03	.01	.00
☐ 302 Marcus Lawton	.20	.10	.02
☐ 303 Rick Cerone	.03	.01	.00
☐ 304 Marty Clary	.03	.01	.00
☐ 305 Eddie Murray	.10	.05	.01
☐ 306 Tom Niedenfuer	.03	.01	.00
☐ 307 Bip Roberts	.03	.01	.00
☐ 308 Jose Guzman	.03	.01	.00
☐ 309 Eric Yelding	.10	.05	.01
☐ 310 Steve Bedrosian	.06	.03	.00
☐ 311 Dwight Smith	.50	.25	.05
☐ 312 Dan Quisenberry	.06	.03	.00
☐ 313 Gus Polidor	.03	.01	.00
☐ 314 Donald Harris FDP	.30	.15	.03
☐ 315 Bruce Hurst	.06	.03	.00
☐ 316 Carney Lansford	.08	.04	.01
☐ 317 Mark Guthrie	.15	.07	.01
☐ 318 Wallace Johnson	.03	.01	.00
☐ 319 Dion James	.03	.01	.00
☐ 320 Dave Stieb	.08	.04	.01
☐ 321 Joe Morgan MG	.03	.01	.00
☐ 322 Junior Ortiz	.03	.01	.00
☐ 323 Willie Wilson	.06	.03	.00
☐ 324 Pete Harnisch	.06	.03	.00
☐ 325 Robby Thompson	.03	.01	.00
☐ 326 Tom McCarthy	.10	.05	.01
☐ 327 Ken Williams	.03	.01	.00
☐ 328 Curt Young	.03	.01	.00
☐ 329 Oddibe McDowell	.06	.03	.00
☐ 330 Ron Darling	.08	.04	.01
☐ 331 Juan Gonzalez	.50	.25	.05
☐ 332 Paul O'Neill	.08	.04	.01
☐ 333 Bill Wegman	.03	.01	.00
☐ 334 Johnny Ray	.06	.03	.00
☐ 335 Andy Hawkins	.03	.01	.00
☐ 336 Ken Griffey Jr.	1.25	.60	.12
☐ 337 Lloyd McClendon	.03	.01	.00
☐ 338 Dennis Lamp	.03	.01	.00
☐ 339 Dave Clark	.03	.01	.00
☐ 340 Fernando Valenzuela	.10	.05	.01
☐ 341 Tom Foley	.03	.01	.00
☐ 342 Alex Trevino	.03	.01	.00
☐ 343 Frank Tanana	.03	.01	.00
☐ 344 George Canale	.15	.07	.01
☐ 345 Harold Baines	.08	.04	.01
☐ 346 Jim Presley	.03	.01	.00
☐ 347 Junior Felix	.30	.15	.03
☐ 348 Gary Wayne	.10	.05	.01
☐ 349 Steve Finley	.10	.05	.01
☐ 350 Bret Saberhagen	.10	.05	.01
☐ 351 Roger Craig MG	.03	.01	.00
☐ 352 Bryn Smith	.06	.03	.00
☐ 353 Sandy Alomar Jr.	.25	.12	.02
☐ 354 Stan Belinda	.10	.05	.01
☐ 355 Marty Barrett	.03	.01	.00
☐ 356 Randy Ready	.03	.01	.00
☐ 357 Dave West	.06	.03	.00
☐ 358 Andres Thomas	.03	.01	.00
☐ 359 Jimmy Jones	.03	.01	.00
☐ 360 Paul Molitor	.08	.04	.01
☐ 361 Randy McCament	.10	.05	.01
☐ 362 Damon Berryhill	.08	.04	.01
☐ 363 Dan Petry	.03	.01	.00
☐ 364 Rolando Roomes	.08	.04	.01
☐ 365 Ozzie Guillen	.06	.03	.00
☐ 366 Mike Heath	.03	.01	.00
☐ 367 Mike Morgan	.03	.01	.00
☐ 368 Bill Doran	.06	.03	.00
☐ 369 Todd Burns	.03	.01	.00
☐ 370 Tim Wallach	.06	.03	.00
☐ 371 Jimmy Key	.06	.03	.00
☐ 372 Terry Kennedy	.03	.01	.00
☐ 373 Alvin Davis	.08	.04	.01
☐ 374 Steve Cummings	.10	.05	.01
☐ 375 Dwight Evans	.08	.04	.01
☐ 376 Checklist 3	.06	.01	.00
☐ 377 Mickey Weston	.10	.05	.01
☐ 378 Luis Salazar	.03	.01	.00
☐ 379 Steve Rosenberg	.03	.01	.00
☐ 380 Dave Winfield	.10	.05	.01
☐ 381 Frank Robinson MG	.08	.04	.01
☐ 382 Jeff Musselman	.03	.01	.00
☐ 383 John Morris	.03	.01	.00
☐ 384 Pat Combs	.30	.15	.03
☐ 385 Fred McGriff AS	.10	.05	.01
☐ 386 Julio Franco AS	.06	.03	.00
☐ 387 Wade Boggs AS	.15	.07	.01
☐ 388 Cal Ripken AS	.10	.05	.01

☐ 389 Robin Yount AS	.15	.07	.01
☐ 390 Ruben Sierra AS	.15	.07	.01
☐ 391 Kirby Puckett AS	.15	.07	.01
☐ 392 Carlton Fisk AS	.08	.04	.01
☐ 393 Bret Saberhagen AS	.08	.04	.01
☐ 394 Jeff Ballard AS	.06	.03	.00
☐ 395 Jeff Russell AS	.06	.03	.00
☐ 396 A.Bartlett Giamatti	.50	.25	.05
(commemorative)			
☐ 397 Will Clark AS	.20	.10	.02
☐ 398 Ryne Sandberg AS	.10	.05	.01
☐ 399 Howard Johnson AS	.08	.04	.01
☐ 400 Ozzie Smith AS	.08	.04	.01
☐ 401 Kevin Mitchell AS	.10	.05	.01
☐ 402 Eric Davis AS	.12	.06	.01
☐ 403 Tony Gwynn AS	.12	.06	.01
☐ 404 Craig Biggio AS	.08	.04	.01
☐ 405 Mike Scott AS	.08	.04	.01
☐ 406 Joe Magrane AS	.06	.03	.00
☐ 407 Mark Davis AS	.06	.03	.00
☐ 408 Trevor Wilson	.03	.01	.00
☐ 409 Tom Brunansky	.08	.04	.01
☐ 410 Joe Boever	.03	.01	.00
☐ 411 Ken Phelps	.03	.01	.00
☐ 412 Jamie Moyer	.03	.01	.00
☐ 413 Brian Dubois	.12	.06	.01
☐ 414 Frank Thomas FDP	.30	.15	.03
☐ 415 Shawon Dunston	.06	.03	.00
☐ 416 Dave Johnson (P)	.12	.06	.01
☐ 417 Jim Gantner	.03	.01	.00
☐ 418 Tom Browning	.06	.03	.00
☐ 419 Beau Allred	.15	.07	.01
☐ 420 Carlton Fisk	.08	.04	.01
☐ 421 Greg Minton	.03	.01	.00
☐ 422 Pat Sheridan	.03	.01	.00
☐ 423 Fred Toliver	.03	.01	.00
☐ 424 Jerry Reuss	.03	.01	.00
☐ 425 Bill Landrum	.03	.01	.00
☐ 426 Jeff Hamilton	.03	.01	.00
☐ 427 Carmen Castillo	.03	.01	.00
☐ 428 Steve Davis	.10	.05	.01
☐ 429 Tom Kelly MG	.03	.01	.00
☐ 430 Pete Incaviglia	.06	.03	.00
☐ 431 Randy Johnson	.03	.01	.00
☐ 432 Damaso Garcia	.03	.01	.00
☐ 433 Steve Olin	.10	.05	.01
☐ 434 Mark Carreon	.06	.03	.00
☐ 435 Kevin Seitzer	.08	.04	.01
☐ 436 Mel Hall	.06	.03	.00
☐ 437 Les Lancaster	.03	.01	.00
☐ 438 Greg Myers	.06	.03	.00
☐ 439 Jeff Parrett	.03	.01	.00
☐ 440 Alan Trammell	.08	.04	.01
☐ 441 Bob Kipper	.03	.01	.00
☐ 442 Jerry Browne	.03	.01	.00
☐ 443 Cris Carpenter	.03	.01	.00
☐ 444 Kyle Abbott FDP	.25	.12	.02
☐ 445 Danny Jackson	.06	.03	.00
☐ 446 Dan Pasqua	.03	.01	.00
☐ 447 Atlee Hammaker	.03	.01	.00
☐ 448 Greg Gagne	.03	.01	.00
☐ 449 Dennis Rasmussen	.03	.01	.00
☐ 450 Rickey Henderson	.20	.10	.02
☐ 451 Mark Lemke	.03	.01	.00
☐ 452 Luis De Los Santos	.08	.04	.01
☐ 453 Jody Davis	.03	.01	.00
☐ 454 Jeff King	.10	.05	.01
☐ 455 Jeffrey Leonard	.06	.03	.00
☐ 456 Chris Gwynn	.06	.03	.00
☐ 457 Gregg Jefferies	.30	.15	.03
☐ 458 Bob McClure	.03	.01	.00
☐ 459 Jim Lefebvre MG	.03	.01	.00
☐ 460 Mike Scott	.08	.04	.01
☐ 461 Carlos Martinez	.20	.10	.02
☐ 462 Denny Walling	.03	.01	.00
☐ 463 Drew Hall	.03	.01	.00
☐ 464 Jerome Walton	1.25	.60	.12
☐ 465 Kevin Gross	.03	.01	.00
☐ 466 Rance Mulliniks	.03	.01	.00
☐ 467 Juan Nieves	.03	.01	.00
☐ 468 Bill Ripken	.03	.01	.00
☐ 469 John Kruk	.06	.03	.00
☐ 470 Frank Viola	.08	.04	.01
☐ 471 Mike Brumley	.06	.03	.00
☐ 472 Jose Uribe	.03	.01	.00
☐ 473 Joe Price	.03	.01	.00
☐ 474 Rich Thompson	.03	.01	.00
☐ 475 Bob Welch	.06	.03	.00
☐ 476 Brad Komminsk	.03	.01	.00
☐ 477 Willie Fraser	.03	.01	.00
☐ 478 Mike LaValliere	.03	.01	.00
☐ 479 Frank White	.06	.03	.00
☐ 480 Sid Fernandez	.08	.04	.01
☐ 481 Garry Templeton	.06	.03	.00
☐ 482 Steve Carter	.12	.06	.01

Always Actively Buying Quality Collections

GEORGIA MUSIC & SPORTS
Dick DeCourcy
1867 Flat Shoals Rd.
Riverdale, GA 30296
404-996-3385

A PERSONAL MESSAGE
TO THE DEALERS OF THE HOBBY
Baseball Cards have been good to us.

Georgia Music & Sports has been a regular advertiser in hobby publications since 1983. We have set up at over 50 shows per year. Both through our ads and the shows we have met many regular customers—for this we are very thankful.

Most of our customers and dealers order from four to six times a month. We try to cultivate repeat business. It is far more important for us to obtain a customer for the long term than ever to think of a quick buck on one deal.

It is not possible to inventory every item in the hobby, but we always try to have on hand Mint sets from the last 10 years as well as unopened, unsearched products from the last 10 years.

We have at present over 350 dealers that order from us every month. We work on the average of 15% profit on most items. Some of our prices may be high and some may be low, but we do try and have the major products always on hand at all times. By having the product, we can save you hours of searching.

We pride ourselves on service . . . we spell service S-P-E-E-D. If you are a regular account and you call in an order today before 2 p.m., we ship it today. Also, 99% of our accounts pay us just as quickly as we ship, the same day they get their product. The rest pay interest.

We will soon be entering our 14th year of business. To those customers who have kept us going for all these years, we give thanks and trust that this union will continue for many years to come. To those new and honorable dealers and store owners who are entering this fast-paced, exciting and growing baseball card hobby, we welcome your business. We have a staff of 11 people to help serve your needs.

Please write or call for our current price list.

Sincerely,

Dick DeCourcy, President
Georgia Music and Sports
MEMBER

Atlanta Area Chamber of Commerce
Atlanta Area Better Business Bureau

Atlanta Area Sports Collectors Association
National Association of Music Merchants

☐ 483	Alejandro Pena	.03	.01	.00	☐ 578	Joe Magrane	.08	.04	.01
☐ 484	Mike Fitzgerald	.03	.01	.00	☐ 579	Art Howe MG	.03	.01	.00
☐ 485	John Candelaria	.06	.03	.00	☐ 580	Joe Carter	.10	.05	.01
☐ 486	Jeff Treadway	.03	.01	.00	☐ 581	Ken Griffey Sr.	.06	.03	.00
☐ 487	Steve Searcy	.03	.01	.00	☐ 582	Rick Honeycutt	.03	.01	.00
☐ 488	Ken Oberkfell	.03	.01	.00	☐ 583	Bruce Benedict	.03	.01	.00
☐ 489	Nick Leyva MG	.03	.01	.00	☐ 584	Phil Stephenson	.10	.05	.01
☐ 490	Dan Plesac	.06	.03	.00	☐ 585	Kal Daniels	.08	.04	.01
☐ 491	Dave Cochrane	.12	.06	.01	☐ 586	Edwin Nunez	.03	.01	.00
☐ 492	Ron Oester	.03	.01	.00	☐ 587	Lance Johnson	.03	.01	.00
☐ 493	Jason Grimsley	.12	.06	.01	☐ 588	Rick Rhoden	.03	.01	.00
☐ 494	Terry Puhl	.03	.01	.00	☐ 589	Mike Aldrete	.03	.01	.00
☐ 495	Lee Smith	.06	.03	.00	☐ 590	Ozzie Smith	.08	.04	.01
☐ 496	Cecil Espy	.03	.01	.00	☐ 591	Todd Stottlemyre	.06	.03	.00
☐ 497	Dave Schmidt	.03	.01	.00	☐ 592	R.J. Reynolds	.03	.01	.00
☐ 498	Rick Schu	.03	.01	.00	☐ 593	Scott Bradley	.03	.01	.00
☐ 499	Bill Long	.03	.01	.00	☐ 594	Luis Sojo	.12	.06	.01
☐ 500	Kevin Mitchell	.20	.10	.02	☐ 595	Greg Swindell	.08	.04	.01
☐ 501	Matt Young	.03	.01	.00	☐ 596	Jose DeJesus	.03	.01	.00
☐ 502	Mitch Webster	.03	.01	.00	☐ 597	Chris Bosio	.06	.03	.00
☐ 503	Randy St.Claire	.03	.01	.00	☐ 598	Brady Anderson	.03	.01	.00
☐ 504	Tom O'Malley	.03	.01	.00	☐ 599	Frank Williams	.03	.01	.00
☐ 505	Kelly Gruber	.06	.03	.00	☐ 600	Darryl Strawberry	.25	.12	.02
☐ 506	Tom Glavine	.06	.03	.00	☐ 601	Luis Rivera	.03	.01	.00
☐ 507	Gary Redus	.03	.01	.00	☐ 602	Scott Garrelts	.06	.03	.00
☐ 508	Terry Leach	.03	.01	.00	☐ 603	Tony Armas	.06	.03	.00
☐ 509	Tom Pagnozzi	.03	.01	.00	☐ 604	Ron Robinson	.03	.01	.00
☐ 510	Dwight Gooden	.20	.10	.02	☐ 605	Mike Scioscia	.03	.01	.00
☐ 511	Clay Parker	.08	.04	.01	☐ 606	Storm Davis	.06	.03	.00
☐ 512	Gary Pettis	.03	.01	.00	☐ 607	Steve Jeltz	.03	.01	.00
☐ 513	Mark Eichhorn	.03	.01	.00	☐ 608	Eric Anthony	1.50	.75	.15
☐ 514	Andy Allanson	.03	.01	.00	☐ 609	Sparky Anderson MG	.06	.03	.00
☐ 515	Len Dykstra	.06	.03	.00	☐ 610	Pedro Guerrero	.08	.04	.01
☐ 516	Tim Leary	.06	.03	.00	☐ 611	Walt Terrell	.03	.01	.00
☐ 517	Roberto Alomar	.08	.04	.01	☐ 612	Dave Gallagher	.03	.01	.00
☐ 518	Bill Krueger	.03	.01	.00	☐ 613	Jeff Pico	.03	.01	.00
☐ 519	Bucky Dent MG	.06	.03	.00	☐ 614	Nelson Santovenia	.03	.01	.00
☐ 520	Mitch Williams	.06	.03	.00	☐ 615	Rob Deer	.06	.03	.00
☐ 521	Craig Worthington	.08	.04	.01	☐ 616	Brian Holman	.08	.04	.01
☐ 522	Mike Dunne	.03	.01	.00	☐ 617	Geronimo Berroa	.06	.03	.00
☐ 523	Jay Bell	.03	.01	.00	☐ 618	Ed Whitson	.03	.01	.00
☐ 524	Daryl Boston	.03	.01	.00	☐ 619	Rob Ducey	.03	.01	.00
☐ 525	Wally Joyner	.08	.04	.01	☐ 620	Tony Castillo	.06	.03	.00
☐ 526	Checklist 4	.06	.01	.00	☐ 621	Melido Perez	.03	.01	.00
☐ 527	Ron Hassey	.03	.01	.00	☐ 622	Sid Bream	.03	.01	.00
☐ 528	Kevin Wickander	.08	.04	.01	☐ 623	Jim Corsi	.03	.01	.00
☐ 529	Greg Harris	.03	.01	.00	☐ 624	Darrin Jackson	.03	.01	.00
☐ 530	Mark Langston	.08	.04	.01	☐ 625	Roger McDowell	.06	.03	.00
☐ 531	Ken Caminiti	.03	.01	.00	☐ 626	Bob Melvin	.03	.01	.00
☐ 532	Cecilio Guante	.03	.01	.00	☐ 627	Jose Rijo	.03	.01	.00
☐ 533	Tim Jones	.06	.03	.00	☐ 628	Candy Maldonado	.03	.01	.00
☐ 534	Louie Meadows	.03	.01	.00	☐ 629	Eric Hetzel	.06	.03	.00
☐ 535	John Smoltz	.08	.04	.01	☐ 630	Gary Gaetti	.08	.04	.01
☐ 536	Bob Geren	.15	.07	.01	☐ 631	John Wetteland	.20	.10	.02
☐ 537	Mark Grant	.03	.01	.00	☐ 632	Scott Lusader	.03	.01	.00
☐ 538	Bill Spiers	.20	.10	.02	☐ 633	Dennis Cook	.10	.05	.01
☐ 539	Neal Heaton	.03	.01	.00	☐ 634	Luis Polonia	.03	.01	.00
☐ 540	Danny Tartabull	.08	.04	.01	☐ 635	Brian Downing	.03	.01	.00
☐ 541	Pat Perry	.03	.01	.00	☐ 636	Jesse Orosco	.03	.01	.00
☐ 542	Darren Daulton	.03	.01	.00	☐ 637	Craig Reynolds	.03	.01	.00
☐ 543	Nelson Liriano	.03	.01	.00	☐ 638	Jeff Montgomery	.06	.03	.00
☐ 544	Dennis Boyd	.03	.01	.00	☐ 639	Tony LaRussa MG	.03	.01	.00
☐ 545	Kevin McReynolds	.08	.04	.01	☐ 640	Rick Sutcliffe	.06	.03	.00
☐ 546	Kevin Hickey	.03	.01	.00	☐ 641	Doug Strange	.12	.06	.01
☐ 547	Jack Howell	.03	.01	.00	☐ 642	Jack Armstrong	.06	.03	.00
☐ 548	Pat Clements	.03	.01	.00	☐ 643	Alfredo Griffin	.03	.01	.00
☐ 549	Don Zimmer MG	.03	.01	.00	☐ 644	Paul Assenmacher	.03	.01	.00
☐ 550	Julio Franco	.06	.03	.00	☐ 645	Jose Oquendo	.03	.01	.00
☐ 551	Tim Crews	.03	.01	.00	☐ 646	Checklist 5	.06	.01	.00
☐ 552	Mike Smith	.12	.06	.01	☐ 647	Rex Hudler	.03	.01	.00
☐ 553	Scott Scudder	.15	.07	.01	☐ 648	Jim Clancy	.03	.01	.00
☐ 554	Jay Buhner	.06	.03	.00	☐ 649	Dan Murphy	.12	.06	.01
☐ 555	Jack Morris	.08	.04	.01	☐ 650	Mike Witt	.06	.03	.00
☐ 556	Gene Larkin	.03	.01	.00	☐ 651	Rafael Santana	.03	.01	.00
☐ 557	Jeff Innis	.10	.05	.01	☐ 652	Mike Boddicker	.03	.01	.00
☐ 558	Rafael Ramirez	.03	.01	.00	☐ 653	John Moses	.03	.01	.00
☐ 559	Andy McGaffigan	.03	.01	.00	☐ 654	Paul Coleman FDP	.30	.15	.03
☐ 560	Steve Sax	.08	.04	.01	☐ 655	Gregg Olson	.25	.12	.02
☐ 561	Ken Dayley	.03	.01	.00	☐ 656	Mackey Sasser	.06	.03	.00
☐ 562	Chad Kreuter	.03	.01	.00	☐ 657	Terry Mulholland	.03	.01	.00
☐ 563	Alex Sanchez	.08	.04	.01	☐ 658	Donell Nixon	.03	.01	.00
☐ 564	Tyler Houston FDP	.40	.20	.04	☐ 659	Greg Cadaret	.03	.01	.00
☐ 565	Scott Fletcher	.03	.01	.00	☐ 660	Vince Coleman	.08	.04	.01
☐ 566	Mark Knudson	.03	.01	.00	☐ 661	Dick Howser TBC'85	.03	.01	.00
☐ 567	Ron Gant	.06	.03	.00	☐ 662	Mike Schmidt TBC'80	.12	.06	.01
☐ 568	John Smiley	.06	.03	.00	☐ 663	Fred Lynn TBC'75	.06	.03	.00
☐ 569	Ivan Calderon	.06	.03	.00	☐ 664	Johnny Bench TBC'70	.10	.05	.01
☐ 570	Cal Ripken	.12	.06	.01	☐ 665	Sandy Koufax TBC'65	.10	.05	.01
☐ 571	Brett Butler	.06	.03	.00	☐ 666	Brian Fisher	.03	.01	.00
☐ 572	Greg Harris	.03	.01	.00	☐ 667	Curt Wilkerson	.03	.01	.00
☐ 573	Danny Heep	.03	.01	.00	☐ 668	Joe Oliver	.15	.07	.01
☐ 574	Bill Swift	.03	.01	.00	☐ 669	Tom Lasorda MG	.06	.03	.00
☐ 575	Lance Parrish	.08	.04	.01	☐ 670	Dennis Eckersley	.08	.04	.01
☐ 576	Mike Dyer	.12	.06	.01	☐ 671	Bob Boone	.06	.03	.00
☐ 577	Charlie Hayes	.08	.04	.01	☐ 672	Roy Smith	.03	.01	.00

☐ 673	Joey Meyer	.03	.01	.00
☐ 674	Spike Owen	.03	.01	.00
☐ 675	Jim Abbott	.50	.25	.05
☐ 676	Randy Kutcher	.03	.01	.00
☐ 677	Jay Tibbs	.03	.01	.00
☐ 678	Kirt Manwaring	.03	.01	.00
☐ 679	Gary Ward	.03	.01	.00
☐ 680	Howard Johnson	.10	.05	.01
☐ 681	Mike Schooler	.06	.03	.00
☐ 682	Dann Bilardello	.03	.01	.00
☐ 683	Kenny Rogers	.10	.05	.01
☐ 684	Julio Machado	.12	.06	.01
☐ 685	Tony Fernandez	.08	.04	.01
☐ 686	Carmelo Martinez	.03	.01	.00
☐ 687	Tim Birtsas	.03	.01	.00
☐ 688	Milt Thompson	.03	.01	.00
☐ 689	Rich Yett	.03	.01	.00
☐ 690	Mark McGwire	.25	.12	.02
☐ 691	Chuck Cary	.03	.01	.00
☐ 692	Sammy Sosa	.35	.17	.03
☐ 693	Calvin Schiraldi	.03	.01	.00
☐ 694	Mike Stanton	.20	.10	.02
☐ 695	Tom Henke	.06	.03	.00
☐ 696	B.J. Surhoff	.06	.03	.00
☐ 697	Mike Davis	.03	.01	.00
☐ 698	Omar Vizquel	.12	.06	.01
☐ 699	Jim Leyland MG	.03	.01	.00
☐ 700	Kirby Puckett	.20	.10	.02
☐ 701	Bernie Williams	.40	.20	.04
☐ 702	Tony Phillips	.03	.01	.00
☐ 703	Jeff Brantley	.12	.06	.01
☐ 704	Chip Hale	.12	.06	.01
☐ 705	Claudell Washington	.06	.03	.00
☐ 706	Geno Petralli	.03	.01	.00
☐ 707	Luis Aquino	.03	.01	.00
☐ 708	Larry Sheets	.03	.01	.00
☐ 709	Juan Berenguer	.03	.01	.00
☐ 710	Von Hayes	.08	.04	.01
☐ 711	Rick Aguilera	.03	.01	.00
☐ 712	Todd Benzinger	.03	.01	.00
☐ 713	Tim Drummond	.12	.06	.01
☐ 714	Marquis Grissom	.50	.25	.05
☐ 715	Greg Maddux	.06	.03	.00
☐ 716	Steve Balboni	.03	.01	.00
☐ 717	Ron Karkovice	.03	.01	.00
☐ 718	Gary Sheffield	.30	.15	.03
☐ 719	Wally Whitehurst	.10	.05	.01
☐ 720	Andres Galarraga	.08	.04	.01
☐ 721	Lee Mazzilli	.03	.01	.00
☐ 722	Felix Fermin	.03	.01	.00
☐ 723	Jeff Robinson	.06	.03	.00
☐ 724	Juan Bell	.15	.07	.01
☐ 725	Terry Pendleton	.03	.01	.00
☐ 726	Gene Nelson	.03	.01	.00
☐ 727	Pat Tabler	.03	.01	.00
☐ 728	Jim Acker	.03	.01	.00
☐ 729	Bobby Valentine MG	.03	.01	.00
☐ 730	Tony Gwynn	.15	.07	.01
☐ 731	Don Carman	.03	.01	.00
☐ 732	Ernest Riles	.03	.01	.00
☐ 733	John Dopson	.03	.01	.00
☐ 734	Kevin Elster	.06	.03	.00
☐ 735	Charlie Hough	.03	.01	.00
☐ 736	Rick Dempsey	.03	.01	.00
☐ 737	Chris Sabo	.08	.04	.01
☐ 738	Gene Harris	.15	.07	.01
☐ 739	Dale Sveum	.03	.01	.00
☐ 740	Jesse Barfield	.08	.04	.01
☐ 741	Steve Wilson	.08	.04	.01
☐ 742	Ernie Whitt	.03	.01	.00
☐ 743	Tom Candiotti	.03	.01	.00
☐ 744	Kelly Mann	.15	.07	.01
☐ 745	Hubie Brooks	.06	.03	.00
☐ 746	Dave Smith	.03	.01	.00
☐ 747	Randy Bush	.03	.01	.00
☐ 748	Doyle Alexander	.03	.01	.00
☐ 749	Mark Parent	.03	.01	.00
☐ 750	Dale Murphy	.12	.06	.01
☐ 751	Steve Lyons	.03	.01	.00
☐ 752	Tom Gordon	.45	.22	.04
☐ 753	Chris Speier	.03	.01	.00
☐ 754	Bob Walk	.03	.01	.00
☐ 755	Rafael Palmeiro	.06	.03	.00
☐ 756	Ken Howell	.03	.01	.00
☐ 757	Larry Walker	.20	.10	.02
☐ 758	Mark Thurmond	.03	.01	.00
☐ 759	Tom Trebelhorn MG	.03	.01	.00
☐ 760	Wade Boggs	.25	.12	.02
☐ 761	Mike Jackson	.03	.01	.00
☐ 762	Doug Dascenzo	.03	.01	.00
☐ 763	Dennis Martinez	.03	.01	.00
☐ 764	Tim Teufel	.03	.01	.00
☐ 765	Chili Davis	.06	.03	.00
☐ 766	Brian Meyer	.08	.04	.01
☐ 767	Tracy Jones	.03	.01	.00

☐ 768	Chuck Crim	.03	.01	.00
☐ 769	Greg Hibbard	.12	.06	.01
☐ 770	Cory Snyder	.08	.04	.01
☐ 771	Pete Smith	.03	.01	.00
☐ 772	Jeff Reed	.03	.01	.00
☐ 773	Dave Leiper	.03	.01	.00
☐ 774	Ben McDonald	1.75	.85	.17
☐ 775	Andy Van Slyke	.08	.04	.01
☐ 776	Charlie Leibrandt	.03	.01	.00
☐ 777	Tim Laudner	.03	.01	.00
☐ 778	Mike Jeffcoat	.03	.01	.00
☐ 779	Lloyd Moseby	.06	.03	.00
☐ 780	Orel Hershiser	.10	.05	.01
☐ 781	Mario Diaz	.03	.01	.00
☐ 782	Jose Alvarez	.03	.01	.00
☐ 783	Checklist 6	.06	.01	.00
☐ 784	Scott Bailes	.03	.01	.00
☐ 785	Jim Rice	.08	.04	.01
☐ 786	Eric King	.03	.01	.00
☐ 787	Rene Gonzales	.03	.01	.00
☐ 788	Frank DiPino	.03	.01	.00
☐ 789	John Wathan MG	.03	.01	.00
☐ 790	Gary Carter	.08	.04	.01
☐ 791	Alvaro Espinoza	.03	.01	.00
☐ 792	Gerald Perry	.06	.03	.00

1990 Topps Wax Box Cards

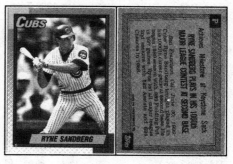

The 1990 Topps wax box cards comprise four different box bottoms with four cards each, for a total of 16 standard-size (2 1/2 by 3 1/2 inch) cards. The front borders are green. The vertically-oriented backs are yellowish green. These cards depict various career milestones achieved during the 1989 season. The card numbers are actually the letters A through P.

		MINT	EXC	G-VG
COMPLETE SET (16)		5.00	2.50	.50
COMMON PLAYER (A-P)		.05	.02	.00

☐	A	Wade Boggs	.40	.20	.04
☐	B	George Brett	.30	.15	.03
☐	C	Andre Dawson	.20	.10	.02
☐	D	Darrell Evans	.10	.05	.01
☐	E	Dwight Gooden	.35	.17	.03
☐	F	Rickey Henderson	.35	.17	.03
☐	G	Tom Lasorda MG	.05	.02	.00
☐	H	Fred Lynn	.10	.05	.01
☐	I	Mark McGwire	.40	.20	.04
☐	J	Dave Parker	.15	.07	.01
☐	K	Jeff Reardon	.10	.05	.01
☐	L	Rick Reuschel	.10	.05	.01
☐	M	Jim Rice	.15	.07	.01
☐	N	Cal Ripken	.25	.12	.02
☐	O	Nolan Ryan	.50	.25	.05
☐	P	Ryne Sandberg	.25	.12	.02

WRITERS & ARTISTS: We are always looking for interesting material for Beckett Monthly. Please send us your articles or ideas. We pay cash for accepted articles and art immediately.

1990 Topps Glossy All-Stars 22

The 1990 Topps Glossy All-Star set contains 22 standard-size (2 1/2 by 3 1/2 inch) glossy cards. The front and back borders are white, and other design elements are red, blue and yellow. This set is almost identical to previous year sets of the same name. One card was included in each 1990 Topps rack pack.

		MINT	EXC	G-VG
COMPLETE SET (22)		4.00	2.00	.40
COMMON PLAYER (1-22)		.10	.05	.01
☐ 1	Tom Lasorda MG	.10	.05	.01
☐ 2	Will Clark	.75	.30	.05
☐ 3	Ryne Sandberg	.25	.10	.02
☐ 4	Howard Johnson	.20	.08	.01
☐ 5	Ozzie Smith	.20	.08	.01
☐ 6	Kevin Mitchell	.30	.12	.02
☐ 7	Eric Davis	.35	.15	.02
☐ 8	Tony Gwynn	.35	.15	.02
☐ 9	Benny Santiago	.20	.08	.01
☐ 10	Rick Reuschel	.10	.05	.01
☐ 11	Don Drysdale CAPT	.15	.06	.01
☐ 12	Tony LaRussa MG	.10	.05	.01
☐ 13	Mark McGwire	.40	.15	.03
☐ 14	Julio Franco	.15	.06	.01
☐ 15	Wade Boggs	.50	.20	.04
☐ 16	Cal Ripken Jr.	.25	.10	.02
☐ 17	Bo Jackson	.75	.30	.05
☐ 18	Kirby Puckett	.35	.15	.02
☐ 19	Ruben Sierra	.35	.15	.02
☐ 20	Terry Steinbach	.15	.06	.01
☐ 21	Dave Stewart	.15	.06	.01
☐ 22	Carl Yastrzemski CAPT	.20	.08	.01

1990 Topps Jumbo Rookies

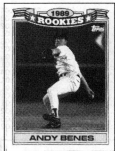 

The 1990 Topps Jumbo Rookies set contains 33 standard-size (2 1/2 by 3 1/2 inch) glossy cards. The front and back borders are white, and other design elements are red, blue and yellow. This set is almost identical to previous year sets of the same name except that it contains 33 cards rather than only 22. One card was included in each 1990 Topps "jumbo" pack. The cards are numbered in alphabetical order.

		MINT	EXC	G-VG
COMPLETE SET (33)		10.00	5.00	1.00
COMMON PLAYER (1-33)		.15	.07	.01
☐ 1	Jim Abbott	1.00	.40	.07
☐ 2	Joey Belle	.50	.20	.04
☐ 3	Andy Benes	.50	.20	.04
☐ 4	Greg Briley	.30	.12	.02
☐ 5	Kevin Brown	.20	.08	.01
☐ 6	Mark Carreon	.20	.08	.01
☐ 7	Mike Devereaux	.20	.08	.01
☐ 8	Junior Felix	.35	.15	.02
☐ 9	Bob Geren	.20	.08	.01
☐ 10	Tom Gordon	.50	.20	.04
☐ 11	Ken Griffey Jr.	1.50	.60	.10
☐ 12	Pete Harnisch	.15	.07	.01
☐ 13	Greg Harris	.15	.07	.01
☐ 14	Greg Hibbard	.20	.08	.01
☐ 15	Ken Hill	.20	.08	.01
☐ 16	Gregg Jefferies	.75	.30	.04
☐ 17	Jeff King	.20	.08	.01
☐ 18	Derek Lilliquist	.20	.08	.01
☐ 19	Carlos Martinez	.25	.12	.02
☐ 20	Ramon Martinez	.30	.12	.02
☐ 21	Bob Milacki	.20	.08	.01
☐ 22	Gregg Olson	.50	.20	.04
☐ 23	Donn Pall	.15	.07	.01
☐ 24	Kenny Rogers	.20	.08	.01
☐ 25	Gary Sheffield	.50	.20	.04
☐ 26	Dwight Smith	.75	.30	.04
☐ 27	Billy Spiers	.30	.12	.02
☐ 28	Omar Vizquel	.20	.08	.01
☐ 29	Jerome Walton	1.00	.40	.07
☐ 30	Dave West	.30	.12	.02
☐ 31	John Wetteland	.30	.12	.02
☐ 32	Steve Wilson	.20	.08	.01
☐ 33	Craig Worthington	.25	.12	.02

1987 Toys'R'Us Rookies

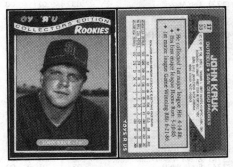

Topps produced this 33-card boxed set for Toys 'R' Us stores. The set is subtitled "Baseball Rookies" and features predominantly younger players. The cards measure 2 1/2" by 3 1/2" and feature a high-gloss, full- color photo of the player inside a black border. The card backs are printed in orange and blue on white card stock.

		MINT	EXC	G-VG
COMPLETE SET (33)		6.00	3.00	.60
COMMON PLAYER (1-33)		.10	.05	.01
☐ 1	Andy Allanson	.10	.05	.01
☐ 2	Paul Assenmacher	.10	.05	.01
☐ 3	Scott Bailes	.10	.05	.01
☐ 4	Barry Bonds	.35	.17	.03
☐ 5	Jose Canseco	1.25	.60	.12
☐ 6	John Cerutti	.10	.05	.01
☐ 7	Will Clark	1.25	.60	.12
☐ 8	Kal Daniels	.50	.25	.05
☐ 9	Jim Deshaies	.15	.07	.01
☐ 10	Mark Eichhorn	.10	.05	.01

☐ 11	Ed Hearn	.10	.05	.01
☐ 12	Pete Incaviglia	.25	.12	.02
☐ 13	Bo Jackson	1.25	.60	.12
☐ 14	Wally Joyner	.60	.30	.06
☐ 15	Charlie Kerfeld	.10	.05	.01
☐ 16	Eric King	.10	.05	.01
☐ 17	John Kruk	.20	.10	.02
☐ 18	Barry Larkin	.50	.25	.05
☐ 19	Mike LaValliere	.10	.05	.01
☐ 20	Greg Mathews	.15	.07	.01
☐ 21	Kevin Mitchell	.60	.30	.06
☐ 22	Dan Plesac	.20	.10	.02
☐ 23	Bruce Ruffin	.15	.07	.01
☐ 24	Ruben Sierra	.75	.35	.07
☐ 25	Cory Snyder	.35	.17	.03
☐ 26	Kurt Stillwell	.20	.10	.02
☐ 27	Dale Sveum	.15	.07	.01
☐ 28	Danny Tartabull	.35	.17	.03
☐ 29	Andres Thomas	.15	.07	.01
☐ 30	Robby Thompson	.15	.07	.01
☐ 31	Jim Traber	.10	.05	.01
☐ 32	Mitch Williams	.25	.12	.02
☐ 33	Todd Worrell	.25	.12	.02

1988 Toys'R'Us Rookies

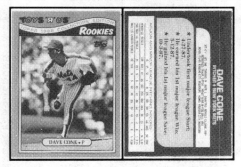

Topps produced this 33-card boxed set for Toys 'R' Us stores. The set is subtitled "Baseball Rookies" and features predominantly younger players. The cards measure 2 1/2" by 3 1/2" and feature a high-gloss, full-color photo of the player inside a blue border. The card backs are printed in pink and blue on white card stock. The cards are numbered on the back and the checklist for the set is found on the back panel of the small collector box. The statistics provided on the card backs cover only three lines, Minor League totals, last season, and Major League totals.

		MINT	EXC	G-VG
	COMPLETE SET (33)	5.00	2.50	.50
	COMMON PLAYER (1-33)	.10	.05	.01
☐ 1	Todd Benzinger	.20	.10	.02
☐ 2	Bob Brower	.10	.05	.01
☐ 3	Jerry Browne	.15	.07	.01
☐ 4	DeWayne Buice	.10	.05	.01
☐ 5	Ellis Burks	1.00	.50	.10
☐ 6	Ken Caminiti	.15	.07	.01
☐ 7	Casey Candaele	.10	.05	.01
☐ 8	Dave Cone	.75	.35	.07
☐ 9	Kelly Downs	.20	.10	.02
☐ 10	Mike Dunne	.10	.05	.01
☐ 11	Ken Gerhart	.15	.07	.01
☐ 12	Mike Greenwell	1.25	.60	.12
☐ 13	Mike Henneman	.20	.10	.02
☐ 14	Sam Horn	.10	.05	.01
☐ 15	Joe Magrane	.25	.12	.02
☐ 16	Fred Manrique	.10	.05	.01
☐ 17	John Marzano	.15	.07	.01
☐ 18	Fred McGriff	1.00	.50	.10
☐ 19	Mark McGwire	1.00	.50	.10
☐ 20	Jeff Musselman	.10	.05	.01
☐ 21	Randy Myers	.25	.12	.02
☐ 22	Matt Nokes	.25	.12	.02
☐ 23	Al Pedrique	.10	.05	.01
☐ 24	Luis Polonia	.15	.07	.01
☐ 25	Billy Ripken	.15	.07	.01

☐ 26	Benny Santiago	.45	.22	.04
☐ 27	Kevin Seitzer	.60	.30	.06
☐ 28	John Smiley	.20	.10	.02
☐ 29	Mike Stanley	.15	.07	.01
☐ 30	Terry Steinbach	.30	.15	.03
☐ 31	B.J. Surhoff	.20	.10	.02
☐ 32	Bobby Thigpen	.20	.10	.02
☐ 33	Devon White	.25	.12	.02

1989 Toys 'R' Us Rookies

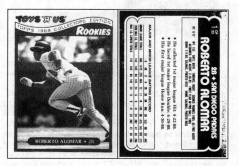

The 1989 Toys 'R' Us Rookies set contains 33 standard-size (2 1/2 by 3 1/2 inch) glossy cards. The fronts are yellow and magenta. The horizontally-oriented backs are sky blue and red, and feature 1988 and career stats. The cards were distributed through Toys 'R' Us stores as a boxed set.

		MINT	EXC	G-VG
	COMPLETE SET (33)	4.50	2.25	.45
	COMMON PLAYER (1-33)	.10	.05	.01
☐ 1	Roberto Alomar	.30	.15	.03
☐ 2	Brady Anderson	.20	.10	.02
☐ 3	Tim Belcher	.20	.10	.02
☐ 4	Damon Berryhill	.30	.15	.03
☐ 5	Jay Buhner	.20	.10	.02
☐ 6	Sherman Corbett	.10	.05	.01
☐ 7	Kevin Elster	.20	.10	.02
☐ 8	Cecil Espy	.10	.05	.01
☐ 9	Dave Gallagher	.20	.10	.02
☐ 10	Ron Gant	.20	.10	.02
☐ 11	Paul Gibson	.10	.05	.01
☐ 12	Mark Grace	1.00	.50	.10
☐ 13	Bryan Harvey	.20	.10	.02
☐ 14	Darrin Jackson	.10	.05	.01
☐ 15	Gregg Jefferies	.75	.35	.07
☐ 16	Ron Jones	.20	.10	.02
☐ 17	Ricky Jordan	.50	.25	.05
☐ 18	Roberto Kelly	.30	.15	.03
☐ 19	Al Leiter	.15	.07	.01
☐ 20	Jack McDowell	.15	.07	.01
☐ 21	Melido Perez	.15	.07	.01
☐ 22	Jeff Pico	.15	.07	.01
☐ 23	Jody Reed	.15	.07	.01
☐ 24	Chris Sabo	.25	.12	.02
☐ 25	Nelson Santovenia	.20	.10	.02
☐ 26	Mackey Sasser	.20	.10	.02
☐ 27	Mike Schooler	.20	.10	.02
☐ 28	Gary Sheffield	.50	.25	.05
☐ 29	Pete Smith	.15	.07	.01
☐ 30	Pete Stanicek	.15	.07	.01
☐ 31	Jeff Treadway	.15	.07	.01
☐ 32	Walt Weiss	.30	.15	.03
☐ 33	Dave West	.25	.12	.02

1983 True Value White Sox

This 23-card set was sponsored by True Value Hardware Stores and features full-color (2 5/8" by 4 1/4") cards of the Chicago White Sox. Most of the set was intended for distribution two cards per game

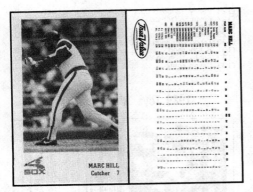

MARC HILL
Catcher 7

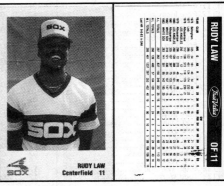

RUDY LAW
Centerfield 11

at selected White Sox Tuesday night home games. The cards are unnumbered except for uniform number given in the lower right corner of the obverse. The card backs contain statistical information in basic black and white. The cards of Harold Baines, Salome Barojas, and Marc Hill were not issued at the park; hence they are more difficult to obtain than the other 20 cards and are marked SP in the checklist below.

	MINT	EXC	G-VG
COMPLETE SET (23)	30.00	15.00	3.00
COMMON PLAYER (1-23)	.35	.17	.03

			MINT	EXC	G-VG
☐	1	Scott Fletcher	.90	.45	.09
☐	3	Harold Baines SP	7.50	3.75	.75
☐	5	Vance Law	.60	.30	.06
☐	7	Marc Hill SP	3.00	1.50	.30
☐	10	Tony LaRussa MG	.75	.35	.07
☐	11	Rudy Law	.35	.17	.03
☐	14	Tony Bernazard	.35	.17	.03
☐	17	Jerry Hairston	.35	.17	.03
☐	19	Greg Luzinski	.75	.35	.07
☐	24	Floyd Bannister	.60	.30	.06
☐	25	Mike Squires	.35	.17	.03
☐	30	Salome Barojas SP	3.00	1.50	.30
☐	31	LaMarr Hoyt	.50	.25	.05
☐	34	Richard Dotson	.50	.25	.05
☐	36	Jerry Koosman	.75	.35	.07
☐	40	Britt Burns	.35	.17	.03
☐	41	Dick Tidrow	.35	.17	.03
☐	42	Ron Kittle	1.00	.50	.10
☐	44	Tom Paciorek	.35	.17	.03
☐	45	Kevin Hickey	.35	.17	.03
☐	53	Dennis Lamp	.35	.17	.03
☐	67	Jim Kern	.35	.17	.03
☐	72	Carlton Fisk	2.00	1.00	.20

1984 True Value White Sox

This 30-card set features full color (2 1/2" by 4") cards of the Chicago White Sox. Most of the set was distributed two cards per game at selected White Sox Tuesday home games. Faust and Minoso were not given out although their cards were available through direct (promotional) contact with them. Brennan and Hulett were not released directly since they were sent down to the minors. The cards are unnumbered except for uniform number given in the lower right corner of the obverse. The card backs contain statistical information in basic black and white.

			MINT	EXC	G-VG
COMPLETE SET (30)			25.00	12.50	2.50
COMMON PLAYER (1-30)			.30	.15	.03

			MINT	EXC	G-VG
☐	1	Juan Agosto	.30	.15	.03
☐	2	Luis Aparicio	2.50	1.25	.25
☐	3	Harold Baines	1.50	.75	.15
☐	4	Floyd Bannister	.50	.25	.05

			MINT	EXC	G-VG
☐	5	Salome Barojas	.30	.15	.03
☐	6	Tom Brennan	1.50	.75	.15
☐	7	Britt Burns	.30	.15	.03
☐	8	Coaching Staff	.30	.15	.03
		(blank back)			
☐	9	Julio Cruz	.30	.15	.03
☐	10	Richard Dotson	.50	.25	.05
☐	11	Jerry Dybzinski	.30	.15	.03
☐	12	Nancy Faust	1.50	.75	.15
		(organist)			
		(blank back)			
☐	13	Carlton Fisk	2.00	1.00	.20
☐	14	Scott Fletcher	.50	.25	.05
☐	15	Jerry Hairston	.30	.15	.03
☐	16	Marc Hill	.30	.15	.03
☐	17	LaMarr Hoyt	.40	.20	.04
☐	18	Tim Hulett	1.50	.75	.15
☐	19	Ron Kittle	.75	.35	.07
☐	20	Tony LaRussa MG	.50	.25	.05
☐	21	Rudy Law	.30	.15	.03
☐	22	Vance Law	.40	.20	.04
☐	23	Greg Luzinski	.60	.30	.06
☐	24	Minnie Minoso	2.00	1.00	.20
☐	25	Tom Paciorek	.30	.15	.03
☐	26	Ron Reed	.30	.15	.03
☐	27	Tom Seaver	2.50	1.25	.25
☐	28	Dave Stegman	.30	.15	.03
☐	29	Mike Squires	.30	.15	.03
☐	30	Greg Walker	.50	.25	.05

1986 True Value

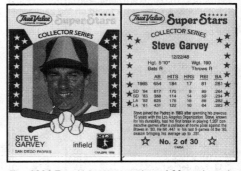

The 1986 True Value set consists of 30 cards each 2 1/2" by 3 1/2" which were printed as panels of four although one of the cards in the panel only pictures a featured product. The complete panel measures 10 3/8" by 3 1/2". The True Value logo is in the upper left corner of the obverse of each card. Supposedly the cards were distributed to customers purchasing 5.00 or more at the store. Cards are frequently found with perforations intact and still in the closed form where only the top card in the folded panel is visible. The card number appears at the bottom of the reverse. Team logos have been surgically removed (airbrushed) from the photos.

	MINT	EXC	G-VG
COMPLETE SET (30)	7.50	3.75	.75
COMMON PLAYER (1-30)	.10	.05	.01

			MINT	EXC	G-VG
☐	1	Pedro Guerrero	.20	.10	.02
☐	2	Steve Garvey	.30	.15	.03
☐	3	Eddie Murray	.30	.15	.03
☐	4	Pete Rose	.50	.25	.05
☐	5	Don Mattingly	.75	.35	.07
☐	6	Fernando Valenzuela	.25	.12	.02
☐	7	Jim Rice	.25	.12	.02
☐	8	Kirk Gibson	.25	.12	.02
☐	9	Ozzie Smith	.25	.12	.02
☐	10	Dale Murphy	.40	.20	.04
☐	11	Robin Yount	.50	.25	.05
☐	12	Tom Seaver	.40	.20	.04
☐	13	Reggie Jackson	.50	.25	.05
☐	14	Ryne Sandberg	.25	.12	.02
☐	15	Bruce Sutter	.15	.07	.01
☐	16	Gary Carter	.20	.10	.02
☐	17	George Brett	.40	.20	.04
☐	18	Rick Sutcliffe	.10	.05	.01
☐	19	Dave Stieb	.10	.05	.01
☐	20	Buddy Bell	.10	.05	.01
☐	21	Alvin Davis	.15	.07	.01
☐	22	Cal Ripken	.25	.12	.02
☐	23	Bill Madlock	.10	.05	.01
☐	24	Kent Hrbek	.15	.07	.01
☐	25	Lou Whitaker	.15	.07	.01
☐	26	Nolan Ryan	.75	.35	.07
☐	27	Dwayne Murphy	.10	.05	.01
☐	28	Mike Schmidt	.60	.30	.06
☐	29	Andre Dawson	.25	.12	.02
☐	30	Wade Boggs	.60	.30	.06

1911 T3 Turkey Red

The cards in this 126-card set measure 5 3/4" by 8". The 1911 "Turkey Red" set of color cabinet style cards, designated T3 in the American Card Catalog, is named after the brand of cigarettes with which it was offered as a premium. Cards 1-50 and 77-126 depict baseball players while the middle series (51-76) portrays boxers. The cards themselves are not numbered but were assigned numbers for ordering purposes by the manufacturer. This list appears on the backs of cards in the 77-126 sub-series and has been used in the checklist below. The boxers (51-76) were formerly assigned a separate catalog number (T9) but have now been returned to the classification to which they properly belong and are indicated in the checklist below by BOX. This attractive set has been reprinted recently in 2 1/2" by 3 1/2" form.

	EX-MT	VG-E	GOOD
COMPLETE SET (126)	34000.	17000.	4000.
COMMON BASEBALL (1-50)	200.00	100.00	20.00
COMMON BOXERS (51-76)	100.00	50.00	10.00
COMMON BASEBALL (77-126)	225.00	110.00	22.00

			EX-MT	VG-E	GOOD
☐	1	M. Brown: Chicago NL	400.00	200.00	40.00
☐	2	Bergen: Brooklyn	200.00	100.00	20.00
☐	3	Leach: Pittsburgh	200.00	100.00	20.00
☐	4	Bresnahan: St.L. NL	350.00	175.00	35.00
☐	5	Crawford: Detroit	400.00	200.00	40.00
☐	6	Chase: New York AL	250.00	125.00	25.00
☐	7	Camnitz: Pittsburgh	200.00	100.00	20.00
☐	8	Clarke: Pittsburgh	350.00	175.00	35.00
☐	9	Cobb: Detroit	4000.00	2000.00	400.00
☐	10	Devlin: New York NL	200.00	100.00	20.00
☐	11	Dahlen: Brooklyn	250.00	125.00	25.00
☐	12	Donovan: Detroit	200.00	100.00	20.00
☐	13	Doyle: New York NL	200.00	100.00	20.00
☐	14	Dooin: Phila. NL	200.00	100.00	20.00
☐	15	Elberfeld: Wash.	200.00	100.00	20.00
☐	16	Evers: Chicago NL	400.00	200.00	40.00
☐	17	Griffith: Cinc.	350.00	175.00	35.00
☐	18	Jennings: Detroit	350.00	175.00	35.00
☐	19	Joss: Cleveland	450.00	225.00	45.00
☐	20	Jordan: Brooklyn	200.00	100.00	20.00
☐	21	Kleinow: New York NL	200.00	100.00	20.00
☐	22	Krause: Phila. AL	200.00	100.00	20.00
☐	23	Lajoie: Cleveland	900.00	450.00	90.00
☐	24	Mitchell: Cincinnati	200.00	100.00	20.00
☐	25	M. McIntyre: Detroit	200.00	100.00	20.00
☐	26	McGraw: New York NL	500.00	250.00	50.00
☐	27	Mathewson: N.Y. NL	1200.00	600.00	150.00
☐	28	H. McIntyre: Brk	200.00	100.00	20.00
☐	29	McConnell: Boston AL	200.00	100.00	20.00
☐	30	Mullin: Detroit	200.00	100.00	20.00
☐	31	Magee: Phila. NL	200.00	100.00	20.00
☐	32	Overall: Chicago NL	200.00	100.00	20.00
☐	33	Pfeister: Chicago NL	200.00	100.00	20.00
☐	34	Rucker: Brooklyn	200.00	100.00	20.00
☐	35	Tinker: Chicago NL	400.00	200.00	40.00
☐	36	Speaker: Boston AL	900.00	450.00	90.00
☐	37	Sallee: St. Louis NL	200.00	100.00	20.00
☐	38	Stahl: Boston AL	200.00	100.00	20.00
☐	39	Waddell: St.Louis AL	450.00	225.00	45.00
☐	40	Willis: St.Louis NL	250.00	125.00	25.00
☐	41	Wiltse: New York NL	200.00	100.00	20.00
☐	42	Young: Cleveland	1000.00	500.00	100.00
☐	43	Out At Third	200.00	100.00	20.00
☐	44	Trying to Catch Him Napping	200.00	100.00	20.00
☐	45	Jordan and Herzog at First	200.00	100.00	20.00
☐	46	Safe At Third	200.00	100.00	20.00
☐	47	Frank Chance At Bat	400.00	200.00	40.00
☐	48	Jack Murray At Bat	200.00	100.00	20.00
☐	49	Close Play At Second	200.00	100.00	20.00
☐	50	Chief Myers At Bat	200.00	100.00	20.00
☐	51	Jim Driscoll BOX	100.00	50.00	10.00
☐	52	Abe Attell BOX	125.00	60.00	12.50
☐	53	Ad. Walgast BOX	100.00	50.00	10.00
☐	54	Johnny Coulon BOX	100.00	50.00	10.00
☐	55	James Jeffries BOX	200.00	100.00	20.00
☐	56	Jack Sullivan BOX (Twin)	125.00	60.00	12.50
☐	57	Battling Nelson BOX	100.00	50.00	10.00
☐	58	Packey McFarland BOX	100.00	50.00	10.00
☐	59	Tommy Murphy BOX	100.00	50.00	10.00
☐	60	Owen Moran BOX	100.00	50.00	10.00
☐	61	Johnny Marto BOX	100.00	50.00	10.00
☐	62	Jimmie Gardner BOX	100.00	50.00	10.00
☐	63	Harry Lewis BOX	100.00	50.00	10.00
☐	64	Wm. Papke BOX	100.00	50.00	10.00
☐	65	Sam Langford BOX	100.00	50.00	10.00
☐	66	Knock-out Brown BOX	100.00	50.00	10.00
☐	67	Stanley Ketchel BOX	150.00	75.00	15.00
☐	68	Joe Jeannette BOX	100.00	50.00	10.00
☐	69	Leach Cross BOX	100.00	50.00	10.00
☐	70	Phil. McGovern BOX	100.00	50.00	10.00
☐	71	Battling Hurley BOX	100.00	50.00	10.00
☐	72	Honey Mellody BOX	100.00	50.00	10.00
☐	73	Al Kaufman BOX	100.00	50.00	10.00
☐	74	Willie Lewis BOX	100.00	50.00	10.00
☐	75	Jack O'Brien BOX "Philadelphia"	125.00	60.00	12.50
☐	76	Jack Johnson BOX	200.00	100.00	20.00
☐	77	Ames: New York NL	225.00	110.00	22.00
☐	78	Baker: Phila. AL (picture probably Jack Barry)	450.00	225.00	45.00
☐	79	Bell: Brooklyn	225.00	110.00	22.00
☐	80	Bender: Phila. AL	450.00	225.00	45.00
☐	81	Bescher: Cincinnati	225.00	110.00	22.00
☐	82	Bransfield: Phila. NL	225.00	110.00	22.00
☐	83	Bridwell: Phila. NL	225.00	110.00	22.00
☐	84	Browne: Wash. and Chicago	225.00	110.00	22.00
☐	85	Burns: Chi. and Cin.	225.00	110.00	22.00
☐	86	Carrigan: Boston AL	225.00	110.00	22.00
☐	87	Collins: Phila. AL	450.00	225.00	45.00
☐	88	Coveleski: Cinc.	225.00	110.00	22.00
☐	89	Criger: New York AL	225.00	110.00	22.00
☐	90	Doolan: Phila. NL	225.00	110.00	22.00

☐ 91	Downey: Cincinnati	225.00	110.00	22.00
☐ 92	Dygert: Phila. AL	225.00	110.00	22.00
☐ 93	Fromme: Cincinnati	225.00	110.00	22.00
☐ 94	Gibson: Pittsburgh	225.00	110.00	22.00
☐ 95	Graham: Boston NL	225.00	110.00	22.00
☐ 96	Groom: Washington	225.00	110.00	22.00
☐ 97	Hoblitzell: Cinc.	225.00	110.00	22.00
☐ 98	Hofman: Chicago NL	225.00	110.00	22.00
☐ 99	Johnson: Washington	1350.00	650.00	150.00
☐ 100	D. Jones: Detroit	225.00	110.00	22.00
☐ 101	Keeler: New York NL	600.00	300.00	60.00
☐ 102	Kling: Chicago NL	225.00	110.00	22.00
☐ 103	Konetchy: St.Louis NL	225.00	110.00	22.00
☐ 104	Lennox: Brooklyn	225.00	110.00	22.00
☐ 105	Lobert: Cincinnati	225.00	110.00	22.00
☐ 106	Lord: Bos. and Chi.	225.00	110.00	22.00
☐ 107	Manning: N.Y. AL	225.00	110.00	22.00
☐ 108	Merkle: New York NL	225.00	110.00	22.00
☐ 109	Moran: Chi. and Phila.	225.00	110.00	22.00
☐ 110	McBride: Washington	225.00	110.00	22.00
☐ 111	Niles: Bos. and Cleve.	225.00	110.00	22.00
☐ 112	Paskert: Cincinnati	225.00	110.00	22.00
☐ 113	Raymond: N.Y. NL	225.00	110.00	22.00
☐ 114	Rhoades: Cleveland	300.00	150.00	30.00
☐ 115	Schlei: New York NL	225.00	110.00	22.00
☐ 116	Schmidt: Detroit	225.00	110.00	22.00
☐ 117	Schulte: Chicago NL	225.00	110.00	22.00
☐ 118	Smith: Chi. and Bos.	225.00	110.00	22.00
☐ 119	Stone: St.L. AL	225.00	110.00	22.00
☐ 120	Street: Washington	225.00	110.00	22.00
☐ 121	Sullivan: Chi. AL	225.00	110.00	22.00
☐ 122	Tenney: New York NL	225.00	110.00	22.00
☐ 123	Thomas: Phila. AL	225.00	110.00	22.00
☐ 124	Wallace: St.Louis AL	400.00	200.00	40.00
☐ 125	Walsh: Chicago AL	450.00	225.00	45.00
☐ 126	Wilson: Pittsburgh	225.00	110.00	22.00

1913 T200 Fatima

The cards in this 16-card set measure 2 5/8" by 5 13/16". The 1913 Fatima Cigarettes issue contains unnumbered glossy surface team cards. Both St. Louis team cards are considered difficult to obtain. A large 13" by 21" unnumbered, heavy cardboard premium issue is also known to exist and is quite scarce. These unnumbered team cards are ordered below by team alphabetical order within league.

		EX-MT	VG-E	GOOD
COMPLETE SET (16)		3000.00	1500.00	300.00
COMMON TEAM (1-16)		150.00	75.00	15.00
☐ 1	Boston AL	200.00	100.00	20.00
☐ 2	Chicago AL	150.00	75.00	15.00
☐ 3	Cleveland AL	150.00	75.00	15.00
☐ 4	Detroit AL	250.00	125.00	25.00
☐ 5	New York AL	500.00	250.00	50.00
☐ 6	Philadelphia AL	150.00	75.00	15.00
☐ 7	St. Louis AL	400.00	200.00	40.00
☐ 8	Washington AL	150.00	75.00	15.00
☐ 9	Boston NL	250.00	125.00	25.00
☐ 10	Brooklyn NL	150.00	75.00	15.00
☐ 11	Chicago NL	150.00	75.00	15.00
☐ 12	Cincinnati NL	150.00	75.00	15.00
☐ 13	New York NL	150.00	75.00	15.00
☐ 14	Philadelphia NL	150.00	75.00	15.00
☐ 15	Pittsburg NL	150.00	75.00	15.00
☐ 16	St. Louis NL	250.00	125.00	25.00

1911 T201 Mecca

The cards in this 50-card set measure 2 1/4" by 4 11/16". The 1911 Mecca Double Folder issue contains unnumbered cards. This issue was one of the first to list statistics of players portrayed on the cards. Each card portrays two players, one when the card is folded, another when the card is unfolded. The card of Dougherty and Lord is considered scarce.

		EX-MT	VG-E	GOOD
COMPLETE SET (50)		4000.00	2000.00	500.00
COMMON PAIR (1-50)		40.00	20.00	4.00
☐ 1	F.Baker and Collins	125.00	60.00	12.50
☐ 2	Barry and Lapp	40.00	20.00	4.00
☐ 3	Bergen and Z.Wheat	75.00	37.50	7.50
☐ 4	Blair and Hartzell	40.00	20.00	4.00
☐ 5	Bresnahan and Huggins	125.00	60.00	12.50
☐ 6	Bridwell and Mathewson	250.00	125.00	25.00
☐ 7	Butler and Abstein	40.00	20.00	4.00
☐ 8	Byrne and F.Clarke	75.00	37.50	7.50
☐ 9	Chance and Evers	150.00	75.00	15.00
☐ 10	Clark and Gaspar	40.00	20.00	4.00
☐ 11	Cobb and S.Crawford	750.00	375.00	75.00
☐ 12	Cole and Kling	40.00	20.00	4.00
☐ 13	Coombs and Thomas	40.00	20.00	4.00
☐ 14	Daubert and Rucker	40.00	20.00	4.00
☐ 15	Dougherty and Lord	300.00	150.00	30.00
☐ 16	Dooin and Titus	40.00	20.00	4.00
☐ 17	Downie and Baker	40.00	20.00	4.00
☐ 18	Dygert and Seymour	40.00	20.00	4.00
☐ 19	Elberfeld and McBride	40.00	20.00	4.00
☐ 20	Falkenberg and Lajoie	125.00	60.00	12.50
☐ 21	Fitzpatrick and Killian	40.00	20.00	4.00
☐ 22	Gardner and Speaker	125.00	60.00	12.50
☐ 23	Gibson and Leach	40.00	20.00	4.00
☐ 24	Graham and Mattern	40.00	20.00	4.00
☐ 25	Hauser and Lush	40.00	20.00	4.00
☐ 26	Herzog and Miller	40.00	20.00	4.00
☐ 27	Hinchman and Hickman	40.00	20.00	4.00
☐ 28	Hofman and M.Brown	75.00	37.50	7.50
☐ 29	Jennings and Summers	75.00	37.50	7.50
☐ 30	Johnson and Ford	40.00	20.00	4.00
☐ 31	McCarty and McGinnity	75.00	37.50	7.50
☐ 32	McGlyn and Barrett	40.00	20.00	4.00
☐ 33	McLean and Grant	40.00	20.00	4.00
☐ 34	Merkle and Wiltse	40.00	20.00	4.00
☐ 35	Meyers and Doyle	40.00	20.00	4.00
☐ 36	Moore and Lobert	40.00	20.00	4.00
☐ 37	Odwell and Downs	40.00	20.00	4.00
☐ 38	Oldring and Bender	75.00	37.50	7.50
☐ 39	Payne and Walsh	75.00	37.50	7.50
☐ 40	Simon and Leifield	40.00	20.00	4.00
☐ 41	Starr and McCabe	40.00	20.00	4.00
☐ 42	Stephens and LaPorte	40.00	20.00	4.00
☐ 43	Stovall and Turner	40.00	20.00	4.00
☐ 44	Street and W.Johnson	300.00	150.00	30.00
☐ 45	Stroud and Donovan	40.00	20.00	4.00
☐ 46	Sweeney and Chase	40.00	20.00	4.00
☐ 47	Thoney and Cicotte	40.00	20.00	4.00
☐ 48	Wallace and Lake	75.00	37.50	7.50
☐ 49	Ward and Foster	40.00	20.00	4.00
☐ 50	Williams and Woodruff	40.00	20.00	4.00

1912 T202 Triple Folders

The cards in this 134-card set measure 2 1/4" by 5 1/4". The 1912 T202 Hassan Triple Folder issue is perhaps the most ingenious baseball card ever issued. The two end cards of each panel are full color, T205-like individual cards whereas the black and white center panel pictures an action photo or portrait. The end cards can be folded across the center panel and stored in this manner. Seventy-six different center panels are known to exist; however, many of the center panels contain more than one combination of end cards. The center panel titles are listed below in alphabetical order while the different combinations of end cards are listed below each center panel as they appear left to right on the front of the card. A total of 132 different card fronts exist. The set price below includes all panel and player combinations listed in the checklist. Back color variations (red or black) also exist. The Birmingham's Home Run card is difficult to obtain as are other cards whose center panel exists with but one combination of end cards. The Devlin with Mathewson end panels on numbers 29A and 74C

picture Devlin as a Giant. Devlin is pictured as a Rustler on 29B and 74D.

	EX-MT	VG-E	GOOD
COMPLETE SET (132)	25000.	12000.	3000.
COMMON PANEL (1-76)	125.00	60.00	12.50

		EX-MT	VG-E	GOOD
☐ 1A	A Close Play at Home: ... Wallace-LaPorte	150.00	75.00	15.00
☐ 1B	A Close Play at Home: ... Wallace-Pelty	150.00	75.00	15.00
☐ 2	A Desperate Slide: .... O'Leary-Cobb	1000.00	500.00	100.00
☐ 3A	A Great Batsman: .... Barger-Bergen	125.00	60.00	12.50
☐ 3B	A Great Batsman: .... Rucker-Bergen	125.00	60.00	12.50
☐ 4	Ambrose McConnell at ..... Bat: Blair-Quinn	125.00	60.00	12.50
☐ 5	A Wide Throw Saves .... Crawford: Mullin-Stanage	150.00	75.00	15.00
☐ 6	Baker Gets His Man: .... Collins-Baker	250.00	125.00	25.00
☐ 7	Birmingham Gets to .... Third: Johnson-Street	350.00	175.00	35.00
☐ 8	Birmingham's Home .... Run: Birmingham-Turner	350.00	175.00	35.00
☐ 9	Bush Just Misses .... Austin: Moran-Magee	125.00	60.00	12.50
☐ 10A	Carrigan Blocks His .... Man: Gaspar-McLean	125.00	60.00	12.50
☐ 10B	Carrigan Blocks His .... Man: Wagner-Carrigan	125.00	60.00	12.50
☐ 11	Catching Him Napping: .... Oakes-Bresnahan	150.00	75.00	15.00
☐ 12	Caught Asleep .... Off First: Bresnahan-Harmon	150.00	75.00	15.00
☐ 13A	Chance Beats Out a .... Hit: Chance-Foxen	200.00	100.00	20.00
☐ 13B	Chance Beats Out a .... Hit: McIntire-Archer	150.00	75.00	15.00
☐ 13C	Chance Beats Out a .... Hit: Overall-Archer	150.00	75.00	15.00
☐ 13D	Chance Beats Out a .... Hit: Rowan-Archer	150.00	75.00	15.00
☐ 13E	Chance Beats Out a .... Hit: Shean-Chance	200.00	100.00	20.00
☐ 14A	Chase Dives into .... Third: Chase-Wolter	125.00	60.00	12.50
☐ 14B	Chase Dives into .... Third: Gibson-Clarke	150.00	75.00	15.00
☐ 14C	Chase Dives into .... Third: Phillippe-Gibson	125.00	60.00	12.50
☐ 15A	Chase Gets Ball Too ...... Late: Egan-Mitchell	125.00	60.00	12.50
☐ 15B	Chase Gets Ball Too ...... Late: Wolter-Chase	125.00	60.00	12.50
☐ 16A	Chase Guarding First: ... Chase-Wolter	125.00	60.00	12.50
☐ 16B	Chase Guarding First: ... Gibson-Clarke	150.00	75.00	15.00
☐ 16C	Chase Guarding First: ... Leifield-Gibson	125.00	60.00	12.50
☐ 17	Chase Ready Squeeze ...... Play: Paskert-Magee	125.00	60.00	12.50
☐ 18	Chase Safe at Third: .... Barry-Baker	150.00	75.00	15.00
☐ 19	Chief Bender Waiting: ...... Bender-Thomas	200.00	100.00	20.00
☐ 20	Clarke Hikes for Home: .... Bridwell-Kling	150.00	75.00	15.00
☐ 21	Close at First: .... Ball-Stovall	125.00	60.00	12.50
☐ 22A	Close at the Plate: .... Walsh-Payne	150.00	75.00	15.00
☐ 22B	Close at the Plate: .... White-Payne	125.00	60.00	12.50
☐ 23	Close at Third (Speak- ...... er): Wood-Speaker	300.00	150.00	30.00
☐ 24	Close at Third .... (Wagner): Wagner-Carrigan	125.00	60.00	12.50
☐ 25A	Collins Easily Safe: .... Byrne-Clarke	150.00	75.00	15.00
☐ 25B	Collins Easily Safe: .... Collins-Baker	250.00	125.00	25.00
☐ 25C	Collins Easily Safe: .... Collins-Murphy	200.00	100.00	20.00
☐ 26	Crawford About	150.00	75.00	15.00
	to Smash: Stanage-Summers			
☐ 27	Cree Rolls Home: .... Daubert-Hummell	125.00	60.00	12.50
☐ 28	Davy Jones' Great .... Slide: Delahanty-Jones	125.00	60.00	12.50
☐ 29A	Devlin Gets His Man: ...... Devlin (Giants)- Mathewson	900.00	450.00	90.00
☐ 29B	Devlin Gets His Man: ...... Devlin (Rustlers)- Mathewson	250.00	125.00	25.00
☐ 29C	Devlin Gets His Man: ...... Fletcher-Mathewson	250.00	125.00	25.00
☐ 29D	Devlin Gets His Man: ...... Meyers-Mathewson	250.00	125.00	25.00
☐ 30A	Donlin Out at First: .... Camnitz-Gibson	125.00	60.00	12.50
☐ 30B	Donlin Out at First: .... Doyle-Merkle	125.00	60.00	12.50
☐ 30C	Donlin Out at First: .... Leach-Wilson	125.00	60.00	12.50
☐ 30D	Donlin Out at First: .... Magee-Dooin	125.00	60.00	12.50
☐ 30E	Donlin Out at First: .... Phillippe-Gibson	125.00	60.00	12.50
☐ 31A	Dooin Gets His Man: ...... Dooin-Doolan	125.00	60.00	12.50
☐ 31B	Dooin Gets His Man: ...... Lobert-Dooin	125.00	60.00	12.50
☐ 31C	Dooin Gets His Man: ...... Titus-Dooin	125.00	60.00	12.50
☐ 32	Easy for Larry: .... Doyle-Merkle	125.00	60.00	12.50
☐ 33	Elberfeld Beats: .... Milan-Elberfeld	125.00	60.00	12.50
☐ 34	Elberfeld Gets His .... Man: Milan-Elberfeld	125.00	60.00	12.50
☐ 35	Engle in a Close Play: ...... Speaker-Engle	200.00	100.00	20.00
☐ 36A	Evers Makes Safe .... Slide: Archer-Evers	200.00	100.00	20.00
☐ 36B	Evers Makes Safe .... Slide: Evers-Chance	250.00	125.00	25.00
☐ 36C	Evers Makes Safe .... Slide: Overall-Archer	150.00	75.00	15.00
☐ 36D	Evers Makes Safe .... Slide: Reulbach-Archer	150.00	75.00	15.00
☐ 36E	Evers Makes Safe .... Slide: Tinker-Chance	500.00	250.00	50.00
☐ 37	Fast Work at Third: .... O'Leary-Cobb	1000.00	500.00	100.00
☐ 38A	Ford Putting Over .... Spitter: Ford-Vaughn	125.00	60.00	12.50
☐ 38B	Ford Putting Over .... Spitter: Sweeney-Ford	125.00	60.00	12.50
☐ 39	Good Play at Third: .... Moriarty-Cobb	1000.00	500.00	100.00
☐ 40	Grant Gets His Man: .... Hoblitzel-Grant	125.00	60.00	12.50
☐ 41A	Hal Chase Too Late: ...... McIntyre-McConnell	125.00	60.00	12.50
☐ 41B	Hal Chase Too Late: ...... Suggs-McLean	125.00	60.00	12.50
☐ 42	Harry Lord at Third: .... Lennox-Tinker	150.00	75.00	15.00
☐ 43	Hartzell Covering: .... Scanlon-Dahlen	125.00	60.00	12.50
☐ 44	Hartzell Strikes Out: .... Groom-Gray	125.00	60.00	12.50
☐ 45	Held at Third: .... Tannehill-Lord	125.00	60.00	12.50
☐ 46	Jake Stahl Guarding: .... Cicotte-Stahl	125.00	60.00	12.50
☐ 47	Jim Delahanty at Bat: ...... Delahanty-Jones	125.00	60.00	12.50
☐ 48A	Just Before the .... Battle: Ames-Meyers	125.00	60.00	12.50
☐ 48B	Just Before the .... Battle: Bresnahan-McGraw	250.00	125.00	25.00
☐ 48C	Just Before the .... Battle: Crandall-Meyers	125.00	60.00	12.50
☐ 48D	Just Before the .... Battle: Devore-Becker	125.00	60.00	12.50

☐ 48E	Just Before the .... Battle: Fletcher-Mathewson	250.00	125.00	25.00

☐ 48E Just Before the 250.00 125.00 25.00
　　Battle:
　　Fletcher-Mathewson
☐ 48F Just Before the 150.00 75.00 15.00
　　Battle:
　　Marquard-Meyers
☐ 48G Just Before the 250.00 125.00 25.00
　　Battle:
　　McGraw-Jennings
☐ 48H Just Before the 250.00 125.00 25.00
　　Battle:
　　Meyers-Mathewson
☐ 48I Just Before the 125.00 60.00 12.50
　　Battle:
　　Snodgrass-Murray
☐ 48J Just Before the 125.00 60.00 12.50
　　Battle:
　　Wiltse-Meyers
☐ 49 Knight Catches Runner: ... 350.00 175.00 35.00
　　Knight-Johnson
☐ 50A Lobert Almost Caught: ... 125.00 60.00 12.50
　　Bridwell-Kling
☐ 50B Lobert Almost Caught: ... 200.00 100.00 20.00
　　Kling-Young
☐ 50C Lobert Almost Caught: ... 125.00 60.00 12.50
　　Mattern-Kling
☐ 50D Lobert Almost Caught: ... 125.00 60.00 12.50
　　Steinfeldt-Kling
☐ 51 Lobert Gets Tenney: 125.00 60.00 12.50
　　Lobert-Dooin
☐ 52 Lord Catches His Man: 125.00 60.00 12.50
　　Tannehill-Lord
☐ 53 McConnell Caught: 125.00 60.00 12.50
　　Richie-Needham
☐ 54 McIntyre at Bat: 125.00 60.00 12.50
　　McIntrye-McConnell
☐ 55 Moriarty Spiked: 125.00 60.00 12.50
　　Willett-Stanage
☐ 56 Nearly Caught: 150.00 75.00 15.00
　　Bates-Bescher
☐ 57 Oldring Almost Home: 125.00 60.00 12.50
　　Lord-Oldring
☐ 58 Schaefer on First: 125.00 60.00 12.50
　　McBride-Milan
☐ 59 Schaefer Steals 150.00 75.00 15.00
　　Second:
　　McBride-Griffith
☐ 60 Scoring from Second: 125.00 60.00 12.50
　　Lord-Oldring
☐ 61A Scrambling Back: 125.00 60.00 12.50
　　Barger-Bergen
☐ 61B Scrambling Back: 125.00 60.00 12.50
　　Wolter-Chase
☐ 62 Speaker Almost Caught: .. 300.00 150.00 30.00
　　Miller-Clarke
☐ 63 Speaker Rounding 450.00 225.00 45.00
　　Third:
　　Wood-Speaker
☐ 64 Speaker Scores: 300.00 150.00 30.00
　　Speaker-Engle
☐ 65 Stahl Safe: 125.00 60.00 12.50
　　Stovall-Austin
☐ 66 Stone About to Swing: 125.00 60.00 12.50
　　Sheckard-Schulte
☐ 67A Sullivan Puts Up High 150.00 75.00 15.00
　　One: Evans-Huggins
☐ 67B Sullivan Puts Up High 125.00 60.00 12.50
　　One: Sweeney-Ford
☐ 68A Sweeney Gets Stahl: 125.00 60.00 12.50
　　Ford-Vaughn
☐ 68B Sweeney Gets Stahl: 125.00 60.00 12.50
　　Sweeney-Ford
☐ 69 Tenney Lands Safely: 125.00 60.00 12.50
　　Raymond-Latham
☐ 70A The Athletic Infield: 150.00 75.00 15.00
　　Barry-Baker
☐ 70B The Athletic Infield: 125.00 60.00 12.50
　　Brown-Graham
☐ 70C The Athletic Infield: 125.00 60.00 12.50
　　Hauser-Konetchy
☐ 70D The Athletic Infield: 125.00 60.00 12.50
　　Krause-Thomas
☐ 71 The Pinch Hitter: 125.00 60.00 12.50
　　Hoblitzel-Egan
☐ 72 The Scissors Slide: 125.00 60.00 12.50
　　Birmingham-Turner
☐ 73A Tom Jones at Bat: 125.00 60.00 12.50
　　Fromme-McLean
☐ 73B Tom Jones at Bat: 125.00 60.00 12.50
　　Gaspar-McLean
☐ 74A Too Late for Devlin: 125.00 60.00 12.50
　　Ames-Meyers
☐ 74B Too Late for Devlin: 125.00 60.00 12.50
　　Crandall-Meyers
☐ 74C Too Late for Devlin: 900.00 450.00 90.00

☐ 74D Too Late for Devlin: 250.00 125.00 25.00
　　Devlin (Giants)-
　　Mathewson
☐ 74E Too Late for Devlin: 150.00 75.00 15.00
　　Devlin (Rustlers)-
　　Mathewson
☐ 74F Too Late for Devlin: 125.00 60.00 12.50
　　Marquard-Meyers
☐ 75A Ty Cobb Steals 1500.00 750.00 150.00
　　Third:
　　Jennings-Cobb
☐ 75B Ty Cobb Steals 1350.00 650.00 150.00
　　Third:
　　Snodgrass-Cobb
☐ 75C Ty Cobb Steals 1350.00 650.00 150.00
　　Third:
　　Stovall-Austin
☐ 76 Wheat Strikes Out: 200.00 100.00 20.00
　　Dahlen-Wheat

T204 Ramly

The cards in this 121-card set measure 2" by 2 1/2". The Ramly baseball series, designated T204 in the ACC, contains unnumbered cards. This set is one of the most distinguished ever produced, containing ornate gold borders around a black and white portrait of each player. There are spelling errors, and two distinct backs, "Ramly" and "TT", are known. Much of the obverse card detail is actually embossed. The players have been alphabetized and numbered for reference in the checklist below.

	EX-MT	VG-E	GOOD
COMPLETE SET (121)	24000.	12000.	3000.
COMMON PLAYER (1-121)	175.00	85.00	18.00

		EX-MT	VG-E	GOOD
☐	1 Whitey Alperman	175.00	85.00	18.00
☐	2 John J. Anderson	175.00	85.00	18.00
☐	3 Jimmy Archer	175.00	85.00	18.00
☐	4 Frank Arellanes	175.00	85.00	18.00
☐	5 Jim Ball (Boston NL)	175.00	85.00	18.00
☐	6 Neal Ball (N.Y. AL)	175.00	85.00	18.00
☐	7 Dave Bancroft	350.00	175.00	35.00
☐	8 Johnny Bates	175.00	85.00	18.00
☐	9 Fred Beebe	175.00	85.00	18.00
☐	10 George Bell	175.00	85.00	18.00
☐	11 Chief Bender	350.00	175.00	35.00
☐	12 Walter Blair	175.00	85.00	18.00
☐	13 Cliff Blankenship	175.00	85.00	18.00
☐	14 Frank Bowerman	175.00	85.00	18.00
☐	15 Kitty Bransfield	175.00	85.00	18.00
☐	16 Roger Bresnahan	350.00	175.00	35.00
☐	17 Al Bridwell	175.00	85.00	18.00
☐	18 Mordecai Brown	350.00	175.00	35.00
☐	19 Fred Burchell	175.00	85.00	18.00
☐	20 Jesse Burkett	450.00	225.00	45.00
☐	21 Robert Byrne	175.00	85.00	18.00
☐	22 Bill Carrigan	175.00	85.00	18.00
☐	23 Frank Chance	400.00	200.00	40.00
☐	24 Charles Chech	175.00	85.00	18.00
☐	25 Eddie Cicotte	225.00	110.00	22.00
☐	26 Otis Clymer	175.00	85.00	18.00
☐	27 Andrew Coakley	175.00	85.00	18.00
☐	28 Eddie Collins	450.00	225.00	45.00
☐	29 Jimmy Collins	450.00	225.00	45.00
☐	30 Wid Conroy	175.00	85.00	18.00
☐	31 Jack Coombs	225.00	110.00	22.00

☐ 32	Doc Crandall	175.00	85.00	18.00
☐ 33	Lou Criger	175.00	85.00	18.00
☐ 34	Harry(Jasper) Davis	175.00	85.00	18.00
☐ 35	Art Devlin	175.00	85.00	18.00
☐ 36	Bill Dineen	175.00	85.00	18.00
☐ 37	Pat Donahue	175.00	85.00	18.00
☐ 38	Mike Donlin	175.00	85.00	18.00
☐ 39	Wild Bill Donovan	175.00	85.00	18.00
☐ 40	Gus Dorner	175.00	85.00	18.00
☐ 41	Joe Dunn	175.00	85.00	18.00
☐ 42	Norman Elberfield	175.00	85.00	18.00
	(sic) Elberfeld			
☐ 43	Johnny Evers	400.00	200.00	40.00
☐ 44	George L. Ewing	175.00	85.00	18.00
☐ 45	George Ferguson	175.00	85.00	18.00
☐ 46	Hobe Ferris	175.00	85.00	18.00
☐ 47	James J. Freeman	175.00	85.00	18.00
☐ 48	Art Fromme	175.00	85.00	18.00
☐ 49	Bob Ganley	175.00	85.00	18.00
☐ 50	Harry (Doc) Gessler	175.00	85.00	18.00
☐ 51	George Graham	175.00	85.00	18.00
☐ 52	Clark Griffith	350.00	175.00	35.00
☐ 53	Roy Hartzell	175.00	85.00	18.00
☐ 54	Charlie Hemphill	175.00	85.00	18.00
☐ 55	Dick Hoblitzell	175.00	85.00	18.00
☐ 56	George (Del) Howard	175.00	85.00	18.00
☐ 57	Harry Howell	175.00	85.00	18.00
☐ 58	Miller Huggins	400.00	200.00	40.00
☐ 59	John Hummel	175.00	85.00	18.00
☐ 60	Walter Johnson	1500.00	750.00	150.00
☐ 61	Charles Jones	175.00	85.00	18.00
☐ 62	Michael Kahoe	175.00	85.00	18.00
☐ 63	Ed Karger	175.00	85.00	18.00
☐ 64	Willie Keeler	450.00	225.00	45.00
☐ 65	Ed Kenotchey	175.00	85.00	18.00
	(sic) Konetchy			
☐ 66	John (Red) Kleinow	175.00	85.00	18.00
☐ 67	John Knight	175.00	85.00	18.00
☐ 68	Vive Lindeman	175.00	85.00	18.00
☐ 69	Hans Loebert	175.00	85.00	18.00
	(sic) Lobert			
☐ 70	Harry Lord	175.00	85.00	18.00
☐ 71	Harry Lumley	175.00	85.00	18.00
☐ 72	Ernie Lush	175.00	85.00	18.00
☐ 73	Rube Manning	175.00	85.00	18.00
☐ 74	James McAleer	175.00	85.00	18.00
☐ 75	Amby McConnell	175.00	85.00	18.00
☐ 76	Moose McCormick	175.00	85.00	18.00
☐ 77	Matthew McIntyre	175.00	85.00	18.00
☐ 78	Larry McLean	175.00	85.00	18.00
☐ 79	Fred Merkle	200.00	100.00	20.00
☐ 80	Clyde Milan	175.00	85.00	18.00
☐ 81	Michael Mitchell	175.00	85.00	18.00
☐ 82	Pat Moran	175.00	85.00	18.00
☐ 83	Harry (Cy) Morgan	175.00	85.00	18.00
☐ 84	Tim Murnane	175.00	85.00	18.00
☐ 85	Danny Murphy	175.00	85.00	18.00
☐ 86	Red Murray	175.00	85.00	18.00
☐ 87	Eustace(Doc) Newton	175.00	85.00	18.00
☐ 88	Simon Nichols	175.00	85.00	18.00
	(sic) Nicholls			
☐ 89	Harry Niles	175.00	85.00	18.00
☐ 90	Bill O'Hara	175.00	85.00	18.00
☐ 91	Charley O'Leary	175.00	85.00	18.00
☐ 92	Dode Paskert	175.00	85.00	18.00
☐ 93	Barney Pelty	175.00	85.00	18.00
☐ 94	Jack Pfeister	175.00	85.00	18.00
☐ 95	Eddie Plank	500.00	250.00	50.00
☐ 96	Jack Powell	175.00	85.00	18.00
☐ 97	Bugs Raymond	175.00	85.00	18.00
☐ 98	Thomas Reilly	175.00	85.00	18.00
☐ 99	Lewis Ritchie	175.00	85.00	18.00
	(sic) Richie			
☐ 100	Nap Rucker	175.00	85.00	18.00
☐ 101	Ed Ruelbach	175.00	85.00	18.00
	(sic) Reulbach			
☐ 102	Slim Sallee	175.00	85.00	18.00
☐ 103	Germany Schaefer	175.00	85.00	18.00
☐ 104	Jimmy Schekard	175.00	85.00	18.00
	(sic) Sheckard			
☐ 105	Admiral Schlei	175.00	85.00	18.00
☐ 106	Frank Schulte	175.00	85.00	18.00
☐ 107	James Sebring	175.00	85.00	18.00
☐ 108	Bill Shipke	175.00	85.00	18.00
☐ 109	Anthony Smith	175.00	85.00	18.00
☐ 110	Tubby Spencer	175.00	85.00	18.00
☐ 111	Jake Stahl	200.00	100.00	20.00
☐ 112	Harry Steinfeldt	175.00	85.00	18.00
☐ 113	Jim Stephens	175.00	85.00	18.00
☐ 114	Gabby Street	175.00	85.00	18.00
☐ 115	William Sweeney	175.00	85.00	18.00
☐ 116	Fred Tenney	175.00	85.00	18.00
☐ 117	Ira Thomas	175.00	85.00	18.00
☐ 118	Joe Tinker	350.00	175.00	35.00
☐ 119	Bob Unglaub	175.00	85.00	18.00
☐ 120	Heine Wagner	175.00	85.00	18.00
☐ 121	Bobby Wallace	350.00	175.00	35.00

T205 Gold Border

The cards in this 208-card set measure 1 1/2" by 2 5/8". The T205 set (ACC designation), also known as the "Gold Border" set, was issued in 1911 in packages of the following cigarette brands: American Beauty, Broadleaf, Cycle, Drum, Hassan, Honest Long Cut, Piedmont, Polar Bear, Sovereign and Sweet Caporal. All the above were products of the American Tobacco Company, and the ads for the various brands appear below the biographical section on the back of each card. There are pose variations noted in the checklist (which is alphabetized and numbered for reference) and there are 12 minor league cards of a more ornate design which are somewhat scarce. The numbers below correspond to alphabetical order within each team by team nickname, i.e., Philadelphia Athletics AL (1-13), St. Louis Browns (14-20), St. Louis Cardinals (21-32), Chicago Cubs (33-51), New York Giants (52-72), Cleveland Naps (73-78), Philadelphia Phillies (79-90), Pittsburgh Pirates (91-103), Cincinnati Reds (104-114), Boston Red Sox (115-122), Boston Rustlers (123-131), Washington Senators (132-139), Brooklyn Superbas (140-153), Detroit Tigers (154-167), Chicago White Sox (168- 182), New York Yankees (183-196), and Minor Leaguers (197- 208). The gold borders of T205 cards chip easily and they are hard to find in "Mint" or even "Near Mint" condition; however they (T205) are not appreciably tougher to find than T206 cards for lesser conditions or grades.

		EX-MT	VG-E	GOOD
COMPLETE SET (209)		27000.	13000.	3500.
COMMON PLAYERS (1-208)		65.00	30.00	7.50
☐ 1	Frank Baker	250.00	125.00	25.00
☐ 2	John J. Barry	65.00	30.00	7.50
☐ 3	Charles A. Bender	200.00	100.00	20.00

□	#	Name			
□	4	Edward T. Collins (mouth closed)	200.00	100.00	20.00
□	5	Edward T. Collins (mouth open)	400.00	200.00	40.00
□	6	James H. Dygert	65.00	30.00	7.50
□	7	Frederick T. Hartsel	65.00	30.00	7.50
□	8	Harry Krause	65.00	30.00	7.50
□	9	Pat'k J. Livingston	65.00	30.00	7.50
□	10	Briscoe Lord	65.00	30.00	7.50
□	11	Daniel Murphy	65.00	30.00	7.50
□	12	Reuben N. Oldring	65.00	30.00	7.50
□	13	Ira Thomas	65.00	30.00	7.50
□	14	William Bailey	65.00	30.00	7.50
□	15	Daniel J. Hoffman	65.00	30.00	7.50
□	16	Frank LaPorte	65.00	30.00	7.50
□	17	B. Pelty	65.00	30.00	7.50
□	18	George Stone	65.00	30.00	7.50
□	19	Roderick J. Wallace (with cap)	200.00	100.00	20.00
□	20	Roderick J. Wallace (without cap)	400.00	200.00	40.00
□	21	Roger Bresnahan (mouth closed)	200.00	100.00	20.00
□	22	Roger Bresnahan (mouth open)	400.00	200.00	40.00
□	23	Frank J. Corridon	65.00	30.00	7.50
□	24	Louis Evans	65.00	30.00	7.50
□	25	Robert Harmon (both ears)	65.00	30.00	7.50
□	26	Robert Harmon (left ear only)	250.00	125.00	25.00
□	27	Arnold J. Hauser	65.00	30.00	7.50
□	28	Miller Huggins	200.00	100.00	20.00
□	29	Edward Konetchy	65.00	30.00	7.50
□	30	John Lush	65.00	30.00	7.50
□	31	Rebel Oakes	65.00	30.00	7.50
□	32	Edward Phelps	65.00	30.00	7.50
□	33	James P. Archer	65.00	30.00	7.50
□	34	Mordecai Brown	200.00	100.00	20.00
□	35	Frank L. Chance	200.00	100.00	20.00
□	36	John J. Evers	200.00	100.00	20.00
□	37	William A. Foxen	65.00	30.00	7.50
□	38	George F. Graham	450.00	225.00	45.00
□	39	John Kling	65.00	30.00	7.50
□	40	Floyd M. Kroh	65.00	30.00	7.50
□	41	Harry McIntire	65.00	30.00	7.50
□	42	Thomas J. Needham	65.00	30.00	7.50
□	43	Orval Overall	65.00	30.00	7.50
□	44	John A. Pfiester	65.00	30.00	7.50
□	45	Edward M. Reulbach	65.00	30.00	7.50
□	46	Lewis Richie	65.00	30.00	7.50
□	47	Frank M. Schulte	65.00	30.00	7.50
□	48	David Shean (Cubs)	450.00	225.00	45.00
□	49	James T. Sheckard	65.00	30.00	7.50
□	50	Harry Steinfeldt	65.00	30.00	7.50
□	51	Joseph B. Tinker	200.00	100.00	20.00
□	52	Leon Ames	65.00	30.00	7.50
□	53	Beals Becker	65.00	30.00	7.50
□	54	Albert Bridwell	65.00	30.00	7.50
□	55	Otis Crandall	65.00	30.00	7.50
□	56	Arthur Devlin	65.00	30.00	7.50
□	57	Joshua Devore	65.00	30.00	7.50
□	58	W.R. Dickson	65.00	30.00	7.50
□	59	Lawrence Doyle	65.00	30.00	7.50
□	60	Arthur Fletcher	65.00	30.00	7.50
□	61	W.A. Latham	65.00	30.00	7.50
□	62	Richard Marquard	200.00	100.00	20.00
□	63	Christy Mathewson	600.00	300.00	60.00
□	64	John J. McGraw	300.00	150.00	30.00
□	65	Fred Merkle	100.00	50.00	10.00
□	66	John T. Meyers	65.00	30.00	7.50
□	67	John J. Murray	65.00	30.00	7.50
□	68	Arthur L. Raymond	250.00	125.00	25.00
□	69	George H. Schlei	65.00	30.00	7.50
□	70	Fred C. Snodgrass	65.00	30.00	7.50
□	71	George Wiltse (both ears)	65.00	30.00	7.50
□	72	George Wiltse (right ear only)	250.00	125.00	25.00
□	73	Neal Ball	65.00	30.00	7.50
□	74	Joseph Birmingham	65.00	30.00	7.50
□	75	Addie Joss	500.00	250.00	50.00
□	76	George T. Stovall	65.00	30.00	7.50
□	77	Terence Turner	250.00	125.00	25.00
□	78	Denton T. Young	550.00	275.00	55.00
□	79	John W. Bates	65.00	30.00	7.50
□	80	Wm. E. Bransfield	65.00	30.00	7.50
□	81	Charles S. Dooin	65.00	30.00	7.50
□	82	Michael Doolan	65.00	30.00	7.50
□	83	Robert Ewing	65.00	30.00	7.50
□	84	Fred Jacklitsch	65.00	30.00	7.50
□	85	John Lobert	65.00	30.00	7.50
□	86	Sherwood R. Magee	65.00	30.00	7.50
□	87	Patrick J. Moran	65.00	30.00	7.50
□	88	George Paskert	65.00	30.00	7.50
□	89	John A. Rowan	250.00	125.00	25.00
□	90	John Titus	65.00	30.00	7.50
□	91	Robert Byrne	65.00	30.00	7.50
□	92	Howard Camnitz	65.00	30.00	7.50
□	93	Fred Clarke	200.00	100.00	20.00
□	94	John Flynn	65.00	30.00	7.50
□	95	George Gibson	65.00	30.00	7.50
□	96	Thomas W. Leach	65.00	30.00	7.50
□	97	Sam Leever	65.00	30.00	7.50
□	98	Albert P. Leifield	65.00	30.00	7.50
□	99	Nicholas Maddox	65.00	30.00	7.50
□	100	John D. Miller	65.00	30.00	7.50
□	101	Charles Phillippe	100.00	50.00	10.00
□	102	Kirb White	250.00	125.00	25.00
□	103	J. Owen Wilson	65.00	30.00	7.50
□	104	Robert H. Bescher	65.00	30.00	7.50
□	105	Thomas W. Downey	65.00	30.00	7.50
□	106	Richard J. Egan	65.00	30.00	7.50
□	107	Arthur Fromme	65.00	30.00	7.50
□	108	Harry L. Gaspar	65.00	30.00	7.50
□	109	Edward L. Grant	250.00	125.00	25.00
□	110	Clark Griffith	200.00	100.00	20.00
□	111	Richard Hoblitzell	65.00	30.00	7.50
□	112	John B. McLean	65.00	30.00	7.50
□	113	Michael Mitchell	65.00	30.00	7.50
□	114	George Suggs	250.00	125.00	25.00
□	115	William Carrigan	65.00	30.00	7.50
□	116	Edward V. Cicotte	100.00	50.00	10.00
□	117	Clyde Engle	65.00	30.00	7.50
□	118	Edward Karger	250.00	125.00	25.00
□	119	John Kleinow	250.00	125.00	25.00
□	120	Tris Speaker	450.00	225.00	45.00
□	121	Jacob G. Stahl	100.00	50.00	10.00
□	122	Charles Wagner	250.00	125.00	25.00
□	123	Edward J. Abbaticchio	65.00	30.00	7.50
□	124	Frederick T. Beck	65.00	30.00	7.50
□	125	G.C. Ferguson	65.00	30.00	7.50
□	126	Wilbur Good	65.00	30.00	7.50
□	127	George F. Graham	65.00	30.00	7.50
□	128	Charles L. Herzog	65.00	30.00	7.50
□	129	A.A. Mattern	65.00	30.00	7.50
□	130	Bayard H. Sharpe	65.00	30.00	7.50
□	131	David Shean (Boston)	65.00	30.00	7.50
□	132	Norman Elberfeld	65.00	30.00	7.50
□	133	Gray	65.00	30.00	7.50
□	134	Robert Groom	65.00	30.00	7.50
□	135	Walter Johnson	900.00	450.00	90.00
□	136	George F. McBride	65.00	30.00	7.50
□	137	J. Clyde Milan	65.00	30.00	7.50
□	138	Herman Schaefer	65.00	30.00	7.50
□	139	Charles E. Street	65.00	30.00	7.50
□	140	Edward B. Barger (full B)	65.00	30.00	7.50
□	141	Edward B. Barger (part B)	250.00	125.00	25.00
□	142	George G. Bell	65.00	30.00	7.50
□	143	William Bergen	65.00	30.00	7.50
□	144	William Dahlen	250.00	125.00	25.00
□	145	Jacob Daubert	100.00	50.00	10.00
□	146	John E. Hummell	65.00	30.00	7.50
□	147	Edgar Lennox	65.00	30.00	7.50
□	148	Pryor McElveen	65.00	30.00	7.50
□	149	G.N. Rucker	65.00	30.00	7.50
□	150	W.D. Scanlan	250.00	125.00	25.00
□	151	Tony Smith	65.00	30.00	7.50
□	152	Zach D. Wheat	200.00	100.00	20.00
□	153	Irvin K. Wilhelm	250.00	125.00	25.00
□	154	Tyrus Raymond Cobb	2000.00	1000.00	250.00
□	155	James Delahanty	65.00	30.00	7.50
□	156	Hugh Jennings	200.00	100.00	20.00
□	157	David Jones	65.00	30.00	7.50
□	158	Thomas Jones	65.00	30.00	7.50
□	159	Edward Killian	65.00	30.00	7.50
□	160	George Moriarity	65.00	30.00	7.50
□	161	George J. Mullin	65.00	30.00	7.50
□	162	Charles O'Leary	65.00	30.00	7.50
□	163	Charles Schmidt	65.00	30.00	7.50
□	164	George Simmons	65.00	30.00	7.50
□	165	Oscar Stanage	65.00	30.00	7.50
□	166	Edgar Summers	65.00	30.00	7.50
□	167	Edgar Willett	65.00	30.00	7.50
□	168	Russell Blackburne	65.00	30.00	7.50
□	169	J. Donohue	200.00	100.00	20.00
□	170A	Patsy Dougherty (white stocking)	200.00	100.00	20.00
□	170B	Patsy Dougherty (red stocking)	65.00	30.00	7.50
□	171	Hugh Duffy	300.00	150.00	30.00
□	172	Frank Lang	65.00	30.00	7.50
□	173	Harry D. Lord	65.00	30.00	7.50
□	174	Ambrose McConnell	65.00	30.00	7.50
□	175	Matthew McIntyre	65.00	30.00	7.50
□	176	Frederick Olmstead	65.00	30.00	7.50
□	177	F. Parent	65.00	30.00	7.50
□	178	Fred Payne	65.00	30.00	7.50

Brian Morris • Paul Lewicki

**102 Watchung Ave.
Montclair, NJ 07042
201-746-9697**

Always buying and selling any and all issues
listed in this book in top conditions prior to 1976.
We specialize in unopened material, scarce, rare and
unusual sets and single cards, as well as Topps,
Bowmans, Play Balls, Goudeys and Tobacco Cards.
Whether you are buying or selling, do it with confidence,
with two of the hobby's leading dealers.

☐ 179	James Scott	65.00	30.00	7.50
☐ 180	Lee Ford Tannehill	65.00	30.00	7.50
☐ 181	Edward Walsh	350.00	175.00	35.00
☐ 182	G.H. White	65.00	30.00	7.50
☐ 183	James Austin	65.00	30.00	7.50
☐ 184	Harold W. Chase	350.00	175.00	35.00
	(Chase only)			
☐ 185	Harold W. Chase	100.00	50.00	10.00
	(Hal Chase)			
☐ 186	Louis Criger	65.00	30.00	7.50
☐ 187	Ray Fisher	250.00	125.00	25.00
☐ 188	Russell Ford	65.00	30.00	7.50
	(dark cap)			
☐ 189	Russell Ford	250.00	125.00	25.00
	(light cap)			
☐ 190	Earl Gardner	65.00	30.00	7.50
☐ 191	Charles Hemphill	65.00	30.00	7.50
☐ 192	Jack Knight	65.00	30.00	7.50
☐ 193	John Quinn	65.00	30.00	7.50
☐ 194	Edward Sweeney	250.00	125.00	25.00
☐ 195	James Vaughn	250.00	125.00	25.00
☐ 196	Harry Wolter	65.00	30.00	7.50
☐ 197	Dr.Merle T. Adkins:	200.00	100.00	20.00
	Baltimore			
☐ 198	John Dunn:	250.00	125.00	25.00
	Baltimore			
☐ 199	George Merritt:	200.00	100.00	20.00
	Buffalo			
☐ 200	Charles Hanford:	200.00	100.00	20.00
	Jersey City			
☐ 201	Forrest D. Cady:	200.00	100.00	20.00
	Newark			
☐ 202	James Frick: Newark	200.00	100.00	20.00
☐ 203	Wyatt Lee: Newark	200.00	100.00	20.00
☐ 204	Lewis McAllister:	200.00	100.00	20.00
	Newark			
☐ 205	John Nee: Newark	200.00	100.00	20.00
☐ 206	James Collins:	400.00	200.00	40.00
	Providence			
☐ 207	James Phelan:	200.00	100.00	20.00
	Providence			
☐ 208	Henry Batch:	200.00	100.00	20.00
	Rochester			

T206 White Border

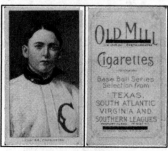

The cards in this 524-card set measure 1 1/2" by 2 5/8". The T206 set was and is the most popular of all the tobacco issues. The set was issued from 1909 to 1911 with sixteen different brands of cigarettes: American Beauty, Broadleaf, Cycle, Carolina Brights,

Drum, El Principe de Gales, Hindu, Lenox, Old Mill, Piedmont, Polar Bear, Sovereign, Sweet Caporal, Tolstoi, Ty Cobb and Uzit. The Ty Cobb brand back is very scarce. The minor league cards are supposedly slightly more difficult to obtain than the cards of the major leaguers, with the Southern League player cards being the most difficult. Minor League players were obtained from the American Association and the Eastern league. Southern League players were obtained from a variety of leagues including the following: South Atlantic League, Southern League, Texas League, and Virginia League. The set price below does not include ultra-expensive Wagner, Plank, Magie error, or Doyle variation.

		EX-MT	VG-E	GOOD
COMPLETE SET (520)		50000.	20000.	6000.
COMMON MAJORS (1-389)		50.00	20.00	5.00
COMMON MINORS (390-475) ...		40.00	20.00	4.00
COMMON SOUTHERN(476-523)		100.00	50.00	10.00
☐	1 Abbaticchio: Pitt.	50.00	20.00	5.00
	Batting follow thru			
☐	2 Abbaticchio: Pitt.	60.00	30.00	6.00
	Batting waiting pitch			
☐	3 Abstein: Pitt.	50.00	20.00	5.00
☐	4 Alperman: Brooklyn	60.00	30.00	6.00
☐	5 Ames: Giants, Port.	60.00	30.00	6.00
☐	6 Ames: Giants, Hands	50.00	20.00	5.00
	over head			
☐	7 Ames: Giants, Hands	60.00	30.00	6.00
	in front of chest			
☐	8 Arellanes: Boston AL	50.00	20.00	5.00
☐	9 Atz: Chicago AL	50.00	20.00	5.00
☐	10 Baker: Phila. AL	200.00	100.00	20.00
☐	11 Ball: Cleveland	50.00	20.00	5.00
☐	12 Ball: N.Y. AL	60.00	30.00	6.00
☐	13 Barbeau: St.L. NL	50.00	20.00	5.00
☐	14 Barry: Phila. AL	50.00	20.00	5.00
☐	15 Bates: Boston NL	60.00	30.00	6.00
☐	16 Beaumont: Boston NL	60.00	30.00	6.00
☐	17 Beck: Boston NL	50.00	20.00	5.00
☐	18 Becker: Boston NL	50.00	20.00	5.00
☐	19 Bell: Brooklyn	50.00	20.00	5.00
	pitching,			
	follow thru)			
☐	20 Bell: Brooklyn, ...	60.00	30.00	6.00
	Hands over head			
☐	21 Bender: Phila. AL	200.00	100.00	20.00
	Portrait			
☐	22 Bender: Phila. AL	175.00	85.00	18.00
	(pitching) trees			
☐	23 Bender: Phila. AL	175.00	85.00	18.00
	(pitching) no trees			
☐	24 Bergen: Brooklyn, ...	50.00	20.00	5.00
	Catching			
☐	25 Bergen: Brooklyn, ...	60.00	30.00	6.00
	Batting			
☐	26 Berger: Cleveland	50.00	20.00	5.00
☐	27 Bescher: Cinc., ...	50.00	20.00	5.00
	Catching fly ball			
☐	28 Bescher: Cinc.	50.00	20.00	5.00
	Portrait			
☐	29 Birmingham: Cleve.	60.00	30.00	6.00
☐	30 Bliss: St.L. NL	50.00	20.00	5.00
☐	31 Bowerman: Bost. NL	60.00	30.00	6.00
☐	32 Bradley: Cleveland, ...	60.00	30.00	6.00
	Portrait			
☐	33 Bradley: Cleveland, ...	50.00	20.00	5.00
	Batting			
☐	34 Bransfield: Phila. NL	60.00	30.00	6.00
☐	35 Bresnahan: St.L. NL, ...	200.00	100.00	20.00
	Portrait			
☐	36 Bresnahan: St.L. NL, ...	175.00	85.00	18.00
	Batting			
☐	37 Bridwell: N.Y. NL, ...	60.00	30.00	6.00
	Portrait			
☐	38 Bridwell: N.Y. NL, ...	50.00	20.00	5.00
	Wearing sweater			
☐	39 G. Brown (sic):	150.00	75.00	15.00
	Chicago NL			
☐	40 G. Brown (sic):	500.00	250.00	50.00
	Washington			
☐	41 M. Brown: Chicago NL ...	200.00	100.00	20.00
	Portrait			
☐	42 M. Brown: Chicago NL ...	175.00	85.00	18.00
	Chicago down			
	front of shirt			
☐	43 M. Brown: Chicago NL, ..	300.00	150.00	30.00

		Cubs across chest			
☐	44	Burch: Brooklyn, ... Fielding	50.00	20.00	5.00
☐	45	Burch: Brooklyn, ... Batting	150.00	75.00	15.00
☐	46	Burns: Chicago AL	50.00	20.00	5.00
☐	47	Bush: Detroit	50.00	20.00	5.00
☐	48	Byrne: St.L. NL	50.00	20.00	5.00
☐	49	Camnitz: Pitt., Arms .... folded over chest	60.00	30.00	6.00
☐	50	Camnitz: Pitt., ... Hands over head	50.00	20.00	5.00
☐	51	Camnitz: Pitt., ... Throwing	50.00	20.00	5.00
☐	52	Campbell: Cinc.	50.00	20.00	5.00
☐	53	Carrigan: Boston AL	50.00	20.00	5.00
☐	54	Chance: Chicago NL, ... Cubs across chest	200.00	100.00	20.00
☐	55	Chance: Chicago NL, ... Chicago down front of shirt	175.00	85.00	18.00
☐	56	Chance: Chicago NL, ... Batting	175.00	85.00	18.00
☐	57	Charles: St.L. NL	50.00	20.00	5.00
☐	58	Chase: N.Y. AL, ... Port. blue bkgd.	90.00	45.00	9.00
☐	59	Chase: N.Y. AL, ... Port., pink bkgd.	175.00	85.00	18.00
☐	60	Chase: N.Y. AL, ... Holding cup	90.00	45.00	9.00
☐	61	Chase: N.Y. AL, ... Throwing, dark cap	90.00	45.00	9.00
☐	62	Chase: N.Y. AL, ... Throwing, white cap	175.00	85.00	18.00
☐	63	Chesbro: N.Y. AL	300.00	150.00	30.00
☐	64	Cicotte: Boston AL	90.00	45.00	9.00
☐	65	Clarke: Pitt., ... Portrait	200.00	100.00	20.00
☐	66	F. Clarke: Pitt.	175.00	85.00	18.00
☐	67	J.J. Clarke: Cleve.	60.00	30.00	6.00
☐	68	Cobb: Detroit, ... Port., red bkgd.	1250.00	600.00	150.00
☐	69	Cobb: Detroit, Port. .... green background	2400.00	1200.00	250.00
☐	70	Cobb: Detroit, Bat .... on shoulder	1350.00	650.00	150.00
☐	71	Cobb: Detroit, Bat .... away from shoulder	1250.00	600.00	150.00
☐	72	Collins: Phila. AL	175.00	85.00	18.00
☐	73	Conroy: Washington, ... Fielding	60.00	30.00	6.00
☐	74	Conroy: Wash., Bat .... on shoulder	50.00	20.00	5.00
☐	75	Covaleski: Phil. NL .... (Harry)	60.00	30.00	6.00
☐	76	Crandall: N.Y. NL, ... without cap	60.00	30.00	6.00
☐	77	Crandall: N.Y. NL, ... sweater and cap	50.00	20.00	5.00
☐	78	Crawford: Detroit, ... Batting	175.00	85.00	18.00
☐	79	Crawford: Detroit, ... Throwing	200.00	100.00	20.00
☐	80	Cree: N.Y. AL	50.00	20.00	5.00
☐	81	Criger: St.L. AL	60.00	30.00	6.00
☐	82	Criss: St.L. AL	60.00	30.00	6.00
☐	83	Dahlen: Brooklyn	300.00	150.00	30.00
☐	84	Dahlen: Bost. NL	90.00	45.00	9.00
☐	85	Davis: Phila. AL	50.00	20.00	5.00
☐	86	G. Davis: Chicago AL	60.00	30.00	6.00
☐	87	H. Davis: Phila. AL	60.00	30.00	6.00
☐	88	Delehanty: Wash.	60.00	30.00	6.00
☐	89	Demmitt: St.L. AL	3000.00	1500.00	300.00
☐	90	Demmitt: N.Y. AL	50.00	20.00	5.00
☐	91	Devlin: N.Y. NL	60.00	30.00	6.00
☐	92	Devore: N.Y. NL	50.00	20.00	5.00
☐	93	Dineen: St.L. AL	50.00	20.00	5.00
☐	94	Donlin: N.Y. NL, ... Fielding	100.00	50.00	10.00
☐	95	Donlin: N.Y. NL, ... Sitting	60.00	30.00	6.00
☐	96	Donlin: N.Y. NL, ... Batting	50.00	20.00	5.00
☐	97	Donohue: Chicago AL	60.00	30.00	6.00
☐	98	Donovan: Detroit, ... Portrait	60.00	30.00	6.00
☐	99	Donovan: Detroit, ... Throwing	50.00	20.00	5.00
☐	100	Dooin: Phila. NL	60.00	30.00	6.00
☐	101	Doolan: Phila. NL, ... Fielding	50.00	20.00	5.00
☐	102	Doolan: Phila. NL, ... Batting	50.00	20.00	5.00
☐	103	Doolin (sic, Doolan): .... Phila. NL,	60.00	30.00	6.00
☐	104	Dougherty: Chic. AL, ... Portrait	60.00	30.00	6.00
☐	105	Dougherty: Chic. AL, ... Fielding	50.00	20.00	5.00
☐	106	Downey: Cinc., ... Batting	50.00	20.00	5.00
☐	107	Downey: Cinc., ... Fielding	50.00	20.00	5.00
☐	108A	Doyle: N.Y. .... (hands over head)	60.00	30.00	6.00
☐	108B	Doyle: N.Y. NAT'L .... (hands over head)	20000.00	10000.00	2500.00
☐	109	Doyle: N.Y. NL, ... Sweater	50.00	20.00	5.00
☐	110	Doyle: N.Y. NL, ... Throwing	60.00	30.00	6.00
☐	111	Doyle: N.Y. NL, ... Bat on shoulder	50.00	20.00	5.00
☐	112	Dubuc: Cin.	50.00	20.00	5.00
☐	113	Duffy: Chicago AL	175.00	85.00	18.00
☐	114	Dunn: Brooklyn	50.00	20.00	5.00
☐	115	Durham: N.Y. NL	60.00	30.00	6.00
☐	116	Dygert: Phila. AL	50.00	20.00	5.00
☐	117	Easterly: Cleveland	50.00	20.00	5.00
☐	118	Egan: Cinc.	50.00	20.00	5.00
☐	119	Elberfeld: Wash., ... Fielding	50.00	20.00	5.00
☐	120	Elberfeld: Wash., ... Portrait	1000.00	500.00	100.00
☐	121	Elberfeld: N.Y. AL, ... Portrait	60.00	30.00	6.00
☐	122	Engle: N.Y. AL	50.00	20.00	5.00
☐	123	Evans: St.L. NL	50.00	20.00	5.00
☐	124	Evers: Chicago NL, ... Portrait	200.00	100.00	20.00
☐	125	Evers: Chicago NL, ... Cubs across chest	300.00	150.00	30.00
☐	126	Evers: Chicago NL, ... Chicago down front of shirt	175.00	85.00	18.00
☐	127	Ewing: Cinc.	60.00	30.00	6.00
☐	128	Ferguson: Boston NL	50.00	20.00	5.00
☐	129	Ferris: St.L. AL	60.00	30.00	6.00
☐	130	Fiene: Chicago AL, ... Portrait	50.00	20.00	5.00
☐	131	Fiene: Chicago AL, ... Throwing	50.00	20.00	5.00
☐	132	Fletcher: N.Y. NL	50.00	20.00	5.00
☐	133	Flick: Cleveland	250.00	125.00	25.00
☐	134	Ford: N.Y. AL	50.00	20.00	5.00
☐	135	Frill: N.Y. AL	50.00	20.00	5.00
☐	136	Fromme: Cinc.	50.00	20.00	5.00
☐	137	Gandil: Chicago AL	90.00	45.00	9.00
☐	138	Ganley: Washington	60.00	30.00	6.00
☐	139	Gasper: Cinc.	50.00	20.00	5.00
☐	140	Geyer: St.L. NL	50.00	20.00	5.00
☐	141	Gibson: Pitt.	60.00	30.00	6.00
☐	142	Gilbert: St.L. NL	60.00	30.00	6.00
☐	143	Goode (sic): Cleve.	60.00	30.00	6.00
☐	144	Graham: Boston NL	50.00	20.00	5.00
☐	145	Graham: St.L. AL	50.00	20.00	5.00
☐	146	Gray: Washington	50.00	20.00	5.00
☐	147	Griffith: Cinc., ... Portrait	200.00	100.00	20.00
☐	148	Griffith: Cinc., ... Batting	175.00	85.00	18.00
☐	149	Groom: Washington	50.00	20.00	5.00
☐	150	Hahn: Chicago AL	60.00	30.00	6.00
☐	151	Hartsel: Phila. AL	50.00	20.00	5.00
☐	152	Hemphill: N.Y. AL	60.00	30.00	6.00
☐	153	Herzog : N.Y. NL	60.00	30.00	6.00
☐	154	Herzog: Boston NL	50.00	20.00	5.00
☐	155	Hinchman: Cleveland	60.00	30.00	6.00
☐	156	Hoblitzell: Cinc.	50.00	20.00	5.00
☐	157	Hoffman: St.L. AL	50.00	20.00	5.00
☐	158	Hofman: Chicago NL	50.00	20.00	5.00
☐	159	Howard: Chicago NL	50.00	20.00	5.00
☐	160	Howell: St.L. AL, ... Portrait	50.00	20.00	5.00
☐	161	Howell: St.L. AL, ... Left hand on hip	50.00	20.00	5.00
☐	162	Huggins: Cinc., ... Portrait	200.00	100.00	20.00
☐	163	Huggins: Cinc., ... Hands to mouth	175.00	85.00	18.00
☐	164	Hulswitt: St.L. NL	50.00	20.00	5.00
☐	165	Hummel: Brooklyn	50.00	20.00	5.00
☐	166	Hunter: Brooklyn	50.00	20.00	5.00
☐	167	Isbell: Chicago AL	60.00	30.00	6.00
☐	168	Jacklitsch: Phila.NL	60.00	30.00	6.00
☐	169	Jennings: Detroit, ... Portrait	200.00	100.00	20.00
☐	170	Jennings: Detroit, ... Yelling	175.00	85.00	18.00
☐	171	Jennings: Detroit, ...	175.00	85.00	18.00

172	Johnson: Washington, ... Dancing for joy	750.00	375.00	75.00
173	Johnson: Washington, ... Portrait Ready to pitch	600.00	300.00	60.00
174	Jones: St.L. AL,	60.00	30.00	6.00
175	Jones: Detroit	50.00	20.00	5.00
176	F. Jones: Chic. AL, Portrait	60.00	30.00	6.00
177	F. Jones: Chic. AL, Hands on hips	60.00	30.00	6.00
178	Jordan: Brooklyn, Portrait	60.00	30.00	6.00
179	Jordan: Brooklyn, Batting	50.00	20.00	5.00
180	Joss: Cleveland, Portrait	300.00	150.00	30.00
181	Joss: Cleveland, Ready to pitch	200.00	100.00	20.00
182	Karger: Cinc.	60.00	30.00	6.00
183	Keeler: N.Y. AL, Portrait	300.00	150.00	30.00
184	Keeler: N.Y. AL, Batting	250.00	125.00	25.00
185	Killian: Detroit, Portrait	60.00	30.00	6.00
186	Killian: Detroit, Pitching	50.00	20.00	5.00
187	Kleinow: N.Y. AL, Batting	60.00	30.00	6.00
188	Kleinow: N.Y. AL, Catching	50.00	20.00	5.00
189	Kleinow: Bost. AL, Catching	300.00	150.00	30.00
190	Kling: Chicago NL	60.00	30.00	6.00
191	Knabe: Phila. NL	50.00	20.00	5.00
192	Knight: N.Y. AL, Portrait	50.00	20.00	5.00
193	Knight: N.Y. AL, Batting	50.00	20.00	5.00
194	Konetchy: St.L. NL, Awaiting low ball	50.00	20.00	5.00
195	Konetchy: St.L. NL, Glove above head	60.00	30.00	6.00
196	Krause: Phila. AL, Portrait	50.00	20.00	5.00
197	Krause: Phila. AL, Pitching	50.00	20.00	5.00
198	Kroh: Chicago NL	50.00	20.00	5.00
199	Lajoie: Cleveland, Portrait	350.00	175.00	35.00
200	Lajoie: Cleveland, Batting	250.00	125.00	25.00
201	Lajoie: Cleveland, Throwing	300.00	150.00	30.00
202	Lake: N.Y. AL	60.00	30.00	6.00
203	Lake: St.L. AL, Hands over head	50.00	20.00	5.00
204	Lake: St.L. AL, Throwing	50.00	20.00	5.00
205	LaPorte: N.Y. AL	50.00	20.00	5.00
206	Latham: N.Y. NL	50.00	20.00	5.00
207	Leach: Pitt., Portrait	60.00	30.00	6.00
208	Leach: Pitt., In fielding position	50.00	20.00	5.00
209	Leifield: Pitt., Batting	50.00	20.00	5.00
210	Leifield: Pitt., Hands behind head	60.00	30.00	6.00
211	Lennox: Brooklyn	50.00	20.00	5.00
212	Liebhardt: Cleve.	60.00	30.00	6.00
213	Lindaman: Boston NL	90.00	45.00	9.00
214	Livingstone: Phila.AL	50.00	20.00	5.00
215	Lobert: Cinc.	60.00	30.00	6.00
216	Lord: Bost. AL	50.00	20.00	5.00
217	Lumley: Brooklyn	60.00	30.00	6.00
218	Lundgren: Chicago NL	350.00	175.00	35.00
219	Maddox: Pitt.	50.00	20.00	5.00
220	Magee: Phila. NL, Portrait	60.00	30.00	6.00
221	Magee: Phila. NL, Batting	50.00	20.00	5.00
222	Magie: Phila. NL (sic) Portrait, name misspelled	10000.00	5000.00	1000.00
223	Manning: N.Y. AL, Batting	60.00	30.00	6.00
224	Manning: N.Y. AL, Hands over head	50.00	20.00	5.00
225	Marquard: N.Y. NL, Portrait	200.00	100.00	20.00
226	Marquard: N.Y. NL, Pitching	175.00	85.00	18.00
227	Marquard: N.Y. NL, Standing	200.00	100.00	20.00
228	Marshall: Brooklyn	50.00	20.00	5.00
229	Mathewson: N.Y. NL, ... Portrait	750.00	375.00	75.00
230	Mathewson: N.Y. NL, ... Pitching, white cap	600.00	300.00	60.00
231	Mathewson: N.Y. NL, ... Pitching, dark cap	500.00	250.00	50.00
232	Mattern: Boston NL	50.00	20.00	5.00
233	McAleese: St.L. AL	50.00	20.00	5.00
234	McBride: Washington	50.00	20.00	5.00
235	McCormick: N.Y. NL	50.00	20.00	5.00
236	McElveen: Brooklyn	50.00	20.00	5.00
237	McGraw: N.Y. NL, Portrait, no cap	300.00	150.00	30.00
238	McGraw: N.Y. NL, Wearing sweater	200.00	100.00	20.00
239	McGraw: N.Y. NL, pointing	250.00	125.00	25.00
240	McGraw: N.Y. NL, Glove on hip	250.00	125.00	25.00
241	McIntyre: Detroit	50.00	20.00	5.00
242	McIntyre: Brooklyn	60.00	30.00	6.00
243	McIntyre: Brooklyn and Chicago NL	50.00	20.00	5.00
244	McLean: Cinc.	50.00	20.00	5.00
245	McQuillan: Phila. NL, Throwing	60.00	30.00	6.00
246	McQuillan: Phila. NL, Batting	50.00	20.00	5.00
247	Merkle: N.Y. NL, Portrait	50.00	20.00	5.00
248	Merkle: N.Y. NL, Throwing	60.00	30.00	6.00
249	Meyers: N.Y. NL	50.00	20.00	5.00
250	Milan: Washington	50.00	20.00	5.00
251	Miller: Pitt.	50.00	20.00	5.00
252	Mitchell: Cinc.	50.00	20.00	5.00
253	Moran: Chicago NL	50.00	20.00	5.00
254	Moriarty: Detroit	50.00	20.00	5.00
255	Mowrey: Cinc.	50.00	20.00	5.00
256	Mullen: Detroit	50.00	20.00	5.00
257	Mullin: Detroit, Throwing	60.00	30.00	6.00
258	Mullin: Detroit, Batting	50.00	20.00	5.00
259	Murphy: Phila. AL, Throwing	60.00	30.00	6.00
260	Murphy: Phila. AL, Bat on shoulder	50.00	20.00	5.00
261	Murray: N.Y. NL, Sweater	50.00	20.00	5.00
262	Murray: N.Y. NL, Bat on shoulder	50.00	20.00	5.00
263	Myers (sic): N.Y. NL, Fielding	50.00	20.00	5.00
264	Myers (sic): N.Y. NL, Batting	50.00	20.00	5.00
265	Needham: Chicago NL	50.00	20.00	5.00
266	Nicholls: Phila. AL	60.00	30.00	6.00
267	Nichols(sic): Phila. AL	50.00	20.00	5.00
268	Niles: Boston AL	60.00	30.00	6.00
269	Oakes: Cinc.	50.00	20.00	5.00
270	O'Hara: St.L. NL	3000.00	1500.00	350.00
271	O'Hara: N.Y. NL.	50.00	20.00	5.00
272	Oldring: Phila. AL, Fielding	60.00	30.00	6.00
273	Oldring: Phila. AL, Bat on shoulder	50.00	20.00	5.00
274	O'Leary: Detroit, Portrait	60.00	30.00	6.00
275	O'Leary: Detroit, Hands on knees	50.00	20.00	5.00
276	Overall: Chicago NL, Portrait	60.00	30.00	6.00
277	Overall: Chicago NL, Pitching, follow thru	50.00	20.00	5.00
278	Overall: Chicago NL, Pitching hiding ball in glove	50.00	20.00	5.00
279	Owen: Chicago AL	60.00	30.00	6.00
280	Parent: Chicago AL	60.00	30.00	6.00
281	Paskert: Cinc.	50.00	20.00	5.00
282	Pastorius: Brooklyn	60.00	30.00	6.00
283	Pattee: Brooklyn	100.00	50.00	10.00
284	Payne: Chicago AL	50.00	20.00	5.00
285	Pelty: St.L. AL, HOR	100.00	50.00	10.00
286	Pelty: St.L. AL, VERT	50.00	20.00	5.00
287	Perring: Cleveland	50.00	20.00	5.00
288	Pfeffer: Chicago NL	50.00	20.00	5.00
289	Pfeister: Chic. NL, Sitting	50.00	20.00	5.00
290	Pfeister: Chic. NL, Pitching	50.00	20.00	5.00

☐ 291	Phelps: St.L. NL	50.00	20.00	5.00
☐ 292	Phillippe: Pitt.	60.00	30.00	6.00
☐ 293	Plank: Phila. AL 12500.00	6000.00	1500.00
☐ 294	Powell: St.L. AL	60.00	30.00	6.00
☐ 295	Powers: Phil. AL	100.00	50.00	10.00
☐ 296	Purtell: Chicago AL	50.00	20.00	5.00
☐ 297	Quinn: N.Y. AL	50.00	20.00	5.00
☐ 298	Raymond: N.Y. NL	50.00	20.00	5.00
☐ 299	Reulbach: Chicago NL, ...	50.00	20.00	5.00
	Pitching			
☐ 300	Reulbach: Chicago NL, ...	100.00	50.00	10.00
	Hands at side			
☐ 301	Rhoades: Cleveland, ...	50.00	20.00	5.00
	Hand in air			
☐ 302	Rhoades: Cleveland, ...	50.00	20.00	5.00
	Ready to pitch			
☐ 303	Rhodes: St.L. NL	50.00	20.00	5.00
☐ 304	Ritchey: Boston NL	60.00	30.00	6.00
☐ 305	Rossman: Detroit	50.00	20.00	5.00
☐ 306	Rucker: Brooklyn, ...	60.00	30.00	6.00
	Portrait			
☐ 307	Rucker: Brooklyn, ...	50.00	20.00	5.00
	Pitching			
☐ 308	Schaefer: Washington	50.00	20.00	5.00
☐ 309	Schaefer: Detroit	60.00	30.00	6.00
☐ 310	Schlei: N.Y. NL, ...	50.00	20.00	5.00
	Sweater			
☐ 311	Schlei: N.Y. NL, ...	50.00	20.00	5.00
	Batting			
☐ 312	Schlei: N.Y. NL, ...	60.00	30.00	6.00
	Fielding			
☐ 313	Schmidt: Detroit, ...	50.00	20.00	5.00
	Portrait			
☐ 314	Schmidt: Detroit, ...	60.00	30.00	6.00
	Throwing			
☐ 315	Schulte: Chicago NL, ...	50.00	20.00	5.00
	Batting, back turned			
☐ 316	Schulte: Chicago NL, ...	60.00	30.00	6.00
	Batting, front pose			
☐ 317	Scott: Chicago AL	50.00	20.00	5.00
☐ 318	Seymour: N.Y. NL, ...	50.00	20.00	5.00
	Portrait			
☐ 319	Seymour: N.Y. NL, ...	50.00	20.00	5.00
	Throwing			
☐ 320	Seymour: N.Y. NL, ...	60.00	30.00	6.00
	Batting			
☐ 321	Shaw: St.L. NL	60.00	30.00	6.00
☐ 322	Sheckard: Chic. NL, ...	50.00	20.00	5.00
	Throwing			
☐ 323	Sheckard: Chic. NL, ...	60.00	30.00	6.00
	Side view			
☐ 324	Shipke: Washington	60.00	30.00	6.00
☐ 325	Smith: Chicago AL	50.00	20.00	5.00
☐ 326	Smith: Chicago and	400.00	200.00	40.00
	Boston AL			
☐ 327	F. Smith: Chicago AL	60.00	30.00	6.00
☐ 328	Happy Smith: Brk.	50.00	20.00	5.00
☐ 329	Snodgrass: N.Y. NL, ...	50.00	20.00	5.00
	Batting			
☐ 330	Snodgrass: N.Y. NL, ...	50.00	20.00	5.00
	Catching			
☐ 331	Spade: Cinc.	60.00	30.00	6.00
☐ 332	Speaker: Boston AL	350.00	175.00	35.00
☐ 333	Spencer: Boston AL	60.00	30.00	6.00
☐ 334	Stahl: Boston AL, ...	50.00	20.00	5.00
	Catching fly ball			
☐ 335	Stahl: Boston AL, ...	50.00	20.00	5.00
	Standing, arms down			
☐ 336	Stanage: Detroit	50.00	20.00	5.00
☐ 337	Starr: Boston NL	50.00	20.00	5.00
☐ 338	Steinfeldt: Chic. NL, ...	60.00	30.00	6.00
	Portrait			
☐ 339	Steinfeldt: Chic. NL, ...	50.00	20.00	5.00
	Batting			
☐ 340	Stephens: St.L. AL	50.00	20.00	5.00
☐ 341	Stone: St.L. AL	60.00	30.00	6.00
☐ 342	Stovall: Cleveland, ...	60.00	30.00	6.00
	Portrait			
☐ 343	Stovall: Cleveland, ...	50.00	20.00	5.00
	Batting			
☐ 344	Street: Washington, ...	50.00	20.00	5.00
	Portrait			
☐ 345	Street: Washington, ...	50.00	20.00	5.00
	Catching			
☐ 346	Sullivan: Chicago AL	60.00	30.00	6.00
☐ 347	Summers: Detroit	50.00	20.00	5.00
☐ 348	Sweeney: N.Y. AL	50.00	20.00	5.00
☐ 349	Sweeney: Bost. NL	50.00	20.00	5.00
☐ 350	L. Tannehill: Chic.AL	60.00	30.00	6.00
☐ 351	Tannehill: Chicago AL	50.00	20.00	5.00
☐ 352	Tannehill: Wash.	50.00	20.00	5.00
☐ 353	Tenney: N.Y. NL, ...	60.00	30.00	6.00
☐ 354	Thomas: Phila. AL	50.00	20.00	5.00
☐ 355	Tinker: Chicago NL, ...	175.00	85.00	18.00
	Ready to hit			

☐ 356	Tinker: Chicago NL, ...	175.00	85.00	18.00
	Bat on shoulder			
☐ 357	Tinker: Chicago NL, ...	200.00	100.00	20.00
	Portrait			
☐ 358	Tinker: Chicago NL, ...	200.00	100.00	20.00
	Hands on knees			
☐ 359	Titus: Phila. NL	50.00	20.00	5.00
☐ 360	Turner: Cleveland	60.00	30.00	6.00
☐ 361	Unglaub: Washington	50.00	20.00	5.00
☐ 362	Waddell: St.L. AL, ...	250.00	125.00	20.00
	Portrait			
☐ 363	Waddell: St.L. AL, ...	200.00	100.00	20.00
	Pitching			
☐ 364	Wagner: Boston AL, ...	100.00	50.00	10.00
	Bat on left shoulder			
☐ 365	Wagner: Boston AL, ...	50.00	20.00	5.00
	Bat on right shoulder			
☐ 366	Wagner: Pitt. ......115000.	55000.	18000.
☐ 367	Wallace: St.L. AL	200.00	100.00	20.00
☐ 368	Walsh: Chicago AL	200.00	100.00	20.00
☐ 369	Warhop: N.Y. AL	50.00	20.00	5.00
☐ 370	Weimer: N.Y. NL	60.00	30.00	6.00
☐ 371	Wheat: Brooklyn	200.00	100.00	20.00
☐ 372	White: Chicago AL, ...	60.00	30.00	6.00
	Portrait			
☐ 373	White: Chicago AL, ...	50.00	20.00	5.00
	Pitching			
☐ 374	Wilhelm: Brooklyn, ...	50.00	20.00	5.00
	Batting			
☐ 375	Wilhelm: Brooklyn, ...	60.00	30.00	6.00
	Hands to chest			
☐ 376	Willett: Detroit, ...	50.00	20.00	5.00
	Batting			
☐ 377	Willetts (sic):	50.00	20.00	5.00
	Detroit, Pitching			
☐ 378	Williams: St.L. AL	60.00	30.00	6.00
☐ 379	Willis: Pitt.	100.00	50.00	10.00
☐ 380	Willis: St.L. NL, ...	90.00	45.00	9.00
	Pitching			
☐ 381	Willis: St.L. NL, ...	90.00	45.00	9.00
	Batting			
☐ 382	Wilson: Pitt.	50.00	20.00	5.00
☐ 383	Wiltse: N.Y. NL, ...	60.00	30.00	6.00
	Portrait			
☐ 384	Wiltse: N.Y. NL, ...	50.00	20.00	5.00
	Sweater			
☐ 385	Wiltse: N.Y. NL, ...	50.00	20.00	5.00
	Pitching			
☐ 386	Young: Cleveland, ...	500.00	250.00	50.00
	Portrait			
☐ 387	Young: Cleveland, ...	400.00	200.00	40.00
	Pitch, front view			
☐ 388	Young: Cleveland, ...	400.00	200.00	40.00
	Pitch, side view			
☐ 389	Zimmerman:	50.00	20.00	5.00
	Chicago NL			
☐ 390	Fred Abbott: Toledo	40.00	20.00	4.00
☐ 391	Merle (Doc) Adkins:	40.00	20.00	4.00
	Baltimore			
☐ 392	John Anderson: Prov.	40.00	20.00	4.00
☐ 393	Herman Armbruster:	40.00	20.00	4.00
	St. Paul			
☐ 394	Harry Arndt: Prov.	40.00	20.00	4.00
☐ 395	Cy Barger: Rochester	40.00	20.00	4.00
☐ 396	John Barry:	40.00	20.00	4.00
	Milwaukee			
☐ 397	Emil H. Batch: Roch.	40.00	20.00	4.00
☐ 398	Jake Beckley: K.C.	175.00	85.00	18.00
☐ 399	Russell Blackburne	40.00	20.00	4.00
	(Lena): Providence			
☐ 400	David Brain: Buffalo	40.00	20.00	4.00
☐ 401	Roy Brashear: K.C.	40.00	20.00	4.00
☐ 402	Fred Burchell:	40.00	20.00	4.00
	Buffalo			
☐ 403	Jimmy Burke: Ind.	40.00	20.00	4.00
☐ 404	John Butler: Roch.	40.00	20.00	4.00
☐ 405	Charles Carr: Ind.	40.00	20.00	4.00
☐ 406	James Peter Casey	40.00	20.00	4.00
	(Doc): Montreal			
☐ 407	Peter Cassidy: Balt.	40.00	20.00	4.00
☐ 408	Wm. Chappelle: Roch.	40.00	20.00	4.00
☐ 409	Wm. Clancy: Buffalo	40.00	20.00	4.00
☐ 410	Joshua Clark: Col.	40.00	20.00	4.00
☐ 411	William Clymer: Col.	40.00	20.00	4.00
☐ 412	Jimmy Collins: Minn.	225.00	110.00	22.00
☐ 413	Bunk Congalton:	40.00	20.00	4.00
	Columbus			
☐ 414	Gavvy Cravath: Minn.	60.00	30.00	6.00
☐ 415	Monte Cross: Ind.	40.00	20.00	4.00
☐ 416	Paul Davidson: Ind.	40.00	20.00	4.00
☐ 417	Frank Delehanty:	40.00	20.00	4.00
	Louisville			
☐ 418	Rube Dessau: Balt.	40.00	20.00	4.00
☐ 419	Gus Dorner: K.C.	40.00	20.00	4.00
☐ 420	Jerome Downs: Minn.	40.00	20.00	4.00

☐ 421	Jack Dunn: Baltimore	40.00	20.00	4.00
☐ 422	James Flanagan: .... Buffalo	40.00	20.00	4.00
☐ 423	James Freeman: Tol.	40.00	20.00	4.00
☐ 424	John Ganzel: Roch.	40.00	20.00	4.00
☐ 425	Myron Grimshaw: Tor. ...	40.00	20.00	4.00
☐ 426	Robert Hall: Balt.	40.00	20.00	4.00
☐ 427	William Hallman: .... Kansas City	40.00	20.00	4.00
☐ 428	John Hannifan: J.C.	40.00	20.00	4.00
☐ 429	Jack Hayden: Ind.	40.00	20.00	4.00
☐ 430	Harry Hinchman: Tol.	40.00	20.00	4.00
☐ 431	Harry C. Hoffman .... (Izzy): Providence	40.00	20.00	4.00
☐ 432	James B. Jackson: .... Baltimore	40.00	20.00	4.00
☐ 433	Joe Kelley: Tor.	225.00	110.00	22.00
☐ 434	Rube Kisinger: Buff. .... (sic) Kissinger	40.00	20.00	4.00
☐ 435	Otto Kruger: Col. .... (sic) Krueger	40.00	20.00	4.00
☐ 436	Wm. Lattimore: Tol.	40.00	20.00	4.00
☐ 437	James Lavender: .... Providence	40.00	20.00	4.00
☐ 438	Carl Lundgren: K.C.	40.00	20.00	4.00
☐ 439	Wm. Malarkey: Buff.	40.00	20.00	4.00
☐ 440	Wm. Maloney: Roch.	40.00	20.00	4.00
☐ 441	Dennis McGann: .... Milwaukee	40.00	20.00	4.00
☐ 442	James McGinley: Tor.	40.00	20.00	4.00
☐ 443	Joe McGinnity: New.	175.00	85.00	18.00
☐ 444	Ulysses McGlynn: .... Milwaukee	40.00	20.00	4.00
☐ 445	George Merritt: J.C.	40.00	20.00	4.00
☐ 446	Wm. Milligan: J.C.	40.00	20.00	4.00
☐ 447	Fred Mitchell: Tor.	40.00	20.00	4.00
☐ 448	Dan Moeller: J.C.	40.00	20.00	4.00
☐ 449	Joseph Herbert Moran: .. Providence	40.00	20.00	4.00
☐ 450	Wm. Nattress: .... Buffalo	40.00	20.00	4.00
☐ 451	Frank Oberlin: Minn.	40.00	20.00	4.00
☐ 452	Peter O'Brien: .... St. Paul	40.00	20.00	4.00
☐ 453	Wm. O'Neil: Minn.	40.00	20.00	4.00
☐ 454	James Phelan: Prov.	40.00	20.00	4.00
☐ 455	Oliver Pickering: .... Minneapolis.	40.00	20.00	4.00
☐ 456	Philip Poland: Balt.	40.00	20.00	4.00
☐ 457	Ambrose Puttman: .... Louisville	40.00	20.00	4.00
☐ 458	Lee Quillen: Minn.	40.00	20.00	4.00
☐ 459	Newton Randall: .... Milwaukee	40.00	20.00	4.00
☐ 460	Louis Ritter: K.C.	40.00	20.00	4.00
☐ 461	Dick Rudolph: Tor.	40.00	20.00	4.00
☐ 462	George Schirm: .... Buffalo	40.00	20.00	4.00
☐ 463	Larry Schlafly: .... Newark	40.00	20.00	4.00
☐ 464	Ossie Schreck: Col. .... (sic) Schreckengost	40.00	20.00	4.00
☐ 465	William Shannon: .... Kansas City	40.00	20.00	4.00
☐ 466	Bayard Sharpe: .... Newark	40.00	20.00	4.00
☐ 467	Royal Shaw: Prov.	40.00	20.00	4.00
☐ 468	James Slagle: Balt.	40.00	20.00	4.00
☐ 469	George Henry Smith: ..... Buffalo	40.00	20.00	4.00
☐ 470	Samuel Strang: Balt.	40.00	20.00	4.00
☐ 471	Luther(Dummy) Taylor: . Buffalo	40.00	20.00	4.00
☐ 472	John Thielman: .... Louisville	40.00	20.00	4.00
☐ 473	John F. White: Buff.	40.00	20.00	4.00
☐ 474	William Wright: Tol.	40.00	20.00	4.00
☐ 475	Irving M. Young: .... Minneapolis	40.00	20.00	4.00
☐ 476	Jack Bastian: .... San Antonio	125.00	60.00	12.50
☐ 477	Harry Bay: Nashv.	125.00	60.00	12.50
☐ 478	Wm. Bernhard: .... Nashville	125.00	60.00	12.50
☐ 479	Ted Breitenstein: .... New Orleans	125.00	60.00	12.50
☐ 480	George(Scoops)Carey: ... Memphis	125.00	60.00	12.50
☐ 481	Cad Coles: Augusta	125.00	60.00	12.50
☐ 482	Wm. Cranston: Memph. ...	125.00	60.00	12.50
☐ 483	Roy Ellam: Nashville	125.00	60.00	12.50
☐ 484	Edward Foster: .... Charleston	125.00	60.00	12.50
☐ 485	Charles Fritz: N.O.	125.00	60.00	12.50
☐ 486	Ed Greminger: Montg.	125.00	60.00	12.50
☐ 487	Guiheen: Portsmouth	125.00	60.00	12.50
☐ 488	William F. Hart .... Little Rock	125.00	60.00	12.50
☐ 489	James Henry Hart: .... Montgomery	125.00	60.00	12.50
☐ 490	J.R. Helm: Columbus ..... (Georgia)	125.00	60.00	12.50
☐ 491	Gordon Hickman: .... Mobile	125.00	60.00	12.50
☐ 492	Buck Hooker: .... Lynchburg	125.00	60.00	12.50
☐ 493	Ernie Howard: Sav.	125.00	60.00	12.50
☐ 494	A.O. Jordan: Atlanta	125.00	60.00	12.50
☐ 495	J.F. Kiernan: .... Columbia	125.00	60.00	12.50
☐ 496	Frank King: Danville	125.00	60.00	12.50
☐ 497	James LaFitte: Macon	125.00	60.00	12.50
☐ 498	Harry Lentz: Little .... Rock (sic) Sentz	125.00	60.00	12.50
☐ 499	Perry Lipe: Richmond	125.00	60.00	12.50
☐ 500	George Manion: .... Columbia	125.00	60.00	12.50
☐ 501	McCauley: Portsmouth ..	125.00	60.00	12.50
☐ 502	Charles B. Miller: .... Dallas	125.00	60.00	12.50
☐ 503	Carlton Molesworth: ...... Birmingham	125.00	60.00	12.50
☐ 504	Dominic Mullaney: .... Jacksonville	125.00	60.00	12.50
☐ 505	Albert Orth: Lynchb.	125.00	60.00	12.50
☐ 506	William Otey: Norf.	125.00	60.00	12.50
☐ 507	George Paige: .... Charleston	125.00	60.00	12.50
☐ 508	Hub Perdue: Nashv.	125.00	60.00	12.50
☐ 509	Archie Persons: .... Montgomery	125.00	60.00	12.50
☐ 510	Edward Reagan: N.O.	125.00	60.00	12.50
☐ 511	R.H. Revelle: Richm.	125.00	60.00	12.50
☐ 512	Isaac Rockenfeld: .... Montgomery	125.00	60.00	12.50
☐ 513	Ray Ryan: Roanoke	125.00	60.00	12.50
☐ 514	Charles Seitz: Norf.	125.00	60.00	12.50
☐ 515	Frank(Shag) Shaughn- .... essy: Roanoke	125.00	60.00	12.50
☐ 516	Carlos Smith: .... Shreveport	125.00	60.00	12.50
☐ 517	Sid Smith: Atlanta	125.00	60.00	12.50
☐ 518	M.R. (Dolly) Stark: .... San Antonio	125.00	60.00	12.50
☐ 519	Tony Thebo: Waco	125.00	60.00	12.50
☐ 520	Woodie Thornton: .... Mobile	125.00	60.00	12.50
☐ 521	Juan Violat: Jackson- ..... ville: (sic) Viola	125.00	60.00	12.50
☐ 522	James Westlake: .... Danville	125.00	60.00	12.50
☐ 523	Foley White: Houston	125.00	60.00	12.50

T207 Brown Background

The cards in this 207-card set measure 1 1/2" by 2 5/8". The T207 set, also known as the "Brown Background" set was issued with Broadleaf, Cycle, Napoleon, Recruit and anonymous (Factories no. 2, 3 or 25) backs in 1912. Broadleaf, Cycle and anonymous backs are difficult to obtain. Although many scarcities and cards with varying degrees of difficulty to obtain exist (see prices below), the Loudermilk, Lewis (Boston NL) and Miller (Chicago

NL) cards are the rarest, followed by Saier and Tyler. The cards are numbered below for reference in alphabetical order by player's name. The complete set price below does include the Lewis variation missing the Braves patch on the sleeve.

			EX-MT	VG-E	GOOD
	COMPLETE SET (208)		27000.00	12500.00	3000.00
	COMMON PLAYER (1-207)		50.00	20.00	5.00
☐	1	Adams: Cleve AL	100.00	50.00	10.00
☐	2	Ainsmith: Wash AL	50.00	20.00	5.00
☐	3	Almeida: Cinc AL	100.00	50.00	10.00
☐	4	Austin: StL AL with StL on shirt	50.00	20.00	5.00
☐	5	Austin: StL AL without StL on shirt	150.00	75.00	15.00
☐	6	Ball: Cleve AL	50.00	20.00	5.00
☐	7	Barger: Brk NL	50.00	20.00	5.00
☐	8	Barry: Phil AL	50.00	20.00	5.00
☐	9	Bauman: Det AL	150.00	75.00	15.00
☐	10	Becker: NY NL	50.00	20.00	5.00
☐	11	Bender: Phil AL	150.00	75.00	15.00
☐	12	Benz: Chi AL	100.00	50.00	10.00
☐	13	Bescher: Cinc AL	50.00	20.00	5.00
☐	14	Birmingham: Cleve AL	100.00	50.00	10.00
☐	15	Blackburne: Chi AL	100.00	50.00	10.00
☐	16	Blanding: Cleve AL	100.00	50.00	10.00
☐	17	Block: Chi AL	50.00	20.00	5.00
☐	18	Bodie: Chi AL	50.00	20.00	5.00
☐	19	Bradley: Bos AL	50.00	20.00	5.00
☐	20	Bresnahan: StL NL	150.00	75.00	15.00
☐	21	Bushelman: Bos AL	100.00	50.00	10.00
☐	22	Butcher: Cleve AL	100.00	50.00	10.00
☐	23	Byrne: Pitt NL	50.00	20.00	5.00
☐	24	Callahan: Chi AL	50.00	20.00	5.00
☐	25	Camnitz: Pitt NL	50.00	20.00	5.00
☐	26	Carey: Pitt NL	150.00	75.00	15.00
☐	27	Carrigan: Bos AL correct back	50.00	20.00	5.00
☐	28	Carrigan: Bos AL Wagner back	200.00	100.00	20.00
☐	29	Chalmers: Phil NL	50.00	20.00	5.00
☐	30	Chance: Chi NL	200.00	100.00	20.00
☐	31	Cicotte: Bos AL	75.00	37.50	7.50
☐	32	Clarke: Cinc NL	50.00	20.00	5.00
☐	33	Cole: Chi AL	50.00	20.00	5.00
☐	34	Collins: Chi AL	250.00	125.00	20.00
☐	35	Coulson: Brk NL	50.00	20.00	5.00
☐	36	Covington: Det AL	50.00	20.00	5.00
☐	37	Crandall: NY NL	50.00	20.00	5.00
☐	38	Cunningham: Wash AL	75.00	37.50	7.50
☐	39	Danforth: Phil AL	50.00	20.00	5.00
☐	40	Daniels: NY AL	50.00	20.00	5.00
☐	41	Daubert: Brk NL	75.00	37.50	7.50
☐	42	Davis: Cleve AL	50.00	20.00	5.00
☐	43	Delahanty: Det AL	50.00	20.00	5.00
☐	44	Derrick: Phil AL	50.00	20.00	5.00
☐	45	Devlin: Bos NL	50.00	20.00	5.00
☐	46	Devore: NY NL	50.00	20.00	5.00
☐	47	Donlin: Pitt NL	100.00	50.00	10.00
☐	48	Donnelly: Bos NL	100.00	50.00	10.00
☐	49	Dooin: Phil NL	50.00	20.00	5.00
☐	50	Downey: Phil NL	100.00	50.00	10.00
☐	51	Doyle: NY NL	50.00	20.00	5.00
☐	52	Drake: Det AL	50.00	20.00	5.00
☐	53	Easterly: Cleve AL	50.00	20.00	5.00
☐	54	Ellis: StL NL	50.00	20.00	5.00
☐	55	Engle: Bos AL	50.00	20.00	5.00
☐	56	Erwin: Brk NL	50.00	20.00	5.00
☐	57	Evans: StL NL	50.00	20.00	5.00
☐	58	Ferry: Pitt NL	50.00	20.00	5.00
☐	59	Fisher: NY AL white cap	150.00	75.00	15.00
☐	60	Fisher: NY AL blue cap	75.00	37.50	7.50
☐	61	Fletcher: NY NL	50.00	20.00	5.00
☐	62	Fournier: Chi AL	100.00	50.00	10.00
☐	63	Fromme: Cinc NL	50.00	20.00	5.00
☐	64	Gainor: Det AL	50.00	20.00	5.00
☐	65	Gardner: Bos AL	50.00	20.00	5.00
☐	66	George: Cleve AL	50.00	20.00	5.00
☐	67	Golden: StL NL	50.00	20.00	5.00
☐	68	Gowdy: Bos NL	50.00	20.00	5.00
☐	69	Graham: Phil NL	100.00	50.00	10.00
☐	70	Graney: Cleve AL	50.00	20.00	5.00
☐	71	Gregg: Cleve AL	100.00	50.00	10.00
☐	72	Hageman: Bos AL	50.00	20.00	5.00
☐	73	Hall: Bos AL	50.00	20.00	5.00
☐	74	Hallinan: St.L. AL	50.00	20.00	5.00
☐	75	E. Hamilton: St.L. AL	50.00	20.00	5.00
☐	76	Harmon: St.L. NL	50.00	20.00	5.00
☐	77	Hartley: NY NL	100.00	50.00	10.00
☐	78	Henriksen, Bos AL	50.00	20.00	5.00
☐	79	Henry: Wash AL	75.00	37.50	7.50
☐	80	Herzog: NY NL	100.00	50.00	10.00
☐	81	Higgins: Brk NL	50.00	20.00	5.00
☐	82	Hoff: NY AL	100.00	50.00	10.00
☐	83	Hogan: StL AL	50.00	20.00	5.00
☐	84	Hooper: Bos AL	400.00	200.00	40.00
☐	85	Houser: Bos AL	100.00	50.00	10.00
☐	86	Hyatt: Pitt NL	100.00	50.00	10.00
☐	87	Johnson: Wash AL	750.00	375.00	75.00
☐	88	Kaler: Cleve AL	50.00	20.00	5.00
☐	89	Kelly: Pitt NL	100.00	50.00	10.00
☐	90	Kirke: Bos NL	100.00	50.00	10.00
☐	91	Kling: Bos NL	50.00	20.00	5.00
☐	92	Knabe: Phil NL	50.00	20.00	5.00
☐	93	Knetzer: Brk NL	50.00	20.00	5.00
☐	94	Konetchy: StL NL	50.00	20.00	5.00
☐	95	Krause: Phil AL	50.00	20.00	5.00
☐	96	Kuhn: Chi AL	100.00	50.00	10.00
☐	97	Kutina: StL AL	100.00	50.00	10.00
☐	98	Lange: Chi AL	100.00	50.00	10.00
☐	99	Lapp: Phil AL	50.00	20.00	5.00
☐	100	Latham: NY NL	50.00	20.00	5.00
☐	101	Leach: Pitt NL	50.00	20.00	5.00
☐	102	Leifield: Pitt NL	50.00	20.00	5.00
☐	103	Lennox: Chi NL	50.00	20.00	5.00
☐	104	Lewis: Bos AL	50.00	20.00	5.00
☐	105A	Lewis: Bos NL (Braves patch on sleeve)	2500.00	1250.00	300.00
☐	105B	Lewis: Bos NL (nothing on sleeve)	2500.00	1250.00	300.00
☐	106	Lively: Det AL	50.00	20.00	5.00
☐	107	Livingston: Cleve AL "A" shirt	200.00	100.00	20.00
☐	108	Livingston: Cleve AL "C" shirt	200.00	100.00	20.00
☐	109	Livingston: Cleve AL "c" shirt	75.00	37.50	7.50
☐	110	Lord: Phil AL	50.00	20.00	5.00
☐	111	Lord: Chi AL	50.00	20.00	5.00
☐	112	Loudermilk: StL NL	2500.00	1250.00	300.00
☐	113	Marquard: NY NL	150.00	75.00	15.00
☐	114	Marsans: Cinc NL	50.00	20.00	5.00
☐	115	McBride: Wash AL	50.00	20.00	5.00
☐	116	McCarthy: Pitt NL	200.00	100.00	20.00
☐	117	McDonald: Bos NL	50.00	20.00	5.00
☐	118	McGraw: NY NL	200.00	100.00	20.00
☐	119	McIntire: Chi NL	50.00	20.00	5.00
☐	120	McIntyre: Chi AL	50.00	20.00	5.00
☐	121	McKechnie: Pitt NL	300.00	150.00	30.00
☐	122	McLean: Cinc NL	50.00	20.00	5.00
☐	123	Milan: Wash AL	50.00	20.00	5.00
☐	124	Miller: Pitt NL	50.00	20.00	5.00
☐	125	Miller: Chi NL	2000.00	1000.00	250.00
☐	126	Miller: Brk NL	100.00	50.00	10.00
☐	127	Miller: Bos NL	100.00	50.00	10.00
☐	128	Mitchell: Cinc NL	50.00	20.00	5.00
☐	129	Mitchell: Cleve AL	90.00	45.00	9.00
☐	130	Mogridge: Chi AL	100.00	50.00	10.00
☐	131	Moore: Phil NL	100.00	50.00	10.00
☐	132	Moran: Phil NL	50.00	20.00	5.00
☐	133	Morgan: Phil AL	50.00	20.00	5.00
☐	134	Morgan: Wash AL	50.00	20.00	5.00
☐	135	Moriarity: Det AL	100.00	50.00	10.00
☐	136	Mullin: Det AL with "D" on cap	90.00	45.00	9.00
☐	137	Mullin: Det AL without "D" on cap	200.00	100.00	20.00
☐	138	Needham: Chi NL	50.00	20.00	5.00
☐	139	Nelson: StL AL	100.00	50.00	10.00
☐	140	Northen: Brk NL	50.00	20.00	5.00
☐	141	Nunamaker: Bos AL	50.00	20.00	5.00
☐	142	Oakes: StL NL	50.00	20.00	5.00
☐	143	O'Brien: Bos AL	50.00	20.00	5.00
☐	144	Oldring: Phil AL	50.00	20.00	5.00
☐	145	Olson: Cleve AL	50.00	20.00	5.00
☐	146	O'Toole: Pitt NL	50.00	20.00	5.00
☐	147	Paskert: Phil NL	50.00	20.00	5.00
☐	148	Pelty: StL AL	100.00	50.00	10.00
☐	149	Perdue: Bos NL	50.00	20.00	5.00
☐	150	Peters: Chi AL	100.00	50.00	10.00
☐	151	Phelan: Cinc NL	100.00	50.00	10.00
☐	152	Quinn: NY AL	50.00	20.00	5.00
☐	153	Ragan: Brk NL	500.00	250.00	50.00
☐	154	Rasmussen: Phil NL	400.00	200.00	40.00
☐	155	Rath: Chi AL	100.00	50.00	10.00
☐	156	Reulbach: Chi NL	50.00	20.00	5.00
☐	157	Rucker: Brk NL	50.00	20.00	5.00
☐	158	Ryan: Cleve AL	100.00	50.00	10.00
☐	159	Saier: Chi NL	750.00	375.00	75.00
☐	160	Scanlon: Phil NL	50.00	20.00	5.00
☐	161	Schaefer: Wash AL	50.00	20.00	5.00
☐	162	Schardt: Brk NL	50.00	20.00	5.00
☐	163	Schulte: Chi NL	50.00	20.00	5.00

☐ 164 Scott: Chi AL	50.00	20.00	5.00
☐ 165 Severeid: Cinc NL	50.00	20.00	5.00
☐ 166 Simon: Pitt NL	50.00	20.00	5.00
☐ 167 Smith: StL NL	50.00	20.00	5.00
☐ 168 Smith: Cinc NL	50.00	20.00	5.00
☐ 169 Snodgrass: NY NL	50.00	20.00	5.00
☐ 170 Speaker: Bos AL	900.00	450.00	90.00
☐ 171 Spratt: Bos NL	50.00	20.00	5.00
☐ 172 Stack: Brk NL	50.00	20.00	5.00
☐ 173 Stanage: Det AL	50.00	20.00	5.00
☐ 174 Steele: StL NL	50.00	20.00	5.00
☐ 175 Steinfeldt: StL NL	50.00	20.00	5.00
☐ 176 Stovall: StL AL	50.00	20.00	5.00
☐ 177 Street: NY AL	50.00	20.00	5.00
☐ 178 Strunk: Phil AL	50.00	20.00	5.00
☐ 179 Sullivan: Chi AL	50.00	20.00	5.00
☐ 180 Sweeney: Bos NL	150.00	75.00	15.00
☐ 181 Tannehill: Chi AL	50.00	20.00	5.00
☐ 182 Thomas: Bos AL	50.00	20.00	5.00
☐ 183 Tinker: Chi NL	150.00	75.00	15.00
☐ 184 Tooley: Brk NL	50.00	20.00	5.00
☐ 185 Turner: Cleve NL	50.00	20.00	5.00
☐ 186 Tyler: Bos NL	750.00	375.00	75.00
☐ 187 Vaughn: NY AL	50.00	20.00	5.00
☐ 188 Wagner: Bos AL	90.00	45.00	9.00
correct back			
☐ 189 Wagner: Bos AL	200.00	100.00	20.00
Carrigan back			
☐ 190 Walker: Wash AL	50.00	20.00	5.00
☐ 191 Wallace: St.L. AL	150.00	75.00	15.00
☐ 192 Warhop: NY AL	50.00	20.00	5.00
☐ 193 Weaver: Chi AL	150.00	75.00	15.00
☐ 194 Wheat: Brk NL	150.00	75.00	15.00
☐ 195 White: Chi AL	100.00	50.00	10.00
☐ 196 Wilie: St.L. NL	75.00	37.50	7.50
☐ 197 Williams: NY AL	50.00	20.00	5.00
☐ 198 Wilson: NY NL	50.00	20.00	5.00
☐ 199 Wilson: Pitt NL	100.00	50.00	10.00
☐ 200 Wiltse: NY NL	50.00	20.00	5.00
☐ 201 Wingo: StL NL	50.00	20.00	5.00
☐ 202 Wolverton: NY AL	50.00	20.00	5.00
☐ 203 Wood: Bos AL	150.00	75.00	15.00
☐ 204 Woodburn: StL NL	100.00	50.00	10.00
☐ 205 Works: Det AL	300.00	150.00	30.00
☐ 206 Yerkes: Bos AL	50.00	20.00	5.00
☐ 207 Zeider: Chi AL	100.00	50.00	10.00

1988 Umpire Cards

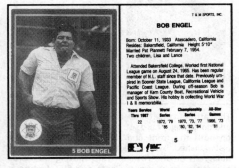

This set of 64 cards was distributed as a small boxed set featuring Major League umpires exclusively. The box itself is blank, white, and silver. The set was produced by T and M Sports under licenses from Major League Baseball and the Major League Umpires Association. The cards are in color and are standard size, 2 1/2" by 3 1/2". Card backs are printed in black on light blue. All the cards are black bordered, but the American Leaguers have a red thin inner border, whereas the National Leaguers have a green thin inner border. A short biographical sketch is given on the back for each umpire. The cards are numbered on the back; the number on the front of each card refers to the umpire's uniform number.

	MINT	EXC	G-VG
COMPLETE SET (64)	10.00	5.00	1.00

COMMON PLAYER (1-64)		.25	.12	.02
☐ 1 Doug Harvey		.35	.17	.03
☐ 2 Lee Weyer		.25	.12	.02
☐ 3 Billy Williams		.25	.12	.02
☐ 4 John Kibler		.25	.12	.02
☐ 5 Bob Engel		.25	.12	.02
☐ 6 Harry Wendelstedt		.35	.17	.03
☐ 7 Larry Barnett		.25	.12	.02
☐ 8 Don Denkinger		.35	.17	.03
☐ 9 Dave Phillips		.35	.17	.03
☐ 10 Larry McCoy		.25	.12	.02
☐ 11 Bruce Froemming		.35	.17	.03
☐ 12 John McSherry		.35	.17	.03
☐ 13 Jim Evans		.25	.12	.02
☐ 14 Frank Pulli		.25	.12	.02
☐ 15 Joe Brinkman		.25	.12	.02
☐ 16 Terry Tata		.25	.12	.02
☐ 17 Paul Runge		.25	.12	.02
☐ 18 Dutch Rennert		.25	.12	.02
☐ 19 Nick Bremigan		.25	.12	.02
☐ 20 Jim McKean		.25	.12	.02
☐ 21 Terry Cooney		.25	.12	.02
☐ 22 Rich Garcia		.25	.12	.02
☐ 23 Dale Ford		.25	.12	.02
☐ 24 Al Clark		.25	.12	.02
☐ 25 Greg Kose		.25	.12	.02
☐ 26 Jim Quick		.25	.12	.02
☐ 27 Ed Montague		.25	.12	.02
☐ 28 Jerry Crawford		.25	.12	.02
☐ 29 Steve Palermo		.25	.12	.02
☐ 30 Durwood Merrill		.25	.12	.02
☐ 31 Ken Kaiser		.45	.22	.04
☐ 32 Vic Voltaggio		.25	.12	.02
☐ 33 Mike Reilly		.25	.12	.02
☐ 34 Eric Gregg		.45	.22	.04
☐ 35 Ted Hendry		.25	.12	.02
☐ 36 Joe West		.25	.12	.02
☐ 37 Dave Pallone		.25	.12	.02
☐ 38 Fred Brocklander		.25	.12	.02
☐ 39 John Shulock		.25	.12	.02
☐ 40 Derryl Cousins		.25	.12	.02
☐ 41 Charlie Williams		.25	.12	.02
☐ 42 Rocky Roe		.25	.12	.02
☐ 43 Randy Marsh		.25	.12	.02
☐ 44 Bob Davidson		.25	.12	.02
☐ 45 Drew Coble		.25	.12	.02
☐ 46 Tim McClelland		.25	.12	.02
☐ 47 Dan Morrison		.25	.12	.02
☐ 48 Rick Reed		.25	.12	.02
☐ 49 Steve Rippley		.25	.12	.02
☐ 50 John Hirshbeck		.25	.12	.02
☐ 51 Mark Johnson		.25	.12	.02
☐ 52 Gerry Davis		.25	.12	.02
☐ 53 Dana DeMuth		.25	.12	.02
☐ 54 Larry Young		.25	.12	.02
☐ 55 Tim Welke		.25	.12	.02
☐ 56 Greg Bonin		.25	.12	.02
☐ 57 Tom Hallion		.25	.12	.02
☐ 58 Dale Scott		.25	.12	.02
☐ 59 Tim Tschida		.25	.12	.02
☐ 60 Dick Stello		.25	.12	.02
☐ 61 All-Star Game		.25	.12	.02
☐ 62 World Series		.25	.12	.02
☐ 63 Jocko Conlan		.60	.30	.06
☐ 64 Checklist Card		.25	.12	.02

1989 Umpires

The 1989 Umpires set contains 63 standard- size (2 1/2 by 3 1/2 inch) cards. The fronts have borderless color photos with AL or NL logos. The backs are grey and include biographical information. The cards were distributed as a boxed set along with a custom album.

	MINT	EXC	G-VG
COMPLETE SET (63)	10.00	5.00	1.00
COMMON PLAYER (1-63)	.25	.12	.02
☐ 1 Doug Harvey	.35	.17	.03
☐ 2 John Kibler	.25	.12	.02
☐ 3 Bob Engel	.25	.12	.02
☐ 4 Harry Wendelstedt	.35	.17	.03
☐ 5 Larry Barnett	.25	.12	.02
☐ 6 Don Denkinger	.35	.17	.03
☐ 7 Dave Phillips	.35	.17	.03
☐ 8 Larry McCoy	.25	.12	.02

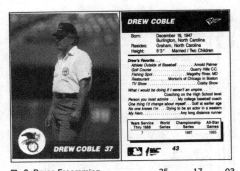

WALLY JOYNER

		MINT	EXC	G-VG

☐ 9	Bruce Froemming	.35	.17	.03
☐ 10	John McSherry	.35	.17	.03
☐ 11	Jim Evans	.25	.12	.02
☐ 12	Frank Pulli	.25	.12	.02
☐ 13	Joe Brinkman	.25	.12	.02
☐ 14	Terry Tata	.25	.12	.02
☐ 15	Nick Bremigan	.25	.12	.02
☐ 16	Jim McKean	.25	.12	.02
☐ 17	Paul Runge	.25	.12	.02
☐ 18	Dutch Rennert	.25	.12	.02
☐ 19	Terry Cooney	.25	.12	.02
☐ 20	Rich Garcia	.25	.12	.02
☐ 21	Dale Ford	.25	.12	.02
☐ 22	Al Clark	.25	.12	.02
☐ 23	Greg Kosc	.25	.12	.02
☐ 24	Jim Quick	.25	.12	.02
☐ 25	Eddie Montague	.25	.12	.02
☐ 26	Jerry Crawford	.25	.12	.02
☐ 27	Steve Palermo	.25	.12	.02
☐ 28	Durwood Merrill	.25	.12	.02
☐ 29	Ken Kaiser	.45	.22	.04
☐ 30	Vic Voltaggio	.25	.12	.02
☐ 31	Mike Reilly	.25	.12	.02
☐ 32	Eric Gregg	.45	.22	.04
☐ 33	Ted Hendry	.25	.12	.02
☐ 34	Joe West	.25	.12	.02
☐ 35	Dave Pallone	.25	.12	.02
☐ 36	Fred Brocklander	.25	.12	.02
☐ 37	John Shulock	.25	.12	.02
☐ 38	Derryl Cousins	.25	.12	.02
☐ 39	Charlie Williams	.25	.12	.02
☐ 40	Rocky Roe	.25	.12	.02
☐ 41	Randy Marsh	.25	.12	.02
☐ 42	Bob Davidson	.25	.12	.02
☐ 43	Drew Coble	.25	.12	.02
☐ 44	Tim McClelland	.25	.12	.02
☐ 45	Dan Morrison	.25	.12	.02
☐ 46	Rick Reed	.25	.12	.02
☐ 47	Steve Rippley	.25	.12	.02
☐ 48	John Hirschbeck	.25	.12	.02
☐ 49	Mark Johnson	.25	.12	.02
☐ 50	Gerry Davis	.25	.12	.02
☐ 51	Dana DeMuth	.25	.12	.02
☐ 52	Larry Young	.25	.12	.02
☐ 53	Tim Welke	.25	.12	.02
☐ 54	Greg Bonin	.25	.12	.02
☐ 55	Tom Hallion	.25	.12	.02
☐ 56	Dale Scott	.25	.12	.02
☐ 57	Tim Tschida	.25	.12	.02
☐ 58	Gary Darling	.25	.12	.02
☐ 59	Mark Hirschbeck	.25	.12	.02
☐ 60	All Star	.25	.12	.02
☐ 61	World Series	.25	.12	.02
☐ 62	Lee Weyer	.25	.12	.02
☐ 63	Connolly/Klem	.50	.25	.05

1988 Upper Deck Samples

This two-card test issue was given away as samples during the summer of 1988 in anticipation of Upper Deck obtaining licenses from Major League Baseball and the Major League Baseball Players Association. Not many were produced (probably less than 25,000 of each) but almost none were thrown away as they were distributed basically only to those who would hold on to them. There are supposedly versions based on where the hologram is printed but the price

below is for the basic variety. These test cards are the same size (2 1/2" by 3 1/2") as the regular issue and are styled similarly. Joyner and Buice were supposedly interested in investing in Upper Deck (conflict of interest prohibited them) and apparently were helpful in getting Upper Deck the necessary licenses. Cards were passed out freely to every dealer at the National Sports Collectors Convention in Atlantic City, New Jersey in August 1988.

		MINT	EXC	G-VG
	COMPLETE SET (2)	40.00	20.00	4.00
	COMMON PLAYER	15.00	7.50	1.50
☐ 1	DeWayne Buice	15.00	7.50	1.50
☐ 700	Wally Joyner	30.00	15.00	3.00

1989 Upper Deck

Ryne Sandberg

This attractive set was introduced in 1989 as an additional major card set. The cards feature full color on both the front and the back. The cards are distinguished by the fact that each card has a hologram on the reverse, thus making the cards essentially copy proof. Cards 668-693 feature a "Collector's Choice" (CC) colorful drawing of a player (by artist Vernon Wells) on the card front and a checklist of that team on the card back. On many cards "Rookie" and team logos can be found with either a "TM" or (R). Cards with missing or duplicate holograms appear to be relatively common and hence there is little, if any, premium value on these "variations." The more significant variations involving changed photos or changed type are listed below. According to the company, the Murphy and Sheridan cards were corrected very early after only 2% of the cards had been produced. This means, for example, that out of 1,000,000 Dale Murphy '89 Upper Deck cards produced there are only 20,000 Murphy error cards. Similarly, the Sheffield was corrected after 15% had been printed; Varsho, Gallego, and Schroeder were corrected after 20%; and Holton, Manrique, and Winningham were corrected 30% of the way through. Collectors should also note that many dealers consider that Upper Deck's "planned" production of 1,000,000 of each player was increased (perhaps even doubled) later in the year due to the explosion in popularity of the Upper Deck cards.

		MINT	EXC	G-VG
	COMPLETE SET (700)	48.00	20.00	5.00
	COMMON PLAYER (1-700)	.06	.03	.00
☐ 1	Ken Griffey Jr.	9.00	3.00	.60
☐ 2	Luis Medina	.30	.15	.03
☐ 3	Tony Chance	.20	.10	.02
☐ 4	Dave Otto	.18	.09	.01
☐ 5	Sandy Alomar Jr. UER	1.50	.75	.15
	(wrong birthdate)			
☐ 6	Rolando Roomes	.30	.15	.03
☐ 7	Dave West	.45	.22	.04
☐ 8	Cris Carpenter	.25	.12	.02
☐ 9	Gregg Jefferies	2.50	1.25	.25
☐ 10	Doug Dascenzo	.20	.10	.02
☐ 11	Ron Jones	.35	.17	.03
☐ 12	Luis De Los Santos	.20	.10	.02
☐ 13A	Gary Sheffield ERR	4.00	2.00	.40
	(SS upside down on card front)			
☐ 13B	Gary Sheffield COR	2.00	1.00	.20
☐ 14	Mike Harkey	.40	.20	.04
☐ 15	Lance Blankenship	.25	.12	.02
☐ 16	William Brennan	.18	.09	.01
☐ 17	John Smoltz	1.00	.50	.10
☐ 18	Ramon Martinez	.75	.30	.05
☐ 19	Mark Lemke	.18	.09	.01
☐ 20	Juan Bell	.30	.15	.03
☐ 21	Rey Palacios	.18	.09	.01
☐ 22	Felix Jose	.30	.15	.03
☐ 23	Van Snider	.25	.12	.02
☐ 24	Dante Bichette	.20	.10	.02
☐ 25	Randy Johnson	.25	.12	.02
☐ 26	Carlos Quintana	.35	.17	.03
☐ 27	Star Rookie Checklist	.06	.01	.00
☐ 28	Mike Schooler	.35	.17	.03
☐ 29	Randy St.Claire	.06	.03	.00
☐ 30	Jerald Clark	.20	.10	.02
☐ 31	Kevin Gross	.06	.03	.00
☐ 32	Dan Firova	.12	.06	.01
☐ 33	Jeff Calhoun	.06	.03	.00
☐ 34	Tommy Hinzo	.06	.03	.00
☐ 35	Ricky Jordan	2.00	1.00	.20
☐ 36	Larry Parrish	.06	.03	.00
☐ 37	Bret Saberhagen UER	.20	.10	.02
	(hit total 931, should be 1031)			
☐ 38	Mike Smithson	.06	.03	.00
☐ 39	Dave Dravecky	.10	.05	.01
☐ 40	Ed Romero	.06	.03	.00
☐ 41	Jeff Musselman	.06	.03	.00
☐ 42	Ed Hearn	.06	.03	.00
☐ 43	Rance Mulliniks	.06	.03	.00
☐ 44	Jim Eisenreich	.06	.03	.00
☐ 45	Sil Campusano	.20	.10	.02
☐ 46	Mike Krukow	.06	.03	.00
☐ 47	Paul Gibson	.12	.06	.01
☐ 48	Mike LaCoss	.06	.03	.00
☐ 49	Larry Herndon	.06	.03	.00
☐ 50	Scott Garrelts	.10	.05	.01
☐ 51	Dwayne Henry	.06	.03	.00
☐ 52	Jim Acker	.06	.03	.00
☐ 53	Steve Sax	.12	.06	.01
☐ 54	Pete O'Brien	.10	.05	.01
☐ 55	Paul Runge	.06	.03	.00
☐ 56	Rick Rhoden	.06	.03	.00
☐ 57	John Dopson	.25	.12	.02
☐ 58	Casey Candaele UER	.06	.03	.00
	(no stats for Astros for '88 season)			
☐ 59	Dave Righetti	.10	.05	.01
☐ 60	Joe Hesketh	.06	.03	.00
☐ 61	Frank DiPino	.06	.03	.00
☐ 62	Tim Laudner	.06	.03	.00
☐ 63	Jamie Moyer	.06	.03	.00
☐ 64	Fred Toliver	.06	.03	.00
☐ 65	Mitch Webster	.06	.03	.00
☐ 66	John Tudor	.10	.05	.01
☐ 67	John Cangelosi	.06	.03	.00
☐ 68	Mike Devereaux	.12	.06	.01
☐ 69	Brian Fisher	.06	.03	.00
☐ 70	Mike Marshall	.10	.05	.01
☐ 71	Zane Smith	.06	.03	.00
☐ 72A	Brian Holton ERR	2.50	1.25	.25
	(photo actually Shawn Hillegas)			
☐ 72B	Brian Holton COR	.30	.15	.03
☐ 73	Jose Guzman	.06	.03	.00
☐ 74	Rick Mahler	.06	.03	.00
☐ 75	John Shelby	.06	.03	.00
☐ 76	Jim Deshaies	.06	.03	.00
☐ 77	Bobby Meacham	.06	.03	.00
☐ 78	Bryn Smith	.10	.05	.01
☐ 79	Joaquin Andujar	.10	.05	.01
☐ 80	Richard Dotson	.06	.03	.00
☐ 81	Charlie Lea	.06	.03	.00
☐ 82	Calvin Schiraldi	.06	.03	.00
☐ 83	Les Straker	.06	.03	.00
☐ 84	Les Lancaster	.06	.03	.00
☐ 85	Allan Anderson	.10	.05	.01
☐ 86	Junior Ortiz	.06	.03	.00
☐ 87	Jesse Orosco	.06	.03	.00
☐ 88	Felix Fermin	.10	.05	.01
☐ 89	Dave Anderson	.06	.03	.00
☐ 90	Rafael Belliard UER	.06	.03	.00
	(wrong birth year)			
☐ 91	Franklin Stubbs	.06	.03	.00
☐ 92	Cecil Espy	.10	.05	.01
☐ 93	Albert Hall	.06	.03	.00
☐ 94	Tim Leary	.10	.05	.01
☐ 95	Mitch Williams	.12	.06	.01
☐ 96	Tracy Jones	.10	.05	.01
☐ 97	Danny Darwin	.06	.03	.00
☐ 98	Gary Ward	.06	.03	.00
☐ 99	Neal Heaton	.06	.03	.00
☐ 100	Jim Pankovits	.06	.03	.00
☐ 101	Bill Doran	.10	.05	.01
☐ 102	Tim Wallach	.10	.05	.01
☐ 103	Joe Magrane	.12	.06	.01
☐ 104	Ozzie Virgil	.06	.03	.00
☐ 105	Alvin Davis	.12	.06	.01
☐ 106	Tom Brookens	.06	.03	.00
☐ 107	Shawon Dunston	.10	.05	.01
☐ 108	Tracy Woodson	.10	.05	.01
☐ 109	Nelson Liriano	.06	.03	.00
☐ 110	Devon White UER	.12	.06	.01
	(doubles total 46, should be 56)			
☐ 111	Steve Balboni	.06	.03	.00
☐ 112	Buddy Bell	.10	.05	.01
☐ 113	German Jimenez	.10	.05	.01
☐ 114	Ken Dayley	.06	.03	.00
☐ 115	Andres Galarraga	.12	.06	.01
☐ 116	Mike Scioscia	.06	.03	.00
☐ 117	Gary Pettis	.06	.03	.00
☐ 118	Ernie Whitt	.06	.03	.00
☐ 119	Bob Boone	.12	.06	.01
☐ 120	Ryne Sandberg	.25	.12	.02
☐ 121	Bruce Benedict	.06	.03	.00
☐ 122	Hubie Brooks	.10	.05	.01
☐ 123	Mike Moore	.10	.05	.01
☐ 124	Wallace Johnson	.06	.03	.00
☐ 125	Bob Horner	.10	.05	.01
☐ 126	Chili Davis	.10	.05	.01
☐ 127	Manny Trillo	.06	.03	.00
☐ 128	Chet Lemon	.06	.03	.00
☐ 129	John Cerutti	.06	.03	.00
☐ 130	Orel Hershiser	.25	.12	.02
☐ 131	Terry Pendleton	.06	.03	.00
☐ 132	Jeff Blauser	.15	.07	.01
☐ 133	Mike Fitzgerald	.06	.03	.00
☐ 134	Henry Cotto	.06	.03	.00
☐ 135	Gerald Young	.10	.05	.01
☐ 136	Luis Salazar	.06	.03	.00
☐ 137	Alejandro Pena	.06	.03	.00
☐ 138	Jack Howell	.06	.03	.00
☐ 139	Tony Fernandez	.10	.05	.01
☐ 140	Mark Grace	2.50	1.25	.25
☐ 141	Ken Caminiti	.06	.03	.00
☐ 142	Mike Jackson	.06	.03	.00
☐ 143	Larry McWilliams	.06	.03	.00
☐ 144	Andres Thomas	.06	.03	.00
☐ 145	Nolan Ryan	2.00	1.00	.20
☐ 146	Mike Davis	.06	.03	.00
☐ 147	DeWayne Buice	.06	.03	.00
☐ 148	Jody Davis	.06	.03	.00
☐ 149	Jesse Barfield	.10	.05	.01
☐ 150	Matt Nokes	.10	.05	.01
☐ 151	Jerry Reuss	.06	.03	.00
☐ 152	Rick Cerone	.06	.03	.00
☐ 153	Storm Davis	.10	.05	.01
☐ 154	Marvell Wynne	.06	.03	.00
☐ 155	Will Clark	1.75	.85	.17
☐ 156	Luis Aguayo	.06	.03	.00
☐ 157	Willie Upshaw	.06	.03	.00
☐ 158	Randy Bush	.06	.03	.00
☐ 159	Ron Darling	.10	.05	.01

☐ 160	Kal Daniels	.10	.05	.01
☐ 161	Spike Owen	.06	.03	.00
☐ 162	Luis Polonia	.06	.03	.00
☐ 163	Kevin Mitchell UER	.60	.30	.06
	('88/total HR's 18/52, should be 19/53)			
☐ 164	Dave Gallagher	.30	.15	.03
☐ 165	Benito Santiago	.20	.10	.02
☐ 166	Greg Gagne	.06	.03	.00
☐ 167	Ken Phelps	.06	.03	.00
☐ 168	Sid Fernandez	.10	.05	.01
☐ 169	Bo Diaz	.06	.03	.00
☐ 170	Cory Snyder	.12	.06	.01
☐ 171	Eric Show	.06	.03	.00
☐ 172	Rob Thompson	.06	.03	.00
☐ 173	Marty Barrett	.06	.03	.00
☐ 174	Dave Henderson	.06	.03	.00
☐ 175	Ozzie Guillen	.10	.05	.01
☐ 176	Barry Lyons	.06	.03	.00
☐ 177	Kelvin Torve	.12	.06	.01
☐ 178	Don Slaught	.06	.03	.00
☐ 179	Steve Lombardozzi	.06	.03	.00
☐ 180	Chris Sabo	.60	.30	.06
☐ 181	Jose Uribe	.06	.03	.00
☐ 182	Shane Mack	.10	.05	.01
☐ 183	Ron Karkovice	.06	.03	.00
☐ 184	Todd Benzinger	.06	.03	.00
☐ 185	Dave Stewart	.15	.07	.01
☐ 186	Julio Franco	.12	.06	.01
☐ 187	Ron Robinson	.06	.03	.00
☐ 188	Wally Backman	.06	.03	.00
☐ 189	Randy Velarde	.10	.05	.01
☐ 190	Joe Carter	.15	.07	.01
☐ 191	Bob Welch	.10	.05	.01
☐ 192	Kelly Paris	.06	.03	.00
☐ 193	Chris Brown	.06	.03	.00
☐ 194	Rick Reuschel	.10	.05	.01
☐ 195	Roger Clemens	.50	.25	.05
☐ 196	Dave Concepcion	.10	.05	.01
☐ 197	Al Newman	.06	.03	.00
☐ 198	Brook Jacoby	.10	.05	.01
☐ 199	Mookie Wilson	.10	.05	.01
☐ 200	Don Mattingly	1.00	.50	.10
☐ 201	Dick Schofield	.06	.03	.00
☐ 202	Mark Gubicza	.10	.05	.01
☐ 203	Gary Gaetti	.10	.05	.01
☐ 204	Dan Pasqua	.06	.03	.00
☐ 205	Andre Dawson	.12	.06	.01
☐ 206	Chris Speier	.06	.03	.00
☐ 207	Kent Tekulve	.06	.03	.00
☐ 208	Rod Scurry	.06	.03	.00
☐ 209	Scott Bailes	.06	.03	.00
☐ 210	Rickey Henderson UER (Throws Right)	.35	.17	.03
☐ 211	Harold Baines	.12	.06	.01
☐ 212	Tony Armas	.10	.05	.01
☐ 213	Kent Hrbek	.12	.06	.01
☐ 214	Darrin Jackson	.12	.06	.01
☐ 215	George Brett	.25	.12	.02
☐ 216	Rafael Santana	.06	.03	.00
☐ 217	Andy Allanson	.06	.03	.00
☐ 218	Brett Butler	.10	.05	.01
☐ 219	Steve Jeltz	.06	.03	.00
☐ 220	Jay Buhner	.25	.12	.02
☐ 221	Bo Jackson	1.50	.75	.15
☐ 222	Angel Salazar	.06	.03	.00
☐ 223	Kirk McCaskill	.06	.03	.00
☐ 224	Steve Lyons	.06	.03	.00
☐ 225	Bert Blyleven	.10	.05	.01
☐ 226	Scott Bradley	.06	.03	.00
☐ 227	Bob Melvin	.06	.03	.00
☐ 228	Ron Kittle	.10	.05	.01
☐ 229	Phil Bradley	.10	.05	.01
☐ 230	Tommy John	.12	.06	.01
☐ 231	Greg Walker	.06	.03	.00
☐ 232	Juan Berenguer	.06	.03	.00
☐ 233	Pat Tabler	.06	.03	.00
☐ 234	Terry Clark	.15	.07	.01
☐ 235	Rafael Palmeiro	.15	.07	.01
☐ 236	Paul Zuvella	.06	.03	.00
☐ 237	Willie Randolph	.10	.05	.01
☐ 238	Bruce Fields	.06	.03	.00
☐ 239	Mike Aldrete	.06	.03	.00
☐ 240	Lance Parrish	.10	.05	.01
☐ 241	Greg Maddux	.20	.10	.02
☐ 242	John Moses	.06	.03	.00
☐ 243	Melido Perez	.15	.07	.01
☐ 244	Willie Wilson	.10	.05	.01
☐ 245	Mark McLemore	.06	.03	.00
☐ 246	Von Hayes	.10	.05	.01
☐ 247	Matt Williams	.30	.15	.03
☐ 248	John Candelaria UER (listed as Yankee for part of '87, should be Mets)	.10	.05	.01

☐ 249	Harold Reynolds	.10	.05	.01
☐ 250	Greg Swindell	.12	.06	.01
☐ 251	Juan Agosto	.06	.03	.00
☐ 252	Mike Felder	.06	.03	.00
☐ 253	Vince Coleman	.15	.07	.01
☐ 254	Larry Sheets	.06	.03	.00
☐ 255	George Bell	.12	.06	.01
☐ 256	Terry Steinbach	.10	.05	.01
☐ 257	Jack Armstrong	.25	.12	.02
☐ 258	Dickie Thon	.06	.03	.00
☐ 259	Ray Knight	.10	.05	.01
☐ 260	Darryl Strawberry	.50	.25	.05
☐ 261	Doug Sisk	.06	.03	.00
☐ 262	Alex Trevino	.06	.03	.00
☐ 263	Jeffrey Leonard	.10	.05	.01
☐ 264	Tom Henke	.10	.05	.01
☐ 265	Ozzie Smith	.20	.10	.02
☐ 266	Dave Bergman	.06	.03	.00
☐ 267	Tony Phillips	.06	.03	.00
☐ 268	Mark Davis	.15	.07	.01
☐ 269	Kevin Elster	.10	.05	.01
☐ 270	Barry Larkin	.20	.10	.02
☐ 271	Manny Lee	.06	.03	.00
☐ 272	Tom Brunansky	.12	.06	.01
☐ 273	Craig Biggio	1.00	.50	.10
☐ 274	Jim Gantner	.06	.03	.00
☐ 275	Eddie Murray	.15	.07	.01
☐ 276	Jeff Reed	.06	.03	.00
☐ 277	Tim Teufel	.06	.03	.00
☐ 278	Rick Honeycutt	.06	.03	.00
☐ 279	Guillermo Hernandez	.10	.05	.01
☐ 280	John Kruk	.10	.05	.01
☐ 281	Luis Alicea	.10	.05	.01
☐ 282	Jim Clancy	.06	.03	.00
☐ 283	Billy Ripken	.06	.03	.00
☐ 284	Craig Reynolds	.06	.03	.00
☐ 285	Robin Yount	.30	.15	.03
☐ 286	Jimmy Jones	.10	.05	.01
☐ 287	Ron Oester	.06	.03	.00
☐ 288	Terry Leach	.10	.05	.01
☐ 289	Dennis Eckersley	.12	.06	.01
☐ 290	Alan Trammell	.15	.07	.01
☐ 291	Jimmy Key	.10	.05	.01
☐ 292	Chris Bosio	.10	.05	.01
☐ 293	Jose DeLeon	.10	.05	.01
☐ 294	Jim Traber	.06	.03	.00
☐ 295	Mike Scott	.15	.07	.01
☐ 296	Roger McDowell	.10	.05	.01
☐ 297	Garry Templeton	.10	.05	.01
☐ 298	Doyle Alexander	.06	.03	.00
☐ 299	Nick Esasky	.12	.06	.01
☐ 300	Mark McGwire UER (doubles total 52, should be 51)	.75	.35	.07
☐ 301	Darryl Hamilton	.25	.12	.02
☐ 302	Dave Smith	.06	.03	.00
☐ 303	Rick Sutcliffe	.10	.05	.01
☐ 304	Dave Stapleton	.10	.05	.01
☐ 305	Alan Ashby	.06	.03	.00
☐ 306	Pedro Guerrero	.12	.06	.01
☐ 307	Ron Guidry	.10	.05	.01
☐ 308	Steve Farr	.06	.03	.00
☐ 309	Curt Ford	.06	.03	.00
☐ 310	Claudell Washington	.10	.05	.01
☐ 311	Tom Prince	.10	.05	.01
☐ 312	Chad Kreuter	.15	.07	.01
☐ 313	Ken Oberkfell	.06	.03	.00
☐ 314	Jerry Browne	.06	.03	.00
☐ 315	R.J. Reynolds	.06	.03	.00
☐ 316	Scott Bankhead	.10	.05	.01
☐ 317	Milt Thompson	.06	.03	.00
☐ 318	Mario Diaz	.10	.05	.01
☐ 319	Bruce Ruffin	.06	.03	.00
☐ 320	Dave Valle	.06	.03	.00
☐ 321A	Gary Varsho ERR (back photo actually Mike Bielecki bunting)	2.50	1.25	.25
☐ 321B	Gary Varsho COR (in road uniform)	.30	.15	.03
☐ 322	Paul Mirabella	.06	.03	.00
☐ 323	Chuck Jackson	.10	.05	.01
☐ 324	Drew Hall	.06	.03	.00
☐ 325	Don August	.10	.05	.01
☐ 326	Israel Sanchez	.10	.05	.01
☐ 327	Denny Walling	.06	.03	.00
☐ 328	Joel Skinner	.06	.03	.00
☐ 329	Danny Tartabull	.12	.06	.01
☐ 330	Tony Pena	.10	.05	.01
☐ 331	Jim Sundberg	.06	.03	.00
☐ 332	Jeff Robinson Pittsburgh Pirates	.10	.05	.01
☐ 333	Oddibe McDowell	.10	.05	.01
☐ 334	Jose Lind	.06	.03	.00
☐ 335	Paul Kilgus	.06	.03	.00
☐ 336	Juan Samuel	.12	.06	.01

337	Mike Campbell	.12	.06	.01
338	Mike Maddux	.06	.03	.00
339	Darnell Coles	.06	.03	.00
340	Bob Dernier	.06	.03	.00
341	Rafael Ramirez	.06	.03	.00
342	Scott Sanderson	.06	.03	.00
343	B.J. Surhoff	.10	.05	.01
344	Billy Hatcher	.06	.03	.00
345	Pat Perry	.06	.03	.00
346	Jack Clark	.12	.06	.01
347	Gary Thurman	.06	.03	.00
348	Tim Jones	.12	.06	.01
349	Dave Winfield	.20	.10	.02
350	Frank White	.10	.05	.01
351	Dave Collins	.06	.03	.00
352	Jack Morris	.10	.05	.01
353	Eric Plunk	.06	.03	.00
354	Leon Durham	.06	.03	.00
355	Ivan DeJesus	.06	.03	.00
356	Brian Holman	.15	.07	.01
357A	Dale Murphy ERR	150.00	75.00	15.00
	(front reverse negative)			
357B	Dale Murphy COR	.75	.35	.07
358	Mark Portugal	.06	.03	.00
359	Andy McGaffigan	.06	.03	.00
360	Tom Glavine	.10	.05	.01
361	Keith Moreland	.06	.03	.00
362	Todd Stottlemyre	.12	.06	.01
363	Dave Leiper	.06	.03	.00
364	Cecil Fielder	.06	.03	.00
365	Carmelo Martinez	.06	.03	.00
366	Dwight Evans	.12	.06	.01
367	Kevin McReynolds	.12	.06	.01
368	Rich Gedman	.06	.03	.00
369	Len Dykstra	.10	.05	.01
370	Jody Reed	.10	.05	.01
371	Jose Canseco UER	1.50	.75	.15
	(strikeout total 391, should be 491)			
372	Rob Murphy	.06	.03	.00
373	Mike Henneman	.06	.03	.00
374	Walt Weiss	.75	.35	.07
375	Rob Dibble	.35	.17	.03
376	Kirby Puckett	.60	.30	.06
	(Mark McGwire in background)			
377	Dennis Martinez	.06	.03	.00
378	Ron Gant	.35	.17	.03
379	Brian Harper	.06	.03	.00
380	Nelson Santovenia	.25	.12	.02
381	Lloyd Moseby	.10	.05	.01
382	Lance McCullers	.10	.05	.01
383	Dave Stieb	.10	.05	.01
384	Tony Gwynn	.35	.17	.03
385	Mike Flanagan	.06	.03	.00
386	Bob Ojeda	.10	.05	.01
387	Bruce Hurst	.10	.05	.01
388	Dave Magadan	.10	.05	.01
389	Wade Boggs	.75	.35	.07
390	Gary Carter	.15	.07	.01
391	Frank Tanana	.06	.03	.00
392	Curt Young	.06	.03	.00
393	Jeff Treadway	.15	.07	.01
394	Darrell Evans	.10	.05	.01
395	Glenn Hubbard	.06	.03	.00
396	Chuck Cary	.06	.03	.00
397	Frank Viola	.15	.07	.01
398	Jeff Parrett	.12	.06	.01
399	Terry Blocker	.12	.06	.01
400	Dan Gladden	.06	.03	.00
401	Louie Meadows	.10	.05	.01
402	Tim Raines	.15	.07	.01
403	Joey Meyer	.10	.05	.01
404	Larry Andersen	.06	.03	.00
405	Rex Hudler	.06	.03	.00
406	Mike Schmidt	.75	.35	.07
407	John Franco	.10	.05	.01
408	Brady Anderson	.30	.15	.03
409	Don Carman	.06	.03	.00
410	Eric Davis	.35	.17	.03
411	Bob Stanley	.06	.03	.00
412	Pete Smith	.10	.05	.01
413	Jim Rice	.12	.06	.01
414	Bruce Sutter	.08	.04	.01
415	Oil Can Boyd	.08	.04	.01
416	Ruben Sierra	.40	.20	.04
417	Mike LaValliere	.06	.03	.00
418	Steve Buechele	.06	.03	.00
419	Gary Redus	.06	.03	.00
420	Scott Fletcher	.06	.03	.00
421	Dale Sveum	.06	.03	.00
422	Bob Knepper	.06	.03	.00
423	Luis Rivera	.06	.03	.00
424	Ted Higuera	.10	.05	.01
425	Kevin Bass	.10	.05	.01
426	Ken Gerhart	.06	.03	.00
427	Shane Rawley	.06	.03	.00
428	Paul O'Neill	.10	.05	.01
429	Joe Orsulak	.06	.03	.00
430	Jackie Gutierrez	.06	.03	.00
431	Gerald Perry	.10	.05	.01
432	Mike Greenwell	1.00	.50	.10
433	Jerry Royster	.06	.03	.00
434	Ellis Burks	.45	.22	.04
435	Ed Olwine	.06	.03	.00
436	Dave Rucker	.06	.03	.00
437	Charlie Hough	.06	.03	.00
438	Bob Walk	.06	.03	.00
439	Bob Brower	.06	.03	.00
440	Barry Bonds	.10	.05	.01
441	Tom Foley	.06	.03	.00
442	Rob Deer	.10	.05	.01
443	Glenn Davis	.15	.07	.01
444	Dave Martinez	.06	.03	.00
445	Bill Wegman	.06	.03	.00
446	Lloyd McClendon	.15	.07	.01
447	Dave Schmidt	.06	.03	.00
448	Darren Daulton	.06	.03	.00
449	Frank Williams	.06	.03	.00
450	Don Aase	.06	.03	.00
451	Lou Whitaker	.12	.06	.01
452	Goose Gossage	.10	.05	.01
453	Ed Whitson	.06	.03	.00
454	Jim Walewander	.10	.05	.01
455	Damon Berryhill	.30	.15	.03
456	Tim Burke	.10	.05	.01
457	Barry Jones	.06	.03	.00
458	Joel Youngblood	.06	.03	.00
459	Floyd Youmans	.06	.03	.00
460	Mark Salas	.06	.03	.00
461	Jeff Russell	.10	.05	.01
462	Darrell Miller	.06	.03	.00
463	Jeff Kunkel	.06	.03	.00
464	Sherman Corbett	.10	.05	.01
465	Curtis Wilkerson	.06	.03	.00
466	Bud Black	.06	.03	.00
467	Cal Ripken Jr.	.20	.10	.02
468	John Farrell	.06	.03	.00
469	Terry Kennedy	.06	.03	.00
470	Tom Candiotti	.06	.03	.00
471	Roberto Alomar	.35	.17	.03
472	Jeff Robinson Detroit Tigers	.10	.05	.01
473	Vance Law	.06	.03	.00
474	Randy Ready UER	.06	.03	.00
	(strikeout total 136, should be 115)			
475	Walt Terrell	.06	.03	.00
476	Kelly Downs	.06	.03	.00
477	Johnny Paredes	.10	.05	.01
478	Shawn Hillegas	.06	.03	.00
479	Bob Brenly	.06	.03	.00
480	Otis Nixon	.06	.03	.00
481	Johnny Ray	.10	.05	.01
482	Geno Petralli	.06	.03	.00
483	Stu Cliburn	.06	.03	.00
484	Pete Incaviglia	.12	.06	.01
485	Brian Downing	.06	.03	.00
486	Jeff Stone	.06	.03	.00
487	Carmen Castillo	.06	.03	.00
488	Tom Niedenfuer	.06	.03	.00
489	Jay Bell	.12	.06	.01
490	Rick Schu	.06	.03	.00
491	Jeff Pico	.10	.05	.01
492	Mark Parent	.12	.06	.01
493	Eric King	.06	.03	.00
494	Al Nipper	.06	.03	.00
495	Andy Hawkins	.06	.03	.00
496	Daryl Boston	.06	.03	.00
497	Ernie Riles	.06	.03	.00
498	Pascual Perez	.10	.05	.01
499	Bill Long UER	.06	.03	.00
	(games started total 70, should be 44)			
500	Kirt Manwaring	.12	.06	.01
501	Chuck Crim	.06	.03	.00
502	Candy Maldonado	.06	.03	.00
503	Dennis Lamp	.06	.03	.00
504	Glenn Braggs	.10	.05	.01
505	Joe Price	.06	.03	.00
506	Ken Williams	.10	.05	.01
507	Bill Pecota	.06	.03	.00
508	Rey Quinones	.06	.03	.00
509	Jeff Bittiger	.12	.06	.01
510	Kevin Seitzer	.20	.10	.02
511	Steve Bedrosian	.10	.05	.01
512	Todd Worrell	.10	.05	.01
513	Chris James	.10	.05	.01
514	Jose Oquendo	.06	.03	.00
515	David Palmer	.06	.03	.00

☐ 516	John Smiley	.06	.03	.00
☐ 517	Dave Clark	.06	.03	.00
☐ 518	Mike Dunne	.06	.03	.00
☐ 519	Ron Washington	.06	.03	.00
☐ 520	Bob Kipper	.06	.03	.00
☐ 521	Lee Smith	.10	.05	.01
☐ 522	Juan Castillo	.06	.03	.00
☐ 523	Don Robinson	.06	.03	.00
☐ 524	Kevin Romine	.06	.03	.00
☐ 525	Paul Molitor	.10	.05	.01
☐ 526	Mark Langston	.15	.07	.01
☐ 527	Donnie Hill	.06	.03	.00
☐ 528	Larry Owen	.06	.03	.00
☐ 529	Jerry Reed	.06	.03	.00
☐ 530	Jack McDowell	.10	.05	.01
☐ 531	Greg Mathews	.06	.03	.00
☐ 532	John Russell	.06	.03	.00
☐ 533	Dan Quisenberry	.10	.05	.01
☐ 534	Greg Gross	.06	.03	.00
☐ 535	Danny Cox	.06	.03	.00
☐ 536	Terry Francona	.06	.03	.00
☐ 537	Andy Van Slyke	.12	.06	.01
☐ 538	Mel Hall	.10	.05	.01
☐ 539	Jim Gott	.06	.03	.00
☐ 540	Doug Jones	.10	.05	.01
☐ 541	Craig Lefferts	.06	.03	.00
☐ 542	Mike Boddicker	.06	.03	.00
☐ 543	Greg Brock	.06	.03	.00
☐ 544	Atlee Hammaker	.06	.03	.00
☐ 545	Tom Bolton	.10	.05	.01
☐ 546	Mike Macfarlane	.12	.06	.01
☐ 547	Rich Renteria	.12	.06	.01
☐ 548	John Davis	.06	.03	.00
☐ 549	Floyd Bannister	.06	.03	.00
☐ 550	Mickey Brantley	.10	.05	.01
☐ 551	Duane Ward	.06	.03	.00
☐ 552	Dan Petry	.06	.03	.00
☐ 553	Mickey Tettleton UER (walks total 175, should be 136)	.12	.06	.01
☐ 554	Rick Leach	.06	.03	.00
☐ 555	Mike Witt	.10	.05	.01
☐ 556	Sid Bream	.06	.03	.00
☐ 557	Bobby Witt	.10	.05	.01
☐ 558	Tommy Herr	.06	.03	.00
☐ 559	Randy Milligan	.12	.06	.01
☐ 560	Jose Cecena	.10	.05	.01
☐ 561	Mackey Sasser	.12	.06	.01
☐ 562	Carney Lansford	.12	.06	.01
☐ 563	Rick Aguilera	.06	.03	.00
☐ 564	Ron Hassey	.06	.03	.00
☐ 565	Dwight Gooden	.40	.20	.04
☐ 566	Paul Assenmacher	.06	.03	.00
☐ 567	Neil Allen	.06	.03	.00
☐ 568	Jim Morrison	.06	.03	.00
☐ 569	Mike Pagliarulo	.10	.05	.01
☐ 570	Ted Simmons	.12	.06	.01
☐ 571	Mark Thurmond	.06	.03	.00
☐ 572	Fred McGriff	.30	.15	.03
☐ 573	Wally Joyner	.25	.12	.02
☐ 574	Jose Bautista	.10	.05	.01
☐ 575	Kelly Gruber	.10	.05	.01
☐ 576	Cecilio Guante	.06	.03	.00
☐ 577	Mark Davidson	.06	.03	.00
☐ 578	Bobby Bonilla UER (total steals 2 in '87, should be 3)	.12	.06	.01
☐ 579	Mike Stanley	.06	.03	.00
☐ 580	Gene Larkin	.06	.03	.00
☐ 581	Stan Javier	.06	.03	.00
☐ 582	Howard Johnson	.20	.10	.02
☐ 583A	Mike Gallego ERR (front reversed negative)	2.50	1.25	.25
☐ 583B	Mike Gallego COR	.30	.15	.03
☐ 584	David Cone	.30	.15	.03
☐ 585	Doug Jennings	.25	.12	.02
☐ 586	Charles Hudson	.06	.03	.00
☐ 587	Dion James	.06	.03	.00
☐ 588	Al Leiter	.20	.10	.02
☐ 589	Charlie Puleo	.06	.03	.00
☐ 590	Roberto Kelly	.35	.17	.03
☐ 591	Thad Bosley	.06	.03	.00
☐ 592	Pete Stanicek	.10	.05	.01
☐ 593	Pat Borders	.12	.06	.01
☐ 594	Bryan Harvey	.20	.10	.02
☐ 595	Jeff Ballard	.25	.12	.02
☐ 596	Jeff Reardon	.10	.05	.01
☐ 597	Doug Drabek	.10	.05	.01
☐ 598	Edwin Correa	.06	.03	.00
☐ 599	Keith Atherton	.06	.03	.00
☐ 600	Dave LaPoint	.06	.03	.00
☐ 601	Don Baylor	.10	.05	.01
☐ 602	Tom Pagnozzi	.10	.05	.01
☐ 603	Tim Flannery	.06	.03	.00
☐ 604	Gene Walter	.06	.03	.00
☐ 605	Dave Parker	.10	.05	.01
☐ 606	Mike Diaz	.06	.03	.00
☐ 607	Chris Gwynn	.12	.06	.01
☐ 608	Odell Jones	.06	.03	.00
☐ 609	Carlton Fisk	.12	.06	.01
☐ 610	Jay Howell	.10	.05	.01
☐ 611	Tim Crews	.06	.03	.00
☐ 612	Keith Hernandez	.12	.06	.01
☐ 613	Willie Fraser	.06	.03	.00
☐ 614	Jim Eppard	.10	.05	.01
☐ 615	Jeff Hamilton	.06	.03	.00
☐ 616	Kurt Stillwell	.06	.03	.00
☐ 617	Tom Browning	.10	.05	.01
☐ 618	Jeff Montgomery	.25	.12	.02
☐ 619	Jose Rijo	.06	.03	.00
☐ 620	Jamie Quirk	.06	.03	.00
☐ 621	Willie McGee	.12	.06	.01
☐ 622	Mark Grant (glove on wrong hand)	.06	.03	.00
☐ 623	Bill Swift	.06	.03	.00
☐ 624	Orlando Mercado	.06	.03	.00
☐ 625	John Costello	.12	.06	.01
☐ 626	Jose Gonzalez	.10	.05	.01
☐ 627A	Bill Schroeder ERR (back photo actually Ronn Reynolds buckling shin guards)	2.50	1.25	.25
☐ 627B	Bill Schroeder COR	.30	.15	.03
☐ 628A	Fred Manrique ERR (back photo actually Ozzie Guillen throwing)	2.50	1.25	.25
☐ 628B	Fred Manrique COR (swinging bat on back)	.30	.15	.03
☐ 629	Ricky Horton	.06	.03	.00
☐ 630	Dan Plesac	.10	.05	.01
☐ 631	Alfredo Griffin	.06	.03	.00
☐ 632	Chuck Finley	.10	.05	.01
☐ 633	Kirk Gibson	.15	.07	.01
☐ 634	Randy Myers	.10	.05	.01
☐ 635	Greg Minton	.06	.03	.00
☐ 636A	Herm Winningham ERR (W1nningham on back)			
☐ 636B	Herm Winningham COR	.30	.15	.03
☐ 637	Charlie Leibrandt	.06	.03	.00
☐ 638	Tim Birtsas	.06	.03	.00
☐ 639	Bill Buckner	.10	.05	.01
☐ 640	Danny Jackson	.10	.05	.01
☐ 641	Greg Booker	.06	.03	.00
☐ 642	Jim Presley	.06	.03	.00
☐ 643	Gene Nelson	.06	.03	.00
☐ 644	Rod Booker	.10	.05	.01
☐ 645	Dennis Rasmussen	.06	.03	.00
☐ 646	Juan Nieves	.06	.03	.00
☐ 647	Bobby Thigpen	.10	.05	.01
☐ 648	Tim Belcher	.20	.10	.02
☐ 649	Mike Young	.06	.03	.00
☐ 650	Ivan Calderon	.10	.05	.01
☐ 651	Oswaldo Peraza	.10	.05	.01
☐ 652A	Pat Sheridan ERR (no position on front)	50.00	25.00	5.00
☐ 652B	Pat Sheridan COR	.25	.12	.02
☐ 653	Mike Morgan	.10	.05	.01
☐ 654	Mike Heath	.06	.03	.00
☐ 655	Jay Tibbs	.06	.03	.00
☐ 656	Fernando Valenzuela	.12	.06	.01
☐ 657	Lee Mazzilli	.06	.03	.00
☐ 658	AL CY: Frank Viola	.12	.06	.01
☐ 659A	AL MVP: Jose Canseco (eagle logo in black)	.50	.25	.05
☐ 659B	AL MVP: Jose Canseco (eagle logo in blue)	.50	.25	.05
☐ 660	AL ROY: Walt Weiss	.12	.06	.01
☐ 661	NL CY: Orel Hershiser	.20	.10	.02
☐ 662	NL MVP: Kirk Gibson	.12	.06	.01
☐ 663	NL ROY: Chris Sabo	.12	.06	.01
☐ 664	ALCS MVP: D.Eckersley	.35	.17	.03
☐ 665	NLCS MVP: O.Hershiser	.20	.10	.02
☐ 666	Great WS Moment (Kirk Gibson's homer)	.12	.06	.01
☐ 667	WS MVP: O.Hershiser	.20	.10	.02
☐ 668	Angels Checklist Wally Joyner	.15	.07	.01
☐ 669	Astros Checklist Nolan Ryan	.35	.17	.03
☐ 670	Athletics Checklist Jose Canseco	.50	.25	.05
☐ 671	Blue Jays Checklist Fred McGriff	.15	.07	.01
☐ 672	Braves Checklist Dale Murphy	.18	.09	.01
☐ 673	Brewers Checklist Paul Molitor	.10	.05	.01
☐ 674	Cardinals Checklist Ozzie Smith	.12	.06	.01

		MINT	EXC	G-VG
☐ 675	Cubs Checklist .... Ryne Sandberg	.12	.06	.01
☐ 676	Dodgers Checklist .... Kirk Gibson	.12	.06	.01
☐ 677	Expos Checklist .... Andres Galaragga	.10	.05	.01
☐ 678	Giants Checklist .... Will Clark	.50	.25	.05
☐ 679	Indians Checklist .... Cory Snyder	.10	.05	.01
☐ 680	Mariners Checklist .... Alvin Davis	.10	.05	.01
☐ 681	Mets Checklist .... Darryl Strawberry	.40	.20	.04
☐ 682	Orioles Checklist .... Cal Ripken	.15	.07	.01
☐ 683	Padres Checklist .... Tony Gwynn	.20	.10	.02
☐ 684	Phillies Checklist .... Mike Schmidt	.35	.17	.03
☐ 685	Pirates Checklist .... Andy Van Slyke UER (96 Junior Ortiz)	.10	.05	.01
☐ 686	Rangers Checklist .... Ruben Sierra	.20	.10	.02
☐ 687	Red Sox Checklist .... Wade Boggs	.35	.17	.03
☐ 688	Reds Checklist .... Eric Davis	.20	.10	.02
☐ 689	Royals Checklist .... George Brett	.15	.07	.01
☐ 690	Tigers Checklist .... Alan Trammell	.10	.05	.01
☐ 691	Twins Checklist .... Frank Viola	.12	.06	.01
☐ 692	White Sox Checklist .... Harold Baines	.10	.05	.01
☐ 693	Yankees Checklist .... Don Mattingly	.50	.25	.05
☐ 694	Checklist 1-100	.06	.01	.00
☐ 695	Checklist 101-200	.06	.01	.00
☐ 696	Checklist 201-300	.06	.01	.00
☐ 697	Checklist 301-400	.06	.01	.00
☐ 698	Checklist 401-500 UER .. 467 Cal Ripkin Jr.	.06	.01	.00
☐ 699	Checklist 501-600 UER .. 543 Greg Booker	.06	.01	.00
☐ 700	Checklist 601-700	.06	.01	.00

1989 Upper Deck Extended

Todd Zeile

The 1989 Upper Deck Extended set contains 100 standard-size (2 1/2 by 3 1/2 inch) cards. The fronts have pure white borders; the backs have recent stats and anti-counterfeit holograms. Both sides feature attractive color photos. The cards were distributed in "high number" packs, along with factory sets, and as a separate set in its own box.

		MINT	EXC	G-VG
COMPLETE SET (100)		36.00	18.00	3.60
COMMON PLAYER (701-800)		.08	.04	.01
☐ 701	Checklist 701-800	.08	.01	.00
☐ 702	Jesse Barfield	.15	.07	.01
☐ 703	Walt Terrell	.08	.04	.01
☐ 704	Dickie Thon	.08	.04	.01
☐ 705	Al Leiter	.15	.07	.01
☐ 706	Dave LaPoint	.08	.04	.01

		MINT	EXC	G-VG
☐ 707	Charlie Hayes	.30	.15	.03
☐ 708	Andy Hawkins	.08	.04	.01
☐ 709	Mickey Hatcher	.08	.04	.01
☐ 710	Lance McCullers	.08	.04	.01
☐ 711	Ron Kittle	.15	.07	.01
☐ 712	Bert Blyleven	.20	.10	.02
☐ 713	Rick Dempsey	.08	.04	.01
☐ 714	Ken Williams	.08	.04	.01
☐ 715	Steve Rosenberg	.20	.10	.02
☐ 716	Joe Skalski	.20	.10	.02
☐ 717	Spike Owen	.08	.04	.01
☐ 718	Todd Burns	.35	.17	.03
☐ 719	Kevin Gross	.08	.04	.01
☐ 720	Tommy Herr	.08	.04	.01
☐ 721	Rob Ducey	.20	.10	.02
☐ 722	Gary Green	.20	.10	.02
☐ 723	Gregg Olson	3.00	1.50	.30
☐ 724	Greg W. Harris	.20	.10	.02
☐ 725	Craig Worthington	.50	.25	.05
☐ 726	Tom Howard	.35	.17	.03
☐ 727	Dale Mohorcic	.08	.04	.01
☐ 728	Rich Yett	.08	.04	.01
☐ 729	Mel Hall	.15	.07	.01
☐ 730	Floyd Youmans	.08	.04	.01
☐ 731	Lonnie Smith	.15	.07	.01
☐ 732	Wally Backman	.08	.04	.01
☐ 733	Trevor Wilson	.20	.10	.02
☐ 734	Jose Alvarez	.20	.10	.02
☐ 735	Bob Milacki	.15	.07	.01
☐ 736	Tom Gordon	3.00	1.50	.30
☐ 737	Wally Whitehurst	.30	.15	.03
☐ 738	Mike Aldrete	.08	.04	.01
☐ 739	Keith Miller	.20	.10	.02
☐ 740	Randy Milligan	.15	.07	.01
☐ 741	Jeff Parrett	.15	.07	.01
☐ 742	Steve Finley	.30	.15	.03
☐ 743	Junior Felix	1.50	.75	.15
☐ 744	Pete Harnisch	.20	.10	.02
☐ 745	Bill Spiers	.60	.30	.06
☐ 746	Hensley Meulens	.60	.30	.06
☐ 747	Juan Bell	.20	.10	.02
☐ 748	Steve Sax	.20	.10	.02
☐ 749	Phil Bradley	.15	.07	.01
☐ 750	Rey Quinones	.08	.04	.01
☐ 751	Tommy Gregg	.08	.04	.01
☐ 752	Kevin Brown	.35	.17	.03
☐ 753	Derek Lilliquist	.30	.15	.03
☐ 754	Todd Zeile	6.50	3.25	.65
☐ 755	Jim Abbott	7.50	3.75	.75
☐ 756	Ozzie Canseco	1.00	.50	.10
☐ 757	Nick Esasky	.20	.10	.02
☐ 758	Mike Moore	.15	.07	.01
☐ 759	Rob Murphy	.08	.04	.01
☐ 760	Rick Mahler	.08	.04	.01
☐ 761	Fred Lynn	.15	.07	.01
☐ 762	Kevin Blankenship	.20	.10	.02
☐ 763	Eddie Murray	.20	.10	.02
☐ 764	Steve Searcy	.20	.10	.02
☐ 765	Jerome Walton	8.50	4.25	.85
☐ 766	Erik Hanson	.30	.15	.03
☐ 767	Bob Boone	.20	.10	.02
☐ 768	Edgar Martinez	.20	.10	.02
☐ 769	Jose DeJesus	.15	.07	.01
☐ 770	Greg Briley	1.50	.75	.15
☐ 771	Steve Peters	.20	.10	.02
☐ 772	Rafael Palmeiro	.20	.10	.02
☐ 773	Jack Clark	.20	.10	.02
☐ 774	Nolan Ryan	4.00	2.00	.40
☐ 775	Lance Parrish	.15	.07	.01
☐ 776	Joe Girardi	.35	.17	.03
☐ 777	Willie Randolph	.15	.07	.01
☐ 778	Mitch Williams	.20	.10	.02
☐ 779	Dennis Cook	.30	.15	.03
☐ 780	Dwight Smith	3.00	1.50	.30
☐ 781	Lenny Harris	.30	.15	.03
☐ 782	Torey Lovullo	.20	.10	.02
☐ 783	Norm Charlton	.20	.10	.02
☐ 784	Chris Brown	.08	.04	.01
☐ 785	Todd Benzinger	.15	.07	.01
☐ 786	Shane Rawley	.08	.04	.01
☐ 787	Omar Vizquel	.30	.15	.03
☐ 788	LaVel Freeman	.50	.25	.05
☐ 789	Jeffrey Leonard	.15	.07	.01
☐ 790	Eddie Williams	.08	.04	.01
☐ 791	Jamie Moyer	.08	.04	.01
☐ 792	Bruce Hurst UER .... (Workd Series)	.15	.07	.01
☐ 793	Julio Franco	.20	.10	.02
☐ 794	Claudell Washington	.15	.07	.01
☐ 795	Jody Davis	.08	.04	.01
☐ 796	Oddibe McDowell	.15	.07	.01
☐ 797	Paul Kilgus	.08	.04	.01
☐ 798	Tracy Jones	.08	.04	.01
☐ 799	Steve Wilson	.20	.10	.02
☐ 800	Pete O'Brien	.15	.07	.01

1990 Upper Deck

Craig Biggio

The 1990 Upper Deck set contains 700 standard-size (2 1/2 by 3 1/2 inch) cards. The front and back borders are white, and both sides feature full color photos. The horizontally-oriented backs have recent stats and anti-counterfeiting holograms. Unlike the 1989 Upper Deck set, the team checklist cards are not grouped numerically at the end of the set, but are mixed in with the first 100 cards.

	MINT	EXC	G-VG
COMPLETE SET (700)	45.00	22.50	4.50
COMMON PLAYER (1-700)	.05	.02	.00

		MINT	EXC	G-VG
☐	1 Star Rookie Checklist	.15	.02	.01
☐	2 Randy Nosek	.15	.02	.01
☐	3 Tom Drees	.25	.12	.02
☐	4 Curt Young	.05	.02	.00
☐	5 Devon White TC	.08	.04	.01
	California Angels			
☐	6 Luis Salazar	.05	.02	.00
☐	7 Von Hayes TC	.08	.04	.01
	Philadelphia Phillies			
☐	8 Jose Bautista	.05	.02	.00
☐	9 Marquis Grissom	.75	.35	.07
☐	10 Orel Hershiser TC	.15	.07	.01
	Los Angeles Dodgers			
☐	11 Rick Aguilera	.05	.02	.00
☐	12 Benito Santiago TC	.10	.05	.01
	San Diego Padres			
☐	13 Deion Sanders	.50	.25	.05
☐	14 Marvell Wynne	.05	.02	.00
☐	15 Dave West	.05	.02	.00
☐	16 Bobby Bonilla TC	.08	.04	.01
	Pittsburgh Pirates			
☐	17 Sammy Sosa	.50	.25	.05
☐	18 Steve Sax TC	.10	.05	.01
	New York Yankees			
☐	19 Jack Howell	.05	.02	.00
☐	20 Mike Schmidt Special	.35	.17	.03
☐	21 Robin Ventura	.75	.35	.07
☐	22 Brian Meyer	.10	.05	.01
☐	23 Blaine Beatty	.20	.10	.02
☐	24 Ken Griffey Jr. TC	.40	.20	.04
	Seattle Mariners			
☐	25 Greg Vaughn	1.50	.75	.15
☐	26 Xavier Hernandez	.15	.07	.01
☐	27 Jason Grimsley	.15	.07	.01
☐	28 Eric Anthony	2.00	1.00	.20
☐	29 Tim Raines TC	.10	.05	.01
	Montreal Expos			
☐	30 David Wells	.05	.02	.00
☐	31 Hal Morris	.10	.05	.01
☐	32 Bo Jackson TC	.35	.17	.03
	Kansas City Royals			
☐	33 Kelly Mann	.15	.07	.01
☐	34 Nolan Ryan Special	.40	.20	.04
☐	35 Scott Service	.15	.07	.01
☐	36 Mark McGwire TC	.25	.12	.02
	Oakland A's			
☐	37 Tino Martinez	.50	.25	.05
☐	38 Chili Davis	.08	.04	.01
☐	39 Scott Sanderson	.05	.02	.00
☐	40 Kevin Mitchell TC	.15	.07	.01
	San Francisco Giants			
☐	41 Lou Whitaker TC	.08	.04	.01

		MINT	EXC	G-VG
	Detroit Tigers			
☐	42 Scott Coolbaugh	.30	.15	.03
☐	43 Jose Cano	.30	.15	.03
☐	44 Jose Vizcaino	.30	.15	.03
☐	45 Bob Hamelin	.80	.40	.08
☐	46 Jose Offerman	1.50	.75	.15
☐	47 Kevin Blankenship	.10	.05	.01
☐	48 Kirby Puckett TC	.20	.10	.02
	Minnesota Twins			
☐	49 Tommy Greene	.50	.25	.05
☐	50 Will Clark Special	.40	.20	.04
☐	51 Rob Nelson	.05	.02	.00
☐	52 Chris Hammond	.15	.07	.01
☐	53 Joe Carter TC	.10	.05	.01
	Cleveland Indians			
☐	54A Ben McDonald ERR	75.00	30.00	6.00
	(no Rookie designation on card front)			
☐	54B Ben McDonald COR	3.50	1.75	.35
☐	55 Andy Benes	.75	.35	.07
☐	56 John Olerud	4.00	1.50	.25
☐	57 Roger Clemens TC	.15	.07	.01
	Boston Red Sox			
☐	58 Tony Armas	.08	.04	.01
☐	59 George Canale	.20	.10	.02
☐	60A Mickey Tettleton TC	3.00	1.00	.25
	Baltimore Orioles (#683 Jamie Weston)			
☐	60B Mickey Tettleton TC	.20	.10	.02
	Baltimore Orioles (#683 Mickey Weston)			
☐	61 Mike Stanton	.20	.10	.02
☐	62 Dwight Gooden TC	.15	.07	.01
	New York Mets			
☐	63 Kent Mercker	.50	.25	.05
☐	64 Francisco Cabrera	.20	.10	.02
☐	65 Steve Avery UER	.50	.25	.05
	(born NJ, should be MI)			
☐	66 Jose Canseco	.60	.30	.06
☐	67 Matt Merullo	.15	.07	.01
☐	68 Vince Coleman TC	.08	.04	.01
	St. Louis Cardinals			
☐	69 Ron Karkovice	.05	.02	.00
☐	70 Kevin Maas	.40	.20	.04
☐	71 Dennis Cook	.15	.07	.01
☐	72 Juan Gonzalez	.75	.35	.07
☐	73 Andre Dawson TC	.10	.05	.01
	Chicago Cubs			
☐	74 Dean Palmer	.35	.17	.03
☐	75 Bo Jackson Special	.50	.25	.05
☐	76 Rob Richie	.15	.07	.01
☐	77 Bobby Rose	.30	.15	.03
☐	78 Brian Dubois	.15	.07	.01
☐	79 Ozzie Guillen TC	.08	.04	.01
	Chicago White Sox			
☐	80 Gene Nelson	.05	.02	.00
☐	81 Bob McClure	.05	.02	.00
☐	82 Julio Franco TC	.08	.04	.01
	Texas Rangers			
☐	83 Greg Minton	.05	.02	.00
☐	84 John Smoltz TC	.10	.05	.01
	Atlanta Braves			
☐	85 Willie Fraser	.05	.02	.00
☐	86 Neal Heaton	.05	.02	.00
☐	87 Kevin Tapani	.20	.10	.02
☐	88 Mike Scott TC	.10	.05	.01
	Houston Astros			
☐	89A Jim Gott ERR	12.00	6.00	1.20
	(photo actually not him)			
☐	89B Jim Gott COR	.15	.07	.01
☐	90 Lance Johnson	.10	.05	.01
☐	91 Robin Yount TC	.15	.07	.01
	Milwaukee Brewers			
☐	92 Jeff Parrett	.05	.02	.00
☐	93 Julio Machado	.20	.10	.02
☐	94 Ron Jones	.08	.04	.01
☐	95 George Bell TC	.08	.04	.01
	Toronto Blue Jays			
☐	96 Jerry Reuss	.05	.02	.00
☐	97 Brian Fisher	.05	.02	.00
☐	98 Kevin Ritz	.20	.10	.02
☐	99 Barry Larkin TC	.10	.05	.01
	Cincinnati Reds			
☐	100 Checklist 1-100	.05	.01	.00
☐	101 Gerald Perry	.05	.02	.00
☐	102 Kevin Appier	.15	.07	.01
☐	103 Julio Franco	.08	.04	.01
☐	104 Craig Biggio	.10	.05	.01
☐	105 Bo Jackson	.60	.30	.06
☐	106 Junior Felix	.35	.17	.03
☐	107 Mike Harkey	.08	.04	.01
☐	108 Fred McGriff	.15	.07	.01
☐	109 Rick Sutcliffe	.08	.04	.01
☐	110 Pete O'Brien	.08	.04	.01

☐ 111	Kelly Gruber	.08	.04	.01
☐ 112	Pat Borders	.05	.02	.00
☐ 113	Dwight Evans	.08	.04	.01
☐ 114	Dwight Gooden	.25	.12	.02
☐ 115	Kevin Batiste	.20	.10	.02
☐ 116	Eric Davis	.25	.12	.02
☐ 117	Kevin Mitchell	.20	.10	.02
☐ 118	Ron Oester	.05	.02	.00
☐ 119	Brett Butler	.08	.04	.01
☐ 120	Danny Jackson	.08	.04	.01
☐ 121	Tommy Gregg	.08	.04	.01
☐ 122	Ken Caminiti	.05	.02	.00
☐ 123	Kevin Brown	.15	.07	.01
☐ 124	George Brett	.15	.07	.01
☐ 125	Mike Scott	.10	.05	.01
☐ 126	Cory Snyder	.10	.05	.01
☐ 127	George Bell	.10	.05	.01
☐ 128	Mark Grace	.40	.20	.04
☐ 129	Devon White	.10	.05	.01
☐ 130	Tony Fernandez	.10	.05	.01
☐ 131	Don Aase	.05	.02	.00
☐ 132	Rance Mulliniks	.05	.02	.00
☐ 133	Marty Barrett	.05	.02	.00
☐ 134	Nelson Liriano	.05	.02	.00
☐ 135	Mark Carreon	.10	.05	.01
☐ 136	Candy Maldonado	.05	.02	.00
☐ 137	Tim Birtsas	.05	.02	.00
☐ 138	Tom Brookens	.05	.02	.00
☐ 139	John Franco	.08	.04	.01
☐ 140	Mike LaCoss	.05	.02	.00
☐ 141	Jeff Treadway	.05	.02	.00
☐ 142	Pat Tabler	.05	.02	.00
☐ 143	Darrell Evans	.08	.04	.01
☐ 144	Rafael Ramirez	.05	.02	.00
☐ 145	Oddibe McDowell	.08	.04	.01
☐ 146	Brian Downing	.05	.02	.00
☐ 147	Curt Wilkerson	.05	.02	.00
☐ 148	Ernie Whitt	.05	.02	.00
☐ 149	Bill Schroeder	.05	.02	.00
☐ 150	Domingo Ramos	.05	.02	.00
☐ 151	Rick Honeycutt	.05	.02	.00
☐ 152	Don Slaught	.05	.02	.00
☐ 153	Mitch Webster	.05	.02	.00
☐ 154	Tony Phillips	.05	.02	.00
☐ 155	Paul Kilgus	.05	.02	.00
☐ 156	Ken Griffey Jr.	1.75	.85	.17
☐ 157	Gary Sheffield	.35	.17	.03
☐ 158	Wally Backman	.05	.02	.00
☐ 159	B.J. Surhoff	.08	.04	.01
☐ 160	Louie Meadows	.05	.02	.00
☐ 161	Paul O'Neill	.10	.05	.01
☐ 162	Jeff McKnight	.20	.10	.02
☐ 163	Alvaro Espinoza	.05	.02	.00
☐ 164	Scott Scudder	.20	.10	.02
☐ 165	Jeff Reed	.05	.02	.00
☐ 166	Gregg Jefferies	.50	.25	.05
☐ 167	Barry Larkin	.10	.05	.01
☐ 168	Gary Carter	.10	.05	.01
☐ 169	Robby Thompson	.05	.02	.00
☐ 170	Rolando Roomes	.08	.04	.01
☐ 171	Mark McGwire	.25	.12	.02
☐ 172	Steve Sax	.10	.05	.01
☐ 173	Mark Williamson	.05	.02	.00
☐ 174	Mitch Williams	.08	.04	.01
☐ 175	Brian Holton	.05	.02	.00
☐ 176	Rob Deer	.08	.04	.01
☐ 177	Tim Raines	.10	.05	.01
☐ 178	Mike Felder	.05	.02	.00
☐ 179	Harold Reynolds	.08	.04	.01
☐ 180	Terry Francona	.05	.02	.00
☐ 181	Chris Sabo	.10	.05	.01
☐ 182	Darryl Strawberry	.30	.15	.03
☐ 183	Willie Randolph	.08	.04	.01
☐ 184	Bill Ripken	.05	.02	.00
☐ 185	Mackey Sasser	.08	.04	.01
☐ 186	Todd Benzinger	.05	.02	.00
☐ 187	Kevin Elster	.08	.04	.01
☐ 188	Jose Uribe	.05	.02	.00
☐ 189	Tom Browning	.08	.04	.01
☐ 190	Keith Miller	.05	.02	.00
☐ 191	Don Mattingly	.60	.30	.06
☐ 192	Dave Parker	.10	.05	.01
☐ 193	Roberto Kelly	.10	.05	.01
☐ 194	Phil Bradley	.08	.04	.01
☐ 195	Ron Hassey	.05	.02	.00
☐ 196	Gerald Young	.05	.02	.00
☐ 197	Hubie Brooks	.08	.04	.01
☐ 198	Bill Doran	.08	.04	.01
☐ 199	Al Newman	.05	.02	.00
☐ 200	Checklist 101-200	.05	.01	.00
☐ 201	Terry Puhl	.05	.02	.00
☐ 202	Frank DiPino	.05	.02	.00
☐ 203	Jim Clancy	.05	.02	.00
☐ 204	Bob Ojeda	.08	.04	.01
☐ 205	Alex Trevino	.05	.02	.00

☐ 206	Dave Henderson	.05	.02	.00
☐ 207	Henry Cotto	.05	.02	.00
☐ 208	Rafael Belliard	.05	.02	.00
☐ 209	Stan Javier	.05	.02	.00
☐ 210	Jerry Reed	.05	.02	.00
☐ 211	Doug Dascenzo	.05	.02	.00
☐ 212	Andres Thomas	.05	.02	.00
☐ 213	Greg Maddux	.08	.04	.01
☐ 214	Mike Schooler	.08	.04	.01
☐ 215	Lonnie Smith	.08	.04	.01
☐ 216	Jose Rijo	.05	.02	.00
☐ 217	Greg Gagne	.05	.02	.00
☐ 218	Jim Gantner	.05	.02	.00
☐ 219	Allan Anderson	.08	.04	.01
☐ 220	Rick Mahler	.05	.02	.00
☐ 221	Jim Deshaies	.05	.02	.00
☐ 222	Keith Hernandez	.10	.05	.01
☐ 223	Vince Coleman	.10	.05	.01
☐ 224	David Cone	.10	.05	.01
☐ 225	Ozzie Smith	.10	.05	.01
☐ 226	Matt Nokes	.08	.04	.01
☐ 227	Barry Bonds	.08	.04	.01
☐ 228	Felix Jose	.05	.02	.00
☐ 229	Dennis Powell	.05	.02	.00
☐ 230	Mike Gallego	.05	.02	.00
☐ 231	Shawon Dunston UER	.10	.04	.01
	('89 stats are Andre Dawson's)			
☐ 232	Ron Gant	.08	.04	.01
☐ 233	Omar Vizquel	.15	.07	.01
☐ 234	Derek Lilliquist	.10	.05	.01
☐ 235	Erik Hanson	.10	.05	.01
☐ 236	Kirby Puckett	.30	.15	.03
☐ 237	Bill Spiers	.30	.15	.03
☐ 238	Dan Gladden	.05	.02	.00
☐ 239	Bryan Clutterbuck	.05	.02	.00
☐ 240	John Moses	.05	.02	.00
☐ 241	Ron Darling	.10	.05	.01
☐ 242	Joe Magrane	.08	.04	.01
☐ 243	Dave Magadan	.08	.04	.01
☐ 244	Pedro Guerrero	.10	.05	.01
☐ 245	Glenn Davis	.10	.05	.01
☐ 246	Terry Steinbach	.08	.04	.01
☐ 247	Fred Lynn	.08	.04	.01
☐ 248	Gary Redus	.05	.02	.00
☐ 249	Ken Williams	.05	.02	.00
☐ 250	Sid Bream	.05	.02	.00
☐ 251	Bob Welch	.08	.04	.01
☐ 252	Bill Buckner	.08	.04	.01
☐ 253	Carney Lansford	.10	.05	.01
☐ 254	Paul Molitor	.10	.05	.01
☐ 255	Jose DeJesus	.05	.02	.00
☐ 256	Orel Hershiser	.12	.06	.01
☐ 257	Tom Brunansky	.10	.05	.01
☐ 258	Mike Davis	.05	.02	.00
☐ 259	Jeff Ballard	.08	.04	.01
☐ 260	Scott Terry	.05	.02	.00
☐ 261	Sid Fernandez	.08	.04	.01
☐ 262	Mike Marshall	.08	.04	.01
☐ 263	Howard Johnson	.12	.06	.01
☐ 264	Kirk Gibson	.12	.06	.01
☐ 265	Kevin McReynolds	.10	.05	.01
☐ 266	Cal Ripken Jr.	.12	.06	.01
☐ 267	Ozzie Guillen	.08	.04	.01
☐ 268	Jim Traber	.05	.02	.00
☐ 269	Bobby Thigpen	.08	.04	.01
☐ 270	Joe Orsulak	.05	.02	.00
☐ 271	Bob Boone	.08	.04	.01
☐ 272	Dave Stewart	.10	.05	.01
☐ 273	Tim Wallach	.08	.04	.01
☐ 274	Luis Aquino	.08	.04	.01
☐ 275	Mike Moore	.08	.04	.01
☐ 276	Tony Pena	.08	.04	.01
☐ 277	Eddie Murray	.12	.06	.01
☐ 278	Milt Thompson	.05	.02	.00
☐ 279	Alejandro Pena	.05	.02	.00
☐ 280	Ken Dayley	.05	.02	.00
☐ 281	Carmen Castillo	.05	.02	.00
☐ 282	Tom Henke	.08	.04	.01
☐ 283	Mickey Hatcher	.05	.02	.00
☐ 284	Roy Smith	.05	.02	.00
☐ 285	Manny Lee	.05	.02	.00
☐ 286	Dan Pasqua	.05	.02	.00
☐ 287	Larry Sheets	.05	.02	.00
☐ 288	Garry Templeton	.08	.04	.01
☐ 289	Eddie Williams	.08	.04	.01
☐ 290	Brady Anderson	.05	.02	.00
☐ 291	Spike Owen	.05	.02	.00
☐ 292	Storm Davis	.08	.04	.01
☐ 293	Chris Bosio	.08	.04	.01
☐ 294	Jim Eisenreich	.05	.02	.00
☐ 295	Don August	.05	.02	.00
☐ 296	Jeff Hamilton	.05	.02	.00
☐ 297	Mickey Tettleton	.08	.04	.01
☐ 298	Mike Scioscia	.05	.02	.00

☐ 299	Kevin Hickey	.05	.02	.00
☐ 300	Checklist 201-300	.05	.01	.00
☐ 301	Shawn Abner	.10	.05	.01
☐ 302	Kevin Bass	.08	.04	.01
☐ 303	Bip Roberts	.05	.02	.00
☐ 304	Joe Girardi	.15	.07	.01
☐ 305	Danny Darwin	.05	.02	.00
☐ 306	Mike Heath	.05	.02	.00
☐ 307	Mike Macfarlane	.05	.02	.00
☐ 308	Ed Whitson	.05	.02	.00
☐ 309	Tracy Jones	.05	.02	.00
☐ 310	Scott Fletcher	.05	.02	.00
☐ 311	Darnell Coles	.05	.02	.00
☐ 312	Mike Brumley	.08	.04	.01
☐ 313	Bill Swift	.05	.02	.00
☐ 314	Charlie Hough	.05	.02	.00
☐ 315	Jim Presley	.05	.02	.00
☐ 316	Luis Polonia	.05	.02	.00
☐ 317	Mike Morgan	.05	.02	.00
☐ 318	Lee Guetterman	.05	.02	.00
☐ 319	Jose Oquendo	.05	.02	.00
☐ 320	Wayne Tolleson	.05	.02	.00
☐ 321	Jody Reed	.05	.02	.00
☐ 322	Damon Berryhill	.10	.05	.01
☐ 323	Roger Clemens	.25	.12	.02
☐ 324	Ryne Sandberg	.15	.07	.01
☐ 325	Benito Santiago	.12	.06	.01
☐ 326	Bret Saberhagen	.12	.06	.01
☐ 327	Lou Whitaker	.10	.05	.01
☐ 328	Dave Gallagher	.05	.02	.00
☐ 329	Mike Pagliarulo	.08	.04	.01
☐ 330	Doyle Alexander	.05	.02	.00
☐ 331	Jeffrey Leonard	.08	.04	.01
☐ 332	Torey Lovullo	.08	.04	.01
☐ 333	Pete Incaviglia	.08	.04	.01
☐ 334	Rickey Henderson	.25	.12	.02
☐ 335	Rafael Palmeiro	.10	.05	.01
☐ 336	Ken Hill	.08	.04	.01
☐ 337	Dave Winfield	.12	.06	.01
☐ 338	Alfredo Griffin	.05	.02	.00
☐ 339	Andy Hawkins	.05	.02	.00
☐ 340	Ted Power	.05	.02	.00
☐ 341	Steve Wilson	.10	.05	.01
☐ 342	Jack Clark	.10	.05	.01
☐ 343	Ellis Burks	.20	.10	.02
☐ 344	Tony Gwynn	.20	.10	.02
☐ 345	Jerome Walton	1.50	.75	.15
☐ 346	Roberto Alomar	.12	.06	.01
☐ 347	Carlos Martinez	.20	.10	.02
☐ 348	Chet Lemon	.05	.02	.00
☐ 349	Willie Wilson	.08	.04	.01
☐ 350	Greg Walker	.05	.02	.00
☐ 351	Tom Bolton	.05	.02	.00
☐ 352	German Gonzalez	.08	.04	.01
☐ 353	Harold Baines	.10	.05	.01
☐ 354	Mike Greenwell	.25	.12	.02
☐ 355	Ruben Sierra	.20	.10	.02
☐ 356	Andres Galarraga	.10	.05	.01
☐ 357	Andre Dawson	.10	.05	.01
☐ 358	Jeff Brantley	.15	.07	.01
☐ 359	Mike Bielecki	.08	.04	.01
☐ 360	Ken Oberkfell	.05	.02	.00
☐ 361	Kurt Stillwell	.05	.02	.00
☐ 362	Brian Holman	.05	.02	.00
☐ 363	Kevin Seitzer	.12	.06	.01
☐ 364	Alvin Davis	.08	.04	.01
☐ 365	Tom Gordon	.75	.35	.07
☐ 366	Bobby Bonilla	.10	.05	.01
☐ 367	Carlton Fisk	.10	.05	.01
☐ 368	Steve Carter	.15	.07	.01
☐ 369	Joel Skinner	.05	.02	.00
☐ 370	John Cangelosi	.05	.02	.00
☐ 371	Cecil Espy	.05	.02	.00
☐ 372	Gary Wayne	.12	.06	.01
☐ 373	Jim Rice	.12	.06	.01
☐ 374	Mike Dyer	.15	.07	.01
☐ 375	Joe Carter	.12	.06	.01
☐ 376	Dwight Smith	.75	.35	.07
☐ 377	John Wetteland	.35	.17	.03
☐ 378	Ernie Riles	.05	.02	.00
☐ 379	Otis Nixon	.05	.02	.00
☐ 380	Vance Law	.05	.02	.00
☐ 381	Dave Bergman	.05	.02	.00
☐ 382	Frank White	.08	.04	.01
☐ 383	Scott Bradley	.05	.02	.00
☐ 384	Israel Sanchez UER (totals don't include '89 stats)	.05	.02	.00
☐ 385	Gary Pettis	.05	.02	.00
☐ 386	Donn Pall	.08	.04	.01
☐ 387	John Smiley	.08	.04	.01
☐ 388	Tom Candiotti	.05	.02	.00
☐ 389	Junior Ortiz	.05	.02	.00
☐ 390	Steve Lyons	.05	.02	.00
☐ 391	Brian Harper	.05	.02	.00

☐ 392	Fred Manrique	.05	.02	.00
☐ 393	Lee Smith	.08	.04	.01
☐ 394	Jeff Kunkel	.05	.02	.00
☐ 395	Claudell Washington	.08	.04	.01
☐ 396	John Tudor	.08	.04	.01
☐ 397	Terry Kennedy	.05	.02	.00
☐ 398	Lloyd McClendon	.05	.02	.00
☐ 399	Craig Lefferts	.05	.02	.00
☐ 400	Checklist 301-400	.05	.01	.00
☐ 401	Keith Moreland	.05	.02	.00
☐ 402	Rich Gedman	.05	.02	.00
☐ 403	Jeff Robinson	.08	.04	.01
☐ 404	Randy Ready	.05	.02	.00
☐ 405	Rick Cerone	.05	.02	.00
☐ 406	Jeff Blauser	.05	.02	.00
☐ 407	Larry Andersen	.05	.02	.00
☐ 408	Joe Boever	.05	.02	.00
☐ 409	Felix Fermin	.05	.02	.00
☐ 410	Glenn Wilson	.05	.02	.00
☐ 411	Rex Hudler	.05	.02	.00
☐ 412	Mark Grant	.05	.02	.00
☐ 413	Dennis Martinez	.05	.02	.00
☐ 414	Darrin Jackson	.05	.02	.00
☐ 415	Mike Aldrete	.05	.02	.00
☐ 416	Roger McDowell	.08	.04	.01
☐ 417	Jeff Reardon	.08	.04	.01
☐ 418	Darren Daulton	.05	.02	.00
☐ 419	Tim Laudner	.05	.02	.00
☐ 420	Don Carman	.05	.02	.00
☐ 421	Lloyd Moseby	.08	.04	.01
☐ 422	Doug Drabek	.08	.04	.01
☐ 423	Lenny Harris	.10	.05	.01
☐ 424	Jose Lind	.05	.02	.00
☐ 425	Dave Johnson (P)	.15	.07	.01
☐ 426	Jerry Browne	.05	.02	.00
☐ 427	Eric Yelding	.10	.05	.01
☐ 428	Brad Komminsk	.05	.02	.00
☐ 429	Jody Davis	.05	.02	.00
☐ 430	Mariano Duncan	.05	.02	.00
☐ 431	Mark Davis	.10	.05	.01
☐ 432	Nelson Santovenia	.05	.02	.00
☐ 433	Bruce Hurst	.08	.04	.01
☐ 434	Jeff Huson	.12	.06	.01
☐ 435	Chris James	.08	.04	.01
☐ 436	Mark Guthrie	.12	.06	.01
☐ 437	Charlie Hayes	.10	.05	.01
☐ 438	Shane Rawley	.05	.02	.00
☐ 439	Dickie Thon	.05	.02	.00
☐ 440	Juan Berenguer	.05	.02	.00
☐ 441	Kevin Romine	.05	.02	.00
☐ 442	Bill Landrum	.05	.02	.00
☐ 443	Todd Frohwirth	.08	.04	.01
☐ 444	Craig Worthington	.10	.05	.01
☐ 445	Fernando Valenzuela	.12	.06	.01
☐ 446	Joey Belle	.75	.35	.07
☐ 447	Ed Whited	.20	.10	.02
☐ 448	Dave Smith	.05	.02	.00
☐ 449	Dave Clark	.05	.02	.00
☐ 450	Juan Agosto	.05	.02	.00
☐ 451	Dave Valle	.05	.02	.00
☐ 452	Kent Hrbek	.10	.05	.01
☐ 453	Von Hayes	.08	.04	.01
☐ 454	Gary Gaetti	.10	.05	.01
☐ 455	Greg Briley	.30	.15	.03
☐ 456	Glenn Braggs	.08	.04	.01
☐ 457	Kirt Manwaring	.05	.02	.00
☐ 458	Mel Hall	.08	.04	.01
☐ 459	Brook Jacoby	.08	.04	.01
☐ 460	Pat Sheridan	.05	.02	.00
☐ 461	Rob Murphy	.05	.02	.00
☐ 462	Jimmy Key	.08	.04	.01
☐ 463	Nick Esasky	.08	.04	.01
☐ 464	Rob Ducey	.05	.02	.00
☐ 465	Carlos Quintana	.08	.04	.01
☐ 466	Larry Walker	.35	.17	.03
☐ 467	Todd Worrell	.10	.05	.01
☐ 468	Kevin Gross	.05	.02	.00
☐ 469	Terry Pendleton	.05	.02	.00
☐ 470	Dave Martinez	.05	.02	.00
☐ 471	Gene Larkin	.05	.02	.00
☐ 472	Len Dykstra	.08	.04	.01
☐ 473	Barry Lyons	.05	.02	.00
☐ 474	Terry Mulholland	.05	.02	.00
☐ 475	Chip Hale	.20	.10	.02
☐ 476	Jesse Barfield	.10	.05	.01
☐ 477	Dan Plesac	.08	.04	.01
☐ 478A	Scott Garrelts ERR (photo actually Bill Bathe)	4.00	1.50	.20
☐ 478B	Scott Garrelts COR	.10	.05	.01
☐ 479	Dave Righetti	.10	.05	.01
☐ 480	Gus Polidor	.05	.02	.00
☐ 481	Mookie Wilson	.08	.04	.01
☐ 482	Luis Rivera	.05	.02	.00
☐ 483	Mike Flanagan	.05	.02	.00

□ 484	Dennis Boyd	.05	.02	.00
□ 485	John Cerutti	.05	.02	.00
□ 486	John Costello	.05	.02	.00
□ 487	Pascual Perez	.08	.04	.01
□ 488	Tommy Herr	.05	.02	.00
□ 489	Tom Foley	.05	.02	.00
□ 490	Curt Ford	.05	.02	.00
□ 491	Steve Lake	.05	.02	.00
□ 492	Tim Teufel	.05	.02	.00
□ 493	Randy Bush	.05	.02	.00
□ 494	Mike Jackson	.05	.02	.00
□ 495	Steve Jeltz	.05	.02	.00
□ 496	Paul Gibson	.05	.02	.00
□ 497	Steve Balboni	.05	.02	.00
□ 498	Bud Black	.05	.02	.00
□ 499	Dale Sveum	.05	.02	.00
□ 500	Checklist 401-500	.05	.01	.00
□ 501	Tim Jones	.05	.02	.00
□ 502	Mark Portugal	.05	.02	.00
□ 503	Ivan Calderon	.08	.04	.01
□ 504	Rick Rhoden	.05	.02	.00
□ 505	Willie McGee	.08	.04	.01
□ 506	Kirk McCaskill	.05	.02	.00
□ 507	Dave LaPoint	.05	.02	.00
□ 508	Jay Howell	.05	.02	.00
□ 509	Johnny Ray	.08	.04	.01
□ 510	Dave Anderson	.05	.02	.00
□ 511	Chuck Crim	.05	.02	.00
□ 512	Joe Hesketh	.05	.02	.00
□ 513	Dennis Eckersley	.10	.05	.01
□ 514	Greg Brock	.05	.02	.00
□ 515	Tim Burke	.08	.04	.01
□ 516	Frank Tanana	.05	.02	.00
□ 517	Jay Bell	.05	.02	.00
□ 518	Guillermo Hernandez	.08	.04	.01
□ 519	Randy Kramer	.10	.05	.01
□ 520	Charles Hudson	.05	.02	.00
□ 521	Jim Corsi	.10	.05	.01
□ 522	Steve Rosenberg	.08	.04	.01
□ 523	Cris Carpenter	.05	.02	.00
□ 524	Matt Winters	.20	.10	.02
□ 525	Melido Perez	.08	.04	.01
□ 526	Chris Gwynn UER (Albeguergue)	.05	.02	.00
□ 527	Bert Blyleven	.10	.05	.01
□ 528	Chuck Cary	.08	.04	.01
□ 529	Daryl Boston	.05	.02	.00
□ 530	Dale Mohorcic	.05	.02	.00
□ 531	Geronimo Berroa	.08	.04	.01
□ 532	Edgar Martinez	.05	.02	.00
□ 533	Dale Murphy	.15	.07	.01
□ 534	Jay Buhner	.08	.04	.01
□ 535	John Smoltz UER (HEA Stadium)	.10	.05	.01
□ 536	Andy Van Slyke	.10	.05	.01
□ 537	Mike Henneman	.05	.02	.00
□ 538	Miguel Garcia	.08	.04	.01
□ 539	Frank Williams	.05	.02	.00
□ 540	R.J. Reynolds	.05	.02	.00
□ 541	Shawn Hillegas	.05	.02	.00
□ 542	Walt Weiss	.10	.05	.01
□ 543	Greg Hibbard	.15	.07	.01
□ 544	Nolan Ryan	.40	.20	.04
□ 545	Todd Zeile	1.75	.85	.17
□ 546	Hensley Meulens	.30	.15	.03
□ 547	Tim Belcher	.10	.05	.01
□ 548	Mike Witt	.08	.04	.01
□ 549	Greg Cadaret	.10	.05	.01
□ 550	Franklin Stubbs	.05	.02	.00
□ 551	Tony Castillo	.08	.04	.01
□ 552	Jeff Robinson	.08	.04	.01
□ 553	Steve Olin	.10	.05	.01
□ 554	Alan Trammell	.10	.05	.01
□ 555	Wade Boggs	.30	.15	.03
□ 556	Will Clark	.60	.30	.06
□ 557	Jeff King	.15	.07	.01
□ 558	Mike Fitzgerald	.05	.02	.00
□ 559	Ken Howell	.05	.02	.00
□ 560	Bob Kipper	.05	.02	.00
□ 561	Scott Bankhead	.08	.04	.01
□ 562A	Jeff Innis ERR (photo actually David West)	4.00	1.50	.20
□ 562B	Jeff Innis COR	.20	.10	.02
□ 563	Randy Johnson	.05	.02	.00
□ 564	Wally Whitehurst	.10	.05	.01
□ 565	Gene Harris	.15	.07	.01
□ 566	Norm Charlton	.10	.05	.01
□ 567	Robin Yount UER (7606 career hits, should be 2606)	.35	.15	.03
□ 568	Joe Oliver	.15	.07	.01
□ 569	Mark Parent	.05	.02	.00
□ 570	John Farrell	.05	.02	.00
□ 571	Tom Glavine	.08	.04	.01
□ 572	Rod Nichols	.10	.05	.01
□ 573	Jack Morris	.10	.05	.01
□ 574	Greg Swindell	.10	.05	.01
□ 575	Steve Searcy	.12	.06	.01
□ 576	Ricky Jordan	.20	.10	.02
□ 577	Matt Williams	.15	.07	.01
□ 578	Mike LaValliere	.05	.02	.00
□ 579	Bryn Smith	.08	.04	.01
□ 580	Bruce Ruffin	.05	.02	.00
□ 581	Randy Myers	.08	.04	.01
□ 582	Rick Wrona	.15	.07	.01
□ 583	Juan Samuel	.10	.05	.01
□ 584	Les Lancaster	.05	.02	.00
□ 585	Jeff Musselman	.05	.02	.00
□ 586	Rob Dibble	.08	.04	.01
□ 587	Eric Show	.05	.02	.00
□ 588	Jesse Orosco	.05	.02	.00
□ 589	Herm Winningham	.05	.02	.00
□ 590	Andy Allanson	.05	.02	.00
□ 591	Dion James	.05	.02	.00
□ 592	Carmelo Martinez	.05	.02	.00
□ 593	Luis Quinones	.05	.02	.00
□ 594	Dennis Rasmussen	.05	.02	.00
□ 595	Rich Yett	.05	.02	.00
□ 596	Bob Walk	.05	.02	.00
□ 597	Andy McGaffigan	.05	.02	.00
□ 598	Billy Hatcher	.05	.02	.00
□ 599	Bob Knepper	.05	.02	.00
□ 600	Checklist 501-600	.05	.01	.00
□ 601	Joey Cora	.08	.04	.01
□ 602	Steve Finley	.10	.05	.01
□ 603	Kal Daniels	.10	.05	.01
□ 604	Gregg Olson	.40	.20	.04
□ 605	Dave Stieb	.10	.05	.01
□ 606	Kenny Rogers	.15	.07	.01
□ 607	Zane Smith	.05	.02	.00
□ 608	Bob Geren	.20	.10	.02
□ 609	Chad Kreuter	.05	.02	.00
□ 610	Mike Smithson	.05	.02	.00
□ 611	Jeff Wetherby	.20	.10	.02
□ 612	Gary Mielke	.10	.05	.01
□ 613	Pete Smith	.05	.02	.00
□ 614	Jack Daugherty	.15	.07	.01
□ 615	Lance McCullers	.05	.02	.00
□ 616	Don Robinson	.05	.02	.00
□ 617	Jose Guzman	.05	.02	.00
□ 618	Steve Bedrosian	.08	.04	.01
□ 619	Jamie Moyer	.05	.02	.00
□ 620	Atlee Hammaker	.05	.02	.00
□ 621	Rick Luecken	.15	.07	.01
□ 622	Greg W. Harris	.12	.06	.01
□ 623	Pete Harnisch	.08	.04	.01
□ 624	Jerald Clark	.05	.02	.00
□ 625	Jack McDowell	.05	.02	.00
□ 626	Frank Viola	.10	.05	.01
□ 627	Teddy Higuera	.08	.04	.01
□ 628	Marty Pevey	.10	.05	.01
□ 629	Bill Wegman	.05	.02	.00
□ 630	Eric Plunk	.05	.02	.00
□ 631	Drew Hall	.05	.02	.00
□ 632	Doug Jones	.08	.04	.01
□ 633	Geno Petralli	.05	.02	.00
□ 634	Jose Alvarez	.05	.02	.00
□ 635	Bob Milacki	.12	.06	.01
□ 636	Bobby Witt	.08	.04	.01
□ 637	Trevor Wilson	.08	.04	.01
□ 638	Jeff Russell	.08	.04	.01
□ 639	Mike Krukow	.05	.02	.00
□ 640	Rick Leach	.05	.02	.00
□ 641	Dave Schmidt	.05	.02	.00
□ 642	Terry Leach	.05	.02	.00
□ 643	Calvin Schiraldi	.05	.02	.00
□ 644	Bob Melvin	.05	.02	.00
□ 645	Jim Abbott	1.50	.75	.15
□ 646	Jaime Navarro	.20	.10	.02
□ 647	Mark Langston	.12	.06	.01
□ 648	Juan Nieves	.05	.02	.00
□ 649	Damaso Garcia	.05	.02	.00
□ 650	Charlie O'Brien	.05	.02	.00
□ 651	Eric King	.05	.02	.00
□ 652	Mike Boddicker	.05	.02	.00
□ 653	Duane Ward	.05	.02	.00
□ 654	Bob Stanley	.05	.02	.00
□ 655	Sandy Alomar Jr.	.35	.17	.03
□ 656	Danny Tartabull	.10	.04	.01
□ 657	Randy McCament	.12	.06	.01
□ 658	Charlie Leibrandt	.05	.02	.00
□ 659	Dan Quisenberry	.08	.04	.01
□ 660	Paul Assenmacher	.05	.02	.00
□ 661	Walt Terrell	.05	.02	.00
□ 662	Tim Leary	.08	.04	.01
□ 663	Randy Milligan	.08	.04	.01
□ 664	Bo Diaz	.05	.02	.00
□ 665	Mark Lemke	.05	.02	.00
□ 666	Jose Gonzalez	.08	.04	.01

☐ 667	Chuck Finley	.08	.04	.01
☐ 668	John Kruk	.08	.04	.01
☐ 669	Dick Schofield	.05	.02	.00
☐ 670	Tim Crews	.05	.02	.00
☐ 671	John Dopson	.05	.02	.00
☐ 672	John Orton	.20	.10	.02
☐ 673	Eric Hetzel	.10	.05	.01
☐ 674	Lance Parrish	.10	.05	.01
☐ 675	Ramon Martinez	.10	.05	.01
☐ 676	Mark Gubicza	.10	.05	.01
☐ 677	Greg Litton	.20	.10	.02
☐ 678	Greg Mathews	.05	.02	.00
☐ 679	Dave Dravecky	.10	.05	.01
☐ 680	Steve Farr	.05	.02	.00
☐ 681	Mike Devereaux	.05	.02	.00
☐ 682	Ken Griffey Sr.	.08	.04	.01
☐ 683A	Mickey Weston ERR (listed as Mickey on card)	9.00	4.50	.90
☐ 683B	Mickey Weston COR	.35	.17	.03
☐ 684	Jack Armstrong	.08	.04	.01
☐ 685	Steve Buechele	.05	.02	.00
☐ 686	Bryan Harvey	.05	.02	.00
☐ 687	Lance Blankenship	.05	.02	.00
☐ 688	Dante Bichette	.05	.02	.00
☐ 689	Todd Burns	.20	.10	.02
☐ 690	Dan Petry	.05	.02	.00
☐ 691	Kent Anderson	.15	.07	.01
☐ 692	Todd Stottlemyre	.08	.04	.01
☐ 693	Wally Joyner	.12	.06	.01
☐ 694	Mike Rochford	.12	.06	.01
☐ 695	Floyd Bannister	.05	.02	.00
☐ 696	Rick Reuschel	.08	.04	.01
☐ 697	Jose DeLeon	.08	.04	.01
☐ 698	Jeff Montgomery	.08	.04	.01
☐ 699	Kelly Downs	.05	.02	.00
☐ 700A	Checklist 601-700 (#683 Jamie Weston)	2.00	.50	.10
☐ 700B	Checklist 601-700 (#683 Mickey Weston)	.10	.05	.01

1989 USPS Legends Stamp Cards

The 1989 USPS Legends Stamp Cards set includes four cards measuring 2 1/2 by 3 9/16 inches. On the fronts, the cards depict the four baseball-related stamp designs which featured actual players. The outer front borders are white; the inner front borders are orange and purple. The vertically-oriented backs are beige and pink. These cards were sold by the U.S. Postal Service as a set (kit) for 7.95 along with the actual stamps, an attractive booklet, and other materials. The first printing of the set was sold out and so a second printing was made. All the stamps in the set are drawings; for example, the Gehrig stamp was painted by noted sports artist, Bart Forbes. All of the stamps except Gehrig (25 cents) are 20-cent stamps.

		MINT	EXC	G-VG
	COMPLETE SET (4)	9.00	4.00	.80
	COMMON PLAYER (1-4)	2.50	1.00	.20
☐ 1	Roberto Clemente Issued August 17, 1984	2.50	1.00	.20
☐ 2	Lou Gehrig Issued June 10, 1989	2.50	1.00	.20
☐ 3	Jackie Robinson Issued August 2, 1982	2.50	1.00	.20
☐ 4	Babe Ruth Issued July 6, 1983	3.00	1.50	.30

1985 Wendy's Tigers

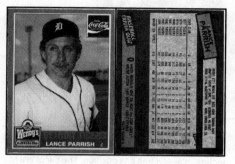

This 22-card set features Detroit Tigers; cards measure 2 1/2" by 3 1/2". The set was co-sponsored by Wendy's and Coca-Cola and was distributed in the Detroit metropolitian area. Coca-Cola purchasers were given a pack which contained three Tiger cards plus a header card. The orange-bordered player photos are different from those used by Topps in their regular set. The cards were produced by Topps as evidenced by the similarity of the card backs with the Topps regular set backs. The set is numbered on the back; the order corresponds to the alphabetical order of the player's names.

		MINT	EXC	G-VG
	COMPLETE SET (22)	9.00	4.50	.90
	COMMON PLAYER (1-22)	.20	.10	.02
☐ 1	Sparky Anderson MG (checklist back)	.60	.30	.06
☐ 2	Doug Bair	.20	.10	.02
☐ 3	Juan Berenguer	.25	.12	.02
☐ 4	Dave Bergman	.20	.10	.02
☐ 5	Tom Brookens	.20	.10	.02
☐ 6	Marty Castillo	.20	.10	.02
☐ 7	Darrell Evans	.50	.25	.05
☐ 8	Barbaro Garbey	.20	.10	.02
☐ 9	Kirk Gibson	1.50	.75	.15
☐ 10	Johnny Grubb	.20	.10	.02
☐ 11	Willie Hernandez	.35	.17	.03
☐ 12	Larry Herndon	.25	.12	.02
☐ 13	Rusty Kuntz	.20	.10	.02
☐ 14	Chet Lemon	.30	.15	.03
☐ 15	Aurelio Lopez	.20	.10	.02
☐ 16	Jack Morris	1.25	.60	.12
☐ 17	Lance Parrish	1.25	.60	.12
☐ 18	Dan Petry	.30	.15	.03
☐ 19	Bill Scherrer	.20	.10	.02
☐ 20	Alan Trammell	1.50	.75	.15
☐ 21	Lou Whitaker	1.00	.50	.10
☐ 22	Milt Wilcox	.20	.10	.02

1982 Wheaties Indians

The cards in this 30-card set measure 2 13/16" by 4 1/8". This set of Cleveland Indians baseball players was co-produced by the Indians baseball club and Wheaties, whose respective logos appear on the front of every card. The cards were given away in groups of 10 as a promotion during games on May 30 (1-10), June 19 (11-20) and July 16, 1982 (21-

LEN
BARKER
Pitcher
WHEATIES

ET THE

R WHEATIES

hiable, irresistible
e crispy, crunchy
heat taste of

ATIES.

ast of Champions

30). The manager (MG), four coaches (CO), and 25 players are featured in a simple format of a color picture, player name and position. The cards are not numbered and the backs contain a Wheaties ad. The set was later sold at the Cleveland Indians gift shop. The cards are ordered below alphabetically within groups of ten as they were issued.

	MINT	EXC	G-VG
COMPLETE SET (30)	12.00	6.00	1.20
COMMON PLAYER (1-30)	.35	.17	.03

		MINT	EXC	G-VG
☐	1 Bert Blyleven	1.00	.50	.10
☐	2 Joe Charboneau	.45	.22	.04
☐	3 Jerry Dybzinski	.35	.17	.03
☐	4 Dave Garcia MG	.35	.17	.03
☐	5 Toby Harrah	.45	.22	.04
☐	6 Ron Hassey	.35	.17	.03
☐	7 Dennis Lewallyn	.35	.17	.03
☐	8 Rick Manning	.35	.17	.03
☐	9 Tommy McCraw CO	.35	.17	.03
☐	10 Rick Waits	.35	.17	.03
☐	11 Chris Bando	.35	.17	.03
☐	12 Len Barker	.45	.22	.04
☐	13 Tom Brennan	.35	.17	.03
☐	14 Rodney Craig	.35	.17	.03
☐	15 Mike Fischlin	.35	.17	.03
☐	16 Johnny Goryl CO	.35	.17	.03
☐	17 Mel Queen CO	.35	.17	.03
☐	18 Lary Sorensen	.35	.17	.03
☐	19 Andre Thornton	.60	.30	.06
☐	20 Eddie Whitson	.45	.22	.04
☐	21 Alan Bannister	.35	.17	.03
☐	22 John Denny	.45	.22	.04
☐	23 Miguel Dilone	.35	.17	.03
☐	24 Mike Hargrove	.60	.30	.06
☐	25 Von Hayes	1.00	.50	.10
☐	26 Bake McBride	.35	.17	.03
☐	27 Jack Perconte	.35	.17	.03
☐	28 Dennis Sommers CO	.35	.17	.03
☐	29 Dan Spillner	.35	.17	.03
☐	30 Rick Sutcliffe	.75	.35	.07

1983 Wheaties Indians

The cards in this 32-card set measure 2 13/16" by 4 1/8". The full color set of 1983 Wheaties Indians is quite similar to the Wheaties set of 1982. The backs, however, are significantly different. They contain complete career playing records of the players. The complete sets were given away at the ball park on May 15, 1983. The set was later made available at the Indians Gift Shop. The manager (MG) and several coaches (CO) are included in the set. The cards below are ordered alphabetically by the subject's name.

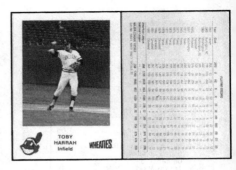

TOBY
HARRAH
Infield
WHEATIES

	MINT	EXC	G-VG
COMPLETE SET (32)	8.00	4.00	.80
COMMON PLAYER (1-32)	.20	.10	.02

		MINT	EXC	G-VG
☐	1 Bud Anderson	.20	.10	.02
☐	2 Jay Baller	.20	.10	.02
☐	3 Chris Bando	.20	.10	.02
☐	4 Alan Bannister	.20	.10	.02
☐	5 Len Barker	.30	.15	.03
☐	6 Bert Blyleven	.75	.35	.07
☐	7 Wil Culmer	.20	.10	.02
☐	8 Miguel Dilone	.20	.10	.02
☐	9 Juan Eichelberger	.20	.10	.02
☐	10 Jim Essian	.20	.10	.02
☐	11 Mike Ferraro MG	.20	.10	.02
☐	12 Mike Fischlin	.20	.10	.02
☐	13 Julio Franco	1.00	.50	.10
☐	14 Ed Glynn	.20	.10	.02
☐	15 Johnny Goryl CO	.20	.10	.02
☐	16 Mike Hargrove	.30	.15	.03
☐	17 Toby Harrah	.30	.15	.03
☐	18 Ron Hassey	.20	.10	.02
☐	19 Neal Heaton	.20	.10	.02
☐	20 Rick Manning	.20	.10	.02
☐	21 Bake McBride	.30	.15	.03
☐	22 Don McMahon CO	.20	.10	.02
☐	23 Ed Napoleon CO	.20	.10	.02
☐	24 Broderick Perkins	.20	.10	.02
☐	25 Dennis Sommers CO	.20	.10	.02
☐	26 Lary Sorensen	.20	.10	.02
☐	27 Dan Spillner	.20	.10	.02
☐	28 Rick Sutcliffe	.75	.35	.07
☐	29 Andre Thornton	.50	.25	.05
☐	30 Manny Trillo	.20	.10	.02
☐	31 George Vukovich	.20	.10	.02
☐	32 Rick Waits	.20	.10	.02

1984 Wheaties Indians

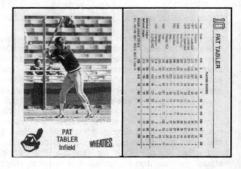

PAT
TABLER
Infield
WHEATIES

The cards in this 29-card set measure 2 13/16" by 4 1/8". For the third straight year, Wheaties distributed a set of Cleveland Indians baseball cards. These over-sized cards were passed out at a Baseball Card Day at the Cleveland Stadium. Similar in appearance to the cards of the past two years, both the Indians and the Wheaties logos appear on the obverse, along with the name, team and position. Cards are numbered on the back by the player's uniform number.

		MINT	EXC	G-VG
	COMPLETE SET (29)	8.00	4.00	.80
	COMMON PLAYER	.20	.10	.02
☐ 2	Brett Butler	.60	.30	.06
☐ 4	Tony Bernazard	.30	.15	.03
☐ 8	Carmelo Castillo	.20	.10	.02
☐ 10	Pat Tabler	.40	.20	.04
☐ 13	Ernie Camacho	.30	.15	.03
☐ 14	Julio Franco	.75	.35	.07
☐ 15	Broderick Perkins	.20	.10	.02
☐ 16	Jerry Willard	.20	.10	.02
☐ 18	Pat Corrales MG	.20	.10	.02
☐ 21	Mike Hargrove	.30	.15	.03
☐ 22	Mike Fischlin	.20	.10	.02
☐ 23	Chris Bando	.20	.10	.02
☐ 24	George Vukovich	.20	.10	.02
☐ 26	Brook Jacoby	.50	.25	.05
☐ 27	Steve Farr	.30	.15	.03
☐ 28	Bert Blyleven	.60	.30	.06
☐ 29	Andre Thornton	.40	.20	.04
☐ 30	Joe Carter	1.25	.60	.12
☐ 31	Steve Comer	.20	.10	.02
☐ 33	Roy Smith	.20	.10	.02
☐ 34	Mel Hall	.50	.25	.05
☐ 36	Jamie Easterly	.20	.10	.02
☐ 37	Don Schulze	.20	.10	.02
☐ 38	Luis Aponte	.20	.10	.02
☐ 44	Neal Heaton	.20	.10	.02
☐ 46	Mike Jeffcoat	.20	.10	.02
☐ 54	Tom Waddell	.20	.10	.02
☐ xx	Indians Coaches: (unnumbered) John Goryl Dennis Sommers Ed Napoleon Bobby Bonds Don McMahon			
☐ xx	Tom-E-Hawk (Mascot) (unnumbered)	.20	.10	.02

1954 Wilson

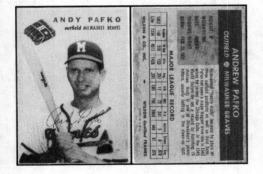

The cards in this 20-card set measure 2 5/8" by 3 3/4". The 1954 "Wilson Weiners" set contains 20 full color, unnumbered cards. The obverse design of a package of hot dogs appearing to fly through the air is a distinctive feature of this set. Uncut sheets have been seen. Cards are numbered below alphabetically by player's name.

		NRMT	VG-E	GOOD
	COMPLETE SET (20)	6500.00	3000.00	750.00
	COMMON PLAYER (1-20)	150.00	75.00	15.00
☐ 1	Roy Campanella	700.00	350.00	70.00
☐ 2	Del Ennis	150.00	75.00	15.00
☐ 3	Carl Erskine	200.00	100.00	20.00
☐ 4	Ferris Fain	150.00	75.00	15.00
☐ 5	Bob Feller	600.00	300.00	60.00
☐ 6	Nelson Fox	300.00	150.00	30.00
☐ 7	Johnny Groth	150.00	75.00	15.00

☐ 8	Stan Hack	150.00	75.00	15.00
☐ 9	Gil Hodges	400.00	200.00	40.00
☐ 10	Ray Jablonski	150.00	75.00	15.00
☐ 11	Harvey Kuenn	250.00	125.00	25.00
☐ 12	Roy McMillan	150.00	75.00	15.00
☐ 13	Andy Pafko	150.00	75.00	15.00
☐ 14	Paul Richards MG	150.00	75.00	15.00
☐ 15	Hank Sauer	150.00	75.00	15.00
☐ 16	Red Schoendienst	400.00	200.00	40.00
☐ 17	Enos Slaughter	450.00	225.00	45.00
☐ 18	Vern Stephens	150.00	75.00	15.00
☐ 19	Sammy White	150.00	75.00	15.00
☐ 20	Ted Williams	2500.00	1250.00	300.00

1985 Woolworth's

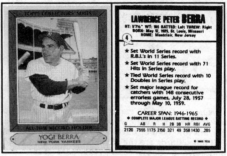

This 44-card set features color as well as black and white cards of All Time Record Holders. The cards are standard size (2 1/2" by 3 1/2") and are printed with blue ink on an orange and white back. The set was produced for Woolworth's by Topps and was packaged in a colorful box which contained a checklist of the cards in the set on the back panel. The numerical order of the cards coincides alphabetically with player's name.

		MINT	EXC	G-VG
	COMPLETE SET (44)	4.00	2.00	.40
	COMMON PLAYER (1-44)	.05	.02	.00
☐ 1	Hank Aaron	.25	.12	.02
☐ 2	Grover C. Alexander	.05	.02	.00
☐ 3	Ernie Banks	.15	.07	.01
☐ 4	Yogi Berra	.20	.10	.02
☐ 5	Lou Brock	.10	.05	.01
☐ 6	Steve Carlton	.10	.05	.01
☐ 7	Jack Chesbro	.05	.02	.00
☐ 8	Ty Cobb	.30	.15	.03
☐ 9	Sam Crawford	.05	.02	.00
☐ 10	Rollie Fingers	.05	.02	.00
☐ 11	Whitey Ford	.10	.05	.01
☐ 12	John Frederick	.05	.02	.00
☐ 13	Frankie Frisch	.05	.02	.00
☐ 14	Lou Gehrig	.30	.15	.03
☐ 15	Jim Gentile	.05	.02	.00
☐ 16	Dwight Gooden	.30	.15	.03
☐ 17	Rickey Henderson	.25	.12	.02
☐ 18	Rogers Hornsby	.10	.05	.01
☐ 19	Frank Howard	.05	.02	.00
☐ 20	Cliff Johnson	.05	.02	.00
☐ 21	Walter Johnson	.15	.07	.01
☐ 22	Hub Leonard	.05	.02	.00
☐ 23	Mickey Mantle	.50	.25	.05
☐ 24	Roger Maris	.15	.07	.01
☐ 25	Christy Mathewson	.10	.05	.01
☐ 26	Willie Mays	.25	.12	.02
☐ 27	Stan Musial	.15	.07	.01
☐ 28	Don Quisenberry	.05	.02	.00
☐ 29	Frank Robinson	.07	.03	.01
☐ 30	Pete Rose	.30	.15	.03
☐ 31	Babe Ruth	.50	.25	.05
☐ 32	Nolan Ryan	.25	.12	.02
☐ 33	George Sisler	.05	.02	.00
☐ 34	Tris Speaker	.10	.05	.01
☐ 35	Ed Walsh	.05	.02	.00
☐ 36	Lloyd Waner	.05	.02	.00
☐ 37	Earl Webb	.05	.02	.00
☐ 38	Ted Williams	.25	.12	.02

		MINT	EXC	G-VG
☐ 39	Maury Wills	.05	.02	.00
☐ 40	Hack Wilson	.05	.02	.00
☐ 41	Owen Wilson	.05	.02	.00
☐ 42	Willie Wilson	.05	.02	.00
☐ 43	Rudy York	.05	.02	.00
☐ 44	Cy Young	.10	.05	.01

1986 Woolworth's

This boxed set of 33 cards was produced by Topps for Woolworth's variety stores. The set features players who hold or have held hitting, home run or RBI titles. Cards are the standard 2 1/2" by 3 1/2" and have a glossy finish. The card fronts are bordered in yellow with the subtitle "Topps Collectors' Series" across the top. The card backs are printed in green and blue ink on white card stock. The custom box gives the set checklist on the back.

		MINT	EXC	G-VG
COMPLETE SET (33)		4.00	2.00	.40
COMMON PLAYER (1-33)		.06	.03	.00
☐ 1	Tony Armas	.06	.03	.00
☐ 2	Don Baylor	.10	.05	.01
☐ 3	Wade Boggs	.60	.30	.06
☐ 4	George Brett	.35	.17	.03
☐ 5	Bill Buckner	.06	.03	.00
☐ 6	Rod Carew	.30	.15	.03
☐ 7	Gary Carter	.20	.10	.02
☐ 8	Cecil Cooper	.10	.05	.01
☐ 9	Darrell Evans	.10	.05	.01
☐ 10	Dwight Evans	.10	.05	.01
☐ 11	George Foster	.10	.05	.01
☐ 12	Bob Grich	.06	.03	.00
☐ 13	Tony Gwynn	.40	.20	.04
☐ 14	Keith Hernandez	.20	.10	.02
☐ 15	Reggie Jackson	.40	.20	.04
☐ 16	Dave Kingman	.10	.05	.01
☐ 17	Carney Lansford	.10	.05	.01
☐ 18	Fred Lynn	.10	.05	.01
☐ 19	Bill Madlock	.06	.03	.00
☐ 20	Don Mattingly	.75	.35	.07
☐ 21	Willie McGee	.15	.07	.01
☐ 22	Hal McRae	.06	.03	.00
☐ 23	Dale Murphy	.35	.17	.03
☐ 24	Eddie Murray	.25	.12	.02
☐ 25	Ben Oglivie	.06	.03	.00
☐ 26	Al Oliver	.06	.03	.00
☐ 27	Dave Parker	.10	.05	.01
☐ 28	Jim Rice	.20	.10	.02
☐ 29	Pete Rose	.45	.22	.04
☐ 30	Mike Schmidt	.50	.25	.05
☐ 31	Gorman Thomas	.10	.05	.01
☐ 32	Willie Wilson	.10	.05	.01
☐ 33	Dave Winfield	.25	.12	.02

1987 Woolworth's Highlights

Topps produced this 33-card set for Woolworth's stores. The set is subtitled "Topps Collectors' Series Baseball Highlights" and consists of high gloss card

fronts with full-color photos. The cards show and describe highlights of the previous season. The card backs are printed in gold and purple and are numbered. The set was sold nationally in Woolworth's for a 1.99 suggested retail price.

		MINT	EXC	G-VG
COMPLETE SET (33)		4.00	2.00	.40
COMMON PLAYER (1-33)		.07	.03	.01
☐ 1	Steve Carlton	.25	.12	.02
☐ 2	Cecil Cooper	.10	.05	.01
☐ 3	Rickey Henderson	.40	.20	.04
☐ 4	Reggie Jackson	.35	.17	.03
☐ 5	Jim Rice	.20	.10	.02
☐ 6	Don Sutton	.20	.10	.02
☐ 7	Roger Clemens	.40	.20	.04
☐ 8	Mike Schmidt	.45	.22	.04
☐ 9	Jesse Barfield	.15	.07	.01
☐ 10	Wade Boggs	.60	.30	.06
☐ 11	Tim Raines	.25	.12	.02
☐ 12	Jose Canseco	.75	.35	.07
☐ 13	Todd Worrell	.15	.07	.01
☐ 14	Dave Righetti	.15	.07	.01
☐ 15	Don Mattingly	.75	.35	.07
☐ 16	Tony Gwynn	.35	.17	.03
☐ 17	Marty Barrett	.07	.03	.01
☐ 18	Mike Scott	.15	.07	.01
☐ 19	Bruce Hurst	.10	.05	.01
☐ 20	Calvin Schiraldi	.07	.03	.01
☐ 21	Dwight Evans	.15	.07	.01
☐ 22	Dave Henderson	.07	.03	.01
☐ 23	Len Dykstra	.10	.05	.01
☐ 24	Bob Ojeda	.07	.03	.01
☐ 25	Gary Carter	.20	.10	.02
☐ 26	Ron Darling	.15	.07	.01
☐ 27	Jim Rice	.20	.10	.02
☐ 28	Bruce Hurst	.10	.05	.01
☐ 29	Darryl Strawberry	.60	.30	.06
☐ 30	Ray Knight	.07	.03	.01
☐ 31	Keith Hernandez	.25	.12	.02
☐ 32	Mets Celebration	.07	.03	.01
☐ 33	Ray Knight	.07	.03	.01

1988 Woolworth's Highlights

Topps produced this 33-card set for Woolworth's stores. The set is subtitled "Topps Collectors' Series Baseball Highlights" and consists of high gloss card fronts with full-color photos. The cards show and describe highlights of the previous season. Cards 19-33 commemorate the World Series with highlights and key players of each game in the series. The card backs are printed in red and blue on white card stock and are numbered. The set was sold nationally in Woolworth's for a 1.99 suggested retail price.

		MINT	EXC	G-VG
COMPLETE SET (33)		4.00	2.00	.40
COMMON PLAYER (1-33)		.05	.02	.00
☐ 1	Don Baylor	.08	.04	.01
☐ 2	Vince Coleman	.12	.06	.01
☐ 3	Darrell Evans	.08	.04	.01
☐ 4	Don Mattingly	.75	.35	.07

☐ 5	Eddie Murray	.20	.10	.02
☐ 6	Nolan Ryan	.75	.35	.07
☐ 7	Mike Schmidt	.50	.25	.05
☐ 8	Andre Dawson	.15	.07	.01
☐ 9	George Bell	.12	.06	.01
☐ 10	Steve Bedrosian	.08	.04	.01
☐ 11	Roger Clemens	.40	.20	.04
☐ 12	Tony Gwynn	.30	.15	.03
☐ 13	Wade Boggs	.50	.25	.05
☐ 14	Benny Santiago	.20	.10	.02
☐ 15	Mark McGwire UER (referenced on card back as NL ROY, sic)	.60	.30	.06
☐ 16	Dave Righetti	.08	.04	.01
☐ 17	Jeffrey Leonard	.05	.02	.00
☐ 18	Gary Gaetti	.08	.04	.01
☐ 19	Frank Viola WS1	.10	.05	.01
☐ 20	Dan Gladden WS1	.05	.02	.00
☐ 21	Bert Blyleven WS2	.10	.05	.01
☐ 22	Gary Gaetti WS2	.10	.05	.01
☐ 23	John Tudor WS3	.08	.04	.01
☐ 24	Todd Worrell WS3	.10	.05	.01
☐ 25	Tom Lawless WS4	.05	.02	.00
☐ 26	Willie McGee WS4	.10	.05	.01
☐ 27	Danny Cox WS5	.08	.04	.01
☐ 28	Curt Ford WS5	.05	.02	.00
☐ 29	Don Baylor WS6	.08	.04	.01
☐ 30	Kent Hrbek WS6	.10	.05	.01
☐ 31	Kirby Puckett WS7	.25	.12	.02
☐ 32	Greg Gagne WS7	.05	.02	.00
☐ 33	Frank Viola WS-MVP	.12	.06	.01

1989 Woolworth's Highlights

The 1989 Woolworth's Highlights set contains 33 standard-size (2 1/2 by 3 1/2 inch) glossy cards. The fronts have red and white borders. The vertically-oriented backs are yellow and red, and describe highlights from the 1988 season including the World Series. The cards were distributed through Woolworth stores as a boxed set.

	MINT	EXC	G-VG
COMPLETE SET (33)	4.00	2.00	.40
COMMON PLAYER (1-33)	.05	.02	.00
☐ 1 Jose Canseco	.75	.35	.07
☐ 2 Kirk Gibson	.20	.10	.02

☐ 3	Frank Viola	.15	.07	.01
☐ 4	Orel Hershiser	.25	.12	.02
☐ 5	Walt Weiss	.20	.10	.02
☐ 6	Chris Sabo	.20	.10	.02
☐ 7	George Bell	.15	.07	.01
☐ 8	Wade Boggs	.50	.25	.05
☐ 9	Tom Browning	.10	.05	.01
☐ 10	Gary Carter	.20	.10	.02
☐ 11	Andre Dawson	.20	.10	.02
☐ 12	John Franco	.10	.05	.01
☐ 13	Randy Johnson	.05	.02	.00
☐ 14	Doug Jones	.05	.02	.00
☐ 15	Kevin McReynolds	.15	.07	.01
☐ 16	Gene Nelson	.05	.02	.00
☐ 17	Jeff Reardon	.10	.05	.01
☐ 18	Pat Tabler	.05	.02	.00
☐ 19	Tim Belcher	.10	.05	.01
☐ 20	Dennis Eckersley	.15	.07	.01
☐ 21	Orel Hershiser	.25	.12	.02
☐ 22	Gregg Jefferies	.50	.25	.05
☐ 23	Jose Canseco	.75	.35	.07
☐ 24	Kirk Gibson	.20	.10	.02
☐ 25	Orel Hershiser	.25	.12	.02
☐ 26	Mike Marshall	.10	.05	.01
☐ 27	Mark McGwire	.50	.25	.05
☐ 28	Rick Honeycutt	.05	.02	.00
☐ 29	Tim Belcher	.10	.05	.01
☐ 30	Jay Howell	.05	.02	.00
☐ 31	Mickey Hatcher	.05	.02	.00
☐ 32	Mike Davis	.05	.02	.00
☐ 33	Orel Hershiser	.25	.12	.02

1931 W517

The cards in this 54-card set measure 3" by 4". This 1931 set of numbered, blank backed cards was placed in the "W" category in the ACC because (1) its producer was unknown and (2) it was issued in strips of three. The photo is black and white but the entire obverse of each card is generally found tinted in tones of sepia, blue, green, yellow, rose, black or gray. The cards are numbered in a small circle on the front. A solid dark line at one end of a card entitled the purchaser to another piece of candy as a prize. There are two different cards of both Babe Ruth and Mickey Cochrane.

	EX-MT	VG-E	GOOD
COMPLETE SET (54)	6500.00	3000.00	700.00
COMMON PLAYER (1-54)	40.00	20.00	4.00
☐ 1 Earl Combs	80.00	40.00	8.00
☐ 2 Pie Traynor	100.00	50.00	10.00
☐ 3 Eddie Rousch	100.00	50.00	10.00
☐ 4 Babe Ruth	1200.00	600.00	150.00
☐ 5 Chalmer Cissell	40.00	20.00	4.00
☐ 6 Bill Sherdel	40.00	20.00	4.00
☐ 7 Bill Shore	40.00	20.00	4.00
☐ 8 George Earnshaw	40.00	20.00	4.00
☐ 9 Bucky Harris	80.00	40.00	8.00

		NRMT	VG-E	GOOD
☐ 10	Charlie Klein	100.00	50.00	10.00
☐ 11	George Kelly	80.00	40.00	8.00
☐ 12	Travis Jackson	80.00	40.00	8.00
☐ 13	Willie Kamm	40.00	20.00	4.00
☐ 14	Harry Heilman	100.00	50.00	10.00
☐ 15	Grover Alexander	125.00	60.00	12.50
☐ 16	Frank Frisch	100.00	50.00	10.00
☐ 17	Jack Quinn	40.00	20.00	4.00
☐ 18	Cy Williams	40.00	20.00	4.00
☐ 19	Kiki Cuyler	80.00	40.00	8.00
☐ 20	Babe Ruth	1500.00	750.00	150.00
☐ 21	Jimmy Foxx	200.00	100.00	20.00
☐ 22	Jimmy Dykes	50.00	25.00	5.00
☐ 23	Bill Terry	100.00	50.00	10.00
☐ 24	Freddy Lindstrom	80.00	40.00	8.00
☐ 25	Hugh Critz	40.00	20.00	4.00
☐ 26	Pete Donahue	40.00	20.00	4.00
☐ 27	Tony Lazzeri	60.00	30.00	6.00
☐ 28	Heine Manush	80.00	40.00	8.00
☐ 29	Chick Hafey	80.00	40.00	8.00
☐ 30	Melvin Ott	150.00	75.00	15.00
☐ 31	Bing Miller	40.00	20.00	4.00
☐ 32	George Haas	40.00	20.00	4.00
☐ 33	Lefty O'Doul	60.00	30.00	6.00
☐ 34	Paul Waner	80.00	40.00	8.00
☐ 35	Lou Gehrig	700.00	350.00	70.00
☐ 36	Dazzy Vance	80.00	40.00	8.00
☐ 37	Mickey Cochrane	125.00	60.00	12.50
☐ 38	Rogers Hornsby	200.00	100.00	20.00
☐ 39	Lefty Grove	150.00	75.00	15.00
☐ 40	Al Simmons	100.00	50.00	10.00
☐ 41	Rube Walberg	40.00	20.00	4.00
☐ 42	Hack Wilson	125.00	60.00	12.50
☐ 43	Art Shires	40.00	20.00	4.00
☐ 44	Sammy Hale	40.00	20.00	4.00
☐ 45	Ted Lyons	80.00	40.00	8.00
☐ 46	Joe Sewell	80.00	40.00	8.00
☐ 47	Goose Goslin	80.00	40.00	8.00
☐ 48	Lou Fonseca	40.00	20.00	4.00
☐ 49	Bob Meusel	50.00	25.00	5.00
☐ 50	Lu Blue	40.00	20.00	4.00
☐ 51	Earl Averill	80.00	40.00	8.00
☐ 52	Eddy Collins	100.00	50.00	10.00
☐ 53	Joe Judge	40.00	20.00	4.00
☐ 54	Mickey Cochrane	125.00	60.00	12.50

W576 1950-56 Callahan HOF

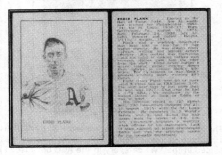

The cards in this 82-card set measure 1 3/4" by 2 1/2". The 1950-56 Callahan Hall of Fame set was issued over a number of years at the Baseball Hall of Fame museum in Cooperstown, New York. New cards were added to the set each year when new members were inducted into the Hall of Fame. The cards with (2) in the checklist exist with two different biographies. The year of each card's first inclusion in the set is also given in parentheses; those not listed parenthetically below were issued in 1950 as well as in all the succeeding years and are hence the most common. Naturally the supply of cards is directly related to how many years a player was included in the set; cards that were not issued until 1955 are much scarcer than those printed all the years between 1950 and 1956. The ACC designation is W576. One frequently finds "complete" sets in the original box; take care to investigate the year of issue, the set may be complete in the sense of all the

cards issued up to a certain year, but not all 82 cards below. For example, a "complete" 1950 set would obviously not include any of the cards marked below with ('52), ('54), or ('55) as none of those cards existed in 1950 since those respective players had not yet been inducted. The complete set price below refers to a set including all 83 cards below. Since the cards are unnumbered, they are numbered below for reference alphabetically by player's name.

		NRMT	VG-E	GOOD
COMPLETE SET (83)		400.00	175.00	45.00
COMMON PLAYER ('50)		1.50	.75	.15
COMMON PLAYER ('52)		3.00	1.50	.30
COMMON PLAYER ('54)		4.00	2.00	.40
COMMON PLAYER ('55)		6.00	3.00	.60
☐ 1	Grover Alexander	3.00	1.50	.30
☐ 2	Cap Anson	2.00	1.00	.20
☐ 3	Frank Baker ('55)	6.00	3.00	.60
☐ 4	Edward Barrow ('54)	4.00	2.00	.40
☐ 5	Chief Bender(2)('54)	4.00	2.00	.40
☐ 6	Roger Bresnahan	1.50	.75	.15
☐ 7	Dan Brouthers	1.50	.75	.15
☐ 8	Mordecai Brown	1.50	.75	.15
☐ 9	Morgan Bulkeley	1.50	.75	.15
☐ 10	Jesse Burkett	1.50	.75	.15
☐ 11	Alexander Cartwright	1.50	.75	.15
☐ 12	Henry Chadwick	1.50	.75	.15
☐ 13	Frank Chance	1.50	.75	.15
☐ 14	Happy Chandler ('52)	25.00	12.50	2.50
☐ 15	Jack Chesbro	1.50	.75	.15
☐ 16	Fred Clarke	1.50	.75	.15
☐ 17	Ty Cobb	40.00	20.00	4.00
☐ 18A	Mickey Cochran ERR (sic, Cochrane)	7.50	3.75	.75
☐ 18B	Mickey Cochrane COR	7.50	3.75	.75
☐ 19	Eddie Collins (2)	2.00	1.00	.20
☐ 20	Jimmie Collins	1.50	.75	.15
☐ 21	Charles Comiskey	1.50	.75	.15
☐ 22	Tom Connolly ('54)	4.00	2.00	.40
☐ 23	Candy Cummings	1.50	.75	.15
☐ 24	Dizzy Dean ('54)	15.00	7.50	1.50
☐ 25	Ed Delahanty	1.50	.75	.15
☐ 26	Bill Dickey ('54)(2)	9.00	4.50	.90
☐ 27	Joe DiMaggio ('55)	75.00	37.50	7.50
☐ 28	Hugh Duffy	1.50	.75	.15
☐ 29	Johnny Evers	1.50	.75	.15
☐ 30	Buck Ewing	1.50	.75	.15
☐ 31	Jimmie Foxx	6.00	3.00	.60
☐ 32	Frank Frisch	2.00	1.00	.20
☐ 33	Lou Gehrig	40.00	20.00	4.00
☐ 34	Charles Gehringer	3.00	1.50	.30
☐ 35	Clark Griffith	1.50	.75	.15
☐ 36	Lefty Grove	4.00	2.00	.40
☐ 37	Gabby Hartnett ('55)	6.00	3.00	.60
☐ 38	Harry Heilmann ('52)	3.00	1.50	.30
☐ 39	Rogers Hornsby	6.00	3.00	.60
☐ 40	Carl Hubbell	2.00	1.00	.20
☐ 41	Hughey Jennings	1.50	.75	.15
☐ 42	Ban Johnson	1.50	.75	.15
☐ 43	Walter Johnson	7.50	3.75	.75
☐ 44	Willie Keeler	1.50	.75	.15
☐ 45	Mike Kelly	2.00	1.00	.20
☐ 46	Bill Klem ('54)	4.00	2.00	.40
☐ 47	Napoleon Lajoie	4.00	2.00	.40
☐ 48	Kenesaw Landis	1.50	.75	.15
☐ 49	Ted Lyons ('55)	6.00	3.00	.60
☐ 50	Connie Mack	2.00	1.00	.20
☐ 51	Walter Maranville('54)	4.00	2.00	.40
☐ 52	Christy Mathewson	7.50	3.75	.75
☐ 53	Tommy McCarthy	1.50	.75	.15
☐ 54	Joe McGinnity	1.50	.75	.15
☐ 55	John McGraw	1.50	.75	.15
☐ 56	Charles Nicholls	1.50	.75	.15
☐ 57	Jim O'Rourke	1.50	.75	.15
☐ 58	Mel Ott	3.00	1.50	.30
☐ 59	Herb Pennock	1.50	.75	.15
☐ 60	Eddie Plank	2.00	1.00	.20
☐ 61	Charles Radbourne	1.50	.75	.15
☐ 62	Wilbert Robinson	1.50	.75	.15
☐ 63	Babe Ruth	75.00	37.50	7.50
☐ 64	Ray Schalk ('55)	6.00	3.00	.60
☐ 65	Al Simmons ('54)	4.00	2.00	.40
☐ 66	George Sisler (2)	2.00	1.00	.20
☐ 67	A.G. Spalding	1.50	.75	.15
☐ 68	Tris Speaker	4.00	2.00	.40
☐ 69	Bill Terry ('54)	6.00	3.00	.60
☐ 70	Joe Tinker	1.50	.75	.15
☐ 71	Pie Traynor	2.00	1.00	.20
☐ 72	Dazzy Vance ('55)	6.00	3.00	.60
☐ 73	Rube Waddell	1.50	.75	.15

☐ 74	Hans Wagner	7.50	3.75	.75
☐ 75	Bobby Wallace ('54)	6.00	3.00	.60
☐ 76	Ed Walsh	1.50	.75	.15
☐ 77	Paul Waner ('52)	5.00	2.50	.50
☐ 78	George Wright	1.50	.75	.15
☐ 79	Harry Wright ('54)	4.00	2.00	.40
☐ 80	Cy Young	4.00	2.00	.40
☐ 81	Museum Interior ('54) (2)	4.00	2.00	.40
☐ 82	Museum Exterior ('54) (2)	4.00	2.00	.40

W605 1955 Robert Gould

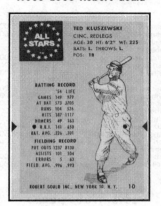

The cards in this 28-card set measure 2 1/2" by 3 1/2". The 1955 Robert F. Gould set of black and white on green cards were toy store cardboard holders for small plastic statues. The statues were attached to the card by a rubber band through two holes on the side of the card. The ACC designation is W605. The cards are numbered in the bottom right corner of the obverse and are blank-backed.

		NRMT	VG-E	GOOD
COMPLETE SET (28)		1250.00	600.00	150.00
COMMON PLAYER (1-28)		25.00	12.50	2.50
☐ 1	Willie Mays	350.00	175.00	35.00
☐ 2	Gus Zernial	25.00	12.50	2.50
☐ 3	Red Schoendienst	75.00	37.50	7.50
☐ 4	Chico Carrasquel	25.00	12.50	2.50
☐ 5	Jim Hegan	25.00	12.50	2.50
☐ 6	Curt Simmons	30.00	15.00	3.00
☐ 7	Bob Porterfield	25.00	12.50	2.50
☐ 8	Jim Busby	25.00	12.50	2.50
☐ 9	Don Mueller	30.00	15.00	3.00
☐ 10	Ted Kluszewski	45.00	22.50	4.50
☐ 11	Ray Boone	25.00	12.50	2.50
☐ 12	Smokey Burgess	30.00	15.00	3.00
☐ 13	Bob Rush	25.00	12.50	2.50
☐ 14	Early Wynn	75.00	37.50	7.50
☐ 15	Bill Bruton	25.00	12.50	2.50
☐ 16	Gus Bell	25.00	12.50	2.50
☐ 17	Jim Finigan	25.00	12.50	2.50
☐ 18	Granny Hamner	25.00	12.50	2.50
☐ 19	Hank Thompson	30.00	15.00	3.00
☐ 20	Joe Coleman	25.00	12.50	2.50
☐ 21	Don Newcombe	45.00	22.50	4.50
☐ 22	Richie Ashburn	60.00	30.00	6.00
☐ 23	Bobby Thomson	45.00	22.50	4.50
☐ 24	Sid Gordon	25.00	12.50	2.50
☐ 25	Gerry Coleman	30.00	15.00	3.00
☐ 26	Ernie Banks	150.00	75.00	15.00
☐ 27	Billy Pierce	35.00	17.50	3.50
☐ 28	Mel Parnell	30.00	15.00	3.00

UNSURE ABOUT CONDITION?
Check out the Beckett Condition Guide in this volume.

1938-39 W711-1

The cards in this 32-card set measure 2" by 3". The 1938-39 Cincinnati Reds Baseball player set was printed in orange and gray tones. Many back variations exist and there are two poses of Vander Meer, portrait (PORT) and an action (ACT) poses. The set was sold at the ballpark and was printed on thin cardboard stock. The cards are unnumbered but have been alphabetized and numbered in the checklist below.

		EX-MT	VG-E	GOOD
COMPLETE SET (32)		600.00	275.00	65.00
COMMON PLAYER (1-32)		12.00	6.00	1.20
☐ 1	Wally Berger (2)	15.00	7.50	1.50
☐ 2	Nino Bongiovanni (39)	50.00	25.00	5.00
☐ 3	Stanley Bordagaray Frenchy (39)	50.00	25.00	5.00
☐ 4	Joe Cascarella (38)	12.00	6.00	1.20
☐ 5	Allen Dusty Cooke (38)	12.00	6.00	1.20
☐ 6	Harry Craft	12.00	6.00	1.20
☐ 7	Ray (Peaches) Davis	12.00	6.00	1.20
☐ 8	Paul Derringer (2)	15.00	7.50	1.50
☐ 9	Linus Frey (2)	12.00	6.00	1.20
☐ 10	Lee Gamble (2)	12.00	6.00	1.20
☐ 11	Ival Goodman (2)	12.00	6.00	1.20
☐ 12	Hank Gowdy	12.00	6.00	1.20
☐ 13	Lee Grissom (2)	12.00	6.00	1.20
☐ 14	Willard Hershberger (2)	12.00	6.00	1.20
☐ 15	Eddie Joost (39)	12.00	6.00	1.20
☐ 16	Wes Livengood (39)	100.00	50.00	10.00
☐ 17	Ernie Lombardi (39)	50.00	25.00	5.00
☐ 18	Frank McCormick	15.00	7.50	1.50
☐ 19	Bill McKechnie (2)	30.00	15.00	3.00
☐ 20	Lloyd Whitey Moore (2)	12.00	6.00	1.20
☐ 21	Billy Myers (2)	12.00	6.00	1.20
☐ 22	Lew Riggs (2)	12.00	6.00	1.20
☐ 23	Eddie Roush COA (38)	40.00	20.00	4.00
☐ 24	Les Scarsella (39)	12.00	6.00	1.20
☐ 25	Gene Schott (38)	12.00	6.00	1.20
☐ 26	Eugene Thompson	12.00	6.00	1.20
☐ 27	Johnny VanderMeer PORT	30.00	15.00	3.00
☐ 28	Johnny VanderMeer ACT	30.00	15.00	3.00
☐ 29	Wm.(Bucky) Walters (2)	15.00	7.50	1.50
☐ 30	Jim Weaver	12.00	6.00	1.20
☐ 31	Bill Werber (39)	12.00	6.00	1.20
☐ 32	Jimmy Wilson (39)	12.00	6.00	1.20

1941 W711-2

The cards in this 34-card set measure 2 1/8" by 2 5/8". The W711-2 Cincinnati Reds set contains unnumbered, black and white cards. This issue is sometimes called the "Harry Hartman" set. The cards are numbered below in alphabetical order by player's name with non-player cards listed at the end.

		EX-MT	VG-E	GOOD
COMPLETE SET (34)		425.00	200.00	40.00
COMMON PLAYER (1-28)		12.00	6.00	1.20
COMMON CARD (29-34)		8.00	4.00	.80
□ 1	Morris Arnovich	12.00	6.00	1.20
□ 2	William (Bill) Baker	12.00	6.00	1.20
□ 3	Joseph Beggs	12.00	6.00	1.20
□ 4	Harry Craft	12.00	6.00	1.20
□ 5	Paul Derringer	18.00	9.00	1.80
□ 6	Linus Frey	12.00	6.00	1.20
□ 7	Ival Goodman	12.00	6.00	1.20
□ 8	Hank Gowdy	15.00	7.50	1.50
□ 9	Witt Guise	12.00	6.00	1.20
□ 10	Willard Hershberger	12.00	6.00	1.20
□ 11	John Hutchings	12.00	6.00	1.20
□ 12	Edwin Joost	12.00	6.00	1.20
□ 13	Ernie Lombardi	50.00	25.00	5.00
□ 14	Frank McCormick	18.00	9.00	1.80
□ 15	Myron McCormick	12.00	6.00	1.20
□ 16	William McKechnie	30.00	15.00	3.00
□ 17	Whitey Moore	12.00	6.00	1.20
□ 18	William (Bill) Myers	12.00	6.00	1.20
□ 19	Elmer Riddle	12.00	6.00	1.20
□ 20	Lewis Riggs	12.00	6.00	1.20
□ 21	James A. Ripple	12.00	6.00	1.20
□ 22	Milburn Shoffner	12.00	6.00	1.20
□ 23	Eugene Thompson	12.00	6.00	1.20
□ 24	James Turner	15.00	7.50	1.50
□ 25	John VanderMeer	25.00	12.50	2.50
□ 26	Bucky Walters	18.00	9.00	1.80
□ 27	Bill Werber	12.00	6.00	1.20
□ 28	James Wilson	12.00	6.00	1.20
□ 29	Results 1940 World Series	8.00	4.00	.80
□ 30	The Cincinati Reds (Title Card)	8.00	4.00	.80
□ 31	The Cincinnati Reds World's Champions (Title Card)	8.00	4.00	.80
□ 32	Debt of Gratitude to Wm. Koehl Co.	8.00	4.00	.80
□ 33	Tell the World About Our Reds	8.00	4.00	.80
□ 34	Harry Hartman	8.00	4.00	.80

1941 W753 Browns

The cards in this 29-card set measure 2 1/8" by 2 5/8". The 1941 W753 set features unnumbered cards of the St. Louis Browns. The cards are numbered below alphabetically by player's name.

		EX-MT	VG-E	GOOD
COMPLETE SET (29)		375.00	175.00	40.00
COMMON PLAYER (1-29)		12.00	6.00	1.20
□ 1	Johnny Allen	12.00	6.00	1.20
□ 2	Elden Auker	12.00	6.00	1.20
□ 3	Donald L. Barnes	12.00	6.00	1.20
□ 4	Johnny Beradino	15.00	7.50	1.50
□ 5	George Caster	12.00	6.00	1.20
□ 6	Harland Clift	12.00	6.00	1.20
□ 7	Roy J. Cullenbine	12.00	6.00	1.20
□ 8	William O. DeWitt	12.00	6.00	1.20
□ 9	Robert Estalella	12.00	6.00	1.20
□ 10	Rick Ferrell	60.00	25.00	5.00

□ 11	Dennis W. Galehouse	12.00	6.00	1.20
□ 12	Joseph L. Grace	12.00	6.00	1.20
□ 13	Frank Grube	12.00	6.00	1.20
□ 14	Robert A. Harris	12.00	6.00	1.20
□ 15	Donald Heffner	12.00	6.00	1.20
□ 16	Fred Hofmann	12.00	6.00	1.20
□ 17	Walter F. Judnich	12.00	6.00	1.20
□ 18	Jack Kramer	12.00	6.00	1.20
□ 19	Chester (Chet) Laabs	12.00	6.00	1.20
□ 20	John Lucadello	12.00	6.00	1.20
□ 21	George H. McQuinn	12.00	6.00	1.20
□ 22	Robert Muncrief Jr.	12.00	6.00	1.20
□ 23	John Niggeling	12.00	6.00	1.20
□ 24	Fritz Ostermueller	12.00	6.00	1.20
□ 25	James (Luke) Sewell	18.00	8.50	1.50
□ 26	Alan C. Strange	12.00	6.00	1.20
□ 27	Bob Swift	12.00	6.00	1.20
□ 28	James (Zack) Taylor	12.00	6.00	1.20
□ 29	Bill Trotter	12.00	6.00	1.20

1941 W754 Cardinals

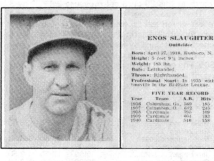

The cards in this 29-card set measure 2 1/8" by 2 5/8". The 1941 W754 set of unnumbered cards features St. Louis Cardinals. The cards are numbered below alphabetically by player's name.

		EX-MT	VG-E	GOOD
COMPLETE SET (29)		475.00	225.00	55.00
COMMON PLAYER (1-29)		12.00	6.00	1.20
□ 1	Sam Breadon	12.00	6.00	1.20
□ 2	Jimmy Brown	12.00	6.00	1.20
□ 3	Mort Cooper	15.00	7.50	1.50
□ 4	Walker Cooper	12.00	6.00	1.20
□ 5	Estel Crabtree	12.00	6.00	1.20
□ 6	Frank Crespi	12.00	6.00	1.20
□ 7	Bill Crouch	12.00	6.00	1.20
□ 8	Mike Gonzalez	12.00	6.00	1.20
□ 9	Harry Gumpert	12.00	6.00	1.20
□ 10	John Hopp	15.00	7.50	1.50
□ 11	Ira Hutchinson	12.00	6.00	1.20
□ 12	Howie Krist	12.00	6.00	1.20
□ 13	Eddie Lake	12.00	6.00	1.20
□ 14	Max Lanier	15.00	7.50	1.50
□ 15	Gus Mancuso	12.00	6.00	1.20
□ 16	Marty Marion	30.00	15.00	3.00
□ 17	Steve Mesner	12.00	6.00	1.20
□ 18	John Mize	60.00	25.00	5.00
□ 19	Terry Moore	20.00	10.00	2.00
□ 20	Sam Nahem	12.00	6.00	1.20

		EX-MT	VG-E	GOOD
☐ 21	Don Padgett	12.00	6.00	1.20
☐ 22	Branch Rickey	60.00	25.00	5.00
☐ 23	Clyde Shoun	12.00	6.00	1.20
☐ 24	Enos Slaughter	60.00	25.00	5.00
☐ 25	Billy Southworth	12.00	6.00	1.20
☐ 26	Coaker Triplett	12.00	6.00	1.20
☐ 27	Buzzy Wares	12.00	6.00	1.20
☐ 28	Lon Warneke	15.00	7.50	1.50
☐ 29	Ernie White	12.00	6.00	1.20

1928 Yuenglings

The cards in this 60-card set measure 1 3/8" by 2 9/16". This black and white, numbered set contains many Hall of Famers. The obverses are the same as those found in sets of E210 and W502. The Paul Waner card, number 45, actually contains a picture of Clyde Barnhardt. Each back contains an offer to redeem pictures of Babe Ruth for ice cream. The ACC designation for this set is F50.

		EX-MT	VG-E	GOOD
COMPLETE SET (60)		1500.00	750.00	150.00
COMMON PLAYER (1-60)		10.00	5.00	1.00
☐ 1	Burleigh Grimes	20.00	10.00	2.00
☐ 2	Walter Reuther	10.00	5.00	1.00
☐ 3	Joe Dugan	12.00	6.00	1.20
☐ 4	Red Faber	20.00	10.00	2.00
☐ 5	Gabby Hartnett	25.00	12.50	2.50

		EX-MT	VG-E	GOOD
☐ 6	Babe Ruth	300.00	150.00	30.00
☐ 7	Bob Meusel	12.00	6.00	1.20
☐ 8	Herb Pennock	20.00	10.00	2.00
☐ 9	George Burns	10.00	5.00	1.00
☐ 10	Joe Sewell	20.00	10.00	2.00
☐ 11	George Uhle	10.00	5.00	1.00
☐ 12	Bob O'Farrell	10.00	5.00	1.00
☐ 13	Rogers Hornsby	60.00	30.00	6.00
☐ 14	Pie Traynor	30.00	15.00	3.00
☐ 15	Clarence Mitchell	10.00	5.00	1.00
☐ 16	Eppa Rixey	20.00	10.00	2.00
☐ 17	Carl Mays	12.00	6.00	1.20
☐ 18	Adolfo Luque	10.00	5.00	1.00
☐ 19	Dave Bancroft	20.00	10.00	2.00
☐ 20	George Kelly	20.00	10.00	2.00
☐ 21	Earl Combs	20.00	10.00	2.00
☐ 22	Harry Heilmann	20.00	10.00	2.00
☐ 23	Ray Schalk	20.00	10.00	2.00
☐ 24	John Mostil	10.00	5.00	1.00
☐ 25	Hack Wilson	30.00	15.00	3.00
☐ 26	Lou Gehrig	150.00	75.00	15.00
☐ 27	Ty Cobb	150.00	75.00	15.00
☐ 28	Tris Speaker	45.00	22.50	4.50
☐ 29	Tony Lazzeri	15.00	7.50	1.50
☐ 30	Waite Hoyt	20.00	10.00	2.00
☐ 31	Sherwood Smith	10.00	5.00	1.00
☐ 32	Max Carey	20.00	10.00	2.00
☐ 33	Gene Hargrave	10.00	5.00	1.00
☐ 34	Miguel Gonzalez	10.00	5.00	1.00
☐ 35	Joe Judge	10.00	5.00	1.00
☐ 36	Sam Rice	20.00	10.00	2.00
☐ 37	Earl Sheely	10.00	5.00	1.00
☐ 38	Sam Jones	10.00	5.00	1.00
☐ 39	Bibb Falk	10.00	5.00	1.00
☐ 40	Willie Kamm	10.00	5.00	1.00
☐ 41	Stan (Bucky) Harris	18.00	9.00	1.80
☐ 42	John McGraw	30.00	15.00	3.00
☐ 43	Art Nehf	10.00	5.00	1.00
☐ 44	Grover C. Alexander	45.00	22.50	4.50
☐ 45	Paul Waner	20.00	10.00	2.00
☐ 46	Bill Terry	30.00	15.00	3.00
☐ 47	Glenn Wright	10.00	5.00	1.00
☐ 48	Earl Smith	10.00	5.00	1.00
☐ 49	Goose Goslin	20.00	10.00	2.00
☐ 50	Frank Frisch	30.00	15.00	3.00
☐ 51	Joe Harris	10.00	5.00	1.00
☐ 52	Cy Williams	12.00	6.00	1.20
☐ 53	Eddie Roush	25.00	12.50	2.50
☐ 54	George Sisler	30.00	15.00	3.00
☐ 55	Ed Rommel	12.00	6.00	1.20
☐ 56	Roger Peckinpaugh	10.00	5.00	1.00
☐ 57	Stanley Coveleskie	20.00	10.00	2.00
☐ 58	Lester Bell	10.00	5.00	1.00
☐ 59	Lloyd Waner	20.00	10.00	2.00
☐ 60	John McInnis	12.00	6.00	1.20

Picture Gallery

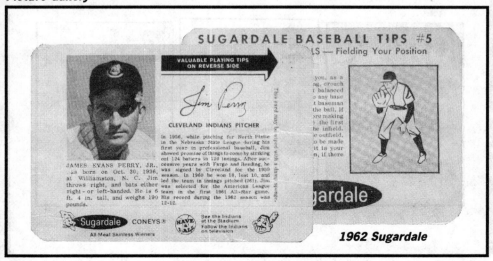

1962 Sugardale

ROY CAMPANELLA
Catcher LOS ANGELES DODGERS

Height: 5'10"   Weight: 218
Home: Glen Cove, New York
Throws: Right   Bats: Right
Born: November 19, 1921

Roy Campanella has been named The Most Valuable Player in the National League on 3 occasions! His finest season was in 1953 when he hit 41 home runs and piled up 142 runs batted in—an all-time high in Dodger history. In his ten campaigns with the Dodgers, Roy has hit 242 homers and only twice has dropped below 20.

MAJOR LEAGUE RECORD

YEAR	CLUB	GAMES	HITS	HR	RBI	AVG.
1948	Dodgers	83	72	9	45	.258
1949	"	130	125	22	82	.287
1950	"	126	123	31	89	.281
1951	"	143	164	33	108	.325
1952	"	128	126	22	97	.269
1953	"	144	162	41	142	.312
1954	"	111	82	19	51	.207
1955	"	123	142	32	107	.318
1956	"	124	85	20	73	.219
1957	"	103	80	13	62	.242

1958 Bell Brand

1959 Morrell

1960 Morrell

1961 Morrell

T200 Fatima Teams

T202 Hassan Trplefolders

T201 Mecca Doublefolders

BECKETT Sports Videos

#1013

#1002

#1001

#1012

#1016

#1004

#1210

#1204

#1207

#1015

Item Number	Description of item	Qty.	Price	Total
#1013	The Boys of Summer: Brooklyn Dodgers (1983)		$14.95	
#1002	Chicago and the Cubs (1987)		$19.95	
#1001	Cincinnati Reds: The Official History (1987)		$19.95	
#1012	Dodger Stadium: The First 25 Years (1987)		$19.95	
#1016	Forever Fenway: 75 Yrs of Red Sox (1987)		$19.95	
#1004	A Giants History: The Tale of Two Cities (1987)		$19.95	
#1210	Grand Slam (1989)		$19.95	
#1204	The History of Baseball (1987)		$29.95	
#1207	Mickey Mantle (1988)		$19.95	
#1015	Pinstripe Power: The 1961 NY Yankees (1986)		$19.95	

*Order as many items as you want! Our flat $2 postage and handling rate covers any size order.

Sub-Total:	
Postage & Handling:*	$2.00
Texas residents please add 8% state sales tax.	
Total:	

New!

☐ **Check here to receive our complete product listing of baseball, football, & basketball videos and other sports products.**

Name _____   Subscriber Acct. # _____
(Please Print)

Address (No P.O. Boxes) _____

City _____   State _____   Zip _____

Payment enclosed via: ☐ Check or Money Order   ☐ VISA/MasterCard

Signature _____

Charge Acct. #_____   Exp. _____

Mail to: Beckett Sports Products, 4887 Alpha Rd, Suite 200, Dallas, TX 75244

EAST TEXAS SPORTS CARDS

P.O. BOX 1334 — 1411 E. RUSK ST.
JACKSONVILLE, TX 75766

Our Quarterly Flyers were a big
hit in 1989. Here are just some
of the items we offered last year:

1989 Upper Deck Factory Sets (1-800) $45
1989 Bowman Wax Boxes $10
1987 Fleer Wax Boxes $45
1988 Donruss Wax Boxes $10

Don't miss out. . .Order yours today! 1 Year: $2   Sample: $1

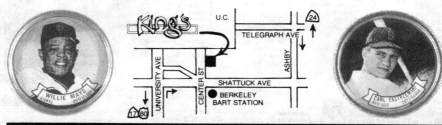

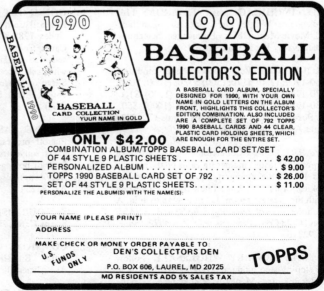

CLASSIFIED ADVERTISING

WANT LISTS APPRECIATED! *Use Guide ** Indicate Condition ** Enclose check/SASE. Money refunded if unavailable or price change. Postage $2.50, minimum order $20. Phone for further information. Thanks! San Francisco Card Exchange, 1316 18th Ave., San Francisco, CA 94122. Phone (415) 665-TEAM.

20% OFF!!! Most cards (*Beckett Monthly* and *Beckett #12* are used for prices). Send want lists, with self-addressed, stamped envelope to Pat's Coins & Cards, 3229 West 24th Street, Erie, PA 16506.

MAILING LIST of baseball card & memorabilia collectors. Adhesive labels. 1000/$29.95; 2000/$57.95; 3000/$84.95. Guaranteed deliverable. Shipped Priority Mail. B&F Sports Cards, Dept. A2, 78 Sixth Avenue, Woonsocket, RI 02895. Phone (401) 765-0934.

BUYING TICKET STUBS, programs, pennants from World Series, All-Star, Super Bowls, championship fights, hockey, basketball playoffs, any sports happening. (602-996-3393). Bob/Ron Adelson, 13447 N. 59th Place, Scottsdale, AZ 85254.

MARK GRACE autographed and numbered 8 card uncut sheet available from the publisher, Baseball Cards-N-More, Kentuckiana's biggest, best and most comprehensive baseball card store. 3900 Shelbyville Road, Louisville KY 40201. (502) 893-0818.

WHEN IN CHICAGO, visit YESTERDAY, 1143 Addison near Wrigley Field. Specializing in Baseball, Movie Memorabilia. Extravagant Selections. Unbelievably Reasonable Prices!

GROUP LOTS: Very Good or better condition. 1960-1969: (250) $170; (500) $320; (1000) $600. 1970-1979: (250) $50; (500) $90; (1000) $160. 1980-1987: (250) $15; (500) $28; (1000) $50. All Postpaid. Bill Henderson's Cards-CL, 2320 Ruger Ave., Janesville, WI 53545.

BIZARRE "Closet Collectibles." Twenty-five of the potential fastest increasing cards on the market. This list of the strangest, most outrageous and kookiest cards is the hottest new form of investing - with the greatest return. Learn how to cash in. A revolution in card investing. Send $3 and an SASE today! Gold Coast Products, P.O. Box 4972, Irvine, CA 92716.

ANYONE CAN BUY WHOLESALE. Follow this step-by-step guide and buy baseball cards at wholesale prices. Money-back guarantee. Save the price of the guide the first purchase. Send $7 plus $1 postage/handling to: Innovative Investments, P.O. Box 5101, Napa, CA 94581.

SAMPLE ISSUE, Baseball Card Broadcaster. Featuring interesting articles, inexpensive advertising, and much more! Published monthly ($7.50/year). Please send 2 stamps to: BCB, Box 1402, Rochester, MI 48308.

STARS, ROOKIES, COMMONS, 70% Retail-Topps, Fleer, Donruss, Score. Send SASE for price list. Garrett's, 1715 Vizedom Road, Hamilton, OH 45013.

AUTOGRAPH REVIEW. 13 years publishing addresses, information. $9.95 annually, 6 issues; Sample $2. 305 Carlton Rd., Syracuse, NY 13207.

*YES! *YES! *YES! *YES! Collectors are making the switch to the world's #1 lowest priced dealer. . .The Baseball Collector Inc. Send 25-cent stamp for our discount pricelist and save BIG! The Baseball Collector Inc., P.O. Box 141-BK, Owingsmills, MD 21117-9998.

CARD COLLECTORS, Save money with "The Card Finder." Write: The Card Finder, 2003 Shady Grove Drive, Bossier City, LA 71112.

TOPPS SETS 1988, 1989, 1990: $19.95 ea. + $2.50 P/H, 6 for $19.75 ea. + $9 P/H, 18 for $19.25 ea. + $20 P/H, 54 for $18.75 ea. + $60 P/H. Bill Henderson's Cards-CL, 2320 Ruger Ave., Janesville, WI 53545.

GOING OUT OF BUSINESS SALE, 1,250,000 Baseball Cards to be liquidated! Inventory includes 1985-88 Topps, Donruss, Fleer, Sportflic Cards, Commons and Stars. Over 10,000 Team sets also available. Prefer to sell entire lot at wholesale price, but welcome large quantity bids. Susan or Urban Seay, P.O. Box 311, Luling, TX 78648, (512) 875-5321 (Day), (512) 875-2597 (Night).

BUYING BASEBALL All-Star, World Series, Playoff programs, yearbooks, ticket stubs, pennants, souvenirs, Super Bowls. Basketball, hockey, football, boxing, all paper material. (602-996-3393). Bob/Ron Adelson, 13447 N. 59th Place, Scottsdale, AZ 85254.

SEE OUR DISPLAY AD on page 441. East Texas Sports Cards, Jacksonville, Texas.

COMMONS WANTED 1956-1977 EX/MT or better. Bill Henderson's Cards-CL, 2320 Ruger Ave., Janesville, WI 53545. 1-608-755-0919.

POLICE/SAFETY SETS: My specialty. Buying, Selling, Trading. Write. Murvin Sterling, 227 Emporia Lane, Duncanville, TX 75116.

ST. LOUIS BASEBALL CARDS
- BILL GOODWIN -
314-892-4737

BUYING
Baseball Cards
& Baseball
Memorabilia

We are paying top prices for your Topps and Bowman Complete Sets, Star Cards, Commons, Goudeys, Tobacco Cards, Hartland Statues, Press Pins, Advertising and other related items.

- Over 4,500 satisfied customers. Numerous financial and hobby references available upon request.

- We have the most competitive buying policy in this industry.

- We are willing to travel or can suggest the easiest means to ship.

- All transactions are completely confidential.

- We guarantee courteous and professional transactions.

Feel free to CALL and discuss what you have for sale anytime.

ST. LOUIS BASEBALL CARDS
- BILL GOODWIN -
"ALWAYS BUYING BASEBALL CARDS & SPORTS MEMORABILIA
Dept. B-12, 5456 Chatfield, St. Louis, Mo. 63129   314-892-4737

EVEN MORE

More color
superstar covers

More answers to
your hobby questions

More monthly profiles on
the big guns in the hobby

More accurate prices
to all the new sets

More hot hobby
art for your
autographing requests

More national rankings
to keep you in the know

More interaction with
fellow collectors
across the country

More informative features
to help you collect better

More explanations to
the hobby's hottest
errors & variations

More fun for
your hobby

FOR LESS!

More updated and comprehensive base-ball card checklists

More collectable superstar photos

More ways to enjoy your baseball cards

More interviews with baseball's current superstars

The best-selling magazine in the hobby just got better. More color, more photos, more enjoyment for less money. More than just a price guide, *Beckett Monthly* is a quality baseball entertainment magazine. Subscribe today!

Beckett Baseball Card Monthly Subscriptions

Name _____ Age _____
(Please Print)

Address _____

City _____ State _____ Zip _____

Type of Subscription: ☐ New Subscription ☐ Renewal

Payment enclosed via: ☐ Check or Money Order ☐ VISA/MasterCard

Signature _____

Acct. # _____ Exp. _____

Check one please:

	Your Price	
1 year (a savings of $10.05 for 12 issues)	**$19.95**	
2 years (a savings of $24.05 for 24 issues)	**$35.95**	All foreign addresses add $18 per year
3 years (a savings of $42.05 for 36 issues)	**$47.95**	for postage. All payments payable in U.S. funds. *Beckett Monthly* is
4 years (a savings of $60.05 for 48 issues)	**$59.95**	published monthly.

Mail to: Beckett Publications, Subscriptions, 4887 Alpha Rd., Suite 200, Dallas, Texas 75244   #12

'TWO' GOOD TO BE TRUE

Two great new magazines in the tradition of
Beckett Baseball Card Monthly.
Up-to-date, accurate, and reliable prices • interesting articles
full-color superstar cover photos • hobby tips • answers to your questions

Beckett Football Card Magazine Subscriptions

Name _____ Age _____

(Please Print)

Address _____

City _____ State _____ Zip _____

Type of Subscription: ☐ New Subscription ☐ Renewal

Payment enclosed via: ☐ Check or Money Order ☐ VISA/MasterCard

Signature _____

Acct. # _____ Exp. _____

Check one please:	Your Price
8 issues (a savings of $8.65)	**$14.95**
16 issues (a savings of $21.25)	**$25.95**
24 issues (a savings of $33.85)	**$36.95**
32 issues (a savings of $46.45)	**$47.95**

All foreign addresses add $12 per 8 issues for postage. All payments payable in U.S. funds.
Beckett Football Card Magazine is published 8 times a year.

Mail to: Beckett Publications, Football Subscriptions, 4887 Alpha Rd., Suite 200,
Dallas, Texas 75244

Beckett Basketball Card Magazine Subscriptions

Name _____ Age _____

(Please Print)

Address _____

City _____ State _____ Zip _____

Type of Subscription: ☐ New Subscription ☐ Renewal

Payment enclosed via: ☐ Check or Money Order ☐ VISA/MasterCard

Signature _____

Acct. # _____ Exp. _____

Check one please:	Your Price
6 issues (a savings of $4.75)	**$12.95**
12 issues (a savings of $13.45)	**$21.95**
18 issues (a savings of $23.15)	**$29.95**
24 issues (a savings of $33.85)	**$36.95**

All foreign addresses add $9 per 6 issues for postage. All payments payable in U.S. funds.
Beckett Basketball Card Magazine is published 6 times a year.

Mail to: Beckett Publications, Basketball Subscriptions, 4887 Alpha Rd., Suite 200,
Dallas, Texas 75244